Washington
Information Directory
2019–2020

Sara Miller McCune founded SAGE Publishing in 1965 to support the dissemination of usable knowledge and educate a global community. SAGE publishes more than 1000 journals and over 800 new books each year, spanning a wide range of subject areas. Our growing selection of library products includes archives, data, case studies and video. SAGE remains majority owned by our founder and after her lifetime will become owned by a charitable trust that secures the company's continued independence.

Los Angeles | London | New Delhi | Singapore | Washington DC | Melbourne

Contents

Reference Boxes and Organization Charts

Each chapter also features a box listing the relevant committee and subcommittee resources in Congress.

Preface

Since 1975, the *Washington Information Directory* has been the essential resource for locating information on governmental and nongovernmental organizations in the national capital region. This trusted and user-friendly directory helps researchers find the right contact at the right organization, whether their interest is consumer product and food safety, equal employment opportunities, finance and investments, housing, immigration, terrorism, or a wealth of other timely topics. The directory allows the user to locate accurate, complete, and current information quickly and easily in a way that free Internet searches cannot.

In updating the *Washington Information Directory* every year, we research each existing organization entry to provide current addresses; phone, fax, TTY, and toll-free numbers; email, web addresses, and social media; and key officers and descriptions. In very recent years, federal office contact information has become increasingly difficult for the public to locate on the open web, but the *Washington Information Directory* continues to be the reliable one-stop resource for navigating our government. Our team painstakingly calls each organization and speaks with a member of its Washington office to obtain information. In directory listings, we include contacts' direct lines whenever possible (many organizations do not publish these numbers on their websites in an attempt to channel all calls through an operator or answering service). When a federal department reorganizes, we assess the new divisions and directorates and reorganize the book, along with providing updated organization charts. Each year we add new government agencies and new nongovernmental organizations, which comprise national organizations and international organizations with Washington offices. Entries are arranged by topic, subtopic, and organization type. The result is an indispensable reference engine that makes finding up-to-date information easy, whether you are using the print edition or navigating the online edition.

Readers will find a comprehensive listing of the members of the 116th Congress as well as a handy "Resources in Congress" box at the beginning of each chapter listing relevant committees and subcommittees for that chapter's topic, along with their website and phone number. Readers may also turn to the first appendix, which offers a complete listing of each 116th Congress committee for which information is available and includes full contact information, leadership, membership, and jurisdictions.

The fully updated chapters of the *Washington Information Directory* are supplemented by two appendices comprising a guide to the members and committees of the 116th Congress; a directory of government websites; a list of governors and other state officials; a list of foreign diplomats and embassies, U.S. ambassadors, and State Department country offices; and current information on the Freedom of Information Act and legislation, and recent Supreme Court cases related to privacy. In the congressional delegation section, we have also included Facebook, Twitter, YouTube, and Instagram information in all members' profiles. Print readers can also search and cross-search across the edition in three ways: through the name index, the organization index, or the subject index.

CQ Press seeks to continue the *Washington Information Directory*'s reputation as an invaluable, comprehensive, and authoritative reference of its kind. We welcome feedback related to the book's quality and functionality, as well as suggestions for future editions.

Laura Notton
Editor

How to Use This Directory

The *Washington Information Directory* is designed to make your search for information quick and easy.

Each chapter covers a broad topic, and within the chapters, information is divided into more specific subject areas. This arrangement allows you to find in one place the departments and agencies of the federal government, congressional committees, and nongovernmental organizations that have the information you need.

The directory divides information sources into three main categories: (1) agencies, (2) Congress, and (3) nongovernmental organizations. There is also a small international organizations category. Each entry includes the name, address, and telephone and fax numbers of the organization; the name and title of the director or the best person to contact for information; press, hotline, and TTY numbers, and email, Internet, Twitter, and Facebook, YouTube, and blog addresses whenever available; and a description of the work performed by the organization. Congressional committees and subcommittees appear in a box at the beginning of each chapter; a full entry for each committee appears in the first appendix.

HOW INFORMATION IS PRESENTED

The following examples represent the three main categories of entries and the other resources provided in the directory. The examples are drawn from the History and Preservation section in Chapter 4, Culture and Religion. (To read the mailing addresses, check the abbreviations at the end of this guide.)

Agencies

In the first category, government agencies are listed. For example, the National Park Service and its acronym appear in bold type. Next, in parentheses, is the name of its parent organization, the Interior Department. Entries may also include the name of an office within the agency, in this case the Office of Cultural Resources.

National Park Service (NPS), (Interior Dept.),
Cultural Resources, Partnerships, and Science,
1849 C St. N.W., #3128, 20240-0001;
(202) 220-4132. Joy Beasley, Associate Director
(Acting).
Web, www.nps.gov/orgs/1345

Oversees preservation of federal historic sites and administration of buildings programs. Programs include the National Register of Historic Places, National Historic and National Landmark Programs, Historic American Building Survey, Historic American Engineering Record, Archeology and Antiquities Act Program, and Technical Preservation Services. Gives grant and aid assistance and tax benefit information to properties listed in the National Register of Historic Places.

Congress

Congressional committees and subcommittees relevant to each chapter are listed in a box in the beginning of each chapter. Each committee's phone number and website are listed here. For a complete listing of congressional committees, including their full contact information, leadership, memberships, and jurisdictions, please refer to the first appendix. Entries that appear under the "Congress" heading within each chapter are agencies under congressional authority, such as the Government Accountability Office or the Library of Congress. Each entry includes a description of the agency's activities relating to the section in which it appears.

Senate Office of Conservation and
Preservation, *S416 CAP, 20510; (202) 224-4550.*
Leona Faust, Director

Develops and coordinates programs related to the conservation and preservation of Senate records and materials for the secretary of the Senate.

Nongovernmental

Thousands of nongovernmental groups have headquarters or legislative offices in or near Washington. Their staffs are often excellent information sources, and these organizations frequently maintain special libraries or information centers. Here is an example of a group with an interest in the preservation of historic sites:

American Battlefield Trust, *1156 15th St. N.W., #900,*
20005; (202) 367-1861. Fax, (202) 367-1865.
James Lighthizer, President.
General email, info@battlefields.org
Web, www.battlefields.org and Twitter, @battlefields

Membership: preservation professionals, historians, conservation activists, and citizens. Preserves endangered Civil War battlefields throughout the United States. Conducts preservation conferences and workshops. Advises local preservation groups. Monitors legislation and regulations at the federal, state, and local levels.

FOR INFORMATION:

CQ Press
An Imprint of SAGE Publications, Inc.
2455 Teller Road
Thousand Oaks, California 91320
E-mail: order@sagepub.com

SAGE Publications Ltd.
1 Oliver's Yard
55 City Road
London, EC1Y 1SP
United Kingdom

SAGE Publications India Pvt. Ltd.
B 1/I 1 Mohan Cooperative Industrial Area
Mathura Road, New Delhi 110 044
India

SAGE Publications Asia-Pacific Pte. Ltd.
18 Cross Street #10-10/11/12
China Square Central
Singapore 048423

Editor: Laura Notton
Researchers: Lisa Bhattacharji,
    Diane Goldenberg-Hart, Linda Fecteau Grimm,
    Vicki Heitsch, Julianna Hellot, Mary Hunter,
    Frances Kerr, Heather Kerrigan, Zeina Mohammed,
    Theresa Munt, Mollie Riegert, Ronald Stouffer,
    Makenzie Winter
Production Editor: Astha Jaiswal
Typesetter: Hurix Digital
Proofreaders: Caryne Brown
Indexers: Joan Shapiro
Cover Designer: Candice Harman
Marketing Manager: Jennifer Jelinski

Printed in Canada

Cover photos: ©istockphoto.com

Library of Congress Cataloging-in-Publication Data

The Library of Congress catalogued the first edition of this title as follows:

Washington information directory. 1975/76—
    Washington. Congressional Quarterly Inc.
    1. Washington, D.C.—Directories.
    2. Washington metropolitan area—Directories.
    3. United States—Executive departments—
    Directories. I. Congressional Quarterly Inc.
F192.3.W33   975.3'0025   75-646321

ISBN: 978-1-5443-5283-1
ISSN: 0887-8064

This book is printed on acid-free paper.

MIX
Paper from
responsible sources
FSC® C004071

19 20 21 22 23 10 9 8 7 6 5 4 3 2 1

Washington
Information Directory
2019–2020

How the *Washington Information Directory* Works

The *Washington Information Directory* (WID) directs your search more efficiently and effectively than any other print or online search. This resource does the hard work of pinpointing the information you need. Here is an example of how to use it to find information on the preservation of historic sites and materials:

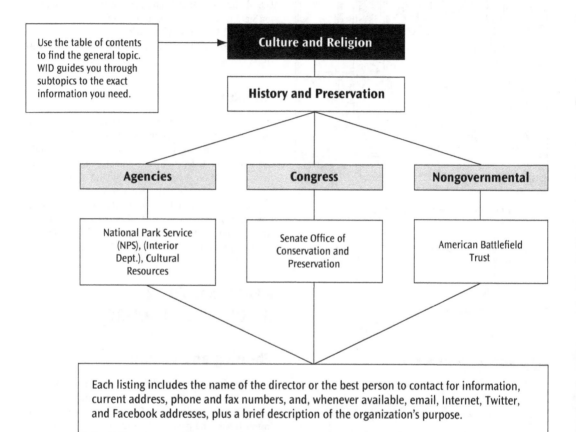

Use the table of contents to find the general topic. WID guides you through subtopics to the exact information you need.

Culture and Religion

History and Preservation

Agencies

Congress

Nongovernmental

National Park Service (NPS), (Interior Dept.), Cultural Resources

Senate Office of Conservation and Preservation

American Battlefield Trust

Each listing includes the name of the director or the best person to contact for information, current address, phone and fax numbers, and, whenever available, email, Internet, Twitter, and Facebook addresses, plus a brief description of the organization's purpose.

Charts and Boxes

This directory includes organization charts to make the hierarchy of federal departments and agencies easy to grasp, as well as reference boxes that provide essential agency contacts and other information. On the topic of historic sites, you can locate the National Park Service within the Interior Department (see chart on p. 305) or consult a list of sites administered by the National Park Service (see box on p. 150). The National Park Service's organization chart appears on page 321. The general organization chart for the federal government appears on page 961.

REFERENCE RESOURCES

Tables of Contents

The table of contents (p. v) lists the directory's chapters and their major subheadings. A list of reference boxes

and organization charts within the chapters is provided on page vii. Each chapter opens with a detailed table of contents, including the boxes and charts that appear in the chapter.

Congressional Information

A section on the 116th Congress, beginning on page 827, provides extensive information about members and committees:

State Delegations. Here (p. 828) you can locate senators, representatives, and delegates by state (or territory) and congressional district.

Committees. These sections list the jurisdictions and memberships of committees and subcommittees of the House (p. 833) and Senate (p. 914), as well as the joint committees of Congress (p. 912). Also included are party leaderships and partisan committees of the House (p. 833) and Senate (p. 927).

Members' Offices. For the House (p. 852) and Senate (p. 928), we provide each member's Capitol Hill office

Map of Capitol Hill

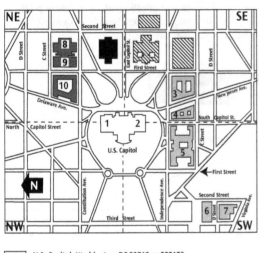

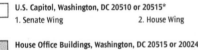

▢ **U.S. Capitol, Washington, DC 20510 or 20515***
1. Senate Wing   2. House Wing

▨ **House Office Buildings, Washington, DC 20515 or 20024**
3. Cannon   4. Longworth
5. Rayburn   6. O'Neill
7. Ford

▨ **Senate Office Buildings, Washington, DC 20510**
 8. Hart   9. Dirksen
10. Russell

■ **Supreme Court, Washington, DC 20543**

▨ **Library of Congress, Washington, DC 20540**

* Mail sent to the U.S. Capitol should bear the zip code of the chamber to which it is addressed.

Note: Dashed lines indicate the city's quadrants, which are noted in the corners of the map.

address, telephone and fax numbers, Internet address, social media (if available), key professional aide, committee assignments, and district office contact information.

House and Senate Caucuses. For congressional caucuses (p. 949), we provide a listing of the most active caucuses with contact information and staff members.

Ready Reference

A section of reference lists, beginning on page 957, provides information on the following subjects:

Government Information on the Internet. Organized by branch of government, this section (p. 956) lists Web addresses for locating information and social media on the White House, cabinet departments, Congress, and the judiciary.

State Government. The list of state officials (p. 963) provides the name, address, and telephone number for each governor, lieutenant governor, secretary of state, attorney general, and state treasurer. It includes a press

contact for the governor and, where applicable, the governor's office representative in Washington, D.C.

Diplomats. The foreign embassies section (p. 977) gives the names, official addresses, and telephone numbers of foreign diplomats in Washington; the names of ranking U.S. diplomatic officials abroad; and the phone numbers for State Department country desk offices.

Federal Laws on Information. This section presents current information on the Freedom of Information Act (p. 995) and privacy legislation (p. 1000).

Indexes

Use the name index (p. 1005) to look up any person listed in the directory. Use the organization index (p. 1045) to find a specific organization or agency. Use the subject index (p. 1095) to locate a particular area of interest. If you need information on a specific topic but do not know a particular source, the index has entries for chapter subsections to help you find where that topic is covered. For example, on the subject of equal employment for women, you can find index entries under Equal Employment Opportunity as well as under Women.

REACHING YOUR INFORMATION SOURCE

Phoning and Faxing

Call information or toll-free numbers first. Often you can get the answer you need without searching any further. If not, an explanation of your query should put you in touch with the person who can answer your question. Rarely will you need to talk to the top administrator.

Offer to fax your query if it is difficult to explain over the phone, but make sure that the person helping you knows to expect your fax. Faxing promptly and limiting your transmission to a single page brings the best results.

Remember that publications and documents are often available from a special office (for federal agencies, see p. 106) and, increasingly, on websites. Ask what is the fastest way to receive the information you need.

Keep in mind the agency or organization, not the name of the director. Personnel changes are common, but for most inquiries you will want to stay within the organization you call, rather than track down a person who may have moved on to a new job.

Concerning congressional questions, first contact one of your members of Congress; representatives have staff assigned to answer questions from constituents. Contact a committee only if you have a technical question that cannot be answered elsewhere.

Writing

Address letters to the director of an office or organization—the contact person listed. Your letter will be directed to the person who can answer your question. Be prepared to follow up by phone.

Using the Internet

Most agencies and governmental organizations have sites on the Internet (for federal departments and agencies, see pp. 114, 958–962) and an email address for general inquiries. Information available from these sources is expanding and is usually free once you are online. However, this approach is not always faster or better than a phone call—Internet connections can be slow, site menus can be complex or confusing, and information can be incomplete or out of date. The office also may be able to alert you to any upcoming changes.

As with faxing, reserve email for inquiries that may be too complex for a phone call, but phone first to establish that someone is ready to help.

ADDRESSES AND AREA CODES

Listings in the directory include full contact information, including telephone area code and, when available, room or suite number and nine-digit zip code. If an office prefers a mailing address that is different from the physical location, we provide both.

Washington, D.C., Addresses

For brevity, entries for agencies, organizations, and congressional offices in the District of Columbia (area code 202) do not include the city as part of the address. Here is the beginning of a typical Washington entry:

Equal Employment Opportunity Commission (EEOC),
131 M St. N.E., 20507; (202) 663-4001.

To complete the mailing address, add "Washington, DC" before the zip code.

Building Addresses

Departments and agencies generally have their own zip codes. Updates to our directory reflect the increasing use of street addresses by the federal government. Federal offices at the following locations are listed by building name or abbreviation:

The White House. Located at 1600 Pennsylvania Ave. N.W., 20500.

Dwight D. Eisenhower Executive Office Building. Located at 17th St. and Pennsylvania Ave. N.W., 20500.

New Executive Office Building. Located at 725 17th St. N.W., 20503.

Main State Department Building. Located at 2201 C St. N.W., 20520.

The Pentagon. Located in Arlington, Virginia, but has a Washington mailing address and different zip codes for each branch of the military.

Navy Annex. Located at Columbia Pike and Southgate Rd., Arlington, VA 20370, but most offices use a Washington mailing address.

U.S. Capitol. Abbreviated as CAP; the letters *H* and *S* before the room number indicate the House or Senate side of the building. Zip codes are 20510 for the Senate, 20515 for the House.

Senate Office Buildings. Mail for delivery to Senate office buildings does not require a street address. The zip code is 20510. Abbreviations, building names, and street locations are as follows:

SDOB	Dirksen Senate Office Bldg., Constitution Ave. between 1st and 2nd Sts. N.E.
SHOB	Hart Senate Office Bldg., 2nd St. and Constitution Ave. N.E.
SROB	Russell Senate Office Bldg., Constitution Ave. between Delaware Ave. and 1st St. N.E.

House Office Buildings. Mail for delivery to House office buildings does not require a street address. The zip code is 20515. Abbreviations, building names, and street locations are as follows:

CHOB	Cannon House Office Bldg., Independence Ave. between New Jersey Ave. and 1st St. S.E.
FHOB	Ford House Office Bldg., 2nd and D Sts. S.W.
LHOB	Longworth House Office Bldg., Independence Ave. between S. Capitol St. and New Jersey Ave. S.E.
OHOB	O'Neill House Office Bldg., 200 C St. S.W. 20024
RHOB	Rayburn House Office Bldg., Independence Ave. between S. Capitol and 1st Sts. S.W.

1

Agriculture, Food, and Nutrition

GENERAL POLICY AND ANALYSIS

Basic Resources

▶**AGENCIES**

Agricultural Marketing Service (AMS) *(Agriculture Dept.), 1400 Independence Ave. S.W., #3069, MS 0201, 20250-0201; (202) 720-4276. Bruce Summers, Administrator; Erin Morris, Associate Administrator, (202) 720-0219. Public Affairs, (202) 720-8998.*
Web, www.ams.usda.gov, Twitter, @USDA_AMS and Facebook, www.facebook.com/usda

Provides domestic and international marketing services to the agricultural industry. Administers marketing, standardization, grading, inspection, and regulatory programs; maintains a market news service to inform producers of price changes; conducts agricultural marketing research and development programs; studies agricultural transportation issues.

Agricultural Marketing Service (AMS) *(Agriculture Dept.), Fair Trade Practices Program, Warehouse and Commodity Management, 1400 Independence Ave. S.W., MS 0506, 20250-0506; (202) 720-2121. Jose R. Gonzalez, Director.*
General email, Jose.Gonzalez@ams.usda.gov
Web, www.fsa.usda.gov/programs-and-services/commodity-operations/warehouse-services/index

Ensures that agriculture facilities are upholding the rules and regulations set forth by the U.S. Warehouse Act and Commodity Credit Corporation contracts. This office is responsible for issuing license and storage agreements and performing warehouse examinations.

Agriculture Dept. (USDA), *1400 Independence Ave. S.W., #200A, 20250-0002; (202) 720-3631. Fax, (202) 720-2166. Sonny Perdue, Secretary. Information, (202) 720-2791. Locator, (202) 720-8732. Press, (202) 720-4623.*
Web, www.usda.gov, Twitter, @USDA and Facebook, www .facebook.com/usda

Serves as principal adviser to the president on agricultural policy; works to increase and maintain farm income and to develop markets abroad for U.S. agricultural products.

Agriculture Dept. (USDA), *Advocacy and Outreach, Whitten Bldg., 1400 Independence Ave. S.W., #520-A, 20250; (202) 720-6350. Fax, (202) 720-7136. Carolyn Parker, Director. Toll-free, (800) 880-4183.*
General email, AdvocacyandOutreach@osec.usda.gov
Web, www.outreach.usda.gov

Develops, manages, and supports programs that provide informatioh, training, and technical assistance to socially disadvantaged farmers and ranchers and small and beginning farmers and ranchers. Administers the Small Farmer Outreach, Training, and Technical Assistance Program and the USDA Farm Worker Initiative. Provides policy guidance and feedback to the department on all outreach-related activities and functions.

Agriculture Dept. (USDA), *National Appeals Division (NAD), 3101 Park Center Dr., #1100, Alexandria, VA 22302; (703) 305-2708. Fax, (703) 305-2825. Steven C. Silverman, Director, (202) 720-3351. TTY, (703) 305-2007.*
General email, nadinfo@usda.gov
Web, www.nad.usda.gov

Conducts impartial administrative appeals hearings and reviews of adverse program decisions for participants of programs administered by the Farm Service Agency, Risk Management Agency, Natural Resources Conservation Service, and Rural Development.

Agriculture Dept. (USDA), *Office of the Chief Economist, Whitten Bldg., 12th and Jefferson Dr. S.W., #112, 20250-3810; (202) 720-4164. Fax, (202) 690-4915. Robert Johansson, Chief Economist. Communications Officer, (202) 720-5447.*
General email, msewadeh@oce.usda.gov
Web, www.usda.gov/oce

Prepares economic and statistical analyses used to plan and evaluate short-range and intermediate-range agricultural policy. Evaluates department policy, proposals, and legislation for their impact on the agricultural economy. Administers department economic agencies, including the Office of Environmental Markets, Office of Risk Assessment and Cost-Benefit Analysis, Office of Energy Policy and New Uses, Climate Change Program Office, and World Agricultural Outlook Board. Publishes the monthly *World Agricultural Supply and Demand Estmates* report.

Agriculture Dept. (USDA), *Office of the Chief Economist, Energy Policy and New Uses, South Bldg., 12th and Jefferson Dr. S.W., #4407, 20250; (202) 401-0461. William Hohenstein, Director (Acting).*
General email, whohenstein@oce.usda.gov
Web, www.usda.gov/oce/energy/index.htm

Develops and coordinates department energy policy, programs, and strategies focusing on renewable energy policy and evaluation, particularly as it relates to biofuels and feedstocks.

Agriculture Dept. (USDA), *Office of the Chief Economist, Environmental Markets, South Bldg., 12th and Jefferson Dr. S.W., #4409, 20250; (202) 720-6698. William Hohenstein, Director (Acting).*
General email, whohenst@oce.usda.gov
Web, www.oem.usda.gov

Supports the development of policies related to emerging markets for water quality, carbon sequestration, wetlands, biodiversity, and other ecosystem services.

Agriculture Dept. (USDA), *Office of the Chief Scientist, 1400 Independence Ave., #338A, 20250; (202) 720-3444. Chavonda Jacobs-Young, Chief Scientist (Acting); Dionne F. Toombs, Director.*
General email, c.jacobsyoung@ars.usda.gov
Web, www.usda.gov/our-agency/staff-offices/office-chief-scientist-ocs

AGRICULTURE RESOURCES IN CONGRESS

For a complete listing of congressional committees, including their full contact information, leadership, membership, and jurisdictions, please refer to the Appendix on pages 827–948.

HOUSE:

House Agriculture Committee, (202) 225-2171.
Web, www.agriculture.house.gov
  Subcommittee on Biotechnology, Horticulture, and Research, (202) 225-2171.
  Subcommittee on Commodity Exchanges, Energy, and Credit, (202) 225-2171.
  Subcommittee on Conservation and Forestry, (202) 225-2171.
  Subcommittee on General Farm Commodities and Risk Management, (202) 225-2171.
  Subcommittee on Livestock and Foreign Agriculture, (202) 225-2171.
  Subcommittee on Nutrition, (202) 225-2171.
House Appropriations Committee, (202) 225-2771.
Web, www.appropriations.house.gov
  Subcommittee on Agriculture, Rural Development, Food and Drug Administration, and Related Agencies, (202) 225-2638.
House Education and the Workforce Committee, (202) 225-4527.
Web, www.edworkforce.house.gov
  Subcommittee on Early Childhood, Elementary, and Secondary Education, (202) 225-4527.
House Energy and Commerce Committee, (202) 225-2927.
Web, www.energycommerce.house.gov
  Subcommittee on Health, (202) 225-2927.
House Foreign Affairs Committee, (202) 225-5021.
Web, www.foreignaffairs.house.gov

House Science, Space, and Technology Committee, (202) 225-6371.
Web, www.science.house.gov
  Subcommittee on Research and Technology, (202) 225-6371.
House Small Business Committee, (202) 225-5821.
Web, www.smallbusiness.house.gov
  Subcommittee on Agriculture, Energy, and Trade, (202) 225-5821.

SENATE:

Senate Agriculture, Nutrition, and Forestry Committee, (202) 224-2035.
Web, www.agriculture.senate.gov
  Subcommittee on Commodities, Risk Management, and Trade, (202) 224-2035.
  Subcommittee on Conservation and Forestry, and Natural Resources, (202) 224-2035.
  Subcommittee on Livestock, Marketing, and Agriculture Security, (202) 224-2035.
  Subcommittee on Nutrition, Agricultural Research, Specialty Crops, (202) 224-2035.
  Subcommittee on Rural Development and Energy, (202) 224-2035.
Senate Appropriations Committee, (202) 224-7257.
Web, www.appropriations.senate.gov
  Subcommittee on Agriculture, Rural Development, Food and Drug Administration, and Related Agencies, (202) 224-8090.

Informs department policy and regulation decisions with scientific research in the areas of agricultural systems and technology, animal health and production, plant health, renewable energy, natural resources, food safety, nutrition, agricultural economics, and rural communities.

Agriculture Dept. (USDA), *People's Garden,* 1400 *Independence Ave. S.W., 20250; (202) 577-7462. Annie Ceccarini, Program Manager. Press, (202) 720-4623. General email, oc.news@usda.gov*

Web, https://peoplesgarden.usda.gov and Twitter, @PeoplesGarden

Works with Agriculture Dept. agencies and offices to promote healthy eating, sustainable agricultural and landscaping practices, and locally produced agricultural products through school gardens, community gardens, urban farms, and small-scale agriculture projects.

Agriculture Dept. (USDA), *Tribal Relations (OTR),* 1400 *Independence Ave. S.W., Room 500-A, 20250;*

(202) 205-2249. Fax, (202) 720-1058. Diane Cullo, Director (Acting). General email, tribal.relations@osec.usda.gov

Web, www.usda.gov/our-agency/staff-offices/office-tribal-relations-otr

Works with American Indians and Alaska Native constituents to develop programs and policies that preserve tribal sovereignty.

Animal and Plant Health Inspection Service (APHIS) *(Agriculture Dept.), Biotechnology Regulatory Services, 4700 River Rd., Unit 147, Riverdale, MD 20737; (301) 851-3877. Michael J. Firko, Deputy Administrator. Applications and regulatory requirements, (301) 851-3886. Compliance, (301) 851-3935. Press, (301) 851-4100.*

Web, www.aphis.usda.gov/aphis/ourfocus/biotechnology

Administers the Coordinated Framework for Regulation of Biotechnology to regulate genetically engineered organisms that may pose a risk to plant health and other agricultural resources; authorizes permits and notifications for the importation, interstate movement, and environmental release of genetically engineered organisms and performs inspections.

Animal and Plant Health Inspection Service (APHIS) *(Agriculture Dept.), International Services, 14th and Independence Ave. S.W., 20250; (202) 799-7132. Cheryle Blakely, Deputy Administrator. Web, www.aphis.usda.gov/aphis/ourfocus/ internationalservices*

Collaborates with foreign partners to control pests and diseases that could harm the U.S.; facilitates safe agricultural trade; ensures effective and efficient management of internationally based programs; invests in international capacity-building with foreign counterparts to prevent the spread of damaging pests and diseases.

Animal and Plant Health Inspection Service (APHIS) *(Agriculture Dept.), Legislative and Public Affairs, South Bldg., 1400 Independence Ave. S.W., #1147, 20250; (202) 799-7030. Bethany Jones, Deputy Administrator, (301) 955-1203. Public Affairs, (301) 851-4100. Web, www.aphis.usda.gov/aphis/banner/contactus/sa_ aphis_contacts/ct_contact_lpa*

Manages communications with Congress, industry stakeholders, trading partners, and the media.

Bureau of Economic and Business Affairs (EB) *(State Dept.), Trade Policy and Negotiations (TPN), Agriculture Policy (AGP), 2201 C St. N.W., #4686, 20520-0002; (202) 647-3090. Fax, (202) 647-1894. Patrick M. Dunn, Director, (202) 647-0133. Web, www.state.gov/e/eb/tpn/agp*

Develops agricultural trade policy; handles questions pertaining to international negotiations on all agricultural products covered by the World Trade Organization (WTO) and bilateral trade agreements. Oversees the distribution of biotechnology outreach funds to promote international acceptance of the technology.

►CONGRESS

For a listing of relevant congressional committees and subcommittees, please see page 3 or the Appendix.

Government Accountability Office (GAO), *Natural Resources and Environment (NRE), 441 G St. N.W., #2T23-A, 20548 (mailing address: 441 G St. N.W., #2T23A, Washington, DC 20548); (202) 512-3841. Mark Gaffigan, Managing Director. Web, www.gao.gov/careers/nre.html*

Audits, analyzes, and evaluates for Congress federal agriculture, food safety, and energy programs; provides guidance on issues including efforts to ensure a reliable and environmentally sound energy supply, land and water resources management, protection of the environment, hazardous and nuclear wastes threat reduction, food safety, and investment in science.

►NONGOVERNMENTAL

American Farm Bureau Federation (AFBF), *600 Maryland Ave. S.W., #1000W, 20024-2520; (202) 406-3600. Fax, (202) 406-3606. Zippy Duvall, President. General email, info@fb.org*

Web, www.fb.org, Twitter, @farmbureau and Facebook, www.facebook.com/AmericanFarmBureau

Federation of state farm bureaus in fifty states and Puerto Rico. Promotes agricultural research. Interests include commodity programs, domestic production, marketing, education, research, financial assistance to the farmer, foreign assistance programs, rural development, the world food shortage, and inspection and certification of food. Monitors legislation and regulations.

Environmental Working Group, *1436 U St. N.W., #100, 20009-3987; (202) 667-6982. Fax, (202) 232-2592. Kenneth A. Cook, President. Web, www.ewg.org and Twitter, @ewg*

Research and advocacy group that studies and publishes reports on a wide range of agricultural and environmental issues, including farm subsidies and industrial pollution. Monitors legislation and regulations.

Equitable Food Initiative, *1875 Connecticut Ave. N.W., 10th Floor, 20009; (202) 730-6672. Peter O'Driscoll, Executive Director. General email, info@equitablefood.org*

Web, http://equitablefood.org, Twitter, @EquitableFood and Facebook, www.facebook.com/EquitableFoodInitiative

Recognizes the contribution of farmworkers in the produce industry while improving agricultural policy and food safety. Creates a network for workers, growers, retailers, and consumers. Promotes improvement of agriculture working conditions, environmental stewardship, and responsible produce growing.

National Assn. of State Depts. of Agriculture, *4350 N. Fairfax Dr., #910, Arlington, VA 22203; (202) 296-9680. Barbara P. Glenn, Chief Executive Officer. General email, nasda@nasda.org*

Web, www.nasda.org and Twitter, @TheNASCUS

Membership: commissioners, secretaries, and directors of agriculture from the fifty states, Puerto Rico, Guam, American Samoa, and the Virgin Islands. Serves as liaison between federal government, state departments, and stakeholders; coordinates agricultural policies and laws; provides data collection, emergency planning, and training; seeks to protect consumers and the environment. Monitors legislation and regulations.

National Council of Agricultural Employers (NCAE), *525 9th St. N.W., #800, 20004; (202) 629-9320. Michael Marsh, Executive Vice President. General email, info@ncaeonline.org*

Web, www.ncaeonline.org and Twitter, @NCAEonline

Membership: employers of agricultural labor. Encourages establishment and maintenance of conditions

Agriculture Department

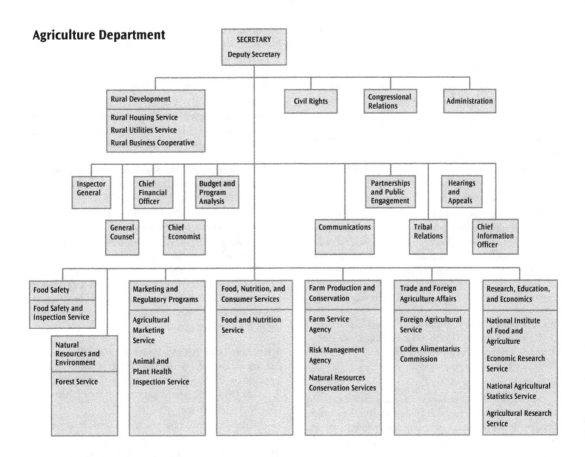

conducive to an adequate supply of domestic and foreign farm labor.

National Farmers Union, *20 F St. N.W., #300, 20001-1560; (202) 554-1600. Fax, (202) 554-1654. Roger Johnson, President.*
General email, info@nfu.org

Web, www.nfu.org, Twitter, @NFUDC and Facebook, www.facebook.com/nationalfarmersunion

Advocates economic and social well-being and quality of life of family farmers, ranchers, fishermen, and consumers and their communities through education, cooperation, and legislation. Encourages sustainable production of food, fiber, feed, and fuel.

National Governors Assn. (NGA), *Natural Resources Committee, 444 N. Capitol St. N.W., #267, 20001-1512; (202) 624-5300. Fax, (202) 624-7814. David Parkhurst, Director; Alex Schaefer, Legislative Director.*
General email, webmaster@nga.org

Web, www.nga.org/cms/center/eet

Monitors legislation and regulations and makes recommendations on agriculture, energy, environment, and natural resource issues to ensure governors' views and priorities are represented in federal policies and regulations.

National Grange, *1616 H St. N.W., 10th Floor, 20006-4999; (202) 628-3507. Fax, (202) 347-1091. Betsy Huber, President, ext. 112. Toll-free, (888) 447-2643.*

General email, info@nationalgrange.org

Web, www.nationalgrange.org and Twitter, @NationalGrange

Membership: farmers and others involved in agricultural production and rural community service activities. Coordinates community service programs with state grange organizations.

National Sustainable Agriculture Coalition, *110 Maryland Ave. N.E., #209, 20002-5622; (202) 547-5754. Fax, (202) 547-1837. Judy Obudzinski, Policy Director (Acting); Margaret Krome, Coalition Director (Acting).*
General email, info@sustainableagriculture.net

Web, www.sustainableagriculture.net, Twitter, @sustainableag and Facebook, www.facebook .com/sustainableag

National alliance of farm, rural, and conservation organizations. Advocates federal policies that promote environmentally sustainable agriculture, natural resources management, and rural community development. Monitors legislation and regulations.

Rural Coalition, *1029 Vermont Ave. N.W., #601, 20005; (202) 628-7160. Fax, (202) 393-1816. Lorette Picciano, Executive Director.*
General email, ruralco@ruralco.org

Web, www.ruralco.org and Twitter, @RuralCo

Alliance of organizations that develop public policies benefiting rural communities. Collaborates with community-based groups on agriculture and rural development issues, including health and the environment, minority farmers, farmworkers, Native Americans' rights, and rural community development. Provides rural groups with technical assistance.

Union of Concerned Scientists, *Food and Environment Program, 1825 K St. N.W., #800, 20006-1232; (202) 223-6133. Fax, (202) 223-6162. Ricardo Salvador, Director.*
General email, ucs@ucsusa.org

Web, www.ucsusa.org/food and Twitter, @cadwego

Promotes a food system that encourages innovative and environmentally sustainable ways of producing high-quality, safe, and affordable food. Focuses on reducing the unnecessary use of antibiotics and strengthening federal oversight of genetically engineered products for food and agriculture and promoting climate-friendly agricultural practices. (Headquarters in Cambridge, Mass.)

Wallace Genetic Foundation, *4910 Massachusetts Ave. N.W., #221, 20016; (202) 966-2932. Fax, (202) 966-3370. Michaela Oldfield, Executive Director.*
General email, wgfdn@aol.com

Web, www.wallacegenetic.org

Supports national and international nonprofits in the areas of sustainable agriculture, agricultural research, preservation of farmland, reduction of environmental toxins, conservation, biodiversity protection, and global climate issues.

Agricultural Research, Education

▶**AGENCIES**

Agricultural Research Service *(Agriculture Dept.), 1400 Independence Ave. S.W., #302A, MS 0300, 20250-0300; (202) 720-3656. Fax, (202) 720-5427. Chavonda Jacobs-Young, Administrator.*
General email, Administrator@ars.usda.gov

Web, www.ars.usda.gov, Twitter, @USDA_ARS and Blog, www.ars.usda.gov/oc/blog/blogposts and Podcast, www.ars.usda.gov/oc/podcasts/index

Conducts research on crops, livestock, poultry, soil and water conservation, agricultural engineering, and control of insects and other pests; develops new uses for farm commodities.

Agricultural Research Service *(Agriculture Dept.), National Plant Germplasm System, 5601 Sunnyside Ave., #4-2212, Beltsville, MD 20705-5139; (301) 504-5541. Fax, (301) 504-6191. Peter K. Bretting, National Program Leader.*
Web, www.ars-grin.gov/npgs

Network of federal and state gene banks that preserve samples of all major field crops and horticultural crops. Collects, preserves, evaluates, and catalogs germplasm and distributes it for specific purposes.

Agriculture Dept. (USDA), *Rural Development, Rural Business–Cooperative Service, 1400 Independence Ave. S.W., #5803-S, MS 3201, 20250-3201; (202) 690-4730. Bette Brand, Administrator. Press, (202) 690-4737.*
Web, www.rd.usda.gov/about-rd/agencies/rural-business-cooperative-service

Annually collects financial and other data from farmer, rancher, and fishery cooperatives; publishes marketing, supply, service, fishery, and bargaining cooperatives data.

Agriculture Dept. (USDA), *Small and Disadvantaged Business Utilization (OSDBU), 1400 Independence Ave. S.W., #1085-S, MS9501, 20250-9501; (202) 720-7117. Michelle Warren, Director (Acting), (202) 720-7835.*
Web, www.dm.usda.gov/smallbus

Provides guidance and technical assistance to small businesses seeking to do business with the USDA; monitors the development and implementation of contracting policies to prevent barriers to small business participation; works with other federal agencies and public/private partners to increase the number of small businesses participating in the contracting arena.

Agriculture Dept. (USDA), *Under Secretary for Research, Education, and Economics (REE), 1400 Independence Ave. S.W., #214W, MS 0110, 20250-0110; (202) 720-5923. Fax, (202) 690-2842. Scott Hutchins, Under Secretary.*
Web, www.ree.usda.gov

Coordinates agricultural research, extension, and teaching programs in the food and agricultural sciences, including human nutrition, home economics, consumer services, agricultural economics, environmental quality, natural and renewable resources, forestry and range management, animal and plant production and protection, aquaculture, and the processing, distribution, marketing, and utilization of food and agricultural products. Oversees the Agricultural Research Service, the National Institute of Food and Agriculture, the Economic Research Service, and the National Agricultural Statistics Service.

Economic Research Service *(Agriculture Dept.), 355 E St. S.W., 20024-8221; (202) 694-5000. Fax, (202) 245-5467. Mary Bohman, Administrator; Greg Pompelli, Associate Administrator.*
General email, service@ers.usda.gov

Web, www.ers.usda.gov and Twitter, @USDA_ERS

Conducts research on economic and policy issues involving food, natural resources, and rural development.

Economic Research Service *(Agriculture Dept.), Market and Trade Economics, 355 E St. S.W., 20024-3221 (mailing address: 1400 Independence Ave. S.W., MS 1800, Washington, DC 20250-0002); (202) 694-5201. Gopi Munisamy, Director.*
Web, www.ers.usda.gov/about-ers/agency-structure/market-and-trade-economics-division-mted

Monitors, evaluates, and conducts research on domestic and foreign economic and policy factors affecting agricultural markets and trade, with a focus on policy and program alternatives, domestic and international markets, commodity analysis and forecasts, international food security, and development of analytical tools and data.

Economic Research Service *(Agriculture Dept.),* **Resource and Rural Economics,** *1400 Independence Ave. S.W., #214W, MS 1800, DC 20250-0; (202) 694-5478. Marca Weinberg, Director.*
Web, www.ers.usda.gov/about-ers/agency-structure/resource-and-rural-economics-division-rred

Conducts research on the interconnectedness of agricultural, energy, climate, and environmental policies; ecosystem services and land use; research and development of agricultural technologies and agricultural productivity; dynamics of farming; rural development; and the well-being of farm and rural households. Collaborates with the department's National Agricultural Statistics Service to implement the annual national Agricultural Resource Management Survey.

Foreign Agricultural Service (FAS) *(Agriculture Dept.),* **Global Analysis,** *1400 Independence Ave. S.W., #4083S, 20250; (202) 720-6301. Fax, (202) 690-1238. Vacant, Deputy Administrator.*
Web, www.fas.usda.gov

Prepares production forecasts, assesses export marketing opportunities, and tracks changes in policies affecting U.S. agricultural trade. Develops and maintains Agriculture Dept.'s data on agricultural production, supply, demand, and trade.

National Agricultural Library *(Agriculture Dept.), 10301 Baltimore Ave., Beltsville, MD 20705-2351; (301) 504-5755. Fax, (301) 504-7042. Paul Wester, Director, (301) 504-5248. TTY, (301) 504-6856.*
General email, agref@usda.gov
Web, www.nal.usda.gov

Principal source of agricultural information in the United States. Makes significant information available to researchers, educators, policymakers, and the public; coordinates with state land-grant and Agriculture Dept. field libraries; promotes international cooperation and exchange of information. Deeper interests include food production, food safety, human nutrition, animal welfare, water quality, rural development, and invasive species. Library hours are 8:30 a.m.–4:30 p.m.

National Agricultural Library *(Agriculture Dept.),* **Alternative Farming Systems Information Center (AFSIC),** *10301 Baltimore Ave., #123, Beltsville, MD 20705-2351; (301) 504-6559. Fax, (301) 504-6927. Bill Thomas, Coordinator.*
General email, agref@usda.gov
Web, www.nal.usda.gov/afsic

Serves individuals and agencies seeking information on sustainability in agriculture, alternative plants and crops, farm energy options, grazing systems and alternative livestock breeds, alternative marketing and business practices, organic production, ecological pest management, and soil and water management.

National Agricultural Statistics Service *(Agriculture Dept.), 1400 Independence Ave. S.W., #5041, MS 2001, 20250-2001; (202) 720-2707. Hubert Hamer, Administrator. Information, (800) 727-9540. Library, (202) 690-8127.*
General email, nass@nass.usda.gov
Web, www.nass.usda.gov and Twitter, @usda_nass

Prepares estimates and reports on production, supply, prices, and other items relating to the U.S. agricultural economy. Reports include statistics on field crops, fruits and vegetables, cattle, hogs, poultry, and related products. Prepares quinquennial national census of agriculture.

National Agricultural Statistics Service *(Agriculture Dept.),* **Census and Survey,** *1400 Independence Ave. S.W., #6306, MS 2020, 20250-2020; (202) 720-4557. Fax, (202) 720-8738. Barbara Rater, Director.*
General email, nass@nass.usda.gov
Web, www.nass.usda.gov

Conducts a quinquennial agricultural census that provides data on crops, livestock, operator characteristics, land use, farm production expenditures, machinery and equipment, and irrigation for counties, states, regions, and the nation.

National Institute of Food and Agriculture (NIFA) *(Agriculture Dept.), Jaime L. Whitten Bldg., 12th St. S.W. and Jefferson Dr., #305A, 20024 (mailing address: 1400 Independence Ave. S.W., MS 2201, Washington, DC 20250-2201); (202) 720-4423. Fax, (202) 720-8987. J. Scott Angle, Director. Communications, (202) 720-4242. Information, (202) 720-2791.*
General email, nifamediarequests@nifa.usda.gov
Web, https://nifa.usda.gov, Twitter, @USDA_NIFA
Blog, https://nifa.usda.gov/newsroom?f%5B0%5D=type%3Ablog

Supports research, education, and extension of issues pertaining to agricultural production, nutrition, food safety, energy independence, and the sustainability of natural resources. Partners with and funds scientists at academic institutions, particularly the land-grant universities, minority-serving institutions, including black colleges and universities, Hispanic-serving institutions, and tribal colleges, as well as government, private, and nonprofit organizations to address critical issues in agriculture, including global food security and hunger, water resources, climate change, sustainable energy, childhood obesity, and food safety. Partners with agricultural extension offices in all counties, states, and territories.

National Institute of Food and Agriculture (NIFA) *(Agriculture Dept.),* **Institute of Bioenergy, Climate, and Environment,** *800 9th St. S.W., #3231, 20024 (mailing address: 1400 Independence Ave. S.W., MS 2210, Washington, DC 20250-2215); (202) 401-4926. Luis Tupas, Deputy Director.*
Web, https://nifa.usda.gov/office/institute-bioenergy-climate-and-environment

Administers programs to address national science priorities that advance energy independence and help agricultural, forest, and range production systems adapt to climate change variables. Provides grants to support the development of sustainable bioenergy production systems, agricultural production systems, and natural resource management activities that are adapted to climate variation and activities that otherwise support sustainable natural resource use.

National Institute of Food and Agriculture (NIFA) *(Agriculture Dept.), Institute of Youth, Family, and Community, 800 9th St. S.W., #4343, 20024 (mailing address: 1400 Independence Ave. S.W., MS 2250, Washington, DC 20250-2225); (202) 720-5305. Fax, (202) 720-3945. Muquarrab Qureshi, Deputy Director.*
Web, https://nifa.usda.gov/office/institute-youth-family-and-community

Provides grants and programmatic training to support youth and family development; partners with county governments, the private sector, and state land-grant universities. Program areas include food and agricultural science education, particularly in minority-serving institutions; childhood nutrition; community food projects; and community service. Includes divisions of Community Education, Family and Consumer Sciences, and Youth and 4-H.

▶**NONGOVERNMENTAL**

National Council of Farmer Cooperatives (NCFC), *50 F St. N.W., #900, 20001-1530; (202) 626-8700. Fax, (202) 626-8722. Charles (Chuck) F. Conner, President; Mary Nowak, Director of Government Affairs.*
General email, info@ncfc.org
Web, www.ncfc.org and Twitter, @FarmerCoop

Membership: cooperative businesses owned and operated by farmers. Conducts educational programs and encourages research on agricultural cooperatives; provides statistics and analyzes trends; presents awards for research papers.

National FFA Organization, *80 M St. S.W., 20003; (646) 491-9060. Steve A. Brown, National FFA Advisor.*
Web, www.ffa.org, Twitter, @NationalFFA and Facebook, www.facebook.com/nationalffa

Membership: local chapters of high school students enrolled in agricultural, food, and natural resources sciences education and agribusiness programs. Coordinates leadership training and other activities with local chapters across the United States. Formerly known as the Future Farmers of America. (Business Center in Indianapolis, Ind.)

Fertilizer and Pesticides

▶**AGENCIES**

Environmental Protection Agency (EPA), *Chemical Safety and Pollution Prevention (OCSPP), 1200 Pennsylvania Ave. N.W., #4146, MC 7101M, 20460; (202) 564-2910. Fax, (202) 564-0801. Vacant, Assistant Administrator; Charlotte Bertrand, Principal Deputy Assistant Administrator (Acting).*

Web, www.epa.gov/aboutepa/about-office-chemical-safety-and-pollution-prevention-ocspp

Registers, controls, and regulates use of pesticides and toxic substances. Manages the Endocrine Disruptor Screening Program, which screens pesticides, chemicals, and environmental contaminants for their potential effect on estrogen, androgen, and thyroid hormone systems.

Environmental Protection Agency (EPA), *Chemical Safety and Pollution Prevention (OCSPP), Pesticide Programs, 1 Potomac Yard, 2777 Crystal Dr., Arlington, VA 22202 (mailing address: 1200 Pennsylvania Ave. N.W., MC 7501P, Washington, DC 20460); (703) 305-7090. Fax, (703) 308-4776. Rick P. Keigwin Jr., Director. National Pesticide Information Center, (800) 858-7378.*
General email, pesticidewebcomments@epa.gov
Web, www.epa.gov/aboutepa/about-office-chemical-safety-and-pollution-prevention-ocspp#opp

Regulates the manufacturing and use of all pesticides, including insecticides, herbicides, rodenticides, disinfectants, and sanitizers, in the United States. Establishes maximum levels for pesticide residues in food. Develops rules that govern labeling and literature accompanying pesticide products. Administers the Integrated Pest Management in Schools and the Pesticide Environmental Stewardship programs. Operates the National Pesticide Information Center (8 a.m.–12 p.m. PST).

Natural Resources Conservation Service *(Agriculture Dept.), Pest Management, 1400 Independence Ave. S.W., #6147, 20250; (202) 253-4376. Joseph K. Bagdon, Pest Management Specialist; Eric S. Hesketh, Pest Management Specialist.*
Web, www.nrcs.usda.gov

Formulates and recommends agency policy in coordination with the Environmental Protection Agency and other Agriculture Dept. agencies for the establishment of standards, procedures, and management of agronomic, forest, and horticultural use of pesticides.

▶**NONGOVERNMENTAL**

Beyond Pesticides, *701 E St. S.E., #200, 20003; (202) 543-5450. Fax, (202) 543-4791. Jay Feldman, Executive Director.*
General email, info@beyondpesticides.org
Web, www.beyondpesticides.org and Twitter, @bpncamp

Coalition of family farmers, farmworkers, consumers, home gardeners, physicians, lawyers, and others concerned about pesticide hazards and safety. Issues information to increase public awareness of environmental, public health, and economic problems caused by pesticide abuse; promotes alternatives to pesticide use, such as organic pest management programs.

Croplife America, *1156 15th St. N.W., #400, 20005-1752; (202) 296-1585. Fax, (202) 463-0474. Christopher Novak, President.*
General email, info@croplifeamerica.org
Web, www.croplifeamerica.org

Membership: pesticide manufacturers. Provides information on pesticide safety, development, and use. Monitors legislation and regulations. (Formerly the American Crop Protection Assn.)

Entomological Society of America, *3 Park Pl., #307, Annapolis, MD 21401-3722; (301) 731-4535. Fax, (301) 731-4538. David Gammel, Executive Director.*
General email, esa@entsoc.org

Web, www.entsoc.org and Twitter, @EntsocAmerica

Advises on crop protection, food chain, and individual and urban health matters dealing with insect pests.

Environmental Working Group, *1436 U St. N.W., #100, 20009-3987; (202) 667-6982. Fax, (202) 232-2592. Kenneth A. Cook, President.*
Web, www.ewg.org and Twitter, @ewg

Research and advocacy organization that studies and reports on the presence of herbicides and pesticides in food and drinking water. Monitors legislation and regulations.

Fertilizer Institute, *425 3rd St. S.W., #950, 20024; (202) 962-0490. Fax, (202) 962-0577. Chris Jahn, President, (202) 515-2700.*
General email, info@tfi.org

Web, www.tfi.org, Twitter, @Fertilizer_Inst and Facebook, www.facebook.com/thefertilizerinstitute

Membership: manufacturers, dealers, and distributors of fertilizer. Provides statistical data and other information concerning the effects of fertilizer and its relationship to world food production, food supply, and the environment.

National Agricultural Aviation Assn., *1440 Duke St., Alexandria, VA 22314; (202) 546-5722. Fax, (202) 546-5726. Andrew D. Moore, Executive Director.*
General email, information@agaviation.org

Web, www.agaviation.org

Membership: agricultural pilots; operating companies that seed, fertilize, and spray land by air; and allied industries. Monitors legislation and regulations. (Affiliated with National Agricultural Aviation Research and Education Foundation.)

National Pest Management Assn., *10460 North St., Fairfax, VA 22030; (703) 352-6762. Fax, (703) 352-3031. Dominique Stumpf, Chief Executive Officer. Toll-free, (800) 678-6722.*
Web, www.npmapestworld.org

Membership: pest control operators. Monitors federal regulations that affect pesticide use; provides members with technical information. Website has a Spanish-language link.

Horticulture and Gardening

▶**AGENCIES**

National Arboretum *(Agriculture Dept.),* *3501 New York Ave. N.E., 20002-1958; (202) 245-4523. Richard T. Olsen, Director, (202) 245-4539.*
Web, www.usna.usda.gov

Maintains public display of plants on 446 acres; provides information and makes referrals concerning cultivated plants (exclusive of field crops and fruits); conducts plant breeding and research; maintains herbarium.

National Arboretum *(Agriculture Dept.), Floral and Nursery Plants Research,* *3501 New York Ave. N.E., #100, 20002; (301) 504-6848. Fax, (301) 504-5096. Margaret Pooler, Research Leader, (301) 504-5218.*
Web, www.ars.usda.gov/northeast-area/washington-dc/national-arboretum/floral-and-nursery-plants-research

Supports research and implementation of new technologies in florist and nursery industries. Areas of research include development of new floral, nursery, and turf plants; detection and control of pathogens in ornamental plants; ornamental plant taxonomy; improvement of nursery production systems; and curation of woody landscape plant germplasm as part of the National Plant Germplasm System.

National Arboretum *(Agriculture Dept.), Gardens Research,* *Jamie L. Whitten Bldg., 1400 Indepencence Ave. S.W. Washington, DC, 20250; (202) 720-3656. Fax, (202) 720-5427. Scott Aker, Supervisory Research Horticulturalist, (202) 245-4533.*
Web, www.ars.usda.gov/northeast-area/washington-dc/national-arboretum/gardens-unit and Twitter, @USDA_ARS

Collects, displays, documents, evaluates, and introduces woody and herbaceous landscape ornamentals; interprets plant collections, display gardens, and Agricultural Research Service and National Arboretum research for the public through signage, exhibits, and programs; and provides educational programs for gardeners and green industry professionals.

Smithsonian Institution, *Botany and Horticulture Library,* *10th St. and Constitution Ave. N.W., #W422, 20560-0166 (mailing address: P.O. Box 37012, MRC 154, Washington, DC 20013-7012); (202) 633-1685. Fax, (202) 786-2866. Robin Everly, Branch Librarian.*
General email, askalibrarian@si.edu

Web, https://library.si.edu/libraries/botany-and-horticulture-library and Twitter, @SmithsonianLibraries

Collection includes books, periodicals, and videotapes on horticulture, garden history, and landscape design. Specializes in American gardens and gardening of the late nineteenth and early twentieth centuries. Open to the public by appointment 9:00 a.m.–4:30 p.m. (Housed at the National Museum of Natural History.)

U.S. Botanic Garden, *100 Maryland Ave. S.W., 20001 (mailing address: 245 1st St. S.W., Washington, DC 20024); (202) 225-8333. Fax, (202) 225-1561. Saharah Moon Chapotin, Executive Director, (202) 225-1110. Horticulture hotline, (202) 226-4785. Press, (202) 226-4145. Program registration information, (202) 225-1116. Special events, (202) 226-7674. Tour line, (202) 226-2055.*
General email, usbg@aoc.gov

Web, www.usbg.gov and Twitter, @USBotanicGarden

Collects, cultivates, and grows various plants for public display and study; identifies botanic specimens and furnishes information on proper growing methods. Conducts horticultural classes and tours.

American Horticultural Society, *River Farm, 7931 E. Boulevard Dr., Alexandria, VA 22308-1300; (703) 768-5700. Fax, (703) 768-8700. Beth Tuttle, President, (703) 768-5700, ext. 123. Member Services, ext. 119.*
General email, webmaster@ahsgardening.org

Web, http://ahsgardening.org, Twitter, @ahs_gardening and Facebook, www.facebook.com/ americanhorticulturalsociety

Promotes the expansion of horticulture in the United States through educational programs for amateur and professional horticulturists. Publishes gardening magazine. Oversees historic house and farm once owned by George Washington, with gardens maintained by staff; house and grounds are rented for special occasions.

American Society for Horticultural Science (ASHS), *1018 Duke St., Alexandria, VA 22314; (703) 836-4606. Michael W. Neff, Executive Director, ext. 106.*
General email, webmaster@ashs.org

Web, www.ashs.org and Twitter, @ASHA_Hort

Membership: educators, government workers, firms, associations, and individuals interested in horticultural science. Promotes scientific research and education in horticulture, including international exchange of information. Publishes the *Journal of the American Society for Horticultural Science.*

AmericanHort, *Washington Office, 525 9th St. N.W., #800, 20004; (202) 789-2900. Fax, (202) 789-1893. Ken Fisher, President, (614) 487-1117.*
General email, hello@AmericanHort.org

Web, www.AmericanHort.org and Twitter, @American_ Hort

Membership: wholesale growers, garden center retailers, landscape firms, and suppliers to the horticultural community. Monitors legislation and regulations on agricultural, environmental, and small business issues; conducts educational seminars on business management for members.

Society of American Florists, *1001 N. Fairfax St., #201, Alexandria, VA 22314; (703) 836-8700. Fax, (703) 836-8705. Kate Penn, Chief Executive Officer. Toll-free, (800) 336-4743.*
Web, https://safnow.org and Twitter, @SAFdelivers

Membership: growers, wholesalers, and retailers in the floriculture and ornamental horticulture industries. Interests include labor, pesticides, the environment, international trade, and toxicity of plants. Mediates industry problems.

Soil and Watershed Conservation

Farm Service Agency (FSA) *(Agriculture Dept.), Conservation and Environmental Programs, 1400 Independence Ave. S.W., Room 4709-S, MS 0513, 20250-0513; (202) 720-6221. Fax, (202) 720-4619. Misty Jones, Director.*
Web, www.fsa.usda.gov

Directs conservation and environmental projects and programs to help farmers and ranchers prevent soil erosion and contamination of natural resources.

National Agricultural Library *(Agriculture Dept.), Water and Agricultural Information Center (WAIC), 10301 Baltimore Ave., 1st Floor, Beltsville, MD 20705-2351; (301) 504-6077. Vacant, Coordinator, (301) 504-6218. Web, www.nal.usda.gov/waic*

Serves individuals and agencies seeking information on water quality and agriculture. Special subject areas include agricultural environmental management, irrigation, water availability, and water quality.

Natural Resources Conservation Service *(Agriculture Dept.), 1400 Independence Ave. S.W., #5105AS, 20250 (mailing address: P.O. Box 2890, Washington, DC 20013-2890); (202) 720-3210. Fax, (202) 720-7690. Mathew Lohr, Chief, (202) 720-7246.*
General email, nrcsdistributioncenter@ia.usda.gov

Web, www.nrcs.usda.gov and Twitter, @USDA_NRCS

Responsible for soil and water conservation programs, including watershed protection, flood prevention, river basin surveys, and resource conservation and development. Provides landowners, operators, state and local units of government, and community groups with technical assistance in carrying out local programs. Inventories and monitors soil, water, and related resource data and resource use trends. Provides information about soil surveys, farmlands, and other natural resources.

American Farmland Trust (AFT), *1150 Connecticut Ave. N.W., #600, 20036; (202) 331-7300. John Piotti, President, (202) 378-1202.*
General email, info@farmland.org

Web, www.farmland.org, Twitter, @farmland and Facebook, www.facebook.com/AmericanFarmland

Works to protect farmland, promote sound farming practices, and keep farmers on the land through local, regional, and national efforts. Works to help farmers implement practices that protect water quality. Conducts independent analyses of policies that affect farmland and advocates government policies that support farmland conservation and keep farms economically viable.

Irrigation Assn., *8280 Willow Oaks Corporate Dr., #400, Fairfax, VA 22031; (703) 536-7080. Fax, (703) 536-7019. Deborah Hamlin, Chief Executive Officer.*

General email, info@irrigation.org

Web, www.irrigation.org

Membership: companies and individuals involved in irrigation, drainage, and erosion control worldwide. Promotes efficient and effective water management through training, education, and certification programs. Interests include economic development and environmental enhancement.

National Assn. of Clean Water Agencies, *1130 Connecticut Ave. N.W., 20036; (202) 833-2672. Fax, (888) 267-9505. Adam Krantz, Chief Executive Officer, (202) 833-4651.*

General email, info@nacwa.org

Web, www.nacwa.org and Twitter, @NACWA

Represents public wastewater treatment works, public and private organizations, law firms representing public clean water agencies, and nonprofit or academic organizations. Interests include water quality and watershed management. Sponsors conferences. Monitors legislation and regulations.

National Assn. of Conservation Districts (NACD), *509 Capitol Court N.E., 20002-4937; (202) 547-6223. Fax, (202) 547-6450. Jeremy Peters, Chief Executive Officer.*

General email, stewardship@nacdnet.org

Web, www.nacdnet.org and Twitter, @NACDconserve

Membership: conservation districts (local subdivisions of state government). Works to promote the conservation of land, forests, and other natural resources. Interests include erosion and sediment control, water quality, and water and flood plain management.

Winrock International, *Washington Office, 2121 Crystal Dr., #500, Arlington, VA 22202; (703) 302-6500. Fax, (703) 302-6512. Rodney Ferguson, President.*

General email, information@winrock.org

Web, www.winrock.org and Twitter, @WinrockIntl

Addresses international water issues through programs targeting sustainable strategies for use and conservation within communities and watersheds. (Headquarters in Little Rock, Ark.)

COMMODITIES, FARM PRODUCE

General

▶**AGENCIES**

Agricultural Marketing Service (AMS) *(Agriculture Dept.), Fair Trade Practices Program, Country of Origin Labeling (COOL), 1400 Independence Ave. S.W., #2614-S, MS 0216, 20250-0216; (202) 720-4486. Randall D. Jones, Deputy Administer of Fair Trade, (202) 720-0219.*

General email, cool@ams.usda.gov

Web, www.ams.usda.gov/rules-regulations/cool

Works with businesses to uphold the origin labeling law, which requires retailers to disclose the source of certain foods, including meats and vegetables, to their customers.

Agricultural Marketing Service (AMS) *(Agriculture Dept.), National Organic Program, 1400 Independence Ave. S.W., Room 2642, STOP 0268, 20250 (mailing address: 1400 Independence Ave. S.W., MS 0268, Washington, DC 20250); (202) 720-3252. Fax, (202) 260-9151. Jennifer Tucker, Deputy Administrator.*

Web, www.ams.usda.gov/about-ams/programs-offices/national-organic-program

Develops national standards and regulations for organically produced agricultural products; accredits certifying agents to certify organic producers and handlers; establishes international organic import and export policies; investigates regulatory violation complaints.

Agricultural Marketing Service (AMS) *(Agriculture Dept.), Transportation and Marketing Programs, 1400 Independence Ave. S.W., #4543, 20250-0264; (202) 690-1300. Arthur Neal, Deputy Administrator.*

Web, www.ams.usda.gov/about-ams/programs-offices/transportation-marketing-program

Promotes efficient, cost-effective marketing and transportation for U.S. agricultural products; sets standards for domestic and international marketing of organic products. Provides exporters with market information, educational services, and regulatory representation.

Agriculture Dept. (USDA), *Under Secretary for Marketing and Regulatory Programs, 1400 Independence Ave. S.W., #228W, MS 0109, 20250-0109; (202) 720-4256. Fax, (202) 720-5775. Gregory (Greg) Ibach, Under Secretary.*

Web, www.usda.gov/our-agency/about-usda/mission-areas

Administers inspection and grading services and regulatory programs for agricultural commodities through the Agricultural Marketing Service and Animal and Plant Health Inspection Service.

Agriculture Dept. (USDA), *Under Secretary for Trade and Foreign Agricultural Affairs, 1400 Independence Ave. S.W., MS 1001, 20250; (202) 720-3935. Ted McKinney, Under Secretary.*

Web, www.fas.usda.gov

Leads on trade policy and international agriculture issues domestically and abroad; facilitates foreign market access and promotes opportunities for U.S. agriculture through trade programs and high-level government negotiations. Oversees the Foreign Agricultural Service.

Animal and Plant Health Inspection Service (APHIS) *(Agriculture Dept.), 1400 Independence Ave. S.W., #312E, MS 3401, 20250-3401; (202) 799-7030. Fax, (202) 720-3982. Kevin A. Shea, Administrator, (202) 799-7017. Customer service, (844) 820-2234. Plants and Plant Products, (877) 770-5990. Press, (301) 851-4100. Veterinary services, (301) 851-3300.*

General email, customerservicecallcenter@aphis.usda.gov

Web, www.aphis.usda.gov and Twitter, @USDA_APHIS

Administers programs in cooperation with the states to prevent the spread of pests and plant diseases; inspects imported animals, flowers, and plants; licenses the manufacture and marketing of veterinary biologics to ensure purity and effectiveness; certifies that U.S. exports are free of pests and disease.

Bureau of Economic and Business Affairs (EB) *(State Dept.), Trade Policy and Negotiations (TPN), Agriculture Policy (AGP), 2201 C St. N.W., #4686, 20520-0002; (202) 647-3090. Fax, (202) 647-1894. Patrick M. Dunn, Director, (202) 647-0133. Web, www.state.gov/e/eb/tpn/agp*

Negotiates bilateral textile trade agreements with foreign governments concerning cotton, wool, and synthetic textile and apparel products.

Commodity Futures Trading Commission, *Three Lafayette Centre, 1155 21st St. N.W., 20581-0001; (202) 418-5000. Fax, (202) 418-5521. J. Christopher Giancarlo, Chair, (202) 418-5030. Toll-free, (866) 366-2382. TTY, (202) 418-5428. General email, questions@cftc.gov Web, www.cftc.gov and Twitter, @CFTC*

Oversees the Commodity Exchange Act, which regulates all commodity futures and options, including agricultural commodities such as wheat, corn, and cotton, to prevent fraudulent trade practices.

Farm Service Agency (FSA) *(Agriculture Dept.), 1400 Independence Ave. S.W., #3086, MS 0506, 20250-0506; (202) 720-3467. Fax, (202) 720-9105. Richard Fordyce, Administrator. Press, (202) 720-7807. Web, www.fsa.usda.gov and Twitter, @usdafsa*

Administers farm commodity programs providing crop loans and purchases; provides crop payments when market prices fall below specified levels; sets acreage allotments and marketing quotas; assists farmers in areas affected by natural disasters.

Farm Service Agency (FSA) *(Agriculture Dept.), Commodity Credit Corp. (CCC), 1400 Independence Ave. S.W., MS 0599, 20250-0571; (202) 720-0402. Fax, (202) 245-4786. Robert Stephenson, Secretary. General email, Robert.Stephenson@wdc.usda.gov Web, www.fsa.usda.gov/about-fsa/structure-and-organization/commodity-credit-corporation/index*

Finances commodity stabilization programs, domestic and export surplus commodity disposal, foreign assistance, storage activities, and related programs.

Foreign Agricultural Service (FAS) *(Agriculture Dept.), 1400 Independence Ave. S.W., #5071S, MS 1001, 20250-1001; (202) 720-3935. Fax, (202) 690-2159. Kenneth Isley, Administrator. Public Affairs, (202) 720-7115. TTY, (202) 720-1786. Web, www.fas.usda.gov and Twitter, @USDAForeignAg*

Promotes exports of U.S. food and agricultural products; represents U.S. agricultural interests in international trade negotiations. Coordinates activities of U.S. representatives in foreign countries who report on crop

and market conditions. Provides programs and services that assist U.S. agricultural exporters with promoting their products overseas. Analyzes world demand and production of various commodities. Monitors sales by private exporters.

Foreign Agricultural Service (FAS) *(Agriculture Dept.), Trade Programs, 1400 Independence Ave. S.W., MS 1020, 20250-1020; (202) 720-9516. Fax, (202) 401-0135. Mark Slupek, Deputy Administrator. Web, www.fas.usda.gov/trade-programs*

Administers programs and provides services that help U.S. exporters develop and maintain international markets for U.S. farm and food products. Provides credit guarantees to encourage financing of commercial exports of U.S. agricultural products.

► **CONGRESS**

For a listing of relevant congressional committees and subcommittees, please see page 3 or the Appendix.

► **NONGOVERNMENTAL**

Commodity Markets Council (CMC), *600 Pennsylvania Ave. S.E., #300, 20003; (202) 547-3035. Jim Newsome, President. Web, www.commoditymkts.org and Twitter, @CommodityMkts*

Federation of commodity futures exchanges, boards of trade, and industry stakeholders, including commodity merchandisers, processors, and refiners; futures commission merchants; food and beverage manufacturers; transportation companies; and financial institutions. Combines members' expertise to formulate positions on market, policy, and contracting issues involving commodities, with an overall goal of facilitating growth in liquidity and transparency in cash and derivative markets. Monitors legislation and regulations. (Formerly the National Grain Trade Council.)

Global Cold Chain Alliance, *241 18th St. S, #620, Arlington, VA 22202; (703) 373-4300. Fax, (703) 373-4301. Corey Rosenbusch, President. General email, email@gcca.org Web, www.gcca.org and Twitter, @gccaorg*

Membership: owners and operators of public refrigerated warehouses. Interests include labor, transportation, taxes, environment, safety, regulatory compliance, and food distribution. Monitors legislation and regulations. (Affiliated with the International Refrigerated Transportation Assn., the International Assn. for Cold Storage Construction, and the International Assn. of Refrigerated Warehouses.)

National Cooperative Business Assn., CLUSA International (NCBA CLUSA), *1775 Eye St. N.W., 8th Floor, 20006; (202) 638-6222. Douglas O'Brien, President. General email, info@ncba.coop Web, www.ncba.coop, Twitter, @NCBA.coop and Facebook, www.facebook.com/NCBACLUSA*

Alliance of cooperatives, businesses, and state cooperative associations. Provides information about starting and managing agricultural cooperatives in the United States and in developing nations. Monitors legislation and regulations.

National Council of Farmer Cooperatives (NCFC), *50 F St. N.W., #900, 20001-1530; (202) 626-8700. Fax, (202) 626-8722. Charles (Chuck) F. Conner, President; Mary Nowak, Director of Government Affairs.*
General email, info@ncfc.org

Web, www.ncfc.org and Twitter, @FarmerCoop

Membership: cooperative businesses owned and operated by farmers. Encourages research on agricultural cooperatives; provides statistics and analyzes trends. Monitors legislation and regulations on agricultural trade, transportation, energy, and tax issues.

Organic Trade Assn., *444 N. Capitol St. N.W., #445A, 20001; (202) 403-8520. Laura Batcha, Executive Director, (202) 403-8512. Media, (202) 403-8514.*
General email, info@ota.com

Web, www.ota.com, Twitter, @OrganicTrade and Facebook, www.facebook.com/OrganicTrade

Membership: growers, shippers, processors, certifiers, farmers' associations, distributors, importers, exporters, consultants, and retailers of organic foods, beverages, ingredients, and fibers. Promotes organic farming processes. Monitors legislation and regulations.

U.S. Agricultural Export Development Council, *2111 Wilson Blvd., #700, Arlington, VA 22201; (703) 556-9290. Lorena Alfaro, Executive Director.*
General email, info@usaedc.org

Web, http://usaedc.org

Membership: agricultural growers and processors, commodity trade associations, farmer cooperatives, and state regional trade groups. Works with the Foreign Agricultural Service on projects to create, expand, and maintain agricultural markets abroad. Sponsors seminars and workshops.

Cotton

►AGENCIES

Farm Service Agency (FSA) *(Agriculture Dept.), Fibers, Peanuts, and Tobacco Analysis, 1400 Independence Ave. S.W., #37605, MS 0515, 20250-0515; (202) 720-3392. Fax, (202) 690-2186. Scott Sanford, Director.*
Web, www.fsa.usda.gov/programs-and-services/economic-and-policy-analysis/fibers-peanuts-tobacco

Develops production adjustment and price support programs to balance supply and demand for cotton, peanuts, and tobacco.

►INTERNATIONAL ORGANIZATIONS

International Cotton Advisory Committee, *1629 K St. N.W., #702, 20006-1636; (202) 463-6660. Fax, (202) 463-6950. Kai Hughes, Executive Director, ext. 116.*
General email, secretariat@icac.org

Web, www.icac.org

Membership: cotton producing and consuming countries. Provides information on cotton production, trade, consumption, stocks, and prices.

►NONGOVERNMENTAL

Cotton Council International, *1521 New Hampshire Ave. N.W., 20036-1203; (202) 745-7805. Fax, (202) 483-4040. Bruce Atherley, Executive Director.*
General email, cottonusa@cotton.org

Web, www.cottonusa.org and Facebook, www.facebook.com/cottonusa.global

Division of National Cotton Council of America. Promotes U.S. raw cotton and cotton-product exports.

Cotton Warehouse Assn. of America, *316 Pennsylvania Ave. S.E., #401, 20003; (202) 544-5875. Fax, (202) 544-5874. Larry Combest, Executive Vice President.*
General email, cwaa@cottonwarehouse.org

Web, http://cottonwarehouse.org

Membership: cotton compress and warehouse operators. Serves as a liaison between members and government agencies; monitors legislation and regulations.

National Cotton Council of America, *Washington Office, 1521 New Hampshire Ave. N.W., 20036-1205; (202) 745-7805. Fax, (202) 483-4040. Reece Langley, Vice President, Washington Operations.*
Web, www.cotton.org and Twitter, @NCottonCouncil

Membership: all segments of the U.S. cotton industry. Provides statistics and information on such topics as cotton history and processing. (Headquarters in Memphis, Tenn.)

Dairy Products and Eggs

►AGENCIES

Agricultural Marketing Service (AMS) *(Agriculture Dept.), Dairy Program, 1400 Independence Ave. S.W., Room 2968, S 0225, 20250-0225; (202) 720-4392. Fax, (202) 690-3410. Dana H. Coale, Deputy Administrator.*
Web, www.ams.usda.gov/about-ams/programs-offices/dairy-program

Email, AskDairy@usda.gov

Administers dairy product marketing, research, and promotion programs; grades dairy products; maintains market news service on daily price changes; sets minimum price that farmers receive for milk. Provides export certification.

Agricultural Marketing Service (AMS) *(Agriculture Dept.), Livestock and Poultry Program, 1400 Independence Ave. S.W., Room S.0292 STOP 0249, 20250-0249 (mailing address: 1400 Independence Ave., MS 0249, Washington, DC 20250); (202) 720-5705. Fax, (202) 720-3499. Jennifer Tucker, Deputy Administrator.*

General email, AskLPS@ams.usda.gov

Web, www.ams.usda.gov/about-ams/programs-offices/livestock-poultry-program

Sets poultry and egg grading standards. Provides promotion and market news services for domestic and international markets.

Farm Service Agency (FSA) *(Agriculture Dept.), Dairy and Sweeteners Analysis, 1400 Independence Ave. S.W., #3752, MS 0516, 20250-0516; (202) 720-4146. Fax, (202) 690-1480. Barbara Fecso, Group Director.*

Web, www.fsa.usda.gov/programs-and-services/economic-and-policy-analysis/dairy-and-sweeteners-analysis

Develops production adjustment and price support programs to balance supply and demand for certain commodities, including dairy products, sugar, and honey.

►NONGOVERNMENTAL

American Butter Institute (ABI), *2107 Wilson Blvd., #600, Arlington, VA 22201-3062; (703) 243-5630. Fax, (703) 841-9328. Tom Balmer, Executive Director, ext. 346.*

General email, info@nmpf.org

Web, www.butterinstitute.org and

Twitter, @butterinstitute

Membership: butter manufacturers, packagers, and distributors. Interests include dairy price supports and programs, packaging and labeling, and imports. Monitors legislation and regulations.

Humane Farm Animal Care, *P.O. Box 82, Middleburg, VA 20118; (703) 435-3883. Fax, (703) 435-3981. Adele Douglass, Chief Executive Officer; Mimi Stein, Executive Director.*

General email, info@certifiedhumane.org

Web, www.certifiedhumane.org,

Twitter, @CertifiedHumane and Facebook, www.facebook.com/CertifiedHumane

Seeks to improve the welfare of farm animals by providing viable, duly monitored standards for humane food production. Administers the Certified Humane Raised and Handled program for meat, poultry, eggs, and dairy products.

International Dairy Foods Assn., *1250 H St. N.W., #900, 20005-3952; (202) 737-4332. Fax, (202) 331-7820. Michael Dykes, President.*

General email, membership@idfa.org

Web, www.idfa.org

Membership: processors, manufacturers, marketers, and distributors of dairy foods in the United States and abroad. Provides members with marketing, public relations, training, and management services. Monitors legislation and regulations. (Affiliated with the Milk Industry Foundation, the National Cheese Institute, and the International Ice Cream Assn.)

National Ice Cream Mix Assn., *2107 Wilson Blvd., #600, Arlington, VA 22201; (703) 243-5630. Fax, (703) 841-9328. Tom Balmer, President.*

Web, www.icecreammix.org

Nonprofit representing the manufacturing industry of ice cream mix, soft serve frozen dessert mix, and shake mix.

National Milk Producers Federation, *2101 Wilson Blvd., #600, Arlington, VA 22201-3062; (703) 243-6111. Fax, (703) 841-9328. Jim Mulhern, Chief Executive Officer.*

General email, info@nmpf.org

Web, www.nmpf.org

Membership: dairy farmer cooperatives. Provides information on development and modification of sanitary regulations, product standards, and marketing procedures for dairy products.

Fruits and Vegetables

►AGENCIES

Agricultural Marketing Service (AMS) *(Agriculture Dept.), Fair Trade Practices Program, Perishable Agricultural Commodities Act (PACA), 1400 Independence Ave. S.W., #1510-S, MS 0242, 20250-0242; (202) 720-4180. Fax, (202) 690-4413. Judith W. Rudman, Director. Toll-free, (800) 495-7222.*

Web, www.ams.usda.gov/rules-regulations/paca

Disputes, PACAdispute@ams.usda.gov

Investigations, PACAInvestigations@ams.usda.gov

License, PACALicense@ams.usda.gov

Partners with fresh and frozen fruit and vegetable businesses to enforce fair business practices and resolve disputes involving inspection certificates, contracts, and bankruptcy payments.

Agricultural Marketing Service (AMS) *(Agriculture Dept.), Specialty Crops Program, 1400 Independence Ave. S.W., #S2077, 20250-0235 (mailing address: 1400 Independence Ave. S.W., MS 0235, Washington, DC 20250); (202) 720-4722. Fax, (202) 720-0016. Sonia Jimenez, Deputy Administrator.*

Web, www.ams.usda.gov/about-ams/programs-offices/specialty-crops-program

Administers research, marketing, promotional, and regulatory programs for fruits, vegetables, nuts, ornamental plants, and other specialty crops; focus includes international markets. Sets grading standards for fresh and processed fruits and vegetables; conducts quality inspections; maintains market news service to inform producers of price changes.

Economic Research Service *(Agriculture Dept.), 355 E St. S.W., 20024-8221; (202) 694-5000. Fax, (202) 245-5467. Mary Bohman, Administrator; Greg Pompelli, Associate Administrator.*

General email, service@ers.usda.gov

Web, www.ers.usda.gov and Twitter, @USDA_ERS

Conducts market research; studies and forecasts domestic supply-and-demand trends for fruits and vegetables.

U.S. Apple Assn., *7600 Leesburg Pike, #400 East, Falls Church, VA 22043; (703) 442-8850. James (Jim) Bair, President.*
General email, info@usapple.org
Web, http://usapple.org and Twitter, @US_Apples

Membership: U.S. commercial apple growers and processors, distributors, exporters, importers, and retailers of apples. Promotes nutrition research and marketing; provides information about apples and nutrition to educators. Monitors legislation and regulations.

United Fresh Produce Assn., *1901 Pennsylvania Ave. N.W., #1100, 20006; (202) 303-3400. Fax, (202) 303-3433. Tom Stenzel, President, (202) 303-3406.*
Web, www.unitedfresh.org and Twitter, @UnitedFresh

Membership: growers, shippers, wholesalers, retailers, food service operators, importers, and exporters involved in producing and marketing fresh fruits and vegetables. Represents the industry before the government and the public sector.

Wine Institute, *Federal and International Public Policy, 601 13th St. N.W., #330 South, 20005-3866; (202) 408-0870. Fax, (202) 371-0061. Charles Jefferson, Vice President.*
Web, www.wineinstitute.org and Twitter, @CalifWines_US

Membership: California wineries and affiliated businesses. Seeks international recognition for California wines; conducts promotional campaigns in other countries. Monitors legislation and regulations. (Headquarters in San Francisco, Calif.)

Grains and Oilseeds

Agricultural Marketing Service (AMS) *(Agriculture Dept.), Federal Grain Inspection Service (FGIS), 1400 Independence Ave. S.W., #3614, 20250-3601; (202) 720-9170. Fax, (202) 690-2333. Dana H. Coale, Administrator (Acting), (202) 720-4392.*
General email, gipsa-webmaster@usda.gov
Web, www.gipsa.usda.gov/fgis/fgis.aspx

Administers inspection and weighing program for barley, canola, corn, flaxseed, oats, rye, sorghum, soybeans, sunflower seed, triticale, wheat, mixed grain, rice, and pulses; conducts quality inspections based on established standards; supervises the official grain inspection and weighing system.

Agricultural Marketing Service (AMS) *(Agriculture Dept.), Livestock and Poultry Program, 1400 Independence Ave. S.W., Room S.0292 STOP 0249, 20250-0249 (mailing address: 1400 Independence Ave., MS 0249, Washington, DC 20250); (202) 720-5705. Fax, (202) 720-3499. Jennifer Tucker, Deputy Administrator.*

General email, AskLPS@ams.usda.gov
Web, www.ams.usda.gov/about-ams/programs-offices/livestock-poultry-program

Administers programs for marketing grain, including rice; maintains market news service to inform producers of grain market situation and daily price changes.

Farm Service Agency (FSA) *(Agriculture Dept.), Feed Grains and Oilseeds Analysis, 1400 Independence Ave. S.W., #3740S, MS 0532, 20250-0532; (202) 720-2711. Fax, (202) 690-2186. Philip Sronce, Group Director.*
Web, www.fsa.usda.gov/programs-and-services/economic-and-policy-analysis/feed-grains-and-oilseeds-analysis

Develops, analyzes, and implements domestic farm policy focusing on corn, soybeans, and other feed grains and oilseeds. Develops production adjustment and price support programs to balance supply and demand for these commodities.

Farm Service Agency (FSA) *(Agriculture Dept.), Food Grains Analysis, 1400 Independence Ave. S.W., MS 0518, 20250-0532; (202) 720-2891. Fax, (202) 690-2186. Thomas F. Tice, Director.*
Web, www.fsa.usda.gov/programs-and-services/economic-and-policy-analysis/food-grains-analysis

Develops marketing loan and contract crop programs in support of food grain commodities, including wheat, rice, and pulse crops.

American Feed Industry Assn. (AFIA), *2101 Wilson Blvd., #810, Arlington, VA 22201; (703) 524-0810. Fax, (703) 524-1921. Joel G. Newman, President; Louise Calderwood, Director of Regulatory Affairs.*
General email, afia@afia.org
Web, www.afia.org and Twitter, @FeedFolks

Membership: more than 5,000 feed manufacturers, pharmaceutical companies, and ingredient suppliers and integrators. Conducts seminars on feed grain production, marketing, advertising, and quality control; interests include international trade. Monitors legislation and regulations.

American Seed Trade Assn. (ASTA), *1701 Duke St., #275, Alexandria, VA 22314-2878; (703) 837-8140. Fax, (703) 837-9365. Andrew (Andy) W. LaVigne, President. Toll-free, (888) 890-7333.*
General email, info@betterseed.org
Web, www.betterseed.org, Twitter, @Better_Seed and Facebook, www.facebook.com/BetterSeedBetterLife

Membership: producers and merchandisers of seeds. Conducts seminars on research developments in corn, sorghum, soybean, and other farm and garden seeds; promotes overseas seed market development.

American Soybean Assn., *Washington Office, 600 Pennsylvania Ave. S.E., #320, 20003-6300; (202) 969-8900. John Gordley, Director, Washington Office, (202) 969-7040.*

General email, membership@soy.org

Web, www.soygrowers.com

Membership: soybean farmers. Promotes expanded world markets and research for the benefit of soybean growers; maintains a network of state and international offices. Monitors legislation and regulations. (Headquarters in St. Louis, Mo.)

Bakery, Confectionery, Tobacco Workers, and Grain Millers International Union, *10401 Connecticut Ave., 4th Floor, Kensington, MD 20895-3940; (301) 933-8600. Fax, (301) 946-8452. David B. Durkee, President.*
General email, bctgmwebmaster@gmail.com

Web, www.bctgm.org and Twitter, @BCTGM

Membership: approximately 120,000 workers from the bakery, confectionery, grain miller, and tobacco industries. Helps members negotiate pay, benefits, and better working conditions; conducts training programs and workshops. Monitors legislation and regulations. (Affiliated with the AFL-CIO.)

Corn Refiners Assn., *1701 Pennsylvania Ave. N.W., #400, 20006-5805; (202) 331-1634. Fax, (202) 331-2054. John Bode, Chief Executive Officer.*
General email, comments@corn.org

Web, https://corn.org and Twitter, @CornRefiners

Promotes research on technical aspects of corn refining and product development; acts as a clearinghouse for members who award research grants to colleges and universities. Monitors legislation and regulations.

National Assn. of Wheat Growers, *415 2nd St. N.E., #200, 20002-4993; (202) 547-7800. Chandler Goule, Chief Executive Officer.*
General email, wheatworld@wheatworld.org

Web, www.wheatworld.org and Twitter, @wheatworld

Federation of state wheat grower associations. Involved with federal farm policy, environmental issues, and the use of biotechnology. Monitors legislation and regulations.

National Corn Growers Assn., Public Policy, *20 F St. N.W., #600, 20001; (202) 628-7001. Fax, (202) 628-1933. Kathy Reding Berrgren, Director of Public Policy.*
General email, corninfo@ncga.com

Web, www.ncga.com, Twitter, @NationalCorn and Facebook, www.facebook.com/corngrowers

Represents the interests of U.S. corn farmers, including in international trade; promotes the use, marketing, and efficient production of corn; conducts research and educational activities; monitors legislation and regulations. (Headquarters in St. Louis, Mo.)

National Grain and Feed Assn., *1400 Crystal Dr., #260, Arlington, VA 22202; (202) 289-0873. Fax, (202) 289-5388. Randall (Randy) C. Gordon, President.*
General email, ngfa@ngfa.org

Web, www.ngfa.org and Twitter, @NGFA

Membership: firms that process, handle, and use U.S. grains and oilseeds in domestic and export markets; commodity futures brokers; and others involved with futures markets. Additional panel resolves disputes over trade and commercial regulations.

National Institute of Oilseed Products, *600 New Hampshire Ave. N.W., #500, 20037; (202) 591-2461. Fax, (202) 591-2445. Leigh Wickersham, Executive Director; John C. Dillard, Legal Counsel, in Washington, D.C.*
General email, niop@kellencompany.com

Web, www.niop.org

Membership: companies and individuals involved in manufacturing and trading oilseed products. Maintains standards for trading and transport of vegetable oils and oilseeds worldwide. (Headquarters in Columbia, S.C.)

National Oilseed Processors Assn., *1300 L St. N.W., #1020, 20005-4168; (202) 842-0463. Fax, (202) 842-9126. Thomas A. Hammer, President.*
General email, jseibert@nopa.org

Web, www.nopa.org

Provides information on oilseed crops, products, processing, and commodity programs; interests include international trade.

North American Export Grain and Oilseed Assn. (NAEGA), *1400 Crystal Dr., #260, Arlington, VA 22202; (202) 682-4030. Fax, (202) 682-4033. Gary C. Martin, President.*
General email, info@naega.org

Web, www.naega.org

Membership: grain and oilseed exporting firms and others interested in the grain export industry. Provides information on grain export and contracting; sponsors foreign seminars. Monitors domestic and international legislation and regulations.

North American Millers' Assn., *1400 Crystal Dr., #650, Arlington, VA 22202; (202) 484-2200. Fax, (202) 488-7416. James A. McCarthy, President.*
General email, generalinfo@namamillers.org

Web, www.namamillers.org, Twitter, @NAMAmillers and Facebook, www.facebook.com/NAMAmillers

Trade association representing the dry corn, wheat, oats, and rye milling industry. Seeks to inform the public, the industry, and government about issues affecting the domestic milling industry. Monitors legislation and regulations.

Soyfoods Assn. of North America, *1101 17th St. N.W., #700, 20036; (202) 659-3520. John H. Cox, Executive Director.*
General email, info@soyfoods.org

Web, www.soyfoods.org and Twitter, @SocialSANA

Membership: large and small soyfood companies, growers and suppliers of soybeans, nutritionists, equipment representatives, food scientists, and retailers. Promotes soybean consumption. Helps establish standards for soyfoods. Monitors legislation and regulations.

U.S. Grains Council, *20 F St. N.W., #600, 20001; (202) 789-0789. Fax, (202) 898-0522. Thomas Sleight, President. General email, grains@grains.org*

Web, www.grains.org and Twitter, @USGC

Membership: barley, corn, DDGS, ethanol, and sorghum producers and exporters; and chemical, machinery, malting, and seed companies interested in feed grain exports. Promotes development of U.S. feed grain markets overseas.

U.S. Wheat Associates, *3103 10th St. North, #300, Arlington, VA 22201; (202) 463-0999. Fax, (571) 386-4854. Vince Peterson, President, (703) 650-0250. General email, infoARL@uswheat.org*

Web, www.uswheat.org and Twitter, @uswheatassoc

Membership: wheat farmers. Develops export markets for the U.S. wheat industry; provides information on wheat production and marketing. Interests include trade policy, food aid, and biotechnology.

USA Rice Federation, *2101 Wilson Blvd., #610, Arlington, VA 22201; (703) 236-2300. Fax, (703) 236-2301. Betsy Ward, Chief Executive Officer. Toll-free, (800) 888-7423. TTY, (703) 236-2310. General email, riceinfo@usarice.com*

Web, www.usarice.com and Twitter, @usaricenews

Membership: rice producers, millers, merchants, and related firms. Provides U.S. and foreign rice trade and industry information; assists in establishing quality standards for rice production and milling. Monitors legislation and regulations.

Sugar

▶AGENCIES

Economic Research Service *(Agriculture Dept.), 355 E St. S.W., 20024-8221; (202) 694-5000. Fax, (202) 245-5467. Mary Bohman, Administrator; Greg Pompelli, Associate Administrator. General email, service@ers.usda.gov*

Web, www.ers.usda.gov and Twitter, @USDA_ERS

Conducts market research; studies and forecasts domestic supply-and-demand trends for sugar and other sweeteners.

Farm Service Agency (FSA) *(Agriculture Dept.), Dairy and Sweeteners Analysis, 1400 Independence Ave. S.W., #3752, MS 0516, 20250-0516; (202) 720-4146. Fax, (202) 690-1480. Barbara Fecso, Group Director. Web, www.fsa.usda.gov/programs-and-services/economic-and-policy-analysis/dairy-and-sweeteners-analysis*

Develops production adjustment and price support programs to balance supply and demand for certain commodities, including dairy products, sugar, and honey.

▶NONGOVERNMENTAL

American Sugar Alliance, *2111 Wilson Blvd., #700, Arlington, VA 22201-3051; (703) 351-5055. Fax, (703) 351-6698. Vickie R. Myers, Executive Director. General email, info@sugaralliance.org*

Web, www.sugaralliance.org and Twitter, @SugarAlliance

National coalition of sugarcane and sugarbeet farmers, processors, refiners, suppliers, workers, and others dedicated to preserving a strong domestic sweetener industry. Monitors legislation and regulations.

American Sugarbeet Growers Assn., *1155 15th St. N.W., #1100, 20005-1756; (202) 833-2398. Fax, (240) 235-4291. Luther Markwart, Executive Vice President. General email, info@americansugarbeet.org*

Web, www.americansugarbeet.org

Membership: sugarbeet growers associations. Serves as liaison to U.S. government agencies, including the Agriculture Dept. and the U.S. Trade Representative; interests include international trade. Monitors legislation and regulations.

Bakery, Confectionery, Tobacco Workers, and Grain Millers International Union, *10401 Connecticut Ave., 4th Floor, Kensington, MD 20895-3940; (301) 933-8600. Fax, (301) 946-8452. David B. Durkee, President. General email, bctgmwebmaster@gmail.com*

Web, www.bctgm.org and Twitter, @BCTGM

Membership: approximately 120,000 workers from the bakery, confectionery, grain miller, and tobacco industries. Helps members negotiate pay, benefits, and better working conditions; conducts training programs and workshops. Monitors legislation and regulations. (Affiliated with the AFL-CIO.)

National Confectioners Assn., *1101 30th St. N.W., #200, 20007; (202) 534-1440. Fax, (202) 337-0637. John H. Downs Jr., President. General email, info@candyusa.com*

Web, www.candyusa.com, Twitter, @CandyUSA and Facebook, www.facebook.com/ NationalConfectionersAssociation

Membership: confectionery manufacturers and suppliers. Provides information on confectionery consumption and nutrition; sponsors educational programs and research on candy technology. Monitors legislation and regulations.

Sugar Assn., *1310 L St. N.W., #860, 20005-4263; (202) 785-1122. Fax, (202) 785-5019. Courtney Gaine, President. General email, sugar@sugar.org*

Web, www.sugar.org and Twitter, @MoreToSugar

Membership: sugar processors, growers, refiners, and planters. Provides nutritional information, public education, and research on sugar.

U.S. Beet Sugar Assn., *50 F St. N.W., #625, 20001; (202) 296-4820. Fax, (202) 331-2065. Brian Baenig, President. General email, USbeet@beetsugar.org*

Web, www.beetsugar.org

Membership: beet sugar processors. Monitors legislation and regulations.

Tobacco and Peanuts

▶**AGENCIES**

Economic Research Service *(Agriculture Dept.), 355 E St. S.W., 20024-8221; (202) 694-5000. Fax, (202) 245-5467. Mary Bohman, Administrator; Greg Pompelli, Associate Administrator. General email, service@ers.usda.gov*

Web, www.ers.usda.gov and Twitter, @USDA_ERS

Conducts market research; studies and forecasts domestic supply-and-demand trends for tobacco.

Farm Service Agency (FSA) *(Agriculture Dept.), Fibers, Peanuts, and Tobacco Analysis, 1400 Independence Ave. S.W., #37605, MS 0515, 20250-0515; (202) 720-3392. Fax, (202) 690-2186. Scott Sanford, Director. Web, www.fsa.usda.gov/programs-and-services/economic-and-policy-analysis/fibers-peanuts-tobacco*

Develops production adjustment and price support programs to balance supply and demand for cotton, peanuts, and tobacco.

▶**NONGOVERNMENTAL**

American Peanut Council, *1500 King St., #301, Alexandria, VA 22314-2737; (703) 838-9500. Fax, (703) 838-9508. Patrick Archer, President, ext. 106. General email, info@peanutsusa.com*

Web, www.peanutsusa.com and Twitter, @pnutsusa

Membership: peanut growers, shellers, brokers, and manufacturers, as well as allied domestic and international companies. Provides information on economic and nutritional value of peanuts; coordinates research; promotes U.S. peanut exports, domestic production, and market development.

Bakery, Confectionery, Tobacco Workers, and Grain Millers International Union, *10401 Connecticut Ave., 4th Floor, Kensington, MD 20895-3940; (301) 933-8600. Fax, (301) 946-8452. David B. Durkee, President. General email, bctgmwebmaster@gmail.com*

Web, www.bctgm.org and Twitter, @BCTGM

Membership: approximately 120,000 workers from the bakery, confectionery, grain miller, and tobacco industries. Helps members negotiate pay, benefits, and better working conditions; conducts training programs and workshops. Monitors legislation and regulations. (Affiliated with the AFL-CIO.)

Cigar Assn. of America, *1100 G St. N.W., #1050, 20005-7405; (202) 223-8204. Fax, (202) 833-0379. Craig P. Williamson, President. General email, cwilliamson@cigarassociation.org*

Web, http://cigarassociation.org and Twitter, @CigarAssoc

Membership: growers and suppliers of cigar leaf tobacco; manufacturers, packagers, importers, and distributors of cigars; and suppliers to the cigar industry. Monitors legislation and regulations.

FARM LOANS, INSURANCE, AND SUBSIDIES

General

▶**AGENCIES**

Agriculture Dept. (USDA), Ombudsperson, *1400 Independence Ave. S.W., 20250; (202) 205-1000. Joanne Dea, Ombudsperson. General email, ombudsperson@usda.gov*

Web, www.usda.gov/our-agency/staff-offices/office-ombudsperson

Works with female and Hispanic farmers and ranchers to address access issues to programs including Farm Service Agency, Rural Development Programs, and Natural Resources Conservation Service.

Agriculture Dept. (USDA), Rural Development, Civil Rights, *1400 Independence Ave. S.W., #1341, MS 0703, 20250-0703; Fax, (202) 692-0279. Sherese C. Paylor, Director (Acting), (202) 692-0097. Complaints, (202) 692-0090. Toll-free, (800) 787-8821. General email, rd.civilrights@wdc.usda.gov*

Web, www.rd.usda.gov/about-rd/offices/civil-rights

Enforces compliance with laws prohibiting discrimination in credit transactions on the basis of sex, marital status, race, color, religion, age, or disability. Ensures equal opportunity in granting Rural Economic and Community Development housing, farm ownership, and operating loans and a variety of community and business program loans.

Agriculture Dept. (USDA), Rural Development, Rural Business–Cooperative Service, *1400 Independence Ave. S.W., #5803-S, MS 3201, 20250-3201; (202) 690-4730. Bette Brand, Administrator. Press, (202) 690-4737. Web, www.rd.usda.gov/about-rd/agencies/rural-business-cooperative-service*

Provides financial assistance, including loans, loan guarantees, and grants to individuals, rural businesses, cooperatives, farmers, and ranchers.

Agriculture Dept. (USDA), Under Secretary for Farm Production and Conservation, *1400 Independence Ave. S.W., MS 0501, 20250-0501; (301) 574-5162. Bill Northey, Under Secretary. Information hotline, (202) 720-2791.*

Web, www.usda.gov/our-agency/about-usda/mission-areas, Twitter, @farmers.gov, Twitter, @BillatUSDA and Facebook, www.facebook.com/farmersgov

Administers programs for agricultural commodity insurance, farm loans, conservation, emergency assistance, and domestic and international food assistance. Oversees the Farm Service Agency, National Resources Conservation Service, and Risk Management Agency.

Farm Credit Administration, *1501 Farm Credit Dr., McLean, VA 22102-5090; (703) 883-4056. Fax, (703) 790-3260. Dallas P. Tonsager, Chief Executive Officer, (703) 883-4000; William J. Hoffman, Chief Operating Officer. TTY, (703) 883-4056.*
General email, info-line@fca.gov
Web, www.fca.gov

Examines and regulates the cooperative Farm Credit System, which comprises farm credit banks, one agricultural credit bank, agricultural credit associations, and federal land credit associations. Oversees credit programs and related services for farmers, ranchers, producers and harvesters of aquatic products, farm-related service businesses, rural homeowners, agricultural and aquatic cooperatives, and rural utilities.

Farm Credit Administration, *Examination, 1501 Farm Credit Dr., McLean, VA 22102-5090; (703) 883-4160. Fax, (703) 883-2978. S. Robert Coleman, Chief Examiner, (703) 883-4246.*
General email, info-line@fca.gov
Web, www.fca.gov/about/offices/offices.html

Enforces and oversees compliance with the Farm Credit Act. Monitors cooperatively owned member banks' and associations' compliance with laws prohibiting discrimination in credit transactions.

Farm Service Agency (FSA) *(Agriculture Dept.), 1400 Independence Ave. S.W., #3086, MS 0506, 20250-0506; (202) 720-3467. Fax, (202) 720-9105. Richard Fordyce, Administrator. Press, (202) 720-7807.*
Web, www.fsa.usda.gov and Twitter, @usdafsa

Oversees farm commodity programs that provide crop loans and purchases. Administers price support programs that provide crop payments when market prices fall below specified levels; conducts programs to help obtain adequate farm and commercial storage and drying equipment for farm products; directs conservation and environmental cost sharing projects and programs to assist farmers during natural disasters and other emergencies.

Farm Service Agency (FSA) *(Agriculture Dept.), Commodity Credit Corp. (CCC), 1400 Independence Ave. S.W., MS 0599, 20250-0571; (202) 720-0402. Fax, (202) 245-4786. Robert Stephenson, Secretary.*
General email, Robert.Stephenson@wdc.usda.gov
Web, www.fsa.usda.gov/about-fsa/structure-and-organization/commodity-credit-corporation/index

Administers and finances the commodity stabilization program through loans, purchases, and supplemental payments; sells through domestic and export markets commodities acquired by the government under this program; administers some aspects of foreign food aid through the Food for Peace program; provides storage facilities.

Farm Service Agency (FSA) *(Agriculture Dept.), Farm Loan Programs, 1400 Independence Ave. S.W., #3605S, MS 0520, 20250-0520; (202) 720-4671. Fax, (202) 690-3573. James Radintz, Deputy Administrator.*
Web, www.fsa.usda.gov/programs-and-services/farm-loan-programs/index

Provides services and loans to beginning farmers and ranchers and administers emergency farm and ranch loan programs.

Farm Service Agency (FSA) *(Agriculture Dept.), Farm Programs, 1400 Independence Ave. S.W., MS 0510, 20250-0510; (202) 720-3175. Fax, (202) 720-4726. Vacant, Deputy Administrator. Press, (202) 720-7807.*
Web, www.fsa.usda.gov/about-fsa/structure-and-organization/farm-programs/index

Administers and manages aid programs for farmers and ranchers, including conservation efforts, disaster relief, marketing loans, and safety-net subsidies. Operates through county offices spread throughout the continental United States, Hawaii, and several American territories.

Farm Service Agency (FSA) *(Agriculture Dept.), Minority and Socially Disadvantaged Farmers Assistance, 1400 Independence Ave. S.W., MS 0503, 20250-0503; (202) 690-1700. Fax, (202) 690-4727. J. Latrice Hill, Director of Outreach. TTY, (202) 720-5132.*
General email, oasdfr@osec.usda.gov
Web, www.fsa.usda.gov

Works with minority and socially disadvantaged farmers who have concerns and questions about loan applications filed with local offices or other Farm Service Agency programs.

Risk Management Agency *(Agriculture Dept.), 1400 Independence Ave. S.W., #6092S, MS 0801, 20250-0801; (202) 690-2803. Fax, (202) 690-2818. Martin Barbre, Administrator. Media, (202) 690-0437.*
General email, rma.cco@rma.usda.gov
Web, www.rma.usda.gov

Operates and manages the Federal Crop Insurance Corp. Provides farmers with insurance against crops lost because of bad weather, insects, disease, and other natural causes.

►CONGRESS

For a listing of relevant congressional committees and subcommittees, please see page 3 or the Appendix.

►NONGOVERNMENTAL

Farm Credit Council, *50 F St. N.W., #900, 20001-1530; (202) 626-8710. Fax, (202) 626-8718. Todd Van Hoose, President, (202) 879-0843.*
Web, www.farmcredit.com and Twitter, @farmcredit

Represents the Farm Credit System, a national financial cooperative that makes loans to agricultural producers, rural homebuyers, farmer cooperatives, and rural utilities. Finances the export of U.S. agricultural commodities.

Farmer Mac, *1999 K St. N.W., 4th Floor, 20006; (202) 872-7700. Fax, (800) 999-1814. Bradford T. Nordholm, President. Toll-free, (800) 879-3276.*
Web, www.farmermac.com

Private corporation chartered by Congress to provide a secondary mortgage market for farm and rural housing loans. Guarantees principal and interest repayment on securities backed by farm and rural housing loans. (Farmer Mac stands for Federal Agricultural Mortgage Corp.)

FOOD AND NUTRITION

General

▶**AGENCIES**

Agricultural Marketing Service (AMS) *(Agriculture Dept.), Science and Technology Program, 1400 Independence Ave. S.W., STOP 0272, 20250 (mailing address: 1400 Independence Ave. S.W., MS 0272, Washington, DC 20250); Ruihong Guo, Deputy Administrator, (202) 720-8556.*
Web, www.ams.usda.gov/about-ams/programs-offices/science-technology-program

Provides scientific, certification, and analytical support service to AMS community programs, federal and state agencies, and the private sector food industry; participates in international food safety organizations. Tests commodities traded with specific countries and regions, including butter, honey, eggs, nuts, poultry, and meat; analyzes nutritional value of U.S. military rations.

Agricultural Research Service *(Agriculture Dept.), 1400 Independence Ave. S.W., #302A, MS 0300, 20250-0300; (202) 720-3656. Fax, (202) 720-5427. Chavonda Jacobs-Young, Administrator.*
General email, Administrator@ars.usda.gov
Web, www.ars.usda.gov, Twitter, @USDA_ARS and Blog, www.ars.usda.gov/oc/blog/blogposts and Podcast, www.ars.usda.gov/oc/podcasts/index

Conducts studies on agricultural problems of domestic and international concern through nationwide network of research centers. Studies include research on human nutrition; livestock production and protection; crop production, protection, and processing; postharvest technology; and food distribution and market value.

Agriculture Dept. (USDA), *Under Secretary for Food, Nutrition, and Consumer Services, 1400 Independence Ave. S.W., #216E, 20250-0106; (202) 720-7711. Fax, (202) 690-3100. Brandon Lipps, Deputy Under Secretary.*
Web, www.fns.usda.gov and Twitter, @USDANutrition

Oversees the Food and Nutrition Service and the Center for Nutrition Policy and Promotion.

Alcohol and Tobacco Tax and Trade Bureau (TTB) *(Treasury Dept.), International Affairs Division, 1310 G St. N.W., #400W, 20005; (202) 453-2260. Fax, (202) 453-2970. Karen E. Welch, Director.*
General email, itd@ttb.gov
Web, www.ttb.gov/offices/iad.shtml

Works with the Office of the United States Trade Representative and federal executive departments to facilitate the import/export trade in beverage and industrial alcohol. Coordinates briefings and other liaison activities for foreign alcohol and tobacco industry members and foreign government officials.

Alcohol and Tobacco Tax and Trade Bureau (TTB) *(Treasury Dept.), Scientific Services Division, 6000 Ammendale Rd., Beltsville, MD 20705-1250; (240) 264-1594. Abdul Mabud, Director.*
Web, www.ttb.gov/offices/ssd.shtml

Provides technical support to the bureau to aid in revenue collection, consumer protection, unfair and unlawful market activities, minimizing technical trade barriers in international trade of regulated products, and facilitating export of U.S. products. Produces scientific data, maintains state laboratories and a well-trained workforce, and continues in the development of new capabilities. Composed of the Beverage Alcohol Laboratory, the Nonbeverage Alcohol Laboratory, the Compliance Laboratory, and the Tobacco Laboratory.

Center for Nutrition Policy and Promotion *(Agriculture Dept.), 3101 Park Center Dr., 10th Floor, Alexandria, VA 22302-1594; (703) 305-7600. Fax, (703) 305-3300. Vacant, Executive Director. Media, (703) 305-2281.*
Web, www.cnpp.usda.gov, Twitter, @MyPlate and Facebook, www.facebook.com/MyPlate

Defines and coordinates nutrition education policy, promotes food and nutrition guidance, and develops nutrition information materials for consumers, policymakers, and professionals in health, education, industry, and media.

Economic Research Service *(Agriculture Dept.), Food Economics, 355 E St. S.W., 20024-3221 (mailing address: 1400 Independence Ave. S.W., MS 1800, Washington, DC 20250-0002); (202) 694-5400. Jayachandran Variyam, Director.*
Web, www.ers.usda.gov/about-ers/agency-structure/food-economics-division-fed

Conducts economic research and analysis on policy issues related to food safety, food prices, and markets; consumer behavior related to food choices, such as food consumption, diet quality, and nutrition; and food and nutrition assistance programs. Provides data and statistics on food prices, food expenditures, and the food supply chain.

Food and Drug Administration (FDA) *(Health and Human Services Dept.), 10903 New Hampshire Ave.,*

Silver Spring, MD 20993; (888) 463-6332. Fax, (301) 847-3536. Dr. Scott Gottlieb, Commissioner. Main Library (White Oak in Silver Spring), (301) 796-2039. Press, (301) 796-4540. Toll-free, (888) 463-6332.
Web, www.fda.gov, Twitter, @US_FDA and Facebook, www.facebook.com/FDA

Protects public health by assessing the safety, effectiveness, and security of human and veterinary drugs, vaccines, and other biological products. Protects the safety and security of the nation's food supply, cosmetics, diet supplements, and products emitting radiation. Regulates tobacco products. Develops labeling and packaging standards; conducts inspections of manufacturers; issues orders to companies to recall and/or cease selling or producing hazardous products; enforces rulings and recommends action to Justice Dept. when necessary. Libraries open to the public; 24-hour advance appointment required.

Food and Drug Administration (FDA) (Health and Human Services Dept.), Center for Food Safety and Applied Nutrition (CFSAN), 5001 Campus Dr., College Park, MD 20740-3835; (240) 402-1600. Fax, (301) 436-2668. Susan T. Mayne, Director.
General email, consumer@fda.gov
Web, www.fda.gov/AboutFDA/CentersOffices/OfficeofFoods/CFSAN

Develops standards of composition and quality of foods (except meat and poultry but including fish); develops safety regulations for food and color additives for foods, cosmetics, and drugs; monitors pesticide residues in foods; conducts food safety and nutrition research; develops analytical methods for measuring food additives, nutrients, pesticides, and chemical and microbiological contaminants; recommends action to Justice Dept.

Food and Drug Administration (FDA) (Health and Human Services Dept.), Nutrition and Food Labeling (ONFL), CPK-1 Bldg., 5100 Paint Branch Pkwy., #4C-095, College Park, MD 20740-3835; (240) 402-2373. Fax, (301) 436-2639. Douglas A. Balentine, Director.
Web, www.fda.gov/Aboutfda/centersoffices/organizationcharts/ucm385139.htm

Scientific and technical component of the Center for Food Safety and Applied Nutrition. Conducts research on nutrients; develops regulations and labeling requirements on infant formulas, medical foods, and dietary supplements, including herbs.

Food and Drug Administration (FDA) (Health and Human Services Dept.), Regulatory Affairs (ORA), White Oak Bldg. 31, 10903 New Hampshire Ave., #3528, Silver Spring, MD 20993; (301) 796-8800. Fax, (301) 847-7942. Melinda K. Plaisier, Associate Commissioner.
Web, www.fda.gov/aboutfda/centersoffices/officeofglobalregulatoryoperationsandpolicy/ora and Twitter, @FDA_ORA

Directs and coordinates the FDA's compliance activities; manages field offices; advises FDA commissioner on domestic and international regulatory policies.

Food and Nutrition Service (Agriculture Dept.), 3101 Park Center Dr., #906, Alexandria, VA 22302-1500; (703) 305-2060. Fax, (703) 305-2908. Brandon Lipps, Administrator. Information, (703) 305-2286.
Web, www.fns.usda.gov and Twitter, @USDANutrition

Administers all Agriculture Dept. domestic food assistance, including the distribution of funds and food for school breakfast and lunch programs (preschool through secondary) to public and nonprofit private schools; the Supplemental Nutrition Assistance Program (SNAP, formerly the food stamp program); and a supplemental nutrition program for women, infants, and children (WIC).

Food and Nutrition Service (Agriculture Dept.), Chief Communications Officer, 3101 Park Center Dr., #926, Alexandria, VA 22302; (703) 305-2281. Fax, (703) 305-2312. Kate Fink, Director of External and Governmental Affairs; Brooke Hardison, Director of Communications (Acting).
Web, www.fns.usda.gov/cga

Provides information concerning the Food and Nutrition Service and its fifteen nutrition assistance programs to the media, program participants, advocates, members of Congress, and the general public. Monitors and analyzes relevant legislation.

Food and Nutrition Service (Agriculture Dept.), Child Nutrition, 3101 Park Center Dr., #640, Alexandria, VA 22302-1500; (703) 305-2054. Cindy Long, Deputy Administrator. Press, (202) 720-4623.
General email, cndinternet@fns.usda.gov
Web, www.fns.usda.gov/school-meals/child-nutrition-programs

Administers the transfer of funds to state agencies for the National School Lunch Program, the School Breakfast Program, the Special Milk Program, the Child and Adult Care Food Program, and the Summer Food Service Program. These programs help fight hunger and obesity by reimbursing organizations such as schools, child care centers, and after-school programs for providing healthy meals to children.

Food and Nutrition Service (Agriculture Dept.), Food Distribution, 3101 Park Center Dr., #504, Alexandria, VA 22302-1500; (703) 305-2680. Fax, (703) 305-2964. Laura Castro, Director.
General email, fdd-pst@fns.usda.gov
Web, www.fns.usda.gov/fdd

Provides food for the National School Lunch Program, the Summer Food Service Program, and the Child and Adult Care Food Program. Administers the Commodity Supplemental Food Program for low-income pregnant and breastfeeding women, new mothers, infants, children, and the elderly. Supplies food to relief organizations for distribution following disasters. Makes commodity food and cash available through the Nutrition Services Incentive Program (formerly the Nutrition Program for the Elderly). Administers the Emergency Food Assistance Program through soup kitchens and food banks and the

Food Safety Resources and Contacts

AGENCIES

Center for Food Safety and Applied Nutrition, Food and Drug Administration (FDA), (Health and Human Services Dept.),
Susan T. Mayne, Director, (888) 723-3366
Office of Analytics and Outreach,
Conrad Choiniere, Director, (240) 402-2413
Office of Food Additive Safety, Dr. Dennis M. Keefe, Director, (240) 402-1200
Office of Food Safety, William Jones, Director, (240) 402-1700
Office of Nutritional Products, Labeling and Dietary Supplements, Douglas A. Balentine, Director, (240) 402-2373

Food Safety and Inspection Service (FSIS), (Agriculture Dept.),
Paul Kiecker, Administrator (Acting), (202) 720-7025
Office of Data Integration and Food Protection, Terri Nintemann, Assistant Administrator, (202) 690-6486

Food Safety Information Center (FSIC), National Agricultural Library, (Agriculture Dept.),
Paul Webster, Director, (301) 504-5248

Office of Ground Water and Drinking Water, Environmental Protection Agency,
Peter Grevatt, Director, (202) 564-8954

Seafood Inspection Program, National Oceanic and Atmospheric Administration (NOAA), (Commerce Dept.),
John Henderschedt, Director, (301) 427-8300

ORGANIZATIONS

Center for Food Safety,
Andrew Kimbrell, Executive Director, (202) 547-9359

Center for Science in the Public Interest,
Lisa Heinzerling, Chair and Director, (202) 332-9110

Food and Water Watch,
Wenonah Hauter, Executive Director, (202) 683-2500

International Food Information Council,
Joseph Clayton, Chief Executive Officer, (202) 296-6540

HOTLINES

FDA Center for Food Safety and Applied Nutrition, (888) SAFEFOOD; (888) 723-3366; www.fda.gov/aboutfda/centersoffices/officeoffoods/cfsan/default.htm

Gateway to Government Food Safety Information, www.foodsafety.gov; www.facebook.com/FoodSafety.gov

Office of Data Integration and Food Protection 24-Hour Emergency Number, (866) 395-9701; www.fsis.usda.gov

Safe Drinking Water Information Hotline, (800) 426-4791; https://water.epa.gov/drink

USDA Meat and Poultry Hotline, (888) 674-6854; mphotline.fsis@usda.gov

---

Food Distribution Program on Indian reservations and to Indian households elsewhere.

Food and Nutrition Service *(Agriculture Dept.),* **National School Lunch Program,** *3101 Park Center Dr., 6th floor, Alexandria, VA 22302; (703) 305-2590. Cindy Long, Deputy Administrator. Communications, (703) 305-2281.*
Web, www.fns.usda.gov/nslp/national-school-lunch-program-nslp

Administers the federal assistance meal program operating in public and nonprofit private schools and residential child care institutions. Provides daily nutritionally balanced and low-cost or free lunches to children.

Food and Nutrition Service *(Agriculture Dept.),* **Policy Support,** *3101 Park Center Dr., #1014, Alexandria, VA 22302-1500; (703) 305-2017. Fax, (703) 305-2576. Richard Lucas, Deputy Associate Administrator.*
Web, www.fns.usda.gov/ops/research-and-analysis

Evaluates federal nutrition assistance programs; provides results to policymakers and program administrators. Funds demonstration grants for state and local nutrition assistance projects.

Food and Nutrition Service *(Agriculture Dept.),* **Special Supplemental Nutrition Program for Women, Infants, and Children (WIC),** *3101 Park Center Dr., #520, Alexandria, VA 22302-1594; (703) 305-2746. Fax, (703) 305-2196. Sarah Widor, Director.*
Web, www.fns.usda.gov/wic

Provides health departments and agencies with federal funding for food supplements and administrative expenses to make food, nutrition education, and health services available to infants, young children, and pregnant, nursing, and postpartum women.

Food and Nutrition Service *(Agriculture Dept.),* **Supplemental Nutrition Assistance Program (SNAP),** *3101 Park Center Dr., #808, Alexandria, VA 22302-1594; (703) 305-2026. Fax, (703) 305-2454. Jessica Shahin, Associate Administrator, (703) 305-2022.*
Web, www.fns.usda.gov/snap

Administers SNAP through state welfare agencies to provide needy persons with Electronic Benefit Transfer cards to increase food purchasing power. Provides matching funds to cover half the cost of EBT card issuance.

Food Safety and Inspection Service *(Agriculture Dept.),* *1400 Independence Ave. S.W., #331E, 20250-3700; (202) 692-4207. Fax, (202) 690-0550. Carmen Rottenberg, Administrator. Consumer inquiries, (800) 535-4555. Press, (202) 720-9113. TTY, (800) 877-8339.*
Web, www.fsis.usda.gov and Twitter, @USDAFoodSafety

Inspects meat, poultry, and egg products moving in interstate commerce for use as human food to ensure that they are safe, wholesome, and accurately labeled. Provides safe handling and labeling guidelines.

Health and Human Services Dept. (HHS), *President's Council on Fitness, Sports, and Nutrition (PCFSN), 1101 Wootton Pkwy., #560, Rockville, MD 20852; (240) 276-9567. Fax, (240) 276-9860. Holli M. Richmond, Executive Director.*
General email, fitness@hhs.gov
Web, www.fitness.gov and Twitter, @FitnessGov

Promotes programs and initiatives that motivate people of all ages, backgrounds, and abilities to lead active, healthy lives through partnerships with the public, private, and nonprofit sectors; provides online information and resources related to fitness, sports, and nutrition; conducts award programs for children and adults and for schools, clubs, and other institutions.

National Agricultural Library *(Agriculture Dept.), Food and Nutrition Information Center (FNIC), 10301 Baltimore Ave., #108, Beltsville, MD 20705-2351; (301) 504-5414. Fax, (301) 504-6409. Wendy Davis, Nutrition and Food Safety Program Leader, (301) 504-6369.*
General email, fnic@ars.usda.gov
Web, www.nal.usda.gov/fnic

Serves primarily educators, health professionals, and consumers seeking information about nutrition assistance programs and general nutrition. Serves as an online provider of science-based information about food and nutrition and links to such information. Lends books and audiovisual materials for educational purposes through interlibrary loans; maintains a database of food and nutrition software and multimedia programs; provides reference services; develops resource lists of health and nutrition publications. Library open to the public.

National Agricultural Library *(Agriculture Dept.), Food Safety Research Information (FSRIO), 10301 Baltimore Ave., #108-B, Beltsville, MD 20705-2351; (301) 504-5515. Wendy Davis, Nutrition and Food Safety Program Leader, (301) 504-6369.*
General email, fsrio@ars.usda.gov
Web, www.nal.usda.gov/fsrio

Provides food safety information to educators, industry, researchers, and the general public. Special subject areas include pathogens and contaminants, sanitation and quality standards, food preparation and handling, and food processing and technology. The center includes the Food Safety Research Information Office, which focuses on providing information and reference services to the research community and the general public.

National Institute of Food and Agriculture (NIFA) *(Agriculture Dept.), Jaime L. Whitten Bldg., 12th St. S.W. and Jefferson Dr., #305A, 20024 (mailing address: 1400 Independence Ave. S.W., MS 2201, Washington, DC 20250-2201); (202) 720-4423. Fax, (202) 720-8987. J. Scott Angle, Director. Communications, (202) 720-4242. Information, (202) 720-2791.*
General email, nifamediarequests@nifa.usda.gov
Web, https://nifa.usda.gov, Twitter, @USDA_NIFA
Blog, https://nifa.usda.gov/newsroom?f%5B0%5D=type%3Ablog

Supports research, education, and extension of issues pertaining to agricultural production, nutrition, food safety, energy independence, and the sustainability of natural resources. Partners with and funds scientists at academic institutions, particularly the land-grant universities, minority-serving institutions, including black colleges and universities, Hispanic-serving institutions, and tribal colleges, as well as government, private, and nonprofit organizations to address critical issues in agriculture, including global food security and hunger, water resources, climate change, sustainable energy, childhood obesity, and food safety. Partners with agricultural extension offices in all counties, states, and territories.

National Institute of Food and Agriculture (NIFA) *(Agriculture Dept.), Institute of Food Production and Sustainability, 800 9th St. S.W., #3305, 20024 (mailing address: 1400 Independence Ave. S.W., MS 2240, Washington, DC 20250-2240); (202) 401-5024. Fax, (202) 401-1782. Parag R. Chitnis, Deputy Director.*
Web, https://nifa.usda.gov/office/institute-food-production-and-sustainability

Enhances food security through productive and sustainable agricultural systems. Includes divisions of Animal Safety, Plant Systems, Protection, Plant Systems Production, and Agriculture Systems.

National Institute of Food and Agriculture (NIFA) *(Agriculture Dept.), Institute of Food Safety and Nutrition, 1400 Independence Ave. S.W., MS 2225, 20250-2225; (202) 702-5004. Fax, (202) 401-4888. Vacant, Deputy Director.*
Web, https://nifa.usda.gov/office/institute-food-safety-and-nutrition

Works toward safe food supply by reducing foodborne illness. Addresses causes of microbial contamination and antimicrobial resistance; educates consumer and food safety professionals; and develops food processing technologies.

National Institute of Food and Agriculture (NIFA) *(Agriculture Dept.), Institute of Youth, Family, and Community, 800 9th St. S.W., #4343, 20024 (mailing address: 1400 Independence Ave. S.W., MS 2250, Washington, DC 20250-2225); (202) 720-5305. Fax, (202) 720-3945. Muquarrab Qureshi, Deputy Director.*
Web, https://nifa.usda.gov/office/institute-youth-family-and-community

Provides grants and programmatic training to support youth and family development; partners with county governments, the private sector, and state land-grant universities. Program areas include food and agricultural science education, particularly in minority-serving institutions; childhood nutrition; community food projects; and community service. Includes divisions of Community Education, Family and Consumer Sciences, and Youth and 4-H.

National Oceanic and Atmospheric Administration (NOAA) *(Commerce Dept.), Seafood Inspection Program, 1315 East-West Hwy., Silver Spring, MD 20910; (301) 427-8300. Fax, (301) 713-1081. John Henderschedt, Director, (301) 427-8314. Toll-free, (800) 422-2750. General email, nmfs.seafood.services@noaa.gov*

Web, www.fisheries.noaa.gov/insight/noaas-seafood-inspection-program

Administers voluntary inspection program for fish products and fish processing plants; certifies fish for wholesomeness, safety, and condition; grades for quality. Conducts training and workshops to help U.S. importers and foreign suppliers comply with food regulations.

►CONGRESS

For a listing of relevant congressional committees and subcommittees, please see page 3 or the Appendix.

►INTERNATIONAL ORGANIZATIONS

Codex Alimentarius Commission, *U.S. Codex Office, 1400 Independence Ave. S.W., South Bldg., #4861, 20250-3700; (202) 205-7760. Fax, (202) 720-3157. Mary Frances Lowe, U.S. Codex Manager; Paulo Almeida, U.S. Associate Manager. Meat and Poultry Hotline, (888) 674-6854. Toll-free TTY, (800) 877-8339. General email, uscodex@fsis.usda.gov*

Web, www.fsis.usda.gov/codex and Twitter, @USDAFoodSafety

Operates within the Food and Agricultural Organization (FAO) and the World Health Organization (WHO) to establish international food and food safety standards and to ensure fair trade practices. Convenes committees in member countries to address specific commodities and issues including labeling, additives in food and veterinary drugs, pesticide residues and other contaminants, and systems for food inspection. (Located in the USDA Food Safety and Inspection Service; international headquarters in Rome at the UN's Food and Agricultural Organization.)

Cultivating New Frontiers in Agriculture (CNFA), *1828 L St. N.W., #710, 20036; (202) 296-3920. Fax, (202) 296-3948. Sylvain Roy, President. General email, info@cnfa.org*

Web, www.cnfa.org

International development organization that has worked in more than 42 countries to provide agricultural solutions to stimulate economic growth and improve livelihoods by cultivating entrepreneurship.

International Food Information Council, *1100 Connecticut Ave. N.W., #430, 20036-4120; (202) 296-6540. Fax, (202) 296-6547. Joseph Clayton, Chief Executive Officer. General email, info@foodinsight.org*

Web, www.foodinsight.org and Twitter, @foodinsight

Membership: food and beverage companies and manufacturers of food ingredients. Provides the media, health professionals, and consumers with science-based information about food safety, health, and nutrition.

►NONGOVERNMENTAL

Academy of Nutrition and Dietetics, *Washington Office, Policy Inititives and Advocacy, 1120 Connecticut Ave. N.W., #460, 20036-3989; (202) 775-8277. Fax, (202) 775-8284. Jeanne Blankenship, Vice President of Policy Initiatives and Advocacy, (312) 899-0040, ext. 6004. Toll-free, (800) 877-0877. General email, govaffairs@eatright.org*

Web, www.eatright.org and Facebook, www.facebook.com/ EatRightNutrition

Press, media@eatright.org

Membership: dietitians and other nutrition professionals. Promotes public health and nutrition; accredits academic programs in clinical nutrition and food service management; sets standards of professional practice. Sponsors the National Center for Nutrition and Dietetics. (Headquarters in Chicago, Ill.)

Center for Science in the Public Interest, *1220 L St. N.W., #300, 20005; (202) 332-9110. Fax, (202) 265-4954. Peter Lurie, President. General email, cspi@cspinet.org*

Web, https://cspinet.org and Twitter, @cspi

Conducts research on food and nutrition. Interests include eating habits, food safety regulations, food additives, organically produced foods, and links between diet and disease. Publishes *Nutrition Action Healthletter.* Monitors U.S. and international policy.

Congressional Hunger Center, *810 7th St. N.E., #02-146, 20002; (202) 547-7022. Fax, (202) 547-7575. Shannon Maynard, Executive Director.*

Web, www.hungercenter.org and Twitter, @HungerCenter

Works to increase public awareness of hunger in the United States and abroad. Develops strategies and trains leaders to combat hunger and facilitates collaborative efforts between organizations.

Council for Responsible Nutrition (CRN), *1828 L St. N.W., #810, 20036-5114; (202) 204-7700. Fax, (202) 204-7701. Steven Mister, President, (202) 240-7676. General email, webmaster@crnusa.org*

Web, www.crnusa.org and Twitter, @CRN_Supplements

Membership: manufacturers, distributors, and ingredient suppliers of dietary supplements. Provides information to members; monitors Food and Drug Administration, Federal Trade Commission, and Consumer Product Safety Commission regulations.

D.C. Central Kitchen, *425 2nd St. N.W., 20001; (202) 234-0707. Michael F. Curtin, Chief Executive Officer, (202) 266-2018.*
Web, www.dccentralkitchen.org and Twitter, @dcck

Distributes food to D.C.-area homeless shelters, transitional homes, low-income schoolchildren, and corner store "food deserts."

Food Allergy Research and Education (FARE), *7901 Jones Branch Dr., #240, McLean, VA 22102; (703) 691-3179. Fax, (703) 691-2713. Lisa Gable, Chief Executive Officer. Toll-free, (800) 929-4040.*
General email, contactfare@foodallergy.org
Web, www.foodallergy.org, Twitter, @FoodAllergyFARE and Facebook, www.facebook.com/FoodAllergyFARE

Membership: dietitians, nurses, physicians, school staff, government representatives, members of the food and pharmaceutical industries, and food-allergy patients and their families. Provides information and educational resources on food allergies and allergic reactions. Offers research grants.

Food and Water Watch, *1616 P St. N.W., #300, 20036; (202) 683-2500. Fax, (202) 683-2501. Wenonah Hauter, Executive Director. Toll-free, (855) 340-8083.*
General email, info@fwwatch.org
Web, www.foodandwaterwatch.org, Twitter, @foodandwater and Facebook, www.facebook .com/FoodandWaterWatch

Consumer organization that advocates stricter water and food safety regulations. Organizes public awareness campaigns and lobbies Congress. Publishes studies of agricultural, food preparation, and drinking water sanitation practices. Chapters in fifteen states and international chapter in Brussels, Belgium.

Food Policy Action, *1436 U St. N.W., #200, 20009; (202) 997-3266. Monica Mills, Executive Director.*
General email, info@foodpolicyaction.org
Web, http://foodpolicyaction.org, Twitter, @FPAction and Facebook, www.facebook.com/FoodPolicyAction

Promotes policies that support healthy food options; works to reduce hunger and improve food access.

Food Research and Action Center (FRAC), *1200 18th St. N.W., #400, 20036; (202) 986-2200. Fax, (202) 986-2525. James D. Weill, President.*
General email, cbsutton@frac.org
Web, www.frac.org, Twitter, @fractweets and Facebook, www.facebook.com/ foodresearchandactioncenter

Public interest advocacy center that works to end hunger and undernutrition in the United States. Offers organizational aid, training, and information to groups seeking to improve or expand federal food programs, including food stamp, child nutrition, and WIC (women, infants, and children) programs; conducts studies relating to hunger and poverty; coordinates network of antihunger organizations. Monitors legislation and regulations.

International Life Sciences Institute (ILSI), *North America, 740 15th St. N.W., #600, 20005; (202) 659-0074. Fax, (202) 659-3859. Stephanie Vidry, Executive Director of Operations.*
General email, info@ilsi.org
Web, www.ilsi.org, Twitter, @ISLI_Global and Facebook, www.facebook.com/ InternationalLifesciencesInstitute

Acts as liaison among scientists from international government agencies, concerned industries, research institutes, and universities regarding the safety of foods and chemical ingredients. Conducts research on caffeine, food coloring, oral health, human nutrition, and other food issues. Promotes international cooperation among scientists.

National Center for Food and Agricultural Policy, *1101 Pennsylvania Ave. N.W., #300, 20004; (202) 429-8422. Fax, (202) 747-7603. Dr. Harry Baumes, Chief Executive Officer.*
General email, info@ncfap.org
Web, www.ncfap.org

Research and educational organization concerned with domestic and international food and agricultural issues. Examines public policy concerning agriculture, food safety and quality, natural resources, and the environment.

National Research Council (NRC), *Agriculture and Natural Resources Board, Keck Center, 500 5th St. N.W., #WS632, 20001; (202) 334-3062. Fax, (202) 334-1978. Robin Schoen, Director.*
General email, banr@nas.edu
Web, http://dels.nas.edu/banr and Twitter, @NASM_Ag

Promotes and oversees research on the environmental impact of agriculture and food sustainability, including forestry, fisheries, wildlife, and the use of land, water, and other natural resources.

Public Citizen, *Health Research Group, 1600 20th St. N.W., 20009-1001; (202) 588-1000. Michael Carome, Director.*
General email, hrg1@citizen.org
Web, www.citizen.org/health-research-group, Twitter, @CitizenHRG and Publications, www.citizen.org/ our-work/health-and-safety/health-research-group-publications

Citizens' interest group that studies and reports on unsafe foods; monitors and petitions the Food and Drug Administration.

School Nutrition Assn., *2900 S. Quincy St., #700, Arlington, VA 22206; (703) 824-3000. Fax, (703) 824-3015. Patricia Montague, Chief Executive Officer. Information, (800) 877-8822.*
General email, servicecenter@schoolnutrition.org
Web, https://schoolnutrition.org and Twitter, @SchoolLunch

Membership: state and national food service workers and supervisors, school cafeteria managers, nutrition educators, industry members, and others interested in school food programs and child nutrition. Offers credentialing and sponsors National School Lunch Week and National School Breakfast Week. (Formerly the American School Food Service Assn.)

Beverages

▶**AGENCIES**

Alcohol and Tobacco Tax and Trade Bureau (TTB) *(Treasury Dept.), 1310 G St. N.W., #300E, Box 12, 20005; (202) 453-2000. Fax, (202) 453-2912. John J. Manfreda, Administrator, ext. 32176. Public Affairs, (202) 453-2180. TTY, (202) 882-9914.*
General email, TTBInternetQuestions@ttb.gov
Web, www.ttb.gov

Regulates the advertising and labeling of alcohol beverages, including the size of containers; enforces federal taxation of alcohol and tobacco. Authorized to refer violations to Justice Dept. for criminal prosecution.

Alcohol and Tobacco Tax and Trade Bureau (TTB) *(Treasury Dept.), Alcohol Labeling and Formulation Division, 1310 G St. N.W., Box 12, 20005; (202) 453-2250. Fax, (202) 453-2300. Janet Scalese, Director. Toll-free, (866) 927-2533.*
General email, alfd@ttb.treas.gov
Web, www.ttb.gov/offices/alfd.shtml

Responsible for tax classification of alcohol beverages, alcohol beverage formula and label compliance with federal laws and regulations, and industry guidance and education on public laws and regulations. Ensures that labels provide consumers with adequate information on the identity and quality of alcohol beverage products.

Alcohol and Tobacco Tax and Trade Bureau (TTB) *(Treasury Dept.), Regulations and Rulings Division, 1310 G St. N.W., #200 East, Box 12, 20005; (202) 453-2265. Amy Greenburg, Director.*
General email, regulations@ttb.gov
Web, www.ttb.gov

Develops guidelines for regional offices responsible for issuing permits for producing gasohol and other ethyl alcohol fuels. Writes and interprets regulations for distilleries that produce ethyl alcohol fuels.

▶**NONGOVERNMENTAL**

American Beverage Assn., *1275 Pennsylvania Ave. N.W., #1100, 20004; (202) 463-6732. Fax, (202) 463-8277. Katherine Lugar, President; Amy E. Hancock, General Counsel Legal and Regulatory Affairs. Press, (202) 463-6770.*
General email, info@ameribev.org
Web, www.ameribev.org, Twitter, @AmeriBev and Facebook, www.facebook.com/AmeriBev

Membership: companies engaged in producing or distributing nonalcoholic beverages and bottled water. Acts as industry liaison with government and the public. (Formerly the National Soft Drink Assn.)

American Beverage Institute, *1090 Vermont Ave. N.W., #800, 20005; (202) 463-7110. Sarah Longwell, Managing Director.*
General email, info@abionline.org
Web, https://abionline.org and Facebook, www.facebook.com/AmericanBeverageInstitute

Promotes responsible alcohol consumption in restaurants and bars. Opposes restrictions on alcohol use. Monitors legislation and regulations.

American Beverage Licensees (ABL), *5101 River Rd., #108, Bethesda, MD 20816-1560; (301) 656-1494. Fax, (301) 656-7539. John Bodnovich, Executive Director. Toll-free, (888) 656-3241.*
General email, info@ablusa.org
Web, www.ablusa.org, Twitter, @ablusa and Facebook, www.facebook.com/ablusa

Membership: state associations of on-premise and off-premise beverage alcohol licensees. Monitors legislation and regulations affecting the alcohol beverage industry.

Beer Institute, *440 1st St. N.W., #350, 20001; (202) 737-2337. Fax, (202) 737-7004. James McGreevy III, President. Toll-free, (800) 379-2739.*
General email, info@beerinstitute.org
Web, www.beerinstitute.org and Twitter, @beerinstitute

Membership: domestic brewers and beer importers and suppliers to the domestic brewing industry. Monitors legislation and regulations.

Distilled Spirits Council of the United States, *1250 Eye St. N.W., #400, 20005-3998; (202) 628-3544. Fax, (202) 682-8888. Chris R. Swonger, President.*
Web, www.discus.org

Membership: manufacturers and marketers of distilled spirits sold in the United States. Provides consumer information on alcohol-related issues and topics. Monitors legislation and regulations.

International Bottled Water Assn. (IBWA), *1700 Diagonal Rd., #650, Alexandria, VA 22314-2864; (703) 683-5213. Fax, (703) 683-4074. Joseph K. Doss, President, (703) 647-4605. Information, 800-WATER-11. Press, (703) 647-4609.*
General email, ibwainfo@bottledwater.org
Web, www.bottledwater.org

Serves as a clearinghouse for industry-related consumer, regulatory, and technical information; interests include international trade. Monitors state and federal legislation and regulations.

National Alcohol Beverage Control Assn. (NABCA), *4401 Ford Ave., #700, Alexandria, VA 22302; (703) 578-4200. Fax, (703) 820-3551. James M. Sgueo, President.*
General email, nabca.info@nabca.org
Web, www.nabca.org and Twitter, @NABCA

Membership: distilleries, importers, brokers, trade associations, and state agencies that control the purchase, distribution, and sale of alcohol beverages. Promotes responsible sale and consumption of these beverages.

Serves as an information clearinghouse. Monitors legislation and regulations.

National Beer Wholesalers Assn., *1101 King St., #600, Alexandria, VA 22314-2944; (703) 683-4300. Fax, (703) 683-8965. Craig A. Purser, President. Toll-free, (800) 300-6417.*
General email, info@nbwa.org

Web, www.nbwa.org and Twitter, @NBWA

Works to enhance the independent beer wholesale industry. Advocates before government and the public; encourages responsible consumption of beer; sponsors programs and services to benefit members; monitors legislation and regulations.

Wine and Spirits Wholesalers of America (WSWA), *805 15th St. N.W., #1120, 20005-2273; (202) 371-9792. Fax, (202) 789-2405. Michelle L. Korsmo, President.*
General email, info@wswa.org

Web, www.wswa.org and Twitter, @wswamedia

Trade association of wholesale distributors of domestic and imported wine and distilled spirits. Provides information on drinking awareness. Represents members' interests before Congress and federal agencies.

Wine Institute, *Federal and International Public Policy, 601 13th St. N.W., #330 South, 20005-3866; (202) 408-0870. Fax, (202) 371-0061. Charles Jefferson, Vice President.*
Web, www.wineinstitute.org and Twitter, @CalifWines_US

Membership: California wineries and affiliated businesses. Seeks international recognition for California wines; conducts promotional campaigns in other countries. Monitors legislation and regulations. (Headquarters in San Francisco, Calif.)

Food Industries

▶NONGOVERNMENTAL

American Bakers Assn. (ABA), *601 Pennsylvania Ave., #230, 20004; (202) 789-0300. Fax, (202) 898-1164. Robb MacKie, President.*
General email, info@americanbakers.org

Web, www.americanbakers.org and Twitter, @AmericanBakers

Membership: wholesale baking companies and their suppliers. Promotes increased consumption of baked goods; provides consumers with nutritional information; conducts conventions. Monitors legislation and regulations.

American Frozen Food Institute, *2345 Crystal Dr., #801, Arlington, VA 22102; (703) 821-0770. Alison Bodor, President.*
General email, info@affi.com

Web, www.affi.org, Twitter, @affi and Facebook, www.facebook.com/AmericanFrozenFoodInstitute

Membership: frozen food packers, distributors, and suppliers. Testifies before Congress and federal agencies.

American Herbal Products Assn., *8630 Fenton St., #918, Silver Spring, MD 20910; (301) 588-1171. Fax, (301) 588-1174. Michael McGuffin, President, ext. 201.*
General email, ahpa@ahpa.org

Web, www.ahpa.org, Twitter, @AHPA1982 and Facebook, www.facebook.com/HerbalProductsAssociation

Membership: U.S. companies and individuals that grow, manufacture, and distribute botanicals and herbal products, including foods, beverages, dietary supplements, and personal care products; associates in education, law, media, and medicine. Supports research; promotes quality standards, consumer access, and self-regulation in the industry. Monitors legislation and regulations.

Bakery, Confectionery, Tobacco Workers, and Grain Millers International Union, *10401 Connecticut Ave., 4th Floor, Kensington, MD 20895-3940; (301) 933-8600. Fax, (301) 946-8452. David B. Durkee, President.*
General email, bctgmwebmaster@gmail.com

Web, www.bctgm.org and Twitter, @BCTGM

Membership: approximately 120,000 workers from the bakery, confectionery, grain miller, and tobacco industries. Helps members negotiate pay, benefits, and better working conditions; conducts training programs and workshops. Monitors legislation and regulations. (Affiliated with the AFL-CIO.)

Food Marketing Institute (FMI), *2345 Crystal Dr., #800, Arlington, VA 22202-4813; (202) 452-8444. Fax, (202) 429-4519. Leslie G. Sarasin, President.*
General email, info@fmi.org

Web, www.fmi.org, Twitter, @FMI_ORG and Facebook, www.facebook.com/FoodMarketingInstitute

Trade association of food retailers and wholesalers. Conducts programs in research, education, industry relations, and public affairs; participates in international conferences. Library open to the public by appointment.

Food Processing Suppliers Assn. (FPSA), *1451 Dolley Madison Blvd., #101, McLean, VA 22101-3850; (703) 761-2600. Fax, (703) 761-4334. David Seckman, President, (703) 663-1200.*
Web, www.fpsa.org, Twitter, @FPSAorg and Facebook, www.facebook.com/FPSAorg

Membership: equipment and ingredient manufacturers, suppliers, and servicers for the food, dairy, and beverage processing industry. Sponsors food engineering scholarships and the biannual Process Expo. (Merger of the International Assn. of Food Industry Suppliers and the Food Processing Machinery Assn.)

Grocery Manufacturers Assn. (GMA), *1001 19th St. North, 7th Floor, Arlington, VA 22209; (571) 378-6760. Fax, 571-378-6759. Geoff Freeman, President.*
General email, info@gmaonline.org

Web, www.gmaonline.org and Twitter, @GroceryMakers

Membership: manufacturers of food, beverage, and consumer packaged goods sold through the retail grocery trade. Interests include holistic waste management solutions, nutritional labeling, ingredient transparency, and the safety and security of the food supply. Supplies industry information to members. Monitors legislation and regulations.

International Foodservice Distributors Assn., *1660 International Dr., #550, McLean, VA 22102; (703) 532-9400. Fax, (703) 880-7117. Mark S. Allen, President, ext. 9933.*
General email, info@ifdaonline.org
Web, www.ifdaonline.org, Twitter, @IFDA and Facebook, www.facebook.com/IFDAOrg

Trade association of foodservice distribution companies that promotes the interests of members in government and industry affairs through research, education, and communication.

NACS: The Assn. for Convenience and Fuel Retailing, *1600 Duke St., 7th Floor, Alexandria, VA 22314-3421; (703) 684-3600. Fax, (703) 836-4564. Henry Armour, President, (703) 518-4282. Toll-free, (800) 966-6227.*
General email, nacs@nacsonline.com
Web, www.nacsonline.com and Twitter, @nacsonline

Membership: convenience store and fuel retailers and industry suppliers. Promotes industry position on labor, tax, environment, alcohol, and food-related issues; conducts research and training programs. Monitors legislation and regulations.

National Automatic Merchandising Assn. (NAMA), **Washington Office,** *1530 Wilson Blvd., #720, Arlington, VA 22209; (571) 346-1901. Fax, (703) 807-2006. Carla Balakgic, President, (312) 346-0370.*
Web, www.namanow.org and Twitter, @NAMAvending

Membership: service companies, equipment manufacturers, and product suppliers for the food and refreshment vending, coffee service, and foodservice management industries. Seeks to advance and promote the automatic merchandising and coffee service industries, provide administrative, logistical, and financial assistance to its members. (Headquarters in Chicago, Ill.)

National Council of Chain Restaurants (NCCR), *1101 New York Ave. N.W., #1200, 20005; (202) 283-7971. Fax, (202) 737-2849. Matthew R. Shay, President; David French, Director of Government Relations. Toll-free, (800) 673-4692.*
General email, contact@nccr.net
Web, www.nrf.com/who-we-are/retail-communities/chain-restaurants-nccr and Twitter, @NRFnews

Trade association representing chain restaurant companies. Affiliated with the National Retail Federation. Monitors legislation and regulations.

National Grocers Assn., *1005 N. Glebe Rd., #250, Arlington, VA 22201-5758; (703) 516-0700. Fax, (703) 516-0115. Peter J. Larkin, President; Molly Pfaffenroth, Director of Government Relations.*
General email, feedback@nationalgrocers.org
Web, www.nationalgrocers.org, Twitter, @NationalGrocers Press, communications@nationalgrocers.org

Trade association that represents independent retail and wholesale grocers. Membership also includes affiliated associations, manufacturers, and service suppliers. Provides members with educational materials through a website, publications, and conferences. Monitors legislation and regulations.

National Pasta Assn. (NPA), *750 National Press Bldg., 529 14th St. N.W., 20045-1806; (202) 591-2459. Fax, (202) 591-2445. Carol Freysinger, Executive Director, (202) 591-2459. General email, info@ilovepasta.org*
Web, www.ilovepasta.org

Membership: U.S. pasta manufacturers, related suppliers, and allied industry representatives. Represents the industry on public policy issues; monitors and addresses technical issues; and organizes events and seminars for the industry.

National Restaurant Assn., *2055 L St. N.W., #700, 20036; (202) 331-5900. Fax, (202) 331-2429. Dawn Sweeney, President. Toll-free, (800) 424-5156.*
General email, askus@restaurant.org
Web, www.restaurant.org and Twitter, @Werrestaurants

Membership: restaurants, cafeterias, clubs, contract feeders, caterers, institutional food services, and other members of the food industry. Supports food service education and research. Monitors legislation and regulations.

North American Meat Institute, *1150 Connecticut Ave. N.W., 12th Floor, 20036; (202) 587-4200. Fax, (202) 587-4300. Julia Anna Potts, President, (202) 587-4262; Eric Mittenthal, Public Affairs, (202) 587-4238. General email, emittenthal@meatinstitute.org*
Web, www.meatinstitute.org, Twitter, @MeatInstitute and Facebook, www.facebook.com/AmericanMeatInstitute

Membership: national and international meat and poultry packers, suppliers, and processors. Provides statistics on meat production and exports. Funds research projects and consumer education programs. Monitors legislation and regulations. (Formed from merger of the North American Meat Assn. and American Meat Institute.)

Shelf-Stable Food Processors Assn. (SFPA), *1150 Connecticut Ave. N.W., 12th Floor, 20036; (202) 587-4200. Fax, (202) 587-4300. Julie Anna Potts, President; Susan Backus, Executive Secretary. General email, info@meatinstitute.org*
Web, www.meatinstitute.org and Twitter, @meatinstitute

Membership: shelf-stable food manufacturers and their suppliers. Provides information on the shelf-stable industry, particularly as it pertains to meat products. (Subsidiary of the North American Meat Institute.)

SNAC International, *1560 Wilson Blvd., #550, Arlington, VA 22209; (703) 836-4500. Fax, (703) 836-8262. Elizabeth Avery, Chief Executive Officer, ext. 204. Toll-free, (800) 628-1334.*
Web, www.snacintl.org and Facebook, www.facebook.com/SNACInternational

Membership: snack food manufacturers and suppliers. Promotes industry sales; compiles statistics; conducts research and surveys; assists members with training and education; provides consumers with industry information. Monitors legislation and regulations.

Tortilla Industry Assn., *1400 N. 14th St., 12th Floor, Arlington, VA 22209; (800) 944-6099. Fax, (800) 944-6177. Jim Kabbani, Executive Director, (703) 819-9550. General email, jkabbaani@tortilla-info.com*
Web, www.tortilla-info.com

Membership: tortilla manufacturers, industry suppliers, and distributors. Promotes tortilla consumption. Provides market research and other industry-related information to its members. Sponsors conferences, seminars, and educational events for the industry.

UNITE HERE, Washington Office, *1775 K St. N.W., #620, 20006-1530; (202) 393-4373. Fax, (202) 223-6213 or (202) 342-2929. Donald Taylor, President.*
Web, www.unitehere.org and Twitter, @unitehere

Membership: workers in the United States and Canada who work in the hotel, gaming, food service, distribution transportation, manufacturing, textile, laundry, and airport industries. Assists members with contract negotiation and grievances; conducts training programs and workshops. Monitors legislation and regulations. (Headquarters in New York. Formed by the merger of the former Union of Needletrades, Textiles and Industrial Employees and the Hotel Employees and Restaurant Employees International Union.)

United Food and Commercial Workers International Union (UFCW), *1775 K St. N.W., 20006-1598; (202) 223-3111. Fax, (202) 728-1803. Anthony (Marc) Perrone, President.*
Web, www.ufcw.org and Twitter, @UFCW

Membership: approximately 1.3 million workers primarily in the retail, meatpacking, food processing, and poultry industries. Interests include health care reform, living wages, retirement security, safe working conditions, and the right to unionize. Monitors legislation and regulations.

World Cocoa Foundation, *1411 K St. N.W., #500, 20005; (202) 737-7870. Fax, (202) 737-7832. Richard Scobey, President.*
General email, wcf@worldcocoa.org
Web, www.worldcocoafoundation.org and Twitter, @WorldCocoa

Promotes a sustainable cocoa economy through economic and social development and environmental conservation in cocoa-growing communities. Helps raise funds for cocoa farmers and increases their access to modern farming practices.

Vegetarianism

▶**NONGOVERNMENTAL**

Compassion Over Killing, *6930 Carroll Ave., #910, Tacoma Park, MD 20912 (mailing address: P.O. Box 9773,*

Washington, DC 20016); (301) 891-2458. Fax, (301) 891-6815. Erica Meier, Executive Director.
General email, info@cok.net
Web, http://cok.net and Twitter, @TryVeg

Animal rights organization that focuses primarily on cruelty to animals in agriculture. Promotes vegetarianism.

Farm Animal Rights Movement (FARM), *10101 Ashburton Lane, Bethesda, MD 20817-1729; (301) 530-1737. Fax, (301) 530-5683. Alex Hershaft, President. Toll-free, 888-FARM-USA.*
General email, info@farmusa.org
Web, www.farmusa.org, www.livevegan.org and Twitter, @FARMUSA

Works to end use of animals for food. Interests include animal protection, consumer health, agricultural resources, and environmental quality. Conducts national educational campaigns, including World Farm Animals Day, the Live Vegan program, and the Great American Meatout. Monitors legislation and regulations.

Vegetarian Resource Group, *P.O. Box 1463, Baltimore, MD 21203-1463; (410) 366-8343. Fax, (410) 366-8804. Charles Stahler, Co-Director; Debra Wasserman, Co-Director.*
General email, vrg@vrg.org
Web, www.vrg.org, Twitter, @VegResourceGrp
Press, press@vrg.org

Works to educate the public on vegetarianism and veganism and issues of health, nutrition, ecology, ethics, and world hunger.

World Food Assistance

▶**AGENCIES**

Agency for International Development (USAID), *Bureau for Food Security, 1300 Pennsylvania Ave. N.W., 20523; (202) 712-0000, Ext. 20189. Fax, (202) 216-3380. Beth Dunford, Assistant Administrator, (202) 712-0658.*
Web, www.usaid.gov/who-we-are/organization/bureaus/bureau-food-security

Administers agricultural development programs, including the Feed the Future initiative. Partners with other U.S. government offices, multilateral institutions, NGOs, the public and private sector, and universities to support country-driven agricultural growth strategies.

Agency for International Development (USAID), *Bureau for Food Security, Farmer-to-Farmer Program, 1300 Pennsylvania Ave. N.W., #2.10-261, 20523; J. Erin Baize, Program Analyst, (202) 712-5711.*
Web, www.usaid.gov/what-we-do/agriculture-and-food-security/supporting-agricultural-capacity-development/john-ogonowski and https://farmer-to-farmer.org and Facebook, www.facebook.com/Farmer2Farmer

Promotes sustainable improvements in food security and agricultural processing, production, and marketing. Provides voluntary assistance to farmers, farm groups, and agribusinesses in developing countries, benefiting approximately one million farmer families in more than 80 countries.

Agriculture Dept. (USDA), *Office of the Chief Economist, World Agricultural Outlook Board, 12th and Jefferson Dr. S.W., Room 112, 20250; (202) 720-2455. Fax, (202) 720-1805. Seth Meyer, Chair.*
Web, www.usda.gov/oce/commodity

Coordinates the department's commodity forecasting program, which develops the official prognosis of supply, utilization, and prices for commodities worldwide. Works with the National Weather Service to monitor the impact of global weather on agriculture.

Bureau of Economic and Business Affairs (EB) *(State Dept.), Trade Policy and Negotiations (TPN), Agriculture Policy (AGP), 2201 C St. N.W., #4686, 20520-0002; (202) 647-3090. Fax, (202) 647-1894. Patrick M. Dunn, Director, (202) 647-0133.*
Web, www.state.gov/e/eb/tpn/agp

Makes recommendations on international food policy issues including effects of U.S. food aid on foreign policy; studies and drafts proposals on the U.S. role in Food for Peace and World Food programs.

Foreign Agricultural Service (FAS) *(Agriculture Dept.), 1400 Independence Ave. S.W., #5071S, MS 1001, 20250-1001; (202) 720-3935. Fax, (202) 690-2159. Kenneth Isley, Administrator. Public Affairs, (202) 720-7115. TTY, (202) 720-1786.*
Web, www.fas.usda.gov and Twitter, @USDAForeignAg

Administers international food programs and provides technical assistance and trade and scientific capacity building support to developing countries.

Foreign Agricultural Service (FAS) *(Agriculture Dept.), Capacity Building and Development, 1400 Independence Ave. S.W., #3008S, MS 1030, 20250-1030; (202) 720-6887. Fax, (202) 720-0069. Jocelyn Brown, Deputy Administrator.*
Web, www.fas.usda.gov

Administers international food assiatance programs and leads the Agriculture Dept.'s efforts to help developing countries improve their agricultural systems and build trade capacity.

National Institute of Food and Agriculture (NIFA) *(Agriculture Dept.), Center for International Programs, 800 9th St. S.W., #2436, 20024 (mailing address: 1400 Independence Ave. S.W., MS 2203, Washington, DC 20250-2203); (202) 720-3801. Fax, (202) 690-2355. Otto Gonzalez, Director.*
Web, https://nifa.usda.gov/office/center-international-programs

Promotes science education in developing economies and shares research to enhance food production and stabilize economies. Interests include agricultural extension, teaching, and research.

State Dept., *Global Food Security, 2201 C St. N.W., #5323, 20520; (202) 647-4027. Caitlin E. Walsh, Special Representative (Acting).*
Web, www.state.gov/s/globalfoodsecurity

Supports country-driven approaches to address the root causes of hunger and poverty, and helps countries transform their own agricultural sectors to grow enough food to sustainably feed their people.

▶**INTERNATIONAL ORGANIZATIONS**

CARE, *Washington Office, 1899 L St. N.W., #500, 20036; (202) 595-2800. Fax, (202) 296-8695. Michelle Nunn, President; David Ray, Vice President of Policy and Advocacy. Toll-free, (800) 422-7385.*
General email, info@care.org
Web, www.care.org and Twitter, @CARE

Works with international governments and communities to ensure sustainable food security and sustainable farming. (U.S. headquarters in Atlanta, Ga.; international headquarters in Geneva, Switzerland.)

Farmer to Farmer, *1472 K. ST., #700, 20005; Morgan Doggett, Communications Manager, (202) 637-6212. Skpye, mdoget2_1.*
General email, AVOP@Partners.net
Web, www.farmer-to-farmer.org, Twitter, @farmertofarmer and Facebook, www.facebook .com/farmer2farmer

Supports farmers and agribusiness professionals in developing countries to improve their livelihoods and food security. Sends volunteers on need-based assignments to provide hands-on training and mentoring in 36 countries. Works with the USAID farmer to farmer program.

Food and Agriculture Organization of the United Nations (FAO), *Washington Office, 2121 K St. N.W., #800B, 20037-0001; (202) 653-2400. Fax, (202) 653-5760. Vimlendra Sharan, Director.*
General email, faolow@fao.org
Web, www.fao.org/north-america/en, Twitter, @FAONorthAmerica and Facebook, www.facebook.com/UNFAO

Offers development assistance; collects, analyzes, and disseminates information; provides policy and planning advice to governments; acts as an international forum for debate on food and agricultural issues, including animal health and production, fisheries, and forestry; encourages sustainable agricultural development and a long-term strategy for the conservation and management of natural resources. Coordinates World Food Day. (International headquarters in Rome.)

International Food Policy Research Institute (IFPRI), *1201 Eye St. N.W., 20005-3915; (202) 862-5600. Fax, (202) 862-5606. Shenggen Fan, Director General.*
General email, ifpri@cgiar.org
Web, www.ifpri.org

Research organization that analyzes the world food situation and suggests ways of making food more available in developing countries. Provides various governments with information on national and international food policy. Sponsors conferences and seminars; publishes research reports. Library open to the public by appointment.

International Fund for Agricultural Development (IFAD), *North American Liaison Office,* *1775 K St. N.W., #500, 20006-1502; (202) 331-9099. Gilbert F. Houngbo, President; Thomas Pesek, Partnership Officer.*
General email, t.pesek@ifad.org
Web, www.ifad.org

Financial institution and specialized agency of the United Nations that provides the rural poor of developing nations with cost-effective ways of overcoming hunger, poverty, and malnutrition. Advocates a community-based approach to reducing rural poverty. (International headquarters in Rome.)

▶ **NONGOVERNMENTAL**

ACDI/VOCA, *50 F St. N.W., #1000, 20001-1530; (202) 469-6000. Fax, (202) 469-6257. Charles J. Hall, President. Toll-free, (800) 929-8622.*
General email, webmaster@acdivoca.org
Web, www.acdivoca.org, Twitter, @acdivoca and Facebook, www.facebook.com/acdivoca

Promotes agribusiness systems that improve production and link farmers to national, regional, and international markets. Partners with farm supply, processing, and marketing cooperatives; farm credit banks; national farmer organizations; and insurance cooperatives. Provides cooperatives with training and technical, management, and marketing assistance; supports farm credit systems, agribusiness, and government agencies in developing countries.

American Red Cross, *National Headquarters,* *431 18th St. N.W., 20006; (202) 303-5000. Gail J. McGovern, President. Headquarters staff directory, (202) 303-5214, ext. 1. Press, (202) 303-5551. Public inquiry, (202) 303-4498. Toll-free, 800-RED-CROSS (733-2767).*
Web, www.redcross.org and Twitter, @RedCross

Humanitarian relief and health education organization chartered by Congress. Provides food and supplies to assist in major disaster and refugee situations worldwide. U.S. delegate of the International Red Cross and Red Crescent Societies in international response efforts.

Bread for the World/Bread for the World Institute, *425 3rd St. S.W., #1200, 20024; (202) 639-9400. Fax, (202) 639-9401. David Beckmann, President. Information, (800) 822-7323.*
General email, bread@bread.org and institute@bread.org
Web, www.bread.org and Twitter, @bread4theworld

Christian citizens' movement that works to eradicate world hunger. Organizes and coordinates political action on issues and public policy affecting the causes of hunger.

Center for Strategic and International Studies, *Global Food Security Project,* *1616 Rhode Island Ave. N.W., 20036; (202) 775-3235. Kimberly Flowers, Director.*
General email, FoodSecurity@csis.org
Web, www.csis.org/programs/global-food-security-project and Twitter, @CSISFood

Conducts research and provides policy guidance on global food security challenges and agricultural development. Interests include the role of technology in increasing production, the importance of integrating nutrition, and economic growth.

Oxfam America, *Policy and Campaigns,* *1101 17th St. N.W., #1300, 20036-4710; (202) 496-1180. Fax, (202) 496-1190. Abby Maxman, President; Paul O'Brien, Vice President for Policy and Campaigns. Information, (800) 776-9326. Press, (202) 496-1169.*
General email, info@oxfamamerica.org
Web, www.oxfamamerica.org and Twitter, @OxfamAmerica

Funds disaster relief and long-term development programs internationally. Organizes grassroots support in the United States for issues affecting global poverty and hunger.

RESULTS, *1101 15th St. N.W., #1200, 20005; (202) 783-4800. Fax, (202) 452-9345. Joanne Carter, Executive Director.*
General email, results@results.org
Web, https://results.org and Twitter, @RESULTS_Tweets

Works to end hunger and poverty nationally and worldwide; encourages grassroots and legislative support of programs and proposals dealing with hunger and hunger-related issues. Monitors legislation and regulations.

Winrock International, *Washington Office,* *2121 Crystal Dr., #500, Arlington, VA 22202; (703) 302-6500. Fax, (703) 302-6512. Rodney Ferguson, President.*
General email, information@winrock.org
Web, www.winrock.org and Twitter, @WinrockIntl

Works to increase economic opportunity; sustain natural resources; protect the environment; and increase long-term productivity, equity, and responsible resource management to benefit the world's poor and disadvantaged communities. Matches innovative approaches in agriculture, natural resources management, clean energy, and leadership development with the unique needs of its partners. Links local individuals and communities with new ideas and technology. (Headquarters in Little Rock, Ark.)

Worldwatch Institute, *1400 16th St. N.W., #430, 20036; (202) 745-8092. Fax, (202) 478-2534. Ed Groark, President (Acting).*
General email, worldwatch@worldwatch.org
Web, www.worldwatch.org and Twitter, @worldwatch

Environmental think tank that studies the environmental, political, and economic links to world population growth and health trends. Interests include food and sustainable agriculture.

LIVESTOCK AND POULTRY

General

▶ **AGENCIES**

Agricultural Marketing Service (AMS) *(Agriculture Dept.), Fair Trade Practices Program, Packers and Stockyards Program, South Bldg., 1400 Independence Ave. S.W., #2055, MS 3601, 20250-3601; (202) 720-0219. Fax, (202) 205-9237. Stuart Frank, Director, (515) 323-2586. Swine Contract Library, (515) 323-2579. General email, PSDWashingtonDC@ams.usda.gov*

Web, www.gipsa.usda.gov/psp/psp.aspx

Swine Contract Library email, SwineContractLibrary@usda.gov

Maintains competition in the marketing of livestock, poultry, and meat by prohibiting deceptive and monopolistic marketing practices; tests market scales and conducts check weighings for accuracy. Maintains the Swine Contract Library.

Agricultural Marketing Service (AMS) *(Agriculture Dept.), Livestock and Poultry Program, 1400 Independence Ave. S.W., Room S.0292 STOP 0249, 20250-0249 (mailing address: 1400 Independence Ave., MS 0249, Washington, DC 20250); (202) 720-5705. Fax, (202) 720-3499. Jennifer Tucker, Deputy Administrator. General email, AskLPS@ams.usda.gov*

Web, www.ams.usda.gov/about-ams/programs-offices/livestock-poultry-program

Administers meat marketing program; maintains market news service to inform producers of meat market situation and daily price changes; develops, establishes, and revises U.S. standards for classes and grades of livestock and meat; grades, examines, and certifies meat and meat products.

Agriculture Dept. (USDA), *Under Secretary for Food Safety, 1400 Independence Ave. S.W., #331E, 20250; (202) 720-7025. Fax, (202) 690-0550. 202 692-4207. Mindy M. Brashears, Deputy Under Secretary. phone, 202 692-4207.*

Web, www.usda.gov/our-agency/about-usda/mission-areas

Develops strategies that ensure the commercial supply of meat, poultry, and egg products is safe, properly labeled, and packaged. Oversees the Food Safety and Inspection Service.

Animal and Plant Health Inspection Service (APHIS) *(Agriculture Dept.), Veterinary Services, 400 N. 8th St., #726, Richmond, VA 23219-4824; (804) 343-2561. Fax, (804) 343-2599. Dr. Jack Shere, Deputy Administrator. General email, jack.a.shere@aphis.usda.gov*

Web, www.aphis.usda.gov/aphis/ourfocus/animalhealth

Works to protect and improve the health, quality, and marketability of our nation's animals and various wildlife and animal products. Creates priorities, objectives, strategies, and field activities for cattle, avian, swine, aquaculture, sheep and goat, equine, and cervid health. Disseminates regulatory information addressing the interstate and importation requirements of genetically engineered animals and insects that may spread animal diseases. Advises on animal health and public issues, including animal welfare, local and commercial livestock, natural resource conservation, and public health; conducts animal health monitoring and surveillance.

Food and Drug Administration (FDA) *(Health and Human Services Dept.), Center for Veterinary Medicine (CVM), 7500 Standish Pl., HFV-1, Rockville, MD 20855-0001; (240) 402-7002. Fax, (240) 276-9001. Steven Solomon, Director. General email, askcvm@fda.hhs.gov*

Web, www.fda.gov/animalveterinary and Twitter, @FDAanimalhealth

Regulates the manufacture and distribution of drugs, food additives, feed, and devices for livestock and pets. Conducts research; works to ensure animal health and the safety of food derived from animals.

Food Safety and Inspection Service *(Agriculture Dept.), 1400 Independence Ave. S.W., #331E, 20250-3700; (202) 692-4207. Fax, (202) 690-0550. Carmen Rottenberg, Administrator. Consumer inquiries, (800) 535-4555. Press, (202) 720-9113. TTY, (800) 877-8339.*

Web, www.fsis.usda.gov and Twitter, @USDAFoodSafety

Inspects meat and poultry products and provides safe handling and labeling guidelines.

▶ **CONGRESS**

For a listing of relevant congressional committees and subcommittees, please see page 3 or the Appendix.

▶ **NONGOVERNMENTAL**

Animal Health Institute, *1325 G St. N.W., #700, 20005-3104; (202) 637-2440. Fax, (202) 393-1667. Alexander S. Mathews, President. Web, www.ahi.org and Twitter, @AnimalsHealthy*

Membership: manufacturers of drugs and other products (including vaccines, pesticides, and vitamins) for pets and food-producing animals. Interests include pet health, livestock health, and disease outbreak prevention. Monitors legislation and regulations.

Compassion Over Killing, *6930 Carroll Ave., #910, Tacoma Park, MD 20912 (mailing address: P.O. Box 9773, Washington, DC 20016); (301) 891-2458. Fax, (301) 891-6815. Erica Meier, Executive Director. General email, info@cok.net*

Web, http://cok.net and Twitter, @TryVeg

Animal rights organization that focuses primarily on cruelty to animals in agriculture. Promotes vegetarianism.

Farm Animal Rights Movement (FARM), *10101 Ashburton Lane, Bethesda, MD 20817-1729; (301) 530-1737. Fax, (301) 530-5683. Alex Hershaft, President. Toll-free, 888-FARM-USA.*

General email, info@farmusa.org

Web, www.farmusa.org, www.livevegan.org and Twitter, @FARMUSA

Works to end use of animals for food. Interests include animal protection, consumer health, agricultural resources, and environmental quality. Conducts national educational campaigns, including World Farm Animals Day, the Live Vegan program, and the Great American Meatout. Monitors legislation and regulations.

Humane Farm Animal Care, P.O. Box 82, Middleburg, VA 20118; (703) 435-3883. Fax, (703) 435-3981. Adele Douglass, Chief Executive Officer; Mimi Stein, Executive Director.

General email, info@certifiedhumane.org

Web, www.certifiedhumane.org, Twitter, @CertifiedHumane and Facebook, www.facebook.com/CertifiedHumane

Seeks to improve the welfare of farm animals by providing viable, duly monitored standards for humane food production. Administers the Certified Humane Raised and Handled program for meat, poultry, eggs, and dairy products.

National Cattlemen's Beef Assn., Washington Office, 1275 Pennsylvania Ave. N.W., #801, 20004; (202) 347-0228. Fax, (202) 638-0607. Kendal Frazier, Chief Executive Officer.

Web, www.beefusa.org

Membership: individual cattlemen, state cattlemen's groups, and breed associations. Provides information on beef research, agricultural labor, beef grading, foreign trade, taxes, marketing, cattle economics, branding, animal health, and environmental management. (Headquarters in Denver, Colo.)

National Chicken Council, 1152 15th St. N.W., #430, 20005-2622; (202) 296-2622. Michael J. Brown, President.

General email, ncc@chickenusa.org

Web, www.nationalchickencouncil.org and Twitter, @chickencouncil

Trade association that represents the vertically integrated producers of 95 percent of the chickens raised and processed for meat in the United States. Monitors domestic and international legislation and regulations.

National Pork Producers Council, 122 C St. N.W., #875, 20001; (202) 347-3600. Fax, (202) 347-5265. Jim Heimerl, President; Nick Giodano, Chief Officer, in Washington, DC.

General email, news@nppc.org

Web, www.nppc.org, Twitter, @NPPC and Facebook, www.facebook.com/NationalPorkProducersCouncil

Membership: pork producers and state pork producer organizations. Interests include pork production, food safety, the environment, trade, and federal regulations. Monitors legislation and regulations. (Headquarters in Des Moines, Iowa.)

National Renderers Assn., 500 Montgomery St., #310, Alexandria, VA 22314; (703) 683-0155. Fax, (571) 970-2279. Nancy Foster, President.

General email, renderers@nationalrenderers.com

Web, http://nationalrenderers.org

Membership: manufacturers of meat meal and tallow. Compiles industry statistics; sponsors research; conducts seminars and workshops. Monitors legislation and regulations.

National Turkey Federation, 1225 New York Ave. N.W., #400, 20005-6404; (202) 898-0100. Fax, (202) 898-0203. Joel Brandenberger, President; Damon Wells, Senior Vice President of Government Relations.

General email, info@turkeyfed.org

Web, www.eatturkey.com, Twitter, @NatlTurkeyFed and Facebook, www.facebook.com/NationalTurkeyFederation

Membership: turkey growers, hatcheries, breeders, and processors. Promotes turkey consumption. Monitors legislation and regulations.

North American Meat Institute, 1150 Connecticut Ave. N.W., 12th Floor, 20036; (202) 587-4200. Fax, (202) 587-4300. Julia Anna Potts, President, (202) 587-4262; Eric Mittenthal, Public Affairs, (202) 587-4238.

General email, emittenthal@meatinstitute.org

Web, www.meatinstitute.org, Twitter, @MeatInstitute and Facebook, www.facebook.com/AmericanMeatInstitute

Membership: national and international meat and poultry packers, suppliers, and processors. Provides statistics on meat production and consumption, livestock, and feed grains. Funds meat research projects and consumer education programs; sponsors conferences and correspondence courses on meat production and processing. Monitors legislation and regulations. (Formed from merger of the North American Meat Assn. and American Meat Institute.)

Shelf-Stable Food Processors Assn. (SFPA), 1150 Connecticut Ave. N.W., 12th Floor, 20036; (202) 587-4200. Fax, (202) 587-4300. Julie Anna Potts, President; Susan Backus, Executive Secretary.

General email, info@meatinstitute.org

Web, www.meatinstitute.org and Twitter, @meatinstitute

Membership: shelf-stable food manufacturers and their suppliers. Provides information on the shelf-stable industry, particularly as it pertains to meat products. (Subsidiary of the North American Meat Institute.)

U.S. Hide, Skin, and Leather Assn. (USHSLA), 1150 Connecticut Ave. N.W., 12th Floor, 20036; (202) 587-4250. Fax, (202) 587-4300. Stephen Sothmann, President.

Web, www.ushsla.org

Membership: producers, brokers, dealers, processors, and exporters of hides and skins. Maintains liaison with allied trade associations and participates in programs on export statistics, hide price reporting, and freight rates; conducts seminars and consumer information programs. (Division of American Meat Institute.)

2

Business and Economics

GENERAL POLICY AND ANALYSIS

Basic Resources

▶ **AGENCIES**

Antitrust Division *(Justice Dept.), Technology and Financial Services,* 450 5th St. N.W., #7700, 20530; (202) 616-5924. Fax, (202) 616-8544. Aaron D. Hoag, Chief. General email, antitrust.atr@usdoj.gov

Web, www.justice.gov/atr/about/ntes.html

Reviews mergers in the areas of information technology, Internet-related businesses, computer hardware and software, high-technology components, manufacturing, professional associations, financial services, and the securities industry.

Bureau of Economic and Business Affairs (EB) *(State Dept.), Commercial and Business Affairs (CBA),* 2201 C St. N.W., #5820, 20520-5820; (202) 647-1625. Fax, (202) 647-3953. Scott Ticknor, Special Representative (Acting). General email, cbaweb@state.gov

Web, www.state.gov/e/eb/cba

Serves as primary contact in the State Dept. for U.S. businesses. Coordinates efforts to facilitate U.S. business interests abroad, ensures that U.S. business interests are given sufficient consideration in foreign policy, and provides assistance to firms with problems overseas (such as claims and trade complaints). Oversees the Global Entrepreneurship Program.

Commerce Dept., *1401 Constitution Ave. N.W., 20230; (202) 482-2000. Wilbur L. Ross, Secretary. Library, (202) 482-1154. Press, (202) 482-4883.*

Web, www.commerce.gov and Twitter, @CommerceGov

Acts as a principal adviser to the president on federal policy affecting industry and commerce; promotes job creation, national economic growth and development, competitiveness, international trade, and technological development; provides business and government with economic statistics, research, and analysis; encourages minority business; promotes tourism. Library open to the public by appointment.

Commerce Dept., *Business Liaison,* 1401 Constitution Ave. N.W., #5062, 20230; (202) 482-1360. Fax, (202) 482-4054. W. Patrick Wilson, Director. General email, businessliaison@doc.gov

Web, www.commerce.gov/doc/os/office-business-liaison

Serves as the federal government's central office for business assistance. Handles requests for information and services as well as complaints and suggestions from businesses; provides a forum for businesses to comment on federal regulations; initiates meetings on policy issues with industry groups, business organizations, trade and small business associations, and the corporate community.

Consumer Product Safety Commission (CPSC), *Economic Analysis,* 4330 East-West Hwy., Bethesda, MD 20814; (301) 504-7705. Fax, (978) 313-1418. Gregory B. Rodgers, Associate Executive Director, (301) 504-7702. Web, www.cpsc.gov

Conducts studies to determine the impact of CPSC's regulations on consumers, the economy, industry, and production. Studies the potential environmental effects of commission actions.

Council of Economic Advisers *(Executive Office of the President),* 725 17th St. N.W., 20502; (202) 395-5084. Fax, (202) 395-5630. Kevin Hassett, Chair; D. J. Nordquist, Chief of Staff. Web, www.whitehouse.gov/cea

Advisory body consisting of three members and supporting staff of economists. Monitors and analyzes the economy and advises the president on economic developments, trends, and policies and on the economic implications of other policy initiatives. Prepares the annual *Economic Report of the President* for Congress. Assesses economic implications of international policy.

Economics and Statistics Administration *(Commerce Dept.),* 1401 Constitution Ave. N.W., #4848, 20230; (202) 482-6607. Fax, (202) 482-0432. Karen Dunn Kelley, Under Secretary. General email, ESAwebmaster@doc.gov

Web, www.commerce.gov/doc/economics-and-statistics-administration and Twitter, @ESAstats

Advises the secretary on economic policy matters, including consumer and capital spending, inventory status, and the short- and long-term outlook in output and unemployment. Seeks to improve economic productivity and growth. Serves as departmental liaison with the Council of Economic Advisers and other government agencies concerned with economic policy. Supervises and sets policy for the Census Bureau and the Bureau of Economic Analysis.

Federal Reserve System, *Board of Governors,* 20th St. and Constitution Ave. N.W., 20551; (202) 452-3000. Jerome H. Powell, Chair; Richard H. Clarida, Vice Chair. Congressional Liaison, (202) 452-3456. Information (meetings), (202) 452-3204. Public Affairs, (202) 452-2955. Publications, (202) 452-3245. TTY, (202) 263-4869. General email, frboard-publicaffairs@frb.gov

Web, www.federalreserve.gov, Twitter, @federalreserve and Facebook, www.facebook.com/federalreserve

Sets U.S. monetary policy. Supervises the Federal Reserve System and influences credit conditions through the buying and selling of Treasury securities in the open market by fixing the amount of reserves depository institutions must maintain and by determining discount rates.

National Economic Council (NEC) *(Executive Office of the President),* The White House, 20502; (202) 456-1111. Larry Kudlow, Director. Web, www.whitehouse.gov

Comprises cabinet members and other high-ranking executive branch officials. Coordinates domestic and international economic policymaking, provides economic policy advice to the president, ensures that policy decisions and programs are consistent with the president's economic goals, and monitors the implementation of the president's economic agenda.

BUSINESS AND ECONOMICS RESOURCES IN CONGRESS

For a complete listing of congressional committees, including their full contact information, leadership, membership, and jurisdictions, please refer to the Appendix on pages 823–944.

HOUSE:

House Agriculture Committee, (202) 225-2171.
Web, agriculture.house.gov
> **Subcommittee on Biotechnology, Horticulture, and Research,** (202) 225-2171.

House Appropriations Committee, (202) 225-2771.
Web, appropriations.house.gov
> **Subcommittee on Commerce, Justice, Science, and Related Agencies,** (202) 225-3351.
> **Subcommittee on Financial Services and General Government,** (202) 225-7245.
> **Subcommittee on Transportation, Housing and Urban Development, and Related Agencies,** (202) 225-2141.

House Budget Committee, (202) 226-7270.
Web, budget.house.gov

House Energy and Commerce Committee, (202) 225-2927.
Web, energycommerce.house.gov
> **Subcommittee on Digital Commerce and Consumer Protection,** (202) 225-2927.
> **Subcommittee on Energy,** (202) 225-2927.
> **Subcommittee on Environment,** (202) 225-2927.
> **Subcommittee on Health,** (202) 225-2927.

House Financial Services Committee, (202) 225-7502.
Web, financialservices.house.gov
> **Subcommittee on Housing and Insurance,** (202) 225-7502.

House Foreign Affairs Committee, (202) 225-5021.
Web, foreignaffairs.house.gov
> **Subcommittee on Terrorism, Nonproliferation, and Trade,** (202) 226-1500.

House Judiciary Committee, (202) 225-3951.
Web, judiciary.house.gov
> **Subcommittee on Courts, Intellectual Property, and the Internet,** (202) 225-5741.
> **Subcommittee on Regulatory Reform, Commercial, and Antitrust Law,** (202) 226-7680.

House Oversight and Government Reform Committee, (202) 225-5074.
Web, oversight.house.gov
> **Subcommittee on Government Operations,** (202) 225-5074.

House Science, Space, and Technology Committee, (202) 225-6371.
Web, science.house.gov
> **Subcommittee on Research and Technology,** (202) 225-6371.

House Small Business Committee, (202) 225-5821.
Web, smallbusiness.house.gov
> **Subcommittee on Agriculture, Energy, and Trade,** (202) 225-5821.
> **Subcommittee on Contracting and Workforce,** (202) 225-5821.
> **Subcommittee on Economic Growth, Tax, and Capital Access,** (202) 225-5821.
> **Subcommittee on Health and Technology,** (202) 225-5821.
> **Subcommittee on Investigations, Oversight, and Regulations,** (202) 225-5821.

House Ways and Means Committee, (202) 225-3625.
Web, waysandmeans.house.gov
> **Subcommittee on Trade,** (202) 225-6649.

National Institute of Standards and Technology (NIST)
(Commerce Dept.), Baldrige Performance Excellence Program, 100 Bureau Dr., MS 1020, Gaithersburg, MD 20899-1020; (301) 975-2036. Fax, (301) 948-3716. Robert Fangmeyer, Director, (301) 975-4781.
General email, baldrige@nist.gov

Web, www.nist.gov/baldrige and Twitter, @BaldrigeProgram

Public–private partnership that educates business, education, and organization leaders on industry-specific best-practices management. Offers organizational assessment tools and criteria.

National Institute of Standards and Technology (NIST)
(Commerce Dept.), Special Programs Office, 100 Bureau Dr., MS 4701, Gaithersburg, MD 20899-4701; (301) 975-4447. Fax, (301) 975-8972. Richard R. Cavanagh, Director. General information, (301) 975-2756.
Web, www.nist.gov/spo

Fosters collaboration among government, military, academic, professional, and private organizations to respond to critical national needs through science-based standards and technology innovation, including the areas of manufacturing and physical infrastructure.

National Institute of Standards and Technology (NIST)
(Commerce Dept.), Standards Services, 100 Bureau Dr., MS 2100, Gaithersburg, MD 20899; (301) 975-4000. Fax, (301) 975-4715. Gordon Gillerman, Director, (301) 975-8406.
General email, sco@nist.gov

Web, www.nist.gov/standardsgov and www.nist.gov/topics/standards

Monitors and participates in industries' development of federal and global standards and standard-enforcement mechanisms. Conducts standards-related research and training and holds workshops for domestic and international audiences. Provides information on industry

JOINT:

Joint Committee on Taxation, (202) 225-3621.
Web, jct.gov

Joint Economic Committee, (202) 224-5171.
Web, jec.senate.gov

SENATE:

Senate Agriculture, Nutrition, and Forestry
    Committee, (202) 224-2035.
Web, agriculture.senate.gov
    Subcommittee on Commodities, Risk
        Management, and Trade, (202) 224-2035.
Senate Appropriations Committee, (202) 224-7257.
Web, appropriations.senate.gov
    Subcommittee on Commerce, Justice,
        Science, and Related Agencies,
        (202) 224-5202.
    Subcommittee on Labor, Health and Human
        Services, Education, and Related Agencies,
        (202) 224-9145.
Senate Banking, Housing, and Urban Affairs
    Committee, (202) 224-7391.
Web, banking.senate.gov
    Subcommittee on Economic Policy,
        (202) 224-7391.
    Subcommittee on Financial Institutions and
        Consumer Protection, (202) 224-7391.
    Subcommittee on National Security and
        International Trade and Finance,
        (202) 224-7391.
    Subcommittee on Securities, Insurance, and
        Investment, (202) 224-7391.
Senate Budget Committee, (202) 224-0642.
Web, budget.senate.gov

Senate Commerce, Science, and Transportation
    Committee, (202) 224-1251.
Web, commerce.senate.gov
    Subcommittee on Consumer Protection, Product
        Safety, Insurance and Data Security,
        (202) 224-1251.
Senate Finance Committee, (202) 224-4515.
Web, finance.senate.gov
    Subcommittee on Energy, Natural Resources, and
        Infrastructure, (202) 224-4515.
    Subcommittee on Fiscal Responsibility and
        Economic Growth, (202) 224-4515.
    Subcommittee on Health Care, (202) 224-4515.
    Subcommittee on International Trade, Customs,
        and Global Competitiveness, (202) 224-4515.
    Subcommittee on Social Security, Pensions and
        Family Policy, (202) 224-4515.
    Subcommittee on Taxation and IRS Oversight,
        (202) 224-4515.
Senate Health, Education, Labor, and Pensions
    Committee, (202) 224-5375.
Web, help.senate.gov
Senate Homeland Security and Governmental Affairs
    Committee, (202) 224-4751.
Web, hsgac.senate.gov
    Permanent Subcommittee on Investigations,
        (202) 224-3721.
Senate Judiciary Committee, (202) 224-5225.
Web, judiciary.senate.gov
    Subcommittee on Antitrust, Competition Policy,
        and Consumer Rights, (202) 224-5444.
    Subcommittee on Oversight, Agency Action,
        Federal Rights, and Federal Courts,
        (202) 224-4224.

standards and specifications, conformity assessment, test methods, domestic and international technical regulations, codes, and recommended practices.

National Security Staff (NSS) *(Executive Office of the President), International Economic Affairs,* The White House, 1600 Pennsylvania Ave., 20504; (202) 456-9281. Fax, (202) 456-9280. Cletus R. Willems, Deputy National Security Adviser.
Web, www.whitehouse.gov/nsc

Advises the president, the National Security Council, and the National Economic Council on all aspects of U.S. foreign policy dealing with U.S. international economic policies.

National Women's Business Council, *409 3rd St. S.W., 5th Floor, 20416; (202) 205-3850. Fax, (202) 205-6825. Nina Roque, Executive Director.*

General email, info@nwbc.gov

Web, www.nwbc.gov and Facebook, www.facebook.com/ NWBCgov

Independent, congressionally mandated council established by the Women's Business Ownership Act of 1988. Reviews the status of women-owned businesses nationwide and makes policy recommendations to the president, Congress, and the Small Business Administration. Assesses the role of the federal government in aiding and promoting women-owned businesses.

Small Business Administration (SBA), *409 3rd St. S.W., 20416-7000; (202) 205-6605. Fax, (202) 205-6802. Linda McMahon, Administrator; Vacant, Deputy Administrator. Locator, (202) 205-6600. Toll-free information (Answer Desk), (800) 827-5722. TTY, (800) 877-8339.*

General email, *answerdesk@sba.gov*

Web, *www.sba.gov* and *Twitter, @SBAgov*

Maintains and strengthens the nation's economy by aiding, counseling, assisting, and protecting the interests of small businesses and by helping families and businesses recover from natural disasters.

Treasury Dept., *1500 Pennsylvania Ave. N.W., #3330, 20220; (202) 622-2000. Fax, (202) 622-6415. Steven Mnuchin, Secretary; Justin Muzinich, Deputy Secretary. Library, (202) 622-0990. Press, (202) 622-2960. TTY, (800) 877-8339.*

General email, *press@treasury.gov*

Web, *https://home.treasury.gov* and *Twitter, @USTreasury*

Serves as chief financial officer of the government and adviser to the president on economic policy. Formulates and recommends domestic and international financial, economic, tax, and broad fiscal policies; manages the public debt; collects monies owed to the U.S. government; supervises national banks and thrifts. Library open to the public by appointment.

Treasury Dept., *Economic Policy, 1500 Pennsylvania Ave. N.W., #3454, 20220; (202) 622-2200. Fax, (202) 622-2633. Diana Furchtgott-Roth, Assistant Secretary (Acting).*

Web, *www.treasury.gov/about/organizational-structure/offices/Pages/Economic-Policy.aspx*

Assists and advises the Treasury secretary in the formulation and execution of domestic and international economic policies and programs; helps prepare economic forecasts for the federal budget.

▶**CONGRESS**

For a listing of relevant congressional committees and subcommittees, please see pages 34–35 or the Appendix.

▶**NONGOVERNMENTAL**

American Business Conference, *1828 L St. N.W., #280, 20036; (202) 822-9300. Fax, (202) 467-4070. John Endean, President; Alfred P. West Jr., Chair.*

General email, *info@americanbusinessconference.org*

Web, *http://americanbusinessconference.org*

Membership: leaders of midsize high-growth companies. Seeks a public policy role for growth companies. Studies capital formation, tax policy, regulatory reform, and international trade.

American Chamber of Commerce Executives, *1330 Braddock Pl., #300, Alexandria, VA 22314; (703) 998-0072. Sheree Anne Kelly, President, (703) 998-3540.*

General email, *info@acce.org*

Web, *www.acce.org, Twitter, @ACCEHQ* and *Facebook, www.facebook.com/ACCEHQ*

Membership: executives of local, state, and international chambers of commerce. Conducts educational programs and conferences for members on topics of interest, including economic development, government relations,

management symposiums, peer networking, industry information and data, and membership drives. Assembles special interest committees for members.

American Council for Capital Formation (ACCF), *1001 Connecticut Ave. N.W., #620, 20036; (202) 293-5811. Mark A. Bloomfield, President. Press, (202) 420-9361.*

General email, *info@accf.org*

Web, *http://accf.org, Twitter, @ACCFmedia* and *Facebook, www.facebook.com/ACCFDC*

Promotes tax, trade, and environmental policies conducive to saving, investment, and economic growth. Affiliated with the ACCF Center for Policy Research, which conducts and funds research on capital formation topics. Monitors legislation and regulations.

American Enterprise Institute (AEI), *1789 Massachusetts Ave. N.W., 20036; (202) 862-5800. Fax, (202) 862-7177. Arthur C. Brooks, President, (202) 419-5213; John Cusey, Vice President of Government Affairs, (202) 828-6021. Press, (202) 862-5829.*

Web, *www.aei.org*

Public policy think tank promoting democracy, free enterprise, and entrepreneurship. Conducts research and sponsors events. Interests include monetary, tax, trade, financial services, and regulatory policy, labor, social security issues, and retirement.

American Society of Assn. Executives (ASAE), *1575 Eye St. N.W., #1100, 20005-1103; (202) 371-0940. Fax, (202) 371-8315. John H. Graham IV, President, (202) 626-2741. Press, (202) 326-9505. Toll-free, (888) 950-2723.*

General email, *ASAEservice@asaecenter.org*

Web, *www.asaecenter.org* and *Twitter, @ASAEcenter*

Membership: managers of trade associations, membership societies, and volunteer organizations. Conducts research and provides educational programs on association management, trends, and developments. Library open to the public.

Americans for Prosperity, *1310 N. Courthouse Rd., #700, Arlington, VA 22201; (703) 224-3200. Fax, (703) 224-3201. Emily Seidel, Chief Executive Officer. Toll-free, (866) 730-0150.*

General email, *info@AFPhq.org*

Web, *www.americansforprosperity.org* and *Twitter, @AFPhq*

Grassroots organization that seeks to educate citizens about economic policy and encourage their participation in the public policy process. Supports limited government and free markets on the local, state, and federal levels. Specific interests include Social Security, trade, and taxes. Monitors legislation and regulations.

Aspen Institute, *2300 N St., N.W., #700, 20037; (202) 736-5800. Fax, (202) 467-0790. Dan Porterfield, President. Press, (202) 736-3849.*

General email, *info@aspeninstitute.org*

Web, *www.aspeninstitute.org* and *Twitter, @AspenInstitute*

Commerce Department

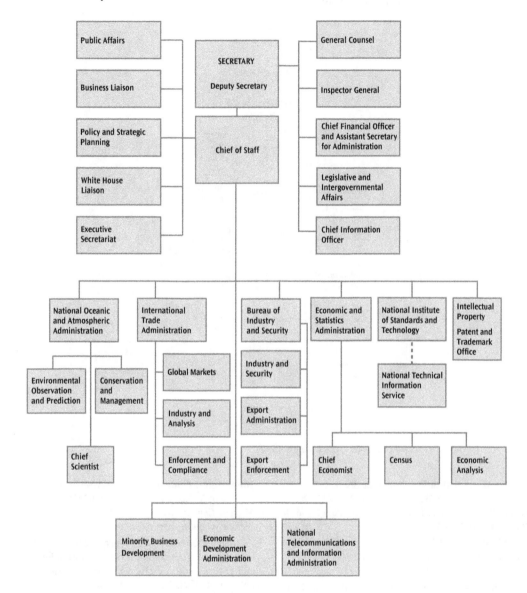

Educational and policy studies organization. Promotes consideration of the public good in a wide variety of policy areas, including business management and economic development. Working with international partners, offers educational seminars, nonpartisan policy forums, public conferences and events, and leadership development initiatives.

Atlas Network, *4075 Wilson Blvd., #310, Arlington, VA 22203; (202) 449-8449. Fax, (202) 280-1259. Brad Lipps, Chief Executive Officer. Press, (202) 449-8441. General email, info@atlasnetwork.org*

Web, www.atlasnetwork.org and Twitter, @AtlasNetwork

Connects free market–oriented think tanks that seek to reform global economic policy. Distributes grants to new

institutes, international student groups, and select partner projects. Administers awards and training programs for free-enterprise organization leaders. Holds forums and events that focus on the advancement of a free-market economic system.

The Brookings Institution, *Center on Regulation and Markets, 1775 Massachusetts Ave. N.W., 20036; Aaron Klein, Policy Director. Web, www.brookings.edu/center/center-on-regulation-and-markets and Twitter, @AaronDKlein*

Research center promoting improvements in regulatory policymaking and efficient and equitable functioning of economic markets; makes regulatory reform recommendations.

Federal Trade Commission

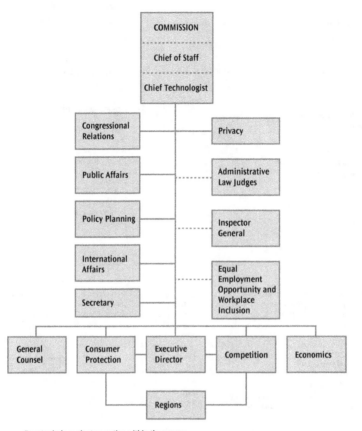

- - - - Denotes independent operation within the agency

The Brookings Institution, *Economic Studies, 1775 Massachusetts Ave. N.W., 20036-2188; (202) 797-6000. Fax, (202) 797-6181. Ted Gayer, Director, (202) 797-6230. Press, (202) 797-6105.*
General email, escomment@brookings.edu

Web, www.brookings.edu/economics and
Twitter, @BrookingsEcon

Sponsors economic research and publishes studies on domestic and international economics, macroeconomics, worldwide economic growth and stability, public finance, industrial organization and regulation, labor economics, social policy, and the economics of human resources.

The Brookings Institution, *Metropolitan Policy Program, 1755 Massachusetts Ave. N.W., 20036; (202) 797-6000. Fax, (202) 797-2965. Amy Liu, Director, (202) 797-2464. Press, (202) 797-6105.*
General email, metro@brookings.edu

Web, www.brookings.edu/metro

Provides research and policy analysis to public, private, and nonprofit leaders to drive economic growth and prosperity. Interests include human capital and economic mobility, industrial innovation and productivity, global marketplace engagement, and infrastructure sustainability.

The Business Council, *1901 Pennsylvania Ave. N.W., #307, 20006; (202) 298-7650. Fax, (202) 785-0296. Marlene Colucci, Executive Director.*
Web, www.thebusinesscouncil.org

Membership: current and former chief executive officers of major corporations. Serves as a forum for business and government to exchange views and explore public policy as it affects U.S. business interests.

The Business Roundtable, *300 New Jersey Ave. N.W., #800, 20001; (202) 872-1260. Fax, (202) 466-3509. Joshua Bolten, President. Press, (202) 496-3289.*
General email, info@brt.org

Web, www.businessroundtable.org and
Twitter, @BizRoundtable

Membership: chief executives of the nation's largest corporations. Examines issues of taxation, antitrust law, corporate governance, international trade, employment policy, and the federal budget. Monitors legislation and regulations.

Business–Higher Education Forum, *2025 M St. N.W., #800, 20036; (202) 367-1189. Fax, (202) 367-2189. Brian K. Fitzgerald, Chief Executive Officer.*

General email, info@bhef.com

Web, www.bhef.com, Twitter, @BHEF

Media, ursula.gross@bhef.org

Membership: chief executive officers of major corporations, foundations, colleges, and universities. Develops and promotes policy positions to enhance U.S. competitiveness. Interests include improving student achievement and readiness for college and work; and strengthening higher education, particularly in the fields of science, technology, engineering, and math.

Center for Study of Public Choice *(George Mason University), Carow Hall, MS 1D3, 4400 University Dr., Fairfax, VA 22030-4444; (703) 993-2330. Fax, (703) 993-2323. Alexander Tabarrok, Director.*

Web, www.gmu.edu/centers/publicchoice

Promotes research in public choice, an interdisciplinary approach to the study of the relationship between economic and political institutions. Interests include constitutional economics, public finance, federalism and local government, econometrics, and trade protection and regulation. Sponsors conferences and seminars.

Committee for Economic Development, *1530 Wilson Blvd., #400, Arlington, VA 22209; (202) 296-5860. Fax, (202) 223-0776. Bernard Bailey, Chief Executive Officer; Joseph J. Minarik, Senior Vice President. Toll-free, (800) 676-7353.*

General email, info@ced.org

Web, www.ced.org and Twitter, @CEDupdate

Nonpartisan, business-led public-policy organization that offers research and analysis. Interests include tax and health care reform, corporate governance and the role of women as administrators, education, immigration, older workers, and international trade.

Competitive Enterprise Institute, *1310 L St. N.W., 7th Floor, 20005; (202) 331-1010. Fax, (202) 331-0640. Kent Lassman, President. Media, (202) 331-2277.*

General email, info@cei.org

Web, https://cei.org and Twitter, @ceidotorg

Advocates free enterprise and limited government. Produces policy analyses on tax, budget, financial services, antitrust, biotechnological, and environmental issues. Monitors legislation and litigates against restrictive regulations through its Free Market Legal Program.

Council on Competitiveness, *900 17th St. N.W., #700, 20006; (202) 682-4292. Fax, (202) 682-5150. Deborah L. Wince-Smith, President; William (Bill) C. Bates, Executive Vice President, (202) 969-3395.*

General email, info@compete.org

Web, www.compete.org and Twitter, @CompeteNow

Nonpartisan peer organization. Membership: chief executives from business, education, and labor. Seeks increased public awareness of issues related to economic competitiveness. Works to set a national action agenda for U.S. competitiveness in global markets.

Economic Policy Institute, *1225 Eye St., #600, 20005; (202) 775-8810. Fax, (202) 775-0819. Thea Lee, President.*

General email, epi@epi.org

Web, www.epi.org

Research and educational organization that publishes analyses on economics, economic development, competitiveness, income distribution, industrial competitiveness, and investment. Conducts public conferences and seminars.

Economic Strategy Institute, *1730 Rhode Island Ave. N.W., #414, 20036; (202) 213-7051. Fax, (202) 965-1104. Clyde V. Prestowitz Jr., President.*

General email, info@econstrat.org

Web, www.econstrat.org and Twitter, @clydeprestowitz

Works to increase U.S. economic competitiveness through research on domestic and international economic policies, industrial and technological developments, and global security issues. Testifies before Congress and government agencies.

Good Jobs First, *1616 P St. N.W., #210, 20036; (202) 232-1616. Greg LeRoy, Executive Director.*

General email, info@goodjobsfirst.org

Web, www.goodjobsfirst.org, Twitter, @GoodJobsFirst and Facebook, www.facebook.com/GoodJobsFirst

Promotes corporate and government accountability in economic development incentives; primary focus is on state and local job subsidies with emerging work on federal development programs and federal regulatory violations data. Maintains Subsidy Tracker database. Includes Good Jobs New York and the Corporate Research Project.

Greater Washington Board of Trade, *800 Connecticut Ave. N.W., #1001, 20006; (202) 857-5900. Fax, (202) 223-2648. Jack McDougle, President.*

General email, info@bot.org

Web, www.bot.org and Twitter, @GWBoardofTrade

Promotes and plans economic growth for the capital region. Supports business-government partnerships, technological training, and transportation planning; promotes international trade; works to increase economic viability of the city of Washington. Monitors legislation and regulations at local, state, and federal levels.

Mercatus Center *(George Mason University), 3434 Washington Blvd., 4th Floor, Arlington, VA 22201; (703) 993-4930. Fax, (703) 993-4935. Tyler Cowen, Director. Information, (800) 815-5711.*

General email, mercatus@mercatus.gmu.edu

Web, www.mercatus.org and Twitter, @tylercowen

Research center that studies sustained prosperity in societies and the conditions that contribute to economic success. Interests include the drivers of social, political, and economic change; international and domestic economic development; entrepreneurship and the institutions that enable it; the benefits and costs of regulatory policy; government performance and transparency; and good governance practices. Also studies the benefits of market-oriented systems using market process analysis. Seeks to bridge the gap between academic research and public policy problems.

National Assn. of Corporate Directors, *1515 N. Courthouse Rd., #1200, Arlington, VA 22201; (571) 367-3700. Fax, (571) 367-3699. Peter Gleason, President.*
General email, join@nacdonline.org
Web, www.nacdonline.org and Twitter, @NACD

Membership: executives of public, private, and nonprofit companies. Serves as a clearinghouse on corporate governance and current board practices. Sponsors seminars, peer forums, research, publications, and board development programs.

National Assn. of Manufacturers (NAM), *State Associations Group, 733 10th St. N.W., #700, 20001; (202) 637-3052. Fax, (202) 637-3182. Amy Rawlings, Executive Director. Toll-free, (800) 814-8468.*
Web, www.nam.org

Membership: employer associations at the regional, state, and local levels. Works to strengthen the U.S. competitive enterprise system. Represents views of the industry on business and economic issues; sponsors conferences and seminars.

National Assn. of State Budget Officers, *444 N. Capitol St. N.W., #642, 20001-1511; (202) 624-5382. Fax, (202) 624-7745. John Hicks, Executive Director, (202) 624-8804.*
General email, nasbo-direct@nasbo.org
Web, www.nasbo.org and Twitter, @NASBO

Membership: state budget and financial officers. Advances state budget practices through research, policy analysis, education, and knowledge sharing. Publishes reports on budget-related issues; shares best practices; provides training and technical assistance. (Affiliate of the National Governors Assn.)

National Economists Club, *P.O. Box 33511, 20033-3511; (703) 493-8824. Michael Chow, Chair; Cliff Waldman, President.*
General email, manager@national-economists.org
Web, www.national-economists.org and
Twitter, @NatlEconClub

Provides venues for scholars, policymakers, business leaders, and public figures to present and defend their views on timely economic topics. Offers members employment and networking opportunities.

Partnership for Public Service, *1100 New York Ave. N.W., #200E, 20005; (202) 775-9111. Fax, (202) 775-8885. Max Stier, President. Press, (202) 775-6868.*
Web, www.ourpublicservice.org and
Twitter, @RPublicService

Membership: large corporations and private businesses, including financial and information technology organizations. Seeks to improve government efficiency, productivity, and management through a cooperative effort of the public and private sectors.

Prosperity Now, *1200 G St. N.W., #400, 20005; (202) 408-9788. Andrea Levere, President.*
General email, hello@prosperitynow.org
Web, https://prosperitynow.org and
Twitter, @prosperitynow

Works to alleviate poverty by expanding economic opportunity and participation, bringing together community practice, public policy, and private markets in new and effective ways. (Formerly Corp. for Enterprise Development.)

U.S. Business and Industry Council (USBIC), *512 C St. N.E., 20002; (202) 266-3980. Fax, (202) 266-3981. Kevin L. Kearns, President.*
Twitter, @KevinLKearns

Membership: owners of privately held manufacturing, farming, processing, and fabricating companies. Advocates energy independence, reindustrialization, and effective use of natural resources and manufacturing capacity. Interests include business tax reduction, the liability crisis, defense and other federal spending, and the trade deficit. Media network distributes op-ed pieces to newspapers and radio stations. (Affiliated with AmericanEconomicAlert.org.)

U.S. Chamber Litigation Center, *1615 H St. N.W., 20062-2000; (202) 463-5337. Fax, (202) 463-5707. John Wood, Senior Vice President.*
General email, litigationcenter@uschamber.com
Web, www.chamberlitigation.com

Public policy law firm of the U.S. Chamber of Commerce. Advocates businesses' positions in court on such issues as antitrust, bankruptcy, and employment, as well as evironmental and constitutional law. Provides businesses with legal assistance and amicus support in legal proceedings before federal courts and agencies.

U.S. Chamber of Commerce, *1615 H St. N.W., 20062-2000; (202) 659-6000. Fax, (202) 463-5327. Thomas J. Donohue, Chief Executive Officer. Customer Service, (800) 638-6582. Press, (202) 463-5682.*
Web, www.uschamber.com and Twitter, @USChamber

Federation of businesses; trade and professional associations; state and local chambers of commerce; and American chambers of commerce abroad. Sponsors programs on management, business confidence, small business, consumer affairs, economic policy, minority business, and tax policy. Monitors legislation and regulations.

U.S. Chamber of Commerce, *Congressional and Public Affairs, 1615 H St. N.W., 20062-2000; (202) 463-5600. Jack Howard, Senior Vice President.*
Web, www.uschamber.com

Advocates businesses' position on government and regulatory affairs. Monitors legislation and regulations on antitrust and corporate policy, product liability, and business-consumer relations.

U.S. Chamber of Commerce, *Economic and Tax Policy, 1615 H St. N.W., 20062-2000; (202) 463-5620. Fax, (202) 463-3174. J. D. Foster, Chief Economist. Press, (202) 463-5682.*
Web, www.uschamber.com/economic-policy

Represents the business community's views on economic policy, including government spending, the federal budget, and tax issues. Forecasts the economy of the United States and other industrialized nations and projects the impact of major policy changes. Studies economic trends and analyzes their effect on the business community.

Coins and Currency

▶AGENCIES

Bureau of Engraving and Printing (BEP) *(Treasury Dept.)*, *14th and C Sts. S.W., 20228; (202) 874-4000. Fax, (202) 874-3177. Leonard R. Olijar, Director. Information, (877) 874-4114. Tours, (202) 874-2330. General email, moneyfactory.info@bep.gov*

Web, www.moneyfactory.gov

Designs, engraves, and prints Federal Reserve notes, military certificates, White House invitations, presidential portraits, and special security documents for the federal government.

Bureau of Engraving and Printing (BEP) *(Treasury Dept.)*, *Mutilated Currency Division*, *14th and C Sts. S.W., #344A, 20018 (mailing address: BEP/MCD, #344A, P.O. Box 37048, Washington, DC 20013); (202) 874-2141. Tryst Hensell, Head, (202) 874-4373. Toll-free, (866) 575-2361. General email, mcdstatus@bep.gov*

Web, www.moneyfactory.gov

Redeems U.S. currency that has been mutilated.

Bureau of the Fiscal Service *(Treasury Dept.)*, *401 14th St. S.W., #545, 20227; (202) 874-7000. Fax, (202) 874-6743. Kim McCoy, Commissioner. Media and congressional inquiries, (202) 504-3535. Public Affairs, (202) 504-3502. Savings Bonds, (844) 284-2676. Web, www.fiscal.treasury.gov, Twitter, @FiscalService and Facebook, www.facebook.com/fiscalservice and Buy and redeem securities online, www.treasurydirect.gov*

Prepares and publishes for the president, Congress, and the public monthly, quarterly, and annual statements of government financial transactions, including reports on U.S. currency and coins in circulation.

Federal Reserve System, Board of Governors, *20th St. and Constitution Ave. N.W., 20551; (202) 452-3000. Jerome H. Powell, Chair; Richard H. Clarida, Vice Chair. Congressional Liaison, (202) 452-3456. Information (meetings), (202) 452-3204. Public Affairs, (202) 452-2955. Publications, (202) 452-3245. TTY, (202) 263-4869. General email, frboard-publicaffairs@frb.gov*

Web, www.federalreserve.gov, Twitter, @federalreserve and Facebook, www.facebook.com/federalreserve

Influences the availability of money as part of its responsibility for monetary policy; maintains reading room for inspection of records that are available to the public.

National Museum of American History *(Smithsonian Institution)*, **National Numismatic Collection,** *14th St. and Constitution Ave. N.W., 20013 (mailing address: P.O. Box 37012, MRC609, Washington, DC 20013-7012); (202) 633-3854. Ellen Feingold, Curator of Numismatic Collection.*

General email, NMHA-NNC@si.edu

Web, http://americanhistory.si.edu/collections/numismatics

Develops and maintains collections of ancient, medieval, modern, U.S., and world coins; U.S. and world currencies; tokens; medals; orders and decorations; and traditional exchange media. Conducts research and responds to public inquiries. Collection can be viewed online.

Treasury Dept., *1500 Pennsylvania Ave. N.W., #3330, 20220; (202) 622-2000. Fax, (202) 622-6415. Steven Mnuchin, Secretary; Justin Muzinich, Deputy Secretary. Library, (202) 622-0990. Press, (202) 622-2960. TTY, (800) 877-8339. General email, press@treasury.gov*

Web, https://home.treasury.gov and Twitter, @USTreasury

Oversees the manufacture of U.S. coins and currency; submits to Congress final reports on the minting of coins or any changes in currency. Library open to the public by appointment.

Treasury Dept., *Treasurer of the United States,* *1500 Pennsylvania Ave. N.W., #2134, 20220; (202) 622-0100. Jovita Carranza, Treasurer.*

Web, www.treasury.gov/about/organizational-structure/offices/Pages/Office-of-the-Treasurer.aspx

Advises the secretary of the Treasury on matters relating to coinage, currency, and the production of other instruments issued by the United States. Has direct oversight over the U.S. Mint, Bureau of Engraving and Printing, and Fort Knox, and is a key liaison with the Federal Reserve. Represents the department in public engagement efforts.

U.S. Mint *(Treasury Dept.)*, *801 9th St. N.W., 8th Floor, 20220; (202) 756-6468. Fax, (202) 756-6160. David J. Ryder, Director. Customer service, (800) 872-6468. Information, (202) 354-7227. Press, (202) 354-7222. TTY, (888) 321-6468. Web, www.usmint.gov, Twitter, @usmint*

General email, usmint-support@usmcatalog.com

Manufactures and distributes all domestic coins; safeguards the government's holdings of precious metals; manufactures and sells commemorative coins and medals of historic interest. Maintains a kiosk at its main building.

▶NONGOVERNMENTAL

Americans for Common Cents, *1900 K St. N.W., 20006-1102; (800) 561-7909. Fax, (202) 408-6399. Mark Weller, Executive Director.*

General email, info@pennies.org

Web, www.pennies.org

Educates policymakers and the public about the penny's impact on the economy. Monitors legislation and regulations to advocate keeping the one-cent coin in the U.S. monetary system.

Federal Budget

▶**AGENCIES**

Bureau of the Fiscal Service *(Treasury Dept.)*, *401 14th St. S.W., #545, 20227; (202) 874-7000. Fax, (202) 874-6743. Kim McCoy, Commissioner. Media and congressional inquiries, (202) 504-3535. Public Affairs, (202) 504-3502. Savings Bonds, (844) 284-2676.*
Web, www.fiscal.treasury.gov, Twitter, @FiscalService and Facebook, www.facebook.com/fiscalservice and Buy and redeem securities online, www.treasurydirect.gov

Borrows to finance federal government operations by selling public debt securities, Treasury notes, and bonds; maintains all records on series EE and HH savings bonds.

Federal Financing Bank *(Treasury Dept.)*, *1500 Pennsylvania Ave. N.W., 20220; (202) 622-2470. Fax, (202) 622-0707. Christopher Tuttle, Chief Financial Officer. General email, FFB@treasury.gov*
Web, www.treasury.gov/ffb

Coordinates federal agency borrowing by purchasing securities issued or guaranteed by federal agencies; funds its operations by borrowing from the Treasury.

Office of Management and Budget (OMB) *(Executive Office of the President)*, *725 17th St. N.W., 20503; (202) 395-3080. Fax, (202) 395-3888. Mick Mulvaney, Director; Russell Vought, Deputy Director of Management. Press, (202) 395-7254.*
Web, www.whitehouse.gov/omb and Twitter, @OMBPress

Prepares the president's annual budget; works with the Council of Economic Advisers and the Treasury Dept. to develop the federal government's fiscal program; oversees administration of the budget; reviews government regulations; coordinates administration procurement and management policy.

Office of Management and Budget (OMB) *(Executive Office of the President)*, *Energy, Science, and Water, 725 17th St. N.W., #8002, 20503; (202) 395-3404. Fax, (202) 395-3049. Jim Herz, Associate Director. Press, (202) 395-7254.*
Web, www.whitehouse.gov/omb

Advises in budget preparation for federal energy, science, and space programs.

Office of Management and Budget (OMB) *(Executive Office of the President)*, *Transportation, 725 17th St. N.W., #9002, 20503; (202) 395-6138. Fax, (202) 395-4797. David Connolly, Chief. Press, (202) 395-7254.*
Web, www.whitehouse.gov/omb

Assists and advises the OMB director on budget preparation, proposed legislation, and evaluations of Transportation Dept. programs, policies, and activities.

Office of Management and Budget (OMB) *(Executive Office of the President)*, *Water and Power, 725 17th St.*

N.W., #8002, 20503; (202) 395-4590. Fax, (202) 395-4817. Kelly Colyar, Chief. Press, (202) 395-7254.
Web, www.whitehouse.gov/omb

Reviews all plans and budgets related to federal or federally assisted water power and related land resource projects.

Treasury Dept., Domestic Finance, Debt Management, *1500 Pennsylvania Ave. N.W., #2417, 20220; (202) 622-1885. Fax, (202) 622-0244. Fred Pietrangeli, Director. General email, Debt.Management@do.treas.gov*
Web, www.treasury.gov/about/organizational-structure/offices/Pages/-Debt-Management.aspx

Provides financial and economic analysis on government financing and Treasury debt management. Coordinates, analyzes, and reviews government borrowing, lending, and investment activities. Determines interest rates for government borrowing and lending programs.

Treasury Dept., Domestic Finance, Policy and Legislative Review, *1120 Vermont Ave. N.W., #916B, 20005; (202) 622-2450. Fax, (202) 622-0427. Vacant, Director. General email, policyandlegislativereview@do.treas.gov*
Web, www.treasury.gov/about/organizational-structure/offices/Pages/-Office-of-Policy-and-Legislative-Review.aspx

Analyzes federal credit program principles and standards, legislation, and proposals related to government borrowing, lending, and investment. Furnishes actuarial and mathematical analysis required for Treasury market financing, the Federal Financing Bank, and other government agencies.

Treasury Dept., Economic Policy, *1500 Pennsylvania Ave. N.W., #3454, 20220; (202) 622-2200. Fax, (202) 622-2633. Diana Furchtgott-Roth, Assistant Secretary (Acting).*
Web, www.treasury.gov/about/organizational-structure/offices/Pages/Economic-Policy.aspx

Assists and advises the Treasury secretary in the formulation and execution of domestic and international economic policies and programs; helps prepare economic forecasts for the federal budget.

▶**CONGRESS**

For a listing of relevant congressional committees and subcommittees, please see pages 34–35 or the Appendix.

Congressional Budget Office, *FHOB, 2nd and D Sts. S.W., 4th Floor, 20515-6925; (202) 226-2600. Keith Hall, Director. Press, (202) 226-2602.*
Web, www.cbo.gov and Twitter, @USCBO

Nonpartisan office that provides the House and Senate with analyses needed for economic and budget decisions, and with the information and estimates required for the congressional budget process.

Government Accountability Office (GAO), *Contracting and National Security Acquisitions (CNSA), 441 G St. N.W., MS 4440-A, 20548; (202) 512-4841. Michele Mackin, Managing Director, (202) 512-4309.*
Web, www.gao.gov

Treasury Department

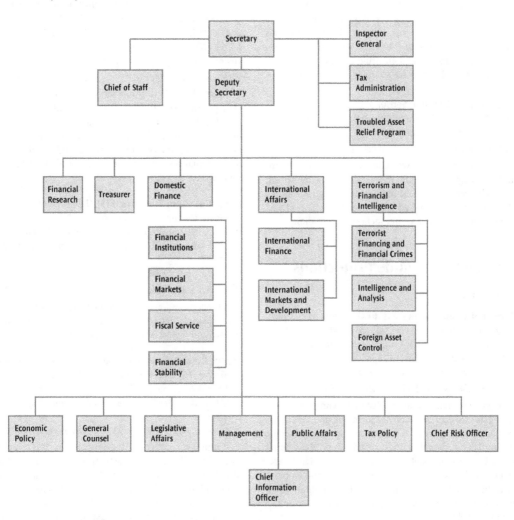

Advises Congress and governmental agencies about federal spending and maximizing investments related to acquisitions and procurements.

Government Accountability Office (GAO), *Financial Management and Assurance (FMA), 441 G St. N.W., #5Q24, 20548; (202) 512-2600. Larry Malenich, Managing Director.*
Web, www.gao.gov/careers/fma.html

Audits the federal government's consolidated financial statements and the statements of several other federal agencies; identifies opportunities to improve accountability for federal assets; issues standards for government audits and federal internal controls.

Office of Management and Budget (OMB) *(Executive Office of the President), Housing, 725 17th St. N.W., #9226, 20503; (202) 395-7874. Fax, (202) 395-1307. Michelle Enger, Deputy Associate Director. Press, (202) 395-7254.*
Web, www.whitehouse.gov/omb

Assists and advises the OMB director in budget preparation, reorganizations, and evaluations of Housing and Urban Development Dept. programs.

▶**NONGOVERNMENTAL**

Committee for a Responsible Federal Budget, *1900 M St. N.W., #850, 20036; (202) 596-3597. Fax, (202) 478-0681. Maya MacGuineas, President.*
General email, info@crfb.org
Web, www.crfb.org and Twitter, @BudgetHawks

Bipartisan nonprofit organization that educates the public about issues that have significant fiscal policy impact. Monitors legislation and regulation. (Affiliated with the New America Foundation.)

Concord Coalition, *1530 Wilson Blvd., #550, Arlington, VA 22209; (703) 894-6222. Robert L. Bixby, Executive Director.*
General email, concordcoalition@concordcoalition.org
Web, www.concordcoalition.org and Twitter, @ConcordC

Nonpartisan grassroots organization dedicated to educating the public about responsible fiscal policy and the causes and consequences of federal budget deficits. Interests include the long-term challenges facing America's entitlement programs, how to build a sound foundation for economic growth, and ensuring that Social Security, Medicare, and Medicaid are secure for all generations.

Taxpayers for Common Sense, *651 Pennsylvania Ave. S.E., 20003; (202) 546-8500. Ryan Alexander, President.*
General email, info@taxpayer.net

Web, www.taxpayer.net and Twitter, @taxpayers

Nonpartisan budget watchdog organization that promotes transparency with federal spending decisions; oversight, regulation, and independent financial audits of federal programs and agencies; and elimination of earmarks, corporate welfare, and ineffective subsidies.

Statistics, Economic Projections

►AGENCIES

Bureau of Economic Analysis (BEA) *(Commerce Dept.),* *4600 Silver Hill Rd., 20233; (202) 606-9900.*
Brian C. Moyer, Director. Congressional Affairs,
(301) 278-9032. Press, (301) 278-9003.
General email, CustomerService@bea.gov

Web, www.bea.gov and Twitter, @BEA_NEWS

Compiles, analyzes, and publishes data on measures of aggregate U.S. economic activity, including gross domestic product; prices by type of expenditure; personal income and outlays; personal savings; corporate profits; capital stock; U.S. international transactions; and foreign investment. Provides statistics of personal income and employment by industry for regions, states, metropolitan areas, and counties. Refers specific inquiries to economic specialists in the field.

Bureau of Labor Statistics (BLS) *(Labor Dept.),*
2 Massachusetts Ave. N.E., #2850, 20212-0001; (202) 691-5200. Fax, (202) 691-7890. Vacant, Commissioner (Acting). Press, (202) 691-5902. TTY, (800) 877-8339.
General email, blsdata_staff@bls.gov

Web, www.bls.gov and Twitter, @BLS_gov

Provides statistical data on the structure and growth of the economy. Publishes reports on these statistical trends, including the *Consumer Price Index, Producer Price Index,* and *Employment and Earnings.*

Bureau of Labor Statistics (BLS) *(Labor Dept.), Prices and Living Conditions (OPLC),* *2 Massachusetts Ave. N.E., #3120, 20212-0001; (202) 691-6960.*
Fax, (202) 691-7080. David M. Friedman, Associate Commissioner. Information, (202) 691-7000.
Web, www.bls.gov/cpi

Collects, processes, analyzes, and disseminates data relating to prices and consumer expenditures; maintains the Consumer Price Index.

Bureau of Labor Statistics (BLS) *(Labor Dept.), Prices and Living Conditions (OPLC), Industrial Prices and Price Index,* *2 Massachusetts Ave. N.E., #3840, 20212-0001; (202) 691-7156. Fax, (202) 691-7753.*
Jeffrey Hill, Assistant Commissioner.
General email, ppi-info@bls.gov

Web, www.bls.gov/ppi

Compiles statistics on energy, apparel, pharmaceuticals, printing, construction materials, and all U.S. products for the Producer Price Index; analyzes movement of prices for natural gas, petroleum, coal, and electric power in the primary commercial and industrial markets. Records changes over time in the prices domestic producers receive.

Bureau of Labor Statistics (BLS) *(Labor Dept.), Productivity and Technology (OPT),* *2 Massachusetts Ave. N.E., #2150, 20212-0001; (202) 691-5618. Fax, (202) 691-5664. Lucy P. Eldridge, Associate Commissioner, (202) 691-6598.*
General email, dipsweb@bls.gov

Web, www.bls.gov/bls/productivity.htm

Develops and analyzes productivity measures for the U.S. business economy and industries, and conducts research on factors affecting productivity.

Census Bureau *(Commerce Dept.), Economic Programs,* *4600 Silver Hill Rd., #8H132, Suitland, MD 20746 (mailing address: 4600 Silver Hill Rd., #8H132, Washington, DC 20233-6000); (301) 763-1858. Ron S. Jarmin, Deputy Director.*
Web, www.census.gov/topics/business-economy.html

Compiles comprehensive statistics on the level and structure of U.S. economic activity and the characteristics of industrial and business establishments at the national, state, and local levels; collects and publishes foreign trade statistics. Explains proper use of data on county business patterns, classification of industries and commodities, and business statistics. Compiles quarterly reports listing financial data for corporations in certain industrial sectors.

Census Bureau *(Commerce Dept.), Economy-Wide Statistics,* *4600 Silver Hill Rd., #8K154, Suitland, MD 20746-2401 (mailing address: 4700 Silver Hill Rd., #8K064, Washington, DC 20233-6500); (301) 763-7643. Kimberly P. Moore, Chief.*
Web, www.census.gov/econ/economywide.html

Provides data of five-year census programs on retail, wholesale, and service industries. Conducts periodic monthly or annual surveys for specific items within these industries.

Census Bureau *(Commerce Dept.), International Trade Management,* *4600 Silver Hill Rd., #5K158, Suitland, MD 20746 (mailing address: 4600 Silver Hill Rd., #6K032, Washington, DC 20233-6700); (301) 763-6937. Fax, (301) 763-6638. Dale C. Kelly, Chief. International trade helpline, (800) 549-0595.*
Web, www.census.gov/foreign-trade/index.html

Provides detailed statistics on all U.S. imports and exports, including petroleum, advanced technology products, and agricultural products; organizes this information by commodity, country, state, district, and port.

Census Bureau *(Commerce Dept.), Manufacturing and Construction, 4600 Silver Hill Rd., #8K151, Suitland, MD 20746 (mailing address: 4600 Silver Hill Rd., Washington, DC 20233); (301) 763-4750. Fax, (301) 763-8398. Edward Watkins, Chief.*
Web, www.census.gov/mcd

Collects, tabulates, and publishes statistics for the manufacturing and construction sectors of the Economic Census.

Council of Economic Advisers *(Executive Office of the President), Statistical Office, 725 17th St. N.W., 20502; (202) 395-5062. Fax, (202) 395-5630. Brian Amorosi, Director.*
Web, www.whitehouse.gov/cea

Compiles and reports aggregate economic data, including national income and expenditures, employment, wages, productivity, production and business activity, prices, money stock, credit, finance, government finance, agriculture, and international statistics.

Economic Research Service *(Agriculture Dept.), 355 E St. S.W., 20024-8221; (202) 694-5000. Fax, (202) 245-5467. Mary Bohman, Administrator; Greg Pompelli, Associate Administrator.*
General email, service@ers.usda.gov
Web, www.ers.usda.gov and Twitter, @USDA_ERS

Conducts market research; studies and forecasts domestic supply-and-demand trends for fruits and vegetables.

Federal Reserve System, *Research and Statistics, 20th and C Sts. N.W., #B3048, 20551; (202) 452-2322. Fax, (202) 452-5296. Stacey Tevlin, Director.*
Web, www.federalreserve.gov/econresdata/rsstaff.htm

Publishes statistical data and analyses on business finance, real estate credit, consumer credit, industrial production, construction, and flow of funds.

Internal Revenue Service (IRS) *(Treasury Dept.), Statistics of Income, 1111 Constitution Ave. N.W., #K-4112, 20224 (mailing address: P.O. Box 2608, Washington, DC 20013-2608); (202) 803-9285. Fax, (202) 803-9393. Tamara Rib, Chief. Publications, (202) 874-0410.*
General email, sis@irs.gov
Web, www.irs.gov/soi-tax-stats-of-income

Provides the public and the Treasury Dept. with statistical information on tax laws. Prepares statistical information for the Commerce Dept. to use in formulating the gross national product (GNP). Publishes *Statistics of Income*, a series available at cost to the public.

International Trade Administration (ITA) *(Commerce Dept.), Industry and Analysis (I&A), Trade Policy and Analysis (OTNA), 1401 Constitution Ave. N.W., #21028,* 20230; (202) 482-3177. Fax, (202) 482-4614. Praveen Dixit, Deputy Assistant Secretary, (202) 482-3177.
Web, www.trade.gov/mas/ian/index.asp

Analyzes international and domestic competitiveness of U.S. industry and component sectors. Assesses impact of regulations on competitive positions. Produces and disseminates U.S. foreign trade and related economic data. Supports U.S. international trade negotiations initiative.

National Agricultural Statistics Service *(Agriculture Dept.), 1400 Independence Ave. S.W., #5041, MS 2001, 20250-2001; (202) 720-2707. Hubert Hamer, Administrator. Information, (800) 727-9540. Library, (202) 690-8127.*
General email, nass@nass.usda.gov
Web, www.nass.usda.gov and Twitter, @usda_nass

Prepares estimates and reports on production, supply, prices, and other items relating to the U.S. agricultural economy. Reports include statistics on field crops, fruits and vegetables, cattle, hogs, poultry, and related products. Prepares quinquennial national census of agriculture.

Securities and Exchange Commission (SEC), *Economic and Risk Analysis, 100 F St. N.E., 20549; (202) 551-6600. Fax, (202) 756-0505. Chyhe Becker, Director (Acting).*
General email, DERA@sec.gov
Web, www.sec.gov/dera

Advises the commission and its staff on economic issues as they pertain to the commission's regulatory activities. Publishes data on trading volume of the stock exchanges; compiles statistics on financial reports of brokerage firms; identifies and analyzes issues, trends, and innovations in the marketplace.

Treasury Dept., *Financial Research, 717 14th St. N.W., 20220; (202) 622-3002. Ken Phelan, Director (Acting).*
Web, www.financialresearch.gov and Twitter, @OFRgov

Conducts research about financial stability and risk management and promotes high-quality financial data, standards, and analysis for the Financial Stability Oversight Council and the public.

Treasury Dept., *Risk Management, 1500 Pennsylvania Ave. N.W., 20220; (202) 622-2983. Vacant, Chief Risk Officer.*
General email, ORM@Treasury.gov
Web, www.treasury.gov/about/organizational-structure/offices/Pages/chief-risk-management.aspx

Recommends policies and promotes programs to the Treasury Dept. and the federal government relating to the management of credit, market, liquidity, operational, and reputational risks.

U.S. International Trade Commission, *Industries, 500 E St. S.W., #504-A, 20436; (202) 205-3296. Fax, (202) 205-3161. Jonathon R. Coleman, Director, (202) 205-3380.*
Web, www.usitc.gov/research_and_analysis/office_industry.htm

Identifies, analyzes, and develops data on economic and technical matters related to the competitive position of the United States in domestic and world markets in agriculture and forest production, chemicals, textiles, energy, electronics, transportation, services and investments, minerals, metals, and machinery.

►CONGRESS

Library of Congress, *Science, Technology, and Business,* *John Adams Bldg., 101 Independence Ave. S.E., #LA 508, 20540-4750; (202) 707-5639. Fax, (202) 707-1925. Ron Bluestone, Chief, (202) 707-0948. Business Reference Services, (202) 707-7934. Science Reference Services, (202) 707-6401. Technical reports, (202) 707-5655.* *Web, www.loc.gov/rr/scitech*

Offers reference service by telephone, by correspondence, and in person. Maintains a collection of more than 3 million reports on science, technology, business management, and economics.

►NONGOVERNMENTAL

American Statistical Assn., *732 N. Washington St., Alexandria, VA 22314-1943; (703) 684-1221. Fax, (703) 684-2037. Ronald Wasserstein, Executive Director.* *Toll-free, (888) 231-3473.* *General email, asainfo@amstat.org* *Web, www.amstat.org*

Membership: statistical practitioners in industry, government, and academia. Supports excellence in the development, application, and dissemination of statistical science through meetings, publications, membership services, education, accreditation, and advocacy.

International Monetary Fund (IMF), *Statistics, 700 19th St. N.W., 20431; (202) 623-7000. Louis Marc Ducharme, Director. Publications, (202) 623-7430.* *General email, statisticsquery@imf.org* *Web, www.imf.org/en/data and eLibrary, www.elibrary .imf.org* *Publications, publications@imf.org*

Publishes monthly *International Financial Statistics (IFS),* which includes comprehensive financial data for most countries, and *Direction of Trade Statistics,* a quarterly publication, which includes the distribution of exports and imports for 1,692 countries. Annual statistical publications include the *Balance of Payments Statistics Yearbook, Direction of Trade Statistics Yearbook, Government Finance Statistics Yearbook,* and *International Financial Statistics Yearbook.* Free online and paid print subscriptions available to the public. All four publications are available on CD-ROM and on the website.

Taxes and Tax Reform

►AGENCIES

Alcohol and Tobacco Tax and Trade Bureau (TTB) *(Treasury Dept.), 1310 G St. N.W., #300E, Box 12, 20005; (202) 453-2000. Fax, (202) 453-2912. John J. Manfreda,* *Administrator, Ext. 32176. Public Affairs, (202) 453-2180. TTY, (202) 882-9914.* *General email, TTBInternetQuestions@ttb.gov* *Web, www.ttb.gov*

Enforces and administers revenue laws relating to firearms, explosives, alcohol, and tobacco.

Internal Revenue Service (IRS) *(Treasury Dept.), 1111 Constitution Ave. N.W., 20224 (mailing address: from outside the U.S.: IRS International Accounts, Philadelphia, PA 19255-0725); (202) 622-5000. Charles Rettig, Commissioner; Terry Lemons, Communications Chief. Phone from outside the U.S., (267) 941-1000. Fax from outside the U.S., (267) 941-1055. Identity theft hotline, (800) 908-4490. Information and assistance, (800) 829-1040. Information for businesses, (800) 829-4933. National Taxpayer Advocates helpline, (877) 777-4778. Press, (202) 317-4000. TTY, (800) 829-4059.* *Web, www.irs.gov, Twitter, @IRSnews and Facebook, www.facebook.com/IRS*

Administers and enforces internal revenue laws and related statutes (except those relating to firearms, explosives, alcohol, and tobacco).

Internal Revenue Service (IRS) *(Treasury Dept.), Art Advisory Panel, 1111 Constitution Ave., #700, C:AP:SO: ART ATTN: AAS, 20024; (305) 982-5364. MariCarmen Cuello, Director (Acting).* *Web, www.irs.gov/Individuals/Art-Appraisal-Services*

Panel of twenty-five art professionals that assists the IRS by reviewing and evaluating taxpayers' appraisals on works of art valued at $50,000 or more involved in federal income, estate, and gift taxes.

Internal Revenue Service (IRS) *(Treasury Dept.), Passthroughs and Special Industries, Excise Tax Branch, 1111 Constitution Ave. N.W., #5314, 20224; (202) 317-3100. Stephanie Bland, Director.* *Web, www.irs.gov*

Administers excise tax programs, including taxes on diesel, gasoline, and special fuels. Advises district offices, internal IRS offices, and general inquirers on tax policy, rules, and regulations.

Internal Revenue Service (IRS) *(Treasury Dept.), Taxpayer Advocate, 1111 Constitution Ave. N.W., #3031, 20224; (202) 622-6100. Fax, (202) 622-7854. Nina E. Olson, National Taxpayer Advocate. Toll-free, (877) 777-4778. TTY, (800) 829-4059.* *Web, https://taxpayeradvocate.irs.gov, Twitter, @IRSnews and Facebook, www.facebook.com/YourVoiceAtIRS*

Helps taxpayers resolve problems with the IRS and recommends changes to prevent the problems. Represents taxpayers' interests in the formulation of policies and procedures.

Multistate Tax Commission, *444 N. Capitol St. N.W., #425, 20001-1538; (202) 650-0300. Gregory S. Matson, Executive Director.* *General email, mtc@mtc.gov* *Web, www.mtc.gov*

Membership: state governments that have enacted the Multistate Tax Compact. Promotes fair, effective, and efficient state tax systems for interstate and international commerce; works to preserve state tax sovereignty. Encourages uniform state tax laws and regulations for multistate and multinational enterprises. Maintains three regional audit offices that monitor compliance with state tax laws and encourage uniformity in taxpayer treatment. Administers program to identify businesses that do not file tax returns with states.

Treasury Dept., *Tax Policy,* *1500 Pennsylvania Ave. N.W., #3120, 20220; (202) 622-0050. Fax, (202) 622-0605. David Kautter, Assistant Secretary.*
Web, www.treasury.gov/about/organizational-structure/ offices/Pages/Tax-Policy.aspx

Formulates and implements domestic and international tax policies and programs; conducts analyses of proposed tax legislation and programs; participates in international tax treaty negotiations; responsible for receipts estimates for the annual budget of the United States.

Treasury Dept., *Tax Policy, International Tax Counsel, 1500 Pennsylvania Ave. N.W., #3058, 20220; (202) 622-1782. Fax, (202) 622-2969. L. G. (Chip) Harter, Deputy Assistant Secretary.*
Web, www.treasury.gov/about/organizational-structure/ offices/Pages/Office-of-the-International-Tax-Counsel.aspx

Analyzes tax policies affecting businesses and international taxation. Negotiates tax treaties with foreign governments and participates in meetings of international organizations. Develops legislative proposals and regulations.

►JUDICIARY

U.S. Tax Court, *400 2nd St. N.W., #134, 20217; (202) 521-0700. Maurice B. Foley, Chief Judge.*
Web, www.ustaxcourt.gov

Tries and adjudicates disputes involving income, estate, and gift taxes and personal holding company surtaxes in cases in which deficiencies have been determined by the Internal Revenue Service.

►NONGOVERNMENTAL

American Enterprise Institute (AEI), *Economic Policy Studies, 1789 Massachusetts Ave. N.W., 20036; (202) 862-5800. Fax, (202) 862-7177. Michael R. Strain, Director, (202) 862-4884.*
Web, www.aei.org and Twitter, @MichaelRStrain

Conducts research on fiscal policy and taxes. Sponsors events.

Americans for Tax Reform, *722 12th St. N.W., #400, 20005; (202) 785-0266. Fax, (202) 785-0261. Grover G. Norquist, President.*
General email, ideas@atr.org
Web, www.atr.org, Twitter, @taxreformer and Twitter, @GroverNorquist

Advocates reduction of federal and state taxes; encourages candidates for public office to pledge their opposition to income tax increases through a national pledge campaign.

The Brookings Institution, *Economic Studies, 1775 Massachusetts Ave. N.W., 20036-2188; (202) 797-6000. Fax, (202) 797-6181. Ted Gayer, Director, (202) 797-6230. Press, (202) 797-6105.*
General email, escomment@brookings.edu
Web, www.brookings.edu/economics and Twitter, @BrookingsEcon

Researches and analyzes U.S. tax policy; provides information to policymakers, journalists, and researchers.

Center on Budget and Policy Priorities, *820 1st St. N.E., #510, 20002; (202) 408-1080. Fax, (202) 408-1056. Robert Greenstein, President.*
General email, center@cbpp.org
Web, www.cbpp.org and Twitter, @CenterOnBudget

Research group that analyzes changes in federal and state programs, such as tax credits, Medicaid coverage, and food stamps, and their effect on low-income and moderate-income households.

Citizens Against Government Waste, *1100 Connecticut Ave. N.W., #650, 20036; (202) 467-5300. Fax, (202) 467-4253. Thomas A. Schatz, President. Media, (202) 467-5318.*
General email, webmaster@cagw.org
Web, www.cagw.org and Twitter, @GovWaste

Taxpayer watchdog group that monitors government spending to identify how waste, mismanagement, and inefficiency in government can be eliminated. Has created criteria to identify pork-barrel spending. Publishes the annual *Congressional Pig Book,* which lists the names of politicians and their pet pork-barrel projects. Monitors legislation and regulations.

Citizens for Tax Justice, *1616 P St. N.W., #200, 20036; (202) 299-1066. Fax, (202) 299-1065. Alan Essig, Executive Director.*
General email, info@ctj.org
Web, www.ctj.org, Twitter, @taxjustice
Press, media@ctj.org

Advocacy organization that works for progressive taxes at the federal, state, and local levels.

Federation of Tax Administrators, *444 N. Capitol St. N.W., #348, 20001; (202) 624-5890. Fax, (202) 624-7888. Gale Garriott, Executive Director.*
Web, www.taxadmin.org

Membership: tax agencies in the fifty states, plus New York City, Philadelphia, and the District of Columbia. Provides information upon written request on tax-related issues, including court decisions and legislation. Conducts research and sponsors workshops.

FreedomWorks, *111 K St. N.E., #600, 20002; (202) 783-3870. Fax, (202) 942-7649. Adam Brandon, President. Toll-free, (888) 564-6273.*

*Web, www.freedomworks.org, Twitter, @FreedomWorks
and Facebook, www.facebook.com/FreedomWorks*

Recruits, educates, trains, and mobilizes citizens to promote lower taxes, less government, and greater economic freedom.

Institute on Taxation and Economic Policy (ITEP), *1616 P St. N.W., #200, 20036; (202) 299-1066. Fax, (202) 299-1065. Alan Essig, Executive Director.*
General email, itep@itep.org

Web, www.itep.org, Twitter, @iteptweets and Facebook, www.facebook.com/instituteontaxation

Research and education organization that promotes tax fairness and sustainability in federal, state, and local tax policy.

National Assn. of Manufacturers (NAM), *Tax and Domestic Economic Policy, 733 10th St. N.W., #700, 20001; (202) 637-3000. Fax, (202) 637-3182. Christopher Netram, Vice President, (202) 637-3077. Press, (202) 637-3096. Toll-free, (800) 814-8468.*
Web, www.nam.org

Represents and acts as advocate for manufacturers on federal tax and budget policies; acts as a spokesperson for manufacturers on fiscal issues in the media; works with the broader business community to advance pro-growth, pro-competitiveness tax policy; conducts conferences. Monitors legislation and regulations.

National Campaign for a Peace Tax Fund, *2121 Decatur Pl. N.W., 20008-1923; (202) 483-3751. Malachy Killbride, Executive Director. Toll-free, (888) 732-2382.*
General email, info@peacetaxfund.org

Web, www.peacetaxfund.org

Supports legislation permitting taxpayers who are conscientiously opposed to military expenditures to have the military portion of their income tax money placed in a separate, nonmilitary fund.

National Tax Assn., *529 14th St. N.W., #750, 20045; (202) 737-3325. Fax, (202) 737-7308. Hana Watkins, Director of Operations.*
General email, natltax@aol.com

Web, www.ntanet.org and Twitter, @NatlTax

Membership: tax lawyers and accountants, academics, legislators, and students. Seeks to advance understanding of tax theory, practice, and policy, as well as other aspects of public finance. Holds conferences and symposiums, including the Annual Conference on Taxation. Publishes the *National Tax Journal.*

National Taxpayers Union, *Communications, 122 C St. N.W., #650, 20001; (703) 683-5700. Peter Sepp, President; Nan Swift, Federal Affairs.*
General email, ntu@ntu.org

Web, www.ntu.org and Twitter, @NTU

Citizens' interest group that promotes tax and spending reduction at all levels of government. Supports constitutional amendments to balance the federal budget and limit taxes.

Tax Analysts, *400 S. Maple Ave., #400, Falls Church, VA 22046; (703) 533-4400. Fax, (703) 533-4444. Cara Griffith, President, (703) 533-4400, ext. 4412. Customer Service, (800) 955-2444.*

Nonpartisan publisher of state, federal, and international tax news and analysis. Advocates tax reforms to develop tax systems that are fair, simple, and efficient. Provides publications to educate tax professionals and the public about tax reform.

The Tax Council, *600 13th St. N.W., #1000, 20005; (202) 822-8062. Fax, (202) 315-3413. Lynda K. Walker, Executive Director, (202) 414-1460.*
General email, general@thetaxcouncil.org

Web, www.thetaxcouncil.org and Twitter, @TheTaxCouncil

Organization of corporations concerned with tax policy and legislation. Interests include tax rate, capital formation, capital gains, foreign source income, and capital cost recovery. (Affiliated with the Tax Council Policy Institute [TCPI].)

Tax Executives Institute, *1200 G St. N.W., #300, 20005-3814; (202) 638-5601. Fax, (202) 638-5607. Eli J. Dicker, Executive Director, (202) 464-8354.*
General email, asktei@tei.org

Web, www.tei.org and Twitter, @TEI_Updates

Membership: accountants, lawyers, and other corporate and business employees dealing with tax issues. Sponsors seminars and conferences on federal, state, local, and international tax issues. Develops and monitors tax legislation, regulations, and administrative procedures.

Tax Foundation, *1325 G. St. N.W., #950, 20005; (202) 464-6200. Scott A. Hodge, President. Press, (202) 464-5120.*
General email, tf@taxfoundation.org

Web, https://taxfoundation.org and Twitter, @taxfoundation

Membership: individuals and businesses interested in federal, state, and local fiscal matters. Conducts research and analysis and prepares reports on taxes and government expenditures. Advocates a simple, transparent, neutral, and stable tax policy.

U.S. Chamber of Commerce, *Economic and Tax Policy, 1615 H St. N.W., 20062-2000; (202) 463-5620. Fax, (202) 463-3174. J. D. Foster, Chief Economist. Press, (202) 463-5682.*
Web, www.uschamber.com/economic-policy

Promotes tax policies that encourage businesses' growth. Opposes tax increases that reduce businesses' ability to grow, invest, and create jobs.

Urban-Brookings Tax Policy Center, *Brookings Institution, 1775 Massachusetts Ave. N.W., 20036; Urban Institute, 2100 M St. N.W., 4th Floor, 20037; Fax, (202) 728-0232. Mark J. Mazur, Director, (202) 261-5500. Brookings Institution Phone, (202) 797-6000. Urban Institute Phone, (202) 833-7200. fax, (202) 728-0232.*
General email, info@taxpolicycenter.org

Web, www.taxpolicycenter.org and Twitter, @TaxPolicyCenter

Consumer Product Safety Commission

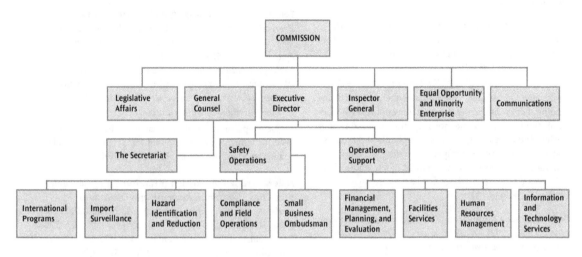

Provides analysis of current and pending tax issues to policymakers, journalists, researchers, and citizens. (Joint venture of the Urban Institute and the Brookings Institution.)

CONSUMER PROTECTION AND EDUCATION

General

►AGENCIES

Civil Division *(Justice Dept.), Consumer Protection,* 450 5th St. N.W., #6400, 20001; (202) 307-0066. Fax, (202) 514-8742. Gus Eylur, Director (Acting).
Web, www.justice.gov/civil/consumer-protection-branch

Enforces consumer protection statutes to protect health, safety, and economic security of consumers. Handles cases in the areas of pharmaceuticals and medical devices, deceptive trade practices and telemarketing fraud, food and dietary supplements, consumer product safety, odometer fraud, tobacco products, and civil defense litigation.

Consumer Product Safety Commission (CPSC), *Small Business Ombudsman,* 4330 East-West Hwy., #800A, Bethesda, MD 20814; (888) 531-9070. Shelby Mathis, Ombudsman, (301) 504-7865. TTY, (301) 595-7054.
General email, sbo@cpsc.gov

Web, www.cpsc.gov and Twitter, @CPSCSmallBiz

Provides guidance and advice to small businesses and small-batch manufacturers about compliance with CPSC laws and regulations as well as technical assistance in resolving problems.

Federal Communications Commission (FCC), *Consumer and Governmental Affairs Bureau (CGB),* 445 12th St.

S.W., #5C758, 20554; (202) 418-1400. Fax, (202) 418-2839. Patrick Webre, Chief. TTY, (888) 835-5322.
General email, cgbweb@fcc.gov

Web, www.fcc.gov/consumer-governmental-affairs and Twitter, @FCC

Develops and implements FCC policies, including disability access. Operates a consumer center that responds to consumer inquiries and complaints. Partners with state, local, and tribal governments in areas of emergency preparedness and implementation of new technologies.

Federal Deposit Insurance Corp. (FDIC), *Consumer and Community Affairs,* 1776 F St. N.W., 6th Floor, 20006; (877) 275-3342. Fax, (703) 254-0222. Elizabeth Ortiz, Deputy Director. Information, 877-ASK-FDIC. TTY, (800) 925-4618.
General email, consumer@fdic.gov

Web, www.fdic.gov/about/contact/directory/index. html#DDCP

Coordinates and monitors complaints filed by consumers against federally insured state banks that are not members of the Federal Reserve System; responds to general banking inquiries; answers questions on deposit insurance coverage.

Federal Maritime Commission (FMC), *Consumer Affairs and Dispute Resolution Services,* 800 N. Capitol St. N.W., #1070, 20573; (202) 523-5807. Fax, (202) 275-0059. Rebecca A. Fenneman, Director. Toll-free, (866) 448-9586.
General email, complaints@fmc.gov

Web, www.fmc.gov/bureaus_offices/consumer_affairs_ and_dispute_resolution_services.aspx

Provides ombudsman, mediation, facilitation, and arbitration services to assist shippers, carriers, marine terminal operators, and the shipping public to resolve commercial cargo shipping disputes. Provides assistance to cruise passengers to resolve disputes with cruise operators for cruises between the United States and international ports. Library open to the public (Monday through Friday, 8:00 a.m.–4:30 p.m.).

Federal Reserve System, *Consumer and Community Affairs, 1709 New York Ave. N.W., 20006; (202) 452-2955. Fax, (202) 452-3849. Eric Belsky, Director. Complaints, (888) 851-1920.* *Web, www.federalreserve.gov/econresdata/ccastaff.htm*

Receives consumer complaints concerning truth-in-lending, fair credit billing, equal credit opportunity, electronic fund transfer, home mortgage disclosure, consumer leasing, and advertising; receives complaints about unregulated practices; refers complaints to district banks. The Federal Reserve monitors enforcement of fair lending laws with regard to state-chartered banks that are members of the Federal Reserve System.

Federal Trade Commission (FTC), *600 Pennsylvania Ave. N.W., 20580; (202) 326-2222. Joseph J. Simons, Chair; David B. Robbins, Executive Director; Noah Joshua Phillips, Commissioner. Press, (202) 326-2180. Congressional Relations, (202) 326-2195. Identity theft hotline, (877) 438-4338. Library, (202) 326-2395.* *Web, www.ftc.gov and Twitter, @FTC*

Promotes policies designed to maintain strong competitive enterprise and consumer protection within the U.S. economic system. Monitors trade practices and investigates cases involving monopoly, unfair restraints, or deceptive practices. Enforces Truth in Lending and Fair Credit Reporting acts. Library open to the public (Monday–Friday, 8:30 a.m.–5:00 p.m.).

Federal Trade Commission (FTC), *Bureau of Consumer Protection, 600 Pennsylvania Ave. N.W., #470, 20580; (202) 326-3280. Fax, (202) 326-3799. Andrew Smith, Director. Complaint hotline, 877-FTC-HELP.* *Web, www.ftc.gov/about-ftc/bureaus-offices/bureau-consumer-protection*

Stops unfair, deceptive, and fraudulent business practices by collecting complaints and conducting investigations, suing companies and people that break the law, developing rules to maintain a fair marketplace, and educating consumers and businesses about their rights and responsibilities.

Federal Trade Commission (FTC), *Bureau of Consumer Protection, Advertising Practices Division, 400 7th Ave. S.W., #10418, 20024; (202) 326-3090. Fax, (202) 326-3259. Mary Engle, Associate Director.* *Web, www.ftc.gov/about-ftc/bureaus-offices/bureau-consumer-protection/our-divisions/division-advertising-practices*

Protects consumers from deceptive and unsubstantiated advertising through law enforcement, public reports, and industry outreach. Focuses on national advertising campaigns for food, dietary supplements and over-the-counter drugs, and medical devices, particularly advertising that makes claims difficult for consumers to evaluate. Monitors alcohol advertising for unfair practices; issues reports on alcohol labeling, advertising, and promotion.

Issues reports on the marketing to children of violent movies, video games, and music recordings.

Federal Trade Commission (FTC), *Bureau of Consumer Protection, Consumer and Business Education Division, 400 7th Ave. S.W., CC-10402, 20024; (202) 326-3650. Fax, (202) 326-3574. Jennifer Leach, Associate Director (Acting). Consumer Response Center, 877-FTC-HELP.* *Web, www.business.ftc.gov and www.ftc.gov/about-ftc/bureaus-offices/bureau-consumer-protection/our-divisions/division-consumer-business*

Develops educational material about FTC activities in order to inform consumers about their rights and to alert businesses about their compliance responsibilities.

Federal Trade Commission (FTC), *Bureau of Consumer Protection, Consumer Response and Operations Division, 600 Pennsylvania Ave. N.W., 20580; (202) 326-2830. Monica Vaca, Associate Director (Acting), (202) 326-2245. Consumer Response Center, 877-FTC-HELP. Consumer Sentinel helpline, (877) 701-9595. FTC Complaint, (877) 382-4357.* *General email, crcmessages@ftc.gov*

Web, www.ftc.gov/about-ftc/bureaus-offices/bureau-consumer-protection/our-divisions/division-consumer-response and Consumer Response Center, www.consumer.ftc.gov and Consumer Sentinel Network, www.ftc.gov/enforcement/consumer-sentinel-network and FTC Complaint Assistant, www.ftccomplaintassistant.gov

Collects and analyzes data in the Consumer Sentinel Network, which provides law enforcement members with access to FTC consumer complaints. Responds to consumer complaints and inquiries received through the Consumer Response Center.

Federal Trade Commission (FTC), *Bureau of Consumer Protection, Enforcement Division, 400 7th Ave. S.W., CC-9423, 20024; (202) 326-2996. Fax, (202) 326-3197. James A. Kohm, Associate Director.* *Web, www.ftc.gov/about-ftc/bureaus-offices/bureau-consumer-protection/our-divisions/division-enforcement*

Enforces consumer protection, including advertising and financial practices, data security, high-tech fraud, and telemarketing and other scams. Coordinates FTC actions with criminal law enforcement agencies; litigates civil actions against those who defraud consumers; and develops, reviews, and enforces a variety of consumer protection rules.

Federal Trade Commission (FTC), *Bureau of Consumer Protection, Marketing Practices Division, 600 Pennsylvania Ave. N.W., 20580; (202) 326-3404. Fax, (202) 326-3395. Lois C. Greisman, Associate Director.* *Web, www.ftc.gov/about-ftc/bureaus-offices/bureau-consumer-protection/our-divisions/division-marketing-practices*

Responds to complaints of consumer fraud in the marketplace, including high-tech Internet and telephone scams, deceptive telemarketing or direct mail marketing schemes, fraudulent business opportunity scams, and violations of the Do Not Call and CAN-SPAM consumer privacy protections.

Federal Trade Commission (FTC), *Bureau of Economics,* *600 Pennsylvania Ave. N.W., 20580; (202) 326-3420. Fax, (202) 326-2380. Bruce Kobayashi, Director. Web, www.ftc.gov/about-ftc/bureaus-offices/bureau-economics*

Provides economic analyses for consumer protection and antitrust investigations, cases, and rulemakings; advises the commission on the effect of government regulations on competition and consumers in various industries; develops special reports on competition, consumer protection, and regulatory issues.

Federal Trade Commission (FTC), *Consumer Response Center, 600 Pennsylvania Ave. N.W., #240, 20580; (202) 326-2830. Fax, (202) 326-2012. Monica Vaca, Associate Director. Do-Not-Call Registry, (888) 382-1222. Identity fraud report line, 877-ID-THEFT. Toll-free, 877-FTC-HELP. TTY, (866) 653-4261. Web, www.consumer.ftc.gov*

Handles complaints about regulations dealing with unfair or deceptive business practices in advertising, credit, marketing, and service industries; educates consumers and businesses about these regulations.

Federal Trade Commission (FTC), *International Affairs, 600 Pennsylvania Ave. N.W., #H494, 20580; (202) 326-2600. Fax, (202) 326-2873. Randolph W. Tritell, Director, (202) 326-3051. Web, www.ftc.gov/about-ftc/bureaus-offices/office-international-affairs*

Assists in the enforcement of antitrust laws and consumer protection by arranging appropriate cooperation and coordination with foreign governments in international cases. Negotiates bilateral and multilateral antitrust and consumer protection agreements and represents the United States in international antitrust policy forums. Assists developing countries in moving toward market-based economies.

Food and Drug Administration (FDA) *(Health and Human Services Dept.), Division of Industry and Consumer Education (DICE), 10903 New Hampshire Ave., Silver Spring, MD 20993; (301) 796-7100. Fax, (301) 847-8149. Elias Mallis, Director, (301) 796-6216. Toll-free, (800) 638-2041. General email, DICE@fda.hhs.gov Web, www.fda.gov/MedicalDevices/ DeviceRegulationandGuidance/ ContactDivisionofIndustryandConsumerEducation*

Responds to questions from consumers of medical devices and radiation-emitting electronic products.

Food and Drug Administration (FDA) *(Health and Human Services Dept.), External Affairs (OEA), White Oak Bldg. 32, 10903 New Hampshire Ave., #5360, Silver Spring, MD 20993; (301) 796-4540. Jennifer Rodriguez, Associate Commissioner (Acting). Consumer inquiries, (888) 463-6332.*

General email, fdaoma@fda.hhs.gov Web, www.fda.gov/AboutFDA/CentersOffices/OC/ OfficeofExternalAffairs

Responds to inquiries on issues related to the FDA. Conducts consumer health education programs for specific groups, including women, older adults, and the educationally and economically disadvantaged. Serves as liaison with national health and consumer organizations.

Food Safety and Inspection Service *(Agriculture Dept.), 1400 Independence Ave. S.W., #331E, 20250-3700; (202) 692-4207. Fax, (202) 690-0550. Carmen Rottenberg, Administrator. Consumer inquiries, (800) 535-4555. Press, (202) 720-9113. TTY, (800) 877-8339. Web, www.fsis.usda.gov and Twitter, @USDAFoodSafety*

Sponsors food safety educational programs to inform the public about measures to prevent foodborne illnesses; sponsors lectures, publications, and public service advertising campaigns. Toll-free hotline answers food safety questions.

General Services Administration (GSA), *USAGov, 1800 F St. N.W., 20405; (844) 872-4681. Fax, (202) 357-0078. Web, www.usa.gov and Web (Spanish), www.gobiernoUSA.gov*

Manages the portal site to U.S. government information, www.usa.gov. Manages kids.gov, a resource that provides government information on education, including primary, secondary, and higher education. Distributes free and low-cost federal publications of consumer interest via the Internet at www.usa.gov and Pueblo.gpo.gov. Assists people with questions about American government agencies, programs, and services via telephone, (800) FED-INFO ([800] 333-4636), or website, http://answers.usa.gov. Operates a contact center to provide information in English or Spanish on all federal government agencies, programs, and services via toll-free telephone, email, and chat. Operated under contract by Sykes in Pennsylvania and Florida. Responds to inquiries about federal programs and services. Gives information about or referrals to appropriate offices.

Securities and Exchange Commission (SEC), *Investor Education and Advocacy, 100 F St. N.E., 20549-0213; (202) 551-6500. Fax, (202) 772-9295. Lori Schock, Director. Toll-free, (800) 732-0330. Web, www.sec.gov/oiea*

Assists individual consumers in investing wisely and avoiding fraud. Provides a variety of services and tools, including publications on mutual funds and annuities, studies and recommendations concerning the evaluation of brokers and advisors, online calculators, and explanations about fees and expenses. Information is also available in Spanish.

Transportation Dept. (DOT), *Aviation Consumer Protection, 1200 New Jersey Ave. S.E., 20590; (202) 366-2220. Norman Strickman, Director, (202) 366-5960. Air travelers with disabilities hotline, (800) 778-4838. TTY, (202) 366-0511. Web, www.transportation.gov/airconsumer*

Consumer Financial Protection Bureau

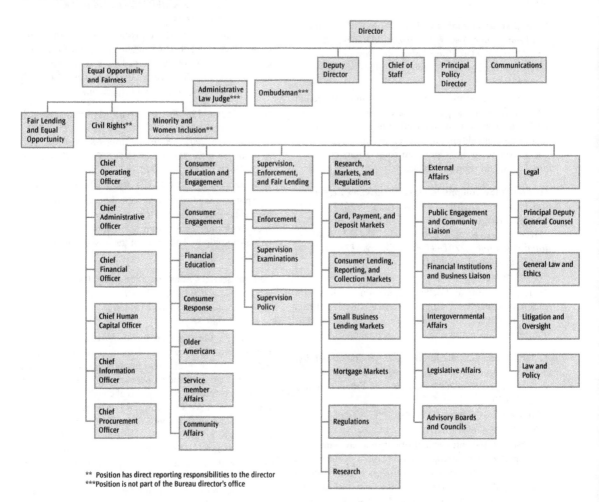

** Position has direct reporting responsibilities to the director
***Position is not part of the Bureau director's office

Processes consumer complaints; advises the secretary on consumer issues; investigates air travel consumer rule violations; educates the public about air travel via reports and website.

Transportation Security Administration (TSA)
(Homeland Security Dept.), Contact Center, 601 S. 12th St., 7th Floor, Arlington, VA 20598; (866) 289-9673. Michelle Cartagena, Program Manager.
General email, tsa-contactcenter@tsa.dhs.gov
Web, www.tsa.gov

Answers questions and collects concerns from the public regarding travel security.

▶**CONGRESS**

For a listing of relevant congressional committees and sub-committees, please see pages 34–35 or the Appendix.

▶**NONGOVERNMENTAL**

American Assn. of Family and Consumer Sciences, *400 N. Columbus St., #202, Alexandria, VA 22314; (703) 706-4600. Fax, (703) 706-4663. Carolyn W. Jackson, Chief Executive Officer, ext. 4611. Toll-free, (800) 424-8080. General email, staff@aafcs.org*
Web, www.aafcs.org, Twitter, @aafcs and Facebook, www.facebook.com/AAFCSheadquarters

Membership: professional home economists. Supports family and consumer sciences education; develops accrediting standards for undergraduate family and consumer science programs; trains and certifies family and consumer science professionals. Monitors legislation and regulations concerning family and consumer issues.

American National Standards Institute (ANSI), *1899 L St. N.W., 11th Floor, 20036; (202) 293-8020. Fax, (202) 293-9287. S. Joe Bhatia, President, (202) 331-3605.*

General email, info@ansi.org

Web, www.ansi.org

Oversees norms and guidelines of many private sectors to strengthen the U.S. market position in a global economy; seeks to protect the health and saftey of consumers and the environment.

Call for Action, *11820 Parklawn Dr., #340, Rockville, MD 20852; (240) 747-0229. Shirley Rooker, President; Eduard Bartholme, Executive Director.*

Web, www.callforaction.org

International network of consumer hotlines affiliated with local broadcast partners. Helps consumers resolve problems with businesses, government agencies, and other organizations through mediation. Provides information on privacy concerns.

CECA Solutions, *2737 Devonshire Pl. N.W., #102, 20008; (202) 468-8440. Fax, (202) 318-0831. Ellen Berman, Chief Executive Officer.*

General email, info@cecarf.org

Web, www.cecarf.org

Conducts consumer education campaigns concerning fuel choices, energy conservation, and legislative and regulatory developments. (Formerly the Consumer Energy Council of America.)

Center for Auto Safety, *1825 Connecticut Ave. N.W., #330, 20009-5708; (202) 328-7700. Fax, (202) 387-0140. Jason K. Levine, Director.*

General email, contact@autosafety.org

Web, www.autosafety.org and Twitter, @Ctr4AutoSafety

Public interest organization that receives written consumer complaints against auto manufacturers; monitors federal agencies responsible for regulating and enforcing auto and highway safety rules.

The Center for Consumer Freedom, *P.O. Box 34557, 20043; (202) 463-7112. Fax, (202) 463-7107. Richard Berman, Executive Director.*

General email, info2consumerfreedom.com

Web, www.consumerfreedom.com and Twitter, @consumerfreedom

Membership: restaurants, food companies, and consumers. Seeks to promote personal freedom and protect consumer choices in lifestyle-related and health-related areas such as diet and exercise. Monitors legislation and regulations.

Center for Digital Democracy, *1875 K St. N.W., 4th Floor, 20006; (202) 986-2220. Jeffrey (Jeff) Chester, Executive Director, (202) 494-7100.*

General email, jeff@democraticmedia.org

Web, www.democraticmedia.org and Twitter, @DigitalDemoc

Tracks and analyzes the online advertising market, including areas affecting public health, news and information, children and adolescents, and financial industries.

Consumer Federation of America, *1620 Eye St. N.W., #200, 20006; (202) 387-6121. Fax, (202) 265-7989.*

Jack Gillis, Executive Director, (202) 939-1018. Press, (202) 737-0766.

General email, cfa@consumerfed.org

Web, https://consumerfed.org and Twitter, @ConsumerFed

Federation of national, regional, state, and local pro-consumer organizations. Promotes consumer interests in banking, credit, and insurance; telecommunications; housing; food, drugs, and medical care; safety; and energy and natural resources development.

Consumers Union of the United States, *Washington Office, 1101 17th St. N.W., #500, 20036; (202) 462-6262. Fax, (202) 265-9548. Marta L. Tellado, President; David Butler, Director, Communications, Washington Office.*

Web, http://consumersunion.org

Independent, nonprofit consumer advocacy group that represents consumer interests before Congress; litigates consumer affairs cases involving government policy, corporate wrongdoing, and harmful products and services. Interests include health care, product safety, energy, government policies, privacy, and banking. Publishes *Consumer Reports* magazine. (Headquarters in Yonkers, N.Y.)

Council of Better Business Bureaus, *3033 Wilson Blvd., #600, Arlington, VA 22201-3843; (703) 276-0100. Fax, (703) 525-8277. Beverly Baskin, President (Acting).*

Web, www.bbb.org/en/us/local-bbb/council-of-better-business-bureaus and Twitter, @bbb_us

Membership: businesses and Better Business Bureaus in the United States and Canada. Promotes ethical business practices and truth in national advertising; mediates disputes between consumers and businesses.

Ethics Research and Compliance Initiative, *2650 Park Tower Dr., #801, Vienna, VA 22180; (703) 647-2185. Fax, (703) 647-2180. Patricia J. Harned, Chief Executive Officer. Information, (800) 777-1285.*

General email, ethics@ethics.org

Web, www.ethics.org and Twitter, @ecinitiative

Nonpartisan research organization that fosters ethical practices among individuals and institutions. Interests include research, knowledge building, education, and advocacy.

Household and Commercial Products Assn., *1667 K St. N.W., #300, 20006; (202) 872-8110. Fax, (202) 223-2636. Stephen (Steve) J. Caldeira, President.*

General email, info@thehcpa.org

Web, www.thehcpa.org and Twitter, @TheHCPA

Provides chemical safety information and consumer education programs; sponsors National Inhalants and Poisons Awareness and Aerosol Education Bureau. Monitors legislation and regulations.

International Business Ethics Institute, *1776 Eye St. N.W., 9th Floor, 20006; (202) 296-6938. Fax, (202) 296-5897. Lori Tansey Martens, President.*

General email, info@business-ethics.org

Web, www.business-ethics.org

Nonpartisan educational organization that promotes business ethics and corporate responsibility.

Knowledge Ecology International (KEI), *1621 Connecticut Ave. N.W., #500, 20009; Fax, (202) 332-2673. James Love, Director, (202) 332-2670. General email, info@keionline.org*

Web, www.keionline.org and Twitter, @jamie_love

Advocates social justice for low-income persons and marginalized groups with consumer access to health care, electronic commerce, competition policy, and information regarding intellectual property rights. Undertakes and publishes research and new ideas; engages in global public interest advocacy; provides technical advice to governments, nongovernmental organizations, and firms.

National Assn. of Consumer Advocates, *1215 17th St. N.W., 5th Floor, 20036; (202) 452-1989. Fax, (202) 452-0099. Ira J. Rheingold, Executive Director, (202) 452-1989 ext. 101. General email, info@consumeradvocates.org*

Web, www.consumeradvocates.org

Membership: consumer advocate attorneys. Seeks to protect the rights of consumers from fraudulent, abusive, and predatory business practices. Provides consumer law training through conferences and publications. Monitors legislation and regulations on banking, credit, and housing laws.

National Assn. of State Utility Consumer Advocates (NASUCA), *8380 Colesville Rd., #101, Silver Spring, MD 20910-6267; (301) 589-6313. Fax, (301) 589-6380. David Springe, Executive Director, (785) 550-7606. General email, nasuca@nasuca.org*

Web, www.nasuca.org

Membership: public advocate offices authorized by states to represent ratepayer interests before state and federal utility regulatory commissions. Monitors legislation and regulatory agencies with jurisdiction over electric utilities, telecommunications, natural gas, and water; conducts conferences. Supports privacy protection for telephone customers.

National Consumers League, *1701 K St. N.W., #1200, 20006; (202) 835-3323. Fax, (202) 835-0747. Sally Greenberg, Executive Director. General email, info@nclnet.org*

Web, www.nclnet.org, Twitter, @ncl_tweets and Facebook, www.facebook.com/nationalconsumersleague

Advocacy group that engages in research and educational activities related to consumer and worker issues. Interests include fraud, privacy, child labor, product safety, and food and drug safety. Web resources include fakechecks.org, fraud.org, lifesmarts.org, sosrx.org, and stopchildlabor.org.

Public Justice Foundation, *1620 L St. N.W., #630, 20036; (202) 797-8600. Fax, (202) 232-7203. F. Paul Bland Jr., Executive Director, ext. 223; Arthur H. Bryant, Chair. Web, www.publicjustice.net and Twitter, @Public_Justice*

Membership: consumer activists, trial lawyers, public interest lawyers, and law professors and students. Litigates to influence corporate and government decisions about products or activities adversely affecting health or safety. Interests include toxic torts, environmental protection, civil rights and civil liberties, workers' safety, consumer protection, and the preservation of the civil justice system. (Formerly Trial Lawyers for Public Justice.)

SAFE KIDS Worldwide, *1255 23rd St. N.W., #400, 20037-1151; (202) 662-0600. Fax, (202) 393-2072. David Strickland, Chair; Torine Creppy, President. General email, gkarton@safekids.org*

Web, www.safekids.org and Twitter, @safekids

Promotes awareness among adults that unintentional injury is the leading cause of death among children ages nineteen and under. Conducts educational programs on childhood injury prevention.

U.S. Chamber of Commerce, *Congressional and Public Affairs, 1615 H St. N.W., 20062-2000; (202) 463-5600. Jack Howard, Senior Vice President. Web, www.uschamber.com*

Monitors legislation and regulations regarding business and consumer issues, including legislation and policies affecting the Federal Trade Commission, the Consumer Product Safety Commission, and other agencies.

U.S. Public Interest Research Group (U.S.PIRG), *Federal Advocacy, 600 Pennsylvania Ave. S.E., #400, 20003; (202) 546-9707. Doug Phelps, Chair; Katie Murtha, Vice President of Federal Government Affairs. General email, uspirg@pirg.org*

Web, www.uspirg.org and Twitter, @uspirg

Conducts research and advocacy on consumer issues, including telephone rates, banking practices, insurance, campaign finance reform, product safety, toxic and solid waste, antibiotic overuse, affordable higher education, and modernizing voter registration; monitors private and governmental actions affecting consumers; supports efforts to challenge consumer fraud and illegal business practices. Serves as national office for state groups. (Headquarters in Denver, Colo.)

Credit Practices

▶**AGENCIES**

Civil Division *(Justice Dept.),* **Consumer Protection,** *450 5th St. N.W., #6400, 20001; (202) 307-0066. Fax, (202) 514-8742. Gus Eylur, Director (Acting). Web, www.justice.gov/civil/consumer-protection-branch*

Files suits to enforce the Truth-in-Lending Act and other federal statutes protecting consumers, generally upon referral by client agencies.

Comptroller of the Currency *(Treasury Dept.),* **Chief Counsel,** *Constitution Center, 400 7th St. S.W., 20506; (202) 649-5400. Fax, (202) 649-6077. Karen Solomon, Chief Counsel. Web, www.occ.gov*

Enforces and oversees compliance by nationally chartered banks with laws prohibiting discrimination in credit transactions on the basis of sex or marital status. Enforces regulations concerning bank advertising; may issue cease-and-desist orders.

Comptroller of the Currency *(Treasury Dept.),* **Compliance and Community Affairs,** *Constitution Center, 400 7th St. S.W., MS 7E512, 20024; (202) 649-5470. Grovetta Gardineer, Senior Deputy Comptroller. Web, https://occ.treas.gov*

Develops policy for enforcing consumer laws and regulations that affect national banks, including the Bank Secrecy (BSA/AML), Truth-in-Lending, Community Reinvestment, and Equal Credit Opportunity acts.

Comptroller of the Currency *(Treasury Dept.),* **Ombudsman,** *Constitution Center, 400 7th St. S.W., MS 10E-12, 20024; (202) 649-5530. Fax, (202) 649-5727. Larry L. Hattix, Ombudsman. Web, www.occ.gov*

Ensures that bank customers and the banks the agency supervises receive fair and expeditious resolution of their concerns.

Consumer Financial Protection Bureau (CFPB), *1700 G St. N.W., 20552; 1990 K St. N.W., 20006; (202) 435-7000. Fax, (855) 237-2392. Kathy Kraninger, Director. RESPA enquiries, (855) 411-2372. Toll-free, (855) 411-2372. TTY, (855) 729-2372. General email, info@consumerfinance.gov Web, www.consumerfinance.gov, Twitter, @cfpb RESPA email, cfpb_respaenquiries@consumerfinance.gov*

An independent government agency created per the Dodd-Frank Act of 2010. Functions include implementing and enforcing federal laws pertaining to mortgages, credit cards, and other consumer financial products and services. Supervises bank and nonbank financial institutions for compliance with consumer financial protection regulations. Accepts consumer complaints about financial products and services. Administers regulations including the Truth in Lending Act (TILA), Real Estate Settlement Procedures Act (RESPA), Fair Debt Collection Practices Act (FDCPA), Electronic Fund Transfer Act (EFTA), and Equal Credit Opportunity Act (ECOA).

Federal Deposit Insurance Corp. (FDIC), *Consumer and Community Affairs, 1776 F St. N.W., 6th Floor, 20006; (877) 275-3342. Fax, (703) 254-0222. Elizabeth Ortiz, Deputy Director. Information, 877-ASK-FDIC. TTY, (800) 925-4618. General email, consumer@fdic.gov Web, www.fdic.gov/about/contact/directory/index .html#DDCP*

Handles complaints concerning truth-in-lending and other fair credit provisions, including charges of discrimination on the basis of sex or marital status.

Federal Deposit Insurance Corp. (FDIC), *Depositor and Consumer Protection, 1776 F St. N.W., #F8000, 20006;* *(202) 898-7088. Fax, (202) 898-3909. Mark Pearce, Director. Web, www.fdic.gov/about/contact/directory/#DDCP*

Examines and supervises federally insured state banks that are not members of the Federal Reserve System to ascertain their safety and soundness.

Federal Reserve System, *Consumer and Community Affairs, 1709 New York Ave. N.W., 20006; (202) 452-2955. Fax, (202) 452-3849. Eric Belsky, Director. Complaints, (888) 851-1920. Web, www.federalreserve.gov/econresdata/ccastaff.htm*

Receives consumer complaints concerning truth-in-lending, fair credit billing, equal credit opportunity, electronic fund transfer, home mortgage disclosure, consumer leasing, and advertising; receives complaints about unregulated practices; refers complaints to district banks. The Federal Reserve monitors enforcement of fair lending laws with regard to state-chartered banks that are members of the Federal Reserve System.

Federal Trade Commission (FTC), *Bureau of Consumer Protection, Financial Practices, 400 7th Ave. S.W., CC-10416, 20024; (202) 326-3224. Fax, (202) 326-3768. Malini Maithal, Associate Director (Acting). Web, www.ftc.gov/about-ftc/bureaus-offices/bureau-consumer-protection/our-divisions/division-financial-practices*

Challenges unfair or deceptive financial practices, including those involving lending, loan servicing, debt negotiation, and debt collection. Enforces specific consumer credit statutes, including the Fair Debt Collection Practices Act, Equal Credit Opportunity Act, Truth-in-Lending Act, Credit Repair Organization Act, Home Ownership and Equity Protection Act, Electronic Fund Transfer Act, Consumer Leasing Act, Holder-In-Due-Course Rule, and Credit Practices Rule. Enforces the Fair Credit Reporting Act, which requires credit bureaus to furnish correct and complete information to businesses evaluating credit, insurance, or job applications.

Federal Trade Commission (FTC), *Bureau of Consumer Protection, Privacy and Identity Protection Division, 600 Pennsylvania Ave. N.W., 20580; (202) 326-2771. Maneesha Mithal, Associate Director. Identity theft hotline, (877) 438-4338. TTY identity theft hotline, (866) 653-4261. Web, www.ftc.gov/about-ftc/bureaus-offices/bureau-consumer-protection/our-divisions/division-privacy-and-identity and Identity theft assistance, www.ftc.gov/idtheft*

Oversees issues related to consumer privacy, credit reporting, identity theft, and information security. Develops policies and enforces the Fair Credit Reporting Act, Gramm-Leach-Bliley Act, and Children's Online Privacy Protection Act.

National Credit Union Administration (NCUA), *Consumer Protection, 1775 Duke St., Alexandria, VA 22314; (703) 518-1140. Fax, (703) 518-6672. J. Biliouris Mathew, Director.*

Federal Deposit Insurance Corporation

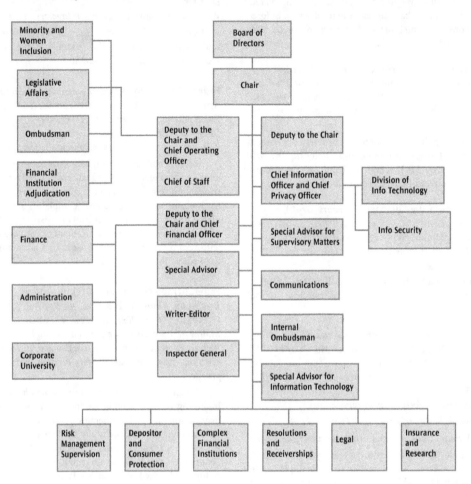

General email, ocfpmail@ncua.gov

Web, www.NCUA.gov/consumers, Twitter, @TheNCUA and Consumer Assistance Center, www.mycreditunion.gov/consumer-assistance-center

Responsible for consumer financial protection compliance policy and rulemaking, fair lending examinations, and consumer financial literacy efforts. Administers the NCUA's Consumer Assistance Center for consumer inquiries and complaints.

National Credit Union Administration (NCUA),
Examination and Insurance, 1775 Duke St., Alexandria, VA 22314-3428; (703) 518-6360. Fax, (703) 518-6499. Larry D. Fazio, Director. Toll-free investment hotline, (800) 755-5999.

General email, eimail@ncua.gov

Web, www.ncua.gov and Twitter, @TheNCUA

Oversees and enforces compliance by federally chartered credit unions with the Truth-in-Lending Act, the Equal Credit Opportunity Act, and other federal statutes protecting consumers.

Small Business Administration (SBA), *Diversity, Inclusion, and Civil Rights,* 409 3rd St. S.W., #6400, 20416; (202) 205-6750. Michele Schimpp, Assistant Administrator. TTY, (800) 877-8339.
Web, www.sba.gov/offices/headquarters/odicr

Reviews complaints based on disability against the Small Business Administration by recipients of its assistance in cases of alleged discrimination in credit transactions; monitors recipients for civil rights compliance.

►NONGOVERNMENTAL

American Bankers Assn. (ABA), *Communications,* 1120 Connecticut Ave. N.W., 20036; (800) 226-5377. Fax, (202) 663-7578. Jeff Sigmund, Senior Vice President, 202 -663-5439.

General email, gjames@aba.com

Web, www.aba.com, Twitter, @ABABankers and Facebook, www.facebook.com/AmericanBankersAssociation

Provides information on a wide range of banking issues and financial management.

American Financial Services Assn. (AFSA), *919 18th St. N.W., #300, 20006-5517; (202) 296-5544. Fax, (202) 223-0321. Chris Stinebert, President. Press, (202) 466-8613.*
General email, info@afsamail.org

Web, www.afsaonline.org, Twitter, @AFSA_DC and Facebook, www.facebook.com/afsaonline

Trade association for the consumer credit industry. Focus includes government relations and consumer education. Monitors legislation and regulations.

Consumer Data Industry Assn., *1090 Vermont Ave. N.W., #200, 20005-4905; (202) 371-0910. Fax, (202) 371-0134. Francis Creighton, Chief Executive Officer. Press, (202) 408-7406.*
General email, cdia@cdiaonline.org

Web, www.cdiaonline.org

Membership: credit reporting, mortgage reporting, and collection service companies. Provides information about credit rights to consumers. Monitors legislation and regulations.

Consumers Union of the United States, *Washington Office, 1101 17th St. N.W., #500, 20036; (202) 462-6262. Fax, (202) 265-9548. Marta L. Tellado, President; David Butler, Director, Communications, Washington Office.*
Web, http://consumersunion.org

Consumer advocacy group active in protecting the privacy of consumers. Interests include credit report accuracy. (Headquarters in Yonkers, N.Y.)

JumpStart Coalition for Personal Finance Literacy, *1001 Connecticut Ave. N.W., #640, 20036; (202) 846-6780. Laura Levine, President.*
General email, info@jumpstart.org

Web, www.jumpstart.org and Twitter, @NatJumpStart

Coalition of organizations that promote financial literacy for pre-K–12 and college-aged students. Offers teacher training programs and online educational materials. Holds annual conferences for financial education professionals. Produces an annual publication that outlines financial education curriculum and topics.

National Assn. of Consumer Advocates, *1215 17th St. N.W., 5th Floor, 20036; (202) 452-1989. Fax, (202) 452-0099. Ira J. Rheingold, Executive Director, (202) 452-1989 ext. 101.*
General email, info@consumeradvocates.org

Web, www.consumeradvocates.org

Membership: consumer advocate attorneys. Seeks to protect the rights of consumers from fraudulent, abusive, and predatory business practices. Provides consumer law training through conferences and publications. Monitors legislation and regulations on banking, credit, and housing laws.

National Retail Federation, *1101 New York Ave. N.W., 20005; (202) 783-7971. Fax, (202) 737-2849. Matthew R. Shay, President; Christopher Baldwin, Chair. Toll-free, (800) 673-4692.*

Web, www.nrf.com, Twitter, @NRFnews and Facebook, www.facebook.com/NationalRetailFederation

Membership: national and state associations of retailers and major retail corporations. Provides information on credit, truth-in-lending laws, and other fair credit practices.

U.S. Public Interest Research Group (U.S.PIRG), *Federal Advocacy, 600 Pennsylvania Ave. S.E., #400, 20003; (202) 546-9707. Doug Phelps, Chair; Katie Murtha, Vice President of Federal Government Affairs.*
General email, uspirg@pirg.org

Web, www.uspirg.org and Twitter, @uspirg

Coordinates grassroots efforts to advance consumer protection laws. Works for the protection of privacy rights, particularly in the area of fair credit reporting. (Headquarters in Denver, Colo.)

Product Safety, Testing

▶AGENCIES

Consumer Product Safety Commission (CPSC), *4330 East-West Hwy., #836, Bethesda, MD 20814; (301) 504-7923. Fax, (301) 504-0461. Ann Marie Buerkle, Chair (Acting); Mary Boyle, Executive Director, (301) 504-7907. Communications, (301) 504-7908. Congressional Relations, (301) 504-7660. National Injury Information Clearinghouse, (301) 504-7921. Product safety hotline, (800) 638-2772. TTY, (301) 595-7054.*
General email, info@cpsc.gov

Web, www.cpsc.gov and Twitter, @USCPSC

Establishes and enforces product safety standards; collects data; studies the causes and prevention of product-related injuries; identifies hazardous products, including imports, and recalls them from the marketplace.

Consumer Product Safety Commission (CPSC), *Communications, 4330 East-West Hwy., #717, Bethesda, MD 20814-4408; (301) 504-7908. Fax, (301) 504-0862. Patty Davis, Director (Acting), (301) 564-6932. Product safety hotline, (800) 638-2772. TTY, (800) 638-8270.*
General email, info@cpsc.gov

Web, www.cpsc.gov

Provides information concerning consumer product safety; works with local and state governments, school systems, and private groups to develop product safety information and education programs. Toll-free hotline accepts consumer complaints on hazardous products and injuries associated with a product and offers recorded information on product recalls and CPSC safety recommendations.

Consumer Product Safety Commission (CPSC), *Compliance and Field Operations, 4330 East-West Hwy., #610, Bethesda, MD 20814; (301) 504-7912. Robert Kaye, Assistant Executive Director, (576) 938-5215.*
Web, www.cpsc.gov

Identifies and acts on defective consumer products; enforces industry compliance with safety standards for domestic and imported products; conducts enforcement litigation. Monitors recall of defective products and issues warnings to consumers.

Consumer Product Safety Commission (CPSC), Engineering Sciences, *5 Research Pl., Rockville, MD 28050; (301) 987-2036. Fax, (978) 367-9122. Joel R. Recht, Associate Executive Director.*
Web, www.cpsc.gov

Develops and evaluates consumer product safety standards, test methods, performance criteria, design specifications, and quality standards; conducts and evaluates engineering tests. Collects scientific and technical data to determine potential hazards of consumer products.

Consumer Product Safety Commission (CPSC), Epidemiology, *4330 East-West Hwy., Bethesda, MD 20814-4408; (301) 504-7671. Fax, (301) 504-0081. Steve Hanway, Associate Executive Director.*
Web, www.cpsc.gov

Collects data on consumer product–related hazards and potential hazards; determines the frequency, severity, and distribution of the various types of injuries and investigates their causes; and assesses the effects of product safety standards and programs on consumer injuries. Conducts epidemiological studies and research in the fields of consumer-related injuries.

Consumer Product Safety Commission (CPSC), Hazard Identification and Reduction, *4330 East-West Hwy., #611, Bethesda, MD 20814-4408; (301) 504-7622. Fax, (301) 504-0038. George Borlase, Associate Executive Director.*
Web, www.cpsc.gov

Establishes labeling and packaging regulations. Develops standards in accordance with the Poison Prevention Packaging Act, the Federal Hazardous Substances Act, the Consumer Products Safety Act, and the Consumer Products Safety Improvement Act.

Consumer Product Safety Commission (CPSC), Health Sciences, *5 Research Pl., #165, Rockville, MD 20850 (mailing address: 4330 East-West Hwy., #600, Bethesda, MD 20814-4408); (301) 987-2240. Fax, (978) 967-8401. Alice Thaler, Associate Executive Director.*
Web, www.cpsc.gov

Evaluates potential health effects and hazards of consumer products and their foreseeable uses and misuses, and performs exposure and risk assessments for product-related hazards.

Consumer Product Safety Commission (CPSC), Laboratory Sciences, *5 Research Pl., Rockville, MD 20850; (301) 987-2037. Fax, (978) 367-1824. Andrew Stadnik, Associate Executive Director.*
Web, www.cpsc.gov

Conducts engineering analyses and testing of consumer products, supports the development of voluntary and mandatory standards, and supports the agency's compliance activities through product safety assessments.

National Injury Information Clearinghouse *(Consumer Product Safety Commission), 4330 East-West Hwy., #820, Bethesda, MD 20814; (301) 504-7921. Fax, (301) 504-0025.*

Shoma Ramaswamy, Program Analyst. To report consumer product-related accidents or injuries, (800) 638-2772. TTY, (301) 595-7054.
General email, clearinghouse@cpsc.gov
Web, www.cpsc.gov/en/About-CPSC/National-Injury-Information-Clearinghouse

Disseminates statistics and information relating to the prevention of death and injury associated with consumer products. Provides injury data from electronic data sources and distributes publications, including hazard analyses, special studies, and data summaries.

▶NONGOVERNMENTAL

American Academy of Pediatrics, *Federal Affairs, 601 13th St. N.W., #400N, 20005; (202) 347-8600. Fax, (202) 393-6137. Mark Del Monte, Chief Executive Officer (Acting). Toll-free information, (800) 336-5475.*
General email, kids1st@aap.org
Web, www.aap.org, Twitter, @AmerAcadPeds and Facebook, www.facebook.com/AmerAcadPeds
Advocacy email, FederalAdvocacy@aap.org

Promotes legislation and regulations concerning child health and safety. Committee on Injury and Poison Prevention drafts policy statements and publishes information on toy safety, poisons, and other issues that affect children and adolescents. (Headquarters in Elk Grove Village, Ill.)

Cosmetic Ingredient Review, *1620 L St. N.W., #1200, 20036-4702; (202) 331-0651. Fax, (202) 331-0088. Dr. Bart Heldreth, Executive Director.*
General email, cirinfo@cir-safety.org
Web, www.cir-safety.org

Voluntary self-regulatory program funded by the Personal Products Council. Reviews and evaluates published and unpublished data to assess the safety of cosmetic ingredients.

Tobacco

▶AGENCIES

Alcohol and Tobacco Tax and Trade Bureau (TTB) *(Treasury Dept.), 1310 G St. N.W., #300E, Box 12, 20005; (202) 453-2000. Fax, (202) 453-2912. John J. Manfreda, Administrator, Ext. 32176. Public Affairs, (202) 453-2180. TTY, (202) 882-9914.*
General email, TTBInternetQuestions@ttb.gov
Web, www.ttb.gov

Enforces and administers existing federal laws and tax code provisions relating to the production and taxation of alcohol and tobacco.

Centers for Disease Control and Prevention (CDC) *(Health and Human Services Dept.), Smoking and Health (OSH), 395 E St. S.W., #9100, 20201; (202) 245-0550. Fax, (202) 245-0554. Simon McNabb, Senior Policy Adviser; Corinne Graffunder, Director. Information, (800) 232-4636.*

General email, tobaccoinfo@cdc.gov

Web, www.cdc.gov/tobacco and
Twitter, @CDCTobaccoFree

Develops, conducts, and supports strategic efforts to protect the public's health in the area of tobacco prevention and control. Funds, trains, and provides technical assistance to states, territories, tribal support centers, and national networks (e.g., National Tobacco Control Program); increases awareness and education about tobacco (e.g., publications, CDC's Smoking & Tobacco Use website, Tips from Former Smokers campaign, earned and digital media); conducts and supports national and international surveillance (e.g., National Youth Tobacco Survey, Global Tobacco Surveillance System).

Food and Drug Administration (FDA) *(Health and Human Services Dept.), Center for Tobacco Products (CTP), White Oak Bldg. 71, 10903 New Hampshire Ave., Room G335, Silver Spring, MD 20993-002; (877) 287-1373. Mitch Zeller, Director.*

General email, askctp@fda.hhs.gov

Web, www.fda.gov/tobaccoproducts and
Twitter, @FDATobacco

Regulates the manufacture, distribution, and marketing of tobacco products.

►NONGOVERNMENTAL

Action on Smoking and Health (ASH), *1250 Connecticut Ave. N.W., 7th. Floor, 20036; (202) 659-4310. Francis Thompson, President; Laurent Huber, Executive Director.*

General email, info@ash.org

Web, www.ash.org, Twitter, @ashorg and Facebook,
www.facebook.com/ASHglobalAction

Blog, https://ash.org/blog

Educational and legal organization that works to protect nonsmokers from cigarette smoking; provides information about smoking hazards and non-smokers' rights.

National Campaign for Tobacco-Free Kids, *1400 Eye St. N.W., #1200, 20005; (202) 296-5469. Fax, (202) 296-5427. Matthew L. Myers, President.*

General email, info@tobaccofreekids.org

Web, www.tobaccofreekids.org and
Twitter, @TobaccoFreeKids

Seeks to reduce tobacco use by children through public policy change and educational programs. Provides technical assistance to state and local programs.

Truth Initiative, *900 G St. N.W., 4th Floor, 20001; (202) 454-5555. Fax, (202) 454-5599. Robin Koval, President.*

General email, press@truthinitiative.org

Web, https://truthinitiative.org and
Twitter, @Truthinitiative

Develops programs to disseminate information on the health effects of tobacco. Provides prevention and cessation services through grants, technical training and assistance, youth activism, partnerships, and community outreach. (Formerly the American Legacy Foundation.)

FINANCE AND INVESTMENTS

General

►AGENCIES

Bureau of the Fiscal Service *(Treasury Dept.), 401 14th St. S.W., #545, 20227; (202) 874-7000. Fax, (202) 874-6743. Kim McCoy, Commissioner. Media and congressional inquiries, (202) 504-3535. Public Affairs, (202) 504-3502. Savings Bonds, (844) 284-2676.*

Web, www.fiscal.treasury.gov, Twitter, @FiscalService and
Facebook, www.facebook.com/fiscalservice and Buy and
redeem securities online, www.treasurydirect.gov

Serves as the government's central financial manager, responsible for cash management and investment of government trust funds, credit administration, and debt collection. Handles central accounting for government fiscal activities; promotes sound financial management practices and increased use of automated payments, collections, accounting, and reporting systems.

Federal Deposit Insurance Corp. (FDIC), *Complex Financial Institutions, 1776 F St. N.W., #F-3080, 20006; (202) 898-7073. Fax, (202) 808-3800. Ricardo (Rick) Delfin, Director.*

Web, www.fdic.gov/about/contact/directory/#OCFI

Reviews and oversees large bank holding companies and nonbank financial companies designated as systemically important by the Financial Stability Oversight Council. Implements orderly liquidations of such companies that fail.

Federal Reserve System, *Financial Stability, 20th and C Sts. N.W., #B2046, 20551; (202) 452-3000. Fax, (202) 263-4852. Andreas Nellie Lehnert, Director; Bora Durdu, Chief of Financial and Macroeconomics Stability Studies.*

Web, www.federalreserve.gov/econresdata/fsprstaff.htm

Identifies and analyzes potential threats to financial stability; monitors financial markets, institutions, and structures; and assesses and recommends policy alternatives to address these threats. Conducts long-term research in banking, finance, and macroeconomics.

Federal Reserve System, *Monetary Affairs, 20th and C Sts. N.W., #B3022B, 20551; (202) 452-3327. Fax, (202) 452-2301. Thomas B. Laubach, Director.*

Web, www.federalreserve.gov/econres/mastaff.htm

Assists the Federal Reserve Board and the Federal Open Market Committee in the conduct of monetary policy, especially in the areas of finance, money and banking, and monetary policy design and implementation. Provides expertise on open market operations, discount window policy, and reserve markets.

Small Business Administration (SBA), *Investments and Innovation, 409 3rd St. S.W., #6300, 20416; (202) 205-6510. Fax, (202) 205-6959. Joseph (Joe) Shepard, Associate Administrator. TTY, (800) 877-8339.*

Web, www.sba.gov/offices/headquarters/ooi

Federal Reserve System

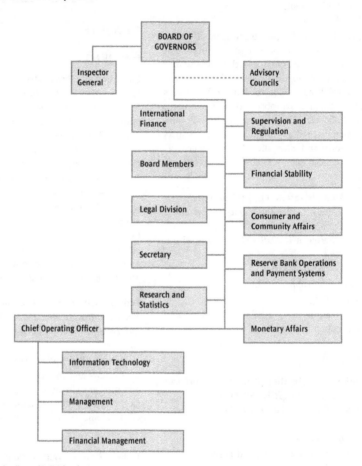

——— Lines of policy and judicial authority
---- Lines of management and administrative authority

Administers and runs the Small Business Investment Company, Small Business Investment Research, and Small Business Technology Transfer programs.

Treasury Dept., *Domestic Finance, Financial Market Policy,* 1500 Pennsylvania Ave. N.W., #5011, 20220; (202) 622-2000. Vacant, Assistant Secretary.
Web, www.treasury.gov/about/organizational-structure/offices/Pages/-Financial-Market-Policy.aspx

Provides analyses and policy recommendations on financial markets, government financing, and securities, tax implications, and related regulations.

▶CONGRESS

For a listing of relevant congressional committees and subcommittees, please see pages 34–35 or the Appendix.

Government Accountability Office (GAO), *Financial Markets and Community Investment (FMCI),* 441 G St. N.W., #5Q24, 20548; (202) 512-8678. Lawrence Evans, Managing Director, (202) 512-4802.
Web, www.gao.gov/careers/fmci.html

Supports congressional efforts to ensure that U.S. financial markets function smoothly and effectively, identifies fraud and abuse, and promotes sound, sustainable community investment by assessing the effectiveness of federal initiatives aimed at small businesses, state and local governments, and communities.

▶NONGOVERNMENTAL

AARP, 601 E St. N.W., 20049; (202) 434-2277. Fax, (202) 434-7946. Jo Ann C. Jenkins, Chief Executive Officer. Library, (202) 434-6233. Membership, (202) 434-7550. Membership, toll-free, (800) 566-0242. Press, (202) 434-2560. Toll-free, (888) 687-2277. TTY, (877) 434-7598. Toll-free Spanish, (877) 342-2277. TTY Spanish, (866) 238-9488.
General email, member@aarp.org

Web, www.aarp.org, Twitter, @AARP and Facebook, www.facebook.com/AARP

Membership: people fifty years of age and older. Offers financial services, including insurance, investment programs, and consumer discounts.

American Institute of Certified Public Accountants, *Washington Office, 1455 Pennsylvania Ave. N.W., 20004-1081; (202) 737-6600. Fax, (202) 638-4512. Mark Peterson, Executive Vice President of Advocacy.*
General email, service@aicpa.org

Web, www.aicpa.org and Twitter, @AICPA

Establishes voluntary professional and ethical regulations for the profession; sponsors conferences and training workshops. Answers technical auditing and accounting questions. (Headquarters in Durham, N.C.)

Americans for Financial Reform, *1615 L St. N.W., #450, 20006; (202) 466-1885. Lisa Donner, Executive Director.*
General email, info@ourfinancialsecurity.org

Web, www.ourfinancialsecurity.org and Twitter, @RealBankReform

Coalition of groups seeking to increase economic transparency and financial institution accountability. Analyzes economic public policies. Interests include protecting consumers, reducing large-bank bailouts, improving the Federal Reserve, regulating Wall Street, and limiting the influence of financial institutions on policy matters. Monitors legislation and regulations.

The Brookings Institution, *Hutchins Center on Fiscal and Monetary Policy, 1775 Massachusetts Ave. N.W., 20036; (202) 238-3115. David Wessel, Director.*
Web, www.brookings.edu/center/the-hutchins-center-on-fiscal-and-monetary-policy and Twitter, @davidmwessel

Research center promoting improvements in and public understanding of fiscal and monetary policies.

Certified Financial Planner Board of Standards, *1425 K St. N.W., #800, 20005; (202) 379-2200. Fax, (202) 379-2299. Kevin R. Keller, Chief Executive Officer.*
Toll-free, (800) 487-1497.
General email, mail@cfpboard.org

Web, www.cfp.net and Twitter, @CFPBoard

Grants certification to professional financial planners through education, examination, and regulation of industry standards. Publishes handbooks and newsletters to advance financial planning ethics and awareness.

Consumer Data Industry Assn., *1090 Vermont Ave. N.W., #200, 20005-4905; (202) 371-0910. Fax, (202) 371-0134. Francis Creighton, Chief Executive Officer. Press, (202) 408-7406.*
General email, cdia@cdiaonline.org

Web, www.cdiaonline.org

Membership: credit reporting, mortgage reporting, and collection service companies. Provides information about credit rights to consumers. Monitors legislation and regulations.

Jump$tart Coalition for Personal Finance Literacy, *1001 Connecticut Ave. N.W., #640, 20036; (202) 846-6780. Laura Levine, President.*
General email, info@jumpstart.org

Web, www.jumpstart.org and Twitter, @NatJumpStart

Coalition of organizations that promote financial literacy for pre-K–12 and college-aged students. Offers teacher training programs and online educational materials. Holds annual conferences for financial education professionals. Produces an annual publication that outlines financial education curriculum and topics.

National Assn. of College and University Business Officers, *1110 Vermont Ave. N.W., #800, 20005; (202) 861-2500. Fax, (202) 861-2583. John D. Walda, President. Toll-free, (800) 462-4916.*
General email, support@nacubo.org

Web, www.nacubo.org and Twitter, @NACUBO

Membership: chief business and financial officers at higher education institutions. Provides members with information on financial management, federal regulations, and other subjects related to the business administration of universities and colleges; conducts workshops on issues such as student aid, institutional budgeting, and accounting.

National Assn. of Investment Companies, *1300 Pennsylvania Ave. N.W., #700, 20004; (202) 204-3001. Fax, (202) 204-3022. Robert L. Greene, President.*
General email, info@naicpe.com

Web, www.naicpe.com

Membership: investment companies that provide minority-owned businesses with venture capital and management guidance. Provides technical assistance; monitors legislation and regulations.

National Assn. of State Auditors, Comptrollers, and Treasurers, *Washington Office, 444 N. Capitol St. N.W., #548, 20001; (202) 624-5451. Fax, (202) 624-5473. Cornelia Chebinou, Washington Director.*
Web, www.nasact.org and Twitter, @nasact

Membership: elected and appointed state and territorial officials who deal with the financial management of state government. Provides training and leadership information on financial management, best practices, and research. Monitors legislation and regulations. (Headquarters in Lexington, Ky.)

National Venture Capital Assn., *25 Massachusetts Ave. N.W., #730, 20001; (202) 864-5920. Fax, (202) 864-5930. Bobby Franklin, President; Cassie Ann Hodges, Director of Communications. Media, (202) 864-5921.*
General email, info@nvca.org

Web, www.nvca.org

Membership: venture capital organizations and individuals and corporate financiers. Promotes understanding of venture capital investment. Facilitates networking opportunities and provides research data on equity investment in emerging growth companies. Monitors legislation.

Banking

▶**AGENCIES**

Community Development Financial Institutions Fund *(Treasury Dept.), 1801 L St. N.W., 6th Floor, 20036*

(mailing address: 1500 Pennsylvania Ave. N.W., Washington, DC 20220); (202) 653-0300. Annie Donovan, Director. Helpline, (202) 653-6421.
General email, cdfihelp@cdfi.treas.gov
Web, www.cdfifund.gov

Provides funds and tax credits to financial institutions to build private markets, create healthy local tax revenues, and expand the availability of credit, investment capital, affordable housing, and financial services in low-income urban, rural, and Native communities.

Comptroller of the Currency *(Treasury Dept.),* Constitution Center, 400 7th St. S.W., 20219; (202) 649-6800. Joseph M. Otting, Comptroller. Press, (202) 649-6870. Information, (800) 613-6743. TDD, (713) 658-0340. TTY, (800) 877-8339.
General email, publicaffairs3@occ.treas.gov
Web, https://occ.treas.gov and Twitter, @USOCC

Charters and examines operations of national banks, federal savings associations, and U.S. operations of foreign-owned banks; establishes guidelines for bank examinations; handles mergers of national banks with regard to antitrust law. Ensures that national banks and savings associations operate in a safe and sound manner, provide fair access to financial services, treat customers fairly, and comply with applicable laws and regulations.

Comptroller of the Currency *(Treasury Dept.), Chief Counsel,* Constitution Center, 400 7th St. S.W., 20506; (202) 649-5400. Fax, (202) 649-6077. Karen Solomon, Chief Counsel.
Web, www.occ.gov

Enforces and oversees compliance by nationally chartered banks with laws prohibiting discrimination in credit transactions on the basis of sex or marital status. Enforces regulations concerning bank advertising; may issue cease-and-desist orders.

Comptroller of the Currency *(Treasury Dept.), Licensing,* Constitution Center, 400 7th St. S.W., #3E-218, 20024; (202) 649-6260. Fax, (202) 649-5728. Stephen A. Lybarger, Deputy Comptroller.
Web, https://occ.treas.gov

Advises the comptroller on policy matters and programs related to bank corporate activities and is the primary decision maker on national bank corporate applications, including charters, mergers and acquisitions, conversions, and operating subsidiaries.

Comptroller of the Currency *(Treasury Dept.), Ombudsman,* Constitution Center, 400 7th St. S.W., MS 10E-12, 20024; (202) 649-5530. Fax, (202) 649-5727. Larry L. Hattix, Ombudsman.
Web, www.occ.gov

Ensures that bank customers and the banks the agency supervises receive fair and expeditious resolution of their concerns.

Comptroller of the Currency *(Treasury Dept.), Public Affairs,* Constitution Center, 400 7th St. S.W., 20506; (202)

649-6870. Fax, (202) 874-4301. Joseph Adamoli, Director; Byran Hubbard, Deputy Comptroller for Public Affairs. Congressional Relations, (202) 649-6737. Customer Assistance Group, (800) 613-6743.
General email, publicaffairs3@occ.treas.gov
Web, www.occ.gov and http://helpwithmybank.gov

Advises the comptroller on banking industry relations, employee communications, Congressional affairs, disclosure, media relations, minority affairs, and publishing.

Federal Deposit Insurance Corp. (FDIC), *550 17th St. N.W., 20429; (703) 562-2222. Fax, (202) 898-3543. Jelena McWilliams, Chair. Press, (202) 898-6993. Toll-free information, (877) 275-3342. TTY, (800) 925-4618.*
Web, www.fdic.gov, Twitter, @FDICgov and Facebook, www.facebook.com/FDICgov

Insures deposits in national banks and state banks. Conducts examinations of insured state banks that are not members of the Federal Reserve System.

Federal Deposit Insurance Corp. (FDIC), *Ombudsman, Virginia Square, L. William Seidman Center, 3501 N. Fairfax Dr., #E-2022, Arlington, VA 22226; (703) 562-6049. Fax, (703) 562-6058. M. Anthony Lowe, Ombudsman. TTY, (800) 925-4618.*
Web, www.fdic.gov/about/contact/directory/#HQOO

An independent, neutral, and confidential source of assistance for the public. Provides answers to the public in the areas of depositor concerns, loan questions, asset information, bank closing issues, and any FDIC regulation or policy.

Federal Deposit Insurance Corp. (FDIC), *Resolutions and Receiverships, 3701 N. Fairfax Dr., #10072, Arlington, VA 22226; (202) 898-6525. Fax, (202) 898-6528. Bret Edwards, Director.*
Web, www.fdic.gov/about/contact/directory/#HQDRR

Plans, executes, and monitors the orderly and least-cost resolution of failing FDIC-insured institutions. Manages remaining liability of the federal savings and deposit insurance funds.

Federal Deposit Insurance Corp. (FDIC), *Risk Management Supervision, 550 17th St. N.W., #5036, 20429; (877) 275-3342. Fax, (202) 898-3638. Doreen R. Eberley, Director.*
Web, www.fdic.gov/about/contact/directory/#HQDSC

Serves as the federal regulator and supervisor of insured state banks that are not members of the Federal Reserve System. Conducts regular examinations and investigations of banks under the jurisdiction of the FDIC; advises bank managers on improving policies and practices. Administers the Bank Insurance Fund, which insures deposits in commercial and savings banks, and the Savings Assn. Insurance Fund, which insures deposits in savings and loan institutions.

Federal Housing Finance Agency (FHFA), *400 7th St. S.W., 20219; (202) 649-3800. Fax, (202) 649-1071. Joseph Otting, Director (Acting). Media, (202) 649-3700. Ombudsman, (888) 665-1474.*

General email, fhfainfo@fhfa.gov

Web, www.fhfa.gov and Twitter, @FHFA

Regulates and works to ensure the financial soundness of Fannie Mae (Federal National Mortgage Assn.), Freddie Mac (Federal Home Loan Mortgage Corp.), and the eleven Federal Home Loan banks. FHFA was formed by a legislative merger of the Office of Federal Housing Enterprise Oversight (OFHEO), the Federal Housing Finance Board, and HUD's Government-sponsored Enterprise (GSE) mission team.

Federal Reserve System, *Board of Governors,* *20th St. and Constitution Ave. N.W., 20551; (202) 452-3000. Jerome H. Powell, Chair; Richard H. Clarida, Vice Chair. Congressional Liaison, (202) 452-3456. Information (meetings), (202) 452-3204. Public Affairs, (202) 452-2955. Publications, (202) 452-3245. TTY, (202) 263-4869. General email, frboard-publicaffairs@frb.gov*

Web, www.federalreserve.gov, Twitter, @federalreserve and Facebook, www.facebook.com/federalreserve

Serves as the central bank and fiscal agent for the government. Examines Federal Reserve banks and state member banks; supervises bank holding companies. Controls wire system transfer operations and supplies currency for depository institutions.

Federal Reserve System, *Reserve Bank Operations and Payment Systems,* *20th St. and Constitution Ave. N.W., MS 190, 20551; (202) 452-2789. Fax, (202) 452-2746. Jeffrey C. Marquardt, Deputy Director.*

Web, www.federalreserve.gov/econresdata/rbopsstaff.htm

Oversees the Federal Reserve banks' provision of financial services to depository institutions and fiscal agency services to the Treasury Dept. and other federal agencies; provides support, such as information technology and financial cost accounting. Develops policies and regulations to foster the efficiency and integrity of U.S. payment systems; works with other central banks and international organizations to improve payment systems more broadly; and conducts research on payment issues.

Federal Reserve System, *Supervision and Regulation,* *20th St. and Constitution Ave. N.W., 20551; (202) 973-6999. Michael Gibson, Director, (202) 452-2495.*

Web, www.federalreserve.gov/econresdata/bsrstaff.htm

Supervises and regulates state banks that are members of the Federal Reserve System; supervises and inspects all bank holding companies; monitors banking practices; approves bank mergers, consolidations, and other changes in bank structure.

National Credit Union Administration (NCUA), *1775 Duke St., Alexandria, VA 22314-3428; (703) 518-6300. Fax, (703) 518-6319. J. Mark McWatters, Chair; Mark A. Treichel, Executive Director, (703) 518-6320. Press, (703) 518-6336. Toll-free, (800) 755-1030. General email, consumerassistance@ncua.gov*

Web, www.ncua.gov, Twitter, @TheNCUA and Facebook, www.facebook.com/NCUAgov

Administers the National Credit Union Share Insurance Fund, which, with the backing of the full faith and credit of the U.S. government, operates and manages the National Credit Union, which insures the deposits of nearly 96 million account holders. Regulates all federally chartered credit unions; charters new credit unions; supervises and examines federal credit unions and insures their member accounts up to $250,000. Insures state-chartered credit unions that apply and are eligible. Manages the Central Liquidity Facility, which supplies emergency short-term loans to members. Conducts research on economic trends and their effect on credit unions and advises the administration's board on economic and financial policy and regulations.

Office of Management and Budget (OMB) *(Executive Office of the President), Housing, Treasury, and Commerce, 725 17th St. N.W., #9201, 20503; (202) 395-4516. Fax, (202) 395-6889. Vacant, Chief. Press, (202) 395-7254.*

Web, www.whitehouse.gov/omb

Monitors the financial condition of deposit insurance funds, including the Bank Insurance Fund, the Savings Assn. Insurance Fund, and the Federal Savings and Loan Insurance Corp. (FSLIC) Resolution Fund. Monitors the Securities and Exchange Commission. Has limited oversight over the Federal Housing Finance Board and the Federal Home Loan Bank System.

Securities and Exchange Commission (SEC), *Corporation Finance, 100 F St. N.E., MS 4613, 20549; (202) 551-3100. Fax, (202) 772-9215. William Hinman, Director.*

Web, www.sec.gov/corpfin

Receives and examines disclosure statements and other information from publicly held companies, including bank holding companies.

Treasury Dept., *Domestic Finance, Financial Institutions,* *1500 Pennsylvania Ave. N.W., #2326, 20220; (202) 622-2610. Fax, (202) 622-4774. Chris Campbell, Assistant Secretary.*

Web, www.treasury.gov/about/organizational-structure/offices/Pages/Financial-Institutions.aspx

Advises the under secretary for domestic finance and the Treasury secretary on financial institutions, banks, and thrifts. Helps formulate policy on financial institutions and government-sponsored enterprises, critical infrastructure protection and compliance policy, and financial education. Oversees the Terrorism Risk Insurance Program and the Community Development Financial Institutions Fund.

Treasury Dept., *Domestic Finance, Financial Institutions Policy,* *1500 Pennsylvania Ave. N.W., #1310, 20220; (202) 622-2000. John Connolly, Senior Policy Advisor, (202) 622-2813. General email, OFIP@treasury.gov*

Web, www.treasury.gov/about/organizational-structure/offices/Pages/-Office-of-Financial-Institutions-Policy.aspx

Coordinates department efforts on all legislation and regulations affecting financial institutions. Develops

Securities and Exchange Commission

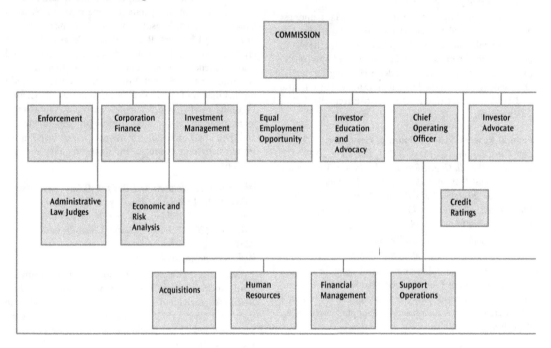

department policy on all matters relating to agencies responsible for supervising financial institutions and financial markets.

Treasury Dept., *Domestic Finance, Financial Stability,* 1500 Pennsylvania Ave. N.W., #2428, 20220; (202) 622-2000. Fax, (202) 622-6415. Vacant, Assistant Secretary. Web, www.treasury.gov/initiatives/financial-stability

Seeks to normalize lending. Provides eligible financial institutions with capital assistance; administers mortgage modification programs. Manages the Troubled Asset Relief Program (TARP).

Treasury Dept., *Special Inspector General for the Troubled Asset Relief Program (SIGTARP),* 1801 L St. N.W., 20220; (202) 622-1419. Fax, (202) 622-4559. Christy Goldsmith Romero, Special Inspector General. Fraud, waste, and abuse hotline, 877-SIG-2009. Press, (202) 927-8940. Web, www.sigtarp.gov and Twitter, @SIGTARP

Conducts, supervises, and coordinates audits and investigations of the purchase, management, and sale of assets under the Troubled Asset Relief Program (TARP).

▶**CONGRESS**

For a listing of relevant congressional committees and subcommittees, please see pages 34–35 or the Appendix.

▶**NONGOVERNMENTAL**

American Bankers Assn. (ABA), *1120 Connecticut Ave. N.W., 20036; (202) 663-5000. Fax, (202) 663-7578. Rob Nichols, President. Information, (800) 226-5377. General email, custserv@aba.com*

Web, www.aba.com, Twitter, @ABABankers and Facebook, www.facebook.com/ AmericanBankersAssociation

Membership: commercial banks. Operates schools to train banking personnel; conducts conferences; formulates government relations policies for the banking community.

American Council of State Savings Supervisors, *1129 20th St. N.W., 9th Floor, 20036; (202) 728-5707. Thomas (Tom) E. Harlow, Executive Director. Web, www.acsss.org*

Membership: supervisors and regulators of state-chartered savings associations; associate members include state-chartered savings associations and state savings banks. Trains state financial regulatory examiners. Monitors legislation and regulations affecting the state-chartered thrift industry.

Assn. for Financial Professionals, *4520 East-West Hwy., #800, Bethesda, MD 20814; (301) 907-2862. Fax, (301) 907-2864. James A. Kaitz, President. Web, www.afponline.org and Twitter, @AFPonline*

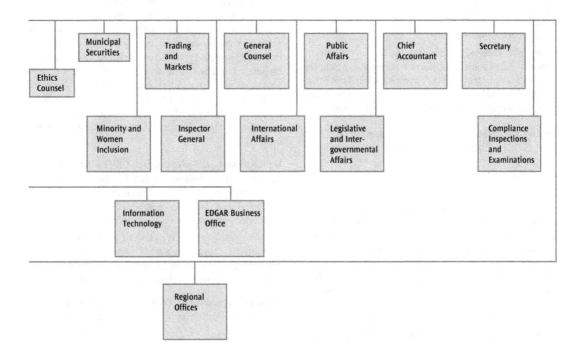

Membership: more than 16,000 members from a wide range of industries throughout all stages of their careers in various aspects of treasury and financial management. Acts as a resource for continuing education, financial tools and publications, career development, certifications, research, representation to legislators and regulators, and the development of industry standards.

BAFT, *1120 Connecticut Ave. N.W., 5th Floor, 20036-3902; (202) 663-7575. Fax, (202) 663-5538. Tod R. Burwell, Chief Executive Officer.*
General email, info@baft.org

Web, www.baft.org

Membership: international financial services providers, including U.S. and non-U.S. commercial banks, financial services companies, and suppliers with major international operations. Interests include international trade, trade finance, payments, compliance, asset servicing, and transaction banking. Monitors and acts as an advocate globally on activities that affect the business of commercial and international banks and nonfinancial companies. (Formerly Bankers' Assn. for Financial Trade.)

Bank Policy Institute (BPI), *600 13th St. N.W., #400, 20005; (202) 289-4322. Greg Baer, Chief Executive Officer.*
General email, info@bpi.com

Web, https://bpi.com and Twitter, @BankPolicy

Membership: universal banks, regional banks and the major foreign banks doing business in the United States. Conduct research and analysis to inform U.S. and global regulators, members of Congress, academics Edgar Business Office, and media through research papers, blog posts, white papers, comment letters, and Congressional testimony. The Business-Innovation-Technology-Security division (BITS), provides a forum for discussing current and emerging technology and innovation, reducing fraud, and improving cybersecurity and risk management practices for the nation's financial sector.

Coalition For Integrity, *1023 15th St. N.W., #300, 20005; (202) 589-1616. Shruti Shah, President.*
General email, administration@coalitionforintegrity.org

Web, www.coalitionforintegrity.org and
Twitter, @unite4integrity

Works to reduce corruption through the promotion of enforcement of international conventions and acting as advocate for global leadership, to increase government transparency and accountability, and to promote private sector integrity. (Formerly Transparency International USA.)

Conference of State Bank Supervisors, *1129 20th St. N.W., 9th Floor, 20036; (202) 296-2840. Fax, (202) 296-1928. John Ryan, President, (202) 728-5724.*
Web, www.csbs.org

Membership: state officials responsible for supervision of state-chartered banking institutions. Conducts educational programs. Monitors legislation and regulations.

Consumer Bankers Assn., *1225 Eye St. N.W., #550, 20005; (202) 552-6380. Richard Hunt, President, (202) 552-6382; Karen Neeley, Regulatory Manager, (202) 552-6393. Media, (202) 552-6371.*
Web, www.consumerbankers.com and
Twitter, @ConsumerBankers

Membership: federally insured financial institutions. Provides information on retail banking, including industry trends. Operates the Graduate School of Retail Bank Management to train banking personnel; conducts research and analysis on retail banking trends; sponsors conferences.

Credit Union National Assn., *Washington Office, 99 M St. S.E., #300, 20003; (202) 638-5777. Jim Nussle, President.*
General email, hello@cuna.coop
Web, www.cuna.org

Confederation of credit unions from every state, the District of Columbia, and Puerto Rico. Represents federal and state chartered credit unions. Monitors legislation and regulations. (Headquarters in Madison, Wisc.)

Electronic Funds Transfer Assn., *4000 Legato Rd., #1100, Fairfax, VA 22033; (571) 318-5556. Fax, (571) 318-5557. Kurt Helwig, President, (571) 318-5555.*
Web, www.efta.org and Twitter, @kurtEFTA

Membership: financial institutions, electronic funds transfer hardware and software providers, automatic teller machine networks, and others engaged in electronic commerce. Promotes electronic payments and commerce technologies; sponsors industry analysis. Monitors legislation and regulations.

Employee Benefit Research Institute, *1100 13th St. N.W., #878, 20005; (202) 659-0670. Fax, (202) 775-6312. Lori Lucas, President.*
General email, info@ebri.org
Web, www.ebri.org

Research institute that focuses on economic security and employee benefit issues. Seeks to raise public awareness about long-term personal financial independence and encourage retirement savings. Does not lobby and does not take public policy positions.

Independent Community Bankers of America, *1615 L St. N.W., #900, 20036; (202) 659-8111. Fax, (202) 659-3604. Preston Kennedy, President. Information, (800) 422-8439.*
General email, info@icba.org
Web, www.icba.org and Twitter, @ICBA

Membership: approximately 5,700 community banks. Interests include farm credit, deregulation, interstate banking, deposit insurance, and financial industry standards.

NACHA: The Electronic Payments Assn., *2550 Wasser Terrace, #400, Herndon, VA 20171; (703) 561-1100.*

Fax, (703) 787-0996. Janet O. Estep, President. Press, (703) 561-3952.
General email, info@nacha.org
Web, www.nacha.org and Twitter, @NACHAOnline

Membership: ACH Network participants. Supports ACH Network growth by managing its development, administration, and governance. Facilitates the expansion and diversification of electronic payments, supporting Direct Deposit and Direct Payment via ACH transactions, including credit and debit transactions; recurring and one-time payments; government, consumer, and business-to-business transactions; international payments; and payments plus payment-related information. Develops operating rules and business practices through its collaborative, self-regulatory model. Sponsors workshops and seminars. (Formerly the National Automated Clearing House Assn.)

National Assn. of Federal Credit Unions (NAFCU), *3138 10th St. North, Arlington, VA 22201-2149; (703) 842-2240. Fax, (703) 522-2734. B. Dan Berger, President, (703) 842-2215. Toll-free, (800) 336-4644.*
Web, www.nafcu.org and Twitter, @NAFCU

Membership: federally chartered credit unions. Issues legislative and regulatory alerts for members and consumers. Sponsors briefings on current financial trends, legislation and regulations, and management techniques.

National Assn. of State Credit Union Supervisors, *1655 N. Fort Myer Dr., #650, Arlington, VA 22209-3113; (703) 528-8351. Fax, (703) 528-3248. Lucy Ito, Chief Executive Officer.*
General email, info@nascus.org
Web, www.nascus.org and Twitter, @NASCUS

Membership: state credit union supervisors, state-chartered credit unions, and credit union leagues. Interests include state regulatory systems; conducts educational programs for examiners. Represents the interests of state agencies to Congress.

National Bankers Assn., *1513 P St. N.W., 20005; (202) 588-5432. Fax, (202) 588-5443. Preston Pinkett III, Chair.*
General email, administration@nationalbankers.org
Web, www.nationalbankers.org and
Twitter, @nationalbankers

Membership: minority-owned and women-owned financial institutions. Monitors legislation and regulations.

National Society of Accountants, *1330 Braddock Pl., #540, Alexandria, VA 22314; (703) 549-6400. Fax, (703) 549-2984. John Rice, Chief Executive Officer, ext. 1313. Toll-free, (800) 966-6679.*
General email, members@nsacct.org
Web, www.nsacct.org and Twitter, @NSAtax

Seeks to improve the accounting profession and to enhance the status of individual practitioners. Sponsors seminars and correspondence courses on accounting, auditing, business law, and estate planning; monitors legislation and regulations affecting accountants and their small-business clients.

Stocks, Bonds, and Securities

▶AGENCIES

Bureau of the Fiscal Service *(Treasury Dept.),*
Legislative and Public Affairs, 401 14th St. S.W., 5th
Floor, 20227; (202) 504-3502. Fax, (202) 874-7016.
Joyce Harris, Director, (202) 504-6760.
Web, www.treasurydirect.gov and www.fiscal.treasury.gov

Plans, develops, and implements communication
regarding Treasury securities.

Federal Reserve System, *Board of Governors,* 20th St.
and Constitution Ave. N.W., 20551; (202) 452-3000.
Jerome H. Powell, Chair; Richard H. Clarida, Vice Chair.
Congressional Liaison, (202) 452-3456. *Information*
(meetings), (202) 452-3204. *Public Affairs,* (202) 452-2955.
Publications, (202) 452-3245. TTY, (202) 263-4869.
General email, frboard-publicaffairs@frb.gov
Web, www.federalreserve.gov, Twitter, @federalreserve and
Facebook, www.facebook.com/federalreserve

Regulates amount of credit that may be extended and
maintained on certain securities in order to prevent excessive use of credit for purchase or carrying of securities.

Securities and Exchange Commission (SEC), 100 F St.
N.E., 20549; (202) 551-2100. Fax, (202) 772-9324.
Jay Clayton, Chair. Investor Information and
Complaints, (202) 551-6551. *Legislative and*
Intergovernmental Affairs, (202) 551-2010. *Personnel*
locator, (202) 551-6000. *Press,* (202) 551-4120. *Toll-free,*
(800) 732-0330. TTY, (800) 877-8339.
General email, chairmanoffice@sec.gov
Web, www.sec.gov

Requires public disclosure of financial and other information about companies whose securities are offered for
public sale, traded on exchanges, or traded over the
counter; issues and enforces regulations to prevent fraud
in securities markets and investigates securities frauds and
violations; supervises operations of stock exchanges and
activities of securities dealers, investment advisers, and
investment companies; regulates purchase and sale of
securities; participates in bankruptcy proceedings involving publicly held companies; has some jurisdiction over
municipal securities trading. Public Reference Section
makes available corporation reports and statements filed
with the SEC. The information is available via the Web
(www.sec.gov/edgar.shtml). Library open to the public by
appointment.

Securities and Exchange Commission (SEC), *Compliance*
Inspections and Examinations, 100 F St. N.E., 20549;
(202) 551-6200. *Peter Driscoll, Director.*
Web, www.sec.gov/ocie/Article/about.html

Analyzes data and conducts examinations in order to
ensure compliance with federal security laws, identify and
monitor risks, improve industry practices, and prevent fraud.

Securities and Exchange Commission (SEC), *Economic*
and Risk Analysis, 100 F St. N.E., 20549; (202) 551-6600.
Fax, (202) 756-0505. *Chyhe Becker, Director (Acting).*

General email, DERA@sec.gov
Web, www.sec.gov/dera

Provides the commission with economic analyses of
proposed rule and policy changes and other information
to guide the SEC in influencing capital markets. Evaluates
the effect of policy and other factors on competition
within the securities industry and among competing securities markets; compiles financial statistics on capital formation and the securities industry.

Securities and Exchange Commission (SEC), *Investor*
Advocate, 100 F St. N.E., 20549; (202) 551-3302.
Rick A. Fleming, Director.
General email, InvestorAdvocate@sec.gov
Web, www.sec.gov/investorad

Considers investors' interests in policymaking;
addresses complaints from retail investors concerning the
commission; studies investor behavior.

Securities and Exchange Commission (SEC), *Office of the*
Whistleblower, 100 F St. N.E., MS 5631, 20549; (202) 551-
4790. Fax, (703) 813-9322. *Jane Norberg, Chief.*
Web, www.sec.gov/whistleblower

Receives information about possible securities law violations and provides information about the whistleblower
program.

Securities and Exchange Commission (SEC), *Trading and*
Markets, 100 F St. N.E., 20549; (202) 551-5777. Fax, (202)
772-9273. *Brett Redfearn, Director.*
General email, tradingandmarkets@sec.gov
Web, www.sec.gov/tm

Oversees and regulates the operations of securities
exchanges, the Financial Industry Regulatory Authority
(FINRA), nationally recognized statistical rating organizations, brokers-dealers, clearing agencies, transfer agents,
alternative trading systems, large traders, security-based
swap dealers, security futures product exchanges, and
securities information processors. Promotes the establishment of a national system for clearing and settling securities transactions. Facilitates the development of a national
market system.

Treasury Dept., *Domestic Finance, Financial Market*
Policy, 1500 Pennsylvania Ave. N.W., #5011, 20220; (202)
622-2000. *Vacant, Assistant Secretary.*
Web, www.treasury.gov/about/organizational-structure/
offices/Pages/-Financial-Market-Policy.aspx

Provides analyses and policy recommendations on
financial markets, government financing, and securities,
tax implications, and related regulations.

▶NONGOVERNMENTAL

American Investment Council, 799 9th St. N.W., #200,
20001; (202) 465-7700. Fax, (202) 639-0209.
Drew Maloney, President.
General email, info@investmentcouncil.org
Web, www.investmentcouncil.org and
Twitter, @AmericaInvests

Advocacy, communications, and research organization and resource center that develops, analyzes, and distributes information about the private equity industry and its contributions to the national and global economy. Monitors legislation and regulations.

Council of Institutional Investors, *1717 Pennsylvania Ave. N.W., #350, 20006; (202) 822-0800. Fax, (202) 822-0801. Ken Bertsch, Executive Director, (202) 261-7098.*
Web, www.cii.org and Twitter, @CouncilInstInv

Membership: pension funds and other employee benefit funds, foundations, and endowments. Studies investment issues that affect pension plan assets. Focuses on corporate governance and shareholder rights. Monitors legislation and regulations.

Financial Industry Regulatory Authority (FINRA), *1735 K St. N.W., 20006-1506; (202) 728-8000. Fax, (202) 728-8075. Robert W. Cook, Chief Executive Officer. Member services, (301) 590-6500. Public disclosure, (800) 289-9999.*
Web, www.finra.org, Twitter, @FINRA_News and Facebook, www.facebook.com/ FinancialIndustryRegulatoryAuthority

Membership: investment brokers and dealers authorized to conduct transactions of the investment banking and securities business under federal and state laws. Serves as the self-regulatory mechanism in the over-the-counter securities market. Operates speakers bureau. (Formerly the National Assn. of Securities Dealers.)

Futures Industry Assn. (FIA), *2001 Pennsylvania Ave. N.W., #600, 20006; (202) 466-5460. Fax, (202) 296-3184. Walter L. Lukken, President.*
General email, info@fia.org
Web, www.fia.org, Twitter, @FIAAmericas and Facebook, www.facebook.com/Futures.Industry .Association

Membership: futures commission merchants, introducing brokers, exchanges, clearinghouses, and others interested in derivative markets. Serves as a forum for discussion of industry issues; engages in regulatory and legislative advocacy; provides market information and statistical data; offers educational programs; works to establish professional and ethical standards for members.

Intercontinental Exchange, *Washington Office, 801 Pennsylvania Ave. N.W., #630, 20004-2685; Alex Albert, Vice President.*
General email, everyone-washington@theice.com
Web, www.intercontinentalexchange.com, Twitter, @ICE_ Markets and Facebook, www.facebook.com/ IntercontinentalExchange

Provides information about risk management services to market participants around the world. Washington office monitors legislation and regulations. (Headquarters in Atlanta, Ga.)

Investment Company Institute, *1401 H St. N.W., #1200, 20005-2148; (202) 326-5800. Fax, (202) 371-5434. Paul Schott Stevens, President. Press, (202) 371-5413.*

General email, matthew.beck@ici.org
Web, www.ici.org and Facebook, www.facebook.com/ici.org

Membership: mutual funds, exchange-traded funds, and closed-end funds registered under the Investment Company Act of 1940 (including investment advisers to and underwriters of such companies) and the unit investment trust industry. Conducts research and disseminates information on issues affecting mutual funds.

Investor Protection Trust, *1020 19th St. N.W., #890, 20036-6123; (202) 775-2112. Don M. Blandin, President.*
General email, iptinfo@investorprotection.org
Web, www.investorprotection.org and Twitter, @IPT_info

Provides noncommercial investment information to consumers to help them make informed investment decisions. Serves as an independent source of noncommercial investor education materials. Operates programs under its own auspices and uses grants to underwrite important initiatives carried out by other organizations.

Municipal Securities Rulemaking Board, *1300 Eye St. N.W., #1000, 20005; (202) 838-1500. Fax, (202) 898-1500. Lynnette Kelly, President.*
General email, MMSRBsupport@mrsb.org
Web, www.msrb.org and Twitter, @MSRB_News

Congressionally chartered self-regulatory organization for the municipal securities market. Regulates municipal securities dealers and municipal advisers and seeks to provide market transparency through the Electronic Municipal Market Access website. Conducts education and outreach. Subject to oversight by the Securities and Exchange Commission.

National Assn. of Bond Lawyers, *601 13th St. N.W., #800-S, 20005-3875; (202) 503-3300. Fax, (202) 637-0217. Linda H. Wyman, Chief Operating Officer, (202) 503-3300 ext. 3306.*
General email, nabl@nabl.org
Web, www.nabl.org and Twitter, @nabldc

Membership: state and municipal finance lawyers. Educates members and others on the law relating to state and municipal bonds and other obligations. Provides advice and comment at the federal, state, and local levels on legislation, regulations, rulings, and court and administrative proceedings regarding public obligations.

National Assn. of Real Estate Investment Trusts, *1875 Eye St. N.W., #600, 20006-5413; (202) 739-9400. Fax, (202) 739-9401. Steven A. Wechsler, President. Toll-free, (800) 362-7348.*
Web, www.reit.com and Twitter, @REITs_NAREIT

Membership: real estate investment trusts and corporations, partnerships, and individuals interested in real estate securities and the industry. Interests include federal taxation, securities regulation, financial standards and reporting standards and ethics, housing and education, and global investment; compiles industry statistics. Monitors federal and state legislation and regulations.

National Investor Relations Institute, *225 Reinekers Lane, #560, Alexandria, VA 22314; (703) 562-7700.*

Fax, (703) 562-7701. Gary LaBranche, President, (703) 562-7676.

General email, niri@niri.org

Web, www.niri.org

Membership: executives engaged in investor relations and financial communications. Provides publications, educational training sessions, and research on investor relations for members; offers conferences and workshops; maintains job placement and referral services for members.

North American Securities Administrators Assn., 750 1st St. N.E., #1140, 20002; (202) 737-0900. Fax, (202) 783-3571. Joseph Brady, Executive Director.

Web, www.nasaa.org

Membership: state, provincial, and territorial securities administrators of the United States, Canada, and Mexico. Serves as the national representative of the state agencies responsible for investor protection. Works to prevent fraud in securities markets and provides a national forum to increase the efficiency and uniformity of state regulation of capital markets. Operates the Central Registration Depository, a nationwide computer link for agent registration and transfers, in conjunction with the National Assn. of Securities Dealers. Monitors legislation and regulations.

Public Company Accounting Oversight Board, 1666 K St. N.W., #800, 20006-2803; (202) 207-9100. Fax, (202) 862-8430. William D. Duhnke III, Chair; Suzanne Kinzer, Chief Administrative Officer, ext. 2139. Information, (202) 591-4135.

Web, www.pcaobus.org and Twitter, @PCAOB_News

Established by Congress to oversee the audits of public companies in order to protect the interests of investors and the public. Also oversees the audits of broker-dealers, including compliance reports filed pursuant to federal securities laws.

Securities Industry and Financial Markets Assn. (SIFMA), Washington Office, 1101 New York Ave. N.W., 8th Floor, 20005; (202) 962-7300. Fax, (202) 962-7305. Kenneth E. Bentsen Jr., Chief Executive Officer.

General email, inquiry@sifma.org

Web, www.sifma.org and Twitter, @SIFMA

Membership: securities firms, banks, and asset managers. Focuses on enhancing the public's trust in markets. Provides educational resources for professionals and investors in the industry. Monitors legislation and regulations. (Headquarters in New York. Merger of the Securities Industry Assn. and the Bond Market Assn.)

Securities Investor Protection Corp. (SIPC), 1667 K St. N.W., #1000, 20006-1620; (202) 371-8300. Fax, (202) 223-1679. Josephine Wang, Chief Executive Officer.

General email, asksipc@sipc.org

Web, www.sipc.org and Twitter, @sipc

Private corporation established by Congress to administer the Securities Investor Protection Act. Acts as a trustee or works with an independent court-appointed trustee to recover funds in brokerage insolvency cases.

Small Business Investor Alliance, 1100 H St. N.W., #1200, 20005; (202) 628-5055. Brett Palmer, President.

General email, info@sbia.org

Web, www.sbia.org and Twitter, @SmallBusinessPE

Membership: private equity, venture capital, and middle market funds that invest in small businesses. Provides training to fund managers and holds industry networking events. Monitors legislation and regulations.

US SIF: The Forum for Sustainable and Responsible Investment, 1660 L St. N.W., #306, 20036; (202) 872-5361. Fax, (202) 775-8686. Lisa Woll, Chief Executive Officer.

Web, www.ussif.org and Twitter, @US_SIF

Membership association promoting sustainable and socially responsible investing. Conducts research, events, and courses on investments considering environmental, social, and corporate governance criteria. Monitors legislation and regulations. (Formerly Social Investment Forum.)

Tangible Assets

▶**AGENCIES**

Commodity Futures Trading Commission, Three Lafayette Centre, 1155 21st St. N.W., 20581-0001; (202) 418-5000. Fax, (202) 418-5521. J. Christopher Giancarlo, Chair, (202) 418-5030. Toll-free, (866) 366-2382. TTY, (202) 418-5428.

General email, questions@cftc.gov

Web, www.cftc.gov and Twitter, @CFTC

Enforces federal statutes relating to commodity futures and options, including gold and silver futures and options. Monitors and regulates gold and silver leverage contracts, which provide for deferred delivery of the commodity and the payment of an agreed portion of the purchase price on margin.

U.S. Mint (Treasury Dept.), 801 9th St. N.W., 8th Floor, 20220; (202) 756-6468. Fax, (202) 756-6160. David J. Ryder, Director. Customer service, (800) 872-6468. Information, (202) 354-7227. Press, (202) 354-7222. TTY, (888) 321-6468.

Web, www.usmint.gov, Twitter, @usmint

General email, usmint-support@usmcatalog.com

Produces and distributes the national coinage so that the nation can conduct trade and commerce. Produces gold, silver, and platinum coins for sale to investors.

▶**NONGOVERNMENTAL**

Precious Metals Assn. of North America, 10340 Democracy Lane, #204, Fairfax, VA 22030; (703) 383-1330. Fax, (703) 383-1332. Paul Miller, Executive Director.

General email, pmiller@mwcapitol.com

Web, www.silverusersassociation.org

Membership: users of silver, including the photographic industry, silversmiths, and other manufacturers. Conducts research on the silver market; monitors government activities in silver; analyzes government statistics on silver consumption and production. Monitors legislation and regulations. (Formerly Silver Users Assn.)

Silver Institute, *1400 Eye St. N.W., #550, 20005; (202) 835-0185. Fax, (202) 835-0155. Michael (Mike) DiRienzo, Executive Director.*
General email, info@silverinstitute.org
Web, www.silverinstitute.org

Membership: companies that mine, refine, fabricate, or manufacture silver or silver-containing products. Conducts research on new technological and industrial uses for silver. Compiles statistics on mining; coinage; and the production, distribution, and use of refined silver.

INDUSTRIAL PRODUCTION, MANUFACTURING

General

▶AGENCIES

Census Bureau *(Commerce Dept.), Manufacturing and Construction, 4600 Silver Hill Rd., #8K151, Suitland, MD 20746 (mailing address: 4600 Silver Hill Rd., Washington, DC 20233); (301) 763-4750. Fax, (301) 763-8398. Edward Watkins, Chief.*
Web, www.census.gov/mcd

Collects, tabulates, and publishes statistics for the manufacturing and construction sectors of the Economic Census.

Economic Development Administration *(Commerce Dept.), 1401 Constitution Ave. N.W., #78006, 20230; (202) 482-5081. Fax, (202) 273-4781. John Fleming, Assistant Secretary. Information, (202) 482-2000. Public Affairs, (202) 482-4085.*
Web, www.eda.gov

Assists U.S. firms in increasing their competitiveness against foreign imports. Certifies eligibility and provides domestic firms and industries adversely affected by increased imports with technical assistance under provisions of the Trade Act of 1974. Administers eleven regional Trade Adjustment Assistance Centers that offer services to eligible U.S. firms.

International Trade Administration (ITA) *(Commerce Dept.), Industry and Analysis (I&A), 1401 Constitution Ave. N.W., #2854, 20230; (202) 482-1461. Fax, (202) 482-5697. James Sullivan, Assistant Secretary (Acting); Anne Driscoll, Deputy Assistant Secretary.*
Web, www.trade.gov/industry

Conducts industry trade analysis. Shapes U.S. trade policy. Participates in trade negotiations. Organizes trade capacity building programs. Evaluates the impact of domestic and international economic and regulatory policies on U.S. manufacturers and service industries.

International Trade Administration (ITA) *(Commerce Dept.), Industry and Analysis (I&A), Manufacturing,* *1401 Constitution Ave. N.W., #28004, 20230; (202) 482-1872. Fax, (202) 482-0856. Ian Steff, Deputy Assistant Secretary.*
Web, www.trade.gov/td/manufacturing and www .manufacturing.gov

Conducts analyses and competitive assessments of high-tech industries, including aerospace, automotive, industrial machinery, medical devices, and the pharmaceutical industry. Develops trade policies for these industries, negotiates market access for U.S. companies, and assists in promoting exports through trade missions, shows, and fairs in major overseas markets.

National Institute of Standards and Technology (NIST) *(Commerce Dept.), Hollings Manufacturing Extension Partnership, 100 Bureau Dr., MS 4800, Gaithersburg, MD 20899-4800; (301) 975-5020. Fax, (301) 963-6556. Carroll Thomas, Director. Toll-free, (800) 637-4634.*
General email, mfg@nist.gov
Web, www.nist.gov/mep

Collaborates with and advises private manufacturers in the United States on innovation strategies, process improvements, green manufacturing, and market diversification.

National Institute of Standards and Technology (NIST) *(Commerce Dept.), Weights and Measures, 100 Bureau Dr., MS 2600, Gaithersburg, MD 20899-2600; (301) 975-2956. Fax, (301) 975-8091. Douglas Olson, Chief; Barbara Turner, Public Relations, (301) 975-4004.*
General email, owm@nist.gov
Web, www.nist.gov/pml/weights-and-measures

Promotes uniform standards among the states for packaging and labeling products and for measuring devices, including scales and commercial measurement instruments; advises manufacturers on labeling and packaging laws and on measuring device standards. Partners with the National Conference on Weights and Measures to develop standards.

▶NONGOVERNMENTAL

American Chemistry Council, *700 2nd St. N.E., 20002; (202) 249-7000. Fax, (202) 249-6100. Calvin (Cal) M. Dooley, President.*
Web, www.americanchemistry.com,
Twitter, @AmChemistry and Facebook, www.facebook .com/AmericanChemistry

Membership: manufacturers of basic industrial chemicals. Provides members with technical research, communications services, and legal affairs counseling. Sponsors research on chemical risk assessments, biomonitoring, and nanotechnology. Interests include environmental safety and health, transportation, energy, and international trade and security. Monitors legislation and regulations.

American Forest and Paper Assn., *Government Affairs, 1101 K St. N.W., #700, 20005; (202) 463-2700. Donna Harman, President; Elizabeth Bartheld, Vice President of Government Affairs.*

General email, info@afandpa.org

Web, http://afandpa.org and Twitter, @ForestandPaoer

Membership: pulp, paper, and paper-based product manufacturers and those in related associations. Interests include tax, housing, environmental, international trade, sustainability, and land-use issues that affect the forest products industry.

American Fuel & Petrochemical Manufacturers, 1800 M St. N.W., # 900 North, 20036; (202) 457-0480. Fax, (202) 457-0486. Chet Thompson, President.

General email, info@afpm.org

Web, www.afpm.org, Twitter, @AFPMonline and Facebook, www.facebook.com/AFPMonline

Membership: petroleum, petrochemical, and refining companies. Interests include allocation, imports, refining technology, petrochemicals, and environmental regulations.

American National Standards Institute (ANSI), 1899 L St. N.W., 11th Floor, 20036; (202) 293-8020. Fax, (202) 293-9287. S. Joe Bhatia, President, (202) 331-3605.

General email, info@ansi.org

Web, www.ansi.org

Administers and coordinates the voluntary U.S. private sector–led consensus standards and conformity assessment system. Serves as the official U.S. representative to the International Organization of Standardization (ISO) and, via the U.S. National Committee, the International Electrotechnical Commission (IEC), and is a U.S. representative to the International Accreditation Forum (IAF).

Assn. for Manufacturing Technology (AMT), 7901 Jones Branch Dr., #900, McLean, VA 22102-4206; (703) 893-2900. Fax, (703) 893-1151. Douglas Woods, President, (703) 827-5202. Toll-free, (800) 524-0475.

General email, amt@amtonline.org

Web, www.amtonline.org and Twitter, @amtonline

Supports the U.S. manufacturing industry; sponsors workshops and seminars; fosters safety and technical standards. Monitors legislation and regulations.

Can Manufacturers Institute, 1730 Rhode Island Ave. N.W., #1000, 20036; (202) 232-4677. Fax, (202) 232-5756. Robert Budway, President.

Web, www.cancentral.com

Represents can manufacturers and suppliers; promotes the use of the can as a form of food and beverage packaging. Conducts market research. Monitors legislation and regulations.

Chlorine Institute Inc., 1300 Wilson Blvd., #525, Arlington, VA 22209; (703) 894-4140. Fax, (703) 894-4130. Frank Reiner, President, (703) 894-4116.

General email, info@cl2.com

Web, www.chlorineinstitute.org and Twitter, @TheChlorineINST

Safety, health, and environmental protection center of the chlor-alkali (chlorine, caustic soda, caustic potash, and hydrogen chloride) industry. Interests include employee health and safety, resource conservation and pollution abatement, control of chlorine emergencies, product specifications, and public and community relations. Publishes technical pamphlets and drawings.

Envelope Manufacturers Assn., 700 S. Washington St., #260, Alexandria, VA 22314; (703) 739-2200. Fax, (703) 739-2209. Maynard H. Benjamin, President.

General email, mhbenjamin@envelope.org

Web, www.envelope.org

Membership: envelope manufacturers and suppliers. Monitors legislation and regulations.

Flexible Packaging Assn., 185 Admiral Cochrane Dr., #105, Annapolis, MD 21401; (410) 694-0800. Fax, (410) 694-0900. Alison Keane, President.

General email, fpa@flexpack.org

Web, www.flexpack.org

Membership: companies that supply or manufacture flexible packaging. Researches packaging trends and technical developments. Compiles industry statistics. Monitors legislation and regulations.

Glass Packaging Institute, 1220 N. Fillmore St., #400, Arlington, VA 22201; (703) 684-6359. Fax, (703) 546-0588. Joseph Cattaneo, President (Acting).

General email, info@gpi.org

Web, www.gpi.org and Twitter, @ChooseGlass

Membership: manufacturers of glass containers and their suppliers. Promotes industry policies to protect the environment, conserve natural resources, and reduce energy consumption; conducts research; monitors legislation affecting the industry. Interests include glass recycling.

Green Seal, 1001 Connecticut Ave. N.W., #827, 20036-5525; (202) 872-6400. Fax, (202) 872-4324. Douglas Gatlin, Chief Executive Officer.

General email, greenseal@greenseal.org

Web, www.greenseal.org and Twitter, @GreenSeal

Grants certification to environmentally sustainable products, services, hotels, restaurants, and other companies.

Household and Commercial Products Assn., 1667 K St. N.W., #300, 20006; (202) 872-8110. Fax, (202) 223-2636. Stephen (Steve) J. Caldeira, President.

General email, info@thehcpa.org

Web, www.thehcpa.org and Twitter, @TheHCPA

Membership: manufacturers, marketers, packagers, and suppliers in the chemical specialties industry. Focus includes cleaning products and detergents, nonagricultural pesticides, disinfectants, automotive and industrial products, polishes and floor finishes, antimicrobials, air care products and candles, and aerosol products. Monitors scientific developments; conducts surveys and research. Monitors legislation and regulations.

Independent Lubricant Manufacturers Assn., 675 N. Washington St., Alexandria, VA 22314; (703) 684-5574. Fax, (703) 350-4919. Holly Alfano, Chief Executive Officer.

General email, ilma@ilma.org

Web, www.ilma.org and Twitter, @ILMATweets

Membership: U.S. and international companies that manufacture automotive, industrial, and metalworking lubricants; associates include suppliers and related businesses. Conducts two workshops and conferences annually; compiles statistics. Monitors legislation and regulations.

Independent Office Products and Furniture Dealers Assn. (IOPFDA), 3601 E. Joppa Rd., Baltimore, MD 21234; (410) 931-8100. Fax, (410) 931-8111. Melissa Ball, President.
General email, info@iopfda.org
Web, www.iopfda.org and www.ofdanet.org

Membership: dealers, manufacturers, wholesalers, manufacturers, representatives, and industry service providers of office products and office furniture. Serves independent dealers and works with their trading partners to develop programs and opportunities that help strengthen the dealer position in the marketplace. Divisions include the Office Furniture Dealers Association (OFDA) and the National Office Products Alliance (NOPA).

Industrial Designers Society of America (IDSA), 555 Grove St., #200, Herndon, VA 20170; (703) 707-6000. Fax, (703) 787-8501. Chris Livaudais, Executive Director.
General email, idsa@idsa.org
Web, www.idsa.org, Twitter, @IDSA and Facebook, www.facebook.com/IDSA.org

Membership: designers of products, equipment, instruments, furniture, transportation, packages, exhibits, information services, and related services, and educators of industrial design. Provides the Bureau of Labor Statistics with industry information. Monitors legislation and regulations.

Industrial Energy Consumers of America, 1776 K St. N.W., #720, 20006; (202) 223-1420. Paul N. Cicio, President, (202) 223-1661.
Web, www.ieca-us.com

National trade association that represents the manufacturing industry and acts as advocate on energy, environmental, and public policy issues. Advocates greater diversity of and lower costs for energy. Monitors legislation and regulations.

Innovation Research Interchange, 2300 Clarendon Blvd., #400, Arlington, VA 22201; (703) 647-2580. Fax, (703) 647-2581. Edward Bernstein, President.
General email, information@iriweb.org
Web, www.iriweb.org, Twitter, @IRIweb and Facebook, www.facebook.com/iriweb

Membership: companies that maintain laboratories for industrial research. Seeks to improve the process of industrial research by promoting cooperative efforts among companies and federal laboratories, between the academic and research communities, and between industry and the government. Monitors legislation and regulations concerning technology, industry, and national competitiveness. (Formerly Industrial Research Institute, Inc.)

International Brotherhood of Electrical Workers (IBEW), 900 7th St. N.W., 20001; (202) 833-7000. Fax, (202) 728-7676. Lonnie Stephenson, International President; Kenneth Cooper, International Secretary-Treasurer.
General email, webmaster@ibew.org
Web, www.ibew.org

Membership: workers in utilities, construction, telecommunications, broadcasting, manufacturing, railroads, and government. Helps members negotiate pay, benefits, and better working conditions; conducts training programs and workshops. Monitors legislation and regulations. (Affiliated with the AFL-CIO.)

International Brotherhood of Teamsters, 25 Louisiana Ave. N.W., 20001-2198; (202) 624-6800. Fax, (202) 624-6918. James P. Hoffa, General President; Christy Bailey, Director of Federal Legislation and Regulation, (202) 624-6993; Bret Caldwell, Director of Communications, (202) 624-6911. Press, (202) 624-6911.
General email, communications@teamster.org
Web, www.teamster.org

Membership: workers in the transportation and construction industries, factories, offices, hospitals, warehouses, and other workplaces. Helps members negotiate pay, benefits, and better working conditions; conducts training programs and workshops. Monitors legislation and regulations.

International Sleep Products Assn., 501 Wythe St., Alexandria, VA 22314-1917; (703) 683-8371. Fax, (703) 683-4503. Ryan Trainer, President.
General email, info@sleepproducts.org
Web, www.sleepproducts.org

Membership: manufacturers of bedding and mattresses. Compiles statistics on the industry. (Affiliated with Sleep Products Safety Council and the Better Sleep Council.)

Laboratory Products Assn., 1114 Fairfax Pl., White Post, VA 22663 (mailing address: P.O. Box 12, Fairfax, VA 22038); (703) 836-1360. Fax, (703) 836-6644. Clark Mulligan, President, Ext. 301.
General email, info@lpanet.org
Web, www.lpanet.org

Membership: manufacturers and distributors of laboratory products and optical instruments. (Affiliated with the Optical Imaging Assn.)

Manufacturers Alliance/MAPI, 1600 Wilson Blvd., #1100, Arlington, VA 22209-2594; (703) 841-9000. David G. Nord, Chair.
Web, www.mapi.net

Membership: companies involved in advanced manufacturing industries, including electronics, telecommunications, precision instruments, computers, and the automotive and aerospace industries. Seeks to increase industrial productivity. Conducts research; organizes discussion councils. Monitors legislation and regulations.

National Assn. of Chemical Distributors (NACD), 1560 Wilson Blvd., #1100, Arlington, VA 22209; (703) 527-6223. Fax, (703) 527-7747. Eric Byer, President.

General email, nacdpublicaffairs@nacd.com

Web, www.nacd.com and Twitter, @NACD_RD

Membership: firms involved in purchasing, processing, blending, storing, transporting, and marketing of chemical products. Provides members with information on such topics as training, safe handling and transport of chemicals, liability insurance, and environmental issues. Manages the NACD Chemical Educational Foundation. Monitors legislation and regulations.

National Assn. of Manufacturers (NAM), 733 10th St. N.W., #700, 20001; (202) 637-3000. Fax, (202) 637-3182. Jay Timmons, President, (202) 637-3106. Toll-free, (800) 814-8468.
General email, manufacturing@nam.org

Web, www.nam.org and Twitter, @ShopFloorNAM

Membership: public and private manufacturing companies. Interests include manufacturing technology, economic growth, international trade, national security, taxation, corporate finance and governance, labor relations, occupational safety, workforce education, health care, energy and natural resources, transportation, and environmental quality. Monitors legislation and regulations.

National Assn. of Manufacturers (NAM), *International Economic Affairs,* 733 10th St. N.W., #700, 20001; (202) 637-3144. Fax, (202) 637-3182. Linda Dempsey, Vice President. Toll-free, (800) 814-8466.
Web, www.nam.org

Represents manufacturing business interests on international economic issues, including trade, international investment, export financing, and export controls.

National Council on Advanced Manufacturing, 2025 M St. N.W., #800, 20036; (202) 367-1247. Fax, (202) 367-2178. Robert (Rusty) Patterson, Chief Executive Officer; Fred Wentzel, Executive Vice President.
General email, wentzelf@nacfam.org

Web, www.nacfam.org

Promotes public policies supportive of advanced manufacturing and industrial modernization conducive to global economic competitiveness. Advocates greater national focus on industrial base modernization, increased investment in plants and equipment, accelerated development and deployment of advanced manufacturing technology, and reform of technical education and training.

Society of Chemical Manufacturers and Affiliates (SOCMA), 1400 Crystal Dr., #630, Arlington, VA 22202; (571) 348-5100. Fax, (571) 348-5138. Jennifer L. Abril, President.
General email, info@socma.com

Web, www.socma.com and Twitter, @socma

Membership: companies that manufacture, distribute, and market organic chemicals; producers of chemical components; and providers of custom chemical services. Interests include international trade, environmental and occupational safety, chemical security, and health issues; conducts workshops and seminars. Promotes commercial opportunities for members. Monitors legislation and regulations.

Society of the Plastics Industry (SPI), 1425 K St. N.W., #500, 20005; (202) 974-5200. Fax, (202) 296-7005. Patricia Davitt Long, President (Acting).
General email, feedback@plasticsindustry.org

Web, www.plasticsindustry.org and
Twitter, @PLASTIC_US

Promotes the plastics industry and its processes, raw materials suppliers, and machinery manufacturers. Monitors legislation and regulations.

Clothing and Textiles

▶**AGENCIES**

International Trade Administration (ITA) *(Commerce Dept.), Industry and Analysis (I&A), Textiles and Apparel (OTEXA),* 1401 Constitution Ave. N.W., #30003, 20230; (202) 482-5078. Fax, (202) 482-2331. Lloyd Wood, Deputy Assistant Secretary, (202) 482-3737; Maria D'Andrea-Yothers, Director, (202) 482-1550.
General email, otexa@trade.gov

Web, http://otexa.trade.gov

Participates in negotiating bilateral textile and apparel import restraint agreements; responsible for export expansion programs and reduction of nontariff barriers for textile and apparel goods; provides data on economic conditions in the domestic textile and apparel markets, including impact of imports.

▶**NONGOVERNMENTAL**

American Apparel and Footwear Assn. (AAFA), 740 6th St. N.W., 3rd and 4th Floors, 20001; (202) 853-9080. Fax, (202) 853-9076. Rick Helfenbein, President. Toll-free, (800) 520-2262.
Web, www.aafaglobal.org, Twitter, @apparelfootwear and Facebook, www.facebook.com/apparelandfootwear

Membership: manufacturers of apparel, sewn products, footwear and their suppliers, importers, and distributors. Provides members with information on the industry, including import and export data. Interests include product flammability and trade promotion. Monitors legislation and regulations.

American Textile Machinery Assn., 201 Park Washington Court, Falls Church, VA 22046-4527; (703) 538-1789. Fax, (703) 241-5603. Clay D. Tyeryar, President.
General email, info@atmanet.org

Web, www.atmanet.org

Membership: U.S.-based manufacturers of textile machinery and related parts and accessories. Interests include competitiveness and expansion of foreign markets. Monitors legislation and regulations.

Dry Cleaning and Laundry Institute, 14700 Sweitzer Lane, Laurel, MD 20707; (301) 622-1900. Fax, (240)

295-4200. Mary Scalco, Chief Executive Officer. Toll-free, (800) 638-2627.
General email, techline@dlionline.org
Web, www.dlionline.org and Twitter, @drylauninst

Membership: dry cleaners and launderers. Conducts research and provides information on products and services. Monitors legislation and regulations.

Footwear Distributors and Retailers of America, 1319 F St. N.W., #700, 20004-1179; (202) 737-5660. Fax, (202) 645-0789. Matt Priest, President.
General email, info@fdra.org
Web, www.fdra.org, Twitter, @FDRA and Facebook, www.facebook.com/FDRADC

Membership: companies that operate shoe retail outlets and wholesale footwear companies with U.S. and global brands. Provides business support and government relations to members. Interests include intellectual property rights, ocean shipping rates, trade with China, and labeling regulations.

National Cotton Council of America, Washington Office, 1521 New Hampshire Ave. N.W., 20036-1205; (202) 745-7805. Fax, (202) 483-4040. Reece Langley, Vice President, Washington Operations.
Web, www.cotton.org and Twitter, @NCottonCouncil

Membership: all segments of the U.S. cotton industry. Formulates positions on trade policy and negotiations; seeks to improve competitiveness of U.S. exports; sponsors programs to educate the public about flammable fabrics. (Headquarters in Memphis, Tenn.)

National Council of Textile Organizations, 1701 K St. N.W., #625, 20006; (202) 822-8028. Fax, (202) 822-8029. Augustine Tantillo, President.
Web, www.ncto.org and Twitter, @NCTO

Membership: U.S. companies that spin, weave, knit, or finish textiles from natural fibers, and associate members from affiliated industries. Interests include domestic and world markets. Monitors legislation and regulations. (Merged with the American Fiber Manufacturers Association.)

Secondary Materials and Recycled Textiles Assn.
(SMART), 3465 Box Hill Corporate Center Dr., Suite H, Abingdon, MD 21009; (443) 640-1050. Fax, (410) 569-3340. Jackie King, Executive Director, ext. 105.
Media, (410) 420-2001.
General email, smartinfo@kingmgmt.org
Web, www.smartasn.org and Twitter, @SMARTTextile

Membership: organizations and individuals involved in producing, shipping, and distributing recycled textiles and other textile products. Sponsors educational programs; publishes newsletters. Monitors legislation and regulations.

UNITE HERE, Washington Office, 1775 K St. N.W., #620, 20006-1530; (202) 393-4373. Fax, (202) 223-6213 or (202) 342-2929. Donald Taylor, President.
Web, www.unitehere.org and Twitter, @unitehere

Membership: workers in the United States and Canada who work in the hotel, gaming, food service, distribution, transportation, manufacturing, textile, laundry, and airport industries. Assists members with contract negotiation and grievances; conducts training programs and workshops. Monitors legislation and regulations. (Headquarters in New York. Formed by the merger of the former Union of Needletrades, Textiles and Industrial Employees and the Hotel Employees and Restaurant Employees International Union.)

Electronics and Appliances

▶NONGOVERNMENTAL

Air-Conditioning, Heating, and Refrigeration Institute
(AHRI), 2311 Wilson Blvd., #400, Arlington, VA 22201; (703) 524-8800. Stephen R. Yurek, President, Ext. 306.
General email, HYilma@ahrinet.org
Web, www.ahrinet.org, Twitter, @ahriengage OR @AHRIconnect and Facebook, www.facebook.com/AHRIconnect?ref=sgm

Membership: manufacturers of gas appliances and equipment for residential and commercial use and related industries. Develops product performance rating standards and administers programs to verify manufacturers' certified ratings. Advocates product improvement; provides market statistics. Monitors legislation and regulations.

American Boiler Manufacturers Assn., 8221 Old Courthouse Rd., #380, Vienna, VA 22182; (703) 356-7172. Scott Lynch, President.
Web, www.abma.com
General email, info@abma.com, Twitter, @ABMABoiler and Facebook, www.facebook.com/ABMABoiler

Membership: manufacturers of boiler systems and boiler-related products, including fuel-burning systems. Interests include energy and environmental issues. Monitors legislation and regulations.

Assn. of Electrical Equipment and Medical Imaging Manufacturers (NEMA), 1300 N. 17th St., #900, Rosslyn, VA 22209-3801; (703) 841-3200. Fax, (703) 841-5900. Kevin Cosgriff, President. Press, (703) 841-3282.
Web, www.nema.org and Twitter, @NEMAupdates

Membership: manufacturers of products used in the generation, transmission, distribution, control, and end use of electricity, including manufacturers of medical diagnostic imaging equipment. Develops technical standards; collects, analyzes, and disseminates industry data. Interests include Smart Grid, high-performance building, carbon footprint, energy storage, and an intelligence portal. Monitors legislation, regulations, and international trade activities.

Consumer Technology Assn., 1919 S. Eads St., Arlington, VA 22202; (703) 907-7600. Fax, (703) 907-7675. Gary Shapiro, President. Press, (703) 907-7650. Toll-free, (866) 858-1555.
General email, cta@cta.tech
Web, https://cta.tech and Twitter, @CTATech

Membership: 2,000 U.S. consumer electronics companies. Promotes the industry; sponsors seminars and conferences; conducts research; consults with member companies. Monitors legislation and regulations. (Affiliated with Electronic Industries Alliance. Formerly Consumer Electronics Assn.)

Electronic Components Industry Assn., *13873 Park Center Rd., Herndon, VA 20171; (571) 323-0294. Fax, (571) 323-0245. Bill Bradford, President. Web, www.ecianow.org*

Membership: manufacturers, distributors, and manufacturer representatives of electronic components and semiconductor products. Provides information and data on industry trends; advocates the authorized sale of electronics components to prevent counterfeit product moving through the supply chain. Monitors legislation and regulations.

National Electrical Contractors Assn., *3 Bethesda Metro Center, #1100, Bethesda, MD 20814; (301) 657-3110. Fax, (301) 215-4500. John M. Grau, Chief Executive Officer. Web, www.necanet.org, Twitter, @necanet and Facebook, www.facebook.com/NECANET*

Membership: electrical contractors who build and service electrical wiring and equipment, including high-voltage construction and service. Represents members in collective bargaining with union workers; sponsors research and educational programs.

Optoelectronics Industry Development Associates, *2010 Massachusetts Ave. N.W., 20036; (202) 416-1474. Fax, (202) 416-6130. Claudia Mazzali, Chair. General email, oida@osa.org*

Web, www.osa.org/industry

Membership: optoelectronics components and systems providers, businesses, and research institutions in North America. Activities include workshops and conferences, industry reports, and advocacy. Monitors legislation and regulations. (Affiliated with The Optical Society.)

Steel, Metalworking, Machinery

▶ AGENCIES

International Trade Administration (ITA) *(Commerce Dept.), Industry and Analysis (I&A), Transportation and Machinery (OTM), 1401 Constitution Ave. N.W., #38032, 20230-0001; (202) 482-0572. Fax, (202) 482-0674. Scott Kennedy, Director, (202) 482-4874. Web, http://trade.gov/td/otm*

Promotes the export of U.S. aerospace, automotive, and machinery products; compiles and analyzes industry data; seeks to secure a favorable position for the U.S. aerospace, auto, and machinery industries in global markets through policy and trade agreements.

▶ NONGOVERNMENTAL

Aluminum Assn., *1400 Crystal Dr., #430, Arlington, VA 22202; (703) 358-2960. Fax, (703) 358-2961.*

Heidi Biggs Brock, President; Curt Wells, Director Regulatory Affairs. Press, (703) 358-2977. General email, info@aluminum.org

Web, www.aluminum.org, Twitter, @AluminumNews and Facebook, www.facebook.com/aluminumAssociation

Represents the aluminum industry. Develops voluntary standards and technical data; compiles statistics concerning the industry. Monitors legislation and regulations.

American Gear Manufacturers Assn., *1001 N. Fairfax St., #500, Alexandria, VA 22314-1587; (703) 684-0211. Fax, (703) 684-0242. Matthew (Matt) Croson, President. General email, website@agma.org*

Web, www.agma.org, Twitter, @agma and Facebook, www .facebook.com/American-Gear.Manufacturers-Association-338851515108

Membership: gear manufacturers, suppliers, and industry consultants. Conducts workshops, seminars, and conferences; develops industry standards; sponsors research. Tracks emerging technologies, including 3D printing, robots and automation, and new materials. Monitors legislation and regulations.

American Institute for International Steel, *1101 King St., #360, Alexandria, VA 22314; (703) 245-8075. Fax, (703) 610-0215. Richard Chriss, President. Web, www.aiis.org*

Membership: importers and exporters of steel, logistics companies, and port authorities. Conducts research and provides analysis on steel market and importing and exporting. Holds annual conferences.

American Iron and Steel Institute (AISI), *Washington Office, 25 Massachusetts Ave. N.W., #800, 20001; (202) 452-7100. Fax, (202) 463-6573. Thomas J. Gibson, President; Kevin Dempsey, Senior Vice President of Public Policy. Press, (202) 452-7116. General email, steelnews@steel.org*

Web, www.steel.org, Twitter, @AISISteel and Facebook, www.facebook.com/aisisteel

Represents the iron and steel industry. Publishes statistics on iron and steel production; promotes the use of steel; conducts research. Monitors legislation and regulations. (Maintains offices in Southfield, Mich., and Pittsburgh, Pa.)

American Iron and Steel Institute, *SteelPAC, 25 Massachusetts Ave. N.W. #800, 20001; Fax, (202) 452-1039. Adam Shaffer, Director of Trade and Economic Policy. Main Contact, (202) 452-7114. Web, www.steel.org/public-policy/steelpac*

Help elect candidates to the U.S. Congress who support AISI's legislative goals of making steel the material of choice and to enhance the competitiveness of the North American steel industry. Political activities include direct lobbying on legislative issues, "grassroots" coalition building, and media communications to ensure the interests of our industry are reflected in policymaking. Acts as advocate to Hill allies, builds new political relationships.

American Wire Producers Assn., *P.O. Box 151387, Alexandria, VA 22315; (703) 299-4434. Fax, (703) 299-4434. Kimberly A. Korbel, Executive Director.*
General email, info@awpa.org

Web, www.awpa.org

Membership: companies that produce carbon, alloy, and stainless steel wire and wire products in the United States, Canada, and Mexico. Interests include imports of rod, wire, and wire products. Publishes survey of the domestic wire industry. Monitors legislation and regulations.

International Assn. of Bridge, Structural, Ornamental, and Reinforcing Iron Workers, *1750 New York Ave. N.W., #400, 20006; (202) 383-4800. Fax, (202) 638-4856. Eric Dean, General President.*
General email, iwmagazine@iwintl.org

Web, www.ironworkers.org and
Twitter, @TheIronWorkers

Membership: approximately 120,000 iron workers. Helps members negotiate pay, benefits, and better working conditions; conducts training programs and workshops. Monitors legislation and regulations. (Affiliated with the AFL-CIO.)

International Assn. of Machinists and Aerospace Workers, *9000 Machinists Pl., Upper Marlboro, MD 20772-2687; (301) 967-4500. Robert Martinez Jr., International President. Information, (301) 967-4520.*
General email, websteward@iamaw.org

Web, www.goiam.org

Membership: machinists in more than 200 industries. Helps members negotiate pay, benefits, and better working conditions; conducts training programs and workshops. Monitors legislation and regulations. (Affiliated with the AFL-CIO, the Canadian Labour Congress, the International Metalworkers Federation, the International Transport Workers' Federation, and the Railway Labor Executives Assn.)

International Brotherhood of Boilermakers, Iron Ship Builders, Blacksmiths, Forgers, and Helpers, *Government Affairs, 1750 New York Ave. N.W., #335, 20006; (202) 756-2868. Fax, (202) 756-2869. Cecile Conroy, Director of Government Affairs, ext.202.*
General email, cconroy@boilermakers.org

Web, https://boilermakers.org

Membership: workers in construction, repair, maintenance, manufacturing, shipbuilding and marine repair, mining and quarrying, railroads, cement kilns, and related industries in the United States and Canada. Helps members negotiate pay, benefits, and better working conditions; conducts training programs and workshops. Monitors legislation and regulations. (Headquarters in Kansas City, Kans.; affiliated with the AFL-CIO.)

Machinery Dealers National Assn., *315 S. Patrick St., Alexandria, VA 22314; (703) 836-9300. Fax, (703) 836-9303. Mark Robinson, Executive Vice President. Toll-free, (800) 872-7807.*

General email, office@mdna.org

Web, www.mdna.org, Twitter, @MDNA_Machines and Facebook, www.facebook.com/Machinery-Dealers-National-Association-270644229632807

Membership: companies that buy and sell used capital equipment. Establishes a code of ethics for members; publishes a buyer's guide that lists members by types of machinery they sell.

Outdoor Power Equipment Institute, *1605 King St., Alexandria, VA 22314; (703) 549-7600. Fax, (703) 549-7604. Kris Kiser, President.*
General email, info@opei.org

Web, www.opei.org and Twitter, @OPEInstitute

Membership: manufacturers of powered lawn and garden maintenance products, components and attachments, and their suppliers. Promotes safe use of outdoor power equipment; keeps statistics on the industry; fosters exchange of information. Monitors legislation and regulations.

Packaging Machinery Manufacturers Institute, *11911 Freedom Dr., #600, Reston, VA 20190; (571) 612-3200. Fax, (703) 243-8556. Jim Pittas, President.*
General email, info@pmmi.org

Web, www.pmmi.org and Twitter, @PMMIorg

Membership: manufacturers of packaging, machinery, packaging-related converting machinery, components, processing materials, and containers. Provides industry information and statistics; offers educational programs to members.

Sheet Metal, Air, Rail, and Transportation Workers (SMART), *1750 New York Ave. N.W., 6th Floor, 20006; (202) 662-0880. Joseph Sellers Jr., General President. Toll-free, (800) 457-7694.*
General email, info@smart-union.org

Web, http://smart-union.org and
Twitter, @smartunionworks

Membership: United States, Puerto Rican, and Canadian workers in the building and construction trades, manufacturing, and the railroad and shipyard industries. Assists members with contract negotiation and grievances; conducts training programs and workshops. Monitors legislation and regulations. (Affiliated with the Sheet Metal and Air Conditioning Contractors' Assn., the AFL-CIO, and the Canadian Labour Congress.)

Specialty Steel Industry of North America, *3050 K St. N.W., #400, 20007; (202) 342-8630. Fax, (202) 342-8451. Dennis Oates, Chair. Toll-free, (800) 982-0355.*
General email, jbrown@kelleydrye.com

Web, www.ssina.com

Membership: manufacturers of products in stainless and other specialty steels. Establishes manufacturing techniques and issues technical guides; operates a hotline for technical questions.

Steel Manufacturers Assn., *1150 Connecticut Ave. N.W., #1125, 20036; (202) 296-1515. Fax, (202) 296-2506. Philip (Phil) K. Bell, President.*

General email, stefanec@steelnet.org

Web, http://steelnet.org

Membership: steel producers and their vendors in North America. Helps members exchange information on technical matters; provides information on the steel industry to the public and government. Monitors legislation and regulations.

United Steelworkers, Legislative, 1155 Connecticut Ave. N.W., #500, 20036; (202) 778-4384. Fax, (202) 419-1486. Holly Hart, Legislative Director, (202) 393-3430. Web, www.usw.org and Twitter, @steelworkers

Membership: more than one million workers in the steel, paper, rubber, energy, chemical, pharmaceutical, and allied industries. Helps members negotiate pay, benefits, and better working conditions; conducts training programs and workshops. Monitors legislation and regulations. (Affiliated with the AFL-CIO; Headquarters in Pittsburgh, Pa.)

INSURANCE

General

▶AGENCIES

Federal Emergency Management Agency (FEMA) (Homeland Security Dept.), Resilience, Federal Insurance and Mitigation Administration, 400 C St. S.W., 20472; (202) 646-2781. Fax, (202) 646-7970. David I. Maurstad, Deputy Associate Administrator. Web, www.fema.gov/what-mitigation/federal-insurance-mitigation-administration

Administers federal insurance programs, including the National Flood Insurance Program, to reduce future losses from floods, earthquakes, tornadoes, and other natural disasters. Makes low-cost flood insurance available to eligible homeowners.

▶CONGRESS

For a listing of relevant congressional committees and subcommittees, please see pages 34–35 or the Appendix.

▶NONGOVERNMENTAL

American Academy of Actuaries, 1850 M St. N.W., #300, 20036; (202) 223-8196. Fax, (202) 872-1948. Shawna Ackerman, President; Mary Downs, Executive Director. General email, guerra@actuary.org

Web, www.actuary.org, Twitter, @Actuary_Dot_Org and Facebook, www.facebook.com/Actuary.Org

Membership: professional actuaries practicing in the areas of life, health, liability, property, and casualty insurance; pensions; government insurance plans; and general consulting. Provides information on actuarial matters, including insurance and pensions; develops professional standards; advises public policymakers.

American Council of Life Insurers, 101 Constitution Ave. N.W., #700, 20001-2133; (202) 624-2000. Susan K. Neely, President. Web, www.acli.com

General email, contact@acli.com, Twitter, @ACLINews and Facebook, www.facebook.com/ACLINews

Membership: life insurance companies authorized to do business in the United States. Conducts research and compiles statistics at state and federal levels. Monitors legislation and regulations.

American Insurance Assn., 555 12th St. N.W., #550, 20004; (202) 828-7100. Fax, (202) 293-1219. John Degnan, President. General email, info@aiadc.org

Web, www.aiadc.org and Twitter, @AIADC

Membership: companies providing property and casualty insurance. Conducts public relations and educational activities; provides information on issues related to property and casualty insurance. Monitors legislation and regulations.

American Society of Pension Professionals and Actuaries, 4245 N. Fairfax Dr., #750, Arlington, VA 22203-1648; (703) 516-9300. Fax, (703) 516-9308. Brian H. Graff, Chief Executive Officer, (703) 516-9300. General email, info@usaretirement.org

Web, www.asppa.org and Twitter, @ASPPA

Membership: administrators, actuaries, advisers, lawyers, accountants, and other financial services professionals who provide consulting and administrative services for employee-based retirement plans. Sponsors educational conferences, webcasts, and credentialing programs for retirement professionals. Monitors legislation and regulations.

Assn. for Advanced Life Underwriting, 11921 Freedom Dr., #1100, Reston, VA 20190; 101 Constitution Ave. N.W., #703 East, 20001; (703) 641-9400. Fax, (703) 641-9885. Marc Cadin, Chief Executive Officer, (703) 641-8149. Toll-free, (888) 275-0092. General email, info@aalu.org

Web, www.aalu.org

Membership: specialized underwriters in the fields of estate analysis, charitable planning, business insurance, pension planning, and employee benefit plans. Monitors legislation and regulations on small-business taxes and capital formation. (Maintains an additional office in Washington, D.C.)

Council of Insurance Agents and Brokers, 701 Pennsylvania Ave. N.W., #750, 20004; (202) 783-4400. Fax, (202) 783-4410. Ken A. Crerar, President, (202) 662-4420. General email, ciab@ciab.com

Web, www.ciab.com and Twitter, @TheCIAB

Represents commercial property and casualty insurance agencies and brokerage firms. Members offer insurance products and risk management services to business, government, and the public.

GAMA International, *3112 Fairview Park Dr., Falls Church, VA 22042; (571) 499-4300. Fax, (571) 499-4302. Bonnie Godsman, Chief Executive Officer, (571) 499-4311. Information, (800) 345-2687.*
General email, gamainternational@gamaweb.com

Web, www.gamaweb.com, Twitter, @GAMAIntl and Facebook, www.facebook.com/gamaintl

Membership: general agents and managers who provide life insurance and related financial products and services. Provides information, education, and training for members.

Independent Insurance Agents and Brokers of America, *127 S. Peyton St., Alexandria, VA 22314; (703) 683-4422. Fax, (703) 683-7556. Robert Rusbuldt, President. Toll-free, (800) 221-7917.*
General email, info@iiaba.net

Web, www.independentagent.com, Twitter, @IndAgent and Facebook, www.facebook.com/independentagent

Provides educational and advisory services; researches issues pertaining to auto, home, business, life, and health insurance; offers cooperative advertising program to members. Political action committee monitors legislation and regulations.

National Assn. of Independent Life Brokerage Agencies, *11325 Random Hills Rd., #110, Fairfax, VA 22030; (703) 884-1525. Fax, (703) 383-6942. Dan LaBert, Chief Executive Officer, (703) 383-3066.*
General email, info@nailba.org

Web, www.nailba.org and Twitter, @NAILBA

Membership: owners of independent life insurance agencies. Fosters the responsible and effective distribution of life and health insurance and related financial services; provides a forum for exchange of information among members. Monitors legislation and regulations.

National Assn. of Insurance and Financial Advisors, *2901 Telestar Court, Falls Church, VA 22042-1205; (703) 770-8102. Fax, (703) 770-8107. Kevin M. Mayeux, Chief Executive Officer, (703) 770-8101. Toll-free, (877) 866-2432.*
General email, membersupport@naifa.org

Web, www.naifa.org and Twitter, @NAIFA

Federation of state and local life underwriters, agents, and financial advisers. Provides information on life and health insurance and other financial services; sponsors education and training programs.

National Assn. of Insurance Commissioners, *Government Relations, 444 N. Capitol St. N.W., #700, 20001-1509; (202) 471-3990. Fax, (816) 460-7493. Eric Cioppa, President, (207) 624-8475; Michael (Mike) F. Consedine, Chief Executive Officer, (202) 471-3390.*
Web, www.naic.org and Twitter, @NAIC

Membership: state insurance commissioners, directors, and supervisors. Provides members with information on legal and market conduct, and financial services; publishes research and statistics on the insurance industry. Monitors legislation and regulations. (Affiliated with the Center for Insurance Policy and Research. Headquarters in Kansas City, Mo.)

National Assn. of Professional Insurance Agents, *419 North Lee St., Alexandria, VA 22314; (703) 836-9340. Fax, (703) 836-1279. Mike Becker, Executive Vice President, (703) 518-1340; Jon Gentile, Vice President of Government Relations, (703) 518-1365. Press, (703) 518-1352.*
General email, web@pianet.org

Web, www.pianet.org and Twitter, @PIANational

Membership: independent insurance agents and brokers. Provides basic and continuing education for agents through courses, seminars, and educational materials. Monitors legislation and regulations.

Nonprofit Risk Management Center, *204 S. King St., Leesburg, VA 20175; (703) 777-3504. Fax, (703) 443-1990. Melanie L. Herman, Executive Director, (202) 785-3891.*
General email, info@nonprofitrisk.org

Web, www.nonprofitrisk.org, Twitter, @nonprofitrisk and Facebook, www.facebook.com/nonprofitrisk

Provides information on insurance and risk management issues through conferences, consulting, online tools, and publications for nonprofit organizations.

Property Casualty Insurers Assn. of America, *Washington Office, 444 N. Capitol St., #801, 20001; (202) 639-0490. Fax, (202) 639-0494. David A. Sampson, Chief Executive Officer.*
Web, www.pciaa.net and Twitter, @PCIAA

Membership: companies providing property and casualty insurance. Monitors legislation and compiles statistics; interests include personal and commercial property and casualty insurance. (Headquarters in Chicago, Ill.)

Reinsurance Assn. of America, *1445 New York Ave. N.W., 7th Floor, 20005; (202) 638-3690. Fax, (202) 638-0936. Franklin W. Nutter, President. Media, (202) 783-8390.*
General email, infobox@reinsurance.org

Web, www.reinsurance.org and Twitter, @TheRAA

Membership: companies writing property and casualty reinsurance. Monitors legislation and regulations.

PATENTS, COPYRIGHTS, AND TRADEMARKS

General

▶ **AGENCIES**

Bureau of Economic and Business Affairs (EB) *(State Dept.),* **Commercial and Business Affairs (CBA),**

International Intellectual Property Enforcement (IPE), 2201 C St. N.W., #4931, 20520-4931; (202) 647-3251. Lisa Dyer, Director.
General email, eb-a-ipe-dl@state.gov
Web, www.state.gov/e/eb/tpp/ipe

Handles multilateral and bilateral policy formulation involving patents, copyrights, and trademarks, and international industrial property of U.S. nationals.

Civil Division *(Justice Dept.),* **Commercial Litigation (OCL),** *Intellectual Property,* 1100 L St. N.W., #11116, 20005; (202) 514-7223. Fax, (202) 307-0345. Gary Hausken, Director.
General email, john.fargo@usdoj.gov
Web, www.justice.gov/civil/intellectual-property-section

Represents the United States in patent, copyright, and trademark cases. Includes the defense of patent infringement suits; legal proceedings to establish government priority of invention; defense of administrative acts of the Register of Copyrights; and actions on behalf of the government involving the use of trademarks.

Patent and Trademark Office *(Commerce Dept.),* Madison Bldg., 600 Dulany St., #10-D44, Alexandria, VA 22314 (mailing address: P.O. Box 1450, Alexandria, VA 22313-1450); (571) 272-1000. Fax, (571) 273-8300. Andrei Iancu, Under Secretary. Customer support, (800) 786-9199. Patent search library, (571) 272-3275. Press, (571) 272-8400. TTY, (800) 877-8339.
Web, www.uspto.gov and Twitter, @USPTO

Grants patents, registers trademarks, and provides patent and trademark information. Library and search file of U.S. and foreign patents available for public use.

U.S. Customs and Border Protection *(Homeland Security Dept.),* **Intellectual Property Rights and Restrictions,** 1300 Pennsylvania Ave. N.W., Mint Annex, 20229; (202) 325-0020. Fax, (202) 572-8744. Charles Steuart, Branch Chief.
General email, hqiprbranch@cbp.dhs.gov
Web, www.cbp.gov

Responsible for customs recordation of registered trademarks and copyrights. Enforces rules and regulations pertaining to intellectual property rights. Coordinates enforcement of International Trade Commission exclusion orders against unfairly competing goods. Determines admissibility of restricted merchandise and cultural properties. Provides support to and coordinates with international organizations and the Office of the U.S. Trade Representative.

▶**CONGRESS**

For a listing of relevant congressional committees and subcommittees, please see pages 34–35 or the Appendix.

Library of Congress, *United States Copyright Office,* 101 Independence Ave. S.E., #403, 20559-6000; (202) 707-8350. Karyn Temple Claggett, Register of Copyrights (Acting). Forms and publications hotline, (202) 707-9100. Information, (202) 707-3000. Toll-free, (877) 476-0778.
Web, www.copyright.gov

Administers the United States copyright laws. Provides information to the public on copyright registration procedures and requirements, and on other Copyright Office services. Registers copyright claims and maintains public records of copyright ownership. Conducts Copyright records searches on a fee basis. Provides information regarding U.S. and foreign copyright laws, but does not give legal advice on copyright matters. Principal advisor to the United States Congress on domestic and international copyright issues.

Library of Congress, *United States Copyright Office, Licensing,* James Madison Memorial Bldg., 101 Independence Ave. S.E., #LM 504, 20557; (202) 707-8150. Fax, (202) 707-0905. James Enzinna, Chief, (202) 708-6801. Information, (202) 707-3000.
General email, licensing@loc.gov
Web, www.copyright.gov/licensing

Administers statutory licensing for cable television companies and satellite carriers, for making and distributing digital audio recording products, and for use of certain noncommercial broadcasting. Collects and distributes royalty payments under the copyright law. Administers Section 115 licensing for making and distributing phonorecords.

▶**JUDICIARY**

U.S. Court of Appeals for the Federal Circuit, 717 Madison Pl. N.W., 20439; (202) 275-8000. Fax, (202) 275-9678. Sharon Prost, Chief Judge; Peter R. Marksteiner, Clerk of the Court, (202) 272-8020. Mediation, (202) 275-8120.
Web, www.cafc.uscourts.gov

Reviews decisions of U.S. Patent and Trademark Office on applications and interferences regarding patents and trademarks; hears appeals on patent infringement cases from district courts.

▶**NONGOVERNMENTAL**

American Intellectual Property Law Assn., 1400 Crystal Dr., #600, Arlington, VA 22202; (703) 415-0780. Fax, (703) 415-0786. Lisa Jorgenson, Executive Director, ext. 347.
General email, aipla@aipla.org
Web, www.aipla.org and Twitter, @aipla

Membership: lawyers practicing in the field of patents, trademarks, and copyrights (intellectual property law). Advises agencies within the U.S. government and other domestic organizations. Holds continuing legal education conferences.

Assn. of American Publishers, *Government Affairs,* 455 Massachusetts Ave. N.W., #700, 20001; (202) 347-3375. Fax, (202) 347-3690. Allan R. Adler, Vice President of Legal and Government Affairs.
General email, info@publishers.org
Web, www.publishers.org and Twitter, @AmericanPublish

Represents U.S. book and journal publishing industry priorities on policy, legislation, and regulatory issues regionally, nationally, and worldwide. Interests include intellectual property rights, worldwide copyright enforcement, digital and new-technology issues, tax and trade, and First Amendment rights.

Intellectual Property Owners Assn., *1501 M St. N.W., #1150, 20005; (202) 507-4500. Fax, (202) 507-4501. Mark Lauroesch, Executive Director; Samantha Aguayo, Director of Government Relations.*
General email, info@ipo.org
Web, www.ipo.org, Twitter, @IPO and Facebook, www .facebook.com/Intellectual-Property-Owners-Association-91943120891/?ref=br_rs

Monitors and acts as advocate for intellectual property legislation. Conducts educational programs to protect intellectual property through patents, trademarks, copyrights, and trade secret laws.

International Anticounterfeiting Coalition, *727 15th St. N.W., 9th Floor, 20005; (202) 223-6667. Robert C. Barchiesi, President.*
General email, iacc@iacc.org
Web, www.iacc.org, Twitter, @IACC_GetReal and Facebook, www.facebook.com/ InternationalAntiCounterfeitingCoalition

Works to combat counterfeiting and piracy by promoting laws, regulations, and directives to render theft of intellectual property unprofitable. Oversees anticounterfeiting programs that increase patent, trademark, copyright, service mark, trade dress, and trade secret protection. Provides information and training to law enforcement officials to help identify counterfeit and pirate products.

International Intellectual Property Alliance, *1818 N St. N.W., 8th Floor, 20036; (202) 355-7900. Fax, (202) 355-7899. Dale Morey, Counsel.*
General email, info@iipa.com
Web, www.iipa.com

Represents U.S. copyright-based industries in efforts to improve international protection of copyrighted materials. Monitors legislation domestically and abroad; promotes enforcement reform abroad.

International Intellectual Property Institute, *209 C St. N.E., 20002; (202) 544-6610. Bruce A. Lehman, President.*
General email, ahirsch@iipi.org
Web, www.iipi.org

Aims to combat patent infringement and eliminate counterfeit products being imported into the U.S. Holds conferences to educate the public on intellectual property rights. Offers training programs and intellectual property guidance for leaders in developing and least developed countries.

National Assn. of Manufacturers (NAM), *Innovation Policy, 733 10th St. N.W., #700, 20001; (202) 637-3000. Fax, (202) 637-3182. Bryan Raymond, Director, (202) 637-3072. Press, (202) 637-3096. Toll-free, (800) 814-8468.*
Web, www.nam.org

Represents manufacturers in government and the media, advocating pro-manufacturing positions on technology policy issues, including cybersecurity, telecommunication, R&D funding, and intellectual property protection; develops policy and legislation on patents, copyrights, trademarks, and trade secrets; works with the broader business community to advance pro-growth, pro-competitiveness technology policy.

National Music Publishers' Assn., *975 F St. N.W., #375, 20004; (202) 393-6672. Fax, (202) 393-6673. David M. Israelite, President.*
General email, pr@nmpa.org
Web, www.nmpa.org and Twitter, @NMPAorg

Works to enforce music copyrights. Sponsors litigation against copyright violators. Monitors and interprets legislation and regulations.

National School Boards Assn., *1680 Duke St., 2nd Floor, Alexandria, VA 22314-3493; (703) 838-6722. Fax, (703) 549-7590. Thomas Gentzel, Executive Director, (703) 838-6730; Frank C. Pugh, President.*
General email, info@nsba.org
Web, www.nsba.org, Twitter, @NSBAComm and Facebook, www.facebook.com/SchoolBoards

Promotes a broad interpretation of copyright law to permit legitimate scholarly use of published and musical works, videotaped programs, and materials for computer-assisted instruction.

Recording Industry Assn. of America, *1025 F St. N.W., 10th Floor, 20004; (202) 775-0101. Fax, (202) 775-7253. Mitch Glazier, Chief Executive Officer.*
Web, www.riaa.com and Twitter, @RIAA

Advocates copyright protection for music artists and opposes censorship. Works to prevent recording piracy, counterfeiting, bootlegging, and unauthorized rentals and imports. Monitors legislation and regulations.

SoundExchange, *733 10th St. N.W., 10th Floor, 20001; (202) 640-5858. Fax, (202) 640-5859. Michael Huppe, President. Press, (202) 559-0558.*
General email, info@soundexchange.com
Web, www.soundexchange.com and Twitter, @SoundExchange

Artists' rights advocacy group that represents record labels and unsigned artists whose work is broadcast on national and global digital radio. Distributes royalties to musicians, performers, and music copyright owners. Monitors legislation and regulations related to digital music licensing.

U.S. Chamber of Commerce, *Congressional and Public Affairs, 1615 H St. N.W., 20062-2000; (202) 463-5600. Jack Howard, Senior Vice President.*
Web, www.uschamber.com

Monitors legislation and regulations on patents, copyrights, and trademarks.

SALES AND SERVICES

General

▶AGENCIES

Census Bureau *(Commerce Dept.), Economy-Wide Statistics,* 4600 Silver Hill Rd., #8K154, Suitland, MD 20746-2401 *(mailing address: 4700 Silver Hill Rd., #8K064, Washington, DC 20233-6500); (301) 763-7643. Kimberly P. Moore, Chief. Web, www.census.gov/econ/economywide.html*

Provides data of five-year census programs on retail, wholesale, and service industries. Conducts periodic monthly or annual surveys for specific items within these industries.

▶NONGOVERNMENTAL

American Society of Appraisers (ASA), *11107 Sunset Hills Rd., #310, Reston, VA 20190; (703) 478-2228. Fax, (703) 742-8471. Bonny Price, Chief Operations Officer, (703) 733-2110. Toll-free, (800) 272-8258. General email, asainfo@appraisers.org*

Web, www.appraisers.org and Twitter, @ASAappraisers

Membership: accredited appraisers of real property, including land, houses, and commercial buildings; business valuation; machinery and technical specialties; yachts; aircraft; public utilities; personal property, including antiques, fine art, residential contents; and gems and jewelry. Affiliate members include students and professionals interested in appraising. Provides technical information; accredits appraisers; provides consumer information programs.

ASIS International, *1625 Prince St., Alexandria, VA 22314-2882; (703) 519-6200. Fax, (703) 519-6299. Peter J. O'Neil, Chief Executive Officer. General email, asis@asisonline.org*

Web, www.asisonline.org and Twitter, @ASIS_Intl

Membership: security administrators who oversee physical and logistical security for private and public organizations, including law enforcement and the military. Develops security standards; offers educational programs and materials on general and industry-specific practices; and administers certification programs. Monitors legislation and regulations.

Assn. of Pool and Spa Professionals, *2111 Eisenhower Ave., #500, Alexandria, VA 22314-4698; (703) 838-0083. Fax, (703) 549-0493. Lawrence Caniglia, President. General email, MemberServices@apsp.org*

Web, www.apsp.org and Twitter, @TheAPSP

Membership: manufacturers, dealers and retailers, service companies, builders, and distributors of pools, spas, and hot tubs. Promotes the industry; provides educational programs for industry professionals; establishes standards for construction and safety. Monitors legislation and regulations.

Convenience Distribution Assn., *11311 Sunset Hills Rd., Reston, VA 20190; (703) 208-3358. Fax, (703) 573-5738. Kimberly Bolin, President, (703) 208-1650. Toll-free, (800) 482-2962. General email, info@cdaweb.net*

Web, www.cdaweb.net and Twitter, @cda_01

Membership: wholesalers, manufacturers, retailers, and brokers who sell or distribute convenience products. Conducts educational programs. Monitors legislation and regulations. (Formerly American Wholesale Marketers Assn.)

Council of Better Business Bureaus, *3033 Wilson Blvd., #600, Arlington, VA 22201-3843; (703) 276-0100. Fax, (703) 525-8277. Beverly Baskin, President (Acting). Web, www.bbb.org/en/us/local-bbb/council-of-better-business-bureaus and Twitter, @bbb_us*

Membership: businesses and Better Business Bureaus in the United States and Canada. Promotes ethical business practices and truth in national advertising; mediates disputes between consumers and businesses.

DECA Inc., *1908 Association Dr., Reston, VA 20191-1594; (703) 860-5000. Fax, (703) 860-4013. Frank Peterson, Executive Director (Acting). General email, info@deca.org*

Web, www.deca.org and Twitter, @DECAInc

Educational organization that helps high school and college students develop skills in marketing, management, finance, hospitality, and entrepreneurship. Promotes business and education partnerships.

Equipment Leasing and Finance Assn., *1625 Eye St. N.W., #850, 20006; (202) 238-3400. Fax, (202) 238-3401. Ralph Petta, President. General email, rjordan@elfaonline.org*

Web, www.elfaonline.org and Twitter, @ELFAOnline

Membership: independent leasing companies, banks, financial service companies, and independent brokers and suppliers to the leasing industry. Promotes the interests of the equipment leasing and finance industry; assists in the resolution of industry problems; encourages standards. Monitors legislation and regulations.

Green Seal, *1001 Connecticut Ave. N.W., #827, 20036-5525; (202) 872-6400. Fax, (202) 872-4324. Douglas Gatlin, Chief Executive Officer. General email, greenseal@greenseal.org*

Web, www.greenseal.org and Twitter, @GreenSeal

Grants certification to environmentally sustainable products, services, hotels, restaurants, and other companies.

Grocery Manufacturers Assn. (GMA), *1001 19th St. North, 7th Floor, Arlington, VA 22209; (571) 378-6760. Fax, 571-378-6759. Geoff Freeman, President. General email, info@gmaonline.org*

Web, www.gmaonline.org and Twitter, @GroceryMakers

Membership: sales and marketing agents and retail merchandisers of food and consumer products worldwide. Sponsors research, training, and educational programs for members and their trading partners. Monitors legislation and regulations.

International Cemetery, Cremation, and Funeral Assn., *107 Carpenter Dr., #100, Sterling, VA 20164; (703) 391-8400. Fax, (703) 391-8416. Nadira E. Baldeliyanage, Executive Director, (703) 391-3403. Information, (800) 645-7700.*
General email, hq@iccfa.com
Web, www.iccfa.com

Membership: owners and operators of cemeteries, crematories, funeral homes, mausoleums, and columbaria. Promotes the building and proper maintenance of modern interment places; promotes high ethical standards in the industry; encourages prearrangement of funerals.

International Council of Shopping Centers, *Global Public Policy, 555 12th St. N.W., #660, 20004; (202) 626-1400. Fax, (202) 626-1418. Tom McGee, President.*
General email, gpp@icsc.org
Web, www.icsc.org

Membership: shopping center owners, developers, managers, retailers, contractors, and others in the industry worldwide. Provides information, including research data. Monitors legislation and regulations. (Headquarters in New York.)

International Franchise Assn., *1900 K St. N.W., #700, 20006; (202) 628-8000. (202) 662-0767. Robert Cresanti, President.*
General email, info@franchise.org
Web, www.franchise.org

Membership: national and international franchisers. Sponsors seminars, workshops, trade shows, and conferences. Monitors legislation and regulations.

NACS: The Assn. for Convenience and Fuel Retailing, *1600 Duke St., 7th Floor, Alexandria, VA 22314-3421; (703) 684-3600. Fax, (703) 836-4564. Henry Armour, President, (703) 518-4282. Toll-free, (800) 966-6227.*
General email, nacs@nacsonline.com
Web, www.nacsonline.com and Twitter, @nacsonline

Membership: convenience store and fuel retailers and industry suppliers. Promotes industry position on labor, tax, environment, alcohol, and food-related issues; conducts research and training programs. Monitors legislation and regulations.

National Assn. of Wholesaler-Distributors, *1325 G St. N.W., #1000, 20005-3100; (202) 872-0885. Fax, (202) 785-0586. Dirk Van Dongen, President.*
General email, naw@naw.org
Web, www.naw.org and Twitter, @NAWorg

Membership: wholesale distributors and trade associations, product sellers, manufacturers, and their insurers. Provides members and government policymakers with research, education, and government relations information. Promotes federal product liability tort reform. Monitors legislation and regulations.

National Retail Federation, *1101 New York Ave. N.W., 20005; (202) 783-7971. Fax, (202) 737-2849. Matthew R. Shay, President; Christopher Baldwin, Chair. Toll-free, (800) 673-4692.*
Web, www.nrf.com, Twitter, @NRFnews and Facebook, www.facebook.com/NationalRetailFederation

Membership: international, national, and state associations of retailers and major retail corporations. Concerned with federal regulatory activities and legislation that affect retailers, including tax, employment, trade, and credit issues. Provides information on retailing through seminars, conferences, and publications.

Personal Care Products Council, *1620 L St. N.W., #1200, 20036; (202) 331-1770. Fax, (202) 331-1969. Lezlee Westine, President.*
Web, www.personalcarecouncil.org; www.cosmeticsinfo.org and Twitter, @PSPCNews

Membership: manufacturers and distributors of finished personal care products. Conducts product safety research and advocacy. Represents the industry at the local, state, and national levels. Interests include legal issues, international trade, legislation, and regulatory policy. (Formerly Cosmetic, Toiletry, and Fragrance Assn.)

Retail Industry Leaders Assn., *1700 N. Moore St., #2250, Arlington, VA 22209-1998; (703) 841-2300. Fax, (703) 841-1184. Sandra (Sandy) Kennedy, President.*
Web, www.rila.org and Twitter, @RILAtweets

Membership: retailers, consumer product manufacturers, and service suppliers in the United States and abroad. Interests include supply chain, trade, finance, asset protection, and workforce issues, and energy. Monitors legislation and regulations. (Formerly International Mass Retail Assn.)

Security Industry Assn., *8405 Colesville Rd., #500, Silver Spring, MD 20910; (301) 804-4700. Fax, (301) 804-4701. Donald (Don) Erickson, Chief Executive Officer, (301) 804-4747.*
General email, info@siaonline.org
Web, www.securityindustry.org and Twitter, @SIAOnline

Membership: manufacturers, service providers, and integrators of electronic security equipment. Sponsors trade shows, develops industry standards, supports educational programs and job training, and publishes statistical research. Monitors legislation and regulations.

Service Station Dealers of America and Allied Trades, *1532 Pointer Ridge Pl., Suite G, Bowie, MD 20716; (301) 390-4405. Fax, (301) 390-3161. Billy Hillmulth, Treasurer, (301) 390-0900.*
General email, rlittlefieldz@wmda.net
Web, www.ssda-at.com and Twitter, @SSDAAT

Membership: state associations of gasoline retailers, repair facilities, car washes, and convenience stores. Interests include environmental issues, retail marketing, oil allocation, imports and exports, prices, and taxation. Monitors legislation and regulations.

Society for Imaging Science and Technology, *7003 Kilworth Lane, Springfield, VA 22151; (703) 642-9090.*

Fax, (703) 642-9094. Suzanne E. Grinnan, Executive Director.

General email, info@imaging.org

Web, www.imaging.org and Twitter, @ImagingOrg

Membership: individuals and companies worldwide in fields of imaging science and technology, including digital printing, electronic imaging, color science, image preservation, photo finishing, prepress technology, and hybrid imaging. Gathers and disseminates technical information; fosters professional development.

Society of Consumer Affairs Professionals in Business (SOCAP International), 625 N. Washington St., #304, Alexandria, VA 22314; (703) 519-3700. Fax, (703) 549-4886. Marjorie Bynum, President, (703) 910-2473.

General email, socap@socap.org

Web, www.socap.org and Twitter, @SOCAP

Membership: managers and supervisors who are responsible for consumer affairs, customer service, market research, and sales and marketing operations. Provides information on customer service techniques, market trends, and industry statistics; sponsors seminars and conferences. Monitors legislation and regulations.

Society of Independent Gasoline Marketers of America (SIGMA), 3930 Pender Dr., #340, Fairfax, VA 22030-0985; (703) 709-7000. Fax, (703) 709-7007. Ryan McNutt, Chief Executive Officer.

General email, sigma@sigma.org

Web, www.sigma.org

Membership: marketers and wholesalers of brand and nonbrand gasoline. Seeks to ensure adequate supplies of gasoline at competitive prices. Monitors legislation and regulations affecting gasoline supply and price.

Specialty Graphic Imaging Assn., 10015 Main St., Fairfax, VA 22031-3489; (703) 385-1335. Fax, (703) 273-0456. Ford Bowers, President. Toll-free, (888) 385-3588.

General email, sgia@sgia.org

Web, www.sgia.org and Twitter, @SGIAGraphic

Provides screen printers, graphic imagers, digital imagers, suppliers, manufacturers, and educators with technical guidebooks, training videos, managerial support, and guidelines for safety programs. Monitors legislation and regulations.

Advertising and Marketing

▶AGENCIES

Federal Highway Administration (FHWA) (Transportation Dept.), Planning, Environment, and Realty, 1200 New Jersey Ave. S.E., #E76-306, 20590; (202) 366-0116. Fax, (202) 366-3713. Gloria M. Shepherd, Associate Administrator.

Web, www.fhwa.dot.gov/real_estate

Administers laws concerning outdoor advertising along interstate and federally aided primary highways.

Federal Trade Commission (FTC), Bureau of Consumer Protection, Advertising Practices Division, 400 7th Ave. S.W., #10418, 20024; (202) 326-3090. Fax, (202) 326-3259. Mary Engle, Associate Director.

Web, www.ftc.gov/about-ftc/bureaus-offices/bureau-consumer-protection/our-divisions/division-advertising-practices

Protects consumers from deceptive and unsubstantiated advertising through law enforcement, public reports, and industry outreach. Focuses on national advertising campaigns for food, dietary supplements and over-the-counter drugs, and medical devices, particularly advertising that makes claims difficult for consumers to evaluate. Monitors alcohol advertising for unfair practices; issues reports on alcohol labeling, advertising, and promotion. Issues reports on the marketing to children of violent movies, video games, and music recordings.

Federal Trade Commission (FTC), Bureau of Consumer Protection, Marketing Practices Division, 600 Pennsylvania Ave. N.W., 20580; (202) 326-3404. Fax, (202) 326-3395. Lois C. Greisman, Associate Director.

Web, www.ftc.gov/about-ftc/bureaus-offices/bureau-consumer-protection/our-divisions/division-marketing-practices

Responds to complaints of consumer fraud in the marketplace, including high-tech Internet and telephone scams, deceptive telemarketing or direct mail marketing schemes, fraudulent business opportunity scams, and violations of the Do Not Call and CAN-SPAM consumer privacy protections.

Food and Drug Administration (FDA) (Health and Human Services Dept.), Prescription Drug Promotion (OPDP), White Oak Bldg. 51, 10903 New Hampshire Ave., #3203, Silver Spring, MD 20993-0002; (301) 796-1200. Fax, (301) 847-8444 or (301) 847-8445. Thomas W. Abrams, Director.

Web, www.fda.gov/aboutfda/centersoffices/officeofmedicalproductsandtobacco/cder/ucm090142.htm

Monitors prescription drug advertising and labeling; investigates complaints; conducts market research on health care communications and drug issues.

▶NONGOVERNMENTAL

Ad Council, 1707 L St. N.W., #600, 20036; (202) 331-9153. Lisa Sherman, President.

General email, info@adcouncil.org

Web, www.adcouncil.org, Twitter, @Adcouncil and Facebook, www.facebook.com/adcouncil

Produces and distributes public service advertisements for nonprofit organizations and federal agencies.

American Advertising Federation, 1101 Vermont Ave. N.W., 5th Floor, 20005; (202) 898-0089. Fax, (202) 898-0159. Amanda Richman, Chair. Toll-free, (800) 999-2231.

General email, aaf@aaf.org

Web, www.aaf.org, Twitter, @AAFNational and Facebook, www.facebook.com/aafnational

Membership: advertising companies (ad agencies, advertisers, media, and services), clubs, associations, and college chapters. A founder of the National Advertising Review Board, a self-regulatory body. Sponsors annual awards for outstanding advertising.

American Assn. of Advertising Agencies, *Government Relations, 1707 L St. N.W., #600, 20036; (202) 331-7345. Fax, (202) 857-3675. Richard (Dick) O'Brien, Executive Vice President.*
General email, wash@aaaadc.org
Web, http://aaaa.org, Twitter, @4As and Facebook, www .facebook.com/aaaaorg
Government relations, GR@4As.org

Co-sponsors the National Advertising Review Board (a self-regulatory body), the Advertising Council, and the Media/Advertising Partnership for a Drug Free America. Monitors legislation and regulations at the federal, state, and local level to protect the agency business and the advertising industry as a whole. (Headquarters in New York.)

Center for Digital Democracy, *1875 K St. N.W., 4th Floor, 20006; (202) 986-2220. Jeffrey (Jeff) Chester, Executive Director, (202) 494-7100.*
General email, jeff@democraticmedia.org
Web, www.democraticmedia.org and
Twitter, @DigitalDemoc

Tracks and analyzes the online advertising market, including areas affecting public health, news and information, children and adolescents, and financial industries.

Color Marketing Group, *1908 Mount Vernon Ave., 3rd Floor, Alexandria, VA 22301; (703) 329-8500.*
Sharon Griffis, Executive Director.
General email, sgriffis@colormarketing.org
Web, https://colormarketing.org and Twitter, @ColorSells

Provides a forum for the exchange of noncompetitive information by color design professionals; seeks to create color forecast information for design and marketing. Holds meetings; sponsors special events in the United States as well as abroad.

CTAM: Cable and Telecommunications Assn. for Marketing, *120 Waterfront St., #200, National Harbor, MD 20745; (301) 485-8900. Fax, (301) 560-4964. Vicki Lins, President, (301) 485-8920.*
General email, info@ctam.com
Web, www.ctam.com and Twitter, @CTAM

Promotes innovation in the cable and related industries in areas of marketing, research, management, and new product development. Sponsors annual marketing and research conferences; interests include international markets.

Culture Marketing Council: The Voice of Hispanic Marketing, *8280 Willow Oaks Corporate Dr., #600, Fairfax, VA 22031; (703) 745-5531. Horacio Gavilán, Executive Director.*
General email, info@culturemarketingcouncil.org
Web, www.culturemarketingcouncil.org,
Twitter, @cmchispanic and Facebook, www.facebook.com/ CultureMarketingCouncil

Works to grow, strengthen, and protect the Hispanic marketing and advertising industry. Strives to increase Hispanics' awareness of market opportunities and enhance professionalism of the industry. (Formerly the Assn. of Hispanic Advertising Agencies .)

Data and Marketing Assn. Nonprofit Federation (DMANF), *225 Reinekers Lane, #325, Alexandria, VA 22314; (202) 861-2498. Xenia (Senny) Boone, Executive Director. Membership and Communications, (202) 861-2427.*
Web, http://nonprofitfederation.org

Membership: businesses and nonprofit organizations using and supporting direct marketing tools. Advocates standards for marketing, focusing on relevance to consumers. Provides research, education, and networking opportunities to members. Operates a service that removes consumer names from unwanted mailing lists. Monitors legislation and regulations. (Formerly the Direct Marketing Association; headquarters in New York.)

International Sign Assn., *1001 N. Fairfax St., #301, Alexandria, VA 22314; (703) 836-4012. Fax, (703) 836-8353. Lori Anderson, President, ext. 116.*
General email, info@signs.org
Web, www.signs.org, Twitter, @ISAsigns and Facebook, www.facebook.com/ISAsigns

Membership: manufacturers and distributors of signs and other visual communications systems. Promotes the sign industry; conducts workshops and seminars; sponsors annual competition.

Outdoor Advertising Assn. of America (OAAA), *1850 M St. N.W., #1040, 20036; (202) 833-5566. Fax, (202) 833-1522. Nancy Fletcher, President.*
General email, info@oaaa.org
Web, www.oaaa.org and Twitter, @YourOAAA

Membership: outdoor advertising companies, operators, suppliers, and affiliates. Serves as a clearinghouse for public service advertising campaigns. Monitors legislation and regulations.

Public Utilities

▶**AGENCIES**

Agriculture Dept. (USDA), *Rural Development, Rural Utilities Service, 1400 Independence Ave. S.W., #5135, MS 1510, 20250-1510; (202) 720-9540. Bette Brand, Administrator (Acting), (202) 690-4730.*
Web, www.rd.usda.gov/about-rd/agencies/rural-utilities-service

Makes loans and loan guarantees to provide electricity, telecommunication systems, and water and waste disposal services to rural areas.

Federal Energy Regulatory Commission (FERC) *(Energy Dept.)*, **Electric Reliability (OER)**, *888 1st St. N.E., #9M-01, 20426; (202) 502-8600. Fax, (202) 219-2836. Andrew Dodge, Director.*
Web, www.ferc.gov/about/offices/oer.asp

Oversees the reliability and security of the nation's bulk power system. Establishes and ensures compliance with reliability and security standards for users, owners, and operators of the bulk power system.

Federal Energy Regulatory Commission (FERC) *(Energy Dept.)*, **Energy Market Regulation (OEMR)**, *888 1st St. N.E., #8A-01, 20426; (202) 502-6700. Fax, (202) 219-2836. Anna Cochrane, Director.*
Web, www.ferc.gov/about/offices/oemr.asp

Advises the Commission and processes caseloads related to the economic regulation of the electric utility, natural gas, and oil industries. Concerns include energy markets, tariffs, and pipeline rates relating to electric utility and natural gas and oil pipeline facilities and services. Analyzes applications for electric public utility corporate transactions, including public utility mergers, issuance of securities, or the assumption of liabilities, to determine if the proposed transactions are consistent with the public interest.

Federal Energy Regulatory Commission (FERC) *(Energy Dept.)*, **Energy Policy and Innovation (OEPI)**, *888 1st St. N.E., #7A-01, 20426; (202) 502-8850. Fax, (202) 219-2836. Jignassa Gadani, Director (Acting).*
Web, www.ferc.gov/about/offices/oepi.asp

Seeks to identify emerging issues affecting wholesale and interstate energy markets. Undertakes outreach to other regulators and industry, conducts studies, and makes recommendations for Commission action with state and federal agencies and the energy industry, taking into account energy and environmental concerns. Interests include renewable energy, efficiency, smart grid technology, transmission issues, electric vehicles, carbon and greenhouse gas issues.

▶ **NONGOVERNMENTAL**

American Gas Assn., *400 N. Capitol St. N.W., #450, 20001-1535; (202) 824-7000. Dave McCurdy, President.*
Web, www.aga.org, Twitter, @aga_naturalgas and Facebook, www.facebook.com/naturalgas

Membership: natural gas utilities and pipeline companies. Interests include all technical and operational aspects of the gas industry. Publishes comprehensive statistical record of the gas industry; conducts national standard testing for gas appliances. Advocates policies that are favorable to increased supplies and lower prices. Monitors legislation and regulations.

American Gas Assn., *Statistics, 400 N. Capitol St. N.W., #450, 20001-1535; (202) 824-7133. Paul Pierson, Manager.*
Web, www.aga.org/events-community/statistics-survey-system and Facebook, www.facebook.com/naturalgas

Issues statistics on the gas utility industry, including supply and reserves.

American Public Power Assn., *2451 Crystal Dr., #1000, Arlington, VA 22202; (202) 467-2900. Fax, (202) 467-2910. Susan Kelly, President.*
Web, www.publicpower.org, Twitter, @publicpowerorg and Facebook, www.facebook.com/americanpublicpower

Membership: local, municipally owned electric utilities nationwide. Represents industry interests before Congress, federal agencies, and the courts; provides educational programs; collects and disseminates information; funds energy research and development projects.

American Water Works Assn., *Government Affairs, 1300 Eye St. N.W., #701W, 20005; (202) 628-8303. Fax, (202) 628-2846. G. Tracy Mehan III, Executive Director.*
General email, custsvc@awwa.org
Web, www.awwa.org

Membership: municipal water utilities, manufacturers of equipment for water industries, water treatment companies, and individuals. Provides information on drinking water treatment and trends and issues affecting water safety; publishes voluntary standards for the water industry; issues policy statements on water supply matters. Monitors legislation and regulations. (Headquarters in Denver, Colo.)

Edison Electric Institute, *701 Pennsylvania Ave. N.W., 20004-2696; (202) 508-5000. Fax, (202) 508-5096. Thomas R. Kuhn, President.*
General email, feedback@eei.org
Web, www.eei.org and Twitter, @Edison_Electric

Membership: investor-owned electric power companies. Interests include electric utility operation and concerns, including conservation and energy management, energy analysis, generation and transmission facilities, fuel resources, the environment, cogeneration and renewable energy resources, safety, reliability, taxes, and regulation matters. Provides information and statistics relating to electric energy; aids member companies in generating and selling electric energy; and conducts information forums.

Edison Electric Institute, *Business Information, 701 Pennsylvania Ave. N.W., 20004-2696; (202) 508-5000. Fax, (202) 508-5599. Steve Frauenheim, Manager; Phil Moeller, Executive Vice President of Business Operations. Press, (202) 508-5659.*
General email, ceisenbrey@eei.org
Web, www.eei.org/resourcesandmedia/products

Publishes information and statistics on electric utility operations, including the *Statistical Yearbook of the Electric Utility Industry*, which contains data on the capacity, generation, sales, customers, revenue, and finances of the electric utility industry. Also reports on environmental and regulatory concerns.

International Brotherhood of Electrical Workers (IBEW), *900 7th St. N.W., 20001; (202) 833-7000. Fax, (202) 728-7676. Lonnie Stephenson, International President; Kenneth Cooper, International Secretary-Treasurer.*
General email, webmaster@ibew.org
Web, www.ibew.org

Membership: workers in utilities, construction, telecommunications, broadcasting, manufacturing, railroads, and government. Helps members negotiate pay, benefits, and better working conditions; conducts training programs and workshops. Monitors legislation and regulations. (Affiliated with the AFL-CIO.)

National Assn. of Regulatory Utility Commissioners, *1101 Vermont Ave. N.W., #200, 20005-3521; (202) 898-2200. Fax, (202) 898-2213. Greg R. White, Executive Director, (202) 898-2208.*
General email, admin@naruc.org

Web, www.naruc.org and Twitter, @narcregions

Membership: members of federal, state, municipal, and international regulatory commissions that have jurisdiction over utilities and carriers. Interests include water, electricity, natural gas, nuclear power, telecommunications, and transportation.

National Assn. of State Utility Consumer Advocates (NASUCA), *8380 Colesville Rd., #101, Silver Spring, MD 20910-6267; (301) 589-6313. Fax, (301) 589-6380. David Springe, Executive Director, (785) 550-7606.*
General email, nasuca@nasuca.org

Web, www.nasuca.org

Membership: public advocate offices authorized by states to represent ratepayer interests before state and federal utility regulatory commissions. Monitors legislation and regulatory agencies with jurisdiction over electric utilities, telecommunications, natural gas, and water; conducts conferences. Supports privacy protection for telephone customers.

National Assn. of Water Companies (NAWC), *2001 L St. N.W., #850, 20036; (202) 833-8383. Fax, (202) 331-7442. Robert F. Powelson, President.*
General email, info@nawc.com

Web, www.nawc.org and Twitter, @MovinH20Forward

Membership: privately owned, regulated water companies. Provides members with information on legislative and regulatory issues and other subjects.

National Hydropower Assn., *601 New Jersey Ave. N.W., #660, 20001; (202) 682-1700. Fax, (202) 682-9478. Linda Church Ciocci, Executive Director.*
General email, help@hydro.org

Web, www.hydro.org

Membership: investor-owned utilities and municipal and independent companies that generate hydroelectric power and power from new water technologies; consulting, engineering, and law firms; and equipment suppliers and manufacturers. Focus includes regulatory relief, public affairs, and coalition building. Monitors legislation and regulations.

National Rural Electric Cooperative Assn. (NRECA), *4301 Wilson Blvd., Arlington, VA 22203-1860; (703) 907-5500. Fax, (703) 907-5511. Jim Matheson, Chief Executive Officer; J. Scott Petersen, Vice President of Communications. Press, (703) 907-5746.*

Web, www.electric.coop, Twitter, @NRECANews and Facebook, www.facebook.com/NRECA.coop

Membership: rural electric cooperative systems and public power and utility districts. Provides members with legislative, legal, and regulatory services. Supports energy and environmental research and offers technical advice and assistance to developing countries.

Utilities Technology Council (UTC), *2511 Jefferson Davis Hwy., #960, Arlington, VA 22202; (202) 872-0030. Fax, (202) 872-1331. Joy Ditto, President.*
General email, marketing@utc.org

Web, www.utc.org and Twitter, @UTCNow

Membership: companies that own, manage, or provide critical telecommunications systems in support of their core business, including energy, gas, and water utility companies, pipeline companies, and radio and international critical infrastructure organizations. Participates in FCC rulemaking proceedings. Interests include fiber security; radio spectrum for fixed and mobile wireless communication; and technological, legislative, and regulatory developments affecting telecommunications operations of energy utilities.

Utility Workers Union of America, *1300 L St. N.W., #1200, 20005; (202) 899-2851. Fax, (202) 899-2852. D. Michael Langford, National President; Mike Coleman, National Secretary-Treasurer; Lee Anderson, Government Affairs Director.*
General email, webmaster@uwua.net

Web, www.uwua.net and Twitter, @The_UWUA

Labor union representing workers in electric, gas, water, and nuclear utility industries. Helps members negotiate pay, benefits, and better working conditions; conducts training programs and workshops. Monitors legislation and regulations. (Affiliated with the AFL-CIO.)

SMALL AND DISADVANTAGED BUSINESS

General

▶**AGENCIES**

Agency for International Development (USAID), *Small and Disadvantaged Business Utilization (OSDBU), 301 4th St., #SA-44 (Room 848), 20024 (mailing address: 1300 Pennsylvania Ave., N.W., Room 848,SA-44, Washington, DC 20523); Mauricio P. Vera, Director, (202) 567-4735. Main, (202) 567-4730.*
General email, osdbu@usaid.gov

Web, www.usaid.gov/who-we-are/organization/ independent-offices/office-small-and-disadvantaged-business-utilization and www.usaid.gov/who-we-are/ organization/independent-offices/office-small-and-disadvantaged-business-utilization-0

Counsels small and minority-owned businesses on how to do business with USAID. Identifies opportunities for small businesses in subcontracting with the agency.

Small Business Administration

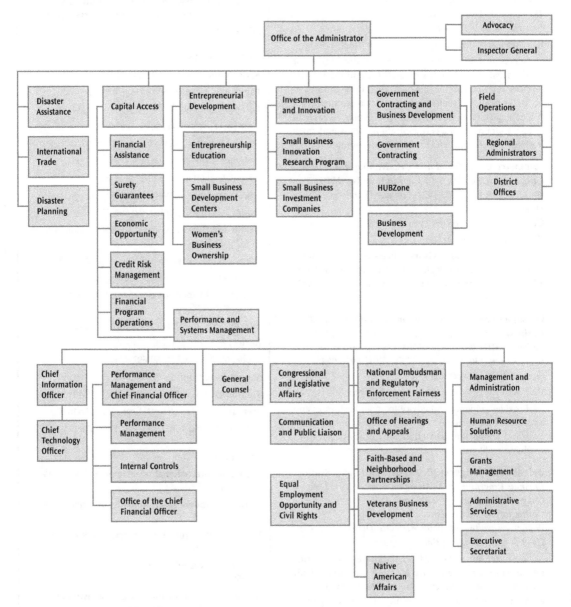

Agriculture Dept. (USDA), *Rural Development, Rural Business–Cooperative Service,* 1400 Independence Ave. S.W., #5803-S, MS 3201, 20250-3201; (202) 690-4730. Bette Brand, Administrator. Press, (202) 690-4737. Web, www.rd.usda.gov/about-rd/agencies/rural-business-cooperative-service

Administers programs that provide the capital, technical support, educational opportunities, and entrepreneurial skills to rural residents to grow businesses or access jobs in agricultural markets. Promotes the use of cooperative businesses. Interests include sustainable renewable energy development; regional food systems development; job creation through recreation and natural resource restoration, conservation, and management; access to broadband.

Agriculture Dept. (USDA), *Small and Disadvantaged Business Utilization (OSDBU),* 1400 Independence Ave. S.W., #1085-S, MS9501, 20250-9501; (202) 720-7117. Michelle Warren, Director (Acting), (202) 720-7835. Web, www.dm.usda.gov/smallbus

Provides guidance and technical assistance to small businesses seeking to do business with the USDA; monitors the development and implementation of contracting policies to prevent barriers to small business participation; works with other federal agencies and public/private partners to increase the number of small businesses participating in the contracting arena.

Commerce Dept., *Business Liaison,* 1401 Constitution Ave. N.W., #5062, 20230; (202) 482-1360. Fax, (202) 482-4054. W. Patrick Wilson, Director.
General email, businessliaison@doc.gov

Web, www.commerce.gov//doc/os/office-business-liaison

Serves as the federal government's central office for business assistance. Handles requests for information and services as well as complaints and suggestions from businesses; provides a forum for businesses to comment on federal regulations; initiates meetings on policy issues with industry groups, business organizations, trade and small business associations, and the corporate community.

Commerce Dept., *Small and Disadvantaged Business Utilization (OSDBU),* 1401 Constitution Ave. N.W., #6411, 20230; (202) 482-1472. LaJuene Desmukes, Director.
General email, osdbu@doc.gov

Web, http://osec.doc.gov/osdbu

An advocacy and advisory office that works toward increasing Commerce Dept. contract awards to small, disadvantaged, women-owned, veteran-owned, and HUB-Zone small businesses.

Consumer Product Safety Commission (CPSC), *Small Business Ombudsman,* 4330 East-West Hwy., #800A, Bethesda, MD 20814; (888) 531-9070. Shelby Mathis, Ombudsman, (301) 504-7865. TTY, (301) 595-7054.
General email, sbo@cpsc.gov

Web, www.cpsc.gov and Twitter, @CPSCSmallBiz

Provides guidance and advice to small businesses and small batch manufacturers about compliance with CPSC laws and regulations as well as technical assistance in resolving problems.

Defense Health Agency (DHA) *(Defense Dept.),* *Small Business Programs,* 7700 Arlington Blvd., #5101, Falls Church, VA 22042-5101; (703) 681-4614.
Cassandra W. Martin, Director.
Web, www.health.mil/About-MHS/OASDHA/Defense-Health-Agency/Small-Business-Program

Seeks to ensure that small businesses have a fair opportunity to compete and be selected for DHA contracts, at both the prime and subcontract levels. Provides information on agency purchases and the contracting process through forums, mentoring programs, and written materials.

Education Dept., *White House Initiative on Asian Americans and Pacific Islanders,* 550 12th St. S.W., 10th Floor, 20202; (202) 245-6418. Fax, (202) 245-7166. Holly Ham, Executive Director; Debra Suarez, Senior Advisor.
General email, whitehouseaapi@ed.gov

Web, http://sites.ed.gov/aapi, Twitter, @whitehouseAAPI and Facebook, www.facebook.com/WhiteHouseAAPI

Works to increase Asian American and Pacific Islander participation in federal business and economic development programs.

Energy Efficiency and Renewable Energy (EERE) *(Energy Dept.),* *Advanced Manufacturing (AMO),* 1000

Small and Disadvantaged Business Contacts at Federal Departments and Agencies

DEPARTMENTS

Agriculture, Vacant, (202) 720-7117

Commerce, LaJuene Desmukes, (202) 482-1472

Defense, James Galvin (Acting), (703) 571-3343

  Air Force, Valerie Muck, (571) 256-8052

  Army, Pamala Calliutt (Acting), (703) 697-2868

  Marine Corps, Dave Dawson, (703) 432-3994

  Navy, Emily Harman, (202) 685-6485

Education, Janet D. Scott, (202) 245-6216

Energy, Charles R. Smith, (202) 586-7377

Health and Human Services, Andrea Brandon (Acting), (202) 690-7300

Homeland Security, Kevin Boshears, (202) 447-5555

  Coast Guard, Kweilin Hollis (Acting), (202) 475-5795

Housing and Urban Development, Jean Lin Pao, (202) 402-5477

Interior, Megan Olsen (Acting), (202) 208-3493

Justice, Bob Connolly, (202) 616-0521

Labor, Gladys Bailey, (202) 693-7244

State, George L. Price, (703) 875-6822

Transportation, Willis A. Morris, (202) 366-1930

Treasury, Pamela Wilson (Acting), (202) 622-1071

Veterans Affairs, Tom Leney, (202) 461-4300

AGENCIES

Agency for International Development, Mauricio Vera, (202) 567-4730

Consumer Product Safety Commission, William Cusey, (301) 504-7945

Environmental Protection Agency, Joan Rodgers, (202) 564-6568

General Services Administration, Charles S. Manger, (855) 672-8472

National Aeronautics and Space Administration, Glenn Delgado, (202) 358-2088

Nuclear Regulatory Commission, Pamela Baker, (301) 415-7380

Small Business Administration, Adriana Menchaca-Gendron, (202) 205-6766

Social Security Administration, Wayne McDonald, (410) 965-7467

Independence Ave. S.W., #5F065, MS EE5A, 20585-0121; (202) 586-9488. Fax, (202) 586-9234. Robert Ivester, Director.
General email, amo_communication@ee.doe.gov

Web, www.energy.gov/eere/amo/advanced-manufacturing-office

Offers financial and technical support to small businesses and individual inventors for establishing technical performance and conducting early development of innovative ideas and inventions that have a significant energy-saving impact and future commercial market potential.

Farm Service Agency (FSA) *(Agriculture Dept.), Minority and Socially Disadvantaged Farmers Assistance,* 1400 *Independence Ave. S.W., MS 0503, 20250-0503; (202) 690-1700. Fax, (202) 690-4727. J. Latrice Hill, Director of Outreach. TTY, (202) 720-5132.*
General email, oasdfr@osec.usda.gov
Web, www.fsa.usda.gov

Works with minority and socially disadvantaged farmers who have concerns and questions about loan applications filed with local offices or other Farm Service Agency programs.

Federal Emergency Management Agency (FEMA) *(Homeland Security Dept.), Resilience, Federal Insurance and Mitigation Administration,* 400 C St. *S.W., 20472; (202) 646-2781. Fax, (202) 646-7970. David I. Maurstad, Deputy Associate Administrator.*
Web, www.fema.gov/what-mitigation/federal-insurance-mitigation-administration

Administers federal flood insurance programs. Makes low-cost flood and crime insurance available to eligible small businesses.

General Services Administration (GSA), *Small Business Utilization,* 1800 F St. N.W., 20405; (202) 501-1021. *Fax, (202) 501-2590. Charles Manger, Associate Administrator. Toll-free, 844-GSA-4111.*
General email, small.business@gsa.gov
Web, www.gsa.gov/acquisition/small-business and *Twitter, @GSAOSBU*

Works to increase small business access to government contract procurement opportunities. Provides policy guidance and direction for GSA Regional Small Business Offices, which offer advice and assistance to businesses interested in government procurement.

Interior Dept. (DOI), *Small and Disadvantaged Business Utilization (OSDBU),* 1849 C St. N.W., Room 4124, 20240; *(202) 208-3493. Fax, (202) 208-7444. Megan Olsen, Director (Acting).*
Web, www.doi.gov/pmb/osdbu

Advocates contracting opportunities for small, small disadvantaged, women-owned, historically underutilized business zones, and service-disabled veteran-owned small businesses and Indian economic enterprises.

Minority Business Development Agency *(Commerce Dept.),* 1401 Constitution Ave. N.W., #5053, 20230; (202) *482-2332. Fax, (202) 482-2500. Chris Garcia, Director (Acting).*
Web, www.mbda.gov and *Twitter, @USMBDA*

Assists minority entrepreneurs one-on-one with financial planning, marketing, management, and technical assistance. Focuses on promoting wealth in minority communities.

National Science Foundation (NSF), *Small Business Innovation Research / Small Business Technology Transfer Program,* 2415 Eisenhower Ave., #E14344, *Alexandria, VA 22134; (703) 292-8050. Fax, (703) 292-9057. Rajesh Mehta, Director, (703) 292-2174.*
General email, sbir@nsf.gov
Web, https://seedfund.nsf.gov

Serves as liaison between the small-business community and NSF offices; awards grants and contracts. Administers the Small Business Innovation Research and Small Business Technology Transfer Programs, which fund research proposals from small science/high technology firms and start-ups. Interests include hard science and technology with high technical risk and potential for significant commercial or societal impact. Offers incentives for commercial development, including NSF-funded research.

National Women's Business Council, *409 3rd St. S.W., 5th Floor, 20416; (202) 205-3850. Fax, (202) 205-6825. Nina Roque, Executive Director.*
General email, info@nwbc.gov
Web, www.nwbc.gov and *Facebook, www.facebook.com/NWBCgov*

Independent, congressionally mandated council established by the Women's Business Ownership Act of 1988. Reviews the status of women-owned businesses nationwide and makes policy recommendations to the president, Congress, and the Small Business Administration. Assesses the role of the federal government in aiding and promoting women-owned businesses.

Small Business Administration (SBA), *409 3rd St. S.W., 20416-7000; (202) 205-6605. Fax, (202) 205-6802. Linda McMahon, Administrator; Vacant, Deputy Administrator. Locator, (202) 205-6600. Toll-free information (Answer Desk), (800) 827-5722. TTY, (800) 877-8339.*
General email, answerdesk@sba.gov
Web, www.sba.gov and *Twitter, @SBAgov*

Provides small businesses with financial and management assistance; offers loans to victims of floods, natural disasters, and other catastrophes; licenses, regulates, and guarantees some financing of small-business investment companies; conducts economic and statistical research on small businesses. SBA Answer Desk is an information and referral service. District or regional offices can be contacted for specific loan information.

Small Business Administration (SBA), *Advocacy,* 409 3rd *St. S.W., 20416; (202) 205-6533. Fax, (202) 205-6928. Major L. Clark III, Chief Counsel (Acting). TTY, (800) 877-8339.*
General email, advocacy@sba.gov
Web, www.sba.gov/offices/headquarters/advocacy

Acts as an advocate for small business viewpoints in regulatory and legislative proceedings. Economic Research Office analyzes the effects of government policies on small businesses and documents the contributions of small business to the economy.

Small Business Administration (SBA), *Capital Access,* 409 3rd St. S.W., #8200, 20416; (202) 205-6657. Fax, (202) 205-7230. William Manger, Associate Administrator. TTY, (800) 877-8339.

Web, www.sba.gov/offices/headquarters/oca

Provides financial assistance to small business, including microloans, surety bond guarantees, investment, and international trade.

Small Business Administration (SBA), *Credit Risk Management,* 409 3rd St. S.W., #8200, 20416; (202) 205-3049. Fax, (202) 205-6831. Susan E. Streich, Director.

Web, www.sba.gov/offices/headquarters/ocrm

Conducts on-site and off-site analysis and reviews of SBA lending partners' activities; reviews the quality of the SBA loan portfolio through trend analysis and assessment of risk indicators.

Small Business Administration (SBA), *Disaster Assistance,* 409 3rd St. S.W., #6050, 20416; (202) 205-6734. Fax, (202) 205-7728. James Rivera, Associate Administrator. Service Center, (800) 659-2955. TTY, (800) 877-8339.

Web, www.sba.gov/offices/headquarters/oda

Provides economic injury loans to small businesses for losses to meet necessary operating expenses, provided the business could have paid these expenses prior to the disaster.

Small Business Administration (SBA), *Diversity, Inclusion, and Civil Rights,* 409 3rd St. S.W., #6400, 20416; (202) 205-6750. Michele Schimpp, Assistant Administrator. TTY, (800) 877-8339.

Web, www.sba.gov/offices/headquarters/odicr

Reviews complaints based on disability against the Small Business Administration by recipients of its assistance in cases of alleged discrimination in credit transactions; monitors recipients for civil rights compliance.

Small Business Administration (SBA), *Entrepreneurial Development,* 409 3rd St. S.W., #6200, 20416; (202) 205-6239. Allen Gutierrez, Associate Administrator. TTY, (800) 877-8339.

General email, oed@sba.gov

Web, www.sba.gov/offices/headquarters/oed

Responsible for business development programs of the offices of the Small Business Development Centers and the offices of Entrepreneurship Education and Women's Business Ownership.

Small Business Administration (SBA), *Entrepreneurial Development, Entrepreneurship Education,* 409 3rd St. S.W., #6200, 20416; (202) 205-6665. Fax, (202) 205-6903. Donald Malcolm Smith, Director. TTY, (800) 877-8339.

Web, www.sba.gov/offices/headquarters/oee

Outreach and education arm of SBA. Provides small businesses with instruction and counseling in marketing, accounting, product analysis, production methods, research and development, and management problems. Provides in-person as well as online training and specialized services for underserved markets.

Small Business Administration (SBA), *Entrepreneurial Development, Small Business Development Centers,* 409 3rd St. S.W., #6400, 20416; (202) 205-6766. Fax, (202) 205-7727. Vacant, Associate Administrator. TTY, (800) 877-8339.

Web, www.sba.gov/offices/headquarters/osbdc

Promotes entrepreneurship, small business growth, and the U.S. economy by providing funding, oversight, and support for the nationwide network of Small Business Development Centers.

Small Business Administration (SBA), *Entrepreneurial Development, Women's Business Ownership,* 409 3rd St. S.W., #6600, 20416; (202) 205-6673. Fax, (202) 205-7287. Kathleen McShane, Assistant Administrator.

General email, womenbusiness@sba.gov

Web, www.sba.gov/offices/headquarters/wbo

Acts as an advocate for current and potential women business owners throughout the federal government and in the private sector. Provides training, counseling, and mentoring through a nationwide network of women's business centers; offers information on national and local resources, including SBA small business programs.

Small Business Administration (SBA), *Government Contracting and Business Development,* 409 3rd St. S.W., #8000, 20416; (202) 205-6459. Fax, (202) 205-5206. Barbara E. Carson, Deputy Associate Administrator. TTY, (800) 877-8339.

Web, www.sba.gov/offices/headquarters/ogc_and_bd

Oversees the Office of Government Contracting and Office of Business Development. Enhances the effectiveness of small business programs to develop policies, regulations, and statutory changes.

Small Business Administration (SBA), *Government Contracting and Business Development, Business Development,* 409 3rd St. S.W., #8800, 20416; (202) 205-5852. Fax, (202) 205-7259. Adriana Menchaca-Gendron, Associate Administrator. TTY, (800) 877-8339.

General email, 8abd@sba.gov

Web, www.sba.gov/offices/headquarters/obd

Coordinates the services provided by private industry, banks, the SBA, and other government agencies—such as business development and management and technical assistance—to increase the number of small businesses owned by socially and economically disadvantaged Americans.

Small Business Administration (SBA), *International Trade,* 409 3rd St. S.W., #2400, 20416; (202) 205-6720. Fax, (202) 205-7272. Peter J. Cazamias Jr., Associate Administrator. TTY, (800) 877-8339.

Web, www.sba.gov/offices/headquarters/oit

Ensures interests of small businesses are considered and reflected in trade negotiations; promotes ability of small businesses to export.

Small Business Administration (SBA), *Investments and Innovation,* 409 3rd St. S.W., #6300, 20416; (202) 205-6510. Fax, (202) 205-6959. Joseph (Joe) Shepard, Associate Administrator. TTY, (800) 877-8339.

Web, www.sba.gov/offices/headquarters/ooi

Administers and runs the Small Business Investment Company, Small Business Investment Research, and Small Business Technology Transfer programs.

Small Business Administration (SBA), *Native American Affairs, 409 3rd St. S.W., #6700, 20416; (202) 205-7364. Fax, (202) 205-6139. Shawn Pensoneau, Assistant Administrator. TTY, (800) 877-8339.*
Web, www.sba.gov/offices/headquarters/naa

Offers tools and resources to increase Native American involvement and opportunities in small business.

Small Business Administration (SBA), *Veterans Business Development, 409 3rd St. S.W., #5700, 20416; (202) 205-6773. Fax, (202) 205-7292. Larry Stubblefield, Associate Administrator. TTY, (800) 877-8339.*
Web, www.sba.gov/offices/headquarters/ovbd

Helps veterans use SBA loans through counseling, procurement, and training programs in entrepreneurship.

▶ **CONGRESS**

For a listing of relevant congressional committees and subcommittees, please see pages 34–35 or the Appendix.

▶ **NONGOVERNMENTAL**

Capital Region Minority Supplier Development Council, *10750 Columbia Pike, #200, Silver Spring, MD 20901; (301) 593-5860. Fax, (301) 593-1364. Sharon R. Pinder, President.*
General email, crmsdc@mddcmsdc.org
Web, http://crmsdc.org and Twitter, @CRMSDC

Certifies minority (Asian, African American, Hispanic, and Native American) business enterprises. Refers corporate buyers to minority suppliers and supports the development, expansion, and promotion of corporate minority supplier development programs. Offers networking opportunities and gives awards. Disseminates statistics and information. Provides consultation services, educational seminars, technical assistance, and training opportunities. (Regional council of the National Minority Supplier Development Council.)

ECDC Enterprise Development Group (EDG), *901 S. Highland St., Arlington, VA 22204; (703) 685-0441. Fax, (703) 685-4200. Tsehaye Teferra, President; Fikru Abebe, Managing Director, ext. 225.*
General email, info@entdevgroup.org
Web, www.entdevgroup.org

Provides microloans to clients in the Washington metropolitan area with low-to-moderate income in order to promote new business enterprises and individual self-sufficiency. Offers business training and pre-loan and post-loan technical assistance to entrepreneurs. Operates a matched savings program for low-income refugees and a car loan program for those with inadequate transportation. An independent subsidiary of the Ethiopian Community Development Council.

Institute for Liberty (IFL), *1250 Connecticut Ave. N.W., #200, 20036; (202) 261-6592. Fax, (877) 350-6147. Andrew Langer, President.*
Web, www.instituteforliberty.org

Seeks to protect small businesses from government over-intrusion. Interests include energy and tax policy, health care, property rights, and Internet freedom. Monitors policy and legislation.

MET Community, *1749 Potomac Greens Dr., Alexandria, VA 22314; (202) 792-9338. Yanire Braña, Executive Director.*
General email, info@metcommunity.org
Web, http://metcommunity.org, Twitter, @metcommunity_us and Facebook, www.facebook.com/METcommunityUS

International organization that promotes mentoring, entrepreneurship, and training among women; educates companies and international communities on diversity, social responsibility, and innovation. Has a presence in eight countries, including Spain, Colombia, Peru, Brazil, and Argentina, and has partnerships with BBVA, World Bank, and BELCORP Foundation.

National Assn. of Investment Companies, *1300 Pennsylvania Ave. N.W., #700, 20004; (202) 204-3001. Fax, (202) 204-3022. Robert L. Greene, President.*
General email, info@naicpe.com
Web, www.naicpe.com

Membership: investment companies that provide minority-owned businesses with venture capital and management guidance. Provides technical assistance; monitors legislation and regulations.

National Assn. of Negro Business and Professional Women's Clubs Inc., *1806 New Hampshire Ave. N.W., 20009; (202) 483-4206. Fax, (202) 462-7253. Diane E. Toppin, President.*
General email, nednambpwcinfo@gmail.com
Web, www.nanbpwc.org and Twitter, @NANBPWC

Promotes and protects the interests of minority business and professional women, serves as advisors to young people seeking to enter business and the professions, provides scholarship support for secondary education, sponsors workshops, and works to improve the quality of life in local and global communities to foster good fellowship. Monitors legislation and regulations.

National Assn. of Women Business Owners, *601 Pennsylvania Ave. N.W., South Bldg., #900, 20004; (202) 609-9817. Fax, (202) 403-3788. Jen Earle, Chief Executive Officer. Toll-free, (800) 556-2826.*
General email, national@nawbo.org
Web, www.nawbo.org and Twitter, @NAWBONational

Promotes the economic, social, and political interests of women business owners through networking, leadership and business development training, and advocacy.

National Black Chamber of Commerce, *4400 Jenifer St. N.W., #331, 20015; (202) 466-6888. Fax, (202) 466-4918. Harry C. Alford, President.*

General email, info@nationalbcc.org

Web, www.nationalbcc.org and
Twitter, @NATIONALBCC

Membership: Black-owned businesses. Educates and trains the Black community in entrepreneurship and other economic areas. Monitors legislation and regulations.

National Cooperative Business Assn., CLUSA International (NCBA CLUSA), *1775 Eye St. N.W., 8th Floor, 20006; (202) 638-6222. Douglas O'Brien, President.*
General email, info@ncba.coop

Web, www.ncba.coop, Twitter, @NCBA.coop and
Facebook, www.facebook.com/NCBACLUSA

Alliance of cooperatives, businesses, and state cooperative associations. Supports development of cooperative businesses; promotes and develops trade among domestic and international cooperatives. Monitors legislation and regulations.

National Federation of Independent Business (NFIB), *Washington Office, 1201 F St. N.W., #200, 20004-1221; (202) 314-2000. Fax, (202) 554-0496. Juanita Duggan, President; Mary Blasinsky, Washington Office Administrator. Press, (202) 554-9000. Toll-free, (800) 634-2669.*
General email, media@nfib.com

Web, www.nfib.com, Twitter, @NFIB and Facebook, www.facebook.com/NFIB

Membership: independent businesses. Monitors public policy issues and legislation affecting small and independent businesses, including taxation, government regulation, labor-management relations, and liability insurance. (Headquarters in Nashville, Tenn.)

National Gay and Lesbian Chamber of Commerce, *1331 F St., #900, 20004; (202) 234-9181. Fax, (202) 234-9185. Justin G. Nelson, President.*
General email, info@nglcc.org

Web, www.nglcc.org, Twitter, @NGLCC and
Facebook, www.facebook.com/NGLCC

Communicates ideas and information for and between businesses and organizations. Works with state and local chambers of commerce and business groups on various issues. Acts as an advocate on behalf of lesbian-, gay-, bisexual-, and transgender-owned businesses; professionals; students of business; and corporations.

National Small Business Assn., *1156 15th St. N.W., #502, 20005; (202) 293-8830. Fax, (202) 872-8543. Todd McCracken, President. Toll-free, (800) 345-6728.*
General email, info@nsba.biz

Web, www.nsba.biz

Membership: manufacturing, wholesale, retail, service, exporting, and other small-business firms and regional small-business organizations. Represents the interests of small business before Congress, the administration, and federal agencies. Services to members include a toll-free legislative hotline and group insurance.

SCORE Assn., *1175 Herndon Pkwy., #900, Herndon, VA 20170; (703) 487-3612. Fax, (703) 487-3066. W. (Ken) Kenneth Yancey Jr., Chief Executive Officer. Information, (800) 634-0245.*
General email, help@score.org

Web, www.score.org and Twitter, @SCOREMentors

Independent volunteer organization funded by the Small Business Administration through which retired, semiretired, and active business executives use their knowledge and experience to counsel small businesses. (Formerly Service Corps of Retired Executives Assn.)

Small Business and Entrepreneurship Council (SBE Council), *200 Lawyers Rd. N.W., #1506, Vienna, VA 22183; (703) 242-5840. Fax, (703) 242-5841. Karen Kerrigan, President.*
General email, info@sbecouncil.org

Web, https://sbecouncil.org and Twitter, @SBECouncil

Membership: U.S. entrepreneurs and business owners. Seeks to protect small business and promotes entrepreneurship. Provides networking opportunities, educational resources, and market intelligence for its members. Monitors legislation and regulations.

Small Business Investor Alliance, *1100 H St. N.W., #1200, 20005; (202) 628-5055. Brett Palmer, President.*
General email, info@sbia.org

Web, www.sbia.org and Twitter, @SmallBusinessPE

Membership: private equity, venture capital, and middle market funds that invest in small businesses. Provides training to fund managers and holds industry networking events. Monitors legislation and regulations.

Small Business Legislative Council, *4800 Hampden Lane, 6th Floor, Bethesda, MD 20814; (301) 652-8302. Paula Calimafde, President; Jackie King, Chair. Press, (301) 951-9351.*
General email, email@sblc.org

Web, http://sblc.org and Twitter, @SBLC_ORG

Membership: trade associations that represent small businesses in the manufacturing, retail, professional and technical services, and agricultural, transportation, tourism, and construction sectors. Monitors and proposes legislation and regulations to benefit small businesses.

U.S. Chamber of Commerce, *Small Business Policy, 1615 H St. N.W., 20062-2000; (202) 463-5498. Fax, (202) 463-3174. Thomas M. Sullivan, Vice President.*
Web, https://uschambersmallbusinessnation.com

Seeks to enhance visibility of small businesses within the national Chamber and the U.S. business community. Provides members with information on national small business programs and legislative issues.

U.S. Hispanic Chamber of Commerce, *1424 K St. N.W., #401, 20015; (202) 842-1212. Fax, (202) 842-3221. Ramiro Cavazos, President. Press, (480) 751-5569.*
General email, info@ushcc.com

Web, www.ushcc.com and Twitter, @USHCC

Membership: Hispanic Chambers of Commerce and business organizations. Monitors legislation. Provides technical assistance to Hispanic business associations and owners. Promotes public policies that enhance the economic development of its members, trade between Hispanic businesses in the United States and Latin America, and partnerships with the larger business community.

U.S. Pan Asian American Chamber of Commerce, *1329 18th St. N.W., 20036; (202) 296-5221. Fax, (202) 296-5225. Susan Au Allen, Chief Executive Officer, (202) 378-1130. Toll-free, (800) 696-7818.*
General email, info@uspaacc.com

Web, www.uspaacc.com and Twitter, @uspacc_ef

Helps Asian American–owned businesses gain access to government and corporate contracts.

U.S. Women's Chamber of Commerce, *700 12th St. N.W., #700, 20005; (202) 607-2488. Margot Dorfman, Chief Executive Officer.*
General email, notify@uswcc.org

Web, www.uswcc.org and Twitter, @uswcc

Provides services and career opportunities to women in business, including networking, leadership training, political advocacy, access to government procurement markets, and technical expertise. Monitors legislation and regulations.

3

Communications and the Media

GENERAL POLICY AND ANALYSIS

Basic Resources

▶AGENCIES

Access Board, *1331 F St. N.W., #1000, 20004-1111; (202) 272-0080. Fax, (202) 272-0081. David M. Capozzi, Executive Director, (202) 272-0010. Toll-free, (800) 872-2253. Toll-free TTY, (800) 993-2822. TTY, (202) 272-0082. General email, info@access-board.gov*
Web, www.access-board.gov

Develops and maintains accessibility requirements for buildings, transit vehicles, telecommunications equipment, medical diagnostic equipment, and electronic and information technology. Provides technical assistance and training on these guidelines and standards. Enforces access standards for federally funded facilities through the Architectural Barriers Act.

Agriculture Dept. (USDA), *Rural Development, Rural Utilities Service, 1400 Independence Ave. S.W., #5135, MS 1510, 20250-1510; (202) 720-9540. Bette Brand, Administrator (Acting), (202) 690-4730.*
Web, www.rd.usda.gov/about-rd/agencies/rural-utilities-service

Administers programs that ensure rural areas have access to affordable, reliable, advanced telecommunications services comparable to those available throughout the rest of the United States.

Federal Communications Commission (FCC), *445 12th St. S.W., 20554; (888) 225-5322. Ajit Pai, Chair, (202) 418-1000. Consumer and Government Affairs, (202) 418-1400. Legislative Affairs, (202) 418-1900. Media Relations, (202) 418-0503. Reference Information Center, (202) 418-0270. Toll-free fax, (866) 418-0232. TTY, (888) 835-5322. Videophone, (844) 432-2275.*
General email, fccinfo@fcc.gov
Web, www.fcc.gov, Twitter, @FCC and Facebook, www.facebook.com/FCC

Regulates interstate and foreign communications by radio, television, wire, cable, microwave, and satellite; consults with other government agencies and departments on national and international matters involving wire and radio telecommunications and with state regulatory commissions on telegraph and telephone matters; reviews applications for construction permits and licenses for such services. Reference Information Center open to the public (except under high-alert status orange and higher).

Federal Communications Commission (FCC), *Economics and Analytics (OEA), 445 12th St. S.W., 20554; (202) 418-2030. Giulia McHenry, Chief (Acting).*
Web, www.fcc.gov/economics-and-analytics

Responsible for expanding the use of economic analysis into commission policymaking, for enhancing the development and use of auctions, and for implementing consistent and effective agency-wide data practices and policies. Provides economic analysis, including cost-benefit analysis,

for rulemakings, transactions, adjudications, and other commission actions; manages FCC auctions in support of and in coordination with FCC Bureaus and Offices; develops policies and strategies to help manage FCC data resources and establishing best practices for data use throughout the FCC in coordination with FCC Bureaus and Offices; and conducts long-term research on ways to improve the commission's policies and processes in each of these areas.

Federal Communications Commission (FCC), *Economics and Analytics (OEA), Auctions, 445 12th St. S.W., 20554; (202) 418-0660. Margaret Wiener, Division Chief (Acting).*
Web, www.fcc.gov/auctions-division#block-menu-block-4

Plans, designs, and conducts all FCC spectrum auctions, including auctions of flexible use licenses in various bands, including the 600 MHz and 700 MHz Bands, Advanced Wireless Services (AWS), and upper microwave bands, and construction permits for over-the-air television and radio services. Implements the commission's incentive auction authority to repurpose spectrum for new uses and conducts reverse auctions to distribute universal service support for fixed and mobile broadband services. Responsible for assuring that all of the commission's auction processes are fair and transparent. In planning for and conducting auctions, the Auctions Division collaborates with the bureaus responsible for regulating and licensing the items to be offered at auction.

Federal Communications Commission (FCC), *Economics and Analytics (OEA), Data, 445 12th St. S.W., 20554; (202) 418-2030. Anne Levine, Deputy Division Chief.*
Web, www.fcc.gov/economics-analytics/data-division#block-menu-block-4

Develops and implements best practices, processes, and standards for data management to meet the needs of commission staff who rely on data to inform policymaking and other core activities of the commission.

Federal Communications Commission (FCC), *Economics and Analytics (OEA), Industry Analysis, 445 12th St. S.W., 20554; (202) 418-2030. Rodger Woock, Division Chief (Acting).*
Web, www.fcc.gov/economics-analytics/industry-analysis-division#block-menu-block-4

Designs and administers significant, economically-relevant data collections used by a variety of FCC bureaus and offices, providing support to bureaus and offices with respect to these data collections as well as support using the data for Continuity of Operations (COOP)/Emergency Response Group (ERG)/Incident Management Team (IMT), and performing analyses and studies.

Federal Communications Commission (FCC), *Economics and Analytics, Economic Analysis (EAD), 445 12th St. S.W., #7-C347, 20554; (202) 418-2030. Fax, (202) 418-2807. Emily Talaga, Division Chief (Acting).*
Web, www.fcc.gov/economics-analytics/economic-analysis-division#block-menu-block-4

Provides analytical and quantitative support as needed to bureaus and offices engaged in rulemakings, transactions, auctions, adjudications, and other matters.

Federal Communications Commission (FCC), Engineering and Technology (OET), 445 12th St. S.W., 7th Floor, 20554; (202) 418-2470. Fax, (202) 418-1944. Julius Knapp, Chief Engineer.
General email, oetinfo@fcc.gov

Web, www.fcc.gov/engineering-%26-technology

Advises the FCC on technical and spectrum matters and assists in developing U.S. telecommunications policy. Identifies and reviews developments in telecommunications and related technologies.

National Telecommunications and Information Administration (NTIA) (Commerce Dept.), 1401 Constitution Ave. N.W., #4898, 20230; (202) 482-2000. Fax, (202) 501-0536. David J. Redl, Assistant Secretary; James C. Wasilewski, Chief of Staff (Acting), (202) 482-1845. Press, (202) 482-7002.
Web, www.ntia.doc.gov, Twitter, @NTIAgov and Facebook, www.facebook.com/ntiagov

Develops domestic and international telecommunications policy for the executive branch; manages federal use of radio spectrum; conducts research on radiowave transmissions and other aspects of telecommunications; serves as information source for federal and state agencies on the efficient use of telecommunications resources.

▶CONGRESS

For a listing of relevant congressional committees and subcommittees, please see page 95 or the Appendix.

Library of Congress, United States Copyright Office, Licensing, James Madison Memorial Bldg., 101 Independence Ave. S.E., #LM 504, 20557; (202) 707-8150. Fax, (202) 707-0905. James Enzinna, Chief, (202) 708-6801. Information, (202) 707-3000.
General email, licensing@loc.gov

Web, www.copyright.gov/licensing

Administers statutory licensing for cable television companies and satellite carriers, for making and distributing digital audio recording products, and for use of certain noncommercial broadcasting. Collects and distributes royalty payments under the copyright law. Administers Section 115 licensing for making and distributing phonorecords.

▶NONGOVERNMENTAL

Accuracy in Media (AIM), 1717 K. St. N.W., #900, 20006; (202) 364-4401. Fax, (202) 364-4098. Donald (Don) K. Irvine, Publisher, ext. 103. Toll-Free, (800) 787-4567.
General email, info@aim.org

Web, www.aim.org, Twitter, @AccuracyInMedia and Facebook, www.facebook.com/AccuracyinMedia

Analyzes print and electronic news media for bias, omissions, and errors in news; approaches media with complaints. Maintains a speakers bureau and a library on political and media topics.

Alliance for Telecommunications Industry Solutions (ATIS), 1200 G St. N.W., #500, 20005; (202) 628-6380. Susan M. Miller, President, (202) 434-8828.
General email, atispr@atis.org

Web, www.atis.org, Twitter, @atisupdates and Facebook, www.facaebook.com/atisdotorg

Develops and promotes the worldwide technical and operations standards for information, entertainment, and communications technologies. Sponsors industry forums; serves as an information clearinghouse. Member of the Inter-American Telecommunication Commission (CITEL). Monitors legislation and regulations.

Center for Media and Public Affairs (CMPA), 2338 S. Queen St., Arlington, VA 22202; (202) 302-5523. S. Robert Lichter, President.
Web, https://cmpa.gmu.edu and Twitter, @CMPAatGMU

Nonpartisan research and educational organization that studies media coverage of social and political issues and campaigns, specifically information about health risks, scientific matters, and presidential campaigns. Conducts surveys; publishes materials and reports. (Affiliated with George Mason University.)

Free Press, Washington Office, 1025 Connecticut Ave. N.W., #1110, 20036; (202) 265-1490. Fax, (202) 265-1489. Craig Aaron, President.
Web, www.freepress.net, Twitter, @freepress and Facebook, www.facebook.com/freepress

Seeks to engage the public in media policymaking. Advocates policies for more competitive and public interest oriented media. (Headquarters in Florence, Mass.)

INCOMPAS, 2025 M St., #800, 20005; (202) 296-6650. Fax, (202) 296-7585. Chip Pickering, Chief Executive Officer.
Web, www.incompas.org, Twitter, @INCOMPAS and Facebook, www.facebook.com/Incompas-196527610405296

Membership: Broadband, cloud, business and enterprise, fiber, international, Internet, tower and backhaul, and wireless providers. Acts as advocate for the competitive telecommunications industry before Congress, the FCC, and state regulatory agencies; sponsors trade shows, conferences, and policy summits. Monitors legislation and regulations. (Formerly COMPTEL.)

Media Institute, 2300 Clarendon Blvd., #602, Arlington, VA 22201; (703) 243-5700. Fax, (703) 243-8808. Richard T. Kapler, President.
General email, info@mediainstitute.org

Web, www.mediainstitute.org

Research foundation that conducts conferences, files court briefs and regulatory comments, and sponsors programs on communications topics. Advocates a competitive media and communications industry and free-speech rights for individuals, media, and corporate speakers.

COMMUNICATIONS AND MEDIA RESOURCES IN CONGRESS

For a complete listing of congressional committees, including their full contact information, leadership, membership, and jurisdictions, please refer to the Appendix on pages 827–948.

HOUSE:

House Administration Committee, (202) 225-8281. Web, cha.house.gov

House Appropriations Committee, (202) 225-2771. Web, appropriations.house.gov

Subcommittee on Labor, Health and Human Services, Education, and Related Agencies, (202) 225-3508.

House Energy and Commerce Committee, (202) 225-2927. Web, energycommerce.house.gov

Subcommittee on Communications and Technology, (202) 225-2927.

House Judiciary Committee, (202) 225-3951. Web, judiciary.house.gov

Subcommittee on the Constitution and Civil Justice, (202) 225-2825.

Subcommittee on Courts, Intellectual Property, and the Internet, (202) 225-5741.

House Oversight and Government Reform Committee, (202) 225-5074. Web, oversight.house.gov

Subcommittee on Information Technology, (202) 225-5074.

House Science, Space, and Technology Committee, (202) 225-6371. Web, science.house.gov

Subcommittee on Research and Technology, (202) 225-6371.

House Small Business Committee, (202) 225-5821. Web, smallbusiness.house.gov

Subcommittee on Health and Technology, (202) 225-5821.

JOINT:

Joint Committee on Printing, (202) 225-2061. Web, cha.house.gov/jointcommittees/joint-committee-on-printing

Joint Committee on the Library of Congress, (202) 225-8281. Web, cha.house.gov/jointcommittees/joint-committee-library

SENATE:

Senate Agriculture, Nutrition, and Forestry Committee, (202) 224-2035. Web, agriculture.senate.gov

Subcommittee on Rural Development and Energy, (202) 224-2035.

Senate Appropriations Committee, (202) 224-7257. Web, appropriations.senate.gov

Subcommittee on Labor, Health and Human Services, Education, and Related Agencies, (202) 224-9145.

Senate Commerce, Science, and Transportation Committee, (202) 224-1251. Web, commerce.senate.gov

Subcommittee on Communications, Technology, Innovation, and the Internet, (202) 224-1251.

Senate Foreign Relations Committee, (202) 224-4651. Web, foreign.senate.gov

Subcommittee on East Asia, The Pacific, and International Cybersecurity Policy, (202) 224-4651.

Senate Judiciary Committee, (202) 224-5225. Web, judiciary.senate.gov

Subcommittee on Antitrust, Competition Policy, and Consumer Rights, (202) 224-5444.

Subcommittee on Crime and Terrorism, (202) 224-5972.

Subcommittee on the Constitution (202) 224-5922.

Senate Rules and Administration Committee, (202) 224-6352. Web, rules.senate.gov

---

Media Matters for America, *P.O. Box 52155, 20091; (202) 756-4100. Fax, (202) 756-4101. Bradley Beychok, President, (202) 756-4100, ext. 165. Press, (202) 772-8195. Web, www.mediamatters.org, Twitter, @mmfa and Facebook, www.facebook.com/Mediamatters*

Web-based research and information center concerned with monitoring and analyzing print, broadcast, cable, radio, and Internet media for inaccurate news and commentary. Seeks to inform journalists and the general public about specific instances of misinformation and provide resources for taking action against false claims.

Media Research Center, *1900 Campus Commons Dr., #600, Reston, VA 20191; (571) 267-3500. Fax, (571)*

375-0099. L. Brent Bozell III, President; David Martin, Executive Vice President. Toll-free, (800) 672-1423. General email, mrc@mrc.org

Web, www.mrc.org, Twitter, @theMRC and Facebook, www.facebook.com/mediaresearchcenter

Conservative media-watch organization working for balanced and responsible news coverage of political issues. Records and analyzes network news programs; analyzes print media; maintains profiles of media executives and library of recordings.

National Captioning Institute, *3725 Concorde Pkwy., #100, Chantilly, VA 20151; Fax, (703) 917-9853.*

Federal Communications Commission

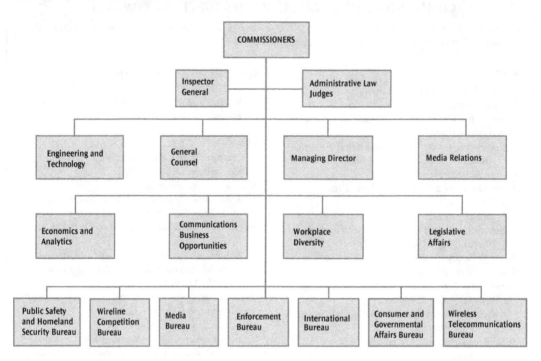

Gene Chao, Chief Executive Officer. Phone/TTY, (703) 917-7600.
General email, mail@ncicap.org

Web, www.ncicap.org

Captions television, cable, webcasting, home video, and DVD programs for the deaf and hard-of-hearing, and produces audio descriptions for the blind on behalf of public and commercial broadcast television networks, cable networks, syndicators, program producers, government agencies, advertisers, and home video distributors. Offers subtitling and language translation services. Produces and disseminates information about the national closed-captioning service and audio-description services.

TDI, P.O. Box 8009, Silver Spring, MD 20907; Claude L. Stout, Executive Director. Phone (voice/video), (301) 563-9112.
General email, info@TDIforaccess.org

Web, https://tdiforaccess.org and Twitter, @TDIforAccess

Membership: individuals, organizations, and businesses that advocate equal access to telecommunications, media, and information technologies for Americans who are deaf and hard of hearing. Interests include closed captioning for television, movies, DVDs, and online videos; emergency access (911); and TTY and Telecommunications Relays Services. Publishes a quarterly magazine and an annual resource directory. Monitors legislation and regulations.

Telecommunications Industry Assn. (TIA), 1320 N. Courthouse Rd., #200, Arlington, VA 22201; (703) 907-7700. Fax, (703) 907-7727. Wesley J. Johnson, Chief

Executive Officer, (703) 907-7702; Cinnamon Rogers, Senior Vice President of Government Affairs, (703) 907-7707.
General email, tia@tiaonline.org

Web, www.tiaonline.org and Twitter, @TIAonline

Trade association for the information and communications technology industry, including broadband, mobile wireless, information technology, networks, cable, satellite, and unified communications. Develops standards; provides market intelligence; analyzes environmental regulations; hosts trade shows and facilitates business opportunities for members. Monitors legislation and regulations.

Cable Services

▶ **AGENCIES**

Federal Communications Commission (FCC), *Media Bureau (MB),* 445 12th St. S.W., 3rd Floor, 20554; (202) 418-7200. Fax, (202) 418-2376. Michelle M. Carey, Chief; Janice Wise, Director of Media Relations, (202) 418-8165.
General email, mediarelations@fcc.gov

Web, www.fcc.gov/media

Makes, recommends, and enforces rules governing cable television and other video distribution services; promotes industry growth, competition, and availability to the public; ensures reasonable rates for consumers in areas that do not have competition in cable service.

Federal Communications Commission (FCC), *Media Bureau (MB), Engineering Division,* 445 12th St. S.W.,

#4-C838, 20554; (202) 418-7000. Fax, (202) 418-1189. John Wong, Chief.
Web, www.fcc.gov/encyclopedia/engineering-division-media-bureau

Provides technical advice for digital television (DTV) transition, latest cable technologies, and spectrum and broadband policies. Oversees the processing of routine cable applications.

Federal Communications Commission (FCC), Media Bureau (MB), Policy Division, 445 12th St. S.W., 20554; (202) 418-2120. Fax, (202) 418-1069. Martha Heller, Chief.
Web, www.fcc.gov/media/policy/policy-division

Conducts proceedings concerning broadcast and cable issues. Facilitates competition in the multichannel video programming marketplace by resolving carriage and other complaints involving access to facilities. Administers FCC's programs for political broadcasting and equal opportunity matters. Interests include children's TV, closed captioning, digital broadcasting, leased access, low-power FM and TV, public broadcasting, and V-chip.

▶**NONGOVERNMENTAL**

CTAM: Cable and Telecommunications Assn. for Marketing, 120 Waterfront St., #200, National Harbor, MD 20745; (301) 485-8900. Fax, (301) 560-4964. Vicki Lins, President, (301) 485-8920.
General email, info@ctam.com

Web, www.ctam.com and Twitter, @CTAM

Promotes innovation in the cable and related industries in areas of marketing, research, management, and new product development. Sponsors annual marketing and research conferences; interests include international markets.

NCTA—The Internet and Television Assn., 25 Massachusetts Ave. N.W., #100, 20001-1413; (202) 222-2300. Fax, (202) 222-2514. Michael K. Powell, President. Government Relations, (202) 222-2410. Press, (202) 222-2350.
General email, info@ncta.com

Web, www.ncta.com, Twitter, @NCTAcable and Facebook, www.facebook.com/NCTAitv

Membership: companies that operate cable television systems, cable television programmers, and manufacturers and suppliers of hardware and software for the industry. Represents the industry before federal regulatory agencies, before Congress, and in the courts; provides management and promotional aids and information on legal, legislative, and regulatory matters. (Formerly the National Cable and Telecommunications Assn.)

Enforcement, Judicial, and Legal Actions

▶**AGENCIES**

Antitrust Division (Justice Dept.), **Telecommunications and Broadband,** 450 5th St. N.W., #7000, 20530; (202)

616-5924. Fax, (202) 514-5399. Scott A. Scheele, Chief. Press, (202) 514-2007.
Web, www.justice.gov/atr/about/tel.html

Investigates and litigates antitrust cases dealing with communications and media. Participates in agency proceedings and rulemaking concerning communications and media; monitors and analyzes legislation.

Federal Bureau of Investigation (FBI) (Justice Dept.), **CALEA Implementation Unit,** Engineering Research Facility, Bldg. 27958A, Quantico, VA 22135; (540) 361-4600. Fax, (540) 361-7082. Marybeth Paglino, Unit Chief, (540) 361-2300.
Web, http://askcalea.fbi.gov

Administers enforcement of the Communications Assistance for Law Enforcement Act (CALEA). Sets standards for telecommunications carriers concerning the development and deployment of electronic surveillance technologies. Promotes cooperation between the telecommunications industry, government entities, and law enforcement officials to develop intercept capabilities required by law enforcement.

Federal Bureau of Prisons (Justice Dept.), **Federal Prison Industries,** 400 1st St. N.W., 20534; (202) 305-3500. Fax, (202) 514-6620. Patrick T. O'Connor, Chief Executive Officer. Customer Service, (800) 827-3168.
Web, www.unicor.gov and www.bop.gov/about/agency/org_fpi.jsp

Administers the inmate-training program operated by the Bureau of Prisons. FPI operates as a wholly owned, self-sustaining government corporation under the trade name UNICOR. FPI employs and provides skills training to Federal inmates in diverse factory settings.

Federal Communications Commission (FCC), Administrative Law Judges, 445 12th St. S.W., #1C768, 20554; (202) 418-2280. Fax, (202) 418-0195. Jane Hinckley Halprin, Chief Judge.
Web, www.fcc.gov/administrative-law-judges

Presides over hearings and issues initial decisions in disputes concerning FCC adjudication proceedings and applications for licensing.

Federal Communications Commission (FCC), Enforcement Bureau (EB), 445 12th St. S.W., 3rd Floor, #7C723, 20554; (202) 418-7450. Fax, (202) 418-2810. Rosemary Harold, Chief. Media Relations, (202) 418-0500. Toll-free, (888) 225-5322.
Web, www.fcc.gov/enforcement#block-menu-block-4

Enforces the provisions of the Communications Act, the FCC's rules and orders, and various licensing terms and conditions. Investigates and responds to potential unlawful conduct to ensure consumer protection, robust competition, efficient and responsible use of the public airwaves, and compliance with public safety-related rules.

▶**NONGOVERNMENTAL**

Federal Communications Bar Assn., 1020 19th St. N.W., #325, 20036-6101; (202) 293-4000. Fax, (202) 293-4317. Kerry Loughney, Executive Director.

General email, fcba@fcba.org

Web, www.fcba.org

Membership: attorneys, nonattorneys, and law students in communications law who practice before the Federal Communications Commission, the courts, and state and local regulatory agencies. Cooperates with the FCC and other members of the bar on legal aspects of communications issues.

Multicultural Media, Telecom, and Internet Council
(MMTC), *1919 Pennsylvania Ave. N.W., #725, 20006; (202) 332-0500. Fax, (202) 332-0503. Maurita Coley Flippin, President.*

General email, info@mmtconline.org

Web, www.mmtconline.org

Membership: lawyers, engineers, broadcasters, cablecasters, telecommunicators, and scholars. Provides pro bono services to the civil rights community on communication policy matters. Represents civil rights groups before the FCC on issues concerning equal opportunity and diversity. Promotes equal opportunity and civil rights in the mass media and telecommunications industries. Operates nonprofit media brokerage and offers fellowships for lawyers and law students interested in FCC practice.

The Software Alliance (BSA), *20 F St. N.W., #800, 20001; (202) 872-5500. Fax, (202) 872-5501. Victoria A. Espinel, President. Toll-free, (888) 667-4722.*

General email, info@bsa.org

Web, www.bsa.org *and Twitter, @BSAnews*

Investigates claims of software theft within corporations, financial institutions, academia, state and local governments, and nonprofit organizations. Provides legal counsel and initiates litigation on behalf of members.

Software and Information Industry Assn. (SIIA), *1090 Vermont Ave. N.W., 6th Floor, 20005-4905; (202) 289-7442. Fax, (202) 289-7097. Jeff (Ken) Joseph, President, (202) 789-4440.*

Web, www.siia.net *and Twitter, @SIIAPolicy*

Membership: software and digital content companies. Conducts an antipiracy program and other intellectual property initiatives.

International and Satellite Communications

▶AGENCIES

Bureau of Economic and Business Affairs (EB) *(State Dept.), International Communications and Information Policy (CIP), 2201 C St. N.W., #4634, 20520-5820; (202) 647-5212. Fax, (202) 647-5957. Robert L. Strayer, Deputy Assistant Secretary.*

Web, www.state.gov/e/eeb/cip

Coordinates U.S. government international communication and information policy. Acts as a liaison for other federal agencies and the private sector in international communications issues. Promotes advancement of information

and communication technology with expanded access and improved efficiency and security; the creation of business opportunities at home and abroad in this sector; resolution of telecommunications trade issues in conjunction with the Office of the U.S. Trade Representative; and the expansion of access to this technology globally.

Federal Communications Commission (FCC),
International Bureau (IB), 445 12th St. S.W., 6th Floor, 20554; (202) 418-0437. Fax, (202) 418-2818. Tom Sullivan, Chief.

General email, contact_ib@fcc.gov

Web, www.fcc.gov/international-bureau *and Blog,* www.fcc.gov/news-events/blog/1621

Coordinates the FCC's international policy activities; represents the FCC in international forums. Licenses international telecommunications carriers, undersea cables, international shortwave broadcasters, and satellite facilities. Coordinates the FCC's collection and dissemination of information on communications and telecommunications policy, regulation, and market developments in other countries and the policies and regulations of international organizations.

Federal Communications Commission (FCC), *Media Bureau (MB), Policy Division, 445 12th St. S.W., 20554; (202) 418-2120. Fax, (202) 418-1069. Martha Heller, Chief.*

Web, www.fcc.gov/media/policy/policy-division

Conducts proceedings concerning post-licensing Direct Broadcast Satellite issues, including the Satellite Home Viewer Improvement Act.

National Telecommunications and Information Administration (NTIA) *(Commerce Dept.), 1401 Constitution Ave. N.W., #4898, 20230; (202) 482-2000. Fax, (202) 501-0536. David J. Redl, Assistant Secretary; James C. Wasilewski, Chief of Staff (Acting), (202) 482-1845. Press, (202) 482-7002.*

Web, www.ntia.doc.gov, Twitter, @NTIAgov *and Facebook, www.facebook.com/ntiagov*

Represents the U.S. telecommunications sector (along with the State Dept.) in negotiating international agreements, including conferences with the International Telecommunication Union.

▶INTERNATIONAL ORGANIZATIONS

Inter-American Telecommunication Commission (CITEL) *(Organization of American States), 1889 F St. N.W., 6th Floor, 20006; (202) 370-4713. Fax, (202) 458-6854. Oscar Léon, Executive Secretary.*

General email, citel@oas.org

Web, www.citel.oas.org *and Twitter, @OEA_Telecom*

Membership: OAS member states and associate members from the telecommunications, Internet, electronic, and media industries, and others. Works with the public and private sectors to facilitate the development of universal telecommunications in the Americas.

▶NONGOVERNMENTAL

Satellite Broadcasting and Communications Assn.
(SBCA), *1100 17th St. N.W., #1150, 20036; (202) 349-3620.*
Fax, (202) 318-2618. Steven Hill, President. Toll-free, (800)
541-5981.
General email, info@sbca.org

Web, www.sbca.org and Twitter, @sbacomm

Membership: owners, operators, manufacturers, dealers, and distributors of satellite receiving stations; software and program suppliers; and others in the satellite services industry. Promotes use of satellite technology for broadcast delivery of video, audio, voice, broadband, and interactive services and as part of the national and global information infrastructure. Monitors legislation and regulations.

Satellite Industry Assn. (SIA), *1200 18th St. N.W., #1001,*
20036; (202) 503-1560. Tom Stroup, President.
General email, info@sia.org

Web, www.sia.org and Twitter, @sia_satellite

Trade association representing global satellite operators, service providers, manufacturers, launch service providers, and ground equipment suppliers. Promotes the benefits and uses of commercial satellite technology. Monitors legislation and regulations, domestically and abroad.

Radio and Television

▶AGENCIES

Broadcasting Board of Governors, *330 Independence*
Ave. S.W., #3300, 20237; (202) 203-4545. Fax, (202) 203-
4585. John F. Lansing, Chief Executive Officer.
Locator, (202) 203-4000. Press, (202) 203-4400.
General email, publicaffairs@bbg.gov

Web, www.bbg.gov and Twitter, @BBGov

Established by Congress to supervise all U.S. government nonmilitary international broadcasting, including Voice of America, Radio and TV Martí, Radio Free Europe/Radio Liberty, Radio Free Asia, and the Middle East Broadcasting Networks (MBN). Assesses the quality and effectiveness of broadcasts with regard to U.S. foreign policy objectives; reports annually to the president and to Congress.

Federal Communications Commission (FCC),
Enforcement Bureau (EB), *445 12th St. S.W., 3rd Floor,*
#7C723, 20554; (202) 418-7450. Fax, (202) 418-2810.
Rosemary Harold, Chief. Media Relations, (202) 418-0500.
Toll-free, (888) 225-5322.

Web, www.fcc.gov/enforcement#block-menu-block-4

Monitors the radio spectrum and inspects broadcast stations; ensures that U.S. radio laws and FCC rules are observed. Develops activities to inform, assist, and educate licensees; provides presentations and information. Manages the Emergency Alert System. Operates the National Call Center in Gettysburg, Pa.

Federal Communications Commission (FCC),
Engineering and Technology (OET), *445 12th St. S.W.,*
7th Floor, 20554; (202) 418-2470. Fax, (202) 418-1944.
Julius Knapp, Chief Engineer.
General email, oetinfo@fcc.gov

Web, www.fcc.gov/engineering-%26-technology

Studies characteristics of radio frequency spectrum. Certifies radios and other electronic equipment to meet FCC standards.

Federal Communications Commission (FCC), *Media*
Bureau (MB), *445 12th St. S.W., 3rd Floor, 20554; (202)*
418-7200. Fax, (202) 418-2376. Michelle M. Carey, Chief;
Janice Wise, Director of Media Relations, (202) 418-8165.
General email, mediarelations@fcc.gov

Web, www.fcc.gov/media

Responsible for the regulation of analog and digital broadcast services. Licenses, regulates, and develops audio and video services in traditional broadcasting and emerging television delivery systems, including digital television (DTV). Processes applications for licensing commercial and noncommercial radio and television broadcast equipment and facilities; handles renewals and changes of ownership; investigates public complaints.

Federal Communications Commission (FCC), *Media*
Bureau (MB), Policy Division, *445 12th St. S.W., 20554;*
(202) 418-2120. Fax, (202) 418-1069. Martha Heller, Chief.
Web, www.fcc.gov/media/policy/policy-division

Conducts proceedings concerning broadcast and cable issues. Facilitates competition in the multichannel video programming marketplace by resolving carriage and other complaints involving access to facilities. Administers FCC's programs for political broadcasting and equal opportunity matters. Interests include children's TV, closed captioning, digital broadcasting, leased access, low-power FM and TV, public broadcasting, and V-chip.

National Endowment for the Arts (NEA), *Media Arts, 400*
7th St. S.W., 20506; (202) 682-5452. Fax, (202) 682-5721.
Jax Deluca, Director, (202) 682-5742. TTY, (202) 682-5496.
Web, www.arts.gov/artistic-fields/media-arts

Awards grants to nonprofit organizations for film, video, and radio productions; supports arts programming broadcast nationally on public television and radio.

▶NONGOVERNMENTAL

Corp. for Public Broadcasting, *401 9th St. N.W., 20004-*
2129; (202) 879-9600. Fax, (202) 879-9700. Patricia de
Stacy Harrison, Chief Executive Officer; Anne Brachman,
Senior Vice President of Government Affairs; Letitia King,
Senior Vice President of Communications.
Comments, (800) 272-2190.
General email, press@cpb.org

Web, www.cpb.org and Twitter, @CPBmedia

Private corporation chartered by Congress under the Public Broadcasting Act of 1967 and funded by the federal government. Helps support the operation of more than 1,400 locally owned and locally operated public television and radio stations nationwide; provides general support for national program production and operation, including content for underserved communities; helps fund projects on U.S. and international news, education, arts, culture, history, and natural history; invests in emerging technologies, such as cable and satellite transmission, the Internet, and broadband communication networks, for use by public media.

National Assn. of Broadcasters (NAB), *1771 N St. N.W., 20036; (202) 429-5300. Gordon H. Smith, President. Communications, (202) 429-5350.*
General email, nab@nab.org

Web, www.nab.org and Twitter, @nabtweets

Membership: radio and television broadcast stations and broadcast networks holding an FCC license or construction permit; associate members include producers of equipment and programs. Assists members in areas of management, engineering, and research. Monitors legislation and regulations.

National Public Radio, *1111 N. Capitol St. N.E., 20002; (202) 513-2000. Fax, (202) 513-3329. Jarl Mohn, President; Elizabeth Jensen, Ombudsman. Press, (202) 513-2300.*
General email, ombudsman@npr.org

Web, www.npr.org

Multimedia news organization composed of 849 member stations operated by 269 member organizations nationwide that are locally owned and operated. Produces and distributes news, music, and entertainment programming in all 50 states. Provides program distribution service via satellite. Represents member stations before Congress, the FCC, and other regulatory agencies. Supported by member station programming fees (about 40 percent of funding); corporate sponsorships; and institutional grants.

Public Broadcasting Service, *2100 Crystal Dr., Arlington, VA 22202; (703) 739-5000. Fax, (703) 739-0775. Paula Kerger, President, (703) 739-5015; Madhulika Sikka, Public Editor, (703) 739-5290.*
General email, pbs@pbs.org

Web, www.pbs.org and Twitter, @PBS

Membership: public television stations nationwide. Selects, schedules, promotes, and distributes national programs; provides public television stations with educational, instructional, and cultural programming; also provides news and public affairs, science and nature, and children's programming. Assists members with technology development and fund-raising.

Telephone and Telegraph

For cellular telephones, see Wireless Telecommunications.

▶**AGENCIES**

Federal Communications Commission (FCC), *Wireline Competition Bureau (WCB), 445 12th St. S.W., #5C343, 20554; (202) 418-1500. Fax, (202) 418-2825. Kris Monteith, Chief (Acting).*
Web, www.fcc.gov/wireline-competition and Blog, www.fcc.gov/news-events/blog/1639

Creates and recommends policy goals, objectives, programs, and plans for the FCC on matters concerning wireline telecommunications. Objectives include promoting competition in wireline services and markets, deregulation, encouraging economically efficient investment in wireline telecommunications infrastructure, expanding the availability of wireline telecommunications services, and fostering economic growth.

General Services Administration (GSA), *Federal Relay Service (FedRelay), 10304 Eaton Pl., Fairfax, VA 22030; (703) 306-6308. Tatyana Mezentseva, Customer Relationship Manager. Customer Service, (800) 877-0996 (Voice/TTY, ASCII, Spanish). Speech-to-Speech, (877) 877-8982. TeleBraille, (866) 893-8340. TTY/ASCII, (800) 877-8339. VCO (Voice Carry Over), (877) 877-6280. Voice, (866) 377-8642.*
General email, ITCSC@gsa.gov

Web, www.gsa.gov/fedrelay and www.federalrelay.us

Provides telecommunications services for conducting official business with and within the federal government to individuals who are deaf or hard of hearing or who have speech disabilities. Federal Relay Service features are Voice, Text Telephone (TTY)/ASCII, HCO, Speech-to-Speech (STS), Spanish, Telebraille, Captioned Telephone Service (CTS), IP Relay, Video Relay Service (VRS), and Relay Conference Captioning (RCC) (including Spanish-to-Spanish captioning). For those with limited English proficiency, contact fas.car@gsa.gov, as services are available in Spanish, Vietnamese, Russian, Portuguese, Polish, Haitian, Creole, and Arabic.

▶**NONGOVERNMENTAL**

NTCA—The Rural Broadband Assn., *4121 Wilson Blvd., #1000, Arlington, VA 22203-1801; (703) 351-2000. Fax, (703) 351-2001. Shirley Bloomfield, Chief Executive Officer, (703) 351-2030.*
General email, pubrelations@ntca.org

Web, www.ntca.org, Twitter, @ntcaconnect and Facebook, www.facebook.com/NTCARuralTelecom

Membership: locally owned and controlled telecommunications cooperatives and companies serving rural and small-town areas. Offers educational seminars, workshops, publications, technical assistance, and various employee benefits programs to members. Monitors legislation and regulations. (Formerly the National Telecommunications Cooperative Assn.)

U.S. Telecom Assn. (USTA), *601 New Jersey Ave. N.W., #600, 20001; (202) 326-7300. Fax, (202) 326-7333. Jonathan Spalter, President.*
General email, policy@ustelecom.org

Web, www.ustelecom.org

Membership: broadband telecommunication service providers and manufacturers and suppliers for these companies. Provides members with information on the industry; conducts webinars; participates in FCC regulatory proceedings.

Wireless Telecommunications

▶ **AGENCIES**

Federal Communications Commission (FCC), *Wireless Telecommunications Bureau (WTB), 445 12th St. S.W., #6160, 20554; (202) 418-0600. Fax, (202) 418-0787. Donald Stockdale, Chief.*
Web, www.fcc.gov/wireless-telecommunications and Blog, www.fcc.gov/news-events/blog/1638

Regulates domestic wireless communications, including cellular telephone, paging, personal communications services, public safety, air and maritime navigation, and other commercial and private radio services. Responsible for implementing the competitive bidding authority for spectrum auctions. Assesses new uses of wireless technologies, including electronic commerce. (Gettysburg office handles all licensing: FCC Wireless Telecommunications Bureau, Spectrum Management Resources and Technologies Division, 1270 Fairfield Rd., Gettysburg, PA 17325; [717] 338-2510.)

▶ **NONGOVERNMENTAL**

CTIA—The Wireless Assn., *1400 16th St. N.W., #600, 20036; (202) 736-3200. Fax, (202) 785-0721. Meredith Baker, President.*
General email, ctiaadministration@ctia.org
Web, www.ctia.org and Twitter, @CTIA

Membership: system operators, equipment manufacturers, engineering firms, and others engaged in the cellular telephone and mobile communications industry in domestic and world markets. Monitors legislation and regulations.

Enterprise Wireless Alliance (EWA), *2121 Cooperative Way, #225, Herndon, VA 20171; (703) 528-5115. Fax, (703) 524-1074. Mark E. Crosby, Chief Executive Officer.*
General email, info@enterprisewireless.org
Web, www.enterprisewireless.org

Membership: enterprise wireless companies, dealers, and trade associations. Serves as an information source on radio frequencies, licensing, new products and technology, and market conditions. Monitors legislation and regulations.

PCIA: The Wireless Infrastructure Assn., *2111 Wilson Blvd., #210, Arlington, VA 22201; (703) 739-0300. Fax, (703) 836-1608. Jonathan Adelstein, President. Information, (800) 759-0300. Press, (703) 462-1445.*
Web, www.wia.org and Twitter, @WIAorg

Represents companies that make up the wireless telecommunications infrastructure industry. Supports wireless communications and information infrastructure.

Utilities Technology Council (UTC), *2511 Jefferson Davis Hwy., #960, Arlington, VA 22202; (202) 872-0030. Fax, (202) 872-1331. Joy Ditto, President.*
General email, marketing@utc.org
Web, www.utc.org and Twitter, @UTCNow

Membership: companies that own, manage, or provide critical telecommunications systems in support of their core business, including energy, gas, and water utility companies, pipeline companies, and radio and international critical infrastructure organizations. Participates in FCC rulemaking proceedings. Interests include fiber security; radio spectrum for fixed and mobile wireless communication; and technological, legislative, and regulatory developments affecting telecommunications operations of energy utilities.

GOVERNMENT INFORMATION

General

▶ **AGENCIES**

General Services Administration (GSA), *Governmentwide Policy, Information, Integrity, and Access, 1800 F St. N.W., #M1E, 20405; (202) 208-0598. Fax, (202) 357-0044. Daniel Pomeroy, Deputy Associate Administrator (Acting).*
Web, www.gsa.gov/about-us/organization/office-of-governmentwide-policy/information-integrity-and-access

Develops, coordinates, and defines ways that electronic and information technology business strategies can assist the Office of Management and Budget and other federal agencies to enhance access to and delivery of information and services to citizens.

General Services Administration (GSA), *Technology Transformation Service, 1800 F St. N.W., 2nd Floor, 20405; (202) 702-0781. Rob Cook, Commissioner.*
General email, tts-info@gsa.gov
Web, www.gsa.gov/tts

Utilizes current methodologies and technologies to improve the way the federal government provides the public with access to information and services. Works to aid agencies in creating services that are more understandable, attainable, and beneficial to the public.

General Services Administration (GSA), *USAGov, 1800 F St. N.W., 20405; (844) 872-4681. Fax, (202) 357-0078. Web, www.usa.gov and Web (Spanish), www.gobiernoUSA.gov*

Manages the portal site to U.S. government information, www.usa.gov. Manages kids.gov, a resource that provides government information on education, including primary, secondary, and higher education. Distributes free and low-cost federal publications of consumer interest via the Internet at www.usa.gov and Pueblo.gpo.gov. Assists people with questions about American government agencies, programs, and services via telephone, (800) FED-INFO ([800] 333-4636), or website, http://answers.usa.gov. Operates a contact center to provide information in English or Spanish on all federal government agencies, programs, and services via toll-free telephone, email, and chat. Operated under contract by Sykes in Pennsylvania and Florida. Responds to inquiries about federal programs and services. Gives information about or referrals to appropriate offices.

Chief Information Officers for Federal Departments and Agencies

DEPARTMENTS

Agriculture, Gary Washington, (202) 720-8833

Commerce, Rod Turk (Acting), (202) 482-4797

Defense, Essye B. Miller (Acting), (703) 695-0348

Air Force, Under Secretary Matthew Donovan, (703) 695-6829

Army, Lt. Gen. Bruce T. Crawford, (703) 695-4366

Navy, Thomas Modly, (703) 695-1840

Education, Jason Gray, (202) 245-6252

Energy, Max Everett, (202) 586-0166

Health and Human Services, Edwin Simcox, (202) 690-6162

Homeland Security, John Zangardi, (202) 282-8000

Housing and Urban Development, David Chow, (202) 708-0306

Interior, Sylvia Burns, (202) 208-6194

Justice, Joseph Klimavicz, (202) 514-0507

Labor, Gundeep Ahluwalia, (202) 693-4446

State, Karen Mummaw (Acting), (202) 647-2889

Transportation, Vacant, (202) 366-9201

Treasury, Eric Olson, (202) 622-1200

Veterans Affairs, James Gfrerer, (202) 461-6910

AGENCIES

Environmental Protection Agency, Vaughn Noga, (202) 564-6665

Federal Communications Commission, Christine Calvosa, (202) 418-7455

Federal Emergency Management Agency, Adrian R. Gardner, (202) 646-3006

Federal Trade Commission, Raghav Vajjhala, (202) 326-2667

General Services Administration, David Shive, (202) 501-1000

Government Accountability Office, Howard Williams Jr., (202) 512-5589

Government Printing Office, Layton Clay (Acting), (202) 512-1040

National Aeronautics and Space Administration, Renee Wynn, (202) 358-1824

National Archives and Records Administration, Swarnali Haldar, (301) 837-1583

National Science Foundation, Douglas A. Balentine, Director, (240) 402-2373

Nuclear Regulatory Commission, David Nelson, (301) 415-7443

Office of Management and Budget, Margie Graves (Acting), (202) 395-3080

Office of Personnel Management, David Garcia, (202) 418-3093

Office of the Director of National Intelligence, John Sherman, (301) 243-1295

Securities and Exchange Commission, Pamela Dyson, (202) 551-8800

Small Business Administration, Maria Roat, (202) 205-6708

Social Security Administration, Rajive K. Mathur, (410) 929-4774

National Archives and Records Administration (NARA), *700 Pennsylvania Ave. N.W., 20408 (mailing address: 8601 Adelphi Rd., College Park, MD 20704-6001); (866) 272-6272. Fax, (202) 357-5901. David S. Ferriero, Archivist of the United States, (202) 357-5900. Communications and marketing, (202) 357-5300. Public programs and events, (202) 357-5000.*
Web, www.archives.gov and Twitter, @USNatArchives

Identifies, preserves, and makes available federal government documents of historic value; administers a network of regional storage centers and archives and operates the presidential library system. Collections include photographs, graphic materials, films, and maps; holdings include records generated by foreign governments (especially in wartime) and by international conferences, commissions, and exhibitions.

National Archives and Records Administration (NARA), *Agency Services, 8601 Adelphi Rd., #3600, College Park, MD 20740-6001; (301) 837-3064. Fax, (301) 837-1617. Jay Trainer, Executive, (301) 837-3064.*
Web, www.archives.gov

Manages the federal record centers throughout the country. Works with the record managers to feed records into the National Archives. Oversees the National Declassification Center, the Office of Government Information Services, and the Information Security Oversight Office.

National Archives and Records Administration (NARA), *Electronic Records Division, 8601 Adelphi Rd., #5320, College Park, MD 20740-6001; (301) 837-0740. Fax, (301) 837-3681. Theodore J. Hull, Director, (301) 837-1824. General email, era.program@nara.gov*
Web, www.archives.gov/records-mgmt/era/technical.html

Preserves, maintains, and makes available electronic records of the U.S. government. Provides researchers with magnetic tape, CD, DVD, and other copies of electronic records on a cost-recovery basis. Offers direct downloads and searches of selected holdings.

National Archives and Records Administration (NARA), *Federal Register, 7 G St. N.W., #A-734, 20401 (mailing address: NF, 8601 Adelphi Rd., College Park, MD 20740-6001); (202) 741-6000. Fax, (202) 741-6012. Oliver A. Potts, Director, (202) 741-6100. TTY, (202) 523-5229. General email, fedreg.info@nara.gov*
Web, www.archives.gov/federal_register/the-federal-register and Twitter, @FedRegister

Informs citizens of their rights and obligations by providing access to the official texts of federal laws, presidential documents, administrative regulations and notices, and descriptions of federal organizations, programs, and activities. Provides online and in-person access to documents on file before their publication. Administers the Electoral College and the constitutional amendment process. Publications available from the U.S. Government Printing Office, (301) 317-3953, http://bookstore.gpo.gov.

National Archives and Records Administration (NARA), *Modern Records Program,* 8601 Adelphi Rd., #2100, College Park, MD 20740; (301) 837-3570. Fax, (301) 837-3697. Laurence N. Brewer, Director, (301) 837-1539.
General email, rm.communications@nara.gov

Administers programs that establish standards, guidelines, and procedures for agency records administration. Manages training programs; inspects records management practices; monitors certain records not contained in National Archives depositories.

National Archives and Records Administration (NARA), *Presidential Libraries,* 8601 Adelphi Rd., #2200, College Park, MD 20740-6001; (301) 837-3250. Fax, (301) 837-3199. Fax, (301) 837-3218. Susan K. Donius, Director (Acting), (202) 357-5376.
Web, www.archives.gov/presidential-libraries and Twitter, @OurPresidents

Administers thirteen presidential libraries. Directs all programs relating to acquisition, preservation, and research use of materials in presidential libraries; conducts oral history projects; publishes finding aids for research sources; provides reference service, including information from and about documentary holdings. Conducts community outreach; oversees museum exhibition programming.

National Archives and Records Administration (NARA), *Reference Services,* 4205 Suitland Rd., Suitland, MD 20746-8001; (301) 778-1600. Christopher Pinkney, Director.
General email, suitland.reference@nara.gov

Web, www.archives.gov/frc/reference-services.html

Provides reference service for unpublished civil and military federal government records. Maintains central catalog of all archival materials. Compiles comprehensive bibliographies of materials related to archival administration and records management. Permits research in American history, archival science, and records management. Maintains collections of the papers of the Continental Congress (1774–1789), U.S. State Dept. diplomatic correspondence (1789–1963), and general records of the U.S. government.

National Archives and Records Administration (NARA), *Research Services,* 8601 Adelphi Rd., #3400, College Park, MD 20740-6001; (301) 837-2000. Fax, (301) 837-3633. Ann A. Cummings, Executive for Research Services, (301) 837-3110. Research customer service, (301) 837-1659. Toll-free, (866) 272-6272.
Web, www.archives.gov/research

Preserves and makes available federal records at fifteen National Archives facilities across the country.

National Security Staff (NSS) *(Executive Office of the President), Strategic Communications and Speechwriting,* Dwight D. Eisenhower Executive Office Bldg., Pennsylvania Ave. and 17th St. N.W., #302, 20500; (202) 456-1414. Ross P. Worthington, Deputy National Security Adviser. Administrative office, (202) 456-9301.
Web, www.whitehouse.gov/the-trump-administration

Advises U.S. government agencies on the direction and theme of the president's message. Assists in the development and coordination of communications programs that disseminate consistent and accurate messages about the U.S. government and policies to the global audience.

National Technical Information Service (NTIS) *(Commerce Dept.),* 5301 Shawnee Rd., Alexandria, VA 22312; (703) 605-6000. Fax, (703) 605-6900. Avi Bender, Director, (703) 605-6400. Bookstore, (703) 605-6040. Customer support, (703) 605-6050. Toll-free, (800) 553-6847. Toll-free customer support, (888) 584-8332. TTY, (703) 487-4639.
General email, info@ntis.gov

Web, www.ntis.gov, Twitter, @NTISInfo and Facebook, www.facebook.com/NTISCustomerContactCenter

Collects and organizes technical, scientific, engineering, and business-related information generated by U.S. and foreign governments and makes it available for commercial use in the private sector. Makes available approximately 3 million works covering research and development, current events, business and management studies, translations of foreign open source reports, foreign and domestic trade, general statistics, environment and energy, health and social sciences, and hundreds of other areas. Provides computer software and computerized data files in a variety of formats, including Internet downloads. Houses the Homeland Security Information Center, a centralized source on major security concerns for health and medicine, food and agriculture, and biochemical war.

Office of Management and Budget (OMB) *(Executive Office of the President), Information and Regulatory Affairs,* 725 17th St. N.W., #10236, 20503; (202) 395-5897. Fax, (202) 395-6102. Neomi Reo, Administrator. Press, (202) 395-7254.
Web, www.whitehouse.gov/omb/information-regulatory-affairs

Oversees implementation and policy development under the Information Technology Reform Act of 1996 and the Paperwork Reduction Act of 1995; focuses on information technology management and substantive information policy, including records management, privacy, and computer security, and the Freedom of Information Act.

▶CONGRESS

For a listing of relevant congressional committees and subcommittees, please see page 95 or the Appendix.

Government Accountability Office (GAO), *Public Affairs,* 441 G St. N.W., Room 7149, 20548; (202) 512-4800. Fax, (202) 512-8546. Charles (Chuck) Young, Managing

Publications Contacts at Federal Departments and Agencies

Many publications for federal departments and agencies may be available through the Government Printing Office (GPO) and the National Technical Information Service (NTIS). For GPO and NTIS contact information, see below.

GENERAL

Government Printing Office (GPO), (202) 512-1800; Toll-free, (866) 512-1800; Fax, (202) 512-2104; www.gpo.gov

House Document Room, (202) 226-5210; https://clerk.house.gov/about/offices_lrc.aspx

Library of Congress, Orders, (202) 707-5093; www.loc.gov/loc/pub

National Technical Information Service (NTIS), (703) 605-6000 or (800) 553-6847; www.ntis.gov/help/order-methods

DEPARTMENTS

Agriculture, Information, (202) 694-5050; Orders via NTIS; www.usda.gov/media

Commerce, Orders via NTIS

Defense, Orders via NTIS; www.defense.gov/pubs

Education, Orders, (877) 433-7827; Fax, (703) 605-6794; www2.ed.gov/about/pubs/intro/index.html

Energy, Orders via NTIS and GPO; www1.eere.energy.gov/library or www.osti.gov/home/ publications

Health and Human Services, Toll-free, (877) 696-6775; www.hhs.gov

Homeland Security, www.dhs.gov/publications-0

Housing and Urban Development, Orders, (800) 767-7468; Fax, (202) 708-2313; www.huduser.org/portal/taxonomy/ term/1

Justice, Orders, (800) 851-3420; www.justice.gov/ publications/publications_a.html

Labor, Statistics orders, (202) 691-5200; Employee benefits, (866) 444-3272; www.dol.gov/ebsa/publications or www.dol.gov/odep/topics/OrderPublications.htm or www.dol.gov/dol/topic/statistics/publications.htm

State, Orders via GPO; www.state.gov/r/pa/ei/rls

Transportation, Orders via NTIS; www.fhwa.dot.gov/ research/publications/periodicals.cfm

Treasury, Orders via NTIS and GPO; www.treasury.gov/ tigta/publications.shtml

Veterans Affairs, www.va.gov/opa/publications

AGENCIES

Census Bureau, Orders, (301) 763-4400; https://census.gov/library/publications.html

Commission on Civil Rights, Orders, (202) 376-8128; www.usccr.gov/pubs

Consumer Product Safety Commission, Orders, (301) 595-7054; www.cpsc.gov/en/Safety-Education/Safety-Guides/General-Information/ Publications-Listing

Corporation for National and Community Service (AmeriCorps), Orders, (800) 942-2677; https://pubs.nationalservice.gov

Energy Information Administration, Orders, (202) 586-8800; www.eia.gov/reports

Environmental Protection Agency, Orders, (800) 490-9198; www.epa.gov/nscep

Equal Employment Opportunity Commission, Orders, (202) 663-4191; TTY, (202) 663-4494; www1.eeoc.gov/eeoc/publications

---

Director, (202) 512-3823. Publications orders, (202) 512-6000.

General email, youngc1@gao.gov

Web, www.gao.gov

Provides information to the public and media on federal programs, reports, and testimonies; organizes press interviews with GAO officials. GAO publications and information about GAO publications are available upon request in print or online.

Government Publishing Office (GPO), *732 N. Capitol St. N.W., 20401; (202) 512-0000. Fax, (202) 512-2104. Vacant, Deputy Director. Public Relations, (202) 512-1957.*

General email, contactcenter@gpo.gov

Web, www.gpo.gov and Twitter, @USGPO

The federal government's official digital secure resource for producing, procuring, cataloging, indexing, authenticating, disseminating, and preserving the official information products of the U.S. government. Responsible for the production and distribution of information products and services for all three branches of the federal government,

including U.S. passports for the State Dept. as well as the official publications of Congress, the White House, and other federal agencies in digital and print formats. Provides for free permanent public access to federal government information through the Federal Digital System (www.fdsys .gov), partnerships with approximately 1,200 libraries nationwide participating in the Federal Depository Library Program, and a secure online bookstore.

Government Publishing Office (GPO), *Contact Center, 732 N. Capitol St. N.W., MS IDCC, 20401; (202) 512-1800. Fax, (202) 512-2104. Lisa Williams, Chief of Distribution and Service Outreach, (202) 512-1065. Toll-free, (866) 512-1800.*

General email, contactcenter@gpo.gov

Web, https://bookstore.gpo.gov/customer-service/contact-us

Provides customer service for the federal government's official digital secure resource for producing, procuring, cataloging, indexing, authenticating, disseminating, and preserving the official information products of the U.S. government.

Federal Communications Commission, Orders, (202) 418-7512; www.fcc.gov

Federal Election Commission, Orders, (800) 424-9530; www.fec.gov/info/publications.shtml

Federal Emergency Management Agency, Toll-free, (800) 480-2520; Fax, (240) 699-0525; or www.ready.gov/publications

Federal Reserve System, Orders, (202) 452-3245; Fax, (202) 728-5886; www.federalreserve.gov/publications/order.htm

Federal Trade Commission, Orders, (877) 382-4357; https://bulkorder.ftc.gov

General Services Administration, Orders, (800) 488-3111; www.gsa.gov/portal/content/101674

Government Accountability Office, Orders, (202) 512-6000; Toll-free, (866) 801-7077; TDD, (202) 512-2537; www.gao.gov/ordering.htm

International Bank for Reconstruction and Development (World Bank), Orders, (703) 661-1580; Toll-free, (800) 645-7247; Fax, (703) 661-1501; www.worldbank.org/reference

International Trade Administration, Orders via NTIS and GPO; https://trade.gov/publications

National Aeronautics and Space Administration, Orders, (202) 358-0000; www.hq.nasa.gov/office/hqlibrary/ic/ic2.htm#pubs

National Archives and Records Administration, Orders, (202) 357-5332; Toll-free, (866) 272-6272; www.archives.gov/publications

National Endowment for the Humanities, Orders, (202) 606-8435

National Park Service, Orders by mail only; www.nps.gov/aboutus/publications.htm

National Science Foundation, Orders, (866) 512-1800; www.nsf.gov/publications

National Transportation Safety Board, Information, (202) 314-6551; www.ntsb.gov/publications/Pages/default.aspx; Post-publication orders via NTIS.

Nuclear Regulatory Commission, Orders, (301) 415-4737 or (800) 397-4209; Orders also from GPO; www.nrc.gov/reading-rm/pdr.html

Occupational Safety and Health Administration, Orders, (202) 693-1888; Fax, (202) 693-2498; www.osha.gov/pls/publications/publication.html

Office of Personnel Management, Orders via GPO; Retirement and insurance information, (202) 606-1800; https://apps.opm.gov/publications

Peace Corps, (202) 692-2250; www.peacecorps.gov/about/open-government/reports/

Securities and Exchange Commission, Orders, (202) 551-4040; Public documents, (202) 551-8090; www.sec.gov/investor/pubs.shtml

Social Security Administration, Orders, (410) 965-2039; Fax, (410) 965-2037; www.ssa.gov/pubs

U.S. Fish and Wildlife Service, Orders, (303) 236-7639; Fax, (303) 236-0845; Orders via NTIS; www.fws.gov/external-affairs/marketing-communications/printing-and-publishing

U.S. Geological Survey, Orders, (888) 275-8747; http://store.usgs.gov

U.S. Institute of Peace, Book orders, (800) 868-8064; Fax, (703) 661-1501; https://bookstore.usip.org

---

Government Publishing Office (GPO), *Security and Intelligent Documents Unit, 732 N. Capitol St. N.W., #C566, 20401; (202) 512-1000. Stephen G. LeBlanc, Deputy Director.*
Web, www.gpo.gov/customers/sid.htm

Works with other federal agencies to ensure the safe and secure design, production, and distribution of security and intelligence documents such as U.S. passports and other secure credentials for federal agencies.

Library of Congress, *Federal Library and Information Network (FEDLINK), John Adams Bldg., 101 Independence Ave. S.E., #LA 217, 20540; (202) 707-4800. Fax, (202) 707-4818. Laurie Neider, Executive Director, (202) 707-4801; Robin Harvey, Editor-in-Chief, (202) 707-4820. FEDLINK Hotline, (202) 707-4900.*
General email, fliccffo@loc.gov
Web, www.loc.gov/flicc

Promotes better utilization of federal library and information resources by seeking to provide the most cost-effective and efficient administrative mechanisms for delivering services and materials to federal libraries and information centers; serves as a forum for discussion of federal library and information policies, programs, and procedures; helps inform Congress, federal agencies, and others concerned with libraries and information centers.

Library of Congress, *Serial and Government Publications, James Madison Memorial Bldg., 101 Independence Ave. S.E., #LM 133, 20540-4760; (202) 707-5690. Teri Sierra, Chief, (202) 707-5277. Current periodical reading room, (202) 707-5691. Reference desk, (202) 707-5208.*
Web, www.loc.gov/rr/news

Operates Newspaper and Current Periodical Reading Room; maintains library's collection of domestic and foreign newspapers, current periodicals, comic books, and current serially issued publications of federal, state, and foreign governments; maintains a selective U.S. federal government publication depository since 1979, a United Nations document collection, and a Federal Advisory Committee (FAC) collection. Responds to written or telephone requests for information on newspapers, periodicals, or government publications, or online through Ask a Librarian. Lends some microfilm through interlibrary loans.

Senate Historical Office, *201 SHOB, 20510; (202) 224-6900. Betty K. Koed, Historian.*
General email, historian@sec.senate.gov
Web, www.senate.gov/art/art_hist_home.htm and
Twitter, @SenateHistory

Serves as an information clearinghouse on Senate history, traditions, and members. Collects, organizes, and distributes to the public unpublished Senate documents; collects and preserves photographs and pictures related to Senate history; conducts an oral history program; advises senators and Senate committees on the disposition of their noncurrent papers and records. Produces publications on the history of the Senate.

U.S. House of Representatives, *Legislative Resource Center, B81 CHOB, 20515-6612; Fax, (202) 226-4362. Ronald (Dale) Thomas, Chief. Bill status, (202) 226-5200.*
General email, info.clerkweb@mail.house.gov
Web, http://clerk.house.gov/about/offices_lrc.aspx

Provides legislative information, records and registration, historical information, and library services to the House and the public. Reading room contains computer terminals where collections may be viewed or printed out. Print publications include a biographical directory, a guide to research collections of former House members, and books on African Americans and women who have served in Congress. Collections include House and Senate journals (1st Congress to present); *Congressional Record* and its predecessors (1st Congress to present); House reports, documents, bills, resolutions, and hearings; Senate reports and documents; U.S. statutes, treaties, the *Federal Register*, U.S. codes, and numerous other documents. (See website or call for a complete list of collections.)

U.S. House of Representatives, *Office of Art and Archives, B53 CHOB, 20515; (202) 226-1300. Fax, (202) 226-4635. Farar P. Elliott, Chief.*
General art email, art@mail.house.gov
General archives email, archives@mail.house.gov
Web, http://history.house.gov and
Twitter, @USHouseHistory

Works with the Office of the Historian to provide access to published documents and historical records of the House. Advises members on the disposition of their records and papers; maintains information on manuscript collections of former members; maintains biographical files on former members; houses photographs and artifacts of former members. Produces publications on Congress and its members.

U.S. House of Representatives, *Office of the Historian, B53 CHOB, 20515; (202) 226-1300. Matthew A. Wasniewski, House Historian.*

General email, history@mail.house.gov
Web, http://history.house.gov and
Twitter, @ushousehistory

Works with the Office of Art and Archives to provide access to published documents and historical records of the House. Conducts historical research. Advises members on the disposition of their records and papers; maintains information on manuscript collections of former members; maintains biographical files on former members. Produces publications on Congress and its members.

► **NONGOVERNMENTAL**

Federation of American Scientists (FAS), *Project on Government Secrecy, 1112 16th St. N.W., #400, 20036; (202) 546-3300. Fax, (202) 675-1010. Steven Aftergood, Project Director.*
General email, fas@fas.org
Web, www.fas.org/issues/government-secrecy

Promotes public access to government information and fosters development of rational information security policies. Works to reduce the scope of government secrecy, including national security classification and declassification policies. Publishes hard-to-find government documents online.

Freedom of Information

► **AGENCIES**

Justice Dept. (DOJ), *Information Policy (OIP), 1425 New York Ave. N.W., #11050, 20530; (202) 514-3642. Fax, (202) 514-1009. Melanie Ann Pustay, Director. Information, (202) 514-2000.*
General email, doj.oip.foia@usdoj.gov
Web, www.justice.gov/oip

Provides federal agencies with advice and policy guidance on matters related to implementing and interpreting the Freedom of Information Act (FOIA). Processes FOIA requests on behalf of the Department's Senior Leadership Offices; adjudicates administrative appeals from Justice Dept. denials of public requests for access to documents; litigates selected FOIA and Privacy Act cases; conducts FOIA training for government agencies.

National Archives and Records Administration (NARA), *Information Security Oversight (ISOO), 700 Pennsylvania Ave. N.W., #100, 20408-0001; (202) 357-5250. Fax, (202) 357-5907. Mark A. Bradley, Director.*
General email, isoo@nara.gov
Web, www.archives.gov/isoo

Receiving guidance from the National Security Council, oversees policy on security classification/declassification on documents and programs for the federal government and industry; develops policies and procedures for sensitive unclassified information.

National Archives and Records Administration (NARA), *National Declassification Center, 8601 Adelphi Rd.,*

Public Affairs Contacts at Federal Departments and Agencies

DEPARTMENTS

Agriculture, Tim Murtaugh, (202) 720-4623

Commerce, James Rockas (Deputy), (202) 482-4883

Defense, Dana W. White, (703) 697-5131

  Air Force, Brig. Gen. Edward W. Thomas Jr., (703) 697-6061

  Army, Brig. Gen. Omar J. Jones, (703) 693-4723

  Marine Corps, Philip J. Kulczewski, (703) 614-4309

  Navy, Capt. Greg Hicks, (703) 697-5342

Education, Nathan Bailey, (202) 401-2000

Energy, Karla Olsen, (202) 586-4940

Health and Human Services, Charmaine Yoest, (202) 690-6344

Homeland Security, Jonathan Rath Hoffman, (202) 282-8010

  Coast Guard, David French, (202) 372-4630

Housing and Urban Development, Amy Thompson, (202) 708-0980

Interior, Paul Ross, (202) 208-6416

Justice, Sarah Isgur Flores, (202) 514-2007

Labor, Jeffrey Y. Grappone, (202) 693-4676

State, Heather Nauert, (202) 647-6088

Transportation, Marianne McInerney, (202) 366-0660

Treasury, Tony Sayegh, (202) 622-2960

Veterans Affairs, John Ullyot, (202) 461-7500

AGENCIES

Agency for International Development, Clayton McCleskey (Acting), (202) 712-4320

Commission on Civil Rights, Brian Walch, (202) 376-8371

Commodity Futures Trading Commission, Erica Richardson, (202) 418-5080

Consumer Product Safety Commission, Joseph Martyak, (301) 504-6932

Corporation for National and Community Service, Samantha Jo Warfield, (202) 606-6775

Environmental Protection Agency, Liz Bowman, (202) 564-4355

Equal Employment Opportunity Commission, Kimberly Smith Brown, (202) 663-4191

Export-Import Bank, Jennifer Hazelton, (202) 565-3200

Farm Credit Administration, Michael A. Stokke, (703) 883-4056

Federal Communications Commission, Brian Hart, (202) 418-0503

Federal Deposit Insurance Corporation, LaJuan Williams-Young, (202) 898-3876

Federal Election Commission, Christian Hilland, (202) 694-1220

Federal Emergency Management Agency, William Booher, (202) 646-4600

Federal Labor Relations Authority, Gina K. Grippando, (202) 218-7776

Federal Mediation and Conciliation Service, John Arnold, (202) 606-5442

Federal Reserve System, Michelle Smith, (202) 452-2955

Federal Trade Commission, Peter Kaplan (Acting), (202) 326-2180

General Services Administration, Ben Kenney, (202) 208-0128

Government Accountability Office, Charles Young, (202) 512-4800

Government Printing Office, Gary Somerset, (202) 512-1957

Institute of Museum and Library Services, Elizabeth Holtan, (202) 653-4757

National Aeronautics and Space Administration, J.D. Harrington, (202) 358-5241

National Archives and Records Administration, Miriam Kleiman, (202) 357-5300

National Capital Planning Commission, Julia Koster, (202) 482-7211

National Credit Union Administration, Ben C. Hardaway, (703) 518-6333

National Endowment for the Arts, Victoria Hutter, (202) 682-5692

National Endowment for the Humanities, Carmen Ingwell, (202) 606-8255

National Institute of Standards and Technology, Gail Porter, (301) 975-3392

National Labor Relations Board, Carmen Torres Spell, (202) 273-1991

National Science Foundation, Amanda Hallberg Greenwell, (703) 292-8070

National Transportation Safety Board, Christopher O'Neil, (202) 314-6100

Nuclear Regulatory Commission, David Castelveter, (301) 415-8200

Occupational Safety and Health Review Commission, Madeleine Pope, (202) 606-5370

Office of Personnel Management, Mark Pekrul, (202) 606-2402

Office of Special Counsel, Jill Gerber, (202) 804-7065

Pension Benefit Guaranty Corporation, Martha Threatt, (202) 326-4343

Securities and Exchange Commission, John Nester, (202) 551-4120

Selective Service System, Lee Alexander, (703) 605-4017

Small Business Administration, Terry Sutherland, (202) 205-6919

Social Security Administration, Mark Hinkle (Acting), (410) 929-4774

U.S. International Trade Commission, Peg O'Laughlin, (202) 205-1819

U.S. Postal Service, Dave Partenheimer, (202) 268-2155

#6350, College Park, MD 20740; (301) 837-0407. Fax, (301) 837-0346. David Mengel, Director (Acting), (301) 837-0585. Released records requests, (301) 837-3510. General email, ndc@nara.gov

Web, www.archives.gov/declassification/ndc

Released records requests email, archives2reference@nara.gov

Directs the review and declassification of records and security-classified materials in the National Archives in accordance with Executive Order 13526 and the Freedom of Information Act; assists other federal archival agencies in declassifying security-classified documents in their holdings. Requests to access newly released records can be submitted through Archives II Reference.

Office of Management and Budget (OMB) *(Executive Office of the President), Information and Regulatory Affairs,* 725 17th St. N.W., #10236, 20503; (202) 395-5897. Fax, (202) 395-6102. Neomi Reo, Administrator. Press, (202) 395-7254.
Web, www.whitehouse.gov/omb/information-regulatory-affairs

Oversees implementation and policy development under the Information Technology Reform Act of 1996 and the Paperwork Reduction Act of 1995; focuses on information technology management and substantive information policy, including records management, privacy, and computer security, and the Freedom of Information Act.

▶**NONGOVERNMENTAL**

American Civil Liberties Union (ACLU), *Washington Legislative Office,* 915 15th St. N.W., 6th floor, 20005; (202) 544-1681. Fax, (202) 546-0738. David Cole, Legal Director. Press, (202) 549-2666.
General email, media@acludc.org

Web, www.aclu.org/legiupdate

Advocates legislation to guarantee constitutional rights and civil liberties. Monitors agency compliance with the Privacy Act and other access statutes. Produces publications. (Headquarters in New York maintains docket of cases.)

American Library Assn., *Washington Office,* 1615 New Hampshire Ave. N.W., 1st Floor, 20009-2520; (202) 628-8410. Fax, (202) 628-8419. Kathi Kromer, Associate Executive Director; Kevin Maher, Deputy Director Government Relations. Information, (800) 941-8478.
General email, alawash@alawash.org

Web, www.ala.org/offices/wo

Advocates public policies that promote public access to government information, open government, and e-Government services. (Headquarters in Chicago, Ill.)

American Society of Access Professionals, 1120 20th St. N.W., #750, 20036; (202) 712-9054. Fax, (202) 216-9646. Claire Shanley, Executive Director.
General email, asap@accesspro.org

Web, www.accesspro.org and Twitter, @ASAPAccessPro

Membership: federal employees, attorneys, journalists, and others working with or interested in access-to-information laws. Seeks to improve the administration of the Freedom of Information Act, the Privacy Act, and other access statutes. Sponsors training workshops and seminars.

Freedom Forum, 555 Pennsylvania Ave. N.W., 20001; (202) 292-6290. Fax, (202) 292-6148. Jan Neuharth, Chief Executive Officer. Toll-free, (888) 639-7386.
Web, www.freedomforum.org

Sponsors training and research that promote free press, free speech, and freedom of information. Interests include the First Amendment and newsroom diversity. Part of the Freedom Forum Insitute.

Radio Television Digital News Assn., 529 14th St. N.W., #1240, 20045; (212) 246-0398. Dan Shelley, Executive Director.
Web, www.rtdna.org and Twitter, @RTDNA

Membership: electronic journalists in radio, television, and all digital media. Sponsors and promotes education and advocacy concerning First Amendment issues, freedom of information, and government secrecy issues; ethics in reporting; improving coverage; implementing technology; and other news industry issues. Radio and Television News Directors Foundation (RTNDF) is the educational arm of the association.

INTERNET AND RELATED TECHNOLOGIES

General

▶**AGENCIES**

National Telecommunications and Information Administration (NTIA) *(Commerce Dept.),* 1401 Constitution Ave. N.W., #4898, 20230; (202) 482-2000. Fax, (202) 501-0536. David J. Redl, Assistant Secretary; James C. Wasilewski, Chief of Staff (Acting), (202) 482-1845. Press, (202) 482-7002.
Web, www.ntia.doc.gov, Twitter, @NTIAgov and Facebook, www.facebook.com/ntiagov

Responsible for oversight of the technical management of the Internet domain name system (DNS) and the Institute for Telecommunication Science (ITS).

▶**CONGRESS**

Library of Congress, *National Digital Information Infrastructure and Preservation Program (NDIIPP),* James Madison Memorial, 101 Independence Ave. S.E., 20540-1300; (202) 707-6530. Fax, (202) 707-0815. Bud Barto, Chief Information Officer; Kim Barnhart, Administrative Assistant.

Oversees development of a national strategy for collecting, archiving, and preserving digital content, and directs the activities of the Information Technology Directorate.

Freedom of Information Contacts at Federal Departments and Agencies

DEPARTMENTS

Agriculture, Alexis Graves, (202) 690-3318

Commerce, Michael Toland, (202) 482-3842

Defense, David Tillotson III, (866) 574-4970

  Air Force, Anh Trinh, (703) 614-8500

  Army, Steven A. Raho, (703) 428-6238

  Marine Corps, Sally Hughes, (703) 614-4008

  Navy, Robin Patterson, (202) 685-0412

Education, Gregory Smith, (202) 401-8365

Energy, Ingrid A. Kolb, (202) 586-5955

Health and Human Services, Michael Marquis, (202) 690-7453

Homeland Security, Sam Kaplan, (202) 343-1743

  Coast Guard, Amanda Ackerson, (202) 475-3522

Housing and Urban Development, Deborah Snowden, (202) 708-3054

Interior, Darrell Strayhorn, (202) 208-5339

Justice, Melanie Tustay, (202) 514-3642

Labor, Ramona Oliver, (202) 693-5391

State, Kellie Robinson, (202) 261-8484

Transportation, Kathy Ray, (202) 366-4542

Treasury, Ryan Law, (202) 622-8098

Veterans Affairs, Dolores Johnson, (202) 632-7233

AGENCIES

Agency for International Development, Angelique M. Crumbly, (202) 712-1371 -, (202) 712-1200

Central Intelligence Agency, Allison Fong, (703) 613-1287

Commission on Civil Rights, Tink Cooper, (202) 514-4210

Commodity Futures Trading Commission, Jonathan Van Doren, (202) 418-5505

Consumer Product Safety Commission, Aboiye Mosheim, amosheim@cpsc.gov; 800-638-2772

Council on Environmental Quality, Howard Sun, (202) 456-6224

Environmental Protection Agency, Larry F. Gottesman, (202) 566-1667

Equal Employment Opportunity Commission, Stephanie D. Garner, (202) 663-4634

Export-Import Bank, Lennell Jackson, (202) 565-3290

Farm Credit Administration, Jane Virga, (703) 883-4071

Federal Communications Commission, Stephanie Kost, (202) 418-1379

Federal Deposit Insurance Corp., M. Anthony Lowe, (703) 562-6040

Federal Election Commission, Robert Kahn, (202) 694-1650

Federal Emergency Management Agency, Vacant, (202) 646-3323

Federal Labor Relations Authority, Vacant, (202) 218-7740

Federal Maritime Commission, Rachel E. Dickon, (202) 523-5725

Federal Reserve, Margaret McCloskey Shanks, (202) 452-2200

Federal Trade Commission, Richard Gold, (202) 326-3355

General Services Administration, Audrey Corbett Brooks, (202) 205-5912

Legal Services Corp., Cheryl DuHart, (202) 295-1500

Merit Systems Protection Board, William D. Spencer, (202) 254-4475

National Aeronautics and Space Administration, Nikki N. Gramian, (202) 358-0625

National Archives and Records Administration, Gary M. Stern, (301) 837-1750

National Credit Union Administration, Linda Dent, (703) 518-6540

National Endowment for the Humanities, Lisette Voyatzis, (202) 606-8322

National Labor Relations Board, Barbara A. O'Neill, (202) 273-3842

National Mediation Board, Mary L. Johnson, (202) 692-5040

National Science Foundation, Justin Guz, (703) 292-2289

National Transportation Safety Board, Melba D. Moye, (202) 314-6540

Nuclear Regulatory Commission, John Moses, (301) 415-1276

Office of Government Ethics, Rachel Dowell, (202) 482-9267

Office of Management and Budget, Heather Walsh, (202) 395-7545

Office of National Drug Control Policy, Michael Passante, (202) 395-6622

Office of Personnel Management, Trina Porter, (202) 606-1153

Office of Science and Technology Policy, Rachael Leonard, (202) 456-6125

Office of the U.S. Trade Representative, Janice Kaye, (202) 395-3419

Peace Corps, D. Miller, (202) 692-1236

Pension Benefit Guaranty Corp., D. Camilla Perry, (202) 326-4040

Securities and Exchange Commission, Barry Walters, (202) 551-7900

Selective Service, Richard S. Flahavan, (703) 605-4005

Small Business Administration, Delorice P. Ford, (202) 401-8203

Social Security Administration, Monica Chyn, (410) 965-1727

U.S. International Trade Commission, Jacqueline N. Gross, (202) 205-1816

Federal Government Websites

CONGRESS

Government Accountability Office, www.gao.gov

House of Representatives, www.house.gov

Library of Congress, www.loc.gov

Senate, www.senate.gov

WHITE HOUSE

General Information, www.whitehouse.gov

DEPARTMENTS

Agriculture, www.usda.gov

Commerce, www.commerce.gov

Defense, www.defense.gov

  Air Force, www.af.mil

  Army, www.army.mil

  Marine Corps, www.marines.mil

  Navy, www.navy.mil

Education, www.ed.gov

Energy, www.energy.gov

Health and Human Services, www.hhs.gov

Homeland Security, www.dhs.gov

  Coast Guard, www.uscg.mil

Housing and Urban Development, www.hud.gov

Interior, www.doi.gov

Justice, www.justice.gov

Labor, www.dol.gov

State, www.state.gov

Transportation, www.transportation.gov

Treasury, www.treasury.gov

Veterans Affairs, www.va.gov

AGENCIES

Agency of International Development, www.usaid.gov

Consumer Product Safety Commission, www.cpsc.gov

Corporation for Public Broadcasting, www.cpb.org

Drug Enforcement Administration, www.dea.gov

Environmental Protection Agency, www.epa.gov

Export-Import Bank, www.exim.gov

Federal Aviation Administration, www.faa.gov

Federal Bureau of Investigation, www.fbi.gov

Federal Communications Commission, www.fcc.gov

Federal Deposit Insurance Corporation, www.fdic.gov

Federal Election Commission, www.fec.gov

Federal Emergency Management Agency, www.fema.gov

Federal Energy Regulatory Commission, www.ferc.gov

Federal Reserve System, www.federalreserve.gov

Federal Trade Commission, www.ftc.gov

Food and Drug Administration, www.fda.gov

General Services Administration, www.gsa.gov

Government Accountability Office, www.gao.gov

Government Publishing Office, www.gpo.gov

Internal Revenue Service, www.irs.gov

National Aeronautics and Space Administration, www.nasa.gov

National Archives and Records Administration, www.archives.gov

National Institute of Standards and Technology, www.nist.gov

National Institutes of Health, www.nih.gov

National Oceanic and Atmospheric Administration, www.noaa.gov; www.climate.gov

National Park Service, www.nps.gov

National Railroad Passenger Corporation (Amtrak), www.amtrak.com

National Science Foundation, www.nsf.gov

National Technical Information Service, www.ntis.gov

National Transportation Safety Board, www.ntsb.gov

Nuclear Regulatory Commission, www.nrc.gov

Occupational Safety and Health Administration, www.osha.gov

Patent and Trademark Office, www.uspto.gov

Peace Corps, www.peacecorps.gov

Pension Benefit Guaranty Corporation, www.pbgc.gov

Securities and Exchange Commission, www.sec.gov

Small Business Administration, www.sba.gov

Smithsonian Institution, www.si.edu

Social Security Administration, www.ssa.gov

U.S. Fish and Wildlife Service, www.fws.gov

U.S. Geological Survey, www.usgs.gov

U.S. International Trade Commission, www.usitc.gov

U.S. Postal Service, www.usps.com

►NONGOVERNMENTAL

Accredited Standards Committee (ASC X12), *8300 Greensboro Dr., #800, McLean, VA 22102; (703) 970-4480. James (Jim) Taylor, Chair.*
General email, info@x12.org

Web, www.x12.org and Twitter, @X12standards

Promotes the development and maintenance of cross-industry Electronic Data Interchange (EDI), XML schemas, and Context Inspired Component Architecture (CICA) standards in electronic commerce that help organizations improve business methods, lower costs, and increase productivity. Provides administrative and technical support. Chartered by the American National Standards Institute. (Formerly Data Interchange Standards Assn.)

American Library Assn., *Washington Office, 1615 New Hampshire Ave. N.W., 1st Floor, 20009-2520; (202) 628-8410. Fax, (202) 628-8419. Kathi Kromer, Associate Executive Director; Kevin Maher, Deputy Director Government Relations. Information, (800) 941-8478. General email, alawash@alawash.org*

Web, www.ala.org/offices/wo

Promotes net neutrality rules that ban blocking, throttling, or degrading of any lawful internet content. Opposes paid prioritization of content; supports preservation of competitive online markets for content and services. (Headquarters in Chicago, Ill.)

Center for Democracy and Technology, *1401 K St. N.W., 2nd Floor, 20005; (202) 637-9800. Fax, (202) 637-0968. Nuala O'Connor, President. Press, (202) 407-8814. General email, info@cdt.org*

Web, https://cdt.org, Twitter, @CenDemTech

Press, press@cdt.org

Promotes and defends privacy and civil liberties on the Internet. Interests include free expression, social networking and access to the Internet, consumer protection, health information privacy and technology, and government surveillance. Monitors legislation and regulations.

Center for Digital Democracy, *1875 K St. N.W., 4th Floor, 20006; (202) 986-2220. Jeffrey (Jeff) Chester, Executive Director, (202) 494-7100. General email, jeff@democraticmedia.org*

Web, www.democraticmedia.org and Twitter, @DigitalDemoc

Seeks to ensure that the public interest is a fundamental part of the digital communications landscape. Conducts public education designed to protect consumer privacy and works to ensure competition in the new media industries, especially at the Federal Trade Commission and the Justice Dept.

Center for Strategic and International Studies, *Technology Policy Program, 1616 Rhode Island Ave. N.W., 20036; (202) 775-3175. Fax, (202) 775-3199. James Andrew Lewis, Director.*

General email, techpolicy@csis.org

Web, www.csis.org/programs/technology-policy-program and Twitter, @CyberCSIS

Conducts and publishes research on emerging technologies, intelligence reform, and space and globalization programs. Interests include cybersecurity, privacy and surveillance, technology and innovation, and Internet governance.

Common Cause, *805 15th St. N.W., #800, 20005; (202) 833-1200. Karen Hobert Flynn, President. Press, (202) 736-5788. General email, CauseNet@commoncause.org*

Web, www.commoncause.org and Twitter, @CommonCause

Nonpartisan citizens' lobby that works to promote laws and regulations safeguarding the free flow of information online. Supports strong open Internet protections; opposes media consolidation.

Computer and Communications Industry Assn. (CCIA), *25 Massachusetts Ave. N.W., 20001; (202) 783-0070. Fax, (202) 783-0534. Edward J. Black, President; Heather Greenfield, Director of Communications. General email, hgreenfield@ccianet.org*

Web, www.ccianet.org and Twitter, @ccianet

Membership: Internet service providers, software providers, and manufacturers and suppliers of computer data processing and communications-related products and services. Interests include Internet freedom, privacy and neutrality, government electronic surveillance, telecommunications policy, tax policy, federal procurement policy, communications and computer industry standards, intellectual property policies, encryption, international trade, and antitrust reform.

Cyber Security Policy and Research Institute *(George Washington University), Tompkins Hall, 725 23rd St. N.W., #106, 20052; (202) 994-5613. Costis Toregas, Director. General email, cspri@gwu.edu*

Web, www.cspri.seas.gwu.edu

Promotes education, research, and policy analysis in the areas of computer security and privacy, computer networks, electronic commerce, e-government, and the cultural aspects of cyberspace.

Family Online Safety Institute, *1440 G St. N.W., 20005; (202) 775-0158. Stephen (Steve) Balkam, Chief Executive Officer. General email, fosi@fosi.org*

Web, www.fosi.org and Twitter, @FOSI

Membership: Internet safety advocates in business, government, academia, the media, and the general public. Identifies risks to children on the Internet; develops and promotes solutions for keeping children safe while protecting free speech. Issues reports on online trends among young people; hosts conferences and other educational events; monitors legislation and regulations internationally. Offices in Washington, D.C., and London.

IDEAlliance, *1800 Diagonal Rd., #320, Alexandria, VA 22314-2862; (703) 837-1070. Fax, (703) 837-1072. Timothy Baechle, Chief Executive Officer.*
General email, info@idealliance.org

Web, www.idealliance.org, Twitter, @Idealliance and Facebook, www.facebook.com/IdeallianceUS

Membership: firms and customers in the visual communications industry, including content and media creators, print and digital service providers, material suppliers, and technology partners. Helps set industry standards for electronic and Web commerce and conducts studies on new information technologies.

Internet Coalition, *1615 L St. N.W., #1100, 20036; (802) 279-3534. Tammy Cota, Executive Director.*
Web, www.theinternetcoalition.com

Membership: companies involved in the online industry, including marketing agencies, consulting and research organizations, entrepreneurs, financial institutions, interactive service providers, software vendors, telecommunications companies, and service bureaus. Promotes consumer confidence and trust in the Internet and monitors the effect of public policy on the Internet and its users with a focus on privacy, taxation, intellectual property, online security, unsolicited email, and content regulation.

Internet Education Foundation, *1440 G St. N.W., 20005; (202) 638-4370. Fax, (202) 637-0968. Tim Lordan, Executive Director.*
General email, tlordan@neted.org

Web, www.neted.org

Sponsors educational initiatives promoting the Internet as a valuable medium for democratic participation, communications, and commerce. Funds the Congressional Internet Caucus Advisory Committee, which works to inform Congress of important Internet-related policy issues. Monitors legislation and regulations.

Internet Engineering Task Force (IETF), *c/o Internet Society (ISOC), 11710 Plaza America Dr., St. 400, Reston, VA 20190-5108; (703) 439-2133. Fax, (703) 326-9881. Portia Wenze-Danley, Administrative Director (Acting).*
General email, iad@ietf.org

Web, www.ietf.org

Membership: network designers, operators, vendors, and researchers from around the world who are concerned with the evolution, smooth operation, and continuing development of the Internet. Establishes working groups to address technical concerns. IETF is an organized activity of the Internet Society. (Headquarters in Fremont, Calif.)

Internet Society (ISOC), *11710 Plaza America Dr., St. 400, Reston, VA 20190-5108; (703) 439-2120. Fax, (703) 326-9881. Andrew Sullivan, President.*
General email, media@isoc.org

Web, www.internetsociety.org, Twitter, @internetsociety and Facebook, www.facebook.com/InternetSociety

Membership: individuals, corporations, nonprofit organizations, and government agencies. Focused on ensuring that the Internet continues to evolve as an open platform for innovation, collaboration, and economic development. Engages in a wide spectrum of Internet issues, including policy, governance, technology, and development and availability of the Internet. Conducts research and educational programs; provides information about the Internet.

National Research Council (NRC), *Computer Science and Telecommunications Board, Keck Center, 500 5th St. N.W., 20001; (202) 334-2605. Fax, (202) 334-2318. Farnam Jahanian, Chair; Jon Eisenberg, Director, (202) 334-2605.*
General email, cstb@nas.edu

Web, http://sites.nationalacademies.org/CSTB

Advises the federal government on technical and public policy issues relating to computing and communications. Research includes computer science, cybersecurity, privacy, the Internet, and electronic voting and voter registration.

Pew Research Center, *Internet, Science, and Technology Project, 1615 L St. N.W., #800, 20036; (202) 419-4300. Fax, (202) 419-8562. Lee Rainie, Director.*
Web, www.pewinternet.org and Twitter, @PewInternet

Conducts research, surveys, and analyses to explore the impact of the Internet on families, communities, teens, education, health care, mobile technologies, and civic and political life. Makes its reports available online for public and academic use. (A project of the Pew Research Center.)

Public Knowledge, *1818 N St. N.W., #410, 20036; (202) 861-0020. Fax, (202) 861-0040. Gene Kimmelman, President, ext. 117.*
General email, pk@publicknowledge.org

Web, www.publicknowledge.org and Twitter, @publicknowledge

Coalition of libraries, educators, scientists, artists, musicians, journalists, lawyers, and consumers interested in intellectual property law and technology policy as it pertains to the Internet and electronic information. Encourages openness, access, and competition in the digital age. Supports U.S. laws and policies that provide incentives to innovators as well as ensure a free flow of information and ideas to the public.

StaySafeOnline.org/National Cyber Security Alliance, *1010 Vermont Ave. N.W., #821, 20005; (202) 570-7431. Kevin Coleman, Executive Director.*
General email, info@staysafeonline.org

Web, www.staysafeonline.org and Twitter, @StaySafeOnline

Public-private partnership that promotes computer safety and responsible online behavior. Designated by the Homeland Security Dept. to provide tools and resources to help home users, small businesses, and schools stay safe online. Online resources include tips, a self-guided cyber security test and checklist, and educational materials.

The Telework Coalition (TelCoa), *204 East St. N.E., 20002; (202) 266-0046. Fax, (202) 465-3776. Chuck Wilsker, President.*

General email, info@telcoa.org

Web, www.telcoa.org and *Twitter, @telcoa*

Promotes telework and access to broadband services to increase productivity and provide employment opportunities for disabled, rural, and older workers, while reducing vehicular travel and energy use. Monitors legislation and regulations.

MEDIA PROFESSIONS AND RESOURCES

General

▶**AGENCIES**

Federal Communications Commission (FCC), Communications Business Opportunities, *445 12th St. S.W., #4A624, 20554; (202) 418-0990. Fax, (202) 418-0235. Sanford S. Williams, Director.*
General email, ocboinfo@fcc.gov

Web, www.fcc.gov/communications-business-opportunities

Provides technical and legal guidance and assistance to the small, minority, and female business communities in the telecommunications industry. Advises the FCC chair on small, minority, and female business issues. Serves as liaison between federal agencies, state and local governments, and trade associations representing small, minority, and female enterprises concerning FCC policies, procedures, rulemaking activities, and increased ownership and employment opportunities.

Federal Communications Commission (FCC), *Media Bureau (MB), Policy Division, Equal Employment Opportunity, 445 12th St. S.W., #3A738, 20554; (202) 418-1450. Fax, (202) 418-1797. Lewis Pulley, Assistant Chief, (202) 418-2120.*
Web, www.fcc.gov/general/equal-employment-opportunity

Responsible for the annual certification of cable television equal employment opportunity compliance. Oversees broadcast employment practices.

National Endowment for the Arts (NEA), *Media Arts, 400 7th St. S.W., 20506; (202) 682-5452. Fax, (202) 682-5721. Jax Deluca, Director, (202) 682-5742. TTY, (202) 682-5496. Web, www.arts.gov/artistic-fields/media-arts*

Awards grants to nonprofit organizations for screen-based projects presented by film, television, video, radio, Internet, mobile technologies, video games, transmedia storytelling, and satellite; supports film and video exhibitions and workshops.

▶**NONGOVERNMENTAL**

Alicia Patterson Foundation, *1100 Vermont Ave. N.W., #900, 20005; (202) 393-5995. Fax, (301) 951-8512. Margaret Engel, Executive Director.*

General email, info@aliciapatterson.org

Web, www.aliciapatterson.org and *Facebook, www.facebook.com/AliciaPattersonFoundation*

Awards fellowships and grants to professional journalists to pursue independent projects of significant interest or continue projects based on their previous investigative work for *The APF Reporter*, a web magazine published by the Foundation.

American News Women's Club, *1607 22nd St. N.W., 20008; (202) 332-6770. Fax, (202) 265-6092. Janis Lamar, President.*
General email, anwclub@comcast.net

Web, www.anwc.org and *Twitter, @NewsWomensClub*

Membership: women in communications. Promotes the advancement of women in all media. Sponsors professional receptions and lectures.

Audiovisual and Integrated Experience Assn. (AVIXA), *11242 Waples Mill Rd., #200, Fairfax, VA 22030; (703) 273-7200. Fax, (703) 278-8082. David Labuskes, Chief Executive Officer. Information, (800) 659-7469.*
General email, membership@avixa.org

Web, www.avixa.org, Twitter, @AVIXA and *Facebook, www.facebook.com/TheAVIXA*

Membership: video and audiovisual dealers, manufacturers and producers, and individuals. Promotes the professional AV communications industry and seeks to enhance members' ability to conduct business successfully through trade shows, education, certification, standards, market research, and government relations. Monitors legislation and regulations. (Formerly Info Comm International.)

Center for Public Integrity, *910 17th St. N.W., #700, 20006; (202) 466-1300. Fax, (202) 466-1102. Jim Morris, Chief Executive Officer (Acting). Media, (202) 481-1205. Web, www.publicintegrity.org, Twitter, @Publici Press, media@publicintegrity.org*

Nonpartisan organization that seeks to produce original investigative journalism on significant issues in the United States and around the world. Organizes and supports investigative journalists committed to transparent and comprehensive reporting. Interests include the environment, public health, public accountability, federal and state lobbying, war profiteering, and financial disclosure.

Communications Workers of America (CWA), *501 3rd St. N.W., 20001; (202) 434-1100. Fax, (202) 434-1279. Christopher M. Shelton, President.*
Web, https://cwa-union.org and *Twitter, @CWAUnion*

Membership: approximately 700,000 workers in telecommunications, journalism, publishing, cable television, electronics, and other fields. Interests include workplace democracy and restoring bargaining rights. Represents members in contract negotiations and grievances; conducts training programs and workshops. Monitors legislation and regulations. (Affiliated with the AFL-CIO.)

Freedom Forum, *555 Pennsylvania Ave. N.W., 20001; (202) 292-6290. Fax, (202) 292-6148. Jan Neuharth, Chief Executive Officer. Toll-free, (888) 639-7386.*
Web, www.freedomforum.org

Sponsors training and research that promote free press, free speech, and freedom of information. Interests include the First Amendment and newsroom diversity. Part of the Freedom Forum Insitute.

The Fuller Project for International Reporting, *1875 Connecticut Ave. N.W., 10th Floor, 20009; Xanthe Scharff, Executive Director.*
General email, info@fullerproject.org
Web, http://fullerproject.org, Twitter, @fullerproject and Facebook, www.facebook.com/FullerProject

Acts as advocate the advancement of women in journalism, photography, filmmaking, and other media professions globally. Acts as advocate and delivers independent investigative articles and videos including political, economic, and military-related content. (Headquarters in Instanbul, Turkey.)

Fund for Investigative Journalism, *529 14th St. N.W., 13th Floor, 20045; (202) 662-7564. Sandy Bergo, Executive Director.*
General email, fundfij@gmail.com
Web, www.fij.org, Twitter, @fundFIJ and Facebook, www.facebook.com/FundFIJ

Provides investigative reporters working outside the protection and backing of major news organizations with grants to cover the expenses of investigative pieces involving corruption, malfeasance, incompetence, and domestic and international societal ills.

International Center for Journalists (ICFJ), *2000 M St. N.W., #250, 20036; (202) 737-3700. Fax, (202) 737-0530. Joyce Barnathan, President.*
General email, editor@icfj.org
Web, www.icfj.org, Twitter, @ICFJ and Facebook, www.facebook.com/ICFJ.org

Fosters international freedom of the press through hands-on training, workshops, seminars, online courses, fellowships, and international exchanges. Offers online mentoring and consulting; publishes media training manuals in various languages.

International Women's Media Foundation (IWMF), *1625 K St. N.W., #1275, 20006; (202) 496-1992. Fax, (202) 496-1977. Elisa Lees Muñoz, Executive Director; Charlotte Fox, Director of Communications.*
General email, info@iwmf.org
Web, http://iwmf.org, Twitter, @IWMF and Facebook, www.facebook.com/IWMFpage

Conducts reporting trips and safety training for women journalists, acts as advocate on behalf of women journalists who work under adverse conditions, and makes grants to support women journalists in their projects and endeavors worldwide.

J-Lab: The Institute for Interactive Journalism, *(202) 255-2571. Jan Schaffer, Executive Director.*
General email, jans@j-lab.org
Web, www.j-lab.org, Twitter, @jlab, Twitter, @janjlab and Facebook, www.facebook.com/InstituteforInteractiveJournalizm

Develops research and discrete projects around new ideas to help journalists and citizens engage in public life. Projects include community news startups, innovations in journalism, news entrepreneurship, participatory and civic journalism, training, and publications.

National Assn. of Black Journalists (NABJ), *1100 Knight Hall, #3100, College Park, MD 20742; (301) 405-0248. Fax, (301) 314-1714. Drew Berry, Executive Director.*
General email, drewnabj@gmail.com
Web, www.nabj.org

Membership: African American students and media professionals. Works to increase recognition and career advancement of minority journalists, to expand opportunities for minority students entering the field, and to promote balanced coverage of the African American community. Sponsors scholarships, internship program, and annual convention.

National Assn. of Government Communicators (NAGC), *201 Park Washington Court, Falls Church, VA 22046-4527; (703) 538-1787. Fax, (703) 241-5603. Dara Rudick, Executive Director (Acting), (703) 834-5550, ext. 100.*
General email, info@nagc.com
Web, https://nagc.com and Twitter, @NAGC

National network of federal, state, and local government communications employees. Provides professional development through public meetings, exhibitions, workshops, and formal courses of instruction. Promotes high standards for the government communications profession and recognizes noteworthy service.

National Assn. of Hispanic Journalists (NAHJ), *1050 Connecticut Ave., 5th Floor, 20036; (202) 853-7760. Fax, (202) 662-7144. Alberto B. Mendoza, Executive Director, (202) 853-7754.*
General email, nahj@nahj.org
Web, www.nahj.org and Twitter, @NAHJ

Membership: professional journalists, educators, students, and others interested in encouraging and supporting the study and practice of journalism and communications by Hispanics. Promotes fair representation and treatment of Hispanics by the media. Provides professional development and computerized job referral service; compiles and updates national directory of Hispanics in the media; sponsors national high school essay contest, journalism awards, and scholarships.

National Federation of Press Women (NFPW), *P.O. Box 3007, Mechanicsville, VA 23116 (mailing address: P.O. Box 5556, Arlington, VA 22205); (804) 746-1033. Fax, (804) 335-1296. Marianne Wolf-Astrauskas, President.*
General email, info@nfpw.org
Web, www.nfpw.org

Membership: communications professionals, both men and women. Provides professional development opportunities for members, including an annual conference.

Media Contacts in Washington, D.C.

MAGAZINES

The Atlantic, 600 New Hampshire Ave. N.W., 20037;
(202) 266-6000

CQ Roll Call Magazine, 77 K St. N.E., 20002-4681;
(202) 650-6500

National Journal, 600 New Hampshire Ave. N.W., 20037;
(202) 266-7900

U.S. News & World Report, 1050 Thomas Jefferson St. N.W.,
4th Floor, 20007; (202) 955-2225

NEWS SERVICES

Agence France-Presse, 1500 K St. N.W., #600, 20005;
(202) 414-0600

Associated Press, 1100 13th St. N.W., #500, 20005;
(202) 641-9000; mediarelations@ap.org

McClatchy, 700 12th St. N.W., #1000, 20005; (202) 383-6000

Reuters, 1333 H St. N.W., #510, 20005; (202) 898-8300

United Press International, 1133 19th St. N.W., #800,
20036; (202) 898-8000

Washington Post News Services & Syndicate, 1301 K St. N.
W., 20071; (202) 334-7666

NEWSPAPERS

New York Times, 1627 Eye St. N.W., #700, 20006;
(202) 862-0300

USA Today, 1575 Eye St. N.W., #350, 20005; (703) 854-6000

Wall Street Journal, 1025 Connecticut Ave. N.W., #800,
20036; (202) 862-9200

Washington City Paper, 734 15th St. N.W., 20005;
(202) 332-2100

Washington Post, 1301 K St. N.W., 20071; (202) 334-6000

Washington Times, 3600 New York Ave. N.E., 20002;
(202) 636-3000

TELEVISION/RADIO NETWORKS

ABC News, 1717 DeSales St. N.W., 20036;
(202) 222-7700

CBS News, 2020 M St. N.W., 20036; (202) 457-4385

CNN, 820 1st St. N.E., 20002; (202) 898-7900

C-SPAN, 400 N. Capitol St. N.W., #650, 20001;
(202) 737-3220

Fox News, 400 N. Capitol St. N.W., #550, 20001;
(202) 824-6300

National Public Radio, 1111 N. Capitol St. N.E., 20002;
(202) 513-2000

NBC News, 4001 Nebraska Ave. N.W., 20016; (202) 885-4111

Public Broadcasting Service, 2100 Crystal Dr., Arlington,
VA 22202; (703) 739-5000

Advocates freedom of the press. Provides cost-effective libel insurance. Monitors legislation and regulations.

National Hispanic Foundation for the Arts (NHFA), *Washington Square, 1050 Connecticut Ave. N.W., 10th Floor, #500, 20036; (202) 293-8330. Fax, (202) 772-3101. Felix Sanchez, Chair.*
General email, info@hispanicarts.org
Web, www.hispanicarts.org and Twitter, @felix_sanchez

Strives to increase the presence of Hispanics in the media, telecommunications, entertainment industries, and performing arts, and to increase programming for the U.S. Latino community. Provides scholarships for Hispanic students to pursue graduate study in the arts.

National Journalism Center, *11480 Commerce Park Dr., #600, Reston, VA 20191; (703) 318-9608. Fax, (703) 318-9122. Elizabeth Donatelli, Executive Director.*
Toll-free, (800) 872-1776.
Web, www.nationaljournalismcenter.org

Sponsors a comprehensive internship program in journalism composed of a series of training seminars that enhance students' knowledge of policy reporting in the areas of economics, education, and business. (Affiliated with Young America's Foundation.)

National Lesbian and Gay Journalists Assn. (NLGJA), *2120 L St. N.W., #850, 20037; (202) 588-9888. Jen Christensen, President.*
General email, info@nlgja.org
Web, www.nlgja.org

Membership: journalists, media professionals, educators, and students working in the news industry. Promotes fair and accurate coverage of lesbian, gay, bisexual, and transgender issues; offers professional development resources; hosts a national conference.

National Press Club, *529 14th St. N.W., 13th Floor, 20045; (202) 662-7500. Fax, (202) 662-7537. Andrea Edney, President. Library and Research Center, (202) 662-7523.*
General email, info@press.org
Web, www.press.org, Twitter, @pressclubdc and Facebook, www.facebook.com/PressClubDC

Membership: reporters, editors, writers, publishers, cartoonists, producers, librarians, and teachers of journalism at all levels. Interests include advancement of professional standards and skills, and the promotion of free expression. Provides networking opportunities and manages an online job listing site for members. Library available to members for research.

National Press Foundation (NPF), *1211 Connecticut Ave. N.W., #310, 20036; (202) 663-7280. Fax, (202) 530-2855. Sandy Johnson, President.*
General email, npf@nationalpress.org
Web, www.nationalpress.org and Twitter, @natpress

Works to enhance the professional competence of journalists through in-career education projects. Sponsors conferences, seminars, fellowships, and awards; conducts public forums and international exchanges. Supports the National Press Club library.

Congressional News Media Galleries

The congressional news media galleries serve as liaisons between members of Congress and their staffs and accredited newspaper, magazine, and broadcasting correspondents. The galleries provide facilities for covering activities of Congress, and gallery staff members ensure that congressional press releases reach appropriate correspondents. Independent committees of correspondents working through the press galleries are responsible for accreditation of correspondents.

House Periodical Press Gallery, H304 CAP, Washington, DC 20515; (202) 225-2941. Robert M. Zatkowski, Director.

House Press Gallery, H315 CAP, Washington, DC 20515; (202) 225-3945. Annie Tin, Director.

House Radio and Television Gallery, H320 CAP, Washington, DC 20515; (202) 225-5214. Olga Ramirez Kornacki, Director.

Press Photographers Gallery, S317 CAP, Washington, DC 20510; (202) 224-6548. Jeffrey S. Kent, Director.

Senate Periodical Press Gallery, S320 CAP, Washington, DC 20510; (202) 224-0265. Justin Wilson, Director.

Senate Press Gallery, S316 CAP, Washington, DC 20510; (202) 224-0241. Laura Lytle, Director.

Senate Radio and Television Gallery, S325 CAP, Washington, DC 20510; (202) 224-6421. Michael Mastrian, Director.

The Newspaper Guild—CWA, 501 3rd St. N.W., 6th Floor, 20001-2797; (202) 434-7177. Fax, (202) 434-1472. Bernard J. Lunzer, President. General email, guild@cwa-union.org

Web, www.newsguild.org, Twitter, @news_guild and Facebook, www.facebook.com/NewsGuild

Membership: journalists, sales and media professionals. Advocates higher standards in journalism; equal employment opportunity in the print, broadcast, wire, and Web media industries; and advancement of members' economic interests. (Affiliated with Communications Workers of America, the AFL-CIO, CLC, and IFJ.)

Pew Research Center, *Journalism and Media Project,* 1615 L St. N.W., #800, 20036; (202) 419-3650. Fax, (202) 419-3699. Amy Mitchell, Director. Press, (202) 419-3650. General email, journalism@pewresearch.org

Web, www.journalism.org and Twitter, @PewJournalism

Evaluates and studies the performance of the press, particularly content analysis using empirical research to quantify what is occurring in the press. Tracks key industry trends. Publishes a daily digest of media news and an annual report on American journalism. (Formerly Project for Excellence in Journalism.)

Society for Technical Communication (STC), 9401 Lee Hwy., #300, Fairfax, VA 22031; (703) 522-4114. Fax, (703) 522-2075. Liz Pohland, Chief Executive Officer; Claudia Ventura, Education Manager.

General email, stc@stc.org

Web, www.stc.org and Twitter, @stc_org

Membership: writers, publishers, educators, editors, illustrators, and others involved in technical communication. Encourages research and develops training programs; aids educational institutions in devising curricula; awards scholarships.

Washington Press Club Foundation, *National Press Club Bldg., 529 14th St. N.W., #1115, 20045; (202) 393-0613. Fax, (202) 662-7040. Deirdre Walch, President.* General email, wpcf@wpcf.org

Web, www.wpcf.org

Seeks to advance professionalism in journalism. Sponsors programs and events to educate students and the public on the role of a free press. Awards paid internships for minorities in D.C.–area newsrooms. Administers an oral history of women in journalism. Sponsors annual Congressional Dinner to welcome Congress back into session.

White House Correspondents' Assn., *600 New Hampshire Ave. N.W., #800, 20037; (202) 266-7453. Fax, (202) 266-7454. Steven Thomma, Executive Director.* General email, director@whca.press

Web, www.whca.net and Twitter, @whca

Membership: reporters with permanent White House press credentials. Acts as a liaison between reporters and White House staff. Sponsors annual WHCA Journalism Awards and Scholarships fund-raising dinner.

Women in Film and Video (WIFV), *4000 Albemarle St. N.W., #305, 20016; (202) 429-9438. Fax, (202) 429-9440. Melissa Houghton, Executive Director.* General email, director@wifv.org

Web, www.wifv.org and Twitter, @WIFVDC

Membership organization dedicated to promoting equal employment opportunities and advancing career development and achievement for women working in all areas of screen-based media and related disciplines.

Women's Institute for Freedom of the Press, *1940 Calvert St. N.W., 20009-1502; (202) 656-0893. Martha Leslie Allen, Director.* General email, mediademocracy@wifp.org

Web, www.wifp.org and Twitter, @WIFP

Conducts research and publishes in areas of communications and the media that are of particular interest to women. Promotes freedom of the press. Publishes a free online directory of media produced by and for women. Partners with the Global Woman PEACE Foundation.

Accreditation in Washington

▶ **AGENCIES**

Defense Dept. (DoD), *Public Affairs,* The Pentagon, #2D961, 20301-1400; (703) 571-3343. Fax, (703) 697-3501. Charles Summers, Assistant to the Secretary of Defense for Public Affairs. Press, (703) 697-5131. Web, www.defense.gov/news

Selects staff of accredited Washington-based media organizations by lottery for rotating assignments with the National Media Pool. Correspondents must be familiar with U.S. military affairs, be available on short notice to deploy to the site of military operations, and adhere to pool ground rules. Issues Pentagon press passes to members of the press regularly covering the Pentagon.

Metropolitan Police Dept., *Office of Communications,* 300 Indiana Ave. N.W., #5126, 20001; (202) 727-4383. Fax, (202) 727-4822. Dustin Sternbeck, Director.
General email, mpd.press@dc.gov
Web, www.mpdc.dc.gov

Serves as connection between the media and the police department.

National Park Service (NPS) *(Interior Dept.),* **National Capital Region,** 1100 Ohio Dr. S.W., 20242; (202) 619-7020. Lisa Mendelson-Ielmini, Regional Director. Permits, (202) 245-4715.
Web, www.nps.gov/ncro

Regional office that administers national parks, monuments, historic sites, and recreation areas in the Washington metropolitan area. Issues special permits required for commercial filming on public park lands. News media representatives covering public events that take place on park lands must notify the Office of Public Affairs and Tourism in advance. A White House, Capitol Hill, metropolitan police, or other policy-agency-issued press pass is required in some circumstances. Commercial filming on park lands requires a special-use permit.

State Dept., *Public Affairs, Foreign Press Centers,* 529 14th St. N.W., #800, 20045; (202) 504-6300. Fax, (202) 504-6334. Benjamin Weber, Director; Martha Klinck, Deputy Director, (202) 504-6354.
Web, https://fpc.state.gov *and Twitter,* @ForeignPressCtr

Provides foreign journalists with access to news sources, including wire services and daily briefings from the White House, State Dept., and Pentagon. Holds live news conferences. Foreign journalists wishing to use the center should check the website for information on what documents to present for admission.

State Dept., *Public Affairs, Press Relations,* 2201 C St. N.W., #2109, 20520-6180; (202) 647-2492.
Robert J. Greenan, Director.
General email, PAPressDuty@state.gov
Web, www.state.gov/media

Each U.S. journalist seeking a long-term building pass must apply in person with a letter from his or her editor or publisher, two application forms (available from the press office), and proof of citizenship. In addition, foreign correspondents need a letter from the embassy of the country in which their organization is based. Applicants should allow three months for security clearance. Members of the press wishing to attend an individual briefing must present a U.S. government-issued photo ID, a media-issued photo ID, or a letter from their employer and photo ID.

White House, *Press Office,* White House, 1600 Pennsylvania Ave. N.W., 20502; (202) 456-2580. Fax, (202) 456-3347. Sarah Huckabee Sanders, Press Secretary. Comments and information, (202) 456-1111. TTY, (202) 456-6213.
General email, whopress@who.eop.gov
Web, www.whitehouse.gov
Briefing Room, http://whitehouse.gov/briefing-room/press-briefings
White House blog, http://whitehouse.gov/blog

Journalists seeking permanent accreditation must meet four criteria. The journalist must be a designated White House correspondent and expected to cover the White House daily; must be accredited by the House and Senate press galleries; must be a resident of the Washington, D.C., area; and must be willing to undergo the required Secret Service background investigation. A journalist's editor, publisher, or employer must write to the press office requesting accreditation. Freelance journalists, cameramen, or technicians wishing temporary accreditation must send letters from at least two news organizations indicating the above criteria.

▶ CONGRESS

House Periodical Press Gallery, H304 CAP, 20515; (202) 225-2941. Robert M. Zatkowski, Director.
General email, periodical.press@mail.house.gov
Web, http://periodical.house.gov

Open by application to periodical correspondents whose chief occupation is gathering and reporting news for periodicals not affiliated with lobbying or membership organizations. Accreditation with the House Gallery covers accreditation with the Senate Gallery. Rotates credentialing duties with the House Periodical Press Gallery every two years.

Senate Periodical Press Gallery, S320CAP, 20510; (202) 224-0265. Fax, (202) 228-3480. Justin Wilson, Director.
General email, periodicals@saa.senate.gov
Web, www.periodicalpress.senate.gov/accreditation

Open by application to periodical correspondents whose chief occupation is gathering and reporting news for periodicals not affiliated with lobbying or membership organizations. Accreditation with the House Gallery covers accreditation with the Senate Gallery. Rotates credentialing duties with the House Periodical Press Gallery every four years.

Senate Press Gallery, S320 CAP, 20004; (202) 224-0241. Fax, (202) 228-1142. Laura Lytle, Director.
General email, Senate_Press_Gallery@SAA.Senate.gov
Web, www.dailypress.senate.gov *and*
Twitter, @SenatePress

Handles accreditation for daily newspapers, wire services, and online publications that cover Congress. Assists correspondents and maintains their access to Senate proceedings.

Senate Radio-Television Gallery, *S325 CAP, 20515; (202) 224-6421. Michael (Mike) Mastrian, Director. General email, senatetvg@saa.senate.gov*

Web, www.radiotv.senate.gov

Determines eligibility for broadcast media credentials in Congress.

►JUDICIARY

Supreme Court of the United States, *1 1st St. N.E., 20543; (202) 479-3000. John G. Roberts Jr., Chief Justice; Kathleen Landin Arberg, Public Information Officer, (202) 479-3211. Visitor information, (202) 479-3030. TTY, (202) 479-3472.*

Web, www.supremecourtus.gov

Journalists seeking to cover the Court should be accredited by either the White House or the House or Senate press galleries, but others may apply by submitting a letter from their editors. Contact the public information office to make arrangements.

Broadcasting

►AGENCIES

Broadcasting Board of Governors, *330 Independence Ave. S.W., #3300, 20237; (202) 203-4545. Fax, (202) 203-4585. John F. Lansing, Chief Executive Officer. Locator, (202) 203-4000. Press, (202) 203-4400. General email, publicaffairs@bbg.gov*

Web, www.bbg.gov and Twitter, @BBGov

Established by Congress to supervise all U.S. government nonmilitary international broadcasting, including Voice of America, Radio and TV Martí, Radio Free Europe/Radio Liberty, Radio Free Asia, and the Middle East Broadcasting Networks (MBN). Assesses the quality and effectiveness of broadcasts with regard to U.S. foreign policy objectives; reports annually to the president and to Congress.

Federal Communications Commission (FCC), *Media Bureau (MB), Policy Division, 445 12th St. S.W., 20554; (202) 418-2120. Fax, (202) 418-1069. Martha Heller, Chief. Web, www.fcc.gov/media/policy/policy-division*

Handles complaints and inquiries concerning the equal time rule, which requires equal broadcast opportunities for all legally qualified candidates for the same office, and other political broadcast, cable, and satellite rules. Interprets and enforces related Communications Act provisions, including the requirement for sponsorship identification of all paid political broadcast, cable, and satellite announcements and the requirement for broadcasters to furnish federal candidates with reasonable access to broadcast time for political advertising. Administers Equal Employment Opportunity (EEO) matters.

►NONGOVERNMENTAL

Alliance for Women in Media Foundation, *1250 24th St. N.W., #300, 20037; (202) 750-3664. Becky Brooks, Executive Director.*

General email, info@allwomeninmedia.org

Web, http://allwomeninmedia.org/foundation, Twitter, @AllWomeninMedia and Facebook, www .facebook.com/allwomeninmedia

Membership: professionals in the media and full-time students in accredited colleges and universities. Promotes industry cooperation and advancement of women. Maintains educational programs, charitable activities, public service campaigns, and scholarships. (Headquarters in Lexington, Ky.)

Broadcast Education Assn. (BEA), *1771 N St. N.W., 20036-2891; (202) 602-0587. Fax, (202) 609-9940. Heather Birks, Executive Director, (202) 602-0584. General email, HELP@BEAweb.org*

Web, www.beaweb.org and Twitter, @BEAWebTweets

Membership: universities, colleges, and faculty members offering specialized training in the radio, television, and electronic media industries. Promotes improvement of curriculum and teaching methods. Fosters working relationships among academics, students, and professionals in the industry. Interests include documentaries, international business and regulatory practices, gender issues, interactive media and emerging technologies, and electronic media law and policy. Administers scholarships in the field.

National Academy of Television Arts and Sciences (NATAS), *National Capital Chesapeake Bay Chapter Office, 11130 Sunrise Valley Dr., #350, Reston, VA 20191; (703) 234-4055. Fax, (703) 435-4390. Carol Wynne, Executive Director.*

General email, info@capitalemmys.org

Web, www.capitalemmys.tv and Twitter, @capitalemmys

Membership: professionals in television and related fields and students in communications. Serves the Virginia, Maryland, and Washington, D.C., television community. Works to upgrade television programming; awards scholarships to junior, senior, or graduate students in communications. Sponsors annual Emmy Awards. (Headquarters in New York.)

National Assn. of Black Owned Broadcasters (NABOB), *1201 Connecticut Ave. N.W., #200, 20036; (202) 463-8970. Fax, (202) 429-0657. James L. Winston, President. General email, info@nabob.org*

Web, www.nabob.org

Membership: minority owners and employees of radio and television stations and telecommunications properties. Provides members and the public with information on the broadcast industry and the FCC. Provides members with legal and advertising research facilities. Monitors legislation and regulations.

National Assn. of Broadcast Employees and Technicians (NABET-CWA), *501 3rd St. N.W., 6th Floor, 20001; (202) 434-1254. Fax, (202) 434-1426. Charlie Braico, President. General email, nabet@nabetcwa.org*

Web, www.nabetcwa.org and Twitter, @NABETCWA

Membership: commercial broadcast, cable television, and radio personnel. Helps members negotiate pay, benefits, and better working conditions; conducts training programs and workshops. Monitors legislation and regulations. (Broadcast and Cable Television Workers Sector of the Communications Workers of America.)

National Assn. of Broadcasters (NAB), *1771 N St. N.W., 20036; (202) 429-5300. Gordon H. Smith, President. Communications, (202) 429-5350.*
General email, nab@nab.org

Web, www.nab.org and Twitter, @nabtweets

Membership: radio and television broadcast stations and broadcast networks holding an FCC license or construction permit; associate members include producers of equipment and programs. Assists members in areas of management, engineering, and research. Monitors legislation and regulations.

Public Broadcasting Service, *2100 Crystal Dr., Arlington, VA 22202; (703) 739-5000. Fax, (703) 739-0775. Paula Kerger, President, (703) 739-5015; Madhulika Sikka, Public Editor, (703) 739-5290.*
General email, pbs@pbs.org

Web, www.pbs.org and Twitter, @PBS

Membership: public television stations nationwide. Selects, schedules, promotes, and distributes national programs; provides public television stations with educational, instructional, and cultural programming; also provides news and public affairs, science and nature, and children's programming. Assists members with technology development and fund-raising.

Radio Free Asia, *2025 M St. N.W., #300, 20036; (202) 530-4900. Kenneth Weinstein, Chair. Press, (202) 530-4976.*
General email, contact@rfa.org

Web, www.rfa.org and Twitter, @RadioFreeAsia

Independent radio, Internet, and television service funded by federal grants to promote and support democracy where public access to a free press is restricted. Broadcasts programs to East Asian countries, including China, Tibet, North Korea, Vietnam, Cambodia, Laos, and Burma; programming includes news, analysis, and specials on political developments, as well as cultural programs.

Radio Free Europe/Radio Liberty, *Washington Office, 1201 Connecticut Ave. N.W., #400, 20036; (202) 457-6900. Fax, (202) 457-6992. Daisy Sindelar, President (Acting); Nenad Pejic, Vice President; Martins Zvaners, Deputy Director of Communications, 202-457-6918. Press, (202) 457-6948.*
General email, zvanersm@rferl.org

Web, www.rferl.org and Twitter, @RFERL

Independent radio, Internet, and television service funded by federal grants to promote and support democracy. Broadcasts programs to 23 countries, including Russia, Afghanistan, Pakistan, Iraq, Iran, and the republics of Central Asia; programming includes news, analysis, and specials on political developments, as well as cultural

programs. Research materials available to the public by appointment. (Headquarters in Prague, Czech Republic.)

Radio Television Digital News Assn., *529 14th St. N.W., #1240, 20045; (212) 246-0398. Dan Shelley, Executive Director.*
Web, www.rtdna.org and Twitter, @RTDNA

Membership: local and network news executives in broadcasting, cable, and other electronic media in more than thirty countries. Serves as information source for members; provides advice on legislative, political, and judicial problems of electronic journalism; conducts international exchanges.

Senate Radio-Television Gallery, *S325 CAP, 20515; (202) 224-6421. Michael (Mike) Mastrian, Director.*
General email, senatetvg@saa.senate.gov

Web, www.radiotv.senate.gov

Membership: broadcast correspondents who cover Congress. Sponsors annual dinner. Acts as a liaison between congressional offices and members of the media, and facilitates broadcast coverage of Senate activities.

Voice of America *(International Broadcasting Bureau), 330 Independence Ave. S.W., 20237; (202) 203-4000. Fax, (202) 203-4960. Amanda Bennett, Director.*
General email, askvoa@voanews.com

Web, www.voanews.com and Twitter, @VOAnews

A multimedia international broadcasting service funded by the U.S. government through the Broadcasting Board of Governors. Broadcasts news, information, educational, and cultural programming to an estimated worldwide audience of more than 134 million people weekly. Programs are produced in more than forty languages.

Walter Kaitz Foundation, *25 Massachusetts Ave. N.W., #100, 20001; (202) 222-2490. Fax, (202) 222-2491. Michelle A. Ray Jr., Executive Director. Press, (202) 222-2350.*
General email, info@walterkaitz.org

Web, www.walterkaitz.org and Twitter, @WalterKaitz

Nonprofit that promotes women, minorities, and veterans working in the media and telecommunications industry. Financially supports and creates programs that provide internships to minority students, educate women on leadership, and advocate diversity in telecommunications. Awards scholarships to professionals in the media and telecommunications industry.

Press Freedom

▶NONGOVERNMENTAL

Reporters Committee for Freedom of the Press, *1156 15th St. N.W., #1020, 20005; (202) 795-9300. Fax, (202) 795-9310. Bruce D. Brown, Executive Director, (202) 795-9301. Legal defense hotline, (800) 336-4243.*
General email, info@rcfp.org

Web, www.rcfp.org, Twitter, @rcfp

Legal defense hotline email, hotline@rcpf.org

Committee of reporters and editors that provides journalists and media lawyers with a 24-hour hotline for media law and freedom of information questions. Provides assistance to journalists and media lawyers in media law court cases, and to student journalists. Produces publications on newsgathering legal issues. Interests include freedom of speech abroad, primarily as it affects U.S. citizens in the press.

Reporters Without Borders (Reporters Sans Frontières), Washington Office, *Southern Railway Bldg., 1500 K St. N.W., #600, 20005 (mailing address: P.O. Box 34032, Washington, DC 20005); (202) 204-5548. Margaux Ewen, Director for North America.*
General email, dcdesk@rsf.org

Web, https://rsf.org, Twitter, @RSF_RWB

Web, https://rsf.org/en/united-states

Defends journalists who have been imprisoned or persecuted while conducting their work. Works to improve the safety of journalists. Advocates freedom of the press internationally through its offices in 11 countries. Sponsors annual events and awards. (Headquarters in Paris, France.)

Student Press Law Center, *1608 Rhode Island Ave. N.W., #211, 20036; (202) 785-5450. Fax, (202) 822-5045. Hadar Harris, Executive Director.*
General email, admin@splc.org

Web, https://splc.org and Twitter, @SPLC

Collects, analyzes, and distributes information on free expression and freedom of information rights of student journalists (print, online, and broadcast) and on violations of those rights in high schools and colleges. Provides free legal advice and referrals to students and faculty advisers experiencing censorship. (Affiliated with the Reporters Committee for Freedom of the Press.)

Women's Institute for Freedom of the Press, *1940 Calvert St. N.W., 20009-1502; (202) 656-0893. Martha Leslie Allen, Director.*
General email, mediademocracy@wifp.org

Web, www.wifp.org and Twitter, @WIFP

Conducts research and publishes in areas of communications and the media that are of particular interest to women. Promotes freedom of the press. Publishes a free online directory of media produced by and for women. Partners with the Global Woman PEACE Foundation.

Print and Online Media

▶**NONGOVERNMENTAL**

American Press Institute (API), *4401 N. Fairfax Dr., #300, Arlington, VA 22203; (571) 366-1200. Thomas (Tom) Rosenstiel, Executive Director, (571) 366-1035.*
General email, hello@pressinstitute.org

Web, www.americanpressinstitute.org and Twitter, @AmPress

Conducts research and training for journalists. Interests include sustaining a free press, and understanding changing audiences, new revenue models, and best practices for journalism in the digital age.

Assn. Media and Publishing, *1090 Vermont Ave. N.W., 6th Floor, 20005-4905; (703) 234-4063. Fax, (703) 435-4390. Mike Marchesano, Executive Director, (646) 568-1309.*
General email, info@associationmediaandpublishing.com

Web, www.siia.net/amp, Twitter, @AssnMediaPub and Facebook, www.facebook.com/ AssociationMediaandPublishing

Membership: association publishers and communications professionals. Works to develop high standards for editorial and advertising content in members' publications. Compiles statistics; bestows editorial and graphics awards; monitors postal regulations. (Formerly Society of National Assn. Publications.)

Assn. of American Publishers, *Government Affairs, 455 Massachusetts Ave. N.W., #700, 20001; (202) 347-3375. Fax, (202) 347-3690. Allan R. Adler, Vice President of Legal and Government Affairs.*
General email, info@publishers.org

Web, www.publishers.org and Twitter, @AmericanPublish

Membership: U.S. publishers of books, scholarly journals, and multiplatform K–12 and higher education course materials. Represents industry priorities on policy, legislation, and regulatory issues regionally, nationally, and worldwide. Interests include intellectual property rights and copyright protection, tax and trade, new technology, educational and library funding, and First Amendment rights.

CQ Press, *2600 Virginia Ave. N.W., #600, 20037; (202) 729-1800. Fax, (202) 729-1940. Blaise R. Simqu, President. Toll-free, (800) 818-7243.*
General email, orders@sagepub.com

Web, https://us.sagepub.com/en-us/nam/cqpress

Publishes books, directories, periodicals, and online products on U.S. government, history, and politics. Products include *U.S. Political Stats, CQ Press Encyclopedia of American Government,* and *CQ Researcher.* (An imprint of SAGE Publishing; Headquarters in Thousand Oaks, Calif.)

Entertainment Software Assn. (ESA), *601 Massachusetts Ave. N.W., #300, 20001; (202) 223-2400. Vacant, President.*
General email, esa@theesa.com

Web, www.theesa.com and Twitter, @theesa

Membership: publishers of interactive entertainment software. Distributes marketing statistics and information. Administers a worldwide antipiracy program. Established an independent rating system for entertainment software. Monitors legislation and regulations. Interests include First Amendment and intellectual property protection efforts.

Essential Information, *1530 P St. N.W., 20005 (mailing address: P.O. Box 19405, Washington, DC 20036); Fax, (202) 234-5176. John Richard, Executive Director.*
General email, info@essential.org

Web, www.essential.org

Provides writers and the public with information on public policy matters; awards grants to investigative reporters; sponsors conference on investigative journalism. Interests include activities of multinational corporations in developing countries.

Graphic Communications Conference of the International Brotherhood of Teamsters (GCC/IBT), *25 Louisiana Ave. N.W., 20001; (202) 508-6660. Fax, (202) 624-8145. George Tedeschi, President.*
General email, kself@gciu.org

Web, www.gciu.org

Membership: approximately 60,000 members of the print and publishing industries, including lithographers, photoengravers, and bookbinders. Assists members with contract negotiation and grievances; conducts training programs and workshops. Monitors legislation and regulations.

IDEAlliance, *1800 Diagonal Rd., #320, Alexandria, VA 22314-2862; (703) 837-1070. Fax, (703) 837-1072. Timothy Baechle, Chief Executive Officer.*
General email, info@idealliance.org

Web, www.idealliance.org, Twitter, @Idealliance and Facebook, www.facebook.com/IdeallianceUS

Membership: firms and customers in the visual communication industry, including content and media creators, print and digital service providers, material suppliers, and technology partners. Assists members in production of color graphics and conducts studies on print media management methods.

Magazine Publishers of America (MPA), *Government Affairs, 1211 Connecticut Ave. N.W., #610, 20036; (202) 296-7277. Linda Thomas Brooks, President, (212) 872-3710.*
Web, www.magazine.org/advocacy

Membership: publishers of consumer magazines. Washington office represents members in all aspects of government relations in Washington and state capitals. Interests include intellectual property, the First Amendment, consumer protection, advertising, and postal, environmental, and tax policy. (Headquarters in New York.)

National Newspaper Publishers Assn. (NNPA), *1816 12th St. N.W., 2nd Floor, 20009; (202) 588-8764. Fax, (202) 588-8960. Denise Rolark Barnes, Chair; Benjamin Chavis Jr., President.*
General email, info@nnpa.org

Web, www.nnpa.org

Membership: newspapers owned by African Americans serving an African American audience. Assists in improving management and quality of the African American press through workshops and merit awards. Sponsors NNPA Media Services, a print and Web advertising-placement and press release distribution service.

News Media Alliance, *4401 Wilson Blvd., #700, Arlington, VA 22203-1867; (571) 366-1000. Fax, (571) 366-1195. David Chavern, President, (571) 366-1100; Paul Boyle, Senior Vice President of Public Policy, (571) 366-1150. Press, (571) 366-1009.*

General email, info@newsmediaalliance.org

Web, www.newsmediaalliance.org, Twitter, @newsalliance and Facebook, www.facebook.com/NewsMediaAlliance

Membership: daily and weekly newspapers, other papers, and online products published in the United States, Canada, other parts of the Western Hemisphere, and Europe. Conducts research and disseminates information on newspaper publishing, including labor relations, legal matters, government relations, technical problems and innovations, telecommunications, economic and statistical data, marketing, and training programs.

NPES: The Assn. for Suppliers of Printing, Publishing, and Converting Technologies, *1899 Preston White Dr., Reston, VA 20191-4367; (703) 264-7200. Fax, (703) 620-0994. Thayer Long, President; Mark Nuzzaco, Vice President of Government Affairs.*
General email, npes@npes.org

Web, www.printtechnologies.org and Twitter, @apt_tech

Trade association representing companies that manufacture and distribute equipment, supplies, systems, software, and services for printing, publishing, and converting.

Open Markets Institute, *1440 G St. N.W., 20005; (240) 888-1638. Barry C. Lynn, Executive Director.*
General email, info@openmarketsinstitute.org

Web, www.openmarketsinstitute.org, Twitter, @openmarkets and Facebook, www.facebook.com/openmarketsinstitute

Think tank promoting public awareness of political and economic monopolization in the U.S.; identifies changes in policy and law, and promotes open discussion with citizens and policymakers regarding political economic challenges, including fair pricing and antitrust laws.

Printing Industries of America (PIA), *Washington Office, 1325 G St. N.W., #500, 20005; (202) 627-6925. Fax, (202) 730-7987. Lisbeth Lyons, Vice President of Government Affairs, ext. 504.*
General email, llyons@printing.org

Web, www.printing.org and Twitter, @PrintInd

Membership: printing firms and businesses that service printing industries. Represents members before Congress and regulatory agencies. Assists members with labor relations, human resources management, and other business management issues. Sponsors graphic arts competition. Monitors legislation and regulations. (Headquarters in Warrendale, Pa.)

Specialized Information Publishers Assn. (SIPA), *1090 Vermont Ave. N.W., 6th Floor, 20005-4905; (202) 289-7442. Fax, (202) 289-7097. Nancy Brand, Managing Director.*
Web, www.siia.net/Divisions/SIPA-Specialized-Information-Publishers-Association

Membership: newsletter publishers, specialized information services, and vendors to that market. Serves as an information clearinghouse and provides educational resources in the field. Monitors legislation and regulations. Library open to the public. (Division of SIIA; formerly the Newsletter and Electronic Publishers Assn.)

4

Culture and Religion

ARTS AND HUMANITIES

General

▶AGENCIES

Federal Council on the Arts and the Humanities, *400 7th St. S.W., 20506; (202) 682-5541. Fax, (202) 682-5721. Mary Anne Carter, Chair (Acting).*
Web, http://arts.gov/artistic-fields/museums/arts-and-artifacts-indemnity-program-domestic-indemnity

Membership: leaders of federal agencies sponsoring arts-related activities. Administers the Arts and Artifacts Indemnity Act, which helps museums reduce the costs of commercial insurance for traveling exhibits.

General Services Administration (GSA), *Design and Construction, Office of the Chief Architect, 1800 F St. N.W., #5400, 20405-0001; (202) 501-1888. David Insinga, Chief Architect.*
General email, david.insinga@gsa.gov
Web, www.gsa.gov/portal/content/104549

Administers the Art in Architecture Program, which commissions publicly scaled works of art for government buildings and landscapes, and the Fine Arts Program, which manages the GSA's collection of fine artwork that has been commissioned for use in government buildings.

John F. Kennedy Center for the Performing Arts, *2700 F St. N.W., 20566-0001; (202) 416-8000. Fax, (202) 416-8524. Deborah F. Rutter, President, (202) 416-8011; David M. Rubenstein, Chair. Performance and ticket information, (202) 467-4600. Toll-free, (800) 444-1324.*
Web, www.kennedy-center.org

National cultural center created by Congress that operates independently; funded in part by federal dollars but primarily through private gifts and sales. Sponsors educational programs; presents American and international performances in theater, music, dance, and film; sponsors the John F. Kennedy Center Education Program, which produces the annual American College Theater Festival; and presents and subsidizes events for young people. The Kennedy Center stages free daily performances open to the public 365 days a year on its Millennium Stage in the Grand Foyer.

National Endowment for the Arts (NEA), *400 7th St. S.W., 20506; (202) 682-5400. Mary Anne Carter, Chair (Acting), (202) 682-5414; Helen Ferre, Public Affairs Director. Press, (202) 682-5570. TTY, (202) 682-5496.*
General email, webmgr@arts.gov
Web, www.arts.gov, Twitter, @NEAarts and Facebook, www.facebook.com/NationalEndowmentfortheArts

Independent grant-making agency. Awards grants to support artistic excellence, creativity, and innovation for the benefit of individuals and communities. Works through partnerships with state arts agencies, local leaders, other federal agencies, and the philanthropic sector. Main funding categories include Art Works (replaces Access to Artistic Excellence and Learning in the Arts for Children and Youth); Challenge America Fast-Track (for art projects in underserved communities); and Our Town (for art projects that contribute to the livability of communities).

National Endowment for the Arts (NEA), *Artist Communities, 400 7th St. S.W., 20506; (202) 682-5428. Fax, (202) 682-5669. Michael Orlove, Director, (202) 682-5469. TTY, (202) 682-5496.*
Web, www.arts.gov/artistic-fields/artist-communities

Awards grants and provides assistance to artist communities for projects that encourage and nurture the development of individual artists.

National Endowment for the Arts (NEA), *Presenting and Multidisciplinary Arts, 400 7th St. S.W., 20506; (202) 682-5428. Fax, (202) 682-5669. Michael Orlove, Director, (202) 682-5969. TTY, (202) 682-5496.*
Web, www.arts.gov/artistic-fields/presenting-multidisciplinary-works

Awards grants to traditional presenting programs as well as artistic works and events that present multiple disciplines, combine or integrate art forms, explore boundaries between art disciplines, and seek to create new forms of expression.

National Endowment for the Humanities (NEH), *400 7th St. S.W., 20506; Fax, (202) 606-8608. John Parrish Peede, Chair, (202) 606-8310; Donna McClish, Librarian, (202) 606-8244. Information, (202) 606-8400. Library, (202) 606-8244. Public Affairs, (202) 606-8446. Toll-free, 800-NEH-1121. Toll-free TTY, (800) 877-8399.*
General email, questions@neh.gov
Web, www.neh.gov, Twitter, @NEHgov and Facebook, www.facebook.com/neh.gov

Independent federal grant-making agency. Awards grants to individuals and institutions for research, scholarship, and educational and public programs (including broadcasts, museum exhibitions, lectures, and symposia) in the humanities (defined as study of archaeology; history; jurisprudence; language; linguistics; literature; philosophy; comparative religion; ethics; history, criticism, and theory of the arts; and humanistic aspects of the social sciences). Funds preservation of books, newspapers, historical documents, and photographs. Library open by appointment only.

Smithsonian Institution, *International Relations and Global Programs, 1100 Jefferson Dr. S.W., #3123, 20560 (mailing address: P.O. Box 37012, Quad MRC 705, Washington, DC 20013-7012); (202) 633-4795. Fax, (202) 786-2557. Molly Fannon, Director.*
General email, global@si.edu
Web, https://global.si.edu and Twitter, @GlobalSI

Fosters the development and coordinates the international aspects of Smithsonian cultural activities; facilitates basic research in history and art and encourages international collaboration among individuals and institutions.

CULTURE AND RELIGION RESOURCES IN CONGRESS

For a complete listing of congressional committees, including their full contact information, leadership, membership, and jurisdictions, please refer to the Appendix on pages 827–948.

HOUSE:

House Administration Committee, (202) 225-8281.
Web, cha.house.gov
House Agriculture Committee, (202) 225-2171.
Web, agriculture.house.gov
House Appropriations Committee,
  (202) 225-2771.
Web, appropriations.house.gov
  Subcommittee on Interior, Environment, and
    Related Agencies, (202) 225-3081.
  Subcommittee on Labor, Health and Human
    Services, Education, and Related Agencies,
    (202) 225-3508.
  Subcommittee on Legislative Branch,
    (202) 226-7252.
House Education and the Workforce Committee,
  (202) 225-4527.
Web, edworkforce.house.gov
  Subcommittee on Early Childhood,
    Elementary, and Secondary Education,
    (202) 225-4527.
  Subcommittee on Higher Education and
    Workforce Development, (202) 225-4527.
House Energy and Commerce Committee,
  (202) 225-2927.
Web, energycommerce.house.gov
  Subcommittee on Communications and
    Technology, (202) 225-2927.
  Subcommittee on Digital Commerce and
    Consumer Protection, (202) 225-2927.
House Judiciary Committee, (202) 225-3951.
Web, judiciary.house.gov
  Subcommittee on the Constitution and Civil
    Justice, (202) 225-2825.
House Natural Resources Committee,
  (202) 225-2761.
Web, naturalresources.house.gov
  Subcommittee on Indian, Insular, and Alaska
    Native Affairs, (202) 226-9725.
House Science, Space, and Technology Committee,
  (202) 225-6371.
Web, science.house.gov
  Subcommittee on Research and Technology,
    (202) 225-6371.
House Ways and Means Committee,
  (202) 225-3625.
Web, waysandmeans.house.gov

JOINT:

Joint Committee on the Library of Congress,
  (202) 225-8281.
Web, cha.house.gov/jointcommittees/joint-committee-
  library

SENATE:

Senate Agriculture, Nutrition, and Forestry
  Committee, (202) 224-2035.
Web, agriculture.senate.gov
  Subcommittee on Nutrition, Agricultural
    Research, Specialty Crops, (202) 224-2035.
Senate Appropriations Committee,
  (202) 224-7257.
Web, appropriations.senate.gov
  Subcommittee on Interior, Environment, and
    Related Agencies, (202) 228-0774.
  Subcommittee on Labor, Health and Human
    Services, Education, and Related Agencies,
    (202) 224-9145.
Senate Banking, Housing, and Urban Affairs
  Committee, (202) 224-7391.
Web, banking.senate.gov
Senate Commerce, Science, and Transportation
  Committee, (202) 224-1251.
Web, commerce.senate.gov
  Subcommittee on Space, Science, and
    Competitiveness, (202) 224-1251.
Senate Energy and Natural Resources Committee,
  (202) 224-4971.
Web, energy.senate.gov
  Subcommittee on National Parks,
    (202) 224-4971.
Senate Finance Committee, (202) 224-4515.
Web, finance.senate.gov
Senate Health, Education, Labor, and Pensions
  Committee, (202) 224-5375.
Web, help.senate.gov
  Subcommittee on Children and Families,
    (202) 224-5375.
Senate Indian Affairs Committee, (202) 224-2251.
Web, indian.senate.gov
Senate Judiciary Committee, (202) 224-5225.
Web, judiciary.senate.gov
Senate Rules and Administration Committee,
  (202) 224-6352.
Web, rules.senate.gov

U.S. Commission of Fine Arts, *401 F St. N.W., #312, 20001-2728; (202) 504-2200. Fax, (202) 504-2195. Earl A. Powell III, Chair; Thomas Luebke, Secretary, tluebke@cfa.gov.*
General email, cfastaff@cfa.gov
Web, www.cfa.gov, Twitter, @CFA_GOV
Georgetown inquiries, georgetown@cfa.gov

Advises the federal and D.C. governments on matters of art and architecture that affect the appearance of the nation's capital.

► **CONGRESS**

For a listing of relevant congressional committees and sub-committees, please see page 124 or the Appendix.

► **NONGOVERNMENTAL**

Americans for the Arts, *1000 Vermont Ave. N.W., 6th Floor, 20005; (202) 371-2830. Fax, (202) 371-0424. Robert L. Lynch, President.*
General email, info@artsusa.org
Web, www.americansforthearts.org

Membership: groups and individuals promoting advancement of the arts and culture in U.S. communities. Provides information on programs, activities, and administration of local arts agencies; on funding sources and guidelines; and on government policies and programs. Conducts, sponsors, and disseminates research on the social, educational, and economic benefits of arts programs. Monitors legislation and regulations.

Assn. of Performing Arts Presenters, *919 18th St., N.W., #650, 20006; (202) 833-2787. Fax, (202) 833-1543. Mario Garcia Durham, President. Toll-free, (888) 820-2787.*
General email, info@artspresenters.org
Web, www.apap365.org and Twitter, @APAP365

Connects performing artists to audiences and communities around the world. Facilitates the work of presenters, artist managers, and consultants through continuing education, regranting programs, and legislative advocacy.

Federation of State Humanities Councils, *1600 Wilson Blvd., #902, Arlington, VA 22209-2511; (703) 908-9700. Fax, (703) 908-9706. Esther Mackintosh, President.*
General email, info@statehumanities.org
Web, www.statehumanities.org, Twitter, @HumFed and Facebook, www.facebook.com/ FederationofStateHumanitiesCouncils

Membership: humanities councils from U.S. states and territories. Provides members with information; forms partnerships with other organizations and with the private sector to promote the humanities. Monitors legislation and regulations.

National Assembly of State Arts Agencies, *1200 18th St. N.W., #1100, 20036; (202) 347-6352. Fax, (202) 737-0526. Pam Breaux, Chief Executive Officer, (202) 347-6352. TTY, (202) 296-0567.*
General email, nasaa@nasaa-arts.org

Web, www.nasaa-arts.org, Twitter, @NASAA_Arts and Facebook, www.facebook.com/NASAA.Arts

Membership: state and territorial arts agencies. Provides members with information, resources, and representation. Interests include arts programs for rural and underserved populations and the arts as a catalyst for economic development. Monitors legislation and regulations.

National Humanities Alliance, *21 Dupont Circle N.W., #800, 20036; (202) 296-4994. Fax, (202) 872-0884. Stephen Kidd, Executive Director, ext. 149.*
General email, humanities@nhalliance.org
Web, www.nhalliance.org, Twitter, @HumanitiesAll and Facebook, www.facebook.com/ NationalHumanitiesAlliance

Represents scholarly and professional humanities associations; associations of museums, libraries, and historical societies; higher education institutions; state humanities councils; and independent and university-based research centers. Promotes the interests of individuals engaged in research, writing, and teaching.

National Humanities Institute (NHI), *P.O. Box 1387, Bowie, MD 20718-1387; (301) 464-4277. Michael P. Federici, President.*
General email, mail@nhinet.org
Web, www.nhinet.org

Promotes research, publishing, and teaching in the humanities. Interests include the effect of the humanities on society. Publishes *Humanitas* journal.

National League of American Pen Women, *1300 17th St. N.W., 20036-1973; (202) 785-1997. Fax, (202) 452-6868. Evelyn B. Wofford, National President.*
General email, contact@nlapw.org
Web, www.nlapw.org, Twitter, @NLAPW and Facebook, www.facebook.com/NLAPW

Promotes the development of the creative talents of professional women in the fields of art, letters, and music composition. Conducts and promotes literary, educational, and charitable activities. Offers scholarships, workshops, and discussion groups.

Performing Arts Alliance, *1211 Connecticut Ave. N.W., #200, 20036 (mailing address: P.O. Box 33001, 1800 M St. N.W., Washington, DC 20033); (202) 207-3850. Fax, (202) 833-1543. Mario Garcia Durham, Executive Director.*
General email, info@thepaalliance.org
Web, www.theperformingartsalliance.org and Twitter, @PAAlliance

Membership: organizations of the professional, non-profit performing arts and presenting fields. Through legislative and grassroots activities, advocates policies favorable to the performing arts and presenting fields.

Provisions Library Resource Center for Arts and Social Change *(George Mason University), Art and Design Bldg., 4400 University Dr., #L002, MS 1C3, Fairfax, VA 22030; (202) 670-7768. Donald H. Russell, Executive Director.*

General email, provisionslibrary@gmail.com

Web, http://provisionslibrary.com and http://soa.gmu.edu/ provisions and Twitter, @ProvisionsLib

Library collection on politics and culture open to the public by appointment. Offers educational and arts programs concerning social change and social justice.

Wolf Trap Foundation for the Performing Arts, *1645 Trap Rd., Vienna, VA 22182-2064; (703) 255-1900. Fax, (703) 255-1905. Arvind Manocha, President. Press, (703) 255-4096. Tickets, (877) 965-3872. TTY, (703) 255-1849.*

General email, wolftrap@wolftrap.org

Web, www.wolftrap.org and Twitter, @wolf_trap

Established by Congress; operates as a public-private partnership between the National Park Service, which maintains the grounds, and the Wolf Trap Foundation, which sponsors performances in theater, music, and dance. Conducts educational programs for children, internships for college students, career-entry programs for young singers, and professional training for teachers and performers.

Education

▶**AGENCIES**

Education Dept., *Innovation and Improvement (OII), Arts in Education National Program, Lyndon Baines Johnson Bldg., 400 Maryland Ave. S.W., #4W214, 20202-5950; (202) 205-1729. Fax, (202) 205-5630. Michelle Johnson Armstrong, Program Manager. General email, michelle.armstrong@ed.gov*

Web, www2.ed.gov/programs/artsnational

Supports national level arts education projects and programs for children and youth, with special emphasis on serving students from low-income families and students with disabilities.

Education Dept., *Innovation and Improvement (OII), Arts in Education—Model Development and Dissemination, Lyndon Baines Johnson Bldg., 400 Maryland Ave. S.W., #4W210, 20202-5950; (202) 401-3576. Fax, (202) 205-5630. Anna Hinton, Director, (202) 260-1816. Toll-free, (800) 872-5327. General email, artsdemo@ed.gov*

Web, www2.ed.gov/programs/artsedmodel

Supports the development of innovative model programs that integrate and strengthen academic performance in core elementary and middle school curricula and that strengthen arts instruction in those grades. Provides grants to local education agencies and nonprofit art organizations. Funds must be used in elementary and middle schools.

Education Dept., *Innovation and Improvement (OII), Arts in Education—Professional Development for Arts Educators, Lyndon Baines Johnson Bldg., 400 Maryland Ave. S.W., #4W214, 20202-5950; (202) 260-2072. Fax, (202) 205-5630. Michelle Johnson Armstrong, Program Manager, (202) 205-1729.*

General email, Michelle.Armstrong@ed.gov

Web, www2.ed.gov/programs/artsedprofdev

Supports the implementation of high-quality professional development model programs in elementary and secondary education for music, dance, drama, and visual arts educators in high-poverty schools. Funds support innovative instructional methods, especially those linked to scientifically based research that integrate standards-based arts instruction with other core academic content.

John F.Kennedy Center for the Performing Arts, *Education, 2700 F St. N.W., 20566-0001; (202) 416-8854. Fax, (202) 416-8728. Mario Rossero, Vice President. Press, (202) 416-8442.*

General email, kced@kennedy-center.org

Web, www.kennedy-center.org/education

Establishes and supports state committees to encourage arts education in schools; promotes community partnerships between performing arts centers and school systems (Partners in Education); provides teachers, artists, and school and arts administrators with professional development classes; offers in-house and touring performances for students, teachers, families, and the general public; arranges artist and company residencies in schools; sponsors the National Symphony Orchestra education program; presents lectures, demonstrations, and classes in the performing arts for the general public; offers internships in arts management; and produces annually the Kennedy Center American College Theater Festival.

John F.Kennedy Center for the Performing Arts, *National Partnerships, 2700 F St. N.W., 20566-0001; (202) 416-8854. Fax, (202) 416-8728. Jordan LaSalle, Director, (202) 416-8850. Press, (202) 416-8442.*

Web, www.kennedy-center.org/education/partners

Supports arts and education institutions throughout the nation by building their capacity to develop and sustain robust arts education programs. Through its two national networks—*Ensuring the Arts for Any Given Child* and *Partners in Education*—it provides professional learning, national peer networking opportunities, and other resources.

National Endowment for the Arts (NEA), *Arts Education, 400 7th St. S.W., 20506; (202) 682-5707. Fax, (202) 682-5002. Ayanna N. Hudson, Director, (202) 682-5515. TTY, (202) 682-5496.*

General email, artseducation@arts.gov

Web, www.arts.gov/artistic-fields/arts-education

Provides grants for curriculum-based arts education for children and youth (generally between ages 5 and 18) in schools or other community-based settings. Projects must provide participatory learning that engages students with accomplished artists and teachers, align with national or state arts education standards, and include assessments of participant learning. Also provides funding to support professional development opportunities for teachers, teaching artists, and other educators.

National Endowment for the Humanities (NEH), *Digital Humanities, 400 7th St. S.W., 20506; (202) 606-8401. Fax, (202) 606-8411. Brett Bobley, Director.*

General email, odh@neh.gov

Web, www.neh.gov/divisions/odh and Twitter, @NEH_ODH

Encourages and supports projects that utilize or study the impact of digital technology on research, education, preservation, access, and public programming in the humanities.

National Endowment for the Humanities (NEH), *Education Programs,* 400 7th St. S.W., 20506; (202) 606-8500. Fax, (202) 606-8394. Carol Peters, Director, (202) 606-8285.

General email, education@neh.gov

Web, www.neh.gov/divisions/education and Twitter, @NEH_Education

Supports the improvement of education in the humanities. Supports classroom resources and faculty training and development.

National Endowment for the Humanities (NEH), *Public Programs,* 400 7th St. S.W., 20506; (202) 606-8269. Fax, (202) 606-8557. Anne-Imelda, Director, (202) 606-8631.

General email, publicpgms@neh.gov

Web, www.neh.gov/divisions/public

Awards grants to libraries, museums, special projects, and media for projects that enhance public appreciation and understanding of the humanities through books and other resources in American library collections. Projects include conferences, exhibitions, essays, documentaries, radio programs, and lecture series.

National Endowment for the Humanities (NEH), *Research Programs,* 400 7th St. S.W., 20506; (202) 606-8200. Fax, (202) 606-8558. Christopher P. Thornton, Director, (202) 606-8286.

General email, research@neh.gov

Web, www.neh.gov/divisions/research

Sponsors fellowship programs for humanities scholars, including summer stipend programs. Provides support to libraries, museums, and independent centers for advanced study.

National Gallery of Art, *Education,* 6th St. and Constitution Ave. N.W., 20565 (mailing address: 2000B S. Club Dr., Landover, MD 20785); (202) 842-6706. Fax, (202) 842-6935. Majorie Johnson, Museum Educator.

General email, EdResources@nga.gov

Web, www.nga.gov/education

Serves as an educational arm of the gallery by providing free programs for schools, families, and adults. Lends audiovisual educational materials free of charge to schools, colleges, community groups, libraries, and individuals. Provides answers to written and telephone inquiries about European and American art.

Smithsonian Center for Learning and Digital Access, 600 Maryland Ave. S.W., #1005W, 20024 (mailing address: P.O. Box 37012, MRC 508, Washington, DC 20013-7012); (202) 633-5330. Fax, (202) 633-5489. Stephanie Norby, Director.

General email, learning@si.edu

Web, https://learninglab.si.edu/about/ SmithsonianCenterforLearningandDigitalAccess and Twitter, @SmithsonianLab

Serves as the Smithsonian's central education office. Provides elementary and secondary teachers with programs, publications, audiovisual materials, regional workshops, and summer courses on using museums and primary source materials as teaching tools. Publishes books and other educational materials for teachers. (Associated with the Smithsonian Learning Lab.)

Smithsonian Institution, *Fellowships and Internships,* 470 L'Enfant Plaza S.W., #7102, 20013-7012 (mailing address: P.O. Box 37012, MRC 902, Washington, DC 20013-7012); (202) 633-7070. Fax, (202) 633-7069. Eric Woodard, Director, (202) 633-7053.

General email, siofi@si.edu

Web, www.smithsonianofi.com and Twitter, @SmithsonianOFI

Provides fellowships to students and scholars for independent research projects in association with members of the Smithsonian professional research staff. Provides central management for all Smithsonian research fellowship programs. Facilitates the Smithsonian's scholarly interactions with universities, museums, and research institutions around the world.

Smithsonian Institution, *Smithsonian Associates,* 1100 Jefferson Dr. S.W., #3077, 20560 (mailing address: P.O. Box 23293, Washington, DC 20026-3293); (202) 633-3030. Fax, (202) 786-2034. Frederica Adelman, Director.

General email, customerservice@smithsonianassociates.org

Web, http://smithsonianassociates.org and Twitter, @SmithsonianTSA

National cultural and educational membership organization that offers courses and lectures for adults and young people. Presents films and offers study tours on subjects related to the arts, humanities, and science; sponsors performances, studio arts workshops, and research.

▶NONGOVERNMENTAL

National Art Education Assn., 901 Prince St., Alexandria, VA 22314; (703) 860-8000. Fax, (703) 860-2960. Deborah B. Reeve, Executive Director, (703) 889-1283. Toll-free, (800) 299-8321.

General email, info@arteducators.org

Web, www.arteducators.org and Twitter, @NAEA

Membership: visual art educators (pre-K through university), school administrators, museum staff, manufacturers and suppliers of art materials. Issues publications on art education theory and practice, research, and current trends; provides technical assistance to art educators. Sponsors awards.

National Assn. for Music Education, 1806 Robert Fulton Dr., Reston, VA 20191-4348; (703) 860-4000. Fax, (703) 860-1531. Mike Blakeslee, Executive Director. Toll-free, (800) 336-3768. Toll-free fax, (888) 275-6232.

General email, memberservices@nafme.org

Web, www.nafme.org and Twitter, @NAfME

Membership: music educators (preschool through university). Holds biennial conference and professional development events. Publishes books and teaching aids for music educators. Monitors legislation and regulations.

National Assn. of Schools of Art and Design, *11250 Roger Bacon Dr., #21, Reston, VA 20190-5248; (703) 437-0700. Fax, (703) 437-6312. Karen Moynahan, Executive Director, (703) 437-0700, ext. 116.*
General email, info@arts-accredit.org

Web, http://nasad.arts-accredit.org

Specialized professional accrediting agency for postsecondary programs in art and design. Conducts and shares research and analysis on topics pertinent to art and design programs and fields of art and design. Offers professional development opportunities for executives of art and design programs.

National Children's Museum, *1300 Pennsylvania Ave. N.W., 20004; (301) 392-2400. Crystal Bowyer, President.*
General email, info@nationalchildrensmuseum.org

Web, www.nationalchildrensmuseum.org,
Twitter, @NatChildrens and Facebook, www.facebook
.com/NationalChildrensMuseum

A cultural and educational institution serving children and families onsite and through national partners and programs. Exhibits and activities focus on the arts, civic engagement, the environment, global citizenship, health and well-being, and play. Affiliated with the Association of Children's Museums Reciprocal Network. (In the process of moving to Washington, D.C., and will reopen in November 2019.)

Wolf Trap Foundation for the Performing Arts, *1645 Trap Rd., Vienna, VA 22182-2064; (703) 255-1900. Fax, (703) 255-1905. Arvind Manocha, President. Press, (703) 255-4096. Tickets, (877) 965-3872. TTY, (703) 255-1849.*
General email, wolftrap@wolftrap.org

Web, www.wolftrap.org and Twitter, @wolf_trap

Established by Congress; operates as a public-private partnership between the National Park Service, which maintains the grounds, and the Wolf Trap Foundation, which sponsors performances in theater, music, and dance. Conducts educational programs for children, internships for college students, career-entry programs for young singers, and professional training for teachers and performers.

Film, Photography, and Broadcasting

▶AGENCIES

National Archives and Records Administration (NARA), Motion Picture, Sound, and Video Branch, *8601 Adelphi Rd., #3360, College Park, MD 20740-6001; (301) 837-1995.*

Fax, (301) 837-3620. Daniel (Dan) X. Rooney, Chief. Holdings questions, (301) 837-0526. TTY, (301) 837-0482.
General email, mopix@nara.gov

Web, www.archives.gov

Selects and preserves audiovisual records produced or acquired by federal agencies; maintains collections from the private sector, including newsreels. Research room open to the public Monday–Saturday, 9:00 a.m.–5:00 p.m.

National Archives and Records Administration (NARA), Still Picture Branch, *8601 Adelphi Rd., NWCS #5360, College Park, MD 20740-6001; (301) 837-0561. Fax, (301) 837-3621. Deborah A Lelansky, Director, (301) 837-1911. Toll-free, (866) 272-6272.*
General email, stillpix@nara.gov

Web, www.archives.gov/research/guides/still-pictures-guide.html

Provides the public with access to and copies of still picture and poster records created or acquired by the federal government; supplies research assistance (both offsite and onsite), finding aids and guides to these materials. Records include still pictures and posters (some in digital format) from more than 200 federal agencies, from the mid-nineteenth century to the present.

National Endowment for the Arts (NEA), *Media Arts, 400 7th St. S.W., 20506; (202) 682-5452. Fax, (202) 682-5721. Jax Deluca, Director, (202) 682-5742. TTY, (202) 682-5496.*
Web, www.arts.gov/artistic-fields/media-arts

Awards grants to nonprofit organizations for screen-based projects presented by film, television, video, radio, Internet, mobile technologies, video games, transmedia storytelling, and satellite; supports film and video exhibitions and workshops.

National Endowment for the Humanities (NEH), *Public Programs, 400 7th St. S.W., 20506; (202) 606-8269. Fax, (202) 606-8557. Anne-Imelda, Director, (202) 606-8631.*
General email, publicpgms@neh.gov

Web, www.neh.gov/divisions/public

Promotes public appreciation of the humanities through support of quality public programs of broad significance, reach, and impact. Awards grants for projects that meet NEH goals and standards, including excellence in content and format, broad public appeal, and wide access to diverse audiences.

▶CONGRESS

For a listing of relevant congressional committees and subcommittees, please see page 124 or the Appendix.

Library of Congress, *Motion Picture, Broadcasting, and Recorded Sound Division, James Madison Memorial Bldg., 101 Independence Ave. S.E., #LM 336, 20540-4690; Gregory Lukow, Chief. Phone, Motion Picture and Broadcasting, (202) 707-8572. Fax, Motion Picture and Television reading room, (202) 707-2371. Phone, Recorded Sound, (202) 707-7833. Fax, Recorded Sound Reference Center, (202) 707-8464.*

General email, Motion Picture and Broadcasting, mpref@loc.gov and *Motion Picture and Broadcasting, www.loc.gov/rr/mopic*

General email, Recorded Sound, rsrc@loc.gov and *Recorded Sound, www.loc/rr/record*

Motion Picture and Broadcasting archives include an extensive range from 1894 to the present of feature films, shorts, animated cartoons, newsreels, television shows, and more. Recorded Sound archives include sound recordings from 1890 to present; tapes the library's concert series and other musical events for radio broadcast; produces recordings of music and poetry for sale to the public. American Film Institute film archives are interfiled with the division's collections. Use of collections restricted to scholars and researchers; reading room open to the public.

Library of Congress, *National Film Preservation Board,* *19053 Mount Pony Rd., Culpeper, VA 22701-7551; (202) 707-5912. Fax, (202) 707-2371. Steve Leggett, Staff Coordinator. TTY, (202) 707-6362.*
Web, www.loc.gov/programs/national-film-preservation-board/about-this-program

Administers the National Film Preservation Plan. Establishes guidelines and receives nominations for the annual selection of twenty-five films of cultural, historical, or aesthetic significance; selections are entered in the National Film Registry to ensure archival preservation in their original form.

Library of Congress, *National Recording Preservation Board,* *101 Independence Ave. S.E., 20540-5698; (202) 707-5912. Fax, (202) 707-2371. Steve Leggett, Staff Coordinator. TTY, (202) 707-6362.*
Web, www.loc.gov/programs/national-recording-preservation-board/about-this-program

Administers the National Recording Preservation Plan aimed at studying the state of and advances in sound recording. Receives nominations for the annual selection of twenty-five recordings demonstrating the range and diversity of American recorded sound heritage. Makes selections to the National Recording Registry.

Library of Congress, *Prints and Photographs Division,* *James Madison Memorial Bldg., 101 Independence Ave. S.E., #LM 337, 20540-4730; (202) 707-6394. Fax, (202) 707-6647. Helena Zinkham, Chief, (202) 707-2922.*
Web, www.loc.gov/rr/print

Maintains Library of Congress's collection of pictorial material not in book format, totaling more than 15 million items. U.S. and international collections include artists' prints; historical prints, posters, and drawings; photographs (chiefly documentary); political and social cartoons; and architectural plans, drawings, prints, and photographs. Reference service provided in the Prints and Photographs Reading Room. Reproductions of nonrestricted material available through the Library of Congress's Photoduplication Service; prints and photographs may be borrowed through the Exhibits Office for exhibits by qualified institutions. A portion of the collections and an overview of reference services are available online.

American Film Institute (AFI), *Silver Theatre and Cultural Center,* *8633 Colesville Rd., Silver Spring, MD 20910-3916; (301) 495-6720. Fax, (301) 495-6777. Ray Barry, Director. Recorded information, (301) 495-6700.*
General email, silverinfo@afi.com
Web, http://afi.com/silver, Twitter, @AFISilver and Facebook, www.facebook.com/AFISilver

Shows films of historical and artistic importance. AFI theater open to the public.

Motion Picture Assn. of America, *1301 K St. N.W., #900E, 20005; (202) 293-1966. Fax, (202) 785-3026. Charles Rivkin, Chief Executive Officer. Anti-piracy hotline, (800) 662-6797.*
General email, ContactUs@mpaa.org
Web, www.mpaa.org and Twitter, @MPAA

Membership: motion picture producers and distributors. Advises state and federal governments on copyrights, censorship, cable broadcasting, and other topics; administers volunteer rating system for motion pictures; works to prevent video piracy.

Special Collections in Mass Media and Culture *(University of Maryland),* *Hornbake Library, 4130 Campus Dr., College Park, MD 20742-7011; (301) 405-9255. Fax, (301) 314-2634. Laura Schnitker, Curator. Reference desk, (301) 405-9212.*
General email, bcast@umd.edu, and Web, www.lib.umd.edu/special/collections/massmedia/home

Maintains library and archives on the history of radio and television. Houses the National Public Broadcasting Archives. Open to the public. (Formerly Library of American Broadcasting.)

Language and Literature

Administration for Children and Families (ACF) *(Health and Human Services Dept.), Administration for Native Americans (ANA), 330 C St. S.W., Room 4126, 20201; (202) 690-7776. Fax, (202) 690-8145. Jeannie Hovland, Commissioner. Toll-free, (877) 922-9262.*
General email, anacomments@acf.hhs.gov
Web, www.acf.hhs.gov/ana

Promotes revitalization and continuation of tribal languages.

National Endowment for the Arts (NEA), *Literature,* *400 7th St. S.W., 20506; (202) 682-5707. Fax, (202) 682-5002. Amy Stolls, Director, (202) 682-5771. TTY, (202) 682-5496.*
General email, literature@arts.gov
Web, www.arts.gov/artistic-fields/literature

Awards grants to published writers, poets, and translators of prose and poetry; awards grants to nonprofit presses, literary magazines, and literature organizations that publish poetry and fiction.

▶CONGRESS

For a listing of relevant congressional committees and sub-committees, please see page 124 or the Appendix.

Library of Congress, *Center for the Book,* James Madison Memorial Bldg., 101 Independence Ave. S.E., #LM 650, 20540; (202) 707-5221. Fax, (202) 707-0269. John Van Oudenaren, Director.
General email, cfbook@loc.gov
Web, www.read.gov/cfb

Seeks to broaden public appreciation of books, reading, literacy, and libraries; sponsors lectures and conferences on the educational and cultural role of the book worldwide, including the history of books and printing, television and the printed word, and the publishing and production of books; cooperates with state centers and with other organizations. Projects and programs are privately funded except for basic administrative support from the Library of Congress.

Library of Congress, *Children's Literature Center,* Thomas Jefferson Bldg., 101 Independence Ave. S.E., #LJ 129, 20540-4620; (202) 707-5535. Fax, (202) 707-4632. Sybille A. Jagusch, Chief, (202) 707-1629.
General email, childref@loc.gov
Web, www.loc.gov/rr/child

Provides reference and information services by telephone, by correspondence, and in person; maintains reference materials on all aspects of the study of children's literature. Serves children indirectly through assistance given to teachers, librarians, and others who work with youth.

Library of Congress, *Main Reading Room,* Thomas Jefferson Bldg., 101 Independence Ave. S.E., #LJ 100, 20540-4660; (202) 707-3399. Fax, (202) 707-1957. Michael North, Head.
Web, www.loc.gov/rr/main

Point of access to the general collection of books and bound periodicals as well as electronic resources, including microform. Offers research orientations.

Library of Congress, *Poetry and Literature Center,* Thomas Jefferson Bldg., 101 Independence Ave. S.E., #A102, 20540-4861; (202) 707-5394. Fax, (202) 707-9946. Robert Casper, Head, (202) 707-1308; Tracy K. Smith, Poet Laureate.
General email, poetry@loc.gov
Web, www.loc.gov/poetry

Advises the library on public literary programs and on the acquisition of literary materials. Sponsors public poetry and fiction readings, lectures, symposia, occasional dramatic performances, and other literary events. Arranges for poets to record readings of their work for the library's tape archive. The poet laureate is appointed annually by the Librarian of Congress on the basis of literary distinction.

Library of Congress, *Rare Book and Special Collections Division,* Thomas Jefferson Bldg., 101 Independence Ave. S.E., #LJ 239, 20540-4740; (202) 707-4144.

Fax, (202) 707-4142. Mark G. Dimunation, Chief, (202) 707-2025.
Web, www.loc.gov/rr/rarebook

Maintains collections of incunabula (books printed before 1501) and other early printed books; early imprints of American history and literature; illustrated books; early Spanish American, Russian, and Bulgarian imprints; Confederate states imprints; libraries of famous personalities (including Thomas Jefferson, Woodrow Wilson, and Oliver Wendell Holmes); special format collections (miniature books, broadsides, almanacs, and pre-1870 copyright records); special interest collections; and special provenance collections. Reference assistance is provided in the Rare Book and Special Collections Reading Room.

Library of Congress, *Young Readers Center,* Thomas Jefferson Bldg., 10 1st St. S.E., #LJ G29, 20540; (202) 707-1950. Fax, (202) 707-0269. Vacant, Head.
General email, yrc@loc.gov
Web, www.read.gov/yrc

Promotes books, reading, literacy, libraries, and the scholarly study of books through affiliates and promotional programs. Places special emphasis on young readers through reading and writing contests.

▶NONGOVERNMENTAL

Alliance Française de Washington, 2142 Wyoming Ave. N.W., 20008-3906; (202) 234-7911. Fax, (202) 234-0125. Sarah Diligenti, Executive Director. Library, (202) 234-7911, ext. 814.
General email, alliance@francedc.org
Web, www.francedc.org, Facebook, www.facebook.com/ AFWDC and Twitter, @francedc?lang=en

Offers courses in French language and literature; presents lectures and cultural events; maintains library of French-language publications for members (restrictions for nonmembers); offers language programs, including on-site corporate language programs.

Center for Applied Linguistics, 4646 40th St. N.W., #200, 20016-1859; (202) 362-0700. Fax, (202) 362-3740. Joel Gómez, President.
General email, info@cal.org
Web, www.cal.org

Research and technical assistance organization that serves as a clearinghouse on application of linguistics to practical language problems. Interests include English as a second language (ESL), teacher training and material development, language education, language proficiency test development, bilingual education, and sociolinguistics.

Center for the Advanced Study of Language (*University of Maryland*), 7005 52nd Ave., College Park, MD 20742; (301) 226-8900. Fax, (301) 226-8811. Steve Fetter, Executive Director (Acting).
General email, info@casl.umd.edu
Web, www.casl.umd.edu and Twitter, @UMDCASL

Conducts research in language and cognition that supports national security; collaborates with government agencies; works to improve the performance of foreign language professionals in the federal government, specifically intelligence. Joint venture with the Defense Dept.

English First, *8001 Forbes Pl., #202, Springfield, VA 22151-2205; (703) 321-8818. Frank McGlynn, Executive Director. Web, www.englishfirst.org*

Seeks to make English the official language of the United States. Advocates policies that make English education available to all children. Monitors legislation and regulations. Opposes multilingual education and governmental policies, including Clinton Executive Order 13166.

Folger Shakespeare Library, *201 E. Capitol St. S.E., 20003-1004; (202) 544-4600. Fax, (202) 544-4623. Michael Witmore, Director. Box Office, (202) 544-7077. General email, info@folger.edu*

Web, www.folger.edu, Twitter, @FolgerLibrary and Facebook, www.facebook.com/folgershakespearelibrary

Maintains major Shakespearean and Renaissance materials; awards fellowships for postdoctoral research; presents concerts, theater performances, poetry and fiction readings, exhibits, and other public events. Offers educational programs for elementary, secondary, high school, college, and graduate school students and teachers. Publishes the Folger Shakespeare editions, *Folger Magazine,* and, in association with the George Washington University, *Shakespeare Quarterly.*

The Herb Block Foundation, *1730 M St. N.W., #1020, 20036; (202) 223-8801. Fax, (202) 223-8804. Marcela Brane, President; Sarah Armstrong Alex, Executive Director. General email, info@herbblock.org*

Web, www.herbblockfoundation.org and Twitter, @TheHerbBlockFdn

Maintains an archive of Herb Block's editorial cartoons through the Library of Congress.

Japan–America Society of Washington, *1819 L St. N.W., Level B2, 20036-3807; (202) 833-2210. Marc Hitzig, Executive Director; Ryan Shaffer, President. General email, info@jaswdc.org*

Web, www.jaswdc.org, Twitter, @jas_wdc and Facebook, www.facebook.com/jas.wdc

Offers lectures and films on Japan; operates a Japanese-language school and an annual nationwide language competition for high school students; partner of the National Cherry Blossom Festival. Maintains library for members.

Joint National Committee for Languages / National Council for Languages and International Studies, *4600 Waverly Ave., Garrett Park, MD 20896 (mailing address: P.O. Box 386, Garrett Park, MD 20896); (202) 580-8684. William P. Rivers, Executive Director. General email, info@languagepolicy.org*

Web, www.languagepolicy.org and Twitter, @JCNLinfo

Coalition of professional organizations in teaching, translation, interpreting, testing, and research. Supports a national policy on language study and international education. Provides forum and clearinghouse for professional language and international education associations. National Council for Languages and International Studies is the political arm.

Linguistic Society of America, *522 21st St. N.W., #120, 20006-5012; (202) 835-1714. Fax, (202) 835-1717. Alyson Reed, Executive Director. General email, lsa@lsadc.org*

Web, www.linguisticsociety.org

Membership: individuals and institutions interested in the scientific analysis of language. Holds linguistic institutes every other year and an annual meeting.

Malice Domestic Ltd., *P.O. Box 8007, Gaithersburg, MD 20898-8007; (301) 730-1675. Verena Rose, Chair; Shawn Reilly Simmons, Public Relations. General email, malicedomesticPR@gmail.com*

Web, www.malicedomestic.org and Facebook, www.facebook.com/Malice-Domestic

Membership: authors and readers of traditional mysteries. Sponsors annual Agatha Awards and an annual convention. Awards grants to unpublished writers in the genre.

National Foreign Language Center *(University of Maryland), 5600 Rivertech Ct., Suite K. Riverdale, MD 20737 (mailing address: P.O. Box 93, Severn Bldg. 810, 5245 Greenbelt Rd., College Park, MD 20742); (301) 405-9828. Fax, (301) 405-9829. Rebecca Rubin Damari, Director of Research. General email, inquiries@nflc.org*

Web, www.nflc.umd.edu and Twitter, @NFLC_UMD

Research and policy organization that develops new strategies for strengthening foreign language competence in the United States. Conducts research on national language needs and assists policymakers in identifying priorities, allocating resources, and designing programs. Interests include the role of foreign language in higher education, national competence in critical languages, ethnic language maintenance, and K–12 and postsecondary language programs.

PEN/Faulkner Foundation, *641 S St. N.W., 3rd Floor, 20001; (202) 898-9063. Fax, (202) 544-4623. Tracy B. McGillivary, President; Gwydion Suilebhan, Executive Director. General email, info@penfaulkner.org*

Web, www.penfaulkner.org and Twitter, @penfaulkner

Sponsors an annual juried award for American fiction. Brings authors to visit public schools to discuss their work. Holds readings by noted authors of American fiction.

U.S. English Inc., *5335 Wisconsin Ave. N.W., #930, 20015; (202) 833-0100. Fax, (202) 833-0108. Mauro E. Mujica, Chair. Toll-free, (800) 787-8216. General email, info@usenglish.org*

Web, www.usenglish.org and Twitter, @usenglishinc

Advocates English as the official language of federal and state government. Affiliate U.S. English Foundation promotes English language education for immigrants.

Museum Education Programs

Alexandria Archaeology, (703) 746-4399

American Alliance of Museums, Museum Assessment Program, (202) 289-1818

Arlington Arts Center, (703) 248-6800

Assn. of Science-Technology Centers, (202) 783-7200

B'nai B'rith Klutznick Museum, (202) 857-6600

C & O Canal, (301) 739-4200

Corcoran Gallery of Art, (202) 994-1700

Daughters of the American Revolution (DAR) Museum, (202) 628-1776

Decatur House, (202) 218-4300

Dumbarton Oaks, (202) 339-6401

Federal Reserve Board Fine Arts Program, (202) 452-3778

Folger Shakespeare Library, (202) 544-4600

Gadsby's Tavern Museum, (703) 746-4242

Institute of Museum and Library Services, (202) 653-4657

J.F.K. Center for the Performing Arts, (202) 467-4600

The Lyceum: Alexandria's History Museum, (703) 746-4994

Mount Vernon, (703) 780-2000

National Arboretum, (202) 245-2726

National Archives, (866) 272-6272

National Building Museum, (202) 272-2448

National Gallery of Art, (202) 737-4215

National Museum of Women in the Arts, (202) 783-5000

Navy Museum, (202) 685-0589

Octagon Museum, (202) 626-7439

Phillips Collection, (202) 387-2151

Smithsonian Institution, (202) 633-1000

  Anacostia Community Museum, (202) 633-4820

  Arthur M. Sackler Gallery, (202) 633-0457

  Center for Education and Museum Studies, (202) 633-5330

  Freer Gallery of Art, (202) 633-0457

  Hirshhorn Museum and Sculpture Garden, (202) 633-4674

  National Air and Space Museum, (202) 633-2214

  National Museum of African Art, (202) 633-4600

  National Museum of American Art, (202) 633-7970

  National Museum of American History, (202) 633-7304

  National Museum of Natural History, (202) 633-2622

  National Museum of the American Indian, (202) 633-6644

  National Portrait Gallery, (202) 633-8300

  Renwick Gallery, (202) 633-7970

Textile Museum, (202) 994-5200

Woodrow Wilson House, (202) 387-4062

The Writer's Center, *4508 Walsh St., Bethesda, MD 20815; (301) 654-8664. Fax, (240) 223-0458. Margaret Meleney, Executive Director.*

General email, post.master@writer.org

Web, www.writer.org and Twitter, @writerscenter

Membership: writers, editors, and interested individuals. Supports the creation, publication, presentation, and dissemination of literary texts. Sponsors workshops in writing. Presents author readings. Maintains a book gallery.

Museums

▶**AGENCIES**

American Art Museum *(Smithsonian Institution), SAMM offices, 790 9th St., N.W. #3100, 20001 (mailing address: MRC 970, Box 37012, Washington, DC 20013-7012); (202) 633-7970. Fax, (202) 633-8424. Stephanie Stebich, Director. Library, (202) 633-8230. Press, (202) 633-8530.*

General email, americanartinfo@si.edu

Web, www.americanart.si.edu, Twitter, @americanart and Facebook, www.facebook.com/americanart

Exhibits and interprets American painting, sculpture, photographs, folk art, and graphic art in the permanent collection and temporary exhibition galleries. Maintains a travelling exhibition program and research and scholar center. Library open to the public. (Includes the Renwick Gallery.)

American Art Museum *(Smithsonian Institution), Renwick Gallery, 17th St. and Pennsylvania Ave. N.W., 20006 (mailing address: Renwick Gallery, MRC 510, P.O. Box 37012, Washington, DC 20013-7012); (202) 633-2850. Robyn Kennedy, Chief Administrator. Information, (202) 633-7970. Press, (202) 633-8530.*

General email, AmericanArtRenwick@si.edu

Web, www.americanart.si.edu/visit/renwick, Twitter, @americanart and Facebook, www.facebookm .com/americanart

Blog, https://americanart.si.edu/blog

Curatorial department of the Smithsonian American Art Museum. Exhibits contemporary American crafts and decorative arts.

Anacostia Community Museum *(Smithsonian Institution), 1901 Fort Pl. S.E., 20020 (mailing address: P.O. Box 37012, MRC 0777, Washington, DC 20013-7012); (202) 633-4820. Fax, (202) 287-3183. Lisa Sasaki, Director (Acting). Press, (202) 633-4876. Public programs, (202) 633-4868. Recorded information, (202) 633-1000. Special events, (202) 633-4867.*

General email, ACMinfo@si.edu

Web, http://anacostia.si.edu and Twitter, @AnacostiaMuseum

Explores, documents, and interprets social and cultural issues that impact contemporary urban communities. Presents changing exhibits and programs.

Drug Enforcement Administration Museum and Visitors Center *(Justice Dept.), 700 Army Navy Dr., Arlington, VA 22202 (mailing address: P.O. Box 2534, Springfield, VA 22152); (202) 307-3463. Fax, (202) 307-8956. Laurie A. Baty, Director. General email, staff@deamuseum.org*

Web, www.deamuseum.org

Seeks to educate the public on the role and impact of federal drug law enforcement through state-of-the-art exhibits, displays, interactive stations, and outreach programs. Admission is free; groups of fifteen or more should call ahead for reservations.

Ford's Theatre National Historic Site, *511 10th St. N.W., 20004 (mailing address: 900 Ohio Dr. S.W., Washington, DC 20024); (202) 426-6924. Fax, (202) 426-1845. Jeff Jones, Site Manager. Recorded ticket information, (202) 638-2941. General email, NACC_FOTH_Interpretation@nps.gov*

Web, www.nps.gov/foth, Twitter, @fordstheatre and Facebook, www.facebook.com/fordstheatrenps

Administered by the National Park Service, which manages Ford's Theatre, Ford's Theatre Museum, and the Peterson House (house where Lincoln died). Presents interpretive talks, exhibits, and tours. Functions as working stage for theatrical productions.

Frederick Douglass National Historic Site, *1411 W St. S.E., 20020; (202) 426-5961. Fax, (202) 426-0880. Julie A. Kutruff, District Manager; Ka'mal McClarin, Site Curator. Group Reservations, (877) 559-6777. Reservations, (877) 444-6777. General email, julie_kutruff@nps.gov*

Web, www.nps.gov/frdo, Twitter, @FredDouglassNPS and Facebook, www.facebook.com/FrederickDouglassNHS

Administered by the National Park Service. Museum of the life and work of abolitionist Frederick Douglass and his family. Offers tours of the home and special programs, such as documentary films, videos, and slide presentations; maintains visitors center and bookstore. Reservations are required for parties of more than ten. Online reservations can be made at www.recreation.gov.

Freer Gallery of Art and Arthur M. Sackler Gallery *(Smithsonian Institution), 1050 Independence Ave. S.W., 20560 (mailing address: P.O. Box 37012, MRC 707, Washington, DC 20013-7012); (202) 633-4880. Fax, (202) 357-4911. Julian Raby, Director. Education Office, (202) 633-0457. Library, (202) 633-0477. Press, (202) 633-0271. Public programs, (202) 633-1000 (recording). TTY, (202) 633-5285. General email, publicaffairsasia@si.edu*

Web, www.asia.si.edu, Twitter, @FreerSackler and Facebook, www.facebook.com/FreerSackler

Exhibits ancient and contemporary Asian art from the Mediterranean to Japan and late nineteenth-century and early twentieth-century American art from its permanent collection, including works by James McNeill Whistler. Presents films, lectures, and concerts. Museum open to the public Monday through Friday, 10:00 a.m.–5:30 p.m.

Hirshhorn Museum and Sculpture Garden *(Smithsonian Institution), 7th St. and Independence Ave. S.W., 20560 (mailing address: P.O. Box 37012, HMSG, MRC 350, Washington, DC 20013-7012); (202) 633-4674. Fax, (202) 633-8835. Melissa Chiu, Director. Press, (202) 633-2807. TTY, (202) 633-8043. General email, hmsginquiries@si.edu*

Web, www.hirshhorn.si.edu and Twitter, @hirshhorn

Preserves and exhibits modern and contemporary art. Offers films, lectures, and tours of the collection. Free and open to the public daily 10:00 a.m.–5:30 p.m.

Institute of Museum and Library Services, *955 L'Enfant Plaza North S.W., #4000, 20024; (202) 653-4657. Fax, (202) 653-4600. Kathryn K. Matthew, Director, (202) 653-4644. Communications and Government Affairs, (202) 653-4757. Library services, (202) 653-4700. Museum services, (202) 653-4789. Grants and policy management, (202) 653-4759. TTY, (202) 653-4614. General email, imlsinfo@imls.gov*

Web, www.imls.gov, Twitter, @US_IMLS and Facebook, www.facebook.com/USIMLS

Independent federal agency established by Congress to assist museums and libraries in increasing and improving their services. Awards grants for the professional development of museum and library staff. Funds research, conferences, and publications.

National Air and Space Museum *(Smithsonian Institution), 6th St. and Independence Ave. S.W., 20560; (202) 633-2214. Fax, (202) 633-8174. Gen. J. R. (Jack) Dailey (USMC, Ret.), Director, (202) 633-2350. Education Office, (202) 633-2540. Library, (202) 633-2320. Tours, (202) 633-2563. TTY, (202) 633-5285. General email, info@si.edu*

Web, www.airandspace.si.edu and Twitter, @airandspace

Maintains the world's largest collection of aviation and space artifacts; exhibits astronautical objects and equipment of historical interest, including the 1903 Wright Flyer, Charles Lindbergh's *Spirit of St. Louis*, the Apollo 11 Command Module *Columbia*, and lunar rock specimens. Planetarium and observatory are available to the public. Library open to the public by appointment.

National Air and Space Museum *(Smithsonian Institution), Steven F. Udvar-Hazy Center, 14390 Air and Space Museum Pkwy., Chantilly, VA 20151; (703) 572-4118. Gen. John R. Dailey, Director, (202) 633-2350. Public Affairs, (202) 633-1000. TTY, (202) 633-5285. General email, info@si.edu*

Web, www.airandspace.si.edu/visit/udvar-hazy-center

Displays and preserves a collection of historical aviation and space artifacts, including the B-29 Superfortress *Enola Gay*, the Lockheed SR-71 Blackbird, the prototype of the Boeing 707, the space shuttle *Discovery*, and a Concorde. Provides a center for research into the history, science, and technology of aviation and space flight. Open to the public daily 10:00 a.m.–5:30 p.m., except December 25.

National Archives and Records Administration (NARA), *National Archives Museum, 701 Constitution Ave. N.W., 20408; (202) 357-5210. Fax, (202) 357-5926. Vacant, Director, (202) 357-5974. Information, (202) 357-5000 ext. 1. Communications and marketing, (202) 357-5300.*
Web, www.archives.gov/museum

Plans and directs activities to acquaint the public with the mission and holdings of the National Archives; conducts behind-the-scenes tours; presents hands-on workshops; develops both traditional and interactive exhibits; produces publications.

National Cryptologic Museum *(National Security Agency), 8290 Colony Seven Rd., Annapolis Junction, MD 20701 (mailing address: 9800 Savage Rd., Fort Meade, MD 20755); (301) 688-5849. Fax, (301) 688-5847. Patrick Weadon, Curator. Library, (301) 688-2145.*
General email, crypto_museum@nsa.gov
Web, www.nsa.gov/about/cryptologic-heritage/museum

Documents the history of the cryptologic profession. Library open to the public.

National Endowment for the Arts (NEA), *Museums, 400 7th St. S.W., 20506; (202) 682-5452. Fax, (202) 682-5721. Wendy Clark, Director, (202) 682-5555.*
TTY, (202) 682-5496.
Web, www.arts.gov/artistic-fields/museums

Awards grants to museums for installing and cataloging permanent and special collections; conducts traveling exhibits; trains museum professionals; conserves and preserves museum collections; and develops arts-related educational programs.

National Gallery of Art, *6th St. and Constitution Ave. N.W., 20565 (mailing address: 2000B S. Club Dr., Landover, MD 20785); (202) 737-4215. Fax, (202) 842-2356. Kaywin Feldman, Director. Library, (202) 842-6511. Press, (202) 842-6353. Visitor services, (202) 842-6691.*
Web, www.nga.gov, Twitter, @ngadc and Facebook, www .facebook.com/nationalgalleryofart

Created by a joint resolution of Congress, the museum is a public-private partnership that collects, preserves, and exhibits European and American paintings, sculpture, and decorative and graphic arts. Offers concerts, demonstrations, lectures, symposia, films, tours, and teacher workshops to enhance exhibitions, the permanent collection, and related topics. Lends art to museums in all fifty states and abroad through the National Lending Service. Publishes a bimonthly calendar of events.

National Museum of African Art *(Smithsonian Institution), 950 Independence Ave. S.W., 20560 (mailing address: P.O. Box 37012, MRC 708, Washington, DC 20013-7012); (202) 633-4600. Fax, (202) 357-4879. Augustus (Gus) Casely-Hayford, Director. General Smithsonian information, (202) 633-4660. Press, (202) 633-4879.*
General email, nmafaweb@si.edu
Web, http://africa.si.edu

Collects, studies, and exhibits traditional and contemporary arts of Africa. Exhibits feature objects from the permanent collection and from private and public collections worldwide. Museum is open 10 a.m.–5:30 p.m. daily except December 25. Library and photo archive open to the public by appointment.

National Museum of American History *(Smithsonian Institution), 14th St. and Constitution Ave. N.W., #4260, MRC 622, 20560-0630 (mailing address: P.O. Box 37012, Washington, DC 20013); (202) 633-3435.*
Fax, (202) 633-4717. Susan Fruchter, Director (Acting). General Smithsonian information, (202) 633-1000. Library, (202) 633-2240. Press, (202) 633-3129. TTY, (202) 633-5285.
General email, info@si.edu
Web, http://americanhistory.si.edu

Collects and exhibits objects representative of American cultural history, applied arts, industry, national and military history, and science and technology. Library open to the public by appointment.

National Museum of American History *(Smithsonian Institution), Culture and Community Life, 12th St. and Constitution Ave. N.W., Room 4212, 20560-0616 (mailing address: P.O. Box 37012, MRC 616, Washington, DC 20013-7012); (202) 633-1707. Fax, (202) 786-2883. Stacey Kluck, Chair. Press, (202) 633-3129.*
General email, info@si.edu
Web, https://americanhistory.si.edu/about/departments/ cultural-and-community-life

Collects and preserves artifacts related to U.S. cultural heritage; supports research, exhibits, performances, and educational programs. Areas of focus include sports, recreation, and leisure; popular culture; music and dance; theater, film, broadcast media, graphic arts, printing, and photographic history.

National Museum of American History *(Smithsonian Institution), National Numismatic Collection, 14th St. and Constitution Ave. N.W., 20013 (mailing address: P.O. Box 37012, MRC609, Washington, DC 20013-7012); (202) 633-3854. Ellen Feingold, Curator of Numismatic Collection.*
General email, NMHA-NNC@si.edu
Web, http://americanhistory.si.edu/collections/numismatics

Develops and maintains collections of ancient, medieval, modern, U.S., and world coins; U.S. and world currencies; tokens; medals; orders and decorations; and traditional exchange media. Conducts research and responds to public inquiries. Collection can be viewed online.

National Museum of Health and Medicine *(Defense Dept.), 2500 Linden Lane, Silver Spring, MD 20910 (mailing address: 2460 Linden Lane, Bldg. 2500, Silver Spring, MD 20910); (301) 319-3300. Fax, (301) 319-3373. Dr. Adrianne Noe, Director. Tours, (301) 319-3312.*
General email, usarmy.detrick.medcom-usamrmc.list .medical-museum@mail.mil
Web, www.medicalmuseum.mil and Twitter, @medicalmuseum

Collects and exhibits medical models, tools, and pathological specimens. Maintains exhibits on military medicine and surgery. Open to the public 10:00 a.m.–5:30 p.m., seven days a week. Study collection available to scholars by appointment.

National Museum of Natural History *(Smithsonian Institution), 10th St. and Constitution Ave. N.W., 20560-0106 (mailing address: P.O. Box 37012, MRC 106, Washington, DC 20013-7012); (202) 633-2664. Fax, (202) 633-0169. Kirk Johnson, Director. General Smithsonian information, (202) 633-1000. Library, (202) 633-1680. Press, (202) 633-2950. TTY, (202) 633-5285. General email, naturalexperience@si.edu*

Web, www.mnh.si.edu and Twitter, @NMNH

Conducts research and maintains exhibitions and collections relating to the natural sciences. Collections are organized into seven research and curatorial departments: anthropology, botany, entomology, invertebrate zoology, mineral sciences, paleobiology, and vertebrate zoology.

National Museum of the American Indian *(Smithsonian Institution), 4th St. and Independence Ave. S.W., 20560; (202) 633-6803. Fax, (202) 633-6920. Kevin Gover, Director, (202) 633-6707. General Smithsonian information, (202) 633-1000. Group reservations, (202) 633-6644. TTY, (202) 633-5285. TTY group reservations, (202) 633-6751. General email, NMAI-info@si.edu*

Web, www.americanindian.si.edu and Twitter, @SmithsonianNMA

Collects, exhibits, preserves, and studies American Indian languages, literature, history, art, and culture. Operates ImagiNations activity center, open to the public. (Affiliated with the George Gustav Heye Center, 1 Bowling Green, New York, NY 10004 and the Cultural Resources Center, 4220 Silver Hill Rd., Suitland, MD 20746.)

National Portrait Gallery *(Smithsonian Institution), 750 9th St. N.W., #410, 20001 (mailing address: P.O. Box 37012, Victor Bldg., MRC 973, Washington, DC 20013-7012); (202) 633-8300. Fax, (202) 633-8243. Kim Sajet, Director, (202) 663-8276; Brandon Fortune, Chief Curator. General Smithsonian information, (202) 633-1000. Library, (202) 633-8230. Press, (202) 633-9889. General email, npgnews@si.edu*

Web, www.npg.si.edu, Twitter, @NPG and Facebook, www.facebook.com/npg.smithsonian

Exhibits paintings, photographs, sculpture, drawings, and prints of individuals who have made significant contributions to the history, development, and culture of the United States. Library open to the public.

National Postal Museum *(Smithsonian Institution), 2 Massachusetts Ave. N.E., 20002 (mailing address: P.O. Box 37012, Washington, DC 20013); (202) 633-5555. Fax, (202) 633-9393. Elliot Gruber, Director. Press, (202) 633-5518. Tours and education, (202) 633-5534. Web, http://postalmuseum.si.edu, Twitter, @PostalMuseum and Facebook, www.facebook .com/SmithsonianNationalPostalMuseum*

Exhibits postal history and stamp collections; provides information on world postal and stamp history.

Naval History and Heritage Command *(Navy Dept.), Navy Art Collection, Washington Navy Yard, 822 Sicard St. S.E., Bldg. 67, 20374 (mailing address: 805 Kidder Breese St. S.E., Washington Navy Yard, DC 20374); (202) 433-3815. Gale Munro, Head Curator. General email, NavyArt@navy.mil*

Web, www.history.navy.mil

Holdings include more than 18,000 paintings, prints, drawings, and sculptures. Artworks depict naval ships, personnel, and action from all eras of U.S. naval history, especially the eras of World War II, the Korean War, and Desert Shield/Storm. Open to the public. Visitors without Defense Dept. or military identification must call in advance. Photo identification required.

Smithsonian Institution, *1000 Jefferson Dr. S.W., 20560 (mailing address: P.O. Box 37012, SIB 153, MRC 010, Washington, DC 20013-7012); (202) 633-1000. David J. Skorton, Secretary; John Davis, Under Secretary for Museums, Education, and Research; Albert G. Horvath, Under Secretary for Finance and Administration. Library, (202) 633-1940. Press (journalists only), (202) 633-2400. General email, info@si.edu*

Web, www.si.edu

Conducts research; publishes results of studies, explorations, and investigations; presents study and reference collections on science, culture, and history; presents exhibitions in the arts, American history, technology, aeronautics and space exploration, and natural history. Smithsonian Institution sites in Washington, D.C., include the Anacostia Community Museum, Archives of American Art, Arthur M. Sackler Gallery, Arts and Industries Building, Freer Gallery of Art, Hirshhorn Museum and Sculpture Garden, National Air and Space Museum, National Museum of African Art, Renwick Gallery, Smithsonian American Art Museum, National Museum of American History, National Museum of the American Indian, National Museum of Natural History, National Portrait Gallery, National Postal Museum, National Zoological Park, S. Dillon Ripley Center, and Smithsonian Institution Building. Libraries open to the public by appointment; library catalogs are available on the Web. Affiliated with more than 175 organizations in 41 states, Panama, and Puerto Rico. Autonomous organizations affiliated with the Smithsonian Institution include John F. Kennedy Center for the Performing Arts, National Gallery of Art, and Woodrow Wilson International Center for Scholars.

Smithsonian Institution, *Smithsonian Museum Support Center, 4210 Silver Hill Rd., MRC 534, Suitland, MD 20746-2863; (301) 238-1026. Fax, (301) 238-3661. Elizabeth (Liz) Dietrich, Management Officer, (301) 238-1010. Library, (301) 238-1030. General email, libmail@si.edu*

Web, https://naturalhistory.si.edu/research/msc

Museum collections management facility dedicated to collections, storage, research, and conservation. Library serves Smithsonian staff, other government agencies, and researchers. Open to the public by appointment.

U.S. Botanic Garden, *100 Maryland Ave. S.W., 20001 (mailing address: 245 1st St. S.W., Washington, DC 20024); (202) 225-8333. Fax, (202) 225-1561.*
Saharah Moon Chapotin, Executive Director, (202) 225-1110. Horticulture hotline, (202) 226-4785. Press, (202) 226-4145. Program registration information, (202) 225-1116. Special events, (202) 226-7674. Tour line, (202) 226-2055.
General email, usbg@aoc.gov

Web, www.usbg.gov and Twitter, @USBotanicGarden

Educates the public on the aesthetic, cultural, economic, therapeutic, and ecological importance of plants to the well-being of humankind.

U.S. Navy Museum *(Naval Historical Center), Bldg. 76, 805 Kidder Breese St. S.E., Washington Navy Yard, DC, 20374-5060; (202) 433-4882. Fax, (202) 433-8200. James H. Bruns, Museum Director; Rear Adm. Samuel Cox (USN, Ret.), Director of Naval History and Heritage Command; Laura Hockensmith, Deputy Director of Education and Public Programs. Tours, (202) 433-6826.*
General email, hhhcpublicaffairs@navy.mil

Web, www.history.navy.mil and Twitter, @USNhistory

Collects, preserves, displays, and interprets historic naval artifacts and artwork. Presents a complete overview of U.S. naval history. Open to the public. Photo identification required.

►CONGRESS

For a listing of relevant congressional committees and subcommittees, please see page 124 or the Appendix.

Library of Congress, *Interpretive Programs, John Adams Bldg., 101 Independence Ave. S.E., #LA G25, 20540; (202) 707-5223. Fax, (202) 707-9063. David Mandel, Chief. Information, (202) 707-5223.*
Web, www.loc.gov/exhibits

Handles exhibits within the Library of Congress; establishes and coordinates traveling exhibits; handles loans of library material.

►NONGOVERNMENTAL

American Alliance of Museums, *2451 Crystal Dr., #1005, Arlington, VA 22202; (202) 289-1818. Fax, (202) 289-6578. Laura L. Lott, President, (202) 289-9110.*
General email, infocenter@aam-us.org

Web, www.aam-us.org, Twitter, @AAMers and Facebook, www.facebook.com/americanmuseums

Membership: individuals, institutions, museums, and museum professionals. Accredits museums; conducts educational programs; promotes international professional exchanges.

Art Services International, *119 Duke St., Alexandria, VA 22314; (703) 548-4554. Fax, (703) 548-3305. Lynn K. Rogerson, Director.*

General email, asi@asiexhibitions.org
Web, www.asiexhibitions.org

Develops, organizes, and circulates fine arts exhibitions throughout the world.

Dumbarton Oaks, *1703 32nd St. N.W., 20007-2961; (202) 339-6400. Fax, (202) 625-0280. Jan M. Ziolkowski, Director. Information, (202) 339-6401.*
General email, museum@doaks.org
Web, www.doaks.org
Tours email, tours@doaks.org

Exhibits Byzantine and pre-Columbian art and artifacts; conducts advanced research and maintains publication programs and library collections in Byzantine and pre-Columbian studies and garden and landscape studies. Offers guided tours of museum and gardens. Gardens open to the public Tuesday through Sunday 2:00–6:00 p.m. in summer, and 2:00–5:00 p.m. in winter (except during inclement weather and on federal holidays; fee charged March 15 through October 31); library open to qualified scholars by advance application. Administered by the trustees for Harvard University.

Hillwood Estate, Museum, and Gardens, *4155 Linnean Ave. N.W., 20008-3806; (202) 686-5807. Fax, (202) 966-7846. Kate Markert, Executive Director, (202) 243-3900. Press, (202) 243-3975.*
General email, info@hillwoodmuseum.org

Web, www.hillwoodmuseum.org and Twitter, @HillwoodMuseum

Former residence of Marjorie Merriweather Post. Maintains and exhibits collection of Russian imperial art, including Fabergé eggs, and eighteenth-century French decorative arts; twelve acres of formal gardens. Gardens and museum open to the public Tuesday through Sunday, 10:00 a.m.–5:00 p.m.; reservations required for large groups.

International Spy Museum, *700 L'Enfant Plaza S.W., 20024; P.O. Box 23137, 20026; (202) 393-7798. Fax, (202) 393-7797. Peter Earnest, Executive Director. Press, (202) 654-0946.*
General email, info@spymuseum.org

Web, www.spymuseum.org, Twitter, @IntlSpyMuseum and Facebook, www.facebook.com/IntlSpyMuseum

Dedicated to educating the public about the tradecraft, history, and contemporary role of espionage, particularly human intelligence, by examining its role in and effect on current and historical events. Offers a collection of international espionage artifacts. (Affiliated with the Malrite Company.)

National Building Museum, *401 F St. N.W., 20001-2637; (202) 272-2448. Fax, (202) 272-2564. Chase W. Rynd, Executive Director, ext. 3109. Press, (202) 272-2448 ext. 3458. Press email, efilar@nbm.org, Web, www.nbm.org and Twitter, @BuildingMuseum*

Celebrates achievements in building, architecture, urban planning, engineering, and historic preservation through educational programs, exhibitions, tours, lectures, workshops, and publications.

National Children's Museum, *1300 Pennsylvania Ave. N.W., 20004; (301) 392-2400. Crystal Bowyer, President. General email, info@nationalchildrensmuseum.org*

Web, www.nationalchildrensmuseum.org, Twitter, @NatChildrens and Facebook, www.facebook.com/NationalChildrensMuseum

A cultural and educational institution serving children and families onsite and through national partners and programs. Exhibits and activities focus on the arts, civic engagement, the environment, global citizenship, health and well-being, and play. Affiliated with the Association of Children's Museums Reciprocal Network. (In the process of moving to Washington, D.C., and will re-open in November 2019.)

National Geographic Museum, *1145 17th St. N.W., 20036-4688; Kathryn Keane, Vice President of Exhibitions. Exhibit information, (202) 857-7588. Tickets and tour information, (202) 857-7700.*

Web, http://nationalgeographic.org/dc and Twitter, @Natgeo

Maintains self-guided exhibits about past and current expeditions, scientific research, and other themes in history and culture. Admission is free; some special exhibitions require ticket purchase.

National Guard Memorial Museum, *1 Massachusetts Ave. N.W., 20001; (202) 789-0031. Fax, (202) 682-9358. Luke Guthrie, Director; Anne Armstrong, Deputy Director, (202) 408-5890. Toll-free, (888) 226-4287.*

General email, ngef@ngaus.org

Web, www.ngef.org/national-guard-memorial-museum, Twitter, @NGMuseum and Facebook, www.facebook.com/NationalGuardMemorialMuseum

Features exhibit areas that explore the National Guard from colonial times through the world wars and the cold war to the modern era through timelines, photographs, artifacts, light, and sound.

National Museum of Civil War Medicine, *48 E. Patrick St., Frederick, MD 21705 (mailing address: P.O. Box 470, Frederick, MD 21705); (301) 695-1864.*
Fax, (301) 695-6823. David Price, Executive Director. General email, info@civilwarmed.org

Web, www.civilwarmed.org and Twitter, @civilwarmed

Maintains artifacts and exhibits pertaining to general and wartime medicine in the 1800s, including dentistry, veterinary medicine, and medical evacuation. Presents information about individual soldiers, surgeons, medics, and nurses. Research department assists with questions about individuals injured in the Civil War.

National Museum of Women in the Arts, *1250 New York Ave. N.W., 20005-3970; (202) 783-5000. Fax, (202) 393-3234. Susan Fisher Sterling, Director; Amy Mannarino, Director of Communications. Information, (800) 222-7270. Library, (202) 783-7338. Press, (202) 783-7373.*
Web, www.nmwa.org and Twitter, @womeninthearts

Acquires, researches, and presents the works of women artists from the Renaissance to the present. Promotes greater representation and awareness of women in the arts. Library open for research to the public by appointment.

National Woman's Party, *144 Constitution Ave. N.E., 20002-5608 (mailing address: P.O. Box 75478, Washington, DC 20013); (202) 546-1210. Fax, (202) 546-3997. Zakiya Thomas, Executive Director. Press, (202) 546-1210, ext. 12.*
General email, info@nationalwomansparty.org

Web, http://nationalwomansparty.org, Twitter, @NatlWomansParty and Facebook, www.facebook.com/NationalWomansParty

Library, library@nationalwomansparty.org

Maintains archives and artifacts documenting women's equality under the law. Interests include the suffragists, the National Women's Party, and the Equal Rights Amendment campaign.

Newseum, *555 Pennsylvania Ave. N.W., 20001; (202) 292-6100. Carrie Christofferson, Executive Director. Press, (202) 292-6200.*
General email, info@newseum.org

Web, www.newseum.org, Twitter, @Newseum and Facebook, www.facebook.com/Newseum

World's only interactive museum of news. Collects items related to the history of news coverage; offers multimedia presentations and exhibits on the past, present, and future of news coverage; emphasizes the importance of the First Amendment to news coverage. (Affiliated with Freedom Forum.)

Octagon Museum, *1799 New York Ave. N.W., 20006-5207; (202) 626-7439. Marci B. Reed, Executive Director. General email, octagonmuseum@aia.org*

Web, www.architectsfoundation.org/octagon-museum, Twitter, @OctagonMuseum and Facebook, www.facebook.com/TheOctagonMuseum

Federal period historic residence open to the public for tours; served as the executive mansion during the War of 1812. Sponsors exhibits, lectures, publications, and educational programs. (Owned by the AIA Foundation [American Institute of Architects].) Guided tours available by appointment. Open for self-guided tours Thursday to Sunday from 1:00 p.m.–4:00 p.m.

Phillips Collection, *1600 21st St. N.W., 20009; (202) 387-2151. Fax, (202) 387-2436. Dorothy Kosinski, Director. Membership, (202) 387-3036. Press, (202) 387-2151, ext. 220. Shop, (202) 387-2151, ext. 239. General email, communications@phillipscollection.org*

Web, www.phillipscollection.org and Twitter, @PhillipsMuseum

Maintains permanent collection of European and American paintings, primarily of the nineteenth through twenty-first centuries, and holds special exhibitions from the same periods. Sponsors lectures, gallery talks, and special events, including Sunday concerts (October–May). Library open to researchers and members.

Society of the Cincinnati, *2118 Massachusetts Ave. N.W., 20008; (202) 785-2040. Fax, (202) 785-0729. Jack*

Duane Warren Jr., Executive Director, ext. 410. Library appointments, ext. 426. Press, ext. 445.
General email, admin@societyofthecincinnati.org
Web, https://societyofthecincinnati.org and
Twitter, @AndersonHouse

Collects and exhibits books, manuscripts, paintings, and other artifacts from the Revolutionary War. Maintains a library for research on the American Revolution. Preserves and operates the Anderson House as a historic landmark and museum.

Textile Museum *(George Washington University), 701 21st St. N.W., 20052; (202) 994-5200. Fax, (202) 483-0994. John Wetenhall, Director.*
General email, museuminfo@gwu.edu
Web, https://museum.gwu.edu and
Twitter, @GWTextileMuseum

Exhibits historic and handmade textiles and carpets with the goal of expanding appreciation of the artistic and cultural importance of the world's textiles. Exhibitions draw from loans and the permanent collection, specializing in the Eastern Hemisphere. Offers annual Fall Symposium, Celebration of Textiles festival, and other programs. Library open to the public during restricted hours Wednesdays and Saturdays.

Tudor Place, *1644 31st St. N.W., 20007; (202) 965-0400. Fax, (202) 965-0164. Mark S. Hudson, Executive Director, ext. 101.*
General email, info@tudorplace.org
Web, www.tudorplace.org and Twitter, @TudorPlace

Operates a historic property, home of Martha Washington's granddaughter and six generations of Custis-Peter family descendants. Seeks to educate the public about American history and culture, focusing on the capital region from the 18th century. Maintains and displays artifacts, maintains a manuscript collection, conducts guided tours, and sponsors educational programs for students and teachers.

U.S. Holocaust Memorial Museum, *100 Raoul Wallenberg Pl. S.W., 20024-2126; (202) 488-0400. Fax, (202) 488-2690. Sara J. Bloomfield, Director. Library, (202) 479-9717. Press, (202) 488-6133. Toll-free, (866) 998-7466. TTY, (202) 488-0406.*
Web, www.ushmm.org and Twitter, @HolocaustMuseum

Preserves documentation about the Holocaust and works to prevent genocide worldwide. Hosts exhibitions and website; conducts public programs, educational outreach, leadership training programs, and Holocaust commemorations; operates the Mandel Center for Advanced Holocaust Studies and the Genocide Prevention Task Force. Library and archives are open to the public.

Woodrow Wilson House *(National Trust for Historic Preservation), 2340 S St. N.W., 20008-4016; (202) 387-4062. Fax, (202) 483-1466. Susan G. Berning, Executive Director (Acting), (202) 695-5561.*

General email, wilsonhouse@woodrowwilsonhouse.org
Web, www.woodrowwilsonhouse.org,
Twitter, @WWilsonHouse
Events, sandrews@woodrowwilsonhouse.org

Georgian Revival home that exhibits state gifts, furnishings, and memorabilia from President Woodrow Wilson's political and postpresidential years.

Music

▶**AGENCIES**

National Endowment for the Arts (NEA), *Music, 400 7th St. S.W., 20506; (202) 682-5438. Fax, (202) 682-5076. Ann Meier Baker, Director, (202) 682-5455. TTY, (202) 682-5496.*
Web, www.arts.gov/artistic-fields/music

Awards grants to support a wide range of music, including classical, opera, contemporary, and jazz. Supports both performing ensembles and music institutions, including chamber music ensembles, opera companies, choruses, early music programs, jazz ensembles, music festivals, and symphony orchestras.

National Museum of American History *(Smithsonian Institution), Culture and Community Life, 12th St. and Constitution Ave. N.W., Room 4212, 20560-0616 (mailing address: P.O. Box 37012, MRC 616, Washington, DC 20013-7012); (202) 633-1707. Fax, (202) 786-2883. Stacey Kluck, Chair. Press, (202) 633-3129.*
General email, info@si.edu
Web, https://americanhistory.si.edu/about/departments/cultural-and-community-life

Preserves American culture and heritage through collections, research, exhibitions, publications, teaching and lectures, and broadcasts. Sponsors Jazz Appreciation Month and a chamber music program. Research areas are open by appointment.

National Symphony Orchestra *(John F. Kennedy Center for the Performing Arts), 2700 F St. N.W., 20566-0004 (mailing address: P.O. Box 101510, Arlington, VA 22210); (202) 416-8000. Fax, (202) 416-8105. Gianandrea Noseda, Music Director; Steven Reineke, Principal Pops Conductor; Deborah Prutter, President. Information and reservations, (202) 467-4600. Toll-free, (800) 444-1324. Tours, (202) 416-8340. Tour accessibility, (202) 416-8727. Tour accessibility TTY, (202) 416-8727. TTY, (202) 416-8524.*
Web, www.kennedy-center.org/nso, Twitter, @kencen and Facebook, www.facebook.com/National.Symphony

Year-round orchestra that presents a full range of symphonic activities: classical, pops, and educational events; national and international tours; recordings; and special events.

▶**CONGRESS**

For a listing of relevant congressional committees and subcommittees, please see page 124 or the Appendix.

Library of Congress, *Motion Picture, Broadcasting, and Recorded Sound Division, James Madison Memorial Bldg., 101 Independence Ave. S.E., #LM 336, 20540-4690; Gregory Lukow, Chief. Phone, Motion Picture and Broadcasting, (202) 707-8572. Fax, Motion Picture and Television reading room, (202) 707-2371. Phone, Recorded Sound, (202) 707-7833. Fax, Recorded Sound Reference Center, (202) 707-8464.*
General email, Motion Picture and Broadcasting, mpref@loc.gov and Motion Picture and Broadcasting, www.loc.gov/rr/mopic

General email, Recorded Sound, rsrc@loc.gov and Recorded Sound, www.loc/rr/record

Maintains library's collection of musical and vocal recordings; tapes the library's concert series and other musical events for radio broadcast; produces recordings of music and poetry for sale to the public. Collection also includes sound recordings (1890–present). Reading room open to the public Monday through Friday, 8:30 a.m.–5:00 p.m.; listening and viewing by appointment only.

Library of Congress, *Music Division, James Madison Memorial Bldg., 101 Independence Ave. S.E., #LM 113, 20540-4710; (202) 707-5503. Fax, (202) 707-0621. Susan H. Vita, Chief, (202) 707-5503. Concert information, (202) 707-5502. Performing Arts Reading Room, (202) 707-5507.*
Web, www.loc.gov/rr/perform

Maintains and services, through the Performing Arts Reading Room, the library's collection of music manuscripts, sheet music, books, and instruments. Coordinates the library's chamber music concert series; produces radio broadcasts and, for sale to the public, recordings of concerts sponsored by the division; issues publications relating to the field of music and to division collections.

Library of Congress, *National Recording Preservation Board, 101 Independence Ave. S.E., 20540-5698; (202) 707-5912. Fax, (202) 707-2371. Steve Leggett, Staff Coordinator. TTY, (202) 707-6362.*
Web, www.loc.gov/programs/national-recording-preservation-board/about-this-program

Administers the National Recording Preservation Plan aimed at studying the state of and advances in sound recording. Receives nominations for the annual selection of twenty-five recordings demonstrating the range and diversity of American recorded sound heritage. Makes selections for the National Recording Registry.

▶**NONGOVERNMENTAL**

American Federation of Musicians, *Government Relations, 5335 Wisconsin Ave. N.W., #440, 20015; Fax, (202) 274-4759. Alfonso Pollard, Director, (202) 274-4756. Toll-free, (800) 762-3444.*
Web, www.afm.org/departments/legislative-office/office-of-government-relations

Seeks to improve the working conditions and salary of musicians. Monitors legislation and regulations affecting musicians and the arts. (Headquarters in New York.)

Future of Music Coalition, *2217 14th St. N.W., 2nd Floor, 20009; (202) 822-2051. Kevin Erickson, Director.*
General email, info@futureofmusic.org

Web, www.futureofmusic.org, Twitter, @future_of_music and Facebook, www.facebook.com/Futureofmusiccoalition

Seeks to educate the media, policymakers, and the public on music technology issues. Identifies and promotes innovative business models that will help musicians and citizens benefit from new technologies.

League of American Orchestras, *Advocacy and Government, 1602 L St. N.W., #611, 20036; (202) 776-0215. Fax, (202) 776-0224. Heather Noonan, Vice President for Advocacy.*
Web, www.americanorchestras.org/advocacy-government .html, Twitter, @OrchLeague and Facebook, www.facebook .com/orchleague

Service and educational organization dedicated to strengthening orchestras. Provides information and analysis on subjects of interest to orchestras through reports, seminars, and other educational forums. Seeks to improve policies that increase public access to orchestral music. Monitors legislation and regulations. (Headquarters in New York.)

National Assn. of Schools of Music, *11250 Roger Bacon Dr., #21, Reston, VA 20190-5248; (703) 437-0700. Fax, (703) 437-6312. Karen Moynahan, Executive Director, (703) 437-0700 x 116.*
General email, info@arts-accredit.org
Web, http://nasm.arts-accredit.org

Specialized professional accrediting agency for postsecondary programs in music. Conducts and shares research and analysis on topics pertinent to music programs and the field of music. Offers professional development opportunities for executives of music programs.

Recording Industry Assn. of America, *1025 F St. N.W., 10th Floor, 20004; (202) 775-0101. Fax, (202) 775-7253. Mitch Glazier, Chief Executive Officer.*
Web, www.riaa.com and Twitter, @RIAA

Membership: creators, manufacturers, and marketers of sound recordings. Educates members about new technology in the music industry; certifies gold, platinum, and multiplatinum recordings; supports parental advisory labels; publishes statistics on the recording industry. Monitors legislation and regulations.

SoundExchange, *733 10th St. N.W., 10th Floor, 20001; (202) 640-5858. Fax, (202) 640-5859. Michael Huppe, President. Press, (202) 559-0558.*
General email, info@soundexchange.com
Web, www.soundexchange.com and Twitter, @SoundExchange

Artists' rights advocacy group that represents record labels and unsigned artists whose work is broadcast on national and global digital radio. Distributes royalties to musicians, performers, and music copyright owners. Monitors legislation and regulations related to digital music licensing.

Theater and Dance

▶**AGENCIES**

Ford's Theatre National Historic Site, *511 10th St. N.W., 20004 (mailing address: 900 Ohio Dr. S.W., Washington, DC 20024); (202) 426-6924. Fax, (202) 426-1845. Jeff Jones, Site Manager. Recorded ticket information, (202) 638-2941.*
General email, NACC_FOTH_Interpretation@nps.gov
Web, www.nps.gov/foth, Twitter, @fordstheatre and Facebook, www.facebook.com/fordstheatrenps

Administered by the National Park Service, which manages Ford's Theatre, Ford's Theatre Museum, and the Peterson House (house where Lincoln died). Presents interpretive talks, exhibits, and tours. Functions as working stage for theatrical productions.

National Endowment for the Arts (NEA), *Dance, 400 7th St. S.W., 20506; (202) 682-5438. Fax, (202) 682-5612. Sara Nash, Director, (202) 682-5791. TTY, (202) 682-5496.*
Web, www.arts.gov/artistic-fields/dance

Awards grants to dance companies and presenters for projects in all dance styles, including ballet, modern dance, jazz, folkloric, tap, hip-hop, and other contemporary forms.

National Endowment for the Arts (NEA), *Theater and Musical Theater, 400 7th St. S.W., 20506; (202) 682-5438. Fax, (202) 682-5612. Greg Reiner, Director, (202) 682-5482. TTY, (202) 682-5496.*
Web, www.arts.gov/artistic-fields/musical-theater

Awards grants to organizations and artists in all venues of theater, including traditional, musical, classical, new plays, works for young audiences, experimental work, community-based work, circus arts, and puppetry.

Smithsonian Institution, *Discovery Theater, 1100 Jefferson Dr. S.W., 20024 (mailing address: Discovery Theater, P.O. Box 23293, Washington, DC 20026-3293); (202) 633-8700. Fax, (202) 633-1322. Roberta Gasbarre, Director.*
General email, info@discoverytheater.org
Web, https://discoverytheater.org

Presents live theatrical performances, including storytelling, dance, music, puppetry, and plays, for young people and their families.

▶**NONGOVERNMENTAL**

Dance/USA, *1029 Vermont Ave. N.W., #400, 20005; (202) 833-1717. Fax, (202) 833-2686. Amy Fitterer, Executive Director.*
General email, danceusa@danceusa.org
Web, www.danceusa.org and Twitter, @DanceUSAorg

Membership: professional dance companies, artists, artist managers, presenters, service organizations, educators, libraries, businesses, and individuals. Advances the art form by addressing the needs, concerns, and interests of the professional dance community through public communications, research and information services, professional development, advocacy, re-granting initiatives, and other projects.

National Assn. of Schools of Dance, *11250 Roger Bacon Dr., #21, Reston, VA 20190-5248; (703) 437-0700. Fax, (703) 437-6312. Karen Moynahan, Executive Director, (703) 437-0700 ext. 116.*
General email, info@arts-accredit.org
Web, http://nasd.arts-accredit.org

Specialized professional accrediting agency for postsecondary programs in dance. Conducts and shares research and analysis on topics pertinent to dance programs and the field of dance. Offers professional development opportunities for executives of dance programs.

National Assn. of Schools of Theatre, *11250 Roger Bacon Dr., #21, Reston, VA 20190-5248; (703) 437-0700. Fax, (703) 437-6312. Karen Moynahan, Executive Director, (703) 437-0700 ext. 116.*
General email, info@arts-accredit.org
Web, http://nast.arts-accredit.org

Specialized professional accrediting agency for postsecondary programs in theatre. Conducts and shares research and analysis on topics pertinent to theatre programs and the field of theatre. Offers professional development opportunities for executives of theatre programs.

National Conservatory of Dramatic Arts, *1556 Wisconsin Ave. N.W., 20007; (202) 333-2202. Raymond (Ray) G. Ficca, President; Nan Kyle Ficca, School Director.*
General email, NCDAdrama@aol.com
Web, www.theconservatory.org and Twitter, @NCDArts

Offers an accredited two-year program in postsecondary professional actor training and a one-year program in advanced professional training. Emphasizes both physical and mental preparedness for acting in the professional entertainment industry.

Shakespeare Theatre Company, *Lansburgh Theatre, 450 7th St. N.W., 20004; Sidney Harmon Hall, 610 F St. N.W., 20004 (mailing address: 516 8th St. S.E., Washington, DC 20003-2834); (202) 547-3230. Fax, (202) 547-0226. Michael Kahn, Artistic Director; Chris Jennings, Executive Director; Michael R. Klein, Chair. Box office, (202) 547-1122. Educational programs, (202) 547-5688. Toll-free, (877) 487-8849. TTY, (202) 546-9606.*
Web, www.shakespearetheatre.org

Professional resident theater that presents Shakespearean and other classical plays. Offers actor training program for youths, adults, and professional actors. Produces free outdoor summer Shakespeare plays and free Shakespeare plays for schools.

Visual Arts

▶**AGENCIES**

National Endowment for the Arts (NEA), *Design, 400 7th St. S.W., 20506; (202) 682-5452. Fax, (202) 682-5721.*

Jen Hughes, Director, (202) 682-5547.
TTY, (202) 682-5496.
Web, www.arts.gov/artistic-fields/design

Provides grants to nonprofit organizations to fund the role of creative design and visual arts in economic revitalization and creating sustainable communities.

National Endowment for the Arts (NEA), *Visual Arts, 400 7th St. S.W., 20506; (202) 682-5442. Fax, (202) 682-5721. Wendy Clark, Director, (202) 682-5555. TTY, (202) 682-5496. Web, www.arts.gov/artistic-fields/visual-arts*

Awards grants to nonprofit organizations for creative works and programs in the visual arts, including painting, sculpture, crafts, video, photography, printmaking, drawing, artists' books, and performance art.

Smithsonian Institution, *Archives of American Art, 750 9th St. N.W., #2200, 20001 (mailing address: P.O. Box 37012, Victor Bldg., #2200, MRC 937, Washington, DC 20013-7012); (202) 633-7940. Fax, (202) 633-7994. Kate Haw, Director, (202) 633-7992. Reference desk, (202) 633-7950. Web, www.aaa.si.edu and Twitter, @ArchivesAmerArt*

Collects and preserves manuscript items, such as notebooks, sketchbooks, letters, and journals; photos of artists and works of art; tape-recorded interviews with artists, dealers, and collectors; exhibition catalogs; directories; and biographies on the history of visual arts in the United States. Library open to scholars and researchers. Reference centers that maintain microfilm copies of a selection of the Archives' collection include New York; Boston; San Francisco; and San Marino, Calif.

State Dept., *Art in Embassies, 2201 C St. N.W., 20520; (703) 875-4202. Vacant, Director. TTY, (703) 875-4182. General email, artinembassies@state.gov*
Web, http://art.state.gov and Twitter, @ArtinEmbassies

Exhibits American art in U.S. ambassadorial residences. Borrows artworks from artists, collectors, galleries, and museums.

►CONGRESS

For a listing of relevant congressional committees and subcommittees, please see page 124 or the Appendix.

Library of Congress, *Prints and Photographs Division, James Madison Memorial Bldg., 101 Independence Ave. S.E., #LM 337, 20540-4730; (202) 707-6394. Fax, (202) 707-6647. Helena Zinkham, Chief, (202) 707-2922. Web, www.loc.gov/rr/print*

Maintains Library of Congress's collection of pictorial material not in book format, totaling more than 15 million items. U.S. and international collections include artists' prints; historical prints, posters, and drawings; photographs (chiefly documentary); political and social cartoons; and architectural plans, drawings, prints, and photographs. Reference service provided in the Prints and Photographs Reading Room. Reproductions of nonrestricted material available through the Library of Congress's Photoduplication Service; prints and photographs may be borrowed through the Exhibits Office for exhibits by qualified institutions. A portion of the collections and an overview of reference services are available online.

►NONGOVERNMENTAL

American Institute of Architects, *1735 New York Ave. N.W., 20006-5292; (202) 626-7300. Fax, (202) 626-7547. Robert A. Ivy, Chief Executive Officer, ext. 7400. Government Advocacy, (202) 626-7480. Press, (202) 626-7457. Toll-free, (800) 242-3837. Alternate Phone, (202) 626-2555. General email, infocentral@aia.org*
Web, www.aia.org, Twitter, @AIANational and Facebook, www.facebook.com/AIANational

Membership: licensed American architects, interns, architecture faculty, engineers, planners, and those in government, manufacturing, or other fields in a capacity related to architecture. Works to advance the standards of architectural education, training, and practice. Promotes the aesthetic, scientific, and practical efficiency of architecture, urban design, and planning; monitors international developments. Offers continuing and professional education programs; sponsors scholarships, internships, and awards. Houses archival collection, including documents and drawings of American architects and architecture. Library open to the public by appointment. Monitors legislation and regulations.

Foundation for Art and Preservation in Embassies (FAPE), *1725 Eye St. N.W., #300, 20006-2423; (202) 349-3724. Fax, (202) 349-3727. Jennifer A. Duncan, Director. General email, info@fapeglobal.org*
Web, www.fapeglobal.org and Facebook, www.facebook .com/FAPEglobal

Works with the State Dept. to contribute fine art for placement in U.S. embassies worldwide.

International Arts and Artists, *9 Hillyer Court N.W., 20008; (202) 338-0680. Fax, (202) 333-0758. Lise Dube-Scherr, President. General email, info@artsandartists.org*
Web, www.artsandartists.org, Twitter, @IAAExchange and Facebook, www.facebook.com/artsandartists

Collects multicultural art and plans art exhibits for museums. Offers affordable print and digital services to artists and organizations. Local gallery, the Hillyer Arts Space, exhibits contemporary art.

National Assn. of Schools of Art and Design, *11250 Roger Bacon Dr., #21, Reston, VA 20190-5248; (703) 437-0700. Fax, (703) 437-6312. Karen Moynahan, Executive Director, (703) 437-0700, ext. 116. General email, info@arts-accredit.org*
Web, http://nasad.arts-accredit.org

Specialized professional accrediting agency for postsecondary programs in art and design. Conducts and shares research and analysis on topics pertinent to art and design programs and fields of art and design. Offers professional development opportunities for executives of art and design programs.

HISTORY AND PRESERVATION

General

▶AGENCIES

Advisory Council on Historic Preservation, *401 F St. N.W., #308, 20001-2637; (202) 517-0200. John M. Fowler, Executive Director.*
General email, achp@achp.gov
Web, www.achp.gov, Twitter, @usachp and Facebook, www.facebook.com/ PreservationTheNextGeneration

Advises the president and Congress on historic preservation; reviews and comments on federal projects and programs affecting historic, architectural, archaeological, and cultural resources. Monitors legislation and regulations.

Bureau of Educational and Cultural Affairs (ECA) *(State Dept.),* **Cultural Heritage Center,** *2200 C St. N.W., 5th Floor, 20037; (202) 632-6197. Cari Enav, Director.*
General email, culprop@state.gov
Web, http://eca.state.gov/cultural-heritage-center, Twitter, @HeritageatState and Facebook, www.facebook .com/usafcp

Protects and preserves ancient and historic monuments, objects, and archaeological sites. Reviews country requests for import restrictions on archaeological or ethnological artifacts and makes recommendations on them to the State Dept. Distributes information to police, customs, museums, dealers, and collectors about cultural heritage objects stolen from archaeological sites, museums, and churches.

Bureau of Engraving and Printing (BEP) *(Treasury Dept.),* *14th and C Sts. S.W., 20228; (202) 874-4000. Fax, (202) 874-3177. Leonard R. Olijar, Director. Information, (877) 874-4114. Tours, (202) 874-2330.*
General email, moneyfactory.info@bep.gov
Web, www.moneyfactory.gov

Provides information on history, design, and engraving of currency; offers public tours; maintains reading room where materials are brought for special research. (For an appointment, write to the BEP's Historical Resource Center at the email below.)

Bureau of Land Management (BLM) *(Interior Dept.),* **Cultural and Paleontological Resources and Tribal Consultation,** *20 M St. S.E., #2134, 20003; (202) 912-7242. Emily Palus, Deputy Division Chief.*
Web, www.blm.gov/programs/cultural-heritage-and-paleontology

Develops bureau policy on historic preservation, archaeological resource protection, consultation with Native Americans, curation of artifacts and records, heritage education, and paleontological resource management.

General Services Administration (GSA), *Design and Construction, Office of the Chief Architect, 1800 F St. N.W., #5400, 20405-0001; (202) 501-1888. David Insinga, Chief Architect.*
General email, david.insinga@gsa.gov
Web, www.gsa.gov/portal/content/104549

Administers the preservation of historic federal buildings.

National Archives and Records Administration (NARA), *Cartographic and Architectural Unit, 8601 Adelphi Rd., #3320, College Park, MD 20740-6001; (301) 837-3200. Fax, (301) 837-3622. Peter F. Brauer, Cartographic Supervisor, (301) 837-2036.*
General email, carto@nara.gov
Web, www.archives.gov/publications/general-info-leaflets/ 26-cartographic.html

Preserves and makes available historical records of federal agencies, including maps, charts, aerial photographs, architectural engineering drawings, patents, lighthouse plans, and ships' plans. Research room open to the public. Records are available for reproduction.

National Archives and Records Administration (NARA), *Preservation Programs, 8601 Adelphi Rd., #2800, College Park, MD 20740-6001; (301) 837-0678. Allison Olson, Director.*
General email, preservation@nara.gov
Web, www.archives.gov/preservation

Manages the preservation program for the 44 National Archives facilities across the country. Develops preservation policy, regulations, and planning. Responsible for conserving and reformatting archival holdings. Ensures that the storage environments are designed and maintained to prolong the life of records. Manages records during emergency preparedness and response for the agency; advises other federal agencies in event of need. Conducts research and testing for materials purchased by and used in the archives, as well as deterioration and preservation processes. Monitors and maintains the condition of the Charters of Freedom.

National Archives and Records Administration (NARA), *Research Services, 8601 Adelphi Rd., #3400, College Park, MD 20740-6001; (301) 837-2000. Fax, (301) 837-3633. Ann A. Cummings, Executive for Research Services, (301) 837-3110. Research customer service, (301) 837-1659. Toll-free, (866) 272-6272.*
Web, www.archives.gov/research

Preserves and makes available federal records at fifteen National Archives facilities across the country.

National Endowment for the Humanities (NEH), *Preservation and Access, 400 7th St. S.W., 20506; (202) 606-8570. Fax, (202) 606-8639. Nadina Gardner, Director, (202) 606-8442.*
General email, preservation@neh.gov
Web, www.neh.gov/divisions/preservation and Twitter, @NEH_PresAccess

Sponsors preservation and access projects, the stabilization and documentation of material culture collections, and the National Digital Newspaper program.

National Museum of American History *(Smithsonian Institution), Curatorial Affairs, 12th St. and Constitution Ave. N.W., 20560 (mailing address: P.O. Box 37012, MRC 664, Washington, DC 20013-7012); (202) 633-3497. Fax, (202) 633-4284. Catherine Eagleton, Associate Director.*
General email, info@si.edu

Web, www.americanhistory.si.edu/about/departments/curatorial-affairs

Conducts research, develops collections, and creates exhibits on American social and public history, based on collections of folk and popular arts, ethnic and craft objects, textiles, coins, costumes and jewelry, ceramics and glass, graphic arts, musical instruments, photographs, technological innovations, appliances, and machines. Research areas are open by appointment.

National Museum of American History *(Smithsonian Institution), Library, 14th St. and Constitution Ave. N.W., R5016, MRC 630, 20560-0630 (mailing address: #5016 Smithsonian Institution, P.O. Box 37012, MRC 360, Washington, DC 20013-7012); (202) 633-3865. Fax, (202) 633-3427. William Baxter, Head Librarian, (202) 633-2067.*
General email, askalibrarian@si.edu

Web, www.library.si.edu/libraries/national-museum-american-history-library

Online catalogue, http://siris-libraries.si.edu/ipac20/ipac .jsp?profile=liball

Supports research on American history, including social, cultural, political, and economic events and development. Maintains collection of trade catalogs and materials about expositions and world fairs. Open to the public by appointment. All library holdings are listed in the online catalog.

National Museum of Health and Medicine *(Defense Dept.), 2500 Linden Lane, Silver Spring, MD 20910 (mailing address: 2460 Linden Lane, Bldg. 2500, Silver Spring, MD 20910); (301) 319-3300. Fax, (301) 319-3373. Dr. Adrianne Noe, Director. Tours, (301) 319-3312.*
General email, usarmy.detrick.medcom-usamrmc.list .medical-museum@mail.mil

Web, www.medicalmuseum.mil and Twitter, @medicalmuseum

Maintains exhibits related to pathology and the history of medicine, particularly military medicine during the Civil War. Open to the public 10:00 a.m.–5:30 p.m., seven days a week. Study collection available for scholars by appointment.

National Park Service (NPS) *(Interior Dept.), 1849 C St. N.W., #3115, 20240; (202) 208-3818. Fax, (202) 208-7889. Paul Daniel Smith, Director (Acting). Press, (202) 208-6843.*

General email, asknps@nps.gov

Web, www.nps.gov and Twitter, @NatlParkService

Administers national parks, monuments, historic sites, and recreation areas.

National Park Service (NPS) *(Interior Dept.), Cultural Resources, Partnerships, and Science, 1849 C St. N.W., #3128, MIB, 20240-0001; (202) 220-4132. Joy Beasley, Associate Director (Acting).*
Web, www.nps.gov/orgs/1345

Oversees preservation of federal historic sites and administration of building programs. Programs include the National Register of Historic Places, National Historic and National Landmark Programs, Historic American Building Survey, Historic American Engineering Record, Archeology and Antiquities Act Program, and Technical Preservation Services. Gives grant and aid assistance and tax benefit information to properties listed in the National Register of Historic Places.

►CONGRESS

For a listing of relevant congressional committees and subcommittees, please see page 124 or the Appendix.

Library of Congress, *Serial and Government Publications, James Madison Memorial Bldg., 101 Independence Ave. S.E., #LM 133, 20540-4760; (202) 707-5690. Teri Sierra, Chief, (202) 707-5277. Current periodical reading room, (202) 707-5691. Reference desk, (202) 707-5208.*
Web, www.loc.gov/rr/news

Collects and maintains information on governmental and nongovernmental organizations that are domestically or internationally based, financed, and sponsored. Responds to written or telephone requests to provide information on the history, structure, operation, and activities of these organizations. Collects and maintains domestic and foreign newspapers and periodicals. Some microfilm materials are available for interlibrary loan through the Library of Congress CALM Division.

Senate Office of Conservation and Preservation, *S416 CAP, 20510; (202) 224-4550. Leona Faust, Director, (202) 224-5730.*

Develops and coordinates programs related to the conservation and preservation of Senate records and materials for the secretary of the Senate.

►NONGOVERNMENTAL

American Battlefield Trust, *1156 15th St. N.W., #900, 20005; (202) 367-1861. Fax, (202) 367-1865. James Lighthizer, President.*
General email, info@battlefields.org

Web, www.battlefields.org and Twitter, @battlefields

Membership: preservation professionals, historians, conservation activists, and citizens. Preserves endangered Civil War battlefields throughout the United States. Conducts preservation conferences and workshops. Advises local preservation groups. Monitors legislation and regulations at the federal, state, and local levels.

American Historical Assn., *777 6th St., N.W., 20001; (202) 544-2422. Fax, (202) 544-8307. James (Jim) Grossman, Executive Director. General email, info@historians.org Web, www.historians.org, Twitter, @AHAHistorians and Facebook, www.facebook.com/AHAHistorians*

Membership: university academics, colleges, museums, historical organizations, libraries and archives, independent historians, students, K–12 teachers, government and business professionals, and individuals interested in history. Interests include academic freedom, professional standards, publication, teaching, professional development, networking, and advocacy. Supports public access to government information; publishes original historical research, journals, bibliographies, historical directories, and a job placement bulletin.

American Institute for Conservation of Historic and Artistic Works, *727 15th St. N.W., #500, 20005-1714; (202) 452-9545. Fax, (202) 452-9328. Eryl P. Wentworth, Executive Director, (202) 661-8060. General email, info@conservation-US.org Web, www.conservation-US.org, Twitter, @conservators and Facebook, www.facebook.com/aiconservation*

Membership: professional conservators, scientists, students, administrators, cultural institutions, collection care professionals, and others. Promotes the knowledge and practice of the conservation of cultural property; supports research; and disseminates information on conservation.

American Studies Assn., *1120 19th St. N.W., #301, 20036-3614; (202) 467-4783. Fax, (202) 467-4786. John F. Stephens, Executive Director. General email, asastaff@theasa.net Web, www.theasa.net and Twitter, @AmeriStudiesAssn*

Fosters the interdisciplinary exchange of ideas about American culture and history in local and global contexts; awards annual prizes for contributions to American studies; provides curriculum resources.

Daughters of the American Revolution, *National Society, 1776 D St. N.W., 20006-5303; (202) 628-1776. Fax, (202) 879-3227. Ann T. Dillon, President General. Web, www.dar.org and Twitter, @TodaysDAR*

Membership: women descended from American Revolutionary War patriots. Conducts historical, educational, and patriotic activities; maintains a genealogical library, fine arts museum, and documentary collection antedating 1830. Library open to the public.

National Conference of State Historic Preservation Officers, *444 N. Capitol St. N.W., #342, 20001-1512; (202) 624-5465. Fax, (202) 624-5419. Erik Hein, Executive Director; Ted Monoson, Director of Government Relations. Web, www.ncshpo.org and Twitter, @NCSHPO*

Membership: state and territorial historic preservation officers and deputy officers. Compiles statistics on programs; monitors legislation and regulations.

National Park Trust, *401 E. Jefferson St., #207, Rockville, MD 20850; (301) 279-7275. Fax, (301) 279-7211. Grace K. Lee, Executive Director. General email, npt@parktrust.org Web, www.parktrust.org and Twitter, @natparktrust*

Protects national parks, wildlife refuges, and historic monuments. Uses funds to purchase private land within or adjacent to existing parks and land suitable for new parks; works with preservation organizations to manage acquired resources.

National Preservation Institute, *P.O. Box 1702, Alexandria, VA 22313; (703) 765-0100. Fax, (703) 768-9350. Jere Gibber, Executive Director; Darwina L. Neal, President. General email, info@npi.org Web, www.npi.org and Facebook, www.facebook.com/ National-Preservation-Institute-273102762795*

Conducts seminars in historic preservation and cultural resource management for those involved in the management, preservation, and stewardship of historic and cultural resources.

National Society of Colonial Dames of America, *2715 Que St. N.W., 20007-3071; (202) 337-2288. Fax, (202) 337-0348. Anna F. Duff, Executive Director. General email, dames@dumbartonhouse.org Web, www.nscda.org and Twitter, @colonialdames*

Membership: descendants of colonists in America before 1750. Conducts historical and educational activities; maintains Dumbarton House, a museum open to the public Tuesday–Sunday; and offers lectures and concerts.

National Society of Colonial Dames XVII Century, *1300 New Hampshire Ave. N.W., 20036-1502; (202) 293-1700. Fax, (202) 466-6099. Leslie Daly Breaux, President General. General email, cd17th@verizon.net Web, www.colonialdames17c.org*

Membership: American women who are lineal descendants of persons who rendered civil or military service and lived in America or one of the British colonies before 1701. Preserves records and shrines; encourages historical research; awards scholarships to undergraduate and graduate students and scholarships in medicine to persons of Native American descent.

National Society of the Children of the American Revolution, *1776 D St. N.W., #224, 20006-5303; (202) 638-3153. Fax, (202) 737-3162. Joanne Zumbrun, Senior National President. General email, hq@nscar.org Web, www.nscar.org*

Membership: descendants, age twenty-two years and under, of American soldiers and patriots of the American Revolution. Conducts historical, educational, and patriotic activities; preserves places of historical interest.

National Trust for Historic Preservation, *2600 Virginia Ave. N.W., #1100, 20037; (202) 588-6000. Fax, (202) 588-6038. Paul Edmondson, President;*

Robin Scullin, Public Affairs. Press, (202) 588-6141.
Toll-free, (800) 944-6847.
General email, info@savingplaces.org
Web, www.preservationnation.org

Conducts seminars, workshops, and conferences on topics related to preservation, including neighborhood conservation, main street revitalization, rural conservation, and preservation law; offers financial assistance through loan and grant programs; provides advisory services; operates historic house sites, which are open to the public; and publishes quarterly magazine and e-newsletters.

Preservation Action, 2020 Pennsylvania Ave. N. W. , #3B, 20006; (202) 463-0970. Fax, (202) 463-1299. Robert Naylor, Program Manager; Bruce MacDougal, Director of Washington Operations.
General email, mail@preservationaction.org
Web, www.preservationaction.org and
Twitter, @PreservationAct

Monitors legislation affecting historic preservation and neighborhood conservation. Maintains a nationwide database of activists. Promotes adequate funding for historic preservation programs and policies that support historic resource protection.

Society for American Archaeology, 1111 14th St. N.W., #800, 20005-5622; (202) 789-8200. Fax, (202) 789-0284. Joe E. Watkins, President.
General email, headquarters@saa.org
Web, www.saa.org and Twitter, @SAAorg

Promotes greater awareness, understanding, and research of archaeology on the American continents; works to preserve and publish results of scientific data and research; serves as information clearinghouse for members.

Archives and Manuscripts

▶**AGENCIES**

National Archives and Records Administration (NARA), 700 Pennsylvania Ave. N.W., 20408 (mailing address: 8601 Adelphi Rd., College Park, MD 20704-6001);
(866) 272-6272. Fax, (202) 357-5901. David S. Ferriero, Archivist of the United States, (202) 357-5900.
Communications and marketing, (202) 357-5300. Public programs and events, (202) 357-5000.
Web, www.archives.gov and Twitter, @USNatArchives

Identifies, preserves, and makes available federal government documents of historic value; administers a network of regional storage centers and archives and operates the presidential library system. Collections include photographs, graphic materials, films, and maps; holdings include records generated by foreign governments (especially in wartime) and by international conferences, commissions, and exhibitions.

National Archives and Records Administration (NARA), *Center for Legislative Archives,* 700 Pennsylvania Ave. N.W., #8E, 20408; (202) 357-5350. Fax, (202) 357-5911. Richard H. Hunt, Director, (202) 357-5472.

General email, legislative.archives@nara.gov
Web, www.archives.gov/legislative and
Twitter, @CongressArchive

Collects and maintains records of congressional committees and legislative files from 1789 to the present. Publishes inventories and guides to these records.

National Archives and Records Administration (NARA), *Electronic Records Division,* 8601 Adelphi Rd., #5320, College Park, MD 20740-6001; (301) 837-0740.
Fax, (301) 837-3681. Theodore J. Hull, Director, (301) 837-1824.
General email, era.program@nara.gov
Web, www.archives.gov/records-mgmt/era/technical.html

Preserves, maintains, and makes available electronic records of the U.S. government. Provides researchers with magnetic tape, CD, DVD, and other copies of electronic records on a cost-recovery basis. Offers direct downloads and searches of selected holdings.

National Archives and Records Administration (NARA), *Presidential Libraries,* 8601 Adelphi Rd., #2200, College Park, MD 20740-6001; (301) 837-3250.
Fax, (301) 837-3199. Fax, (301) 837-3218.
Susan K. Donius, Director (Acting), (202) 357-5376.
Web, www.archives.gov/presidential-libraries and
Twitter, @OurPresidents

Administers thirteen presidential libraries. Directs all programs relating to acquisition, preservation, and research use of materials in presidential libraries; conducts oral history projects; publishes finding aids for research sources; provides reference service, including information from and about documentary holdings. Conducts community outreach; oversees museum exhibition programming.

National Archives and Records Administration (NARA), *Reference Services,* 4205 Suitland Rd., Suitland, MD 20746-8001; (301) 778-1600. Christopher Pinkney, Director.
General email, suitland.reference@nara.gov
Web, www.archives.gov/frc/reference-services.html

Provides reference service for unpublished civil and military federal government records. Maintains central catalog of all archival materials. Compiles comprehensive bibliographies of materials related to archival administration and records management. Permits research in American history, archival science, and records management. Maintains collections of the papers of the Continental Congress (1774–1789), U.S. State Dept. diplomatic correspondence (1789–1963), and general records of the U.S. government.

National Archives and Records Administration (NARA), *Textual Reference Archives,* 700 Pennsylvania Ave. N.W., #G13, 20408; (202) 357-5287. Fax, (202) 357-5934. Trevor K. Plante, Branch Chief, (202) 357-5287;
Dennis M. Edelin, Section Chief, (202) 357-5266.
General email, archives1reference@nara.gov
Web, www.archives.gov

Provides access to the textual records of the Executive and Judicial Branches of the federal government located in

National Park Service Sites in the Capital Region

The National Park Service administers most parks, circles, and monuments in the District of Columbia, as well as sites in nearby Maryland, Virginia, and West Virginia. For information on facilities not listed here, visit www.nps.gov/parks.html.

Go to www.recreation.gov for information on visiting and making reservations at federal recreation sites nationwide.

Antietam National Battlefield, (301) 432-5124

Arlington House, Robert E. Lee Memorial, (703) 235-1530

C & O Canal National Historical Park, (301) 739-4200

Great Falls Area (C & O Canal Maryland), (301) 767-3714

Catoctin Mountain Park, (301) 663-9388

Clara Barton National Historic Site, (301) 320-1410

Ford's Theatre National Historic Site, (202) 426-6924

Fort Washington Park (includes Piscataway Park), (301) 763-4600

Frederick Douglass National Historic Site, (202) 426-5961

George Washington Memorial Parkway (includes memorials to Theodore Roosevelt, Lyndon Johnson, and U.S. Marine Corps), (703) 289-2500

Glen Echo Park, (301) 634-2222

Great Falls Park, Virginia, (703) 757-3103

Greenbelt Park, (301) 344-3948

Harpers Ferry National Historical Park, (304) 535-6029

Manassas National Battlefield Park, (703) 361-1339

Mary McLeod Bethune Council House National Historic Site, (202) 673-2402

Monocacy National Battlefield, (301) 662-3515

National Mall (includes presidential and war memorials and Pennsylvania Avenue National Historic Site), (202) 426-6841

President's Park (White House), (202) 208-1631

Prince William Forest Park, (703) 221-7181

Rock Creek Park, (202) 895-6000

Thomas Stone National Historic Site, (301) 392-1776

Wolf Trap National Park for the Performing Arts, (703) 255-1800

General email, nhprc@nara.gov

Web, www.archives.gov/nhprc

Awards grants to nonprofit institutions, educational institutions, and local and state governments to preserve and make accessible historical records, including the papers of nationally significant Americans. Helps preserve electronic records and digitize and publish online collections.

National Museum of American History (*Smithsonian Institution*), *Archives Center, 14th St. and Constitution Ave. N.W., 20560-0601 (mailing address: P.O. Box 37012, NMAH MRC 601, Washington, DC 20013-7012); (202) 633-3270. Fax, (202) 312-1990. Robert Horton, Assistant Director. Press, (202) 633-3129. TTY, (202) 357-1729.*
General email, archivescenter@si.edu

Web, www.americanhistory.si.edu/archives

Acquires, organizes, preserves, and makes available for research the museum's archival and documentary materials relating to American history and culture. Three-dimensional objects and closely related documents are in the care of curatorial divisions. Research areas are open by appointment.

Smithsonian Institution, *Archives of American Art, 750 9th St. N.W., #2200, 20001 (mailing address: P.O. Box 37012, Victor Bldg., #2200, MRC 937, Washington, DC 20013-7012); (202) 633-7940. Fax, (202) 633-7994. Kate Haw, Director, (202) 633-7992. Reference desk, (202) 633-7950.*
Web, www.aaa.si.edu and Twitter, @ArchivesAmerArt

Collects and preserves manuscript items, such as notebooks, sketchbooks, letters, and journals; photos of artists and works of art; tape-recorded interviews with artists, dealers, and collectors; exhibition catalogs; directories; and biographies on the history of visual arts in the United States. Library open to scholars and researchers. Reference centers that maintain microfilm copies of a selection of the Archives' collection include New York; Boston; San Francisco; and San Marino, Calif.

▶CONGRESS

For a listing of relevant congressional committees and subcommittees, please see page 124 or the Appendix.

Library of Congress, *Main Reading Room, Thomas Jefferson Bldg., 101 Independence Ave. S.E., #LJ 100, 20540-4660; (202) 707-3399. Fax, (202) 707-1957. Michael North, Head.*
Web, www.loc.gov/rr/main

Point of access to the general collection of books and bound periodicals as well as electronic resources including microform. Offers research orientations.

Library of Congress, *Manuscript Division, James Madison Memorial Bldg., 101 Independence Ave. S.E., #LM 101, 20540-4680; (202) 707-5383. Fax, (202) 707-7791. Jeff Flannery, Chief. Reading room, (202) 707-5387.*
Web, www.loc.gov/rr/mss

Maintains, describes, and provides reference service on the library's manuscript collections, including the papers

---

the National Archives in Washington, D.C., and College Park, Md. Makes reproductions for a fee.

National Historical Publications and Records Commission (*National Archives and Records Administration*), *700 Pennsylvania Ave. N.W., #114, 20408-0001; (202) 357-5010. Fax, (202) 357-5914. Christopher Eck, Executive Director, (202) 357-5010; Lucy Barber, Deputy Executive Director, (202) 357-5306. Toll-free, (866) 272-6272.*

of U.S. presidents and other eminent Americans. Manuscript reading room primarily serves serious scholars and researchers; historians and reference librarians are available for consultation.

Library of Congress, *Microform and Electronic Resources Center,* *Thomas Jefferson Bldg., 101 Independence Ave. S.E., #LJ 139, 20540-4660; (202) 707-4773. Fax, (202) 707-1957. James P. Sweany, Head.*
Web, www.loc.gov/rr/main.ccc.htm/microform

Has custody of and services the library's general microform collection. Provides work stations for searching the library's online catalog and accessing the Internet. Open to the public, hours posted on the website.

Library of Congress, *National Digital Information Infrastructure and Preservation Program (NDIIPP),* *James Madison Memorial Bldg., 101 Independence Ave. S.E., 20540-1300; (202) 707-6530. Fax, (202) 707-0815. Bud Barto, Chief Information Officer; Kim Barnhart, Administrative Assistant.*

Oversees development of a national strategy for collecting, archiving, and preserving digital content, and directs the activities of the Information Technology Directorate.

Library of Congress, *Preservation Directorate, 101 Independence Ave. S.E., 20540; (202) 707-1840. Fenella France, Director, (202) 707-2922. General email, preserve@loc.gov*
Web, www.loc.gov/preservation

Responsible for preserving book and paper materials in the library's collections.

Senate Historical Office, *201 SHOB, 20510; (202) 224-6900. Betty K. Koed, Historian. General email, historian@sec.senate.gov*
Web, www.senate.gov/art/art_hist_home.htm and Twitter, @SenateHistory

Serves as an information clearinghouse on Senate history, traditions, and members. Collects, organizes, and distributes to the public unpublished Senate documents; collects and preserves photographs and pictures related to Senate history; conducts an oral history program; advises senators and Senate committees on the disposition of their noncurrent papers and records. Produces publications on the history of the Senate.

U.S. House of Representatives, *Office of Art and Archives, B53 CHOB, 20515; (202) 226-1300. Fax, (202) 226-4635. Farar P. Elliott, Chief. General art email, art@mail.house.gov General archives email, archives@mail.house.gov*
Web, http://history.house.gov and Twitter, @USHouseHistory

Works with the Office of the Historian to provide access to published documents and historical records of the House. Advises members on the disposition of their records and papers; maintains information on manuscript collections of former members; maintains biographical files on former members; houses photographs and artifacts of former members. Produces publications on Congress and its members.

U.S. House of Representatives, *Office of the Historian, B53 CHOB, 20515; (202) 226-1300. Matthew A. Wasniewski, House Historian. General email, history@mail.house.gov*
Web, http://history.house.gov and Twitter, @ushousehistory

Works with the Office of Art and Archives to provide access to published documents and historical records of the House. Conducts historical research. Advises members on the disposition of their records and papers; maintains information on manuscript collections of former members; maintains biographical files on former members. Produces publications on Congress and its members.

▶**NONGOVERNMENTAL**

Assassination Archives and Research Center, *962 Wayne Ave., #910, Silver Spring, MD 20910; (301) 565-0249. James Lesar, President. General email, aarc@aarclibrary.org*
Web, www.aarclibrary.org and Twitter, @aarclibrary

Acquires, preserves, and disseminates information on political assassinations. Materials and information available on website and by request through mail. On-site access available to the public by appointment only.

Moorland-Spingarn Research Center (MSRC) *(Howard University), 500 Howard Pl. N.W., #263, 20059; (202) 806-7275. Fax, (202) 806-5903. Rhea Ballard-Thrower, Executive Director, (202) 806-7236; Celia C. Daniel, Librarian, (202) 806-7446. Library, (202) 806-7250.*
Web, http://library.howard.edu/MSRC and Twitter, @MoorlandHU

Comprehensive repository for the documentation of the history and culture of people of African descent in Africa, the Americas, and other parts of the world; collects, preserves, and makes available for research a wide range of resources chronicling the black experience.

National Security Archive *(George Washington University), Gelman Library, 2130 H St. N.W., #701, 20037; (202) 994-7000. Fax, (202) 994-7005. Thomas Blanton, Director. General email, nsarchiv@gwu.edu*
Web, www.nsarchive.org

Research institute and library that provides information on U.S. foreign and economic policy and national security affairs. Maintains and publishes collection of declassified and unclassified documents obtained through the Freedom of Information Act. Archive open to the public by appointment. Website has a Russian-language link.

Society of the Cincinnati, *2118 Massachusetts Ave. N.W., 20008; (202) 785-2040. Fax, (202) 785-0729. Jack Duane Warren Jr., Executive Director, ext. 410. Library appointments, ext. 426. Press, ext. 445.*

General email, admin@societyofthecincinnati.org

Web, https://societyofthecincinnati.org and
Twitter, @AndersonHouse

Collects and preserves American manuscripts and books from the 1700s. Specializes in documents and artifacts related to the American Revolution.

Genealogy

▶**AGENCIES**

National Archives and Records Administration (NARA),
700 Pennsylvania Ave. N.W., 20408 (mailing address: 8601 Adelphi Rd., College Park, MD 20704-6001);
(866) 272-6272. Fax, (202) 357-5901. David S. Ferriero, Archivist of the United States, (202) 357-5900.
Communications and marketing, (202) 357-5300. Public programs and events, (202) 357-5000.
Web, www.archives.gov and *Twitter, @USNatArchives*

Makes available resources for genealogy research, including military, passport, immigration, census, and land records. Holds genealogy consultations at the Microfilm Research desk one Saturday every month. Genealogy lectures and workshops are available nationwide; events may be found on the National Archives calendar www .archives.gov/calendar.

National Archives and Records Administration (NARA),
Textual Reference Archives, 700 Pennsylvania Ave. N.W., #G13, 20408; (202) 357-5287. Fax, (202) 357-5934. Trevor K. Plante, Branch Chief, (202) 357-5287; Dennis M. Edelin, Section Chief, (202) 357-5266. General email, archives1reference@nara.gov

Web, www.archives.gov

Assists individuals interested in researching record holdings of the National Archives, including genealogical records; issues research cards to researchers who present photo identification. Users must be at least fourteen years of age.

▶**CONGRESS**

For a listing of relevant congressional committees and subcommittees, please see page 124 or the Appendix.

Library of Congress, *Local History and Genealogy Reference Services, Thomas Jefferson Bldg., 101 Independence Ave. S.E., #LJ 100, 20540-4660; (202) 707-3399. Fax, (202) 707-1957. James P. Sweany, Head. Web, www.loc.gov/rr/genealogy*

Provides reference and referral service on topics related to local history, genealogy, and heraldry throughout the United States.

▶**NONGOVERNMENTAL**

Daughters of the American Revolution, *National Society, 1776 D St. N.W., 20006-5303; (202) 628-1776. Fax, (202) 879-3227. Ann T. Dillon, President General. Web, www.dar.org* and *Twitter, @TodaysDAR*

Membership: women descended from American Revolutionary War patriots. Maintains a genealogical library, which is open to the public.

National Genealogical Society, *6400 Arlington Blvd., #810, Falls Church, VA 22042; (703) 525-0050. Fax, (703) 525-0052. Ben Spratling, President. Toll-free, (800) 473-0060. General email, ngs@ngsgenealogy.org*

Web, www.ngsgenealogy.org, Twitter, @ngsgenealogy and *Facebook, www.facebook.com/ngsgenealogy*

Encourages study of genealogy and publication of all records that are of genealogical interest. Provides online courses and an in-depth home study program; holds an annual conference.

National Museum of Civil War Medicine, *48 E. Patrick St., Frederick, MD 21705 (mailing address: P.O. Box 470, Frederick, MD 21705); (301) 695-1864. Fax, (301) 695-6823. David Price, Executive Director. General email, info@civilwarmed.org*

Web, www.civilwarmed.org and *Twitter, @civilwarmed*

Assists individuals with questions about ancestors injured in the Civil War.

National Society Daughters of the American Colonists,
2205 Massachusetts Ave. N.W., 20008-2813; (202) 667-3076. Fax, (202) 667-0571. Mary C. Armstrong, President. General email, admin@nsdac.org

Web, www.nsdac.org

Membership: women descended from men and women who were resident in or gave civil or military service to the colonies prior to the Revolutionary War. Maintains library of colonial and genealogical records, open to the public by appointment.

Washington D.C. Family History Center, *10000 Stoneybrook Dr., Kensington, MD 20895; (301) 587-0042. Linda Christensen, Director. General email, info@wdcfhc.org*

Web, www.wdcfhc.org

Maintains genealogical library for research. Collection includes international genealogical index, family group record archives, microfiche registers, and the Family Search Computer Program (www.familysearch.org). Library open to the public. (Sponsored by the Church of Jesus Christ of Latter-day Saints.)

Specific Cultures

▶**AGENCIES**

Center for Folklife and Cultural Heritage *(Smithsonian Institution), 600 Maryland Ave. S.W., #2001, 20024 (mailing address: P.O. Box 37012, MRC 520, Washington, DC 20013-7012); (202) 633-6440. Fax, (202) 633-6474. Michael Atwood Mason, Director, (202) 633-1141. General email, folklife@si.edu*

Web, https://folklife.si.edu and *Twitter, @SmithsonianFolk*

Promotes and conducts research into traditional U.S. cultures and foreign folklife traditions; produces folkways recordings, films, videos, and educational programs; presents annual Smithsonian Folklife Festival in Washington, D.C.

Interior Dept. (DOI), *Indian Arts and Crafts Board (IACB),* 1849 C St. N.W., #2528-MIB, 20240-0001; (202) 208-3773. Fax, (202) 208-5196. Meridith Z. Stanton, Director. Toll-free, (888) 278-3253.
General email, iacb@ios.doi.gov
Web, www.doi.gov/iacb and Facebook, www.facebook.com/ IndianArtsandCraftsBoard

Advises Native American artisans and craft guilds; produces a source directory on arts and crafts of Native Americans (including Alaska Natives); maintains museums of native crafts in Montana, South Dakota, and Oklahoma; provides information on the Indian Arts and Crafts Act.

National Museum of the American Indian *(Smithsonian Institution),* 4th St. and Independence Ave. S.W., 20560; (202) 633-6803. Fax, (202) 633-6920. Kevin Gover, Director, (202) 633-6707. General Smithsonian information, (202) 633-1000. Group reservations, (202) 633-6644. TTY, (202) 633-5285. TTY group reservations, (202) 633-6751.
General email, NMAI-info@si.edu
Web, www.americanindian.si.edu and Twitter, @SmithsonianNMA

Collects, exhibits, preserves, and studies American Indian languages, literature, history, art, and culture. Operates ImagiNations activity center, open to the public. (Affiliated with the George Gustav Heye Center, 1 Bowling Green, New York, NY 10004 and the Cultural Resources Center, 4220 Silver Hill Rd., Suitland, MD 20746.)

▶**CONGRESS**

For a listing of relevant congressional committees and subcommittees, please see page 124 or the Appendix.

Library of Congress, *American Folklife Center,* Thomas Jefferson Bldg., 101 Independence Ave. S.E., #LJ G53, 20540-4610; (202) 707-5510. Fax, (202) 707-2076. Elizabeth (Betsy) Peterson, Director, (202) 202-1745. Folklife events, (202) 707-5510. Reading room, (202) 707-5510.
General email, folklife@loc.gov
Web, www.loc.gov/folklife

Coordinates national, regional, state and local government, and private folklife activities; contracts with individuals and groups for research and field studies in American folklife and for exhibits and workshops; maintains the National Archive of Folk Culture (an ethnographic collection of American and international folklore, grassroots oral histories, and ethnomusicology) and the Veterans History Project (a collection of oral histories and documentary materials from veterans of World Wars I and II and the Korean, Vietnam, and Persian Gulf wars). Conducts internships at the archive; lectures; sponsors year-round concerts of traditional and ethnic music.

American Folklife Center Reading Room is located in room #LJ G43.

▶**NONGOVERNMENTAL**

David S. Wyman Institute for Holocaust Studies, 1200 G St. N.W., #800, 20005; (202) 434-8994. Rafael Medoff, Director.
General email, info@wymaninstitute.org
Web, www.wymaninstitute.org

Educates the public about U.S. response to Nazism and the Holocaust through scholarly research, public events and exhibits, publications, conferences, and educational programs.

National Council for the Traditional Arts, 8757 Georgia Ave., #450, Silver Spring, MD 20910; (301) 565-0654. Fax, (301) 565-0472. Lora Bottinelli, Executive Director, ext. 11.
General email, info@ncta-usa.org
Web, www.ncta-usa.org and Twitter, @NCTA1933

Seeks to celebrate and honor arts of cultural and ethnic significance, including music, crafts, stories, and dance. Promotes artistic authenticity in festivals, national and international tours, concerts, radio and television programs, CD recordings, and films. Works with national parks and other institutions to create, plan, and present cultural events, exhibits, and other programs. Sponsors the annual National Folk Festival.

National Endowment for the Arts (NEA), *Folk and Traditional Arts,* 400 7th St. S.W., 20506; (202) 682-5428. Fax, (202) 682-5669. Clifford Murphy, Director, (202) 682-5726. TTY, (202) 682-5496.
Web, www.arts.gov/artistic-fields/folk-traditional-arts

Awards grants to the folk and traditional arts that are rooted in and reflective of the cultural life of communities.

National Hispanic Foundation for the Arts (NHFA), Washington Square, 1050 Connecticut Ave. N.W., 10th Floor, #500, 20036; (202) 293-8330. Fax, (202) 772-3101. Felix Sanchez, Chair.
General email, info@hispanicarts.org
Web, www.hispanicarts.org and Twitter, @felix_sanchez

Strives to increase the presence of Hispanics in the media, telecommunications, entertainment industries, and performing arts, and to increase programming for the U.S. Latino community. Provides scholarships for Hispanic students to pursue graduate study in the arts.

National Italian American Foundation, 1860 19th St. N.W., 20009; (202) 387-0600. Fax, (202) 387-0800. Jerry Jones, Chief of Staff, (202) 939-3102. Press, (202) 387-0600.
General email, information@niaf.org
Web, www.niaf.org

Membership: U.S. citizens of Italian ancestry. Promotes recognition of Italian American contributions to American society; funds cultural events, educational symposia, antidefamation programs, and grants and scholarships;

serves as an umbrella organization for local Italian American clubs throughout the United States.

Pew Research Center, Hispanic Trends Project, 1615 L St. N.W., #800, 20036; (202) 419-4300. Fax, (202) 419-3608. Mark Hugo Lopez, Director. Press, (202) 419-4372. Web, www.pewhispanic.org and Twitter, @PewHispanic

Seeks to improve understanding of the U.S. Hispanic population and its impact on the nation, as well as explore Latino views on a range of social matters and public policy issues, including public opinion, identity, and trends in voting, immigration, work, and education. Conducts public opinion surveys and other studies that are made available to the public. (A project of the Pew Research Center.)

Washington Area

▶AGENCIES

National Capital Planning Commission, 401 9th St. N.W., North Lobby, #500N, 20004; (202) 482-7200. Fax, (202) 482-7272. Marcel Acosta, Executive Director. General email, info@ncpc.gov Web, www.ncpc.gov

Central planning agency for the federal government in the national capital region, which includes the District of Columbia and suburban Maryland and Virginia. Reviews and approves plans for the preservation of certain historic and environmental features in the national capital region, including the annual federal capital improvement plan.

National Park Service (NPS) (Interior Dept.), National Capital Region, 1100 Ohio Dr. S.W., 20242; (202) 619-7020. Lisa Mendelson-Ielmini, Regional Director. Permits, (202) 245-4715. Web, www.nps.gov/ncro

Provides visitors with information on Washington-area parks, monuments, and Civil War battlefields; offers press services for the media and processes special event applications and permits.

White House Visitor Center (President's Park), 1450 Pennsylvania Ave. N.W., 20230; (202) 208-1631. Fax, (202) 208-1643. Peter Lonsway, Park Manager; Kathy Langley, Visitor Center Manager; John Stanwich, National Park Service White House Liaison, (202) 619-6344. TTY, (800) 877-8339. General email, presidents_park@nps.gov Web, www.nps.gov/whho and Twitter, @PresParkNPS

Administered by the National Park Service. Educates visitors about the White House through videos, exhibits, and historical artifacts. Public tours of the White House are available to those who submit requests to their member of Congress and are accepted up to six months in advance. (Ellipse Visitor Pavilion Complex located just west of the intersection of 15th and E Sts. N.W.)

▶CONGRESS

For a listing of relevant congressional committees and subcommittees, please see page 124 or the Appendix.

Senate Commission on Art, S411 CAP, 20510; (202) 224-2955. Melinda Smith, Curator of the Senate. General email, curator@sec.senate.gov Web, www.senate.gov/art/art_hist_home.htm

Accepts artwork and historical objects for display in Senate office buildings and the Senate wing of the Capitol. Maintains and exhibits Senate collections (paintings, sculptures, furniture, and manuscripts); oversees and maintains old Senate and Supreme Court chambers.

▶NONGOVERNMENTAL

Assn. for Preservation of Historic Congressional Cemetery, 1801 E St. S.E., 20003-2499; (202) 543-0539. Fax, (202) 449-8364. Paul Williams, President. General email, staff@congressionalcemetery.org Web, www.congressionalcemetery.org and Twitter, @CongCemetery

Administers and maintains the Washington Parish Burial Ground (commonly known as the Congressional Cemetery). Tours available Saturdays at 11:00 a.m. in warm weather. See website for tour information.

D.C. Preservation League, 1221 Connecticut Ave. N.W., #5A, 20036; (202) 783-5144. Fax, (202) 783-5596. Rebecca A. Miller, Executive Director. General email, info@dcpreservation.org Web, www.dcpreservation.org

Participates in planning and preserving buildings and sites in Washington, D.C. Programs include protection and enhancement of the city's landmarks; educational lectures, tours, and seminars; and technical assistance to neighborhood groups. Monitors legislation and regulations.

Historical Society of Washington, D.C., 555 Pennsylvania Ave. N.W., 20001-3746; (202) 249-3955. John Suau, Executive Director; Anne McDonough, Library and Collections Director; Jane Levey, Programs and Exhibits Director. Library, (202) 249-3955. General email, info@dchistory.org Web, www.dchistory.org and Twitter, @DCHistory

Maintains research collections on the District of Columbia. Publishes Washington History magazine. Research library open to the public by appointment.

Martin Luther King Jr. Memorial Library, Washingtoniana Division, 4340 Connecticut Ave. N.W. Washington, DC, 20008; (202) 727-1213. Kerrie Cotten Williams, Manager of Special Collections. General email, wash.dcpl@dc.gov Web, www.dclibrary.org/research/washingtoniana

Maintains reference collections of District of Columbia current laws and regulations, history, and culture. Collections include biographies; travel books; memoirs and diaries; family, church, government, and institutional histories;

maps (1612–present); plat books; city, telephone, and real estate directories (1822–present); census schedules; newspapers (1800–present), including the Washington Evening Star microfilm (1852–1981) and microfilm of several other historic newspapers dating back to 1800, and a collection of clippings and photographs (1940–1981); periodicals; and oral history materials on local neighborhoods, ethnic groups, and businesses.

National Mall Coalition, *9507 Overlea Dr., Rockville, MD 20850 (mailing address: P.O. Box 4709, Rockville, MD 20849); (301) 335-8490. Fax, (301) 340-3947. Judy Scott Feldman, Chair. General email, jfeldman@nationalmallcoalition.org Web, www.nationalmallcoalition.org*

Coalition of architects, historians, educators, and citizens promoting the protection and long-range vision planning of the National Mall in Washington, D.C.

Supreme Court Historical Society, *224 E. Capitol St. N.E., 20003; (202) 543-0400. Fax, (202) 547-7730. David T. Pride, Executive Director. Web, http://supremecourthistory.org*

Acquires, preserves, and displays historic items associated with the Court; conducts and publishes scholarly research. Conducts lecture programs; promotes and supports educational activities about the Court.

Tudor Place, *1644 31st St. N.W., 20007; (202) 965-0400. Fax, (202) 965-0164. Mark S. Hudson, Executive Director, ext. 101. General email, info@tudorplace.org Web, www.tudorplace.org and Twitter, @TudorPlace*

Operates a historic property, home of Martha Washington's granddaughter and six generations of Custis-Peter family descendants. Seeks to educate the public about American history and culture, focusing on the capital region from the 18th century. Maintains and displays artifacts, maintains a manuscript collection, conducts guided tours, and sponsors educational programs for students and teachers.

U.S. Capitol Historical Society, *200 Maryland Ave. N.E., 20002; (202) 543-8919. Fax, (202) 525-2790. Jane L. Campbell, President, ext. 12; William C. di Giacomantonio, Chief Historian, ext. 27. Information, (800) 887-9318. General email, uschs@uschs.org Web, https://uschs.org, Twitter, @USCapHis and Twitter, @CapitolHistory*

Membership: members of Congress, individuals, and organizations interested in the preservation of the history and traditions of the U.S. Capitol. Conducts historical research; offers tours, lectures, workshops, and films; holds events involving members of Congress; publishes an annual historical calendar.

White House Historical Assn., *740 Jackson Pl. N.W., 20006 (mailing address: P.O. Box 27624, Washington, DC 20038-7624); (202) 737-8292. Fax, (202) 789-0440.*

Stewart D. McLaurin, President. Toll-free for purchases, (800) 555-2451. General email, customerservice@whha.org Web, www.whitehousehistory.org and Twitter, @WhiteHouseHstry

Seeks to enhance the understanding and appreciation of the White House. Publishes books on the White House, its inhabitants, its artworks, its furnishings, and its history. Net proceeds from book sales, videos and DVDs, traveling exhibits, the museum shop, and gift shop go toward the purchase of historic items for the White House permanent collection.

PHILANTHROPY, PUBLIC SERVICE, AND VOLUNTEERISM

General

▶AGENCIES

AmeriCorps *(Corp. for National and Community Service), 250 E St. S.W., 20024-3208; (202) 606-5000. Fax, (202) 606-3475. Barbara Stewart, Chief Executive Officer. Local TTY, (202) 606-3472. TTY, (800) 833-3722. Volunteer recruiting information, (800) 942-2677. General email, info@cns.gov Web, www.nationalservice.gov/programs/americorps, Twitter, @AmeriCorps and Facebook, www.facebook.com/ americorps*

Provides Americans age seventeen and older with opportunities to serve their communities on a full-time or part-time basis. Participants work in the areas of education, public safety, human needs, and the environment and earn education awards for college or vocational training.

AmeriCorps *(Corp. for National and Community Service), National Civilian Community Corps, 250 E St. S.W., 20024-3208; (202) 606-5000. Fax, (202) 606-3462. Gina Cross, Director (Acting), (202) 606-3233. Local TTY, (202) 565-2799. TTY, (800) 833-3722. Volunteer recruiting information, (800) 942-2677. General email, info@cns.gov Web, www.nationalservice.gov/programs/americorps/ americorps-nccc, Twitter, @AmeriCorpsNCCC and Facebook, www.facebook.com/AmeriCorpsNCCC*

Provides a ten-month residential service and leadership program for men and women ages eighteen to twenty-four of all social, economic, and educational backgrounds. Works to restore and preserve the environment. Working in teams of eight to ten, members provide disaster relief, fight forest fires, restore homes and habitats after natural disasters, and work in a variety of other service projects in every state.

AmeriCorps *(Corp. for National and Community Service), State and National Program, 250 E St. S.W., 20024-3208; (202) 606-5000. Chester Spellman, Director.*

TTY, (800) 833-3722. Volunteer recruiting information, (800) 942-2677.

General email, questions@americorps.gov

Web, www.nationalservice.gov/programs/americorps/ americorps-state-and-national, Twitter, @nationalservice

Grants email, AmeriCorpsGrants@cns.gov

AmeriCorps State administers and oversees Ameri-Corps funding distributed to governor-appointed state commissions, which distribute grants to local organizations and to such national organizations as Habitat for Humanity. AmeriCorps National provides grants directly to national public and nonprofit organizations that sponsor service programs, Indian tribes, and consortia formed across two or more states, including faith-based and community organizations, higher education institutions, and public agencies.

AmeriCorps *(Corp. for National and Community Service), Volunteers in Service to America (VISTA),* 250 E St. S.W., 20024-3208; (202) 606-5000. Fax, (202) 565-2789. Eileen Conoboy, Director (Acting). TTY, (800) 833-3722. Volunteer recruiting information, (800) 942-2677.

General email, questions@americorps.gov

Web, www.americorps.gov/programs/americorps/ americorps-vista, Twitter, @AmeriCorpsVISTA and Facebook, www.facebook.com/AmeriCorpsVISTA

Assigns full-time volunteers to public and private non-profit organizations for one year to alleviate poverty in local communities. Volunteers receive a living allowance, health care, and other benefits and their choice of a post-service stipend or education award.

Corp. for National and Community Service, 250 E St. N.W., 20525; (202) 606-5000. Fax, (202) 606-3460. Barbara Stewart, Chief Executive Officer. Press, (202) 606-6775. TTY, (800) 833-3722. Volunteer recruiting information, (800) 942-2677.

General email, info@cns.gov

Web, www.nationalservice.gov and Twitter, @nationalservice

Partners people of all ages with national and community-based organizations, schools, faith-based groups, and local agencies to assist with community needs in education, the environment, public safety, homeland security, and other areas. Programs include AmeriCorps-VISTA (Volunteers in Service to America), AmeriCorps-NCCC (National Civilian Community Corps), and the Senior Corps, among others.

Federal Emergency Management Agency (FEMA) *(Homeland Security Dept.), Resilience, National Preparedness, Individual and Community Preparedness,* Techworld Bldg., 800 K St. N.W., #5127, 20472-3630; (202) 786-9557. Natalie F. Enclade, Director. Flood insurance information, (888) 379-9531. Storm shelter information, (866) 222-3580.

General email, citizencorps@dhs.gov

Web, www.ready.gov/citizen-corps

Conducts research on individual, business, and community preparedness. Administers Citizen Corps, a national network of state, territory, tribal, and local councils that coordinate with local first responders to develop community-specific public education, outreach, training, and volunteer opportunities that address community preparedness and resiliency.

Peace Corps, 1111 20th St. N.W., 20526; (202) 692-1040. Fax, (202) 692-8400. Josephine (Jody) Olsen, Director. Information, (855) 855-1961. Press, (202) 692-2230.

Web, www.peacecorps.gov and Twitter, @PeaceCorps

Promotes world peace, friendship, and mutual understanding between the United States and developing nations. Administers volunteer programs to assist developing countries in education, the environment, health (particularly HIV awareness and prevention), small business development, agriculture, and urban youth development.

Senior Corps *(Corp. for National and Community Service), Retired and Senior Volunteer Program, Foster Grandparent Program, and Senior Companion Program,* 250 E. St. S.W., 20525; (202) 606-5000. Deborah Cox Roush, Director. National service information hotline, (800) 942-2677. Press, (202) 606-6775. General email, info@cns.gov

Web, www.nationalservice.gov/programs/senior-corps, Twitter, @SeniorCorps and Facebook, www.facebook.com/ SeniorCorps

Network of programs that help older Americans find service opportunities in their communities, including the Retired and Senior Volunteer Program, which encourages older citizens to use their talents and experience in community service; the Foster Grandparent Program, which gives older citizens opportunities to work with exceptional children and children with special needs; and the Senior Companion Program, which recruits older citizens to help homebound adults, especially seniors, with special needs.

► **CONGRESS**

For a listing of relevant congressional committees and subcommittees, please see page 124 or the Appendix.

► **NONGOVERNMENTAL**

Arca Foundation, 1308 19th St. N.W., 20036; (202) 822-9193. Anna Lefer Kuhn, Executive Director. General email, proposals@arcafoundation.org

Web, www.arcafoundation.org

Awards grants to nonprofit organizations for philanthropic endeavors in the areas of social equity and justice. Interests include corporate accountability, and civic participation domestically and internationally.

Assn. of Direct Response Fundraising Counsel (ADRFCO), 1319 F St. N.W., #402, 20004; (202) 293-9640. Fax, (202) 887-9699. Robert S. Tigner, General Counsel. General email, adrfco@msn.com

Web, www.adrfco.org

Membership: businesses in the direct response fundraising industry. Establishes standards of ethical practice in such areas as ownership of direct mail donor lists and mandatory disclosures by fund-raising counsel. Educates nonprofit organizations and the public on direct response fundraising. Represents members' interests before the federal and state governments.

Assn. of Fundraising Professionals (AFP), *4300 Wilson Blvd., #300, Arlington, VA 22203-4168; (703) 684-0410. Fax, (703) 684-0540. Mike Geiger, President. Information, (800) 666-3863.*
General email, afp@afpnet.org
Web, www.afpnet.org

Membership: individuals who serve as fundraising executives for nonprofit institutions or as members of counseling firms engaged in fund-raising management. Promotes ethical standards; offers workshops; provides resources for member certification; monitors legislation and regulations. AFP Foundation promotes philanthropy and volunteerism. Library open to the public by appointment.

Best Buddies International, *Capitol Region, 6231 Leesburg Pike, #310, Falls Church, VA 22044; (703) 533-9420. Fax, (703) 533-9423. Karen Glasser, Regional Director. Information, (800) 892-8339.*
General email, capitolregion@bestbuddies.org
Web, www.bestbuddies.org/capitolregion and Twitter, @BestBuddies

Volunteer organization that provides companionship, integrated employment, and leadership development programs to people with intellectual disabilities worldwide. (Headquarters in Miami, Fla.)

BoardSource, *750 9th St. N.W., #650, 20001; (202) 349-2500. Fax, (202) 349-2599. Anne Wallestad, Chief Executive Officer. Media, (202) 349-2583. Toll-free, (877) 892-6273.*
Web, www.boardsource.org and Twitter, @BoardSource

Works to improve the effectiveness of nonprofit organizations by strengthening their boards of directors. Operates an information clearinghouse; publishes materials on governing nonprofit organizations; assists organizations in conducting training programs, workshops, and conferences for board members and chief executives.

Capital Research Center, *1513 16th St. N.W., 20036; (202) 483-6900. Fax, (202) 483-6990. Scott Walter, President; Kristen Eastlick, Vice President for Programs, (202) 462-2052.*
General email, contact@capitalresearch.org
Web, https://capitalresearch.org and Twitter, @capitalresearch

Conservative think tank that researches funding sources, especially foundations, charities, and other nonprofits, of public interest and advocacy groups. Analyzes the impact these groups have on public policy. Publishes findings in newsletters and reports.

Caring Institute, *228 7th St. S.E., 20003; (202) 547-4273. Fax, (202) 546-4510. Kathleen Halamandaris, President.*
General email, info@caring.org
Web, http://caring.org

Promotes selflessness and public service. Recognizes the achievements of individuals who have demonstrated a commitment to serving others. Operates the Frederick Douglass Museum and Hall of Fame for Caring Americans. Sponsors the National Caring Award and offers internships to high school and college students.

The Congressional Award, *379 FHOB, 20515 (mailing address: P.O. Box 77440, Washington, DC 20013-7440); (202) 226-0130. Fax, (202) 226-0131. Erica Wheelan Heyse, National Director. Toll-free, (888) 802-9273.*
General email, information@congressionalaward.org
Web, http://congressionalaward.org and Twitter, @theaward

Nonpartisan noncompetitive program established by Congress that recognizes the achievements of young people ages thirteen and one-half to twenty-three. Participants are awarded certificates or medals for setting and achieving goals in four areas: volunteer public service, personal development, physical fitness, and expeditions and exploration.

The Corps Network, *1275 K St. N.W., #1050, 20005; (202) 737-6272. Fax, (202) 737-6277. Mary Ellen Sprenkel, President.*
Web, http://corpsnetwork.org and Twitter, @TheCorpsNetwork

Membership: youth corps programs. Produces publications and workshops on starting and operating youth corps and offers technical assistance programs. Holds annual conference. Monitors legislation and regulations.

Council of Better Business Bureaus, *Wise Giving Alliance, 3033 Wilson Blvd., #600, Arlington, VA 22201-3843; (703) 276-0100. Fax, (703) 525-8277. H. Art Taylor, President.*
General email, give@council.bbb.org
Web, www.give.org and Twitter, @wisegiving

Serves as a donor information service on national charities. Evaluates charities in relation to Better Business Bureau standards for charitable solicitation, which address charity finances, solicitations, fund-raising practices, and governance. Produces quarterly guide that summarizes these findings.

Council on Foundations, *1255 23rd St. N.W., #200, 20037; (703) 879-0600. Kathleen Enright, President. Toll-free, (800) 673-9036.*
General email, membership@cof.org
*Web, www.cof.org and Twitter, @COF_*

Membership: independent community, family, and public-sponsored and company-sponsored foundations; corporate giving programs; and foundations in other countries. Promotes responsible and effective philanthropy through educational programs, publications, government relations, and promulgation of a set of principles and practices for effective grant making.

Earth Share, *7735 Old Georgetown Rd., #510, Bethesda, MD 20814; (240) 333-0300. Fax, (240) 333-0301. Vacant, President. Information, (800) 875-3863.*

General email, info@earthshare.org

Web, www.earthshare.org and *Twitter, @EarthShare*

Federation of environmental and conservation organizations. Works with government and private payroll contribution programs to solicit contributions to member organizations for environmental research, education, and community programs. Provides information on establishing environmental giving options in the workplace.

Evangelical Council for Financial Accountability, *440 W. Jubal Early Dr., #100, Winchester, VA 22601-6319; (540) 535-0103. Fax, (540) 535-0533. Dan Busby, President. Information, (800) 323-9473.*
General email, info@ecfa.org

Web, www.ecfa.org and *Twitter, @ecfa*

Membership: charitable, religious, international relief, and educational nonprofit U.S.–based organizations committed to evangelical Christianity. Assists members in making appropriate public disclosure of their financial practices and accomplishments. Certifies organizations that conform to standards of financial integrity and Christian ethics.

Exponent Philanthropy, *1720 N St. N.W., 20036; (202) 580-6560. Fax, (202) 580-6579. Henry L. Berman, Chief Executive Officer. Toll-free, (888) 212-9922.*
General email, info@exponentphilanthropy.org

Web, www.exponentphilanthropy.org and
Twitter, @exponentphil

Membership: donors, trustees, consultants, and employees of philanthropic foundations that have few or no staff. Offers educational programs and publications, referrals, networking opportunities, and liability insurance to members. (Formerly the Assn. of Small Foundations.)

Foundation Center, *Washington Office, 1627 K St. N.W., 3rd Floor, 20006-1708; (202) 331-1400. Fax, (202) 331-1739. Kim Patton, Director.*
General email, kpb@foundationcenter.org

Web, www.foundationcenter.org/washington, Twitter, @FCWashington and *Facebook, www.facebook .com/foundationcenter*

GrantSpace, http://grantspace.org

Publishes foundation guides and electronic databases. Serves as a clearinghouse on foundations and corporate giving, nonprofit management, fund-raising, and grants for individuals. Provides training and seminars on fund-raising and grant writing. Operates libraries in Atlanta, Cleveland, New York, San Francisco, and Washington, D.C.; library catalog available on the website. Libraries open to the public. (Headquarters in New York.)

General Federation of Women's Clubs, *1734 N St. N.W., 20036-2990; (202) 347-3168. Fax, (202) 835-0246. Patricia Budka, Chief of Operations. Toll-free, (800) 443-4392.*
General email, gfwc@gfwc.org

Web, www.gfwc.org and *Twitter, @GFWCHQ*

Nondenominational, nonpartisan international organization of women volunteers. Interests include conservation, education, international and public affairs, domestic violence awareness and prevention, and the arts.

Good360, *675 N. Washington St., #330, Alexandria, VA 22314; (703) 836-2121. Fax, (877) 798-3192. Howard Sherman, Chief Executive Officer.*
General email, press@good360.org

Web, www.good360.org, Twitter, @Good360 and
Facebook, www.facebook.com/Good360.org

Online product-donation marketplace that seeks to meet the needs of nonprofit organizations by encouraging corporations to donate new and like-new manufactured products to domestic and international charities. Works with companies to develop in-kind giving programs, coordinates distribution to nonprofit agencies, and provides reporting and impact stories. Cause-neutral, services any vetted, approved nonprofit, church, or school.

GuideStar by Candid, *1250 H St. N.W., #1150, 20005; Jacob Harold, President. Toll-free, (800) 421-8656.*
General email, community@guidestar.org

Web, www.guidestar.org and *Twitter, @GuideStarUSA*

Public charity that curates a database gathering and distributing information about IRS-registered nonprofit organizations. Reports on organizations' purpose, impact, finances, and legitimacy.

Habitat for Humanity International, *Government Relations and Advocacy, 1310 L St. N.W., #350, 20005; (202) 628-9171. Fax, (202) 628-9169. Chris Vincent, Vice President of Advocacy and Government Relations.*
General email, advocacy@habitat.org

Web, www.habitat.org/about/advocacy

Christian ministry that seeks to eliminate poverty housing. Helps people attain housing through home construction, rehabilitation and repairs, and increased access to improved shelter through programs. Offers housing support services that enable low-income families to make improvements on their homes. Works in more than 70 countries.

Independent Sector, *1602 L St. N.W., #900, 20036; (202) 467-6100. Fax, (202) 467-6101. Dan Cardinali, Chief Executive Officer.*
General email, info@independentsector.org

Web, www.independentsector.org, Twitter, @IndSector and
Facebook, www.facebook.com/IndependentSector

Membership: corporations, foundations, and national voluntary, charitable, and philanthropic organizations. Advocates supportive government policies and encourages volunteering, giving, and best practice not-for-profit nonpartisan initiatives by the private sector for public causes.

The Links Inc., *1200 Massachusetts Ave. N.W., 20005-4501; (202) 842-8686. Fax, (202) 842-4020. Gwendolyn Boyd, Executive Director (Acting), Ext. 211.*
General email, info@linksinc.org

Web, www.linksinc.org, Twitter, @linksinc and
Facebook, www.facebook.com/thelinksinc

Predominantly African American women's volunteer service organization that works to enrich, sustain, and ensure the culture and economic survival of African Americans and other persons of African ancestry. Areas of focus are services to youth, the arts, national trends and service, international trends and services, and health and human services. Programs are implemented via sharing of public information, education, economic development, and public policy campaigns.

Lutheran Volunteer Corps, *1226 Vermont Ave. N.W., 20005; (202) 387-3222. Fax, (202) 667-0037. Deirdre Bagley, President.*
General email, outreach@lutheranvolunteercorps.org
Web, www.lutheranvolunteercorps.org and Twitter, @LVCorps

Administers volunteer program in selected U.S. cities; coordinates activities with health and social service agencies, educational institutions, and environmental groups. Places volunteers in full-time positions in direct service, community organizing, advocacy, and public policy.

Mars Foundation, *6885 Elm St., McLean, VA 22101; (703) 821-4900. Fax, (703) 448-9678. Sue Martin, Assistant Secretary; O. O. Otih, Secretary-Treasurer.*

Awards grants in education, arts, health care concerns, animal wildlife environment, and history.

National Committee for Responsive Philanthropy, *1900 L St. N.W., #825, 20036; (202) 387-9177. Fax, (202) 332-5084. Aaron Dorfman, President. Publications, (202) 387-9177 ext. 21.*
General email, info@ncrp.org
Web, www.ncrp.org, Twitter, @NCRP and Facebook, www .facebook.com/NCRPcommunity

Directs philanthropic giving to benefit the socially, economically, and politically disenfranchised; acts as advocate for groups that represent the poor, minorities, and women. Conducts research; organizes local coalitions. Monitors legislation and regulations.

National Conference on Citizenship (NCOC), *1900 L St. N.W., #800, 20036; (202) 601-7096. Sterling Speirn, Chief Executive Officer.*
General email, conference@ncoc.net
Web, https://ncoc.org, Twitter, @NCoC and Facebook, www.facebook.com/NCoC1

Congressionally chartered nonpartisan nonprofit that supports the Civic Health Initiative. Encourages citizens to participate in civic services. Holds annual conferences to promote public-service activities in local communities. Produces the *Civic Health Index* to measure civic engagement.

National Peace Corps Assn., *1900 L St. N.W., #610, 20036-5002; (202) 293-7728. Fax, (202) 293-7554. Glenn Blumhorst, President.*
General email, ncpa@peacecorpsconnect.org
Web, www.peacecorpsconnect.org and Twitter, @pcorpsconnect

Membership: returned Peace Corps volunteers, staff, and interested individuals. Promotes a global perspective in the United States; seeks to educate the public about the

---

Faith-Based and Neighborhood Partnerships Contacts at Federal Departments and Agencies

White House Office of Faith-Based and Neighborhood Partnerships, (202) 456-3394, www.whitehouse.gov/ presidential-actions/executive-order-establishment-white-house-faith-opportunity-initiative

DEPARTMENTS

Agriculture, Michelle Wert, (202) 720-1176; www.rd.usda.gov/about-rd/initiatives/faith-based-and-neighborhood-partnerships-fbnp

Commerce, Vacant

Education, Angel Rush, (202) 401-1876; https://sites.ed.gov/fbnp

Health and Human Services, Shannon Royce, (202) 358-3595; www.hhs.gov/partnerships

Homeland Security, Misty Angel, Director (Acting), (202) 646-3487; www.dhs.gov/dhs-center-faith-based-neighborhood-partnerships

Housing and Urban Development, Richard Youngblood, (202) 708-2404; www.hud.gov/offices/fbci

Justice, Vacant, (202) 305-7462; https://ojp.gov/fbnp

Labor, Vacant, (202) 693-6017; www.dol.gov/cfbnp

State, Vacant, www.state.gov/s/rga

Veterans Affairs, Stephen B. Dillard, (202) 461-7689; www.va.gov/cfbnpartnerships

AGENCIES

Agency for International Development, Timothy Lavelle (Acting); www.usaid.gov/faith-based-and-community-initiatives

Corporation for National and Community Service, www.nationalservice.gov/special-initiatives/ communities/faith-based-and-other-community-initiatives-and-neighborhood

---

developing world; supports Peace Corps programs; maintains a network of returned volunteers.

Nexus Global Youth Summit, *1400 16th St. N.W., #710, 20036; (202) 265-4300. Jonah Wittkamper, President. Andrew Lea-Zucher, City Ambassador, in Washington, D.C. General email, info@nexusyouthsummit.org*
Web, www.nexusyouthsummit.com and Facebook, www .facebook.com/nexusyouthsummit

Seeks to increase the philanthropic efforts of young investors and entrepreneurs. Holds summits for philanthropists and social entrepreneurs to network and discuss their current projects. Affiliated with Search for Common Ground and The Giving Back Fund.

Philanthropy Roundtable, *1120 20th St. N.W., #550 South, 20036; (202) 822-8333. Fax, (202) 822-8325. Adam Meyerson, President.*
General email, main@philanthropyroundtable.org
Web, www.philanthropyroundtable.org

Membership: individual donors, foundation trustees and staff, and corporate giving officers. Helps donors achieve their charitable objectives by offering counsel and peer-to-peer exchange opportunities.

Points of Light Institute, *1440 G St. N.W., 20005; (404) 979-2900. Fax, (404) 979-2901. Natalye Paquin, Chief Executive Officer. Press, (202) 729-8282.*
General email, info@pointsoflight.org
Web, www.pointsoflight.org and Twitter, @PointsofLight

Promotes mobilization of people for volunteer community service aimed at solving social problems. Through HandsOn Network regional centers, offers technical assistance, training, and information services to nonprofit organizations, public agencies, corporations, and others interested in volunteering. (Headquarters in Atlanta, Ga.)

United Way Worldwide, *701 N. Fairfax St., Alexandria, VA 22314-2045; (703) 836-7112. Fax, (703) 519-0097. Brian A. Gallagher, President.*
Web, www.unitedway.org and Twitter, @UnitedWay

Membership: independent United Way organizations in 41 countries and territories, including 1,150 in the United States. Provides staff training; fund-raising, planning, and communications assistance; resource management; and national public service advertising. Activities support education, financial stability, and health.

Urban Institute, *Center on Nonprofits and Philanthropy, 500 L'Enfant Plaza S.W., 20024; (202) 833-7200. Shena Ashley, Vice President.*
Web, www.urban.org/center/cnp

Conducts and disseminates research on the role and impact of nonprofit organizations and philanthropy.

Volunteers of America, *1660 Duke St., Alexandria, VA 22314; (703) 341-5000. Fax, (703) 341-7000. Michael King, President. Toll-free, (800) 899-0089.*
General email, info@voa.org
Web, www.voa.org and Twitter, @Vol_of_America

Faith-based organization that promotes local human services and outreach programs. Facilitates individual and community involvement. Focuses on children at risk, abused and neglected children, older adults, homeless individuals, people with disabilities, veterans, and those formerly incarcerated.

W. O'Neil Foundation, *5454 Wisconsin Ave., #730, Chevy Chase, MD 20815; (301) 656-5848. Helene O'Neil Shere, President.*

Awards grants primarily to Roman Catholic organizations providing programs and basic needs of the poor, such as food, clothing, shelter, and basic medical care, both nationally and internationally.

Youth Service America, *1050 Connecticut Ave. N.W., #65525, 20035-5525; (202) 296-2992. Fax, (202) 296-4030. Steven A. Culbertson, President.*
General email, outreach@ysa.org
Web, www.ysa.org and Twitter, @youthservice

Advocates youth service at national, state, and local levels. Promotes opportunities for young people to be engaged in community service. Sponsors Global Youth Service Day. Hosts database of U.S. volunteer opportunities.

Washington Area

▶ **NONGOVERNMENTAL**

Boy Scouts of America, *National Capitol Area Council, Marriott Scout Service Center, 9190 Rockville Pike, Bethesda, MD 20814-3897; (301) 530-9360. Fax, (301) 564-9513. Craig Poland, Scout Executive, (301) 214-9101.*
Web, www.NCACBSA.org and Twitter, @NCACBSA

Educational service organization for youth that supports more than 1,700 local units that provide quality youth programs, including cub scouting, boy scouting, venturing, and exploring. National Capitol Area Council covers the Washington, D.C., metro area, sixteen counties in Maryland and Virginia, and the U.S. Virgin Islands. (Headquarters in Irving, Tex.)

Eugene and Agnes E. Meyer Foundation, *1250 Connecticut Ave. N.W., #800, 20036; (202) 483-8294. Fax, (202) 328-6850. Nicky Goren, President.*
General email, ngoren@meyerfdn.org
Web, www.meyerfoundation.org and Twitter, @MeyerFoundation

Seeks to improve the quality of life in Washington, D.C. Awards grants to nonprofit organizations in four program areas: education, employment, asset building, and housing.

Eugene B. Casey Foundation, *16308 Crabbs Branch Way, Rockville, MD 20855; (301) 948-6500. Betty Brown Casey, Trustee.*

Philanthropic organization that supports the arts, education, and social services in the metropolitan Washington area.

The Herb Block Foundation, *1730 M St. N.W., #1020, 20036; (202) 223-8801. Fax, (202) 223-8804. Marcela Brane, President; Sarah Armstrong Alex, Executive Director.*
General email, info@herbblock.org
Web, www.herbblockfoundation.org and Twitter, @TheHerbBlockFdn

Awards grants to charitable and educational programs that combat discrimination and poverty and promote citizen involvement in government. Provides scholarships to individuals seeking to attend community colleges in the Washington, D.C., area. Awards prizes for excellence in editorial cartooning to serve as as a tool for freedom and to address social issues.

Humane Rescue Alliance, *1201 New York Ave N.E., 20002; P.O. Box 96312, 20090-6312; (202) 576-6664. Claudia Roll, Director of Operations. Adoption center, (202) 723-5730. 24-hour animal cruelty and emergency*

hotline, (202) 723-5730. Spay and neuter center,
(202) 608-1356.
General email, adopt@washhumane.org
Web, www.humanerescuealliance.org,
Twitter, @HumaneRescue
Press, matt.williams@warl.org

Congressionally chartered animal welfare agency and open-access animal shelter. Promotes pet adoption; offers low-cost spay and neuter services and trap-and-neuter programs. Operates the D.C. Animal Care and Control.

International Order of the Rainbow For Girls,
Washington Assembly, (301) 460-3088. Allie R., Advisor.
Web, www.gomarylandrainbow.org

Membership: girls ages 11 through 20. Promotes leadership training through community service and volunteerism. Includes local assemblies throughout the United States. (Headquarters in McAlester, Okla.)

Junior League of Washington, *3039 M St. N.W., 20007;*
(202) 337-2001. Tycely Williams, President.
General email, office@jlw.org
Web, www.jlw.org

Educational and charitable women's organization that promotes volunteerism and works for community improvement through leadership of trained volunteers. Interests include promoting volunteerism and developing the potential of women. Current emphasis is on literacy. (Assn. of Junior Leagues International headquarters in New York.)

Morris and Gwendolyn Cafritz Foundation, *1825 K St.*
N.W., #1400, 20006; (202) 223-3100. Fax, (202) 296-7567.
Calvin Cafritz, Chair; Mardell Moffett, Executive Director.
General email, info@cafritzfoundation.org
Web, www.cafritzfoundation.org

Awards grants to educational, arts, and social services institutions in the metropolitan Washington area.

Quota International, *1420 21st St. N.W., 20036;*
(202) 331-9694. Fax, (202) 331-4395. Nancy Fitzpatrick,
Executive Director.
General email, staff@quota.org
Web, www.quotainternational.org and
Twitter, @QuotaIntl

International service organization that links members in twelve countries in a worldwide network of service and friendship. Interests include deaf, hard-of-hearing, and speech-impaired individuals and disadvantaged women and children. Maintains the We Share Foundation, a charitable organization.

Washington Regional Assn. of Grantmakers, *1400 16th*
St. N.W., #740, 20036; (202) 939-3440. Fax, (202) 939-3442.
Tamara Lucas Copeland, President, (202) 939-3441.
General email, info@washingtongrantmakers.org
Web, www.washingtongrantmakers.org and
Twitter, @WRAGtweets

Network of funders that partners with agencies and nongovernmental organizations in the Washington, D.C.,

region. Identifies and implements new and innovative forms of philanthropy. Shares best practices. Advocates collective philanthropic community in the region and publishes issue briefs.

RECREATION AND SPORT

General

▶**AGENCIES**

Bureau of Land Management (BLM) *(Interior Dept.),*
Recreation and Visitor Services, 20 M St. S.E., 6th Floor,
20003 (mailing address: 1849 C St. N.W., MS 6224,
Washington, DC 20240); (202) 912-7094.
Fax, (202) 245-0050. Andy Tenney, Division Chief,
(202) 912-7094; Dennis Byrd, Outdoor Recreation Planner,
(202) 912-7252.
Web, www.blm.gov/programs/recreation

Develops recreation opportunities and visitor services on public lands.

Health and Human Services Dept. (HHS), *President's*
Council on Fitness, Sports, and Nutrition (PCFSN), 1101
Wootton Pkwy., #560, Rockville, MD 20852;
(240) 276-9567. Fax, (240) 276-9860. Holli M. Richmond,
Executive Director.
General email, fitness@hhs.gov
Web, www.fitness.gov and Twitter, @FitnessGov

Promotes programs and initiatives that motivate people of all ages, backgrounds, and abilities to lead active, healthy lives through partnerships with the public, private, and nonprofit sectors; provides online information and resources related to fitness, sports, and nutrition; conducts award programs for children and adults and for schools, clubs, and other institutions.

National Park Service (NPS) *(Interior Dept.), 1849 C St.*
N.W., #3115, 20240; (202) 208-3818. Fax, (202) 208-7889.
Paul Daniel Smith, Director (Acting).
Press, (202) 208-6843.
General email, asknps@nps.gov
Web, www.nps.gov and Twitter, @NatlParkService

Oversees coordination, planning, and financing of public outdoor recreation programs at all levels of government. Conducts recreation research surveys; administers financial assistance program to states for planning and development of outdoor recreation programs. (Some lands designated as national recreation areas are not under NPS jurisdiction.)

▶**NONGOVERNMENTAL**

American Canoe Assn., *503 Sophia St., #100,*
Fredericksburg, VA 22401; (540) 907-4460.
Wade Blackwood, Executive Director, (540) 907-4460
ext. 111; Christopher (Chris) Stec, Chief Operating Officer,
(540) 907-4460 ext. 110.

General email, aca@americancanoe.org

Web, www.americancanoe.org, Twitter, @AmericanCanoe and Facebook, www.facebook.com/Paddlesport

Membership: individuals and organizations interested in the promotion of canoeing, kayaking, and other paddle sports. Works to preserve the nation's recreational waterways. Sponsors programs in safety education, competition, recreation, public awareness, conservation, and public policy. Monitors legislation and regulations.

American Gaming Assn., 799 9th St. N.W., #700, 20001; (202) 552-2675. Fax, (202) 552-2676. Bill Miller, President; Grace Bennett, Government Relations Manager.

General email, info@americangaming.org

Web, www.americangaming.org, Twitter, @AmerGamingAssn and Facebook, www .facebook.com/americangaming

Membership: casinos, casino and gaming equipment manufacturers, and financial services companies. Compiles statistics and serves as an information clearinghouse on the gaming industry. Administers a task force to study gambling addiction, raise public awareness of the condition, and develop assistance programs for it. Monitors legislation and regulations.

American Hiking Society, 8605 2nd Ave., Silver Spring, MD 20910; (301) 565-6704. Fax, (301) 565-6714. Kathryn (Kate) Van Waes, Executive Director. Toll-free, (800) 972-8608.

General email, info@americanhiking.org

Web, https://americanhiking.org, Twitter, @AmericanHiking and Facebook, www.facebook .com/AmericanHiking

Membership: individuals and clubs interested in preserving America's trail system and protecting the interests of hikers and other trail users. Sponsors research on trail construction and a trail maintenance summer program. Provides information on outdoor volunteer opportunities on public lands.

American Recreation Coalition, 1200 G St. N.W., #650, 20005; (202) 682-9530. Fax, (202) 682-9529. Derrick A. Crandall, President.

General email, bnasta@funoutdoors.com

Web, www.funoutdoors.com, Twitter, @AmerRecreation and Facebook, www.facebook.com/American-Recreation-Coalition-164907310233438

Membership: recreation industry associations, recreation enthusiast groups, and leading corporations in the recreation products and services sectors. Promotes health and well-being through outdoor recreation. Monitors regulations and legislation.

American Sportfishing Assn., 1001 N. Fairfax St., #501, Alexandria, VA 22314; (703) 519-9691. Fax, (703) 519-1872. Glenn Hughes, President, (703) 519-9691, ext. 245.

General email, ASAcomm@asafishing.org

Web, www.asafishing.org and Twitter, @ASAfishing

Works to ensure healthy and sustainable fisheries resources and to expand market growth for its members through increased participation in sportfishing. Programs include Keep America Fishing and the Fish America Foundation.

Boat U.S. (Boat Owners Assn. of the United States), 5323 Port Royal Rd., Springfield, VA 22151; (703) 461-2878. Fax, (703) 461-2847. Scott Croft, Director of Public Relations, (703) 461-2864.

General email, govtaffairs@boatus.com

Web, www.boatus.com and Twitter, @BoatUS

Membership: owners of recreational boats. Represents boat-owner interests before the federal, state, and local governments.

Club Managers Assn. of America, 1733 King St., Alexandria, VA 22314; (703) 739-9500. Fax, (703) 739-0124. Jeffrey (Jeff) Morgan, Chief Executive Officer.

General email, cmaa@cmaa.org

Web, https://cmaanet.org

Membership: managers of membership clubs. Promotes the profession of club management through education and other assistance.

Disabled Sports USA, 451 Hungerford Dr., #608, Rockville, MD 20850; (301) 217-0960. Fax, (301) 217-0968. Glenn Merry, Executive Director, (301) 217-9838.

General email, info@dsusa.org

Web, www.disabledsportsusa.org and Twitter, @DisabledSportsUSA

Offers nationwide sports rehabilitation programs in more than forty summer and winter sports; promotes independence, confidence, and fitness through programs for people with permanent disabilities, including wounded service personnel; conducts workshops and competitions through community-based chapters; participates in world championships.

FishAmerica Foundation, 1001 N. Fairfax St., #501, Alexandria, VA 22314; (703) 519-9691. Fax, (703) 519-1872. Vacant, Grants Manager, (703) 519-9691, ext. 247.

General email, fafgrants@asafishing.org

Web, www.fishamerica.org, Twitter, @fafgrants and Facebook, www.facebook.com/FishAmerica

Invests in local communities to restore habitat, improve water quality, and advance fisheries research to increase sportfish populations and sportfishing opportunities. (Affiliated with the American Sportfishing Assn.)

National Aeronautic Assn., Reagan Washington National Airport, Hangar 7, #202, 20001-6015; (703) 416-4888. Fax, (703) 416-4877. Greg Principato, President.

General email, naa@naa.aero

Web, www.naa.aero and Facebook, www.facebook.com/NationalAeronauticAssociation

Membership: persons interested in development of general and sporting aviation, including skydiving, commercial and military aircraft, and spaceflight. Supervises sporting aviation competitions; administers awards in aviation.

National Center for Bicycling & Walking, *Project for Public Spaces, 2599 Ontario Rd. N.W., 200090; (202) 518-0524. Mark Plotz, Program Manager, (202) 518-0524, ext. 224.*
General email, info@bikewalk.org
Web, www.bikewalk.org

Promotes bicycle use; conducts research, planning, and training projects; develops safety education and public information materials; offers consulting services for long-range planning and policy analysis. Works to increase public awareness of the benefits and opportunities of bicycling and walking. (Headquarters in New York.)

National Club Assn., *1201 15th St. N.W., #450, 20005; (202) 822-9822. Fax, (202) 822-9808. Henry Wallmeyer, President.*
General email, info@nationalclub.org
Web, www.nationalclub.org and Twitter, @NatlClubAssn

Promotes the interests of private, social, and recreational clubs. Monitors legislation and regulations.

National Collegiate Athletic Assn. (NCAA), *Government Relations, 1 Dupont Circle N.W., #310, 20036-1139; (202) 293-3050. Fax, (202) 293-3075. Abe L. Frank, Director, ext. 2122.*
Web, www.ncaa.org

Membership: colleges and universities, conferences, and organizations interested in the administration of intercollegiate athletics. Certifies institutions' athletic programs; compiles records and statistics; produces publications and television programs; administers youth development programs; awards student athletes with postgraduate scholarships and degree-completion grants. (Headquarters in Indianapolis, Ind.)

National Football League Players Assn., *1133 20th St. N.W., #600, 20036; (202) 463-2200. Fax, (202) 756-9310. DeMaurice Smith, Executive Director.*
Toll-free, (800) 372-2000.
Web, www.nflpa.com, Twitter, @NFLPA and Facebook, www.facebook.com/NFLPA

Membership: professional football players. Represents members in matters concerning wages, hours, and working conditions. Provides assistance to charitable and community organizations. Sponsors programs and events to promote the image of professional football and its players.

National Indian Gaming Assn. (NIGA), *224 2nd St. S.E., 20003; (202) 546-7711. Fax, (202) 546-1755. Jason Giles, Executive Director, (202) 548-3810.*
General email, questions@indiangaming.org
Web, www.indiangaming.org and Facebook, www .facebook.com/NIGAIndianGaming

Membership: more than 180 Indian nations as well as other organizations, tribes, and businesses engaged in gaming enterprises. Operates as a clearinghouse for tribes, policymakers, and the public on Indian gaming issues and tribal community development.

National Recreation and Park Assn., *22377 Belmont Ridge Rd., Ashburn, VA 20148-4501; (703) 858-0784. Fax, (703) 858-0794. Barbara Tulipane, Chief Executive Officer, (703) 858-2140. Toll-free, (800) 626-6772.*
General email, customerservice@nrpa.org
Web, www.nrpa.org, Twitter, @nrpa_news and Facebook, www.facebook.com/ NationalRecreationandParkAssociation

Membership: park and recreation professionals and interested citizens. Promotes support and awareness of park, recreation, and leisure services; advances environmental and conservation efforts; facilitates development, expansion, and management of resources; provides technical assistance for park and recreational programs; and provides professional development to members. Monitors legislation and regulations.

Road Runners Club of America, *1501 Lee Hwy., #140, Arlington, VA 22209; (703) 525-3890. Fax, (703) 525-3891. Jean Knaack, Executive Director.*
General email, office@rrca.org
Web, www.rrca.org and Twitter, @RRCAnational

Develops and promotes road races and fitness programs, including the Kids Run the Nation Program and the Women's Distance Festival. Issues guidelines on road races concerning safety, legal issues, and runners with disabilities. Facilitates communication between clubs.

Society of Health and Physical Educators (SHAPE) America, *1900 Association Dr., Reston, VA 20191-1598; (703) 476-3400. Fax, (703) 476-9527. Stephanie A. Morris, Chief Executive Officer. Toll-free, (800) 213-7193.*
General email, info@shapeamerica.org
Web, www.shapeamerica.org and Twitter, @SHAPE_ America

Membership: teachers and others who work with school health, physical education, athletics, recreation, dance, and safety education programs (kindergarten through postsecondary levels). Member associations are National Assn. for Girls and Women in Sport, American Assn. for Health Education, National Dance Assn., National Assn. for Sport and Physical Education, and American Assn. for Physical Activity and Recreation.

Special Olympics International Inc., *1133 19th St. N.W., 20036-3604; (202) 628-3630. Fax, (202) 824-0200. Mary Davis, Chief Executive Officer; Timothy P. Shriver, Chair. Toll-free, (800) 700-8585.*
General email, info@specialolympics.org
Web, www.specialolympics.org and Twitter, @SpecialOlympics

Offers individuals with intellectual disabilities opportunities for year-round sports training; sponsors athletic competition for 4 million athletes worldwide in twenty-two individual and Olympic-type team sports.

StopPredatoryGambling.org, *100 Maryland Ave. N.E., #310, 20002; (202) 567-6996. Les Bernal, Executive Director, (202) 567-6996, ext. 1.*

General email, mail@stoppredatorygambling.org

Web, www.stoppredatorygambling.org

Seeks to end government support of exploitive forms of gambling. Compiles information on the personal, social, economic, and public health impacts of gambling and disseminates it to citizens and policymakers at the local, state, and national levels. Monitors legislation and regulations.

U.S. Eventing Assn. (USEA), *525 Old Waterford Rd. N.W., Leesburg, VA 20176-2050; (703) 779-0440.*
Fax, (703) 779-0550. Rob Burk, Chief Executive Officer, (703) 779-9895.
General email, info@useventing.com

Web, www.useventing.com and Twitter, @useventing

Membership: individuals interested in eventing, an Olympic-recognized equestrian sport featuring dressage, cross-country, and show jumping. Registers all national events to ensure that they meet the standards set by the U.S. Equestrian Federation. Sponsors three-day events for members from beginner novice to Olympic levels. Provides educational materials on competition, riding, and care of horses.

U.S. Olympic Committee, *Government Relations, 1100 H St. N.W., #600, 20005; (202) 466-3399.*
Fax, (202) 466-5068. David Francis, Associate Director; Jennifer Gallagher, Manager.
General email, communications@usoc.org

Web, www.teamusa.org

Responsible for training, entering, and underwriting U.S. teams in the Olympic, Paralympic, Pan American, and Parapan Games. Supports the bid of U.S. cities to host the Games; recognizes the national governing body of each sport in these games. Promotes international athletic competition. (Headquarters in Colorado Springs, Colo.)

U.S. Parachute Assn., *5401 Southpoint Centre Blvd., Fredericksburg, VA 22407-2612; (540) 604-9740.*
Fax, (540) 604-9741. Edward Scott, Executive Director, ext. 325.
General email, uspa@uspa.org

Web, www.uspa.org and Twitter, @skydiveusa

Membership: individuals and organizations interested in skydiving. Develops safety procedures; maintains training programs; issues skydiving licenses and ratings; certifies skydiving instructors; sanctions national competitions; and documents record attempts. Offers liability insurance to members. Monitors legislation and regulations.

RELIGION

General

► NONGOVERNMENTAL

American Assn. of Pastoral Counselors, *9504A Lee Hwy., Fairfax, VA 22031-2303 (mailing address: P.O. Box 3030, Oakton, VA 22124); (703) 385-6967. Fax, (703) 884-9165. Tere Tyner Canzoneri, President.*

General email, info@aapc.org

Web, www.aapc.org

Membership: mental health professionals with training in both religion and the behavioral sciences. Nonsectarian organization that accredits pastoral counseling centers, certifies pastoral counselors, and approves training programs.

American Friends Service Committee (AFSC), *Public Policy, 1822 R St. N.W., 20009-1604; (202) 483-3341. Fax, (202) 232-3197. R. Aura Kanegis, Director.*
General email, advocacy@afsc.org

Web, www.afsc.org/national-office-public-policy-and-advocacy-oppa, Twitter, @afsc_org and Facebook, www.facebook.com/AmericanFriendsServiceCommittee

Education, outreach, and advocacy office for the AFSC, an independent organization affiliated with the Religious Society of Friends (Quakers) in America. Sponsors domestic and international service, development, justice, and peace programs. Priorities include Iraq, Israel/Palestine, civil rights and liberties, and economic justice in the United States. Interests include peace education; arms control and disarmament; social and economic justice; gay and lesbian rights, racism, sexism, and civil rights; refugees and immigration policy; crisis response and relief efforts; and international development efforts, especially in Central America, the Middle East, and southern Africa. (Headquarters in Philadelphia, Pa.)

American Humanist Assn., *1821 Jefferson Pl. N.W., 20036; (202) 238-9088. Fax, (202) 238-9003. Sunil Panikkath, President; Roy Speckhardt, Executive Director. Toll-free, (800) 837-3792.*
General email, aha@americanhumanist.org

Web, https://americanhumanist.org, Twitter, @americanhumanist and Facebook, www.facebook.com/americanhumanist

Seeks to educate the public about humanism and bring humanists together for mutual support and action. Defends the civil liberties and constitutional freedoms of humanists and leads both local and national humanist organizations toward progressive societal change.

American Islamic Congress, *1031 15th St. N.W., #243, 20005; (202) 595-3160. Zainab Al-Suwaij, Executive Director.*
General email, info@aicongress.org

Web, www.aicongress.org, Twitter, @aicongress?lang=en and Facebook, www.facebook.com/AmericanIslamicCongress

Independent, nonpartisan initiative of American Muslims challenging negative perceptions of Muslims by advocating interethnic and interfaith understanding. Promotes open multicultural society and civil liberties; advocates women's equality, free expression, and nonviolence. Encourages the denouncement of terrorism, extremism, and hate speech within the Muslim community. Maintains offices in Tunisia and Iraq.

American Jewish Committee, *Government and International Affairs, 1156 15th St. N.W., 20005;*

(202) 785-4200. David Harris, Chief Executive Officer; Jason Isaacson, Managing Director of Government and International Affairs.
General email, washington@ajc.org

Web, www.ajc.org, Twitter, @AJCGlobal and Facebook, www.facebook.com/AJCGlobal

Human relations agency devoted to protecting civil and religious rights for all people. Interests include church-state issues, research on energy security, Israel and the Middle East, the security and well-being of Jewish diasporic communities worldwide, immigration, social discrimination, civil and women's rights, education, and international cooperation for peace and human rights. (Headquarters in New York.)

Americans United for Separation of Church and State, *1310 L St. N.W., #200, 20005; (202) 466-3234. Fax, (202) 466-2587. Gary Carleton, Managing Director.*
General email, americansunited@au.org

Web, www.au.org and Twitter, @americansunited

Citizens' interest group. Opposes federal and state aid to parochial schools; works to ensure religious neutrality in public schools; supports free religious exercise; initiates litigation; maintains speakers bureau. Monitors legislation and regulations.

B'nai B'rith International, *1120 20th St. N.W., #300N, 20036; (202) 857-6600. Fax, (202) 857-2700. Daniel S. Mariaschin, Executive Vice President. Media, (202) 857-6699. Toll-free, (888) 388-4224.*
General email, info@bnaibrith.org

Web, www.bnaibrith.org and Twitter, @BnaiBrith

International Jewish organization that promotes the security and continuity of the Jewish people and the State of Israel; defends human rights; combats anti-Semitism; and promotes Jewish identity through cultural activities. Interests include strengthening family life and the education and training of youth, providing broad-based services for the benefit of senior citizens, and advocacy on behalf of Jews throughout the world.

Baptist Joint Committee for Religious Liberty, *200 Maryland Ave. N.E., 3rd Floor, 20002; (202) 544-4226. Fax, (202) 544-2094. Amanda Tyler, Executive Director.*
General email, bjc@bjconline.org

Web, www.bjconline.org and Twitter, @BJContheHill

Membership: Baptist conventions and conferences. Interests include religious liberty, separation of church and state, First Amendment religious issues, and government regulation of religious institutions. Files court briefs, leads educational programs, and monitors legislation.

Baptist World Alliance, *405 N. Washington St., Falls Church, VA 22046; (703) 790-8980. Fax, (703) 893-5160. Elijah Brown, General Secretary.*
General email, bwa@bwanet.org

Web, www.bwanet.org and Twitter, @TheBWA

International Baptist organization. Conducts religious teaching and works to create a better understanding among nations. Organizes development efforts and disaster relief worldwide. Interests include human rights and religious liberty.

Catholic Information Center, *1501 K St. N.W., #175, 20005; (202) 783-2062. Rev. Charles Trulls, Director.*
General email, events@cicdc.org

Web, www.cicdc.org and Twitter, @CICDC

Catholic cultural center, hosts lectures and events, offers free counseling services. Includes Catholic bookstore and chapel.

Chaplain Alliance for Religious Liberty, *P.O. Box 151353, Alexandria, VA 22315; (571) 293-2427. Fax, (910) 221-2226. Col. Phil Wright (USA, Ret.), Executive Director; Capt. Craig Muehler (USN, Ret.), Chair.*
General email, info@chaplainalliance.org

Web, http://chaplainalliance.org

Membership: military chaplains and others who support orthodox Christian doctrines. Seeks to ensure that all chaplains and those they serve may exercise their religious liberties without fear of reprisal. Interests include the conflict between official protection for gays in the military and orthodox Christian teachings. Issues press releases; grants media interviews; monitors legislation and regulations.

Christian Science Committee on Publication, *Federal Office, 444 N. Capitol St. N.W., #601, 20001; (202) 296-2190. Tessa E.B. Frost, Director of Federal Government Affairs.*
General email, federal@christianscience.com

Web, www.christianscience.com/member-resources/committee-on-publication

Public service organization that provides information on the religious convictions and practices of Christian Scientists.

Conference of Major Superiors of Men (CMSM), *7300 Hanover Dr., #304, Greenbelt, MD 20770; (301) 588-4030. Fax, (240) 650-3597. Rev. Mark Padrez, Executive Director.*
General email, postmaster@cmsm.org

Web, https://cmsm.org

National representative body for more than 17,000 men in 240 religious and apostolic communities in the United States, including foreign missionaries. Collaborates with U.S. bishops and other key groups and organizations that serve church and society.

Council on American–Islamic Relations, *453 New Jersey Ave. S.E., 20003-4034; (202) 488-8787. Fax, (202) 488-0833. Nihad Awad, National Executive Director; Ibrahim Hooper, Communications, (202) 744-7726.*
General email, info@cair.com

Web, http://cair.com and Twitter, @CAIRNational

Promotes the understanding of Islam to the American public. Seeks to empower the Muslim community in the United States and protect civil liberties through political and social activism.

Episcopal Church, *Government Relations,* 110 Maryland Ave. N.E., #309, 20002; (202) 547-7300. Fax, (202) 547-4457. Rebecca Linder Blachly, Director. Toll-free, (800) 334-7620. Web, www.episcopalchurch.org/eppn, www .episcopalchurch.org/office/office-government-relations and Twitter, @TheEPPN

Informs Congress, the executive branch, and governmental agencies about the actions and resolutions of the Episcopal Church. Monitors legislation and regulations. (Denominational headquarters in New York.)

Ethics and Public Policy Center, 1730 M St. N.W., #910, 20036; (202) 682-1200. Fax, (202) 408-0632. M. Edward Whelan III, President. General email, ethics@eppc.org

Web, www.eppc.org and Twitter, @EPPCdc

Considers implications of Judeo-Christian moral tradition for domestic and foreign policymaking.

Evangelical Lutheran Church in America, *Advocacy,* 218 D St. S.E., 20001; (202) 783-7507. Rev. Amy Reumann, Director. Toll-free, (800) 638-3522. General email, washingtonoffice@elca.org

Web, www.elca.org/advocacy and Twitter, @ELCAadvocacy

Represents the church's ministries, relationships, projects, and relief efforts on behalf of underrepresented people in order to effect policy change. Monitors and responds to proposed legislation and regulations. (Headquarters in Chicago, Ill.)

Faith in Public Life, P.O. Box 33668, 20033; (202) 499-4083. Fax, (202) 315-0469. Rev. Jennifer Butler, Chief Executive Officer. General email, info@faithinpubliclife.org

Web, www.faithinpubliclife.org and Twitter, @FaithinPublicLife

Provides organizing and communications support to diverse faith leaders and organizations working to further justice and the common good in public policy; designs and implements coalitions and initiatives to promote faith as a force for the common good.

General Board of Church and Society of the United Methodist Church, 100 Maryland Ave. N.E., 20002; (202) 488-5600. Fax, (202) 488-5619. Rev. Susan Henry-Crowe, General Secretary, (202) 488-5629. Press, (202) 488-5630. General email, gbcs@umcjustice.org

Web, www.umc-gbcs.org, Twitter, @UMCjustice and Facebook, www.facebook.com/umcjustice

One of four international general program boards of the United Methodist Church. Provides training and educational resources to member churches on social concerns. Monitors legislation and regulations. (Has offices at the Church Center for the United Nations.)

General Conference of Seventh-day Adventists, 12501 Old Columbia Pike, Silver Spring, MD 20904-6600; (301) 680-6000. Ted N. C. Wilson, President;

Williams Costa Jr., Director of Communications. Press, (301) 680-6315. General email, info@contact.adventist.org

Web, www.adventist.org, Twitter, @adventistchurch and Facebook, www.facebook.com/TheAdventistChurch

World headquarters of the Seventh-day Adventist Church. Interests include education, health care, humanitarian relief, and religious liberty. Supplies educational tools for the blind and the hard of hearing. Operates hospitals and schools worldwide. Organizes community service-oriented youth groups.

Institute on Religion and Democracy, 1023 15th St. N.W., #601, 20005-2601; (202) 682-4131. Fax, (202) 682-4136. Mark Tooley, President. General email, info@theird.org

Web, www.theird.org, Twitter, @theIRD and Facebook, www.facebook.com/TheIRD

Interdenominational bipartisan organization that supports democratic and constitutional forms of government consistent with the values of Christianity. Serves as a resource center to promote Christian perspectives on U.S. national and foreign policy questions. Interests include international conflicts, religious liberties, and the promotion of democratic forms of government in the United States and worldwide.

Interfaith Alliance, 2101 L St. N.W., #40, 20037; (202) 466-0567. Fax, (202) 857-3977. Rabbi Jack Moline, President. General email, info@interfaithalliance.org

Web, www.interfaithalliance.org, Twitter, @intrfthalliance and Facebook, www.facebook.com/interfaithalliance

Membership: seventy-five faith traditions, including Protestant, Catholic, Jewish, and Muslim clergy, laity, and others who favor a positive, nonpartisan role for religious faith in public life, as well as for those who follow no faith tradition. Advocates mainstream religious values; promotes tolerance and social opportunity; opposes the use of religion to promote political extremism at national, state, and local levels. Monitors legislation and regulations.

International Religious Liberty Assn., 12501 Old Columbia Pike, Silver Spring, MD 20904-6600; (301) 680-6686. Fax, (301) 680-6695. John R. Nay, President; Ganoune Diop, Secretary General. General email, info@irla.org

Web, www.irla.org, Twitter, @irla-usa and Facebook, www .facebook.com/irla.hq

Seeks to preserve and expand religious liberty and freedom of conscience; advocates separation of church and state; sponsors international and domestic meetings and congresses.

Islamic Society of North America (ISNA), *Office of Interfaith and Community Alliances,* 110 Maryland Ave. N.E., #304, 20002; (202) 544-6565. Fax, (703) 464-7326. Omer Bin Abdullah, Communications, (703) 742-8108. General email, info@isna.net

Web, www.isna.net

Conducts outreach to grassroots organizations and engages in joint programs with other religious organizations, including the National Council of Churches, the United States Conference of Catholic Bishops, and the Union for Reform Judaism. Seeks to promote a positive image of Islam and Muslims to national political leaders and strong relationships with U.S. congressional staff and federal government officials. Serves as an outreach resource to the American Muslim community. (Headquarters in Plainfield, Ind.)

Jesuit Conference, *Social and International Ministries,* *1016 16th St. N.W., 4th Floor, 20036; (202) 462-0400. Fax, (202) 328-9212. Timothy Kesecki, President; Sean Michaelson, Executive Secretary.* *General email, usjc@jesuit.org*

Web, www.jesuits.org and Twitter, @jesuitnews

Information and advocacy organization of Jesuits and laypersons concerned with peace and social justice issues. Interests include peace and disarmament, domestic poverty, socially responsible investing, and migration and immigration.

Jewish Federations of North America, *Washington Office, (202) 785-5900. William Daroff, Director.* *General email, dc@JewishFederations.org*

Web, www.jewishfederations.org and Facebook, www .facebook.com/jfederations

Acts as advocate for the 148 Jewish federations across the United States on issues of concern, including long-term care, families at risk, and naturally occurring retirement communities. Offers marketing, communications, and public relations support; coordinates a speakers bureau. (Headquarters in New York.)

Jewish Women International, *1129 20th St. N.W., #801, 20036; (202) 857-1300. Fax, (202) 857-1380. Loribeth Weinstein, Chief Executive Officer. Toll-free, (800) 343-2823.* *General email, jwi@jwi.org*

Web, www.jwi.org, Facebook, www.facebook.com/ jewishwomeninternational and Twitter, @JewishWomenIntl

Membership: Jewish women, supporters, and partners in the United States and Canada. Interests include empowerment of women and girls, ending domestic and sexual violence, financial literacy and economic security, and highlighting women's leadership at multigenerational intersections.

Leadership Conference of Women Religious, *8737 Colesville Rd., #610, Silver Spring, MD 20910; (301) 588-4955. Fax, (301) 587-4575. Carol Zinn, Executive Director.* *Web, www.lcwr.org*

Membership: Roman Catholic women who are the principal administrators of their congregations in the United States and around the world. Offers programs and support to members; conducts research; serves as an information clearinghouse.

Loyola Foundation, *10335 Democracy Lane, #202, Fairfax, VA 22030; (571) 435-9401. Fax, (571) 435-9402. A. Gregory McCarthy IV, Executive Director.* *General email, info@loyolafoundation.org*

Web, www.loyolafoundation.org

Assists overseas Catholic mission activities. Awards grants to international missionaries and Catholic dioceses for vehicle and equipment purchase and construction.

Maryknoll Office for Global Concerns *(Catholic Foreign Mission Society of America), 200 New York Ave. N.W., 20001; (202) 832-1780. Fax, (202) 832-5195. Susan Gunn, Director (Acting).* *General email, ogc@maryknoll.org*

Web, www.maryknollogc.org

Conducts education and advocacy for international policies that promote peace, social justice, and ecological integrity. (Headquarters in Maryknoll, N.Y.)

Mennonite Central Committee, *Washington Office, 920 Pennsylvania Ave. S.E., 20003; (202) 544-6564. Fax, (202) 544-2820. Rachelle Lyndaker Schlabach, Executive Director, (202) 544-6564, ext. 6112.* *General email, mccwash@mcc.org*

Web, http://mcc.org/get-involved/advocacy/washington

Christian organization engaged in service and development projects. Monitors legislation and regulations affecting issues of interest to Mennonite and Brethren in Christ churches. Interests include human rights in developing countries, military spending, the environment, world hunger, poverty, and civil and religious liberties. (Headquarters in Akron, Pa.)

Muslim Public Affairs Council, *Washington Office, 1020 16th St. N.W., 20036; (202) 547-7701. Fax, (202) 547-7704. Salam Al-Marayati, National President; Hoda Hawa, Washington Office Director.* *General email, hello@mpac.org*

Web, www.mpac.org and Twitter, @mpac_national

Policy advocacy group seeking an accurate portrayal of Islam and Muslims in the media and popular culture. Comments and provides background information to journalists and other media professionals to inform public opinion. (Headquarters in Los Angeles, Calif.)

National Assn. of Evangelicals, *P.O. Box 23269, 20026; (202) 479-0815. Leith Anderson, President.* *General email, info@nae.net*

Web, www.nae.net and Twitter, @NAEvangelicals

Membership: evangelical denominations, nonprofits, churches, schools, and individuals. Works to connect and represent Christian evangelical denominations, nonprofits, churches, schools, and individuals. Interests include church and faith; family; religious liberty; economic policy; church-state relations; immigration and refugee policy; and world relief efforts. Provides networking opportunities and commissions chaplains. Monitors legislation and regulations.

National Clergy Council, *109 2nd St. N.E., 20002; (202) 737-1776. Fax, (202) 546-6864. Peggy Nienaber, Executive Director.*

General email, faith@faithandlibertyDC.org

Web, www.faithandlibertyDC.org

Informal network of conservative and traditional Christian clergy and heads of religious organizations and societies. Advocates injecting religious morality into public policy debates. Monitors legislation and regulations.

National Council of Catholic Women, *200 N. Glebe Rd., #725, Arlington, VA 22203; (703) 224-0990. Fax, (703) 224-0991. Andrea Cecilli, Executive Director; Maribeth Stewart Blogoslawski, President. Toll-free, (800) 506-9407.*

General email, nccw01@nccw.org

Web, www.nccw.org, Twitter, @NCCW1920 and Facebook, www.facebook.com/ nationalcouncilofcatholicwomen

Roman Catholic women's organization. Provides education and information to Catholic women regarding social issues. Interests include women and poverty, employment, family life, abortion, care for older adults, world hunger, global water supplies, genetic engineering research, pornography, capital punishment, immigration, domestic violence, and human trafficking. Special programs include volunteer respite care, leadership training for women, mentoring of mothers, and drug and alcohol abuse education. Monitors legislation and regulations.

National Council of Churches, *110 Maryland Ave. N.E., #108, 20002-5603; (202) 544-2350. Fax, (202) 543-1297. Jim Winkler, President, (202) 481-6684.*

General email, info@nationalcouncilofchurches.us

Web, www.nationalcouncilofchurches.us, Twitter, @nccusa and Facebook, www.facebook.com/ nationalcouncilofchurches

Membership: thirty-eight Protestant, Anglican, and Orthodox denominations. Interests include interreligious relations, racial and social equality; social welfare, economic justice, environmental justice, peace, and international issues, with a focus on peacemaking and mass incarceration issues; and church-state relations.

National Council of Jewish Women, *Washington Office, 2055 L St. N.W., #650, 20036; (202) 296-2588. Fax, (202) 331-7792. Jody Rabhan, Director of Washington Operations.*

General email, action@ncjwdc.org

Web, www.ncjw.org, Twitter, @NCJW and Facebook, www .facebook.com/NCJWInc

Progressive Jewish women's membership organization. Activities include education, community service, and advocacy. Interests include women's issues, reproductive, civil, and constitutional rights, child care, judicial nominations, religion-state separation, and human needs funding issues. (Headquarters in New York.)

NCSEJ: National Coalition Supporting Eurasian Jewry, *1120 20th St. N.W, #300N, 20006-3413; (202) 898-2500.*

Fax, (202) 898-0822. Mark B. Levin, Executive Director; Daniel Rubin, Chair.

General email, ncsj@ncsj.org

Web, www.ncsej.org, Twitter, @NCSEJ and Facebook, www.facebook.com/thencsej

Advocacy group promoting political and religious freedom on behalf of Jews in Russia, Ukraine, the Baltic states, and Eurasia. Works with community and government leadership in the United States and in the former Soviet Union addressing issues of anti-Semitism, community relations, and promotion of democracy, tolerance, and U.S. engagement in the region.

Operation Understanding DC, *3000 Connecticut Ave. N.W., #335, 20008; (202) 234-6832. Fax, (202) 234-6669. Yolanda Savage-Narva, Executive Director.*

General email, info@oudc.org

Web, www.oudc.org and Twitter, @OU_DC

African American and Jewish youth education program promoting leadership and antidiscrimination.

Orthodox Union, *Advocacy Center, 820 1st St. N.E., #730, 20002; (202) 513-6484. Fax, (202) 513-6497. Nathan Diament, Executive Director.*

General email, info@ouadvocacy.org

Web, www.ou.org/public_affairs

Works to protect Orthodox Jewish interests and freedoms through dissemination of policy briefings to government officials. Encourages Jewish law and a traditional perspective on public policy issues. Coordinates grassroots activities. (Headquarters in New York.)

Pew Research Center, *Religion and Public Life Project, 1615 L St. N.W., #800, 20036; (202) 419-4550. Fax, (202) 419-4559. Alan Cooperman, Director. Media, (202) 419-4564.*

General email, religion@pewresearch.org

Web, www.pewforum.org and Twitter, @PewReligion

Nonpartisan organization that seeks to explore the impact of religion on public affairs, political behavior, the law, domestic policy, and international affairs. Conducts polling and independent research; serves as a clearinghouse and forum on these issues. Delivers findings to journalists, government officials, and other interested groups. (A Pew Research Center project.)

Presbyterian Mission (U.S.A.), *Office of Public Witness, 100 Maryland Ave. N.E., #410, 20002; (202) 543-1126. Fax, (202) 543-7755. Rev. Jimmie Ray Hawkins II, Director. Toll-free, (800) 728-7228.*

General email, ga_washington_office@pcusa.org

Web, www.presbyterianmission.org/ministries/washington and Twitter, @Presbyterian

Provides information on the views of the general assembly of the Presbyterian Church on public policy issues; monitors legislation affecting issues of concern. Interests include budget priorities, foreign policy, arms control, civil rights, religious liberty, church-state relations, economic justice, environmental justice, and public policy issues affecting women. (Headquarters in Louisville, Ky.)

Progressive National Baptist Convention Inc., *601 50th St. N.E., 20019; (202) 396-0558. Fax, (202) 398-4998. Timothy Stewart, President. Toll-free, (800) 876-7622. General email, office@pnbc.org*

Web, www.pnbc.org

Baptist denomination that supports missionaries, implements education programs, and acts as advocate for civil and human rights.

Public Religion Research Institute, *1023 15th St. N.W., 9th Floor, 20005; (202) 238-9424. Fax, (202) 238-9427. Robert P. Jones, Chief Executive Officer, (202) 238-9426. Press, (202) 674-9215. General email, info@publicreligion.org*

Web, www.publicreligion.org and Twitter, @publicreligion

Nonpartisan nonprofit that conducts surveys and publishes research on the junction of public life and religion. Serves as a resource to help journalists and the public understand the impact of religion on American life and discussions on public policy.

Religious Action Center of Reform Judaism, *Union for Reform Judaism, 2027 Massachusetts Ave. N.W., 20036; (202) 387-2800. Fax, (202) 667-9070. Rabbi Jonah Pesner, Director. General email, rac@rac.org*

Web, www.rac.org and Twitter, @TheRAC

Religious and educational organization that mobilizes the American Jewish community on legislative and social concerns. Interests include economic justice, civil rights, religious liberty, and international peace.

Sojourners, *408 C St. N.E., 20002; (202) 328-8842. Fax, (202) 328-8757. Robert (Rob) Wilson-Black, Chief Executive Officer; Elizabeth Denlinger Reaves, Director. Press, (202) 328-8842. Toll-free, (800) 714-7474. General email, sojourners@sojo.net*

Web, https://sojo.net and Twitter, @Sojourners

Membership: Catholics, Protestants, Evangelicals, and other interested Christians. Grassroots network that focuses on social injustices and the intersection of faith, politics, and culture. (Merger of Sojourners and Call to Renewal.)

U.S. Conference of Catholic Bishops (USCCB), *3211 4th St. N.E., 20017; (202) 541-3000. Fax, (202) 541-3166. James Rogers, Chief Communications Officer, (202) 541-3201. Order placement toll-free, (800) 235-8722. Web, www.usccb.org and Twitter, @USCCB*

Serves as a forum for bishops to exchange ideas, debate concerns of the church, and draft responses to religious and social issues. Provides information on doctrine and policies of the Roman Catholic Church; develops religious education and training programs; formulates policy positions on social issues, including the economy, employment, federal budget priorities, voting rights, energy, health, housing, rural affairs, international military and political matters, human rights, the arms race, global economics, and immigration and refugee policy.

United Church of Christ, *Washington Office, 100 Maryland Ave. N.E., #330, 20002; (202) 543-1517. Fax, (202) 543-5994. Sandra (Sandy) Sorensen, Director. Web, www.ucc.org and Twitter, @unitedchurch*

Studies public policy issues and promotes church policy on these issues; organizes legislative advocacy to address church views. Interests include health care, international peace, economic justice, the environment, climate change, civil rights, and immigration. (Headquarters in Cleveland, Ohio.)

Washington Ethical Society, *7750 16th St. N.W., 20012; (202) 882-6650. Amanda Poppei, Senior Leader. General email, wes@ethicalsociety.org*

Web, www.ethicalsociety.org and Twitter, @EthicalDC

A humanistic religious community that sets standards, distributes ethical culture materials, trains leaders, awards grants, publishes statements on moral issues and public policy, and coordinates national projects such as youth programs. (Affiliated with the American Ethical Union and the Unitarian Universalist Assn.)

Women's Alliance for Theology, Ethics, and Ritual (WATER), *8121 Georgia Ave., #310, Silver Spring, MD 20910; (301) 589-2509. Fax, (301) 589-3150. Diann L. Neu, Co-Director; Mary E. Hunt, Co-Director. General email, water@hers.com*

Web, www.waterwomensalliance.org and Twitter, @watervoices

Feminist theological organization that focuses on issues concerning women and religion. Interests include social issues; work skills for women with disabilities; human rights in Latin America; and liturgies, rituals, counseling, and research.

TRAVEL AND TOURISM

General

▶**AGENCIES**

Bureau of Consular Affairs (CA) *(State Dept.), Passport Services, 600 19 St. N.W., #6826, 20006; (202) 647-9584. Brenda Sprague, Deputy Assistant Secretary. National Passport Information Center, (877) 487-2778. Web, https://travel.state.gov/content/passports/en/passports.html*

National Passport Information Center, NPIC@state.gov

Creates passports and provides information and resources to citizens about how to obtain, replace, and change a U.S. passport.

Bureau of Consular Affairs (CA) *(State Dept.), Special Issuance Agency, 600 19th St. N.W., #3.200, 20006; (202) 485-8244. Jennifer Walsh, Director. National Passport Information Center, (877) 487-2778. Web, http://travel.state.gov*

Administers passport laws and issues passports. (Most branches of the U.S. Postal Service and most U.S. district and state courts are authorized to accept applications and payment for passports and to administer the required oath to U.S. citizens. Completed applications are sent from the post office or court to the nearest State Dept. regional passport office for processing.)

International Trade Administration (ITA) *(Commerce Dept.), Industry and Analysis (I&A), National Travel and Tourism (NTTO), 1401 Constitution Ave. N.W., #10003, 20230-0001; (202) 482-0140. Fax, (202) 482-2887. Isabel Hill, Executive Director, (202) 482-5120.*
General email, ntto@trade.gov

Web, http://travel.trade.gov

Fosters international tourism trade development, including public-private partnerships; represents the United States in tourism-related meetings with foreign government officials. Assembles, analyzes, and disseminates data and statistics on travel and tourism to and from the United States.

National Park Service (NPS) *(Interior Dept.), National Tourism Program, 1849 C St. N.W., #1357, 20240; (202) 354-6472. Fax, (202) 371-5179. Donald Leadbetter, Chief.*
General email, donald_leadbetter@nps.gov

Web, www.nps.gov/orgs/1365/index.htm

Directs and supports the National Park Service's tourism program. Acts as liaison to government departments and agencies on tourism issues. Serves as the primary contact for national and international travel and tourism industry officials and professionals.

▶ **CONGRESS**

For a listing of relevant congressional committees and subcommittees, please see page 124 or the Appendix.

▶ **NONGOVERNMENTAL**

American Hotel and Lodging Assn., *1250 Eye St. N.W., #1100, 20005-3931; (202) 289-3100. Fax, (202) 289-3199. William (Chip) Rogers, President.*
General email, info@ahla.com

Web, https://ahla.com, Twitter, @ahla and Facebook, www .facebook.com/hotelassociation

Membership: state and city partner lodging associations. Provides operations, technical, educational, marketing, and communications services to members. Monitors legislation and regulations.

American Resort Development Assn., *1201 15th St. N.W., #400, 20005-2842; (202) 371-6700. Fax, (202) 289-8544. Howard Nusbaum, President.*
Web, www.arda.org

Membership: U.S. and international developers, builders, financiers, marketing companies, and others involved in resort, recreational, and community development. Serves as an information clearinghouse; monitors federal and state legislation affecting land, time-share, and community development industries.

American Society of Travel Agents (ASTA), *675 N. Washington St., #490, Alexandria, VA 22314-2963; (703) 739-2782. Fax, (703) 739-3268. Zane Kerby, President, (703) 739-6804. Toll-free, (800) 275-2782.*
General email, askasta@asta.org

Web, www.asta.org and Twitter, @ASTAAdvisors

Membership: representatives of the travel industry. Works to safeguard the traveling public against fraud, misrepresentation, and other unethical practices. Offers training programs for travel agents. Consumer affairs department offers help for anyone with a travel complaint against a member of the association.

Center for Responsible Travel (CREST), *1225 Eye St. N.W., #600, 20005; (202) 347-9203, ext. 417. Fax, (202) 775-0819. Martha Honey, Director.*
General email, staff@responsibletravel.org

Web, www.responsibletravel.org and Twitter, @CRESTResTravel

Designs, monitors, evaluates, and seeks to improve ecotourism and sustainable tourism principles and practices.

Cruise Lines International Assn., *1201 F St. N.W., #250, 20004; (202) 759-9370. Fax, (202) 759-9344. Kelly Craighead, President.*
General email, info@cruising.org

Web, www.cruising.org

Membership: more than fifty cruise lines as well as other cruise industry professionals. Advises domestic and international regulatory organizations on shipping policy. Works with U.S. and international agencies to promote safety, public health, security, medical facilities, environmental awareness, and passenger protection. Monitors legislation and regulations.

Destinations International, *2025 M St. N.W., #500, 20036-3309; (202) 296-7888. Fax, (202) 296-7889. Don Welsh II, Chief Executive Officer; Caitlyn Blizzard, Communications Director, (202) 835-4202.*
General email, info@destinationinternational.org

Web, https://destinationsinternational.org

Membership: travel- and tourism-related businesses, convention and meeting professionals, and tour operators. Encourages business travelers and tourists to visit local historic, cultural, and recreational areas; assists in meeting preparations. Monitors legislation and regulations.

Global Business Travel Assn., *1101 King St., #500, Alexandria, VA 22314; (703) 684-0836. Fax, (703) 342-4324. Michael (Mike) McCormick, Executive Director, (703) 236-1129.*
General email, info@gbta.org

Web, www.gbta.org and Twitter, @GlobalBTA

Membership: corporate travel managers and travel service suppliers. Promotes educational advancement of members and provides a forum for exchange of information on U.S. and international travel. Monitors legislation and regulations.

Hostelling International USA—American Youth Hostels, *8401 Colesville Rd., #600, Silver Spring, MD 20910-9663; (301) 495-1240. Fax, (240) 650-2094. Russell Hedge, Chief Executive Officer.*
General email, members@hiusa.org
Web, www.hiusa.org and Twitter, @HIUSA

Seeks to improve cultural understanding through a nationwide network of hostels and travel-based programs. Provides opportunities for outdoor recreation and inexpensive educational travel and accommodations through hostelling. Member of the International Youth Hostel Federation.

International Assn. of Amusement Parks and Attractions, *Advocacy and Safety, 1448 Duke St., Alexandria, VA 22314; (703) 299-5758. Fax, (703) 836-4801. Randy Davis, Senior Vice President of Safety and Advocacy, (703) 299-5753. Press, (703) 299-5127.*
General email, gr@iaapa.org
Web, www.iaapa.org/Safety-and-Advocacy

Membership: companies from around the world in the amusement parks and attractions industry. Monitors legislation and regulations. (Headquarters in Orlando, Fla.)

Passenger Vessel Assn., *103 Oronoco St., #200, Alexandria, VA 22314; (703) 518-5005. Fax, (703) 518-5151. John R. Groundwater, Executive Director, ext. 22. Toll-free, (800) 807-8360.*
General email, pvainfo@passengervessel.com
Web, www.passengervessel.com

Membership: owners, operators, and suppliers for U.S. and Canadian passenger vessels and international vessel companies. Interests include insurance, safety and security, and U.S. congressional impact on dinner and excursion boats, car and passenger ferries, overnight cruise ships, and riverboat casinos. Monitors legislation and regulations.

U.S. Travel Assn., *1100 New York Ave. N.W., #450, 20005-3934; (202) 408-8422. Fax, (202) 408-1255. Roger Dow, President. Media, (202) 408-2183.*
General email, feedback@ustravel.org
Web, www.USTravel.org, Twitter, @USTravel and Project Time Off, www.projecttimeoff.com

Membership: travel-related companies and associations, state tourism offices, convention and visitors bureaus. Advocates increased travel to and within the United States; conducts research, provides marketing, and hosts trade shows. Monitors legislation and regulations.

UNITE HERE, *Washington Office, 1775 K St. N.W., #620, 20006-1530; (202) 393-4373. Fax, (202) 223-6213 or (202) 342-2929. Donald Taylor, President.*
Web, www.unitehere.org and Twitter, @unitehere

Membership: workers in the United States and Canada who work in the hotel, gaming, food service, distribution, transportation, manufacturing, textile, laundry, and airport industries. Assists members with contract negotiation and grievances; conducts training programs and workshops. Monitors legislation and regulations. (Headquarters in New York. Formed by the merger of the former Union of Needletrades, Textiles and Industrial Employees and the Hotel Employees and Restaurant Employees International Union.)

5

Education

GENERAL POLICY AND ANALYSIS

Basic Resources

▶AGENCIES

Education Dept., *Lyndon Baines Johnson Bldg., 400 Maryland Ave. S.W., #7W301, 20202-0001; (202) 401-3000. Fax, (202) 260-7867. Elizabeth (Betsy) DeVos, Secretary; Carlos G. Muñiz, General Counsel, (202) 401-6000. Federal Student Aid Information Center, (800) 433-3243. Fraud, Waste, and Abuse hotline, (800) 647-8733. Information Resource Center, (202) 401-2000. Press, (202) 401-1576. Publications, (877) 433-7827. Toll-free, (800) 872-5327. TTY, (800) 877-8339.*
Web, www.ed.gov and Twitter, @usedgov

Establishes education policy and acts as principal adviser to the president on education matters; administers and coordinates most federal assistance programs on education.

Education Dept., *Educational Technology (OET), Lyndon Baines Johnson Bldg., 400 Maryland Ave. S.W., #5W114, 20202; (202) 401-1444. Jim Blew, Director (Acting).*
General email, tech@ed.gov
Web, www.tech.ed.gov and Twitter, @OfficeofEdTech

Develops national educational policy and advocates the transition from print-based to digital learning.

Education Dept., *International Affairs, Lyndon Baines Johnson Bldg., 400 Maryland Ave. S.W., #6W108, 20202-0001; (202) 401-0430. Fax, (202) 401-2508. Maureen McLaughlin, Director, (202) 401-8964.*
General email, international.affairs@ed.gov
Web, www.ed.gov/international

Responsible for the overall coordination of the Education Dept.'s international presence. Works with department program offices, support units, and senior leadership as well as with external partners, including other federal agencies, state and local agencies, foreign governments, international organizations, and the private sector.

Education Dept., *Legislative and Congressional Affairs (OLCA), Lyndon Baines Johnson Bldg., 400 Maryland Ave. S.W., #6W315, 20202-3500; (202) 401-0020. Fax, (202) 401-1438. Peter Oppenheim, Assistant Secretary.*
General email, olcainquiries@ed.gov
Web, www2.ed.gov/about/offices/list/olca

Directs and supervises all legislative activities of the Education Dept. Participates on legislation and regulation development teams within the department and provides legislative history behind the current law.

Educational Resources Information Center (ERIC) *(Education Dept.), 550 12th St. S.W., 7th Floor, 20202-5950; (800) 538-3742. Erin Pollard, Program Director.*
General email, ericrequests@ed.gov
Web, http://eric.ed.gov

Coordinates an online national information system of education literature and resources. Provides a centralized bibliographic and full-text database of journal articles and other published and unpublished materials. Available at no charge to educators worldwide. Managed by the Applied Engineering Management Corp.

National Library of Education *(Education Dept.), 400 Maryland Ave. S.W., 20202-5721; (202) 205-5015. Fax, (202) 401-0547. Barbara Holton, Deputy Director, (202) 205-4410. Information, (800) 424-1616. Reference, (202) 205-5015. TTY, (800) 877-8339.*
General email, askalibrarian@ed.gov
Web, http://ies.ed.gov/ncee/projects/nle

Federal government's main resource center for education information. Provides information, statistical, and referral services to the Education Dept. and other government agencies, the education community, and the public. Library open to the public by appointment only.

▶CONGRESS

For a listing of relevant congressional committees and subcommittees, please see page 174 or the Appendix.

Government Accountability Office (GAO), *Education, Workforce, and Income Security (EWIS), 441 G St. N.W., #5910, 20548; (202) 512-7215. Barbara D. Bovbjerg, Managing Director.*
Web, www.gao.gov/careers/ewis.html

Assists Congress in analyzing the efficiency and effectiveness of federal agency programs that foster the development, education, and skill attainment of children and adults; provide benefits and protections for workers, families, veterans, and those with disabilities; ensure an adequate and secure retirement for an aging population.

▶NONGOVERNMENTAL

American Council on Education (ACE), *Division of Government and Public Affairs, 1 Dupont Circle N.W., 20036; Daniel Madzelen, Assistant Vice President; Steven Bloom, Director of State Relations. Main, (202) 939-9300, ext. 2.*
Web, www.acenet.edu/advocacy/Pages/default.aspx
Public Affairs, HENA@acenet.edu

Coordinates and publicizes higher education to the federal government. Communicates information on educational concerns and ACE policies to the media, college and university officials, and the general public. Monitors legislation and regulations. Supports immigration, labor and employment, and veterans legislation,

Aspen Institute, *2300 N St., N.W., #700, 20037; (202) 736-5800. Fax, (202) 467-0790. Dan Porterfield, President. Press, (202) 736-3849.*
General email, info@aspeninstitute.org
Web, www.aspeninstitute.org and
Twitter, @AspenInstitute

Educational and policy studies organization. Promotes consideration of the public good in a wide variety of policy areas, including education. Working with international

EDUCATION RESOURCES IN CONGRESS

For a complete listing of congressional committees, including their full contact information, leadership, membership, and jurisdictions, please refer to the Appendix on pages 827–948.

HOUSE:

House Administration Committee, (202) 225-8281. Web, cha.house.gov

House Agriculture Committee, (202) 225-2171. Web, agriculture.house.gov

 Subcommittee on Biotechnology, Horticulture, and Research, (202) 225-2171.

House Appropriations Committee, (202) 225-2771. Web, appropriations.house.gov

 Subcommittee on Interior, Environment, and Related Agencies, (202) 225-3081.

 Subcommittee on Labor, Health and Human Services, Education, and Related Agencies, (202) 225-3508.

 Subcommittee on Legislative Branch, (202) 226-7252.

House Armed Services Committee, (202) 225-4151. Web, armedservices.house.gov

 Subcommittee on Military Personnel, (202) 225-7560.

House Education and the Workforce Committee, (202) 225-4527. Web, edworkforce.house.gov

 Subcommittee on Early Childhood, Elementary, and Secondary Education, (202) 225-4527.

 Subcommittee on Higher Education and Workforce Development, (202) 225-4527.

House Natural Resources Committee, (202) 225-2761. Web, naturalresources.house.gov

House Oversight and Government Reform Committee, (202) 225-5074. Web, oversight.house.gov

 Subcommittee on Information Technology, (202) 225-5074.

House Science, Space, and Technology Committee, (202) 225-6371. Web, science.house.gov

 Subcommittee on Research and Technology, (202) 225-6371.

JOINT:

Joint Committee on the Library of Congress, (202) 225-8281. Web, cha.house.gov/jointcommittees/joint-committee-library

SENATE:

Senate Agriculture, Nutrition, and Forestry Committee, (202) 224-2035. Web, agriculture.senate.gov

 Subcommittee on Nutrition, (202) 224-2035.

Senate Appropriations Committee, (202) 224-7257. Web, appropriations.senate.gov

 Subcommittee on Interior, Environment, and Related Agencies, (202) 228-0774.

 Subcommittee on Labor, Health and Human Services, Education, and Related Agencies, (202) 224-9145.

 Subcommittee on Legislative Branch, (202) 224-3477.

Senate Armed Services Committee, (202) 224-3871. Web, armed-services.senate.gov

 Subcommittee on Personnel, (202) 224-3871.

Senate Banking, Housing, and Urban Affairs Committee, (202) 224-7391. Web, banking.senate.gov

Senate Commerce, Science, and Transportation Committee, (202) 224-1251. Web, commerce.senate.gov

 Subcommittee on Space, Science, and Competitiveness, (202) 224-1251.

Senate Health, Education, Labor, and Pensions Committee, (202) 224-5375. Web, help.senate.gov

 Subcommittee on Children and Families, (202) 224-5375.

Senate Indian Affairs Committee, (202) 224-2251. Web, indian.senate.gov

Senate Rules and Administration Committee, (202) 224-6352. Web, rules.senate.gov

partners, offers educational seminars, nonpartisan policy forums, public conferences and events, and leadership development initiatives.

The Brookings Institution, *Brown Center on Education Policy, 1775 Massachusetts Ave. N.W., 20036; (202) 797-2472. Michael Hansen, Director. Web, www.brookings.edu/center/brown-center-on-education-policy and Twitter, @BrookingsEd*

Research center promoting education policymaking. Interests include the impact of curriculum, school accountability, class size, instructional technology, student loans, preschool education, public pensions, teacher evaluation, school districts contributions, and the academic achievement of U.S. students on international assessments.

Center for Education Reform, *1455 Pennsylvania Ave. N.W., #250, 20004; (202) 750-0016. Fax, (202) 290-2492.*

Education Department

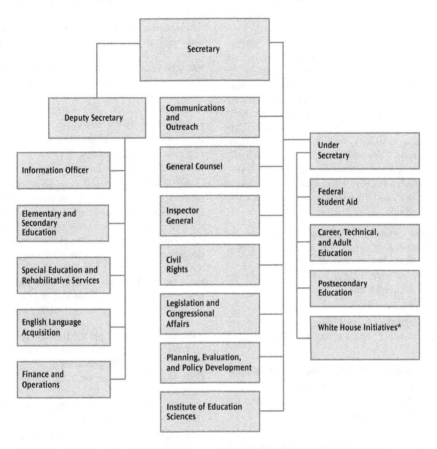

* White House Initiatives will be included in a future reorganization of the Office of Communications and Outreach. The initiatives are Center for Faith and Opportunity Initiatives, White House Initiative on American Indian and Alaska Native Education, White House Initiative on Asian Americans and Pacific Islanders, White House Initiative on Educational Excellence for Hispanics, White House Initiative on Educational Excellence for African Americans, and White House Initiative on Historically Black Colleges and Universities.

Jeanne Allen, Chief Executive Officer.
Toll-free, (800) 521-2118.
General email, christina@edreform.com

Web, www.edreform.com and Twitter, @edreform

Research and informational organization that promotes education reform through grassroots advocacy. Interests include charter school laws, school choice programs, teacher qualifications, and educational standards. Website serves as a networking forum for parents, educators, policymakers, and others interested in education reform, providing news reports and information on education seminars throughout the country.

Center for Law and Education, *7011 8th St. N.W.,*
20012; (202) 986-3000. Fax, (202) 986-6648.
Paul Weckstein, Co-Director, (202) 986-3000, ext. 101;
Kathleen Boundy, Co-Director (located in Boston).
General email, cle@cleweb.org

Web, www.cleweb.org

Works to advance the right of all students nationally, in particular those from low-income families, to a high-

quality education. Focuses on assessments, testing, and tracking; rights of students with disabilities (including special education); students with limited English proficiency, including bilingual education; implementation of key parent participation provisions under Title 1; vocational education; excessive/discriminatory discipline; and the education of youth in juvenile justice facilities. (Headquarters in Boston, Mass.)

National Assn. of State Boards of Education, *333 John Carlyle St., #530, Alexandria, VA 22314; (703) 684-4000. Robert Hull, President, (703) 740-4837; Megan Blanco, Senior Policy Associate, (703) 740-4827.*
General email, boards@nasbe.org

Web, www.nasbe.org, Twitter, @nasbe

Publications, publications@nasbe.org

Membership: members of state boards of education, state board attorneys, and executives of state boards. Works to strengthen state boards as the preeminent educational policymaking bodies for students and citizens.

National Governors Assn. (NGA), *Center for Best Practices, Education Division,* 444 N. Capitol St. N.W., #267, 20001-1512; (202) 624-7801. Aaliyah Samuel, Director.
Web, www.nga.org/cms/center/edu

Provides information, research, policy analysis, and technical assistance to governors and their staff in the areas of early childhood, K–12, and postsecondary education. Focus areas include early education access, readiness, and quality; teacher and principal preparation, evaluation, and professional development; postsecondary education standards and assessments, including Common Core Standards, Science, Technology, Engineering, and Math (STEM), and ready assessments; competency-based learning and charter schools; higher education and career training access, success, and affordability; and finance, data, and accountability.

National Research Council (NRC), *Testing and Assessment Board,* Keck Center, 500 5th St. N.W., 11th Floor, 20001; (202) 334-3776. Fax, (202) 334-2210. Colleen Hartman, Director; James H. Crocker, Vice-Chair.
General email, bota1@nas.edu
Web, http://sites.nationalacademies.org/dbasse/bota

Assists policymakers by providing scientific expertise about critical issues of testing and assessment in education and the workplace.

National School Public Relations Assn., 15948 Derwood Rd., Rockville, MD 20855; (301) 519-0496. Fax, (301) 519-0494. Richard D. Bagin, Executive Director.
General email, info@nspra.org
Web, www.nspra.org

Membership: educators and individuals interested in improving communications in education. Works to improve communication between educators and the public on the needs of schools. Provides educators with information on public relations and policy developments.

Internships, Fellowships, Grants

▶**AGENCIES**

Bureau of Educational and Cultural Affairs (ECA) *(State Dept.),* **Global Educational Programs,** 2200 C St. N.W., #4CC17, 20520; (202) 632-6342. Anthony D. Koliha, Director, (202) 632-6345.
Web, http://eca.state.gov/about-bureau-0/organizational-structure/office-global-educational-programs

Administers the Hubert H. Humphrey Fellowship Program, the Community College Initiative Program, and the Benjamin A. Gilman International Scholarship Program, and programs for the exchange and professional development of secondary school teachers and educators.

Harry S. Truman Scholarship Foundation, 712 Jackson Pl. N.W., 20006-4901; (202) 395-4831. Fax, (202) 395-6995. Andrew Rich, Executive Secretary, (202) 395-3545.
General email, office@truman.gov
Web, www.truman.gov and Twitter, @TrumanApp

Memorial to Harry S. Truman established by Congress. Provides students preparing for careers in public service with graduate school scholarship funding. (Candidates are nominated by their respective colleges or universities while in their third year of undergraduate study.)

National Endowment for the Arts (NEA), 400 7th St. S.W., 20506; (202) 682-5400. Mary Anne Carter, Chair (Acting), (202) 682-5414; Helen Ferre, Public Affairs Director. Press, (202) 682-5570. TTY, (202) 682-5496.
General email, webmgr@arts.gov
Web, www.arts.gov, Twitter, @NEAarts and Facebook, www.facebook.com/ NationalEndowmentfortheArts

Independent grant-making agency. Awards grants to support artistic excellence, creativity, and innovation for the benefit of individuals and communities. Works through partnerships with state arts agencies, local leaders, other federal agencies, and the philanthropic sector. Main funding categories include Art Works (replaces Access to Artistic Excellence and Learning in the Arts for Children and Youth); Challenge America Fast-Track (for art projects in underserved communities); and Our Town (for art projects that contribute to the livability of communities).

National Endowment for the Humanities (NEH), 400 7th St. S.W., 20506; Fax, (202) 606-8608. John Parrish Peede, Chair, (202) 606-8310; Donna McClish, Librarian, (202) 606-8244. Information, (202) 606-8400. Library, (202) 606-8244. Public Affairs, (202) 606-8446. Toll-free, 800-NEH-1121. Toll-free TTY, (800) 877-8399.
General email, questions@neh.gov
Web, www.neh.gov, Twitter, @NEHgov and Facebook, www.facebook.com/neh.gov

Independent federal grant-making agency. Awards grants to individuals and institutions for research, scholarship, and educational and public programs (including broadcasts, museum exhibitions, lectures, and symposia) in the humanities (defined as study of archaeology; history; jurisprudence; language; linguistics; literature; philosophy; comparative religion; ethics; history, criticism, and theory of the arts; and humanistic aspects of the social sciences). Funds preservation of books, newspapers, historical documents, and photographs. Library open by appointment only.

National Endowment for the Humanities (NEH), *Education Programs,* 400 7th St. S.W., 20506; (202) 606-8500. Fax, (202) 606-8394. Carol Peters, Director, (202) 606-8285.
General email, education@neh.gov
Web, www.neh.gov/divisions/education and Twitter, @NEH_Education

Offers seminars and institutes for higher education faculty, school teachers, and independent scholars. Promotes research and development.

National Science Foundation (NSF), *Education and Human Resources Directorate,* 2415 Eisenhower Ave., Room C11000, Alexandria, VA 22314; (703) 292-8600.

Fax, (703) 292-9179. Karen Marrongelle, Assistant Director.

Web, www.nsf.gov/dir/index.jsp?org=ehr

Provides fellowships and grants for graduate research and teacher education, instructional materials, and studies on the quality of existing science and mathematics programs. Participates in international studies.

National Science Foundation (NSF), *Graduate Education Division, 2415 Eisenhower Ave., Room W11200, Alexandria, VA 22314; (703) 292-8630. Fax, (703) 292-9048. Nirmala Kannankutty, Director (Acting). TTY, (800) 281-8749.*

Web, www.nsf.gov/div/index.jsp?div=dge

Supports activities to strengthen the education of research scientists and engineers; promotes career development; offers predoctoral fellowships and traineeships for study and research.

President's Commission on White House Fellowships, *712 Jackson Pl. N.W., 20503; (202) 395-4522. Fax, (202) 395-6179. Robert (Mike) Duncan, Director. General email, whitehousefellows@whf.eop.gov*

Web, www.whitehouse.gov/participate/fellows

Nonpartisan commission that provides professionals from all sectors of national life with the opportunity to observe firsthand the processes of the federal government. Fellows work for one year as special assistants to cabinet members or to principal members of the White House staff. Qualified applicants have demonstrated superior accomplishments early in their careers and have a commitment to leadership and public service.

Smithsonian Institution, *Fellowships and Internships, 470 L'Enfant Plaza S.W., #7102, 20013-7012 (mailing address: P.O. Box 37012, MRC 902, Washington, DC 20013-7012); (202) 633-7070. Fax, (202) 633-7069. Eric Woodard, Director, (202) 633-7053. General email, siofi@si.edu*

Web, www.smithsonianofi.com and Twitter, @SmithsonianOFI

Administers internships and fellowships in residence for study and research at the Smithsonian Institution in history of science and technology, American and cultural history, history of art, anthropology, evolutionary and systematic biology, environmental sciences, astrophysics and astronomy, earth sciences, and tropical biology.

Woodrow Wilson International Center for Scholars, *1300 Pennsylvania Ave. N.W., 20004-3027; (202) 691-4000. Fax, (202) 691-4001. Jane Harman, President, (202) 691-4202. Press, (202) 691-4217. General email, wwics@wilsoncenter.org*

Web, www.wilsoncenter.org, Twitter, @thewilsoncenter

Fellowship information, fellowships@wilsoncenter.org

Library, library.email@wilsoncenter.org

Supports research in the social studies and humanities. Awards fellowships to individuals from a wide variety of backgrounds, including academia, government, the non-profit sector, and the corporate world. Hosts public policy

and senior scholars who conduct research and write in a variety of disciplines. Offers grant competitions through regional programs, including the Asia Program, the Kennan Institute, East European Studies, and the Canada Institute. Library open for scholars.

▶NONGOVERNMENTAL

American Architectural Foundation, *740 15th St. N.W., 20005; (202) 787-1010. Marci B. Reed, Executive Director. General email, info@archfoundation.org*

Web, www.archfoundation.org

Seeks to advance the quality of American architecture. Provides design leadership training and techinical assistance. Awards grants for architecture-oriented projects.

American Assn. of University Women (AAUW), *1310 L St. N.W., #1000, 20005; (202) 785-7700. Fax, (202) 872-1425. Kimberly (Kim) Churches, Chief Executive Officer, ext. 7767. Toll-free, (800) 326-2289. TTY, (202) 785-7777. General email, connect@aauw.org*

Web, www.aauw.org, Twitter, @aauw and Facebook, www.facebook.com/AAUW.National

Awards fellowships and grants to women for various areas of study and educational pursuit. Offers fellowships to women coming to the United States for one year of graduate study. Awards grants to women returning to school for postbaccalaureate education or professional development.

American Political Science Assn. (APSA), *Congressional Fellowship Program, 1527 New Hampshire Ave. N.W., 20036-1206; (202) 483-2512. Fax, (202) 483-2657. Janna Deitz, Program Director, (202) 483-2520. General email, cfp@apsanet.org*

Web, www.apsanet.org/cfp

Places midcareer political scientists, journalists, faculty of medical schools (Robert Wood Johnson Fellowships, Health and Aging Policy Fellowships), and federal executives in congressional offices and committees for nine-month fellowships. Individual government agencies nominate federal executive participants.

Ashoka: Innovators for the Public, *1700 N. Moore St., #2000, Arlington, VA 22209; (703) 527-8300. Fax, (703) 527-8383. Bill Drayton, Chief Executive Officer. General email, info@ashoka.org*

Web, www.ashoka.org and Twitter, @Ashoka

Supports fellowships for individuals with ideas for social change and entrepreneurship in seventy developing nations. Provides fellows with research support, organizational networking, legal counseling, economic support, and business consulting. Seeks to educate the public about the developing world and the work of its fellows.

Center for the Study of the Presidency and Congress, *601 13th St. N.W., #1050N, 20005; (202) 872-9800. Fax, (202) 872-9811. Glenn C. Nye, President. General email, hurst.renner@thepresidency.org*

Web, www.thepresidency.org and Twitter, @CSPC_DC

Provides fellowships to undergraduate and graduate students studying the U.S. presidency, the public policy-making process, the presidential relations with Congress, allies, the media, and the public.

Congressional Black Caucus Foundation, *1720 Massachusetts Ave. N.W., 20036-1903; (202) 263-2800. Fax, (202) 263-0842. Elsie L. Scott, President (Acting). General email, info@cbcfinc.org*

Web, www.cbcfinc.org and Twitter, @CBCFInc

Conducts public policy research on issues of concern to African Americans. Sponsors internships and scholarships, as well as fellowship programs in which professionals and academic candidates work on congressional committees and subcommittees.

Council for International Exchange of Scholars, *1400 K St. N.W., #700, 20005; (202) 686-4000. Fax, (202) 686-4029. Sarah Ilchman, Chief. General email, scholars@iie.org*

Web, www.cies.org and Twitter, @FulbrightPrgrm

Cooperates with the U.S. government in administering Fulbright grants for university teaching and advanced research abroad. (A division of the Institute of International Education.)

Education Trust, *1250 H St. N.W., #700, 20005; (202) 293-1217. Fax, (202) 293-2605. John B. King Jr., President. General email, lsingleton@edtrust.org*

Web, www.edtrust.org and Twitter, @EdTrust

Researches and disseminates data on student achievement. Provides assistance to school districts, colleges, and other organizations to raise student achievement, especially among poor and minority students. Monitors legislation and regulations.

Eisenhower Institute, *818 Connecticut Ave. N.W., #800, 20006; (202) 628-4444. Fax, (202) 628-4445. Susan Eisenhower, Chair Emeritus; Patrick Cochran, Program Manager. General email, ei@gettysburg.edu*

Web, www.eisenhowerinstitute.org

Provides scholarships, fellowships, internships, and other sponsored opportunities for students to participate in dialogue with prominent figures and to pursue study of public policy and related fields. (Affiliated with Gettysburg College in Gettysburg, Pa.)

Foundation Center, *Washington Office, 1627 K St. N.W., 3rd Floor, 20006-1708; (202) 331-1400. Fax, (202) 331-1739. Kim Patton, Director. General email, kpb@foundationcenter.org*

Web, www.foundationcenter.org/washington, Twitter, @FCWashington and Facebook, www.facebook .com/foundationcenter

GrantSpace, http://grantspace.org

Publishes foundation guides and electronic databases. Serves as a clearinghouse on foundations and corporate giving, nonprofit management, fund-raising, and grants

for individuals. Provides training and seminars on fund-raising and grant writing. Operates libraries in Atlanta, Cleveland, New York, San Francisco, and Washington, D.C.; library catalog available on the website. Libraries open to the public. (Headquarters in New York.)

The Fund for American Studies (TFAS), *1706 New Hampshire Ave. N.W., 20009; (202) 986-0384. Fax, (202) 986-0390. Roger R. Ream, President. General email, info@tfas.org*

Web, www.tfas.org, Twitter, @TFASorg and Facebook, www.facebook.com/TFASorg

Sponsors internships for college students on comparative political and economic systems, business and government affairs, political journalism, philanthropy, and voluntary service; grants scholarships. Interests include political and economic freedoms.

Grantmakers in Health, *1100 Connecticut Ave. N.W., #1200, 20036; (202) 452-8331. Fax, (202) 452-8340. Faith Mitchell, President. General email, info@gih.org*

Web, www.gih.org and Twitter, @GIHealth

Seeks to increase the capacity of health foundations and giving programs to enhance public health and health education. Fosters information exchange among grantmakers. Publications include a bulletin on current news in health and human services.

The Herb Block Foundation, *1730 M St. N.W., #1020, 20036; (202) 223-8801. Fax, (202) 223-8804. Marcela Brane, President; Sarah Armstrong Alex, Executive Director. General email, info@herbblock.org*

Web, www.herbblockfoundation.org and Twitter, @TheHerbBlockFdn

Awards grants to charitable and educational programs that combat discrimination and poverty and promote citizen involvement in government. Provides scholarships to individuals seeking to attend community colleges in the Washington, D.C., area. Awards prizes for excellence in editorial cartooning to serve as as a tool for freedom and to address social issues.

Institute for Responsible Citizenship, *1227 25th St. N.W., 6th Floor, 20037; (202) 660-2501. William A. Keyes, President. Web, www.theinstitute.net and Facebook, www.facebook .com/responsiblecitizenship*

Offers grants, internships, and leadership courses for African American men scholars. Academic areas for internships include art, business, finance, philanthropy, education, government, healthcare, science, technology, law, public relations, and religion.

Institute of Current World Affairs, *1779 Massachusetts Ave. N.W., #605, 20036; (202) 364-4068. Gregory Feifer, Executive Diretor.*

General email, icwa@icwa.org

Web, www.icwa.org, Twitter, @ICWAnews and *Facebook, www.facebook.com/ InstituteOfCurrentWorldAffairs*

Offers two-year fellowships to support the independent study of international region-specific issues. Fellows write monthly newsletters to update the institute on their progress and findings. Presents public events on international topics.

Institute of International Education, *National Security Education Program, 4800 Mark Center Dr., #08F09-02, Alexandria, VA 22350-7000 (mailing address: P.O. Box 20010, Arlington, VA 22209); (571) 256-0711. Fax, (703) 692-2615. Michael A. Nugent, Director. Boren Awards information, (800) 618-6737.*

General email, nsep@nsep.gov

Web, www.nsep.gov

Administers Boren Awards and Language Flagship programs; provides scholarships, fellowships, and institutional grants to students and academics with an interest in foreign affairs and national security.

Marine Technology Society, *1100 H St. N.W., #LL-100, 20005; (202) 717-8705. Fax, (202) 347-4302. Kathleen Herndon, Executive Director.*

General email, membership@mtsociety.org

Web, www.mtsociety.org

Provides scholarships to high school and postsecondary students in marine-related programs with focus in marine technology, marine engineering, and marine science.

National Journalism Center, *11480 Commerce Park Dr., #600, Reston, VA 20191; (703) 318-9608. Fax, (703) 318-9122. Elizabeth Donatelli, Executive Director. Toll-free, (800) 872-1776.*

Web, www.nationaljournalismcenter.org

Sponsors a comprehensive internship program in journalism composed of a series of training seminars that enhance students' knowledge of policy reporting in the areas of economics, education, and business. (Affiliated with the Young America's Foundation.)

The Washington Center for Internships and Academic Seminars, *1333 16th St. N.W., 20036-2205; (202) 238-7900. Fax, (202) 238-7700. Christopher Norton, President. Information, (800) 486-8921.*

General email, info@twc.edu

Web, www.twc.edu and *Twitter, @TWCInternships*

Arranges congressional, agency, and public service internships for college undergraduate students for credit. Sponsors classes and lectures as part of the internship program. Scholarships and stipends available. Fee for internship and housing assistance.

Women's Research and Education Institute (WREI), *3808 Brighton Court, Alexandria, VA 22305; (703) 302-0754. Susan Scanlan, President, (202) 280-2718.*

General email, wrei@wrei.org

Web, www.wrei.org

Provides data and analysis of issues affecting women and their families to policymakers, the press, and the public. Its Women in the Military project acts as an advocate on policy issues affecting women in uniform through publications and conferences.

Professional Development, Interests, and Benefits

▶**AGENCIES**

Education Dept., *Innovation and Improvement (OII), Arts in Education—Professional Development for Arts Educators, Lyndon Baines Johnson Bldg., 400 Maryland Ave. S.W., #4W214, 20202-5950; (202) 260-2072. Fax, (202) 205-5630. Michelle Johnson Armstrong, Program Manager, (202) 205-1729.*

General email, Michelle.Armstrong@ed.gov

Web, www2.ed.gov/programs/artsedprofdev

Supports the implementation of high-quality professional development model programs in elementary and secondary education for music, dance, drama, and visual arts educators in high-poverty schools. Funds support innovative instructional methods, especially those linked to scientifically based research that integrate standards-based arts instruction with other core academic content.

Education Dept., *Innovation and Improvement (OII), Teacher Quality Programs (TQP), Lyndon Baines Johnson Bldg., 400 Maryland Ave. S.W., #4W306, 20202-5950; (202) 260-2614. Venitia Richardson, Director, (202) 260-2614.*

General email, Venitia.Richardson@ed.gov

Web, www2.ed.gov/about/offices/list/oii/tqp

Supports the implementation of recruitment, preparation, and professional development programs for teachers and principals.

▶**NONGOVERNMENTAL**

American Assn. of Colleges for Teacher Education, *1307 New York Ave. N.W., #300, 20005-4701; (202) 293-2450. Fax, (202) 457-8095. Lynn M. Gangone, President, (202) 478-4505.*

General email, aacte@aacte.org

Web, www.aacte.org, Twitter, @aacte and *Facebook, www .facebook.com/aacte*

Membership: colleges and universities with teacher education programs. Informs members about state and federal policies affecting teacher education and about professional issues such as accreditation, certification, and assessment. Collects and analyzes information on education.

American Assn. of School Administrators, *1615 Duke St., Alexandria, VA 22314; (703) 528-0700. Daniel A. Domenech, Executive Director, (703) 875-0722.*

General email, info@aasa.org

Web, www.aasa.org, Twitter, @aasahq and *Facebook, www.facebook.com/AASApage*

Membership: more than 13,000 educational leaders, including superintendents, chief executive officers, senior-level school administrators, and professors, as well as aspiring school system leaders. Seeks to support and develop effective school system leaders through publications and professional development workshops.

American Federation of School Administrators, *1101 17th St. N.W., #408, 20036-4704; (202) 986-4209. Fax, (202) 986-4211. Ernest A. Logan, President; Paul Wolostsky, Executive Director.*
General email, afsa@afsaadmin.org

Web, www.afsaadmin.org, Twitter, @ASFAUnion and Facebook, www.facebook.com/AFSAUnion

Membership: approximately 20,000 school administrators, including principals, vice principals, directors, and supervisors in the United States, Puerto Rico, and U.S. Virgin Islands. Helps members negotiate pay, benefits, and better working conditions; conducts training programs and workshops. Monitors legislation and regulations. (Affiliated with the AFL-CIO.)

American Federation of Teachers (AFT), *555 New Jersey Ave. N.W., 20001-2079; (202) 879-4400. Randi Weingarten, President.*
General email, online@aft.org

Web, www.aft.org, Twitter, @AFTUnion and Facebook, www.facebook.com/AFTUnion

Membership: 1.5 million public school teachers and staff, higher education faculty and staff, state and local government employees, and nurses and health care professionals. Assists members with contract negotiation and grievances; conducts training programs and workshops. Monitors legislation and regulations. (Affiliated with the AFL-CIO.)

American Political Science Assn. (APSA), *1527 New Hampshire Ave. N.W., 20036-1206; (202) 483-2512. Fax, (202) 483-2657. Steven Rathgeb Smith, Executive Director.*
General email, apsa@apsanet.org

Web, www.apsanet.org, Twitter, @APSAtweets and Facebook, www.facebook.com/likeAPSA

Membership: political scientists, primarily college and university professors. Promotes scholarly inquiry into all aspects of political science, including international affairs and comparative government. Works to increase public understanding of politics; provides services to facilitate and enhance research, teaching, and professional development of its members. Seeks to improve the status of women and minorities in the profession. Offers congressional fellowships, workshops, and awards.

ASCD, *1703 N. Beauregard St., Alexandria, VA 22311-1714; (703) 578-9600. Fax, (703) 575-5400. Deborah Delisle, Executive Director. Information, (800) 933-2723.*
General email, member@ascd.org

Web, www.ascd.org and Twitter, @ASCD

Membership: professional educators internationally, including superintendents, supervisors, principals, teachers, professors of education, and school board members. Develops professional development programs, products, and services for educators. Holds an annual conference; offers webinars, consulting services, books, and other publications. (Formerly the Assn. for Supervision and Curriculum Development.)

Assn. of School Business Officials International, *44790 Maynard Sq., #200, Ashburn, VA 20147; (703) 478-0405. Fax, (703) 478-0205. John Musso, Executive Director. Toll-free, (866) 682-2729.*
General email, asboreq@asbointl.org

Web, www.asbointl.org and Twitter, @ASBOINTL

Membership: administrators, directors, and others involved in school business management. Provides news and information concerning management best practices and the effective use of educational resources. Hosts conferences; sponsors research; monitors legislation and regulations.

Assn. of Teacher Educators, *11350 Random Hills Rd., #800, PMB 6, Fairfax, VA 22030 (mailing address: P.O. Box 793, Manassas, VA 20113); (703) 659-1708. Fax, (703) 595-4792. David A. Ritchey, Executive Director. General email, info@ate1.org*

Web, www.ate1.org and Twitter, @AssocTeacherEd

Membership: individuals and public and private agencies involved with teacher education. Seeks to improve teacher education at all levels; conducts workshops and conferences; produces and disseminates publications.

Council for Advancement and Support of Education, *1307 New York Ave. N.W., #1000, 20005-4701; (202) 328-2273. Fax, (202) 387-4973. Sue Cunningham, President; Brian Flahaven, Senior Director of Advocacy. General email, memberservicecenter@case.org*

Web, www.case.org and Twitter, @CASEAdvance

Membership: two-year and four-year colleges, universities, and independent schools. Offers professional education and training programs to members; advises members on institutional advancement issues, including fundraising, public relations programs, government relations, and management. Library open to professional members by appointment.

Council of Chief State School Officers, *1 Massachusetts Ave. N.W., #700, 20001-1431; (202) 336-7000. Fax, (202) 408-8072. Carissa Moffat Miller, Executive Director. Press, (202) 336-7034. General email, communications@ccsso.org*

Web, http://ccsso.org and Twitter, @CCSSO

Membership: the public officials who head departments of elementary and secondary education in the states, the District of Columbia, the Department of Defense Education Activity, and five U.S. extrastate jurisdictions. Provides leadership, advocacy, and technical assistance on major educational issues. Seeks member consensus on major educational issues and acts as advocate on issue positions to civic and professional organizations, federal agencies, Congress, and the public.

Federal Education Assn., *1201 16th St. N.W., #117, 20036; (202) 822-7850. Fax, (202) 822-7867. Chuck McCarter, President.*
General email, fea@feaonline.org

Web, www.feaonline.org and Twitter, @FedEdAssoc

Membership: teachers and personnel of Defense Dept. schools for military dependents in the United States and abroad. Provides professional development through workshops and publications. Monitors legislation and regulations.

International Assn. for Continuing Education and Training (IACET), *2201 Cooperative Way, #600, Herndon, VA 20171; (703) 763-0705. Fax, (703) 634-6274. Joe McClary, Chief Executive Officer, ext. 101. General email, info@iacet.org*

Web, www.iacet.org, Twitter, @IACETorg and Facebook, www.facebook.com/IACETOrg

Membership: education and training organizations and individuals who use the Continuing Education Unit. (The C.E.U. is defined as ten contact hours of participation in an organized continuing education program that is noncredit.) Authorizes organizations that issue the C.E.U.; develops criteria and guidelines for use of the C.E.U.

National Assn. of Biology Teachers, *11 Main St., Suite D, Warrenton, VA 20186 (mailing address: P.O. Box 3363, Warrenton, VA 20188); (703) 264-9696. Fax, (202) 962-3939. Jaclyn Reeves-Pepin, Executive Director, (703) 264-9696 ext. 4. Information, (888) 501-6228. General email, office@nabt.org*

Web, www.nabt.org

Membership: biology teachers and others interested in life sciences education at the elementary, secondary, and collegiate levels. Provides professional development opportunities through its publication program, summer workshops, conventions, and national award programs.

National Assn. of Secondary School Principals, *1904 Association Dr., Reston, VA 20191-1537; (703) 860-0200. JoAnn D. Bartoletti, Executive Director. Toll-free, (800) 253-7746.*

Web, www.nassp.org and Twitter, @nassp

Membership: principals and assistant principals of middle schools and senior high schools, both public and private, and college-level teachers of secondary education. Conducts training programs for members; serves as clearinghouse for information on secondary school administration. Student activities office provides student councils, student activity advisers, and national and junior honor societies with information on national associations.

National Business Education Assn., *1914 Association Dr., Reston, VA 20191-1596; (703) 860-8300. Fax, (703) 620-4483. Janet M. Treichel, Executive Director, (703) 860-8300, ext. 11. General email, nbea@nbea.org*

Web, www.nbea.org and Twitter, @NBEA

Membership: business education teachers and others interested in the field. Provides information on business education; offers teaching materials; sponsors conferences. Monitors legislation and regulations affecting business education.

National Council on Teacher Quality, *1440 G St. N.W., #8193, 20005; (202) 393-0020. Fax, (202) 393-0095. Kate Walsh, President. General email, help@pathtoteach.org*

Web, www.nctq.org, Twitter, @NCTQ and Facebook, www.facebook.com/teacherquality and Path to Teach, www.pathtoteach.org

Advocacy group for teacher quality and effectiveness. Interests include state and district teacher policy reform. Reviews and reports on national teacher training programs, layoff policies, teacher contracts, and state performance. Analyzes school board policies, teacher performance evaluations, and salary schedules to aid dialogue between school officials and teachers unions.

National Education Assn. (NEA), *1201 16th St. N.W., 20036-3290; (202) 833-4000. Fax, (202) 822-7974. Lily Eskelson Garcia, President; John C. Stocks, Executive Director. Press, (202) 822-7823. Web, www.nea.org and Twitter, @NEAToday*

Membership: more than 3.2 million educators from preschool to university graduate programs. Promotes the interest of the profession of teaching and the cause of education in the United States. Monitors legislation and regulations at state and national levels.

National Institute for School Leadership, Inc. (NISL), *2121 K St. N.W., #700, 20037; (202) 449-5060. Fax, (202) 293-1560. Jason Dougal, Chief Executive Officer, (202) 378-2212. General email, info@ncee.org*

Web, www.nisl.org and Twitter, @nislorg

Offers research-based professional development programs designed to give principals the knowledge and skills they need to be instructional leaders and improve student achievement in their schools. (Subsidiary of National Center on Education and the Economy [NCEE].)

National Science Teachers Assn., *1840 Wilson Blvd., Arlington, VA 22201-3000; (703) 243-7100. Fax, (703) 243-7177. David L. Evans, Executive Director. Web, www.nsta.org*

Membership: science teachers from elementary through college levels. Provides forum for exchange of information. Monitors legislation and regulations.

NEA Foundation, *1201 16th St. N.W., #416, 20036-3207; (202) 822-7840. Fax, (202) 822-7779. Harriet Sanford, President. General email, NEAFoundation@nea.org*

Web, www.neafoundation.org, Twitter, @NEAFoundation and Facebook, www.facebook.com/theneafoundation

Offers grants and programs to public educators to improve teaching techniques, increase classroom innovations, and otherwise further professional development.

Grant areas include science, technology, engineering, and mathematics teaching and learning, with a current special emphasis on "green" grants. Program specialties include strategies for improving achievement rates for poor and minority students.

NRTA: AARP's Educator Community, *601 E St. N.W., 20049; (202) 434-2380. Fax, (202) 434-3439. Emily Allen, Vice President. Information, (888) 687-2277.*
General email, gruiz@aarp.org

Web, www.aarp.org/nrta

Membership: active and retired teachers, other school personnel (elementary through postsecondary), and those interested in education and learning over age fifty. Provides members with information on relevant national issues. Provides state associations of retired school personnel with technical assistance. (Formerly the National Retired Teachers Assn.)

TESOL International Assn., *1925 Ballenger Ave., #550, Alexandria, VA 22314-6820; (703) 836-0774.*
Fax, (703) 836-7864. Christopher Powers, Executive Director, ext. 505. Information, (888) 891-0041.
General email, info@tesol.org

Web, www.tesol.org and Twitter, @TESOL_Assn

Provides professional development programs and career services for teachers of English to speakers of other languages. Sponsors professional development programs and provides career management services.

Research

▶AGENCIES

Institute of Education Sciences *(Education Dept.), 550 12th S.W. St., 20024; (202) 245-6940. Fax, (202) 245-6113. Mark Schneider, Director. Library, (202) 205-4945.*
General email, contact.ies@ed.gov

Web, https://ies.ed.gov, Twitter, @IESResearch and Facebook, www.facebook.com/IESResearch

Provides scientific evidence on which to ground education practice and policy through the work of four centers dealing with education research, education statistics, education evaluation and regional assistance, and special education research. Funds studies on ways to improve academic achievement, conducts large-scale evaluations of federal education programs, and reports a wide array of statistics on the condition of education. Library open 9:00 a.m.–5:00 p.m.

Institute of Education Sciences *(Education Dept.), National Center for Education Evaluation and Regional Assistance (NCEE), 550 12th St. S.W., 20024;*
(202) 245-6940. Fax, (202) 245-6113. Matthew Soldner, Commissioner, (202) 245-8385.
Web, https://ies.ed.gov/ncee and Twitter, @IESResearch

Conducts large-scale evaluations and provides research-based technical assistance and information about high-quality research to educators and policymakers. Programs include What Works Clearinghouse, Regional Educational Laboratories Program, and the ERIC library of education research and resources.

Institute of Education Sciences *(Education Dept.), National Center for Education Research (NCER), 550 12th St. S.W., 20004; (202) 245-6940. Fax, (202) 245-6113. Elizabeth Eisner, Commissioner.*
Web, https://ies.ed.gov/ncer

Supports research to improve student outcomes and education quality; supports training programs to prepare researchers to conduct high-quality scientific-education research.

Institute of Education Sciences *(Education Dept.), National Center for Education Statistics (NCES), 550 12th St. S.W., #4061, 20202; (202) 403-5551.*
Fax, (202) 245-6101. James L. Woodworth, Commissioner. Web, https://nces.ed.gov, Twitter, @EdNCES and Facebook, www.facebook.com/EdNCES

Primary federal entity for collecting and analyzing data related to education. Administers the National Assessment of Educational Progress (NAEP), the "Nation's Report Card."

Institute of Education Sciences *(Education Dept.), National Center for Special Education Research (NCSER), 550 12th St. S.W., #4144, 20024; (202) 245-6940. Fax, (202) 245-6113. Elizabeth Albro, Commissioner, (202) 245-8201.*
Web, http://ies.ed.gov/ncser

Sponsors a comprehensive program of special education research designed to expand the knowledge and understanding of infants, toddlers, and children with disabilities.

National Library of Education *(Education Dept.), 400 Maryland Ave. S.W., 20202-5721; (202) 205-5015.*
Fax, (202) 401-0547. Barbara Holton, Deputy Director, (202) 205-4410. Information, (800) 424-1616. Reference, (202) 205-5015. TTY, (800) 877-8339.
General email, askalibrarian@ed.gov

Web, http://ies.ed.gov/ncee/projects/nle

Provides information and answers questions on education statistics and research. Collection focuses on education research, but also includes fields such as law, public policy, economics, urban affairs, and sociology. Includes current and historical Education Dept. publications. Library open to the public by appointment only.

▶NONGOVERNMENTAL

American Councils for International Education: ACTR/ ACCELS, *1828 L St. N.W., #1200, 20036; (202) 833-7522. Lorne Craner, President, ext. 101.*
General email, general@americancouncils.org

Web, www.americancouncils.org, Twitter, @AC_Global and Facebook, www.facebook.com/AmericanCouncils

Advances education and research worldwide through international programs focused on academic exchange, professional training, distance learning, curriculum and test development, delivery of technical assistance, research, evaluation, and institution building.

American Educational Research Assn., *1430 K St. N.W., #1200, 20005; (202) 238-3200. Fax, (202) 238-3250. Felice J. Levine, Executive Director, (202) 238-3200, ext. 201.*
General email, members@aera.net
Web, www.aera.net, Twitter, @ AERA_EdResearch and Facebook, www.facebook.com/AERA_EdResearch

Membership: educational researchers affiliated with universities and colleges, school systems, think tanks, and federal and state agencies. Publishes original research in education; sponsors publication of reference works in educational research; conducts continuing education programs; studies status of women and minorities in the education field.

American Institutes for Research, *1000 Thomas Jefferson St. N.W., 20007; (202) 403-5000. Fax, (855) 459-6213. David Myers, President. Press, (202) 403-6347. TTY, (877) 334-3499.*
General email, inquiry@air.org
Web, www.air.org and Twitter, @AIR_Info

Conducts research on educational evaluation and improvement. Develops and implements assessment and testing services that improve student education as well as meet the requirements set forth by state and federally mandated programs.

The Brookings Institution, *Governance Studies, 1755 Massachusetts Ave. N.W., 20036; (202) 797-6090. Fax, (202) 797-6144. Darrell M. West, Director, (202) 797-6481. Information, (202) 797-6000. Press, (202) 797-6105.*
Web, www.brookings.edu/governance

Conducts research and provides policy recommendations on topics in education.

Council on Governmental Relations, *1200 New York Ave. N.W., #460, 20005; (202) 289-6655. Fax, (202) 289-6698. Wendy Streitz, President, ext. 111. Web, www.cogr.edu*

Membership: research universities, institutes, and medical colleges maintaining federally supported programs. Advises members and makes recommendations to government agencies regarding policies and regulations affecting federally funded university research.

Knowledge Alliance, *777 6th St. N.W., #500, 20001; (202) 770-2218. Michele McLaughlin, President.*
General email, michele@knowledgeall.net
Web, www.knowledgeall.net and Twitter, @KnowledgeAll

Membership: university-based educational research and development organizations, educational entrepreneurs, and technical assistance providers. Promotes use of scientifically based solutions for improving teaching and learning. (Formerly the National Education Knowledge Industry Assn.)

National Assn. of Independent Colleges and Universities, *1025 Connecticut Ave. N.W., #700, 20036-5405; (202) 785-8866. Fax, (202) 835-0003. David L. Warren, President.*

General email, geninfo@naicu.edu
Web, www.naicu.edu and Twitter, @NAICUtweets

Membership: liberal arts colleges, research universities, church-related and faith-related institutions, historically black colleges and universities, women's colleges, performing and visual arts institutions, two-year colleges; graduate schools of law, medicine, engineering, business, and other professions. Tracks campus trends, conducts research, analyzes higher-education issues, and helps coordinate state-level activities. Interests include federal policies that affect student aid, taxation, and government regulation. Monitors legislation and regulations.

RAND Corp., *Washington Office, 1200 S. Hayes St., Arlington, VA 22202-5050; (703) 413-1100. Fax, (703) 413-8111. Nicholas Burger, Director; Anita Chandra, Director for Social and Economic Well-Being, ext. 5323.*
Web, www.rand.org

Conducts research on education policy. (Headquarters in Santa Monica, Calif.)

LIBRARIES, TECHNOLOGY, AND EDUCATIONAL MEDIA

General

▶AGENCIES

Dibner Library of the History of Science and Technology *(Smithsonian Institution), 12th St. and Constitution Ave. N.W., NMAH 1041, MRC 672, 20560 (mailing address: P.O. Box 37012, MRC 154, Washington, DC 20013-7012); (202) 633-3872. Lilla Vekerdy, Head of Special Collections. Press, (202) 633-1522.*
General email, Dibnerlibrary@si.edu
Web, www.library.si.edu/libraries/dibner-library-history-science-and-technology

Collection includes major holdings in the history of science and technology dating from the fifteenth century to the nineteenth century. Extensive collections in engineering, transportation, chemistry, mathematics, physics, electricity, and astronomy. Open to the public by appointment.

Education Dept., *Educational Technology (OET), Lyndon Baines Johnson Bldg., 400 Maryland Ave. S.W., #5W114, 20202; (202) 401-1444. Jim Blew, Director (Acting).*
General email, tech@ed.gov
Web, www.tech.ed.gov and Twitter, @OfficeofEdTech

Develops national educational policy and advocates the transition from print-based to digital learning.

Institute of Museum and Library Services, *955 L'Enfant Plaza North S.W., #4000, 20024; (202) 653-4657. Fax, (202) 653-4600. Kathryn K. Matthew, Director, (202) 653-4644. Communications and Government Affairs, (202) 653-4757. Library services, (202) 653-4700.*

Museum services, (202) 653-4789. Grants and policy management, (202) 653-4759. TTY, (202) 653-4614. General email, imlsinfo@imls.gov

Web, www.imls.gov, Twitter, @US_IMLS and Facebook, www.facebook.com/USIMLS

Awards grants to help museums and libraries make their services and resources more accessible for all as well as grants to improve the care of museum collections and the recruitment, training, and development of library and museum staff. All types of libraries and museums are eligible, including African American history and culture museums, and institutions serving Native American, Hawaiian, and Alaskan tribal communities. Collects data, forms strategic partnerships, and advises policymakers and other federal agencies on museum, library, and information services.

National Archives and Records Administration (NARA), *National Archives Museum, 701 Constitution Ave. N.W., 20408; (202) 357-5210. Fax, (202) 357-5926. Vacant, Director, (202) 357-5974. Information, (202) 357-5000 ext. 1. Communications and marketing, (202) 357-5300. Web, www.archives.gov/museum*

Produces teaching packets that feature National Archives historic documents and online educational tools.

National Archives and Records Administration (NARA), *Presidential Libraries, 8601 Adelphi Rd., #2200, College Park, MD 20740-6001; (301) 837-3250. Fax, (301) 837-3199. Fax, (301) 837-3218. Susan K. Donius, Director (Acting), (202) 357-5376. Web, www.archives.gov/presidential-libraries and Twitter, @OurPresidents*

Administers thirteen presidential libraries. Directs all programs relating to acquisition, preservation, and research use of materials in presidential libraries; conducts oral history projects; publishes finding aids for research sources; provides reference service, including information from and about documentary holdings. Conducts community outreach; oversees museum exhibition programming.

National Endowment for the Humanities (NEH), *Digital Humanities, 400 7th St. S.W., 20506; (202) 606-8401. Fax, (202) 606-8411. Brett Bobley, Director. General email, odh@neh.gov*

Web, www.neh.gov/divisions/odh and Twitter, @NEH_ODH

Encourages and supports projects that utilize or study the impact of digital technology on research, education, preservation, access, and public programming in the humanities.

National Endowment for the Humanities (NEH), *Public Programs, 400 7th St. S.W., 20506; (202) 606-8269. Fax, (202) 606-8557. Anne-Imelda Radice, Director, (202) 606-8631. General email, publicpgms@neh.gov*

Web, www.neh.gov/divisions/public

Awards grants to libraries, museums, special projects, and media for projects that enhance public appreciation and understanding of the humanities through books and other resources in American library collections. Projects include conferences, exhibitions, essays, documentaries, radio programs, and lecture series.

Smithsonian Center for Learning and Digital Access, *600 Maryland Ave. S.W., #1005W, 20024 (mailing address: P.O. Box 37012, MRC 508, Washington, DC 20013-7012); (202) 633-5330. Fax, (202) 633-5489. Stephanie Norby, Director. General email, learning@si.edu*

Web, https://learninglab.si.edu/about/ SmithsonianCenterforLearningandDigitalAccess and Twitter, @SmithsonianLab

Serves as the Smithsonian's central education office. Provides elementary and secondary teachers with programs, publications, audiovisual materials, regional workshops, and summer courses on using museums and primary source materials as teaching tools. Publishes books and other educational materials for teachers. (Associated with the Smithsonian Learning Lab.)

Smithsonian Institution, *Office of the Director, Libraries, National Museum of Natural History, 10th St. and Constitution Ave. N.W., Room 29, 20560 (mailing address: P.O. Box 37012, MRC 154, Washington, DC 20013-7012); (202) 633-2240. Nancy E. Gwinn, Director. Web, http://library.si.edu and Twitter, @SILibraries*

Unites twenty libraries into one system supported by an online catalog of the combined collections. Maintains collection of general reference, biographical, and interdisciplinary materials; serves as an information resource on institution libraries and museum studies. Open to the public by appointment.

▶CONGRESS

For a listing of relevant congressional committees and subcommittees, please see page 174 or the Appendix.

Library of Congress, *101 Independence Ave. S.E., 20559-6000; (202) 707-5000. Carla Hayden, Librarian of Congress. General reference, (202) 707-3000. Reading room, (202) 707-3399. Office of communications, (202) 707-2905. Visitor information, (202) 707-8000. Web, www.loc.gov, Twitter, @librarycongress and Facebook, www.facebook.com/libraryofcongress and Copyright information, www.copyright.gov and General reference, www.loc.gov//rr/askalib and Legislative information, www.congress.gov*

The nation's library.

Library of Congress, *Main Reading Room, Thomas Jefferson Bldg., 101 Independence Ave. S.E., #LJ 100, 20540-4660; (202) 707-3399. Fax, (202) 707-1957. Michael North, Head. Web, www.loc.gov/rr/main*

Point of access to the general collection of books and bound periodicals as well as electronic resources, including microform. Offers research orientations.

Libraries at Federal Departments and Agencies

DEPARTMENTS

Agriculture, (301) 504-5755

Commerce, (202) 482-1154

Defense, (703) 695-1992

Education, (202) 205-5015

Energy (Main), (202)-586-0945

Energy (Law), (202)-586-0945

Health and Human Services (Law), (202) 619-0190

Homeland Security, (831) 272-2437

Housing and Urban Development, (202) 708-2370

Interior, (202) 208-5815

Justice, (202) 305-3000

Labor, (202) 693-6600

State, (202) 647-1099

Transportation, (202) 366-3282

Treasury, (202) 622-2000

Veterans Affairs, (202) 461-7573

AGENCIES

Agency for International Development, (202) 712-0579

Commission on Civil Rights, (202) 376-8110

Commodity Futures Trading Commission, (202) 418-5593

Consumer Product Safety Commission, (301) 504-7923

Drug Enforcement Administration, (202) 307-8932

Environmental Protection Agency, (202) 566-0556

Equal Employment Opportunity Commission, (202) 663-4630

Export-Import Bank, (202) 565-3980

Federal Communications Commission, (202) 418-0450

Federal Deposit Insurance Corporation, (202) 898-3631

Federal Election Commission, (202) 326-2395

Federal Labor Relations Authority, www.flra.gov/ history_index

Federal Maritime Commission, (202) 523-5762

Federal Reserve Board, (202) 452-2018

Federal Trade Commission, (202) 326-2395

Government Accountability Office (Law), (202) 512-5941

International Bank for Reconstruction and Development (World Bank)/International Monetary Fund, (202) 473-2000 / (202) 623-7054

Merit Systems Protection Board, (202) 653-7200

National Aeronautics and Space Administration, (202) 358-0168

National Archives and Records Administration, (301) 837-3415

National Credit Union Administration (Law), (703) 518-6546

National Endowment for the Humanities, (202) 606-8244

National Institutes of Health, (301) 496-1080

National Labor Relations Board, (202) 273-3720

National Library of Medicine, (301) 594-5983

National Science Foundation, (703) 292-7830

Nuclear Regulatory Commission, (301) 415-6239

Occupational Safety and Health Review Commission, (202) 606-5729

Overseas Private Investment Corporation, (202) 336-8488

Peace Corps, (202) 692-1236

Postal Regulatory Commission, (202) 789-6800

Securities and Exchange Commission, (202) 551-5450

Small Business Administration Law Library, (202) 401-8203

Smithsonian Institution, (202) 633-2240

American Art and Portrait Gallery, (202) 633-8230

Botany and Horticulture, (202) 633-1685

Cooper Hewitt Design Museum, (202) 849-8330

Dibner Library of the History of Science and Technology, (202) 633-3872

Freer Gallery of Art, (202) 633-0477

Hirshhorn Museum, (202) 633-2774

John Wesley Powell Library of Anthropology, (202) 633-1640

National Air and Space Museum, (202) 633-2320

National Museum of African American History, (202) 633-7498

National Museum of African Art, (202) 633-4680

National Museum of American History, (202) 633-3865

National Museum of the American Indian, (301) 238-1376

National Museum of Natural History, (202) 633-1680

National Postal Museum, (202) 633-5543

National Zoological Park, (202) 633-1030

Social Security Administration, (410) 965-1727

U.S. International Trade Commission, www.usitc.gov/ elearning/hts/library/htms/resources1.htm

Main Library, (202) 205-2630

Law, (202) 205-3287

Library of Congress Divisions and Programs

African and Middle Eastern Division, (202) 707-7937

American Folklife Center, (202) 707-5510

Asian Division, (202) 707-3766

Business Reference Services, (202) 707-3156

Cataloging Distribution Service, (202) 707-6100 or (855) 266-1884

Center for the Book, (202) 707-5221

Children's Literature Center, (202) 707-5535

Copyright Office, (877) 476-0778

Electronic Resources Center, (202) 707-3370

European Division, (202) 707-4515

Federal Library and Information Center Committee, (202) 707-4800

Geography and Map Division, (202) 707-6277

Hispanic Division, (202) 707-5397

Humanities and Social Science Division, (202) 707-3399

Interlibrary Loan Division (CALM), (202) 707-5444

Interpretive Programs, (202) 707-5223

Law Library, (202) 707-5079

Law Library Reading Room, (202) 707-5080

Local History and Genealogy Reference Services, (202) 707-3399

Manuscript Division, (202) 707-5387

Mary Pickford Theater, (202) 707-5677

Microform Reading Room, (202) 707-4773

Motion Picture, Broadcasting, and Recorded Sound Division, Audio-Visual, (202) 707-5840; Moving Image, (202) 707-8572; Recorded Sound, (202) 707-7833

Music Reference, Performing Arts Reading Room (202) 707-5507

National Library Service for the Blind and Physically Handicapped, (202) 707-5100

Poetry and Literature Center, (202) 707-5394

Preservation Directorate, (202) 707-5000

Prints and Photographs Division, (202) 707-6394

Rare Book and Special Collections Division, (202) 707-3448

Science, Technology and Business Division, (202) 707-5639

Serial and Government Publications Division, (202) 707-5690

►NONGOVERNMENTAL

American Library Assn., Washington Office, *1615 New Hampshire Ave. N.W., 1st Floor, 20009-2520; (202) 628-8410. Fax, (202) 628-8419. Kathi Kromer, Associate Executive Director; Kevin Maher, Deputy Director Government Relations. Information, (800) 941-8478. General email, alawash@alawash.org*

Web, www.ala.org/offices/wo

Educational organization of librarians, trustees, and educators. Washington office monitors legislation and regulations on libraries and information science. Seeks to maintain and increase federal government funding of libraries and services. (Headquarters in Chicago, Ill.)

Assn. of Research Libraries (ARL), *21 Dupont Circle N.W., #800, 20036-1118; (202) 296-2296. Fax, (202) 872-0884. Mary Lee Kennedy, Executive Director. General email, webmgr@arl.org*

Web, www.arl.org and Twitter, @ARLnews

Membership: major research libraries, mainly at universities, in the United States and Canada. Interests include development of library resources in all formats, subjects, and languages; computer information systems and other bibliographic tools; management of research libraries; preservation of library materials; worldwide information policy; public access to federally funded research; and publishing and scholarly communication.

Audiovisual and Integrated Experience Assn. (AVIXA), *11242 Waples Mill Rd., #200, Fairfax, VA 22030; (703) 273-7200. Fax, (703) 278-8082. David Labuskes, Chief Executive Officer. Information, (800) 659-7469. General email, membership@avixa.org*

Web, www.avixa.org, Twitter, @AVIXA and Facebook, www.facebook.com/TheAVIXA

Membership: manufacturers, dealers, and specialists in educational communications products. Provides educators with information on federal funding for audiovisual, video, and computer equipment and materials; monitors trends in educational technology; conducts audiovisual trade shows worldwide. (Formerly Info Comm International.)

The Brookings Institution, Center for Technology Innovation, *1775 Massachusetts Ave. N.W., 20036; (202) 797-6090. Darrell M. West, Director, (202) 797-6481. Web, www.brookings.edu/about/center-for-technology-innovation*

Research center promoting policymaking and public debate about technology innovation, including digital infrastructure, the mobile economy, e-governance, digital media and entertainment, cybersecurity and privacy, digital medicine, and virtual education.

Coalition for Networked Information, *21 Dupont Circle N.W., #800, 20036; (202) 296-5098. Fax, (202) 872-0884. Clifford A. Lynch, Executive Director. General email, info@cni.org*

Web, www.cni.org and Twitter, @cni_org

Membership: higher education, publishing, network and telecommunications, information technology, and libraries and library organizations, as well as government agencies and foundations. Promotes networked information technology, scholarly communication, intellectual productivity, and education.

Consortium for School Networking (CoSN), 1325 G St. N.W., #420, 20005; (202) 861-2676. Fax, (202) 393-2011. Keith R. Krueger, Chief Executive Officer. Certification hotline, (202) 524-8464. Membership hotline, (202) 558-0059. Toll-free, (866) 267-8747.
General email, info@cosn.org

Web, http://cosn.org and Twitter, @CoSN

Membership: teachers and school officials who support educational technology for grades K–12. Grants certification to educators who are fluent in technology and promote the role of technology in teaching. Assists schools in implementing educational technologies. Holds an annual policy summit to support legislation that affects technology education.

Council on Library and Information Resources, 2221 S. Clark St., Arlington, VA 22202; (202) 939-4750. Fax, (202) 600-9628. Charles Henry, President.
General email, contact@clir.org

Web, www.clir.org and Twitter, @CLIRnews

Acts on behalf of the nation's libraries, archives, and universities to develop and encourage collaborative strategies for preserving the nation's intellectual heritage; seeks to strengthen its information systems and learning environments.

Digital Promise, 1001 Connecticut Ave. N.W., #830, 20036; (202) 450-3675. Karen Cator, President.
General email, contact@digitalpromise.org

Web, www.digitalpromise.org

Assists educators, technology developers, and researchers in applying and creating educational technologies that improve student learning. Grants microcredentials to teachers and equips schools with mobile learning technology.

Folger Shakespeare Library, 201 E. Capitol St. S.E., 20003-1004; (202) 544-4600. Fax, (202) 544-4623. Michael Witmore, Director. Box Office, (202) 544-7077.
General email, info@folger.edu

Web, www.folger.edu, Twitter, @FolgerLibrary and Facebook, www.facebook.com/folgershakespearelibrary

Maintains major Shakespearean and Renaissance materials; awards fellowships for postdoctoral research; presents concerts, theater performances, poetry and fiction readings, exhibits, and other public events. Offers educational programs for elementary, secondary, high school, college, and graduate school students and teachers. Publishes the Folger Shakespeare editions, Folger Magazine, and, in association with the George Washington University, Shakespeare Quarterly.

Gallaudet University, Library, 800 Florida Ave. N.E., 20002-3695; Sarah Hamrick, Director of Library Public Services, (202) 651-5214; Michael (Mike) Olson, Senior Archivist. Videophone, (202) 779-9478.
General email, library.help@gallaudet.edu

Web, www.gallaudet.edu/library.html and Facebook, www.facebook.com/GallaudetLibrary

Maintains extensive special collection on deafness, including archival materials relating to deaf cultural history and Gallaudet University.

Libraries Without Borders, Washington Office, 1342 Florida Ave. N.W., 20009; (703) 705-9321. Patrick Weil, Chair; Adam Echelman, Executive Director.
General email, admin@librarieswithoutborders.org

Web, www.librarieswithoutborders.org, Twitter, @BSF_Intl and Facebook, www.facebook.com/LibrariesWithoutBorders

Disseminates information globally, provides access to knowledge, education, and training, and promotes libraries and book distribution. Provides citizens in poor areas access to information with the aim of combating poverty and social inequality.

Lubuto Library Partners, 5614 Connecticut Ave N.W., #368, 20015-2604; (202) 558-5609. Jane Kinney Meyers, President.
General email, webmail@lubuto.org

Web, www.lubuto.org

International development organization that focuses on library development for youth in southern African countries. Works with public and private libraries and other partners to construct an open-access library collection and accessible services for children and youth in southern Africa. Sponsors library programs to foster education in the arts and technology; offers services for children with disabilities.

National Assn. for Music Education, 1806 Robert Fulton Dr., Reston, VA 20191-4348; (703) 860-4000. Fax, (703) 860-1531. Mike Blakeslee, Executive Director. Toll-free, (800) 336-3768. Toll-free fax, (888) 275-6232.
General email, memberservices@nafme.org

Web, www.nafme.org and Twitter, @NAfME

Publishes books and teaching aids for music educators, parents, and administrators.

Newseum Institute, 555 Pennsylvania Ave. N.W., 20001; (202) 292-6100. Barbara McCormack, Vice President of Education, (202) 292-6200.
General email, media@newseum.org

Web, www.newseuminstitute.org and Twitter, @NewseumInst

Affiliated with the Freedom Forum and Newsuem as an education and outreach partner. Offers programs and learning platforms for current central debates and political issues within journalism and religion.

Special Libraries Assn., 7918 Jones Branch Dr., #300, McLean, VA 22102; (703) 647-4900. Fax, (703) 506-3266. Amy Lestition Burke, Executive Director.
General email, sla@sla.org

Web, www.sla.org and Twitter, @SLAhq

Membership: librarians and information managers serving institutions that use or produce information in specialized areas, including business, engineering, law, the arts and sciences, government, museums, and universities. Conducts professional development programs, research projects, and an annual conference. Monitors legislation and regulations.

POSTSECONDARY EDUCATION

General

▶ **AGENCIES**

Education Dept., *Postsecondary Education (OPE),* Lyndon Baines Johnson Bldg., 400 Maryland Ave. S.W., 20202; (202) 453-6914. Fax, (202) 502-7677. Diane Jones, Assistant Secretary (Acting). TTY, (800) 437-0833.
Web, www2.ed.gov/about/offices/list/ope and
Twitter, @EDPostsecondary

Formulates federal postsecondary education policy. Administers federal assistance programs for public and private postsecondary institutions; provides financial support for faculty development, construction of facilities, and improvement of graduate, continuing, cooperative, and international education; awards grants and loans for financial assistance to eligible students.

Education Dept., *Postsecondary Education (OPE), Fund for the Improvement of Postsecondary Education (FIPSE),* Lyndon Baines Johnson Bldg., 400 Maryland Ave. S.W., #4W120, 20202; (202) 453-6914.
Fax, (202) 502-7877. Ralph Hines, Director.
General email, fipse@ed.gov
Web, www.ed.gov/about/offices/list/ope/fipse

Works to improve postsecondary education by administering grant competitions.

Education Dept., *Postsecondary Education (OPE), Higher Education Programs (HEP),* Lyndon Baines Johnson Bldg., 400 Maryland Ave. S.W., 20202; (202) 453-6808. Vacant, Deputy Assistant Secretary.
Web, www2.ed.gov/about/offices/list/ope/hep.html

Administers programs to increase access to postsecondary education for low-income first-generation students and students with disabilities. Supports higher education facilities and programs through financial support to eligible institutions, and management of programs that recruit and prepare low-income students for successful completion of college. Programs include seven TRIO programs, institutional development programs for minority-serving institutions, and the Fund for the Improvement of Postsecondary Education.

Education Dept., *Postsecondary Education (OPE), Higher Education Programs (HEP), Institutional Service, Minority Science and Engineering Improvement Program,* Lyndon Baines Johnson Bldg., 400 Maryland Ave. S.W., 4th Floor, 20202; (202) 453-7913. Bernadette Hence, Senior Program Manager.
General email, OPE.MSEIP@ed.gov
Web, www2.ed.gov/programs/iduesmsi/index.html

Provides grants to predominantly minority institutions to effect long-range improvement in science and engineering education and to increase the flow of underrepresented ethnic minorities, particularly minority women, into science and engineering careers.

Education Dept., *Postsecondary Education (OPE), Higher Education Programs (HEP), International and Foreign Language Education,* Lyndon Baines Johnson Bldg., 400 Maryland Ave. S.W., #3E200, 20202; (202) 453-6950. Fax, (202) 453-5780. Cheryl Gibbs, Deputy Assistant Secretary (Acting).
Web, www2.ed.gov/about/offices/list/ope/iegps and
Twitter, @GoGlobalED

Advises the Assistant Secretary for Postsecondary Education on matters affecting postsecondary, international, and foreign language education. Responsible for encouraging and promoting the study of foreign languages and cultures of other countries at the elementary, secondary, and postsecondary levels in the United States. Administers programs that increase expertise in foreign languages and area or international studies, and coordinates with related international and foreign language education programs of other federal agencies.

National Institutes of Health (NIH) *(Health and Human Services Dept.), Intramural Training and Education (OITE),* 2 Center Dr., Bldg. 2, #2E04, MSC 0230, Bethesda, MD 20892-0240; (301) 496-2427. Fax, (301) 594-9606. Sharon Milgram, Director, (301) 594-2053.
General email, trainingwww@mail.nih.gov
Web, www.training.nih.gov

Administers programs and initiatives to recruit and develop individuals who participate in research training activities on the NIH's campuses. Maintains an interactive website for the various research training programs. Supports the training mission of the NIH Intramural Research Program through placement, retention, support, and tracking of trainees at all levels, as well as program delivery and evaluation. Administers the NIH Academy, the Summer Internship Program, the Undergraduate Scholarship Program, the Graduate Partnerships Program, and the Postbac and Technical Intramural Research Training Award programs.

▶ **CONGRESS**

For a listing of relevant congressional committees and subcommittees, please see page 174 or the Appendix.

▶ **NONGOVERNMENTAL**

Accuracy in Academia (AIA), 4200 Wisconsin Ave. N.W., 2081420016 (mailing address: P.O. Box 5647, Derwood, MD 20855); (202) 364-4401 or (240) 686-5964.

Fax, (202) 364-4098 (240) 686-5964. Malcolm A. Kline, Executive Director.
General email, info@academia.org

Web, www.academia.org, Twitter, @CampusReport and Facebook, www.facebook.com/AccuracyinAcademia

Seeks to eliminate political bias in university education, particularly discrimination against students, faculty, or administrators on the basis of political beliefs. Reports on bias in education. Publishes a monthly newsletter.

ACT Inc. (American College Testing, *Washington Office,*
1 Dupont Circle N.W. #340, 20036-1170; (202) 223-2318.
Fax, (202) 293-2223. Tom Lindsley, Director of Federal Government Relations, ext. 1.
Web, www.act.org, Twitter, @ACTStudent and Facebook, www.facebook.com/theacttest

Administers ACT assessment planning and examination for colleges and universities. Provides more than one hundred assessment, research, information, and program management services in the areas of education and workforce development to elementary and secondary schools, colleges, professional associations, businesses, and government agencies. (Headquarters in Iowa City, Iowa.)

American Assn. of Colleges of Pharmacy, *1400 Crystal Dr., #300, Arlington, VA 22202; (703) 739-2330.*
Fax, (703) 836-8982. Lucinda L. Maine, Executive Vice President, ext. 1021.
General email, mail@aacp.org

Web, www.aacp.org, Twitter, @AACPharmacy and Facebook, www.facebook.com/AACPharmacy

Membership: teachers and administrators representing colleges of pharmacy accredited by the American Council on Pharmaceutical Education. Sponsors educational programs; conducts research; provides career information; helps administer the Pharmacy College Admissions Test.

American Assn. of Collegiate Registrars and Admissions Officers, *1108 16th St. N.W., #400, 20036; (202) 293-9161.*
Fax, (202) 872-8857. Michael Reilly, Executive Director.
General email, info@aacrao.org

Web, www.aacrao.org, Twitter, @aacrao and Facebook, www.facebook.com/AACROA

Membership: degree-granting postsecondary institutions, government agencies, higher education coordinating boards, private education organizations, and education-oriented businesses. Promotes higher education and contributes to the professional development of members working in admissions, enrollment management, financial aid, institutional research, records, and registration. Uses research, technology, and training to maintain compliance standards.

American Assn. of Community Colleges, *1 Dupont Circle N.W., #700, 20036; (202) 728-0200. Fax, (202) 833-2467. Walter G. Bumphus, President.*
Web, www.aacc.nche.edu, Twitter, @Comm_College and Facebook, www.facebook.com/CommCollege

Membership: accredited two-year community technical and junior colleges, corporate foundations, international associates, and institutional affiliates. Studies include policies for lifelong education, workforce training programs and partnerships, international curricula, enrollment trends, and cooperative programs with public schools and communities. (Affiliated with the Council for Resource Development.)

American Assn. of State Colleges and Universities, *1307 New York Ave. N.W., 5th Floor, 20005; (202) 293-7070.*
Fax, (202) 296-5819. Mildred Garcia, President, (202) 478-4647.
General email, info@aascu.org

Web, www.aascu.org, Twitter, @AASCU and Facebook, www.facebook.com/aascu

Membership: presidents and chancellors of state colleges and universities. Promotes equity in education and fosters information exchange among members. Interests include student financial aid, international education programs, academic affairs, teacher education, and higher education access and affordability. Monitors legislation and regulations.

American Assn. of University Professors (AAUP), *1133 19th St. N.W., #200, 20036; (202) 737-5900.*
Fax, (202) 737-5526. Julie Schmid, Executive Director, (202) 594-3644.
General email, aaup@aaup.org

Web, www.aaup.org, Twitter, @AAUP and Facebook, www.facebook.com/AAUPNational

Membership: college and university faculty members. Defends faculties' and professional staffs' academic freedom and tenure; advocates collegial governance; assists in the development of policies ensuring due process. Conducts workshops and education programs. Monitors legislation and regulations.

American Conference of Academic Deans, *1818 R St. N.W., 20009; (202) 884-7419. Fax, (202) 265-9532. Laura Matthias, Executive Director, (202) 884-7419.*
General email, info@acad.org

Web, http://acad.org, Twitter, @ACADeans and Facebook, www.facebook.com/American-Conference-of-Academic-Deans/1524110051145574

Membership: academic administrators of two- and four-year accredited colleges, universities, and community colleges (private and public). Fosters information exchange among members on college curricular and administrative issues.

American Council of Trustees and Alumni, *1730 M St. N.W., #600, 20036-4525; (202) 467-6787.*
Fax, (202) 467-6784. Michael B. Poliakoff, President.
Toll-free, (800) 258-6648.
General email, info@goacta.org

Web, www.goacta.org, Twitter, @goacta and Facebook, www.facebook.com/GoActa

Membership: college and university alumni and trustees interested in promoting academic freedom and

Colleges and Universities in the Washington Metropolitan Area

American University, 4400 Massachusetts Ave. N.W., 20016. Switchboard, (202) 885-1000. Sylvia M. Burwell, President, (202) 885-2121

Catholic University of America, 620 Michigan Ave. N.E., 20064. Switchboard, (202) 319-5000. John Garvey, President, (202) 319-5100

Corcoran School of the Arts and Design, George Washington University, 500 17th St. N.W., 20006. Switchboard, (202) 994-1700. Sanjit Sethi, Director, (202) 994-1700

Gallaudet University, 800 Florida Ave. N.E., 20002. Switchboard, (202) 651-5393 (voice and TTY). Roberta (Bobbi) Cordano, President, (202) 651-5005 (voice and TTY)

George Mason University, 4400 University Dr., Fairfax, VA 22030. Switchboard, (703) 993-1000. Ángel Cabrera, President, (703) 993-8700

George Washington University, 2121 Eye St. N.W., 20052. Switchboard, (202) 994-1000. Thomas J. LeBlanc, President, (202) 994-6500

George Washington University at Mount Vernon Campus, 2100 Foxhall Rd. N.W., 20007. Switchboard, (202) 242-6670. Rachelle S. Heller, Associate Provost, (202) 242-6698

Georgetown University, 3700 O St. N.W., 20057. Switchboard, (202) 687-0100. John J. DeGioia, President, (202) 687-4134

Howard University, 2400 6th St. N.W., 20059. Switchboard, (202) 806-6100. Wayne A.I. Frederick, President, (202) 806-2500

The Institute of World Politics, 1521 16th St. N.W., 20036-1464. Switchboard, (202) 462-2101. John Lenczowski, President, (202) 462-2101 ext. 333

Marymount University, 2807 N. Glebe Rd., Arlington, VA 22207. Switchboard, (703) 522-5600. Matthew D. Shank, President, (703) 284-1598

Paul H. Nitze School of Advanced International Studies (SAIS), Johns Hopkins University, 1740 Massachusetts Ave. N.W., 20036. Switchboard, (202) 663-5600. Vali R. Nasr, Dean, (202) 663-5624

Strayer University, 2303 Dulles Station Blvd., Herndon, VA 20171. Switchboard, (888) 311-0355. Brian W. Jones, President, (888) 311-0355

Trinity Washington University, 125 Michigan Ave. N.E., 20017. Switchboard, (202) 884-9000. Patricia A. McGuire, President, (202) 884-9050

University of Maryland, College Park, MD 20742. Switchboard, (301) 405-1000. Wallace D. Loh, President, (301) 405-5803

University of the District of Columbia, 4200 Connecticut Ave. N.W., 20008. Switchboard, (202) 274-5000. Ronald Mason Jr., President, (202) 274-6016

University of Virginia (Northern Virginia Center), 7054 Haycock Rd., Falls Church, VA 22043. Switchboard, (703) 536-1100. Steve Laymon, Dean, (434) 982-5206

Virginia Tech (Northern Virginia Center), 7054 Haycock Rd., Falls Church, VA 22043 Switchboard, (703) 538-8324. Kenneth H. Wong, Director of Northern Virginia Campus, (703) 538-8310

Virginia Theological Seminary, 3737 Seminary Rd., Alexandria, VA 22304. Switchboard, 703-370-6600. The Very Rev. Ian S. Markham, Dean, (703) 461-1701

Washington Adventist University, 7600 Flower Ave., Takoma Park, MD 20912. Switchboard, (800) 835-4212. Weymouth Spence, President, (301) 891-4128

Wesley Theological Seminary, 4500 Massachusetts Ave. N.W., 20016. Switchboard, (202) 885-8600. Rev. Dr. David McAllister-Wilson, President, (202) 885-8611

---

excellence. Seeks to help alumni and trustees direct their financial contributions to programs that will raise educational standards at their alma maters. Promotes the role of alumni and trustees in shaping higher-education policies.

American Council on Education (ACE), *1 Dupont Circle N.W., #800, 20036-1193; (202) 939-9300. Ted Mitchell, President. Public Affairs, (202) 939-9365.*
General email, comments@acenet.edu

Web, www.acenet.edu, Twitter, @ACEducation and Facebook, www.facebook.com/AmericanCouncilEducation

Membership: presidents of universities and other education institutions. Conducts and publishes research; maintains offices dealing with government relations, women and minorities in higher education, management of higher-education institutions, adult learning and educational credentials (academic credit for nontraditional learning, especially in the armed forces), leadership development, and international education.

Assn. of American Colleges and Universities (AACU), *1818 R St. N.W., 20009; (202) 387-3760.*
Fax, (202) 265-9532. Lynn Pasquerella, President.
General email, information@aacu.org

Web, www.aacu.org, Twitter, @aacu and Facebook, www.facebook.com/Association-of-American-Colleges-and-Universities-48308128458

Membership: two-year and four-year public and private colleges, universities, and postsecondary consortia. Works to develop effective academic programs and improve undergraduate curricula and services. Seeks to encourage, enhance, and support student achievement through liberal education for all students, regardless of academic specialization or intended career.

The Assn. of American Law Schools, *1614 20th St. N.W., 20009-1001; (202) 296-8851. Fax, (202) 296-8869. Judith Areen, Executive Director.*
General email, aals@aals.org

Web, www.aals.org and Twitter, @TheAALS

Membership: law schools, subject to approval. Membership criteria include high-quality academic programs, faculty, scholarship, and students; academic freedom; diversity of people and viewpoints; and emphasis on public service. Hosts meetings and workshops; publishes a directory of law teachers. Acts as advocate on behalf of legal education; monitors legislation and judicial decisions.

Assn. of American Universities, *1200 New York Ave. N.W., #550, 20005; (202) 408-7500. Fax, (202) 408-8184. Mary Sue Coleman, President.*
Web, www.aau.edu and Twitter, @AAUniversities

Membership: public and private universities in the United States and Canada with emphasis on graduate and professional education and research. Fosters information exchange among presidents of member institutions.

Assn. of Catholic Colleges and Universities, *1 Dupont Circle N.W., #650, 20036; (202) 457-0650. Fax, (202) 728-0977. Michael Galligan-Stierle, President, ext. 222. General email, accu@accunet.org*
Web, www.accunet.org and Twitter, @CatholicHighrEd

Membership: regionally accredited American Catholic colleges and universities. Offers affiliated status for selected international Catholic universities. Acts as a clearinghouse for information on Catholic institutions of higher education.

Assn. of Collegiate Schools of Architecture, *1735 New York Ave. N.W., 3rd Floor, 20006; (202) 785-2324. Fax, (202) 628-0448. Michael J. Monti, Executive Director. General email, info@acsa-arch.org*
Web, www.acsa-arch.org and Twitter, @ACSAUpdate

Membership: U.S. and Canadian institutions that offer at least one accredited architecture degree program. Conducts workshops and seminars for architecture school faculty; presents awards for student and faculty excellence in architecture; publishes a guide to architecture schools in North America.

Assn. of Community College Trustees (ACCT), *1101 17th St. N.W., #300, 20036; (202) 775-4667. Fax, (202) 223-1297. J. Noah Brown, President. General email, acctinfo@acct.org*
Web, www.acct.org and Twitter, @CCTrustees

Provides members of community college governing boards with training in educational programs and services. Monitors federal education programs and acts as advocate on behalf of community colleges and their trustees.

Assn. of Governing Boards of Universities and Colleges, *1133 20th St. N.W., #300, 20036; (202) 296-8400. Fax, (202) 223-7053. Richard D. Legon, President. Toll-free, (800) 356-6317.*
Web, www.agb.org and Twitter, @AGBtweets

Membership: presidents, boards of trustees, regents, commissions, and other groups governing colleges, universities, and institutionally related foundations. Interests include the relationship between the president and board of trustees and other subjects relating to governance.

Assn. of Jesuit Colleges and Universities, *1 Dupont Circle N.W., #405, 20036-1140; (202) 862-9893. Fax, (202) 862-8523. Rev. Michael J. Sheeran, President. General email, info@ajcunet.edu*
Web, www.ajcunet.edu, Twitter, @jesuitcolleges and Facebook, www.facebook.com/jesuitcolleges

Membership: American Jesuit colleges and universities. Monitors government regulatory and policymaking activities affecting higher education. Publishes the AJCU Directory and a monthly newsletter. Promotes national and international cooperation among Jesuit higher-education institutions.

Assn. of Public and Land-Grant Universities, *1307 New York Ave. N.W., #400, 20005-4722; (202) 478-6040. Fax, (202) 478-6046. Peter McPherson, President, (202) 478-6060. General email, info@aplu.org*
Web, www.aplu.org and Twitter, @APLU_News

Membership: land-grant colleges; state and public research universities. Serves as clearinghouse on issues of public higher education.

Business–Higher Education Forum, *2025 M St. N.W., #800, 20036; (202) 367-1189. Fax, (202) 367-2189. Brian K. Fitzgerald, Chief Executive Officer. General email, info@bhef.com*
Web, www.bhef.com, Twitter, @BHEF
Press, ursula.gross@bhef.org

Membership: chief executive officers of major corporations, foundations, colleges, and universities. Develops and promotes policy positions to enhance U.S. competitiveness. Interests include improving student achievement and readiness for college and work; and strengthening higher education, particularly in the fields of science, technology, engineering, and math.

Career Education Colleges and Universities (CECU), *1530 Wilson Blvd., #1050, Arlington, VA 22209; (571) 970-3941. Fax, (571) 970-6753. Steve Gunderson, President, (571) 970-3954.*
Web, www.career.org and Twitter, @CECUed

Membership: private postsecondary colleges and career schools in the United States. Works to expand the accessibility of postsecondary career education and to improve the quality of education offered by member institutions. (Formerly Career College Assn.)

College Board, *Advocacy and Policy, 1919 M St. N.W., #300, 20034; (202) 741-4700. Fax, (202) 223-7035. Stephanie Sanford, Chief of Global Policy and External Relations. Communications Office, (212) 713-8052. Toll-free, (866) 630-9305.*
Web, www.collegeboard.org and Twitter, @CollegeBoard

Membership: colleges and universities, secondary schools, school systems, and education associations. Provides direct student support programs and professional development for educators; conducts policy analysis and research; and advocates public policy positions that support educational excellence and promote student access to higher education. (Headquarters in New York.)

Consortium of Universities for Global Health, *1608 Rhode Island Ave. N.W., #240, 20036; (202) 974-6363. Fax, (202) 833-5078. Dr. Keith Martin, Executive Director. General email, info@cugh.org*

Web, www.cugh.org and Twitter, @CUGHnews

Assists in regulating curricula and standards for university global health programs. Coordinates academic partnerships between national universities and international educational institutions in developing countries.

Council for Advancement and Support of Education, *1307 New York Ave. N.W., #1000, 20005-4701; (202) 328-2273. Fax, (202) 387-4973. Sue Cunningham, President; Brian Flahaven, Senior Director of Advocacy. General email, memberservicecenter@case.org*

Web, www.case.org and Twitter, @CASEAdvance

Membership: two-year and four-year colleges, universities, and independent schools. Offers professional education and training programs to members; advises members on institutional advancement issues, including fundraising, public relations programs, government relations, and management. Library open to professional members by appointment.

Council for Christian Colleges & Universities, *321 8th St. N.E., 20002; (202) 546-8713. Fax, (202) 546-8913. Shirley V. Hoogstra, President; Shapri LoMaglio, Vice President of Government Relations. General email, council@cccu.org*

Web, www.cccu.org and Twitter, @cccuorg

Membership: accredited four-year Christian liberal arts colleges. Offers faculty development conferences on faith and the academic disciplines. Coordinates annual gathering of college administrators. Sponsors internship/seminar programs for students at member colleges. Promotes Christian-affiliated higher education. Interests include religious and educational freedom.

Council of Graduate Schools, *1 Dupont Circle N.W., #230, 20036-1173; (202) 223-3791. Fax, (202) 331-7157. Suzanne T. Ortega, President. General email, general_inquiries@cgs.nche.edu*

Web, http://cgsnet.org and Twitter, @CGSGradEd

Membership: private and public colleges and universities with significant involvement in graduate education, research, and scholarship. Produces publications and information about graduate education; provides a forum for member schools to exchange information and ideas.

Council of Independent Colleges, *1 Dupont Circle N.W., #320, 20036-1142; (202) 466-7230. Fax, (202) 466-7238. Richard Ekman, President. General email, cic@cic.nche.edu*

Web, www.cic.edu

Membership: independent liberal arts colleges and universities, and higher education affiliates and organizations. Sponsors development programs for college presidents, deans, and faculty members and communications officers on topics such as leadership, financial management, academic quality, visibility, and other issues crucial to high-quality education and independent liberal arts colleges. Holds workshops and annual meetings, conducts research, and produces publications.

Council on Social Work Education, *1701 Duke St., #200, Alexandria, VA 22314-3457; (703) 683-8080. Fax, (703) 683-8099. Darla Spence Coffey, President. General email, info@cswe.org*

Web, www.cswe.org and Twitter, @CSocialWorkEd

Membership: educational and professional institutions, social welfare agencies, and private citizens. Promotes high-quality education in social work. Accredits social work programs.

DECA Inc., *1908 Association Dr., Reston, VA 20191-1594; (703) 860-5000. Fax, (703) 860-4013. Frank Peterson, Executive Director (Acting). General email, info@deca.org*

Web, www.deca.org and Twitter, @DECAInc

Educational organization that helps high school and college students develop skills in marketing, management, finance, hospitality, and entrepreneurship. Promotes business and education partnerships.

Educational Testing Service (ETS), *Communications and Public Affairs, 1800 K St. N.W., #900, 20006-2202; (202) 659-0616. Fax, (202) 457-8687. Walt MacDonald, President. TTY, (202) 659-8067. General email, etsinfo@ets.org*

Web, www.ets.org

Administers examinations for admission to educational programs and for graduate and licensing purposes; conducts instructional programs in testing, evaluation, and research in education fields. Washington office handles government and professional relations. Fee for services. (Headquarters in Princeton, N.J.)

NASPA: Student Affairs Administrators in Higher Education, *111 K St. N.E., 10th Floor, 20002; (202) 265-7500. Fax, (202) 898-5737. Kevin Kruger, President, (202) 702-4651, ext. 1175. General email, office@naspa.org*

Web, www.naspa.org, Twitter, @NASPAtweets and Facebook, www.facebook.com/naspaFB

Membership: student affairs administrators, deans, faculty, and graduate and undergraduate students at 2,100 campuses, representing 25 countries. Seeks to develop leadership and improve practices in student affairs administration. Initiates and supports programs and legislation to improve student affairs administration.

National Assn. for College Admission Counseling, *1050 N. Highland St., #400, Arlington, VA 22201; (703) 836-2222. Fax, (703) 243-9375. Joyce E. Smith, Chief Executive Officer, (703) 299-6828. Information, (800) 822-6285. General email, info@nacacnet.org*

Web, www.nacacnet.org and Twitter, @NACAC

Membership: high school guidance counselors, independent counselors, college and university admissions officers, and financial aid officers. Promotes and funds research on admission counseling and on the transition from high school to college. Acts as advocate for student rights in college admissions. Sponsors national college fairs and continuing education for members.

National Assn. of College and University Attorneys, *1 Dupont Circle N.W., #620, 20036-1182; (202) 833-8390. Fax, (202) 296-8379. Kathleen Curry Santora, Chief Executive Officer, ext. 4.*
General email, nacua@nacua.org
Web, www.nacua.org and Twitter, @NACUAtweets

Provides information on legal developments affecting postsecondary education. Operates a clearinghouse through which in-house and external legal counselors are able to network with their counterparts on current legal problems.

National Assn. of College and University Business Officers, *1110 Vermont Ave. N.W., #800, 20005; (202) 861-2500. Fax, (202) 861-2583. John D. Walda, President. Toll-free, (800) 462-4916.*
General email, support@nacubo.org
Web, www.nacubo.org and Twitter, @NACUBO

Membership: chief business and financial officers at higher-education institutions. Provides members with information on financial management, federal regulations, and other subjects related to the business administration of universities and colleges; conducts workshops on issues such as student aid, institutional budgeting, and accounting.

National Assn. of Independent Colleges and Universities, *1025 Connecticut Ave. N.W., #700, 20036-5405; (202) 785-8866. Fax, (202) 835-0003. David L. Warren, President.*
General email, geninfo@naicu.edu
Web, www.naicu.edu and Twitter, @NAICUtweets

Membership: liberal arts colleges, research universities, church-related and faith-related institutions, historically black colleges and universities, women's colleges, performing and visual arts institutions, two-year colleges; graduate schools of law, medicine, engineering, business, and other professions. Tracks campus trends, conducts research, analyzes higher-education issues, and helps coordinate state-level activities. Interests include federal policies that affect student aid, taxation, and government regulation. Monitors legislation and regulations.

National Council of University Research Administrators, *1015 18th St. N.W., #901, 20036; (202) 466-3894. Fax, (202) 223-5573. Kathleen Larmett, Executive Director.*
General email, info@ncura.edu
Web, www.ncura.edu, Twitter, @NCURA and Facebook, www.facebook.com/ncura1959

Membership: individuals involved in grant administration at colleges, universities, and teaching hospitals.

Encourages development of effective policies and procedures in the administration of these programs.

Network of Schools of Public Policy, Affairs, and Administration (NASPAA), *1029 Vermont Ave. N.W., #1100, 20005-3517; (202) 628-8965. Fax, (202) 626-4978. Laurel McFarland, Executive Director, (202) 628-8965 ext. 105.*
General email, naspaa@naspaa.org
Web, www.naspaa.org, Twitter, @naspaa and Facebook, www.facebook.com/naspaaglobal

Membership: universities involved in education, research, and training in public management in the United States and internationally.

Washington Higher Education Secretariat, *1 Dupont Circle N.W., #800, 20036-1110; (202) 939-9310. Fax, (202) 833-4760. Ted Mitchell, Chair.*
General email, whs@acenet.edu
Web, www.whes.org

Membership: national higher-education association chief executives representing the different sectors and functions in postsecondary institutions. Provides forum for discussion on national and local education issues. (Coordinated by the president of the American Council on Education.)

College Accreditation

Many college-based or university-based independent postsecondary education programs are accredited by member associations. See specific headings and associations within the chapter.

►AGENCIES

Education Dept., *Accreditation Group, 1990 K St. N.W., #8065, 20006-8509; (202) 453-6128. Herman Bounds Jr., Director.*
General email, aslrecordsmanager@ed.gov
Web, www.ed.gov/accreditation

Reviews accrediting agencies and state approval agencies that seek initial or renewed recognition by the secretary; provides the National Advisory Committee on Institutional Quality and Integrity with staff support.

►NONGOVERNMENTAL

Accrediting Commission of Career Schools and Colleges, *2101 Wilson Blvd., #302, Arlington, VA 22201; (703) 247-4212. Fax, (703) 247-4533. Michale S. McComis, Executive Director, (703) 247-4520.*
General email, info@accsc.org
Web, www.accsc.org, Twitter, @ACCSCAccredits and Facebook, www.facebook.com/accscaccreditation

Serves as the national accrediting agency for private postsecondary institutions offering occupational and vocational programs. Sponsors workshops and meetings on academic excellence and ethical practices in career education.

Accrediting Council for Continuing Education and Training (ACCET), 1722 N St. N.W., 20036; (202) 955-1113. Fax, (202) 955-1118. William V. Larkin, Executive Director, ext. 105.
General email, info@accet.org

Web, www.accet.org

Peer-reviewed accrediting agency for noncollegiate continuing education and training institutions. Establishes standards, policies, and procedures to identify best education and training practices.

Accrediting Council for Independent Colleges and Schools (ACICS), 750 1st St. N.E., #980, 20002-4223; (202) 336-6780. Fax, (202) 842-2593. Michelle Edwards, President; Perliter Walters-Gilliam, Vice President of Accreditation.
General email, info@acics.org

Web, www.acics.org, Twitter, @ACICSaccredits and Facebook, www.facebook.com/ACICSaccredits

Accredits postsecondary institutions offering programs of study through the master's degree level that are designed to train and educate persons for careers or professions where business applications and concepts constitute or support the career or professional activity. Promotes educational excellence and ethical business practices in its member schools.

American Academy for Liberal Education (AALE), 1200 G St. N.W., #883, 20005; (202) 389-6550. Mary Ann A. Powers, Executive Director.
General email, aaleinfo@aale.org

Web, www.aale.org

Accredits colleges, universities, and charter schools whose general education program in the liberal arts meets the academy's accreditation requirements. Provides support for institutions that maintain substantial liberal arts programs and desire to raise requirements to meet AALE standards.

Council for Higher Education Accreditation, 1 Dupont Circle N.W., #510, 20036; (202) 955-6126. Fax, (202) 955-6129. Judith S. Eaton, President.
General email, chea@chea.org

Web, www.chea.org, www.cheainternational.org and Twitter, @CHEAnews

Advocates voluntary self-regulation of colleges and universities through accreditation; conducts recognition processes for accrediting organizations; coordinates research, debate, and processes that improve accreditation; mediates disputes and fosters communications among accrediting bodies and the higher education community.

Council for the Accreditation of Educator Preparation, 1140 19th St., #400, 20036; (202) 223-0077. Fax, (202) 296-6620. Christoper Koch, President.
General email, caep@caepnet.org

Web, http://ncate.org and Twitter, @caepupdates

Evaluates and accredits schools and departments of education at colleges and universities. Publishes list of accredited institutions and standards for accreditation. (Formerly National Council for Accreditation of Teacher Education.)

Council on Education for Public Health, 1010 Wayne Ave., #220, Silver Spring, MD 20910; (202) 789-1050. Laura Rasar King, Executive Director.
Web, https://ceph.org and Twitter, @CEPHtweets

Accredits schools of public health and undergraduate and graduate programs in public health.

Distance Education and Accrediting Commission (DEAC), 1101 17th St. N.W., #808, 20036; (202) 234-5100. Fax, (202) 332-1386. Leah K. Matthews, Executive Director.
General email, info@deac.org

Web, www.deac.org

Membership: accredited distance education and online institutions. Accredits distance education and online institutions that offer high school diplomas, postsecondary education programs, and degree programs through to the doctoral level. Recognized by the U.S. Department of Education and the Council for Higher Education Accreditation.

National Architectural Accrediting Board Inc., 1735 New York Ave. N.W., 20006; (202) 783-2007. Fax, (202) 783-2822. Helen Combs Dreiling, Executive Director (Acting).
General email, info@naab.org

Web, www.naab.org and Twitter, @NAABNews

Accredits Bachelor, Master, and Doctor of Architecture degree programs in the United States; assists organizations in other countries to develop accreditation standards.

National Assn. of Schools of Dance, 11250 Roger Bacon Dr., #21, Reston, VA 20190-5248; (703) 437-0700. Fax, (703) 437-6312. Karen Moynahan, Executive Director, (703) 437-0700 x 116.
General email, info@arts-accredit.org

Web, http://nasd.arts-accredit.org

Specialized professional accrediting agency for postsecondary programs in dance. Conducts and shares research and analysis on topics pertinent to dance programs and the field of dance. Offers professional development opportunities for executives of dance programs.

National Assn. of Schools of Music, 11250 Roger Bacon Dr., #21, Reston, VA 20190-5248; (703) 437-0700. Fax, (703) 437-6312. Karen Moynahan, Executive Director, (703) 437-0700, ext. 116.
General email, info@arts-accredit.org

Web, http://nasm.arts-accredit.org

Specialized professional accrediting agency for postsecondary programs in music. Conducts and shares research and analysis on topics pertinent to music programs and the field of music. Offers professional development opportunities for executives of music programs.

National Assn. of Schools of Theatre, *11250 Roger Bacon Dr., #21, Reston, VA 20190-5248; (703) 437-0700. Fax, (703) 437-6312. Karen Moynahan, Executive Director, (703) 437-0700, ext. 116.*
General email, info@arts-accredit.org
Web, http://nast.arts-accredit.org

Specialized professional accrediting agency for postsecondary programs in theatre. Conducts and shares research and analysis on topics pertinent to theatre programs and the field of theatre. Offers professional development opportunities for executives of theatre programs.

Network of Schools of Public Policy, Affairs, and Administration (NASPAA), *1029 Vermont Ave. N.W., #1100, 20005-3517; (202) 628-8965. Fax, (202) 626-4978. Laurel McFarland, Executive Director, (202) 628-8965, ext. 105.*
General email, naspaa@naspaa.org
Web, www.naspaa.org, Twitter, @naspaa and Facebook, www.facebook.com/naspaaglobal

Accredits master's degree programs in public affairs, public policy, and public administration.

Financial Aid to Students

▶AGENCIES

Education Dept., Federal Student Aid, *830 1st St. N.E., 20202; (202) 377-3000. Fax, (202) 275-5000. Wayne Johnson, Chief Operating Officer. FSA customer service, (800) 433-7327. Student Aid Information Center, (800) 433-3243. TTY, (800) 730-8913.*
Web, https://studentaid.ed.gov/sa

Administers federal loan, grant, and work-study programs for postsecondary education to eligible individuals. Administers the Pell Grant Program, the Perkins Loan Program, the Stafford Student Loan Program (Guaranteed Student Loan)/PLUS Program, the College Work-Study Program, the Supplemental Loans for Students (SLS), and the Supplemental Educational Opportunity Grant Program.

Education Dept., Health Education Assistance Loan Program, *12501 Ardennes Ave., #200, Rockville, MD 20857; (844) 509-8957. Tawana Lewis, Supervisor.*
General email, heal@ed.gov
Web, www.ifap.ed.gov/HEALInfo/HEALInfo.html

Insures loans provided by private lenders to students attending eligible health professions schools under the Public Health Service Act. New loans to student borrowers have been discontinued. Refinancing has been terminated.

Education Dept., Postsecondary Education (OPE), Higher Education Programs (HEP), Institutional Service, *Lyndon Baines Johnson Bldg., 400 Maryland Ave. S.W., 2nd Floor, 20202; (202) 453-6914. Fax, (202) 502-7699. Vacant, Deputy Assistant Secretary, (202) 453-6808.*

General email, OPE_Institutional_Development@ed.gov
Web, www2.ed.gov/about/offices/list/ope/idues

Provides financial and administrative support for limited resource institutions serving minority and financially disadvantaged students. Administers programs authorized under the Higher Education Act of 1965 and its subsequent amendments. Title III programs include support for Historically Black Colleges and Universities, American Indian Tribally Controlled Colleges and Universities, and Minority Science and Engineering Improvement Program. Title V programs strengthen institutions serving Hispanic and other low-income students. Title VII supports the implementation and evaluation of and shares findings of innovative educational reform ideas.

Education Dept., Postsecondary Education (OPE), Higher Education Programs (HEP), Student Service, *Lyndon Baines Johnson Bldg., 400 Maryland Ave. S.W., 20202; (202) 453-6914. Fax, (202) 502-7857. Lynda Byrd-Johnson, Senior Director.*
General email, OPE_TRIO@ed.gov
Web, www2.ed.gov/about/offices/list/ope/student-service.html

Administers grant programs (TRIO) for low-income, potential first-generation students and individuals with disabilities from middle school to graduate school, in addition to programs focused on college readiness, campus-based child care, and graduate fellowships. TRIO programs include Educational Opportunity Centers, Upward Bound, Upward Bound Math and Science, Talent Search, Student Support Services, Ronald E. McNair Postbaccalaureate Achievement Program, TRIO training program, and Veterans Upward Bound.

▶NONGOVERNMENTAL

College Board, Advocacy and Policy, *1919 M St. N.W., #300, 20034; (202) 741-4700. Fax, (202) 223-7035. Stephanie Sanford, Chief of Global Policy and External Relations. Communications Office, (212) 713-8052. Toll-free, (866) 630-9305.*
Web, www.collegeboard.org and Twitter, @CollegeBoard

Membership: colleges and universities, secondary schools, school systems, and education associations. Provides direct student support programs and professional development for educators; conducts policy analysis and research; and advocates public policy positions that support educational excellence and promote student access to higher education. (Headquarters in New York.)

Education Finance Council, *440 First St., #560, 20001; (202) 955-5510. Debra J. Chromy, President.*
General email, info@efc.org
Web, www.efc.org

Membership: Nonprofit and state-based higher-education finance organizations. Participates in the Federal Family Education Loan Program (FFELP). Works to maintain and expand student access to higher education through tax-exempt funding for loans.

National Assn. of Student Financial Aid Administrators, *1801 Pennsylvania Ave. N.W., #850, 20006-3606; (202) 785-0453. Fax, (202) 785-1487. Justin Draeger, President.*

General email, info@nasfaa.org

Web, www.nasfaa.org and Twitter, @nasfaa

Membership: more than 20,000 financial aid professionals at nearly 3,000 colleges, universities, and career schools. Interests include student aid legislation, regulatory analysis, and training for financial aid administrators.

National Council of Higher Education Resources, *1100 Connecticut Ave. N.W., #1200, 20036-4110; (202) 822-2106. Fax, (202) 822-2143. James P. Bergeron, President.*

General email, info@nchelp.us

Web, www.ncher.us and Twitter, @ncher_us

Membership: agencies and organizations involved in servicing and collecting federal student loans and providing debt management, financial literacy, student loan counseling, and other college access and success services. Fosters information exchange among members.

Student Aid Alliance, *1 Dupont Circle N.W., #800, 20036-1193; (202) 939-9359. Fax, (202) 833-4762. Ted Mitchell, ACE President, (202) 939-9300; David L. Warren, NAICU President, (202) 785-8866; Jon Sansmith, ACE Director of Government Relations, (202) 939-9359.*

Web, studentaidalliance.org and Twitter, @StuAidAlliance

Membership: more than seventy organizations representing students, administrators, and faculty members from all sectors of higher education. Seeks to ensure adequate funding of federal aid programs. Monitors legislation and regulations. (Co-chaired by the National Assn. of Independent Colleges and Universities [NAICU] and the American Council on Education [ACE].)

PRESCHOOL, ELEMENTARY, SECONDARY EDUCATION

General

▶**AGENCIES**

Defense Dept. (DoD), *Education Activity, 4800 Mark Center Dr., Alexandria, VA 22350-1400; (571) 372-0590. Fax, (571) 372-5829. Thomas M. Brady, Director.*

General email, dodea.director@hq.dodea.edu

Web, www.dodea.edu

Civilian office that maintains school system for dependents of all military personnel and eligible civilians in the United States and abroad. Develops uniform curriculum and educational standards; monitors student performance and school accreditation.

Education Dept., *Elementary and Secondary Education (OESE), Lyndon Baines Johnson Bldg., 400 Maryland Ave. S.W., #3W315, 20202; (202) 401-0113.*

Fax, (202) 205-0310. Frank Brogan, Assistant Secretary (Acting).

General email, oese@ed.gov

Web, www2.ed.gov/about/offices/list/oese

Administers federal assistance programs for preschool, elementary, and secondary education (both public and private). Program divisions include Student Achievement and School Accountability (including Title I aid for disadvantaged children); Migrant Education; Impact Aid; School Support and Rural Programs; Early Learning; Safe and Healthy Students; and Academic Improvement and Teacher Quality Programs.

Education Dept., *Elementary and Secondary Education (OESE), Academic Improvement and Teacher Quality Programs, Lyndon Baines Johnson Bldg., 400 Maryland Ave. S.W., #3E314, 20202; (202) 260-8228. Fax, (202) 260-8969. Sylvia Lyles, Director, (202) 260-2551.*

General email, oese@ed.gov

Web, www2.ed.gov/about/offices/list/oese/aitq

Provides financial assistance to state and local educational agencies, community and faith-based organizations, and other entities to support activities to recruit and retain high-quality teaching staff and to strengthen the quality of elementary and secondary education. Divided into four program groups: the Academic Improvement Program, the High School Programs, the Teacher Quality Program, and Literacy Programs; implements programs providing support for reopening and rebuilding schools in areas impacted by natural disasters; implements the 21st Century Community Learning Centers, which provide academic enrichment opportunities during nonschool hours for students attending high-poverty and low-performing schools.

Education Dept., *Elementary and Secondary Education (OESE), Impact Aid, Lyndon Baines Johnson Bldg., 400 Maryland Ave. S.W., #3E105, 20202-6244; (202) 260-3858. Marilyn Hall, Director. Toll-free fax, (866) 799-1273.*

General email, impact.aid@ed.gov

Web, www2.ed.gov/about/offices/list/oese/impactaid

Provides funds for elementary and secondary educational activities to school districts in federally impacted areas (where federal activities such as military bases enlarge staff and reduce taxable property).

Education Dept., *Elementary and Secondary Education (OESE), Indian Education Programs, Lyndon Baines Johnson Bldg., 400 Maryland Ave. S.W., #3E205, 20202-6335; (202) 260-3774. Fax, (202) 260-7779. Tara Ramsey, Director (Acting), (202) 401-0767.*

General email, indian.education@ed.gov

Web, www2.ed.gov/about/offices/list/oese/oie

Aids local school districts with programs for Native American and Alaska Native students.

Education Dept., *Elementary and Secondary Education (OESE), Migrant Education, Lyndon Baines Johnson Bldg., 400 Maryland Ave. S.W., #3E317, LBJ, 20202-6135; (202) 260-1164. Fax, (202) 205-0089. Lisa Gillette, Director.*

Web, www2.ed.gov/programs/mep/index.html

Administers grant programs that provide academic and supportive services to the children of families who migrate to find work in the agricultural and fishing industries.

Education Dept., *Elementary and Secondary Education (OESE), Safe and Healthy Students (OSHS),* Lyndon Baines Johnson Bldg., 400 Maryland Ave. S.W., #3E-245, 20202-6135; (202) 453-6777. Fax, (202) 453-6742. Paul Kesner, Director (Acting).
General email, oese@ed.gov

Web, www2.ed.gov/about/offices/list/oese/oshs

Develops policy for the department's drug and violence prevention initiatives for students in elementary and secondary schools and institutions of higher education. Provides financial assistance for drug and violence prevention activities. Coordinates education efforts in drug and violence prevention with those of other federal departments and agencies.

Education Dept., *Elementary and Secondary Education (OESE), Safe and Healthy Students (OSHS), Education for Homeless Children and Youth Program,* Lyndon Baines Johnson Bldg., 400 Maryland Ave. S.W., 20202-6132; (202) 453-6777. Fax, (202) 260-7764. John McLaughlin, Program Coordinator.
General email, HomelessEd@ed.gov

Web, www2.ed.gov/programs/homeless

Provides formula grants to education agencies in the states, Puerto Rico, and through the Bureau of Indian Affairs to Native Americans to educate homeless children and youth and to establish an office of coordinator of education for homeless children and youth in each jurisdiction.

Education Dept., *Elementary and Secondary Education (OESE), School Support and Rural Programs (SSRP),* Lyndon Baines Johnson Bldg., 400 Maryland Ave. S.W., #3W205, 20202-6400; (202) 401-0039. Fax, (202) 205-5870. David Cantrell, Director.
Web, www2.ed.gov/about/offices/list/oese/sst

Provides a coordinated strategy for focusing federal resources on supporting improvements in schools; promotes development and implementation of comprehensive improvement plans that direct resources toward improved achievement for all students.

Education Dept., *Elementary and Secondary Education (OESE), State Support,* Lyndon Baines Johnson Bldg., 400 Maryland Ave. S.W., #3W202, FB-6, 20202-6132; (202) 260-0826. Fax, (202) 260-7764. Vacant, Deputy Director.
General email, oese@ed.gov

Web, www2.ed.gov/about/offices/list/oese/oss

Administers programs that provide financial assistance to local and state education agencies, including Title I, Part A grants to local educational agencies along with several other major programs, including Title II, Title III, The School Improvement Grants, Race To The Top, the State Assessment Grant program, and the Enhanced Assessment Grant program.

Education Dept., *English Language Acquisition (OELA),* Lyndon Baines Johnson Bldg., 400 Maryland Ave. S.W., #5E106, 20202-6510; (202) 401-1461. Fax, (202) 260-1292. José A. Viana, Assistant Deputy Secretary.
Web, www2.ed.gov/about/offices/list/oela

Provides grants for the professional development of teachers of English learners and administers the Native American/Alaska-Native Children in School Program and National Professional Development Discretionary Grant Programs.

Education Dept., *Innovation and Improvement (OII),* Lyndon Baines Johnson Bldg., 400 Maryland Ave. S.W., #4W300, 20202-0001; (202) 205-4500. Fax, (202) 205-4123. Margo Anderson, Associate Assistant Deputy Secretary.
Web, http://sites.ed.gov/oii/oii-program-offices and Twitter, @ED_OII

Provides grants for innovative K–12 educational practices in areas such as alternative routes to teacher certification, traditional teaching of American history, financial literacy and economic education, and arts in education.

Education Dept., *Innovation and Improvement (OII), Arts in Education National Program,* Lyndon Baines Johnson Bldg., 400 Maryland Ave. S.W., #4W214, 20202-5950; (202) 205-1729. Fax, (202) 205-5630. Michelle Johnson Armstrong, Program Manager.
General email, michelle.armstrong@ed.gov

Web, www2.ed.gov/programs/artsnational

Supports national level arts education projects and programs for children and youth, with special emphasis on serving students from low-income families and students with disabilities.

Education Dept., *Innovation and Improvement (OII), Arts in Education—Model Development and Dissemination,* Lyndon Baines Johnson Bldg., 400 Maryland Ave. S.W., #4W210, 20202-5950; (202) 401-3576. Fax, (202) 205-5630. Anna Hinton, Director, (202) 260-1816. Toll-free, (800) 872-5327.
General email, artsdemo@ed.gov

Web, www2.ed.gov/programs/artsedmodel

Supports the development of innovative model programs that integrate and strengthen academic performance in core elementary and middle school curricula and that strengthen arts instruction in those grades. Provides grants to local education agencies and nonprofit art organizations. Funds must be used in elementary and middle schools.

Education Dept., *Innovation and Improvement (OII), Charter Schools Program,* Lyndon Baines Johnson Bldg., 400 Maryland Ave. S.W., 20202; (202) 205-4500. Stefan Huh, Director.
Web, https://innovation.ed.gov/what-we-do/charter-schools

Funds the creation of new public charter schools, location of suitable facilities, and national initiatives that support charter schools; disseminates information about effective practices within charter schools.

Education Dept., *Innovation and Improvement (OII),*
Education Innovation and Research (EIR), *Lyndon*
Baines Johnson Bldg., 400 Maryland Ave. S.W., 20202;
(202) 453-7122. Kelly Terpak, Director (Acting).
General email, eir@ed.gov

Web, https://innovation.ed.gov/what-we-do/innovation/
education-innovation-and-research-eir

Provides funding to create, develop, implement, replicate, or take to scale entrepreneurial, evidence-based, field-initiated innovations to improve student achievement and attainment for high-need students.

Health and Human Services Dept. (HHS), *Head Start*
(OHS), 330 C St. S.W., 8th Floor, 20201; (202) 205-8573.
Deborah Bergeron, Director. Information, (866) 763-6481.
Web, www.acf.hhs.gov/ohs, Twitter, @HeadStartgov and
Facebook, www.facebook.com/HeadStartgov

Awards grants to nonprofit and for-profit organizations and local governments for operating community Head Start programs (comprehensive development programs for children, ages birth to five, of low-income families); manages parent and child centers, Early Childhood Learning and Knowledge Centers (ECLKC), for families with children up to age five. Conducts research and manages demonstration programs, including those under the Comprehensive Child Care Development Act of 1988; administers the Child Development Associate scholarship program, which trains individuals for careers in child development, often as Head Start teachers.

National Assessment Governing Board, *800 N. Capitol*
St. N.W., #825, 20002-4233; (202) 357-6938.
Fax, (202) 357-6945. Lisa Stooksberry, Deputy Executive
Director. Toll-free, (877) 997-6938.
General email, nagb@ed.gov

Web, www.nagb.org and Twitter, @GovBoard

Independent board of local, state, and federal officials, educators, and others appointed by the secretary of education and funded under the National Assessment of Educational Progress (NAEP) program. Sets policy for NAEP, a series of tests measuring achievements of U.S. students since 1969.

United States Presidential Scholars Program
(Education Dept.), 400 Maryland Ave. S.W., #5E228,
20202-8173; (202) 401-0961. Fax, (202) 260-7465.
Simone M. Olson, Executive Director. Toll-free, 800-USA-
LEARN.
General email, Presidential.Scholars@ed.gov

Web, www2.ed.gov/programs/psp and Twitter, @usedgov

Honorary recognition program that selects 161 graduating high school seniors who demonstrate outstanding achievement in academics, community service, artistic ability, leadership, and career and technical fields.

► **CONGRESS**

For a listing of relevant congressional committees and subcommittees, please see page 174 or the Appendix.

► **NONGOVERNMENTAL**

Achieve, Inc., *1919 M St. N.W., #450, 20036;*
(202) 419-1540. Michael (Mike) Cohen, President,
(202) 419-1566.
Web, www.achieve.org, Twitter, @AchieveInc and
Facebook, www.facebook.com/pages/Achieve/46050812271

Bipartisan organization that seeks to raise academic standards, improve performance assessments, and strengthen personal accountability among young people. Encourages high school graduates to pursue postsecondary education and rewarding careers. Monitors legislation and regulations.

Afterschool Alliance, *1101 14th St. N.W., #700, 20005;*
(202) 347-2030. Fax, (202) 347-2092. Jodi Grant, Executive
Director. Press, (202) 371-1999.
General email, info@afterschoolalliance.org

Web, www.afterschoolalliance.org,
Twitter, @afterschool4all and Facebook, www.facebook
.com/afterschoolalliancedc

Advocacy group that campaigns for afterschool programs. Partners include Congressional and local government leaders. Trains selected Afterschool Ambassadors to educate policymakers about afterschool programs. Publishes reports supporting afterschool daycare.

Alliance for Excellent Education, *1201 Connecticut Ave.*
N.W., #901, 20036; (202) 828-0828. Fax, (202) 828-0821.
Deborah Delisle, President.
Web, www.all4ed.org, Twitter, @all4ed and
Facebook, www.facebook.com/All4ed

Policy and advocacy organization that promotes secondary education reform, with a focus on the most at-risk students. Works to increase public awareness through webinars, conferences, reports, publications, and press releases. Monitors legislation and regulations.

Assn. for Childhood Education International, *1875*
Connecticut Ave. N.W., 10th Floor, 20009; (202) 372-9986.
Fax, (202) 372-9989. Diane Whitehead, Executive Director.
Information, (800) 423-3563.
General email, headquarters@acei.org

Web, www.acei.org and Twitter, @ChildhoodEdIntl

Membership: educators, parents, and professionals who work with children (infancy to adolescence). Works to promote the rights, education, and well-being of children worldwide. Holds annual conference.

Center for Inspired Teaching, *1436 U St. N.W., #400,*
20009; (202) 462-1956. Fax, (202) 462-1905. Mary Kadera,
Executive Director (Acting).
General email, info@inspiredteaching.org

Web, http://inspiredteaching.org and
Twitter, @InspireTeach

Promotes teaching skills that make the most of children's innate desire to learn. Provides professional development through course, mentoring, new teacher certification and residency programs, school partnerships, and a demonstration charter school.

Center on Education Policy, 2100 Pennsylvania Ave. N.W., #310, 20052; (202) 994-9050. Fax, (202) 994-8859. Maria Voles Ferguson, Executive Director.
General email, cep-dc@cep-dc.org

Web, www.cep-dc.org and Twitter, @CEPDC

Acts as advocate for public education. Interests include the federal role in education and the status and effects of state high school exit examinations. Provides expert advice upon request. Works with many other education, business, state, and civic organizations. Monitors local, state, and federal legislation and regulations.

Character Education Partnership, 1634 Eye St. N.W., #550, 20006; (202) 296-7743. Fax, (202) 296-7779. Doug Karr, President, ext. 20.
General email, information@character.org

Web, http://character.org and Twitter, @CharacterDotOrg

Promotes the integration of character development in schools and education. Trains education professionals to support character development and social-emotional learning skills, and decrease student behavioral problems. Sponsors an annual forum and publication on effective character education practices.

Council for Professional Recognition, 2460 16th St. N.W., 20009-3547; (202) 265-9090. Fax, (202) 265-9161. Valora Washington, Chief Executive Officer.
Toll-free, (800) 424-4310.
CDA Candidates email, cdafeedback@cda.org, Web, www .cdacouncil.org and Twitter, @cdacouncil

Promotes high standards for early childhood teachers. Awards credentials to family day care, preschool, home visitor, and infant-toddler caregivers. Administers the Child Development Associate National Credentialing Program, designed to assess and credential early childhood education professionals.

Council of Chief State School Officers, 1 Massachusetts Ave. N.W., #700, 20001-1431; (202) 336-7000. Fax, (202) 408-8072. Carissa Moffat Miller, Executive Director. Press, (202) 336-7034.
General email, communications@ccsso.org

Web, http://ccsso.org and Twitter, @CCSSO

Membership: the public officials who head departments of elementary and secondary education in the states, the District of Columbia, the Department of Defense Education Activity, and five U.S. extrastate jurisdictions. Provides leadership, advocacy, and technical assistance on major educational issues. Seeks member consensus on major educational issues and advocates issue positions to civic and professional organizations, federal agencies, Congress, and the public.

Council of the Great City Schools, 1331 Pennsylvania Ave. N.W., #1100N, 20004-1758; (202) 393-2427. Fax, (202) 393-2400. Michael (Mike) Casserly, Executive Director.
Web, www.cgcs.org and Twitter, @GreatCitySchls

Membership: superintendents and school board members of large urban school districts. Provides research, legislative, and support services for members; interests include elementary and secondary education and school finance.

DECA Inc., 1908 Association Dr., Reston, VA 20191-1594; (703) 860-5000. Fax, (703) 860-4013. Frank Peterson, Executive Director (Acting).
General email, info@deca.org

Web, www.deca.org and Twitter, @DECAInc

Educational organization that helps high school and college students develop skills in marketing, management, finance, hospitality, and entrepreneurship. Promotes business and education partnerships.

Editorial Projects in Education, Inc., 6935 Arlington Rd., #100, Bethesda, MD 20814-5233; (301) 280-3100. Fax, (301) 280-3200. Michele J. Givens, President.
Toll-free, (800) 346-1834.
Web, www.edweek.org

Promotes awareness of important issues in K–12 education among professionals and the public. Publishes the journal Education Week, books, special reports, and video productions on topics of interest to educators.

Family, Career, and Community Leaders of America, 1910 Association Dr., Reston, VA 20191-1584; (703) 476-4900. Fax, (703) 439-2662. Sandy Spavone, Executive Director.
General email, national@fcclainc.org

Web, www.fcclainc.org and Twitter, @NationalFCCLA

National vocational student organization that helps students through grade 12 address personal, family, work, and social issues through family and consumer sciences education.

Institute for Educational Leadership (IEL), 4301 Connecticut Ave. N.W., #100, 20008; (202) 822-8405. Fax, (202) 872-4050. Johan Uvin, President.
General email, iel@iel.org

Web, www.iel.org, Twitter, @IELconnects and Facebook, www.facebook.com/IELconnects

Works with educators, human services personnel, government officials, and association executives to improve educational opportunities for youths; conducts research on education issues.

National Assn. for College Admission Counseling, 1050 N. Highland St., #400, Arlington, VA 22201; (703) 836-2222. Fax, (703) 243-9375. Joyce E. Smith, Chief Executive Officer, (703) 299-6828.
Information, (800) 822-6285.
General email, info@nacacnet.org

Web, www.nacacnet.org and Twitter, @NACAC

Membership: high school guidance counselors, independent counselors, college and university admissions officers, and financial aid officers. Promotes and funds research on admission counseling and on the transition from high school to college. Acts as advocate for student rights in college admissions. Sponsors national college fairs and continuing education for members.

National Assn. for the Education of Young Children, *1313 L St. N.W., #500, 20005; (202) 232-8777. Fax, (202) 328-1846. Rhian Evans Allvin, Chief Executive Officer, ext. 8819. Information, (800) 424-2460.*
General email, help@naeyc.org

Web, www.naeyc.org and Twitter, @NAEYC

Membership: early childhood teachers, administrators, college faculty, and directors of early childhood programs at the state and local levels. Works to improve the education of and the quality of services to children from birth through age eight. Sponsors professional development opportunities for early childhood educators. Offers an accreditation program and conducts two conferences annually; issues publications.

National Assn. of Elementary School Principals, *1615 Duke St., Alexandria, VA 22314; (703) 684-3345. Fax, (703) 549-5568. L. Earl Franks, Executive Director, (703) 684-3345 Ext 250. Toll-free, (800) 386-2377. Toll-free fax, (800) 396-2377.*
General email, naesp@naesp.org

Web, www.naesp.org and Twitter, @naesp

Membership: elementary school and middle school principals. Conducts workshops for members on federal and state policies and programs and on professional development. Offers assistance in contract negotiations.

National Assn. of Secondary School Principals, *1904 Association Dr., Reston, VA 20191-1537; (703) 860-0200. JoAnn D. Bartoletti, Executive Director. Toll-free, (800) 253-7746.*
Web, www.nassp.org and Twitter, @nassp

Membership: principals and assistant principals of middle schools and senior high schools, both public and private, and college-level teachers of secondary education. Conducts training programs for members; serves as clearinghouse for information on secondary school administration. Student activities office provides student councils, student activity advisers, and national and junior honor societies with information on national associations.

National Center on Education and the Economy (NCEE), *2121 K St. N.W., #700, 20037; (202) 379-1800. Fax, (202) 293-1560. Anthony Makay, President.*
General email, info@ncee.org

Web, www.ncee.org and Twitter, @CtrEdEcon

Partnership of states, school districts, corporations, foundations, and nonprofit organizations that provides research, analysis, advocacy, tools, and technical assistance to improve the nation's school systems, student performances, and training for the workplace. (Administers the National Institute for School Leadership.)

National Council for the Social Studies (NCSS), *8555 16th St., #500, Silver Spring, MD 20910; (301) 588-1800. Fax, (301) 588-2049. Lawrence Paska, Executive Director, (301) 850-7451. Publications, (800) 683-0812.*
General email, information@ncss.org

Web, www.socialstudies.org and Twitter, @NCSSNetwork

Membership: curriculum developers, educational administrators, state supervisors, and social studies educators, including K–12 classroom teachers and university professors of history, political science, geography, economics, civics, psychology, sociology, and anthropology. Promotes the teaching of social studies; encourages research; sponsors publications; works with other organizations to advance social studies education.

National Head Start Assn., *1651 Prince St., Alexandria, VA 22314; (703) 739-0875. Fax, (703) 739-0878. Yasmina S. Vinci, Executive Director. Toll-free, (866) 677-8724.*
Web, www.nhsa.org

Membership: organizations that represent Head Start children, families, and staff. Recommends strategies on issues affecting Head Start programs; provides training and professional development opportunities. Monitors legislation and regulations.

National PTA, *1250 N. Pitt St., Alexandria, VA 22314; (703) 518-1200. Fax, (703) 836-0942. Nathan R. Monell, Executive Director. Toll-free, (800) 307-4782.*
General email, info@pta.org

Web, www.pta.org, Twitter, @NationalPTA and Facebook, www.facebook.com/ParentTeacherAssociation

Membership: parent-teacher associations at the preschool, elementary, and secondary levels. Washington office represents members' interests on education, funding for education, parent involvement, child protection and safety, comprehensive health care for children, AIDS, the environment, children's television and educational technology, child care, and nutrition.

National School Boards Assn., *1680 Duke St., 2nd Floor, Alexandria, VA 22314-3493; (703) 838-6722. Fax, (703) 549-7590. Thomas Gentzel, Executive Director, (703) 838-6730; Frank C. Pugh, President.*
General email, info@nsba.org

Web, www.nsba.org, Twitter, @NSBAComm and Facebook, www.facebook.com/SchoolBoards

Federation of state school board associations. Interests include funding of public education, local governance, and quality of education programs. Sponsors seminars, an annual conference, and an information center. Publishes a monthly journal and various newsletters. Monitors legislation and regulations. Library open to the public by appointment.

Reading Is Fundamental, *750 1st St. N.E., #920, 20002; (202) 536-3400. Fax, (202) 536-3518. Alicia Levi, President. Information, 877-RIF-READ. Press, (202) 536-3458.*
General email, contactus@rif.org

Web, www.rif.org and Twitter, @RIFWEB

Conducts programs and workshops to motivate young people to read. Provides young people in low-income neighborhoods with free books and parents with services to encourage reading at home.

School Nutrition Assn., *2900 S. Quincy St., #700, Arlington, VA 22206; (703) 824-3000. Fax, (703) 824-3015.*

Patricia Montague, Chief Executive Officer.
Information, (800) 877-8822.
General email, servicecenter@schoolnutrition.org

Web, https://schoolnutrition.org and
Twitter, @SchoolLunch

Membership: state and national food service workers and supervisors, school cafeteria managers, nutrition educators, industry members, and others interested in school food programs and child nutrition. Offers credentialing and sponsors National School Lunch Week and National School Breakfast Week. (Formerly the American School Food Service Assn.)

Teach for America, *Washington Office,* 1805 7th St. N.W., 7th Floor, 20001; (202) 552-2400.
Fax, (202) 371-9272. Adele Fabrikant, Executive Director.
Information, (800) 832-1230.
General email, admissions@teachforamerica.org

Web, www.teachforamerica.org/where-we-work/dc-region and Twitter, @TFADCRegion

A national teacher corps of recent college graduates who teach in underfunded urban and rural public schools. Promotes outstanding teaching methodologies and educational equity. Monitors legislation and regulations. (Headquarters in New York.)

Thomas B. Fordham Institute, *National Office,* 1016 16th St. N.W., 8th Floor, 20036; (202) 223-5452.
Fax, (202) 223-9226. Michael J. Petrilli, President.
General email, thegadfly@edexcellence.net

Web, https://edexcellence.net and
Twitter, @educationgadfly

Advocates education reform to improve the quality of children's school systems. Researches and analyzes education policy issues. Brings scholars to the Capitol to brainstorm solutions to national education issues with education policy experts. Distributes an online course that educates the public about fundamental education policies that affect young students. Publishes the newsletter *The Education Gadfly Weekly.*

Private, Parochial, and Home Schooling

▶**AGENCIES**

Education Dept., *Innovation and Improvement (OII),*
Lyndon Baines Johnson Bldg., 400 Maryland Ave. S.W.,
#4W300, 20202-0001; (202) 205-4500. Fax, (202) 205-4123.
Margo Anderson, Associate Assistant Deputy Secretary.
Web, http://sites.ed.gov/oii/oii-program-offices and
Twitter, @ED_OII

Supports the establishment of charter schools, magnet schools, and other public and nonpublic education alternatives. Serves as liaison and resource to the nonpublic education community.

Education Dept., *Innovation and Improvement (OII),*
Non-Public Education, Lyndon Baines Johnson Bldg., 400

Maryland Ave. S.W., 20202-5940; (202) 401-1365.
Maureen Dowling, Director, (202) 260-7820.
General email, onpe@ed.gov

Web, https://innovation.ed.gov/what-we-do/nonpublic-education

Acts as liaison between the department and the non-public school community, including private, state, and home schools.

▶**NONGOVERNMENTAL**

Americans United for Separation of Church and State,
1310 L St. N.W., #200, 20005; (202) 466-3234.
Fax, (202) 466-2587. Gary Carleton, Managing Director.
General email, americansunited@au.org

Web, www.au.org and Twitter, @americansunited

Citizens' interest group. Opposes federal and state aid to parochial schools; works to ensure religious neutrality in public schools; supports free religious exercise; initiates litigation; maintains speakers bureau. Monitors legislation and regulations.

Council for American Private Education, 1300
Pennsylvania Ave. N.W., #190-433, 20004; (301) 916-8460.
Fax, (301) 916-8485. Michael Shuttloffel, Executive Director.
General email, cape@capenet.org

Web, http://capenet.org

Coalition of national private school associations serving private elementary and secondary schools. Acts as a liaison between private education and government, other educational organizations, the media, and the public. Seeks greater access to private schools for all families. Monitors legislation and regulations.

Home School Legal Defense Assn., P.O. Box 3000,
Purcellville, VA 20134-9000; (540) 338-5600.
Fax, (540) 301-5881. J. Michael Smith, President.
General email, info@hslda.org

Web, www.hslda.org and Twitter, @HSLDA

Membership: families who practice home schooling. Provides members with legal consultation and defense. Initiates civil rights litigation on behalf of members. Monitors legislation and regulations.

National Assn. of Independent Schools, *Government Relations,* 1129 20th St. N.W., #800, 20036-3425;
(202) 973-9700. Fax, (888) 316-3862. Donna Orem,
President, (202) 973-9711. Press, (202) 973-9717.
General email, generalinfo@nais.org

Web, www.nais.org

Membership: independent elementary and secondary schools in the United States and abroad. Provides statistical and educational information to members. Monitors legislation and regulations.

National Catholic Educational Assn., 1005 N. Glebe Rd.,
#525, Arlington, VA 22201; (571) 257-0010.
Fax, (703) 243-0025. Thomas W. Burnford, President.
Toll-free, (800) 711-6232.

General email, nceatalk@ncea.org

Web, www.ncea.org and Twitter, @NCEATALK

Membership: Catholic schools (preschool through college and seminary) and school administrators. Provides consultation services to members for administration, curriculum, continuing education, religious education, campus ministry, boards of education, and union and personnel negotiations; conducts workshops and conferences; supports federal aid for private education. (Affiliated with the Assn. of Catholic Colleges and Universities.)

National PTA, *1250 N. Pitt St., Alexandria, VA 22314; (703) 518-1200. Fax, (703) 836-0942. Nathan R. Monell, Executive Director. Toll-free, (800) 307-4782.*
General email, info@pta.org

Web, www.pta.org, Twitter, @NationalPTA and Facebook, www.facebook.com/ParentTeacherAssociation

Membership: parent-teacher associations at the preschool, elementary, and secondary levels. Coordinates the National Coalition for Public Education, which opposes tuition tax credits and vouchers for private education.

U.S. Conference of Catholic Bishops (USCCB), *Secretariat of Catholic Education, 3211 4th St. N.E., 20017-1194; (202) 541-3132. Fax, (202) 541-3390.*
Sr. Mary Pat Donoghue, Executive Director.
Web, www.usccb.org/beliefs-and-teachings/how-we-teach/catholic-education

Represents Catholic bishops in the United States in public policy educational issues.

SPECIAL GROUPS IN EDUCATION

Gifted and Talented

▶**NONGOVERNMENTAL**

Council for Exceptional Children (CEC), *2900 Crystal Dr., #100, Arlington, VA 22202-3557; (703) 620-3660. Fax, (703) 264-9494. Alexander T. Graham, Executive Director. Toll-free, (888) 232-7733. TTY, (866) 915-5000.*
General email, service@cec.sped.org

Web, www.cec.sped.org and Twitter, @CECMembership

Membership association that acts as advocate on behalf of children with disabilities and gifts and talents as well as special educators. Sets professional standards for the field; publishes books, journals, newsletters, and other resources; and offers professional development for teachers and administrators, including an annual convention. Sponsors the Yes I Can! Awards for children with disabilities who excel. Monitors legislation and regulations.

National Assn. for Gifted Children, *1331 H St. N.W., #1001, 20005; (202) 785-4268. Fax, (202) 785-4248. M. Rene Islas, Executive Director.*
General email, nagc@nagc.org

Web, www.nagc.org and Twitter, @NAGCGIFTED

Membership: teachers, administrators, state coordinators, and parents. Acts as advocate for increased federal support for intellectually and creatively gifted children in public and private schools. Produces publications and conducts training for educators and parents.

Learning and Physically Disabled

▶**AGENCIES**

Education Dept., *Special Education and Rehabilitative Services (OSERS), Lyndon Baines Johnson Bldg., 400 Maryland Ave. S.W., 20202-7100 (mailing address: 400 Maryland Ave. S.W., Washington, DC 20202-7000); (202) 245-7468 (main phone is voice and TTY accessible). Fax, (202) 245-7638. Johnny Collett, Assistant Secretary.*
Web, www2.ed.gov/about/offices/list/osers

Administers federal assistance programs for the education and rehabilitation of people with disabilities through the Office of Special Education Programs and the Rehabilitation Services Administration; maintains a national information clearinghouse for people with disabilities. Provides information on federal legislation and programs and national organizations concerning individuals with disabilities.

Education Dept., *Special Education and Rehabilitative Services (OSERS), Special Education Programs (OSEP), Lyndon Baines Johnson Bldg., 400 Maryland Ave. S.W., 20202-7100; (202) 245-7459. Fax, (202) 245-7323. Laurie VanderPloeg, Director.*
Web, www2.ed.gov/about/offices/list/osers/osep

Responsible for special education programs and services designed to meet the needs and develop the full potential of children from infancy through age 21. Programs include support for training of teachers and other professional personnel; grants for research; financial aid to help states initiate and improve their resources; and media services and captioned films for hearing-impaired persons.

Institute of Education Sciences *(Education Dept.), National Center for Special Education Research (NCSER), 550 12th St. S.W., #4144, 20024; (202) 245-6940. Fax, (202) 245-6113. Elizabeth Albro, Commissioner, (202) 245-8201.*
Web, http://ies.ed.gov/ncser

Sponsors a comprehensive program of special education research designed to expand the knowledge and understanding of infants, toddlers, and children with disabilities.

John F. Kennedy Center for the Performing Arts, *VSA and Accessibility, 2700 F St. N.W., 20566 (mailing address: P.O. Box 101510, Arlington, VA 22210); (202) 416-8898. Fax, (202) 416-4840. Betty Siegel, Director.*
General email, access@kennedy-center.org

Web, www.kennedy-center.org/education

Initiates and supports research and program development providing arts training and programming for persons with disabilities to make classrooms and communities more inclusive. Provides technical assistance and training to VSA

Arts state organizations; acts as an information clearing-house for arts and persons with disabilities.

Office of Personnel Management (OPM), *Veterans Services, 1900 E St. N.W., #7439, 20415; (202) 606-3602. Fax, (202) 606-6017. Hakeem Basheerud-Deen, Director. Web, www.opm.gov/policy-data-oversight/veterans-services*

Provides outreach to colleges and universities on Schedule A hiring authorities for people with disabilities.

Smithsonian Institution, *Accessibility Program, 14th St. and Constitution Ave. N.W., #1050, 20013-7012 (mailing address: P.O. Box 37012, NMAH, MRC 607, Washington, DC 20013-7012); (202) 633-2921. Fax, (202) 633-4352. Elizabeth (Beth) Ziebarth, Director. General email, access@si.edu*

Web, www.si.edu/Accessibility

Coordinates the Smithsonian's efforts to improve accessibility of its programs and facilities to visitors and staff with disabilities. Serves as a resource for museums and individuals nationwide.

▶ CONGRESS

For a listing of relevant congressional committees and sub-committees, please see page 174 or the Appendix.

Library of Congress, *National Library Service for the Blind and Physically Handicapped, 1291 Taylor St. N.W., 20542 (mailing address: Library of Congress, Washington, DC 20542); (202) 707-5100. Fax, (202) 707-0712. Karen Keninger, Director. Toll-free, (888) 657-7323. General email, nls@loc.gov*

Web, www.loc.gov/nls

Braille email, braille@loc.gov

Administers a national program of free library services for persons with physical disabilities in cooperation with regional and subregional libraries. Produces and distributes full-length books and magazines in recorded form and in Braille. Reference section answers questions relating to blindness and physical disabilities and on library services available to persons with disabilities.

▶ NONGOVERNMENTAL

Assn. for Education and Rehabilitation of the Blind and Visually Impaired, *1703 N. Beauregard St., #440, Alexandria, VA 22311; (703) 671-4500. Fax, (703) 671-6391. Louis M. Tutt, Executive Director. Toll-free, (877) 492-2708. General email, aer@aerbvi.org*

Web, www.aerbvi.org and Twitter, @AERBVI

Membership: professionals who work in all phases of education and rehabilitation of children and adults who are blind and visually impaired. Provides support and professional development opportunities through conferences, continuing education, and publications. Issues professional recognition awards and student scholarships. Monitors legislation and regulations.

Assn. of University Centers on Disabilities (AUCD), *1100 Wayne Ave., #1000, Silver Spring, MD 20910; (301) 588-8252. Fax, (301) 588-2842. Andrew J. Imparato, Executive Director. General email, aucdinfo@aucd.org*

Web, www.aucd.org and Twitter, @AUCDNews

Network of facilities that diagnose and treat the developmentally disabled. Trains graduate students and professionals in the field; helps state and local agencies develop services. Interests include interdisciplinary training and services, early screening to prevent developmental disabilities, and development of equipment and programs to serve persons with disabilities.

Council for Exceptional Children (CEC), *2900 Crystal Dr., #100, Arlington, VA 22202-3557; (703) 620-3660. Fax, (703) 264-9494. Alexander T. Graham, Executive Director. Toll-free, (888) 232-7733. TTY, (866) 915-5000. General email, service@cec.sped.org*

Web, www.cec.sped.org and Twitter, @CECMembership

Membership association that acts as advocate on behalf of children with disabilities and gifts and talents as well as special educators. Sets professional standards for the field; publishes books, journals, newsletters, and other resources; and offers professional development for teachers and administrators, including an annual convention. Sponsors the Yes I Can! Awards for children with disabilities who excel. Monitors legislation and regulations.

Council for Opportunity in Education, *1025 Vermont Ave. N.W., #900, 20005-3516; (202) 347-7430. Fax, (202) 347-0786. Maureen Hoyler, President, ext. 321. Web, www.coenet.us and Twitter, @COETalk*

Membership: more than 1,000 colleges and agencies. Works in conjunction with colleges and agencies that host the federally funded TRIO programs, designed to help low-income, first-generation immigrants, students with disabilities, and veterans enroll in and graduate from college.

Gallaudet University, *800 Florida Ave. N.E., 20002-3695; (202) 651-5000. Roberta (Bobbi) Cordano, President, (202) 651-5005. Web, www.gallaudet.edu, Twitter, @GallaudetU and Facebook, www.facebook.com/gallaudetu*

Offers undergraduate, graduate, and doctoral degree programs for deaf, hard-of-hearing, and hearing students. Conducts research; maintains the Laurent Clerc National Deaf Education Center and demonstration preschool, elementary (Kendall Demonstration Elementary School), and secondary (Model Secondary School for the Deaf) programs. Sponsors the Center for Global Education, National Deaf Education Network and Clearinghouse, and the Cochlear Implant Education Center. Links to each department's video phone are at www.gallaudet.edu/about_gallaudet/contact_us.html.

National Assn. of Private Special Education Centers, *601 Pennsylvania Ave. N.W., South Bldg., #900, 20004; (202) 434-8225. Fax, (202) 434-8224. Sherry L. Kolbe, Executive Director.*

General email, napsec@napsec.org

Web, www.napsec.org

Represents private special education programs, residential therapeutic centers, and early intervention services at the preschool, elementary, and secondary levels and postsecondary levels, as well as adult programs. Acts as advocate for greater education opportunities for children, youth, and adults with disabilities.

National Assn. of State Directors of Special Education, *225 Reinkers Lane, #420, Alexandria, VA 22314; (703) 519-3800. Fax, (703) 519-3808. Bill East, Executive Director, (703) 519-3800, ext. 301.*

General email, nasdse@nasdse.org

Web, www.nasdse.org

Membership: state directors of special education and others interested in special education policy. Monitors legislation, regulations, policy, and research affecting special education.

Minorities and Women

► **AGENCIES**

Bureau of Indian Education (BIE) *(Interior Dept.),* *1849 C St. N.W., MS 3609-MIB, 20240; (202) 208-6123. Tony L. Dearman, Director.*

Web, www.bie.edu, Twitter, @BureauIndianEdu and Facebook, www.facebook.com/Bureauofindianeducation

Operates schools and promotes school improvement for Native Americans, including people with disabilities. Provides assistance to Native American pupils in public schools. Aids Native American college students. Sponsors adult education programs designed specifically for Native Americans.

Civil Rights Division *(Justice Dept.),* *Educational Opportunities (EOS), 601 D St. N.W., #4300, 20530; (202) 514-4092. Fax, (202) 514-8337. Shaheena Simons, Chief. Toll-free, (877) 292-3804.*

General email, education@usdoj.gov

Web, www.justice.gov/crt/educational-opportunities-section

Initiates litigation to ensure equal opportunities in public education; enforces laws dealing with civil rights in public education.

Education Dept., *Civil Rights (OCR), Lyndon Baines Johnson Bldg., 400 Maryland Ave. S.W., #4E313, 20202-1100; (202) 453-5900. Fax, (202) 453-6012. Kenneth L. Marcus, Assistant Secretary. Toll-free, (800) 421-3481. TTY, (800) 877-8339.*

General email, ocr@ed.gov

Web, www2.ed.gov/ocr and Twitter, @EDcivilrights

Enforces laws prohibiting use of federal funds for education programs or activities that discriminate on the basis of race, color, sex, national origin, age, or disability; authorized to discontinue funding.

Education Dept., *Elementary and Secondary Education (OESE), Indian Education Programs, Lyndon Baines Johnson Bldg., 400 Maryland Ave. S.W., #3E205, 20202-6335; (202) 260-3774. Fax, (202) 260-7779. Tara Ramsey, Director (Acting), (202) 401-0767.*

General email, indian.education@ed.gov

Web, www2.ed.gov/about/offices/list/oese/oie

Aids local school districts with programs for Native American and Alaska Native students.

Education Dept., *Elementary and Secondary Education (OESE), Migrant Education, Lyndon Baines Johnson Bldg., 400 Maryland Ave. S.W., #3E317, LBJ, 20202-6135; (202) 260-1164. Fax, (202) 205-0089. Lisa Gillette, Director.*

Web, www2.ed.gov/programs/mep/index.html

Administers grant programs that provide academic and supportive services to the children of families who migrate to find work in the agricultural and fishing industries.

Education Dept., *Postsecondary Education (OPE), Higher Education Programs (HEP), Institutional Service, Lyndon Baines Johnson Bldg., 400 Maryland Ave. S.W., 2nd Floor, 20202; (202) 453-6914. Fax, (202) 502-7699. Vacant, Deputy Assistant Secretary, (202) 453-6808.*

General email, OPE_Institutional_Development@ed.gov

Web, www2.ed.gov/about/offices/list/ope/idues

Provides financial and administrative support for limited resource institutions serving minority and financially disadvantaged students. Administers programs authorized under the Higher Education Act of 1965 and its subsequent amendments. Title III programs include support for Historically Black Colleges and Universities, American Indian Tribally Controlled Colleges and Universities, and Minority Science and Engineering Improvement Program. Title V programs strengthen institutions serving Hispanic and other low-income students. Title VII supports the implementation and evaluation of and shares findings of innovative educational reform ideas.

Education Dept., *Postsecondary Education (OPE), Higher Education Programs (HEP), Institutional Service, Minority Science and Engineering Improvement Program, Lyndon Baines Johnson Bldg., 400 Maryland Ave. S.W., 4th Floor, 20202; (202) 453-7913. Bernadette Hence, Senior Program Manager.*

General email, OPE.MSEIP@ed.gov

Web, www2.ed.gov/programs/iduesmsi/index.html

Provides grants to predominantly minority institutions to effect long-range improvement in science and engineering education and to increase the flow of underrepresented ethnic minorities, particularly minority women, into science and engineering careers.

Education Dept., *White House Initiative on American Indian and Alaska Natives Education, Lyndon Baines Johnson Bldg., 400 Maryland Ave. S.W., #4W116, 20002; (202) 453-6600. Fax, (202) 453-5635. Ron Lessard, Executive Director (Acting), (202) 453-5509.*

Web, http://sites.ed.gov/whiaiane and
Twitter, @WhiteHouseAIAN

Supports activities that expand and improve educational opportunities for American Indians and Alaska Native students. Interests include reducing the student dropout rate, strengthening tribal colleges and universities, and helping students acquire industry-recognized credentials for job attainment and advancement. Supports teaching native languages and histories at all educational levels.

Education Dept., *White House Initiative on Asian Americans and Pacific Islanders,* 550 12th St. S.W., 10th Floor, 20202; (202) 245-6418. Fax, (202) 245-7166. Holly Ham, Executive Director; Debra Suarez, Senior Advisor.
General email, whitehouseaapi@ed.gov
Web, http://sites.ed.gov/aapi, Twitter, @whitehouseAAPI and Facebook, www.facebook.com/WhiteHouseAAPI

Works to increase Asian American and Pacific Islander participation in federal education programs. Supports institutions of higher education through two-year grants to improve academic programs, institutional management, and fiscal stability.

Education Dept., *White House Initiative on Educational Excellence for African Americans,* Lyndon Baines Johnson Bldg., 400 Maryland Ave. S.W., 20202; (202) 205-9853. Vacant, Executive Director; Monique S. Toussaint, Senior Advisor.
General email, WHIEEAA@ed.gov
Web, http://sites.ed.gov/whieeaa and Twitter, @WhiteHouseIEEAA

Promotes high-quality education for African Americans by improving access to learning opportunities for educators and administrators, supporting efforts to increase the number of African American teachers and administrators, enhancing investments in early care and education programs, reinforcing connections to rigorous K–12 courses and increasing access to critical supports, and helping to increase the number of African American students applying to, persisting in, and successfully completing college.

Education Dept., *White House Initiative on Educational Excellence for Hispanics,* Lyndon Baines Johnson Bldg., 400 Maryland Ave. S.W., #4W108, 20202-3601; (202) 401-1411. Fax, (202) 401-8377. Emmanuel Caudillo, Senior Advisor.
General email, whieeh@ed.gov
Web, http://sites.ed.gov/hispanic-initiative and Twitter, @HispanicEd

Promotes high-quality education for Hispanic communities and the participation of Hispanics in federal education programs. Disseminates information on educational resources. Promotes parental involvement, engagement of the business community, early learning programs, and enrollment in college. Works directly with communities nationwide in public-private partnerships.

Education Dept., *White House Initiative on Historically Black Colleges and Universities,* Lyndon Baines Johnson Bldg., 400 Maryland Ave. S.W., #7E306, 20202;

(202) 453-5634. Fax, (202) 453-5632. Johnathan Holifield, Executive Director; Arthur McMahan, Senior Associate Director, (202) 453-7750.
General email, oswhi-hbcu@ed.gov
Web, http://sites.ed.gov/whhbcu

Seeks to expand the participation of the black college community in the programs of the federal government and to engage the private sector to help achieve this objective. Hosts annual conference. Provides information about federal contracts, grants, scholarships, fellowships, and other resources available to historically black colleges and universities.

U.S. Commission on Civil Rights, *Civil Rights Evaluation,* 1331 Pennsylvania Ave. N.W., #1150, 20425; (202) 376-7700. Fax, (202) 376-7754. Katherine Culliton-Gonzalez, Director. Complaints Unit hotline, (202) 376-8513. TTY, (800) 877-8339.
Web, www.usccr.gov

Researches federal policy on education, including desegregation. Library open to the public.

►CONGRESS

For a listing of relevant congressional committees and subcommittees, please see page 174 or the Appendix.

►NONGOVERNMENTAL

American Assn. of University Women (AAUW), 1310 L St. N.W., #1000, 20005; (202) 785-7700. Fax, (202) 872-1425. Kimberly (Kim) Churches, Chief Executive Officer, ext. 7767. Toll-free, (800) 326-2289. TTY, (202) 785-7777.
General email, connect@aauw.org
Web, www.aauw.org, Twitter, @aauw and Facebook, www.facebook.com/AAUW.National

Membership: graduates of accredited colleges, universities, and recognized foreign institutions. Interests include equity for women and girls in education, the workplace, health care, and the family.

American Indian Higher Education Consortium, 121 Oronoco St., Alexandria, VA 22314; (703) 838-0400. Fax, (703) 838-0388. Carrie L. Billy, President.
General email, info@aihec.org
Web, http://aihec.org, Twitter, @aihec and Facebook, www.facebook.com/American-Indian-Higher-Education-Consortium-206472546110004/timeline

Membership: tribal colleges and universities (TCUs). Objectives include increased financial support for TCUs, equitable participation in the land-grant system, expanded technology programs in Indian Country, and development of an accrediting body for postsecondary institutions that serve American Indians.

Assn. of American Colleges and Universities (AACU), 1818 R St. N.W., 20009; (202) 387-3760. Fax, (202) 265-9532. Lynn Pasquerella, President.

General email, information@aacu.org

Web, www.aacu.org, Twitter, @aacu and Facebook, www
.facebook.com/Association-of-American-Colleges-and-
Universities-48308128458

Serves as clearinghouse for information on women professionals in higher education. Interests include women's
studies, women's centers, and women's leadership and professional development.

Assn. of Public and Land-Grant Universities, *Office for
Access and Success: The Advancement of Public Black
Colleges and Hispanic Serving Institutions, 1307 New
York Ave. N.W., #400, 20005-4722; (202) 478-6040.
Fax, (202) 478-6046. Peter McPherson, President.*
General email, info@aplu.org

Web, www.aplu.org and Twitter, @APLU_News

Seeks to improve equity, access, and successful outcomes at all public and land-grant universities with a special
focus on underserved students and minority-serving institutions. Conducts research, provides advocacy, implements
programs, and provides capacity building for such institutions; acts as a liaison between these institutions, the federal
government, and private associations. Monitors legislation
and regulations.

Clare Booth Luce Policy Institute, *112 Elden St., Suite P,
Herndon, VA 20170; (703) 318-0730. Fax, (703) 318-8867.
Michelle Easton, President. Toll-free, (888) 891-4288.*
General email, info@cblpi.org

Web, http://cblpi.org and Twitter, @CBLPI

Seeks to engage young women through student programs promoting conservative values and leadership.
Offers mentoring, internship, and networking opportunities for young women.

Council for Opportunity in Education, *1025 Vermont
Ave. N.W., #900, 20005-3516; (202) 347-7430.
Fax, (202) 347-0786. Maureen Hoyler, President, ext. 321.*
Web, www.coenet.us and Twitter, @COETalk

Membership: more than 1,000 colleges and agencies.
Works in conjunction with colleges and agencies that host
the federally funded TRIO programs, designed to help low-
income, first-generation immigrants, students with disabilities, and veterans enroll in and graduate from college.

Hispanic Assn. of Colleges and Universities,
*Washington Office, Government Affairs, 1 Dupont Circle
N.W., #430, 20036; (202) 833-8361. (202) 467-0893.
Fax, (202) 261-5082. Antonio R. Flores, President.*
General email, dcgr@hacu.net

Web, www.hacu.net

Membership: Hispanic-serving institutions (HSIs) and
other higher education institutions committed to improving the quality of schools for Hispanics in the United States,
Puerto Rico, Latin America, and Spain. Focuses on increased
federal funding for HSIs; partnerships with government
agencies and industry; faculty development and research;
technological assistance; and financial aid and internships
for Hispanic students. (Headquarters in San Antonio, Tex.)

Institute for Responsible Citizenship, *1227 25th St.
N.W., 6th Floor, 20037; (202) 660-2501. William A. Keyes,
President.*
Web, www.theinstitute.net and Facebook, www.facebook
.com/responsiblecitizenship

Offers grants, internships, and leadership courses
for African American men scholars. Academic areas for
internships include art, business, finance, philanthropy,
education, government, health care, science, technology,
law, public relations, and religion.

League of United Latin American Citizens, *1133 19th St.
N.W., #1000, 20036; (202) 833-6130. Fax, (202) 833-6135.
Sidney Benavides, Chief Executive Officer, Ext. 108.*
General email, info@lulac.org

Web, www.lulac.org

Seeks to increase the number of minorities, especially
Hispanics, attending postsecondary schools; supports legislation to increase educational opportunities for Hispanics and other minorities; provides scholarship funds and
educational and career counseling.

NAACP Legal Defense and Educational Fund, Inc.,
*Washington Office, 700 14th St., #600, 20005;
(202) 682-1300. Todd A. Cox, Director of Policy.*
Web, www.naacpldf.org and Twitter, @NAACP_LDF

Civil rights litigation group that provides legal information about civil rights and advice on educational discrimination against women and minorities; monitors
federal enforcement of civil rights laws. Not affiliated with
the NAACP. (Headquarters in New York.)

National Alliance of Black School Educators, *310
Pennsylvania Ave. S.E., 20003; (202) 608-6310.
Fax, (202) 608-6319. Marietta English, President,
(410) 358-6600. Toll-free, (800) 221-2654.*
General email, info@nabse.org

Web, www.nabse.org

Seeks to increase the academic achievement of all children, in particular those of African American descent, by
developing and recommending educational policy. Provides professional development, networking, advocacy,
and research and development opportunities for educators and school administrators, including workshops and
conferences. Disseminates new instructional and learning
strategies.

**National Assn. for Equal Opportunity in Higher
Education (NAFEO),** *110 Maryland Ave. N.E., 20002;
(202) 552-3300. Fax, (202) 552-3330. Lezli Baskerville,
President.*
Web, www.nafeonation.org and Twitter, @_NAFEO

Membership: historically and predominantly black colleges and universities, including public, private, land-grant,
two-year, four-year, graduate, and professional schools.
Represents and acts as advocate on behalf of its member
institutions and the students, faculty, and alumni they serve.
Operates a national research and resource center on blacks
in higher education.

National Assn. for the Advancement of Colored People (NAACP), *Washington Bureau, 1156 15th St. N.W., #915, 20005; (202) 463-2940. Fax, (202) 463-2953. Derrick Johnson, President.*
General email, washingtonbureau@naacpnet.org

Web, www.naacp.org and Twitter, @NAACP

Membership: persons interested in civil rights for all minorities. Works for equal opportunity for minorities in all areas, including education; seeks to ensure a high-quality desegregated education for all through litigation and legislation. (Headquarters in Baltimore, Md.)

National Assn. of Colored Women's and Youth Clubs Inc. (NACWYC), *1601 R St. N.W., 20009-6420; (202) 667-4080. Sharon R. Bridgeforth, President.*
General email, ematthews@nacwcya.org

Web, www.nacwc.org

Seeks to promote education, protect and enforce civil rights, raise the standard of family living, promote interracial understanding, and enhance leadership development. Awards scholarships; conducts programs in education, social service, and philanthropy.

National Hispanic Foundation for the Arts (NHFA), *Washington Square, 1050 Connecticut Ave. N.W., 10th Floor, #500, 20036; (202) 293-8330. Fax, (202) 772-3101. Felix Sanchez, Chair.*
General email, info@hispanicarts.org

Web, www.hispanicarts.org and Twitter, @felix_sanchez

Strives to increase the presence of Hispanics in the media, telecommunications, entertainment industries, and performing arts, and to increase programming for the U.S. Latino community. Provides scholarships for Hispanic students to pursue graduate study in the arts.

National Indian Education Assn. (NIEA), *1514 P St. N.W., Suite B, 20005; (202) 544-7290. Fax, (202) 544-7293. Diana Cournoyer, Executive Director (Acting).*
General email, niea@niea.org

Web, www.niea.org, Twitter, @WereNIEA and Facebook, www.facebook.com/NIEAFanPage

Represents American Indian, Alaska Native, and Native Hawaiian educators and students. Seeks to improve educational opportunities and resources for those groups nationwide while preserving their traditional cultures and values. Monitors legislation and regulations.

National Society of Black Engineers, *205 Daingerfield Rd., Alexandria, VA 22314; (703) 549-2207. Fax, (703) 683-5312. Karl Reid, Executive Director.*
General email, info@nsbe.org

Web, www.nsbe.org and Twitter, @NSBE

Membership: Black engineers and college students studying engineering. Offers academic excellence programs, scholarships, leadership training, and professional and career development opportunities. Activities include tutorial programs, group study sessions, high school/junior high outreach programs, technical seminars and workshops, career fairs, and an annual convention.

National Women's Law Center, *11 Dupont Circle N.W., #800, 20036; (202) 588-5180. Fax, (202) 588-5185. Fatima Gross Graves, President.*
General email, info@nwlc.org

Web, www.nwlc.org, Twitter, @nwlc and Facebook, www.facebook.com/nwlc

Works to protect and advance the rights of women and girls at work, in school, and beyond. Maintains programs that focus on enforcing Title IX's provisions for equal treatment in education and narrowing the gender gap in athletics and the technology-oriented workplace. Other interests include equal pay and benefits, sexual harassment laws, the right to family leave, child care and early learning, poverty and income support, and the preservation of diversity in the workplace.

Operation Understanding DC, *3000 Connecticut Ave. N.W., #335, 20008; (202) 234-6832. Fax, (202) 234-6669. Yolanda Savage-Narva, Executive Director.*
General email, info@oudc.org

Web, www.oudc.org and Twitter, @OU_DC

African American and Jewish youth education program promoting leadership and antidiscrimination.

UnidosUS, *1126 16th St. N.W., #600, 20036-4845; (202) 785-1670. Fax, (202) 776-1792. Janet Murguía, President.*
General email, info@unidos.org

Web, www.unidosus.org, Twitter, @WeAreUnidosUS and Facebook, www.facebook.com/Weareunidosus

Provides research, policy analysis, and advocacy on educational status and needs of Hispanics; promotes education reform benefiting Hispanics; develops and tests community-based models for helping Hispanic students succeed in school. Interests include counseling, testing, and bilingual, vocational, preschool through postsecondary, and migrant education. (Formerly the National Council of La Raza.)

United Negro College Fund (UNCF), *1805 7th St. N.W., 20001 (mailing address: P.O. Box 10444, Fairfax, VA 22031-0444); (202) 810-0200. Fax, (202) 810-0224. Michael L. Lomax, President. Toll-free, (800) 331-2244.*
Web, www.uncf.org and Twitter, @UNCF

Membership: private colleges and universities with historically black enrollment. Raises money for member institutions; monitors legislation and regulations.

Younger Women's Task Force, *1310 L St. N.W., #1000, 20005; (202) 785-7700. Fax, (202) 872-1425. Kimberly Churches, Chief Executive Officer. Toll-free, (800) 326-2289. TTY, (202) 785-7777.*
General email, ywtf@aauw.org

Web, www.aauw.org/membership/ywtf and Twitter, @ywtf

Grassroots organization that encourages young women to engage in political activism on issues directly affecting them. Provides leadership training and a local and national network for peer mentoring. (Sponsored by the American Assn. of University Women.)

SPECIAL TOPICS IN EDUCATION

Bilingual and Multicultural

▶AGENCIES

Bureau of Educational and Cultural Affairs (ECA) *(State Dept.), English Language Programs, 2200 C St. N.W., #4B16, 20520; (202) 632-9272. Joseph Bookbinder, Director, (202) 632-9281.*
General email, americanenglish@state.gov
Web, http://eca.state.gov/about-bureau-0/organizational-structure/office-english-language-programs
https://americanenglish.state.gov

Promotes the learning and teaching of American English around the world in order to foster mutual understanding between the people of other countries and the people of the United States.

Education Dept., *English Language Acquisition (OELA), Lyndon Baines Johnson Bldg., 400 Maryland Ave. S.W., #5E106, 20202-6510; (202) 401-1461. Fax, (202) 260-1292. José A. Viana, Assistant Deputy Secretary.*
Web, www2.ed.gov/about/offices/list/oela

Provides grants for the professional development of teachers of English learners and administers the Native American/Alaska-Native Children in School Program and National Professional Development Discretionary Grant Programs.

Education Dept., *Postsecondary Education (OPE), Higher Education Programs (HEP), International and Foreign Language Education, Lyndon Baines Johnson Bldg., 400 Maryland Ave. S.W., #3E200, 20202; (202) 453-6950. Fax, (202) 453-5780. Cheryl Gibbs, Deputy Assistant Secretary (Acting).*
Web, www2.ed.gov/about/offices/list/ope/iegps and Twitter, @GoGlobalED

Advises the Assistant Secretary for Postsecondary Education on matters affecting postsecondary, international, and foreign language education. Responsible for encouraging and promoting the study of foreign languages and cultures of other countries at the elementary, secondary, and postsecondary levels in the United States. Administers programs that increase expertise in foreign languages and area or international studies, and coordinates with related international and foreign language education programs of other federal agencies.

▶NONGOVERNMENTAL

National Assn. for Bilingual Education, *c/o Ana G. Mendez University System, 11006 Veirs Mills Rd., #L-1, Wheaton, MD 20902; (240) 450-3700. Fax, (240) 450-3799. Santiago V. Wood, National Executive Director.*
General email, nabe@nabe.org
Web, www.nabe.org and Twitter, @NABEorg

Membership: educators, policymakers, paraprofessionals, parents, personnel, students, and researchers.

Works to strengthen educational programs for non-English-speaking students and to promote foreign language education among American students. Conducts annual conference and workshops; publishes research.

National Clearinghouse for English Language Acquisition (NCELA), *Language Instruction Educational Programs, 4340 East-West Hwy., #1100, Bethesda, MD 20814; (301) 828-1515. Fax, (301) 828-1506. Patricia Garcia-Arena, Project Director.*
General email, askncela@manhattanstrategy.com
Web, https://ncela.ed.gov

Collects, analyzes, and disseminates information relating to the effective education of linguistically and culturally diverse learners in the United States. Supports the Office of English Language Acquisition, Language Enhancement, and Academic Achievement for Limited English Proficient Students (OELA) in its mission to respond to Title III educational needs, and implement No Child Left Behind (NCLB) as it applies to English language learners. Supports networking among state-level administrators of Title III programs. Serves other stakeholders involved in English learner education, including teachers and other practitioners, parents, university faculty, administrators and federal policymakers. Authorized under Title III of the No Child Left Behind Act of 2001 (NCLB). Since October 2018, NCELA has been operated by Manhattan Strategy Group, under contract from the Education Dept.

National Foreign Language Center *(University of Maryland), 5600 Rivertech Ct., Suite K, Riverdale, MD 20737 (mailing address: P.O. Box 93, Severn Bldg. 810, 5245 Greenbelt Rd., College Park, MD 20742); (301) 405-9828. Fax, (301) 405-9829. Rebecca Rurbin Damari, Director of Research.*
General email, inquiries@nflc.org
Web, www.nflc.umd.edu and Twitter, @NFLC_UMD

Research and policy organization that develops new strategies for strengthening foreign language competence in the United States. Conducts research on national language needs and assists policymakers in identifying priorities, allocating resources, and designing programs. Interests include the role of foreign language in higher education, national competence in critical languages, ethnic language maintenance, and K–12 and postsecondary language programs.

National Research Council (NRC), *Testing and Assessment Board, Keck Center, 500 5th St. N.W., 11th Floor, 20001; (202) 334-3776. Fax, (202) 334-2210. Colleen Hartman, Director; James H. Crocker, Vice-Chair.*
General email, bota1@nas.edu
Web, http://sites.nationalacademies.org/dbasse/bota

Seeks to ensure fairness and accuracy in the testing of students with disabilities and English learners.

TESOL International Assn., *1925 Ballenger Ave., #550, Alexandria, VA 22314-6820; (703) 836-0774. Fax, (703) 836-7864. Christopher Powers, Executive Director, ext. 505. Information, (888) 891-0041.*

General email, info@tesol.org

Web, www.tesol.org and *Twitter, @TESOL_Assn*

Provides professional development programs and career services for teachers of English to speakers of other languages. Sponsors professional development programs and provides career management services.

U.S. English Inc., *5335 Wisconsin Ave. N.W., #930, 20015; (202) 833-0100. Fax, (202) 833-0108. Mauro E. Mujica, Chair. Toll-free, (800) 787-8216.*

General email, info@usenglish.org

Web, www.usenglish.org and *Twitter, @usenglishinc*

Advocates English as the official language of federal and state governments. Affiliate U.S. English Foundation promotes English language education for immigrants.

World Learning, *Global Development and Exchange Programs, 1015 15th St. N.W., 7th Floor, 20005-2065; (202) 408-5420. Fax, (202) 408-5397. Carol Jenkins, President, (202) 464-6643. Toll-free, (800) 858-0292. TTY, (202) 408-5420, ext. 711.*

General email, development@worldlearning.org

Web, www.worldlearning.org and *Twitter, @WorldLearning*

Provides training for English language teachers and other education professionals. Increases access to and the quality of basic education. Administered by World Learning's Division of International Development and Exchange Programs. Administers field-based study abroad programs, which offer semester and summer programs for high school, college, and graduate students.

Citizenship Education

▶**NONGOVERNMENTAL**

American Press Institute (API), *4401 N. Fairfax Dr., #300, Arlington, VA 22203; (571) 366-1200. Thomas (Tom) Rosenstiel, Executive Director, (571) 366-1035.*

General email, hello@pressinstitute.org

Web, www.americanpressinstitute.org and *Twitter, @AmPress*

Supports student programs that focus on newspaper readership and an appreciation of the First Amendment as ways of developing engaged and literate citizens.

Close Up Foundation, *1330 Braddock Pl., #400, Alexandria, VA 22314-1952; (703) 706-3300. Fax, (703) 706-0001. Timothy S. Davis, President. Toll-free, (800) 256-7387.*

General email, info@closeup.org

Web, https://closeup.org and *Twitter, @CloseUp_DC*

Sponsors weeklong programs on American government in Washington, D.C., for middle and high school students.

Horatio Alger Assn. of Distinguished Americans, *99 Canal Center Plaza, #320, Alexandria, VA 22314;*

(703) 684-9444. Fax, (703) 684-9445. Terrence J. Giroux, Executive Director.

General email, association@horatioalger.org

Web, www.horatioalger.org, Twitter, @HoratioAlgerUS and *Facebook, www.facebook.com/HoratioAlgerUS*

Educates young people about the economic and personal opportunities available in the American free enterprise system. Conducts seminars on careers in public and community service; operates internship program. Presents the Horatio Alger Youth Award to outstanding high school students and the Horatio Alger Award to professionals who have overcome adversity to achieve success in their respective fields. Awards college scholarships to individuals who have overcome adversity.

League of Women Voters Education Fund (LWV), *1730 M St. N.W., #1000, 20036-4508; (202) 429-1965. Fax, (202) 429-0854. Virginia Kase, Chief Executive Officer.*

General email, lwv@lwv.org

Web, www.lwv.org/education-fund

Education and research organization established by the League of Women Voters of the United States. Promotes citizen knowledge of and involvement in representative government; conducts citizen education on current public policy issues; seeks to increase voter registration and turnout; sponsors candidate forums and debates.

National 4-H Council, *7100 Connecticut Ave., Chevy Chase, MD 20815-4999; (301) 961-2800. Fax, (202) 720-8987. J. Scott Angle, Director, (202) 720-4423. Press, (202) 702-4651.*

Web, www.4-h.org, Twitter, @4H and *Facebook, www.facebook.com/4-h*

4-H membership: young people across America learning leadership, citizenship, life skills, science, healthy living, and food security. National 4-H Council strengthens and complements the 4-H Youth Development Program of the Agricultural Dept.'s cooperative extension system of state land-grant universities. Interests include 4-H afterschool, healthy lifestyle, science engineering and technology, food security, and citizenship in governance. In the United States, 4-H programs are implemented by 109 land-grant universities and more than 3,000 cooperative extension offices. Outside the United States, 4-H programs operate through independent, country-led organizations in more than 50 countries.

Washington Workshops Foundation, *2101 L St., #400, 20037; (202) 965-3434. Fax, (202) 965-1018. Tom Crossan, President. Information, (800) 368-5688.*

General email, info@workshops.org

Web, www.workshops.org and *Twitter, @WorkshopsWire*

Educational foundation that provides introductory seminars on American government and politics to junior and senior high school students, including the congressional seminars for high school students.

Continuing, Vocational, and Adult Education

►AGENCIES

Education Dept., *Career, Technical, and Adult Education (OCTAE),* 550 12th St. S.W., 11th Floor, 20202-7100 (mailing address: 400 Maryland Ave. S.W., P-OCTAE, Washington, DC 20202-7100); (202) 245-7700. Fax, (202) 245-7838. Scott Stump, Assistant Secretary.
General email, octae@ed.gov

Web, www2.ed.gov/about/offices/list/ovae

Administers programs pertaining to adult education and literacy, career and technical education, and community colleges.

Education Dept., *Career, Technical, and Adult Education (OCTAE), Academic and Technical Education,* 550 12th St. S.W., #11059, 20202-7100 (mailing address: 400 Maryland Ave. S.W., P-OCTAE, DATE, Washington, DC 20202-7100); (202) 245-7700. Fax, (202) 245-7838. Sharon Miller, Director, (202) 245-7846.
General email, octae@ed.gov

Web, www2.ed.gov/about/offices/list/ovae/pi/cte

Establishes national initiatives that help states implement career and technical education programs. Administers state formula and discretionary grant programs under the Carl D. Perkins Career and Technical Education Act.

Education Dept., *Career, Technical, and Adult Education (OCTAE), Adult Education and Literacy,* 550 12th St. S.W., 11th Floor, 20202-7100 (mailing address: 400 Maryland Ave. S.W., P-OCTAE, DAEL, Washington, DC 20202); (202) 245-7700. Fax, (202) 245-7838. Cheryl L. Keenan, Director, (202) 245-7810.
General email, octae@ed.gov

Web, www2.ed.gov/about/offices/list/ovae/pi/AdultEd

Administers adult education programs for reading, writing, math, English language proficiency, and problem solving. Provides funding to state and local education agencies to implement and improve adult education and literacy activities.

►NONGOVERNMENTAL

Accrediting Council for Continuing Education and Training (ACCET), 1722 N St. N.W., 20036; (202) 955-1113. Fax, (202) 955-1118. William V. Larkin, Executive Director, ext. 105.
General email, info@accet.org

Web, www.accet.org

Seeks to identify, evaluate, and enhance the delivery of continuing education and training programs. Offers professional development through workshops, conferences, and Webinars.

Assn. for Career and Technical Education (ACTE), 1410 King St., Alexandria, VA 22314; (703) 683-3111.

Fax, (703) 683-7424. LeAnn Wilson, Executive Director. Information, (800) 826-9972.
General email, acte@acteonline.org

Web, www.acteonline.org and Twitter, @actecareertech

Membership: teachers, students, supervisors, administrators, and others working or interested in career and technical education (middle school through postgraduate). Interests include the impact of high school graduation requirements on career and technical education; private sector initiatives; and the improvement of the quality and image of career and technical education. Offers an annual convention and other professional development opportunities. Monitors legislation and regulations.

Career Education Colleges and Universities (CECU), 1530 Wilson Blvd., #1050, Arlington, VA 22209; (571) 970-3941. Fax, (571) 970-6753. Steve Gunderson, President, (571) 970-3954.
Web, www.career.org and Twitter, @CECUed

Acts as an information clearinghouse on trade and technical schools. (Formerly Career College Assn.)

Covenant House, *Washington Office,* 2001 Mississippi Ave. S.E., 20020; (202) 610-9600. Madye Henson, President.
Web, http://covenanthousedc.org and
Twitter, @CovenantHouseDC

Protects young people suffering from homelessness, abuse, and neglect. Provides services including GED and adult education and job readiness. (Affiliated with Covenant House International.)

National Assn. of State Directors of Career Technical Education Consortium, 8484 Georgia Ave., #620, Silver Spring, MD 20910; (301) 588-9630. Fax, (301) 576-7115. Kimberly A. Green, Executive Director, (301) 588-9630 ext. 12; Austin Estes, Senior Policy Associate.
General email, info@careertech.org

Web, www.careertech.org

Membership: state career education agency heads, senior staff, and business, labor, and other education officials. Advocates state and national policy to strengthen career technical education and workforce development. Monitors legislation and regulations.

SkillsUSA, 14001 SkillsUSA Way, Leesburg, VA 20176-5494; (703) 777-8810. Fax, (703) 777-8999. Timothy W. Lawrence, Executive Director, ext. 601. Educational Resources, (800) 321-8422. Toll-free, (844) 875-4557.
General email, anyinfo@skillsusa.org

Web, www.skillsusa.org and Twitter, @SkillsUSA

Membership: students, teachers, and administrators of trade, industrial, technical, and health occupations programs at public high schools, vocational schools, and two-year and four-year colleges. Promotes strong work skills, workplace ethics, understanding of free enterprise, and lifelong education. (Formerly Vocational Industrial Clubs of America.)

University Professional & Continuing Education Assn. (UPCEA), 1 Dupont Circle N.W., #615, 20036; (202) 659-3130. Fax, (202) 785-0374. Robert J. Hansen, Chief Executive Officer.

General email, info@upcea.edu

Web, www.upcea.edu and *Twitter, @UPCEA*

Membership: higher education institutions and non-profit organizations involved in postsecondary continuing education. Prepares statistical analyses and produces data reports for members; recognizes accomplishments in the field. Monitors legislation and regulations.

Literacy, Basic Skills

▶AGENCIES

AmeriCorps *(Corp. for National and Community Service), Volunteers in Service to America (VISTA),* 250 E St. S.W., 20024-3208; (202) 606-5000. Fax, (202) 565-2789. Eileen Conoboy, Director (Acting). TTY, (800) 833-3722. Volunteer recruiting information, (800) 942-2677.

General email, questions@americorps.gov

Web, www.americorps.gov/programs/americorps/ americorps-vista, Twitter, @AmeriCorpsVISTA and *Facebook, www.facebook.com/AmeriCorpsVISTA*

Assigns volunteers to local and state education departments, to public agencies, and to private nonprofit organizations that have literacy programs. Other activities include tutor recruitment and training and the organization and expansion of local literacy councils, workplace literacy programs, and intergenerational literacy programs.

Education Dept., *Career, Technical, and Adult Education (OCTAE), Adult Education and Literacy,* 550 12th St. S.W., 11th Floor, 20202-7100 (mailing address: 400 Maryland Ave. S.W., P-OCTAE, DAEL, Washington, DC 20202); (202) 245-7700. Fax, (202) 245-7838. Cheryl L. Keenan, Director, (202) 245-7810.

General email, octae@ed.gov

Web, www2.ed.gov/about/offices/list/ovae/pi/AdultEd

Provides state and local education agencies and the general public with information on establishing, expanding, improving, and operating adult education and literacy programs. Emphasizes basic and life skills attainment, English literacy, and high school completion. Awards grants to state education agencies for adult education and literacy programs, including workplace and family literacy.

▶CONGRESS

For a listing of relevant congressional committees and subcommittees, please see page 174 or the Appendix.

Library of Congress, *Center for the Book,* James Madison Memorial Bldg., 101 Independence Ave. S.E., #LM 650, 20540; (202) 707-5221. Fax, (202) 707-0269. John Van Oudenaren, Director.

General email, cfbook@loc.gov

Web, www.read.gov/cfb

Promotes family and adult literacy; encourages the study of books and stimulates public interest in books, reading, and libraries; sponsors publication of a directory describing national organizations that administer literacy programs. Affiliated state centers sponsor projects and hold events that call attention to the importance of literacy.

Library of Congress, *Young Readers Center,* Thomas Jefferson Bldg., 10 1st St. S.E., #LJ G29, 20540; (202) 707-1950. Fax, (202) 707-0269. Vacant, Head.

General email, yrc@loc.gov

Web, www.read.gov/yrc

Promotes books, reading, literacy, libraries, and the scholarly study of books through affiliates and promotional programs. Places special emphasis on young readers through reading and writing contests.

▶NONGOVERNMENTAL

AFL-CIO Working for America Institute *(WAI),* 815 16th St. N.W., 20006; (202) 508-3717. Fax, (202) 508-3719. Brad Markell, Executive Director. Main Switchboard, (202) 637-5000. Press, (202) 637-5018.

General email, info@workingforamerica.org

Web, www.workingforamerica.org

Provides labor unions, employers, education agencies, and community groups with technical assistance for workplace education programs focusing on adult literacy, basic skills, and job training. Interests include new technologies and workplace innovations.

Assn. for Talent Development (ATD), 1640 King St., 3rd Floor, Alexandria, VA 22314; (703) 683-8100. Fax, (703) 683-1523. Tony Bingham, Chief Executive Officer. Toll-free, (800) 628-2783.

General email, customercare@astd.org

Web, www.astd.org, Twitter, @atd and *Facebook, www .facebook.com/ATD*

Membership: trainers and human resource development specialists. Publishes information on workplace literacy.

Center for Applied Linguistics, 4646 40th St. N.W., #200, 20016-1859; (202) 362-0700. Fax, (202) 362-3740. Joel Gómez, President.

General email, info@cal.org

Web, www.cal.org

Research and technical assistance organization that serves as a clearinghouse on application of linguistics to practical language problems. Interests include English as a second language (ESL), teacher training and material development, language education, language proficiency test development, bilingual education, and sociolinguistics.

First Book, 1319 F St. N.W., #1000, 20004-1155; (202) 393-1222. Fax, (202) 628-1258. Kyle Zimmer, President. Toll-free, (866) 732-3669.

General email, staff@firstbook.org

Web, www.firstbook.org, Twitter, @FirstBook and *Facebook, www.facebook.com/FirstBook*

Donates and sells books to programs serving children of low-income families. Organizes fund-raisers to support and promote literacy programs.

General Federation of Women's Clubs, *1734 N St. N.W., 20036-2990; (202) 347-3168. Fax, (202) 835-0246. Patricia Budka, Chief of Operations. Toll-free, (800) 443-4392. General email, gfwc@gfwc.org*

Web, www.gfwc.org and Twitter, @GFWCHQ

Nondenominational, nonpartisan international organization of women volunteers. Develops literacy projects in response to community needs; sponsors tutoring.

National Coalition for Literacy, *P.O. Box 2932, 20013-2932; (202) 363-3684. Deborah Kennedy, President. General email, ncl@ncladvocacy.org*

Web, www.national-coalition-literacy.org and Twitter, @NCLAdvocacy

Members: national organizations concerned with adult education. Promotes adult education, family literacy, and English language acquisition in the United States.

Reading Is Fundamental, *750 1st St. N.E., #920, 20002; (202) 536-3400. Fax, (202) 536-3518. Alicia Levi, President. Information, 877-RIF-READ. Press, (202) 536-3458. General email, contactus@rif.org*

Web, www.rif.org and Twitter, @RIFWEB

Conducts programs and workshops to motivate young people to read. Provides young people in low-income neighborhoods with free books and parents with services to encourage reading at home.

Science and Mathematics Education

▶**AGENCIES**

Education Dept., *Postsecondary Education (OPE), Higher Education Programs (HEP), Institutional Service, Minority Science and Engineering Improvement Program, Lyndon Baines Johnson Bldg., 400 Maryland Ave. S.W., 4th Floor, 20202; (202) 453-7913. Bernadette Hence, Senior Program Manager. General email, OPE.MSEIP@ed.gov*

Web, www2.ed.gov/programs/iduesmsi/index.html

Provides grants to predominantly minority institutions to effect long-range improvement in science and engineering education and to increase the flow of underrepresented ethnic minorities, particularly minority women, into science and engineering careers.

National Aeronautics and Space Administration (NASA), *Education, 300 E St. S.W., 4th Floor, 20546; (202) 358-0103. Fax, (202) 358-3048. Mike Kincaid, Associate Administrator. General email, education@nasa.gov*

Web, http://nasa.gov/offices/education/about and Twitter, @NASAedu

Coordinates NASA's education programs and activities to meet national educational needs and ensure a sufficient talent pool to preserve U.S. leadership in aeronautical technology and space science.

National Oceanic and Atmospheric Administration (NOAA) *(Commerce Dept.), National Sea Grant College Program, 1315 East-West Hwy., SSMC-3, 11th Floor, Silver Spring, MD 20910; (301) 734-1066. Fax, (301) 713-0799. Jonathan Pennock, Director, (301) 734-1089. General email, SGweb@noaa.gov*

Web, www.seagrant.noaa.gov and Twitter, @SeaGrant

Provides grants, primarily to colleges and universities, for marine resource development; sponsors undergraduate and graduate education and the training of technicians at the college level.

National Science Foundation (NSF), *Education and Human Resources Directorate, 2415 Eisenhower Ave., Room C11000, Alexandria, VA 22314; (703) 292-8600. Fax, (703) 292-9179. Karen Marrongelle, Assistant Director.*

Web, www.nsf.gov/dir/index.jsp?org=ehr

Develops and supports programs to strengthen science and mathematics (STEM) education.

National Science Foundation (NSF), *Human Resource Development Division, 2415 Eisenhower Ave., Room E11400, Alexandria, VA 22134; (703) 292-8640. Fax, (703) 292-9019. Jermelina Tupas, Director (Acting). Web, www.nsf.gov/div/index.jsp?div=hrd*

Supports and encourages participation in scientific and engineering (STEM) education and research by women, minorities, and people with disabilities. Awards grants and scholarships.

National Science Foundation (NSF), *National Center for Science and Engineering Statistics, 2415 Eisenhower Ave., Room 1400, Alexandria, VA 22134; (703) 292-8780. Fax, (703) 292-9092. Emilda B. Rivers, Director. Web, www.nsf.gov/statistics*

Supports education and training of researchers in the use of large-scale nationally representative data sets.

National Science Foundation (NSF), *Undergraduate Education Division, 2415 Eisenhower Ave., Room W11100, Alexandria, VA 22134; (703) 292-8670. Fax, (703) 292-9015. Robin Wright, Director, (703) 292-8637. Web, www.nsf.gov/div/index.jsp?div=DUE*

Promotes education in science, technology, engineering, and mathematics (STEM) at two-year and four-year colleges and universities.

Office of Science and Technology Policy (OSTP) *(Executive Office of the President), Science, Eisenhower Executive Office Bldg., 1650 Pennsylvania Ave. N.W., 20504; (202) 456-4444. Fax, (202) 456-6027. Lloyd Whitman, Assistant Director. General email, info@ostp.gov*

Web, www.ostp.gov

Evaluates the effectiveness of science education programs, which include environment, life sciences, physical sciences and engineering, and social, behavioral, and educational sciences.

►NONGOVERNMENTAL

American Assn. for the Advancement of Science (AAAS), Education and Human Resources Programs, *1200 New York Ave. N.W., 6th Floor, 20005; (202) 326-6670 (voice and TTY accessible). Fax, (202) 371-9849.*
Shirley M. Malcom, Director, (202) 326-6720.
General email, ehr@aaas.org

Web, www.aaas.org/program/education-and-human-resources

Membership: scientists, scientific organizations, students, and professionals interested in science, engineering mathematics, and technology education. Focuses on expanding science education opportunities for women, minorities, and people with disabilities.

American Assn. of Physics Teachers, *1 Physics Ellipse, 5th Floor, College Park, MD 20740-3845; (301) 209-3311. Fax, (301) 209-0845. Beth A. Cunningham, Executive Officer.*
General email, eo@aapt.org

Web, www.aapt.org, Twitter, @AAPTHQ and Facebook, www.facebook.com/AAPTHQ

Membership: physics teachers and others interested in physics education. Seeks to advance the institutional and cultural role of physics education. Sponsors seminars and conferences; provides educational information and materials. (Affiliated with the American Institute of Physics.)

American Society for Engineering Education, *1818 N St. N.W., #600, 20036-2479; (202) 331-3500. Fax, (202) 265-8504. Norman L. Fortenberry, Executive Director, (202) 331-3545. Press, (202) 331-5767.*
Web, www.asee.org and Twitter, @ASEE_DC

Membership: engineering faculty and administrators, professional engineers, government agencies, and engineering colleges, corporations, and professional societies. Conducts research, conferences, and workshops on engineering education. Monitors legislation and regulations.

Assn. for Women in Science, *1667 K St., N.W., #800, 20006; (202) 588-8175. Karene Richards, Executive Director (Acting).*
General email, awis@awis.org

Web, www.awis.org and Twitter, @AWISNational

Promotes equal opportunity for women in scientific professions; provides career and funding information. Provides educational scholarships for women in science. Interests include international development.

Assn. of Science-Technology Centers, *818 Connecticut Ave. N.W., 7th Floor, 20006-2734; (202) 783-7200. Fax, (202) 783-7207. Cristin Dorgelo, President, (202) 783-7200, ext. 115.*
General email, info@astc.org

Web, www.astc.org and Twitter, @ScienceCenters

Membership: more than 600 science centers, science museums, and similar operations in forty-seven countries. Strives to enhance the ability of its members to engage visitors in science activities and explorations of scientific phenomena. Sponsors conferences and informational exchanges on interactive exhibits, hands-on science experiences, and educational programs for children, families, teachers, and older audiences; publishes journal; compiles statistics; provides technical assistance for museums; speaks for science centers before Congress and federal agencies.

Challenger Center for Space Science Education, *422 1st St. S.E., 3rd Floor, 20003; (202) 827-1580. Fax, (202) 827-0031. Lance Bush, President. Toll-free, (800) 969-5747.*
General email, info@challenger.org

Web, www.challenger.org, Twitter, @ChallengerCtr

Press, press@challenger.org

Educational organization designed to stimulate interest in science, math, and technology among middle school and elementary school students. Students participate in interactive mission simulations that require training and classroom preparation. Sponsors Challenger Learning Centers across the United States, Canada, the United Kingdom, and Korea.

EarthEcho International, *2101 L St. N.W., #800, 20037; (202) 350-3190. Fax, (202) 857-3977. Philippe Cousteau, President. Press, (202) 870-1818.*
General email, info@earthecho.org

Web, www.earthecho.org and Twitter, @EarthEcho

Education resource center that helps students identify environmental issues in their communities and take action to solve them. Holds expeditions to South Florida to investigate the impact of human activity on its natural ecosystems. Provides teachers with learning materials to engage students with real-world data. Specializes in dead zones.

Entomological Society of America, *3 Park Pl., #307, Annapolis, MD 21401-3722; (301) 731-4535. Fax, (301) 731-4538. David Gammel, Executive Director.*
General email, esa@entsoc.org

Web, www.entsoc.org and Twitter, @EntsocAmerica

Membership: entomology researchers, teachers, extension service personnel, administrators, marketing representatives, research technicians, consultants, students, and hobbyists. Sponsors symposia, conferences, journals, and continuing education seminars.

International Technology and Engineering Educators Assn., *1914 Association Dr., #201, Reston, VA 20191-1539; (703) 860-2100. Fax, (703) 860-0353. Steven A. Barbato, Executive Director.*
General email, iteea@iteea.org

Web, www.iteea.org

Membership: technology education teachers, supervisors, teacher educators, and individuals studying to be technology education teachers (elementary school through university level). Technology education includes the curriculum areas of manufacturing, construction, communications, transportation, robotics, energy, design, and engineering.

Marine Technology Society, *1100 H St. N.W., #LL-100, 20005; (202) 717-8705. Fax, (202) 347-4302. Kathleen Herndon, Executive Director.*
General email, membership@mtsociety.org
Web, www.mtsociety.org

Provides scholarships to high school and postsecondary students in marine-related programs with focus in marine technology, marine engineering, and marine science.

Mathematical Assn. of America, *1529 18th St. N.W., 20036-1358; (202) 387-5200. Fax, (204) 396-5647. Michael Pearson, Executive Director.*
Information, (800) 331-1622.
General email, maaservice@maa.org
Web, www.maa.org

Membership: mathematics professors and individuals worldwide with a professional interest in mathematics. Seeks to improve the teaching of collegiate mathematics. Conducts professional development programs.

National Assn. of Biology Teachers, *11 Main St., Suite D, Warrenton, VA 20186 (mailing address: P.O. Box 3363, Warrenton, VA 20188); (703) 264-9696. Fax, (202) 962-3939. Jaclyn Reeves-Pepin, Executive Director, (703) 264-9696 ext. 4.*
Information, (888) 501-6228.
General email, office@nabt.org
Web, www.nabt.org

Membership: biology teachers and others interested in life sciences education at the elementary, secondary, and collegiate levels. Interests include teaching standards, science curriculum, and issues affecting biology and life sciences education.

National Council of Teachers of Mathematics, *1906 Association Dr., Reston, VA 20191-1502; (703) 620-9840. Fax, (703) 476-2970. Ken Krehbiel, Executive Director. Toll-free, (800) 235-7566.*
General email, nctm@nctm.org
Web, www.nctm.org, Twitter, @NCTM and Facebook, www.facebook.com/TeachersofMathematics

Membership: mathematics educators, researchers, students, and other interested persons. Works for the improvement of classroom instruction at all levels. Serves as forum and information clearinghouse on issues related to mathematics education. Offers educational materials and conferences. Monitors legislation and regulations.

National Geographic Society, *1145 17th St. N.W., 20036-4688; (202) 857-7000. Fax, (202) 775-6141. Tracy R. Wolstencroft, President. Library, (202) 857-7783. Press, (202) 857-7027. Publication information, (800) 647-5463. Publication information TTY, (800) 548-9797.*
Web, www.nationalgeographic.org,
Twitter, @NatGeoExplorers and Facebook, www.facebook .com/natgeoexplorers

Educational and scientific organization. Publishes *National Geographic, National Geographic Adventure, National Geographic Traveler, National Geographic Kids,* and *National Geographic Little Kids* magazines; produces maps, books, and films; maintains a museum; offers film-lecture series; produces television specials and the National Geographic Channel. Library open to the public.

National Research Council (NRC), *Life Sciences Board, Keck Center, 500 5th St. N.W., 6th Floor, 20001; (202) 334-2187. Fax, (202) 334-1289. Fran Sharples, Director; James P. Collins, Chair.*
General email, bls@nas.edu
Web, http://dels.nas.edu/bls

Oversees studies on undergradute level biology education.

National Research Council (NRC), *Science Education Board, Keck Center, 500 5th St. N.W., 20001; (202) 334-2164. Fax, (202) 334-2210. Heidi Schweingruber, Director, (202) 334-2009; Adam Gamoran, Chair.*
General email, bose@nas.edu
Web, http://nas.edu/bose

Promotes science education in schools and informal learning environments, such as science museums, aquariums, nature centers, and social networks. Provides guidance in federal legislation, particularly as it relates to STEM education.

National Science Foundation (NSF), *Graduate Education Division, 2415 Eisenhower Ave., Room W11200, Alexandria, VA 22314; (703) 292-8630. Fax, (703) 292-9048. Nirmala Kannankutty, Director (Acting). TTY, (800) 281-8749.*
Web, www.nsf.gov/div/index.jsp?div=dge

Supports activities to strengthen the education of research scientists and engineers; promotes career development.

National Science Teachers Assn., *1840 Wilson Blvd., Arlington, VA 22201-3000; (703) 243-7100. Fax, (703) 243-7177. David L. Evans, Executive Director.*
Web, www.nsta.org

Membership: science teachers from elementary through college levels. Seeks to improve science education. Monitors legislation and regulations.

National Society of Black Engineers, *205 Daingerfield Rd., Alexandria, VA 22314; (703) 549-2207. Fax, (703) 683-5312. Karl Reid, Executive Director.*
General email, info@nsbe.org
Web, www.nsbe.org and Twitter, @NSBE

Membership: Black engineers and college students studying engineering. Offers academic excellence programs, scholarships, leadership training, and professional and career development opportunities. Activities include tutorial programs, group study sessions, high school/junior high outreach programs, technical seminars and workshops, career fairs, and an annual convention.

Smithsonian Science Education Center, *901 D St. S.W., #704-B, 20024; (202) 633-2972. Fax, (202) 287-2070. Carol L. O'Donnell, Director.*
General email, ScienceEducation@si.edu
Web, https://ssec.si.edu and Twitter, @SmithsonianScie

Works to establish effective science programs for all students. Disseminates research information; develops curriculum materials; seeks to increase public support for change of science education through the development of strategic partnerships.

Society for Science and the Public, *1719 N St. N.W., 20036; (202) 785-2255. Fax, (202) 785-3751. Maya Ajmera, Chief Executive Officer. Toll-free, (800) 552-4412. Web, www.societyforscience.org*

Twitter, @Society4Science

General email, ssp@societyforscience.org

Promotes understanding and appreciation of science and the role it plays in human advancement. Sponsors science competitions and other science education programs in schools; awards scholarships. Publishes *Science News* and *Science News for Kids*. Provides funds and training to select U.S. science and math teachers who serve under-resourced students.

6

Employment and Labor

GENERAL POLICY AND ANALYSIS

Basic Resources

▶**AGENCIES**

Labor Dept. (DOL), *200 Constitution Ave. N.W., 20210;* *(202) 693-6000. Fax, (202) 693-6681. R. Alexander Acosta, Secretary, (202) 693-6000; Patrick Pizzella, Deputy Secretary, (202) 693-6002. Library, (202) 693-6600. Toll-free, (866) 487-2365. TTY, (877) 889-5627.* General email, talktodol@dol.gov

Web, www.dol.gov, Twitter, @USDOL and Facebook, www .facebook.com/departmentoflabor

Promotes and develops the welfare of U.S. wage earners; administers federal labor laws; acts as principal adviser to the president on policies relating to wage earners, working conditions, and employment opportunities. Library open to the public, 8:15 a.m–4:45 p.m.

Labor Dept. (DOL), *Administrative Law Judges, 800 K St. N.W., #400N, 20001-8002; (202) 693-7300. Fax, (202) 693-7365. Stephen R. Henley, Chief Administrative Law Judge, (202) 693-7542; Patricia Coleman, Chief Docket Clerk, (202) 693-7300; Angel Perez, Director of Program Operations, (202) 693-7542.* General email, OALJ-Questions@dol.gov

Web, www.oalj.dol.gov

Presides over formal hearings to determine violations of minimum wage requirements, overtime payments, compensation benefits, employee discrimination, grant performance, alien certification, employee protection, the Sarbanes-Oxley Act, and health and safety regulations set forth under numerous statutes, executive orders, and regulations. With few exceptions, hearings are required to be conducted in accordance with the Administrative Procedure Act.

Labor Dept. (DOL), *Administrative Review Board, 200 Constitution Ave. N.W., #N5404, 20210 (mailing address: 200 Constitution Ave. N.W., #S5220, Washington, DC 20210); (202) 693-6200. Fax, (202) 693-6220. William Thomas Barto, Chair.* *Web, www.dol.gov/arb*

Issues final decisions for the secretary of labor on appeals from decisions of the administrator of the Wage and Hour Division and the Office of Administrative Law Judges under a broad range of federal labor laws, including nuclear, environmental, safety and security, financial, and transportation whistle-blower protection provisions; contract compliance laws; child labor laws; immigration laws; migrant and seasonal agricultural worker protection laws; the McNamara O'Hara Service Contract Act; and the Davis-Bacon Act.

▶**CONGRESS**

For a listing of relevant congressional committees and subcommittees, please see page 218 or the Appendix.

Government Accountability Office (GAO), *Education, Workforce, and Income Security (EWIS), 441 G St. N.W., #5910, 20548; (202) 512-7215. Barbara D. Bovbjerg, Managing Director.* *Web, www.gao.gov/careers/ewis.html*

Assists Congress in analyzing the efficiency and effectiveness of federal agency programs that foster the development, education, and skill attainment of children and adults; provide benefits and protections for workers, families, veterans, and those with disabilities; ensure an adequate and secure retirement for an aging population.

▶**NONGOVERNMENTAL**

AFL-CIO (American Federation of Labor–Congress of Industrial Organizations), *815 16th St. N.W., 20006; (202) 637-5000. Fax, (202) 637-5058. Richard L. Trumka, President. Press, (202) 637-5018.* *Web, www.aflcio.org, Twitter, @AFLCIO and Facebook, www.facebook.com/aflcio* Press, pressclips@aflcio.org

Voluntary federation of national and international labor unions in the United States. Represents members before Congress and other branches of government. Each member union conducts its own contract negotiations. Library (located in Silver Spring, Md.) open to the public.

American Enterprise Institute (AEI), *1789 Massachusetts Ave. N.W., 20036; (202) 862-5800. Fax, (202) 862-7177. Arthur C. Brooks, President, (202) 419-5213; John Cusey, Vice President of Government Affairs, (202) 828-6021. Press, (202) 862-5829.* *Web, www.aei.org*

Research and educational organization that studies trends in employment, earnings, the environment, health care, and income in the United States.

Employment Policies Institute, *1090 Vermont Ave. N.W., #800, 20005-4605; (202) 463-7650. Fax, (202) 463-7107. Michael Saltsman, Managing Director.* General email, info@epionline.org

Web, www.epionline.org

Sponsors and conducts research on public policy and employment. Opposes raising the minimum wage. Monitors legislation and regulations.

Good Jobs First, *1616 P St. N.W., #210, 20036; (202) 232-1616. Greg LeRoy, Executive Director.* General email, info@goodjobsfirst.org

Web, www.goodjobsfirst.org, Twitter, @GoodJobsFirst and Facebook, www.facebook.com/GoodJobsFirst

Promotes corporate and government accountability in economic development incentives; primary focus is on state and local job subsidies with emerging work on federal development programs and federal regulatory violations data. Maintains Subsidy Tracker database. Includes Good Jobs New York and the Corporate Research Project.

HR Policy Assn., *1100 13th St. N.W., #850, 20005-4090; (202) 789-8670. Fax, (202) 789-0064. Daniel V. Yager, President.*

EMPLOYMENT AND LABOR RESOURCES IN CONGRESS

For a complete listing of congressional committees, including their full contact information, leadership, membership, and jurisdictions, please refer to the Appendix on pages 827–948.

HOUSE:

House Agriculture Committee, (202) 225-2171.
Web, agriculture.house.gov
  Subcommittee on Biotechnology, Horticulture, and Research, (202) 225-2171.
House Appropriations Committee, (202) 225-2771.
Web, appropriations.house.gov
  Subcommittee on Labor, Health and Human Services, Education, and Related Agencies, (202) 225-3508.
House Armed Services Committee, (202) 225-4151.
Web, armedservices.house.gov
  Subcommittee on Military Personnel, (202) 225-7560.
House Education and the Workforce Committee, (202) 225-4527.
Web, edworkforce.house.gov
  Subcommittee on Health, Employment, Labor, and Pensions, (202) 225-4527.
  Subcommittee on Higher Education and Workforce Development, (202) 225-4527.
  Subcommittee on Workforce Protections, (202) 225-4527.
House Judiciary Committee, (202) 225-3951.
Web, judiciary.house.gov
  Subcommittee on Immigration and Border Security, (202) 225-3926.
House Oversight and Government Reform Committee, (202) 225-5074.
Web, oversight.house.gov
  Subcommittee on Government Operations, (202) 225-5074.
House Small Business Committee, (202) 225-5821.
Web, smallbusiness.house.gov
  Subcommittee on Contracting and Workforce, (202) 225-5821.
House Veterans' Affairs Committee, (202) 225-3527.
Web, veterans.house.gov
  Subcommittee on Economic Opportunity, (202) 226-5491.
House Ways and Means Committee, (202) 225-3625.
Web, waysandmeans.house.gov
  Subcommittee on Human Resources, (202) 225-1025.
  Subcommittee on Social Security, (202) 225-9263.

JOINT:

Joint Economic Committee, (202) 224-5171.
Web, jec.senate.gov

SENATE:

Senate Agriculture, Nutrition, and Forestry Committee, (202) 224-2035.
Web, agriculture.senate.gov
  Subcommittee on Commodity Exchanges, Energy, and Credit (202) 224-2035.
Senate Appropriations Committee, (202) 224-7257.
Web, appropriations.senate.gov
  Subcommittee on Labor, Health and Human Services, Education, and Related Agencies, (202) 224-9145.
Senate Finance Committee, (202) 224-4515.
Web, finance.senate.gov
  Subcommittee on International Trade, Customs, and Global Competitiveness, (202) 224-4515.
  Subcommittee on Social Security, Pensions and Family Policy, (202) 224-4515.
  Subcommittee on Taxation and IRS Oversight, (202) 224-4515.
Senate Health, Education, Labor, and Pensions Committee, (202) 224-5375.
Web, help.senate.gov
  Subcommittee on Employment and Workplace Safety, (202) 224-5375.
  Subcommittee on Primary Health and Retirement Security, (202) 224-5375.
Senate Homeland Security and Governmental Affairs Committee, (202) 224-4751.
Web, hsgac.senate.gov
  Permanent Subcommittee on Investigations, (202) 224-3721.
  Subcommittee on Regulatory Affairs and Federal Management, (202) 224-4551.
Senate Judiciary Committee, (202) 224-5225.
Web, judiciary.senate.gov
  Subcommittee on Border Security and Immigration, (202) 224-7840.
Senate Small Business and Entrepreneurship Committee, (202) 224-5175.
Web, sbc.senate.gov
Senate Special Committee on Aging, (202) 224-5364.
Web, aging.senate.gov

General email, info@hrpolicy.org

Web, www.hrpolicy.org

Promotes discussion of human resource policy and practice, including strategies and initiatives that promote job growth, employment security, and competitiveness.

National Assn. of Professional Employer Organizations, *707 N. Saint Asaph St., Alexandria, VA 22314; (703) 836-0466. Fax, (703) 836-0976. Pat Cleary, President, (703) 739-8163.*

General email, info@napeo.org

Web, www.napeo.org

Membership: professional employer organizations. Provides code of ethics. Conducts research; sponsors seminars and conferences for members. Monitors legislation and regulations.

National Fund for Workforce Solutions, *1730 Rhode Island Ave., #712, 20036; (202) 223-8994. Elicia Wilson, Chief Administrative Officer; Fred Detrick, President.*

Web, https://nationalfund.org, Twitter, @National_Fund and Facebook, www.facebook.com/NFWorkforce

Partners with employers, individuals, and philanthropic organizations to promote better economic opportunities and prosperous communities. Acts as advocate for policies that help workers, local employers, and economic growth.

People's Action, *1101 17th St. N.W.,#1220, 20036-4721; (202) 263-4520. George Goehl, Director.*

Web, https://peoplesaction.org, Twitter, @PplsAction and Facebook, www.facebook.com/pplsaction

Advocates policies to help working people. Supports improved employee benefits, including health care, child care, and paid family leave; promotes lifelong education and training of workers. Seeks full employment, higher wages, and increased productivity. Monitors legislation and regulations. Merger of Campaign for America's Future, Alliance for a Just Society, and Center for Health, Environment, and Justice. (Headquartered in Chicago, Ill.).

Urban Institute, *Center on Labor, Human Services, and Population, 500 L'Enfant Plaza S.W., 20024; (202) 833-7200. Fax, (202) 463-8522. Signe-Mary McKernan, Vice President.*

Web, www.urban.org/policy-centers/center-labor-human-services-and-population

Analyzes employment and income trends, studies how the U.S. population is growing, and evaluates programs dealing with homelessness, child welfare, and job training. Other areas of interest include immigration, mortality, sexual and reproductive health, adolescent risk behavior, child care, domestic violence, and youth development.

International Issues

▶**AGENCIES**

Bureau of Democracy, Human Rights, and Labor (DRL) *(State Dept.), 2201 C St. N.W., #7827, 20520-7812;*

(202) 647-1337. Fax, (202) 647-5283. Marc Susser, Senior Advisor.

Web, www.state.gov/j/drl, Twitter, @StateDRL and Facebook, www.facebook.com/StateDRL

Blog, https://blogs.state.gov/latest-stories

Implements U.S. policies relating to human rights, labor, and religious freedom; prepares annual review of human rights worldwide.

Bureau of Democracy, Human Rights, and Labor (DRL) *(State Dept.), International Labor Affairs (ILA), 1800 G St. N.W., #2422, 20006; (202) 663-3569. Stephen Moody, Director.*

Web, www.state.gov/j/drl/ila

Works with organized labor, nongovernmental organizations, international organizations, and corporations to monitor and promote worker rights throughout the world. Contributes to U.S. foreign policy goals related to democracy promotion, trade, development, and human rights.

Bureau of Democracy, Human Rights, and Labor (DRL) *(State Dept.), Multilateral and Global Affairs (MLGA), Business and Human Rights Team (BHR), 2401 E St. N.W., 20037; (202) 663-3661. Jason A. Donovan, Director.*

General email, IFBHR@state.gov

Web, www.state.gov/j/drl

Works with companies, nongovernmental organizations, and governments to provide corporate contributions to global prosperity while ensuring companies operate in a manner that protects against human rights abuses.

Bureau of Educational and Cultural Affairs (ECA) *(State Dept.), Private Sector Exchange, 2200 C St. N.W., #5BB11, 20520; (202) 632-9386. Fax, (202) 632-2701. Kevin Saba, Deputy Assistant Secretary (Acting), (202) 632-6193.*

General email, jvisas@state.gov

Web, http://eca.state.gov/about-bureau-0/organizational-structure/office-private-sector-exchange

Administers the Exchange Visitor Program to allow non-immigrants to participate in work-based and study-based exchange programs in the United States.

Bureau of International Labor Affairs (ILAB) *(Labor Dept.), 200 Constitution Ave. N.W., #S2235, 20210; (202) 693-4770. Fax, (202) 693-4780. Martha E. Newton, Deputy Under Secretary; Mark A. Mittelhauser, Associate Deputy Under Secretary.*

General email, Contact-ILAB@dol.gov

Web, www.dol.gov/ilab

Assists in formulating international economic and trade policies affecting American workers. Represents the United States in trade negotiations. Helps administer the United States labor attaché program. Carries out overseas technical assistance projects. Represents the United States in various international organizations. Houses the Office of Trade Agreement Implementation, which is responsible for overseeing the implementation of the labor provisions of free trade agreements.

Labor Department

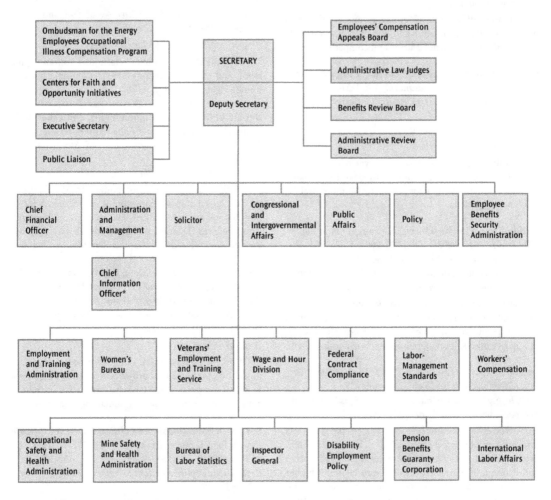

*Indicates direct access to the Secretary

Bureau of International Labor Affairs (ILAB) *(Labor Dept.), Child Labor, Forced Labor, and Human Trafficking (OCFT), 200 Constitution Ave. N.W., #S5307, 20210; (202) 693-4843. Fax, (202) 693-4830. Marcia Eugenio, Director.*
Web, www.dol.gov/agencies/ilab/our-work/child-forced-labor-trafficking

General email, globalkids@dol.gov

Conducts research and reporting to inform U.S. foreign policy, trade policy, and cooperation initiatives to combat child labor, forced labor, and human trafficking; works with foreign governments, organizations, and businesses to build capacity and strategies for responding to exploitive labor practices.

Bureau of International Labor Affairs (ILAB) *(Labor Dept.), Economic and Labor Research (OELR), 200 Constitution Ave. N.W., Room S5205, 20210; (202) 693-4802. Fax, (202) 693-4851. Ken Swinnerton, Director (Acting).*

General email, Contact-OTLA@dol.gov

Web, www.dol.gov/agencies/ilab/about-us/mission# mission-offices and Maps and data, www.dol.gov/ilab/map and Reports and publications, www.dol.gov/ilab/reports/ search/?q=oelr

Conducts research on the effects of international trade and economic policies and developments on earnings, employment, and working conditions of American workers, cross-country comparative and macroeconomic analyses, and methods of ensuring compliance with international workers' rights.

Bureau of International Labor Affairs (ILAB) *(Labor Dept.), International Relations (OIR), 200 Constitution Ave. N.W., #S5317, 20210; (202) 693-4855. Fax, (202) 693-4860. Robert B. Shepard, Director.*
General email, Contact-OIR@dol.gov

Web, www.dol.gov/agencies/ilab/about-us/mission

Provides administrative support for U.S. participation in the International Labor Organization (ILO) and Asian

Pacific Economic Cooperation (APEC) and at the Paris-based Organisation for Economic Cooperation and Development (OECD). Provides research on labor and employment in other countries. Facilitates information sharing between Labor Dept. and other countries.

Bureau of International Labor Affairs (ILAB) *(Labor Dept.), International Relations (OIR), International Visitors Program, 200 Constitution Ave. N.W., #S5303, 20210; (202) 693-4793. Patricia Butler, International Program Specialist.*
General email, butler.patricia@dol.gov
Web, www.dol.gov/ilab/diplomacy/fvp.htm

Works with the State Dept., the Agency for International Development, and other agencies in arranging visits and training programs for foreign officials interested in U.S. labor and trade laws and practices, worker training programs, and employment services.

Bureau of International Labor Affairs (ILAB) *(Labor Dept.), Trade and Labor Affairs (OTLA), 200 Constitution Ave. N.W., #S5317, 20210; (202) 693-4802. Fax, (202) 693-4851. Matthew Levin, Director.*
General email, Contact-OTLA@dol.gov
Web, www.dol.gov/ilab

Coordinates international technical cooperation in support of the labor provisions in free trade agreements. Provides services, information, expertise, and technical cooperation programs that support the Labor Dept.'s foreign policy objectives. Administers the U.S. government's responsibilities under the North American Free Trade Agreement on Labor Cooperation and labor chapters of U.S. regional and bilateral free trade agreements. Provides technical assistance for postconflict reconstruction and reintegration activities in countries key to U.S. security. Provides technical assistance globally to help countries observe international labor standards. Supports HIV/AIDS workplace preventive education in countries around the world.

Employment and Training Administration (ETA) *(Labor Dept.), Trade Adjustment Assistance (OTAA), 200 Constitution Ave. N.W., N-5428, 20210 (mailing address: 200 Constitution Ave. N.W., #12-200, Washington, DC 20210); (202) 693-3560. Fax, (202) 693-3584. Norris T. Tyler III, Administrator. Toll-free, (888) 365-6822.*
General email, taa.petition@dol.gov
Web, www.doleta.gov/tradeact

Assists American workers who are totally or partially unemployed because of increased imports or a shift in production; offers training, job search and relocation assistance, weekly benefits at state unemployment insurance levels, and other reemployment services.

President's Committee on the International Labor Organization *(Labor Dept.), 200 Constitution Ave. N.W., #2235, 20210; (202) 693-4808. Fax, (202) 693-4780. R. Alexander Acosta, Secretary of Labor; Martha E. Newman, Deputy Under Secretary for International Affairs; Robert B. Shepard, Director of International Relations. Toll free, (866) 487-2365.*

General email, contact-ILAB@dol.gov
Web, www.dol.gov/ilab/diplomacy/pc-ilo-page1.htm

Advisory committee that directs U.S. participation in the International Labor Organization; composed of government, employer, and worker representatives, including secretaries of labor, commerce, and state, the president's national security adviser, the president's national economic adviser, and the presidents of the AFL-CIO and the U.S. Council of International Business. Formulates and coordinates policy on the International Labor Organization (ILO); advises the president and the secretary of labor.

▶**CONGRESS**

For a listing of relevant congressional committees and subcommittees, please see page 218 or the Appendix.

▶**INTERNATIONAL ORGANIZATIONS**

International Labour Organization (ILO), *Washington Office, 900 19th St., 20006; (202) 617-3952. Fax, (202) 617-3960. Kevin Cassidy, Director; Jennifer Mansey, Public Policy & Communications officer.*
General email, washington@ilo.org
Web, www.ilo.org/washington and Twitter, @ILRF

Works toward advancing social justice through the promotion of international labor standards, employment, social protection, and social dialogue. Carries out research and technical cooperation and advisory services under these four major themes and related subthemes, including labor statistics, wages, occupational safety and health and other working conditions, social security, eradication of child labor and forced labor, equality of treatment in employment and occupation, freedom of association, and bargaining rights. Liaison office for the United States and multilateral organizations in Washington, D.C. (Headquarters in Geneva.)

World Bank, *Human Development Network, 1818 H St. N.W., 20433; (202) 473-1000. Annette Dixon, Vice President.*
Web, www.worldbank.org

Assists developing countries in delivering effective and affordable health care, education, and social services. Interests include poverty reduction, income protection, nutrition, jobs access, health coverage, and basic education.

▶**NONGOVERNMENTAL**

Fair Labor Assn. (FLA), *1111 19th St. N.W., #401, 20036; (202) 898-1000. Fax, (202) 898-9050. Sharon Waxman, Chief Executive Officer.*
General email, info@fairlabor.org
Web, www.fairlabor.org and Twitter, @FairLaborAssoc

Membership: consumer, human, and labor rights groups; apparel and footwear manufacturers and retailers; and colleges and universities. Seeks to protect the rights of workers in the United States and worldwide. Concerns include sweatshop practices, forced labor, child labor, and worker health and benefits. Monitors workplace conditions and reports findings to the public. Develops capacity for sustainable labor compliance.

Immigration Works USA, *737 8th St. S.E., #201, 20003; (202) 506-4541. Fax, (202) 595-8962. Tamar Jacoby, President. Press, (202) 506-4541.*
General email, info@immigrationworksusa.org
Web, www.immigrationworksusa.org and
Twitter, @ImmigWorksUSA

Coalition of business owners that seeks to educate the public about the benefits of immigration and build support for bringing immigration policy in line with the country's labor needs. Monitors legislation and regulations.

International Labor Rights Forum, *1634 Eye St. N.W., #1000, 20006; (202) 347-4100. Fax, (202) 347-4885. Judy Gearhart, Executive Director, ext. 106.*
General email, laborrights@ilrf.org
Web, www.laborrights.org and Twitter, @ILRF

Promotes the enforcement of international labor rights through policy advocacy; acts as advocate for better protection of workers. Concerns include child labor, sweatshops, and exploited workers. Monitors legislation and regulations on national and international levels.

NumbersUSA, *Capitol Hill Office, 11 D St. S.E., 1st Floor, 20003; 1400 Crystal Dr., #240, Arlington, VA 22209; (202) 543-1341. Fax, (202) 543-3147. Roy Beck, President; Rosemary Jenks, Vice President of Government Affairs. Donations, (703) 816-8820.*
General email, info@numbersusa.com
Web, www.numbersusa.com, Twitter, @NumbersUSA and Facebook, www.facebook.com/numbersusa

Public policy organization that favors immigration reduction as a way of promoting economic justice for American workers. Monitors legislation and regulations.

Solidarity Center, *1130 Connecticut Ave. N.W., #800, 20036; (202) 974-8383. Fax, (202) 974-8384. Shawna Bader-Blau, Executive Director. Press, (202) 974-8369.*
General email, information@solidaritycenter.org
Web, www.solidaritycenter.org and
Twitter, @solidaritycntr

Provides assistance to free and democratic trade unions worldwide. Provides trade union leadership courses in collective bargaining, union organization, trade integration, labor-management cooperation, union administration, and political theories. Sponsors social and community development projects; focus includes child labor, human and worker rights, and the role of women in labor unions. (Affiliated with the AFL-CIO.)

Labor Standards and Practices

▶**AGENCIES**

Bureau of Labor Statistics (BLS) *(Labor Dept.),*
Compensation and Working Conditions (OCWC),
2 Massachusetts Ave. N.E., #4130, 20212; (202) 691-6300.
Fax, (202) 691-6310. Kristen Monaco, Associate Commissioner.
Web, www.bls.gov

Conducts annual survey of occupational requirements, including the physical demands, environmental conditions, training requirements, and cognitive requirements of work.

Housing and Urban Development Dept. (HUD), *Davis Bacon and Labor Standards, 451 7th St. S.W., Room 7122, 20410; (202) 708-0370. Fax, (202) 619-8022. Pamela Glekas-Spring, Director, (202) 402-4449.*
Web, www.hud.gov/program_offices/davis_bacon_and_ labor_standards

Seeks to ensure that laborers on HUD-assisted construction projects are paid prevailing wages by contractors. Administers and enforces labor standards provisions within the Davis-Bacon and related acts, the Copeland Act, and Contract Work Hours and Safety Standards Act, and the maintenance wage requirements of the U.S. Housing Act of 1937.

Labor Dept. (DOL), *Wage and Hour Division (WHD), 200 Constitution Ave. N.W., #S3502, 20210; (202) 693-0051. Fax, (202) 693-1406. Bryan Jarret, Administrator (Acting). Press, (202) 693-4676. TTY, (877) 889-5627.*
Web, www.dol.gov/whd and Twitter, @WHD_DOL

Enforces the minimum-wage, overtime pay, record keeping, and child labor requirements of the Fair Labor Standards Act, the Migrant and Seasonal Agricultural Worker Protection Act, the Employee Polygraph Protection Act, the Family and Medical Leave Act, and a number of employment standards and worker protections as provided in several immigration-related statutes. Also enforces the wage garnishment provisions of the Consumer Credit Protection Act; and the prevailing wage requirements of the Davis-Bacon Act, the Service Contract Act, and other statutes applicable to federal contracts for construction and the provision of goods and services.

Labor Dept. (DOL), *Wage and Hour Division (WHD), Fair Labor Standards Act Enforcement, 200 Constitution Ave. N.W., #3516, 20210; (202) 693-0067.*
Fax, (202) 693-1387. Derrick J. Witherspoon, Branch Chief, (202) 693-0067.
Web, www.dol.gov/whd/flsa

Issues interpretations and rulings of the Fair Labor Standards Act of 1938. Interests include minimum wage, overtime pay, hours worked, record keeping, and child labor.

Labor Dept. (DOL), *Wage and Hour Division (WHD), Family and Medical Leave, 200 Constitution Ave. N.W., #S3502, 20210; (202) 693-0066. Fax, (202) 693-1387. Helen M. Applewhaite, Branch Chief, (202) 693-0066. Press, (202) 693-4676.*
Web, www.dol.gov/whd/fmla

Oversees implementation of the Family and Medical Leave Act, which entitles eligible employees of covered employers to take unpaid job-protected leave for specified family and medical reasons with continuation of group health insurance coverage.

Labor Dept. (DOL), *Wage and Hour Division (WHD),* *Government Contracts Enforcement,* 200 Constitution Ave. N.W., #S3502, 20210; (202) 693-0064. Fax, (202) 693-1087. Michelle King, Director (Acting), (202) 693-0574. Toll-free, (866) 487-9243.
Web, www.dol.gov/whd/govcontracts

Enforces the Davis-Bacon Act, the Walsh-Healey Public Contracts Act, the Contract Work Hours and Safety Standards Act, the Service Contract Act, and other related government contract labor standards statutes.

Labor Dept. (DOL), *Wage and Hour Division (WHD),* *Immigration,* 200 Constitution Ave. N.W., 20210; (202) 693-0071. Jennifer Amore, Branch Chief.
Web, www.dol.gov/whd/immigration

Enforces certain provisions under the Immigration and Nationality Act (INA), including labor standards protections for certain temporary nonimmigrant workers and inspection for compliance with the employment eligibility record-keeping requirements.

Labor Dept. (DOL), *Wage and Hour Division (WHD),* *Wage Determination,* 200 Constitution Ave. N.W., #S3502, 20210; (202) 693-0571. Olivia Jones, Branch Chief, (202) 693-0571.
Web, www.dol.gov/whd

Issues prevailing wage determinations under the Service Contract Act of 1965 and other regulations pertaining to wage determination.

▶**CONGRESS**

For a listing of relevant congressional committees and subcommittees, please see page 218 or the Appendix.

▶**NONGOVERNMENTAL**

Fair Labor Assn. (FLA), 1111 19th St. N.W., #401, 20036; (202) 898-1000. Fax, (202) 898-9050. Sharon Waxman, Chief Executive Officer.
General email, info@fairlabor.org
Web, www.fairlabor.org and Twitter, @FairLaborAssoc

Membership: consumer, human, and labor rights groups; apparel and footwear manufacturers and retailers; and colleges and universities. Seeks to protect the rights of workers in the United States and worldwide. Concerns include sweatshop practices, forced labor, child labor, and worker health and benefits. Monitors workplace conditions and reports findings to the public. Develops capacity for sustainable labor compliance.

National Whistleblowers Center (NWC), P.O. Box 25074, 20027; (202) 342-1903. Stephen M. Kohn, Executive Director.
General email, contact@whistleblowers.org
Web, www.whistleblowers.org

Protects employees who legally disclose information about illegal activities of employers. Advocates policy reform for whistle-blowers. Educates the public on whistle-blower rights and assists whistle-blowers in finding attorneys. Coordinates a speakers bureau.

Trabajadores Unidos de Washington DC—Workers United of Washington DC (TUWDC), 1419 V St. N.W., #305, 20009; (202) 299-0162. Arturo Griffiths, Executive Director, (202) 445-0411.
General email, info.tuwdc@gmail.com
Web, www.tuwdc.org, Twitter, @tu_wdc and Facebook, www.facebook.com/tuwdc.org

Seeks to advance solutions to challenges faced by D.C.–area day laborers, low-wage workers, and migrant workers, including working conditions, discrimination, wage theft, and workplace safety.

Statistics and Information

▶**AGENCIES**

Bureau of International Labor Affairs (ILAB) *(Labor Dept.), Economic and Labor Research (OELR),* 200 Constitution Ave. N.W., Room S5205, 20210; (202) 693-4802. Fax, (202) 693-4851. Ken Swinnerton, Director (Acting).
General email, Contact-OTLA@dol.gov
Web, www.dol.gov/agencies/ilab/about-us/mission#mission-offices and Maps and data, www.dol.gov/ilab/map and Reports and publications, www.dol.gov/ilab/reports/search/?q=oelr

Conducts research on the effects of international trade and economic policies and developments on earnings, employment, and working conditions of American workers, cross-country comparative and macroeconomic analyses, and methods of ensuring compliance with international workers' rights.

Bureau of Labor Statistics (BLS) *(Labor Dept.),* 2 Massachusetts Ave. N.E., #2850, 20212-0001; (202) 691-5200. Fax, (202) 691-7890. Vacant, Commissioner (Acting). Press, (202) 691-5902. TTY, (800) 877-8339.
General email, blsdata_staff@bls.gov
Web, www.bls.gov and Twitter, @BLS_gov

Collects, analyzes, and publishes data on labor economics, including employment, unemployment, hours of work, wages, employee compensation, prices, consumer expenditures, labor-management relations, productivity, technological developments, and occupational safety and health. Publishes reports on these statistical trends, including the *Consumer Price Index, Producer Price Index,* and *Employment and Earnings.*

Bureau of Labor Statistics (BLS) *(Labor Dept.), Compensation and Working Conditions (OCWC),* 2 Massachusetts Ave. N.E., #4130, 20212; (202) 691-6300. Fax, (202) 691-6310. Kristen Monaco, Associate Commissioner.
Web, www.bls.gov

Compiles data on occupational safety and health, wages and benefits, and occupational requirements.

Bureau of Labor Statistics (BLS) *(Labor Dept.), Compensation and Working Conditions (OCWC), Compensation Levels and Trends,* 2 Massachusetts Ave.

Personnel Offices at Federal Departments and Agencies

Job seekers interested in additional information can explore federal government career opportunities through the government's official employment information system website, www.usajobs.gov.

DEPARTMENTS

Agriculture, (202) 720-8732

Commerce, (202) 482-4807

Education, 1-800-872-5327

Energy, (202) 586-8734

Health and Human Services, (202) 690-6191

Homeland Security, (202) 282-8000

  Coast Guard, (202) 543-8313

Housing and Urban Development, (202) 402-3139

Interior, (202) 208-3100

Justice, (202) 514-3101

Labor, (202) 693-7600

State, (202) 261-8175

Transportation, (202) 366-4088

Treasury, (202) 927-4800

Veterans Affairs, (202) 461-7750

AGENCIES

Administrative Office of the U.S. Courts, (202) 502-3800

Commodity Futures Trading Commission, (202) 418-5009

Consumer Product Safety Commission, (301) 504-7925

Corporation for National and Community Service, (202) 606-6736

Defense Logistics Agency, (571)-767-6427

Environmental Protection Agency, (202) 564-4606

Equal Employment Opportunity Commission, (202) 663-4306

Export-Import Bank, (202) 565-3300

Farm Credit Administration, (703) 883-4200

Federal Communications Commission, (202) 418-0100

Federal Deposit Insurance Corporation, (877) 275-3342

Federal Election Commission, (202) 694-1080

Federal Emergency Management Agency, (866) 896-8003

Federal Labor Relations Authority, (202) 218-7979

Federal Mediation and Conciliation Service, (202) 606-5460

Federal Reserve Board, (202) 452-3880

Federal Trade Commission, (202) 326-2021

Food and Drug Administration, (240) 402-4500

General Services Administration, (202) 501-0398

Government Accountability Office, (202) 512-5811

Government Printing Office, (202) 512-1308

Health Resources and Services Administration, (301) 443-5895

National Aeronautics and Space Administration, (202) 358-1998

National Archives and Records Administration, (314) 801-0587

National Credit Union Administration, (703) 518-6510

National Endowment for the Arts, (202) 682-5405

National Endowment for the Humanities, (202) 606-8415

National Institutes of Health, (301) 496-2404

National Labor Relations Board, (202) 273-3900

National Mediation Board, (202) 692-5010

National Science Foundation, (703) 292-8180

National Transportation Safety Board, (202) 314-6000

Nuclear Regulatory Commission, (301) 415-7400

Office of Personnel Management, (202) 606-1800

Peace Corps, (202) 692-1200

Securities and Exchange Commission, (202) 551-7500

Small Business Administration, (202) 205-6600

Smithsonian Institution, (202) 633-6370

Social Security Administration, (800) 772-1213; TTY, (800) 325-0778

Transportation Security Administration, (877) 872-7990

U.S. International Trade Commission, (202) 205-2651

U.S. Postal Service, (877) 477-3273

N.E., #4160, 20212-0001; (202) 691-6199. Hilery Z. Simpson, Assistant Commissioner. TTY, (202) 691-5200. Web, www.bls.gov/ncs/summary.htm

Compiles data on wages and benefits. Develops the National Compensation Survey. Analyzes, distributes, and disseminates information on occupational earnings, benefits, and compensation trends.

Bureau of Labor Statistics (BLS) *(Labor Dept.),* **Compensation and Working Conditions (OCWC),** *Occupational Safety and Health Statistics,* 2 Massachusetts

Ave. N.E., #3180, 20212-0001; (202) 691-6170. Fax, (202) 691-6196. Vacant, Assistant Commissioner. General email, iifstaff@bls.gov Web, www.bls.gov/iif

Compiles and publishes statistics on occupational injuries, illnesses, and fatalities.

Bureau of Labor Statistics (BLS) *(Labor Dept.),* **Current Employment Statistics (CES), National,** 2 Massachusetts Ave. N.E., #4840, 20212-0001; (202) 691-6555. Fax, (202) 691-6641. Angie Clinton, Branch Chief.

General email, cesinfo@bls.gov

Web, www.bls.gov/ces

Surveys business and government agencies and publishes detailed industry data on employment, hours, and earnings of workers on nonfarm payrolls. Estimates are produced for the nation.

Bureau of Labor Statistics (BLS) *(Labor Dept.), Current Employment Statistics (CES), State and Area, 2* Massachusetts Ave. N.E., #4170, 20212; (202) 691-6559. Christopher D. Manning, Chief.

General email, sminfo@bls.gov

Web, www.bls.gov/sae

Surveys business agencies and publishes detailed industry data on employment, hours, and earnings of workers on nonfarm payrolls. Estimates are produced for states and selected metropolitan areas.

Bureau of Labor Statistics (BLS) *(Labor Dept.), Employment and Unemployment Statistics (OEUS),* 2 Massachusetts Ave. N.E., #4945, 20212-0022; (202) 691-6400. Fax, (202) 691-6425. Michael W. Horrigan, Associate Commissioner. Press, (202) 691-5902.

General email, cpsinfo@bls.gov

Web, www.bls.gov/bls/employment.htm

Monitors employment and unemployment trends on national and local levels; compiles data on worker and industry employment and earnings.

Bureau of Labor Statistics (BLS) *(Labor Dept.), Employment and Unemployment Statistics (OEUS), Current Employment Analysis,* 2 Massachusetts Ave. N.E., #4675, 20212; (202) 691-6459. Fax, (202) 691-6459. Julie Hatch Maxfield, Assistant Commissioner, (202) 691-5473. Current Population Survey, (202) 691-6378. Local area unemployment statistics, (202) 691-6392. Press, (202) 691-5902.

General email, lausinfo@bls.gov

Web, www.bls.gov/lau

Issues labor force and unemployment statistics for states, counties, metropolitan statistical areas, cities with populations of 25,000 or more, and the United States as a whole.

Bureau of Labor Statistics (BLS) *(Labor Dept.), Employment and Unemployment Statistics (OEUS), Industry Employment Statistics,* 2 Massachusetts Ave. N.E., #4860, 20212; (202) 691-5440. Fax, (202) 691-6644. Kenneth W. Robertson, Assistant Commissioner.

General email, oesinfo@bls.gov

Web, www.bls.gov/emp

Produces monthly employment statistics, quarterly wage data, business employment dynamics statistics, and job openings and labor turnover statistics.

Bureau of Labor Statistics (BLS) *(Labor Dept.), Productivity and Technology (OPT), 2 Massachusetts Ave. N.E., #2150, 20212-0001; (202) 691-5618.*

Fax, (202) 691-5664. Lucy P. Eldridge, Associate Commissioner, (202) 691-6598.

General email, dipsweb@bls.gov

Web, www.bls.gov/bls/productivity.htm

Develops and analyzes productivity measures for the U.S. business economy and industries, and conducts research on factors affecting productivity.

Employment and Training Administration (ETA) *(Labor Dept.), Unemployment Insurance (OUI), 200* Constitution Ave. N.W., #S4524, 20210; (202) 693-3032. Fax, (202) 693-3229. Gay M. Gilbert, Administrator.

Web, https://ows.doleta.gov/unemploy

Provides guidance and oversight with respect to federal and state unemployment compensation. Compiles statistics on state unemployment insurance programs. Studies unemployment issues related to benefits.

Occupational Safety and Health Administration (OSHA) *(Labor Dept.), Statistical Analysis, 200 Constitution Ave. N.W., #N3507, 20210; (202) 693-2300. Dave Schmidt, Director.*

Web, www.osha.gov/dts/osa and www.osha.gov/oshstats

Compiles and provides all statistical data for OSHA, such as occupational injury and illness records, which are used in setting standards and making policy.

▶**CONGRESS**

For a listing of relevant congressional committees and subcommittees, please see page 218 or the Appendix.

Unemployment Benefits

▶**AGENCIES**

Employment and Training Administration (ETA) *(Labor Dept.), Trade Adjustment Assistance (OTAA), 200* Constitution Ave. N.W., N-5428, 20210 (mailing address: 200 Constitution Ave. N.W., #12-200, Washington, DC 20210); (202) 693-3560. Fax, (202) 693-3584. Norris T. Tyler III, Administrator. Toll-free, (888) 365-6822.

General email, taa.petition@dol.gov

Web, www.doleta.gov/tradeact

Assists American workers who are totally or partially unemployed because of increased imports or a shift in production; offers training, job search and relocation assistance, weekly benefits at state unemployment insurance levels, and other reemployment services.

Employment and Training Administration (ETA) *(Labor Dept.), Unemployment Insurance (OUI), 200* Constitution Ave. N.W., #S4524, 20210; (202) 693-3032. Fax, (202) 693-3229. Gay M. Gilbert, Administrator.

Web, https://ows.doleta.gov/unemploy

Directs and reviews the state-administered system that provides income support for unemployed workers nationwide; advises state and federal employment security agencies on wage-loss, worker dislocation, and adjustment assistance compensation programs.

►CONGRESS

For a listing of relevant congressional committees and sub-committees, please see page 218 or the Appendix.

►NONGOVERNMENTAL

National Assn. of State Workforce Agencies, *444 N. Capitol St. N.W., #300, 20001; (202) 434-8020. Fax, (202) 434-8033. Scott Sanders, Executive Director, (202) 434-8022. General email, naswa@naswa.org*

Web, www.naswa.org and Twitter, @naswaorg

Membership: state workforce agency administrators. Informs members of employment training programs, unemployment insurance programs, employment services, labor market information, and legislation. Provides unemployment insurance and workforce development professionals with opportunities for networking and information exchange.

EMPLOYMENT AND TRAINING PROGRAMS

General

►AGENCIES

Employment and Training Administration (ETA) *(Labor Dept.), 200 Constitution Ave. N.W., #S2307, 20210; (202) 693-2772. Molly E. Conway, Assistant Secretary (Acting). Press, (215) 861-5100. Toll-free employment and training hotline, 877-US2-JOBS. TTY, (877) 889-5627. General email, etapagemaster@dol.gov*

Web, www.doleta.gov

Administers federal government job training and worker dislocation programs, federal grants to states for public employment service programs, and unemployment insurance benefits, primarily through state and local workforce development systems.

Employment and Training Administration (ETA) *(Labor Dept.), Workforce Investment (OWI), 200 Constitution Ave. N.W., #C4526, 20210; (202) 693-3980. Fax, (202) 693-3981. Amanda Ahlstrand, Administrator. Web, www.doleta.gov/etainfo/wrksys/*

Provides workers with information, job search assistance, and training. Helps employers acquire skilled workers. Provides national leadership, oversight, policy guidance, and technical assistance under the Workforce Innovation and Opportunity Act. Oversees programs administered through the One-Stop delivery system assisting communities, businesses, and job seekers, including dislocated and transitioning workers, disadvantaged youth, veterans, individuals with disabilities, migrant and seasonal farmworkers, and Native Americans, in a changing global economy.

Employment and Training Administration (ETA) *(Labor Dept.), Workforce Investment (OWI), Adult Services, 200 Constitution Ave. N.W., #S4209, 20210; (202) 693-3046. Fax, (202) 693-3817. Robert Kight, Chief. Web, www.doleta.gov/Programs*

Provides targeted job training services for migrant and seasonal farm workers, Native Americans, older workers, veterans, and the disabled. Aims to increase the employment, job retention, earnings, and career advancement of U.S. workers.

Employment and Training Administration (ETA) *(Labor Dept.), Workforce Investment (OWI), Division of Strategic Investment, 200 Constitution Ave. N.W., #C4518, 20210; (202) 693-3949. Fax, (202) 693-3890. Robin Fernkas, Chief. General email, businessrelations@dol.gov*

Web, www.doleta.gov/etainfo/wrksys/dinap.cfm#DSI

Serves as liaison between business and industry and the workforce investment system, a network of state and local resources that connects workers to job opportunities and helps businesses recruit, train, and maintain a skilled workforce. Manages the High Growth Job Training Initiative with the goal of preparing workers for high-growth and high-demand jobs. Targeted industries include advanced manufacturing, aerospace, biotechnology, health care, and information technology, construction, hospitality, transportation, and energy.

Employment and Training Administration (ETA) *(Labor Dept.), Workforce Investment (OWI), National Programs, Tools, and Technical Assistance, 200 Constitution Ave. N.W., #C-4510, 20210-3945; (202) 693-3045. Fax, (202) 693-3015. Steve Rietzke, Chief. TTY, (877) 889-5627.*

Web, www.doleta.gov/etainfo/wrksys/dinap.cfm#DNPTTA and WorkforceGPS, www.workforcegps.org

Oversees and provides support for implementation of employment and training services to targeted populations, including National Farmworker Jobs Program; migrant and seasonal farmworker Monitor Advocate activities; and services for individuals with disabilities, including the Disability Employment Initiative; Work Opportunity Tax Credit; and Senior Community Service Employment Program. Provides workers and businesses with labor market information and online career information to help connect skilled workers to businesses. Oversees and provides support for grants to states to produce labor market information; sponsors and oversees the agency's technical assistance platform for use by workforce development professionals, WorkforceGPS.

Health Resources and Services Administration (HRSA) *(Health and Human Services Dept.), Bureau of Health Workforce (BHW), 5600 Fishers Lane, #11 West Wing, Rockville, MD 20857; (301) 443-5794. Fax, (301) 443-0463. Dr. Luis Padilla, Associate Administrator. Web, www.hrsa.gov/about/organization/bureaus/bhw*

Supports primary care and public health education and practice. Supports recruitment of health care professionals, including nursing and allied health professionals, for underserved populations. Administers categorical training

programs, scholarship and loan programs, and minority and disadvantaged assistance programs. Oversees National Practitioner Data Bank.

Housing and Urban Development Dept. (HUD), *Davis Bacon and Labor Standards, 451 7th St. S.W., Room 7122, 20410; (202) 708-0370. Fax, (202) 619-8022. Pamela Glekas-Spring, Director, (202) 402-4449. Web, www.hud.gov/program_offices/davis_bacon_and_labor_standards*

Partnership between HUD and the Labor Dept. that assists low-income housing residents in obtaining job training and employment.

► **CONGRESS**

For a listing of relevant congressional committees and subcommittees, please see page 218 or the Appendix.

► **NONGOVERNMENTAL**

AFL-CIO Working for America Institute *(WAI), 815 16th St. N.W., 20006; (202) 508-3717. Fax, (202) 508-3719. Brad Markell, Executive Director. Main Switchboard, (202) 637-5000. Press, (202) 637-5018. General email, info@workingforamerica.org*

Web, www.workingforamerica.org

Provides technical assistance to labor unions, employers, education agencies, and community groups for workplace programs focusing on dislocated workers, economically disadvantaged workers, and skill upgrading. Interests include new technologies and workplace innovations.

D.C. Central Kitchen, *425 2nd St. N.W., 20001; (202) 234-0707. Michael F. Curtin, Chief Executive Officer, (202) 266-2018. Web, www.dccentralkitchen.org and Twitter, @dcck*

Administers the Culinary Jobs Training program for unemployed, homeless, or formerly incarcerated men and women.

Goodwill Industries International, *15810 Indianola Dr., Rockville, MD 20855; (301) 530-6500. Fax, (301) 530-1516. Steven C. Preston, President. Toll-free, (800) 466-3945. General email, contactus@goodwill.org*

Web, www.goodwill.org, Twitter, @GoodwillIntl and Facebook, www.facebook.com/GoodwillIntl

Serves youth, seniors, veterans, and people with disabilities, criminal records, and other specialized needs by providing education and career services and training, as well as job placement opportunities and post-employment support.

Graduate School USA, *Center for Leadership Management, 600 Maryland Ave. S.W., 20024-2520; (202) 314-3300. Fax, (866) 221-6761. Cynthia Hawkins, Director. TTY, (888) 744-2717. General email, customersupport@graduateschool.edu*

Web, www.graduateschool.edu/content/clm

Trains federal employees with managerial potential for executive positions in the government. Leadership programs serve employees at levels from GS4 through SES.

Institute for Credentialing Excellence, *2025 M St. N.W., #800, 20036-3309; (202) 367-1165. Fax, (202) 367-2165. Denise Roosendaal, Executive Director. General email, info@credentialingexcellence.org*

Web, www.credentialingexcellence.org, Twitter, @ICE_Excellence and Facebook, www.facebook.com/credentialingexcellence

Membership: certifying agencies and other groups that issue credentials for professions and occupations. Promotes public understanding of competency assurance certification programs. Oversees commission that establishes certification program standards. Monitors regulations.

National Assn. of State Workforce Agencies, *444 N. Capitol St. N.W., #300, 20001; (202) 434-8020. Fax, (202) 434-8033. Scott Sanders, Executive Director, (202) 434-8022. General email, naswa@naswa.org*

Web, www.naswa.org and Twitter, @naswaorg

Membership: state employment security administrators. Informs members of federal legislation on job placement, veterans affairs, and employment and training programs. Distributes labor market information; trains new state administrators and executive staff. Provides employment and training professionals with opportunities for networking and information exchange.

National Assn. of Workforce Boards (NAWB), *1155 15th St. N.W., #350, 20005; (202) 857-7900. Fax, (202) 857-7955. Ronald (Ron) Painter, Chief Executive Officer, (202) 857-7900, ext. 101. General email, nawb@nawb.org*

Web, www.nawb.org and Twitter, @Workforceinvest

Membership: private industry councils and state job training coordinating councils established under the Job Training Partnership Act of 1982 (renamed Workforce Boards under the Workforce Investment Act). Interests include job training opportunities for youth and unemployed, economically disadvantaged, and dislocated workers; and private sector involvement in federal employment and training policy. Provides members with technical assistance; holds conferences and seminars.

National Assn. of Workforce Development Professionals (NAWDP), *1155 15th St. N.W., #350, 20005; (202) 589-1790. Fax, (202) 589-1799. Melissa Robbins, Chief Executive Officer. Toll-free, (877) 202-2472. General email, info@nawdp.org*

Web, www.nawdp.org and Twitter, @NAWDP

Membership: professionals and policymakers in the employment and training field. Promotes professionalism, information exchange, networking, and professional growth in the workforce development field. Monitors legislation and regulations.

National Governors Assn. (NGA), *Center for Best Practices, Economic, Human Services, and Workforce Programs, 444 N. Capitol St. N.W., #267, 20001-1512; (202) 624-5345. Fax, (202) 624-7829. Martin Simon, Director (Acting). Web, www.nga.org/cms/center/ehsw*

Provides information, research, policy analysis, technical assistance, and resource development for governors and their staff across a range of policy issues. Promotes economic development and innovation; workforce development focused on industry-based strategies; pathways to employment and populations with special needs; and human services for children, youth, low-income families, and people with disabilities.

The Telework Coalition (TelCoa), *(202) 266-0046. Fax, (202) 465-3776. Chuck Wilsker, President. General email, info@telcoa.org*

Web, www.telcoa.org and Twitter, @telcoa

Promotes telework and access to broadband services to increase productivity and provide employment opportunities for disabled, rural, and older workers, while reducing vehicular travel and energy use. Monitors legislation and regulations.

U.S. Chamber of Commerce, *Center for Education and Workforce, 1615 H St. N.W., 20062-2000; (202) 463-5525. Fax, (202) 887-3424. Cheryl A. Oldham, Vice President. General email, education@uschamber.com*

Web, www.uschamberfoundation.org

Works with U.S. Chamber of Commerce members on workforce development issues, including educational reform, human resources, and job training.

U.S. Conference of Mayors, *Workforce Development Council, 1620 Eye St. N.W., 4th Floor, 20006; (202) 293-7330. Fax, (202) 293-2352. Kathleen Amoroso, Assistant Executive Director for Jobs, Education, and the Workforce Development Council, (202) 861-6723. Web, www.uscmwdc.org*

Offers technical assistance to members participating in federal job training programs; monitors related legislation; acts as an information clearinghouse on employment and training programs.

Worldwide ERC (Employee Relocation Council), *4401 Wilson Blvd., #510, Arlington, VA 22203; (703) 842-3400. Fax, (703) 436-9630. Peggy Smith, President, (703) 842-3407. General email, CustomerCare@worldwideerc.org*

Web, www.worldwideerc.org and Twitter, @WorldwideERC

Membership: corporations that relocate employees and moving, real estate, and relocation management companies. Researches and recommends policies that provide a smooth transition for relocated employees and their families. Holds conferences and issues publications on employee relocation issues.

Aliens

▶**AGENCIES**

Employment and Training Administration (ETA) *(Labor Dept.), Foreign Labor Certification (OFLC), 375 E St., #12-200, 20210 (mailing address: 200 Constitution Ave.*

N.W., #12-200, Washington, DC 20210); (202) 693-3010. Fax, (202) 693-2768. William Thompson, Administrator (Acting). Web, www.foreignlaborcert.doleta.gov

Sets national policies and guidelines for carrying out the responsibilities of the secretary of labor pursuant to the Immigration and Nationality Act regarding the admission of foreign workers to the United States for both temporary and permanent employment; certifies whether U.S. workers are available for positions for which admission of foreign workers is sought and whether employment of foreign nationals will adversely affect the wages and working conditions of similarly employed U.S. workers.

Apprenticeship Programs

▶**AGENCIES**

Employment and Training Administration (ETA) *(Labor Dept.), Office of Apprenticeship (OA), 200 Constitution Ave. N.W., #N5311, 20210-0001; (202) 693-2796. Fax, (202) 693-3799. John V. Ladd, Administrator. General email, oa.administrator@dol.gov*

Web, www.dol.gov/featured/apprenticeship

Alternate email, Apprenticeship.USA@dol.gov

Advises the secretary of labor on the role of apprenticeship programs in employment training and on safety standards for those programs; encourages sponsors to include these standards in planning apprenticeship programs. Promotes establishment of apprenticeship programs in private industry and the public sector.

Employment and Training Administration (ETA) *(Labor Dept.), Workforce Investment (OWI), Youth Services, 200 Constitution Ave. N.W., #N4508, 20210; (202) 693-3030. Fax, (202) 693-3861. Jen Troke, Director. General email, youthservices@dol.gov*

Web, www.doleta.gov/etainfo/wrksys/dinap.cfm#DYS

Administers youth grant programs designed to enhance youth education, encourage school completion, and provide career and apprenticeship opportunities. Oversees the Going Home: Serious and Violent Offender Reentry Initiative and YouthBuild.

Dislocated Workers

▶**AGENCIES**

Employment and Training Administration (ETA) *(Labor Dept.), Workforce Investment (OWI), 200 Constitution Ave. N.W., #C4526, 20210; (202) 693-3980. Fax, (202) 693-3981. Amanda Ahlstrand, Administrator. Web, www.doleta.gov/etainfo/wrksys/*

Provides workers with information, job search assistance, and training. Oversees programs administered through the One-Stop delivery system assisting job seekers, including dislocated and transitioning workers.

Selected Internships and Other Opportunities in the Washington Metropolitan Area

For congressional internships, contact members' offices. For opportunities at federal agencies, visit www.usajobs.gov/StudentsAndGrads. For information on changes to the federal internship program, see www.opm.gov/policy-data-oversight/hiring-authorities/students-recent-graduates.

American Assn. for the Advancement of Science, Yolanda Scott George, (202) 326-6677; www.aaas.org

American Civil Liberties Union, Adina Ellis, (202) 544-1681; www.aclu.org

American Farm Bureau Federation, Marty Tatman, (202) 406-3682; www.fb.org

American Federation of Teachers, Donna Kimbrue, (202) 879-4439; www.aft.org

American Red Cross, Ashley Turner, (202) 303-5214; www.redcross.org

Americans for the Arts, Terry Cangelosi, (202) 371-2830; www.americansforthearts.org

Amnesty International, Richard Eastmond, (202) 544-0200; www.amnestyusa.org

B'nai B'rith International, Eric Fusfield, (202) 857-6613; www.bnaibrith.org

Carnegie Institution of Washington, Cady Canapp, (202) 939-1113; www.carnegiescience.edu

Center for Responsive Politics, Internship Coordinator, (202) 857-0044; www.opensecrets.org

Center for Science in the Public Interest, Colleen O'Day, (202) 332-9110; www.cspinet.org

Children's Defense Fund, Mamie Berry, (202) 662-3507; www.childrensdefense.org

Common Cause, Patricia Bennett, (202) 833-1200; www.commoncause.org

Council on Hemispheric Affairs, Larry Birns, (202) 223-4975; www.coha.org

C-SPAN, Teresa Easley, (202) 737-3220; www.c-span.org

Democratic National Committee, Internship Coordinator, (202) 863-8000; www.democrats.org

Friends of the Earth, Internship Coordinator, (202) 783-7400; www.foe.org

Inter-American Dialogue, Tamar Solnik, (202) 822-9002; www.thedialogue.org

International Assn. of Chiefs of Police, Ryan Daugirda, (800) 843-4227, ext. 851; www.theiacp.org

Middle East Institute, Internship Coordinator, (202) 785-1141; www.mei.edu

Motion Picture Assn. of America, Internship Coordinator, (202) 293-1966; www.mpaa.org

National Academy of Sciences, Internship Coordinator, (202) 334-2000; www.nasonline.org

National Assn. for Equal Opportunity in Higher Education, Internship Coordinator, (202) 552-3300; www.nafeonation.org

National Assn. for the Advancement of Colored People, Internship Coordinator, (202) 463-2940; www.naacpdc.org

National Assn. of Broadcasters, Internship Coordinator, (202) 429-3928; www.nab.org

National Center for Missing & Exploited Children, Susan Herbert Peacock, (877) 446-2632; www.missingkids.com

National Geographic Society, Yvonne Perry, (202) 857-7000; www.nationalgeographic.com

National Governors Assn., Asha Pinkney Gillus, (202) 624-5300; www.nga.org

National Head Start Assn., Julie Antoniou, (703) 739-0875; www.nhsa.org

National Law Center on Homelessness and Poverty, Janelle Fernandez, (202) 638-2535; www.nlchp.org

National Organization for Women, Internship Coordinator, (202) 628-8669; www.now.org

National Public Radio, Internship Coordinator, (202) 513-2000; www.npr.org

National Trust for Historic Preservation, Carla Washinko, (202) 588-6000; www.preservationnation.org

National Wildlife Federation, Courtney Cochran, (703) 438-6265; www.nwf.org

The Nature Conservancy, Mike Tetreault, (301) 897-8570; www.nature.org; @nature_careers

Points of Light Institute, Joselyn Cassidy, (404) 979-2913; www.pointsoflight.org

Radio Free Europe/Radio Liberty, Internship Coordinator, (202) 457-6900; www.rferl.org; DCinternships@rferl.org

Republican National Committee, Internship Coordinator, (202) 863-8630; www.gop.com; Internships@gop.com

Special Olympics International, Andrea Cahn, (202) 408-2640; www.specialolympics.org

U.S. Chamber of Commerce, Megan Bartlett, (202) 659-6000; www.uschamber.com

United Negro College Fund, Mary Williams, (202) 810-0258; Fax, (855) 237-9601; www.uncf.org

---

Employment and Training Administration (ETA) *(Labor Dept.), Workforce Investment (OWI), Adult Services, 200 Constitution Ave. N.W., #S4209, 20210; (202) 693-3046. Fax, (202) 693-3817. Robert Kight, Chief. Web, www.doleta.gov/Programs*

Responsible for adult training and services for dislocated workers funded under the Workforce Investment Act; examines training initiatives.

▶**NONGOVERNMENTAL**

National Assn. of Workforce Boards (NAWB), *1155 15th St. N.W., #350, 20005; (202) 857-7900. Fax, (202) 857-7955. Ronald (Ron) Painter, Chief Executive Officer, (202) 857-7900, ext. 101. General email, nawb@nawb.org Web, www.nawb.org and Twitter, @Workforceinvest*

Membership: private industry councils and state job training coordinating councils established under the Job Training Partnership Act of 1982 (renamed Workforce Boards under the Workforce Investment Act). Interests include job training opportunities for youth and unemployed, economically disadvantaged, and dislocated workers; and private sector involvement in federal employment and training policy. Provides members with technical assistance; holds conferences and seminars.

National Governors Assn. (NGA), *Center for Best Practices, Economic, Human Services, and Workforce Programs,* *444 N. Capitol St. N.W., #267, 20001-1512; (202) 624-5345. Fax, (202) 624-7829. Martin Simon, Director (Acting). Web, www.nga.org/cms/center/ehsw*

Provides technical assistance to members participating in employment and training activities for dislocated workers.

Migrant and Seasonal Farm Workers

▶**AGENCIES**

Employment and Training Administration (ETA) *(Labor Dept.), Workforce Investment (OWI), 200 Constitution Ave. N.W., #C4526, 20210; (202) 693-3980. Fax, (202) 693-3981. Amanda Ahlstrand, Administrator. Web, www.doleta.gov/etainfo/wrksys/*

Provides workers with information, job search assistance, and training. Oversees programs administered through the One-Stop delivery system assisting job seekers, including migrant and seasonal farmworkers.

Employment and Training Administration (ETA) *(Labor Dept.), Workforce Investment (OWI), Adult Services, 200 Constitution Ave. N.W., #S4209, 20210; (202) 693-3046. Fax, (202) 693-3817. Robert Kight, Chief. Web, www.doleta.gov/Programs*

Provides targeted job training services for migrant and seasonal farm workers.

Employment and Training Administration (ETA) *(Labor Dept.), Workforce Investment (OWI), National Farmworker Jobs Program, 200 Constitution Ave. N.W., #4518, 20210-3945; (202) 693-3045. Fax, (202) 693-3015. Steven Rietzke, Chief. General email, NFJP@dol.gov Web, www.doleta.gov/farmworker/*

Provides funds for programs that help migrant and seasonal farm workers and their families find better jobs in agriculture and other areas. Services include occupational training, education, and job development and placement. Partners with states to provide services. Provides grants to assist with permanent and temporary housing.

Labor Dept. (DOL), *Wage and Hour Division (WHD), Farm Labor, 200 Constitution Ave. N.W., #S3502, 20210; (202) 693-0070. Fax, (202) 693-1387. Jennifer Amore, Branch Chief, (202) 693-0070. Toll-free, (866) 487-9243. Web, www.dol.gov/whd/ag*

Administers and enforces the Migrant and Seasonal Agricultural Worker Protection Act, which protects migrant and seasonal agricultural workers from substandard labor practices by farm labor contractors, agricultural employers, and agricultural associations. Also enforces the provisions of the Immigration and Nationality Act that pertain to the employment of H-2A visa workers and U.S. workers in corresponding employment; the temporary labor camp and field sanitation standards of the Occupational Safety and Health Act; and the standards pertaining to employment in agriculture of the Fair Labor Standards Act.

▶**NONGOVERNMENTAL**

Assn. of Farmworker Opportunity Programs, *1120 20th St. N.W., #3005, 20036; (202) 384-1754. Daniel Sheehan, Executive Director. General email, rcrumley@afop.org Web, www.afop.org and Twitter, @AFOPNational*

Represents state-level organizations that provide job training and other services and support to migrant and seasonal farm workers. Monitors legislation and conducts research.

Migrant Legal Action Program, *1001 Connecticut Ave. N.W., #915, 20036-5524; (202) 775-7780. Fax, (202) 775-7784. Roger C. Rosenthal, Executive Director. General email, mlap@mlap.org Web, www.mlap.org and Facebook, www.facebook.com/ MigrantLegalActionProgram*

Supports and assists local legal services, migrant education, migrant health issues, and other organizations and private attorneys with respect to issues involving the living and working conditions of migrant farm workers. Monitors legislation and regulations.

Older Workers

▶**AGENCIES**

Employment and Training Administration (ETA) *(Labor Dept.), Senior Community Service Employment Program, 200 Constitution Ave. N.W., #C4510, 20210; (202) 693-3980. Fax, (202) 693-3817. Amanda Ahlstrand, Administrator. Web, www.doleta.gov/seniors*

Provides funds for part-time community service work-training programs; the programs pay minimum wage and are operated by national sponsoring organizations and state and territorial governments. The program is aimed at unemployed economically disadvantaged persons age fifty-five and over.

▶**NONGOVERNMENTAL**

AARP, *601 E St. N.W., 20049; (202) 434-2277. Fax, (202) 434-7946. Jo Ann C. Jenkins, Chief Executive Officer. Library, (202) 434-6233. Membership, (202) 434-7550. Membership, toll-free, (800) 566-0242.*

Press, (202) 434-2560. Toll-free, (888) 687-2277. TTY, (877) 434-7598. Toll-free Spanish, (877) 342-2277. TTY Spanish, (866) 238-9488.

General email, member@aarp.org

Web, www.aarp.org, Twitter, @AARP and Facebook, www.facebook.com/AARP

Membership: people fifty years of age and older. Provides members with training, employment information, and volunteer programs.

Experience Works, Inc., 4401 Wilson Blvd., #210, Arlington, VA 22203; (703) 522-7272. Fax, (703) 522-0141. Sally Boofer, Chief Executive Officer. Toll-free, (866) 397-9757.

Web, www.experienceworks.org and Facebook, www.facebook.com/ExperienceWorks

Trains and places older adults in the workforce. Seeks to increase awareness of issues affecting older workers and build support for policies and legislation benefiting older adults. Maintains a help line for those unemployed who are fifty-five and older.

National Council on Aging, Senior Community Service Employment Program, 251 18th St. South, #500, Arlington, VA 22202; (571) 527-3900. Fax, (571) 527-3901. Jim Seith, Director.

General email, info@ncoa.org

Web, www.ncoa.org/economic-security/matureworkers/scsep

Operates a grant through funding from the U.S. Labor Dept. under the authority of the Older Americans Act to provide workers age fifty-five and over with community service employment and training opportunities in their resident communities.

Workers with Disabilities

▶AGENCIES

Education Dept., Special Education and Rehabilitative Services (OSERS), Rehabilitation Services Administration (RSA), Lyndon Baines Johnson Bldg., 400 Maryland Ave. S.W., 20202-7100; (202) 245-7468. Fax, (202) 245-7591. Carol Dobak, Deputy Commissioner (Acting).

Web, www2.ed.gov/about/offices/list/osers/rsa

Coordinates and directs federal services for eligible persons with physical or mental disabilities, with emphasis on programs that promote employment opportunities. Provides vocational training and job placement; supports projects with private industry; administers grants for the establishment of supported-employment programs.

Employment and Training Administration (ETA) (Labor Dept.), Workforce Investment (OWI), 200 Constitution Ave. N.W., #C4526, 20210; (202) 693-3980. Fax, (202) 693-3981. Amanda Ahlstrand, Administrator.

Web, www.doleta.gov/etainfo/wrksys/

Provides workers with information, job search assistance, and training. Oversees programs administered through the One-Stop delivery system assisting job seekers, including individuals with disabilities.

Labor Dept. (DOL), Disability Employment Policy (ODEP), 200 Constitution Ave. N.W., #S1303, 20210; (202) 693-7880. Fax, (202) 693-7888. Nathan Mehrens, Deputy Assistant Secretary for Policy, (202) 693-5959. Toll-free, 866-ODEP-DOL (633-7365). TTY, (877) 889-5627.

General email, odep@dol.gov

Web, www.dol.gov/odep

Influences disability employment policy by developing and promoting the use of evidence-based disability employment policies and practices, building collaborative partnerships, and delivering data on employment of people with disabilities.

Office of Personnel Management (OPM), Veterans Services, 1900 E St. N.W., #7439, 20415; (202) 606-3602. Fax, (202) 606-6017. Hakeem Basheerud-Deen, Director.

Web, www.opm.gov/policy-data-oversight/veterans-services

Provides federal employees and transitioning military service members and their families, federal human resources professionals, and hiring managers with information on employment opportunities with the federal government. Administers the Disabled Veterans Affirmative Action Program.

U.S. AbilityOne Commission, 1401 S. Clark St., #715, Arlington, VA 22202-3259; (703) 603-2100. Fax, (703) 603-0655. Tina Ballard, Executive Director. Toll-free, (800) 999-5963.

General email, info@abilityone.gov

Web, www.abilityone.gov

Presidentially appointed committee. Determines which products and services are suitable for federal procurement from qualified nonprofit agencies that employ people who are blind or have other significant disabilities; seeks to increase employment opportunities for these individuals. (Formerly Committee for Purchase from People Who Are Blind or Severely Disabled.)

▶NONGOVERNMENTAL

Business Leadership Network (USBLN), 3000 Potomac Ave., #101, Alexandria, VA 22305; (800) 706-2710. Fax, (800) 706-1335. Jill Houghton, Chief Executive Officer.

General email, info@disabilityIN.org

Web, www.disabilityin.org and Twitter, @DisabilityIN

Advocates inclusion of people with disabilities in the workplace, supply chain, and marketplaces; provides information on disability inclusion business practices.

Center for Employment and Economic Well-Being, 1133 19th St. N.W., #400, 20036; (202) 682-0100. Fax, (202) 204-0071. Kerry Desjardins, Policy Associate; Russ Sykes, Director.

Web, https://aphsa.org/CEEWB/default.aspx and Twitter, @APHSA1

Works to identify the best practices and resources that will help move low-income individuals into sustainable careers. Supports public policies that provide the opportunities for individuals, families, and communities to

Equal Employment Opportunity Commission

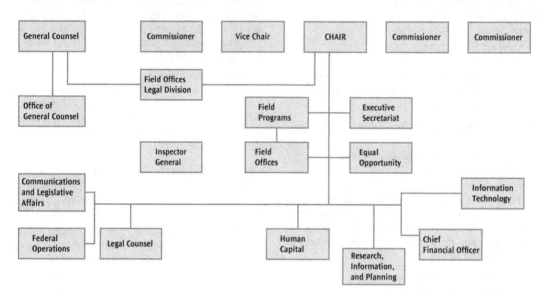

succeed in the workforce. (Affiliated with the American Public Human Services Association.)

Youth

Employment and Training Administration (ETA) *(Labor Dept.), Workforce Investment (OWI), Youth Services,* 200 Constitution Ave. N.W., #N4508, 20210; (202) 693-3030. Fax, (202) 693-3861. Jen Troke, Director. General email, youthservices@dol.gov

Web, www.doleta.gov/etainfo/wrksys/dinap.cfm#DYS

Administers youth grant programs designed to enhance youth education, encourage school completion, and provide career and apprenticeship opportunities. Oversees the Going Home: Serious and Violent Offender Reentry Initiative and YouthBuild.

Forest Service *(Agriculture Dept.), Youth Conservation Corps,* 201 14th St. S.W., 20024 (mailing address: 1400 Independence Ave. S.W., MS 1125, Washington, DC 20250-1125); (202) 205-0650. Merlene Mazyck, Program Manager. Toll-free, (800) 832-1355. General email, mmazyck@fs.fed.us

Web, www.fs.fed.us/working-with-us/opportunities-for-young-people/youth-conservation-corps-opportunities

Administers, with the National Park Service and the Fish and Wildlife Service, the Youth Conservation Corps, a summer employment and training public works program for youths ages fifteen to eighteen. The program is conducted in national parks, in national forests and grasslands, and on national wildlife refuges.

Labor Dept. (DOL), *Job Corps,* 200 Constitution Ave. N.W., #N4463, 20210; (202) 693-3000.

Fax, (202) 693-2767. Lenita Jacobs-Simmons, National Director. Information, (800) 733-5627. TTY, (877) 889-5627. General email, national_office@jobcorps.gov

Web, www.dol.gov/general/topic/training/jobcorps and Facebook, www.facebook.com/doljobcorps

Provides job training for disadvantaged youth at residential centers. Most of the centers are managed and operated by corporations and nonprofit organizations.

Labor Dept. (DOL), *Wage and Hour Division (WHD), Child Labor,* 200 Constitution Ave. N.W., #3516, 20210; (202) 693-0067. Fax, (202) 693-1387. Derrick J. Witherspoon, Branch Chief, (202) 693-0067. Press, (202) 693-0185. Toll-free, (866) 487-9243. Web, www.dol.gov/whd/childlabor.htm

Administers and enforces child labor, special minimum wage, and other provisions of Section 14 of the Fair Labor Standards Act.

The Corps Network, 1275 K St. N.W., #1050, 20005; (202) 737-6272. Fax, (202) 737-6277. Mary Ellen Sprenkel, President. Web, http://corpsnetwork.org and Twitter, @TheCorpsNetwork

Membership: youth corps programs. Produces publications and workshops on starting and operating youth corps and offers technical assistance programs. Holds annual conference. Monitors legislation and regulations.

Covenant House, *Washington Office,* 2001 Mississippi Ave. S.E., 20020; (202) 610-9600. Madye Henson, President. Web, http://covenanthousedc.org and Twitter, @CovenantHouseDC

Equal Employment Opportunity Contacts at Federal Departments and Agencies

DEPARTMENTS

Agriculture, Winona Lake Scott (Acting), (202) 720-3808

Commerce, Tinisha Agramonte, (202) 482-0625

Defense, Tyvonia Ward, (703) 604-9710

Air Force, James H. Carlock Jr., (240) 612-4357

Army, James Braxton Sr., (202) 761-8707

Marine Corps, Paula E. Bedford, (571) 256-8301

Navy, Celina Kline, (901) 874-2507

Education, Michael A. Chew, (202) 401-0691

Energy, Neil Schuldenfrei, (202) 586-2218

Health and Human Services, Cynthia Richardson-Crooks, (202) 690-6555

Homeland Security, Carl Lucas, (202) 357-7700

Coast Guard, Francine Williams, (202) 372-4260

Housing and Urban Development, John P. Benison, (202) 708-3362

Interior, John W. Burden, (202) 208-5693

Justice, Richard Toscano, (202) 616-4800

Labor, Samuel Rhames, (202) 693-6500

State, Gregory B. Smith, (202) 647-9295

Transportation, Charles E. James Sr., (202) 366-4648

Treasury, Mariam G. Harvey, (202) 622-0316

Veterans Affairs, A'ngela D. Dunn, (202) 461-4131

AGENCIES

Commission on Civil Rights, Vacant, (202) 376-8582

Commodity Futures Trading Commission, Vacant, (202) 418-5151

Consumer Product Safety Commission, Kathleen Buttrey, (301) 504-7771

Corporation for National and Community Service, Tasha Stewart, (202) 606-6913

Environmental Protection Agency, Tanya Lawrence, Deputy Director (Acting), (202) 564-2916

Equal Employment Opportunity Commission, Erica D. White-Dunston, (202) 663-7081

Export-Import Bank, Patrease Jones-Brown, (202) 565-3591

Farm Credit Administration, Thais Burlew, (703) 883-4290

Federal Communications Commission, Linda Miller, (202) 418-1799

Federal Deposit Insurance Corporation, Anthony Pagano, (703) 562-6062

Federal Election Commission, Kevin Salley, (202) 694-1229

Federal Emergency Management Agency, Regis Phelan (Acting), (202) 212-3535

Federal Energy Regulatory Commission (FERC), Madeline H. Lewis, (202) 502-8120

Federal Labor Relations Authority, Gina Grippando, (202) 218-7740

Federal Maritime Commission, Howard F. Jimenez, (202) 523-5859

Federal Mediation and Conciliation Service, Denise Patterson McKenney, (202) 606-5448

Federal Reserve Board, Sheila Clark, (202) 452-2883

Federal Trade Commission, Kevin D. Williams, (202) 326-2196

General Services Administration, Madeline Caliendo, (202) 501-0767

Merit Systems Protection Board, Jerry Beat, (202) 254-4405

National Aeronautics and Space Administration, Tom Luedtke (Associate), (202) 358-2167

National Credit Union Administration, Monica Hughes Davy, (703) 518-1650

National Endowment for the Humanities, Adam Wolfson (Acting), (202) 606-8231

National Labor Relations Board, Brenda V. Harris, (202) 273-3891

National Science Foundation, Rhonda J. Davis, (703) 292-8020

National Transportation Safety Board, Fara D. Guest, (202) 314-6190

Office of Personnel Management, LaShonn M. Woodland, (202) 606-2460

Peace Corps, Laara Manler, (202) 692-2139

Securities and Exchange Commission, Peter Henry, (202) 551-6040

Small Business Administration, Larry Stubblefield, (202) 205-6750

Smithsonian Institution, Rudy D. Watley, (202) 633-6430

Social Security Administration, Claudia J. Postell (Acting), (410) 965-3318

U.S. International Trade Commission, Altivia Jackson, (202) 205-2239

U.S. Postal Service, Eloise Lance, (202) 268-3820

Protects young people suffering from homelessness, abuse, and neglect. Provides services including GED and adult education and job readiness. (Affiliated with Covenant House International.)

EQUAL EMPLOYMENT OPPORTUNITY

General

▶AGENCIES

Agriculture Dept. (USDA), *Rural Development, Civil Rights,* 1400 Independence Ave. S.W., #1341, MS 0703, 20250-0703; Fax, (202) 692-0279. Sherese C. Paylor, Director (Acting), (202) 692-0097.
Complaints, (202) 692-0090. Toll-free, (800) 787-8821.
General email, rd.civilrights@wdc.usda.gov

Web, www.rd.usda.gov/about-rd/offices/civil-rights

Processes Equal Employment Opportunity complaints for Rural Development employees, former employees, and applicants. Enforces compliance with the Equal Credit Opportunity Act, which prohibits discrimination on the basis of sex, marital status, race, color, religion, disability, or age in rural housing, utilities, and business programs. Provides civil rights training to Rural Development's national, state, and field staffs.

Civil Rights Division *(Justice Dept.), Employment Litigation (ELS),* 601 D St. N.W., #4040, 20579; (202) 514-3831. Fax, (202) 514-1005. Delora L. Kennebrew, Chief. Library, (202) 514-3775. TTY, (202) 514-6780.
Web, www.justice.gov/crt/employment-litigation-section

Investigates, negotiates, and litigates allegations of employment discrimination by public schools, universities, state and local governments, and federally funded employers; has enforcement power.

Equal Employment Opportunity Commission (EEOC), 131 M St. N.E., 20507; (202) 663-4001.
Fax, (202) 663-4110. Victoria Lipnic, Chair (Acting).
Library, (202) 663-4630. Toll-free information, (800) 669-4000. Training Institute, (703) 291-0880.
Training Institute toll-free, (866) 446-0940. Training Institute TTY, (800) 828-1120. TTY, (202) 663-4494.
General email, info@eeoc.gov

Web, www.eeoc.gov

Training Institute email, eeoc.traininginstitute@eeoc.gov

Works to end job discrimination by private and government employers based on race, color, religion, sex, national origin, disability, or age. Works to protect employees against reprisal for protest of employment practices alleged to be unlawful in hiring, promotion, firing, wages, and other terms and conditions of employment. Works for increased employment of persons with disabilities, affirmative action by the federal government, and an equitable work environment for employees with mental and physical disabilities. Enforces Title VII of the Civil Rights Act of 1964, as amended, which includes the Pregnancy Discrimination Act; Americans with Disabilities Act; Age Discrimination in Employment Act; Equal Pay Act; Genetic Information Nondiscrimination Act (GINA); and, in the federal sector, rehabilitation laws. Receives charges of discrimination; attempts conciliation or settlement; can bring court action to force compliance; has review and appeals responsibility in the federal sector. Library open to the public by appointment only.

Equal Employment Opportunity Commission (EEOC), *Field Programs,* 131 M St. N.E., 5th Floor, 20507; (202) 663-4801. Fax, (202) 663-7190. Nicholas Inzeo, Director.
Web, www.eeoc.gov/field

Provides guidance and technical assistance through 15 district offices to employees who suspect discrimination and to employers who are working to comply with equal employment laws.

Federal Communications Commission (FCC), *Media Bureau (MB), Policy Division, Equal Employment Opportunity,* 445 12th St. S.W., #3A738, 20554; (202) 418-1450. Fax, (202) 418-1797. Lewis Pulley, Assistant Chief, (202) 418-2120.
Web, www.fcc.gov/general/equal-employment-opportunity

Responsible for the annual certification of cable television equal employment opportunity compliance. Oversees broadcast employment practices.

Labor Dept. (DOL), *Civil Rights Center (CRC),* 200 Constitution Ave. N.W., #N4123, 20210; (202) 693-6500. Fax, (202) 693-6505. Naomi M. Barry-Perez, Director. TTY, (800) 877-8339.
General email, civilrightscenter@dol.gov

Web, www.dol.gov/oasam/programs/crc

Resolves complaints of workplace discrimination on the basis of race, color, religion, sex, national origin, age, or disability in programs funded by the department. Library open to the public.

Labor Dept. (DOL), *Federal Contract Compliance Programs (OFCCP),* 200 Constitution Ave. N.W., #C3325, 20210; (202) 693-0137. Fax, (202) 693-1304. Craig E. Leen, Director, (202) 693-0101. Toll-free, (800) 397-6251. TTY, (202) 693-0103.
General email, OFCCP-Public@dol.gov

Web, www.dol.gov/ofccp

Monitors and enforces government contractors' compliance with federal laws and regulations on equal employment opportunities and affirmative action, including employment rights of minorities, women, persons with disabilities, and disabled and Vietnam-era veterans.

Office of Personnel Management (OPM), *Veterans Services,* 1900 E St. N.W., #7439, 20415; (202) 606-3602. Fax, (202) 606-6017. Hakeem Basheerud-Deen, Director.
Web, www.opm.gov/policy-data-oversight/veterans-services

Administers the Disabled Veterans Affirmative Action Program.

U.S. Commission on Civil Rights, *Civil Rights Evaluation,* 1331 Pennsylvania Ave. N.W., #1150, 20425;

(202) 376-7700. Fax, (202) 376-7754. Katherine Culliton-Gonzalez, Director. Complaints Unit hotline, (202) 376-8513. TTY, (800) 877-8339.
Web, www.usccr.gov

Researches federal policy in areas of equal employment and job discrimination; monitors the economic status of minorities and women, including their employment and earnings. Library open to the public.

▶ CONGRESS

For a listing of relevant congressional committees and subcommittees, please see page 218 or the Appendix.

▶ NONGOVERNMENTAL

Equal Employment Advisory Council, 1501 M St. N.W., #400, 20005; (202) 629-5650. Fax, (202) 629-5651. Joseph S. Lakis, President.
General email, info@cwc.org
Web, www.eeac.org

Membership: principal equal employment officers and lawyers. Files amicus curiae (friend of the court) briefs; conducts research and provides information on equal employment law and policy. Monitors legislation and regulations.

Minorities

▶ AGENCIES

Bureau of Indian Affairs (BIA) (Interior Dept.), Indian Energy and Economic Development (IEED), 1849 C. St. N.W., Room 4152, 20240; (202) 219-0740.
Fax, (202) 208-4564. Jack R. Stevens, Director (Acting), (202) 208-6764.
Web, www.bia.gov/as-ia/ieed

Develops policies and programs to promote the achievement of economic goals for members of federally recognized tribes who live on or near reservations. Provides job training; assists those who have completed job training programs in finding employment; provides loan guarantees; and enhances contracting opportunities for individuals and tribes.

Education Dept., White House Initiative on Asian Americans and Pacific Islanders, 550 12th St. S.W., 10th Floor, 20202; (202) 245-6418. Fax, (202) 245-7166. Holly Ham, Executive Director; Debra Suarez, Senior Advisor.
General email, whitehouseaapi@ed.gov
Web, http://sites.ed.gov/aapi, Twitter, @whitehouseAAPI and Facebook, www.facebook.com/WhiteHouseAAPI

Works to expand Asian American and Pacific Islander federal employment opportunities. Ensures that workers' rights are protected and upheld.

Employment and Training Administration (ETA) (Labor Dept.), Workforce Investment (OWI), Indian and Native American Programs, 200 Constitution Ave. N.W., #S4209, 20210; (202) 693-3046. Fax, (202) 693-3817. Athena Brown, Chief, (202) 693-3737.

Web, www.doleta.gov/etainfo/wrksys/dinap.cfm#DINAP

Administers grants for training and employment-related programs to promote employment opportunity; provides unemployed, underemployed, and economically disadvantaged Native Americans and Alaska and Hawaiian Natives with funds for training, job placement, and support services.

▶ NONGOVERNMENTAL

AFL-CIO, Asian Pacific American Labor Alliance (APALA), 815 16th St. N.W., 2nd Floor, 20006; (202) 508-3733. Alvina Yeh, Executive Director.
General email, apala@apalanet.org
Web, www.apalanet.org, Twitter, @APALAnational and Facebook, www.facebook.com/APALAnational

Membership: Asian American and Pacific Islander (AAPI) union members. Represents regional Asia–Pacific Rim labor activists in a national scope and assists in union member issues. Interests include gender analysis, youth participation, civil and human rights within the AAPI community.

American Assn. for Access, Equity, and Diversity (AAAED), 1701 Pennsylvania Ave. N.W., #200, 20006; (202) 349-9855. Fax, (202) 355-1399. Shirley J. Wilcher, Executive Director. Toll-free, (866) 562-2233.
General email, info@aaaed.org
Web, www.aaaed.org, Twitter, @affirmativeat and Facebook, www.facebook.com/theaaaed

Membership: professional managers in the areas of affirmative action, equal opportunity, diversity, and human resources. Sponsors education, research, and training programs. Acts as a liaison with government agencies involved in equal opportunity compliance. Maintains ethical standards for the profession. (Formerly the American Assn. for Affirmative Action.)

Blacks in Government, 3005 Georgia Ave. N.W., 20001-3807; (202) 667-3280. Fax, (202) 667-3705. Doris H. Sartor, President.
General email, bignational@bignet.org
Web, www.bignet.org and Twitter, @BigNational

Advocacy organization for public employees. Promotes equal opportunity and career advancement for African American government employees; provides career development information; seeks to eliminate racism in the federal workforce; sponsors programs, business meetings, and social gatherings; represents interests of African American government workers to Congress and the executive branch; promotes voter education and registration.

Center for Equal Opportunity, 7700 Leesburg Pike, #231, Falls Church, VA 22043; (703) 442-0066.
Fax, (703) 442-0449. Roger Clegg, President; Linda Chavez, Chair; Rudy Gersten, Executive Director.
General email, comment@ceousa.org
Web, www.ceousa.org and Twitter, @ceousa

Research organization concerned with issues of race, ethnicity, and assimilation; opposes racial preferences in employment or education, contracting, and other areas. Monitors legislation and regulations.

Coalition of Black Trade Unionists, 1155 Connecticut Ave. N.W., #500, 20036 (mailing address: P.O. Box 66268, Washington, DC 20035); (202) 778-3318.
Fax, (202) 419-1486. Terrence L. Melvin, President.
General email, cbtu@cbtu.org

Web, http://cbtu.org and Twitter, @CBTU72

Monitors legislation affecting African American and other minority trade unionists. Focuses on equal employment opportunity, unemployment, and voter education and registration.

Conference of Minority Transportation Officials, 100 M St. S.E., #917, 20003; (202) 506-2917. A. Bradley Mims, Chief Executive Officer.
General email, info@comto.org

Web, www.comto.org, Twitter, @COMTO_National and Facebook, www.facebook.com/Conference-Of-Minority-Transportation-Officials-COMTO-330029463789014

Forum for minority professionals working in the transportation sector. Provides opportunities and reinforces networks through advocacy, training, and professional development for minorities in the industry.

Labor Council for Latin American Advancement, 815 16th St. N.W., 3rd Floor, 20006; (202) 508-6919.
Fax, (202) 508-6922. Hector E. Sanchez, Executive Director.
General email, headquarters@lclaa.org

Web, www.lclaa.org, Twitter, @LCLAA and Facebook, www.facebook.com/LCLAA

Membership: Hispanic trade unionists. Encourages equal employment opportunity, voter registration, and participation in the political process. (Affiliated with the AFL-CIO and the Change to Win Federation.)

NAACP Legal Defense and Educational Fund, Inc., Washington Office, 700 14th St., #600, 20005; (202) 682-1300. Todd A. Cox, Director of Policy.
Web, www.naacpldf.org and Twitter, @NAACP_LDF

Civil rights litigation group that provides legal information about civil rights legislation and advice on employment discrimination against women and minorities; monitors federal enforcement of equal opportunity rights laws. Not affiliated with the NAACP. (Headquarters in New York.)

National Assn. for the Advancement of Colored People (NAACP), Washington Bureau, 1156 15th St. N.W., #915, 20005; (202) 463-2940. Fax, (202) 463-2953.
Derrick Johnson, President.
General email, washingtonbureau@naacpnet.org

Web, www.naacp.org and Twitter, @NAACP

Membership: persons interested in civil rights for all minorities. Advises individuals with employment discrimination complaints. Seeks to eliminate job discrimination and to bring about full employment for all Americans through legislation and litigation. (Headquarters in Baltimore, Md.)

National Assn. of Hispanic Federal Executives, P.O. Box 14514, 20044; (202) 315-3942. Al Gallegos, National President; Luis Espinoza, President of the Washington, D.C., Chapter.
General email, president@nahfe.org

Web, https://nahfe.org

Works to ensure that the needs of the Hispanic American community are addressed in the policymaking levels of the federal government by promoting career and learning opportunities for qualified Hispanics in the federal GS/GM-12/15 grade levels and the Senior Executive Service policymaking positions.

National Assn. of Negro Business and Professional Women's Clubs Inc., 1806 New Hampshire Ave. N.W., 20009; (202) 483-4206. Fax, (202) 462-7253.
Diane E. Toppin, President.
General email, nednambpwcinfo@gmail.com

Web, www.nanbpwc.org and Twitter, @NANBPWC

Promotes and protects the interests of minority business and professional women, serves as advisors to young people seeking to enter business and the professions, provides scholarship support for secondary education, sponsors workshops, and works to improve the quality of life in local and global communities to foster good fellowship. Monitors legislation and regulations.

National Lesbian and Gay Journalists Assn. (NLGJA), 2120 L St. N.W., #850, 20037; (202) 588-9888.
Jen Christensen, President.
General email, info@nlgja.org

Web, www.nlgja.org

Works within the journalism industry to foster fair and accurate coverage of lesbian, gay, bisexual, and transgender issues. Opposes workplace bias against all minorities and provides professional development for its members.

National Urban League, Washington Bureau, 2901 14th St. N.W., 20009; (202) 265-8200. George H. Lambert Jr., Affiliate Chief Executive Officer.
Web, http://nul.iamempowered.com/affiliate/greater-washington-urban-league

Federal advocacy division of social service organization concerned with the social welfare of African Americans and other minorities. Testifies before congressional committees and federal agencies on equal employment; studies and evaluates federal enforcement of equal employment laws and regulations. (Headquarters in New York.)

Society of American Indian Government Employees, (410) 802-2190. Fredericka Joseph, Chair.
General email, chair@saige.org

Web, https://saige.org

Facebook, Facebook

Supports equal employment opportunities for American Indians and Alaska Natives in the government workforce. Monitors legislation and policies. (Headquarters in Skiatook, Okla.)

UnidosUS, *1126 16th St. N.W., #600, 20036-4845; (202) 785-1670. Fax, (202) 776-1792. Janet Murguía, President. General email, info@unidos.org*

Web, www.unidosus.org, Twitter, @WeAreUnidosUS and Facebook, www.facebook.com/Weareunidosus

Provides research, policy analysis, and advocacy on Hispanic employment status and programs; provides Hispanic community-based groups with technical assistance to help develop effective employment programs with strong educational components. Works to promote understanding of Hispanic employment needs in the private sector. Interests include women in the workplace, affirmative action, equal opportunity employment, and youth employment. Monitors federal employment legislation and regulations. (Formerly the National Council of La Raza.)

Washington Government Relations Group, *1325 G St. N.W., #500, 20005; (202) 449-7651. Fax, (202) 449-7701. Marcus Sebastian Mason, President. General email, info@wgrginc.org*

Web, www.wgrginc.org

Works to enrich the careers and leadership abilities of African American government relations professionals working in business, financial institutions, law firms, trade associations, and nonprofit organizations. Increases dialogue between members and senior-level policymakers to produce public policy solutions.

Older Adults

▶**NONGOVERNMENTAL**

AARP, *601 E St. N.W., 20049; (202) 434-2277. Fax, (202) 434-7946. Jo Ann C. Jenkins, Chief Executive Officer. Library, (202) 434-6233. Membership, (202) 434-7550. Membership, toll-free, (800) 566-0242. Press, (202) 434-2560. Toll-free, (888) 687-2277. TTY, (877) 434-7598. Toll-free Spanish, (877) 342-2277. TTY Spanish, (866) 238-9488. General email, member@aarp.org*

Web, www.aarp.org, Twitter, @AARP and Facebook, www .facebook.com/AARP

Membership: people fifty years of age and older. Promotes a multigenerational workforce and seeks to prevent age discrimination in the workplace.

National Caucus and Center on Black Aging, Inc., *1220 L St. N.W., #800, 20005-2407; (202) 637-8400. Fax, (202) 347-0895. Karyne Jones, President. General email, support@ncba-aged.org*

Web, www.ncba-aged.org and Twitter, @NCBADC

Concerned with issues that affect older Black Americans and other minorities. Sponsors employment and housing programs for older adults and education and training for professionals in gerontology. Monitors legislation and regulations.

Women

▶**AGENCIES**

Women's Bureau *(Labor Dept.), 200 Constitution Ave. N.W., #S3002, 20210; (202) 693-6710. Fax, (202) 693-6725. Patricia G. Greene, Director; Joan Harrigan-Farrelly, Deputy Director; Erica Wright, Deputy Director. Information, (800) 827-5335. General email, Womens.Bureau@dol.gov*

Web, www.dol.gov/wb

Monitors women's employment issues. Promotes employment opportunities for women; sponsors workshops, job fairs, symposia, demonstrations, and pilot projects. Offers technical assistance; conducts research and provides publications on issues that affect working women; represents working women in international forums.

▶**NONGOVERNMENTAL**

Assn. for Women in Science, *1667 K St., N.W., #800, 20006; (202) 588-8175. Karene Richards, Executive Director (Acting). General email, awis@awis.org*

Web, www.awis.org and Twitter, @AWISNational

Promotes equal opportunity for women in scientific professions; provides career and funding information. Provides educational scholarships for women in science. Interests include international development.

Business and Professional Women's Foundation, *1030 15th St. N.W., #B1, Room 148, 20005; (202) 293-1100. Fax, (202) 861-0298. Roslyn Ridgeway, Chair. General email, foundation@bpwfoundation.org*

Web, www.bpwfoundation.org and Twitter, @WomenMisbehavin

Works to eliminate barriers to the full participation of women in the workplace. Interests include pay equity, work-life balance, women veterans, and green jobs for women. Conducts research; provides issue briefs and other publications; monitors legislation and regulations.

Coalition of Labor Union Women, *815 16th St. N.W., 2nd Floor South, 20006-1119; (202) 508-6969. Fax, (202) 508-6968. Elise Bryant, President; Carol S. Rosenblatt, Executive Director, (202) 508-6951. General email, getinfo@cluw.org*

Web, http://cluw.org and Twitter, @CLUWNational

Seeks to make unions more responsive to the needs of women in the workplace; advocates affirmative action and the active participation of women in unions. Monitors legislation and regulations.

Federally Employed Women, *455 Massachusetts Ave. N.W., 20001 (mailing address: P.O. Box 306, Washington, DC 20001); (202) 898-0994. Fax, (202) 898-1535. Karen Rainey, President. General email, few@few.org*

Web, www.few.org and Facebook, www.facebook.com/ federallyemployedwomen

Membership: women and men who work for the federal government. Works to eliminate sex discrimination in government employment and to increase job opportunities for women; offers training programs. Monitors legislation and regulations.

Institute for Women's Policy Research (IWPR), *1200 18th St. N.W., #301, 20036; (202) 785-5100.*
Fax, (202) 833-4362. Heidi Hartmann, President.
General email, iwpr@iwpr.org
Web, www.iwpr.org, Twitter, @IWPResearch and Facebook, www.facebook.com/iwpresearch

Public policy research organization that focuses on women's issues, including family and work balance and employment and wages.

NAACP Legal Defense and Educational Fund, Inc.,
Washington Office, 700 14th St., #600, 20005;
(202) 682-1300. Todd A. Cox, Director of Policy.
Web, www.naacpldf.org and Twitter, @NAACP_LDF

Civil rights litigation group that provides legal information about civil rights legislation and advice on employment discrimination against women and minorities; monitors federal enforcement of equal opportunity rights laws. Not affiliated with the NAACP. (Headquarters in New York.)

National Assn. of Women Business Owners, *601 Pennsylvania Ave. N.W., South Bldg., #900, 20004; (202) 609-9817. Fax, (202) 403-3788. Jen Earle, Chief Executive Officer. Toll-free, (800) 556-2826.*
General email, national@nawbo.org
Web, www.nawbo.org and Twitter, @NAWBONational

Promotes the economic, social, and political interests of women business owners through networking, leadership and business development training, and advocacy.

National Partnership for Women and Families, *1875 Connecticut Ave. N.W., #650, 20009-5731; (202) 986-2600. Fax, (202) 986-2539. Debra L. Ness, President; Debbie Wilkes, Chief of Staff.*
General email, info@nationalpartnership.org
Web, www.nationalpartnership.org

Advocacy organization that promotes fairness in the workplace. Publishes and disseminates information in print and on the Web to heighten awareness of work and family issues. Monitors legislative activity and pending Supreme Court cases and argues on behalf of family issues before Congress and in the courts.

National Women's Law Center, *11 Dupont Circle N.W., #800, 20036; (202) 588-5180. Fax, (202) 588-5185. Fatima Gross Graves, President.*
General email, info@nwlc.org
Web, www.nwlc.org, Twitter, @nwlc and Facebook, www.facebook.com/nwlc

Works to protect and advance the rights of women and girls at work, in school, and beyond. Maintains programs that focus on enforcing Title IX's provisions for equal treatment in education and narrowing the gender gap in athletics and the technology-oriented workplace. Other interests include equal pay and benefits, sexual harassment

laws, the right to family leave, child care and early learning, poverty and income support, and the preservation of diversity in the workplace.

Women in Film and Video (WIFV), *4000 Albemarle St. N.W., #305, 20016; (202) 429-9438. Fax, (202) 429-9440. Melissa Houghton, Executive Director.*
General email, director@wifv.org
Web, www.wifv.org and Twitter, @WIFVDC

Membership organization dedicated to promoting equal employment opportunities and advancing career development and achievement for women working in all areas of screen-based media and related disciplines.

Workers with Disabilities

▶**AGENCIES**

Equal Employment Opportunity Commission (EEOC), *131 M St. N.E., 20507; (202) 663-4001. Fax, (202) 663-4110. Victoria Lipnic, Chair (Acting). Library, (202) 663-4630. Toll-free information, (800) 669-4000. Training Institute, (703) 291-0880. Training Institute toll-free, (866) 446-0940. Training Institute TTY, (800) 828-1120. TTY, (202) 663-4494.*
General email, info@eeoc.gov
Web, www.eeoc.gov
Training Institute email, eeoc.traininginstitute@eeoc.gov

Works for increased employment of persons with disabilities, affirmative action by the federal government, and an equitable work environment for employees with mental and physical disabilities.

Equal Employment Opportunity Commission (EEOC), *Legal Counsel, Americans with Disabilities Act Policy Division, 131 M St. N.E., 20507; (202) 663-4665. Fax, (202) 663-6034. Christopher J. Kuczynski, Assistant Legal Counsel. TTY, (202) 663-7026.*
Web, www.eeoc.gov

Provides interpretations, opinions, and technical assistance on the ADA provisions and the provisions of the Genetic Information Nondiscrimination Act (GINA) relating to employment.

Labor Dept. (DOL), *Disability Employment Policy (ODEP), 200 Constitution Ave. N.W., #S1303, 20210; (202) 693-7880. Fax, (202) 693-7888. Nathan Mehrens, Deputy Assistant Secretary for Policy, (202) 693-5959. Toll-free, 866-ODEP-DOL (633-7365). TTY, (877) 889-5627.*
General email, odep@dol.gov
Web, www.dol.gov/odep

Promotes employment opportunties for people with disabilities.

▶**NONGOVERNMENTAL**

Assn. of People Supporting Employment First (APSE), *7361 Calhoun Pl., #680, Rockville, MD 20855;*

(301) 279-0060. Fax, (301) 279-0075. Jenny Stonemeir, Executive Director (Acting).
General email, cesp@apse.org

Web, www.apse.org and Twitter, @nationalaspse

Advocates opportunities for equitable employment for those with disabilities. Monitors legislation and regulations.

HUMAN RESOURCES

General

▶ AGENCIES

National Science Foundation (NSF), *Education and Human Resources Directorate,* 2415 Eisenhower Ave., Room C11000, Alexandria, VA 22314; (703) 292-8600. Fax, (703) 292-9179. Karen Marrongelle, Assistant Director.
Web, www.nsf.gov/dir/index.jsp?org=ehr

Supports the development of a diverse and well-prepared STEM workforce through a variety of education and research programs.

National Science Foundation (NSF), *Human Resource Development Division,* 2415 Eisenhower Ave., Room E11400, Alexandria, VA 22134; (703) 292-8640. Fax, (703) 292-9019. Jermelina Tupas, Director (Acting).
Web, www.nsf.gov/div/index.jsp?div=hrd

Supports programs and activities to increase participation of minorities, women, and people with disabilities in the STEM workforce.

Office of Personnel Management (OPM), *Human Resources Solutions,* 1900 E St. N.W., #2469F, 20415-1000; (202) 606-0900. Fax, (202) 606-9200. Joseph S. Kennedy, Associate Director.
Web, www.opm.gov/about-us/our-people-organization/program-divisions/human-resources-solutions

Manages federal human resources policy, including staffing, compensation, benefits, labor relations, and position classification.

▶ CONGRESS

For a listing of relevant congressional committees and subcommittees, please see page 218 or the Appendix.

▶ NONGOVERNMENTAL

American Assn. for Access, Equity, and Diversity (AAAED), 1701 Pennsylvania Ave. N.W., #200, 20006; (202) 349-9855. Fax, (202) 355-1399. Shirley J. Wilcher, Executive Director. Toll-free, (866) 562-2233.
General email, info@aaaed.org

Web, www.aaaed.org, Twitter, @affirmativeat and Facebook, www.facebook.com/theaaaed

Membership: professional managers in the areas of affirmative action, equal opportunity, diversity, and human resources. Sponsors education, research, and training programs. Acts as a liaison with government agencies involved

in equal opportunity compliance. Maintains ethical standards for the profession. (Formerly the American Assn. for Affirmative Action.)

American Assn. for the Advancement of Science (AAAS), *Education and Human Resources Programs,* 1200 New York Ave. N.W., 6th Floor, 20005; (202) 326-6670 (voice and TTY accessible). Fax, (202) 371-9849.
Shirley M. Malcom, Director, (202) 326-6720.
General email, ehr@aaas.org

Web, www.aaas.org/program/education-and-human-resources

Works to increase and provide information on the status of women, minorities, and people with disabilities in the STEM workforce in order to keep the science, engineering mathematics, and technology sectors competitive.

American Staffing Assn., 277 S. Washington St., #200, Alexandria, VA 22314-3675; (703) 253-2020. Fax, (703) 253-2053. Richard A. Wahlquist, President, (703) 253-2020.
Web, https://americanstaffing.net and Twitter, @StaffingTweets

Membership: companies supplying other companies with workers on a temporary or permanent basis, with outsourcing, with human resources, and with professional employer organizations (PEOs) arrangements. Monitors legislation and regulations. Encourages the maintenance of high ethical standards and provides public relations and educational support to members.

Assn. for Talent Development (ATD), 1640 King St., 3rd Floor, Alexandria, VA 22314; (703) 683-8100. Fax, (703) 683-1523. Tony Bingham, Chief Executive Officer. Toll-free, (800) 628-2783.
General email, customercare@astd.org

Web, www.astd.org, Twitter, @atd and Facebook, www.facebook.com/ATD

Membership: trainers and human resource development specialists. Promotes workplace training programs and human resource development. Interests include productivity, leadership development, and employee retraining and performance improvement. Holds conferences; publishes information about employee learning and development; provides online training. (Formerly American Society for Training and Development.)

Employee Assistance Professionals Assn., 4350 N. Fairfax Dr., #740, Arlington, VA 22203; (703) 387-1000. Fax, (703) 522-4585. Tamara Cagney, President.
General email, info@eapassn.org

Web, www.eapassn.org

Membership: professionals in the workplace who assist employees and their family members with personal and behavioral problems, including health, marital, family, financial, alcohol, drug, legal, emotional, stress, or other personal problems that adversely affect employee job performance and productivity.

HR Policy Assn., 1100 13th St. N.W., #850, 20005-4090; (202) 789-8670. Fax, (202) 789-0064. Daniel V. Yager, President.

National Labor Relations Board

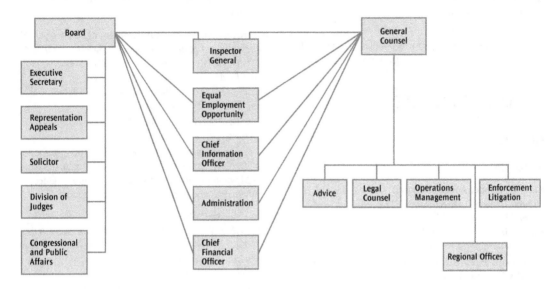

General email, info@hrpolicy.org

Web, www.hrpolicy.org

Membership: chief human resource officers in charge of employee relations. Promotes advancement of the human resource profession; interests include health care, executive compensation, labor law and labor relations, employment rights, immigration, executive compensation, impact of artifical intelligence on work, regulatory reform and enforcement, and retirement security.

Human Resources Research Organization (HumRRO), *66 Canal Center Plaza, #700, Alexandria, VA 22314-1578; (703) 549-3611. Fax, (703) 549-2860. Suzanne Tsacoumis, President.*
Web, www.humrro.org, Twitter, @HumRROorg and Facebook, www.facebook.com/Human-Resources-Research-Organization-HumRRO-161583990533313

Studies, designs, develops, surveys, and evaluates personnel systems, chiefly in the workplace. Interests include personnel selection and promotion, career progression, performance appraisal, training, program evaluation, leadership assessment, and human capital analytics.

International Public Management Assn. for Human Resources (IPMA-HR), *1617 Duke St., Alexandria, VA 22314; (703) 549-7100. Fax, (703) 684-0948. Neil Reichenberg, Executive Director.*
General email, ipma@ipma-hr.org
Web, www.ipma-hr.org, Twitter, @IPMAHR and Facebook, www.facebook.com/International-Public-Management-Association-for-Human-Resources-IPMA-HR-38098732966

Provides public sector human resource professionals with industry news, jobs, policies, resources, education, and professional development opportunities.

National Assn. of Manufacturers (NAM), *Infrastructure, Innovation, and Human Resources Policy, 733 10th St.*

N.W., #700, 20001; (202) 637-3155. Fax, (202) 637-3182. Robyn Boerstling, Vice President. Alternate phone, (202) 637-3000.
Web, www.nam.org

Interests include health care, Social Security, employee benefits, cost containment, mandated benefits, Medicare, and other federal programs that affect employers. Opposed to government involvement in health care.

Society for Human Resource Management, *1800 Duke St., Alexandria, VA 22314-3499; (703) 548-3440. Fax, (703) 535-6490. Johnny C. Taylor Jr., President. Information, (800) 283-7476. Press, (703) 535-6260. General email, shrm@shrm.org*
Web, https://shrm.org and Twitter, @SHRM

Membership: human resource management professionals. Provides human resource training and certification exams. Monitors legislation and regulations concerning recruitment, training, and employment practices; occupational safety and health; compensation and benefits; employee and labor relations; and equal employment opportunity. Sponsors seminars and conferences.

LABOR-MANAGEMENT OPPORTUNITY

General

▶AGENCIES

Defense Dept. (DoD), *National Committee for Employer Support of the Guard and Reserve, 4800 Mark Center Dr., #03E25, Arlington, VA 22350-1200; (703) 882-3747. Capt. Juliet Perkins (USN), Director; Craig M. McKinley, National Chair. Toll-free, (800) 336-4590.*

General email, osd.USERRA@mail.mil

Web, www.esgr.mil

Public Affairs email, osd.esgr-pa@mail.mil

Works to gain and maintain employer support for National Guard and Reserve service by recognizing outstanding support and providing service members and employers with information on applicable law. Volunteers provide free education, consultation, and, if necessary, mediation between employers and National Guard and Reserve service members.

Federal Mediation and Conciliation Service (FMCS), *250 E St. S.W., 7th Floor, 20427; (202) 606-8100. Fax, (202) 606-4251. Gary Hattal, Deputy Director, Field Operations. Public Affairs, (202) 606-8100.*

General email, feedback@fmcs.gov

Web, www.fmcs.gov, Twitter, @FMCS_USA and Facebook, www.facebook.com/fmcs.usa

Independent agency formed under the Labor-Management Relations Act of 1947 (Taft-Hartley Act), which assists labor and management representatives in dispute resolution and conflict management through voluntary mediation and arbitration services; mediates collective bargaining contract negotiation; awards competitive grants to joint labor-management initiatives; trains other federal agencies in mediating administrative disputes and formulating rules and regulations under the Administrative Dispute Resolution Act of 1996 and the Negotiated Rulemaking Act of 1996; provides training to unions and management in cooperative processes; provides international consulting and training to more than 60 countries. Headquartered in Washington, D.C., with offices across the country.

Labor Dept. (DOL), *Labor-Management Standards (OLMS), 200 Constitution Ave. N.W., #N1519, 20210; (202) 693-0125. Fax, (202) 693-1344. Arthur F. Rosenfeld, Director (Acting), (202) 693-0123.*

General email, olms-public@dol.gov

Web, www.dol.gov/olms

Administers and enforces the Labor-Management Reporting and Disclosure Act of 1959 (Landrum-Griffin Act), which guarantees union members certain rights; sets rules for electing union officers, handling union funds, and using trusteeships; requires unions, union officers and employees, employers, and labor consultants to file financial and other reports with the Labor Dept. Administers relevant sections of the Civil Service Reform Act of 1978 and the Foreign Service Act of 1980. Administers the employee protection provisions of the Federal Transit law.

National Labor Relations Board (NLRB), *1015 Half St. S.E., 20570-0001; (202) 273-1000. John F. Ring, Chair; Peter B. Robb, General Counsel; Roxanne Rothschild, Executive Secretary (Acting). Library, (202) 273-3720. Press and public information, (202) 273-1991. Toll-free, (844) 762-6572. TTY, (866) 315-6572.*

Web, www.nlrb.gov and Twitter, @NLRB

Administers the National Labor Relations Act. Works to prevent and remedy unfair labor practices by employers and labor unions; conducts elections among employees to

---

AFL-CIO

DEPARTMENTS

Communications, Amaya Smith, Director, (202) 637-5393

Government Affairs, William Samuel, Director, (202) 637-5320

International, Cathy Feingold, Director, (202) 637-5050

Legal Dept., Craig Becker, General Counsel, (202) 637-5155

Office of the President, Richard L. Trumka, President, (202) 637-5231

Organizing, Lynn Rodenhuis, Director, (202) 639-6225

Political, Michael Podhorzer, Director, (202) 637-5104

Safety and Health, Margaret Seminario, Director, (202) 637-5366

TRADE AND INDUSTRIAL SECTORS

Building and Construction Trades, Sean McGarvey, President, (202) 347-1461

Maritime Trades, Michael Sacco, President, (202) 628-6300

Metal Trades, James V. Hart, President, (202) 508-3705

Professional Employees, Paul E. Almeida, President, (202) 638-0320

Transportation Trades, Larry I. Willis, President, (202) 628-9262

Union Label and Service Trades, Richard Kline, President, (202) 508-3700

---

determine whether they wish to be represented by a labor union for collective bargaining purposes. Complaints may be filed in field offices by calling the toll-free line. Library open to the public.

National Mediation Board, *1301 K St. N.W., #250E, 20005-7011; (202) 692-5000. Fax, (202) 692-5082. Kyle Fortson, Chair. Information, (202) 692-5050. TTY, (202) 692-5001.*

General email, infoline@nmb.gov

Web, www.nmb.gov

Mediates labor disputes in the railroad and airline industries; determines and certifies labor representatives for those industries. Library open by appointment.

►CONGRESS

For a listing of relevant congressional committees and subcommittees, please see page 218 or the Appendix.

►NONGOVERNMENTAL

AFL-CIO (American Federation of Labor–Congress of Industrial Organizations), *815 16th St. N.W., 20006;*

(202) 637-5000. Fax, (202) 637-5058. Richard L. Trumka, President. Press, (202) 637-5018.
Web, www.aflcio.org, Twitter, @AFLCIO and Facebook, www.facebook.com/aflcio
Press, pressclips@aflcio.org

Voluntary federation of national and international labor unions in the United States. Represents members before Congress and other branches of government. Each member union conducts its own contract negotiations. Library (located in Silver Spring, Md.) open to the public.

AFL-CIO Working America, 815 16th St. N.W., 20006; (202) 637-5137. Karen Nussbaum, Founding Director; Matt Morrison, Executive Director.
General email, info@workingamerica.org
Web, www.workingamerica.org, Twitter, @workingamerica and Facebook, www.facebook .com/WorkingAmerica

Acts as advocate on behalf of nonunion workers at the community, state, and national levels. Seeks to secure better jobs, health care, education, and retirement benefits for these workers. Monitors legislation and regulations. (A community affiliate of the AFL-CIO.)

AFL-CIO, *Asian Pacific American Labor Alliance (APALA),* 815 16th St. N.W., 2nd Floor, 20006; (202) 508-3733. Alvina Yeh, Executive Director.
General email, apala@apalanet.org
Web, www.apalanet.org, Twitter, @APALAnational and Facebook, www.facebook.com/APALAnational

Membership: Asian American and Pacific Islander (AAPI) union members. Represents regional Asia–Pacific Rim labor activists in a national scope and assists in union member issues. Trains union members in areas including organization, development, and political advocacy.

Air Line Pilots Assn., International, 1625 Massachusetts Ave. N.W., #800, 20036; (703) 689-2270. Capt. Joe DePete, President. Press, (703) 481-4440. Toll-free, (888) 359-2572.
General email, alpaemail@alpa.org
Web, www.alpa.org, Twitter, @wearealpa and Facebook, www.facebook.com/WeAreAlpa

Membership: airline pilots in the United States and Canada. Promotes air travel safety; assists investigations of aviation accidents. Publishes the *Air Line Pilot Magazine.* Monitors legislation and regulations. (Affiliated with the AFL-CIO and the Canadian Labour Conference.)

American Federation of Musicians, *Government Relations,* 5335 Wisconsin Ave. N.W., #440, 20015; Fax, (202) 274-4759. Alfonso Pollard, Director, (202) 274-4756. Toll-free, (800) 762-3444.
Web, www.afm.org/departments/legislative-office/office-of-government-relations

Seeks to improve the working conditions and salary of musicians. Monitors legislation and regulations affecting musicians and the arts. (Headquarters in New York.)

Assn. of Flight Attendants–CWA, 501 3rd St. N.W., 20001-2797; (202) 434-1300. Fax, (202) 434-1319. Sara Nelson, President. Press, (202) 550-5520. Toll-free, (800) 424-2401.

General email, info@afacwa.org
Web, www.afacwa.org and Twitter, @afa_cwa

Membership: approximately 60,000 flight attendants. Helps members negotiate pay, benefits, and better working conditions; conducts training programs and workshops. Monitors legislation and regulations. (Affiliated with the AFL-CIO.)

Bakery, Confectionery, Tobacco Workers, and Grain Millers International Union, 10401 Connecticut Ave., 4th Floor, Kensington, MD 20895-3940; (301) 933-8600. Fax, (301) 946-8452. David B. Durkee, President.
General email, bctgmwebmaster@gmail.com
Web, www.bctgm.org and Twitter, @BCTGM

Membership: approximately 120,000 workers from the bakery, confectionery, grain miller, and tobacco industries. Helps members negotiate pay, benefits, and better working conditions; conducts training programs and workshops. Monitors legislation and regulations. (Affiliated with the AFL-CIO.)

The Center for Union Facts, 1090 Vermont Ave. N.W., #800, 20005; (202) 463-7100. Fax, (202) 463-7107. Richard Berman, Executive Director.
Web, www.unionfacts.com

Seeks to educate businesses, union members, and the public about the labor movement's political activities, specifically those of union officials. Interests include management of union dues. Monitors legislation and regulations.

Coalition of Black Trade Unionists, 1155 Connecticut Ave. N.W., #500, 20036 (mailing address: P.O. Box 66268, Washington, DC 20035); (202) 778-3318. Fax, (202) 419-1486. Terrence L. Melvin, President.
General email, cbtu@cbtu.org
Web, http://cbtu.org and Twitter, @CBTU72

Monitors legislation affecting African American and other minority trade unionists. Focuses on equal employment opportunity, unemployment, and voter education and registration.

Coalition of Labor Union Women, 815 16th St. N.W., 2nd Floor South, 20006-1119; (202) 508-6969. Fax, (202) 508-6968. Elise Bryant, President; Carol S. Rosenblatt, Executive Director, (202) 508-6951.
General email, getinfo@cluw.org
Web, http://cluw.org and Twitter, @CLUWNational

Seeks to make unions more responsive to the needs of women in the workplace; advocates affirmative action and the active participation of women in unions. Monitors legislation and regulations.

Communications Workers of America (CWA), 501 3rd St. N.W., 20001; (202) 434-1100. Fax, (202) 434-1279. Christopher M. Shelton, President.
Web, https://cwa-union.org and Twitter, @CWAUnion

Membership: approximately 700,000 workers in telecommunications, journalism, publishing, cable television, electronics, and other fields. Interests include workplace democracy and restoring bargaining rights. Represents members in contract negotiations and grievances; conducts training programs and workshops. Monitors legislation and regulations. (Affiliated with the AFL-CIO.)

Federal Education Assn., *1201 16th St. N.W., #117, 20036; (202) 822-7850. Fax, (202) 822-7867. Chuck McCarter, President.*
General email, fea@feaonline.org
Web, www.feaonline.org and Twitter, @FedEdAssoc

Membership: teachers and personnel of Defense Dept. schools for military dependents in the United States and abroad. Helps members negotiate pay, benefits, and better working conditions.

International Assn. of Bridge, Structural, Ornamental, and Reinforcing Iron Workers, *1750 New York Ave. N.W., #400, 20006; (202) 383-4800. Fax, (202) 638-4856. Eric Dean, General President.*
General email, iwmagazine@iwintl.org
Web, www.ironworkers.org and Twitter, @TheIronWorkers

Membership: approximately 120,000 iron workers. Helps members negotiate pay, benefits, and better working conditions; conducts training programs and workshops. Monitors legislation and regulations. (Affiliated with the AFL-CIO.)

International Assn. of Fire Fighters, *1750 New York Ave. N.W., #300, 20006-5395; (202) 737-8484. Fax, (202) 737-8418. Harold A. Schaitberger, General President.*
General email, pr@tburn.iaff.org
Web, www.i aff.org, Twitter, @IAFFNewsDesk and Facebook, www.facebook.com/IAFFonline

Membership: more than 310,000 professional firefighters and emergency medical personnel. Assists members with contract negotiation and grievances; conducts training programs and workshops. Monitors legislation and regulations. (Affiliated with the AFL-CIO and the Canadian Labour Congress.)

International Assn. of Heat and Frost Insulators and Allied Workers, *9602 Martin Luther King Hwy., Lanham, MD 20706-1839; (301) 731-9101. Fax, (301) 731-5058. James McCourt, General President.*
General email, hfi@insulators.org
Web, www.insulators.org and Twitter, @InsulatorsUnion

Membership: approximately 30,000 workers in insulation industries. Helps members negotiate pay, benefits, and better working conditions; conducts training programs and workshops. Monitors legislation and regulations. (Affiliated with the AFL-CIO.)

International Assn. of Machinists and Aerospace Workers, *9000 Machinists Pl., Upper Marlboro, MD 20772-2687; (301) 967-4500. Robert Martinez Jr., International President. Information, (301) 967-4520.*
General email, websteward@iamaw.org
Web, www.goiam.org

Membership: machinists in more than 200 industries. Helps members negotiate pay, benefits, and better working conditions; conducts training programs and workshops. Monitors legislation and regulations. (Affiliated with the AFL-CIO, the Canadian Labour Congress, the International Metalworkers Federation, the International Transport Workers' Federation, and the Railway Labor Executives Assn.)

International Assn. of Machinists and Aerospace Workers, *Transportation Communications Union, 3 Research Pl., Rockville, MD 20850-3279; (301) 948-4910. Robert A. Scardelletti, President.*
General email, info@iamaw.org
Web, www.goiam.org/index.php/tcunion

Membership: approximately 46,000 railway workers. Assists members with contract negotiation and grievances; conducts training programs and workshops. Monitors legislation and regulations. (Affiliated with the AFL-CIO and Canadian Labour Congress.)

International Brotherhood of Boilermakers, Iron Ship Builders, Blacksmiths, Forgers, and Helpers, *Government Affairs, 1750 New York Ave. N.W., #335, 20006; (202) 756-2868. Fax, (202) 756-2869. Cecile Conroy, Director of Government Affairs, ext. 202.*
General email, cconroy@boilermakers.org
Web, https://boilermakers.org

Membership: workers in construction, repair, maintenance, manufacturing, shipbuilding and marine repair, mining and quarrying, railroads, cement kilns, and related industries in the United States and Canada. Helps members negotiate pay, benefits, and better working conditions; conducts training programs and workshops. Monitors legislation and regulations. (Headquarters in Kansas City, Kans.; affiliated with the AFL-CIO.)

International Brotherhood of Electrical Workers (IBEW), *900 7th St. N.W., 20001; (202) 833-7000. Fax, (202) 728-7676. Lonnie Stephenson, International President; Kenneth Cooper, International Secretary-Treasurer.*
General email, webmaster@ibew.org
Web, www.ibew.org

Membership: workers in utilities, construction, telecommunications, broadcasting, manufacturing, railroads, and government. Helps members negotiate pay, benefits, and better working conditions; conducts training programs and workshops. Monitors legislation and regulations. (Affiliated with the AFL-CIO.)

International Brotherhood of Teamsters, *25 Louisiana Ave. N.W., 20001-2198; (202) 624-6800. Fax, (202) 624-6918. James P. Hoffa, General President; Christy Bailey, Director of Federal Legislation and Regulation, (202) 624-6993; Bret Caldwell, Director of Communications, (202) 624-6911. Press, (202) 624-6911.*
General email, communications@teamster.org
Web, www.teamster.org

Membership: workers in the transportation and construction industries, factories, offices, hospitals, warehouses, and other workplaces. Helps members negotiate pay, benefits, and better working conditions; conducts training programs and workshops. Monitors legislation and regulations.

International Longshore and Warehouse Union (ILWU),
Washington Office, *1025 Connecticut Ave. N.W., #507,*
20036; (202) 463-6265. Fax, (202) 467-4875.
Lindsay McLaughlin, Legislative Director.
General email, bianca.blomquist@ilwu.org
Web, www.ilwu.org

Membership: longshore and warehouse personnel. Helps members negotiate pay, benefits, and better working conditions; conducts training programs and workshops. Monitors legislation and regulations. (Headquarters in San Francisco, Calif.)

International Longshoremen's Assn., Washington Office,
1101 17th St. N.W., #400, 20036-4704; (202) 955-6304.
Fax, (202) 955-6048. John Bowers Jr., Executive Director.
General email, iladc@aol.com
Web, www.ilaunion.org

Membership: approximately 65,000 longshore personnel. Helps members negotiate pay, benefits, and better working conditions; conducts training programs and workshops. Monitors legislation and regulations. (Headquarters in New Jersey; affiliated with the AFL-CIO.)

International Union of Bricklayers and Allied
Craftworkers, *620 F St. N.W., 20004; (202) 783-3788.*
James Boland, President. Toll-free, (888) 880-8222.
General email, askbac@bacweb.org
Web, www.bacweb.org

Membership: bricklayers, stonemasons, and other skilled craftworkers in the building industry. Helps members negotiate pay, benefits, and better working conditions; conducts training programs and workshops. Monitors legislation and regulations. (Affiliated with the AFL-CIO and the International Masonry Institute.)

International Union of Operating Engineers, *1125 17th*
St. N.W., 20036; (202) 429-9100. Fax, (202) 778-2688.
James T. Callahan, General President.
Web, www.iuoe.org

Membership: approximately 400,000 operating engineers, including heavy equipment operators, mechanics, and surveyors in the construction industry, and stationary engineers, including operations and building maintenance staff. Represents members in negotiating pay, benefits, and better working conditions; conducts training programs and workshops. Monitors legislation and regulations in the U.S. and Canada. (Affiliated with the AFL-CIO.)

International Union of Painters and Allied Trades,
7234 Parkway Dr., Hanover, MD 21076; (410) 564-5900.
Fax, (866) 656-4124. Kenneth Rigmaiden, General President.
General email, mail@iupat.org
Web, www.iupat.org, Twitter, @GoIUPAT and
Facebook, www.facebook.com/GoIUPAT

Membership: more than 140,000 painters, glaziers, floor covering installers, sign makers, show decorators, and workers in allied trades in the United States and Canada. Helps members negotiate pay, benefits, and better working conditions; conducts training programs and workshops. Monitors legislation and regulations. (Affiliated with the AFL-CIO.)

Labor Council for Latin American Advancement, *815*
16th St. N.W., 3rd Floor, 20006; (202) 508-6919.
Fax, (202) 508-6922. Hector E. Sanchez, Executive Director.
General email, headquarters@lclaa.org
Web, www.lclaa.org, Twitter, @LCLAA and
Facebook, www.facebook.com/LCLAA

Membership: Hispanic trade unionists. Encourages equal employment opportunity, voter registration, and participation in the political process. (Affiliated with the AFL-CIO and the Change to Win Federation.)

Laborers' International Union of North America, *905*
16th St. N.W., 20006-1765; (202) 737-8320.
Fax, (202) 737-2754. Terry O'Sullivan, President.
Web, www.liuna.org, Twitter, @LIUNA and
Facebook, www.facebook.com/
LaborersInternationalUnionofNorthAmerica

Membership: more than 500,000 construction workers; federal, state, and local government employees; health care professionals; mail handlers; custodial service personnel; shipbuilders; and hazardous waste handlers. Helps members negotiate pay, benefits, and better working conditions; conducts training programs and workshops. Monitors legislation and regulations. (Affiliated with the AFL-CIO.)

National Assn. of Manufacturers (NAM), *Infrastructure,*
Innovation, and Human Resources Policy, 733 10th St.
N.W., #700, 20001; (202) 637-3155. Fax, (202) 637-3182.
Robyn Boerstling, Vice President. Alternate phone,
(202) 637-3000.
Web, www.nam.org

Provides information on corporate industrial relations, including collective bargaining, labor standards, international labor relations, productivity, employee benefits, health care, and other current labor issues; monitors legislation and regulations.

National Right to Work Committee, *8001 Braddock Rd.,*
#500, Springfield, VA 22160; (703) 321-9820.
Fax, (703) 321-7342. Mark Mix, President. Information,
(800) 325-7892.
General email, info@nrtwc.org
Web, www.nrtwc.org, Twitter, @Right2Work and
Facebook, www.facebook.com/NationalRightToWork

Citizens' organization opposed to compulsory union membership. Supports right-to-work legislation.

National Right to Work Legal Defense and Education
Foundation, *8001 Braddock Rd., #600, Springfield, VA*
22160; (703) 321-8510. Fax, (703) 321-9613. Mark Mix,
President. Toll-free, (800) 336-3600.

General email, info@nrtw.org

Web, www.nrtw.org

Provides free legal aid for employees in cases of compulsory union membership abuses.

The Newspaper Guild—CWA, *501 3rd St. N.W., 6th Floor, 20001-2797; (202) 434-7177. Fax, (202) 434-1472. Bernard J. Lunzer, President.*

General email, guild@cwa-union.org

Web, www.newsguild.org, Twitter, @news_guild and Facebook, www.facebook.com/NewsGuild

Membership: journalists, sales and media professionals. Advocates higher standards in journalism; equal employment opportunity in the print, broadcast, wire, and Web media industries; and advancement of members' economic interests. (Affiliated with Communications Workers of America, the AFL-CIO, CLC, and IFJ.)

Operative Plasterers' and Cement Masons' International Assn. of the United States and Canada, *9700 Patuxent Woods Dr., #200, Columbia, MD 21046; (301) 623-1000. Fax, (301) 623-1032. Daniel E. Stepano, President.*

General email, opcmiaintl@opcmia.org

Web, www.opcmia.org and Twitter, @opcmiaint

Membership: approximately 58,000 cement masons and plasterers. Helps members negotiate pay, benefits, and better working conditions; conducts training programs and workshops. Monitors legislation and regulations. (Affiliated with the AFL-CIO.)

Public Service Research Council, *320-D Maple Ave. East, Vienna, VA 22180-4742; (703) 242-3575. Fax, (703) 242-3579. David Y. Denholm, President.*

General email, info@psrconline.org

Web, www.psrconline.org

Independent nonprofit research and educational organization. Studies labor unions and labor issues with emphasis on employment in the public sector. Monitors legislation and regulations.

Seafarers International Union of North America, *5201 Auth Way, Camp Springs, MD 20746-4275; (301) 899-0675. Fax, (301) 899-7355. Michael Sacco, President. Press, (301) 899-0675, ext. 4300.*

Web, www.seafarers.org and Twitter, @SeafarersUnion

Represents professional U.S. merchant mariners sailing aboard U.S.-flag vessels in the deep sea, Great Lakes, and inland trades; works to protect members' job security.

Service Employees International Union, *1800 Massachusetts Ave. N.W., 20036; (202) 730-7000. Fax, (202) 429-5563. Mary Kay Henry, President. Press, (202) 730-7162. Toll-free, (800) 424-8592.*

General email, media@seiu.org

Web, www.seiu.org and Twitter, @SEIU

Membership: approximately 2.2 million members in Canada, the United States, and Puerto Rico among health care, public services, and property services employees.

Promotes better wages, health care, and job security for workers. Monitors legislation and regulations.

Sheet Metal, Air, Rail, and Transportation Workers (SMART), *1750 New York Ave. N.W., 6th Floor, 20006; (202) 662-0880. Joseph Sellers Jr., General President. Toll-free, (800) 457-7694.*

General email, info@smart-union.org

Web, http://smart-union.org and Twitter, @smartunionworks

Membership: United States, Puerto Rican, and Canadian workers in the building and construction trades, manufacturing, and the railroad and shipyard industries. Assists members with contract negotiation and grievances; conducts training programs and workshops. Monitors legislation and regulations. (Affiliated with the Sheet Metal and Air Conditioning Contractors' Assn., the AFL-CIO, and the Canadian Labour Congress.)

Solidarity Center, *1130 Connecticut Ave. N.W., #800, Washington, DC, 20036; (202) 974-8383. Fax, (202) 974-8384. Shawna Bader-Blau, Executive Director. Press, (202) 974-8369.*

General email, information@solidaritycenter.org

Web, www.solidaritycenter.org and Twitter, @solidaritycntr

Provides assistance to free and democratic trade unions worldwide. Provides trade union leadership courses in collective bargaining, union organization, trade integration, labor-management cooperation, union administration, and political theories. Sponsors social and community development projects; focus includes child labor, human and worker rights, and the role of women in labor unions. (Affiliated with the AFL-CIO.)

U.S. Chamber of Commerce, *Employment Policy, 1615 H St. N.W., 20062-2000; (202) 463-5522. Fax, (202) 463-3194 and (202) 463-5901. Glenn Spencer, Senior Vice President.*

General email, laborpolicy@uschamber.com

Web, www.uschamber.com/labor-immigration-and-employee-benefits and ADA information, www.uschamber.com/health-reform

Immigration news, http://immigration.uschamber.com

Formulates and analyzes chamber policy in the areas of labor law, employment nondiscrimination, minimum wage and wage-hour, occupational safety and health, immigration, labor-management relations, work-family issues and leave mandates, and emerging international labor policy issues. Monitors legislation and regulations affecting labor-management relations.

UNITE HERE, *Washington Office, 1775 K St. N.W., #620, 20006-1530; (202) 393-4373. Fax, (202) 223-6213 or (202) 342-2929. Donald Taylor, President.*

Web, www.unitehere.org and Twitter, @unitehere

Membership: workers in the United States and Canada who work in the hotel, gaming, food service, distibution, transportation, manufacturing, textile, laundry, and airport industries. Assists members with contract negotiation and grievances; conducts training programs and workshops. Monitors legislation and regulations. (Headquarters in New York. Formed by the merger of the former Union of Needletrades, Textiles and Industrial Employees and the Hotel Employees and Restaurant Employees International Union.)

United Auto Workers (UAW), *Washington Office, 1757 N St. N.W., 20036; (202) 828-8500. Fax, (202) 293-3457. Josh Nassar, Legislative Director.*
Web, www.uaw.org and Twitter, @uaw

Membership: approximately 400,000 active and 600,000 retired North American workers in aerospace, automotive, defense, manufacturing, steel, technical, and other industries. Assists members with contract negotiations and grievances; conducts training programs and workshops. Monitors legislation and regulations. (Headquarters in Detroit, Mich.)

United Food and Commercial Workers International Union (UFCW), *1775 K St. N.W., 20006-1598; (202) 223-3111. Fax, (202) 728-1803. Anthony (Marc) Perrone, President.*
Web, www.ufcw.org and Twitter, @UFCW

Membership: approximately 1.3 million workers primarily in the retail, meatpacking, food processing, and poultry industries. Interests include health care reform, living wages, retirement security, safe working conditions, and the right to unionize. Monitors legislation and regulations.

United Mine Workers of America, *18354 Quantico Gateway Dr., #200, Triangle, VA 22172-1779; (703) 291-2400. Cecil E. Roberts, President. General email, info@umwa.org*
Web, www.umwa.org and Twitter, @MineWorkers

Membership: coal miners and other mining workers. Represents members in collective bargaining with industry. Conducts educational, housing, and health and safety training programs; monitors federal coal-mining safety programs.

United Steelworkers, Legislative, *1155 Connecticut Ave. N.W., #500, 20036; (202) 778-4384. Fax, (202) 419-1486. Holly Hart, Legislative Director, (202) 393-3430.*
Web, www.usw.org and Twitter, @steelworkers

Membership: more than one million workers in the steel, paper, rubber, energy, chemical, pharmaceutical, and allied industries. Helps members negotiate pay, benefits, and better working conditions; conducts training programs and workshops. Monitors legislation and regulations. (Affiliated with the AFL-CIO; Headquarters in Pittsburgh, Pa.)

Utility Workers Union of America, *1300 L St. N.W., #1200, 20005; (202) 899-2851. Fax, (202) 899-2852. D. Michael Langford, National President; Mike Coleman, National Secretary-Treasurer; Lee Anderson, Government Affairs Director. General email, webmaster@uwua.net*
Web, www.uwua.net and Twitter, @The_UWUA

Labor union representing workers in electric, gas, water, and nuclear utility industries. Helps members negotiate pay, benefits, and better working conditions; conducts training programs and workshops. Monitors legislation and regulations. (Affiliated with the AFL-CIO.)

PENSIONS AND BENEFITS

General

▶**AGENCIES**

Advisory Council on Employee Welfare and Pension Benefit Plans (ERISA Advisory Council) *(Labor Dept.), 200 Constitution Ave. N.W., #S2524, 20210; (202) 693-6309. Fax, (202) 219-5526. Jeanne Klinefelter Wilson, Deputy Executive Secretary, (202) 693-8300. Toll-free, (866) 444-3272.*
Web, www.dol.gov/agencies/ebsa/about-ebsa/about-us/erisa-advisory-council

Advises and makes recommendations to the secretary of labor under the Employee Retirement Income Security Act of 1974 (ERISA).

Bureau of Labor Statistics (BLS) *(Labor Dept.), Compensation and Working Conditions (OCWC), 2 Massachusetts Ave. N.E., #4130, 20212; (202) 691-6300. Fax, (202) 691-6310. Kristen Monaco, Associate Commissioner.*
Web, www.bls.gov

Conducts quarterly surveys of wages and benefits; data used for the quarterly *Employment Cost Index*, the quarterly *Employer Costs for Employee Compensation*, and annual reports on the incidence and provisions of employee benefits.

Employee Benefits Security Administration *(Labor Dept.), 200 Constitution Ave. N.W., #S2524, 20210; (202) 693-8300. Fax, (202) 219-5526. Preston Rutledge, Assistant Secretary; Timothy Hauser, Deputy Assistant Secretary for Programs. Toll-free, (866) 444-3272.*
Web, www.dol.gov/ebsa

Administers, regulates, and enforces private employee benefit plan standards established by the Employee Retirement Income Security Act of 1974 (ERISA), with particular emphasis on fiduciary obligations; receives and maintains required reports from employee benefit plan administrators pursuant to ERISA.

Federal Retirement Thrift Investment Board, *77 K St. N.E., #1000, 20002; (202) 942-1600. Ravindra Deo, Executive Director. Toll-free, (877) 968-3778. TTY, (877) 847-4385.*
Web, www.frtib.gov

Administers the Thrift Savings Plan, a tax-deferred, defined contribution plan that permits federal employees and members of the uniformed services to save for additional retirement security under a program similar to private 401(k) plans.

Internal Revenue Service (IRS) *(Treasury Dept.)*, *Joint Board for the Enrollment of Actuaries*, *1111 Constitution Ave. N.W., SE:RPO, REFM, Park 4, 4th Floor, 20224;*
Patrick McDonough, Executive Director;
Chet Andrzejewski, Chair.
General email, nhqjbea@irs.gov
Web, www.irs.gov/tax-professionals/enrolled-actuaries

Joint board, with members from the departments of Labor and Treasury and the Pension Benefit Guaranty Corp., established under the Employee Retirement Income Security Act of 1974 (ERISA). Promulgates regulations for the enrollment of pension actuaries; examines applicants and grants certificates of enrollment; disciplines enrolled actuaries who have engaged in misconduct in the discharge of duties under ERISA.

Office of Personnel Management (OPM), *Retirement Operations, 1900 E St. N.W., #2H28, 20415;*
(724) 794-2005. Fax, (724) 794-4323.
Kenneth J. Zawodny Jr., Associate Director,
(724) 794-7759; Tia Butler, Deputy Associate Director.
Toll-free, (888) 767-6738. TTY, (855) 887-4957.
General email, retire@opm.gov
Web, www.opm.gov/retire

Provides civil servants with information and assistance on federal retirement payments.

Pension Benefit Guaranty Corp., *1200 K St. N.W., 20005-4026 (mailing address: P.O. Box 151750, Alexandria, VA 22315-1750); (202) 326-4000. Fax, (202) 326-4047.*
Alice Maroni, Chief Management Officer. Customer Service, (800) 400-7242. General legal inquiries,
(202) 326-4020. Locator, (202) 326-4110. TTY, (800) 877-8339, ask to connect to (800) 400-7242.
Web, www.pbgc.gov and Twitter, @USPBGC

Self-financed U.S. government corporation. Insures private-sector defined benefit pension plans; guarantees payment of retirement benefits subject to certain limitations established in the Employee Retirement Income Security Act of 1974 (ERISA). Provides insolvent multiemployer pension plans with financial assistance to enable them to pay guaranteed retirement benefits.

Railroad Retirement Board, *Legislative Affairs, 1310 G St. N.W., #500, 20005-3004; (202) 272-7742.*
Fax, (202) 272-7728. Beverly Britton-Fraser, Director.
Toll-free, (877) 772-5772.
General email, ola@rrb.gov/org/ogc/ola.asp
Web, https://rrb.gov/OurAgency/OfficeofGeneralCounsel/ OfficeofLegislativeAffair

Assists congressional offices with inquiries on retirement, spouse, survivor, unemployment, and sickness benefits for railroad employees and retirees. Assists with legislation. (Headquarters in Chicago, Ill.)

►CONGRESS

For a listing of relevant congressional committees and subcommittees, please see page 218 or the Appendix.

►NONGOVERNMENTAL

AARP, *601 E St. N.W., 20049; (202) 434-2277.*
Fax, (202) 434-7946. Jo Ann C. Jenkins, Chief Executive Officer. Library, (202) 434-6233. Membership,
(202) 434-7550. Membership, toll-free, (800) 566-0242.
Press, (202) 434-2560. Toll-free, (888) 687-2277. TTY,
(877) 434-7598. Toll-free Spanish, (877) 342-2277. TTY Spanish, (866) 238-9488.
General email, member@aarp.org
Web, www.aarp.org, Twitter, @AARP and Facebook, www .facebook.com/AARP

Researches and testifies on private, federal, and other government employee pension legislation and regulations; conducts seminars; provides information on preretirement preparation.

Alliance for Retired Americans, *815 16th St. N.W., 4th Floor, 20006-4104; (202) 637-5399. Fax, (202) 637-5398.*
Robert Roach Jr., President. Membership, (800) 333-7212.
Web, https://retiredamericans.org, Twitter, @ActiveRetirees and Facebook, www.facebook.com/retiredamericans

Alliance of retired members of unions affiliated with the AFL-CIO, senior citizen clubs, associations, councils, and other groups. Seeks to nationalize health care services and to strengthen benefits to older adults, including improved Social Security payments, secure social and economic justice including civil rights, and education and health programs. (Affiliate of the AFL-CIO.)

American Academy of Actuaries, *1850 M St. N.W., #300, 20036; (202) 223-8196. Fax, (202) 872-1948.*
Shawna Ackerman, President; Mary Downs, Executive Director.
General email, guerra@actuary.org
Web, www.actuary.org, Twitter, @Actuary_Dot_Org and Facebook, www.facebook.com/Actuary.Org

Membership: professional actuaries practicing in the areas of life, health, liability, property, and casualty insurance; pensions; government insurance plans; and general consulting. Provides information on actuarial matters, including insurance and pensions; develops professional standards; advises public policymakers.

American Benefits Council, *1501 M St. N.W., #600, 20005; (202) 289-6700. Fax, (202) 289-4582.*
James A. Klein, President; Diann Howland, Vice President Legislative Affairs.
General email, info@abcstaff.org
Web, www.americanbenefitscouncil.org,
Twitter, @benefitscouncil and Facebook, www.facebook .com/benefitscouncil

Membership: employers, consultants, banks, and service organizations. Informs members of employee benefits,

Occupational Safety and Health Administration

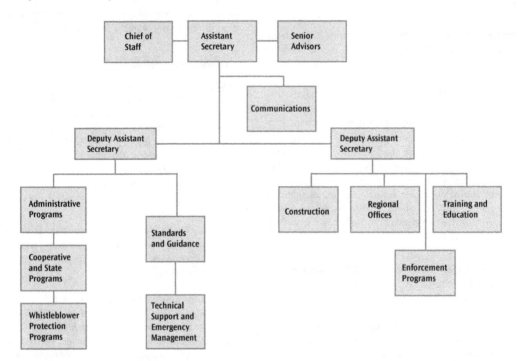

including private pension benefits, health benefits, and compensation.

American Society of Pension Professionals and Actuaries, *4245 N. Fairfax Dr., #750, Arlington, VA 22203-1648; (703) 516-9300. Fax, (703) 516-9308. Brian H. Graff, Chief Executive Officer, (703) 516-9300. General email, info@usaretirement.org*

Web, www.asppa.org and Twitter, @ASPPA

Membership: administrators, actuaries, advisers, lawyers, accountants, and other financial services professionals who provide consulting and administrative services for employee-based retirement plans. Sponsors educational conferences, webcasts, and credentialing programs for retirement professionals. Monitors legislation and regulations.

The Brookings Institution, *Economic Studies, 1775 Massachusetts Ave. N.W., 20036-2188; (202) 797-6000. Fax, (202) 797-6181. Ted Gayer, Director, (202) 797-6230. Press, (202) 797-6105. General email, escomment@brookings.edu*

Web, www.brookings.edu/economics and Twitter, @BrookingsEcon

Promotes efforts to make retirement saving easier and improve retirement income prospects for American workers.

The Brookings Institution, *Retirement Security Project, 1775 Massachusetts Ave. N.W., 20036; (202) 797-6000. William Gale, Director. Press, (202) 797-6105. Web, www.brookings.edu/about/projects/ retirementsecurity*

Promotes policy solutions for improving retirement income and financial security for middle-income and low-income workers who do not have access to employer-sponsored retirement savings plans or traditional pensions.

Council of Institutional Investors, *1717 Pennsylvania Ave. N.W., #350, 20006; (202) 822-0800. Fax, (202) 822-0801. Ken Bertsch, Executive Director, (202) 261-7098.*

Web, www.cii.org and Twitter, @CouncilInstInv

Membership: pension funds and other employee benefit funds, foundations, and endowments. Studies investment issues that affect pension plan assets. Focuses on corporate governance and shareholder rights. Monitors legislation and regulations.

Employee Benefit Research Institute, *1100 13th St. N.W., #878, 20005; (202) 659-0670. Fax, (202) 775-6312. Lori Lucas, President. General email, info@ebri.org*

Web, www.ebri.org

Research organization serving as an employee benefits information source on health, welfare, and retirement issues. Does not lobby and does not take public policy positions.

Employers Council on Flexible Compensation, *1220 L St. N.W., #100-417, 20005-4018; (202) 659-4300. Fax, (202) 618-6060. Martin Trussell, Executive Director. General email, info@ecfc.org*

Web, www.ecfc.org and Twitter, @GoECFC

Advocates tax-advantaged, private-employer benefit programs. Supports the preservation and expansion of employee choice in savings and pension plans. Monitors legislation and regulations. Interests include cafeteria plans and 401(k) plans.

ERISA Industry Committee, *701 8th St. N.W., #610, 20001; (202) 789-1400. Annette Guarisco Fildes, President, (202) 627-1910.*
General email, memberservices@eric.org
Web, www.eric.org

Membership: large major U.S. employers. Advocates members' positions on employee retirement, health care coverage, and welfare benefit plans. Monitors legislation and regulations.

National Assn. of Manufacturers (NAM), *Infrastructure, Innovation, and Human Resources Policy, 733 10th St. N.W., #700, 20001; (202) 637-3155. Fax, (202) 637-3182. Robyn Boerstling, Vice President. Alternate phone, (202) 637-3000.*
Web, www.nam.org

Interests include health care, cost containment, mandated benefits, Medicare, and other federal programs that affect employers. Opposed to government involvement in health care and proposed expansion of health care liability.

National Institute on Retirement Security, *1612 K St. N.W., #500, 20006; (202) 457-8190. Diane Oakley, Executive Director.*
General email, info@nirsonline.org
Web, www.nirsonline.org and Twitter, @nirsonline

Researches retirement security policies and educates the public and policymakers about the positive impact of benefit pension plans. Advocates broader, more defined retirement plans.

Pension Rights Center, *1730 M St. N.W., #1000, 20036; (202) 296-3776. Karen W. Ferguson, Director. Toll-free, (888) 420-6550.*
General email, kgarrett@pensionrights.org
Web, www.pensionrights.org and Twitter, @PensionRights

Works to preserve and expand pension rights; provides information and technical assistance on pension law.

ProtectSeniors.Org, *601 Pennsylvania Ave., South Bldg., #900, 20004; (202) 434-8193. Fax, (540) 439-9570. Jim Casey, President; Paul Miller, Executive Director. Toll-free, (800) 398-3044.*
General email, info@protectseniors.org
Web, www.protectseniors.org and Twitter, @ProtectSeniors

Aims to illegalize the corporate discontinuation of promised health care benefits after employees have retired. Acts as advocate against pension stripping. Monitors legislation and regulation.

U.S. Chamber of Commerce, *Employment Policy, 1615 H St. N.W., 20062-2000; (202) 463-5522. Fax, (202) 463-3194 and (202) 463-5901. Glenn Spencer, Senior Vice President.*
General email, laborpolicy@uschamber.com
Web, www.uschamber.com/labor-immigration-and-employee-benefits and ADA information, www.uschamber.com/health-reform
Immigration news, http://immigration.uschamber.com

Formulates and analyzes chamber policy in the areas of health care, pensions and retirement plans, Social Security, and Medicare. Monitors legislation and regulations affecting employee benefits.

United Mine Workers of America, *Health and Retirement Funds, 2121 K St. N.W., #350, 20037-1801; (202) 521-2200. Fax, (202) 521-2394. Lorraine Lewis, Executive Director, (202) 521-2320. Call Center, (800) 291-1425.*
General email, health1@umwafunds.org
Web, www.umwafunds.org

Labor-management trust fund that provides health and retirement benefits to coal miners. Health benefits are provided to pensioners, their dependents, and, in some cases, their survivors.

Urban Institute, *Income and Benefits Policy Center, 500 L'Enfant Plaza S.W., 20024; (202) 833-7200. Fax, (202) 833-4388. Gregory Acs, Vice President.*
Web, www.urban.org/center/ibp
Retirement policy, http://urban.org/retirement_policy

Studies how public policy influences behavior and the economic well-being of families, particularly the disabled, the elderly, and those with low incomes.

Women's Institute for a Secure Retirement (WISER), *1001 Connecticut Ave. N.W., #730, 20036; (202) 393-5452. Fax, (202) 393-5890. Cindy Hounsell, President.*
General email, info@wiserwomen.org
Web, www.wiserwomen.org and Twitter, @WISERWomen

Provides information on women's retirement issues. Monitors legislation and regulations.

WORKPLACE SAFETY AND HEALTH

General

▶**AGENCIES**

Bureau of Labor Statistics (BLS) *(Labor Dept.), Compensation and Working Conditions (OCWC), 2 Massachusetts Ave. N.E., #4130, 20212; (202) 691-6300. Fax, (202) 691-6310. Kristen Monaco, Associate Commissioner.*
Web, www.bls.gov

Compiles data on occupational safety and health.

Environment, Health, Safety, and Security (EHSS) *(Energy Dept.), Health and Safety, 1000 Independence Ave. S.W., AU-10-GTN, 20585; (301) 903-5926. Fax, (301) 903-3445. Patricia R. Worthington, Director.*
Web, http://energy.gov/ehss/organizational-chart/office-health-and-safety

Establishes hazardous-material worker safety and health requirements and expectations for the Energy Dept. and assists in their implementation. Conducts and supports domestic and international hazardous material health studies and programs. Supports the Labor Dept. in the implementation of the Energy Employees Occupational Illness Compensation Program Act (EEOICPA).

Federal Mine Safety and Health Review Commission (FMSHRC), *1331 Pennsylvania Ave. N.W., #520N, 20004-1710; (202) 434-9905. Fax, (202) 434-9906. Lisa Boyd, Executive Director; Michael G. Young, Chair (Acting). TTY, (202) 434-4000, ext. 293.*
General email, fmshrc@fmshrc.gov
Web, www.fmshrc.gov

Independent agency established by the Federal Mine Safety and Health Act of 1977. Holds fact-finding hearings and issues orders affirming, modifying, or vacating the labor secretary's enforcement actions regarding mine safety and health. Reading room open to the public by appointment.

Mine Safety and Health Administration *(Labor Dept.), 201 12th St. South, #401, Arlington, VA 22202-5450; (202) 693-9400. Fax, (202) 693-9801. David G. Zatezalo, Assistant Secretary. Toll-free, (800) 746-1553.*
General email, ASKMSHA@dol.gov
Web, www.msha.gov and Twitter, @MSHA_DOL

Administers and enforces the health and safety provisions of the Federal Mine Safety and Health Act of 1977.

National Institute for Occupational Safety and Health (NIOSH) *(Centers for Disease Control and Prevention), 395 E St. S.W., Patriots Plaza 1, #9200, 20201; (202) 245-0625. Dr. John Howard, Director. Information, (800) 232-4636. TTY, (888) 232-6348.*
General email, cdcinfo@cdc.gov
Web, www.cdc.gov/niosh

Entity within the Centers for Disease Control and Prevention in Atlanta. Supports and conducts research on occupational safety and health issues; provides technical assistance and training; develops recommendations for the Labor Dept. Operates an occupational safety and health bibliographic database.

Occupational Safety and Health Administration (OSHA) *(Labor Dept.), 200 Constitution Ave. N.W., #S2315, 20210; (202) 693-2000. Fax, (202) 693-1659. Loren Sweatt, Assistant Secretary (Acting). Emergency hotline, (800) 321-6742. TTY, (877) 889-5627.*
Web, www.osha.gov, Twitter, @OSHA_DOL and Facebook, www.facebook.com/pages/US-Department-of-Labor-Occupational-Safety-and-Health-Administration/110034312373653

Sets and enforces rules and regulations for workplace safety and health. Implements the Occupational Safety and Health Act of 1970. Provides federal agencies and private industries with compliance guidance and assistance. Website has a Spanish-language link.

Occupational Safety and Health Administration (OSHA) *(Labor Dept.), Communications, 200 Constitution Ave. N.W., #N3647, 20210; (202) 693-1999.*

Fax, (202) 693-1635. Francis Meilinger, Director. Emergency hotline, (800) 321-6742.
Web, www.osha.gov/as

Develops strategies, products, and materials to promote public understanding of OSHA standards, regulations, guidelines, policies, and activities to improve the safety and health of employees.

Occupational Safety and Health Administration (OSHA) *(Labor Dept.), Construction, 200 Constitution Ave. N.W., #N3468, 20210; (202) 693-2020. Fax, (202) 693-1689. Scott Ketcham, Director (Acting).*
Web, www.osha.gov/doc

Provides technical expertise to OSHA's enforcement personnel; initiates studies to determine causes of construction accidents; works with the private sector to promote construction safety and training and to identify, reduce, and eliminate construction-related hazards.

Occupational Safety and Health Administration (OSHA) *(Labor Dept.), Cooperative and State Programs, 200 Constitution Ave. N.W., #N3700, 20210; (202) 693-2020. Fax, (202) 693-1689. Douglas Kalinowski, Director.*
Web, www.osha.gov/dcsp

Implements OSHA's cooperative programs, coordinates the agency's compliance assistance and outreach activities, coordinates the agency's relations with state plan states; oversees OSHA international issues; and coordinates small business assistance outreach.

Occupational Safety and Health Administration (OSHA) *(Labor Dept.), Enforcement Programs, 200 Constitution Ave. N.W., #N3119, 20210; (202) 693-2100. Fax, (202) 693-1681. Vacant, Director; Dionne Williams, Director of Health Enforcement, (202) 693-2190; Arthur Buchanan, Director of General Industry and Agriculture Enforcement, (202) 893-1850; Patrick Kapust, Deputy Director. Emergency, (800) 321-6742. TTY, (877) 889-5627. Whistle-blower hotline, (800) 321-6742. Whistle-blower protection, (202) 693-2199.*
Web, www.osha.gov/dep/enforcement/dep_offices.html

Develops, interprets, and provides guidance for compliance safety standards for agency field personnel, private employees, and employers.

Occupational Safety and Health Administration (OSHA) *(Labor Dept.), Maritime and Agriculture, 200 Constitution Ave. N.W., #N3609, 20210-0001; (202) 693-2222. Fax, (202) 693-1663. Amy Wangdahl, Office Director, ext. 32066.*
Web, www.osha.gov/dts/maritime/mission.html

Writes occupational safety and health standards and guidance products for the maritime industry and agriculture.

Occupational Safety and Health Administration (OSHA) *(Labor Dept.), Standards and Guidance, 200 Constitution Ave. N.W., #N3718, 20210; (202) 693-1950. Fax, (202) 693-1678. William Perry, Director.*
Web, www.osha.gov/dsg

Develops new or revised occupational health standards for toxic, hazardous, and carcinogenic substances;

biological and safety hazards; or other harmful physical agents, such as vibration, noise, and radiation.

Occupational Safety and Health Review Commission, *1120 20th St. N.W., 9th Floor, 20036-3457; (202) 606-5100. Fax, (202) 606-5050. Heather L. MacDougall, Chair, (202) 606-5364. TTY, (877) 889-5627.*
Web, www.oshrc.gov

Independent executive branch agency that adjudicates disputes between private employers and the Occupational Safety and Health Administration arising under the Occupational Safety and Health Act of 1970.

▶**CONGRESS**

For a listing of relevant congressional committees and subcommittees, please see page 218 or the Appendix.

▶**NONGOVERNMENTAL**

American Industrial Hygiene Assn., *3141 Fairview Park Dr., #777, Falls Church, VA 22042-4507; (703) 849-8888. Fax, (703) 207-3561. Lawrence (Larry) D. Sloan, Chief Executive Officer.*
General email, infonet@aiha.org
Web, www.aiha.org, Twitter, @AIHA and Facebook, www .facebook.com/aihaglobal

Membership: scientists and engineers who practice industrial hygiene in government, labor, academic institutions, and independent organizations. Promotes health and safety standards in the workplace and the community; conducts research to identify potential dangers; educates workers about job-related risks; monitors safety regulations. Interests include international standards and information exchange.

Fair Labor Assn. (FLA), *1111 19th St. N.W., #401, 20036; (202) 898-1000. Fax, (202) 898-9050. Sharon Waxman, Chief Executive Officer.*
General email, info@fairlabor.org
Web, www.fairlabor.org and Twitter, @FairLaborAssoc

Membership: consumer, human, and labor rights groups; apparel and footwear manufacturers and retailers; and colleges and universities. Seeks to protect the rights of workers in the United States and worldwide. Concerns include sweatshop practices, forced labor, child labor, and worker health and benefits. Monitors workplace conditions and reports findings to the public. Develops capacity for sustainable labor compliance.

International Safety Equipment Assn. (ISEA), *1901 N. Moore St., #808, Arlington, VA 22209-1702; (703) 525-1695. Fax, (703) 528-2148. Charles D. Johnson, President.*
General email, isea@safetyequipment.org
Web, www.safetyequipment.org

Trade organization that drafts industry standards for employees' and emergency responders' personal safety and protective equipment; encourages development and use of proper equipment to deal with workplace hazards;

participates in international standards activities, especially in North America. Monitors legislation and regulations.

Migrant Legal Action Program, *1001 Connecticut Ave. N.W., #915, 20036-5524; (202) 775-7780. Fax, (202) 775-7784. Roger C. Rosenthal, Executive Director. General email, mlap@mlap.org*
Web, www.mlap.org and Facebook, www.facebook.com/ MigrantLegalActionProgram

Monitors legislation, regulations, and enforcement activities of the Environmental Protection Agency and the Occupational Safety and Health Administration in the area of pesticide use as it affects the health of migrant farm workers. Litigates cases concerning living and working conditions experienced by migrant farm workers. Works with local groups on implementation of Medicaid block grants.

National Assn. of Manufacturers (NAM), *Infrastructure, Innovation, and Human Resources Policy, 733 10th St. N.W., #700, 20001; (202) 637-3155. Fax, (202) 637-3182. Robyn Boerstling, Vice President. Alternate phone, (202) 637-3000.*
Web, www.nam.org

Conducts research, develops policy, and informs members of toxic injury compensation systems, and occupational safety and health legislation, regulations, and standards internationally. Offers mediation service to business members.

Public Citizen, *Health Research Group, 1600 20th St. N.W., 20009-1001; (202) 588-1000. Michael Carome, Director.*
General email, hrg1@citizen.org
Web, www.citizen.org/health-research-group, Twitter, @CitizenHRG and Publications, www.citizen.org/ our-work/health-and-safety/health-research-group- publications

Citizens' interest group that studies and reports on occupational diseases; monitors the Occupational Safety and Health Administration and participates in OSHA enforcement proceedings.

Workers' Compensation

▶**AGENCIES**

Bureau of Labor Statistics (BLS) *(Labor Dept.), Compensation and Working Conditions (OCWC), Occupational Safety and Health Statistics, 2 Massachusetts Ave. N.E., #3180, 20212-0001; (202) 691-6170. Fax, (202) 691-6196. Vacant, Assistant Commissioner.*
General email, iifstaff@bls.gov
Web, www.bls.gov/iif

Compiles and publishes statistics on occupational injuries, illnesses, and fatalities.

Labor Dept. (DOL), *Benefits Review Board, 200 Constitution Ave. N.W., #N5101, 20210 (mailing address: 200 Constitution Ave. N.W., #S5220, Washington, DC*

20210); (202) 693-6300. Fax, (202) 693-6310.
Betty Jean Hall, Chair.
Web, www.dol.gov/brb/welcome.html

Reviews appeals of workers seeking benefits under the Longshore and Harbor Workers' Compensation Act and its extensions, including the District of Columbia Workers' Compensation Act, and Title IV (Black Lung Benefits Act) of the Federal Coal Mine Health and Safety Act.

Labor Dept. (DOL), *Employees' Compensation Appeals Board,* 200 Constitution Ave. N.W., #N5416, 20210 (mailing address: 200 Constitution Ave. N.W., #S5220, Washington, DC 20210); (202) 693-6377.
Fax, (202) 693-6367. Christopher James Godfrey, Chair, (202) 693-6377. DOL Contact Center, (866) 487-2365.
Web, www.dol.gov/ecab/welcome.html and www.dol.gov/appeals

Reviews and determines appeals of final determinations of benefit claims made by the Office of Workers' Compensation Programs under the Federal Employees' Compensation Act.

Labor Dept. (DOL), *Workers' Compensation Programs (OWCP),* 200 Constitution Ave. N.W., #S3524, 20210; (202) 343-5580. Fax, (202) 693-1378. Julia K. Hearthway, Director.
Web, www.dol.gov/owcp

Administers four federal workers' compensation programs: the Federal Employees' Compensation Program, the Longshore and Harbor Workers' Compensation Program, the Black Lung Benefits Program, and the Energy Employees Occupational Illness Compensation Program.

Workers Compensation (OWCP) *(Labor Dept.),* **Coal Mine Workers' Compensation,** 200 Constitution Ave.

N.W., #C3520, 20210 (mailing address: DCMWC, P.O. Box 8307, London, KY 40742-8307); (202) 693-0046.
Fax, (202) 693-1395. Michael A. Chance, Director. Toll-free Federal Black Lung Program, (800) 347-2502. TTY, (877) 889-5627.
General email, DCMWC-public@dol.gov
Web, www.dol.gov/owcp/dcmwc

Provides direction for administration of the black lung benefits program. Adjudicates all black lung claims; certifies benefit payments and maintains black lung beneficiary rolls.

►**NONGOVERNMENTAL**

American Insurance Assn., 555 12th St. N.W., #550, 20004; (202) 828-7100. Fax, (202) 293-1219. John Degnan, President.
General email, info@aiadc.org
Web, www.aiadc.org and Twitter, @AIADC

Membership: companies providing property and casualty insurance. Offers information on workers' compensation legislation and regulations; conducts educational activities. Monitors legislation and regulations.

National Assn. of Manufacturers (NAM), *Infrastructure, Innovation, and Human Resources Policy,* 733 10th St. N.W., #700, 20001; (202) 637-3155. Fax, (202) 637-3182. Robyn Boerstling, Vice President. Alternate phone, (202) 637-3000.
Web, www.nam.org

Conducts research, develops policy, and informs members of workers' compensation law; provides feedback to government agencies.

7

Energy

GENERAL POLICY AND ANALYSIS

Basic Resources

▶AGENCIES

Agriculture Dept. (USDA), *Office of the Chief Economist, Energy Policy and New Uses,* South Bldg., 12th and Jefferson Dr. S.W., #4407, 20250; (202) 401-0461. William Hohenstein, Director (Acting).
General email, whohenstein@oce.usda.gov
Web, www.usda.gov/oce/energy/index.htm

Develops and coordinates department energy policy, programs, and strategies focusing on renewable energy policy and evaluation, particularly as it relates to biofuels and feedstocks.

Energy Dept. (DOE), 1000 Independence Ave. S.W., #7A257, 20585; (202) 586-6210. Fax, (202) 586-4403. Rick Perry, Secretary. Locator, (202) 586-5000. Press, (202) 586-4940. TTY, (800) 877-8339.
General email, thesecretary@hq.doe.gov
Web, www.energy.gov

Decides major energy policy issues and acts as principal adviser to the president on energy matters, including strategic reserves and nuclear power; acts as principal spokesperson for the department.

Energy Dept. (DOE), *Advanced Research Projects Agency (ARPA-E),* 1000 Independence Ave. S.W., 20585; (202) 287-1005. Fax, (202) 287-5450. Chanette Armstrong, Principal Deputy Director.
General email, ARPA-E@hq.doe.gov
Web, www.arpa-e.energy.gov and Twitter, @ARPAE

Seeks to advance energy technologies that are too early for private-sector investment yet have the potential to radically improve U.S. economic prosperity, national security, and environmental well-being. Provides energy researchers with funding, technical assistance, and market readiness through a competitive project selection process and active program management.

Energy Dept. (DOE), *Deputy Secretary,* 1000 Independence Ave. S.W., #7B252, 20585; (202) 586-5500. Fax, (202) 586-7210. Dan Brouillette, Deputy Secretary. Locator, (202) 586-5000. Press, (202) 586-4940.
Web, www.energy.gov

Serves as chief operations officer. Manages departmental programs in conservation and renewable energy, fossil energy, energy research, the Energy Information Administration, nuclear energy, civilian radioactive waste management, and the power marketing administrations.

Energy Dept. (DOE), *Economic Impact and Diversity,* 1000 Independence Ave. S.W., #5B110, 20585; (202) 586-8383. Fax, (202) 586-3075. Hon. James E. Campos, Principal Deputy Director.
Web, www.energy.gov/diversity/office-economic-impact-and-diversity

Advises the secretary on the impacts of energy policies, programs, regulations, and other departmental actions on underrepresented communities; minority educational institutions; and minority, small, and women-owned business enterprises.

Energy Dept. (DOE), *Energy Policy and Systems Analysis (EPSA),* 1000 Independence Ave. S.W., #7C034, 20585; (202) 586-0945. Fax, (202) 586-0900. Carol Battershell, Principal Deputy Director.
Web, www.energy.gov/epsa

Principal energy policy adviser to the secretary and deputy secretary on domestic energy policy development and implementation, as well as Energy Dept. policy analysis and activities. Supports the Energy Dept. White House interagency process, providing data collection, analysis, stakeholder engagement, and data synthesis.

Energy Dept. (DOE), *Energy Policy and Systems Analysis (EPSA), Energy Security,* 1000 Independence Ave. S.W., 20585; (202) 586-4800. Fax, (202) 586-0900. Carol Battershell, Deputy Director for Energy Security (Acting).
Web, www.energy.gov/epsa

Serves as principal adviser to the secretary, deputy secretary, and under secretary in formulating and evaluating departmental policy. Reviews programs, budgets, regulations, and legislative proposals to ensure consistency with departmental policy.

Energy Dept. (DOE), *Technology Transitions (OTT),* 1000 Independence Ave. S.W., 20585; (202) 586-5000. Conner Prochaska, Director.
General email, OTT@hq.doe.gov
Web, https://energy.gov/technologytransitions/office-technology-transitions

Develops policies and establishes partnerships with the commercial sector to translate agency energy technology research and innovation into products and services for the private sector.

Energy Dept. (DOE), *Under Secretary of Energy,* 1000 Independence Ave. S.W., S-4, 20585; (202) 586-0505. Mark W. Menezes, Under Secretary.
Web, www.energy.gov/contributors/mark-w-menezes

Serves as the department's principal advisor on energy policy and on existing and emerging energy technologies.

Energy Dept. (DOE), *Under Secretary of Science,* 1000 Independence Ave. S.W., S-4, 20585; (202) 586-0505. Paul M. Dabbar, Under Secretary.
Web, www.energy.gov/contributors/paul-m-dabbar and Twitter, @ScienceUnderSec

Serves as the department's principal adviser on fundamental energy research, energy technologies, and science. Administers programs for nuclear and high-energy particle physics, basic energy, advanced computing, fusion, and biological and environmental research. Manages the department's national labs and user facilities.

Environment, Health, Safety, and Security (EHSS) *(Energy Dept.),* 1000 Independence Ave. S.W., #7G040,

20585; (202) 586-4399. Fax, (202) 586-5605.
Matthew Moury, Associate Under Secretary.
General email, AUUserSupport@hq.doe.gov

Web, https://energy.gov/ehss/environment-health-safety-security

Develops policy and establishes standards to ensure safety and health protection in all department activities. Coordinates and integrates health, safety, environment, and security enforcement at the Energy Dept. Responsible for policy development, technical assistance, safety analysis, education, and training. Addresses federal employee, contractor, and subcontractor concerns related to the environment, safety, health, security, quality, and management.

Environment, Health, Safety, and Security (EHSS) *(Energy Dept.), Environmental Protection and Environmental Safety & Health Reporting, 1000 Independence Ave. S.W., #6B-128, 20585; (202) 586-4399. Fax, (202) 586-7330. Michael J. Silverman, Director.*

Web, www.energy.gov/ehss/organizational-chart/office-environmental-protection-sustainability-support-corporate-safety

Establishes policies and guidance for environmental protection and compliance; provides technical assistance to departmental program and field offices in complying with environmental requirements.

Federal Energy Regulatory Commission (FERC) *(Energy Dept.), 888 1st St. N.E., 20426; (202) 502-6088. Fax, (202) 502-8612. Neil Chatterjee, Chair, (202) 502-6477. eLibrary questions, (202) 502-6652. Enforcement hotline, (202) 502-8390. Enforcement toll-free, (888) 889-8030. Press, (202) 502-8680. Toll-free, (866) 208-3372. TTY, (202) 502-8659. General email, customer@ferc.gov*

Web, www.ferc.gov, Twitter, @FERC and Facebook, www.facebook.com/FERC.gov

Independent agency that regulates the interstate transmission of electricity, natural gas, and oil, including approving rates and charges. Reviews proposals to build liquefied natural gas terminals and interstate natural gas pipelines and approves siting. Licenses and inspects nonfederal hydroelectric projects. Regulates the sale of natural gas for resale in interstate commerce and wholesale interstate sales of electricity. Ensures the reliability of high-voltage interstate transmission systems. Establishes accounting and financial reporting requirements for regulated utilities. Studies and recommends policies and regulations.

Federal Energy Regulatory Commission (FERC) *(Energy Dept.), Energy Market Regulation (OEMR), 888 1st St. N.E., #8A-01, 20426; (202) 502-6700. Fax, (202) 219-2836. Anna Cochrane, Director.*

Web, www.ferc.gov/about/offices/oemr.asp

Advises the Commission and processes caseloads related to the economic regulation of the electric utility, natural gas, and oil industries. Concerns include energy markets, tariffs, and pipeline rates relating to electric utility and natural gas and oil pipeline facilities and services. Analyzes

applications for electric public utility corporate transactions, including public utility mergers, issuance of securities, or the assumption of liabilities, to determine if the proposed transactions are consistent with the public interest.

Federal Energy Regulatory Commission (FERC) *(Energy Dept.), Energy Policy and Innovation (OEPI), 888 1st St. N.E., #7A-01, 20426; (202) 502-8850. Fax, (202) 219-2836. Jignassa Gadani, Director (Acting).*

Web, www.ferc.gov/about/offices/oepi.asp

Seeks to identify emerging issues affecting wholesale and interstate energy markets. Undertakes outreach to other regulators and industry, conducts studies, and makes recommendations for Commission action with state and federal agencies and the energy industry, taking into account energy and environmental concerns. Interests include renewable energy, efficiency, smart grid technology, transmission issues, electric vehicles, carbon and greenhouse gas issues.

National Institute of Standards and Technology (NIST) *(Commerce Dept.), Special Programs Office, 100 Bureau Dr., MS 4701, Gaithersburg, MD 20899-4701; (301) 975-4447. Fax, (301) 975-8972. Richard R. Cavanagh, Director. General information, (301) 975-2756.*

Web, www.nist.gov/spo

Fosters collaboration among government, military, academic, professional, and private organizations to respond to critical national needs through science-based standards and technology innovation, including energy concerns.

National Nuclear Security Administration (NNSA) *(Energy Dept.), Emergency Operations, 1000 Independence Ave. S.W., #GH060, 20585; (202) 586-9892. Fax, (202) 586-3904. Hon. Charles L. Hopkins III, Associate Administrator.*

Web, www.energy.gov/nnsa/nnsa-offices/emergency-operations

Works to ensure coordinated Energy Dept. responses to energy-related emergencies. Recommends policies to mitigate the effects of energy-supply crises on the United States; recommends government responses to energy emergencies.

Office of Management and Budget (OMB) *(Executive Office of the President), Energy, Science, and Water, 725 17th St. N.W., #8002, 20503; (202) 395-3404. Fax, (202) 395-3049. Jim Herz, Associate Director. Press, (202) 395-7254.*

Web, www.whitehouse.gov/omb

Advises and assists the president in preparing the budget for energy programs; coordinates OMB energy policy and programs.

Office of Science *(Energy Dept.), 1000 Independence Ave. S.W., #7B058, 20585; (202) 586-5430. Fax, (202) 586-4120. Vacant, Director; J. Stephen Binkley, Deputy Director of Science Programs.*

Web, https://science.energy.gov and Twitter, @doescience

Advises the secretary on the department's physical science research and energy research and development programs; the use of multipurpose laboratories (except weapons laboratories); and education and training for basic

ENERGY RESOURCES IN CONGRESS

For a complete listing of congressional committees, including their full contact information, leadership, membership, and jurisdictions, please refer to the Appendix on pages 827–948.

HOUSE:

House Appropriations Committee, (202) 225-2771.
Web, appropriations.house.gov
  Subcommittee on Energy and Water Development, and Related Agencies, (202) 225-3421.
  Subcommittee on Interior, Environment, and Related Agencies, (202) 225-3081.
House Armed Services Committee, (202) 225-4151.
Web, armedservices.house.gov
  Subcommittee on Readiness, (202) 226-8979.
House Education and the Workforce Committee, (202) 225-4527.
Web, edworkforce.house.gov
  Subcommittee on Workforce Protections, (202) 225-4527.
House Energy and Commerce Committee, (202) 225-2927.
Web, energycommerce.house.gov
  Subcommittee on Energy, (202) 225-2927.
  Subcommittee on Environment, (202) 225-2927.
House Foreign Affairs Committee, (202) 225-5021.
Web, foreignaffairs.house.gov
House Natural Resources Committee, (202) 225-2761.
Web, naturalresources.house.gov
  Subcommitee on Water, Power, and Oceans (202) 225-8331.

House Oversight and Government Reform Committee, (202) 225-5074.
  Subcommittee on Interior, Engergy, and Environment, (202) 225-5074.
House Science, Space, and Technology Committee, (202) 225-6371.
Web, science.house.gov
  Subcommittee on Energy, (202) 225-6371.
House Small Business Committee, (202) 225-5821.
Web, smallbusiness.house.gov
  Subcommittee on Agriculture, Energy, and Trade, (202) 225-5821.
House Transportation and Infrastructure Committee, (202) 225-9446.
Web, transportation.house.gov
  Subcommittee on Railroads, Pipelines, and Hazardous Materials, (202) 226-0727.
  Subcommittee on Water Resources and Environment, (202) 225-4360.
House Ways and Means Committee, (202) 225-3625.
Web, waysandmeans.house.gov
  Subcommittee on Trade, (202) 225-6649.

JOINT:
Joint Committee on Taxation, (202) 225-3621.
Web, jct.gov

and applied research activities. Manages the department's high-energy and nuclear physics programs and the fusion energy program. Conducts environmental and health-related research and development programs, including studies of energy-related pollutants and hazardous materials.

▶**CONGRESS**

For a listing of relevant congressional committees and subcommittees, please see pages 255–256 or the Appendix.

Government Accountability Office (GAO), *Natural Resources and Environment (NRE), 441 G St. N.W., #2T23-A, 20548 (mailing address: 441 G St. N.W., #2T23A, Washington, DC 20548); (202) 512-3841. Mark Gaffigan, Managing Director.*
Web, www.gao.gov/careers/nre.html

Audits, analyzes, and evaluates for Congress federal agriculture, food safety, and energy programs; provides guidance on issues including efforts to ensure a reliable and environmentally sound energy supply, land and water resources management, protection of the environment, hazardous and nuclear wastes threat reduction, food safety, and investment in science.

▶**NONGOVERNMENTAL**

American Assn. of Blacks in Energy (AABE), *1625 K St. N.W., #405, 20006; (202) 371-9530. Fax, (202) 371-9218. Paula R. Glover, President.*
General email, info@aabe.org
Web, www.aabe.org, Twitter, @_AABE and Facebook, www.facebook.com/AABENational

Encourages participation of African Americans and other minorities in energy research and in formulating energy policy. Provides financial aid and scholarships to African American students who pursue careers in energy-related fields. Promotes greater awareness in private and public sectors of the impacts of energy policy on minority communities.

Aspen Institute, *2300 N St., N.W., #700, 20037; (202) 736-5800. Fax, (202) 467-0790. Dan Porterfield, President. Press, (202) 736-3849.*
General email, info@aspeninstitute.org
Web, www.aspeninstitute.org and Twitter, @AspenInstitute

Educational and policy studies organization. Promotes consideration of the public good in a wide variety

Joint Economic Committee, (202) 224-5171.
Web, jec.senate.gov

SENATE:

Senate Agriculture, Nutrition, and Forestry Committee, (202) 224-2035.
Web, agriculture.senate.gov
    Subcommittee on Rural Development and Energy, (202) 224-2035.
Senate Appropriations Committee, (202) 224-7257.
Web, appropriations.senate.gov
    Subcommittee on Energy and Water Development, (202) 224-8119.
    Subcommittee on Interior, Environment, and Related Agencies, (202) 228-0774.
Senate Commerce, Science, and Transportation Committee, (202) 224-1251.
Web, commerce.senate.gov
    Subcommittee on Oceans, Fisheries, and Coast Guard, (202) 224-1251.
    Subcommittee on Space, Science, and Competitiveness, (202) 224-1251.
Senate Energy and Natural Resources Committee, (202) 224-4971.
Web, energy.senate.gov
    Subcommittee on Energy, (202) 224-4971.
    Subcommittee on Water and Power, (202) 224-4971.

Senate Environment and Public Works Committee, (202) 224-6176.
Web, epw.senate.gov
    Subcommittee on Clean Air and Nuclear Safety, (202) 224-6176.
    Subcommittee on Fisheries, Water, and Wildlife, (202) 224-6176.
Senate Finance Committee, (202) 224-4515.
Web, finance.senate.gov
    Subcommittee on Energy, Natural Resources, and Infrastructure, (202) 224-4515.
Senate Foreign Relations Committee, (202) 224-4651.
Web, foreign.senate.gov
    Subcommittee on Multilateral International Development, Multilateral Institutions, and International Economic, Energy, and Environmental Policy, (202) 224-4651.
Senate Health, Education, Labor, and Pensions Committee, (202) 224-5375.
Web, help.senate.gov
    Subcommittee on Employment and Workplace Safety, (202) 224-5375.
Senate Homeland Security and Governmental Affairs Committee, (202) 224-4751.
Web, hsgac.senate.gov

---

of policy areas, including energy and the environment. Working with international partners, offers educational seminars, nonpartisan policy forums, public conferences and events, and leadership development initiatives.

CECA Solutions, *2737 Devonshire Pl. N.W., #102, 20008; (202) 468-8440. Fax, (202) 318-0831. Ellen Berman, Chief Executive Officer.*
General email, info@cecarf.org
Web, www.cecarf.org

Analyzes economic and social effects of energy policies and advances interests of residential and small business consumers. Builds consensus on energy policy issues among public- and private-sector organizations, state and local groups, businesses, utilities, consumers, environmentalists, government agencies, and others. Interests include clean and sustainable fuels, distributed generation of electricity, and reliable electric systems. (Formerly the Consumer Energy Council of America.)

Center for Strategic and International Studies, Energy and National Security Program, *1616 Rhode Island Ave. N.W., 20036; (202) 775-3115. Sarah Ladislaw, Director.*
General email, lhyland@csis.org
Web, www.csis.org/programs/energy-and-national-security-program and Twitter, @CSISEnergy

Conducts and publishes research on energy policy and technology.

Edison Electric Institute, *701 Pennsylvania Ave. N.W., 20004-2696; (202) 508-5000. Fax, (202) 508-5096. Thomas R. Kuhn, President.*
General email, feedback@eei.org
Web, www.eei.org and Twitter, @Edison_Electric

Membership: investor-owned electric power companies. Interests include electric utility operation and concerns, including conservation and energy management, energy analysis, resources and environment, cogeneration and renewable energy resources, safety, reliability, taxes, and regulation matters.

Energy Bar Assn., *2000 M St. N.W., #715, 20036; (202) 223-5625. Fax, (202) 833-5596. Lisa A. Levine, Chief Executive Officer.*

Energy Department

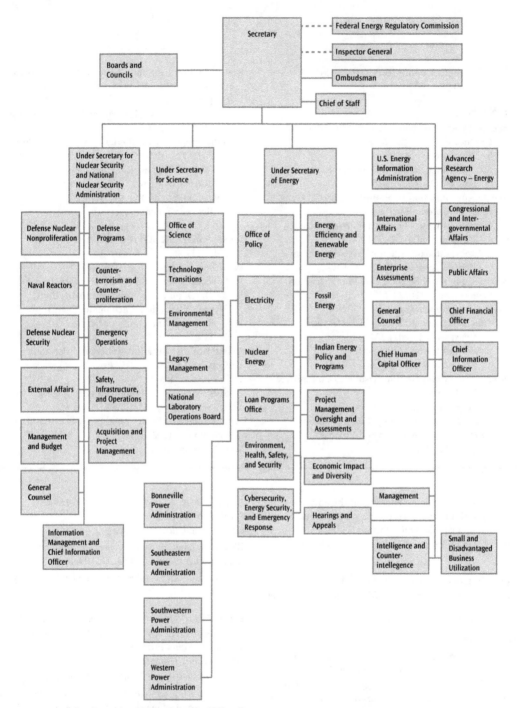

- - - - - - - Indicates a support or advisory relationship with the unit

General email, admin@eba-net.org

Web, www.eba-net.org

Membership: lawyers interested in all areas of energy law. Interests include administration of laws covering production, development, conservation, transmission, and economic regulation of energy.

Energy Future Coalition, *1750 Pennsylvania Ave. N.W., #300, 20006; (202) 463-1947. Pete Ogden, Executive Director. General email, info@energyfuturecoalition.org*

Web, www.energyfuturecoalition.org

Nonpartisan public policy alliance that seeks to bridge the differences among business, labor, and environmental groups and identify energy policy options with broad political support. Interests include development of a national electricity transmission plan to bring renewable resources to market, and reduction of energy waste. Receives support from the United Nations Foundation.

Environmental and Energy Study Institute (EESI), *1020 19th St. N.W., #650, 20036-6101; (202) 628-1400. Fax, (202) 204-5244. Carol Werner, Executive Director, (202) 662-1881.*
General email, info@eesi.org
Web, www.eesi.org and Twitter, @eesionline

Nonpartisan policy education and analysis group established by members of Congress to foster informed debate on environmental and energy issues. Interests include policies for sustainable development, energy, sustainable bioenergy, climate change, agriculture, transportation, and fiscal policy reform.

Industrial Energy Consumers of America, *1776 K St. N.W., #720, 20006; (202) 223-1420. Paul N. Cicio, President, (202) 223-1661.*
Web, www.ieca-us.com

National trade association that represents the manufacturing industry and acts as advocate on energy, environmental, and public policy issues. Advocates greater diversity of and lower costs for energy. Monitors legislation and regulations.

National Assn. of Energy Service Companies, *1615 M St. N.W., #800, 20036-3213; (202) 822-0950. Fax, (202) 822-0955. Timothy D. Unruh, Executive Director, (571) 337-4056.*
General email, info@naesco.org
Web, www.naesco.org and Twitter, @NaescoNews

Membership: companies that design, manufacture, finance, and install energy efficiency and renewable energy equipment; energy efficiency and renewable energy services companies; and government officials. Acts as advocate for and serves as a clearinghouse on energy efficiency strategies. Monitors legislation and regulations.

National Assn. of State Energy Officials (NASEO), *1300 N. 17th St., #1275, Arlington, VA 22209; (703) 299-8800. Fax, (703) 299-6208. David Terry, Executive Director.*
General email, energy@naseo.org
Web, www.naseo.org and Twitter, @NASEO_Energy

Membership: senior officials from each state and territory, plus affiliates from public and private sectors. Seeks to improve energy programs, provide policy analysis, and act as an information clearinghouse. Interests include efficiency, renewables, building codes, emergency preparedness, and fuel production and distribution.

National Governors Assn. (NGA), *Center for Best Practices, Environment, Energy, and Transportation Division, 444 N. Capitol St. N.W., #267, 20001-1512; (202) 624-5300. Fax, (202) 624-7829. Sue Gander, Director.*
General email, webmaster@nga.org
Web, www.nga.org/cms/center/eet

Identifies best practices for energy, land use, environment, and transportation issues and shares them with the states.

National Governors Assn. (NGA), *Natural Resources Committee, 444 N. Capitol St. N.W., #267, 20001-1512; (202) 624-5300. Fax, (202) 624-7814. David Parkhurst, Director; Alex Schaefer, Legislative Director.*
General email, webmaster@nga.org
Web, www.nga.org/cms/center/eet

Monitors legislation and regulations and makes recommendations on agriculture, energy, environment, and natural resource issues to ensure governors' views and priorities are represented in federal policies and regulations.

National Research Council (NRC), *Energy and Environmental Systems Board, Keck Center, 500 5th St. N.W., #W917, 20001; (202) 334-2045. K. John Holmes, Director.*
Web, http://sites.nationalacademies.org/DEPS/BEES

Conducts studies in order to advise the federal government and the private sector about issues in energy and environmental technology, and related public policy. Focuses on energy supply and demand technologies and systems, including resource extraction through mining and drilling, energy conversion, distribution and delivery, and efficiency of use; environmental consequences of energy related activities; environmental systems and controls in areas related to fuel production, energy conversion, transmission, and use; and other issues relating to national security and defense. Sponsors studies, workshops, symposia, and a variety of information dissemination activities.

RAND Corp., *Washington Office, 1200 S. Hayes St., Arlington, VA 22202-5050; (703) 413-1100. Fax, (703) 413-8111. Nicholas Burger, Director; Anita Chandra, Director for Social and Economic Well-Being, ext. 5323.*
Web, www.rand.org

Analyzes the effects of existing and proposed energy policies on the environment. (Headquarters in Santa Monica, Calif.)

U.S. Chamber of Commerce, *Environment, Technology, and Regulatory Affairs, 1615 H St. N.W., 20062-2000; (202) 463-5533. Neil Bradley, Executive Vice President.*
General email, environment@uschamber.com
Web, www.uschamber.com/etra and Twitter, @Regulations

Develops policy on all issues affecting energy, including alternative energy, emerging technologies, regulatory affairs, energy taxes, telecommunications, and onshore and offshore mining of energy resources.

Data and Statistics

▶**AGENCIES**

Census Bureau *(Commerce Dept.), Special Reimbursable Surveys Branch, 4600 Silver Hill Rd., #6H047, Suitland, MD 20746 (mailing address: 4600 Silver Hill Rd., #6H047,*

Washington, DC 20233); (301) 763-4639. Mary Susan Bucci, Chief.
Web, www.census.gov

Collects and tabulates data for the Manufacturing Energy Consumption Survey for the Energy Dept. concerning combustible and noncombustible energy resources for the U.S. manufacturing sector. Collects data on quarterly plant capacity utilization within the manufacturing and printing sector.

Energy Information Administration (EIA) *(Energy Dept.),* 1000 Independence Ave. S.W., #2H027, 20585; (202) 586-4361. Fax, (202) 586-0329. Linda Capuano, Administrator. Information, (202) 586-8800.
General email, infoctr@eia.gov

Web, www.eia.gov

Collects and publishes data on national and international energy reserves, financial status of energy-producing companies, production, demand, consumption, and other areas; provides long- and short-term analyses of energy trends and data.

Energy Information Administration (EIA) *(Energy Dept.),* **Electricity, Coal, Nuclear, and Renewable Analysis,** 1000 Independence Ave. S.W., #2H073, EI50, 20585; (202) 586-2432. Jim Diefenderfer, Director.
Web, www.eia.gov

Collects data, compiles statistics, and prepares analyses and forecasts on domestic coal supplies, electric power supplies, uranium supplies and markets, and alternative energy supplies, including biomass, solar, wind, waste, wood, and alcohol. Directs collection of spent fuel data and validation of spent nuclear fuel discharge data for the Civilian Radioactive Waste Management Office. Prepares analyses and forecasts on the availability, production, prices, processing, transportation, and distribution of nuclear energy, both domestically and internationally.

Energy Information Administration (EIA) *(Energy Dept.),* **Energy Analysis,** 1000 Independence Ave. S.W., #2H073, 20585; (202) 586-2222. Fax, (202) 586-3045. Ian Mead, Assistant Administrator.
Web, www.eia.gov/analysis

Analyzes and forecasts alternative energy futures. Develops, applies, and maintains modeling systems for analyzing the interactions of demand, conversion, and supply for all energy sources and their economic and environmental impacts. Concerned with emerging energy markets and U.S. dependence on petroleum imports.

Energy Information Administration (EIA) *(Energy Dept.),* **Energy Consumption and Efficiency Analysis,** 1000 Independence Ave. S.W., 20585; (202) 586-1762. James Turnure, Director.
Web, www.eia.gov

Collects and provides data on energy consumption in the residential, commercial, and industrial sectors. Prepares analyses on energy consumption by sector and fuel type, including the impact of conservation measures.

Energy Information Administration (EIA) *(Energy Dept.),* **Energy Consumption and Efficiency Statistics,** 1000 Independence Ave. S.W., #2F073, 20585; (202) 586-3548. Thomas Leckey, Director (Acting).
Web, www.eia.gov

Conducts national energy consumption surveys and publishes energy consumption data and analysis.

Energy Information Administration (EIA) *(Energy Dept.),* **Energy Statistics,** 1000 Independence Ave. S.W., #2G020, 20585; (202) 586-6012. Fax, (202) 586-9739. Thomas Leckey, Assistant Administrator, (202) 586-3548. General email, infoctr@eia.doe.gov

Web, www.eia.gov

Conducts survey, statistical methods, and integration activities related to energy consumption and efficiency; electricity; nuclear and renewable energy; oil, gas, and coal supply; and petroleum and biofuels. Manages EIA data collection program and the quality control for statistical reports.

Energy Information Administration (EIA) *(Energy Dept.),* **Integrated and International Energy Analysis,** 1000 Independence Ave. S.W., MS EI35, 20585; (202) 586-1284. Fax, (202) 586-3045. Angelina LaRose, Director.
Web, www.eia.gov

Compiles, interprets, and reports international energy statistics and U.S. energy data for international energy organizations. Analyzes international energy markets; makes projections concerning world prices and trade for energy sources, including oil, natural gas, coal, and electricity; monitors world petroleum market to determine U.S. vulnerability.

Energy Information Administration (EIA) *(Energy Dept.),* **National Energy Information Center,** 1000 Independence Ave. S.W., 20585; (202) 586-6537. Fax, (202) 586-3045. Gina Pearson, Assistant Administrator for Communications. General email, infoctr@eia.doe.gov

Web, www.eia.gov

Serves as the information point of contact for federal, state, and local governments; academia, businesses, and industry; foreign governments and international organizations; the news media; and the public. Manages and oversees the Energy Information Administration's public website, printed publications, and a customer contact center.

Energy Information Administration (EIA) *(Energy Dept.),* **Oil, Gas, and Coal Supply Statistics,** 1000 Independence Ave. S.W., #BE072, 20585; (202) 586-0957. Deborah Coaxum, Director. General email, infoctr@eia.doe.gov

Web, www.eia.gov/about/eia_offices.cfm

Collects and publishes weekly, monthly, and annual estimates of domestic natural gas, coal, and upstream oil. Performs analyses of the natural gas, coal, and upstream oil industries, including consumption, prices, and storage levels.

Energy Information Administration (EIA) *(Energy Dept.), Petroleum and Biofuel Statistics,* 1000 *Independence Ave. S.W., #BG041, 20585; (202) 586-4615. Robert Merriam, Director.*
General email, infoctr@eia.doe.gov
Web, www.eia.gov/about/eia_offices.cfm

Collects, compiles, interprets, and publishes data on domestic production, distribution, and prices of crude oil and refined petroleum products; analyzes and projects availability of petroleum supplies.

▶NONGOVERNMENTAL

American Gas Assn., *Statistics,* 400 N. Capitol St. N.W., #450, 20001-1535; (202) 824-7133. *Paul Pierson, Manager.*
Web, www.aga.org/events-community/statistics-survey-system/ and Facebook, www.facebook.com/naturalgas

Issues statistics on the gas utility industry, including supply and reserves.

American Petroleum Institute, *Statistics,* 1220 L St. N.W., 20005-4070; (202) 682-8000. Fax, (202) 962-4730. *Hazem Arafa, Director, ext. 8506.*
General email, apidata@api.org
Web, www.api.org/products-and-services/statistics

Provides basic statistical information on petroleum industry operations, market conditions, and environmental, health, and safety performance. Includes data on supply and demand of crude oil and petroleum products, exports and imports, refinery operations, drilling activities and costs, environmental expenditures, injuries, illnesses and fatalities, oil spills, and emissions.

National Mining Assn., *Communications,* 101 Constitution Ave. N.W., #500E, 20001-2133; (202) 463-2600. Fax, (202) 463-2666. *M. Richardson (Rich) Nolan, Senior Vice President of Government and Political Affairs.*
Web, www.nma.org

Collects, analyzes, and distributes statistics on the mining industry, including statistics on the production, transportation, and consumption of coal and hard rock minerals.

Energy Conservation

▶AGENCIES

Energy Efficiency and Renewable Energy (EERE) *(Energy Dept.),* 1000 *Independence Ave. S.W., #6A013, MS EE1, 20585; (202) 586-9220. Daniel Simmons, Assistant Secretary. Information, (877) 337-3463. Press, (202) 586-4940.*
General email, eereic@ee.doe.gov
Web, www.energy.gov/eere/office-energy-efficiency-renewable-energy

Administers financial and technical assistance for state energy programs, weatherization for low-income households, and implementation of energy conservation measures

by schools, hospitals, local governments, and public care institutions and federal facilities.

Energy Efficiency and Renewable Energy (EERE) *(Energy Dept.), Advanced Manufacturing (AMO),* 1000 *Independence Ave. S.W., #5F065, MS EE5A, 20585-0121; (202) 586-9488. Fax, (202) 586-9234. Robert Ivester, Director.*
General email, amo_communication@ee.doe.gov
Web, www.energy.gov/eere/amo/advanced-manufacturing-office

Conducts research and disseminates information to increase energy end-use efficiency, promote renewable energy use and industrial applications, and reduce the volume of industrial and municipal waste.

Energy Efficiency and Renewable Energy (EERE) *(Energy Dept.), Building Technologies (BTO),* 1000 *Independence Ave. S.W., MS EE2J, 20585; (202) 586-9127. Fax, (202) 586-4617. David Nemtzow, Director.*
General email, Buildings@ee.doe.gov
Web, www.energy.gov/eere/buildings/building-technologies-office

Funds research to reduce commercial and residential building energy use. Programs include research and development, equipment standards and analysis, and technology validation and market introduction.

Energy Efficiency and Renewable Energy (EERE) *(Energy Dept.), Federal Energy Management Program (FEMP),* 1000 *Independence Ave. S.W., MS EE5F, 20585; (202) 586-5772. Fax, (202) 586-3000. Leslie Nichols, Strategic Director.*
Web, http://energy.gov/eere/femp/federal-energy-management-program

Provides federal agencies with information and technology services to implement energy conservation measures. Areas include finance and contract assistance, purchase of energy-efficient products, design and operation of buildings, and vehicle fleet management.

Energy Efficiency and Renewable Energy (EERE) *(Energy Dept.), Vehicle Technologies (VTO),* 1000 *Independence Ave. S.W., #5G030, 20585; (202) 586-8055. Fax, (202) 586-7409. David Howell, Deputy Director.*
Web, www.energy.gov/eere/vehicles/vehicle-technologies-office

Works with the motor vehicle industry to develop technologies for improved vehicle fuel efficiency and cleaner fuels.

Energy Efficiency and Renewable Energy (EERE) *(Energy Dept.), Weatherization and Intergovernmental Programs (WIP),* 1000 *Independence Ave. S.W., MS EE5W, 20585; (202) 586-1510. Fax, (202) 586-1233. Anna Garcia, Director.*
General email, monica.areval@nrel.gov
Web, www.eere.energy.gov/wip

Supports private and government efforts to improve the energy efficiency of buildings and transportation. Promotes accelerated market penetration of energy efficiency and renewable energy technologies. Provides funding and technical assistance to state and local governments and Indian tribes. Administers weatherization assistance program that assists elderly and low-income persons to make their homes energy efficient. Reviews building codes that promote energy efficiency in buildings.

Housing and Urban Development Dept. (HUD), *Community Planning and Development, Environment and Energy, 451 7th St. S.W., #7212, 20410; (202) 708-1201. Fax, (202) 708-3363. Danielle Schopp, Director, (202) 402-4442.*
Web, www.hud.gov/program_offices/comm_planning/library/energy

Develops policies promoting energy efficiency, conservation, and renewable sources of supply in housing and community development programs.

National Institute of Standards and Technology (NIST) *(Commerce Dept.), Engineering Laboratory, 100 Bureau Dr., MS 8600, Gaithersburg, MD 20899-8600; (301) 975-5900. Fax, (301) 975-4032. Howard H. Harary, Director.*
General email, el@nist.gov
Web, www.nist.gov/el

Develops measurement techniques, test methods, and mathematical models to encourage energy conservation in large buildings. Interests include refrigeration, lighting, infiltration and ventilation, heating and air conditioning, indoor air quality, and heat transfer in the building envelope.

▶CONGRESS

For a listing of relevant congressional committees and subcommittees, please see pages 255–256 or the Appendix.

▶NONGOVERNMENTAL

Alliance to Save Energy, *1850 M St. N.W., #610, 20036; (202) 857-0666. Jason Hartke, President; Ben Evans, Vice President Government Affairs, (202) 530-2222.*
General email, info@ase.org
Web, www.ase.org, Twitter, @ToSaveEnergy and Facebook, www.facebook.com/alliancetosaveenergy

Coalition of business, government, environmental, and consumer leaders who promote the efficient and clean use of energy to benefit consumers, the environment, the economy, and national security. Conducts programs addressing energy efficiency in commercial and residential buildings, utilities, appliances, and equipment, industry, and education. International programs provide technical and financial assistance to national and local partners.

American Council for an Energy-Efficient Economy (ACEEE), *529 14th St. N.W., #600, 20045-1000; (202) 507-4000. Fax, (202) 429-2248. Steven Nadel, Executive Director, (202) 507-4011.*
General email, aceeeinfo@aceee.org
Web, http://aceee.org and Twitter, @ACEEEdc

Independent research organization concerned with energy policy, technologies, and conservation. Interests include consumer information, energy efficiency in buildings and appliances, improved transportation efficiency, industrial efficiency, utility issues, and conservation in developing countries.

Building Codes Assistance Project, *1850 M St. N.W., #610, 20036; (202) 530-2211. Maureen Guttman, President.*
General email, info@bcapcodes.org
Web, www.bcap-energy.org and Twitter, @BCAPOCEAN

Advocacy group that supports and enforces national building energy codes. Assists cities, states, and countries in complying with federal energy efficiency codes, including planning, technical assistance, and training. Provides outreach and coordination activities to provide information about current code data and cost analysis to policymakers. International interests include India, the Asia–Pacific region, Ukraine, and arid regions.

Environmental Defense Fund, *Washington Office, 1875 Connecticut Ave. N.W., #600, 20009-5728; (202) 387-3500. Fax, (202) 234-6049. Fred Krupp, President. Information, (800) 684-3322.*
Web, www.edf.org/offices/washington-dc and Twitter, @EnvDefenseFund

Citizens' interest group staffed by lawyers, economists, and scientists. Provides information on energy issues and advocates energy conservation measures. Interests include China and the Amazon rain forest. Provides utilities and environmental organizations with research and guidance on energy conservation. (Headquarters in New York.)

Friends of the Earth (FOE), *1101 15th St. N.W., 11th Floor, 20005; (202) 783-7400. Fax, (202) 783-0444. Erich Pica, President. Toll-free, (877) 843-8687.*
Web, www.foe.org, Twitter, @foe_us and Facebook, www.facebook.com/foe.us

Environmental advocacy group. Interests include climate disruption, renewable energy resources, and air and water pollution. Specializes in federal budget and tax issues related to the environment, including the Keystone XL pipeline, World Bank, and U.S. Export-Import Bank.

National Insulation Assn. (NIA), *516 Herdon Parkway #D, Reston, VA 20170; (703) 464-6422. Fax, (703) 464-5896. Michele M. Jones, Executive Vice President, ext. 119. Toll-free, (877) 968-7642.*
General email, niainfo@insulation.org
Web, www.insulation.org

Membership: open-shop and union contractors, distributors, laminators, fabricators, and manufacturers that provide thermal insulation, insulation accessories, and components to the commercial, mechanical, and industrial markets. Provides information to members on industry trends and technologies, and offers service contacts for consumers. Monitors legislation and regulations.

North American Insulation Manufacturers Assn., *11 Canal Center Plaza, #103, Alexandria, VA 22314; (703) 684-0084. Fax, (703) 684-0427. Curt Rich, President. General email, sfitzgerald-redd@naima.org*

Web, www.naima.org, Twitter, @knowinsulation and Facebook, www.facebook.com/insulationinstitute

Membership: manufacturers of insulation products for use in homes, commercial buildings, and industrial facilities. Provides information on the use of insulation for thermal efficiency, sound control, and fire safety; monitors research in the industry. Interests include energy efficiency and sustainability. Monitors legislation and regulations.

Power Shift Network, *1875 Connecticut Ave. N.W., 10th Floor, 20009; Joy Carmona, Executive Director (Acting). General email, theteam@powershift.org*

Web, https://powershift.org, Twitter, @powershiftnet and Facebook, www.facebook.com/PowerShiftNetwork

Membership: youth-based organizations that support sustainable energy. Trains youth leaders to have a larger impact on their local communities. Campaigns for clean energy bills. Holds conferences on climate change and sustainable energy options. Interests include activism on college campuses and environmental justice. (Formerly the Energy Action Coalition.)

Resources for the Future, *1616 P St. N.W., 20036-1400; (202) 328-5000. Fax, (202) 939-3460. Richard G. Newell, President. Library, (202) 328-5089. Press, (202) 328-5168. General email, info@rff.org*

Web, www.rff.org and Twitter, @rff

Research organization that conducts independent studies on economic and policy aspects of energy, environment, conservation, and natural resource management issues worldwide. Interests include climate change, energy, natural resource issues in developing countries, and public health.

Sierra Club, *Legislative Office, 50 F St. N.W., 8th Floor, 20001; (202) 547-1141. Fax, (202) 547-6009. Melinda Pierce, Legislative Director; Bob Bingaman, National Organizing Director, (202) 675-7904; Michael Brune, Executive Director. General email, information@sierraclub.org*

Web, www.sierraclub.org

Citizens' interest group that promotes protection and responsible use of the Earth's ecosystems and its natural resources. Focuses on combating global warming/greenhouse effect through energy conservation, efficient use of renewable energy resources, auto efficiency, and constraints on deforestation. Monitors federal, state, and local legislation relating to the environment and natural resources. (Headquarters in Oakland, Calif.)

Worldwatch Institute, *1400 16th St. N.W., #430, 20036; (202) 745-8092. Fax, (202) 478-2534. Ed Groark, President (Acting). General email, worldwatch@worldwatch.org*

Web, www.worldwatch.org and Twitter, @worldwatch

Focuses on an interdisciplinary approach to solving global environmental problems. Interests include energy conservation, renewable resources, solar power, and energy use in developing countries.

International Trade and Cooperation

▶AGENCIES

Bureau of Energy Resources (ENR) *(State Dept.), 2201 C St. N.W., #4428, 20520; (202) 647-8543. John McCarrick, Special Envoy and Coordinator for International Energy Affairs (Acting), (202) 647-8543.*

Web, www.state.gov/e/enr, Twitter, @EnergyAtState Blog, https://blogs.state.gov/tags/economic-and-energy-issues

Manages the global energy economy through diplomacy between energy producers and consumers, and stimulates the market forces toward the advancement of sustainable, renewable energy sources.

Bureau of Energy Resources (ENR) *(State Dept.), Policy Analysis and Public Diplomacy, 2201 C St. N.W., #4422, 20520; (202) 647-2879. Fax, (202) 647-7431. Chris Davy, Director, (202) 647-3016.*

Web, www.state.gov/e/enr

Seeks to put energy security interests at the forefront of U.S. foreign policy. Objectives include increasing energy diplomacy with major producers and consumers; stimulating market forces toward energy development and reconstruction, with an emphasis on alternative energies and electricity; and promoting good governance and increased transparency to improve commercially viable and environmentally sustainable access to people without energy services.

Bureau of International Security and Nonproliferation (ISN) *(State Dept.), Nuclear Energy, Safety, and Security Affairs (NESS), 2201 C St. N.W., #3320, 20520; (202) 647-4061. Richard K. Stratford, Director, (202) 647-4061.*

Web, www.state.gov/t/isn/offices/ness/index.htm

Coordinates and supervises international nuclear energy policy for the State Dept.; promotes adherence to technical conventions regarding peaceful uses of nuclear energy.

Energy Dept. (DOE), *Energy Policy and Systems Analysis (EPSA), Energy Security, 1000 Independence Ave. S.W., 20585; (202) 586-4800. Fax, (202) 586-0900. Carol Battershell, Deputy Director for Energy Security (Acting).*

Web, www.energy.gov/epsa

Advises the assistant secretary and Energy Dept. leadership on energy demand and supply, energy efficiency, energy research and development, and the environment, including air quality and climate. Provides analysis for the development of domestic and international energy policy. Responds to energy market disruptions and emergencies. Recommends science and technology policies.

Energy Dept. (DOE), *International Affairs, 1000 Independence Ave. S.W., #7C016, MS IA1, 20585; (202) 586-5800. Fax, (202) 586-0861. Theodore J. Garrish, Assistant Secretary.*
Web, www.energy.gov/ia/office-international-affairs

Advises the Energy Dept. leadership in the development of a national policy concerning domestic and international energy matters. Coordinates the varied interests of the department's divisions and other government organizations. Negotiates and manages international energy agreements. Develops and promotes international partnerships for deployment of greenhouse gas abatement technologies.

Energy Information Administration (EIA) *(Energy Dept.), Integrated and International Energy Analysis, 1000 Independence Ave. S.W., MS EI35, 20585; (202) 586-1284. Fax, (202) 586-3045. Angelina LaRose, Director.*
Web, www.eia.gov

Compiles, interprets, and reports international energy statistics and U.S. energy data for international energy organizations. Analyzes international energy markets; makes projections concerning world prices and trade for energy sources, including oil, natural gas, coal, and electricity; monitors world petroleum market to determine U.S. vulnerability.

International Trade Administration (ITA) *(Commerce Dept.), Industry and Analysis (I&A), Energy and Environmental Industries (OEEI), 1400 Constitution Ave. N.W., #4053, 20230; (202) 482-5225. Adam O'Malley, Director, (202) 482-4850.*
Web, www.trade.gov/td/energy

Promotes global competitiveness of U.S. energy and environmental companies. Conducts analyses of these two sectors and of overseas trade and investment opportunities and trade barriers affecting them. Develops strategies for removing foreign trade barriers and improving investment conditions. Organizes conferences and workshops.

National Nuclear Security Administration (NNSA) *(Energy Dept.), Emergency Operations, 1000 Independence Ave. S.W., #GH060, 20585; (202) 586-9892. Fax, (202) 586-3904. Hon. Charles L. Hopkins III, Associate Administrator.*
Web, www.energy.gov/nnsa/nnsa-offices/emergency-operations

Monitors international energy situations as they affect domestic market conditions; recommends policies on and government responses to energy emergencies; represents the United States in the International Energy Agency's emergency programs and NATO civil emergency preparedness activities.

Nuclear Energy (NE) *(Energy Dept.), International Nuclear Energy Policy and Cooperation, 1000 Independence Ave. S.W., #5A-143, 20585; (202) 586-5253. Fax, (202) 586-8353. Vacant, Deputy Assistant Secretary; SarahLennon, Associate Deputy Assistent Director.*
Web, www.energy.gov/ne/nuclear-reactor-technologies/international-nuclear-energy-policy-and-cooperation

Responsible for the Energy Dept.'s international civilian nuclear energy activities, including research, development and demonstration cooperation, international framework and partnership development, and international nuclear energy policy.

Nuclear Regulatory Commission, *International Programs, 11555 Rockville Pike, MS 04E21, Rockville, MD 20852; (301) 415-1780. Nader Marnish, Director.*
Web, www.nrc.gov/about-nrc/organization/oipfuncdesc.html

Coordinates application review process for exports and imports of nuclear materials, facilities, and components. Makes recommendations on export-import licensing upon completion of review process. Conducts related policy reviews.

Office of Science *(Energy Dept.), 1000 Independence Ave. S.W., #7B058, 20585; (202) 586-5430. Fax, (202) 586-4120. Vacant, Director; J. Stephen Binkley, Deputy Director of Science Programs.*
Web, https://science.energy.gov and Twitter, @doescience

Coordinates energy research, science, and technology programs among producing and consuming nations; analyzes existing international research and development activities; pursues international collaboration in research and in the design, development, construction, and operation of new facilities and major scientific experiments; participates in negotiations for international cooperation activities.

U.S. International Trade Commission, *Natural Resources and Energy, 500 E St. S.W., #511F, 20436; (202) 205-3419. Fax, (202) 205-2217. Robert (Bob) Carr, Chief, (202) 205-3042.*
General email, cynthia.foreso@usitc.gov
Web, www.usitc.gov

Advisory fact-finding agency on tariffs, commercial policy, and foreign trade matters. Analyzes data on oil, crude petroleum, petroleum products, natural gas and its products, and coal and its products (including all forms of coke) traded internationally; investigates effects of tariffs on certain chemical and energy imports.

▶ **CONGRESS**

For a listing of relevant congressional committees and subcommittees, please see pages 255–256 or the Appendix.

▶ **INTERNATIONAL ORGANIZATIONS**

European Union, *Delegation to the United States of America, 2175 K St. N.W., 20037; (202) 862-9500. Fax, (202) 429-1766. David O'Sullivan, Ambassador.*
General email, delegation-usa-info@eeas.europa.eu
Web, www.euintheus.org and Twitter, @EUintheUS

Information and public affairs office in the United States for the European Union. Advances energy policy cooperation and strategies between the United States and Europe; interests include renewable and clean energy, foreign oil dependence, and green technologies. (Headquarters in Brussels.)

▶NONGOVERNMENTAL

Atlantic Council, *Global Energy Center,* *1101 15th St. N.W., 10th Floor, 20005-5503; (202) 463-7226. Fax, (202) 463-4590. Randolph Bell, Director. Press, (202) 778-4967. General email, press@program/global.energy.org* *Web, www.atlanticcouncil.org and Twitter, ACGlobalEnergy*

Seeks to create common understanding of critical energy and environmental issues through nonpartisan policy analysis and recommendations. Studies and makes policy recommendations on the economic, political, and security aspects of energy supply and international environment issues.

U.S. Energy Assn., *1300 Pennsylvania Ave. N.W., #550, Mailbox 142, 20004-3022; (202) 312-1230. Fax, (202) 682-1682. Barry K. Worthington, Executive Director. General email, reply@usea.org* *Web, www.usea.org and Twitter, @USEnergyAssn*

Membership: energy-related organizations, including professional, trade, and government groups. Participates in the World Energy Council (headquartered in London). Sponsors seminars and conferences on energy resources, policy management, technology, utilization, and conservation.

Winrock International, *Washington Office,* *2121 Crystal Dr., #500, Arlington, VA 22202; (703) 302-6500. Fax, (703) 302-6512. Rodney Ferguson, President. General email, information@winrock.org* *Web, www.winrock.org and Twitter, @WinrockIntl*

Works to sustain natural resources and protect the environment. Matches innovative approaches in agriculture, natural resource management, clean energy, and leadership development with the unique needs of its partners. (Headquarters in Little Rock, Ark.)

ELECTRICITY

General

▶AGENCIES

Energy Dept. (DOE), *Electricity Delivery and Energy Reliability (OE),* *1000 Independence Ave. S.W., #8H033, 20585; (202) 586-1411. Fax, (202) 586-1472. Bruce Walker, Assistant Secretary. General email, OEwebmaster@hq.doe.gov* *Web, https://energy.gov/oe/office-electricity-delivery-and-energy-reliability*

Develops electricity policies and programs that shape electricity system planning and market operations; develops technologies to improve the grid infrastructure that provides electricity to homes, offices, and factories.

Energy Dept. (DOE), *Power Marketing Liaison Office,* *1000 Independence Ave. S.W., #8G037, 20585;*

(202) 586-5581. Fax, (202) 586-6261. Michael D. McElhany, Assistant Administrator. *Web, www.wapa.gov*

Serves as a liaison among the Southeastern, Southwestern, and Western area power administrations; other federal agencies; and Congress. Coordinates marketing of electric power from federally owned hydropower projects.

National Institute of Standards and Technology (NIST) *(Commerce Dept.),* *Smart Grid,* *100 Bureau Dr., MS 8200, Gaithersburg, MD 20899-8200; (301) 975-5987. Fax, (301) 975-4091. Chris Greer, Director, (301) 975-5919. General email, smartgrid@nist.gov* *Web, www.nist.gov/smartgrid*

Develops interoperable standards to govern operations and future growth of the national Smart Grid, a planned electricity system that will add digital technology to electricity grids throughout the United States to channel their electric currents at an anticipated lower cost and higher efficiency. Works with manufacturers, consumers, energy providers, and regulators to ensure cohesion throughout the Smart Grid infrastructure.

Tennessee Valley Authority, *Government Affairs,* *500 N. Capitol St. N.W., #220, 20001; (202) 898-2999. Fax, (202) 898-2998. William D. (Bill) Johnson, President. General email, tvainfo@tva.gov* *Web, www.tva.gov and Twitter, @TVAnews*

Federal corporation that coordinates resource conservation, development, and land-use programs in the Tennessee River Valley. Uses fossil fuel, nuclear, and hydropower sources to generate and supply wholesale power to municipal and cooperative electric systems, federal installations, and some industries.

▶CONGRESS

For a listing of relevant congressional committees and subcommittees, please see pages 255–256 or the Appendix.

▶NONGOVERNMENTAL

American Coalition for Clean Coal Electricity (ACCCE), *1069 West Broad St., #913, Falls Church, VA 22046; (202) 459-4800. Fax, (202) 459-4897. Michelle Bloodworth, President. General email, info@americaspower.org* *Web, www.americaspower.org, Twitter, @AmericasPower and Facebook, www.facebook.com/AmericasPower*

Membership: coal, railroad, and electric utility companies and suppliers. Educates the public, regulators, and policymakers about economic, technological, and scientific research on energy resources employed in generating electricity. Promotes the use of coal in generating electricity and supports development of carbon-sequestration and clean-coal technologies for minimizing coal's environmental impacts.

Assn. of Electrical Equipment and Medical Imaging Manufacturers (NEMA), *1300 N. 17th St., #900, Rosslyn,*

Federal Energy Regulatory Commission

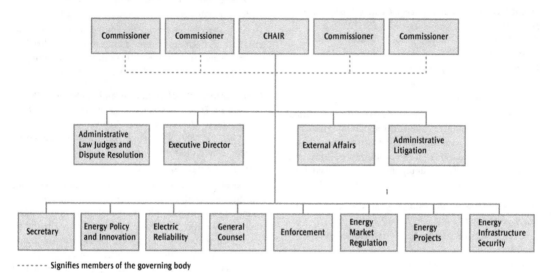

- - - - - - Signifies members of the governing body

VA 22209-3801; (703) 841-3200. Fax, (703) 841-5900. *Kevin Cosgriff, President. Press, (703) 841-3282. Web, www.nema.org and Twitter, @NEMAupdates*

Membership: manufacturers of products used in the generation, transmission, distribution, control, and end use of electricity, including manufacturers of medical diagnostic imaging equipment. Develops technical standards; collects, analyzes, and disseminates industry data. Interests include Smart Grid, high-performance building, carbon footprint, energy storage, and an intelligence portal. Monitors legislation, regulations, and international trade activities.

Electric Power Supply Assn., *1401 New York Ave. N.W., #950, 20005-2110; (202) 628-8200. Fax, (202) 628-8260. John Shelk, President. Web, www.epsa.org*

Membership: power generators active in U.S. and global markets, power marketers, and suppliers of goods and services to the industry. Promotes competition in the delivery of electricity to consumers.

Electricity Consumers Resource Council (ELCON), *1101 K St. N.W., #700, 20005; (202) 682-1390. Devin Hartman, President. General email, elcon@elcon.org Web, www.elcon.org*

Membership: large industrial users of electricity. Promotes development of coordinated federal, state, and local policies concerning electrical supply for industrial users; studies rate structures and their impact on consumers.

National Electrical Contractors Assn., *3 Bethesda Metro Center, #1100, Bethesda, MD 20814; (301) 657-3110. Fax, (301) 215-4500. John M. Grau, Chief Executive Officer. Web, www.necanet.org, Twitter, @necanet and Facebook, www.facebook.com/NECANET*

Membership: electrical contractors who build and service electrical wiring and equipment, including high-voltage construction and service. Represents members in collective bargaining with union workers; sponsors research and educational programs.

National Hydropower Assn., *601 New Jersey Ave. N.W., #660, 20001; (202) 682-1700. Fax, (202) 682-9478. Linda Church Ciocci, Executive Director. General email, help@hydro.org Web, www.hydro.org*

Membership: investor-owned utilities and municipal and independent companies that generate hydroelectric power and power from new water technologies; consulting, engineering, and law firms; and equipment suppliers and manufacturers. Focus includes regulatory relief, public affairs, and coalition building. Monitors legislation and regulations.

Research and Development

▶ **AGENCIES**

National Institute of Standards and Technology (NIST) *(Commerce Dept.), Quantum Measurement Division, 100 Bureau Dr., MS 8420, Gaithersburg, MD 20899-8420; (301) 975-3210. Fax, (301) 990-3038. Yuri Ralchenko, Chief (Acting). Web, www.nist.gov/pml/div684*

Conducts research to characterize and define performance parameters of electrical/electronic systems, components, and materials; applies research to advance measurement instrumentation and the efficiency of electric power transmission and distribution; develops and maintains national electrical reference standards, primarily for power, energy, and related measurements, to assist in the development of new products and promote international competitiveness.

Office of Science *(Energy Dept.), Fusion Energy Sciences (FES),* 19901 Germantown Rd., #SC24, Germantown, MD 20874-1290 (mailing address: Germantown Bldg., 1000 Independence Ave. S.W., #SC24, Washington, DC 20585); (301) 903-4941. Fax, (301) 903-8584. James W. Van Dam, Associate Director (Acting).
Web, http://science.energy.gov/fes

Conducts research and development on fusion energy for electric power generation.

► **NONGOVERNMENTAL**

Electric Power Research Institute (EPRI), *Washington Office,* 1325 G St. N.W., #1080, 20005; (202) 293-7518. Fax, (202) 296-5436. Barbara Bauman Tyran, Executive Director of Government Relations, (202) 293-7513.
General email, askepri@askepri.com

Web, www.epri.com and *Twitter, @EPRINews*

Membership: investor-owned and municipally owned electric utilities and rural cooperatives. Conducts research and development in power generation and delivery technologies, including fossil fuel, nuclear, and renewable energy sources used by electric utilities. Studies energy management and utilization, including conservation and environmental issues. (Headquarters in Palo Alto, Calif.)

FOSSIL FUELS

General

► **AGENCIES**

Fossil Energy (FE) *(Energy Dept.),* 1000 Independence Ave. S.W., #4G084, 20585-1290; (202) 586-6660. Fax, (202) 586-5146. Steven Winberg, Assistant Secretary.
Web, www.fe.doe.gov

http://energy.gov/fe/office-fossil-energy, Twitter, @fossilenergygov and *Facebook, www.facebook .com/FossilEnergy*

Responsible for policy and management of high-risk, long-term research and development in recovering, converting, and using fossil energy, including coal, petroleum, oil shale, and unconventional sources of natural gas. Handles the petroleum reserve and the naval petroleum and oil shale reserve programs; oversees the Clean Coal Program to design and construct environmentally clean coal-burning facilities.

U.S. Geological Survey (USGS) *(Interior Dept.), Energy Resources Program,* 12201 Sunrise Valley Dr., MS 913, Reston, VA 20192-0002 (mailing address: 913 National Center, Reston, VA 20192); (703) 648-6470; (703) 648-6471. Fax, (703) 648-5464. Walter Scott Guidroz, Program Coordinator.
General email, gd-energypubs@usgs.gov

Web, http://energy.usgs.gov

Conducts research on geologically based energy resources of the United States and the world, including assessments of the quality, quantity, and geographic locations of natural gas, oil, gas hydrates, geothermal, and coal resources. Estimates energy resource availability and recoverability, including hydraulic fracturing ("fracking"); and conducts research on the deleterious environmental impacts of energy resource occurrence and use.

► **CONGRESS**

For a listing of relevant congressional committees and subcommittees, please see pages 255–256 or the Appendix.

► **NONGOVERNMENTAL**

Diesel Technology Forum, 5291 Corporate Dr., #102, Frederick, MD 21703-2875; (301) 668-7230. Fax, (301) 668-7234. Allen Schaeffer, Executive Director; Kristen Gifford, Communications.
General email, dtf@dieselforum.org

Web, www.dieselforum.org and *Twitter, @DieselTechForum*

Represents diesel interests, with a focus on environmental protection. Advocates use of diesel engines. Supports energy research and advises policymakers. Monitors legislation and regulations.

Coal

► **AGENCIES**

Bureau of Land Management (BLM) *(Interior Dept.), Solid Minerals,* 20 M St. S.E., #2134 LM, 20003 (mailing address: 1849 C St. N.W., WO 320, Washington, DC 20240); (202) 912-7113. Fax, (202) 912-7199. Mitchell Leverette, Chief.
Web, www.blm.gov

Evaluates and classifies coal resources on federal lands; develops and administers leasing programs. Supervises coal-mining operations on federal lands; oversees pre- and postlease operations, including production phases of coal development. Oversees implementation of the Mining Law of 1872 and the Mineral Materials Act of 1955.

Federal Mine Safety and Health Review Commission (FMSHRC), 1331 Pennsylvania Ave. N.W., #520N, 20004-1710; (202) 434-9905. Fax, (202) 434-9906. Lisa Boyd, Executive Director; Michael G. Young, Chair (Acting). TTY, (202) 434-4000, ext. 293.
General email, fmshrc@fmshrc.gov

Web, www.fmshrc.gov

Independent agency established by the Federal Mine Safety and Health Act of 1977. Holds fact-finding hearings and issues orders affirming, modifying, or vacating the labor secretary's enforcement actions regarding mine safety and health. Reading room open to the public by appointment.

Interior Dept. (DOI), *Surface Mining Reclamation and Enforcement (OSMRE),* 1849 C St. N.W., #4513, 20240; (202) 208-4006. Fax, (202) 219-3106. Glenda H. Owens,

Director (Acting). Press, (202) 208-2565. TTY, (202) 208-2694.

General email, getinfo@osmre.gov

Web, www.osmre.gov, Twitter, @OSMRE and Facebook, www.facebook.com/OSMRE

Administers the Surface Mining Control and Reclamation Act of 1977. Establishes and enforces national standards for the regulation and reclamation of surface coal mining and the surface effects of underground coal mining; oversees state implementation of these standards.

Mine Safety and Health Administration (*Labor Dept.*), 201 12th St. South, #401, Arlington, VA 22202-5450; (202) 693-9400. Fax, (202) 693-9801. David G. Zatezalo, Assistant Secretary. Toll-free, (800) 746-1553.

General email, ASKMSHA@dol.gov

Web, www.msha.gov and Twitter, @MSHA_DOL

Administers and enforces the health and safety provisions of the Federal Mine Safety and Health Act of 1977. Monitors underground mining and processing operations of minerals, including minerals used in construction materials; produces educational materials in engineering; and assists with rescue operations following mining accidents.

▶NONGOVERNMENTAL

American Coalition for Clean Coal Electricity (ACCCE), 1069 West Broad St., #913, Falls Church, VA 22046; (202) 459-4800. Fax, (202) 459-4897. Michelle Bloodworth, President.

General email, info@americaspower.org

Web, www.americaspower.org, Twitter, @AmericasPower and Facebook, www.facebook.com/AmericasPower

Membership: coal, railroad, and electric utility companies and suppliers. Educates the public, regulators, and policymakers about economic, technological, and scientific research on energy resources employed in generating electricity. Promotes the use of coal in generating electricity and supports development of carbon-sequestration and clean-coal technologies for minimizing coal's environmental impacts.

American Coke and Coal Chemicals Institute, 25 Massachusetts Ave. N.W., #800, 20001; (724) 772-1167. Fax, (866) 422-7794. David C. Ailor, President.

General email, information@accci.org

Web, www.accci.org

Membership: producers of metallurgical coke and coal; tar distillers and coal chemical producers; coke and coal brokers; equipment, materials, and service suppliers to the coke industry; builders of coke ovens and coke by-product plants. Maintains committees on coke, coal chemicals, manufacturing, environment, safety and health, human resources, quality, governmental relations, and international affairs.

Assn. of Bituminous Contractors, Inc., 815 Connecticut Ave., #620, 20037; (202) 785-4440. William H. Howe, General Counsel.

Membership: independent and general contractors that build coal mines. Represents members before the

Federal Mine Safety and Health Review Commission and in collective bargaining with the United Mine Workers of America.

Bituminous Coal Operators' Assn., 1776 Eye St. N.W., #245, 20006; (202) 783-3195. Michael O. McKown, President.

General email, lpatrickbcoa@aol.com

Membership: firms that mine bituminous coal. Represents members in collective bargaining with the United Mine Workers of America.

National Coal Council, 1101 Pennsylvania Ave. N.W., #300, 20004; (202) 756-4524. Fax, (202) 688-2201. Janet Gellici, Chief Executive Officer, (602) 717-5112.

General email, info@ncc1.org

Web, www.nationalcoalcouncil.org and Twitter, @CoalCouncil

Membership: individuals appointed by the secretary of energy. Represents coal consumers and producers, transporters, engineering firms, equipment and supply vendors, academics, consultants, NGOs, and public officials. Monitors federal policies.

National Mining Assn., 101 Constitution Ave. N.W., #500 East, 20001-2133; (202) 463-2600. Fax, (202) 463-2666. Harold P. (Hal) Quinn Jr., President. Press, (202) 463-2642.

General email, webmaster@nma.org

Web, www.nma.org

Membership: coal producers, coal sales and transportation companies, equipment manufacturers, consulting firms, coal resource developers and exporters, coal-burning electric utility companies, and other energy companies. Collects, analyzes, and distributes industry statistics; conducts special studies of competitive fuels, coal markets, production and consumption forecasts, and industry planning. Interests include exports, coal leasing programs, coal transportation, environmental issues, health and safety, national energy policy, slurry pipelines, and research and development, including synthetic fuels. Monitors legislation and regulation. (Merged with Coal Exporters Assn. of the United States.)

United Mine Workers of America, 18354 Quantico Gateway Dr., #200, Triangle, VA 22172-1779; (703) 291-2400. Cecil E. Roberts, President.

General email, info@umwa.org

Web, www.umwa.org and Twitter, @MineWorkers

Membership: coal miners and other mining workers. Represents members in collective bargaining with industry. Conducts educational, housing, and health and safety training programs; monitors federal coal-mining safety programs.

Oil and Natural Gas

▶AGENCIES

Bureau of Land Management (BLM) (*Interior Dept.*), *Fluid Minerals*, 20 M St. S.E., #2134LM, 20003;

(202) 912-7143. Fax, (202) 912-7194. Steven Wells, Division Chief.
Web, www.blm.gov

Evaluates and classifies oil, natural gas, and geothermal resources on federal lands; develops and administers leasing programs. Supervises extraction of oil (including from oil shale deposits), natural gas, and geothermal energy resources on federal lands; oversees prelease and postlease operations, including production phases of oil and natural gas development; oversees federal land-leasing reforms.

Bureau of Ocean Energy Management (BOEM) *(Interior Dept.), Strategic Resources,* 1849 C St. N.W., MS DM5238, 20240; (202) 208-3515. Fax, (202) 513-0775. Renee Orr, Chief.
General email, boempublicaffairs@boem.gov
Web, www.boem.gov

Develops and implements the Five-Year Outer Continental Shelf (OCS) Oil and Natural Gas Leasing Program; oversees assessments and inventories of oil, gas, and other mineral resources. Conveys access to marine minerals; maintains official maps and geographic data; conducts economic evaluations that ensure fair market value for OCS leases. Leads efforts to identify and mitigate the financial risks associated with offshore lease activities.

Bureau of Safety and Environmental Enforcement (BSEE) *(Interior Dept.),* 1849 C St. N.W., MS 5438, 20240-0001; (202) 208-3985. Scott A. Angelle, Director.
General email, bseepublicaffairs@bsee.gov

Web, www.bsee.gov, Twitter, @BSEEgov and Facebook, www.facebook.com/BSEEgov and YouTube, www.youtube.com/user/bseegov

Responsible for inspections, enforcement, and safety of offshore oil and gas operations. Functions include the development and enforcement of safety and environmental regulations, research, inspections, offshore regulatory and compliance programs, oil spill response, and training of inspectors and industry professionals.

Bureau of Safety and Environmental Enforcement (BSEE) *(Interior Dept.), Offshore Regulatory Programs (OORP),* 1849 C St. N.W., MS DM5438, 20240-0001; (202) 208-3985. Douglas Morris, Chief.
General email, bseepublicaffairs@bsee.gov

Web, www.bsee.gov/what-we-do/offshore-regulatory-programs

Develops standards, regulations, and compliance programs governing Outer Continental Shelf oil, gas, and minerals exploration and operations. Purview includes safety management programs, safety and pollution prevention research, technology assessments, standards for inspections and enforcement policies, and accident investigation practices.

Fossil Energy (FE) *(Energy Dept.), Oil and Natural Gas,* 1000 Independence Ave. S.W., #3E028, 20585; (202) 586-5600. Fax, (202) 586-6221. Shawn Bennett, Associate Deputy Assistant Secretary.
Web, www.fe.doe.gov

Responsible for research and development programs in oil and gas exploration, production, processing, and storage; studies ways to improve efficiency of oil recovery in depleted reservoirs; coordinates and evaluates research and development among government, universities, and industrial research organizations.

Fossil Energy (FE) *(Energy Dept.), Petroleum Reserves,* Forrestal Bldg., 1000 Independence Ave. S.W., FE-40, 20585; (202) 586-4410. Douglas MacIntyre, Deputy Assistant Secretary (Acting).
Web, www.energy.gov/fe/services/petroleum-reserves

Manages programs that provide the United States with strategic and economic protection against disruptions in oil supplies, including the Strategic Petroleum Reserves, the Northeast Home Heating Oil Reserve, and the Naval Petroleum and the Northeast Gasoline Supply Reserve.

▶NONGOVERNMENTAL

American Fuel & Petrochemical Manufacturers, 1800 M St. N.W., #900 North, 20036; (202) 457-0480. Fax, (202) 457-0486. Chet Thompson, President.
General email, info@afpm.org
Web, www.afpm.org, Twitter, @AFPMonline and Facebook, www.facebook.com/AFPMonline

Membership: petroleum, petrochemical, and refining companies. Interests include allocation, imports, refining technology, petrochemicals, and environmental regulations.

American Petroleum Institute, 200 Massachusetts Ave. N.W., #1100, 20001-5571; (202) 682-8000. Mike Sommers, President. Press, (202) 682-8114.
Web, www.api.org, Twitter, API@Energy and Facebook, www.facebook.com/TheAmericanPetroleumInstitute

Membership: producers, refiners, marketers, pipeline operators, and transporters of oil, natural gas, and related products such as gasoline. Provides information on the industry, including data on exports and imports, taxation, transportation, weekly refinery operations and inventories, and drilling activity and costs; conducts research on petroleum and publishes statistical and drilling reports. Develops equipment and operating standards. Certifies compliance of equipment manufacturing and of environmental and occupational safety and health management systems.

American Public Gas Assn. (APGA), 201 Massachusetts Ave. N.E., #C4, 20002-4988; (202) 464-2742. Fax, (202) 464-0246. Bert Kalisch, President. Toll-free, (800) 927-4204.
General email, apga@apga.org
Web, www.apga.org, Twitter, @APGA and Facebook, www.facebook.com/publicgas

Membership: municipally owned gas distribution systems. Provides information on federal developments affecting natural gas. Promotes efficiency and works to protect the interests of public gas systems. Sponsors workshops and conferences.

Center for Liquefied Natural Gas, *1620 Eye St. N.W., #700, 20006; (202) 289-2253. Fax, (202) 962-4753. Charlie Riedl, Executive Director, (202) 839-3002. Web, https://lngfacts.org and Twitter, @LNGfacts*

Membership: liquefied natural gas producers, shippers, terminal operators and developers, and energy trade associations. Provides general and technical information on liquefied natural gas. Monitors legislation and regulations.

Compressed Gas Assn., *14501 George Carter Way, #103, Chantilly, VA 20151-1788; (703) 788-2700. Fax, (703) 961-1831. Richard Gottwald, President. General email, cga@cganet.com*

Web, www.cganet.com

Membership: all segments of the compressed gas industry, including producers and distributors of compressed and liquefied gases. Promotes and coordinates technical development and standardization of the industry. Monitors legislation and regulations.

Gas Technology Institute (GTI), *Policy and Regulatory Affairs, 1250 H St. N.W., #880, 20005; (847) 768-0511. Richard Kaelin, Executive Director of Washington Operations. General email, washingtonops@gti.energy*

Web, www.gastechnology.org and Twitter, @GasTechnology

Membership: all segments of the natural gas industry, including producers, pipelines, and distributors. Conducts research and develops new technology for gas customers and the industry. (Headquarters in Des Plaines, Ill.)

Independent Petroleum Assn. of America, *119 Lake Shore Dr., Cross Junction, VA 22625; (202) 857-4722. Fax, (202) 857-4799. Barry Russell, Chief Executive Officer. Web, www.ipaa.org, Twitter, @IPAAaccess and Facebook, www.facebook.com/IPAAaccess*

Membership: independent oil and natural gas producers; service companies; and others with interests in domestic exploration, development, and production of oil and natural gas. Interests include leasing, prices and taxation, foreign trade, environmental restrictions, and improved recovery methods.

International Assn. of Drilling Contractors (IADC), *Government and Regulatory Affairs, 1667 K St. N.W., #420, 20006; (202) 293-0670. Fax, (202) 872-0047. Jason McFarland, President, (713) 292-1945. General email, info@iadc.org*

Web, www.iadc.org and Twitter, @DC_Magazine

Membership: oil and gas drilling contractors, oil and gas producers, and others in the industry worldwide. Promotes safe exploration and production of hydrocarbons, advances in drilling technology, and preservation of the environment. Monitors legislation and regulations. (Headquarters in Houston, Tex.)

International Liquid Terminals Assn. (ILTA), *1005 N. Glebe Rd., #600, Arlington, VA 22201; (703) 875-2011. Fax, (703) 875-2018. Kathryn Clay, President.*

General email, info@ilta.org

Web, www.ilta.org

Membership: commercial operators of for-hire bulk liquid terminals and tank storage facilities, including those for crude oil and petroleum. Promotes the safe and efficient handling of various types of bulk liquid commodities. Sponsors workshops and seminars and publishes directories. Monitors legislation and regulations.

Interstate Natural Gas Assn. of America, *20 F St. N.W., #450, 20001; (202) 216-5900. Donald F. Santa Jr., President. Press, (202) 216-5913. Web, www.ingaa.org*

Press, media@ingaa.org

Membership: U.S. interstate, Canadian, and Mexican interprovincial natural gas pipeline companies. Commissions studies and provides legislative and regulatory information on the natural gas pipeline industry.

National Ocean Industries Assn., *1120 G St. N.W., #900, 20005; (202) 347-6900. Fax, (202) 347-8650. Randall Luthi, President. General email, jwilliams@noia.org*

Web, www.noia.org and Twitter, @oceanindustries

Membership: manufacturers, producers, suppliers, and support and service companies involved in marine, offshore, and ocean work. Interests include offshore oil and gas supply and production, pursuit of offshore renewable-energy opportunities, environmental safeguards, equipment supply, gas transmission, navigation, research and technology, and shipyards.

National Petroleum Council, *1625 K St. N.W., #600, 20006-1656; (202) 393-6100. Fax, (202) 331-8539. Marshall W. Nichols, Executive Director; Gregory L. Armstrong, Chair. General email, info@npc.org*

Web, www.npc.org

Federally chartered, privately funded advisory committee to the secretary of energy on matters relating to the petroleum industry, including oil and natural gas. Publishes reports concerning technical aspects of the oil and gas industries.

National Propane Gas Assn., *1899 L St. N.W., #350, 20036-4623; (202) 466-7200. Fax, (202) 466-7205. Richard R. Roldan, President, (202) 355-1388. General email, info@npga.org*

Web, www.npga.org and Twitter, @NPGApropane

Membership: retail marketers, producers, wholesale distributors, appliance and equipment manufacturers, equipment fabricators, and distributors and transporters of liquefied petroleum gas. Conducts research, safety, and educational programs; provides statistics on the industry.

National Research Council (NRC), *Gulf Research Program, Keck Center, 500 5th St. N.W., 20001; (202) 334-2138. Lauren Alexander Augustine, Executive Director.*

General email, gulfprogram@nas.edu

Web, www.nationalacademies.org/gulf and
Twitter, @NASEM_Gulf

Promotes oil system safety and the protection of human
health and the environment in the Gulf of Mexico and
other U.S. outer continental shelf areas.

Natural Gas Supply Assn., *1620 Eye St. N.W., #700, 20006;
(202) 326-9300. Fax, (202) 326-9308. Dena Wiggins,
President.*
Web, www.ngsa.org

Membership: major and independent producers of
domestic natural gas. Interests include the production,
consumption, marketing, and regulation of natural gas.
Monitors legislation and regulations.

NGVAmerica (Natural Gas Vehicles for America), *400 N.
Capitol St. N.W., 20001; (202) 824-7360.
Fax, (202) 824-9160. Daniel Gage, President;
Allison Cunningham, Director of Government Affairs.*
General email, pkerkhoven@ngvamerica.org

Web, www.ngvamerica.org, Twitter, @NGVamerican and
Facebook, www.facebook.com/NGVAmerica

Membership: natural gas distributors and producers;
automobile and engine manufacturers; natural gas vehicle
product and service suppliers; research and development
organizations; enviromental groups; and state and local
government agencies. Advocates installation of natural gas
and biomethane fuel stations and development of industry
standards. Helps market new products and equipment
related to compressed natural gas (CNG), liquefied natural
gas (LNG), and biomethane-powered vehicles.

Oil Change International, *714 G St. S.E., #202, 20003;
(202) 518-9029. Fax, (202) 330-5952. Stephen Kretzmann,
Executive Director. Press, (202) 316-3499.*
General email, info@priceofoil.org

Web, www.priceofoil.org

Advocates national and global clean energy policies with
a focus on fossil fuels. Researches the fossil fuel industry and
publishes reports aimed to debate the use of oil, gas, and coal.
Campaigns against fossil fuel developments.

Petroleum Marketers Assn. of America (PMAA), *1901 N.
Fort Myer Dr., #500, Arlington, VA 22209-1604;
(703) 351-8000. Fax, (703) 351-9160. Rob Underwood,
President.*
General email, info@pmaa.org

Web, www.pmaa.org and Twitter, @pmaa_47

Membership: state and regional associations representing independent branded and nonbranded marketers of
petroleum products. Provides information on all aspects of
petroleum marketing. Monitors legislation and regulations.

**Society of Independent Gasoline Marketers of America
(SIGMA),** *3930 Pender Dr., #340, Fairfax, VA 22030-0985;
(703) 709-7000. Fax, (703) 709-7007. Ryan McNutt, Chief
Executive Officer.*
General email, sigma@sigma.org

Web, www.sigma.org

Membership: marketers and wholesalers of brand and
nonbrand gasoline. Seeks to ensure adequate supplies of
gasoline at competitive prices. Monitors legislation and
regulations affecting gasoline supply and price.

Pipelines

▶**AGENCIES**

Federal Energy Regulatory Commission (FERC) *(Energy
Dept.), Energy Market Regulation (OEMR), 888 1st St.
N.E., #8A-01, 20426; (202) 502-6700. Fax, (202) 219-2836.
Anna Cochrane, Director.*
Web, www.ferc.gov/about/offices/oemr.asp

Establishes and enforces maximum rates and charges
for oil and natural gas pipelines; establishes oil pipeline
operating rules; issues certificates for and regulates construction, sale, and acquisition of natural gas pipeline facilities. Ensures compliance with the Natural Gas Policy Act,
the Natural Gas Act, and other statutes.

Federal Energy Regulatory Commission (FERC) *(Energy
Dept.), Energy Projects (OEP), 888 1st St. N.E., #6A-01,
20426; (202) 502-8700. Fax, (202) 219-0205. Terry Turpin,
Director.*
Web, www.ferc.gov/about/offices/oep.asp

Focuses on the engineering and environmental aspects
of siting and development of new gas pipeline projects;
authorizes and monitors hydroelectric projects for compliance and to safeguard the public.

National Transportation Safety Board (NTSB), *Railroad,
Pipeline, and Hazardous Materials Investigations, 490
L'Enfant Plaza East S.W., 20594; (202) 314-6463.
Fax, (202) 688-2569. Robert Hall, Director.
Press, (202) 314-6100.*
Web, www.ntsb.gov/about/organization/RPHM

Investigates hazardous materials and petroleum pipeline accidents.

**Pipeline and Hazardous Materials Safety
Administration** *(Transportation Dept.), Hazardous
Materials Safety, 1200 New Jersey Ave. S.E., #E21-317,
20590; (202) 366-4488. Fax, (202) 366-5713.
William S. (Bill) Schoonover, Associate Administrator.
Hazardous Materials Information Center, (800) 467-4922.*
General email, phmsa.hmhazmatsafety@dot.gov

Web, https://cms.phmsa.dot.gov/about-phmsa/offices/
office-hazardous-materials-safety

Designates fuels, chemicals, and other substances as
hazardous materials and regulates their transportation in
interstate commerce. Provides technical assistance on hazardous waste materials transportation safety and security
to state and local governments. Gathers and analyzes incident data from carriers transporting hazardous materials.

**Pipeline and Hazardous Materials Safety
Administration** *(Transportation Dept.), Pipeline Safety,
1200 New Jersey Ave. S.E., E24-455, 20590; (202) 366-4595.*

Fax, (202) 366-4566. Alan K. Mayberry, Associate Administrator.
General email, phmsa.pipelinesafety@dot.gov
Web, www.phmsa.dot.gov/about-phmsa/offices/office-pipeline-safety

Issues and enforces federal regulations for oil, natural gas, and petroleum products pipeline safety. Inspects pipelines and oversees risk management by pipeline operators.

▶ **NONGOVERNMENTAL**

Assn. of Oil Pipe Lines (AOPL), 900 17th St. N.W., #600, 20006; (202) 408-7970. Fax, (202) 280-1949. Andrew J. Black, President. Media, (202) 292-4509.
General email, aopl@aopl.org
Web, www.aopl.org

Membership: owners and operators of oil pipelines. Analyzes industry statistics. Monitors legislation and regulations.

Interstate Natural Gas Assn. of America, 20 F St. N.W., #450, 20001; (202) 216-5900. Donald F. Santa Jr., President. Press, (202) 216-5913.
Web, www.ingaa.org
Press, media@ingaa.org

Membership: U.S. interstate, Canadian, and Mexican interprovincial natural gas pipeline companies. Commissions studies and provides legislative and regulatory information on the natural gas pipeline industry.

NUCLEAR ENERGY

General

▶ **AGENCIES**

Nuclear Regulatory Commission, 11555 Rockville Pike, MS 016G4, Rockville, MD 20852; (301) 415-7000. Fax, (301) 415-3504. Kristine L. Svinicki, Chair. 24-hour emergency, (301) 816-5100. Fraud, waste, and abuse hotline, (800) 233-3497. Press, (301) 415-8200. Public Document Room, (301) 397-4209. Safety & Security, (800) 695-7403. Toll-free, (800) 368-5642. TTY, (301) 415-5575.
General email, opa@nrc.gov
Web, www.nrc.gov, Twitter, @NRCgov and Facebook, www.facebook.com/nrcgov

Regulates commercial uses of nuclear energy; responsibilities include licensing, inspection, and enforcement; monitors and regulates the imports and exports of nuclear material and equipment.

Nuclear Regulatory Commission, Public Affairs, 11555 Rockville Pike, MS 016D3, Rockville, MD 20852-2738; (301) 415-8200. Fax, (301) 415-3716. David Castelveter, Director.
General email, opa.resource@nrc.gov
Web, www.nrc.gov/about-nrc/public-affairs.html

Provides the public and the news media with information about the Nuclear Regulatory Commission's programs, policy decisions, and activities, primarily through social media and by issuing news releases and distributing commission speeches, fact sheets, and brochures. Follows news coverage of the agency and responds to media and public inquiries.

Tennessee Valley Authority, Government Affairs, 500 N. Capitol St. N.W., #220, 20001; (202) 898-2999. Fax, (202) 898-2998. William D. (Bill) Johnson, President.
General email, tvainfo@tva.gov
Web, www.tva.gov and Twitter, @TVAnews

Coordinates resource conservation, development, and land-use programs in the Tennessee River Valley. Produces and supplies wholesale power to municipal and cooperative electric systems, federal installations, and some industries; interests include nuclear power generation.

▶ **CONGRESS**

For a listing of relevant congressional committees and subcommittees, please see pages 255–256 or the Appendix.

▶ **NONGOVERNMENTAL**

American Physical Society, Washington Office, Office of Government Affairs, 529 14th St. N.W., #1050, 20045-2001; (202) 662-8700. Fax, (202) 662-8711. Francis Slakey, Chief Government Affairs Officer; Mark Elsesser, Legislative Affairs, (202) 662-8710. Press Secretary, (202) 662-8702.
General email, oga@aps.org
Web, www.aps.org, Twitter, @APSphysics and Facebook, www.facebook.com/apsphysics

Scientific and educational society of educators, students, citizens, and scientists, including industrial scientists. Sponsors studies on issues of public concern related to physics, such as reactor safety and energy use. Informs members of national and international developments. (Headquarters in College Park, Md.)

Nuclear Energy Institute, 1201 F St. N.W., #1100, 20004; (202) 739-8000. Fax, (202) 785-4019. Maria Korsnick, President.
General email, NEIGA_Nuclearenergy@nei.org
Web, www.nei.org, Twitter, @NEI and Facebook, www.facebook.com/NuclearEnergyInstitute
Press, media@nei.org

Membership: utilities; industries; labor, service, and research organizations; law firms; universities; and government agencies interested in peaceful uses of nuclear energy, including the generation of electricity. Acts as a spokesperson for the nuclear power industry; provides information on licensing and plant siting, research and development, safety and security, waste disposal, and legislative and policy issues.

Nuclear Information and Resource Service, 6930 Carroll Ave., #340, Takoma Park, MD 20912-4446;

(301) 270-6477. Fax, (301) 270-4291. Timothy Judson, Executive Director.

General email, nirsnet@nirs.org

Web, www.nirs.org and Facebook, www.facebook.com/NIRSnet

Information and networking clearinghouse for environmental activists and other individuals concerned about nuclear power plants, radioactive waste, and radiation and sustainable energy issues. Initiates large-scale organizing and public education campaigns and provides technical and strategic expertise to environmental groups. Library open to the public by appointment.

Public Citizen, *Energy Program, 215 Pennsylvania Ave. S.E., 20003-1155; (202) 546-4996. Tyson Slocum, Director.*

General email, energy@citizen.org

Web, www.citizen.org/cmep

Public interest group that promotes energy efficiency and renewable energy technologies; opposes nuclear energy. Interests include nuclear plant safety and energy policy issues.

Union of Concerned Scientists, *Global Security, 1825 K St. N.W., #800, 20006-1232; (202) 223-6133. Fax, (202) 223-6162. David Wright, Co-Director; Lisbeth Gronlund, Co-Director.*

General email, ucs@ucsusa.org

Web, www.ucsusa.org

An independent public interest group of scientists and citizens concerned with U.S. energy policy, including nuclear energy economics and power plant safety and security. Monitors the performance of nuclear power plants and their regulators; evaluates the economics of nuclear power relative to other low-carbon energy resources. (Headquarters in Cambridge, Mass.)

Licensing and Plant Siting

▶ **AGENCIES**

Environment, Health, Safety, and Security (EHSS) *(Energy Dept.), 1000 Independence Ave. S.W., #7G040, 20585; (202) 586-4399. Fax, (202) 586-5605. Matthew Moury, Associate Under Secretary.*

General email, AUUserSupport@hq.doe.gov

Web, https://energy.gov/ehss/environment-health-safety-security

Develops corporate security policy and standards affecting nuclear weapons facilities, nuclear materials, and classified information and provides security assistance to field elements in planning site protection strategies.

Federal Emergency Management Agency (FEMA) *(Homeland Security Dept.), Resilience, National Preparedness, Technological Hazards, 400 C St. S.W., MS 3600, 20472-3025; (202) 646-3158. Fax, (703) 308-0324. Michael Casey, Director.*

Web, www.fema.gov/technological-hazards-division

Reviews off-site preparedness for commercial nuclear power facilities; evaluates emergency plans before plant licensing and submits findings to the Nuclear Regulatory Commission.

Nuclear Regulatory Commission, *New Reactors, 11545 Rockville Pike, MS T6F15, Rockville, MD 20852; (301) 415-1897. Fax, (301) 415-6323. Frederick Brown, Director; Vonna Ordaz, Deputy Director.*

Web, www.nrc.gov/about-nrc/organization/nrofuncdesc.html

Licenses and regulates nuclear power plants that use new designs; approves siting of new plants.

Nuclear Regulatory Commission, *Nuclear Material Safety and Safeguards (NMSS), 11555 Rockville Pike, Rockville, MD 20852; (301) 415-0595. Scott Moore, Director (Acting).*

Web, www.nrc.gov/about-nrc/organization/nmssfuncdesc.html

Licenses all nuclear facilities and materials except power reactors; directs principal licensing and regulation activities for the management of nuclear waste.

Nuclear Regulatory Commission, *Nuclear Reactor Regulation, 11555 Rockville Pike, MS O13H16M, Rockville, MD 20852; (301) 415-1270. Fax, (301) 415-8333. Ho Nieh, Director.*

Web, www.nrc.gov/about-nrc/organization/nrrfuncdesc.html

Licenses nuclear power plants and operators.

Research and Development

▶ **AGENCIES**

Nuclear Energy (NE) *(Energy Dept.), 1000 Independence Ave. S.W., #5A143, E-1, 20585; (202) 586-2240. Fax, (202) 586-4403. Vacant, Assistant Secretary; Edward McGinnis, Deputy Assistant Secretary.*

Web, www.energy.gov/ne/office-nuclear-energy and Facebook, www.facebook.com/NuclearEnergyGov and Blog, www.energy.gov/ne/listings/ne-blog-archive

Responsible for nuclear technology research and development, management of the Energy Dept.'s nuclear technology infrastructure, uranium activities, and fuel cycle issues. Supports nuclear education, including university reactor instrumentation and equipment upgrades and general support to nuclear engineering programs at U.S. universities. Leads U.S. participation in the Global Nuclear Energy Partnership, which seeks to demonstrate a more proliferation-resistant closed fuel cycle and increase the safety and security of nuclear energy.

Nuclear Energy (NE) *(Energy Dept.), Fuel Cycle Research Technologies, 1000 Independence Ave. S.W., #5A-107, 20585; (202) 586-8105. Fax, (202) 586-0541. John Herczeg, Deputy Assistant Secretary.*

Nuclear Regulatory Commission

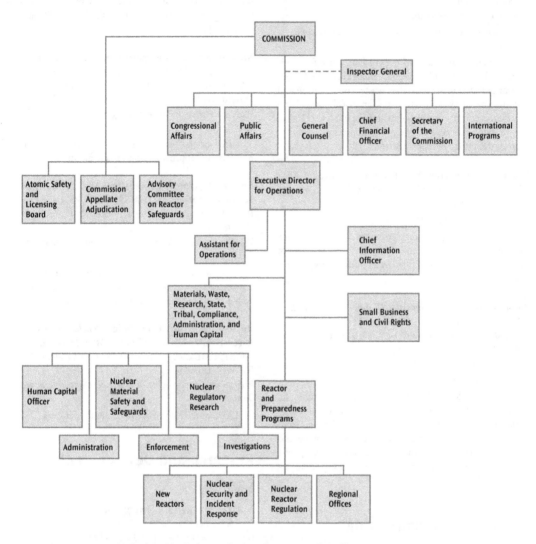

- - - Indicates a support or advisory relationship with the unit rather than a direct reporting relationship

General email, fuelcells@ee.doe.gov

Web, www.energy.gov/ne/nuclear-reactor-technologies

Organizes and conducts research and development through five initiatives: Fuel Cycle Options; Advanced Fuels; Separations and Waste Forms; Used Fuel Disposition; and Material Protection, Control, and Accountability Technologies. Seeks to implement safe strategies for management, storage, and permanent disposal solutions.

Nuclear Energy (NE) *(Energy Dept.), International Nuclear Energy Policy and Cooperation, 1000 Independence Ave. S.W., #5A-143, 20585; (202) 586-5253. Fax, (202) 586-8353. Vacant, Deputy Assistant Secretary; Sarah Lennon, Associate Deputy Assistent Director.*
Web, www.energy.gov/ne/nuclear-reactor-technologies/ international-nuclear-energy-policy-and-cooperation

Responsible for the Energy Dept.'s international civilian nuclear energy activities, including research, development and demonstration cooperation, international framework and partnership development, and international nuclear energy policy.

Nuclear Regulatory Commission, *Nuclear Regulatory Research, 11555 Rockville Pike, 2 White Flat, Rockville, MD 20952; (301) 415-1902. Raymond Furstenau, Director. Web, www.nrc.gov/about-nrc/organization/resfuncdesc.html*

Plans, recommends, and implements nuclear regulatory research, standards development, and resolution of safety issues for nuclear power plants and other facilities regulated by the Nuclear Regulatory Commission; develops and promulgates all technical regulations.

Office of Science *(Energy Dept.), Fusion Energy Sciences (FES), 19901 Germantown Rd., #SC24, Germantown, MD*

20874-1290 (mailing address: Germantown Bldg., 1000 Independence Ave. S.W., #SC24, Washington, DC 20585); (301) 903-4941. Fax, (301) 903-8584. James W. Van Dam, Associate Director (Acting).
Web, http://science.energy.gov/fes

Conducts research and development on fusion energy for electric power generation.

▶NONGOVERNMENTAL

National Research Council (NRC), *Nuclear and Radiation Studies Board,* Keck Center, 500 5th St. N.W., 20001; (202) 334-3066. Fax, (202) 334-3077.
Charles Ferguson, Chair; Ourania Kosti, Senior Program Officer.
General email, nrsb@nas.edu
Web, http://dels.nas.edu/nrsb

Oversees studies on safety, security, technical efficacy, and other policy and societal issues arising from the application of nuclear and radiation-based technologies, including exposure to radiation, malevolent uses of nuclear and radiation-based technologies, and risks and benefits of nuclear and radiation-based applications.

Safety, Security, and Waste Disposal

▶AGENCIES

Defense Nuclear Facilities Safety Board, 625 Indiana Ave. N.W., #700, 20004-2901; (202) 694-7000. Fax, (202) 208-6518. Bruce Hamilton, Chair. Information, (202) 694-7000. Toll-free, (800) 788-4016.
General email, mailbox@dnfsb.gov
Web, www.dnfsb.gov

Independent board created by Congress and appointed by the president to provide external oversight of Energy Dept. defense nuclear weapons production facilities and make recommendations to the secretary of energy regarding public health and safety.

Environment, Health, Safety, and Security (EHSS) *(Energy Dept.),* 1000 Independence Ave. S.W., #7G040, 20585; (202) 586-4399. Fax, (202) 586-5605. Matthew Moury, Associate Under Secretary.
General email, AUUserSupport@hq.doe.gov
Web, https://energy.gov/ehss/environment-health-safety-security

Implements nuclear safety management programs, and fire protection and natural phenomena hazard control requirements; ensures protection of workers, the public, and the environment from the hazards associated with nuclear operations; resolves nuclear safety, facility safety, and quality assurance issues.

Environmental Management (EM) *(Energy Dept.),* 1000 Independence Ave. S.W., #EM-31, 20585; (202) 586-7709. Fax, (301) 903-7236. Anne M. White, Assistant Secretary. DOE switchboard, (202) 586-5000. TTY, (800) 877-8339.

General email, EM.WebContentManager@em.doe.gov
Web, www.energy.gov/em/office-environmental-management

Manages Energy Dept. programs that treat, stabilize, and dispose of radioactive waste, including that generated from the decontamination and decommissioning of Energy Dept. facilities and sites. Works to develop a reliable national system for low-level waste management and techniques for treatment and immobilization of waste from former nuclear weapons complex sites. Provides technical assistance to states and Regional Disposal Compacts on the safe and effective management of commercially generated wastes.

Environmental Protection Agency (EPA), *Air and Radiation (OAR), Radiation and Indoor Air,* 1200 Pennsylvania Ave. N.W., #5426, MC 6608T, 20460; (202) 343-9320. Fax, (202) 564-1408. Jonathan Edwards, Director.
Web, www.epa.gov/aboutepa/about-office-air-and-radiation-oar#oria

Ensures the safe disposal of radioactive waste. Administers the nationwide Environmental Radiation Ambient Monitoring System (RadNet), which analyzes environmental radioactive contamination. Fields a Radiological Emergency Response Team to respond to radiological incidents.

Federal Emergency Management Agency (FEMA) *(Homeland Security Dept.),* 500 C St. S.W., 20472; (202) 646-3900. Fax, (202) 212-5889. William B. Long, Administrator. Disaster TTY, (800) 427-5593. FEMA helpline, (800) 621-3362. Locator, (202) 646-2500. Press, (202) 646-3272. Toll-free, 800-621-FEMA. TTY, (800) 462-7585.
General email, femaopa@dhs.gov
Web, www.fema.gov, Twitter, @fema and Facebook, www.facebook.com/FEMA

Assists state and local governments responding to and recovering from natural, technological, and attack-related emergencies, including in communities where accidents at nuclear power facilities have occurred and communities surrounding accidents involving transportation of radioactive materials; operates the National Emergency Training Center. Coordinates emergency preparedness, mitigation, response, and recovery activities, and planning for all federal agencies and departments.

National Transportation Safety Board (NTSB), *Railroad, Pipeline, and Hazardous Materials Investigations,* 490 L'Enfant Plaza East S.W., 20594; (202) 314-6463. Fax, (202) 688-2569. Robert Hall, Director. Press, (202) 314-6100.
Web, www.ntsb.gov/about/organization/RPHM

Investigates accidents involving the transportation of hazardous materials.

Nuclear Regulatory Commission, *Advisory Committee on Reactor Safeguards,* 11545 Rockville Pike, Rockville, MD 20852 (mailing address: Nuclear Regulatory Commission, MS T2E26, Washington, DC 20555-0001);

(301) 415-7360. Fax, (301) 415-5589. Andrea Veil, Executive Director.
Web, www.nrc.gov/about-nrc/organization/acrsfuncdesc .html

Advises the commission on the licensing and operation of production and utilization facilities and related safety issues, the adequacy of proposed reactor safety standards, and technical and policy issues related to the licensing of evolutionary and passive plant designs. Reports on the NRC Safety Research Program. Reviews Energy Dept. nuclear activities and facilities and provides technical advice to the Energy Dept.'s Nuclear Safety Board upon request.

Nuclear Regulatory Commission, Enforcement, 11555 Rockville Pike, MS O4A 15A, Rockville, MD 20852; (301) 415-2741. Fax, (301) 415-3431. George Wilson, Director (Acting). 24-hour operations, (301) 816-5100. Toll-free hotline, (800) 695-7403.
General email, allegation@nrc.gov

Web, www.nrc.gov/about-nrc/regulatory/enforcement.html

Oversees the development and implementation of policies and programs that enforce the commission's procedures concerning public health and safety. Identifies and takes action against violators.

Nuclear Regulatory Commission, Investigations, 11555 Rockville Pike, MS O3F1, Rockville, MD 20852; (301) 415-2373. Fax, (301) 415-2370.
Edward (Andy) Shuttleworth, Director.
Web, www.nrc.gov/about-nrc/organization/oifuncdesc .html

Develops policy, procedures, and standards for investigations of licensees, applicants, and their contractors or vendors concerning wrongdoing. Refers substantiated criminal cases to the Justice Dept. Informs the commission's leadership about investigations concerning public health and safety.

Nuclear Regulatory Commission, Nuclear Material Safety and Safeguards (NMSS), 11555 Rockville Pike, Rockville, MD 20852; (301) 415-0595. Scott Moore, Director (Acting).
Web, www.nrc.gov/about-nrc/organization/nmssfuncdesc .html

Regulates commercial nuclear reactors; storage, transportation and disposal of high-level radioactive waste and spent nuclear fuel; and the transportation of radioactive materials regulated under the Atomic Energy Act. Develops and implements policies for uranium recovery, conversion, and enrichment activities; fuel fabrication and development; and transportation of nuclear materials, including certification of transport containers and reactor spent fuel storage.

Nuclear Regulatory Commission, Nuclear Reactor Regulation, 11555 Rockville Pike, MS O13H16M, Rockville, MD 20852; (301) 415-1270. Fax, (301) 415-8333. Ho Nieh, Director.
Web, www.nrc.gov/about-nrc/organization/nrrfuncdesc .html

Conducts safety inspections of nuclear reactors. Regulates nuclear materials used or produced at nuclear power plants.

Nuclear Regulatory Commission, Nuclear Regulatory Research, 11555 Rockville Pike, 2 White Flat, Rockville, MD 20952; (301) 415-1902. Raymond Furstenau, Director.
Web, www.nrc.gov/about-nrc/organization/resfuncdesc .html

Plans, recommends, and implements resolution of safety issues for nuclear power plants and other facilities regulated by the Nuclear Regulatory Commission.

Nuclear Regulatory Commission, Nuclear Security and Incident Response, 11601 Landsdown St., #3WFN09D20, N. Bethesda, MD 20852; (301) 287-3734.
Fax, (301) 287-9351. Brian Holian, Director.
Emergency, (301) 816-5100. Nonemergency, (800) 695-7403.
Web, www.nrc.gov/about-nrc/organization/nsirfuncdesc .html

Evaluates technical issues concerning security at nuclear facilities. Develops and directs the commission's response to incidents. Serves as point of contact with Homeland Security Dept., Energy Dept., Federal Emergency Management Agency, and intelligence and law enforcement offices and other agencies.

Nuclear Waste Technical Review Board, 2300 Clarendon Blvd., #1300, Arlington, VA 22201-3367; (703) 235-4473. Fax, (703) 235-4495. Nigel Mote, Executive Director, (703) 235-4490.
General email, info@nwtrb.gov

Web, www.nwtrb.gov

Independent board of scientists and engineers nominated by the Academy of Sciences and appointed by the president to review, evaluate, and report on Energy Dept. development of waste disposal systems and repositories for spent fuel and high-level radioactive waste. Oversees siting, packaging, and transportation of waste, in accordance with the amendments to the Nuclear Waste Policy Act of 1987.

Pipeline and Hazardous Materials Safety Administration (Transportation Dept.), Hazardous Materials Safety, 1200 New Jersey Ave. S.E., #E21-317, 20590; (202) 366-4488. Fax, (202) 366-5713. William S. (Bill) Schoonover, Associate Administrator. Hazardous Materials Information Center, (800) 467-4922. General email, phmsa.hmhazmatsafety@dot.gov

Web, https://cms.phmsa.dot.gov/about-phmsa/offices/ office-hazardous-materials-safety

Issues safety regulations and exemptions for the transportation of hazardous materials; works with the International Atomic Energy Agency on standards for international shipments of radioactive materials.

▶ **NONGOVERNMENTAL**

Union of Concerned Scientists, Nuclear Power, 1825 K St. N.W., #800, 20006; (202) 223-6133. Fax, (202) 223-6162. Edwin Lyman, Director (Acting).

General email, ucs@ucsusa.org

Web, www.ucsusa.org/nuclear-power

An independent public interest group of scientists and citizens concerned with U.S. nuclear power policy and ability to respond to nuclear accidents. Interests include nuclear waste storage, storage facility security measures, safe generation of fissure chain reactions, and reactor design.

RENEWABLE ENERGIES, ALTERNATIVE FUELS

General

▶AGENCIES

Bureau of Energy Resources (ENR) *(State Dept.),* 2201 C St. N.W., #4428, 20520; (202) 647-8543. John McCarrick, Special Envoy and Coordinator for International Energy Affairs (Acting), (202) 647-8543.
Web, www.state.gov/e/enr, Twitter, @EnergyAtState
Blog, https://blogs.state.gov/tags/economic-and-energy-issues

Manages the global energy economy through diplomacy between energy producers and consumers, and stimulates the market forces toward the advancement of sustainable, renewable energy sources.

Bureau of Land Management (BLM) *(Interior Dept.),* **Energy, Minerals, and Realty Management,** 1849 C St. N.W., #5625, 20240; (202) 208-4201. Fax, (202) 208-4800. Michael Nedd, Assistant Director.
Web, www.blm.gov/programs/energy-and-minerals

Develops and administers policy, guidance, and performance oversight for the renewable energy program, including wind, solar, and geothermal energy; the fluid minerals program, including oil, gas, and helium; the solid minerals programs, including mining law, coal, oil shale, and salable minerals; the lands and realty programs; and the Public Land Survey System. Provides national leadership and develops national partnerships with organizations interested in energy, minerals, and realty management.

Energy Efficiency and Renewable Energy (EERE) *(Energy Dept.),* 1000 Independence Ave. S.W., #6A013, MS EE1, 20585; (202) 586-9220. Daniel Simmons, Assistant Secretary. Information, (877) 337-3463. Press, (202) 586-4940.
General email, eereic@ee.doe.gov
Web, www.energy.gov/eere/office-energy-efficiency-renewable-energy

Develops and manages programs to improve markets for renewable energy sources, including solar, biomass, wind, geothermal, and hydropower, and to increase efficiency of energy use among residential, commercial, transportation, utility, and industrial users.

Energy Efficiency and Renewable Energy (EERE) *(Energy Dept.),* **Fuel Cell Technologies (FCTO),** 1000

Independence Ave. S.W., #5G082, 20585; (202) 586-3388. Fax, (202) 586-2373. Sunita Satyapal, Director, (202) 586-2336.
General email, fuelcells@ee.doe.gov
Web, http://energy.gov/eere/fuelcells/fuel-cell-technologies-office

Works with industry, academia, nonprofit institutions, national labs, government agencies, and other Energy Dept. offices to promote the use of hydrogen, fuel cells, and related technologies.

Office of Science *(Energy Dept.),* **Basic Energy Sciences (BES),** 19901 Germantown Rd., #SC22, Germantown, MD 20874-1290 (mailing address: Germantown Bldg., 1000 Independence Ave. S.W., #SC22, Washington, DC 20585); (301) 903-3081. Fax, (301) 903-6594. Harriet Kung, Director.
General email, sc.bes@science.doe.gov
Web, http://science.energy.gov/bes

Supports research to understand, predict, and control matter and energy at electronic, atomic, and molecular levels to provide foundations for new energy technology.

Office of Science *(Energy Dept.),* **Biological and Environmental Research (BER), Climate and Environmental Sciences Division (CESD),** 19901 Germantown Rd., #SC23.1, Germantown, MD 20874-1290 (mailing address: Germantown Bldg., 1000 Independence Ave. S.W., #SC23.1, Washington, DC 20585); (301) 903-4775. Gerald Geernaert, Director.
Web, http://science.energy.gov/ber/research/cesd

Supports research on atmospheric systems, terrestrial ecosystems, and subsurface biogeochemistry as well as Earth system modeling and regional and global climate change modeling to improve predictive understanding of Earth's climate and environmental systems in order to inform development of sustainable solutions to energy challenges.

▶CONGRESS

For a listing of relevant congressional committees and subcommittees, please see pages 255–256 or the Appendix.

▶NONGOVERNMENTAL

American Council on Renewable Energy (ACORE), 1600 K St. N.W., #650, 20006 (mailing address: P.O. Box 33518, Washington, DC 20003); (202) 393-0001. Gregory Wetstone, President. Media, (202) 777-7548, ext. 3.
General email, info@acore.org
Web, http://acore.org, Twitter, @ACORE and Facebook, www.facebook.com/AmericanCouncilOnRenewableEnergy

Membership: professional service firms, government officials, universities, financial institutions, nonprofits, and renewable energy industries and associations. Publishes research to educate the media and the public about renewable electricity, hydrogen, and fuels. Interests include solar power, wind power, biofuels, biomass, geothermal power, marine energy, hydroelectric power, waste-to-energy, and waste heat-to-power.

Electric Power Supply Assn., *1401 New York Ave. N.W., #950, 20005-2110; (202) 628-8200. Fax, (202) 628-8260. John Shelk, President.*
Web, www.epsa.org

Membership: companies that generate electricity, steam, and other forms of energy using a broad spectrum of fossil fuel–fired and renewable technologies.

Fuel Cell and Hydrogen Energy Assn., *1211 Connecticut Ave. N.W., #650, 20036; (202) 261-1337.*
Morry Markowitz, President.
General email, info@fchea.org
Web, www.fchea.org, Twitter, @FCHEA_News and Facebook, www.facebook.com/FCHEA

Membership: industry, small businesses, government agencies, and nonprofit organizations. Promotes use of hydrogen as an energy carrier; fosters the development and application of fuel cell and hydrogen technologies.

Institute for the Analysis of Global Security, *7811 Montrose Rd., #505, Potomac, MD 20854-3363; Gal Luft, Co-Director; Anne Korin, Co-Director.*
Toll-free, (866) 713-7527.
General email, info@iags.org
Web, www.iags.org

Seeks to promote public awareness of the link between energy and security; explores options for strengthening the world's energy security, including approaches to reducing the strategic importance of oil. Conducts and publishes research; hosts conferences; monitors legislation and regulations.

SRI International, *Washington Office, 1100 Wilson Blvd., #2800, Arlington, VA 22209; (703) 524-2053. Fax, (703) 247-8569. William Jeffrey, Executive Director. Web, www.sri.com and Twitter, @SRI_Intl*

Conducts energy-related research and development. Interests include power generation, fuel and solar cells, clean energy storage, and advanced batteries. (Headquarters in Menlo Park, Calif.)

Biofuels

▶AGENCIES

Energy Efficiency and Renewable Energy (EERE) *(Energy Dept.), Bioenergy Technologies Office (BETO), 1000 Independence Ave. S.W., MS EE3B, #5H021, 20585; (202) 586-5188. Jonathan Male, Director.*
General email, eere_bioenergy@ee.doe.gov
Web, https://energy.gov/eere/bioenergy

Partners with public and private stakeholders to develop and demonstrate technologies for producing cost-competitive advanced biofuels from nonfood biomass resources, including cellulosic biomass, algae, and wet waste.

National Institute of Food and Agriculture (NIFA) *(Agriculture Dept.), Institute of Bioenergy, Climate, and Environment, 800 9th St. S.W., #3231, 20024 (mailing address: 1400 Independence Ave. S.W., MS 2210, Washington, DC 20250-2215); (202) 401-4926. Luis Tupas, Deputy Director.*
Web, https://nifa.usda.gov/office/institute-bioenergy-climate-and-environment

Administers programs to address national science priorities that advance energy independence and help agricultural, forest, and range production systems adapt to climate change variables. Provides grants to support the development of sustainable bioenergy production systems, agricultural production systems, and natural resource management activities that are adapted to climate variation and activities that otherwise support sustainable natural resource use.

Office of Science *(Energy Dept.), Biological and Environmental Research (BER), 19901 Germantown Rd., #SC23, Germantown, MD 20874-1290 (mailing address: Germantown Bldg., 1000 Independence Ave. S.W., #SC23, Washington, DC 20585); (301) 903-3251. Fax, (301) 903-5051. Sharlene Weatherwax, Associate Director.*
General email, sc.ber@science.doe.gov
Web, http://science.energy.gov/ber

Advances biological and environmental research and provides scientific user facilities to support innovation in energy security and environmental responsibility.

Office of Science *(Energy Dept.), Biological and Environmental Research (BER), Biological Systems Science Division (BSSD), 19901 Germantown Rd., #SC23.2, Germantown, MD 20874-1290 (mailing address: Germantown Bldg., 1000 Independence Ave. S.W., #SC23.2, Washington, DC 20585); (301) 903-5469. Fax, (301) 903-0567. Todd Anderson, Director.*
Web, http://science.energy.gov/ber/research/bssd

Supports research and technology development to achieve predictive systems-level understanding of complex biological systems, including redesign of microbes and plants for sustainable biofuel production, improved carbon storage, and contaminent remediation. Areas of research include genomic science, bioimaging technology, biological systems, and radiological sciences.

Office of Science *(Energy Dept.), Biological and Environmental Research (BER), Biological Systems Science Division (BSSD), Genomic Science Program, 19901 Germantown Rd., #SC72, Germantown, MD 20874-1290; (301) 903-5469. Fax, (301) 903-0567. Catherine (Cathy) Ronning, Program Manager.*
Web, http://genomicscience.energy.gov

Supports research using microbial and plant genomic data, high-throughput technologies, and modeling and simulation to develop predictive understanding of biological systems behavior relevant to solving energy and environmental challenges.

▶NONGOVERNMENTAL

Biomass Thermal Energy Council (BTEC), *1211 Connecticut Ave. N.W., #650, 20036-2701; (202) 596-3974. Fax, (202) 223-5537. Jeff Serfass, Executive Director.*
General email, info@biomassthermal.org
Web, www.biomassthermal.org and Twitter, @BiomassThermal

Membership: biomass fuel producers, appliance manufacturers and distributors, supply chain companies, and nonprofit organizations that seek to advance the use of biomass for heat and other thermal energy applications. Conducts research, public education, and advocacy for the biomass thermal energy industry. Monitors legislation and regulations.

Hearth, Patio, and Barbecue Assn. (HPBA), *1901 N. Moore St., #600, Arlington, VA 22209-1708; (703) 522-0086. Fax, (703) 522-0548. Jack Goldman, President.*
General email, hpbamail@hpba.org
Web, www.hpba.org and Twitter, @HPBA

Membership: all sectors of the hearth products industry. Provides industry training programs to its members on the safe and efficient use of alternative fuels and appliances. Works with the Hearth Education Foundation, which certifies gas hearth, fireplace, pellet stove, and wood stove appliances and venting design specialists.

Methanol Institute, *225 Reinekers Lane, #205, Alexandria, VA 22315; (703) 248-3636. Greg Dolan, Chief Executive Officer.*
General email, mi@methanol.org
Web, www.methanol.org

Membership: global methanol producers and related industries. Encourages use of methanol fuels and development of chemical-derivative markets. Monitors legislation and regulations.

Renewable Fuels Assn., *425 3rd St. S.W., #1150, 20024; (202) 289-3835. Fax, (202) 289-7519. Geoff Cooper, President.*
General email, info@ethanolrfa.org
Web, www.ethanolrfa.org and Twitter, @EthanolRFA

Membership: companies and state governments involved in developing the domestic ethanol industry. Distributes publications on ethanol performance. Monitors legislation and regulations.

Geothermal Energy

▶AGENCIES

Energy Efficiency and Renewable Energy (EERE) *(Energy Dept.), Geothermal Technologies (GTO), 1000 Independence Ave. S.W., MS 5E066, 20585; (202) 287-1818. Susan Hamm, Director.*
General email, geothermal@ee.doe.gov
Web, www.energy.gov/eere/geothermal

Responsible for research and technology development of geothermal energy resources. Conducts outreach to state energy offices and consumers.

U.S. Geological Survey (USGS) *(Interior Dept.), Volcano Hazards Program, 12201 Sunrise Valley Dr., MS 904, Reston, VA 20192-0002; (703) 648-4773. Fax, (703) 648-5483. Charles W. Mandeville, Program Coordinator.*
General email, vscweb@usgs.gov
Web, http://volcanoes.usgs.gov

Provides staff support to the U.S. Geological Survey through programs in volcano hazards.

▶NONGOVERNMENTAL

Geothermal Energy Assn., *P.O. Box 5619, Baltimore, MD 21210; (443) 739-5155. Karl Gawell, Executive Director.*
Web, www.geo-energy.org and Twitter, @geoenergist

Membership: American companies who promote the national and global advancement of geothermal energy. Represents and supports energy policies that improve the geothermal energy industry. Holds a forum to discuss geothermal issues and advancing geothermal technologies. Researches geothermal industry statistics and provides educational outreach to the public.

Solar, Ocean, and Wind Energy

▶AGENCIES

Bureau of Ocean Energy Management (BOEM) *(Interior Dept.), 1849 C St. N.W., 20240; (202) 208-6474. Walter Cruickshank, Director (Acting).*
General email, boempublicaffairs@boem.gov
Web, www.boem.gov, Twitter, @BOEM_DOI and Facebook, www.facebook.com/BureauOfOceanEnergyManagement

Manages development of U.S. Outer Continental Shelf energy and mineral resources.

Bureau of Ocean Energy Management (BOEM) *(Interior Dept.), Renewable Energy Programs (OREP), 45600 Woodland Rd., VAM-OREP, Sterling, VA 20166; (703) 787-1300. Fax, (703) 787-1708. James Bennett, Chief.*
General email, boempublicaffairs@boem.gov
Web, www.boem.gov/Renewable-Energy

Grants leases, easements, and rights-of-way for orderly, safe, and environmentally responsible renewable energy development activities on the Outer Continental Shelf, including offshore wind and hydrokinetic projects.

Energy Efficiency and Renewable Energy (EERE) *(Energy Dept.), Solar Energy Technologies (SETO), SunShot Initiative, 950 L'Enfant Plaza, 6th Floor, 20585 (mailing address: 1000 Independence Ave. S.W., Washington, DC 20585); (202) 287-1862. Fax, (202) 586-8148. Charlie Gay, Director.*
General email, solar@ee.doe.gov
Web, www.energy.gov/eere/sunshot

Supports research and development of solar technologies of all types through national laboratories and partnerships with industries and universities. Seeks to make solar energy cost-effective through research, manufacturing, and market solutions.

Energy Efficiency and Renewable Energy (EERE) *(Energy Dept.), Water Power Technologies (WPTO), 1000 Independence Ave. S.W., #5H072, MS EE2B, 20585; (202) 586-7595. Alejandro Moreno, Director.*
General email, alejandro.moreno@ee.doe.gov

Web, https://energy.gov/eere/water/water-power-technologies-office

Supports research, development, deployment, and commercialization of water power technologies.

Energy Efficiency and Renewable Energy (EERE) *(Energy Dept.), Wind Energy Technologies (WETO), 1000 Independence Ave. S.W., 20585; (202) 586-5348. Valerie Reed, Director (Acting).*
Web, www.energy.gov/eere/wind/wind-energy-technologies-office

Supports research, development, deployment, and commercialization of wind energy technologies.

► CONGRESS

For a listing of relevant congressional committees and subcommittees, please see pages 255–256 or the Appendix.

► NONGOVERNMENTAL

American Wind Energy Assn., *1501 M St. N.W., #900, 20005-1700; (202) 383-2500. Fax, (202) 383-2505. Tom Kieman, Chief Executive Officer; Diane Miller, Vice President of Public Affairs.*
General email, windmail@awea.org

Web, www.awea.org and Twitter, @AWEA

Membership: manufacturers, developers, operators, and distributors of wind machines; utility companies; and others interested in wind energy. Advocates wind energy as an alternative energy source; makes industry data available to the public and to federal and state legislators. Promotes export of wind energy technology.

National Ocean Industries Assn., *1120 G St. N.W., #900, 20005; (202) 347-6900. Fax, (202) 347-8650. Randall Luthi, President.*
General email, jwilliams@noia.org

Web, www.noia.org and Twitter, @oceanindustries

Membership: manufacturers, producers, suppliers, and support and service companies involved in marine, offshore, and ocean work. Interests include ocean thermal energy and new energy sources.

Solar Electric Light Fund, *1612 K St. N.W., #300, 20006; (202) 234-7265. Fax, (202) 328-9512. Robert A. (Bob) Freling, Executive Director.*
General email, info@self.org

Web, www.self.org and Twitter, @solarfund

Promotes and develops solar rural electrification and energy self-sufficiency in developing countries. Assists developing-world communities and governments in acquiring and installing decentralized household and community solar electric systems.

Solar Energy Industries Assn., *1425 K St. N.W., #1000, 20005; (202) 682-0556. Fax, (202) 682-0559. Abigail Ross Hopper, Chief Executive Officer; Katherine Gensler, Vice President of Regulatory Affairs, (202) 556-2873. Press, (202) 556-2872.*
General email, info@seia.org

Web, www.seia.org and Twitter, @SEIA

Membership: industries with interests in the production and use of solar energy. Promotes growth of U.S. and international markets. Interests include photovoltaic, solar thermal power, and concentrating solar power. Conducts conferences. Monitors legislation and regulations.

8

Environment and
Natural Resources

GENERAL POLICY AND ANALYSIS

Basic Resources

▶AGENCIES

Agriculture Dept. (USDA), *Under Secretary for Natural Resources and Environment,* 1400 Independence Ave. S.W., #240E, 20250-0108; (202) 720-7173. Fax, (202) 720-0632. Jim Hubbard, Under Secretary.
Web, www.usda.gov/our-agency/about-usda/mission-areas

Formulates and promulgates policy relating to environmental activities and management of natural resources. Oversees the Forest Service and the Natural Resources Conservation Service.

Council on Environmental Quality *(Executive Office of the President),* 730 Jackson Pl. N.W., 20503; (202) 395-5750. Fax, (202) 456-6546. Christy Goldfuss, Managing Director.
Web, www.whitehouse.gov/ceq

Develops environmental priorities; advises and assists the president on national and international environmental policy; evaluates, coordinates, and mediates federal activities on the environment; prepares the president's yearly environmental quality report to Congress.

Environmental Protection Agency (EPA), *1200 Pennsylvania Ave. N.W., #3000, MC 1101A, 20460; (202) 564-4700. Fax, (202) 501-1450. Andrew Wheeler, Administrator (Acting); Andrew R. Wheeler, Deputy Administrator. EPA switchboard, (202) 272-0167. Press, (202) 564-4355. TTY, (800) 877-8339.*
Web, www.epa.gov

Administers federal environmental policies, research, and regulations; provides information on environmental subjects, including water pollution, pollution prevention, hazardous and solid waste disposal, air and noise pollution, pesticides and toxic substances, and radiation.

Environmental Protection Agency (EPA), *Policy,* 1200 Pennsylvania Ave. N.W., #1804A, 20460; (202) 564-4332. Fax, (202) 501-1688. Brittany Bolen, Associate Administrator.
General email, policyoffice@epa.gov
Web, www.epa.gov/aboutepa/about-office-policy-op

Coordinates agency policy development and standard-setting activities through four divisions: Regulatory Policy and Management, the National Center for Environmental Economics, Strategic Environmental Management, and Sustainable Communities.

Environmental Protection Agency (EPA), *Research and Development (ORD), National Center for Environmental Assessment,* 1 Potomac Yard, 2777 Crystal Dr., Arlington, VA 22202 (mailing address: 1200 Pennsylvania Ave. N.W., MC 8601P, Washington, DC 20460); (202) 564-7903. Tina Bahadori, Director.
Web, www.epa.gov/aboutepa/about-national-center-environmental-assessment-ncea

Evaluates animal and human health data to define environmental health hazards and estimate risk to humans. Conducts research and prepares reports and assessments.

Environmental Protection Agency (EPA), *Science Advisory Board,* 1300 Pennsylvania Ave. N.W., #31150, 20004-4164 (mailing address: 1200 Pennsylvania Ave. N.W., MC 1400R, Washington, DC 20460); (202) 564-2221. Fax, (202) 565-2098. Thomas Carpenter, Designated Federal Officer, (202) 564-4885; Tom Brennan, Director (Acting).
General email, sab@epa.gov
Web, https://yosemite.epa.gov/sab/sabpeople.nsf/WebCommittees/BOARD and www.epa.gov/aboutepa/about-science-advisory-board-sab-and-sab-staff-office

Coordinates nongovernment scientists and engineers who advise the administrator on scientific and technical aspects of environmental problems and issues. Evaluates EPA research projects, the technical basis of regulations and standards, and policy statements.

Federal Highway Administration (FHWA) *(Transportation Dept.), Planning, Environment, and Realty,* 1200 New Jersey Ave. S.E., #E76-306, 20590; (202) 366-0116. Fax, (202) 366-3713. Gloria M. Shepherd, Associate Administrator.
Web, www.fhwa.dot.gov/real_estate

Works with developers and municipalities to ensure conformity with the National Environmental Policy Act (NEPA) project development process.

Interior Dept. (DOI), 1849 C St. N.W., MS 7328, 20240; (202) 208-7351. David Bernhardt, Secretary; George Franchois, Librarian, (202) 282-5815. Employee directory, (202) 208-3100. Library, (202) 208-5815. Press, (202) 208-6416.
General email, feedback@ios.doi.gov
Web, www.doi.gov, Twitter, @Interior and Facebook, www.facebook.com/USInterior and Blog, www.doi.gov/blog

Principal U.S. conservation agency. Manages most federal land; responsible for conservation and development of mineral and water resources; responsible for conservation, development, and use of fish and wildlife resources; operates recreation programs for federal parks, refuges, and public lands; preserves and administers the nation's scenic and historic areas; reclaims arid lands in the West through irrigation; administers Native American lands and develops relationships with tribal governments. Reference library open to the public 7:45 a.m.–5:00 p.m.

Interior Dept. (DOI), *Communications,* 1849 C St. N.W., #6312, 20240; (202) 208-6416. Fax, (202) 208-5133. Russell Newell, Deputy Director, (202) 208-6232. Employee Directory, (202) 208-3100.
General email, interior_press@ios.doi.gov
Web, http://doi.gov/news

Issues press releases about Interior Dept. events and announcements. Provides information to the general public, tourists, businesses, Native Americans, governments, and others.

Interior Dept. (DOI), *Environmental Policy and Compliance (OEPC),* 1849 C St. N.W., MS 5538, 20240; (202) 208-3891. Michaela Noble, Director, (202) 208-3891, ext. 1.
Web, www.doi.gov/oepc

Provides leadership on a national and regional level for environmental policies and compliance for U.S. resource management and conservation; ensures compliance with the National Environmental Policy Act (NEPA), regulations, and reporting requirements; manages funding for long-term cleanup of hazardous materials; oversees Interior Dept.'s protection and recovery activities for natural and cultural resources and historic properties during emergency response efforts.

Interior Dept. (DOI), *Policy Analysis (PPA),* 1849 C St. N.W., MS 3530, 20240; (202) 208-5978. Fax, (202) 208-4867. Susan Combs, Assistant Secretary; Greg Renkes, Director.
Web, www.doi.gov/ppa

Provides cross-cutting policy planning and analysis to support decision making and policies across the Department; makes recommendations and develops policy options for resolving natural resource problems.

Maritime Administration *(Transportation Dept.), Office of Environment,* West Bldg., 1200 New Jersey Ave. S.E., W28-342, 20590; (202) 366-1931. Fax, (202) 366-6988. Michael Carter, Associate Administrator (Acting).
Web, www.maritime.dot.gov/ports/office-environment/office-environment

Focuses on environmental stewardship, maritime safety, and maritime security; maritime research and development; and maritime international and domestic rules, regulations, and standards. Provides environmental support for America's Marine Highway Program and ensures compliance with the National Environmental Policy Act. Advises Maritime Administrator on domestic and international environmental policies that affect maritime transportation.

National Institute of Environmental Health Sciences (NIEHS) *(National Institutes of Health), Washington Office,* 31 Center Dr., #B1C02, MSC 2256, Bethesda, MD 20892-2256; (301) 496-3511. Fax, (301) 496-0563. Linda S. Birnbaum, Director, (919) 541-3201; Jed R. Bullock, Legislative Liaison. Information, (919) 541-3345.
General email, webcenter@niehs.nih.gov
Web, www.niehs.nih.gov, Twitter, @NIEHS and Facebook, www.facebook.com/NIH.NIEHS

Conducts and supports research on the human effects of various environmental exposures, expanding the scientific basis for making public health decisions based on the potential toxicity of environmental agents. (Most operations located in Research Triangle, N.C.)

National Institute of Standards and Technology (NIST) *(Commerce Dept.), Special Programs Office,* 100 Bureau Dr., MS 4701, Gaithersburg, MD 20899-4701; (301) 975-4447. Fax, (301) 975-8972. Richard R. Cavanagh, Director. General information, (301) 975-2756.
Web, www.nist.gov/spo

Fosters collaboration among government, military, academic, professional, and private organizations to respond to critical national needs through science-based standards and technology innovation, including environmental concerns.

National Oceanic and Atmospheric Administration (NOAA) *(Commerce Dept.), Performance, Risk, and Social Science (PRSS),* 1315 East-West Hwy., Silver Spring, MD 20910; (301) 713-1632. Fax, (301) 713-0585. Tony Wilhelm, Director, (240) 533-9012.
General email, PPI.SocSci@noaa.gov
Web, www.performance.noaa.gov

Oversees NOAA's performance, risk, and social science divisions. Provides business intelligence, quarterly performance updates, risk assessments, social science research, strategic planning, and budget analysis to NOAA leadership.

Office of Management and Budget (OMB) *(Executive Office of the President), Water and Power,* 725 17th St. N.W., #8002, 20503; (202) 395-4590. Fax, (202) 395-4817. Kelly Colyar, Chief. Press, (202) 395-7254.
Web, www.whitehouse.gov/omb

Reviews all plans and budgets related to federal or federally assisted water power and related land resource projects.

▶**CONGRESS**

For a listing of relevant congressional committees and subcommittees, please see pages 283–284 or the Appendix.

Government Accountability Office (GAO), *Natural Resources and Environment (NRE),* 441 G St. N.W., #2T23-A, 20548 (mailing address: 441 G St. N.W., #2T23A, Washington, DC 20548); (202) 512-3841. Mark Gaffigan, Managing Director.
Web, www.gao.gov/careers/nre.html

Audits, analyzes, and evaluates for Congress federal agriculture, food safety, and energy programs; provides guidance on issues including efforts to ensure a reliable and environmentally sound energy supply, land and water resources management, protection of the environment, hazardous and nuclear wastes threat reduction, food safety, and investment in science.

▶**NONGOVERNMENTAL**

Aspen Institute, 2300 N St., N.W., #700, 20037; (202) 736-5800. Fax, (202) 467-0790. Dan Porterfield, President. Press, (202) 736-3849.
General email, info@aspeninstitute.org
Web, www.aspeninstitute.org and
Twitter, @AspenInstitute

Educational and policy studies organization. Promotes consideration of the public good in a wide variety of policy

ENVIRONMENTAL RESOURCES IN CONGRESS

For a complete listing of congressional committees, including their full contact information, leadership, membership, and jurisdictions, please refer to the Appendix on pages 827–948.

HOUSE:

House Agriculture Committee, (202) 225-2171.
Web, agriculture.house.gov
  Subcommittee on Biotechnology, Horticulture,
    and Research, (202) 225-2171.
  Subcommittee on Conservation and Forestry,
    (202) 225-2171.
  Subcommittee on Livestock and Foreign
    Agriculture, (202) 225-2171.
House Appropriations Committee, (202) 225-2771.
Web, appropriations.house.gov
  Subcommittee on Agriculture, Rural
    Development, Food and Drug
    Administration, and Related Agencies,
    (202) 225-2638.
  Subcommittee on Commerce, Justice, Science,
    and Related Agencies, (202) 225-3351.
  Subcommittee on Energy and Water
    Development and Related Agencies,
    (202) 225-3421.
  Subcommittee on Interior, Environment, and
    Related Agencies, (202) 225-3081.
House Energy and Commerce Committee,
  (202) 225-2927.
Web, energycommerce.house.gov
  Subcommittee on Environment, (202) 225-2927.
House Natural Resources Committee,
  (202) 225-2761.
Web, naturalresources.house.gov
  Subcommittee on Energy and Mineral Resources,
    (202) 225-9297.

  Subcommittee on Federal Lands,
    (202) 226-7736.
  Subcommittee on Indian, Insular, and Alaska
    Native Affairs, (202) 226-9725.
  Subcommittee on Oversight and Investigation,
    (202) 225-7107.
  Subcommittee on Water, Power, and Oceans,
    (202) 225-8331.
**House Oversight and Government Reform
  Committee,** (202) 225-5074.
Web, oversight.house.gov
  Subcommittee on Interior, Energy, and
    Environment, (202) 225-5074.
House Science, Space, and Technology Committee,
  (202) 225-6371.
Web, science.house.gov
  Subcommittee on Environment,
    (202) 225-6371.
  Subcommittee on Research and Technology,
    (202) 225-6371.
House Small Business Committee, (202) 225-5821.
Web, smallbusiness.house.gov
**House Transportation and Infrastructure
  Committee,** (202) 225-9446.
Web, transportation.house.gov
  Subcommittee on Coast Guard and Maritime
    Transportation, (202) 226-3552.
  Subcommittee on Railroads, Pipelines, and
    Hazardous Materials, (202) 226-0727.
  Subcommittee on Water Resources and
    Environment, (202) 225-4360.

---

areas, including energy and the environment. Working with international partners, offers educational seminars, nonpartisan policy forums, public conferences and events, and leadership development initiatives.

Earth Share, *7735 Old Georgetown Rd., #510, Bethesda, MD 20814; (240) 333-0300. Fax, (240) 333-0301. Vacant, President. Information, (800) 875-3863.*
General email, info@earthshare.org

Web, www.earthshare.org and Twitter, @EarthShare

Federation of environmental and conservation organizations. Works with government and private payroll contribution programs to solicit contributions to member organizations for environmental research, education, and community programs. Provides information on establishing environmental giving options in the workplace.

EarthEcho International, *2101 L St. N.W., #800, 20037; (202) 350-3190. Fax, (202) 857-3977. Philippe Cousteau, President. Press, (202) 870-1818.*

General email, info@earthecho.org

Web, www.earthecho.org and Twitter, @EarthEcho

Education resource center that helps students identify environmental issues in their communities and take action to solve them. Holds expeditions to South Florida to investigate the impact of human activity on its natural ecosystems. Provides teachers with learning materials to engage students with real-world data. Specializes in dead zones.

Environment America, *Federal Advocacy Office, 600 Pennsylvania Ave. S.E., #400, 20003; (202) 683-1250. Fax, (202) 543-6489. Margie Alt, Executive Director.*
Web, www.environmentamerica.org and
Twitter, @EnvAm

Coordinates grassroots efforts to advance environmental and consumer protection laws; conducts research on environmental issues, including global warming, clean energy, preservation and conservation, clean water and air, and toxic pollution; compiles reports and disseminates

SENATE:

Senate Agriculture, Nutrition, and Forestry Committee, (202) 224-2035.

Web, agriculture.senate.gov

Subcommittee on Conservation, Forestry, and Natural Resources, (202) 224-2035.

Subcommittee on Livestock, Marketing, and Agriculture Security, (202) 224-2035.

Subcommittee on Rural Development and Energy, (202) 224-2035.

Senate Appropriations Committee, (202) 224-7257.

Web, appropriations.senate.gov

Subcommittee on Agriculture, Rural Development, Food and Drug Administration, and Related Agencies, (202) 224-8090.

Subcommittee on Commerce, Justice, Science, and Related Agencies, (202) 224-5202.

Subcommittee on Energy and Water Development, (202) 224-8119.

Subcommittee on Interior, Environment, and Related Agencies, (202) 228-0774.

Senate Commerce, Science, and Transportation Committee, (202) 224-1251.

Web, commerce.senate.gov

Subcommittee on Oceans, Atmosphere, Fisheries, and the Coast Guard, (202) 224-1251.

Senate Energy and Natural Resources Committee, (202) 224-4971.

Web, energy.senate.gov

Subcommittee on Energy, (202) 224-4971.

Subcommittee on National Parks, (202) 224-4971.

Subcommittee on Public Lands, Forests, and Mining, (202) 224-4971.

Subcommittee on Water and Power, (202) 224-4971.

Senate Environment and Public Works Committee, (202) 224-6176.

Web, epw.senate.gov

Subcommittee on Clean Air and Nuclear Safety, (202) 224-6176.

Subcommittee on Fisheries, Water, and Wildlife, (202) 224-6176.

Subcommittee on Superfund, Waste Management, and Regulatory Oversight, (202) 224-6176.

Subcommittee on Transportation and Infrastructure, (202) 224-6176.

Senate Finance Committee, (202) 224-4515.

Web, finance.senate.gov

Subcommittee on Energy, Natural Resources, and Infrastructure, (202) 224-4515.

Senate Foreign Relations Committee, (202) 224-4651.

Web, foreign.senate.gov

Subcommittee on Mulitlateral International Development, Multilateral Institutions, and International Economic, Energy, and Environmental Policy, (202) 224-4651.

Senate Indian Affairs Committee, (202) 224-2251.

Web, indian.senate.gov

Senate Small Business and Entrepreneurship Committee, (202) 224-5175.

Web, sbc.senate.gov

---

information on such issues; drafts and monitors environmental laws; testifies on behalf of proposed environmental legislation. (Headquarters in Boston.)

Environmental and Energy Study Institute (EESI), *1020 19th St. N.W., #650, 20036-6101; (202) 628-1400. Fax, (202) 204-5244. Carol Werner, Executive Director, (202) 662-1881. General email, info@eesi.org*

Web, www.eesi.org and Twitter, @eesionline

Nonpartisan policy education and analysis group established by members of Congress to foster informed debate on environmental and energy issues. Interests include policies for sustainable development, energy, sustainable bioenergy, climate change, agriculture, transportation, and fiscal policy reform.

Environmental Council of the States, *50 F St. N.W., #350, 20001; (202) 266-4920. Fax, (202) 266-4937. Don Welsh, Executive Director, (202) 266-4929.*

General email, ecos@ecos.org

Web, www.ecos.org and Twitter, @ECOStates

Works to improve the environment by providing for the exchange of ideas and experiences among states and territories; fosters cooperation and coordination among environmental management professionals.

Environmental Defense Fund, *Washington Office, 1875 Connecticut Ave. N.W., #600, 20009-5728; (202) 387-3500. Fax, (202) 234-6049. Fred Krupp, President. Information, (800) 684-3322.*

Web, www.edf.org/offices/washington-dc and Twitter, @EnvDefenseFund

Citizens' interest group staffed by lawyers, economists, and scientists. Takes legal action on environmental issues; provides information on pollution prevention, environmental health, wetlands, toxic substances, acid rain, tropical rain forests, and litigation of water pollution standards. (Headquarters in New York.)

Environmental Protection Agency

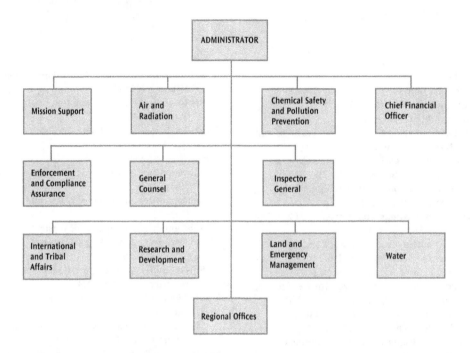

Environmental Law Institute, *1730 M St. N.W., #700, 20036; (202) 939-3800. Fax, (202) 939-3868. Scott Fulton, President.*
Web, www.eli.org and Twitter, @eliorg

Conducts policy studies on the environment and sustainability. Publishes materials on environmental issues, sponsors education and training courses and conferences on environmental law, issues policy recommendations, and provides technical assistance in the United States and abroad.

Environmental Working Group, *1436 U St. N.W., #100, 20009-3987; (202) 667-6982. Fax, (202) 232-2592. Kenneth A. Cook, President.*
Web, www.ewg.org and Twitter, @ewg

Research and advocacy group that studies and publishes reports on a wide range of agricultural and environmental issues, including farm subsidies and industrial pollution. Monitors legislation and regulations.

Friends of the Earth (FOE), *1101 15th St. N.W., 11th Floor, 20005; (202) 783-7400. Fax, (202) 783-0444. Erich Pica, President. Toll-free, (877) 843-8687.*
Web, www.foe.org, Twitter, @foe_us and Facebook, www.facebook.com/foe.us

Environmental advocacy group. Interests include climate and energy, oceans and water, food and emerging technology, and economic drivers of environmental degradation. Specializes in federal budget and tax issues related to the environment, sustainable food systems, corporate power, and natural resources.

Green America, *1612 K St. N.W., #600, 20006; (202) 872-5307. Fax, (202) 331-8166. Alisa Gravitz, President. Information, (800) 584-7336. Press, (202) 872-5310. General email, info@greenamerica.org*
Web, www.greenamerica.org and Twitter, @greenamerica

Educates consumers and businesses about social and environmental responsibility. Publishes a directory of environmentally and socially responsible businesses and a financial planning guide for investment.

GreenLatinos, *801 Pennsylvania Ave. N.W., #1010, 20004; (202) 230-2070. Mark Magaña, President. General email, jeanettealcaraz@greenlatinos.org*
Web, www.greenlatinos.org, Twitter, @GreenLatino and Facebook, www.facebook.com/GreenLatinos

Provides a platform for Latino leaders to convene and address national, regional, and local environmental, natural resource, and conservation issues affecting Latinos in the United States.

League of Conservation Voters (LCV), *740 15th St. N.W., 7th Floor, 20005; (202) 785-8683. Fax, (202) 835-0491. Gene Karpinski, President.*
Web, www.lcv.org and Twitter, @LCVoters

Supports the environmental movement by advocacy for sound environmental policies and helping elect environmentally concerned candidates to public office. Publishes the National Environmental Scorecard and Presidential Report Card.

National Council for Science and the Environment, *740 15th St. N.W., #900, 20005; (202) 596-3428. Michelle Wyman, Executive Director, (202) 851-3144. General email, ncse@ncseglobal.org*

Web, www.ncseglobal.org, Twitter, @NCSEglobal and Facebook, www.facebook.com/ncseglobal

Coordinates programs that bring together individuals, institutions, and communities to discuss environmental education, research, and public policy decisions affecting the environment.

National Governors Assn. (NGA), *Center for Best Practices, Environment, Energy, and Transportation Division, 444 N. Capitol St. N.W., #267, 20001-1512; (202) 624-5300. Fax, (202) 624-7829. Sue Gander, Director. General email, webmaster@nga.org*

Web, www.nga.org/cms/center/eet

Identifies best practices for energy, land use, environment, and transportation issues and shares them with the states.

National Governors Assn. (NGA), *Natural Resources Committee, 444 N. Capitol St. N.W., #267, 20001-1512; (202) 624-5300. Fax, (202) 624-7814. David Parkhurst, Director; Alex Schaefer, Legislative Director. General email, webmaster@nga.org*

Web, www.nga.org/cms/center/eet

Monitors legislation and regulations and makes recommendations on agriculture, energy, environment, and natural resource issues to ensure governors' views and priorities are represented in federal policies and regulations.

National Research Council (NRC), *Energy and Environmental Systems Board, Keck Center, 500 5th St. N.W., #W917, 20001; (202) 334-2045. K. John Holmes, Director.*

Web, http://sites.nationalacademies.org/DEPS/BEES

Conducts studies in order to advise the federal government and the private sector about issues in energy and environmental technology, and related public policy. Focuses on energy supply and demand technologies and systems, including resource extraction through mining and drilling, energy conversion, distribution and delivery, and efficiency of use; environmental consequences of energy-related activities; environmental systems and controls in areas related to fuel production, energy conversion, transmission, and use; and other issues relating to national security and defense. Sponsors studies, workshops, symposia, and a variety of information-dissemination activities.

National Research Council (NRC), *Environmental Change and Society Board, Keck Center, 500 5th St. N.W., 20001; (202) 334-3218. Fax, (202) 334-3751. Toby Warden, Director, (202) 334-3453; Kristie Lee Ebi, Chair. General email, BECS@nas.edu*

Web, http://sites.nationalacademies.org/DBASSE/BECS

Conducts research on the interactions between human activities and the environment, including climate variation, resource use and decision making, adaptation to change, and risk and resilience.

Natural Resources Defense Council, *Washington Office, 1152 15th St. N.W., #300, 20005; (202) 289-6868. Fax, (202) 289-1060. Ed Yoon, Director of Policy Advocacy; Ana Cohen, Director of Government Affairs. General email, nrdcinfo@nrdc.org*

Web, www.nrdc.org, Twitter, @NRDC and Facebook, www.facebook.com/nrdc.org

Environmental organization staffed by lawyers and scientists who conduct litigation and research. Interests include air, water, land use, forests, toxic materials, natural resources management and conservation, preservation of endangered plant species, and ozone pollution. Website has a Spanish-language link. (Headquarters in New York.)

Nature Conservancy, *4245 N. Fairfax Dr., #100, Arlington, VA 22203-1606; (703) 841-5300. Fax, (703) 841-1283. Mark Tercek, Chief Executive Officer; Kacky Andrews, Executive Vice President of Global Strategies. Information, (800) 628-6860. General email, comment@tnc.org*

Web, www.nature.org, Twitter, @nature_org and Facebook, www.facebook.com/thenatureconservancy

Press, ghenrich-koenis@tnc.org

Maintains an international system of natural sanctuaries; acquires land to protect endangered species and habitats. Collaborates with other conservation organizations, country and local governments, corporations, indigenous peoples and communities, and individuals such as fishermen, ranchers, and farmers to create management plans for natural areas.

Pew Environment Group, *901 E St. N.W., 20004-2008; (202) 552-2000. Fax, (202) 552-2299. Rebecca W. Rimel, President; Josh Reichert, Managing Director Environmental Group. General email, media@pewtrusts.org*

Web, www.pewenvironment.org and Twitter, @pewenvironment

Identifies and publicizes environmental issues at the international, national, and local levels, with the goal of strengthening environmental policies and practices. Interests include climate change, clean air, endangered species, global warming, hazardous chemicals, national park pollution, and campaign finance reform. Opposes efforts to weaken environmental laws. Monitors legislation and regulations.

Pinchot Institute for Conservation, *1400 16th St. N.W., #350, 20036; (202) 797-6580. Fax, (202) 797-6583. William C. Price, President.*

Web, www.pinchot.org

Seeks to advance forest conservation and sustainable natural resources management nationally through research and analysis, education and technical assistance, and development of conservation leaders.

Public Employees for Environmental Responsibility (PEER), *962 Wayne Ave., #610, Silver Spring, MD 20910; (202) 265-7337. Fax, (202) 265-4192. Jeff Ruch, Executive Director.*

General email, info@peer.org

Web, www.peer.org and Twitter, @PEERorg

Service organization for public citizens and employees of federal, state, and local resource management agencies. Defends legal rights of public employees who speak out concerning natural resource management and environmental protection issues. Monitors enforcement of environmental protection laws.

Resources for the Future, *1616 P St. N.W., 20036-1400; (202) 328-5000. Fax, (202) 939-3460. Richard G. Newell, President. Library, (202) 328-5089. Press, (202) 328-5168.*
General email, info@rff.org

Web, www.rff.org and Twitter, @rff

Engages in research and education on environmental and natural resource issues, including forestry, multiple use of public lands, costs and benefits of pollution control, endangered species, environmental risk management, energy and national security, and climate resources. Interests include hazardous waste, the Superfund, and biodiversity. Publishes research findings; offers academic fellowships. Library open to the public by appointment.

Sierra Club, *Legislative Office, 50 F St. N.W., 8th Floor, 20001; (202) 547-1141. Fax, (202) 547-6009. Melinda Pierce, Legislative Director; Bob Bingaman, National Organizing Director, (202) 675-7904; Michael Brune, Executive Director.*
General email, information@sierraclub.org

Web, www.sierraclub.org

Citizens' interest group that promotes protection of natural resources. Interests include the Clean Air Act; the Arctic National Wildlife Refuge; protection of national forests, parks, and wilderness; toxins; global warming; promotion of responsible international trade; and international development lending reform. Monitors legislation and regulations. (Headquarters in Oakland, Calif.)

U.S. Chamber of Commerce, *Environment, Technology, and Regulatory Affairs, 1615 H St. N.W., 20062-2000; (202) 463-5533. Neil Bradley, Executive Vice President.*
General email, environment@uschamber.com

Web, www.uschamber.com/etra and Twitter, @Regulations

Monitors operations of federal departments and agencies responsible for environmental programs, policies, regulatory issues, and food safety. Analyzes and evaluates legislation and regulations that affect the environment.

Global Warming and Climate Change

▶**AGENCIES**

Agriculture Dept. (USDA), *Office of the Chief Economist, Climate Change Program, South Bldg., 12th and Jefferson Dr. S.W., #4407, 20250; (202) 720-6698.*
William Hohenstein, Director.
General email, whohenst@oce.usda.gov

Web, www.usda.gov/oce/climate_change/index.htm

Develops department responses to climate change, particularly as it impacts agriculture, forests, grazing lands, and rural communities; coordinates activities with other federal agencies to align climate change strategy goals and policy.

Bureau of Oceans and International Environmental and Scientific Affairs (OES) *(State Dept.), Global Change (EGC), 2201 C St. N.W., #2480, 20520; (202) 647-3984. Trigg Talley, Director.*
General email, ClimateComms@State.gov

Web, www.state.gov/e/oes/climate

Addresses climate change challenges through international policy, agreements, and partnerships.

Economic Research Service *(Agriculture Dept.), 355 E St. S.W., 20024-8221; (202) 694-5000. Fax, (202) 245-5467. Mary Bohman, Administrator; Greg Pompelli, Associate Administrator.*
General email, service@ers.usda.gov

Web, www.ers.usda.gov and Twitter, @USDA_ERS

Provides research and economic information to the USDA. Interests include economic and policy issues involving food, farm practices and management, natural resources, and rural development. Website offers a briefing room on global climate change and other environmental topics.

Environmental Protection Agency (EPA), *Air and Radiation (OAR), Atmospheric Programs, Climate Change Division, 1200 Pennsylvania Ave. N.W., #5426, MC 6207A, 20460; (202) 343-9876. Fax, (202) 343-2342. Paul M. Gunning, Director.*
General email, hargrove.anne@epa.gov

Web, www.epa.gov/aboutepa/about-office-air-and-radiation-oar#oap

Works to address global climate change and the associated risks to human health and the environment. Analyzes greenhouse gas emissions and reduction options. Educates the public on climate change and provides climate analysis and strategies to policymakers, experts, and U.S. climate negotiators.

National Oceanic and Atmospheric Administration (NOAA) *(Commerce Dept.), Climate Program Office (CPO), 1315 East-West Hwy., SSMC-3, Room 12124, Silver Spring, MD 20910; (301) 734-1263. Fax, (301) 713-0515. Wayne Higgins, Director.*
General email, oar.cpo.office@noaa.gov

Web, www.cpo.noaa.gov

Manages NOAA-funded research programs that focus on climate science and assessments on a regional, national, and international scale.

National Oceanic and Atmospheric Administration (NOAA) *(Commerce Dept.), Ocean Acidification Program (OAP), 1315 East-West Hwy., #10356, Silver Spring, MD 20910; (301) 734-1075. Elizabeth (Libby) Jewett, Director.*
General email, noaa.oceanacidification@noaa.gov

Web, www.oceanacidification.noaa.gov and Twitter, @OA_NOAA

Monitors changes in ocean chemistry due to the continued acidification of the oceans and Great Lakes, and assesses the socioeconomic impacts. Maintains relationships with scientists, resource managers, stakeholders, policymakers, and the public to implement adaptation strategies and monitor the biological responses of ecologically and economically important species. Operates from NOAA's Office of Oceanic and Atmospheric Research.

Office of Science *(Energy Dept.), Biological and Environmental Research (BER), Climate and Environmental Sciences Division (CESD),* 19901 Germantown Rd., #SC23.1, Germantown, MD 20874-1290 (mailing address: Germantown Bldg., 1000 Independence Ave. S.W., #SC23.1, Washington, DC 20585); (301) 903-4775. Gerald Geernaert, Director.
Web, http://science.energy.gov/ber/research/cesd

Supports research on atmospheric systems, terrestrial ecosystems, and subsurface biogeochemistry as well as Earth system modeling and regional and global climate change modeling to improve predictive understanding of Earth's climate and environmental systems in order to inform development of sustainable solutions to energy challenges.

U.S. Geological Survey (USGS) *(Interior Dept.), Land Resources,* 12201 Sunrise Valley Dr., MS 516, Reston, VA 20192; (703) 648-4215. Fax, (703) 648-7031.
T. Douglas Beard Jr., Associate Director (Acting).
Web, www.usgs.gov/mission-areas/land-resources

Supports the science community with its long-term observational networks and extensive databases encompassing the fields of climate history, land-use and land-cover change, and carbon and nutrient cycles.

▶**CONGRESS**

For a listing of relevant congressional committees and subcommittees, please see pages 283–284 or the Appendix.

▶**NONGOVERNMENTAL**

Antarctic and Southern Ocean Coalition, *1320 19th St. N.W., 5th Floor, 20036; (202) 234-2480. Claire Christian, Executive Director.*
General email, secretariat@asoc.org
Web, www.asoc.org and Twitter, @AntarcticaSouth

Promotes research on the impact of climate change on the Antarctic region.

The Brookings Institution, *Climate and Energy Economics Project, 1775 Massachusetts Ave. N.W., 20036; (202) 797-6000. Warwick McKibbin, Co-Director; Pete Wilcoxen, Co-Director. Press, (202) 797-6105.*
Web, www.brookings.edu/about/projects/climate-energy-economics

Promotes economically efficient approaches to mitigating human impacts on climate change, including cap-and-trade.

The Brookings Institution, *Economic Studies, 1775 Massachusetts Ave. N.W., 20036-2188; (202) 797-6000. Fax, (202) 797-6181. Ted Gayer, Director, (202) 797-6230. Press, (202) 797-6105.*
General email, escomment@brookings.edu
Web, www.brookings.edu/economics and Twitter, @BrookingsEcon

Promotes environmentally sound and economically efficient climate policy, with a focus on the economics of domestic cap-and-trade approaches and global agreement.

Center for Climate and Energy Solutions, *2101 Wilson Blvd., #550, Arlington, VA 22201; (703) 516-4146. Fax, (703) 841-1422. Bob Perciasepe, President.*
Web, www.c2es.org and Twitter, @C2ES_org

Independent organization that issues information and promotes discussion by policymakers on the science, economics, and policy of climate change.

Climate Institute, *1201 New York Ave. N.W., #410, 20005; (202) 552-0163. John C. Topping, President.*
General email, info@climate.org
Web, http://climate.org and Twitter, @Climate_Inst

Educates the public and policymakers on climate change, the greenhouse effect, global warming, and the depletion of the ozone layer. Assesses climate change risks and develops strategies on mitigating climate change in developing countries and in North America.

The Climate Reality Project, *750 9th St. N.W., #520, 20001; (202) 567-6800. Fax, (202) 628-1445. Ken Berlin, President.*
General email, info@climatereality.com
Web, www.climaterealityproject.org and Twitter, @ClimateReality

Aims to reduce carbon emissions, supports taxing oil and coal companies that emit large amounts of carbon, and educates the public on climate change and its relation to carbon pollution.

CO2 Coalition, *1621 N. Kent St., #603, Arlington, VA 22209; (571) 970-3180. William Happer, President.*
General email, info@co2coalition.org
Web, http://co2coalition.org and Twitter, @co2coalition

Educates leaders, policymakers, and the public about climate change and impact of carbon dioxide reduction.

Global Green USA, *Washington Office, 820 1st St. N.E., #LL-180, 20002; (202) 380-3440. Chris Weiss, Director of Washington, D.C., Environmental Network.*
General email, cweiss@globalgreen.org
Web, www.globalgreen.org/washington-dc, www.dcen.net, Twitter, @globalgreen and Facebook, www.facebook.com/globalgreenfans

Offers research and community-based projects to educate people about the environment and encourage improved environmental policy. Interests include climate change solutions, green building for affordable housing and schools, energy efficiency and clean energy, protection of natural resources, and recycling. (Headquarters in Santa Monica,

Calif.) (U.S. national affiliate of Mikhail Gorbachev's Green Cross International.)

National Research Council (NRC), *Atmospheric Sciences and Climate Board, Keck Center, 500 5th St. N.W., #602, 20001; (202) 334-3512. Fax, (202) 334-3825. Amanda Staudt, Director; A. R. (Ravi) Ravishankara, Chair.*
General email, basc@nas.edu
Web, www.dels.nas.edu/basc

Supports research on climate change, air pollution, and severe weather in order to address environmental policies, human health, emergency management, energy choices, manufacturing decisions, construction codes, and agricultural methods.

Physicians for Social Responsibility (PSR), *1111 14th St. N.W., #700, 20005; (202) 667-4260. Fax, (202) 667-4201. Jeff Carter, Executive Director.*
General email, psrnatl@psr.org
Web, www.psr.org and Twitter, @psrenvironment

Membership: doctors, nurses, health scientists, and concerned citizens. Works to slow, stop, and reverse global warming and degradation of the environment. Conducts public education programs, monitors policy, and serves as a liaison with other concerned groups.

Resources for the Future, *1616 P St. N.W., 20036-1400; (202) 328-5000. Fax, (202) 939-3460. Richard G. Newell, President. Library, (202) 328-5089. Press, (202) 328-5168.*
General email, info@rff.org
Web, www.rff.org and Twitter, @rff

Research organization that conducts independent studies on economic and policy aspects of energy, environment, conservation, and natural resource management issues worldwide. Interests include climate change, energy, natural resource issues in developing countries, and public health.

Science and Environmental Policy Project (SEPP), *P.O. Box 1126, Springfield, VA 22151; (703) 978-6025. Ken Haapala, President.*
General email, info@sepp.org
Web, www.sepp.org

Works to clarify environmental problems and provide effective, economical solutions. Encourages use of scientific knowledge when making health or environmental public policy decisions. Disseminates research and policy papers by skeptics of global warming.

Union of Concerned Scientists, *Climate and Energy Program, 1825 K St. N.W., #800, 20006-1232; (202) 223-6133. Fax, (202) 223-6162. Angela Ledford Anderson, Director.*
General email, ucs@ucsusa.org
Web, www.ucsusa.org

Promotes clean energy and global warming emissions reduction. Advocates international policy responses to the threat of global climate change.

Wallace Genetic Foundation, *4910 Massachusetts Ave. N.W., #221, 20016; (202) 966-2932. Fax, (202) 966-3370. Michaela Oldfield, Executive Director.*
General email, wgfdn@aol.com
Web, www.wallacegenetic.org

Supports national and international nonprofits in the areas of sustainable agriculture, agricultural research, preservation of farmland, reduction of environmental toxins, conservation, biodiversity protection, and global climate issues.

International Issues

▶AGENCIES

Bureau of Oceans and International Environmental and Scientific Affairs (OES) *(State Dept.), 2201 C St. N.W., #3880, 20520-7818; (202) 647-1554. Fax, (202) 647-0217. Marcia Bernicat, Principal Deputy Assistant Secretary.*
Web, www.state.gov/e/oes, Twitter, @StateDeptOES and Facebook, www.facebook.com/StateDepartment.OES

Concerned with foreign policy as it affects natural resources and the environment, human health, the global climate, energy production, and oceans and fisheries.

Bureau of Oceans and International Environmental and Scientific Affairs (OES) *(State Dept.), Conservation and Water (ECW), 2201 C St. N.W., #2657, 20520; (202) 647-4683. Fax, (202) 647-1052. Christine Dawson, Director, (202) 647-4683.*
General email, waterteam@state.gov
Web, www.state.gov/e/oes/ecw

Represents the United States in international affairs relating to ecology and conservation issues. Interests include wildlife, tropical forests, coral reefs, and biological diversity.

Bureau of Oceans and International Environmental and Scientific Affairs (OES) *(State Dept.), Environmental Quality and Transboundary Issues (EQT), 2201 C St. N.W., #2726, 20520; (202) 647-9831. Fax, (202) 647-1052. Brian Doherty, Director.*
Web, www.state.gov/e/oes/eqt

Advances U.S. interests internationally regarding multilateral environmental organizations, chemical and hazardous waste and other pollutants, and bilateral and regional environmental policies.

Bureau of Oceans and International Environmental and Scientific Affairs (OES) *(State Dept.), Policy and Public Outreach (PPO), 2201 C St. N.W., #2880, 20520; (202) 647-4658. Susan Cleary, Director.*
Web, www.state.gov/e/oes/policy

Integrates oceans, environment, polar, science, technology, and health issues into U.S. foreign policy, and works to address these issues in the media, NGOs, the private sector, and Congress.

Environmental Protection Agency (EPA), *International and Tribal Affairs (OITA),* 1200 Pennsylvania Ave. N.W., #31106, MC 2610R, 20460; (202) 564-6600. Fax, (202) 565-2407. Jane Nishida, Principal Deputy Assistant Administrator.
General email, oita.contactus@epa.gov
Web, www.epa.gov/aboutepa/about-office-international-and-tribal-affairs-oita

Coordinates the agency's work on international environmental issues and programs, including management of bilateral agreements and participation in multilateral organizations and negotiations. Works to strengthen public health and environmental programs on tribal lands, emphasizing helping tribes administer their own environment programs.

Forest Service *(Agriculture Dept.), International Programs,* 1 Thomas Circle N.W., #400, 20005; (202) 644-4600. Fax, (202) 644-4603. Valdis E. Mezainis, Director, (202) 644-4621.
Web, www.fs.fed.us/global

Responsible for the Forest Service's involvement in international forest conservation efforts. Analyzes international resource issues; promotes information exchange; provides planning and technical assistance. Interested in sustainable forest management, covering illegal logging, climate change, and migratory species.

Interior Dept. (DOI), *International Affairs (OIA),* 1849 C St. N.W., MS 3559, 20240; (202) 208-5479. Fax, (202) 513-7728. Karen Senhadji, Director.
Web, www.doi.gov//intl

Focuses on international conservation and management of wildlife and natural resources, protection of cultural resources, cooperation on indigenous affairs, and monitoring of natural hazards, including volcanoes and earthquakes.

International Trade Administration (ITA) *(Commerce Dept.), Industry and Analysis (I&A), Energy and Environmental Industries (OEEI),* 1400 Constitution Ave. N.W., #4053, 20230; (202) 482-5225. Adam O'Malley, Director, (202) 482-4850.
Web, www.trade.gov/td/energy

Works to facilitate and increase export of U.S. environmental technologies, including goods and services. Conducts market analysis, business counseling, and trade promotion.

▶ **CONGRESS**

For a listing of relevant congressional committees and subcommittees, please see pages 283–284 or the Appendix.

▶ **INTERNATIONAL ORGANIZATIONS**

International Conservation Caucus Foundation (ICCF), 25786 Georgetown Station, 20027; (202) 471-4222. John B. Gantt, President.

General email, hq@iccfoundation.us
Web, www.iccfoundation.us, Twitter, @TheICCFGroup and Facebook, www.facebook.com/theiccfgroup

Seeks to improve U.S. efforts in international conservation. Coordinates between policymakers and conservationists to address ecosystem issues. Holds the International Conservation Gala and congressional briefing series. Administers awards to activists. Manages the Ocean Caucus Foundation to protect sea life.

International Joint Commission, *United States and Canada, U.S. Section,* 1717 H St. N.W., #801, 20440; (202) 736-9000. Fax, (202) 632-2006. Charles Lawson, Secretary; Frank Bevacqua, Public Information Officer, (202) 736-9024.
General email, bevacquaf@washington.ijc.org
Web, www.ijc.org

Prevents and resolves disputes between the United States and Canada on transboundary water and air resources. Investigates issues upon request of the governments of the United States and Canada. Reviews applications for water resource projects. (Canadian section in Ottawa; Great Lakes regional office in Windsor, Ontario.)

International Union for the Conservation of Nature, *Washington D.C. Office,* 1630 Connecticut Ave. N.W., 3rd Floor, 20009; (202) 387-4826. Fax, (202) 387-4823. Frank Hawkins, Director.
General email, deborah.good@iucn.org
Web, www.iucn.org/usa

Membership: world governments, their environmental agencies, and nongovernmental organizations. Studies conservation issues from local to global levels. Helps provide links for members and partners around the world to key U.S.-based institutions, such as the U.S. Government and its agencies, the World Bank, the Global Environment Facility, the Inter-American Development Bank, the United Nations, and other organizations. Interests include protected areas, forests, oceans, polar regions, biodiversity, species survival, environmental law, sustainable use of resources, and the impact of trade on the environment. Hosts a number of IUCN staff, programs, and initiatives concerned with global conservation and sustainable development issues. (Headquarters in Gland, Switzerland.)

Organization of American States (OAS), *Sustainable Development,* 1889 F St. N.W., #710, 20006; (202) 458-3567. Fax, (202) 458-3560. Cletus Springer, Director, ext. 9084.
General email, sustainable_dev@oas.org
Web, www.oas.org/en/sedi/dsd

Promotes integrated and sustainable development of natural resources in OAS member states through the design and implementation of policies, programs, and partnerships. Interests include integrated management of shared water resources, hazard risk management, sustainable cities, biodiversity protection, sustainable energy, and environmental law.

►NONGOVERNMENTAL

Conservation International, *2011 Crystal Dr., #500, Arlington, VA 22202; (703) 341-2400. Fax, (703) 553-0654. Peter Seligmann, Chair; M. Sanjayan, Chief Executive Officer; Jennifer Morris, President. Toll-free, (800) 429-5660.*
General email, community@conservation.org

Web, www.conservation.org and Twitter, @ConservationOrg

Works to conserve tropical rain forests through economic development; promotes exchange of debt relief for conservation programs that involve local people and organizations. Interests include fresh water, food, biodiversity, climate, health, and cultural services. Provides private groups and governments with information and technical advice on conservation efforts and collaborates with business and government in these efforts; supports conservation data gathering in the Americas, Europe, Africa, Asia, and the Caribbean, as well as the oceans.

Environmental Investigation Agency (EIA), *P.O. Box 53343, 20009; (202) 483-6621. Fax, (202) 986-8626. Alexander (Sascha) von Bismarck, Director.*
General email, info@eia-global.org

Web, www.eia-global.org and Twitter, @EIAEnvironment

Works to expose international environmental crime, including illegal trade of wildlife, illegal logging, and sale of ozone-depleting substances. Monitors legislation and regulations. Also maintains an office in London.

Greenpeace USA, *702 H St. N.W., #300, 20001; (202) 462-1177. Fax, (202) 462-4507. Annie Leonard, Executive Director. Toll-free, (800) 722-6995.*
General email, info@wdc.greenpeace.org

Web, www.greenpeace.org, Twitter, @greenpeaceusa and Facebook, www.facebook.com/greenpeaceusa

Seeks to expose global environmental problems and to promote solutions through nonviolent direct action, lobbying, and creative communication. Interests include forests, oceans, toxins, global warming, disarmament, and genetic engineering. (International office in Amsterdam, The Netherlands.)

Institute for Policy Studies, *1301 Connecticut Ave. N.W., #600, 20036; (202) 234-9382. Fax, (202) 387-7915. John Cavanagh, Executive Director.*
General email, info@ips-dc.org

Web, www.ips-dc.org, Twitter, @IPS_DC and Facebook, www.facebook.com/InstituteforPolicyStudies

Research and educational think tank focused on social justice and security, especially equality, ecological sustainability, and peace. Interests include environmental protection, sustainable energy solutions, the impact of fossil fuels on climate change, and clean air, land, water, and food.

Species Survival Network (SSN), *2100 L St. N.W., 20037; (301) 956-8027. Ann Michels, Executive Director.*

General email, info@ssn.org

Web, http://ssn.org

Coalition of organizations seeking to enforce the Convention on International Trade in Endangered Species of Wild Fauna and Flora (CITES). Acts as advocate against exploitation, injury, cruel treatment, and possible extinction of native animals and plants caused by global trade. Researches and analyzes policies to educate the public on their potential impact on the environment.

Winrock International, *Washington Office, 2121 Crystal Dr., #500, Arlington, VA 22202; (703) 302-6500. Fax, (703) 302-6512. Rodney Ferguson, President.*
General email, information@winrock.org

Web, www.winrock.org and Twitter, @WinrockIntl

Works to sustain natural resources and protect the environment. Matches innovative approaches in agriculture, natural resource management, clean energy, and leadership development with the unique needs of its partners. (Headquarters in Little Rock, Ark.)

World Resources Institute, *10 G St. N.E., #800, 20002; (202) 729-7600. Fax, (202) 729-7610. Andrew Steer, President, (202) 729-7676. Press, (202) 729-7736.*
Web, www.wri.org and Twitter, @worldresources

Conducts research on environmental problems and studies the interrelationships of natural resources, economic growth, and human needs. Interests include forestry and land use, renewable energy, fisheries, and sustainable agriculture. Assesses environmental policies of aid agencies.

World Wildlife Fund (WWF), *1250 24th St. N.W., 20037-1193 (mailing address: P.O. Box 97180, Washington, DC 20090-7180); (202) 293-4800. Fax, (202) 293-9211. Carter S. Roberts, President.*
General email, membership@wwfus.org

Web, www.worldwildlife.org and Twitter, @World_Wildlife

Conducts scientific research and analyzes policy on environmental and conservation issues, including pollution reduction, land use, forestry and wetlands management, parks, soil conservation, and sustainable development. Supports projects to promote biological diversity and to save endangered species and their habitats, including tropical forests in Latin America, Asia, and Africa. Awards grants and provides technical assistance to local conservation groups.

Worldwatch Institute, *1400 16th St. N.W., #430, 20036; (202) 745-8092. Fax, (202) 478-2534. Ed Groark, President (Acting).*
General email, worldwatch@worldwatch.org

Web, www.worldwatch.org and Twitter, @worldwatch

Focuses on an interdisciplinary approach to solving global environmental problems. Interests include energy conservation, renewable resources, solar power, and energy use in developing countries.

ANIMALS AND PLANTS

General

▶AGENCIES

Animal and Plant Health Inspection Service (APHIS)
(Agriculture Dept.), Investigative and Enforcement Services, 4700 River Rd., #85, Riverdale, MD 20737-1234; (301) 851-2948. Fax, (301) 734-4328. Steven Bennett, Director, (301) 851-2948.
Web, www.aphis.usda.gov/aphis/ourfocus/business-services/ies

Provides investigative and enforcement services and leadership, direction, and support for compliance activities within the service.

Animal and Plant Health Inspection Service (APHIS)
(Agriculture Dept.), Plant Protection and Quarantine, 1400 Independence Ave. S.W., #302E, 20250; (202) 799-7163. Fax, (202) 690-0472. Osama El-Lissy, Deputy Administrator. Anti-smuggling hotline, (800) 877-3835.
General email, aphis.web@aphis.usda.gov
Web, www.aphis.usda.gov/plant_health

Encourages compliance with regulations that safeguard agriculture and natural resources from the risks associated with the entry, establishment, or spread of animal and plant pests and noxious weeds. Methods include requirements for the import and export of plants and plant products; partnership agreements with industry groups, community organizations, and government entities; and public education and outreach.

National Zoological Park *(Smithsonian Institution),* 3001 Connecticut Ave. N.W., 20008 (mailing address: DEVS, P.O. Box 37012, MRC 5516, Washington, DC 20013-7012); (202) 633-4888 (recorded information line). Fax, (202) 673-4836. Steven Monfort, Executive Director. Friends of the Zoo, (202) 633-3038. Library, (202) 633-2922. Press, (202) 633-3055. TTY, (202) 673-7800. Zoo police, (202) 633-4134.
Web, www.nationalzoo.si.edu, Twitter, @NationalZoo and Facebook, www.facebook.com/nationalzoo

Maintains a public zoo. Conducts research on animal behavior, ecology, nutrition, reproductive physiology, pathology, and veterinary medicine; operates an annex near Front Royal, Va., for the propagation and study of endangered species. Houses a unit of the Smithsonian Institution library open to qualified researchers by appointment. Interlibrary loans available.

U.S. Customs and Border Protection *(Homeland Security Dept.), Agricultural Program and Trade Liaison Office,* 1300 Pennsylvania Ave. N.W., #2.5B, 20229; (202) 344-3298. Fax, (202) 344-1442. Kevin Harriger, Executive Director.
Web, www.cbp.gov

Responsible for safeguarding the nation's animal and natural resources from pests and disease through inspections at ports of entry and beyond.

▶CONGRESS

For a listing of relevant congressional committees and subcommittees, please see pages 283–284 or the Appendix.

▶NONGOVERNMENTAL

Animal Health Institute, 1325 G St. N.W., #700, 20005-3104; (202) 637-2440. Fax, (202) 393-1667. Alexander S. Mathews, President.
Web, www.ahi.org and Twitter, @AnimalsHealthy

Membership: manufacturers of drugs and other products (including vaccines, pesticides, and vitamins) for pets and food-producing animals. Interests include pet health, livestock health, and disease outbreak prevention. Monitors legislation and regulations.

National Research Council (NRC), *Agriculture and Natural Resources Board,* Keck Center, 500 5th St. N.W., #WS632, 20001; (202) 334-3062. Fax, (202) 334-1978. Robin Schoen, Director.
General email, banr@nas.edu
Web, http://dels.nas.edu/banr and Twitter, @NASM_Ag

Promotes and oversees research on the environmental impact of agriculture and food sustainability, including forestry, fisheries, wildlife, and the use of land, water, and other natural resources.

Animal Rights and Welfare

▶AGENCIES

Animal and Plant Health Inspection Service (APHIS)
(Agriculture Dept.), Animal Care, 4700 River Rd., #84, Riverdale, MD 20737-1234; (301) 851-3751. Fax, (301) 734-4978. Bernadette Juarez, Deputy Administrator.
General email, ace@aphis.usda.gov
Web, www.aphis.usda.gov/animal_welfare

Administers laws for the breeding, exhibition, and care of animals raised for sale and research and transported commercially. Enforces the Animal Welfare Act and Horse Protection Act; accepts animal welfare complaints.

Animal and Plant Health Inspection Service (APHIS)
(Agriculture Dept.), Center for Animal Welfare, 4700 River Rd., #84, Riverdale, MD 20737; (301) 851-3751. Fax, (301) 734-4978. Elizabeth Goldentyer, Associate Deputy Director.
General email, ace@aphis.usda.gov
Web, www.aphis.usda.gov/aphis/ourfocus/animalwelfare/CAW

Provides guidance on policy development and analysis, education and outreach, and scientific research related to animal welfare issues, especially in support of the Animal

Welfare Act and the Horse Protection Act. (Headquarters in Kansas City, Mo.)

National Agricultural Library *(Agriculture Dept.),* *Animal Welfare Information Center (AWIC), 10301 Baltimore Ave., #118, Beltsville, MD 20705; (301) 504-6212. Kristina Adams, Coordinator, (301) 504-5486.*
General email, awic@ars.usda.gov

Web, www.nal.usda.gov/awic

Provides information for improved animal care and use in research, testing, teaching, and exhibition.

National Institutes of Health (NIH) *(Health and Human Services Dept.), Animal Care and Use (OACU), 31 Center Dr., Bldg. 31, #B1C37, MSC 2252, Bethesda, MD 20892-2252; (301) 496-5424. Fax, (301) 480-8298. Stephen Denny, Director (Acting).*
General email, secoacu@od.nih.gov

Web, http://oacu.oir.nih.gov

Provides guidance for the humane care and use of animals in the intramural research program at NIH.

National Institutes of Health (NIH) *(Health and Human Services Dept.), Laboratory Animal Welfare (OLAW), 6705 Rockledge Dr., RLK1, #360, MSC 7982, Bethesda, MD 20892-7982; (301) 496-7163. Fax, (301) 480-3394. Patricia A. Brown, Director.*
General email, olaw@mail.nih.gov

Web, https://olaw.nih.gov/home.htm

Develops and monitors policy on the humane care and use of animals in research conducted by any public health service entity.

▶**CONGRESS**

For a listing of relevant congressional committees and subcommittees, please see pages 283–284 or the Appendix.

▶**NONGOVERNMENTAL**

Alley Cat Allies, *7920 Norfolk Ave., #600, Bethesda, MD 20814-2525; (240) 482-1980. Fax, (240) 482-1990. Becky Robinson, President.*
General email, info@alleycat.org

Web, www.alleycat.org, Twitter, @AlleyCatAllies and Facebook, www.facebook.com/AlleyCatAllies

Clearinghouse for information on feral and stray cats. Advocates the trap-neuter-return method to reduce feral cat populations.

American Humane Assn., *1400 16th St. N.W., #360, 20036; (202) 841-6080. Fax, (202) 450-2335. Robin R. Ganzert, President. Toll-free, (800) 227-4645.*
General email, info@americanhumane.org

Web, www.americanhumane.org, Twitter, @AmericanHumane and Facebook, www.facebook.com/americanhumane

Membership: animal shelters, humane organizations, child protection agencies, government agencies, and individuals. Prepares model state legislation on child abuse and

its prevention; publishes surveys on child and animal abuse and state abuse laws.

American Physiological Society, *6120 Executive Blvd., #600, Rockville, MD 20852-4911; (301) 634-7164. Fax, (301) 634-7241. Scott Steen, Executive Director, (301) 634-7118.*
Web, www.the-aps.org and Twitter, @APSPhysiology

Works to establish standards for the humane care and use of laboratory animals.

Americans for Medical Progress, *444 N. Capitol St. N.W., #417, 20001; (202) 624-8810. Paula Clifford, Executive Director, (202) 624-8812.*
General email, amp@amprogress.org

Web, www.amprogress.org and Twitter, @CureDisease

Promotes and protects animal-based medical research. Serves as a media resource by fact-checking claims of animal rights groups. Conducts public education campaigns on the link between animal research and medical advances.

Animal Welfare Institute, *900 Pennsylvania Ave. S.E., 20003 (mailing address: P.O. Box 3650, Washington, DC 20027); (202) 337-2332. Fax, (202) 446-2131. Cathy Liss, President.*
General email, awi@awionline.org

Web, www.awionline.org

Works to improve conditions for animals in laboratories, on farms, in commerce, in homes, and in the wild. Promotes efforts to end horse slaughter. Monitors legislation and regulations. (Merged with the Society for Animal Protective Legislation.)

Compassion Over Killing, *6930 Carroll Ave., #910, Tacoma Park, MD 20912 (mailing address: P.O. Box 9773, Washington, DC 20016); (301) 891-2458. Fax, (301) 891-6815. Erica Meier, Executive Director.*
General email, info@cok.net

Web, http://cok.net and Twitter, @TryVeg

Animal rights organization that focuses primarily on cruelty to animals in agriculture. Promotes vegetarianism.

Doris Day Animal League, *1255 23rd St. N.W., 20037; (202) 452-1100. Vacant, Executive Director.*
General email, info@ddal.org

Web, www.ddal.org

Seeks to reduce the inhumane treatment of animals through legislative initiatives, education, and programs. Works with all levels of government to pass new protection laws and strengthen existing ones. (Affiliated with the Humane Society of the United States.)

Farm Animal Rights Movement (FARM), *10101 Ashburton Lane, Bethesda, MD 20817-1729; (301) 530-1737. Fax, (301) 530-5683. Alex Hershaft, President. Toll-free, 888-FARM-USA.*
General email, info@farmusa.org

Web, www.farmusa.org, www.livevegan.org and Twitter, @FARMUSA

Works to end use of animals for food. Interests include animal protection, consumer health, agricultural resources, and environmental quality. Conducts national educational campaigns, including World Farm Animals Day, the Live Vegan program, and the Great American Meatout. Monitors legislation and regulations.

Humane Farm Animal Care, *P.O. Box 82, Middleburg, VA 20118; (703) 435-3883. Fax, (703) 435-3981. Adele Douglass, Chief Executive Officer; Mimi Stein, Executive Director.*
General email, info@certifiedhumane.org
Web, www.certifiedhumane.org,
Twitter, @CertifiedHumane and Facebook, www.facebook.com/CertifiedHumane

Seeks to improve the welfare of farm animals by providing viable, duly monitored standards for humane food production. Administers the Certified Humane Raised and Handled program for meat, poultry, eggs, and dairy products.

Humane Rescue Alliance, *1201 New York Ave N.E., 20002; P.O. Box 96312, 20090-6312; (202) 576-6664. Claudia Roll, Director of Operations. Adoption center, (202) 723-5730. 24-hour animal cruelty and emergency hotline, (202) 723-5730. Spay and neuter center, (202) 608-1356.*
General email, adopt@washhumane.org
Web, www.humanerescuealliance.org,
Twitter, @HumaneRescue
Press, matt.williams@warl.org

Congressionally chartered animal welfare agency and open-access animal shelter. Promotes pet adoption; offers low-cost spay and neuter services and trap-and-neuter programs. Operates the D.C. Animal Care and Control.

Humane Society Legislative Fund, *1255 23rd St. N.W., #455, 20037; (202) 676-2314. Fax, (202) 676-2300. Sara Amundson, President. Press, (301) 548-7778. Donations, (800) 876-5170.*
General email, humanesociety@hslf.org
Web, www.hslf.org, Twitter, @HSLegFund and Facebook, www.facebook.com/humanelegislation

Works to pass state and federal laws protecting animals from cruelty and suffering; educates the public about animal protection issues and supports humane candidates for office. (Lobbying arm of the Humane Society of the United States.)

Humane Society of the United States, *1255 23rd St. N.W., #450, 20037; (202) 452-1100. Fax, (202) 778-6132. Kitty Block, President (Acting). Toll-free, (866) 720-2676. Web, www.humanesociety.org, Twitter, @HumaneSociety and Facebook, www.facebook.com/humanesociety*

Citizens' interest group that sponsors programs in pet and equine protection, disaster preparedness and response, wildlife and habitat protection, animals in research, and farm animal welfare. Interests include legislation to protect pets, provide more humane treatment for farm animals, strengthen penalties for illegal animal fighting, and curb abusive sport hunting practices such as trophy hunting, baiting, and hounding.

National Assn. for Biomedical Research, *1100 Vermont Ave. N.W., #1100, 20005; (202) 857-0540. Fax, (202) 659-1902. Matthew Bailey, President.*
General email, info@nabr.org
Web, www.nabr.org

Membership: scientific and medical professional societies, academic institutions, and research-oriented corporations involved in the use of animals in biomedical research. Supports the humane use of animals in medical research, education, and product-safety assessment. Monitors legislation and regulations.

National Research Council (NRC), *Institute for Laboratory Animal Research, Keck Center, 500 5th St. N.W., #645, 20001; (202) 334-2590. Fax, (202) 334-1687. Gregory Symmes, Director; Magaret S. Landi, Chair.*
Web, www.dels.nas.edu/ilar

Develops and makes available scientific and technical information on laboratory animals and other biological research resources for the scientific community, institutional animal care and use committees, the federal government, science educators and students, and the public.

Physicians Committee for Responsible Medicine (PCRM), *5100 Wisconsin Ave. N.W., #400, 20016; (202) 686-2210. Fax, (202) 686-2216. Neal Barnard, President. Press, 202–527-7316.*
General email, pcrm@pcrm.org
Web, www.pcrm.org and Twitter, @PCRM

Investigates alternatives to animal use in medical research experimentation, product testing, and education.

Fish

▶**AGENCIES**

Atlantic States Marine Fisheries Commission, *1050 N. Highland St., #200 A-N, Arlington, VA 22201; (703) 842-0740. Fax, (703) 842-0741. Robert E. Beal, Executive Director.*
General email, info@asmfc.org
Web, www.asmfc.org

Interstate compact commission of marine fisheries representatives from fifteen states along the Atlantic seaboard. Assists states in developing joint fisheries programs; works with other fisheries organizations and the federal government on environmental, natural resource, and conservation issues.

Environment and Natural Resources Division *(Justice Dept.), Wildlife and Marine Resources, 601 D St. N.W., 3rd Floor, 20004 (mailing address: P.O. Box 7415, Ben Franklin Station, Washington, DC 20044-7369); (202) 305-0210. Fax, (202) 305-0275. Seth M. Barsky, Section Chief. Web, www.justice.gov/enrd/wildlife-and-marine-resources-section*

Supervises civil cases under federal maritime law and other laws protecting marine fish and mammals.

Environmental Protection Agency (EPA), *Water (OW),* *1200 Pennsylvania Ave. N.W., MC 4101M, 20460; (202) 564-5700. David Ross, Assistant Administrator.*
Web, www.epa.gov/aboutepa/about-office-water

Monitors water pollution to promote healthy fish habitats. Issues fish and shellfish advisories and promotes safe eating guidelines.

Forest Service *(Agriculture Dept.),* **Watershed, Fish, Wildlife, Air, and Rare Plants,** *201 14th St. S.W., 35C, 20024 (mailing address: 1400 Independence Ave. S.W., MS 1121, Washington, DC 20250-1121); (202) 205-1671. Fax, (202) 644-4806. Robert (Rob) Harper, Director.*
General email, rharper@fs.fed.us
Web, www.fs.fed.us/biology

Provides national policy direction and management for watershed, fish, wildlife, air, and rare plants programs on lands managed by the Forest Service.

Interior Dept. (DOI), *Assistant Secretary for Fish, Wildlife, and Parks,* *1849 C St. N.W., #3160, 20240; (202) 208-4416. Fax, (202) 208-4684. Margaret Everson, Assistant Secretary, (202) 208-4545.*
Web, www.doi.gov

Responsible for programs associated with the development, conservation, and use of fish, wildlife, recreational, historical, and national park system resources. Coordinates marine environmental quality and biological resources programs with other federal agencies. Oversees the U.S. Fish and Wildlife Service and National Park Service.

National Oceanic and Atmospheric Administration (NOAA) *(Commerce Dept.),* *1401 Constitution Ave. N.W., #5128, 20230; (202) 482-3436. Fax, (202) 408-9674. Timothy Gallaudet, Under Secretary (Acting). Library, (301) 713-2600. Press, (202) 482-6090.*
Web, www.noaa.gov and Twitter, @NOAA

Conducts research in marine and atmospheric sciences; surveys resources of the sea; analyzes economic aspects of fisheries operations; develops and implements policies on international fisheries; provides states with grants to conserve coastal zone areas; protects marine mammals; provides colleges and universities with grants for research, education, and marine advisory services.

National Oceanic and Atmospheric Administration (NOAA) *(Commerce Dept.),* **National Marine Fisheries Service (NMFS),** *1315 East-West Hwy., 14th floor, Silver Spring, MD 20910; (301) 427-8000. Fax, (301) 713-1940. Chris Oliver, Assistant Administrator. Press, (301) 427-8003.*
Web, www.nmfs.noaa.gov and Twitter, @NOAAFisheries

Administers marine fishing regulations, including offshore fishing rights and international agreements; conducts marine resources research; studies use and management of these resources; administers the Magnuson-Stevens Fishery Conservation and Management Act; manages and protects marine resources, especially endangered species and marine mammals, within the exclusive economic zone.

U.S. Fish and Wildlife Service *(Interior Dept.),* *1849 C St. N.W., #3358, 20240; (202) 208-4717. Fax, (202) 208-6965. Margaret Everson, Principal Deputy Director. Press, (703) 358-2220. Toll-free, (800) 344-9453.*
General email, fisheries@fws.gov
Web, www.fws.gov and Twitter, @USFWS

Works with federal and state agencies and nonprofits to conserve, protect, and enhance fish and wildlife and their habitats for the continuing benefit of the American people.

U.S. Fish and Wildlife Service *(Interior Dept.),* **Endangered Species,** *5275 Leesburg Pike, Falls Church, VA 22041; (703) 358-2171. Fax, (202) 208-5618. Bridget Fahey, Chief.*
Web, www.fws.gov/endangered and Twitter, @USFWSEndsp

Administers federal policy on fish and wildlife under the Endangered Species Act, Marine Mammal Protection Act, Fish and Wildlife Coordination Act, Oil Pollution Act, and other environmental laws. Reviews all federal and federally licensed projects to determine environmental effects on fish and wildlife. Responsible for maintaining the endangered species list and for protecting and restoring species to healthy numbers.

U.S. Fish and Wildlife Service *(Interior Dept.),* **Fisheries and Aquatic Conservation,** *5275 Leesburg Pike, MS FAC-3C018A, Falls Church, VA 22041-3803; (703) 358-1792. Fax, (703) 358-2847. David Hoskins, Assistant Director.*
General email, fisheries@fws.gov
Web, www.fws.gov/fisheries and Twitter, @USFWSFisheries

Develops, manages, and protects interstate and international fisheries, including fisheries of the Great Lakes, fisheries on federal lands, aquatic ecosystems, endangered species of fish, and anadromous species. Administers the National Fish Hatchery System and the National Fish and Wildlife Resource Management Offices, as well as the Habitat and Conservation and Environmental Quality Divisions.

U.S. Geological Survey (USGS) *(Interior Dept.),* **Ecosystems,** *12201 Sunrise Valley Dr., MS 300, Reston, VA 20192-0002; (703) 648-4051. Fax, (703) 648-7031. Anne E. Kinsinger, Associate Director.*
Web, www.usgs.gov/ecosystems

Conducts research and monitoring to develop and convey an understanding of ecosystem function and distributions, physical and biological components, and trophic dynamics for freshwater, terrestrial, and marine ecosystems and the human, fish, and wildlife communities they support. Subject areas include invasive species, endangered species and habitats, genetics and genomics, and microbiology.

► **CONGRESS**

For a listing of relevant congressional committees and subcommittees, please see pages 283–284 or the Appendix.

American Fisheries Society (AFS), *425 Barlow Pl., #110, Bethesda, MD 20814-2144; (301) 897-8616. Fax, (301) 897-8096. Douglas Austen, Executive Director, ext. 208. Bookstore, (301) 897-8616 ext. 231.*
General email, main@fisheries.org
Web, https://fisheries.org, Twitter, @AmFisheriesSoc and Facebook, www.facebook.com/AmericanFisheriesSociety

Membership: biologists and other scientists interested in fisheries. Promotes the fisheries profession, the advancement of fisheries science, and conservation of renewable aquatic resources. Monitors legislation and regulations.

Assn. of Fish and Wildlife Agencies, *1100 1st St. N.E., #825, 20001; (202) 838-3474. Fax, (202) 350-9869. Ron Regan, Executive Director. Press, (202) 838-3461.*
General email, info@fishwildlife.org
Web, www.fishwildlife.org, Twitter, @fishwildlife and Facebook, www.facebook.com/FishWildlifeAgencies

Membership: state, provincial, and territorial fish and wildlife management agencies in the United States, Canada, and Mexico. Encourages balanced, research-based fish and wildlife resource management. Monitors legislation and regulations.

National Fish and Wildlife Foundation, *1133 15th St. N.W., #1100, 20005; (202) 857-0166. Fax, (202) 857-0162. Jeff Trandahl, Executive Director.*
General email, info@nfwf.org
Web, www.nfwf.org, Twitter, @NFWFnews and Facebook, www.facebook.com/FishandWildlife

Forges partnerships between the public and private sectors in support of national and international conservation activities that identify and root out causes of environmental problems that affect fish, wildlife, and plants.

National Fisheries Institute, *7918 Jones Branch Dr., #700, McLean, VA 22102; (703) 752-8882. John Connelly, President. Press, (703) 752-8891.*
General email, contact@nfi.org
Web, www.aboutseafood.com and Twitter, @NFImedia

Membership: vessel owners and distributors, processors, wholesalers, importers, traders, and brokers of fish and shellfish. Monitors legislation and regulations on fisheries. Advocates eating seafood for health benefits.

Ocean Conservancy, *1300 19th St. N.W., 8th Floor, 20036; (202) 429-5609. Fax, (202) 872-0619. Janis Jones, President. Toll-free, (800) 519-1541.*
General email, membership@oceanconservancy.org
Web, www.oceanconservancy.org, Twitter, @OurOcean and Facebook, www.facebook.com/oceanconservancy

Works to prevent the overexploitation of living marine resources, including fisheries, and to restore depleted marine wildlife populations through research, education, and science-based advocacy.

Trout Unlimited, *1777 N. Kent St., #100, Arlington, VA 22209; (703) 522-0200. Fax, (703) 284-9400. Chris Wood, President, (703) 284-9403. Toll-free, (800) 834-2419.*
Web, www.tu.org and Twitter, @TroutUnlimited

Membership: individuals interested in the protection and restoration of cold-water fish and their habitat. Sponsors research projects with federal and state fisheries agencies; administers programs for water-quality surveillance and cleanup of streams and lakes. Monitors legislation and regulations.

Wildlife and Marine Mammals

Animal and Plant Health Inspection Service (APHIS) *(Agriculture Dept.), Wildlife Services, 1400 Independence Ave. S.W., #1624S, 20250-3402; 4700 River Rd., Riverdale, MD 20737; (202) 799-7095. Fax, (202) 690-0053. Janet Bucknall, Deputy Administrator.*
Web, www.aphis.usda.gov/wildlife_damage

Works to minimize damage caused by wildlife to crops and livestock, natural resources, and human health and safety. Removes or eliminates predators and nuisance birds. Interests include aviation safety and coexistence of people and wildlife in suburban areas. Oversees the National Wildlife Research Center in Ft. Collins, Colo.

Environment and Natural Resources Division *(Justice Dept.), Wildlife and Marine Resources, 601 D St. N.W., 3rd Floor, 20004 (mailing address: P.O. Box 7415, Ben Franklin Station, Washington, DC 20044-7369); (202) 305-0210. Fax, (202) 305-0275. Seth M. Barsky, Section Chief.*
Web, www.justice.gov/enrd/wildlife-and-marine-resources-section

Responsible for criminal enforcement and civil litigation under federal fish and wildlife conservation statutes, including protection of wildlife, fish, and plant resources within U.S. jurisdiction, and management and restoration of Florida Everglades. Monitors interstate and foreign commerce of these resources.

Forest Service *(Agriculture Dept.), Watershed, Fish, Wildlife, Air, and Rare Plants, 201 14th St. S.W., 35C, 20024 (mailing address: 1400 Independence Ave. S.W., MS 1121, Washington, DC 20250-1121); (202) 205-1671. Fax, (202) 644-4806. Robert (Rob) Harper, Director.*
General email, rharper@fs.fed.us
Web, www.fs.fed.us/biology

Provides national policy direction and management for watershed, fish, wildlife, air, and rare plants programs on lands managed by the Forest Service.

Interior Dept. (DOI), *Assistant Secretary for Fish, Wildlife, and Parks, 1849 C St. N.W., #3160, 20240; (202) 208-4416. Fax, (202) 208-4684. Margaret Everson, Assistant Secretary, (202) 208-4545.*
Web, www.doi.gov

Responsible for programs associated with the development, conservation, and use of fish, wildlife, recreational, historical, and national park system resources. Coordinates marine environmental quality and biological resources programs with other federal agencies. Oversees the U.S. Fish and Wildlife Service and National Park Service.

Marine Mammal Commission, *4340 East-West Hwy., #700, Bethesda, MD 20814; (301) 504-0087. Fax, (301) 504-0099. Peter O. Thomas, Executive Director.*
General email, mmc@mmc.gov
Web, www.mmc.gov

Established by Congress to ensure protection and conservation of marine mammals and the ecosystems of which they are a part. Supports research and makes recommendations to federal agencies to ensure that their activities are consistent with the provisions of the Marine Mammal Protection Act.

Migratory Bird Conservation Commission, *5275 Leesburg Pike, Falls Church, VA 22041-3803 (mailing address: 5275 Leesburg Pike, MS 3N053, Falls Church, VA 22041-3803); (703) 358-1713. Fax, (703) 358-2223. A. Eric Alvarez, Secretary.*
General email, mbcc@fws.gov
Web, www.fws.gov/refuges/realty/mbcc.html

Established by the Migratory Bird Conservation Act of 1929. Decides which areas to purchase for use as migratory bird refuges and the price at which they are acquired.

National Oceanic and Atmospheric Administration (NOAA) *(Commerce Dept.), 1401 Constitution Ave. N.W., #5128, 20230; (202) 482-3436. Fax, (202) 408-9674. Timothy Gallaudet, Under Secretary (Acting). Library, (301) 713-2600. Press, (202) 482-6090.*
Web, www.noaa.gov and Twitter, @NOAA

Conducts research in marine and atmospheric sciences; surveys resources of the sea; analyzes economic aspects of fisheries operations; develops and implements policies on international fisheries; provides states with grants to conserve coastal zone areas; protects marine mammals; provides colleges and universities with grants for research, education, and marine advisory services.

National Oceanic and Atmospheric Administration (NOAA) *(Commerce Dept.), Protected Resources (OPR), 1315 East-West Hwy., 13th Floor, Silver Spring, MD 20910; (301) 427-8400. Fax, (301) 713-0376. Donna Wieting, Director.*
Web, www.nmfs.noaa.gov/pr and
Twitter, @NOAAfisheries

Administers the Endangered Species Act and the Marine Mammal Protection Act. Provides guidance on the conservation and protection of marine mammals, threatened and endangered marine and anadromous species, and their habitat. Develops national guidelines and policies for the implementation of the Acts, including recovery of protected species, review and issuance of permits and authorization under the Acts, and consultations with other agencies on federal actions that may affect protected species or their habitat. Prepares and reviews management and recovery plans and environmental impact analysis.

U.S. Fish and Wildlife Service *(Interior Dept.), 1849 C St. N.W., #3358, 20240; (202) 208-4717. Fax, (202) 208-6965.*

Margaret Everson, Principal Deputy Director. Press, (703) 358-2220. Toll-free, (800) 344-9453.
General email, fisheries@fws.gov
Web, www.fws.gov and Twitter, @USFWS

Works with federal and state agencies and nonprofits to conserve, protect, and enhance fish and wildlife and their habitats for the continuing benefit of the American people.

U.S. Fish and Wildlife Service *(Interior Dept.), Bird Habitat Conservation, 5275 Leesburg Pike, MS MB, Falls Church, VA 22041; (703) 358-1784. Fax, (703) 358-2217. Vacant, Division Chief.*
Web, www.fws.gov/birds and Twitter, @usfwsBirds

Coordinates U.S. activities with Canada and Mexico to protect waterfowl habitats, restore waterfowl populations, and set research priorities under the North American Waterfowl Management Plan.

U.S. Fish and Wildlife Service *(Interior Dept.), Endangered Species, 5275 Leesburg Pike, Falls Church, VA 22041; (703) 358-2171. Fax, (202) 208-5618. Bridget Fahey, Chief.*
Web, www.fws.gov/endangered and
Twitter, @USFWSEndsp

Administers federal policy on fish and wildlife under the Endangered Species Act, Marine Mammal Protection Act, Fish and Wildlife Coordination Act, Oil Pollution Act, and other environmental laws. Reviews all federal and federally licensed projects to determine environmental effects on fish and wildlife. Responsible for maintaining the endangered species list and for protecting and restoring species to healthy numbers.

U.S. Fish and Wildlife Service *(Interior Dept.), National Wildlife Refuge System, 1849 C St., #3349, 20240; (202) 208-5333. Cynthia Martinez, Chief. Toll-free, (800) 344-9453.*
Web, www.fws.gov/refuges and Twitter, @USFWSRefuges

Determines policy for the management of wildlife. Manages the National Wildlife Refuge System and land acquisition for wildlife refuges.

U.S. Geological Survey (USGS) *(Interior Dept.), Ecosystems, 12201 Sunrise Valley Dr., MS 300, Reston, VA 20192-0002; (703) 648-4051. Fax, (703) 648-7031. Anne E. Kinsinger, Associate Director.*
Web, www.usgs.gov/ecosystems

Conducts research and monitoring to develop and convey an understanding of ecosystem function and distributions, physical and biological components, and trophic dynamics for freshwater, terrestrial, and marine ecosystems and the human, fish, and wildlife communities they support. Subject areas include invasive species, endangered species and habitats, genetics and genomics, and microbiology.

▶ **CONGRESS**

For a listing of relevant congressional committees and subcommittees, please see pages 283–284 or the Appendix.

▶ NONGOVERNMENTAL

Animal Welfare Institute, *900 Pennsylvania Ave. S.E., 20003 (mailing address: P.O. Box 3650, Washington, DC 20027); (202) 337-2332. Fax, (202) 446-2131. Cathy Liss, President.*
General email, awi@awionline.org
Web, www.awionline.org

Works to preserve species threatened with extinction and protect wildlife from inhumane means of capture. Promotes efforts to end whaling and shark finning. Programs include preserving American wild horses and promoting nonlethal wildlife management solutions. Monitors legislation and regulations. (Merged with the Society for Animal Protective Legislation.)

Antarctic and Southern Ocean Coalition, *1320 19th St. N.W., 5th Floor, 20036; (202) 234-2480. Claire Christian, Executive Director.*
General email, secretariat@asoc.org
Web, www.asoc.org and Twitter, @AntarcticaSouth

Works to protect the fragile environment and biodiversity of the Antarctic continent, including krill conservation, in the Southern Ocean.

Assn. of Fish and Wildlife Agencies, *1100 1st St. N.E., #825, 20001; (202) 838-3474. Fax, (202) 350-9869. Ron Regan, Executive Director. Press, (202) 838-3461.*
General email, info@fishwildlife.org
Web, www.fishwildlife.org, Twitter, @fishwildlife and Facebook, www.facebook.com/FishWildlifeAgencies

Membership: state, provincial, and territorial fish and wildlife management agencies in the United States, Canada, and Mexico. Encourages balanced, research-based fish and wildlife resource management. Monitors legislation and regulations.

Defenders of Wildlife, *1130 17th St. N.W., 20036; (202) 682-9400. Fax, (202) 682-1331. Jamie Rappaport Clark, President. Toll-free, (800) 385-9712.*
General email, memberservices@defenders.org
Web, www.defenders.org and Twitter, @Defenders

Advocacy group that works to protect wild animals, marine life, and plant life in their natural communities. Interests include endangered species and biodiversity. Monitors legislation and regulations.

Ducks Unlimited, *Governmental Affairs, 444 N. Capital St. N.W., 20001; (202) 347-1530. Roger Hoyt, President; Dan Wrinn, Director of Public Policy.*
Web, www.ducks.org

Promotes waterfowl and other wildlife conservation through activities aimed at developing and restoring natural nesting and migration habitats. (Headquarters in Memphis, Tenn.)

Humane Society of the United States, *1255 23rd St. N.W., #450, 20037; (202) 452-1100. Fax, (202) 778-6132. Kitty Block, President (Acting). Toll-free, (866) 720-2676.*
Web, www.humanesociety.org, Twitter, @HumaneSociety and Facebook, www.facebook.com/humanesociety

Works for the humane treatment and protection of animals. Interests include protecting endangered wildlife and marine mammals and their habitats and ending inhumane or cruel conditions in zoos.

Jane Goodall Institute, *1595 Spring Hill Rd., #550, Vienna, VA 22182; (703) 682-9220. Fax, (703) 682-9312. Carlos Drews, Chief Operating Officer.*
Web, www.janegoodall.org

Seeks to increase primate habitat conservation, expand noninvasive primate research, and promote activities that ensure the well-being of primates. (Affiliated with Jane Goodall Institutes in Canada, Europe, Asia, and Africa.)

National Audubon Society, *Public Policy, 1200 18th St. N.W., #500, 20036; (202) 861-2242. Teresa Christopher, Vice President for Conservation and Operations.*
General email, audubonaction@audubon.org
Web, www.audubon.org and Twitter, @audobonsociety

Citizens' interest group that promotes environmental conservation and education, focusing on birds and their habitats. Provides information on bird science, water resources, public lands, rangelands, forests, parks, wildlife conservation, and the National Wildlife Refuge System. Operates state offices, local chapters, and nature centers nationwide. (Headquarters in New York.)

National Fish and Wildlife Foundation, *1133 15th St. N.W., #1100, 20005; (202) 857-0166. Fax, (202) 857-0162. Jeff Trandahl, Executive Director.*
General email, info@nfwf.org
Web, www.nfwf.org, Twitter, @NFWFnews and Facebook, www.facebook.com/FishandWildlife

Forges partnerships between the public and private sectors in support of national and international conservation activities that identify and root out causes of environmental problems that affect fish, wildlife, and plants.

National Wildlife Federation, *11100 Wildlife Center Dr., Reston, VA 20190-5362 (mailing address: P.O. Box 1583, Merrifield, VA 22116-1583); (703) 438-6000. Fax, (703) 438-3570. Collin O'Mara, President. Information, (800) 822-9919. Press, (202) 797-6634.*
General email, info@nwf.org
Web, www.nwf.org, Twitter, @NWF and Facebook, www.facebook.com/NationalWildlife and YouTube, www.youtube.com/user/NationalWildlife
Blog, https://blog.nwf.org/

Promotes conservation of natural resources; provides information on the environment and resource management; takes legal action on environmental issues.

National Wildlife Refuge Assn., *1001 Connecticut Ave. N.W., #905, 20036; (202) 417-3803. Geoffrey Haskett, President; Caroline Brouwer, Government Affairs.*
General email, nwra@refugeassociation.org
Web, www.refugeassociation.org, Twitter, @WildRefuge and Facebook, www.facebook.com/RefugeAssociation

Works to improve management and protection of the National Wildlife Refuge System by providing information to administrators, Congress, and the public. Advocates adequate funding and improved policy guidance for the Refuge System; assists individual refuges with particular needs.

Ocean Conservancy, *1300 19th St. N.W., 8th Floor, 20036; (202) 429-5609. Fax, (202) 872-0619. Janis Jones, President. Toll-free, (800) 519-1541.*
General email, membership@oceanconservancy.org
Web, www.oceanconservancy.org, Twitter, @OurOcean and Facebook, www.facebook.com/oceanconservancy

Works to conserve the diversity and abundance of life in the oceans and coastal areas, to prevent the overexploitation of living marine resources and the degradation of marine ecosystems, and to restore depleted marine wildlife populations and their ecosystems.

Wildlife Habitat Council, *8737 Colesville Rd., #800, Silver Spring, MD 20910; (301) 588-8994. Fax, (301) 588-4629. Margaret O'Gorman, President, (301) 588-4219.*
General email, whc@wildlifehc.org
Web, www.wildlifehc.org and Twitter, @WildlifeHC

Membership: corporations, conservation groups, local governments, and academic institutions. Seeks to increase the quality and amount of wildlife habitat on corporate, private, and public lands. Builds partnerships between corporations and conservation groups to find solutions that balance economic growth with a healthy, biodiverse, and sustainable environment. Provides technical assistance and educational programs; fosters collaboration among members.

The Wildlife Society, *425 Barlow Pl., #200, Bethesda, MD 20814-2144; (301) 897-9770. Fax, (301) 530-2471. Ed Thompson, Chief Executive Officer.*
General email, tws@wildlife.org
Web, www.wildlife.org and Twitter, @wildlifesociety

Membership: wildlife biologists and resource management specialists. Provides information on management techniques, sponsors conferences, maintains list of job opportunities for members.

World Wildlife Fund (WWF), *1250 24th St. N.W., 20037-1193 (mailing address: P.O. Box 97180, Washington, DC 20090-7180); (202) 293-4800. Fax, (202) 293-9211. Carter S. Roberts, President.*
General email, membership@wwfus.org
Web, www.worldwildlife.org and Twitter, @World_Wildlife

International conservation organization that supports and conducts scientific research and conservation projects to promote biological diversity and to save endangered species and their habitats. Awards grants for habitat protection.

POLLUTION AND TOXINS

General

▶AGENCIES

Army Corps of Engineers *(Defense Dept.), 441 G St. N.W., #3K05, 20314-1000; (202) 761-0001. Fax, (202)*

761-4463. Lt. Gen. Todd T. Semonite (USA), Chief of Engineers. Press, (202) 761-0011.
General email, hq-publicaffairs@usace.army.mil
Web, www.usace.army.mil and Twitter, @USACEHQ

Cleans sites contaminated with hazardous, toxic, or radioactive waste and material.

Environment and Natural Resources Division *(Justice Dept.), Environmental Defense (EDS), 601 D St. N.W., #8000, 20004 (mailing address: P.O. Box 7611, Washington, DC 20044); (202) 514-2701. Fax, (202) 616-2426. Letitia J. Grishaw, Chief.*
Web, www.justice.gov/enrd/environmental-crimes-section

Conducts litigation on air, water, noise, pesticides, solid waste, toxic substances, Superfund, and wetlands in cooperation with the Environmental Protection Agency; represents the EPA in suits involving judicial review of EPA actions; represents the U.S. Army Corps of Engineers in cases involving dredge-and-fill activity in navigable waters and adjacent wetlands; represents the Coast Guard in oil and hazardous spill cases; defends all federal agencies in environmental litigation.

Environment and Natural Resources Division *(Justice Dept.), Environmental Enforcement (EES), 601 D St. N.W., #2121, 20004 (mailing address: P.O. Box 7611, Ben Franklin Station, Washington, DC 20044-7611); (202) 514-2701. Fax, (202) 514-0097. Thomas A. Mariani, Chief.*
Web, www.justice.gov/enrd/environmental-enforcement-section

Conducts civil enforcement actions on behalf of the United States for all environmental protection statutes, including air, water, pesticides, hazardous waste, wetland matters investigated by the Environmental Protection Agency, and other civil environmental enforcement.

Environmental Protection Agency (EPA), *1200 Pennsylvania Ave. N.W., #3000, MC 1101A, 20460; (202) 564-4700. Fax, (202) 501-1450. Andrew Wheeler, Administrator (Acting); Andrew R. Wheeler, Deputy Administrator. EPA switchboard, (202) 272-0167. Press, (202) 564-4355. TTY, (800) 877-8339.*
Web, www.epa.gov

Administers federal environmental policies, research, and regulations; provides information on environmental subjects, including water pollution, pollution prevention, hazardous and solid waste disposal, air and noise pollution, pesticides and toxic substances, and radiation.

Environmental Protection Agency (EPA), *Chemical Safety and Pollution Prevention (OCSPP), 1200 Pennsylvania Ave. N.W., #4146, MC 7101M, 20460; (202) 564-2910. Fax, (202) 564-0801. Vacant, Assistant Administrator; Charlotte Bertrand, Principal Deputy Assistant Administrator (Acting).*
Web, www.epa.gov/aboutepa/about-office-chemical-safety-and-pollution-prevention-ocspp

Studies and makes recommendations for regulating chemical substances under the Toxic Substances Control Act. Compiles list of chemical substances subject to the act.

Environmental Protection Agency (EPA), *Chemical Safety and Pollution Prevention (OCSPP), Pollution Prevention and Toxics,* 1200 Pennsylvania Ave. N.W., #4146, MC 7401M, 20460; (202) 564-3810. Fax, (202) 564-0575. Jeffrey Morris, Director. Toxic substance hotline, (202) 554-1404.
Web, www.epa.gov/aboutepa/about-office-chemical-safety-and-pollution-prevention-ocspp

Manages programs on pollution prevention and new and existing chemicals in the marketplace such as asbestos, lead, mercury, formaldehyde, PFOAs, and PCBs. Programs include the High Production Volume Challenge Program, Sustainable Futures, the Green Chemistry Program, Green Suppliers Network, the High Production Volume Challenge Program, Design for the Environment, and the Chemical Right-to-Know Initiative. Selects and implements control measures for new and existing chemicals that present a risk to human health and the environment. Oversees and manages regulatory evaluation and decision-making processes. Evaluates alternative remedial control measures under the Toxic Substances Control Act and makes recommendations concerning the existence of unreasonable risk from exposure to chemicals, including pesticides and fungicides. Develops generic and chemical-specific rules for new chemicals. Operates the toxic substance hotline.

Environmental Protection Agency (EPA), *Children's Health Protection (OCHP),* 1301 Constitution Ave., #1144, MC 1107T, 20460; (202) 564-2188. Fax, (202) 564-2733. Dr. Ruth A. Etzel, Director.
Web, www2.epa.gov/aboutepa/about-office-childrens-health-protection-ochp and www.epa.gov/children

Supports and facilitates the EPA's efforts to protect children's health from environmental risks through safe chemicals management. Provides leadership on interagency Healthy Homes Work Group and Healthy School Environments Initiative. Offers grants through the Office of Children's Health Protection and Environmental Education (OCHPEE).

Environmental Protection Agency (EPA), *Enforcement and Compliance Assurance (OECA),* 1200 Pennsylvania Ave. N.W., #3204, MC 2201A, 20460; (202) 564-2440. Fax, (202) 501-3842. Susan Bodine, Assistant Administrator.
Web, www.epa.gov/aboutepa/about-office-enforcement-and-compliance-assurance-oeca

Enforces laws that protect public health and the environment from hazardous materials, pesticides, and toxic substances. Implements the Clean Air Act, Clean Water Act, Comprehensive Environmental Response, Compensation and Liability Act, Emergency Planning and Community Right-to-Know Act, Federal Insecticide, Fungicide, and Rodenticide Act, Marine Protection, Research, and Sanctuaries Act, National Environmental Policy Act, Oil Pollution Act, Resource Conservation and Recovery Act, Safe Drinking Water Act, and Toxic Substances Control Act.

Environmental Protection Agency (EPA), *Enforcement and Compliance Assurance (OECA), Environmental Justice,* 1200 Pennsylvania Ave. N.W., #2201A, 20460;

(202) 564-2515. Fax, (202) 501-0936. Matthew Tejada, Director. Hotline, (800) 962-6215.
Web, www.epa.gov/aboutepa/about-office-enforcement-and-compliance-assurance-oeca#oej

Works to protect human health and the environment in communities overburdened with environmental pollution by implementing justice programs, policies, and activities.

Environmental Protection Agency (EPA), *Land and Emergency Management (OLEM), Federal Facilities Restoration and Reuse,* 1 Potomac Yard, 2777 S. Crystal Dr., Arlington, VA 22202 (mailing address: 1200 Pennsylvania Ave. N.W., #5106R, Washington, DC 20460); (202) 564-2307. Paul Leonard, Director (Acting).
Web, www.epa.gov/fedfac

Works with the Defense Dept., Energy Dept., and other federal offices for more effective and less costly cleanup and reuse of federal facilities.

Environmental Protection Agency (EPA), *Land and Emergency Management (OLEM), Resource Conservation and Recovery,* 1 Potomac Yard, 2777 S. Crystal Dr., Arlington, VA 22202 (mailing address: 1200 Pennsylvania Ave. N.W., #5301P, Washington, DC 20460); (703) 308-8895. Fax, (703) 308-0513. Barnes Johnson, Director.
Web, www.epa.gov/aboutepa/about-office-land-and-emergency-management#orcr

Protects human health and the environment by ensuring responsible national management of hazardous and nonhazardous waste. Administers the Resource Conservation and Recovery Act.

Environmental Protection Agency (EPA), *Research and Development (ORD),* 1200 Pennsylvania Ave. N.W., #41222, MC 8101R, 20460; (202) 564-6620. Fax, (202) 565-2430. Jennifer Orme-Zavaleta, Principal Deputy Assistant Administrator.
Web, www2.epa.gov/aboutepa/about-office-research-and-development-ord

Develops scientific data and methods to support EPA standards and regulations. Conducts exposure and risk assessments. Researches applied and long-term technologies to reduce risks from pollution.

▶**CONGRESS**

For a listing of relevant congressional committees and subcommittees, please see pages 283–284 or the Appendix.

▶**NONGOVERNMENTAL**

The Brookings Institution, *Climate and Energy Economics Project,* 1775 Massachusetts Ave. N.W., 20036; (202) 797-6000. Warwick McKibbin, Co-Director; Pete Wilcoxen, Co-Director. Press, (202) 797-6105.
Web, www.brookings.edu/about/projects/climate-energy-economics

Promotes economically efficient approaches to mitigating human impacts on climate change, including cap-and-trade.

National Research Council (NRC), *Environmental Studies and Toxicology Board,* Keck Center, 500 5th St. N.W., 20001; (202) 334-3591. Clifford S. Duke, Director; William H. Farland, Chair.
General email, best@nas.edu

Web, http://dels.nas.edu/best

Conducts research on environmental pollution problems affecting human health, human impacts on the environment, and the assessment and management of related risks to human health and the environment. Seeks to improve environmental decision making and public understanding of environmental issues.

Physicians for Social Responsibility (PSR), 1111 14th St. N.W., #700, 20005; (202) 667-4260. Fax, (202) 667-4201. Jeff Carter, Executive Director.
General email, psrnatl@psr.org

Web, www.psr.org and Twitter, @psrenvironment

Membership: doctors, nurses, health scientists, and concerned citizens. Works to protect the public and environment from toxic chemicals. Conducts public education programs, monitors policy, and serves as a liaison with other concerned groups.

Air Pollution

▶AGENCIES

Environmental Protection Agency (EPA), *Air and Radiation (OAR),* 1200 Pennsylvania Ave. N.W., #5426, MC 6101A, 20460; (202) 564-7404. Fax, (202) 564-1408. Bill Wehrum, Assistant Administrator; Elizabeth Shaw, Principal Deputy Assistant Administrator.
Web, www.epa.gov/aboutepa/about-office-air-and-radiation-oar

Develops national programs, policies, and regulations for controlling air pollution and radiation exposure. Administers air quality standards and planning programs of the Clean Air Act Amendment of 1990. Operates the Air and Radiation Docket and Information Center. Supervises the Office of Air Quality Planning and Standards in Durham, N.C., which develops air quality standards and provides information on air pollution control issues, including industrial air pollution. Administers the Air Pollution Technical Information Center in Research Triangle Park, N.C., which collects and provides technical literature on air pollution.

Environmental Protection Agency (EPA), *Air and Radiation (OAR), Atmospheric Programs,* 1200 Pennsylvania Ave. N.W., #5426, MC 6201A, 20460; (202) 343-9140. Fax, (202) 343-2210. Sarah W. Dunham, Director.
Web, www.epa.gov/aboutepa/about-office-air-and-radiation-oar#oap

Responsible for acid rain, ozone layer protection, climate change, and regional air quality programs. Examines strategies for preventing atmospheric pollution and mitigating climate change. Administers public-private partnerships, such as ENERGY STAR.

Environmental Protection Agency (EPA), *Air and Radiation (OAR), Atmospheric Programs, Climate Change Division,* 1200 Pennsylvania Ave. N.W., #5426, MC 6207A, 20460; (202) 343-9876. Fax, (202) 343-2342. Paul M. Gunning, Director.
General email, hargrove.anne@epa.gov

Web, www.epa.gov/aboutepa/about-office-air-and-radiation-oar#oap

Implements voluntary programs to reduce non–carbon dioxide emissions.

Environmental Protection Agency (EPA), *Air and Radiation (OAR), Transportation and Air Quality,* 1200 Pennsylvania Ave. N.W., #5426, MC 6401A, 20460; (202) 564-1682. Fax, (202) 564-1408. Christopher Grundler, Director.
General email, otaq@epa.gov

Web, www3.epa.gov/otaq and www.epa.gov/aboutepa/about-office-air-and-radiation-oar#otaq and NVFEL, www3.epa.gov/nvfel

Promotes reduction of air pollution and greenhouse gas emissions from automobiles, trucks, buses, farm and construction equipment, lawn and garden equipment, marine engines, aircraft, and locomotives. Establishes national air quality standards for on-road and nonroad mobiles and develops fuel efficiency programs. Supervises the National Vehicle and Fuel Emissions Laboratory (NVFEL) in Ann Arbor, Mich., which provides emissions testing services to aid the development of certifications, enforcement actions, test procedures, and rulemaking.

Federal Aviation Administration (FAA) *(Transportation Dept.), Policy, International Affairs, and Environment (APL), Environment and Energy Research and Development,* 800 Independence Ave. S.W., #900W, 20591; (202) 267-3576. Fax, (202) 267-5594. Kevin Welsh, Executive Director.
Web, www.faa.gov/about/office_org/headquarters_offices/apl/research

Develops government standards for aircraft noise and emissions.

▶CONGRESS

For a listing of relevant congressional committees and subcommittees, please see pages 283–284 or the Appendix.

▶NONGOVERNMENTAL

Alliance for Responsible Atmospheric Policy, 2111 Wilson Blvd., 8th Floor, Arlington, VA 22201; (703) 243-0344. Fax, (703) 243-2874. Kevin Fay, Executive Director.
General email, fay@alliancepolicy.org

Web, www.alliancepolicy.org and Twitter, @Atmospolicy

Coalition of users and producers of chlorofluorocarbons (CFCs). Seeks further study of the stratospheric ozone depletion theory. Coordinates industry participation in the development of economically and environmentally beneficial international and domestic atmospheric policies.

Center for Auto Safety, *1825 Connecticut Ave. N.W., #330, 20009-5708; (202) 328-7700. Fax, (202) 387-0140. Jason K. Levine, Director.*
General email, contact@autosafety.org

Web, www.autosafety.org and Twitter, @Ctr4AutoSafety

Public interest organization that conducts research on air pollution caused by auto emissions; monitors fuel economy regulations.

Center for Clean Air Policy, *750 1st St. N.E., #1025, 20002; (202) 408-9260. Fax, (202) 408-8896. Allison Bender-Corbett, Executive Director.*
General email, general@ccap.org or tassistant@ccap.org

Web, http://ccap.org and Twitter, @CleanAirPolicy

Membership: international policymakers, climate negotiators, corporations, environmentalists, and academicians. Analyzes economic and environmental effects of air pollution and related environmental problems. Serves as a liaison among government, corporate, community, and environmental groups.

Climate Institute, *1201 New York Ave. N.W., #410, 20005; (202) 552-0163. John C. Topping, President.*
General email, info@climate.org

Web, http://climate.org and Twitter, @Climate_Inst

Educates the public and policymakers on climate change, the greenhouse effect, global warming, and the depletion of the ozone layer. Assesses climate change risks and develops strategies on mitigating climate change in developing countries and in North America.

The Climate Reality Project, *750 9th St. N.W., #520, 20001; (202) 567-6800. Fax, (202) 628-1445. Ken Berlin, President.*
General email, info@climatereality.com

Web, www.climaterealityproject.org and Twitter, @ClimateReality

Aims to reduce carbon emissions, supports taxing oil and coal companies that emit large amounts of carbon, and educates the public on climate change and its relation to carbon pollution.

Environmental Defense Fund, *Washington Office, 1875 Connecticut Ave. N.W., #600, 20009-5728; (202) 387-3500. Fax, (202) 234-6049. Fred Krupp, President. Information, (800) 684-3322.*
Web, www.edf.org/offices/washington-dc and Twitter, @EnvDefenseFund

Citizen interest group staffed by lawyers, economists, and scientists. Conducts research and provides information on pollution prevention, environmental health, and the Clean Air Act. (Headquarters in New York.)

Manufacturers of Emission Controls Assn., *2200 Wilson Blvd., #310, Arlington, VA 22201; (202) 296-4797. Rasto Brezny, Executive Director.*
General email, asantos@meca.org

Web, www.meca.org and Twitter, @MECAforCleanAir

Membership: manufacturers of motor vehicle emission control equipment. Provides information on emission technology and industry capabilities.

National Assn. of Clean Air Agencies (NACAA), *444 N. Capitol St. N.W., #307, 20001; (202) 624-7864. Fax, (202) 624-7863. Miles Keogh, Executive Director.*
General email, 4cleanair@4cleanair.org

Web, www.4cleanair.org

Membership: air pollution control agencies nationwide. Seeks to improve effective management of air resources by encouraging the exchange of information among air pollution control officials. Monitors federal regulations; publishes reports and analyses; develops model rules for states and localities.

National Research Council (NRC), *Atmospheric Sciences and Climate Board, Keck Center, 500 5th St. N.W., #602, 20001; (202) 334-3512. Fax, (202) 334-3825. Amanda Staudt, Director; A. R. (Ravi) Ravishankara, Chair.*
General email, basc@nas.edu

Web, www.dels.nas.edu/basc

Supports research on climate change, air pollution, and severe weather in order to address environmental policies, human health, emergency management, energy choices, manufacturing decisions, construction codes, and agricultural methods.

Hazardous Materials

▶AGENCIES

Agency for Toxic Substances and Disease Registry (ATSDR) *(Health and Human Services Dept.), Washington Office, 1200 Pennsylvania Ave. N.W., MC 5202P, 20460; Steve A. Jones, Regional Director, (703) 603-8729, (800) 232-4436.*
Web, www.atsdr.cdc.gov/dro/hq.html, Twitter, @CDCEnvironment and Facebook, www.facebook.com/ToxZone

Works with federal, state, and local agencies to prevent, minimize, or eliminate adverse effects of exposure to toxic substances at spill and waste disposal sites. Maintains a registry of persons exposed to hazardous substances and of diseases and illnesses resulting from exposure to hazardous or toxic substances. Conducts public health assessments, health studies, surveillance activities, and health education training. Maintains inventory of hazardous substances and registry of sites closed or restricted because of contamination by hazardous material. (Headquarters in Atlanta, Ga.)

Defense Dept. (DoD), *Sustainment, 3400 Defense Pentagon, #1E518, 20301-3500; (703) 697-1369. Fax, (703) 693-0555. Robert H. McMahon, Assistant Secretary.*
Web, www.acq.osd.mil/eie

Oversees and provides guidance on logistics, maintenance, material readiness, strategic mobility, and sustainment for all Defense Dept. domestic and overseas installations.

Energy Dept. (DOE), *Legacy Management, 1000 Independence Ave. S.W., #6E-041, 20585; (202) 586-7550. Fax, (202) 586-8403. Carmelo Melendez, Director. General email, LM@hq.doe.gov*

Web, www.energy.gov/lm/office-legacy-management

Mitigates community impacts resulting from the cleanup of legacy waste, including radioactive and chemical waste, environmental contamination, and hazardous material. Oversees the legacy waste from the Cold War and World War II; makes legacy records and information accesible to the public.

Environment and Natural Resources Division *(Justice Dept.), Environmental Enforcement (EES), 601 D St. N.W., #2121, 20004 (mailing address: P.O. Box 7611, Ben Franklin Station, Washington, DC 20044-7611); (202) 514-2701. Fax, (202) 514-0097. Thomas A. Mariani, Chief.* Web, www.justice.gov/enrd/environmental-enforcement-section

Represents the United States in civil cases under environmental laws that involve the handling, storage, treatment, transportation, and disposal of hazardous waste. Recovers federal money spent to clean up hazardous waste sites or sues defendants to clean up sites under Superfund.

Environmental Protection Agency (EPA), *Chemical Safety and Pollution Prevention (OCSPP), Pollution Prevention and Toxics, 1200 Pennsylvania Ave. N.W., #4146, MC 7401M, 20460; (202) 564-3810. Fax, (202) 564-0575. Jeffrey Morris, Director. Toxic substance hotline, (202) 554-1404.* Web, www.epa.gov/aboutepa/about-office-chemical-safety-and-pollution-prevention-ocspp

Assesses the health and environmental hazards of existing chemical substances and mixtures; collects information on chemical use, exposure, and effects; maintains inventory of existing chemical substances; reviews new chemicals and regulates the manufacture, distribution, use, and disposal of harmful chemicals. Implements the Toxic Substances Control Act and the Pollution Prevention Act. Selects and implements control measures for new and existing chemicals that present a risk to human health and the environment. Oversees and manages regulatory evaluation and decision-making processes. Evaluates alternative remedial control measures under the Toxic Substances Control Act and makes recommendations concerning the existence of unreasonable risk from exposure to chemicals, including pesticides and fungicides. Develops generic and chemical-specific rules for new chemicals. Operates the toxic substance hotline.

Environmental Protection Agency (EPA), *Emergency Management, 1200 Pennsylvania Ave. N.W., MC 5104A, 20460; (202) 564-8600. Reggie Cheatham, Director, (202) 564-8003. Toll-free call center, (800) 424-8802.* Web, www.epa.gov/emergency-response

Develops and administers chemical emergency preparedness and prevention programs; reviews effectiveness of programs; prepares community right-to-know regulations. Provides guidance materials, technical assistance, and training. Implements the preparedness and community right-to-know provisions of the Superfund Amendments and Reauthorization Act of 1986.

Environmental Protection Agency (EPA), *Enforcement and Compliance Assurance (OECA), Site Remediation Enforcement, 1200 Pennsylvania Ave. N.W., #2251A, 20460; (202) 564-5110. Fax, (202) 564-0094. Cyndy Mackey, Director.* Web, www.epa.gov/aboutepa/about-office-enforcement-and-compliance-assurance-oeca#osre

Requires those responsible for hazardous waste sites to clean up or reimburse the EPA for cleanup. Enforces national hazardous waste cleanup programs, including Superfund programs, Resource Conservation and Recovery Act, Oil Pollution Act, and underground storage tank systems.

Environmental Protection Agency (EPA), *Land and Emergency Management (OLEM), 1200 Pennsylvania Ave. N.W., MC 5101T, 20460; (202) 566-0200. Fax, (202) 566-0207. Barry Breen, Assistant Administrator (Acting). National Response Center, (800) 424-8802. Superfund information hotline, (800) 424-9346. TTY, (202) 272-0165.* Web, www2.epa.gov/aboutepa/about-office-land-and-emergency-management-olem

Administers and enforces the Superfund act and manages the handling, cleanup, and disposal of hazardous wastes.

Environmental Protection Agency (EPA), *Land and Emergency Management (OLEM), Brownfields and Land Revitalization, 1300 Pennsylvania Ave. N.W., #5105T, 20460; (202) 566-2777. David Lloyd, Director.* Web, www.epa.gov/land-revitalization and www.epa.gov/brownfields

Provides grants and technical assistance to communities, states, tribes, and other stakeholders needing resources to prevent, assess, safely clean up, and sustainably reuse brownfields and formerly contaminated properties.

Environmental Protection Agency (EPA), *Land and Emergency Management (OLEM), Superfund Remediation and Technology Innovation, 1 Potomac Yard, 2777 Crystal Dr., Arlington, VA 22202 (mailing address: 1200 Pennsylvania Ave. N.W., #5201P, Washington, DC 20460); (703) 603-8960. Jim Woolford, Director.* Web, www.epa.gov/superfund and www.epa.gov/aboutepa/about-office-land-and-emergency-management#osrt

Responsible for Superfund and contaminated land cleanup; responds to environmental emergencies, oil spills, and natural disasters.

Environmental Protection Agency (EPA), *Land and Emergency Management (OLEM), Underground Storage Tanks, 1300 Pennsylvania Ave N.W., 7th Floor, 20460 (mailing address: 1200 Pennsylvania Ave. N.W., #5401R, Washington, DC 20460); (202) 564-2564. Carolyn Hoskinson, Director.* Web, www.epa.gov/ust and www.epa.gov/aboutepa/about-office-land-and-emergency-management#oust

Interior Department

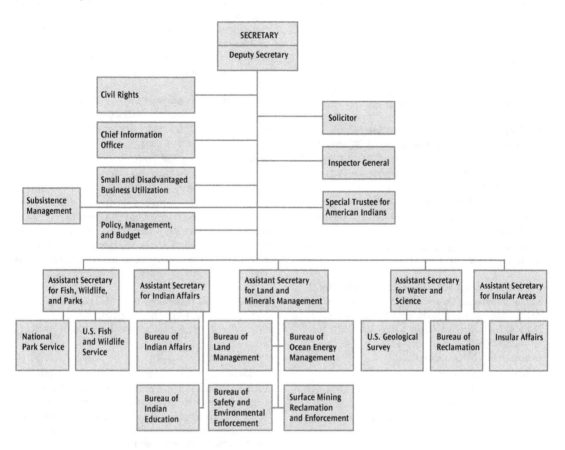

Carries out regulations for underground storage tank systems storing petroleum and certain hazardous substances to prevent groundwater contamination.

Federal Aviation Administration (FAA) *(Transportation Dept.), Security and Hazardous Materials Safety (ASH),* 800 Independence Ave. S.W., #300E, 20591; (202) 267-7211. Fax, (202) 267-8496. Claudio Manno, Associate Administrator.
Web, www.faa.gov/about/office_org/headquarters_offices/ash

Seeks to ensure air transportation safety by preventing hazardous materials accidents aboard aircraft and protecting FAA employees and facilities from criminal and terrorist acts.

Housing and Urban Development Dept. (HUD), *Lead Hazard Control and Healthy Homes,* 451 7th St. S.W., #8236, 20410; (202) 708-0310. Fax, (202) 708-0014. Matthew Ammon, Director, (202) 402-4337.
Web, www.hud.gov/program_offices/healthy_homes and *Twitter, @HUDHealthyHomes*

Advises HUD offices, other agencies, health authorities, and the housing industry on lead poisoning prevention. Develops regulations for lead-based paint; conducts research; makes grants to state and local governments for lead hazard reduction and inspection of housing.

Interior Dept. (DOI), *Natural Resource Damage Assessment and Restoration Program,* 1849 C St. N.W., MS 5538, 20240; (202) 208-4863. Stephen Glomb, Director.
Web, www.doi.gov/restoration

Works to restore natural resources that have been compromised as a result of oil spills or hazardous substances released into the environment.

Pipeline and Hazardous Materials Safety Administration *(Transportation Dept.),* 1200 New Jersey Ave. S.E., #E27-300, 20590; (202) 366-4433. Fax, (202) 366-3666. Howard (Skip) Elliott, Administrator. Hazardous Materials Information Center, (800) 467-4922. To report an incident, (800) 424-8802.
General email, phmsa.administrator@dot.gov
Web, www.phmsa.dot.gov and *Twitter, @PHMSA_DOT*

Oversees the safe and secure movement of hazardous materials to industry and consumers by all modes of transportation, including pipelines. Works to eliminate transportation-related deaths and injuries. Promotes transportation solutions to protect communities and the environment.

Pipeline and Hazardous Materials Safety Administration *(Transportation Dept.), Hazardous Materials Safety,* 1200 New Jersey Ave. S.E., #E21-317,

20590; (202) 366-4488. Fax, (202) 366-5713.
William S. (Bill) Schoonover, Associate Administrator.
Hazardous Materials Information Center, (800) 467-4922.
General email, phmsa.hmhazmatsafety@dot.gov
Web, https://cms.phmsa.dot.gov/about-phmsa/offices/
office-hazardous-materials-safety

Designates substances as hazardous materials and regulates their transportation in interstate commerce; coordinates international standards regulations.

Pipeline and Hazardous Materials Safety Administration (Transportation Dept.), Pipeline Safety, 1200 New Jersey Ave. S.E., E24-455, 20590; (202) 366-4595. Fax, (202) 366-4566. Alan K. Mayberry, Associate Administrator.
General email, phmsa.pipelinesafety@dot.gov
Web, www.phmsa.dot.gov/about-phmsa/offices/office-pipeline-safety

Issues and enforces federal regulations for hazardous liquids pipeline safety.

U.S. Coast Guard (USCG) (Homeland Security Dept.), National Response Center, 2100 2nd St. S.W., #2111B, 20593-0001; (202) 372-2097. Fax, (202) 267-1322. Dana S. Tulis, Director. Hotline, (800) 424-8802. Local, (202) 267-2675. TTY, (202) 267-4477.
General email, NRC@uscg.mil
Web, www.nrc.uscg.mil

Maintains 24-hour hotline for reporting oil, biological, radiological, and chemical discharges in the environment. Notifies appropriate federal officials to reduce the effects of accidents.

►CONGRESS

For a listing of relevant congressional committees and subcommittees, please see pages 283–284 or the Appendix.

►NONGOVERNMENTAL

Alliance of Hazardous Materials Professionals, 1300 Piccard Dr. # LL14, Rockville, MD 20850; (301) 329-6850. Fax, (301) 990-9771. Charles W. L. Deale, Executive Director; Carl Heinlein, Government Affairs - AHMP Liaison.
General email, info@ahmpnet.org
Web, www.ahmpnet.org and Twitter, @AHMPros

Membership: professionals who work with hazardous materials and environmental, health, and safety issues. Offers professional development and networking opportunities to members. Members must be certified by the Institute of Hazardous Materials Management (IHMM).

Chlorine Institute Inc., 1300 Wilson Blvd., #525, Arlington, VA 22209; (703) 894-4140. Fax, (703) 894-4130. Frank Reiner, President, (703) 894-4116.
General email, info@cl2.com
Web, www.chlorineinstitute.org and
Twitter, @TheChlorineINST

Safety, health, and environmental protection center of the chlor-alkali (chlorine, caustic soda, caustic potash, and hydrogen chloride) industry. Interests include employee health and safety, resource conservation and pollution abatement, control of chlorine emergencies, product specifications, and public and community relations. Publishes technical pamphlets and drawings.

Dangerous Goods Advisory Council, 7501 Greenway Center Dr., #760, Greenbelt, MD 20770; (202) 289-4550. Fax, (202) 289-4074. Vaughn Arthur, President.
General email, info@dgac.org
Web, www.dgac.org and Twitter, @DGAC_HMAC

Membership: shippers, carriers, container manufacturers and conditioners, emergency response and spill cleanup companies, and trade associations. Promotes safety in the domestic and international transportation of hazardous materials. Provides information and educational services; sponsors conferences, workshops, and seminars. Advocates uniform hazardous materials regulations. Also known as the Hazardous Materials Advisory Council.

Environmental Technology Council, 1112 16th St. N.W., #420, 20036; (202) 783-0870. Fax, (202) 737-2038. David R. Case, Executive Director. Press, (202) 783-0870, ext. 202.
Web, www.etc.org

Membership: environmental service firms. Interests include the recycling, detoxification, and disposal of hazardous and industrial waste and cleanup of contaminated industrial sites; works to encourage permanent and technology-based solutions to environmental problems. Provides the public with information.

Institute of Hazardous Materials Management (IHMM), 9210 Corporate Blvd., Rockville, MD 20850; (301) 984-8969. Fax, (301) 984-1516. Eugene Gilbert, Executive Director.
General email, info@ihmm.org
Web, www.ihmm.org and Twitter, @TheIHMM

Seeks to educate professionals and the general public about proper handling of hazardous materials; issues certifications. Administers the Certified Hazardous Materials Manager program, the Certified Hazardous Materials Practitioner program, the Certified Dangerous Goods Professsional (CDGP), and the Certified Dangerous Goods Trainer (CDGT).

Rachel Carson Council Inc., 8600 Irvington Ave., Bethesda, MD 20817; (301) 214-2400. Robert Musil, President, (301) 493-4571.
General email, office@rachelcarsoncouncil.org
Web, www.rachelcarsoncouncil.org and
Twitter, @RachelCarsonDC

Acts as a clearinghouse for information on pesticides and alternatives to their use; maintains extensive data on toxicity and the effects of pesticides on humans, domestic animals, and wildlife. Library open to the public by appointment.

Radiation Protection

►AGENCIES

Environmental Protection Agency (EPA), *Air and Radiation (OAR),* 1200 Pennsylvania Ave. N.W., #5426, MC 6101A, 20460; (202) 564-7404. Fax, (202) 564-1408. Bill Wehrum, Assistant Administrator; Elizabeth Shaw, Principal Deputy Assistant Administrator.
Web, www.epa.gov/aboutepa/about-office-air-and-radiation-oar

Develops national programs, policies, and regulations for controlling air pollution and radiation exposure. Administers air quality standards and planning programs of the Clean Air Act Amendment of 1990. Operates the Air and Radiation Docket and Information Center. Supervises the Office of Air Quality Planning and Standards in Durham, N.C., which develops air quality standards and provides information on air pollution control issues, including industrial air pollution. Administers the Air Pollution Technical Information Center in Research Triangle Park, N.C., which collects and provides technical literature on air pollution.

Environmental Protection Agency (EPA), *Air and Radiation (OAR), Radiation and Indoor Air,* 1200 Pennsylvania Ave. N.W., #5426, MC 6608T, 20460; (202) 343-9320. Fax, (202) 564-1408. Jonathan Edwards, Director.
Web, www.epa.gov/aboutepa/about-office-air-and-radiation-oar#oria

Establishes standards to regulate the amount of radiation discharged into the environment from uranium mining and milling projects and other activities that result in radioactive emissions. Oversees the National Air and Radiation Environmental Laboratory in Montgomery, Ala.

Food and Drug Administration (FDA) *(Health and Human Services Dept.), Center for Devices and Radiological Health (CDRH),* White Oak Bldg. 66, 10903 New Hampshire Ave., Silver Spring, MD 20993; (301) 796-5900. Fax, (301) 847-8510. Jeffrey E. Shuren, Director.
General email, jeff.shuren@fda.hhs.gov
Web, www.fda.gov/medicaldevices and www.fda.gov/AboutFDA/CentersOffices/OfficeofMedicalProductsandTobacco/CDRH

Administers national programs to control exposure to radiation; establishes standards for emissions from consumer and medical products; conducts factory inspections; provides physicians and consumers with guidelines on radiation-emitting products. Conducts research, training, and educational programs.

►CONGRESS

For a listing of relevant congressional committees and subcommittees, please see pages 283–284 or the Appendix.

►NONGOVERNMENTAL

National Council on Radiation Protection and Measurements (NCRP), 7910 Woodmont Ave., #400, Bethesda, MD 20814-3095; (301) 657-2652. Fax, (301) 907-8768. Kathryn D. Held, President; Jerold T. Bushberg Jr., Senior Vice President.
General email, ncrp@ncrponline.org
Web, www.ncrponline.org and Twitter, @NCRP_Bethesda

Nonprofit organization chartered by Congress that collects and analyzes information and provides recommendations on radiation protection and measurement. Studies radiation emissions from household items and from office and medical equipment. Holds annual conference; publishes reports on radiation protection and measurement.

National Research Council (NRC), *Nuclear and Radiation Studies Board,* Keck Center, 500 5th St. N.W., 20001; (202) 334-3066. Fax, (202) 334-3077. Charles Ferguson, Chair; Ourania Kosti, Senior Program Officer.
General email, nrsb@nas.edu
Web, http://dels.nas.edu/nrsb

Oversees studies on safety, security, technical efficacy, and other policy and societal issues arising from the application of nuclear and radiation-based technologies, including generation, use, remediation, and disposition of nuclear materials and radioactive wastes.

Recycling and Solid Waste

►AGENCIES

Environmental Protection Agency (EPA), *Land and Emergency Management (OLEM), Resource Conservation and Recovery,* 1 Potomac Yard, 2777 S. Crystal Dr., Arlington, VA 22202 (mailing address: 1200 Pennsylvania Ave. N.W., #5301P, Washington, DC 20460); (703) 308-8895. Fax, (703) 308-0513. Barnes Johnson, Director.
Web, www.epa.gov/aboutepa/about-office-land-and-emergency-management#orcr

Through the Reduce, Reuse, Recycle program, provides information to communities about conserving energy and the natural environment, reducing waste, and recycling electronics and appliances.

►CONGRESS

For a listing of relevant congressional committees and subcommittees, please see pages 283–284 or the Appendix.

►NONGOVERNMENTAL

American Chemistry Council, 700 2nd St. N.E., 20002; (202) 249-7000. Fax, (202) 249-6100. Calvin M. (Cal) Dooley, President.
Web, www.americanchemistry.com,
Twitter, @AmChemistry and Facebook, www.facebook.com/AmericanChemistry

Membership: manufacturers of basic industrial chemicals. Seeks to increase plastics recycling; conducts research on disposal of plastic products; sponsors research on waste-handling methods, incineration, and degradation; supports programs that test alternative waste management technologies. Monitors legislation and regulations.

Assn. of State and Territorial Solid Waste Management Officials (ASTSWMO), *1101 17th St. N.W., #707, 20036; (202) 640-1060. Fax, (202) 331-3254. Dania Rodriguez, Executive Director.*
Web, www.astswmo.org and Twitter, @ASTSWMO

Membership: state and territorial solid waste management officials. Works with the Environmental Protection Agency to develop policy affecting waste, materials management, and remediation.

Energy Recovery Council, *2200 Wilson Blvd., #310, Arlington, VA 22201; (202) 467-6240. Edward (Ted) Michaels, President.*
General email, tmichaels@energyrecoverycouncil.org
Web, www.energyrecoverycouncil.org

Membership: companies that design, build, and operate resource recovery facilities. Promotes integrated solutions to municipal solid waste management issues. Encourages the use of waste-to-energy technology.

Environmental Technology Council, *1112 16th St. N.W., #420, 20036; (202) 783-0870. Fax, (202) 737-2038. David R. Case, Executive Director. Press, (202) 783-0870, ext. 202.*
Web, www.etc.org

Membership: environmental service firms. Interests include the recycling, detoxification, and disposal of hazardous and industrial waste and cleanup of contaminated industrial sites; works to encourage permanent and technology-based solutions to environmental problems. Provides the public with information.

EPS Industry Alliance, *1298 Cronson Blvd., #201, Crofton, MD 21114; (410) 451-8340. Fax, (410) 451-8343. Betsy Bowers, Executive Director. Toll-free, (800) 607-3772. General email, info@epsindustry.org*
Web, www.epsindustry.org

Membership: companies that recycle foam packaging material (expanded polystyrene). Coordinates national network of collection centers for postconsumer foam packaging products; helps to establish new collection centers.

Foodservice Packaging Institute (FPI), *7700 Leesburg Pike, #421, Falls Church, VA 22043; (703) 592-9889. Fax, (703) 592-9864. Lynn Dyer, President, (571) 255-4211. General email, jgoldman@fpi.org*
Web, www.fpi.org, Twitter, @FPIHQ and Facebook, www.facebook.com/FoodservicePackagingInstitute

Membership: manufacturers, suppliers, and distributors of disposable products used in food service, packaging, and consumer products. Promotes the use of disposables for commercial and home use.

Glass Packaging Institute, *1220 N. Fillmore St., #400, Arlington, VA 22201; (703) 684-6359. Fax, (703) 546-0588. Joseph Cattaneo, President (Acting). General email, info@gpi.org*
Web, www.gpi.org and Twitter, @ChooseGlass

Membership: manufacturers of glass containers and their suppliers. Promotes industry policies to protect the environment, conserve natural resources, and reduce energy consumption; conducts research; monitors legislation affecting the industry. Interests include glass recycling.

Institute for Local Self-Reliance, *1710 Connecticut Ave. N.W., 4th Floor, 20009; (202) 898-1610. Fax, (202) 898-1612. Neil N. Seldman, President, (202) 898-1610, ext. 5210.*
General email, info@ilsr.org
Web, www.ilsr.org, Twitter, @ilsr and Facebook, www.facebook.com/localselfreliance

Advocates the development of a materials policy at local, state, and regional levels to reduce per capita consumption of raw materials and to shift from dependence on fossil fuels to reliance on renewable resources.

Institute of Scrap Recycling Industries, Inc., *1250 H St. N.W., #400, 20005; (202) 662-8500. Fax, (202) 626-0900. Robin K. Wiener, President.*
General email, isri@isri.org
Web, www.isri.org, Twitter, @ISRI and Facebook, www.facebook.com/isri1987

Represents processors, brokers, and consumers of scrap and recyclable paper, glass, plastic, textiles, rubber, ferrous and nonferrous metals, and electronics.

National Waste and Recycling Assn., *1550 Crystal Dr., #804, Arlington, VA 22202; (202) 244-4700. Fax, (202) 966-4824. Darrel Smith, President, (202) 364-3730. Toll-free, (800) 424-2869. General email, info@wasterecycling.org*
Web, https://wasterecycling.org

Membership: organizations engaged in refuse collection, processing, and disposal. Provides information on solid and hazardous waste recycling and waste equipment, organics and composting, waste-based energy, and emerging technologies; sponsors workshops. A merger of Environmental Industry Assns. and its sub-associations, the National Solid Waste Management Assn. and the Waste Equipment Technology Assn.

PaintCare Inc., *901 New York Ave. N.W., 20001; (855) 724-6809. Fax, (855) 358-2020. Marjaneh Zarrehparvar, Executive Director, (202) 719-3683. Press, (415) 606-3211. General email, info@paintcare.org*
Web, www.paintcare.org

Assists paint manufacturers in planning programs to help recycle or dispose of unneeded paint. Organizes paint drop-off locations. Supports statewide paint stewardship laws.

Secondary Materials and Recycled Textiles Assn. (SMART), *3465 Box Hill Corporate Center Dr., Suite H, Abingdon, MD 21009; (443) 640-1050. Fax, (410) 569-3340. Jackie King, Executive Director, ext. 105. Press, (410) 420-2001. General email, smartinfo@kingmgmt.org*
Web, www.smartasn.org and Twitter, @SMARTTextile

Membership: organizations and individuals involved in producing, shipping, and distributing recycled textiles and other textile products. Sponsors educational programs; publishes newsletters. Monitors legislation and regulations.

Solid Waste Assn. of North America (SWANA), *1100 Wayne Ave., #650, Silver Spring, MD 20910-7219; (301) 585-2898. Fax, (301) 589-7068. David Biderman, Executive Director. Toll-free, (800) 467-9262.*
General email, membership@swana.org
Web, https://swana.org and Twitter, @SWANA

Membership: government and private industry officials who manage municipal solid waste programs. Interests include waste reduction, collection, recycling (including of electronics), combustion, and disposal. Conducts training and certification programs. Operates solid waste information clearinghouse. Monitors legislation and regulations.

U.S. Conference of Mayors, *Municipal Waste Management Assn., 1620 Eye St. N.W., 4th Floor, 20006; (202) 293-7330. Fax, (202) 429-2352. Judy Sheahan, Assistant Executive Director for Environmental Policy, (202) 861-6775.*
General email, info@usmayors.org
Web, www.usmayors.org/mwma

Membership: mayors of cities with populations of 30,000 or more, local governments, and private companies involved in planning and developing solid waste management programs, including pollution prevention, waste-to-energy, and recycling. Interests include Superfund, brownfields, air and water quality, and waste-to-energy technologies. Assists communities with financing, environmental assessments, and associated policy implementation.

Water Pollution

▶**AGENCIES**

Bureau of Safety and Environmental Enforcement (BSEE) *(Interior Dept.), 1849 C St. N.W., MS 5438, 20240-0001; (202) 208-3985. Scott A. Angelle, Director.*
General email, bseepublicaffairs@bsee.gov
Web, www.bsee.gov, Twitter, @BSEEgov and Facebook, www.facebook.com/BSEEgov and YouTube, www.youtube.com/user/bseegov

Responsible for inspections, enforcement, and safety of offshore oil and gas operations. Functions include the development and enforcement of safety and environmental regulations, research, inspections, offshore regulatory and compliance programs, oil spill response, and training of inspectors and industry professionals.

Bureau of Safety and Environmental Enforcement (BSEE) *(Interior Dept.), Environmental Compliance Division (ECD), 45600 Woodland Rd., Sterling, VA 20166; (703) 787-1567. David S. Fish (USCG, Ret.), Chief.*
General email, bseepublicaffairs@bsee.gov
Web, www.bsee.gov/resources-tools/compliance

Responsible for monitoring and improving industry's compliance with environmental standards, by reviewing

and enforcing permits, laws, and regulations during the Outer Continental Shelf (OCS) operations.

Bureau of Safety and Environmental Enforcement (BSEE) *(Interior Dept.), Offshore Regulatory Programs (OORP), 1849 C St. N.W., MS DM5438, 20240-0001; (202) 208-3985. Douglas Morris, Chief.*
General email, bseepublicaffairs@bsee.gov
Web, www.bsee.gov/what-we-do/offshore-regulatory-programs

Develops standards, regulations, and compliance programs governing Outer Continental Shelf oil, gas, and minerals exploration and operations. Purview includes safety management programs, safety and pollution prevention research, technology assessments, standards for inspections and enforcement policies, and accident investigation practices.

Bureau of Safety and Environmental Enforcement (BSEE) *(Interior Dept.), Oil Spill Preparedness Division (OSPD), 45600 Woodland Rd., Sterling, VA 20166; (703) 787-1569. Eric Miller, Chief (Acting).*
General email, bseepublicaffairs@bsee.gov
Web, www.bsee.gov/what-we-do/oil-spill-preparedness

Reviews oil spill response plans and executes team training and exercises, and inspects response equipment and resources.

Bureau of Safety and Environmental Enforcement (BSEE) *(Interior Dept.), Safety and Incident Investigations Division (SIID), 1849 C St. N.W., #5438, 20240; (202) 208-4005. Stacey Noem, National Program Manager.*
General email, bseepublicaffairs@bsee.gov
Web, www.bsee.gov/what-we-do/incident-investigations

Manages the National Investigations Program, which conducts investigations of major offshore incidents as outlined in the Outer Continental ShelfLands Act (OCSLA).

Environmental Protection Agency (EPA), *Land and Emergency Management (OLEM), Underground Storage Tanks, 1300 Pennsylvania Ave N.W., 7th Floor, 20460 (mailing address: 1200 Pennsylvania Ave. N.W., #5401R, Washington, DC 20460); (202) 564-2564. Carolyn Hoskinson, Director.*
Web, www.epa.gov/ust and www.epa.gov/aboutepa/about-office-land-and-emergency-management#oust

Carries out regulations for underground storage tank systems storing petroleum and certain hazardous substances to prevent groundwater contamination.

Environmental Protection Agency (EPA), *Water (OW), 1200 Pennsylvania Ave. N.W., MC 4101M, 20460; (202) 564-5700. David Ross, Assistant Administrator.*
Web, www.epa.gov/aboutepa/about-office-water

Implements the Clean Water Act and portions of the Ocean Dumping Ban Act, Marine Plastics Pollution Research and Control Act, London Dumping Convention, and the International Convention for the Prevention of Pollution from Ships.

Environmental Protection Agency (EPA), *Water (OW),*
Ground Water and Drinking Water, 1200 Pennsylvania
Ave. N.W., #2104, MC 4601M, 20460; (202) 564-3750.
Fax, (202) 564-3753. Peter C. Grevatt, Director, (202) 564-
8954. Toll-free hotline, (800) 426-4791.
General email, ogwdw.web@epa.gov

Web, www2.epa.gov/aboutepa/about-office-water#ground

Develops standards for the quality of drinking water
supply systems; regulates underground injection of waste
and protection of groundwater wellhead areas under the
Safe Drinking Water Act; provides information on public
water supply systems.

Environmental Protection Agency (EPA), *Water (OW),*
Science and Technology, 1200 Pennsylvania Ave. N.W.,
#5231, MC 4301M, 20460; (202) 566-0430. Fax, (202) 566-
0441. Deborah Nagle, Director (Acting), (202) 566-0430.
General email, ost.comments@epa.gov

Web, www2.epa.gov/aboutepa/about-office-water#science

Develops and coordinates water pollution control programs for the Environmental Protection Agency. Assists
state and regional agencies in establishing water quality
standards and planning local water resources management.
Develops guidelines for industrial and municipal wastewater discharge. Provides grants for water quality monitoring
and swimming advisories at recreational coastal and Great
Lakes beaches. Formulates shellfish protection policies and
issues fish advisories.

Environmental Protection Agency (EPA), *Water (OW),*
Wastewater Management, 1200 Pennsylvania Ave. N.W.,
#7116A, MC 4201M, 20460; (202) 564-0748. Fax, (202)
501-2238. Andrew Sawyers, Director.
Web, www2.epa.gov/aboutepa/about-office-
water#wastewater

Oversees the issuance of water permits. Responsible for
the Pretreatment Program regulating industrial discharges
to local sewage treatment. Oversees the State Revolving
Funds Program, which provides assistance for the construction of wastewater treatment plants. Implements programs for prevention of water pollution, including the
Clean Watersheds Needs Survey, National Pollutent Discharge Elimination System (NPDES), U.S.–Mexico Border
Water Infrastructure Grant Program, and WaterSense.

Environmental Protection Agency (EPA), *Water (OW),*
Wastewater Management, Sustainable Water
Infrastructure, 1200 Pennsylvania Ave. N.W., #7119A,
MC 4204M, 20460; (202) 564-5385. Fax, (202) 501-2346.
Raffael Stein, Director.
Web, www2.epa.gov/aboutepa/about-office-
water#wastewater and www.epa.gov/sustainable-water-
infrastructure

Directs programs to assist in the design and construction of municipal sewage systems. Develops programs to
ensure efficient operation and maintenance of municipal
wastewater treatment facilities.

National Drinking Water Advisory Council
(Environmental Protection Agency), 1200 Pennsylvania

Ave. N.W., #4100T, MC 4606M, 20460; (202) 564-4029.
Jennifer McClain, Deputy Director.
Web, www.epa.gov/ndwac

Membership: members of the general public, state and
local agencies, and private groups. Advises the EPA administrator on activities, functions, and policies relating to
implementation of the Safe Drinking Water Act.

**National Oceanic and Atmospheric Administration
(NOAA)** *(Commerce Dept.),* **Response and Restoration**
(ORR), 1305 East-West Hwy., 10th Floor, Bldg. 4, Silver
Spring, MD 20910; (202) 533-0391. Fax, (301) 713-4389.
David Westerholm, Director, (240) 533-0385.
General email, orr.webmaster@noaa.gov

Web, www.response.restoration.noaa.gov and
Twitter, @NOAACleanCoasts

Provides information on damage to marine ecosystems
caused by pollution and debris. Offers information on spill
trajectory projections and chemical hazard analyses.
Researches trends of toxic contamination on U.S. coastal
regions.

U.S. Coast Guard (USCG) *(Homeland Security Dept.),*
Marine Environmental Response Policy, 2703 Martin
Luther King Jr. Ave. S.E., CG-721, 20593; (202) 372-2234.
Capt. Ricardo B. Alonso, Chief.
Web, www.dco.uscg.mil/Our-Organization/Assistant-
Commandant-for-Response-Policy-CG-5R/Office-of-
Incident-Management-Preparedness-CG-5RI/Marine-
Envir

Oversees cleanup operations after spills of oil and other
hazardous substances in U.S. waters, on the Outer Continental Shelf, and in international waters. Reviews coastal
zone management and enforces international standards for
pollution prevention and response.

U.S. Coast Guard (USCG) *(Homeland Security Dept.),*
National Pollution Funds Center, 2703 Martin Luther
King Jr. Ave. S.E., MS 7605, 20593-7605; (202) 795-6003.
Fax, (202) 795-6900. William R. Grawe, Director.
Web, www.uscg.mil/npfc

Certifies pollution liability coverage for vessels and
companies involved in oil exploration and transportation
in U.S. waters and on the Outer Continental Shelf. Ensures
adequacy of funds to respond to oil spills and deters future
spills by managing the Oil Spill Liability Trust Fund.

U.S. Coast Guard (USCG) *(Homeland Security Dept.),*
National Response Center, 2100 2nd St. S.W., #2111B,
20593-0001; (202) 372-2097. Fax, (202) 267-1322.
Dana S. Tulis, Director. Hotline, (800) 424-8802. Local,
(202) 267-2675. TTY, (202) 267-4477.
General email, NRC@uscg.mil

Web, www.nrc.uscg.mil

Maintains 24-hour hotline for reporting oil, biological,
radiological, and chemical discharges in the environment.
Notifies appropriate federal officials to reduce the effects
of accidents.

▶CONGRESS

For a listing of relevant congressional committees and sub-committees, please see pages 283–284 or the Appendix.

▶NONGOVERNMENTAL

Assn. of Clean Water Administrators, *1634 Eye St. N.W., #750, 20006; (202) 756-0605. Fax, (202) 793-2600. Julia Anastasio, Executive Director.*
General email, memberservices@acwa-us.org
Web, www.acwa-us.org and Twitter, @cleanwaterACWA

Membership: state and interstate water quality regulators. Represents the states' concerns on implementation, funding, and reauthorization of the Clean Water Act. Monitors legislation and regulations.

Clean Water Action, *1444 Eye St. N.W., #400, 20005; (202) 895-0420. Fax, (202) 895-0438. Robert (Bob) Wendelgass, Chief Executive Officer.*
General email, cwa@cleanwater.org
Web, https://cleanwateraction.org and Twitter, @cleanh2oaction

Citizens' organization interested in clean, safe, and affordable water. Works to influence public policy through education, technical assistance, and grassroots organizing. Interests include toxins and pollution, drinking water, water conservation, sewage treatment, pesticides, mass burn incineration, bay and estuary protection, and consumer water issues. Monitors legislation and regulations.

Clean Water Network, *600 Pennsylvania Ave. S.E., #400, 20003; (303) 573-3871, ext. 395. Kristine Oblock, Coordinator.*
Web, www.clean-water-network.org and Twitter, @CleanWaterNet

Advocacy coalition of local and national groups that support clean waterways. Provides resources for organizers to protect waterways against human-caused pollution. (Affiliated with Environment America.)

National Assn. of Clean Water Agencies, *1130 Connecticut Ave., 20036; (202) 833-2672. Fax, (888) 267-9505. Adam Krantz, Chief Executive Officer, (202) 833-4651.*
General email, info@nacwa.org
Web, www.nacwa.org and Twitter, @NACWA

Represents public wastewater treatment works, public and private organizations, law firms representing public clean water agencies, and nonprofit or academic organizations. Interests include water quality and watershed management. Sponsors conferences. Monitors legislation and regulations.

Ocean Conservancy, *1300 19th St. N.W., 8th Floor, 20036; (202) 429-5609. Fax, (202) 872-0619. Janis Jones, President. Toll-free, (800) 519-1541.*
General email, membership@oceanconservancy.org
Web, www.oceanconservancy.org, Twitter, @OurOcean and Facebook, www.facebook.com/oceanconservancy

Works to protect the health of oceans and seas. Advocates policies that restrict discharge of pollutants harmful to marine ecosystems.

Water Environment Federation, *601 Wythe St., Alexandria, VA 22314-1994; (703) 684-2400. Fax, (703) 684-2492. Eileen O'Neill, Executive Director, (703) 684-2430. Toll-free, (800) 666-0206.*
General email, csc@wef.org
Web, www.wef.org and Twitter, @WEForg

Membership: civil and environmental engineers, wastewater treatment plant operators, scientists, government officials, and others concerned with water quality. Works to preserve and improve water quality worldwide. Provides the public with technical information and educational materials. Monitors legislation and regulations.

Water Research Foundation, *1199 N. Fairfax St., #900, Alexandria, VA 22314-1445; (571) 384-2100. Peter Grevatt, Chief Executive Officer, (571) 384-2094.*
General email, info@WaterRF.org
Web, www.waterrf.org, Twitter, @WaterResearch and Facebook, www.facebook.com/waterenvironmentRF

Conducts research and promotes technology to treat and recover materials from wastewater, stormwater, and seawater, including water, nutrients, energy, and biosolids. (Headquarters in Denver, Colo.)

RESOURCES MANAGEMENT

General

▶AGENCIES

Bureau of Land Management (BLM) *(Interior Dept.), Resources and Planning, 1849 C St. N.W., #5646, 20240; (202) 208-4896. Fax, (202) 208-5000. Kristin Bail, Assistant Director.*
Web, www.blm.gov/programs/planning-and-nepa

Manages more than 245 million acres of public land and about 700 million acres of subsurface mineral estate for several uses. Develops and implements natural resource programs for renewable resources use and protection, including management of forested land, rangeland, soil and water quality, recreation, and cultural programs.

Interior Dept. (DOI), *1849 C St. N.W., MS 7328, 20240; (202) 208-7351. David Bernhardt, Secretary; George Franchois, Librarian, (202) 282-5815. Employee directory, (202) 208-3100. Library, (202) 208-5815. Press, (202) 208-6416.*
General email, feedback@ios.doi.gov
Web, www.doi.gov, Twitter, @Interior and Facebook, www.facebook.com/USInterior and Blog, www.doi.gov/blog

Manages most federal land through its component agencies. Responsible for conservation and development of mineral, water, and fish and wildlife resources. Operates recreation programs for federal parks, refuges, and public lands. Preserves and administers scenic and historic areas.

Administers Native American lands and develops relationships with tribal governments. Reference library open to the public 7:45 a.m.–5:00 p.m.

Tennessee Valley Authority, *Government Affairs, 500 N. Capitol St. N.W., #220, 20001; (202) 898-2999. Fax, (202) 898-2998. William D. (Bill) Johnson, President.*
General email, tvainfo@tva.gov

Web, www.tva.gov and Twitter, @TVAnews

Coordinates resource conservation, development, and land-use programs in the Tennessee River Valley. Activities include forestry and wildlife development.

U.S. Fish and Wildlife Service *(Interior Dept.),* **Bird Habitat Conservation,** *5275 Leesburg Pike, MS MB, Falls Church, VA 22041; (703) 358-1784. Fax, (703) 358-2217. Vacant, Division Chief.*
Web, www.fws.gov/birds and Twitter, @usfwsBirds

Membership: government and private-sector conservation experts. Works to protect, restore, and manage wetlands and other habitats for migratory birds and other animals and to maintain migratory bird and waterfowl populations.

▶ **NONGOVERNMENTAL**

The Conservation Fund, *1655 N. Fort Myer Dr., #1300, Arlington, VA 22209-3199; (703) 525-6300. Fax, (703) 525-4610. Lawrence A. (Larry) Selzer, President.*
General email, webmaster@conservationfund.org

Web, www.conservationfund.org and Twitter, @ConservationFnd

Creates partnerships with the private sector, nonprofit organizations, and public agencies to promote land and water conservation. Operates land trusts, identifies real estate for conservation, and runs loan programs.

Izaak Walton League of America, *707 Conservation Lane, Gaithersburg, MD 20878-2983; (301) 548-0150. Fax, (301) 548-0146. Scott Kovarovics, Executive Director. Toll-free, (800) 453-5463.*
General email, info@iwla.org

Web, www.iwla.org, Twitter, @IWLA_org and Facebook, www.facebook.com/iwla.org

Grassroots organization that promotes conservation of natural resources and the environment. Interests include air and water pollution, farmland conservation, clean and renewable energy, wildlife habitat protection, and instilling conservation ethics in outdoor recreationists.

National Audubon Society, *Public Policy, 1200 18th St. N.W., #500, 20036; (202) 861-2242. Teresa Christopher, Vice President for Conservation and Operations.*
General email, audubonaction@audubon.org

Web, www.audubon.org and Twitter, @audubonsociety

Citizens' interest group that promotes environmental conservation and education, focusing on birds and their habitats. Provides information on bird science, water resources, public lands, rangelands, forests, parks, wildlife conservation, and the National Wildlife Refuge System.

Operates state offices, local chapters, and nature centers nationwide. (Headquarters in New York.)

National Research Council (NRC), *Agriculture and Natural Resources Board, Keck Center, 500 5th St. N.W., #WS632, 20001; (202) 334-3062. Fax, (202) 334-1978. Robin Schoen, Director.*
General email, banr@nas.edu

Web, http://dels.nas.edu/banr and Twitter, @NASM_Ag

Promotes and oversees research on the environmental impact of agriculture and food sustainability, including forestry, fisheries, wildlife, and the use of land, water, and other natural resources.

National Sustainable Agriculture Coalition, *110 Maryland Ave. N.E., #209, 20002-5622; (202) 547-5754. Fax, (202) 547-1837. Judy Obudzinski, Policy Director (Acting); Margaret Krome, Coalition Director (Acting).*
General email, info@sustainableagriculture.net

Web, www.sustainableagriculture.net, Twitter, @sustainableag and Facebook, www.facebook.com/sustainableag

National alliance of farm, rural, and conservation organizations. Advocates federal policies that promote environmentally sustainable agriculture, natural resources management, and rural community development. Monitors legislation and regulations.

National Wildlife Federation, *11100 Wildlife Center Dr., Reston, VA 20190-5362 (mailing address: P.O. Box 1583, Merrifield, VA 22116-1583); (703) 438-6000. Fax, (703) 438-3570. Collin O'Mara, President. Information, (800) 822-9919. Press, (202) 797-6634.*
General email, info@nwf.org

Web, www.nwf.org, Twitter, @NWF and Facebook, www.facebook.com/NationalWildlife and YouTube, www.youtube.com/user/NationalWildlife

Blog, https://blog.nwf.org/

Promotes conservation of natural resources; provides information on the environment and resource management; takes legal action on environmental issues.

Renewable Natural Resources Foundation, *6010 Executive Blvd., 5th Floor, N. Bethesda, MD 20852-3827; (301) 770-9101. Fax, (301) 770-9104. Robert D. Day, Executive Director.*
General email, info@rnrf.org

Web, www.rnrf.org

Consortium of professional, scientific, and education organizations working to advance scientific and public education in renewable natural resources. Encourages the application of sound scientific practices to resource management and conservation. Fosters interdisciplinary cooperation among its member organizations.

U.S. Chamber of Commerce, *Environment, Technology, and Regulatory Affairs, 1615 H St. N.W., 20062-2000; (202) 463-5533. Neil Bradley, Executive Vice President.*
General email, environment@uschamber.com

Web, www.uschamber.com/etra and Twitter, @Regulations

Develops policy on all issues affecting the production, use, and conservation of natural resources, including fuel and nonfuel minerals, timber, water, public lands, onshore and offshore energy, wetlands, and endangered species.

Winrock International, *Washington Office, 2121 Crystal Dr., #500, Arlington, VA 22202; (703) 302-6500. Fax, (703) 302-6512. Rodney Ferguson, President.*
General email, information@winrock.org
Web, www.winrock.org and Twitter, @WinrockIntl

Works with communities and governments to foster fair resource use, incentives for sustainable land use, and alternative income strategies to reduce pressure on natural resources. (Headquarters in Little Rock, Ark.)

Forests and Rangelands

▶**AGENCIES**

Forest Service *(Agriculture Dept.), 201 14th St. S.W., 20024 (mailing address: 1400 Independence Ave. S.W., MS 1144, Washington, DC 20250-0003); (202) 205-1661. Fax, (202) 205-1765. Vicki Christiansen, Chief. Press, (202) 205-1134. Toll-free, (800) 832-1355.*
Web, www.fs.fed.us, Twitter, @forestservice and Facebook, www.facebook.com/USForestService

Manages national forests and grasslands for outdoor recreation and sustained yield of renewable natural resources, including timber, water, forage, fish, and wildlife. Cooperates with state and private foresters; conducts forestry research.

Forest Service *(Agriculture Dept.), Fire and Aviation Management, 201 14th St. S.W., 3rd Floor, 3 Central, 20024 (mailing address: 1400 Independence Ave. S.W., MS 1107, Washington, DC 20250-0003); (202) 205-0808. Fax, (703) 605-1401. Shawna Legarza, Director.*
Web, www.fs.fed.us/fire

Responsible for aviation and fire management programs, including fire control planning and prevention, suppression of fires, and the use of prescribed fires. Provides state foresters with financial and technical assistance for fire protection in forests and on rural lands.

Forest Service *(Agriculture Dept.), International Programs, 1 Thomas Circle N.W., #400, 20005; (202) 644-4600. Fax, (202) 644-4603. Valdis E. Mezainis, Director, (202) 644-4621.*
Web, www.fs.fed.us/global

Responsible for the Forest Service's involvement in international forest conservation efforts. Analyzes international resource issues; promotes information exchange; provides planning and technical assistance. Interested in sustainable forest management, covering illegal logging, climate change, and migratory species.

Forest Service *(Agriculture Dept.), National Forest System, 201 14th St. S.W., 5th Floor, 20024; (202) 205-1523. Fax, (202) 649-1180. Chris French, Deputy Chief (Acting).*
Web, www.fs.fed.us

Manages 193 million acres of forests and rangelands. Products and services from these lands include timber, water, forage, wildlife, minerals, and recreation.

Forest Service *(Agriculture Dept.), Research and Development, 201 14th St. S.W., #2NW, 20024 (mailing address: 1400 Independence Ave. S.W., Washington, DC 20250); (202) 205-1665. Fax, (202) 205-1530. Alex Friend, Deputy Chief. Toll-free, (800) 832-1355.*
Web, www.fs.fed.us/research

Conducts biological, physical, and economic research related to forestry, including studies on harvesting methods, acid deposition, international forestry, the effects of global climate changes on forests, and forest products. Provides information on the establishment, improvement, and growth of trees, grasses, and other forest vegetation. Works to protect forest resources from fire, insects, diseases, and animal pests. Examines the effect of forest use activities on water quality, soil erosion, and sediment production. Conducts continuous forest survey and analyzes outlook for future supply and demand.

Forest Service *(Agriculture Dept.), State and Private Forestry, 201 14th St. S.W., #3NW, 20024 (mailing address: 1400 Independence Ave. S.W., MS 1109, Washington, DC 20250-1109); (202) 205-1657. Fax, (202) 205-1174. Patricia Hirami, Deputy Chief (Acting).*
Web, www.fs.fed.us

Assists state and private forest owners with the protection and management of 574 million acres of forest and associated watershed lands. Assistance includes fire control, protecting forests from insects and diseases, land-use planning, developing multiple-use management, and improving practices in harvesting, processing, and marketing of forest products.

Forest Service *(Agriculture Dept.), Youth Conservation Corps, 201 14th St. S.W., 20024 (mailing address: 1400 Independence Ave. S.W., MS 1125, Washington, DC 20250-1125); (202) 205-0650. Merlene Mazyck, Program Manager. Toll-free, (800) 832-1355.*
General email, mmazyck@fs.fed.us
Web, www.fs.fed.us/working-with-us/opportunities-for-young-people/youth-conservation-corps-opportunities

Administers, with the National Park Service and the Fish and Wildlife Service, the Youth Conservation Corps, a summer employment and training public works program for youths ages fifteen to eighteen. The program is conducted in national parks, in national forests and grasslands, and on national wildlife refuges.

Smithsonian Tropical Research Institute, *Forest Global Earth Observatory (ForestGEO), 10th St. and Constitution Ave. N.W., MRC 166, 20560; (202) 633-0666. Fax, (202) 786-2563. Stuart J. Davies, Director.*
General email, ForestGEO@si.edu
Web, https://forestgeo.si.edu and Twitter, @ForestGEO

Conducts long-term forest research and contributes to the scientific community through training, grants, and partnerships with international organizations. Uses research to monitor impacts of climate change and to guide natural resource policy. (Formerly Center for Tropical Forest Science.)

►CONGRESS

For a listing of relevant congressional committees and sub-committees, please see pages 283–284 or the Appendix.

►NONGOVERNMENTAL

American Forests, *1220 L St. N.W., #750, 20005; (202) 737-1944. Fax, (202) 737-2457. Jad Daley, President.*
General email, info@americanforests.org
Web, www.americanforests.org,
Twitter, @AmericanForests and Facebook,
www.facebook.com/AmericanForests

Citizens' interest group that promotes protection and responsible management of forests and natural resources. Provides information on conservation, public land policy, and urban forestry. Promotes an international tree-planting campaign to help mitigate global warming. Monitors legislation and regulations.

Forest Resources Assn., *1901 Pennsylvania Ave. N.W., #303, 20006; (202) 296-3937. Fax, (202) 296-0562. Deb Hawkinson, President.*
General email, info@forestresources.org
Web, www.forestresources.org, Twitter, @forestresources and Facebook, www.facebook.com/ForestResourcesAssociation

Membership: suppliers, brokers, transporters, and consumers of unprocessed wood products, as well as businesses that serve the forest products supply chain. Provides information on the safe, efficient, and sustainable harvest of forest products and their transport from woods to mill; works to ensure continued access to the timberland base. Monitors legislation and regulations.

International Wood Products Assn., *4214 King St., Alexandria, VA 22302; (703) 820-6696. Fax, (703) 820-8550. Cindy L. Squires, Executive Director.*
General email, info@iwpawood.org
Web, www.iwpawood.org

Membership: companies that handle imported wood products. Encourages environmentally responsible forest management and international trade in wood products. Sponsors research and environmental education on tropical forestry.

National Assn. of Conservation Districts (NACD), *509 Capitol Court N.E., 20002-4937; (202) 547-6223. Fax, (202) 547-6450. Jeremy Peters, Chief Executive Officer.*
General email, stewardship@nacdnet.org
Web, www.nacdnet.org and Twitter, @NACDconserve

Membership: conservation districts (local subdivisions of state government). Works to promote the conservation of land, forests, and other natural resources. Interests include forestry and wildlife and range management.

National Assn. of State Foresters, *444 N. Capitol St. N.W., #540, 20001; (202) 624-5415. Fax, (202) 624-5407. Jay Farrell, Executive Director.*
General email, info@stateforesters.org
Web, www.stateforesters.org and Twitter, @StateForesters

Membership: directors of state forestry agencies from all states, the District of Columbia, and U.S. territories. Interests include forest management, employment generated by forestry and forest products, and climate change. Monitors legislation and regulations.

National Lumber and Building Material Dealers Assn., *2025 M St. N.W., #800, 20036-3309; (202) 367-1169. Jonathan M. Paine, President.*
General email, info@dealer.org
Web, www.dealer.org

Membership: federated associations of retailers in the lumber and building material industries. Supports forest conservation programs and environmental safety.

Pinchot Institute for Conservation, *1400 16th St. N.W., #350, 20036; (202) 797-6580. Fax, (202) 797-6583. William C. Price, President.*
Web, www.pinchot.org

Seeks to advance forest conservation and sustainable natural resources management nationally through research and analysis, education and technical assistance, and development of conservation leaders.

Save America's Forests, *4 Library Court S.E., 20003; (202) 544-9219. Carl Ross, Executive Director.*
General email, info@saveamericasforests.org
Web, www.saveamericasforests.org

Coalition of environmental and public interest groups, scientists, businesses, and individuals. Advocates comprehensive nationwide laws and international policies to prevent deforestation and to protect forest ecosystems and indigenous rights.

Society of American Foresters, *10100 Laureate Way, Bethesda, MD 20814-2198; (301) 897-8720. Fax, (301) 897-3690. Louise Murgia, Chief Operating Officer. Toll-free, (866) 897-8720.*
General email, info@safnet.org
Web, www.eforester.org and Twitter, @foresters

Association of forestry professionals. Provides technical information on forestry, accredits forestry programs in universities and colleges, and publishes scientific forestry journals.

Sustainable Forestry Initiative, *2121 K St. N.W., #750, 20037; (202) 596-3450. Fax, (202) 596-3451. Kathy Abusow, President.*
General email, info@sfiprogram.org
Web, www.sfiprogram.org and Twitter, @sfiprogram

Works to ensure protection of forests while continuing to produce wood and paper products as needed by the economy. Encourages perpetual growing and harvesting of trees and protection of wildlife, plants, soil, water, and air quality. Seeks to mitigate illegal logging. Interests include the economic, environmental, cultural, and legal issues related to forestry.

The Wilderness Society, *1615 M St. N.W., 20036; (202) 833-2300. Fax, (202) 429-3958. Jamie Williams, President. Toll-free, (800) 843-9453.*
General email, action@tws.org
Web, www.wilderness.org and Twitter, @wilderness

Promotes preservation of wilderness and the responsible management of federal lands, including national parks and forests, wilderness areas, wildlife refuges, and land administered by the Interior Dept.'s Bureau of Land Management.

Land Resources

►**AGENCIES**

Bureau of Land Management (BLM) *(Interior Dept.), 1849 C St.:N.W., #5665, 20240; (202) 208-3801. Fax, (202) 208-5242. Brian Steed, Deputy Director of Policy and Programs. Press, (202) 208-6913. TTY, (800) 877-8339.*
Web, www.blm.gov, Twitter, @BLMNational and Facebook, www.facebook.com/BLMNational and YouTube, www.youtube.com/user/BLMNational

Manages public lands and federally owned mineral resources, including oil, gas, and coal. Resources managed and leased include wildlife habitats, timber, minerals, open space, wilderness areas, forage, and recreational resources. Surveys federal lands and maintains public land records.

Bureau of Land Management (BLM) *(Interior Dept.), Lands, Realty, and Cadastral Survey, 1849 C St. N.W., #2134LM, 20003; (202) 912-7088. Fax, (202) 912-7199. Robert Jolley, Division Chief, (202) 912-7350.*
Web, www.blm.gov/programs/lands-and-realty

Oversees use, acquisition, and disposal of public lands. Conducts the Public Lands Survey; authorizes rights-of-way on public lands for uses that include roads, power lines, and wind and solar facilities.

Bureau of Reclamation *(Interior Dept.), 1849 C St. N.W., MS 7069-MIB, 20240-0001; (202) 513-0501. Fax, (202) 513-0309. Brenda Burman, Commissioner; Shelby Hagenauer, Deputy Commissioner. Press, (202) 513-0575.*
Web, www.usbr.gov, Twitter, @usbr and Facebook, www.facebook.com/bureau.of.reclamation and YouTube, www.youtube.com/user/reclamation

Responsible for acquisition, administration, management, and disposal of lands in seventeen western states associated with bureau water resource development projects. Provides overall policy guidance for land use, including agreements with public agencies for outdoor recreation, fish and wildlife enhancement, and land-use authorizations such as leases, licenses, permits, and rights of way. Interests include increasing water-based outdoor recreation facilities and opportunities.

Environmental Protection Agency (EPA), *Land and Emergency Management (OLEM), 1200 Pennsylvania Ave. N.W., MC 5101T, 20460; (202) 566-0200. Fax, (202) 566-0207. Barry Breen, Assistant Administrator (Acting). National Response Center, (800) 424-8802. Superfund information hotline, (800) 424-9346. TTY, (202) 272-0165.*
Web, www2.epa.gov/aboutepa/about-office-land-and-emergency-management-olem

Administers and enforces the Resource Conservation and Recovery Act and the Brownfields Program and Superfund.

Environmental Protection Agency (EPA), *Land and Emergency Management (OLEM), Brownfields and Land Revitalization, 1300 Pennsylvania Ave. N.W., #5105T, 20460; (202) 566-2777. David Lloyd, Director.*
Web, www.epa.gov/land-revitalization and www.epa.gov/brownfields

Provides grants and technical assistance to communities, states, tribes, and other stakeholders needing resources to prevent, assess, safely clean up, and sustainably reuse brownfields and formerly contaminated properties.

Environmental Protection Agency (EPA), *Land and Emergency Management (OLEM), Resource Conservation and Recovery, 1 Potomac Yard, 2777 S. Crystal Dr., Arlington, VA 22202 (mailing address: 1200 Pennsylvania Ave. N.W., #5301P, Washington, DC 20460); (703) 308-8895. Fax, (703) 308-0513. Barnes Johnson, Director.*
Web, www.epa.gov/aboutepa/about-office-land-and-emergency-management#orcr

Protects human health and the environment by ensuring responsible national management of hazardous and nonhazardous waste. Administers the Resource Conservation and Recovery Act.

Housing and Urban Development Dept. (HUD), *Community Planning and Development, Environment and Energy, 451 7th St. S.W., #7212, 20410; (202) 708-1201. Fax, (202) 708-3363. Danielle Schopp, Director, (202) 402-4442.*
Web, www.hud.gov/program_offices/comm_planning/library/energy

Issues policies and sets standards for environmental and land-use planning and environmental management practices. Oversees HUD implementation of requirements on environment, historic preservation, archaeology, flood plain management, wetlands protection, environmental justice (ensuring that the environment and human health are fairly protected for all people/Executive Order 12898), coastal zone management, sole source aquifers, farmland protection, endangered species, airport clear zones, explosive hazards, and noise.

Interior Dept. (DOI), *Assistant Secretary for Land and Minerals Management, 1849 C St. N.W., MS 6628, 20240; (202) 208-6734. Joseph (Joe) Balash, Assistant Secretary.*
Web, www.doi.gov

Directs and supervises the Bureau of Land Management; the Bureau of Ocean Energy Management, Regulation, and

Enforcement; Bureau of Safety and Environmental Enforcement; and the Office of Surface Mining. Supervises programs associated with land-use planning, onshore and offshore minerals, surface mining reclamation and enforcement, and Outer Continental Shelf minerals management.

Interior Dept. (DOI), *Board of Land Appeals (IBLA),* 801 *N. Quincy St., #300, Arlington, VA 22203; (703) 235-3750. Fax, (703) 235-8349. James F. Roberts, Chief Administrative Judge (Acting).*
General email, ibla@oha.doi.edu

Web, www.doi.gov/oha/organization/ibla

Adjunct office of the interior secretary that decides appeals from decisions rendered by the Bureau of Land Management; Bureau of Ocean Energy Management, Regulation, and Enforcement; Office of Surface Mining and Reclamation Enforcement; and Bureau of Indian Affairs concerning the use and disposition of public lands and minerals. (Board is separate and independent from bureaus and offices whose decisions it reviews.)

Interior Dept. (DOI), *Surface Mining Reclamation and Enforcement (OSMRE),* 1849 *C St. N.W., #4513, 20240; (202) 208-4006. Fax, (202) 219-3106. Glenda H. Owens, Director (Acting). Press, (202) 208-2565. TTY, (202) 208-2694.*
General email, getinfo@osmre.gov

Web, www.osmre.gov, Twitter, @OSMRE and Facebook, www.facebook.com/OSMRE

Regulates surface mining of coal and surface effects of underground coal mining. Responsible for reclamation of abandoned coal mine lands.

Interior Dept. (DOI), *Wildland Fire (OWF),* 1849 *C St. N.W., MS 2660, 20240; (202) 208-2719. Fax, (202) 606-3150. Jeff Rupert, Director.*
General email, wildlandfire@ios.doi.gov

Web, www.doi.gov/wildlandfire and Twitter, @DOIWildlandFire

Oversees all wildland fire management programs, policies, budgets, and information technology in order to manage risk to firefighters, communities, and landscapes. Bridges the individual fire programs of the four land management bureaus; supports the wildland fire needs of the bureau.

Natural Resources Conservation Service *(Agriculture Dept.),* 1400 *Independence Ave. S.W., #5105AS, 20250 (mailing address: P.O. Box 2890, Washington, DC 20013-2890); (202) 720-3210. Fax, (202) 720-7690. Mathew Lohr, Chief, (202) 720-7246.*
General email, nrcsdistributioncenter@ia.usda.gov

Web, www.nrcs.usda.gov and Twitter, @USDA_NRCS

Responsible for soil and water conservation programs, including watershed protection, flood prevention, river basin surveys, and resource conservation and development. Provides landowners, operators, state and local units of government, and community groups with technical assistance in carrying out local programs. Website has a Spanish-language link.

Tennessee Valley Authority, *Government Affairs,* 500 *N. Capitol St. N.W., #220, 20001; (202) 898-2999. Fax, (202) 898-2998. William D. (Bill) Johnson, President.*
General email, tvainfo@tva.gov

Web, www.tva.gov and Twitter, @TVAnews

Coordinates resource conservation, development, and land-use programs in the Tennessee River Valley. Provides information on land usage in the region.

U.S. Geological Survey (USGS) *(Interior Dept.),* **Land Change Science Program,** 12201 *Sunrise Valley Dr., MS 516, Reston, VA 20192-0002; (703) 648-5320. Fax, (703) 648-6953. Debra A. Willard, Program Co-Coordinator; Brad Reed, Program Co-Coordinator.*
Web, http://usgs.gov/land-resources/land-change-science-program?qt-programs-l2-landing-page=0#qt-programs-l2-landing-page

Conducts research on land cover and documents land change; develops tools to support resource allocation decisions.

U.S. Geological Survey (USGS) *(Interior Dept.),* **Land Resources,** 12201 *Sunrise Valley Dr., MS 516, Reston, VA 20192; (703) 648-4215. Fax, (703) 648-7031. T. Douglas Beard Jr., Associate Director (Acting).*
Web, www.usgs.gov/mission-areas/land-resources

Supports the science community with its long-term observational networks and extensive databases emcompassing the fields of climate history, land-use and land-cover change, and carbon and nutrient cycles.

►CONGRESS

For a listing of relevant congressional committees and subcommittees, please see pages 283–284 or the Appendix.

►NONGOVERNMENTAL

American Geosciences Institute, 4220 *King St., Alexandria, VA 22302-1502; (703) 379-2480. Fax, (703) 379-7563. Allyson K. Anderson Book, Executive Director, ext. 202.*
General email, agi@americangeosciences.org

Web, www.americangeosciences.org and Twitter, @AGI_Updates

Membership: earth science societies and associations. Provides education and outreach. Maintains computerized database of the world's geoscience literature (available to the public for a fee). Monitors legislation and regulations.

American Resort Development Assn., 1201 *15th St. N.W., #400, 20005-2842; (202) 371-6700. Fax, (202) 289-8544. Howard Nusbaum, President.*
Web, www.arda.org

Membership: U.S. and international developers, builders, financiers, marketing companies, and others involved in resort, recreational, and community development. Serves as an information clearinghouse; monitors federal and state legislation affecting land, time share, and community development industries.

Land Trust Alliance, *1250 H St. N.W., #600, 20005; (202) 638-4725. Fax, (202) 638-4730. Andrew Bowman, President, (202) 800-2250.*
General email, info@lta.org

Web, www.landtrustalliance.org and Twitter, @ltalliance

Membership: organizations and individuals who work to conserve land resources. Serves as a forum for the exchange of information; conducts research and public education programs. Monitors legislation and regulations.

National Assn. of Conservation Districts (NACD), *509 Capitol Court N.E., 20002-4937; (202) 547-6223. Fax, (202) 547-6450. Jeremy Peters, Chief Executive Officer.*
General email, stewardship@nacdnet.org

Web, www.nacdnet.org and Twitter, @NACDconserve

Membership: conservation districts (local subdivisions of state government). Works to promote the conservation of land, forests, and other natural resources. Interests include forestry, water, flood plain, wildlife, and range management.

Public Lands Council, *1275 Pennsylvania Ave. N.W., #801, 20004; (202) 347-0228. Fax, (202) 638-0607. Bob Skinner, President; Ethan Lane, Executive Director, ext. 126.*
Web, www.publiclandscouncil.org and Twitter, @PLCranching

Membership: cattle and sheep ranchers who hold permits and leases to graze livestock on public lands. (Affiliated with the National Cattlemen's Beef Association and the American Sheep Industry Association, and the Association of National Grasslands.)

Scenic America, *727 15th St. N.W., #1100, 20005-6029; (202) 792-1300. Mark Falzone, President.*
General email, max.ashburn@scenic.org

Web, www.scenic.org and Twitter, @ScenicAmerica

Membership: national, state, and local groups concerned with land-use control, growth management, and landscape protection. Works to enhance the scenic quality of America's communities and countryside. Provides information and technical assistance on scenic byways, tree preservation, economics of aesthetic regulation, billboard and sign control, scenic areas preservation, and growth management.

Wallace Genetic Foundation, *4910 Massachusetts Ave. N.W., #221, 20016; (202) 966-2932. Fax, (202) 966-3370. Michaela Oldfield, Executive Director.*
General email, wgfdn@aol.com

Web, www.wallacegenetic.org

Supports national and international nonprofits in the areas of sustainable agriculture, agricultural research, preservation of farmland, reduction of environmental toxins, conservation, biodiversity protection, and global climate issues.

The Wilderness Society, *1615 M St. N.W., 20036; (202) 833-2300. Fax, (202) 429-3958. Jamie Williams, President. Toll-free, (800) 843-9453.*

General email, action@tws.org

Web, www.wilderness.org and Twitter, @wilderness

Promotes preservation of wilderness and the responsible management of federal lands, including national parks and forests, wilderness areas, wildlife refuges, and land administered by the Interior Dept.'s Bureau of Land Management.

Metals and Minerals

▶AGENCIES

Bureau of Land Management (BLM) *(Interior Dept.), Energy, Minerals, and Realty Management, 1849 C St. N.W., #5625, 20240; (202) 208-4201. Fax, (202) 208-4800. Michael Nedd, Assistant Director.*
Web, www.blm.gov/programs/energy-and-minerals

Develops and administers policy, guidance, and performance oversight for the renewable energy program, including wind, solar, and geothermal energy; the fluid minerals program, including oil, gas, and helium; the solid minerals programs, including mining law, coal, oil shale, and salable minerals; the lands and realty programs; and the Public Land Survey System. Provides national leadership and develops national partnerships with organizations interested in energy, minerals, and realty management.

Bureau of Safety and Environmental Enforcement (BSEE) *(Interior Dept.), Offshore Regulatory Programs (OORP), 1849 C St. N.W., MS DM5438, 20240-0001; (202) 208-3985. Douglas Morris, Chief.*
General email, bseepublicaffairs@bsee.gov

Web, www.bsee.gov/what-we-do/offshore-regulatory-programs

Develops standards, regulations, and compliance programs governing Outer Continental Shelf oil, gas, and minerals exploration and operations. Purview includes safety management programs, safety and pollution prevention research, technology assessments, standards for inspections and enforcement policies, and accident investigation practices.

Interior Dept. (DOI), *Assistant Secretary for Land and Minerals Management, 1849 C St. N.W., MS 6628, 20240; (202) 208-6734. Joseph (Joe) Balash, Assistant Secretary.*
Web, www.doi.gov

Directs and supervises the Bureau of Land Management; the Bureau of Ocean Energy Management, Regulation, and Enforcement; Bureau of Safety and Environmental Enforcement; and the Office of Surface Mining. Supervises programs associated with land-use planning, onshore and offshore minerals, surface mining reclamation and enforcement, and Outer Continental Shelf minerals management.

Interior Dept. (DOI), *Board of Land Appeals (IBLA), 801 N. Quincy St., #300, Arlington, VA 22203; (703) 235-3750. Fax, (703) 235-8349. James F. Roberts, Chief Administrative Judge (Acting).*
General email, ibla@oha.doi.edu

Web, www.doi.gov/oha/organization/ibla

Adjunct office of the interior secretary that issues final decisions concerning the Surface Mining Control and Reclamation Act of 1977. (Board is separate and independent from bureaus and offices whose decisions it reviews.)

Interior Dept. (DOI), *Natural Resources Revenue (ONRR), Washington Office, 1849 C St. N.W., MS 5134, 20240; (202) 513-0603. Fax, (202) 513-0682.*
Gregory J. (Greg) Gould, Director. Press, (202) 513-0600.
Web, www.onrr.gov, Twitter, @DOINRR and
Facebook, www.facebook.com/DOIONRR

Manages revenues associated with federal offshore and federal and American Indian onshore mineral leases, as well as revenues received through offshore renewable energy efforts. Collects and disburses all natural resources revenues.

U.S. Geological Survey (USGS) *(Interior Dept.), Global Minerals Analysis, 12201 Sunrise Valley Dr., MS 991, Reston, VA 20192-0002; (703) 648-4976. Fax, (703) 648-7757. Steven D. Textoris, Chief.*
Web, http://minerals.usgs.gov/minerals

Collects, analyzes, and disseminates information on ferrous and nonferrous metals, including gold, silver, platinum group metals, iron, iron ore, steel, chromium, and nickel.

U.S. Geological Survey (USGS) *(Interior Dept.), Mineral Resources Program, 12201 Sunrise Valley Dr., MS 913, Reston, VA 20192-0002; (703) 648-6108. Fax, (703) 648-6057. Thomas C. Crafford, Program Coordinator.*
General email, minerals@usgs.gov
Web, https://minerals.usgs.gov/ and
Twitter, @USGSMinerals

Coordinates mineral resource activities for the Geological Survey, including research and information on U.S. and international mineral resources, baseline information on earth materials, and geochemical and geophysical instrumentation and applications.

►**CONGRESS**

For a listing of relevant congressional committees and subcommittees, please see pages 283–284 or the Appendix.

►**NONGOVERNMENTAL**

Mineralogical Society of America, *3635 Concorde Pkwy., #500, Chantilly, VA 20151-1110; (703) 652-9950. Fax, (703) 652-9951. J. Alexander Speer, Executive Director.*
General email, jaspeer@minsocam.org
Web, www.minsocam.org

Membership: mineralogists, petrologists, crystallographers, geochemists, educators, students, and others interested in mineralogy. Conducts research; sponsors educational programs; promotes industrial application of mineral studies.

National Mining Assn., *101 Constitution Ave. N.W., #500 East, 20001-2133; (202) 463-2600. Fax, (202) 463-2666. Harold P. (Hal) Quinn Jr., President. Press, (202) 463-2642.*
General email, webmaster@nma.org
Web, www.nma.org

Membership: domestic producers of coal and industrial-agricultural minerals and metals; manufacturers of mining equipment; engineering and consulting firms; and financial institutions. Interests include mine-leasing programs, mine health and safety, research and development, public lands, and minerals availability. Monitors legislation and regulations.

Native American Trust Resources

►**AGENCIES**

Administration for Children and Families (ACF) *(Health and Human Services Dept.), Administration for Native Americans (ANA), 330 C St. S.W., Room 4126, 20201; (202) 690-7776. Fax, (202) 690-8145. Jeannie Hovland, Commissioner. Toll-free, (877) 922-9262.*
General email, anacomments@acf.hhs.gov
Web, www.acf.hhs.gov/ana

Awards grants to assist tribes with resources to develop legal and organizational capacities to protect their natural environments.

Bureau of Indian Affairs (BIA) *(Interior Dept.), Indian Energy and Economic Development (IEED), 1849 C. St. N.W., Room 4152, 20240; (202) 219-0740. Fax, (202) 208-4564. Jack R. Stevens, Director (Acting), (202) 208-6764.*
Web, www.bia.gov/as-ia/ieed

Assists tribes with environmentally responsible exploration, development, and management of energy and mineral resources to generate new jobs and sustainable tribal economies.

Bureau of Indian Affairs (BIA) *(Interior Dept.), Indian Services (OIS), 1849 C St. N.W., MS 3645-MIB, 20240; (202) 513-7642. Fax, (202) 208-2648. Debrah McBride, Deputy Bureau Director (Acting). Public Affairs, (202) 208-3710.*
Web, www.bia.gov/bia/ois

Assists tribal and Indian landowners with managing natural and energy trust resources; builds and maintains housing, transportation, energy, and irrigation infrastructure; and provides law enforcement protection, corrections, and administration of justice services on federal Indian lands.

Bureau of Indian Affairs (BIA) *(Interior Dept.), Trust Services (OTS), 1849 C St. N.W., MS 4620-MIB, 20240; (202) 208-5831. Fax, (202) 219-1255. Johnna Blackhair, Deputy Bureau Director.*
Web, www.bia.gov/bia/ots

Assists in developing and managing bureau programs involving Native American trust resources (agriculture, forestry, wildlife, water, irrigation, real property management probate, and title records).

Bureau of Land Management (BLM) *(Interior Dept.), Energy, Minerals, and Realty Management, 1849 C St.*

N.W., #5625, 20240; (202) 208-4201. Fax, (202) 208-4800. Michael Nedd, Assistant Director.

Web, www.blm.gov/programs/energy-and-minerals

Provides leadership to the Bureau of Land Management's trust management for Indian minerals operations, surveys, and trust patent preparation.

Environment and Natural Resources Division, Justice Dept. (DOJ), Indian Resources (IRS), 601 D St. N.W., #3507, 20004 (mailing address: P.O. Box 7611, L'Enfant Plaza, Washington, DC 20044); (202) 305-0269. Fax, (202) 305-0275. S. Craig Alexander, Chief.

Web, www.justice.gov/enrd/Indian-resources-section

Represents the United States in suits, including trust violations, brought on behalf of individual Native Americans and Native American tribes against the government. Also represents the United States as trustee for Native Americans in court actions involving protection of Native American land and resources.

Environmental Protection Agency (EPA), Water (OW), 1200 Pennsylvania Ave. N.W., MC 4101M, 20460; (202) 564-5700. David Ross, Assistant Administrator.

Web, www.epa.gov/aboutepa/about-office-water

Works with American Indian tribes to implement the Safe Drinking Water Act and improve access to safe drinking water on tribal lands.

Interior Dept. (DOI), 1849 C St. N.W., MS 7328, 20240; (202) 208-7351. David Bernhardt, Secretary; George Franchois, Librarian, (202) 282-5815. Employee directory, (202) 208-3100. Library, (202) 208-5815. Press, (202) 208-6416.

General email, feedback@ios.doi.gov

Web, www.doi.gov, Twitter, @Interior and Facebook, www.facebook.com/USInterior and Blog, www.doi.gov/blog

Principal U.S. conservation agency. Manages most federal land, including Native American lands; develops relationships with tribal governments. Reference library open to the public 7:45 a.m.–5:00 p.m.

Interior Dept. (DOI), Natural Resources Revenue (ONRR), Washington Office, 1849 C St. N.W., MS 5134, 20240; (202) 513-0603. Fax, (202) 513-0682. Gregory J. (Greg) Gould, Director. Press, (202) 513-0600.

Web, www.onrr.gov, Twitter, @DOINRR and Facebook, www.facebook.com/DOIONRR

Manages revenues associated with federal offshore and federal and American Indian onshore mineral leases, as well as revenues received through offshore renewable energy efforts. Collects and disburses all natural resources revenues.

Interior Dept. (DOI), Office of the Solicitor, Indian Affairs, 1849 C St. N.W., MS 6511, 20240; (202) 208-3401. Fax, (202) 219-1791. Eric Shepard, Associate Solicitor.

Web, www.doi.gov/solicitor/headquarters

Advises the Bureau of Indian Affairs and the secretary of the interior on all legal matters, including its trust responsibilities toward Native Americans and their natural resources.

▶CONGRESS

For a listing of relevant congressional committees and subcommittees, please see pages 283–284 or the Appendix.

▶NONGOVERNMENTAL

Native American Rights Fund, Washington Office, 1514 P St. N.W., Suite D, Rear entrance, 20005; (202) 785-4166. Fax, (202) 822-0068. John E. Echohawk, Executive Director; Joel Williams, Managing Attorney.

Web, www.narf.org and Facebook, www.facebook.com/NativeAmericanRightsFund

Provides Native Americans and Alaska Natives with legal assistance in land claims, water rights, hunting, and other areas. Practices federal Indian law. (Headquarters in Boulder, Colo.)

Ocean and Coastal Resources

▶AGENCIES

Bureau of Oceans and International Environmental and Scientific Affairs (OES) (State Dept.), 2201 C St. N.W., #3880, 20520-7818; (202) 647-1554. Fax, (202) 647-0217. Marcia Bernicat, Principal Deputy Assistant Secretary.

Web, www.state.gov/e/oes, Twitter, @StateDeptOES and Facebook, www.facebook.com/StateDepartment.OES

Promotes water security, peaceful cooperation on polar issues, and sustainable ocean policy.

Bureau of Oceans and International Environmental and Scientific Affairs (OES) (State Dept.), Marine Conservation (OMC), 2201 C St. N.W., #2758, 20520; (202) 647-2335. William Gibbons-Fly, Director.

Web, www.state.gov/e/oes/ocns/fish

Handles the management, conservation, and restoration of living marine resources. Seeks to maintain a healthy and productive marine environment and ecosystems.

Bureau of Safety and Environmental Enforcement (BSEE) (Interior Dept.), Safety Enforcement Division (SED), 45600 Woodland Rd., Sterling, VA 20166; (202) 208-6184. Jennifer Mehaffey, Chief (Acting).

General email, bseepublicaffairs@bsee.gov

Web, www.bsee.gov/what-we-do/safety-enforcement

Inspects, monitors, and enforces safety regulations of offshore companies to ensure compliance and conservation of offshore resources.

Environmental Protection Agency (EPA), Water (OW), 1200 Pennsylvania Ave. N.W., MC 4101M, 20460; (202) 564-5700. David Ross, Assistant Administrator.

Web, www.epa.gov/aboutepa/about-office-water

Restores and maintains oceans, watersheds, and their aquatic ecosystems. Implements the Clean Water Act and portions of the Coastal Zone Act, Ocean Dumping Ban Act, Marine Protection Act, Shore Protection Act, Marine Plastics Pollution Research and Control Act, and the

International Convention for the Prevention of Pollution from Ships.

National Oceanic and Atmospheric Administration (NOAA) *(Commerce Dept.), National Marine Sanctuaries, 1305 East-West Hwy., 11th Floor, Silver Spring, MD 20910; (301) 713-3125. Fax, (301) 713-0404. Rebecca Holyoke, Director, (240) 533-0685.*
General email, sanctuaries@noaa.gov

Web, www.sanctuaries.noaa.gov and Twitter, @santuaries

Administers the National Marine Sanctuary Program, which seeks to protect the ecology and the recreational and cultural resources of marine and Great Lakes waters.

National Oceanic and Atmospheric Administration (NOAA) *(Commerce Dept.), National Ocean Service (NOS), 1305 East-West Hwy., SSMC4, #9149, Silver Spring, MD 20910; (301) 713-3074. Fax, (301) 713-4269. Nicole LaBoeuf, Assistant Administrator (Acting). Press, (301) 713-3066.*
General email, nos.info@noaa.gov

Web, www.oceanservice.noaa.gov

Manages charting and geodetic services, oceanography and marine services, coastal resource coordination, and marine survey operations; conducts environmental cleanup of coastal pollution.

National Oceanic and Atmospheric Administration (NOAA) *(Commerce Dept.), Ocean Acidification Program (OAP), 1315 East-West Hwy., #10356, Silver Spring, MD 20910; (301) 734-1075. Elizabeth (Libby) Jewett, Director.*
General email, noaa.oceanacidification@noaa.gov

Web, www.oceanacidification.noaa.gov and Twitter, @OA_NOAA

Monitors changes in ocean chemistry due to the continued acidification of the oceans and Great Lakes, and assesses the socioeconomic impacts. Maintains relationships with scientists, resource managers, stakeholders, policymakers, and the public to implement adaptation strategies and monitor the biological responses of ecologically and economically important species. Operates from NOAA's Office of Oceanic and Atmospheric Research.

National Oceanic and Atmospheric Administration (NOAA) *(Commerce Dept.), Oceanic and Atmospheric Research (OAR), 1315 East-West Hwy., Silver Spring, MD 20910; (301) 713-2458. Craig N. McLean, Assistant Administrator.*
Web, http://research.noaa.gov and Twitter, @NOAAResearch

Works to protect, restore, and manage coastal and ocean resources through ecosystem-based management.

U.S. Geological Survey (USGS) *(Interior Dept.), Coastal and Marine Hazards and Resources, 12201 Sunrise Valley Dr., MS 905, Reston, VA 20192; (703) 648-6422. Fax, (703) 648-5464. John W. Haines, Program Coordinator.*
Web, http://marine.usgs.gov

Handles resource assessment, exploration research, and marine geologic and environmental studies on U.S. coastal regions and the Outer Continental Shelf.

▶**CONGRESS**

For a listing of relevant congressional committees and subcommittees, please see pages 283–284 or the Appendix.

▶**NONGOVERNMENTAL**

Blue Frontier Campaign, *1530 P St. N.W., 20005 (mailing address: P.O. Box 19367, Washington, DC 20036); (202) 387-8030. Fax, (202) 234-5176. David Helvarg, Executive Director.*
General email, info@bluefront.org

Web, www.bluefront.org and Twitter, @Blue_Frontier

Promotes ocean conservation. Seeks to strengthen unity among ocean conservationists and encourage public awareness at the local, regional, and national levels.

Coastal States Organization, *444 N. Capitol St. N.W., #638, 20001; (202) 508-3860. Fax, (202) 508-3843. Bradley Watson, Executive Director, (202) 508-3844.*
General email, cso@coastalstates.org

Web, www.coastalstates.org

Nonpartisan organization that represents governors of thirty-five U.S. coastal states, territories, and commonwealths on management of coastal, Great Lakes, and marine resources. Interests include ocean dumping, coastal pollution, wetlands preservation and restoration, national oceans policy, and the Outer Continental Shelf. Gathers and analyzes data to assess state coastal needs; sponsors and participates in conferences and workshops.

Joint Ocean Commission Initiative, *c/o Meridian Institute, 1800 M St. N.W., #400N, 20036; (202) 354-6444. Fax, (202) 354-6441. John Ehrmann, Senior Partner.*
General email, lcantral@merid.org

Web, www.jointoceancommission.org and Twitter, @JointOceanCL

Provides policy information on ocean conservation and releases Ocean Policy Report Cards that analyze the effectiveness of policy initiatives on ocean and coast protection. (Formed by the U.S. Commission on Ocean Policy and the Pew Oceans Commission.)

Marine Technology Society, *1100 H St. N.W., #LL-100, 20005; (202) 717-8705. Fax, (202) 347-4302. Kathleen Herndon, Executive Director.*
General email, membership@mtsociety.org

Web, www.mtsociety.org

Membership: scientists, engineers, technologists, and others interested in marine science, technology, and education.

National Ocean Industries Assn., *1120 G St. N.W., #900, 20005; (202) 347-6900. Fax, (202) 347-8650. Randall Luthi, President.*

National Park Service

General email, jwilliams@noia.org

Web, www.noia.org and Twitter, @oceanindustries

Membership: manufacturers, producers, suppliers, and support and service companies involved in marine, offshore, and ocean work. Interests include offshore oil and gas supply and production, deep-sea mining, ocean thermal energy, and new energy sources.

National Research Council (NRC), *Gulf Research Program,* Keck Center, 500 5th St. N.W., 20001; (202) 334-2138. Lauren Alexander Augustine, Executive Director.
General email, gulfprogram@nas.edu

Web, www.nationalacademies.org/gulf and Twitter, @NASEM_Gulf

Promotes oil system safety and the protection of human health and the environment in the Gulf of Mexico and other U.S. outer continental shelf areas.

National Research Council (NRC), *Ocean Studies Board,* Keck Center, 500 5th St. N.W., MS 607, 20001; (202) 334-
2714. Fax, (202) 334-2885. Larry A. Mayer, Chair; Susan Roberts, Director.
General email, osbfeedback@nas.edu

Web, http://dels.nas.edu/osb

Conducts research to understand, manage, and conserve coastal and marine environments. Areas of interest include the ocean's role in the global climate system, technology and infrastructure needs for ocean research, ocean-related aspects of national security, fisheries science and management, and ocean education.

Oceana, 1025 Connecticut Ave. N.W., 20036; (202) 833-3900. Fax, (202) 833-2070. Andrew F. Sharpless, Chief Executive Officer. Toll-free, 877-7-OCEANA.
General email, info@oceana.org

Web, www.oceana.org, Twitter, @Oceana and Facebook, www.facebook.com/oceana

Promotes ocean conservation both nationally and internationally; pursues policy changes to reduce pollution and protect fish, marine mammals, and other forms of sea life.

Conducts specific scientific, legal, policy, and advocacy campaigns. Monitors legislation and regulations.

Parks and Recreation Areas

►AGENCIES

Bureau of Land Management (BLM) *(Interior Dept.), Cultural and Paleontological Resources and Tribal Consultation, 20 M St. S.E., #2134, 20003; (202) 912-7242. Emily Palus, Deputy Division Chief.*
Web, www.blm.gov/programs/cultural-heritage-and-paleontology

Identifies and manages cultural heritage and recreation programs on public lands.

Bureau of Land Management (BLM) *(Interior Dept.), Recreation and Visitor Services, 20 M St. S.E., 6th Floor, 20003 (mailing address: 1849 C St. N.W., MS 6224, Washington, DC 20240); (202) 912-7094. Fax, (202) 245-0050. Andy Tenney, Division Chief, (202) 912-7094; Dennis Byrd, Outdoor Recreation Planner, (202) 912-7252. Web, www.blm.gov/programs/recreation*

Develops recreation opportunities and visitor services on public lands.

Bureau of Reclamation *(Interior Dept.), 1849 C St. N.W., MS 7069-MIB, 20240-0001; (202) 513-0501. Fax, (202) 513-0309. Brenda Burman, Commissioner; Shelby Hagenauer, Deputy Commissioner. Press, (202) 513-0575.*
Web, www.usbr.gov, Twitter, @usbr and Facebook, www.facebook.com/bureau.of.reclamation and YouTube, www.youtube.com/user/reclamation

Responsible for acquisition, administration, management, and disposal of lands in seventeen western states associated with bureau water resource development projects. Provides overall policy guidance for land use, including agreements with public agencies for outdoor recreation, fish and wildlife enhancement, and land-use authorizations such as leases, licenses, permits, and rights of way. Interests include increasing water-based outdoor recreation facilities and opportunities.

Forest Service *(Agriculture Dept.), Recreation, Heritage, and Volunteer Resources, 201 14th St. S.W., 5SW, 20024 (mailing address: 1400 Independence Ave. S.W., MS 1125, Washington, DC 20250-0003); (202) 205-1240. Fax, (703) 605-5131. Vacant, Director.*
Web, www.fs.fed.us/recreation

Develops policy and sets guidelines on administering national forests and grasslands for recreational purposes. (The Forest Service administers some of the lands designated as national recreation areas.)

Interior Dept. (DOI), *Assistant Secretary for Fish, Wildlife, and Parks, 1849 C St. N.W., #3160, 20240; (202) 208-4416. Fax, (202) 208-4684. Margaret Everson, Assistant Secretary, (202) 208-4545.*
Web, www.doi.gov

Responsible for programs associated with the development, conservation, and use of fish, wildlife, recreational, historical, and national park system resources. Coordinates marine environmental quality and biological resources programs with other federal agencies. Oversees the U.S. Fish and Wildlife Service and National Park Service.

National Park Service (NPS) *(Interior Dept.), 1849 C St. N.W., #3115, 20240; (202) 208-3818. Fax, (202) 208-7889. Paul Daniel Smith, Director (Acting). Press, (202) 208-6843.*
General email, asknps@nps.gov
Web, www.nps.gov and Twitter, @NatlParkService

Oversees coordination, planning, and financing of public outdoor recreation programs at all levels of government. Conducts recreation research surveys; administers financial assistance program to states for planning and development of outdoor recreation programs. (Some lands designated as national recreation areas are not under NPS jurisdiction.)

National Park Service (NPS) *(Interior Dept.), Policy, 1201 Eye St. N.W., 7th Floor, 20005 (mailing address: 1849 C St. N.W., Washington, DC 20240); (202) 354-3950. Fax, (202) 371-5189. Alma Ripps, Chief, (202) 354-3951. Web, www.nps.gov/applications/npspolicy/index.cfm*

Researches and develops management policy on matters relating to the National Park Service; makes recommendations on the historical significance of national trails and landmarks.

Tennessee Valley Authority, *Government Affairs, 500 N. Capitol St. N.W., #220, 20001; (202) 898-2999. Fax, (202) 898-2998. William D. (Bill) Johnson, President.*
General email, tvainfo@tva.gov
Web, www.tva.gov and Twitter, @TVAnews

Operates Land Between the Lakes, a national recreation and environmental education area located in western Kentucky and Tennessee.

U.S. Fish and Wildlife Service *(Interior Dept.), National Wildlife Refuge System, 1849 C St., #3349, 20240; (202) 208-5333. Cynthia Martinez, Chief. Toll-free, (800) 344-9453.*
Web, www.fws.gov/refuges and Twitter, @USFWSRefuges

Manages the National Wildlife Refuge System. Most refuges are open to public use; activities include bird and wildlife watching, fishing, hunting, and environmental education.

►CONGRESS

For a listing of relevant congressional committees and subcommittees, please see pages 283–284 or the Appendix.

►NONGOVERNMENTAL

American Hiking Society, *8605 2nd Ave., Silver Spring, MD 20910; (301) 565-6704. Fax, (301) 565-6714. Kathryn (Kate) Van Waes, Executive Director. Toll-free, (800) 972-8608.*

General email, info@americanhiking.org

Web, https://americanhiking.org,
Twitter, @AmericanHiking and Facebook, www.facebook
.com/AmericanHiking

Membership: individuals and clubs interested in preserving America's trail system and protecting the interests of trail users. Provides information on outdoor volunteer opportunities on public lands.

American Recreation Coalition, *1200 G St. N.W., #650, 20005; (202) 682-9530. Fax, (202) 682-9529. Derrick A. Crandall, President.*
General email, bnasta@funoutdoors.com

Web, www.funoutdoors.com, Twitter, @AmerRecreation and Facebook, www.facebook.com/American-Recreation-Coalition-164907310233438

Membership: recreation industry associations, recreation enthusiast groups, and leading corporations in the recreation products and services sectors. Promotes health and well-being through outdoor recreation. Monitors regulations and legislation.

National Park Foundation, *1110 Vermont Ave. N.W., #200, 20005; (202) 796-2500. Fax, (202) 796-2509. Will Shafroth, President; Bryan Traubert, Chair.*
General email, ask-npf@nationalparks.org

Web, www.nationalparks.org and Twitter, @GoParks

Encourages private-sector support of the national park system; provides grants and sponsors educational and cultural activities. Chartered by Congress and chaired by the Interior secretary.

National Park Trust, *401 E. Jefferson St., #207, Rockville, MD 20850; (301) 279-7275. Fax, (301) 279-7211. Grace K. Lee, Executive Director.*
General email, npt@parktrust.org

Web, www.parktrust.org and Twitter, @natparktrust

Protects national parks, wildlife refuges, and historic monuments. Uses funds to purchase private land within or adjacent to existing parks and land suitable for new parks; works with preservation organizations to manage acquired resources.

National Parks Conservation Assn., *777 6th St. N.W., #700, 20001-3723; (202) 223-6722. Fax, (202) 454-3333. Theresa Pierno, President. Information, (800) 628-7275.*
General email, npca@npca.org

Web, www.npca.org and Twitter, @npca

Citizens interest group that seeks to protect national parks and other park system areas.

National Recreation and Park Assn., *22377 Belmont Ridge Rd., Ashburn, VA 20148-4501; (703) 858-0784. Fax, (703) 858-0794. Barbara Tulipane, Chief Executive Officer, (703) 858-2140. Toll-free, (800) 626-6772.*
General email, customerservice@nrpa.org

Web, www.nrpa.org, Twitter, @nrpa_news and Facebook, www.facebook.com/ NationalRecreationandParkAssociation

Membership: park and recreation professionals and interested citizens. Promotes support and awareness of park, recreation, and leisure services; advances environmental and conservation efforts; facilitates development, expansion, and management of resources; provides technical assistance for park and recreational programs; and provides professional development to members. Monitors legislation and regulations.

Rails-to-Trails Conservancy, *2121 Ward Court N.W., 5th Floor, 20037; (202) 331-9696. Fax, (202) 223-9257. Ryan Chao, President. Press, (202) 974-5155.*
Web, www.railstotrails.org and Twitter, @railstotrails

Promotes the conversion of abandoned railroad corridors into hiking and biking trails for public use. Provides public education programs and technical and legal assistance. Publishes trail guides. Monitors legislation and regulations.

Scenic America, *727 15th St. N.W., #1100, 20005-6029; (202) 792-1300. Mark Falzone, President.*
General email, max.ashburn@scenic.org

Web, www.scenic.org and Twitter, @ScenicAmerica

Membership: national, state, and local groups concerned with land-use control, growth management, and landscape protection. Works to enhance the scenic quality of America's communities and countryside. Provides information and technical assistance on scenic byways, tree preservation, economics of aesthetic regulation, billboard and sign control, scenic areas preservation, and growth management.

Student Conservation Assn., *4245 N. Fairfax Dr., #825, Arlington, VA 22203; (703) 524-2441. Fax, (703) 524-2451. Jaime Berman Matyas, President.*
General email, DCinfo@thesca.org

Web, www.thesca.org and Twitter, @the_sca

Service organization that provides youth and adults with opportunities for training and work experience in natural resource management and conservation. Volunteers serve in national parks, forests, wildlife refuges, and other public lands.

The Wilderness Society, *1615 M St. N.W., 20036; (202) 833-2300. Fax, (202) 429-3958. Jamie Williams, President. Toll-free, (800) 843-9453.*
General email, action@tws.org

Web, www.wilderness.org and Twitter, @wilderness

Promotes preservation of wilderness and the responsible management of federal lands, including national parks and forests, wilderness areas, wildlife refuges, and land administered by the Interior Dept.'s Bureau of Land Management.

World Wildlife Fund (WWF), *1250 24th St. N.W., 20037-1193 (mailing address: P.O. Box 97180, Washington, DC 20090-7180); (202) 293-4800. Fax, (202) 293-9211. Carter S. Roberts, President.*
General email, membership@wwfus.org

Web, www.worldwildlife.org and Twitter, @World_Wildlife

International conservation organization that provides funds and technical assistance for establishing and maintaining parks.

Water Resources

▶**AGENCIES**

Agriculture Dept. (USDA), *Rural Development, Rural Utilities Service,* 1400 Independence Ave. S.W., #5135, MS 1510, 20250-1510; (202) 720-9540. Bette Brand, Administrator (Acting), (202) 690-4730.
Web, www.rd.usda.gov/about-rd/agencies/rural-utilities-service

Makes loans and provides technical assistance for development, repair, and replacement of water and waste disposal systems in rural areas.

Army Corps of Engineers *(Defense Dept.),* 441 G St. N.W., #3K05, 20314-1000; (202) 761-0001. Fax, (202) 761-4463. Lt. Gen. Todd T. Semonite (USA), Chief of Engineers. Press, (202) 761-0011.
General email, hq-publicaffairs@usace.army.mil
Web, www.usace.army.mil and *Twitter, @USACEHQ*

Provides local governments with disaster relief, flood control, navigation, and hydroelectric power services.

Bureau of Reclamation *(Interior Dept.),* 1849 C St. N.W., MS 7069-MIB, 20240-0001; (202) 513-0501. Fax, (202) 513-0309. Brenda Burman, Commissioner; Shelby Hagenauer, Deputy Commissioner. Press, (202) 513-0575.
Web, www.usbr.gov, Twitter, @usbr and *Facebook, www.facebook.com/bureau.of.reclamation* and *YouTube, www.youtube.com/user/reclamation*

Administers federal programs for water and power resource development and management in seventeen western states; oversees municipal and industrial water supplies, hydroelectric power generation, irrigation, flood control, water quality improvement, river regulation, fish and wildlife enhancement, and outdoor recreation. Water resource development projects include dams, power plants, and canals.

Environmental Protection Agency (EPA), *Water (OW),* 1200 Pennsylvania Ave. N.W., MC 4101M, 20460; (202) 564-5700. David Ross, Assistant Administrator.
Web, www.epa.gov/aboutepa/about-office-water

Monitors drinking water safety and restores and maintains oceans, watersheds, and their aquatic ecosystems. Implements the Clean Water Act and Safe Drinking Water Act.

Environmental Protection Agency (EPA), *Water (OW), Wetlands, Oceans, and Watersheds,* 1200 Pennsylvania Ave. N.W., #7301, MC 4501T, 20004; (202) 566-1146. Fax, (202) 566-1147. John Goodin, Director (Acting), (202) 566-1373.

General email, ow-owow-internet-comments@epa.gov
Web, www2.epa.gov/aboutepa/about-office-water#wetlands

Coordinates federal policies affecting marine and freshwater ecosystems, including watersheds, coastal ecosystems, and wetlands. Regulates and monitors ocean dumping and seeks to minimize polluted runoff and restore impaired waters. Manages dredge-and-fill program under section 404 of the Clean Water Act. Promotes public awareness of resource preservation and management.

Interior Dept. (DOI), *Assistant Secretary for Water and Science,* 1849 C St. N.W., #6641, MS 6341, 20240; (202) 208-3186. Fax, (202) 208-6948. Timothy R. (Tim) Petty, Assistant Secretary, (202) 513-0535.
Web, www.doi.gov

Administers departmental water, scientific, and research activities. Directs and supervises the Bureau of Reclamation and the U.S. Geological Survey.

Interstate Commission on the Potomac River Basin, 30 W. Gude Dr., #450, Rockville, MD 20850; (301) 984-1908. Carlton Haywood, Executive Director, ext. 105.
General email, info@icprb.org
Web, www.potomacriver.org

Nonregulatory interstate compact commission established by Congress to control and reduce water pollution and to restore and protect living resources in the Potomac River and its tributaries. Monitors water quality; assists metropolitan water utilities; seeks innovative methods for solving water supply and land resource problems. Provides information and educational materials on the Potomac River basin.

National Agricultural Library *(Agriculture Dept.), Water and Agricultural Information Center (WAIC),* 10301 Baltimore Ave., 1st Floor, Beltsville, MD 20705-2351; (301) 504-6077. Vacant, Coordinator, (301) 504-6218.
Web, www.nal.usda.gov/waic

Serves individuals and agencies seeking information on water quality and agriculture. Special subject areas include agricultural environmental management, irrigation, water availability, and water quality.

Smithsonian Environmental Research Center *(Smithsonian Institution),* 647 Contees Wharf Rd., Edgewater, MD 21037-0028 (mailing address: P.O. Box 28, Edgewater, MD 21037-0028); (443) 482-2200. Fax, (443) 482-2380. Anson H. (Tuck) Hines, Director, (443) 482-2208. Press, (443) 482-2325.
Web, https://serc.si.edu and *Twitter, @SmithsonianEnv*

Serves as a research center on water ecosystems in the coastal zone.

Tennessee Valley Authority, *Government Affairs,* 500 N. Capitol St. N.W., #220, 20001; (202) 898-2999. Fax, (202) 898-2998. William D. (Bill) Johnson, President.
General email, tvainfo@tva.gov
Web, www.tva.gov and *Twitter, @TVAnews*

Coordinates resource conservation, development, and land-use programs in the Tennessee River Valley. Operates the river control system; projects include flood control, navigation development, and multiple-use reservoirs.

U.S. Geological Survey (USGS) *(Interior Dept.), Water,* 12201 Sunrise Valley Dr., MS 436, Reston, VA 20192-0002; (703) 648-4557. Fax, (703) 648-5002.
Donald Walter (Don) Cline, Associate Director.
Web, http://water.usgs.gov

Administers the Water Resources Research Act of 1990. Monitors and assesses the quantity and quality of the nation's freshwater resources; collects, analyzes, and disseminates data on water use and the effect of human activity and natural phenomena on hydrologic systems; assesses sources and behavior of contaminants in the water environment, and develops tools to improve management and understanding of water resources. Provides federal agencies, state and local governments, international organizations, and foreign governments with scientific and technical assistance.

►**CONGRESS**

For a listing of relevant congressional committees and subcommittees, please see pages 283–284 or the Appendix.

►**NONGOVERNMENTAL**

American Rivers, 1101 14th St. N.W., #1400, 20005; (202) 347-7550. William Robert (Bob) Irvin, President. Toll-free, (877) 347-7550.
General email, akober@americanrivers.org
Web, www.americanrivers.org, Twitter, @americanrivers and Facebook, www.facebook.com/AmericanRivers

Works to preserve and protect the nation's river systems through public information and advocacy. Collaborates with grassroots river and watershed groups, other conservation groups, sporting and recreation groups, businesses, local citizens, and various federal, state, and tribal agencies. Monitors legislation and regulations.

American Water Works Assn., *Government Affairs,* 1300 Eye St. N.W., #701W, 20005; (202) 628-8303. Fax, (202) 628-2846. G. Tracy Mehan III, Executive Director.
General email, custsvc@awwa.org
Web, www.awwa.org

Membership: municipal water utilities, manufacturers of equipment for water industries, water treatment companies, and individuals. Provides information on drinking water treatment and trends and issues affecting water safety; publishes voluntary standards for the water industry; issues policy statements on water supply matters. Monitors legislation and regulations. (Headquarters in Denver, Colo.)

Assn. of State Drinking Water Administrators (ASDWA), 1401 Wilson Blvd., #1225, Arlington, VA 22209; (703) 812-9505. Fax, (703) 812-9506. Alan Roberson, Executive Director.
General email, info@asdwa.org
Web, www.asdwa.org and Twitter, @ASDWorg

Membership: state officials responsible for the drinking water supply and enforcement of safety standards. Monitors legislation and regulations.

Center for Water Security and Cooperation, 1701 Pennsylvania Ave. N.W., #300, 20006; (202) 796-8672. Alexandra Campbell-Ferrari, Executive Director.
General email, cwsc@ourwatersecurity.org
Web, www.ourwatersecurity.org, Twitter, @WaterLawyers and Facebook, www.facebook.com/TheCWSC

Nonpartisan organization dedicated to water security and management. Develops and facilitates policy to protect access to water and sewer services. Fosters cooperation and diplomacy in the approach to water security and rights.

Environmental Defense Fund, *Washington Office,* 1875 Connecticut Ave. N.W., #600, 20009-5728; (202) 387-3500. Fax, (202) 234-6049. Fred Krupp, President.
Information, (800) 684-3322.
Web, www.edf.org/offices/washington-dc and Twitter, @EnvDefenseFund

Citizens' interest group staffed by lawyers, economists, and scientists. Takes legal action on environmental issues; provides information on pollution prevention, environmental health, water resources, water marketing, and sustainable fishing. (Headquarters in New York.)

Irrigation Assn., 8280 Willow Oaks Corporate Dr., #400, Fairfax, VA 22031; (703) 536-7080. Fax, (703) 536-7019. Deborah Hamlin, Chief Executive Officer.
General email, info@irrigation.org
Web, www.irrigation.org

Membership: companies and individuals involved in irrigation, drainage, and erosion control worldwide. Promotes efficient and effective water management through training, education, and certification programs. Interests include economic development and environmental enhancement.

Izaak Walton League of America, 707 Conservation Lane, Gaithersburg, MD 20878-2983; (301) 548-0150. Fax, (301) 548-0146. Scott Kovarovics, Executive Director.
Toll-free, (800) 453-5463.
General email, info@iwla.org
Web, www.iwla.org, Twitter, @IWLA_org and Facebook, www.facebook.com/iwla.org

Grassroots organization that promotes conservation of natural resources and the environment. Coordinates a citizen action program to monitor and improve the condition of local streams.

National Assn. of Conservation Districts (NACD), 509 Capitol Court N.E., 20002-4937; (202) 547-6223. Fax, (202) 547-6450. Jeremy Peters, Chief Executive Officer.
General email, stewardship@nacdnet.org
Web, www.nacdnet.org and Twitter, @NACDconserve

Membership: conservation districts (local subdivisions of state government). Develops national policies and works to promote the conservation of water resources. Interests include erosion and sediment control and control of nonpoint source pollution.

National Assn. of Flood and Stormwater Management Agencies (NAFSMA), *1333 H St. N.W., 1000 West, 20005 (mailing address: P.O. Box 56764, Washington, DC 20040); (202) 289-8625. Fax, (202) 530-3389. Susan Gilson, Executive Director.*
General email, info@nafsma.org
Web, www.nafsma.org

Membership: state, county, and local governments, and special flood management districts concerned with management of water resources. Interests include stormwater management, disaster assistance, flood insurance, and federal flood management policy. Monitors legislation and regulations.

National Research Council (NRC), *Water Science and Technology Board,* *Keck Bldg., 500 5th St. N.W., #607, 20001; (202) 334-3422. Fax, (202) 334-1377. Catherine Kling, Chair; Elizabeth Eide, Director.*
General email, wstb@nas.edu
Web, http://dels.nas.edu/wstb

Supports science, engineering, economics, and policy research for the efficient management and use of water resources.

National Water Resources Assn. (NWRA), *4 E St. S.E., 20003; (202) 698-0693. Fax, (202) 698-0694. Ron Thompson, President; Ian Lyle, Executive Vice President.*
General email, nwra@nwra.org
Web, http://nwra.org, Twitter, @NWRA_Water and Facebook, www.facebook.com/NWRAWater

Membership: conservation and irrigation districts, municipalities, and others interested in water resources. Works for the development and maintenance of water resources and a sustainable water supply. Represents interests of members before Congress and regulatory agencies.

Rural Community Assistance Partnership (RCAP), *1701 K St. N.W., #700, 20006; (202) 408-1273. Fax, (202) 408-8165. Nathan Ohle, Executive Director. Toll-free, (800) 321-7227.*
General email, info@rcap.org
Web, https://rcap.org and Twitter, @RCAPInc

Provides expertise to rural communities on wastewater disposal, protection of groundwater supply, and access to safe drinking water. Targets communities with predominantly low-income or minority populations. Offers outreach policy analysis, training, and technical assistance to elected officials and other community leaders, utility owners and operators, and residents.

Water Environment Federation, *601 Wythe St., Alexandria, VA 22314-1994; (703) 684-2400. Fax, (703) 684-2492. Eileen O'Neill, Executive Director, (703) 684-2430. Toll-free, (800) 666-0206.*
General email, csc@wef.org
Web, www.wef.org and Twitter, @WEForg

Membership: civil and environmental engineers, wastewater treatment plant operators, scientists, government officials, and others concerned with water quality. Works to preserve and improve water quality worldwide. Provides the public with technical information and educational materials. Monitors legislation and regulations.

Water Research Foundation, *1199 N. Fairfax St., #900, Alexandria, VA 22314-1445; (571) 384-2100. Peter Grevatt, Chief Executive Officer, (571) 384-2094.*
General email, info@WaterRF.org
Web, www.waterrf.org, Twitter, @WaterResearch and Facebook, www.facebook.com/waterenvironmentRF

Conducts research and promotes technology to treat and recover materials from wastewater, stormwater, and seawater, including water, nutrients, energy, and biosolids. (Headquarters in Denver, Colo.)

9

Government Operations

GENERAL POLICY AND ANALYSIS

Basic Resources

▶**AGENCIES**

Administrative Conference of the United States (ACUS),
*1120 20th St. N.W., #706 South, 20036; (202) 480-2080.
Matthew L. Wiener, Executive Director, (202) 480-2104.
General email, info@acus.gov*
*Web, www.acus.gov, Twitter, @ACUSgov and
Facebook, www.facebook.com/ACUSgov*

Independent federal agency consisting of federal officials and experts from the private sector and academia; promotes efficiency and fairness in government procedures, regulatory programs, and grant and benefit administration. Conference committees include the Committee on Adjudication, Committee on Administration and Management, Committee on Collaborative Governance, Committee on Judicial Review, Committee on Regulation, and Committee on Rulemaking.

Domestic Policy Council (*Executive Office of the
President*), *The White House, 20502; (202) 456-5594.
Fax, (202) 456-3342. Joe Grogan, Director.*
*Web, www.whitehouse.gov/get-involved/internships/
presidential-departments*

Comprises cabinet officials and staff members. Coordinates the domestic policymaking process to facilitate the implementation of the president's domestic agenda throughout federal agencies in such major domestic policy areas as agriculture, education, energy, environment, health, housing, labor, and veterans affairs.

Executive Office of the President, *Intergovernmental
Affairs, 1600 Pennsylvania Ave. N.W., 20502; (202) 456-
1414. Fax, (202) 456-1641. Douglas L. Hoelscher, Director.
TTY, (202) 456-6213.*
Web, www.whitehouse.gov

Seeks to build relationships with constituents and to connect citizens with their elected officials.

Executive Office of the President, *Public Liaison,
Dwight D. Eisenhower Executive Office Bldg., #110, 20502;
(202) 456-1414. Fax, (202) 456-1641. Timothy Pataki,
Director. TTY, (202) 456-6213.*
Web, www.whitehouse.gov

Promotes presidential priorities through outreach to concerned constituencies and public interest groups.

General Services Administration (GSA), *Administration
(OAS), 1800 F St. N.W., 20405; (202) 527-0095.
Bob Stafford, Chief Administrative Services Officer. FOIA
Requester Service Center, 855-675-FOIA.*
*Web, www.gsa.gov/about-us/organization/office-of-
administrative-services*

Manages all aspects of the Freedom of Information Act (FOIA) program; responsible for the management of executive correspondence, maintaining the agency's internal directives, setting travel and charge card policies, and developing workplace initiatives.

General Services Administration (GSA),
*Governmentwide Policy, Acquisition Policy, 1800 F St.
N.W., 20405; (202) 501-1043. Jeffrey A. (Jeff) Koses, Deputy
Chief Acquisition Officer.*
*General email, askacquisition@gsa.gov and
FARPolicy@gsa.gov*
Web, www.gsa.gov/portal/category/101099

Develops and implements federal government acquisition policies and procedures; administers Federal Acquisition Regulation (FAR) for civilian agencies. Manages several GSA-specific and governmentwide acquisition database systems.

General Services Administration (GSA), *Technology
Transformation Service, 1800 F St. N.W., 2nd Floor,
20405; (202) 702-0781. Rob Cook, Commissioner.*
General email, tts-info@gsa.gov
Web, www.gsa.gov/tts

Utilizes current methodologies and technologies to improve the way the federal government provides the public with access to information and services. Works to aid agencies in creating services that are more understandable, attainable, and beneficial to the public.

General Services Administration (GSA), *USAGov, 1800
F St. N.W., 20405; (844) 872-4681. Fax, (202) 357-0078.*
*Web, www.usa.gov and Web (Spanish),
www.gobiernoUSA.gov*

Manages the portal site to U.S. government information, www.usa.gov. Manages kids.gov, a resource that provides government information on education, including primary, secondary, and higher education. Distributes free and low-cost federal publications of consumer interest via the Internet at www.usa.gov and Pueblo.gpo.gov. Assists people with questions about American government agencies, programs, and services via telephone, (800) FED-INFO ([800] 333-4636), or website, http://answers.usa.gov. Operates a contact center to provide information in English or Spanish on all federal government agencies, programs, and services via toll-free telephone, email, and chat. Operated under contract by Sykes in Pennsylvania and Florida. Responds to inquiries about federal programs and services. Gives information about or referrals to appropriate offices.

Office of Administration (*Executive Office of the
President*), *725 17th St. N.W., #240, 20503; (202) 456-
2861. Monica Block, Director (Acting).*
Web, www.whitehouse.gov/the-trump-administration

Provides administrative support services to the Executive Office of the President, including financial management and information technology support, human resources management, library and research assistance, facilities management, procurement, printing and graphics support, security, and mail and messenger operations.

Office of Management and Budget (OMB) (*Executive
Office of the President*), *725 17th St. N.W., 20503; (202)*

395-3080. Fax, (202) 395-3888. Mick Mulvaney, Director; Russell Vought, Deputy Director of Management. Press, (202) 395-7254.

Web, www.whitehouse.gov/omb and Twitter, @OMBPress

Works with other federal agencies to develop and maintain the website ExpectMore.gov, which uses the Program Assessment Rating Tool (PART) to gauge the effectiveness of federal programs. Holds programs accountable for improving their performance and management.

Office of Management and Budget (OMB) *(Executive Office of the President), Information and Regulatory Affairs, 725 17th St. N.W., #10236, 20503; (202) 395-5897. Fax, (202) 395-6102. Neomi Reo, Administrator. Press, (202) 395-7254.*

Web, www.whitehouse.gov/omb/information-regulatory-affairs

Oversees development of federal regulatory programs. Supervises agency information management activities in accordance with the Paperwork Reduction Act of 1995, as amended; reviews agency analyses of the effect of government regulatory activities on the U.S. economy.

Office of Management and Budget (OMB) *(Executive Office of the President), Statistical and Science Policy, 725 17th St. N.W., #10201, 20503; (202) 395-3093. Fax, (202) 395-7245. Nancy Potok, Chief. Press, (202) 395-7254.*

Web, www.whitehouse.gov/omb

Carries out the statistical policy and coordination functions under the Paperwork Reduction Act of 1995; develops long-range plans for improving federal statistical programs; develops policy standards and guidelines for statistical data collection, classification, and publication; evaluates statistical programs and agency performance.

Regulatory Information Service Center *(General Services Administration), 1800 F St. N.W., #2219F, 20405; (202) 482-7340. Fax, (202) 482-7360. Scott D. Anderson, Administrator (Acting).*

General email, risc@gsa.gov

Web, www.gsa.gov/risc and Twitter, @USGSA

Provides the president, Congress, and the public with information on federal regulatory policies and their effects on society; recommends ways to make regulatory information more accessible to government officials and the public. Publishes the Unified Agenda of Federal Regulatory and Deregulatory Actions. See www.reginfo.gov for information about government regulations.

▶CONGRESS

For a listing of relevant congressional committees and sub-committees, please see pages 320–321 or the Appendix.

Government Accountability Office (GAO), *Strategic Issues (SI), 441 G St. N.W., #2040C, 20548; (202) 512-6806. J. Christopher Mihm, Managing Director.*

Web, www.gao.gov/careers/strategicissues.html

Audits, analyzes, and evaluates intergovernmental relations activities, federal grants and regulations, tax issues, census activities, and the nation's overall financial condition.

Library of Congress, *Federal Research Division, John Adams Bldg., 101 Independence Ave. S.E., #LA 5281, 20540-4840; (202) 707-3900. Fax, (202) 707-3920. Mukta Ohri, Chief.*

General email, frds@loc.gov

Web, www.loc.gov/rr/frd

Provides research and analytical support to federal agencies and authorized federal contractors.

▶NONGOVERNMENTAL

American Political Science Assn. (APSA), *1527 New Hampshire Ave. N.W., 20036-1206; (202) 483-2512. Fax, (202) 483-2657. Steven Rathgeb Smith, Executive Director.*

General email, apsa@apsanet.org

Web, www.apsanet.org, Twitter, @APSAtweets and Facebook, www.facebook.com/likeAPSA

Membership: political scientists, primarily college and university professors. Promotes scholarly inquiry into all aspects of political science, including international affairs and comparative government. Acts as liaison with federal agencies, Congress, and the public. Offers congressional fellowships, workshops, and awards. Provides information on political science issues.

The Brookings Institution, *Governance Studies, 1755 Massachusetts Ave. N.W., 20036; (202) 797-6090. Fax, (202) 797-6144. Darrell M. West, Director, (202) 797-6481. Information, (202) 797-6000. Press, (202) 797-6105.*

Web, www.brookings.edu/governance

Explores the formal and informal political institutions of democratic governments to assess how they govern, how their practices compare, and how citizens and government servants can advance sound government.

Center for Regulatory Effectiveness (CRE), *1823 Jefferson Pl. N.W., #500, 20036; (202) 265-2383. James J. (Jim) Tozzi, Executive Director.*

General email, contact@thecre.com

Web, www.thecre.com

Clearinghouse for methods to improve the federal regulatory process and public access to data and information used to develop federal regulations. Conducts analyses of the activities of the OMB Office of Information and Regulatory Affairs and serves as a regulatory watchdog over executive branch agencies. Acts as advocate on regulatory issues.

Center for the Study of the Presidency and Congress, *601 13th St. N.W., #1050N, 20005; (202) 872-9800. Fax, (202) 872-9811. Glenn C. Nye, President.*

General email, hurst.renner@thepresidency.org

Web, www.thepresidency.org and Twitter, @CSPC_DC

Membership: college students, government officials, and business leaders interested in the presidency, government, and politics. Conducts conferences, lectures, and

GOVERNMENT OPERATIONS RESOURCES IN CONGRESS

For a complete listing of congressional committees, including their full contact information, leadership, membership, and jurisdictions, please refer to the Appendix on pages 827–948.

HOUSE:

House Administration Committee, (202) 225-8281.
Web, cha.house.gov

House Appropriations Committee, (202) 225-2771.
Web, appropriations.house.gov

Subcommittee on Commerce, Justice, Science, and Related Agencies, (202) 225-3351.

Subcommittee on Financial Services and General Government, (202) 225-7245.

Subcommittee on Legislative Branch, (202) 226-7252.

House Budget Committee, (202) 226-7270.
Web, budget.house.gov

House Education and the Workforce Committee, (202) 225-4527.
Web, edworkforce.house.gov

Subcommittee on Workforce Protections, (202) 225-4527.

House Energy and Commerce Committee, (202) 225-2927.
Web, energycommerce.house.gov

Subcommittee on Oversight and Investigations, (202) 225-2927.

House Ethics Committee, (202) 225-7103.
Web, ethics.house.gov

House Financial Services Committee, (202) 225-7502.
Web, financialservices.house.gov

Subcommittee on Oversight and Investigations, (202) 225-7502.

House Homeland Security Committee, (202) 226-8417.
Web, homeland.house.gov

Subcommittee on Oversight and Management Efficiency, (202) 226-8417.

House Judiciary Committee, (202) 225-3951.
Web, judiciary.house.gov

Subcommittee on the Constitution and Civil Justice, (202) 225-2825.

House Oversight and Government Reform Committee, (202) 225-5074.
Web, oversight.house.gov

Subcommittee on Government Operations, (202) 225-5074.

Subcommittee on Health Care, Benefits, and Administrative Rules, (202) 225-5074.

Subcommittee on Interior, Energy, and Environment, (202) 225-5074.

House Rules Committee, (202) 225-9191.
Web, rules.house.gov

House Science, Space, and Technology Committee, (202) 225-6371.
Web, science.house.gov

Subcommittee on Oversight, (202) 225-6371.

House Small Business Committee, (202) 225-5821.
Web, smallbusiness.house.gov

---

symposiums on domestic, economic, and foreign policy issues. Publishes papers, essays, books, and reports on various aspects of the presidency and Congress.

Partnership for Public Service, *1100 New York Ave. N.W., #200E, 20005; (202) 775-9111. Fax, (202) 775-8885. Max Stier, President. Press, (202) 775-6868. Web, www.ourpublicservice.org and Twitter, @RPublicService*

Membership: large corporations and private businesses, including financial and information technology organizations. Seeks to improve government efficiency, productivity, and management through a cooperative effort of the public and private sectors.

Buildings and Services

▶**AGENCIES**

General Services Administration (GSA), *1800 F St. N.W., 20405; (202) 501-0800. Emily W. Murphy, Administrator; Allison F. Brigati, Deputy Administrator; Carol F. Ochoa, Inspector General. Web, www.gsa.gov, Twitter, @usgsa and Facebook, www.facebook.com/GSA*

Establishes policies for managing federal government property, including construction and operation of buildings and procurement and distribution of supplies and equipment; manages transportation, telecommunications, and office space for federal employees. Manages disposal of surplus federal property. Responsible for www.USA.gov.

General Services Administration (GSA), *Asset and Transportation Management, 1800 F St. N.W., 20405; (202) 501-1777. Fax, (202) 273-4670. Alexander Kurien, Deputy Associate Administrator, (202) 969-4073. Web, www.gsa.gov/portal/category/21400*

Seeks to improve the management and control of procured transportation services governmentwide, promoting regulatory flexibility and business incentives and tools. Works to direct efficient use of assests through efficient policy formation for travel, employee relocation, personal and real property, motor vehicles, aircraft, transportation, and mail.

General Services Administration (GSA), *Catalog of Federal Domestic Assistance (CFDA), 2200 Crystal City Dr., Crystal Park 1, Arlington, VA 22202; 1800 F St. N.W., 20405-0001; (703) 605-2119. Michael Stephenson, Director. Help Desk, (866) 606-8220. Federal Service Desk, www.fsd.gov*

Subcommittee on Investigations, Oversight, and
Regulations, (202) 225-5821.
House Veterans' Affairs Committee, (202) 225-3527.
Web, veterans.house.gov
Subcommittee on Oversight and Investigations,
(202) 225-3569.
House Ways and Means Committee, (202) 225-3625.
Web, waysandmeans.house.gov
Subcommittee on Oversight, (202) 225-9263.

SENATE:

Senate Appropriations Committee, (202) 224-7257.
Web, appropriations.senate.gov
Subcommittee on Commerce, Justice, Science,
and Related Agencies, (202) 224-5202.
Subcommittee on Financial Services and General
Government, (202) 224-1133.
Subcommittee on Legislative Branch,
(202) 224-3477.
Senate Budget Committee, (202) 224-0642.
Web, www.budget.senate.gov
Senate Environment and Public Works Committee,
(202) 224-6176.
Web, epw.senate.gov
Subcommittee on Superfund, Waste Management,
and Regulatory Oversight, (202) 224-6176.
Subcommittee on Transportation and
Infrastructure, (202) 224-6176.

Senate Finance Committee, (202) 224-4515.
Web, finance.senate.gov
Subcommittee on Fiscal Responsibility and
Economic Growth, (202) 224-4515.
Senate Homeland Security and Governmental Affairs
Committee, (202) 224-4751.
Web, hsgac.senate.gov
Permanent Subcommittee on Investigations,
(202) 224-3721.
Subcommittee on Federal Spending,
Oversight, and Emergency Management,
(202) 224-7155.
Subcommittee on Regulatory Affairs and Federal
Management, (202) 224-4551.
Senate Judiciary Committee, (202) 224-5225.
Web, judiciary.senate.gov
Subcommittee on Oversight, Agency Action,
Federal Rights, and Federal Courts,
(202) 224-4224.
Senate Rules and Administration Committee,
(202) 224-6352.
Web, rules.senate.gov
Senate Select Committee on Ethics,
(202) 224-2981.
Web, ethics.senate.gov
Senate Small Business and Entrepreneurship
Committee, (202) 224-5175.
Web, sbc.senate.gov

Disseminates information on federal assistance programs available to state and local governments through the CFDA website. Information includes all types of federal aid and explains types of assistance, eligibility requirements, application processes, and suggestions for writing proposals. Catalog may be downloaded from the CFDA website. Printed version may be ordered from the Superintendent of Documents, U.S. Government Printing Office, Washington, DC 20402; (202) 512-1800, or toll-free, (866) 512-1800; or online at http://bookstore.gpo.gov.

General Services Administration (GSA), *Federal Acquisition Service, 1800 F St. N.W., 20405; (202) 357-5844. Alan Thomas Jr., Commissioner. National Customer Service Center (NCSC), (800) 488-3111 and NCSCcustomer.service@gsa.gov.*
General email, contactfas@gsa.gov
Web, www.gsa.gov/fas and Twitter, @FAS_Outreach

Responsible for providing federal agencies with common-use goods and nonpersonal services and for procurement and online acquisition tools, transportation and travel management, and motor vehicle management.

General Services Administration (GSA),
Governmentwide Policy, 1800 F St. N.W., 20405; (202)

549-2430. Fax, (202) 208-1224. Jessica Salmoiraghi, Associate Administrator.
Web, www.gsa.gov/ogp

Coordinates GSA policymaking activities, including areas of personal and real property, travel and transportation, acquisition (internal GSA and governmentwide), information technology, regulatory information, and use of federal advisory committees; promotes collaboration between government and the private sector in developing policy and management techniques; works to integrate acquisition, management, and disposal of government property.

General Services Administration (GSA), *National Capital Region (NCR), 301 7th St. S.W., #7022, 20024; (202) 708-9100. Fax, (202) 708-9966. Scott Anderson, Regional Administrator.*
Web, www.gsa.gov/about-us/regions/welcome-to-the-national-capital-region-11

Provides federal agencies with office space and property management services, assisted acquisition services, telecommunication and network services, energy conservation and recycling services, and property management services; has equal status with regional offices.

White House Offices

OFFICE OF THE PRESIDENT

President, Donald J. Trump

 1600 Pennsylvania Ave. N.W., 20500; (202) 456-1414, Fax (202) 456-2461;

 Web, www.whitehouse.gov;

 Email, president@whitehouse.gov

Chief of Staff, Mick Mulvaney (Acting), (202) 456-1414

Advance and Operations, Vacant, Director, (202) 456-1414

Cabinet Secretary, Bill McGinley, Director, (202) 456-1414

Communications, Vacant, Director, (202) 456-1414

Correspondence, Vacant, Director, (202) 456-1414

Counsel, Pat Cipollone, Chief White House Counsel, (202) 456-1414

House Liaison, Joyce Meyer, Deputy Assistant to the President, (202) 456-1414

Intergovernmental Affairs and Public Engagement, John DeStefano, Assistant to the President, (202) 456-1414

Legislative Affairs, Marc T. Short, Assistant to the President, (202) 456-1414

Management and Administration, Marcia Lee Kelly, Assistant to the President, (202) 456-1414

Media Affairs, Helen Aguirre Ferré, Director, (202) 456-6238

National Intelligence, Daniel Coats, Director, (703) 733-8600

National Security Advisor, John Bolton, (202) 456-1414

Presidential Personnel, John DeStefano, Assistant to the President, (202) 456-9713

Press Secretary, Sarah Huckabee Sanders, (202) 456-2580

Scheduling and Advance, Robert Peede Jr, Director, (202) 456-1414

Speechwriting, Stephen Miller, Director, (202) 456-1414

Staff Secretary, Derek Lyons, (202) 456-2702

U.S. Secret Service (Homeland Security), Randolph Alles, Director, (202) 406-5708

White House Fellows, Elizabeth Dial Pinkerton, Director, (202) 395-4522

White House Military Office, Daniel Walsh, Director, (202) 456-1414

OFFICE OF THE FIRST LADY

First Lady, Melania Trump

 1600 Pennsylvania Ave. N.W., 20500; (202) 456-1414; Web, www.whitehouse.gov/people/melania-trump

Chief of Staff, Lindsay Reynolds, Chief of Staff, 202-456-1414

Communications, Stephanie Grisham, Director; Vacant, Press Secretary (202) 456-1414

OFFICE OF THE VICE PRESIDENT

Vice President, Michael R. Pence, 1600 Pennsylvania Ave. N.W., 20500; (202) 456-1414,

 Web, www.whitehouse.gov/administration/vice-president-pence;

 Email, vice.president@whitehouse.gov

Chief of Staff, Nick Ayers, Chief of Staff, (202) 456-1414

Communications, Jarrod Agen, Director, (202) 456-1414

Wife of the Vice President, Karen Pence, (202) 456-1414

General Services Administration (GSA), *Portfolio Management and Real Estate,* 301 7th St. S.W., 20407; (202) 708-5334. Fax, (202) 208-0033. Chris Wisner, Director.

Web, www.gsa.gov/portal/category/22181

Provides execution, oversight and guidance for governmentwide real property asset management plans and related activities, including the use and disposal of excess real property and the acquisition of leased assets. Promotes and assesses compliance with management policies and regulations for the effective and efficient stewardship of federal real property assets and alternative workplaces.

General Services Administration (GSA), *Public Buildings Services,* 1800 F St. N.W., #6459, 20405; (202) 501-1100. Dan Mathews, Commissioner.

Web, www.gsa.gov/pbs

Administers the acquisition, construction, maintenance, and operation of buildings owned or leased by the federal government. Manages and disposes of federal real estate.

General Services Administration (GSA), *Urban Development/Good Neighbor Program,* 1800 F St. N.W., #3341, 20405-0001; (202) 501-1856. Fax, (202) 501-3393. Francis (Frank) Giblin, Program Manager, (202) 494-9236.

Web, www.gsa.gov/urbandevelopment and *Twitter, @GSA_urbdev*

Advises on locations, designs, and renovations of federal facilities in central business areas, historic districts, and local redevelopment areas where they can anchor or promote community development. Collaborates with local and national civic and other organizations. Serves as clearinghouse for good practices.

Ethics in Government

►AGENCIES

Administrative Conference of the United States (ACUS), *1120 20th St. N.W., #706 South, 20036; (202) 480-2080. Matthew L. Wiener, Executive Director, (202) 480-2104.*

The Cabinet of Donald J. Trump

The president's cabinet includes the vice president and the heads of fifteen executive departments. In addition, every president has discretion to elevate any number of other government officials to cabinet-rank status. The cabinet is primarily an advisory group.

VICE PRESIDENT

Michael R. Pence, Vice President, (202) 456-1414;
Web, www.whitehouse.gov/administration/
vice-president-pence;
Email, vice.president@whitehouse.gov

EXECUTIVE DEPT. CABINET MEMBERS

Agriculture, Sonny Perdue, Secretary, (202) 720-6630;
Web, www.usda.gov

Commerce, Wilbur Ross, Secretary, (202) 482-2000;
Web, www.commerce.gov; Email, TheSec@doc.gov

Defense, Patrick M. Shanahan, Secretary (Acting),
(703) 571-3343; Web, www.defense.gov

Education, Betsy DeVos, (202) 401-3000; Web, www.ed.gov

Energy, Rick Perry, Secretary, (202) 586-6210;
Web, www.energy.gov

Health and Human Services, Alex M. Azar II, Secretary,
(202) 690-7000; Web, www.hhs.gov

Homeland Security, Kevin McAleenan, Secretary (Acting),
(202) 282-8000; Web, www.dhs.gov

Housing and Urban Development, Ben Carson, Secretary,
(202) 708-0417; Web, www.hud.gov

Interior, David Bernhardt, Secretary (Acting),
(202) 208-3100; Web, www.doi.gov

Justice, William Pelham Barr, Attorney General,
(202) 514-2000; Web, www.justice.gov

Labor, Alexander Acosta, Secretary, (202) 693-6000;
Web, www.dol.gov

State, Michael Pompeo, Secretary, (202) 647-4000;
Web, www.state.gov

Transportation, Elaine Chao, Secretary, (202) 366-4000;
Web, www.dot.gov

Treasury, Steven Mnuchin, Secretary, (202) 622-2000;
Web, www.treasury.gov

Veterans Affairs, Robert Wilkie, Secretary, (202) 461-4800;
Web, www.va.gov

OTHER CABINET-RANK OFFICIALS

Council of Economic Advisers, Kevin Hassett, Chair,
(202) 456-1414; Web, www.whitehouse.gov/cea

Environmental Protection Agency, Andrew R. Wheeler,
Administrator, (202) 564-4700; Web, www.epa.gov

Office of Management and Budget, Mick Mulvaney,
Director, (202) 395-3080;
Web, www.whitehouse.gov/omb

Office of the White House Chief of Staff, Mick Mulvaney,
Chief of Staff (Acting), (202) 456-1414;
Web, www.whitehouse.gov

Small Business Administration, Linda McMahon,
Administrator, (202) 205-6708; Web, www.sba.gov

United States Mission to the United Nations,
Jonathan Cohen, Ambassador (Acting), (212) 415-4050

U.S. Trade Representative, Robert Lighthizer,
Ambassador, (202) 395-6890; Web, www.ustr.gov

General email, info@acus.gov

Web, www.acus.gov, Twitter, @ACUSgov and Facebook, www.facebook.com/ACUSgov

Independent federal agency consisting of federal officials and experts from the private sector and academia; promotes efficiency and fairness in government procedures, regulatory programs, and grant and benefit administration. Conference committees include the Committee on Adjudication, Committee on Administration and Management, Committee on Collaborative Governance, Committee on Judicial Review, Committee on Regulation, and Committee on Rulemaking.

Criminal Division *(Justice Dept.), Public Integrity (PIN), 1400 New York Ave. N.W., #12000, 20005; (202) 514-1412. AnnaLou Tirol, Chief (Acting).*
Web, www.justice.gov/criminal/pin

Conducts investigations of wrongdoing in selected cases that involve alleged corruption of public office or violations of election law by public officials, including members of Congress.

U.S. Office of Government Ethics, *1201 New York Ave. N.W., #500, 20005-3917; (202) 482-9300. Fax, (202) 482-9237. Emory A. Rounds III, Director. Press, (202) 482-9274. TTY, (800) 877-8339.*
General email, contactoge@oge.gov
Web, www.oge.gov

Ensures that executive branch ethics programs are in compliance with applicable ethics laws and regulations. Administers executive branch policies relating to financial disclosure, employee conduct, and conflict-of-interest laws. Works to prevent conflicts of interest on the part of federal employees and to resolve those that do occur. Provides educational materials and training; conducts outreach to the general public, the private sector, and civil society; shares model practices with and provides technical assistance to state, local, and foreign governments and international organizations; manages email list service to notify federal ethics officials of changes in law and regulations.

U.S. Office of Special Counsel, *1730 M St. N.W., #218, 20036-4505; (202) 804-7000. Fax, (202) 254-3711. Henry Kerner, Special Counsel; Ellen Chubin Epstein,*

Government Accountability Office

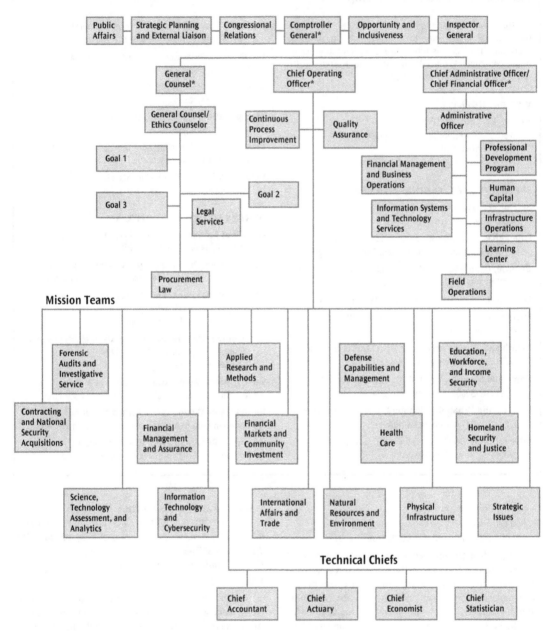

*The Executive Committee

Principal Deputy Special Counsel; Zachary Kurz, Communications Director; Catherine McMullen, Chief, Disclosure Unit. Issues relating to the Hatch Act, (800) 854-2824. Press, (202) 804-7065. Prohibited personnel practices, (800) 872-9855. TTY, (800) 877-8339. Whistleblower disclosure hotline, (800) 572-9855.

Web, www.osc.gov

General email, info@osc.gov

Investigates allegations of prohibited personnel practices and prosecutes individuals who violate federal statutes and regulations governing federal employees, military veterans, and reservists. Receives and refers federal employee disclosures of waste, fraud, inefficiency, mismanagement, and other violations in the federal government. Enforces the Hatch Act, which limits political activity by most federal and District of Columbia employees.

▶ CONGRESS

For a listing of relevant congressional committees and subcommittees, please see pages 320–321 or the Appendix.

Government Accountability Office (GAO), *441 G St. N.W., 20548; (202) 512-5500. Fax, (202) 512-5507. Gene L. Dodaro, Comptroller General. Congressional Relations, (202) 512-4400. Information, (202) 512-3000. Publications and documents, (202) 512-6000. General email, contact@gao.gov*

Web, www.gao.gov and Twitter, @USGAO

Independent, nonpartisan agency in the legislative branch. Serves as the investigating agency for Congress; carries out legal, accounting, auditing, and claims settlement functions; makes recommendations for more effective government operations; makes reports available to Congress and the public.

Government Accountability Office (GAO), *General Counsel, 441 G St. N.W., MS 7182, 20548; (202) 512-5400. Fax, (202) 512-7703. Thomas H. Armstrong, General Counsel. Web, www.gao.gov/legal*

Adjudicates challenges to the proposed or actual awards of government contracts; renders decisions and opinions on matters of appropriations law; provides legal expertise in support of GAO's functions.

▶ **NONGOVERNMENTAL**

Citizens Against Government Waste, *1100 Connecticut Ave. N.W., #650, 20036; (202) 467-5300. Fax, (202) 467-4253. Thomas A. Schatz, President. Media, (202) 467-5318. General email, webmaster@cagw.org*

Web, www.cagw.org and Twitter, @GovWaste

Taxpayer watchdog group that monitors government spending to identify how waste, mismanagement, and inefficiency in government can be eliminated. Has created criteria to identify pork-barrel spending. Publishes the annual *Congressional Pig Book*, which lists the names of politicians and their pet pork-barrel projects. Monitors legislation and regulations.

Citizens for Responsibility and Ethics in Washington (CREW), *1101 K St. N.W., #201, 20005; (202) 408-5565. Fax, (202) 588-5020. Noah Bookbinder, Executive Director. General email, info@citizensforethics.org*

Web, www.citizensforethics.org and Twitter, @CREWcrew

Promotes ethics and accountability in government and public life. Investigates, reports, and litigates government misconduct. Seeks to enforce government disclosure of information.

Federation of American Scientists (FAS), *Project on Government Secrecy, 1112 16th St. N.W., #400, 20036; (202) 546-3300. Fax, (202) 675-1010. Steven Aftergood, Project Director. General email, fas@fas.org*

Web, www.fas.org/issues/government-secrecy

Promotes public access to government information and fosters development of rational information security policies. Works to reduce the scope of government secrecy, including national security classification and declassification policies. Publishes hard-to-find government documents online.

Fund for Constitutional Government (FCG), *122 Maryland Ave. N.E., 20002; (202) 546-3799. Fax, (202) 543-3156. Conrad Martin, Executive Director. General email, info@fcgonline.org*

Web, www.fcgonline.org

Promotes an open and accountable government. Seeks to expose and correct corruption in the federal government and private sector through research and public education. Sponsors the Electronic Privacy Information Center, the Government Accountability Project, the Project on Government Oversight, and OpenTheGovernment.org.

Government Accountability Project (GAP), *1612 K St. N.W., #1100, 20006; (202) 457-0034. Fax, (202) 457-0059. Louis Clark, Executive Director. General email, info@whistleblower.org*

Web, www.whistleblower.org, Twitter, @GovAcctProj and Facebook, www.facebook.com/pg/ GovernmentAccountabilityProject

Membership: federal employees, union members, professionals, and interested citizens. Provides legal and strategic counsel to employees in the public and private sectors who seek to expose corporate and government actions that are illegal, wasteful, or repressive; aids such employees in personnel action taken against them; assists grassroots organizations investigating corporate wrongdoing, government inaction, or corruption. Promotes policy and legal reforms of whistleblower laws. (Formerly the National Whistleblower Center.)

Project on Government Oversight, *1100 G St. N.W., #500, 20005-3806; (202) 347-1122. Fax, (202) 347-1116. Danielle Brian, Executive Director. General email, info@pogo.org*

Web, www.pogo.org and Twitter, @POGOBlog

Public interest organization that works to expose waste, fraud, abuse, and conflicts of interest in all aspects of federal spending.

Sunlight Foundation, *1440 G St. N.W., 20005; (202) 742-1520. Fax, (202) 742-1524. John Wonderlich, Executive Director. General email, info@sunlightfoundation.com*

Web, https://sunlightfoundation.com and Twitter, @SunFoundation

Utilizes new information technology to make government more transparent and accountable. Projects include Sunlight Labs, Sunlight Reporting Group, http://PoliticalPartyTime.org, and http://influenceexplorer.com. Offers "OpenGov grants" for innovative projects that liberate or use municipal government data and tutorials for media and citizens on the role of money in politics.

Executive Reorganization

▶AGENCIES

Office of Management and Budget (OMB) *(Executive Office of the President), Performance and Personnel Management, 725 17th St. N.W., #7236, 20503; (202) 395-5017. Fax, (202) 395-5738. Margaret Weichert, Deputy Assistant Director. Press, (202) 395-7254.*
Web, www.whitehouse.gov/omb/performance

Examines, evaluates, and suggests improvements for agencies and programs within the Office of Personnel Management and the Executive Office of the President.

Office of Management and Budget (OMB) *(Executive Office of the President), President's Management Council, Dwight D. Eisenhower Executive Office Bldg., #216, 20503; Fax, (202) 395-6102. Jeffery Price, Council Contact. Press, (202) 395-7254.*
Web, www.whitehouse.gov/omb and www.gsa.gov/portal/content/133811

Membership: chief operating officers of federal government departments and agencies. Responsible for implementing the management improvement initiatives of the administration. Develops and oversees improved governmentwide management and administrative systems; formulates long-range plans to promote these systems; works to resolve interagency management problems and to implement reforms.

▶CONGRESS

For a listing of relevant congressional committees and subcommittees, please see pages 320–321 or the Appendix.

CENSUS, POPULATION DATA

General

▶AGENCIES

Census Bureau *(Commerce Dept.), 4600 Silver Hill Rd., #8H001, Suitland, MD 20746 (mailing address: 4600 Silver Hill Rd., #8H001, Washington, DC 20233-0100); (301) 763-2135. Steven Dillingham, Director. Information, (800) 923-8282. Library, (301) 763-2511. Press, (301) 763-3030. TTY, (800) 877-8339.*
General email, pio@census.gov
Web, www.census.gov and Twitter, @uscensusbureau

Conducts surveys and censuses (including the decennial census of population, the American Community Survey, the economic census, and census of governments); collects and analyzes demographic, social, economic, housing, foreign trade, and data on governmental data; publishes statistics for use by federal, state, and local governments, Congress, businesses, planners, and the public. Provides online resources and data analysis tools. Library open to the public Monday through Friday, 9:30 a.m.–3:30 p.m.

Census Bureau *(Commerce Dept.), Customer Liaison and Marketing Services, North Bldg., 4600 Silver Hill Rd., #8H180, Suitland, MD 20746 (mailing address: Customer Service, Bureau of the Census, MS 0801, Washington, DC 20233-0500); (301) 763-4636. Fax, (301) 763-6831. Misty Reed, Chief (Acting). Orders, (800) 923-8282. Press, (301) 763-3030.*
General email, clmso.call.center.help@census.gov
Web, www.census.gov/clo/www/clo.html

Main contact for information about the Census Bureau's products and services. Census data and maps on counties, municipalities, and other small areas are available on the website and in libraries.

Census Bureau *(Commerce Dept.), Decennial Census, 4600 Silver Hill Rd., #8H122, Suitland, MD 20746 (mailing address: 4600 Silver Hill Rd., #8H122, Washington, DC 20233-7000); (301) 763-4668. Albert E. Fontenot Jr., Associate Director. Press, (301) 763-3030. Toll-free, (800) 923-8282.*
Web, www.census.gov/programs-surveys/decennial-census/about.html

Provides data from the decennial census (including general plans and procedures); economic, demographic, and population statistics; and information on trends. Conducts preparation for the next census.

Census Bureau *(Commerce Dept.), Fertility and Family Statistics, 4600 Silver Hill Rd., #7H371, Suitland, MD 20746-8500 (mailing address: 4600 Silver Hill Rd., #7H371, Washington, DC 20233); (301) 763-2416. Rose Kreider, Chief.*
Web, www.census.gov/topics/health/fertility.html and www.census.gov/topics/families.html

Provides data and statistics on fertility and family composition. Conducts census and survey research on the number of children, household composition, and living arrangements of women in the United States, especially working mothers. Conducts studies on child care and child well-being.

Census Bureau *(Commerce Dept.), Geography, 4600 Silver Hill Rd., 4th Floor, Suitland, MD 20746 (mailing address: 4600 Silver Hill Rd., 4th Floor, Washington, DC 20233-7400); (301) 763-1128. Fax, (301) 763-4710. Deirdre Dalpiaz Bishop, Chief.*
General email, geo.geography@census.gov
Web, www.census.gov/geo

Manages the MAF TIGER system, a nationwide geographic and address database; prepares maps for use in conducting censuses and surveys and for showing their results geographically; determines names and current boundaries of legal geographic units; defines names and boundaries of selected statistical areas; develops geographic code schemes; maintains computer files of area measurements, geographic boundaries, and map features with address ranges.

Census Bureau *(Commerce Dept.), Population, 4600 Silver Hill Rd., #6H174, Suitland, MD 20746 (mailing address: 4600 Silver Hill Rd., #6H174, Washington, DC*

20233-8800); (301) 763-2071. Fax, (301) 763-2516. Karen Battle, Chief.

General email, pop@census.gov

Web, www.census.gov/programs-surveys/popproj.html

Prepares population estimates and projections for national, state, and local areas and congressional districts. Provides data on demographic and social statistics in the following areas: families and households, marital status and living arrangements, farm population, migration and mobility, population distribution, ancestry, fertility, child care, race and ethnicity, language patterns, school enrollment, educational attainment, and voting.

Census Bureau *(Commerce Dept.), Social, Economic, and Housing Statistics,* 4600 Silver Hill Rd., #7H174, Suitland, MD 20746 (mailing address: 4600 Silver Hill Rd., #7H174, Washington, DC 20233-8500); (301) 763-3195. Fax, (301) 763-3232. David G. Waddington, Chief.

Web, www.census.gov/topics/housing.html

Develops statistical programs for the decennial census, the American Community Survey, and for other surveys on housing, income, poverty, and the labor force. Collects and explains the proper use of economic, social, and demographic data. Responsible for the technical planning, analysis, and publication of data from current surveys, including the decennial census, the American Community Survey, the American Housing Survey, the Current Population Survey, and the Survey of Income and Program Participation.

▶**CONGRESS**

For a listing of relevant congressional committees and subcommittees, please see pages 320–321 or the Appendix.

▶**NONGOVERNMENTAL**

Population Assn. of America, 8630 Fenton St., #722, Silver Spring, MD 20910; (301) 565-6710. Fax, (301) 565-7850. John Casterline, President; Noreen Goldman, Vice President.

Web, www.populationassociation.org and Twitter, @PopAssocAmerica

Membership: university, government, and industry researchers in demography. Publishes newsletters, monitors legislation and related government activities, and supports collaboration of demographers. Holds annual technical sessions to present papers on domestic and international population issues and statistics.

Population Reference Bureau, 1875 Connecticut Ave. N.W., #520, 20009-5728; (202) 483-1100. Fax, (202) 328-3937. Jeffrey Jordan, President. Media, (202) 939-5407. Toll-free, (800) 877-9881.

General email, popref@prb.org

Web, www.prb.org and Twitter, @PRBdata

Educational organization engaged in information dissemination, training, and policy analysis on domestic and international population trends and issues. Interests include international development and family planning programs, the environment, and U.S. social and economic policy.

Urban Institute, *Center on Labor, Human Services, and Population,* 500 L'Enfant Plaza S.W., 20024; (202) 833-7200. Fax, (202) 463-8522. Signe-Mary McKernan, Vice President.

Web, www.urban.org/policy-centers/center-labor-human-services-and-population

Analyzes employment and income trends, studies how the U.S. population is growing, and evaluates programs dealing with homelessness, child welfare, and job training. Other areas of interest include immigration, mortality, sexual and reproductive health, adolescent risk behavior, child care, domestic violence, and youth development.

CIVIL SERVICE

General

▶**AGENCIES**

National Archives and Records Administration (NARA), *Information Security Oversight (ISOO),* 700 Pennsylvania Ave. N.W., #100, 20408-0001; (202) 357-5250. Fax, (202) 357-5907. Mark A. Bradley, Director.

General email, isoo@nara.gov

Web, www.archives.gov/isoo

Receiving guidance from the National Security Council, oversees policy on security classification on documents for the federal government and industry; monitors performance of all security classification/declassification programs for the federal government and industry; develops policies and procedures for sensitive unclassified information. Evaluates implementation, advises department and agency heads of corrective actions, and prepares an annual report to the president.

Office of Personnel Management (OPM), 1900 E St. N.W., #5A09, 20415-0001; (202) 606-1800. Fax, (202) 606-2573. Margaret Weichert, Director (Acting). Press, (202) 606-2402. TTY, (800) 877-8339.

Web, www.opm.gov, Twitter, @USOPM and Facebook, www.facebook.com/USOPM

Administers civil service rules and regulations; sets policy for personnel management, labor-management relations, workforce effectiveness, and employment within the executive branch; manages federal personnel activities, including recruitment, pay comparability, and benefit programs.

Office of Personnel Management (OPM), *Data Analysis Group,* 1900 E St. N.W., #2449, 20415-0001; (202) 606-1909. Fax, (202) 606-1719. Bob Heim, Group Manager.

General email, fedstats@opm.gov

Web, www.opm.gov/policy-data-oversight/data-analysis-documentation/federal-employment-reports

Official government source of statistics on the government workforce. Produces information and analyses for the Office of Personnel Management, Congress, and

Human Resources for Federal Departments and Agencies

DEPARTMENTS

Agriculture, Roberta Jeanquart, (202) 720-3585

Commerce, Kevin E. Mahoney, (202) 482-4807

Defense, William H. Booth, (703) 571-3343

Education, Cassandra Cuffee-Graves, (202) 453-5588

Energy, Tonya M. Mackey (Acting), (202) 586-1234

Health and Human Services, Christine Major, (202) 690-6191

Homeland Security, Chip Fulghum, (202) 282-8000

Housing and Urban Development, Towanda Brooks, (202) 708-0940

Interior, LC Williams, (202) 208-3100

Justice, Mari Barr Santangelo, (202) 514-4350

Labor, Sydney Rose, (202) 693-7600

State, William E. Todd (Acting), (202) 647-9898

Transportation, Susan Schwartz, (202) 366-4088

Treasury, J. Trevor Norris, (202) 622-2000

AGENCIES

Agency for International Development, Bob Leavitt, (202) 712-1234

Commodity Futures Trading Commission, Karen Leydon, (202) 418-5007

Environmental Protection Agency, Linda L. Gray, (202) 564-4606

Federal Communications Commission, Tom Green, (202) 418-0116

Federal Election Commission, Edward W. Holder (Acting), (202) 694-1007

Federal Energy Regulatory Commission, Alyssa Asonye, (202) 502-6300

Federal Maritime Commission, Todd Cole, (202) 523-5773

Federal Mediation and Conciliation Service, Traci Coddington, (202) 606-5466

Federal Trade Commission, Vicki A. Barber, (202) 326-2700

General Services Administration, Antonia Harris, (202) 501-0398

Government Accountability Office, Bill White, (202) 512-5811

National Credit Union Assn., Cheryl Eyre, (703) 518-6510

National Endowment for the Arts, Craig McCord, (202) 682-5405

National Endowment for the Humanities, Anthony Mitchell, (202) 606-8415

National Labor Relations Board, Chonita Young, (202) 273-3900

National Science Foundation, Dianne M. Campbell Krieger, (703) 292-8180

National Transportation Safety Board, Emily Carroll, (202) 314-6233

Nuclear Regulatory Commission, Miriam Cohen, (301) 415-7400

Securities and Exchange Commission, Lacey Dingman, (202) 551-7500

Smithsonian Institution, James Douglas, (202) 633-6370

U.S. International Trade Commission, Eric Mozie, (202) 205-2651

---

the public on statistical aspects of the federal civilian workforce, including trends in composition, grade levels, minority employment, sizes of agencies, and salaries.

Office of Personnel Management (OPM), *Veterans Services, 1900 E St. N.W., #7439, 20415; (202) 606-3602. Fax, (202) 606-6017. Hakeem Basheerud-Deen, Director. Web, www.opm.gov/policy-data-oversight/veterans-services*

Monitors federal agencies' personnel practices and develops policies and programs for veterans.

State Dept., *Bureau of Human Resources, 2201 C St. N.W., #6218, 20520; (202) 647-9898. Fax, (202) 647-5080. Carol Z. Perez, Director General. Web, www.state.gov/m/dghr*

Manages human resource policies for the department's Foreign and Civil Service employees in the areas of recruitment, assignment evaluation, promotion, discipline, career development, and retirement.

State Dept., *Bureau of Human Resources, Family Liaison, 2201 C St. N.W., #1239, 20520-0108; (202) 647-1076. Fax, (202) 647-1670. Susan Frost, Director. Toll-free, (800) 440-0397. General email, flo@state.gov Web, www.state.gov/m/dghr/flo*

Works to improve the quality of life of U.S. government employees and their family members assigned to, or returning from, a U.S. embassy or consulate abroad. Areas of interest are education and youth, family member employment, and support services for personal and past crises, including evacuations. Manages the worldwide Community Liaison Office program.

U.S. Office of Special Counsel, *1730 M St. N.W., #218, 20036-4505; (202) 804-7000. Fax, (202) 254-3711. Henry Kerner, Special Counsel; Ellen Chubin Epstein, Principal Deputy Special Counsel; Zachary Kurz, Communications Director; Catherine McMullen, Chief,*

Disclosure Unit. Issues relating to the Hatch Act, (800) 854-2824. Press, (202) 804-7065. Prohibited personn, (800) 872-9855. TTY, (800) 877-8339. Whistleblower disclosure hotline, (800) 572-9855.

Web, www.osc.gov

General email, info@osc.gov

Interprets federal laws, including the Hatch Act, concerning political activities allowed by certain federal employees; investigates allegations of Hatch Act violations and conducts prosecutions. Investigates and prosecutes complaints under the Whistleblower Protection Act.

►CONGRESS

For a listing of relevant congressional committees and subcommittees, please see pages 320–321 or the Appendix.

►NONGOVERNMENTAL

American Federation of Government Employees (AFGE), *80 F St. N.W., 20001; (202) 737-8700. Fax, (202) 639-6490. J. David Cox, President, (202) 639-6435; Tom Kahn, Director of Legislative and Political Affairs, (202) 639-6404. Membership, (202) 639-6410. Press, (202) 639-6453.*

General email, comments@afge.org

Web, www.afge.org

Membership: approximately 670,000 federal and District of Columbia government employees. Provides legal services to members; assists members with contract negotiations and grievances. Monitors legislation and regulations. (Affiliated with the AFL-CIO.)

Blacks in Government, *3005 Georgia Ave. N.W., 20001-3807; (202) 667-3280. Fax, (202) 667-3705. Doris H. Sartor, President.*

General email, bignational@bignet.org

Web, www.bignet.org and Twitter, @BigNational

Advocacy organization for public employees. Promotes equal opportunity and career advancement for African American government employees; provides career development information; seeks to eliminate racism in the federal workforce; sponsors programs, business meetings, and social gatherings; represents interests of African American government workers to Congress and the executive branch; promotes voter education and registration.

Federal Managers Assn., *1641 Prince St., Alexandria, VA 22314-2818; (703) 683-8700. Fax, (703) 683-8707. Renee M. Johnson, National President; Todd V. Wells, Executive Director, ext. 102.*

General email, info@fedmanagers.org

Web, www.fedmanagers.org

Seeks to improve the effectiveness of federal supervisors and managers and the operations of the federal government. Interests include cost-effective government restructuring, competitive civil service pay and benefits, and maintaining the core values of the civil service.

Federally Employed Women, *455 Massachusetts Ave. N.W., 20001 (mailing address: P.O. Box 306, Washington,*

DC 20001); (202) 898-0994. Fax, (202) 898-1535. Karen Rainey, President.

General email, few@few.org

Web, www.few.org and Facebook, www.facebook.com/ federallyemployedwomen

Membership: women and men who work for the federal government. Works to eliminate sex discrimination in government employment and to increase job opportunities for women; offers training programs. Monitors legislation and regulations.

Senior Executives Assn., *77 K St. N.E., #2600, 20002; (202) 971-3300. Fax, (202) 971-3317. Bill Valdez, President.*

General email, action@seniorexecs.org

Web, https://seniorexecs.org and Twitter, @seniorexecs

Professional association representing Senior Executive Service members and other federal career executives. Sponsors professional education. Interests include management improvement. Monitors legislation and regulations.

Dismissals and Disputes

►AGENCIES

Merit Systems Protection Board, *1615 M St. N.W., 5th Floor, 20419; (202) 653-7200. Fax, (202) 653-7130. Dennis Kirk, Chair; Jennifer R. Everling, Clerk of the Board (Acting). Message line, (202) 254-4800. MSPB Inspector General hotline, (800) 424-9121. TTY, (800) 877-8339.*

General email, mspb@mspb.gov

Web, www.mspb.gov

Independent quasi-judicial agency that handles hearings and appeals involving federal employees; protects the integrity of federal merit systems and ensures adequate protection for employees against abuses by agency management. Library open to the public by appointment.

Merit Systems Protection Board, *Appeals Counsel, 1615 M St. N.W., 20419; (202) 653-7200. Fax, (202) 653-7130. Susan Swafford, Director.*

General email, mspb@mspb.gov

Web, www.mspb.gov/appeals/appeals.htm

Analyzes and processes petitions for review of appeals decisions from the regional offices; prepares opinions and orders for board consideration; analyzes and processes cases that are reopened and prepares proposed depositions.

Merit Systems Protection Board, *Policy and Evaluations, 1615 M St. N.W., 20419; (202) 653-7200. Fax, (202) 653-7130. James M. Read, Director, (202) 254-4464; James Tsugawa, Deputy Director, (202) 254-4506. Information, (202) 254-4496. TTY, (800) 877-8339.*

General email, studies@mspb.gov

Web, www.mspb.gov

Conducts studies on the civil service and other executive branch merit systems; reports to the president and Congress on whether federal employees are adequately protected against political abuses and prohibited personnel

Financial Officers for Federal Departments and Agencies

DEPARTMENTS

Agriculture, Lynn Moaney (Acting), (202) 720-0727

Commerce, Tom Gilman, (202) 482-4951

Defense, David L. Norquist, (703) 545-6700

Air Force, John Roth, (703) 697-1974

Army, John E. Whitley, (703) 614-4356

Navy, Thomas W. Harker, (703) 697-2325

Education, Douglas Webster, (202) 245-8176

Energy, Randall Henrickson, (202) 586-4171

Health and Human Services, Sheila Conley, (202) 690-6396

Homeland Security, Stacy Marcott (Acting), (202) 447-5751

Coast Guard, Rear Adm. Andrew J. Tiongson, (202) 372-3470

Housing and Urban Development, Irving L. Dennis, (202) 708-1946

Interior, Scott Cameron, (202) 208-6593

Justice, Leigh Benda, (202) 307-0623

Labor, Geoffrey Kenyon, (202) 693-6800

State, Christopher Flaggs, (202) 647-4000

Transportation, Lana T. Hurdle, (202) 366-9191

Treasury, Joseph M. Otting, Comptroller of the Currency, (202) 649-6400

Veterans Affairs, Edward Murray (Acting), (202) 461-6600

AGENCIES

Advisory Council on Historic Preservation, Ismail D. Ahmed, (202) 517-0204

Agency for International Development, Reginald Mitchell, (202) 712-0000

Central Intelligence Agency, Vacant, (703) 482-0623

Commission on Civil Rights, TinaLouise Martin, (202) 376-8364

Commodity Futures Trading Commission, Mary Jean Buhler, (202) 418-5089

Consumer Product Safety Commission, Jay Hoffman, (301) 504-7207

Corporation for National and Community Service, Robert McCarty, (202) 606-7503

Corporation for Public Broadcasting, William P. Tayman, (202) 879-9600

Environmental Protection Agency, Vacant, (202) 564-1151

Equal Employment Opportunity Commission, Germaine P. Roseboro, (202) 663-4900

Export-Import Bank, David M. Sena, (202) 565-3946

Farm Credit Administration, Stephen G. Smith, (703) 883-4275

Federal Bureau of Investigation, Richard L. Haley II, (202) 324-3000

Federal Communications Commission, Kathleen Heuer, (202) 418-4560

Federal Deposit Insurance Corporation, Steven O. App, (202) 898-8732

Federal Election Commission, Gilbert Ford (Acting), (202) 694-1315

Federal Emergency Management Agency, Mary Comans, (202) 646-2500

Federal Energy Regulatory Commission, William Douglas Foster Jr., (202) 502-6118

Federal Home Loan Mortgage Corporation (Freddie Mac), James G. MacKey, (703) 903-2000

Federal Maritime Commission, Leonard Ballard, (202) 523-5770

---

practices. Conducts annual oversight review of the Office of Personnel Management.

Merit Systems Protection Board, *Washington Regional Office, 1901 S. Bell St., #950, Arlington, VA 22202; (703) 756-6250. Fax, (703) 756-7112. Hon. Jeremiah Cassidy, Regional Director.*
General email, washingtonregionaloffice@mspb.gov
Web, www.mspb.gov

Hears and decides appeals of adverse personnel actions (such as removals, suspensions for more than fourteen days, and reductions in grade or pay), retirement, and performance-related actions for federal civilian employees who work in the Washington, D.C., area, Virginia, North Carolina, or in overseas areas not covered by other regional board offices. Federal civilian employees who work outside

Washington should contact the Merit Systems Protection Board regional office in their area.

Office of Personnel Management (OPM), *Employee Services, Partnership and Labor Relations, Employee Accountability, 1900 E St. N.W., #7H28H, 20415-0001; (202) 606-2930. Fax, (202) 606-2613. Debra Buford, Manager.*
General email, er@opm.gov
Web, www.opm.gov/er

Develops, implements, and interprets policy on governmentwide employee relations. Intervenes in or seeks reconsideration of erroneous third-party decisions.

Office of Personnel Management (OPM), *General Counsel, 1900 E St. N.W., #7347, 20415-0001; (202)*

Federal Mediation and Conciliation Service,
Prasad Kotiswaran, (202) 606-8100

Federal National Mortgage Association (Fannie Mae),
David Benson, (202) 752-7000

Federal Trade Commission, David Rebich,
(202) 326-2201

General Services Administration, Gerard Badorrek,
(202) 501-1721

Government Accountability Office, Karl Maschino,
(202) 512-5800

**International Bank for Reconstruction and
Development (World Bank),** Joaquim Levy,
(202) 473-1000

John F. Kennedy Center for the Performing Arts,
Lynne Pratt, (202) 416-8000

Merit Systems Protection Board, Kevin J. Nash,
(202) 653-7263

National Academy of Sciences, Mary Didi Salmon,
(202) 334-2000

National Aeronautics and Space Administration,
Andrew Hunter (Acting), (202) 358-0001

National Archives and Records Administration,
Colleen Murphy (Acting), (301) 837-2000

National Credit Union Administration, Rendell L. Jones,
(703) 518-6570

National Endowment for the Arts, Heidi Ren,
(202) 682-5491

National Endowment for the Humanities, Sean Doss,
(202) 606-8336

National Labor Relations Board, Mehul Parekh,
(202) 208-3000

National Mediation Board, Samantha T. Jones (Assistant),
(202) 692-5010

National Railroad Passenger Corporation (Amtrak),
William Feidt, (202) 906-4020

National Science Foundation, Teresa Grancorvitz,
(703) 292-4435

National Transportation Safety Board, Edward Benthall,
(202) 314-6000

Nuclear Regulatory Commission, Maureen Wylie,
(301) 415-7322

Occupational Safety and Health Review Commission,
Debra A. Hall, (202) 606-5380

Office of Management and Budget, Mick Mulvaney,
(202) 395-3080

Office of Personnel Management, Don Pierce,
(202) 606-5040

Overseas Private Investment Corporation,
Mildred Callear, (202) 336-8400

Peace Corps, Jacqueline P Carey,
(202) 692-1600

Pension Benefit Guaranty Corporation, Patricia Kelly,
(202) 326-4170

Postal Regulatory Commission, Stacy L. Ruble,
(202) 789-6800

Securities and Exchange Commission, Caryn Kauffman
(Acting), (202) 551-8834

Small Business Administration, Tim Gribben,
(202) 205-6449

Smithsonian Institution, Vacant, (202) 633-6370

Social Security Administration, Michelle King,
(410) 965-7748

U.S. International Trade Commission, Lois Chandler,
(202) 205-3098

U.S. Postal Service, Joseph R. Corbett,
(202) 268-5272

606-1700. Fax, (202) 606-2609. *Vacant, General Counsel;
Kathie Ann Whipple, Deputy General Counsel.
Web, www.opm.gov/about-us/our-people-organization/
office-of-the-general-counsel*

Represents the federal government before the Merit
Systems Protection Board, other administrative tribunals,
and the courts.

U.S. Office of Special Counsel, *1730 M St. N.W., #218,
20036-4505; (202) 804-7000. Fax, (202) 254-3711.
Henry Kerner, Special Counsel; Ellen Chubin Epstein,
Principal Deputy Special Counsel; Zachary Kurz,
Communications Director; Catherine McMullen, Chief,
Disclosure Unit. Issues relating to the Hatch Act, (800)
854-2824. Press, (202) 804-7065. Prohibited personnel
practices, (800) 872-9855. TTY, (800) 877-8339.
Whistleblower disclosure hotline, (800) 572-9855.*

*Web, www.osc.gov
General email, info@osc.gov*

Investigates allegations of prohibited personnel practices, including reprisals against whistleblowers (federal
employees who disclose waste, fraud, inefficiency, and
wrongdoing by supervisors of federal departments and
agencies). Initiates necessary corrective or disciplinary
action. Enforces the Hatch Act, which limits political activity by most federal and District of Columbia
employees.

▶ JUDICIARY

U.S. Court of Appeals for the Federal Circuit, *717
Madison Pl. N.W., 20439; (202) 275-8000. Fax, (202)
275-9678. Sharon Prost, Chief Judge; Peter R. Marksteiner,*

Clerk of the Court, (202) 272-8020. Mediation, (202) 275-8120.
Web, www.cafc.uscourts.gov

Reviews decisions of the Merit Systems Protection Board.

Hiring, Recruitment, and Training

▶AGENCIES

General Services Administration (GSA), *Federal Acquisition Institute, Bldg. 270, 9830 Flagler Rd., Ft. Belvoir, VA 22060-5565 (mailing address: 9820 Belvoir Rd., Bldg. 270, Ft. Belvoir, VA 22060); (703) 805-2333. Jeffrey Birch, Director.*
General email, contact@fai.gov

Web, www.fai.gov and www.gsa.gov/portal/content/118227

Fosters development of a professional acquisition workforce governmentwide; collects and analyzes acquisition workforce data; helps agencies identify and recruit candidates for the acquisitions field; develops instructional materials; evaluates training and career development programs.

Office of Personnel Management (OPM), *Classification and Assessment Policy, 1900 E St. N.W., #6500, 20415-0001; (202) 606-3600. Fax, (202) 606-4891. April Davis, Manager.*
General email, fedclass@opm.gov

Web, www.opm.gov

Develops job classification standards for occupations in the general schedule and federal wage system.

Office of Personnel Management (OPM), *Human Resources Solutions, 1900 E St. N.W., #2469F, 20415-1000; (202) 606-0900. Fax, (202) 606-9200. Joseph S. Kennedy, Associate Director.*
Web, www.opm.gov/about-us/our-people-organization/ program-divisions/human-resources-solutions

Manages federal human resources policy, including staffing, compensation, benefits, labor relations, and position classification.

Office of Personnel Management (OPM), *Merit System Accountability and Compliance, 1900 E St. N.W., #6484, 20415-5100; (202) 606-2980. Fax, (202) 606-5056. Mark W. Lambert, Associate Director.*
Web, www.opm.gov/about-us/our-people-organization/ program-divisions/merit-system-accountability-and-compliance

Responsible for training and curriculum development programs for government executives and supervisors.

Office of Personnel Management (OPM), *National Background Investigations Bureau, 1900 E St. N.W., #2H31, 20415-0001; (202) 606-1800. Fax, (202) 606-2390. Charles Phalen, Director, (202) 606-0948. TTY, (202) 606-2532.*
General email, FISinquiries@opm.gov
Web, www.opm.gov/investigations

Initiates and conducts investigations of new federal employees.

Office of Personnel Management (OPM), *Veterans Services, 1900 E St. N.W., #7439, 20415; (202) 606-3602. Fax, (202) 606-6017. Hakeem Basheerud-Deen, Director.*
Web, www.opm.gov/policy-data-oversight/veterans-services

Provides federal employees and transitioning military service members and their families, federal human resources professionals, and hiring managers with information on employment opportunities with the federal government.

Office of Personnel Management (OPM), *Veterans Services, Intergovernmental Personnel Act Mobility Program, 1900 E St. N.W., #7463, 20415-0001; (202) 606-1155. Fax, (202) 606-4430. Gregory Snowden, Program Head.*
General email, ipa@opm.gov

Web, www.opm.gov/programs/ipa

Implements temporary personnel exchanges between federal agencies and nonfederal entities, including state and local governments, institutions of higher education, and other organizations.

State Dept., *Bureau of Human Resources, Career Development and Assignments, 2121 Virginia Ave. N.W., #4100, 20522 (mailing address: HR/CDA, Washington, DC 20520-6258); (202) 663-8094. Fax, (202) 663-0994. David Burns, Director.*
Web, www.state.gov

Coordinates programs related to the professional development of American members of the Foreign Service, including career development and assignment counseling programs, training, and presidential appointments and resignations.

▶NONGOVERNMENTAL

Society of American Indian Government Employees, *(410) 802-2190. Fredericka Joseph, Chair.*
General email, chair@saige.org

Web, https://saige.org

Facebook, Facebook

Fosters the recruitment, development, and advancement of American Indians and Alaska Natives in the government workforce. Promotes communication among its members. Serves as an information clearinghouse. Coordinates training and conferences for government employees on issues concerning American Indians and Alaska Natives. Monitors legislation and policies. (Headquarters in Skiatook, Okla.)

Labor-Management Relations

▶AGENCIES

Federal Labor Relations Authority, *1400 K St. N.W., 20424-0001; (202) 218-7770. Fax, (202) 482-6526. Colleen Duffy Kiko, Chair; William Tosick, Executive Director, (202) 218-7791. Press, (202) 218-7776.*
Web, www.flra.gov

Oversees the federal labor-management relations program; administers the law that protects the right of non-postal federal employees to organize, bargain collectively, and participate through labor organizations of their own choosing.

Federal Service Impasses Panel *(Federal Labor Relations Authority)*, *1400 K St. N.W., #200, 20424-0001; (202) 218-7790. Fax, (202) 482-6674. Kimberly Moseley, Executive Director; Mark A. Carter, Chair.*
Web, www.flra.gov/components-offices/components/federal-service-impasses-panel-fsip-or-panel

Assists in resolving contract negotiation impasses over conditions of employment between federal agencies and labor organizations representing federal employees.

Office of Personnel Management (OPM), *Employee Services, Accountability and Workforce Relations, 1900 E St. N.W., #7H28, 20415-0001; (202) 606-2930. Fax, (202) 606-2613. Timothy F. Curry, Deputy Associate Director.*
Web, www.opm.gov/about-us/our-people-organization/program-divisions/employee-services

Develops policy for government agencies and unions regarding employee-management and labor-management relations.

Office of Personnel Management (OPM), *General Counsel, 1900 E St. N.W., #7347, 20415-0001; (202) 606-1700. Fax, (202) 606-2609. Vacant, General Counsel; Kathie Ann Whipple, Deputy General Counsel.*
Web, www.opm.gov/about-us/our-people-organization/office-of-the-general-counsel

Advises the government on law and legal policy relating to federal labor-management relations; represents the government before the Merit Systems Protection Board.

▶NONGOVERNMENTAL

American Foreign Service Assn. (AFSA), *2101 E St. N.W., 20037; (202) 338-4045. Fax, (202) 338-6820.*
Barbara Stephenson, President. Press, (202) 944-5508.
General email, member@afsa.org
Web, www.afsa.org, Twitter, @afsatweets and Facebook, www.facebook.com/afsapage

Membership: active and retired foreign service employees of federal agencies. Represents active duty foreign service personnel in labor-management negotiations; seeks to ensure adequate resources for foreign service operations and personnel. Monitors legislation and regulations related to foreign service personnel and retirees.

National Alliance of Postal and Federal Employees (NAPFE), *1640 11th St. N.W., 20001-5008; (202) 939-6325. Fax, (202) 939-6392. Janice F. Robinson, President.*
General email, info@napfe.org
Web, www.napfe.com

Membership: approximately 70,000 postal and federal employees. Helps members negotiate pay, benefits, equal opportunity, and better working conditions; conducts training programs and workshops. Monitors legislation and regulations.

National Assn. of Government Employees (NAGE), *Washington Office, 1020 N. Fairfax St., #200, Alexandria, VA 22314; (703) 519-0300. Fax, (703) 519-0311. David J. Holway, National President. Toll-free, (866) 412-7790.*
Web, www.nage.org

Membership: federal government employees. Helps members negotiate pay, benefits, and better working conditions; conducts training programs and workshops. Monitors legislation and regulations. (Affiliated with Service Employees International Union. Headquarters in Quincy, Mass.)

National Federation of Federal Employees, *1225 New York Ave. N.W., #450, 20005; (202) 216-4420. Fax, (202) 898-1861. Randy L. Erwin, National President.*
General email, nffenews@nffe.org
Web, www.nffe.org and Twitter, @NFFE_Union

Membership: approximately 100,000 employees throughout various agencies within the federal government. Helps members negotiate pay, benefits, and better working conditions; conducts training programs and workshops. Monitors legislation and regulations. (Affiliated with International Assn. of Machinists & Aerospace Workers, AFL-CIO.)

National Treasury Employees Union (NTEU), *1750 H St. N.W., 20006; (202) 572-5500. Fax, (202) 572-5644. Tony Reardon, President.*
General email, nteu-pr@nteu.org
Web, www.nteu.org and Twitter, @NTEUnews

Membership: approximately 150,000 employees from the Treasury Dept. and thirty other federal agencies and departments. Helps members negotiate pay, benefits, and better working conditions; conducts training programs and workshops. Monitors legislation and regulations.

Public Service Research Council, *320-D Maple Ave. East, Vienna, VA 22180-4742; (703) 242-3575. Fax, (703) 242-3579. David Y. Denholm, President.*
General email, info@psrconline.org
Web, www.psrconline.org

Independent nonprofit research and educational organization. Studies labor unions and labor issues with emphasis on employment in the public sector. Monitors legislation and regulations.

Pay and Employee Benefits

▶AGENCIES

Labor Dept. (DOL), *Workers' Compensation Programs (OWCP), Federal Employees' Compensation (DFEC), 200 Constitution Ave. N.W., #S3524, #S3512, 20210; (202) 693-0040. Antonio Rios, Director, (202) 693-0040. Toll-free, (866) 692-7487 (customers should contact their district office first, www.dol.gov/owcp/dfec/regs/compliance/wc.htm). TTY, (877) 889-5627.*
Web, www.dol.gov/owcp/dfec

Administers the Federal Employees Compensation Act, which provides disability compensation for federal

Inspectors General for Federal Departments and Agencies

Departmental and agency inspectors general are responsible for identifying and reporting program fraud and abuse, criminal activity, and unethical conduct in the federal government. In the legislative branch the Government Accountability Office also has fraud and abuse hotlines: (202) 512-7470. Check www.ignet.gov for additional listings.

DEPARTMENTS

Agriculture, Hon. Phyllis Fong, (202) 720-8001;
Hotline, (800) 424-9121

Commerce, Hon. Peggy E. Gustafson, (202) 482-4661;
Hotline, (800) 482-5197

Defense, Hon. Glenn A. Fine (Acting), (703) 604-8300;
Hotline, (800) 424-9098

Education, Hon. Kathleen Tighe, (202) 245-6900;
Hotline, (800) 647-8733; Fax, (202) 245-7047

Energy, Hon. April Stephenson (Acting), (202) 586-1818;
Hotline, (800) 541-1625

Health and Human Services, Hon. Daniel Levinson,
(202) 619-3148;
Hotline, (800) 447-8477

Homeland Security and FEMA, Hon. John Roth,
(202) 254-4100;
Hotline, (800) 323-8603

Housing and Urban Development, Hon. Helen Albert,
(202) 708-0430;
Hotline, (800) 347-3735; Fax, (202) 708-4829

Interior, Hon. Mary L. Kendall (Acting), (202) 208-5745;
Hotline, (800) 424-5081

Justice, Hon. Michael E. Horowitz, (202) 514-3435;
Hotline, (800) 869-4499

Labor, Hon. Scott Dahl, (202) 693-5100;
Hotline, (800) 347-3756

State, Hon. Steve Linick, (202) 663-0340;
Hotline, (800) 409-9926

Transportation, Hon. Calvin L. Scovel III, (202) 366-1959;
Hotline, (800) 424-9071

Treasury, Hon. Eric M. Thorson, (202) 622-1090;
Hotline, (800) 359-3898

Veterans Affairs, Hon. Michael J. Missal, (202) 461-4720;
Hotline, (800) 488-8244

AGENCIES

Agency for International Development,
Hon. Ann Calvaresi Barr, (202) 712-1150;
Hotline, (800) 230-6539

Appalachian Regional Commission, Hon. Hubert Sparks,
(202) 884-7675;
Hotline, (800) 532-4611

Board of Governors of the Federal Reserve System,
Hon. Mark Bialek, (202) 973-5000;
Hotline, (800) 827-3340; Fax, (202) 973-5044

Central Intelligence Agency, Hon. Christopher R. Sharpley
(Acting), (703) 874-2553;
Hotline, (703) 482-0623

Commodity Futures Trading Commission,
Hon. A. Roy Lavik, (202) 418-5110;
Hotline, (202) 418-5510

Consumer Financial Protection Bureau,
Hon. Mark Bialek, (202) 973-5000;
Hotline, (800) 827-3340

Consumer Product Safety Commission, Hon. Christopher
W. Dentel, (301) 504-7906;
Hotline, (301) 504-7906

Defense Intelligence Agency, Hon. Kristi Waschull,
(202) 231-1000;
Hotline, (202) 231-5554

Elections Assistance Commission, Hon. Patricia Layfield,
(301) 734-3104;
Hotline, (866) 552-0004

Environmental Protection Agency,
Hon. Arthur A. Elkins Jr., (202) 566-0847;
Hotline, (888) 546-8740

Equal Employment Opportunity Commission,
Hon. Milton A. Mayo Jr., (202) 663-4327;
Hotline, (800) 849-4230

Export-Import Bank of the United States,
Hon. Mark L. Greenblatt, (202) 565-3908;
Hotline, (888) 644-3946

Farm Credit Administration, Hon. Wendy R. Laguarda,
(703) 883-4030;
Hotline, (800) 437-7322

Federal Communications Commission,
Hon. David L. Hunt, (202) 418-0470;
Hotline, (888) 863-2244

Federal Deposit Insurance Corporation,
Hon. Jay N. Lerner, (703) 562-2035;
Hotline, (800) 964-3342

Federal Election Commission, Hon. J. Cameron Thurber
(Deputy), (202) 694-1015;
Hotline, (800) 964-3342

Federal Housing Finance Agency,
Hon. Laura S. Wertheimer, (202) 730-0881;
Hotline, (800) 793-7724

Federal Labor Relations Authority,
Hon. Dana Rooney-Fisher, (202) 218-7744;
Hotline, (800) 331-3572

Federal Maritime Commission, Hon. Jon Hatfield,
(202) 523-5863;
Hotline, (202) 523-5865

Federal Trade Commission, Hon. Roslyn A. Mazer, (202) 326-3295; Hotline, (202) 326-2800

General Services Administration, Hon. Carol Fortine Ochoa, (202) 501-0450; Hotline, (800) 424-5210

Government Accountability Office, Hon. Adam Trzeciak, (202) 512-5748; Hotline, (800) 743-7574

Legal Services Corporation, Hon. Jeffrey E. Schanz, (202) 295-1660; Hotline, (800) 678-8868

National Aeronautics and Space Administration, Hon. Paul K. Martin, (202) 358-1220; Hotline, (800) 424-9183

National Credit Union Administration, Hon. James Hagen, (703) 518-6350; Hotline, (703) 518-6357

National Geospatial-Intelligence Agency, Hon. Joseph Composto, (571) 557-5400; Hotline, (800) 380-7729

National Labor Relations Board, Hon. David P. Berry, (202) 273-1960; Hotline, (800) 736-2983

National Reconnaissance Office, Hon. Susan S. Gibson, (703) 808-1205; Hotline, (703) 808-1644

National Science Foundation, Hon. Allison Lerner, (703) 292-7100; Hotline, (800) 428-2189

National Security Agency, Hon. Robert P. Storch, (301) 688-6327; Hotline, (301) 688-6311

Nuclear Regulatory Commission, Hon. Hubert T. Bell, (301) 415-5930; Hotline, (800) 233-3497

Office of Personnel Management, Hon. Norbert Vint (Acting), (202) 606-1200; Hotline, (877) 499-7295

Office of the Inspector General of the Intelligence Community, Hon. Wayne Stone (Acting), (571) 204-8149; Hotline, (855) 731-3260

Pension Benefit Guaranty Corporation, Hon. Robert Westbrooks, (202) 326-4030; Hotline, (800) 303-9737

Postal Regulatory Commission, Hon. Jack Callender, (202) 789-6817; Hotline, (202) 789-6817

Securities and Exchange Commission, Hon. Carl W. Hoecker, (202) 551-6061; Hotline, (877) 442-0854

Small Business Administration, Hon. Hannibal Ware (Acting), (202) 205-6586; Hotline, (800) 767-0385

Social Security Administration, Hon. Gale Stallworth Stone (Acting), (410) 966-8385; Hotline, (800) 269-0271

Special Inspector General for Afghanistan Reconstruction, Hon. John F. Sopko, (703) 545-6000; Hotline, (866) 329-8893

Special Inspector General for the Troubled Asset Relief Program, Hon. Christy Goldsmith Romero, (202) 622-1419; Hotline, (877) 744-2009

Treasury Inspector General for Tax Administration, Hon. J. Russell George, (202) 622-6500; Hotline, (800) 366-4484

U.S. International Trade Commission, Hon. Philip M. Heneghan, (202) 205-2210; Hotline, (800) 358-8530

U.S. Postal Service, Hon. Tammy Whitcomb (Acting), (703) 248-2100; Hotline, (888) 877-7644

OTHER FEDERAL AGENCIES

Amtrak, Hon. Thomas J. Howard, (202) 906-4600; Hotline, (800) 468-5469

Architect of the Capitol, Hon. Christopher P. Failla, (202) 593-1948; Hotline, (877) 489-8583

Corporation for National and Community Service, Hon. Deborah Jeffrey, (202) 606-9390; Hotline, (800) 452-8210

Corporation for Public Broadcasting, Hon. Mary Mitchelson, (202) 879-9660; Hotline, (800) 599-2170

Government Printing Office, Hon. Michael A. Raponi, (202) 512-0039; Hotline, (800) 743-7574

Library of Congress, Hon. Kurt W. Hyde, (202) 707-6314; Hotline, (202) 707-6306

National Archives, Hon. James E. Springs, (301) 837-3000; Hotline, (800) 786-2551

National Endowment for the Arts, Hon. Ronald Stith, (202) 682-5402; Hotline, (877) 535-7448

National Endowment for the Humanities, Hon. Laura Davis, (202) 606-8574; Hotline, (877) 786-7598

Peace Corps, Hon. Kathy A. Buller, (202) 692-2900; Hotline, (800) 233-5874

Smithsonian Institution, Hon. Cathy Helm, (202) 633-7050; Hotline, (202) 252-0321

U.S. Capitol Police, Hon. Fay F. Ropella, (202) 593-4555; Hotline, (866) 906-2446

employees, including wage replacement benefits, medical treatment, vocational rehabilitation, and other benefits.

Office of Personnel Management (OPM), *Employee Services,* 1900 E St. N.W., #7460 MM, 20415; (202) 606-2520. Mark D. Reinhold, Associate Director.
Web, www.opm.gov/about-us/our-people-organization/program-divisions/employee-services

Develops federal human resource systems for pay and leave, employee development, staffing, recruiting, hiring, Factor Evaluation System (FES) policy, and labor and employee relations, senior executive services, veterans' services, and performance management.

Office of Personnel Management (OPM), *Federal Prevailing Rate Advisory Committee,* 1900 E St. N.W., #5H27, 20415; (202) 606-2858. Jill Nelson, Chair.
General email, pay-leave-policy@opm.gov

Web, www.opm.gov/about-us/our-people-organization/organizational-contacts/federal-prevailing-rate-advisory-committee

Advises OPM on the governmentwide administration of Federal Wage System employees.

Office of Personnel Management (OPM), *Healthcare and Insurance, Federal Employee Insurance Operations,* 1900 E St. N.W., #3425, 20415; (202) 606-4995. Fax, (202) 606-4640. Alan Spielman, Director; Edwin DeHarde, Assistant Director, (202) 606-0522.
Web, www.opm.gov/insure

Administers group life insurance for federal employees and retirees; negotiates rates and benefits with health insurance carriers; settles disputed claims. Administers the Federal Employees' Health Benefits (FEHB), the Federal Employees' Group Life Insurance (FEGLI), the Federal Long Term Care Insurance (FLTCIP), Federal Employee Dental and Vision Benefits (FEDVIP), and the Flexible Spending Accounts (FSA) programs.

Office of Personnel Management (OPM), *Pay and Leave,* 1900 E St. N.W., #7H31, 20415; (202) 606-2838. Fax, (202) 606-4264. Brenda Roberts, Deputy Associate Director.
General email, pay-leave-policy@opm.gov

Web, www.opm.gov/policy-data-oversight/pay-leave

Develops and maintains governmentwide agency regulations pertaining to pay and leave. Responsible for the General Schedule and locality pay adjustment process for white-collar federal workers. Supports the Federal Salary Council and the president's "pay agent" (composed of the directors of OPM and the Office of Management and Budget and the secretary of labor). Annual report of the pay agent and General Schedule pay rates are available on OPM's website. Supports the Federal Prevailing Rate Advisory Committee and provides regulations and policies for the administration of the federal wage system for blue-collar federal employees.

Office of Personnel Management (OPM), *Retirement Operations,* 1900 E St. N.W., #2H28, 20415; (724) 794-2005. Fax, (724) 794-4323. Kenneth J. Zawodny Jr., Associate Director, (724) 794-7759; Tia Butler, Deputy Associate Director. Toll-free, (888) 767-6738. TTY, (855) 887-4957.

General email, retire@opm.gov
Web, www.opm.gov/retire

Administers the civil service and federal employees' retirement systems; responsible for monthly annuity payments and other benefits; organizes and maintains retirement records; distributes information on retirement and on insurance programs for annuitants.

Office of Personnel Management (OPM), *Work-Life,* 1900 E St. N.W., #7456, 20415-2000; (202) 606-0846. Julie Brill, Manager.
General email, worklife@opm.gov
Web, www.opm.gov/policy-data-oversight/worklife

Sets policy and guidelines for federal agencies in establishing and maintaining programs on the federal telework program, employee assistance programs, the Federal Child Care Subsidy Program, and health and wellness.

State Dept., *Bureau of Administration, Allowances,* 2401 E St. N.W., #L314/SA-1, 20522-0103; (202) 663-1121. Fax, (202) 261-8707. Cheryl N. Johnson, Director.
General email, Allowances@state.gov
Web, http://aoprals.state.gov

Develops and coordinates policies, regulations, standards, and procedures to administer the governmentwide allowances and benefits program abroad under the State Dept. Standardized Regulations. Compiles statistics of living costs, hardship differentials, and danger pay allowances to compensate U.S. Government civilian employees while on assignments abroad.

State Dept., *Medical Services,* 2401 E St. N.W., #L218, 20522-0102; (202) 663-1649. Fax, (202) 663-1613. Mark J. Cohen, Medical Director (Acting).
Web, www.state.gov/m/med

Operates a worldwide primary health care system for U.S. citizen employees, and eligible family members, of participating U.S. government agencies. Conducts physical examinations of Foreign Service officers and candidates; provides clinical services; assists with medical evacuation of patients overseas.

Treasury Dept., *Management, DC Pensions,* 1500 Pennsylvania Ave. N.W., 20220; (202) 622-0800. Fax, (202) 622-1763. Nancy Ostrowski, Director.
General email, DCPensions@treasury.gov
Web, www.treasury.gov/about/organizational-structure/offices/Pages/D.C.-Pensions.aspx

Funds and distributes the District of Columbia Judges' Retirement Plan and the federal portion of the District of Columbia's retirement plans for teachers, police officers, and firefighters as required by Title XI of the Balanced Budget Act of 1997 law.

▶ NONGOVERNMENTAL

National Active and Retired Federal Employees Assn. (NARFE), 606 N. Washington St., Alexandria, VA 22314-1914; (703) 838-7760. Fax, (703) 838-7785. Kenneth Thomas, President. Member relations, (800) 456-8410.

Office of Personnel Management

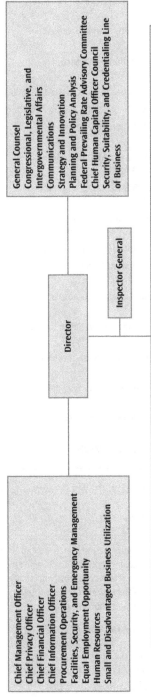
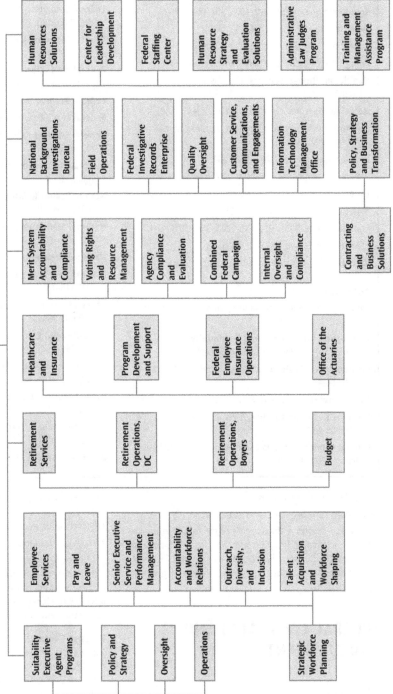

Director

Chief Management Officer
Chief Privacy Officer
Chief Financial Officer
Chief Information Officer
Procurement Operations
Facilities, Security, and Emergency Management
Equal Employment Opportunity
Human Resources
Small and Disadvantaged Business Utilization

General Counsel
Congressional, Legislative, and Intergovernmental Affairs
Communications
Strategy and Innovation
Planning and Policy Analysis
Federal Prevailing Rate Advisory Committee
Chief Human Capital Officer Council
Security, Suitability, and Credentialing Line of Business

Inspector General

Human Resources Solutions
Center for Leadership Development
Federal Staffing Center
Human Resource Strategy and Evaluation Solutions
Administrative Law Judges Program
Training and Management Assistance Program

National Background Investigations Bureau
Field Operations
Federal Investigative Records Enterprise
Quality Oversight
Customer Service, Communications, and Engagements
Information Technology Management Office
Policy, Strategy and Business Transformation
Contracting and Business Solutions

Merit System Accountability and Compliance
Voting Rights and Resource Management
Agency Compliance and Evaluation
Combined Federal Campaign
Internal Oversight and Compliance

Healthcare and Insurance
Program Development and Support
Federal Employee Insurance Operations
Office of the Actuaries

Retirement Services
Retirement Operations, DC
Retirement Operations, Boyers
Budget

Employee Services
Pay and Leave
Senior Executive Service and Performance Management
Accountability and Workforce Relations
Outreach, Diversity, and Inclusion
Talent Acquisition and Workforce Shaping

Suitability Executive Agent Programs
Policy and Strategy
Oversight
Operations

Strategic Workforce Planning

Procurement Officers for Federal Departments and Agencies

DEPARTMENTS

Agriculture, Lisa M. Wilusz, (202) 720-9448

Commerce, Barry Berkowitz, (202) 482-4248

Defense, Shay D. Assad, (703) 695-4235

Education, Angela Billups, (202) 245-6995

Energy, Paul Bosco, (202) 586-1784

Health and Human Services, Lisa Davis, (202) 260-6713

Homeland Security, Soraya Correa, (202) 447-5300

Housing and Urban Development, Keith W. Surber (Acting), (202) 402-2909

Interior, Megan Olsen, (202) 513-7554

Justice, Christopher V. Henshaw, (202) 616-3613

Labor, Carl Campbell, (202) 693-4028

State, Corey Rindner, (703) 516-1689

Transportation, Willie H. Smith, (202) 366-4271

Treasury, Iris B. Cooper, (202) 622-1678

Veterans Affairs, Rick Lemmon (Acting), (202) 632-7806

AGENCIES

Consumer Product Safety Commission, Akram Ahmad (Acting), (301) 504-7884

Corporation for National and Community Service, Henrietta Young (Acting), (202) 606-6988

Environmental Protection Agency, Kimberly Patrick, (202) 564-4310

Export-Import Bank, Mark Pitra, (202) 565-3338

Farm Credit Administration, A. Jerome Fowlkes, (703) 883-4378

Federal Communications Commission, Dawn Digiorgio (Acting), (202) 418-1933

Federal Deposit Insurance Corporation, Michael J. Rubino, (202) 942-0376

Federal Emergency Management Agency, Bobby McCane, (202) 942-0376

Federal Maritime Commission, Katona Bryan-Wade, (202) 523-5900

Federal Mediation and Conciliation Service, Cynthia Washington, (202) 606-5477

Federal Reserve System, Michell C. Clark, (202) 452-3000

Federal Trade Commission, Nancy Moreno, (202) 326-3667

General Services Administration, Jeff Koses, (703) 605-5535

National Aeronautics and Space Administration, William P. McNally, (202) 358-2090

National Labor Relations Board, Lasharn Hamilton, (202) 273-4210

National Mediation Board, Samantha T. Jones, (202) 692-5010

National Science Foundation, Jeffery Lupis, (703) 292-7944

Nuclear Regulatory Commission, James C. Corbett, (301) 415-8725

Office of Personnel Management, Juan Arratia, (202) 606-0698

Securities and Exchange Commission, Vance Cathell, (202) 551-8385

Small Business Administration, Kristian Jovanovic, (202) 205-6459

Social Security Administration, Seth P. Binstock, (410) 965-7748

U.S. International Trade Commission, Debra Bridge, (202) 205-2004

U.S. Postal Service, Tom Samra, (202) 268-3389

General email, hq@narfe.org

Web, www.narfe.org and Twitter, @NARFEHQ

Works to preserve the integrity of the federal employee retirement systems. Provides members with information about benefits for retired federal employees and for survivors of deceased federal employees. Monitors legislation and regulations.

FEDERAL CONTRACTS AND PROCUREMENT

General

▶**AGENCIES**

Defense Contract Audit Agency *(Defense Dept.),* 8725 *John Jay Kingman Rd., #2135, Fort Belvoir, VA 22060-6219; (703) 767-3200. Fax, (703) 767-3267. Anita Bales,*

Director. Media, (703) 697-5131. DCAA OIG hotline, (571) 448-3135.

General email, dcaaweb@dcaa.mil

Web, www.dcaa.mil

Performs all contract audits for the Defense Dept. Provides Defense Dept. personnel responsible for procurement and contract administration with accounting and financial advisory services regarding the negotiation, administration, and settlement of contracts and subcontracts.

Defense Contract Management Agency *(Defense Dept.),* *14501 George Carter Way, 2nd Floor, Chantilly, VA 20151; (571) 521-1600. Vice Adm. David H. Lewis (USN), Director. FOIA, (804) 734-1488. Media, (804) 734-1492. Web, www.dcma.mil and Twitter, @DCMAnews*

Ensures the integrity of the contracting process, and provides a broad range of contract-procurement management services, including cost and pricing, quality assurance, contract administration and termination, and small business support.

Defense Dept. (DoD), *Armed Services Board of Contract Appeals,* 5109 Leesburg Pike, Skyline 6, 7th Floor, Falls Church, VA 22041-3208; (703) 681-8500. Fax, (703) 681-8535. Judge John J. Thrasher, Chair; Catherine A. Stanton, General Counsel.
General email, asbca.recorder@mail.mil
Web, www.asbca.mil

Adjudicates disputes arising under Defense Dept. contracts.

Defense Health Agency (DHA) *(Defense Dept.),* **Small Business Programs,** 7700 Arlington Blvd., #5101, Falls Church, VA 22042-5101; (703) 681-4614.
Cassandra W. Martin, Director.
Web, www.health.mil/About-MHS/OASDHA/Defense-Health-Agency/Small-Business-Program

Seeks to ensure that small businesses have a fair opportunity to compete and be selected for DHA contracts, at both the prime and subcontract levels. Provides information on agency purchases and the contracting process through forums, mentoring programs, and written materials.

General Services Administration (GSA), *Civilian Board of Contract Appeals (CBCA),* 1800 M St. N.W., 6th Floor, 20036; (202) 606-8800. Fax, (202) 606-0019. Jeri K. Somers, Chair.
Web, www.gsa.gov/about-us/organization/civilian-board-of-contract-appeals-overview

Presides over various disputes involving Federal executive branch agencies. Resolves contract disputes between government contractors and agencies under the Contract Dispute Act.

General Services Administration (GSA), *Federal Procurement Data System–Next Generation (FPDS-NG),* 1800 F St. N.W., 20405; (866) 606-8220. Vacant, Director. Help Desk, (800) 488-3111.
General email, mashelpdesk@gsa.gov
Web, www.fpds.gov/fpdsng_cms/index.php/en/ and www.gsa.gov/portal/content/157105

Service contracted out by GSA that collects procurement data from all federal government contracts and disseminates these data via the Internet. Reports include agency identification, products or services purchased, dollar obligation, principal place of performance, and contractor identification; also provides socioeconomic indicators such as business size and business ownership type.

General Services Administration (GSA), **Governmentwide Policy, Acquisition Policy,** 1800 F St. N.W., 20405; (202) 501-1043. Jeffrey A. (Jeff) Koses, Deputy Chief Acquisition Officer.
General email, askacquisition@gsa.gov and FARPolicy@gsa.gov
Web, www.gsa.gov/portal/category/101099

Conducts pre-award and post-award contract reviews; suspends and debars contractors for unsatisfactory performance; coordinates and promotes governmentwide career management and training programs for contracting personnel.

General Services Administration (GSA), *Small Business Utilization,* 1800 F St. N.W., 20405; (202) 501-1021. Fax, (202) 501-2590. Charles Manger, Associate Administrator. Toll-free, 844-GSA-4111.
General email, small.business@gsa.gov
Web, www.gsa.gov/acquisition/small-business and Twitter, @GSAOSBU

Works to increase small business access to government contract procurement opportunities. Provides policy guidance and direction for GSA Regional Small Business Offices, which offer advice and assistance to businesses interested in government procurement.

Interior Dept. (DOI), *Small and Disadvantaged Business Utilization (OSDBU),* 1849 C St. N.W., Room 4124, 20240; (202) 208-3493. Fax, (202) 208-7444. Megan Olsen, Director (Acting).
Web, www.doi.gov/pmb/osdbu

Advocates contracting opportunities for small, small disadvantaged, women-owned, historically underutilized business zones, and service-disabled veteran-owned small businesses and Indian economic enterprises.

Labor Dept. (DOL), *Federal Contract Compliance Programs (OFCCP),* 200 Constitution Ave. N.W., #C3325, 20210; (202) 693-0137. Fax, (202) 693-1304. Craig E. Leen, Director, (202) 693-0101. Toll-free, (800) 397-6251. TTY, (202) 693-0103.
General email, OFCCP-Public@dol.gov
Web, www.dol.gov/ofccp

Monitors and enforces government contractors' compliance with federal laws and regulations on equal employment opportunities and affirmative action, including employment rights of minorities, women, persons with disabilities, and disabled and Vietnam-era veterans.

Labor Dept. (DOL), *Wage and Hour Division (WHD),* *Government Contracts Enforcement,* 200 Constitution Ave. N.W., #S3502, 20210; (202) 693-0064. Fax, (202) 693-1087. Michelle King, Director (Acting), (202) 693-0574. Toll-free, (866) 487-9243.
Web, www.dol.gov/whd/govcontracts

Enforces the Davis-Bacon Act, the Walsh-Healey Public Contracts Act, the Contract Work Hours and Safety Standards Act, the Service Contract Act, and other related government contract labor standards statutes.

Minority Business Development Agency *(Commerce Dept.),* 1401 Constitution Ave. N.W., #5053, 20230; (202) 482-2332. Fax, (202) 482-2500. Chris Garcia, Director (Acting).
Web, www.mbda.gov and Twitter, @USMBDA

Assists minority business owners in obtaining federal loans and contract awards; produces an annual report on federal agencies' performance in procuring from minority-owned businesses.

Office of Management and Budget (OMB) *(Executive Office of the President),* **Federal Procurement Policy,** 725 17th St. N.W., #9013, 20503; Leslie Field, Deputy Administrator.
Web, www.whitehouse.gov/omb/management/office-federal-procurement-policy

Oversees and coordinates government procurement policies, regulations, and procedures. Responsible for cost accounting rules governing federal contractors and subcontractors. Interests include effective use of competition, cost-effective contracting for vehicles, and managing a useful information technology system for federal procurement managers.

Small Business Administration (SBA), *Government Contracting and Business Development,* 409 3rd St. S.W., #8000, 20416; (202) 205-6459. Fax, (202) 205-5206. Barbara E. Carson, Deputy Associate Administrator. TTY, (800) 877-8339.
Web, www.sba.gov/offices/headquarters/ogc_and_bd

Oversees the Office of Government Contracting and Office of Business Development. Enhances the effectiveness of small business programs to develop policies, regulations, and statutory changes.

Small Business Administration (SBA), *Government Contracting and Business Development, Government Contracting,* 409 3rd St. S.W., #8800, 20416; (202) 205-6460. Fax, (202) 205-7324. Barbara E. Carson, Deputy Associate Administrator. TTY, (800) 877-8339.
Web, www.sba.gov/offices/headquarters/ogc

Seeks to maximize participation by small, disadvantaged, and woman-owned businesses in federal government contract awards and large prime subcontract awards. Advocates on behalf of small business in the federal procurement world.

U.S. AbilityOne Commission, 1401 S. Clark St., #715, Arlington, VA 22202-3259; (703) 603-2100. Fax, (703) 603-0655. Tina Ballard, Executive Director. Toll-free, (800) 999-5963.
General email, info@abilityone.gov
Web, www.abilityone.gov

Presidentially appointed committee. Determines which products and services are suitable for federal procurement from qualified nonprofit agencies that employ people who are blind or have other significant disabilities; seeks to increase employment opportunities for these individuals. (Formerly Committee for Purchase from People Who Are Blind or Severely Disabled.)

▶CONGRESS

For a listing of relevant congressional committees and subcommittees, please see pages 320–321 or the Appendix.

Government Accountability Office (GAO), *Contracting and National Security Acquisitions (CNSA),* 441 G St. N.W., MS 4440-A, 20548; (202) 512-4841. Michele Mackin, Managing Director, (202) 512-4309.
Web, www.gao.gov

Advises Congress and governmental agencies about federal spending and maximizing investments related to acquisitions and procurements.

Government Accountability Office (GAO), *General Counsel,* 441 G St. N.W., MS 7182, 20548; (202) 512-5400.

Fax, (202) 512-7703. Thomas H. Armstrong, General Counsel.
Web, www.gao.gov/legal

Adjudicates challenges to the proposed or actual awards of government contracts; renders decisions and opinions on matters of appropriations law; provides legal expertise in support of GAO's functions.

▶NONGOVERNMENTAL

Coalition for Government Procurement, 1990 M St. N.W., #450, 20036; (202) 331-0975. Fax, (202) 521-3533. Roger D. Waldron, President, (202) 315-1051.
General email, info@thecgp.org
Web, http://thecgp.org and Twitter, @TheCGPOrg

Alliance of business firms that sell to the federal government. Seeks equal opportunities for businesses to sell to the government; monitors practices of the General Services Administration and government procurement legislation and regulations.

National Contract Management Assn. (NCMA), 21740 Beaumeade Circle, #125, Ashburn, VA 20147; (571) 382-0082. Fax, (703) 448-0939. Kraig Conrad, Chief Executive Officer, (571) 382-1123. Toll-free, (800) 344-8096.
General email, ncma@ncmahq.org
Web, www.ncmahq.org, Twitter, @NCMA and Facebook, www.facebook.com/NCMAHQ

Membership: individuals concerned with administering, procuring, negotiating, and managing government and commercial contracts and subcontracts. Sponsors the Certified Professional Contracts Manager Program and various educational and professional programs.

NIGP: The Institute for Public Procurement, 2411 Dulles Corner Park, #350, Herndon, VA 20171; (703) 736-8900. Fax, (703) 736-9644. Rick Grimm, Chief Executive Officer, ext. 235. Information, (800) 367-6447.
Web, www.nigp.org and Facebook, www.facebook.com/OfficialNIGP

Membership: governmental purchasing departments, agencies, and organizations at the federal, state, and local levels in the United States, Canada, and internationally. Provides public procurement officers with technical assistance and information, training seminars, and professional certification. (Formerly the National Institute of Governmental Purchasing.)

Professional Services Council (PSC), 4401 Wilson Blvd., #1110, Arlington, VA 22203; (703) 875-8059. Fax, (703) 875-8922. David Berteau, President.
Web, www.pscouncil.org and Twitter, @PSCSpeaks

Membership: associations and firms that provide local, state, federal, and international governments with professional, engineering, and technical services. Analyzes the process by which the government awards contracts to private firms. Monitors legislation and regulations.

POSTAL SERVICE

General

▶AGENCIES

U.S. Postal Service (USPS), *475 L'Enfant Plaza S.W., 20260-0001; (202) 268-2000. Fax, (202) 268-5211. Megan J. Brennan, Postmaster General. General information, (800) 275-8777. Library, (202) 268-2906. Press, (202) 268-6524. TTY, (800) 877-8339. Web, www.usps.com and Twitter, @USPS*

Offers postal service throughout the country as an independent establishment of the executive branch. Library open to the public by appointment.

U.S. Postal Service (USPS), *Inspection Service, 475 L'Enfant Plaza S.W., #3100, 20260-2100; (202) 268-4264. Fax, (202) 268-7316. Gary Barksdale, Chief Postal Inspector (Acting). Fraud and abuse hotline, (877) 876-2455. Press, (202) 268-3700. Web, http://postalinspectors.uspis.gov and Twitter, @USPIpressroom*

Investigates violations of postal laws, such as theft of mail or posted valuables, assaults on postal employees, organized crime in postal-related matters, and prohibited mailings. Conducts internal audits; investigates postal activities to determine effectiveness of procedures; monitors compliance of individual post offices with postal regulations. (Headquarters in Chicago, Ill.)

▶CONGRESS

For a listing of relevant congressional committees and sub-committees, please see pages 320–321 or the Appendix.

Consumer Services

▶AGENCIES

Postal Regulatory Commission, *Public Affairs and Government Relations, 901 New York Ave. N.W., #200, 20268; (202) 789-6800. Fax, (202) 789-6891. Ann C. Fisher, Director. General email, prc-pagr@prc.gov Web, www.prc.gov/offices/pagr*

Supports public outreach and education and media relations; provides information for consumers and responds to their inquiries. Informal complaints regarding individual rate and service inquiries are referred to the Consumer Advocate of the Postal Service.

Employee and Labor Relations

▶AGENCIES

U.S. Postal Service (USPS), *Employee Resource Management, 475 L'Enfant Plaza S.W., #9840,*

20260-4200; (202) 268-3783. Fax, (202) 268-5605. Simon Storey, Vice President. Web, www.usps.com

Drafts and implements employment policies and practices and safety and health guidelines.

U.S. Postal Service (USPS), *Labor Relations, 475 L'Enfant Plaza S.W., #9014, 20260-4100; (202) 268-7447. Fax, (202) 268-3074. Douglas A. Tulino, Vice President. Web, www.usps.com*

Handles collective bargaining and contract administration for the U.S. Postal Service.

▶NONGOVERNMENTAL

American Postal Workers Union (APWU), *1300 L St. N.W., 20005; (202) 842-4200. Fax, (202) 842-4297. Mark Dimondstein, President, (202) 842-4250. Web, www.apwu.org, Twitter, @APWUnational and Facebook, www.facebook.com/apwunational*

Membership: more than 200,000 postal employees and retirees, including clerks, motor vehicle operators, maintenance operators, and retirees. Assists members with contract negotiation and grievances; conducts training programs and workshops. Monitors legislation and regulations. (Affiliated with the Postal, Telegraph, and Telephone International and the AFL-CIO.)

National Alliance of Postal and Federal Employees (NAPFE), *1640 11th St. N.W., 20001-5008; (202) 939-6325. Fax, (202) 939-6392. Janice F. Robinson, President. General email, info@napfe.org Web, www.napfe.com*

Membership: approximately 70,000 postal and federal employees. Helps members negotiate pay, benefits, equal opportunity, and better working conditions; conducts training programs and workshops. Monitors legislation and regulations.

National Assn. of Letter Carriers, *100 Indiana Ave. N.W., 20001-2144; (202) 393-4695. Fredric V. Rolando, President. Web, www.nalc.org and Twitter, @NALC_National*

Membership: union letter carriers working for, or retired from, the U.S. Postal Service. Assists members with contract negotiation and grievances; conducts training programs and workshops. Monitors legislation and regulations. (Affiliated with the AFL-CIO and the Union Network International.)

National Assn. of Postal Supervisors, *1727 King St., #400, Alexandria, VA 22314-2753; (703) 836-9660. Fax, (703) 836-9665. Brian J. Wagner, President. General email, napshq@naps.org Web, www.naps.org and Twitter, @napshq*

Membership: present and retired postal supervisors, managers, and postmasters. Management association that cooperates with other postal management associations, unions, and the U.S. Postal Service to improve the efficiency of the postal service; promotes favorable working conditions and broader career opportunities for all postal employees; provides members with information on current functions and legislative issues of the postal service.

National Rural Letter Carriers' Assn., *1630 Duke St., Alexandria, VA 22314-3467; (703) 684-5545. Fax, (703) 518-0677. Ronnie W. Sutts, President.*
Web, www.nrlca.org

Membership: more than 100,000 rural letter carriers working for, or retired from, the U.S. Postal Service. Seeks to improve rural mail delivery. Negotiates labor agreements affecting members; conducts training programs and workshops. Monitors legislation and regulations.

National Star Route Mail Contractors Assn., *324 E. Capitol St. N.E., 20003-3897; (202) 543-1661. Fax, (202) 543-8863. John V. (Skip) Maraney, Executive Director. Toll-free, (800) 543-1661.*
General email, eyoung-scales@nsrmca.net
Web, www.starroutecontractors.org

Membership: contractors for highway mail transport and selected rural route deliverers. Acts as liaison between contractors and the U.S. Postal Service, Transportation Dept., Labor Dept., and Congress concerning contracts, wages, and other issues. Monitors legislation and regulations.

United Postmasters and Managers of America, *8 Herbert St., Alexandria, VA 22305-2600; (703) 683-9027. Fax, (703) 683-0923. Daniel Heins, President.*
General email, information@unitedpma.org
Web, www.unitedpma.org and Twitter, @UPMA15

Membership: present and former postmasters and postal managers of the United States. Promotes the postal service and the welfare of its members. Assists postmasters facing discipline or other adverse actions. Monitors legislation and regulations. (Formerly the National Association of Postmasters of the United States.)

Mail Rates and Classification

▶**AGENCIES**

Postal Regulatory Commission, *901 New York Ave. N.W., #200, 20268-0001; (202) 789-6800. Fax, (202) 789-6891. Robert G. Taub, Chair.*
General email, prc-dockets@prc.gov
Web, www.prc.gov

Independent agency with regulatory oversight over the U.S. Postal Service. Develops and maintains regulations concerning postal rates; consults with the Postal Service on delivery service standards and performance measures; consults with the State Dept. on international postal policies; prevents anticompetitive postal practices; and adjudicates complaints.

U.S. Postal Service (USPS), *Mail Entry and Payment Technology, 475 L'Enfant Plaza S.W., #2P836, 20260-0911; (202) 268-6406. Fax, (202) 268-8273. Marc McCrery, Vice President (Acting).*
Web, www.usps.com and Business services, www.usps.com/business

Implements policies governing the acceptance and verification of business mail by the U.S. Postal Service.

U.S. Postal Service (USPS), *Pricing and Costing, 475 L'Enfant Plaza S.W., #4100, 20260-5014; (202) 268-8116. Fax, (202) 268-6251. Sharon Owens, Vice President.*
Web, www.usps.com

Sets prices for U.S. Postal Service product lines using competitive pricing methods.

U.S. Postal Service (USPS), *Product Classification, 475 L'Enfant Plaza S.W., #4446, 20260-5015; (202) 268-3789. Fax, (202) 268-3888. Lizbeth (Liz) Dobbins, Manager.*
Web, www.usps.com

Issues policy statements on domestic mail classification matters. Ensures the accuracy of policies developed by the Postal Regulatory Commission with respect to domestic mail classification schedules.

▶**NONGOVERNMENTAL**

Alliance of Nonprofit Mailers, *1211 Connecticut Ave. N.W., #610, 20036-2705; (202) 462-5132. Fax, (202) 462-0423. Stephen Kearney, Executive Director.*
General email, alliance@nonprofitmailers.org
Web, www.nonprofitmailers.org, Facebook, www.facebook.com/AllianceNM and Twitter, @NonProfitMailer

Works to maintain reasonable mail rates for nonprofit organizations. Represents member organizations before Congress, the U.S. Postal Service, the Postal Regulatory Commission, and federal courts on nonprofit postal rate and mail classification issues, nondiscrimination relative to commercial mailers, and the external discipline of the Consumer Price Index cap.

Assn. for Postal Commerce (POSTCOM), *1800 Diagonal Rd., #600, Alexandria, VA 22314; (703) 524-0096. Fax, (703) 997-2414. Michael Plunkett, President.*
General email, info@postcom.org
Web, www.postcom.org and Twitter, @PostCom2

Membership: companies and organizations interested in mail as a medium for advertising and product delivery. Provides members with information about postal news worldwide, postal policy, postal rates, and legislation regarding postal regulations. Monitors legislation and regulations.

DMA Nonprofit Federation, *225 Reinekers Lane, #325, Alexandria, VA 22314; (202) 861-2498. Fax, (202) 628-4383. Xenia Boone, General Counsel. Alternate phone, (202) 861-2427.*
General email, aosgood@the-dma.org
Web, www.nonprofitfederation.org

Membership: nonprofit organizations and their suppliers that rely on nonprofit mail and other marketing channels, including digital, email, and telephone, to reach donors. Serves as a liaison between members and the U.S. Postal Service; represents members' interests before regulatory agencies; monitors legislation and regulations. Hosts conferences on fund-raising across marketing channels.

Parcel Shippers Assn. (PSA), *P.O. Box 450, Oxon Hill, MD 20750; (571) 257-7617. Fax, (301) 749-8684. Paul Kovlakas, President. General email, psa@parcelshippers.org*

Web, www.parcelshippers.org

Voluntary organization of business firms concerned with the shipment of parcels. Works to improve parcel post rates and service; represents members before the Postal Regulatory Commission in matters regarding parcel post rates. Monitors legislation and regulations.

Stamps, Postal History

▶AGENCIES

National Postal Museum *(Smithsonian Institution),* 2 *Massachusetts Ave. N.E., 20002 (mailing address: P.O. Box 37012, Washington, DC 20013); (202) 633-5555. Fax, (202) 633-9393. Elliot Gruber, Director. Press, (202) 633-5518. Tours and education, (202) 633-5534. Web, http://postalmuseum.si.edu, Twitter, @PostalMuseum and Facebook, www.facebook.com/SmithsonianNationalPostalMuseum*

Exhibits postal history and stamp collections; provides information on world postal and stamp history.

U.S. Postal Service (USPS), *Citizens' Stamp Advisory Committee, 475 L'Enfant Plaza S.W., #3300, 20260-3501; (202) 268-2000. Janet Klug, Chair. Web, http://about.usps.com/who-we-are/csac/welcome.htm*

Reviews stamp subject nominations, which are open to the public. Develops the annual Stamp Program and makes subject and design recommendations to the Postmaster General.

U.S. Postal Service (USPS), *Stamp Services, 475 L'Enfant Plaza S.W., #3300, 20260-3501; (202) 268-3326. Fax, (202) 268-4965. William Gicker Jr., Director (Acting). Web, www.usps.com*

Manages the stamp selection function; develops the basic stamp preproduction design; manages relationship with stamp collecting community.

PUBLIC ADMINISTRATION

General

▶AGENCIES

Office of Management and Budget (OMB) *(Executive Office of the President), President's Management Council, Dwight D. Eisenhower Executive Office Bldg., #216, 20503; Fax, (202) 395-6102. Jeffery Price, Council Contact. Press, (202) 395-7254. Web, www.whitehouse.gov/omb and www.gsa.gov/portal/content/133811*

Membership: chief operating officers of federal government departments and agencies. Responsible for implementing the management improvement initiatives of the administration. Develops and oversees improved governmentwide management and administrative systems; formulates long-range plans to promote these systems; works to resolve interagency management problems and to implement reforms.

President's Commission on White House Fellowships, *712 Jackson Pl. N.W., 20503; (202) 395-4522. Fax, (202) 395-6179. Robert (Mike) Duncan, Director. General email, whitehousefellows@whf.eop.gov*

Web, www.whitehouse.gov/participate/fellows

Nonpartisan commission that provides professionals from all sectors of national life with the opportunity to observe firsthand the processes of the federal government. Fellows work for one year as special assistants to cabinet members or to principal members of the White House staff. Qualified applicants have demonstrated superior accomplishments early in their careers and have a commitment to leadership and public service.

▶CONGRESS

For a listing of relevant congressional committees and subcommittees, please see pages 320–321 or the Appendix.

▶NONGOVERNMENTAL

American Society for Public Administration, *1730 Rhode Island Ave. N.W., #500, 20036; (202) 393-7878. Fax, (202) 638-4952. William P. Shields Jr., Executive Director, (202) 585-4307. General email, info@aspanet.org*

Web, www.aspanet.org, Twitter, @ASPANational and Facebook, www.facebook.com/ASPANational

Membership: government administrators, public officials, educators, researchers, and others interested in public administration. Presents awards to distinguished professionals in the field; sponsors workshops and conferences; disseminates information about public administration. Promotes high ethical standards for public service.

Assn. of Government Accountants, *2208 Mount Vernon Ave., Alexandria, VA 22301; (703) 684-6931. Fax, (703) 548-9367. Ann M. Ebberts, Chief Executive Officer. Toll-free, (800) 242-7211. General email, agamembers@agacgfm.org*

Web, www.agacgfm.org and Twitter, @AGACGFM

Membership: professionals engaged in government accounting, auditing, budgeting, and information systems. Sponsors education, research, and conferences; administers certification program.

Federally Employed Women, *455 Massachusetts Ave. N.W., 20001 (mailing address: P.O. Box 306, Washington, DC 20001); (202) 898-0994. Fax, (202) 898-1535. Karen Rainey, President. General email, few@few.org*

Web, www.few.org and Facebook, www.facebook.com/federallyemployedwomen

Membership: women and men who work for the federal government. Works to eliminate sex discrimination in government employment and to increase job opportunities for women; offers training programs. Monitors legislation and regulations.

International City/County Management Assn. (ICMA), *777 N. Capitol St. N.E., #500, 20002-4201; (202) 289-4262. Fax, (202) 962-3500. Marc Ott, Executive Director, ext. 3528. Member services and information, (202) 962-3680. Toll-free, (800) 745-8780.*
General email, membership@icma.org

Web, www.icma.org

Membership: appointed managers and administrators of cities, towns, counties, and other local governments around the world; local government employees; academics; and other individuals with an interest in local government. Provides member support, publications, data and information, peer and results-oriented assistance, and training and professional development to members and others to help build sustainable communities. Sponsors workshops, regional summits, and an annual conference. Publishes resources for local government management professionals.

International Public Management Assn. for Human Resources (IPMA-HR), *1617 Duke St., Alexandria, VA 22314; (703) 549-7100. Fax, (703) 684-0948. Neil Reichenberg, Executive Director.*
General email, ipma@ipma-hr.org

Web, www.ipma-hr.org, Twitter, @IPMAHR and Facebook, www.facebook.com/International-Public-Management-Association-for-Human-Resources-IPMA-HR-38098732966

Membership: personnel professionals from federal, state, and local governments. Provides information on training procedures, management techniques, and legislative developments on the federal, state, and local levels.

National Academy of Public Administration, *1600 K St. N.W., #400, 20006; (202) 347-3190. Teresa W. Gerton, President, (202) 204-3615.*
General email, academy@napawash.org

Web, www.napawash.org and Twitter, @napawash

Membership: scholars and administrators in public management. Chartered by Congress to assist federal, state, and local government agencies, public officials, and foundations with government and management challenges.

National Foundation for Women Legislators, *1727 King St., #300, Alexandria, VA 22314; (703) 518-7931. Jody Thomas, Executive Director.*
General email, nfwl@womenlegislators.org

Web, www.womenlegislators.org,
Twitter, @womenlegislators and Facebook,
www.facebook.com/womenlegislators

Provides leadership development and networking resources to elected women leaders at the city, state, and federal levels of government.

National Women's Political Caucus, *1001 Connecticut Ave., #1020, 20036 (mailing address: P.O. Box 50476,*

Washington, DC 20091); (202) 785-1100. Donna Lent, President; Diedre Malone, Communications.
General email, info@nwpc.org

Web, www.nwpc.org, Twitter, @NWPCnational and Facebook, www.facebook.com/NWPC.fb

Seeks to increase the number of women in policymaking positions in federal, state, and local government. Identifies, recruits, trains, and supports pro-choice women candidates for public office. Monitors agencies and provides names of qualified women for high-level and mid-level appointments.

Network of Schools of Public Policy, Affairs, and Administration (NASPAA), *1029 Vermont Ave. N.W., #1100, 20005-3517; (202) 628-8965. Fax, (202) 626-4978. Laurel McFarland, Executive Director, (202) 628-8965 ext. 105.*
General email, naspaa@naspaa.org

Web, www.naspaa.org, Twitter, @naspaa and Facebook, www.facebook.com/naspaaglobal

Serves as a clearinghouse for information on education in public administration, public policy, and public affairs programs in colleges and universities.

Women in Government Relations, *1420 New York Ave. N.W., #500, 20005; (202) 868-6797. Emily Bardach, Executive Director, (703) 299-8547.*
General email, info@wgr.org

Web, www.wgr.org and Twitter, @WGRDC

Membership: professionals in business, trade associations, and government whose jobs involve governmental relations at the federal, state, or local level. Serves as a forum for exchange of information among its members.

STATE AND LOCAL GOVERNMENT

General

▶**AGENCIES**

General Services Administration (GSA), *Catalog of Federal Domestic Assistance (CFDA), 2200 Crystal City Dr., Crystal Park 1, Arlington, VA 22202; 1800 F St. N.W., 20405-0001; (703) 605-2119. Michael Stephenson, Director. Help Desk, (866) 606-8220.*
Federal Service Desk, www.fsd.gov

Disseminates information on federal assistance programs available to state and local governments through the CFDA website. Information includes all types of federal aid and explains types of assistance, eligibility requirements, application processes, and suggestions for writing proposals. Catalog may be downloaded from the CFDA website. Printed version may be ordered from the Superintendent of Documents, U.S. Government Printing Office, Washington, DC 20402; (202) 512-1800, or toll-free, (866) 512-1800; or online at http://bookstore.gpo.gov.

Multistate Tax Commission, *444 N. Capitol St. N.W., #425, 20001-1538; (202) 650-0300. Gregory S. Matson, Executive Director.*

General email, mtc@mtc.gov

Web, www.mtc.gov

Membership: state governments that have enacted the Multistate Tax Compact. Promotes fair, effective, and efficient state tax systems for interstate and international commerce; works to preserve state tax sovereignty. Encourages uniform state tax laws and regulations for multistate and multinational enterprises. Maintains three regional audit offices that monitor compliance with state tax laws and encourage uniformity in taxpayer treatment. Administers program to identify businesses that do not file tax returns with states.

Office of Management and Budget (OMB) *(Executive Office of the President), Federal Financial Management, 725 17th St. N.W., #6025, 20503; Fax, (202) 395-3952. Mark Reger, Controller (Acting). Press, (202) 395-7254. Web, www.whitehouse.gov/omb/management/office-federal-financial-management*

Facilitates exchange of information on financial management standards, techniques, and processes among officers of state and local governments.

State Justice Institute, *11951 Freedom Dr., #1020, Reston, VA 20190; (571) 313-8843. Fax, (571) 313-1173. Jonathan D. Mattiello, Executive Director. General email, contact@sji.gov*

Web, www.sji.gov and Twitter, @statejustice

Awards grants to state courts and to state agencies for programs that improve state courts' judicial administration. Maintains judicial information clearinghouses and establishes technical resource centers; conducts educational programs; delivers technical assistance.

▶**CONGRESS**

For a listing of relevant congressional committees and subcommittees, please see pages 320–321 or the Appendix.

▶**NONGOVERNMENTAL**

American Legislative Exchange Council (ALEC), *2900 Crystal Dr., 6th Floor, Arlington, VA 22202; (703) 373-0933. Fax, (703) 373-0927. Lisa B. Nelson, Chief Executive Officer, ext. 240; Michael Bowman, Vice President of Policy, ext. 245. Media, (571) 482-5035. General email, membership@alec.org*

Web, www.alec.org, Twitter, @ALEC_states and Facebook, www.facebook.com/alec.states

Nonpartisan educational and research organization for state legislators. Conducts research and provides information and model state legislation on public policy issues. Supports the development of state policies to limit government, expand free markets, promote economic growth, and preserve individual liberty.

The Brookings Institution, *Metropolitan Policy Program, 1755 Massachusetts Ave. N.W., 20036; (202) 797-6000. Fax, (202) 797-2965. Amy Liu, Director, (202) 797-2464. Press, (202) 797-6105.*

Local Government in the Washington Metropolitan Area

DISTRICT OF COLUMBIA

Executive Office of the Mayor,
Muriel Bowser, Mayor
John A. Wilson Bldg.
1350 Pennsylvania Ave. N.W., #316, 20004;
  (202) 727-2643; Fax, (202) 727-0505;
Email, eom@dc.gov;
Web, mayor.dc.gov

MARYLAND

Montgomery County,
Ike Leggett, County Executive
101 Monroe St., 2nd Floor, Rockville, MD 20850;
  (240) 777-0311; Fax, (240) 777-2517;
Email, ocemail@montgomerycountymd.gov;
Web, www.montgomerycountymd.gov/exec

Prince George's County,
Rushern L. Baker III, County Executive
14741 Gov. Oden Bowie Dr., 2nd Floor, Upper Marlboro,
  MD 20772; (301) 952-4131; Fax, (301) 952-5148;
Email, countyexecutive@co.pg.md.us;
Web, www.princegeorgescountymd.gov

VIRGINIA

Arlington County,
Mark Schwartz, County Manager
2100 Clarendon Blvd., Arlington, VA 22201;
  (703) 228-3120; Fax, (703) 228-3218;
Email, countymanager@arlingtonva.us;
Web, www.arlingtonva.us

City of Alexandria,
Allison Silberberg, Mayor
301 King St., Room 1900, Alexandria, VA 22314;
  (703) 746-4357; Fax, (703) 838-6426;
Email, alexvamayor@aol.com;
Web, www.alexandriava.gov

City of Falls Church,
Wyatt Shields, City Manager, 300 Park Ave., #303E, Falls
  Church, VA 22046; (703) 248-5004; Fax,
  (703) 248-5146;
Email, city-manager@fallschurchva.gov;
Web, www.fallschurchva.gov

Fairfax County,
Brian Hill, County Executive
12000 Government Center Pkwy.,
  #552, Fairfax, VA 22035; (703) 324-2531;
  Fax, (703) 324-3956;
Email, 703fairfax@fairfaxcounty.gov;
Web, www.fairfaxcounty.gov

General email, metro@brookings.edu

Web, www.brookings.edu/metro

Helps U.S. cities and metropolitan areas study and reform their economic, fiscal, and social policies. Conducts research at the national, state, and local levels.

Coalition of Northeastern Governors (CONEG), *Policy Research Center, Inc., 400 N. Capitol St. N.W., #382, 20001; (202) 624-8450. Jay Lucey, Executive Director.*

General email, info@coneg.org

Web, http://coneg.org

Membership: governors of seven northeastern states (Connecticut, Maine, Massachusetts, New Hampshire, New York, Rhode Island, and Vermont). Addresses shared interests in regional energy, economic development, transportation, and the environment; serves as an information clearinghouse on regional and federal issues; facilitates joint action among member states. Secretariat to the New England Governors & Eastern Canadian Premiers and to the Northeast Committee on Environment.

Council of State Governments (CSG), *Washington Office, 444 N. Capitol St. N.W., #401, 20001; (202) 624-5460. Fax, (202) 624-5452. David Adkins, Executive Director; Andy Karellas, Director of Federal Affairs. Media, (859) 244-8246.*

General email, membership@csg.org

Web, www.csg.org, www.csg.org/federal_affairs.aspx and Twitter, @CSGovts

Membership: governing bodies of states, commonwealths, and territories and various affiliated national organizations of state officials. Promotes interstate, federal-state, and state-local cooperation; interests include education, transportation, human services, housing, natural resources, and economic development. Provides services to affiliates and associated organizations, including the National Assn. of State Treasurers, National Assn. of Government Labor Officials, and other state administrative organizations in specific fields. Monitors legislation and executive policy. (Headquarters in Lexington, Ky.)

Government Finance Officers Assn. (GFOA), *Federal Liaison Center, 660 N. Capitol St., #410, 20001; (202) 393-8020. Fax, (202) 393-0780. Emily S. Brock, Director, (202) 393-8467.*

General email, federalliaison@gfoa.org

Web, www.gfoa.org and Twitter, @GFOA

Membership: state and local government finance managers. Offers training and publications in public financial management. Conducts research in public fiscal management, design and financing of government programs, and formulation and analysis of government fiscal policy. (Headquarters in Chicago, Ill.)

International City/County Management Assn. (ICMA), *777 N. Capitol St. N.E., #500, 20002-4201; (202) 289-4262. Fax, (202) 962-3500. Marc Ott, Executive Director, ext. 3528. Member services and information, (202) 962-3680. Toll-free, (800) 745-8780.*

General email, membership@icma.org

Web, www.icma.org

Membership: appointed managers and administrators of cities, towns, counties, and other local governments around the world; local government employees; academics; and other individuals with an interest in local government. Provides member support, publications, data and information, peer and results-oriented assistance, and training and professional development to members and others to help build sustainable communities. Sponsors workshops, regional summits, and an annual conference. Publishes resources for local government management professionals.

International Municipal Lawyers Assn. (IMLA), *51 Monroe St., #404, Rockville, MD 20850; (202) 466-5424. Fax, (202) 785-0152. Chuck Thompson, General Counsel, ext. 7110.*

General email, info@imla.org

Web, www.imla.org

Membership: local government attorneys and public law practitioners. Acts as a research service for members in all areas of municipal law; participates in litigation of municipal and constitutional law issues.

National Assn. of Bond Lawyers, *601 13th St. N.W., #800-S, 20005-3875; (202) 503-3300. Fax, (202) 637-0217. Linda H. Wyman, Chief Operating Officer, (202) 503-3300 ext. 3306.*

General email, nabl@nabl.org

Web, www.nabl.org and Twitter, @nabldc

Membership: state and municipal finance lawyers. Educates members and others on the law relating to state and municipal bonds and other obligations. Provides advice and comment at the federal, state, and local levels on legislation, regulations, rulings, and court and administrative proceedings regarding public obligations.

National Assn. of Counties (NACo), *600 N. Capitol St. N.W., #400, 20001; (202) 393-6226. Matthew D. Chase, Executive Director. Press, (202) 942-4220. Toll-free, (888) 407-6226.*

General email, dcox@naco.org

Web, www.naco.org and Twitter, @NACoTweets

Membership: county governments and county officials and their staffs through NACo's affiliates. Conducts research, supplies information, and provides technical and public affairs assistance on issues affecting counties. Interests include homeland security, drug abuse, access to health care, and public-private partnerships. Monitors legislation and regulations.

National Assn. of Regional Councils (NARC), *660 N. Capitol St. N.W., #440, 20001; (202) 986-1032. Leslie Wollack, Executive Director, (202) 618-5696.*

General email, info@narc.org

Web, narc.org and Twitter, @narcregions

Membership: regional councils of local governments, councils of government, and metropolitan planning organizations. Works to improve local governments' intergovernmental planning and coordination at the regional level. Interests include transportation, economic and community development, workforce development, housing, aging, energy, environment, public safety, and emergency management.

National Assn. of Secretaries of State, *444 N. Capitol St. N.W., #401, 20001; (202) 624-3525. Fax, (202) 624-3527. Leslie Reynolds, Executive Director.*
General email, nass@sso.org

Web, www.nass.org and Twitter, @Nassorg

Organization of secretaries of state and lieutenant governors or other comparable state officials from the fifty states, the District of Columbia, Guam, Puerto Rico, and the U.S. Virgin Islands. Interests include budget and finance, elections and voting, state business services and licensing, e-government, and state heritage, including a digital archives initiative.

National Assn. of State Auditors, Comptrollers, and Treasurers, *Washington Office, 444 N. Capitol St. N.W., #548, 20001; (202) 624-5451. Fax, (202) 624-5473. Cornelia Chebinou, Washington Director.*
Web, www.nasact.org and Twitter, @nasact

Membership: elected and appointed state and territorial officials who deal with the financial management of state government. Provides training and leadership information on financial management, best practices, and research. Monitors legislation and regulations. (Headquarters in Lexington, Ky.)

National Assn. of State Budget Officers, *444 N. Capitol St. N.W., #642, 20001-1511; (202) 624-5382. Fax, (202) 624-7745. John Hicks, Executive Director, (202) 624-8804. General email, nasbo-direct@nasbo.org*

Web, www.nasbo.org and Twitter, @NASBO

Membership: state budget and financial officers. Advances state budget practices through research, policy analysis, education, and knowledge sharing. Publishes reports on budget-related issues; shares best practices; provides training and technical assistance. (Affiliate of the National Governors Assn.)

National Assn. of Towns and Townships (NATaT), *1901 Pennsylvania Ave. N.W., #700, 20006; (202) 331-8500. Jennifer Imo, Federal Director.*
General email, info@natat.org

Web, www.natat.org

Membership: towns, townships, small communities, and others interested in supporting small-town government. Provides local government officials from small jurisdictions with technical assistance, educational services, and public policy support; conducts research and coordinates training for local government officials nationwide. Interests include tax benefits for local public service volunteers, local economic development, water and wastewater infrastructure, transportation improvements, and allocation of federal resources. (Affiliated with National Center for Small Communities.)

National Black Caucus of Local Elected Officials (NBC/LEO), *National League of Cities, 660 N. Capitol St. N.W., 20001; (202) 626-3000. Leon Andrews, Director for Race,*

Equity, and Leadership, (202) 626-3039. Information, (877) 827-2385.
General email, constituencygroups@nlc.org
Web, www.nlc.org

Membership: Black elected officials at the local level and other interested individuals. Seeks to increase Black participation on the National League of Cities' steering and policy committees. Informs members on issues, and plans strategies to achieve objectives through legislation and direct action. Interests include cultural diversity, local government and community participation, housing, economics, job training, the family, and human rights.

National Black Caucus of State Legislators, *444 N. Capitol St. N.W., #622, 20001; (202) 624-5457. Fax, (202) 508-3826. Juanzena Johnson, Executive Director.*
Web, www.nbcsl.org

Membership: Black state legislators. Promotes effective leadership among Black state legislators through education, research, and training; serves as an information network and clearinghouse for members.

National Conference of State Legislatures, *Washington Office, 444 N. Capitol St. N.W., #515, 20001; (202) 624-5400. Fax, (202) 737-1069. William Pound, Executive Director. General email, info@ncsl.org*

Web, www.ncsl.org and Twitter, @NCSLorg

Coordinates and represents state legislatures at the federal level; conducts research, produces videos, and publishes reports in areas of interest to state legislatures; conducts an information exchange program on intergovernmental relations; sponsors seminars for state legislators and their staffs. Interests include unfunded federal mandates, state-federal law conflict, and fiscal integrity. Monitors legislation and regulations. (Headquarters in Denver, Colo.)

National Foundation for Women Legislators, *1727 King St., #300, Alexandria, VA 22314; (703) 518-7931. Jody Thomas, Executive Director.*
General email, nfwl@womenlegislators.org

Web, www.womenlegislators.org,
Twitter, @womenlegislators and Facebook,
www.facebook.com/womenlegislators

Provides leadership development and networking resources to elected women leaders at the city, state, and federal levels of government.

National Governors Assn. (NGA), *444 N. Capitol St. N.W., #267, 20001-1512; (202) 624-5300. Scott Pattison, Executive Director. Press, (202) 624-5313. General email, info@nga.org*

Web, www.nga.org and Twitter, @NatGovsAssoc

Membership: governors of states, commonwealths, and territories. Provides members with policy and technical assistance. Makes policy recommendations to Congress and the president on community and economic development; education; international trade and foreign relations; energy and the environment; health care and welfare reform; agriculture; transportation, commerce, and technology;

communications; criminal justice; public safety; and work-force development.

National League of Cities, 660 N. Capitol St. N.W., #450, 20001; (202) 626-3000. Fax, (202) 626-3043. Clarence Anthony, Executive Director, (202) 626-3010. Toll-free, (877) 827-2385.
General email, info@nlc.org
Web, www.nlc.org

Membership: cities and state municipal leagues. Provides city leaders with training, technical assistance, and publications; investigates needs of local governments in implementing federal programs that affect cities. Holds two annual conferences; conducts research; sponsors awards. Monitors legislation and regulations. (Affiliates include National Black Caucus of Local Elected Officials.)

NIGP: The Institute for Public Procurement, 2411 Dulles Corner Park, #350, Herndon, VA 20171; (703) 736-8900. Fax, (703) 736-9644. Rick Grimm, Chief Executive Officer, ext. 235. Information, (800) 367-6447.
Web, www.nigp.org and Facebook, www.facebook.com/OfficialNIGP

Membership: governmental purchasing departments, agencies, and organizations at the federal, state, and local levels in the United States, Canada, and internationally. Provides public procurement officers with technical assistance and information, training seminars, and professional certification. (Formerly the National Institute of Governmental Purchasing.)

Public Risk Management Assn. (PRIMA), 700 S. Washington St., #218, Alexandria, VA 22314; (703) 528-7701. Fax, (703) 739-0200. Marshall W. Davies, Executive Director, (703) 253-1265.
General email, info@primacentral.org
Web, www.primacentral.org

Membership: state and local governments and their risk management practitioners, including benefits and insurance managers, and private sector organizations. Develops and teaches cost-effective management techniques for handling public liability issues; promotes professional development of its members. Gathers and disseminates information about risk management to public and private sectors.

Public Technology Institute (PTI), 660 N. Capitol St. N.W., #400, Alexandria, VA 20001; (202) 626-2400. Alan R. Shark, Executive Director, (202) 626-2445. Press, (202) 626-2432.
General email, info@pti.org
Web, www.pti.org and Twitter, @Public_Tech

Cooperative research, development, and technology-transfer organization of cities and counties in North America. Assists local governments in increasing efficiency, reducing costs, improving services, and developing public enterprise programs to help local officials create revenues and serve citizens. Participates in international conferences.

Stateline.org, 901 E St. N.W., 7th Floor, 20004-2008; (202) 552-2000. Fax, (202) 552-2299. Scott Greenberger, Executive Editor. Press, (202) 540-6507.

General email, editor@stateline.org
Web, www.pewtrusts.org/en/research-and-analysis/blogs/stateline/about

Independent online news site and forum. Encourages debate on state-level issues such as health care, tax and budget policy, the environment, and immigration. (Part of the Pew Charitable Trust.)

U.S. Conference of Mayors, 1620 Eye St. N.W., 4th Floor, 20006; (202) 293-7330. Fax, (202) 293-2352. J. Thomas (Tom) Cochran, Executive Director.
General email, info@usmayors.org
Web, www.usmayors.org and Twitter, @usmayors

Membership: mayors of cities with populations of 30,000 or more. Promotes city-federal cooperation; publishes reports and conducts meetings on federal programs, policies, and initiatives that affect urban and suburban interests. Serves as a clearinghouse for information on urban and suburban problems. (Approximately 1,400 U.S. cities.)

Women In Government, 444 N. Capitol St. N.W., #401, 20001; (202) 434-4850. Lucy Gettman, Executive Director, (202) 434-4852.
Web, www.womeningovernment.org and Twitter, @WomenInGovt

Membership: women state legislators. Seeks to enhance the leadership role of women policymakers by providing issue education and leadership training. Sponsors seminars and conducts educational research.

Washington Area

►CONGRESS

For a listing of relevant congressional committees and sub-committees, please see pages 320–321 or the Appendix.

►NONGOVERNMENTAL

Metropolitan Washington Council of Governments, 777 N. Capitol St. N.E., #300, 20002-4239; (202) 962-3200. Fax, (202) 962-3201. Chuck Bean, Executive Director, (202) 962-3260. Press, (202) 962-3250.
General email, ccogdtp@mwcog.org
Web, www.mwcog.org

Membership: local governments in the Washington area, plus members of the Maryland and Virginia legislatures and the U.S. Congress and the Department of Homeland Security. Analyzes and develops regional responses to issues such as the environment, affordable housing, economic development, health, population growth, human and social services, public safety, and transportation.

Walter E. Washington Convention Center Authority, 801 Mt. Vernon Pl. N.W., 20001; (202) 249-3000. Fax, (202) 249-3397. Gregory A. O'Dell, Chief Executive Officer. Information, (800) 368-9000. Press, (202) 249-3217.
Web, www.dcconvention.com and Twitter, @TheEventsDC

Promotes national and international conventions, meetings, and trade shows; hosts sports, entertainment, and special events; fosters redevelopment of downtown Washington.

10 Health

GENERAL POLICY AND ANALYSIS

Basic Resources

▶**AGENCIES**

Agency for Health Care Research and Quality (AHCRQ) *(Health and Human Services Dept.), (Research and Quality),* 5600 Fishers Lane, 7th Floor, Rockville, MD 20857; (301) 427-1364. Fax, (301) 427-1873. *Gopal Khanna, Director,* (301) 427-1200. Congressional Affairs, (301) 427-1214. Press, (301) 427-1864. Public inquiries, (301) 427-1104. TTY, (888) 586-6340.
General email, info@ahrq.gov

Web, www.ahrq.gov/cpi/centers/ockt/index.html, Twitter, @AHRQNews and Facebook, www.facebook.com/ahrq.gov

Works to improve the quality, safety, effectiveness, and efficiency of health care in the United States. Promotes improvements in clinical practices and in organizing, financing, and delivering health care services. Conducts and supports comparative effectiveness research, demonstration projects, evaluations, and training; disseminates information on a wide range of activities.

Assistant Secretary for Health (OASH) *(Health and Human Services Dept.),* 200 Independence Ave. S.W., #715G, 20201; (202) 690-7694. *Dr. Brett P. Giroir, Assistant Secretary (Acting).* Communications, (202) 205-1842.
General email, ASH@hhs.gov

Web, www.hhs.gov/ash and Twitter, @hhsgov

Develops public health policy recommendations across Health and Human Services Dept offices. Oversees the Office of the Surgeon General and Commissioned Corps of the U.S. Public Health Service.

Assistant Secretary for Health (OASH) *(Health and Human Services Dept.), Disease Prevention and Health Promotion (ODPHP),* 1101 Wootton Pkwy., #LL100, Rockville, MD 20852; (240) 453-8280. Fax, (240) 453-8282. *Dr. Donald Wright, Director.*
General email, odphpinfo@hhs.gov

Web, www.health.gov

Develops national policies for disease prevention, clinical preventive services, and health promotion; assists the private sector and agencies with disease prevention, clinical preventive services, and health promotion activities.

Assistant Secretary for Health (OASH) *(Health and Human Services Dept.), National Health Information Center (NHIC),* 1100 Wootton Pkwy., #LL100, Rockville, MD 20852 (mailing address: P.O. Box 1133, Washington, DC 20013-1133); (240) 453-8280. Fax, (240) 453-8282. *Dr. Donald Wright, Director.*
General email, healthfinder@nhic.org and info@nhic.org

Web, www.health.gov/nhic and www.healthfinder.gov

A project of the Office of Disease Prevention and Health Promotion; provides referrals on health topics and resources. Maintains a calendar of National Health Observances.

Assistant Secretary for Health (OASH) *(Health and Human Services Dept.), Surgeon General,* Tower Bldg., 1101 Wootton Pkwy., Plaza Level 1, #100, Rockville, MD 20852 (mailing address: Tower Bldg., Plaza Level 1, #100, 1101 Wooton Pkwy., Rockville, MD 20852); (240) 276-8853. Fax, (240) 453-6141. *Vice Adm. (Dr.) Jerome M. Adams, Surgeon General.* Press, (202) 202-0143.
Web, www.surgeongeneral.gov and Twitter, @Surgeon_General

Directs activities of the Office of the Assistant Secretary for Health. Serves as the secretary's principal adviser on health concerns; exercises specialized responsibilities in various health areas, including domestic and global health. Advises the public on smoking, AIDS, immunization, diet, nutrition, disease prevention, and other general health issues, including responses to bioterrorism. Oversees activities of all members of the Commissioned Corps of the U.S. Public Health Service.

Centers for Disease Control and Prevention (CDC) *(Health and Human Services Dept.), Washington Office,* 395 E St. S.W., #9100, 20201; (202) 245-0600. Fax, (202) 245-0602. *Robert Redfield, Director; Dr. Mitchell (Mitch) Wolfe, Director, Washington Office (Acting).* Public inquiries, (800) 232-4636. TTY, (888) 232-6348.
General email, cdcwashington@cdc.gov

Web, www.cdc.gov/washington and Twitter, @CDCgov

Collaborates with state and local health departments to further health promotion; prevention of disease, injury, and disability; and preparedness for new health threats. Monitors the health of individuals, detects and investigates health problems, conducts research to enhance prevention, develops and acts as advocate for public health policies, implements prevention strategies, promotes healthy behaviors, fosters safe and healthful environments, and provides leadership and training. (Headquarters in Atlanta, Ga.)

Health and Human Services Dept. (HHS), 200 Independence Ave. S.W., 20201; (202) 690-7000. Fax, (202) 690-7203. *Alex M. Azar II, Secretary.* Public Affairs, (202) 690-6343. Toll-free, (877) 696-6775. TTY, (800) 877-8339.
General email, secretary@hhs.gov

Web, www.hhs.gov, Twitter, @HHSGov and Facebook, www.facebook.com/HHS

Acts as principal adviser to the president on health and welfare plans, policies, and programs of the federal government. Encompasses eleven operating divisions, including eight agencies in the U.S. Public Health Service and three human services agencies, including the Centers for Medicare and Medicaid Services, the Administration for Children and Families, the National Institutes of Health, and the Centers for Disease Control and Prevention.

Health and Human Services Dept. (HHS), *Civil Rights (OCR), Conscience and Religious Freedom Division,* 200 Independence Ave. S.W., 20201; *Roger Severino, Civil*

Rights Director. Toll-free, (800) 368-1019. TTY, (800) 537-7697.

General email, OCRMail@hhs.gov

Web, www.hhs.gov/conscience/index.html

Works to protect and enforce laws and regulations that protect the conscience and the free exercise of religion and prohibit coercion and religious discrimination in HHS-funded or -conducted programs and activities.

Health and Human Services Dept. (HHS), *National Center for Health Statistics, National Committee on Vital and Health Statistics (NCVHS),* 3311 Toledo Rd., Hyattsville, MD 20782; (301) 458-4715. Fax, (301) 458-4022. Rebecca Hines, Executive Secretary.

General email, vgh4@cdc.gov

Web, www.ncvhs.hhs.gov

Statutory public advisory body on health data statistics and national health information policy. Serves as a national forum on health data. Aims to accelerate the evolution of public and private health information systems toward more uniform, shared data standards within the context of privacy and security concerns.

Health and Human Services Dept. (HHS), *National Coordinator for Health Information Technology (ONC),* 330 C St. S.W., Floor 7, 20201; (202) 690-7151. Fax, (202) 690-6079. Dr. Don Rucker, National Coordinator.

General email, onc.request@hhs.gov

Web, www.healthit.gov and Twitter, @ONC_HealthIT

Coordinates nationwide efforts to implement information technology that allows for electronic use and exchange of health information. Goals include ensuring security for patient health information, improving health care quality, and reducing health care costs.

Health and Human Services Dept. (HHS), *Planning and Evaluation (ASPE),* 200 Independence Ave. S.W., #415F, 20201; (202) 690-7858. Fax, (202) 690-7383. Brenda Destro, Deputy Assistant Secretary.

General email, osaspeinfo@hhs.gov

Web, https://aspe.hhs.gov and Twitter, @HHS_ASPE

Advises the secretary on policy development in health, disability, human services, data, and science, and provides advice and analysis on economic policy. Manages strategic and legislative planning and reviews regulations. Conducts research and evaluation studies, develops policy analyses, and estimates the cost and benefits of policy alternatives under consideration by the department or Congress.

Health and Human Services Dept. (HHS), *Planning and Evaluation (ASPE), Health Policy,* 200 Independence Ave. S.W., #447D, 20201; (202) 690-6870. Vacant, Deputy Assistant Secretary.

Web, https://aspe.hhs.gov/office-health-policy-hp

Develops, analyzes and coordinates health policy issues for secretary, including assisting in development and review of regulations and budgets and legislation and assisting in survey design efforts.

Health and Human Services Dept. (HHS), *Planning and Evaluation (ASPE), Science and Data Policy,*

200 Independence Ave. S.W., #444E, 20201; (202) 690-7100. Laina Bush, Deputy Assistant Secretary, (202) 690-7100.

Web, https://aspe.hhs.gov/office-science-and-data-policy

Provides analysis on public health science policy and data policy issues and initiatives to the department.

Health and Human Services Dept. (HHS), *Preparedness and Response (ASPR),* 200 Independence Ave. S.W., #638-G, 20201; (202) 205-2882. Dr. Robert Kadlec, Assistant Secretary.

Web, www.phe.gov/Preparedness/Pages/default.aspx and Twitter, @PHEgov

Serves as the secretary's principal adviser on matters relating to bioterrorism and public health emergencies. Directs activities of HHS relating to the protection of the civilian population from acts of bioterrorism and other public health emergencies.

Health Resources and Services Administration (HRSA) *(Health and Human Services Dept.),* 5600 Fishers Lane, #13N192, Rockville, MD 20857; (301) 443-2216. Fax, (301) 443-1246. George Sigounas, Administrator. Press, (301) 443-3376. TTY, (877) 897-9910.

General email, askhrsa.gov

Web, www.hrsa.gov and Twitter, @HRSAgov

Administers federal health service programs related to access, quality, equity, and cost of health care. Supports state and community efforts to deliver care to underserved areas and groups with special health needs. Oversees organ, bone marrow, and cord blood donation; compensates individuals harmed by vaccination; and maintains databases that protect against health care malpractice, waste, fraud, and abuse.

Health Resources and Services Administration (HRSA) *(Health and Human Services Dept.), Rural Health Policy (FORHP),* 5600 Fishers Lane, #17W45, Rockville, MD 20857; (301) 443-0835. Fax, (301) 443-2803. Tom Morris, Associate Administrator.

General email, tmorris@hrsa.gov

Web, www.hrsa.gov/rural-health/index.html

Works with federal agencies, states, and the private sector to develop solutions to health care problems in rural communities. Administers grants to rural communities and supports rural health services research. Studies the effects of Medicare and Medicaid programs on rural access to health care.

National Aeronautics and Space Administration (NASA), *Chief Health and Medical Officer,* 300 E St. S.W., 20546; (202) 358-2390. Fax, (202) 358-3349. Dr. James D. Polk, Chief Health and Medical Officer.

Web, www.nasa.gov/offices/ochmo

Ensures the health and safety of NASA employees in space and on the ground. Develops health and medical policy, establishes guidelines for health and medical practices, oversees health care delivery, and monitors human and animal research standards within the agency.

National Center for Health Statistics (NCHS) *(Centers for Disease Control and Prevention),* 3311 Toledo Rd., #7204,

---

HEALTH RESOURCES IN CONGRESS

For a complete listing of congressional committees, including their full contact information, leadership, membership, and jurisdictions, please refer to the Appendix on pages 827–948.

HOUSE:

House Agriculture Committee, (202) 225-2171.
Web, agriculture.house.gov
    Subcommittee on Nutrition, (202) 225-2171.
House Appropriations Committee, (202) 225-2771.
Web, appropriations.house.gov
    Subcommittee on Agriculture, Rural Development, Food and Drug Administration, and Related Agencies, (202) 225-2638.
    Subcommittee on Labor, Health and Human Services, Education, and Related Agencies, (202) 225-3508.
House Armed Services Committee, (202) 225-4151.
Web, armedservices.house.gov
    Subcommittee on Military Personnel, (202) 225-7560.
House Budget Committee, (202) 226-7270.
Web, budget.house.gov
House Education and the Workforce Committee, (202) 225-4527.
Web, edworkforce.house.gov
    Subcommittee on Health, Employment, Labor, and Pensions, (202) 225-4527.
    Subcommittee on Workforce Protections, (202) 225-4527.
House Energy and Commerce Committee, (202) 225-2927.
Web, energycommerce.house.gov
    Subcommittee on Environment, (202) 225-2927.
    Subcommittee on Health, (202) 225-2927.

House Foreign Affairs Committee, (202) 225-5021.
Web, foreignaffairs.house.gov
    Subcommittee on Africa, Global Health, Global Human Rights, and International Organizations, (202) 226-7812.
House Natural Resources Committee, (202) 225-2761.
Web, naturalresources.house.gov
House Oversight and Government Reform Committee, (202) 225-5074.
Web, oversight.house.gov
    Subcommittee on Health Care, Benefits, and Administrative Rules, (202) 225-5074.
House Science, Space, and Technology Committee, (202) 225-6371.
Web, science.house.gov
    Subcommittee on Research and Technology, (202) 225-6371.
House Small Business Committee, (202) 225-5821.
Web, smallbusiness.house.gov
    Subcommittee on Health and Technology, (202) 225-5821.
House Veterans' Affairs Committee, (202) 225-3527.
Web, veterans.house.gov
    Subcommittee on Health, (202) 225-9154.
House Ways and Means Committee, (202) 225-3625.
Web, waysandmeans.house.gov
    Subcommittee on Health, (202) 225-3943.

Hyattsville, MD 20782-2064; (301) 458-4800. Fax, (301) 458-4020. Sayeedha Uddin, Executive Secretary, (301) 458-4303. Toll-free CDC information, (800) 232-4636. Web, www.cdc.gov/nchs

Compiles, analyzes, and disseminates national statistics on population health characteristics, health facilities and human resources, health costs and expenditures, and health hazards. Interests include international health statistics.

National Institute for Occupational Safety and Health (NIOSH) *(Centers for Disease Control and Prevention),* 395 E St. S.W., Patriots Plaza 1, #9200, 20201; (202) 245-0625. Dr. John Howard, Director. Information, (800) 232-4636. TTY, (888) 232-6348.
General email, cdcinfo@cdc.gov

Web, www.cdc.gov/niosh

Supports and conducts research on occupational safety and health issues; provides technical assistance and training; organizes international conferences and symposia; develops

recommendations for the Labor Dept. Operates occupational safety and health bibliographic databases; publishes documents on occupational safety and health.

National Institute of Standards and Technology (NIST) *(Commerce Dept.), Special Programs Office,* 100 Bureau Dr., MS 4701, Gaithersburg, MD 20899-4701; (301) 975-4447. Fax, (301) 975-8972. Richard R. Cavanagh, Director. General information, (301) 975-2756.
Web, www.nist.gov/spo

Fosters collaboration among government, military, academic, professional, and private organizations to respond to critical national needs through science-based standards and technology innovation, including areas of health.

National Institutes of Health (NIH) *(Health and Human Services Dept.),* 1 Center Dr., Bldg. 1, #344, MSC 0188, Bethesda, MD 20892-0148; (301) 496-4000. Fax, (301) 496-0017. Dr. Francis S. Collins, Director;

SENATE:

Senate Agriculture, Nutrition, and Forestry
  Committee, (202) 224-2035.
Web, agriculture.senate.gov
  Subcommittee on Rural Development and
    Energy, (202) 224-2035.
  Subcommittee on Nutrition, Agricultural
    Research, Specialty Crops, (202) 224-2035.
Senate Appropriations Committee, (202) 224-7257.
Web, appropriations.senate.gov
  Subcommittee on Agriculture, Rural
    Development, Food and Drug
    Administration, and Related Agencies,
    (202) 224-8090.
  Subcommittee on Labor, Health and Human
    Services, Education, and Related Agencies,
    (202) 224-9145.
Senate Armed Services Committee,
  (202) 224-3871.
Web, armed-services.senate.gov
  Subcommittee on Personnel, (202) 224-3871.
Senate Banking, Housing, and Urban Affairs
  Committee, (202) 224-7391.
Web, banking.senate.gov
Senate Budget Committee, (202) 224-0642.
Web, budget.senate.gov
Senate Commerce, Science, and Transportation
  Committee, (202) 224-1251.
Web, commerce.senate.gov
  Subcommittee on Consumer Protections,
    Product Safety, Insurance and Data Security,
    (202) 224-1251.

Senate Environment and Public Works Committee,
  (202) 224-6176.
Web, epw.senate.gov
  Subcommittee on Clean Air and Nuclear Safety,
    (202) 224-6176.
  Subcommittee on Superfund, Waste Management,
    and Regulatory Oversight, (202) 224-6176.
  Subcommittee on Transportation and
    Infrastructure, (202) 224-6176.
Senate Finance Committee, (202) 224-4515.
Web, finance.senate.gov
  Subcommittee on Health Care, (202) 224-4515.
Senate Health, Education, Labor, and Pensions
  Committee, (202) 224-5375.
Web, help.senate.gov
  Subcommittee on Children and Families,
    (202) 224-5375.
  Subcommittee on Employment and Workplace
    Safety, (202) 228-5375.
  Subcommittee on Primary Health and
    Retirement Security, (202) 224-5375.
Senate Indian Affairs Committee, (202) 224-2251.
Web, indian.senate.gov
Senate Judiciary Committee, (202) 224-5225.
Web, judiciary.senate.gov
  Subcommittee on Crime and Terrorism,
    (202) 224-5972.
Senate Small Business and Entrepreneurship
  Committee, (202) 224-5175.
Web, sbc.senate.gov
Senate Special Committee on Aging, (202) 224-5364.
Web, aging.senate.gov

Dr. Lawrence A. Tabak, Deputy Director. Press, (301) 496-5787. TTY, (301) 402-9612.
Web, www.nih.gov

Supports and conducts biomedical research into the causes and prevention of diseases and furnishes information to health professionals and the public. Comprises research institutes and other components (the National Library of Medicine, the National Center for Advancing Translational Sciences, the John E. Fogarty International Center, and 27 institutes, including the National Cancer Institute; the National Institute of Allergy and Infectious Diseases; the National Heart, Lung, and Blood Institute; and the National Institute of Diabetes and Digestive and Kidney Diseases). All institutes are located in Bethesda, except the National Institute of Environmental Health Sciences, P.O. Box 12233, Research Triangle Park, N.C. 27709.

National Institutes of Health (NIH) *(Health and Human Services Dept.), Science Policy (OSP), 6705 Rockledge Dr., MSC 7985, Bethesda, MD 20892-7985; (301) 496-9838.*

Fax, (301) 496-9839. Carrie D. Wolinetz, Associate Director, (301) 496-2122.
General email, sciencepolicy@od.nih.gov
Web, http://osp.od.nih.gov

Advises the NIH director on science policy issues affecting the medical research community. Participates in the development of new policy and program initiatives. Monitors and coordinates agency planning and evaluation activities. Plans and implements a comprehensive science education program. Develops and implements NIH policies and procedures for the safe conduct of recombinant DNA and other biotechnology activities.

State Dept., *Medical Services, 2401 E St. N.W., #L218, 20522-0102; (202) 663-1649. Fax, (202) 663-1613.*
Mark J. Cohen, Medical Director (Acting).
Web, www.state.gov/m/med

Operates a worldwide primary health care system for U.S. citizen employees, and eligible family members, of participating U.S. government agencies. Conducts physical examinations of Foreign Service officers and candidates; provides clinical services; assists with medical evacuation of patients overseas.

▶**CONGRESS**

For a listing of relevant congressional committees and sub-committees, please see pages 362–363 or the Appendix.

Government Accountability Office (GAO), *Health Care (HC),* 441 G St. N.W., #5A21, 20548; (202) 512-7114. *Nikki Clowers, Managing Director, (202) 512-4010. Web, www.gao.gov/careers/healthcare.html*

Provides analyses, recommendations, and policy options to Congress and the executive branch for all federal government health programs, including those administered by the Defense (TRICARE), Health and Human Services, and Veterans Affairs Depts.

▶**NONGOVERNMENTAL**

Alliance for Health Policy, 1444 Eye St. N.W., #910, 20005-6573; (202) 789-2300. *Sarah J. Dash, President. General email, info@allhealthpolicy.org*

Web, www.allhealthpolicy.org, Twitter, @AllHealthPolicy and Facebook, www.facebook.com/allhealthpoicy.org

Nonpartisan organization that advocates health care reform, including cost containment and coverage for all. Sponsors conferences, forums and seminars for journalists, business leaders, policymakers, and the public. Seeks to be a source for unbiased health policy information.

Altarum Institute, 2000 M St. N.W., #400, 20036; (202) 828-5100. *Fax, (202) 728-9469. Linc Smith, President; Christin Hitchcock, Manager of Contracts and Procurement, (734) 302-4742. Toll-free, (888) 776-5187. Web, www.altarum.org, Twitter, @Altarum and Facebook, www.facebook.com/altarum*

Nonprofit health systems research and consulting organization focusing on health care delivery and financing issues that impact the health of diverse populations. (Head-quarters in Ann Arbor, Mich.)

American Public Health Assn., 800 Eye St. N.W., 20001-3710; (202) 777-2742. *Fax, (202) 777-2534. Dr. Georges C. Benjamin, Executive Director. TTY, (202) 777-2500. General email, comments@apha.org*

Web, www.apha.org and Twitter, @PublicHealth

Membership: health providers, educators, environmentalists, policymakers, and health officials at all levels working both within and outside of governmental organizations and educational institutions. Works to protect communities from serious, preventable health threats. Strives to ensure that community-based health promotion and disease prevention activities and preventive health services are universally accessible in the United States. Develops standards for scientific procedures in public health.

American Red Cross, *Government Relations,* 431 18th St. N.W., 20006; (202) 303-4371. *Cherae Bishop, Senior Vice President of Government Relations. General email, governmentrelations@redcross.org*

Web, www.redcross.org/about-us/governance/government-relations.html

Works to create, through legislative and regulatory initiatives, a pubic-policy environment that will forward the mission and objectives of the American Red Cross.

Assn. of State and Territorial Health Officials, 2231 Crystal Dr., #450, Arlington, VA 22202; (202) 371-9090. *Fax, (571) 527-3189. Michael Fraser, Executive Director, (202) 371-3142. Web, www.astho.org, www.statepublichealth.org and Twitter, @astho*

Membership: executive officers of state and territorial public health departments. Serves as legislative review agency and information source for members. Monitors legislation and regulations.

The Brookings Institution, *Center for Health Policy,* 1775 Massachusetts Ave. N.W., 20036; (703) 524-3513. *Paul Ginsburg, Director. General email, paul.ginsburg@usc.edu*

Web, www.brookings.edu/center/center-for-health-policy

Research center promoting healthcare policy and affordable health care. Interests include Medicare spending and delivery, implementation of the Affordable Healthcare Act and health insurance marketplaces, prescription drug reimbursement, and long-term care.

The Brookings Institution, *Economic Studies,* 1775 Massachusetts Ave. N.W., 20036-2188; (202) 797-6000. *Fax, (202) 797-6181. Ted Gayer, Director, (202) 797-6230. Press, (202) 797-6105. General email, escomment@brookings.edu*

Web, www.brookings.edu/economics and Twitter, @BrookingsEcon

Studies federal health care issues and health programs, including Medicare, Medicaid, and long-term care.

Grantmakers in Health, 1100 Connecticut Ave. N.W., #1200, 20036; (202) 452-8331. *Fax, (202) 452-8340. Faith Mitchell, President. General email, info@gih.org*

Web, www.gih.org and Twitter, @GIHealth

Seeks to increase the capacity of health foundations and giving programs to enhance public health and health education. Fosters information exchange among grantmakers. Publications include a bulletin on current news in health and human services.

Health Policy Institute *(Georgetown University),* 3300 Whitehaven St. N.W., #5000, Box 571444, 20057-1485; (202) 687-0880. *Fax, (202) 687-3110. Toni McRae, Administrative Assistant. Web, http://ihcrp.georgetown.edu and Twitter, @GUPublicPolicy*

Research branch of Georgetown University's McCourt School of Public Policy. Interests include quality of care and outcomes research, health care financing, the uninsured, federal health insurance reforms, and the impact of changes in the health care market on providers and patients.

Healthcare Leadership Council, *750 9th St. N.W., #500, 20001; (202) 452-8700. Fax, (202) 296-9561. Mary R. Grealy, President.*
Web, www.hlc.org and Twitter, @HealthInFocus

Membership: health care leaders who examine major health issues, including access and affordability. Works to implement new public policies.

Henry J. Kaiser Family Foundation, *Washington Office, 1330 G St. N.W., 20005; (202) 347-5270. Fax, (202) 347-5274. Drew Altman, President.*
Web, www.kff.org and Twitter, @KaiserFamFound

Offers information on major health care issues. Conducts research and communications programs. Monitors legislation and regulations. (Headquarters in Menlo Park, Calif. Not affiliated with Kaiser Permanente or Kaiser Industries.)

National Assn. of Counties (NACo), *600 N. Capitol St. N.W., #400, 20001; (202) 393-6226. Matthew D. Chase, Executive Director. Press, (202) 942-4220. Toll-free, (888) 407-6226.*
General email, dcox@naco.org
Web, www.naco.org and Twitter, @NACoTweets

Promotes federal understanding of county governments' role in providing, funding, and overseeing health services at the local level. Interests include indigent health care, Medicaid and Medicare, prevention of and services for HIV infection and AIDS, long-term care, mental health, maternal and child health, and traditional public health programs conducted by local health departments. Monitors legislation and regulations.

National Assn. of County and City Health Officials, *1201 Eye St. N.W., 4th Floor, 20005; (202) 783-5550. Fax, (202) 783-1583. Lori Freeman, Chief Executive Officer, (202) 507-4271.*
General email, info@naccho.org
Web, www.naccho.org and Twitter, @NACCHOalerts

Represents the nation's local health departments. Develops resources and programs to support local public health practices and systems. Submits health policy proposals to the federal government.

National Committee for Quality Assurance, *1100 13th St. N.W., 3rd Floor, 20005; (202) 955-3500. Fax, (202) 955-3599. Margaret E. O'Kane, President. Toll-free information on health plans and accreditation, (888) 275-7585.*
Web, www.ncqa.org and Twitter, @NCQA

Provides information on the quality of health care provided by health care institutions and individual providers. Assesses and reports on managed care plans through accreditation and performance measurement programs.

National Governors Assn. (NGA), *Center for Best Practices, Health Division, 444 N. Capitol St. N.W., #267, 20001-1512; (202) 624-5343. Fax, (202) 624-7825. Hemi Tewarson, Director. Information, (202) 624-5300.*
Web, www.nga.org/cms/center/health

Covers issues in the areas of health care service delivery and reform, including payment reform, health workforce planning, quality improvement, and public health and behavioral health integration within the medical delivery system. Other focus areas include Medicaid cost containment, state employee and retiree health benefits, maternal and child health, prescription drug abuse prevention, and health insurance exchange planning.

National Health Council, *1730 M St. N.W., #500, 20036-4561; (202) 785-3910. Fax, (202) 785-5923. Marc M. Boutin, Chief Executive Officer.*
General email, info@nhcouncil.org
Web, www.nationalhealthcouncil.org and Twitter, @NHcouncil

Membership: voluntary health agencies, associations, and business, insurance, and government groups interested in health. Conducts research on health and health-related issues. Monitors legislation and regulations.

National Quality Forum, *1030 15th St. N.W., #800, 20005; (202) 783-1300. Fax, (202) 783-3434. Shantanu Agrawal, President. Press, (202) 478-9326.*
General email, info@qualityforum.org
Web, www.qualityforum.org

Works to improve the quality of health care in the United States by setting national priorities and goals for performance improvement, endorsing national consensus standards for measuring and publicly reporting on performances, and promoting the attainment of national goals through education and outreach programs.

National Research Council (NRC), *Health and Medicine Division, Keck Center, 500 5th St. N.W., 20001; (202) 334-2352. Fax, 202-334 1412. Clyde J. Behney, Executive Director.*
General email, HMD-NASEM@nas.edu
Web, www.nationalacademies.org/hmd and Twitter, @NASEM_Health

Advises the government and public sector on matters relating to medical research, care, and education; examines policy matters relating to health care and public health.

National Research Council (NRC), *Health Care Services Board, Keck Center, 500 5th St. N.W., #W712, 20001; (202) 334-2001. Fax, (202) 334-2647. Sharyl Nass, Board Director; David Blumethal, Chair.*
Web, http://www.nationalacademies.org/hmd/About-HMD/Leadership-Staff/HMD-Staff-Leadership-Boards/Board-on-Health-Care-Services.aspx

Advises policymakers about the healthcare system in general as well as financing, effectiveness, workforce, and delivery of health care.

Health and Human Services Department

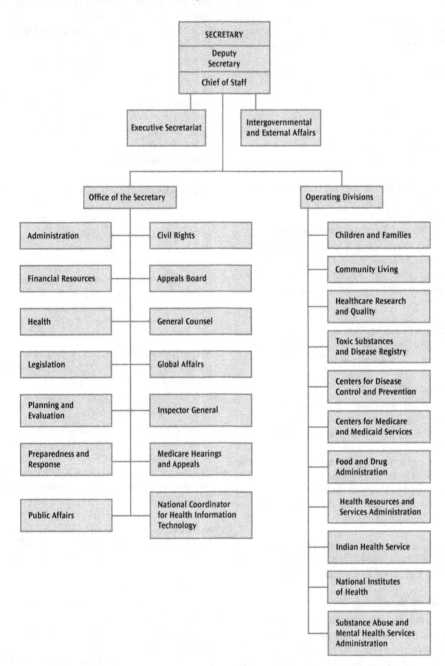

National Research Council (NRC), *Health Sciences Policy Board,* Keck Center, 500 5th St. N.W., 20001; (202) 334-1888. Fax, (202) 334-1329. Andrew Pope, Director. *General email, hsp@nas.edu*

Web, www.nationalacademies.org/hmd

Oversees research and activities related to basic biomedical and clinical research, including the role of science in policy and decision making; the education of health and research professionals and the general public, the preparedness, resilience, and sustainability of communities; biomedical ethics.

National Research Council (NRC), *Human-Systems Integration Board,* Keck Center, 500 5th St. N.W., 11th Floor, 20001; (202) 334-3453. Fax, (202) 334-2210. Toby Warden, Director. *General email, bohsi@nas.edu*

Web, http://sites.nationalacademies.org/dbasse/bohsi

Conducts studies on human factors and human-systems integration. Areas of research include home health care and disability and rehabilitation research.

National Research Council (NRC), *Population Health and Public Health Practice Board,* Keck Center, 500 5th St. N.W., 20001; (202) 334-2383. Fax, (202) 334-2939. Rose Marie Martinez, Director.
General email, bph@nas.edu

Web, www.nationalacademies.org/hmd

Supports research on public health, including vaccine safety, pandemic preparedness issues, smoking cessation, health disparities, and reducing environmental and occupational hazards.

National Vaccine Information Center, 21525 Ridgetop Circle, #100, Sterling, VA 20166; (703) 938-0342. Fax, (571) 313-1268. Barbara Loe Fisher, President; Theresa Wrangham, Executive Director.
General email, contactnvic@gmail.com

Web, www.nvic.org, Twitter, @NVICLoeDown and Facebook, www.facebook.com/national.vaccine .information.center

Educational organization that supports informed vaccination decisions, including the option to forgo vaccination. Provides assistance to parents of children who have experienced vaccine reactions and publishes information on diseases and vaccines. Monitors vaccine research, legislation, and regulations.

Public Citizen, *Health Research Group,* 1600 20th St. N.W., 20009-1001; (202) 588-1000. Michael Carome, Director.
General email, hrg1@citizen.org

Web, www.citizen.org/health-research-group, Twitter, @CitizenHRG and Publications, www.citizen.org/ our-work/health-and-safety/health-research-group-publications

Citizens' interest group that conducts policy-oriented research on health care issues. Interests include hospital quality and costs, doctors' fees, physician discipline and malpractice, state administration of Medicare programs, workplace safety and health, unnecessary surgery, comprehensive health planning, dangerous drugs, carcinogens, and medical devices. Favors a single-payer (Canadian-style) comprehensive health program.

RAND Corp., *Health Care Division, Washington Office,* 1200 S. Hayes St., Arlington, VA 22202-5050; (703) 413-1100. Fax, (703) 413-8111. Peter S. Hussey, Director. Press, (703) 414-4795.
General email, RANDHealthCare@rand.org

Web, www.rand.org/health-care/about.html and Twitter, @RANDHealth

Research organization that assesses health issues, including alternative reimbursement schemes for health care. Interests include health care costs and quality, military health, obesity, chronic disease prevention, and public health preparedness. Monitors national and international trends. (Headquarters in Santa Monica, Calif.)

Regulatory Affairs Professionals Society, 5635 Fishers Lane, #400, Rockville, MD 20852; (301) 770-2920 ext. 200. Fax, (301) 841-7956. Paul Brooks, Executive Director.
General email, raps@raps.org

Web, www.raps.org and Twitter, @RAPSorg

Membership: regulatory professionals in the medical device, pharmaceutical, and biotechnology product sectors worldwide. Promotes the safety and effectiveness of health care products. Supports the regulatory profession with resources, including education and certification. Monitors legislation and regulations.

Urban Institute, *Health Policy Center,* 500 L'Enfant Plaza S.W., 20024; (202) 833-7200. Genevieve M. Kenney, Vice President; Stephen Zuckerman, Vice President.
Web, www.urban.org/policy-centers/health-policy-center

Analyzes trends and underlying causes of changes in health insurance, coverage access to care, and use of health care services by the U.S. population. Researches and analyzes select health issues, including private insurance; the uninsured; Medicaid, Medicare, and the State Children's Health Insurance Program (SCHIP); disability and long-term care; vulnerable populations; and health care reform.

Global Health

▶AGENCIES

Agency for International Development (USAID), *Bureau for Global Health,* 1300 Pennsylvania Ave. N.W., #3.64, 20523-3100; (202) 712-4120. Fax, (202) 216-3485. Alma Crumm Golden, Senior Deputy Assistant Administrator.
Web, www.usaid.gov/what-we-do/global-health

Participates in global efforts to stabilize world population growth and support women's reproductive rights. Focus includes family planning; reproductive health care; infant, child, and maternal health; and prevention of sexually transmitted diseases, especially AIDS. Conducts demographic and health surveys; educates girls and women.

Agency for International Development (USAID), *Bureau for Global Health, Family Planning and Reproductive Health,* 1300 Pennsylvania Ave. N.W., #3.06-011, 20523-3600; (202) 712-4120. Fax, (202) 216-3485. Alma Crumm Golden, Senior Deputy Assistant Administrator. Press, (202) 712-4320.
General email, pi@usaid.gov

Web, www.usaid.gov/what-we-do/global-health/family-planning, Twitter, usaidgh and Facebook, www.facebook.com/usaidgh

Advances and supports family planning and reproductive health programs in more than 30 countries.

Assistant Secretary for Health (OASH) *(Health and Human Services Dept.), Global Affairs (OGA),* 200 Independence Ave. S.W., #639H, 20201; (202) 690-6174. (202) 260-0399. Fax, (202) 690-7127. Garrett Grigsby, Assistant Secretary (Acting).

General email, globalhealth@hhs.gov

Web, www.globalhealth.gov and Twitter, @hhsgov

Engages with multilateral organizations, foreign governments, ministries of health, civil society groups, and the private sector to advance policies that protect and promote health nationally and worldwide.

Bureau of Oceans and International Environmental and Scientific Affairs (OES) *(State Dept.), International Health and Biodefense (IHB), 2201 C St. N.W., #2734, 20520; (202) 647-1318. Jerry Mallory, Director.*

Web, www.state.gov/e/oes/intlhealthbiodefense

Advances the Global Health Security Agenda and focuses on issues including pandemic preparedness, new outbreaks of disease, new international policy discussions, and the impact of science and technology, medicine, and public health.

Fogarty International Center (FIC) *(National Institutes of Health), 31 Center Dr., MSC 2220, Bethesda, MD 20892-2220; (301) 496-1415. Fax, (301) 402-2173.*
Dr. Roger I. Glass, Director.
General email, ficinfo@nih.gov

Web, www.fic.nih.gov, Twitter, @fogarty_NIH and Facebook, www.facebook.com/fogarty.nih

Promotes and supports international scientific research and training to reduce disparities in global health. Leads formulation and implementation of international biomedical research and policy. Supports the conduct of research in high-priority global health areas, including infectious diseases such as HIV/AIDS, and helps build research capacity in the developing world.

Food and Drug Administration (FDA) *(Health and Human Services Dept.), International Programs (OIP), White Oak Bldg. 31/32, 10903 New Hampshire Ave., Silver Spring, MD 20993; (301) 796-4600. Fax, (301) 595-7937. Mary Lou Valdez, Associate Commissioner.*
Web, www.fda.gov/AboutFDA/CentersOffices/ OfficeofGlobalRegulatoryOperationsandPolicy/ OfficeofInternationalPrograms/ucm245229.htm and www.fda.gov/AboutFDA/CentersOffices/ OfficeofGlobalRegulatoryOperationsandPolicy/ OfficeofInternationalPrograms

Serves as FDA's liaison with foreign counterpart agencies, international organizations, and the U.S. diplomatic corps. Gathers and assesses information to inform decisions about FDA-regulated product imports. Seeks to advance global public health through distribution of health information, coordination of public health strategies, and promotion of public safety. Seeks to harmonize regulatory standards. Provides technical assistance.

▶**INTERNATIONAL ORGANIZATIONS**

Pan American Health Organization, *525 23rd St. N.W., 20037; (202) 974-3000. Fax, (202) 974-3663. Dr. Carissa F. Etienne, Director.*
Web, www.paho.org and Twitter, @PAHOWHO

Works to extend health services to underserved populations of its member countries and to control or eradicate communicable diseases; promotes cooperation among governments to solve public health problems. (Regional Office for the Americas of the World Health Organization, which is headquartered in Geneva, Switzerland.)

▶**NONGOVERNMENTAL**

Consortium of Universities for Global Health, *1608 Rhode Island Ave. N.W., #240, 20036; (202) 974-6363. Fax, (202) 833-5078. Dr. Keith Martin, Executive Director.*
General email, info@cugh.org

Web, www.cugh.org and Twitter, @CUGHnews

Assists universities in sharing resources and research on global health challenges. Coordinates academic partnerships between national universities and international educational institutions in developing countries. Develops national and global health centers.

Global Health Council, *1875 K St. N.W., 4th Floor, 20006; (703) 717-5251. Fax, (703) 717-5215. Loyce Pace, Executive Director.*
General email, membership@globalhealth.org

Web, www.globalhealth.org and Twitter, @GlobalHealthOrg

Membership: students, health care professionals, NGOs, foundations, corporations, and academic institutions. Works to secure the information and resources for improved global health.

National Research Council (NRC), *Global Health Board, Keck Center, 500 5th St. N.W., 20001; (202) 334-3967. Fax, (202) 334-3861. Ann Kerth, Chair; Julie Pavlin, Director.*
General email, HMD-NASEM@nas.edu

Web, www.nationalacademies.org/hmd/About-HMD/ Leadership-Staff/HMD-Staff-Leadership-Boards/Board-on-Global-Health.aspx

Carries out activities related to international health policy and health concerns of developing countries; main focus is public health programs for prevention and control of disease and disability.

World Bank, *Human Development Network, 1818 H St. N.W., 20433; (202) 473-1000. Annette Dixon, Vice President.*
Web, www.worldbank.org

Assists developing countries in delivering effective and affordable health care, education, and social services. Interests include poverty reduction, income protection, nutrition, jobs access, health coverage, and basic education.

Health Insurance, Managed Care

▶**AGENCIES**

Centers for Medicare and Medicaid Services (CMS) *(Health and Human Services Dept.), Center for Consumer Information and Insurance Oversight*

(CCIIO), 200 Independence Ave. S.W., #739H, 20001; (202) 690-6360. Fax, (443) 380-6928. Randolph (Randy) Pate, Director. Affordable Care hotline, (888) 393-2789.
General email, healthins@hhs.gov

Web, www.cms.gov/cciio

Assists states in reviewing insurance rates, including oversight of administrative costs as a percentage of expenditures for medical care (medical loss ratio); provides guidance and oversight for state-based insurance exchanges; administers the pre-existing condition insurance plan, the temporary high-risk pool program, and the early retiree reinsurance program; compiles and maintains data for an Internet portal providing information on insurance options.

Centers for Medicare and Medicaid Services (CMS) (Health and Human Services Dept.), Center for Medicare, 7500 Security Blvd., C5-01-14, Baltimore, MD 21244; (410) 786-0550. Demetrios Kouzoukas, Director. Information, (410) 786-3000.
Web, www.cms.gov/medicare/medicare.html

Manages the traditional fee-for-service Medicare program, which includes the development of payment policy and management of Medicare fee-for-service contractors.

►CONGRESS

For a listing of relevant congressional committees and subcommittees, please see pages 362–363 or the Appendix.

►NONGOVERNMENTAL

America's Health Insurance Plans (AHIP), 601 Pennsylvania Ave. N.W., South Bldg., #500, 20004; (202) 778-3200. Fax, (202) 331-7487. Matt Eyles, President, ext. 6372. Press, (202) 778-8494.
General email, ahip@ahip.org; info@ahip.org

Web, www.ahip.org, Twitter, @AHIPCoverage and Facebook, www.facebook.com/AHIP/?fref=ts

Membership: companies providing medical expense, long-term care, disability income, dental, supplemental, and stop-loss insurance and reinsurance to consumers, employers, and public purchasers. Advocates evidence-based medicine, targeted strategies for giving all Americans access to health care, and health care cost savings through regulatory, legal, and other reforms. Provides educational programs and legal counsel. Monitors legislation and regulations. (Merger of the American Assn. of Health Plans and Health Insurance Assn. of America.)

American Medical Assn. (AMA), Government Relations, 25 Massachusetts Ave. N.W., #600, 20001-7400; (202) 789-7400. Fax, (202) 789-7485. Dr. Patrice A. Harris, President. Toll-free, (800) 621-8335.
Web, www.ama-assn.org and
Twitter, @AmericanMedicalAssn

Membership: physicians, residents, and medical students. Interests include cost, quality, and access to health care; and physician payment and delivery innovation.

Monitors legislation and regulations. (Headquarters in Chicago, Ill.)

Autism Speaks, Washington Office, 1990 K St. N.W., 2nd Floor, 20006; (202) 955-3111. Angela Geiger, President. Toll-free, (888) 288-4762.
General Email, NationalCapitolArea@AutismSpeaks.org, Web, www.autismspeaks.org and Twitter, @autismspeaks

Advocates insurance reform to maximize coverage for evidence-based treatments for autism and autism spectrum disorders.

Blue Cross and Blue Shield Assn., Washington Office, 1310 G St. N.W., 20005; (202) 626-4780. Fax, (202) 626-4833. Scott Serota, President. Press, (202) 626-8625.
General email, press@bcbsa.com

Web, www.bcbs.com and Twitter, @BCBSAssociation

Owns the Blue Cross and Blue Shield names and marks (brands) and grants several types of licenses to use them; also conducts trade association activities and operates businesses to support its license holders. (Headquarters in Chicago, Ill.)

Council for Affordable Health Coverage (CAHC), 440 1st St. N.W., #430, 20001; (202) 808-8852. Jennifer Steger, Senior Director, Government Affairs.
Web, www.cahc.net, Twitter, @C4AHC and Facebook, www.facebook.com/c4ahc

Membership: insurers, employers, patients, consumers, pharmaceutical manufacturers, and providers. Coalition promoting competitive and transparent market solutions to America's health care problems. Promotes reform measures, including health savings accounts, tax equity, universal access, medical price disclosure prior to treatment, and caps on malpractice awards. Monitors legislation and regulations at state and federal levels.

Employee Benefit Research Institute, 1100 13th St. N.W., #878, 20005; (202) 659-0670. Fax, (202) 775-6312. Lori Lucas, President.
General email, info@ebri.org

Web, www.ebri.org

Research organization serving as an employee benefits information source on health, welfare, and retirement issues. Does not lobby and does not take public policy positions.

Employers Council on Flexible Compensation, 1220 L St. N.W., #100-417, 20005-4018; (202) 659-4300. Fax, (202) 618-6060. Martin Trussell, Executive Director.
General email, info@ecfc.org

Web, www.ecfc.org and Twitter, @GoECFC

Represents employers who have or are considering flexible compensation plans. Supports the preservation and expansion of employee choice in health insurance coverage. Monitors legislation and regulations.

Families USA, 1225 New York Ave. N.W., #800, 20005; (202) 628-3030. Fax, (202) 347-2417. Frederick Isasi, Executive Director.

General email, info@familiesusa.org

Web, www.familiesusa.org and *Twitter, @FamiliesUSA*

Interests include health care, the Affordable Care Act, Social Security, Medicare, and Medicaid. Offers Enrollment Assister Resource Centers to help consumers and businesses obtain high-quality, affordable health care. Monitors legislation and regulations affecting the elderly. Focuses on communities of color.

Galen Institute, *P.O. Box 130, Paeonian Springs, VA 20129; (703) 687-4665. Fax, (703) 687-4675. Grace-Marie Turner, President.*
General email, galen@galen.org

Web, www.galen.org, Twitter, @galeninstitute and *Facebook, www.facebook.com/GalenInstitute*

Provides ideas and information on health care financing and advancing consumer choice in health care. Advocates health savings accounts, competition among private plans in Medicare, and other free-market health reform ideas.

The HSA Coalition, *2121 K St. N.W., 20006; (202) 271-3959. Fax, (202) 478-0903. Vacant, President.*
General email, contact@hsacoalition.org

Web, www.hsacoalition.org, Twitter, @thehsacoalition and *Facebook, www.facebook.com/thehsacoalition*

Analyzes health savings accounts' policies and issues. Monitors and regulates legislation to protect and expand the number of Americans who could choose to have a health savings account (HSA).

National Academy of Social Insurance, *1200 New Hampshire Ave. N.W., #830, 20036; (202) 452-8097. Fax, (202) 452-8111. William J. Arnone, Chief Executive Officer.*
General email, nasi@nasi.org

Web, www.nasi.org

Promotes research and education on Social Security, Medicare, health care financing, and related public and private programs; assesses social insurance programs and their relationship to other programs; supports research and leadership development. Acts as a clearinghouse for social insurance information.

National Assn. of Health Underwriters, *1212 New York Ave. N.W., #1100, 20005; (202) 552-5060. Fax, (202) 747-6820. Janet Trautwein, Executive Vice President, (202) 888-0832. Press, (202) 595-3074.*
General email, info@nahu.org

Web, www.nahu.org and *Twitter, @nahudotorg*

Membership: licensed health insurance agents, brokers, consultants, and benefit professionals. Offers continuing education programs as well as business-development tools. Promotes private sector health insurance. Monitors legislation and regulations.

National Business Group on Health, *20 F St. N.W., #200, 20001-6705; (202) 558-3000. Fax, (202) 628-9244. Brian J. Marcotte, President, (202) 558-3005.*

General email, info@businessgrouphealth.org

Web, www.businessgrouphealth.org and *Twitter, @NBGHemployers*

Membership: large corporations with an interest in health care benefits. Interests include reimbursement policies, disease prevention and health promotion, hospital cost containment, health care planning, corporate education, Medicare, and retiree medical costs. Monitors legislation and regulations.

National Coalition on Health Care, *1111 14th St. N.W., #900, 20005; (202) 638-7151. John Rother, Chief Executive Officer.*
Web, www.nchc.org and *Twitter, @NC_HC*

Membership: insurers, labor organizations, large and small businesses, consumer groups, and health care providers. Acts as advocate for affordable high quality health care. Monitors legislation and regulations.

National Health Care Anti-Fraud Assn., *1220 L St. N.W., #600, 20005; (202) 659-5955. Fax, (202) 785-6764. Louis Saccoccio, Chief Executive Officer; Leigh McKenna, Senior Director of Government and Public Affairs.*
General email, nhcaa@nhcaa.org

Web, www.nhcaa.org

Membership: health insurance companies and regulatory and law enforcement agencies. Members work to identify, investigate, and prosecute individuals and groups defrauding health care reimbursement systems. Offers education and training for fraud investigators, including medical identity theft. Sponsors the Institute for Health Care Fraud Prevention.

ProtectSeniors.Org, *601 Pennsylvania Ave., South Bldg., #900, 20004; (202) 434-8193. Fax, (540) 439-9570. Jim Casey, President; Paul Miller, Executive Director. Toll-free, (800) 398-3044.*
General email, info@protectseniors.org

Web, www.protectseniors.org and *Twitter, @ProtectSeniors*

Aims to illegalize the corporate discontinuation of promised health care benefits after employees have retired. Acts as advocate against pension stripping. Monitors legislation and regulation.

Society of Professional Benefit Administrators, *2 Wisconsin Circle, #670, Chevy Chase, MD 20815; (301) 718-7722. Fax, (301) 718-9440. Anne Lennan, President.*
General email, info@spbatpa.org

Web, https://spbatpa.org and *Twitter, @spbatpa*

Membership: third-party administration firms that manage employee benefit plans for client employers. Interests include health care regulations, employee benefits, revision of Medicare programs, and health care cost containment. Monitors industry trends, government compliance requirements, and developments in health care financing.

Centers for Medicare and Medicaid Services

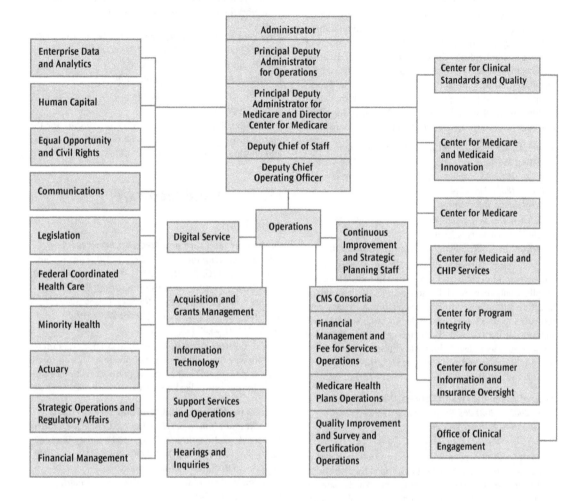

Enterprise Data and Analytics	Administrator	Center for Clinical Standards and Quality
Human Capital	Principal Deputy Administrator for Operations	Center for Medicare and Medicaid Innovation
Equal Opportunity and Civil Rights	Principal Deputy Administrator for Medicare and Director Center for Medicare	Center for Medicare
Communications	Deputy Chief of Staff	Center for Medicaid and CHIP Services
Legislation	Deputy Chief Operating Officer	Center for Program Integrity

(Organization chart boxes:)

Enterprise Data and Analytics · Human Capital · Equal Opportunity and Civil Rights · Communications · Legislation · Federal Coordinated Health Care · Minority Health · Actuary · Strategic Operations and Regulatory Affairs · Financial Management

Administrator · Principal Deputy Administrator for Operations · Principal Deputy Administrator for Medicare and Director Center for Medicare · Deputy Chief of Staff · Deputy Chief Operating Officer

Digital Service · Operations · Continuous Improvement and Strategic Planning Staff

Acquisition and Grants Management · Information Technology · Support Services and Operations · Hearings and Inquiries

CMS Consortia · Financial Management and Fee for Services Operations · Medicare Health Plans Operations · Quality Improvement and Survey and Certification Operations

Center for Clinical Standards and Quality · Center for Medicare and Medicaid Innovation · Center for Medicare · Center for Medicaid and CHIP Services · Center for Program Integrity · Center for Consumer Information and Insurance Oversight · Office of Clinical Engagement

Hospitals

►AGENCIES

Centers for Medicare and Medicaid Services (CMS)
(Health and Human Services Dept.), Center for Clinical Standards and Quality (CCSQ), Quality and Safety Oversight Group, 7500 Security Blvd., C2-21-16, Baltimore, MD 21244-1850; (410) 786-9493. Fax, (410) 786-0194. Karen Tritz, Director (Acting); Tenille Rogers, Deputy Director.
Web, www.cms.gov/About-CMS/Agency-Information/ CMSLeadership/Office_CCSQ.html

Enforces health care and safety standards for hospitals, nursing homes, and other health care facilities.

►CONGRESS

For a listing of relevant congressional committees and sub-committees, please see pages 362–363 or the Appendix.

►NONGOVERNMENTAL

America's Essential Hospitals, *401 Ninth St. N.W., #900, 20004; (202) 585-0100. Dr. Bruce Siegel, President; Carlos Jackson, Vice President Legislative Affairs. General email, info@essentialhospitals.org*
Web, https://essentialhospitals.org, Twitter, @OurHospitals and Facebook, www.facebook.com/essentialhospitals

Membership: city and county public hospitals, state universities, and hospital districts and authorities. Interests include Medicaid patients and vulnerable populations, including AIDS patients, the homeless, the mentally ill, and non-English–speaking patients. Holds annual regional meetings. Monitors legislation and regulations. (Formerly National Assn. of Public Hospitals and Health Systems.)

American Hospital Assn., *Washington Office,* Two City Center, 800 10th St. N.W., #400, 20001-4956; (202) 638-1100. Richard J. (Rick) Pollack, President, ext. 4625. Information, (800) 424-4301.

Web, www.aha.org, Twitter, @AHAhospitals and Facebook, www.facebook.com/ahahospitals

Membership: hospitals, other inpatient care facilities, outpatient centers, Blue Cross plans, areawide planning agencies, regional medical programs, hospital schools of nursing, and individuals. Conducts research and education projects in such areas as provision of comprehensive care, hospital economics, hospital facilities and design, and community relations; participates with other health care associations in establishing hospital care standards. Monitors legislation and regulations. (Headquarters in Chicago, Ill.)

American Medical Rehabilitation Providers Assn. (AMRPA), *529 14th St., N.W., # 750, 20045; (202) 591-2469. Fax, (202) 223-1925. John Ferraro, Executive Director. Toll-free, (888) 346-4624.*
General email, info@amrpa.org
Web, www.amrpa.org, Twitter, @AMRPA and Facebook, www.facebook.com/ AmericanMedicalRehabilitationProvidersAssociation

Association representing a membership of freestanding rehabilitation hospitals and rehabilitation units of general hospitals, outpatient rehabilitation facilities, skilled-nursing facilities, and others. Provides leadership, advocacy, and resources to develop medical rehabilitation services and supports for persons with disabilities and others in need of services. Acts as a clearinghouse for information to members on the nature and availability of services. Monitors legislation and regulations.

Assn. of Academic Health Centers, *1400 16th St. N.W., #720, 20036; (202) 265-9600. Fax, (202) 265-7514. Dr. Steven L. Kanter, President.*
Web, www.aahcdc.org and Twitter, @aahcdc

Membership: academic health centers (composed of a medical school, a teaching hospital, and at least one other health professional school or program). Participates in studies and public debates on health professionals' training and education, patient care, and biomedical research.

Children's Hospital Assn., *Washington Office, 600 13th St. N.W., #500, 20005; (202) 753-5500. Fax, (202) 347-5147. Mark Wietecha, President.*
Web, www.childrenshospitals.org, Twitter, @hospitals4kids and Facebook, www.facebook.com/childrenshospitals

Membership: more than 220 children's hospitals nationwide. Acts as a resource for pediatric data and analytics for clinical and operational performance. Monitors state and federal issues on clinical care, education, research, and advocacy. (Merger of the Child Health Corporation of America, National Assn. of Children's Hospitals and Related Institutions, and National Assn. of Children's Hospitals.)

Federation of American Hospitals, *750 9th St. N.W., #600, 20001-4524; (202) 624-1500. Fax, (202) 737-6462. Charles N. Kahn III, President. Press, (202) 624-1527. General email, info@fah.org*
Web, www.fah.org, Twitter, @FedAmerHospital and Facebook, www.facebook.com/FedAmHospitals

Membership: investor-owned or federally owned or managed community hospitals and health systems. Interests include national health care issues, such as cost containment, Medicare and Medicaid, the tax code, and the hospital workforce. Monitors legislation and regulations.

Physician Hospitals of America, *2025 M St. N.W., #800, 20036; (202) 367-1113. Fax, (202) 367-2113. John Richardson, Executive Director. General email, info@physicianhospitals.org*
Web, www.physicianhospitals.org and Twitter, @physicianhosp

Membership organization acting as advocate for the physician-owned hospital industry; provides networking and continuing-education opportunities.

Medicaid and Medicare

▶**AGENCIES**

Centers for Medicare and Medicaid Services (CMS) *(Health and Human Services Dept.), 200 Independence Ave. S.W., #314G, 20201; (202) 619-0630. Fax, (202) 690-6262. Seema Verma, Administrator; Brady Brookes, Deputy Chief of Staff. Information, (410) 786-3000. Toll-free, (877) 267-2323. TTY, (866) 226-1819.*
Web, www.cms.gov

Administers Medicare (a health insurance program for persons with disabilities or age sixty-five or older who are eligible to participate) and Medicaid (a health insurance program for persons judged unable to pay for health services).

Centers for Medicare and Medicaid Services (CMS) *(Health and Human Services Dept.), Center for Clinical Standards and Quality (CCSQ), 7500 Security Blvd., S3-02-01, Baltimore, MD 21244; (410) 786-6841. Fax, (410) 786-6857. Dr. Kate Goodrich, Director.*
Web, www.cms.gov/About-CMS/Agency-Information/ CMSLeadership/Office_CCSQ.html

Develops, establishes, and enforces standards that regulate the quality of care of hospitals and other health care facilities under Medicare and Medicaid programs. Administers operations of survey and peer review organizations that enforce health care standards, primarily for institutional care.

Centers for Medicare and Medicaid Services (CMS) *(Health and Human Services Dept.), Center for Clinical Standards and Quality (CCSQ), Nursing Homes (DNH), 7500 Security Blvd., C2-23-17, Baltimore, MD 21244; (410) 786-7818. Fax, (410) 786-0194. Evan Shulman, Director (Acting).*
Web, www.cms.gov/About-CMS/Agency-Information/ CMSLeadership/Office_CCSQ.html

Monitors compliance of nursing homes with government standards. Focus includes quality of care, environmental conditions, and participation in Medicaid and Medicare programs.

Centers for Medicare and Medicaid Services (CMS) *(Health and Human Services Dept.), Center for Medicaid and CHIP Services (CMCS), 7500 Security Blvd.,*

C5-21-17, Baltimore, MD 21244; (202) 690-7428.
Chris Traylor, Deputy Administrator (Acting).
Web, www.cms.gov/About-CMS/Agency-Information/
CMSLeadership/office_CMCSC.html and
www.medicaid.gov

Administers and monitors Medicaid programs to ensure program quality and financial integrity; promotes beneficiary awareness and access to services.

Centers for Medicare and Medicaid Services (CMS)
(Health and Human Services Dept.), Center for Medicaid and CHIP Services (CMCS), Disabled and Elderly Health Programs Group (DEHPG), 7500 Security Blvd., S2-14-26, Baltimore, MD 21244; (410) 786-0325.
Michael (Mike) Nardone, Director.
Web, www.medicaid.gov

Reviews all benefit and pharmacy state plan amendments for all Medicaid populations, Medicaid managed-care delivery systems, home-based and community-based services, and long-term services. Supports transformation grant programs, including Money Follows the Person and the Balancing Incentive Program.

Centers for Medicare and Medicaid Services (CMS)
(Health and Human Services Dept.), Center for Medicare, 7500 Security Blvd., C5-01-14, Baltimore, MD 21244; (410) 786-0550. Demetrios Kouzoukas, Director.
Information, (410) 786-3000.
Web, www.cms.gov/medicare/medicare.html

Manages the contractual framework for the Medicare program; establishes and enforces performance standards for contractors who process and pay Medicare claims. Issues regulations and guidelines for administration of the Medicare program.

Centers for Medicare and Medicaid Services (CMS)
(Health and Human Services Dept.), Center for Medicare and Medicaid Innovation (CMMI), 7500 Security Blvd., WB-06-05, Baltimore, MD 21244; (410) 786-3028.
Fax, (410) 786-0487. Adam Boehler, Director;
Amy Bassano, Deputy Director.
General email, innovate@cms.hhs.gov
Web, https://innovation.cms.gov/ and
Twitter, @CMSInnovates

Established pursuant to the Affordable Care Act of 2010 to explore innovative approaches to Medicare, Medicaid, and CHIP health care delivery and administration, with the goal of improving health outcomes and lowering costs. Solicits input from health care providers, the business community, patients and families, and other interested parties in order to indentify best practices. Funds state demonstration projects to evaluate integrated care and payment approaches.

Centers for Medicare and Medicaid Services (CMS)
(Health and Human Services Dept.), Center for Medicare, Chronic Care Management (DCCM), 7500 Security Blvd., C5-05-27, Baltimore, MD 21244; (410) 786-4533. Fax, (410) 786-0765. Jana Lindquist, Director, (410) 786-9374.
Web, www.cms.gov/About-CMS/Agency-Information/
OMH/equity-initiatives/chronic-care-management.html

Administers coverage policy and payment for Medicare patients with two or more chronic conditions expected to last at least 12 months or until the death of the patient.

Centers for Medicare and Medicaid Services (CMS)
(Health and Human Services Dept.), Center for Program Integrity (CPI), 7500 Security Blvd., AR-18-50, Baltimore, MD 21244; (410) 786-1892. Alec Alexander, Deputy Administrator.
Web, www.cms.gov/About-CMS/Agency-Information/
CMSLeadership/Office_CPI.html

Acts as the central office for all statewide Medicare and Medicaid programs and CHIP integrity fraud and abuse issues. Promotes Medicare and Medicaid program integrity and CHIP by reviewing policies, monitoring programs, and colloborating with other stakeholders, including the Justice Dept. and state law enforcement agencies.

Centers for Medicare and Medicaid Services (CMS)
(Health and Human Services Dept.), Enterprise Data and Analytics (OEDA), 7500 Security Blvd., B2-29-04, Baltimore, MD 21244; (410) 786-6384.
Allison M. Oelschlaeger, Director, (202) 690-8257;
Andrew (Andy) Shatto, Deputy Director.
Web, www.cms.gov/About-CMS/Agency-Information/
CMSLeadership/Office-OEDA.html

Serves as primary federal statistical office for disseminating economic data on Medicare and Medicaid.

Centers for Medicare and Medicaid Services (CMS)
(Health and Human Services Dept.), Strategic Operations and Regulatory Affairs (OSORA), 7500 Security Blvd., C4-26-05, Baltimore, MD 21244; (410) 786-9327. Kathleen Cantwell, Director.
Web, www.cms.gov/About-CMS/Agency-Information/
CMSLeadership/Office_OSORA.html

Manages CMS decision-making and regulatory processes; provides leadership and advocacy in relation to official policy matters. Coordinates the preparation of manuals and other policy instructions of CMS programs.

Health Resources and Services Administration (HRSA)
(Health and Human Services Dept.), Rural Health Policy (FORHP), 5600 Fishers Lane, #17W45, Rockville, MD 20857; (301) 443-0835. Fax, (301) 443-2803. Tom Morris, Associate Administrator.
General email, tmorris@hrsa.gov
Web, www.hrsa.gov/rural-health/index.html

Studies the effects of Medicare and Medicaid programs on rural access to health care.

▶**CONGRESS**

For a listing of relevant congressional committees and subcommittees, please see pages 362–363 or the Appendix.

▶**NONGOVERNMENTAL**

AARP, 601 E St. N.W., 20049; (202) 434-2277. Fax, (202) 434-7946. Jo Ann C. Jenkins, Chief Executive Officer.
Library, (202) 434-6233. Membership, (202) 434-7550.

Membership, toll-free, (800) 566-0242. Press, (202) 434-2560. Toll-free, (888) 687-2277. TTY, (877) 434-7598. Toll-free Spanish, (877) 342-2277. TTY Spanish, (866) 238-9488.

General email, member@aarp.org

Web, www.aarp.org, Twitter, @AARP and Facebook, www.facebook.com/AARP

Membership: people fifty years of age and older. Monitors legislation and regulations and disseminates information to members concerning Medicaid and Medicare.

Families USA, *1225 New York Ave. N.W., #800, 20005; (202) 628-3030. Fax, (202) 347-2417. Frederick Isasi, Executive Director.*

General email, info@familiesusa.org

Web, www.familiesusa.org and Twitter, @FamiliesUSA

Interests include health care, the Affordable Care Act, Social Security, Medicare, and Medicaid. Offers Enrollment Assister Resource Centers to help consumers and businesses obtain high-quality, affordable health care. Monitors legislation and regulations affecting the elderly. Focuses on communities of color.

Federation of American Hospitals, *750 9th St. N.W., #600, 20001-4524; (202) 624-1500. Fax, (202) 737-6462. Charles N. Kahn III, President. Press, (202) 624-1527.*

General email, info@fah.org

Web, www.fah.org, Twitter, @FedAmerHospital and Facebook, www.facebook.com/FedAmHospitals

Membership: investor-owned for-profit hospitals and health care systems. Studies Medicaid and Medicare reforms. Maintains speakers bureau; compiles statistics on investor-owned hospitals. Monitors legislation and regulations.

Medicare Rights Center, *1441 Eye St. N.W., #1105, 20005; (202) 637-0961. Fax, (202) 637-0962. Joe Baker, President. Helpline, (800) 333-4114.*

General email, info@medicarerights.org

Web, www.medicarerights.org and Twitter, @medicarerights

Advocates affordable health care for seniors and people with disabilities. Educates the public on medicare rights and benefits. Provides free Medicare counseling, as well as courses and training to health care professionals. Monitors legislation and regulations.

National Committee to Preserve Social Security and Medicare, *111 K St. N.E., #700, 20002; (202) 216-0420. Fax, (202) 216-0446. Max Richtman, President. Press, (202) 216-8378. Senior hotline/Legislative updates, (800) 998-0180.*

General email, webmaster@ncpssm.org

Web, www.ncpssm.org, Twitter, @NCPSSM and Facebook, www.facebook.com/NationalCommittee

Educational and advocacy organization that focuses on Social Security and Medicare programs and on related income security and health issues. Interests include retirement income protection, health care reform, and the quality of life of seniors. Monitors legislation and regulations.

Medical Devices and Technology

▶**AGENCIES**

Access Board, *1331 F St. N.W., #1000, 20004-1111; (202) 272-0080. Fax, (202) 272-0081. David M. Capozzi, Executive Director, (202) 272-0010. Toll-free, (800) 872-2253. Toll-free TTY, (800) 993-2822. TTY, (202) 272-0082. General email, info@access-board.gov*

Web, www.access-board.gov

Develops and maintains accessibility requirements for buildings, transit vehicles, telecommunications equipment, medical diagnostic equipment, and electronic and information technology. Provides technical assistance and training on these guidelines and standards. Enforces access standards for federally funded facilities through the Architectural Barriers Act.

Armed Forces Radiobiology Research Institute *(Defense Dept.), 4301 Jones Bridge Rd., Bethesda, MD 20889; (301) 295-0530. Fax, (301) 295-9477. Capt. John Gilstad (USN), Director. Public Affairs, (301) 295-1214.*

Web, www.usuhs.edu/afrri

Serves as the principal ionizing radiation radiobiology research laboratory under the jurisdiction of the Uniformed Services University of the Health Sciences. Educates and trains radiation biologists. Participates in international conferences and projects.

Food and Drug Administration (FDA) *(Health and Human Services Dept.), Center for Devices and Radiological Health (CDRH), White Oak Bldg. 66, 10903 New Hampshire Ave., Silver Spring, MD 20993; (301) 796-5900. Fax, (301) 847-8510. Jeffrey E. Shuren, Director. General email, jeff.shuren@fda.hhs.gov*

Web, www.fda.gov/medicaldevices and www.fda.gov/AboutFDA/CentersOffices/OfficeofMedicalProductsandTobacco/CDRH

Evaluates safety, efficacy, and labeling of medical devices; classifies devices; establishes performance standards; assists in legal actions concerning medical devices; coordinates research and testing; conducts training and educational programs. Accredits and certifies mammography facilities and personnel. Maintains an international reference system to facilitate trade in devices. Library open to the public.

Food and Drug Administration (FDA) *(Health and Human Services Dept.), Combination Products (OCP), White Oak Bldg. 32, 10903 New Hampshire Ave., Hub/Mail Room #5129, Silver Spring, MD 20993; (301) 796-8930. Fax, (301) 847-8619. Thinh X. Nguyen, Director. General email, combination@fda.gov*

Web, www.fda.gov/CombinationProducts

Seeks to streamline the processing of complex drug-device, drug-biologic, and device-biologic combination products. Responsibilities cover the entire regulatory life cycle of combination products, including jurisdiction decisions as well as the timeliness and effectiveness of premarket review, and the consistency and appropriateness of postmarket regulation. Responsible for the classification of medical or biological products.

Food and Drug Administration (FDA) *(Health and Human Services Dept.), Division of Industry and Consumer Education (DICE), 10903 New Hampshire Ave., Silver Spring, MD 20993; (301) 796-7100. Fax, (301) 847-8149. Elias Mallis, Director, (301) 796-6216. Toll-free, (800) 638-2041.*
General email, DICE@fda.hhs.gov

Web, www.fda.gov/MedicalDevices/ DeviceRegulationandGuidance/ ContactDivisionofIndustryandConsumerEducation

Serves as liaison between small-business manufacturers of medical devices and the FDA. Assists manufacturers in complying with FDA regulatory requirements; sponsors seminars.

National Institute of Biomedical Imaging and Bioengineering (NIBIB) *(National Institutes of Health), 9000 Rockville Pike, Bldg. 31, #1C14, Bethesda, MD 20892; (301) 496-8859. Fax, (301) 480-0679. Bruce Tromberg, Director.*
General email, info@nibib.nih.gov

Web, www.nibib.nih.gov, Twitter, @NIBIBgov and Facebook, www.facebook.com/nibibgov

Conducts and supports research and development of biomedical imaging and bioengineering techniques and devices to improve the prevention, detection, and treatment of disease.

▶ NONGOVERNMENTAL

Advanced Medical Technology Assn., *701 Pennsylvania Ave. N.W., #800, 20004-2654; (202) 783-8700. Fax, (202) 783-8750. Scott Whitaker, President.*
General email, info@advamed.org

Web, www.advamed.org, Twitter, @advamedupdate and Facebook, www.facebook.com/Advamed

Membership: manufacturers of medical devices, diagnostic products, and health care information systems. Interests include safe and effective medical devices; conducts educational seminars. Monitors legislation, regulations, and international issues.

American Assn. for Homecare, *241 18th St. South, #500, Arlington, VA 22202; (202) 372-0107. Fax, (202) 835-8306. Thomas Ryan, President, (202) 372-0753. Toll-free, (866) 289-0492.*
General email, info@aahomecare.org

Web, www.aahomecare.org, Twitter, @aahomecare and Facebook, www.facebook.com/aahomecare?ref=hl

Membership: home medical equipment manufacturers and home health care service providers. Works to serve the medical needs of Americans who require oxygen equipment and therapy, mobility assistive technologies, medical supplies, inhalation drug therapy, home infusion, and other home medical services. Provides members with education, training, and information about industry trends. Monitors legislation and regulations.

American College of Radiology, *Government Relations, 505 9th St. N.W., #910, 20004; (800) 227-5463. Joshua Cooper Jr., Senior Director of Government Relations; Michael Peters, Director of Legislative and Regulatory Affairs. Government Relations, (202) 223-1670.*
General email, info@acr.org

Web, www.acr.org

Membership: certified radiologists and medical physicists in the United States and Canada. Develops programs in radiation protection, technologist training, practice standards, and health care insurance; maintains a placement service for radiologists; participates in international conferences. (Headquarters in Reston, Va.)

American Institute of Ultrasound in Medicine, *14750 Sweitzer Lane, #100, Laurel, MD 20707-5906; (301) 498-4100. Glynis V. Harvey, Chief Executive Officer. Toll-free, (800) 638-5352.*
General email, admin@aium.org

Web, www.aium.org, Twitter, @AIUM_Ultrasound and Facebook, www.facebook.com/AIUMultrasound

Membership: medical professionals who use ultrasound technology in their practices. Promotes multidisciplinary research and education on safe and effective use of diagnostic ultrasound through conventions and educational programs. Develops guidelines for accreditation. Monitors international research.

American Medical Informatics Assn., *4720 Montgomery Lane, #500, Bethesda, MD 20814; (301) 657-1291. Fax, (301) 657-1296. Dr. Douglas B. Fridsma, President.*
General email, mail@amia.org

Web, www.amia.org, Twitter, @AMIAinformatics and Facebook, www.facebook.com/AIMAinformatics

Membership: medical professionals and students interested in informatics. Studies and pursues effective uses of biomedical data, information, and knowledge for scientific inquiry, problem solving, and decision making to improve human health. Applications include basic and applied research, clinical services, consumer services, and public health.

American Orthotic and Prosthetic Assn., *330 John Carlyle St., #200, Alexandria, VA 22314-5760 (mailing address: P.O. Box 34711, Alexandria, VA 22334); (571) 431-0876. Fax, (571) 431-0899. Eve Lee, Executive Director, (571) 431-0802.*
General email, info@aopanet.org

Web, www.aopanet.org and Twitter, @AmericanOandP

Membership: companies that manufacture or supply artificial limbs and braces, and patient-care professionals who fit and supervise device use.

American Roentgen Ray Society, *44211 Slatestone Court, Leesburg, VA 20176-5109; (703) 729-3353. Fax, (703) 729-4839. Susan B. Cappitelli, Executive Director. Toll-free, (866) 940-2777.*
General email, info@arrs.org

Web, www.arrs.org and Twitter, @ARRS_Radiology

Membership: physicians and researchers in radiology and allied sciences. Publishes research; conducts conferences; presents scholarships and awards; monitors international research.

Board of Registered Polysomnographic Technologists, *1420 New York Ave., N.W., 5th Floor, 20005; (703) 610-9020. Fax, (703) 610-0229. Jim Magruder, Executive Director.*
General email, info@brpt.org
Web, www.brpt.org

Provides credentialing and certification for polysomnographic technologists. Offers continuing-education programs and education opportunities.

Health Industry Distributors Assn., *310 Montgomery St., Alexandria, VA 22314-1516; (703) 549-4432. Fax, (703) 549-6495. Matthew Rowan, President.*
General email, hida@hida.org
Web, www.hida.org and Twitter, @HIDAorg

Membership: medical products distributors. Sponsors and conducts trade shows and training seminars. Monitors legislation and regulations.

National Research Council (NRC), *Nuclear and Radiation Studies Board, Keck Center, 500 5th St. N.W., 20001; (202) 334-3066. Fax, (202) 334-3077. Charles Ferguson, Chair; Ourania Kosti, Senior Program Officer.*
General email, nrsb@nas.edu
Web, http://dels.nas.edu/nrsb

Oversees studies on safety, security, technical efficacy, and other policy and societal issues arising from the application of nuclear and radiation-based technologies, including medical applications.

Program for Appropriate Technology in Health (PATH), *Washington Office, 455 Massachusetts Ave. N.W., #1000, 20001; (202) 822-0033. Fax, (202) 457-1466. Steve Davis, President.*
General email, info@path.org
Web, www.path.org

Develops, tests, and implements health technologies and strategies for low-resource countries. Works with community groups, other nongovernmental organizations, governments, companies, and UN agencies to expand the most successful programs. Interests include reproductive health, immunization, maternal-child health, emerging and epidemic diseases, and nutrition. (Headquarters in Seattle, Wash.)

Rehabilitation Engineering and Assistive Technology Society of North America (RESNA), *1560 Wilson Blvd., #850, Arlington, VA 22209; (703) 524-6686. Fax, (703) 524-6630. Andrea Van Hook, Executive Director (Acting).*
General email, info@resna.org
Web, www.resna.org and Twitter, @RESNAorg

Membership: engineers, health professionals, assistive technologists, persons with disabilities, and others. Promotes and supports developments in rehabilitation engineering and technology; acts as an information clearinghouse. (RESNA stands for Rehabilitation Engineering and Assistive Technology Society of North America.)

Nursing Homes and Hospices

▶ AGENCIES

Centers for Medicare and Medicaid Services (CMS) *(Health and Human Services Dept.), Center for Clinical Standards and Quality (CCSQ), Continuing Care Providers (DCCP), 7500 Security Blvd., C2-21-16, Baltimore, MD 21244-1850; (410) 786-4857. Fax, (410) 786-0194. Peggye Wilkerson, Director.*
Web, www.cms.gov/About-CMS/Agency-Information/CMSLeadership/Office_CCSQ.html

Monitors compliance with government standards of psychiatric hospitals and long-term and intermediate care facilities, including residential treatment facilities, community mental health centers, intermediate care facilities for mental retardation, outpatient rehabilitation facilities, home health care, hospice care, portable X-ray units, dialysis facilities, and outpatient physical, language, and speech therapy facilities. Focus includes quality of care, environmental conditions, and participation in Medicaid and Medicare programs. Coordinates health care programs for the mentally challenged.

Centers for Medicare and Medicaid Services (CMS) *(Health and Human Services Dept.), Center for Clinical Standards and Quality (CCSQ), Nursing Homes (DNH), 7500 Security Blvd., C2-23-17, Baltimore, MD 21244; (410) 786-7818. Fax, (410) 786-0194. Evan Shulman, Director (Acting).*
Web, www.cms.gov/About-CMS/Agency-Information/CMSLeadership/Office_CCSQ.html

Monitors compliance of nursing homes with government standards. Focus includes quality of care, environmental conditions, and participation in Medicaid and Medicare programs.

Centers for Medicare and Medicaid Services (CMS) *(Health and Human Services Dept.), Center for Clinical Standards and Quality (CCSQ), Quality and Safety Oversight Group, 7500 Security Blvd., C2-21-16, Baltimore, MD 21244-1850; (410) 786-9493. Fax, (410) 786-0194. Karen Tritz, Director (Acting); Tenille Rogers, Deputy Director.*
Web, www.cms.gov/About-CMS/Agency-Information/CMSLeadership/Office_CCSQ.html

Enforces health care and safety standards for nursing homes and other long-term care facilities.

▶ NONGOVERNMENTAL

AARP, *Federal Health and Family Advocacy, 601 E St. N.W., 20049; (202) 434-3770. Megan O'Reilly, Director for Health and Family Advocacy, (202) 434-6987.*
Web, www.aarp.org

Maintains the Legal Counsel for the Elderly, which acts as advocate on behalf of older residents of the District of Columbia who reside in nursing homes and board and care homes. Monitors legislation and regulations.

American College of Health Care Administrators, *1101 Connecticut Ave. N.W., #450, 20036; (202) 536-5120. Bill McGinley, President, (800) 561-3148 ext. 705. Toll-free, (800) 561-3148.*
General email, info@achca.org

Web, www.achca.org, Twitter, @ACHCA and Facebook, www.facebook.com/The-American-College-of-Health=Care-Administrators-326597784597/

Membership: administrators of long-term health care organizations and facilities, including home health care programs, hospices, day care centers for the elderly, nursing and hospital facilities, retirement communities, assisted-living communities, and mental health care centers. Conducts research on statistical characteristics of nursing home and other medical administrators; conducts seminars and workshops; offers education courses; provides certification for administrators.

American Health Care Assn., *1201 L St. N.W., 20005; (202) 842-4444. Fax, (202) 842-3860. Mark Parkinson, President. Press, (202) 898-2814. Publication orders, (800) 321-0343.*
General email, help@hctrendtracker.com

Web, www.ahcancal.org, Twitter, @ahcancal and Facebook, www.facebook.com/ahcancal

Association of facility-based long-term and post–acute care providers and affiliates of state health organizations. Advocates high-quality care and services for frail, elderly, and disabled Americans, communicating with government, business leaders, and the general public. Provides information, education, and administrative tools. Monitors legislation and regulations.

Hospice Foundation of America, *1707 L St. N.W., #220, 20036; (202) 457-5811. Fax, (202) 457-5815. Amy Tucci, President. Toll-free, (800) 854-3402.*
General email, hfaoffice@hospicefoundation.org

Web, www.hospicefoundation.org and Facebook, www.facebook.com/hospicefoundation

Acts as an advocate for the hospice style of health care through ongoing programs of public education and training, information dissemination, and research.

National Assn. for Home Care and Hospice, *228 7th St. S.E., 20003; (202) 547-7424. Fax, (202) 547-3540. William A. Dombi, President.*
General email, info@nahc.org

Web, www.nahc.org and Twitter, @OfficialNAHC

Membership: hospice, home care, and private-duty providers and other community service organizations assisting those with chronic health problems or life-threatening illness. Works to educate and provide information for the public on hospice and home care. Interests include Medicare, Medicaid, and other insurance for home care and hospice. Monitors legislation and regulations.

National Center for Assisted Living, *1201 L St. N.W., 20005; (202) 842-4444. Fax, (202) 842-3860. Scott Tittle, Executive Director. Public Affairs, (202) 898-2825.*
General email, ncal@ncal.org

Web, www.ahcancal.org/ncal and Twitter, @ahcancal

Membership: assisted living professionals. Provides networking opportunities and professional development; hosts educational seminars and an annual convention. Provides free resources for consumers looking into assisted living and other long-term care resources. Monitors legislation and regulations. (Affiliated with American Health Care Assn.)

National Consumer Voice for Quality Long-Term Care (NCCNHR), *1001 Connecticut Ave. N.W., #632, 20036; (202) 332-2275. Fax, (866) 230-9789. Lori O. Smetanka, Executive Director, ext. 206; Amity Overall Laib, National Long-Term Care Ombudsman Resource Center Director.*
General email, info@theconsumervoice.org

Web, www.theconsumervoice.org and Facebook, www.facebook.com/theconsumervoice

Advocates high-quality care and quality of life for consumers in all long-term care settings. Promotes citizen participation in all aspects of nursing homes; acts as clearinghouse for nursing home advocacy. Hosts National Long-Term Care Ombudsman Resource Center.

National Hospice and Palliative Care Organization, *1731 King St., Alexandria, VA 22314; (703) 837-1500. Fax, (703) 837-1233. Edo (Don) Banach, President; Amanda Bow, Communications Director. Press, (703) 837-3139. Toll-free consumer information and referral helpline, (800) 658-8898.*
General email, nhpco_info@nhpco.org

Web, www.nhpco.org, Twitter, @NHPCO_news and Facebook, www.facebook.com/NHPCO and Consumer information, www.caringinfo.org

Membership: institutions and individuals providing hospice and palliative care and other interested organizations and individuals. Promotes supportive care for the terminally ill and their families; sets hospice program standards; provides information on hospices. Monitors legislation and regulations.

National Long-Term Care Ombudsman Resource Center, *1001 Connecticut Ave. N.W. #632, 20036; (202) 332-2275. Fax, (202) 332-2949. Amity Overall Laib, Director.*
General email, ombudcenter@theconsumervoice.org

Web, www.ltcombudsman.org

Provides technical assistance, management guidance, policy analysis, and program development information on behalf of state and substate ombudsman programs. (Affiliate of the National Consumer Voice for Quality Long-Term Care.)

Food and Drug Administration

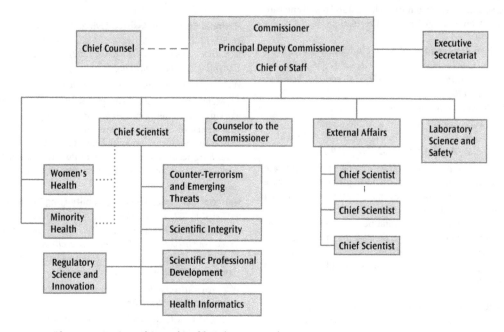

- – – Direct report to General Counsel Health and Human Services
········ Indirect report to the Office of Chief Scientist

Pharmaceuticals

▶**AGENCIES**

Food and Drug Administration (FDA) *(Health and Human Services Dept.)*, *10903 New Hampshire Ave., Silver Spring, MD 20993; (888) 463-6332. Fax, (301) 847-3536. Dr. Scott Gottlieb, Commissioner. Main Library (White Oak in Silver Spring), (301) 796-2039. Press, (301) 796-4540. Toll-free, (888) 463-6332.*
Web, www.fda.gov, Twitter, @US_FDA and Facebook, www.facebook.com/FDA

Protects public health by assessing the safety, effectiveness, and security of human and veterinary drugs, vaccines, and other biological products. Protects the safety and security of the nation's food supply, cosmetics, diet supplements, and products emitting radiation. Regulates tobacco products. Develops labeling and packaging standards; conducts inspections of manufacturers; issues orders to companies to recall and/or cease selling or producing hazardous products; enforces rulings and recommends action to Justice Dept. when necessary. Libraries open to the public; 24-hour advance appointment required.

Food and Drug Administration (FDA) *(Health and Human Services Dept.)*, *Center for Drug Evaluation and Research (CDER)*, *White Oak Bldg. 51, 10903 New Hampshire Ave., #6133, Silver Spring, MD 20993; (301) 796-5400. Fax, (301) 595-7910. Dr. Janet Woodcock, Director. Press, (301) 796-3700.*

General email, druginfo@fda.hhs.gov
Web, www.fda.gov/drugs and www.fda.gov/AboutFDA/CentersOffices/OfficeofMedicalProductsandTobacco/CDER

Reviews and approves applications to investigate and market new drugs; monitors prescription drug advertising; works to harmonize drug approval internationally.

Food and Drug Administration (FDA) *(Health and Human Services Dept.)*, *Center for Drug Evaluation and Research (CDER), Biostatistics (OB)*, *White Oak Bldg. 21, 10903 New Hampshire Ave., #3554, Silver Spring, MD 20993; (301) 796-1700. Fax, (301) 796-9734. Lisa LaVange, Director.*
Web, www.fda.gov/aboutfda/centersoffices/officeofmedicalproductsandtobacco/cder/ucm166250.htm

Conducts research and provides information on statistical methodology for drug regulation and development.

Food and Drug Administration (FDA) *(Health and Human Services Dept.)*, *Center for Drug Evaluation and Research (CDER), Generic Drugs (OGD)*, *White Oak Bldg. 75, 10903 New Hampshire Ave., #1692, Silver Spring, MD 20993; (240) 402-7920. Fax, (301) 595-1147. Dr. Kathleen Uhl, Director, (240) 402-7921.*
General email, genericdrugs@fda.hhs.gov
Web, www.fda.gov/AboutFDA/CentersOffices/OfficeofMedicalProductsandTobacco/CDER /ucm119100.htm

Oversees generic drug review process to ensure the safety and effectiveness of approved drugs.

Food and Drug Administration (FDA) *(Health and Human Services Dept.), Center for Drug Evaluation and Research (CDER), New Drugs (OND), White Oak Bldg. 22, 10903 New Hampshire Ave., #6311, Silver Spring, MD 20993; (301) 796-0700. Fax, (301) 796-9856. Dr. Janet Woodcock, Director (Acting). Web, www.fda.gov/AboutFDA/CentersOffices/ OfficeofMedicalProductsandTobacco/CDER/ ucm184426.htm*

Provides regulatory oversight for investigational studies during drug development; makes decisions regarding marketing approval for new innovator and non-generic drugs, including decisions related to changes to already marketed products.

Food and Drug Administration (FDA) *(Health and Human Services Dept.), Center for Drug Evaluation and Research (CDER), Pharmaceutical Quality (OPQ), White Oak Bldg. 21, 10903 New Hampshire Ave., Silver Spring, MD 20993; (301) 796-2400. Fax, (301) 796-9996. Michael Kopcha, Director. General email, CDER-OPQ-Inquiries@fda.hhs.gov Web, www.fda.gov/AboutFDA/CentersOffices/ OfficeofMedicalProductsandTobacco/CDER/ucm4183 47.htm*

Reviews the critical quality attributes and manufacturing processes of new drugs, establishes quality standards to ensure safety and efficacy, and facilitates new drug development.

Food and Drug Administration (FDA) *(Health and Human Services Dept.), Orphan Products Development (OOPD), White Oak Bldg. 32, 10903 New Hampshire Ave., #5295, Silver Spring, MD 20993-0002; (301) 796-8660. Fax, (301) 847-8621. Dr. Janet W. Maynard, Director. General email, orphan@fda.hhs.gov Web, www.fda.gov/ForIndustry/ DevelopingProductsforRareDiseasesConditions*

Promotes the development of drugs, devices, and alternative medical food therapies for rare diseases or conditions. Coordinates activities on the development of orphan drugs among federal agencies, manufacturers, and patient advocacy organizations.

Food and Drug Administration (FDA) *(Health and Human Services Dept.), Prescription Drug Promotion (OPDP), White Oak Bldg. 51, 10903 New Hampshire Ave., #3203, Silver Spring, MD 20993-0002; (301) 796-1200. Fax, (301) 847-8444 or (301) 847-8445. Thomas W. Abrams, Director. Web, www.fda.gov/aboutfda/centersoffices/ officeofmedicalproductsandtobacco/cder/ucm090142.htm*

Monitors prescription drug advertising and labeling; investigates complaints; conducts market research on health care communications and drug issues.

Food and Drug Administration (FDA) *(Health and Human Services Dept.), Regulatory Affairs (ORA), White Oak Bldg. 31, 10903 New Hampshire Ave., #3528, Silver Spring, MD 20993; (301) 796-8800. Fax, (301) 847-7942. Melinda K. Plaisier, Associate Commissioner.*

Web, www.fda.gov/aboutfda/centersoffices/ officeofglobalregulatoryoperationsandpolicy/ora and Twitter, @FDA_ORA

Directs and coordinates the FDA's compliance activities; manages field offices; advises FDA commissioner on domestic and international regulatory policies.

National Institutes of Health (NIH) *(Health and Human Services Dept.), Dietary Supplements (ODS), 6100 Executive Blvd., #3B01, MSC-7517, Bethesda, MD 20892-7517; (301) 435-2920. Fax, (301) 480-1845. Joseph Betz, Director (Acting). General email, ods@nih.gov Web, http://ods.od.nih.gov and Twitter, @NIH_ODS*

Reviews scientific evidence on the safety and efficacy of dietary supplements. Conducts, promotes, and coordinates scientific research within the NIH relating to dietary supplements. Conducts and supports conferences, workshops, and symposia and publishes research results on scientific topics related to dietary supplements.

▶ **NONGOVERNMENTAL**

American Assn. of Colleges of Pharmacy, *1400 Crystal Dr., #300, Arlington, VA 22202; (703) 739-2330. Fax, (703) 836-8982. Lucinda L. Maine, Executive Vice President, ext. 1021. General email, mail@aacp.org Web, www.aacp.org, Twitter, @AACPharmacy and Facebook, www.facebook.com/AACPharmacy*

Represents and acts as advocate for pharmacists in the academic community. Conducts programs and activities in cooperation with other national health and higher education associations.

American Pharmacists Assn., *2215 Constitution Ave. N.W., 20037-2985; (202) 628-4410. Fax, (202) 783-2351. Thomas Menighan, Chief Executive Officer, (202) 429-7567. Information, (800) 237-2742. Library, (202) 429-7524. General email, infocenter@aphanet.org Web, www.pharmacist.com and Twitter, @pharmacists*

Membership: practicing pharmacists, pharmaceutical scientists, and pharmacy students. Promotes professional education and training; publishes scientific journals and handbooks on nonprescription drugs; monitors international research. Library open to the public by appointment.

American Society for Pharmacology and Experimental Therapeutics, *1801 Rockville Pike, #210, Rockville, MD 20852-1633; (301) 634-7060. Fax, (301) 634-7061. Judith Siuciak, Executive Director. General email, info@aspet.org Web, www.aspet.org, Twitter, @ASPET and Facebook, www.facebook.com/ASPETpage*

Membership: researchers and teachers involved in basic and clinical pharmacology primarily in the United States and Canada.

American Society of Consultant Pharmacists (ASCP),
*1240 N. Pitt St., #300, Alexandria, VA 22314-3563; (703)
739-1300. Fax, (202) 408-1101. Chad Worz, Executive
Director. Toll-free, (800) 355-2727.*
General email, info@ascp.com

Web, www.ascp.com and Twitter, @ASCPharm

Membership: dispensing and clinical pharmacists with
expertise in therapeutic medication management for geriatric patients; provides services to long-term care facilities,
institutions, and hospices as well as older adults in assisted-
living and home-based care. Monitors legislation and regulations.

American Society of Health-System Pharmacists (ASHP),
*4500 East-West Hwy., #900, Bethesda, MD 20814; (301)
657-3000. Fax, (301) 657-6232. Paul W. Abramowitz, Chief
Executive Officer. Toll-free, (866) 279-0681.*
Web, www.ashp.org and Twitter, @ASHPOfficial

Membership: pharmacists who practice in organized
health care settings such as hospitals, health maintenance
organizations, and long-term care facilities. Publishes reference materials and provides educational programs and conferences. Accredits pharmacy residency and pharmacy
technician training programs. Monitors legislation and regulations.

Assn. for Accessible Medicines, *601 New Jersey Ave.,
N.W., #850, 20001; (202) 249-7100. Fax, (202) 249-7105.
Chester (Chip) Davis Jr., President.*
General email, info@gphaonline.org

*Web, http://accessiblemeds.org, Twitter, @AccessibleMeds
and Facebook, www.facebook.com/accessiblemeds*

Membership: manufacturers and distributors of generic
pharmaceuticals and pharmaceutical chemicals and suppliers of goods and services to the generic pharmaceutical
industry. Attempts to increase availability and public awareness of safe, effective generic medicines. Monitors legislation
and regulations. (Formerly the Generic Pharmaceutical
Assn.)

Consumer Healthcare Products Assn., *1625 Eye St. N.W.,
#600, 20006; (202) 429-9260. Fax, (202) 223-6835.
Scott Melville, President; John F. Gay, Senior Vice President
of Government Affairs. Press and public affairs, (202)
429-3520.*
General email, mtringale@chpa.org

Web, https://chpa.org and Twitter, @CHPA

Membership: manufacturers and marketers of nonprescription medicines and nutritional supplements; associate
members include suppliers, advertising agencies, research
and testing laboratories, and others. Promotes the role of
self-medication in health care. Monitors legislation and
regulations.

Healthcare Distribution Alliance, *901 N. Glebe Rd.,
#1000, Arlington, VA 22203; (703) 787-0000. Fax, (703)
812-5282. John M. Gray, President.*
Web, www.hda.org and Twitter, @HDAconnect

Membership: distributors and manufacturers of pharmaceutical and health-related products and information.

Serves as a forum on major industry issues. Researches and
disseminates information on distribution issues and management practices. Monitors legislation and regulations.

National Assn. of Chain Drug Stores, *1776 Wilson Blvd.,
#200, Arlington, VA 22209; (703) 549-3001. Fax, (703) 836-
4869. Steven Anderson, President.*
General email, contactus@nacds.org

Web, www.nacds.org and Twitter, @NACDS

Membership: chain drug retailers; associate members
include manufacturers, suppliers, publishers, and advertising agencies. Provides information on the pharmacy profession, community pharmacy practice, and retail prescription
drug economics. Monitors legislation and regulations.

National Community Pharmacists Assn., *100
Daingerfield Rd., Alexandria, VA 22314; (703) 683-8200.
Fax, (703) 683-3619. B. Douglas Hoey, Chief Executive
Officer, ext. 2648. Membership, (800) 544-7447.*
General email, info@ncpanet.org

*Web, www.ncpanet.org, Twitter, @Commpharmacy and
Facebook, www.facebook.com/commpharmacy?ref=nf*

Membership: independent pharmacy owners, including independent pharmacies, independent pharmacy fran-
chises, and independent chains. Promotes the interests of
independent community pharmacists to compete in the
health care market. Monitors legislation and regulations.

National Pharmaceutical Council, *1717 Pennsylvania
Ave., #800, 20006; (202) 827-2100. Fax, (202) 827-0314.
Dan Leonard, President, (202) 827-2080.*
General email, info@npcnow.org

Web, www.npcnow.org and Twitter, @npcnow

Membership: pharmaceutical manufacturers that
research and produce trade-name prescription medication
and other pharmaceutical products. Sponsors and conducts scientific analyses of the use of pharmaceuticals and
the clinical and economic value of innovation.

Parenteral Drug Assn. (PDA), *4350 East-West Hwy., #600,
Bethesda, MD 20814; (301) 656-5900. Fax, (301) 986-0296.
Richard Johnson, President, ext. 123.*
General email, info@pda.org

Web, www.pda.org

Membership: scientists involved in the development,
manufacture, quality control, and regulation of pharma-
ceuticals/biopharmaceuticals and related products. Provides science, technology, and regulatory information and
education to the pharmaceutical and biopharmaceutical
community. Influences FDA regulatory process.

Pharmaceutical Care Management Assn., *325 7th St.
N.W. 9th Floor, 20004; (202) 756-5700. Fax, (202) 756-
5708. JC Scott, President.*
General email, info@pcmanet.org

Web, www.pcmanet.org and Twitter, @pcmanet

Membership: companies providing managed care
pharmacy and pharmacy benefits management. Promotes
legislation, research, education, and practice standards that
foster high-quality, affordable pharmaceutical care.

Pharmaceutical Research and Manufacturers of America, *950 F St. N.W., #300, 20004; (202) 835-3400. Steve Ubl, President. Press, (202) 835-3460.*
Web, www.phrma.org and Twitter, @PhRMA

Membership: research-based pharmaceutical and biotechnology companies that orginate, develop, and manufacture prescription drugs. Advocates public policies that encourage discovery of new medicines. Provides consumer information on drug abuse, the safe and effective use of prescription medicines, and developments in important areas, including the treatment of HIV/AIDS.

U.S. Pharmacopeial Convention, *12601 Twinbrook Pkwy., Rockville, MD 20852-1790; (301) 881-0666. Fax, (301) 816-8148. Dr. Ronald Piervincenzi, Chief Executive Officer. Toll-free, (800) 227-8772.*
General email, custsvc@usp.org

Web, www.usp.org and Twitter, @uspharmacopeia

Establishes and revises standards for drug strength, quality, purity, packaging, labeling, and storage of prescription and over-the-counter medications. Publishes drug use information, official drug quality standards, patient education materials, and consumer drug references. Interests include international standards. (Offices in Switzerland, India, China, and Brazil.)

HEALTH PROFESSIONS

General

▶ **AGENCIES**

Centers for Medicare and Medicaid Services (CMS) *(Health and Human Services Dept.), Center for Clinical Standards and Quality (CCSQ), 7500 Security Blvd., S3-02-01, Baltimore, MD 21244; (410) 786-6841. Fax, (410) 786-6857. Dr. Kate Goodrich, Director.*
Web, www.cms.gov/About-CMS/Agency-Information/CMSLeadership/Office_CCSQ.html

Oversees professional review and other medical review programs; establishes guidelines; prepares issue papers relating to legal aspects of professional review and quality assurance.

Education Dept., *Health Education Assistance Loan Program, 12501 Ardennes Ave., #200, Rockville, MD 20857; (844) 509-8957. Tawana Lewis, Supervisor.*
General email, heal@ed.gov

Web, www.ifap.ed.gov/HEALInfo/HEALInfo.html

Insures loans provided by private lenders to students attending eligible health professions schools under the Public Health Service Act. New loans to student borrowers have been discontinued. Refinancing has been terminated.

Health Resources and Services Administration (HRSA) *(Health and Human Services Dept.), Bureau of Health Workforce (BHW), 5600 Fishers Lane, #11 West Wing, Rockville, MD 20857; (301) 443-5794. Fax, (301) 443-0463. Dr. Luis Padilla, Associate Administrator.*
Web, www.hrsa.gov/about/organization/bureaus/bhw

Supports primary care and public health education and practice. Supports recruitment of health care professionals, including nursing and allied health professionals, for underserved populations. Administers categorical training programs, scholarship and loan programs, and minority and disadvantaged assistance programs. Oversees National Practitioner Data Bank.

Health Resources and Services Administration (HRSA) *(Health and Human Services Dept.), Bureau of Health Workforce (BHW), National Practitioner Data Bank (NPDB), 15036 Conference Center Dr., Chantilly, VA 10832; (301) 443-2300. Fax, (703) 803-1964. Dave Loewenstein, Division Director, (301) 443-8263. Information, (800) 767-6732.*
General email, help@npdb.hrsa.gov

Web, www.npdb.hrsa.gov

Provides information on reports of malpractice payments, adverse state licensure, clinical privileges, and society membership actions (only to eligible entities, including state licensing boards, hospitals, and other health care entities) about physicians, dentists, and other licensed health care practitioners.

Health Resources and Services Administration (HRSA) *(Health and Human Services Dept.), National Health Service Corps (NHSC), 5600 Fishers Lane, #8-05, Rockville, MD 20857; (301) 443-4021. Fax, (301) 443-2080. Israil Ali, Associate Administrator. Toll-free, (800) 221-9393. TTY, (877) 897-9910.*
Web, www.nhsc.hrsa.gov and Twitter, @NHSCorps

Supplies communities experiencing a shortage of health care personnel with doctors and other medical professionals.

Health Resources and Services Administration (HRSA) *(Health and Human Services Dept.), National Health Service Corps (NHSC), Clinician Recruitment and Services, 5600 Fishers Lane, Rockville, MD 20857; (301) 594-4400. Fax, (301) 594-4981. Mary Wakefield, Director. Toll-free, (800) 221-9393.*
Web, www.nhsc.hrsa.gov and Twitter, @NHSCorps

Supplies communities experiencing a shortage of health care personnel with doctors and other medical professionals. Provides educational financial aid incentives for service.

National Institute of Biomedical Imaging and Bioengineering (NIBIB) *(National Institutes of Health), 9000 Rockville Pike, Bldg. 31, #1C14, Bethesda, MD 20892; (301) 496-8859. Fax, (301) 480-0679. Bruce Tromberg, Director.*
General email, info@nibib.nih.gov

Web, www.nibib.nih.gov, Twitter, @NIBIBgov and Facebook, www.facebook.com/nibibgov

Offers multidisciplinary training programs for scientists and engineers at all stages of their careers in bioimaging and bioengineering.

National Institute of General Medical Sciences (NIGMS) *(National Institutes of Health), Training, Workforce Development, and Diversity, 45 Center Dr., Bldg. 45, #2AS37, MSC 6200, Bethesda, MD 20892-6200; (301) 594-3900. Fax, (301) 480-2753. Dr. Alison Gammie, Director.*

Web, http://nigms.nih.gov/training

Administers research and research training programs aimed at increasing the number of minority biomedical scientists. Funds grants, fellowships, faculty development awards, and development of research facilities.

Uniformed Services University of the Health Sciences *(Defense Dept.), 4301 Jones Bridge Rd., Bethesda, MD 20814-4799; (301) 295-3013. Fax, (301) 295-1960. Dr. Richard W. Thomas, President. Registrar, (301) 295-3199. Toll-free information, (800) 515-5257.*

General email, president@usuhs.edu

Web, www.usuhs.mil and Twitter, @USUhealthsci

An accredited four-year medical and postgraduate dental school under the auspices of the Defense Dept. Awards doctorates and master's degrees in health-related and science-related fields.

►CONGRESS

For a listing of relevant congressional committees and subcommittees, please see pages 362–363 or the Appendix.

►NONGOVERNMENTAL

Aerospace Medical Assn., *320 S. Henry St., Alexandria, VA 22314-3579; (703) 739-2240. Fax, (703) 739-9652. Jeffery C. Sventek, Executive Director.*

General email, inquiries@asma.org

Web, www.asma.org, Twitter, @Aero_Med and Facebook, www.facebook.com/ AerospaceMedicalAssociation

Membership: physicians, flight surgeons, aviation medical examiners, flight nurses, scientists, technicians, and specialists in clinical, operational, and research fields of aerospace medicine. Promotes programs to improve aerospace medicine and maintain safety in aviation by examining and monitoring the health of aviation personnel; members may consult in aircraft investigation and cockpit design.

AFT Healthcare, *555 New Jersey Ave. N.W., 20001; (202) 879-4400. Fax, (202) 879-4545. Randi Weingarten, President.*

General email, afthealthcare@aft.org

Web, www.aft.org/healthcare, Twitter, @AFTHealthcare and Facebook, www.facebook.com/AFTunion

Membership: teachers, public employees, and nurses and other health care workers. Assists members with contract negotiation and grievances; conducts training programs and workshops. Monitors legislation and regulations. (Division of the American Federation of Teachers.)

Alliance for Academic Internal Medicine, *330 John Carlyle St., #610, Alexandria, VA 22314; (703) 341-4540. Fax, (703) 519-1893. Dr. D. Craig Brater, President; Bergitta E. Cotroneo, Executive Vice President.*

General email, aaim@im.org

Web, www.im.org, Twitter, @AAIMonline and Facebook, www.facebook.com/AAIMonline

Membership: program directors, clerkship directors, administrators, and chairs of internal medicine departments at all U.S. medical schools and several affiliated teaching hospitals. Provides services, training, and educational and research opportunities for leaders in internal medicine departments. Monitors legislation and regulations.

American Assn. of Colleges of Pharmacy, *1400 Crystal Dr., #300, Arlington, VA 22202; (703) 739-2330. Fax, (703) 836-8982. Lucinda L. Maine, Executive Vice President, ext. 1021.*

General email, mail@aacp.org

Web, www.aacp.org, Twitter, @AACPharmacy and Facebook, www.facebook.com/AACPharmacy

Represents and acts as advocate for pharmacists in the academic community. Conducts programs and activities in cooperation with other national health and higher education associations.

American College of Health Care Administrators, *1101 Connecticut Ave. N.W., #450, 20036; (202) 536-5120. Bill McGinley, President, (800) 561-3148 ext. 705. Toll-free, (800) 561-3148.*

General email, info@achca.org

Web, www.achca.org, Twitter, @ACHCA and Facebook, www.facebook.com/The-American-College-of-Health=Care-Administrators-326597784597/

Membership: administrators of long-term health care organizations and facilities, including home health care programs, hospices, day care centers for the elderly, nursing and hospital facilities, retirement communities, assisted living communities, and mental health care centers. Conducts research on statistical characteristics of nursing home and other medical administrators; conducts seminars and workshops; offers education courses; provides certification for administrators.

American College of Radiology, *Government Relations, 505 9th St. N.W., #910, 20004; (800) 227-5463. Joshua Cooper Jr., Senior Director of Government Relations; Michael Peters, Director of Legislative and Regulatory Affairs. Government Relations, (202) 223-1670.*

General email, info@acr.org

Web, www.acr.org

Membership: certified radiologists and medical physicists in the United States and Canada. Develops programs in radiation protection, technologist training, practice standards, and health care insurance; maintains a placement service for radiologists; participates in international conferences. (Headquarters in Reston, Va.)

American Health Lawyers Assn., *1620 Eye St. N.W., 6th Floor, 20006-4010; (202) 833-1100. Fax, (202) 833-1105. David S. Cade, Chief Executive Officer, (202) 833-0777. General email, info@healthlawyers.org*

Web, www.healthlawyers.org

Public interest email, publicinterest@healthlawyers.org

Membership: corporate, institutional, and government lawyers interested in the health field; law students; and health professionals. Serves as an information clearinghouse on health law; sponsors health law educational programs and seminars.

American Institute of Ultrasound in Medicine, *14750 Sweitzer Lane, #100, Laurel, MD 20707-5906; (301) 498-4100. Glynis V. Harvey, Chief Executive Officer. Toll-free, (800) 638-5352.*

General email, admin@aium.org

Web, www.aium.org, Twitter, @AIUM_Ultrasound and Facebook, www.facebook.com/AIUMultrasound

Membership: medical professionals who use ultrasound technology in their practices. Promotes multidisciplinary research and education on safe and effective use of diagnostic ultrasound through conventions and educational programs. Develops guidelines for accreditation. Monitors international research.

American Medical Group Assn., *One Prince St., Alexandria, VA 22314-3318; (703) 838-0033. Fax, (703) 548-1890. Dr. Jerry W. Penso, President, ext. 356. Web, www.amga.org, Twitter, @theAMGA and Facebook, www.facebook.com/theAMGA*

Membership: medical group and health system organizations. Compiles statistics on group practice and clinical best practices. Sponsors a foundation for research and education programs. Advocates the multispecialty group practice model of health care delivery. Provides educational and networking programs and publications, benchmarking data services, and financial and operations assistance. Monitors legislation and regulations.

American Speech-Language-Hearing Assn. (ASHA), *2200 Research Blvd., Rockville, MD 20850-3289; 444 N. Capitol St. N.W., #715, 20001; (202) 624-5951. Fax, (301) 296-8500. Arlene Pietranton, Chief Executive Officer. Press, (301) 296-8732. Toll-free for Action Center, (800) 498-2071 (voice and TTY accessible). Toll-free for nonmembers, (800) 638-8255.*

General email, nsslha@asha.org

Web, www.asha.org and Twitter, @ASHAWeb

Membership: specialists in speech-language pathology and audiology. Sponsors professional education programs; acts as accrediting agent for graduate programs; certifies audiologists and speech-language pathologists. (National office in Rockville, Md.)

AMSUS—Society of Federal Health Professionals, *12154 Darnstown Rd., #506, Gaithersburg, MD 20878; (301) 897-8800. Fax, (301) 530-5446. Brig. Gen. John M. Cho (USA, Ret.), Executive Director. Toll-free, (800) 761-9320.*

General email, amsus@amsus.org

Web, www.amsus.org and Twitter, @AMSUS

Membership: health professionals, including nurses, dentists, pharmacists, and physicians, who work or have worked for the U.S. Public Health Service, the VA, or the Army, Navy, Air Force, Guard, and Reserves, and students. Works to improve all phases of federal health services.

Assn. for Healthcare Philanthropy, *2511 Jefferson Davis Hwy., #810, Arlington, VA 22202; (703) 532-6243. Fax, (703) 532-7170. Alice Ayers, President.*

General email, ahp@ahp.org

Web, www.ahp.org and Twitter, @AHPIntl

Membership: hospital and health care executives who manage fund-raising activities and organizations and individuals who provide consulting services for such activities. Acts as a clearinghouse on philanthropy and offers programs, services, and publications and e-communications to members.

Assn. for Prevention Teaching and Research, *1001 Connecticut Ave. N.W., #610, 20036; (202) 463-0550. Fax, (202) 463-0555. Allison L. Lewis, Executive Director. Toll-free, (866) 520-2787.*

General email, info@aptrweb.org

Web, www.aptrweb.org and Twitter, @APTRupdate

Membership: faculty, researchers, residents, and students within schools of medicine, schools of public health, schools of nursing, schools of pharmacy, physician assistant programs, graduate programs for public health, and health agencies. Works to advance population-based and public health education, research, and service by linking supporting members from the academic prevention community. Develops curricular resources and professional development programs. (Formerly the Assn. of Teachers of Preventive Medicine.)

Assn. for Professionals in Infection Control and Epidemiology (APIC), *1400 Crystal Dr., #900, Arlington, VA 22202; (202) 789-1890. Katrina Crist, Chief Executive Officer, (202) 789-1890. Toll-free, (800) 650-9570.*

General email, info@apic.org

Web, www.apic.org

Membership: infection prevention health practitioners, including nurses, physicians, public health professionals, epidemiologists, microbiologists, and medical technologists. Monitors legislation and regulations.

Assn. of Schools and Programs of Public Health, *1900 M St. N.W., #710, 20036; (202) 296-1099. Fax, (202) 296-1252. Laura Magaña Valladares, President, (202) 296-1099, ext. 120.*

General email, info@aspph.org

Web, www.aspph.org and Twitter, @ASPPHtweets

Membership: deans, faculty, and students of accredited graduate schools of public health. Promotes improved education and training of professional public health personnel; interests include disease prevention, health promotion, and international health.

Assn. of Schools of Allied Health Professions, *122 C St. N.W., #200, 20001; (202) 237-6481. Fax, (202) 237-6485. John Colbert, Executive Director.*
General email, thomas@asahp.org

Web, www.asahp.org and Twitter, @ASAHPDC

Membership: two-year and four-year colleges and academic health science centers with allied health professional training programs; administrators, educators, and practitioners; and professional societies. Serves as information resource; works with the Health and Human Services Dept. to conduct surveys of allied health-education programs. Interests include health promotion and disease prevention, ethics in health care, and the participation of women and persons with disabilities in allied health. Monitors legislation and regulations.

Assn. of University Programs in Health Administration (AUPHA), *1730 M St. N.W., #407, 20036; (202) 763-7283. Gerald Glandon, President.*
General email, aupha@aupha.org

Web, www.aupha.org and Twitter, @AUPHA

Membership: university-based educational programs, faculty, practitioners, and provider organizations. Works to improve the field of health care management and practice by educating entry-level professional managers.

Health Volunteers Overseas, *1900 L St. N.W., #310, 20036; (202) 296-0928. Fax, (202) 296-8018. Nancy A. Kelly, Executive Director.*
General email, info@hvousa.org

Web, www.hvousa.org

Operates training programs in developing countries for health professionals who wish to teach low-cost health care delivery practices.

Healthcare Financial Management Assn., *Washington Office, 1090 Vermont Ave. N.W., #500, 20005; (202) 296-2920. Fax, (202) 849-3645. Richard Gundling, Senior Vice President. Information, (800) 252-4362.*
General email, memberservice@hfma.org

Web, www.hfma.org and Twitter, @hfmaorg

Membership: health care financial management specialists. Offers educational programs; provides information on financial management of health care. (Headquarters in Westchester, Ill.)

Hispanic-Serving Health Professions Schools, *11 Main St., #D, Warrenton, VA 20186; (202) 808-3480. Fax, (202) 962-3939. Dr. Norma Perez, President.*
General email, hshps@hshps.org

Web, www.hshps.org and Twitter, @HSHPS96

Seeks to increase representation of Hispanics in all health care professions through academic development, initiatives, and training. Monitors legislation and regulations.

National Assn. of County and City Health Officials, *1201 Eye St. N.W., 4th Floor, 20005; (202) 783-5550. Fax, (202) 783-1583. Lori Freeman, Chief Executive Officer, (202) 507-4271.*

General email, info@naccho.org

Web, www.naccho.org and Twitter, @NACCHOalerts

Membership: city, county, and district health officers. Provides members with information on national, state, and local health developments. Works to develop the technical competence, managerial capacity, and leadership potential of local public health officials.

National Assn. of Healthcare Access Management, *2025 M St. N.W., #800, 20036-3309; (202) 367-1125. Fax, (202) 367-2125. Kirsten Shaffer, Executive Director.*
General email, info@naham.org

Web, www.naham.org and Twitter, @mynaham

Promotes professional growth and recognition of health care patient access managers, who handle hospital patient admissions, registration, finance, and patient relations; provides instructional videotapes; sponsors educational programs.

Physicians for Human Rights, *Washington Office, 1110 Vermont Ave. N.W., 5th Floor, 20005; (202) 728-5335. Fax, (202) 728-3053. Michael Payne, Senior Policy Associate; Donna McKay, Advocacy Officer.*
General email, phrusa@phrusa.org

Web, www.physiciansforhumanrights.org and Twitter, @P4HR

Mobilizes doctors, nurses, health specialists, scientists, and others to promote health and human rights globally. (Headquarters in New York City.)

Society of Health and Physical Educators (SHAPE) America, *1900 Association Dr., Reston, VA 20191-1598; (703) 476-3400. Fax, (703) 476-9527. Stephanie A. Morris, Chief Executive Officer. Toll-free, (800) 213-7193.*
General email, info@shapeamerica.org

Web, www.shapeamerica.org and Twitter, @SHAPE_America

Membership: health educators and allied health professionals in community and volunteer health agencies, educational institutions, and businesses. Develops health education programs; monitors legislation and regulations.

Chiropractors

▶**NONGOVERNMENTAL**

American Chiropractic Assn., *1701 Clarendon Blvd., #200, Arlington, VA 22209; (703) 276-8800. Fax, (703) 243-2593. Karen Silberman, Executive Vice President. Press, (703) 812-0226.*
General email, memberinfo@acatoday.org

Web, www.acatoday.org, Twitter, @ACAtoday and Facebook, www.facebook.com/acatoday.org

Association of chiropractic physicians. Promotes standards of care. Interests include health care coverage, sports injuries, physical fitness, internal disorders, and orthopedics. Supports foundation for chiropractic education and research. Maintains a legal action fund to sue on behalf of patients whose insurers deny them coverage of chiropractic services. Monitors legislation and regulations.

Foundation for the Advancement of Chiropractic Tenets and Science, *6400 Arlington Blvd., #800, Falls Church, VA 22042; (703) 528-5000. Fax, (703) 528-5023. George Curry, President. Toll-free, (800) 423-4690. General email, chiro@chiropractic.org*

Web, www.chiropractic.org

Offers financial aid for education and research programs in colleges and independent institutions; studies chiropractic services in the United States; provides international relief and development programs. (Affiliate of the International Chiropractors Assn.)

International Chiropractors Assn., *6400 Arlington Blvd., #800, Falls Church, VA 22042; (703) 528-5000. Fax, (703) 528-5023. Ron Hendrickson, Executive Director, (571) 765-7560. Toll-free, (800) 423-4690. General email, info@chiropractic.org*

Web, www.chiropractic.org

Membership: chiropractors, students, educators, and laypersons. Seeks to increase public awareness of chiropractic care. Supports research on health issues; administers scholarship program; monitors legislation and regulations.

North American Spine Assn., *Washington Office, 300 New Jersey Ave N.W., 20001; (202) 575-2020. Jeffrey Wang, President, (323) 442-5303. Toll-free, (888) 960-6277.*

Web, www.spine.org and Twitter, @NASSspine

Membership: physicians, nurse practitioners, nurses, physician assistants, chiropractors, physical therapists, researchers, other health care professionals with an interest in the spine. Monitors legislation and regulations.

Dentists

▶**AGENCIES**

Veterans Health Administration (VHA) *(Veterans Affairs Dept.), Dentistry, 810 Vermont Ave. N.W., 10NC7, 20420; (202) 632-8342. Dr. Patricia Arola, Assistant Under Secretary.*

Web, www.va.gov/dental

Administers and coordinates VA oral health care programs; dental care delivered in a VA setting; administration of oral research, education, and training for VA oral health personnel; delivery of care to VA patients in private practice settings.

▶**NONGOVERNMENTAL**

American College of Dentists, *839-J Quince Orchard Blvd., Gaithersburg, MD 20878-1614; (301) 977-3223. Theresa S. Gonzales, Executive Director. General email, office@acd.org*

Web, www.acd.org, Twitter, @College1920 and Facebook, www.facebook.com/College1920

Honorary society of dentists. Fellows are elected based on their contributions to education, research, dentistry,

and community and civic organizations. Organizes ethics seminars, award programs, online courses on leadership and dental ethics, and speaker series.

American Dental Education Assn., *655 K St. N.W., #800, 20001; (202) 289-7201. Fax, (202) 289-7204. Dr. Richard W. Valachovic, President; Christina McWilson Thomas, Director of Government Affairs. General email, adea@adea.org*

Web, www.adea.org and Twitter, @adeaweb

Membership: U.S. and Canadian dental schools; advanced, hospital, and allied dental education programs; corporations; and faculty and students. Works to influence education, research, and the delivery of oral health care for the improvement of public health. Provides information on dental teaching and research and on admission requirements of U.S. dental schools; publishes a monthly journal and newsletter. Monitors legislation and regulations.

Dental Trade Alliance, *4350 N. Fairfax Dr., #220, Arlington, VA 22203; (703) 379-7755. Fax, (703) 931-9429. Gary W. Price, Chief Executive Officer. General email, contact@dentaltradealliance.org*

Web, www.dentaltradealliance.org

Membership: dental laboratories and distributors and manufacturers of dental equipment and supplies. Collects and disseminates statistical and management information; conducts studies, programs, and projects of interest to the industry; acts as liaison with government agencies.

International Assn. for Dental Research, *1619 Duke St., Alexandria, VA 22314-3406; (703) 548-0066. Fax, (703) 548-1883. Dr. Christopher H. Fox, Executive Director. General email, research@iadr.org*

Web, www.iadr.org and Facebook, www.facebook.com/DentalResearch

Membership: professionals engaged in dental research worldwide. Conducts annual convention, conferences, and symposia.

National Dental Assn., *6411 Ivy Lane, #703, Greenbelt, MD 20770; (240) 241-4448. Fax, (240) 297-9181. LaVette C. Henderson, Deputy Executive Director. General email, info@ndaonline.org*

Web, www.ndaonline.org and Twitter, @NDA1913

Promotes the interests of ethnic minority dentists through recruitment, educational and financial services, and federal legislation and programs.

Medical Researchers

▶**AGENCIES**

National Institutes of Health (NIH) *(Health and Human Services Dept.), Intramural Training and Education (OITE), 2 Center Dr., Bldg. 2, #2E04, MSC 0230, Bethesda, MD 20892-0240; (301) 496-2427. Fax, (301) 594-9606. Sharon Milgram, Director, (301) 594-2053.*

General email, trainingwww@mail.nih.gov

Web, www.training.nih.gov

Administers programs and initiatives to recruit and develop individuals who participate in research training activities on the NIH's campuses. Maintains an interactive website for the various research training programs. Supports the training mission of the NIH Intramural Research Program through placement, retention, support, and tracking of trainees at all levels, as well as program delivery and evaluation. Administers the NIH Academy, the Summer Internship Program, the Undergraduate Scholarship Program, the Graduate Partnerships Program, and the Postbac and Technical Intramural Research Training Award programs.

▶NONGOVERNMENTAL

Alliance for Regenerative Medicine, *1900 L. St. N.W., # 735, 20036; Janet Lynch Lambert, Chief Executive Officer.*
General email, info@alliancerm.org

Web, www.alliancerm.org, Twitter, @alliancerm and Facebook, www.facebook.com/Alliance-for-Regenerative-Medicine-377427548983535

Press, lscull@alliancerm.org

Membership: nationally recognized patient advocacy organizations, academic research institutions, companies, health insurers, financial institutions, foundations, and individuals with life-threatening illnesses and disorders. Acts as advocate for research and technologies in regenerative medicine, including stem cell research and somatic cell nuclear transfer; seeks to increase public understanding. (Formerly Coalition for the Advancement of Medical Research.)

American Assn. for Clinical Chemistry, *900 7th St. N.W., #400, 20001; (202) 857-0717. Fax, (202) 833-4576. Janet Kreizman, Chief Executive Officer. Toll-free, (800) 892-1400.*
General email, info@aacc.org

Web, www.aacc.org, Twitter, @_AACC and Facebook, www.facebook.com/AmerAssocforClinChem

International society of chemists, physicians, and other scientists specializing in clinical chemistry. Provides educational and professional development services; presents awards for outstanding achievement. Monitors legislation and regulations.

American Assn. of Immunologists, *1451 Rockville Pike, #650, Rockville, MD 20852; (301) 634-7178. Fax, (301) 634-7887. M. Michele Hogan, Executive Director.*
General email, infoaai@aai.org

Web, www.aai.org, Twitter, @ImmunologyAAI and Facebook, www.facebook.com/ImmunologyAAI

Membership: scientists working in virology, bacteriology, biochemistry, genetics, immunology, and related disciplines. Conducts training courses and workshops; compiles statistics; participates in international conferences; publishes *The Journal of Immunology*. Monitors legislation and regulations.

American Assn. of Pharmaceutical Scientists, *2107 Wilson Blvd., #700, Arlington, VA 22201-3042; (703) 243-2800. Fax, (703) 243-9532. Walt Marlowe, Executive Director, (703) 248-4701. Customer Service, (877) 998-2277. Public Relations, (703) 248-4740.*
General email, aaps@aaps.org

Web, www.aaps.org, Twitter, @AAPSComms and Facebook, www.facebook.com/americanassociationofpharmaeuticalscientists?filter=1

Membership: pharmaceutical scientists from biomedical, biotechnological, and health care fields. Promotes pharmaceutical sciences as an industry. Represents scientific interests within academia and public and private institutions. Provides forums for scientists to engage in dialogue, networking, and career development. Monitors legislation and regulations.

American Medical Writers Assn., *30 W. Gude Dr., #525, Rockville, MD 20850-4347; (240) 238-0940. Fax, (301) 294-9006. Susan Krug, Executive Director, ext. 109; Shari Rager, Deputy Director, ext. 107.*
General email, amwa@amwa.org

Web, www.amwa.org, Twitter, @AmMedWriters and Facebook, www.facebook.com/amwa.org

Membership: Provides professional education and additional services to writers, editors, and others in the field of biomedical communication, via workshops, conferences, and online. Also facilitates on-site corporate training.

American Society for Clinical Laboratory Science (ASCLS), *1861 International Dr., #200, McLean, VA 22102; (571) 748-3770. Jim Flanigan, Executive Vice President. Press, (571) 748-3771.*
General email, ascls@ascls.org

Web, www.ascls.org, Twitter, @ASCLS and Facebook, www.facebook.com/ASCLS

Membership: clinical laboratory scientists. Conducts continuing-education programs for clinical laboratory scientists and laboratory practitioners. Monitors legislation and regulations.

American Society for Clinical Pathology, *Washington Office, 1225 New York Ave. N.W., #350, 20005-6156; (202) 408-1110. Fax, (202) 408-1101. Jeff Jacobs, Chief Officer for Science, Technology, and Policy, ext. 2290; Matthew (Matt) Schulze, Director of the Center for Public Policy, ext. 2285. Customer service for members, (800) 267-2727.*
General email, info@ascp.org

Web, www.ascp.org

Membership: pathologists, residents, and other physicians; clinical scientists; registered certified medical technologists; and technicians. Promotes continuing education, educational standards, and research in pathology. Monitors legislation, regulations, and international research. (Headquarters in Chicago, Ill.)

Assn. of Accredited Naturopathic Medical Colleges, *1717 K St. N.W., #900, 20006; (800) 345-7454. Fraser Smith, Executive Director.*

General email, info@aanmc.org

Web, www.aanmc.org and Twitter, @AANMC

Membership: accredited schools of naturopathic medicine. Provides database of practicing naturopathic physicians and information on how to become a licensed naturopathic doctor.

Assn. of Public Health Laboratories, 8515 Georgia Ave., #700, Silver Spring, MD 20910; (240) 485-2745. Fax, (240) 485-2700. Scott J. Becker, Executive Director, (240) 485-2747. Press, (240) 485-2793.
General email, info@aphl.org

Web, www.aphl.org and Twitter, @APHL

Membership: state and local public health, environmental, agricultural, and food safety laboratories. Offers technical assistance to member laboratories; sponsors educational programs for public health and clinical laboratory practitioners; develops systems for electronic exchange of lab data; develops laboratory system in under-resourced countries. Works with the CDC, FDA, EPA, and other federal partners to support disease detection and surveillance, laboratory response to health crises, quality drinking water, and other public health services.

Board of Registered Polysomnographic Technologists, 1420 New York Ave., N.W., 5th Floor, 20005; (703) 610-9020. Fax, (703) 610-0229. Jim Magruder, Executive Director.
General email, info@brpt.org

Web, www.brpt.org

Provides credentialing and certification for polysomnographic technologists. Offers continuing-education programs and education opportunities.

Society of Research Administrators International (SRA International), 1560 Wilson Blvd., #310, Arlington, VA 22209; (703) 741-0140. Fax, (703) 741-0142. Ellen Lupinski Quinn, Chief Operating Officer, ext. 213.
General email, info@srainternational.org

Web, www.srainternational.org and
Twitter, @SocietyRAIntl

Membership: scientific and medical research administrators in the United States and other countries. Educates the public about the profession; offers professional development services; sponsors mentoring and awards programs.

Society of Toxicology, 11190 Sunrise Valley Dr., #300, Reston, VA 20191; (703) 438-3115. Fax, (703) 438-3113. Leigh Ann Burns Naas, President.
General email, sothq@toxicology.org

Web, www.toxicology.org and Twitter, @SOToxicology

Membership: scientists from academic institutions, government, and industry worldwide who work in toxicology. Promotes professional development, exchange of information, and research to advance toxicological science.

Nurses and Physician Assistants

►AGENCIES

National Institute of Nursing Research (NINR) *(National Institutes of Health),* Bldg. 31, 31 Center Dr., #5B10, MSC 2178, Bethesda, MD 20892-2178; (301) 496-0207. Fax, (301) 480-4969. Ann Cashion, Director, (301) 496-8230.
General email, info@ninr.nih.gov

Web, www.ninr.nih.gov and Twitter, @NINR

Provides grants and awards for nursing research and research training. Research focus includes health promotion and disease prevention, quality of life, health disparities, and end-of-life issues.

►NONGOVERNMENTAL

American Academy of Physician Assistants (AAPA), 2318 Mill Rd., #1300, Alexandria, VA 22314-1552; (703) 836-2272. Fax, (703) 684-1924. Jennifer L. (Jenna) Dorn, Chief Executive Officer, ext. 4303.
General email, aapa@aapa.org

Web, www.aapa.org, Twitter, @aapaorg and
Facebook, www.facebook.com/AAPA.org

Advocacy email, advocacy@aapa.org

Membership: physician assistants and physician assistant students. Sponsors continuing medical education programs for recertification of physician assistants; offers malpractice insurance. Interests include health care reform, quality of care, research, and laws and regulations affecting physician assistant practice and patients. Monitors legislation and regulations.

American Assn. of Colleges of Nursing, 655 K. St. N.W., #750, 20001; (202) 463-6930. Fax, (202) 785-8320. Deborah Trautman, President, ext. 227.
General email, info@aacnnursing.org

Web, www.aacnnursing.org, Twitter, @AACNursing and Facebook, www.facebook.com/AACNursing

Promotes high-quality baccalaureate and graduate nursing education; works to secure federal support of nursing education, nursing research, and student financial assistance; operates databank providing information on enrollments, graduations, salaries, and other conditions in nursing higher education. Interests include international practices.

American College of Nurse-Midwives, 8403 Colesville Rd., #1550, Silver Spring, MD 20910-6374; (240) 485-1800. Fax, (240) 485-1818. Sheri A. Sesay-Tufflour, Chief Executive Officer, (240) 485-1810; Amy Kohl, Director of Government Affairs, (240) 485-1806.
General email, info@acnm.org

Web, www.midwife.org, Twitter, @ACNMmidwives and
Facebook, www.facebook.com/ACNMmidwives

Membership: certified nurse-midwives and certified midwives who preside at deliveries and provide postnatal care or primary gynecological care. Establishes clinical practice studies. Interests include preventive health care for women.

American Nurses Assn., *8515 Georgia Ave., #400, Silver Spring, MD 20910; (301) 628-5000. Fax, (301) 628-5001. Loressa Cole, Chief Executive Officer. Toll-free, (800) 284-2378.*
General email, info@ana.org
Web, http://nursingworld.org, Twitter, @RNAction, Twitter, @ANANursingWorld and Facebook, www.facebook.com/AmericanNursesAssociation

Membership: registered nurses. Promotes high standards of nursing practice, the rights of nurses in the workplace, and a positive and realistic view of nursing. Affiliated organizations include the American Nurses Foundation, the American Academy of Nursing, and the American Nurses Credentialing Center. Monitors legislation and regulations.

National Assn. of Nurse Practitioners in Women's Health, *505 C St. N.E., 20002; (202) 543-9693 ext. 1. Fax, (202) 543-9858. Gay Johnson, Chief Executive Officer, (202) 543-9693, ext. 3.*
General email, info@npwh.org
Web, www.npwh.org and Twitter, @NPWH

Develops standards for nurse practitioner training and practices. Sponsors and provides accreditation of women's health nurse practitioner continuing education programs. Provides the public and government with information on nurse practitioner education, practice, and women's health issues.

National Black Nurses Assn., *8630 Fenton St., #910, Silver Spring, MD 20910-3803; (301) 589-3200. Fax, (301) 589-3223. Millicent Gorham, Executive Director.*
General email, info@nbna.org
Web, www.nbna.org and Twitter, @NbnaInc

Membership: Black nurses from the United States, the eastern Caribbean, and Africa. Fosters improvement in the level of care available to minorities, conducts continuing education programs, and builds relationships with public and private agencies and organizations to exert influence on laws and programs. Conducts and publishes research.

Physical and Occupational Therapy

▶NONGOVERNMENTAL

American Occupational Therapy Assn., *4720 Montgomery Lane, #200, Bethesda, MD 20814-3449; (301) 652-6611. Fax, (301) 652-7711. Sherry Keramidas, Executive Director. TTY, (800) 377-8555.*
Web, www.aota.org and Twitter, @AOTAInc

Membership: occupational therapists, occupational therapy assistants, and students. Associate members include businesses and organizations supportive of occupational therapy. Accredits educational programs and credentials occupational therapists. Supports research and sponsors scholarships, grants, and fellowships. Monitors legislation and regulations.

American Physical Therapy Assn., *1111 N. Fairfax St., Alexandria, VA 22314-1488; (703) 684-2782. Fax, (703) 684-7343. Justin Moore, Chief Executive Officer. Information, (800) 999-2782.*
General email, memberservices@apta.org
Web, www.apta.org, Twitter, @APTAtweets and Facebook, www.facebook.com/AmericanPhysicalTherapyAssociation

Membership: physical therapists, assistants, and students. Establishes professional standards and accredits physical therapy programs; seeks to improve physical therapy education, practice, and research.

Physicians

▶NONGOVERNMENTAL

American Academy of Family Physicians (AAFP), Washington Office, *1133 Connecticut Ave. N.W., #1100, 20036-4342; (202) 232-9033. Fax, (202) 232-9044. R. Shawn Martin, Vice President for Practice Advancement and Advocacy. Toll-free, (888) 794-7481.*
General email, capitol@aafp.org
Web, www.aafp.org, Twitter, @aapf and Facebook, www.facebook.com/familymed

Membership: family physicians, family practice residents, and medical students. Sponsors continuing medical education programs; promotes family practice residency programs. Monitors legislation and regulations. (Headquarters in Leawood, Kans.)

American Academy of Orthopaedic Surgeons, Government Relations, *317 Massachusetts Ave. N.E., 1st Floor, 20002; (202) 546-4430. Fax, (202) 546-5051. Graham H. Newson, Director.*
General email, dc@aaos.org
Web, www.aaos.org/Advocacy and Twitter, @AAOSAdvocacy

Membership: orthopaedic surgeons and musculoskeletal care professionals. Offers continuing education activities; publishes scientific and medical journals and electronic resources. Engages in health policy and acts as advocate on behalf of orthopaedic surgeons and patients. (Headquarters in Rosemont, Ill.)

American Academy of Otolaryngology—Head and Neck Surgery (AAO-HNS), *1650 Diagonal Rd., Alexandria, VA 22314-2857; (703) 836-4444. Fax, (703) 684-4288. Dr. Gavin Setzen, President; Dr. James C. Denneny III, Chief Executive Officer. Press, (703) 535-3762.*
General email, memberservices@entnet.org
Web, www.entnet.org, Twitter, @AAOHNS and Facebook, www.facebook.com/AAOHNS

Membership: otolaryngologists—head and neck surgeons. Supports the advancement of scientific medical research. Provides continuing medical education for members. Monitors legislation, regulations, and international research.

American Assn. of Colleges of Osteopathic Medicine,
7700 Old Georgetown Rd.,#250, Bethesda, MD 20814; (301) 968-4100. Fax, (301) 968-4101. Stephen C. Shannon, President.
General email, webmaster@aacom.org
Web, www.aacom.org, Twitter, @AACOMGR and Facebook, www.facebook.com/ AmericanAssociationcollegesOsteopathicMedicine

Administers a centralized application service for osteopathic medical colleges; supports an increase in the number of minority and economically disadvantaged students in osteopathic colleges; maintains an information database; sponsors recruitment programs. Monitors legislation and regulations.

American Assn. of Naturopathic Physicians, *300 New Jersey Ave. N.W., #900, 20001; (202) 237-8150. Fax, (202) 237-5213. Laura Farr, Executive Director, (202) 849-6306.*
General email, member.services@naturopathic.org
Web, www.naturopathic.org

Membership: naturopathic physicians who are licensed as primary health care providers. Promotes naturopathic physician education and acceptance of naturopathic medicine in the nation's health care system.

American Assn. of Neurological Surgeons, *Government Affairs, 25 Massachusetts Ave.,. N.W., #610, 20001; (202) 628-2072. Fax, (202) 628-5264. Katie O. Orrico, Director, Washington Office.*
General email, info@aans.org
Web, www.aans.org/en/Advocacy/About-the-Washington-Office, Twitter, @neurosurgery and Facebook, www.facebook.com/AANSNeuro

Research and education association dedicated to advancing the specialty of neurological surgery; advocates neurosurgeons' interests in public policy. Publishes the *Journal of Neurosurgery* and other publications and resources. (Headquarters in Rolling Meadows, Ill.)

American College of Cardiology, *Heart House, 2400 N St. N.W., 20037; (202) 375-6000 ext. 5603. Fax, (202) 375-7000. Thomas W. Attebery, Chief Executive Officer; Cathleen C. Gates, Chief Operating Officer. Press, (202) 375-6523. Toll-free, (800) 253-4636 ext. 5603.*
General email, resource@acc.org
Web, www.acc.org, Twitter, @accintouch and Facebook, www.facebook.com/ AmericanCollegeofCardiology

Membership: physicians, surgeons, and scientists specializing in cardiovascular health care. Sponsors programs in continuing medical education; collaborates with national and international cardiovascular organizations.

American College of Emergency Physicians, *Public Affairs, 2121 K St. N.W., #325, 20037-1801; (202) 728-0610. Fax, (202) 728-0617. Dean Wilkerson, Executive Director, (800) 798-1822, ext. 3200; Laura Wooster, Associate Executive Director, (202) 728-0610, ext. 3016. Toll-free, (800) 320-0610.*

Web, www.acep.org, Twitter, @acepnow and Facebook, www.facebook.com/ACEPFan
Public Affairs, publicaffairs@acep.org

Membership: physicians, residents, and interns. Interests include health care reform, Medicare and Medicaid legislation and regulations, medical liability, overcrowding in emergency departments, access to emergency care, bioterrorism and terrorism preparedness, managed care, and adult and pediatric emergencies. Disseminates public education materials. (Headquarters in Dallas, Tex.)

American College of Obstetricians and Gynecologists, *409 12th St. S.W., 20024-9998 (mailing address: P.O. Box 70620, Washington, DC 20024-9998); (202) 638-5577. Dr. Lisa M. Hollier, Executive Vice President (Acting). Toll-free, (800) 673-8444.*
General email, communications@acog.org
Web, www.acog.org, Twitter, @acognews and Facebook, www.facebook.com/ACOGNational

Membership: medical specialists in obstetrics and gynecology. Disseminates standards of clinical practice and promotes patient involvement in medical care. Provides mentorship programs and educational guidelines. Monitors legislation, regulations, and international research on maternal and child health care.

American College of Oral and Maxillofacial Surgeons (ACOMS), *2025 M St. N.W., #800, 20036; (202) 367-1182. Steven C. Kemp, Executive Director.*
General email, info@acoms.org
Web, www.acoms.org, Twitter, @theACOMS and Facebook, www.facebook.com/theACOMS

Professional association serving the specialty of oral and maxillofacial surgery, the surgical arm of dentistry. Provides continuing education courses; holds an annual conference. Publishes the journal *Oral Surgery, Oral Medicine, Oral Pathology, Oral Radiology.* (Headquarters in Rosemont, Ill.)

American College of Osteopathic Surgeons, *1680 Duke St., #500, Alexandria, VA 22314; (703) 684-0416. Fax, (703) 684-3280. Linda Taliaferro, Chief Executive Officer, (571) 551-2005. Toll-free, (800) 888-1312 ext. 108. General Inquires, (571) 551-2008.*
General email, info@facos.org
Web, www.facos.org, Twitter, @AcoSurgeons and Facebook, www.facebook.com/American-College-of-Osteopathic-Surgeons-ACOS-502454306437329

Membership: osteopathic surgeons in disciplines of neurosurgery, thoracic surgery, cardiovascular surgery, urology, plastic surgery, and general surgery. Offers members continuing surgical education programs and use of the ACOS-sponsored coding and reimbursement online database. Monitors legislation and regulations.

American College of Preventive Medicine, *455 Massachusetts Ave. N.W., #200, 20001; (202) 466-2044. Donna Grande, Chief Executive Officer, ext. 118; Kate McFayden, Government Affairs, ext. 107.*

General email, info@acpm.org

Web, www.acpm.org, Twitter, @ACPM_HQ and Facebook, www.facebook.com/AmericanCollegeOfPreventiveMedicine

Membership: physicians in general preventive medicine, public health, international health, occupational medicine, and aerospace medicine. Provides educational opportunities; advocates public policies consistent with scientific principles of the discipline; supports the investigation and analysis of issues relevant to the field. Monitors legislation and regulations.

American College of Surgeons, *Advocacy and Health Policy, 20 F St. N.W., #1000, 20001; (202) 337-2701. Fax, (202) 337-4271. Christian Shalgian, Director, (202) 337-2701; Dr. Frank Opelka, Medical Director of Quality and Health Policy; Dr. Patrick Bailey, Medical Director of Advocacy.*

General email, ahp@facs.org

Web, www.facs.org/advocacy

Monitors legislation and regulations concerning surgery; conducts continuing education programs and sponsors scholarships for graduate medical education. Interests include hospital cancer programs, trauma care, hospital accreditation, and international research. (Headquarters in Chicago, Ill.)

American Health Quality Assn., *7918 Jones Branch Dr., #300, McLean, VA 22102; Alison Shafer Teitelbaum, Executive Director.*

General email, info@ahqa.org

Web, www.ahqa.org, Twitter, @AHQA and Facebook, www.facebook.com/AHQA.org

National network of private Quality Improvement Organizations (QIOs) that seek to improve health care provider performance through quality improvement, technical assistance, provider performance measurement feedback, teaching self-assessment techniques, responding to consumer complaints and appeals, and initiating community-based quality improvement programs. Monitors legislation and regulations.

American Medical Assn. (AMA), *Government Relations, 25 Massachusetts Ave. N.W., #600, 20001-7400; (202) 789-7400. Fax, (202) 789-7485. Dr. Patrice A. Harris, President. Toll-free, (800) 621-8335.*

Web, www.ama-assn.org and Twitter, @AmericanMedicalAssn

Membership: physicians, residents, and medical students. Provides information on the medical profession and health care; cooperates in setting standards for medical schools and hospital intern and residency training programs; offers physician placement service and counseling on management practices; provides continuing medical education. Interests include international research and peer review. Monitors legislation and regulations. (Headquarters in Chicago, Ill.)

American Osteopathic Assn., *Advocacy Center, 1090 Vermont Ave. N.W., #500, 20005; (202) 349-8250.*

Fax, (202) 544-3525. David J. Pugach, Senior Vice President of Public Policy. Toll-free, (888) 626-9262.

General email, info@osteopathic.org

Web, www.osteopathic.org/about/advocacy, Twitter, @AOAforDOs and Facebook, www.facebook/com/osteopathicphysicians

Membership: osteopathic physicians. Promotes public health, education, and research; accredits osteopathic educational institutions. Monitors legislation and regulations. (Headquarters in Chicago, Ill.)

American Podiatric Medical Assn., *9312 Old Georgetown Rd., Bethesda, MD 20814; (301) 581-9200. Fax, (301) 530-2752. Dr. James R. Christina, Chief Executive Officer; Dr. Dennis R. Frisch, President.*

Web, www.apma.org, Twitter, @APMA and Facebook, www.facebook.com/theAPMA

Membership: podiatrists in affiliated and related societies. Interests include advocacy in legislative affairs, health policy and practice, scientific meetings, and public education.

American Psychiatric Assn., *800 Maine Ave. S.W., #900, 20024; (202) 559-3900. Dr. Saul Levin, Medical Director. Press, (202) 459-9732. Publishing toll-free, (800) 368-5777. Toll-free, (888) 357-7924.*

General email, apa@psych.org

Web, www.psychiatry.org, Twitter, @APAPsychiatric and Facebook, www.facebook.com/AmericanPsychiatricAssocition

Membership: psychiatrists. Promotes availability of high-quality psychiatric care; provides the public with information; assists state and local agencies; conducts educational programs for professionals and students in the field; participates in international meetings and research. Library open to members.

American Roentgen Ray Society, *44211 Slatestone Court, Leesburg, VA 20176-5109; (703) 729-3353. Fax, (703) 729-4839. Susan B. Cappitelli, Executive Director. Toll-free, (866) 940-2777.*

General email, info@arrs.org

Web, www.arrs.org and Twitter, @ARRS_Radiology

Membership: physicians and researchers in radiology and allied sciences. Publishes research; conducts conferences; presents scholarships and awards; monitors international research.

American Society of Addiction Medicine, *11400 Rockville Pike, #200, Rockville, MD 20852; (301) 656-3920. Fax, (301) 656-3815. Penny Mills, Executive Vice President, (301) 547-4105.*

General email, email@asam.org

Web, www.asam.org and Twitter, @ASAMorg

Membership: physicians and medical students. Supports the study and provision of effective treatment and care for people with alcohol and drug dependencies; educates physicians. Monitors legislation and regulations.

American Society of Nuclear Cardiology (ASNC), *9302 Lee Hwy., #120, Fairfax, VA 22031; (703) 459-2555.*

Fax, (301) 215-7113. Kathleen Flood, Chief Executive Officer.

General email, info@asnc.org

Web, www.asnc.org and Twitter, @MyASNC

Membership: physicians, scientists, technologists, and other professionals engaged in nuclear cardiology practice or research. Provides professional education programs; establishes standards and guidelines for training and practice; promotes research worldwide. Works with agreement states to monitor user-licensing requirements of the Nuclear Regulatory Commission.

American Society of Transplant Surgeons, 2461 S. Clark St., #640, Arlington, VA 22202; (703) 414-7870. Fax, (703) 414-7874. Kim Gifford, Executive Director.

General email, asts@asts.org

Web, www.asts.org and Twitter, @ASTSchimera

Promotes education and research on organ and tissue transplantation for patients with end-stage organ failure. Provides information for policy decisions affecting the practice of transplantation. Offers professional development for transplant colleagues.

Assn. of American Medical Colleges (AAMC), 655 K St. N.W., #100, 20001-2399; (202) 828-0600. Fax, (202) 828-1125. Dr. Darrell G. Kirch, President.

General email, aacas@aamc.org

Web, www.aamc.org and Twitter, @AAMCtoday

Membership: accredited U.S. and Canadian schools of medicine, teaching hospitals, health systems, academic and scientific societies, medical students and faculty, and residents and resident physicians. Administers Medical College Admission Test.

Clerkship Directors in Internal Medicine, 330 John Carlyle St., #610, Alexandria, VA 22314; (703) 341-4540. Fax, (703) 519-1893. Amy Shaheen, President.

General email, AAIM@im.org

Web, www.im.org/p/cm/ld/fid=235

Membership: directors of third-year and fourth-year internal medicine clerkships at U.S. and Canadian medical schools. (Affiliated with Alliance for Academic Internal Medicine.)

College of American Pathologists, Advocacy Division, 1001 G St. N.W., #425 West, 20001; (202) 354-7100. Fax, (202) 354-8101. John H. Scott, Vice President, Advocacy. Information, (800) 392-9994.

Web, www.cap.org and Twitter, @Pathologists

Membership: physicians who are board certified in clinical or anatomic pathology. Accredits laboratories and provides them with proficiency testing programs; promotes the practice of pathology and laboratory medicine worldwide. Monitors legislation and regulations. (Headquarters in Northfield, Ill.)

National Medical Assn., 8403 Colesville Rd., #820, Silver Spring, MD 20910; (202) 347-1895. Martin Hamlette, Executive Director.

Web, www.nmanet.org and Twitter, @NationalMedAssn

Membership: physicians of African descent. Supports increased participation of minorities in the health professions, especially medicine.

Physician Hospitals of America, 2025 M St. N.W., #800, 20036; (202) 367-1113. Fax, (202) 367-2113. John Richardson, Executive Director.

General email, info@physicianhospitals.org

Web, www.physicianhospitals.org and Twitter, @physicianhosp

Membership organization advocating the physician-owned hospital industry; provides networking and continuing education opportunities.

Physicians Committee for Responsible Medicine (PCRM), 5100 Wisconsin Ave. N.W., #400, 20016; (202) 686-2210. Fax, (202) 686-2216. Neal Barnard, President. Press, 202–527-7316.

General email, pcrm@pcrm.org

Web, www.pcrm.org and Twitter, @PCRM

Membership: health care professionals, medical students, and laypersons interested in preventive medicine, nutrition, and higher standards in research. Conducts clinical research, educational programs, and public information campaigns; advocates more effective and compassionate health-related policies in government and in public and private institutions.

Society of Thoracic Surgeons, Advocacy, 20 F St. N.W., #310C, 20001-1230; (202) 787-1230. Fax, (202) 280-1477. Natalie Boden, Director of Communications, (312) 202-5819; Courtney Yohe, Director of Government Relations.

General email, advocacy@sts.org

Web, www.sts.org/advocacy and Twitter, @STS_CTsurgery

Membership: surgeons, researchers, and allied health care professionals in cardiothoracic surgery. Monitors legislation and regulations. (Headquarters in Chicaco, Ill.)

Veterinarians

▶AGENCIES

Animal and Plant Health Inspection Service (APHIS) (Agriculture Dept.), Veterinary Services, 400 N. 8th St., #726, Richmond, VA 23219-4824; (804) 343-2561. Fax, (804) 343-2599. Dr. Jack Shere, Deputy Administrator.

General email, jack.a.shere@aphis.usda.gov

Web, www.aphis.usda.gov/aphis/ourfocus/animalhealth

Regulates veterinary biologics, including vaccines, bacterins, antisera, diagnostic kits, and other products of biological origin, to ensure that the veterinary biologics available for the diagnosis, prevention, and treatment of animal diseases are pure, safe, potent, and effective. Provides veterinary training materials and veterinarian accreditation.

Food and Drug Administration (FDA) (Health and Human Services Dept.), Center for Veterinary Medicine (CVM), 7500 Standish Pl., HFV-1, Rockville, MD 20855-0001; (240) 402-7002. Fax, (240) 276-9001. Steven Solomon, Director.

General email, askcvm@fda.hhs.gov

Web, www.fda.gov/animalveterinary and *Twitter, @FDAanimalhealth*

Regulates the manufacture and distribution of drugs, food additives, feed, and devices for livestock and pets. Conducts research; works to ensure animal health and the safety of food derived from animals.

National Zoological Park *(Smithsonian Institution),* *3001 Connecticut Ave. N.W., 20008 (mailing address: DEVS, P.O. Box 37012, MRC 5516, Washington, DC 20013-7012); (202) 633-4888 (recorded information line). Fax, (202) 673-4836. Steven Monfort, Executive Director. Friends of the Zoo, (202) 633-3038. Library, (202) 633-2922. Press, (202) 633-3055. TTY, (202) 673-7800. Zoo police, (202) 633-4134.*

Web, www.nationalzoo.si.edu, Twitter, @NationalZoo and *Facebook, www.facebook.com/nationalzoo*

Conducts research on animal behavior, ecology, nutrition, reproductive physiology, pathology, and veterinary medicine. Houses a unit of the Smithsonian Institution library open to qualified researchers by appointment. Interlibrary loans available.

American Veterinary Medical Assn., *Governmental Relations, 1910 Sunderland Pl. N.W., 20036-1642; (202) 789-0007. Fax, (202) 842-4360. Dr. Mark Lutschaunig, Director. Toll-free, (800) 321-1473.*

General email, avmagrd@avma.org

Web, www.avma.org and *Twitter, @AVMAvets*

Monitors legislation and regulations that influence animal and human health and advance the veterinary medical profession. (Headquarters in Schaumburg, Ill.)

Assn. of American Veterinary Medical Colleges (AAVMC), *655 K St., #725, 20005-3536; (202) 371-9195. Fax, (202) 842-0773. Dr. Andrew T. Maccabe, Chief Executive Officer.*

Web, www.aavmc.org and *Twitter, @AAVMC*

Membership: U.S., Canadian, and international schools and colleges of veterinary medicine, departments of comparative medicine, and departments of veterinary science in agricultural colleges. Produces veterinary reports; provides information about scholarships and continuing education programs and sponsors conferences on veterinary medical issues.

Vision Care

National Eye Institute (NEI) *(National Institutes of Health), 31 Center Dr., #6A32, MSC 2510, Bethesda, MD 20892-2510; (301) 496-5248. Fax, (301) 402-1065. Dr. Paul A. Sieving, Director.*

General email, 2020@nei.nih.gov

Web, www.nei.nih.gov and *Twitter, @NatEyeInstitute*

Conducts and supports research, training, health information dissemination, and other programs with respect to blinding eye diseases, visual disorders, mechanisms of visual function, preservation of sight, and the special health problems and requirements of the blind.

American Academy of Ophthalmology, *Governmental Affairs, 20 F St. N.W., #400, 20001-6701; (202) 737-6662. Fax, (202) 737-7061. Catherine G. (Cathy) Cohen, Vice President.*

General email, politicalaffairs@aao.org

Web, www.aao.org, Twitter, @AcedemyEyeSmart and *Facebook, www.facebook.com/AcedemyEyeSmart*

Membership: eye physicians and surgeons. Provides information on eye diseases. Monitors legislation, regulations, and international research. (Headquarters in San Francisco, Calif.)

American Board of Opticianry and National Contact Lens Examiners Board, *6506 Loisdale Rd., #330, Springfield, VA 22150; (703) 719-5800. Fax, (703) 719-9144. James Morris, Executive Director. Toll-free, (800) 296-1379.*

General email, mail@abo-ncle.org

Web, http://abo-ncle.org and *Facebook, www.facebook .com/opticiancertification*

Establishes standards for opticians who dispense eyeglasses and contact lenses. Administers voluntary professional exams and awards certification to opticians and ophthalmic professionals; maintains registry of certified eyeglass and contact lens dispensers. Adopts and enforces continuing education requirements; assists state licensing boards; approves educational offerings for recertification requirements.

American Optometric Assn., *Washington Office, 1505 Prince St., #300, Alexandria, VA 22314-2874; (703) 739-9200. Fax, (703) 739-9497. Jon Hymes, Executive Director, (703) 837-1371. Information, (800) 365-2219.*

General email, jfhymes@aoa.org

Web, www.aoa.org and *Twitter, @AOAConnect*

Membership: optometrists, optometry students, and paraoptometric assistants and technicians in a federation of state, student, and armed forces optometric associations. Sets professional standards and provides research and information on eye care to the public. Monitors legislation and regulations and acts as liaison with international optometric groups and government optometrists; conducts continuing education programs for optometrists and provides information on eye care. (Headquarters in St. Louis, Mo.)

American Society of Cataract and Refractive Surgery, *4000 Legato Rd., #700, Fairfax, VA 22033; (703) 591-2220. Fax, (703) 591-0614. Thomas W. Samuelson, President; Nick Mamalis, Vice President.*

Web, www.ascrs.org and *Twitter, @ASCRStweets*

Membership: more than 9,000 ophthalmologists who specialize in cataract and refractive surgery. Offers educational programs and services to its members. Monitors regulations affecting ophthalmic practices. Sponsors independent research. Maintains a foundation dedicated to improving public understanding of ophthalmology and providing eye care to underserved parts of the world.

Assn. for Research in Vision and Ophthalmology (ARVO), 1801 Rockville Pike, #400, Rockville, MD 20852-5622; (240) 221-2900. Fax, (240) 221-0370. Iris M. Rush, Executive Director.

General email, arvo@arvo.org

Web, www.arvo.org and Twitter, @ARVOinfo

Promotes eye and vision research; issues awards for significant research and administers research grant program.

Assn. of Schools and Colleges of Optometry, 6110 Executive Blvd., #420, Rockville, MD 20852; (301) 231-5944. Fax, (301) 770-1828. Dawn Mancuso, Executive Director.

General email, cdoyle@opted.org

Web, www.opted.org and Twitter, @OptometricED

Membership: U.S. and Puerto Rican optometry schools and colleges and foreign affiliates. Provides information about the Optometry College Admission Test to students. Supports the international development of optometric education. Monitors legislation and regulations.

Eye Bank Assn. of America, 1101 17th St. N.W., 20036; (202) 775-4999. Fax, (202) 429-6036. Kevin P. Corcoran, President.

General email, info@restoresight.org

Web, www.restoresight.org

Membership: eye banks in Brazil, Canada, England, Japan, Saudi Arabia, Taiwan, and the United States. Sets and enforces medical standards for processing, storing, evaluating, and distributing ocular and corneal tissue for transplantation; seeks to increase donations to eye, tissue, and organ banks; conducts training and certification programs for eye bank technicians; compiles statistics; accredits eye banks.

International Eye Foundation, 10801 Connecticut Ave., Kensington, MD 20895; (240) 290-0263. Fax, (240) 290-0269. Victoria M. Sheffield, President.

General email, ief@iefusa.org

Web, www.iefusa.org, Twitter, @iefusa and Facebook, www.facebook.com/iefusa

Operates blindness prevention programs focusing on cataracts, trachoma, "river blindness," and childhood blindness, including vitamin A deficiency. Provides affordable ophthalmic instruments, equipment, and supplies to eye hospitals in developing countries to help lower surgical costs. Works to strengthen management and financial sustainability of eye hospitals and clinics in developing countries. Works with the World Health Organization, ministries of health, and international and indigenous organizations in Africa, Asia, Latin America, and eastern Europe to promote eye care.

Lab Division, 225 Reinekers Lane, #700, Alexandria, VA 22314; (703) 548-4560. Fax, (703) 548-4580. Ashley Mills, Chief Executive Officer. Toll-free, (866) 826-0290.

General email, info@thevisioncouncil.org

Web, www.thevisioncouncil.org/members/optical-lab-division

Membership: optical laboratories. Promotes the eyewear industry; collects and disseminates lab performance data; sponsors conferences. Monitors legislation and regulations. (Affiliated with The Vision Council.)

The Vision Council, 225 Reinekers Lane, #700, Alexandria, VA 22314; (703) 548-4560. Fax, (703) 548-4580. Ashley Mills, Chief Executive Officer. Toll-free, (866) 826-0290.

General email, info@thevisioncouncil.org

Web, www.thevisioncouncil.org and Twitter, @opticalindustry

Sponsors trade shows and public relations programs for the ophthalmic industry. Educates the public on developments in the optical industry. Represents manufacturers and distributors of optical products and equipment.

HEALTH SERVICES FOR SPECIAL GROUPS

General

▶**AGENCIES**

Education Dept., Special Education and Rehabilitative Services (OSERS), Rehabilitation Services Administration (RSA), Lyndon Baines Johnson Bldg., 400 Maryland Ave. S.W., 20202-7100; (202) 245-7468. Fax, (202) 245-7591. Carol Dobak, Deputy Commissioner (Acting).

Web, www2.ed.gov/about/offices/list/osers/rsa

Allocates funds to state agencies and nonprofit organizations for programs serving eligible physically and mentally disabled persons; services provided by these funds include medical and psychological treatment as well as the establishment of supported-employment programs.

Eunice Kennedy Shriver National Institute of Child Health and Human Development (NICHD) (National Institutes of Health), National Center for Medical Rehabilitation Research (NCMRR), 6710B Rockledge Dr., Bldg. 6710B, Room 2107, MSC 7002, Bethesda, MD 20817; (301) 496-0295. Fax, (301) 480-3854. Alison Cernich, Director.

Web, www.nichd.nih.gov/about/org/ncmrr

Supports research to foster the development of scientific knowledge needed to enhance the health, productivity, independence, and quality of life of persons with disabilities. Supports research and research training on pathophysiology and management of chronically injured nervous and musculoskeletal systems (including stroke, traumatic brain injury, spinal cord injury, and orthopedic conditions); repair and recovery of motor and cognitive function; functional plasticity, adaptation, and windows of opportunity for rehabilitative interventions; rehabilitative strategies; pediatric rehabilitation; secondary conditions associated with chronic disabilities; improved diagnosis, assessment, and outcome measures; and development of orthotics, prosthetics, and other assistive technologies and devices.

Federal Bureau of Prisons *(Justice Dept.),* **Health Services,** *320 1st St. N.W., #454, 20534; (202) 307-3055. Fax, (202) 514-6620. Dr. Deborah G. Schult, Assistant Director.*
Web, www.bop.gov/about/agency/org_hsd.jsp

Administers health care and treatment programs for prisoners in federal institutions.

Health Resources and Services Administration (HRSA) *(Health and Human Services Dept.),* **Bureau of Primary Health Care (BPHC),** *5600 Fishers Lane, #16W29, Rockville, MD 20857; (301) 594-4110. Fax, (301) 594-4072. James Macrae, Associate Administrator. Helpline, (877) 974-2742.*
Web, www.bphc.hrsa.gov

Funds health centers in underserved communities; develops health policies and programs to increase primary and preventive healthcare access and eliminate health disparities.

National Institute on Deafness and Other Communication Disorders (NIDCD) *(National Institutes of Health),* *31 Center Dr., #3C02, MSC 2320, Bethesda, MD 20892-2320; (301) 827-8183. Fax, (301) 402-0018. Judith Cooper Jr., Director (Acting), (301) 402-0900. Evenings and weekends, (301) 496-3315. Interpreter service, (301) 496-1807. Toll-free, (800) 241-1044. TTY, (800) 241-1055.*
General email, nidcdinfo@nidcd.nih.gov
Web, www.nidcd.nih.gov and Twitter, @nidcd

Conducts and supports research and research training and disseminates information on hearing disorders and other communication processes, including diseases that affect hearing, balance, smell, taste, voice, speech, and language. Monitors international research.

National Institute on Minority Health and Health Disparities (NIMHD) *(National Institutes of Health),* *2 Democracy Plaza, 6707 Democracy Blvd., #800, MSC 5465, Bethesda, MD 20892-5465; (301) 402-1366. Fax, (301) 480-4049. Dr. Eliseo J. Perez-Stable, Director.*
General email, nimhdinfor@nimhd.nih.gov
Web, www.nimhd.nih.gov and Twitter, @NIMHD

Promotes minority health and leads, coordinates, supports, and assesses the NIH's effort to eliminate health disparities. Conducts and supports basic clinical, social, and behavioral research; promotes research infrastructure and training; fosters emerging programs; disseminates information; and reaches out to minority and other communities suffering from health disparities.

U.S. Immigration and Customs Enforcement (ICE) *(Homeland Security Dept.),* **ICE Health Service Corps,** *500 12th St. S.W., 2nd Floor, 20536; (202) 732-4600. Dr. Stewart D. Smith, Assistant Director, (202) 732-3047. Web, www.ice.gov/about/offices/enforcement-removal-operations/ihs*

Consists of U.S. Public Health Service commissioned officers, federal civil servants, and contract support staff. Administers ICE's detainee health care program, providing direct care to detained aliens at designated facilities and overseeing medical care at other detention facilities.

►CONGRESS

For a listing of relevant congressional committees and subcommittees, please see pages 362–363 or the Appendix.

►NONGOVERNMENTAL

Assn. of Clinicians for the Underserved (ACU), *1420 Spring Hill Rd., #600, Tysons Corner, VA 22102; (844) 422-8247. Fax, (703) 562-8801. Craig Kennedy, Executive Director.*
General email, acu@clinicians.org
Web, www.clinicians.org and Twitter, @ACUunderserved

Membership: clinicians, advocates, and health care organizations. Works to improve the health of underserved populations and eliminate health disparities in the United States. Educates and supports health care clinicians serving these populations. Interests include health care access, transdisciplinary approaches to health care, workforce development and diversity, pharmaceutical access, and health information technology.

Catholic Health Assn. of the United States, *1875 Eye St. N.W., #1000, 20006; (202) 296-3993. Fax, (202) 296-3997. Sister Carol Keehan, President.*
Web, www.chausa.org and Twitter, @TheCHAUSA

Concerned with the health care needs of the poor and disadvantaged. Promotes health care reform, including universal insurance coverage, and more cost-effective, affordable health care.

National Assn. of Community Health Centers, *7501 Wisconsin Ave., #1100W, Bethesda, MD 20814; (301) 347-0400. Fax, (301) 347-0459. Tom Van Coverden, President. Web, www.nachc.org and Twitter, @NACHC*

Membership: community, migrant, public housing, and homeless health centers. Represents America's federally qualified health centers. Seeks to ensure the continued development of community health care programs through policy analysis, research, technical assistance, publications, education, and training.

National Health Law Program, *Washington Office,* *1444 Eye St. N.W., #1105, 20005; (202) 289-7661. Fax, (202) 289-7724. Elizabeth G. Taylor, Executive Director.*
General email, nhelpdc@healthlaw.org
Web, www.healthlaw.org

Organization of lawyers representing the economically disadvantaged and minorities. Offers technical assistance, workshops, seminars, and training for health law specialists.

Issues include health care reform, Medicaid, child and adolescent health, and disability and reproductive rights.

Minority Health

▶AGENCIES

Agency for Health Care Research and Quality (AHCRQ) *(Health and Human Services Dept.)*, *(Research and Quality)*, 5600 Fishers Lane, 7th Floor, Rockville, MD 20857; (301) 427-1364. Fax, (301) 427-1873. Gopal Khanna, Director, (301) 427-1200. Congressional Affairs, (301) 427-1214. Press, (301) 427-1864. Public inquiries, (301) 427-1104. TTY, (888) 586-6340. General email, info@ahrq.gov
Web, www.ahrq.gov/cpi/centers/ockt/index.html, Twitter, @AHRQNews and Facebook, www.facebook.com/ahrq.gov

Researches health care quality among minorities. Identifies and devises solutions for disparities in access to care, diagnosis, and treatment of illness. Provides health care professionals with research on minority health.

Assistant Secretary for Health (OASH) *(Health and Human Services Dept.)*, *Minority Health (OMH)*, 1101 Wootton Pkwy., #600, Rockville, MD 20852; (240) 453-2882. Fax, (240) 453-2883. Alexis D. Bakos, Deputy Assistant Secretary. Information, (800) 444-6472. General email, info@minorityhealth.gov
Web, http://minorityhealth.hhs.gov and Twitter, @MinorityHealth

Oversees the implementation of the secretary's Task Force on Black and Minority Health and legislative mandates; develops programs to meet the health care needs of minorities; awards grants to coalitions of minority community organizations.

Centers for Medicare and Medicaid Services (CMS) *(Health and Human Services Dept.)*, *Minority Health (OMH)*, 7500 Security Blvd., S2-12-17, Baltimore, MD 21244; (410) 786-6842. Cara V. James, Director, (410) 786-2773.
Web, www.cms.gov/About-CMS/Agency-Information/CMSLeadership/Office_OMH.html

Seeks to reduce inequalities in health outcomes of racial and ethnic minority populations. Manages disparities data and evaluates impact; coordinates minority health initiatives within the agency; serves as the liaison to other agency offices of minority health.

Education Dept., *White House Initiative on Asian Americans and Pacific Islanders*, 550 12th St. S.W., 10th Floor, 20202; (202) 245-6418. Fax, (202) 245-7166. Holly Ham, Executive Director; Debra Suarez, Senior Advisor.
General email, whitehouseaapi@ed.gov
Web, http://sites.ed.gov/aapi, Twitter, @whitehouseAAPI and Facebook, www.facebook.com/WhiteHouseAAPI

Works to increase Asian American and Pacific Islander participation in federal health programs. Interests include reducing health risks, improving assess to high-quality health care, and promoting healthful living.

Food and Drug Administration (FDA) *(Health and Human Services Dept.)*, *Minority Health (OMH)*, White Oak Campus, 10903 New Hampshire Ave., Silver Spring, MD 20993; (240) 402-5084. Fax, (301) 847-3536. Capt. Richardae Araojo, Director, (301) 796-1152. General email, omh@fda.hhs.gov
Web, www.fda.gov/aboutfda/centersoffices/oc/officeofminorityhealth/default.htm, www.fda.gov/forconsumers/byaudience/minorityhealth and Twitter, @FDAOMH

Serves as the principal adviser to the Commissioner on minority health and health disparities. Provides leadership and direction in identifying agency actions that can help reduce health disparities, including the coordination of efforts across the agency. Promotes effective communication and the dissemination of information to the public, particularly underserved, vulnerable populations.

Health and Human Services Dept. (HHS), *Civil Rights (OCR)*, 200 Independence Ave. S.W., #509F, 20201; (202) 619-0403. Fax, (202) 619-3437. Roger Severino, Director. Toll-free, (800) 368-1019. TTY, (800) 537-7697. General email, OCRMail@hhs.gov
Web, www.hhs.gov/ocr

Administers and enforces laws prohibiting discrimination on the basis of race, color, sex, national origin, religion, age, or disability in programs receiving federal funds from the department; authorized to discontinue funding. Enforces the Health Insurance Portability and Accountability Act (HIPAA), Privacy, Security, and Breach Notification rules, and the Patient Safety Act and Rules.

Health and Human Services Dept. (HHS), *Minority Health (OMH)*, Tower Oaks Bldg., 1101 Wootton Pkwy., #600, Rockville, MD 20852; (240) 453-2882. Fax, (240) 453-2883. Capt. Felicia Collins, Director. Information, (800) 444-6472. TTY, (301) 251-1432. General email, info@minorityhealth.hhs.gov
Web, www.hhs.gov/ash/public-health-offices/index.html

Promotes improved health among racial and ethnic minority populations. Advises the Health and Human Services Dept. secretary and the Office of Public Health and Science on public health program activities affecting American Indian and Alaska Native, Black/African American, Asian American, Pacific Islander, Native Hawaiian, and Hispanic populations. Awards grants to programs and projects that address minority health issues, including prevention projects to administer health promotion, education, and disease-prevention programs.

Health and Human Services Dept. (HHS), *Minority Health Resource Center (OMH Resource Center)*, 8400 Corporate Dr., #500, Landover, MD 20785; (301) 251-1797. Fax, (301) 251-2160. Candice Ahwah Gonzalez, Project Director. Information, (800) 444-6472. TTY, (301) 251-1432.

National Institutes of Health

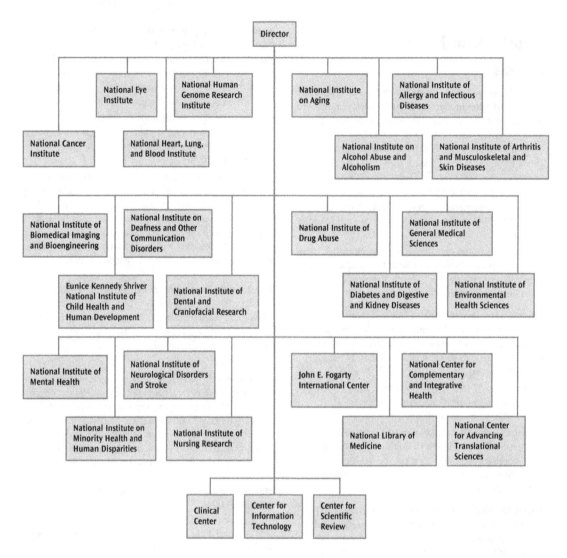

General email, info@minorityhealth.hhs.gov

Web, www.minorityhealth.hhs.gov/omh/browse.aspx?lvl=
1&lvlid=3

Serves as a national resource and referral service on minority health issues. Provides information on health topics such as substance abuse, cancer, heart disease, violence, diabetes, HIV/AIDS, and infant mortality. Provides free services, including customized database searches, publications, and referrals regarding American Indian and Alaska Native, African American, Asian American and Pacific Islander, and Hispanic populations.

Health Resources and Services Administration (HRSA) *(Health and Human Services Dept.), Bureau of Primary Health Care (BPHC), 5600 Fishers Lane, #16W29, Rockville, MD 20857; (301) 594-4110. Fax, (301) 594-4072. James Macrae, Associate Administrator. Helpline, (877) 974-2742.*
Web, www.bphc.hrsa.gov

Advises the associate administrator for primary care on public health activities affecting ethnic, racial, and other minority groups, including migrant and seasonal farmworkers, homeless persons, persons living in public housing, older adults, and women.

Health Resources and Services Administration (HRSA) *(Health and Human Services Dept.), Health Equity (OHE), 5600 Fishers Lane, #1270, Rockville, MD 20857; (301) 443-2964. Fax, (301) 443-7853. Michelle Allender, Director.*
General email, ask@hrsa.gov

Web, www.hrsa.gov/about/organization/bureaus/ohe

Sponsors programs and activities that address the special health needs of socially disadvantaged and underserved populations. Advises the administrator on minority health issues affecting the Health Resources and Services Administration (HRSA) and policy development; collects data on minority health activities within HRSA; represents HRSA programs affecting the health of racial and ethnic minorities to the health community and organizations in the public, private, and international sectors.

Indian Health Service (IHS) *(Health and Human Services Dept.)*, 5600 Fishers Lane, Rockville, MD 20857; (301) 443-3593. Rear Adm. Michael D. Weahkee, Principal Deputy. TTY, (301) 443-6394.

Web, www.ihs.gov, Twitter, @IIHSgov and Facebook, www.facebook.com/IndianHealthService

Acts as the health advocate for and operates hospitals and health centers that provide preventive, curative, and community health care for Native Americans and Alaska Natives.

National Institute on Minority Health and Health Disparities (NIMHD) *(National Institutes of Health)*, 2 Democracy Plaza, 6707 Democracy Blvd., #800, MSC 5465, Bethesda, MD 20892-5465; (301) 402-1366. Fax, (301) 480-4049. Dr. Eliseo J. Perez-Stable, Director.

General email, nimhdinfor@nimhd.nih.gov

Web, www.nimhd.nih.gov and Twitter, @NIMHD

Promotes minority health and leads, coordinates, supports, and assesses the NIH's effort to eliminate health disparities. Conducts and supports basic clinical, social, and behavioral research; promotes research infrastructure and training; fosters emerging programs; disseminates information; and reaches out to minority and other communities suffering from health disparities.

▶ NONGOVERNMENTAL

Asian and Pacific Islander American Health Forum, *Government Relations*, 1629 K St. N.W., #400, 20006; (202) 466-7772. Fax, (202) 296-0610. Kathy Ko Chin, President.

General email, info@apiahf.org

Web, www.apiahf.org and Twitter, @apiahf

Works to improve the health status of and access to care by Asian Americans and Pacific Islanders and to address health disparities, including disability and mental health, HIV/AIDS, smoking, and cancer. Monitors legislation in the areas of health, politics, and social and economic issues that affect Asian Americans, native Hawaiians, and Pacific Islanders. (Headquarters in Oakland, Calif.)

Black Women's Health Imperative, 55 M St. S.E., #940, 20003; (202) 548-4000. Fax, (202) 543-9743. Linda Goler Blount, President.

General email, imperative@bwhi.org

Web, www.bwhi.org and Twitter, @blkwomenshealth

Provides the tools and information for African American women to prevent health problems, to recognize symptoms and early warning signs, and to understand all of the options available for their specific health situations. Achieves these ends through community outreach, advocacy, resources and research, education, and mobilization. (Formerly the National Black Women's Health Project.)

National Alliance for Hispanic Health, 1501 16th St. N.W., 20036-1401; (202) 387-5000. Fax, (202) 797-4353.

Jane L. Delgado, President. Toll-free, (866) 783-2645. Toll-free in Spanish, (866) 783-2645.

General email, membership@healthyamericas.org

Web, www.healthyamericas.org and Twitter, @Health4Americas

Acts as advocate and conducts research to improve the health of Hispanics; promotes research and philanthropy; develops capacity of community-based health and social service organizations. Educates consumers on family and prenatal health, diabetes, depression, ADHD, immunization, HIV/AIDS, women's health, osteoporosis, tobacco control, and environmental health.

National Black Nurses Assn., 8630 Fenton St., #910, Silver Spring, MD 20910-3803; (301) 589-3200. Fax, (301) 589-3223. Millicent Gorham, Executive Director.

General email, info@nbna.org

Web, www.nbna.org and Twitter, @NbnaInc

Membership: Black nurses from the United States, the eastern Caribbean, and Africa. Fosters improvement in the level of care available to minorities.

National Council of Urban Indian Health, 924 Pennsylvania Ave. S.E., 20003; (202) 544-0344. Fax, (202) 544-9394. Francys Crevier, Executive Director.

Web, www.ncuih.org, Twitter, @NCUIH_Official and Facebook, www.facebook.com/NCUIH

Membership: Indian health care providers. Supports accessible, high-quality health care programs for American Indians and Alaska Natives living in urban communities. Provides education and training. Monitors legislation and funding.

National Hispanic Medical Assn., 1920 L St. N.W., #725, 20036; (202) 628-5895. Fax, (202) 628-5898. Dr. Elena V. Rios, President.

General email, nhma@nhmamd.org

Web, www.nhmamd.org and Twitter, @NHMAmd

Provides policymakers and health care providers with information and support to strengthen the delivery of health care to Hispanic communities in the United States. Areas of interest include high-quality care and increased opportunities in medical education for Latinos. Works with federal officials, other Hispanic advocacy groups, and Congress to eliminate disparities in health care for minorities.

National Minority AIDS Council (NMAC), 1000 Vermont Ave. N.W., #200, 20005; (202) 870-0918. Paul A. Kawata, Executive Director, (202) 277-2777.

General email, communications@nmac.org

Web, www.nmac.org

Works to build the capacity of small faith- and community-based organizations delivering HIV/AIDS services in communities of color. Holds national conferences; administers treatment and research programs and training; disseminates electronic and printed resource materials; conducts public policy advocacy.

Older Adults

►AGENCIES

Centers for Medicare and Medicaid Services (CMS)
(Health and Human Services Dept.), Center for Clinical Standards and Quality (CCSQ), Nursing Homes (DNH), 7500 Security Blvd., C2-23-17, Baltimore, MD 21244; (410) 786-7818. Fax, (410) 786-0194. Evan Shulman, Director *(Acting).*
Web, www.cms.gov/About-CMS/Agency-Information/ CMSLeadership/Office_CCSQ.html

Monitors compliance of nursing homes with government standards. Focus includes quality of care, environmental conditions, and participation in Medicaid and Medicare programs.

Centers for Medicare and Medicaid Services (CMS)
(Health and Human Services Dept.), Center for Medicaid and CHIP Services (CMCS), Disabled and Elderly Health Programs Group (DEHPG), 7500 Security Blvd., S2-14-26, Baltimore, MD 21244; (410) 786-0325.
Michael (Mike) Nardone, Director.
Web, www.medicaid.gov

Reviews all benefit and pharmacy state plan amendments for all Medicaid populations, Medicaid managed-care delivery systems, home-based and community-based services, and long-term services. Supports transformation grant programs, including Money Follows the Person and the Balancing Incentive Program.

National Institute on Aging (NIA) *(National Institutes of Health),* 31 Center Dr., Bldg. 31, #5C27, MSC 2292, Bethesda, MD 20892-2292; (301) 496-9265. Fax, (301) 496-2525. Dr. Richard J. Hodes, Director. Alzheimer's Disease Education and Referral Center, (800) 438-4380. Communications and Public Liaison, (301) 496-1752. Information Center, (800) 222-2225. TTY, (800) 222-4225.
General email, niaic@nih.gov
Web, www.nia.nih.gov and Twitter, @Alzheimers_NIH

Conducts and supports biomedical, social, and behavioral research and training related to the aging process and the diseases and special problems of the aged. Manages the Alzheimer's Disease Education and Referral Center (www.alzheimers.nia.nih.gov).

Veterans Health Administration (VHA) *(Veterans Affairs Dept.), Geriatrics and Extended Care,* 810 Vermont Ave. N.W., #10P4G, 20420; (202) 461-6750. Fax, (202) 495-5167. Dr. Scotte Hartronft, Chief Consultant (Acting); Thomas E. Edes, Executive Director.
Web, www.va.gov/geriatrics

Administers research, educational, and clinical health care programs in geriatrics at VA and community nursing homes, personal care homes, VA domiciliaries, state veterans' homes, and in home-based and other noninstitutional care.

►NONGOVERNMENTAL

AARP, 601 E St. N.W., 20049; (202) 434-2277. Fax, (202) 434-7946. Jo Ann C. Jenkins, Chief Executive Officer. Library, (202) 434-6233. Membership, (202) 434-7550. Membership, toll-free, (800) 566-0242. Press, (202) 434-2560. Toll-free, (888) 687-2277. TTY, (877) 434-7598. Toll-free Spanish, (877) 342-2277. TTY Spanish, (866) 238-9488.
General email, member@aarp.org
Web, www.aarp.org, Twitter, @AARP and Facebook, www.facebook.com/AARP

Membership: people fifty years of age and older. Promotes healthy living for older adults and disseminates information about the Affordable Care Act and health care laws, health products, health and life insurance, and brain and mental health. Offers member discounts on health care needs, including prescriptions and glasses.

AARP, *Federal Health and Family Advocacy,* 601 E St. N.W., 20049; (202) 434-3770. Megan O'Reilly, Director for Health and Family Advocacy, (202) 434-6987.
Web, www.aarp.org

Maintains the Legal Counsel for the Elderly, which acts as advocate on behalf of older residents of the District of Columbia who reside in nursing homes and board and care homes. Monitors legislation and regulations.

Alliance for Aging Research, 1700 K St. N.W., #740, 20006; (202) 293-2856. Sue Peschin, President.
General email, info@agingresearch.org
Web, www.agingresearch.org, Twitter, @Aging_Research and Facebook, www.facebook.com/ AllianceforAgingResearch

Membership: senior corporate and foundation executives, science leaders, and congressional representatives. Citizen advocacy organization that seeks to improve the health and independence of older Americans through public and private research. Monitors legislatioon and research.

Alliance for Retired Americans, 815 16th St. N.W., 4th Floor, 20006-4104; (202) 637-5399. Fax, (202) 637-5398. Robert Roach Jr., President. Membership, (800) 333-7212.
Web, https://retiredamericans.org, Twitter, @ActiveRetirees and Facebook, www.facebook.com/retiredamericans

Supports expansion of Medicare, improved health programs, national health care, and reduced cost of drugs. Nursing Home Information Service provides information on nursing home standards and regulations. Monitors legislation and regulations. (Affiliate of the AFL-CIO.)

Alzheimer's Assn., *Public Policy Office,* 1212 New York Ave., #800, 20005-6105; (202) 393-7737. Rachel Conant, Senior Political Director, ext. 7121; Robert J. Egge, Chief of Public Policy, ext. 8660. Toll-free, (866) 865-0270. Helpline, (800) 272-3900.

General email, advocateinfo@alz.org

Web, www.alz.org and Twitter, www.twitter.com/
alzassociation and Facebook, www.facebook.com/actionalz
and Virtual library, www.alz.org/library

Offers family support services and educates the public
about Alzheimer's disease, a neurological disorder mainly
affecting the brain tissue in older adults. Promotes research
and long-term care protection; maintains liaison with
Alzheimer's associations abroad. Monitors legislation and
regulations. (Headquarters in Chicago, Ill.)

American Assn. for Geriatric Psychiatry, 6728 Old
McLean Village Dr., McLean, VA 22101; (703) 556-9222.
Fax, (703) 556-8729. Christopher N. Wood, Executive
Officer, (703) 556-9222, ext. 142.
General email, main@aagponline.org

Web, www.aagponline.org, Twitter, @GeriPsyc and
Facebook, www.facebook.com/American-Association-for-
geriatric-Psychiatry-AAGP

Works to improve the practice of geriatric psychiatry
and mental health through education, research, and advocacy, and support for career development for clinicians,
educators, and researchers. Monitors legislation and regulations. Publishes the American Journal of Geriatric Psychiatry.

American Society of Consultant Pharmacists (ASCP),
1240 N. Pitt St., #300, Alexandria, VA 22314-3563; (703)
739-1300. Fax, (202) 408-1101. Chad Worz, Executive
Director. Toll-free, (800) 355-2727.
General email, info@ascp.com

Web, www.ascp.com and Twitter, @ASCPharm

Membership: dispensing and clinical pharmacists with
expertise in therapeutic medication management for geriatric patients; provides services to long-term care facilities,
institutions, and hospices as well as older adults in assisted
living and home-based care. Monitors legislation and regulations.

Gerontological Society of America, 1220 L St. N.W.,
#901, 20005-4018; (202) 842-1275. Fax, (202) 587-5860.
James Appleby, Executive Director, (202) 587-2821.
General email, geron@geron.org

Web, www.geron.org and Twitter, @geronsociety

Scientific organization of researchers, educators, and
professionals in the field of aging. Promotes the study of
aging and the application of research to public policy. Interests include health and civic engagement.

Leading Age, 2519 Connecticut Ave. N.W., 20008-1520;
(202) 783-2242. Fax, (202) 783-2255. Katie Smith Sloan,
Chief Executive Officer.
General email, info@leadingage.org

Web, www.leadingage.org

Membership: nonprofit nursing homes, housing, and
health-related facilities for the elderly sponsored by religious, fraternal, labor, private, and governmental organizations. Conducts research on long-term care for the elderly;
sponsors institutes and workshops on accreditation, financing, and institutional life. Monitors legislation and regulations.

National Assn. for Home Care and Hospice, 228 7th St.
S.E., 20003; (202) 547-7424. Fax, (202) 547-3540.
William A. Dombi, President.
General email, info@nahc.org

Web, www.nahc.org and Twitter, @OfficialNAHC

Membership: hospice, home care, and private-duty
providers. Advocates the rights of the aged, disabled, and
ill to remain independent in their own homes as long as
possible. Monitors legislation and regulations.

National Caucus and Center on Black Aging, Inc., 1220
L St. N.W., #800, 20005-2407; (202) 637-8400. Fax, (202)
347-0895. Karyne Jones, President.
General email, support@ncba-aged.org

Web, www.ncba-aged.org and Twitter, @NCBADC

Concerned with issues that affect older Black Americans
and other minorities. Sponsors employment and housing
programs for older adults and education and training for
professionals in gerontology. Monitors legislation and regulations.

National Council on Aging, 251 18th St. South, #500,
Arlington, VA 22202; (571) 527-3900. Fax, (571) 527-3901.
James P. (Jim) Firman, President, ext. 1. Eldercare
locator, (800) 677-1116. Press, (571) 527-3914.
General email, info@ncoa.org

Web, www.ncoa.org, Twitter, @NCOAging and
Facebook, www.facebook.com/NCOAging

Promotes the physical, mental, and emotional health of
older persons and studies adult day care and community-
based long-term care. Monitors legislation and regulations.

National Hispanic Council on Aging, 2201 12th St. N.W.,
#101, 20009; (202) 347-9733. Fax, (202) 347-9735.
Yanira Cruz, President.
General email, nhcoa@nhcoa.org

Web, www.nhcoa.org and Twitter, @NHCOA

Membership: senior citizens, health care workers, professionals in the field of aging, and others in the United
States and Puerto Rico who are interested in topics related
to Hispanics and aging. Provides research training, policy
analysis, consulting, and technical assistance; sponsors
seminars, workshops, and management internships.

**National Long-Term Care Ombudsman Resource
Center,** 1001 Connecticut Ave. N.W. #632, 20036; (202)
332-2275. Fax, (202) 332-2949. Amity Overall Laib,
Director.
General email, ombudcenter@theconsumervoice.org

Web, www.ltcombudsman.org

Provides technical assistance, management guidance,
policy analysis, and program development information on
behalf of state and substate ombudsman programs. (Affiliate of the National Consumer Voice for Quality Long-Term
Care.)

Prenatal, Maternal, and Child Health Care

▶**AGENCIES**

Assistant Secretary for Health (OASH) *(Health and Human Services Dept.)*, *Adolescent Health (OAH)*, 1101 Wootton Pkwy., #700, Rockville, MD 20852; (240) 453-2846. Evelyn Kappeler, Director.
General email, oah.gov@hhs.gov

Web, www.hhs.gov/ash/oah

Supports and evaluates teen pregnancy prevention programs; implements the Pregnancy Assistance Fund; coordinates HHS efforts related to adolescent health promotion and disease prevention.

Centers for Medicare and Medicaid Services (CMS) *(Health and Human Services Dept.)*, *Center for Medicaid and CHIP Services (CMCS)*, 7500 Security Blvd., C5-21-17, Baltimore, MD 21244; (202) 690-7428. Chris Traylor, Deputy Administrator (Acting).
Web, www.cms.gov/About-CMS/Agency-Information/CMSLeadership/office_CMCSC.html and www.medicaid.gov

Develops health care policies and programs for needy children under Medicaid; works with the Public Health Service and other related agencies to coordinate the department's child health resources. (Known as the Children's Health Insurance Program.)

Environmental Protection Agency (EPA), *Children's Health Protection (OCHP)*, 1301 Constitution Ave., #1144, MC 1107T, 20460; (202) 564-2188. Fax, (202) 564-2733. Dr. Ruth A. Etzel, Director.
Web, www2.epa.gov/aboutepa/about-office-childrens-health-protection-ochp and www.epa.gov/children

Supports and facilitates the EPA's efforts to protect children's health from environmental risks through safe chemicals management. Provides leadership on interagency Healthy Homes Work Group and Healthy School Environments Initiative. Offers grants through the Office of Children's Health Protection and Environmental Education (OCHPEE).

Eunice Kennedy Shriver National Institute of Child Health and Human Development (NICHD) *(National Institutes of Health)*, 31 Center Dr., Bldg. 31, #2A03, MSC 2425, Bethesda, MD 20892-2425 (mailing address: NICHD Information Resource Center, P.O. Box 3006, Rockville, MD 20847); (301) 496-1848. Fax, (301) 402-1104. Dr. Diana W. Bianchi, Director. Press, (301) 496-5133. Toll-free, (800) 370-2943. Toll-free fax, (866) 760-5947.
General email, nichdinformationresourcescenter @mail.nih.gov

Web, www.nichd.nih.gov, Twitter, @NICHD_NIH and Facebook, www.facebook.com/nichdgov

Supports and conducts research in biomedical, behavioral, and social sciences related to child and maternal health, medical rehabilitation, and reproductive sciences.

Interests include demography, social sciences, and population dynamics; male/female fertility and infertility; developing and evaluating contraceptive methods; safety and efficacy of pharmaceuticals for pregnant women, infants, and children; maternal/pediatric HIV/AIDS infections (including HIV/AIDS and Zika), transmission, and treatment associated infections; pediatric growth and endocrine research; child development and behavior; developmental biology, typical and atypical development; intellectual and developmental disabilities; gynecologic health conditions, including pelvic floor disorders; pregnancy, labor, and delivery; fetal and infant health; sudden infant death syndrome (SIDS); childhood injury and critical illness; genetics, genomics, and rare diseases; epidemiology and biostatistics; health behavior; medical rehabilitation, including brain injury, stroke, and spinal cord injury, cerebral palsy, and spina bifida.

Eunice Kennedy Shriver National Institute of Child Health and Human Development (NICHD) *(National Institutes of Health)*, *Child Development and Behavior Branch (CDBB)*, 6710B Rockledge Dr., Bldg. 6710B, Room 2422, MSC 7002, Bethesda, MD 20817; (301) 402-7886. Andrew Bremer, Chief (Acting).
Web, www.nichd.nih.gov/about/org/der/branches/cdbb

Develops scientific initiatives and supports research and research training relevant to the psychological, neurobiological, language, behavioral, and educational development and health of children. Major research areas include behavioral pediatrics, health promotion, cognitive development, behavioral neuroscience, psychobiology, early learning and school readiness, language and bilingualism, biliteracy, math and science cognition and learning, learning disabilities, social and emotional development, and child and family processes.

Eunice Kennedy Shriver National Institute of Child Health and Human Development (NICHD) *(National Institutes of Health)*, *Developmental Biology and Structural Variation Branch (DBSVB)*, 6710B Rockledge Dr., Bldg. 6710B, Room 2441, MSC 7002, Bethesda, MD 20817; (301) 496-5541. Fax, (301) 480-0303. James Coulombe, Chief.
Web, www.nichd.nih.gov/about/org/der/branches/dbsvb

Supports research and training focused on understanding the biological processes that control normal embryonic development, as well as the mechanisms that underlie molecular susceptibility and etiology of structural birth defects. Major program areas for the branch include developmental genetics, systems developmental biology, early embryonic development and differentiation, biophysics/biomechanics of development, developmental neurobiology and neural crest differentiation, organogenesis, regeneration and regenerative medicine, stem cells and induced pluripotent stem cells, and structural birth defects.

Eunice Kennedy Shriver National Institute of Child Health and Human Development (NICHD) *(National Institutes of Health)*, *Maternal and Pediatric Infectious Disease Branch (MPIDB)*, 6710B Rockledge Dr., Bldg.

6710B, Room 2113, MSC 7002, Bethesda, MD 20817; (301) 435-6868. Fax, (301) 480-3882. Dr. Rohan Hazra, Chief. Web, www.nichd.nih.gov/about/org/der/branches/mpidb

Supports and conducts research into the epidemiology, natural history, pathogenesis, transmission, treatment, and prevention of infectious diseases, including congenital infections such as Zika and cytomegalovirus; tropical diseases specifically affecting children and pregnant women; and vaccine-preventable disease in infants, children, adolescents, and women.

Eunice Kennedy Shriver National Institute of Child Health and Human Development (NICHD) *(National Institutes of Health), Obstetric and Pediatric Pharmacology and Therapeutics Branch (OPPTB),* 6710B Rockledge Dr., Bldg.6710B, Room 2113, MSC 7002, Bethesda, MD 20817; (301) 435-6868. Fax, (301) 480-3882. Dr. Rohan Hazra, Chief (Acting). Web, www.nichd.nih.gov/about/org/der/branches/opptb

Promotes basic, translational, and clinical research to improve the safety and efficacy of therapeutics, primarily pharmaceuticals, and to ensure centralization and coordination of research, clinical trials, and drug development activities for obstetric and pediatric populations. Develops and supports an understanding of how to appropriately treat disease during pregnancy, infancy, childhood, and adolescence using therapeutic approaches, to assure that medications are appropriately tested for dosing, safety, and effectiveness within their target populations.

Eunice Kennedy Shriver National Institute of Child Health and Human Development (NICHD) *(National Institutes of Health), Pediatric Growth and Nutrition Branch (PGNB),* 6710B Rockledge Dr., Bldg. 6710B, Room 2444, MSC 7002, Bethesda, MD 20817; (301) 402-7886. Andrew Bremer, Chief. Web, www.nichd.nih.gov/about/org/der/branches/pgnb

Supports research on understanding basic and clinical aspects of growth and development, including the biological processes that underlie normal growth and development, as well as research on how these biological processes go awry. Major research programs include how nutrition promotes healthy growth and development; lactation and breastfeeding; the causes of obesity in childhood and sequelae of childhood obesity in adulthood; the genetic, nutritional, and hormonal antecedents of bone health and the origins of osteoporosis; the neuroendocrine basis of growth and the onset of puberty; and the development of the hypothalamo-pituitary adrenal, gonadal, and thyroid axes.

Eunice Kennedy Shriver National Institute of Child Health and Human Development (NICHD) *(National Institutes of Health), Pediatric Trauma and Critical Illness Branch (PTCIB),* 6710B Rockledge Dr., Bldg. 6710B, Room 2336, MSC 7002, Bethesda, MD 20817; (301) 496-1514. Valerie Maholmes, Chief. Web, www.nichd.nih.gov/about/org/der/branches/ptcib

Supports research and research training focused on preventing, treating, and reducing all forms of childhood trauma, injury, and critical illness across the continuum of care. Topics of interest include respiratory failure,

multiple organ dysfunction syndrome, traumatic brain injury, sepsis, end-of-life issues in pediatric intensive care unit populations, child maltreatment, violence, and other causes of severe traumatic injury.

Eunice Kennedy Shriver National Institute of Child Health and Human Development (NICHD) *(National Institutes of Health), Pregnancy and Perinatology Branch (PPB),* 6710B Rockledge Dr., Bldg. 6710B, Room 2320, MSC 7002, Bethesda, MD 20817; (301) 496-5577. Dr. Caroline Signore, Branch Chief (Acting). Web, www.nichd.nih.gov/about/org/der/branches/ppb

Supports research to improve the health of women before, during, and after pregnancy; reduce the number of preterm births and other birth complications; increase infant survival free from disease and disability; and ensure the long-term health of mothers and their children. Supports training grants for medical researchers in maternal-fetal medicine, neonatology, and related fields.

Food And Drug Administration (FDA) *(Health and Human Services Dept.), Pediatric Therapeutics (OPT),* White Oak Bldg. 32, 10903 New Hampshire Ave., Silver Spring, MD 20993-0002; (301) 796-8659. Fax, (301) 847-8640. Dr. Susan McCune, Director. General email, opt@fda.hhs.gov Web, www.fda.gov/AboutFDA/CentersOffices/ OfficeofMedicalProductsandTobacco/ OfficeofScienceandHealthCoordination/ucm2018186.htm

Works to provide timely access to medical products proven to be safe and effective for children. Designs clinical studies that expand the knowledge of pediatrics.

Health Resources and Services Administration (HRSA) *(Health and Human Services Dept.), Maternal and Child Health Bureau (MCHB),* 5600 Fishers Lane, #18W, Rockville, MD 20857; (301) 443-2170. Fax, (301) 480-1312. Aaron Lopata, Chief Medical Officer; Michael Warren, Associate Administrator. Web, www.mchb.hrsa.gov

Administers programs for prenatal, maternal, and child health care. Funds block grants to states for mothers and children and for children with special health needs; awards funding for research training, genetic disease testing, counseling and information dissemination, hemophilia diagnostic and treatment centers, and demonstration projects to improve the health of mothers and children. Interests also include emergency medical services for children, universal newborn hearing screening, and traumatic brain injury.

Health Resources and Services Administration (HRSA) *(Health and Human Services Dept.), National Vaccine Injury Compensation Program (VICP),* 5600 Fishers Lane, Parklawn Bldg., #11C-26, Rockville, MD 20857; (800) 338-2382. Dr. Avril Houston, Director (Acting). Web, www.hrsa.gov/vaccinecompensation

Provides a no-fault alternative to the traditional legal system for resolving vaccine injury petitions for individuals thought to be injured by certain childhood vaccines; including rotavirus vaccine; diphtheria and tetanus toxoids and pertussis vaccine; measles, mumps, and rubella vaccine; varicella, hepatitis A and B, HiB vaccine; oral polio and inactivated polio vaccines; and influenza, pneumococcal conjugate, meningococcal, and human papillomavirus vaccines.

▶**NONGOVERNMENTAL**

American Academy of Child and Adolescent Psychiatry, *3615 Wisconsin Ave. N.W., 20016-3007; (202) 966-7300. Fax, (202) 464-0131. Heidi B. Fordi, Executive Director. General email, communications@aacap.org*

Web, www.aacap.org, Twitter, @aacap and Facebook, www.facebook.com/American-Academy-of-Child-Adolescent-Psychiatry/1454598665751

Government Affairs, gov@aacap.org

Membership: child and adolescent psychiatrists trained to promote healthy development and to evaluate, diagnose, and treat children, adolescents, and families affected by mental illness. Sponsors annual meeting and review for medical board examinations. Provides information on child and adolescent development and mental illnesses. Monitors international research and U.S. legislation concerning children with mental illness.

American Academy of Pediatrics, *Federal Affairs, 601 13th St. N.W., #400N, 20005; (202) 347-8600. Fax, (202) 393-6137. Mark Del Monte, Chief Executive Officer (Acting). Toll-free information, (800) 336-5475. General email, kids1st@aap.org*

Web, www.aap.org, Twitter, @AmerAcadPeds and Facebook, www.facebook.com/AmerAcadPeds

Advocacy email, FederalAdvocacy@aap.org

Advocates maternal and child health legislation and regulations. Interests include increased access and coverage for persons under age twenty-one, immunizations, injury prevention, environmental hazards, child abuse, emergency medical services, biomedical research, Medicaid, disabilities, pediatric AIDS, substance abuse, and nutrition. (Headquarters in Elk Grove Village, Ill.)

American College of Nurse-Midwives, *8403 Colesville Rd., #1550, Silver Spring, MD 20910-6374; (240) 485-1800. Fax, (240) 485-1818. Sheri A. Sesay-Tufflour, Chief Executive Officer, (240) 485-1810; Amy Kohl, Director of Government Affairs, (240) 485-1806. General email, info@acnm.org*

Web, www.midwife.org, Twitter, @ACNMmidwives and Facebook, www.facebook.com/ACNMmidwives

Membership: certified nurse-midwives and certified midwives who preside at deliveries and provide postnatal care or primary gynecological care. Establishes clinical practice studies. Interests include preventive health care for women.

American College of Obstetricians and Gynecologists, *409 12th St. S.W., 20024-9998 (mailing address: P.O. Box 70620, Washington, DC 20024-9998); (202) 638-5577. Dr. Lisa M. Hollier, Executive Vice President (Acting). Toll-free, (800) 673-8444.*

General email, communications@acog.org

Web, www.acog.org, Twitter, @acognews and Facebook, www.facebook.com/ACOGNational

Membership: medical specialists in obstetrics and gynecology. Disseminates standards of clinical practice and promotes patient involvement in medical care. Provides mentorship programs and educational guidelines. Monitors legislation, regulations, and international research on maternal and child health care.

Assn. of Maternal and Child Health Programs (AMCHP), *1825 K St. N.W., #250, 20006; (202) 775-0436. Fax, (202) 478-5120. Jonathan Webb, Chief Executive Officer. General email, info@amchp.org*

Web, www.amchp.org and Twitter, @DC_AMCHP

Membership: state public health leaders and others. Works to improve the health and well-being of women, children, and youth, including those with special health care needs and their families.

Assn. of Women's Health, Obstetric, and Neonatal Nurses (AWHONN), *1800 M St. N.W.,#7405, 20036; (202) 261-2400. Fax, (202) 728-0575. Suzanne C. Berry, Chief Executive Officer. Customer Service, (800) 354-2268. Toll-free, (800) 673-8499. General email, customerservice@awhonn*

Web, www.awhonn.org and Twitter, @AWHONN

Promotes the health of women and newborns. Provides nurses with information and support. Produces educational materials and legislative programs.

Children's Defense Fund, *25 E St. N.W., 20001; (202) 628-8787. Fax, (202) 662-3510. Marian Wright Edelman, President Emerita; Max Lesko, National Executive Director. Toll-free, (800) 233-1200. General email, cdfinfo@childrensdefense.org*

Web, www.childrensdefense.org and Twitter, @ChildDefender

Advocacy group concerned with programs for children and youth. Assesses adequacy of the Early and Periodic Screening, Diagnosis, and Treatment Program for Medicaid-eligible children. Promotes adequate prenatal care for adolescent and lower-income women; works to prevent adolescent pregnancy.

Children's Dental Health Project (CDHP), *1020 19th St. N.W., #400, 20036; (202) 833-8288. Meg Booth, Executive Director, (202) 833-8288. Press, (202) 417-3600. General email, info@cdhp.org*

Web, www.cdhp.org and Twitter, @Teeth_Matter

Coalition comprising policymakers, dental care professionals, and individuals seeking innovative and cost-effective solutions for improving children's dental health. Provides information to policymakers, oral health care providers, and media about dental care provisions of the Affordable Care Act; monitors Medicaid and other insurance programs; promotes prevention strategies.

Children's Hospital Assn., *Washington Office,* 600 13th St. N.W., #500, 20005; (202) 753-5500. *Fax, (202) 347-5147. Mark Wietecha, President.*
Web, www.childrenshospitals.org, Twitter, @hospitals4kids and Facebook, www.facebook.com/childrenshospitals

Promotes education and research on child health care related to more than 220 children's hospitals in the United States and internationally; compiles statistics and provides information on pediatric hospitalizations. (Merger of the Child Health Corporation of America, National Assn. of Children's Hospitals and Related Institutions, and National Assn. of Children's Hospitals.)

Guttmacher Institute, *Public Policy,* 1301 Connecticut Ave. N.W., #700, 20036-3902; (202) 296-4012. *Fax, (202) 223-5756. Rachel Benson Gold, Vice President of Public Policy; Heather D. Boonstra, Director of Public Policy.* Toll-free, (877) 823-0262.
General email, policyinfo@guttmacher.org
Web, www.guttmacher.org and Twitter, @Guttmacher

Conducts research, policy analysis, and public education in reproductive health issues, including maternal and child health. (Headquarters in New York.)

Healthy Teen Network, 1501 St. Paul St., #114, Baltimore, MD 21202; (410) 685-0410. *Fax, (410) 685-0481. Janet Max, President (Acting).*
General email, info@healthyteennetwork.org
Web, www.healthyteennetwork.org and Twitter, @healthyteen

Membership: health and social work professionals, community and state leaders, and individuals. Promotes services to prevent and resolve problems associated with adolescent sexuality, pregnancy, and parenting. Helps to develop stable and supportive family relationships through program support and evaluation. Monitors legislation and regulations.

Lamaze International, 2025 M St. N.W., #800, 20036-3309; (202) 367-1128. *Fax, (202) 367-2128. Linda Harmon, Executive Director.*
General email, info@lamaze.org
Web, www.lamaze.org, Twitter, @LamazeOnline and Facebook, www.facebook.com/LamazeChildbirth

Membership: supporters of the Lamaze philosophy of childbirth, including parents, physicians, childbirth educators, and other health professionals. Trains and certifies Lamaze educators. Provides referral service for parents seeking Lamaze classes.

March of Dimes, *Government Affairs,* 1550 Crystal Dr., #1300, Arlington, VA 22202; (202) 659-1800. *Fax, (202) 296-2964. Cynthia Pellegrini, Senior Vice President for Public Policy and Government Affairs; Nikki Garro, Director of Public Policy Research.* Toll-free, (888) 663-4637.
Web, www.marchofdimes.org/advocacy-and-government-affairs-issues-and-advocacy-priorities.aspx and Twitter, @MarchofDimes

Works to prevent birth defects, low birth weight, and infant mortality. Awards grants for research and provides funds for treatment of birth defects. Medical services grantees provide prenatal counseling. Monitors legislation and regulations. (Headquarters in White Plains, N.Y.)

The National Alliance to Advance Adolescent Health, 1615 M St. N.W., #290, 20036; (202) 223-1500. *Margaret A. McManus, President.*
General email, jshorr@thenationalalliance.org
Web, www.thenationalalliance.org and Twitter, @TheNatlAlliance

Seeks to increase adolescents' access to integrated physical, behavioral, and sexual health care to reduce health risk behaviors, identify health problems earlier, and equip adolescents to manage their health conditions. Promotes expanded comprehensive clinical and community prevention health strategies for adolescents.

National Assn. of School Psychologists, 4340 East-West Hwy., #402, Bethesda, MD 20814; (301) 657-0270. *Fax, (301) 657-0275. Kathleen Minke, Executive Director.* Toll-free, (866) 331-6277.
General email, kcowan@naspweb.org
Web, www.nasponline.org and Twitter, @nasponline

Membership: graduate education students and professors, school psychologists, supervisors of school psychological services, and others who provide mental health services for children in school settings. Provides professional education and development to members. Provides school safety and crisis response direct services. Fosters information exchange; advises local, state, and federal policymakers and agencies that develop children's mental health educational services. Develops professional ethics and standards.

National Center for Education in Maternal and Child Health, 3300 Whitehaven St. N.W., 20007-2292 *(mailing address: Georgetown University, Box 571272, Washington, DC 20057-1272); Fax, (202) 784-9777. Rochelle Mayer, Director, (202) 784-9552; Olivia Pickett, Director of Library Services.*
General email, mchgroup@georgetown.edu
Web, www.ncemch.org and Twitter, @NCEMCH

Collects and disseminates information about maternal and child health to health professionals and the general public. Carries out special projects for the U.S. Maternal and Child Health Bureau. Library open to the public by appointment. (Affiliated with McCourt School of Public Policy, Georgetown University.)

National Organization on Fetal Alcohol Syndrome, 1200 Eton Court N.W., 3rd Floor, 20007; (202) 785-4585. *Fax, (202) 466-6456. Tom Donaldson, President. Information, (800) 666-6327.*
General email, information@nofas.org
Web, www.nofas.org and Twitter, @nofas_usa

Works to eradicate fetal alcohol syndrome and alcohol-related birth defects through public education, conferences,

Information Sources on Women's Health

AIDSinfo (NIH), (800) 448-0440; www.aidsinfo.nih.gov

American College of Obstetricians and Gynecologists, (202) 638-5577; www.acog.org

American Society for Reproductive Medicine, (205) 978-5000; www.asrm.org

Breast Cancer Network of Strength, After Breast Cancer Diagnosis, (414) 977-1780; www.abcdbreastcancersupport.org

Guttmacher Institute, (202) 296-4012; Toll-free, (877) 823-0262; www.guttmacher.org

Healthfinder (HHS), www.healthfinder.gov

Health Resources and Services Administration (HRSA), Maternal and Child Health (HHS), (301) 443-2170; www.mchb.hrsa.gov

Lamaze International, (202) 367-1128; www.lamaze.org

Medline (NIH), https://medlineplus.gov/women.html

National Breast Cancer Coalition, (202) 296-7477; Toll-free, (800) 622-2838; www.breastcancerdeadline2020.org

National Cancer Institute (NIH), (800) 422-6237; www.cancer.gov

National Institute of Aging (NIH), Information Center, (800) 222-2225, TTY, (800) 222-4225; www.nia.nih.gov

National Osteoporosis Foundation, (202) 223-2226; Toll-free, (800) 231-4222; www.nof.org

National Research Center for Women and Families, (202) 223-4000; www.center4research.org

National Women's Health Information Center (HHS), (800) 994-9662; www.womenshealth.gov

National Women's Health Network, (202) 682-2640; www.nwhn.org

Planned Parenthood Federation of America, (202) 973-4800; www.plannedparenthood.org

U.S. National Library of Medicine (NIH), Communications, (301) 594-5983; www.nlm.nih.gov

Women's Mental Health Consortium, National Institute of Mental Health (NIH), (866) 615-6464; www.nimh.nih.gov; wmhcny.org

---

medical school curricula, and partnerships with federal programs interested in fetal alcohol syndrome.

Zero to Three: National Center for Infants, Toddlers, and Families, *1255 23rd St. N.W., #350, 20037; (202) 638-1144. Fax, (202) 638-0851. Matthew Melmed, Executive Director. Publications, (800) 899-4301.*
General email, 0to3@presswarehouse.com

Web, www.zerotothree.org and Twitter, @zerotothree

Works to improve infant health, mental health, and development. Sponsors training programs for professionals, offers fellowships, and publishes books, curricula, assessment tools, videos, and practical guidebooks. Provides private and government organizations with information on early childhood development issues.

Women's Health

▶**AGENCIES**

Assistant Secretary for Health (OASH) *(Health and Human Services Dept.), Women's Health (OWH), 200 Independence Ave. S.W., #712E, 20201; (202) 690-7650. Fax, (202) 205-2631. Dr. Dorothy Fink, Director. Information, (800) 994-9662. TTY, (888) 220-5446.*
General email, womenshealth@hhs.gov

Web, www.womenshealth.gov, www.girlshealth.gov and Twitter, @womenshealth

Promotes better health for girls and women as well as health equity through sex/gender-specific approaches. Methods include educating health professionals and motivating behavior change in consumers through the dissemination of health information.

Eunice Kennedy Shriver National Institute of Child Health and Human Development (NICHD) *(National Institutes of Health), Gynecologic Health and Disease Branch (GHDB), 6710B Rockledge Dr., Bldg. 6710B, Room 2440, MSC 7002, Bethesda, MD 20817; (301) 480-1646. Fax, (301) 480-3668. Dr. Lisa Halvorson, Chief.*
Web, www.nichd.nih.gov/about/org/der/branches/ghdb

Supports basic, translational, and clinical programs and research training programs related to gynecologic health throughout the reproductive life span, beginning at puberty and extending through early menopause. Areas of interest include menstrual disorders, uterine fibroids, endometriosis, ovarian cysts and polycystic ovary syndrome, pelvic floor disorders, as well as studies of the mechanisms underlying chronic pelvic pain, vulvodynia, and dysmenorrhea. Obstetric fistula and female genital cutting are also of interest as they apply to both international and immigrant communities, and the role of genomics and epigenomics in elucidating etiology and providing novel approaches for treatment options in an array of gynecologic disorders are also of interest.

Eunice Kennedy Shriver National Institute of Child Health and Human Development (NICHD) *(National Institutes of Health), Pediatric Growth and Nutrition Branch (PGNB), 6710B Rockledge Dr., Bldg. 6710B, Room 2444, MSC 7002, Bethesda, MD 20817; (301) 402-7886. Andrew Bremer, Chief.*
Web, www.nichd.nih.gov/about/org/der/branches/pgnb

Supports research to understand basic and clinical aspects of growth and development, including the biological processes that underlie normal growth and development, as well as research on how these biological processes go awry. Major research programs include how nutrition promotes healthy growth and development; lactation and breastfeeding; the causes of obesity in childhood and sequelae of childhood obesity in adulthood; the genetic, nutritional, and hormonal antecedents of bone health and the origins of osteoporosis; the neuroendocrine basis of growth and the onset of puberty; and the development of the hypothalamo-pituitary adrenal, gonadal, and thyroid axes.

Food and Drug Administration (FDA) *(Health and Human Services Dept.), Women's Health (OWH),* White Oak Bldg. 32, 10903 New Hampshire Ave., #2333, Silver Spring, MD 20993; (301) 796-9440. Fax, (301) 847-8604. *Kaveeta P. Vasisht, Associate Commissioner (Acting).*
General email, marsha.henderson@fda.hhs.gov

Web, www.fda.gov/AboutFDA/CentersOffices/OC/ OfficeofWomensHealth and Twitter, @FDAWomen

Supports scientific research on women's health and collaborates with other government agencies and national organizations to sponsor scientific and consumer outreach on women's health issues. Interests include breast cancer, cardiovascular disease, diabetes, pregnancy, menopause, and the safe use of medications.

Health Resources and Services Administration (HRSA) *(Health and Human Services Dept.), Women's Health (OWH),* 5600 Fishers Lane, Rockville, MD 20857; (301) 443-8664. Sabrina Matoff-Stepp, Director. Toll-free, (800) 221-9393.
Web, www.hrsa.gov/about/organization/bureaus/owh

Works to improve health care by reducing sex- and gender-based disparities. Support dissemination of information on topics related to women's health, including health insurance and violence prevention.

National Institutes of Health (NIH) *(Health and Human Services Dept.), Research on Women's Health (ORWH),* 6707 Democracy Blvd., #400, MSC 5484, Bethesda, MD 20892-5484; (301) 402-1770. Fax, (301) 402-1798. *Dr. Janine Austin Clayton, Director.*
General email, ORWHinfo@mail.nih.gov

Web, http://orwh.od.nih.gov and Twitter, @NIH_ORWH

Collaborates with NIH institutes and centers to establish NIH goals and policies for research related to women's health and sex-based or gender-based studies of the differences between women and men. Supports expansion of research on diseases, conditions, and disorders that affect women; monitors inclusion of women and minorities in clinical research; develops opportunities and support for recruitment and advancement of women in biomedical careers.

Women's Health Initiative (WHI), 2 Rockledge Center, 6701 Rockledge Dr., #9192, MS 7913, Bethesda, MD 20892-7935; (301) 435-6667. Fax, (301) 480-5158. Shari Ludham, WHI Contact. Information, (301) 592-8573. Press, (301) 496-4236.

General email, helpdesk@whi.org

Web, www.whi.org

Supports clinical trials and observational studies to improve understanding of the causes and prevention of major diseases affecting the health of women. Interests include cardiovascular disease, cancer, fractures, and hormone therapy. Sponsored by the National Heart, Lung, and Blood Institute (NHLBI).

▶**NONGOVERNMENTAL**

Assn. of Women's Health, Obstetric, and Neonatal Nurses (AWHONN), 1800 M St. N.W.,#7405, 20036; (202) 261-2400. Fax, (202) 728-0575. Suzanne C. Berry, Chief Executive Officer. Customer Service, (800) 354-2268. Toll-free, (800) 673-8499.
General email, customerservice@awhonn

Web, www.awhonn.org and Twitter, @AWHONN

Promotes the health of women and newborns. Provides nurses with information and support. Produces educational materials and legislative programs.

Black Women's Health Imperative, 55 M St. S.E., #940, 20003; (202) 548-4000. Fax, (202) 543-9743. *Linda Goler Blount, President.*
General email, imperative@bwhi.org

Web, www.bwhi.org and Twitter, @blkwomenshealth

Provides the tools and information for African American women to prevent health problems, to recognize symptoms and early warning signs, and to understand all of the options available for their specific health situations. Achieves these ends through community outreach, advocacy, resources and research, education, and mobilization. (Formerly the National Black Women's Health Project.)

Institute for Women's Policy Research (IWPR), 1200 18th St. N.W., #301, 20036; (202) 785-5100. Fax, (202) 833-4362. Heidi Hartmann, President.
General email, iwpr@iwpr.org

Web, www.iwpr.org, Twitter, @IWPResearch and Facebook, www.facebook.com/iwpresearch

Public policy research organization that focuses on women's issues, including health care and comprehensive family and medical leave programs.

National Center for Health Research, 1001 Connecticut Ave. N.W., #1100, 20036; (202) 223-4000. Fax, (202) 223-4242. Diana Zuckerman, President.
General email, info@center4research.org

Web, www.center4research.org and Twitter, @NC4HR

Utilizes scientific and medical research to improve the quality of women's lives and the lives of family members. Seeks to educate policymakers about medical and scientific research through hearings, meetings, and publications. Affiliated with the Cancer Prevention and Treatment Fund.

National Women's Health Network, 1413 K St. N.W., 4th Floor, 20005; (202) 682-2640. Fax, (202) 682-2648. *Cynthia Pearson, Executive Director.*

General email, nwhn@nwhn.org

Web, www.nwhn.org, Twitter, @TheNWHN and Facebook, www.facebook.com/TheNWHN

Health questions, healthquestions@nwhn.org

Acts as an information clearinghouse on women's health issues; monitors federal health policies and legislation. Interests include older women's health issues, sexual and reproductive health, contraception, menopause, abortion, unsafe drugs, AIDS, breast cancer, and universal health.

Society for Women's Health Research, *1025 Connecticut Ave. N.W., #1104, 20036; (202) 223-8224. Fax, (202) 833-3472. Amy M. Miller, President.*

General email, info@swhr.org

Web, https://swhr.org and Twitter, @SWHR

Promotes public and private funding for women's health research and changes in public policies affecting women's health. Seeks to advance women as leaders in the health professions and to inform policymakers, educators, and the public of research outcomes. Sponsors meetings; produces reports; conducts educational campaigns.

WomenHeart: National Coalition for Women With Heart Disease, *1100 17th St. N.W., #500, 20036; (202) 728-7199. Fax, (202) 688-2861. Vacant, Chief Executive Officer. Spanish hotline, (800) 676-6002.*

General email, mail@womenheart.org

Web, www.womenheart.org and Twitter, @WomenHeartOrg

Patient-centered organization that seeks to advance women's heart health through advocacy, community education, and patient support.

HEALTH TOPICS: RESEARCH AND ADVOCACY

General

▶**AGENCIES**

Assistant Secretary for Health (OASH) *(Health and Human Services Dept.), Human Research Protections (OHRP), Tower Bldg., 1101 Wootton Pkwy., #200, Rockville, MD 20852; (240) 453-6900. Fax, (240) 453-6909. Dr. Jerry Menikoff, Director. Toll-free, (866) 447-4777.*

General email, ohrp@hhs.gov

Web, www.hhs.gov/ohrp

Promotes the rights, welfare, and well-being of subjects involved in research conducted or supported by the Health and Human Services Dept.; helps to ensure that research is carried out in accordance with federal regulations by providing clarification and guidance, developing educational programs and materials, and maintaining regulatory oversight.

Eunice Kennedy Shriver National Institute of Child Health and Human Development (NICHD) *(National Institutes of Health), Division of Extramural Research*

(DER), 6710B Rockledge Dr., Bldg. 6710B, Room 2134, MSC 7002, Bethesda, MD 20817; (301) 496-8535. Dr. Della Hann, Director.

Web, www.nichd.nih.gov/about/org/der

Develops, implements, and coordinates cross-cutting, multidisciplinary research activities within NICHD's broad research portfolio, which includes biological, behavioral, and clinical research related to conception and pregnancy; normal and abnormal development in childhood; reproductive health; and population dynamics across the life span. Coordinates and funds research and training programs across the United States and many other countries through grants and contracts.

Food and Drug Administration (FDA) *(Health and Human Services Dept.), Center for Biologics Evaluation and Research (CBER), White Oak Bldg. 71, 10903 New Hampshire Ave., Silver Spring, MD 20993; (240) 402-8000. Fax, (301) 595-1310. Dr. Peter Marks, Director. Press and publications, (240) 402-7800. Toll-free, (800) 435-4709.*

Web, www.fda.gov/AboutFDA/CentersOffices/OfficeofMedicalProductsandTobacco/CBER and Twitter, @FDACBER

Regulates biological products for human use under applicable federal laws, including the Public Health Service Act and Federal Food Drug and Cosmetic Act. Interests include blood and blood products, vaccines, allergenics, gene therapies, human cells, tissues and cellular and tissue-based products.

Health Resources and Services Administration (HRSA) *(Health and Human Services Dept.), Healthcare Systems Bureau (HSB), Transplantation (DoT), 5600 Fishers Lane, #8W, Rockville, MD 20857; (301) 443-7577. Fax, (301) 594-6095. Frank Hollomon, Director (Acting).*

General email, donation@hrsa.gov

Web, www.organdonor.gov

Implements provisions of the National Organ Transplant Act. Provides information on federal programs involved in transplantation; supports the national network for deceased donor organ procurement and matching; maintains information on transplant recipients; awards grants to increase organ donation and transplantation.

Health Resources and Services Administration (HRSA), Healthcare Systems Bureau (HSB), *5600 Fishers Lane, Rockville, MD 20857; (301) 443-3300. Cheryl R. Dammons, Associate Administrator.*

Web, www.hrsa.gov/about/organization/bureaus/hsb/index.html

Administers programs in areas of public health, including organ donation and transplantation, poison control, bone marrow and cord blood transplantation, drug pricing, injury compensation, and Hansen's disease (leprosy).

Mark O. Hatfield Clinical Research Center *(National Institutes of Health), 10 Center Dr., Bethesda, MD 20892; (301) 496-4000. Dr. James K. Gilman, Chief Executive Officer, (301) 496-4114. Admissions, (301) 496-3315. Patient recruitment, (800) 411-1222.*

Web, http://clinicalcenter.nih.gov

Provides inpatient and outpatient care and conducts clinical research. Promotes the application of scientific laboratory research to benefit patient health and medical care. With the Warren Grant Magnuson Clinical Center, forms the NIH Clinical Center.

National Heart, Lung, and Blood Institute (NHLBI)
(National Institutes of Health), 31 Center Dr., Bldg. 31, #5A48, MSC 2486, Bethesda, MD 20892-2486; (301) 592-8573. Fax, (301) 402-0818. Dr. Gary H. Gibbons, Director, (301) 496-5166. Press, (301) 496-4236.
General email, nhlbiinfo@nhlbi.nih.gov
Web, www.nhlbi.nih.gov, Twitter, @nih_nhlbi and Facebook, www.facebook.com/NHLBI

Collects and disseminates information on diseases of the heart, lungs, and blood, with an emphasis on disease prevention. Works with patients, families, health care professionals, scientists, community organizations, and the media to promote the application of research results to address public health needs. Promotes international collaboration in its educational programs for scientists and clinicians.

National Institute of General Medical Sciences (NIGMS)
(National Institutes of Health), 45 Center Dr., #3AN44E, MSC 6200, Bethesda, MD 20892-6200; (301) 496-7301. Fax, (301) 402-0156. Jon R. Lorsch, Director.
General email, info@nigms.nih.gov
Web, www.nigms.nih.gov, Twitter, @NIGMS and Facebook, www.facebook.com/nigms.nih.gov

Primarily supports basic biomedical research and training that lays the foundation for advances in disease diagnosis, treatment, and prevention. Areas of special interest include bioinformatics, cell biology, developmental biology, physiology, biological chemistry genetics, and computational biology.

National Institute of General Medical Sciences (NIGMS)
(National Institutes of Health), Training, Workforce Development, and Diversity, 45 Center Dr., Bldg. 45, #2AS37, MSC 6200, Bethesda, MD 20892-6200; (301) 594-3900. Fax, (301) 480-2753. Dr. Alison Gammie, Director.
Web, http://nigms.nih.gov/training

Administers research and research training programs aimed at increasing the number of minority biomedical scientists. Funds grants, fellowships, faculty development awards, and development of research facilities.

National Institutes of Health (NIH) *(Health and Human Services Dept.),* 1 Center Dr., Bldg. 1, #344, MSC 0188, Bethesda, MD 20892-0148; (301) 496-4000. Fax, (301) 496-0017. Dr. Francis S. Collins, Director; Dr. Lawrence A. Tabak, Deputy Director. Press, (301) 496-5787. TTY, (301) 402-9612.
Web, www.nih.gov

Supports and conducts biomedical research on the causes and prevention of diseases; furnishes health professionals and the public with information.

National Institutes of Health (NIH) *(Health and Human Services Dept.), Center for Information Technology*
(CIT), 6555 Rock Spring Dr., #3G04, Bethesda, MD 20817; (301) 496-4357. Fax, (301) 402-1754. Andrea T. Norris, Director. Toll Free, (888) 319-4357. TTY, (301) 496-8294.
Web, http://cit.nih.gov

Responsible for incorporating computers into biomedical research information, technology, security, and administrative procedures of the NIH.

National Institutes of Health (NIH) *(Health and Human Services Dept.), Center for Scientific Review (CSR),* 6701 Rockledge Dr., #3030, MSC 7768, Bethesda, MD 20892-7776; (301) 435-1111. Fax, (301) 480-3965. Noni Byrnes, Director, (301) 435-1023.
Web, www.csr.nih.gov

Conducts scientific merit review of research grant and fellowship applications submitted to the NIH. Participates in formulating grant and award policies.

National Institutes of Health (NIH) *(Health and Human Services Dept.), National Center for Advancing Translational Sciences (NCATS),* 1 Democracy Plaza, 9th Floor, #900, 6701 Democracy Blvd., MSC 4874, Bethesda, MD 20892-4874 (mailing address: Use zip code 20817 for express mail.); (301) 594-8966. Dr. Christopher P. Austin, Director. Press, (301) 435-0888.
General email, info@ncats.nih.gov
Web, www.ncats.nih.gov

Works in partnership with regulatory, academic, nonprofit, and private sectors to identify and overcome hurdles that slow the development of effective treatments and cures.

National Institutes of Health (NIH) *(Health and Human Services Dept.), National Center for Complementary and Integrative Health (NICCIH),* 9000 Rockville Pike, MSC282, Bethesda, MD 20892; (301) 435-6826. Fax, (301) 402-4741. Dr. Helene Langevin, Director.
Information, (888) 644-6226. TTY, (866) 464-3615.
General email, info@nccih.nih.gov
Web, www.nccih.nih.gov

Conducts and supports research on complementary and alternative medicine; trains researchers and disseminates information to practitioners and the public.

National Institutes of Health (NIH) *(Health and Human Services Dept.), Stem Cell Task Force,* 9000 Rockville Pike, 31 Center Dr., Bldg. 31, #8A52, MSC2540, Bethesda, MD 20892-2540; (301) 496-3167. Dr. Walter J. Koroshetz, Chair.
General email, stemcell@mail.nih.gov
Web, http://stemcells.nih.gov

The federal government's primary source for stem cell research, policy, and funding. Enables and speeds the pace of stem cell research by identifying resources and developing measures to enhance such resources.

National Library of Medicine *(National Institutes of Health),* 8600 Rockville Pike, Bldg. 38, #2E17, MSC 3808, Bethesda, MD 20894; (301) 496-6308. Fax, (301) 402-1384. Dr. Patricia Flatley Brennan, Director, (301) 496-6221.

Local and International, (301) 594-5983. TTY, (800) 735-2258.

General email, custserv@nlm.nih.gov

Web, www.nlm.nih.gov, Twitter, @nlm_news and PubMed Central, www.ncbi.nlm.nih.gov/pmc

Offers medical library services and computer-based reference service to the public, health professionals, libraries in medical schools and hospitals, and research institutions. Operates a toxicology information service for the scientific community, industry, and federal agencies. Assists medical libraries through the National Network of Libraries of Medicine. Assists in the improvement of basic library resources. Reading room open to the public Monday through Friday, 8:30 a.m.–5:00 p.m.

National Library of Medicine *(National Institutes of Health), Health Information Programs Development,* 8600 Rockville Pike, Bldg. 38, #2S20, MSC 12, Bethesda, MD 20894; (301) 496-2311. Fax, (301) 496-4450. Michael F. Huerta, Director, (301) 496-8834.

General email, custserv@nlm.nih.gov

Web, www.nlm.nih.gov

Facilitates worldwide use of the library's medical databases through agreements with individual nations, international organizations, and commercial vendors. Helps the library acquire and share international biomedical literature.

National Library of Medicine *(National Institutes of Health), Lister Hill National Center for Biomedical Communications,* 8600 Rockville Pike, Bldg. 38A, #07N707, Bethesda, MD 20894; (301) 496-4441. Dr. Clement McDonald, Director. Visitor Center, (301) 496-7771.

Web, http://lhncbc.nlm.nih.gov

A research and development division of the National Library of Medicine. Conducts and supports research and development in the dissemination of high-quality imagery, medical language processing, high-speed access to biomedical information, intelligent database systems development, multimedia visualization, knowledge management, data mining, machine-assisted indexing, terminology, and data structure and standards for exchanging clinical data.

National Library of Medicine *(National Institutes of Health), National Center for Biotechnology Information,* 8600 Rockville Pike, Bldg. 38A, 8th Floor, Bethesda, MD 20892; (301) 435-5978. Fax, (301) 480-4559. Dr. James Ostell, Director.

General email, info@ncbi.nlm.nih.gov

Web, www.ncbi.nlm.nih.gov and Pub Med Central, www.pubmedcentral.nih.gov

Creates automated systems for storing and analyzing knowledge of molecular biology and genetics. Develops new information technologies to aid in understanding the molecular processes that control human health and disease. Conducts basic research in computational molecular biology. Sponsors PubMed Central, a publicly accessible digital archive of life sciences journal literature.

Naval Medical Research Center *(Defense Dept.),* 503 Robert Grant Ave., #1W28, Silver Spring, MD 20910-7500; (301) 319-7403. Fax, (301) 319-7424. Capt. Adam W. Armstrong (USN), Commanding Officer.

General email, svc.pao.nmrc@med.navy.mil

Web, www.med.navy.mil/sites/nmrc and Facebook, www.facebook.com/NavalMedicalRC

Performs basic and applied biomedical research in areas of military importance, including infectious diseases, hyperbaric medicine, wound repair enhancement, environmental stress, and immunobiology. Provides support to field laboratories and naval hospitals; monitors research internationally.

NIH Clinical Center *(National Institutes of Health),* 10 Center Dr., #6-2551, Bethesda, MD 20892-1504; (301) 496-4000. Fax, (301) 402-2984. Dr. James K. Gilman, Director, (301) 496-4114. Communications, (301) 496-2563.

Web, www.cc.nih.gov, Twitter, @NIHClinicalCntr and Facebook, www.facebook.com/NIHClinicalCenter

Serves as a clinical research center for the NIH; patients are referred by physicians and self-referred throughout the United States and overseas.

Walter Reed Army Institute of Research *(Defense Dept.),* 503 Robert Grant Ave., Silver Spring, MD 20910-7500; (301) 319-9000. Fax, (301) 319-9549. Col. Deydre S. Teyhen, Commander. Public Affairs Officer, (301) 319-9471. Reference Librarian, (301) 319-9555.

General email, usarmy.detrick.medcom-wrair.mbx.public-affairs@mail.mil

Web, www.wrair.army.mil and Twitter, @wrair

Provides research, education, and training in support of the Defense Dept.'s health care system. Develops vaccines and drugs to prevent and treat infectious diseases. Other research efforts include surveillance of naturally occurring infectious diseases of military importance and study of combat casualty care (blood loss, resuscitation, and brain and other organ system trauma), battle casualties, operational stress, sleep deprivation, and medical countermeasures against biological and chemical agents.

►CONGRESS

For a listing of relevant congressional committees and subcommittees, please see pages 362–363 or the Appendix.

►NONGOVERNMENTAL

Academy Health, 1666 K St. N.W., #1100, 20006; (202) 292-6700. Fax, (202) 292-6800. Dr. Lisa A. Simpson, President; Lauren Gerlach, Director.

Web, www.academyhealth.org, Twitter, @AcademyHealth and Facebook, www.facebook.com/AcademyHealth

Membership: individuals and organizations with an interest in health services research, including health policymakers, universities, private research organizations, professional associations, consulting firms, advocacy organizations, insurers, managed care companies, health care systems, and pharmaceutical companies. Serves as an information clearinghouse on health services research and policy; communicates with policymakers concerning state and federal health policies; works to increase public and private funding for health services research, including comparative effectiveness and public health systems and services research. Offers professional development and training programs for health services researchers and policymakers. Monitors legislation and regulations. (Formerly Academy for Health Services Research and Health Policy.)

American Clinical Laboratory Assn., *1100 New York Ave. N.W., #725 West, 20005; (202) 637-9466. Julie Khani, President; Sharon West, Vice President of Legal and Regulatory Affairs.*
General email, info@acla.com
Web, www.acla.com, Twitter, @ACLAlabs and Facebook, www.facebook.com/ACLAlabs

Membership: laboratories and laboratory service companies. Advocates laws and regulations that recognize the role of laboratory services in cost-effective health care. Works to ensure the confidentiality of patient test results. Provides education, information, and research materials to members. Monitors legislation and regulations.

American Physiological Society, *6120 Executive Blvd., #600, Rockville, MD 20852-4911; (301) 634-7164. Fax, (301) 634-7241. Scott Steen, Executive Director, (301) 634-7118.*
Web, www.the-aps.org and Twitter, @APSPhysiology

Membership: physiologists, students, and laypersons interested in physiology. Researches how the body and its organ systems function. Promotes scientific research, education, and dissemination of information through publication of peer-reviewed journals; monitors international research. Works to establish standards for the humane care and use of laboratory animals. Offers travel fellowships for scientific meetings; encourages minority participation in physiological research. Publishes fourteen scientific journals and a newsletter.

American Trauma Society, *201 Park Washington Court, Falls Church, VA 22046; (703) 538-3544. Fax, (703) 241-5603. Suzanne M. Prentiss, Executive Director. Toll-free, (800) 556-7890.*
General email, info@amtrauma.org
Web, www.amtrauma.org and Twitter, @ATSTrauma

Seeks to prevent trauma and improve its treatment. Coordinates programs aimed at reducing the incidence and severity of trauma; sponsors research; provides training to nurses and others involved in the trauma field. Provides support to trauma survivors. Monitors legislation and regulations.

Center for Applied Proteomics and Molecular Medicine *(George Mason University), 10900 University Blvd., Bull Run Hall, #325, Manassas, VA 20110 (mailing address: 10900 University Blvd., #325, MS1A9, Manassas, VA 20110); (703) 993-9526. Fax, (703) 993-8606.*

Lance A. Liotta, Co-Director; Emanuel Petricoin III, Co-Director.
General email, phackett@gmu.edu
Web, http://capmm.gmu.edu

Conducts translational medical research in order to tailor treatment to individual patients. Participates in clinical trials.

Council on Education for Public Health, *1010 Wayne Ave., #220, Silver Spring, MD 20910; (202) 789-1050. Laura Rasar King, Executive Director.*
Web, https://ceph.org and Twitter, @CEPHtweets

Works to strengthen public health programs through research and other means.

Foundation for the National Institutes of Health, *11400 Rockville Pike, #600, Bethesda, MD 20852; (301) 402-5311. Fax, (301) 480-2752. Maria C. Freire, President, (301) 443-1811.*
General email, foundation@fnih.org
Web, www.fnih.org, Twitter, @FNIH_Org and Facebook, www.facebook.com/FNIHorg

Established by Congress to support the NIH's mission of developing new knowledge through biomedical research. Works to foster collaborative relationships in education, research, and related activities between the NIH, industry, academia, and nonprofit organizations; supports basic and clinical research to advance medical knowledge; supports training and advanced education programs for future researchers; and invests in educational programs related to medical research.

Howard Hughes Medical Institute, *4000 Jones Bridge Rd., Chevy Chase, MD 20815-6789; (301) 215-8500. Fax, (301) 215-8863. Erin O'Shea, President.*
Web, www.hhmi.org, Twitter, @HHMINEWS and Facebook, www.facebook.com/HowardHughesMed

Conducts biomedical research programs in major academic medical centers, hospitals, and universities. Areas of research include cell biology, computational biology, genetics, immunology, neuroscience, and structural biology. Maintains a grants program in science education, including precollege, undergraduate, graduate, and postgraduate levels. Supports selected biomedical researchers in foreign countries.

Institute for Alternative Futures (IAF), *2800 Eisehower Ave., #220, Alexandria, VA 22314-5204; (703) 684-5880. Fax, (703) 684-0640. Jonathan Peck, President.*
General email, futurist@altfutures.org
Web, www.altfutures.org and Facebook, www.facebook.com/Institute-for-Alternative-Futures-227831155314

Research and educational organization that explores the implications of future developments in various fields and facilitates planning efforts. Works with state and local governments, Congress, international organizations, federal government, and regional associations; conducts seminars. Interests include pharmaceutical research, health care, telecommunications, artificial intelligence, energy, the environment, and sustainability.

International Epidemiology Institute, *1455 Research Blvd., #550, Rockville, MD 20850; (301) 424-1054. Fax, (301) 424-1053. William J. Blot, Chief Executive Officer.*
General email, info@iei.us
Web, www.iei.us

Investigates biomedical problems and environmental health issues for the public and private sectors, universities, and other institutions. Conducts studies and clinical trials. Helps identify potential risks and benefits associated with new medicines and new medical devices, including implants. (Affiliated with Vanderbilt University in Nashville, Tenn.)

Johns Hopkins University Applied Physics Laboratory, *Research and Exploratory Development, 11100 Johns Hopkins Rd., Laurel, MD 20723-6099; (240) 228-5000. Jim Schatz, Head. Press, (240) 228-5020.*
Web, www.jhuapl.edu/ourwork/red

Research and development laboratory that seeks to improve warfighter survivability, sustainment, and performance through battlefield trauma prevention and mitigation, along with medical device evaluation and development. Programs include improvement of soldier protection equipment, the development of a neurally integrated upper extremity prosthetic, and blast-related traumatic brain injury research.

National Center for Healthy Housing, *10320 Little Patuxent Pkwy., #500, Columbia, MD 21044; (410) 992-0712. Fax, (443) 539-4150. Amanda Reddy, Executive Director, (443) 539-4152.*
General email, info@nchh.org
Web, www.nchh.org and Twitter, @NCHH

Collects, analyzes, and distributes information on creating and maintaining safe and healthful housing. Provides technical assistance and training to public health, housing, and environmental professionals. Interests include aging in place for older adults, radon, allergens, pest management, and lead poisoning.

National Institute of Environmental Health Sciences (NIEHS) *(National Institutes of Health), Washington Office, 31 Center Dr., #B1C02, MSC 2256, Bethesda, MD 20892-2256; (301) 496-3511. Fax, (301) 496-0563. Linda S. Birnbaum, Director, (919) 541-3201; Jed R. Bullock, Legislative Liaison. Information, (919) 541-3345.*
General email, webcenter@niehs.nih.gov
Web, www.niehs.nih.gov, Twitter, @NIEHS and Facebook, www.facebook.com/NIH.NIEHS

Conducts and supports research on the human effects of various environmental exposures, expanding the scientific basis for making public health decisions based on the potential toxicity of environmental agents. (Most operations located in Research Triangle, N.C.)

Research!America, *241 18th St. South, #501, Alexandria, VA 22202; (703) 739-2577. Fax, (703) 739-2372. Mary Woolley, President.*
General email, info@researchamerica.org
Web, www.researchamerica.org and Twitter, @ResearchAmerica

Membership: academic institutions, professional societies, voluntary health organizations, corporations, and individuals interested in promoting medical research. Provides information on the benefits of medical and health research and seeks to increase funding for research. Monitors legislation and regulations.

Science Communication Network, *4405 East-West Hwy., #601, Bethesda, MD 20814; (301) 654-6665. Amy Kostant, Executive Director.*
General email, info@sciencecom.org
Web, http://sciencecommunicationnetwork.org

Conducts educational workshops to give environmental health scientists the media tools to enable their work to be accurately reported to the public and journalists. Focuses on issues including environmental health and reproductive health connections; effects of energy exploration on health, including fracking; population health disparities; environmental contaminant links to autoimmune diseases, such as allergies; diseases of aging such as Parkinson's disease and dementia; and health effects associated with climate change.

SRI International, *Washington Office, 1100 Wilson Blvd., #2800, Arlington, VA 22209; (703) 524-2053. Fax, (703) 247-8569. William Jeffrey, Executive Director.*
Web, www.sri.com and Twitter, @SRI_Intl

Research and consulting organization. Conducts studies on biotechnology, genetic engineering, drug metabolism, cancer, toxicology, disease control systems, and other areas of basic and applied research; monitors international research. (Headquarters in Menlo Park, Calif.)

Alternative Medicine

▶**AGENCIES**

Food and Drug Administration (FDA) *(Health and Human Services Dept.), Center for Food Safety and Applied Nutrition (CFSAN), 5001 Campus Dr., College Park, MD 20740-3835; (240) 402-1600. Fax, (301) 436-2668. Susan T. Mayne, Director.*
General email, consumer@fda.gov
Web, www.fda.gov/AboutFDA/CentersOffices/OfficeofFoods/CFSAN

Develops standards for dietary supplements taken as part of alternative medicine treatments.

National Cancer Institute (NCI) *(National Institutes of Health), Cancer Treatment and Diagnosis (DCTD), Cancer Complementary and Alternative Medicine (OCCAM), 9609 Medical Center Dr., Room 5W136, Rockville, MD 20850; (240) 276-6595. Fax, (240) 276-7888. Dr. Jeffrey D. White, Director. Press, (301) 496-6641. TTY, (800) 332-8615.*

General email, ncioccam1-r@mail.nih.gov

Web, https://cam.cancer.gov

Investigates approaches to cancer therapy using complementary and alternative medicine. Conducts research on lifestyle modifications, including diet, exercise, and mind-body approaches, for their impact on cancer outcomes.

National Institutes of Health (NIH) *(Health and Human Services Dept.), National Center for Complementary and Integrative Health (NICCIH),* 9000 Rockville Pike, MSC282, Bethesda, MD 20892; (301) 435-6826. Fax, (301) 402-4741. Dr. Helene Langevin, Director. Information, (888) 644-6226. TTY, (866) 464-3615. General email, info@nccih.nih.gov

Web, www.nccih.nih.gov

Works with the Food and Drug Administration (FDA) to develop regulations for the research and use of alternative medicine.

▶**NONGOVERNMENTAL**

American Assn. of Naturopathic Physicians, 300 New Jersey Ave. N.W., #900, 20001; (202) 237-8150. Fax, (202) 237-5213. Laura Farr, Executive Director, (202) 849-6306. General email, member.services@naturopathic.org

Web, www.naturopathic.org

Membership: naturopathic physicians who are licensed as primary health care providers. Promotes the combination of modern medicine and natural and traditional therapies, including therapeutic nutrition, botanical medicine, homeopathy, and natural childbirth.

American Assn. of Pharmaceutical Scientists, 2107 Wilson Blvd., #700, Arlington, VA 22201-3042; (703) 243-2800. Fax, (703) 243-9532. Walt Marlowe, Executive Director, (703) 248-4701. Customer Service, (877) 998-2277. Public Relations, (703) 248-4740. General email, aaps@aaps.org

Web, www.aaps.org, Twitter, @AAPSComms and Facebook, www.facebook.com/ americanassociationofpharmaeuticalscientists?filter=1

Through its philanthropic arm, the American Association of Pharmaceutical Scientists Foundation, provides funding to advance research, education, and training for therapies, drug development, and manufacturing.

American Music Therapy Assn., 8455 Colesville Rd., #1000, Silver Spring, MD 20910; (301) 589-3300. Fax, (301) 589-5175. Lee Grossman, Executive Director. General email, info@musictherapy.org

Web, www.musictherapy.org, Twitter, @AMTAInc and Facebook, www.facebook.com/AMTAinc

Promotes the therapeutic use of music by approving degree programs and clinical training sites, establishing professional competencies and clinical practice standards for music therapists, and conducting research in the music therapy field.

Assn. of Accredited Naturopathic Medical Colleges, 1717 K St. N.W., #900, 20006; (800) 345-7454. Fraser Smith, Executive Director. General email, info@aanmc.org

Web, www.aanmc.org and Twitter, @AANMC

Promotes naturopathic and medical education, research, and teaching.

Arthritis, Bone Diseases

▶**AGENCIES**

National Institute of Arthritis and Musculoskeletal and Skin Diseases (NIAMS) *(National Institutes of Health),* 31 Center Dr., Bldg. 31, #4C32, MS 2350, Bethesda, MD 20892-2350; (301) 496-4484. Fax, (301) 718-6366. Robert H. Carter, Director (Acting), (301) 496-3651. Health information, (877) 226-4267. TTY, (301) 565-2966. General email, niamsinfo@mail.nih.gov

Web, www.niams.nih.gov and Twitter, @NIH_NIAMS

Conducts and funds research on arthritis, rheumatic, skin, muscle, and bone diseases and musculoskeletal disorders. Funds national arthritis centers.

National Institute of Arthritis and Musculoskeletal and Skin Diseases (NIAMS) *(National Institutes of Health), Information Clearinghouse,* 1 AMS Circle, Bethesda, MD 20892-3675; (301) 495-4484. Fax, (301) 718-6366. Anita Linde, Director (Acting). Toll-free, (877) 226-4267. TTY, (301) 565-2966. General email, niamsinfo@mail.nih.gov

Web, www.niams.nih.gov

Supports medical research into the causes, treatment, and prevention of diseases of the bones, muscles, joints, and skin. Provides general information on health conditions and referrals to organizations.

National Institutes of Health (NIH) *(Health and Human Services Dept.), Osteoporosis and Related Bone Diseases (ORBD),* 2 AMS Circle, Bethesda, MD 20892; (202) 223-0344. Fax, (202) 293-2356. Dr. Robert Carter, Director (Acting). Toll-free, (800) 624-2663. TTY, (202) 466-4315. General email, NIHBoneInfo@mail.nih.gov

Web, www.bones.nih.gov

Provides patients, health professionals, and the public with resources and information on metabolic bone diseases, including osteoporosis, Paget's disease of bone, and osteogenesis imperfecta. Seeks to increase the awareness, knowledge, and understanding of the prevention, early detection, and treatment of osteoporosis and related bone diseases.

▶**NONGOVERNMENTAL**

American Society for Bone and Mineral Research (ASBMR), 2025 M St. N.W., #800, 20036-3309; (202) 367-1161. Fax, (202) 367-2161. Ann L. Elderkin, Executive Director, (202) 367-1161.

General email, asbmr@asbmr.org

Web, www.asbmr.org, Twitter, @ASBMR and *Facebook, www.facebook.com/ASBMR*

Membership: scientists and physicians who study bone and mineral metabolism and related fields. Promotes public awareness of bone diseases. Publishes the *Journal of Bone and Mineral Research* and the *Primer on the Metabolic Bone Diseases and Disorders of Mineral Metabolism.* Awards grants for member research.

National Osteoporosis Foundation, *251 18th St., #630, Arlington, VA 22202; (703) 647-3000. Fax, (703) 414-3742. Elizabeth Thompson, Chief Executive Officer. Toll-free, (800) 231-4222.*

General email, info@nof.org

Web, www.nof.org and *Twitter, @osteoporosisNOF*

Volunteer health organization that seeks to prevent osteoporosis and related bone fractures, to promote lifelong bone health, to improve the lives of those affected by osteoporosis, and to find a cure through programs of awareness, advocacy, and public health education and research. Monitors legislation and international research.

Osteogenesis Imperfecta Foundation, *804 W. Diamond Ave., #210, Gaithersburg, MD 20878; (301) 947-0083. Fax, (301) 947-0456. Tracy Smith Hart, Chief Executive Officer. Toll-free, (844) 889-7579.*

General email, bonelink@oif.org

Web, www.oif.org and *Twitter, @OIFoundation*

Provides health care professionals and patients with information about osteogenesis imperfecta (OI), also known as brittle bone disease; offers research grants; promotes public policy that supports people living with OI.

Blood, Bone Marrow

▶**AGENCIES**

National Heart, Lung, and Blood Institute (NHLBI) *(National Institutes of Health), Blood Diseases and Resources Division (DBDR), 6701 Rockledge Dr., #9030, MSC 7950, Bethesda, MD 20892-7950; (301) 435-0080. Fax, (301) 480-0867. Dr. W. Keith Hoots, Director. Public Affairs, (301) 496-4236.*

Web, www.nhlbi.nih.gov/about/org/dbdr and *Twitter, @NHLBI_BloodDiv*

Supports research and training on the causes, diagnosis, treatment, and prevention of nonmalignant blood diseases and research in transfusion medicine and blood banking, stem cell biology, and blood supply adequacy and safety. Provides biospecimens and cellular resources to the scientific community.

National Heart, Lung, and Blood Institute (NHLBI) *(National Institutes of Health), Blood Diseases and Resources Division (DBDR), Blood Epidemiology and Clinical Therapeutics Branch, 6701 Rockledge Dr., #9142, MSC 7950, Bethesda, MD 20892-7950; (301) 435-0065. Fax, (301) 480-1046. Dr. Simone Glynn, Branch Chief.*

Web, www.nhlbi.nih.gov/about/org/dbdr

Responsible for oversight, support, and stimulation of epidemiologic, clinical, and implementation research throughout the spectrum of blood science. Branch responsibilities include oversight, support, and stimulation of epidemiologic health services and observational clinical research; oversight, support, and stimulation of therapeutic and interventional clinical trials (T2 Research); acquisition and maintenance of expertise in clinical study and trial design and administration on behalf of the Division; oversight, support, and stimulation of implementation science and research (T3 Research); training of blood science workforce; and scientific liaison for epidemiologic, clinical, and implementation research across the Division, NHLBI, NIH, and partner federal agencies.

National Heart, Lung, and Blood Institute (NHLBI) *(National Institutes of Health), Blood Diseases and Resources Division (DBDR), Molecular, Cellular, and Systems Blood Science Branch, 6701 Rockledge Dr., #90930, Bethesda, MD 20892-7950; (301) 435-0070. Fax, (301) 480-1016. Yu-Chang Yang, Branch Chief.*

Web, www.nhlbi.nih.gov/about/org/dbdr

Provides oversight, support, and stimulation of fundamental basic research and early stage laboratory translation of the biology of blood, the blood forming elements, and the interface between each of the latter with other cellular and organ systems. Branch responsibilities include oversight, support, and stimulation of discovery science focused on the explication of the physiology and pathophysiology of blood, bone marrow, and blood vessels; oversight support and stimulation of systems of biological approaches to understanding the critical role of blood/bone marrow/ vascular endothelium in animal and human organs and organisms; oversight, support, and stimulation of the application of fundamental genetics, proteomic and metabolomic tools to understanding hematologic physiology and pathophysiology; administration of and liaison to the HNLBI/NIH resources related to basic research in nonneoplastic hematology; and fostering scientific communication across the Division, NHLBI, NIH, and partner federal agencies.

National Heart, Lung, and Blood Institute (NHLBI) *(National Institutes of Health), Blood Diseases and Resources Division (DBDR), Translational Blood Science and Resource Branch, 6701 Rockledge Dr., #90930, Bethesda, MD 20892-7950; (301) 435-0050. Fax, (301) 480-1046. Traci Heath Mondoro, Branch Chief. Press, (301) 496-4236.*

Web, www.nhlbi.nih.gov/about/org/dbdr

Provides oversight, support, and stimulation of translational research throughout the spectrum of blood science, as well as the resources required to support heart, lung, blood, and sleep research. Branch responsibilities include oversight, support, and stimulation of postdiscovery science, preclinical research, and early phase clinical studies and trials (TI, T2 Research); oversight, support, and stimulation of SBIR/STTR initiatives in the blood sciences; administration of and liaison to NHLBI resources related to translational research; training of the blood science workforce; and scientific liaison for translation research across the Division, NHLBI, NIH, and partner federal agencies.

National Heart, Lung, and Blood Institute (NHLBI) *(National Institutes of Health), Health Information Center,* 31 Center Dr., Bldg. 31, Bethesda, MD 20892-2480 (mailing address: P.O. Box 30105, Bethesda, MD 20824-0105); (301) 592-8573. Lenora Johnson, Director, (301) 496-4236.
General email, nhlbiInfo@nhlbi.nih.gov
Web, www.nhlbi.nih.gov/health/contact

Provides public and patient education materials on the prevention and treatment of heart, lung, and blood diseases.

National Institute of Diabetes and Digestive and Kidney Diseases (NIDDK) *(National Institutes of Health), Kidney, Urologic, and Hematologic Diseases (KUH),* 2 Democracy Plaza, 6707 Democracy Blvd., #625, MSC 5458, Bethesda, MD 20892; (301) 496-6325. Fax, (301) 480-3510. Dr. Robert A. Star, Director. Information, (800) 891-5390. Press, (301) 496-3583.
Web, www.niddk.nih.gov

Supports basic research on and clinical studies of the states of blood cell formation, mobilization, and release. Interests include anemia associated with chronic diseases, iron and white blood cell metabolism, and genetic control of hemoglobin.

Warren Grant Magnuson Clinical Center *(National Institutes of Health), Transfusion Medicine,* 10 Center Dr., Bldg. 10, #1C711, MSC-1184, Bethesda, MD 20892-1184; (301) 496-4506. Fax, (301) 402-1360. Dr. Harvey G. Klein, Department Chief, (301) 496-9702. Press, (301) 496-2563.
Web, http://clinicalcenter.nih.gov/dtm and Twitter, @NIHClinicalCntr

Supplies blood and blood components for research and patient care. Provides training programs and conducts research in the preparation and transfusion of blood and blood products. Research topics include hepatitis, automated cell separation, immunohematology, and AIDS transmittal through transfusions.

▶**NONGOVERNMENTAL**

AABB, 4550 Montgomery Ave., #700, North Tower, Bethesda, MD 20814; (301) 907-6977. Fax, (301) 907-6895. Debra BenAvram, Chief Executive Officer. Press, (301) 215-6526.
General email, aabb@aabb.org
Web, www.aabb.org, Twitter, @aabb and Facebook, www.facebook.com/pages/AABB/57750581473

Membership: Physicians, nurses, scientists, researchers, administrators medical technologists and other health care providers; hospital and community blood centers, transfusion and transplantation services, and individuals involved in transfusion and transplantation medicine and related biological therapies. Develops and implements standards, accreditation and educational programs, and services that optimize patient and donor care and safety. Encourages the voluntary donation of blood and other tissues and organs through education and public information. (Formerly the American Assn. of Blood Banks.)

American Red Cross, *National Headquarters,* 431 18th St. N.W., 20006; (202) 303-5000. Gail J. McGovern, President. Headquarters staff directory, (202) 303-5214, ext. 1. Press, (202) 303-5551. Public inquiry, (202) 303-4498. Toll-free, 800-RED-CROSS (733-2767).
Web, www.redcross.org and Twitter, @RedCross

Humanitarian relief and health education organization chartered by Congress; provides services in the United States and internationally, when requested. Collects blood and maintains blood centers; conducts research; operates the national bone marrow registry and a rare-donor registry. Serves as U.S. member of the International Federation of Red Cross and Red Crescent Societies.

Cancer

▶**AGENCIES**

National Cancer Institute (NCI) *(National Institutes of Health),* 9609 Medical Center Dr., MSC 9760, Bethesda, MD 20892-9760; (800) 422-6237. Fax, (301) 402-0338. Dr. Norman (Ned) Sharpless, Director, (301) 496-5615. Press, (301) 496-6641.
Web, www.cancer.gov, Twitter, @theNCI and Facebook, www.facebook.com/cancer.gov

Conducts and funds research on the causes, diagnosis, treatment, prevention, control, and biology of cancer and the rehabilitation of cancer patients; administers the National Cancer Program; coordinates international research activities. Sponsors regional and national cancer information services.

National Cancer Institute (NCI) *(National Institutes of Health), Cancer Biology (DCB),* 9609 Medical Center Dr., MSC 9747, Bethesda, MD 20892; (240) 276-6180. Fax, (240) 276-7861. Dinah Singer, Director.
Web, www.cancer.gov/about-nci/organization/dcb

Supports and provides funding for basic research in cancer biology at academic institutions and research foundations. Interests include immunology, hematology, DNA, tumors biology, and structural biology.

National Cancer Institute (NCI) *(National Institutes of Health), Cancer Control and Population Sciences (DCCPS),* 9609 Medical Center Dr., MSC 9764, Bethesda, MD 20892-9760; (240) 276-6636. Robert Croyle, Director, (240) 276-6690.
Web, https://cancercontrol.cancer.gov and Twitter, @NCICancerCtrl

Researches the causes and distribution of cancer in populations, supports the development and delivery of effective interventions, and monitors and analyzes cancer trends in all segments of the population.

National Cancer Institute (NCI) *(National Institutes of Health), Cancer Epidemiology and Genetics (DCEG),*

9609 Medical Center Dr., MSC 9776, Bethesda, MD 20892; (240) 276-7150. Dr. Stephen J. Chanock, Director.
General email, ncicontactdceg@mail.nih.gov
Web, https://dceg.cancer.gov and
Twitter, @NCIEpiTraining

Researches the causes of cancer and pathways to prevention through epidemiologic, clinical, and laboratory observations.

National Cancer Institute (NCI) *(National Institutes of Health), Cancer Prevention,* 9609 Medical Center Dr., Bethesda, MD 20892; (240) 276-7120. Dr. Deborah Winn, Director (Acting).
Web, http://prevention.cancer.gov and
Twitter, @NCIprevention

Seeks to plan, direct, implement, and monitor cancer research focused on early detection, cancer risk, chemoprevention, and supportive care. Focuses on intervention in the process of carcinogenesis to prevent development into invasive cancer. Supports various approaches, from preclinical discovery and development of biomarkers and chemoprevention agents, including pharmaceuticals and micronutrients, to Phase III clinical testing. Programs are carried out with other National Cancer Institute divisions, NIH institutes, and federal and state agencies.

National Cancer Institute (NCI) *(National Institutes of Health), Cancer Treatment and Diagnosis (DCTD),* Bldg. 31, 31 Center Dr., Room 3A-44, Bethesda, MD 20892; (240) 781-3320. Fax, (240) 541-4515. Dr. James H. Doroshow, Director.
General email, ncidctdinfo@mail.nih.gov
Web, https://dctd.cancer.gov

Seeks to take prospective detection and treatment leads, facilitate their paths to clinical application, and expedite the initial and subsequent large-scale testing of new agents, biomarkers, imaging tests, and other therapeutic interventions, including radiation, surgery, and immunotherapy.

National Cancer Institute (NCI) *(National Institutes of Health), Cancer Treatment and Diagnosis (DCTD), Biometric Research Program,* 9609 Medical Center Dr., #5W110, Rockville, MD 20850; (240) 276-6041. Fax, (240) 276-7888. Dr. Lisa Meier McShane, Associate Director (Acting), (240) 276-6037.
General email, brb@brb.nci.nih.gov
Web, https://brb.nci.nih.gov

Supports cancer research on carcinogenesis and systems pharmacology, and identifies molecular targets, resistance mechanisms and effective new drugs, drug combinations, and biomarkers mechanisms.

National Cancer Institute (NCI) *(National Institutes of Health), Cancer Treatment and Diagnosis (DCTD), Cancer Complementary and Alternative Medicine (OCCAM),* 9609 Medical Center Dr., Room 5W136, Rockville, MD 20850; (240) 276-6595. Fax, (240) 276-7888. Dr. Jeffrey D. White, Director. Press, (301) 496-6641. TTY, (800) 332-8615.

General email, ncioccam1-r@mail.nih.gov
Web, https://cam.cancer.gov

Investigates approaches to cancer therapy using complimentary and alternative medicine. Conducts research on lifestyle modifications, including diet, exercise, and mind-body approaches, for their impact on cancer outcomes.

National Cancer institute (NCI) *(National Institutes of Health), Cancer Treatment and Diagnosis (DCTD), Cancer Diagnosis Program,* 31 Center Dr., Bldg 31-3A-44, Bethesda, MD 20892; (240) 781-3320. Fax, (240) 541-4515. Dr. James Doroshaw, Division Director, (240) 781-3320.
General email, ncidctdinfo@mail.nih.gov
Web, https://cdp.cancer.gov

Funds cancer resources and research for the development of innovative in vitro diagnostics and novel diagnostic technologies in order to improve cancer detection, evaluation, and treatment.

National Cancer Institute (NCI) *(National Institutes of Health), Cancer Treatment and Diagnosis (DCTD), Cancer Therapy Evaluation Program,* 9609 Medical Center Dr., Bethesda, MD 20892; (240) 276-6515. Fax, (240) 276-7891. Dr. Meg Mooney, Associate Director (Acting), (240) 276-5904.
General email, NCINCTNRFA.mail.nih.gov
Web, https://ctep.cancer.gov

Supports cancer research by funding and sponsoring clinical trials to evaluate new anticancer agents, with an emphasis on translational research on molecular targets and drug effects.

National Cancer Institute (NCI) *(National Institutes of Health), Cancer Treatment and Diagnosis (DCTD), Developmental Therapeutics Program,* 9609 Medical Center Dr., Bethesda, MD 20892-9735; (240) 276-5949. Jerry M. Collins, Associate Director.
General email, ncidtpinfo@mail.nih.gov
Web, https://dtp.cancer.gov

Provides resources about new cancer therapeutic agents and services to public and private research communities; makes grants to fund drug discovery and biochemical pharmacology research.

National Cancer Institute (NCI) *(National Institutes of Health), Cancer Treatment and Diagnosis (DCTD), Translational Research Program,* 9609 Medical Center Dr., #3W110, MSC 9726, Bethesda, MD 20892; (240) 276-5730. Fax, (240) 276-7881. Dr. Toby T. Hecht, Associate Director, (240) 276-5730 ext. 1.
General email, ncitrp-r@mail.nih.gov
Web, https://trp.cancer.gov

Administers SPORE grants (the Specialized Programs of Research Excellence). Encourages the study of organ-specific cancers, blood malignancies, and other cancers. Promotes and funds interdisciplinary research and information exchange between basic and clinical science to move basic research findings from the laboratory to applied settings involving patients and populations. Encourages laboratory and clinical scientists to work collaboratively to plan, design, and implement research programs on cancer prevention, detection, diagnosis, treatment, and control.

National Cancer Institute (NCI) *(National Institutes of Health), Center for Cancer Research (CCR), Bldg. 31, 31 Center Dr., Room 3A11, Bethesda, MD 20892; (240) 760-6400. Dr. Tom Misteli, Director, (240) 760-6400.*
Web, https://ccr.cancer.gov and Twitter, @NCIResearchCtr

Supports clinical cancer research, with a focus on individual genes and proteins, drug discovery, biomedical devices and technology, and advances in treatment.

National Cancer Institute (NCI) *(National Institutes of Health), Communications and Public Liaison, 9609 Medical Center Dr., #MSC 9760, Bethesda, MD 20892-9760; (240) 276-6600. Fax, (240) 276-7680. Peter Garrett, Director.*
General email, nciocpl@mail.nih.gov
Web, www.cancer.gov.aboutnci/organization/ocpl and Twitter, @theNCI

Collects and disseminates scientific information on cancer biology, etiology, screening, prevention, treatment, and supportive care for patients, caregivers, health professionals, researchers, advocates, and media. Provides core communications for cancer information.

President's Cancer Panel, *c/o National Cancer Institute, 9000 Rockville Pike, Bldg. 31, B2B37, MSC 2590, Bethesda, MD 20892; (240) 781-3430. Dr. Abby Sandler, Executive Secretary.*
General email, prescancerpanel@nih.gov
Web, https://prescancerpanel.cancer.gov and Twitter, @PresCancerPanel

Presidentially appointed committee that monitors and evaluates the National Cancer Program; reports to the president and Congress.

▶**NONGOVERNMENTAL**

American Cancer Society, *Cancer Action Network, 555 11th St. N.W., #300, 20004; (202) 661-5700. Fax, (202) 661-5750. Christopher W. Hansen, President; Gary M. Greeley, Chief Executive Officer.*
Web, www.fightcancer.org, Twitter, @ACSCAN and Facebook, www.facebook.com/ACSCAN

Supports evidence-based policy and legislation designed to eliminate cancer as a major health problem; works to encourage elected officials and candidates to make cancer a top national priority. Monitors legislation and regulations. (Headquarters in Atlanta, Ga.)

American Childhood Cancer Organization, *6868 Distribution Dr., Beltsville, MD 20705 (mailing address: P.O. Box 498, Kensington, MD 20895-0498); Ruth I. Hoffman, Chief Executive Officer, (202) 262-9949 (c); Jamie Bloyd, Director of Government Affairs, (859) 948-4626 (c). Toll-free, (855) 858-2226. Ruth Hoffman, (855) 858-2226 ext. 104.*

General email, staff@acco.org
Web, www.acco.org, Twitter, @aacorg and Facebook, www.facebook.com/americanchildhoodcancer

Membership: families of children with cancer, survivors of childhood cancer, and health and education professionals. Serves as an information and educational network; sponsors self-help groups for parents of children and adolescents with cancer. Monitors legislation and regulations.

American Institute for Cancer Research, *1560 Wilson Blvd., #1000, Arlington, VA 22209 (mailing address: P.O. Box 97167, Washington, DC 20090-7167); (202) 328-7744. Fax, (202) 328-7226. Marilyn Gentry, President; Kelly B. Browning, Chief Executive Officer, ext. 3026. Toll-free, (800) 843-8114.*
General email, aicrweb@aicr.org
Web, www.aicr.org, Twitter, @aicrtweets and Facebook, www.facebook.com/AmericanInstituteforCancerResearch

Funds research and fellowship programs on the relationship of nutrition, physical activity, and weight management to cancer risk. Interprets scientific literature; sponsors education programs on cancer prevention.

American Society for Radiation Oncology (ASTRO), *251 18th St. South, 8th Floor, Arlington, VA 22202; (703) 502-1550. Fax, (703) 502-7852. Laura Thevenot, Chief Executive Officer, (703) 839-7302.*
General email, information@astro.org
Web, www.astro.org and Twitter, @ASTRO_org

Radiation oncology, biology, and physics organization that seeks to improve patient care through education, clinical practice, the advancement of science, and advocacy.

American Society of Clinical Oncology (ASCO), *2318 Mill Rd., #800, Alexandria, VA 22314; (571) 483-1300. Fax, (703) 299-0255. Clifford A. Hudis, Chief Executive Officer.*
General email, info@conquer.com
Web, www.asco.org and Twitter, @ASCO

Membership: physicians and scientists specializing in cancer prevention, treatment, education, and research. Promotes exchange of information in clinical research and patient care relating to all stages of cancer; monitors international research.

Assn. of Community Cancer Centers, *1801 Research Blvd., #400, Rockville, MD 20850; (301) 984-9496. Fax, (301) 770-1949. Christian G. Downs, Executive Director.*
Web, www.accc-cancer.org and Twitter, @ACCCBuzz

Membership: individuals from community hospitals involved in multidisciplinary cancer programs, including physicians, administrators, nurses, medical directors, pharmacists, and other members of the cancer care team. Supports comprehensive cancer care for all. Monitors legislation and regulations.

Cancer Support Community, *734 15th St. N.W., #300, 20005; (202) 659-9709. Fax, (202) 974-7999.*

Kim Thiboldeaux, *Chief Executive Officer;* Linda House, *President.* Toll-free, (888) 793-9355.
General email, help@cancersupportcommunity.org

Web, www.cancersupportcommunity.org and Twitter, @CancerSupportHQ

Research and advocacy organization providing support services to those facing cancer. Research and Training Institute supports cancer-related psychosocial, behavioral, and surviorship research.

Leukemia and Lymphoma Society, *National Capital Area Chapter,* *3601 Eisenhower Ave., #450, Alexandria, VA 22304; (703) 399-2900. Fax, (703) 399-2901. Beth Gorman, Executive Director, (703) 339-2909. Information, (800) 955-4572.*
Web, www.lls.org, Twitter, @LLSusa and Facebook, www.facebook.com/LLSUSA

Voluntary health organization that funds blood cancer research, education, and patient services. Seeks to find cures for leukemia, lymphoma, Hodgkin's disease, and myeloma, and to improve the quality of life of patients and their families. Local chapters provide blood cancer patients with disease and treatment information, financial assistance, counseling, and referrals. (Headquarters in White Plains, N.Y.)

Lung Cancer Alliance, *1700 K St. N.W., #660, 20006; (202) 463-2080. Laurie Fenton Ambrose, President. Press, (202) 742-1428. Toll-free helpline, (800) 298-2436.*
General email, info@lungcanceralliance.org

Web, www.lungcanceralliance.org

Advocates lung cancer research and access to screenings, treatments, diagnostics, and testing. Provides information about lung cancer risks and early detection.

National Breast Cancer Coalition, *1010 Vermont Ave. N.W., #900, 20005; (202) 296-7477. Fax, (202) 265-6854. Frances M. (Fran) Visco, President. Toll-free, (800) 622-2838. Press, (202) 973-0593.*
General email, info@breastcancerdeadline2020.org

Web, www.breastcancerdeadline2020.org and Twitter, @Deadline2020

Membership: organizations, local coalitions, and individuals. Supports increasing funding for breast cancer research; monitors how funds are spent; seeks to expand access to quality health care for all; and ensures that trained advocates influence all decision making that impacts breast cancer.

National Coalition for Cancer Survivorship, *8455 Colesville Rd., #930, Silver Spring, MD 20910; (301) 650-9127. Fax, (301) 565-9670. Shelley Fuld Nasso, Chief Executive Officer. Toll-free information and publications, (877) 622-7937.*
General email, info@canceradvocacy.org

Web, www.canceradvocacy.org, Twitter, @CancerAdvocacy and Facebook, www.facebook.com/cancersurvivorship

Membership: survivors of cancer (newly diagnosed, in treatment, and living beyond cancer), their families and friends, health care providers, and support organizations.

Distributes information, including the Cancer Survival Toolbox, about living with cancer diagnosis and treatment; offers free publications and resources that help enable individuals to take charge of their own care or the care of others.

Ovarian Cancer Research Alliance, *1101 14th St., #850, 20005; (202) 331-1332. Fax, (202) 331-2292. Audra Moran, President. Toll-free, (866) 399-6262.*
General email, info@ocrahope.org

Web, www.ocrahope.org

Acts as an advocate at the federal and state levels for adequate and sustained funding for ovarian cancer research and awareness programs. Promotes legislation that would improve the quality of life and access to care for all cancer patients. Provides information and resources for survivors, women at risk, and health providers.

Dental Care

▶**AGENCIES**

National Institute of Dental and Craniofacial Research (NIDCR) *(National Institutes of Health), 31 Center Dr., Bldg. 31, #2C39, MS 2290, Bethesda, MD 20892-2190; (301) 496-3571. Fax, (301) 402-2185. Martha J. Somerman, Director. Press, (301) 496-4261. Toll-free, (866) 232-4528.*
General email, nidcrinfo@mail.nih.gov

Web, www.nidcr.nih.gov

Conducts and funds clinical research and promotes training and career development in oral, dental, and craniofacial health. Monitors international research and evaluates its implications for public policy.

▶**NONGOVERNMENTAL**

American Dental Assn. (ADA), *Government Relations, 1111 14th St. N.W., #1100, 20005; (202) 898-2424. Michael Graham, Senior Vice President Government and Public Affairs. General, (202) 898-2400.*
General email, adpac@ada.org

Web, www.ada.org/en/advocacy and Twitter, @AmerDentalAssn

Conducts research, provides dental education materials, compiles statistics on dentistry and dental care. Monitors legislation and regulations. (Headquarters in Chicago, Ill.)

Children's Dental Health Project (CDHP), *1020 19th St. N.W., #400, 20036; (202) 833-8288. Meg Booth, Executive Director, (202) 833-8288. Press, (202) 417-3600.*
General email, info@cdhp.org

Web, www.cdhp.org and Twitter, @Teeth_Matter

Coalition comprising policymakers, dental care professionals, and individuals seeking innovative and cost-effective solutions for improving children's dental health. Provides information to policymakers, oral health care providers, and media about dental care provisions of the Affordable Care Act; monitors Medicaid and other insurance programs; promotes prevention strategies.

International Assn. for Dental Research, *1619 Duke St., Alexandria, VA 22314-3406; (703) 548-0066. Fax, (703) 548-1883. Dr. Christopher H. Fox, Executive Director. General email, research@iadr.org*

Web, www.iadr.org and Facebook, www.facebook.com/DentalResearch

Membership: professionals engaged in dental research worldwide. Conducts annual convention, conferences, and symposia.

Dermatology, Skin Disorders

►AGENCIES

National Institute of Arthritis and Musculoskeletal and Skin Diseases (NIAMS) *(National Institutes of Health), 31 Center Dr., Bldg. 31, #4C32, MS 2350, Bethesda, MD 20892-2350; (301) 496-4484. Fax, (301) 718-6366. Robert H. Carter, Director (Acting), (301) 496-3651. Health information, (877) 226-4267. TTY, (301) 565-2966. General email, niamsinfo@mail.nih.gov*

Web, www.niams.nih.gov and Twitter, @NIH_NIAMS

Supports research on the causes and treatment of skin diseases, including psoriasis, eczema, and acne.

►NONGOVERNMENTAL

American Academy of Dermatology, *Government Affairs, 1445 New York Ave. N.W., #800, 20005; (202) 842-3555. Fax, (202) 842-4355. Barbara Greenan, Senior Director of Advocacy and Policy, (202) 712-2602. General email, govtaffairs@aad.org*

Web, www.aad.org, Twitter, @ADDmember and Facebook, www.facebook.com/AADmember

Membership: practicing dermatologists. Promotes the science and art of medicine and surgery related to the skin, hair, and nails. Advocates high-quality dermatologic care and higher standards of care. Monitors legislation and regulations. (Headquarters in Rosemon, Ill.)

American Academy of Facial Plastic and Reconstructive Surgery (AAFPRS), *310 S. Henry St., Alexandria, VA 22314; (703) 299-9291. Fax, (703) 299-8898. Steven J. Jurich, Executive Vice President, ext. 231. General email, info@aafprs.org*

Web, www.aafprs.org, Twitter, @AAFPRS and Facebook, www.facebook.com/AAFPRS

Membership: facial plastic and reconstructive surgeons and other board-certified surgeons whose focus is surgery of the face, head, and neck. Promotes research and study in the field. Helps train residents in facial plastic and reconstructive surgery; offers continuing medical education. Sponsors scientific and medical meetings, international symposia, fellowship training program, seminars, and workshops. Provides videotapes on facial plastic and reconstructive surgery.

Melanoma Research Foundation, *1411 K St. N.W., #800, 20005; (202) 347-9675. Fax, (202) 347-9678. Klyleigh Li*

Pira, Chief Executive Officer. Helpline, (877) 673-6460. Toll-free, (800) 673-1290. General email, klipira@melanoma.org

Web, www.melanoma.org

Educates patients, caregivers, and physicians about the diagnosis, prevention, and treatment of melanoma; advocates medical research for effective treatments.

Diabetes, Digestive Diseases

►AGENCIES

National Diabetes Information Clearinghouse *(National Institutes of Health), Bldg. 31, 31 Center Dr., #9A04, MSC 2560, Bethesda, MD 20892-2560; (800) 860-8747. Fax, (301) 634-0716. Dr. Judith Fradkin, Director, (301) 496-7349. TTY, (866) 569-1162. General email, healthinfo@niddk.nih.gov*

Web, www.niddk.nih.gov/health-information/diabetes and Twitter, @NIDDKgov

Provides health professionals and the public with information on the symptoms, causes, treatments, and general nature of diabetes.

National Digestive Diseases Information Clearinghouse *(National Institutes of Health), Bldg. 31, 31 Center Dr., #9A04, MSC 2560, Bethesda, MD 20892; (800) 860-8747. Fax, (301) 634-0716. Dr. Stephen James, Director, (301) 594-7680. TTY, (866) 569-1162. General email, healthinfo@niddk.nih.gov*

Web, www.niddk.nih.gov/health-information/digestive-diseases and Twitter, @NIDDKgov

Provides health professionals and the public with information on the symptoms, causes, treatments, and general nature of digestive diseases and ailments.

National Institute of Diabetes and Digestive and Kidney Diseases (NIDDK) *(National Institutes of Health), 31 Center Dr., Bldg. 31, #9A52, MS 2560, Bethesda, MD 20892-2560; (301) 496-5741. Fax, (301) 402-2125. Dr. Griffin P. Rodgers, Director. Press, (301) 496-3583. TTY, (866) 569-1162. General email, healthinfo@niddk.nih.gov*

Web, www.niddk.nih.gov, Twitter, @NIDDKgov and Facebook, www.facebook.com/National-Institute-of-Diabetes-and-Digestive-and-Kidney-Diseases-NIDDK-159778759845

Conducts and supports basic and clinical research and research training on diabetes and other endocrine and metabolic diseases, digestive diseases, nutrition, obesity, and kidney, urologic, and hematologic diseases. Website provides evidence-based health information.

National Institute of Diabetes and Digestive and Kidney Diseases (NIDDK) *(National Institutes of Health), Diabetes, Endocrinology, and Metabolic Diseases (DEM), 2 Democracy Plaza, 6707 Democracy Blvd., #683, MSC 2560, Bethesda, MD 20892; (301) 496-7349.*

Fax, (301) 480-3503. Dr. Philip Smith, Director (Acting), (301) 594-8816. Press, (301) 496-3583.
Web, www.niddk.nih.gov

Provides research funding and support for basic and clinical research in the areas of type 1 and type 2 diabetes and other metabolic disorders, including cystic fibrosis; endocrinology and endocrine disorders; obesity, neuroendocrinology, and energy balance; and development, metabolism, and basic biology of liver, fat, and endocrine tissues.

National Institute of Diabetes and Digestive and Kidney Diseases (NIDDK) *(National Institutes of Health), Digestive Diseases and Nutrition (DDN), 2 Democracy Plaza, 6707 Democracy Blvd., #677, MSC 5450, Bethesda, MD 20892-5450; (301) 594-7680. Fax, (301) 480-8300. Stephen P. James, Director. Press, (301) 496-3583.*
Web, www.niddk.nih.gov

Awards grants and contracts to support basic and clinical research related to digestive diseases and nutrition, as well as training and career development. Conducts and supports research concerning liver and biliary diseases; pancreatic diseases; gastrointestinal disease, including neuroendocrinology, motility, immunology, absorption, and transport in the gastrointestinal tract; nutrient metabolism; obesity; and eating disorders.

▶NONGOVERNMENTAL

American Diabetes Assn. (ADA), *2451 Crystal Dr., #900, Arlington, VA 22202; (703) 549-1500. Tracey D. Brown, Chief Executive Officer; Dr. LaShawn McIver, Senior Vice President of Government Affairs and Advocacy. Press, (703) 299-2053. Toll-free, (800) 342-2383.*
General email, askada@diabetes.org
Web, www.diabetes.org,
Twitter, @AmericanDiabetesAssociation and Facebook, www.facebook.com/AmericanDiabetesAssociation

Works to improve access to quality care and to eliminate discrimination against people because of their diabetes. Provides local affiliates with education, information, and referral services. Conducts and funds research on diabetes. Monitors international research. Monitors legislation and regulations.

American Gastroenterological Assn., *4930 Del Ray Ave., Bethesda, MD 20814; (301) 654-2055. Fax, (301) 654-5920. Tom Serena, Executive Vice President. Press, (301) 272-1603.*
General email, member@gastro.org
Web, www.gastro.org, Twitter, @amergastroassno and Facebook, www.facebook.com/AmerGastroAssn

Membership: 17,000 gastroenterology clinicians, scientists, health care professionals, and educators. Sponsors scientific research on digestive diseases; disseminates information on new methods of prevention and treatment. Monitors legislation and regulations. (Affiliated with the Foundation of Digestive Health and Nutrition.)

Endocrine Society, *2055 L St. N.W., #600, 20036; (202) 971-3636. Fax, (202) 736-9705. Barbara Byrd Keenan, Chief Executive Officer. Toll-free, (888) 363-6274.*
General email, info@endocrine.org
Web, www.endocrine.org

Membership: scientists, doctors, health care educators, clinicians, nurses, and others interested in endocrine glands and their disorders. Promotes endocrinology research and clinical practice; sponsors seminars and conferences; gives awards and travel grants.

JDRF, *Advocacy, 1400 K St. N.W., #1212, 20005; (202) 371-9746. Cynthia Rice, Senior Vice President of Advocacy and Policy, ext. 3004159. Toll-free, (800) 533-1868.*
General email, advocacy@jdrf.org
Web, www.jdrf.org

Conducts research, education, and public awareness programs aimed at improving the lives of people with type 1 (juvenile) diabetes and finding a cure for diabetes and its related complications. Monitors legislation and regulations. (Formerly the Juvenile Diabetes Research Foundation.) (Headquarters in New York.)

Family Planning and Population

▶AGENCIES

Agency for International Development (USAID), *Bureau for Global Health, Family Planning and Reproductive Health, 1300 Pennsylvania Ave. N.W., #3.06-011, 20523-3600; (202) 712-4120. Fax, (202) 216-3485. Alma Crumm Golden, Senior Deputy Assistant Administrator. Press, (202) 712-4320.*
General email, pi@usaid.gov
Web, www.usaid.gov/what-we-do/global-health/family-planning, Twitter, usaidgh and Facebook, www.facebook.com/usaidgh

Advances and supports family planning and reproductive health programs in more than 30 countries.

Assistant Secretary for Health (OASH) *(Health and Human Services Dept.), Adolescent Health (OAH), 1101 Wootton Pkwy., #700, Rockville, MD 20852; (240) 453-2846. Evelyn Kappeler, Director.*
General email, oah.gov@hhs.gov
Web, www.hhs.gov/ash/oah

Supports and evaluates teen pregnancy prevention programs; implements the Pregnancy Assistance Fund; coordinates HHS efforts related to adolescent health promotion and disease prevention.

Assistant Secretary for Health (OASH) *(Health and Human Services Dept.), Population Affairs (OPA), 200 Independence Ave. S.W., 20201; (240) 453-2800. Fax, (240) 453-2801. Dr. Diane Foley, Deputy Assistant Secretary. Press, (202) 205-0143.*
General email, opa@hhs.gov
Web, www.hhs.gov/opa and Twitter, @opa1

Responsible for Title X Family Planning Program, which provides family planning services, health screening services, and screening for STDs (including HIV) to all who want and need them, with priority given to low-income persons; the Title XX Adolescent Family Life Program, including demonstration projects to develop, implement, and evaluate program interventions to promote abstinence from sexual activity among adolescents and to provide comprehensive health care, education, and social services to pregnant and parenting adolescents; and planning, monitoring, and evaluating population research.

Census Bureau *(Commerce Dept.), Fertility and Family Statistics, 4600 Silver Hill Rd., #7H371, Suitland, MD 20746-8500 (mailing address: 4600 Silver Hill Rd., #7H371, Washington, DC 20233); (301) 763-2416. Rose Kreider, Chief.*
Web, www.census.gov/topics/health/fertility.html and www.census.gov/topics/families.html

Provides data and statistics on fertility and family composition. Conducts census and survey research on the number of children, household composition, and living arrangements of women in the United States, especially working mothers. Conducts studies on child care and child well-being.

Eunice Kennedy Shriver National Institute of Child Health and Human Development (NICHD) *(National Institutes of Health), Contraceptive Research Branch (CRB), 6710B Rockledge Dr., Bldg. 6710B, Room 2432, MSC 7002, Bethesda, MD 20817; (301) 827-4663. Fax, (301) 480-1972. Daniel Johnston, Chief.*
Web, www.nichd.nih.gov/about/org/der/branches/crb

Develops and supports research and research training programs in effects of contraceptive use on human health; development of new and improved methods of contraception; and targeted studies to improve the development of new and improved methods of contraception. Major research areas include contraceptive research and development and prevention of HIV transmission/acquisition through better understanding of reproductive health.

Eunice Kennedy Shriver National Institute of Child Health and Human Development (NICHD) *(National Institutes of Health), Fertility and Infertility Branch (FI), 6710B Rockledge Dr., Bldg. 6710B, Room 2350, MSC 7002, Bethesda, MD 20817; (301) 435-6970. Fax, (301) 480-3885. Louis DePaolo, Chief.*
Web, www.nichd.nih.gov/about/org/der/branches/fib

Encourages, enables, and supports scientific research aimed at alleviating human infertility, discovering new ways to control fertility, and expanding knowledge of processes that underlie human reproduction. Funds basic and clinical studies that enhance understanding of normal reproduction and reproductive pathophysiology, as well as enable the development of more effective strategies for the diagnosis, management, and prevention of conditions that compromise fertility.

Eunice Kennedy Shriver National Institute of Child Health and Human Development (NICHD) *(National*

Institutes of Health), Population Dynamics Branch (PDB), 6710B Rockledge Dr., Bldg. 6710B, Room 2206, MSC 7002, Bethesda, MD 20817; (301) 496-1175. Fax, (301) 480-3863. Rebecca L. Clark, Chief.
Web, www.nichd.nih.gov/about/org/der/branches/pdb

Conducts research and research training in demography, which includes the study of human populations, including fertility, mortality and morbidity, migration, population distribution, nuptiality, family demography, population growth and decline, and the causes and consequences of demographic change; reproductive health, including behavioral and social science research on sexually transmitted diseases, HIV/AIDS, family planning, and infertility; and in population health, which focuses on human health, productivity, behavior, and development at the population level using methods including inferential statistics, natural experiments, policy experiments, statistical modeling, and gene/environment interaction studies.

▶ **NONGOVERNMENTAL**

Advocates for Youth, *1325 G. St. N.W., #980, 20005; (202) 419-3420. Fax, (202) 419-1448. Debra Hauser, President.*
General email, information@advocatesforyouth.org
Web, www.advocatesforyouth.org,
Twitter, @AdvocatesTweets and Facebook, www.facebook.com/Advocates4Youth

Seeks to reduce the incidence of unintended teenage pregnancy, sexually transmitted infections, and HIV through public education, training and technical assistance, research, and media programs.

American Society for Reproductive Medicine, J. *Benjamin Younger Office of Public Affairs, 409 12th St. S.W., 20024-2188; (202) 863-2494. Sean B. Tipton, Public Affairs Director.*
General email, advocacy@asrm.dc.org
Web, www.asrm.org and Twitter, @repromed

Membership: obstetrician/gynecologists, urologists, reproductive endocrinologists, embryologists, mental health professionals, internists, nurses, practice administrators, laboratory technicians, pediatricians, research scientists, and veterinarians. Seeks to educate health care professionals, policymakers, and the public on the science and practice of reproductive medicine and associated legal and ethical issues. Monitors legislation and regulations. (Headquarters in Birmingham, Ala.)

Guttmacher Institute, *Public Policy, 1301 Connecticut Ave. N.W., #700, 20036-3902; (202) 296-4012. Fax, (202) 223-5756. Rachel Benson Gold, Vice President of Public Policy; Heather D. Boonstra, Director of Public Policy. Toll-free, (877) 823-0262.*
General email, policyinfo@guttmacher.org
Web, www.guttmacher.org and Twitter, @Guttmacher

Conducts research, policy analysis, and public education in reproductive health, fertility regulation, population, and related areas of U.S. and international health. (Headquarters in New York.)

National Abortion Federation (NAF), *1090 Vermont Ave. N.W., # 1000, 20005; (202) 667-5881. Fax, (202) 667-5890. Vicki Saporta, President. NAF Hotline, (800) 772-9100. General email, naf@prochoice.org*

Web, www.prochoice.org and Twitter, @NatAbortionFed

Professional association of abortion providers in the United States, Canada, and Mexico City. Offers information on medical, legal, and social aspects of abortion; sets quality standards for abortion care. Conducts training and accredited continuing medical education. Runs a toll-free hotline for women seeking information or referrals. Monitors legislation and regulations.

National Family Planning and Reproductive Health Assn., *1025 Vermont Ave., #800, 20005; (202) 293-3114. Fax, (202) 293-1990. Clare Coleman, President. General email, info@nfprha.org*

Web, www.nfprha.org

Represents family planning providers, including nurses, nurse practitioners, administrators, and other health care professionals nationwide. Provides advocacy, education, and training for those in the family planning and reproductive health care field. Interests include family planning for the low-income and uninsured, and reducing rates of unintended pregnancy.

Planned Parenthood Federation of America, *Public Policy, 1110 Vermont Ave. N.W., #300, 20005; (202) 973-4800. Fax, (202) 296-3242. Dr. Leana Wen, President; Vacant, Vice President Government Relations. Press, (202) 261-4433. Toll-free, (800) 230-7526.*

Web, www.plannedparenthood.org and Twitter, @PPFA

Educational, research, and medical services organization. Washington office conducts research and monitors legislation on health care topics, including reproductive health, women's health, contraception, family planning, abortion, and global health. (Headquarters in New York accredits affiliated local centers, which offer medical services, birth control, and family planning information.)

Population Action International, *1300 19th St. N.W., #200, 20036; (202) 557-3400. Fax, (202) 728-4177. Suzanne Ehlers, President. General email, info@pailorg*

Web, www.pai.org

Promotes population stabilization through public education and universal access to voluntary family planning. Library open to the public by appointment.

Population Connection, *2120 L St. N.W., #500, 20037; (202) 332-2200. Fax, (202) 332-2302. John Seager, President. Toll-free, (800) 767-1956. General email, info@populationconnection.org*

Web, www.populationconnection.org and Twitter, @popconnect

Membership: persons interested in sustainable world populations. Promotes the expansion of domestic and international family planning programs; supports a voluntary population stabilization policy and women's access to abortion and family planning services; works to protect the earth's resources and environment. (Formerly Zero Population Growth.)

Population Institute, *105 2nd St. N.E., 20002; (202) 544-3300. Fax, (202) 544-0068. Robert Walker, President; William Ryson, Chief Operating Officer. General email, info@populationinstitute.org*

Web, www.populationinstitute.org and Twitter, @PopInstitute

Promotes voluntary family planning and reproductive health services. Seeks to increase public awareness of social, economic, and environmental consequences of rapid population growth. Advocates a balance between global population and natural resources to policymakers in developing and industrialized nations. Recruits and trains population activists.

Population Reference Bureau, *1875 Connecticut Ave. N.W., #520, 20009-5728; (202) 483-1100. Fax, (202) 328-3937. Jeffrey Jordan, President. Press, (202) 939-5407. Toll-free, (800) 877-9881. General email, popref@prb.org*

Web, www.prb.org and Twitter, @PRBdata

Educational organization engaged in information dissemination, training, and policy analysis on domestic and international population trends and issues. Interests include international development and family planning programs, the environment, and U.S. social and economic policy.

Power to Decide, *1776 Massachusetts Ave. N.W., #200, 20036; (202) 478-8500. Fax, (202) 478-8588. Ginny Ehrlich, Chief Executive Officer. General email, info@powertodecide.org*

Web, www.powertodecide.org and Twitter, @powertodecide

Nonpartisan initiative that seeks to reduce the U.S. teen and unplanned pregnancy rates. Provides education and information regarding contraception. (Formerly the National Campaign to Prevent Teen and Unplanned Pregnancy.)

Genetics, Genetic Disorders

►AGENCIES

Eunice Kennedy Shriver National Institute of Child Health and Human Development (NICHD) *(National Institutes of Health), Intellectual and Developmental Disabilities Branch (IDDB), 6710B Rockledge Dr., Bldg. 6710B, Room 2328, MSC 7002, Bethesda, MD 20817; (301) 496-1383. Fax, (301) 480-5665. Dr. Melissa Ann Parisi, Chief.*

Web, www.nichd.nih.gov/about/org/der/branches/iddb

Supports research projects, training programs, and research centers dedicated understanding, preventing, and ameliorating intellectual and developmental disabilities. Major research areas include common and rare neuromuscular and neurodevelopmental disorders, such as Down, Fragile X, and Rett syndromes; inborn errors of metabolism; autism spectrum disorders; and conditions currently and soon-to-be detectable through newborn screening.

Health Resources and Services Administration (HRSA)
(Health and Human Services Dept.), Maternal and Child Health Bureau (MCHB), 5600 Fishers Lane, #18W, Rockville, MD 20857; (301) 443-2170. Fax, (301) 480-1312. Aaron Lopata, Chief Medical Officer; Michael Warren, Associate Administrator.
Web, www.mchb.hrsa.gov

Awards funds, including demonstration grants, to develop or enhance regional, local, and state genetic screening, diagnostic, counseling, and follow-up programs; assists states in their newborn screening programs; provides funding for regional hemophilia treatment centers; and supports comprehensive care for individuals and families with Cooley's anemia, and those with sickle cell anemia identified through newborn screening.

National Human Genome Research Institute (NHGRI)
(National Institutes of Health), 31 Center Dr., Bldg. 31, #4B09, MSC 2152, Bethesda, MD 20892-2152; (301) 496-0844. Fax, (301) 402-4831. Dr. Eric D. Green, Director. Information, (301) 496-0844.
Web, www.genome.gov, Facebook, www.facebook.com/ genome.gov and Twitter, @genome_gov

Conducts and funds a broad range of studies aimed at understanding the structure and function of the human genome and its role in health and disease. Supports the development of resources and technology that will accelerate genome research and its application to human health. Studies the ethical, legal, and social implications of genome research, and supports the training of investigators, as well as the dissemination of genome information to the public and to health professionals.

National Institute of Allergy and Infectious Diseases (NIAID)
(National Institutes of Health), Allergy, Immunology, and Transplantation (DAIT), 5601 Fishers Lane, #7C13, MS 9828, Rockville, MD 20852; (301) 496-1886. Fax, (301) 402-0175. Dr. Daniel Rotrosen, Director.
Web, www.niaid.nih.gov/about/dait

Supports extramural basic and clinical research to increase understanding of the causes and mechanisms that lead to the development of immunologic diseases and to expand knowledge that can be applied to developing improved techniques of diagnosis, treatment, and prevention. Interests include lupus; allergic diseases, such as asthma, hay fever, and contact dermatitis; and acute and chronic inflammatory disorders.

National Institute of General Medical Sciences (NIGMS)
(National Institutes of Health), Genetics and Developmental Biology (GDB), 45 Center Dr., #2AS25K, MSC 6200, Bethesda, MD 20892-6200; (301) 594-0943. Fax, (301) 480-2228. Dorit Zuk, Division Director.
General email, info@nigms.nih.gov
Web, www.nigms.nih.gov/about/overview/Pages/GDB.aspx

Supports research and research training in genetics. Maintains Human Genetic Cell Repository; distributes cell lines and DNA samples to research scientists.

National Institutes of Health (NIH)
(Health and Human Services Dept.), Biotechnology Activities (OBA), 6705 Rockledge Dr., #750, MSC 7985, Bethesda, MD 20892; (301) 496-9838. Fax, (301) 496-9839. Dr. Jessica Tucker, Director, (301) 451-4431.
General email, oba-osp@od.nih.gov
Web, https://osp.od.nih.gov/biosafety-biosecurity-and-emerging-biotechnology/

Reviews requests submitted to the NIH involving genetic testing, recombinant DNA technology, xenotransplantation, and biosecurity; develops and implements research guidelines for safe conduct of DNA-related research. Monitors scientific progress in human genetics.

▶NONGOVERNMENTAL

Center for Sickle Cell Disease
(Howard University), 1840 7th St. N.W., #203, 20001; (202) 865-8292. Fax, (202) 232-6719. Juan Saloman-Andonie, Administrative Director, (202) 865-8287.
General email, sicklecell@howard.edu
Web, http://huhealthcare.com/healthcare/hospital/ specialty-services/sickle-cell-disease-center

Screens and tests for sickle cell disease; conducts research; promotes public education and community involvement; provides counseling, patient care, and transition support from pediatric to adult care services.

Cystic Fibrosis Foundation,
4550 Montgomery Ave., #1100N, Bethesda, MD 20814; (301) 951-4422. Fax, (301) 951-6378. Dr. Preston W. Campbell III, President. Information, (800) 344-4823.
General email, info@cff.org
Web, www.cff.org and Twitter, @CF_Foundation

Conducts research on cystic fibrosis, a genetic disease affecting the respiratory and digestive systems. Focuses on medical research to identify a cure and to improve quality of life for those living with cystic fibrosis.

Genetic Alliance,
4301 Connecticut Ave. N.W., #404, 20008-2369; (202) 966-5557. Fax, (202) 966-8553. Sharon Terry, Chief Executive Officer.
General email, info@geneticalliance.org
Web, www.geneticalliance.org and Twitter, @GeneticAlliance

Coalition of government, industry, advocacy organizations, and private groups that seeks to advance genetic research and its applications. Promotes increased funding for research, improved access to services, and greater support for emerging technologies, tests, and treatments. Acts as an advocate on behalf of individuals and families living with genetic conditions.

Genetics Society of America,
6120 Executive Blvd., #550, Rockville, MD 20852; (240) 880-2000. Tracey A. DePellegrin, Executive Director.

General email, society@genetics-gsa.org

Web, www.genetics-gsa.org and *Twitter, @GeneticsGSA*

Facilitates professional cooperation among persons conducting research in and teaching genetics. Advocates research funding; sponsors meetings; and publishes scholarly research journals.

Kennedy Institute of Ethics *(Georgetown University),* *Healy Hall, 37th and O Sts. N.W., 4th Floor, 20057; (202) 687-8099. David Sulmasy, Director (Acting). Library, (202) 687-3885.*

General email, kennedyinstitute@georgetown.edu

Web, https://kennedyinstitute.georgetown.edu, Twitter, @kieatgu and *Facebook, www.facebook.com/ KennedyInstituteofEthics*

Carries out teaching and research on medical ethics, including legal and ethical definitions of death, allocation of health resources, and recombinant DNA and human gene therapy. Sponsors the annual Intensive Bioethics Course. Conducts international programs. Serves as the home of the Bioethics Research Library at Georgetown University (http://bioethics.georgetown.edu) and the National Information Resource on Ethics and Human Genetics (http://genthx.georgetown.edu). Provides free reference assistance and bibliographic databases covering all ethical issues in health care, genetics, and biomedical research. Publishes the *Kennedy Institute of Ethics Journal.* Library open to the public.

March of Dimes, *Government Affairs, 1550 Crystal Dr., #1300, Arlington, VA 22202; (202) 659-1800. Fax, (202) 296-2964. Cynthia Pellegrini, Senior Vice President for Public Policy and Government Affairs; Nikki Garro, Director of Public Policy Research. Toll-free, (888) 663-4637.*

Web, www.marchofdimes.org/advocacy-and-government-affairs-issues-and-advocacy-priorities.aspx and *Twitter, @MarchofDimes*

Works to prevent and treat birth defects. Awards grants for research and provides funds for treatment of birth defects. Monitors legislation and regulations. (Headquarters in White Plains, N.Y.)

Osteogenesis Imperfecta Foundation, *804 W. Diamond Ave., #210, Gaithersburg, MD 20878; (301) 947-0083. Fax, (301) 947-0456. Tracy Smith Hart, Chief Executive Officer. Toll-free, (844) 889-7579.*

General email, bonelink@oif.org

Web, www.oif.org and *Twitter, @OIFoundation*

Provides health care professionals and patients with information about osteogenesis imperfecta (OI), also known as brittle bone disease; offers research grants; promotes public policy that supports people living with OI.

Heart Disease, Strokes

▶**AGENCIES**

National Heart, Lung, and Blood Institute (NHLBI) *(National Institutes of Health), Cardiovascular Sciences*

Division (DCVS), *6701 Rockledge Dr., #8128, Bethesda, MD 20892; (301) 435-0422. Fax, (301) 480-7971. Dr. David C. Goff Jr., Director, (301) 435-0422. Press, (301) 496-4236.*

General email, lauerm@nhlbi.nih.gov

Web, www.nhlbi.nih.gov/about/divisions/division-cardiovascular-sciences

Supports basic, clinical, population, and health services research on the causes, prevention, and treatment of cardiovascular disease and technology development. Interests include disease and risk factor patterns in populations; clinical trials of interventions; and genetic, behavioral, sociocultural, environmental, and health-systems factors of disease risk and outcomes.

National Heart, Lung, and Blood Institute (NHLBI) *(National Institutes of Health), Health Information Center, 31 Center Dr., Bldg. 31, Bethesda, MD 20892-2480 (mailing address: P.O. Box 30105, Bethesda, MD 20824-0105); (301) 592-8573. Lenora Johnson, Director, (301) 496-4236.*

General email, nhlbilnfo@nhlbi.nih.gov

Web, www.nhlbi.nih.gov/health/contact

Acquires, maintains, and disseminates information on cholesterol, high blood pressure, heart attack awareness, and asthma to the public and health professionals.

National Institute of Neurological Disorders and Stroke (NINDS) *(National Institutes of Health), 31 Center Dr., Bldg. 31, #8A52, MS 2540, Bethesda, MD 20824; (301) 496-3167. Fax, (301) 402-2186. Dr. Walter J. Koroshetz, Director. Information, (301) 496-5751. Toll-free, (800) 352-9424.*

Web, www.ninds.nih.gov, Twitter, @NINDSnews and *Facebook, www.facebook.com/NINDSandPartners*

Conducts research and disseminates information on the causes, prevention, diagnosis, and treatment of neurological disorders and stroke; supports basic and clinical research in related scientific areas. Provides research grants to public and private institutions and individuals. Operates a program of contracts for the funding of research and research-support efforts.

▶**NONGOVERNMENTAL**

American Heart Assn., *Federal Advocacy, 1150 Connecticut Ave. N.W., #300, 20036; (202) 785-7900. Sue Nelson, Vice President of Federal Advocacy, (202) 785-7912; Kristy Anderson, Government Relations Advisor, (202) 785-7927.*

Web, www.heart.org

Membership: physicians, scientists, and other interested individuals. Supports research, patient advocacy, treatment, and community service programs that provide information about heart disease and stroke; participates in international conferences and research. Monitors legislation and regulations. (Headquarters in Dallas, Texas.)

WomenHeart: National Coalition for Women With Heart Disease, *1100 17th St. N.W., #500, 20036; (202)*

728-7199. Fax, (202) 688-2861. Vacant, Chief Executive Officer. Spanish hotline, (800) 676-6002.
General email, mail@womenheart.org

Web, www.womenheart.org and
Twitter, @WomenHeartOrg

Patient-centered organization that seeks to advance women's heart health through advocacy, community education, and patient support.

HIV and AIDS

▶AGENCIES

Assistant Secretary for Health (OASH) *(Health and Human Services Dept.), HIV/AIDS and Infectious Disease Policy (OHAIDP),* 330 C St. S.W., #L001, 20201; (202) 795-7697. Fax, (202) 691-2102. Tammy Beckham, Director.
Web, www.hhs.gov/ash/ohaidp

HIV/AIDS information, http://aids.gov and
Twitter, @AIDSgov

Advises the Assistant Secretary for Health and senior Health and Human Services officials on the implementation and development of policies, programs, and activities related to HIV/AIDS, viral hepatitis, other infectious diseases of public health signicance, and blood safety and availability.

Assistant Secretary for Health (OASH) *(Health and Human Services Dept.), Minority Health (OMH),* 1101 Wootton Pkwy., #600, Rockville, MD 20852; (240) 453-2882. Fax, (240) 453-2883. Alexis D. Bakos, Deputy Assistant Secretary. Information, (800) 444-6472.
General email, info@minorityhealth.gov

Web, http://minorityhealth.hhs.gov and
Twitter, @MinorityHealth

Awards grants to minority AIDS education and prevention projects.

Centers for Disease Control and Prevention (CDC) *(Health and Human Services Dept.), Washington Office,* 395 E St. S.W., #9100, 20201; (202) 245-0600. Fax, (202) 245-0602. Robert Redfield, Director; Dr. Mitchell (Mitch) Wolfe, Director, Washington Office (Acting). Public inquiries, (800) 232-4636. TTY, (888) 232-6348.
General email, cdcwashington@cdc.gov

Web, www.cdc.gov/washington and Twitter, @CDCgov

Conducts research to prevent and control acquired immune deficiency syndrome (AIDS); promotes public awareness through guidelines for health care workers, educational packets for schools, and monthly reports on incidences of AIDS. (Headquarters in Atlanta, Ga.)

Eunice Kennedy Shriver National Institute of Child Health and Human Development (NICHD) *(National Institutes of Health), Maternal and Pediatric Infectious Disease Branch (MPIDB),* 6710B Rockledge Dr., Bldg.

6710B, Room 2113, MSC 7002, Bethesda, MD 20817; (301) 435-6868. Fax, (301) 480-3882. Dr. Rohan Hazra, Chief.
Web, www.nichd.nih.gov/about/org/der/branches/mpidb

Supports and conducts domestic and international research related to the epidemiology, diagnosis, clinical manifestations, pathogenesis, transmission, treatment, and prevention of HIV infection and its complications in infants, children, adolescents, and pregnant and non-pregnant women. Investigates the effects of HIV and other infectious agents and their therapies on pregnant women, pregnancy outcomes, fetuses, and children, and the impact of pregnancy on the course of HIV disease and other infectious diseases.

Food and Drug Administration (FDA) *(Health and Human Services Dept.), Center for Drug Evaluation and Research (CDER),* White Oak Bldg. 51, 10903 New Hampshire Ave., #6133, Silver Spring, MD 20993; (301) 796-5400. Fax, (301) 595-7910. Dr. Janet Woodcock, Director. Press, (301) 796-3700.
General email, druginfo@fda.hhs.gov

Web, www.fda.gov/drugs and www.fda.gov/AboutFDA/ CentersOffices/OfficeofMedicalProductsandTobacco/CDER

Approves new drugs for AIDS and AIDS-related diseases. Reviews and approves applications to investigate and market new drugs; works to harmonize drug approval internationally.

Health Resources and Services Administration (HRSA) *(Health and Human Services Dept.), HIV/AIDS Bureau (HAB),* 5600 Fishers Lane, #09W37, Rockville, MD 20857; (301) 443-1993. Laura Cheever, Associate Administrator.
Web, www.hab.hrsa.gov

Administers grants to support health care programs for AIDS patients, including those that reimburse low-income patients for drug expenses. Provides patients with AIDS and HIV-related disorders with ambulatory and community-based care. Conducts AIDS/HIV education and training activities for health professionals.

National Institute of Allergy and Infectious Diseases (NIAID) *(National Institutes of Health), HIV/AIDS,* 5601 Fishers Lane, #8D33, MS 9831, Rockville, MD 20852; (301) 496-9112. Fax, (301) 402-1505. Carl W. Dieffenbach, Director.
Web, www.niaid.nih.gov/about/daids

Supports extramural basic and clinical research to better understand HIV and how it causes disease; find new tools to prevent HIV infection, including a preventative vaccine; develop new and more effective treatments for people infected with HIV; and work toward a cure.

National Institute of Mental Health (NIMH) *(National Institutes of Health), AIDS Research Division (DAR),* 5601 Fishers Lane, Room 8D20, Rockville, MD 20852; (240) 627-3874. Dianne M. Rausch, Director.
General email, drausch@mail.nih.gov

Web, www.nimh.nih.gov/about/organization/dar

Supports research programs that reduce the incidence of HIV/AIDS worldwide and decrease the burden of living with HIV/AIDS.

National Institutes of Health (NIH) *(Health and Human Services Dept.), AIDS Research (OAR),* 5601 Fishers Lane, #2F40, MSC 9310, Rockville, MD 20852; (301) 496-0357. Fax, (301) 496-2119. Dr. Maureen M. Goodenow, Director. General email, oarinfo@nih.gov

Web, www.oar.nih.gov

Responsible for the scientific, budgetary, legislative, and policy elements of the NIH AIDS research program. Plans, coordinates, evaluates, and funds all NIH AIDS research.

State Dept., *U.S. Global AIDS Coordinator and Health Diplomacy,* 1800 G St. N.W., SA-22 #10300, 20037; (202) 663-2440. Fax, (202) 663-2979. Deborah L. Birx, Coordinator, (202) 633-2579. Press, (202) 663-1151. General email, SGACPublicAffairs@state.gov

Web, www.state.gov/s/gac and *President's Plan for AIDS Relief,* www.pepfar.gov

Oversees and coordinates all U.S. international HIV/AIDS activities, including implementation of the President's Emergency Plan for AIDS Relief.

Walter Reed Army Institute of Research *(Defense Dept.), U.S. Military HIV Research Program,* 6720A Rockledge Dr., #400, Bethesda, MD 20817; (301) 500-3600. Fax, (301) 500-3666. Robert Gramzinski, Director. General email, info@hivresearch.org

Web, www.hivresearch.org and *Twitter, @MHRPinfo*

Conducts HIV research, encompassing vaccine development, prevention, disease surveillance, and care and treatment options.

Warren Grant Magnuson Clinical Center *(National Institutes of Health), Transfusion Medicine,* 10 Center Dr., Bldg. 10, #1C711, MSC-1184, Bethesda, MD 20892-1184; (301) 496-4506. Fax, (301) 402-1360. Dr. Harvey G. Klein, Department Chief, (301) 496-9702. Press, (301) 496-2563. Web, http://clinicalcenter.nih.gov/dtm and *Twitter, @NIHClinicalCntr*

Supplies blood and blood components for patient care and research. Conducts research on diseases transmissible by blood, primarily AIDS and hepatitis.

▶**NONGOVERNMENTAL**

The AIDS Institute, 1705 DeSales St. N.W., #700, 20036; (202) 835-8373. Fax, (202) 835-8368. Carl Schmid, Deputy Executive Director for Public Policy and Advocacy. General email, info@theaidsinstitute.org

Web, www.theaidsinstitute.org and *Twitter, @TheAIDSInstitute*

Conducts research and disseminates information on health care and HIV issues. Develops and promotes policy aimed at improving the health and welfare of children, youth, and families affected by HIV. Provides training and technical assistance to health care providers and consumers. Monitors legislation ahd regulations. Program office is in Tampa, Florida.

AIDS United, 1101 14th St. N.W., #300, 20005; (202) 408-4848. Fax, (202) 408-1818. Jesse Milan Jr., President, (202) 876-2817. General email, aidsaction@aidsaction.org

Web, www.aidsunited.org, *Twitter, @Aids-United* and *Facebook, www.facebook.com/AIDSUnited*

Channels resources to community-based organizations to fight HIV/AIDS at the local level. Provides grants, capacity building, policy and advocacy, plus technical assistance and research to nearly 400 organizations, principally for prevention efforts.

American Red Cross, *National Headquarters,* 431 18th St. N.W., 20006; (202) 303-5000. Gail J. McGovern, President. Headquarters staff directory, (202) 303-5214, ext. 1. Press, (202) 303-5551. Public inquiry, (202) 303-4498. Toll-free, 800-RED-CROSS (733-2767). Web, www.redcross.org and *Twitter, @RedCross*

Humanitarian relief and health education organization chartered by Congress. Conducts public education campaigns on HIV/AIDS. Operates worldwide vaccination program. Serves as U.S. member of the International Federation of Red Cross and Red Crescent Societies.

Children's AIDS Fund, 1329 Shepard Dr., #7, Sterling, VA 20164 (mailing address: P.O. Box 16433, Washington, DC 20041); (703) 433-1560. Fax, (703) 433-1561. Anita M. Smith, President. General email, info@childrensaidsfund.org

Web, http://childrensaidsfund.org

Provides care, services, resources, referrals, and education to children and their families affected by HIV disease. Focuses on children from birth through age 24 who are infected with HIV, have been orphaned by HIV, or will potentially be orphaned by HIV.

DKT International, 1701 K St. N.W., #900, 20006; (202) 223-8780. Fax, (202) 223-8786. Christopher H. Purdy, President. Press, (646) 964-4446. General email, info@dktinternational.org

Web, www.dktinternational.org and *Twitter, @dktchangeslives*

Supports HIV/AIDS prevention by managing international social marketing campaigns for contraceptives. Assists in family planning and providing safe abortions. Interests include high-risk populations in developing countries.

The Foundation for AIDS Research (amfAR), *Public Policy,* 1100 Vermont Ave. N.W., #600, 20005; (202) 331-8600. Fax, (202) 331-8606. Gregorio Millett, Director. General email, info@amfar.org

Web, www.amfar.org, *Twitter, @amfAR* and *Facebook, www.facebook.com/amfarthefoundationforaidsresearch*

Supports funding for basic biomedical and clinical AIDS research; promotes AIDS prevention education worldwide; advocates effective AIDS-related public policy. Monitors legislation, regulations, and international research. (Headquarters in New York.)

Human Rights Campaign (HRC), *1640 Rhode Island Ave. N.W., 20036-3278; (202) 216-1500. Fax, (202) 347-5323. Chad Griffin, President. Toll-free, (800) 777-4723. TTY, (202) 216-1572.*
General email, hrc@hrc.org
Web, www.hrc.org, Twitter, @HRC and Facebook, www.facebook.com/humanrightscampaign

Promotes legislation to fund HIV/AIDS research and educates the LGBT community and our allies about the realities of HIV prevention, treatment, and care.

National Minority AIDS Council (NMAC), *1000 Vermont Ave. N.W., #200, 20005; (202) 870-0918. Paul A. Kawata, Executive Director, (202) 277-2777.*
General email, communications@nmac.org
Web, www.nmac.org

Works to build the capacity of small faith- and community-based organizations delivering HIV/AIDS services in communities of color. Holds national conferences; administers treatment and research programs and training; dissem inates electronic and printed resource materials; conducts public policy advocacy.

Infectious Diseases, Allergies

▶**AGENCIES**

Assistant Secretary for Health (OASH) *(Health and Human Services Dept.), HIV/AIDS and Infectious Disease Policy (OHAIDP), 330 C St. S.W., #L001, 20201; (202) 795-7697. Fax, (202) 691-2102. Tammy Beckham, Director.*
Web, www.hhs.gov/ash/ohaidp
HIV/AIDS information, http://aids.gov and Twitter, @AIDSgov

Advises the Assistant Secretary for Health and senior Health and Human Services officials on the implementation and development of policies, programs, and activities related to HIV/AIDS, viral hepatitis, other infectious diseases of public health signicance, and blood safety and availability.

Eunice Kennedy Shriver National Institute of Child Health and Human Development (NICHD) *(National Institutes of Health), Maternal and Pediatric Infectious Disease Branch (MPIDB), 6710B Rockledge Dr., Bldg. 6710B, Room 2113, MSC 7002, Bethesda, MD 20817; (301) 435-6868. Fax, (301) 480-3882. Dr. Rohan Hazra, Chief.*
Web, www.nichd.nih.gov/about/org/der/branches/mpidb

Supports and conducts research into the epidemiology, natural history, pathogenesis, transmission, treatment, and prevention of infectious diseases, including congenital infections such as Zika and cytomegalovirus; tropical diseases specifically affecting children and pregnant women; and vaccine-preventable disease in infants, children, adolescents, and women.

Health and Human Services Dept. (HHS), *National Vaccine Program (NVPO), 200 Independence Ave. S.W.,* *#715H, 20201; (202) 690-5566. Tammy R. Beckham, Director (Acting).*
General email, nvpo@hhs.gov
Web, www.hhs.gov/nvpo, www.vaccines.gov and Twitter, @HHSvaccines

Coordinates with federal offices about vaccine and immunization activities. Carries out National Vaccine Plan goals to prevent infectious diseases.

National Institute of Allergy and Infectious Diseases (NIAID) *(National Institutes of Health), 5601 Fishers Lane, MSC 9806, Bethesda, MD 20892-9806; (301) 496-5717. Fax, (301) 402-3573. Dr. Anthony S. Fauci, Director. Press, (301) 402-1663. Toll-free health and research information, (866) 284-4107. TTY health and research information, (800) 877-8339.*
General email, ocpostoffice@niaid.nih.gov
Web, www.niaid.nih.gov, Twitter, @NIAIDNews and Facebook, www.facebook.com/niaid.nih

Conducts research and supports research worldwide on the causes of infectious and immune-mediated diseases to develop better means of prevention, diagnosis, and treatment.

National Institute of Allergy and Infectious Diseases (NIAID) *(National Institutes of Health), Allergy, Immunology, and Transplantation (DAIT), 5601 Fishers Lane, #7C13, MS 9828, Rockville, MD 20852; (301) 496-1886. Fax, (301) 402-0175. Dr. Daniel Rotrosen, Director.*
Web, www.niaid.nih.gov/about/dait

Supports extramural basic and clinical research to increase understanding of the causes and mechanisms that lead to the development of immunologic diseases and to expand knowledge that can be applied to developing improved techniques of diagnosis, treatment, and prevention. Interests include lupus; allergic diseases, such as asthma, hay fever, and contact dermatitis; and acute and chronic inflammatory disorders.

National Institute of Allergy and Infectious Diseases (NIAID) *(National Institutes of Health), Microbiology and Infectious Diseases (DMID), 5601 Fishers Lane, #7G51, MS 9826, Rockville, MD 20892; (301) 435-3385. Emily Erbelding, Director.*
Web, www.niaid.nih.gov/about/dmid

Supports extramural basic and clinical research to control and prevent diseases caused by virtually all human infectious agents except HIV by providing funding and resources for researchers.

▶**NONGOVERNMENTAL**

Allergy and Asthma Network, *8229 Boone Blvd., #260, Vienna, VA 22182-2661; (703) 641-9595. Fax, (703) 288-5271. Tonya Winders, President. Information, (800) 878-4403.*
General email, info@allergyasthmanetwork.org
Web, www.allergyasthmanetwork.org, Twitter, @AllergyAsthmaHQ and Facebook, www.facebook.com/AllergyAsthmaHQ

Membership: families dealing with asthma and allergies. Works to eliminate suffering and death due to asthma, allergies, and related conditions through education, advocacy, and community outreach.

Asthma and Allergy Foundation of America (AAFA), *8201 Corporate Dr., #1000, Landover, MD 20785; (202) 466-7643. Fax, (202) 466-8940. Kenneth Mendez, President. Information, (800) 727-8462.*
General email, info@aafa.org

Web, www.aafa.org and Twitter, @AAFANational

Provides information on asthma and allergies; awards research grants to asthma and allergic disease professionals; offers in-service training to allied health professionals, child care providers, and others.

Food Allergy Research and Education (FARE), *7901 Jones Branch Dr., #240, McLean, VA 22102; (703) 691-3179. Fax, (703) 691-2713. Lisa Gable, Chief Executive Officer. Toll-free, (800) 929-4040.*
General email, contactfare@foodallergy.org

Web, www.foodallergy.org, Twitter, @FoodAllergyFARE and Facebook, www.facebook.com/FoodAllergyFARE

Membership: dietitians, nurses, physicians, school staff, government representatives, members of the food and pharmaceutical industries, and food-allergy patients and their families. Provides information and educational resources on food allergies and allergic reactions. Offers research grants.

National Center for Biodefense and Infectious Diseases *(George Mason University), 10650 Pyramid Pl., MS 1J5, Manassas, VA 20110; (703) 993-4265. Fax, (703) 993-4280. Charles Bailey, Executive Director.*
General email, cbailey2@gmu.edu

Web, http://ncbid.gmu.edu and http://cos.gmu.edu

Researches and develops diagnostics and treatments for emerging infectious diseases as well as those pathogens that could be used as terrorist weapons that require special containment. Manages a graduate education program.

National Foundation for Infectious Diseases, *7201 Wisconsin Ave., #750, Bethesda, MD 20814; (301) 656-0003. Fax, (301) 907-0878. Marla Dalton, Executive Director.*
General email, info@nfid.org

Web, www.nfid.org, Twitter, @NFIDvaccines and Facebook, www.facebook.com/nfidvaccines

Works to educate the public and health care professionals about the causes, treatment, and prevention of infectious diseases.

Kidney Disease

▶AGENCIES

National Institute of Diabetes and Digestive and Kidney Diseases (NIDDK) *(National Institutes of Health), 31 Center Dr., Bldg. 31, #9A52, MS 2560, Bethesda, MD 20892-2560; (301) 496-5741. Fax, (301) 402-2125.*

Dr. Griffin P. Rodgers, Director. Press, (301) 496-3583. TTY, (866) 569-1162.
General email, healthinfo@niddk.nih.gov

Web, www.niddk.nih.gov, Twitter, @NIDDKgov and Facebook, www.facebook.com/National-Institute-of-Diabetes-and-Digestive-and-Kidney-Diseases-NIDDK-159778759845

Conducts and supports basic and clinical research and research training on diabetes and other endocrine and metabolic diseases, digestive diseases, nutrition, obesity, and kidney, urologic, and hematologic diseases. Website provides evidence-based health information.

National Institute of Diabetes and Digestive and Kidney Diseases (NIDDK) *(National Institutes of Health), Kidney, Urologic, and Hematologic Diseases (KUH), 2 Democracy Plaza, 6707 Democracy Blvd., #625, MSC 5458, Bethesda, MD 20892; (301) 496-6325. Fax, (301) 480-3510. Dr. Robert A. Star, Director. Information, (800) 891-5390. Press, (301) 496-3583.*
Web, www.niddk.nih.gov

Funds research on the prevention, diagnosis, and treatment of renal disorders. Conducts research and reviews grant proposals concerning maintenance therapy for persons with chronic kidney, urologic, and renal diseases.

National Institute of Diabetes and Digestive and Kidney Diseases (NIDDK) *(National Institutes of Health), National Kidney and Urologic Diseases Information Clearinghouse, 3 Information Way, Bethesda, MD 20892-3580; (301) 496-3583. Fax, (703) 738-7422. Kathy Kranzfelder, Director. Information, (800) 860-8747. Press, (301) 496-3583. TTY, (866) 569-1162.*
General email, nkudic@info.niddk.nih.gov

Web, www.niddk.nih.gov/health-information/health-communication-programs/niddk-information-clearinghouses/Pages/default.aspx

Supplies health care providers and the public with information on the symptoms, causes, treatments, and general nature of kidney and urologic diseases.

▶NONGOVERNMENTAL

American Kidney Fund, *11921 Rockville Pike, #300, Rockville, MD 20852; LaVarne A. Burton, Chief Executive Officer; Deborah Darcy, Director of Government Relations. Helpline, (866) 300-2900. Toll-free, (800) 638-8299.*
General email, helpline@kidneyfund.org

Web, http://kidneyfund.org, Twitter, @KidneyFund and Facebook, www.facebook.com/AmericanKidneyFund

Provides direct financial support to dialysis and kidney transplant patients in need; supports health education and kidney disease prevention efforts. Monitors legislation and regulations.

American Society of Nephrology (ASN), *1510 H St. N.W., #800, 20005; (202) 640-4660. Fax, (202) 637-9793. Dr. Mark Rosenberg, President.*
General email, email@asn-online.org

Web, www.asn-online.org and Twitter, @ASNKidney

Membership: health professionals who specialize in kidney disease. Holds the annual Kidney Week meeting for members to share research. Advocates awareness of kidney disease. Publishes the *Journal of the American Society of Nephrology* and the *Clinical Journal of the American Society of Nephrology*. Offers online courses and information on training programs for nephrologists. Awards grants and fellowships to members who conduct research on kidney disease treatment and prevention.

National Kidney Foundation, *Government Relations,* *5335 Wisconsin Ave. N.W., #300, 20015-2078; (202) 244-7900. Fax, (202) 244-7405. Michele Anthony, Executive Director. Information, (800) 622-9010.*
General email, infowdc@kidney.org
Web, www.kidney.org; www.kidneywdc.org

Supports funding for kidney dialysis and other forms of treatment for kidney disease; provides information on detection and screening of kidney diseases; supports organ transplantation programs. Monitors legislation, regulations, and international research. (Headquarters in New York.)

Lung Disease

▶**AGENCIES**

National Heart, Lung, and Blood Institute (NHLBI) *(National Institutes of Health), Health Information Center, 31 Center Dr., Bldg. 31, Bethesda, MD 20892-2480 (mailing address: P.O. Box 30105, Bethesda, MD 20824-0105); (301) 592-8573. Lenora Johnson, Director, (301) 496-4236.*
General email, nhlbilnfo@nhlbi.nih.gov
Web, www.nhlbi.nih.gov/health/contact

Acquires, maintains, and disseminates information on asthma and other lung ailments.

National Heart, Lung, and Blood Institute (NHLBI) *(National Institutes of Health), Lung Diseases Division (DLD), 2 Rockledge Center, 6701 Rockledge Dr., #10042, MS 7952, Bethesda, MD 20892; (301) 435-0233. Fax, (301) 480-3547. James P. Kiley, Director.*
Web, www.nhlbi.nih.gov/about/divisions/division-lung-diseases and Twitter, @NHLB_LungDiv

Plans, implements, and monitors research and training programs in lung diseases and sleep disorders, including research on causes, diagnosis, treatments, prevention, and health education. Interests include COPD, genetics, cystic fibrosis, asthma, bronchopulmonary dysplasia, immunology, respiratory neurobiology, sleep-disordered breathing, critical care and acute lung injury, developmental biology and pediatric pulmonary diseases, immunologic and fibrotic pulmonary disease, rare lung disorders, pulmonary vascular disease, and pulmonary complications of AIDS and tuberculosis.

▶**NONGOVERNMENTAL**

American Lung Assn., *1331 Pennsylvania Ave. N.E., #1425N, 20004 (mailing address: 211 East Lombard St., Baltimore, MD 21202); (302) 565-2073.*

Harold P. Wimmer, President; Dina Gordon, Executive Director, (302) 565-2073. Toll-free, (800) 586-4872.
General email, info@lung.org
Web, www.lung.org and Twitter, @LungAssociation

Promotes improved lung health and the prevention of lung disease through research, education, and advocacy. Interests include antismoking campaigns; lung-related biomedical research; air pollution; and all lung diseases, including asthma, COPD, and lung cancer. (Headquarters in Chicago, Ill.)

Cystic Fibrosis Foundation, *4550 Montgomery Ave., #1100N, Bethesda, MD 20814; (301) 951-4422. Fax, (301) 951-6378. Dr. Preston W. Campbell III, President. Information, (800) 344-4823.*
General email, info@cff.org
Web, www.cff.org and Twitter, @CF_Foundation

Conducts research on cystic fibrosis, a genetic disease affecting the respiratory and digestive systems. Focuses on medical research to identify a cure and to improve quality of life for those living with cystic fibrosis.

Lung Cancer Alliance, *1700 K St. N.W., #660, 20006; (202) 463-2080. Laurie Fenton Ambrose, President. Press, (202) 742-1428. Toll-free helpline, (800) 298-2436.*
General email, info@lungcanceralliance.org
Web, www.lungcanceralliance.org

Advocates lung cancer research and access to screenings, treatments, diagnostics, and testing. Provides information about lung cancer risks and early detection.

Neurological and Muscular Disorders

▶**AGENCIES**

Eunice Kennedy Shriver National Institute of Child Health and Human Development (NICHD) *(National Institutes of Health), Intellectual and Developmental Disabilities Branch (IDDB), 6710B Rockledge Dr., Bldg. 6710B, Room 2328, MSC 7002, Bethesda, MD 20817; (301) 496-1383. Fax, (301) 480-5665. Dr. Melissa Ann Parisi, Chief.*
Web, www.nichd.nih.gov/about/org/der/branches/iddb

Supports research projects, training programs, and research centers dedicated to understanding, preventing, and ameliorating intellectual and developmental disabilities. Major research areas include common and rare neuromuscular and neurodevelopmental disorders, such as Down, Fragile X, and Rett syndromes; inborn errors of metabolism; autism spectrum disorders; and conditions currently and soon-to-be detectable through newborn screening.

National Institute of Mental Health (NIMH) *(National Institutes of Health), Neuroscience and Basic Behavioral Science Division (DNBBS), 6001 Executive Blvd., #7204, MSC 9645, Rockville, MD 20892; (301) 443-3563. Fax, (301) 443-1731. Linda S. Brady, Director.*
Web, www.nimh.nih.gov/about/organization/dnbbs

Supports research programs in the areas of basic neuroscience, genetics, basic behavioral science, research training, resource development, drug discovery, and research dissemination. Responsible for ensuring that relevant basic science knowledge is generated to create improved diagnosis, treatment, and prevention of mental and behavioral disorders.

National Institute of Neurological Disorders and Stroke (NINDS) *(National Institutes of Health), 31 Center Dr., Bldg. 31, #8A52, MS 2540, Bethesda, MD 20824; (301) 496-3167. Fax, (301) 402-2186. Dr. Walter J. Koroshetz, Director. Information, (301) 496-5751. Toll-free, (800) 352-9424. Web, www.ninds.nih.gov, Twitter, @NINDSnews and Facebook, www.facebook.com/NINDSandPartners*

Conducts research and disseminates information on the causes, prevention, diagnosis, and treatment of neurological disorders and stroke; supports basic and clinical research in related scientific areas. Provides research grants to public and private institutions and individuals. Operates a program of contracts for the funding of research and research-support efforts.

▶**NONGOVERNMENTAL**

Alzheimer's Assn., *Public Policy Office, 1212 New York Ave., #800, 20005-6105; (202) 393-7737. Rachel Conant, Senior Political Director, ext. 7121; Robert J. Egge, Chief of Public Policy, ext. 8660. Toll-free, (866) 865-0270. Helpline, (800) 272-3900.*
General email, advocateinfo@alz.org

Web, www.alz.org and Twitter, www.twitter.com/ alzassociation and Facebook, www.facebook.com/actionalz and Virtual library, www.alz.org/library

Offers family support services and educates the public about Alzheimer's disease, a neurological disorder mainly affecting the brain tissue in older adults. Promotes research and long-term care protection; maintains liaison with Alzheimer's associations abroad. Monitors legislation and regulations. (Headquarters in Chicago, Ill.)

American Academy of Orthopaedic Surgeons, *Government Relations, 317 Massachusetts Ave. N.E., 1st Floor, 20002; (202) 546-4430. Fax, (202) 546-5051. Graham H. Newson, Director.*
General email, dc@aaos.org

Web, www.aaos.org/Advocacy and Twitter, @AAOSAdvocacy

Membership: orthopaedic surgeons and musculoskeletal care professionals. Offers continuing education activities; publishes scientific and medical journals and electronic resources. Engages in health policy and acts as advocate on behalf of orthopaedic surgeons and patients. (Headquarters in Rosemont, Ill.)

Autism Speaks, *Washington Office, 1990 K St. N.W., 2nd Floor, 20006; (202) 955-3111. Angela Geiger, President. Toll-free, (888) 288-4762.*
General email, NationalCapitolArea@AutismSpeaks.org

Web, www.autismspeaks.org and Twitter, @autismspeaks

Science and advocacy organization that funds biomedical research to determine the causes, prevention, treatments, and cure for autism.

Brain Injury Assn. of America, *1608 Spring Hill Rd., #110, Vienna, VA 22182; (703) 761-0750. Fax, (703) 761-0755. Susan H. Connors, President. Information, (800) 444-6443. General email, info@biausa.org*
Web, www.biausa.org and Twitter, @biaamerica

Works to improve the quality of life for persons with traumatic brain injuries and for their families. Promotes the prevention of head injuries through public awareness and education programs. Offers state-level support services for individuals and their families. Monitors legislation and regulations.

CHADD: The National Resource on ADHD, *4601 Presidents Dr., #300, Lanham, MD 20706; (301) 306-7070. Fax, (301) 306-7090. Belynda L. Gauthier, President. Toll-free, (800) 233-4050.*
Web, www.chadd.org and Twitter, @CHADD_ADHD

Membership: health care and mental health professionals, educators, and individuals with ADHD or ADHD-related symptoms. Conducts advocacy and outreach to policymakers at the state and federal levels in areas including health care reform, bullying in schools, and mental health parity. The affiliated National Research Center is a CDC-funded clearinghouse for evidence-based information about ADHD.

Epilepsy Foundation, *8301 Professional Pl. East, #230, Landover, MD 20785-2356; (301) 459-3700. Fax, (301) 577-2684. Phillip Gattone, Chief Executive Officer. Information, (800) 332-1000. Spanish language, (866) 748-8008.*
General email, contactus@efa.org
Web, www.epilepsy.com and Twitter, @EpilepsyFdn

Promotes research and treatment of epilepsy; makes research grants; disseminates information and educational materials. Affiliates provide direct services for people with epilepsy and make referrals when necessary.

National Multiple Sclerosis Society, *Washington Chapter, 1800 M St. N.W., #B50 North, 20036; (202) 296-5363. Fax, (202) 296-3425. Chartese Berry, Chapter President, (202) 375-5616. Toll-free, (800) 344-4867. General email, info-dcmd@nmss.org*
Web, www.msandyou.org

Seeks to advance medical knowledge of multiple sclerosis, a disease of the central nervous system; disseminates information worldwide. (Headquarters in New York.)

North American Spine Assn., *Washington Office, 300 New Jersey Ave N.W., 20001; (202) 575-2020. Jeffrey Wang, President, (323) 442-5303. Toll-free, (888) 960-6277. Web, www.spine.org and Twitter, @NASSspine*

Supports research and advocacy for quality, ethical, evidence-based spine care for patients.

Society for Neuroscience, *1121 14th St. N.W., #1010, 20005; (202) 962-4000. Fax, (202) 962-4941. Marty Saggese, Executive Director.*

General email, info@sfn.org

Web, www.sfn.org and Twitter, @SfNtweets

Membership: scientists and physicians worldwide who research the brain, spinal cord, and nervous system. Interests include the molecular and cellular levels of the nervous system; systems within the brain, such as vision and hearing; and behavior produced by the brain. Promotes education in the neurosciences and the application of research to treat nervous system disorders.

Spina Bifida Assn., *1600 Wilson Blvd., #800, Arlington, VA 22209 (mailing address: P.O. Box 17427, Arlington, VA 22216); (202) 944-3285. Fax, (202) 944-3295. Sara Struwe, Chief Executive Officer, ext. 12. Information, (800) 621-3141.*

General email, sbaa@sbaa.org

Web, http://spinabifidaassociation.org and Twitter, @SpinaBifidaAssn

Membership: individuals with spina bifida, their supporters, and concerned professionals. Offers educational programs, scholarships, and support services; acts as a clearinghouse; provides referrals and information about treatment and prevention. Serves as U.S. member of the International Federation for Hydrocephalus and Spina Bifida, which is headquartered in Geneva, Switzerland. Monitors legislation and regulations.

United Cerebral Palsy (UCP), *1825 K St. N.W., #600, 20006; (202) 776-0406. Fax, (202) 776-0414. Armando Contreras, President. Information, (800) 872-5827.*

Web, www.ucp.org and Twitter, @UCPnational

National network of state and local affiliates that assists individuals with cerebral palsy and other developmental disabilities and their families. Provides parent education, early intervention, employment services, family support and respite programs, therapy, assistive technology, and vocational training.

Nutrition

▶**AGENCIES**

Center for Nutrition Policy and Promotion *(Agriculture Dept.), 3101 Park Center Dr., 10th Floor, Alexandria, VA 22302-1594; (703) 305-7600. Fax, (703) 305-3300. Vacant, Executive Director. Press, (703) 305-2281.*

Web, www.cnpp.usda.gov, Twitter, @MyPlate and Facebook, www.facebook.com/MyPlate

Defines and coordinates nutrition education policy, promotes food and nutrition guidance, and develops nutrition information materials for consumers, policymakers, and professionals in health, education, industry, and media.

Eunice Kennedy Shriver National Institute of Child Health and Human Development (NICHD) *(National Institutes of Health), Pediatric Growth and Nutrition Branch (PGNB), 6710B Rockledge Dr., Bldg. 6710B, Room 2444, MSC 7002, Bethesda, MD 20817; (301) 402-7886. Andrew Bremer, Chief.*

Web, www.nichd.nih.gov/about/org/der/branches/pgnb

Supports research to understand basic and clinical aspects of growth and development, including the biological processes that underlie normal growth and development, as well as research on how these biological processes go awry. Major research programs include how nutrition promotes healthy growth and development; lactation and breastfeeding; the causes of obesity in childhood and sequelae of childhood obesity in adulthood; the genetic, nutritional, and hormonal antecedents of bone health and the origins of osteoporosis; the neuroendocrine basis of growth and the onset of puberty; and the development of the hypothalamo-pituitary adrenal, gonadal, and thyroid axes.

Food and Drug Administration (FDA) *(Health and Human Services Dept.), Center for Food Safety and Applied Nutrition (CFSAN), 5001 Campus Dr., College Park, MD 20740-3835; (240) 402-1600. Fax, (301) 436-2668. Susan T. Mayne, Director.*

General email, consumer@fda.gov

Web, www.fda.gov/AboutFDA/CentersOffices/OfficeofFoods/CFSAN

Conducts research about dietary supplements and nutrition in general.

National Agricultural Library *(Agriculture Dept.), Food and Nutrition Information Center (FNIC), 10301 Baltimore Ave., #108, Beltsville, MD 20705-2351; (301) 504-5414. Fax, (301) 504-6409. Wendy Davis, Nutrition and Food Safety Program Leader, (301) 504-6369.*

General email, fnic@ars.usda.gov

Web, www.nal.usda.gov/fnic

Serves primarily educators, health professionals, and consumers seeking information about nutrition assistance programs and general nutrition. Serves as an online provider of science-based information about food and nutrition and links to such information. Lends books and audiovisual materials for educational purposes through interlibrary loans; maintains a database of food and nutrition software and multimedia programs; provides reference services; develops resource lists of health and nutrition publications. Library open to the public.

National Institute of Diabetes and Digestive and Kidney Diseases (NIDDK) *(National Institutes of Health), Digestive Diseases and Nutrition (DDN), 2 Democracy Plaza, 6707 Democracy Blvd., #677, MSC 5450, Bethesda, MD 20892-5450; (301) 594-7680. Fax, (301) 480-8300. Stephen P. James, Director. Press, (301) 496-3583.*

Web, www.niddk.nih.gov

Awards grants and contracts to support basic and clinical research related to digestive diseases and nutrition, as well as training and career development. Conducts and supports research concerning liver and biliary diseases; pancreatic diseases; gastrointestinal disease, including neuroendocrinology, motility, immunology, absorption, and transport in the gastrointestinal tract; nutrient metabolism; obesity; and eating disorders.

National Institute of Diabetes and Digestive and Kidney Diseases (NIDDK) *(National Institutes of Health), Nutrition Research (ONR), 2 Democracy Plaza, 6707 Democracy Blvd., #677, MS 5450, Bethesda, MD 20892; (301) 594-3988. Fax, (301) 480-3768. Dr. Christopher J. Lynch, Director. General email, nutritionresearch@mail.nih.gov*

Web, www.niddk.nih.gov/about-niddk/offices-divisions/office-nutrition-research

Supports research on nutritional requirements, dietary fiber, obesity, eating disorders, energy regulation, clinical nutrition, trace minerals, and basic nutrient functions.

National Institute of Food and Agriculture (NIFA) *(Agriculture Dept.), Institute of Food Safety and Nutrition, 1400 Independence Ave. S.W., MS 2225, 20250-2225; (202) 702-5004. Fax, (202) 401-4888. Vacant, Deputy Director. Web, https://nifa.usda.gov/office/institute-food-safety-and-nutrition*

Promotes programs to improve citizens' health through better nutrition, reducing childhood obesity, and improving food quality.

National Institutes of Health (NIH) *(Health and Human Services Dept.), Dietary Supplements (ODS), 6100 Executive Blvd., #3B01, MSC-7517, Bethesda, MD 20892-7517; (301) 435-2920. Fax, (301) 480-1845. Joseph Betz, Director (Acting). General email, ods@nih.gov*

Web, http://ods.od.nih.gov and Twitter, @NIH_ODS

Reviews scientific evidence on the safety and efficacy of dietary supplements. Conducts, promotes, and coordinates scientific research within the NIH relating to dietary supplements. Conducts and supports conferences, workshops, and symposia and publishes research results on scientific topics related to dietary supplements.

▶**NONGOVERNMENTAL**

Academy of Nutrition and Dietetics, *Washington Office, Policy Inititives and Advocacy, 1120 Connecticut Ave. N.W., #460, 20036-3989; (202) 775-8277. Fax, (202) 775-8284. Jeanne Blankenship, Vice President of Policy Initiatives and Advocacy, (312) 899-0040, ext. 6004. Toll-free, (800) 877-0877. General email, govaffairs@eatright.org*

Web, www.eatright.org and Facebook, www.facebook.com/EatRightNutrition

Press, media@eatright.org

Membership: dietitians and other nutrition professionals. Promotes public health and nutrition; accredits academic programs in clinical nutrition and food service management; sets standards of professional practice. Sponsors the National Center for Nutrition and Dietetics. (Headquarters in Chicago, Ill.)

American Society for Nutrition, *9211 Corporate Blvd., #300, Rockville, MD 20850; (240) 428-3650. Fax, (240) 404-6797. John E. Courtney, Executive Officer. General email, info@nutrition.org*

Web, www.nutrition.org and Twitter, @nutritionorg

Membership: nutritional research scientists and practitioners, including clinical nutritionists. Supports and advocates research on the role of human nutrition in health and disease; encourages undergraduate and graduate nutrition education; supports minority affairs; offers awards for research. (Merger of the American Society for Clinical Nutrition and the American Society for Nutritional Sciences.)

American Society for Parenteral and Enteral Nutrition (ASPEN), *8401 Colesville Rd., #510, Silver Spring, MD 20910-3805; (301) 587-6315. Fax, (301) 587-2365. Wanda Johnson, Chief Executive Director, ext. 126. General email, aspen@nutrition.org*

Web, www.nutritioncare.org, Twitter, @ASPENWEB and Facebook, www.facebook.com/nutritioncare.org

Membership: health care professionals who provide patients with intravenous nutritional support during hospitalization and rehabilitation at home. Develops nutrition guidelines; provides educational materials; conducts annual meetings.

Eating Disorders Coalition for Research, Policy, and Action, *P.O. Box 96503-98807, 20090; (202) 543-9570. Fax, (646) 417-6378. David Jaffe, Executive Director. General email, manager@eatingdisorderscoalition.org*

Web, www.eatingdisorderscoalition.org and Twitter, @EDCoalition

Seeks greater national and federal recognition of eating disorders. Promotes recognition of eating disorders as a public health priority and the implementation of more accessible treatment and more effective prevention programs. Monitors legislation and regulations.

Obesity Society, *1110 Bonifant St., #500, Silver Spring, MD 20910; (301) 563-6526. Fax, (301) 563-6595. Dr. Steven B. Heymsfield, President; Anthony Comuzzie, Executive Director; Laura Tester Meyer, Chief Operating Officer. Web, www.obesity.org, Twitter, @ObesitySociety and Facebook, www.facebook.com/TheObesitySociety*

Promotes research, education, and advocacy to better understand, prevent, and treat obesity. Informs the medical community and the public of new advances.

Sleep Disorders

▶**AGENCIES**

National Heart, Lung, and Blood Institute (NHLBI) *(National Institutes of Health), Lung Diseases Division (DLD), National Center on Sleep Disorders Research (NCSDR), 6701 Rockledge Dr., #10170, MS 7952, Bethesda, MD 20892; (301) 435-0199. Fax, (301) 480-3451. Michael J. Twery, Program Director. Web, www.nhlbi.nih.gov/about/org/ncsdr*

Supports research and training related to sleep and circadian rhythm risks contributing to heart, lung, and blood disorders. Serves as a point of contact and coordination for sleep research and education across NIH, several federal agencies, and outside organizations.

▶NONGOVERNMENTAL

American Sleep Apnea Assn., *641 S St. N.W., 3rd Floor, 20001-5196; (888) 293-3650. Adam Amdur, Chief Patient Officer, (305) 773-8877.*
General email, asaa@sleepapnea.org
Web, www.sleepapnea.org, Twitter, @sleepapnea.org and Facebook, www.facebook.com/sleepapnea.org

Promotes continuing improvements in treatments for sleep apnea and acts as advocate on behalf of sleep apnea patients. Monitors legislation and regulations.

Circadian Sleep Disorders Network, *4619 Woodfield Rd., Bethesda, MD 20814; Peter Mansbach, President.*
General email, csd-n@csd-n.org
Web, www.circadiansleepdisorders.org and Twitter, @CSD_N

Seeks to increase awareness of circadian sleep disorders among the medical community and general public. Acts as advocate for accommodation of patients in education and employment.

National Sleep Foundation, *1010 N. Glebe Rd., #420, Arlington, VA 22201; (703) 243-1697. Fax, (202) 347-3472. David Cloud, Chief Executive Officer.*
General email, nsf@sleepfoundation.org
Web, www.sleepfoundation.org and Twitter, @sleepfoundation

Supports sleep-related public education and research to understand sleep problems and sleep disorders, including insomnia, sleep apnea, and narcolepsy. Works to prevent sleep-related accidents, especially those that involve driving. Monitors legislation and regulations related to sleep, alertness, and safety, such as hours-of-service rules for commercial drivers.

National Sleep Foundation, *Sleep for Kids, 1010 N. Glebe Rd., #310, Arlington, VA 22201; General email, nsf@sleepfoundation.org*
Web, www.sleepforkids.org

Provides information about the importance of sleep for children and sleep disorders, and tips for parents and teachers to help school-age children develop good sleep habits.

Substance Abuse

▶AGENCIES

Education Dept., *Elementary and Secondary Education (OESE), Safe and Healthy Students (OSHS), Lyndon Baines Johnson Bldg., 400 Maryland Ave. S.W., #3E-245, 20202-6135; (202) 453-6777. Fax, (202) 453-6742. Paul Kesner, Director (Acting).*

General email, oese@ed.gov
Web, www2.ed.gov/about/offices/list/oese/oshs

Develops policy for the department's drug and violence prevention initiatives for students in elementary and secondary schools and institutions of higher education. Provides financial assistance for drug and violence prevention activities. Coordinates education efforts in drug and violence prevention with those of other federal departments and agencies.

National Drug Control Policy (ONDCP) *(Executive Office of the President), President's Commission on Combating Drug Addiction and the Opioid Crisis, The White House, Washington, DC, 20500; (202) 456-1111. James W. Carroll, Director.*
General email, commission@ondcp.eop.gov
Web, www.whitehouse.gov/ondcp/presidents-commission

Conducts research and studies around ways to combat and treat drug abuse, addiction, and the opioid crisis that affects communities across the United States.

National Institute on Alcohol Abuse and Alcoholism (NIAAA) *(National Institutes of Health), 5635 Fishers Lane, MSC 9304, Bethesda, MD 20892-9304; (301) 443-3885. Fax, (301) 443-7043. Dr. George F. Koob, Director. Press, (301) 443-3860.*
General email, niaaaweb-r@exchange.nih.gov
Web, www.niaaa.nih.gov

Supports basic and applied research on preventing and treating alcoholism and alcohol-related problems; conducts research and disseminates findings on alcohol abuse and alcoholism. Participates in U.S. and international research.

National Institute on Drug Abuse (NIDA) *(National Institutes of Health), 6001 Executive Blvd., #5213, MSC-9561, Bethesda, MD 20892-9581; (301) 443-1124. Fax, (301) 480-2485. Dr. Nora Volkow, Director. Press, (301) 443-6245.*
Web, www.drugabuse.gov

Conducts and sponsors research on the prevention, effects, and treatment of drug abuse. Monitors international policy and research.

Substance Abuse and Mental Health Services Administration (SAMHSA) *(Health and Human Services Dept.), 5600 Fishers Lane, Rockville, MD 20852; (240) 276-2000. Fax, (240) 489-1450. Elinore F. McCance-Katz, Assistant Secretary. Hotline, (800) 662-4357. Information, (877) 726-4727. Toll-free, (800) 487-4889.*
General email, samhsainfo@samhsa.hhs.gov
Web, www.samhsa.gov and Twitter, @samhsagov

Provides and manages block grants and special programmatic funding aimed at reducing the impact of substance abuse and mental illness on communities. Provides states, providers, communities, and the public with information about behavioral health issues and prevention/treatment approaches. Administers substance abuse and mental health treatment referral service: (800) 662-4357 or www.samhsa.gov/treatment. Offers behavioral health publications and other resources: http://store.samhsa.gov/home or P.O. Box 2345, Rockville, MD 20847.

Substance Abuse and Mental Health Services Administration (SAMHSA) *(Health and Human Services Dept.), Center for Substance Abuse Prevention (CSAP), 5600 Fishers Lane, Rockville, MD 20852; (240) 276-2420. Fax, (301) 480-8480. Luis Vaquez, Director (Acting). Information, (877) 726-4727. TTY, (800) 487-4889. Workplace helpline, 800-WORKPLACE; (800) 967-5752. Web, www.samhsa.gov/about-us/who-we-are/offices-centers/csap*

Demonstrates, evaluates, and disseminates strategies for preventing alcohol and drug abuse. Operates the National Clearinghouse for Alcohol and Drug Information, which provides information, publications, and grant applications for programs to prevent substance abuse. (Clearinghouse address: http://store.samhsa.gov or P.O. Box 2345, Rockville, MD 20847; toll-free phone, (800) 729-6686.)

Substance Abuse and Mental Health Services Administration (SAMHSA) *(Health and Human Services Dept.), Center for Substance Abuse Treatment (CSAT), 5600 Fishers Lane, Rockville, MD 20852; (240) 276-1660. Fax, (301) 480-6596. Anne Herron, Director (Acting). Information, (877) 726-4727. Publications, (877) 726-4727. Treatment referral, (800) 662-4357. TTY, (800) 487-4889. Web, www.samhsa.gov/about-us/who-we-are/offices-centers/csat*

Develops and supports policies and programs that improve and expand treatment services for alcoholism, substance abuse, and addiction. Administers grants that support private and public addiction prevention and treatment services. Evaluates alcohol treatment programs and other drug treatment programs and delivery systems.

▶**INTERNATIONAL ORGANIZATIONS**

International Commission for the Prevention of Alcoholism and Drug Dependency, *12501 Old Columbia Pike, Silver Spring, MD 20904; (301) 680-6719. Fax, (301) 680-6707. Yves Daccord, Director-general; Katia Reinart, Director of North American Region, (301) 680-6833. General email, the_icpa@hotmail.com*

Web, http://icpaworld.org

Membership: health officials, physicians, educators, clergy, and judges worldwide. Promotes scientific research on prevention of alcohol and drug dependencies; provides information about medical effects of alcohol and drugs; conducts world congresses. (Health Ministries Dept. of the General Conference of Seventh-Day Adventists.)

▶**NONGOVERNMENTAL**

American Society of Addiction Medicine, *11400 Rockville Pike, #200, Rockville, MD 20852; (301) 656-3920. Fax, (301) 656-3815. Penny Mills, Executive Vice President, (301) 547-4105.*

General email, email@asam.org

Web, www.asam.org and Twitter, @ASAMorg

Membership: physicians and medical students. Supports the study and provision of effective treatment and care for people with alcohol and drug dependencies; educates physicians. Monitors legislation and regulations.

Assn. for Addiction Professionals (AAP), *44 Canal Center Plaza, #301, Alexandria, VA 22314; (703) 741-7686. Fax, (800) 377-1136. Cynthia Moreno Tuohy, Executive Director. Information, (800) 548-0497. General email, naadac2@naadac.org*

Web, www.naadac.org and Twitter, @NAADACorp

Membership: professionals in the addiction field. Supports professional development by providing educational resources, certification programs, workshops, and conferences for treatment professionals. (Formerly National Assn. of Alcoholism and Drug Abuse Counselors.)

Drug Policy Alliance, *National Affairs, 1620 Eye St. N.W., #925, 20006; (202) 683-2030. Fax, (202) 216-0803. Maria McFarland Sánchez-Moreno, Executive Director. General email, contact@drugpolicy.org*

Web, www.drugpolicy.org and Twitter, @DrugPolicyOrg

Supports reform of current drug control policy; seeks to broaden debate on drug policy to include considering alternatives to incarceration, expanding lawful maintenance therapies, and restoring constitutional protections; advocates medical treatment to control drug abuse; opposes random drug testing; studies drug policy in other countries. Sponsors the biennial International Conference on Drug Policy Reform. Monitors legislation and regulations. (Headquarters in New York.)

Drug Strategies, *2101 L St. N.W., #800, 20037; (415) 638-6600. Mathea Falco, President. General email, drugstrategies@gmail.com*

Web, www.drugstrategies.com

Researches effectiveness of drug abuse prevention, treatment, and education. Supports effective practices and educates the public on treating substance abuse. Special interests include teenagers and prescription pill abuse.

Mothers Against Drunk Driving (MADD), *Government Affairs, 1200 18th St. N.W., #700, 20036; (202) 688-1193. Fax, (972) 869-2206. J.T. Griffin, Chief Government Affairs Officer; Frank Harris, State Legislative Affairs Manager, (202) 688-1194. 24-hour helpline, 877-MADD-HELP. Toll-free, (877) 275-6233. General email, policy@madd.org*

Web, www.madd.org, Twitter, @MADDOnline and Facebook, www.facebook.com/MADD.Official

Advocacy group that seeks to stop drunk driving and prevent underage drinking. Monitors legislation and regulations. (Headquarters in Irving, Tex.)

National Assn. of State Alcohol and Drug Abuse Directors (NASADAD), *1919 Pennsylvania Ave. N.W.,*

#M250, 20006; (202) 293-0090. Fax, (202) 293-1250. Robert (Rob) Morrison, Executive Director, ext. 4862. General email, dcoffice@nasadad.org

Web, http://nasadad.org

Provides information on drug abuse treatment and prevention; contracts with federal and state agencies for design of programs to fight and prevent drug abuse.

Treatment Communities of America (TCA), *2200 Pennsylvania Ave. N.W., #4075E, 20037; (202) 296-3503. Patricia Clay, Executive Director. Web, www.treatmentcommunitiesofamerica.org*

Membership: nonprofit organizations that provide substance abuse and mental health treatment and rehabilitation. Provides policy analysis and educates the public on substance abuse and treatment issues. Promotes the interests of therapeutic communities, their clients, and staffs. Monitors legislation and regulations.

MENTAL HEALTH

General

▶**AGENCIES**

National Institute of Mental Health (NIMH) *(National Institutes of Health), 6001 Executive Blvd., #6200, MSC 9663, Bethesda, MD 20892-9663; (301) 443-4513. Fax, (301) 443-4279. Dr. Joshua A. Gordon, Director, (301) 443-3673. Toll-free, (866) 615-6464. Toll-free TTY, (866) 415-8051. TTY, (301) 443-8431. General email, nimhinfo@nih.gov*

Web, www.nimh.nih.gov, Twitter, @NIMHgov and Facebook, www.facebook.com/nimhgov

Conducts research on the cause, diagnosis, treatment, and prevention of mental disorders; provides information on mental health problems and programs. Participates in international research.

National Institute of Mental Health (NIMH) *(National Institutes of Health), Neuroscience and Basic Behavioral Science Division (DNBBS), 6001 Executive Blvd., #7204, MSC 9645, Rockville, MD 20892; (301) 443-3563. Fax, (301) 443-1731. Linda S. Brady, Director. Web, www.nimh.nih.gov/about/organization/dnbbs*

Supports research programs in the areas of basic neuroscience, genetics, basic behavioral science, research training, resource development, drug discovery, and research dissemination. Responsible for ensuring that relevant basic science knowledge is generated to create improved diagnosis, treatment, and prevention of mental and behavioral disorders.

National Institute of Mental Health (NIMH) *(National Institutes of Health), Research on Disparities and Global Mental Health (ORDGMH), 6001 Executive Blvd., #7213, MSC 9659, Bethesda, MD 20892; (301) 443-2847.*

Fax, (301) 443-9877. Andrea Beckel-Mitchener, Director (Acting). Web, www.nimh.nih.gov/about/organization/gmh

Funds and oversees research to identify trends and gaps in the areas of mental health disparities, women's mental health, and global mental health. Supports research training for minorities in the mental health field; supports development of the mental health research workforce in low- and middle-income countries.

National Institute of Mental Health (NIMH) *(National Institutes of Health), Services and Intervention Research Division (DSIR), 6001 Executive Blvd., Room 7141, MS 9629, Rockville, MD 20852; (301) 435-0371. Robert K. Heinssen, Director. Web, www.nimh.nih.gov/about/organization/dsir*

Supports research programs to evaluate the effectiveness of pharmacologic, psychosocial, somatic, rehabilitative, and combination interventions on mental and behavior disorders; conducts mental health services research.

National Institute of Mental Health (NIMH) *(National Institutes of Health), Translational Research Division (DTR), 6001 Executive Blvd., #8128, MSC 9032, Bethesda, MD 20892; (301) 451-3029. Fax, (301) 480-4415. Dr. Sarah H. Lisanby, Director. Web, www.nimh.nih.gov/about/organization/dtr*

Directs, plans, and supports programs of research and research training that translate knowledge from basic science to discover the etiology, pathophysiology, and trajectory of mental disorders and develops effective interventions for children and adults. Supports integrative, multidisciplinary research on the following areas: the phenotype characterization and risk factors for psychiatric disorders; neurobehavioral mechanisms of psychopathology; trajectories of risk and resilience based on the interactive influences of genetics, brain development, environment, and experience; and design and testing of innovative psychosocial, psychopharmacologic, and somatic treatment interventions.

National Institutes of Health (NIH) *(Health and Human Services Dept.), Behavioral and Social Sciences Research (OBSSR), Bldg. 31, 31 Center Dr., #B1C19, Bethesda, MD 20892-0183; (301) 402-1146. Fax, (301) 402-1150. Dr. William Riley, Director. Web, http://obssr.od.nih.gov and Twitter, @NIHOBSSR*

Works to advance behavioral and social sciences training, to integrate a biobehavioral perspective across the NIH, and to improve communication among scientists and with the public. Develops funding initiatives for research and training. Sets priorities for research. Provides training and career development opportunities for behavioral and social scientists. Links minority students with mentors. Organizes cultural workshops and lectures.

Substance Abuse and Mental Health Services Administration (SAMHSA) *(Health and Human Services Dept.), 5600 Fishers Lane, Rockville, MD 20852; (240) 276-2000. Fax, (240) 489-1450. Elinore F. McCance-Katz,*

Assistant Secretary. Hotline, (800) 662-4357. Information, (877) 726-4727. Toll-free, (800) 487-4889.
General email, samhsainfo@samhsa.hhs.gov

Web, www.samhsa.gov and Twitter, @samhsagov

Provides and manages block grants and special programmatic funding aimed at reducing the impact of substance abuse and mental illness on communities. Provides states, providers, communities, and the public with information about behavioral health issues and prevention/treatment approaches. Administers substance abuse and mental health treatment referral service: (800) 662-4357 or www.samhsa.gov/treatment. Offers behavioral health publications and other resources: http://store.samhsa.gov/home or P.O. Box 2345, Rockville, MD 20847.

Substance Abuse and Mental Health Services Administration (SAMHSA) *(Health and Human Services Dept.), Center for Mental Health Services (CMHS), 5600 Fishers Lane, Rockville, MD 20852; (240) 276-1310. Fax, (240) 276-1320. Anita Everett, Director (Acting). Information, (877) 726-4727. Treatment referral, (800) 662-4357. TTY, (800) 487-4889.*
Web, www.samhsa.gov/about-us/who-we-are/offices-centers/cmhs

Works with federal agencies, tribal entities and territories, and state and local governments to demonstrate, evaluate, and disseminate service delivery models to treat mental illness, promote mental health, and prevent the developing or worsening of mental illness. Operates the National Mental Health Information Center.

Veterans Health Administration (VHA) *(Veterans Affairs Dept.), Mental Health Services, 810 Vermont Ave. N.W., MS 10P4M, 20420; (202) 461-4170. Fax, (202) 495-5933. Marsden McGuire, Deputy Chief Consultant; Vashtie Reedy, Management Program Analyst, (202) 461-7309. Coaching Into Care Toll-free, (888) 823-7458.*
Web, www.mentalhealth.va.gov and Coaching Into Care Web, www.mirecc.va.gov/coaching

Develops ambulatory and inpatient psychiatry and psychology programs for the mentally ill and for drug and alcohol abusers; programs are offered in VA facilities and twenty-one Veterans Integrated Services Networks. Incorporates special programs for veterans suffering from posttraumatic stress disorders, serious mental illness, addictive disorders, and homelessness.

▶**CONGRESS**

For a listing of relevant congressional committees and subcommittees, please see pages 362–363 or the Appendix.

▶**NONGOVERNMENTAL**

Active Minds, *2001 S St. N.W., #630, 20009; (202) 332-9595. Alison Malmon, Executive Director, ext. 101. Press, (202) 332-9595, ext. 109.*
General email, info@activeminds.org

Web, www.activeminds.org, Twitter, @active_minds and Facebook, www.facebook.com/activemindsinc

Supports student-run chapters nationwide to help promote youth mental health awareness on college campuses. Offers mental health and mental illness information and resources.

American Academy of Child and Adolescent Psychiatry, *3615 Wisconsin Ave. N.W., 20016-3007; (202) 966-7300. Fax, (202) 464-0131. Heidi B. Fordi, Executive Director.*
General email, communications@aacap.org

Web, www.aacap.org, Twitter, @aacap and Facebook, www.facebook.com/American-Academy-of-Child-Adolescent-Psychiatry/1454598665751

Government Affairs, gov@aacap.org

Membership: child and adolescent psychiatrists trained to promote healthy development and to evaluate, diagnose, and treat children, adolescents, and families affected by mental illness. Sponsors annual meeting and review for medical board examinations. Provides information on child and adolescent development and mental illnesses. Monitors international research and U.S. legislation concerning children with mental illness.

American Assn. for Geriatric Psychiatry, *6728 Old McLean Village Dr., McLean, VA 22101; (703) 556-9222. Fax, (703) 556-8729. Christopher N. Wood, Executive Officer, (703) 556-9222, ext. 142.*
General email, main@aagponline.org

Web, www.aagponline.org, Twitter, @GeriPsyc and Facebook, www.facebook.com/American-Association-for-geriatric-Psychiatry-AAGP

Works to improve the practice of geriatric psychiatry and mental health through education, research, and advocacy, and support for career development for clinicians, educators, and researchers. Monitors legislation and regulations. Publishes the *American Journal of Geriatric Psychiatry.*

American Assn. of Pastoral Counselors, *9504A Lee Hwy., Fairfax, VA 22031-2303 (mailing address: P.O. Box 3030, Oakton, VA 22124); (703) 385-6967. Fax, (703) 884-9165. Tere Tyner Canzoneri, President.*
General email, info@aapc.org

Web, www.aapc.org

Membership: mental health professionals with training in both religion and the behavioral sciences. Nonsectarian organization that accredits pastoral counseling centers, certifies pastoral counselors, and approves training programs.

American Assn. of Suicidology, *5221 Wisconsin Ave. N.W., 20015; (202) 237-2280. Fax, (202) 237-2282. Colleen J. Creighton, Executive Director. Suicide prevention lifeline, 800-273-TALK (8255).*
General email, info@suicidology.org

Web, www.suicidology.org, Twitter, @AAsuicidolgy and Facebook, www.facebook.com/AASuicidology

Membership: educators, researchers, suicide prevention centers, school districts, volunteers, and survivors affected by suicide. Works to understand and prevent suicide; provides suicide prevention training, serves as an information clearinghouse.

American Foundation for Suicide Prevention, *Public Policy, 440 1st St. N.W., #300, 20001; (202) 449-3600. Fax, (202) 449-3601. John Madigan, Vice President of Public Policy, ext. 103. National Suicide Prevention Lifeline, (800) 273-8255.*
General email, info@afsp.org
Web, https://afsp.org

Seeks to understand and prevent suicide through research, education, and advocacy. Provides programs and resources for survivors of suicide loss and people at risk, funds scientific research, offers educational programs for professionals, educates the public about mood disorders and suicide prevention, and promotes policies that impact suicide and prevention. Monitors legislation and regulations. (Headquarters in New York, N.Y.)

American Mental Health Counselors Assn., *107 S. West St., #779, Alexandria, VA 22314; (703) 548-6002. Fax, (703) 548-5233. Joel E. Miller, Executive Director. Toll-free, (800) 326-2642.*
Web, www.amhca.org, Twitter, @AMHCA1 and Facebook, www.facebook.com/amhca

Membership: professional counselors and graduate students in the mental health field. Sponsors leadership training and continuing-education programs for professionals in the field of mental health counseling; holds annual conference. Monitors legislation and regulations.

American Psychiatric Assn., *800 Maine Ave. S.W., #900, 20024; (202) 559-3900. Dr. Saul Levin, Medical Director. Press, (202) 459-9732. Publishing toll-free, (800) 368-5777. Toll-free, (888) 357-7924.*
General email, apa@psych.org
Web, www.psychiatry.org, Twitter, @APAPsychiatric and Facebook, www.facebook.com/ AmericanPsychiatricAssocition

Membership: psychiatrists. Promotes availability of high-quality psychiatric care; provides the public with information; assists state and local agencies; conducts educational programs for professionals and students in the field; participates in international meetings and research. Library open to members.

American Psychological Assn., *750 1st St. N.E., 20002-4242; (202) 336-5500. Fax, (202) 336-5502. Arthur C. Evans Jr., Chief Executive Officer. Library, (202) 336-5640. Toll-free, (800) 374-2721.*
General email, practise@apa.org
Web, www.apa.org, Twitter, @APA and Facebook, www.facebook.com/AmericanPsychologicalAssociation

Membership: professional psychologists, educators, and behavioral research scientists. Supports research, training, and professional services; works toward improving the qualifications, competence, and training programs of psychologists. Monitors international research and U.S. legislation on mental health. Library open to the public by appointment.

American Psychosomatic Society, *6728 Old McLean Village Dr., McLean, VA 22101-3906; (703) 556-9222. Fax, (703) 556-8729. Laura E. Degnon, Executive Director.*
General email, info@psychosomatic.org
Web, www.psychosomatic.org and Twitter, @connectAPS

Advances and disseminates scientific understanding of relationships among biological, psychological, social, and behavioral factors in medicine through publications, annual meetings, conferences, and interest groups. Offers educational resources and sponsors awards and scholarships.

Anxiety and Depression Assn. of America, *8701 Georgia Ave., #412, Silver Spring, MD 20910; (240) 485-1001. Fax, (240) 485-1035. Susan K. Gurley, Executive Director. Press, (240) 485-1016.*
General email, information@adaa.org
Web, www.adaa.org and Twitter, @Got_Anxiety

Membership: clinicians and researchers who treat and study anxiety and depression disorders; individuals with these disorders and their families; and other interested individuals. Promotes prevention, treatment, and cure of anxiety and depression disorders by disseminating information, linking individuals to treatment, and encouraging research and advancement of scientific knowledge.

Assn. of Black Psychologists, *7119 Allentown Rd., #203, Ft. Washington, MD 20744; (301) 449-3082. Fax, (301) 449-3084. Huberta Jackson-Lowman, President.*
General email, abpsi@abpsi.org
Web, www.abpsi.org and Twitter, @ABPsiSC

Membership: psychologists, psychology students, and others in the mental health field. Develops policies and resources to foster mental health in the African American community; holds annual convention.

Bazelon Center for Mental Health Law, *1101 15th St. N.W., #1212, 20005; (202) 467-5730. Fax, (202) 223-0409. Holly O'Donnell, Chief Executive Officer.*
General email, communications@bazelon.org
Web, www.bazelon.org and Twitter, @BazelonCenter

Public interest law firm. Works to establish and advance the legal rights of children and adults with mental disabilities and ensure their equal access to services and resources needed for full participation in community life. Provides technical support to lawyers and other advocates. Conducts test case litigation to defend rights of persons with mental disabilities. Conducts policy analysis, builds coalitions, issues advocacy alerts, publishes handbooks, and maintains advocacy resources online. Monitors legislation and regulations.

Eating Disorders Coalition for Research, Policy, and Action, *P.O. Box 96503-98807, 20090; (202) 543-9570. Fax, (646) 417-6378. David Jaffe, Executive Director.*
General email, manager@eatingdisorderscoalition.org
Web, www.eatingdisorderscoalition.org and Twitter, @EDCoalition

Seeks greater national and federal recognition of eating disorders. Promotes recognition of eating disorders as a public health priority and the implementation of more accessible treatment and more effective prevention programs. Monitors legislation and regulations.

Mental Health America, *500 Montgomery St., #820, Alexandria, VA 22314; (703) 684-7722. Fax, (703) 684-5968. Paul Gionfriddo, President. Information, (800) 969-6642.*
General email, info@mentalhealthamerica.net
Web, www.mentalhealthamerica.net

Works to increase accessible and appropriate care for adults and children with mental disorders. Informs and educates public about mental illnesses and available treatment. Supports research on illnesses and services.

National Action Alliance for Suicide Prevention, *1025 Thomas Jefferson St. N.W., #700W, 20007; (202) 572-3737. Robert W. Turner, Co-Chair; Dr. Carolyn M. Clancy, Co-Chair. Hotline, (800) 273-8255.*
General email, info@actionalliance.org
Web, www.actionallianceforsuicideprevention.org and Twitter, @Action_Alliance

Seeks to advance the National Strategy for Suicide Prevention (NSSP) and reduce the rate of suicide. Advocates that health care reform include suicide prevention methods and improve data on suicide.

National Alliance on Mental Illness (NAMI), *3803 N. Fairfax Dr., #100, Arlington, VA 22203; (703) 524-7600. Fax, (703) 524-9094. Mary Giliberti, Chief Executive Officer. Toll-free, (800) 950-6264.*
General email, info@nami.org
Web, www.nami.org and Twitter, @NAMICommunicate

Membership: mentally ill individuals and their families and caregivers. Works to eradicate mental illness and improve the lives of those affected by brain disorders; sponsors public education and advocacy. Monitors legislation and regulations.

National Assn. for Behavioral Healthcare, *900 17th St. N.W., #420, 20006-2507; (202) 393-6700. Fax, (202) 783-6041. Mark J. Covall, President.*
General email, nabh@nabh.org
Web, www.nabh.org

Membership: behavioral health care systems that provide inpatient, residential, and outpatient treatment and prevention and care programs for children, adolescents, adults, and older adults with mental and substance use disorders.

National Assn. of School Psychologists, *4340 East-West Hwy., #402, Bethesda, MD 20814; (301) 657-0270. Fax, (301) 657-0275. Kathleen Minke, Executive Director. Toll-free, (866) 331-6277.*
General email, kcowan@naspweb.org
Web, www.nasponline.org and Twitter, @nasponline

Membership: graduate education students and professors, school psychologists, supervisors of school psychological services, and others who provide mental health services

for children in school settings. Provides professional education and development to members. Provides school safety and crisis response direct services. Fosters information exchange; advises local, state, and federal policymakers and agencies that develop children's mental health educational services. Develops professional ethics and standards.

National Assn. of State Mental Health Program Directors, *66 Canal Center Plaza, #302, Alexandria, VA 22314-1591; (703) 739-9333. Fax, (703) 548-9517. Brian Hepburn, Executive Director.*
Web, www.nasmhpd.org

Membership: officials in charge of state mental health agencies. Compiles data on state mental health programs. Fosters collaboration among members; provides technical assistance and consultation. Maintains research institute. Operates under a cooperative agreement with the National Governors Association. (Affiliated with NASMHPD Research Institute, Inc., Falls Church, Va.)

National Council for Behavioral Health, *1400 K St. N.W., #400, 20005; (202) 684-7457. Fax, (202) 386-9391. Linda Rosenberg, President.*
General email, communications@thenationalcouncil.org
Web, www.TheNationalCouncil.org,
Twitter, @nationalcouncil and Facebook, www.facebook .com/TheNationalCouncil

Membership: community mental health agencies and state community mental health associations. Conducts research on community mental health activities; provides information, technical assistance, and referrals. Operates a job bank; publishes newsletters and a membership directory. Monitors legislation and regulations affecting community mental health facilities. (Formerly National Council for Community Behavioral Healthcare.)

National Register of Health Service Psychologists, *1200 New York Ave. N.W., #800, 20005; (202) 783-7663. Fax, (202) 347-0550. Morgan T. Sammons, Executive Director.*
Web, www.nationalregister.org

Credentials and promotes health service psychologists that meet the National Register's requirements. Conducts biannual investigations of ethical behavior of health service psychologists. Maintains a database of licensed and accredited health service psychologists. Sponsors free continuing-education programs. Monitors legislation and regulations related to health care reform.

Psychiatric Rehabilitation Assn., *7918 Jones Branch Dr., #300, McLean, VA 22101; (703) 442-2078. Fax, (703) 506-3266. Lee K. Lowery, Managing Director.*
General email, info@psychrehabassociation.org
Web, www.uspra.org and Twitter, @PsychRehab

Membership: agencies, mental health practitioners, researchers, policymakers, family groups, and consumer organizations. Supports the community adjustment of persons with psychiatric disabilities. Promotes the role of rehabilitation in mental health systems; opposes discrimination based on mental disability. Certifies psychosocial rehabilitation practitioners.

The Treatment Advocacy Center, *200 N. Glebe Rd., #801, Arlington, VA 22203; (703) 294-6001. Fax, (703) 294-6010. John Snook, Executive Director. Press, (703) 294-6003. General email, info@treatmentadvocacycenter.org*

Web, www.treatmentadvocacycenter.org and *Twitter, @TreatmentAdvCtr*

Works to eliminate legal and other barriers to treatment of severe mental illness.

Treatment Communities of America (TCA), *2200 Pennsylvania Ave. N.W., #4075E, 20037; (202) 296-3503. Patricia Clay, Executive Director. Web, www.treatmentcommunitiesofamerica.org*

Membership: nonprofit organizations that provide substance abuse and mental health treatment and rehabilitation. Provides policy analysis and educates the public on substance abuse and treatment issues. Promotes the interests of therapeutic communities, their clients, and staffs. Monitors legislation and regulations.

11

Housing and Development

GENERAL POLICY AND ANALYSIS

Basic Resources

►AGENCIES

Agriculture Dept. (USDA), *Rural Development, External Affairs,* 1400 Independence Ave. S.W., MS 0705, 20250-0705; Maria Wheat, Director; Freddie Mack, Deputy Director. Congressional inquiries, (202) 720-0999. Press, (202) 690-0498.
Web, www.rd.usda.gov/about-rd/offices/legislative-public-affairs

Disseminates information to the media and general public about policy matters related to housing and rural development.

Economic Development Administration *(Commerce Dept.),* 1401 Constitution Ave. N.W., #78006, 20230; (202) 482-5081. Fax, (202) 273-4781. John Fleming, Assistant Secretary. Information, (202) 482-2000. Public Affairs, (202) 482-4085.
Web, www.eda.gov

Advises the commerce secretary on domestic economic development. Administers development assistance programs that provide financial and technical aid to economically distressed areas to stimulate economic growth and create jobs. Awards public works and technical assistance grants to public institutions, nonprofit organizations, and Native American tribes; assists state and local governments with economic adjustment problems caused by long-term or sudden economic dislocation.

Housing and Urban Development Dept. (HUD), 451 7th St. S.W., #10000, 20410; (202) 708-1112. Fax, (202) 619-8365. Benjamin S. (Ben) Carson, Secretary; Brian Montgomery, Deputy Secretary (Acting); Helen Albert, Inspector General, (202) 708-0430. Congressional and Intergovernmental Relations, (202) 708-0005. Locator, (202) 401-0388. Public Affairs, (202) 708-0980. TTY, (202) 708-1455.
Web, www.hud.gov, Twitter, @HUDGOV and Facebook, www.facebook.com/HUD

Responsible for federal programs concerned with housing needs, fair housing opportunities, and improving and developing the nation's urban and rural communities. Administers mortgage insurance, rent subsidy, preservation, rehabilitation, and antidiscrimination in housing programs. Advises the president on federal policy and makes legislative recommendations on housing and community development issues.

Housing and Urban Development Dept. (HUD), *Policy Development and Research,* 451 7th St. S.W., #8100, 20410-6000; P.O. Box 23268, 20026-3268; (202) 708-1600. Todd M. Richardson, General Deputy Assistant Secretary. Toll-free, (800) 245-2691. Toll-free TTY, (800) 245-2691.
General email, helpdesk@huduser.gov
Web, www.huduser.gov/portal/home

Studies ways to improve the effectiveness and equity of HUD programs; analyzes housing and urban issues, including national housing goals, the operation of housing financial markets, the management of housing assistance programs, and statistics on federal and housing insurance programs; conducts the American Housing Survey; develops policy recommendations to improve federal housing programs. Works to increase the affordability of rehabilitated and newly constructed housing through technological and regulatory improvements.

Office of Management and Budget (OMB) *(Executive Office of the President),* *Housing,* 725 17th St. N.W., #9226, 20503; (202) 395-7874. Fax, (202) 395-1307. Michelle Enger, Deputy Associate Director. Press, (202) 395-7254.
Web, www.whitehouse.gov/omb

Assists and advises the OMB director in budget preparation, reorganizations, and evaluations of Housing and Urban Development Dept. programs.

►CONGRESS

For a listing of relevant congressional committees and subcommittees, please see page 441 or the Appendix.

►NONGOVERNMENTAL

Housing and Development Law Institute, 630 Eye St. N.W., 20001-3736; (202) 289-3400. Fax, (202) 289-3401. Lisa L. Walker, Chief Executive Officer.
General email, hdli@hdli.org
Web, www.hdli.org

Membership organization that assists agencies and developers in public and affordable housing and community development in addressing common legal concerns and problems; publishes a quarterly compilation of nationwide case law affecting housing agencies; conducts seminars on legal issues and practices in the housing and community development field.

National Assn. of Housing and Redevelopment Officials, 630 Eye St. N.W., 20001-3736; (202) 289-3500. Fax, (202) 289-8181. Adrianna Todman, Chief Executive Officer. Toll-free, (877) 866-2476.
General email, nahro@nahro.org
Web, www.nahro.org and Twitter, @NAHROnational

Membership: housing, community, and urban development practitioners and organizations, and state and local government agencies and personnel. Works with federal government agencies to improve community development and affordable and public housing programs; conducts training programs.

National Center for Healthy Housing, 10320 Little Patuxent Pkwy., #500, Columbia, MD 21044; (410) 992-0712. Fax, (443) 539-4150. Amanda Reddy, Executive Director, (443) 539-4152.
General email, info@nchh.org
Web, www.nchh.org and Twitter, @NCHH

Collects, analyzes, and distributes information on creating and maintaining safe and healthful housing. Provides technical assistance and training to public health, housing, and environmental professionals. Interests include aging in place for older adults, radon, allergens, pest management, and lead poisoning.

Research and Statistics

▶ AGENCIES

Census Bureau *(Commerce Dept.), Social, Economic, and Housing Statistics, 4600 Silver Hill Rd., #7H174, Suitland, MD 20746 (mailing address: 4600 Silver Hill Rd., #7H174, Washington, DC 20233-8500); (301) 763-3195. Fax, (301) 763-3232. David G. Waddington, Chief.*
Web, www.census.gov/topics/housing.html

Publishes decennial census of housing and the American Housing Survey, which describe housing inventory characteristics. Also publishes a quarterly survey of market absorption. Survey on housing vacancy is available on the website.

Housing and Urban Development Dept. (HUD), *Economic Affairs, 451 7th St. S.W., #8204, 20410-6000; (202) 402-5899. Fax, (202) 708-1159. Kurt Usowski, Deputy Assistant Secretary, (202) 904-6972.*
Web, www.hud.gov

Assembles data on housing markets and subsidized housing programs; conducts housing statistical surveys, analyzes housing finance markets; analyzes economic effects of HUD regulations; gathers local housing market intelligence; and conducts other economic research.

Housing and Urban Development Dept. (HUD), *Policy Development and Research, 451 7th St. S.W., #8100, 20410-6000; P.O. Box 23268, 20026-3268; (202) 708-1600. Todd M. Richardson, General Deputy Assistant Secretary. Toll-free, (800) 245-2691. Toll-free TTY, (800) 245-2691.*
General email, helpdesk@huduser.gov
Web, www.huduser.gov/portal/home

Assesses and maintains information on housing needs, market conditions, and programs; conducts research on housing and community development issues such as building technology, economic development, and urban planning.

Housing and Urban Development Dept. (HUD), *Policy Development and Research, HUD USER, 451 7th St. S.W., #8110, 20026-3268; Fax, (703) 742-7889. Rachelle Levitt, Project Manager. Locator, (202) 401-0388. Toll-free, (800) 245-2691. Toll-free TTY, (800) 927-7589.*
General email, helpdesk@huduser.gov
Web, www.huduser.org, Twitter, @HUDUSERnews and Facebook, www.facebook.com/HUD-User-183685747712

Research information service and clearinghouse for HUD research reports. Provides information on past and current HUD research; maintains HUD USER, an in-house database. Extensive collection of publications and

documents available online. Clearinghouse help desk open Monday–Friday, 8:30 a.m.–5:00 p.m.

Housing and Urban Development Dept. (HUD), *Program Evaluation Division, 451 7th St. S.W., #8120, 20410; (202) 402-6139. Carol S. Star, Director.*
General email, carol.s.star@hud.gov
Web, www.hud.gov

Conducts research, program evaluations, and demonstrations for all HUD housing, community development, and fair housing and equal opportunity programs.

COMMUNITY AND REGIONAL DEVELOPMENT

General

▶ AGENCIES

Bureau of Indian Affairs (BIA) *(Interior Dept.), Indian Services (OIS), 1849 C St. N.W., MS 3645-MIB, 20240; (202) 513-7642. Fax, (202) 208-2648. Debrah McBride, Deputy Bureau Director (Acting). Public Affairs, (202) 208-3710.*
Web, www.bia.gov/bia/ois

Assists tribal and Indian landowners with managing natural and energy trust resources; builds and maintains housing, transportation, energy, and irrigation infrastructure; and provides law enforcement protection, corrections, and administration of justice services on federal Indian lands.

Community Development Financial Institutions Fund *(Treasury Dept.), 1801 L St. N.W., 6th Floor, 20036 (mailing address: 1500 Pennsylvania Ave. N.W., Washington, DC 20220); (202) 653-0300. Annie Donovan, Director. Helpline, (202) 653-6421.*
General email, cdfihelp@cdfi.treas.gov
Web, www.cdfifund.gov

Provides funds and tax credits to financial institutions to build private markets, create healthy local tax revenues, and expand the availability of credit, investment capital, affordable housing, and financial services in low-income urban, rural, and Native communities.

Defense Dept. (DoD), *Economic Adjustment, 2231 Crystal Dr., #520, Arlington, VA 22202-4704; (703) 697-2130. Fax, (703) 607-0170. Patrick J. O'Brien, Director, (703) 697-2123.*
Web, www.oea.gov and Twitter, @OEAGov

Assists communities where defense activities are being expanded. Serves as the staff for the Economic Adjustment Committee, an interagency group that coordinates federal technical and financial transition assistance to localities.

Education Dept., *White House Initiative on Asian Americans and Pacific Islanders, 550 12th St. S.W., 10th Floor, 20202; (202) 245-6418. Fax, (202) 245-7166.*

HOUSING AND DEVELOPMENT RESOURCES IN CONGRESS

For a complete listing of congressional committees, including their full contact information, leadership, membership, and jurisdictions, please refer to the Appendix on pages 827–948.

HOUSE:

House Agriculture Committee, (202) 225-2171.
Web, agriculture.house.gov
    Subcommittee on Commodity Exchanges, Energy, and Credit, (202) 225-2171.
    Subcommittee on Conservation and Forestry, and Natural Resources, (202) 225-2171.

House Appropriations Committee, (202) 225-2771.
Web, appropriations.house.gov
    Subcommittee on Agriculture, Rural Development, Food and Drug Administration, and Related Agencies, (202) 225-2638.
    Subcommittee on Financial Services and General Government, (202) 225-7245.
    Subcommittee on Transportation, Housing and Urban Development, and Related Agencies, (202) 225-2141.

House Budget Committee, (202) 226-7270.
Web, budget.house.gov

House Financial Services Committee, (202) 225-7502.
Web, financialservices.house.gov
    Subcommittee on Capital Markets, Securities, and Investment, (202) 225-7502.
    Subcommittee on Financial Institutions and Consumer Credit, (202) 225-7502.
    Subcommittee on Housing and Insurance, (202) 225-7502.
    Subcommittee on Monetary Policy and Trade, (202) 225-7502.
    Subcommittee on Oversight and Investigations, (202) 225-7502.

House Small Business Committee, (202) 225-5821.
Web, smallbusiness.house.gov
    Subcommittee on Agriculture, Energy, and Trade, (202) 225-5821.

House Transportation and Infrastructure Committee, (202) 225-9446.
Web, transportation.house.gov
    Subcommittee on Economic Development, Public Buildings, and Emergency Management, (202) 225-3014.

House Ways and Means Committee, (202) 225-3625.
Web, waysandmeans.house.gov
    Subcommittee on Oversight, (202) 225-9263.

SENATE:

Senate Agriculture, Nutrition, and Forestry Committee, (202) 224-2035.
Web, agriculture.senate.gov
    Subcommittee on Rural Development and Energy, (202) 224-2035.

Senate Appropriations Committee, (202) 224-7257.
Web, appropriations.senate.gov
    Subcommittee on Agriculture, Rural Development, Food and Drug Administration, and Related Agencies, (202) 224-8090.
    Subcommittee on Financial Services and General Government, (202) 224-1133.
    Subcommittee on Transportation, Housing and Urban Development, and Related Agencies, (202) 224-7281.

Senate Banking, Housing, and Urban Affairs Committee, (202) 224-7391.
Web, banking.senate.gov
    Subcommittee on Economic Policy, (202) 224-7391.
    Subcommittee on Financial Institutions and Consumer Protection, (202) 224-7391.
    Subcommittee on Housing, Transportation, and Community Development, (202) 224-7391.
    Subcommittee on Securities, Insurance, and Investment, (202) 224-7391.

Senate Budget Committee, (202) 224-0642.
Web, budget.senate.gov

Senate Environment and Public Works Committee, (202) 224-6176.
Web, epw.senate.gov

Senate Finance Committee, (202) 224-4515.
Web, finance.senate.gov

Senate Homeland Security and Governmental Affairs Committee, (202) 224-4751.
Web, hsgac.senate.gov

Senate Indian Affairs Committee, (202) 224-2251.
Web, indian.senate.gov

Senate Judiciary Committee, (202) 224-5225.
Web, judiciary.senate.gov
    Subcommittee on the Constitution, (202) 224-5922.

Senate Small Business and Entrepreneurship Committee, (202) 224-5175.
Web, sbc.senate.gov

Senate Special Committee on Aging, (202) 224-5364.
Web, aging.senate.gov

Housing and Urban Development Department

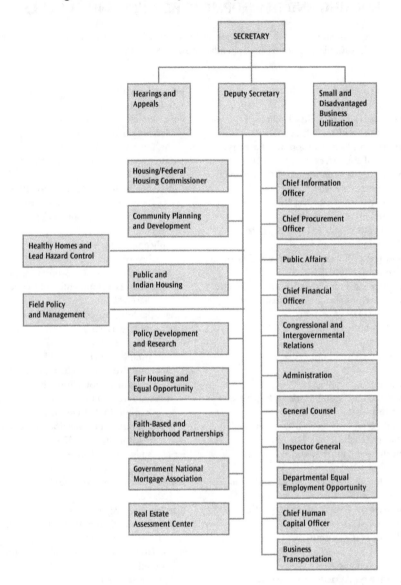

```
                              SECRETARY

        Hearings and         Deputy Secretary        Small and
        Appeals                                       Disadvantaged
                                                      Business
                                                      Utilization

        Housing/Federal
        Housing Commissioner                  Chief Information
                                              Officer

        Community Planning
        and Development                       Chief Procurement
                                              Officer
Healthy Homes and
Lead Hazard Control                           Public Affairs

        Public and
        Indian Housing                        Chief Financial
                                              Officer
Field Policy
and Management                                Congressional and
                                              Intergovernmental
        Policy Development                    Relations
        and Research
                                              Administration
        Fair Housing and
        Equal Opportunity
                                              General Counsel

        Faith-Based and
        Neighborhood Partnerships             Inspector General

        Government National
        Mortgage Association                   Departmental Equal
                                              Employment Opportunity

        Real Estate                           Chief Human
        Assessment Center                     Capital Officer

                                              Business
                                              Transportation
```

Holly Ham, Executive Director; Debra Suarez, Senior Advisor.

General email, whitehouseaapi@ed.gov

Web, http://sites.ed.gov/aapi, Twitter, @whitehouseAAPI and Facebook, www.facebook.com/WhiteHouseAAPI

Works to increase Asian American and Pacific Islander participation in federal housing and community development programs. Interests include creating sustainable communities by connecting housing to jobs and helping to build clean-energy communities.

Housing and Urban Development Dept. (HUD),
Community Planning and Development,
451 7th St. S.W., #7100, 20410; (202) 708-2690.
Fax, (202) 708-3336. Neal J. Rackleff, Assistant
Secretary; David Woll, Principal Deputy Assistant Secretary.
Web, www.hud.gov/program_offices/comm_planning

Provides cities and states with community and economic development and housing assistance, including community development block grants. Encourages public-private partnerships in urban development and private sector initiatives. Oversees enterprise zone development program.

Housing and Urban Development Dept. (HUD),
Community Planning and Development, Block Grant
Assistance, 451 7th St. S.W., #7286, 20410; (202) 708-3587.
Fax, (202) 401-2044. Claudette Fernandez, Director.
Web, www.hud.gov/program_offices/comm_planning/
communitydevelopment

Provides grants on a formula basis to states, cities, and urban counties to be used for a wide range of eligible community development activities selected by the grantee.

Housing and Urban Development Dept. (HUD), *Community Planning and Development, Block Grant Assistance, Entitlement Communities Division, 451 7th St. S.W., #7282, 20410; (202) 708-1577. Fax, (202) 401-2044. Steve Johnson, Director.*
Web, www.hudexchange.info/programs/cdbg-entitlement

Provides entitled cities and counties with block grants to provide housing, community, revitalization, and economic opportunity for low-income and moderate-income people.

Housing and Urban Development Dept. (HUD), *Community Planning and Development, Block Grant Assistance, States and Small Cities Division, 451 7th St. S.W., #7184, 20410; (202) 708-1322. Fax, (202) 401-2044. Vacant, Director; James Hoemann, Deputy Director, (202) 402-5716.*
Web, www.hud.gov/program_offices/comm_planning/communitydevelopment

Provides states with grants for distribution to small cities (fewer than 50,000 persons) and small counties (fewer than 200,000 persons) that do not receive funding through the Entitlement Community Development Block Grant Program. Funds benefit low-income and moderate-income persons, eliminate slums and blighted conditions, or meet other urgent community development needs. All states (except Hawaii), plus Puerto Rico, receive State Community Development Block Grant (CDBG) program funding. In Hawaii, HUD provides funding directly to the local governments. A separate program also provides funding to the Insular Areas.

Housing and Urban Development Dept. (HUD), *Community Planning and Development, Economic Development, 451 7th St. S.W., #7136, 20410; (202) 708-4091. Fax, (202) 708-7543. Vacant, Deputy Assistant Secretary, (202) 708-2690.*
Web, www.hud/topics/economicdevelopment

Manages economic development programs, including Empowerment Zones/Renewal Communities, Rural Housing and Economic Development, and Brownfields Economic Development Initiatives. Encourages private-public partnerships for development through neighborhood development corporations. Formulates policies and legislative proposals on economic development.

Housing and Urban Development Dept. (HUD), *Community Planning and Development, Environment and Energy, 451 7th St. S.W., #7212, 20410; (202) 708-1201. Fax, (202) 708-3363. Danielle Schopp, Director, (202) 402-4442.*
Web, www.hud.gov/program_offices/comm_planning/library/energy

Issues policies and sets standards for environmental and land-use planning and for environmental management practices. Develops policies promoting energy efficiency,

conservation, and renewable sources of supply in housing and community development programs.

Housing and Urban Development Dept. (HUD), *Community Planning and Development, Technical Assistance and Management, 451 7th St. S.W., #7228, 20410; (202) 708-3176. Fax, (202) 708-4275. Vacant, Director.*
Web, www.hud.gov/program_offices/comm_planing/about/cpdta

Develops program policies and designs and implements technical assistance plans for state and local governments for use in community planning and development programs.

Housing and Urban Development Dept. (HUD), *Field Policy and Management, 451 7th St. S.W., #7108, 20410; (202) 708-2426. Fax, (202) 708-1558. Matthew F. Hunter, Assistant Deputy Secretary, (202) 402-6512.*
Web, www.hud.gov/program_offices/field_policy_mgt

Acts as liaison and coordinates all activities between the Office of Community Planning and Development and regional and field offices; evaluates the performance of regional and field offices. Conducts policy analyses and evaluations of community planning and development programs, including the Community Development Block Grant Program, the Empowerment Zones/Enterprise Communities Program, and the McKinney Act programs.

►CONGRESS

For a listing of relevant congressional committees and subcommittees, please see page 441 or the Appendix.

►NONGOVERNMENTAL

American Planning Assn., *1030 15th St. N.W., #750W, 20005; (202) 349-1016. Fax, (202) 872-0643. Joel Albizo, Chief Executive Director.*
Web, www.planning.org, Twitter, @APA_Planning and Facebook, www.facebook.com/AmericanPlanningAssociation

Membership: professional planners and others interested in urban, suburban, and rural planning. Serves as a clearinghouse for planners. Sponsors professional development workshops conducted by the American Institute of Certified Planners. Prepares studies and technical reports; conducts seminars and conferences. (Headquarters in Chicago, Ill.)

American Resort Development Assn., *1201 15th St. N.W., #400, 20005-2842; (202) 371-6700. Fax, (202) 289-8544. Howard Nusbaum, President.*
Web, www.arda.org

Membership: U.S. and international developers, builders, financiers, marketing companies, and others involved in resort, recreational, and community development. Serves as an information clearinghouse; monitors federal and state legislation affecting land, time share, and community development industries.

APPA: Leadership in Educational Facilities, *1643 Prince St., Alexandria, VA 22314-2818; (703) 684-1446. Fax, (703) 549-2772. E. Lander Medlin, Executive Vice President, (703) 542-3829.*
General email, webmaster@appa.org
Web, www.appa.org and Twitter, @APPA_facilities

Membership: professionals involved in the administration, maintenance, planning, and development of buildings and facilities used by colleges and universities, K–12 private and public schools, museums, libraries, and other educational institutions. Interests include maintenance and upkeep of housing facilities. Provides information on campus energy management programs and campus accessibility for people with disabilities. (Formerly the Assn. of Higher Education Facilities Officers.)

Center for Community Change, *1536 U St. N.W., 20009; (202) 339-9300. Fax, (202) 387-4892. Dorian Warren, President.*
General email, info@communitychange.org
Web, https://communitychange.org and Twitter, @communitychange

Works to strengthen grassroots organizations that help low-income people, working-class people, and minorities develop skills and resources to improve their communities and change the policies and institutions that affect their lives. Monitors legislation and regulations.

Council of State Community Development Agencies, *600 Eye St. N.W., 20001; (202) 293-5820. Fax, (202) 466-2122. Dianne E. Taylor, Executive Director.*
General email, coscda@coscda.org
Web, http://coscda.org

Membership: directors and staff of state community development agencies. Promotes common interests among the states, including community and economic development, housing, homelessness, infrastructure, and state and local planning.

Institute for Local Self-Reliance, *1710 Connecticut Ave. N.W., 4th Floor, 20009; (202) 898-1610. Fax, (202) 898-1612. Neil N. Seldman, President, (202) 898-1610, ext. 5210.*
General email, info@ilsr.org
Web, www.ilsr.org, Twitter, @ilsr and Facebook, www.facebook.com/localselfreliance

Conducts research and provides technical assistance on environmentally sound economic development for government, small businesses, and community organizations. Advocates policies that enable communities to invest in and support locally owned telecommunications infrastructure, small, independent businesses, diverting organic waste from the waste stream, and local ownership and deployment of renewable energy resources, including economic analyses of solar and wind at a variety of scalable levels.

International Information on Site Planning, *715 G St. S.E., 20003; (202) 546-2322. Fax, (202) 546-2722. Beatriz de Winthuysen Coffin, Director.*
General email, iisitep@aol.com
Web, www.iisp-insitu.com

Directs research and provides information on site planning development and design of sites and buildings; conducts study and travel programs.

KaBOOM!, *4301 Connecticut Ave. N.W., #ML-1, 20008; (202) 659-0215. Fax, (202) 659-0210. James Siegal, Chief Executive Officer; Bruce Bowman, President. Press, (202) 464-6167.*
General email, webmaster@kaboom.org
Web, www.kaboom.org, Twitter, @kaboom and Facebook, www.facebook.com/kaboom

Offers grants to develop and manage playgrounds in low-income communities. Publishes research on public policy and the impact of play areas in neighborhoods.

Local Initiatives Support Corp., *Washington Office, 1825 K St. N.W., #1100, 20006; (202) 739-9284. Fax, (202) 785-4850. Ramon Jacobson, Director (Acting), (202) 739-9273.*
General email, abuck@lisc.org
Web, www.liscdc.org

Provides community development corporations and nonprofit organizations with financial and technical assistance to build affordable housing and revitalize distressed neighborhoods. (Headquarters in New York.)

National Assn. of Conservation Districts (NACD), *509 Capitol Court N.E., 20002-4937; (202) 547-6223. Fax, (202) 547-6450. Jeremy Peters, Chief Executive Officer.*
General email, stewardship@nacdnet.org
Web, www.nacdnet.org and Twitter, @NACDconserve

Membership: conservation districts (local subdivisions of state government). Works to promote the conservation of land, forests, and other natural resources. Interests include rural development and urban and community conservation.

National Assn. of Counties (NACo), *Community and Economic Development, 660 N. Capitol St. N.W., #400, 20001; (202) 393-6226. Deborah Cox, Deputy Executive, (202) 942-4286; Daria Daniel, Associate Legislative Director, (202) 942-4212.*
Web, www.naco.org/topics/community-economic-development

Membership: county governments. Conducts research and provides information on community development block grants, assisted low-income housing, and other housing and economic development programs. Monitors legislation and regulations.

National Assn. of Development Organizations, *400 N. Capitol St. N.W., #388, 20001; (202) 624-7806. Fax, (202) 624-8813. Joe McKinney, Executive Director, (202) 624-5947.*
General email, info@nado.org
Web, www.nado.org

Membership: organizations interested in regional, local, and rural economic development. Provides information on federal, state, and local development programs and revolving loan funds; sponsors conferences and training.

National Assn. of Housing and Redevelopment Officials, *630 Eye St. N.W., 20001-3736; (202) 289-3500. Fax, (202) 289-8181. Adrianna Todman, Chief Executive Officer. Toll-free, (877) 866-2476.*
General email, nahro@nahro.org

Web, www.nahro.org and Twitter, @NAHROnational

Membership: housing, community, and urban development practitioners and organizations, and state and local government agencies and personnel.

National Assn. of Regional Councils (NARC), *660 N. Capitol St. N.W., #440, 20001; (202) 986-1032. Leslie Wollack, Executive Director, (202) 618-5696.*
General email, info@narc.org

Web, narc.org and Twitter, @narcregions

Membership: regional councils of local governments and metropolitan planning organizations. Works with member local governments to encourage areawide economic growth and cooperation between public and private sectors, with emphasis on community development.

National Community Development Assn., *1825 K St. N.W., #515, 20006; (202) 587-2772. Fax, (202) 887-5546. Vicki Watson, Executive Director.*
Web, www.ncdaonline.org and Twitter, @NCDAonline

Membership: local governments that administer federally supported community and economic development, housing, and human service programs.

National Trust for Historic Preservation, *2600 Virginia Ave. N.W., #1100, 20037; (202) 588-6000. Fax, (202) 588-6038. Paul Edmondson, President; Robin Scullin, Public Affairs. Press, (202) 588-6141. Toll-free, (800) 944-6847.*
General email, info@savingplaces.org

Web, www.preservationnation.org

Conducts seminars, workshops, and conferences on topics related to preservation, including neighborhood conservation, main street revitalization, rural conservation, and preservation law; offers financial assistance through loan and grant programs; provides advisory services; operates historic house sites, which are open to the public; and publishes quarterly magazine and e-newsletters.

Partners for Livable Communities, *1429 21st St. N.W., 20036; (202) 887-5990. Robert H. McNulty, President.*
General email, mbourne@livable.org

Web, www.livable.org

Promotes working partnerships among public, private, and governmental sectors to improve the quality of life and economic development at local and regional levels. Conducts conferences and workshops; maintains referral clearinghouse; provides technical assistance.

Scenic America, *727 15th St. N.W., #1100, 20005-6029; (202) 792-1300. Mark Falzone, President.*
General email, max.ashburn@scenic.org

Web, www.scenic.org and Twitter, @ScenicAmerica

Membership: national, state, and local groups concerned with land-use control, growth management, and landscape protection. Works to enhance the scenic quality of America's communities and countryside. Provides information and technical assistance on scenic byways, tree preservation, economics of aesthetic regulation, billboard and sign control, scenic areas preservation, and growth management.

Smart Growth America, *1152 15th St. N.W., #450, 20005; (202) 207-3355. Fax, (202) 207-3349. Calvin Gladney, President.*
General email, info@smartgrowthamerica.org

Web, https://smartgrowthamerica.org and Twitter, @SmartGrowthUSA

Coalition of advocacy groups that supports citizen-driven planning that coordinates development, transportation, revitalization of older areas, and preservation of open space and the environment.

The Woodson Center, *1625 K St. N.W., #1200, 20006; (202) 518-6500. Fax, (202) 588-0314. Robert L. Woodson Sr., President.*
General email, info@woodsoncenter.org

Web, http://woodsoncenter.org and Twitter, @woodsoncenter

Provides community and faith-based organizations with training, technical assistance, and additional sources of support. Addresses issues such as youth violence, substance abuse, teen pregnancy, homelessness, joblessness, poor education, and deteriorating neighborhoods.

Rural Areas

▶ **AGENCIES**

Agriculture Dept. (USDA), *Rural Development, 1400 Independence Ave. S.W., #206W, 20250-0107; (202) 720-4581. Joel C. Baxley, Assistant to the Secretary (Acting).*
Web, www.rd.usda.gov and Twitter, @usdaRD

Acts as chief adviser to the secretary on agricultural credit and related matters; coordinates rural development policies and programs throughout the federal government; supervises the Rural Utilities Service, Rural Housing Service, and Rural Business-Cooperative Service.

Agriculture Dept. (USDA), *Rural Development, Rural Business–Cooperative Service, 1400 Independence Ave. S.W., #5803-S, MS 3201, 20250-3201; (202) 690-4730. Bette Brand, Administrator. Press, (202) 690-4737.*
Web, www.rd.usda.gov/about-rd/agencies/rural-business-cooperative-service

Administers community development programs that provide technical assistance and help communities and regions to establish strategic, long-term economic development goals.

Agriculture Dept. (USDA), *Rural Development, Rural Housing Service, 1400 Independence Ave. S.W., #5014, MS 0701, 20250-0701; (202) 692-0268. Joel Blaxley, Administrator. Toll-free, (800) 414-1226.*
Web, www.rd.usda.gov/about-rd/agencies/rural-housing-service and Loan information, www.rdhomeloans.usda.gov

Offers financial assistance to apartment dwellers and homeowners in rural areas; provides funds to construct or improve single-family and multifamily housing and community facilities.

Agriculture Dept. (USDA), *Rural Development, Rural Utilities Service, 1400 Independence Ave. S.W., #5135, MS 1510, 20250-1510; (202) 720-9540. Bette Brand, Administrator (Acting), (202) 690-4730.*
Web, www.rd.usda.gov/about-rd/agencies/rural-utilities-service

Makes loans and loan guarantees to rural electric and telephone companies providing service in rural areas. Administers the Rural Telephone Bank, which provides supplemental financing from federal sources. Makes loans for economic development and creation of jobs in rural areas, for water and waste disposal, and for distance learning and telemedicine.

Farm Service Agency (FSA) *(Agriculture Dept.), Farm Loan Programs, 1400 Independence Ave. S.W., #3605S, MS 0520, 20250-0520; (202) 720-4671. Fax, (202) 690-3573. James Radintz, Deputy Administrator.*
Web, www.fsa.usda.gov/programs-and-services/farm-loan-programs/index

Supports rural development through farm program loans, including real estate, farm production, and emergency loans.

National Agricultural Library *(Agriculture Dept.), Rural Information Center (RIC), 10301 Baltimore Ave., #123, Beltsville, MD 20705-2351; (800) 633-7701. Mary Louise Reynnells, Coordinator, (301) 504-5293.*
General email, ric@ars.usda.gov
Web, www.nal.usda.gov/ric

Provides services for rural communities, local officials, organizations, businesses, and rural citizens in the interest of maintaining rural areas. Interests include community development, tourism promotion, water quality, recycling, and technology transfer.

►CONGRESS

For a listing of relevant congressional committees and subcommittees, please see page 441 or the Appendix.

►NONGOVERNMENTAL

Farm Credit Council, *50 F St. N.W., #900, 20001-1530; (202) 626-8710. Fax, (202) 626-8718. Todd Van Hoose, President, (202) 879-0843.*
Web, www.farmcredit.com and Twitter, @farmcredit

Represents the Farm Credit System, a national financial cooperative that makes loans to agricultural producers, rural homebuyers, farmer cooperatives, and rural utilities. Finances the export of U.S. agricultural commodities.

Irrigation Assn., *8280 Willow Oaks Corporate Dr., #400, Fairfax, VA 22031; (703) 536-7080. Fax, (703) 536-7019. Deborah Hamlin, Chief Executive Officer.*
General email, info@irrigation.org
Web, www.irrigation.org

Membership: companies and individuals involved in irrigation, drainage, and erosion control worldwide. Promotes efficient and effective water management through training, education, and certification programs. Interests include economic development and environmental enhancement.

National Cooperative Business Assn., CLUSA International (NCBA CLUSA), *1775 Eye St. N.W., 8th Floor, 20006; (202) 638-6222. Douglas O'Brien, President.*
General email, info@ncba.coop
Web, www.ncba.coop, Twitter, @NCBA.coop and Facebook, www.facebook.com/NCBACLUSA

Alliance of cooperatives, businesses, and state cooperative associations. Provides information about starting and managing agricultural cooperatives in the United States and in developing nations. Monitors legislation and regulations.

National Council of Farmer Cooperatives (NCFC), *50 F St. N.W., #900, 20001-1530; (202) 626-8700. Fax, (202) 626-8722. Charles F. (Chuck) Conner, President; Mary Nowak, Director of Government Affairs.*
General email, info@ncfc.org
Web, www.ncfc.org and Twitter, @FarmerCoop

Membership: cooperative businesses owned and operated by farmers. Encourages research on agricultural cooperatives; provides statistics and analyzes trends. Monitors legislation and regulations on agricultural trade, transportation, energy, and tax issues.

National Rural Electric Cooperative Assn. (NRECA), *4301 Wilson Blvd., Arlington, VA 22203-1860; (703) 907-5500. Fax, (703) 907-5511. Jim Matheson, Chief Executive Officer; J. Scott Petersen, Vice President of Communications. Press, (703) 907-5746.*
Web, www.electric.coop, Twitter, @NRECANews and Facebook, www.facebook.com/NRECA.coop

Membership: rural electric cooperative systems and public power and utility districts. Provides members with legislative, legal, and regulatory services. Supports energy and environmental research and offers technical advice and assistance to developing countries.

National Rural Housing Coalition, *1331 G St. N.W., 10th Floor, 20005; (202) 393-5229. Fax, (202) 393-3034. Stan Keasling, President.*
General email, nrhc@ruralhousingcoalitions.org
Web, www.ruralhousingcoalition.org

Advocates improved housing for low-income rural families; works to increase public awareness of rural housing problems; administers the Self-Help Housing Fund, Farm Worker Housing Fund, Rural Community Assistance Fund, and HUD Task Force. Monitors legislation and regulations.

National Sustainable Agriculture Coalition, *110 Maryland Ave. N.E., #209, 20002-5622; (202) 547-5754. Fax, (202) 547-1837. Judy Obudzinski, Policy Director (Acting); Margaret Krome, Coalition Director (Acting).*

General email, info@sustainableagriculture.net

Web, www.sustainableagriculture.net,

Twitter, @sustainableag and Facebook,
www.facebook.com/sustainableag

National alliance of farm, rural, and conservation organizations. Advocates federal policies that promote environmentally sustainable agriculture, natural resources management, and rural community development. Monitors legislation and regulations.

NTCA—The Rural Broadband Assn., *4121 Wilson Blvd., #1000, Arlington, VA 22203-1801; (703) 351-2000. Fax, (703) 351-2001. Shirley Bloomfield, Chief Executive Officer, (703) 351-2030.*

General email, pubrelations@ntca.org

Web, www.ntca.org, Twitter, @ntcaconnect and
Facebook, www.facebook.com/NTCARuralTelecom

Membership: locally owned and controlled telecommunications cooperatives and companies serving rural and small-town areas. Offers educational seminars, workshops, publications, technical assistance, and various employee benefits programs to members. Monitors legislation and regulations. (Formerly the National Telecommunications Cooperative Assn.)

Rural Coalition, *1029 Vermont Ave. N.W., #601, 20005; (202) 628-7160. Fax, (202) 393-1816. Lorette Picciano, Executive Director.*

General email, ruralco@ruralco.org

Web, www.ruralco.org and Twitter, @RuralCo

Alliance of organizations that develop public policies benefiting rural communities. Collaborates with community-based groups on agriculture and rural development issues, including health and the environment, minority farmers, farmworkers, Native Americans' rights, and rural community development. Provides rural groups with technical assistance.

Rural Community Assistance Partnership (RCAP), *1701 K St. N.W., #700, 20006; (202) 408-1273. Fax, (202) 408-8165. Nathan Ohle, Executive Director. Toll-free, (800) 321-7227.*

General email, info@rcap.org

Web, https://rcap.org and Twitter, @RCAPInc

Provides expertise to rural communities on wastewater disposal, protection of groundwater supply, and access to safe drinking water. Targets communities with predominantly low-income or minority populations. Offers outreach policy analysis, training, and technical assistance to elected officials and other community leaders, utility owners and operators, and residents.

Specific Regions

▶AGENCIES

Appalachian Regional Commission, *1666 Connecticut Ave. N.W., #700, 20009-1068; (202) 884-7700. Fax, (202)* 884-7691. Scott T. Hamilton, Executive Director; Tim Thomas, Federal Co-Chair. Press, (202) 884-7771.

General email, info@arc.gov

Web, www.arc.gov

Federal-state-local partnership for economic development of the region, including West Virginia and parts of Alabama, Georgia, Kentucky, Maryland, Mississippi, New York, North Carolina, Ohio, Pennsylvania, South Carolina, Tennessee, and Virginia. Plans and provides technical and financial assistance and coordinates federal and state efforts for economic development of Appalachia.

Interstate Commission on the Potomac River Basin, *30 W. Gude Dr., #450, Rockville, MD 20850; (301) 984-1908. Carlton Haywood, Executive Director, ext. 105.*

General email, info@icprb.org

Web, www.potomacriver.org

Nonregulatory interstate compact commission established by Congress to control and reduce water pollution and to restore and protect living resources in the Potomac River and its tributaries. Monitors water quality; assists metropolitan water utilities; seeks innovative methods to solve water supply and land resource problems. Provides information and educational materials on the Potomac River basin.

National Capital Planning Commission, *401 9th St. N.W., North Lobby, #500N, 20004; (202) 482-7200. Fax, (202) 482-7272. Marcel Acosta, Executive Director.*

General email, info@ncpc.gov

Web, www.ncpc.gov

Central planning agency for the federal government in the national capital region, which includes the District of Columbia and suburban Maryland and Virginia. Reviews and approves plans for the physical growth and development of the national capital area, using environmental, historic, and land-use criteria.

Tennessee Valley Authority, *Government Affairs, 500 N. Capitol St. N.W., #220, 20001; (202) 898-2999. Fax, (202) 898-2998. William D. (Bill) Johnson, President.*

General email, tvainfo@tva.gov

Web, www.tva.gov and Twitter, @TVAnews

Federal corporation that coordinates resource conservation, development, and land-use programs in the Tennessee River Valley. Uses fossil fuel, nuclear, and hydropower sources to generate and supply wholesale power to municipal and cooperative electric systems, federal installations, and some industries.

▶NONGOVERNMENTAL

Greater Washington Board of Trade, *800 Connecticut Ave. N.W., #1001, 20006; (202) 857-5900. Fax, (202) 223-2648. Jack McDougle, President.*

General email, info@bot.org

Web, www.bot.org and Twitter, @GWBoardofTrade

Promotes and plans economic growth for the capital region. Supports business-government partnerships, technological training, and transportation planning; promotes international trade; works to increase economic viability of the city of Washington. Monitors legislation and regulations at local, state, and federal levels.

New England Council, *Washington Office,* *331 Constitution Ave. N.E., 20002; (202) 547-0048. Fax, (202) 547-9149. James T. Brett, President; Peter Phipps, Vice President of Federal Affairs.*
General email, necouncil@newenglandcouncil.com
Web, https://newenglandcouncil.com,
Twitter, @NECouncil and Facebook, www.facebook.com/ newenglandcouncil

Provides information on business and economic issues concerning New England; serves as liaison between the New England congressional delegations and business community. (Headquarters in Boston, Mass.)

Northeast–Midwest Institute, *50 F St. N.W., #950, 20001; (202) 544-5200. Fax, (202) 544-0043. Michael Goff, President, (202) 464-4010.*
General email, info@nemw.org
Web, www.nemw.org

Public policy research organization that promotes the economic vitality and environmental sustainability of the northeast and midwest regions. Interests include distribution of federal funding to regions, economic development, human resources, energy, and natural resources.

Urban Areas

► **AGENCIES**

General Services Administration (GSA), *Urban Development/Good Neighbor Program, 1800 F St. N.W., #3341, 20405-0001; (202) 501-1856. Fax, (202) 501-3393. Francis (Frank) Giblin, Program Manager, (202) 494-9236.*
Web, www.gsa.gov/urbandevelopment and Twitter, @GSA_urbdev

Advises on locations, designs, and renovations of federal facilities in central business areas, historic districts, and local redevelopment areas where they can anchor or promote community development. Collaborates with local and national civic and other organizations. Serves as clearinghouse for good practices.

Housing and Urban Development Dept. (HUD), *Community Planning and Development, Affordable Housing Programs, 451 7th St. S.W., #7164, 20410; (202) 708-2684. Fax, (202) 708-1744. Virginia Sardone, Director.*
Web, www.hud.gov/program_offices/comm_planning/ affordablehousing

Coordinates with cities to convey publicly owned, abandoned property to low-income families in exchange for their commitment to repair, occupy, and maintain the property.

► **NONGOVERNMENTAL**

Assn. of Metropolitan Planning Organizations, *444 N. Capitol St., #345, 20001; (202) 624-3680. Fax, (202) 624-3685. DeLania Hardy, Executive Director.*
General email, ampo@ampo.org
Web, www.ampo.org and Twitter, @ASSOC_MPOS

Membership: more than 385 metropolitan councils of elected officials and transportation professionals responsible for planning local transportation systems. Provides a forum for professional and organizational development; sponsors conferences and training programs.

International Downtown Assn., *910 17th St. N.W., #1050, 20007; (202) 393-6801. David T. Downey, President, (202) 798-5922.*
General email, customerservice@downtown.org
Web, www.ida-downtown.org

Membership: organizations, corporations, public agencies, and individuals interested in the development and management of city downtown areas. Supports cooperative efforts between the public and private sectors to revitalize downtowns and adjacent neighborhoods; provides members with information, technical assistance, and advice.

Milton S. Eisenhower Foundation, *1875 Connecticut Ave. N.W., #410, 20009; (202) 234-8104. Fax, (202) 234-8484. Alan Curtis, President.*
General email, tfelder@eisenhowerfoundation.org
Web, www.eisenhowerfoundation.org

Strives to help urban communities combat violence by supporting programs with proven records of success. Provides funding, technical assistance, evaluation, and supervision to communities wishing to replicate successful programs.

National Assn. for the Advancement of Colored People (NAACP), *Washington Bureau,* *1156 15th St. N.W., #915, 20005; (202) 463-2940. Fax, (202) 463-2953. Derrick Johnson, President.*
General email, washingtonbureau@naacpnet.org
Web, www.naacp.org and Twitter, @NAACP

Membership: persons interested in civil rights for all minorities. Works to eliminate discrimination in housing and urban affairs. Interests include programs for urban redevelopment, urban homesteading, and low-income housing. Supports programs that make affordable rental housing available to minorities and that maintain African American ownership of urban and rural land. (Headquarters in Baltimore, Md.)

National Assn. of Neighborhoods, *1300 Pennsylvania Ave. N.W., #700, 20004; (202) 332-7766. Ricardo C. Byrd, Executive Director.*
General email, info@nanworld.org
Web, www.nanworld.org

Federation of neighborhood groups that provides technical assistance to local governments, neighborhood groups, and businesses. Seeks to increase influence of grassroots groups on decisions affecting neighborhoods; sponsors training workshops promoting neighborhood awareness.

National League of Cities, 660 N. Capitol St. N.W., #450, 20001; (202) 626-3000. Fax, (202) 626-3043. Clarence Anthony, Executive Director, (202) 626-3010. Toll-free, (877) 827-2385.
General email, info@nlc.org
Web, www.nlc.org

Membership: cities and state municipal leagues. Aids city leaders in developing programs; investigates needs of local governments in implementing federal community development programs.

National Urban League, Washington Bureau, 2901 14th St. N.W., 20009; (202) 265-8200. George H. Lambert Jr., Affiliate Chief Executive Officer.
Web, http://nul.iamempowered.com/affiliate/greater-washington-urban-league

Federal advocacy division of social service organization concerned with the social welfare of African Americans and other minorities. Conducts legislative and policy analysis on housing and urban affairs. Operates a job network. (Headquarters in New York.)

NeighborWorks America, 999 N. Capitol St. N.E., #900, 20002; (202) 760-4000. Fax, (202) 376-2600. Marietta Rodriguez, President.
General email, editor@nw.org
Web, www.nw.org, Twitter, @neighborworks and Facebook, www.facebook.com/NeighborWorksAmerica

Chartered by Congress to assist localities in developing and operating local neighborhood-based programs designed to reverse decline in urban residential neighborhoods and rural communities. Oversees the National NeighborWorks Network, an association of local nonprofit organizations concerned with urban and rural development.

Urban Institute, Metropolitan Housing and Communities Policy Center, 500 L'Enfant Plaza S.W., 20024; (202) 833-7200. Mary K. Cunningham, Vice President.
Web, www.urban.org/center/met

Research center that deals with urban problems. Researches federal, state, and local policies; focus includes community development block grants, neighborhood rehabilitation programs, and housing issues.

Urban Land Institute, 2001 L St. N.W., #200, 20036; (202) 624-7000. Fax, (202) 624-7140. W. Edward (Ed) Walter, Global Chief Executive Officer. Information, (800) 321-5011.
General email, Customerservice@uli.org
Web, www.uli.org and Twitter, @UrbanLandInst

Membership: land developers, planners, state and federal agencies, financial institutions, home builders, consultants, and Realtors. Provides responsible leadership in the use of land to enhance the total environment; monitors trends in new community development.

CONSTRUCTION

General

▶**NONGOVERNMENTAL**

American Public Works Assn., Washington Office, 1275 K St. N.W., #750, 20005; (202) 408-9541. Andrea Eales, Director of Government Affairs, (202) 218-6730.
General email, apwa.washington@gmail.com
Web, www.apwa.net and Twitter, @APWATweets

Membership: engineers, architects, and others who maintain and manage public works facilities and services. Conducts research and education and promotes exchange of information on transportation and infrastructure-related issues. (Headquarters in Kansas City, Mo.)

American Subcontractors Assn., 1004 Duke St., Alexandria, VA 22314-3588; (703) 684-3450. Fax, (703) 836-3482. Richard Bright, Chief Operating Officer, ext. 1335.
General email, asaoffice@asa-hq.com
Web, www.asaonline.com and Twitter, @ASAupdate

Membership: construction subcontractors, specialty contractors, and their suppliers. Addresses business, contract, and payment issues affecting all subcontractors. Interests include procurement laws, payment practices, and lien laws. Monitors legislation and regulations.

Associated Builders and Contractors, 440 1st St. N.W., #200, 20001; (202) 595-1505. Michael Bellaman, President.
General email, gotquestion@abc.org
Web, www.abc.org and Twitter, @ABCNational

Membership: construction contractors engaged primarily in nonresidential construction, subcontractors, and suppliers. Sponsors apprenticeship, safety, and training programs. Provides labor relations information; compiles statistics. Monitors legislation and regulations.

Associated General Contractors of America, 2300 Wilson Blvd., #300, Arlington, VA 22201; (703) 548-3118. Fax, (703) 548-3119. Stephen E. Sandherr, Chief Executive Officer.
General email, info@agc.org
Web, www.agc.org and Twitter, @AGCofA

Membership: general contractors engaged primarily in nonresidential construction; subcontractors; suppliers; accounting; insurance and bonding; and law firms. Conducts training programs, conferences, seminars, and market development activities for members. Produces position papers on construction issues. Monitors legislation and regulations.

Construction Management Assn. of America (CMAA), 7926 Jones Branch Dr., #800, McLean, VA 22102-3303; (703) 356-2622. Fax, (703) 356-6388. Andrea Rutledge, President.

General email, info@cmaanet.org

Web, https://cmaanet.org and Twitter, @CMAA_HQ

Promotes the development of construction management as a profession through publications, education, a certification program, and an information network. Serves as an advocate for construction management in the legislative, executive, and judicial branches of government.

Construction Specifications Institute (CSI), *123 N. Pitt St., #450, Alexandria, VA 22314; (800) 689-2900. Fax, (703) 684-0465. Mark Dorsey, Chief Executive Officer.*

General email, csi@csinet.org

Web, http://CSIResources.org and Twitter, @CSIConstruction

Membership: architects, engineers, contractors, and others in the construction industry. Promotes construction technology; publishes reference materials to help individuals prepare construction documents; sponsors certification programs for construction specifiers and manufacturing representatives.

Mechanical Contractors Assn. of America, *1385 Piccard Dr., Rockville, MD 20850; (301) 869-5800. Fax, (301) 990-9690. John R. Gentille, Chief Executive Officer.*

General email, help@mcaa.org

Web, www.mcaa.org

Membership: mechanical contractors and members of related professions. Seeks to improve building standards and codes. Provides information, publications, and training programs; conducts seminars and annual convention. Monitors legislation and regulations.

National Assn. of Home Builders (NAHB), *1201 15th St. N.W., 20005-2800; (202) 266-8200. Fax, (202) 266-8400. Jerry Howard, Executive Officer, (800) 368-5242, ext. 8257. Press, (202) 266-8254. Toll-free, (800) 368-5242.*

General email, info@nahb.org

Web, www.nahb.org and Twitter, @NAHBhome

Membership: contractors, builders, architects, engineers, mortgage lenders, and others interested in home building and residential real estate construction. Participates in updating and developing building codes and standards; offers technical information. Interests include environmental and land-use policies. Monitors legislation and regulations.

National Assn. of Minority Contractors, *910 17th St. N.W., #413, 20006; (202) 296-1600. Fax, (202) 296-1644. Wendell Stemley, National President.*

General email, info@namcnational.org

Web, www.namcnational.org and Twitter, @NAMCNational

Membership: minority businesses and related firms, women contractors, strategic alliances, and individuals serving those businesses in the construction industry. Advises members on commercial and government contracts; provides technical assistance and industry-specific training; provides bid information on government contracts.

Monitors legislation and regulations. Acts as advocate for legislative changes.

National Assn. of Plumbing-Heating-Cooling Contractors, *180 S. Washington St., #100, Falls Church, VA 22046; (703) 237-8100. Fax, (703) 237-7442. Michael Copp, Executive Vice President. Information, (800) 533-7694.*

General email, naphcc@naphcc.org

Web, www.phccweb.org and Twitter, @phccnatl

Provides education and training for the plumbing and HVACR industry. Offers career information, internships, and scholarship programs for business and engineering students to encourage careers in the plumbing and mechanical contracting field. Promotes health, safety, and protection of the environment.

National Electrical Contractors Assn., *3 Bethesda Metro Center, #1100, Bethesda, MD 20814; (301) 657-3110. Fax, (301) 215-4500. John M. Grau, Chief Executive Officer.*

Web, www.necanet.org, Twitter, @necanet and Facebook, www.facebook.com/NECANET

Membership: electrical contractors who build and service electrical wiring and equipment, including high-voltage construction and service. Represents members in collective bargaining with union workers; sponsors research and educational programs.

National Research Council (NRC), *Infrastructure and the Constructed Environment Board, Keck Center, 500 5th St. N.W., #WS938, 20001; (202) 334-3505. Fax, (202) 334-3718. Cameron Oskvig, Chair.*

General email, bice@nas.edu

Web, http://sites.nationalacademies.org/deps/bice/index.htm

Advises the government, the private sector, and the public on technology, science, and public policy related to the design, construction, operations, maintenance, security, and evaluation of buildings, facilities, and infrastructure systems; the relationship between the constructed and natural environments and their interaction with human activities; the effects of natural and man-made hazards on constructed facilities and infrastructure; and the interdependencies of infrastructure systems, including power, water, transportation, telecommunications, wastewater, and buildings.

National Utility Contractors Assn. (NUCA), *3925 Chain Bridge Rd., #300, Fairfax, VA 22030; (703) 358-9300. Fax, (703) 358-9307. Bill Hillman, Chief Executive Officer.*

General email, nuca@nuca.com

Web, www.nuca.com

Membership: contractors who perform water, sewer, and other underground utility construction. Sponsors conferences; conducts surveys. Monitors public works legislation and regulations.

Sheet Metal and Air Conditioning Contractors' National Assn., *4201 Lafayette Center Dr., Chantilly, VA 20151-1219; Capitol Hill Office, 305 4th St. N.E., 20002-5815;*

(703) 803-2980. Fax, (703) 803-3732. Vincent R. Sandusky, Chief Executive Officer, (703) 803-2985. Capitol Hill, (202) 547-8202.

General email, info@smacna.org

Web, www.smacna.org

Membership: unionized sheet metal and air conditioning contractors. Provides information on standards and installation and fabrication methods. Interests include energy efficiency and sustainability.

U.S. Green Building Council, 2101 L St. N.W., #500, 20037; (202) 742-3792. Fax, (202) 828-5110. Mahesh Ramanujam, Chief Exeutive Officer. Toll-free, (800) 795-1747.

General email, LEEDinfo@usgbc.org

Web, www.usgbc.org and Twitter, @USGBC

Promotes buildings that are environmentally responsible, profitable, and healthy. Rates green buildings in order to accelerate implementation of environmentally friendly design practices.

Architecture and Design

▶AGENCIES

General Services Administration (GSA), *Design and Construction, Office of the Chief Architect,* 1800 F St. N.W., #5400, 20405-0001; (202) 501-1888. David Insinga, Chief Architect.

General email, david.insinga@gsa.gov

Web, www.gsa.gov/portal/content/104549

Administers the Design Excellence Program, which reviews designs of federal buildings and courthouses.

▶NONGOVERNMENTAL

American Architectural Foundation, 740 15th St. N.W., 20005; (202) 787-1010. Marci B. Reed, Executive Director.

General email, info@archfoundation.org

Web, www.archfoundation.org

Seeks to advance the quality of American architecture. Works to increase public awareness and understanding and to apply new technology to create more humane environments. Acts as liaison between the profession and the public. Operates the historic Octagon Museum.

American Institute of Architects, 1735 New York Ave. N.W., 20006-5292; (202) 626-7300. Fax, (202) 626-7547. Robert A. Ivy, Chief Executive Officer, ext. 7400. Government Advocacy, (202) 626-7480. Press, (202) 626-7457. Toll-free, (800) 242-3837. Alternate Phone, (202) 626-2555.

General email, infocentral@aia.org

Web, www.aia.org, Twitter, @AIANational and Facebook, www.facebook.com/AIANational

Membership: licensed American architects, interns, architecture faculty, engineers, planners, and those in government, manufacturing, or other fields in a capacity related to architecture. Works to advance the standards

of architectural education, training, and practice. Promotes the aesthetic, scientific, and practical efficiency of architecture, urban design, and planning; monitors international developments. Offers continuing and professional education programs; sponsors scholarships, internships, and awards. Houses archival collection, including documents and drawings of American architects and architecture. Library open to the public by appointment. Monitors legislation and regulations.

American Society of Interior Designers, 1152 15th St. N.W., #910, 20006; (202) 546-3480. Fax, (202) 546-3240. Randy W. Fiser, Chief Executive Officer.

General email, asid@asid.org

Web, www.asid.org and Twitter, @asid

Offers certified professional development courses addressing the technical, professional, and business needs of designers; bestows annual scholarships, fellowships, and awards; supports licensing efforts at the state level.

American Society of Landscape Architects, 636 Eye St. N.W., 20001-3736; (202) 898-2444. Fax, (202) 898-1185. Nancy Somerville, Executive Vice President, (202) 216-2339. Toll-free, (888) 999-2752.

General email, info@asla.org

Web, www.asla.org and Twitter, @NationalASLA

Membership: professional landscape architects. Advises government agencies on land-use policy and environmental matters. Accredits university-level programs in landscape architecture; conducts professional education seminars for members.

AmericanHort, *Washington Office,* 525 9th St. N.W., #800, 20004; (202) 789-2900. Fax, (202) 789-1893. Ken Fisher, President, (614) 487-1117.

General email, hello@AmericanHort.org

Web, www.AmericanHort.org and Twitter, @American_Hort

Serves as an information clearinghouse on the technical aspects of nursery and landscape business and design.

Assn. of Collegiate Schools of Architecture, 1735 New York Ave. N.W., 3rd Floor, 20006; (202) 785-2324. Fax, (202) 628-0448. Michael J. Monti, Executive Director.

General email, info@acsa-arch.org

Web, www.acsa-arch.org and Twitter, @ACSAUpdate

Membership: U.S. and Canadian institutions that offer at least one accredited architecture degree program. Conducts workshops and seminars for architecture school faculty; presents awards for student and faculty excellence in architecture; publishes a guide to architecture schools in North America.

Industrial Designers Society of America (IDSA), 555 Grove St., #200, Herndon, VA 20170; (703) 707-6000. Fax, (703) 787-8501. Chris Livaudais, Executive Director.

General email, idsa@idsa.org

Web, www.idsa.org, Twitter, @IDSA and Facebook, www.facebook.com/IDSA.org

Membership: designers of products, equipment, instruments, furniture, transportation, packages, exhibits, information services, and related services, and educators of industrial design. Provides the Bureau of Labor Statistics with industry information. Monitors legislation and regulations.

Landscape Architecture Foundation, *1200 17th St. N.W., #210, 20036; (202) 331-7070. Fax, (202) 331-7079. Barbara Deutsch, Chief Executive Officer, (202) 331-7070. General email, rbooher@lafoundation.org*

Web, www.lafoundation.org, Twitter, @lafoundation and Facebook, www.facebook.com/lafoundation.org

Conducts research and provides educational and scientific information on sustainable landscape architecture and development and related fields. Awards scholarships and fellowships.

National Architectural Accrediting Board Inc., *1735 New York Ave. N.W., 20006; (202) 783-2007. Fax, (202) 783-2822. Helen Combs Dreiling, Executive Director (Acting). General email, info@naab.org*

Web, www.naab.org and Twitter, @NAABNews

Accredits Bachelor, Master, and Doctor of Architecture degree programs in the United States; assists organizations in other countries to develop accreditation standards.

National Assn. of Landscape Professionals, *12500 Fair Lakes Circle, #200, Fairfax, VA 22033; (703) 736-9666. Fax, (703) 322-2066. Sabeena Hickman, Chief Executive Officer, (703) 736-9666, ext. 208; Lisa Styker, Director of Communications, (540) 729-2114. Toll-free, (800) 395-2522. General email, info@landscapeprofessionals.org*

Web, www.landscapeprofessionals.org and Twitter, @the_nalp

Membership: lawn care professionals, exterior maintenance contractors, installation/design/building professionals, and interiorscapers. Provides members with education, business management and marketing tools, and networking opportunities. Offers certification program. Focus is the green industry. Monitors legislation.

National Assn. of Schools of Art and Design, *11250 Roger Bacon Dr., #21, Reston, VA 20190-5248; (703) 437-0700. Fax, (703) 437-6312. Karen Moynahan, Executive Director, (703) 437-0700, ext. 116. General email, info@arts-accredit.org*

Web, http://nasad.arts-accredit.org

Specialized professional accrediting agency for postsecondary programs in art and design. Conducts and shares research and analysis on topics pertinent to art and design programs and fields of art and design. Offers professional development opportunities for executives of art and design programs.

National Council of Architectural Registration Boards (NCARB), *1801 K St. N.W., #700-K, 20006-1310; (202) 783-6500. Fax, (202) 783-0290. Michael J. Armstrong,*

Chief Executive Officer. Customer Service, (202) 879-0520. Web, www.ncarb.org and Twitter, @NCARB

Membership: state architectural registration boards. Develops examinations used in the United States and its territories for licensing architects; certifies architects.

Society for Marketing Professional Services, *123 N. Pitt St., #400, Alexandria, VA 22314-3133; (703) 549-6117. Fax, (703) 549-2498. Michael V. Geary, Chief Executive Officer, ext. 221. Information, (800) 292-7677. General email, info@smps.org*

Web, www.smps.org and Twitter, @SMPSHQ

Membership: individuals who provide professional services to the building industry. Assists individuals who market design services in the areas of architecture, engineering, planning, interior design, landscape architecture, and construction management. Provides seminars, workshops, and publications for members. Maintains job banks.

Codes, Standards, and Research

▶**AGENCIES**

Access Board, *1331 F St. N.W., #1000, 20004-1111; (202) 272-0080. Fax, (202) 272-0081. David M. Capozzi, Executive Director, (202) 272-0010. Toll-free, (800) 872-2253. Toll-free TTY, (800) 993-2822. TTY, (202) 272-0082. General email, info@access-board.gov*

Web, www.access-board.gov

Develops and maintains accessibility requirements for buildings, transit vehicles, telecommunications equipment, medical diagnostic equipment, and electronic and information technology. Provides technical assistance and training on these guidelines and standards. Enforces access standards for federally funded facilities through the Architectural Barriers Act.

Energy Efficiency and Renewable Energy (EERE) *(Energy Dept.), Building Technologies (BTO), 1000 Independence Ave. S.W., MS EE2J, 20585; (202) 586-9127. Fax, (202) 586-4617. David Nemtzow, Director. General email, Buildings@ee.doe.gov*

Web, www.energy.gov/eere/buildings/building-technologies-office

Funds research to reduce commercial and residential building energy use. Programs include research and development, equipment standards and analysis, and technology validation and market introduction.

Environmental Protection Agency (EPA), *Air and Radiation (OAR), Radiation and Indoor Air, 1200 Pennsylvania Ave. N.W., #5426, MC 6608T, 20460; (202) 343-9320. Fax, (202) 564-1408. Jonathan Edwards, Director. Web, www.epa.gov/aboutepa/about-office-air-and-radiation-oar#oria*

Establishes standards for measuring radon. Develops model building codes for state and local governments.

Provides states and building contractors with technical assistance and training on radon detection and mitigation. Oversees the Radiation and Indoor Environments Laboratory in Las Vegas, Nev. Administers the Clean Air Act.

Federal Housing Administration (FHA) *(Housing and Urban Development Dept.), Manufactured Housing Programs, 451 7th St. S.W., #9162, 20410-8000; (202) 402-7112. Fax, (202) 708-4213. Teresa Payne, Administrator (Acting). Consumer complaints, (800) 927-2891.*
General email, mhs@hud.gov

Web, www.hud.gov/program_officer/housing/rmra/mhsl/mhs.home

Establishes and maintains standards for selection of new materials and methods of construction; evaluates technical suitability of products and materials; develops uniform, preemptive, and mandatory national standards for manufactured housing; enforces standards through design review and quality control inspection of factories; administers a national consumer protection program. Handles dispute resolution.

Housing and Urban Development Dept. (HUD), *Lead Hazard Control and Healthy Homes, 451 7th St. S.W., #8236, 20410; (202) 708-0310. Fax, (202) 708-0014. Matthew Ammon, Director, (202) 402-4337.*
Web, www.hud.gov/program_offices/healthy_homes and Twitter, @HUDHealthyHomes

Advises HUD offices, other agencies, health authorities, and the housing industry on lead poisoning prevention. Develops regulations for lead-based paint; conducts research; makes grants to state and local governments for lead hazard reduction and inspection of housing.

National Institute of Standards and Technology (NIST) *(Commerce Dept.), 100 Bureau Dr., Bldg. 101, #A1134, Gaithersburg, MD 20899-1000 (mailing address: 100 Bureau Dr., MS 1000, Gaithersburg, MD 20899); (301) 975-2300. Fax, (301) 869-8972. Walter Copan, Under Secretary. TTY, (800) 877-8339.*
General email, director@nist.gov

Web, www.nist.gov

Provides services to support National Safety Construction Team Act investigations to assess building performance, emergency response, and evacuation procedures.

National Institute of Standards and Technology (NIST) *(Commerce Dept.), Engineering Laboratory, 100 Bureau Dr., MS 8600, Gaithersburg, MD 20899-8600; (301) 975-5900. Fax, (301) 975-4032. Howard H. Harary, Director.*
General email, el@nist.gov

Web, www.nist.gov/el

Performs analytical, laboratory, and field research in the area of building technology and its applications for building usefulness, safety, and economy; produces performance criteria and evaluation, test, and measurement methods for building owners, occupants, designers, manufacturers, builders, and federal, state, and local regulatory authorities. Researches architecture, materials construction, energy production and distribution, and manufacturing to develop recommendations for constructing buildings that maximize safety, withstand earthquakes and other natural disasters, and are energy efficient. Contributes standards and codes development; provides performance metrics, measurement and testing methods, and protocols; and evaluates systems and practices.

U.S. Fire Administration *(Federal Emergency Management Agency), 16825 S. Seton Ave., Emmitsburg, MD 21727-8998; (301) 447-1000. Fax, (301) 447-1441. G. Keith Bryant, Administrator, (202) 646-4223. Press, (301) 447-1853. Toll-free, (800) 238-3358.*
Web, www.usfa.fema.gov and Twitter, @usfire

Conducts research and collects, analyzes, and disseminates data on combustion, fire prevention, firefighter safety, and the management of fire prevention organizations; studies and develops arson-prevention programs and fire-prevention codes; maintains the National Fire Incident Reporting System.

▶NONGOVERNMENTAL

American Society of Civil Engineers (ASCE), *1801 Alexander Bell Dr., Reston, VA 20191-4400; Washington Office, 101 Constitution Ave., #375E, 20001; (202) 789-7850. Fax, (202) 789-7859. Thomas W. Smith III, Executive Director. Toll-free, (800) 548-2723. Press, (202) 789-7853.*
General email, customercare.asce.org

Web, www.asce.org and Twitter, @ascetweets

Membership: professionals and students in civil engineering. Develops standards by consensus for construction documents and building codes, and standards for civil engineering education, licensure, and ethics. Organizes international conferences; maintains technical and professional reference materials; hosts e-learning sites. Advocates improvements in public infrastructure; monitors legislation and regulations.

American Society of Heating, Refrigerating, and Air Conditioning Engineers (ASHRAE), *Government Affairs, 1255 23rd St. N.W., #825, 20037; (202) 833-1830. Fax, (202) 833-0118. Doug Read, Director.*
General email, ashre@ashrae.org

Web, www.ashrae.org and Twitter, @ashraenews

Membership: engineers and others involved with the heating, ventilation, air conditioning, and refrigeration industry in the United States and abroad, including students. Sponsors research, meetings, and educational activities. Develops industry standards; publishes technical data. Monitors legislation and regulations. (Headquarters in Atlanta, Ga.)

Asphalt Roofing Manufacturers Assn., *529 14th St. N.W., #750, 20045; (202) 591-2450. Fax, (202) 591-2445. Reed Hitchcock, Executive Vice President.*
General email, info@asphaltroofing.org

Web, www.asphaltroofing.org

Membership: manufacturers of bitumen-based roofing products. Assists in developing local building codes and standards for asphalt roofing products. Provides technical information; supports research. Monitors legislation and regulations.

Assn. of Pool and Spa Professionals, *2111 Eisenhower Ave., #500, Alexandria, VA 22314-4698; (703) 838-0083. Fax, (703) 549-0493. Lawrence Caniglia, President.*
General email, MemberServices@apsp.org
Web, www.apsp.org and Twitter, @TheAPSP

Membership: manufacturers, dealers and retailers, service companies, builders, and distributors of pools, spas, and hot tubs. Promotes the industry; provides educational programs for industry professionals; establishes standards for construction and safety. Monitors legislation and regulations.

Building Codes Assistance Project, *1850 M St. N.W., #610, 20036; (202) 530-2211. Maureen Guttman, President.*
General email, info@bcapcodes.org
Web, www.bcap-energy.org and Twitter, @BCAPOCEAN

Advocacy group that supports and enforces national building energy codes. Assists cities, states, and counties in complying with federal energy efficiency codes, including planning, technical assistance, and training. Provides outreach and coordination activities to provide information about current code data and cost analysis to policymakers. International interests include India, the Asia–Pacific region, Ukraine, and arid regions.

Center for Auto Safety, *1825 Connecticut Ave. N.W., #330, 20009-5708; (202) 328-7700. Fax, (202) 387-0140. Jason K. Levine, Director.*
General email, contact@autosafety.org
Web, www.autosafety.org and Twitter, @Ctr4AutoSafety

Monitors Federal Trade Commission warranty regulations and HUD implementation of federal safety and construction standards for manufactured mobile homes.

Home Innovation Research Labs, *400 Prince George's Blvd., Upper Marlboro, MD 20774; (301) 249-4000. Fax, (301) 430-6180. J. Michael Luzier, President. Toll-free, (800) 638-8556.*
Web, www.homeinnovation.com and Twitter, @HomeResearchLab

Conducts contract research and product labeling and certification for U.S. industry, government, and trade associations related to home building and light commercial industrial building. Interests include energy conservation, new technologies, international research, public health issues, affordable housing, special needs housing for the elderly and persons with disabilities, building codes and standards, land development, and environmental issues. (Independent subsidiary of the National Assn. of Home Builders [NAHB].)

International Code Council, *500 New Jersey Ave. N.W., 6th Floor, 20001-2070; (202) 370-1800. Fax, (202) 783-2348. Dominic Sims, Chief Executive Officer. Toll-free, (888) 422-7233.*
General email, carecenter@iccsafe.org
Web, www.iccsafe.org, Twitter, @IntlCodeCouncil and Facebook, www.facebook.com/InternationalCodeCouncil

Membership association dedicated to building safety and sustainability. Develops codes used to construct residential and commercial buildings, including homes and schools. Offers "green" standards accreditation for businesses providing energy-efficient and sustainable infrastructure.

National Fire Protection Assn., *Government Affairs, 50 F St. N.W., #625, 20001; (202) 898-0222. Fax, (202) 898-0044. Seth Statler, Government Affairs Director. Toll-free, (800) 344-3555.*
General email, wdc@nfpa.org
Web, www.nfpa.org, Twitter, @NFPA and Facebook, www.facebook.com/theNFPA

Membership: individuals and organizations interested in fire protection. Develops and updates fire protection codes and standards; sponsors technical assistance programs; collects fire data statistics. Monitors legislation and regulations. (Headquarters in Quincy, Mass.)

National Institute of Building Sciences, *1090 Vermont Ave. N.W., #700, 20005-4950; (202) 289-7800. Fax, (202) 289-1092. Lakisha Ann Woods, President.*
General email, nibs@nibs.org
Web, www.nibs.org and Twitter, @NIBS_news

Public-private partnership authorized by Congress to improve the regulation of building construction, facilitate the safe introduction of innovative building technology, and disseminate performance criteria and other technical information.

Materials and Labor

▶**NONGOVERNMENTAL**

American Coatings Assn., *901 New York Ave. N.W., #300 West, 20001; (202) 462-6272. Fax, (202) 462-8549. J. Andrew (Andy) Doyle, President, (202) 462-3932.*
General email, members@paint.org
Web, www.paint.org and Facebook, www.facebook.com/AmericanCoatingsAssociation

Membership: paint and coatings manufacturers, raw materials suppliers, distributors, and other industry professionals. Provides educational and public outreach programs for the industry; interests include health, safety, and the environment. Monitors legislation and regulations.

American Concrete Pavement Assn. (ACPA), *Washington Office, 500 New Jersey Ave. N.W., 20001; (202) 638-2272 (c). Fax, (202) 638-2688. Leif Wathne, Executive Vice President of Practice Advancement and Advocacy, (202) 638-2272.*
General email, acpa@acpa.org
Web, www.acpa.org, Twitter, @PaveConcrete and Facebook, www.facebook.com/American-Concrete-Pavement-Association-152937364784177

Represents the concrete pavement industry. Promotes use of concrete for airport, highway, street, and local road pavements. Provides members with project assistance, educational workshops, and training programs. Researches concrete pavement design, construction, and rehabilitation. (Headquarters in Rosemont, Ill.)

American Forest and Paper Assn., *Government Affairs,* *1101 K St. N.W., #700, 20005; (202) 463-2700.* *Donna Harman, President; Elizabeth Bartheld, Vice President of Government Affairs.*
General email, info@afandpa.org
Web, http://afandpa.org and Twitter, @ForestandPaoer

Membership: wood and specialty products manufacturers and those in related associations. Interests include tax, housing, environmental, international trade, natural resources, and land-use issues that affect the wood and paper products industry.

Architectural Woodwork Institute, *46179 Westlake Dr., #120, Potomac Falls, VA 20165-5874; (571) 323-3636. Fax, (571) 323-3630. Philip Duvic, Executive Vice President.*
General email, info@awinet.org
Web, www.awinet.org and Twitter, @AWInational

Membership: architectural woodworkers, suppliers, design professionals, and students. Promotes the use of architectural woodworking; establishes industry standards; conducts seminars and workshops.

Asphalt Roofing Manufacturers Assn., *529 14th St. N.W., #750, 20045; (202) 591-2450. Fax, (202) 591-2445. Reed Hitchcock, Executive Vice President.*
General email, info@asphaltroofing.org
Web, www.asphaltroofing.org

Membership: manufacturers of bitumen-based roofing products. Assists in developing local building codes and standards for asphalt roofing products. Provides technical information; supports research. Monitors legislation and regulations.

Assn. of the Wall and Ceiling Industries, *513 W. Broad St., #210, Falls Church, VA 22046-3257; (703) 538-1600. Fax, (703) 534-8307. Steven A. Etkin, Executive Vice President.*
General email, awci@awci.org
Web, www.awci.org and Twitter, @AWCI_INFO

Membership: contractors and suppliers working in the wall and ceiling industries. Sponsors conferences and seminars. Monitors legislation and regulations.

The Brick Industry Assn., *12007 Sunrise Valley Dr., #430, Reston, VA 20191; (703) 620-0010. Fax, (703) 620-3928. Raymond W. Leonhard, President, (703) 674-1533.*
General email, brickinfo@bia.org
Web, www.gobrick.com and Twitter, @BrickIndustry

Membership: manufacturers and distributors of clay brick. Provides technical expertise and assistance; promotes bricklaying vocational education programs; maintains collection of technical publications on brick masonry construction. Monitors legislation and regulations.

Building Systems Councils of the National Assn. of Home Builders, *1201 15th St. N.W., 7th Floor, 20005-2800; Fax, (202) 266-8141. Devin Perry, Director, (202) 266-8577. Toll-free, (800) 368-5242, ext. 8577.*
Web, www.nahb.org and Twitter, @NAHBhome

Membership: manufacturers and suppliers of home building products and services. Represents all segments of the industry. Assists in developing National Assn. of Home Builders policies regarding building codes, legislation, and government regulations affecting manufacturers of model-code-compliant, factory-built housing (includes concrete, log, timber, modular, and panelized); sponsors educational programs; conducts plant tours of member operations.

Composite Panel Assn., *19465 Deerfield Ave., #306, Leesburg, VA 20176; (703) 724-1128. Fax, (703) 724-1588. Jackson Morrill, President, ext. 243.*
General email, admin@decorativesurfaces.org
Web, www.CompositePanel.org and Twitter, @theDecorSurface

Membership: manufacturers of particleboard, medium-density fiberboard, and hardboard engineered woodsiding/trim, and decorative surfaces in North America. Promotes use of these materials; conducts industry education; offers a certification program for recycled and low-emitting products (Eco-Certified Composite [ECC] Sustainability and Certification Program). Monitors legislation and regulations.

Decorative Hardwoods Assn., *42777 Trade West Dr., Sterling, VA 20166; (703) 435-2900. Fax, (703) 435-2573. Clifford (Kip) Howlett, President.*
General email, Resources@decorativehardwoods.org
Web, www.decorativehardwoods.org

Membership: manufacturers, distributors, wholesalers, suppliers, and sales agents of hardwood, plywood, veneer, and engineered wood flooring. Disseminates business information; sponsors workshops and seminars; issues certifications; conducts research.

Door and Hardware Institute, *14150 Newbrook Dr., #200, Chantilly, VA 20151-2232; (703) 222-2010. Fax, (703) 222-2410. Jerry S. Heppes, Chief Executive Officer, (703) 222-0972.*
General email, info@dhi.org
Web, www.dhi.org

Membership: companies and individuals that manufacture or distribute doors and related fittings. Promotes the industry. Interests include building security, life safety and exit devices, and compliance with the Americans with Disabilities Act. Monitors legislation and regulations.

Gypsum Assn., *962 Wayne Ave., #620, Silver Spring, MD 20910; (301) 277-8686. Fax, (301) 277-8747. Stephen H. Meima, Executive Director. Publications, (888) 264-2665.*

General email, info@gypsum.org

Web, www.gypsum.org

Membership: manufacturers of gypsum wallboard and other gypsum panel proucts. Assists members, code officials, builders, designers, and others with technical problems and building code questions; publishes *Fire Resistance Design Manual* referenced by major building codes; conducts safety programs for member companies. Monitors legislation and regulations.

International Assn. of Bridge, Structural, Ornamental, and Reinforcing Iron Workers, *1750 New York Ave. N.W., #400, 20006; (202) 383-4800. Fax, (202) 638-4856. Eric Dean, General President.*

General email, iwmagazine@iwintl.org

Web, www.ironworkers.org and Twitter, @TheIronWorkers

Membership: approximately 120,000 iron workers. Helps members negotiate pay, benefits, and better working conditions; conducts training programs and workshops. Monitors legislation and regulations. (Affiliated with the AFL-CIO.)

International Assn. of Heat and Frost Insulators and Allied Workers, *9602 Martin Luther King Hwy., Lanham, MD 20706-1839; (301) 731-9101. Fax, (301) 731-5058. James McCourt, General President.*

General email, hfi@insulators.org

Web, www.insulators.org and Twitter, @InsulatorsUnion

Membership: approximately 30,000 workers in insulation industries. Helps members negotiate pay, benefits, and better working conditions; conducts training programs and workshops. Monitors legislation and regulations. (Affiliated with the AFL-CIO.)

International Brotherhood of Boilermakers, Iron Ship Builders, Blacksmiths, Forgers, and Helpers, Government Affairs, *1750 New York Ave. N.W., #335, 20006; (202) 756-2868. Fax, (202) 756-2869. Cecile Conroy, Director of Government Affairs, ext. 202.*

General email, cconroy@boilermakers.org

Web, https://boilermakers.org

Membership: workers in construction, repair, maintenance, manufacturing, shipbuilding and marine repair, mining and quarrying, railroads, cement kilns, and related industries in the United States and Canada. Helps members negotiate pay, benefits, and better working conditions; conducts training programs and workshops. Monitors legislation and regulations. (Headquarters in Kansas City, Kans.; affiliated with the AFL-CIO.)

International Brotherhood of Electrical Workers (IBEW), *900 7th St. N.W., 20001; (202) 833-7000. Fax, (202) 728-7676. Lonnie Stephenson, International President; Kenneth Cooper, International Secretary-Treasurer.*

General email, webmaster@ibew.org

Web, www.ibew.org

Membership: workers in utilities, construction, telecommunications, broadcasting, manufacturing, railroads, and government. Helps members negotiate pay, benefits,

and better working conditions; conducts training programs and workshops. Monitors legislation and regulations. (Affiliated with the AFL-CIO.)

International Brotherhood of Teamsters, *25 Louisiana Ave. N.W., 20001-2198; (202) 624-6800. Fax, (202) 624-6918. James P. Hoffa, General President; Christy Bailey, Director of Federal Legislation and Regulation, (202) 624-6993; Bret Caldwell, Director of Communications, (202) 624-6911. Press, (202) 624-6911.*

General email, communications@teamster.org

Web, www.teamster.org

Membership: workers in the transportation and construction industries, factories, offices, hospitals, warehouses, and other workplaces. Helps members negotiate pay, benefits, and better working conditions; conducts training programs and workshops. Monitors legislation and regulations.

International Union of Bricklayers and Allied Craftworkers, *620 F St. N.W., 20004; (202) 783-3788. James Boland, President. Toll-free, (888) 880-8222.*

General email, askbac@bacweb.org

Web, www.bacweb.org

Membership: bricklayers, stonemasons, and other skilled craftworkers in the building industry. Helps members negotiate pay, benefits, and better working conditions; conducts training programs and workshops. Monitors legislation and regulations. (Affiliated with the AFL-CIO and the International Masonry Institute.)

International Union of Operating Engineers, *1125 17th St. N.W., 20036; (202) 429-9100. Fax, (202) 778-2688. James T. Callahan, General President.*

Web, www.iuoe.org

Membership: approximately 400,000 operating engineers, including heavy equipment operators, mechanics, and surveyors in the construction industry, and stationary engineers, including operations and building maintenance staff. Represents members in negotiating pay, benefits, and better working conditions; conducts training programs and workshops. Monitors legislation and regulations in the U.S. and Canada. (Affiliated with the AFL-CIO.)

International Union of Painters and Allied Trades, *7234 Parkway Dr., Hanover, MD 21076; (410) 564-5900. Fax, (866) 656-4124. Kenneth Rigmaiden, General President.*

General email, mail@iupat.org

Web, www.iupat.org, Twitter, @GoIUPAT and Facebook, www.facebook.com/GoIUPAT

Membership: more than 140,000 painters, glaziers, floor covering installers, signmakers, show decorators, and workers in allied trades in the United States and Canada. Helps members negotiate pay, benefits, and better working conditions; conducts training programs and workshops. Monitors legislation and regulations. (Affiliated with the AFL-CIO.)

Kitchen Cabinet Manufacturers Assn., *1899 Preston White Dr., Reston, VA 20191-5435; (703) 264-1690. Fax, (703) 620-6530. Betsy Natz, Chief Executive Officer.*
General email, info@kcma.org

Web, www.kcma.org and Twitter, @KCMAorg

Represents cabinet manufacturers and suppliers to the industry. Provides government relations, management statistics, marketing information, and plant tours. Administers cabinet testing and certification programs.

National Concrete Masonry Assn., *13750 Sunrise Valley Dr., Herndon, VA 20171-4662; (703) 713-1900. Fax, (703) 713-1910. Robert D. Thomas, President.*
General email, info@ncma.org

Web, www.ncma.org, Twitter, @ConcreteMasonry and Facebook, www.facebook.com/ NationalConcreteMasonryAssociation

Membership: producers and suppliers of concrete, masonry, and related goods and services. Conducts research; provides members with technical, marketing, government relations, and communications assistance.

National Glass Assn. (NGA), *1945 Old Gallows Rd., #750, Vienna, VA 22182; (703) 442-4890. Fax, (703) 442-0630. Nicole Harris, President. Toll-free, (866) 342-5642.*
Web, www.glass.org, Twitter, @NatGlassAssoc and Facebook, www.facebook.com/NationalGlassAssociation

Membership: companies in the flat (architectural and automotive) glass industry. Provides education and training programs to promote quality workmanship, ethics, and safety standards in the architectural, automotive, and window and door glass industries. Acts as a clearinghouse for information and links professionals with job listings, suppliers, and technical support. Monitors legislation and regulations.

National Insulation Assn. (NIA), *516 Herdon Parkway #D, Reston, VA 20170; (703) 464-6422. Fax, (703) 464-5896. Michele M. Jones, Executive Vice President, ext. 119. Toll-free, (877) 968-7642.*
General email, niainfo@insulation.org

Web, www.insulation.org

Membership: open-shop and union contractors, distributors, laminators, fabricators, and manufacturers that provide thermal insulation, insulation accessories, and components to the commercial, mechanical, and industrial markets. Provides information to members on industry trends and technologies, and offers service contacts for consumers. Monitors legislation and regulations.

National Lumber and Building Material Dealers Assn., *2025 M St. N.W., #800, 20036-3309; (202) 367-1169. Jonathan M. Paine, President.*
General email, info@dealer.org

Web, www.dealer.org

Membership: federated associations of retailers in the lumber and building material industries. Provides statistics training and networking opportunities to members. Monitors legislation and regulations.

North American Insulation Manufacturers Assn., *11 Canal Center Plaza, #103, Alexandria, VA 22314; (703) 684-0084. Fax, (703) 684-0427. Curt Rich, President.*
General email, sfitzgerald-redd@naima.org

Web, www.naima.org, Twitter, @knowinsulation and Facebook, www.facebook.com/insulationinstitute

Membership: manufacturers of insulation products for use in homes, commercial buildings, and industrial facilities. Provides information on the use of insulation for thermal efficiency, sound control, and fire safety; monitors research in the industry. Interests include energy efficiency and sustainability. Monitors legislation and regulations.

Operative Plasterers' and Cement Masons' International Assn. of the United States and Canada, *9700 Patuxent Woods Dr., #200, Columbia, MD 21046; (301) 623-1000. Fax, (301) 623-1032. Daniel E. Stepano, President.*
General email, opcmiaintl@opcmia.org

Web, www.opcmia.org and Twitter, @opcmiaint

Membership: approximately 58,000 cement masons and plasterers. Helps members negotiate pay, benefits, and better working conditions; conducts training programs and workshops. Monitors legislation and regulations. (Affiliated with the AFL-CIO.)

Portland Cement Assn., *Washington Office, 1150 Connecticut Ave. N.W., #500, 20036-4104; (202) 408-9494. Fax, (202) 408-0877. Michael Ireland, Chief Executive Officer, (847) 972-9004; Rachael Derby, Vice President of Government Affairs, (202) 719-1983.*
Web, www.cement.org and Twitter, @PCA_Daily

Membership: producers of portland cement. Monitors legislation and regulations. (Headquarters in Skokie, Ill.)

Roof Coatings Manufacturers Assn., *529 14th St. N.W., #750, 20045; (202) 591-2452. Fax, (202) 591-2445. Matt Coffindaffer, Executive Director, (202) 207-0919.*
General email, questions@roofcoatings.org

Web, www.roofcoatings.org

Membership: firms, partnerships, and corporations that manufacture or supply cold-applied protective roof coatings. Provides guidance on building codes and standards and technical developments. Affiliated with the Reflective Roof Coatings Institute.

Sheet Metal, Air, Rail, and Transportation Workers (SMART), *1750 New York Ave. N.W., 6th Floor, 20006; (202) 662-0880. Joseph Sellers Jr., General President. Toll-free, (800) 457-7694.*
General email, info@smart-union.org

Web, http://smart-union.org and Twitter, @smartunionworks

Membership: United States, Puerto Rican, and Canadian workers in the building and construction trades, manufacturing, and the railroad and shipyard industries. Assists members with contract negotiation and grievances; conducts training programs and workshops. Monitors legislation and regulations. (Affiliated with the Sheet Metal and Air Conditioning Contractors' Assn., the AFL-CIO, and the Canadian Labour Congress.)

FIRE PREVENTION AND CONTROL

General

▶AGENCIES

Forest Service *(Agriculture Dept.), Fire and Aviation Management,* 201 14th St. S.W., 3rd Floor, 3 Central, 20024 (mailing address: 1400 Independence Ave. S.W., MS 1107, Washington, DC 20250-0003); (202) 205-0808. Fax, (703) 605-1401. Shawna Legarza, Director. Web, www.fs.fed.us/fire

Responsible for aviation and fire management programs, including fire control planning and prevention, suppression of fires, and the use of prescribed fires. Provides state foresters with financial and technical assistance for fire protection in forests and on rural lands.

Interior Dept. (DOI), *Wildland Fire (OWF),* 1849 C St. N.W., MS 2660, 20240; (202) 208-2719. Fax, (202) 606-3150. Jeff Rupert, Director. General email, wildlandfire@ios.doi.gov Web, www.doi.gov/wildlandfire and Twitter, @DOIWildlandFire

Oversees all wildland fire management programs, policies, budgets, and information technology in order to manage risk to firefighters, communities, and landscapes. Bridges the individual fire programs of the four land management bureaus; supports the wildland fire needs of the bureau.

National Institute of Standards and Technology (NIST) *(Commerce Dept.), Engineering Laboratory,* 100 Bureau Dr., MS 8600, Gaithersburg, MD 20899-8600; (301) 975-5900. Fax, (301) 975-4032. Howard H. Harary, Director. General email, el@nist.gov Web, www.nist.gov/el

Conducts basic and applied research on fire and fire resistance of construction materials; develops testing methods, standards, design concepts, and technologies for fire protection and prevention.

U.S. Fire Administration *(Federal Emergency Management Agency),* 16825 S. Seton Ave., Emmitsburg, MD 21727-8998; (301) 447-1000. Fax, (301) 447-1441. G. Keith Bryant, Administrator, (202) 646-4223. Press, (301) 447-1853. Toll-free, (800) 238-3358. Web, www.usfa.fema.gov and Twitter, @usfire

Conducts research and collects, analyzes, and disseminates data on combustion, fire prevention, firefighter safety, and the management of fire prevention organizations; studies and develops arson-prevention programs and fire-prevention codes; maintains the National Fire Incident Reporting System.

U.S. Fire Administration *(Federal Emergency Management Agency), National Fire Academy,* 16825 S. Seton Ave., Emmitsburg, MD 21727-8998; (301) 447-1117. Fax, (301) 447-1441. Tonya Hoover, Superintendent, (301) 447-1117. General email, usfa-webmaster@fema.dhs.gov Web, www.usfa.dhs.gov/training/nfa

Trains fire officials and related professionals in fire-prevention and management, current firefighting technologies, and the administration of fire prevention organizations.

▶NONGOVERNMENTAL

International Assn. of Fire Chiefs, 4795 Meadow Wood Lane, #100, Chantilly, VA 20151; (703) 273-0911. Fax, (703) 273-9363. Mark Light, Chief Executive Officer, (703) 537-4808. Web, www.iafc.org, Twitter, @IAFC and Facebook, www.facebook.com/firechiefs

Membership: fire service chiefs and chief officers. Conducts research on fire control; testifies before congressional committees. Monitors legislation and regulations affecting fire safety codes.

International Assn. of Fire Fighters, 1750 New York Ave. N.W., #300, 20006-5395; (202) 737-8484. Fax, (202) 737-8418. Harold A. Schaitberger, General President. General email, pr@tburn.iaff.org Web, www.i aff.org, Twitter, @IAFFNewsDesk and Facebook, www.facebook.com/IAFFonline

Membership: more than 310,000 professional firefighters and emergency medical personnel. Assists members with contract negotiation and grievances; conducts training programs and workshops. Monitors legislation and regulations. (Affiliated with the AFL-CIO and the Canadian Labour Congress.)

National Fire Protection Assn., *Government Affairs,* 50 F St. N.W., #625, 20001; (202) 898-0222. Fax, (202) 898-0044. Seth Statler, Government Affairs Director. Toll-free, (800) 344-3555. General email, wdc@nfpa.org Web, www.nfpa.org, Twitter, @NFPA and Facebook, www.facebook.com/theNFPA

Membership: individuals and organizations interested in fire protection. Develops and updates fire protection codes and standards; sponsors technical assistance programs; collects fire data statistics. Monitors legislation and regulations. (Headquarters in Quincy, Mass.)

HOUSING

General

▶AGENCIES

Housing and Urban Development Dept. (HUD), *Housing Office,* 451 7th St. S.W., #9100, 20410; (202) 708-2601. Fax, (202) 708-1403. Brian D. Montgomery, Assistant

Secretary & FHA Commissioner, (202) 402-5430.
TTY, (202) 708-1455.
Web, www.hud.gov/program_offices/housing

Administers housing programs, including the production, financing, and management of housing; directs preservation and rehabilitation of the housing stock; manages regulatory programs.

▶CONGRESS

For a listing of relevant congressional committees and subcommittees, please see page 441 or the Appendix.

▶NONGOVERNMENTAL

Habitat for Humanity International, *Government Relations and Advocacy,* 1310 L St. N.W., #350, 20005; (202) 628-9171. Fax, (202) 628-9169. Chris Vincent, Vice President of Advocacy and Government Relations.
General email, advocacy@habitat.org
Web, www.habitat.org/about/advocacy

Christian ministry that seeks to eliminate poverty housing. Helps people attain housing through home construction, rehabilitation and repairs, and increased access to improved shelter through programs. Offers housing support services that enable low-income families to make improvements on their homes. Works in more than 70 countries.

National Community Stabilization Trust (NCST), 910 17th St. N.W., #500A, 20006; (202) 223-3237. Robert Grossinger, President. Press, (214) 710-3411.
General email, info@stabilizationtrust.org
Web, www.stabilizationtrust.org and Twitter, @_NCST

Assists local housing providers in acquiring, vacant, abandoned, and foreclosed properties from financial institutions to build new affordable living properties. Manages funds for community stabilization programs from public and private investors. Coordinates management and rehabilitation of foreclosed properties. Works with housing organizations to solve policy issues.

National Housing and Rehabilitation Assn., 1400 16th St. N.W., #420, 20036; (202) 939-1750. Fax, (202) 265-4435. Peter H. Bell, President, (202) 939-1741; Thom Amdur, Executive Director, (202) 939-1753.
General email, info@housingonline.com
Web, www.housingonline.com

Membership: historic rehabilitation businesses, development firms and organizations, and city, state, and local agencies concerned with affordable multifamily housing. Monitors government policies affecting multifamily development and rehabilitation.

National Housing Conference (NHC), 1900 M St. N.W., #550, 20036; (202) 466-2121. Fax, (202) 466-2122. David M. Dworkin, President; Tristan Breaux, Director of Policy. Press, (202) 466-2121, ext. 240.
General email, info@nhc.org
Web, www.nhc.org and Twitter, @natlhousingconf

Membership: state and local housing officials, community development specialists, builders, bankers, lawyers, civic leaders, tenants, architects and planners, labor and religious groups, and national housing and housing-related organizations. Mobilizes public support for community development and affordable housing programs; conducts educational sessions. Supports the Center for Housing Policy, NHC's research affiliate.

National Leased Housing Assn., 1900 L St. N.W., #300, 20036; (202) 785-8888. Fax, (202) 785-2008. Denise B. Muha, Executive Director.
General email, info@hudnlha.com
Web, www.hudnlha.com and Twitter, @leasedhousing

Membership: public and private organizations and individuals concerned with multifamily low and moderate income and government-assisted housing programs. Conducts training seminars. Monitors legislation and regulations.

National Low Income Housing Coalition, 1000 Vermont Ave., #500, 20005; (202) 662-1530. Fax, (202) 393-1973. Diane Yentel, President, ext. 225.
General email, info@nlihc.org
Web, www.nlihc.org and Twitter, @NLIHC

Membership: organizations and individuals that support low-income housing. Works to end the affordable housing crisis in America. Interests include the needs of the lowest-income people and those who are homeless. Monitors legislation and regulations.

Fair Housing, Special Groups

▶AGENCIES

Housing and Urban Development Dept. (HUD), *Community Planning and Development, HIV/AIDS Housing,* 451 7th St. S.W., #7248, 20410; (202) 708-1943. Rita Flegel, Director.
General email, HOPWA@hud.gov
Web, www.hud.gov/program_offices/comm_planning/aidshousing, Twitter, @HUD_HOPWA and HOPWA information, www.hudexchange.info/programs/hopwa

Makes grants to local communities, states, and nonprofit organizations for projects that benefit low-income persons living with HIV/AIDS and their families. Manages the Housing Opportunities for Persons With AIDS (HOPWA) program.

Housing and Urban Development Dept. (HUD), *Fair Housing and Equal Opportunity,* 451 7th St. S.W., #5100, 20410-2000; (202) 708-4252. Fax, (202) 708-4483. Anna Maria Farias, Assistant Secretary. Housing discrimination hotline, (800) 669-9777.
Web, http://program_offices/fair_housing_equal_opp

Monitors compliance with legislation requiring equal opportunities in housing for minorities, persons with disabilities, and families with children. Monitors compliance with construction codes to accommodate people with disabilities in multifamily dwellings. Hotline answers inquiries about housing discrimination.

Housing and Urban Development Dept. (HUD), *Fair Housing Initiative Programs*, 451 7th St. S.W., #5222, 20410; (202) 402-7095. Fax, (202) 708-4445.
Myron P. Newry, Director.
General email, AllAboutFHIP@hud.gov
Web, www.hud.gov/program_offices/fair_housing_equal_opp/partners/FHIP/fhip

Awards grants to public and private organizations and to state and local agencies. Funds projects that educate the public about fair housing rights; investigates housing discrimination complaints. Programs are designed to prevent or eliminate discriminatory housing practices.

Public and Indian Housing *(Housing and Urban Development Dept.)*, *Native American Programs*, 451 7th St. S.W., #4126, 20410-5000; (202) 401-7914. Fax, (202) 401-7909. Heidi J. Frechette, Deputy Assistant Secretary, (202) 402-7914.
Web, http://portal.hud.gov/hudportal/HUD?src=/program_offices/public_indian_housing/ih

Administers federal assistance for Native American tribes. Assistance programs focus on housing and community and economic development through competitive and formula grants. Funds for approved activities are provided directly to tribes or Alaska Native villages or to a tribally designated housing authority.

▶ NONGOVERNMENTAL

National American Indian Housing Council, 122 C St. N.W., #350, 20001; (202) 789-1754. Fax, (202) 789-1758. *Tony Walters, Executive Director, (202) 454-0928.*
Toll-free, (800) 284-9165.
General email, info@naihc.net
Web, www.naihc.net and Twitter, @naihc_national

Membership: Native American housing authorities. Clearinghouse for information on Native American housing issues; works for safe and sanitary dwellings for Native American and Alaska Native communities; monitors policies of the Housing and Urban Development Dept. and housing legislation; provides members with training and technical assistance in managing housing assistance programs.

National Assn. for the Advancement of Colored People (NAACP), *Washington Bureau*, 1156 15th St. N.W., #915, 20005; (202) 463-2940. Fax, (202) 463-2953.
Derrick Johnson, President.
General email, washingtonbureau@naacpnet.org
Web, www.naacp.org and Twitter, @NAACP

Membership: persons interested in civil rights for all minorities. Works to eliminate discrimination in housing and urban affairs. Supports programs that make affordable rental housing available to minorities and that maintain African American ownership of land. (Headquarters in Baltimore, Md.)

National Assn. of Real Estate Brokers, 9831 Greenbelt Rd., #309, Lanham, MD 20706; (301) 552-9340. Fax, (301) 552-9216. *Jeffrey Hicks, President; Antoine Thompson, National Executive Director.*
General email, nareb@nareb.com
Web, www.nareb.com and Twitter, @REALIST_NAREB

Membership: minority real estate brokers, appraisers, contractors, property managers, and salespersons. Works to prevent discrimination in housing policies and practices; conducts seminars on contracting and federal policy.

National Fair Housing Training Academy, 600 Maryland Ave. S.W., #027, 20024; (202) 314-3422. Fax, (202) 314-3556. *Amy Peters, Director.*
General email, Support@nfhta.org
Web, www.nfhta.org and Twitter, @nfhta

Provides fair housing and civil rights training and education to federal, state, and local agencies, educators, attorneys, advocates, and other fair housing professionals. (Sponsored and funded by the Housing and Urban Development Dept.)

National Multifamily Housing Council, 1775 Eye St. N.W., #1100, 20006; (202) 974-2300. Fax, (202) 775-0112. *Douglas Bibby, President, (202) 974-2323.*
General email, info@nmhc.org
Web, www.nmhc.org

Membership: owners, financiers, managers, and developers of multifamily housing. Serves as a clearinghouse on rent control, condominium conversion, taxes, fair housing, and environmental issues.

National Rural Housing Coalition, 1331 G St. N.W., 10th Floor, 20005; (202) 393-5229. Fax, (202) 393-3034. *Stan Keasling, President.*
General email, nrhc@ruralhousingcoalitions.org
Web, www.ruralhousingcoalition.org

Advocates improved housing for low-income rural families; works to increase public awareness of rural housing problems; administers the Self-Help Housing Fund, Farm Worker Housing Fund, Rural Community Assistance Fund, and HUD Task Force. Monitors legislation and regulations.

UnidosUS, 1126 16th St. N.W., #600, 20036-4845; (202) 785-1670. Fax, (202) 776-1792. *Janet Murguía, President.*
General email, info@unidos.org
Web, www.unidosus.org, Twitter, @WeAreUnidosUS and Facebook, www.facebook.com/Weareunidosus

Helps Hispanic community-based groups obtain funds, develop and build low-income housing and community facilities, and develop and finance community economic development projects; conducts research and provides policy analysis on the housing status and needs of Hispanics; monitors legislation on fair housing and government funding for low-income housing. (Formerly the National Council of La Raza.)

Public and Subsidized Housing

▶AGENCIES

Federal Housing Administration (FHA) *(Housing and Urban Development Dept.), Housing Assistance and Grant Administration,* 451 7th St. S.W., #6134, 20410-8000; (202) 708-3000. Fax, (202) 708-3104.
Catherine Brennan, Director.
Web, http://portal.hud.gov/hudportal/HUD?src=/program_offices/housing/mfh/hsgmfbus/abouthaga

Directs and oversees the housing assistance and grant programs, including project-based Section 8 housing assistance, Section 202/811 capital advance and project rental assistance programs, the Assisted-Living Conversion Program (ALCP), rent supplements, service coordinator, and congregate housing services grant programs.

Federal Housing Administration (FHA) *(Housing and Urban Development Dept.), Housing Assistance Contract Administration Oversight,* 451 7th St. S.W., #6151, 20410-8000; (202) 708-2677. Fax, (202) 708-1300.
Kerry Hickman, Director; Lewis Suiter, Deputy Director.
Web, http://portal.hud.gov/hudportal/HUD?src=/program_offices/housing/mfh/hsgmfbus/abouthacao

Administers Section 8 contracts and other rental subsidy programs. Ensures that Section 8 subsidized properties meet the department's goal of providing decent, safe, and sanitary housing to low-income families.

Housing and Urban Development Dept. (HUD), *Community Planning and Development, Affordable Housing Programs,* 451 7th St. S.W., #7164, 20410; (202) 708-2684. Fax, (202) 708-1744. Virginia Sardone, Director.
Web, www.hud.gov/program_offices/comm_planning/affordablehousing

HOME program helps to expand the supply of decent, affordable housing for low-income and very-low-income families by providing grants to states and local governments to help renters, new home buyers, or existing homeowners. SHOP program provides funds for nonprofit organizations to purchase home sites and develop or improve the infrastructure needed to facilitate sweat equity and volunteer-based homeownership programs for low-income families.

Housing and Urban Development Dept. (HUD), *Community Planning and Development, Rural Housing and Economic Development (RHED),* 451 7th St. S.W., #7240, 20410; (202) 708-2290. Fax, (202) 708-7543. Jackie Williams, Director. TTY, (202) 708-1455.
Web, www.hudexchange.info/programs/rhed

Promotes decent housing and economic opportunities for low-income and middle-income individuals; offers rental, homebuyer, and homeowner assistance and resources for homeless persons, youth, and veterans.

Public and Indian Housing *(Housing and Urban Development Dept.),* 451 7th St. S.W., #4100, 20410-0800; (202) 708-0950. Fax, (202) 619-8478. Dominique Blom, General Deputy Assistant Secretary; Vacant, Assistant Secretary. TTY, (202) 708-1455.

General email, daniella.d.mungo@hud.gov
Web, https://portal.hud.gov/program_offices/public_Indian_housing

Seeks to ensure that safe, decent, and affordable housing is available to low-income and Native American families, the elderly, and persons with disabilities.

Public and Indian Housing *(Housing and Urban Development Dept.), Housing Voucher Management and Operations,* 451 7th St. S.W., #920, 20410; (202) 402-6050. Fax, (202) 708-0690. Rebecca Primeaux, Director.
Web, http://portal.hud.gov/hudportal/HUD?src=/program_offices/public_indian_housing

Administers certificate and housing voucher programs and moderate rehabilitation authorized by Section 8 of the Housing Act of 1937, as amended. Provides rental subsidies to lower-income families.

Public and Indian Housing *(Housing and Urban Development Dept.), Public Housing and Voucher Programs,* 451 7th St. S.W., #4130, 20410-5000; (202) 708-2815. Fax, (202) 708-0690. Danielle Bastarache, Deputy Assistant Secretary, (202) 402-5264. Information Service, (202) 708-0744. Section 8, (202) 708-0477.
Web, http://portal.hud.gov/hudportal/HUD?src=/program_offices/public_indian_housing

Establishes policies and procedures for low-income public housing and rental assistance programs, including special needs for the elderly and disabled, standards for rental and occupancy, utilities and maintenance engineering, and financial management.

Public and Indian Housing *(Housing and Urban Development Dept.), Public Housing Investments,* 451 7th St. S.W., #4130, 20410-0050; (202) 401-8812. Fax, (202) 401-2370. Robert Mulderig, Deputy Assistant Secretary (Acting), (202) 402-4780.
Web, http://portal.hud.gov/hudportal/HUD?src=/program_offices/public_indian_housing

Establishes development policies and procedures for low-income housing programs, including criteria for site approval and construction standards; oversees administration of the Capital Fund for modernizing existing public housing, the Choice Neighborhood Program, and the Moving to Work demonstration program for public housing authorities. Administers the HOPE VI Program and manages the Special Applications Center.

Real Estate Assessment Center (REAC) *(Housing and Urban Development Dept.),* 550 12th St. S.W., #100, 20410; (202) 475-7949. Donald J. Lavoy, Deputy Assistant Secretary. Information, (202) 708-1112. Toll-free, (888) 245-4860. TTY, (202) 708-1455. phone, (202) 475-7949.
General email, reac_tac@hud.gov
Web, www.hud.gov/reac

Conducts physical inspections and surveys of resident satisfaction in publicly owned, insured, or subsidized housing. Assesses financial condition and management operations of public housing agencies.

▶NONGOVERNMENTAL

Council of Large Public Housing Authorities, *455 Massachusetts Ave. N.W., #425, 20001; (202) 638-1300. Fax, (202) 638-2364. Sunia Zaterman, Executive Director. General email, clpha@clpha.org*

Web, http://clpha.org

Works to preserve and improve public housing through advocacy, research, policy analysis, and public education.

Enterprise Community Partners, *10 G St. N.E., #580, 20002; (410) 964-1230. Fax, (410) 964-1376. Laurel Blatchford, President; David Bowers, Vice President. Toll-free, (800) 624-4298.*

Web, www.enterprisecommunity.org

Works with local groups to help provide decent, affordable housing for low-income individuals and families, including green affordable housing. Works to link public transit to affordable housing.

Housing Assistance Council, *1025 Vermont Ave. N.W., #606, 20005-3516; (202) 842-8600. Fax, (202) 347-3441. David Lipsetz, Chief Executive Officer. General email, hac@ruralhome.org*

Web, www.ruralhome.org, Twitter, @RuralHome and Facebook, www.facebook.com/HousingAssistanceCouncil

Operates in rural areas and in cities of fewer than 25,000 citizens. Advises low-income and minority groups seeking federal assistance for improving rural housing and community facilities; studies and makes recommendations for federal, state, and local housing policies; makes low-interest loans for housing programs for low-income and minority groups living in rural areas, including Native Americans and farm workers; publishes technical guides and reports on rural housing issues.

Public Housing Authorities Directors Assn., *511 Capitol Court N.E., #200, 20002-4937; (202) 546-5445. Fax, (202) 546-4381. Timothy G. Kaiser, Executive Director. Web, www.phada.org and Twitter, @PHADA*

Membership: executive directors of public housing authorities. Serves as liaison between members and the Housing and Urban Development Dept. and Congress; conducts educational seminars and conferences. Monitors legislation and regulations.

Urban Institute, *Metropolitan Housing and Communities Policy Center, 500 L'Enfant Plaza S.W., 20024; (202) 833-7200. Mary K. Cunningham, Vice President. Web, www.urban.org/center/met*

Research center that deals with urban problems. Researches housing policy problems, including housing management, public housing programs, finance, and rent control.

Senior Living

▶NONGOVERNMENTAL

AARP, *601 E St. N.W., 20049; (202) 434-2277. Fax, (202) 434-7946. Jo Ann C. Jenkins, Chief Executive Officer.*

Library, (202) 434-6233. Membership, (202) 434-7550. Membership, toll-free, (800) 566-0242. Press, (202) 434-2560. Toll-free, (888) 687-2277. TTY, (877) 434-7598. Toll-free Spanish, (877) 342-2277. TTY Spanish, (866) 238-9488.

General email, member@aarp.org

Web, www.aarp.org, Twitter, @AARP and Facebook, www.facebook.com/AARP

Promotes safe and affordable housing for older adults, including safe communities, physical disability accomodation, adequate transportation options, and access to grocery stores, doctors, and community activities.

American Seniors Housing Assn., *5225 Wisconsin Ave. N.W., #502, 20015; (202) 237-0900. Fax, (202) 237-1616. David Schless, President, (202) 885-5560. General email, info@seniorshousing.org*

Web, www.seniorshousing.org

Membership: development, finance, and operation professionals working in seniors apartments, independent and assisted living communities, and retirement communities. Promotes the advancement of quality seniors housing and health care through research, education, and monitoring legislation and regulations.

Argentum, *1650 King St., #602, Alexandria, VA 22314; (703) 894-1805. Fax, (703) 894-1831. James Balda, President. Press, (703) 562-1185. General email, info@argentum.org*

Web, www.argentum.org

Represents operators of communities for seniors, including independent-living, assisted-living, and Alzheimer's care facilities, but not including nursing homes or hospices. Promotes the development of standards and increased awareness for the senior living industry. Provides members with information on policy, funding access, and quality of care. Interests include informed choice, safe environments, caring and competent staff, and funding alternatives to increase accessibility to senior communities. Monitors legislation and regulations. (Formerly Assisted Living Federation of America.)

B'nai B'rith International, *Center for Senior Services, 1120 20th St. N.W., #300N, 20036; (202) 857-6535. Fax, (202) 857-6531. Mark D. Olshan, Director. Toll-free, (866) 999-6596. General email, seniors@bnaibrith.org*

Web, www.bnaibrith.org

Acts as an advocate on behalf of the aging population in America. Works with local groups to sponsor federally assisted housing for independent low-income senior citizens and persons with disabilities, regardless of race or religion.

Leading Age, *2519 Connecticut Ave. N.W., 20008-1520; (202) 783-2242. Fax, (202) 783-2255. Katie Smith Sloan, Chief Executive Officer. General email, info@leadingage.org*

Web, www.leadingage.org

Membership: nonprofit nursing homes, housing, and health-related facilities for the elderly. Provides research and technical assistance for providers of long-term care for the elderly. Monitors legislation and regulations.

National Caucus and Center on Black Aging, Inc., *1220 L St. N.W., #800, 20005-2407; (202) 637-8400. Fax, (202) 347-0895. Karyne Jones, President.*
General email, support@ncba-aged.org

Web, www.ncba-aged.org and Twitter, @NCBADC

Concerned with issues that affect older Black Americans and other minorities. Sponsors employment and housing programs for older adults and education and training for professionals in gerontology. Monitors legislation and regulations.

National Council on Aging, *251 18th St. South, #500, Arlington, VA 22202; (571) 527-3900. Fax, (571) 527-3901. James P. (Jim) Firman, President, ext. 1. Eldercare locator, (800) 677-1116. Press, (571) 527-3914.*
General email, info@ncoa.org

Web, www.ncoa.org, Twitter, @NCOAging and Facebook, www.facebook.com/NCOAging

Serves as an information clearinghouse on aging. Works to ensure quality housing for older persons. Monitors legislation and regulations.

REAL ESTATE

General

▶ AGENCIES

Bureau of Land Management (BLM) *(Interior Dept.),* **Lands, Realty, and Cadastral Survey,** *1849 C St. N.W., #2134LM, 20003; (202) 912-7088. Fax, (202) 912-7199. Robert Jolley, Division Chief, (202) 912-7350.*
Web, www.blm.gov/programs/lands-and-realty

Oversees use, acquisition, and disposal of public lands. Conducts the Public Lands Survey; authorizes rights-of-way on public lands for uses that include roads, power lines, and wind and solar facilities.

Federal Highway Administration (FHWA) *(Transportation Dept.), Planning, Environment, and Realty,* *1200 New Jersey Ave. S.E., #E76-306, 20590; (202) 366-0116. Fax, (202) 366-3713. Gloria M. Shepherd, Associate Administrator.*
Web, www.fhwa.dot.gov/real_estate

Works with developers and municipalities to ensure conformity with the National Environmental Policy Act (NEPA) project development process.

▶ CONGRESS

For a listing of relevant congressional committees and subcommittees, please see page 441 or the Appendix.

▶ NONGOVERNMENTAL

American Land Title Assn., *1800 M St. N.W., #300S, 20036; (202) 296-3671. Fax, (202) 223-5843. Kelly L. Romeo, Vice President, ext. 224. Toll-free, (800) 787-2582. Toll-free Fax, 800–329-2582.*
General email, service@alta.org

Web, www.alta.org and Twitter, @ALTAonline

Membership: land title insurance underwriting companies, abstracters, lawyers, and title insurance agents. Searches, reviews, and insures land titles to protect real estate investors, including home buyers and mortgage lenders; provides industry information. Monitors legislation and regulations.

American Land Trust Assn, *TIPAC, 1800 M. St. N.W., #3005, 20036; (202) 296-3671. Nicole Reppert, Director of Political Affairs, ext. 233.*
Web, www.alta/advocacy/tipac.cfm

PAC representing the land title industry. Raises money to elect and reelect candidates that support and understand the issues affecting the land title industry.

American Resort Development Assn., *1201 15th St. N.W., #400, 20005-2842; (202) 371-6700. Fax, (202) 289-8544. Howard Nusbaum, President.*
Web, www.arda.org

Membership: U.S. and international developers, builders, financiers, marketing companies, and others involved in resort, recreational, and community development. Serves as an information clearinghouse; monitors federal and state legislation.

American Society of Appraisers (ASA), *11107 Sunset Hills Rd., #310, Reston, VA 20190; (703) 478-2228. Fax, (703) 742-8471. Bonny Price, Chief Operations Officer, (703) 733-2110. Toll-free, (800) 272-8258.*
General email, asainfo@appraisers.org

Web, www.appraisers.org and Twitter, @ASAappraisers

Membership: accredited appraisers of real property, including land, houses, and commercial buildings; business valuation; machinery and technical specialties; yachts; aircraft; public utilities; personal property, including antiques, fine art, residential contents; and gems and jewelry. Affiliate members include students and professionals interested in appraising. Provides technical information; accredits appraisers; provides consumer information programs.

Appraisal Foundation, *1155 15th St. N.W., #1111, 20005; (202) 347-7722. Fax, (202) 347-7727. David S. Bunton, President.*
General email, info@appraisalfoundation.org

Web, www.appraisalfoundation.org and Twitter, @uspap

Ensures that real estate appraisers are qualified to offer their services by promoting uniform appraisal standards and establishing education, experience, and examination requirements.

Appraisal Institute, *Government Relations, 440 1st St. N.W., #880, 20001; (202) 298-6449. Fax, (202) 298-5547.*

William (Bill) Garber, Director of Government and External Relations, (202) 298-5597.
General email, insidethebeltway@appraisalinstitute.org
Web, www.appraisalinstitute.org

Provides Congress, regulatory agencies, and the executive branch with information on real estate appraisal matters. (Headquarters in Chicago, Ill.)

Assn. of Foreign Investors in Real Estate, 1300 Pennsylvania Ave. N.W., 20004-3020; (202) 312-1400. Fax, (202) 312-1401. Gunnar Branson, Chief Executive Officer.
General email, afireinfo@afire.org
Web, www.afire.org

Represents foreign institutions that are interested in the laws, regulations, and economic trends affecting the U.S. real estate market. Informs the public and the government of the contributions foreign investment makes to the U.S. economy. Examines current issues and organizes seminars for members.

Manufactured Housing Institute, 1655 Ft. Meyer Dr., #104, Arlington, VA 22209; (703) 558-0400. Fax, (703) 558-0401. Richard A. Jennison, President; Lesli Gooch, Government Affairs.
General email, info@mfghome.org
Web, www.manufacturedhousing.org

Represents community owners and developers, financial lenders, and builders, suppliers, and retailers of manufactured and modular homes. Provides information on manufactured and modular home construction standards, finance, site development, property management, and marketing.

National Assn. of Home Builders (NAHB), 1201 15th St. N.W., 20005-2800; (202) 266-8200. Fax, (202) 266-8400. Jerry Howard, Executive Officer, (800) 368-5242, ext. 8257. Press, (202) 266-8254. Toll-free, (800) 368-5242.
General email, info@nahb.org
Web, www.nahb.org and Twitter, @NAHBhome

Membership: contractors, builders, architects, engineers, mortgage lenders, and others interested in home building and residential real estate construction. Offers educational programs and information on housing policy in the United States. Monitors legislation and regulations.

National Assn. of Real Estate Brokers, 9831 Greenbelt Rd., #309, Lanham, MD 20706; (301) 552-9340. Fax, (301) 552-9216. Jeffrey Hicks, President; Antoine Thompson, National Executive Director.
General email, nareb@nareb.com
Web, www.nareb.com and Twitter, @REALIST_NAREB

Membership: minority real estate brokers, appraisers, contractors, property managers, and salespersons. Works to prevent discrimination in housing policies and practices; conducts seminars on contracting and federal policy.

National Assn. of Real Estate Investment Trusts, 1875 Eye St. N.W., #600, 20006-5413; (202) 739-9400. Fax, (202) 739-9401. Steven A. Wechsler, President. Toll-free, (800) 362-7348.
Web, www.reit.com and Twitter, @REITs_NAREIT

Membership: real estate investment trusts and corporations, partnerships, and individuals interested in real estate securities and the industry. Interests include federal taxation, securities regulation, financial standards and reporting standards and ethics, housing and education, and global investment; compiles industry statistics. Monitors federal and state legislation and regulations.

National Assn. of Realtors, *Government Affairs,* 500 New Jersey Ave. N.W., 11th Floor, 20001-2020; (202) 383-1000. Fax, (202) 383-7580. Jerry Smaby, Senior Vice President. Toll-free, (800) 874-6500.
Web, www.realtor.org and Twitter, @askNAR

Sets professional standards, trademark regulations, and code of ethics for the real estate business; promotes education, research, and exchange of information. Interests include housing markets, property rights, and federal housing finance and insurance programs and agencies. Monitors legislation and regulations. (Headquarters in Chicago, Ill.)

The Real Estate Roundtable, 801 Pennsylvania Ave. N.W., #720, 20004; (202) 639-8400. Fax, (202) 639-8442. Jeffrey D. DeBoer, President.
General email, info@rer.org
Web, www.rer.org

Membership: real estate owners, advisers, builders, investors, lenders, and managers. Serves as forum for public policy issues, including taxes, energy, homeland security, the environment, capital, credit, and investments.

Society of Industrial and Office Realtors, 1201 New York Ave. N.W., #350, 20005-6126; (202) 449-8200. Fax, (202) 216-9325. Thomas E. McCormick III, Chief Executive Officer, (202) 449-8202.
General email, admin@sior.com
Web, www.sior.com and Twitter, @SIORglobal

Membership: commercial and industrial real estate brokers worldwide. Certifies brokers; sponsors seminars and conferences; mediates and arbitrates business disputes for members; sponsors a speakers bureau. (Affiliated with the National Assn. of Realtors.)

Mortgages and Finance

▶AGENCIES

Agriculture Dept. (USDA), *Rural Development, Rural Housing Service,* 1400 Independence Ave. S.W., #5014, MS 0701, 20250-0701; (202) 692-0268. Joel Blaxley, Administrator. Toll-free, (800) 414-1226.
Web, www.rd.usda.gov/about-rd/agencies/rural-housing-service and Loan information, www.rdhomeloans.usda.gov

Makes loans and grants in rural communities (population under 20,000) to low-income borrowers, including the elderly and persons with disabilities, for buying, building, or improving single-family and multifamily houses. Makes

Federal Housing Finance Agency

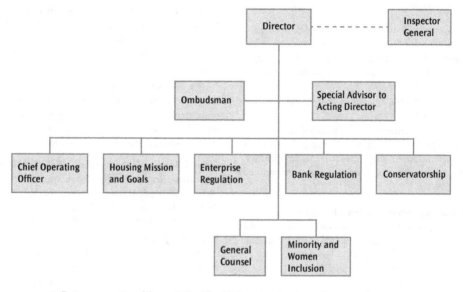

– – – – – Indicates a support or advisory relationship with the unit rather than a direct reporting relationship

grants for rehabilitating homes and making health and safety improvements.

Comptroller of the Currency *(Treasury Dept.),* **Chief Counsel,** *Constitution Center, 400 7th St. S.W., 20506; (202) 649-5400. Fax, (202) 649-6077. Karen Solomon, Chief Counsel.*
Web, www.occ.gov

Enforces and oversees compliance by nationally chartered banks with laws prohibiting discrimination in credit transactions on the basis of sex or marital status. Enforces regulations concerning bank advertising; may issue cease-and-desist orders.

Consumer Financial Protection Bureau (CFPB), *1700 G St. N.W., 20552; 1990 K St. N.W., 20006; (202) 435-7000. Fax, (855) 237-2392. Kathy Kraninger, Director. RESPA enquiries, (855) 411-2372. Toll-free, (855) 411-2372. TTY, (855) 729-2372.*
General email, info@consumerfinance.gov
Web, www.consumerfinance.gov, Twitter, @cfpb
RESPA email, cfpb_respaenquiries@consumerfinance.gov

Responsible for helping home buyers become better shoppers for settlement services and eliminating kickbacks and referral fees that unnecessarily increase the costs of certain settlement services. Administers mortgage regulations including the Ability-to-Repay/Qualified Mortgage rule, which prohibits certain predatory lending practices and requires mortgage creditors to make a reasonable and good-faith effort to verify a borrower's ability to repay a loan.

Fannie Mae *(Federal Housing Finance Agency), 1100 15th St. N.W., 20005; (202) 752-7000. Fax, (240) 699-3893.*

Hugh R. Frater, Chief Executive Officer (Acting). Information for consumers, (800) 232-6643.
Web, www.fanniemae.com, www.fhfa.gov, Twitter, @FannieMae and Facebook, www.facebook.com/ fanniemae

Congressionally chartered, shareholder-owned corporation under conservatorship of the Federal Housing Finance Agency. Makes mortgage funds available by buying conventional and government-insured mortgages in the secondary mortgage market; raises capital through sale of short-term and long-term obligations, mortgages, and stock; issues and guarantees mortgage-backed securities; administers the mortgage fraud program. (Fannie Mae stands for Federal National Mortgage Assn.)

Federal Housing Administration (FHA) *(Housing and Urban Development Dept.), 451 7th St. S.W., #9100, 20410; (202) 708-2601. Fax, (202) 708-1624. Brian Montgomery, Commissioner.*
Web, http://portal.hud.gov/hudportal/HUD?src=/ program_offices/housing/fhahistory

Provides mortage insurance on loans made by approved lenders for single and multifamily homes and hospitals.

Federal Housing Administration (FHA) *(Housing and Urban Development Dept.), Multifamily Housing, 451 7th St. S.W., #6106, 20410; (202) 708-7220. Fax, (202) 708-2583. C. Lamar Seats, Deputy Assistant Secretary.*
Web, http://portal.hud.gov/hudportal/HUD?src=/ program_offices/housing/mfh/hsgmfbus/aboutdas

Determines risk and administers programs associated with government-insured mortgage programs, architectural procedures, and land development programs for multifamily housing. Administers the Rural Rental Housing

Program and the development of congregate housing facilities that provide affordable housing, adequate space for meals, and supportive services.

Federal Housing Administration (FHA) *(Housing and Urban Development Dept.), Multifamily Housing Production,* 451 7th St. S.W., #6134, 20410-8000; (202) 708-1142. Fax, (202) 708-3104. Patricia M. Burke, Director *(Acting). TTY, (202) 708-1455.*
Web, www.hud.gov/program_offices/housing/mfh/ hsgmfbus/aboutmfd

Establishes procedures for the origination of FHA-insured mortgages for multifamily housing. Administers the mortgage insurance programs for rental, cooperative, and condominium housing, nursing homes, and assisted living systems.

Federal Housing Administration (FHA) *(Housing and Urban Development Dept.), Single Family Housing,* 451 7th St. S.W., #9282, 20410; (202) 708-3175. Fax, (202) 708-2582. Gisele Roget, Deputy Assistant Secretary.
Web, http://portal.hud.gov/hudportal/HUD?src=/ program_offices/housing/sfh

Determines risk and administers programs associated with government-insured mortgage programs for single family housing. Administers requirements to obtain and maintain federal government approval of mortgages.

Federal Housing Administration (FHA) *(Housing and Urban Development Dept.), Single Family Program Development,* 451 7th St. S.W., #9278, 20410-8000; (202) 708-2121. Fax, (202) 708-4308. Elissa Saunders, Director.
Web, http://portal.hud.gov/hudportal/HUD?src=/ program_offices/housing/sfh

Establishes procedures for mortgage insurance programs related to the purchase or rehabilitation of single family homes.

Federal Housing Administration (FHA) *(Housing and Urban Development Dept.), Title I Insurance,* 451 7th St. S.W., #9266, 20410; (202) 708-2121. Fax, (202) 708-4308. Kevin Stevens, Director.
Web, http://portal.hud.gov/hudportal/HUD?src=/ program_offices/housing/sfh/title

Sets policy for Title I loans on manufactured home and property improvement loans. Provides information to borrowers and lenders on policy issues.

Federal Housing Finance Agency (FHFA), 400 7th St. S.W., 20219; (202) 649-3800. Fax, (202) 649-1071. Joseph Otting, Director (Acting). Media, (202) 649-3700. Ombudsman, (888) 665-1474.
General email, fhfainfo@fhfa.gov
Web, www.fhfa.gov and Twitter, @FHFA

Regulates and works to ensure the financial soundness of Fannie Mae (Federal National Mortgage Assn.), Freddie Mac (Federal Home Loan Mortgage Corp.), and the eleven Federal Home Loan banks. FHFA was formed by a legislative merger of the Office of Federal Housing Enterprise Oversight (OFHEO), the Federal Housing Finance Board,

and HUD's Government-sponsored Enterprise (GSE) mission team.

Federal Housing Finance Agency (FHFA), *Enterprise Regulation,* 400 7th St. S.W., 20219; (202) 649-3809. Fax, (202) 777-1206. Nina Nichols, Deputy Director.
General email, DeputyDirector-Enterprises@FHFA.gov
Web, www.fhfa.gov

Responsible for ensuring that Fannie Mae and Freddie Mac are adequately capitalized and operate in a safe and sound manner. Supervision includes programs for accounting and disclosure, capital adequacy, examination, financial analysis, and supervision infrastructure.

Federal Housing Finance Agency (FHFA), *Federal Home Loan Bank Regulation (FHLBank Regulation),* 400 7th St. S.W., 20219; (202) 649-3808. Fax, (202) 649-3500. Andre D. Galeano, Deputy Director.
General email, DeputyDirector-FHLBanks@FHFA.gov
Web, www.fhfa.gov

Responsible for ensuring that the Federal Home Loan Banks operate in a fiscally sound manner, have adequate capital, and are able to raise funds in capital markets. Conducts safety and soundness examinations, Affordable Housing Program examinations, examination and supervisory policy and program development, FHLBank analysis, risk modeling, risk monitoring and information management, and risk analysis and research.

Freddie Mac *(Federal Housing Finance Agency),* 8200 Jones Branch Dr., McLean, VA 22102-3110; (703) 903-2000. Fax, (703) 903-3495. Donald H. Layton, Chief Executive Officer. Homeowners hotline, (800) 373-3343. Press, (703) 903-3933. Toll-free, (800) 424-5401.
Web, www.freddiemac.com, www.fhfa.gov,
Twitter, @FreddieMac and Facebook, www.facebook.com/ FreddieMac

Chartered by Congress to support homeownership and rental housing by increasing the flow of funds for residential mortgages and mortgage-related securities. Purchases loans from lenders to replenish their supply of funds so that they may make more mortgage loans to borrowers. (Freddie Mac stands for Federal Home Loan Mortgage Corp.)

Ginnie Mae *(Housing and Urban Development Dept.),* 425 3rd St. S.W., #500, 20024 (mailing address: 451 7th St. S.W., #B-133, Washington, DC 20410); (202) 708-0926. Fax, (202) 485-0206. Maren Kasper, Executive Vice President. Hotline, (888) 446-6434.
Web, www.ginniemae.gov and Twitter, @GinnieMaeGov

Supports government housing objectives by expanding affordable housing finance via secondary markets for multi-family and single-family residential, hospital, and nursing home mortgages. The wholly owned government corporation serves as a vehicle for channeling funds from domestic and global capital markets into the U.S. mortgage market through mortgage-backed securities programs and helps to increase the supply of credit available for housing. Guarantees privately issued securities backed by Federal Housing Administration, Veterans Affairs Dept., USDA Rural Development, and HUD's Office of Public and Indian

Resources for Mortgage Financing and Other Housing Assistance

The following agencies and organizations offer consumer information pertaining to mortgages and other housing issues.

Center for Responsible Lending, Washington, D.C., office, (202) 349-1850; www.responsiblelending.org

Center on Budget and Policy Priorities, (202) 408-1080; www.cbpp.org

Consumer Federation of America, (202) 387-6121; www.consumerfed.org

Council for Affordable and Rural Housing, (703) 837-9001; www.carh.org

Fannie Mae, (202) 752-7000; www.fanniemae.com

Freddie Mac, (703) 903-2000; www.freddiemac.com

Housing and Urban Development Dept., (202) 708-1112; www.hud.gov

Housing Assistance Council, (202) 842-8600; www.ruralhome.org

Mortgage Bankers Assn., (202) 557-2700; www.mbaa.org

National Assn. of Development Companies, (202) 349-0070; www.nadco.org

National Assn. of Home Builders, (800) 368-5242; www.nahb.org

National Assn. Of Local Housing Finance Agencies, (202) 367-1197; www.nalhfa.org

National Assn. of Realtors, (202) 383-1000; www.nar.realtor

National Council of State Housing Agencies, (202) 624-7710; www.ncsha.org

National Housing Conference, (202) 466-2121; www.nhc.org

National Housing Trust, (202) 333-8931; www.nhtinc.org

National Leased Housing Assn., (202) 785-8888; www.hudnlha.com

National Low Income Housing Coalition, (202) 662-1530; www.nlihc.org

National Reverse Mortgage Lenders Assn., (202) 939-1760; www.reversemortgage.org or www.nrmlaonline.org

NeighborhoodWorks America, (202) 760-4000; www.nw.org

Smart Growth America, (202) 207-3355; www.smartgrowthamerica.org

Urban Institute, (202) 833-7200; www.urban.org

Housing mortgages. (Ginnie Mae stands for Government National Mortgage Assn.)

Housing and Urban Development Dept. (HUD), *Housing Office, 451 7th St. S.W., #9100, 20410; (202) 708-2601. Fax, (202) 708-1403. Brian D. Montgomery, Assistant Secretary & FHA Commissioner, (202) 402-5430. TTY, (202) 708-1455.*
Web, www.hud.gov/program_offices/housing

Administers all Federal Housing Administration (FHA) mortgage insurance programs; approves and monitors all lending institutions that conduct business with HUD.

Small Business Administration (SBA), *Disaster Assistance, 409 3rd St. S.W., #6050, 20416; (202) 205-6734. Fax, (202) 205-7728. James Rivera, Associate Administrator. Service Center, (800) 659-2955. TTY, (800) 877-8339.*
Web, www.sba.gov/offices/headquarters/oda

Provides low-interest disaster loans to homeowners and renters to repair or replace real estate, personal property, machinery and equipment, inventory and business assets that have been damaged or destroyed in a declared disaster.

Veterans Benefits Administration (VBA) *(Veterans Affairs Dept.), Loan Guaranty Service, 1800 G St., #851, 20006 (mailing address: 810 Vermont Ave. N.W., Washington, DC 20420); (202) 632-8862. Fax, (202) 495-5798. Jeffrey F. London, Director.*
Web, www.benefits.va.gov/homeloans

Guarantees private institutional financing of home loans (including manufactured-home loans) for veterans; provides disabled veterans with direct loans and grants for specially adapted housing; administers a direct loan program for Native American veterans living on trust land.

▶**CONGRESS**

For a listing of relevant congressional committees and subcommittees, please see page 441 or the Appendix.

▶**NONGOVERNMENTAL**

American Bankers Assn. (ABA), *1120 Connecticut Ave. N.W., 20036; (202) 663-5000. Fax, (202) 663-7578. Rob Nichols, President. Information, (800) 226-5377. General email, custserv@aba.com*
Web, www.aba.com, Twitter, @ABABankers and Facebook, www.facebook.com/ AmericanBankersAssociation

Membership: insured depository institutions involved in finance, including community banking. Provides information on issues that affect the industry. Monitors economic issues affecting savings institutions; publishes real estate lending survey. Monitors legislation and regulations. (America's Community Bankers merged with the American Banking Assn.)

Center for Responsible Lending, *Washington Office, 910 17th St. N.W., #500, 20006; (202) 349-1850. Fax, (202) 289-9009. Michael Calhoun, President. Web, www.responsiblelending.org and Twitter, @CRLONLINE*

Seeks to protect homeownership and family wealth by working to eliminate abusive financial practices. Conducts studies on lending practices, assists consumer attorneys, and provides information to policymakers. Provides a Web-based archive of information for public use. Monitors legislation and regulations at state and federal levels.

Consumer Data Industry Assn., *1090 Vermont Ave. N.W., #200, 20005-4905; (202) 371-0910. Fax, (202) 371-0134. Francis Creighton, Chief Executive Officer. Press, (202) 408-7406. General email, cdia@cdiaonline.org Web, www.cdiaonline.org*

Membership: credit reporting, mortgage reporting, and collection service companies. Provides information about credit rights to consumers. Monitors legislation and regulations.

Farmer Mac, *1999 K St. N.W., 4th Floor, 20006; (202) 872-7700. Fax, (800) 999-1814. Bradford T. Nordholm, President. Toll-free, (800) 879-3276. Web, www.farmermac.com*

Private corporation chartered by Congress to provide a secondary mortgage market for farm and rural housing loans. Guarantees principal and interest repayment on securities backed by farm and rural housing loans. (Farmer Mac stands for Federal Agricultural Mortgage Corp.)

Mortgage Bankers Assn., *1919 M St. N.W., 5th Floor, 20036; (202) 557-2700. Robert D. Broeksmit, President. Information, (800) 793-6222. Web, www.mba.org, Twitter, @MBAMortgage and Facebook, www.facebook.com/mbamortgage*

Membership: institutions involved in real estate finance. Maintains School of Mortgage Banking; collects statistics on the industry. Conducts seminars and workshops in specialized areas of mortgage finance. Monitors legislation and regulations.

National Assn. of Affordable Housing Lenders, *1025 Connecticut Ave. N.W., #710, 20036; (202) 293-9850. Benson (Buzz) Roberts, President. General email, naahl@naahl.org Web, www.naahl.org and Twitter, @NAAHCOC*

Membership: lenders who specialize in providing private capital for affordable housing and community development in low- and moderate-income areas.

National Assn. of Consumer Advocates, *1215 17th St. N.W., 5th Floor, 20036; (202) 452-1989. Fax, (202) 452-0099. Ira J. Rheingold, Executive Director, (202) 452-1989 ext. 101. General email, info@consumeradvocates.org Web, www.consumeradvocates.org*

Membership: consumer advocate attorneys. Seeks to protect the rights of consumers from fraudulent, abusive, and predatory business practices. Provides consumer law training through conferences and publications. Monitors legislation and regulations on banking, credit, and housing laws.

National Assn. of Home Builders (NAHB), *1201 15th St. N.W., 20005-2800; (202) 266-8200. Fax, (202) 266-8400. Jerry Howard, Executive Officer, (800) 368-5242, ext. 8257. Press, (202) 266-8254. Toll-free, (800) 368-5242. General email, info@nahb.org Web, www.nahb.org and Twitter, @NAHBhome*

Membership: contractors, builders, architects, engineers, mortgage lenders, and others interested in home building and residential real estate construction. Interests include policies to stimulate the housing market, taxation, and mortgage financing. Monitors legislation and regulations.

National Assn. of Local Housing Finance Agencies, *2025 M St. N.W., #800, 20036-3309; (202) 367-1197. Fax, (202) 367-2197. Jonathan Paine, Executive Director, (202) 367-2496; Heather Voorman, Policy Director. General email, info@nalhfa.org Web, www.nalhfa.org and Twitter, @NALHFAnews*

Membership: professionals of city and county governments, nonprofits, and private firms that finance affordable housing. Provides professional development programs in new housing finance and other areas. Monitors legislation and regulations.

National Council of State Housing Agencies, *444 N. Capitol St. N.W., #438, 20001; (202) 624-7710. Fax, (202) 624-5899. Stockton Williams, Executive Director. General email, info@ncsha.org Web, www.ncsha.org, Twitter, @HomeEverything and Facebook, www.facebook.com/National-Council-of-State-Housing-Agencies-NCSHA-73339029343*

Membership: state housing finance agencies. Promotes greater opportunities for lower-income people to rent or buy affordable housing.

National Reverse Mortgage Lenders Assn., *1400 16th St. N.W., #420, 20036; (202) 939-1760. Fax, (202) 265-4435. Peter H. Bell, President, (202) 939-1741. General email, dhicks@dworbell.com Web, www.nrmlaonline.org*

National trade association for firms that originate, service, and invest in reverse mortgages. Monitors legislation and regulations.

Property Management

▶**AGENCIES**

Federal Housing Administration (FHA) *(Housing and Urban Development Dept.), Asset Management and Portfolio Oversight, 451 7th St. S.W., #6162, 20410; (202)*

708-2059. Fax, (202) 708-3104. Brian Murray, Director (Acting).
Web, http://portal.hud.gov/hudportal/HUD?src=/program_offices/housing/mfh/hsgmfbus/aboutam

Oversees HUD management, ownership, and sale of properties, which HUD owns by virtue of default and foreclosure or for which HUD is mortgagee-in-possession.

Federal Housing Administration (FHA) *(Housing and Urban Development Dept.),* *Procurement Management,* 451 7th St. S.W., #2222, 20410; (202) 402-7127. Fax, (202) 708-2698. Amelia McCormick, Director.
Web, http://portal.hud.gov

Develops and implements policies and procedures and conducts contract administration for the Office of Housing and the Federal Housing Administration headquarters' procurement actions.

▶NONGOVERNMENTAL

Building Owners and Managers Assn. International, 1101 15th St. N.W., #800, 20005; (202) 408-2662. Fax, (202) 326-6377. Henry Chamberlain, President, (202) 326-6325.
General email, info@boma.org
Web, www.boma.org and Twitter, @BOMAIntl

Membership: office building owners and managers. Reviews changes in model codes and building standards; conducts seminars and workshops on building operation and maintenance issues; sponsors educational and training programs. Monitors legislation and regulations.

Community Associations Institute, 6402 Arlington Blvd., #500, Falls Church, VA 22042; (703) 970-9220. Fax, (703) 970-9558. Tom Skiba, Chief Executive Officer.
Toll-free, (888) 224-4321.
General email, cai-info@ACIonline.org
Web, www.caionline.org and Twitter, @CAIsocial

Membership: homeowner associations, builders, lenders, owners, managers, Realtors, insurance companies, and public officials. Provides members with information on creating, financing, and maintaining common facilities and services in condominiums and other planned developments.

NAIOP Commercial Real Estate Development Assn., 2355 Dulles Corner Blvd., #750, Herndon, VA 20171; (703) 904-7100. Fax, (703) 904-7942.
Thomas J. (Tom) Bisacquino, President, (703) 904-7100, ext. 104.
Web, www.naiop.org and Twitter, @NAIOP

Membership: developers, planners, designers, builders, financiers, and managers of industrial and office properties. Provides research and continuing education programs. Monitors legislation and regulations on capital gains, real estate taxes, impact fees, growth management, environmental issues, and hazardous waste liability.

National Apartment Assn., 4300 Wilson Blvd., #800, Arlington, VA 22203; (703) 518-6141. Fax, (703) 248-9440. Robert (Bob) Pinnegar, President, (703) 797-0686.

General email, webmaster@naahq.org
Web, www.naahq.org and Twitter, @NAAhq

Membership: state and local associations of owners, managers, investors, developers, and builders of apartment houses or other rental properties. Conducts educational and professional certification programs. Monitors legislation and regulations.

National Assn. of Housing and Redevelopment Officials, 630 Eye St. N.W., 20001-3736; (202) 289-3500. Fax, (202) 289-8181. Adrianna Todman, Chief Executive Officer. Toll-free, (877) 866-2476.
General email, nahro@nahro.org
Web, www.nahro.org and Twitter, @NAHROnational

Conducts studies and provides training and certification in the operation and management of rental housing.

National Assn. of Housing Cooperatives, 1120 20th St. N.W., #750, 20036-3441; (202) 737-0797. Fax, (202) 216-9646. Mik Bauer, Executive Director.
General email, info@nahc.coop
Web, www.coophousing.org and Twitter, @NAHC1960

Membership: housing cooperative professionals and organizations that provide services to housing cooperatives. Promotes housing cooperatives; provides technical assistance in all phases of cooperative housing; sponsors educational programs and on-site training; provides legal service referrals; monitors legislation; maintains an information clearinghouse on housing cooperatives. Online resources include a directory of financial, legal, and management services experts in the housing cooperative community.

National Center for Housing Management, 11350 Random Hills Rd., #811, Fairfax, VA 22030; (800) 368-5625. Fax, (904) 372-2324. Paul Votto, President.
General email, service@nchm.org
Web, www.nchm.org and Twitter, @TheNCHM

Private corporation created by executive order to meet housing management and training needs. Conducts research, demonstrations, and educational and training programs in all types of multifamily housing management. Develops and implements certification systems for housing management programs.

National Cooperative Business Assn., CLUSA International (NCBA CLUSA), 1775 Eye St. N.W., 8th Floor, 20006; (202) 638-6222. Douglas O'Brien, President.
General email, info@ncba.coop
Web, www.ncba.coop, Twitter, @NCBA.coop and Facebook, www.facebook.com/NCBACLUSA

Alliance of cooperatives, businesses, and state cooperative associations. Provides information about starting and managing housing cooperatives. Monitors legislation and regulations.

National Multifamily Housing Council, 1775 Eye St. N.W., #1100, 20006; (202) 974-2300. Fax, (202) 775-0112. Douglas Bibby, President, (202) 974-2323.

General email, info@nmhc.org

Web, www.nmhc.org

Membership: owners, financiers, managers, and developers of multifamily housing. Advocates policies and programs at the federal, state, and local levels to increase the supply and quality of multifamily units in the United States; serves as a clearinghouse on rent control, condominium conversion, taxes, fair housing, and environmental issues.

Property Management Assn., *7508 Wisconsin Ave., 4th Floor, Bethesda, MD 20814; (301) 657-9200. Fax, (301) 907-9326. Tom Cohn, Executive Vice President.*
General email, info@pma-dc.org

Web, www.pma-dc.org and *Twitter, @PMAAssociation*

Membership: property managers and firms that offer products and services needed in the property management field. Promotes information exchange on property management practices.

12

International Affairs

GENERAL POLICY AND ANALYSIS

Basic Resources

►**AGENCIES**

Bureau of Intelligence and Research (INR) *(State Dept.),* 2201 C St. N.W., #6468, 20520-6531; (202) 647-9177. Fax, (202) 736-4688. Ellen E. McCarthy, Assistant Secretary.
Web, www.state.gov/s/inr

Coordinates foreign policy–related research, analysis, and intelligence programs for the State Dept. and other federal agencies.

Bureau of International Organization Affairs (IO) *(State Dept.),* 2201 C St. N.W., #6323, 20520-6319; (202) 647-9600. Fax, (202) 647-9722. Kevin Moley, Assistant Secretary. Press, (202) 647-6899.
General email, IOmailbox@state.gov
Web, www.state.gov/p/io and Twitter, @State_IO

Coordinates and develops policy guidelines for U.S. participation in the United Nations and in other international organizations and conferences.

Bureau of International Organization Affairs (IO) *(State Dept.), International Conferences,* 2401 E St. N.W., Room H436, 20522; (202) 663-1024. Mark J. Biedlingmaier, Director.
Web, www.state.gov/p/io

Coordinates U.S. participation in multilateral conferences and accredits delegations.

Bureau of International Organization Affairs (IO) *(State Dept.), United Nations Political Affairs (UNP),* 2201 C St. N.W., #1828, 20520-6319; (202) 647-2393. Fax, (202) 647-0039. Joseph Manso, Director.
Web, www.state.gov/p/io

Deals with UN political and institutional matters and international security affairs.

Bureau of Oceans and International Environmental and Scientific Affairs (OES) *(State Dept.), Policy and Public Outreach (PPO),* 2201 C St. N.W., #2880, 20520; (202) 647-4658. Susan Cleary, Director.
Web, www.state.gov/e/oes/policy

Integrates oceans, environment, polar, science, technology, and health issues into U.S. foreign policy, and works to address these issues in the media, NGOs, the private sector, and Congress.

Defense Dept. (DoD), *International Security Affairs,* 2000 Defense Pentagon, #3C889, 20301-2000; (703) 697-2788. Fax, (703) 697-3279. Kathryn Wheelbarger, Assistant Secretary (Acting).
Web, http://policy.defense.gov/OUSDPOffices/ASDforInternationalSecurityAffairs

Advises the secretary of defense and recommends policies on regional security issues in the Middle East, Africa, Russia/Eurasia, and Europe/NATO.

National Security Staff (NSS) *(Executive Office of the President), International Economic Affairs,* The White House, 1600 Pennsylvania Ave., 20504; (202) 456-9281. Fax, (202) 456-9280. Cletus R. Willems, Deputy National Security Adviser.
Web, www.whitehouse.gov/nsc

Advises the president, the National Security Council, and the National Economic Council on all aspects of U.S. foreign policy dealing with U.S. international economic policies.

State Dept., 2201 C St. N.W., 20520; (202) 647-4000. Fax, (202) 647-3340. Michael R. (Mike) Pompeo, Secretary. Press, (202) 647-2492.
Web, www.state.gov, Twitter, @StateDept
Facebook, www.facebook.com/usdos and YouTube, www.youtube.com/user/statevideo
Blog, https://blogs.state.gov

Directs and coordinates U.S. foreign relations and interdepartmental activities of the U.S. government overseas.

State Dept., *Policy Planning,* 2201 C St. N.W., #7311, 20520; (202) 647-2972. Fax, (202) 647-0844. Kiron K. Skinner, Director.
General email, policyplanning@state.gov
Web, www.state.gov/s/p

Advises the secretary and other State Dept. officials on foreign policy matters.

State Dept., *Religion and Global Affairs,* 2201 C St. N.W., 20520; (202) 647-1459. Douglas M. (Doug) Padgett, Unit Chief.
General email, RGAOffice@state.gov
Web, www.state.gov/s/rga, Twitter, @SpecialRepRGA and Facebook, www.facebook.com/USDOSrga?fref=ts

Advises the Secretary on policy matters as they relate to religion; supports State Dept. posts and bureaus in their efforts to assess religious dynamics and engage religious actors; serves as point of entry for individuals who would like to engage the State Dept. on matters of religion and global affairs.

State Dept., *Under Secretary for Civilian Security, Democracy, and Human Rights,* 2201 C St. N.W., #7261, 20520; (202) 647-6240. Fax, (202) 647-0753. Vacant, Under Secretary; Ian H. Boyd, Executive Assistant, (202) 647-7818.
Web, www.state.gov/j

Advises the secretary on transnational issues. Divisions include Democracy, Human Rights, and Labor; International Narcotics and Law Enforcement; Conflict and Stabilization Operations; Population, Refugees, and Migration; Counterterrorism; Global Criminal Justice; and Monitor and Combat Trafficking in Persons.

State Dept., *Under Secretary for Management,* 2201 C St. N.W., #7207, 20520; (202) 647-1500. Fax, (202) 647-0168. William E. Todd, Under Secretary (Acting).
Web, www.state.gov/m

Serves as principal adviser to the secretary on management matters, including budgetary, administrative, and personnel policies of the department and the Foreign Service. Oversees the Bureau of Administration, Bureau of Budget and Planning, Bureau of the Comptroller and Global Financial Services, Bureau of Consular Affairs, Bureau of Diplomatic Security, Bureau of Human Resources, Bureau of Information Resource Management, Bureau of Overseas Buildings Operations, Director of Diplomatic Reception Rooms, Foreign Service Institute, Office of Management Policy, Rightsizing, and Innovation, Office of Medical Services, and Office of White House Liaison.

State Dept., *Under Secretary for Political Affairs,* 2201 C St. N.W., #7250, 20520; (202) 647-0995. Fax, (202) 647-4780. David Hale, Under Secretary, (202) 647-2471. Web, www.state.gov/p

Manages regional and bilateral policy issues and assists in the overall direction of the department. Oversees the Africa, East Asia and the Pacific, Europe and Eurasia, Near East, South and Central Asia, Western Hemisphere, and International Organizations bureaus.

State Dept., *Under Secretary for Public Diplomacy and Public Affairs,* 2201 C St. N.W., #5932, 20520; (202) 647-9199. Fax, (202) 647-9140. Vacant, Under Secretary (Acting); Michelle Giuda, Assistant Secretary. Web, www.state.gov and Twitter, @UnderSecPD

Seeks to broaden public affairs discussion on foreign policy with U.S. citizens, media, and institutions. Divisions include Education and Cultural Affairs, International Information Programs, Public Affairs, Strategic Counterterrorism Communications, and Policy, Planning, and Resources.

▶CONGRESS

For a listing of relevant congressional committees and subcommittees, please see pages 474–475 or the Appendix.

Government Accountability Office (GAO), *International Affairs and Trade (IAT),* 441 G St. N.W., #4T21, 20548; (202) 512-4128. Thomas Melito, Managing Director. Web, www.gao.gov/careers/iat.html

Audits, analyzes, and evaluates international programs and trade; evaluates economic, political, and security problems worldwide. In addition to federal departments, oversight work includes U.S. Agency for International Development, Office of the U.S. Trade Representative, Broadcasting Board of Governors, North Atlantic Treaty Organization, World Bank, International Monetary Fund, and United Nations.

House Democracy Partnership, 2246 RHOB, 20515; (202) 225-4561. Fax, (202) 225-1166. Rep. Peter Roskam, Chair; Jeff Billman, Staff Director. General email, jeff.billman@mail.house.gov Web, https://hdp.house.gov and Twitter, @house_democracy

Provides advice to members and staff of parliaments of select countries that have established or are developing democratic governments.

▶INTERNATIONAL ORGANIZATIONS

International Monetary Fund (IMF), *700 19th St. N.W., 20431; 1900 Pennsylvania Ave. N.W., 20431; (202) 623-7000. Fax, (202) 623-4661. Christine Lagarde, Managing Director; Adam Lerrick, U.S. Executive Director. Legislative Affairs, (202) 623-6220. Press, (202) 623-7100.* Web, www.imf.org

International organization of 188 member countries that promotes policies for financial stability and economic growth, works to prevent financial crises, and helps members solve balance-of-payment problems through loans funded by member contributions.

Organisation for Economic Co-operation and Development (OECD), *Washington Center, 1776 Eye St. N.W., #450, 20006; (202) 785-6323. Fax, (202) 315-2508. Will Davis, Head of Center, (202) 822-3869.* General email, washington.contact@oecd.org

Web, www.oecd.org/washington and Twitter, @oced_washington

Membership: thirty-four nations, including Australia, Canada, Japan, Mexico, New Zealand, the United States, and western European nations. Serves as a forum for government officials to exchange information on their countries' policies. (Headquarters in Paris.)

Organization of American States (OAS), *17th St. and Constitution Ave. N.W., 20006; Administration Bldg., 19th St. and Constitution Ave. N.W., 20006; General Secretariat Bldg., 1889 F St. N.W., 20006; (202) 370-5000. Fax, (202) 458-3967. Luis Almagro Lemes, Secretary General. Library, (202) 458-6041.* General email, ai@oas.org

Web, www.oas.org and Twitter, @oas_official

Membership: the United States, Canada, and all independent Latin American and Caribbean countries. Funded by quotas paid by member states and by contributions to special multilateral funds. Works to promote democracy, eliminate poverty, and resolve disputes among member nations. Provides member states with technical and advisory services in cultural, educational, scientific, social, and economic areas. Library open to the public (at 19th and Constitution).

United Nations Information Center, *1775 K St. N.W., #500, 20006; (202) 331-8670. Fax, (202) 331-9191. Mary Kirtley Waters, Director.* General email, unicdc@unic.org

Web, www.unicwash.org and Twitter, @unicdc

Lead United Nations (UN) office in Washington. Serves as a resource for information and materials about the United Nations.

INTERNATIONAL AFFAIRS RESOURCES IN CONGRESS

For a complete listing of congressional committees, including their full contact information, leadership, membership, and jurisdictions, please refer to the Appendix on pages 827–948.

HOUSE:

House Appropriations Committee, (202) 225-2771.
Web, appropriations.house.gov

Subcommittee on Commerce, Justice, Science, and Related Agencies, (202) 225-3351.

Subcommittee on Interior, Environment, and Related Agencies, (202) 225-3081.

Subcommittee on State, Foreign Operations, and Related Programs, (202) 225-2041.

House Armed Services Committee, (202) 225-4151.
Web, armedservices.house.gov

Subcommittee on Strategic Forces, (202) 225-1967.

House Energy and Commerce Committee, (202) 225-2927.
Web, energycommerce.house.gov

Subcommittee on Digital Commerce and Consumer Protection, (202) 225-2927.

House Financial Services Committee, (202) 225-7502.
Web, financialservices.house.gov

Subcommittee on Monetary Policy and Trade, (202) 225-7502.

House Foreign Affairs Committee, (202) 225-5021.
Web, foreignaffairs.house.gov

Subcommittee on Africa, Global Health, Global Human Rights, and International Organizations, (202) 226-7812.

Subcommittee on Asia and the Pacific, (202) 226-7825.

Subcommittee on Europe, Eurasia, and Emerging Threats, (202) 226-6434.

Subcommittee on Terrorism, Nonproliferation, and Trade, (202) 226-1500.

Subcommittee on the Middle East and North Africa, (202) 225-3345.

Subcommittee on the Western Hemisphere, (202) 226-9980.

House Homeland Security Committee, (202) 226-8417.
Web, homeland.house.gov

Subcommittee on Border and Maritime Security, (202) 226-8417.

House Judiciary Committee, (202) 225-3951.
Web, judiciary.house.gov

Subcommittee on Crime, Terrorism, Homeland Security, and Investigations, (202) 225-5727.

Subcommittee on Immigration and Border Security, (202) 225-3926.

House Natural Resources Committee, (202) 225-2761.
Web, naturalresources.house.gov

Subcommittee on Water, Power, and Oceans, (202) 225-8331.

House Oversight and Government Reform Committee, (202) 225-5074.
Web, oversight.house.gov

Subcommittee on National Security, (202) 225-5074.

House Permanent Select Committee on Intelligence, (202) 225-4121.
Web, intelligence.house.gov

Subcommittee on Research and Technology, (202) 225-6371.

Subcommittee on Space, (202) 225-6371.

House Science, Space, and Technology Committee, (202) 225-6371.
Web, science.house.gov

House Small Business Committee, (202) 225-5821.
Web, smallbusiness.house.gov

Subcommittee on Agriculture, Energy, and Trade, (202) 225-5821.

Subcommittee on Economic Growth, Tax, and Capital Access, (202) 225-5821.

▶NONGOVERNMENTAL

American Enterprise Institute (AEI), *Foreign and Defense Policy Studies, 1789 Massachusetts Ave. N.W., 20036; (202) 862-5800. Fax, (202) 862-7177. Danielle Pletka, Senior Vice President, (202) 862-7184. Web, www.aei.org and Twitter, @dpletka*

Research and educational organization that conducts conferences, seminars, and debates and sponsors research on international affairs.

American Foreign Policy Council, *509 C St. N.E., 20002; (202) 543-1006. Fax, (202) 543-1007. Herman Pirchner Jr., President.*

General email, afpc@afpc.org

Web, http://afpc.org, Twitter, @afpc and Facebook, www.facebook.com/americanforeignpolicycouncil

Provides policymakers with information on foreign policy issues and options. Assists international leaders in establishing democracies. Holds meetings between Congressional officials and officials in other countries. Publishes articles on current foreign affairs. Interests include terrorism in Europe and Asia, the Russia–China alliance, and nuclear weapons.

Aspen Institute, *2300 N St., N.W., #700, 20037; (202) 736-5800. Fax, (202) 467-0790. Dan Porterfield, President. Press, (202) 736-3849.*

House Transportation and Infrastructure
Committee, (202) 225-9446.
Web, transportation.house.gov
  Subcommittee on Coast Guard and Maritime
  Transportation, (202) 226-3552.
House Ways and Means Committee,
(202) 225-3625.
Web, waysandmeans.house.gov
  Subcommittee on Trade, (202) 225-6649.

JOINT:

Joint Economic Committee, (202) 224-5171.
Web, jec.senate.gov

SENATE:

Senate Appropriations Committee, (202) 224-7257.
Web, appropriations.senate.gov
  Subcommittee on State, Foreign Operations, and
  Related Programs, (202) 224-7284.
Senate Armed Services Committee, (202) 224-3871.
Web, armed-services.senate.gov
  Subcommittee on Seapower, (202) 224-3871.
Senate Banking, Housing, and Urban Affairs
Committee, (202) 224-7391.
Web, banking.senate.gov
  Subcommittee on National Security and
  International Trade and Finance,
  (202) 224-7391.
Senate Commerce, Science, and Transportation
Committee, (202) 224-1251.
Web, commerce.senate.gov
  Subcommittee on Oceans, Atmosphere, Fisheries,
  and the Coast Guard, (202) 224-1251.
Senate Energy and Natural Resources Committee,
(202) 224-4971.
Web, energy.senate.gov
Senate Finance Committee, (202) 224-4515.
Web, finance.senate.gov

Subcommittee on International Trade,
  Customs, and Global Competitiveness,
  (202) 224-4515.
Senate Foreign Relations Committee, (202) 224-4651.
Web, foreign.senate.gov
  Subcommittee on Africa and Global Health
  Policy, (202) 224-4651.
  Subcommittee on East Asia, the Pacific, and
  International Cybersecurity Policy,
  (202) 224-4651.
  Subcommittee on Europe and Regional Security
  Cooperation, (202) 224-4651.
  Subcommittee on Multilateral International
  Development, Multilateral Institutions, and
  International Economic, Energy, and
  Environmental Policy, (202) 224-4651.
  Subcommittee on Near East, South Asia,
  Central Asia, and Counterterrorism,
  (202) 224-4651.
  Subcommittee on State Department and USAID
  Management, International Operations, and
  Bilateral International Development,
  (202) 224-4651.
  Subcommittee on Western Hemisphere,
  Transnational Crime, Civilian Security,
  Democracy, Human Rights, and Global
  Women's Issues, (202) 224-4651.
Senate Homeland Security and Governmental Affairs
Committee, (202) 224-4751.
Web, hsgac.senate.gov
Senate Judiciary Committee, (202) 224-5225.
Web, judiciary.senate.gov
  Subcommittee on Crime and Terrorism,
  (202) 224-5972.
  Subcommittee on Border Security and
  Immigration, (202) 224-7840.
  Subcommittee on Privacy, Technology, and the
  Law, (202) 224-4521.

General email, info@aspeninstitute.org
Web, www.aspeninstitute.org and
Twitter, @AspenInstitute

Educational and policy studies organization. Promotes consideration of the public good in a wide variety of policy areas, including international relations and homeland security. Working with international partners, offers educational seminars, nonpartisan policy forums, public conferences and events, and leadership development initiatives.

Atlantic Council, 1030 15th St. N.W., 12th Floor, 20005; (202) 463-7226. Fax, (202) 463-7241. Frederick Kempe, President. Press, (202) 778-4967.

General email, info@atlanticcouncil.org
Web, www.atlanticcouncil.org and
Twitter, @ATLANTICCOUNCIL

Conducts studies and makes policy recommendations on U.S. foreign security and international economic policies in the Atlantic and Pacific communities; sponsors conferences and educational exchanges.

The Brookings Institution, Foreign Policy Studies, 1775 Massachusetts Ave. N.W., 20036; (202) 797-6003. Fax, (202) 797-6004. Bruce Jones, Director. Press, (202) 797-6105.
Web, www.brookings.edu/foreign-policy

State Department

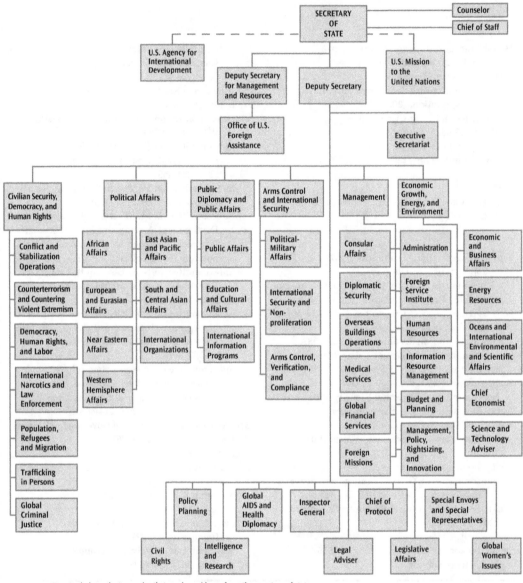

— — — Denotes independent agencies that receive guidance from the secretary of state

Conducts studies on foreign policy, national security, regional and global affairs, and economic policies. Includes five policy centers: Center for Middle East Policy, the Center for East Asia Policy Studies, the Center on the United States and Europe, Center for 21st Century Security and Intelligence, and the John L. Thornton China Center.

The Brookings Institution, *Project on International Order and Strategy, 1775 Massachusetts Ave. N.W., 20036; (202) 540-7759. Thomas Wright, Senior Fellow, (202) 797-6072. Press, (202) 797-6103.*
Web, www.brookings.edu/about/projects/international-order-strategy

Fosters research, policy engagement, and debate on international order and strategy. Interests include the rise of new powers on the international stage, the diffusion of political and military power, Western economic difficulties, challenges in the Middle East, and territorial disputes in Asia.

Center for International Policy, *2000 M St. N.W., #720, 20036; (202) 232-3317. Fax, (202) 232-3440. Salih Booker, Executive Director.*
General email, cip@ciponline.org
Web, www.ciponline.org and Twitter, @CIPonline

Research and educational organization concerned with peace and security worldwide. Special interests include military spending, U.S. intelligence policy, and U.S. policy toward Asia, Colombia, and Cuba. Publishes the *International Policy Report*.

Center for Strategic and International Studies, *1616 Rhode Island Ave. N.W., 20036; (202) 887-0200. Fax, (202) 775-3199. John J. Hamre, Chief Executive Officer. Press, (202) 775-3199.*
General email, webmaster@csis.org
Web, www.csis.org and Twitter, @CSIS

A bipartisan organization that seeks to advance global security and prosperity by providing strategic insights and practical policy solutions to decision makers. Expertise includes defense and international security, emerging global issues, and regional transformation.

Center for the Advanced Study of Language *(University of Maryland), 7005 52nd Ave., College Park, MD 20742; (301) 226-8900. Fax, (301) 226-8811. Steve Fetter, Executive Director (Acting).*
General email, info@casl.umd.edu
Web, www.casl.umd.edu and Twitter, @UMDCASL

Conducts research in language and cognition that supports national security; collaborates with government agencies; works to improve the performance of foreign language professionals in the federal government, specifically intelligence. Joint venture with the Defense Dept.

Center for the National Interest, *1025 Connecticut Ave. N.W., #1200, 20036-5651; (202) 887-1000. Fax, (202) 887-5222. Dimitri K. Simes, President; Paul J. Saunders, Executive Director.*
General email, info@cftni.org
Web, https://cftni.org and Twitter, @CFTNI

Works to develop new principles for U.S. global engagement and security; energy security and climate change; immigration and national security; and U.S. relations with China, Japan, the Middle East, Russia, and America's European allies. Publishes a bimonthly magazine.

Citizens for Global Solutions, *5 Thomas Circle, 20005; (202) 546-3950. Vacant, Chief Executive Officer.*
General email, info@globalsolutions.org
Web, http://globalsolutions.org, Twitter, @GlobalSolutions and Facebook, www.facebook.com/citizensforglobalsolutions

Encourages U.S. global engagement on a broad range of foreign policy issues, including UN reform, international law and justice, health and the environment, international institutions, and peace and security.

The Conservative Caucus (TCC), *332 W. Lee Hwy., #221, Warrenton, VA 20816; (540) 219-4536. Peter J. Thomas, Chair.*
General email, info@conservativeusa.org
Web, www.conservativeusa.org and Twitter, @ConservCaucus

Legislative interest organization that promotes grassroots activity on national defense and foreign policy.

Council on Foreign Relations, *Washington Office, 1777 F St. N.W., 20006; (202) 509-8400. Fax, (202) 509-8490. Richard N. Haass, President; James M. Lindsay, Senior Vice President.*
General email, communications@cfr.org
Web, www.cfr.org and Twitter, @CFR_org

Promotes understanding of U.S. foreign policy and international affairs. Awards research grants through its International Affairs Fellowship Program. Publishes *Foreign Affairs* bimonthly. (Headquarters in New York.)

Ethics and Public Policy Center, *1730 M St. N.W., #910, 20036; (202) 682-1200. Fax, (202) 408-0632. M. Edward Whelan III, President.*
General email, ethics@eppc.org
Web, www.eppc.org and Twitter, @EPPCdc

Considers implications of Judeo-Christian moral tradition for domestic and foreign policymaking. Conducts research and holds conferences on foreign policy, including the role of the U.S. military abroad.

Freedom House, *1850 M St. N.W., 11th Floor, 20036; (202) 296-5101. Fax, (202) 293-2840. Michael J. Abramowitz, President. Press, (202) 747-7035.*
General email, info@freedomhouse.org
Web, www.freedomhouse.org, Twitter, @FreedomHouseDC and Facebook, www.facebook.com/FreedomHouseDC

Independent watchdog organization promoting civil society; democratic governance; women's rights; LGBTI rights; elections; intergovernmental bodies; free markets; the rule of law; independent media, including Internet freedom; and U.S. engagement in international affairs through education, advocacy, and training initiatives. Collects and analyzes data on political rights and civil liberties worldwide; publishes comparative surveys and reports; sponsors conferences and training programs.

Friends Committee on National Legislation (FCNL), *245 2nd St. N.E., 20002-5795; (202) 547-6000. Fax, (202) 547-6019. Diane Randall, Executive Secretary. Recorded information, (202) 547-4343. Toll-free, (800) 630-1330.*
General email, fcnl@fcnl.org
Web, www.fcnl.org, Twitter, @FCNL and Facebook, www.facebook.com/quakerlobby

Seeks to broaden public interest and affect legislation and policy concerning regional and global institutions, peace processes, international development, and the work of the United Nations. (Affiliated with the Religious Society of Friends [Quakers].)

Institute for Policy Studies, *1301 Connecticut Ave. N.W., #600, 20036; (202) 234-9382. Fax, (202) 387-7915. John Cavanagh, Executive Director.*
General email, info@ips-dc.org
Web, www.ips-dc.org, Twitter, @IPS_DC and Facebook, www.facebook.com/InstituteforPolicyStudies

Research and educational think tank focused on social justice and security, especially equality, ecological sustainability, and peace. Interests include foreign policy, income inequality, and human rights.

Institute for Policy Studies, *Foreign Policy in Focus,*
1301 Connecticut Ave. N.W., #600, 20036; (202) 234-9382.
Fax, (202) 387-7915. John Feffer, Director.
General email, fpif@ips-dc.org

Web, www.fpif.org, Twitter, @FPIF and Facebook,
www.facebook.com/ForeignPolicyInFocus

Think tank that provides analysis of U.S. foreign policy
and international affairs and recommends progressive policy alternatives. Publishes reports; organizes briefings for
the public, media, and policymakers. Interests include climate change, global poverty, nuclear weapons, terrorism,
and military conflict.

Institute of Current World Affairs, *1779 Massachusetts*
Ave. N.W., #605, 20036; (202) 364-4068. Gregory Feifer,
Executive Diretor.
General email, icwa@icwa.org

Web, www.icwa.org, Twitter, @ICWAnews and
Facebook, www.facebook.com/
InstituteOfCurrentWorldAffairs

Offers two-year fellowships to support the independent
study of international region-specific issues. Fellows write
monthly newsletters to update the institute on their progress and findings. Presents public events on international
topics.

Institute of World Politics, *1521 16th St. N.W., 20036-*
1464; (202) 462-2101. Fax, (202) 464-0335.
John Lenczowski, President. Toll-free, (888) 566-9497.
General email, info@iwp.edu

Web, www.iwp.edu, Twitter, @theIWP and
Facebook, www.facebook.com/theiwp

Offers master's degree and professional education in
national security, statecraft, and international affairs.

International Center, *1001 North Carolina Ave. S.E.,*
20003 (mailing address: P.O. Box 41720, Arlington, VA
22204); (202) 285-4328. Virginia Foote, President.
General email, theinternationalcenter@theintlcenter.org

Web, www.theintlcenter.org

Research, advocacy, and aid organization concerned
with U.S. foreign policy in developing countries. Project
arms include trade and investment between the United
States and Vietnam, reforestation and agroforestry training
in Central America and the Caribbean, rehabilitation services and equipment for Cambodians with disabilities,
land-mine clearance and school upgrades in Vietnam, and
youth sports exchange programs.

International Foundation for Electoral Systems (IFES),
2011 Crystal Dr., 10th Floor, Arlington, VA 22202; (202)
350-6700. Fax, (202) 350-6701. Anthony Banbury,
President.
General email, media@ifes.org

Web, www.ifes.org, Twitter, @IFES1987 and
Facebook, www.facebook.com/IFES1987

Nonpartisan organization providing professional support to electoral democracies, both emerging and mature.
Through fieldwork and applied research and advocacy,
strives to promote citizen participation, transparency, and
accountability in political life and civil society.

International Republican Institute (IRI), *1225 Eye St.*
N.W., #800, 20005; (202) 408-9450. Dan Twining,
President.
General email, info@iri.org

Web, www.iri.org, Twitter, @IRIGlobal and
Facebook, www.facebook.com/
InternationalRepublicanInstitute

Created under the National Endowment for Democracy Act. Fosters democratic self-rule through closer ties
and cooperative programs with political parties and other
nongovernmental institutions overseas.

Just Foreign Policy, *4410 Massachusetts Ave. N.W., #290,*
20016; (202) 448-2898. Robert Naiman, Policy Director.
General email, info@justforeignpolicy.org

Web, www.justforeignpolicy.org, Twitter, @justfp and
Facebook, www.facebook.com/justforeignpolicy

Nonpartisan membership organization that seeks to
influence U.S. foreign policy through education, organization, and mobilization of citizens. Advocates cooperation,
international law, and diplomacy as means to achieve a just
foreign policy.

National Democratic Institute for International Affairs
(NDI), *455 Massachusetts Ave. N.W., 8th Floor, 20001-*
2621; (202) 728-5500. Derek Mitchell, President. Toll-free
fax, (888) 875-2887.
General email, contactndi@ndi.org

Web, www.ndi.org, Twitter, @NDI and Facebook,
www.facebook.com/National.Democratic.Institute

Conducts nonpartisan international programs to help
maintain and strengthen democratic institutions worldwide. Focuses on party building, governance, and electoral
systems.

National Endowment for Democracy, *1025 F St. N.W.,*
#800, 20004; (202) 378-9700. Fax, (202) 378-9407.
Carl Gershman, President; J. William (Bill) Leonard, Chief
Operating Officer; Jodi Herman, Vice President of
Government Relations and Public Affairs.
General email, info@ned.org

Web, www.ned.org, Twitter, @NEDemocracy and
Facebook, www.facebook.com/National.Endowment.for
.Democracy

Grant-making organization that receives funding from
Congress. Awards grants to private organizations involved
in democratic development abroad, including the areas of
democratic political processes; pluralism; and education,
culture, and communications.

National Security Archive *(George Washington*
University), Gelman Library, 2130 H St. N.W., #701,
20037; (202) 994-7000. Fax, (202) 994-7005.
Thomas Blanton, Director.
General email, nsarchiv@gwu.edu

Web, www.nsarchive.org

Research institute and library that provides information on U.S. foreign and economic policy and national security affairs. Maintains and publishes collection of declassified and unclassified documents obtained through the Freedom of Information Act. Archive open to the public by appointment. Website has a Russian-language link.

Partnership for a Secure America (PSA), *1129 20th St. N.W., #500, 20036; (202) 293-8580. Nathan Sermonis, Executive Director.*
General email, info@psaonline.org

Web, www.psaonline.org and Twitter, @PSAonline

Supports a bipartisan approach to foreign policy issues. Researches and publishes reports on international policies and their impact on foreign relations. Organizes conferences for political parties to debate and develop consensus on issues.

Paul H. Nitze School of Advanced International Studies, *1740 Massachusetts Ave. N.W., 20036; (202) 663-5600. Fax, (202) 663-5647. Vali Nasr, Dean. Press, (202) 663-5620. Toll free, (877) 548-9274.*
General email, sais.dc.admissions@jhu.edu

Web, www.sais-jhu.edu and Twitter, @SAISHopkins

Offers graduate and nondegree programs in international relations, economics, public policy, regional and functional studies, and foreign languages. Sponsors the Johns Hopkins Foreign Policy Institute and several other research centers. (Affiliated with Johns Hopkins University.)

Pew Research Center, *Global Attitudes and Trends Project, 1615 L St. N.W., #800, 20036; (202) 419-4400. Fax, (202) 419-4399. Richard Wike, Director. Press, (202) 419-4372.*
General email, info@pewglobal.org

Web, www.pewglobal.org and Twitter, @PewGlobal

Conducts public opinion surveys about world affairs and makes results available to journalists, academics, policymakers, and the public. Attempts to gauge attitudes in every region of the world toward globalization, democracy, trade, terrorism, and other key issues. (A Pew Research Center project.)

The Truman Center for National Policy, *1250 Eye St., #500, 20005; (202) 216-9723. Fax, (202) 682-1818. Jenna Ben-Yehuda, President.*
General email, info@TrumanCenter.org

Web, http://trumancenter.org

Public policy research and educational organization that serves as a forum for development of national policy alternatives. Leads discussion and advances policies aimed at promoting U.S. global engagement and leadership in the 21st century. Focus on issues such as cybersecurity and defense energy. (Partner of the Truman National Security Project.)

Truman National Security Project, *1250 Eye St. N.W., #500, 20005; (202) 216-9723. Fax, (202) 682-1818. Jenna Ben-Yehuda, President.*

General email, info@trumanproject.org

Web, http://trumanproject.org and Twitter, @TrumanProject

Membership: veterans and policy and political leaders. Forum for development of national policy alternatives. Promotes national security policy coordination, strengthening the U.S. military and intelligence, foreign affairs and diplomacy, democracy, and open trade. (Partner of the Truman Center for National Policy.)

U.S. Global Leadership Coalition (USGLC), *1129 20th St. N.W., #600, 20036; (202) 689-8911. Fax, (202) 689-8910. Liz Schrayer, President. Press, (202) 730-4163.*
General email, info@usglc.org

Web, www.usglc.org and Twitter, @UGLC

Advocates strengthening the International Affairs Budget. Seeks to combat global terrorism, diseases, and poverty. Interests include emerging world markets, developing countries, and humanitarian aid. Holds summits and publishes annual reports on global policy issues and proposals.

Women's Foreign Policy Group, *1801 F St. N.W., 3rd Floor, 20006; (202) 429-2692. Patricia Ellis, President Emeritus; Kimberly (Kim) Kahnhauser Freeman, Executive Director.*
General email, programs@wfpg.org

Web, www.wfpg.org and Twitter, @wfpg

Promotes women's leadership and women's interests in international affairs professions. Conducts policy programs, mentoring, and research.

World Affairs Councils of America, *1200 18th St. N.W., #902, 20036; (202) 833-4557. Fax, (202) 833-4555. Bill Clifford, President.*
General email, waca@worldaffairscouncils.org

Web, www.worldaffairscouncils.org and Twitter, @WACAmerica

Nonpartisan network that supports and represents local councils dedicated to educating the public on international issues at a grassroots level. Holds a national annual conference for member councils of each state. Coordinates expert speaker arrangements for small communities and provides fellowships for international business leaders. Supports programs that educate high school students on global affairs.

Diplomats and Foreign Agents

▶**AGENCIES**

Bureau of Diplomatic Security (DS) *(State Dept.), 2201 C St. N.W., #6316, 20520; (202) 647-6290. Fax, (571) 345-2527. Michael Evanoff, Assistant Secretary.*
General email, DSPublicAffairs@state.gov

Web, www.state.gov/m/ds, Twitter, @StateDeptDSS and Facebook, www.facebook.com/StateDeptDSS

Provides a secure environment for conducting U.S. diplomacy and promoting American interests abroad and in the United States.

Bureau of Diplomatic Security (DS) (State Dept.), Countermeasures, *1801 N. Lynn St., #23L04, Rosslyn, VA 22209; (571) 345-3836. Todd J. Brown, Deputy Assistant Secretary.*
Web, www.state.gov/m/ds

Supervises development of the Overseas Security Policy Board security standards and department policies associated with the physical and technical security of U.S. diplomatic missions around the world. Oversees the Diplomatic Courier Service to ensure secure and expeditious delivery of classified material to U.S. diplomatic missions globally.

Bureau of Diplomatic Security (DS) (State Dept.), Diplomatic Security Service (DSS), *1801 N. Lynn St., 23rd Floor, Rosslyn, VA 22209; (571) 345-3815. Fax, (202) 647-0122. Christian J. Schurman, Principal Deputy Assistant Secretary. Diplomatic Service Command Center, (571) 345-3146. Public Affairs, (571) 345-2502.*
Web, www.state.gov/m/ds/c66769.htm

Oversees the safety and security of all U.S. government employees at U.S. embassies and consulates abroad. Responsible for the safety of the secretary of state and all foreign dignitaries below head of state level who are visiting the United States.

Bureau of Diplomatic Security (DS) (State Dept.), Security Technology (ST), *1400 Wilson Blvd., 1st Floor, #SA14, Rosslyn, VA 22209; (703) 312-3667. John Fitzsimmons, Assistant Director.*
Web, www.state.gov/m/ds

Provides advanced cyber threat analysis, incident detection and response, cyber investigative support, and emerging technology solutions for U.S. embassies.

Foreign Service Institute (State Dept.), *4000 Arlington Blvd., Arlington, VA 22204-1500 (mailing address: U.S. Department of State, Washington, DC 20522-4201); (703) 302-6729. Fax, (703) 302-7227. Amb. Daniel B. Smith, Director. Student messages and course information, (703) 302-7144.*
General email, FSIPublicAffairs@state.gov
Web, www.state.gov/m/fsi and Twitter, @FSIatState

Provides training for U.S. government personnel involved in foreign affairs agencies, including employees of the State Dept., USAID, and the Defense Dept. Includes the Schools of Applied Information Technology, Language Studies, Leadership and Management, and Professional and Area Studies as well as the Transition Center and the Assn. for Diplomatic Studies and Training.

National Security Division (Justice Dept.), Foreign Agents Registration Unit, *Constitution Square Bldg. 3, 175 N St. N.E., #1300, 20002; (202) 233-0776; (202) 233-0777. Fax, (202) 233-2147. Heather H. Hunt, Chief.*
General email, fara.public@usdoj.gov
Web, www.fara.gov

Receives and maintains the registration of agents representing foreign countries, companies, organizations, and individuals. Compiles semiannual report on foreign agent registrations. Foreign agent registration files are open for public inspection.

State Dept., Bureau of Administration, Overseas Schools, *2401 E St. N.W., #H328/SA1, 20522-0103; (202) 261-8200. Fax, (202) 261-8224. Thomas P. Shearer, Director.*
General email, OverseasSchools@state.gov
Web, www.state.gov/m/a/os

Promotes high-quality educational opportunities at the elementary and secondary school levels for dependents of American citizens carrying out the programs and interests of the U.S. government abroad.

State Dept., Bureau of Human Resources, Family Liaison, *2201 C St. N.W., #1239, 20520-0108; (202) 647-1076. Fax, (202) 647-1670. Susan Frost, Director. Toll-free, (800) 440-0397.*
General email, flo@state.gov
Web, www.state.gov/m/dghr/flo

Works to improve the quality of life of U.S. government employees and their family members assigned to, or returning from, a U.S. embassy or consulate abroad. Areas of interest are education and youth, family member employment, and support services for personal and past crises, including evacuations. Manages the worldwide Community Liaison Office program.

State Dept., Chief of Protocol, *2201 C St. N.W., #1238, 20520; (202) 647-2663 during business hours, (202) 647-1512 after business hours. Fax, (202) 647-3980. Sean P. Lawler, Chief. Press, (202) 647-2681.*
General email, ProtocolHelp@state.gov
Web, www.state.gov/s/cpr and Twitter, @US_Protocol

Serves as principal adviser to the president, vice president, secretary, and other high-ranking government officials on matters of diplomatic procedure governed by law or international customs and practice.

State Dept., Foreign Missions, *2201 C St. N.W., #2236, 20520; (202) 647-3417. Fax, (202) 736-4145. Clifton C. (Cliff) Seagroves, Director (Acting).*
General email, ofminfo@state.gov
Web, www.state.gov/ofm

Regulates the benefits, privileges, and immunities granted to foreign missions and their personnel in the United States on the basis of the treatment accorded U.S. missions abroad and considerations of national security and public safety.

▶ **CONGRESS**

For a listing of relevant congressional committees and subcommittees, please see pages 474–475 or the Appendix.

▶ **NONGOVERNMENTAL**

American Foreign Service Assn. (AFSA), *2101 E St. N.W., 20037; (202) 338-4045. Fax, (202) 338-6820. Barbara Stephenson, President. Press, (202) 944-5508.*
General email, member@afsa.org
Web, www.afsa.org, Twitter, @afsatweets and Facebook, www.facebook.com/afsapage

Membership: active and retired foreign service employees of the State Dept., International Broadcasting Board, Agency for International Development, Foreign Commercial Service, and Foreign Agricultural Service. Offers scholarship programs; maintains club for members; represents active duty foreign service personnel in labor-management negotiations. Seeks to ensure adequate resources for foreign service operations and personnel. Conducts outreach programs to educate the public on diplomacy. Interests include business-government collaboration and international trade. Monitors legislation and regulations related to foreign service personnel and retirees.

Council of American Ambassadors, *888 17th St. N.W., #306, 20006-3312; (202) 296-3757. Fax, (202) 296-0926. Timothy A. Chorba, President; Kathleen Sheehan, Executive Director.*
General email, council@americanambassadors.org

Web, https://americanambassadors.org

Membership: U.S. ambassadors. Seeks to educate the public on foreign policy issues affecting the national interest. Hosts discussions, lectures, and conferences. Offers fellowships for students and foreign service personnel.

Executive Council on Diplomacy, *818 Connecticut Ave. N.W., 12th Floor, 20006-2702; (202) 466-5199. Fax, (202) 872-8696. Solveig Spielmann, Executive Director.*
General email, ecd@diplomacycouncil.org

Web, www.diplomacycouncil.org

Brings foreign diplomats from international organizations such as the United Nations and World Bank into contact with their U.S. counterparts. Provides a forum for discussion on issues such as agriculture, international trade, education, and the arts.

Institute for the Study of Diplomacy *(Georgetown University), 1316 36th St. N.W., 20007; (202) 965-5735. Fax, (202) 965-5811. Amb. Barbara K. Bodine, Director. Toll-free, (877) 703-4660.*
Web, http://isd.georgetown.edu, Twitter, @GUDiplomacy and Facebook, www.facebook.com/GUdiplomacy

Part of the Edmund A. Walsh School of Foreign Service. Focuses on the practical implementation of foreign policy objectives; draws on academic research and the concrete experience of diplomats and other members of the policy community.

Humanitarian Aid

▶**AGENCIES**

Administration for Children and Families (ACF) *(Health and Human Services Dept.), Refugee Resettlement (ORR), Mary E. Switzer Bldg., 330 C St. S.W., Room 5123, 20201; (202) 401-9246. Fax, (202) 401-0981. Jonathan Hayes, Director (Acting). Parent Hotline, (800) 203-7001.*
Web, www.acf.hhs.gov/orr

Directs a domestic resettlement program for refugees; reimburses states for costs incurred in giving refugees monetary and medical assistance; awards funds to voluntary resettlement agencies for providing refugees with monetary assistance and case management.

Agency for International Development (USAID), *Bureau for Democracy, Conflict, and Humanitarian Assistance, U.S. Foreign Disaster Assistance (OFDA), 1300 Pennsylvania Ave. N.W., 8th Floor, 20523-8602; (202) 712-0841. Fax, (202) 216-3191. Carol Chan, Director (Acting). General email, ofdainquiries@ofda.gov*

Web, www.usaid.gov/who-we-are/organization/bureaus/ bureau-democracy-conflict-and-humanitarian-assistance/ office-us, Twitter, @theOFDA and Facebook, www.facebook.com/USAID.OFDA

OFDA Press, USAIDressOfficers@usaid.gov

Administers disaster relief and preparedness assistance to foreign countries to save lives and alleviate human suffering. Aids displaced persons in disaster situations and helps other countries manage natural disasters and complex emergencies.

Agency for International Development (USAID), *Transition Initiatives (OTI), 1300 Pennsylvania Ave. N.W., #B3.06-124, 20523-8602; (202) 712-0284. Stephen Lennon, Director, (202) 712-1409. Public Affairs, (202) 712-4320.*
General email, DCHA.OTIOutreachMailList@usaid.gov

Web, www.usaid.gov/political-transition-initiatives and Twitter, @USAIDOTI

Provides efficient short-term assistance to countries in crisis in order to stabilize their governments.

Assistant Secretary for Health (OASH) *(Health and Human Services Dept.), Global Affairs (OGA), 200 Independence Ave. S.W., #639H, 20201; (202) 690-6174. (202) 260-0399. Fax, (202) 690-7127. Garrett Grigsby, Assistant Secretary (Acting).*
General email, globalhealth@hhs.gov

Web, www.globalhealth.gov and Twitter, @hhsgov

Represents the Health and Human Services Dept. before other governments, U.S. government agencies, international organizations, and the private sector on international and refugee health issues. Promotes international cooperation; provides health-related humanitarian and developmental assistance. Serves as the primary liaison to the World Health Organization.

Bureau of Population, Refugees, and Migration (PRM) *(State Dept.), 2201 C St. N.W., #6825, 20520-5824; (202) 647-7630. Fax, (202) 647-8162. Vacant, Assistant Secretary, (202) 647-5982; Carol T. O'Connell, Principal Deputy Assistant Secretary.*
Web, www.state.gov/j/prm, Twitter, @StatePRM and Facebook, www.facebook.com/State.PRM

Press, PRMPress@state.gov

Develops and implements policies and programs on matters relating to international refugees, internally displaced persons, and victims of conflict, including repatriation and resettlement programs; funds and monitors overseas relief, assistance, and repatriation programs; manages refugee admission to the United States.

State Dept., U.S. Foreign Assistance Resources, *2201 C St. N.W., #5923, 20520; (202) 647-2527. Fax, (202) 647-2529. Eric Ueland, Director, (202) 647-2604.*
Web, www.state.gov/f

Works to ensure the strategic and effective allocation, management, and use of foreign assistance resources.

State Dept., U.S. Global AIDS Coordinator and Health Diplomacy, *1800 G St. N.W., SA-22 #10300, 20037; (202) 663-2440. Fax, (202) 663-2979. Deborah L. Birx, Coordinator, (202) 633-2579. Press, (202) 663-1151.*
General email, SGACPublicAffairs@state.gov
Web, www.state.gov/s/gac and President's Plan for AIDS Relief, www.pepfar.gov

Oversees and coordinates all U.S. international HIV/AIDS activities, including implementation of the President's Emergency Plan for AIDS Relief.

►CONGRESS

For a listing of relevant congressional committees and subcommittees, please see pages 474–475 or the Appendix.

►INTERNATIONAL ORGANIZATIONS

The Global Fund for Children, *1411 K St. N.W., #1200, 20005; (202) 331-9003. Fax, (202) 331-9004. John Hecklinger, Chief Executive Officer.*
General email, info@globalfundforchildren.org
Web, www.globalfundforchildren.org, Twitter, @Global4Children and Facebook, www.facebook.com/GlobalFundforChildren

Funds grassroots organizations that help impoverished, abused, and refugee children in foreign countries. Assists in management, planning, and networking between other organizations. Holds workshops for grantees to share knowledge, experience, and practices aimed at helping vulnerable children.

International Assn. for Human Values, *Washington Office, 2401 15th St. N.W., 20009; (202) 250-3405. Fax, (202) 747-6543. Filiz Odabas-Geldiay, Executive Director.*
General email, usa@iahv.org
Web, www.iahv.org/us-en and Facebook, www.facebook.com/iafhv

Humanitarian organization offering programs to promote nonviolence and service projects. Interests include youth empowerment, leadership, disaster relief and rehabilitation, sustainable rural and community development, women's empowerment, veterans' trauma relief, and prisoner reform programs.

International Committee of the Red Cross (ICRC), *Washington Office, 1100 Connecticut Ave. N.W., #500, 20036; (202) 587-4600. Peter Maurer, President; Alexandra Boivin, Head of U.S. Delegation;*

Elizabeth Gorman Shaw, Media Contact, (202) 361-1566. Press, (202) 361-1566.
General email, washington_was@icrc.org
Web, www.icrc.org

Serves as the ICRC's main point of contact with U.S. authorities on issues concerning operations and international humanitarian law. Supports efforts internationally to help people affected by armed conflict. Visits people held by the U.S. government in Guantánamo Bay, Cuba. (Headquarters in Geneva, Switzerland.)

International Organization for Migration (IOM), *Washington Office, 1752 N St. N.W., #700, 20036; (202) 862-1826. Fax, (202) 862-1879. Luca Dall'Oglio, Chief of Mission, ext. 229; William Lacy Swing, Director General.*
General email, iomwashingtonRMF@iom.int
Web, www.iom.int/countries/united-states-america and Twitter, @UNmigration

Nonpartisan organization that plans and operates resource mobilization functions (RMF), including refugee resettlement, national migration, and humanitarian assistance to displaced populations at the request of its member governments. Advises governments on migration policies, supports victims of human trafficking, assists returning migrants, and raises awareness about the benefits of migration. Recruits skilled professionals for developing countries. (Headquarters in Geneva, Switzerland.)

Jesuit Refugee Service / USA, *1016 16th St. N.W., #500, 20036; (202) 462-0400. Fax, (202) 328-9212. Joan Rosenhauer, National Director; Giuliana McPherson, Policy Director.*
General email, jrsusa@jesuit.org
Web, www.jrsusa.org

U.S. Jesuit organization that aids refugees and other forcibly displaced persons worldwide, through accompaniment, advocacy, and service. Mobilizes the U.S. Jesuit response to forced displacement; provides advocacy and funding support to programs throughout the world. Monitors refugee and immigration legislation. (International headquarters in Rome.)

U.S. Fund for the United Nations Children's Fund (UNICEF), *Public Policy and Advocacy, 1775 K St. N.W., #360, 20006; (202) 296-4242. Fax, (202) 296-4060. Mark Engman, Senior Director, (202) 802-9102. Toll-free, (800) 367-5437.*
General email, washington@unicefusa.org
Web, www.unicefusa.org/campaigns/public-policy-advocacy and Twitter, @UNICEFUSA

Serves as the information reference service on UNICEF; advocates policies to advance the well-being of the world's children. Interests include international humanitarian assistance, U.S. volunteerism, child survival, and international health. (Headquarters in New York.)

United Nations High Commissioner for Refugees (UNHCR), *Washington Office, 1800 Massachusetts Ave. N.W., #500, 20036; (202) 296-5191. Fax, (202) 296-5660. Matthew Reynolds, Regional Representative.*

International Disaster Relief Organizations

Action Against Hunger, (212) 967-7800;
www.actionagainsthunger.org

American Jewish Joint Distribution Committee,
(212) 687-6200; www.jdc.org

American Red Cross, (800) 733-2767 or (202) 303-5214;
www.redcross.org

AmeriCares, (203) 658-9500; www.americares.org

CARE, (202) 595-2800; www.care.org

Catholic Relief Services, (888) 277-7575; www.crs.org

Child Fund, (800) 776-6767; www.childfund.org

Church World Service, (800) 297-1516 or (574) 264-3102;
www.cwsglobal.org

Direct Relief International, (805) 964-4767 or
(800) 676-1638; www.directrelief.org

Episcopal Relief and Development, (855) 312-4325;
www.episcopalrelief.org

Health Right International, (212) 226-9890;
www.healthright.org

InterAction, (202) 667-8227; www.interaction.org

International Federation of Red Cross/Red Crescent,
(212) 338-0161; www.ifrc.org

International Medical Corps, (310) 826-7800;
www.internationalmedicalcorps.org

International Rescue Committee, (212) 551-3000;
www.rescue.org

Islamic Relief USA, (855) 447-1001; www.irusa.org

Lutheran World Relief, (800) 597-5972; www.lwr.org

Mercy Corps, (800) 292-3355; www.mercycorps.org

Operation USA, 323.413.2353; www.opusa.org

Oxfam America, (800) 776-9326; www.oxfamamerica.org

Pan American Health Organization, (202) 974-3000;
www.paho.org/disasters

Save the Children, (800) 728-3843;
www.savethechildren.org

UNICEF, (800) 367-5437; www.unicefusa.org

World Food Programme (UN), (202) 627-3737;
www.wfp.org

World Vision, (888) 511-6548; www.worldvision.org

General email, usawa@unhcr.org

Web, www.unhcrwashington.org and Twitter, @Refugees

Works with governments and voluntary organizations to protect and assist refugees worldwide. Promotes long-term alternatives to refugee camps, including voluntary repatriation, local integration, and resettlement overseas. (Headquarters in Geneva, Switzerland.)

▶NONGOVERNMENTAL

American Red Cross, *National Headquarters, 431 18th St. N.W., 20006; (202) 303-5000. Gail J. McGovern, President. Headquarters staff directory, (202) 303-5214, ext. 1. Press, (202) 303-5551. Public inquiry, (202) 303-4498. Toll-free, 800-RED-CROSS (733-2767).*

Web, www.redcross.org and Twitter, @RedCross

Humanitarian organization chartered by Congress to provide domestic and international disaster relief and to act as a medium of communication between the U.S. armed forces and their families in time of war and personnel emergencies. Provides shelter, food, emotional support, supplies, funds, and technical assistance for relief in domestic and major international disasters through the International Federation of Red Cross and Red Crescent Societies.

Center for Civilians in Conflict, *1828 L St., #1050, 20036; (202) 558-6958. Federico Borello, Executive Director.*

General email, info@civiliansinconflict.org

Web, https://civiliansinconflict.org

Media, phendricks@civiliansinconflict.org

Acts as advocate to national governments and militaries for recognition, compensation, and other assistance to civilians they have harmed in armed conflicts.

Christian Relief Services, *8301 Richmond Hwy., #900, Alexandria, VA 22309; (703) 317-9086. Fax, (703) 317-9690. Paul Krizek, Executive Director. Information, 800-33-RELIEF. TTY, (800) 828-1140.*

General email, info@christianrelief.org

Web, http://christianrelief.org

Promotes economic development and the alleviation of poverty in urban areas of the United States, Appalachia, Native American reservations, Haiti, Mexico, Honduras, Lithuania, the Czech Republic, and Africa. Donates medical supplies and food; administers housing, hospital, and school construction programs; provides affordable housing for low-income individuals and families.

Evangelical Lutheran Church in America, *Advocacy, 218 D St. S.E., 20001; (202) 783-7507. Rev. Amy Reumann, Director. Toll-free, (800) 638-3522.*

General email, washingtonoffice@elca.org

*Web, www.elca.org/advocacy and
Twitter, @ELCAadvocacy*

Lutheran Immigration and Refugee Service responds to people caught in conflict and facing persecution, acts as advocate for their needs and interests, helps people access resources for basic human needs, works with foster care programs for minors, offers legal assistance, and develops new and innovative service programs and partnerships. (Headquarters in Chicago, Ill.)

Health Volunteers Overseas, *1900 L St. N.W., #310, 20036; (202) 296-0928. Fax, (202) 296-8018. Nancy A. Kelly, Executive Director.*
General email, info@hvousa.org

Web, www.hvousa.org

Operates training programs in developing countries for health professionals who wish to teach low-cost health care delivery practices.

International Rescue Committee, *Public Policy and Advocacy, 1730 M St. N.W., #505, 20036; David Milband, President. Media, (646) 761-0307. Central office (NYC), (212) 551-3000.*
General email, advocacy@theIRC.org

Web, www.rescue.org

Provides worldwide emergency aid, protection, resettlement services, educational support, and advocacy for refugees, displaced persons, and victims of oppression and violent conflict; recruits volunteers. (Headquarters in New York.)

National Council of Churches, *110 Maryland Ave. N.E., #108, 20002-5603; (202) 544-2350. Fax, (202) 543-1297. Jim Winkler, President, (202) 481-6684.*
General email, info@nationalcouncilofchurches.us

Web, www.nationalcouncilofchurches.us, Twitter, @nccusa and Facebook, www.facebook.com/ nationalcouncilofchurches

Works to foster cooperation among Christian congregations across the nation in programs concerning poverty, racism, family, environment, and international humanitarian objectives.

Oxfam America, *Policy and Campaigns, 1101 17th St. N.W., #1300, 20036-4710; (202) 496-1180. Fax, (202) 496-1190. Abby Maxman, President; Paul O'Brien, Vice President for Policy and Campaigns. Information, (800) 776-9326. Press, (202) 496-1169.*
General email, info@oxfamamerica.org

Web, www.oxfamamerica.org and Twitter, @OxfamAmerica

Funds disaster relief and long-term development programs internationally. Organizes grassroots support in the United States for issues affecting global poverty, including climate change, aid reform, and corporate transparency. (Headquarters in Boston, Mass.)

Program for Appropriate Technology in Health (PATH), *Washington Office, 455 Massachusetts Ave. N.W., #1000, 20001; (202) 822-0033. Fax, (202) 457-1466. Steve Davis, President.*
General email, info@path.org

Web, www.path.org

Develops, tests, and implements health technologies and strategies for low-resource countries. Works with community groups, other nongovernmental organizations, governments, companies, and UN agencies to expand the most successful programs. Interests include reproductive health, immunization, maternal-child health, emerging and epidemic diseases, and nutrition. (Headquarters in Seattle, Wash.)

Refugees International, *2001 S St. N.W., #700, 20009; (202) 828-0110. Fax, (202) 828-0819. Eric Schwartz, President. Press, (202) 540-7026. Toll-free, (800) 733-8433.*
General email, ri@refugeesinternational.org

Web, www.refugeesinternational.org and Twitter, @RefugeesIntl

Advocates assistance and protection for displaced people worldwide. Conducts field studies to identify basic needs and makes recommendations to policymakers and aid agencies.

Salvation Army Disaster Service, *2626 Pennsylvania Ave. N.W., 20037-1618; (202) 756-2600. Fax, (202) 679-5568. Rebecca Chestnutt, Disaster Director.*
General email, rebecca.chestnutt@uss.salvationarmy.org

Web, http://disaster.salvationarmyusa.org and Twitter, @SalArmyEDS

Provides U.S. and international disaster victims and rescuers with emergency support, including food, clothing, and counseling services.

U.S. Committee for Refugees and Immigrants, *2231 Crystal Dr., #350, Arlington, VA 22202-3794; (703) 310-1130. Fax, (703) 769-4241. Eskinder Negash, Chief Executive Officer; Stacie Blake, Director of Government Relations. Press, (703) 310-1166.*
General email, uscri@uscridc.org

Web, www.refugees.org and Twitter, USCridc

Defends rights of refugees in the United States and abroad. Helps immigrants and refugees adjust to American society; assists in resettling recently arrived immigrants and refugees; offers information, counseling services, and temporary living accommodations through its member agencies nationwide; issues publications on refugees and refugee resettlement; collects and disseminates information on refugee issues. Monitors legislation and regulations.

U.S. Conference of Catholic Bishops (USCCB), *Migration and Refugee Services, 3211 4th St. N.E., 20017; (202) 541-3352. Fax, (202) 541-3399. Bill Canny, Executive Director, (202) 541-3169.*
General email, mrs@usccb.org

Web, www.usccb.org/mrs

Acts as advocate for immigrants, refugees, migrants, and victims of human trafficking. Works with legislative and executive branches of the U.S. government and with national and international organizations such as the U.N. High Commissioner for Refugees to promote fair and responsive immigration and refugee policy.

Women for Women International, *2000 M St. N.W., #200, 20036; (202) 737-7705. Fax, (202) 737-7709. Laurie Adams, Chief Executive Officer.*
General email, general@womenforwomen.org

Web, www.womenforwomen.org and Twitter, @WomenforWomen

Helps women in war-torn regions rebuild their lives through financial and emotional support, job skills training, rights education, access to capital, and assistance for small-business development.

World Vision, *Advocacy, 300 Eye St. N.E., 20002; (202) 572-6300. Fax, (202) 572-6480. Magaret Schuler, Senior Vice President of International Programs; Robert (Bob) Zachritz, Vice President of Advocacy and Government Relations. Press, (202) 679-1620.*
General email, info@worldvision.org

Web, www.worldvision.org, Washington, DC, www.worldvisionusprograms.org/national_capital.php and *Twitter, @WorldVisionUSA*

Christian humanitarian and development organization that works with children, their families, and their communities worldwide. Interests include social injustice and the causes of poverty. Provides emergency disaster relief and long-term development programs domestically and abroad. (Headquarters in Seattle, Wash.)

Information and Exchange Programs

▶ AGENCIES

Broadcasting Board of Governors, *330 Independence Ave. S.W., #3300, 20237; (202) 203-4545. Fax, (202) 203-4585. John F. Lansing, Chief Executive Officer. Locator, (202) 203-4000. Press, (202) 203-4400.*
General email, publicaffairs@bbg.gov

Web, www.bbg.gov and *Twitter, @BBGov*

Established by Congress to supervise all U.S. government nonmilitary international broadcasting, including Voice of America, Radio and TV Martí, Radio Free Europe/Radio Liberty, Radio Free Asia, and the Middle East Broadcasting Networks (MBN). Assesses the quality and effectiveness of broadcasts with regard to U.S. foreign policy objectives; reports annually to the president and to Congress.

Bureau of Educational and Cultural Affairs (ECA) *(State Dept.), 2200 C St. N.W., #5BB17/, 20522; (202) 632-6445. (202) 632-6452. Fax, (202) 632-2701. Marie Royce, Assistant Secretary.*
General email, ecawebsitesmail@state.gov

Web, www.eca.state.gov, Twitter, @ECAatState and *Facebook, www.facebook.com/ExchangeProgramsAtState*

Seeks to promote mutual understanding between the people of the United States and other countries through international educational and training programs. Promotes personal, professional, and institutional ties between private citizens and organizations in the United States and abroad; presents U.S. history, society, art, and culture to overseas audiences.

Bureau of Educational and Cultural Affairs (ECA) *(State Dept.), Academic Exchange Programs, 2200 C St. N.W.,* #4B06, 20520; (202) 632-3234. Mary Kirk, Director. *Fulbright Program, (202) 632-3238.*
Web, http://eca.state.gov/about-bureau-0/organizational-structure/office-academic-exchanges

Provides opportunities for international study and research from the undergraduate through postdoctoral and professional levels. Works with the Fulbright Program, Global Undergraduate Exchange Program, Edmund S. Muskie Graduate Fellowship Program, and Study of the United States Institutes.

Bureau of Educational and Cultural Affairs (ECA) *(State Dept.), Citizen Exchanges, 2200 C St. N.W., #3B16, 20520; (202) 632-6062. Karl Stoltz, Director, (202) 632-6062.*
General email, professionalexchange@state.gov

Web, https://eca.state.gov/about-bureau/organizational-structure/office-citizen-exchanges

Provides professional, youth, cultural, and sports exchange opportunities for U.S. and foreign participants.

Bureau of Educational and Cultural Affairs (ECA) *(State Dept.), English Language Programs, 2200 C St. N.W., #4B16, 20520; (202) 632-9272. Joseph Bookbinder, Director, (202) 632-9281.*
General email, americanenglish@state.gov

Web, http://eca.state.gov/about-bureau-0/organizational-structure/office-english-language-programs
https://americanenglish.state.gov

Promotes the learning and teaching of American English around the world in order to foster mutual understanding between the people of other countries and the people of the United States.

Bureau of Educational and Cultural Affairs (ECA) *(State Dept.), Global Educational Programs, 2200 C St. N.W., #4CC17, 20520; (202) 632-6342. Anthony D. Koliha, Director, (202) 632-6345.*
Web, http://eca.state.gov/about-bureau-0/organizational-structure/office-global-educational-programs

Monitors the flow of international students to the United States and of U.S. students to other countries. Administers the Hubert H. Humphrey Fellowship Program, the Community College Initiative Program, and the Benjamin A. Gilman International Scholarship Program.

Bureau of Educational and Cultural Affairs (ECA) *(State Dept.), International Visitors, 2200 C St. N.W., #3B06, 20520; (202) 632-6383. Anne Grimes, Director. International Visitors Leadership Program, (202) 632-3283.*
Web, http://eca.state.gov/about-bureau-0/organizational-structure/office-international-visitors

Seeks to build mutual understanding between the United States and other nations through short-term visits to the United States for current and emerging foreign leaders.

Bureau of Educational and Cultural Affairs (ECA) *(State Dept.), Policy and Evaluation, 2200 C St. N.W., #5E02, 20520; (202) 632-2742. Stephen A. Guice, Head (Acting).*

General email, ecaevaluation@state.gov

Web, https://eca.state.gov/about-bureau/organizational-structure/office-policy-and-evaluation

Evaluates Bureau programs and measures performance to ensure quality and consistency. Houses the Cultural Heritage Center.

Bureau of Educational and Cultural Affairs (ECA) (State Dept.), Private Sector Exchange, 2200 C St. N.W., #5BB11, 20520; (202) 632-9386. Fax, (202) 632-2701. Kevin Saba, Deputy Assistant Secretary (Acting), (202) 632-6193.

General email, jvisas@state.gov

Web, http://eca.state.gov/about-bureau-0/organizational-structure/office-private-sector-exchange

Administers the Exchange Visitor Program to allow non-immigrants to participate in work-based and study-based exchange programs in the United States.

Bureau of International Information Programs (IIP) (State Dept.), 2201 C St. N.W., SA-5, 20520; (202) 632-9942. Fax, (202) 632-9901. Nicole Chulick, Coordinator (Acting).

General email, Contact_IIP@state.gov

Web, www.state.gov/r/iip and Twitter, @IIPState

Implements strategic communications programs—including Internet and print publications, traveling and electronically transmitted speaker programs, and information resource services—that reach key international audiences and support department initiatives. Explains U.S. foreign policy. Develops governmentwide technology policies that help disseminate this information.

National Institute of Standards and Technology (NIST) (Commerce Dept.), International and Academic Affairs, 100 Bureau Dr., MS 1090, Gaithersburg, MD 20899-1090; (301) 975-6478. Fax, (301) 975-3530. Claire M. Saundry, Director, (301) 975-2386. TTY, (301) 975-8295.

General email, inquiries@nist.gov

Web, www.nist.gov/iaao

Represents the institute in international functions involving science and technology; coordinates programs with foreign institutions; assists scientists from foreign countries who visit the institute for consultation. Administers a postdoctoral research associates program and oversees NIST's cooperation with academic institutions and researchers.

Voice of America (International Broadcasting Bureau), 330 Independence Ave. S.W., 20237; (202) 203-4000. Fax, (202) 203-4960. Amanda Bennett, Director.

General email, askvoa@voanews.com

Web, www.voanews.com and Twitter, @VOAnews

A multimedia international broadcasting service funded by the U.S. government through the Broadcasting Board of Governors. Broadcasts news, information, educational, and cultural programming to an estimated worldwide audience of more than 134 million people weekly. Programs are produced in more than forty languages.

▶ NONGOVERNMENTAL

Alliance for International Exchange, 1828 L St. N.W., #1150, 20036; (202) 293-6141. Fax, (202) 293-6144. Ilir Zherka, Executive Director.

General email, msahlu@alliance-exchange.org

Web, www.alliance-exchange.org, Twitter, @AllianceExchange and Facebook, www.facebook.com/AllianceIntlExchange

Promotes public policies that support the growth of international exchange between the United States and other countries. Provides professional representation, resource materials, publications, and public policy research for those involved in international exchanges.

American Bar Assn. (ABA), International Legal Exchange Program (ILEX), 1050 Connecticut Ave. N.W., #400, 20036; (202) 662-1660. Fax, (202) 662-1669. Jinny Choi, International Projects Manager, (202) 662-1675.

General email, intlex@staff.abanet.org

Web, www.americanbar.org/groups/international_law/initiatives_awards/international_legal_exchange

Facilitates entry into the United States for foreign lawyers offered training in U.S. law firms. Serves as designated U.S. government overseer for the J-1 visa and accepts applications from foreign lawyers. Houses the International Legal Resource Center.

American Council of Young Political Leaders, 1030 15th St. N.W., #580 West, 20005; (202) 857-0999. Libby Rosenbaum, Chief Executive Officer, (202) 448-9331.

General email, info@acypl.org

Web, http://acypl.org, Twitter, @ACYPL and Facebook, www.facebook.com/ACYPL

Bipartisan political education organization that promotes understanding among young elected leaders and political professionals around the world. Designs and manages international educational exchanges.

American Councils for International Education: ACTR/ACCELS, 1828 L St. N.W., #1200, 20036; (202) 833-7522. Lorne Craner, President, ext. 101.

General email, general@americancouncils.org

Web, www.americancouncils.org, Twitter, @AC_Global and Facebook, www.facebook.com/AmericanCouncils

Conducts educational exchanges for high school, university, and graduate school students as well as scholars with the countries of Africa, eastern Europe, Eurasia, southeast Europe, and the Middle East.

Atlas Corps, 99 M St., S.E., 4th Floor, 20003; (202) 391-0694. Scott Beale, Chief Executive Officer.

General email, info@atlascorps.org

Web, www.atlascorps.org and Twitter, @atlascorps

Provides U.S. fellowships to international leaders in public service and leaders of social issues in order to globally promote innovation in the nonprofit sector.

Business–Higher Education Forum, 2025 M St. N.W., #800, 20036; (202) 367-1189. Fax, (202) 367-2189. Brian K. Fitzgerald, Chief Executive Officer.

General email, info@bhef.com

Web, www.bhef.com, Twitter, @BHEF

Press, ursula.gross@bhef.org

Membership: chief executive officers of major corporations, museums, colleges, and universities. Promotes the development of industry-university alliances around the world. Provides countries in central and eastern Europe with technical assistance in enterprise development, management training, market economics, education, and infrastructure development.

Center for Intercultural Education and Development (Georgetown University), 3300 Whitehaven St. N.W., #1000, 20007 (mailing address: P.O. Box 579400, Washington, DC 20007); (202) 687-1400. Fax, (202) 687-2555. Chantal Santelices, Executive Director, (202) 687-1918.

General email, cied@georgetown.edu

Web, http://cied.georgetown.edu and Twitter, @GeorgetownCIED

Designs and administers programs aimed at improving the quality of lives of economically disadvantaged people; provides technical education, job training, leadership skills development, and business management training; runs programs in Central America, the Caribbean, Central Europe, the Middle East, and Southeast Asia.

Council for International Exchange of Scholars, 1400 K St. N.W., #700, 20005; (202) 686-4000. Fax, (202) 686-4029. Sarah Ilchman, Chief.

General email, scholars@iie.org

Web, www.cies.org and Twitter, @FulbrightPrgrm

Cooperates with the U.S. government in administering Fulbright grants for university teaching and advanced research abroad. (A division of the Institute of International Education.)

English-Speaking Union, Washington Office, 3610 Albemarle St. N.W., 20008; (202) 244-6140. Fax, (202) 333-8258. Heather B. McCabe, President.

General email, washingtondc@esuus.org

Web, www.esuus.org/washingtondc

Member organization for individuals interested in international educational and cultural exchange programs with countries in which English is a major language. Presents programs on the culture and history of the English-speaking world; sponsors annual Shakespeare competition among Washington metropolitan area schools. (National headquarters in New York.)

Global Ties U.S., 1250 H St. N.W., #305, 20005; (202) 842-1414. Fax, (202) 289-4625. Katherine Brown, President.

General email, info@globaltiesus.org

Web, www.globaltiesus.org and Twitter, @GlobalTiesUS

Members coordinate international exchange programs and bring international visitors to communities throughout the United States. Provides its members, from all 50 states and more than 20 countries, with connections, leadership development, and professional resources. (Formerly National Council for International Visitors.)

Graduate School USA, International Institute, 600 Maryland Ave. S.W., #320, 20024-2520; (202) 314-3508. Nina Bankova, Director. TTY, (888) 744-2717.

General email, intlinst@graduateschool.edu

Web, www.graduateschool.edu/content/ii

Offers professional development training and educational services to foreign and domestic audiences, including federally funded exchange program participants, foreign governments, international organizations, nongovernmental agencies, academia, and employees of U.S. agencies engaged in international activities. Provides tailored programs in the areas of capacity building, professional and educational exchanges, and governance.

Institute of International Education, Washington Office, 1400 K St. N.W., #700, 20005-2403; (202) 898-0600. Fax, (202) 326-7754. Allan Goodman, President.

Web, www.iie.org/en/Why-IIE/Offices/Washington-DC and Facebook, www.facebook.com/IIEglobal

Educational exchange, scholarship, and training organization that arranges professional programs for international visitors; conducts training courses in energy, environment, journalism, human resource development, educational policy and administration, and business-related fields; provides developing countries with short-term and long-term technical assistance in human resource development; arranges professional training and support for staff of human rights organizations; sponsors fellowships and applied internships for midcareer professionals from developing countries; manages programs sending U.S. teachers, undergraduate and graduate students, and professionals abroad; implements contracts and cooperative agreements for the State Dept., the U.S. Agency for International Development, foreign governments, philanthropic foundations, multilateral banks, and other organizations. (Headquarters in New York.)

International Arts and Artists, 9 Hillyer Court N.W., 20008; (202) 338-0680. Fax, (202) 333-0758. Lise Dubé-Scherr, President.

General email, info@artsandartists.org

Web, www.artsandartists.org, Twitter, @IAAExchange and Facebook, www.facebook.com/artsandartists

Assists international artists and institutions in obtaining visas. Provides international internships and training programs. Offers an exchange program for artists to travel and complete international art-related internships.

International Research and Exchanges Board (IREX), 1275 K St. N.W., #600, 20005; (202) 628-8188. Fax, (202) 628-8189. Kristin Lord, President.

General email, communications@irex.org

Web, www.irex.org, Twitter, @IREXintl and Facebook, www.facebook.com/irexinternational

Provides programs, grants, and consulting expertise in more than 100 countries to improve the quality of education, strengthen independent media, and foster pluralistic civil society development.

Libraries Without Borders, *Washington Office, 1342 Florida Ave. N.W., 20009; (703) 705-9321. Patrick Weil, Chair; Adam Echelman, Executive Director.*
General email, admin@librarieswithoutborders.org

Web, www.librarieswithoutborders.org, Twitter, @BSF_Intl and Facebook, www.facebook.com/ LibrariesWithoutBorders

Disseminates information globally, provides access to knowledge, education, and training, and promotes libraries and book distribution. Provides citizens in poor areas access to information with the aim of combating poverty and social inequality.

Meridian International Center, *1630 Crescent Pl. N.W., 20009; (202) 667-6800. Fax, (202) 667-1475. Amb. Stuart W. Holliday, President. Toll-free, (800) 424-2974.*
General email, info@meridian.org

Web, www.meridian.org

Conducts international educational and cultural programs; provides foreign visitors and diplomats in the United States with services, including cultural orientation, seminars, and language assistance. Offers international exhibitions for Americans.

NAFSA: Assn. of International Educators, *1307 New York Ave. N.W., 8th Floor, 20005-4701; (202) 737-3699. Fax, (202) 737-3657. Esther Brimmer, Executive Director. Publications, (866) 538-1927.*
General email, inbox@nafsa.org

Web, www.nafsa.org and Twitter, @NAFSA

Membership: individuals engaged in the field of international education and exchange at the postsecondary level. Promotes educational opportunities across national boundaries. Sets and upholds standards of good practice and provides professional education and training.

Radio Free Asia, *2025 M St. N.W., #300, 20036; (202) 530-4900. Kenneth Weinstein, Chair. Press, (202) 530-4976.*
General email, contact@rfa.org

Web, www.rfa.org and Twitter, @RadioFreeAsia

Independent radio, Internet, and television service funded by federal grants to promote and support democracy where public access to a free press is restricted. Broadcasts programs to East Asian countries, including China, Tibet, North Korea, Vietnam, Cambodia, Laos, and Burma; programming includes news, analysis, and specials on political developments, as well as cultural programs.

Radio Free Europe/Radio Liberty, *Washington Office, 1201 Connecticut Ave. N.W., #400, 20036; (202) 457-6900. Fax, (202) 457-6992. Daisy Sindelar, President (Acting); Nenad Pejic, Vice President; Martins Zvaners, Deputy Director of Communications, 202–457-6918. Press, (202) 457-6948.*
General email, zvanersm@rferl.org

Web, www.rferl.org and Twitter, @RFERL

Independent radio, Internet, and television service funded by federal grants to promote and support democracy. Broadcasts programs to 23 countries, including Russia, Afghanistan, Pakistan, Iraq, Iran, and the republics of Central Asia; programming includes news, analysis, and specials on political developments, as well as cultural programs. Research materials available to the public by appointment. (Headquarters in Prague, Czech Republic.)

Sister Cities International, *915 15th St. N.W., 4th Floor, 20005; (202) 347-8630. Fax, (202) 393-6524. Roger-Mark De Souza, President, (202) 321-8422.*
General email, info@sistercities.org

Web, https://sistercities.org and Twitter, @SisterCitiesInt

A network of more than 2,300 partnerships between U.S. and foreign cities. Promotes global cooperation at the municipal level, cultural understanding, and economic stimulation through exchanges of citizens, ideas, and materials. Serves as information clearinghouse for economic and sustainability issues and as program coordinator for trade missions. Sponsors youth programs.

World Learning, *Global Development and Exchange Programs, 1015 15th St. N.W., 7th Floor, 20005-2065; (202) 408-5420. Fax, (202) 408-5397. Carol Jenkins, President, (202) 464-6643. Toll-free, (800) 858-0292. TTY, 711.*
General email, development@worldlearning.org

Web, www.worldlearning.org and Twitter, @WorldLearning

Assists public and private organizations engaged in international cooperation and business. Works with governments and private counterparts to support foreign professional exchanges. Develops tailored technical training programs for midcareer professionals. Provides technical expertise, management support, travel, and business development services. Administers programs that place international exchange students in U.S. colleges and universities. Implements youth exchanges focused on leadership, current issues, and peacebuilding. Administered by World Learning's Division of International Development and Exchange Programs. Administers field-based study abroad programs, which offer semester and summer programs for high school, college, and graduate students.

Youth for Understanding USA, *6856 Eastern Ave. N.W., #310, 20012; (202) 774-5200. Fax, (202) 588-7571. Scott Messing, President. Teen information, (800) 833-6243.*
General email, info@yfu.org

Web, www.yfuusa.org and Twitter, @yfu_usa

Educational organization that administers international exchange programs, primarily for high school students. Administers scholarship programs that sponsor student exchanges.

War, Conflict, and Peacekeeping

►AGENCIES

Agency for International Development (USAID), *Bureau for Democracy, Conflict, and Humanitarian Assistance,*

1300 Pennsylvania Ave. N.W., #8.6-0.84, 20523-8601; (202) 712-0100. Tim Ziemer, Assistant Administrator (Acting). Web, www.usaid.gov/who-we-are/organization/bureaus/ bureau-democracy-conflict-and-humanitarian-assistance

Manages U.S. foreign disaster assistance, emergency and developmental food aid, democracy programs, conflict management programs, and programs to assist countries transitioning out of crises. Assists U.S. voluntary organizations, schools, and hospitals abroad. Serves as USAID's liaison to the U.S. military.

Agency for International Development (USAID), *Bureau for Democracy, Conflict, and Humanitarian Assistance, Conflict Management and Mitigation (CMM), 1300 Pennsylvania Ave. N.W., #5.10A, 20523; (202) 712-0000, Ext. 21228. Veeraya (Kate) Somvongsiri, Deputy Assistant Administrator (Acting).*

General email, conflict@usaid.gov

Web, www.usaid.gov/who-we-are/organization/bureaus/ bureau-democracy-conflict-and-humanitarian-assistance/ office-0

Supports USAID's work as it relates to conflict management, fragility, political instability, and extremism. Applies best practices of conflict management to areas such as democracy and governance, economic growth, natural resource management, and peace-building efforts.

Bureau of Conflict and Stabilization Operations (CSO) *(State Dept.), 2201 C St., N.W. #SA-9, 20522; (202) 472-8509. Denise Natali, Assistant Secretary.*

General email, csopublic@state.gov

Web, www.state.gov/j/cso, Twitter, @StateCSO and Facebook, www.facebook.com/stateCSO

Advances U.S. national security by working with partners in select countries to mitigate and prevent violent conflict. Conducts conflict analysis to identify factors contributing to mass violence or instability; develops prioritized strategies to address these factors; provides experienced leadership and technical experts to operationalize U.S. government and host-nation plans. Provides funding and training.

Bureau of International Narcotics and Law Enforcement Affairs (INL) *(State Dept.), Criminal Justice and Assistance Partnerships (CAP), 2401 E St. N.W., #L505, 20037; (202) 634-1415. Vacant, Director.*

Web, www.state.gov/j/inl/offices/index.htm

Works with international governments to build or improve justice systems to prevent or eliminate transnational crime, strengthen governance, and prevent conflict; builds capacity of countries deploying police to UN and regional peacekeeping operations.

Bureau of International Organization Affairs (IO) *(State Dept.), Peace Support Operations, Sanctions, and Counterterrorism (PSC), 2201 C St. N.W., #1827, 20520; (202) 736-7733. Fax, (202) 647-9722. John D. Cockrell, Director (Acting).*

Web, www.state.gov/p/io

Works with the United Nations to implement peacekeeping operations; manages State Dept. coordination of counterterrorism issues in the UN system.

Bureau of Political-Military Affairs (PM) *(State Dept.), 2201 C St. N.W., #6212, 20520; (202) 647-7199. Fax, (202) 736-4779. Mark String, Deputy Assistant Secretary. Web, www.state.gov/t/pm*

Liaison between the State Dept. and Defense Dept. Provides policy direction in the areas of international security, security assistance, military operations, defense strategy and policy, military use of space, and defense trade.

Bureau of Political-Military Affairs (PM) *(State Dept.), Global Programs and Initiatives (GPI), 2025 E St. N.W., 20520; (202) 453-8380. Michael L. Smith, Director. Web, www.state.gov/t/pm/gpi*

Facilitates training and equipping of international peacekeepers; supports programs that enable international cooperation on security issues, including UN and regional peacekeeping operation capabilities, aircraft policy and diplomatic clearance for foreign state aircraft and naval vessels seeking to enter U.S. territory, port security and sea access, and foreign partners assistance for addressing emergent challenges to their security.

State Dept., *Policy Planning, 2201 C St. N.W., #7311, 20520; (202) 647-2972. Fax, (202) 647-0844. Kiron K. Skinner, Director.*

General email, policyplanning@state.gov

Web, www.state.gov/s/p

Advises the secretary and other State Dept. officials on foreign policy matters, including international peacekeeping and peace enforcement operations.

►**CONGRESS**

For a listing of relevant congressional committees and subcommittees, please see pages 474–475 or the Appendix.

►**NONGOVERNMENTAL**

Act Now to Stop War and End Racism (ANSWER) Coalition, *617 Florida Ave. N.W., Lower Level, 20001; (202) 265-1948. Fax, (202) 280-1022. Sarah Sloan, National Staff Coordinator. Press, (202) 265-1948. General email, info@answercoalition.org*

Web, www.answercoalition.org and Facebook, www.facebook.com/AnswerCoalition

Works to end war and conflict, with an emphasis on the Middle East and Somalia. Conducts demonstrations with other peace and anti-war groups, especially ethnic and cultural identity groups concerned with ending racism.

Carnegie Endowment for International Peace, *1779 Massachusetts Ave. N.W., 20036-2103; (202) 483-7600. Fax, (202) 483-1840. William J. Burns, President. General email, info@carnegieendowment.org*

Web, http://carnegieendowment.org and Twitter, @CarnegieEndow

Global network of policy research centers in Russia, China, Europe, the Middle East, India, and the United States. Conducts research on international affairs and U.S. foreign policy in order to promote peace. Program activities cover a broad range of military, political, and economic issues; sponsors panel discussions.

Center for Advanced Defense Studies, *1100 H St. N.W., #750, 20005; (202) 289-3332. David Johnson, Executive Director.*
General email, info@c4ads.org
Web, https://c4ads.org, Twitter, @C4ADS
media, communications@c4ads.org

Analyzes global data and publishes reports on international conflict and security concerns. Conducts field research in conflict areas.

Conflict Solutions International, *1629 K St. N.W., #300, 20006; (202) 349-3972. Vacant, President.*
General email, info@csiorg.org
Web, www.csiorg.org and Facebook, www.facebook.com/ConflictSolutionsInternational

All-volunteer nonpartisan organization that reviews and analyzes global issues to support ending violent conflict. Holds forums to educate the public and increase awareness of religious movements, civil conflict, and independence groups. Interests include relations between the United States and Cuba, including negotiations to release political prisoners.

Enough Project, *1420 K St. N.W., #200, 20005; (202) 580-7690. John Prendergast, Director.*
General email, info@enoughproject.org
Web, www.enoughproject.org and Twitter, @enoughproject

Research and policy organization aimed at protecting peace and human rights in African conflict zones; countering armed groups and violent kleptocratic regimes; preventing transnational crime and terror; and ending the trafficking of ivory, gold, diamonds, conflict minerals, and other natural resources. Conducts field research in conflict zones, develops and advocates for policy recommendations, supports social movements in affected countries, and mobilizes public campaigns.

Fourth Freedom Forum, *Washington Office, 1101 14th St. N.W., #900, 20005; (202) 802-9393. Eelco Kessels, Executive Director.*
General email, globalct@gmail.com
Web, www.globalcenter.org

Conducts research and training to advance global cooperation to address transnational threats, including terrorism, nuclear proliferation, and drug trafficking.

Friends Committee on National Legislation (FCNL), *245 2nd St. N.E., 20002-5795; (202) 547-6000. Fax, (202) 547-6019. Diane Randall, Executive Secretary. Recorded information, (202) 547-4343. Toll-free, (800) 630-1330.*
General email, fcnl@fcnl.org
Web, www.fcnl.org, Twitter, @FCNL and Facebook, www.facebook.com/quakerlobby

Supports world disarmament; international cooperation; domestic, economic, peace, and social justice issues; and improvement in relations between the United States and the former Soviet Union. Opposes conscription. Affiliated with the Religious Society of Friends (Quakers).

Fund for Peace, *1101 14th St. N.W., #1020, 20005; (202) 223-7940. J.J. Messner, Executive Director.*
Web, www.fundforpeace.org, Twitter, @fundforpeace and Facebook, www.facebook.com/fund4peace

Promotes international sustainable security. Produces the Failed States Index and the Conflict Assessment System Tool (CAST) that gathers information for determining conflict risk. Works with policymakers, government agencies, nonprofits, journalists, and private organizations to advocate nonviolent conflict resolution. Interests include early warning, election violence, and preventing violence against women.

International Center on Nonviolent Conflict (ICNC), *1775 Pennsylvania Ave., 20038; (202) 416-4720. Fax, (202) 466-5918. Hardy Merriman, President.*
General email, icnc@nonviolent-conflict.org
Web, www.nonviolent-conflict.org, Twitter, @civilresistance and Facebook, www.facebook.com/CivilResistance

Advocates nonviolent methods to protect international human rights and democracy. Supports research and education to broaden these methods. Holds seminars on successful nonviolent conflict practices.

International Crisis Group, *Washington Office, 1629 K St. N.W., #450, 20006; (202) 785-1601. Robert Malley, President.*
General email, washington@crisisgroup.org
Web, www.crisisgroup.org

Private, multinational organization that seeks to prevent international conflict. Writes and distributes reports and raises funds. (Headquarters in Brussels.)

International Peace and Security Institute (IPSI), *5225 Wisconsin Ave. N.W., #104, 20015; (202) 966-5901. Deborah Mancini, Executive Director.*
General email, info@ipsinstitute.org
Web, www.ipsinstitute.org, Twitter, @IPSInstitute and Facebook, www.facebook.com/IPSInstituteDC

Researches and analyzes global conflict. Holds educational symposiums and offers training programs to promote peacebuilding skills. Publishes weekly reports on international conflict management and current affairs.

International Stability Operations Assn. (ISOA), *17251 Eye St. N.W., #300, 20006 (mailing address: 1714 Corwin Dr., Silver Spring, MD 20910); (703) 336-3940. Howard (Howie) Lind, President.*
General email, howielind@stability-operations.org
Web, www.stability-operations.org

Membership: private-sector service companies involved in all sectors of peace and stability operations around the world, including mine clearance, logistics, security, training, and emergency humanitarian aid. Works to institute standards and codes of conduct. Monitors legislation.

Refugees International, *2001 S St. N.W., #700, 20009; (202) 828-0110. Fax, (202) 828-0819. Eric Schwartz, President. Media, (202) 540-7026. Toll-free, (800) 733-8433.*
General email, ri@refugeesinternational.org
Web, www.refugeesinternational.org and Twitter, @RefugeesIntl

Advocates assistance and protection for displaced people worldwide. Conducts field studies to identify basic needs and makes recommendations to policymakers and aid agencies.

Search for Common Ground (SFCG), *1730 Rhode Island Ave. N.W., #1101, 20036; (202) 265-4300. Fax, (202) 232-6718. Shamil Idriss, President. Press, (202) 572-6289.*
*Web, www.sfcg.org, Twitter, @SFCG_*
General email, webinfo@sfcg.org

International nonprofit that seeks to end global violent conflict at a grassroots level. Provides mediation services and training for youth and women activists. Produces print and video media to encourage discussions on how to solve issues nonviolently. Supports theater and sports programs for youth in politically disadvantaged areas.

U.S. Conference of Catholic Bishops (USCCB), *International Justice and Peace, 3211 4th St. N.E., 20017-1194; (202) 541-3160. Fax, (202) 541-3339. Lucas Koach, Director.*
General email, jphdmail@usccb.org
Web, www.usccb.org/about/international-justice-and-peace

Works with the U.S. State Dept., foreign government offices, and international organizations on issues of peace, justice, and human rights.

U.S. Institute of Peace, *2301 Constitution Ave. N.W., 20037; (202) 457-1700. Fax, (202) 429-6063. Stephen J. Hadley, Chair; Nancy Lindborg, President. Press, (202) 429-3869.*
General email, info@usip.org
Web, www.usip.org and Twitter, @USIP

Independent, nonpartisan institution established by Congress. Aims to prevent and resolve violent international conflicts, promote post-conflict stability, and increase peace-building capacity, tools, and intellectual capital worldwide. Provides training, analysis, and other resources to people, organizations, and governments working to build world peace.

Win Without War, *1 Thomas Circle N.W., #700 20005; (202) 656-4999. Stephen Miles, Executive Director, (504) 289-3594.*
General email, info@winwithoutwar.org
Web, www.winwithoutwar.org and Twitter, @winwithoutwar

Network of activists and national organizations promoting international cooperation and agreements as the best means for securing peace. Encourages U.S. foreign policies of counterterrorism and weapons nonproliferation, but opposes unilateral military preemption.

IMMIGRATION AND NATURALIZATION

General

▶**AGENCIES**

Administration for Children and Families (ACF) *(Health and Human Services Dept.), Refugee Resettlement (ORR), Mary E. Switzer Bldg., 330 C St. S.W., Room 5123, 20201; (202) 401-9246. Fax, (202) 401-0981. Jonathan Hayes, Director (Acting). Parent Hotline, (800) 203-7001.*
Web, www.acf.hhs.gov/orr

Directs a domestic resettlement program for refugees; reimburses states for costs incurred in giving refugees monetary and medical assistance; awards funds to voluntary resettlement agencies for providing refugees with monetary assistance and case management.

Bureau of Consular Affairs (CA) *(State Dept.), Visa Services, 2401 E St. N.W., #6811, 20522-0106; (202) 647-9584. Edward J. Ramotowski, Deputy Assistant Secretary. National Visa Center (immigrant inquiries), (603) 334-0700. National Visa Center (nonimmigrant inquiries), (603) 334-0888.*
Web, http://travel.state.gov/content/visas/en.html

Supervises visa issuance system, which is administered by U.S. consular offices abroad.

Civil Division *(Justice Dept.), Immigration Litigation (OIL), 1331 Pennsylvania Ave. N.W., #7025S, 20004 (mailing address: P.O. Box 878, Ben Franklin Station, Washington, DC 20044); (202) 616-4930. Fax, (202) 307-8837. David McConnell, Director.*
Web, www.justice.gov/civil/office-immigration-litigation

Handles most civil litigation arising under immigration and nationality laws.

Executive Office for Immigration Review *(Justice Dept.), 5107 Leesburg Pike, #2600, Falls Church, VA 22041; (703) 305-0169. James McHenry, Director. TTY, (800) 828-1120. Case Information System, (800) 898-7180. Employer Sanctions and Antidiscrimination Cases, (703) 305-0864. Justice Dept., (202) 514-2000. Legislative and Public Affairs, (703) 305-0289.*
Web, www.justice.gov/eoir, Twitter, @DOJ_EOIR and Facebook, www.facebook.com/doj.eoir

Quasi-judicial body that includes the Board of Immigration Appeals and offices of the chief immigration judge and the chief administration hearing officer. Interprets immigration laws; conducts hearings and hears appeals on immigration issues.

U.S. Citizenship and Immigration Services (USCIS)
(Homeland Security Dept.), 20 Massachusetts Ave. N.W.,
20529; (800) 375-5283. L. Francis Cissna, Director.
Customer Service Center, (800) 375-5283. Press, (202) 272-
1200. TTY, (800) 767-1833.
Web, www.uscis.gov and Twitter, @USCIS

Responsible for the administration of immigration and
naturalization adjudication functions and establishing
immigration services policies and priorities.

U.S. Coast Guard (USCG) *(Homeland Security Dept.), Law
Enforcement,* CG-MLE, 2703 Martin Luther King Jr. Ave.
S.E., MS 7516, 20593-7516; (202) 372-2161.
Capt. Timothy (Tim) Brown, Chief.

Interdicts illegal migrants at sea and assists in repatriation.

▶**CONGRESS**

*For a listing of relevant congressional committees and sub-
committees, please see pages 474–475 or the Appendix.*

▶**INTERNATIONAL ORGANIZATIONS**

International Catholic Migration Commission (ICMC),
Washington Office, 3211 4th St. N.E., #141, 20017-1194;
(202) 541-3389. Msgr. Anne Therese Gallagher, President;
Limnyuy Konglim, Head of U.S. Liaison Office.
General email, info@icmc.net

Web, www.icmc.net

Supports ICMC's worldwide programs by liaising with
the U.S. government, nongovernmental organizations, and
the American public. Works with refugees, internally displaced persons, migrants, asylum seekers, and trafficking
victims. Responds to refugees' immediate needs while
working for return to and reintegration in their home
country, local integration, or resettlement in a third country. (Headquarters in Geneva, Switzerland.)

International Organization for Migration (IOM),
Washington Office, 1752 N St. N.W., #700, 20036; (202)
862-1826. Fax, (202) 862-1879. Luca Dall'Oglio, Chief of
Mission, ext. 229; William Lacy Swing, Director General.
General email, iomwashingtonRMF@iom.int

*Web, www.iom.int/countries/united-states-america and
Twitter, @UNmigration*

Nonpartisan organization that plans and operates
resource mobilization functions (RMF), including refugee
resettlement, national migration, and humanitarian assistance to displaced populations at the request of its member
governments. Advises governments on migration policies,
supports victims of human trafficking, assists returning
migrants, and raises awareness about the benefits of migration. Recruits skilled professionals for developing countries. (Headquarters in Geneva, Switzerland.)

▶**NONGOVERNMENTAL**

American Immigration Lawyers Assn., 1331 G St. N.W.,
#300, 20005-3142; (202) 507-7600. Fax, (202) 783-7853.
Benjamin Johnson, Executive Director.

General email, membership@aila.org

*Web, http://aila.org, Twitter, @ailanational and
Facebook, www.facebook.com/AILANational*

Association for lawyers interested in immigration law.
Provides information and continuing education programs
on immigration law and policy; offers workshops and conferences. Acts as advocate for a fair and just immigration
law policy. Monitors legislation and regulations.

Center for Immigration Studies, 1629 K St. N.W., #600,
20006; (202) 466-8185. Fax, (202) 466-8076.
Mark Krikorian, Executive Director.
General email, center@cis.org

Web, www.cis.org and Twitter, @wwwCISorg

Nonpartisan organization that conducts research and
policy analysis of the economic, social, demographic, and
environmental impact of immigration on the United
States. Sponsors symposiums.

Ethiopian Community Development Council, Inc., 901
S. Highland St., Arlington, VA 22204; (703) 685-0510.
Fax, (703) 685-0529. Tsehaye Teferra, President.
General email, info@ecdcus.org

Web, www.ecdcus.org and Twitter, @ECDCUS

Seeks to improve quality of life for African immigrants
and refugees in the United States through local and
national programs. Interests include the resettlement and
acculturation of refugees, health education, and cultural
outreach for communities. Also provides business loans
and management training for minority-owned and
women-owned businesses in the Washington metropolitan
area.

Federation for American Immigration Reform (FAIR),
25 Massachusetts Ave. N.W., #330, 20001; (202) 328-7004.
Fax, (202) 387-3447. Daniel A. Stein, President.
Toll-free, (877) 627-3247.
General email, fair@fairus.org

*Web, www.fairus.org, Twitter, @FAIRImmigration and
Facebook, www.facebook.com/FAIRImmigration*

Organization of individuals interested in immigration
reform. Monitors immigration laws and policies.

Immigration Works USA, 737 8th St. S.E., #201, 20003;
(202) 506-4541. Fax, (202) 595-8962. Tamar Jacoby,
President. Press, (202) 506-4541.
General email, info@immigrationworksusa.org

*Web, www.immigrationworksusa.org and
Twitter, @ImmigWorksUSA*

Coalition of business owners that seeks to educate the
public about the benefits of immigration and build support
for bringing immigration policy in line with the country's
labor needs. Monitors legislation and regulations.

Institute for the Study of International Migration
(Georgetown University), 3300 Whitehaven St. N.W., 3rd
Floor, 20007; (202) 687-2558. Fax, (202) 687-2541.
Katharine M. Donato, Director.

General email, isim@georgetown.edu

Web, http://isim.georgetown.edu, Twitter, @GUMigration and Facebook, www.facebook.com/ISIM.Georgetown

Researches international migration policy, cause, and conflict through the study of social, economic, environmental, and political dimensions of international migration. Administers academic certificates to students in subjects such as Refugee and Humanitarian Emergencies and Human Rights Law. Offers scholarship programs for international researchers and students to study independent topics. (Part of the School of Foreign Service.)

Lutheran Immigration and Refugee Service, *Advocacy, 110 Maryland Ave. N.E., #505-507, 20001; (202) 381-1030. Fax, (410) 230-2890. Javier Cuebas, Director of Advocacy. General email, dc@lirs.org*

Web, www.lirs.org, Twitter, @LIRSorg and Facebook, www.facebook.com/LIRSorg

Resettles refugees and provides them with case management, job training, English language, and legal assistance. Provides specialized foster care services for unaccompanied refugee youth and facilitates the reunification of unaccompanied immigrant children in federal custody with their parents or relatives. Funds and provides technical assistance to local projects that offer social and legal services to immigrants and refugees, particularly those in immigration detention. (Headquarters in Baltimore, Md.)

Migration Policy Institute, *1400 16th St. N.W., #300, 20036; (202) 266-1940. Fax, (202) 266-1900. Andrew Selee, President, (202) 266-1933. General email, info@migrationpolicy.org*

Web, www.migrationpolicy.org

Nonpartisan think tank that studies the movement of people within the United States and worldwide. Provides analysis, development, and evaluation of migration, integration, and refugee policies at local, national, and international levels.

National Immigration Forum, *50 F St. N.W., #300, 20001; (202) 347-0040. Fax, (202) 347-0058. Ali Noorani, Executive Director. Press, (202) 383-5987. General email, media@immigrationforum.org*

Web, www.immigrationforum.org, Twitter, @NatImmForum and Facebook, www.facebook.com/NationalImmigrationForum

Pro-immigration advocacy organization that provides policy analysis, research, and updates on immigration policy developments to members and allies across the country. Monitors legislation and regulations related to immigrants and immigration. Works with broad cross-section of immigrant-advocacy, immigrant-serving, religious, business, and labor organizations to advance policies welcoming to immigrants.

NumbersUSA, *Capitol Hill Office, 11 D St. S.E., 1st Floor, 20003; 1400 Crystal Dr., #240, Arlington, VA 22209; (202) 543-1341. Fax, (202) 543-3147. Roy Beck, President; Rosemary Jenks, Vice President of Government Affairs. Donations, (703) 816-8820.*

General email, info@numbersusa.com

Web, www.numbersusa.com, Twitter, @NumbersUSA and Facebook, www.facebook.com/numbersusa

Public policy organization that favors immigration reduction as a way of promoting economic justice for American workers. Monitors legislation and regulations.

Pew Research Center, *Hispanic Trends Project, 1615 L St. N.W., #800, 20036; (202) 419-4300. Fax, (202) 419-3608. Mark Hugo Lopez, Director. Press, (202) 419-4372. Web, www.pewhispanic.org and Twitter, @PewHispanic*

Seeks to improve understanding of the U.S. Hispanic population and its impact on the nation, as well as explore Latino views on a range of social matters and public policy issues, including public opinion, identity, and trends in voting, immigration, work, and education. Conducts public opinion surveys and other studies that are made available to the public. (A project of the Pew Research Center.)

U.S. Committee for Refugees and Immigrants, *2231 Crystal Dr., #350, Arlington, VA 22202-3794; (703) 310-1130. Fax, (703) 769-4241. Eskinder Negash, Chief Executive Officer; Stacie Blake, Director of Government Relations. Press, (703) 310-1166. General email, uscri@uscridc.org*

Web, www.refugees.org and Twitter, USCridc

Defends rights of refugees in the United States and abroad. Helps immigrants and refugees adjust to American society; assists in resettling recently arrived immigrants and refugees; offers information, counseling services, and temporary living accommodations through its member agencies nationwide; issues publications on refugees and refugee resettlement; collects and disseminates information on refugee issues. Monitors legislation and regulations.

U.S. Conference of Catholic Bishops (USCCB), *Migration and Refugee Services, 3211 4th St. N.E., 20017; (202) 541-3352. Fax, (202) 541-3399. Bill Canny, Executive Director, (202) 541-3169. General email, mrs@usccb.org*

Web, www.usccb.org/mrs

Acts as advocate for immigrants, refugees, migrants, and victims of human trafficking. Works with legislative and executive branches of the U.S. government and with national and international organizations such as the U.N. High Commissioner for Refugees to promote fair and responsive immigration and refugee policy.

UnidosUS, *1126 16th St. N.W., #600, 20036-4845; (202) 785-1670. Fax, (202) 776-1792. Janet Murguía, President. General email, info@unidos.org*

Web, www.unidosus.org, Twitter, @WeAreUnidosUS and Facebook, www.facebook.com/Weareunidosus

Provides research, policy analysis, and advocacy relating to immigration policy and programs. Monitors federal legislation on immigration, legalization, employer sanctions, employment discrimination, and eligibility of immigrants for federal benefit programs. Assists community-based groups involved in immigration and education services and educates employers about immigration laws. (Formerly the National Council of La Raza.)

INTERNATIONAL LAW AND AGREEMENTS

General

► **AGENCIES**

Bureau of Economic and Business Affairs (EB) *(State Dept.), Trade Policy and Programs (TPP), Bilateral Trade Affairs (BTA)*, 2201 C St. N.W., #4452, 20520; (202) 647-3784. Fax, (202) 647-6540. Robert D. Manogue, Director, (202) 647-4017.
Web, www.state.gov/e/eb/tpn/bta

Develops, negotiates, and implements free trade agreements, trade and investment framework agreements, and trade preference programs.

Bureau of Economic and Business Affairs (EB) *(State Dept.), Transportation Affairs (TRA), Aviation Negotiations (AN)*, 2201 C St. N.W., #3425, 20520-5820; (202) 647-5843. Fax, (202) 647-9143. Paul A. Brown, Director.
Web, www.state.gov/e/eb/tra

Manages bilateral aviation relationships; works with the Transporation Dept. and private sector to negotiate bilateral agreements to support and improve commercial aviation.

Bureau of International Narcotics and Law Enforcement Affairs (INL) *(State Dept.), Anticrime Programs*, 2401 E St. N.W., #L600, 20037; (202) 663-1860. Susan Snyder, Director.
Web, www.state.gov/j/inl/offices/index.htm

Works with international governments to combat international organized crime, high-level corruption, money-laundering, terrorist financing, cyber and intellectual property crimes, threats to border security, narcotics trafficking, and other smuggling and trafficking crimes.

Bureau of International Organization Affairs (IO) *(State Dept.), Peace Support Operations, Sanctions, and Counterterrorism (PSC)*, 2201 C St. N.W., #1827, 20520; (202) 736-7733. Fax, (202) 647-9722. John D. Cockrell, Director (Acting).
Web, www.state.gov/p/io

Structures and enforces United Nations sanctions so that they be effective and humane, and builds support for peacekeeping and sanctions from Congress and private organizations.

Bureau of Political-Military Affairs (PM) *(State Dept.), Security Negotiations and Agreements (SNA)*, 2201 C St. N.W., #3242, 20520; (202) 647-0622. Curtis E. Velasquez, Deputy Director.
Web, www.state.gov/t/pm/c17194.htm

Negotiates and oversees implementation of international security agreements, including defense cooperation agreements, burden-sharing and facilities access agreements, transit and overflight arrangements, and state flights agreements, in order to facilitate the deployment and movement of U.S. forces and materiel abroad and provide protections for U.S. service members operating overseas.

Federal Bureau of Investigation (FBI) *(Justice Dept.), International Operations Division*, 935 Pennsylvania Ave. N.W., #7825, 20535; (202) 324-5904. Fax, (202) 324-5292. George L. Piro, Assistant Director.
Web, www.fbi.gov/about/leadership-and-structure/international-operations

Supports FBI involvement in international investigations; oversees liaison offices in U.S. embassies abroad. Maintains contacts with other federal agencies, Interpol, foreign police and security officers based in Washington, DC, and national law enforcement associations.

Internal Revenue Service (IRS) *(Treasury Dept.), Criminal Investigation*, 1111 Constitution Ave. N.W., #2501, 20224; (202) 317-3200. Don Fort, Chief. Tax fraud hotline, (800) 829-0433.
Web, www.irs.gov/uac/criminal-enforcement-1 and Twitter, @IRSnews

Manages the Offshore Voluntary Disclosure Program to allow taxpayers to disclose previously undisclosed offshore accounts and assets.

National Telecommunications and Information Administration (NTIA) *(Commerce Dept.)*, 1401 Constitution Ave. N.W., #4898, 20230; (202) 482-2000. Fax, (202) 501-0536. David J. Redl, Assistant Secretary; James C. Wasilewski, Chief of Staff (Acting), (202) 482-1845. Press, (202) 482-7002.
Web, www.ntia.doc.gov, Twitter, @NTIAgov and Facebook, www.facebook.com/ntiagov

Represents the U.S. telecommunications sector (along with the State Dept.) in negotiating international agreements, including conferences with the International Telecommunication Union.

State Dept., *Global Criminal Justice*, 2201 C St. N.W., #7419A, 20520; (202) 647-5072. Fax, (202) 736-4465. Beth Van Schaack, Deputy.
Web, www.state.gov/j/gcj and Twitter, @StateDept_GCJ

Oversees U.S. stance on the creation of courts and other judicial mechanisms to bring perpetrators of crimes under international law to justice. Engages in diplomacy with foreign governments whose nationals have been captured in the war on terrorism. Has primary responsibility for policy on Iraqi war crimes.

State Dept., *Office of the Legal Adviser*, 2201 C St. N.W., #6421, 20520-6310; (202) 647-5036. Jennifer Gillian Newstead, Legal Adviser.
Web, www.state.gov/s/l

Provides the secretary and the department with legal advice on domestic and international problems; participates in international negotiations; represents the U.S. government in international litigation and in international conferences related to legal issues.

State Dept., *Office of the Legal Adviser, International Claims and Investment Disputes, 2430 E St. N.W., #203, 20520; (202) 776-8360. Fax, (202) 776-8389. Lisa J. Grosh, Assistant Legal Adviser, (202) 776-8325.*
Web, www.state.gov/s/l/c3433.htm

Handles claims by foreign governments and their nationals against the U.S. government, as well as claims against the State Dept. for negligence under the Federal Tort Claims Act. Administers the Iranian claims program and negotiates agreements with other foreign governments on claims settlements.

State Dept., *Office of the Legal Adviser, Law Enforcement and Intelligence, 2201 C St. N.W., #5419, 20520; (202) 647-5111. Fax, (202) 647-4802. Thomas B. Heinemann, Assistant Legal Adviser, (202) 647-5654.*
Web, www.state.gov

Negotiates extradition treaties, legal assistance treaties in criminal matters, and other agreements relating to international criminal matters.

State Dept., *Office of the Legal Adviser, Treaty Affairs, 2201 C St. N.W., #5420, 20520; (202) 647-1345. Fax, (202) 647-9844. Michael J. Mattler, Assistant Legal Adviser, (202) 647-1092.*
General email, treatyoffice@state.gov
Web, www.state.gov/s/l/treaty

Provides legal advice on treaties and other international agreements, including constitutional questions, drafting, negotiation, and interpretation of treaties; maintains records of treaties and executive agreements.

Transportation Dept. (DOT), *International Aviation, 1200 New Jersey Ave. S.E., #W86-316, 20590; (202) 366-2423. Fax, (202) 366-3694. Brian Hedberg, Director, (202) 366-7783.*
Web, www.transportation.gov/policy/aviation-policy/office-international-aviation

Responsible for international aviation regulation and negotiations, including fares, tariffs, and foreign licenses; represents the United States at international aviation meetings.

U.S. Coast Guard (USCG) *(Homeland Security Dept.), Law Enforcement, CG-MLE, 2703 Martin Luther King Jr. Ave. S.E., MS 7516, 20593-7516; (202) 372-2161. Capt. Timothy (Tim) Brown, Chief.*

Oversees enforcement of federal laws and treaties and other international agreements to which the United States is party on, over, and under the high seas and waters subject to the jurisdiction of the United States.

▶ **CONGRESS**

For a listing of relevant congressional committees and subcommittees, please see pages 474–475 or the Appendix.

▶ **INTERNATIONAL ORGANIZATIONS**

INTERPOL Washington *(Justice Dept.), 950 Pennsylvania Ave., 20530-0001; (202) 616-9000. Fax, (202) 616-8400. Wayne Salzgaber, Director.*
Web, www.justice.gov/interpol-washington, Twitter, @TheJusticeDept and Facebook, www.facebook.com/DOJ

U.S. representative to INTERPOL; participates in international investigations on behalf of U.S. police; coordinates the exchange of investigative information on crimes, including drug trafficking, counterfeiting, missing persons, and terrorism. Coordinates law enforcement requests for investigative assistance in the United States and abroad. Assists with extradition processes. Serves as liaison between foreign and U.S. law enforcement agencies at federal, state, and local levels. (Headquarters in Lyons, France.)

▶ **NONGOVERNMENTAL**

American Arbitration Assn., *Government Relations, 1120 Connecticut Ave. N.W., #490, 20036; S. Pierre Paret, Vice President. Toll-free, (800) 778-7879.*
Web, www.adr.org and Twitter, @adrorg

Provides dispute resolution services and information. Administers international arbitration and mediation systems. (Headquarters in New York.)

American Bar Assn. (ABA), *International Law, 1050 Connecticut Ave. N.W., 20036; (202) 662-1660. Fax, (202) 662-1669. Christina Heid, Section Director, (202) 662-1034. General email, intlaw@americanbar.org*
Web, www.americanbar.org/groups/international_law and Twitter, @ABInternatl

Monitors and makes recommendations concerning developments in the practice of international law that affect ABA members and the public. Conducts programs, including International Legal Exchange, and produces publications covering the practice of international law.

American Bar Assn. (ABA), *Rule of Law Initiative, 1050 Connecticut Ave. N.W., #450, 20036; (202) 662-1950. Fax, (202) 662-1597. Alberto Mora, Director. General email, rol@americanbar.org*
Web, www.americanbar.org/advocacy/rule_of_law.html, Twitter, @ABARuleofLaw and Facebook, www.facebook.com/ABA.Rule.of.Law.Initiative

Promotes the rule of law and specific legal reforms in developing countries throughout the world; recruits volunteer legal professionals from the United States and western Europe. Interests include human rights, anti-corruption initiatives, criminal law, efforts against human trafficking, judicial reform, legal education reform, civic education, reforming the legal profession, and women's rights.

American Society of International Law, *2223 Massachusetts Ave. N.W., 20008-2864; (202) 939-6001. Fax, (202) 797-7133. Mark D. Agrast, Executive Director. Library, (202) 939-6001.*
Web, www.asil.org and Twitter, @asilorg

U.S. Customs and Border Protection

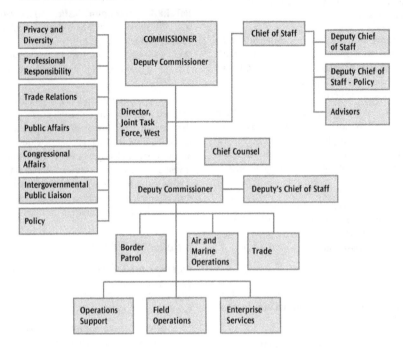

Membership: lawyers, academics, corporate counsel, judges, representatives of government and nongovernmental organizations, international civil servants, students, and others interested in international law. Conducts research and study programs on international law. Holds an annual meeting on current issues in international law. Library open to the public 9:00 a.m.–4:00 p.m.

Antarctic and Southern Ocean Coalition, *1320 19th St. N.W., 5th Floor, 20036; (202) 234-2480. Claire Christian, Executive Director.*
General email, secretariat@asoc.org
Web, www.asoc.org and Twitter, @AntarcticaSouth

Promotes effective implementation of the Antarctic Treaty System aimed at peaceful and free scientific research in the region.

Codex Alimentarius Commission, U.S. Codex Office, *1400 Independence Ave. S.W., South Bldg., #4861, 20250-3700; (202) 205-7760. Fax, (202) 720-3157. Mary Frances Lowe, U.S. Codex Manager; Paulo Almeida, U.S. Associate Manager. Meat and Poultry Hotline, (888) 674-6854. Toll-free TTY, (800) 877-8339.*
General email, uscodex@fsis.usda.gov
Web, www.fsis.usda.gov/codex and Twitter, @USDAFoodSafety

Operates within the Food and Agricultural Organization (FAO) and the World Health Organization (WHO) to establish international food and food safety standards and to ensure fair trade practices. Convenes committees in member countries to address specific commodities and issues, including labeling, additives in food and veterinary drugs, pesticide residues and other contaminants, and systems for food inspection. (Located in the USDA Food Safety and Inspection Service; international headquarters in Rome at the UN's Food and Agricultural Organization.)

Inter-American Bar Assn., *1889 F ST. N.W., #355, 20006; (202) 466-5944. Fax, (202) 466-5946.*
Ulises Montoya Alberti, Secretary General.
General email, iaba@iaba.org
Web, www.iaba.org and Twitter, @IABA_FIA

Membership: lawyers and bar associations in the Western Hemisphere with associate members in Europe. Works to promote uniformity of national and international laws; holds conferences; makes recommendations to national governments and organizations. Library open to the public by appointment only.

International Law Institute, *1055 Thomas Jefferson St. N.W., #M-100, 20007; (202) 247-6006. Fax, (202) 247-6010. Kim Phan, Executive Director.*
General email, info@ili.org
Web, www.ili.org

Performs scholarly research, offers training programs, and provides technical assistance in the areas of international law and economic development. Sponsors international conferences.

World Justice Project (WJP), *1025 Vermont Ave. N.W., #1200, 20005; (202) 407-9330. Fax, (202) 747-5816. Elizabeth Andersen, Executive Director.*
General email, wjp@worldjusticeproject.org
Web, www.worldjusticeproject.org and Twitter, @TheWJP

Supports the international rule of law in order to enforce civil and criminal justice, open government, and absence of corruption. Publishes journals and researches the rule of law and its influence on international economies and politics. Produces the annual Rule of Law Index, which measures countries' effectiveness at practicing the rule of law. Holds conferences and other outreach activities to advance practical solutions to strengthen the rule of law.

Americans Abroad

▶ AGENCIES

Bureau of Consular Affairs (CA) *(State Dept.),* 2201 C St. N.W., #6826, 20520-4818; (202) 647-9584. Fax, (202) 647-9622. Carl C. Risch, Assistant Secretary. Assistance to U.S citizens overseas, (888) 407-4747 in United States and Canada or (202) 501-4444 if overseas during business hours or (202) 647-4000 after hours. National Passport Information Center (fees are charged for calls to this number, (877) 487-2778 with credit card. Press, (202) 485-6150.
Web, https://travel.state.gov, Twitter, @TravelGov and Facebook, www.facebook.com/travelgov
Blog, https://blogs.state.gov

Issues passports to U.S. citizens and visas to immigrants and nonimmigrants seeking to enter the United States. Provides protection, assistance, and documentation for U.S. citizens abroad.

Bureau of Consular Affairs (CA) *(State Dept.), Children's Issues,* 2201 C. St. N.W., 9th Floor, #SA17, 20522-1709; Ted Coley, Director, (202) 485-6262. Phone (U.S. and Canada), (888) 407-4747. Phone (outside U.S.), (202) 501-4444. Abduction fax, (202) 485-6221. Prevention fax, (202) 485-6222.
General email, AskCI@state.gov
Web, http://travel.state.gov/content/childabduction/en.html
Abduction email, PreventAbduction1@state.gov

Assists with consular aspects of children's services and fulfills U.S. treaty obligations relating to the abduction of children. Advises foreign service posts on international parental child abduction and intercountry adoption.

Bureau of Consular Affairs (CA) *(State Dept.), Fraud Prevention,* 600 19th St. N.W., #8-206, 20522; (202) 485-6750. Brett Pomainville, Director, (202) 485-6754.
Web, https://travel.state.gov

Provides resources, tools, and information to consular officials in order to identify and prevent passport and visa fraud.

Bureau of Consular Affairs (CA) *(State Dept.), Overseas Citizens Services (OCS),* 600 19th St. N.W., 10th Floor, #SA17, 20006; (888) 407-4747. Fax, (202) 647-3732. Michelle Bernier-Toth, Managing Director, (202) 485-6046. Call Center, (888) 407-4747. From overseas, (202) 501-4444.
Web, http://travel.state.gov

Handles matters involving protective services for Americans abroad, including arrests, assistance in death cases, loans, medical emergencies, welfare and whereabouts

inquiries, travel warnings and consular information, nationality and citizenship determination, document issuance, judicial and notarial services, estates, property claims, third-country representation, and disaster assistance.

Bureau of Consular Affairs (CA) *(State Dept.), Overseas Citizens Services (OCS), Legal Affairs,* 600 19th St. N.W., #SA17A, 20037; (202) 485-6180. Fax, (202) 485-8033. Corrin Ferber, Director. Recorded consular information, (202) 647-5225. Toll-free, (888) 407-4747.
General email, ask-ocs-l-attyreplies@state.gov
Web, http://travel.state.gov

Offers guidance concerning the administration and enforcement of laws on citizenship and on the appropriate documentation of Americans traveling and residing abroad; gives advice on legislative matters, including implementation of new laws, and on treaties and agreements; reconsiders the acquisition and loss of U.S. citizenship in complex cases; and administers the overseas federal benefits program.

Bureau of Consular Affairs (CA) *(State Dept.), Passport Services,* 600 19 St. N.W., #6826, 20006; (202) 647-9584. Brenda Sprague, Deputy Assistant Secretary. National Passport Information Center, (877) 487-2778.
Web, https://travel.state.gov/content/passports/en/passports.html
National Passport Information Center, NPIC@state.gov

Creates passports and provides information and resources to citizens about how to obtain, replace, and change a U.S. passport.

Bureau of Consular Affairs (CA) *(State Dept.), Special Issuance Agency,* 600 19th St. N.W., #3.200, 20006; (202) 485-8244. Jennifer Walsh, Director. National Passport Information Center, (877) 487-2778.
Web, http://travel.state.gov

Maintains a variety of records received from the Overseas Citizens Services, including consular certificates of witness to marriage and reports of birth and death. (Individuals wishing to apply for a U.S. passport may seek additional information via the phone number or web address listed above.)

Foreign Claims Settlement Commission of the United States *(Justice Dept.),* 600 E St. N.W., #6002, 20579 (mailing address: 601 D St. N.W., #10300, Washington, DC 20579); (202) 616-6975. Fax, (202) 616-6993. Patrick Hovakimian, Commissioner; Sylvia Becker, Commissioner.
General email, info.fcsc@usdoj.gov
Web, www.justice.gov/fcsc

Processes claims by U.S. nationals against foreign governments for property losses sustained.

National Security Division *(Justice Dept.), Justice for Victims of Overseas Terrorism,* 950 Pennsylvania Ave. N.W., 20530; (202) 233-0701. Heather Cartwright, Director.
General email, nsd.ovt@usdoj.gov
Web, www.justice.gov/nsd-ovt

Monitors the investigation and prosecution of terrorist attacks against U.S. citizens abroad; works with other Justice Dept. offices to ensure that the rights of victims are respected.

State Dept., *Office of the Legal Adviser, International Claims and Investment Disputes*, *2430 E St. N.W., #203, 20520; (202) 776-8360. Fax, (202) 776-8389. Lisa J. Grosh, Assistant Legal Adviser, (202) 776-8325.*
Web, www.state.gov/s/l/c3433.htm

Handles claims by U.S. government and citizens against foreign governments; handles claims by owners of U.S. flag vessels for reimbursements of fines, fees, licenses, and other direct payments for illegal seizures by foreign governments in international waters under the Fishermen's Protective Act.

Boundaries

▶AGENCIES

Bureau of Western Hemisphere Affairs *(State Dept.)*, *Canadian Affairs*, *2201 C St. N.W., #3918, 20520; (202) 647-2170. Fax, (202) 647-4088. Cynthia Kierscht, Director.*
Web, www.state.gov/p/wha

Advises the secretary on Canadian affairs. Acts as liaison between the United States and Canada in international boundary and water matters as defined by binational treaties and agreements. Also involved with border health and environmental issues, political and defense cooperation, and economics and trade.

Bureau of Western Hemisphere Affairs *(State Dept.)*, *Mexican Affairs*, *2201 C St. N.W., #3924, 20520-6258; (202) 647-8766. Fax, (202) 647-5752. Colleen Hoey, Director, (202) 647-8186.*
Web, www.state.gov/p/wha

Advises the secretary on Mexican affairs. Acts as liaison between the United States and Mexico in international boundary and water matters as defined by binational treaties and agreements. Also involved with border health and environmental issues, new border crossings, and significant modifications to existing crossings.

Saint Lawrence Seaway Development Corp.
(Transportation Dept.), 1200 New Jersey Ave. S.E., #E311, 20590; (202) 366-0091. Fax, (202) 366-7147. Craig H. Middlebrook, Deputy Administrator.
Toll-free, (800) 785-2779.
General email, slsdc@dot.gov
Web, www.seaway.dot.gov

Operates and maintains the Saint Lawrence Seaway within U.S. territorial limits; conducts development programs and coordinates activities with its Canadian counterpart.

▶INTERNATIONAL ORGANIZATIONS

International Boundary Commission, *United States and Canada, U.S. Section*, *1717 H St. N.W., #845, 20006; (202)*

736-9100. Fax, (202) 254-0008. Kyle K. Hipsley, Commissioner, (202) 736-9102.
General email, hipsleyk@ibcusca.org
Web, www.internationalboundarycommission.org

Defines and maintains the international boundary line between the United States and Canada. Rules on applications for approval of projects affecting boundary or transboundary waters. Assists the United States and Canada in protecting the transboundary environment. Alerts the governments to emerging issues that may give rise to bilateral disputes. Jointly reports to the U.S. and Canadian governments on an annual basis. (Canadian section in Ottawa.)

International Joint Commission, *United States and Canada, U.S. Section*, *1717 H St. N.W., #801, 20440; (202) 736-9000. Fax, (202) 632-2006. Charles Lawson, Secretary; Frank Bevacqua, Public Information Officer, (202) 736-9024.*
General email, bevacquaf@washington.ijc.org
Web, www.ijc.org

Handles disputes concerning the use of boundary waters; negotiates questions dealing with the rights, obligations, and interests of the United States and Canada along the border; establishes procedures for the adjustment and settlement of questions. (Canadian section in Ottawa; Great Lakes regional office in Windsor, Ontario.)

Extradition and Prisoner Transfer

▶AGENCIES

Criminal Division *(Justice Dept.)*, *Enforcement Operations (OEO), International Prisoner Transfer Program*, *John C. Keeney Bldg., 1301 New York Ave. N.W., 10th Floor, 20005; (202) 514-3173. Fax, (202) 514-9003. Jennifer A.H. Hodge, Director of Enforcement Operations; Vaugn A Ary, Director of International Affairs.*
Web, www.justice.gov/criminal-oeo/international-prisoner-transfer-program

Implements prisoner transfer treaties with foreign countries.

Criminal Division *(Justice Dept.)*, *International Affairs (OIA)*, *1301 New York Ave. N.W., #800, 20005; (202) 514-0000. Fax, (202) 514-0080. Vaughn A. Ary, Director. Citizen phone line, (202) 353-4641.*
General email, criminal.division@usdoj.gov
Web, www.justice.gov/criminal-oia

Performs investigations necessary for extradition of fugitives from the United States and other nations. Handles U.S. and foreign government requests for mutual legal assistance, including documentary evidence.

State Dept., *Office of the Legal Adviser, Law Enforcement and Intelligence*, *2201 C St. N.W., #5419, 20520; (202) 647-5111. Fax, (202) 647-4802. Thomas B. Heinemann, Assistant Legal Adviser, (202) 647-5654.*
Web, www.state.gov

Negotiates and approves extradition of fugitives between the United States and other nations.

Fishing, Law of the Sea

►AGENCIES

Bureau of Oceans and International Environmental and Scientific Affairs (OES) *(State Dept.), Marine Conservation (OMC), 2201 C St. N.W., #2758, 20520;* (202) 647-2335. *William Gibbons-Fly, Director.*
Web, www.state.gov/e/oes/ocns/fish

Promotes food security through sustainable fisheries.

Bureau of Oceans and International Environmental and Scientific Affairs (OES) *(State Dept.), Oceans and Polar Affairs (OPA), 2201 C St. N.W., #2665, 20520;* (202) 647-3925. *Fax, (202) 647-4353. Evan T. Bloom, Director.*
Web, www.state.gov/e/oes/ocns/opa

Promotes U.S. interests in ocean and polar affairs through implementation of the Law of the Sea Convention, participation in international conferences, and negotiation of formal agreements.

National Oceanic and Atmospheric Administration (NOAA) *(Commerce Dept.), National Marine Fisheries Service (NMFS), 1315 East-West Hwy., 14th floor, Silver Spring, MD 20910; (301) 427-8000. Fax, (301) 713-1940. Chris Oliver, Assistant Administrator. Press, (301) 427-8003.*
Web, www.nmfs.noaa.gov and Twitter, @NOAAFisheries

Administers marine fishing regulations, including offshore fishing rights and international agreements.

U.S. Coast Guard (USCG) *(Homeland Security Dept.), Law Enforcement, CG-MLE, 2703 Martin Luther King Jr. Ave. S.E., MS 7516, 20593-7516; (202) 372-2161. Capt. Timothy (Tim) Brown, Chief.*

Enforces domestic fisheries laws and international fisheries agreements.

►CONGRESS

For a listing of relevant congressional committees and subcommittees, please see pages 474–475 or the Appendix.

Human Rights

►AGENCIES

Bureau of Democracy, Human Rights, and Labor (DRL) *(State Dept.), 2201 C St. N.W., #7827, 20520-7812; (202) 647-1337. Fax, (202) 647-5283. Marc Susser, Senior Advisor.*
Web, www.state.gov/j/drl, Twitter, @StateDRL and Facebook, www.facebook.com/StateDRL
Blog, https://blogs.state.gov/latest-stories

Implements U.S. policies relating to human rights, labor, and religious freedom; prepares annual review of human rights worldwide.

Bureau of Democracy, Human Rights, and Labor (DRL) *(State Dept.), International Labor Affairs (ILA), 1800 G St. N.W., #2422, 20006; (202) 663-3569. Stephen Moody, Director.*
Web, www.state.gov/j/drl/ila

Works with organized labor, nongovernmental organizations, international organizations, and corporations to monitor and promote worker rights throughout the world. Contributes to U.S. foreign policy goals related to democracy promotion, trade, development, and human rights.

Bureau of Democracy, Human Rights, and Labor (DRL) *(State Dept.), International Religious Freedom (IRF), 2201 C St. N.W., #2428, 20520; (202) 647-1237. Samuel D. Brownback, Ambassador at Large; Daniel L. Nadel, Director.*
Web, www.state.gov/j/drl/irf and Twitter, @State_IRF

Monitors religious persecution and discrimination worldwide, recommends and implements regional policies, and develops programs to promote religious freedom.

Bureau of Democracy, Human Rights, and Labor (DRL) *(State Dept.), Multilateral and Global Affairs (MLGA), Business and Human Rights Team (BHR), 2401 E St. N.W., 20037; (202) 663-3661. Jason A. Donovan, Director. General email, IFBHR@state.gov*
Web, www.state.gov/j/drl

Works with companies, nongovernmental organizations, and governments to provide corporate contributions to global prosperity while ensuring companies operate in a manner that protects against human rights abuses.

Bureau of International Organization Affairs (IO) *(State Dept.), Human Rights and Humanitarian Affairs (HRH), 2401 E St. N.W., #L409, 20037; (202) 663-1176. William Mozdzierz, Director.*
Web, www.state.gov/p/io

Works with UN bodies to advance U.S. policy relating to human rights, democracy promotion, humanitarian assistance, women's issues, indigenous issues, and social affairs.

Criminal Division *(Justice Dept.), Human Rights and Special Prosecutions (HRSP), John C. Keeney Bldg., 1301 New York Ave. N.W., #200, 20530; (202) 616-2492. Fax, (202) 616-2491. Teresa McHenry, Chief; Eli M. Rosenbaum, Director of Human Rights Enforcement Strategy and Policy.*
Web, www.justice.gov/criminal-hrsp

Tracks war criminals within the United States with connections to world genocidal conflicts; investigates and prosecutes human rights violators for torture, war crimes, recruitment or use of child soldiers, female genital mutilation, international antiquities trafficking, and immigration and naturalization fraud. Handles legal action to ensure denaturalization and/or deportation.

State Dept., *Global Women's Issues, 2201 C St. N.W., #7532, 20520; (202) 647-7285. Fax, (202) 647-7288. Rahima Kandahari, Director.*
Web, www.state.gov/s/gwi and Twitter, @GenderAtState

Works to promote the human rights of women within U.S. foreign policy. Participates in international organizations and conferences; advises other U.S. agencies; disseminates information.

State Dept., *Monitor and Combat Trafficking in Persons,* 2025 E St. N.W., #3054, 20520; (202) 453-8478. *Fax, (202) 312-9637. John C. Raymond, Ambassador. General email, tipoutreach@state.gov*

Web, www.state.gov/g/tip and Twitter, @JTIP_State

Combats trafficking in persons domestically and internationally. Publishes annual *Trafficking in Persons Report,* which assesses the progress of other governments, analyzes best practices and new data, and summarizes U.S. efforts to combat human trafficking at home. Funds programs that provide related law enforcement training, offer comprehensive victim services, and raise public awareness.

U.S. Commission on International Religious Freedom, 732 N. Capitol St. N.W., #A714, 20401; (202) 523-3240. *Fax, (202) 523-5020. Erin Singshinsuk, Executive Director. General email, media@uscirf.gov*

Web, www.uscirf.gov and Twitter, @USCIRF

Agency created by the International Religious Freedom Act of 1998 to monitor religious freedom worldwide and to advise the president, the secretary of state, and Congress on how best to promote it.

▶**CONGRESS**

For a listing of relevant congressional committees and subcommittees, please see pages 474–475 or the Appendix.

▶**NONGOVERNMENTAL**

American Bar Assn. (ABA), *Rule of Law Initiative,* 1050 *Connecticut Ave. N.W., #450, 20036; (202) 662-1950. Fax, (202) 662-1597. Alberto Mora, Director. General email, rol@americanbar.org*

Web, www.americanbar.org/advocacy/rule_of_law.html, Twitter, @ABARuleofLaw and Facebook, www.facebook.com/ABA.Rule.of.Law.Initiative

Promotes the rule of law and specific legal reforms in developing countries throughout the world; recruits volunteer legal professionals from the United States and western Europe. Interests include human rights, anti-corruption initiatives, criminal law, efforts against human trafficking, judicial reform, legal education reform, civic education, reforming the legal profession, and women's rights.

Amnesty International USA, *Washington National Office,* 600 Pennsylvania Ave. S.E., 5th Floor, 20003; (202) 544-0200. Fax, (202) 546-7142. Margaret Huang, Executive Director. Press, (202) 509-8194. Toll-free, 800-AMNESTY. *General email, aiusa@aiusa.org*

Web, www.amnestyusa.org and Twitter, @amnesty

International organization that investigates, exposes, and responds to human rights abuses. Works for the release of men and women imprisoned anywhere in the world for their beliefs, political affiliation, color, ethnic origin, sex, language, or religion, provided they have neither used nor advocated violence. Opposes torture and the death penalty; urges fair and prompt trials for all political prisoners. (U.S. headquarters in New York.)

Center for Human Rights and Humanitarian Law, 4300 *Nebraska Ave. N.W., 20016; (202) 274-4180. Macarena Saez, Director, (202) 274-4388. General email, humlaw@wcl.american.edu*

Web, www.wcl.american.edu/impact/initiatives-programs/center and Twitter, @humanrts

Seeks to promote human rights and humanitarian law. Establishes training programs for judges, lawyers, and law schools; assists emerging democracies and other nations in developing laws and institutions that protect human rights; organizes conferences with public and private institutions. (Affiliated with the Washington College of Law at American University.)

Center of Concern, 1627 K St. N.W., 11th Floor, 20006; *(202) 635-2757. Lester A. Myers, President, (202) 421-1181. General email, coc@coc.org*

Web, www.educationforjustice.org and Twitter, @CenterofConcern

Independent, interdisciplinary organization that conducts social analysis, theological reflection, policy advocacy, and public education on issues of international justice and peace from the perspective of a Catholic social tradition.

ChildFund International, *Washington Office,* 1200 18th *St. N.W., #718, 20036; (804) 756-2700. Fax, (202) 682-3481. Anne Lynam Goddard, President; Cheri Dahl, Executive Director, U.S. Programs. Toll-free, (800) 776-6767. General email, questions@childfund.org*

Web, www.childfund.org and Twitter, @ChildFund

Works internationally to ensure the survival, protection, and development of children. Promotes the improvement in quality of life of children within the context of family, community, and culture. Helps children in unstable situations brought on by war, natural disasters, and other high-risk circumstances. (Headquarters in Richmond, Va.)

FAIR Girls, 2021 L St. N.W., #254, 20036; (202) 520-9777. *Erin Andrews, Executive Director. Crisis hotline, (855) 900-3247. National trafficking hotline, (888) 373-7888. General email, info@fairgirls.org*

Web, www.fairgirls.org

Provides interventionist holistic care for survivors of trafficking who identify as girls or young women through prevention education and policy advocacy. Works to eradicate human trafficking and create improved outcomes for survivors.

Free the Slaves, 1320 19th St. N.W., #600, 20036; (202) *775-7480. Fax, (202) 775-7485. Alison Kiehl Friedman, Executive Director (Acting).*

General email, info@freetheslaves.net

Web, http://freetheslaves.net, Twitter, @FreeTheSlaves and Facebook, www.facebook.com/FreetheSlaves

Conducts field operations in India, Nepal, Haiti, Ghana, Congo, and Senegal to liberate slaves and help them rebuild their lives and advocacy initiatives in the United States and overseas to change the economic, legal, and social conditions that allow modern slavery to exist. Partners with governments, international institutions, faith communities, and the business community to engage their assistance in creating an enabling environment for antislavery projects. Develops new monitoring and evaluation methods to establish slavery prevalence and programmatic impact.

Genocide Watch *(George Mason University),* School of Conflict Analysis, 3351 N. Fairfax Dr., MS 4D3, Arlington, VA 22201; (703) 993-8749. Fax, (703) 993-1302. Gregory H. Stanton, Founding President. General email, president@genocidewatch.org

Web, www.genocidewatch.com and Twitter, @genocide_watch

Educates the public and policymakers about the causes, processes, and warning signs of genocide; seeks to create the institutions and the political will to prevent and stop genocide and to bring perpetrators of genocide to justice. (Coordinator of the Alliance Against Genocide.)

GoodWeave USA, *1111 14th St. N.W., #820, 20005; (202) 234-9050. Fax, (202) 234-9056. Nina Smith, Chief Executive Officer.* General email, info@goodweave.org

Web, www.goodweave.org and Twitter, @GoodWeave

International human rights organization working to end child labor in Indian, Nepalese, and Afghanistani global supply chains. Inspects and certifies workplace conditions. Runs schools and rehabilitation centers for former child workers.

Human Rights First, *Washington Office, 805 15th St. N.W., #900, 20005-2207; (202) 547-5692. Fax, (202) 543-5999. Michael Breen, President. Press, (202) 370-3319.* General email, press@humanrightsfirst.org

Web, www.humanrightsfirst.org, Twitter, @humanrights1st and Facebook, www.facebook .com/humanrightsfirst

Promotes human rights as guaranteed by the International Bill of Human Rights. Mobilizes activists and the legal community to pressure the U.S. government and private companies to respect human rights and rule of the law. Advocates American leadership to secure core freedoms worldwide.

Human Rights Watch, *Washington Office, 1630 Connecticut Ave. N.W., #500, 20009; (202) 612-4321. Fax, (202) 612-4333. Sarah Margon, Washington Director.* General email, hrwdc@hrw.org

Web, www.hrw.org/tag/washington-dc, Twitter, @hrw and Facebook, www.facebook.com/HumanRightsWatch

International, nonpartisan human rights organization that monitors human rights violations worldwide, subdivided into five regional concentrations—Africa, the Americas, Asia, Europe and Central Asia, and the Middle East and North Africa. Coordinates thematic projects on women's rights, LGBT rights, arms, children's rights, health and disability rights, business and human rights, counterterrorism, and international justice. Conducts fact-finding missions in more than 90 countries around the world; publicizes violations and encourages international protests; maintains file on human rights violations. (Headquarters in New York.)

International Assn. of Official Human Rights Agencies (IAOHRA), *444 N. Capitol St. N.W., #237, 20001; (202) 624-5410. Robin S. Toma, President, (213) 738-2788.* General email, iaohra@sso.org

Web, www.iaohra.org

Works with government and human rights agencies worldwide to promote civil and human rights, including elimination of unlawful discrimination in employment, housing, education, and public accommodations. Offers management training for human rights executives and civil rights workshops for criminal justice agencies; develops training programs in investigative techniques, settlement and conciliation, and legal theory. Serves as an information clearinghouse on human rights laws and enforcement.

International Justice Mission, *P.O. Box 58147, 20037-8147; (703) 465-5495. Fax, (703) 465-5499. Sean Litton, President.* General email, contact@ijm.org

Web, www.ijm.org

Seeks to help people suffering injustice and oppression who cannot rely on local authorities for relief. Documents and monitors conditions of abuse and oppression, educates churches and the public about abuses, and mobilizes intervention on behalf of victims.

Jubilee Campaign USA, *9689-C Main St., Fairfax, VA 22031; (703) 503-0791. Fax, (703) 503-0792. Ann Buwalda, Executive Director. Toll-free, (877) 654-4331.* General email, jubilee@jubileecampaign.org

Web, www.jubileecampaign.org

Promotes human rights and religious liberty for ethnic and religious minorities in countries that oppress them. Advocates the release of prisoners of conscience and revising laws to achieve this. Especially interested in ending the exploitation of children.

Physicians for Human Rights, *Washington Office, 1110 Vermont Ave. N.W., 5th Floor, 20005; (202) 728-5335. Fax, (202) 728-3053. Michael Payne, Senior Policy Associate; Donna McKay, Advocacy Officer.* General email, phrusa@phrusa.org

Web, www.physiciansforhumanrights.org and Twitter, @P4HR

Investigates and seeks to end human rights abuses. Issues reports and press releases; conducts training programs on health and human rights issues; acts as advocate before policymakers. (Headquarters in New York City.)

Polaris Project, *P.O. Box 65323, 20035; (202) 790-6300. Fax, (202) 745-1119. Bradley Myles, Chief Executive Officer. 24-hour hotline, (888) 373-7888.*
General email, info@polarisproject.org
Web, www.polarisproject.org and Twitter, @Polaris_Project

Fights human trafficking at the local, national, and international levels with an emphasis on policy advocacy and survivor support. Operates the 24-hour National Human Trafficking Resource Center Hotline for victims, law enforcement agencies, and others.

Robert F. Kennedy Human Rights, *1300 19th St. N.W., #750, 20036-1651; (202) 463-7575. Fax, (202) 463-6606. Kerry Kennedy, President. Media, (646) 809-0120.*
General email, communications@rfkhumanrights.org
Web, https://rfkhumanrights.org and
Twitter, @RFKHumanRights

Presents annual book, journalism, and human rights awards and carries out programs that support the work of the human rights award laureates in their countries. Investigates and reports on human rights; campaigns to heighten awareness of these issues, stop abuses, and encourage governments, international organizations, and corporations to adopt policies that ensure respect for human rights. Provides training for human rights advocates.

Torture Abolition and Survivors Support Coalition International (TASSC), *4121 Harewood Rd. N.E., Suite B, 20017-1597; (202) 529-2991. Fax, (202) 529-8334. Léonce Byimana, Executive Director.*
General email, info@tassc.org
Web, www.tassc.org and Twitter, @TASSCintl

Coalition of torture survivors seeking to end torture through public education and political advocacy. Provides resources and information to survivors of torture and their families.

U.S. Conference of Catholic Bishops (USCCB), *International Justice and Peace, 3211 4th St. N.E., 20017-1194; (202) 541-3160. Fax, (202) 541-3339. Lucas Koach, Director.*
General email, jphdmail@usccb.org
Web, www.usccb.org/about/international-justice-and-peace

Works with the U.S. State Dept., foreign government offices, and international organizations on issues of peace, justice, and human rights.

Narcotics Trafficking

▶**AGENCIES**

Bureau of International Narcotics and Law Enforcement Affairs (INL) *(State Dept.), 2201 C St. N.W., #7826, 20520-7512; (202) 647-8464.*
Kirsten Dawn Madison, Assistant Secretary.
Web, www.state.gov/j/inl, Twitter, @StateINL and Facebook, www.facebook.com/StateINL
Blog, https://blogs.state.gov/latest-stories?field_issues_tid=6373&field_region_tid=All&keys=&=Apply

Coordinates efforts to establish and facilitate stable criminal justice systems in order to strengthen international law enforcement and judicial effectiveness, bolster cooperation in legal affairs, and support the rule of law, while respecting human rights. Seeks to disrupt the overseas production and trafficking of illicit drugs by means of counterdrug and anticrime assistance and coordination with foreign nations and international organizations.

Defense Dept. (DoD), *Counternarcotics and Global Threats, 2500 Defense Pentagon, #5C653, 20301-2500; (703) 697-7202. Fax, (703) 692-6947. Thomas Alexander, Deputy Assistant Secretary.*
Web, http://policy.defense.gov/OUSDP-Offices/ASD-for-Special-Operations-Low-Intensity-Conflict/Counternarcotics-and-Global-Threats

Coordinates and monitors Defense Dept. support of civilian drug law enforcement agencies and interagency efforts to detect and monitor the maritime and aerial transit of illegal drugs into the United States. Represents the secretary on drug control matters outside the department.

Drug Enforcement Administration (DEA) *(Justice Dept.), 700 Army-Navy Dr., Arlington, VA 22202 (mailing address: 8701 Morrissette Dr., MS AES, Springfield, VA 22152); Fax, (202) 307-4540. Uttam Dhillon, Administrator (Acting). Phone (Command Center), (202) 307-8000. D.C. Division office, (202) 305-8500. General information, (202) 307-1000. Press, (202) 307-7977.*
Web, www.dea.gov

Assists foreign narcotics agents; cooperates with the State Dept., embassies, the Agency for International Development, and international organizations to strengthen narcotics law enforcement and to reduce supply and demand in developing countries; trains and advises narcotics enforcement officers in developing nations.

Internal Revenue Service (IRS) *(Treasury Dept.), Criminal Investigation, 1111 Constitution Ave. N.W., #2501, 20224; (202) 317-3200. Don Fort, Chief. Tax fraud hotline, (800) 829-0433.*
Web, www.irs.gov/uac/criminal-enforcement-1 and Twitter, @IRSnews

Lends support in counterterrorism and narcotics investigations conducted in conjunction with other law enforcement agencies, both foreign and domestic.

U.S. Coast Guard (USCG) *(Homeland Security Dept.), Law Enforcement, CG-MLE, 2703 Martin Luther King Jr. Ave. S.E., MS 7516, 20593-7516; (202) 372-2161. Capt. Timothy (Tim) Brown, Chief.*

Combats smuggling of narcotics and other drugs into the United States via the Atlantic and Pacific Oceans and the Gulf of Mexico. Works with U.S. Customs and Border Protection on drug law enforcement.

U.S. Customs and Border Protection *(Homeland Security Dept.), Border Patrol, 1300 Pennsylvania Ave. N.W., #6.5E, 20229; (202) 344-2050. Fax, (202) 344-3140. Carla L. Provost, Chief.*
Web, www.cbp.gov/border-security/along-us-borders/overview

International Trade Administration

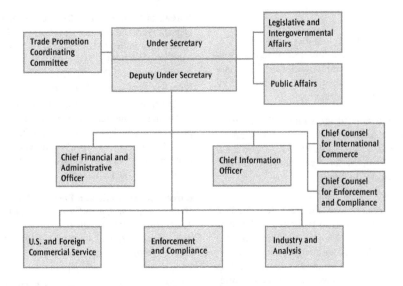

Mobile uniformed law enforcement arm of the Homeland Security Dept. Primary mission is to detect and prevent the illegal trafficking of people and contraband across U.S. borders.

U.S. Customs and Border Protection *(Homeland Security Dept.)*, **Field Operations**, *1300 Pennsylvania Ave. N.W., #2.4A, 20229; (202) 344-1620. Fax, (202) 344-2777. Todd Owen, Executive Assistant Commissioner. Press, (202) 344-1700.*
Web, www.cbp.gov/border-security/ports-entry

Interdicts and seizes contraband, including narcotics and other drugs, at the U.S. border.

U.S. Immigration and Customs Enforcement (ICE) *(Homeland Security Dept.),* 500 12th St. S.W., 20536; (202) 732-3000. Fax, (202) 732-3080. Ronald D. Vitiello, Director (Acting). Hotline to report suspicious activity, (866) 347-2423. Press, (202) 732-4242. TTY, (802) 872-6196.*
Web, www.ice.gov and Twitter, @ICEgov

Investigates narcotics smuggling, including money laundering, document and identity fraud, and immigration enforcement; interdicts flow of narcotics into the United States.

INTERNATIONAL TRADE AND DEVELOPMENT

General

▶ **AGENCIES**

Agriculture Dept. (USDA), *Under Secretary for Trade and Foreign Agricultural Affairs,* 1400 Independence Ave.

S.W., MS 1001, 20250; (202) 720-3935. Ted McKinney, Under Secretary.
Web, www.fas.usda.gov

Leads on trade policy and international agriculture issues domestically and abroad; facilitates foreign market access and promotes opportunities for U.S. agriculture through trade programs and high-level government negotiations. Oversees the Foreign Agricultural Service.

Alcohol and Tobacco Tax and Trade Bureau (TTB) *(Treasury Dept.),* **International Affairs Division,** *1310 G St. N.W., #400W, 20005; (202) 453-2260. Fax, (202) 453-2970. Karen E. Welch, Director.*
General email, itd@ttb.gov

Web, www.ttb.gov/offices/iad.shtml

Works with the Office of the United States Trade Representative and federal executive departments to facilitate the import/export trade in beverage and industrial alcohol. Coordinates briefings and other liaison activities for foreign alcohol and tobacco industry members and foreign government officials.

Antitrust Division *(Justice Dept.),* **International,** *450 5th St. N.W., #1100, 20530; (202) 514-5816. Fax, (202) 514-4508. Lynda K. Marshall, Chief.*
Web, www.justice.gov/atr

Acts as the division's liaison with foreign governments and international organizations, including the European Union, regarding antitrust enforcement and competition issues. Works with the State Dept. to exchange information with foreign governments concerning investigations involving foreign corporations and nationals.

Bureau of Economic and Business Affairs (EB) *(State Dept.),* 2201 C St. N.W., #4932, 20520-5820; (202) 647-7971. Fax, (202) 647-5713. Manisha Singh, Assistant Secretary.

Web, www.state.gov/e/eb, Twitter, @EconAtState and *Facebook, www.facebook.com/EconAtState*

Blog, https://blogs.state.gov/issues/economic-and-business-issues

Formulates and implements policies related to U.S. economic relations with foreign countries, including international business practices, communications and information, trade, finance, investment, development, natural resources, energy, and transportation.

Bureau of Economic and Business Affairs (EB) *(State Dept.), Commercial and Business Affairs (CBA),* 2201 C St. N.W., #5820, 20520-5820; (202) 647-1625. Fax, (202) 647-3953. Scott Ticknor, Special Representative (Acting).
General email, cbaweb@state.gov

Web, www.state.gov/e/eb/cba

Serves as primary contact in the State Dept. for U.S. businesses. Coordinates efforts to facilitate U.S. business interests abroad, ensures that U.S. business interests are given sufficient consideration in foreign policy, and provides assistance to firms with problems overseas (such as claims and trade complaints). Oversees the Global Entrepreneurship Program.

Bureau of Economic and Business Affairs (EB) *(State Dept.), Counter Threat Finance and Sanctions (TFS),* 2201 C St. N.W., #4657, 20520; (202) 647-7677. David Meale, Deputy Assistant Secretary (Acting).
Web, www.state.gov/e/eb/tfs

Coordinates efforts to create, modify, or terminate unilateral sanctions regimes on countries such as such as Iran, Syria, and Cuba as appropriate to the changing international situation; builds international support for combating terrorist finance; provides foreign policy guidance to the Treasury and Commerce Depts. on specific commercial business, export, import, and general licensing issues.

Bureau of Economic and Business Affairs (EB) *(State Dept.), Counter Threat Finance and Sanctions (TFS), Sanctions Policy and Implementation (SPI),* 2201 C St. N.W., #4657, 20520; (202) 647-7489. Fax, (202) 647-4064. David Meale, Director.
Web, www.state.gov/e/eb/tfs/spi

Develops and implements U.S. economic sanctions of embargoed countries. Coordinates U.S. participation in multilateral strategic trade control and revisions related to the export of strategically critical high-technology goods. Cooperates with the Commerce, Defense, and Treasury Depts. regarding export controls.

Bureau of Economic and Business Affairs (EB) *(State Dept.), Trade Policy and Negotiations (TPN),* 2201 C St. N.W., #4652, 20520-5820; (202) 647-5991. Peter D. Haas, Deputy Assistant Secretary (Acting).
General email, ebtpn@state.gov

Web, www.state.gov/e/eb/tpn

Develops and administers policies and programs on international trade, including trade negotiations and agreements, import relief, unfair trade practices, trade relations with developing countries, export development, and export controls (including controls imposed for national security or foreign policy purposes).

Bureau of Economic and Business Affairs (EB) *(State Dept.), Trade Policy and Negotiations (TPN), Agriculture Policy (AGP),* 2201 C St. N.W., #4686, 20520-0002; (202) 647-3090. Fax, (202) 647-1894. Patrick M. Dunn, Director, (202) 647-0133.
Web, www.state.gov/e/eb/tpn/agp

Develops agricultural trade policy; handles questions pertaining to international negotiations on all agricultural products covered by the World Trade Organization (WTO) and bilateral trade agreements. Oversees the distribution of biotechnology outreach funds to promote international acceptance of the technology.

Bureau of Economic and Business Affairs (EB) *(State Dept.), Trade Policy and Programs (TPP), Bilateral Trade Affairs (BTA),* 2201 C St. N.W., #4452, 20520; (202) 647-3784. Fax, (202) 647-6540. Robert D. Manogue, Director, (202) 647-4017.
Web, www.state.gov/e/eb/tpn/bta

Develops, negotiates, and implements free trade agreements, trade and investment framework agreements, and trade preference programs.

Bureau of Economic and Business Affairs (EB) *(State Dept.), Trade Policy and Programs (TPP), Multilateral Trade Affairs (MTA),* 2201 C St. N.W., #4725, Washington, DC; (202) 647-6324. Fax, (202) 647-0892. Amy E. Holman, Director.
Web, www.state.gov/e/eb/tpn/mta

Leads the State Dept. trade policy activities in multilateral institutions, including the World Trade Organization, World Customs Organization, and Organization for Economic Cooperation and Development. Provides technical expertise in regional and bilateral trade negotiations, including labor, environment, services, government procurement, customs, trade remedies and enforcement, textiles, standards, regulatory cooperation, and trade capacity building.

Bureau of Economic and Business Affairs (EB) *(State Dept.), Transportation Affairs (TRA),* 2201 C St. N.W., #3425, 20520-5820; (202) 647-4045. Hugo Y. Yon, Deputy Assistant Secretary (Acting).
Web, www.state.gov/e/eb/tra

Supports the U.S. global transportation industry; negotiates international air services agreements; works with other departments on safe transportation infrastructure policies. Oversees the offices of Aviation Negotiations and Transportation Policy.

Bureau of Industry and Security (BIS) *(Commerce Dept.),* 14th St. and Constitution Ave. N.W., #3898, 20230; (202) 482-1455. Daniel O. Hill, Deputy Under Secretary (Acting). Export licensing information, (202) 482-4811. Press, (202) 482-2721.
Web, www.bis.doc.gov and Twitter, @BISgov

Administers the Export Administration Act; coordinates export administration programs of federal departments and agencies; maintains control lists and performs export licensing for the purposes of national security, foreign policy, and short supply. Monitors impact of foreign boycotts on the United States; ensures availability of goods and services essential to industrial performance on contracts for national defense. Assesses availability of foreign products and technology to maintain control lists and licensing.

Census Bureau *(Commerce Dept.)*, **International Trade Management,** *4600 Silver Hill Rd., #5K158, Suitland, MD 20746 (mailing address: 4600 Silver Hill Rd., #6K032, Washington, DC 20233-6700); (301) 763-6937. Fax, (301) 763-6638. Dale C. Kelly, Chief. International trade helpline, (800) 549-0595.*
Web, www.census.gov/foreign-trade/index.html

Provides data on all aspects of foreign trade in commodities. Compiles information for 240 trading partners, including China, Japan, and Mexico, through all U.S. states and ports. Publishes the monthly economic indicator, U.S. International Trade in Goods and Services, in conjunction with the U.S. Bureau of Economic Analysis.

Federal Maritime Commission (FMC), *International Affairs, 800 N. Capitol St. N.W., 20573-0001; (202) 523-5725. Fax, (202) 523-0014. Michael A. Khouri, Chair (Acting); Karen V. Gregory, Managing Director. Library, (202) 523-5762. TTY, (800) 877-8339.*
General email, inquiries@fmc.gov
Web, www.fmc.gov and Twitter, @FMC_gov

Regulates the foreign ocean shipping of the United States; reviews agreements (on rates, services, and other matters) filed by ocean common carriers for compliance with shipping statutes and grants limited antitrust immunity. Monitors the laws and practices of foreign governments that could have a discriminatory or otherwise adverse impact on shipping conditions in the United States. Enforces special regulatory requirements applicable to ocean common carriers owned or controlled by foreign governments (controlled carriers). Adjudicates claims filed by regulated entities and the shipping public. Library open to the public (Monday–Friday, 8:00 a.m.–4:30 p.m.).

Federal Trade Commission (FTC), *International Affairs, 600 Pennsylvania Ave. N.W., #H494, 20580; (202) 326-2600. Fax, (202) 326-2873. Randolph W. Tritell, Director, (202) 326-3051.*
Web, www.ftc.gov/about-ftc/bureaus-offices/office-international-affairs

Assists in the enforcement of antitrust laws and consumer protection by arranging appropriate cooperation and coordination with foreign governments in international cases. Negotiates bilateral and multilateral antitrust and consumer protection agreements and represents the United States in international antitrust policy forums. Assists developing countries in moving toward market-based economies.

Foreign Agricultural Service (FAS) *(Agriculture Dept.), 1400 Independence Ave. S.W., #5071S, MS 1001, 20250-1001; (202) 720-3935. Fax, (202) 690-2159. Kenneth Isley,*

Administrator. Public Affairs, (202) 720-7115. TTY, (202) 720-1786.
Web, www.fas.usda.gov and Twitter, @USDAForeignAg

Expands and maintains access to foreign markets for U.S. agricultural products by removing trade barriers and enforcing U.S. rights under existing trade agreements. Works with foreign governments, international organizations, and the Office of the U.S. Trade Representative to establish international standards and rules to improve accountability and predictability for agricultural trade.

International Trade Administration (ITA) *(Commerce Dept.), 1401 Constitution Ave. N.W., #3850, 20230; (202) 482-2867. Gilbert B. Kaplan, Under Secretary. Trade information, (800) 872-8723.*
Web, www.trade.gov

Seeks to strengthen the competitiveness of U.S. industry, promote trade and investment, and ensure fair trade and compliance with trade law and agreements.

International Trade Administration (ITA) *(Commerce Dept.), Enforcement and Compliance (E&C), 1401 Constitution Ave. N.W., #3099B, 20230; (202) 482-1780. Fax, (202) 482-0947. Gary Taverman, Assistant Secretary (Acting); Christian Marsh, Deputy Assistant Secretary. Communications, (202) 482-0063.*
General email, ECcommunications@trade.gov
Web, http://trade.gov/enforcement

Safeguards and enhances the competitive strength of U.S. industries against unfair trade through the enforcement of U.S. antidumping duty (AD) and countervailing duty (CVD) trade laws and ensures compliance with trade agreements negotiated on behalf of U.S. industries. Promotes the creation and maintenance of U.S. jobs and economic growth by supporting the negotiation of international trade agreements to open foreign markets. Administers the Foreign Trade Zones program and certain sector-specific agreements and programs, such as the Steel Import Monitoring and Analysis licensing program.

International Trade Administration (ITA) *(Commerce Dept.), Global Markets, 1401 Constitution Ave. N.W., Room 38006, 20230; (202) 482-5777. Fax, (202) 482-5444. Ian Steff, Assistant Secretary; Holly Vineyard, Deputy Assistant Secretary, (202) 482-4651.*
Web, www.trade.gov/markets

Develops and implements trade and investment policies affecting countries, regions, or international organizations to improve U.S. market access abroad. Provides information and analyses of foreign market barriers and economic conditions to the U.S. private sector; monitors foreign compliance with trade agreements signed with the United States.

International Trade Administration (ITA) *(Commerce Dept.), Global Markets, North and Central America, 1401 Constitution Ave. N.W., Room 30013, #3826, 20230; (202) 482-6452. Fax, (202) 482-5013. Geri Word, Director.*
Web, www.trade.gov/markets

Coordinates Commerce Dept. activities and assists U.S. business regarding export to Mexico, Canada, Central

America, and the Caribbean. Helps negotiate and ensures compliance with U.S. free trade agreements, including NAFTA (North American Free Trade Agreement) and the Dominican Republic–Central American Free Trade Agreement (CAFTA-DR).

International Trade Administration (ITA) *(Commerce Dept.), Global Markets, SelectUSA, 1401 Constitution Ave. N.W., Room 1235, MC3128, 20230-0001; (202) 482-0829. Fax, (202) 482-3643. Brian Lenihan, Deputy Director. Call Center, (202) 482-6800.*
General email, info@selectusa.gov
Web, http://selectusa.gov

Manages foreign direct investment promotion and encourages U.S. companies to expand, add new facilities, and bring back jobs from abroad. Facilitates investor inquiries, conducts outreach to foreign investors, provides support for state and local governments' investment promotion efforts, and serves as an ombudsman in Washington, DC, for the international investment community. Website available in eight languages.

International Trade Administration (ITA) *(Commerce Dept.), Global Markets, U.S. and Foreign Commercial Service, 1401 Constitution Ave. N.W., Room 38006, 20230; (202) 482-5777. Dale Tasharski, Deputy Director General (Acting).*
Web, www.trade.gov/cs

Promotes the export of U.S. goods and services; protects and advocates U.S. business interests abroad; provides counseling and information on overseas markets, international contacts, and trade promotion.

International Trade Administration (ITA) *(Commerce Dept.), Industry and Analysis (I&A), 1401 Constitution Ave. N.W., #2854, 20230; (202) 482-1461. Fax, (202) 482-5697. James Sullivan, Assistant Secretary (Acting); Anne Driscoll, Deputy Assistant Secretary.*
Web, www.trade.gov/industry

Seeks to strengthen the international competitiveness of U.S. businesses; coordinates export promotion programs and trade missions; compiles and analyzes trade data. Divisions focus on basic industries, service industries and finance, technology and aerospace, consumer goods, tourism, and environmental technologies exports.

International Trade Administration (ITA) *(Commerce Dept.), Industry and Analysis (I&A), National Travel and Tourism (NTTO), 1401 Constitution Ave. N.W., #10003, 20230-0001; (202) 482-0140. Fax, (202) 482-2887. Isabel Hill, Executive Director, (202) 482-5120.*
General email, ntto@trade.gov
Web, http://travel.trade.gov

Fosters international tourism trade development, including public-private partnerships; represents the United States in tourism-related meetings with foreign government officials. Assembles, analyzes, and disseminates data and statistics on travel and tourism to and from the United States.

International Trade Administration (ITA) *(Commerce Dept.), Industry and Analysis (I&A), Trade Policy and Analysis (OTNA), 1401 Constitution Ave. N.W., #21028, 20230; (202) 482-3177. Fax, (202) 482-4614. Praveen Dixit, Deputy Assistant Secretary, (202) 482-3177.*
Web, www.trade.gov/mas/ian/index.asp

Monitors and analyzes U.S. international trade and competitive performance, foreign direct investment in the United States, and international economic factors affecting U.S. trade; identifies future trends and problems.

International Trade Administration (ITA) *(Commerce Dept.), Industry and Analysis (I&A), Trade Promotion Programs and Strategic Partnerships, 1401 Constitution Ave. N.W., #800-RRB, 20230; (202) 482-5927. Fax, (202) 482-7800. Anne Grey, Executive Director of Trade Promotion Programs, (202) 482-5927; Jamie Merriman, Director of Strategic Partnerships.*
General email, partners@trade.gov
Web, http://2016.export.gov/strategicpartnerships

Supports the entry of U.S. industries into new markets by establishing domestic forums to showcase U.S. goods for foreign purchasers through the International Buy Program (IBP), and certifying international forums to connect U.S. exporters with overseas clients through the Trade Fair Certification Program. Creates opportunities for U.S. firms to meet on a one-to-one basis with foreign industry executives and government officials to establish sales channels through the Trade Missions Program. The Strategic Partnership Program works in conjunction with private corporations, trade associations, and educational institutions to leverage combined resources to further U.S. exports.

National Institute of Food and Agriculture (NIFA) *(Agriculture Dept.), Center for International Programs, 800 9th St. S.W., #2436, 20024 (mailing address: 1400 Independence Ave. S.W., MS 2203, Washington, DC 20250-2203); (202) 720-3801. Fax, (202) 690-2355. Otto Gonzalez, Director.*
Web, https://nifa.usda.gov/office/center-international-programs

Promotes science education in developing economies and shares research to enhance food production and stabilize economies. Interests include agricultural extension, teaching, and research.

National Institute of Standards and Technology (NIST) *(Commerce Dept.), Standards Services, 100 Bureau Dr., MS 2100, Gaithersburg, MD 20899; (301) 975-4000. Fax, (301) 975-4715. Gordon Gillerman, Director, (301) 975-8406.*
General email, sco@nist.gov
Web, www.nist.gov/standardsgov and www.nist.gov/topics/standards

Monitors and participates in industries' development of federal and global standards and standard-enforcement mechanisms. Conducts standards-related research and training and holds workshops for domestic and international audiences. Provides information on industry standards and specifications, conformity assessment, test methods, domestic and international technical regulations, codes, and recommended practices.

President's Export Council *(Commerce Dept.), 1401 Constitution Ave. N.W., #4043, 20230; (202) 482-1124. Fax, (202) 482-4452. Israel Hernandez, Executive Director (Acting); Ian Steff, Assistant Secretary for Global Markets (Acting).*
Web, www.trade.gov/pec

Advises the president on all aspects of export trade, including export controls, promotion, and expansion. Composed of up to 28 private-sector leaders in business, agriculture, and federal, state, and local government.

Small Business Administration (SBA), *International Trade, 409 3rd St. S.W., #2400, 20416; (202) 205-6720. Fax, (202) 205-7272. Peter J. Cazamias Jr., Associate Administrator. TTY, (800) 877-8339.*
Web, www.sba.gov/offices/headquarters/oit

Offers instruction, assistance, and information on exporting through counseling and conferences. Helps businesses gain access to export financing through loan guarantee programs.

State Dept., *Under Secretary for Economic Growth, Energy, and the Environment, 2201 C St. N.W., #7256, 20520-7512; (202) 647-7575. Fax, (202) 647-0675. Manisha Sing, Under Secretary, (202) 647-7674; Vacant, Executive Assistant.*
Web, www.state.gov/e

Advises the secretary on formulation and implementation of international economic policies and programs, including international monetary and financial affairs, trade, telecommunications, energy, agriculture, commodities, investments, and international transportation issues. Coordinates economic summit meetings. Oversees the Bureau of Economic and Business Affairs, Bureau of Energy Resources, Bureau of Oceans and International Environmental and Scientific Affairs, Office of the Chief Economist, and Office of the Science and Technology Adviser.

Trade Promotion Coordinating Committee, *14th St. and Constitution Ave. N.W., #31027, 20230; (202) 482-5455. Fax, (202) 482-4137. Wilbur L. Ross, Secretary of Commerce; Patrick Kirwan, Director.*
Web, http://2016.export.gov/advocacy/eg_main_022762. asp and Twitter, @ExportGov

Coordinates all export promotion and export financing activities of the U.S. government. Composed of heads of the departments of Commerce, State, Treasury, Defense, Homeland Security, Interior, Agriculture, Labor, Transportation, and Energy, OMB, U.S. Trade Representative, National Security Council/National Economic Council, EPA, Small Business Administration, AID, Export-Import Bank, Overseas Private Investment Corporation, and the U.S. Trade and Development Agency. Secretary of Commerce is the chair.

Treasury Dept., *International Affairs, International Trade, 1500 Pennsylvania Ave. N.W., #5204, 20220; (202)* 622-2000. Fax, (202) 622-1731. Lailee Moghtader, Director, (202) 622-1819.
Web, www.treasury.gov/about/organizational-structure/ offices/International-Affairs/Pages/trade.aspx

Formulates Treasury Dept. foreign trade policies and coordinates them with other agencies through the U.S. Trade Representative.

Treasury Dept., *Terrorism and Financial Intelligence, Foreign Assets Control, 1500 Pennsylvania Ave. N.W., Treasury Annex, 20220; (202) 622-2490. Fax, (202) 622-1657. Andrea E. Gacki, Director. Hotline, (800) 540-6322. Licensing Division, (202) 622-2480.*
General email, ofac_feedback@do.treas.gov
Web, www.treasury.gov/about/organizational-structure/ offices/Pages/Office-of-Foreign-Assets-Control.aspx

Administers and enforces economic and trade sanctions against targeted foreign countries and regimes, terrorists, international narcotics traffickers, transnational criminal organizations, and those engaged in activities related to the proliferation of weapons of mass destruction. Acts under presidential wartime and national emergency powers, as well as under authority granted by specific legislation, to impose controls on transactions and freeze foreign assets under U.S. jurisdiction.

U.S. Customs and Border Protection *(Homeland Security Dept.), 1300 Pennsylvania Ave. N.W., #4.4A, 20229; (202) 325-8000. Fax, (202) 344-1380. Kevin K. McAleenan, Commissioner. Information, (877) 227-5511. Press, (202) 344-1700. TTY, (800) 877-8339.*
Web, www.cbp.gov and Twitter, @cbp

Collects import and export data for international trade statistics. Library open to the public by appointment.

U.S. Customs and Border Protection *(Homeland Security Dept.), Commercial Targeting and Analysis Center, 1300 Pennsylvania Ave. N.W., 20229; (202) 325-6586. Christopher Robertson, Branch Chief.*
General email, ctac@cdp.dhs.gov
Web, www.cbp.gov

Facilitates information sharing among participating government agencies to prevent, deter, interdict, and investigate violations of U.S. import and export laws.

U.S. Foreign Trade Zones Board *(Commerce Dept.), 1401 Constitution Ave. N.W., #21013, 20230; (202) 482-2862. Fax, (202) 482-0002. Andrew McGilvray, Executive Secretary.*
Web, www.trade.gov/ftz

Authorizes public and private corporations to establish foreign trade zones to which foreign and domestic goods can be brought without being subject to customs duties.

U.S. International Trade Commission, *500 E St. S.W., 20436; (202) 205-2000. Fax, (202) 708-2431. David S. Johanson, Chair. Press, (202) 205-1819. Reference Library, (202) 205-2630. TTY, (202) 205-1810.*
Web, www.usitc.gov

Provides Congress, the president, and the U.S. trade representative with technical information and advice on trade and tariff matters. Determines the impact of imports on U.S. industries in antidumping and countervailing duty investigations. Directs actions against certain unfair trade practices, such as intellectual property infringement. Investigates and reports on U.S. industries and the global trends that affect them. Publishes the Harmonized Tariff Schedule of the United States. Library open to the public.

U.S. International Trade Commission, *Industries, 500 E St. S.W., #504-A, 20436; (202) 205-3296. Fax, (202) 205-3161. Jonathon R. Coleman, Director, (202) 205-3380. Web, www.usitc.gov/research_and_analysis/office_industry.htm*

Identifies, analyzes, and develops data on economic and technical matters related to the competitive position of the United States in domestic and world markets in agriculture and forest production, chemicals, textiles, energy, electronics, transportation, services and investments, minerals, metals, and machinery.

U.S. Trade and Development Agency, *1101 Wilson Blvd., #1100, Arlington, VA 22209-3901; (703) 875-4357. Fax, (703) 875-4009. Thomas R. Hardy, Director (Acting). General email, info@ustda.gov*

Web, www.ustda.gov and Twitter, @USTDA

Assists U.S. companies exporting to developing and middle-income countries. Provides grants for feasibility studies. Offers technical assistance and identifies commercial opportunities in these countries.

U.S. Trade Representative *(Executive Office of the President), 600 17th St. N.W., #205, 20508; (202) 395-6890. Fax, (202) 395-4656. Amb. Robert E. Lighthizer, U.S. Trade Representative. Press, (202) 395-3230. General email, correspondence@ustr.eop.gov*

Web, www.ustr.gov

Serves as principal adviser to the president and primary trade negotiator on international trade policy. Develops and coordinates U.S. trade policy, including commodity and direct investment matters, import remedies, East-West trade policy, U.S. export expansion policy, and the implementation of MTN (Multilateral Trade Negotiations) agreements. Conducts international trade negotiations and represents the United States in World Trade Organization (WTO) matters.

U.S. Trade Representative *(Executive Office of the President), Intergovernmental Affairs and Public Engagement (IAPE), 600 17th St. N.W., #107, 20508; (202) 395-2870. Fax, (202) 395-4656. Vacant, Assistant U.S. Trade Representative. General email, IAPE@ustr.eop.gov*

Web, www.ustr.gov/about-us/policy-offices/intergovernmental-affairs

Leads the U.S. Trade Representative's public outreach efforts to state and local governments; business and agricultural communities; and labor, environmental, and consumer groups. Oversees the U.S. Trade Advisory Committee system.

▶CONGRESS

For a listing of relevant congressional committees and subcommittees, please see pages 474–475 or the Appendix.

Government Accountability Office (GAO), *International Affairs and Trade (IAT), 441 G St. N.W., #4T21, 20548; (202) 512-4128. Thomas Melito, Managing Director. Web, www.gao.gov/careers/iat.html*

Audits, analyzes, and evaluates international programs and trade; evaluates economic, political, and security problems worldwide. In addition to federal departments, oversight work includes U.S. Agency for International Development, Office of the U.S. Trade Representative, Broadcasting Board of Governors, North Atlantic Treaty Organization, World Bank, International Monetary Fund, and United Nations.

▶JUDICIARY

U.S. Court of Appeals for the Federal Circuit, *717 Madison Pl. N.W., 20439; (202) 275-8000. Fax, (202) 275-9678. Sharon Prost, Chief Judge; Peter R. Marksteiner, Clerk of the Court, (202) 272-8020. Mediation, (202) 275-8120. Web, www.cafc.uscourts.gov*

Reviews decisions concerning the International Trade Commission.

▶INTERNATIONAL ORGANIZATIONS

European Union, *Delegation to the United States of America, 2175 K St. N.W., 20037; (202) 862-9500. Fax, (202) 429-1766. David O'Sullivan, Ambassador. General email, delegation-usa-info@eeas.europa.eu*

Web, www.euintheus.org and Twitter, @EUintheUS

Information and public affairs office in the United States for the European Union. Advances transatlantic trade policies and direct foreign investment; negotiates the Transatlantic Trade and Investment Partnership (TTIP). (Headquarters in Brussels.)

Food and Agriculture Organization of the United Nations (FAO), *Washington Office, 2121 K St. N.W., #800B, 20037-0001; (202) 653-2400. Fax, (202) 653-5760. Vimlendra Sharan, Director. General email, faolow@fao.org*

Web, www.fao.org/north-america/en, Twitter, @FAONorthAmerica and Facebook, www.facebook.com/UNFAO

Offers development assistance; collects, analyzes, and disseminates information; provides policy and planning advice to governments; acts as an international forum for debate on food and agricultural issues, including animal health and production, fisheries, and forestry; encourages sustainable agricultural development and a long-term strategy for the conservation and management of natural resources. Coordinates World Food Day. (International headquarters in Rome.)

International Economic Development Council, *734 15th St. N.W., #900, 20005; (202) 223-7800. Fax, (202) 223-4745. Jeffrey Finkle, President; Tanner Bokor, Press Director, (202) 639-9104. Press, (202) 639-9104.*
General email, mail@iedconline.org

Web, www.iedconline.org, Twitter, @IEDCtweets and Facebook, www.facebook.com/iedcONLINE

Membership: public economic development directors, chamber of commerce staff, utility executives, academicians, and others who design and implement development programs. Provides information to members on job creation, attraction, and retention.

Organisation for Economic Co-operation and Development (OECD), *Washington Center, 1776 Eye St. N.W., #450, 20006; (202) 785-6323. Fax, (202) 315-2508. Will Davis, Head of Center, (202) 822-3869.*
General email, washington.contact@oecd.org

Web, www.oecd.org/washington and Twitter, @oced_washington

Membership: thirty-four nations, including Australia, Canada, Japan, Mexico, New Zealand, the United States, and western European nations. Funded by membership contributions. Serves as a forum for members to exchange information and coordinate their economic policies; compiles statistics. Washington Center sells OECD publications and software; maintains a reference library that is open to the public. (Headquarters in Paris.)

Organization of American States (OAS), *Economic Development, 1889 F St. N.W., #750, 20006; (202) 370-9953. Fax, (202) 458-3561. Maryse Robert, Director.*
General email, mrobert@oas.org

Web, www.oas.org/en/sedi/desd

Responsible for matters related to economic development in the hemisphere, with a focus on micro, small, and medium-sized enterprises. Works to promote economic growth, social inclusion, competition, and innovation.

The SEEP Network (The Small Enterprise Education and Promotion Network), *1621 N. Kent St., #900, Arlington, VA 22209; (202) 534-1400. Fax, (703) 276-1433. Sharon D'Onofrio, Executive Director. Press, (202) 534-1402.*
General email, seep@seepnetwork.org

Web, https://seepnetwork.org and Twitter, @TheSEEPNetwork

Membership: international organizations seeking to end poverty. Promotes inclusive markets and financial systems to improve impoverished areas. Conducts research on industry trends, opinions, and practices in developing countries. Interests include financial services and business development.

Trans-Atlantic Business Council, *1601 K St. N.W., 20001; (202) 778-9073. Fax, (202) 778-9100. Bart Gordon, U.S. Director.*
Web, http://transatlanticbusiness.org and Twitter, @TABC_Council

Membership: American companies with operations in Europe and European companies with operations in the United States. Promotes a barrier-free transatlantic market that contributes to economic growth, innovation, and security.

World Bank, *1818 H St. N.W., 20433; (202) 473-1000. Fax, (202) 477-6391. Kristalina Georgieva, President (Acting); Erik Bethel, U.S. Executive Director (Acting); David Theis, Media contact. Anticorruption hotline, (202) 458-7677. Press, (202) 473-7660. Publications, (800) 645-7247 or (703) 661-1580.*
General email, info_us@worldbank.org

Web, www.worldbank.org/en/country/unitedstates and Twitter, @worldbank

International development institution funded by government membership subscriptions and borrowings on private capital markets. Aims to end extreme poverty and advance education, health, and economies. Finances economic development projects in agriculture, environmental protection, education, public utilities, telecommunications, water supply, sewerage, public health, and other areas.

▶NONGOVERNMENTAL

Ashoka: Innovators for the Public, *1700 N. Moore St., #2000, Arlington, VA 22209; (703) 527-8300. Fax, (703) 527-8383. Bill Drayton, Chief Executive Officer.*
General email, info@ashoka.org

Web, www.ashoka.org and Twitter, @Ashoka

Supports fellowships for individuals with ideas for social change and entrepreneurship in seventy developing nations. Provides fellows with research support, organizational networking, legal counseling, economic support, and business consulting. Seeks to educate the public about the developing world and the work of its fellows.

Assn. of Foreign Investors in Real Estate, *1300 Pennsylvania Ave. N.W., 20004-3020; (202) 312-1400. Fax, (202) 312-1401. Gunnar Branson, Chief Executive Officer.*
General email, afireinfo@afire.org

Web, www.afire.org

Represents foreign institutions that are interested in the laws, regulations, and economic trends affecting the U.S. real estate market. Informs the public and the government of the contributions foreign investment makes to the U.S. economy. Examines current issues and organizes seminars for members.

Assn. of Women in International Trade, *100 M St. S.E., #600, 20003 (mailing address: P.O. Box 76825, Washington, DC 20013); (202) 869-3795. Lisa Schroeter, President.*
General email, info@wiit.org

Web, www.wiit.org and Twitter, @wiit_dc

Membership: women and men from all sectors concerned with international trade, including import-export firms, government, corporations, and nonprofit organizations. Provides members with opportunities for professional development. Maintains job bank and sponsors mentoring program.

British–American Business Assn., *P.O. Box 16482, 20041; (202) 293-0010. Fax, (202) 296-3332. Patricia A. Karhuse, Executive Director.*
General email, info@babawashington.org
Web, www.babawashington.org and Twitter, @BABADC

Organization dedicated to the development of business relations between the United Kingdom and the United States.

The Brookings Institution, *Global Economy and Development Studies, 1775 Massachusetts Ave. N.W., 20036; (202) 797-6000. Fax, (202) 797-6004. Kemal Dervis, Director. Communications, (202) 797-6421.*
General email, globalmedia@brookings.edu
Web, www.brookings.edu/global

Facilitates international policy debate on globalization, poverty reduction, global economy, and public goods.

Center for Global Development, *2055 L St. N.W., #500, 20036; (202) 416-4000. Fax, (202) 416-4050. Masood Ahmed, President. Press, (202) 416-4040.*
General email, info@cgdev.org
Web, www.cgdev.org and Twitter, @CGDev

Works to reduce global poverty and inequality through policy-oriented research and active engagement on development issues with policymakers and the public. Conducts independent research to develop practical ideas for global prosperity.

Center for International Private Enterprise, *1211 Connecticut Ave. N.W., #700, 20036; (202) 721-9200. Fax, (202) 721-9250. Andrew Wilson, Executive Director.*
General email, info@cipe.org
Web, www.cipe.org and Twitter, @CIPEglobal

Promotes global democratic development through private enterprise and market-oriented reform. Supported by the National Endowment for Democracy, works with business leaders, policymakers, and journalists to build civic institutions. Key program areas include anticorruption, access to information, the informal sector and property rights, and women and youth. (Affiliated with the U.S. Chamber of Commerce.)

Cultivating New Frontiers in Agriculture (CNFA), *1828 L St. N.W., #710, 20036; (202) 296-3920. Fax, (202) 296-3948. Sylvain Roy, President.*
General email, info@cnfa.org
Web, www.cnfa.org

International development organization that has worked in more than 42 countries to provide agricultural solutions to stimulate economic growth and improve livelihoods by cultivating entrepreneurship.

Economic Strategy Institute, *1730 Rhode Island Ave. N.W., #414, 20036; (202) 213-7051. Fax, (202) 965-1104. Clyde V. Prestowitz Jr., President.*
General email, info@econstrat.org
Web, www.econstrat.org and Twitter, @clydeprestowitz

Works to increase U.S. economic competitiveness through research on domestic and international economic policies, industrial and technological developments, and global security issues. Testifies before Congress and government agencies.

Federation of International Trade Assns., *11654 Plaza America Dr., #120, Reston, VA 20190; (703) 634-3482. Kimberly Park, President.*
General email, info@fita.org
Web, www.fita.org

Membership: local, regional, and national trade associations throughout North America that have an international mission. Works to increase North American exports.

Global Business Dialogue, *1717 Pennsylvania Ave., 20006; (202) 463-5074. Fax, (202) 463-5074. R.K. Morris, President.*
General email, comments@gbdinc.org
Web, www.gbdinc.org

Promotes discussion of trade and investment within the global business community.

Institute for Sustainable Communities, *Washington Office, 888 17th St. N.W., #610, 20006; (202) 777-7575. Fax, (202) 777-7577. George Hamilton, President.*
General email, isc@iscvt.org
Web, www.iscvt.org, Twitter, @SustainableComm and Facebook, www.facebook.com/SustainableComm

Provides training and technical assistance to communities around the world to engage citizens in developing and implementing plans for a sustainable future. Interests include civil and human rights, public health, arms control, and environmental and consumer affairs. Aids groups in making better use of resources, such as access to the media and coalition building. (Headquarters in Montpelier, Vt.)

International Business Ethics Institute, *1776 Eye St. N.W., 9th Floor, 20006; (202) 296-6938. Fax, (202) 296-5897. Lori Tansey Martens, President.*
General email, info@business-ethics.org
Web, www.business-ethics.org

Works to increase public awareness and dialogue about international business ethics issues through various educational resources and activities. Works with companies to assist them in establishing effective international ethics programs.

International Executive Service Corps (IESC), *1900 M St. N.W., #500, 20036; (202) 589-2600. David Hartingh, President.*
General email, iesc@iesc.org
Web, www.iesc.org

Promotes self-sustainable economic growth in developing countries. Implements financial and management programs to improve trade, technology, and tourism. Includes the Geekcorps division to assist in managing technical programs.

National Assn. of Manufacturers (NAM), *International Economic Affairs, 733 10th St. N.W., #700, 20001; (202)*

637-3144. Fax, (202) 637-3182. Linda Dempsey, Vice President. Toll-free, (800) 814-8466.
Web, www.nam.org

Represents manufacturing business interests on international economic issues, including trade, international investment, export financing, and export controls.

National Customs Brokers and Forwarders Assn. of America, 1200 18th St. N.W., #901, 20036; (202) 466-0222. Fax, (202) 466-0226. Megan Montgomery, Executive Vice President.
General email, recep@ncbfaa.org
Web, www.ncbfaa.org

Membership: customs brokers and freight forwarders in the United States. Fosters information exchange within the industry. Monitors legislation and regulations.

National Foreign Trade Council, 1625 K St. N.W., #200, 20006-1604; (202) 887-0278. Fax, (202) 452-8160. Rufus Yerxa, President.
General email, nftcinformation@nftc.org
Web, www.nftc.org, Twitter, @NFTC and Facebook, www.facebook.com/National-Foreign-Trade-Council-105955409792

Membership: U.S. companies engaged in international trade and investment. Advocates open international trading, export expansion, and policies to assist U.S. companies competing in international markets. Provides members with information on international trade topics. Sponsors seminars and conferences.

U.S. Chamber of Commerce, International Affairs Division, 1615 H St. N.W., 20062-2000; (202) 463-5460. Fax, (202) 463-3114. Myron Brilliant, Executive Vice President.
Web, www.uschamber.com/international-affairs-division and Twitter, @ChamberGlobal

Provides liaison with network of U.S. chambers of commerce abroad; administers bilateral business councils; responsible for international economic policy development; informs members of developments in international affairs, business economics, and trade; sponsors seminars and conferences. Monitors legislation and regulations.

United States Council for International Business, Policy and Government Affairs, 1400 K St. N.W., #525, 20005; (202) 371-1316. Fax, (202) 371-8249. Robert Mulligan, Senior Vice President, (202) 682-7375.
General email, info@uscib.org
Web, www.uscib.org and Twitter, @USCIB

Membership: multinational corporations, service companies, law firms, and business associations. Represents U.S. business positions before intergovernmental bodies, foreign governments, and business communities. Promotes an open system of world trade, finance, and investment. (Headquarters in New York.)

Urban Institute, Center on International Development and Governance, 500 L'Enfant Plaza S.W., 20024; (202) 833-7200. Charles Cadwell, Vice-President.

General email, idginfo@urban.org
Web, www.urban.org/center/idg

Promotes economic and democratic development in developing and transition countries. Conducts research and works with government officials, international development agencies, and international financial institutions to provide technical assistance toward local governance, service delivery, and public finance.

Washington International Trade Assn., 1300 Pennsylvania Ave. N.W., #G-329, 20004-3014; (202) 312-1600. Fax, (202) 312-1601. Kenneth I. (Ken) Levinson, Executive Director.
General email, wita@wita.org
Web, https://wita.org and Twitter, @WITA_DC

Membership: trade professionals. Conducts programs and provides neutral forums to discuss international trade issues. Monitors legislation and regulations.

Development Assistance

▶**AGENCIES**

Agency for International Development (USAID), Bureau for Democracy, Conflict, and Humanitarian Assistance, 1300 Pennsylvania Ave. N.W., #8.6-0.84, 20523-8601; (202) 712-0100. Tim Ziemer, Assistant Administrator (Acting).
Web, www.usaid.gov/who-we-are/organization/bureaus/bureau-democracy-conflict-and-humanitarian-assistance

Manages U.S. foreign disaster assistance, emergency and developmental food aid, democracy programs, conflict management programs, and programs to assist countries transitioning out of crises. Assists U.S. voluntary organizations, schools, and hospitals abroad. Serves as USAID's liaison to the U.S. military.

Agency for International Development (USAID), Bureau for Economic Growth, Education, and Environment, 1300 Pennsylvania Ave. N.W., #3.9, 20523-3900; (202) 712-0670. Fax, (202) 216-3239. Michelle Bekkering, Senior Deputy Assistant Administrator.
Web, www.usaid.gov/who-we-are/organization/bureaus/bureau-economic-growth-education-and-environment

Assists with the economic growth of developing countries by providing policy, technical, and financial assistance for cost-effective, reliable energy programs and other infrastructure. Works to foster increased capability of foreign missions to collaborate with governments, entrepreneurs, and other local institutions and individuals to encourage country-based assistance programs. Divisions focus on economic growth, including business, microenterprise development, and institutional reform; the environment and energy use; human capacity development, including education and training; and women in development.

Agency for International Development (USAID), Bureau for Economic Growth, Education, and Environment, Education, 1300 Pennsylvania Ave. N.W., #3.08-095, 20523-3901; Robert Burch, Director. Main Switchboard, (202) 712-0000, Ext. 63427.

General email, officeofeducation@usaid.gov

Web, www.usaid.gov/education

Provides field support, technical leadership, and research to help foreign missions and countries manage and develop their human resources. Improves the means of basic and higher education as well as training. Administers the USAID Participant Training Program, which provides students and midcareer professionals from developing countries with academic and technical training, and the Entrepreneur International Initiative, a short-term training/trade program that matches developing-country entrepreneurs with their American counterparts to familiarize them with American goods, services, and technology.

Agency for International Development (USAID), *Bureau for Food Security, 1300 Pennsylvania Ave. N.W., 20523; (202) 712-0000, Ext. 20189. Fax, (202) 216-3380. Beth Dunford, Assistant Administrator, (202) 712-0658. Web, www.usaid.gov/who-we-are/organization/bureaus/ bureau-food-security*

Administers agricultural development programs, including the Feed the Future initiative. Partners with other U.S. government offices, multilateral institutions, NGOs, the public and private sector, and universities to support country-driven agricultural growth strategies.

Agency for International Development (USAID), *Bureau for Food Security, Farmer-to-Farmer Program, 1300 Pennsylvania Ave. N.W., #2.10-261, 20523; J. Erin Baize, Program Analyst, (202) 712-5711. Web, www.usaid.gov/what-we-do/agriculture-and-food- security/supporting-agricultural-capacity-development/ john-ogonowski*

https://farmer-to-farmer.org/ and Facebook, www.facebook.com/Farmer2Farmer

Promotes sustainable improvements in food security and agricultural processing, production, and marketing. Provides voluntary assistance to farmers, farm groups, and agribusinesses in developing countries, benefiting approximately one million farmer families in more than 80 countries.

Agency for International Development (USAID), *Bureau for Global Health, 1300 Pennsylvania Ave. N.W., #3.64, 20523-3100; (202) 712-4120. Fax, (202) 216-3485. Alma Crumm Golden, Senior Deputy Assistant Administrator. Web, www.usaid.gov/what-we-do/global-health*

Participates in global efforts to stabilize world population growth and support women's reproductive rights. Focus includes family planning; reproductive health care; infant, child, and maternal health; and prevention of sexually transmitted diseases, especially AIDS. Conducts demographic and health surveys; educates girls and women.

Bureau of International Organization Affairs (IO) *(State Dept.), Economic and Development Affairs (EDA), 2201 C St. N.W., #2830, 20520; (202) 647-1545. Margaret H. Bond, Director. Web, www.state.gov/p/io*

Works with the United Nations Food and Agricultural Organization, World Food Program, and World Health Organization to implement U.S. policy initiatives on human security, with particular focus on economic growth and sustainable development, global food security, and global health issues

Criminal Division *(Justice Dept.), International Criminal Investigative Training Assistance Program (ICITAP), 1331 F St. N.W., #500, 20530; Gregory Ducot, Director (Acting). Main, (202) 305-8190. Web, www.justice.gov/criminal-icitap*

Works with foreign governments to develop professional and transparent law enforcement institutions that protect human rights, combat corruption, and reduce the threat of transnational crime and terrorism. Provides international development assistance that supports both national security and foreign policy objectives.

Millennium Challenge Corp., *1099 14th St. N.W., #700, 20005-3550; (202) 521-3600. Jonathan Nash, Chief Executive Officer. Legislative Affairs, (202) 521-3880. General email, web@mcc.gov Web, www.mcc.gov and Twitter, @MCCgov*

Government corporation that provides financial assistance to developing nations that encourage economic freedom. Funds are used for agricultural development, education, enterprise and private-sector development, governance, health, and building trade capacity. Monitors legislation and regulations.

Peace Corps, *1111 20th St. N.W., 20526; (202) 692-1040. Fax, (202) 692-8400. Josephine (Jody) Olsen, Director. Information, (855) 855-1961. Press, (202) 692-2230. Web, www.peacecorps.gov and Twitter, @PeaceCorps*

Promotes world peace, friendship, and mutual understanding between the United States and developing nations. Administers volunteer programs to assist developing countries in education, the environment, health (particularly HIV awareness and prevention), small business development, agriculture, and urban youth development.

State Dept., *Global Food Security, 2201 C St. N.W., #5323, 20520; (202) 647-4027. Caitlin E. Walsh, Special Representative (Acting). Web, www.state.gov/s/globalfoodsecurity*

Supports country-driven approaches to address the root causes of hunger and poverty, and helps countries transform their own agricultural sectors to grow enough food to sustainably feed their people.

▶INTERNATIONAL ORGANIZATIONS

CARE, *Washington Office, 1899 L St. N.W., #500, 20036; (202) 595-2800. Fax, (202) 296-8695. Michelle Nunn, President; DavidRay, Vice President of Policy and Advocacy. Toll-free, (800) 422-7385. General email, info@care.org Web, www.care.org and Twitter, @CARE*

Assists the developing world's poor through emergency assistance and community self-help programs that focus on sustainable development, agriculture, agroforestry, water and sanitation, health, family planning, and income generation. Community-based efforts are centered on providing resources to poor women. (U.S. headquarters in Atlanta, Ga.; international headquarters in Geneva, Switzerland.)

Grameen Foundation, *1400 K St., #550, 20005; (202) 628-3560. Fax, (202) 628-2341. Steve Hollingworth, President. Web, www.grameenfoundation.org and Twitter, @GrameenFdn*

Seeks to eliminate poverty by providing microfinance and technology products and services in sub-Saharan Africa, Asia, the Middle East and North Africa (MENA) region, Latin America, and the Caribbean. Develops mobile phone–based solutions that address "information poverty" among the poor, providing tools, information, and services in the fields of health, agriculture, financial services, and livelihood creation. Focuses on assistance to women seeking to start or expand their own businesses.

International Development Assn., *1818 H St. N.W., MSN MCG5-501, 20433; (202) 473-1000. Idah Tswary-Riddihough, Director; Lisa Finneran, Senior Adviser. Web, www.ida.worldbank.org*

Affiliate of the World Bank funded by membership contributions and transfers of funds from the World Bank. Provides long-term, low-interest, and interest-free loans and grants to the poorest countries.

Quota International, *1420 21st St. N.W., 20036; (202) 331-9694. Fax, (202) 331-4395. Nancy Fitzpatrick, Executive Director. General email, staff@quota.org Web, www.quotainternational.org and Twitter, @QuotaIntl*

International service organization that links members in twelve countries in a worldwide network of service and friendship. Interests include deaf, hard-of-hearing, and speech-impaired individuals and disadvantaged women and children. Maintains the We Share Foundation, a charitable organization.

TechnoServe, *1777 N. Kent St., #1100, Arlington, VA 22209; (202) 785-4515. Fax, (202) 785-4544. Will Warshauer, President. Donor Support, (800) 999-6757. Press, (202) 650-5713. General email, info@technoserve.org Web, www.technoserve.org and Twitter, @technoserve*

International nonprofit that assists entrepreneurs in poor and developing countries. Provides access to technology, information, and resources that connect business owners to suppliers and industry networks to increase their revenue. Specializes in farming and agricultural enterprises.

United Nations Development Programme (UNDP), *Washington Office, 1775 K St. N.W., #500, 20006; (202) 331-9130. Fax, (202) 331-9363. Achim Steiner, Administrator; Paul Clayman, Director.*

General email, undp.washington@undp.org Web, www.us.undp.org/ and Twitter, @UNDPDC

Funded by voluntary contributions from national governments. Administers United Nations support for economic and social development in developing countries, democratic governance, poverty reduction, crisis prevention and recovery, energy and the environment, and HIV/AIDS. (Headquarters in New York.)

United Way Worldwide, *701 N. Fairfax St., Alexandria, VA 22314-2045; (703) 836-7112. Fax, (703) 519-0097. Brian A. Gallagher, President. Web, www.unitedway.org and Twitter, @UnitedWay*

Membership: independent United Way organizations in 41 countries and territories, including 1,150 in the United States. Provides staff training; fund-raising, planning, and communications assistance; resource management; and national public service advertising. Activities support education, financial stability, and health.

Women for Women International, *2000 M St. N.W., #200, 20036; (202) 737-7705. Fax, (202) 737-7709. Laurie Adams, Chief Executive Officer. General email, general@womenforwomen.org Web, www.womenforwomen.org and Twitter, @WomenforWomen*

Helps women in war-torn regions rebuild their lives through financial and emotional support, job skills training, rights education, access to capital, and assistance for small business development.

World Bank, *Human Development Network, 1818 H St. N.W., 20433; (202) 473-1000. Annette Dixon, Vice President. Web, www.worldbank.org*

Assists developing countries in delivering effective and affordable health care, education, and social services. Interests include poverty reduction, income protection, nutrition, jobs access, health coverage, and basic education.

▶ **NONGOVERNMENTAL**

ACDI/VOCA, *50 F St. N.W., #1000, 20001-1530; (202) 469-6000. Fax, (202) 469-6257. Charles J. Hall, President. Toll-free, (800) 929-8622. General email, webmaster@acdivoca.org Web, www.acdivoca.org, Twitter, @acdivoca and Facebook, www.facebook.com/acdivoca*

Recruits professionals for voluntary, short-term technical assistance to cooperatives, environmental groups, and agricultural enterprises in developing countries and emerging democracies. Interests include poverty reduction, community stabilization, and market integration. Promotes rural finance for micro-sized to medium-sized enterprises.

Adventist Development and Relief Agency, *12501 Old Columbia Pike, Silver Spring, MD 20904; (301) 680-6380. Fax, (301) 680-6370. Jonathan Duffy, President. Toll-free, (800) 424-2372.*

General email, hello@adra.org

Web, www.adra.org, Twitter, @ADRAIntl and Facebook, www.facebook.com/joinADRA

Worldwide humanitarian agency of the Seventh-day Adventist Church. Works to alleviate poverty in developing countries and responds to disasters. Sponsors activities that improve health, foster economic and social well-being, and build self-reliance.

American Jewish World Service, *Government Affairs,* *1001 Connecticut Ave. N.W., #1200, 20036-3405; (202) 379-4300. Rori Kramer, Director of Government Affairs, (202) 379-4270. Toll-free, (800) 889-7146.* *Web, www.ajws.org/get-involved/ajws-in-your-community/washington-dc/ and Twitter, @ajws*

International development organization that works to alleviate poverty and promote human rights around the world. Provides grants to grassroots organizations; offers volunteer services, advocacy, and education for society building, sustainable development, and protection of human rights. Promotes global citizenship within the Jewish community. (Headquarters in New York.)

Bikes for the World, *11720 Parklawn Dr., Rockville, MD 20852; (703) 740-7856. Fax, (703) 525-0931. Taylor Jones, Executive Director.* *General email, office@bikesfortheworld.org* *Web, www.bikesfortheworld.org and Twitter, @bikeftworld*

Collects unwanted bicycles and related paraphernalia in the United States and delivers them to low-cost community development programs assisting the poor in developing countries.

Center for Intercultural Education and Development *(Georgetown University), 3300 Whitehaven St. N.W., #1000, 20007 (mailing address: P.O. Box 579400, Washington, DC 20007); (202) 687-1400. Fax, (202) 687-2555. Chantal Santelices, Executive Director, (202) 687-1918.* *General email, cied@georgetown.edu* *Web, http://cied.georgetown.edu and Twitter, @GeorgetownCIED*

Designs and administers programs aimed at improving the quality of lives of economically disadvantaged people; provides technical education, job training, leadership skills development, and business management training; runs programs in Central America, the Caribbean, Central Europe, the Middle East, and Southeast Asia.

Development Gateway, *1110 Vermont Ave. N.W., #500, 20005; (202) 572-9200. Josh Powell, Chief Executive Officer.* *General email, info@developmentgateway.org* *Web, www.developmentgateway.org*

Provides international and grassroots development organizations with visual translations of data and analysis. Assists in applying data-based solutions to policies. Seeks to improve evaluation, decision making, and management of international development efforts.

Foundation for International Community Assistance **(FINCA),** *1201 15th St. N.W., 8th Floor, 20005; (202) 682-1510. Fax, (202) 318-3090. Rupert Scofield, President.* *General email, info@finca.org* *Web, www.finca.org, Twitter, @FINCA and Facebook, www.facebook.com/FINCA.International*

Provides financial services to low-income entrepreneurs outside the United States in order to create jobs, build assets, and improve standards of living. Delivers microfinance products and services through a network of wholly owned programs in Africa, Eurasia, the Middle East, and Latin America, operating on commercial principles of performance and sustainability. Focuses efforts on those living on less than $2.50/day, with a loan portfolio of approximately $1 billion estimated to reach about one million people worldwide.

Global Communities, *8601 Georgia Ave., #300, Silver Spring, MD 20910-3440; (301) 587-4700. Fax, (301) 587-7315. David A. Weiss, President.* *General email, mailbox@globalcommunities.org* *Web, www.globalcommunities.org*

Works under contract with the Agency for International Development, United Nations, and World Bank to strengthen local government housing departments abroad.

Institute for State Effectiveness, *1050 30th St. N.W., 20007; (202) 298-5959. Fax, (202) 298-5564. Claire Lockhart, Director.* *General email, info@effectivestates.org* *Web, www.effectivestates.org, Twitter, @effectivestates and Facebook, www.facebook.com/Institute-for-State-Effectiveness-611501212244248*

Aims to improve international government accountability by creating policies and educating local leaders and citizens on successful accountability practices. Studies how nations build accountable governments and creates similar tools for developing countries and leaders.

InterAction, *1400 16th St. N.W., #210, 20036; (202) 667-8227. Samuel A. Worthington, Chief Executive Officer; Vacant, President.* *General email, ia@interaction.org* *Web, www.interaction.org and Twitter, @InterActionOrg*

Alliance of nearly 200 U.S.-based international development and humanitarian nongovernmental organizations. Provides a forum for exchange of information on development assistance issues, including food aid and other relief services, migration, and refugee affairs. Monitors legislation and regulations.

International Center for Research on Women, *1120 20th St. N.W., #500N, 20036; (202) 797-0007. Fax, (202) 797-0020. Sarah Degnan Kambou, President.* *General email, info@icrw.org* *Web, www.icrw.org, Twitter, @ICRW and Facebook, www.facebook.com/ICRWDC*

Advances gender equality and human rights, fights poverty, and promotes sustainable economic and social development through research, program implementation, information gathering, publications, and strategic media outreach. Conducts empirical research and promotes practical, evidence-based solutions that enable women to control their own lives and fully participate in their societies.

Leadership Initiatives, *Youth Development Programs,* *4410 Massachusetts Ave., #236, 20016; (202) 738-1115. Fax, (202) 280-1221. Marshall Bailly, Executive Director. General email, info@lichange.org*

Web, www.BeTheChangeNow.org

Offers entrepreneurship training and leadership courses to individuals in developing countries. Connects high school students to international leaders to solve local business issues. Interests include mentoring orphans and youth. Focuses on communities in Nigeria, Namibia, and the Philippines.

Millennium Institute, *2200 Pennsylvania Ave. N.W., 4th floor East Tower, 20037; (202) 507-5820. Hans R. Herren, President. General email, info@millennium-institute.org*

Web, www.millennium-institute.org and Twitter, @millenniuminst

Research and international development organization that provides computer modeling services for planning and building a sustainable economic and ecological future.

National Peace Corps Assn., *1900 L St. N.W., #610, 20036-5002; (202) 293-7728. Fax, (202) 293-7554. Glenn Blumhorst, President. General email, ncpa@peacecorpsconnect.org*

Web, www.peacecorpsconnect.org and Twitter, @pcorpsconnect

Membership: returned Peace Corps volunteers, staff, and interested individuals. Promotes a global perspective in the United States; seeks to educate the public about the developing world; supports Peace Corps programs; maintains a network of returned volunteers.

Oxfam America, *Policy and Campaigns, 1101 17th St. N.W., #1300, 20036-4710; (202) 496-1180. Fax, (202) 496-1190. Abby Maxman, President; Paul O'Brien, Vice President for Policy and Campaigns. Information, (800) 776-9326. Press, (202) 496-1169. General email, info@oxfamamerica.org*

Web, www.oxfamamerica.org and Twitter, @OxfamAmerica

Funds disaster relief and long-term development programs internationally. Organizes grassroots support in the United States for issues affecting global poverty, including climate change, aid reform, and corporate transparency. (Headquarters in Boston, Mass.)

PYXERA Global, *99 M St. S.E., #400, 20003; (202) 872-0933. Fax, (202) 872-0923. Deirdre White, Chief Executive Officer. General email, info@pyxeraglobal.org*

Web, www.pyxeraglobal.org and Twitter, @PYXERAGlobal

Recruits and coordinates public, private, and volunteer resources to strengthen small and medium-sized businesses and the institutions, governments, and industries that drive economic growth in emerging markets through five practice areas: global citizenship and volunteerism, supply chain development, tourism development, security and economic recovery, and access to finance for development. (Formerly CDC Development Solutions.)

Salvation Army World Service Office, *615 Slaters Lane, Alexandria, VA 22314 (mailing address: P.O. Box 1428, Alexandria, VA 22313); (703) 684-5500. Fax, (703) 684-5536. Lt. Col. Thomas Bowers, National Secretary; Lt. Col. Jacalyn Bowers, Assistant National Secretary. Media, (703) 647-4796. General email, SAWSO.Communications@usn.salvation army.org*

Web, www.sawso.org

Works in Eastern Europe, Latin America, the Caribbean, Africa, Asia, and the South Pacific to provide technical assistance to local Salvation Army programs of health services, vocational and business training, literacy, microenterprise, and relief and reconstruction assistance. (International headquarters in London.)

Vital Voices Global Partnership, *1625 Massachusetts Ave. N.W., #300, 20036; (202) 861-2625. Fax, (202) 296-4142. Alyse Nelson, Chief Executive Officer. General email, info@vitalvoices.org*

Web, www.vitalvoices.org and Twitter, @VitalVoices

Worldwide organization of volunteers with governmental, corporate, or other leadership expertise that trains and mentors emerging women leaders in Asia, Africa, Eurasia, Latin America and the Caribbean, and the Middle East. Seeks to expand women's political participation and representation, increase women's entrepreneurship and business leadership, and combat human rights violations affecting women.

World Cocoa Foundation, *1411 K St. N.W., #500, 20005; (202) 737-7870. Fax, (202) 737-7832. Richard Scobey, President. General email, wcf@worldcocoa.org*

Web, www.worldcocoafoundation.org and Twitter, @WorldCocoa

Promotes a sustainable cocoa economy through economic and social development and environmental conservation in cocoa-growing communities. Helps raise funds for cocoa farmers and increases their access to modern farming practices.

World Learning, *Global Development and Exchange Programs, 1015 15th St. N.W., 7th Floor, 20005-2065; (202) 408-5420. Fax, (202) 408-5397. Carol Jenkins, President, (202) 464-6643. Toll-free, (800) 858-0292. TTY, 711. General email, development@worldlearning.org*

Web, www.worldlearning.org and Twitter, @WorldLearning

Partners with nongovernmental organizations, government institutions, schools, universities, and others to strengthen local capacity and performance. Develops training programs that prepare local organizations to lead development initiatives. Provides technical assistance, mentoring, and small-grant funding. Administered by World Learning's Division of International Development and Exchange Programs.

Finance, Investment, and Monetary Affairs

►AGENCIES

Bureau of Economic Analysis (BEA) *(Commerce Dept.),* *4600 Silver Hill Rd., 20233; (202) 606-9900.* *Brian C. Moyer, Director. Congressional Affairs, (301) 278-9032. Press, (301) 278-9003.* *General email, CustomerService@bea.gov* *Web, www.bea.gov and Twitter, @BEA_NEWS*

Compiles, analyzes, and publishes data on measures of aggregate U.S. economic activity, including gross domestic product; prices by type of expenditure; personal income and outlays; personal savings; corporate profits; capital stock; U.S. international transactions; and foreign investment. Provides statistics of personal income and employment by industry for regions, states, metropolitan areas, and counties. Refers specific inquiries to economic specialists in the field.

Bureau of Economic Analysis (BEA) *(Commerce Dept.),* *Direct Investment Division, 4600 Silver Hill Rd., 20233; (301) 278-9591. Patricia Abaroa, Chief.* *General email, internationalaccounts@bea.gov* *Web, www.bea.gov*

Compiles statistics on foreign direct investment in the United States and U.S. direct investment abroad.

Bureau of Economic Analysis *(Commerce Dept.),* *International Economics, Balance of Payments Division, 4600 Silver Hill Rd., 20233; (301) 278-9585. Kristy Howell, Chief.* *General email, internationalaccounts@bea.gov* *Web, www.bea.gov/international*

Compiles, analyzes, and publishes quarterly and annual statistics on the U.S. international transactions accounts and the U.S. international investment position accounts. Publishes a monthly release with U.S. Census Bureau on U.S. trade in goods and services. Conducts research and analysis on the international economic accounts.

Bureau of Economic and Business Affairs (EB) *(State Dept.), International Finance and Development (IFD), 2201 C St. N.W., #4880, 20520; (202) 647-4632. Fax, (202) 647-7453. Roland F. de Marcellus, Deputy Assistant Secretary (Acting).* *Web, www.state.gov/e/eb/ifd*

Formulates and implements policies related to multinational investment and insurance; activities of the World Bank and regional banks in the financial development of various countries; bilateral aid; international monetary reform; international antitrust cases; and international debt, banking, and taxation.

Bureau of Economic and Business Affairs (EB) *(State Dept.), International Finance and Development (IFD), Development Finance (ODF), 2201 C St. N.W., #4871, 20520; (202) 647-9427. Fax, (202) 647-5585. Roland F. de Marcellus, Director (Acting), (202) 647-9426.* *Web, www.state.gov/e/eb/ifd/odf*

Fosters development of new markets overseas, supports export opportunities, and seeks to strengthen U.S. international economic ties. Works with international bank organizations, including the World Bank, to promote U.S. economic policies.

Bureau of Economic and Business Affairs (EB) *(State Dept.), International Finance and Development (IFD), Investment Affairs (OIA), 2201 C St. N.W., #4669, 20520-5820; (202) 736-4907. Fax, (202) 647-0320. Michael K. Tracton, Director.* *General email, eb-a-oia-dl@state.gov* *Web, www.state.gov/e/eb/ifd/oia*

Develops U.S. investment policy. Makes policy recommendations regarding multinational enterprises and the expropriation of and compensation for U.S. property overseas. Negotiates bilateral and multilateral investment agreements. Coordinates the State Dept.'s position with respect to the Committee for Foreign Investments in the United States.

Bureau of Economic and Business Affairs (EB) *(State Dept.), International Finance and Development (IFD), Monetary Affairs (OMA), 2201 C St. N.W., #4880, 20520; (202) 647-9497. Fax, (202) 647-7453. Jessica M. Webster, Director.* *General email, eb-a-oma-dl@state.gov* *Web, www.state.gov/e/eb/ifd/oma*

Monitors global macroeconomic developments and identifies financial trends and potential crises in countries affecting U.S. interests. Formulates debt relief policies and negotiates debt relief agreements.

Committee on Foreign Investment in the United States *(Treasury Dept.), 1500 Pennsylvania Ave. N.W., #5221, 20220; (202) 622-1860. Fax, (202) 622-0391. Stephen (Steve) Hanson, Staff Chair.* *General email, cfius@treasury.gov* *Web, www.treasury.gov/cfius*

Reviews foreign acquisition of U.S. companies and determines whether they pose national security threats. Conducts investigations into such acquisitions.

Export-Import Bank of the United States, *811 Vermont Ave. N.W., 20571; (202) 565-3946. Fax, (202) 565-3380. Jeffrey Gerrish, Chair. Press, (202) 565-3200. Toll-free hotline, (800) 565-3946. TTY, (202) 565-3377.* *Web, www.exim.gov*

Independent agency of the U.S. government with 12 regional offices. Aids in financing exports of U.S. goods and services; guarantees export loans made by commercial lenders, working capital guarantees, and export credit insurance; conducts an intermediary loan program. National Contact Center advises businesses in using U.S. government export programs.

Federal Reserve System, *International Finance, 20th and C Sts. N.W., #B1242C, 20551-0001; (202) 452-3770. Fax, (202) 452-6424. Steven B. Kamin, Director. Press, (202) 452-3799.*
Web, www.federalreserve.gov/econresdata/ifstaff.htm

Provides the Federal Reserve's board of governors with economic analyses of international developments. Compiles data on exchange rates.

Overseas Private Investment Corp., *1100 New York Ave. N.W., 20527; (202) 336-8400. Fax, (202) 336-7949. David Bohigian, President (Acting). Anticorruption hotline, (202) 712-1023. Information, (202) 336-8799. Press, (202) 336-8460.*
General email, info@opic.gov
Web, www.opic.gov

Provides assistance through political risk insurance, direct loans, and loan guarantees to qualified U.S. private investors to support their investments in emerging markets. Offers preinvestment information and counseling. Provides insurance against the risks of expropriation, political violence, and inconvertibility of local currency.

Securities and Exchange Commission (SEC), *International Affairs, 100 F St. N.E., MS 1004, 20549; (202) 551-6690. Fax, (202) 772-9281. Racquel Fox, Director.*
Web, www.sec.gov/oia

Promotes investor protection, cross-border securities transactions, and fair, efficient, and transparent markets by advancing international regulatory and enforcement cooperation, promoting the adoption of high regulatory standards worldwide, and formulating technical assistance programs to strengthen the regulatory structure in global finance markets. Works with a global network of securities regulators and law enforcement authorities to facilitate cross-border regulatory compliance and help ensure that international borders are not used to escape detection and prosecution of fraudulent securities activities. Provides the commission and SEC staff with advice and assistance in international enforcement and regulatory efforts.

Treasury Dept., *International Affairs, 1500 Pennsylvania Ave. N.W., #3432, 20220; (202) 622-1270. Fax, (202) 622-0417. David Malpass, Under Secretary. Press, (202) 622-2920.*
Web, www.treasury.gov/about/organizational-structure/ offices/Pages/Office-Of-International-Affairs.aspx

Coordinates and implements U.S. international economic and financial policy in cooperation with other government agencies. Works to improve the international monetary and investment system; monitors international gold and foreign exchange operations; coordinates development lending; coordinates Treasury Dept. participation in foreign investment in the United States; studies international monetary, economic, and financial issues; analyzes data on international transactions.

Treasury Dept., *International Affairs, African Nations, 1500 Pennsylvania Ave. N.W., 20220; (202) 622-2156. Eric Meyer, Deputy Assistant Secretary.*
Web, www.treasury.gov/about/organizational-structure/ offices/Pages/–Africa.aspx

Develops and guides economic policy and loan and development programs toward 49 sub-Saharan African economies.

Treasury Dept., *International Affairs, East Asia, 1500 Pennsylvania Ave. N.W., #3217, 20220; (202) 622-2000. Robert Kaproth, Deputy Assistant Secretary, (202) 622-0132; Leslie Hull, Director, (202) 622-4644.*
Web, www.treasury.gov/about/organizational-structure/ offices/Pages/East-Asia.aspx

Provides economic analysis of countries in East Asia, including Australia, China, Hong Kong, Japan, the Koreas, Mongolia, New Zealand, the Pacific Islands, and Taiwan. Plays a role in managing the U.S.–China Strategic and Economic Dialogue and U.S. engagement with Asian regional initiatives.

Treasury Dept., *International Affairs, Europe and Eurasia, 1500 Pennsylvania Ave N.W., #4138, 20220; (202) 622-2722. Elizabeth Berry, Deputy Assistant Secretary, (202) 622-5795; Brian McCauley, Director.*
Web, www.treasury.gov/about/organizational-structure/ offices/Pages/–Europe-and-Eurasia.aspx

Guides and develops economic policies toward more than 50 economies in Europe and Eurasia.

Treasury Dept., *International Affairs, International Monetary Policy, 1500 Pennsylvania Ave. N.W., #3034, 20220; (202) 622-2129. Andy Baukol, Deputy Assistant Secretary.*
Web, www.treasury.gov/resource-center/international/int-monetary-fund/Pages/imf_policy.aspx

Provides policy analysis and recommendations with respect to U.S. participation in the International Monetary Fund, an international organization made up of 189 countries working toward global fiscal unity.

Treasury Dept., *International Affairs, Investment Negotiations, 1500 Pennsylvania Ave. N.W., #5419, 20220; (202) 622-1749. Fax, (202) 622-0967. Anthony Ieronimo, Director.*
Web, www.treasury.gov/about/organizational-structure/ offices/Pages/-Trade-and-Investment-Policy.aspx

Heads the U.S. delegation to the Participants and Working Party on Export Credits and Credit Guarantees of the Organization for Economic Cooperation and Development, negotiating agreements to reduce subsidies in export credit support. Negotiates bilateral investment treaties (BITs) and the investment portion of free trade agreements (FTAs) with foreign governments.

Treasury Dept., *International Affairs, Investment Security, 1500 Pennsylvania Ave. N.W., #5221, 20220; (202) 622-1860. Fax, (202) 622-9212. Thomas Feddo, Deputy*

Assistant Secretary, (202) 622-7222; Brian Reissaus, Director of Investment Review and Investigation; Laura Black, Director of Policy and International Relations; Vacant, Director of Mitigation, Monitoring and Enforcement. General email, cifius@do.treas.gov

Web, www.treasury.gov/about/organizational-structure/offices/Pages/-Investment-Security.aspx

Oversees U.S. open investment initiatives. Responsible for the implementation of the Treasury Dept.'s responsibilities as chair of the Committee on Foreign Investment in the United States.

Treasury Dept., International Affairs, Middle East and North Africa, 1500 Pennsylvania Ave. N.W., #3218A, 20220; (202) 622-2156. Fax, (202) 622-0431. Eric Meyer, Deputy Assistant Secretary; Anthony Marcus, Director, (202) 622-6565.

Web, www.treasury.gov/about/organizational-structure/offices/Pages/-Middle-East-and-North-Africa.aspx

Represents the department in the World Bank, International Monetary Fund in the region, and other international institutions that address economic, financial, and development matters. Provides economic analyses of the Middle East (stretching from Morocco to Iran and from Yeman to Turkey) and North Africa.

Treasury Dept., International Affairs, Multilateral Development Bank Operations and Policy, 1500 Pennsylvania Ave. N.W., #3205, 20220; (202) 622-5052. Fax, (202) 622-0664. Mathew Haarsager, Deputy Assistant Secretary.

Web, www.treasury.gov/about/organizational-structure/offices/Pages/Development-Policy-and-Debt.aspx

Leads economic growth and poverty reduction efforts in developing countries by providing funds to multilateral development banks; advises the department and the department banks on reforms and innovative financing proposals; formulates the U.S. position on issues facing debtor countries.

Treasury Dept., International Affairs, South and Southeast Asia, 1500 Pennsylvania Ave. N.W., #3218B, 20220; (202) 622-2000. Seth Bleiweis, Director, (202) 622-8236.

Web, www.treasury.gov/about/organizational-structure/offices/Pages/South-and-Southeast-Asia.aspx

Provides economic analysis of 19 countries in south and southeast Asia. Represents the department in the World Bank, International Monetary Fund, and Asian Development Bank. Leads on issues related to India, including representing the United States in the new U.S.–India Economic and Financial Partnership, and has responsibility for Dept.'s engagement with the Asia Pacific Economic Cooperation (APEC) forum and Association of South East Asian Nations (ASEAN).

Treasury Dept., International Affairs, Technical Assistance, 1750 Pennsylvania Ave. N.W., 8th Floor, 20006; (202) 622-7610. Fax, (202) 622-5879. William Larry McDonald, Deputy Assistant Secretary, (202) 622-5504; Jason Orlando, Director, (202) 622-5792.

General email, info@ota.treas.gov

Web, www.treasury.gov/about/organizational-structure/offices/Pages/Technical-Assistance-.aspx

Works with finance ministries and central banks of developing and transition countries to improve their ability to manage public finances and safeguard their financial sectors by promoting effective revenue policies, strengthening ministries of finance, providing assistance with domestic government securities, and combating economic crimes, including tax evasion, money laundering, terrorism financing, and supporting the development of strong financial sectors.

Treasury Dept., International Affairs, Western Hemisphere, 1500 Pennsylvania Ave. N.W., #3037, 20220; (202) 622-4262. Michael Kaplan, Deputy Assistant Secretary, (202) 622-4262; Matthew Malloy, Director, (202) 622-5795.

Web, www.treasury.gov/about/organizational-structure/offices/Pages/-Western-Hemisphere.aspx

Responsible for economic analysis, financial diplomacy, and U.S. policy initiatives in 35 countries in Latin America, the Caribbean, and Canada.

►CONGRESS

For a listing of relevant congressional committees and subcommittees, please see pages 474–475 or the Appendix.

►INTERNATIONAL ORGANIZATIONS

Coalition for Integrity, 1023 15th St. N.W., #300, 20005; (202) 589-1616. Shruti Shah, President. General email, administration@coalitionforintegrity.org

Web, www.coalitionforintegrity.org and Twitter, @unite4integrity

Institute of International Finance, 1333 H St. N.W., #800 East, 20005-4770; (202) 857-3600. Fax, (202) 775-1430. Timothy D. Adams, President. General email, info@iif.com

Web, www.iif.com and Twitter, @IIF

Global association of financial institutions. Provides analysis and research on emerging markets. Identifies and analyzes regulatory, financial, and economic policy issues. Promotes the development of sound financial systems with particular emphasis on emerging markets.

Inter-American Development Bank, 1300 New York Ave. N.W., 20577; (202) 623-1000. Fax, (202) 623-3096. Luis Alberto Moreno, President; Annette Pedrosa, U.S. Executive Director. Library, (202) 623-3211. Press, (202) 623-1555.

Web, www.iadb.org, Twitter, @the_IDB and Facebook, www.facebook.com/IADB.org

Promotes, through loans and technical assistance, the investment of public and private capital in member countries of Latin America and the Caribbean for social and economic development purposes. Facilitates economic integration of the Latin American region, operating the

Inter-American Investment Corporation and the Multilateral Investment Fund. Library open to the public by appointment.

Intercontinental Exchange, *Washington Office, 801 Pennsylvania Ave. N.W., #630, 20004-2685; Alex Albert, Vice President.*
General email, everyone-washington@theice.com
Web, www.intercontinentalexchange.com, Twitter, @ICE_Markets and Faceebook, www.facebook.com/IntercontinentalExchange

Provides information about risk-management services to market participants around the world. Washington office monitors legislation and regulations. (Headquarters in Atlanta, Ga.)

International Centre for Settlement of Investment Disputes (ICSID), *1818 H St. N.W., MS C3-300, 20433; (202) 458-1534. Fax, (202) 522-2615. Meg Kinnear, Secretary General, (202) 473-5531.*
General email, ICSIDsecretariat@worldbank.org
Web, www.worldbank.org/icsid

Handles the conciliation and arbitration of investment disputes between contracting states and foreign investors. Has more than 140 member states and is affiliated with the World Bank.

International Finance Corp., *2121 Pennsylvania Ave. N.W., 20433; (202) 473-1000. Philippe Le Houérou, Chief Executive Officer. Press, (202) 473-9336.*
Web, www.ifc.org

A member of the World Bank Group that lends to private-sector companies and financial institutions. Works with the private sector to encourage entrepreneurship and build sustainable businesses: advising them on a wide range of issues, including environmental, social, and governance standards, energy and efficiency, and supply chains. Helps expand access to critical finance for individuals and micro, small, and medium enterprises through its work with financial intermediary clients.

International Monetary Fund (IMF), *700 19th St. N.W., 20431; 1900 Pennsylvania Ave. N.W., 20431; (202) 623-7000. Fax, (202) 623-4661. Christine Lagarde, Managing Director; Adam Lerrick, U.S. Executive Director. Legislative Affairs, (202) 623-6220. Media, (202) 623-7100.*
Web, www.imf.org

International organization of 188 member countries that promotes policies for financial stability and economic growth, works to prevent financial crises, and helps members solve balance-of-payment problems through loans funded by member contributions.

International Monetary Fund (IMF), *Statistics, 700 19th St. N.W., 20431; (202) 623-7000. Louis Marc Ducharme, Director. Publications, (202) 623-7430.*
General email, statisticsquery@imf.org
Web, www.imf.org/en/data and eLibrary, www.elibrary.imf.org
Publications, publications@imf.org

Publishes monthly *International Financial Statistics (IFS)*, which includes comprehensive financial data for most countries, and *Direction of Trade Statistics*, a quarterly publication, which includes the distribution of exports and imports for 1,692 countries. Annual statistical publications include the *Balance of Payments Statistics Yearbook*, *Direction of Trade Statistics Yearbook*, *Government Finance Statistics Yearbook*, and *International Financial Statistics Yearbook*. Free online and paid print subscriptions available to the public. All four publications are available on the website.

Multilateral Investment Guarantee Agency, *1818 H St. N.W., 20433; (202) 458-2538. Fax, (202) 522-0316. Keiko Honda, Executive Vice President, (202) 473-2503. Press, (202) 458-9771.*
General email, migainquiry@worldbank.org
Web, www.miga.org and Twitter, @MIGA

World Bank affiliate that encourages foreign investment in developing countries. Provides guarantees against losses due to currency transfer, expropriation, war, civil disturbance, breach of contract, and the nonhonoring of a sovereign financial obligation. Provides dispute resolution services for guaranteed investments to prevent disruptions to developmentally beneficial projects. Membership open to World Bank member countries.

World Bank, *1818 H St. N.W., 20433; (202) 473-1000. Fax, (202) 477-6391. Kristalina Georgieva, President (Acting); Erik Bethel, U.S. Executive Director (Acting); David Theis, Media contact. Anticorruption hotline, (202) 458-7677. Press, (202) 473-7660. Publications, (800) 645-7247 or (703) 661-1580.*
General email, info_us@worldbank.org
Web, www.worldbank.org/en/country/unitedstates and Twitter, @worldbank

International organization encouraging the flow of public and private foreign investment into developing countries through low-interest loans, credits, and grants; collects data on selected economic indicators, world trade, and external public debt. Consists of The International Bank for Reconstruction and Development, The International Development Assn., The International Finance Corporation, The Multilateral Investment Guarantee Agency, and The International Centre for Settlement of Investment Dispute.

▶**NONGOVERNMENTAL**

BAFT, *1120 Connecticut Ave. N.W., 5th Floor, 20036-3902; (202) 663-7575. Fax, (202) 663-5538. Tod R. Burwell, Chief Executive Officer.*
General email, info@baft.org
Web, www.baft.org

Membership: international financial services providers, including U.S. and non–U.S. commercial banks, financial services companies, and suppliers with major international operations. Interests include international trade, trade finance, payments, compliance, asset servicing, and transaction banking. Monitors and acts as an advocate globally on activities that affect the business of commercial and international banks and nonfinancial companies. (Formerly Bankers' Assn. for Financial Trade.)

Bretton Woods Committee, *1701 K St. N.W., #950, 20006; (202) 331-1616. Fax, (202) 785-9423. Randy S. Rodgers, Executive Director.*
General email, info@brettonwoods.org
Web, www.brettonwoods.org and
Twitter, @BrettonWoodsCom

Works to increase public understanding of the World Bank, the regional development institutions, the International Monetary Fund, and the World Trade Organization.

Coalition for Employment Through Exports, *1625 K St. N.W., #200, 20006; (202) 296-6107. Fax, (202) 296-9709. John Hardy Jr., President.*
General email, info@usaexport.org
Web, http://usaexport.org

Membership: major U.S. exporters and banks. Works to ensure adequate lending authority for the Export-Import Bank and other trade finance facilities as well as competitive export financing policies for the United States.

Financial Transparency Coalition, *2000 M St. N.W., #720, 20036; (202) 232-3317. Sargon Nissan, Director.*
General email, info@financialtransparency.org
Web, https://financialtransparency.org, Twitter, @FinTrCo and Facebook, www.facebook.com/FinancialTransparencyCoalition

Research and educational organization concerned with improving international financial transparency in order to decrease illicit financial flows. Encourages multinational corporations to report their profits and taxes, create open information sources on beneficial ownership, and automate tax information exchange.

Global Financial Integrity (GFI), *1100 17th St. N.W., #505, 20036; (202) 293-0740. Fax, (202) 293-1720. Raymond Baker, President, (202) 293-0740, ext. 226. Press, (202) 293-0740, ext. 231.*
General email, gfi@gfintegrity.org
Web, www.gfintegrity.org and Twitter, @GFI_Tweets

Nonprofit that researches and acts as advocate against illicit financial flows between foreign countries. Publishes reports that analyze illegal monetary transfers around the world. Assists developing countries in applying policies to prevent illicit transactions due to drug trafficking, political corruption, money laundering, and terrorist funding.

Microcredit Summit Campaign, *1101 15th St. N.W., #1200, 20005; (202) 637-9600. Fax, (202) 452-9356. Larry Reed, Director; Joanne Carter, Executive Director.*
General email, info@microcreditsummit.org

Membership: microfinance institutions, organizations, practitioners, and advocates aiming to provide international poor families with credit for self-employment and financial and business services. Specializes in helping women in poor families become financially self-sustainable. Holds annual summits to discuss successful microfinance practices that combat global poverty.

Organization for International Investment, *1225 19th St. N.W., #501, 20036; (202) 659-1903. Fax, (202) 659-2293. Nancy McLernon, President.*
General email, jsamford@ofii.org;ralexander@ofii.org
Web, www.ofii.org and Twitter, @ofii

Membership: U.S. subsidiaries of international companies. Provides data on international investment in the United States, including reports on exports, tax revenue, and job creation. Monitors legislation and regulations concerning the business operations of U.S. subsidiaries.

Peterson Institute for International Economics (PIIE), *1750 Massachusetts Ave. N.W., 20036-1903; (202) 328-9000. Fax, (202) 659-3225. Adam S. Posen, President. Press, (202) 454-1334.*
General email, comments@piie.com
Web, www.petersoninstitute.org and Twitter, @PIIE

Conducts studies and makes policy recommendations on international economic issues, including monetary affairs, trade, investment, energy, exchange rates, commodities, and North–South and East–West economic relations.

REGIONAL AFFAIRS

See also Foreign Embassies, U.S. Ambassadors, and Country Desk Offices (Appendix).

Africa

For North Africa, see Near East and South Asia.

▶**AGENCIES**

Agency for International Development (USAID), *Bureau for Africa, 1300 Pennsylvania Ave. N.W., #4.08C, 20523-4801; (202) 712-0500. Cheryl L. Anderson, Deputy Assistant Administrator; Ramsey Day, Senior Deputy Assistant Director.*
Web, www.usaid.gov/who-we-are/organization/bureaus/bureau-africa

Advises the USAID administrator on U.S. policy toward developing countries in Africa.

Bureau of African Affairs *(State Dept.), 2201 C St. N.W., #6234A, 20520-3430; (202) 647-2530. Fax, (202) 647-6301. Tibor P. Nagy Jr., Assistant Secretary.*
Web, www.state.gov/p/af, Twitter, @AsstSecStateAF and Facebook, www.facebook.com/DOSAfricanAffairs
Blog, https://blogs.state.gov/regions/africa

Advises the secretary on U.S. policy toward sub-Saharan Africa. Directors, assigned to different regions in Africa, aid the assistant secretary.

Bureau of African Affairs *(State Dept.), Central African Affairs, 2201 C St. N.W., #4244, 20520-2902; (202) 663-0535. Fax, (202) 647-1726. Rafael Foley, Director (Acting), (202) 647-6491.*
Web, www.state.gov/p/af

Includes Burundi, Cameroon, Central African Republic, Chad, the Democratic Republic of Congo, the Republic of Congo, Equatorial Guinea, Gabon, Rwanda, and São Tomé and Príncipe.

Bureau of African Affairs *(State Dept.), East African Affairs, 2201 C St. N.W., #4248, 20520; (202) 647-8852. Fax, (202) 647-0810. Vincent Spera, Director (Acting), (202) 647-5220.*
Web, www.state.gov/p/af

Includes Comoros, Djibouti, Eritrea, Ethiopia, Kenya, Madagascar, Mauritius, Seychelles, Somalia, Tanzania, and Uganda.

Bureau of African Affairs *(State Dept.), Southern African Affairs, 2201 C St. N.W., #4236, 20520; (202) 647-9836. Fax, (202) 647-5007. Matthew T. Harrington, Deputy Assistant Secretary, (202) 647-2447.*
Web, www.state.gov/p/af

Includes Angola, Botswana, Lesotho, Malawi, Mozambique, Namibia, South Africa, Swaziland, Zambia, and Zimbabwe.

Bureau of African Affairs *(State Dept.), Special Envoy for Sudan and South Sudan, 2201 C St. N.W., #1460, 20520; (202) 647-5066. Brian Shukan, Director.*
Web, www.state.gov/s/sudan, Twitter, @SUSSESSS and Facebook, www.facebook.com/US.Special.Envoy.for.Sudan

Represents the U.S. government's interests in Sudan and Darfur/South Sudan.

Bureau of African Affairs *(State Dept.), West African Affairs, 2201 C St. N.W., #4246, 20520-3430; (202) 647-3395. Fax, (202) 647-4855. Sandra E. Clark, Director, (202) 647-2638.*
Web, www.state.gov/p/af

Includes Benin, Burkina Faso, Cape Verde, Côte d'Ivoire, the Gambia, Ghana, Guinea, Guinea-Bissau, Liberia, Mali, Mauritania, Niger, Nigeria, Senegal, Sierra Leone, and Togo.

Defense Dept. (DoD), *International Security Affairs, 2000 Defense Pentagon, #3C889, 20301-2000; (703) 697-2788. Fax, (703) 697-3279. Kathryn Wheelbarger, Assistant Secretary (Acting).*
Web, http://policy.defense.gov/OUSDPOffices/ASDforInternationalSecurityAffairs

Advises the secretary of defense and recommends policies on regional security issues in the Middle East, Africa, Russia/Eurasia, and Europe/NATO.

Defense Dept. (DoD), *International Security Affairs, Africa, 2000 Defense Pentagon, 20301-2000; (703) 697-2788. Alan Patterson, Deputy Assistant Secretary; Todd Coker, Principal Director.*
Web, www.defense.gov

Advises the assistant secretary for international security affairs on matters dealing with Africa.

United States African Development Foundation (USADF), *1400 Eye St. N.W., #1000, 20005-2248; (202) 233-8800. Fax, (202) 673-3810. C.D. Glin, President. Press, (202) 673-3916, ext. 8811.*

General email, info@usadf.gov
Web, www.usadf.gov, Twitter, @USADF and Facebook, www.facebook.com/USADF

Established by Congress to work with and fund organizations and individuals involved in community-based development projects in Africa. Gives preference to projects involving extensive participation by local Africans. Work focuses on conflict and postconflict areas.

► **CONGRESS**

For a listing of relevant congressional committees and subcommittees, please see pages 474–475 or the Appendix.

Library of Congress, *African and Middle Eastern Division, Thomas Jefferson Bldg., 101 Independence Ave. S.E., #LJ 220, 20540-4660; (202) 707-7937. Fax, (202) 252-3180. Mary-Jane Deeb, Chief, (202) 707-1221. Reading room, (202) 707-4188.*
General email, amed@loc.gov
Web, www.loc.gov/rr/amed

Maintains collections of African, Near Eastern, and Hebraic material. Prepares bibliographies and special studies relating to Africa and the Middle East. Reference service and reading rooms available to the public. (Need reader's card to use.)

► **INTERNATIONAL ORGANIZATIONS**

World Bank, *Africa Region, 1818 H St. N.W., 20433; (202) 473-1000. Hafez Ghanem, Vice President; Steven Shalita, Communications Manager, (202) 458-1042.*
General email, africateam@worldbank.org
Web, www.worldbank.org/en/region/afr and Twitter, @WorldBankAfrica

Aims to reduce poverty in middle-income countries and creditworthy poorer countries by promoting sustainable development through low-interest loans, zero to low-interest credits, grants, guarantees, risk management products, and analytical and advisory services. Priorities in Africa include education, health, public administration, infrastructure, financial and private sector development, agriculture, and environmental and natural resource management.

► **NONGOVERNMENTAL**

Africa Faith and Justice Network (AFJN), *3025 4th St. N.E., #122, 20017; (202) 817-3670. Fax, (202) 817-3671. Rev. Aniedi Okure, Executive Director.*
General email, afjn@afjn.org
Web, www.afjn.org, Twitter, @AFJN-DC and Facebook, www.facebook.com/AfricaFaithandJusticeNetwork

Acts as an advocate with Catholic missionary congregations and Africa-focused coalitions for U.S. economic and political policies that benefit Africa. Promotes the Catholic view of peace building, human rights, and social justice. Interests include ending armed conflict, equitable trade with and investment in Africa, and sustainable development. Monitors legislation and regulations.

Africare, *440 R St. N.W., 20001-1935; (202) 462-3614. Fax, (202) 387-1034. Robert L. Mallett, President.*
General email, info@africare.org
Web, www.africare.org, Twitter, @africare and Facebook, www.facebook.com/Africare

Seeks to improve the quality of life in rural Africa through development of water resources, increased food production, and delivery of health services.

The Brookings Institution, *Global Economy and Development Studies, Africa Growth Initiative, 1775 Massachusetts Ave. N.W., 20036; (202) 797-6000. Fax, (202) 797-6004. Amadou Sy, Director.*
General email, AGI@Brookings.edu
Web, www.brookings.edu/about/projects/africa-growth

Conducts policy research and analysis focusing on sustainable economic growth in Africa. Interests include financial development, risks to growth including climate change and epidemics, trade and regional integration, governance transparency, reduction of gender barriers, and youth employment.

Corporate Council on Africa, *1100 17th St. N.W., #1200, 20036; (202) 835-1115. Fax, (202) 263-3525. Florizelle (Florie) Liser, President.*
General email, cca@corporatecouncilonafrica.com
Web, www.corporatecouncilonafrica.com and Twitter, @CorpCnclAfrica

Membership: American corporations working with African agriculture, energy, finance, health, trade, communication technology, and security industries. Promotes business relations between the United States and Africa. Facilitates government and business advancements in Africa's trade industry. Monitors legislation and regulations that impact African commercial relations.

Lubuto Library Partners, *5614 Connecticut Ave N.W., #368, 20015-2604; (202) 558-5609. Jane Kinney Meyers, President.*
General email, webmail@lubuto.org
Web, www.lubuto.org

International development organization that focuses on library development for youth in southern African countries. Works with public and private libraries and other partners to construct an open-access library collection and accessible services for children and youth in southern Africa. Sponsors library programs to foster education in the arts and technology; offers services for children with disabilities.

Sudan Sunrise, *10508 James Wren Way, Fairfax, VA 22030; (202) 499-6984. Tom Prichard, Executive Director.*
General email, info@sudansunrise.org
Web, http://sudansunrise.org and Twitter, @SudanSunrise

Supports schools and education programs for children of various religions, tribes, and communities in Sudan and South Sudan.

East Asia and Pacific

▶**AGENCIES**

Agency for International Development (USAID), *Bureau for Asia, 1300 Pennsylvania Ave. N.W., 20523-4900; (202) 712-0200. Fax, (202) 216-3386. Gloria Steele, Senior Deputy Assistant Administrator.*
Web, www.usaid.gov/who-we-are/organization/bureaus/bureau-asia

Advises the USAID administrator on U.S. economic development policy in Asia.

Bureau of East Asian and Pacific Affairs *(State Dept.), 2201 C St. N.W., #6205, 20520-6205; (202) 647-9596. Patrick Murphy, Principal Deputy Assistant Secretary. Press, (202) 647-2538.*
Web, www.state.gov/p/eap, Twitter, @USAsiaPacific and Facebook, www.facebook.com/USAsiaPacific
Blog, https://blogs.state.gov/latest-stories?field_region_tid=1580

Advises the secretary on U.S. policy toward East Asian and Pacific countries. Directors assigned to specific countries within the bureau aid the assistant secretary.

Bureau of East Asian and Pacific Affairs *(State Dept.), Australia, New Zealand, and Pacific Island Affairs, 2201 C St. N.W., #4318, 20520; (202) 736-4659. Fax, (202) 647-0118. Nicholas Dean, Director.*
Web, www.state.gov/p/eap

Bureau of East Asian and Pacific Affairs *(State Dept.), Chinese and Mongolian Affairs, 2201 C St. N.W., #4318, 20520; (202) 647-6796. Fax, (202) 736-7809. Hanscom Smith, Director, (202) 647-6787.*
Web, www.state.gov/p/eap

Bureau of East Asian and Pacific Affairs *(State Dept.), Japanese Affairs, 2201 C St. N.W., #4206, 20520; (202) 647-2913. Edwin (Ted) Saeger, Director.*
Web, www.state.gov/p/eap

Bureau of East Asian and Pacific Affairs *(State Dept.), Korean Affairs, 2201 C St. N.W., #4206, 20520; (202) 647-7719. Joy Yamamoto, Director.*
Web, www.state.gov/p/eap

Bureau of East Asian and Pacific Affairs *(State Dept.), Mainland Southeast Asia Affairs, 2201 C St. N.W., #5206, 20520-6310; (202) 647-4495. Fax, (202) 647-3069. Mark Tesone, Director.*
Web, www.state.gov/p/eap

Includes Burma, Cambodia, Laos, Thailand, and Vietnam.

Bureau of East Asian and Pacific Affairs *(State Dept.), Maritime Southeast Asia Affairs, 2201 C St. N.W., #5210, 20520; (202) 647-2143. Fax, (202) 736-4559. Mark Clark, Director.*
Web, www.state.gov/p/eap

Includes the Philippines, Malaysia, Brunei, Indonesia, East Timor, and Singapore.

Bureau of East Asian and Pacific Affairs *(State Dept.),* **North Korea Affairs,** *2201 C St. N.W., #7321, 20520-5209; (202) 647-5569. Stephen Biegun, Special Representative for North Korea.*
Web, www.state.gov/p/eap

Bureau of East Asian and Pacific Affairs *(State Dept.),* **Taiwan Coordination,** *2201 C St. N.W., #4312, 20520; (202) 647-7711. James Heller, Director.*
Web, www.state.gov/p/eap

Defense Dept. (DoD), *Asian and Pacific Security Affairs, 2700 Defense Pentagon, #5D688, 20301-2400; (703) 695-4175. Randall Shriver, Assistant Secretary; David Helvey, Principal Deputy Assistant Secretary. Press, (703) 697-5131.*
Web, http://policy.defense.gov/OUSDPoffices/ ASDforAsianandPacificSecurityAffairs

Advises the under secretary of defense on matters dealing with Asia and the Pacific.

Defense Dept. (DoD), *East Asia Security Affairs, 2700 Defense Pentagon, #5D688, 20301-2700; (703) 695-4175. Kelly Magsamen, Deputy Assistant Secretary.*
Web, http://policy.defense.gov/OUSDP-Offices/ASD-for-Asian-and-Pacific-Security-Affairs

Advises the under secretary of defense on matters dealing with China, Japan, Mongolia, North and South Korea, and Taiwan.

Japan–United States Friendship Commission, *1201 15th St. N.W., #330, 20005-2842; (202) 653-9800. Fax, (202) 653-9802. Paige Cottingham-Streater, Executive Director.*
General email, jusfc@jusfc.gov
Web, www.jusfc.gov

Independent agency established by Congress that makes grants and administers funds and programs promoting educational and cultural exchanges between Japan and the United States.

▶CONGRESS

For a listing of relevant congressional committees and subcommittees, please see pages 474–475 or the Appendix.

Congressional–Executive Commission on China, *243 FHOB, 20515; (202) 226-3766. Fax, (202) 226-3804. Rep. Christopher H. Smith, Co-Chair; Sen. Marco Rubio, Co-Chair; Elyse Anderson, Staff Director, (202) 226-3821. General email, infocecc@mail.house.gov*
Web, www.cecc.gov and Twitter, @CECCgov

Independent agency created by Congress. Membership includes individuals from the executive and legislative branches. Monitors human rights and the development of the rule of law in the People's Republic of China. Submits an annual report to the president and Congress.

Library of Congress, *Asian Division, Thomas Jefferson Bldg., 101 Independence Ave. S.E., #LJ 150, 20540; (202) 707-3766. Fax, (202) 252-1724. Dongfang Shao, Chief, (202) 707-5919. Reading room, (202) 707-5426.*
Web, www.loc.gov/rr/asian

Maintains collections of Asian-American Pacific, Chinese, Korean, Japanese, Southeast Asian, South Asian, and Tibetan and Mongolian material. Reference service is provided in the Asian Reading Room, room #150.

U.S.–China Economic and Security Review Commission, *444 N. Capitol St. N.W., #602, 20001; (202) 624-1407. Fax, (202) 624-1406. Daniel Peck, Executive Director. General email, contact@uscc.gov*
Web, www.uscc.gov and Twitter, @USCC_GOV

Investigates the national security implications of the bilateral trade and economic relationship between China and the United States. Makes recommendations to Congress based on its findings.

▶INTERNATIONAL ORGANIZATIONS

World Bank, *East Asia and Pacific Region, 1818 H St. N.W., C9th Floor, 20433; (202) 473-1000. Victoria Kwakwa, Vice President; Alejandro Cedeno, Communications Manager, (202) 473-4709. General email, mmontemayor@worldbank.org*
Web, www.worldbank.org/en/region/eap and Twitter, @WB_AsiaPacific

Works to fight poverty and improve the living standards of low- and middle-income people in the countries of East Asia and the Pacific by providing loans, policy advice, technical assistance, and knowledge-sharing services. Areas of interest include finance, economic development, education, water supply, agriculture, public health, and environmental protection.

▶NONGOVERNMENTAL

American Institute in Taiwan, *1700 N. Moore St., #1700, Arlington, VA 22209-1385; (703) 525-8474. Fax, (703) 841-1385. Amb. James F. (Jim) Moriarty, Chair; John J. Norris Jr., Managing Director.*
Web, www.ait.org.tw/en, Twitter, @AIT.Social.Media and Facebook, www.facebook.com/AIT.Social.Media

Chartered by Congress to coordinate commercial, cultural, and other activities between the people of the United States and Taiwan. Represents U.S. interests and maintains offices in Taiwan.

Asia Foundation, *Washington Office, 1779 Massachusetts Ave. N.W., #815, 20036; (202) 588-9420. Fax, (202) 588-9409. Nancy Yuan, Director.*
General email, dc.general@asiafoundation.org
Web, www.asiafoundation.org and Twitter, @Asia_Foundation

Provides grants and technical assistance in Asia and the Pacific Islands (excluding the Middle East). Seeks to strengthen legislatures, legal and judicial systems, market economies, the media, and nongovernmental organizations. (Headquarters in San Francisco, Calif.)

Asia Policy Point (APP), *1730 Rhode Island Ave. N.W., #414, 20036; (202) 822-6040. Fax, (202) 822-6044. Mindy Kotler, Director.*

General email, asiapolicyhq@gmail.com

Web, www.jiaponline.org

Blog, http://newasiapolicypoint.blogspot.com

Studies Japanese and Northeast Asian security and public policies as they relate to the United States. Researches and analyzes issues affecting Japan's relationship with the West. (Formerly the Japan Information Access Project.)

Asia Society Policy Institute, *Washington Office, 1779 Massachusetts Ave., #810, 20036; (202) 833-2742. Fax, (202) 833-0189. Wendy Cutler, Managing Director.*

General email, asiadc@asiasociety.org

Web, www.asiasociety.org and Twitter, @AsiaPolicy

Membership: individuals, organizations, and corporations interested in Asia and the Pacific (excluding the Middle East). Focuses on United States and Asia foreign policy issues. Sponsors seminars and lectures on political, economic, and cultural issues. (Headquarters in New York.)

The Brookings Institution, *Center for East Asia Policy Studies, 1775 Massachusetts Ave. N.W., 20036; (202) 238-3104. Richard C. Bush, Director.*

Web, www.brookings.edu/center/center-for-east-asia-policy-studies and Twitter, @richardbushiii

Conducts research, analysis, and exchange to enhance policy development on political, security, and economic issues in East Asia. Administers a visiting fellowship program annually. Interests include Taiwan relations; U.S.–ROK relations; Japanese politics and foreign policies; U.S.-China strategic relations; and Southeast Asia's growing strategic, economic, and diplomatic importance.

The Brookings Institution, *John L. Thornton China Center, 1775 Massachusetts Ave. N.W., 20036; (202) 797-6103. Cheng Li, Director.*

Web, www.brookings.edu/center/john-l-thornton-china-center and Twitter, @brookingschina

Research center promoting policies concerning China and its increasingly greater role in foreign affairs. Interests include secure energy sources, economic reforms, social and economic inequality, and citizen participation in government.

East–West Center, *Washington Office, 1819 L St. N.W., #600, 20036; (202) 293-3995. Fax, (202) 293-1402. Satu P. Limaye, Director.*

General email, washington@eastwestcenter.org

Web, www.eastwestcenter.org/ewc-in-washington

Promotes strengthening of relations and understanding among countries and peoples of Asia, the Pacific, and the United States. Plans to undertake substantive programming activities, including collaborative research, training, seminars, and outreach; publications; and congressional study groups. (Headquarters in Honolulu, Hawaii.)

Eurasia Foundation, *1350 Connecticut Ave. N.W., #1000, 20036-1730; (202) 234-7370. Fax, (202) 234-7377. Lisa Coll, President.*

General email, info@eurasia.org

Web, www.eurasia.org and Twitter, @EFNetwork

Operates in Eurasia, the Middle East, and China. Provides capacity building, entrepreneurship training, advocacy education, social entrepreneurship training, and fellowship exchanges to support small business growth, local institutional performance, the responsiveness of local governments, and the leadership of young people.

Formosan Assn. for Public Affairs, *552 7th St. S.E., 20003; (202) 547-3686. Fax, (202) 543-7891. Michael Kuo, President.*

Web, www.fapa.org and Facebook, www.facebook.com/FormosanAssociationforPublicAffairs

Political group that advocates the independence of Taiwan and promotes democracy. Seeks to improve relations between the United States and Taiwan. Educates the public, policymakers, and the media about current issues in Taiwan. Monitors legislation and regulations related to Taiwan's relationship with the United States.

Heritage Foundation, *Asian Studies Center, 214 Massachusetts Ave. N.E., 20002-4999; (202) 546-4400. Fax, (202) 675-1779. Walter Lohman, Director. Press, (202) 675-1761.*

General email, info@heritage.org

Web, www.heritage.org/asia

Conducts research and provides information on U.S. policies in Asia and the Pacific. Interests include economic and security issues in the Asia Pacific region. Hosts speakers and visiting foreign policy delegations; sponsors conferences.

International Campaign for the Rohingya, *P.O. Box 48698, 20002-0698; (617) 596-6158. Simon Billenness, Executive Director.*

Web, www.rohingyacampaign.org and Twitter, @Rohingya_ICR

Acts as advocate for the Rohingya people with international organizations, governments, corporations, and civil society through education. Works to reduce genocide through the "No Business With Genocide" campaign by building a global movement to hold corporations accountable and put pressure on corporations in key sectors to stop supporting regimes complicit in genocide and crimes against humanity.

Jamestown Foundation, *1310 L St. N.W., #810, 20005; (202) 483-8888. Fax, (202) 483-8337. Glen E. Howard, President.*

General email, pubs@jamestown.org

Web, www.jamestown.org, Twitter, @JamestownTweets and Facebook, www.facebook.com/The-Jamestown-Foundation

Provides policymakers with information about events and trends in societies that are strategically or tactically important to the United States and that frequently restrict access to such information. Serves as an alternative source to official or intelligence channels, especially with regard to Eurasia, China, and terrorism. Publishes the *Militant Leadership Monitor,* covering leaders of major insurgencies and militant movements.

Japan–America Society of Washington, *1819 L St. N.W., Level B2, 20036-3807; (202) 833-2210. Marc Hitzig, Executive Director; Ryan Shaffer, President.*
General email, info@jaswdc.org
Web, www.jaswdc.org, Twitter, @jas_wdc and Facebook, www.facebook.com/jas.wdc

Conducts programs on U.S.–Japan political, security, and economic issues. Cultural programs include lectures, a Japanese-language school, and assistance to Japanese performing artists. Maintains library for members. Participates in National Cherry Blossom Festival.

Taipei Economic and Cultural Representative Office (TECRO), *4201 Wisconsin Ave. N.W., 20016; (202) 895-1800. Fax, (202) 966-0825. Stanley Kao, Representative. Press, (202) 895-1850.*
General email, usa@mofa.gov.tw
Web, www.taiwanembassy.org/us_en/index.html and Twitter, @TECRO_USA

Represents political, economic, and cultural interests of the government of the Republic of China (Taiwan) in the United States.

U.S.–Asia Institute, *232 E. Capitol St. N.E., 20003; (202) 544-3181. Fax, (202) 747-5889. Mary Sue Bissell, Executive Director.*
General email, usai@usasiainstitute.org
Web, www.usasiainstitute.org and Twitter, @usasiainstitute

Organization of individuals interested in Asia. Encourages dialogue among political and business leaders in the United States and Asia. Interests include foreign policy, international trade, Asian and American cultures, education, and employment. Conducts research and sponsors conferences and workshops in cooperation with the State Dept. to promote greater understanding between the United States and Asian nations.

U.S.–China Business Council, *1818 N St. N.W., #200, 20036-2470; (202) 429-0340. Fax, (202) 775-2476. Craig Allen, President.*
General email, info@uschina.org
Web, www.uschina.org and Twitter, @USChinaBusiness

Member-supported organization that represents U.S. companies engaged in business relations with the People's Republic of China. Participates in U.S. policy issues relating to China and other international trade. Publishes research reports. (Maintains offices in Beijing and Shanghai.)

United States–Indonesia Society, *1625 Massachusetts Ave. N.W., #550, 20036-2260; (202) 232-1400. Fax, (202) 232-7300. David (Dave) Merrill, President.*
General email, usindo@usindo.org
Web, www.usindo.org and Twitter, @USINDO

Seeks to strengthen relations between the United States and Indonesia. Educates and holds forums on economic and political trends in Indonesia. Grants scholarships and fellowships to students and professionals to travel from or to the United States and Indonesia.

Europe

(Includes the Baltic states)

▶**AGENCIES**

Agency for International Development (USAID), *Bureau for Europe and Eurasia, 301 4th St. S.W., #247, 20523 (mailing address: 1300 Pennsylvania Ave. N.W., Washington, DC 20521); (202) 567-4020. Fax, (202) 567-4256. Brock Bierman, Assistant Administrator.*
Web, www.usaid.gov/who-we-are/organization/bureaus/bureau-europe-and-eurasia

Advises the USAID administrator on U.S. economic development policy in Europe and Eurasia.

Bureau of European and Eurasian Affairs (EUR) *(State Dept.), 2201 C St. N.W., #6226, 20520; (202) 647-4876. Fax, (202) 647-5716. A. Wess Mitchell, Assistant Secretary, (202) 647-9626. Press, (202) 647-5116.*
Web, www.state.gov/p/eur

Advises the secretary on U.S. policy toward European and Eurasian countries. Directors assigned to specific countries within the bureau aid the assistant secretary.

Bureau of European and Eurasian Affairs *(State Dept.), Central European Affairs, 2201 C St. N.W., #4230, 20520; (202) 647-1484. Fax, (202) 647-5117. Amy Carnie, Deputy Director, (202) 647-2005.*
Web, www.state.gov/p/eur

Includes Austria, Bulgaria, Czech Republic, Hungary, Liechtenstein, Poland, Romania, Slovak Republic, Slovenia, and Switzerland.

Bureau of European and Eurasian Affairs *(State Dept.), European Security and Political Affairs, 2201 C St. N.W., #6511, 20520; (202) 647-1626. Fax, (202) 647-1369. Joseph Manso, Director.*
Web, www.state.gov/p/eur

Coordinates and advises, with the Defense Dept. and other agencies, the U.S. mission to NATO and the U.S. delegation to the Organization for Security and Cooperation in Europe regarding political, military, and arms control matters.

Bureau of European and Eurasian Affairs *(State Dept.), European Union and Regional Affairs, 2201 C St. N.W., #5424, 20520; (202) 647-3246. Fax, (202) 647-9959. Jeffrey Giauque, Director (Acting).*
Web, www.state.gov/p/eur

Handles all matters concerning the European Union, with emphasis on trade issues. Monitors export controls and economic activities for the North Atlantic Treaty Organization and the Organization for Security and Cooperation in Europe.

Bureau of European and Eurasian Affairs *(State Dept.), Nordic and Baltic Affairs, 2201 C St. N.W., #5428, 20520; (202) 647-5669. Fax, (202) 736-4170. Ian Campbell, Director, (202) 647-6556.*
Web, www.state.gov/p/eur

Includes Denmark, Estonia, Finland, Iceland, Latvia, Lithuania, Norway, and Sweden.

Bureau of European and Eurasian Affairs *(State Dept.),* *South Central European Affairs,* 2201 C St. N.W., #5219, 20520; (202) 647-0608. Fax, (202) 647-1838. *Susan K. Falatko, Director (Acting).* *Web, www.state.gov/p/eur*

Includes Albania, Bosnia-Herzegovina, Croatia, Kosovo, Macedonia, Serbia, and Montenegro.

Bureau of European and Eurasian Affairs *(State Dept.),* *Southern European Affairs,* 2201 C St. N.W., #5511, 20520; (202) 647-6112. Fax, (202) 647-5087. *Yuri Kim, Director, (202) 647-6994.* *Web, www.state.gov/p/eur*

Includes Cyprus, Greece, and Turkey.

Bureau of European and Eurasian Affairs *(State Dept.),* *Special Envoy for Holocaust Issues,* 2201 C St. N.W., #6219, 20520-6219; (202) 647-4753. Thomas K. Yazdgerdi, *Special Envoy.* *Web, www.state.gov/p/eur/rt/hlcst*

Bureau of European and Eurasian Affairs *(State Dept.),* *Western European Affairs,* 2201 C St. N.W., #5218, 20520; (202) 647-1469. Fax, (202) 647-3459. Robert Faucher, *Director.* *Web, www.state.gov/p/eur*

Includes Andorra, Belgium, Bermuda, France, Ireland, Italy, Luxembourg, Malta, Monaco, the Netherlands, Portugal, San Marino, Spain, the United Kingdom, and the Vatican.

Defense Dept. (DoD), *International Security Affairs,* 2000 Defense Pentagon, #3C889, 20301-2000; (703) 697-2788. Fax, (703) 697-3279. Kathryn Wheelbarger, Assistant Secretary (Acting). *Web, http://policy.defense.gov/OUSDPOffices/ ASDforInternationalSecurityAffairs*

Advises the secretary of defense and recommends policies on regional security issues in the Middle East, Africa, Russia/Eurasia, and Europe/NATO.

Defense Dept. (DoD), *International Security Affairs,* *European and NATO Policy,* 2000 Defense Pentagon, #5B652, 20301-2000; (703) 695-5553. James J. Townsend, *Deputy Assistant Secretary (Acting); Rachel Ellehuus,* *Principal Director.* *Web, www.defense.gov*

Advises the assistant secretary for international security affairs on matters dealing with Europe and NATO.

▶ **CONGRESS**

For a listing of relevant congressional committees and subcommittees, please see pages 474–475 or the Appendix.

Library of Congress, *European Division, Thomas Jefferson Bldg., 101 Independence Ave. S.E., #LJ 249, 20540;*

(202) 707-5414. Fax, (202) 707-8482. Grant Harris, Chief, (202) 707-5859. Reference desk, (202) 707-4515. *General email, eurref@loc.gov* *Web, www.loc.gov/rr/european*

Provides reference service on the library's European collections (except collections on Spain, Portugal, and the British Isles). Prepares bibliographies and special studies relating to European countries, including Russia and the other states of the former Soviet Union and eastern bloc. Maintains current unbound Slavic language periodicals and newspapers, which are available at the European Reference Desk. Recommends materials for acquisition.

▶ **INTERNATIONAL ORGANIZATIONS**

European Parliament Liaison Office, 2175 K St. N.W., #600, 20037; (202) 862-4734. Antoine Ripoll, Director, (202) 862-4731. *General email, epwashington@ep.europa.eu* *Web, www.europarl.europa.eu/us and* *Twitter, @EPWashingtonDC*

Acts as the contact point between the European Parliament and the U.S. Congress. Seeks to intensify working relations between the European Parliament and the U.S. Congress at all levels, particularly between corresponding committees of jurisdiction, and between European Parliament lawmakers and U.S. regulators. Represents the Parliament's viewpoint to the U.S. administration and Congress. Principal issues addressed are human rights, the threat of terrorism, economic growth, and environmental protection.

European Union, *Delegation to the United States of* *America,* 2175 K St. N.W., 20037; (202) 862-9500. Fax, (202) 429-1766. David O'Sullivan, Ambassador. *General email, delegation-usa-info@eeas.europa.eu* *Web, www.euintheus.org and Twitter, @EUintheUS*

Information and public affairs office in the United States for the European Union. Provides social policy data on the European Union and provides statistics and information on member countries, including those related to energy, economics, development and cooperation, commerce, agriculture, industry, and technology. (Headquarters in Brussels.)

World Bank, *Europe and Central Asia Region,* 1818 H St. N.W., 20433; (202) 473-1000. Cyril Muller, Vice President; Carl Hanlon, Communications Manager. *General email, eca@worldbank.org* *Web, www.worldbank.org/en/region/eca and* *Twitter, @WorldBankECA*

Works to fight poverty and improve the living standards of low- and middle-income people in the countries of eastern Europe by providing loans, policy advice, technical assistance, and knowledge-sharing services. Areas of interest include finance, economic development, education, water supply, agriculture, public health, and environmental protection.

▶ NONGOVERNMENTAL

American Hellenic Institute, *1220 16th St. N.W., 20036-3202; (202) 785-8430. Fax, (202) 785-5178. Nick Larigakis, President.*
General email, info@ahiworld.org

Web, http://ahiworld.org, Twitter, @AmericanHellenicInst and Facebook, www.facebook.com/AmericanHellenicInstitute and Library Portal, www.ahiworld.org/ahif-library

Works to strengthen relations between Greece, Cyprus, Turkey, southeastern Europe, and the United States and within the American Hellenic community.

British American Security Information Council (BASIC), *1725 DeSales St. N.W., #600, 20036; Paul Ingram, Executive Director.*
General email, basicuk@basicint.org

Web, www.basicint.org and Twitter, @basic_int

Independent analysis and advocacy organization that researches global security issues, including nuclear policies, military strategies, armaments, and disarmament. Assists in the development of global security policies, promotes public awareness, and facilitates exchange of information on both sides of the Atlantic. (UK office is in London.)

The Brookings Institution, Center on the United States and Europe, *1775 Massachusetts Ave. N.W., 20036; (202) 540-7785. Kemal Kirisci, Senior Fellow.*
Web, www.brookings.edu/center/center-on-the-united-states-and-europe and Twitter, @kemalkirisci

Research center promoting U.S.–Europe policy. Interests include transformation of the European Union, engagement strategies for the Balkans, Caucasus, Russia, Turkey, and Ukraine, and NATO and European security. Holds seminars and public forums on policy-relevant issues.

Center for European Policy Analysis, *1725 Pennsylvania Ave. N.W., #400, 20004; (202) 551-9200. Peter B. Doran, President. Media, (202) 551-9202.*
General email, info@cepa.org

Web, http://cepa.org and Twitter, @cepa

Researches public policy in Central and Eastern European countries and seeks to improve their relations with the United States. Holds conferences on issues affecting transnational business, economy, security, and energy resources.

German American Business Council, *2000 M St. N.W., #335, 20036; (202) 955-5595. Ulrich Gamerdinger, President.*
General email, gabc@gabcwashington.com

Web, http://gabcwashington.com

Promotes transatlantic business dialogue between Germany and the United States through improved communication between embassies, industry, governments, and academia.

German Marshall Fund of the United States, *1744 R St. N.W., 20009; (202) 683-2650. Fax, (202) 265-1662. Karen Donfried, President.*
General email, info@gmfus.org

Web, www.gmfus.org and Twitter, @gmfus

American institution created by a gift from Germany as a permanent memorial to Marshall Plan aid. Seeks to stimulate exchange of ideas and promote transatlantic cooperation. Awards grants to promote the study of international and domestic policies; supports comparative research and debate on key issues.

Irish National Caucus, *P.O. Box 15128, 20003-0849; (202) 544-0568. Fax, (202) 488-7537. Fr. Sean McManus, President.*
General email, support@irishnationalcaucus.org

Web, www.irishnationalcaucus.org

Educational organization concerned with protecting human rights in Northern Ireland. Seeks to end anti-Catholic discrimination in Northern Ireland through implementation of the McBride Principles, initiated in 1984. Advocates nonviolence and supports the peace process in Northern Ireland. Monitors legislation and regulations.

Joint Baltic American National Committee (JBANC), *400 Hurley Ave., Rockville, MD 20850; (301) 340-1954. Karl Altau, Managing Director.*
General email, jbanc@jbanc.org

Web, www.jbanc.org, Twitter, @JBANCchatter and Facebook, www.facebook.com/JointBalticAmericanNationalCommittee

Washington representative of the Estonian, Latvian, and Lithuanian American communities in the United States; acts as a representative on issues affecting the Baltic states.

Trans-Atlantic Business Council, *1601 K St. N.W., 20001; (202) 778-9073. Fax, (202) 778-9100. Bart Gordon, U.S. Director.*
Web, http://transatlanticbusiness.org and Twitter, @TABC_Council

Membership: American companies with operations in Europe and European companies with operations in the United States. Promotes a barrier-free transatlantic market that contributes to economic growth, innovation, and security.

Latin America, Canada, and the Caribbean

▶ AGENCIES

Agency for International Development (USAID), *Bureau for Latin America and the Caribbean, 1300 Pennsylvania Ave. N.W., #5.09, 20523-5900; (202) 712-4760. Fax, (202) 216-3012. Steve Olive, Senior Deputy Assistant Administrator. Press, (202) 712-5952.*
Web, www.usaid.gov/who-we-are/organization/bureaus/bureau-latin-america-and-caribbean

Advises the USAID administrator on U.S. policy toward developing Latin American and Caribbean countries. Designs and implements assistance programs for developing nations.

Bureau of Western Hemisphere Affairs *(State Dept.),* *2201 C St. N.W., #6262, 20520; (202) 647-5780.* *Julie J. Chung, Principal Deputy Assistant Secretary. Press, (202) 647-0842.* *Web, www.state.gov/p/wha, Twitter, @WHAAsstSecty* *Blog, https://blogs.state.gov/latest-stories?field_region_tid=1583 and YouTube, www.youtube.com/user/whabureau*

Advises the secretary on U.S. policy toward North, Central, and South America. Directors assigned to specific regions within the bureau aid the assistant secretary.

Bureau of Western Hemisphere Affairs *(State Dept.),* **Andean Affairs,** *2201 C St. N.W., #4915, 20520; (202) 647-1715. Keith Mines, Director.* *Web, www.state.gov/p/wha*

Includes Bolivia, Colombia, Ecuador, Peru, and Venezuela.

Bureau of Western Hemisphere Affairs *(State Dept.),* **Brazilian and Southern Cone Affairs,** *2201 C St. N.W., #4258, 20520; (202) 647-1926. Fax, (202) 736-7825. Bruce W. Friedman, Director (Acting), (202) 647-1774.* *Web, www.state.gov/p/wha*

Includes Argentina, Brazil, Chile, Paraguay, and Uruguay.

Bureau of Western Hemisphere Affairs *(State Dept.),* **Canadian Affairs,** *2201 C St. N.W., #3918, 20520; (202) 647-2170. Fax, (202) 647-4088. Cynthia Kierscht, Director.* *Web, www.state.gov/p/wha*

Bureau of Western Hemisphere Affairs *(State Dept.),* **Caribbean Affairs,** *2201 C St. N.W., #4262, 20520-6258; (202) 736-4350. Fax, (202) 647-2901. Steve Royster, Deputy Director, (202) 736-4766.* *Web, www.state.gov/p/wha*

Includes Antigua and Barbuda, Aruba, Bahamas, Barbados, Dominica, Dominican Republic, Grenada, Guyana, Jamaica, Netherlands Antilles, St. Kitts and Nevis, St. Lucia, St. Vincent and the Grenadines, Suriname, and Trinidad and Tobago.

Bureau of Western Hemisphere Affairs *(State Dept.),* **Central American Affairs,** *2201 C St. N.W., #5906, 20520; (202) 647-0087. Fax, (202) 647-2597. Peter Brennan, Director.* *Web, www.state.gov/p/wha*

Includes Belize, Costa Rica, El Salvador, Guatemala, Honduras, Nicaragua, and Panama.

Bureau of Western Hemisphere Affairs *(State Dept.),* **Cuban Affairs,** *2201 C St. N.W., #3234, 20520; (202) 647-9272. Fax, (202) 647-7095. Timothy P. Zuniga-Brown, Coordinator, (202) 453-8464.* *Web, www.state.gov/p/wha*

Bureau of Western Hemisphere Affairs *(State Dept.),* **Haitian Affairs,** *2201 C St. N.W., #6262, 20520-6258; (202) 647-4736. Allen Greenberg, Director.* *General email, HaitiSpecialCoordinator@state.gov* *Web, www.state.gov/p/wha/ci/ha/hsc*

Coordinates assistance to Haiti. Oversees U.S. government engagement with Haiti, including implementation of a reconstruction strategy in partnership with the Haitian government.

Bureau of Western Hemisphere Affairs *(State Dept.),* **Mexican Affairs,** *2201 C St. N.W., #3924, 20520-6258; (202) 647-8766. Fax, (202) 647-5752. Colleen Hoey, Director, (202) 647-8186.* *Web, www.state.gov/p/wha*

Bureau of Western Hemisphere Affairs *(State Dept.),* **U.S. Mission to the Organization of American States,** *2201 C St. N.W., #5914, 20520-6258; (202) 647-9376. Fax, (202) 647-6973. Carols Trujillo, U.S. Permanent Representative.* *Web, www.state.gov/p/wha*

Formulates U.S. policy and represents U.S. interests at the Organization of American States (OAS).

Defense Dept. (DoD), *International Security Affairs,* **Western Hemisphere,** *2000 Defense Pentagon, #3E806, 20301-2000; (703) 697-7200. Fax, (703) 697-6602. Sergio de la Peña, Deputy Assistant Secretary.* *Web, www.defense.gov*

Advises the assistant secretary for international security affairs on inter-American matters; aids in the development of U.S. policy toward Latin America.

Inter-American Foundation, *1331 Pennsylvania Ave. N.W., #1200 North, 20004; (202) 360-4530.* *Paloma Adams-Allen, President.* *General email, inquiries@iaf.gov* *Web, www.iaf.gov, Twitter, @IAFgrassroots and Facebook, www.facebook.com/iafgrassroots*

Supports small-scale Latin American and Caribbean social and economic development efforts through grassroots development programs, grants, and fellowships.

International Trade Administration (ITA) *(Commerce Dept.), Global Markets, North and Central America,* *1401 Constitution Ave. N.W., Room 30013, #3826, 20230; (202) 482-6452. Fax, (202) 482-5013. Geri Word, Director.* *Web, www.trade.gov/markets*

Coordinates Commerce Dept. activities and assists U.S. business regarding export to Mexico, Canada, Central America, and the Caribbean. Helps negotiate and ensures compliance with U.S. free trade agreements, including NAFTA (North American Free Trade Agreement) and the Dominican Republic–Central American Free Trade Agreement (CAFTA-DR).

▶ **CONGRESS**

For a listing of relevant congressional committees and subcommittees, please see pages 474–475 or the Appendix.

Library of Congress, *Hispanic Division, Thomas Jefferson Bldg., 101 Independence Ave. S.E., #LJ 240, 20540-4850; (202) 707-5400. Fax, (202) 707-2005. Suzanne Schadl, Chief, (202) 707-5400. Reference staff and reading room, (202) 707-5397.*
Web, www.loc.gov/rr/hispanic

Orients researchers and scholars in the area of Iberian, Latin American, Caribbean, and U.S. Latino studies. All major subject areas are represented with emphasis on history, literature, and the social sciences. Primary and secondary source materials are available in the library's general collections for the study of all periods, from pre-Columbian to the present. The collection includes the "Archive of Hispanic Literature on Tape" with recordings of nearly 700 authors reading their own material, available in the reading room and with a select number of recordings available for streaming online as the collection is being digitized.

▶ INTERNATIONAL ORGANIZATIONS

Inter-American Development Bank, *1300 New York Ave. N.W., 20577; (202) 623-1000. Fax, (202) 623-3096. Luis Alberto Moreno, President; Annette Pedrosa, U.S. Executive Director. Library, (202) 623-3211. Press, (202) 623-1555.*
Web, www.iadb.org, Twitter, @the_IDB and Facebook, www.facebook.com/IADB.org

Promotes, through loans and technical assistance, the investment of public and private capital in member countries of Latin America and the Caribbean for social and economic development purposes. Facilitates economic integration of the Latin American region, operating the Inter-American Investment Corporation and the Multilateral Investment Fund. Library open to the public by appointment.

Inter-American Telecommunication Commission (CITEL) *(Organization of American States), 1889 F St. N.W., 6th Floor, 20006; (202) 370-4713. Fax, (202) 458-6854. Oscar Léon, Executive Secretary.*
General email, citel@oas.org
Web, www.citel.oas.org and Twitter, @OEA_Telecom

Membership: OAS member states and associate members from the telecommunications, Internet, electronic, and media industries, and others. Works with the public and private sectors to facilitate the development of universal telecommunications in the Americas.

Organization of American States (OAS), *17th St. and Constitution Ave. N.W., 20006; Administration Bldg., 19th St. and Constitution Ave. N.W., 20006; General Secretariat Bldg., 1889 F St. N.W., 20006; (202) 370-5000. Fax, (202) 458-3967. Luis Almagro Lemes, Secretary General. Library, (202) 458-6041.*
General email, ai@oas.org
Web, www.oas.org and Twitter, @oas_official

Membership: the United States, Canada, and all independent Latin American and Caribbean countries. Funded by quotas paid by member states and by contributions to special multilateral funds. Works to promote democracy, eliminate poverty, and resolve disputes among member nations. Provides member states with technical and advisory services in cultural, educational, scientific, social, and economic areas. Library open to the public (at 19th and Constitution).

United Nations Economic Commission for Latin America and the Caribbean (CEPAL), *Washington Office, 1825 K St. N.W., #1120, 20006-1210; (202) 596-3713. Inés Bustillo, Director.*
General email, eclacwash@eclac.org
Web, www.cepal.org/en/headquarters-and-offices/eclac-washington-dc and Twitter, @eclac_un

Membership: Latin American, Caribbean, and some industrially developed Western nations. Seeks to strengthen economic relations between countries both within and outside Latin America through research and analysis of socioeconomic problems, training programs, and advisory services to member governments. (Headquarters in Santiago, Chile.)

World Bank, *Latin America and the Caribbean Region, 1818 H St. N.W., 20433; (202) 473-1000. Axel Van Trotsenburg, Vice President; Candyce Rocha, Communications Manager, (202) 458-4963.*
Web, www.worldbank.org/lac

Works to fight poverty and improve the living standards of poor and middle-income people in the countries of Latin America and the Caribbean by providing loans, policy advice, technical assistance, and knowledge-sharing services. Areas of interest include finance, economic development, education, water supply, agriculture, and infrastructure, public health, and environmental protection.

▶ NONGOVERNMENTAL

Americas Society / Council of the Americas, *Washington Office, 1615 L St. N.W., #250, 20036; (202) 659-8989. Fax, (202) 659-7755. Susan Segal, President; Eric Farnsworth, Vice President, in Washington, D.C..*
Web, www.as-coa.org and Twitter, @ASCOA

Membership: businesses with interests and investments in Latin America. Seeks to expand the role of private enterprise in development of the region. (Headquarters in New York.)

Council on Hemispheric Affairs, *2501 Calvert St. N.W., #401, 20008; (202) 223-4975. Fax, (202) 223-4979. Larry R. Birns, Director.*
General email, coha@coha.org
Web, www.coha.org and Twitter, @COHAofficial

Seeks to expand interest in inter-American relations and increase press coverage of Latin America and Canada. Monitors U.S., Latin American, and Canadian relations, with emphasis on human rights, trade, growth of democratic institutions, freedom of the press, and hemispheric economic and political developments; provides educational materials and analyzes issues. Issues annual survey on human rights and freedom of the press. Publishes a biweekly newsletter.

Group of Fifty (Grupo de los Cincuenta), *1300 19th St. N.W., #200, 20036; (202) 808-3360. Andres Naim, Chief Executive Officer. Toll-free, (888) 798-2366.*
General email, Contact@G-50.org

Web, www.g-50.org

Membership: business leaders who own Latin American enterprises. Holds an annual forum to improve networking between business executives and to promote economic growth in Latin America.

Guatemala Human Rights Commission/USA, *3321 12th St. N.E., 20017-4008; (202) 529-6599. Annie Bird, Director (Acting).*
General email, ghrc-usa@ghrc-usa.org

Web, www.ghrc-usa.org and Twitter, @GHRCUSA

Provides information and collects and makes available reports on human rights violations in Guatemala; publishes a quarterly report of documented cases of specific abuses. Takes on special projects and leads delegations to further sensitize the public and the international community to human rights abuses in Guatemala.

Inter-American Dialogue, *1155 15th St. N.W., #800, 20005; (202) 822-9002. Fax, (202) 822-9553. Michael Shifter, President.*
General email, iad@thedialogue.org

Web, www.thedialogue.org, Twitter, @The_Dialogue and Facebook, www.facebook.com/InterAmericanDialogue

Serves as a forum for communication and exchange among leaders of the Americas. Provides analyses and policy recommendations on issues of hemispheric concern. Interests include economic integration, trade, and the strengthening of democracy in Latin America. Hosts private and public exchanges; sponsors conferences and seminars; publishes daily newsletter, *Latin America Advisor.*

Latin America Working Group, *2029 P St. N.W., #301, 20036; (202) 546-7010. Fax, (202) 543-7647. Lisa Haugaard, Executive Director.*
General email, lawg@lawg.org

Web, www.lawg.org, Twitter, @lawgaction and Facebook, www.facebook.com/lawgaction

Represents more than sixty organizations concerned with Latin America. Encourages U.S. policies toward Latin America that promote human rights, justice, peace, and sustainable development.

Pan American Development Foundation, *1889 F St. N.W., 2nd Floor, 20006; (202) 458-3969. Fax, (202) 458-6316. Katie Taylor, Executive Director. Donations, (877) 572-4484.*
Web, www.padf.org and Twitter, @PADForg

Works with the public and private sectors to improve the quality of life throughout the Caribbean and Latin America. Associated with the Organization of American States (OAS).

Partners of the Americas, *1424 K St. N.W., #700, 20005-2410; (202) 628-3300. Fax, (202) 628-3306. John McPhail, President.*
General email, info@partners.net

Web, www.partners.net and Twitter, @PartnersAmericas

Membership: chapters, individuals, and organizations in the United States, Latin America, Brazil, and the Caribbean. Sponsors technical assistance projects and cultural exchanges between the United States, Latin America, Brazil, and the Caribbean; supports self-help projects in food security and agricultural development, sport for development, youth and children, climate change and environmental protection, professional leadership exchanges, civil society and governance, and women and gender equality.

U.S.–Mexico Chamber of Commerce, *6800 Versar Center, #450, Springfield, VA 22151 (mailing address: P.O. Box 14414, Washington, DC 20044); (703) 752-4751. Fax, (703) 642-1088. Albert C. Zapanta, President.*
General email, info@usmcoc.org

Web, www.usmcoc.org and Twitter, @USMCOC

Promotes trade and investment between the United States and Mexico. Provides members with information and expertise on conducting business between the two countries as pertains to NAFTA. Serves as a clearinghouse for information.

Washington Office on Latin America, *1666 Connecticut Ave. N.W., #400, 20009; (202) 797-2171. Fax, (202) 797-2172. Matt Clausen, President.*
General email, wola@wola.org

Web, www.wola.org, Twitter, @WOLA_org

Press, press@wola.org

Acts as a liaison between government policymakers and groups and individuals concerned with human rights and U.S. policy in Latin America and the Caribbean. Serves as an information resource center; monitors legislation.

Near East and South Asia

(Includes North Africa)

▶**AGENCIES**

Agency for International Development (USAID), Afghanistan and Pakistan Affairs, *1300 Pennsylvania Ave. N.W., #5.6-027, 20523; (202) 712-5002. Karen L. Freeman, Assistant Administrator. Main Switchboard, (202) 712-0000 (Ask Operator for Ext. 25931).*
General email, infoafghanistan@usaid.gov

Web, www.usaid.gov/who-we-are/organization/independent-offices/office-afghanistan-and-pakistan-affairs

Advises the USAID administrator on U.S. economic development policy in Afghanistan and Pakistan.

Agency for International Development (USAID), *Bureau for Asia,* 1300 Pennsylvania Ave. N.W., 20523-4900; (202) 712-0200. Fax, (202) 216-3386. Gloria Steele, Senior Deputy Assistant Administrator.
Web, www.usaid.gov/who-we-are/organization/bureaus/bureau-asia

Advises the USAID administrator on U.S. economic development policy in Asia.

Agency for International Development (USAID), *Bureau for Middle East,* 1300 Pennsylvania Ave. N.W., #4.09-006, 20523-4900; (202) 712-0300. Michael T. Harvey, Assistant Administrator, (202) 712-0084.
Web, www.usaid.gov/who-we-are/organization/bureaus/bureau-middle-east

Advises the USAID administrator on U.S. economic development policy in the Middle East.

Bureau of Near Eastern Affairs *(State Dept.),* 2201 C St. N.W., #6242, 20520-6243; (202) 647-7207. Fax, (202) 736-4462. David M. Satterfield, Assistant Secretary (Acting), (202) 647-7207.
Web, www.state.gov/p/nea

Advises the secretary on U.S. policy toward countries of the Near East and North Africa. Directors assigned to specific countries within the bureau aid the assistant secretary.

Bureau of Near Eastern Affairs *(State Dept.),* **Arabian Peninsula Affairs,** 2201 C St. N.W., #4224, 20520-6243; (202) 647-6184. Ellen J. Germain, Director.
General email, nea-arp-dl@state.gov
Web, www.state.gov/p/nea

Includes Bahrain, Kuwait, Oman, Qatar, Saudi Arabia, United Arab Emirates, and Yemen.

Bureau of Near Eastern Affairs *(State Dept.),* **Assistance Coordination,** 2430 E St. N.W., Central, 20037; (202) 776-8367. Theresa Grencik, Director.
Web, www.state.gov/p/nea

Oversees U.S. foreign assistance and aid to the Middle East and North Africa and establishes programs that advance U.S. policy priorities.

Bureau of Near Eastern Affairs *(State Dept.),* **Egypt Affairs,** 2201 C St. N.W., #5256, 20520; (202) 647-8078. Fax, (202) 482-1632. Oliver B. John, Director (Acting).
Web, www.state.gov/p/nea

Bureau of Near Eastern Affairs *(State Dept.),* **Iranian Affairs,** 2201 C St. N.W., #1058, 20520; (202) 647-5544. Steven Fagin, Director.
Web, www.state.gov/p/nea

Bureau of Near Eastern Affairs *(State Dept.),* **Iraq Affairs,** 2201 C St. N.W., #4827, 20520; (202) 647-9405. Fax, (202) 736-4464. Peter T. Shea, Director.
Web, www.state.gov/p/nea

Bureau of Near Eastern Affairs *(State Dept.),* **Israel and Palestinian Affairs,** 2201 C St. N.W., #6251, 20520; (202) 647-3672. Fax, (202) 736-4461. Amanda Pilz, Director (Acting).
Web, www.state.gov/p/nea

Bureau of Near Eastern Affairs *(State Dept.),* **Levant Affairs,** 2201 C St. N.W., #4241, 20520-6243; (202) 647-1018. Fax, (202) 647-0989. Eric Gaudiosi, Director.
Web, www.state.gov/p/nea

Includes Jordan, Lebanon, and Syria.

Bureau of Near Eastern Affairs *(State Dept.),* **Maghreb Affairs,** 2201 C St. N.W., #4440, 20520-6243; (202) 647-4679. Fax, (202) 485-2843. Joshua Harris, Director (Acting).
Web, www.state.gov/p/nea

Includes Algeria, Libya, Morocco, Tunisia, and Mauritania.

Bureau of South and Central Asian Affairs *(State Dept.),* 2201 C St. N.W., #6254, 20520-6258; (202) 736-4325. Fax, (202) 736-4333. Alice G. Wells, Principal Deputy Assistant Secretary.
Web, www.state.gov/p/sca, Twitter, @State_SCA
Blog, https://blogs.state.gov/region/south-and-central-asia

Advises the secretary on U.S. policy toward South and Central Asian countries. Directors assigned to specific countries within the bureau aid the assistant secretary.

Bureau of South and Central Asian Affairs *(State Dept.),* **Afghanistan Affairs,** 2201 C St. N.W., #1880, 20520-6258; (202) 647-6708. Fax, (202) 736-4650. John Ginkel, Director.
Web, www.state.gov/p/sca

Bureau of South and Central Asian Affairs *(State Dept.),* **India Affairs,** 2201 C St. N.W., #5251, 20520-6243; (202) 647-1114. Fax, (202) 736-4463. Sean B. Stein, Director.
Web, www.state.gov/p/sca

Bureau of South and Central Asian Affairs *(State Dept.),* **Nepal, Sri Lanka, Bangladesh, Bhutan, and Maldives Affairs,** 2201 C St. N.W., #5250, 20520-6243; (202) 647-1613. Fax, (202) 647-1183. David Richelsoph, Director, (202) 647-1116.
Web, www.state.gov/p/sca

Bureau of South and Central Asian Affairs *(State Dept.),* **Pakistan Affairs,** 2201 C St. N.W., #1861, 20520-6258; (202) 647-6711. David Ranz, Director.
Web, www.state.gov/p/sca

Defense Dept. (DoD), *Afghanistan, Pakistan, and Central Asia Security Affairs,* 2700 Defense Pentagon, #5D652, 20301; (703) 695-4175. Fax, (703) 697-7044. Colin F. Jackson, Deputy Assistant Secretary, (703) 614-5411.
Web, https://policy.defense.gov/ASDforAsianandPacificSecurityAffair

Advises the under secretary of defense on matters dealing with Afghanistan, Pakistan, and Central Asia.

Defense Dept. (DoD), *International Security Affairs,* 2000 Defense Pentagon, #3C889, 20301-2000; (703) 697-2788. Fax, (703) 697-3279. Kathryn Wheelbarger, Assistant Secretary (Acting).
Web, http://policy.defense.gov/OUSDPOffices/ASDforInternationalSecurityAffairs

Advises the secretary of defense and recommends policies on regional security issues in the Middle East, Africa, Russia/Eurasia, and Europe/NATO.

Defense Dept. (DoD), *International Security Affairs, Middle East,* 2000 *Defense Pentagon, #5B712, 20301-2000; (703) 697-1335. Fax, (703) 693-6795. Michael Mulroy, Deputy Assistant Secretary.*
Web, www.defense.gov

Advises the assistant secretary for international security affairs on matters dealing with the Middle East and South Asia.

Defense Dept. (DoD), *South and Southeast Asia Security Affairs,* 2700 *Defense Pentagon, #5D688, 20301-2700; (703) 695-4175. Joseph Felter, Deputy Assistant Secretary.*
Web, http://policy.defense.gov/OUSDPOffices/ASDforAsianandPacificSecurityAffairs.aspx

Advises the under secretary of defense on matters dealing with nations of Southeast Asia, Australia, Timor-Leste, New Zealand, Pacific Island States, and bilateral security relations with India and all other South Asian countries.

▶ CONGRESS

For a listing of relevant congressional committees and subcommittees, please see pages 474–475 or the Appendix.

Library of Congress, *African and Middle Eastern Division,* Thomas Jefferson Bldg., 101 Independence Ave. S.E., #LJ 220, 20540-4660; (202) 707-7937. Fax, (202) 252-3180. Mary-Jane Deeb, Chief, (202) 707-1221. Reading room, (202) 707-4188.
General email, amed@loc.gov
Web, www.loc.gov/rr/amed

Maintains collections of African, Near Eastern, and Hebraic material. Prepares bibliographies and special studies relating to Africa and the Middle East. Reference service and reading rooms available to the public. (Need reader's card to use.)

Library of Congress, *Asian Division,* Thomas Jefferson Bldg., 101 Independence Ave. S.E., #LJ 150, 20540; (202) 707-3766. Fax, (202) 252-1724. Dongfang Shao, Chief, (202) 707-5919. Reading room, (202) 707-5426.
Web, www.loc.gov/rr/asian

Maintains collections of Asian-American Pacific, Chinese, Korean, Japanese, Southeast Asian, South Asian, and Tibetan and Mongolian material. Reference service is provided in the Asian Reading Room, room #150.

▶ INTERNATIONAL ORGANIZATIONS

League of Arab States, *Washington Office,* 1100 17th St. N.W., #602, 20036; (202) 265-3210. Fax, (202) 331-1525. Amb. Salah Sarhan, Chief Representative.
General email, arableague@aol.com
Web, www.arableague-us.org

Membership: Arab countries in the Near East, North Africa, and the Indian Ocean. Coordinates members' policies in political, cultural, economic, and social affairs; mediates disputes among members and between members and third parties. Washington office maintains the Arab Information Center. (Headquarters in Cairo.)

Southeast Asia Resource Action Center (SEARAC), 1628 16th St. N.W., 3rd Floor, 20009; (202) 601-2960. Fax, (202) 667-6449. Quyen Dinh, Executive Director.
General email, searac@searac.org
Web, www.searac.org and Twitter, @SEARC

Works to advance Cambodian, Hmong, Laotian, and Vietnamese refugee rights through leadership and advocacy training. Collects and analyzes data on Southeast Asian Americans; publishes reports.

World Bank, *Middle East and North Africa Region,* 1818 H St. N.W., 20433; (202) 473-1000. Ferid Belhaj, Vice President; Will Stebbins, Communications Manager.
General email, mnateam@worldbank.org
Web, www.worldbank.org/en/region/mena and Twitter, @WorldBankMENA

Works to fight poverty and improve the living standards of low- and middle-income people in the countries of the Middle East and North Africa by providing loans, policy advice, technical assistance, and knowledge-sharing services. Areas of interest include finance, economic development, education, water supply, agriculture, public health, and environmental protection.

World Bank, *South Asia Region,* 1818 H St. N.W., 20433; (202) 473-1000. Hartwig Schafer, Vice President; Elana Karaban, Communications Manager, (202) 473-9277.
Web, www.worldbank.org/en/region/sar and Twitter, @WorldBankSAsia

Works to fight poverty and improve the living standards of low- and middle-income people in the countries of South Asia by providing loans, policy advice, technical assistance, and knowledge-sharing services. Areas of interest include finance, economic development, education, water supply, agriculture, public health, and environmental protection.

▶ NONGOVERNMENTAL

American Israel Public Affairs Committee, 251 H St. N.W., 20001-2017; (202) 639-5200. Howard Kohr, Executive Director.
General email, information@aipac.org
Web, www.aipac.org, Twitter, @AIPAC and Facebook, www.facebook.com/aipac

Works to maintain and improve relations between the United States and Israel. Holds educational seminars.

American Jewish Committee, *Project Interchange,* 1156 15th St. N.W., 20005; (202) 833-0025. Fax, (202) 331-7702. Robin S. Levenston, Executive Director, (202) 785-5468.
General email, pi@projectinterchange.org
Web, www.projectinterchange.org, Twitter, @projinterchange and Facebook, www.facebook.com/projectinterchange

Sponsors policymakers, industry leaders, journalists, and scholars to travel to Israel to meet and take part in seminars with Israeli government officials, business leaders, and academics to learn about current developments and issues affecting education, immigration, human rights, and the economy in Israel.

American Kurdish Information Network (AKIN), *2722 Connecticut Ave. N.W., #12, 20008-5366; (202) 483-6444. Kani Xulam, Director.*
General email, akin@kurdistan.org

Web, http://kurdistan.org, Twitter, @AKINinfo and Facebook, www.facebook.com/FreeKurdistan

Membership: Americans of Kurdish origin, recent Kurdish immigrants and refugees, and others. Collects and disseminates information about the Kurds, an ethnic group living in parts of Turkey, Iran, Iraq, and Syria. Monitors human rights abuses against Kurds; promotes self-determination in Kurdish homelands; fosters Kurdish American friendship and understanding.

American Near East Refugee Aid (ANERA), *1111 14th St. N.W., #400, 20005; (202) 266-9700. Fax, (202) 266-9701. Sean Carroll, President.*
General email, anera@anera-jwg.org

Web, www.anera.org and Twitter, @ANERAorg

Works with local institutions and partner organizations to provide sustainable development, health, education, and employment programs to Palestinian and Lebanese communities and impoverished families throughout the Middle East. Delivers humanitarian aid during emergencies. (Field offices in the West Bank, Gaza, and Lebanon.)

AMIDEAST, *2025 M St. N.W., #600, 20036-3363; (202) 776-9600. Fax, (202) 776-7000. Mondher Ben Ayed, President.*
General email, inquiries@amideast.org

Web, www.amideast.org and Twitter, @AMIDEASThq

Promotes understanding and cooperation between Americans and the people of the Middle East and North Africa through education, information, and development programs in the region. Produces educational material to help improve teaching about the Middle East and North Africa in American schools and colleges.

Asia Society Policy Institute, *Washington Office,* *1779 Massachusetts Ave., #810, 20036; (202) 833-2742. Fax, (202) 833-0189. Wendy Cutler, Managing Director.*
General email, asiadc@asiasociety.org

Web, www.asiasociety.org and Twitter, @AsiaPolicy

Membership: individuals, organizations, and corporations interested in Asia and the Pacific (excluding the Middle East). Focuses on United States and Asia foreign policy issues. Sponsors seminars and lectures on political, economic, and cultural issues. (Headquarters in New York.)

B'nai B'rith International, *1120 20th St. N.W., #300N, 20036; (202) 857-6600. Fax, (202) 857-2700. Daniel S. Mariaschin, Executive Vice President. Media, (202) 857-6699. Toll-free, (888) 388-4224. General email, info@bnaibrith.org*

Web, www.bnaibrith.org and Twitter, @BnaiBrith

International Jewish organization that promotes the security and continuity of the Jewish people and the State of Israel; defends human rights; combats anti-Semitism; and promotes Jewish identity through cultural activities. Interests include strengthening family life and the education and training of youth, providing broad-based services for the benefit of senior citizens, and advocacy on behalf of Jews throughout the world.

The Brookings Institution, *Center for Middle East Policy,* *1775 Massachusetts Ave. N.W., 20036; (202) 797-2463. Natan Sachs, Director.*
Web, www.brookings.edu/center/center-for-middle-east-policy and Twitter, @dbyman

Research center promoting policymaking on the Middle East. Interests include the Israeli–Palestinian conflict, the Iran nuclear deal, civil war in Syria, Libya and Yemen, refugees and reconstruction, trends in political Islam, combatting extremism and terrorism, and U.S. strategies in the Middle East.

Center for Contemporary Arab Studies (*Georgetown University*), *241 Intercultural Center, 37th and O Sts. N.W., 20057-1020; (202) 687-5793. Fax, (202) 687-7001. Rochelle Davis, Director, (202) 687-5648.*
General email, ccasinfo@georgetown.edu

Web, http://ccas.georgetown.edu and Twitter, @ccasGU

The master's program at Georgetown University; sponsors lecture series, seminars, and conferences. Conducts a community outreach program that assists secondary school teachers in the development of instructional materials on the Middle East; promotes the study of the Arabic language in area schools.

Center for Democracy and Human Rights in Saudi Arabia, *1629 K St. N.W., #300, 20006; (202) 558-5552. Fax, (202) 536-5210. Ali Alyami, Executive Director, (202) 413-0084.*
General email, cdhr@cdhr.info

Web, http://cdhr.info and Twitter, @CDHRSA

Monitors relations between the United States and Saudi Arabia. Promotes democratic reform of Saudi policies and studies the global impact of current events in Saudi Arabia. Interests include women's rights, religious and press freedom, secular judiciary systems, and government accountability. Holds conferences to analyze Saudi polices, international relations, current events, and strict interpretations of Islam. Educates the public, policymakers, and the media on related issues.

Center for Strategic and International Studies, *Middle East Program,* *1616 Rhode Island Ave. N.W., 20036; (202) 775-3179. Jon B. Alterman, Director.*
General email, middleeastprogram@csis.org

Web, www.csis.org/programs/middle-east-program and Twitter, @CSISMidEast

Conducts research and publishes on regional trends in the Middle East. Interests include political, social, and economic change in North Africa, Asian strategies toward the Middle East, shifting dynamics in the Gulf, and radicalism and insurgencies. Publishes a montly newsletter and holds conferences.

Eurasia Foundation, *1350 Connecticut Ave. N.W., #1000, 20036-1730; (202) 234-7370. Fax, (202) 234-7377. Lisa Coll, President.*
General email, info@eurasia.org
Web, www.eurasia.org and Twitter, @EFNetwork

Operates in Eurasia, the Middle East, and China. Provides capacity building, entrepreneurship training, advocacy education, social entrepreneurship training, and fellowship exchanges to support small business growth, local institutional performance, the responsiveness of local governments, and the leadership of young people.

Foundation for Middle East Peace, *1319 18th St. N.W., 20036; (202) 835-3650. Fax, (202) 835-3651. Lara Friedman, President.*
General email, info@fmep.org
Web, www.fmep.org, Twitter, @FMEP and Facebook, www.facebook.com/Foundation-for-Middle-East-Peace-82038934261

Educational organization that seeks to promote understanding and resolution of the Israeli-Palestinian conflict. Provides media with information; and awards grants to organizations and activities that contribute to the solution of the conflict.

Hollings Center for International Dialogue, *2101 L St. N.W., #800, 20037; (202) 833-5090. Michael Carroll, Executive Director.*
General email, info@hollingscenter.org
Web, www.hollingscenter.org and Twitter, @HollingsCenter

Holds conferences to encourage mutual understanding and policy debate between the U.S. and Muslim-oriented regions in North Africa, the Middle East, and South Asia. Participants include younger generation leaders, academics, government officials, and business leaders. Awards grants for independent study of issues that arise between the U.S. and Muslim-dominated territories.

Institute for Palestine Studies, *Washington Office, 3501 M St. N.W., 20007-2624; (202) 342-3990. Fax, (202) 342-3927. Julia Pitner, Executive Director.*
General email, ipsdc@palestine-studies.org
Web, www.palestine-studies.org, Twitter, @PalStudies and Facebook, www.facebook.com/palstudies

Scholarly research institute that specializes in the history and development of the Palestine problem, the Arab–Israeli conflict, and their peaceful resolution. Conducts educational outreach, holds panels and lectures for the public, and produces a quarterly journal. (Maintains offices in Beirut and Jerusalem.)

Institute of Turkish Studies *(Georgetown University), 3300 Whitehaven St. N.W., #3100, 20007; (202) 687-0292. Fax, (202) 687-3780. Sinan Ciddi, Executive Director.*
General email, itsdirector@turkishstudies.org
Web, www.turkishstudies.org, Twitter, @TurkishStudies and Facebook, www.facebook.com/instituteofturkishstudies

Independent grant-making organization that supports and encourages the development of Turkish studies in American colleges and universities. Awards grants to individual scholars and educational institutions in the United States. (Housed within the Edmund A. Walsh School of Foreign Service.)

Middle East Institute, *1319 18th St. N.W., 20036; Oman Library, 1761 N St. N.W., 20036; (202) 785-1141. Paul Salem, President, (202) 785-1141. Library, (202) 785-1141, ext. 222. Press, (202) 785-1141, ext. 236.*
General email, info@mei.edu
Web, www.mei.edu and Twitter, @paulsalem

Membership: individuals interested in the Middle East. Seeks to broaden knowledge of the Middle East through research, conferences and seminars, language classes, lectures, and exhibits. Library open to members and the press Monday through Friday 10:00 a.m.–5:00 p.m.

Middle East Media Research Institute (MEMRI), *P.O. Box 27837, 20038-7837; (202) 955-9070. Steve Emerson, Executive Director.*
General email, memri@memri.org
Web, www.memri.org

Explores the Middle East through the region's media. Seeks to inform the debate over U.S. policy in the Middle East.

Middle East Policy Council, *1730 M St. N.W., #512, 20036-4505; (202) 296-6767. Fax, (202) 296-5791. Hon. Richard J. Schmierer, President.*
General email, info@mepc.org
Web, www.mepc.org, Twitter, @MidEastPolicy and Facebook, www.facebook.com/mideastpolicy

Encourages public discussion and understanding of issues affecting U.S. policy in the Middle East. Sponsors conferences for the policy community; conducts educational outreach program; publishes journal and an e-newsletter.

National Council on U.S.–Arab Relations, *1730 M St. N.W., #503, 20036; (202) 293-6466. Fax, (202) 293-7770. John Duke Anthony, President.*
General email, info@ncusar.org
Web, http://ncusar.org, Twitter, @NCUSAR and Facebook, www.facebook.com/NCUSAR

Educational organization that works to improve mutual understanding between the United States and the Middle East and North Africa (MENA) region. Serves as a clearinghouse on Arab issues and maintains speakers bureau. Coordinates trips for U.S. professionals and congressional delegations to the MENA region.

National U.S.–Arab Chamber of Commerce, *1201 15th St. N.W., #205, 20036; (202) 289-5920. Fax, (202) 289-5938. David Hamod, President.*
General email, info@nusacc.org
Web, www.nusacc.org and Twitter, @nusacc

Promotes trade between the United States and the Middle East and North Africa (MENA) region. Offers members informational publications, research and certification services, and opportunities to meet with international delegations. Operates four regional offices.

New Israel Fund, *Washington Office,* *2100 M St. N.W., #619, 20037; (202) 842-0900. Fax, (202) 842-0991. Daniel Sokatch, Chief Executive Officer; Tali Herskowitz, Washington Regional Director, (202) 513-7870. General email, dc@nif.org*

Web, www.nif.org, Twitter, @NewIsraelFund and Facebook, www.facebook.com/newisraelfund

International philanthropic partnership of North Americans, Israelis, and Europeans. Supports activities that defend civil and human rights, promote Jewish–Arab equality and coexistence, advance the status of women, nurture tolerance, bridge social and economic gaps, encourage government accountability, and assist citizen efforts to protect the environment. Makes grants and provides capacity-building assistance to Israeli public interest groups; trains civil rights lawyers. (Headquarters in New York City.)

Project on Middle East Democracy (POMED), *1730 Rhode Island Ave. N.W., #617, 20036; (202) 828-9660. Fax, (202) 828-9661. Stephen McInerney, Executive Director. Press, (202) 828-9600, ext. 23. General email, todd.ruffner@pomed.org*

Web, www.pomed.org and Twitter, @POMED

Researches and publishes reports to educate policymakers on methods the United States can use to build democracies in the Middle East. Holds conferences to address United States–Middle East policy issues. Advocates democracy in the Middle East and supports pro-democracy foreign policies.

S. Daniel Abraham Center for Middle East Peace, *633 Pennsylvania Ave. N.W., 5th Floor, 20004; (202) 624-0850. Fax, (202) 624-0855. S. Daniel Abraham, Chair; Robert Wexler, President. General email, info@centerpeace.org*

Web, www.centerpeace.org and Twitter, @AbrahamCenter

Membership: Middle Eastern policymakers, U.S. government officials, and international business leaders. Serves as a mediator to encourage a peaceful resolution to the Arab–Israeli conflict; sponsors travel to the region, diplomatic exchanges, and conferences for Middle Eastern and U.S. leaders interested in the peace process.

United Palestinian Appeal (UPA), *1330 New Hampshire Ave. N.W., #104, 20036-6350; (202) 659-5007. Fax, (202) 296-0224. Saleem F. Zaru, Executive Director. Toll-free, (855) 659-5007. General email, contact@helppupa.org*

Web, www.helpUPA.org and Twitter, @UPAConnect

An American charitable organization dedicated to improving the quality of life for Palestinians in the Middle East, particularly those in the West Bank, the Gaza Strip, and refugee camps. Provides funding for community development projects, health care, education, children's services, and emergency relief. Funded by private donations from individuals and foundations in the United States and the Middle East and North Africa (MENA) region.

Washington Institute for Near East Policy, *1111 19th St. N.W., #500, 20036; (202) 452-0650. Fax, (202) 223-5364. Robert Satloff, Executive Director. Web, www.washingtoninstitute.org and Twitter, @washinstitute*

Research and educational organization that seeks to improve the effectiveness of U.S. policy in the Middle East by promoting debate among policymakers, journalists, and scholars.

Russia and New Independent States

For the Baltic states, see Europe.

▶AGENCIES

Agency for International Development (USAID), *Bureau for Europe and Eurasia,* *301 4th St. S.W., #247, 20523 (mailing address: 1300 Pennsylvania Ave. N.W., Washington, DC 20521); (202) 567-4020. Fax, (202) 567-4256. Brock Bierman, Assistant Administrator. Web, www.usaid.gov/who-we-are/organization/bureaus/bureau-europe-and-eurasia*

Advises the USAID administrator on U.S. economic development policy in Europe and Eurasia.

Bureau of European and Eurasian Affairs (EUR) *(State Dept.), 2201 C St. N.W., #6226, 20520; (202) 647-4876. Fax, (202) 647-5716. A. Wess Mitchell, Assistant Secretary, (202) 647-9626. Press, (202) 647-5116. Web, www.state.gov/p/eur*

Advises the secretary on U.S. policy toward European and Eurasian countries. Directors assigned to specific countries within the bureau aid the assistant secretary.

Bureau of European and Eurasian Affairs *(State Dept.), Caucasus Affairs and Regional Conflicts, 2201 C St. N.W., #4220, 20520-7512; (202) 647-8741. Fax, (202) 736-7915. Alicia Allison, Director. Web, www.state.gov/p/eur*

Includes Armenia, Azerbaijan, Georgia, and conflict regions.

Bureau of European and Eurasian Affairs *(State Dept.), Russian Affairs, 2201 C St. N.W., #4417, 20520-7512; (202) 647-9806. Fax, (202) 647-8980. Nicholas Berliner, Director. Web, www.state.gov/p/eur*

Bureau of European and Eurasian Affairs *(State Dept.), Ukraine, Moldova, and Belarus Affairs, 2201 C St. N.W., #4427, 20520-7512; (202) 647-6750. Fax, (202) 647-3506. Bradley A. Freden, Director. Web, www.state.gov/p/eur*

Bureau of South and Central Asian Affairs *(State Dept.), Central Asian Affairs, 2201 C St. N.W., #1880, 20520;*

(202) 647-6745. Fax, (202) 736-4650. Walter S. Reid, Director.
Web, www.state.gov/p/sca

Includes Kazakhstan, Kyrgyzstan, Tajikistan, Turkmenistan, and Uzbekistan.

Defense Dept. (DoD), *International Security Affairs, 2000 Defense Pentagon, #3C889, 20301-2000; (703) 697-2788. Fax, (703) 697-3279. Kathryn Wheelbarger, Assistant Secretary (Acting).*
Web, http://policy.defense.gov/OUSDPOffices/ ASDforInternationalSecurityAffairs

Advises the secretary of defense and recommends policies on regional security issues in the Middle East, Africa, Russia/Eurasia, and Europe/NATO.

Defense Dept. (DoD), *International Security Affairs, Russia, Ukraine, and Eurasia, 2000 Defense Pentagon, 20301-2000; (703) 571-0231. Laura K. Cooper, Deputy Assistant Secretary (Acting).*
Web, www.defense.gov

Advises the assistant secretary for international security affairs on matters dealing with Russia, Ukraine, and Eurasia.

►CONGRESS

For a listing of relevant congressional committees and subcommittees, please see pages 474–475 or the Appendix.

Library of Congress, *European Division, Thomas Jefferson Bldg., 101 Independence Ave. S.E., #LJ 249, 20540; (202) 707-5414. Fax, (202) 707-8482. Grant Harris, Chief, (202) 707-5859. Reference desk, (202) 707-4515.*
General email, eurref@loc.gov
Web, www.loc.gov/rr/european

Provides reference service on the library's European collections (except collections on Spain, Portugal, and the British Isles). Prepares bibliographies and special studies relating to European countries, including Russia and the other states of the former Soviet Union and eastern bloc. Maintains current unbound Slavic language periodicals and newspapers, which are available at the European Reference Desk. Recommends materials for acquisition.

►INTERNATIONAL ORGANIZATIONS

World Bank, *Europe and Central Asia Region, 1818 H St. N.W., 20433; (202) 473-1000. Cyril Muller, Vice President; Carl Hanlon, Communications Manager.*
General email, eca@worldbank.org
Web, www.worldbank.org/en/region/eca and Twitter, @WorldBankECA

Works to fight poverty and improve the living standards of low- and middle-income people in the countries of eastern Europe and central Asia, including states of the former Soviet Union, by providing loans, policy advice, technical assistance, and knowledge-sharing services. Interests include finance, economic development, education, water supply, agriculture, public health, and environmental protection.

►NONGOVERNMENTAL

Armenian Assembly of America, *734 15th St., #500, 20005; (202) 393-3434. Fax, (202) 638-4904. Bryan Ardouny, Executive Director.*
General email, info@aaainc.org
Web, www.armenian-assembly.org and Twitter, @aramac.dc

Promotes public understanding and awareness of Armenian issues; advances research and data collection and disseminates information on the Armenian people; advocates greater Armenian American participation in the American democratic process; works to alleviate human suffering of Armenians.

Armenian National Committee of America, *1711 N St. N.W., 20036; (202) 775-1918. Fax, (202) 223-7964. Aram Hamparian, Executive Director.*
General email, anca@anca.org
Web, www.anca.org and Twitter, @ANCA_DC

Armenian American grassroots political organization. Works to advance concerns of the Armenian American community. Interests include strengthening U.S.–Armenian relations.

Center for Strategic and International Studies, *Russia and Eurasia Program, 1616 Rhode Island Ave. N.W., 20036; (202) 887-0200. Olga Oliker, Director.*
Web, www.csis.org/programs/russia-and-eurasia-program and Twitter, @CSISRussia

Conducts and publishes research on regional security, domestic politics, economic development, trade and transit, defense and high technology, and energy in Russia and former Soviet Union states, as well as political and economic relationships between the states and other critical geopolitical groups.

Center on Global Interests, *1050 Connecticut Ave. N.W., #500, 20036; (202) 973-2832. Nikolai Zlobin, President.*
General email, info@globalinterests.org
Web, www.globalinterests.org, Twitter, @CGI_DC
Media, okuzmina@globalinterests.org

Research center that analyzes and publishes reports on foreign relations. Specializes in U.S. and Russian affairs. Holds international conferences to educate policymakers and the media on global challenges, economies, policies, and conflict.

Eurasia Foundation, *1350 Connecticut Ave. N.W., #1000, 20036-1730; (202) 234-7370. Fax, (202) 234-7377. Lisa Coll, President.*
General email, info@eurasia.org
Web, www.eurasia.org and Twitter, @EFNetwork

Operates in Eurasia, the Middle East, and China. Provides capacity building, entrepreneurship training, advocacy education, social entrepreneurship training, and fellowship exchanges to support small business growth, local institutional performance, the responsiveness of local governments, and the leadership of young people.

Institute for European, Russian, and Eurasian Studies *(George Washington University), 1957 E St. N.W., 20052-0001; (202) 994-6340. Peter Rollberg, Director.*
General email, ieresgwu@email.gwu.edu

Web, https://ieres.elliott.gwu.edu, Twitter, @IERES_GWU and Facebook, www.facebook.com/ieresgwu

Studies and researches European, Russian, and Eurasian affairs. Sponsors a master's program in European and Eurasian studies. (Affiliated with the George Washington University Elliott School of International Affairs.)

Jamestown Foundation, *1310 L St. N.W., #810, 20005; (202) 483-8888. Fax, (202) 483-8337. Glen E. Howard, President.*
General email, pubs@jamestown.org

Web, www.jamestown.org, Twitter, @JamestownTweets and Facebook, www.facebook.com/The-Jamestown-Foundation

Provides policymakers with information about events and trends in societies that are strategically or tactically important to the United States and that frequently restrict access to such information. Serves as an alternative source to official or intelligence channels, especially with regard to Eurasia, China, and terrorism. Publishes the *Militant Leadership Monitor*, covering leaders of major insurgencies and militant movements.

Kennan Institute, *1 Woodrow Wilson Plaza, 1300 Pennsylvania Ave. N.W., 20004-3027; (202) 691-4000. Fax, (202) 691-4247. Matthew Rojansky, Director.*
General email, kennan@wilsoncenter.org

Web, www.wilsoncenter.org/program/kennan-institute, Twitter, @kennaninstitute and Facebook, www.facebook.com/Kennan.Institute

Offers residential research scholarships to academic scholars and to specialists from government, media, and the private sector for studies to improve American knowledge about Russia, Ukraine, Central Asia, and the Caucasus. Sponsors lectures; publishes reports; promotes dialogue between academic specialists and policymakers. (Affiliated with the Woodrow Wilson International Center for Scholars.)

NCSEJ: National Coalition Supporting Eurasian Jewry, *1120 20th St. N.W, #300N, 20006-3413; (202) 898-2500. Fax, (202) 898-0822. Mark B. Levin, Executive Director; Daniel Rubin, Chair.*
General email, ncsj@ncsj.org

Web, www.ncsej.org, Twitter, @NCSEJ and Facebook, www.facebook.com/thencsej

Membership: national Jewish organizations and local federations. Coordinates efforts by members to aid Jews in the former Soviet Union.

U.S.–Russia Business Council, *1101 17th St. N.W., #600, 20036; (202) 739-9180. Fax, (202) 659-5920. Daniel A. Russell, President. Press, (202) 739-9187.*

General email, info@usrbc.org

Web, www.usrbc.org

Membership: U.S. companies involved in trade and investment in Russia. Promotes commercial ties between the United States and Russia; provides business services. Monitors legislation and regulations. (Maintains office in Moscow.)

U.S.–Ukraine Foundation, Washington Office, *1090 Vermont Ave. N.W., #600, 20005; (202) 789-4467. Fax, (202) 280-1989. Nadia K. McConnell, President.*
General email, info@usukraine.org

Web, www.usukraine.org and Twitter, @usukraine

Encourages and facilitates democratic and human rights development and free market reform in the Ukraine. Creates and sustains communications channels between the United States and Ukraine. Manages the U.S.–Ukraine Community Partnerships Project. (Maintains office in Kiev, Ukraine.)

Ukrainian National Information Service, Washington Office, *311 Massachusetts Ave. N.E., Lower Level, 20002; (202) 547-0018. Fax, (202) 547-0019. Michael Sawkiw Jr., Director.*
General email, unis@ucca.org

Web, www.ucca.org and Twitter, @UkrCongComAm

Information bureau of the Ukrainian Congress Committee of America in New York. Monitors U.S. policy and foreign assistance to Ukraine. Supports educational, cultural, and humanitarian activities in the Ukranian-American community. (Headquarters in New York.)

U.S. Territories and Associated States

▶**AGENCIES**

Interior Dept. (DOI), Insular Affairs (OIA), *1849 C St. N.W., MS 2429, 20240; (202) 208-4736. Fax, (202) 208-5226. Douglas W. Domenech, Assistant Secretary for Insular Areas; Nikolao Pula, Director.*
Web, www.doi.gov/oia

Promotes economic, social, and political development of U.S. territories (Guam, American Samoa, the U.S. Virgin Islands, and the Commonwealth of the Northern Mariana Islands). Supervises federal programs for the Freely Associated States (Federated States of Micronesia, Republic of the Marshall Islands, and Republic of Palau).

National Conference of Puerto Rican Women, *1220 L St. N.W., #100-177, 20005; Michelle Centeno, National President; Milagros V. McGuire, President of the Washington, D.C., Chapter.*
General email, nacoprw_nationalpress55@aol.com

Web, www.nacoprw.org

Nonprofit, nonpartisan organization promoting the participation of Puerto Rican and other Hispanic women in their economic, social, and political life. Provides training, mentorship, and leadership development at the local and national level through workshops and institutes; provides scholarships to Hispanic individuals.

► CONGRESS

For a listing of relevant congressional committees and subcommittees, please see pages 474–475 or the Appendix.

American Samoa's Delegate to Congress, *1339 LHOB, 20515; (202) 225-8577. Fax, (202) 225-8757. Aumua Amata C. Radewagen, Delegate.*
Web, http://radewagen.house.gov, Twitter, @repamata and Facebook, www.facebook.com/aumnaamata

Represents American Samoa in Congress.

Guam's Delegate to Congress, *1632 HOB, 20515; (202) 225-1188. Fax, (202) 226-0341. Michael San Nicolas, Delegate.*
Web, https://sannicolas.house.gov

Represents Guam in Congress.

Northern Mariana Islands' Delegate to Congress, *2411 RHOB, 20515; (202) 225-2646. Fax, (202) 226-4249. Gregorio Sablan, Delegate. Toll-free, (877) 446-3465. Web, www.sablan.house.gov*

Represents the Northern Mariana Islands in Congress.

Puerto Rican Resident Commissioner, *1609 LHOB, 20515; (202) 225-2615. Fax, (202) 225-2154. Jenniffer Gonzalez-Colon, Resident Commissioner.*

Web, http://gonzalez-colon.house.gov and Twitter, @repjenniffer

Represents the Commonwealth of Puerto Rico in Congress.

Virgin Islands' Delegate to Congress, *2404 RHOB, 20515; (202) 225-1790. Fax, (202) 225-5517. Stacey Plaskett, Delegate.*
General email, samantha.roberts@mail.house.gov
Web, http://plaskett.house.gov and Twitter, @StaceyPlaskett

Represents the Virgin Islands in Congress.

► NONGOVERNMENTAL

Commonwealth of Puerto Rico Federal Affairs Administration, *1100 17th St. N.W., #800, 20036; (202) 778-0710. Fax, (202) 778-0721. Carlos R. Mercader, Executive Director.*
General email, info@prfaa.pr.gov
Web, http://prfaa.pr.gov and Twitter, @PRFAA

Represents the governor and the government of the Commonwealth of Puerto Rico before Congress and the executive branch; conducts research; serves as official press information center for the Commonwealth of Puerto Rico. Monitors legislation and regulations.

13 ⚖

Law and Justice

GENERAL POLICY AND ANALYSIS

Basic Resources

▶AGENCIES

Justice Dept. (DOJ), *950 Pennsylvania Ave. N.W., #4400, 20530-0001; (202) 514-2001. Fax, (202) 307-6777. William Barr, Attorney General; Jeffrey A. Rosen, Deputy Attorney General. Information and switchboard, (202) 514-2000. Library, (202) 514-3775. Public Affairs, (202) 514-2007. Public comments, (202) 353-1555. General email, askdoj@usdoj.gov Web, www.justice.gov and Twitter, @DOJATJ*

Serves as counsel for the U.S. government. Represents the government in enforcing the law in the public interest. Plays key role in protecting against criminals and subversion, in ensuring healthy competition of business in U.S. free enterprise system, in safeguarding the consumer, and in enforcing drug, immigration, and naturalization laws. Plays a significant role in protecting citizens through effective law enforcement, crime prevention, crime detection, and prosecution and rehabilitation of offenders. Conducts all suits in the Supreme Court in which the United States is concerned. Represents the government in legal matters generally, furnishing legal advice and opinions to the president, the cabinet, and the heads of executive departments, as provided by law. Justice Dept. organization includes divisions on antitrust, civil law, civil rights, criminal law, environment and natural resources, and taxes, as well as the Bureau of Alcohol, Tobacco, Firearms, and Explosives; Drug Enforcement Administration; Executive Office for Immigration Review; Federal Bureau of Investigation; Federal Bureau of Prisons; Foreign Claims Settlement Commission; Office of Justice Programs; U.S. Attorneys; U.S. Marshals Service; U.S. Parole Commission; and U.S. Trustees.

Justice Dept. (DOJ), *Legal Policy (OLP), 950 Pennsylvania Ave. N.W., #4234, 20530-0001; (202) 514-4601. Fax, (202) 514-2424. Beth A. Williams, Assistant Attorney General. Web, www.justice.gov/olp*

Develops and implements the Justice Dept.'s major policy initiatives, often with the cooperation of other offices within the department and among other agencies. Works with Office of Legislative Affairs to promote the department's policies in Congress.

Justice Dept. (DOJ), *Solicitor General, 950 Pennsylvania Ave. N.W., #5143, 20530-0001; (202) 514-2203. Fax, (202) 514-9769. Noel Francisco, Solicitor General. Information on pending cases, (202) 514-2217. Web, www.justice.gov/osg*

Represents the federal government before the Supreme Court of the United States.

National Security Division *(Justice Dept.), 950 Pennsylvania Ave. N.W., #7339, 20530; (202) 514-2401.*

Fax, (202) 514-9836. John Demers, Assistant Attorney General. Press, (202) 514-2007. General email, nsd.public@usdoj.gov Web, www.justice.gov/nsd

Provides legal assistance and advice, in coordination with the Office of Legal Counsel as appropriate, to all branches of government on matters of national security law and policy.

Office of Justice Programs (OJP) *(Justice Dept.), 810 7th St. N.W., 20531; (202) 307-5933. Fax, (202) 514-7805. Matt M. Dummermuth, Principal Deputy Assistant Attorney General. Press, (202) 307-0703. General email, askojp@ncjrs.gov Web, https://ojp.gov, Twitter, @OJPgov and Facebook, www.facebook.com/DOJOJP*

Provides federal leadership, coordination, and assistance in developing the nation's capacity to prevent and control crime, administer justice, and assist crime victims. Includes the Bureau of Justice Assistance, which supports state and local criminal justice strategies; the Bureau of Justice Statistics, which collects, analyzes, and disseminates criminal justice data; the National Institute of Justice, which is the primary research and development agency of the Justice Dept.; the Office of Juvenile Justice and Delinquency Prevention, which supports state and local efforts to combat juvenile crime and victimization; the Office of Victims of Crime, which provides support for crime victims and leadership to promote justice and healing for all crime victims; and the Community Capacity Development Office, which provides resources to support community-based anticrime efforts.

State Justice Institute, *11951 Freedom Dr., #1020, Reston, VA 20190; (571) 313-8843. Fax, (571) 313-1173. Jonathan D. Mattiello, Executive Director. General email, contact@sji.gov Web, www.sji.gov and Twitter, @statejustice*

Awards grants to state courts and to state agencies for programs that improve state courts' judicial administration. Maintains judicial information clearinghouses and establishes technical resource centers; conducts educational programs; delivers technical assistance.

▶CONGRESS

For a listing of relevant congressional committees and subcommittees, please see pages 542–543 or the Appendix.

▶JUDICIARY

Administrative Office of the U.S. Courts, *1 Columbus Circle N.E., 20544-0001; (202) 502-2600. James C. Duff, Director. Web, www.uscourts.gov*

Provides administrative support to the federal courts, including the procurement of supplies and equipment; the administration of personnel, budget, and financial control services; and the compilation and publication of statistical data and reports on court business. Implements the policies of the Judicial Conference of the United States and supports its committees. Recommends plans and strategies to manage court business. Procures needed resources, legislation, and other assistance for the judiciary from Congress and the executive branch.

Administrative Office of the U.S. Courts, *Court Services Division, 1 Columbus Circle N.E., 20544-0001; (202) 502-1500. Mary Louise Mitterhoff, Chief. Public Affairs, (202) 502-2600.*
Web, www.uscourts.gov

Provides staff, policy, legal, operational, and program support for the appeals, district, and U.S. bankruptcy courts.

Federal Judicial Center, *1 Columbus Circle N.E., 20002-8003; (202) 502-4160. Fax, (202) 502-4099. John S. Cooke, Director. Library, (202) 502-4156. Public Affairs, (202) 502-4250.*
Web, www.fjc.gov

Conducts research on the operations of the federal court system; develops and conducts continuing education and training programs for judges and judicial personnel; and makes recommendations to improve the administration of the courts.

Judicial Conference of the United States, *1 Columbus Circle N.E., #7430, 20544; (202) 502-2400. Fax, (202) 502-3019. John G. Roberts Jr., Chief Justice of the United States; James C. Duff, Director. Public Affairs, (202) 502-2600.*
Web, www.uscourts.gov

Serves as the policymaking and governing body for the administration of the federal judicial system; advises Congress on the creation of new federal judgeships. Interests include international judicial relations.

Supreme Court of the United States, *1 1st St. N.E., 20543; (202) 479-3000. John G. Roberts Jr., Chief Justice; Kathleen Landin Arberg, Public Information Officer, (202) 479-3211. Visitor information, (202) 479-3030. TTY, (202) 479-3472.*
Web, www.supremecourtus.gov

Highest appellate court in the federal judicial system. Interprets the U.S. Constitution, federal legislation, and treaties. Provides information on new cases filed, the status of pending cases, and admissions to the Supreme Court Bar. Library open to Supreme Court bar members only.

▶**NONGOVERNMENTAL**

American Bar Assn. (ABA), *Governmental Affairs, 1050 Connecticut Ave. N.W., #400, 20036; (202) 662-1760. Fax, (202) 662-1762. Holly Cook, Director, (202) 662-1860.*
General email, louise.neu@americanbar.org
Web, www.americanbar.org/groups/departments_offices/ government_affairs_office.html

Acts as advocate before Congress, the executive branch, and other governmental entities on issues of importance to the legal profession. Publishes the *ABA Washington Letter*, a monthly online legislative analysis; and *ABA Washington Summary*, a daily online publication.

American Tort Reform Assn., *1101 Connecticut Ave. N.W., #400, 20036-4351; (202) 682-1163. Fax, (202) 682-1022. Sherman Joyce, President.*
Web, www.atra.org and Twitter, @AMTortReform

Membership: businesses, associations, trade groups, professional societies, and individuals interested in reforming the civil justice system in the United States. Develops model state legislation and position papers on tort liability and reform. Monitors legislation, regulations, and legal rulings.

Aspen Institute, *2300 N St., N.W., #700, 20037; (202) 736-5800. Fax, (202) 467-0790. Dan Porterfield, President. Press, (202) 736-3849.*
General email, info@aspeninstitute.org
Web, www.aspeninstitute.org and Twitter, @AspenInstitute

Educational and policy studies organization. Brings together individuals from diverse backgrounds to discuss how to deal with long-standing philosophical disputes and contemporary social challenges in law and justice.

The Federalist Society, *1776 Eye St. N.W., #300, 20006; (202) 822-8138. Fax, (202) 296-8061. Eugene B. Meyer, President.*
General email, info@fed-soc.org
Web, www.fedsoc.org, Twitter, @FedSoc and Facebook, www.facebook.com/Federalist.Society

Promotes conservative and libertarian principles among lawyers, judges, law professors, law students, and the general public. Sponsors lectures, debates, seminars, fellowships, and awards programs.

Government Accountability Project (GAP), *1612 K St. N.W., #1100, 20006; (202) 457-0034. Fax, (202) 457-0059. Louis Clark, Executive Director.*
General email, info@whistleblower.org
Web, www.whistleblower.org, Twitter, @GovAcctProj and Facebook, www.facebook.com/pg/ GovernmentAccountabilityProject

Membership: federal employees, union members, professionals, and interested citizens. Supports and represents employee whistle-blowers. Works to ensure that whistle-blower disclosures about improper government and industry actions that are harmful to the environment, public health, national security, food safety, the financial sector, and several other areas are defended and heard. Represents whistle-blower clients in legal actions and operates attorney referral service through National Whistleblower Legal Defense and Education Fund. (Formerly the National Whistleblower Center.)

Justice Policy Institute, *1012 14th St. N.W., #600, 20005; (202) 558-7974. Fax, (202) 558-7978. Marc Schindler, Executive Director, (202) 568-6569. Press, (202) 888-6748.*

LAW AND JUSTICE RESOURCES IN CONGRESS

For a complete listing of congressional committees, including their full contact information, leadership, membership, and jurisdictions, please refer to the Appendix on pages 827–948.

HOUSE:

House Administration Committee, (202) 225-8281.
Web, cha.house.gov
House Appropriations Committee, (202) 225-2771.
Web, appropriations.house.gov
    Subcommittee on Commerce, Justice, Science,
      and Related Agencies, (202) 225-3351.
    Subcommittee on Homeland Security,
      (202) 225-5834.
House Education and the Workforce Committee,
    (202) 225-4527.
Web, edworkforce.house.gov
    Subcommittee on Workforce Protections,
      (202) 225-4527.
House Energy and Commerce Committee,
    (202) 225-2927.
Web, energycommerce.house.gov
    Subcommittee on Digital Commerce and
      Consumer Protection, (202) 225-2927.
    Subcommittee on Energy, (202) 225-2927.
    Subcommittee on Health, (202) 225-2927.
House Ethics Committee, (202) 225-7103.
Web, ethics.house.gov
House Financial Services Committee,
    (202) 225-7502.
Web, financialservices.house.gov
    Subcommittee on Financial Institutions
      and Consumer Credit,
      (202) 225-7502.
House Homeland Security Committee,
    (202) 226-8417.
Web, homeland.house.gov
    Subcommittee on Border and Maritime
      Security, (202) 226-8417.

House Judiciary Committee, (202) 225-3951.
Web, judiciary.house.gov
    Subcommittee on the Constitution and Civil
      Justice, (202) 225-2825.
    Subcommittee on Courts, Intellectual Property,
      and the Internet, (202) 225-5741.
    Subcommittee on Crime, Terrorism,
      Homeland Security, and Investigations,
      (202) 225-5727.
    Subcommittee on Immigration and Border
      Security, (202) 225-3926.
    Subcommittee on Regulatory Reform,
      Commercial, and Antitrust Law,
      (202) 226-7680.
House Natural Resources Committee,
    (202) 225-2761.
Web, naturalresources.house.gov
    Subcommittee on Energy and Mineral Resources,
      (202) 225-9297.
House Oversight and Government Reform
    Committee, (202) 225-5074.
Web, oversight.house.gov
    Subcommittee on Government Operations,
      (202) 225-5074.
House Small Business Committee,
    (202) 225-5821.
Web, smallbusiness.house.gov
    Subcommittee on Health and Technology,
      (202) 225-5821.
House Ways and Means Committee,
    (202) 225-3625.
Web, waysandmeans.house.gov
    Subcommittee on Human Resources,
      (202) 225-1025.

General email, info@justicepolicy.org

Web, www.justicepolicy.org, Twitter, @JusticePolicy and Facebook, www.facebook.com/JusticePolicy

Research, advocacy, and policy development organization. Analyzes current and emerging adult and juvenile criminal justice problems; educates the public about criminal justice issues; provides technical assistance to communities seeking to reform incarceration policies. Interests include new prison construction, alternatives to incarceration, antigang legislation, and curfew laws.

National Center for State Courts, *Government Relations, 111 2nd St. N.E., 20002; (202) 684-2622. Fax, (757) 220-0449. S. Kay Farley, Executive Director; Michael Buenger, Executive Vice President, (757) 259-1831. Toll-free, (800) 616-6164.*

General email, govrel@ncsc.org

Web, www.ncsc.org

Works to improve state court systems through research, technical assistance, and training programs. Monitors legislation affecting court systems; interests include state-federal jurisdiction, family law, criminal justice, court administration, international agreements, and automated information systems. Serves as secretariat for eleven state court organizations, including the Conference of Chief Justices, Conference of State Court Administrators, American Judges Assn., and National Assn. for Court Management. (Headquarters in Williamsburg, Va.)

RAND Corp., Washington Office, *1200 S. Hayes St., Arlington, VA 22202-5050; (703) 413-1100. Fax, (703) 413-8111. Nicholas Burger, Director;*

SENATE:

Senate Agriculture, Nutrition, and Forestry Committee, (202) 224-2035.
Web, agriculture.senate.gov

Subcommittee on Livestock, Marketing, and Agriculture Security, (202) 224-2035.

Senate Appropriations Committee, (202) 224-7257.
Web, appropriations.senate.gov

Subcommittee on Commerce, Justice, Science, and Related Agencies, (202) 224-5202.

Subcommittee on Homeland Security, (202) 224-8244.

Senate Commerce, Science, and Transportation Committee, (202) 224-1251.
Web, commerce.senate.gov

Subcommittee on Consumer Protection, Product Safety, Insurance and Data Security, (202) 224-1251.

Subcommittee on Oceans, Atmosphere, Fisheries, and the Coast Guard, (202) 224-1251.

Senate Finance Committee, (202) 224-4515.
Web, finance.senate.gov

Subcommittee on Taxation and IRS Oversight, (202) 224-4515.

Senate Foreign Relations Committee, (202) 224-4651.
Web, foreign.senate.gov

Subcommittee on Western Hemisphere, Transnational Crime, Civilian Security, Democracy, Human Rights, and Global Women's Issues, (202) 224-4651.

Senate Health, Education, Labor, and Pensions Committee, (202) 224-5375.
Web, help.senate.gov

Subcommittee on Children and Families, (202) 224-5375.

Subcommittee on Employment and Workplace Safety, (202) 224-5375.

Senate Homeland Security and Governmental Affairs Committee, (202) 224-4751.
Web, hsgac.senate.gov

Permanent Subcommittee on Investigations, (202) 224-3721.

Senate Indian Affairs Committee, (202) 224-2251.
Web, indian.senate.gov

Senate Judiciary Committee, (202) 224-5225.
Web, judiciary.senate.gov

Subcommittee on Antitrust, Competition Policy, and Consumer Rights, (202) 224-5444.

Subcommittee on the Constitution, (202) 224-5922.

Subcommittee on Crime and Terrorism, (202) 224-5972.

Subcommittee on Border Security and Immigration, (202) 224-7840.

Subcommittee on Oversight, Agency Action, Federal Rights, and Federal Courts, (202) 224-4224.

Subcommittee on Privacy, Technology, and the Law, (202) 224-4521.

Senate Rules and Administration Committee, (202) 224-6352.
Web, rules.senate.gov

Senate Select Committee on Ethics, (202) 224-2981.
Web, ethics.senate.gov

Senate Small Business and Entrepreneurship Committee, (202) 224-5175.
Web, sbc.senate.gov

Senate Special Committee on Aging, (202) 224-5364.
Web, aging.senate.gov

Anita Chandra, Director for Social and Economic Well-Being, ext. 5323.
Web, www.rand.org

Analyzes current problems of the American civil and criminal justice systems and evaluates recent and pending changes and reforms. (Headquarters in Santa Monica, Calif.)

U.S. Chamber of Commerce, *Congressional and Public Affairs, 1615 H St. N.W., 20062-2000; (202) 463-5600. Jack Howard, Senior Vice President.*
Web, www.uschamber.com

Federation of individuals, firms, corporations, trade and professional associations, and local, state, and regional chambers of commerce. Monitors legislation and regulations in administrative law, antitrust policy, civil justice reform, and product liability reform.

U.S. Chamber of Commerce, *Institute for Legal Reform, 1615 H St. N.W., 20062-2000; (202) 463-5724. Fax, (202) 463-5302. Lisa A. Rickard, President.*
General email, ilr@uschamber.com
Web, http://instituteforlegalreform.org and Twitter, @LegalReform

Works to reform state and federal civil justice systems. Strives to reduce excessive litigation. Hosts public forums on legal and tort reform.

Urban Institute, *Justice Policy Center, 500 L'Enfant Plaza S.W., 20024; (202) 833-7200. Fax, (202) 659-8985. Nancy G. La Vigne, Vice President.*
Web, www.urban.org/center/jpc

Conducts research and evaluation designed to improve justice and public safety policies and practices at the

Justice Department

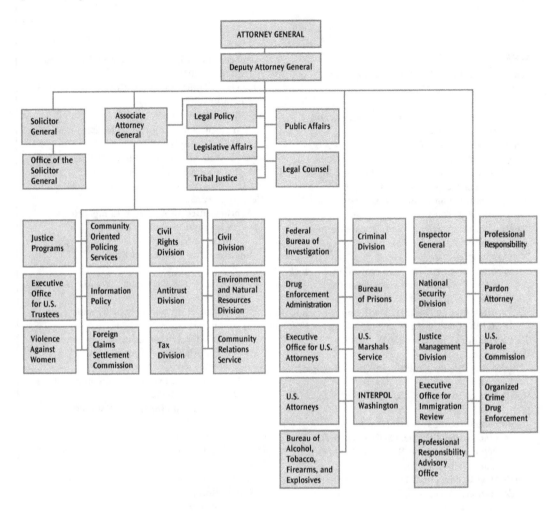

national, state, and local levels. Works with practitioners, public officials, and community groups to generate evidence on effectiveness of existing programs and to provide guidance on improvements.

Dispute Resolution

▶ AGENCIES

Justice Dept. (DOJ), *Community Relations Service (CRS),* 600 E St. N.W., #6000, 20530; (202) 305-2935. Gerri Ratliff, Deputy Director.
General email, askcrs@usdoj.gov
Web, www.justice.gov/crs

Works with state and local governments, private and public organizations, civil rights groups, and local community leaders to promote conflict resolution for community challenges arising from differences of race, color, national origin, gender, gender identity, sexual orientation, religion, and disability. Assists communities in developing local mechanisms and community capacity to

prevent tension and violent hate crimes from occurring in the future.

Justice Dept. (DOJ), *Legal Policy (OLP), Interagency Alternative Dispute Resolution Working Group,* 950 Pennsylvania Ave. N.W., #4529, 20530-0001; Beth A. Williams, Assistant Attorney General.
General email, ADRWeb@usdoj.gov
Web, www.adr.gov

Division of the office of the associate attorney general. Coordinates Justice Dept. activities related to dispute resolution. Responsible for alternative dispute resolution (ADR) policy and training. Manages the Interagency ADR Working Group.

Occupational Safety and Health Review Commission,
1120 20th St. N.W., 9th Floor, 20036-3457; (202) 606-5100. Fax, (202) 606-5050. Heather L. MacDougall, Chair, (202) 606-5364. TTY, (877) 889-5627.
Web, www.oshrc.gov

Independent executive branch agency that adjudicates disputes between private employers and the Occupational Safety and Health Administration arising under the Occupational Safety and Health Act of 1970.

►NONGOVERNMENTAL

American Arbitration Assn., *Government Relations,* 1120 Connecticut Ave. N.W., #490, 20036; S. Pierre Paret, Vice President. Toll-free, (800) 778-7879.
Web, www.adr.org and Twitter, @adrorg

Provides alternative dispute resolution services to governments and the private sector. (Headquarters in New York.)

American Bar Assn. (ABA), *Dispute Resolution,* 1050 Connecticut Ave. N.W., #400, 20036; (202) 662-1680. Fax, (202) 662-1683. Linda Warren Seely, Director, (202) 662-1685.
General email, dispute@americanbar.org
Web, www.americanbar.org/groups/dispute_resolution, Twitter, @ABA_DR and Facebook, www.facebook.com/ABADisputeResolution1

Provides training and resources to lawyers, law students, mediators, and arbitrators on dispute resolution.

Call for Action, 11820 Parklawn Dr., #340, Rockville, MD 20852; (240) 747-0229. Shirley Rooker, President; Eduard Bartholme, Executive Director.
Web, www.callforaction.org

International network of consumer hotlines affiliated with local broadcast partners. Helps consumers resolve problems with businesses, government agencies, and other organizations through mediation. Provides information on privacy concerns.

Center for Dispute Settlement, 1666 Connecticut Ave. N.W., #525, 20009-1039; (202) 265-9572. Fax, (202) 332-3951. Linda R. Singer, President.
General email, admin@cdsusa.org
Web, www.cdsusa.org and Twitter, @CdsCenter

Designs, implements, and evaluates alternative and nonjudicial methods of dispute resolution. Mediates disputes. Provides training in dispute resolution for public and private institutions, individuals, and communities.

Council of Better Business Bureaus, *Dispute Resolution,* 3033 Wilson Blvd., #600, Arlington, VA 22201-3843; (703) 276-0100. Fax, (703) 525-8277. Jennifer Raleigh, Senior Vice President of Enterprise Programs.
General email, contactdr@council.bbb.org
Web, www.bbb.org/council/bbb-dispute-handling-and-resolution

Administers mediation and arbitration programs through Better Business Bureaus nationwide to assist in resolving disputes between businesses and consumers. Assists with unresolved disputes between car owners and automobile manufacturers. Maintains pools of certified arbitrators nationwide. Provides mediation training.

Judicial Appointments

►AGENCIES

Justice Dept. (DOJ), *Legal Policy (OLP),* 950 Pennsylvania Ave. N.W., #4234, 20530-0001; (202) 514-4601. Fax, (202) 514-2424. Beth A. Williams, Assistant Attorney General.
Web, www.justice.gov/olp

Investigates and processes prospective candidates for presidential appointment (subject to Senate confirmation) to the federal judiciary.

►CONGRESS

For a listing of relevant congressional committees and subcommittees, please see pages 542–543 or the Appendix.

►JUDICIARY

Administrative Office of the U.S. Courts, 1 Columbus Circle N.E., 20544-0001; (202) 502-2600. James C. Duff, Director.
Web, www.uscourts.gov

Supervises all administrative matters of the federal court system, except the Supreme Court. Transmits to Congress the recommendations of the Judicial Conference of the United States concerning creation of federal judgeships and other legislative proposals.

Judicial Conference of the United States, 1 Columbus Circle N.E., #7430, 20544; (202) 502-2400. Fax, (202) 502-3019. John G. Roberts Jr., Chief Justice of the United States; James C. Duff, Director. Public Affairs, (202) 502-2600.
Web, www.uscourts.gov

Serves as the policymaking and governing body for the administration of the federal judicial system; advises Congress on the creation of new federal judgeships. Interests include international judicial relations.

►NONGOVERNMENTAL

Alliance for Justice, 11 Dupont Circle N.W., #500, 20036-1213; (202) 822-6070. Nan Aron, President.
General email, alliance@afj.org
Web, www.afj.org, Twitter, @AFJustice and Facebook, www.facebook.com/AllianceforJustice

Monitors candidates for vacancies in the federal judiciary; independently reviews nominees' records; maintains statistics on the judiciary.

BUSINESS AND TAX LAW

Antitrust

►AGENCIES

Antitrust Division *(Justice Dept.),* 950 Pennsylvania Ave. N.W., #3109, 20530-0001; (202) 514-2401.

General Counsels for Federal Departments and Agencies

DEPARTMENTS

Agriculture, Stephen Vaden (Acting), (202) 720-3351

Commerce, Peter Davidson, (202) 482-4772

Defense, William S. Castle (Acting), (703) 695-3341

  Air Force, Thomas E. Ayres, (703) 697-0941

  Army, James E. McPherson, (703) 697-9235

  Navy, Anne M. Brennan (Acting), (703) 614-1994

Education, Carlos G. Muñiz, (202) 401-6000

Energy, Eric J. Fygi, (202) 586-5281

Health and Human Services, Robert P. Charrow, (202) 690-7741

Homeland Security, John Mitnick, (202) 282-9822

Housing and Urban Development, Paul Compton, (202) 708-2240

Interior, Daniel Jorjani, (202) 208-4423

Justice, Jean King, (703) 305-0470

Labor, Kate O'Scannlain, (202) 693-5260

State, Richard C. Visek, 202-647-4000

Transportation, Steven G. Bradbury, (202) 366-4702

Treasury, Brent J. McIntosh, (202) 622-2000

Veterans Affairs, James M. Byrne, (202) 632-7718

AGENCIES

Advisory Council on Historic Preservation, Javier Marques (202) 517-0200; jmarques@achp.gov

Agency for International Development, David H. Moore, (202) 712-0900

Central Intelligence Agency, Courtney Simmons Elwood, (703) 482-0623

Commission on Civil Rights, Maureen Rudolph, (202) 376-7622

Commodity Futures Trading Commission, Daniel J. Davis, (202) 418-5649

Consumer Product Safety Commission, Mary Boyle, (301) 504-7859

Corporation for National Service, Tim Noelker, (202) 606-5000

Environmental Protection Agency, Matthew Z. Leopold, (202) 564-8040

Equal Employment Opportunity Commission, Vacant, (202) 663-4702

Farm Credit Administration, Charles R. Rawls, (703) 883-4021

Federal Communications Commission, Thomas M. Johnson, Jr., (202) 418-1700

Federal Deposit Insurance Corporation, Nick Podsiadly, (703) 562-2037

Federal Election Commission, Lisa J. Stevenson (Acting), (202) 694-1650

Federal Emergency Management Agency, Adrian Sevier, (202) 646-2500

Federal Energy Regulatory Commission, James Danly, (202) 502-6000

Federal Labor Relations Authority, Vacant, (202) 218-7910

Fax, (202) 616-2645. Makan Delrahim, Assistant Attorney General. Press, (202) 514-2007.

General email, antitrust.atr@usdoj.gov

Web, www.usdoj.gov/atr and Twitter, @JusticeATR

Enforces antitrust laws to prevent monopolies and unlawful restraint of trade; has civil and criminal jurisdiction; coordinates activities with the Bureau of Competition of the Federal Trade Commission.

Antitrust Division (Justice Dept.), **Antitrust Documents Group,** 450 5th St. N.W., #1024, 20530; (202) 514-2481. Fax, (202) 514-3763. Kenneth Hendricks, Chief.

General email, atrdocsgrp@usdoj.gov

Web, www.justice.gov/atr/antitrust-foia

Maintains files and handles requests for information on federal civil and criminal antitrust cases; provides the president and Congress with copies of statutory reports prepared by the division on a variety of competition-related issues; issues opinion letters on whether certain business activity violates antitrust laws.

Antitrust Division (Justice Dept.), **Defense, Industrials, and Aerospace,** 450 5th St. N.W., #8700, 20530;

(202) 307-0924. Fax, (202) 514-9033. Maribeth Petrizzi, Chief.

Web, www.justice.gov/atr/about/lit2.html

Investigates and litigates cases involving defense, waste industries, avionics and aeronautics, road and highway construction, metals and mining, industrial equipment, and banking.

Antitrust Division (Justice Dept.), **Healthcare and Consumer Products,** 450 5th St. N.W., #4700, 20530; (202) 307-0001. Fax, (202) 307-5802. Peter J. Mucchetti, Chief.

Web, www.justice.gov/atr/about-division/litigation-i-section

Investigates and litigates cases involving health care, paper, pulp, timber, food products, cosmetics and hair care, bread, beer, appliances, and insurance.

Antitrust Division (Justice Dept.), **Media, Entertainment, and Professional Services,** 450 5th St. N.W., #4000, 20530-0001; (202) 305-8376. Fax, (202) 514-7308. Owen M. Kendler, Chief.

General email, ATR.LitIII.Information@usdoj.gov

Web, www.justice.gov/atr/about/lit3.html

Federal Maritime Commission, Tyler J. Wood, (202) 523-5740

Federal Mediation and Conciliation Service, Michael J. Bartlett, (202) 606-3737

Federal Reserve System, Dawn Starr, (202) 452-8090

Federal Trade Commission, David Shonka (Acting), (202) 326-2424

General Services Administration, Jack St. John (Acting), (202) 501-2200

International Bank for Reconstruction and Development (World Bank), Sandie Okoro, (202) 473-1000

Merit Systems Protection Board, Katherine Smith, (202) 653-7171

National Aeronautics and Space Administration, Sumara M. Thompson-King, (202) 358-2450

National Credit Union Administration, Michael J. McKenna, (703) 518-6540

National Endowment for the Arts, India Pinkney, (202) 682-5418

National Endowment for the Humanities, Michael McDonald, (202) 606-8322

National Labor Relations Board, Peter B. Robb, (202) 273-3700

National Mediation Board, Mary Johnson, (202) 692-5040

National Railroad Passenger Corporation (Amtrak), Eleanor D. Acheson, (202) 906-4600

National Science Foundation, Lawrence Rudolph, (703) 292-8060

National Transportation Safety Board, Kathleen Silbaugh, (202) 314-6080

Nuclear Regulatory Commission, Marion Zobler, (301) 415-1743

Occupational Safety and Health Review Commission, Nadine N. Mancini, (202) 606-5410

Office of Personnel Management, Vacant (202) 606-1700

Overseas Private Investment Corporation, William Doffermyre, (202) 336-8400

Peace Corps, Robert Shanks, (855) 855-1961

Pension Benefit Guaranty Corporation, Judith Starr, (202) 326-4400

Postal Regulatory Commission, David A. Trissell, (202) 789-6820

Securities and Exchange Commission, Robert B. Stebbins, (202) 551-5100

Small Business Administration, Chris Pilkerton, (202) 205-6642

Smithsonian Institution, Judith E. Leonard, (202) 633-5115

Social Security Administration, Asheesh Agarwal, (410) 965-1234

U.S. International Trade Commission, Dominic Bianchi, (202) 708-5403 or (202) 205-2000

U.S. Postal Service, Thomas J. Marshall, (202) 268-2950

Investigates and litigates certain antitrust cases involving such commodities as movies, radio, TV, newspapers, performing arts, sports, and credit and debit cards. Handles certain violations of antitrust laws that involve patents, copyrights, and trademarks. Deals with mergers and acquisitions.

Antitrust Division *(Justice Dept.), Technology and Financial Services, 450 5th St. N.W., #7700, 20530; (202) 616-5924. Fax, (202) 616-8544. Aaron D. Hoag, Chief. General email, antitrust.atr@usdoj.gov*

Web, www.justice.gov/atr/about/ntes.html

Investigates and litigates certain antitrust cases involving financial institutions, including securities, commodity futures, computer hardware and software, professional associations, and high-technology component manufacturing; participates in agency proceedings and rulemaking in these areas; monitors and analyzes legislation.

Antitrust Division *(Justice Dept.), Telecommunications and Broadband, 450 5th St. N.W., #7000, 20530; (202) 616-5924. Fax, (202) 514-5399. Scott A. Scheele, Chief. Press, (202) 514-2007.*

Web, www.justice.gov/atr/about/tel.html

Investigates and litigates antitrust cases dealing with communications and media, including mobile wireless services, broadband Internet, satellite communications services, voice communication services, video programming distribution, and business telecommunications services.

Antitrust Division *(Justice Dept.), Transportation, Energy, and Agriculture (TEA), 450 5th St. N.W., #8004, 20530; (202) 616-5924. Fax, (202) 307-2784. Kathleen S. O'Neill, Chief.*

Web, www.justice.gov/atr/about/tea.html

Responsible for civil antitrust enforcement, competition advocacy, and competition policy in the area of domestic and international aviation, bus and leisure travel, railroads, trucking, and ocean shipping, hotels, restaurants, and travel services, electricity, oil-field services, food products, crops, seeds, fish and livestock, and agricultural biotech. Participates in proceedings before the Federal Energy Regulatory Commission, Environmental Protection Agency, Agriculture Dept., Energy Dept., State Dept., Commerce Dept., Transportation Dept., and the Federal Maritime Commission.

Comptroller of the Currency *(Treasury Dept.),*
Constitution Center, 400 7th St. S.W., 20219; (202) 649-6800. Joseph M. Otting, Comptroller. Press, (202) 649-6870. Information, (800) 613-6743. TDD, (713) 658-0340. TTY, (800) 877-8339.
General email, publicaffairs3@occ.treas.gov
Web, https://occ.treas.gov and Twitter, @USOCC

Charters and examines operations of national banks, federal savings associations, and U.S. operations of foreign-owned banks; establishes guidelines for bank examinations; handles mergers of national banks with regard to antitrust law. Ensures that national banks and savings associations operate in a safe and sound manner, provide fair access to financial services, treat customers fairly, and comply with applicable laws and regulations.

Federal Communications Commission (FCC), *Wireline Competition Bureau (WCB), 445 12th St. S.W., #5C343, 20554; (202) 418-1500. Fax, (202) 418-2825. Kris Monteith, Chief (Acting).*
Web, www.fcc.gov/wireline-competition and Blog, www.fcc.gov/news-events/blog/1639

Regulates mergers involving common carriers (wireline facilities that furnish interstate communications services).

Federal Deposit Insurance Corp. (FDIC), *Risk Management Supervision, 550 17th St. N.W., #5036, 20429; (877) 275-3342. Fax, (202) 898-3638. Doreen R. Eberley, Director.*
Web, www.fdic.gov/about/contact/directory/#HQDSC

Studies and analyzes applications for mergers, consolidations, acquisitions, and assumption transactions between insured banks.

Federal Energy Regulatory Commission (FERC) *(Energy Dept.), 888 1st St. N.E., 20426; (202) 502-6088. Fax, (202) 502-8612. Neil Chatterjee, Chair, (202) 502-6477. eLibrary questions, (202) 502-6652. Enforcement hotline, (202) 502-8390. Enforcement toll-free, (888) 889-8030. Press, (202) 502-8680. Toll-free, (866) 208-3372. TTY, (202) 502-8659. General email, customer@ferc.gov*
Web, www.ferc.gov, Twitter, @FERC and Facebook, www.facebook.com/FERC.gov

Regulates mergers, consolidations, and acquisitions of electric utilities; regulates the acquisition of interstate natural gas pipeline facilities.

Federal Reserve System, *Supervision and Regulation, 20th St. and Constitution Ave. N.W., 20551; (202) 973-6999. Michael Gibson, Director, (202) 452-2495.*
Web, www.federalreserve.gov/econresdata/bsrstaff.htm

Approves bank mergers, consolidations, and other alterations in bank structure.

Federal Trade Commission (FTC), *600 Pennsylvania Ave. N.W., 20580; (202) 326-2222. Joseph J. Simons, Chair; David B. Robbins, Executive Director; Noah Joshua Phillips, Commissioner. Press, (202) 326-2180. Congressional Relations, (202) 326-2195. Identity theft hotline, (877) 438-4338. Library, (202) 326-2395.*
Web, www.ftc.gov and Twitter, @FTC

Promotes policies designed to maintain strong competitive enterprise and consumer protection within the U.S. economic system. Monitors trade practices and investigates cases involving monopoly, unfair restraints, or deceptive practices. Enforces Truth in Lending and Fair Credit Reporting acts. Library open to the public (Monday–Friday, 8:30 a.m.–5:00 p.m.).

Federal Trade Commission (FTC), *Bureau of Competition, 600 Pennsylvania Ave. N.W., #CC-5422, 20580; (202) 326-3300. Fax, (202) 326-2884. Bruce Hoffman, Director.*
General email, antitrust@ftc.gov
Web, www.ftc.gov/about-ftc/bureaus-offices/bureau-competition

Enforces antitrust laws and investigates possible violations, mergers and acquisitions, and anticompetitive practices; seeks voluntary compliance and pursues civil judicial remedies; reviews premerger filings; coordinates activities with the Antitrust Division of the Justice Dept. Library open to the public (Monday–Friday, 8:30 a.m.–5:00 p.m.).

Federal Trade Commission (FTC), *Bureau of Competition, Anticompetitive Practices (ACP), 400 7th St. S.W., #5417, 20024; (202) 326-2641. Fax, (202) 326-3496. Geoffrey Green, Assistant Director. Toll-free, (877) 382-4357.*
General email, antitrust@ftc.gov
Web, www.ftc.gov/about-ftc/bureaus-offices/bureau-competition

Investigates nonmerger anticompetitive practices in real estate and a variety of other industries. Interests include intellectual property and professional and regulatory boards.

Federal Trade Commission (FTC), *Bureau of Competition, Compliance, 400 7th St. S.W., #8416, 20024; (202) 326-2861. Fax, (202) 326-3396. Roberta S. Baruch, Assistant Director.*
General email, bccompliance@ftc.gov
Web, www.ftc.gov/about-ftc/bureaus-offices/bureau-competition

Monitors and enforces competition orders and oversees required remediations in company conduct. Investigates possible violations of the Hart-Scott-Rodino Act.

Federal Trade Commission (FTC), *Bureau of Competition, Health Care Division, 400 7th St. S.W., #7245, 20024; (202) 326-3759. Fax, (202) 326-3384. Markus H. Meier, Assistant Director.*
Web, www.ftc.gov/about-ftc/bureaus-offices/bureau-competition

Investigates and litigates nonmerger anticompetitive practices among physicians, hospitals, and health insurers in the health care industry, including the pharmaceutical industry. Works against pay-for-delay agreements among pharmaceutical companies that insulate brand-name drugs from competition with lower-cost generic drugs.

Federal Trade Commission (FTC), *Bureau of Competition, Honors Paralegal Program, 400 7th St.*

Federal Maritime Commission

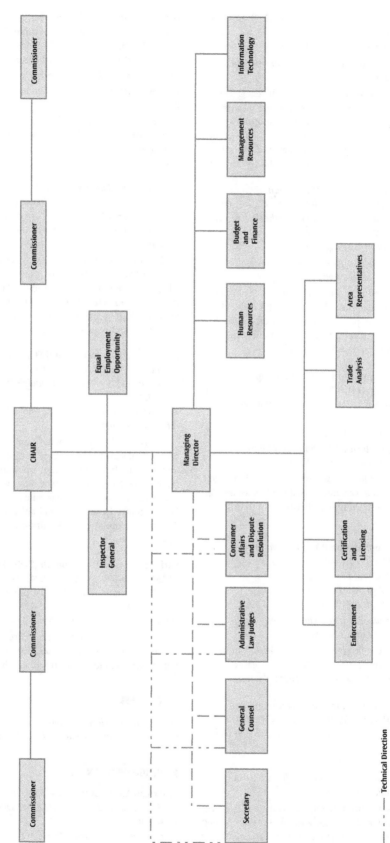

S.W., #8310, 20024; (202) 326-2750. Fax, (202) 326-3496. Kimberly Burris, Coordinator.

General email, honorsparalegals@ftc.gov

Web, www.ftc.gov/about-ftc/careers-ftc/work-ftc/honors-paralegal-program

Administers paralegal program for individuals considering a career in law, economics, business, or public service. Honors paralegals are given significant responsibility and hands-on experience while assisting attorneys and economists in the investigation and litigation of antitrust matters. Applicants are appointed for 14-month to four-year terms.

Federal Trade Commission (FTC), Bureau of Competition, Mergers I, 400 7th St. S.W., #6226, 20024; (202) 326-3106. Fax, (202) 326-2655. Michael Moiseyev, Assistant Director.

General email, antitrust@ftc.gov

Web, www.ftc.gov/about-ftc/bureaus-offices/bureau-competition/inside-bureau-competition

Investigates and litigates antitrust violations in mergers and acquisitions, primarily in the health care–related industries, including pharmaceutical manufacturing and distribution and medical devices. Also handles scientific, industrial, defense, and technology industries.

Federal Trade Commission (FTC), Bureau of Competition, Mergers II, 400 7th Ave. S.W., #7414, 20024; (202) 326-3505. Fax, (202) 326-2071. Dominic Vote, Assistant Director.

General email, antitrust@ftc.gov

Web, www.ftc.gov/about-ftc/bureaus-offices/bureau-competition/inside-bureau-competition

Investigates and litigates antitrust violations in mergers and acquisitions in the chemicals, coal mining, technology, entertainment, and computer hardware and software industries.

Federal Trade Commission (FTC), Bureau of Competition, Mergers III, 400 7th Ave. S.W., #7616, 20024; (202) 326-2563. Fax, (202) 326-3383. Peter Richman, Assistant Director.

General email, antitrust@ftc.gov

Web, www.ftc.gov/about-ftc/bureaus-offices/bureau-competition/inside-bureau-competition

Investigates and litigates antitrust violations in mergers and acquisitions concerning the oil and gas, ethanol, industrial spray equipment, and energy industries.

Federal Trade Commission (FTC), Bureau of Competition, Mergers IV, 400 7th Ave. S.W., #6418, 20024; (202) 326-3680. Fax, (202) 326-2286. Kevin Hahm, Assistant Director.

General email, antitrust@ftc.gov

Web, www.ftc.gov/about-ftc/bureaus-offices/bureau-competition/inside-bureau-competition

Investigates and litigates antitrust violations in mergers and acquisitions concerning hospitals, the grocery food product industry, the media, funeral homes, and consumer goods.

Federal Trade Commission (FTC), Bureau of Competition, Premerger Notification (PNO), 400 7th Ave. S.W., #5301, 20024; (202) 326-2740. Fax, (202) 326-2624. Robert L. Jones, Assistant Director, (202) 326-2740.

General email, antitrust@ftc.gov

Web, www.ftc.gov/enforcement/premerger-notification-program

Reviews premerger filings under the Hart-Scott-Rodino Act for the FTC and Justice Dept. Coordinates investigative work with federal and state agencies; participates in international projects.

Federal Trade Commission (FTC), Bureau of Economics, 600 Pennsylvania Ave. N.W., 20580; (202) 326-3420. Fax, (202) 326-2380. Bruce Kobayashi, Director.

Web, www.ftc.gov/about-ftc/bureaus-offices/bureau-economics

Provides economic analyses for consumer protection and antitrust investigations, cases, and rulemakings; advises the commission on the effect of government regulations on competition and consumers in various industries; develops special reports on competition, consumer protection, and regulatory issues.

Federal Trade Commission (FTC), International Affairs, 600 Pennsylvania Ave. N.W., #H494, 20580; (202) 326-2600. Fax, (202) 326-2873. Randolph W. Tritell, Director, (202) 326-3051.

Web, www.ftc.gov/about-ftc/bureaus-offices/office-international-affairs

Assists in the enforcement of antitrust laws and consumer protection by arranging appropriate cooperation and coordination with foreign governments in international cases. Negotiates bilateral and multilateral antitrust and consumer protection agreements and represents the United States in international antitrust policy forums. Assists developing countries in moving toward market-based economies.

Surface Transportation Board (STB), 395 E St. S.W., #1220, 20423-0001; (202) 245-0245. Fax, (202) 245-0458. Ann D. Begeman, Chair. Library, (202) 245-0288. Press, (202) 245-0238. TTY, (800) 877-8339.

Web, www.stb.gov/stb/index.html

Regulates rail rate disputes, railroad consolidations, rail line construction proposals, line abandonments, and rail car service. Library open to the public.

►CONGRESS

For a listing of relevant congressional committees and subcommittees, please see pages 542–543 or the Appendix.

►NONGOVERNMENTAL

American Antitrust Institute (AAI), 1025 Connecticut Ave. N.W., #1000, 20036; (202) 828-1226. Diana L. Moss, President.

Web, www.antitrustinstitute.org and

Twitter, @AntitrustInst

Pro-antitrust organization that provides research and policy analysis to journalists, academic researchers, lawyers, economists, businesspeople, government officials, courts, and the general public. Seeks to educate the public on the importance of fair competition. Monitors legislation and regulations on competition-oriented policies.

The Business Roundtable, *300 New Jersey Ave. N.W., #800, 20001; (202) 872-1260. Fax, (202) 466-3509. Joshua Bolten, President. Press, (202) 496-3289.*
General email, info@brt.org
Web, www.businessroundtable.org and
Twitter, @BizRoundtable

Membership: chief executives of the nation's largest corporations. Examines issues of concern to business, including antitrust law.

U.S. Chamber Litigation Center, *1615 H St. N.W., 20062-2000; (202) 463-5337. Fax, (202) 463-5707. John Wood, Senior Vice President.*
General email, litigationcenter@uschamber.com
Web, www.chamberlitigation.com

Public policy law firm of the U.S. Chamber of Commerce. Advocates businesses' positions in court on such issues as antitrust, bankruptcy, and employment, environmental, and constitutional law. Provides businesses with legal assistance and amicus support in legal proceedings before federal courts and agencies.

Bankruptcy

►**AGENCIES**

Executive Office for U.S. Trustees *(Justice Dept.), 441 G St. N.W., #6150, 20530; (202) 307-1399. Fax, (202) 307-0672. Clifford J. White III, Director, (202) 307-1391.*
General email, ustrustee.program@usdoj.gov
Web, www.justice.gov/ust

Handles the administration and oversight of bankruptcy and liquidation cases filed under the Bankruptcy Reform Act, including detecting and combating bankruptcy fraud. Provides individual U.S. trustee offices with administrative and management support.

►**CONGRESS**

For a listing of relevant congressional committees and subcommittees, please see pages 542–543 or the Appendix.

►**NONGOVERNMENTAL**

American Bankruptcy Institute, *66 Canal Center Plaza, #600, Alexandria, VA 22314-1592; (703) 739-0800. Fax, (866) 921-1027. Samuel J. Gerdano, Executive Director.*

General email, support@abiworld.org
Web, www.abi.org, Twitter, @abiworld and
Facebook, www.facebook.com/
TheAmericanBankruptcyInstitute

Membership: lawyers, federal and state legislators, and representatives of accounting and financial services firms, lending institutions, credit organizations, and consumer groups. Provides information and educational services on insolvency, reorganization, and bankruptcy issues; sponsors conferences, seminars, and workshops.

National Assn. of Consumer Bankruptcy Attorneys, *2200 Pennsylvania Ave. N.W., 4th Floor, 20037; (800) 499-9040. Fax, (866) 408-9515. Maureen Thompson, Legislative Director; Dan Labert, Executive Director.*
General email, admin@nacba.org
Web, www.nacba.org and Twitter, @NACBAorg

Advocates on behalf of consumer debtors and their attorneys. Files amicus briefs on behalf of parties in the U.S. courts of appeal and Supreme Court, and provides educational programs and workshops for attorneys. Monitors legislation and regulations.

U.S. Chamber Litigation Center, *1615 H St. N.W., 20062-2000; (202) 463-5337. Fax, (202) 463-5707. John Wood, Senior Vice President.*
General email, litigationcenter@uschamber.com
Web, www.chamberlitigation.com

Public policy law firm of the U.S. Chamber of Commerce. Advocates businesses' positions in court on such issues as antitrust, bankruptcy, and employment, environmental, and constitutional law. Provides businesses with legal assistance and amicus support in legal proceedings before federal courts and agencies.

Tax Violations

►**AGENCIES**

Internal Revenue Service (IRS) *(Treasury Dept.),* **Criminal Investigation,** *1111 Constitution Ave. N.W., #2501, 20224; (202) 317-3200. Don Fort, Chief. Tax fraud hotline, (800) 829-0433.*
Web, www.irs.gov/uac/criminal-enforcement-1 and
Twitter, @IRSnews

Investigates money laundering, criminal violations of the tax law, and related financial crimes.

Internal Revenue Service (IRS) *(Treasury Dept.),* **Procedures and Administration,** *1111 Constitution Ave. N.W., #5503, 20224; (202) 317-3400. Fax, (202) 317-5374. Drita Tonuzi, Deputy Chief Counsel for Operations; Kathy Zuba, Associate Chief Administrative Counsel. Press, (202) 317-4000.*
Web, www.irs.gov

Oversees field office litigation of civil cases that involve underpayment of taxes when the taxpayer chooses to challenge the determinations of the IRS in the U.S. Tax Court, or when the taxpayer chooses to pay the amount in question and sue the IRS for a refund. Reviews briefs and defense letters prepared by field offices for tax cases; drafts legal advice memos; prepares tax litigation advice memoranda; coordinates litigation strategy. Makes recommendations concerning appeal and certiorari. Prepares tax regulations, rulings, and other published guidance regarding the Internal Revenue Code, as enacted.

Tax Division *(Justice Dept.)*, *950 Pennsylvania Ave. N.W., #4141, 20530-0001; (202) 514-2901. Fax, (202) 514-5479. Richard E. Zuckerman, Assistant Attorney General, (202) 514-2901.*
Web, www.justice.gov/tax

Authorizes prosecution of all criminal cases involving tax violations investigated and developed by the Internal Revenue Service (IRS); represents the IRS in civil litigation except in U.S. Tax Court proceedings; represents other agencies, including the Defense and Interior Depts., in cases with state or local tax authorities.

▶CONGRESS

For a listing of relevant congressional committees and subcommittees, please see pages 542–543 or the Appendix.

▶JUDICIARY

U.S. Tax Court, *400 2nd St. N.W., #134, 20217; (202) 521-0700. Maurice B. Foley, Chief Judge.*
Web, www.ustaxcourt.gov

Tries and adjudicates disputes involving income, estate, and gift taxes and personal holding company surtaxes in cases in which deficiencies have been determined by the Internal Revenue Service.

▶NONGOVERNMENTAL

American Bar Assn. (ABA), *Taxation, 1050 Connecticut Ave. N.W., #400, 20036; (202) 662-8670. Fax, (202) 662-8682. John A. Thorner, Director, (202) 662-8677.*
General email, tax@americanbar.org
Web, www.americanbar.org/groups/taxation

Studies and recommends policies on taxation; provides information on tax issues; sponsors continuing legal education programs; monitors tax laws and legislation.

CIVIL RIGHTS

General

▶AGENCIES

Civil Rights Division *(Justice Dept.)*, *950 Pennsylvania Ave. N.W., #5643, 20530-0001; (202) 514-4609. Fax, (202) 514-0293. Eric S. Dreiband, Assistant Attorney General. Press, (202) 514-2007. TTY, (202) 514-0716.*
General email, complaint@usdoj.gov
Web, www.justice.gov/crt and Twitter, @TheJusticeDept

Enforces federal civil rights laws prohibiting discrimination on the basis of race, color, religion, sex, disability, age, or national origin in voting, education, employment, credit, housing, public accommodations and facilities, credit, and federally assisted programs.

Civil Rights Division *(Justice Dept.)*, *Disability Rights (DRS), 950 Pennsylvania Ave. N.W., 20530; (202) 307-0663. Fax, (202) 307-1197. Rebecca Bond, Chief. Information and ADA specialist, (800) 514-0301. TTY, (800) 514-0383.*
Web, www.justice.gov/crt/disability-rights-section

Litigates cases under Titles I, II, and III of the Americans with Disabilities Act, which prohibits discrimination on the basis of disability in places of public accommodation and in all activities of state and local government. Provides technical assistance to businesses and individuals affected by the law.

Civil Rights Division *(Justice Dept.)*, *Educational Opportunities (EOS), 601 D St. N.W., #4300, 20530; (202) 514-4092. Fax, (202) 514-8337. Shaheena Simons, Chief. Toll-free, (877) 292-3804.*
General email, education@usdoj.gov
Web, www.justice.gov/crt/educational-opportunities-section

Initiates litigation to ensure equal opportunities in public education; enforces laws dealing with civil rights in public education.

Education Dept., *Civil Rights (OCR), Lyndon Baines Johnson Bldg., 400 Maryland Ave. S.W., #4E313, 20202-1100; (202) 453-5900. Fax, (202) 453-6012. Kenneth L. Marcus, Assistant Secretary. Toll-free, (800) 421-3481. TTY, (800) 877-8339.*
General email, ocr@ed.gov
Web, www2.ed.gov/ocr and Twitter, @EDcivilrights

Enforces laws prohibiting use of federal funds for education programs or activities that discriminate on the basis of race, color, sex, national origin, age, or disability; authorized to discontinue funding.

Health and Human Services Dept. (HHS), *Civil Rights (OCR), 200 Independence Ave. S.W., #509F, 20201; (202) 619-0403. Fax, (202) 619-3437. Roger Severino, Director. Toll-free, (800) 368-1019. TTY, (800) 537-7697.*
General email, OCRMail@hhs.gov
Web, www.hhs.gov/ocr

Administers and enforces laws prohibiting discrimination on the basis of race, color, sex, national origin, religion, age, or disability in programs receiving federal funds from the department; authorized to discontinue funding. Enforces the Health Insurance Portability and Accountability Act (HIPAA), Privacy, Security, and Breach Notification rules, and the Patient Safety Act and Rules.

U.S. Commission on Civil Rights, *1331 Pennsylvania Ave. N.W., #1150, 20425; (202) 376-7700. Fax, (202) 376-7672. Catherine Lhamon, Chair; Mauro Albert Morales, Staff Director. Press, (202) 376-8371. TTY, (202) 372-8116.*

General email, publicaffairs@usccr.gov

Web, www.usccr.gov, Twitter, @USCCRgov

Civil right complaints email, referrals@usccr.gov

Assesses federal laws, policies, and legal developments to determine the nature and extent of denial of equal protection under the law on the basis of race, color, religion, sex, national origin, age, or disability in employment, voting rights, education, administration of justice, and housing. Issues reports and makes recommendations to the president and Congress; serves as national clearinghouse for civil rights information; receives civil rights complaints and refers them to the appropriate federal agency for action. Library open to the public.

U.S. Commission on Civil Rights, *Civil Rights Evaluation, 1331 Pennsylvania Ave. N.W., #1150, 20425; (202) 376-7700. Fax, (202) 376-7754. Katherine Culliton-Gonzalez, Director. Complaints Unit hotline, (202) 376-8513. TTY, (800) 877-8339.*

Web, www.usccr.gov

Develops national civil rights policy and enforcement of federal civil rights laws; studies alleged deprivations of voting rights and alleged discrimination based on race, color, religion, sex, age, disability, or national origin, or in the administration of justice.

▶**CONGRESS**

For a listing of relevant congressional committees and subcommittees, please see pages 542–543 or the Appendix.

▶**NONGOVERNMENTAL**

American Assn. for Access, Equity, and Diversity (AAAED), *1701 Pennsylvania Ave. N.W., #200, 20006; (202) 349-9855. Fax, (202) 355-1399. Shirley J. Wilcher, Executive Director. Toll-free, (866) 562-2233.*

General email, info@aaaed.org

Web, www.aaaed.org, Twitter, @affirmativeat and Facebook, www.facebook.com/theaaaed

Membership: professional managers in the areas of affirmative action, equal opportunity, diversity, and human resources. Sponsors education, research, and training programs. Acts as a liaison with government agencies involved in equal opportunity compliance. Maintains ethical standards for the profession. (Formerly the American Assn. for Affirmative Action.)

Lawyers' Committee for Civil Rights Under Law, *1500 K St., #900, 20005-2124; (202) 662-8600. Fax, (202) 783-0857. Kristen Clarke, Executive Director. Toll-free, (888) 299-5227.*

General email, info@lawyerscommittee.org

Web, www.lawyerscommittee.org, Twitter, @LawyersComm and Facebook, www.facebook.com/lawyerscommittee

Provides minority groups and the poor with legal assistance in such areas as voting rights, employment discrimination, education, environment, and equal access to government services and benefits.

Leadership Conference on Civil and Human Rights, *1620 L St. N.W., #1100, 20036; (202) 466-3311. Fax, (202) 466-3435. Vanita Gupta, President. Press, (202) 869-0398.*

General email, info@civilrights.org

Web, www.civilrights.org, Twitter, @civilrightsorg and Facebook, www.facebook.com/civilandhumanrights

Coalition of national organizations representing minorities, women, labor, older Americans, people with disabilities, and religious groups. Works for enactment and enforcement of civil rights, human rights, and social welfare legislation; acts as clearinghouse for information on civil rights legislation and regulations.

NAACP Legal Defense and Educational Fund, Inc., *Washington Office, 700 14th St., #600, 20005; (202) 682-1300. Todd A. Cox, Director of Policy.*

Web, www.naacpldf.org and Twitter, @NAACP_LDF

Civil rights litigation group that provides legal information on civil rights issues, including employment, housing, and educational discrimination; monitors federal enforcement of civil rights laws. Not affiliated with the NAACP. (Headquarters in New York.)

National Coalition Building Institute, *Metro Plaza Bldg., 8403 Colesville Rd., #1100, Silver Spring, MD 20910; (240) 638-2813. Cherie Brown, Chief Executive Officer.*

General email, info@ncbi.org

Web, www.ncbi.org and Twitter, @NCBIworld

Offers national and global leadership workshops and programs that combat racism and prejudice. Publishes reports on effective practices in reducing racism in education and the workplace.

Poverty and Race Research Action Council, *740 15th St. N.W., #300, 20005; (202) 866-0703. Fax, (202) 842-2885. Philip Tegeler, Executive Director.*

General email, info@prrac.org

Web, www.prrac.org and Twitter, @PRRAC_DC

Facilitates cooperative links between researchers and activists who work on race and poverty issues. Publishes bimonthly *Poverty & Race* newsletter and a civil rights history curriculum guide. Policy research areas include housing, education, and health disparities.

Rainbow PUSH Coalition, *Public Policy Institute, Government Relations and Telecommunications Project, 727 15th St. N.W., #200, 20005; (301) 256-8587. Fax, (202) 393-1495. Jesse L. Jackson Sr., President; Steve Smith, Executive Director; Frank Watkins, Director of Public Policy. Press, (773) 373-3366.*

General email, info@rainbowpush.org

Web, https://rainbowpush.org/washington-dc and Twitter, @RPCoalition

Independent civil rights organization concerned with public policy toward political, economic, and social justice for women, workers, and minorities. (Headquarters in Chicago, Ill.)

Selected Minorities-Related Resources

ADVOCACY AND ANTIDISCRIMINATION

American-Arab Anti-Discrimination Committee, (202) 244-2990; www.adc.org

Anti-Defamation League, (212) 885-7700; www.adl.org

Arab American Institute, (202) 429-9210; www.aaiusa.org

Human Rights Campaign, (202) 628-4160; www.hrc.org

Japanese American Citizens League, (202) 223-1240; www.jacl.org

Mexican American Legal Defense and Education Fund, (202) 293-2828; www.maldef.org

NAACP (National Assn. for the Advancement of Colored People), (202) 463-2940; www.naacp.org

National Council of La Raza, (202) 785-1670; www.nclr.org

National Gay and Lesbian Task Force, (202) 393-5177; www.thetaskforce.org

National Organization for Women, (202) 628-8669; www.now.org

Organization of Asian Pacific Americans, (formerly the Organization of Chinese Americans), (202) 223-5500; www.ocanational.org

Rainbow/PUSH Coalition, 301-256-8587; www.rainbowpush.org

BUSINESS AND LABOR

Business and Professional Women USA, (202) 293-1100; www.bpwfoundation.org

Council of Federal EEO and Civil Rights Executives, (800) 669-4000; www.eeoc.gov

Minority Business Development Agency, (202) 482-2332; www.mbda.gov

National Assn. of Hispanic Federal Executives Inc., (202) 315-3942; www.nahfe.org

National Assn. of Minority Contractors, (202) 296-1600; www.namcnational.org

National Assn. of Women Business Owners, (800) 556-2926; www.nawbo.org

National Black Chamber of Commerce, (202) 466-6888; www.nationalbcc.org

National U.S.-Arab Chamber of Commerce, (202) 289-5920; www.nusacc.org

U.S. Hispanic Chamber of Commerce, (202) 842-1212; www.ushcc.com

U.S. Pan Asian American Chamber of Commerce, (202) 296-5221; www.uspaacc.com

EDUCATION

American Assn. for Access, Equity and Diversity (formerly the American Assn. for Affirmative Action), (202) 349-9855; www.aaaed.org

American Indian Higher Education Consortium, (703) 838-0400; www.aihec.org

Assn. of American Colleges and Universities, (202) 387-3760; www.aacu.org

Assn. of Research Libraries, (202) 296-2296; www.arl.org/diversity

African Americans

▶NONGOVERNMENTAL

Joint Center for Political and Economic Studies, *633 Pennsylvania Ave. N.W., 20004; (202) 789-3500. Fax, (202) 789-6390. Spencer Overton, President.*
General email, info@jointcenter.org
Web, www.jointcenter.org and Twitter, @JointCenter

Documents and analyzes the political and economic status of African Americans, focusing on political participation, economic advancement, and health policy. Publishes *Focus Magazine* annually; disseminates information through forums and conferences.

National Assn. for the Advancement of Colored People (NAACP), *Washington Bureau, 1156 15th St. N.W., #915, 20005; (202) 463-2940. Fax, (202) 463-2953. Derrick Johnson, President.*
General email, washingtonbureau@naacpnet.org
Web, www.naacp.org and Twitter, @NAACP

Membership: persons interested in civil rights for all minorities. Seeks, through legal, legislative, and direct action, to end discrimination in all areas, including discriminatory practices in the administration of justice. Studies and recommends policy on court administration and jury selection. Maintains branch offices in many state and federal prisons. (Headquarters in Baltimore, Md.)

National Assn. of Colored Women's and Youth Clubs Inc. (NACWYC), *1601 R St. N.W., 20009-6420; (202) 667-4080. Sharon R. Bridgeforth, President.*
General email, ematthews@nacwcya.org
Web, www.nacwc.org

Seeks to promote education, protect and enforce civil rights, raise the standard of family living, promote interracial understanding, and enhance leadership development. Awards scholarships; conducts programs in education, social service, and philanthropy.

National Black Caucus of Local Elected Officials (NBC/ LEO), *National League of Cities, 660 N. Capitol St. N.W., 20001; (202) 626-3000. Leon Andrews, Director for Race, Equity, and Leadership, (202) 626-3039. Information, (877) 827-2385.*

National Assn. for Equal Opportunity in Higher Education, (202) 552-3300; www.nafeonation.org

GOVERNMENT, LAW, AND PUBLIC POLICY

Asian American Justice Center, (202) 296-2300; www.advancingjustice-aajc.org

Blacks in Government, (202) 667-3280; www.bignet.org

Congressional Black Caucus Foundation, Inc., (202) 263-2800; www.cbcfinc.org

Congressional Hispanic Caucus Institute, (202) 543-1771; www.chci.org

Council on American-Islamic Relations, (202) 488-8787; www.cair.com

Institute for Women's Policy Research, (202) 785-5100; www.iwpr.org

Joint Center for Political and Economic Studies, (202) 789-3500; www.jointcenter.org

Leadership Conference on Civil Rights, (202) 466-3311; www.civilrights.org

National Congress on American Indians, (202) 466-7767; www.ncai.org

National Women's Law Center, (202) 588-5180; www.nwlc.org

National Women's Political Caucus, (202) 785-1100; www.nwpc.org

Society of American Indian Government Employees, www.saige.org

HEALTH

Asian and Pacific Islander American Health Forum, (202) 466-7772; www.apiahf.org

National Alliance for Hispanic Health, (202) 387-5000; www.hispanichealth.org

National Black Nurses Assn., (301) 589-3200; www.nbna.org

National Council of Urban Indian Health, (202) 544-0344; www.ncuih.org

National Hispanic Medical Assn., (202) 628-5895; www.nhmamd.org

National Minority AIDS Council, (202) 853-1846; www.nmac.org

MEDIA

Center for Digital Democracy, (202) 986-2220; www.democraticmedia.org

International Women's Media Foundation, (202) 496-1992; www.iwmf.org

Minority Media and Telecommunications Council, (202) 332-0500; www.mmtconline.org

National Assn. of Black Owned Broadcasters, (202) 463-8970; www.nabob.org

National Assn. of Hispanic Journalists, contact@nahj.org; www.nahj.org

National Lesbian and Gay Journalists Assn., (202) 588-9888; www.nlgja.org

---

General email, constituencygroups@nlc.org

Web, www.nlc.org

Membership: Black elected officials at the local level and other interested individuals. Seeks to increase Black participation on the National League of Cities' steering and policy committees. Informs members on issues and plans strategies for achieving objectives through legislation and direct action. Interests include cultural diversity, local government and community participation, housing, economics, job training, the family, and human rights.

National Black Caucus of State Legislators, *444 N. Capitol St. N.W., #622, 20001; (202) 624-5457. Fax, (202) 508-3826. Juanzena Johnson, Executive Director.*

Web, www.nbcsl.org

Membership: Black state legislators. Interests include legislation and public policies that impact the general welfare of African American consituents within respective jurisdictions.

National Black Justice Coalition, *P.O. Box 71395, 20024; (202) 319-1552. Fax, (202) 319-7365.*

Sharon J. Lettman-Hicks, Chief Executive Officer; David J. Johns, Executive Director.

General email, info@nbjc.org

Web, www.nbjc.org

Seeks equality for Black lesbian, gay, bisexual, and transgender people by fighting racism and homophobia through education initiatives.

National Council of Negro Women, *633 Pennsylvania Ave. N.W., 20004-2605; (202) 737-0120. Fax, (202) 737-0476. Ingrid Saunders Jones, Chair; Janice Mathis, Executive Director.*

General email, info@ncnw.org

Web, www.ncnw.org and Twitter, @NCNWHQ

Seeks to advance opportunities for African American women, their families, and communities through research, advocacy, and national and community-based programs in the United States and Africa.

National Urban League, *Washington Bureau, 2901 14th St. N.W., 20009; (202) 265-8200. George H. Lambert Jr., Affiliate Chief Executive Officer.*

Web, http://nul.iamempowered.com/affiliate/greater-washington-urban-league

Federal advocacy division of social service organization concerned with the social welfare of African Americans and other minorities. Seeks elimination of racial segregation and discrimination; monitors legislation, policies, and regulations to determine impact on minorities; interests include employment, health, welfare, education, housing, and community development. (Headquarters in New York.)

Hispanics

▶NONGOVERNMENTAL

League of United Latin American Citizens, *1133 19th St. N.W., #1000, 20036; (202) 833-6130. Fax, (202) 833-6135. Sidney Benavides, Chief Executive Officer, ext. 108.*
General email, info@lulac.org
Web, www.lulac.org

Seeks full social, political, economic, and educational rights for Hispanics in the United States. Programs include housing projects for the poor, employment and training for youth and women, and political advocacy on issues affecting Hispanics, including immigration. Affiliated with LULAC National Educational Service Centers (LNESCs), which award scholarships. Holds exposition open to the public.

Mexican American Legal Defense and Educational Fund, *National Public Policy, 1016 16th St. N.W., #100, 20036; (202) 293-2828. Thomas A. Saenz, President; Andrea Senteno, Legislative Staff Attorney. General information, (213) 629-2512.*
General email, info@maldef.org
Web, www.maldef.org/about/offices/washington_dc

Works with Congress and the White House to promote legislative advocacy for minority groups. Interests include equal employment, voting rights, bilingual education, immigration, and discrimination. Monitors legislation and regulations. (Headquarters in Los Angeles, Calif.)

U.S. Conference of Catholic Bishops (USCCB), *Cultural Diversity in the Church, 3211 4th St. N.E., 20017-1194; (202) 541-3150. Fax, (202) 541-5417. Mar Munoz-Visoso, Executive Director.*
General email, cdha@usccb.org
Web, www.usccb.org/issues-and-action/cultural-diversity
and Twitter, USCulturalDiver

Acts as an information clearinghouse on communications and pastoral and liturgical activities; serves as liaison for other church institutions and government and private agencies; provides information on legislation; acts as advocate for their five intercultural competencies (African-Americans, Asian/Pacific Islanders, Hispanic/Latino, Native Americans, and Pastoral Care of Migrants, Refugees and Travelers) within the National Conference of Catholic Bishops.

UnidosUS, *1126 16th St. N.W., #600, 20036-4845; (202) 785-1670. Fax, (202) 776-1792. Janet Murguía, President.*
General email, info@unidos.org
Web, www.unidosus.org, Twitter, @WeAreUnidosUS and Facebook, www.facebook.com/Weareunidosus

Seeks to reduce poverty of and discrimination against Hispanic Americans. Offers assistance to Hispanic community-based organizations. Conducts research and policy analysis. Interests include education, employment and training, asset development, immigration, language access issues, civil rights, and housing and community development. Monitors legislation and regulations. (Formerly the National Council of La Raza.)

Lesbian, Gay, Bisexual, and Transgender People

▶NONGOVERNMENTAL

Dignity USA, *Washington Office, 721 8th St. S.E., 20003 (mailing address: P.O. Box 15279, Washington, DC 20003-0279); (202) 546-2235. Fax, (202) 521-3954. Chris Pett, President.*
General email, dignity@dignitywashington.org
Web, www.dignitywashington.org

Membership: gay, lesbian, bisexual, and transgender Catholics, their families, and friends. Works to promote spiritual development, social interaction, educational outreach, and acceptance within the Catholic community. Sponsors a Spanish language affiliate group, Grupo Latino. (Headquarters in Medford, Mass.)

Gay & Lesbian Victory Fund and Leadership Institute, *1225 Eye St. N.W., #525, 20005; (202) 842-8679. Fax, (202) 289-3863. Annise Parker, President.*
Web, www.victoryfund.org, Twitter, @VictoryFund and Facebook, www.facebook.com/victoryfund

Supports the candidacy of openly LGBTQ individuals in federal, state, and local elections.

Gay and Lesbian Activists Alliance of Washington (GLAA), *P.O. Box 75265, 20013; (202) 797-4421. Bobbi Strang, President.*
General email, equal@glaa.org
Web, www.glaa.org and Twitter, @glaadc

Advances the rights of gays, lesbians, and transgender people within the Washington community.

Human Rights Campaign (HRC), *1640 Rhode Island Ave. N.W., 20036-3278; (202) 216-1500. Fax, (202) 347-5323. Chad Griffin, President. Toll-free, (800) 777-4723. TTY, (202) 216-1572.*
General email, hrc@hrc.org
Web, www.hrc.org, Twitter, @HRC and Facebook, www.facebook.com/humanrightscampaign

Provides campaign support and educates the public to ensure the rights of lesbian, gay, bisexual, and transgender people at home, work, school, and in the community. Works to prohibit workplace discrimination based on sexual orientation and gender identity, combat hate crimes, and fund AIDS research, care, and prevention.

National Black Justice Coalition, *P.O. Box 71395, 20024; (202) 319-1552. Fax, (202) 319-7365.*

Sharon J. Lettman-Hicks, *Chief Executive Officer;* David J. Johns, *Executive Director.*
General email, info@nbjc.org
Web, www.nbjc.org

Seeks equality for Black lesbian, gay, bisexual, and transgender people by fighting racism and homophobia through education initiatives.

National Center for Transgender Equality (NCTE), *1133 19th St. N.W., #302, 20036; (202) 642-4542. Mara Keisling, Executive Director.*
General email, ncte@transequality.org
Web, www.transequality.org and Twitter, @TransEquality

Works to advance the equality of transgender people through advocacy, collaboration, and empowerment, and to make them safe from discrimination and violence. Provides resources to local efforts nationwide.

National Lesbian and Gay Journalists Assn. (NLGJA), *2120 L St. N.W., #850, 20037; (202) 588-9888. Jen Christensen, President.*
General email, info@nlgja.org
Web, www.nlgja.org

Works within the journalism industry to foster fair and accurate coverage of lesbian, gay, bisexual, and transgender issues. Opposes workplace bias against all minorities and provides professional development for its members.

National LGBTQ Task Force, *1325 Massachusetts Ave. N.W., #600, 20005-4164; (202) 393-5177. Fax, (202) 393-2241. Rea Carey, Executive Director, (202) 639-6302.*
General email, thetaskforce@thetaskforce.org
Web, www.thetaskforce.org, Twitter, @TheTaskForce and Facebook, www.facebook.com/thetaskforce

Works toward equal rights for the lesbian, gay, bisexual, and transgender community. Trains activists working at the state and local levels. Conducts research and public policy analysis. Monitors legislation. (Formerly National Gay and Lesbian Task Force [NGLTF].)

National Organization for Women (NOW), *1100 H St. N.W., #300, 20005; (202) 628-8669. Toni Van Pelt, President. TTY, (202) 331-9002.*
General email, now@now.org
Web, www.now.org and Twitter, @NationalNOW

Membership: women and men interested in feminist civil rights. Promotes the development and enforcement of legislation prohibiting discrimination on the basis of sexual orientation.

Parents, Families, and Friends of Lesbians and Gays (PFLAG), *1828 L St. N.W., #660, 20036; (202) 467-8180. Fax, (202) 467-8194. Brian Bond, Executive Director.*
General email, info@pflag.org
Web, www.pflag.org and Twitter, @PFLAG

Promotes the health and well-being of gay, lesbian, transgender, and bisexual persons, their families, and their friends through support, education, and advocacy. Works to change public policies and attitudes toward gay, lesbian,

transgender, and bisexual persons. Monitors legislation and regulations.

Supporting and Mentoring Youth Advocates and Leaders (SMYAL), *410 7th St. S.E., 20003-2707; (202) 546-5940. Fax, (202) 330-5839. Sultan Shakir, Executive Director, (202) 567-3151.*
General email, supporterinfo@smyal.org
Web, https://smyal.org and Twitter, @SMYALDMV

Provides support to youth who are lesbian, gay, bisexual, transgender, intersex, or who may be questioning their sexuality. Facilitates youth center and support groups; promotes HIV/AIDS awareness; coordinates public education programs about homophobia. (Formerly Sexual Minority Youth Assistance League [SMYAL].)

Woodhull Freedom Foundation, *1601 18th St. N.W., #4, 20009; (888) 960-3332. Fax, (202) 330-5282. Ricci Joy Levy, President.*
General email, info@woodhullfoundation.org
Web, www.woodhullfoundation.org and Twitter, @woodhullsfa

Advocacy group for sexual and gender identity. Interests include reducing discrimination based on family structure. Presents awards to activists who advance sexual freedom as a human right. Holds annual summits to share experiences and solutions to current human rights issues related to sex, gender, and family. Monitors legislation and regulation on sexual freedom.

Native Americans

▶ **AGENCIES**

Administration for Children and Families (ACF) *(Health and Human Services Dept.)*, **Administration for Native Americans (ANA),** *330 C St. S.W., Room 4126, 20201; (202) 690-7776. Fax, (202) 690-8145. Jeannie Hovland, Commissioner. Toll-free, (877) 922-9262.*
General email, anacomments@acf.hhs.gov
Web, www.acf.hhs.gov/ana

Awards grants for locally determined social and economic development strategies; promotes Native American economic and social self-sufficiency; funds tribes and Native American and Native Hawaiian organizations; provides grant funding for community development projects. Commissioner chairs the Intradepartmental Council on Indian Affairs, which coordinates Native American–related programs.

Bureau of Indian Affairs (BIA) *(Interior Dept.)*, *1849 C St. N.W., MS 4606-MIB, 20240; (202) 208-5116. Fax, (202) 208-6334. Darryl Lacounte, Director (Acting). Press, (202) 208-3710.*
Web, www.bia.gov

Works with federally recognized Indian tribal governments and Alaska Native communities in a government-to-government relationship. Encourages and supports tribes' efforts to govern themselves and to provide needed programs and services on the reservations. Manages land held in trust for Indian tribes and individuals. Funds educational benefits, road construction and maintenance, social services, police protection, economic development efforts, and special assistance to develop governmental and administrative skills.

Interior Dept. (DOI), *Assistant Secretary for Indian Affairs, 1849 C St. N.W., MS-4660-MIB, 20240; (202) 208-7163. Fax, (202) 208-5320. John Tahsuda III, Principal Deputy Assistant Secretary.*
Web, www.doi.gov

Administers laws and regulations relating to Indian tribes, individual Indian tribal members, and Indian affairs. Oversees the Bureau of Indian Affairs and Bureau of Indian Education.

Justice Dept. (DOJ), *Tribal Justice (OTJ), 950 Pennsylvania Ave. N.W., 20530-0001; (202) 514-8812. Tracy Toulou, Director.*
Web, www.justice.gov/otj

Serves as the Justice Dept.'s point of contact for communication with Indian tribes and their concerns. Collaborates with federal and other government agencies to promote consistent, informed governmentwide policies, operations, and initiatives related to Indian tribes.

Tribal Justice and Safety *(Justice Dept.), 950 Pennsylvania Ave. N.W., 20530; (202) 514-8812. Tracy Toulou, Director. Grants management hotline, (888) 549-9901, option 3.*
General email, tribalgrants@usdoj.gov
Web, www.justice.gov/tribal

Represents tribal community interests, including law enforcement policy, communications, detention facilities, federal prosecution in Indian country, tribal court development, domestic violence, drug courts and substance abuse, federal litigation involving tribes, and civil rights. Coordinates assistance grant funding from across various Justice Dept. offices and agencies.

▶CONGRESS

For a listing of relevant congressional committees and sub-committees, please see pages 542–543 or the Appendix.

▶JUDICIARY

U.S. Court of Federal Claims, *717 Madison Pl. N.W., 20005; (202) 357-6400. Fax, (202) 357-6401. Margaret M. Sweeney, Chief Judge; Lisa Reyes, Clerk of the Court. Press, (202) 357-6643.*
Web, www.uscfc.uscourts.gov

Deals with Native American tribal claims against the government that are founded on the Constitution, congressional acts, government regulations, and contracts. Examples include congressional reference cases; patent cases; claims for land, water, and mineral rights; and the accounting of funds held for Native Americans under various treaties.

▶NONGOVERNMENTAL

National Congress of American Indians, *Embassy of Tribal Nations, 1516 P St. N.W., 20005; (202) 466-7767. Fax, (202) 466-7797. Jacqueline Johnson Pata, Executive Director, ext. 218.*
General email, ncai@ncai.org
Web, www.ncai.org and Twitter, @NCAI1944

Membership: American Indian and Alaska Native tribal governments and individuals. Provides information and serves as general advocate for tribes. Monitors legislative and regulatory activities affecting Native American affairs.

Native American Rights Fund, *Washington Office, 1514 P St. N.W., Suite D, Rear entrance, 20005; (202) 785-4166. Fax, (202) 822-0068. John E. Echohawk, Executive Director; Joel Williams, Managing Attorney.*
Web, www.narf.org and Facebook, www.facebook.com/NativeAmericanRightsFund

Provides Native Americans and Alaska Natives with legal assistance in land claims, water rights, hunting, and other areas. Practices federal Indian law. (Headquarters in Boulder, Colo.)

Navajo Nation, *Washington Office, 750 1st St. N.E., #1010, 20002; (202) 682-7390. Fax, (202) 682-7391. Jackson Brossy, Executive Director; Jonathon Nez, President.*
General email, info@nnwo.org
Web, www.nnwo.org, Twitter, @nnwodc and Facebook, www.facebook.com/nnwodc

Monitors legislation and regulations affecting the Navajo people; serves as an information clearinghouse on the Navajo Nation. (Headquarters in Window Rock, Ariz.)

Older Adults

▶AGENCIES

Administration for Community Living (ACL) *(Health and Human Services Dept.), Administration on Aging (AOA), Mary E. Switzer Bldg., 330 C St. S.W., 20201; (202) 619-0724. Edwin L. Walker, Deputy Assistant Secretary. Eldercare locator, (800) 677-1116. Press, (202) 357-3507. TTY, (800) 877-8339.*
Web, www.acl.gov/about-acl/administration-aging

Advocacy agency for older Americans and their concerns. Collaborates with tribal organizations, community and national organizations, and state and area agencies to implement grant programs and services designed to improve the quality of life for older Americans, such as information and referral, adult day care, elder abuse prevention, home-delivered meals, in-home care, transportation, and services for caregivers.

▶CONGRESS

For a listing of relevant congressional committees and sub-committees, please see pages 542–543 or the Appendix.

►NONGOVERNMENTAL

60 Plus, *515 King St., #315, Alexandria, VA 22314; (703) 807-2070. Fax, (703) 807-2073. James (Jim) L. Martin, Chair, (571) 216-1928.*
General email, info@60plus.org
Web, www.60plus.org, Twitter, @60plusAssoc and Facebook, www.facebook.com/60Plus.org

Acts as advocate for the rights of senior citizens. Interests include free enterprise, less government regulation, and tax reform. Works to eliminate estate taxes. Publishes rating system of members of Congress. Monitors legislation and regulations.

AARP Foundation, *Legal Advocacy, 601 E St. N.W., 20049; (202) 434-2060. William (Bill) Alvarado Rivera, Senior Vice President of Litigation.*
General email, litigation@aarp.org
Web, www.aarp.org/aarp-foundation/our-work/legal-advocacy, Twitter, @AARPFoundation and Facebook, www.facebook.com/AARPFoundation

Advocates the legal rights of citizens age fifty years and older. Addresses age discrimination in the workplace; consumer and financial fraud and utilities issues; employee benefits, including pensions; investor protection; health, including long-term services and supports, Medicaid, Medicare, and prescription drug affordability; housing, including predatory mortgage lending and livable communities; low-income benefits, including the Supplemental Nutrition Assistance Program; and voting rights.

Justice in Aging, *1444 Eye St. N.W., #1100, 20005; (202) 289-6976. Fax, (202) 289-7224. Kevin Prindiville, Executive Director.*
General email, nsclc@nsclc.org
Web, www.justiceinaging.org and Twitter, @justiceinacing

Provides training, technical assistance, and litigation for attorneys representing the elderly poor and persons with disabilities. Represents clients before Congress and federal departments and agencies. Focus includes Social Security, Medicare, Medicaid, long-term care residents' rights, home health care, pensions, and protective services. Funded by the Administration on Aging and various charitable foundations. Formerly National Senior Citizens Law Center.

National Hispanic Council on Aging, *2201 12th St. N.W., #101, 20009; (202) 347-9733. Fax, (202) 347-9735. Yanira Cruz, President.*
General email, nhcoa@nhcoa.org
Web, www.nhcoa.org and Twitter, @NHCOA

Membership: senior citizens, health care workers, professionals in the field of aging, and others in the United States and Puerto Rico who are interested in topics related to Hispanics and aging. Provides research training, policy analysis, consulting, and technical assistance; sponsors seminars, workshops, and management internships.

Seniors Coalition, *1250 Connecticut Ave. N.W., #200, 20036-2643; (202) 261-3594. Fax, (866) 728-5450. Joseph L. Bridges, Chief Executive Officer.*
General email, tsc@senior.org
Web, http://senior.org

Seeks to protect the quality of life and economic well-being of older Americans. Interests include health care, Social Security, taxes, pharmaceutical issues, and Medicare. Conducts seminars and monitors legislation and regulations.

Other Minority Groups

►AGENCIES

Education Dept., *White House Initiative on Asian Americans and Pacific Islanders, 550 12th St. S.W., 10th Floor, 20202; (202) 245-6418. Fax, (202) 245-7166. Holly Ham, Executive Director; Debra Suarez, Senior Advisor.*
General email, whitehouseaapi@ed.gov
Web, http://sites.ed.gov/aapi, Twitter, @whitehouseAAPI and Facebook, www.facebook.com/WhiteHouseAAPI

Ensures that Asian Americans and Pacific Islanders have equal access to federal programs and services. Methods include expanding language access and increasing enforcement efforts to combat discrimination.

►NONGOVERNMENTAL

American–Arab Anti-Discrimination Committee (ADC), *1705 DeSales St. N.W., #500, 20036; (202) 244-2990. Fax, (202) 333-6470. Samer E. Khalaf, President.*
General email, adc@adc.org
Web, www.adc.org and Twitter, @adctweets

Nonpartisan and nonsectarian organization that promotes and seeks to protect the human rights and cultural heritage of Americans of Arab descent. Works to combat discrimination against Arab Americans in employment, education, and political life and to prevent stereotyping of Arabs in the media. Monitors legislation and regulations.

Anti-Defamation League, *Washington Office, 1100 Connecticut Ave. N.W., #1020, 20036; (202) 452-8310. Fax, (202) 296-2371. Kenneth Jacobson, Deputy National Director.*
General email, washington-dc@adl.org
Web, www.adl.org and Twitter, @ADL_WashDC

Seeks to combat anti-Semitism and other forms of bigotry. Interests include discrimination in employment, housing, voting, and education; U.S. foreign policy in the Middle East; and the treatment of Jews worldwide. Monitors legislation and regulations affecting Jewish interests and the civil rights of all Americans. (Headquarters in New York.)

Asian Americans Advancing Justice (AAJC), *1620 L St. N.W., #1050, 20036; (202) 296-2300. Fax, (202) 296-2318. John C. Yang, President.*
General email, information@advancingequality.org
Web, www.advancingjustice_aajc.org and Twitter, @AAAJ_AAJC

Works to advance the human and civil rights of Asian Americans and other minority groups through advocacy, public policy, public education, and litigation. Promotes civic engagement at the local, regional, and national levels. Interests include affirmative action, hate crimes, media diversity, census, broadband and telecommunications, youth advocacy, immigrant rights, language access, and voting rights.

Japanese American Citizens League, *Washington Office, 1629 K St. N.W., #400, 20006; (202) 223-1240. David Inoue, Executive Director.*
General email, dc@jacl.org
Web, www.jacl.org

Monitors legislative and regulatory activities affecting the rights of Japanese Americans. Supports civil rights of all Americans, with a focus on Asian and Asian Pacific Americans. (Headquarters in San Francisco, Calif.)

Muslim Public Affairs Council, *Washington Office, 1020 16th St. N.W., 20036; (202) 547-7701. Fax, (202) 547-7704. Salam Al-Marayati, National President; Hoda Hawa, Washington Office Director.*
General email, hello@mpac.org
Web, www.mpac.org and Twitter, @mpac_national

Promotes the civil rights of American Muslims and the integration of Islam into American pluralism; assists victims of hate crimes; advises government agencies on national security and civil rights issues. (Headquarters in Los Angeles, Calif.)

OCA: Asian Pacific American Advocates, *1322 18th St. N.W., 20036-1803; (202) 223-5500. Fax, (202) 296-0540. Ken Lee, Chief Executive Officer.*
General email, oca@ocanational.org
Web, www.ocanational.org, Twitter, @OCANational and Facebook, www.facebook.com/OCAnatl

Advocacy group seeking to advance the social, political, and economic well-being of Asian Pacific Americans in the United States.

Organization of Chinese American Women, *P.O. Box 3443, Oakton, VA 22124; (301) 907-3898. Fax, (301) 907-3899. Donna Byler, Executive Director.*
General email, info@ocawwomen.org
Web, www.ocawwomen.org

Promotes equal rights and opportunities for Chinese and other Asian Pacific American women in professional and nonprofessional fields. Provides members with leadership and skills training and newly arrived immigrants with career development.

Women

▶**NONGOVERNMENTAL**

Independent Women's Forum (IWF), *119 Lake Shore Dr., Cross Junction, VA 22625; (202) 857-5201. Fax, (202) 429-9574. Carrie Lukas, President.*

General email, info@iwf.org
Web, www.iwf.org, Twitter, @IWF and Facebook, www.facebook.com/independentwomensforum

Membership: women and men interested in advancing limited government, equality under the law, property rights, free markets, strong families, and a powerful and effective national defense and foreign policy. Publishes policy papers; makes appearances on radio and television broadcasts; maintains speakers bureau. Interests include school choice, Social Security, health care reform, and democracy promotion and women's human rights in the Middle East.

Institute for Women's Policy Research (IWPR), *1200 18th St. N.W., #301, 20036; (202) 785-5100. Fax, (202) 833-4362. Heidi Hartmann, President.*
General email, iwpr@iwpr.org
Web, www.iwpr.org, Twitter, @IWPResearch and Facebook, www.facebook.com/iwpresearch

Public policy research organization that focuses on women's issues, including the status of women in the United States and discrimination based on gender, race, or ethnicity.

International Center for Research on Women, *1120 20th St. N.W., #500N, 20036; (202) 797-0007. Fax, (202) 797-0020. Sarah Degnan Kambou, President.*
General email, info@icrw.org
Web, www.icrw.org, Twitter, @ICRW and Facebook, www.facebook.com/ICRWDC

Advances gender equality and human rights, fights poverty, and promotes sustainable economic and social development through research, program implementation, information gathering, publications, and strategic media outreach. Conducts empirical research and promotes practical, evidence-based solutions that enable women to control their own lives and fully participate in their societies.

Jewish Women International, *1129 20th St. N.W., #801, 20036; (202) 857-1300. Fax, (202) 857-1380. Loribeth Weinstein, Chief Executive Officer. Toll-free, (800) 343-2823.*
General email, jwi@jwi.org
Web, www.jwi.org, Facebook, www.facebook.com/jewishwomeninternational and Twitter, @JewishWomenIntl

Membership: Jewish women, supporters, and partners in the United States and Canada. Interests include empowerment of women and girls, ending domestic and sexual violence, financial literacy and economic security, and highlighting women's leadership at multigenerational intersections.

National Organization for Women (NOW), *1100 H St. N.W., #300, 20005; (202) 628-8669. Toni Van Pelt, President. TTY, (202) 331-9002.*
General email, now@now.org
Web, www.now.org and Twitter, @NationalNOW

Membership: women and men interested in feminist civil rights. Uses traditional and nontraditional forms of political activism, including nonviolent civil disobedience, to improve the status of all women regardless of age, income, sexual orientation, or race. Maintains liaisons with counterpart organizations worldwide.

National Partnership for Women and Families, *1875 Connecticut Ave. N.W., #650, 20009-5731; (202) 986-2600. Fax, (202) 986-2539. Debra L. Ness, President; Debbie Wilkes, Chief of Staff.*
General email, info@nationalpartnership.org
Web, www.nationalpartnership.org

Advocacy organization that promotes reproductive health and rights, access to affordable health care, and policies that create equal opportunities for women and families. Publishes and disseminates information in print and on the Web to heighten awareness of work and family issues. Monitors legislative activity and pending Supreme Court cases and argues on behalf of family issues before Congress and in the courts.

National Woman's Party, *144 Constitution Ave. N.E., 20002-5608 (mailing address: P.O. Box 75478, Washington, DC 20013); (202) 546-1210. Fax, (202) 546-3997. Zakiya Thomas, Executive Director. Press, (202) 546-1210, ext. 12.*
General email, info@nationalwomansparty.org
Web, http://nationalwomansparty.org,
Twitter, @NatlWomansParty and Facebook,
www.facebook.com/NationalWomansParty
Library, library@nationalwomansparty.org

Maintains archives and artifacts documenting women's equality under the law. Interests include the suffragists, the National Women's Party, and the Equal Rights Amendment campaign.

National Women's Law Center, *11 Dupont Circle N.W., #800, 20036; (202) 588-5180. Fax, (202) 588-5185. Fatima Gross Graves, President.*
General email, info@nwlc.org
Web, www.nwlc.org, Twitter, @nwlc and Facebook, www.facebook.com/nwlc

Works to expand and protect women's legal rights through advocacy and public education. Interests include reproductive rights, health, education, employment, income security, and family support.

YWCA USA, *1020 19th St. N.W., #750, 20036; (202) 467-0801. Fax, (202) 467-0802. Alejandra Y. Castillo, Chief Executive Officer.*
General email, info@ywca.org
Web, www.ywca.org and Twitter, @ywcausa

Strives to empower women and girls and to eliminate racism. Provides services and programs concerning child care and youth development, economic empowerment, global awareness, health and fitness, housing and shelter, leadership development, racial justice and human rights, and violence prevention. (YWCA stands for Young Women's Christian Association.)

CONSTITUTIONAL LAW AND CIVIL LIBERTIES

General

▶**AGENCIES**

Justice Dept. (DOJ), *Legal Counsel (OLC), 950 Pennsylvania Ave. N.W., #5218, 20530-0001; (202) 514-2051. Fax, (202) 514-0539. Steven A. Engel, Assistant Attorney General.*
Web, www.justice.gov/olc

Advises the attorney general, the president, and executive agencies on questions regarding constitutional law.

U.S. Commission on Civil Rights, *1331 Pennsylvania Ave. N.W., #1150, 20425; (202) 376-7700. Fax, (202) 376-7672. Catherine Lhamon, Chair; Mauro Albert Morales, Staff Director. Press, (202) 376-8371. TTY, (202) 372-8116.*
General email, publicaffairs@usccr.gov
Web, www.usccr.gov, Twitter, @USCCRgov
Civil right complaints email, referrals@usccr.gov

Assesses federal laws, policies, and legal developments to determine the nature and extent of denial of equal protection under the law on the basis of race, color, religion, sex, national origin, age, or disability in employment, voting rights, education, administration of justice, and housing. Issues reports and makes recommendations to the president and Congress; serves as national clearinghouse for civil rights information; receives civil rights complaints and refers them to the appropriate federal agency for action. Library open to the public.

▶**CONGRESS**

For a listing of relevant congressional committees and sub-committees, please see pages 542–543 or the Appendix.

▶**JUDICIARY**

Supreme Court of the United States, *1 1st St. N.E., 20543; (202) 479-3000. John G. Roberts Jr., Chief Justice; Kathleen Landin Arberg, Public Information Officer, (202) 479-3211. Visitor information, (202) 479-3030. TTY, (202) 479-3472.*
Web, www.supremecourtus.gov

Highest appellate court in the federal judicial system. Interprets the U.S. Constitution, federal legislation, and treaties. Provides information on new cases filed, the status of pending cases, and admissions to the Supreme Court Bar. Library open to Supreme Court bar members only.

▶**NONGOVERNMENTAL**

American Civil Liberties Union (ACLU), *District of Columbia, 915 15th St. N.W., 2nd Floor, 20005; (202) 457-0800. Monica Hopkins, Executive Director.*

General email, info@aclu.org

Web, www.acludc.org, Twitter, @ACLU_DC and Facebook, www.facebook.com/aclu.dc

Seeks to protect the civil liberties of the citizens, including federal employees, of the District of Columbia. Interests include First Amendment rights, privacy, and due process.

American Civil Liberties Union (ACLU), *Washington Legislative Office, 915 15th St. N.W., 6th Floor, 20005; (202) 544-1681. Fax, (202) 546-0738. David Cole, Legal Director. Press, (202) 549-2666.*

General email, media@acludc.org

Web, www.aclu.org/legiupdate

Focuses on constitutional rights and civil liberties, minority and women's rights, gay and lesbian rights, and privacy; supports legalized abortion, opposes government-sponsored school prayer and legislative restrictions on television content. Washington office monitors legislative and regulatory activities and public policy. Library open to the public by appointment. (Headquarters in New York maintains docket of cases.)

American Constitution Society for Law and Policy, *1899 L St. N.W., #200, 20036; (202) 393-6181. Fax, (202) 393-6189. Caroline Fredrickson, President.*

General email, info@acslaw.org

Web, www.acslaw.org, Twitter, @acslaw and Facebook, www.facebook.com/acslaw

National association of lawyers, law students, judges, legal scholars, and policymakers that promotes a progressive vision of constitutional law and public policy. Produces issue briefs and publications. Organizes lectures, conferences, seminars, and two annual student competitions.

Center for Democracy and Technology, *1401 K St. N.W., 2nd Floor, 20005; (202) 637-9800. Fax, (202) 637-0968. Nuala O'Connor, President. Press, (202) 407-8814.*

General email, info@cdt.org

Web, https://cdt.org, Twitter, @CenDemTech

Press, press@cdt.org

Promotes civil liberties and democratic values in computer and communications media, both in the United States and abroad. Interests include free speech, privacy, and open access to the Internet. Monitors legislation and regulations.

Center for Individual Rights, *1100 Connecticut Ave. N.W., #625, 20036; (202) 833-8400. Fax, (202) 833-8410. Terence (Terry) J. Pell, President.*

General email, cir@cir-usa.org

Web, www.cir-usa.org

Public interest law firm that provides free representation to individuals who cannot afford adequate legal counsel in cases raising constitutional questions of individual rights. Interests include freedom of speech and religious expression, civil rights, and Congress's enumerated powers.

The Constitution Project (TCP), *1200 18th St. N.W., #1000, 20036; (202) 580-6920. Fax, (202) 580-6929.*

Virginia (Ginny) E. Sloan, President, (202) 580-6920, ext. 923.

General email, info@constitutionproject.org

Web, https://constitutionproject.org and Twitter, @ConPro

Think tank that brings together policy experts and legal practitioners from across the political and ideological spectrum to address current constitutional challenges. Interests include checks and balances, counterterrorism policies and practices, criminal discovery, data collection and privacy, the death penalty, DNA collection, government surveillance and searches, immigration, right to counsel, sentencing, and transparency and accountability. Hosts discussions and online forums; issues written reports and press releases. (Affiliated with the Project on Government Oversight.)

Constitutional Accountability Center, *1200 18th St. N.W., #501, 20036; (202) 296-6889. Fax, (202) 296-6895. Elizabeth B. Wydra, President.*

General email, cac@theusconstitution.org

Web, https://theusconstitution.org and Twitter, @MyConstitution

Nonprofit think tank, law firm, and advocacy group that supports Constitutional rights and freedoms by working with courts, the government, and academic professionals. Publishes books and reports on Constitutional issues. Manages cases related to Constitutional law. Interests include civil rights, citizenship, corporations, and the environment.

Electronic Privacy Information Center (EPIC), *1718 Connecticut Ave. N.W., #200, 20009; (202) 483-1140. Fax, (202) 483-1248. Marc Rotenberg, President.*

General email, info@epic.org

Web, www.epic.org and Twitter, @EPICprivacy

Public interest research center. Conducts research and conferences on domestic and international civil liberties issues, including privacy, free speech, information access, computer security, and encryption; litigates cases. Monitors legislation and regulations. Operates an online bookstore.

Ethics and Public Policy Center, *1730 M St. N.W., #910, 20036; (202) 682-1200. Fax, (202) 408-0632. M. Edward Whelan III, President.*

General email, ethics@eppc.org

Web, www.eppc.org and Twitter, @EPPCdc

Examines current issues of jurisprudence, especially those relating to constitutional interpretation.

Institute for Justice, *901 N. Glebe Rd., #900, Arlington, VA 22203; (703) 682-9320. Fax, (703) 682-9321. Scott G. Bullock, President.*

General email, general@ij.org

Web, www.ij.org, Twitter, @IJ and Facebook, www.facebook.com/instituteforjustice

Sponsors seminars to train law students, grassroots activists, and practicing lawyers in applying advocacy strategies in public-interest litigation. Seeks to protect individuals from arbitrary government interference in free speech, private property rights, parental school choice, and economic liberty. Litigates cases.

National Organization for Women (NOW), *1100 H St. N.W., #300, 20005; (202) 628-8669. Toni Van Pelt, President. TTY, (202) 331-9002.*
General email, now@now.org
Web, www.now.org and Twitter, @NationalNOW

Membership: women and men interested in civil rights for women. Works to end discrimination based on gender, to preserve abortion rights, and to pass an equal rights amendment to the Constitution.

Newseum Institute, *First Amendment Center, 555 Pennsylvania Ave. N.W., 20001; (202) 292-6290. Ken Paulson, President; Gene Policinski, Chief Operating Officer, (615) 727-1600.*
General email, ken.paulson@mtsu.edu
Web, www.newseuminstitute.org/first-amendment-center, Twitter, @1stAmendmentCtr and Facebook, www.facebook.com/firstamendmentcenter

Provides educational resources about First Amendment freedoms. Serves as a nonpartisan forum for the study and exploration of free-expression issues, including freedom of speech, the press, religion, and the rights to assemble and to petition the government. Co-sponsors, with the Newseum, the Religious Freedom Education Project. The center is an operating program of the Freedom Forum and is associated with the Diversity Institute and has offices in the John Seigenthaler Center at Vanderbilt University in Nashville, Tenn., and at the Newseum in Washington, D.C.

Open Society Foundations (OSF), *Washington Office, 1730 Pennsylvania Ave. N.W., 7th Floor, 20006; (202) 721-5600. Fax, (202) 530-0128. Lora Lumpe, Advocacy Director.*
General email, info@osi-dc.org
Web, www.soros.org/initiatives/washington

Addresses violations of civil liberties in the United States. Interests include criminal and civil justice reform, global economic policies, and women's rights. (Headquarters in New York. Affiliated with the Soros Foundation Network.)

Abortion and Reproductive Issues

▶**NONGOVERNMENTAL**

Catholics for Choice, *1436 U St. N.W., #301, 20009-3997; (202) 986-6093. Fax, (202) 332-7995. Jon O'Brien, President.*
General email, cfc@catholicsforchoice.org
Web, www.catholicsforchoice.org and Twitter, @Catholics4Choice

Works to change church positions and public policies that limit individual freedom, particularly those related to sexuality and reproduction. Provides the public, policymakers, and groups working for change with information and analysis.

Center for Law and Religious Freedom, *8001 Braddock Rd., #302, Springfield, VA 22151; (703) 642-1070. Kimberlee W. Colby, Director.*
General email, clshq@clsnet.org
Web, clsnet.org/center/about and Twitter, @CLS_HQ

Provides legal assistance and advocacy on anti-abortion and religious-freedom issues. Monitors legislation and regulations. (Affiliated with the Christian Legal Society.)

Feminists for Life of America, *P.O. Box 151567, Alexandria, VA 22315; Serrin M. Foster, President.*
General email, info@feministsforlife.org
Web, www.feministsforlife.org, Twitter, @feminists4life! and Facebook, www.facebook.com/FeministsForLife

Membership: women and men who are against abortion and in favor of feminism. Opposes abortion, euthanasia, and capital punishment; seeks to redress economic and social conditions that cause women to choose abortion.

March for Life Education and Defense Fund, *1012 14th St. N.W., #300, 20005; (202) 234-3300. Fax, (202) 234-3350. Jeanne F. Mancini, President.*
General email, info@marchforlife.org
Web, www.marchforlife.org and Twitter, @March_for_Life

Membership: individuals and organizations that support government action prohibiting abortion. Sponsors annual march in Washington each January 22. Monitors legislation and regulations.

NARAL Pro-Choice America, *1725 Eye St. N.W., #900, 20006; (202) 973-3000. Fax, (202) 973-3096. Ilyse Hogue, President. Press, (202) 973-3000 ext. 2.*
Web, www.prochoiceamerica.org and Twitter, @NARAL

Membership: persons who support using the political process to guarantee women a range of reproductive choices, including preventing unintended pregnancy, bearing healthy children, and choosing legal abortion. (Formerly National Abortion and Reproductive Rights Action League.)

National Abortion Federation (NAF), *1090 Vermont Ave. N.W., #1000, 20005; (202) 667-5881. Fax, (202) 667-5890. Vicki Saporta, President. NAF Hotline, (800) 772-9100.*
General email, naf@prochoice.org
Web, www.prochoice.org and Twitter, @NatAbortionFed

Membership: abortion providers. Seeks to ensure that abortion is safe, legal, and accessible.

National Committee for a Human Life Amendment, *P.O. Box 34116, 20043; (202) 393-0703. Brian Duggan, Executive Director.*
General email, info@nchla.org
Web, www.humanlifeaction.org and Twitter, @HumanLifeAction

Supports legislation and a constitutional amendment prohibiting abortion.

National Organization for Women (NOW), *1100 H St. N.W., #300, 20005; (202) 628-8669. Toni Van Pelt, President. TTY, (202) 331-9002.*

U.S. Courts

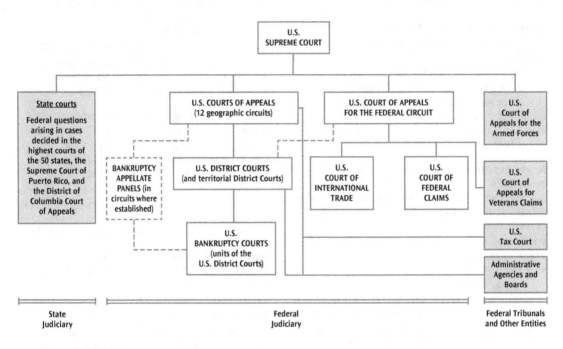

```
                                    ┌─────────────────┐
                                    │      U.S.        │
                                    │  SUPREME COURT   │
                                    └─────────────────┘
```

State courts	U.S. COURTS OF APPEALS (12 geographic circuits)	U.S. COURT OF APPEALS FOR THE FEDERAL CIRCUIT	U.S. Court of Appeals for the Armed Forces
Federal questions arising in cases decided in the highest courts of the 50 states, the Supreme Court of Puerto Rico, and the District of Columbia Court of Appeals	BANKRUPTCY APPELLATE PANELS (in circuits where established) · U.S. DISTRICT COURTS (and territorial District Courts)	U.S. COURT OF INTERNATIONAL TRADE · U.S. COURT OF FEDERAL CLAIMS	U.S. Court of Appeals for Veterans Claims
	U.S. BANKRUPTCY COURTS (units of the U.S. District Courts)		U.S. Tax Court · Administrative Agencies and Boards

State Judiciary   **Federal Judiciary**   **Federal Tribunals and Other Entities**

General email, now@now.org

Web, www.now.org and Twitter, @NationalNOW

Membership: women and men interested in civil rights for women. Works to preserve abortion rights.

National Right to Life Committee, *512 10th St. N.W., 20004-1401; (202) 626-8800. Fax, (202) 737-9189. Carol Tobias, President. Press, (202) 626-8825.*

General email, nrlc@nrlc.org

Web, www.nrlc.org

Press, mediarelations@nrlc.org

Association of fifty state right-to-life organizations. Opposes abortion, infanticide, and euthanasia; supports legislation prohibiting abortion except when the life of the mother is endangered. Operates an information clearinghouse and speakers bureau. Monitors legislation and regulations.

National Women's Health Network, *1413 K St. N.W., 4th Floor, 20005; (202) 682-2640. Fax, (202) 682-2648. Cynthia Pearson, Executive Director.*

General email, nwhn@nwhn.org

Web, www.nwhn.org, Twitter, @TheNWHN and Facebook, www.facebook.com/TheNWHN

Health questions, healthquestions@nwhn.org

Advocacy organization interested in women's health. Seeks to preserve legalized abortion; monitors legislation and regulations; testifies before Congress.

Religious Coalition for Reproductive Choice, *1413 K St. N.W., 14th Floor, 20005; (202) 628-7700. Fax, (202) 628-7716. Delia Allen-O'Brien, Executive of Operations and Finance.*

General email, operations@rcrc.org

Web, www.rcrc.org and Twitter, @RCRChoice

Coalition of religious groups favoring birth control, sexuality education, and access to legal abortion. Opposes constitutional amendments and federal and state legislation restricting access to abortion services in most cases. Monitors legislation and regulations.

U.S. Conference of Catholic Bishops (USCCB), *Secretariat of Pro-Life Activities, 3211 4th St. N.E., 20017-1194; (202) 541-3070. Fax, (202) 541-3054. Tom Grenchik, Executive Director. Publications, (800) 235-8722.*

General email, prolife@usccb.org

Web, www.usccb.org/prolife

Provides information on the position of the Roman Catholic Church on abortion. Monitors legislation on abortion, embryonic stem-cell research, human cloning, and related issues. Promotes alternatives to abortion.

Claims Against the Government

▶ **AGENCIES**

Civil Division *(Justice Dept.), Commercial Litigation (OCL), National Courts, 1100 L St. N.W., #12124, 20530; (202) 514-7300. Fax, (202) 307-0972. Robert E. Kirschman Jr., Director.*

Web, www.justice.gov/civil/national-courts-section-0

Represents the United States in the U.S. Court of Federal Claims. Practice areas include government contracts, constitutional claims, government pay and personnel suits, veterans and other benefits appeals, and international trade and tariff matters.

Civil Division *(Justice Dept.), Torts Branch, Aviation and Admiralty Litigation,* 1425 New York Ave. N.W., #10100, 20005 (mailing address: P.O. Box 14271, Washington, DC 20044-4271); (202) 616-4100. Fax, (202) 616-4002. Barry Benson, Director.
Web, www.justice.gov/civil/torts/aa/t-aa.html

Represents the federal government in civil suits concerning the maritime industry and aviation and admiralty incidents and accidents.

Environment and Natural Resources Division *(Justice Dept.),* 950 Pennsylvania Ave. N.W., #2143, 20530-0001; (202) 514-2701. Fax, (202) 514-5331. Jeffrey Bossert Clark, Assistant Attorney General. Press, (202) 514-2007.
General email, press@usdoj.gov
Web, www.justice.gov/enrd

Represents the United States in the U.S. Court of Federal Claims in cases arising from acquisition of property, Indian rights and claims, and environmental challenges to federal programs and activities.

Environment and Natural Resources Division, *Justice Dept. (DOJ), Indian Resources (IRS),* 601 D St. N.W., #3507, 20004 (mailing address: P.O. Box 7611, L'Enfant Plaza, Washington, DC 20044); (202) 305-0269. Fax, (202) 305-0275. S. Craig Alexander, Chief.
Web, www.justice.gov/enrd/Indian-resources-section

Represents the United States in suits, including trust violations, brought on behalf of individual Native Americans and Native American tribes against the government.

State Dept., *Office of the Legal Adviser, International Claims and Investment Disputes,* 2430 E St. N.W., #203, 20520; (202) 776-8360. Fax, (202) 776-8389. Lisa J. Grosh, Assistant Legal Adviser, (202) 776-8325.
Web, www.state.gov/s/l/c3433.htm

Handles claims by U.S. government and citizens against foreign governments, as well as claims by foreign governments and their nationals against the U.S. government; negotiates international claims agreements. Handles claims against the State Dept. for negligence (under the Federal Tort Claims Act) and claims by owners of U.S. flag vessels due to illegal seizures by foreign governments in international waters (under the Fishermen's Protective Act).

Tax Division *(Justice Dept.),* 950 Pennsylvania Ave. N.W., #4141, 20530-0001; (202) 514-2901. Fax, (202) 514-5479. Richard E. Zuckerman, Assistant Attorney General, (202) 514-2901.
Web, www.justice.gov/tax

Represents the United States and its officers in all civil and criminal litigation arising under the internal revenue laws, other than proceedings in the U.S. Tax Court.

Supreme Court Justices

CHIEF JUSTICE
John G. Roberts Jr.
Appointed chief justice by President George W. Bush, sworn in Sept. 29, 2005.

ASSOCIATE JUSTICES
in order of appointment

Anthony M. Kennedy
Appointed by President Ronald Reagan, sworn in Feb. 18, 1988.

Clarence Thomas
Appointed by President George H.W. Bush, sworn in Oct. 23, 1991.

Ruth Bader Ginsburg
Appointed by President Bill Clinton, sworn in Aug. 10, 1993.

Stephen G. Breyer
Appointed by President Bill Clinton, sworn in Aug. 3, 1994.

Samuel A. Alito Jr.
Appointed by President George W. Bush, sworn in Jan. 31, 2006.

Sonia Sotomayor
Appointed by President Barack Obama, sworn in Aug. 8, 2009.

Elena Kagan
Appointed by President Barack Obama, sworn in Aug. 7, 2010.

Neil Gorsuch
Appointed by President Donald J. Trump, sworn in Apr. 10, 2017.

Brett Kavanaugh
Appointed by President Donald J. Trump, sworn in Oct. 6, 2018.

►CONGRESS

For a listing of relevant congressional committees and subcommittees, please see pages 542–543 or the Appendix.

►JUDICIARY

U.S. Court of Federal Claims, 717 Madison Pl. N.W., 20005; (202) 357-6400. Fax, (202) 357-6401. Margaret M. Sweeney, Chief Judge; Lisa Reyes, Clerk of the Court. Press, (202) 357-6643.
Web, www.uscfc.uscourts.gov

Renders judgment on any nontort claims for monetary damages against the United States founded upon the Constitution, statutes, government regulations, and government contracts. Examples include compensation for taking of property, claims arising under construction and supply contracts, certain patent cases, cases involving the refund of federal taxes, and statutory claims made by foreign governments against the United States. Hears cases involving Native American claims.

Privacy

▶ AGENCIES

Office of Management and Budget (OMB) *(Executive Office of the President), Information and Regulatory Affairs, 725 17th St. N.W., #10236, 20503; (202) 395-5897. Fax, (202) 395-6102. Neomi Reo, Administrator. Press, (202) 395-7254.*
Web, www.whitehouse.gov/omb/information-regulatory-affairs

Oversees implementation of the Privacy Act of 1974 and other privacy-related and security-related statutes. Issues guidelines and regulations.

▶ CONGRESS

For a listing of relevant congressional committees and sub-committees, please see pages 542–543 or the Appendix.

▶ NONGOVERNMENTAL

American Library Assn., Washington Office, *1615 New Hampshire Ave. N.W., 1st Floor, 20009-2520; (202) 628-8410. Fax, (202) 628-8419. Kathi Kromer, Associate Executive Director; Kevin Maher, Deputy Director Government Relations. Information, (800) 941-8478. General email, alawash@alawash.org*
Web, www.ala.org/offices/wo

Works with public interest groups, think tanks, and the private sector to promote privacy rights; opposes government warrantless searches of browser histories. (Headquarters in Chicago, Ill.)

Center for Democracy and Technology, *1401 K St. N.W., 2nd Floor, 20005; (202) 637-9800. Fax, (202) 637-0968. Nuala O'Connor, President. Press, (202) 407-8814. General email, info@cdt.org*
Web, https://cdt.org, Twitter, @CenDemTech
Press, press@cdt.org

Promotes and defends privacy and civil liberties on the Internet. Interests include free expression, social networking and access to the Internet, consumer protection, health information privacy and technology, and government surveillance. Monitors legislation and regulations.

Communications Workers of America (CWA), *501 3rd St. N.W., 20001; (202) 434-1100. Fax, (202) 434-1279. Christopher M. Shelton, President.*
Web, https://cwa-union.org and Twitter, @CWAUnion

Membership: telecommunications, broadcast, and printing and publishing workers. Opposes electronic monitoring of productivity, eavesdropping by employers, and misuse of drug and polygraph tests.

Future of Privacy Forum, *1400 Eye St. N.W., #450, 20005; (202) 768-8950. John Verdi, Vice President of Policy.*

General email, info@fpf.org
Web, www.fpf.org, Twitter, @futureofprivacy and Facebook, www.facebook.com/FutureofPrivacy

Think tank focusing on privacy; encourages consensus on ethical norms, policies, and practices regarding information and technology privacy.

National Consumers League, *1701 K St. N.W., #1200, 20006; (202) 835-3323. Fax, (202) 835-0747. Sally Greenberg, Executive Director. General email, info@nclnet.org*
Web, www.nclnet.org, Twitter, @ncl_tweets and Facebook, www.facebook.com/nationalconsumersleague

Advocacy group concerned with privacy rights of consumers. Interests include credit and financial records, medical records, direct marketing, telecommunications, and workplace privacy.

Religious Freedom

▶ AGENCIES

Health and Human Services Dept. (HHS), *Civil Rights (OCR), Conscience and Religious Freedom Division, 200 Independence Ave. S.W., 20201; Roger Severino, Civil Rights Director. Toll-free, (800) 368-1019. TTY, (800) 537-7697. General email, OCRMail@hhs.gov*
Web, www.hhs.gov/conscience/index.html

Works to protect and enforce laws and regulations that protect the conscience and the free exercise of religion and prohibit coercion and religious discrimination in HHS-funded or -conducted programs and activities.

▶ NONGOVERNMENTAL

Americans for Religious Liberty, *P.O. Box 6656, Silver Spring, MD 20916; (301) 460-1111. Edd Doerr, President. General email, arlinc@verizon.net*
Web, www.arlinc.org

Educational organization concerned with issues involving the separation of church and state. Opposes government-sponsored school prayer and tax support for religious institutions; supports religious neutrality in public education; defends abortion rights. Provides legal services in litigation cases. Maintains speakers bureau.

Americans United for Separation of Church and State, *1310 L St. N.W., #200, 20005; (202) 466-3234. Fax, (202) 466-2587. Gary Carleton, Managing Director. General email, americansunited@au.org*
Web, www.au.org and Twitter, @americansunited

Citizens' interest group that opposes government-sponsored prayer in public schools and tax aid for parochial schools.

Becket Fund for Religious Liberty, *1200 New Hampshire Ave. N.W., #700, 20036; (202) 955-0095. Fax, (202)*

Privacy Resources

For general information and additional privacy contacts visit www.identitytheft.gov. See government agencies' individual websites for their privacy policies and freedom of information procedures.

AGENCIES AND CONGRESS

Federal Trade Commission, Identity Theft, www.ftc.gov/idtheft; Privacy Initiatives, www.ftc.gov/privacy-policy; hotline, (877) 438-4338

House Judiciary Committee, Subcommittee on the Constitution and Civil Justice, (202) 225-3951; www.judiciary.house.gov

National Do-Not-Call Registry, toll-free, (888) 382-1222 www.fcc.gov/encyclopedia/do-not-call-list

Office of Management and Budget (concerning the Privacy Act), (202) 395-3647; www.fpc.gov/resources/office-of-management-and-budget

Senate Judiciary Committee, (202) 224-5225 (Majority), (202) 224-7703 (Minority); www.judiciary.senate.gov

U.S. Postal Service, (800) 275-8777; http://about.usps.com/who-we-are/privacy-policy/privacy-policy-highlights.htm

NONGOVERNMENTAL

American Bar Association, Lawyer Referral Service, (202) 662-1000 or (800) 285-2221; www.americanbar.org/groups/legal_services/flh-home.html

American Civil Liberties Union, (202) 546-0738; www.aclu.org/technology-and-liberty

Call for Action, (240) 747-0229; www.callforaction.org

Center for Democracy and Technology, (202) 637-9800; www.cdt.org

Center for National Security Studies, (202) 721-5650; www.cnss.org

Center for Study of Responsive Law, (202) 387-8030; www.csrl.org

Consumer Data Industry Association, (202) 371-0910; www.cdiaonline.org

Consumers Union of the United States, (202) 462-6262; www.consumersunion.org

Direct Marketing Assn., Do-Not-Call Registry, (202) 955-5030; www.thedma.org

Electronic Privacy Information Center (EPIC), (202) 483-1140; www.epic.org

Health Privacy Project, (202) 637-9800; www.cdt.org/health-privacy

National Consumers League, (202) 835-3323; www.nclnet.org

U.S. Postal Inspection Service, (877) 876-2455; https://postalinspectors.uspis.gov

U.S. Public Interest Research Group (USPIRG), (202) 546-9707; www.uspirg.org

---

955-0090. *William Mumma, President; Montse Alvarado, Executive Director. Press, (202) 349-7226.*

Web, www.becketlaw.org and Twitter, @TheBecketFund

Public interest law firm that promotes freedom of expression for people of all faiths. Works to ensure that people and institutions of all faiths, domestically and abroad, are entitled to a voice in public affairs.

Center for Law and Religious Freedom, *8001 Braddock Rd., #302, Springfield, VA 22151; (703) 642-1070. Kimberlee W. Colby, Director.*

General email, clshq@clsnet.org

Web, clsnet.org/center/about and Twitter, @CLS_HQ

Provides legal assistance and advocacy on anti-abortion and religious-freedom issues. Monitors legislation and regulations. (Affiliated with the Christian Legal Society.)

Christian Legal Society, *8001 Braddock Rd., #302, Springfield, VA 22151; (703) 642-1070. David Nammo, Chief Executive Officer, ext. 501.*

General email, clshq@clsnet.org

Web, www.christianlegalsociety.org and Twitter, @CLS_HQ

Membership: Christian lawyers, judges, paralegals, law professors, law students, and others. Interests include the

defense of religious freedom and the provision of legal aid to the poor.

International Religious Liberty Assn., *12501 Old Columbia Pike, Silver Spring, MD 20904-6600; (301) 680-6686. Fax, (301) 680-6695. John R. Nay, President; Ganoune Diop, Secretary General.*

General email, info@irla.org

Web, www.irla.org, Twitter, @irla-usa and Facebook, www.facebook.com/irla.hq

Seeks to preserve and expand religious liberty and freedom of conscience; advocates separation of church and state; sponsors international and domestic meetings and congresses.

National Assn. of Evangelicals, *P.O. Box 23269, 20026; (202) 479-0815. Leith Anderson, President.*

General email, info@nae.net

Web, www.nae.net and Twitter, @NAEvangelicals

Membership: evangelical churches, organizations (including schools), and individuals. Supports religious freedom. Monitors legislation and regulations.

Newseum Institute, *Religious Freedom Center, 555 Pennsylvania Ave. N.W., 20001; (202) 292-6447. Charles C. Haynes, Director, (202) 292-6293; Kristin Farrington, Executive Director, (202) 292-6473.*

General email, religion@newseum.org

Web, www.religiousfreedomcenter.org and

Twitter, @RelFreedomCenter

Nonpartisan national initiative focused on educating the public about the religious liberty principles of the First Amendment.

Separation of Powers

▶**NONGOVERNMENTAL**

Public Citizen, *Litigation Group,* *1600 20th St. N.W., 20009-1001; (202) 588-1000. Allison Zieve, Director of Litigation. Press, (202) 588-7741.*

General email, litigation@citizen.org

Web, www.citizen.org/litigation

Conducts litigation for Public Citizen, a citizens' interest group, in cases involving separation of powers; represents individuals and groups with similar interests.

CRIMINAL LAW

General

▶**AGENCIES**

Bureau of International Narcotics and Law Enforcement Affairs (INL) *(State Dept.), Anticrime Programs,* *2401 E St. N.W., #L600, 20037; (202) 663-1860. Susan Snyder, Director.*

Web, www.state.gov/j/inl/offices/index.htm

Works with international governments to combat international organized crime, high-level corruption, money laundering, terrorist financing, cyber and intellectual property crimes, threats to border security, narcotics trafficking, and other smuggling and trafficking crimes.

Bureau of International Narcotics and Law Enforcement Affairs (INL) *(State Dept.), Criminal Justice and Assistance Partnerships (CAP),* *2401 E St. N.W., #L505, 20037; (202) 634-1415. Vacant, Director.*

Web, www.state.gov/j/inl/offices/index.htm

Develops partnerships with U.S. state and local law enforcement, departments of corrections, and justice organizations to provide technical expertise to support criminal justice development and reform.

Criminal Division *(Justice Dept.),* *950 Pennsylvania Ave. N.W., 20530-0001; (202) 514-1152. Fax, (202) 616-0762. Brian Benczkowski, Assistant Attorney General. Department comment line, (202) 353-1555. Public Affairs, (202) 514-2007. TTY, (800) 877-8339.*

General email, Criminal.Division@usdoj.gov

Web, www.justice.gov/criminal

Enforces all federal criminal laws except those specifically assigned to the antitrust, civil rights, environment and natural resources, and tax divisions of the Justice

Dept. Supervises and directs U.S. attorneys in the field on criminal matters and litigation; supervises international extradition proceedings. Coordinates federal enforcement efforts against white-collar crime, fraud, and child pornography; handles civil actions under customs, liquor, narcotics, gambling, and firearms laws; coordinates enforcement activities against organized crime. Directs the National Asset Forfeiture Program for seizing the proceeds of criminal activity. Investigates and prosecutes criminal offenses involving public integrity and subversive activities, including treason, espionage, and sedition; Nazi war crimes; and related criminal offenses. Handles all civil cases relating to internal security and counsels federal departments and agencies regarding internal security matters. Drafts responses on proposed and pending criminal law legislation.

Criminal Division *(Justice Dept.), Capital Case Section (CCS),* *950 Pennsylvania Ave. N.W., 20530; (202) 514-2000. Rich Burns, Chief (Acting).*

Web, www.justice.gov/criminal/capital-case-section

Promotes consistency and fairness in the application of the death penalty throughout the United States; provides expertise and resources for federal prosecutors involved with capital cases.

Federal Bureau of Investigation (FBI) *(Justice Dept.),* *935 Pennsylvania Ave. N.W., #7176, 20535-0001; (202) 324-3000. Christopher Wray, Director. Information, (202) 324-3000. Press, (202) 324-3691.*

Web, www.fbi.gov, Twitter, @FBI and *Facebook, www.facebook.com/FBI*

Investigates all violations of federal criminal laws except those assigned specifically to other federal agencies. Exceptions include alcohol, counterfeiting, and tobacco violations (Justice Dept. and Commerce Dept.); customs violations and illegal entry of aliens (Homeland Security Dept.); and postal violations (U.S. Postal Service). Priorities include protecting the United States against terror attacks; protecting civil rights; combating public corruption at all levels, transnational/national criminal organizations and enterprises, white-collar crime, and significant violent crime; and supporting federal, state, local, and international partners. Services to other law enforcement agencies include fingerprint identifications, laboratory services, police training, and access to the National Crime Information Center (a communications network among federal, state, and local police agencies).

Federal Bureau of Investigation (FBI) *(Justice Dept.), Criminal Investigative Division (CID),* *935 Pennsylvania Ave. N.W., #3012, 20535; (202) 324-4260. Fax, (202) 324-0027. Robert Johnson, Assistant Director.*

Web, www.fbi.gov/investigate/violent-crime

Investigates mass killings, sniper murders, serial killings, criminal street gangs, crimes against children, child prostitution, bank robberies and other violent robberies, carjackings, kidnappings, fugitives and missing persons, crimes on Indian reservations, and assaults and threats of assault on the president and other federal officials.

Federal Bureau of Investigation (FBI) *(Justice Dept.)*, *Critical Incident Response Group (CIRG), Strategic Information and Operations Center (SIOC)*, *935 Pennsylvania Ave. N.W., #5712, 20535; (202) 323-3300. Fax, (202) 323-2212. John Barrios, Chief, (202) 323-2015. Press, (202) 324-3691. Secure line, (202) 323-2214. Toll-free, (877) 324-6324.*
General email, sioc@ic.fbi.gov

Web, www.fbi.gov/about-us/cirg/sioc

Serves as a twenty-four-hour crisis management and information processing center. Coordinates initial and crisis response investigations of violations of federal law relating to terrorism, sabotage, espionage, treason, sedition, and other matters affecting national security.

Office of Justice Programs (OJP) *(Justice Dept.)*, *National Institute of Justice (NIJ), 810 7th St. N.W., 7th Floor, 20531; (202) 307-0765. Fax, (202) 307-6394. David B. Muhlhausen, Director. Press, (202) 307-0703. General email, ojp.ocom.@usdoj.gov*

Web, www.nij.gov and Facebook, www.facebook.com/ OJPNIJ

Conducts research on all aspects of criminal justice, including crime prevention, enforcement, adjudication, and corrections; evaluates programs; develops model programs using new techniques. Serves as an affiliated institute of the United Nations Crime Prevention and Criminal Justice Program (UNCPCJ); studies transnational issues, especially within the Western Hemisphere. Maintains the National Criminal Justice Reference Service, which provides information on criminal justice research topics, including community policing, faith-based initiatives, self-protection, gang crime, hate crime, property crime, terrorism, human trafficking, and violent crime: (800) 851-3420; in Maryland, (301) 519-5500; Web, www.ncjrs.gov. Sponsors the National Missing and Unidentified Persons System, a clearinghouse for missing persons and unidentified decedent records: http://NamUs.gov.

▶CONGRESS

For a listing of relevant congressional committees and subcommittees, please see pages 542–543 or the Appendix.

▶INTERNATIONAL ORGANIZATIONS

INTERPOL Washington *(Justice Dept.)*, *950 Pennsylvania Ave., 20530-0001; (202) 616-9000. Fax, (202) 616-8400. Wayne Salzgaber, Director.*
Web, www.justice.gov/interpol-washington, Twitter, @TheJusticeDept and Facebook, www.facebook.com/DOJ

U.S. representative to INTERPOL; participates in international investigations on behalf of U.S. police; coordinates the exchange of investigative information on crimes, including drug trafficking, counterfeiting, missing persons, and terrorism. Coordinates law enforcement requests for investigative assistance in the United States and abroad. Assists with extradition processes. Serves as

liaison between foreign and U.S. law enforcement agencies at federal, state, and local levels. (Headquarters in Lyons, France.)

▶NONGOVERNMENTAL

American Bar Assn. (ABA), *Criminal Justice, 1050 Connecticut Ave. N.W., #400, 20036; (202) 662-1500. Fax, (202) 662-1501. Kevin Scruggs, Director, (202) 662-1503.*
General email, crimjustice@americanbar.org

Web, www.americanbar.org/groups/criminal_justice.html and Twitter, @ABAJS

Responsible for all matters pertaining to criminal law and procedure for the association. Studies and makes recommendations on all facets of the criminal and juvenile justice systems, including sentencing, juries, pretrial procedures, grand juries, and white-collar crime. (Headquarters in Chicago, Ill.)

Justice Research and Statistics Assn., *1000 Vermont Ave. N.W., #450, 20005; (202) 842-9330. Fax, (202) 448-1723. Jeffrey Sedgewick, Executive Director.*
General email, cjinfo@jrsa.org

Web, www.jrsa.org, Twitter, @JRSAinfo and Facebook, www.facebook.com/Justice-Research-and-Statistics-Association-139560619431173

Promotes nonpartisan research and analysis to inform criminal and juvenile justice policy and decision making. Disseminates policy- and justice-related research and information to the justice community, and convenes informational seminars on new research, programs, and technologies.

National Crime Prevention Council, *2614 Chapel Lake Dr., Suite B, Gambrills, MD 21054; (443) 292-4565. Ordway P. Burden, President.*
Web, www.ncpc.org, Twitter, @McGruffatNCPC and Facebook, www.facebook.com/McGruff

Educates public on crime prevention through media campaigns, supporting materials, and training workshops; sponsors McGruff public service campaign; runs demonstration programs in schools.

National Criminal Justice Assn., *720 7th St. N.W., 3rd Floor, 20001; (202) 628-8550. Fax, (202) 448-1723. Chris Asplen, Executive Director, (202) 448-1712; Bethany Broida, Communications, (202) 448-1713. Press, (202) 448-1713.*
General email, info@ncja.org

Web, www.ncja.org and Twitter, @thencja

Membership: criminal and juvenile justice organizations and professionals. Represents state, tribal, and local governments. Provides members and interested individuals with technical assistance and information, including crime prevention and crime control issues.

Child Abuse, Domestic Violence, and Sexual Assault

►AGENCIES

Air Force Dept. *(Defense Dept.), Sexual Assault Prevention and Response (SAPR) (AF/CVS), 1690 Air Force Pentagon, 20330-1670; (202) 767-7272. Maj. Gen. James C. Johnson, Director of the Integrated Resilience Office. Helpline, (877) 995-5247. Public Affairs, (703) 697-3039.*
General Email, whs.mc-alex.wso.mbx.SAPRO@mail.mil and Web, www.af.mil/SAPR.aspx

Works to eliminate the occurance of sexual assault in the Air Force, and acts as advocate for recovery and prevention.

Criminal Division *(Justice Dept.), Child Exploitation and Obscenity Section (CEOS), 1400 New York Ave. N.W., 6th Floor, 20005; (202) 514-5780. Fax, (202) 514-1793. Steven J. Grocki, Chief.*
Web, www.justice.gov/criminal-ceos

Enforces federal child exploitation, obscenity, and pornography laws; prosecutes cases involving violations of these laws, including international trafficking and kidnapping. Maintains collection of briefs, pleadings, and other material for use by federal, state, and local prosecutors. Assists the U.S. Attorney's Office with investigations, trials, and appeals pertaining to these offenses. Advises and trains law enforcement personnel, federal prosecutors, and Justice Dept. officials.

Criminal Division *(Justice Dept.), Child Exploitation and Obscenity Section (CEOS), Project Safe Childhood, 810 7th St. N.W., 20531; General email, AskDOJ@usdoj.gov*
Web, www.justice.gov/psc

Combines law enforcement efforts, community action, and public awareness to combat child exploitation, particularly in regard to child pornography, online enticement, child sex tourism, commercial sexual exploitation, and sexual exploitation in Indian Country. Offers resources and publications.

Criminal Division *(Justice Dept.), Organized Crime and Gang Section (OCGS), 1301 New York Ave. N.W., #700, 20005; (202) 514-3594. Fax, (202) 514-3601. David L. Jaffe, Chief (Acting).*
General email, criminaldivision@usdoj.gov
Web, www.justice.gov/criminal-ocgs

Maintains responsibility over all domestic violent crime–related statutes within the U.S. code.

Defense Dept. (DoD), *Sexual Assault Prevention and Response, 4800 Mark Center Dr., #07G21, Alexandria, VA 22350; (571) 372-2657. Rear Adm. Ann M. Burkhardt, Director. Hotline, (877) 995-5247.*
General email, whc.mc-alex.wso.mbx.SAPRO@mail.mil
Web, www.sapr.mil and www.myduty.mil

Serves as the single point of accountability for the Defense Dept.'s sexual assault policy. Responsible for improving prevention, enhancing reporting and response, and holding perpetrators appropriately accountable.

Justice Dept. (DOJ), *Elder Justice Initiative (EJI), 950 Pennsylvania Ave. N.W., 20530; Andy Mao, Coordinator. Eldercare locator helpline, (800) 677-1116.*
General email, elder.justice@usdoj.gov
Web, www.justice.gov/elderjustice and Rural and tribal resources, www.justice.gov/elderjustice/rural-and-tribal-resources

Coordinates the Dept.'s elder justice efforts, including law enforcement actions against nursing homes that provide substandard services to Medicare and Medicaid beneficiaries; develops resources and information to enhance federal, state, and local efforts to prevent and combat elder abuse, neglect, and financial exploitation.

Justice Dept. (DOJ), *Violence Against Women (OVW), 145 N St. N.E., #10W.121, 20530; (202) 307-6026. Fax, (202) 305-2589. Katie Sullivan, Deputy Director (Acting); Mary Frances Bowley, Executive Director. National Domestic Violence Hotline, 800-799-SAFE. TTY, (202) 307-2277.*
General email, ovw.info@usdoj.gov
Web, www.justice.gov/ovw and Twitter, @OVWJustice

Seeks more effective policies and services to combat domestic violence, sexual assault, stalking, and other crimes against women. Helps administer grants to states to fund shelters, crisis centers, and hotlines, and to hire law enforcement officers, prosecutors, and counselors specializing in cases of sexual violence and other violent crimes against women.

Office of Justice Programs (OJP) *(Justice Dept.), National Institute of Justice (NIJ), 810 7th St. N.W., 7th Floor, 20531; (202) 307-0765. Fax, (202) 307-6394. David B. Muhlhausen, Director. Press, (202) 307-0703.*
General email, ojp.ocom.@usdoj.gov
Web, www.nij.gov and Facebook, www.facebook.com/OJPNIJ

Conducts research on all aspects of criminal justice, including AIDS issues for law enforcement officials. Studies on rape and domestic violence available from the National Criminal Justice Reference Service: (800) 851-3420; in Maryland, (301) 519-5500; Web, www.ncjrs.gov.

Office of Justice Programs (OJP) *(Justice Dept.), Sex Offender Sentencing, Monitoring, Apprehending, Registering, and Tracking (SMART), 810 7th St. N.W., 20531; (202) 514-4689. Fax, (202) 616-2906. Laura L. Rogers, Director.*
General email, AskSMART@usdoj.gov
Web, www.smart.gov

Administers the standards for the Sex Offender Registration and Notification Program. Administers grant programs, including those relating to sex offender registration and notification. Works with and provides technical assistance to states, principal U.S. territories, local governments, tribal governments, and other public and private entities involved in activities related to sex offender registration or notification or to other measures for the protection of children or other members of the public from sexual abuse or exploitation.

▶ NONGOVERNMENTAL

American Bar Assn. (ABA), *Center on Children and the Law,* *1050 Connecticut Ave. N.W., #400, 20036; (202) 662-1720. Vacant, Director; Kathleen McNaught, Assistant Director.*
General email, ctrchildlaw@americanbar.org
Web, www.americanbar.org/groups/child_law.html, Twitter, @ABACCL and Facebook, www.facebook.com/abaCCL

Provides state and private child welfare organizations with training and technical assistance. Interests include child abuse and neglect, adoption, foster care, and medical neglect.

National Center for Missing and Exploited Children, *333 John Carlyle St., #125, Alexandria, VA 22314-5767; (703) 224-2150. Fax, (703) 224-2122. John F. Clark, Chief Executive Officer. Toll-free hotline, (800) 843-5678.*
Web, www.missingkids.com and Twitter, @MissingKids

Private organization that assists parents and citizens' groups in locating and safely returning missing children; offers technical assistance to law enforcement agencies; coordinates public and private missing children programs; maintains database that coordinates information on missing children.

National Coalition Against Domestic Violence, *Public Policy, 2000 M St. N.W., #480, 20036; (202) 714-7662. Rachel Graber, Public Policy Manager, (202) 714-7662. National Domestic Violence Hotline, (800) 799-7233 (SAFE). TTY, (800) 787-3224.*
General email, publicpolicy@ncadv.org
Web, www.ncadv.org, Twitter, @NCADV and Facebook, www.facebook.com/NationalCoalitionAgainstDomesticViolence

Monitors legislation and public policy initiatives concerning victims and survivors of domestic violence. Work includes empowering victims, promoting and coordinating direct services, and educating the public about domestic violence. Offers the Cosmetic & Reconstructive Support Program to survivors. (Headquarters in Denver, Colo.)

National Network to End Domestic Violence (NNEDV), *1325 Massachusetts Ave. N.W., 7th Floor, 20005; (202) 543-5566. Fax, (202) 543-5626. Kim Gandy, President. National Domestic Violence Hotline, (800) 799-7233. TTY, (800) 787-3224.*
Web, www.nnedv.org and Twitter, @nnedv

Represents state domestic violence coalitions at the federal level. Operates as advocate for stronger legislation against domestic violence.

Rape, Abuse, and Incest National Network (RAINN), *1220 L St. N.W., #505, 20005; (202) 544-1034. Fax, (202) 544-3556. Scott Berkowitz, President. National Sexual Assault hotline, (800) 656-4673. Press, (202) 544-5537.*

General email, info@rainn.org
Web, www.rainn.org and Twitter, @RAINN

Links sexual assault victims to confidential local services through national sexual assault hotline. Operates the Defense Dept.'s sexual assault helpline. Provides extensive public outreach and education programs nationwide on sexual assault prevention, prosecution, and recovery. Promotes national policy efforts to improve services to victims.

Stop Child Predators, *5185 MacArthur Blvd., #575, 20016; (202) 248-7052. Fax, (202) 248-4427. Stacie D. Rumenap, President.*
General email, info@stopchildpredators.org
Web, www.stopchildpredators.org and Twitter, @StopPredators

Advocacy organization that seeks to protect children from crime and hold their victimizers accountable. Works with victims' families, law enforcement, and decision makers to develop effective policies and solutions. Goals include establishing penalty enhancements for those who commit sexual offenses against children and creating an integrated nationwide sex offender registry.

Cyber Crime

▶ AGENCIES

Criminal Division *(Justice Dept.),* **Computer Crime and Intellectual Property Section (CCIPS),** *1301 New York Ave. N.W., #600, 20530; (202) 514-1026. Fax, (202) 514-6113. John Lynch, Chief. Public Affairs, (202) 514-2007.*
Web, www.justice.gov/criminal-ccips

Investigates and litigates criminal cases involving computers, intellectual property, and the Internet. Administers the Computer Crime Initiative, a program designed to combat electronic penetrations, data theft, and cyberattacks on critical information systems. Provides specialized technical and legal assistance to other Justice Dept. divisions; coordinates international efforts; formulates policies and proposes legislation on computer crime and intellectual property issues.

Federal Bureau of Investigation (FBI) *(Justice Dept.),* **Cyber Division,** *935 Pennsylvania Ave. N.W., #5835, 20535; (202) 324-7770. Fax, (202) 324-2840. Matt Gorham Jr., Assistant Director.*
Web, www.fbi.gov/about-us/investigate/cyber

Coordinates the investigations of federal violations in which the Internet or computer networks are exploited for terrorist, foreign government-sponsored intelligence, or criminal activities, including copyright violations, fraud, pornography, child exploitation, and malicious computer intrusions.

U.S. Immigration and Customs Enforcement (ICE) *(Homeland Security Dept.),* **Cyber Crimes Center (C3),** *500 12th St. S.W., 20536; (703) 293-8005. Fax, (703) 293-9127. Dave Denton, Associate Deputy Assistant Director. Press, (202) 732-4242.*
Web, www.ice.gov/cyber-crimes

Focuses on the investigation of international Internet crimes, such as money laundering, financing of terrorist activities, child sexual exploitation, human smuggling and trafficking, intellectual property rights violations, identity and document fraud, illegal arms trafficking, and drug trafficking.

U.S. Secret Service *(Homeland Security Dept.), Criminal Investigative Division, 950 H St. N.W., #5000, 20223; (202) 406-9330. Fax, (202) 406-5016. Vacant, Special Agent-in-Charge.*
Web, www.secretservice.gov/investigation

Plans, reviews, and coordinates criminal investigations involving reports of telecommunications and computer crimes.

Drug Control

▶ **AGENCIES**

Criminal Division *(Justice Dept.), Narcotic and Dangerous Drugs Section (NDDS), 145 N St. N.E., 20530; (202) 514-0917. Fax, (202) 514-6112. Arthur G. Wyatt, Chief.*
Web, www.justice.gov/criminal/ndds

Investigates and prosecutes participants in criminal syndicates involved in the large-scale importation, manufacture, shipment, or distribution of illegal narcotics and other dangerous drugs. Trains agents and prosecutors in the techniques of major drug litigation.

Defense Dept. (DoD), *Counternarcotics and Global Threats, 2500 Defense Pentagon, #5C653, 20301-2500; (703) 697-7202. Fax, (703) 692-6947. Thomas Alexander, Deputy Assistant Secretary.*
Web, http://policy.defense.gov/OUSDP-Offices/ASD-for-Special-Operations-Low-Intensity-Conflict/Counternarcotics-and-Global-Threats

Advises the secretary on Defense Dept. policies and programs in support of federal counternarcotics operations and the implementation of the president's national drug control policy.

Drug Enforcement Administration (DEA) *(Justice Dept.), 700 Army-Navy Dr., Arlington, VA 22202 (mailing address: 8701 Morrissette Dr., MS AES, Springfield, VA 22152); Fax, (202) 307-4540. Uttam Dhillon, Administrator (Acting). Phone (Command Center), (202) 307-8000. D.C. Division office, (202) 305-8500. General information, (202) 307-1000. Press, (202) 307-7977.*
Web, www.dea.gov

Enforces federal laws and statutes relating to narcotics and other dangerous drugs, including addictive drugs, depressants, stimulants, and hallucinogens; manages the National Narcotics Intelligence System in cooperation with federal, state, and local officials; investigates violations and regulates legal trade in narcotics and dangerous drugs. Provides school and community officials with drug abuse policy guidelines. Provides information on drugs and drug abuse.

Federal Bureau of Investigation (FBI) *(Justice Dept.), 935 Pennsylvania Ave. N.W., #7176, 20535-0001; (202) 324-3000. Christopher Wray, Director. Information, (202) 324-3000. Press, (202) 324-3691.*
Web, www.fbi.gov, Twitter, @FBI and Facebook, www.facebook.com/FBI

Shares responsibility with the Drug Enforcement Administration for investigating violations of federal criminal drug laws; investigates organized crime involvement with illegal narcotics trafficking.

Food and Drug Administration (FDA) *(Health and Human Services Dept.), Center for Drug Evaluation and Research (CDER), White Oak Bldg. 51, 10903 New Hampshire Ave., #6133, Silver Spring, MD 20993; (301) 796-5400. Fax, (301) 595-7910. Dr. Janet Woodcock, Director. Press, (301) 796-3700.*
General email, druginfo@fda.hhs.gov
Web, www.fda.gov/drugs and www.fda.gov/AboutFDA/CentersOffices/OfficeofMedicalProductsandTobacco/CDER

Makes recommendations to the Justice Dept.'s Drug Enforcement Administration on narcotics and dangerous drugs to be controlled.

Internal Revenue Service (IRS) *(Treasury Dept.), Criminal Investigation, 1111 Constitution Ave. N.W., #2501, 20224; (202) 317-3200. Don Fort, Chief. Tax fraud hotline, (800) 829-0433.*
Web, www.irs.gov/uac/criminal-enforcement-1 and Twitter, @IRSnews

Lends support in counterterrorism and narcotics investigations conducted in conjunction with other law enforcement agencies, both foreign and domestic.

National Drug Control Policy (ONDCP) *(Executive Office of the President), 1800 G St. N.W., 20006; (202) 395-6700. Fax, (202) 395-6708. James W. Carroll, Director (Acting).*
Web, www.whitehouse.gov/ondcp and Twitter, @ONDCP

Establishes policies and oversees the implementation of a national drug control strategy with the goal of reducing illicit drug use, manufacturing, trafficking, and drug-related crimes, violence, and health consequences. Coordinates the international and domestic antidrug efforts of executive branch agencies and ensures that such efforts sustain and complement state and local antidrug activities. Advises the president and the National Security Council on drug control policy. (Clearinghouse address: P.O. Box 6000, Rockville, MD 20849-6000.)

Office of Justice Programs (OJP) *(Justice Dept.), Bureau of Justice Assistance (BJA), 810 7th St. N.W., 4th Floor, 20531; (202) 616-6500. Fax, (202) 305-1367. John Adler, Director. Media, (202) 307-0703.*
General email, askbja@usdoj.gov
Web, www.bja.gov and Facebook, www.facebook.com/DOJBJA

Awards grants and provides eligible state, local, and tribal governments with training and technical assistance to enforce laws relating to narcotics and other dangerous drugs.

►NONGOVERNMENTAL

Drug Policy Alliance, National Affairs, 1620 Eye St. N.W., #925, 20006; (202) 683-2030. Fax, (202) 216-0803. Maria McFarland Sánchez-Moreno, Executive Director. General email, contact@drugpolicy.org

Web, www.drugpolicy.org and Twitter, @DrugPolicyOrg

Supports reform of current drug control policy; seeks to broaden debate on drug policy to include considering alternatives to incarceration, expanding lawful mainte- nance therapies, and restoring constitutional protections; advocates medical treatment to control drug abuse; opposes random drug testing; studies drug policy in other countries. Sponsors the biennial International Conference on Drug Policy Reform. Monitors legislation and regula- tions. (Headquarters in New York.)

Marijuana Policy Project, P.O. Box 77492, Capitol Hill, 20013; (202) 462-5747. Fax, (202) 232-0442. Steve Hawkins, Executive Director. General email, info@mpp.org

Web, www.mpp.org, Twitter, @MarijuanaPolicy and Facebook, www.facebook.com/MarijuanaPolicyProject

Promotes reform of marijuana policies and regula- tions. Opposes the prohibition of responsible growing and use of marijuana by adults. Interests include allowing doc- tors to recommend marijuana to seriously ill patients and eliminating criminal penalties for marijuana use.

National Assn. of State Alcohol and Drug Abuse Directors (NASADAD), 1919 Pennsylvania Ave. N.W., #M250, 20006; (202) 293-0090. Fax, (202) 293-1250. Robert (Rob) Morrison, Executive Director, ext. 4862. General email, dcoffice@nasadad.org

Web, http://nasadad.org

Provides information on drug abuse treatment and prevention; contracts with federal and state agencies for design of programs to fight and prevent drug abuse.

National Organization for the Reform of Marijuana Laws (NORML), 1100 H St. N.W., #830, 20005; (202) 483- 5500. Fax, (202) 483-0057. Eric Altieri, Executive Director; Randy Quast, Chair. General email, norml@norml.org

Web, www.norml.org

Works to reform federal, state, and local marijuana laws and policies. Educates the public and conducts litiga- tion on behalf of marijuana consumers. Monitors legisla- tion and regulations.

RAND Corp., Drug Policy Research Center, Washington Office, 1200 S. Hayes St., Arlington, VA 22202-5050; (703) 413-1100. Fax, (703) 413-8111. Beau Kilmer, Co-Director; Rosalie Liccardo Pacula, Co-Director. General email, dprc@rand.org

Web, www.rand.org/well-being/justice-policy/centers/ dprc.html

Studies and analyzes the nation's drug problems and policies. Emphasis on empirical research and policy recom- mendations; interests include international and local policy,

trafficking, interdiction, modeling and forecasting, preven- tion, and treatment. Provides policymakers with informa- tion. (Headquarters in Santa Monica, Calif.)

Environmental Crime

►AGENCIES

Environment and Natural Resources Division (Justice Dept.), 950 Pennsylvania Ave. N.W., #2143, 20530-0001; (202) 514-2701. Fax, (202) 514-5331. Jeffrey Bossert Clark, Assistant Attorney General. Press, (202) 514-2007. General email, press@usdoj.gov

Web, www.justice.gov/enrd

Handles civil suits involving the federal government in all areas of the environment and natural resources; han- dles some criminal suits involving pollution control, wild- life protection, stewardship of public lands, and natural resources.

Environment and Natural Resources Division (Justice Dept.), Environmental Crimes (ECS), 601 D St. N.W., 2nd Floor, 20004 (mailing address: P.O. Box 7611, Washington, DC 20044); (202) 305-0321. Deborah L. Harris, Chief. Web, www.justice.gov/enrd/environmental-crimes-section

Conducts criminal enforcement actions on behalf of the United States for all environmental protection statutes, including air, water, pesticides, hazardous waste, wetland matters investigated by the Environmental Protection Agency, and other criminal environmental enforcement. Supervises criminal cases under federal maritime law and other laws protecting marine fish and mammals. Focuses on smugglers and black-market dealers of protected wildlife.

Environment and Natural Resources Division (Justice Dept.), Environmental Defense (EDS), 601 D St. N.W., #8000, 20004 (mailing address: P.O. Box 7611, Washington, DC 20044); (202) 514-2701. Fax, (202) 616- 2426. Letitia J. Grishaw, Chief. Web, www.justice.gov/enrd/environmental-crimes-section

Conducts litigation on air, water, noise, pesticides, solid waste, toxic substances, Superfund, and wetlands in cooperation with the Environmental Protection Agency; represents the EPA in suits involving judicial review of EPA actions; represents the U.S. Army Corps of Engineers in cases involving dredge-and-fill activity in navigable waters and adjacent wetlands; represents the Coast Guard in oil and hazardous spill cases; defends all federal agen- cies in environmental litigation.

Environment and Natural Resources Division (Justice Dept.), Environmental Enforcement (EES), 601 D St. N.W., #2121, 20004 (mailing address: P.O. Box 7611, Ben Franklin Station, Washington, DC 20044-7611); (202) 514- 2701. Fax, (202) 514-0097. Thomas A. Mariani, Chief. Web, www.justice.gov/enrd/environmental-enforcement- section

Conducts civil enforcement actions on behalf of the United States for all environmental protection statutes, including air, water, pesticides, hazardous waste, wetland matters investigated by the Environmental Protection Agency, and other civil environmental enforcement.

Environment and Natural Resources Division *(Justice Dept.), Wildlife and Marine Resources, 601 D St. N.W., 3rd Floor, 20004 (mailing address: P.O. Box 7415, Ben Franklin Station, Washington, DC 20044-7369); (202) 305-0210. Fax, (202) 305-0275. Seth M. Barsky, Section Chief. Web, www.justice.gov/enrd/wildlife-and-marine-resources-section*

Responsible for criminal enforcement and civil litigation under federal fish and wildlife conservation statutes, including protection of wildlife, fish, and plant resources within U.S. jurisdiction, and management and restoration of Florida Everglades. Monitors interstate and foreign commerce of these resources.

Environment and Natural Resources Division, *Justice Dept. (DOJ), Indian Resources (IRS), 601 D St. N.W., #3507, 20004 (mailing address: P.O. Box 7611, L'Enfant Plaza, Washington, DC 20044); (202) 305-0269. Fax, (202) 305-0275. S. Craig Alexander, Chief. Web, www.justice.gov/enrd/Indian-resources-section*

Represents the United States in suits, including trust violations, brought on behalf of individual Native Americans and Native American tribes against the government. Also represents the United States as trustee for Native Americans in court actions involving protection of Native American land and resources.

Environmental Protection Agency (EPA), *Enforcement and Compliance Assurance (OECA), Criminal Enforcement, Forensics, and Training, 1200 Pennsylvania Ave. N.W., MS 2201A, 20460; (202) 564-2480. Henry Barnet, Director. Web, www.epa.gov/aboutepa/about-office-enforcement-and-compliance-assurance-oeca and Twitter, @EPAJustice*

Investigates violations of environmental laws and provides technical and forensic services for civil and criminal investigations and council for legal and policy matters. Enforcement activities target the most serious water, air, and chemical hazards.

Environmental Defense Fund, *Washington Office, 1875 Connecticut Ave. N.W., #600, 20009-5728; (202) 387-3500. Fax, (202) 234-6049. Fred Krupp, President. Information, (800) 684-3322. Web, www.edf.org/offices/washington-dc and Twitter, @EnvDefenseFund*

Citizens' interest group staffed by lawyers, economists, and scientists. Takes legal action on environmental issues; provides information on pollution prevention, environmental health, wetlands, toxic substances, acid rain, tropical rain forests, sustainable fishing, clean energy, and litigation of water pollution standards. (Headquarters in New York.)

Gun Control

Bureau of Alcohol, Tobacco, Firearms, and Explosives (ATF) *(Justice Dept.), 99 New York Ave. N.E., 20226; (202) 648-7080. Thomas E. Brandon, Deputy Director. Firearm theft hotline, (800) 930-9275. Illegal firearm activity hotline, (800) 283-4867. General email, ATFTips@atf.gov*

Web, www.atf.gov and Twitter, @ATFHQ

Enforces and administers laws to eliminate illegal possession and use of firearms. Investigates criminal violations and regulates legal trade, including imports and exports. Receives reports of illegal firearms activity and firearm theft.

Brady Center to Prevent Gun Violence, *840 1st St. N.E., #400, 20002; (202) 370-8100. Fax, (202) 370-8102. Kris Brown, President. Press, (202) 370-8128. Web, www.bradycampaign.org and Twitter, @Bradybuzz*

Educational, research, and legal action organization that seeks to allay gun violence, especially among children. Library open to the public.

Coalition to Stop Gun Violence, *805 15th St. N.W., #502, 20005; (202) 408-0061. Mike Beard, President Emeritus; Joshua (Josh) Horwitz, Executive Director. General email, csgv@csgv.org*

Web, www.csgv.org and Twitter, @CSGV

Membership: 47 national organizations and individual supporters. Works to reduce gun violence by fostering effective community and national action.

Educational Fund to Stop Gun Violence, *805 15th St. N.W., #502, 20005; (202) 408-7560. Josh Horwitz, Executive Director; Andrew Patrick, Communications. General email, efsgv@efsgv.org*

Web, http://efsgv.org and Twitter, @EFSGV

Group of national organizations, including faith-based groups, child welfare advocates, public health professionals, and social justice organizations, that seeks to reduce gun violence through research and education. Monitors legislation and regulations. (Affiliated with the Coalition to Stop Gun Violence.)

Gun Owners of America, *8001 Forbes Pl., #202, Springfield, VA 22151; (703) 321-8585. Fax, (703) 321-8408. Erich Pratt, Executive Director. Web, www.gunowners.org*

Seeks to preserve the right to bear arms and to protect the rights of law-abiding gun owners. Administers foundation that provides gun owners with legal assistance in suits against the federal government. Monitors legislation, regulations, and international agreements.

National Rifle Assn. of America (NRA), *11250 Waples Mill Rd., Fairfax, VA 22030; (703) 267-3820. Fax, (703)*

267-3976. *Wayne LaPierre, Chief Executive Officer; Oliver North, President.* Toll-free, (800) 672-3888. *Web, www.nra.org and Twitter, @NRA*

Membership: target shooters, hunters, gun collectors, gunsmiths, police officers, and others interested in firearms. Promotes shooting sports and recreational shooting and safety; studies and makes recommendations on firearms laws. Opposes gun control legislation. (Affiliated with the Institute for Legislative Action, the NRA's lobbying arm.)

Juvenile Justice

▶AGENCIES

Education Dept., *Elementary and Secondary Education (OESE), State Support,* *Lyndon Baines Johnson Bldg., 400 Maryland Ave. S.W., #3W202, FB-6, 20202-6132; (202) 260-0826. Fax, (202) 260-7764. Vacant, Deputy Director. General email, oese@ed.gov*

Web, www2.ed.gov/about/offices/list/oese/oss

Funds state and local institutions responsible for providing neglected or delinquent children with free public education.

Office of Justice Programs (OJP) *(Justice Dept.), Juvenile Justice and Delinquency Prevention (OJJDP),* *810 7th St. N.W., 20531; (202) 307-5911. Fax, (301) 240-5830. Caren Harp, Administrator. Clearinghouse, (800) 851-3420. Web, www.ojjdp.gov, Twitter, @OJPOJJDP and Facebook, www.facebook.com/OJPOJJDP*

Administers federal programs related to prevention and treatment of juvenile delinquency; missing and exploited children; child victimization; and training, technical assistance, and research and evaluation in these areas. Operates the Juvenile Justice Clearinghouse. Sponsors the National Criminal Justice Reference Service ((800) 851-3420).

Office of Justice Programs (OJP) *(Justice Dept.), National Institute of Justice (NIJ),* *810 7th St. N.W., 7th Floor, 20531; (202) 307-0765. Fax, (202) 307-6394. David B. Muhlhausen, Director. Press, (202) 307-0703. General email, ojp.ocom.@usdoj.gov*

Web, www.nij.gov and Facebook, www.facebook.com/ OJPNIJ

Maintains the National Criminal Justice Reference Service, which provides data and information on juvenile justice research topics, including child protection, juvenile courts, missing children, gangs, bullying, school safety, and mentoring: (800) 851-3420; in Maryland, (301) 519-5500; Web, www.ncjrs.gov.

▶NONGOVERNMENTAL

Coalition for Juvenile Justice, *1319 F St. N.W., #402, 20004; (202) 467-0864. Fax, (202) 887-0738. Naomi Smoot, Executive Director, ext. 113.*

General email, info@juvjustice.org

Web, http://juvjustice.org and Twitter, @4juvjustice

Nationwide coalition of governor-appointed advisory groups, practitioners, and volunteers. Seeks to improve juvenile justice and to prevent children and youth from becoming involved in the courts. Issues include the removal of youth from adult jails and lockups and attention to the disproportionate number of youth of color in the juvenile justice system.

Justice Research and Statistics Assn., *1000 Vermont Ave. N.W., #450, 20005; (202) 842-9330. Fax, (202) 448-1723. Jeffrey Sedgewick, Executive Director. General email, cjinfo@jrsa.org*

Web, www.jrsa.org, Twitter, @JRSAinfo and Facebook, www.facebook.com/Justice-Research-and-Statistics-Association-139560619431173

Promotes nonpartisan research and analysis to inform criminal and juvenile justice policy and decision making. Disseminates policy- and justice-related research and information to the justice community, and convenes informational seminars on new research, programs, and technologies.

Organized Crime

▶AGENCIES

Criminal Division *(Justice Dept.), Narcotic and Dangerous Drugs Section (NDDS),* *145 N St. N.E., 20530; (202) 514-0917. Fax, (202) 514-6112. Arthur G. Wyatt, Chief.*

Web, www.justice.gov/criminal/ndds

Investigates and prosecutes participants in criminal syndicates involved in the large-scale importation, manufacture, shipment, or distribution of illegal narcotics and other dangerous drugs. Trains agents and prosecutors in the techniques of major drug litigation.

Criminal Division *(Justice Dept.), Organized Crime and Gang Section (OCGS),* *1301 New York Ave. N.W., #700, 20005; (202) 514-3594. Fax, (202) 514-3601. David L. Jaffe, Chief (Acting).*

General email, criminaldivision@usdoj.gov

Web, www.justice.gov/criminal-ocgs

Enforces federal criminal laws when subjects under investigation are alleged racketeers or part of syndicated criminal operations or gangs; coordinates efforts of federal, state, and local law enforcement agencies against organized crime, including emerging international groups; formulates violent crime and gang prosecution policy; maintains responsibility over all firearms-related statutes within the U.S. code. Cases include extortion, murder, bribery, fraud, money laundering, narcotics, labor racketeering, and violence that disrupts the criminal justice process.

Federal Bureau of Investigation (FBI) *(Justice Dept.), Criminal Investigative Division (CID), Organized Crime,* *935 Pennsylvania Ave. N.W., #3352, 20535-0001;*

(202) 324-5625. Fax, (202) 324-0880. Maxwell Marker, Section Chief, Eastern Hemisphere; Marlin Ritzman, Section Chief, Western Hemisphere.
Web, www.fbi.gov/about-us/investigate/organizedcrime

Coordinates all FBI organized-crime investigations. Determines budget, training, and resource needs for investigations, including those related to international organized crime. Conducts undercover operations, surveillance, and multiagency investigations, and works with international partners.

Other Violations

▶AGENCIES

Bureau of Alcohol, Tobacco, Firearms, and Explosives (ATF) (Justice Dept.), 99 New York Ave. N.E., 20226; (202) 648-7080. Thomas E. Brandon, Deputy Director. Firearm theft hotline, (800) 930-9275. Illegal firearm activity hotline, (800) 283-4867.
General email, ATFTips@atf.gov

Web, www.atf.gov and Twitter, @ATFHQ

Performs law enforcement functions relating to alcohol (beer, wine, distilled spirits), tobacco, arson, explosives, and destructive devices; investigates criminal violations and regulates legal trade.

Criminal Division (Justice Dept.), Election Crimes, 1400 New York Ave. N.W., #12100, 20005; (202) 514-1412. Anna Lou Tirol, Chief (Acting), (202) 514-1178. Press, (202) 514-2007.
Web, www.justice.gov/criminal/pin

Supervises enforcement of federal criminal laws related to campaigns and elections. Oversees investigation of deprivation of voting rights; intimidation and coercion of voters; denial or promise of federal employment or other benefits; illegal political contributions, expenditures, and solicitations; and all other election violations referred to the division.

Criminal Division (Justice Dept.), Fraud Section (FRD), 1400 New York Ave. N.W., #4100, 20530; (202) 514-7023. Fax, (202) 514-7021. Robert Zink, Chief (Acting).
Web, www.justice.gov/criminal-fraud

Administers federal enforcement activities related to fraud and white-collar crime. Focuses on frauds against government programs, transnational and multidistrict fraud, and cases involving the security and commodity exchanges, banking practices, and consumer victimization.

Criminal Division (Justice Dept.), Money Laundering and Asset Recovery Section (MLARS), 1400 New York Ave. N.W., #10100, 20005; (202) 514-1263. Fax, (202) 514-5522. Deborah Connor, Chief.
Web, www.justice.gov/criminal-mlars

Investigates and prosecutes money laundering and criminal and civil forfeiture offenses involving illegal transfer of funds within the United States and from the United States to other countries. Oversees and coordinates legislative policy proposals. Advises U.S. attorneys' offices in multidistrict money laundering and criminal and civil forfeiture prosecutions. Represents Justice Dept. in international anti-money laundering and criminal and civil forfeiture initiatives.

Criminal Division (Justice Dept.), Organized Crime and Gang Section (OCGS), 1301 New York Ave. N.W., #700, 20005; (202) 514-3594. Fax, (202) 514-3601. David L. Jaffe, Chief (Acting).
General email, criminaldivision@usdoj.gov

Web, www.justice.gov/criminal-ocgs

Reviews and advises on prosecutions of criminal violations concerning the operation of employee benefit plans in the private sector, labor-management relations, the operation of employee pension and health care plans, and internal affairs of labor unions.

Federal Bureau of Investigation (FBI) (Justice Dept.), Economic Crimes, 935 Pennsylvania Ave. N.W., #3925, 20535; (202) 324-6352. Fax, (202) 324-9147. Francine Gross, Chief. Press, (202) 324-3691.
Web, www.fbi.gov

Investigates, reduces, and prevents significant financial crimes against individuals, businesses, and industries by safeguarding the integrity and credibility of corporations, securities and commodities markets, investment vehicles, and the insurance industry. Reinforces compliance in the corporate world and promotes investor confidence in the United States financial markets. Categorizes the frauds it investigates into four separate classifications: corporate fraud, securities and commodities fraud, insurance fraud (non-health care related), and mass marketing fraud.

National Security Division (Justice Dept.), Counterintelligence and Export Control, 950 Pennsylvania Ave. N.W., 20530; (202) 514-1057. Fax, (202) 514-8714. Joy Bratt, Chief.
General email, nsd.public@usdoj.gov

Web, www.justice.gov/nsd

Supervises the investigation and prosecution of cases affecting national security, foreign relations, and the export of military and strategic commodities and technology. Has executive responsibility for authorizing the prosecution of cases under criminal statutes relating to espionage, sabotage, neutrality, and atomic energy. Provides legal advice to U.S. Attorneys' offices and investigates agencies on federal statutes concerning national security. Coordinates criminal cases involving the application of the Classified Information Procedures Act. Administers and enforces the Foreign Agents Registration Act of 1938 and related disclosure statutes.

National Security Division (Justice Dept.), Counterterrorism, 950 Pennsylvania Ave. N.W., 20530; (202) 514-1057. Fax, (202) 514-8714. Michael J. Mullaney, Chief.
General email, nsd.public@usdoj.gov

Web, www.justice.gov/nsd/counterterrorism-section

Seeks to assist, through investigation and prosecution, in preventing and disrupting acts of terrorism anywhere in the world that impact significant U.S. interests and persons.

National Security Division *(Justice Dept.), Law and Policy, 950 Pennsylvania Ave. N.W., 20530; (202) 514-7941. Brad Wiegmann, Deputy Assistant Attorney General. General email, nsd.justice@usdoj.gov*

Web, www.justice.gov/nsd

Provides legal assistance and advice on matters of national security law.

Securities and Exchange Commission (SEC), *Office of the Whistleblower, 100 F St. N.E., MS 5631, 20549; (202) 551-4790. Fax, (703) 813-9322. Jane Norberg, Chief.*

Web, www.sec.gov/whistleblower

Receives information about possible securities law violations and provides information about the whistle-blower program.

U.S. Customs and Border Protection *(Homeland Security Dept.), Field Operations, 1300 Pennsylvania Ave. N.W., #2.4A, 20229; (202) 344-1620. Fax, (202) 344-2777. Todd Owen, Executive Assistant Commissioner. Press, (202) 344-1700.*

Web, www.cbp.gov/border-security/ports-entry

Combats smuggling of funds; enforces statutes relating to the processing and regulation of people, carriers, cargo, and mail into and out of the United States. Investigates counterfeiting, child pornography, commercial fraud, and Internet crimes.

U.S. Postal Service (USPS), *Inspection Service, 475 L'Enfant Plaza S.W., #3100, 20260-2100; (202) 268-4264. Fax, (202) 268-7316. Gary Barksdale, Chief Postal Inspector (Acting). Fraud and abuse hotline, (877) 876-2455. Press, (202) 268-3700.*

Web, http://postalinspectors.uspis.gov and Twitter, @USPIpressroom

Protects mail, postal funds, and property from criminal violations of postal laws, such as mail fraud or distribution of obscene materials. (Headquarters in Chicago, Ill.)

U.S. Secret Service *(Homeland Security Dept.), 950 H St. N.W., #8000, 20223; (202) 406-5000. Fax, (202) 406-5246. James M. Murray, Director. Information, (202) 406-5708. Press, (202) 406-5708.*

Web, www.secretservice.gov and Twitter, @SecretService

Investigates violations of laws relating to counterfeiting of U.S. currency; financial crimes, including access device fraud, financial institution fraud, identity theft, and computer fraud; and computer-based attacks on the financial, banking, and telecommunications infrastructure.

U.S. Secret Service *(Homeland Security Dept.), Criminal Investigative Division, 950 H St. N.W., #5000, 20223; (202) 406-9330. Fax, (202) 406-5016. Vacant, Special Agent-in-Charge.*

Web, www.secretservice.gov/investigation

Investigates crimes associated with financial institutions. Jurisdiction includes bank fraud, access device fraud

involving credit and debit cards, telecommunications and computer crimes, fraudulent identification, fraudulent government and commercial securities, and electronic funds transfer fraud.

International Anticounterfeiting Coalition, *727 15th St. N.W., 9th Floor, 20005; (202) 223-6667. Robert C. Barchiesi, President. General email, iacc@iacc.org*

Web, www.iacc.org, Twitter, @IACC_GetReal and Facebook, www.facebook.com/ InternationalAntiCounterfeitingCoalition

Works to combat counterfeiting and piracy by promoting laws, regulations, and directives to render theft of intellectual property unprofitable. Oversees anticounterfeiting programs that increase patent, trademark, copyright, service mark, trade dress, and trade-secret protection. Provides information and training to law enforcement officials to help identify counterfeit and pirate products.

Stalking Resource Center, *2000 M St. N.W., #480, 20036; (202) 467-8700. Fax, (202) 467-8701. Mai Fernandez, Executive Director. Referrals, (855) 484-2846. General email, src@ncvc.org*

Web, www.victimsofcrime.org/our-programs/stalking-resource-center and Twitter, @CrimeVictimsOrg

Acts as an information clearinghouse on stalking. Works to raise public awareness of the dangers of stalking. Encourages the development and implementation of multidisciplinary responses to stalking in local communities, and policy and protocol enhancements for the criminal justice system. Offers practitioner training and technical assistance. (Affiliated with the National Center for Victims of Crime.)

Sentencing and Corrections

►AGENCIES

Federal Bureau of Prisons *(Justice Dept.), 320 1st St. N.W., 20534; (202) 307-3198. Fax, (202) 514-6620. Hugh J. Hurwitz, Director (Acting), (202) 307-3250. Inmate locator service, (202) 307-3126. Press, (202) 514-6551.*

Web, www.bop.gov, Twitter, @BOPCareers and Facebook, www.facebook.com/BOPCareers

Supervises operations of federal correctional institutions, community treatment facilities, and commitment and management of federal inmates; oversees contracts with local institutions for confinement and support of federal prisoners. Regional offices are responsible for administration; central office in Washington coordinates operations and issues standards and policy guidelines. Central office includes Federal Prison Industries, a government corporation providing prison-manufactured goods and services for sale to federal agencies, and the National Institute of

Corrections, an information and technical assistance center on state and local corrections programs.

Federal Bureau of Prisons *(Justice Dept.),* **Health** *Services, 320 1st St. N.W., #454, 20534; (202) 307-3055. Fax, (202) 514-6620. Dr. Deborah G. Schult, Assistant Director.*
Web, www.bop.gov/about/agency/org_hsd.jsp

Administers health care and treatment programs for prisoners in federal institutions.

Federal Bureau of Prisons *(Justice Dept.),* **National** *Institute of Corrections, 320 1st St. N.W., #5007, 20534; (202) 307-3106. Fax, (202) 514-6620. Shaina Vanek, Deputy Director (Acting). Toll-free, (800) 995-6423. Web, https://nicic.gov and www.bop.gov/about/agency/org_ nic.jsp*

Provides training, technical assistance, information clearinghouse services, and policy/program development assistance to federal, state, and local corrections agencies.

Justice Dept. (DOJ), *Pardon Attorney, RFK Bldg., 950 Pennsylvania Ave., 20530 (mailing address: 145 N St. N.E., #5E508, Washington, DC 20530); (202) 616-6070. Fax, (202) 616-6069. Rosalind Sargent-Burns, Deputy Pardon Attorney.*
General email, USpardonattorney@usdoj.gov
Web, www.justice.gov/pardon

Advises the president on the exercise of executive clemency power, including pardons, commutations of sentence, remissions of fine or restitution, and reprieves. Receives and reviews petitions to the president for all forms of executive clemency, including pardons and sentence reductions; initiates investigations and prepares the deputy attorney general's recommendations to the president on petitions.

Office of Justice Programs (OJP) *(Justice Dept.),* **Bureau** *of Justice Assistance (BJA), 810 7th St. N.W., 4th Floor, 20531; (202) 616-6500. Fax, (202) 305-1367. John Adler, Director. Media, (202) 307-0703.*
General email, askbja@usdoj.gov
Web, www.bja.gov and Facebook, www.facebook.com/ DOJBJA

Provides states and communities with funds and technical assistance for corrections demonstration projects.

Office of Justice Programs (OJP) *(Justice Dept.),* **National** *Institute of Justice (NIJ), 810 7th St. N.W., 7th Floor, 20531; (202) 307-0765. Fax, (202) 307-6394.*
David B. Muhlhausen, Director. Press, (202) 307-0703.
General email, ojp.ocom.@usdoj.gov
Web, www.nij.gov and Facebook, www.facebook.com/ OJPNIJ

Conducts research on all aspects of criminal justice, including crime prevention, enforcement, adjudication, and corrections; seeks to reduce incarceration and probation while maintaining public safety and holding offenders accountable. Maintains the National Criminal Justice Reference Service, which provides information on corrections research topics, including jails and prisons, inmate

assistance, parole and probations, recidivism, and reentry: (800) 851-3420; in Maryland, (301) 519-5500; Web, www .ncjrs.gov.

U.S. Parole Commission *(Justice Dept.), 90 K St. N.E., 3rd Floor, 20530; (202) 346-7000. Fax, (202) 357-1085. Patricia K. Cushwa, Chair (Acting).*
General email, public.inquiries@usdoj.gov
Web, www.justice.gov/uspc
Press, uspc.media@usdoj.gov

Makes release and revocation decisions for all federal prisoners serving sentences of more than one year for offenses committed before November 1, 1987, and for D.C. Code offenders serving parolable offenses or subject to a term of supervised release.

U.S. Sentencing Commission, *1 Columbus Circle N.E., #2-500 South Lobby, 20002-8002; (202) 502-4500. Fax, (202) 502-4699. Kenneth P. Cohen, Staff Director. Help-line, (202) 502-4545.*
General email, pubaffairs@ussc.gov
Web, www.ussc.gov and Twitter, @TheUSSCgov

Establishes sentencing guidelines and policy for all federal courts, including guidelines prescribing the appropriate form and severity of punishment for those convicted of federal crimes. Provides training and research on sentencing-related issues. Serves as an information resource.

▶ JUDICIARY

Administrative Office of the U.S. Courts, *1 Columbus Circle N.E., 20544-0001; (202) 502-2600. James C. Duff, Director.*
Web, www.uscourts.gov

Supervises all administrative matters of the federal court system, except the Supreme Court; collects statistical data on business of the courts.

Administrative Office of the U.S. Courts, *Probation and Pretrial Services, 1 Columbus Circle N.E., #4-300, 20544-0001; (202) 502-1600. Fax, (202) 502-1677. Matthew G. Rowland, Assistant Director.*
Web, www.uscourts.gov/services-forms/probation-and-pretrial-services

Determines the resource and program requirements of the federal and pretrial services system. Provides policy guidance, program evaluation services, management and technical assistance, and training to probation and pretrial services officers.

▶ NONGOVERNMENTAL

American Bar Assn. (ABA), *Criminal Justice, 1050 Connecticut Ave. N.W., #400, 20036; (202) 662-1500. Fax, (202) 662-1501. Kevin Scruggs, Director, (202) 662-1503.*
General email, crimjustice@americanbar.org
Web, www.americanbar.org/groups/criminal_justice.html and Twitter, @ABAJS

Studies and makes recommendations on all aspects of the correctional system, including overcrowding in prisons and the privatization of prisons and correctional institutions. (Headquarters in Chicago, Ill.)

American Civil Liberties Union Foundation, *National Prison Project, 915 15th St. N.W., 7th Floor, 20005; (202) 393-4930. Fax, (202) 393-4931. David C. Fathi, Director, (202) 548-6603.*
Web, www.aclu.org/issues/prisoners-rights and Twitter, @DavidCFathi

Litigates on behalf of prisoners through class action suits. Seeks to improve prison conditions and the penal system; serves as resource center for prisoners' rights.

American Correctional Assn. (ACA), *206 N. Washington St., #200, Alexandria, VA 22314; (703) 224-0000. Fax, (703) 224-0179. James A. Gondles Jr., Executive Director, (703) 224-0103. Information, (800) 222-5646.*
Web, www.aca.org, Twitter, @ACAinfo and Facebook, www.facebook.com/AmericanCorrectionalAssociation

Membership: corrections professionals in all aspects of corrections, including juvenile and adult facilities, community facilities, and academia; affiliates include state and regional corrections associations in the United States and Canada. Conducts and publishes research; provides state and local governments with technical assistance; certifies corrections professionals. Offers professional development courses and accreditation programs. Monitors legislation and regulation. Interests include criminal justice issues, correctional standards, and accreditation programs. Library open to the public.

Amnesty International USA, *Washington National Office, 600 Pennsylvania Ave. S.E., 5th Floor, 20003; (202) 544-0200. Fax, (202) 546-7142. Margaret Huang, Executive Director. Media, (202) 509-8194. Toll-free, 800-AMNESTY.*
General email, aiusa@aiusa.org
Web, www.amnestyusa.org and Twitter, @amnesty

International organization that opposes retention or reinstitution of the death penalty; advocates humane treatment of all prisoners. (U.S. headquarters in New York.)

Death Penalty Information Center, *1701 K St. N.W., #205, 20006; (202) 289-2275. Robert Dunham, Executive Director. Press, (202) 289-4022.*
General email, dpic@deathpenaltyinfo.org
Web, www.deathpenaltyinfo.org and Twitter, @DPinfoCtr

Provides the media and public with analysis and information on issues concerning capital punishment. Conducts briefings for journalists; prepares reports; issues press releases.

Families Against Mandatory Minimums, *1100 H St. N.W., #1000, 20005; (202) 822-6700. Fax, (202) 822-6704. Kevin Ring, President.*
General email, famm@famm.org
Web, www.famm.org and Twitter, @FAMMFoundation

Seeks to repeal statutory mandatory minimum prison sentences. Works to increase public awareness of inequity of mandatory minimum sentences through grassroots efforts and media outreach programs.

NAACP Legal Defense and Educational Fund, Inc., *Washington Office, 700 14th St., #600, 20005; (202) 682-1300. Todd A. Cox, Director of Policy.*
Web, www.naacpldf.org and Twitter, @NAACP_LDF

Civil rights litigation group that supports abolition of capital punishment; assists attorneys representing prisoners on death row; focuses public attention on race discrimination in the application of the death penalty. Not affiliated with the NAACP. (Headquarters in New York.)

National Center on Institutions and Alternatives, *7130 Rutherford Rd., Baltimore, MD 21244; (443) 780-1300. Fax, (410) 597-9656. Herbert J. Hoelter, Chief Executive Officer.*
General email, info@ncianet.org
Web, www.ncianet.org and Twitter, @NCIA_Baltimore

Seeks to reduce incarceration as primary form of punishment imposed by criminal justice system; advocates use of extended community service, work-release, and halfway house programs; operates youth and adult residential programs; provides defense attorneys and courts with specific recommendations for sentencing and parole. (Affiliated with the Augustus Institute. Headquarters in Baltimore, Md.)

National Coalition to Abolish the Death Penalty, *80 M St. S.E., 20036; (703) 957-8198. Diann Rust-Tierney, Executive Director; Gregory Joseph, Program Director, (646) 346-4289. 90 Million Strong, (202) 331-4090.*
General email, admin-info@ncadp.org
Web, www.ncadp.org, Twitter, @ncadp and Facebook, www.facebook.com/ncadp

Membership: organizations and individuals opposed to the death penalty. Maintains collection of death penalty research. Provides training, resources, and conferences. Works with families of murder victims; tracks execution dates. Launched the 90 Million Strong campaign to form a coalition of partners who oppose the death penalty. Monitors legislation and regulations.

Prison Fellowship Ministries, *44180 Riverside Pkwy., Lansdowne, VA 20176; (703) 478-0100. James J. Ackerman, Chief Executive Officer. Toll-free, (800) 206-9764.*
General email, info@pfm.org
Web, www.pfm.org and Twitter, @prisonfellowship

Religious organization that ministers to prisoners and ex-prisoners, victims, and the families involved. Offers counseling, seminars, and support for readjustment after release; works to increase the fairness and effectiveness of the criminal justice system.

The Sentencing Project, *1705 DeSales St. N.W., 8th Floor, 20036; (202) 628-0871. Fax, (202) 628-1091. Marc Mauer, Executive Director.*

General email, staff@sentencingproject.org

Web, www.sentencingproject.org and Twitter, @SentencingProj

Engages in research and advocacy on criminal justice policy issues, including sentencing, incarceration, juvenile justice, racial disparity, alternatives to incarceration, and felony disenfranchisement. Publishes research.

Victim Assistance

Federal Bureau of Investigation (FBI) *(Justice Dept.)*, *Victim Assistance*, 935 Pennsylvania Ave. N.W., #3329, 20535; (202) 324-1339. Fax, (202) 324-2113. *Kathryn McKay Turman, Assistant Director.*
General email, victim.assistance@fbi.gov

Web, www.fbi.gov/stats-services/victim_assistance

Ensures that victims of crimes investigated by the FBI are identified, offered assistance, and given information about case events. Manages the Victim Assistance Program in the fifty-six FBI field offices as well as the FBI's international offices. Trains agents and personnel to work with victims. Coordinates resources and services to victims in cases of terrorism and crimes against citizens that occur outside the United States. Coordinates with other federal agencies on behalf of victims.

Justice Dept. (DOJ), *Elder Justice Initiative (EJI)*, 950 Pennsylvania Ave. N.W., 20530; Andy Mao, Coordinator. Eldercare locator helpline, (800) 677-1116.
General email, elder.justice@usdoj.gov

Web, www.justice.gov/elderjustice and Rural and tribal resources, www.justice.gov/elderjustice/rural-and-tribal-resources

Makes available training and resources for elder abuse victim specialists; maintains a victim resource locator to help victims and their families identify support and other resources.

Justice Dept. (DOJ), *Violence Against Women (OVW)*, 145 N St. N.E., #10W.121, 20530; (202) 307-6026. Fax, (202) 305-2589. Katie Sullivan, Deputy Director (Acting); Mary Frances Bowley, Executive Director. National Domestic Violence Hotline, 800-799-SAFE. TTY, (202) 307-2277.
General email, ovw.info@usdoj.gov

Web, www.justice.gov/ovw and Twitter, @OVWJustice

Seeks more effective policies and services to combat domestic violence, sexual assault, stalking, and other crimes against women. Helps administer grants to states to fund shelters, crisis centers, and hotlines, and to hire law enforcement officers, prosecutors, and counselors specializing in cases of sexual violence and other violent crimes against women.

National Security Division *(Justice Dept.)*, *Justice for Victims of Overseas Terrorism*, 950 Pennsylvania Ave.

N.W., 20530; (202) 233-0701. Heather Cartwright, Director.
General email, nsd.ovt@usdoj.gov

Web, www.justice.gov/nsd-ovt

Monitors the investigation and prosecution of terrorist attacks against U.S. citizens abroad; works with other Justice Dept. offices to ensure that the rights of victims are respected.

Office of Justice Programs (OJP) *(Justice Dept.)*, *National Institute of Justice (NIJ)*, 810 7th St. N.W., 7th Floor, 20531; (202) 307-0765. Fax, (202) 307-6394. *David B. Muhlhausen, Director. Press, (202) 307-0703.*
General email, ojp.ocom.@usdoj.gov

Web, www.nij.gov and Facebook, www.facebook.com/OJPNIJ

Researches victimization trends and evaluates victim advocacy programs. Maintains the National Criminal Justice Reference Service, which provides data and information on victim research topics, including intervention, restorative justice, and victimization of special populations: (800) 851-3420; in Maryland, (301) 519-5500; Web, www.ncjrs.gov.

Office of Justice Programs (OJP) *(Justice Dept.)*, *Victims of Crime (OVC)*, 810 7th St. N.W., 8th Floor, 20531; (202) 307-5983. Fax, (202) 514-6383. Darlene Hutchinson Biehl, Director. Resource Center, (800) 851-3420 or TTY, (301) 240-6310. Victim hotline, (800) 331-0075 or TTY, (800) 553-2508.
General email, askovc@ojp.gov

Web, www.ovc.gov, Twitter, @OJPOVC and Facebook, www.facebook.com/OJPOVC

Works to advance the rights of and improve services to the nation's crime victims. Supports programs and initiatives to assist other federal agencies, state and local governments, tribal governments, private nonprofit organizations, and the international community in their efforts to aid victims of violent and nonviolent crime. Provides emergency funding and services for victims of terrorism and mass violence and victims of human trafficking. Funds the development of training and technical assistance for victim service providers and other professionals through the Training and Technical Assistance Center, (866) 682-8822 or TTY (866) 682-8880. Funds demonstration projects and coordinates annual observances of National Crime Victims' Rights Week. Website has a Spanish-language link.

FAIR Girls, 2021 L St. N.W., #254, 20036; (202) 520-9777. Erin Andrews, Executive Director. Crisis hotline, (855) 900-3247. National trafficking hotline, (888) 373-7888.
General email, info@fairgirls.org

Web, www.fairgirls.org

Provides interventionist holistic care for survivors of trafficking who identify as girls or young women through prevention education and policy advocacy. Works to eradicate human trafficking and create improved outcomes for survivors.

National Assn. of Crime Victim Compensation Boards, *P.O. Box 16003, Alexandria, VA 22302; (703) 780-3200. Dan Eddy, Executive Director.*
General email, dan.eddy@nacvcb.org
Web, www.nacvcb.org

Provides state compensation agencies with training and technical assistance. Provides public information on victim compensation.

National Center for Missing and Exploited Children, *333 John Carlyle St., #125, Alexandria, VA 22314-5767; (703) 224-2150. Fax, (703) 224-2122. John F. Clark, Chief Executive Officer. Toll-free hotline, (800) 843-5678.*
Web, www.missingkids.com and Twitter, @MissingKids

Works with law enforcement, social service agencies, and mental health agencies to provide support networks for child victims and their families; offers legal resources for attorneys and families.

National Center for Victims of Crime, *2000 M St. N.W., #480, 20036; (202) 467-8700. Fax, (202) 467-8701. Mai Fernandez, Executive Director.*
Web, www.victimsofcrime.org

Works with victims' groups and criminal justice agencies to protect the rights of crime victims through state and federal statutes and policies. Promotes greater responsiveness to crime victims through training and education; provides research and technical assistance in the development of victim-related legislation.

National Coalition Against Domestic Violence, *Public Policy, 2000 M St. N.W., #480, 20036; (202) 714-7662. Rachel Graber, Public Policy Manager, (202) 714-7662. National Domestic Violence Hotline, (800) 799-7233 (SAFE). TTY, (800) 787-3224.*
General email, publicpolicy@ncadv.org
Web, www.ncadv.org, Twitter, @NCADV and Facebook, www.facebook.com/ NationalCoalitionAgainstDomesticViolence

Monitors legislation and public policy initiatives concerning victims and survivors of domestic violence. Work includes empowering victims, promoting and coordinating direct services, and educating the public about domestic violence. Offers the Cosmetic & Reconstructive Support Program to survivors. (Headquarters in Denver, Colo.)

National Organization for Victim Assistance, *510 King St., #424, Alexandria, VA 22314; (703) 535-6682. Fax, (703) 535-5500. Richard Barajas, Executive Director. Toll-free and referral line, (800) 879-6682.*
Web, www.trynova.org

Membership: persons involved with victim and witness assistance programs, criminal justice professionals, researchers, crime victims, and others interested in victims' rights. Monitors legislation; provides victims and victim support programs with technical assistance, referrals, and program support; provides information on victims' rights.

Rape, Abuse, and Incest National Network (RAINN), *1220 L St. N.W., #505, 20005; (202) 544-1034. Fax, (202)*

544-3556. Scott Berkowitz, President. National Sexual Assault hotline, (800) 656-4673. Press, (202) 544-5537. General email, info@rainn.org
Web, www.rainn.org and Twitter, @RAINN

Links sexual assault victims to confidential local services through national sexual assault hotline. Operates the Defense Dept.'s sexual assault helpline. Provides extensive public outreach and education programs nationwide on sexual assault prevention, prosecution, and recovery. Promotes national policy efforts to improve services to victims.

Stalking Resource Center, *2000 M St. N.W., #480, 20036; (202) 467-8700. Fax, (202) 467-8701. Mai Fernandez, Executive Director. Referrals, (855) 484-2846.*
General email, src@ncvc.org
Web, www.victimsofcrime.org/our-programs/stalking-resource-center and Twitter, @CrimeVictimsOrg

Acts as an information clearinghouse on stalking. Works with professionals and organizations to provide victim-centered responses to stalking; develops and enhances services for victims of stalking. Offers confidential referrals for crime victims. Provides training events on topics including intimate partner violence, sexual assault, technology use and stalking, investigating and prosecuting stalking, safety planning, and coordinated community response. (Affiliated with the National Center for Victims of Crime.)

LAW ENFORCEMENT

General

▶AGENCIES

Bureau of International Narcotics and Law Enforcement Affairs (INL) *(State Dept.), Anticrime Programs, 2401 E St. N.W., #L600, 20037; (202) 663-1860. Susan Snyder, Director.*
Web, www.state.gov/j/inl/offices/index.htm

Supports a global network of International Law Enforcement Academies to combat international drug trafficking, criminality, and terrorism.

Community Oriented Policing Services (COPS) *(Justice Dept.), 145 N St. N.E., 20530 (mailing address: for overnight delivery, use zip code 20002); (202) 616-2888. Fax, (202) 616-2914. Phil Keith, Director. Press, (202) 514-9079. Response Center, (800) 421-6770. Toll Free, (800) 421-6770.*
General email, askCopsRC@usdoj.gov
Web, https://cops.usdoj.gov and Twitter, @COPSOffice

Awards grants to tribal, state, and local law enforcement agencies to hire and train community policing professionals, acquire and deploy crime-fighting technologies, and develop and test policing strategies. Community policing emphasizes crime prevention through partnerships between law enforcement and citizens.

Criminal Division *(Justice Dept.), International Criminal Investigative Training Assistance Program (ICITAP),*

1331 F St. N.W., #500, 20530; Gregory Ducot, Director (Acting). Main, (202) 305-8190.
Web, www.justice.gov/criminal-icitap

Works with foreign governments to develop professional and transparent law enforcement institutions that protect human rights, combat corruption, and reduce the threat of transnational crime and terrorism. Provides international development assistance that supports both national security and foreign policy objectives.

Federal Bureau of Investigation (FBI) *(Justice Dept.),* **Partner Engagement,** *935 Pennsylvania Ave. N.W., #7128, 20535; (202) 324-7126. Kerry Sleeper, Assistant Director.*
General email, olec@leo.gov

Web, www.fbi.gov/about/partnerships/office-of-partner-engagement

Advises FBI executives on the use of state and local law enforcement and resources in criminal, cyber, and counterterrorism investigations. Coordinates the bureau's intelligence-sharing and technological efforts with state and local law enforcement. Serves as a liaison with the Homeland Security Dept. and other federal entities.

Federal Law Enforcement Training Center (FLETC) *(Homeland Security Dept.),* **National Capital Region (NCR),** *1717 H St. N.W., 7th Floor, #16, 20006; (202) 233-0260. Fax, (202) 233-0258. Thomas J. Walters, Director, (912) 267-2070.*
General email, FLETC-WashingtonOffice@dhs.gov

Web, www.fletc.gov/washington-operations-wo, Twitter, @FLETC and Facebook, www.facebook.com/fletc

Trains federal law enforcement personnel. Provides services to state, local, tribal, and international law enforcement agencies. (Headquarters in Glynco, Ga.)

Federal Trade Commission (FTC), *Bureau of Consumer Protection, Consumer Response and Operations Division,* *600 Pennsylvania Ave. N.W., 20580; (202) 326-2830. Monica Vaca, Associate Director (Acting), (202) 326-2245. Consumer Response Center, 877-FTC-HELP. Consumer Sentinel helpline, (877) 701-9595. FTC Complaint, (877) 382-4357.*
General email, crcmessages@ftc.gov

Web, www.ftc.gov/about-ftc/bureaus-offices/bureau-consumer-protection/our-divisions/division-consumer-response and Consumer Response Center, www.consumer.ftc.gov and Consumer Sentinel Network, www.ftc.gov/enforcement/consumer-sentinel-network and FTC Complaint Assistant, www.ftccomplaintassistant.gov

Collects and analyzes data in the Consumer Sentinel Network, which provides law enforcement members with access to FTC consumer complaints. Responds to consumer complaints and inquiries received through the Consumer Response Center.

Financial Crimes Enforcement Network *(Treasury Dept.),* *P.O. Box 39, Vienna, VA 22183-0039; (703) 905-3591. Fax, (703) 905-3690. Kenneth A. Blanco, Director. Press, (703) 905-3770. Resource Center, (800) 767-2825.*

General email, frc@fincen.gov
Web, www.fincen.gov

Administers an information network in support of federal, state, and local law enforcement agencies in the prevention and detection of terrorist financing, money-laundering operations, and other financial crimes. Administers the Bank Secrecy Act.

Interior Dept. (DOI), *Law Enforcement and Security (OLES), 1849 C St. N.W., MS 3428-MIB, 20240; (202) 208-6319. Fax, (202) 208-1185. Darren Cruzan, Director. Watch Office, (202) 208-4108.*
Web, www.doi.gov/pmb/oles

Develops law enforcement staffing models; establishes departmental training requirements and monitors their implementation; oversees the hiring of key law enforcement and security personnel; and reviews law enforcement and security budgets.

Office of Justice Programs (OJP) *(Justice Dept.),* **Bureau of Justice Assistance (BJA),** *810 7th St. N.W., 4th Floor, 20531; (202) 616-6500. Fax, (202) 305-1367. John Adler, Director. Press, (202) 307-0703.*
General email, askbja@usdoj.gov

Web, www.bja.gov and Facebook, www.facebook.com/DOJBJA

Provides funds to eligible state and local governments and to nonprofit organizations for criminal justice programs, primarily those that combat drug trafficking and other drug-related crime.

Office of Justice Programs (OJP) *(Justice Dept.),* **National Institute of Justice (NIJ),** *810 7th St. N.W., 7th Floor, 20531; (202) 307-0765. Fax, (202) 307-6394. David B. Muhlhausen, Director. Press, (202) 307-0703.*
General email, ojp.ocom.@usdoj.gov

Web, www.nij.gov and Facebook, www.facebook.com/OJPNIJ

Develops practices and policies that improve performance in law enforcement personnel and criminal justice agencies; evaluates ways to limit deaths and injuries of law enforcement and suspects; seeks to expand the use of DNA evidence and forensic science. Maintains the National Criminal Justice Reference Service, which provides information on various law enforcement topics, including crime mapping, crime scene investigation, profiling, community policing, training, and stress management: (800) 851-3420; in Maryland, (301) 519-5500; Web, www.ncjrs.gov.

Transportation Security Administration (TSA) *(Homeland Security Dept.),* **Office of Law Enforcement, Federal Air Marshal Service,** *TSA-18, 601 S. 12th St., Arlington, VA 20598-6018; (703) 487-3400. Fax, (703) 487-3405. Roderick Allison, Director.*
Web, www.tsa.gov/about-tsa/office-law-enforcement

Protects air security in the United States. Promotes public confidence in the U.S. civil aviation system. Deploys marshals on flights around the world to detect and deter hostile acts targeting U.S. air carriers, airports, passengers, and crews.

U.S. Marshals Service *(Justice Dept.)*, *2604 Jefferson Davis Hwy., CS-3, #1200, Alexandria, VA 22301; (202) 307-9100. Fax, (703) 603-7021. David Anderson, Deputy Director (Acting). TTY, (202) 307-5012.*
General email, us.marshals@usdoj.gov

Web, www.usmarshals.gov

Acts as the enforcement arm of the federal courts and U.S. attorney general. Responsibilities include court and witness security, prisoner custody and transportation, prisoner support, maintenance and disposal of seized and forfeited property, and special operations. Administers the Federal Witness Security Program. Apprehends fugitives, including those wanted by foreign nations and believed to be in the United States; oversees the return of fugitives apprehended abroad and wanted by U.S. law enforcement. Carries out the provisions of the Adam Walsh Child Protection and Safety Act.

▶**CONGRESS**

For a listing of relevant congressional committees and subcommittees, please see pages 542–543 or the Appendix.

▶**NONGOVERNMENTAL**

Feminist Majority Foundation, *National Center for Women and Policing, 1600 Wilson Blvd., #801, Arlington, VA 22209; (703) 522-2214. Fax, (703) 522-2219. Eleanor Smeal, President; Vacant, Director.*
General email, womencops@feminist.org

Web, http://womenandpolicing.com

Seeks to increase the number of women at all ranks of policing and law enforcement. (Headquarters in Beverly Hills, Calif.)

International Assn. of Chiefs of Police, *44 Canal Center Plaza, #200, Alexandria, VA 22314; (703) 836-6767. Fax, (703) 836-4543. Vince Talucci, Executive Director. Toll-free, (800) 843-4227.*
General email, information@theiacp.org

Web, www.theiacp.org, Twitter, @TheIACP and Facebook, www.facebook.com/TheIACP

Membership: foreign and U.S. police executives and administrators at federal, state, and local levels. Consults and conducts research on all aspects of police activity; conducts training programs and develops educational aids; conducts public education programs.

International Assn. of Chiefs of Police, *Advisory Committee for Patrol and Tactical Operations, 44 Canal Center Plaza, #200, Alexandria, VA 22314; (703) 836-6767. Sabrina Rhodes, Staff Liaison. Toll-free, (800) 843-4227.*
General email, committees@theiacp.org

Web, www.theiacp.org/workinggroup/Committee/patrol-and-tactical-operations-committee

Membership: foreign and U.S. police executives and administrators. Maintains liaison with civil defense and emergency service agencies in the United States and other nations; prepares guidelines for police cooperation with emergency and disaster relief agencies during emergencies.

National Organization of Black Law Enforcement Executives, *4609 Pinecrest Office Park Dr., Suite F, Alexandria, VA 22312-1442; (703) 658-1529. Fax, (703) 658-9479. Dwayne A. Crawford, Executive Director.*
Web, www.noblenational.org and Twitter, @noblenatl

Membership: African American police chiefs and senior law enforcement executives. Works to increase community involvement in the criminal justice system and to enhance the role of African Americans in law enforcement. Provides urban police departments with assistance in police operations, community relations, and devising strategies to sensitize the criminal justice system to the problems of the African American community.

National Sheriffs' Assn., *1450 Duke St., Alexandria, VA 22314-3490; (703) 836-7827. Fax, (703) 838-5349. Jonathan Thompson, Executive Director. Toll-free, (800) 424-7827.*
General email, nsamail@sheriffs.org

Web, www.sheriffs.org, Twitter, @NationalSheriff and Facebook, www.facebook.com/Nationalsheriffsassociation

Membership: sheriffs and other municipal, state, and federal law enforcement officers. Conducts research and training programs for members in law enforcement, court procedures, and corrections. Publishes *Sheriff* magazine and an e-newsletter.

Police Executive Research Forum, *1120 Connecticut Ave. N.W., #930, 20036; (202) 466-7820. Fax, (202) 466-7826. Chuck Wexler, Executive Director, (202) 454-8326. TTY, (202) 466-2670.*
General email, perf@policeforum.org

Web, www.policeforum.org

Membership: law enforcement executives. Conducts research on law enforcement issues and disseminates criminal justice and law enforcement information.

Police Foundation, *1201 Connecticut Ave. N.W., #200, 20036-2636; (202) 833-1460. Fax, (202) 659-9149. Jim Burch, President (Acting).*
General email, info@policefoundation.org

Web, www.policefoundation.org and Twitter, @PoliceFound

Research and education foundation that conducts studies to improve police procedures; provides technical assistance for innovative law enforcement strategies, including community-oriented policing.

LEGAL PROFESSIONS AND RESOURCES

General

▶**AGENCIES**

Executive Office for U.S. Attorneys *(Justice Dept.), 950 Pennsylvania Ave. N.W., #2242, 20530-0001; (202)*

514-2000. Fax, (202) 252-1415. James (Jim) A. Crowley IV, Director.

Web, www.justice.gov/usao/eousa

Provides the offices of U.S. attorneys with technical assistance and supervision in areas of legal counsel, personnel, and training. Publishes the *U.S. Attorneys' Manual* and *United States Attorneys' Bulletin*. Administers the Attorney General's Office of Legal Education, which conducts workshops and seminars to develop the litigation skills of the department's attorneys in criminal and civil trials. Develops and implements Justice Dept. procedures for collecting criminal fines.

Justice Dept. (DOJ), *Legal Policy (OLP),* 950 Pennsylvania Ave. N.W., #4234, 20530-0001; (202) 514-4601. Fax, (202) 514-2424. Beth A. Williams, Assistant Attorney General.

Web, www.justice.gov/olp

Works to improve the availability and quality of legal defense for vulnerable populations; seeks fair and just outcomes for those facing financial and other disadvantages effectively and efficiently. Works collaboratively with local, state, tribal, and federal participants to implement solutions.

Justice Dept. (DOJ), *Professional Responsibility (OPR),* 950 Pennsylvania Ave. N.W., #3266, 20530-0001; (202) 514-3365. Fax, (202) 514-5050. Corey Amundson, Counsel.

General email, opr.complaints@usdoj.gov

Web, www.justice.gov/opr

Receives and reviews allegations of misconduct by Justice Dept. attorneys; refers cases that warrant further review to appropriate investigative agency or unit; makes recommendations to the attorney general for action on certain misconduct cases.

Legal Services Corp., 3333 K St. N.W., 3rd Floor, 20007-3522; (202) 295-1500. Fax, (202) 337-6797. James J. Sandman, President, (202) 295-1555. Public reading room, (202) 295-1502.

General email, rauscherc@lsc.gov

Web, www.lsc.gov and Twitter, @lsctweets

Independent federal corporation established by Congress. Awards grants to local agencies that provide the poor with legal services. Library open to the public by appointment only.

▶NONGOVERNMENTAL

American Assn. for Justice, 777 6th St. N.W., #200, 20001; (202) 965-3500. Fax, (202) 342-5484. Linda Lipsen, Chief Executive Officer, ext. 8305. Toll-free, (800) 424-2725.

General email, help@justice.org

Web, www.justice.org, Twitter, @JusticeDotOrg and Facebook, www.facebook.com/JusticeDotOrg

Membership: attorneys, judges, law professors, and students. Interests include aspects of legal and legislative activity relating to the adversary system and trial by jury, victims' rights, property and casualty insurance, revisions of federal rules of evidence, criminal code, jurisdictions of courts, juries, and consumer law. (Formerly the Assn. of Trial Lawyers of America.)

American Bar Assn. (ABA), 1050 Connecticut Ave. N.W., #400, 20036; (202) 662-1000. Fax, (202) 662-1757. Robert (Bob) Carlson, President; Jack L. Rives, Executive Director. Information, (800) 285-2221. Library, (202) 662-1015.

Web, www.americanbar.org, Twitter, @abaesq and Facebook, www.facebook.com/AmericanBarAssociation

Membership: lawyers, law students, and individuals interested in law. Provides resources to law professionals, accredits law schools, and establishes ethical codes. Composed of the Governmental Affairs Office, Public Services Division, Government and Public Sector Lawyers Division, International Law and Practice Section, Criminal Justice Section, Taxation Section, Individual Rights and Responsibilities Section, Dispute Resolution Section, Administrative Law and Regulatory Practice Section, Rule of Law Initiative, and others. (Headquarters in Chicago, Ill.)

American Bar Assn. (ABA), *Commission on Disability Rights,* 1050 Connecticut Ave. N.W., #400, 20036; (202) 662-1570. Fax, (202) 442-3439. Amy L. Allbright, Director; Robert T. Gonzales, Chair.

General email, cdr@americanbar.org

Web, www.americanbar.org/groups/diversity/ disabilityrights, Twitter, @ABADisability and Facebook, www.facebook.com/ABA.CDR

Promotes the rule of law for persons with mental, physical, and sensory disabilities and their full and equal participation in the legal profession. Offers online resources, publications, and continuing education opportunities on disability law topics and engages in national initiatives to remove barriers to the education, employment, and advancement of lawyers with disabilities.

American Bar Assn. (ABA), *International Law,* 1050 Connecticut Ave. N.W., 20036; (202) 662-1660. Fax, (202) 662-1669. Christina Heid, Section Director, (202) 662-1034.

General email, intlaw@americanbar.org

Web, www.americanbar.org/groups/international_law and Twitter, @ABInternatl

Monitors and makes recommendations concerning developments in the practice of international law that affect ABA members and the public. Conducts programs, including International Legal Exchange, and produces publications covering the practice of international law.

American Bar Assn. (ABA), *International Legal Exchange Program (ILEX),* 1050 Connecticut Ave. N.W., #400, 20036; (202) 662-1660. Fax, (202) 662-1669. Jinny Choi, International Projects Manager, (202) 662-1675.

General email, intlex@staff.abanet.org

Web, www.americanbar.org/groups/international_law/ initiatives_awards/international_legal_exchange

Facilitates entry into the United States for foreign lawyers offered training in U.S. law firms. Serves as designated U.S. government overseer for the J-1 visa and accepts applications from foreign lawyers. Houses the International Legal Resource Center.

American Health Lawyers Assn., *1620 Eye St. N.W., 6th Floor, 20006-4010; (202) 833-1100. Fax, (202) 833-1105. David S. Cade, Chief Executive Officer, (202) 833-0777.*
General email, info@healthlawyers.org

Web, www.healthlawyers.org

Public interest email, publicinterest@healthlawyers.org

Membership: corporate, institutional, and government lawyers interested in the health field; law students; and health professionals. Serves as an information clearing-house on health law; sponsors health law educational programs and seminars.

American Immigration Lawyers Assn., *1331 G St. N.W., #300, 20005-3142; (202) 507-7600. Fax, (202) 783-7853. Benjamin Johnson, Executive Director.*
General email, membership@aila.org

Web, http://aila.org, Twitter, @ailanational and Facebook, www.facebook.com/AILANational

Association for lawyers interested in immigration law. Provides information and continuing education programs on immigration law and policy; offers workshops and conferences. Operates as advocate for a fair and just immigration law policy. Monitors legislation and regulations.

American Inns of Court Foundation, *225 Reinekers Lane, #770, Alexandria, VA 22314; (703) 684-3590. Brig. Gen. Malinda E. Dunn (USA, Ret.), Executive Director, ext. 102. Toll-free, (800) 233-3590.*
General email, info@innsofcourt.org

Web, http://home.innsofcourt.org, Twitter, @innsofcourt and Facebook, www.facebook.com/AmericanInnsofCourt

Promotes professionalism, ethics, civility, and legal skills of judges, lawyers, academicians, and law students in order to improve the quality and efficiency of the legal profession.

The Assn. of American Law Schools, *1614 20th St. N.W., 20009-1001; (202) 296-8851. Fax, (202) 296-8869. Judith Areen, Executive Director.*
General email, aals@aals.org

Web, www.aals.org and Twitter, @TheAALS

Membership: law schools, subject to approval. Membership criteria include high-quality academic programs, faculty, scholarship, and students; academic freedom; diversity of people and viewpoints; and emphasis on public service. Hosts meetings and workshops; publishes a directory of law teachers. Acts as advocate on behalf of legal education; monitors legislation and judicial decisions.

Assn. of Corporate Counsel, *1001 G St., N.W., #300W, 20001; (202) 293-4103. Fax, (202) 293-4701. Veta T. Richardson, President.*
Web, www.acc.com and Twitter, @ACCinhouse

Membership: practicing lawyers in corporate law departments, associations, and in legal departments of other private-sector organizations. Provides information on corporate law issues, including securities, health and safety, the environment, intellectual property, litigation, international legal affairs, pro bono work, and labor benefits. Monitors legislation and regulations, with primary focus on issues affecting in-house attorneys' ability to practice law. (Formerly American Corporate Counsel Assn.)

Assn. of Transportation Law Professionals, *P.O. Box 5407, Annapolis, MD 21403; (410) 268-1311. Fax, (410) 268-1322. Lauren Michalski, Executive Director.*
General email, info@atlp.org

Web, www.atlp.org

Membership: Transportation attorneys and company counsel, government officials, and industry practitioners. Provides members with continuing educational development in transportation law and practice.

Energy Bar Assn., *2000 M St. N.W., #715, 20036; (202) 223-5625. Fax, (202) 833-5596. Lisa A. Levine, Chief Executive Officer.*
General email, admin@eba-net.org

Web, www.eba-net.org

Membership: lawyers interested in all areas of energy law. Interests include administration of laws covering production, development, conservation, transmission, and economic regulation of energy.

Equal Employment Advisory Council, *1501 M St. N.W., #400, 20005; (202) 629-5650. Fax, (202) 629-5651. Joseph S. Lakis, President.*
General email, info@cwc.org

Web, www.eeac.org

Membership: principal equal employment officers and lawyers. Files amicus curiae (friend of the court) briefs; conducts research and provides information on equal employment law and policy. Monitors legislation and regulations.

Federal Bar Assn., *1220 N. Fillmore St., #444, Arlington, VA 22201; (571) 481-9100. Fax, (571) 481-9090. Stacey King, Executive Director.*
General email, fba@fedbar.org

Web, www.fedbar.org, Twitter, @federalbar and Facebook, www.facebook.com/FederalBar

Membership: attorneys employed by the federal government or practicing before federal courts or agencies. Concerns include professional ethics, legal education (primarily continuing education), and legal services.

Federal Circuit Bar Assn., *1620 Eye St. N.W., #801, 20006; (202) 466-3923. Fax, (202) 833-1061. James E. Brookshire, Executive Director, (202) 558-2421.*
General email, brookshire1@fedcirbar.org

Web, www.fedcirbar.org

Represents practitioners before the Court of Appeals for the Federal Circuit. Fosters discussion between different groups within the legal community; sponsors regional seminars; publishes a scholarly journal.

Hispanic National Bar Assn. (HNBA), *1020 19th St. N.W., #505, 20036; (202) 223-4777. Fax, (202) 503-3403. Alba Cruz-Hacker, Executive Director.*
General email, nationaloffice@hnba.com

Web, www.hnba.com and Twitter, @HNBANews

Membership: Hispanic American attorneys, judges, law professors, paralegals, and law students. Seeks to increase professional opportunities in law for Hispanic Americans and to increase Hispanic American representation in law schools. (Affiliated with National Hispanic Leadership Agenda and the American Bar Assn.)

Inter-American Bar Assn., *1889 F ST. N.W., #355, 20006; (202) 466-5944. Fax, (202) 466-5946.*
Ulises Montoya Alberti, Secretary General.
General email, iaba@iaba.org

Web, www.iaba.org and Twitter, @IABA_FIA

Membership: lawyers and bar associations in the Western Hemisphere with associate members in Europe. Works to promote uniformity of national and international laws; holds conferences; makes recommendations to national governments and organizations. Library open to the public by appointment only.

International Law Institute, *1055 Thomas Jefferson St. N.W., #M-100, 20007; (202) 247-6006. Fax, (202) 247-6010. Kim Phan, Executive Director.*
General email, info@ili.org

Web, www.ili.org

Performs scholarly research, offers training programs, and provides technical assistance in the areas of international law and economic development. Sponsors international conferences.

Lawyers for Civil Justice, *1530 Wilson Blvd., #1030, Arlington, VA 22209; (202) 429-0045. Fax, (202) 429-6982. Andrea B. Looney, Executive Director, (202) 429-0045.*
Web, www.lfcj.com and Twitter, @LCJReform

Membership: defense lawyers and corporate counsel. Interests include tort reform, litigation cost containment, and tort and product liability. Monitors legislation and regulations affecting civil justice reform.

National Assn. of Attorneys General, *1850 M St. N.W., 12th Floor, 20036; (202) 326-6000. Chris Toth, Executive Director; Marjorie Sharpe, Communications Director, (202) 326-6021. Press, (202) 326-6047.*
General email, feedback@naag.org

Web, www.naag.org and Twitter, @NatlAssnAttysGen

Membership: attorneys general of the states, territories, and commonwealths. Fosters interstate cooperation on legal and law enforcement issues, conducts policy research and analysis, and facilitates communication between members and all levels of government.

National Assn. of Bond Lawyers, *601 13th St. N.W., #800-S, 20005-3875; (202) 503-3300. Fax, (202) 637-0217. Linda H. Wyman, Chief Operating Officer, (202) 503-3300 ext. 3306.*
General email, nabl@nabl.org

Web, www.nabl.org and Twitter, @nabldc

Membership: state and municipal finance lawyers. Educates members and others on the law relating to state and municipal bonds and other obligations. Provides advice and comment at the federal, state, and local levels on legislation,

regulations, rulings, and court and administrative proceedings regarding public obligations.

National Assn. of College and University Attorneys, *1 Dupont Circle N.W., #620, 20036-1182; (202) 833-8390. Fax, (202) 296-8379. Kathleen Curry Santora, Chief Executive Officer, ext. 4.*
General email, nacua@nacua.org

Web, www.nacua.org and Twitter, @NACUAtweets

Provides information on legal developments affecting postsecondary education. Operates a clearinghouse through which in-house and external legal counselors are able to network with their counterparts on current legal problems.

National Assn. of Consumer Bankruptcy Attorneys, *2200 Pennsylvania Ave. N.W., 4th Floor, 20037; (800) 499-9040. Fax, (866) 408-9515. Maureen Thompson, Legislative Director; Dan LaBert, Executive Director.*
General email, admin@nacba.org

Web, www.nacba.org and Twitter, @NACBAorg

Acts as advocate on behalf of consumer debtors and their attorneys. Files amicus briefs on behalf of parties in the U.S. courts of appeal and Supreme Court, and provides educational programs and workshops for attorneys. Monitors legislation and regulations.

National Assn. of Criminal Defense Lawyers, *1660 L St. N.W., 12th Floor, 20036; (202) 872-8600. Fax, (202) 872-8690. Norman L. Reimer, Executive Director, (202) 465-7623.*
General email, assist@nacdl.org

Web, www.nacdl.org and Twitter, @NACDL

Volunteer bar association of criminal defense attorneys and their local, state, and international affiliates. Provides members with continuing education, a brief bank, an ethics hotline, and specialized assistance in such areas as forensic science. Offers free legal assistance to members threatened with sanctions. Interests include eliminating mandatory minimum sentencing, forensic lab reform, death penalty reform, protection of privacy rights, indigent defense reform, overcriminalization, and civil liberties. Monitors legislation and regulations.

National Bar Assn., *1816 12th St. N.W., 20009 (mailing address: P.O. Box 90500, Washington, DC 20090); (202) 842-3900. Fax, (202) 842-3901. Joseph Drayton, President.*
General email, communications@nationalbar.org

Web, www.nationalbar.org and Twitter, @nationalbar

Membership: primarily African-American attorneys, legal professionals, judges, and law students. Interests include legal education and improvement of the judicial process. Sponsors legal education seminars in all states that require continuing legal education for lawyers.

National Court Reporters Assn., *12030 Sunrise Valley Dr., #400, Reston, VA 20191; (703) 556-6272. Fax, (703) 391-0629. Laura Butler, Executive Manager, (703) 584-9032. Toll-free, (800) 272-6272.*
General email, msic@ncra.org

Web, www.ncra.org and Twitter, @NCRA

Membership organization that offers certification and continuing education for court reporting and captioning. Acts as a clearinghouse on technology and information for and about court reporters; certifies legal video specialists. Monitors legislation and regulations.

National District Attorneys Assn. (NDAA), *1400 Crystal Dr., #330, Arlington, VA 22202; (703) 549-9222. Fax, (703) 836-3195. Nelson O. Bunn, Executive Director, (703) 519-1666.*
Web, www.ndaa.org and Twitter, @ndaajustice

Membership: prosecutors. Sponsors conferences and workshops on such topics as criminal justice, district attorneys, the courts, child abuse, national traffic laws, community prosecution, violence against women, gun violence, and others; conducts research; provides information, training, and technical assistance to prosecutors; and analyzes policies related to improvements in criminal prosecution.

National Legal Aid and Defender Assn., *1901 Pennsylvania Ave. N.W., #500, 20006; (202) 452-0620. Fax, (202) 872-1031. Jo-Ann Wallace, President, ext. 206. General email, info@nlada.org*
Web, www.nlada.org and Twitter, @NLADA

Membership: national organizations and individuals providing indigent clients, including prisoners, with legal aid and defender services. Serves as a clearinghouse for member organizations; provides training and support services.

Women's Bar Assn., *2020 Pennsylvania Ave. N.W., #446, 20006; (202) 639-8880. Fax, (202) 639-8889. Carol Montoya, Executive Director. General email, admin@wbadc.org*
Web, www.wbadc.org and Twitter, @WBADC

Membership: women and men who are judges, attorneys in the public and private sectors, law students, and lawyers at home who remain professionally active. Promotes appointment of members to positions in the judiciary and legislative policies that foster the advancement of women.

Data and Research

▶**AGENCIES**

Community Oriented Policing Services (COPS) *(Justice Dept.), 145 N St. N.E., 20530 (mailing address: for overnight delivery, use zip code 20002); (202) 616-2888. Fax, (202) 616-2914. Phil Keith, Director. Press, (202) 514-9079. Response Center, (800) 421-6770. Toll Free, (800) 421-6770. General email, askCopsRC@usdoj.gov*
Web, https://cops.usdoj.gov and Twitter, @COPSOffice

Provides publications and other educational materials on a wide range of law enforcement concerns and community policing topics.

Justice Dept. (DOJ), *Elder Justice Initiative (EJI), 950 Pennsylvania Ave. N.W., 20530; Andy Mao, Coordinator. Eldercare locator helpline, (800) 677-1116. General email, elder.justice@usdoj.gov*
Web, www.justice.gov/elderjustice and Rural and tribal resources, www.justice.gov/elderjustice/rural-and-tribal-resources

Provides access to a database containing bibliographic information for thousands of scientific, legal, and general elder abuse and financial exploitation articles and reviews.

Justice Dept. (DOJ), *National Criminal Justice Reference Service (NCJRS), P.O. Box 6000, Rockville, MD 20849-6000; (800) 851-3420. Fax, (301) 240-5830. General email, responsecenter@ncjrs.gov*
Web, www.ncjrs.gov

Offers justice and drug-related information and resources to support research, policy, and program development. Curates the NCJRS Virtual Library.

Office of Justice Programs (OJP) *(Justice Dept.), Bureau of Justice Statistics (BJS), 810 7th St. N.W., 2nd Floor, 20531; (202) 307-0765. Fax, (202) 307-5846. Jeffrey H. Anderson, Director; Kara McCarthy, Public Affairs, (202) 307-1241. Toll-free, (800) 851-3420. General email, askbjs@usdoj.gov*
Web, www.bjs.gov and Twitter, @BJSgov

Collects, evaluates, publishes, and provides statistics on criminal justice. Data available from the National Criminal Justice Reference Service: P.O. Box 6000, Rockville, Md., 20849-6000; toll-free, (800) 851-3420; international callers, (301) 519-5500; TTY (877) 712-9279; and from the National Archive of Criminal Justice Data in Ann Arbor, Mich., (800) 999-0960.

Office of Justice Programs (OJP) *(Justice Dept.), National Institute of Justice (NIJ), 810 7th St. N.W., 7th Floor, 20531; (202) 307-0765. Fax, (202) 307-6394. David B. Muhlhausen, Director. Press, (202) 307-0703. General email, ojp.ocom.@usdoj.gov*
Web, www.nij.gov and Facebook, www.facebook.com/OJPNIJ

Conducts research on all aspects of criminal justice, including crime prevention, enforcement, adjudication, and corrections; evaluates programs; develops model programs using new techniques. Serves as an affiliated institute of the United Nations Crime Prevention and Criminal Justice Programme (UNCPCJ); studies transnational issues. Maintains the National Criminal Justice Reference Service, which provides information on criminal justice, including activities of the Office of National Drug Control Policy and law enforcement in Latin America: (800) 851-3420 or (301) 519-5500; Web, www.ncjrs.gov.

▶**CONGRESS**

For a listing of relevant congressional committees and subcommittees, please see pages 542–543 or the Appendix.

Library of Congress, *Law Library, James Madison Memorial Bldg., 101 Independence Ave. S.E., #LM 240,*

20540; (202) 707-5065. Fax, (202) 707-1820. Jane Sanchez, Law Librarian, (202) 707-9825. Reading room, (202) 707-5080. Reference, (202) 707-5079.
Web, www.loc.gov/law, Twitter, @LawLibCongress and Facebook, www.facebook.com/lawlibraryofcongress

Maintains collections of foreign, international, and comparative law texts organized jurisdictionally by country. Covers all legal systems, including common, civil, Roman, canon, religious, and ancient and medieval law. Services include a public reading room; a microtext facility, with readers and printers for microfilm and microfiche; and foreign law/rare book reading areas. Staff of legal specialists is competent in approximately forty languages; does not provide advice on legal matters.

▶**JUDICIARY**

Administrative Office of the U.S. Courts, 1 Columbus Circle N.E., 20544-0001; (202) 502-2600. James C. Duff, Director.
Web, www.uscourts.gov

Supervises all administrative matters of the federal court system, except the Supreme Court; prepares statistical data and reports on the business of the courts, including reports on juror utilization; caseloads of federal, public, and community defenders; and types of cases adjudicated.

Administrative Office of the U.S. Courts, Data and Analysis, 1 Columbus Circle N.E., #2-250, 20544; (202) 502-3900. Gary Yakimob, Chief. Public Affairs, (202) 502-2600.
Web, www.uscourts.gov

Compiles information and statistics from civil, criminal, appeals, and bankruptcy cases. Publishes statistical reports on court management; juror utilization; federal offenders; equal access to justice; the Financial Privacy Act; caseloads of federal, public, and community defenders; and types of cases adjudicated.

Supreme Court of the United States, Library, 1 1st St. N.E., 20543; (202) 479-3177. Fax, (202) 479-3477. Linda Maslow, Librarian.
Web, www.supremecourt.gov

Maintains collection of Supreme Court documents dating from the mid-1800s. Records, briefs, and depository documents available for public use.

▶**NONGOVERNMENTAL**

Federal Bar Assn., 1220 N. Fillmore St., #444, Arlington, VA 22201; (571) 481-9100. Fax, (571) 481-9090. Stacey King, Executive Director.
General email, fba@fedbar.org
Web, www.fedbar.org, Twitter, @federalbar and Facebook, www.facebook.com/FederalBar

Conducts research and programs in fields that include tax, environment, veterans health, intellectual property, Social Security, transportation, Native American, antitrust, immigration, and international law.

Justice Research and Statistics Assn., 1000 Vermont Ave., #450, 20005; (202) 842-9330. Fax, (202) 448-1723. Jeffrey Sedgwick, Executive Director.
General email, cjinfo@jrsa.org
Web, www.jrsa.org and Twitter, @JRSAinfo

Provides information on the collection, analysis, dissemination, and use of data concerning crime and criminal justice at the state level; serves as liaison between the Justice Dept. Bureau of Justice Statistics and the states; develops standards for states on the collection, analysis, and use of statistics. Offers courses in criminal justice and in research and evaluation methodologies in conjunction with its annual conference.

National Consumer Law Center, Washington Office, 1001 Connecticut Ave. N.W., #510, 20036-5528; (202) 452-6252. Fax, (202) 296-4062. Richard DuBois, Executive Director; Lauren Saunders, Associate Director, Washington Office, ext. 105.
General email, consumerlaw@nclc.org
Web, www.nclc.org and Twitter, @NCLC4consumers

Provides lawyers funded by the Legal Services Corp. with research and assistance; provides lawyers with training in consumer and energy law. (Headquarters in Boston, Mass.)

PUBLIC INTEREST LAW

General

▶**AGENCIES**

Justice Dept. (DOJ), 950 Pennsylvania Ave. N.W., #4400, 20530-0001; (202) 514-2001. Fax, (202) 307-6777. William Barr, Attorney General; Rod Rosenstein, Deputy Attorney General. Information and switchboard, (202) 514-2000. Library, (202) 514-3775. Public Affairs, (202) 514-2007. Public comments, (202) 353-1555.
General email, askdoj@usdoj.gov
Web, www.justice.gov and Twitter, @DOJATJ

Serves as counsel for the U.S. government. Represents the government in enforcing the law in the public interest. Plays key role in protecting against criminals and subversion, in ensuring healthy competition of business in U.S. free enterprise system, in safeguarding the consumer, and in enforcing drug, immigration, and naturalization laws. Plays a significant role in protecting citizens through effective law enforcement, crime prevention, crime detection, and prosecution and rehabilitation of offenders. Conducts all suits in the Supreme Court in which the United States is concerned. Represents the government in legal matters generally, furnishing legal advice and opinions to the president, the cabinet, and the heads of executive departments, as provided by law. Justice Dept. organization includes divisions on antitrust, civil law, civil rights, criminal law, environment and natural resources, and taxes, as well as the Bureau of Alcohol, Tobacco, Firearms, and Explosives; Drug Enforcement Administration; Executive Office for

Immigration Review; Federal Bureau of Investigation; Federal Bureau of Prisons; Foreign Claims Settlement Commission; Office of Justice Programs; U.S. Attorneys; U.S. Marshals Service; U.S. Parole Commission; and U.S. Trustees.

Legal Services Corp., *3333 K St. N.W., 3rd Floor, 20007-3522; (202) 295-1500. Fax, (202) 337-6797.*
James J. Sandman, President, (202) 295-1555. Public reading room, (202) 295-1502.
General email, rauscherc@lsc.gov

Web, www.lsc.gov and Twitter, @lsctweets

Independent federal corporation established by Congress. Awards grants to local agencies that provide the poor with legal services. Library open to the public by appointment only.

► **CONGRESS**

For a listing of relevant congressional committees and subcommittees, please see pages 542–543 or the Appendix.

► **NONGOVERNMENTAL**

Alliance for Justice, *11 Dupont Circle N.W., #500, 20036-1213; (202) 822-6070. Nan Aron, President.*
General email, alliance@afj.org

Web, www.afj.org, Twitter, @AFJustice and Facebook, www.facebook.com/AllianceforJustice

Membership: public interest lawyers and advocacy, environmental, civil rights, and consumer organizations. Promotes reform of the legal system to ensure access to the courts; monitors selection of federal judges; works to preserve the rights of nonprofit organizations to advocate on behalf of their constituents.

Appleseed, *1111 19th St. N.W., #200, 20034; (202) 347-7960. Fax, (202) 347-7961. Deirdre Flaherty, President.*
General email, appleseed@appleseednetwork.org

Web, www.appleseednetwork.org

Network of seventeen public interest justice centers in the United States and Mexico advocating reforms designed to provide greater access to economic opportunity, fair courts, criminal justice, housing, education, food, and accountable government.

Bazelon Center for Mental Health Law, *1101 15th St. N.W., #1212, 20005; (202) 467-5730. Fax, (202) 223-0409. Holly O'Donnell, Chief Executive Officer.*
General email, communications@bazelon.org

Web, www.bazelon.org and Twitter, @BazelonCenter

Public interest law firm. Works to establish and advance the legal rights of children and adults with mental disabilities and ensure their equal access to services and resources needed for full participation in community life. Provides technical support to lawyers and other advocates. Conducts test case litigation to defend rights of persons with mental disabilities. Conducts policy analysis, builds coalitions, issues advocacy alerts, publishes handbooks, and maintains advocacy resources online. Monitors legislation and regulations.

Becket Fund for Religious Liberty, *1200 New Hampshire Ave. N.W., #700, 20036; (202) 955-0095. Fax, (202) 955-0090. William Mumma, President; Montse Alvarado, Executive Director. Press, (202) 349-7226.*
Web, www.becketlaw.org and Twitter, @TheBecketFund

Public interest law firm that promotes freedom of expression for people of all faiths. Works to ensure that people and institutions of all faiths, domestically and abroad, are entitled to a voice in public affairs.

Brady Center to Prevent Gun Violence, *840 1st St. N.E., #400, 20002; (202) 370-8100. Fax, (202) 370-8102. Kris Brown, President. Media, (202) 370-8128.*
Web, www.bradycampaign.org and Twitter, @Bradybuzz

Public interest organization that works for gun control legislation and serves as an information clearinghouse. Monitors legislation and regulations.

Center for Individual Rights, *1100 Connecticut Ave. N.W., #625, 20036; (202) 833-8400. Fax, (202) 833-8410. Terence (Terry) J. Pell, President.*
General email, cir@cir-usa.org

Web, www.cir-usa.org

Public interest law firm that provides free representation to individuals who cannot afford adequate legal counsel in cases raising constitutional questions of individual rights. Interests include freedom of speech and religious expression, civil rights, and Congress's enumerated powers.

Center for Law and Education, *7011 8th St. N.W., 20012; (202) 986-3000. Fax, (202) 986-6648. Paul Weckstein, Co-Director, (202) 986-3000, ext. 101; Kathleen Boundy, Co-Director (located in Boston).*
General email, cle@cleweb.org

Web, www.cleweb.org

National advocacy organization committed to improving education of low-income students. Works with students, parents, their advocates, and members of the school community to implement and effectuate school and district level changes. Focuses on school and district reform and civil rights; uses multiforum advocacy (legislative, administrative advocacy, and litigation, as needed) on behalf of low-income individuals. (Headquarters in Boston, Mass.)

Center for Law and Social Policy (CLASP), *1200 18th St. N.W., #200, 20036; (202) 906-8000. Fax, (202) 842-2885. Olivia Golden, Executive Director.*
General email, aparker@clasp.org

Web, www.clasp.org and Twitter, @CLASP_DC

Public policy organization with expertise in national, state, and local policy affecting low-income Americans. Seeks to improve the economic security and educational and workforce prospects of low-income children, youth, adults, and families.

Center for Study of Responsive Law, *1530 P St. N.W., 20005 (mailing address: P.O. Box 19367, Washington, DC*

20036); (202) 387-8030. Fax, (202) 234-5176. John Richard, Administrator.
General email, info@csrl.org

Web, http://csrl.org

Consumer-interest clearinghouse that conducts research and holds conferences on public interest law. Interests include white-collar crime, the environment, occupational health and safety, the postal system, banking deregulation, insurance, freedom of information policy, and broadcasting.

Christian Legal Society, 8001 Braddock Rd., #302, Springfield, VA 22151; (703) 642-1070. David Nammo, Chief Executive Officer, ext. 501.
General email, clshq@clsnet.org

Web, www.christianlegalsociety.org and Twitter, @CLS_HQ

Membership: Christian lawyers, judges, paralegals, law professors, law students, and others. Interests include the defense of religious freedom and the provision of legal aid to the poor.

Civil Rights Clinic (Georgetown University), 600 New Jersey Ave. N.W., #532, 20001; (202) 661-6739. Fax, (202) 662-9634. Aderson Francois, Director.
General email, civilrightsclinic@georgetown.edu

Web, www.law.georgetown.edu/academics/academic-programs/clinical-programs/our-clinics/civil-rights-clinic/index.cfm

Public-interest law firm funded by Georgetown University Law Center. Studies federal administrative law and federal court litigation. Gives graduate fellows an opportunity to work on unique, large-scale projects. Interests include civil rights and voting rights.

Electronic Privacy Information Center (EPIC), 1718 Connecticut Ave. N.W., #200, 20009; (202) 483-1140. Fax, (202) 483-1248. Marc Rotenberg, President.
General email, info@epic.org

Web, www.epic.org and Twitter, @EPICprivacy

Public-interest research center. Conducts research and conferences on domestic and international civil liberties issues, including privacy, free speech, information access, computer security, and encryption; litigates cases. Monitors legislation and regulations. Operates an online bookstore.

Institute for Justice, 901 N. Glebe Rd., #900, Arlington, VA 22203; (703) 682-9320. Fax, (703) 682-9321. Scott G. Bullock, President.
General email, general@ij.org

Web, www.ij.org, Twitter, @IJ and Facebook, www.facebook.com/instituteforjustice

Sponsors seminars to train law students, grassroots activists, and practicing lawyers in applying advocacy strategies in public-interest litigation. Seeks to protect individuals from arbitrary government interference in free speech, private property rights, parental school choice, and economic liberty. Litigates cases.

Institute for Public Representation, 600 New Jersey Ave. N.W., #312, 20001; (202) 662-9535. Fax, (202) 662-9634. Hope Babcock, Co-Director; Vacant, Co-Director.
General email, gulcipr@law.georgetown.edu

Web, http://scholarship.law.georgetown.edu/ipr

Blog, instituteforpublicrepresentation.org

Public interest law firm funded by Georgetown University Law Center that studies federal administrative law and federal court litigation. Gives graduate fellows an opportunity to work on unique, large-scale projects. Interests include First Amendment and media law, environmental law, and general public interest matters.

Mexican American Legal Defense and Educational Fund, **National Public Policy,** 1016 16th St. N.W., #100, 20036; (202) 293-2828. Thomas A. Saenz, President; Andrea Senteno, Legislative Staff Attorney. General information, (213) 629-2512.
General email, info@maldef.org

Web, www.maldef.org/about/offices/washington_dc

Provides Mexican Americans and other Hispanics with high-impact litigation in the areas of employment, education, immigration rights, and voting rights. Monitors legislation and regulations. (Headquarters in Los Angeles, Calif.)

Migrant Legal Action Program, 1001 Connecticut Ave. N.W., #915, 20036-5524; (202) 775-7780. Fax, (202) 775-7784. Roger C. Rosenthal, Executive Director.
General email, mlap@mlap.org

Web, www.mlap.org and Facebook, www.facebook.com/MigrantLegalActionProgram

Provides both direct representation to farmworkers and technical assistance and support to health, education, and legal services programs for migrants. Monitors legislation and regulations.

National Consumer Law Center, **Washington Office,** 1001 Connecticut Ave. N.W., #510, 20036-5528; (202) 452-6252. Fax, (202) 296-4062. Richard DuBois, Executive Director; Lauren Saunders, Associate Director, Washington Office, ext. 105.
General email, consumerlaw@nclc.org

Web, www.nclc.org and Twitter, @NCLC4consumers

Provides lawyers funded by the Legal Services Corp. with research and assistance; researches problems of low-income consumers and develops alternative solutions. (Headquarters in Boston, Mass.)

National Health Law Program, **Washington Office,** 1444 Eye St. N.W., #1105, 20005; (202) 289-7661. Fax, (202) 289-7724. Elizabeth G. Taylor, Executive Director.
General email, nhelpdc@healthlaw.org

Web, www.healthlaw.org

Organization of lawyers representing the economically disadvantaged and minorities. Offers technical assistance, workshops, seminars, and training for health law specialists. Issues include health care reform, Medicaid, child and adolescent health, and disability and reproductive rights.

National Law Center on Homelessness and Poverty,
2000 M St. N.W., #210, 20036; (202) 638-2535. Fax, (202)
628-2737. Maria Foscarinis, Executive Director.
General email, email@nlchp.org

Web, www.nlchp.org and Twitter, @nichphomeless

Legal advocacy group that works to prevent and end homelessness through impact litigation, legislation, and education. Conducts research on homelessness issues. Acts as a clearinghouse for legal information and technical assistance. Monitors legislation and regulations.

National Legal Aid and Defender Assn., *1901*
Pennsylvania Ave. N.W., #500, 20006; (202) 452-0620.
Fax, (202) 872-1031. Jo-Ann Wallace, President, ext. 206.
General email, info@nlada.org

Web, www.nlada.org and Twitter, @NLADA

Membership: national organizations and individuals providing indigent clients, including prisoners, with legal aid and defender services. Serves as a clearinghouse for member organizations; provides training and support services.

Public Citizen, *Litigation Group, 1600 20th St. N.W.,*
20009-1001; (202) 588-1000. Allison Zieve, Director of
Litigation. Press, (202) 588-7741.
General email, litigation@citizen.org

Web, www.citizen.org/litigation

Conducts litigation for Public Citizen, a consumer advocacy group, in the areas of consumer rights, access to courts, health and safety, government and corporate accountability, and separation of powers; represents other individuals and nonprofit groups with similar interests.

Public Justice Foundation, *1620 L St. N.W., #630,*
20036; (202) 797-8600. Fax, (202) 232-7203.

F. Paul Bland Jr., Executive Director, ext. 223;
Arthur H. Bryant, Chair.
Web, www.publicjustice.net and Twitter, @Public_Justice

Membership: consumer activists, trial lawyers, public interest lawyers, and law professors and students. Litigates to influence corporate and government decisions about products or activities adversely affecting health or safety. Interests include toxic torts, environmental protection, civil rights and civil liberties, workers' safety, consumer protection, and the preservation of the civil justice system. (Formerly Trial Lawyers for Public Justice.)

Street Law, Inc., *1010 Wayne Ave., #870, Silver Spring,*
MD 20910; (301) 589-1130. Fax, (301) 589-1131.
Lee Arbetman, Executive Director.
General email, learnmore@streetlaw.org

Web, www.streetlaw.org and Twitter, @StreetLawInc

International educational organization that promotes public understanding of law, the legal system, democracy, and human rights. Provides curriculum materials, training, and technical assistance to secondary school systems, law schools, departments of corrections, juvenile justice systems, bar associations, community groups, and state, local, and foreign governments.

Washington Legal Foundation, *2009 Massachusetts Ave.*
N.W., 20036; (202) 588-0302. Fax, (202) 588-0371.
Constance Claffey Larcher, Chief Executive Officer.
General email, info@wlf.org

Web, www.wlf.org and Twitter, @WLF

Public interest law and policy center. Seeks a legal and regulatory environment supportive of free enterprise through litigation, education, and advocacy. Interests include free-market principles, limited government, and civil liberties.

14 Military Personnel and Veterans

GENERAL POLICY AND ANALYSIS

Basic Resources

▶ **AGENCIES**

Air Force Dept. *(Defense Dept.), Air Force Personnel Center (AFPC)*, 1040 Air Force Pentagon, #4D950, 20330-1040; (703) 695-6770. Maj. Gen. Brian T. Kelly, Commander. Public Affairs, (210) 565-2334.
General email, afpc.pa.task@us.af.mil
Web, www.afpc.af.mil, Twitter, @AFCareers and Facebook, www.facebook.com/AirForcePersonnelCenter

Implements and evaluates Air Force military and civilian personnel policies; serves as the principal adviser to the Air Force personnel director on civilian personnel matters and programs. (Headquarters in Tex.)

Air Force Dept. *(Defense Dept.), Manpower, Personnel, and Services*, 1040 Air Force Pentagon, #4E168, 20330-1040; (703) 697-6088. Lt. Gen. Brian T. Kelly, Deputy Chief of Staff.
Web, www.af.mil

Military office that coordinates military and civilian personnel policies of the Air Force Dept.

Air Force Dept. *(Defense Dept.), Manpower, Personnel, and Services, Military Force Management Policy*, 1400 W. Perimeter Rd., #4770, Joint Base Andrews, MD 20762; (703) 695-6770. Maj. Gen. Robert D. Labrutta, Director; Mark Engelbaum, Executive Director.
Web, www.afpc.af.mil

Establishes department management policies regarding the accession, assignment, evaluation, skills analysis and management, promotion, readiness, retraining, separation, and retirement of Air Force military and civilian personnel. Oversees total force contingency, mobilization, training management, and rated force policy. (Headquarters in Tex.)

Army Dept. *(Defense Dept.), G-1*, 300 Army Pentagon, #2E446, 20310-0300; (703) 697-8060. Fax, (703) 695-1631. Lt. Gen. Thomas C. Seamands (USA), Deputy Chief of Staff, G-1.
Web, www.armyg1.army.mil

Military office that coordinates military and civilian personnel policies of the Army Dept.

Defense Dept. (DoD), *Community and Public Outreach*, 1400 Defense Pentagon, 2E984, 20301-1400; (703) 693-2337. Fax, (703) 697-2577. Col. Paul Haverstick, Deputy Assistant Secretary (Acting). Toll-free (Military OneSource), (800) 342-9647. Press, (703) 697-5131. Public Affairs, (703) 571-3343.
Web, www.defense.gov

Administers Pentagon tours; hosts Joint Civilian Orientation Conference (JCOC), enabling senior American business, education, and community leaders to engage with military personnel; replies to inquiries from the general public; serves as primary liaison to national veterans and military organizations.

Defense Dept. (DoD), *Military Personnel Policy*, 4000 Defense Pentagon, #5A678, 20301-4000; (703) 571-0116. Fax, (703) 571-0120. Lernes Hebert (USNAF, Ret.), Deputy Assistant Secretary (Acting).
Web, https://prhome.defense.gov

Military office that coordinates military personnel policies of the Defense Dept. and reviews military personnel policies of the individual services.

Defense Dept. (DoD), *Personnel and Readiness*, 4000 Defense Pentagon, #3E986, 20301-4000; (703) 695-5254. Fax, (703) 571-5363. Vacant, Under Secretary. Military OneSource international, (800) 342-9647. Military OneSource international collect, (703) 253-7599. Military OneSource Toll-free, (800) 342-9647.
Web, http://prhome.defense.gov and Military OneSource, www.militaryonesource.mil

Coordinates civilian and military personnel policies of the Defense Dept. and reviews personnel policies of the individual services. Handles equal opportunity policies; serves as focal point for all readiness issues. Administers Military OneSource, a 24/7 toll-free information and referral telephone service for matters relating to education, financial aid, relocation, housing, child care, counseling, and other employee concerns. Military OneSource is available worldwide to military personnel and their families.

Defense Dept. (DoD), *Public Affairs*, The Pentagon, #2D961, 20301-1400; (703) 571-3343. Fax, (703) 697-3501. Charles Summers, Assistant to the Secretary of Defense for Public Affairs. Press, (703) 697-5131.
Web, www.defense.gov/news

Responds to public inquiries concerning Defense Dept. mission, activities, policies, and personnel.

Navy Dept. *(Defense Dept.), Military Personnel, Plans, and Policy*, 701 S. Courthouse Rd., Arlington, VA 22204; (703) 604-6155. Fax, (703) 604-5943. Rear Adm. Robert (Fritz) Burke (USN), Director.
Web, www.navy.mil

Military office that coordinates naval personnel policies, including promotions, professional development, and compensation, for officers and enlisted personnel.

Navy Dept. *(Defense Dept.), Naval Personnel*, 701 S. Courthouse Rd., Arlington, VA 22204; (703) 604-2863. Fax, (703) 604-5942. Vice Adm. Robert P. Burke (USN), Chief. Toll-free, (866) 827-5672. TTY, (866) 297-1971.
General email, UASKPC@navy.mil
Web, www.navy.mil/cno, Twitter, @usnpeople and Facebook, www.facebook.com/usnpeople

Responsible for planning and programming of manpower and personnel resources, budgeting for Navy personnel, developing systems to manage total force manpower and personnel resources, and assignment of Navy personnel. (Office based in Millington, Tenn.)

▶ **CONGRESS**

For a listing of relevant congressional committees and subcommittees, please see page 594 or the Appendix.

MILITARY PERSONNEL AND VETERANS RESOURCES IN CONGRESS

For a complete listing of congressional committees, including their full contact information, leadership, membership, and jurisdictions, please refer to the Appendix on pages 827–948.

HOUSE:

House Appropriations Committee, (202) 225-2771.
Web, appropriations.house.gov
  Subcommittee on Defense, (202) 225-2847.
  Subcommittee on Military Construction, Veterans Affairs, and Related Agencies, (202) 225-3047.
House Armed Services Committee, (202) 225-4151.
Web, armedservices.house.gov
  Subcommittee on Emerging Threats and Capabilities, (202) 226-2843.
  Subcommittee on Military Personnel, (202) 225-7560.
  Subcommittee on Oversight and Investigations, (202) 226-5048.
  Subcommittee on Readiness, (202) 226-8979.
  Subcommittee on Seapower and Protection Forces, (202) 226-2211.
  Subcommittee on Strategic Forces, (202) 225-1967.
  Subcommittee on Tactical Air and Land Forces, (202) 225-4440.
House Financial Services Committee, (202) 225-7502.
Web, financialservices.house.gov
  Subcommittee on Financial Institutions and Consumer Credit, (202) 225-7502.
  Subcommittee on Housing and Insurance, (202) 225-7502.
  Subcommittee on Oversight and Investigations, (202) 225-7502.
House Foreign Affairs Committee, (202) 225-5021.
Web, foreignaffairs.house.gov
House Oversight and Government Reform Committee, (202) 225-5074.
Web, oversight.house.gov
  Subcommittee on National Security, (202) 225-5074.
House Transportation and Infrastructure Committee, (202) 225-9446.
Web, transportation.house.gov
  Subcommittee on Coast Guard and Maritime Transportation, (202) 226-3552.

House Veterans' Affairs Committee, (202) 225-3527.
Web, veterans.house.gov
  Subcommittee on Disability Assistance and Memorial Affairs, (202) 225-9164.
  Subcommittee on Economic Opportunity, (202) 226-5491.
  Subcommittee on Health, (202) 225-9154.
  Subcommittee on Oversight and Investigations, (202) 225-3569.

SENATE:

Senate Appropriations Committee, (202) 224-7257.
Web, appropriations.senate.gov
  Subcommittee on Defense, (202) 224-6688.
  Subcommittee on Military Construction, Veterans Affairs, and Related Agencies, (202) 224-8224.
Senate Armed Services Committee, (202) 224-3871.
Web, armed-services.senate.gov
  Subcommittee on Airland, (202) 224-3871.
  Subcommittee on Cybersecurity, (202) 224-3871.
  Subcommittee on Emerging Threats and Capabilities, (202) 224-3871.
  Subcommittee on Personnel, (202) 224-3871.
  Subcommittee on Readiness and Management Support, (202) 224-3871.
  Subcommittee on Seapower, (202) 224-3871.
  Subcommittee on Strategic Forces, (202) 224-3871.
Senate Banking, Housing, and Urban Affairs Committee, (202) 224-7391.
Web, banking.senate.gov
  Subcommittee on Financial Institutions and Consumer Protection, (202) 224-7391.
Senate Foreign Relations Committee, (202) 224-4651.
Web, foreign.senate.gov
Senate Homeland Security and Governmental Affairs Committee, (202) 224-4751.
Web, hsgac.senate.gov
Senate Veterans' Affairs Committee, (202) 224-9126.
Web, veterans.senate.gov

► **NONGOVERNMENTAL**

Air Force Assn. (AFA), *1501 Lee Hwy., #400, Arlington, VA 22209-1198; (703) 247-5800. Fax, (703) 247-5853. Lt. Gen. Bruce Wright (USAF, Ret.), President. Press, (703) 247-5850. Toll-free, (800) 727-3337.*
General email, membership@afa.org
Web, www.afa.org, Twitter, @AirForceAssoc and Facebook, www.facebook.com/AirForceAssociation

Membership: civilians and active duty, reserve, retired, and cadet personnel of the Air Force. Informs members and the public of developments in the aerospace field. Monitors legislation and Defense Dept. policies. Library on aviation history open to the public by appointment.

Air Force Sergeants Assn. (AFSA), *5211 Auth Rd., Suitland, MD 20746; (301) 899-3500. Fax, (301) 899-8136. Keith A. Reed, Executive Officer. Toll-free, (800) 638-0594.*

General email, staff@hqafsa.org

Web, www.hqafsa.org and Twitter, @hqafsa.org

Membership: active duty, reserve, National Guard, and retired enlisted Air Force personnel. Monitors and advocates legislation and policies that promote quality of life benefits for its members. Offers scholarships to dependent children of enlisted Air Force members.

Noncommissioned Officers Assn., *National Capital Office,* P.O. Box 3085, Oakton, VA 22124; (703) 549-0311. Fax, (703) 549-0245. Vincent W. Patton III, President; Jon Ostrowski, Executive Director for Government Affairs. Toll-free, (800) 662-2620.

General email, tkish@ncoadc.org

Web, www.ncoausa.org

Congressionally chartered fraternal organization of active duty, reserve, guard, and retired enlisted military personnel. Sponsors job fairs to assist members in finding employment. Monitors legislation and regulations. (Headquarters in Selma, Tex.)

U.S. Army Warrant Officers Assn., *462 Herndon Pkwy., #207,* Herndon, VA 20170-5235; (703) 742-7727. Fax, (703) 742-7728. CWO John (Jack) DuTeil (USA, Ret.), Executive Director. Toll-free, (800) 587-2962.

General email, usawoaed@verizon.net

Web, http://usawoa.org

Membership: active duty, guard, reserve, and retired and former warrant officers. Monitors and makes recommendations to Defense Dept., Army Dept., and Congress on policies and programs affecting Army warrant officers and their families. Provides professional development programs for members.

United Service Organizations (USO), *2111 Wilson Blvd., #1200,* Arlington, VA 22201-7677 (mailing address: P.O. Box 96860, Washington, DC 20077); (703) 908-6400. Fax, (703) 908-6402. J.D. Crouch II, President. Toll-free, (888) 484-3876.

Web, www.uso.org and Twitter, @the_USO

Voluntary civilian organization chartered by Congress. Provides military personnel and their families in the United States and overseas with social, educational, and recreational programs.

DEFENSE PERSONNEL

Chaplains

▶**AGENCIES**

Air Force Dept. *(Defense Dept.), Chief of Chaplains,* 1380 Air Force Pentagon, 20330; (571) 256-7729. Fax, (571) 256-7642. Maj. Gen. Steven A. Schiacki, Chief of Chaplains. General email, usaf.pentagon.af.hc.mbx.workflow@mail.mil

Web, www.airforce.com/careers/specialty-careers/chaplain, Twitter, @AirForceChaplainCorps and Facebook, www.facebook.com/AirForceChaplainCorps

Oversees chaplains and religious services within the Air Force; maintains liaison with religious denominations.

Army Dept. *(Defense Dept.), Chief of Chaplains,* 2700 Army Pentagon, #3E524, 20310-2700; (703) 695-1133. Fax, (703) 695-9834. Maj. Gen. Paul Hurley (USA), Chief of Chaplains.

Web, www.army.mil/chaplaincorpsnet

Oversees chaplains and religious services within the Army; maintains liaison with religious denominations.

Defense Dept. (DOD), *Armed Forces Chaplains Board,* OUSD (P&R) MPP-AFCB, 4000 Defense Pentagon, #2E341, 20301-4000; (703) 697-9015. Rear Adm. Margaret Kibben (USN), Chair; Col. Jay S. Johns (USNG), Executive Director.

General email, osd.afcb5120@mail.mil

Web, http://prhome.defense.gov/M-RA/MPP/AFCB

Membership: chiefs and deputy chiefs of chaplains of the armed services; works to coordinate religious policies and services among the military branches.

Marine Corps *(Defense Dept.), Chaplain,* 3000 Navy Pentagon, 20350; (703) 614-9280. Fax, (703) 695-3431. Rear Adm. Gregory N. Todd (USN), Chaplain.

Web, www.hqmc.marines.mil/Agencies/HeadquartersandServiceBattalion/chaplainoffice.aspx

Oversees chaplains and religious services within the Marine Corps; maintains liaison with religious denominations.

National Guard Bureau *(Defense Dept.), Chaplain Services,* 111 S. George Mason Dr., Arlington, VA 22204; (703) 607-8657. Fax, (703) 607-5295. Brig. Gen Kenneth (Ed) Brandt (ARNG), Director.

General email, ng.ncr.arng.mbx.office-of-the-chaplain@mail.mil

Web, www.nationalguard.mil

Represents the Chief National Guard Bureau on all aspects of the chaplains' mission. Directs and oversees the activities and policies of the National Guard Chaplain Services. Oversees chaplains and religious services within the National Guard; maintains liaison with religious denominations.

Navy Dept. *(Defense Dept.), Chief of Chaplains,* 2000 Navy Pentagon, #5E270, 20350-1000; (703) 614-4043. Rear Adm. Brent W. Scott (USN), Chief.

Web, www.navy.mil/local/crb, www.navy.mil/local/chaplaincorps, Twitter, @NavyChaplains and Facebook, www.facebook.com/ChiefofNavyChaplains

Oversees chaplains and religious services within the Navy; maintains liaison with religious denominations.

U.S. Coast Guard (USCG) *(Homeland Security Dept.), Chaplain,* CG-00A, 2703 Martin Luther King Jr. Ave. S.E., MS 7000, 20593-7000; (202) 372-4434. Fax, (202) 372-8305. Capt. Thomas J. Walcott, Chaplain.

General email, HQS-SMB-CG-00A-ChaplainOffice@uscg.mil

Web, www.uscg.mil/Leadership/Senior-Leadership/Chaplain-of-the-Coast-Guard/

Oversees chaplains and religious services within the Coast Guard; maintains liaison with religious denominations.

▶NONGOVERNMENTAL

Chaplain Alliance for Religious Liberty, P.O. Box 151353, Alexandria, VA 22315; (571) 293-2427. Fax, (910) 221-2226. Col. Phil Wright (USA, Ret.), Executive Director; Capt. Craig Muehler (USN, Ret.), Chair.
General email, info@chaplainalliance.org

Web, http://chaplainalliance.org

Membership: military chaplains and others who support orthodox Christian doctrines. Seeks to ensure that all chaplains and those they serve may exercise their religious liberties without fear of reprisal. Interests include the conflict between official protection for gays in the military and orthodox Christian teachings. Issues press releases; grants media interviews; monitors legislation and regulations.

Military Chaplains Assn. of the United States of America, 5541 Lee Hwy., Arlington, VA 22207-7056 (mailing address: P.O. Box 7056, Arlington, VA 22207-7056); (703) 533-5890. Maj. Gen. Razz Waff (USA, Ret.), Executive Director; Stephen Stott, Administrative Director.
General email, chaplains@mca-usa.org

Web, www.mca-usa.org

Membership: chaplains of all faiths in all branches of the armed services and chaplains of veterans affairs and civil air patrol. Provides training opportunities for chaplains and a referral service concerning chaplains and chaplaincy.

National Conference on Ministry to the Armed Forces, P.O. Box 7572, Arlington, VA 22207-9998; (703) 608-2100. Capt. John (Jack) H. Lea III (CHC USN, Ret.), Executive Director.
General email, info@ncmaf.com

Web, www.ncmaf.net and Twitter, @NCMAForg

Connects member faith groups and religious diversity with the armed forces and Veterans Affairs Dept. chaplaincies.

National Conference on Ministry to the Armed Forces, *Endorsers Conference for Veterans Affairs Chaplaincy,* P.O. Box 7572, Arlington, VA 22207-9998; (703) 608-2100. Sarah Lammert, Chair.
General email, info@ncmaf.com

Web, www.ncmaf.net and Twitter, @NCMAForg

Endorses clergy-persons for service as chaplains to VA hospitals. Liaises between the American religious community and the Veterans Affairs Dept.

Civilian Employees

▶AGENCIES

Army Dept. *(Defense Dept.), Civilian Personnel,* 300 Army Pentagon, #2D484, 20310-0300; (703) 614-8143. Michael Reheuser, Assistant G-1 for Civilian Personnel.
Web, www.asamra.army.mil/org_cslmo.html

Develops and reviews Army civilian personnel policies and advises the Army leadership on civilian personnel matters.

Army Dept. *(Defense Dept.), Diversity and Leadership,* 111 Army Pentagon, #2A332, 20310-0111; (703) 614-5332. Fax, (703) 614-5279. Warren S. Whitlock, Deputy Assistant Secretary.
Web, www.asamra.army.mil/org_diversity.cfm

Civilian office that administers equal employment opportunity and civil rights programs and policies for civilian employees of the Army.

Defense Dept. (DoD), *Employment and Compensation,* 4800 Mark Center Dr., #06F15, SCTP Division, Alexandria, VA 22350-1100; (703) 882-5196. Hong Miller, Director.
Web, www.dcpas.osd.mil/EC

Manages workforce restructuring programs for Defense Dept. civilians, including downsizing, placement, voluntary early retirement, and transition assistance programs.

Marine Corps *(Defense Dept.), Human Resources and Organizational Management,* Code ARH, 3000 Marine Corps Pentagon, #2C253, 20350-3000; Mann Hall, 2004 Barnett Ave., Quantico, VA 22134; (703) 614-8371. William I. Whaley, Director. Phone (Quantico), (703) 784-2049.
General email, hromdir@usmc.mil

Web, www.hqmc.marines.mil/hrom/unit-home/HRONSFArlingtonOffice

Develops and implements personnel and equal employment opportunity programs for civilian employees of the Marine Corps headquarters.

Navy Dept. *(Defense Dept.), Civilian Human Resources,* 614 Sicard St. S.E., #100, 20374-5072; (703) 695-2633. Paige Hinkle-Bowles, Deputy Assistant Secretary. Toll-free, (800) 378-4559.
General email, donhrfaq@navy.mil

Web, www.secnav.navy.mil/donhr/Pages/default.aspx and Facebook, www.facebook.com/NavyOCHR

Civilian office that develops and reviews Navy and Marine Corps civilian personnel and equal opportunity programs and policies.

U.S. Coast Guard (USCG) *(Homeland Security Dept.), Human Resources Directorate,* CG-1, 2703 Martin Luther King Jr. Ave. S.E., MS 7907, 20593-7907; (202) 475-5002. Rear Adm. William G. Kelly, Assistant Commandant.
Web, www.uscg.mil/hr

Responsible for hiring, recruiting, and training all military and nonmilitary Coast Guard personnel. Administers employee benefits.

Equal Opportunity

►AGENCIES

Air Force Dept. *(Defense Dept.), Equal Opportunity (EO),* 1602 California Ave., #217, Joint Base Andrews, MD 20762; (240) 612-4357. Cyrus A. Salazar, Director. Affirmative employment program, (240) 612-1365. Disability and reasonable accommodation, (240) 612-4006. Discrimination and sexual harrasment hotline, (888) 231-4058.
General email, audie.k.sanders.civ@mail.mil
Web, www.af.mil/Equal-Opportunity

Office that develops and administers Air Force equal opportunity programs and policies for civilians and military personnel.

Army Dept. *(Defense Dept.), Diversity and Leadership,* 111 Army Pentagon, #2A332, 20310-0111; (703) 614-5332. Fax, (703) 614-5279. Warren S. Whitlock, Deputy Assistant Secretary.
Web, www.asamra.army.mil/org_diversity.cfm

Develops policy and conducts program reviews for the Dept. of Army Civilian Equal Employment Opportunity and Affirmative Employment Programs.

Civil Rights Division *(Justice Dept.), Employment Litigation (ELS),* 601 D St. N.W., #4040, 20579; (202) 514-3831. Fax, (202) 514-1005. Delora L. Kennebrew, Chief. Library, (202) 514-3775. TTY, (202) 514-6780.
Web, www.justice.gov/crt/employment-litigation-section

Enforces the Uniform Services Employment and Reemployment Rights Act, which prohibits employers from discriminating or retaliating against an employee due to past, current, or future military obligation.

Defense Dept. (DoD), *Defense Advisory Committee on Women in the Services,* 4800 Mark Center Dr., #04J25-01, Alexandria, VA 22350-9000; (703) 697-2122. Fax, (703) 614-6233. Col. Toya Davis (USA), Military Director.
General email, osd.pentagon.ousd-p-r.mbx.dacowits@mail.mil
Web, http://dacowits.defense.gov

Provides the DoD with advice and recommendations on matters and policies relating to the recruitment and retention, treatment, employment, integration, and well-being of highly qualified professional women in the armed forces.

Defense Dept. (DoD), *Diversity Management and Equal Opportunity,* 4000 Defense Pentagon, #5D641, 20301-4000; (703) 571-9321. Fax, (703) 571-9338.
F. Michael Sena, Director (Acting).
Web, http://diversity.defense.gov

Formulates equal employment opportunity policy for the Defense Dept.

Marine Corps *(Defense Dept.), Equal Opportunity and Diversity Management,* MRA (MPE), 3280 Russell Rd., 4th Floor, Quantico, VA 22134-5103; (703) 784-9372. (703) 432-2472. Fax, (703) 784-9814. Alfrita Jones, Deputy.
Web, www.marines.mil/special-staff/equal-opportunity-adviser

Military office that develops, monitors, and administers Marine Corps equal opportunity and diversity programs.

Navy Dept. *(Defense Dept.), Civilian Human Resources,* 614 Sicard St. S.E., #100, 20374-5072; (703) 695-2633. Paige Hinkle-Bowles, Deputy Assistant Secretary. Toll-free, (800) 378-4559.
General email, donhrfaq@navy.mil
Web, www.secnav.navy.mil/donhr/Pages/default.aspx and Facebook, www.facebook.com/NavyOCHR

Civilian office that develops and reviews Navy and Marine Corps civilian personnel and equal opportunity programs and policies.

Navy Dept. *(Defense Dept.), Diversity and Inclusion,* 701 S. Courthouse Rd., #3R180, Arlington, VA 22204; (703) 604-5004. Fax, (703) 604-5943. Capt. Candace Eckert (USN), Special Assistant to Chief of Naval Personnel; Jessica Milam, Director of Women's Policy.
Web, www.navy.com/who-we-are/diversity

Military office that develops and administers Navy diversity programs and policies.

U.S. Coast Guard (USCG) *(Homeland Security Dept.), Civil Rights Directorate,* Commandant, CG-00H, 2703 Martin Luther King Jr. Ave. S.E., MS 7000, 20593-7000; (202) 372-4500. Terri A. Dickerson, Director.
General email, OCR@uscg.mil
Web, www.uscg.mil/Resources/Civil-Rights/

Administers equal opportunity regulations and programs for Coast Guard military and civilian personnel.

►NONGOVERNMENTAL

Human Rights Campaign (HRC), 1640 Rhode Island Ave. N.W., 20036-3278; (202) 216-1500. Fax, (202) 347-5323. Chad Griffin, President. Toll-free, (800) 777-4723. TTY, (202) 216-1572.
General email, hrc@hrc.org
Web, www.hrc.org, Twitter, @HRC and Facebook, www.facebook.com/humanrightscampaign

Promotes legislation affirming the rights of lesbian, gay, bisexual, and transgender people. Focus includes discrimination in the military.

Minerva Center, 20 Granada Rd., Pasadena, MD 21122-2708; (410) 437-5379. Linda Grant DePauw, Director.
General email, lgdepauw@gmail.com

Encourages the study of women in war and women and the military. Focus includes current U.S. servicewomen, women veterans, women in war and the military abroad, and the preservation of artifacts, oral history, and first-hand accounts of women's experience in military service.

Family Services

▶AGENCIES

Air Force Dept. *(Defense Dept.), Military and Family Support Center,* 1191 Menoher Dr., Joint Base Andrews, MD 20762; (301) 981-7087. Fax, (301) 981-9215. *Rose Anderson, Chief.*
Web, www.andrewsfss.com

Military policy office that monitors and reviews services provided to Air Force families and civilian employees with family concerns at Joint Base Andrews; oversees Airmen and Family Readiness Centers.

Defense Dept. (DoD), *Education Activity,* 4800 Mark Center Dr., Alexandria, VA 22350-1400; (571) 372-0590. Fax, (571) 372-5829. *Thomas M. Brady, Director.*
General email, dodea.director@hq.dodea.edu
Web, www.dodea.edu

Civilian office that maintains school system for dependents of all military personnel and eligible civilians in the United States and abroad. Develops uniform curriculum and educational standards; monitors student performance and school accreditation.

Defense Dept. (DoD), *Resources and Oversight,* 4000 Defense Pentagon, #2E319, 20301-4000; (703) 571-2373. *Carolee Van Horn, Director.*
Web, www.defense.gov

Coordinates policies related to quality of life of military personnel and their families.

Marine Corps *(Defense Dept.), Marine and Family Programs,* M and RA (MF), 3280 Russell Rd., Quantico, VA 22134-5103; (703) 784-9501. Fax, (703) 432-9269. *Marie C. Balocki, Director.*
Web, www.usmc-mccs.org

Sponsors family service centers located on major Marine Corps installations. Oversees the administration of policies affecting the quality of life of Marine Corps military families. Administers relocation assistance programs.

Navy Dept. *(Defense Dept.), Personnel Readiness and Community Support,* 701 S. Courthouse Rd., Arlington, VA 22204; (703) 604-5045. *James N. Stewart, Under Secretary for Personnel and Readiness; Jim Coffman, Chief Information Officer.*
Web, www.npc.navy.mil

Acts as liaison between D.C. area and Navy quality of life programs located in Tenn., which provide naval personnel and families being sent overseas with information and support; addresses problems of abuse and sexual assault within families; helps Navy spouses find employment; facilitates communication between Navy families and Navy officials; and assists in relocating Navy families during transition from military to civilian life.

U.S. Coast Guard (USCG) *(Homeland Security Dept.), Health, Safety, and Work-Life,* CG-11, 2703 Martin Luther King Jr. Ave. S.E., 20593; (202) 475-5130. Fax, (202) 475-5906. *Rear Adm. Erica G. Schwartz, Director.*

General email, germaine.y.jefferson@uscg.mil
Web, www.dcms.uscg.mil/Our-Organization/Assistant-Commandant-for-Human-Resources-CG-1/Health-Safety-and-Work-Life-CG-11/

Oversees all health, safety, and work-life aspects of the Coast Guard, including individual and family support programs.

▶CONGRESS

For a listing of relevant congressional committees and subcommittees, please see page 594 or the Appendix.

▶NONGOVERNMENTAL

Air Force Aid Society, 1550 Crystal Dr., #809, Arlington, VA 22202; (703) 972-2650. *Lt. Gen. John D. Hopper Jr. (USAF, Ret.), Chief Executive Officer.*
General email, afas@afas-hq.org
Web, www.afas.org, Twitter, @AFASHQ
Emergency assistance email, ea@afas-hq.org

Membership: Air Force active duty, reserve, and retired military personnel and their dependents. Provides active duty and retired Air Force military personnel with personal emergency loans for basic needs, travel, or dependents' health expenses; assists families of active duty, deceased, or retired Air Force personnel with postsecondary education grants.

American Red Cross, *Service to the Armed Forces, Military Families,* 431 18th St. N.W., 20006; (202) 303-5000, ext. 2. Fax, (202) 303-0216. *Koby L. Langley, Senior Vice President. Emergency communication services,* (877) 272-7337.
Web, www.redcross.org/about-us/our-work/military-families.html

Provides emergency services for active duty armed forces personnel and their families, including verified communications, financial assistance, information and referral, and counseling. Mandated by Congress to contact military personnel in family emergencies; provides military personnel with verification of family situations for emergency leave applications.

Armed Forces Hostess Assn., 6604 Army Pentagon, #1E541, Arlington, VA 20310; (703) 614-0350; (703) 614-0485. Fax, (703) 697-5542. *Elaine Freeman, President.*
General email, usarmy.pentagon.hqda-sptsvcs.mbx.afha@mail.mil
Web, https://sswafha.hqda.pentagon.mil

Volunteer office staffed by retirees and spouses of military personnel of all armed services. Serves as an information clearinghouse for military and civilian Defense Dept. families; maintains information on military bases in the United States and abroad; issues information handbook for families in the Washington area.

Army Distaff Foundation (Knollwood), 6200 Oregon Ave. N.W., 20015-1543; (202) 541-0492. Fax, (202) 364-2856. *Maj. Gen. Timothy P. McHale (USA, Ret.), Chief Executive*

Officer; Col. Paul W. Bricker (USA, Ret.), Chief Operating Officer. Admission, (202) 541-0149. Information, (800) 541-4255.
General email, dschrag@armydistaff.org
Web, www.armydistaff.org

Nonprofit continuing care retirement community for career military officers and their families. Provides retirement housing and health care services.

Army Emergency Relief, 2530 Crystal Dr., #13161, Alexandria, VA 22202; (703) 428-0000.
Lt. Gen. Raymond V. Mason (USA, Ret.), Executive Director. Toll-free, (866) 878-6372.
General email, aer@aerhq.org
Web, www.aerhq.org, Twitter, @aerhq and Facebook, www.facebook.com/AERHQ

Provides emergency financial assistance to retirees and to soldiers and family members of the U.S. Army, Army Reserves, and National Guard who are on extended active duty; provides scholarships to further the education of service members' spouses and dependents.

EX-POSE: Ex-Partners of Servicemembers for Equality, P.O. Box 11191, Alexandria, VA 22312-0191; (703) 941-5844. Fax, (703) 212-6951. Sue Arroyo, Office Staff; Janice Stucki, Office Staff.
General email, expose1980@gmail.com
Web, www.ex-pose.org

Membership: military members, retirees, current/former spouses and their children. Educates military couples going through divorce. Provides explanation of possible legal interests and legal entitlements depending on the length of marriage. Open Tuesday and Wednesday, 10:00 a.m–3:00 p.m.

Fisher House Foundation, 12300 Twinbrook Pkwy., #410, Rockville, MD 20852; (301) 294-8560. Fax, (301) 294-8562. David A. Coker, President. Toll-free, (888) 294-8560.
General email, info@fisherhouse.org
Web, www.fisherhouse.org, Twitter, @FisherHouseFdtn and Facebook, www.facebook.com/FisherHouse

Builds new houses on the grounds of major military and VA hospitals to enable families of hospitalized service members to stay within walking distance. Donates the Fisher Houses to the U.S. government. Administers the Hero Miles Program, which uses donated frequent flier miles to purchase airline tickets for hospitalized service members and their families. Provides scholarships for military children.

Freedom Alliance, 22570 Markey Court, #240, Dulles, VA 20166; (703) 444-7940. Fax, (703) 444-9893.
Tom Kilgannon, President. Toll-free, (800) 475-6620.
General email, info@freedomalliance.org
Web, www.freedomalliance.org,
Twitter, @FreedomAlliance and Facebook, www.facebook.com/FreedomAlliance

Promotes strong national defense and honors military service. Awards monetary grants to wounded troops; assists soldiers and their families with housing and travel expenses; provides active duty troops with meals, clothing, entertainment, and other comforts. Provides college scholarships to children of those killed or permanently disabled in an operations mission or training accident.

Marine Corps League, 3619 Jefferson Davis Hwy., #115, Stafford, VA 22554 (mailing address: P.O. Box 3070, Merrifield, VA 22116); (703) 207-9588. Fax, (703) 207-0047. Robert J. Borka, Chief Operating Officer.
Web, www.mclnational.org and Twitter, @MCL_HQ

Membership: active duty, retired, and reserve Marine Corps groups. Promotes the interests of the Marine Corps and works to preserve its traditions. Administers programs related to veteran homelessness, injured veterans, and youth programs; founded and runs Toys For Tots. Monitors legislation and regulations.

National Military Family Assn., 3601 Eisenhower Ave., #425, Alexandria, VA 22304; (703) 931-6632. Fax, (703) 931-4600. Gail McGinn, Chair; Joyce Raezer, Executive Director.
General email, info@militaryfamily.org
Web, www.militaryfamily.org

Membership: active duty and retired military, National Guard, and reserve personnel of all U.S. uniformed services, civilian personnel, families, and other interested individuals. Works to improve the quality of life for military families.

Naval Services FamilyLine, 1043 Harwood St. S.E., #100, Bldg. 154, Washington Navy Yard, DC 20374-5067; (202) 433-2333. Fax, (202) 433-4622. Leanna McCollum, Chair. Toll-free, (877) 673-7773.
General email, info@nsfamilyline.org
Web, www.nsfamilyline.org, Facebook, www.facebook.com/nsfamilyline and Twitter, @nsfamilyline

Offers support services to spouses of Navy personnel; disseminates information on all aspects of military life; fosters sense of community among sea service personnel and their families.

Navy–Marine Corps Relief Society, 875 N. Randolph St., #225, Arlington, VA 22203-1977; (703) 696-4904. Adm. Charles (Steve) S. Abbot (USN, Ret.), President. Toll-free, (800) 654-8364.
General email, communications@nmcrs.org
Web, www.nmcrs.org and Facebook, www.facebook.com/NMCRS

Assists active duty and retired Navy and Marine Corps personnel and their families in times of need. Disburses interest-free loans and grants. Provides educational scholarships and loans; visiting nurse services; and other services, including combat casualty assistance, thrift shops, budget counseling, and volunteer training.

Our Military Kids, Inc., 6861 Elm St., #2-A, McLean, VA 22101; (703) 734-6654. Fax, (703) 734-6503. Rod Clapper, Executive Director. Toll-free, (866) 691-6654.
General email, omkinquiry@ourmilitarykids.org
Web, www.ourmilitarykids.org

Provides grants for extracurricular activities for school-aged children of deployed and severely injured soldiers, including Reserve and National Guard military personnel.

Financial Services

▶AGENCIES

Air Force Dept. *(Defense Dept.), Financial Management and Comptroller (SAF/FM),* 1130 Air Force Pentagon, #4E978, 20330-1130; (703) 697-1974. John P. Roth, Assistant Secretary; Maj. Jason L. Coleman, Senior Military Assistant.
General email, usaf.pentagon.saf-fm.mbx.saf-fm-workflow@mail.mil
Web, www.saffm.hq.af.mil, Twitter, @USAFComptroller and Facebook, www.facebook.com/USAFComptroller

Provides financial management and analysis to the secretary of the Air Force; directs program and budget development; oversees acquisition and operational cost analysis. Provides resources, financial services, and decision support to deliver air, space, and cyber capabilities to the nation.

Defense Dept. (DoD), *Accounting and Finance Policy Analysis,* 1100 Defense Pentagon, #3D150, 20301-1100; (703) 571-1396. Kim Laurunce, Director.
Web, www.defense.gov

Develops accounting policy for the Defense Dept. federal management regulation.

▶CONGRESS

For a listing of relevant congressional committees and subcommittees, please see page 594 or the Appendix.

▶NONGOVERNMENTAL

Armed Forces Benefit Assn., 909 N. Washington St., Alexandria, VA 22314; (703) 549-4455. Fax, (703) 706-5961. Gen. Ralph (Ed) E. Eberhart (USAF, Ret.), President. Toll-free, (800) 776-2322.
General email, info@afba.com
Web, www.afba.com and Twitter, @AFBAbenefits

Membership: active duty and retired personnel of the uniformed services, federal civilian employees, government contractors, first responders, and family members. Offers low-cost life, health, and long-term care insurance and financial, banking, and investment services worldwide.

Army and Air Force Mutual Aid Assn., 102 Sheridan Ave., Fort Myer, VA 22211-1110; (703) 707-4600. Fax, (888) 210-4882. Maj. Walt Lincoln (USA, Ret.), President. Toll-free, (888) 961-5427.
General email, info@aafmaa.com
Web, www.aafmaa.com

Private organization that offers member and family life insurance, financial, and survivor assistance services to all ranks of Army, Air Force, Coast Guard, Marine Corps, and Navy who are active duty; Guard, Reserve, USAFA, USCGA, USMA, USMMA, and USNA cadets or midshipmen; ROTC contract/scholarship cadets; and retirees.

Army Emergency Relief, 2530 Crystal Dr., #13161, Alexandria, VA 22202; (703) 428-0000.
Lt. Gen. Raymond V. Mason (USA, Ret.), Executive Director. Toll-free, (866) 878-6372.
General email, aer@aerhq.org
Web, www.aerhq.org, Twitter, @aerhq and Facebook, www.facebook.com/AERHQ

Provides emergency financial assistance to retirees and to soldiers and family members of the U.S. Army, Army Reserves, and National Guard who are on extended active duty; provides scholarships to further the education of service members' spouses and dependents.

Defense Credit Union Council, 1627 Eye St. N.W., #935, 20006; (202) 734-5007. Fax, (202) 821-1329. Anthony R. Hernandez, President.
General email, admin@dcuc.org
Web, www.dcuc.org

Trade association of credit unions serving the Defense Dept.'s military and civilian personnel. Works with the National Credit Union Administration to solve problems concerning the operation of credit unions for the military community; maintains liaison with the Defense Dept.

The Enlisted Assn., Washington Office, 1800 Diagonal Rd., #600, Alexandria, VA 22314; (703) 684-1981. Fax, (703) 548-4876. Deirdre Parke Holleman, Executive Director. Toll-free, (800) 554-8732. VA caregiver support, (855) 260-3274.
General email, info@treadc.org
Web, www.trea.org and Twitter, @Tenlisteda1

Membership: enlisted personnel of the armed forces, including active duty, reserve, guard, and retirees. Runs scholarship, legislative, and veterans service programs, including food assistance, disaster relief, disability assistance, vocational education training, and prostheses and canine dogs for wounded veterans. (Also known as Retired Enlisted Assn.; headquarters in Aurora, Colo.)

Health Care

▶AGENCIES

Air Force Dept. *(Defense Dept.), Sexual Assault Prevention and Response (SAPR) (AF/CVS),* 1690 Air Force Pentagon, 20330-1670; (202) 767-7272. Maj. Gen. James C. Johnson, Director of the Integrated Resilience Office. Helpline, (877) 995-5247. Public Affairs, (703) 697-3039.
General email, whs.mc-alex.wso.mbx.SAPRO@mail.mil
Web, www.af.mil/SAPR.aspx

Works to eliminate the occurance of sexual assault in the Air Force, and acts as advocate for recovery and prevention.

Air Force Dept. *(Defense Dept.), Surgeon General (AF/SG),* 1780 Air Force Pentagon, #4E114, 20330-1780;

(703) 692-6800. Lt. Gen. Dorothy A. Hogg, Surgeon General. Congressional and Public Affairs, (703) 681-7921. General email, usaf.pentagon.af-sg.mbx.af-sg-public-affairs@mail.mil

Web, www.airforcemedicine.af.mil, Twitter, @USAFHealth and Facebook, www.facebook.com/AirForceMedicalService

Directs the provision of medical and dental services for Air Force personnel and their beneficiaries.

Army Dept. *(Defense Dept.), Command Policy and Programs,* 300 Army Pentagon, 20310-0300; (703) 692-1281. Lt. Col. David J. Deppmeier (USA), Chaplain; Lt. Col. Jerome (Jerry) Pionk (USA), Director of Public Affairs. Web, www.asamra.army.mil/mission.cfm

Develops policies and initiatives to enhance soldiers' health, fitness, and morale, with the goal of improving personnel readiness and institutional strength of the army. Interests include weight control and suicide prevention.

Army Dept. *(Defense Dept.), Surgeon General,* 7700 Arlington Blvd., #4SW112, Falls Church, VA 22042-5140; (703) 681-3000. Fax, (703) 681-3167. Lt. Gen. (Dr.) Nadja Y. West (USA), Surgeon General. General email, OTSGWebPublisher@amedd.army.mil

Web, www.armymedicine.army.mil and Twitter, @ArmyMedicine

Directs the provision of medical and dental services for Army personnel and their dependents.

Army Dept. *(Defense Dept.), Warrior Transition Command,* 2530 Crystal Dr., 10th Floor, Arlington, VA 22202; (703) 428-7118. Fax, (703) 325-0291. Col. Christopher Toner, Commander. Wounded soldier and family hotline, (800) 984-8523. Web, www.wtc.army.mil and Twitter, @armyWTC

Provides leadership, command, and control for wounded soldiers' health and welfare, military administrative requirements, and readiness. Collaborates with medical providers in order to facilitate quality care, disposition, and transition. Supports the needs of wounded warriors and their families; supports the professional growth of all personnel.

Army Dept. *(Defense Dept.), Wounded Warrior Program (AW2),* 2530 Crystal Dr., 10th Floor, Arlington, VA 22202; (877) 393-9058. Fax, (703) 325-1516. Col. Terence J. Johnson (USA), Director. Overseas, (312) 221-9113. General email, AW2@conus.army.mil

Assists and acts as advocate for severely disabled and ill soldiers, veterans, and their families. Provides each soldier with a personal AW2 advocate. Tracks and monitors severely disabled soldiers beyond their medical retirement.

Assistant Secretary for Health (OASH) *(Health and Human Services Dept.), Surgeon General, Commissioned Corps of the U.S. Public Health Service (PHS), Division of Commissioned Corps Personnel and Readiness (DCCPR),* 1101 Wootton Pkwy., Plaza Level, #100, Rockville, MD 20852; (240) 453-6000. Fax, (240) 453-6109.

Rear Adm. Joan Hunter, Director. Recruitment, (800) 279-1605. General email, CCHelpDesk@hhs.gov

Web, www.usphs.gov

Recruitment email, Corpsrecruitment@hhs.gov

Responsible for the overall force management, operations, and deployment readiness and response of the Commissioned Corps of the U.S. Public Health Service. Manages officer medical records and evaluations, recruitment, and calls to active duty.

Defense Dept. (DoD), *Force Health Protection and Readiness,* 7700 Arlington Blvd., #5101, Falls Church, VA 22042; (703) 681-8456. Thomas McCaffery, Assistant Secretary of Defense and Health Affairs (Acting). General email, FHPR.communications@tma.osd.mil

Web, http://health.mil

Advises the secretary of defense on measures to improve the health of deployed forces. Maintains communication between the Defense Dept., service members, veterans, and their families.

Defense Dept. (DoD), *Health Affairs, Clinical Program Policy,* 1200 Defense Pentagon, #3E1082, 20301-1200; (703) 681-1708. Fax, (703) 681-3655. Dr. Jack W. Smith, Director.

Web, www.health.mil

Develops policies for the medical benefits programs for active duty and retired military personnel and dependents in the Defense Dept.

Defense Dept. (DoD), *National Intrepid Center of Excellence,* 4860 South Palmer Rd., Bethesda, MD 20889; Capt. (Dr.) Walter M. Greenhalgh (USN), Director. 24-hour helpline, (301) 319-3600. General email, dha.bethesda.ncr-medical.mbx.nicoe@mail.mil

Web, www.nicoe.capmed.mil

Provides evaluation, treatment planning, research, and education for service members and their families dealing with the interactions of mild traumatic brain injury and psychological health conditions. Primary patient population is active duty service members who are not responding to current therapy; provider-referral required.

Defense Health Agency (DHA) *(Defense Dept.),* 7700 Arlington Blvd., #5101, Falls Church, VA 22042-5101; (703) 681-1730. Vice Adm. (Dr.) Raquel C. Bono (USN), Director. Web, www.health.mil/About-MHS/OASDHA/Defense-Health-Agency

Combat support agency directing medical services for the Army, Navy, Air Force, and Marine Corps. Administers the TRICARE health plan providing medical, dental, and pharmacy programs worldwide to service members, retirees, and their families. Manages inpatient facilities and associated clinics in the national capital region.

Marine Corps *(Defense Dept.), Marine and Family Programs,* M and RA (MF), 3280 Russell Rd., Quantico,

VA 22134-5103; (703) 784-9501. Fax, (703) 432-9269. Marie C. Balocki, Director.

Web, www.usmc-mccs.org

Military office that directs Marine Corps health care, family violence, and drug and alcohol abuse policies and programs.

Naval Medical Research Center *(Defense Dept.), 503 Robert Grant Ave., #1W28, Silver Spring, MD 20910-7500; (301) 319-7403. Fax, (301) 319-7424.* Capt. Adam W. Armstrong (USN), Commanding Officer. General email, svc.pao.nmrc@med.navy.mil

Web, www.med.navy.mil/sites/nmrc and Facebook, www .facebook.com/NavalMedicalRC

Performs basic and applied biomedical research in areas of military importance, including infectious diseases, hyperbaric medicine, wound repair enhancement, environmental stress, and immunobiology. Provides support to field laboratories and naval hospitals; monitors research internationally.

Navy Dept. *(Defense Dept.), Manpower and Reserve Affairs, Health Affairs, 1000 Navy Pentagon, #4D548, 20350-1000; (703) 693-0238. Fax, (703) 697-1475.* Capt. Mary Jenkins (USN), Director.

Web, www.navy.mil

Reviews medical programs for Navy and Marine Corps military personnel and develops and reviews policies relating to these programs.

Navy Dept. *(Defense Dept.), Patient Administration/ TriCare Operations, 7700 Arlington Blvd., #5113, Falls Church, VA 22042; (703) 681-9025.* Shelly Huffman, Head of TriCare Operations; Lt. Cmdr. Sean Morris, Patient Administration.

Web, www.med.navy.mil

Military office that interprets and oversees the implementation of Navy health care policy. Assists in the development of eligibility policy for medical benefits programs for Navy and Marine Corps military personnel.

Navy Dept. *(Defense Dept.), Surgeon General, 7700 Arlington Blvd., #5113, Falls Church, VA 22042-5113; (703) 681-9025. Fax, (703) 681-9527.* Vice Adm. C. Forrest Faison III (USN), Surgeon General. Phone (after hours), (202) 714-0131. fax, (703) 681-9527. Public Affairs, (703) 681-9038.

Web, www.med.navy.mil

Directs the provision of medical and dental services for Navy and Marine Corps personnel and their dependents; oversees the Navy's Bureau of Medicine and Surgery.

U.S. Coast Guard (USCG) *(Homeland Security Dept.), Health, Safety, and Work-Life, CG-11, 2703 Martin Luther King Jr. Ave. S.E., 20593; (202) 475-5130. Fax, (202) 475-5906.* Rear Adm. Erica G. Schwartz, Director. General email, germaine.y.jefferson@uscg.mil

Web, www.dcms.uscg.mil/Our-Organization/Assistant-Commandant-for-Human-Resources-CG-1/Health-Safety-and-Work-Life-CG-11/

Oversees all health, safety, and work-life aspects of the Coast Guard, including the operation of medical and dental clinics and sick bays on ships. Investigates Coast Guard accidents, such as the grounding of ships and downing of aircraft. Oversees all work-life–related programs, including health promotion, mess halls and galleys, and individual and family support programs.

Walter Reed Army Institute of Research *(Defense Dept.), 503 Robert Grant Ave., Silver Spring, MD 20910-7500; (301) 319-9000. Fax, (301) 319-9549.* Col. Deydre S. Teyhen, Commander. Public Affairs Officer, (301) 319-9471. Reference Librarian, (301) 319-9555. General email, usarmy.detrick.medcom-wrair.mbx.public-affairs@mail.mil

Web, www.wrair.army.mil and Twitter, @wrair

Provides research, education, and training in support of the Defense Dept.'s health care system. Develops vaccines and drugs to prevent and treat infectious diseases. Other research efforts include surveillance of naturally occurring infectious diseases of military importance and study of combat casualty care (blood loss, resuscitation, and brain and other organ system trauma), battle casualties, operational stress, sleep deprivation, and medical countermeasures against biological and chemical agents.

▶ **NONGOVERNMENTAL**

AMSUS—Society of Federal Health Professionals, *12154 Darnstown Rd., #506, Gaithersburg, MD 20878; (301) 897-8800. Fax, (301) 530-5446.* Brig. Gen. John M. Cho (USA, Ret.), Executive Director. Toll-free, (800) 761-9320. General email, amsus@amsus.org

Web, www.amsus.org and Twitter, @AMSUS

Membership: health professionals, including nurses, dentists, pharmacists, and physicians, who work or have worked for the U.S. Public Health Service, the VA, or the Army, Navy, Air Force, Guard, and Reserves, and students. Works to improve all phases of federal health services.

CAUSE (Comfort for America's Uniformed Services), *1100 N. Glebe Rd., #373, Arlington, VA 22201 (mailing address: 4201 Wilson Blvd., #110-284, Arlington, VA 22203); (703) 591-4965. Fax, (703) 591-0066.* Theresa Rudacille, Executive Director. General email, info@cause-usa.org

Web, http://cause-usa.org and Twitter, @Cause_USA

Provides comfort items and organizes recreational programs for U.S. military service personnel undergoing medical treatment or recuperating in government hospitals or rehabilitation facilities.

Commissioned Officers Assn. of the U.S. Public Health Service, *8201 Corporate Dr., #1170, Landover, MD 20785; (301) 731-9080. Fax, (301) 731-9084.* Col. James (Jim) T. Currie (USA, Ret.), Executive Director. Web, http://coausphs.org and Twitter, @COAUSPHS

Membership: commissioned officers of the U.S. Public Health Service. Supports improvements to public health, especially through the work of the PHS Commissioned Corps. Sponsors conferences and training workshops. Monitors legislation and regulations.

Injured Marine Semper Fi Fund/Semper Fi Fund, *715 Broadway St., Quantico, VA 22134 (mailing address: Wounded Warrior Center Bldg., H49, Box 555193, Camp Pendleton, CA 92055-5193); (703) 640-0181. Fax, (703) 640-0192. Karen Guenther, President. General email, info@semperfifund.org*

Web, www.semperfifund.org, Twitter, @SemperFiFund and Facebook, www.facebook.com/semperfifund

With its program America's First, provides financial assistance and lifetime support to post-9/11 combat-wounded, critically ill, and catastrophically injured members of all branches of the U.S. Armed Forces and their families, ensuring that they have the resources needed during recovery and transition back to their communities.

Missing in Action, Prisoners of War

►**AGENCIES**

Air Force Dept. *(Defense Dept.), Manpower, Personnel, and Services, 1040 Air Force Pentagon, #4E168, 20330-1040; (703) 697-6088. Lt. Gen. Brian T. Kelly, Deputy Chief of Staff. Web, www.af.mil*

Military office that responds to inquiries about missing in action (MIA) personnel for the Air Force; refers inquiries to the Military Personnel Center at Randolph Air Force Base in San Antonio, Texas.

Bureau of East Asian and Pacific Affairs *(State Dept.), Mainland Southeast Asia Affairs, 2201 C St. N.W., #5206, 20520-6310; (202) 647-4495. Fax, (202) 647-3069. Mark Tesone, Director. Web, www.state.gov/p/eap*

Handles issues related to Americans missing in action in Indochina; serves as liaison with Congress, international organizations, and foreign governments on developments in these countries.

Defense Dept. (DoD), *Defense POW/MIA Accounting, 241 18th St. South, #800, Arlington, VA 22202; (703) 699-1102. Fax, (703) 602-1890. Kelly K. McKeague, Director; Rear Adm. Jon C. Kreitz (USN), Deputy Director. Press, (703) 699-1420. Web, www.dpaa.mil*

Civilian office responsible for policy matters relating to prisoners of war and missing personnel issues. Represents the Defense Dept. before Congress, the media, veterans organizations, and prisoner of war and missing personnel families.

Defense Dept. (DoD), *Public Affairs, The Pentagon, #2D961, 20301-1400; (703) 571-3343. Fax, (703) 697-3501. Charles Summers, Assistant to the Secretary of Defense for Public Affairs. Press, (703) 697-5131. Web, www.defense.gov/news*

Responds to public inquiries concerning Defense Dept. personnel.

Marine Corps *(Defense Dept.), Casualty Assistance Section, 2008 Elliott Rd., Quantico, VA 22134-5102; (703) 784-9512. Fax, (703) 784-4134. Gerald Castle, Head. Toll-free, (800) 847-1597. General email, casualty.section@usmc.mil*

Web, http://usmc-mccs.org/services/benefits/casualty-assistance

Military office that acts as liaison for inquiries about missing in action (MIA) personnel for the Marine Corps and distributes information about Marine Corps MIAs to the next of kin.

Navy Dept. *(Defense Dept.), Naval Personnel, 701 S. Courthouse Rd., Arlington, VA 22204; (703) 604-2863. Fax, (703) 604-5942. Vice Adm. Robert P. Burke (USN), Chief. Toll-free, (866) 827-5672. TTY, (866) 297-1971. General email, UASKPC@navy.mil*

Web, www.navy.mil/cno, Twitter, @usnpeople and Facebook, www.facebook.com/usnpeople

Military office that responds to inquiries about missing in action (MIA) personnel for the Navy and distributes information about Navy MIAs. (Office based in Millington, Tenn.)

►**CONGRESS**

For a listing of relevant congressional committees and subcommittees, please see page 594 or the Appendix.

►**NONGOVERNMENTAL**

National League of Families of American Prisoners and Missing in Southeast Asia, *5673 Columbia Pike, #100, Falls Church, VA 22041; (703) 465-7432. Fax, (703) 465-7433. Ann Mills-Griffith, Chair. General email, powmiafam@aol.com*

Web, www.pow-miafamilies.org

Membership: family members of MIAs and POWs and returned POWs of the Vietnam War are voting members; nonvoting associate members include veterans and other interested people. Works for the release of all prisoners of war, an accounting of the missing, and repatriation of the remains of those who have died serving their country in Southeast Asia. Works to raise public awareness of these issues; maintains regional and state coordinators.

Pay and Compensation

►**AGENCIES**

Air Force Dept. *(Defense Dept.), Manpower, Personnel, and Services, Military Compensation Policy Division, 1500 Perimeter Rd., #4790, Joint Base Andrews, MD 20762; (240) 612-4022. Col. Brian A. Anderson, Chief. Web, www.afpc.af.mil*

Military office that develops and administers Air Force policy regarding personnel travel, entitlements, housing allowances, uniforms, leave and absence, and compensation.

Army Dept. *(Defense Dept.), Military Compensation, 111 Army Pentagon, #2E469, 20310-0111; (703) 697-1482. Fax, (703) 693-7072. Jerilyn (Jeri) B. Busch, SES, Director. Customer service, (888) 332-7411.*
Web, http://militarypay.defense.gov

Military office that provides oversight of the development and administration of and compliance with Army military personnel pay and compensation policies.

Army Dept. *(Defense Dept.), My Army Benefits, 2530 Crystal Dr., #6000, Arlington, VA 22202; (703) 286-2560. Fax, (703) 601-0057. Brig. Gen. Henry L. Huntley, Director. Toll-free, (888) 721-2769.*
General email, usarmy.pentagon.hqda-des-g1.mbx.help-my-army-benefits@mail.mil
Web, http://myarmybenefits.us.army.mil

Military office that provides Army benefits information.

Defense Dept. (DoD), *Military Compensation, 4000 Defense Pentagon, #3D1067, 20301-4000; (703) 693-1058. Jerilyn (Jeri) B. Busch, Director.*
Web, http://militarypay.defense.gov

Promulgates military pay and compensation policies to the uniformed services and advises the secretary of defense on military compensation policy.

Marine Corps *(Defense Dept.), Military Manpower Policy, 3280 Russell Rd., Quantico, VA 22134-5105; (703) 784-9352. Fax, (703) 784-9812. Brig. Gen. William Swann, Director.*
General email, manpower@usmc.mil
Web, www.quantico.marines.mil/Offices-Staff/G-1-Manpower

Military office that develops and administers Marine Corps personnel pay and compensation policies.

Navy Dept. *(Defense Dept.), Military Pay and Compensation Policy, 701 S. Courthouse Rd., Arlington, VA 22204; (703) 604-4718. David Haldeman, Branch Head.*
General email, nxag_n130@navy.mil
Web, www.navy.com/what-to-expect/navy-benefits-compensation-and-pay

Military office that develops and administers Navy military pay, compensation, and personnel policies.

► **NONGOVERNMENTAL**

Fleet Reserve Assn. (FRA), *125 N. West St., Alexandria, VA 22314-2754; (703) 683-1400. Fax, (703) 549-6610. Thomas J. Snee, National Executive Director, (703) 683-1400, ext. 101. Membership/Customer Service, (800) 372-1924.*
General email, fra@fra.org
Web, www.fra.org, Twitter, @FRAHQ and Facebook, www.facebook.com/FRA.org/?ref=br_tf

Membership: current and former enlisted members of the Navy, Marine Corps, and Coast Guard. Interests include health care, pay, benefits, and quality-of-life

programs for sea services personnel. Monitors legislation and regulations.

Recruitment

► **AGENCIES**

Air Force Dept. *(Defense Dept.), Air Force Personnel Center (AFPC), Force Management, 1400 W. Perimeter Rd., #4710, Joint Base Andrews, 20762; (240) 612-4040. Col. Gerald (Jerry) Diaz, Chief.*
Web, www.afpc.af.mil/Force-Development/

Military office that gives active-duty enlisted personnel information about available force management courses. Supports military and civilian developmental education courses and distance learning courses.

Air Force Dept. *(Defense Dept.), Manpower and Reserve Affairs (SAF/MR), 1670 Air Force Pentagon, #4E1020, 20330-1670; (703) 697-2302. Shon J. Manasco, Assistant Secretary. Public Affairs, (703) 697-5828.*
General email, usaf.pentagon.saf-mr.mbx.saf-mr-workflow-all@mail.mil
Web, www.af.mil/About-Us/Biographies/Display/Article/1391994/shon-j-manasco

Civilian office that oversees manpower, military, and civilian personnel, Reserve component affairs, and readiness support for the Air Force.

Army Dept. *(Defense Dept.), Manpower and Reserve Affairs, 111 Army Pentagon, #2E460, 20310-0111; (703) 697-9253. Fax, (703) 692-9000. Sgt. Maj. Tamara Gregory, Senior Enlisted Advisor.*
Web, www.asamra.army.mil

Civilian office that reviews policies and programs for Army personnel and reserves; makes recommendations to the secretary of the Army. Oversees training, military preparedness, and mobilization for all civilians and active and reserve members of the Army.

Defense Dept. (DoD), *Accession Policy, 4000 Defense Pentagon, #3D1066, 20301-4000; (703) 695-5525. Stephanie P. Miller, Director; Chris Arendt, Deputy Director.*
Web, www.defense.gov

Military office that monitors Defense Dept. recruiting programs and policies, including advertising, market research, and enlistment standards. Coordinates with the individual services on recruitment of military personnel.

Defense Dept. (DoD), *Manpower and Reserve Affairs, 1500 Defense Pentagon, #2E556, 20301-1500; (703) 697-6631. Fax, (703) 697-1682. Stephanie Barna, Assistant Secretary (Acting).*
Web, www.people.mil

Civilian office that addresses all policy matters pertaining to the six reserve components of the military services. Develops and delivers civilian and military personnel policy and implements human resource solutions that support the Total Force and mission readiness.

Marine Corps *(Defense Dept.)*, **Human Resources and Organizational Management**, *Code ARH, 3000 Marine Corps Pentagon, #2C253, 20350-3000; Mann Hall, 2004 Barnett Ave., Quantico, VA 22134; (703) 614-8371. William I. Whaley, Director. Phone (Quantico), (703) 784-2049.*
General email, hromdir@usmc.mil

Web, www.hqmc.marines.mil/hrom/unit-home/ HRONSFArlingtonOffice

Develops and implements personnel and equal employment opportunity programs to recruit, develop, and maintain the workforce at Marine Corps headquarters.

Marine Corps *(Defense Dept.)*, **Manpower and Reserve Affairs**, *James Wesley Marsh Center, 3280 Russell Rd., Bldg. 3280, Quantico, VA 22134; (703) 784-9012. Lt. Gen. Michael Rocco (USMC), Deputy Commandant.*
Web, www.manpower.usmc.mil

Oversees planning, directing, coordinating, and supervising of both active and reserve Marine Corps forces.

Marine Corps *(Defense Dept.)*, **Recruiting Command**, *3280 Russell Rd., Quantico, VA 22134-5105; (703) 784-9454. Maj. Gen. James W. Bierman (USMC), Commanding General. After work hours, (703) 675-7901.*
General email, mcrcpa@marines.usmc.mil

Web, www.mcrc.marines.mil

Military office that administers and executes policies for Marine Corps officer and enlisted recruitment programs.

Navy Dept. *(Defense Dept.)*, **Manpower and Reserve Affairs**, *1000 Navy Pentagon, #4E590, 20350-1000; (703) 695-4333. Fax, (703) 614-4103. Gregory J. Slavonic, Assistant Secretary.*
Web, www.navy.mil

Civilian office that oversees the recruitment of active and reserve Navy personnel, government civilians, contractors, and volunteers.

Selective Service System, *1515 Wilson Blvd., #400, Arlington, VA 22209-2425; (703) 605-4100. Fax, (703) 605-4106. Donald M. Benton, Director. Locator, (703) 605-4000. Toll-free, (888) 655-1825. TTY, (800) 877-8339. TTY Español, (800) 845-6136.*
General email, information@sss.gov

Web, www.sss.gov and Twitter, @sss_gov

Supplies the armed forces with manpower when authorized; registers male citizens of the United States ages eighteen to twenty-five. In an emergency, would institute a draft and would provide alternative service assignments to men classified as conscientious objectors.

U.S. Coast Guard (USCG) *(Homeland Security Dept.)*, **Human Resources Directorate**, *CG-1, 2703 Martin Luther King Jr. Ave. S.E., MS 7907, 20593-7907; (202) 475-5002. Rear Adm. William G. Kelly, Assistant Commandant.*
Web, www.uscg.mil/hr

Responsible for hiring, recruiting, and training all military and nonmilitary Coast Guard personnel. Administers employee benefits.

Retirement, Separation

▶**AGENCIES**

Armed Forces Retirement Home—Washington, *140 Rock Creek Church Rd. N.W., 20011-8400 (mailing address: 3700 N. Capitol St. N.W., Washington, DC 20011-8400); (800) 422-9988. (202) 541-5501. Fax, (202) 541-7519. Stephen T. Rippe, Chief Operating Officer.*
General email, admissions@afrh.gov

Web, www.afrh.gov

Gives domiciliary and medical care to retired members of the armed services or career service personnel unable to earn a livelihood. Formerly known as U.S. Soldiers' and Airmen's Home. (Armed Forces Retirement Home in Gulfport, Miss., reopened in 2010.)

Army Dept. *(Defense Dept.)*, **Retirement Services**, *251 18th St. South, #210, Arlington, VA 22202-3531; (703) 571-7232. Fax, (703) 601-0120. Mark Overberg (USA, Ret.), Director. Alternate phone, (703) 545-2637.*
General email, ArmyRSO@mail.mil

Web, https://soldierforlife.army.mil/retirement

Military office that makes retirement policy and oversees retirement programs for Army military personnel.

Defense Dept. *(DoD)*, **Military Compensation**, *4000 Defense Pentagon, #3D1067, 20301-4000; (703) 693-1058. Jerilyn (Jeri) B. Busch, Director.*
Web, http://militarypay.defense.gov

Develops retirement policies and reviews administration of retirement programs for all Defense Dept. military personnel.

Marine Corps *(Defense Dept.)*, **Retired Services**, *3280 Russell Rd., Quantico, VA 22134-5103; (703) 784-9312. Fax, (703) 784-9834. Maj. Gen. Bradley S. James, Commander; Gregg T. Habel, Executive Director. Toll-free, (800) 336-4649.*
Web, www.marines.mil/General-Special-Staff/G1/AAU/ Separations

Military office that administers retirement programs and benefits for Marine Corps retirees and the Marine Corps retirement community survivor benefit plan.

Marine Corps *(Defense Dept.)*, **Separation and Retirement**, *3280 Russell Rd., Quantico, VA 22134-5103; (703) 784-9304. Fax, (703) 784-9834. Col. Steven M. Hanscom (USMC, Ret.), Head.*
Web, www.marines.mil

Military office that processes Marine Corps military personnel retirements and separations but does not administer benefits.

▶**NONGOVERNMENTAL**

Army Distaff Foundation (Knollwood), *6200 Oregon Ave. N.W., 20015-1543; (202) 541-0492. Fax, (202) 364-2856. Maj. Gen. Timothy P. McHale (USA, Ret.), Chief Executive Officer; Col. Paul W. Bricker (USA, Ret.), Chief Operating*

Officer. Admission, (202) 541-0149. Information, (800) 541-4255.
General email, dschrag@armydistaff.org
Web, www.armydistaff.org

Nonprofit continuing care retirement community for career military officers and their families. Provides retirement housing and health care services.

MILITARY EDUCATION AND TRAINING

General

▶**AGENCIES**

Air Force Dept. *(Defense Dept.), Air Force Personnel Center (AFPC), 1040 Air Force Pentagon, #4D950, 20330-1040; (703) 695-6770. Maj. Gen. Brian T. Kelly, Commander. Public Affairs, (210) 565-2334.*
General email, afpc.pa.task@us.af.mil
Web, www.afpc.af.mil, Twitter, @AFCareers and Facebook, www.facebook.com/AirForcePersonnelCenter

Supervises operations and policies of all professional military education, including continuing education programs. Oversees operations and policies of Air Force service schools, including technical training for newly enlisted Air Force personnel. (Headquarters in Tex.)

Air Force Dept. *(Defense Dept.), Air Force Personnel Center (AFPC), Force Management Integration, 1660 Air Force Pentagon, #5E818, 20330-1660; (703) 614-4751. Fax, (703) 693-4244. Jeffrey R. Mayo, Deputy Assistant Secretary.*
Web, www.afpc.af.mil

Civilian office that monitors and reviews education policies of the U.S. Air Force Academy at Colorado Springs and officer candidates' training and Reserve Officers Training Corps (ROTC) programs for the Air Force. Advises the secretary of the Air Force on education matters, including graduate education, voluntary education programs, and flight, specialized, and recruit training.

Army Dept. *(Defense Dept.), Military Personnel Management, 300 Army Pentagon, #1D429, 20310-0300; (703) 695-5871. Fax, (703) 695-6012. Maj. Gen. Jason T. Evans (USA), Director.*
Web, www.army.mil

Military office that supervises operations and policies of the U.S. Military Academy and officer candidates' training and Reserve Officers Training Corps (ROTC) programs. Advises the chief of staff of the Army on academy and education matters.

Army Dept. *(Defense Dept.), Training Development Directorate, 2221 Adams Ave., Fort Lee, VA 23801-2102; (804) 765-1471. Lt. Col. Alex Shimabukuro (USA), Deputy Director.*

General email, usarmy.lee.tradoc.mbx.leee-scoe-g3-mailbox@mail.mil
Web, www.cascom.army.mil/g_staff/g3/tdd.htm

Military office that plans and monitors program resources for active duty and reserve unit training readiness programs.

Civil Air Patrol National Capital Wing, *200 McChord St. S.W., #111, Joint Base Anacostia-Bolling, 20032; (202) 767-4405. Col. Janon Ellis, Wing Commander.*
General email, info@natcapwing.org
Web, www.natcapwg.cap.gov and Twitter, @NatCapWing

Official auxiliary of the U.S. Air Force. Sponsors a cadet training and education program for junior and senior high school age students. Conducts emergency services, homeland security missions, and an aerospace education program. (Headquarters at Maxwell Air Force Base, Ala.)

Defense Acquisition University *(Defense Dept.), 9820 Belvoir Rd., Fort Belvoir, VA 22060-5565; (703) 805-3360. Fax, (703) 805-2639. James P. Woolsey, President. Toll-free, (866) 568-6924.*
General email, DAUhelp@dau.mil
Web, www.dau.mil and Twitter, @DAUNow

Academic institution that offers courses to military and civilian personnel who specialize in acquisition and procurement. Conducts research to support and improve management of defense systems acquisition programs.

Defense Dept. (DoD), *Accession Policy, 4000 Defense Pentagon, #3D1066, 20301-4000; (703) 695-5525. Stephanie P. Miller, Director; Chris Arendt, Deputy Director.*
Web, www.defense.gov

Reviews and develops education policies of the service academies, service schools, graduate and voluntary education programs, education programs for active duty personnel, tuition assistance programs, and officer candidates' training and Reserve Officers Training Corps (ROTC) programs for the Defense Dept. Advises the secretary of defense on education matters.

Defense Dept. (DoD), *Force Education and Training, 4000 Defense Pentagon, #1E537, 20301-4000; (703) 695-2618. Fax, (703) 692-2855. Fred Drummond, Deputy Assistant Secretary.*
Web, http://prhome.defense.gov

Develops, reviews, and analyzes legislation, policies, plans, programs, resource levels, and budgets for the training of military personnel and military units. Develops the substantive-based framework, working collaboratively across the defense, federal, academic, and private sectors, for the global digital knowledge environment. Manages with other government agencies the sustainability and modernization of DoD training ranges.

Dwight D. Eisenhower School for National Security and Resource Strategy *(Defense Dept.), Fort Lesley J. McNair, 408 4th Ave. S.W., Bldg. 59, 20319-5062; (202) 685-4278. Fax, (202) 685-4339. Brig. Gen. Kyle W. Robinson (USAF), Commandant. Administration, (202) 685-4333.*

General email, university-registrar@ndu.edu

Web, http://es.ndu.edu

Division of National Defense University. Offers professional level courses for senior military officers and senior civilian government officials. Academic program focuses on management of national resources, mobilization, and industrial preparedness. (Formerly known as the Industrial College of the Armed Forces.)

Marine Corps *(Defense Dept.)*, *Alfred M. Gray Research Center*, *2040 Broadway St., Quantico, VA 22134; (703) 784-2240. Paul Weber, Deputy Director, (703) 432-5058. Archives, (703) 784-4685. Library, (703) 784-4409.*
Web, http://grc-usmcu.libguides.com/gray-research-center

Supports the professional, military, educational, and academic needs of the students and faculty of the Marine Corps University. Acts as a central research facility for marines in operational units worldwide. Houses the library and archives of the Marine Corps.

Marine Corps *(Defense Dept.)*, *Training and Education Command*, *1019 Elliot Rd., Quantico, VA 22134-5001; (703) 784-3730. (703) 784-0245. Fax, (703) 784-0012. Maj. Gen. William F. Mullen, Commanding General.*
Web, www.tecom.marines.mil

Military office that develops and implements training and education programs for regular and reserve personnel and units.

National Defense University *(Defense Dept.)*, *Fort Lesley J. McNair, 300 5th Ave. S.W., Bldg. 62, #305A, 20319-5066; (202) 685-4700. Fax, (202) 685-3935. Vice Adm. Fritz Roegge (USN), President. Press, (202) 685-3140. General email, NDUWebmaster@ndu.edu*

Web, www.ndu.edu, Twitter, @NDU_EDU and Facebook, www.facebook.com/ndu.edu

Specialized university sponsored by the Joint Chiefs of Staff to prepare individuals for senior executive duties in the national security establishment. Offers master of science degrees in national resource strategy, national security strategy, joint campaign planning and strategy, and government information leadership; a master of arts degree in strategic security studies; and nondegree and certificate programs and courses.

National War College *(Defense Dept.)*, *Fort Lesley J. McNair, 300 D St. S.W., Bldg. 61, 20319-5078; (202) 685-3674. Fax, (202) 685-6461. Brig. Gen. Chad T. Manske (USAF), Commandant.*
Web, http://nwc.ndu.edu

Division of National Defense University. Offers professional level courses for senior military officers, senior civilian government officials, and foreign officers. Academic program focuses on the formulation and implementation of national security policy and military strategy.

Navy Dept. *(Defense Dept.)*, *Manpower and Reserve Affairs*, *1000 Navy Pentagon, #4E590, 20350-1000; (703) 695-4333. Fax, (703) 614-4103. Gregory J. Slavonic, Assistant Secretary.*
Web, www.navy.mil

Civilian office that reviews policies of the U.S. Naval Academy, Navy and Marine Corps service schools, and officer candidates' training and Reserve Officer Training Corps (ROTC) programs. Advises the secretary of the Navy on education matters, including voluntary education programs.

U.S. Naval Academy *(Defense Dept.)*, *121 Blake Rd., Annapolis, MD 21402-5000; (410) 293-1000. Fax, (410) 293-3133. Vice Adm. Walter (Ted) Carter Jr. (USN), Superintendent; Capt. Stephen B. Latta (USN, Ret.), Dean of Admissions; Capt. Robert B. Chadwick II (USMC), Commandant of Midshipmen. Admissions/Candidate guidance, (410) 293-1858. Public Affairs, (410) 293-1520. Visitor information, (410) 293-8687.*
General email, pao@usna.edu

Web, www.usna.edu, Twitter, @NavalAcademy and Admissions, www.usna.edu/Admissions

Provides undergraduate education for young men and women who have been nominated by members of their state's congressional delegation or, in some cases, the president or vice president of the United States. Graduates receive bachelor of science degrees and are commissioned as either an ensign in the U.S. Navy or a second lieutenant in the U.S. Marine Corps.

Uniformed Services University of the Health Sciences *(Defense Dept.)*, *4301 Jones Bridge Rd., Bethesda, MD 20814-4799; (301) 295-3013. Fax, (301) 295-1960. Dr. Richard W. Thomas, President. Registrar, (301) 295-3199. Toll-free information, (800) 515-5257.*
General email, president@usuhs.edu

Web, www.usuhs.mil and Twitter, @USUhealthsci

An accredited four-year medical and postgraduate dental school under the auspices of the Defense Dept. Awards doctorates and master's degrees in health-related and science-related fields.

►CONGRESS

For a listing of relevant congressional committees and subcommittees, please see page 594 or the Appendix.

►NONGOVERNMENTAL

Assn. of Military Colleges and Schools of the U.S., *12332 Washington Brice Rd., Fairfax, VA 22033; (703) 272-8406. Col. Ray Rottman (USAF, Ret.), Executive Director.*
General email, amcsus@cox.net

Web, www.amcsus.org and Twitter, @CharacterisKey

Membership: nonfederal military colleges and universities, junior colleges, and preparatory secondary schools that emphasize character development, leadership, and knowledge. Interests include Reserve Officers Training Corps (ROTC). Publishes a newsletter; sponsors an annual meeting and outreach activities. Represents member schools before the Defense Dept., Education Dept., and the general public.

George and Carol Olmsted Foundation, *80 East Jefferson St., #300B, Falls Church, VA 22046; (703) 536-3500. Maj.*

Gen. Bruce K. Scott (USA, Ret.), President. Toll-free, (877) 656-7833.

General email, scholars@olmstedfoundation.org

Web, www.olmstedfoundation.org and Twitter, @OlmstedScholars

Administers grants for two years of graduate study overseas, including foreign language study, for selected officers of the armed forces.

Military Order of the World Wars, 435 N. Lee St., Alexandria, VA 22314-2301; (703) 683-4911. Fax, (703) 683-4501. Brig. Gen. Arthur B. Morrill III (USAF, Ret.), Chief of Staff.

General email, chiefofstaff@moww.org

Web, www.moww.org and Facebook, www.facebook.com/militaryorder

Membership: retired and active duty commissioned officers, warrant officers, and flight officers. Supports a strong national defense; supports patriotic education in schools; presents awards to outstanding Junior and Senior Reserve Officers Training Corps (ROTC) cadets, Boy Scouts, and Girl Scouts.

National Research Council (NRC), Air Force Studies Board, Keck Center, 500 5th St. N.W., 9th Floor, 20001; (202) 334-2000. Gen. Douglas M. Fraser (USAF, Ret.), Chair; Ellen Chou, Director.

Web, http://nationalacademies.org/afsb

Supports activities related to the development of science and technology within the Air Force. Interests of study include fuel efficiency, acquisition processes, and assuring the future scientific and technical qualification of Air Force personnel.

Navy League of the United States, 2300 Wilson Blvd., #200, Arlington, VA 22201-5424; (703) 528-1775. Fax, (703) 528-2333. James Bruns, National Executive Director. Toll-free, (800) 356-5760.

General email, service@navyleague.org

Web, www.navyleague.org, Twitter, @NavyLeagueUS and Facebook, www.facebook.com/NavyLeagueUS

Membership: retired and reserve military personnel and civilians interested in the U.S. Navy, Marine Corps, Coast Guard, and Merchant Marine. Distributes literature, provides speakers, and conducts seminars to promote interests of the sea services. Sponsors Naval Sea Cadet Corps and Navy League Sea Cadet Corps for young people ages eleven through eighteen. Graduates are eligible to enter the Navy at advanced pay grades. Monitors legislation.

Servicemembers Opportunity Colleges, 2300 Dulles Station Blvd., Herndon, VA 20171; (800) 892-7205. Jeffrey Carpenter, Director, ext. 700.

Web, http://gosoced.org

Partnership of higher education associations, educational institutions, the Defense Dept., and the military services. Offers courses for credit and degree programs to military personnel and their families stationed in the United States and around the world.

MILITARY GRIEVANCES AND DISCIPLINE

General

▶AGENCIES

Air Force Dept. (Defense Dept.), Inspector General (SAF/IG), Complaints Resolution Directorate, Joint Base Anacostia-Bolling, Carpenter Bldg., 5683 Castle Ave., 20032; (210) 565-3200. Lt. Gen. Stayce D. Harris, Inspector General. Hotline, (202) 404-5262. Hotline toll-free, (800) 538-8429.

General email, AFPC.IG@us.af.mil

Web, www.afpc.af.mil/inspector-general/

Hotline, usaf.ighotline@mail.mil

Military office that handles intelligence oversight; criminal investigations; counterintelligence operations; complaints; and fraud, waste, and abuse programs. Oversees the Air Force Inspection Agency and Air Force Office of Special Investigations.

Air Force Dept. (Defense Dept.), Manpower and Reserve Affairs (SAF/MR), Air Force Review Boards Agency (AFRBA), 1500 W. Perimeter Rd., #3700, Joint Base Andrew, MD 20762-7002; (240) 612-5400. Fax, (240) 612-6016. P. Philip Deavel, Director.

Web, www.af.mil/About-Us/Fact-Sheets/Display/Article/104511/air-force-review-boards-agency

Civilian office that responds to complaints from Air Force military and civilian personnel and assists in seeking corrective action.

Army Dept. (Defense Dept.), Army Review Boards Agency, 251 18th St. South, #385, Arlington, VA 22202-3531; (703) 545-6900. Fax, (703) 601-0703. Francine Blackmon, Deputy Assistant Secretary.

Web, http://arba.army.pentagon.mil

Civilian office that administers boards reviewing appeals cases. Administers the Army Grade Determination Review Board, Army Board for Correction of Military Records, Disability Rating Review Board, Discharge Review Board, Army Clemency and Parole Board, Physical Disability Review Board, and Physical Disability Appeals Board, Army Corrections Command Board, and the Army Suitability Evaluation Board.

Defense Dept. (DoD), Diversity Management and Equal Opportunity, 4000 Defense Pentagon, #5D641, 20301-4000; (703) 571-9321. Fax, (703) 571-9338. F. Michael Sena, Director (Acting).

Web, http://diversity.defense.gov

Evaluates civil rights complaints from military personnel, including issues of sexual harassment and recruitment.

Defense Dept. (DoD), Legal Policy, 4000 Defense Pentagon, #2C548A, 20301-4000; (703) 697-3387. Vacant, Director; Lt. Col. Reggie D. Yager, Deputy Director.

Web, www.defense.gov

Coordinates policy in a variety of personnel-related areas, including the Members Civil Relief Act, legal assistance, political activities, and corrections.

Defense Dept. (DoD), *Sexual Assault Prevention and Response,* *4800 Mark Center Dr., #07G21, Alexandria, VA 22350; (571) 372-2657. Rear Adm. Ann M. Burkhardt, Director. Hotline, (877) 995-5247.*
General email, whc.mc-alex.wso.mbx.SAPRO@mail.mil
Web, www.sapr.mil and www.myduty.mil

Serves as the single point of accountability for the Defense Dept.'s sexual assault policy. Responsible for improving prevention, enhancing reporting and response, and holding perpetrators appropriately accountable.

Defense Legal Services Agency *(Defense Dept.),* **General Counsel,** *1600 Defense Pentagon, #3E788, 20301-1600; (703) 695-3341. Paul C. Ney Jr., General Counsel (Acting).*
Web, www.dod.mil/dodgc

Provides legal guidance to the Air Force, Army, Navy, and other Defense Dept. agencies. Administers programs governing military standards and conduct.

Marine Corps *(Defense Dept.),* **Inspector General of the Marine Corps,** *701 S. Courthouse Rd., Bldg. 12, #1J165, Arlington, VA 22204; (703) 604-4660. Fax, (703) 604-1006. Brig. Gen. David A. Ottignon (USMC), Inspector General. Complaint hotline, (866) 243-3887.*
General email, ORGMB_IGMC_ADMIN@usmc.mil
Web, www.hqmc.marines.mil/igmc

Military office that investigates complaints from Marine Corps personnel and assists in seeking corrective action.

Navy Dept. *(Defense Dept.),* **Manpower and Reserve Affairs,** *1000 Navy Pentagon, #4E590, 20350-1000; (703) 695-4333. Fax, (703) 614-4103. Gregory J. Slavonic, Assistant Secretary.*
Web, www.navy.mil

Civilian office that receives complaints from Navy and Marine Corps military personnel and assists in seeking corrective action.

▶**CONGRESS**

For a listing of relevant congressional committees and subcommittees, please see page 594 or the Appendix.

Correction of Military Records

▶**AGENCIES**

Air Force Dept. *(Defense Dept.),* **Air Force Personnel Center (AFPC), Board for the Correction of Military Records (AFBCMR),** *1500 W. Perimeter Rd., #3700, Joint Base Andrews, MD 20762; (240) 612-5379. Fax, (240) 612-5619. Troy McIntosh, Executive Director, (240) 612-5392.*
General email, usaf-pentagon.saf-mr.mbx.saf-mrbc@mail.mil
Web, www.afpc.af.mil/board-for-correction-of-military-records

Civilian board that reviews appeals for corrections to Air Force personnel records and makes recommendations to the secretary of the Air Force.

Army Dept. *(Defense Dept.),* **Board for the Correction of Military Records,** *251 18th St. South, #385, Arlington, VA 22202-3523; (703) 545-6900. Fax, (703) 601-0703. Sarah Bercaw, Director.*
Web, http://arba.army.pentagon.mil

Civilian board that reviews appeals for corrections to Army personnel records and makes recommendations to the secretary of the Army under Section 1552 of Title 10 of the U.S. Code.

Defense Dept. (DoD), *Legal Policy,* *4000 Defense Pentagon, #2C548A, 20301-4000; (703) 697-3387. Vacant, Director; Lt. Col. Reggie D. Yager, Deputy Director.*
Web, www.defense.gov

Coordinates policy for armed services boards charged with correcting military records.

Navy Dept. *(Defense Dept.),* **Board for Correction of Naval Records,** *701 S. Courthouse Rd., Bldg. 12, #1001, Arlington, VA 22204-2490; (703) 604-6884. Fax, (703) 604-3437. Elizabeth Hill, Executive Director.*
General email, BCNR@navy.mil
Web, www.secnav.navy.mil/mra/bcnr/Pages/default.aspx
Applications, BCNR_Application@navy.mil

Civilian board that reviews appeals for corrections to Navy and Marine Corps personnel records and makes recommendations to the secretary of the Navy.

U.S. Coast Guard (USCG) *(Homeland Security Dept.),* **Board for Correction of Military Records,** *245 Murray Lane, MS 485, 20528; (202) 447-4099. Fax, (202) 447-3111. Julia Andrews, Chair.*
General email, cgbcmr@dhs.gov
Web, www.uscg.mil/Resources/legal/BCMR/

Civilian board (an adjunct to the U.S. Coast Guard) that reviews appeals for corrections to Coast Guard personnel records and makes recommendations to the general counsel of the Homeland Security Dept.

Legal Proceedings

▶**AGENCIES**

Air Force Dept. *(Defense Dept.),* **Judge Advocate General (JAG),** *1420 Air Force Pentagon, 20330-1420; (703) 614-5732. Lt. Gen. Jeffrey A. Rockwell, Judge Advocate General.*
General email, usaf.pentagon.af-ja.mbx.workflow@mail.mil
Web, www.afjag.af.mil

Military office that prosecutes and defends Air Force personnel during military legal proceedings. Gives legal advice and assistance to Air Force personnel.

Army Dept. *(Defense Dept.),* **Army Clemency and Parole Board,** *Crystal Square 5, 251 18th St. South, #385,*

Arlington, VA 22202-3531; (703) 571-0532. Fax, (703) 601-0493. Alexander Conyers, Chair.
General email, army.arbainquiry@mail.mil
Web, http://arba.army.pentagon.mil/clemency-parole.cfm

Conducts clemency, parole, and mandatory supervised release hearings for eligible Army prisoners.

Army Dept. *(Defense Dept.)*, **Judge Advocate General,** 2200 Army Pentagon, #3E542, 20310-2200; (703) 697-5151. Fax, (703) 697-1059. Lt. Gen. Charles Pede (USA), Judge Advocate General. Service desk, (703) 693-0000.
Web, www.army.mil/jagc

Military policy office for the field offices that prosecute and defend Army personnel during military legal proceedings. Serves as an administrative office for military appeals court, which hears legal proceedings involving Army personnel.

Defense Dept. (DoD), *Court of Appeals for the Armed Forces,* 450 E St. N.W., 20442-0001; (202) 761-1448. Fax, (202) 761-4672. Joseph Perlak, Clerk of the Court. Library, (202) 761-1466.
Web, www.armfor.uscourts.gov

Serves as the appellate court for cases involving dishonorable or bad conduct discharges, confinement of a year or more, and the death penalty, and for cases certified to the court by the judge advocate general of an armed service. Less serious cases are reviewed by the individual armed services. Library open to the public.

Marine Corps *(Defense Dept.)*, **Judge Advocate,** 3000 Marine Corps Pentagon, #4D558, 20350-3000; (703) 614-8661. Fax, (703) 693-3208. Col. Eric R. Kleis Jr. (USMC), Deputy Staff Judge Advocate. Legal assistance, (703) 792-7442.
Web, www.hqmc.marines.mil/sja

Military office that administers legal proceedings involving Marine Corps personnel.

Navy Dept. *(Defense Dept.)*, **Judge Advocate General,** 1322 Patterson Ave. S.E., #3000, Washington Navy Yard, DC 20374-5066; (703) 614-7420. Fax, (703) 697-4610. Vice Adm. John G. Hannick III (USN), Judge Advocate General. Press, (202) 685-5275.
Web, www.jag.navy.mil and Facebook, www.facebook.com/navyjag

Military office that administers the Judge Advocate General's Corps, which conducts legal proceedings involving Navy and Marine Corps personnel.

Military Police and Corrections

▶**AGENCIES**

Army Dept. *(Defense Dept.)*, **Provost Marshal General, Operations Division,** 2800 Army Pentagon, DAPM-MPO, #MF748, 20310-2800; (703) 693-9478. Fax, (703) 693-6580. Maj. Gen. David P. Glaser (USA), Chief, (703) 693-9478.
Web, www.army.mil/opmg and Twitter, @ArmyOPMG

Develops policies and supports military police and corrections programs in all branches of the U.S. Army. Operates the Military Police Management Information System (MPMIS), which automates incident reporting and tracks information on facilities, staff, and inmates, including enemy prisoners of war.

Defense Dept. (DoD), *Legal Policy,* 4000 Defense Pentagon, #2C548A, 20301-4000; (703) 697-3387. Vacant, Director; Lt. Col. Reggie D. Yager, Deputy Director.
Web, www.defense.gov

Coordinates and reviews Defense Dept. policies and programs relating to deserters.

MILITARY HISTORY AND HONORS

General

▶**AGENCIES**

Air Force Dept. *(Defense Dept.)*, **Air Force History and Museum Programs,** 1190 Air Force Pentagon, #4E1062, 20330-1190 (mailing address: 3 Brookley Ave., Box 94 Joint Base Anacostia-Bolling, Washington, DC 20032); (703) 697-5600. Walter (Walt) A. Grudzinskas, Director. Historian, (202) 404-2264. Reference Section, (202) 404-2261.
General email, usaf.pentagon.af-ho.mbx.afhso-research@mail.mil
Web, www.afhistoryandmuseums.af.mil and www.afhistory.af.mil

Publishes histories, studies, monographs, and reference works; directs worldwide Air Force History and Museums Program and provides guidance to the Air Force Historical Research Agency at Maxwell Air Force Base in Alabama, Air Force Historical Support Division in Washington, D.C., and National Museum of the USAF in Ohio; supports Air Force Air Staff agencies and responds to inquiries from the public and the U.S. government.

Air Force Dept. *(Defense Dept.)*, **Historical Studies Office (AFHSO),** Joint Base Anacostia-Bolling, 20 MacDill Blvd. S.E., #207, 20032 (mailing address: 3 Brookley Ave, Box 94, JBAB Washington, DC 20032); (202) 404-2264. Mary Dysart, Research Agency Commander; Walter A. Grudzinskas, Director of Air Force History and Museums. Reference desk, (334) 953-5697.
General email, AFHRA.NEWS@us.af.mil
Web, www.afhra.af.mil

Supports the Director of Air Force History and Museums and conducts research and analysis of the service's major operational activities. Publishes books, monographs, studies, and reports covering the history of the Air Force. (Connected with the Air Force Historical Research Agency located at Maxwell Air Force Base, Alabama.)

Army Dept. *(Defense Dept.)*, **Institute of Heraldry,** 9325 Gunston Rd., Bldg. 1466, #S113, Fort Belvoir, VA 22060-5579; (703) 806-0055. Fax, (703) 806-4964. Charles Mugno, Director.

General email, TIOHWebmaster@us.army.mil

Web, www.tioh.hqda.pentagon.mil

Furnishes heraldic services to the armed forces and other U.S. government agencies, including the Executive Office of the President. Responsible for research, design, development, and standardization of official symbolic items, including seals, decorations, medals, insignia, badges, flags, and other items awarded to or authorized for official wear or display by government personnel and agencies. Limited research and information services on these items are provided to the general public.

Army Dept. *(Defense Dept.), U.S. Army Center of Military History,* Fort Lesley J. McNair, Collins Hall, 102 4th Ave., Bldg. 35, 20319-5060; (202) 685-2706. Fax, (202) 685-4570. Charles Bowrey, Executive Director.

Library, (202) 685-3573.

Web, www.history.army.mil

Publishes the official history of the Army. Provides information on Army history; coordinates Army museum system and art program. Works with Army school system to ensure that history is included in curriculum. Provides heraldic products and services in support of federal government. Sponsors professional appointments, fellowships, and awards. Library open to researchers for archival research Monday through Thursday, 8:00 a.m.–4:00 p.m., and Friday 8:00 a.m.–12:00 noon; not a lending library.

Defense Dept. (DoD), *Center for Military History,* 1777 N. Kent St., #5000, Arlington, VA 22209; Erin R. Mahan, Chief Historian.

Web, http://history.defense.gov

Researches and writes historical accounts of the office of the secretary of defense; coordinates historical activities of the Defense Dept. and prepares special studies at the request of the secretary.

Defense Dept. (DoD), *Joint History Office,* 9999 Defense Pentagon, #1A466, 20318-9999; (703) 695-2137. Fax, (703) 614-6243. John F. Shortal, Director.

General email, john.f.shortal.civ@mail.mil

Web, www.jcs.mil/about/joint-staff-history

Provides historical support services to the chair of the Joint Chiefs of Staff and the Joint Staff, including research; writes the official history of the Joint Chiefs. Supervises field programs encompassing nine Unified Commands.

Marine Corps *(Defense Dept.), History Division,* Simmons Center, 2044 Broadway St., Quantico, VA 22134; (703) 432-4877. Jay Hatton, Director (Acting). Archives, (703) 784-4685. Reference, (703) 432-4874.

General email, history.division@usmcu.edu

Web, www.mcu.usmc.mil/historydivision

Writes official histories of the corps for government agencies and the public; answers inquiries about Marine Corps history.

National Archives and Records Administration (NARA), *Reference Services,* 4205 Suitland Rd., Suitland, MD 20746-8001; (301) 778-1600. Christopher Pinkney, Director.

General email, suitland.reference@nara.gov

Web, www.archives.gov/frc/reference-services.html

Contains Army records from the Revolutionary War to the Vietnam War, Navy records from the Revolutionary War to the Korean War, and Air Force records from 1947 to 1954. Handles records captured from enemy powers at the end of World War II and a small collection of records captured from the Vietnamese. Conducts research in response to specific inquiries; makes records available for reproduction or examination in research room.

National Museum of American History *(Smithsonian Institution), Armed Forces History,* 14th St. and Constitution Ave. N.W., NMAH-4032, MRC 620, 20560-0620; (202) 633-3950. Jennifer Locke Jones, Chair.

Web, https://americanhistory.si.edu/about/departments/armed-forces-history/collections

Maintains collections relating to the history of the U.S. armed forces, U.S. military technology, and the American flag; includes manuscripts, documents, correspondence, uniforms, small arms and weapons, and other personal memorabilia of armed forces personnel of all ranks. Research areas are open by appointment.

National Museum of Health and Medicine *(Defense Dept.),* 2500 Linden Lane, Silver Spring, MD 20910 (mailing address: 2460 Linden Lane, Bldg. 2500, Silver Spring, MD 20910); (301) 319-3300. Fax, (301) 319-3373. Dr. Adrianne Noe, Director. Tours, (301) 319-3312.

General email, usarmy.detrick.medcom-usamrmc.list.medical-museum@mail.mil

Web, www.medicalmuseum.mil and

Twitter, @medicalmuseum

Maintains exhibits related to pathology and the history of medicine, particularly military medicine during the Civil War. Open to the public 10:00 a.m.–5:30 p.m., seven days a week. Study collection available for scholars by appointment.

Naval History and Heritage Command *(Navy Dept.),* 805 Kidder Breese St. S.E., Washington Navy Yard, DC 20374-5060; (202) 433-7880. Fax, (202) 781-0021. Rear Adm. Samuel Cox (USN, Ret.), Director. Archives, (202) 433-3224. Art Gallery, (202) 433-3815. Library, (202) 433-4132. Museum, (202) 433-4882. Press, (202) 685-0581.

General email, NHHCPublicAffairs@navy.mil

Web, www.history.navy.mil, Twitter, @USNHistory and Facebook, www.facebook.com/USNHistory

Produces publications on naval history. Maintains historical files on Navy ships, operations, shore installations, and aviation. Collects Navy art, artifacts, and photographs. Library, archives, museum, and gallery are open to the public.

Naval History and Heritage Command *(Navy Dept.),* *Navy Art Collection,* Washington Navy Yard, 822 Sicard St. S.E., Bldg. 67, 20374 (mailing address: 805 Kidder Breese St. S.E., Washington Navy Yard, DC 20374); (202) 433-3815. Gale Munro, Head Curator.

General email, NavyArt@navy.mil

Web, www.history.navy.mil

Holdings include more than 18,000 paintings, prints, drawings, and sculptures. Artworks depict naval ships, personnel, and action from all eras of U.S. naval history, especially the eras of World War II, the Korean War, and Desert Shield/Storm. Open to the public. Visitors without Defense Dept. or military identification must call in advance. Photo identification required.

U.S. Coast Guard (USCG) (Homeland Security Dept.), Historian, *CG-09224, 2703 Martin Luther King Jr. Ave. S.E., MS 7816, 20593-7816; (202) 372-4651. Fax, (202) 372-4984. Scott Price, Chief Historian.*

General email, History@uscg.mil

Web, www.uscg.mil/Historians-Office/

Collects and maintains Coast Guard historical artifacts and documents. Archives are available to the public by appointment only.

U.S. Navy Museum *(Naval Historical Center), Bldg. 76, 805 Kidder Breese St. S.E., Washington Navy Yard, DC 20374-5060; (202) 433-4882. Fax, (202) 433-8200. James H. Bruns, Museum Director; Rear Adm. Samuel Cox (USN, Ret.), Director of Naval History and Heritage Command; Laura Hockensmith, Deputy Director of Education and Public Programs. Tours, (202) 433-6826.*

General email, hhhcpublicaffairs@navy.mil

Web, www.history.navy.mil and Twitter, @USNhistory

Collects, preserves, displays, and interprets historic naval artifacts and artwork. Presents a complete overview of U.S. naval history. Open to the public. Photo identification required.

▶**NONGOVERNMENTAL**

Air Force Historical Foundation, *602 California Ave., #F162, Joint Base Andrews, MD 20762 (mailing address: P.O. Box 790, Clinton, MD 20735-0790); (301) 736-1959. Lt. Col. James (Jim) A. Vertenten (USAF, Ret.), Executive Director, (703) 395-7261.*

General email, ed@afhistory.org

Web, www.afhistory.org

Membership: individuals interested in the history of the U.S. Air Force and U.S. air power. Bestows awards on Air Force Academy and Air War College students and to other active duty personnel. Funds research and publishes books on aviation and Air Force history.

American Battlefield Trust, *1156 15th St. N.W., #900, 20005; (202) 367-1861. Fax, (202) 367-1865. James Lighthizer, President.*

General email, info@battlefields.org

Web, www.battlefields.org and Twitter, @battlefields

Membership: preservation professionals, historians, conservation activists, and citizens. Preserves endangered Civil War battlefields throughout the United States. Conducts preservation conferences and workshops. Advises local preservation groups. Monitors legislation and regulations at the federal, state, and local levels.

Marine Corps Heritage Foundation, *18900 Jefferson Davis Hwy., Triangle, VA 22172; (703) 640-7965. Fax, (703) 640-9546. Maj. Gen. James A. Kessler Jr. (USMC, Ret.), President. Toll-free, (800) 397-7585.*

General email, info@marineheritage.org

Web, www.marineheritage.org

Preserves and promotes Marine Corps history through education, awards, and publications. Offers funding for the study of Marine Corps history. Funds the ongoing expansion of the National Museum of the Marine Corps.

Military Order of the World Wars, *435 N. Lee St., Alexandria, VA 22314-2301; (703) 683-4911. Fax, (703) 683-4501. Brig. Gen. Arthur B. Morrill III (USAF, Ret.), Chief of Staff.*

General email, chiefofstaff@moww.org

Web, www.moww.org and Facebook, www.facebook.com/ militaryorder

Membership: retired and active duty commissioned officers, warrant officers, and flight officers. Presents awards to outstanding Reserve Officers Training Corps (ROTC) cadets; gives awards to Boy Scouts and Girl Scouts; conducts youth leadership conferences.

Minerva Center, *20 Granada Rd., Pasadena, MD 21122-2708; (410) 437-5379. Linda Grant DePauw, Director.*

General email, lgdepauw@gmail.com

Encourages the study of women in war and women and the military. Focus includes current U.S. servicewomen, women veterans, women in war and the military abroad, and the preservation of artifacts, oral history, and first-hand accounts of women's experience in military service.

National Guard Educational Foundation, *1 Massachusetts Ave. N.W., 20001; (202) 789-0031. Fax, (202) 682-9358. Anne Armstrong, Deputy Director, (202) 408-5890; Ryan Trainor, Archivist, (202) 408-5887. Library, (202) 408-5890. Toll-free, (888) 226-4287.*

General email, ngef@ngef.org

Web, www.ngef.org

Promotes public awareness of the National Guard by providing information about its history and traditions. Museum and library open to the public.

National Guard Memorial Museum, *1 Massachusetts Ave. N.W., 20001; (202) 789-0031. Fax, (202) 682-9358. Luke Guthrie, Director; Anne Armstrong, Deputy Director, (202) 408-5890. Toll-free, (888) 226-4287.*

General email, ngef@ngaus.org

Web, www.ngef.org/national-guard-memorial-museum, Twitter, @NGMuseum and Facebook, www.facebook.com/ NationalGuardMemorialMuseum

Features exhibit areas that explore the National Guard from colonial times through the world wars and the cold war to the modern era through timelines, photographs, artifacts, light, and sound.

National Museum of American Jewish Military History, *1811 R St. N.W., 20009; (202) 265-6280. Fax, (202) 462-3192. Greg Byrne, Director. Tours, (202) 265-6280.*

General email, nmajmh@nmajmh.org

Web, www.nmajmh.org

Collects, preserves, and displays memorabilia of Jewish men and women in the military; conducts research; sponsors seminars; provides information on the history of Jewish participation in the U.S. armed forces.

Naval Historical Foundation, *1306 Dahlgren Ave. S.E., Washington Navy Yard, DC 20374-5055 (mailing address: P.O. Box 15304, Washington, DC 20043); (202) 678-4333. Fax, (703) 580-5280. Dale Lumme, Executive Director. Toll-free, (888) 880-0102.*

General email, info@navyhistory.org

Web, www.navyhistory.org and Twitter, @USNavyHistory

Collects private documents and artifacts relating to naval history; maintains collection on deposit with the Library of Congress for public reference; conducts oral history and heritage speakers programs; raises funds to support the Navy Museum and historical programs.

Cemeteries and Memorials

►AGENCIES

Air Force Memorial Foundation, *1 Air Force Memorial Dr., Arlington, VA 22204; (703) 462-4358. (703) 695-3592. Zachary Steele, Events and Outreach Coordinator.*

General email, afmemorial@mail.mil

Web, www.afdw.af.mil/afmemorial and Facebook, www.facebook.com/AirForceMemorial

Oversees daily management of and directs event planning and fund-raising in support of the Air Force Memorial.

American Battle Monuments Commission, *Courthouse Plaza 2, 2300 Clarendon Blvd., #500, Arlington, VA 22201-3367; (703) 696-6900. William M. Matz Jr., Secretary, (703) 696-6902.*

General email, info@abmc.gov

Web, www.abmc.gov and Facebook, www.facebook.com/abmcpage

Manages twenty-four military cemeteries overseas and certain memorials in the United States; provides next of kin with grave site and related information.

Army Dept. *(Defense Dept.), Arlington National Cemetery, Interment Services, Arlington, VA 22211; (877) 907-8585. Karen Durham-Aguilera, Executive Director. Fax (for documents), (571) 256-3334.*

Email (for documents), arlingtoncemetery.isb@mail.mil and Web, www.arlingtoncemetery.mil

Arranges interment services and provides eligibility information for burials at Arlington National Cemetery.

National Cemetery Administration *(Veterans Affairs Dept.), 810 Vermont Ave. N.W., #43A1, 20420; (202) 461-6112. Fax, (202) 273-6709. Randy C. Reeves, Under Secretary for Memorial Affairs. Information on burial eligibility, (800) 827-1000.*

Web, www.cem.va.gov

https://gravelocator.cem.va.gov and Twitter, @VANatCemeteries

Administers VA national cemeteries; furnishes markers and headstones for deceased veterans; administers state grants to establish, expand, and improve veterans' cemeteries. Provides presidential memorial certificates to next of kin.

►CONGRESS

For a listing of relevant congressional committees and subcommittees, please see page 594 or the Appendix.

►NONGOVERNMENTAL

U.S. Navy Memorial Foundation, *701 Pennsylvania Ave. N.W., #123, 20004-2608; (202) 380-0710. Fax, (202) 737-2308. Rear Adm. Frank Thorp IV (USN, Ret.), President. Toll-free, (800) 821-8892.*

General email, bosuch@navymemorial.org

Web, www.navymemorial.org and Twitter, @Navymemorial

Educational foundation authorized by Congress. Focuses on U.S. naval history; built and supports the national Navy memorial to honor those who serve or have served in the sea services.

Women in Military Service for America Memorial Foundation, *P.O. Box 420560, 20042-0560; (703) 533-1155. Fax, (703) 931-4208. Maj. Gen. Dee Ann McWilliams (USA, Ret.), President; LTC Marilla Cushman (USA, Ret.), Director of Development and Public Relations. Information, (800) 222-2294. The Women's Memorial, (703) 892-2606.*

General email, hq@womensmemorial.org

Web, www.womensmemorial.org and Twitter, @wimsatweets

Authorized by Congress to create, build, and operate the national memorial to honor women who serve or have served in the U.S. armed forces from the Revolutionary War to the present. Mailing address is for donations. Memorial is located at the Gateway at Arlington National Cemetery.

Ceremonies, Military Bands

►AGENCIES

Air Force Dept. *(Defense Dept.), Air Force Bands, 1690 Air Force Pentagon, Room 1D887, 20330-1690; (202) 767-4310. CMSgt. William E. Marr, Chief Manager. Public Affairs, (703) 693-0019.*

Web, www.music.af.mil, Twitter, @USAFBands and Facebook, www.facebook.com/AirFoceBands

Disseminates information to the public regarding various Air Force bands, including their schedules and performances. Oversees policy, training, and personnel assignments for Air Force bands.

Army Dept. *(Defense Dept.), Army Field Band, 4214 Field Band Dr., #5330, Fort Meade, MD 20755-7055; (301) 677-6586. Lt. Col. Jim R. Keene (USA), Commander.*

General email, usarmyfieldband@mail.mil

Web, http://armyfieldband.com

Supports the Army by providing musical services for official military ceremonies and community events. Sponsors vocal and instrumental clinics for high school and college students.

Army Dept. *(Defense Dept.), Ceremonies and Special Events,* Fort Lesley J. McNair, 103 3rd Ave., 20319-5058; (202) 685-2993. Ronald Chaney, Ceremonies Chief. *Web, www.mdwhome.mdw.army.mil/ceremonial-support/requesting-ceremonial-support and Twitter, @MDW-USARMY*

Coordinates and schedules public ceremonies and special events, including appearances of all armed forces bands and honor guards.

Army Dept. *(Defense Dept.), The U.S. Army Band,* Attn: TUSAB, 400 McNair Rd., Fort Myer, VA 22211-1306; (703) 696-3718. Fax, (703) 696-0279. Col. Andrew J. Esch (USA), Commander. Music Library, (703) 696-3648. *Web, www.usarmyband.com and Twitter, @thearmyband*

Supports the Army by providing musical services for official military ceremonies and community events.

Defense Dept. (DoD), *Community and Public Outreach,* 1400 Defense Pentagon, 2E984, 20301-1400; (703) 693-2337. Fax, (703) 697-2577. Col. Paul Haverstick, Deputy Assistant Secretary (Acting). Toll-free (Military OneSource), (800) 342-9647. Press, (703) 697-5131. Public Affairs, (703) 571-3343. *Web, www.defense.gov*

Administers requests for ceremonial bands and other military assets for public events.

Marine Corps *(Defense Dept.), Marine Band,* Marine Barracks Annex, 7th St. and K St. S.E., 20003 (mailing address: Marine Barracks Washington, 8th St. and Eye St. S.E., Washington, DC 20390); (202) 433-5809. Fax, (202) 433-4752. Col. Jason K. Fettig, Director. Concert information, (202) 433-4011. National tours, (703) 614-1405. *General email, marineband.communication@usmc.mil*

Web, www.marineband.marines.mil and Facebook, www.facebook.com/marineband

Provides music for the U.S. President and the Commandant of the Marine Corps. Supports the Marine Corps by providing musical services for official military ceremonies and community events.

Navy Dept. *(Defense Dept.), Navy Band,* 617 Warrington Ave. S.E., Washington Navy Yard, DC 20374-5054; (202) 433-3676. Fax, (202) 433-4108. Capt. Kenneth Collins (USN), Commanding Officer. Auditions, (202) 433-2840. Information, (202) 433-3366. Public Affairs, (202) 433-4777. *General email, NavyBand.Public.Affairs@navy.mil*

Web, www.navyband.navy.mil, Twitter, @usnavyband and Facebook, www.facebook.com/usnavyband

Supports the Navy by providing musical services for official military ceremonies and community events.

U.S. Naval Academy *(Defense Dept.), Band,* 101 Buchanan Rd., Annapolis, MD 21402-1258; (410) 293-3282. Fax, (410) 293-2116. Lt. Cmdr. Patrick K. Sweeten, Director. Concert information, (410) 293-1257. Press, (410) 293-1262. *General email, bandrops@usna.edu*

Web, www.usna.edu/USNABand and Twitter, @USNAband

The Navy's oldest continuing musical organization. Supports the Navy by providing musical services for official military ceremonies and community events.

U.S. Naval Academy *(Defense Dept.), Drum and Bugle Corps,* U.S. Naval Academy, Alumni Hall, 675 Decatur Rd., Annapolis, MD 21402-5086; (410) 293-3602. Fax, (410) 293-4508. Jeff Weir, Corps Director. *General email, weir@usna.edu*

Web, www.usna.edu/USNADB

One of the oldest drum and bugle corps in the United States. The all-midshipmen drum and bugle corps plays for Brigade of Midshipmen at sporting events, pep rallies, parades, and noon formations. Supports the Navy by providing musical services for official military ceremonies and community events.

RESERVES AND NATIONAL GUARD

General

▶**AGENCIES**

Air Force Dept. *(Defense Dept.), Air Force Reserve Command (AFRC),* 1150 Air Force Pentagon, #4E138, 20330-1150; (703) 695-9225. Lt. Gen. Richard W. Scobee, Chief. Public Affairs, (478) 327-1748. *Public Affairs email, afrc.paworkflow@us.af.mil, Web, www.afrc.af.mil, Twitter, @USAFReserve and Facebook, www.facebook.com/usairforcereserve*

Units of commissioned officers and enlisted airmen who are ready for active duty and are performing specialized missions and operations for the Air Force. (Headquarters in Ga.)

Air Force Dept. *(Defense Dept.), Manpower and Reserve Affairs,* 1660 Air Force Pentagon, #5D742, 20330-1660; (703) 697-6375. Fax, (703) 695-2701. Vacant, Deputy Assistant Secretary. *Web, www.af.mil*

Civilian-led office responsible for overseeing the Air Force Reserve and developing policies concerning manpower, military and civilian personnel issues, Reserve component affairs, and readiness support for the Air Force. (Headquarters in Ga.)

Air Force Dept. *(Defense Dept.), Manpower and Reserve Affairs (SAF/MR),* 1670 Air Force Pentagon, #4E1020, 20330-1670; (703) 697-2302. Shon J. Manasco, Assistant Secretary. Public Affairs, (703) 697-5828.

General email, usaf.pentagon.saf-mr.mbx.saf-mr-workflow-all@mail.mil

Web, www.af.mil/About-Us/Biographies/Display/Article/1391994/shon-j-manasco

Civilian office that oversees manpower, military, and civilian personnel, Reserve component affairs, and readiness support for the Air Force.

Army Dept. *(Defense Dept.), Army Reserve,* 2400 Army Pentagon, #3E562, 20310-2400; (703) 695-1784. Lt. Gen. Charles D. Luckey (USA), Chief. Web, www.usar.army.mil and Twitter, @USArmyReserve

Military office that monitors legislative affairs as well as coordinates and directs Army Reserve matters (excluding the Army National Guard).

Army Dept. *(Defense Dept.), Manpower and Reserve Affairs,* 111 Army Pentagon, #2E460, 20310-0111; (703) 697-9253. Fax, (703) 692-9000. Sgt. Maj. Tamara Gregory, Senior Enlisted Advisor. Web, www.asamra.army.mil

Civilian office that reviews policies and programs for Army personnel and reserves; makes recommendations to the secretary of the Army. Oversees training, military preparedness, and mobilization for all civilians and active and reserve members of the Army.

Defense Dept. (DoD), *Manpower and Reserve Affairs,* 1500 Defense Pentagon, #2E556, 20301-1500; (703) 697-6631. Fax, (703) 697-1682. Stephanie Barna, Assistant Secretary (Acting). Web, www.people.mil

Civilian office that addresses all policy matters pertaining to the six reserve components of the military services. Develops and delivers civilian and military personnel policy and implements human resource solutions that support the Total Force and mission readiness.

Defense Dept. (DoD), *National Committee for Employer Support of the Guard and Reserve,* 4800 Mark Center Dr., #03E25, Arlington, VA 22350-1200; (703) 882-3747. Capt. Juliet Perkins (USN), Director; Craig M. McKinley, National Chair. Toll-free, (800) 336-4590. General email, osd.USERRA@mail.mil

Web, www.esgr.mil

Public Affairs email, osd.esgr-pa@mail.mil

Works to gain and maintain employer support for National Guard and Reserve service by recognizing outstanding support and providing service members and employers with information on applicable law. Volunteers provide free education, consultation, and, if necessary, mediation between employers and National Guard and Reserve service members.

Marine Corps *(Defense Dept.), Manpower and Reserve Affairs,* James Wesley Marsh Center, 3280 Russell Rd., Bldg. 3280, Quantico, VA 22134; (703) 784-9012. Lt. Gen. Michael Rocco (USMC), Deputy Commandant. Web, www.manpower.usmc.mil

Oversees planning, directing, coordinating, and supervising of both active and reserve Marine Corps forces.

Marine Corps *(Defense Dept.), Reserve Affairs,* 3280 Russell Rd., Quantico, VA 22134-5103; (703) 784-9350. Fax, (703) 784-9805. Col. Morris Rowe (USMC), Director. General email, SMB_HQMC_HROMDIR@usmc.mil Web, www.marines.mil

Military office that coordinates and directs Marine Corps Reserve matters.

National Guard Bureau *(Defense Dept.),* 111 George Mason Dr., Arlington, Va, 22204; (703) 607-3643. Fax, (703) 607-1313. Gen. Joseph L. Lengyel (USA), Chief. Press, (703) 607-6767. General email, ng.NCR.mbx.gomailbox@mail.mil Web, www.nationalguard.mil and Twitter, @nationalguard

Military office that oversees and coordinates activities of the Air National Guard and Army National Guard.

National Guard Bureau *(Defense Dept.), Air National Guard,* 1000 Airforce Pentagon, #4E126, 20330; (703) 614-8033. Lt. Gen. L. Scott Rice (ANG), Director. Web, www.ang.af.mil and Facebook, www.facebook.com/AirNationalGuard

Military office that coordinates and directs Air National Guard matters.

National Guard Bureau *(Defense Dept.), Army National Guard,* 111 S. George Mason Dr., Arlington, VA 22204; (703) 607-7000. Fax, (703) 607-7088. Lt. Gen. Timothy J. Kadavy (ARNG), Director. Public Affairs, (703) 601-6767. Web, www.nationalguard.mil

Military office that coordinates and directs Army National Guard matters.

National Guard Bureau *(Defense Dept.), Chaplain Services,* 111 S. George Mason Dr., Arlington, VA 22204; (703) 607-8657. Fax, (703) 607-5295. Brig. Gen. Kenneth (Ed) Brandt (ARNG), Director. General email, ng.ncr.arng.mbx.office-of-the-chaplain@mail.mil Web, www.nationalguard.mil

Represents the Chief National Guard Bureau on all aspects of the chaplains' mission. Directs and oversees the activities and policies of the National Guard Chaplain Services. Oversees chaplains and religious services within the National Guard; maintains liaison with religious denominations.

Navy Dept. *(Defense Dept.), Manpower and Reserve Affairs,* 1000 Navy Pentagon, #4E590, 20350-1000; (703) 695-4333. Fax, (703) 614-4103. Gregory J. Slavonic, Assistant Secretary. Web, www.navy.mil

Civilian office that oversees the recruitment of active and reserve Navy personnel, government civilians, contractors, and volunteers.

Navy Dept. *(Defense Dept.), Navy Reserve,* 2000 Navy Pentagon, CNO-N095, #4E426, 20350-2000; (703) 693-5757. Vice Adm. Luke M. McCollum (USN), Chief. Duty office, (757) 445-8506.

Web, www.navy.com/about/about-reserve.html and *Twitter, @navy_reserve*

Military office that coordinates and directs Navy Reserve matters. (Headquarters in Norfolk, Va.)

Navy Dept. *(Defense Dept.), Reserve Affairs, 1000 Navy Pentagon, #4D548, 20350-1000; (703) 614-1327. Fax, (703) 693-4959. Dennis Biddick, Deputy Assistant Secretary. Web, www.navy.mil*

Civilian office that reviews Navy and Marine Corps Reserve policies.

U.S. Coast Guard (USCG) *(Homeland Security Dept.), Reserve and Military Personnel, CG-13, 2703 Martin Luther King Jr. Ave. S.E., MS 7907, 20593-7097; (202) 475-5420. Matthew W. Sibley, Director; George M. Williamson, Master Chief. General email, cgreserve@uscg.mil*

Web, www.reserve.uscg.mil

The Reservist *magazine, TheReservist@uscg.mil*

Develops and oversees military personnel policy programs to recruit, train, and support all U.S. Coast Guard reserve and active duty forces. Publishes *The Reservist* magazine.

▶**NONGOVERNMENTAL**

Assn. of Civilian Technicians (ACT), *12620 Lake Ridge Dr., Lake Ridge, VA 22192-2354; (703) 494-4845. Fax, (703) 494-0961. Terry W. Garnett, National President. Web, www.actnat.com*

Membership: federal civil service employees of the National Guard and Title 5 federal employees. Represents members before federal agencies and Congress.

Assn. of the U.S. Navy, *3601 Eisenhower Ave., #110, Alexandria, VA 22304; (703) 548-5800. Fax, (703) 683-3647. Rear Adm. Christopher Cole (USN Ret.), Chief Executive Officer. Toll-free, (877) 628-9411. General email, info@ausn.org*

Web, www.ausn.org and *Twitter, @AUSNTweets*

Membership: active duty and retired Navy and Navy Reserve officers and their families and persons interested in the U.S. Navy. Supports and promotes U.S. military and naval policies, particularly the interests of Navy personnel and Navy veterans. Offers education programs, reviews of officer and enlisted records, and scholarships for the education of family members. Provides the public with information on national security issues. Assists members with Navy careers, military retirement, and veterans' benefits.

Assn. of the United States Army, *2425 Wilson Blvd., Arlington, VA 22201; (703) 841-4300. Fax, (703) 525-9039. Gen. Carter Ham (USA Ret.), President, (703) 907-2603. Information, (800) 336-4570. General email, info@ausa.org*

Web, www.ausa.org and *Twitter, @AUSAorg*

Membership: civilians and active duty and retired members of the armed forces. Conducts symposia on defense issues and researches topics that affect the military.

Enlisted Assn. of the National Guard of the United States, *1 Massachusetts Ave. N.W., #880, 20001; (703) 519-3846. Fax, (703) 519-3849. Frank Yoakum, Executive Director. Information, (800) 234-3264. General email, eangus@eangus.org*

Web, www.eangus.org

Membership: active duty and retired enlisted members and veterans of the National Guard. Promotes a strong national defense and National Guard. Sponsors scholarships, conducts seminars, and provides information concerning members and their families.

National Guard Assn. of the United States, *1 Massachusetts Ave. N.W., 20001-1431; (202) 789-0031. Fax, (202) 682-9358. Brig. Gen. Roy Robinson (ARNG, Ret.), President, (202) 408-5894. General email, ngaus@ngaus.org*

Web, www.ngaus.org and *Twitter, @NGAUS1878*

Membership: active duty and retired officers of the National Guard. Works to promote a strong national defense and to maintain a strong, ready National Guard.

Reserve Officers Assn. of the United States, *1 Constitution Ave. N.E., 20002-5618; (202) 479-2200. Fax, (202) 547-1641. Jeff Philips, Executive Director, (202) 646-7701. Information, (800) 809-9448. General email, roainfo@roa.org*

Web, www.roa.org and *Twitter, @ReserveOfficer*

Membership: active duty and inactive commissioned and noncommissioned officers of all uniformed services. Supports continuation of a reserve force to enhance national security. Monitors legislation and regulations.

VETERANS

General

▶**AGENCIES**

Armed Forces Retirement Home—Washington, *140 Rock Creek Church Rd. N.W., 20011-8400 (mailing address: 3700 N. Capitol St. N.W., Washington, DC 20011-8400); (800) 422-9988. (202) 541-5501. Fax, (202) 541-7519. Stephen T. Rippe, Chief Operating Officer. General email, admissions@afrh.gov*

Web, www.afrh.gov

Gives domiciliary and medical care to retired members of the armed services or career service personnel unable to earn a livelihood. Formerly known as U.S. Soldiers' and Airmen's Home. (Armed Forces Retirement Home in Gulfport, Miss., reopened in 2010.)

Center for Minority Veterans *(Veterans Affairs Dept.), 810 Vermont Ave. N.W., #436, MC 00M, 20420; (202) 461-6191. Fax, (202) 273-7092. Stephen P. Dillard, Director. Web, www.va.gov/centerforminorityveterans*

Advises the secretary on adoption and implementation of policies and programs affecting minority veterans,

Veterans Affairs Department

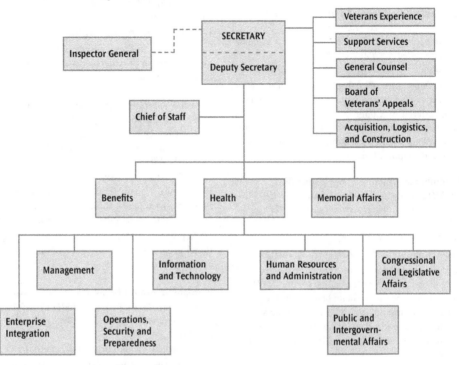

specifically Pacific Islander, Asian American, African American, Hispanic/Latino, and Native American, including American Indian, Alaska Native, and Native Hawaiian veterans.

Center for Women Veterans *(Veterans Affairs Dept.),* *810 Vermont Ave. N.W., #435, MC 00W, 20420; (202) 461-6193. Fax, (202) 273-7092. Vacant, Director; Anna D. Crenshaw, Deputy Director.*
General email, 00w@va.gov

Web, www.va.gov/womenvet

Advises the secretary on policy on matters related to women veterans; recognizes the service and contributions of women veterans and women in the military.

Navy Dept. *(Defense Dept.), Council of Review Boards,* *720 Kennon St. S.E., Bldg. 36, #309, Washington Navy Yard, DC 20374-5023; (202) 685-6408. Fax, (202) 685-6610. Jeffrey Riehl (USMC, Ret.), Director.*
General email, crsc@navy.mil

Web, www.secnav.navy.mil/mra/CORB/pages/home.aspx

Includes the Naval Clemency and Parole Board, which reviews cases of Navy and Marine Corps prisoners; the Naval Discharge Review Board, which considers former service members' less-than-honorable discharge for potential upgrade; the Physical Evaluation Board, which makes determinations about physical fitness for continuation of military service; and the Combat-Related Special Compensation Board, which makes determinations about combat-related conditions and appropriate compensation. All boards make recommendations to the secretary of the Navy.

Veterans Affairs Dept. (VA), *810 Vermont Ave. N.W., MC 00, 20420; (202) 461-4800. Fax, (202) 495-5463. Robert Wilkie, Secretary; James G. Byrne, Deputy Secretary (Acting). Benefits, (800) 827-1000. Crisis line, (800) 273-8255, option 1. Health care, (877) 222-8387. Press, (202) 461-7600. Toll-free, (844) 698-2311.*
Web, www.va.gov, Twitter, @DeptVetAffairs
Information System (IRIS), https://iris.va.gov

Administers programs benefiting veterans, including disability compensation, pensions, education, home loans, insurance, vocational rehabilitation, medical care at veterans' hospitals and outpatient facilities, and burial benefits.

Veterans Affairs Dept. (VA), *Enterprise Integration, 810 Vermont Ave. N.W., #300, MS 008, 20420; (202) 461-5800. Fax, (202) 273-5993. D. Melissa Glynn, Assistant Secretary.*
General email, vacontactopp@va.gov

Web, www.va.gov/op3

Serves as the single departmentwide repository, clearinghouse, and publication source for veterans' demographic and statistical information. Provides advice and support to the secretary in the areas of strategic planning, policy development, program analysis and management, and data governance.

▶ **CONGRESS**

For a listing of relevant congressional committees and subcommittees, please see page 594 or the Appendix.

►**NONGOVERNMENTAL**

American Legion, *Legislative Affairs, 1608 K St. N.W., 20006; (202) 861-2700. Fax, (202) 861-2786. Derek Fronaberger, Deputy Director of Legislative Affairs, (202) 263-2990. Media, (202) 263-2991. Web, www.legion.org and Twitter, @AmericanLegion*

Membership: honorably discharged veterans who served on active duty during periods of declared military conflict. Chartered by Congress to assist veterans with claims for benefits; offers a large array of programs and services for veterans and their families. (National headquarters in Indianapolis, Ind.)

AMVETS (American Veterans), *4647 Forbes Blvd., Lanham, MD 20706; (301) 459-9600. Fax, (301) 459-7924. Joseph Chenelly, Executive Director. Toll-free, (877) 726-8387. General email, amvets@amvets.org Web, www.amvets.org and Twitter, @AMVETSHQ*

Membership: those who are serving or have served honorably in any branch of the military from WWII to the present. Helps members obtain benefits and services; participates in community programs; operates a volunteer service that donates time to hospitalized veterans and warrior transition programs. Monitors legislation and regulations.

Military Officers Assn. of America, *201 N. Washington St., Alexandria, VA 22314-2539; (703) 549-2311. Lt. Gen. Dana Atkins (USAF, Ret.), President. Information, (800) 234-6622. General email, msc@moaa.org Web, www.moaa.org*

Membership: officers, former officers, and surviving spouses of officers of the uniformed services. Assists members, their dependents, and survivors with military personnel matters, including service status and retirement problems; provides employment assistance. Monitors legislation affecting active duty officers, retirees, and veterans' affairs, health, and military compensation issues.

Military Order of the Purple Heart of the U.S.A., *5413 Backlick Rd., Suite B, Springfield, VA 22151-3960; (703) 642-5360. Fax, (703) 642-1841. Lt. Col. Ernesto Hernandez III (USMC, Ret.), National Adjutant. Toll-free, (888) 668-1656. General email, communications@purpleheart.org Web, www.purpleheart.org*

Membership: veterans awarded the Purple Heart for combat wounds. Chartered by Congress to assist veterans and their families. Conducts service and welfare work on behalf of disabled and needy veterans and their families, especially those requiring claims assistance, those who are homeless, and those requiring employment assistance. Organizes volunteers to provide assistance to hospitalized veterans at VA medical facilities and State Veterans Homes.

National Coalition for Homeless Veterans, *1730 M. St. N.W., #705, 20036; (202) 546-1969. Fax, (202) 546-2063.* Kathryn Monet, Executive Director. Toll-free, 800-VET-HELP. Toll-free fax, (888) 233-8582. General email, info@nchv.org Web, www.nchv.org and Twitter, @NCHVorg

Faith-based organization providing technical assistance to service providers; acts as advocate on behalf of homeless veterans.

National Veterans Legal Services Program, *1600 K St. N.W., #500, 20006 (mailing address: P.O. Box 65762, Washington, DC 20035); (202) 265-8305. Fax, (202) 328-0063. Barton F. Stichman, Executive Director; Ronald B. Abrams, Counsel. General email, info@nvlsp.org Web, www.nvlsp.org, Twitter, @Lawyer4Warriors and Facebook, www.facebook.com/LawyersServingWarriors and YouTube, www.youtube.com/user/LawyersServing*

Represents the interests of veterans through educational programs, advocacy, public policy programming, and litigation.

Vietnam Veterans of America, *8719 Colesville Rd., #100, Silver Spring, MD 20910-3710; (301) 585-4000. Fax, (301) 585-0519. John P. Rowan, President. Information, (800) 882-1316. General email, communications@vva.org Web, www.vva.org and Twitter, @VVAmerica*

Congressionally chartered membership organization that provides information on legislation that affects Vietnam-era veterans and their families. Engages in legislative and judicial advocacy in areas relevant to Vietnam-era veterans. Provides information concerning benefits and initiates programs that ensure access to education and employment opportunities. Promotes full accounting of POWs and MIAs.

Appeals of VA Decisions

►**AGENCIES**

Defense Dept. (DoD), *Legal Policy, 4000 Defense Pentagon, #2C548A, 20301-4000; (703) 697-3387. Vacant, Director; Lt. Col. Reggie D. Yager, Deputy Director. Web, www.defense.gov*

Coordinates policy in a variety of personnel-related areas, including the Members Civil Relief Act, legal assistance, political activities, and corrections.

Navy Dept. *(Defense Dept.), Council of Review Boards, 720 Kennon St. S.E., Bldg. 36, #309, Washington Navy Yard, DC 20374-5023; (202) 685-6408. Fax, (202) 685-6610. Jeffrey Riehl (USMC, Ret.), Director. General email, crsc@navy.mil Web, www.secnav.navy.mil/mra/CORB/pages/home.aspx*

Military office that administers boards that review appeal cases for the Navy and the Marine Corps. Composed of the Physical Evaluation Board, the Naval Discharge Review Board, the Naval Clemency and Parole

Board, the Combat-Related Special Compensation (CRSC) Branch, and the Board for Decorations and Medals.

Veterans Affairs Dept. (VA), *Board of Veterans Appeals,* *425 Eye St. N.W., 20001 (mailing address: P.O. Box 27063, Washington, DC 20038); (800) 923-8387. Fax, (844) 678-8979. Cheryl L. Mason, Chair. Claims status, (202) 565-5436.* *Web, www.bva.va.gov*

Final appellate body within the department; reviews claims for veterans benefits on appeal from agencies of original jurisdiction. Decisions of the board are subject to review by the U.S. Court of Appeals for Veterans Claims.

▶JUDICIARY

U.S. Court of Appeals for the Federal Circuit, *717 Madison Pl. N.W., 20439; (202) 275-8000. Fax, (202) 275-9678. Sharon Prost, Chief Judge; Peter R. Marksteiner, Clerk of the Court, (202) 272-8020. Mediation, (202) 275-8120.* *Web, www.cafc.uscourts.gov*

Reviews decisions concerning the Veterans' Judicial Review Provisions.

U.S. Court of Appeals for Veterans Claims, *625 Indiana Ave. N.W., #900, 20004-2950; (202) 501-5970. Fax, (202) 501-5848. Robert N. Davis, Chief Judge; Gregory O. Block, Clerk of the Court.* *Web, www.uscourts.cavc.gov and Twitter, @UscavcL*

Independent court that reviews decisions of the VA's Board of Veterans Appeals concerning benefits. Focuses primarily on disability benefits claims.

▶NONGOVERNMENTAL

American Legion, *Claims Services, Veterans Affairs, and Rehabilitation Division, 1608 K St. N.W., 20006; (202) 861-2700. Fax, (202) 833-4452. Louis J. Celli Jr., Director.* *Web, www.legion.org*

Membership: honorably discharged veterans who served during declared military conflicts. Assists veterans with appeals before the Veterans Affairs Dept. for compensation and benefits claims.

American Legion, *Discharge Review and Correction Boards Unit, 1608 K St. N.W., 20006-2847; (202) 861-2700. Fax, (202) 833-4452. Alex Zhang, Assistant Director.* *Web, www.legion.org*

Membership: honorably discharged veterans who served during declared military conflicts. Represents before the Defense Dept. former military personnel seeking to upgrade less-than-honorable discharges and to correct alleged errors in military records.

Disabled American Veterans, *National Service and Legislative Headquarters, 807 Maine Ave. S.W., 20024-2410; (202) 554-3501. Fax, (202) 554-3581. J. Marc Burgess, National Adjutant; Dennis R. Nixon, National Commander. Toll-free, (877) 872-3289.* *Web, www.dav.org*

Oversees regional offices in assisting disabled veterans with claims, benefits, and appeals, including upgrading less-than-honorable discharges. Monitors legislation. (Headquarters in Cold Spring, Ky.)

National Veterans Legal Services Program, *1600 K St. N.W., #500, 20006 (mailing address: P.O. Box 65762, Washington, DC 20035); (202) 265-8305. Fax, (202) 328-0063. Barton F. Stichman, Executive Director; Ronald B. Abrams, Counsel.* *General email, info@nvlsp.org* *Web, www.nvlsp.org, Twitter, @Lawyer4Warriors and Facebook, www.facebook.com/LawyersServingWarriors and YouTube, www.youtube.com/user/LawyersServing*

Represents the interests of veterans through educational programs, advocacy, public policy programming, and litigation.

Veterans of Foreign Wars of the United States, *200 Maryland Ave. N.E., 20002-5724; (202) 543-2239. Fax, (202) 543-6719. B.J. Lawrence, Commander-in-Chief; Robert E. Wallace, Executive Director. Helpline, (800) 839-1899. Member Service Center, 833-VFW-VETS.* *General email, vfw@vfw.org* *Web, www.vfw.org and Twitter, @VFWHQ*

Assists veterans and their dependents and survivors with appeals before the Veterans Affairs Dept. for benefits claims. Assists with cases in the U.S. Court of Appeals for Veterans Claims. (Headquarters in Kansas City, Mo.)

Benefits

▶AGENCIES

Center for Women Veterans *(Veterans Affairs Dept.), 810 Vermont Ave. N.W., #435, MC 00W, 20420; (202) 461-6193. Fax, (202) 273-7092. Vacant, Director; Anna D. Crenshaw, Deputy Director.* *General email, 00w@va.gov* *Web, www.va.gov/womenvet*

Seeks to ensure that women veterans receive benefits and services on par with those of male veterans.

Veterans Affairs Dept. (VA), *Intergovernmental Affairs, 810 Vermont Ave. N.W., #915, 20420; (202) 461-7402. Fax, (202) 273-5716. Thayer Verschoor, Executive Director; Shirley Williams, Program Assistant, (202) 461-7088.* *Web, www.va.gov*

Responds to veterans' complaints concerning VA benefits and services. Answers questions about policy and makes referrals to other VA offices, as appropriate.

Veterans Benefits Administration (VBA) *(Veterans Affairs Dept.), 1800 G St. N.W., #520, 20223 (mailing address: 810 Vermont Ave. N.W., #520, Washington, DC 20420); (202) 461-9300. Fax, (202) 275-3591. Paul R. Lawrence, Under Secretary. Toll-free insurance hotline, (800) 669-8477.* *Web, www.vba.va.gov and Twitter, @VaVetBenefits*

Administers nonmedical benefits programs for veterans and their dependents and survivors. Benefits include veterans' compensation (including disability compensation) and pensions, survivors' benefits, education and rehabilitation assistance, home loan benefits, insurance coverage, and burials.

Veterans Benefits Administration (VBA) *(Veterans Affairs Dept.), Compensation Service, 810 Vermont Ave. N.W., #645, MS 21, 20420; (202) 461-9700. Fax, (202) 530-9094. Beth Murphy, Director. Toll-free, (800) 827-1000.*
Web, www.benefits.va.gov/compensation/

Administers disability payments; handles claims for burial and plot allowances by veterans' survivors. Provides information on and assistance with benefits legislated by Congress for veterans of active military, naval, or air service.

► **CONGRESS**

For a listing of relevant congressional committees and subcommittees, please see page 594 or the Appendix.

► **NONGOVERNMENTAL**

American Red Cross, *Service to the Armed Forces, Military Families, 431 18th St. N.W., 20006; (202) 303-5000, ext. 2. Fax, (202) 303-0216. Koby L. Langley, Senior Vice President. Emergency communication services, (877) 272-7337.*
Web, www.redcross.org/about-us/our-work/military-families.html

Assists veterans and their dependents with claims for benefits on a limited basis; supports medical care and rehabilitation services at military and veterans hospitals.

Blinded Veterans Assn., *125 N. West St., Alexandria, VA 22314; (202) 371-8880. Fax, (202) 371-8258. Joseph Bogart, Executive Director. Toll-free, (800) 669-7079.*
General email, bva@bva.org
Web, www.bva.org and Twitter, @BlindedVeterans

Chartered by Congress to assist veterans with claims for benefits. Seeks out blinded veterans to make them aware of benefits and services available to them.

Fleet Reserve Assn. (FRA), *125 N. West St., Alexandria, VA 22314-2754; (703) 683-1400. Fax, (703) 549-6610. Thomas J. Snee, National Executive Director, (703) 683-1400, ext. 101. Membership/Customer Service, (800) 372-1924.*
General email, fra@fra.org
Web, www.fra.org, Twitter, @FRAHQ and Facebook, www.facebook.com/FRA.org/?ref=br_tf

Recognized by the Veterans Affairs Dept. to assist veterans and widows of veterans with benefit claims. Monitors legislation and regulations.

Jewish War Veterans of the U.S.A., *1811 R St. N.W., 20009; (202) 265-6280. Fax, (202) 234-5662. Herb Rosenbleeth, National Executive Director.*
General email, jwv@jwv.org
Web, www.jwv.org and Twitter, @JewishWarVets

Recognized by the Veterans Affairs Dept. to assist veterans with claims for benefits. Offers programs in community relations and services, foreign affairs, national defense, and veterans affairs. Monitors legislation and regulations that affect veterans.

Noncommissioned Officers Assn., *National Capital Office, P.O. Box 3085, Oakton, VA 22124; (703) 549-0311. Fax, (703) 549-0245. Vincent W. Patton III, President; Jon Ostrowski, Executive Director for Government Affairs. Toll-free, (800) 662-2620.*
General email, tkish@ncoadc.org
Web, www.ncoausa.org

Congressionally chartered and accredited by the Veterans Affairs Dept. to assist veterans and widows of veterans with claims for benefits. Monitors legislation and regulations. (Headquarters in Selma, Tex.)

Paralyzed Veterans of America, *801 18th St. N.W., 20006-3517; (202) 872-1300. Carl Blake Jr., Executive Director; David Zurfluh, National President. Hotline, (800) 232-1782. Information, (800) 424-8200. TTY, (800) 795-4327.*
General email, info@pva.org
Web, www.pva.org and Twitter, @PVA1946

Congressionally chartered veterans service organization that assists veterans with claims for benefits. Distributes information on special education for paralyzed veterans; acts as advocate for high-quality care and supports and raises funds for medical research.

Veterans for Common Sense, *1140 3rd St. N.E., #2138, 20002; (202) 750-5430. Anthony Hardie, Director, (608) 239-4658.*
General email, info@veteransforcommonsense.org
Web, www.veteransforcommonsense.org and Twitter, @Vets4CommonSens

Grassroots policy advocacy nonprofit that aims to protect veterans benefits and rights. Monitors legislation and regulations.

Veterans of Foreign Wars of the United States, *200 Maryland Ave. N.E., 20002-5724; (202) 543-2239. Fax, (202) 543-6719. B.J. Lawrence, Commander-in-Chief; Robert E. Wallace, Executive Director. Helpline, (800) 839-1899. Member Service Center, 833-VFW-VETS.*
General email, vfw@vfw.org
Web, www.vfw.org and Twitter, @VFWHQ

Chartered by Congress to assist veterans with claims for benefits, including disability compensation, education, and pensions. Inspects VA health care facilities and cemeteries. Monitors medical updates and employment practices regarding veterans. (Headquarters in Kansas City, Mo.)

Veterans of Modern Warfare, *#33107, P.O. Box 96503, 20090; Joseph F. Morgan, President. Suicide hotline, (800) 273-8255. Toll-free, (888) 445-9891.*
General email, info@vmwusa.org and Twitter, @VMWUSA

Chapter-based membership organization. Provides information and assistance in obtaining benefits to all veterans, including active duty and National Guard and Reserve components, as well as any veteran who has served in the U.S. Armed Forces since August 2, 1990. Acts as advocate for veterans.

Education, Economic Opportunity

▶AGENCIES

Office of Personnel Management (OPM), *Veterans Services, 1900 E St. N.W., #7439, 20415; (202) 606-3602. Fax, (202) 606-6017. Hakeem Basheerud-Deen, Director. Web, www.opm.gov/policy-data-oversight/veterans-services*

Provides federal employees and transitioning military service members and their families, federal human resources professionals, and hiring managers with information on employment opportunities with the federal government. Administers the Disabled Veterans Affirmative Action Program.

Small Business Administration (SBA), *Veterans Business Development, 409 3rd St. S.W., #5700, 20416; (202) 205-6773. Fax, (202) 205-7292. Larry Stubblefield, Associate Administrator. TTY, (800) 877-8339. Web, www.sba.gov/offices/headquarters/ovbd*

Helps veterans use SBA loans through counseling, procurement, and training programs in entrepreneurship.

Veterans Benefits Administration (VBA) *(Veterans Affairs Dept.), Education Service, 1800 G St. N.W., #601, 20006 (mailing address: 810 Vermont Ave. N.W., #520, Washington, DC 20420); (202) 461-9800. Charmine Bogue II, Director (Acting). Bill information, (888) 442-4551. Web, www.benefits.va.gov/gibill*

Administers VA's education program, including financial support for veterans' education and for spouses and dependent children of deceased and disabled veterans; provides eligible veterans and dependents with educational assistance under the G.I. Bill and Veterans Educational Assistance Program. Provides postsecondary institutions with funds, based on their enrollment of eligible veterans.

Veterans Benefits Administration (VBA) *(Veterans Affairs Dept.), Loan Guaranty Service, 1800 G St., #851, 20006 (mailing address: 810 Vermont Ave. N.W., Washington, DC 20420); (202) 632-8862. Fax, (202) 495-5798. Jeffrey F. London, Director. Web, www.benefits.va.gov/homeloans*

Guarantees private institutional financing of home loans (including manufactured home loans) for veterans; provides disabled veterans with direct loans and grants for specially adapted housing; administers a direct loan program for Native American veterans living on trust land.

Veterans Benefits Administration (VBA) *(Veterans Affairs Dept.), Vocational Rehabilitation and Employment Service, 1800 G St. N.W., 20006 (mailing address: 810 Vermont Ave. N.W., #520, Washington, DC 20420); (202) 461-9600. Fax, (202) 275-5122. William (Will) Streitberger, Director. Web, www.benefits.va.gov/vocrehab/index.asp*

Administers VA's vocational rehabilitation and employment program, which provides service-disabled veterans with services and assistance; helps veterans to become employable and to obtain and maintain suitable employment.

Veterans' Employment and Training Service *(Labor Dept.), 200 Constitution Ave. N.W., #S1325, 20210; (202) 693-4700. Fax, (202) 693-4755. Sam Shellenberger, Deputy Assistant Secretary for Operations; Vacant, Deputy Assistant Secretary for Policy. Toll-free, (800) 487-2365. Web, www.dol.gov/vets and Twitter, @VETS_DOL*

Works with and monitors state employment offices to see that preference is given to veterans seeking jobs; advises the secretary on veterans' issues.

▶CONGRESS

For a listing of relevant congressional committees and subcommittees, please see page 594 or the Appendix.

▶NONGOVERNMENTAL

Blinded Veterans Assn., *125 N. West St., Alexandria, VA 22314; (202) 371-8880. Fax, (202) 371-8258. Joseph Bogart, Executive Director. Toll-free, (800) 669-7079. General email, bva@bva.org*

Web, www.bva.org and Twitter, @BlindedVeterans

Provides blind and disabled veterans with vocational rehabilitation.

Council for Opportunity in Education, *1025 Vermont Ave. N.W., #900, 20005-3516; (202) 347-7430. Fax, (202) 347-0786. Maureen Hoyler, President, ext. 321. Web, www.coenet.us and Twitter, @COETalk*

Membership: more than 1,000 colleges and agencies. Works in conjunction with colleges and agencies that host the federally funded TRIO programs, designed to help low-income first-generation immigrants, students with disabilities, and veterans enroll in and graduate from college.

National Assn. of State Workforce Agencies, *444 N. Capitol St. N.W., #300, 20001; (202) 434-8020. Fax, (202) 434-8033. Scott Sanders, Executive Director, (202) 434-8022. General email, naswa@naswa.org*

Web, www.naswa.org and Twitter, @naswaorg

Membership: state employment security administrators. Provides veterans employment and training professionals with opportunities for networking and information exchange. Monitors legislation and regulations that affect veterans employment and training programs involving state employment security agencies.

Paralyzed Veterans of America, *801 18th St. N.W., 20006-3517; (202) 872-1300. Carl Blake Jr., Executive Director; David Zurfluh, National President. Hotline, (800) 232-1782. Information, (800) 424-8200. TTY, (800) 795-4327. General email, info@pva.org*

Web, www.pva.org and Twitter, @PVA1946

Congressionally chartered veterans service organization that assists veterans with claims for benefits. Promotes access to educational and public facilities and to public transportation for people with disabilities; seeks modification of workplaces.

Health Care, VA Hospitals

▶AGENCIES

Army Dept. *(Defense Dept.), Wounded Warrior Program (AW2), 2530 Crystal Dr., 10th Floor, Arlington, VA 22202; (877) 393-9058. Fax, (703) 325-1516. Col. Terence J. Johnson (USA), Director. Overseas, (312) 221-9113. General email, AW2@conus.army.mil*

Assists and acts as advocate for severely disabled and ill soldiers, veterans, and their families. Provides each soldier with a personal AW2 advocate. Tracks and monitors severely disabled soldiers beyond their medical retirement.

Veterans Health Administration (VHA) *(Veterans Affairs Dept.), 810 Vermont Ave. N.W., #800, 20420 (mailing address: 810 Vermont Ave. N.W., #520, Washington, DC 20420); (202) 461-7000. Fax, (202) 273-7090. Dr. Richard Stone, Executive In Charge. Toll-free, (877) 222-8387. Web, www.va.gov/health and Twitter, @VeteransHealth*

Oversees all health care policies for all eligible veterans. Recommends policy and administers medical and hospital services for eligible veterans. Publishes guidelines on treatment of veterans exposed to Agent Orange.

Veterans Health Administration (VHA) *(Veterans Affairs Dept.), Academic Affiliations, 811 Vermont Ave., #4, 20420 (mailing address: 810 Vermont Ave. N.W., #520, Washington, DC 20420); (202) 461-9490. Fax, (202) 461-9855. Dr. Marjorie Bowman, Chief Officer. Web, www.va.gov/oaa/*

Administers education and training programs for health professionals, students, and residents through partnerships with affiliated academic institutions.

Veterans Health Administration (VHA) *(Veterans Affairs Dept.), Dentistry, 810 Vermont Ave. N.W., 10NC7, 20420; (202) 632-8342. Dr. Patricia Arola, Assistant Under Secretary. Web, www.va.gov/dental*

Administers and coordinates VA oral health care programs; dental care delivered in a VA setting; administration of oral research, education, and training for VA oral health personnel; delivery of care to VA patients in private practice settings.

Veterans Health Administration (VHA) *(Veterans Affairs Dept.), Geriatrics and Extended Care, 810 Vermont Ave. N.W., #10P4G, 20420; (202) 461-6750. Fax, (202) 495-5167. Dr. Scotte Hartronft, Chief Consultant (Acting); Thomas E. Edes, Executive Director. Web, www.va.gov/geriatrics*

Administers research, educational, and clinical health care programs in geriatrics at VA and community nursing homes, in personal care homes, in VA domiciliaries, in state veterans' homes, and in home-based and other non-institutional care.

Veterans Health Administration (VHA) *(Veterans Affairs Dept.), Health Policy and Planning, 810 Vermont Ave. N.W., 10P1, 20420; (202) 461-7100. Fax, (202) 273-9030. Lucille Beck, Assistant Deputy Under Secretary. General email, VHAHQ.OPPWebmaster@va.gov Web, www.va.gov/healthpolicyplanning*

Advises on the development, implementation, and impact of VHA policy, strategic planning, and data management. Develops policy, programs, and funds initiatives within the Veterans Affairs Dept. that advance the health of veterans in rural America.

Veterans Health Administration (VHA) *(Veterans Affairs Dept.), Mental Health Services, 810 Vermont Ave. N.W., MS 10P4M, 20420; (202) 461-4170. Fax, (202) 495-5933. Marsden McGuire, Deputy Chief Consultant; Vashtie Reedy, Management Program Analyst, (202) 461-7309. Coaching Into Care Toll-free, (888) 823-7458. Web, www.mentalhealth.va.gov and Coaching Into Care Web, www.mirecc.va.gov/coaching*

Develops ambulatory and inpatient psychiatry and psychology programs for the mentally ill and for drug and alcohol abusers; programs are offered in VA facilities and twenty-one Veterans Integrated Service Networks. Incorporates special programs for veterans suffering from posttraumatic stress disorders, serious mental illness, addictive disorders, and homelessness.

Veterans Health Administration (VHA) *(Veterans Affairs Dept.), Patient Care Services, 810 Vermont Ave. N.W., 20420; (202) 461-7800. Fax, (202) 495-5243. Dr. Maria L. Lorente, Assistant Deputy Under Secretary (Acting); Dr. Jane Kim, Deputy Chief Officer (Acting). Web, www.patientcare.va.gov*

Manages clinical programs of the VA medical care system, including rehabilitation and recovery, diagnosis and therapy, palliative care, disease prevention, and health promotion.

Veterans Health Administration (VHA) *(Veterans Affairs Dept.), Readjustment Counseling Service, 1717 H St. N.W., #444, 20006; (202) 461-6525. Fax, (202) 495-6206. Michael W. Fisher, Chief Officer. Toll-free, (877) 927-8387. Web, www.va.gov and VA Center, www.vetcenter.va.gov*

Responsible for community-based centers for veterans, service members, and military families nationwide. Provides outreach and counseling services for readjustment counseling, military sexual trauma causes, and bereavement counseling services. Offers Mobile Vet Centers that focus on services that help veterans make the transition between military and civilian life.

Veterans Health Administration (VHA) *(Veterans Affairs Dept.), Research and Development, 810 Vermont Ave.*

N.W., (10P9), MS 10P9, 20420; (202) 443-5600. Fax, (202) 495-6196. Dr. Rachel B. Ramoni, Chief Officer.

General email, vha10P9ordops@va.gov

Web, www.research.va.gov

Formulates and implements policy for the research and development program of the Veterans Health Administration; advises the under secretary for health on research-related matters and on management of the VA's health care system; represents the VA in interactions with external organizations in matters related to biomedical and health services research.

Veterans Health Administration (VHA) *(Veterans Affairs Dept.),* **Voluntary Service,** *810 Vermont Ave. N.W., 10B2A, 20420; (202) 461-7300. Fax, (202) 495-6208. Sabrina Clark, Director.*

General email, VHACO10B2AStaff@va.gov

Web, www.volunteer.va.gov

Supervises volunteer programs in VA medical centers.

►CONGRESS

For a listing of relevant congressional committees and subcommittees, please see page 594 or the Appendix.

►NONGOVERNMENTAL

American Red Cross, *Service to the Armed Forces,* **Military Families,** *431 18th St. N.W., 20006; (202) 303-5000, ext. 2. Fax, (202) 303-0216. Koby L. Langley, Senior Vice President. Emergency communication services, (877) 272-7337.*

Web, www.redcross.org/about-us/our-work/military-families.html

Assists veterans and their dependents with claims for benefits on a limited basis; supports medical care and rehabilitation services at military and veterans hospitals.

Army Distaff Foundation (Knollwood), *6200 Oregon Ave. N.W., 20015-1543; (202) 541-0492. Fax, (202) 364-2856. Maj. Gen. Timothy P. McHale (USA, Ret.), Chief Executive Officer; Col. Paul W. Bricker (USA, Ret.), Chief Operating Officer. Admission, (202) 541-0149. Information, (800) 541-4255.*

General email, dschrag@armydistaff.org

Web, www.armydistaff.org

Nonprofit continuing care retirement community for career military officers and their families. Provides retirement housing and health care services.

Disabled American Veterans, *National Service and* **Legislative Headquarters,** *807 Maine Ave. S.W., 20024-2410; (202) 554-3501. Fax, (202) 554-3581. J. Marc Burgess, National Adjutant; Dennis R. Nixon, National Commander. Toll-free, (877) 872-3289.*

Web, www.dav.org

Chartered by Congress to assist veterans with claims for benefits; represents veterans seeking to correct alleged errors in military records. Assists families of veterans with disabilities. (Headquarters in Cold Spring, Ky.)

Marine Corps League, *3619 Jefferson Davis Hwy., #115, Stafford, VA 22554 (mailing address: P.O. Box 3070, Merrifield, VA 22116); (703) 207-9588. Fax, (703) 207-0047. Robert J. Borka, Chief Operating Officer.*

Web, www.mclnational.org and Twitter, @MCL_HQ

Membership: active duty, retired, and reserve Marine Corps groups. Chartered by Congress to assist veterans with claims for benefits. Operates a volunteer service program in VA hospitals. assists veterans and their survivors. Monitors legislation and regulations.

National Assn. of Veterans Affairs Physicians and Dentists, *P.O. Box 15418, Arlington, VA 22215-0418; (866) 836-3520. Fax, (540) 972-1728. Dr. Samuel V. Spagnolo, President.*

General email, info@navapd.org

Web, www.navapd.org

Seeks to improve the quality of care and conditions at VA hospitals. Monitors legislation and regulations on veterans' health care.

National Conference on Ministry to the Armed Forces, *Endorsers Conference for Veterans Affairs Chaplaincy, P.O. Box 7572, Arlington, VA 22207-9998; (703) 608-2100. Sarah Lammert, Chair.*

General email, info@ncmaf.com

Web, www.ncmaf.net and Twitter, @NCMAForg

Endorses clergy-persons for service as chaplains to VA hospitals. Liaises between the American religious community and the Veterans Affairs Dept.

Paralyzed Veterans of America, *801 18th St. N.W., 20006-3517; (202) 872-1300. Carl Blake Jr., Executive Director; David Zurfluh, National President. Hotline, (800) 232-1782. Information, (800) 424-8200. TTY, (800) 795-4327.*

General email, info@pva.org

Web, www.pva.org and Twitter, @PVA1946

Congressionally chartered veterans service organization. Consults with the Veterans Affairs Dept. on the establishment and operation of spinal cord injury treatment centers.

Veterans of Foreign Wars of the United States, *200 Maryland Ave. N.E., 20002-5724; (202) 543-2239. Fax, (202) 543-6719. B.J. Lawrence, Commander-in-Chief; Robert E. Wallace, Executive Director. Helpline, (800) 839-1899. Member Service Center, 833-VFW-VETS.*

General email, vfw@vfw.org

Web, www.vfw.org and Twitter, @VFWHQ

Chartered by Congress to assist veterans with claims for benefits, including disability compensation, education, and pensions. Inspects VA health care facilities and cemeteries. Monitors medical updates and employment practices regarding veterans. (Headquarters in Kansas City, Mo.)

Vietnam Veterans of America, *Veterans Health* **Council,** *8719 Colesville Rd., #100, Silver Spring, MD 20910-3710; (301) 585-4000, ext. 148. Fax, (301) 585-3180. Dr. Arthur (Tom) Shelton, Executive Director. Toll-free, (800) 882-1316.*

General email, vhc@vva.org

Web, www.vva.org/?s=veterans+health+council

Health education and information network for veterans and their families.

Spouses, Dependents, Survivors

►AGENCIES

Air Force Dept. *(Defense Dept.), Manpower, Personnel, and Services, 1040 Air Force Pentagon, #4E168, 20330-1040; (703) 697-6088. Lt. Gen. Brian T. Kelly, Deputy Chief of Staff.*
Web, www.af.mil

Military office that responds to inquiries concerning deceased Air Force personnel and their beneficiaries; refers inquiries to the Military Personnel Center at Randolph Air Force Base in San Antonio, Texas.

Marine Corps *(Defense Dept.), Casualty Assistance Section, 2008 Elliott Rd., Quantico, VA 22134-5102; (703) 784-9512. Fax, (703) 784-4134. Gerald Castle, Head. Toll-free, (800) 847-1597.*
General email, casualty.section@usmc.mil

Web, http://usmc-mccs.org/services/benefits/casualty-assistance

Confirms beneficiaries of deceased Marine Corps personnel for benefits distribution.

Veterans Health Administration (VHA) *(Veterans Affairs Dept.), Readjustment Counseling Service, 1717 H St. N.W., #444, 20006; (202) 461-6525. Fax, (202) 495-6206. Michael W. Fisher, Chief Officer. Toll-free, (877) 927-8387. Web, www.va.gov and VA Center, www.vetcenter.va.gov*

Offers bereavement counseling to parents, spouses, siblings, and children of armed forces personnel who died in service to their country and to family members of reservists and those in the National Guard who died while federally activated. Services include outreach, counseling, and referrals. Counseling provided without cost at community-based Vet Centers. Offers Mobile Vet Centers that focus on services that help veterans make the transition between military and civilian life.

►NONGOVERNMENTAL

American Gold Star Mothers Inc., *2128 Leroy Pl. N.W., 20008-1893; (202) 265-0991. Becky Christmas, President.*
General email, AGSM@goldstarmoms.com

Web, http://goldstarmoms.com, Twitter, @AGSM_National and Facebook, www.facebook.com/American-Gold-Stat-Mothers-National-Official-108308072594520

Membership: mothers who have lost sons or daughters in military service. Members serve as volunteers in VA hospitals and around the country.

Army and Air Force Mutual Aid Assn., *102 Sheridan Ave., Fort Myer, VA 22211-1110; (703) 707-4600. Fax, (888) 210-4882. Maj. Walt Lincoln (USA, Ret.), President. Toll-free, (888) 961-5427.*
General email, info@aafmaa.com

Web, www.aafmaa.com

Private service organization that offers member and family insurance services to U.S. armed forces personnel. Recognized by the Veterans Affairs Dept. as assisting veterans and their survivors with claims for benefits.

EX-POSE: Ex-Partners of Servicemembers for Equality, *P.O. Box 11191, Alexandria, VA 22312-0191; (703) 941-5844. Fax, (703) 212-6951. Sue Arroyo, Office Staff; Janice Stucki, Office Staff.*
General email, expose1980@gmail.com

Web, www.ex-pose.org

Membership: military members, retirees, current/former spouses and their children. Educates military couples going through divorce. Provides explanation of possible legal interests and legal entitlements depending on the length of marriage. Open Tuesday and Wednesday, 10:00 a.m.–3:00 p.m.

Marine Corps League, *3619 Jefferson Davis Hwy., #115, Stafford, VA 22554 (mailing address: P.O. Box 3070, Merrifield, VA 22116); (703) 207-9588. Fax, (703) 207-0047. Robert J. Borka, Chief Operating Officer.*
Web, www.mclnational.org and Twitter, @MCL_HQ

Membership: active duty, retired, and reserve Marine Corps groups. Chartered by Congress to assist veterans with claims for benefits. Operates a volunteer service program in VA hospitals. Assists veterans and their survivors. Monitors legislation and regulations.

Tragedy Assistance Program for Survivors, Inc. (TAPS), *3033 Wilson Blvd., 3rd Floor, Arlington, VA 22201; (202) 588-8277. Fax, (571) 385-2524. Bonnie Carroll, President. Toll-free 24-hour crisis intervention hotline, (800) 959-8277.*
General email, info@taps.org

Web, www.taps.org and Twitter, @TAPSorg

Offers emotional support to those who have lost a loved one in military service. Has caseworkers who act as liaisons to military and veterans agencies. Provides 24/7 resource and information help line. Hosts Good Grief camps for children, seminars for adults, and online and in-person support groups. Publishes a quarterly magazine on grief and loss.

15

National and
Homeland Security

GENERAL POLICY AND ANALYSIS

Basic Resources

▶AGENCIES

Air Force Dept. *(Defense Dept.)*, *1670 Air Force Pentagon, #4E878, 20330-1670; (703) 697-7376. Heather A. Wilson, Secretary. Press, (703) 695-0640. Public Inquiries, (703) 697-3039.*
Web, www.af.mil, Twitter, @usairforce and Facebook, www.facebook.com/USairforce

Civilian office that develops and reviews Air Force national security policies in conjunction with the chief of staff of the Air Force and the secretary of defense.

Air Force Dept. *(Defense Dept.)*, *Chief of Staff (CSAF), 1670 Air Force Pentagon, 20330-1670; (703) 697-9225. Fax, (703) 693-9297. Gen. David L. Goldfein, Chief of Staff.*
Web, www.af.mil/AboutUs/AirForceSeniorLeaders/CSAF.aspx, Twitter, @GenDaveGoldfein and Facebook, www.facebook.com/CSAFOfficial

Military office that develops and directs Air Force national security policies in conjunction with the Secretary of the Air Force, Secretary of Defense, National Security Council, and the president.

Air Force Dept. *(Defense Dept.)*, *Information Dominance and Chief Information Officer, 1800 Air Force Pentagon, #4E1050, 20330-1800; (703) 695-6829. William Marion, Chief Information Officer (Acting). Press, (703) 695-0640.*
General email, usaf.pentagon.saf-cio-a6.mbx.saf-cio-a6-cag-workflow@mail.mil
Web, www.safcioa6.af.mil

Responsible for cyberspace policymaking, planning, programming, and evaluating performance of the Air Force's command, control, communications, and computer (C-4) system; advises on information technology, cyberspace, and national security systems.

Army Dept. *(Defense Dept.)*, *101 Army Pentagon, #3E700, 20310-0101; (703) 695-1717. Fax, (703) 697-8036. Mark T. Esper, Secretary.*
Web, www.army.mil and Twitter, @USArmy

Civilian office that develops and reviews Army national security policies in conjunction with the chief of staff of the Army and the secretary of defense.

Army Dept. *(Defense Dept.)*, *Chief of Staff, 200 Army Pentagon, #3E672, 20310-0200; (703) 697-0900. Fax, (703) 614-5268. Gen. Mark A. Milley (USA), Chief of Staff.*
Web, www.army.mil and Twitter, @GENMarkMilley

Military office that develops and administers Army national security policies in conjunction with the secretary of the Army and the secretary of defense.

Defense Dept. (DoD), *1000 Defense Pentagon, #3E880, 20301-1000; (703) 692-7100. Fax, (703) 571-8951.*

David Norquist, Deputy Secretary (Acting); Patrick Shanahan, Secretary (Acting). Information, (703) 571-3343. Pentagon operator, (703) 545-6700. Press, (703) 697-5131. Tours, (703) 697-1776.
Web, www.defense.gov and Twitter, @DeptofDefense

Civilian office that develops national security policies and has overall responsibility for administering national defense; responds to public and congressional inquiries about national defense matters.

Defense Dept. (DoD), *Chief Information Officer, 6000 Defense Pentagon, #3E1030, 20301-6000; (703) 695-0348. Fax, (703) 695-4647. Dana Deasy, Chief Information Officer.*
Web, http://dodcio.defense.gov

Civilian office with policy oversight for all command, control, and communications matters.

Defense Dept. (DoD), *Command, Control, Communications, and Computers/Cyber, 8000 Joint Staff Pentagon, #1E1044, 20318-6000; (703) 695-3562. Lt. Gen. Bradford J. Shwedo III (USAF), Director.*
Web, www.jcs.mil/Directorates/J6%7CC4Cyber.aspx

Advises the secretary of defense on policy for command, control, communications, and computer/cyber matters throughout the Defense Dept.

Defense Dept. (DoD), *Homeland Defense and Global Security, 2600 Defense Pentagon, #3C852A, 20301-2600; (703) 697-7728. Fax, (703) 693-6338. Kenneth P. Rapuano, Assistant Secretary.*
Web, http://policy.defense.gov/OUSDP-Offices/ASD-for-Homeland-Defense-Global-Security/

Develops and coordinates national security and defense strategies and advises on the resources, forces, and contingency plans necessary to implement those strategies. Ensures the integration of defense strategy into the department's resource allocation and force structure development. Evaluates the capability of forces to accomplish defense strategy. Also serves as primary liaison between the Defense Dept. and the Homeland Security Dept. Supervises all Defense Dept. homeland defense activities.

Defense Dept. (DoD), *Joint Chiefs of Staff, 9999 Defense Pentagon, #2D932, 20318-9999; (703) 697-9121. Fax, (703) 697-6002. Gen. Joseph F. Dunford Jr. (USM), Chair. Media, (703) 697-4272.*
Web, www.jcs.mil

Joint military staff office that assists the president, the National Security Council, and the secretary of defense in developing national security policy and in coordinating operations of the individual armed services.

Defense Dept. (DoD), *Policy, 2000 Defense Pentagon, #3E806, 20301; (703) 697-7200. Fax, (703) 697-6602. John C. Rood, Under Secretary; David Trachtenberg, Deputy Under Secretary.*
Web, http://policy.defense.gov

Civilian office responsible for policy matters relating to international security issues and political-military affairs. Oversees such areas as arms control, foreign military sales, intelligence collection and analysis, and NATO and regional security affairs.

Defense Dept. (DoD), *Special Operations and Low-Intensity Conflict,* 2500 Defense Pentagon, #3C852A, 20301-2500; (703) 695-9667. Fax, (703) 693-6335. *Owen West, Assistant Secretary.*
Web, http://policy.defense.gov/OUSDP-Offices/ASD-for-Special-Operations-Low-Intensity-Conflict

Serves as special staff assistant and civilian adviser to the secretary of defense on matters related to special operations and international terrorism.

Defense Dept. (DoD), *Sustainment,* 3400 Defense Pentagon, #1E518, 20301-3500; (703) 697-1369. Fax, (703) 693-0555. *Robert H. McMahon, Assistant Secretary.*
Web, www.acq.osd.mil/eie

Oversees and provides guidance on logistics, maintenance, material readiness, strategic mobility, and sustainment for all Defense Dept. domestic and overseas installations.

Homeland Security Dept. (DHS), 3801 Nebraska Ave. N.W., 20528; 301 7th St. S.W., MS0501, 20528; (202) 282-8000. (202) 447-5890. Fax, (202) 447-5437. *Kevin K. McAleenan, Secretary (Acting); Claire M. Grady, Deputy Secretary (Acting); Jonathan Hoffman, Communications Director,* (202) 282-8852.
General email, DHSExecSec@hq.dhs.gov
Web, www.dhs.gov and Twitter, @DHSgov

Responsible for the development and coordination of a comprehensive national strategy to protect the United States against terrorist attacks and other threats and hazards.

Marine Corps *(Defense Dept.),* **Commandant,** *Marine Corps Headquarters, 3000 Marine Corps Pentagon, #2C253, 20350-3000; (703) 614-2500. Fax, (703) 697-7246. Gen. Robert B. Neller (USMC), Commandant. Information,* (703) 614-2500.
Web, www.hqmc.marines.mil/cmc/home.aspx and Twitter, @GenRobertNeller

Military office that develops and directs Marine Corps national security policies in conjunction with the secretary of defense and the secretary of the Navy.

National Institute of Standards and Technology (NIST) *(Commerce Dept.),* **Special Programs Office,** 100 Bureau Dr., MS 4701, Gaithersburg, MD 20899-4701; (301) 975-4447. Fax, (301) 975-8972. *Richard R. Cavanagh, Director. General information,* (301) 975-2756.
Web, www.nist.gov/spo

Fosters collaboration among government, military, academic, professional, and private organizations to respond to critical national needs through science-based standards and technology innovation, including areas of homeland security and cybersecurity.

National Security Council (NSC) *(Executive Office of the President),* *The White House,* 20504; (202) 456-1414.

John Bolton, National Security Advisor. Press, (202) 456-9271.
Web, www.whitehouse.gov/nsc

Advises the president on domestic, foreign, and military policies relating to national security.

National Security Staff (NSS) *(Executive Office of the President),* **Defense Policy and Strategy,** *The White House, 1600 Pennsylvania Ave., 20504; (202) 456-9191. Fax, (202) 456-9190. Charles M. Kupperman, Deputy National Security Adviser.*
Web, www.whitehouse.gov/nsc

Advises the assistant to the president for national security affairs on matters concerning defense policy.

Navy Dept. *(Defense Dept.),* 1200 Navy Pentagon, #4D652, 20350-1000; (703) 697-7391. Richard V. Spencer, Secretary; Thomas Modly, Under Secretary.
General email, secnavypa.fct@navy.mil
Web, www.navy.mil, Twitter, @USNavy and Facebook, www.facebook.com/USNavy

Civilian office that develops and reviews Navy and Marine Corps national security policies in conjunction with the chief of naval operations, the commandant of the Marine Corps, and the secretary of defense.

Navy Dept. *(Defense Dept.),* **Naval Operations,** 2000 Navy Pentagon, #4E658, 20350-2000; (703) 695-5664. Fax, (703) 693-9408. Adm. John Richardson (USN), Chief.
Web, www.navy.mil/cno and Twitter, @NavalOperations

Military office that develops Navy national security policies in conjunction with the secretary of defense and the secretary of the Navy and in cooperation with the commandant of the Marine Corps.

State Dept., *Foreign Missions,* 2201 C St. N.W., #2236, 20520; (202) 647-3417. Fax, (202) 736-4145. *Clifton (Cliff) C. Seagroves, Director (Acting).*
General email, ofminfo@state.gov
Web, www.state.gov/ofm

Authorized to control the numbers, locations, and travel privileges of foreign diplomats and diplomatic staff in the United States.

Transportation Security Administration (TSA) *(Homeland Security Dept.),* **Security Policy and Industry Engagement,** *TSA-28, 601 S. 12th St., Arlington, VA 20598-6028; (571) 227-1417. Fax, (571) 227-2932. Eddie Mayenschein, Assistant Administrator.*
Web, www.tsa.gov

Formulates policy and shares information related to security in various segments of the transportation industry, including commercial airports, commercial airlines, general aviation, mass transit and passenger rail, freight rail, maritime, highway and motor carrier, pipeline and air cargo. Coordinates with the U.S. Coast Guard.

U.S. Coast Guard (USCG) *(Homeland Security Dept.),* *2703 Martin Luther King Jr. Ave. S.E., MS 7000,*

NATIONAL AND HOMELAND SECURITY RESOURCES IN CONGRESS

For a complete listing of congressional committees, including their full contact information, leadership, membership, and jurisdictions, please refer to the Appendix on pages 000–000.

HOUSE:

House Appropriations Committee, (202) 225-2771.
Web, appropriations.house.gov
Subcommittee on Defense, (202) 225-2847.
Subcommittee on Energy and Water
Development and Related Agencies,
(202) 225-3421.
Subcommittee on Financial Services and General
Government, (202) 225-7245.
Subcommittee on Homeland Security,
(202) 225-5834.
Subcommittee on Interior, Environment, and
Related Agencies, (202) 225-3081.
Subcommittee on Military Construction,
Veterans Affairs, and Related Agencies,
(202) 225-3047.
Subcommittee on State, Foreign Operations, and
Related Programs, (202) 225-2041.
House Armed Services Committee,
(202) 225-4151.
Web, armedservices.house.gov
Subcommittee on Emerging Threats and
Capabilities, (202) 226-2843.
Subcommittee on Military Personnel,
(202) 225-7560.
Subcommittee on Readiness,
(202) 226-8979.
Subcommittee on Strategic Forces,
(202) 225-1967.
Subcommittee on Tactical Air and Land Forces,
(202) 225-4440.
House Energy and Commerce Committee,
(202) 225-2927.
Web, energycommerce.house.gov
Subcommittee on Health, (202) 225-2927.
House Financial Services Committee,
(202) 225-7502.
Web, financialservices.house.gov
Subcommittee on Housing and Insurance,
(202) 225-7502.
House Foreign Affairs Committee,
(202) 225-5021.
Web, foreignaffairs.house.gov

Subcommittee on Terrorism, Nonproliferation,
and Trade, (202) 226-1500.
House Homeland Security Committee,
(202) 226-8417.
Web, homeland.house.gov
Subcommittee on Border and Maritime Security,
(202) 226-8417.
Subcommittee on Counterterrorism and
Intelligence, (202) 226-8417.
Subcommittee on Cybersecurity and
Infrastructure Protection,
(202) 226-8417.
Subcommittee on Emergency Preparedness,
Response and Communications,
(202) 226-8417.
Subcommittee on Oversight and
Management Efficiency,
(202) 226-8417.
Subcommittee on Transportation and Protective
Security, (202) 226-8417.
House Judiciary Committee, (202) 225-3951.
Web, judiciary.house.gov
Subcommittee on the Constitution and Civil
Justice, (202) 225-2825.
Subcommittee on Crime, Terrorism,
Homeland Security, and Investigations,
(202) 225-5727.
Subcommittee on Immigration and Border
Security, (202) 225-3926.
**House Oversight and Government Reform
Committee,** (202) 225-5074.
Web, oversight.house.gov
Subcommittee on National Security,
(202) 225-5074.
House Permanent Select Committee on Intelligence,
(202) 225-4121.
Web, intelligence.house.gov
Subcommittee on CIA, (202) 225-4121.
Subcommittee on Department of Defense
Intelligence and Overhead Architecture,
(202) 225-4121.
Subcommittee on Emerging Threats,
(202) 225-4121.

20593-7000; (202) 372-4000. Fax, (202) 372-8302.
Adm. Karl L. Schultz, Commandant. Public
Affairs, (202) 372-4600.
Web, www.uscg.mil and Twitter, @USCG

Provides homeland security for U.S. harbors, ports, and coastlines. Implements heightened security measures for commercial, tanker, passenger, and merchant vessels. Enforces federal laws on the high seas and navigable waters of the United States and its possessions; maintains

a state of military readiness to assist the Navy in time of war or when directed by the president.

U.S. Coast Guard (USCG) *(Homeland Security Dept.),*
Response Policy, CG-5E, 2703 Martin Luther Jr. Ave. S.W.,
MS 7516, 20593; (202) 372-2014. (202) 372-2011. Rear
Adm. Anthony (Jack) Vogt, Assistant Commandant.
Web, www.dco.uscg.mil/Our-Organization/Assistant-
Commandant-for-Response-Policy-CG-5R/

Subcommittee on NSA and Cybersecurity,
(202) 225-4121.
Subcommittee on Research and Technology,
(202) 225-6371.
House Science, Space, and Technology Committee,
(202) 225-6371.
Web, science.house.gov
House Transportation and Infrastructure
Committee, (202) 225-9446.
Web, transportation.house.gov
Subcommittee on Economic Development,
Public Buildings, and Emergency
Management, (202) 225-3014.

SENATE:
Senate Appropriations Committee,
(202) 224-7257.
Web, appropriations.senate.gov
Subcommittee on Defense, (202) 224-6688.
Subcommittee on Energy and Water
Development, (202) 224-8119.
Subcommittee on Financial Services and General
Government, (202) 224-1133.
Subcommittee on Homeland Security,
(202) 224-8244.
Subcommittee on Interior, Environment, and
Related Agencies, (202) 228-0774.
Subcommittee on Military Construction,
Veterans Affairs, and Related Agencies,
(202) 224-8224.
Subcommittee on State, Foreign Operations, and
Related Programs, (202) 224-7284.
Senate Armed Services Committee,
(202) 224-3871.
Web, armed-services.senate.gov
Subcommittee on Airland, (202) 224-3871.
Subcommittee on Cybersecurity, (202) 224-3871.
Subcommittee on Emerging Threats and
Capabilities, (202) 224-3871.
Subcommittee on Personnel, (202) 224-3871.
Subcommittee on Readiness and Management
Support, (202) 224-3871.
Subcommittee on Seapower, (202) 224-3871.

Subcommittee on Strategic Forces,
(202) 224-3871.
Senate Banking, Housing, and Urban Affairs
Committee, (202) 224-7391.
Web, banking.senate.gov
Subcommittee on National Security and
International Trade and Finance,
(202) 224-7391.
Senate Environment and Public Works Committee,
(202) 224-6176.
Web, epw.senate.gov
Subcommittee on Clean Air and Nuclear Safety,
(202) 224-6176.
Subcommittee on Transportation and
Infrastructure, (202) 224-6176.
Senate Foreign Relations Committee,
(202) 224-4651.
Web, foreign.senate.gov
Subcommittee on Western Hemisphere,
Transnational Crime, Civilian Security,
Democracy, Human Rights, and Global
Women's Issues, (202) 224-4651.
Senate Homeland Security and Governmental Affairs
Committee, (202) 224-4751.
Web, hsgac.senate.gov
Permanent Subcommittee on Investigations,
(202) 224-3721.
Subcommittee on Federal Spending,
Oversight, and Emergency Management,
(202) 224-7155.
Subcommittee on Regulatory Affairs and Federal
Management, (202) 224-4551.
Senate Judiciary Committee, (202) 224-5225.
Web, judiciary.senate.gov
Subcommittee on the Constitution,
(202) 224-5922.
Subcommittee on Crime and Terrorism,
(202) 224-5972.
Subcommittee on Border Security and
Immigration, (202) 224-7840.
Senate Select Committee on Intelligence,
(202) 224-1700.
Web, intelligence.senate.gov

Operates the Coast Guard National Response Center; participates in defense operations and homeland security; assists with law enforcement/drug interdictions.

► **CONGRESS**

For a listing of relevant congressional committees and subcommittees, please see pages 608–609 or the Appendix.

Government Accountability Office (GAO), *Defense Capabilities and Management (DCM), 441 G St. N.W., #4440B, 20548; (202) 512-4300. Cathleen A. Berrick, Managing Director.*
Web, www.gao.gov/careers/dcm.html

Provides analyses, recommendations, and policy options to Congress in areas of defense, including planning and force structure, readiness and training, warfighter support, emerging threats, irregular warfare, homeland defense, strategic human-capital management, logistics, infrastructure, business operations, and budgeting.

Government Accountability Office (GAO), *Homeland Security and Justice (HSJ),* 441 G St. N.W., #6H19, 20548; (202) 512-8777. Charles M. Johnson Jr., Managing Director.
Web, www.gao.gov/careers/hsj.html

Audits, analyzes, and evaluates for Congress federal administration of homeland security and justice areas and national preparedness programs and activities.

▶**NONGOVERNMENTAL**

Air Force Assn. (AFA), 1501 Lee Hwy., #400, Arlington, VA 22209-1198; (703) 247-5800. Fax, (703) 247-5853. Lt. Gen. Bruce Wright (USAF, Ret.), President. Press, (703) 247-5850. Toll-free, (800) 727-3337.
General email, membership@afa.org
Web, www.afa.org, Twitter, @AirForceAssoc and Facebook, www.facebook.com/AirForceAssociation

Membership: civilians and active duty, reserve, retired, and cadet personnel of the Air Force. Informs members and the public of developments in the aerospace field. Monitors legislation and Defense Dept. policies. Library on aviation history open to the public by appointment.

American Conservative Union (ACU), 1331 H St. N.W., #500, 20005; (202) 347-9388. Fax, (202) 347-9389. Dan Schneider, Executive Director; Michi Iljazi, Director of Government Affairs.
General email, contact@conservative.org
Web, http://conservative.org, Twitter, @ACUConservative and Facebook, www.facebook.com/ACUConservative

Legislative interest organization concerned with national defense policy, legislation related to nuclear weapons, U.S. strategic position vis-à-vis the former Soviet Union, missile defense programs, U.S. troops under UN command, and U.S. strategic alliance commitments.

American Enterprise Institute (AEI), *Foreign and Defense Policy Studies,* 1789 Massachusetts Ave. N.W., 20036; (202) 862-5800. Fax, (202) 862-7177. Danielle Pletka, Senior Vice President, (202) 862-7184.
Web, www.aei.org and Twitter, @dpletka

Research and educational organization that conducts conferences, seminars, and debates and sponsors research on national security, defense policy, and arms control.

American Security Council Foundation, 1300 Pennsylvania Ave. N.W., #700, 20004; (202) 204-2541. John McIntosh, Director of Operations.
General email, info@ascfusa.org
Web, www.ascfusa.org, Twitter, @ASCFUSA and Facebook, www.facebook.com/ascfusa
Press, press@ascfusa.org

Nonpartisan organization that promotes developing and maintaining military, economic, and diplomatic strength to preserve national security. Monitors legislation and conducts educational activities.

American Security Project, 1201 Pennsylvania Ave. N.W., #520, 20004; Brig. Gen. Stephen A. Cheney (USMC, Ret.), Chief Executive Officer. Phone/Press, (202) 347-4267.
General email, press@americansecurityproject.org
Web, www.americansecurityproject.org, Twitter, @AmSecProject and Facebook, www.facebook.com/AmSecProject

Nonprofit, nonpartisan organization that educates the public on the advancement of national security. Distributes research on security issues to the media, publications, and events. Promotes action and holds meetings to discuss new national security strategies.

ASIS International, 1625 Prince St., Alexandria, VA 22314-2882; (703) 519-6200. Fax, (703) 519-6299. Peter J. O'Neil, Chief Executive Officer.
General email, asis@asisonline.org
Web, www.asisonline.org and Twitter, @ASIS_Intl

Membership: security administrators who oversee physical and logistical security for private and public organizations, including law enforcement and the military. Develops security standards; offers educational programs and materials on general and industry-specific practices; and administers certification programs. Monitors legislation and regulations.

Aspen Institute, 2300 N St., N.W., #700, 20037; (202) 736-5800. Fax, (202) 467-0790. Dan Porterfield, President. Press, (202) 736-3849.
General email, info@aspeninstitute.org
Web, www.aspeninstitute.org and Twitter, @AspenInstitute

Educational and policy studies organization. Promotes consideration of the public good in a wide variety of policy areas, including international relations and homeland security. Working with international partners, offers educational seminars, nonpartisan policy forums, public conferences and events, and leadership development initiatives.

Assn. of the United States Army, 2425 Wilson Blvd., Arlington, VA 22201; (703) 841-4300. Fax, (703) 525-9039. Gen. Carter Ham (USA Ret.), President, (703) 907-2603. Information, (800) 336-4570.
General email, info@ausa.org
Web, www.ausa.org and Twitter, @AUSAorg

Membership: civilians and active duty and retired members of the armed forces. Conducts symposia on defense issues and researches topics that affect the military.

Atlantic Council, 1030 15th St. N.W., 12th Floor, 20005; (202) 463-7226. Fax, (202) 463-7241. Frederick Kempe, President. Press, (202) 778-4967.
General email, info@atlanticcouncil.org
Web, www.atlanticcouncil.org and Twitter, @ATLANTICCOUNCIL

Conducts studies and makes policy recommendations on U.S. foreign security and international economic policies in the Atlantic and Pacific communities; sponsors conferences and educational exchanges.

Defense Department

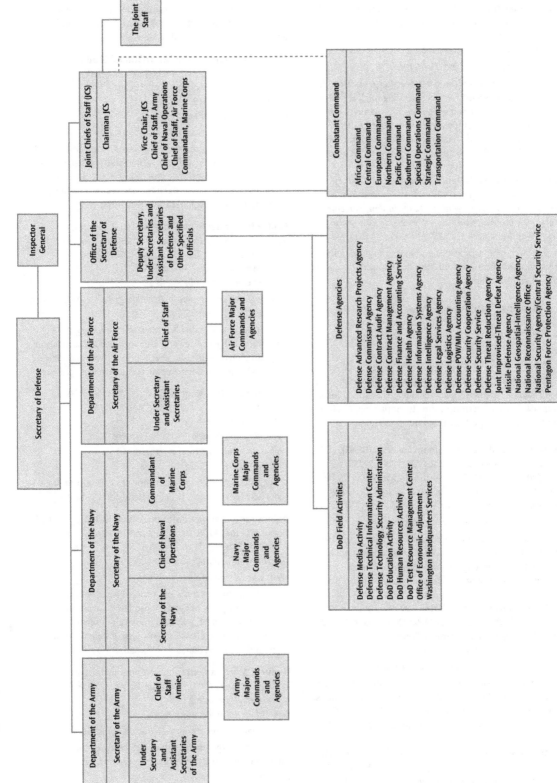

Secretary of Defense

Inspector General

Department of the Army
Secretary of the Army
Under Secretary and Assistant Secretaries of the Army
Chief of Staff Armies
Army Major Commands and Agencies

Department of the Navy
Secretary of the Navy
Chief of Naval Operations
Commandant of Marine Corps
Navy Major Commands and Agencies
Marine Corps Major Commands and Agencies

Department of the Air Force
Secretary of the Air Force
Under Secretary and Assistant Secretaries
Chief of Staff
Air Force Major Commands and Agencies

Office of the Secretary of Defense
Deputy Secretary, Under Secretaries and Assistant Secretaries of Defense and Other Specified Officials

Joint Chiefs of Staff (JCS)
Chairman JCS
Vice Chair, JCS
Chief of Staff, Army
Chief of Naval Operations
Chief of Staff, Air Force
Commandant, Marine Corps

The Joint Staff

Combatant Command
Africa Command
Central Command
European Command
Northern Command
Pacific Command
Southern Command
Special Operations Command
Strategic Command
Transportation Command

DoD Field Activities
Defense Media Activity
Defense Technical Information Center
Defense Technology Security Administration
DoD Education Activity
DoD Human Resources Activity
DoD Test Resource Management Center
Office of Economic Adjustment
Washington Headquarters Services

Defense Agencies
Defense Advanced Research Projects Agency
Defense Commissary Agency
Defense Contract Audit Agency
Defense Contract Management Agency
Defense Finance and Accounting Service
Defense Health Agency
Defense Information Systems Agency
Defense Intelligence Agency
Defense Legal Services Agency
Defense Logistics Agency
Defense POW/MIA Accounting Agency
Defense Security Cooperation Agency
Defense Security Service
Defense Threat Reduction Agency
Joint Improvised-Threat Defeat Agency
Missile Defense Agency
National Geospatial-Intelligence Agency
National Reconnaissance Office
National Security Agency/Central Security Service
Pentagon Force Protection Agency

-------- Indicates a support or advisory relationship with the unit rather than a direct reporting relationship

British American Security Information Council (BASIC), *1725 DeSales St. N.W., #600, 20036; Paul Ingram, Executive Director.*
General email, basicuk@basicint.org

Web, www.basicint.org and Twitter, @basic_int

Independent analysis and advocacy organization that researches global security issues, including nuclear policies, military strategies, armaments, and disarmament. Assists in the development of global security policies, promotes public awareness, and facilitates exchange of information on both sides of the Atlantic. (UK office is in London.)

The Brookings Institution, *Center for 21st Century Security and Intelligence, 1775 Massachusetts Ave. N.W., 20036; (202) 797-6103. Michael E. O'Hanlon, Director.*
Web, www.brookings.edu/center/center-for-21st-century-security-and-intelligence and Twitter, @MichaelEOHanlon

Research center promoting policymaking on defense, arms control and nonproliferation, cybersecurity, arms control, and intelligence.

The Brookings Institution, *Foreign Policy Studies, 1775 Massachusetts Ave. N.W., 20036; (202) 797-6003. Fax, (202) 797-6004. Bruce Jones, Director. Press, (202) 797-6105.*
Web, www.brookings.edu/foreign-policy

Research and educational organization that focuses on major national security topics, including U.S. armed forces, weapons decisions, terrorism threats, employment policies, and the security aspects of U.S. foreign relations.

Business Executives for National Security (BENS), *1030 15th St. N.W., #200 East, 20005; (202) 296-2125. Fax, (202) 296-2490. Gen. Norton A. Schwartz (USAF, Ret.), Chief Executive Officer. Media, (202) 481-1148.*
General email, bens@bens.org

Web, www.bens.org and Twitter, @BENS_org

Monitors legislation on national security issues from a business perspective; holds conferences, congressional forums, and other meetings on national security issues; works with other organizations on defense policy issues.

Center for Naval Analyses (CNA), *3003 Washington Blvd., Arlington, VA 22201-2117; (703) 824-2000. Fax, (703) 824-2942. Katherine A.W. McGrady, President.*
General email, inquiries@cna.org

Web, www.cna.org and Twitter, @CNA_org

Conducts research on homeland security and defense, weapons acquisitions, tactical problems, naval operations, and air traffic management. Parent organization is CNA, which also operates CNA Institute for Public Research.

Center for Security Policy, *2020 Pennsylvania Ave. N.W., #189, 20006; (202) 835-9077. Fax, (202) 835-9066. Frank J. Gaffney Jr., Executive Chair, (202) 835-9077, ext. 1006; Fred Fleitz, President.*
General email, info@securefreedom.org

Web, www.centerforsecuritypolicy.org and Twitter, @securefreedom

Educational institution concerned with U.S. defense and foreign policy. Interests include arms control compliance and verification policy and technology transfer policy.

Center for Strategic and International Studies, *1616 Rhode Island Ave. N.W., 20036; (202) 887-0200. Fax, (202) 775-3199. John J. Hamre, Chief Executive Officer. Media, (202) 775-3199.*
General email, webmaster@csis.org

Web, www.csis.org and Twitter, @CSIS

A bipartisan organization that seeks to advance global security and prosperity by providing strategic insights and practical policy solutions to decision makers. Expertise includes defense and international security, emerging global issues, and regional transformation.

Center for Strategic and International Studies, *Technology Policy Program, 1616 Rhode Island Ave. N.W., 20036; (202) 775-3175. Fax, (202) 775-3199. James Andrew Lewis, Director.*
General email, techpolicy@csis.org

Web, www.csis.org/programs/technology-policy-program and Twitter, @CyberCSIS

Conducts and publishes research on emerging technologies, intelligence reform, and space and globalization programs. Interests include cybersecurity, privacy and surveillance, technology and innovation, and Internet governance.

The Conservative Caucus (TCC), *332 W. Lee Hwy., #221, Warrenton, VA 20816; (540) 219-4536. Peter J. Thomas, Chair.*
General email, info@conservativeusa.org

Web, www.conservativeusa.org and Twitter, @ConservCaucus

Legislative interest organization that promotes grassroots activity on national defense and foreign policy.

Defense Orientation Conference Assn. (DOCA), *9245 Old Keene Mill Rd., #100, Burke, VA 22015-4202; (703) 451-1200. Robert J. Jans, President.*
General email, doca@doca.org

Web, www.doca.org

Membership: citizens interested in national defense. Under the auspices of the Defense Dept., promotes continuing education of members on national security issues through visits to embassies and tours of defense installations in the United States and abroad.

Henry L. Stimson Center, *1211 Connecticut Ave. N.W., 8th Floor, 20036; (202) 223-5956. Fax, (202) 238-9604. Brian Finlay, President.*
General email, info@stimson.org

Web, www.stimson.org and Twitter, @StimsonCenter

Research organization that studies arms control and international security, focusing on policy, technology, and politics.

Hudson Institute, *National Security Studies, 1201 Pennsylvania Ave. N.W., 4th Floor, 20004; (202) 974-2400. Fax, (202) 974-2410. Kenneth R. Weinstein, Chief Executive Officer. Press, (202) 974-2417.*

Homeland Security Department

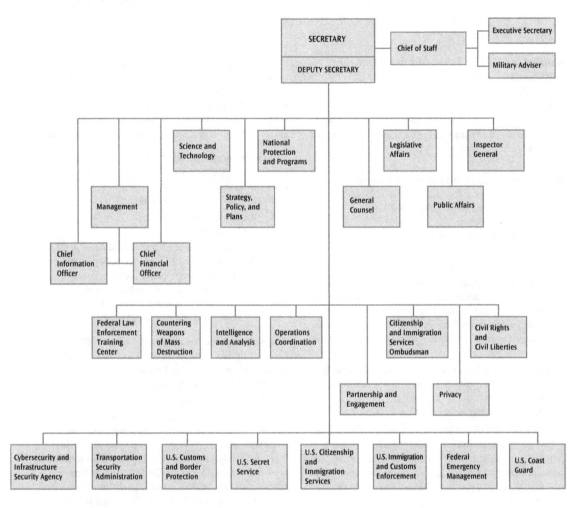

General email, info@hudson.org

Web, www.hudson.org, Twitter, @HudsonInstitute and Facebook, www.facebook.com/HudsonInstitutePoliticalStudies

Public policy research organization that conducts studies on U.S. overseas bases, U.S.–NATO relations, and missile defense programs. Focuses on long-range implications for U.S. national security.

Institute for Science and International Security, *440 1st St. N.W., #800, 20001; (202) 547-3633. David Albright, President.*

General email, isis@isis-online.org

Web, www.isis-online.org and Facebook, www.facebook.com/Institute-for-Science-and-International-Security-351457957011/?ref=br_rs

Analyzes scientific and policy issues affecting national and international security, including the spread of nuclear weapons, the problems of war, regional and global arms races, and the environmental, health, and safety hazards of nuclear weapons production.

Institute of International Education, *National Security Education Program,* *4800 Mark Center Dr., #08F09-02, Alexandria, VA 22350-7000 (mailing address: P.O. Box 20010, Arlington, VA 22209); (571) 256-0711. Fax, (703) 692-2615. Michael A. Nugent, Director. Boren Awards information, (800) 618-6737.*

General email, nsep@nsep.gov

Web, www.nsep.gov

Administers Boren Awards and Language Flagship programs; provides scholarships, fellowships, and institutional grants to students and academics with an interest in foreign affairs and national security.

Jewish Institute for National Security Affairs (JINSA), *1101 14th St. N.W., #1110, 20005; (202) 667-3900. Michael Makovsky, Executive Director.*

General email, info@jinsa.org

Web, www.jinsa.org

Seeks to educate the public about the importance of effective U.S. defense capability and inform the U.S. defense and foreign affairs community about Israel's role in Mediterranean and Middle Eastern affairs. Sponsors lectures and conferences; facilitates dialogue between security policymakers, military officials, diplomats, and the general public.

National Institute for Public Policy, *9302 Lee Hwy., #750, Fairfax, VA 22031-1214; (703) 293-9181. Fax, (703) 293-9198. Keith B. Payne, President. Web, www.nipp.org*

Studies public policy and its relation to national security. Interests include arms control, strategic weapons systems and planning, and foreign policy.

National Security Archive *(George Washington University), Gelman Library, 2130 H St. N.W., #701, 20037; (202) 994-7000. Fax, (202) 994-7005. Thomas Blanton, Director. General email, nsarchiv@gwu.edu Web, www.nsarchive.org*

Research institute and library that provides information on U.S. foreign and economic policy and national security affairs. Maintains and publishes collection of declassified and unclassified documents obtained through the Freedom of Information Act. Archive open to the public by appointment. Website has a Russian-language link.

Partnership for a Secure America (PSA), *1129 20th St. N.W., #500, 20036; (202) 293-8580. Nathan Sermonis, Executive Director. General email, info@psaonline.org Web, www.psaonline.org and Twitter, @PSAonline*

Supports a bipartisan approach to national security policies and issues. Researches and publishes reports on national security threats such as terrorism. Organizes conferences for political parties to debate and develop consensus on issues.

RAND Corp., *Homeland Security Operational Analysis Center (HSOAC), 1200 S. Hayes St., Arlington, VA 22202; (703) 413-1100. Terrence Kelly, Director, ext. 4905. Web, www.rand.org/hsrd/hsoac.html*

Federally funded research development center (FFRDC) chartered to provide independent analysis of homeland security issues. Conducts research, works to promote dialogue, and provides executive education through workshops, conferences, publications and reports, and outreach programs.

RAND Corp., *Washington Office, 1200 S. Hayes St., Arlington, VA 22202-5050; (703) 413-1100. Fax, (703) 413-8111. Nicholas Burger, Director; Anita Chandra, Director for Social and Economic Well-Being, ext. 5323. Web, www.rand.org*

Conducts research on national security issues, including political/military affairs of the former Soviet Union and U.S. strategic policy. Research focuses on citizen preparedness, defense strategy, and military force planning. (Headquarters in Santa Monica, Calif.)

The Truman Center for National Policy, *1250 Eye St., #500, 20005; (202) 216-9723. Fax, (202) 682-1818. Jenna Ben-Yehuda, President. General email, info@TrumanCenter.org Web, http://trumancenter.org*

Public policy research and educational organization that serves as a forum for development of national policy alternatives. Leads discussion and advances policies aimed at promoting U.S. global engagement and leadership in the 21st century. Focus on issues such as cybersecurity and defense energy. (Partner of the Truman National Security Project.)

Truman National Security Project, *1250 Eye St. N.W., #500, 20005; (202) 216-9723. Fax, (202) 682-1818. Jenna Ben-Yehuda, President. General email, info@trumanproject.org Web, http://trumanproject.org and Twitter, @TrumanProject*

Membership: veterans and policy and political leaders. Forum for development of national policy alternatives. Promotes national security policy coordination, strengthening the U.S. military and intelligence, foreign affairs and diplomacy, democracy, and open trade. (Partner of the Truman Center for National Policy.)

Women in International Security (WIIS), *1301 Connecticut Ave. N.W., #750, 20036; (202) 684-6010. Chantal de Jonge Oudraat, President. General email, info@wiisglobal.org Web, http://wiisglobal.org and Twitter, @WIIS_Global*

Seeks to advance the leadership and professional development of women in the field of international peace and security decision and policymaking. Maintains a database of women foreign and defense policy specialists worldwide; organizes conferences in the United States and elsewhere; disseminates information on jobs, internships, and fellowships. Has chapters in the United States and international affiliates. (Affiliated with SIPRI North America.)

Civil Rights and Liberties

▶**AGENCIES**

Homeland Security Dept. (DHS), *Civil Rights and Civil Liberties (CRCL), 245 Murray Lane S.W., Bldg. 410, MS 0190, 20528-0190; (202) 401-1474. Fax, (202) 401-4708. Cameron Quinn, Civil Rights and Civil Liberties Officer. Toll-free, (866) 644-8360. Toll-free TTY, (866) 644-8361. General email, crcl@dhs.gov Web, www.dhs.gov/topic/civil-rights-and-civil-liberties Facebook, CivilRightsAndCivilLiberties*

Provides legal and policy advice to the secretary and senior officers of the department on civil rights and civil liberties issues; maintains dialogue with minority communities; investigates and resolves complaints filed by members of the public.

Homeland Security Dept. (DHS), *Privacy Office, 245 Murray Lane, Bldg. 110, 20528-0655; (202) 343-1717.*

Fax, (202) 343-4010. Jonathan Cantor, Chief Privacy Officer (Acting).

General email, privacy@dhs.gov

Web, www.dhs.gov/privacy-office

Responsible for ensuring that department policies and use of technology sustain individual privacy. Makes annual report to Congress and enforces the provisions of the 1974 Privacy Act and evaluates legislative and regulatory proposals involving collection, use, and disclosure of personal information by the federal government.

National Security Agency (NSA) *(Defense Dept.), Civil Liberties and Privacy, 9800 Savage Rd., #6272, Fort Meade, MD 20755-6000; (301) 688-6311. Rebecca (Becky) Richards, Civil Liberties and Privacy Officer.*

Web, www.nsa.gov/about/civil-liberties

Advises the director of the NSA to ensure that privacy and civil liberties protections are inherent in strategic decisions, particularly in the areas of technology and processes. Seeks to increase transparency.

Office of Management and Budget (OMB) *(Executive Office of the President), Information and Regulatory Affairs, 725 17th St. N.W., #10236, 20503; (202) 395-5897. Fax, (202) 395-6102. Neomi Reo, Administrator. Press, (202) 395-7254.*

Web, www.whitehouse.gov/omb/information-regulatory-affairs

Oversees implementation of the Privacy Act of 1974 and other privacy-related and security-related statutes. Issues guidelines and regulations.

▶**CONGRESS**

For a listing of relevant congressional committees and subcommittees, please see pages 608–609 or the Appendix.

▶**NONGOVERNMENTAL**

American Civil Liberties Union (ACLU), *Washington Legislative Office, 915 15th St. N.W., 6th floor, 20005; (202) 544-1681. Fax, (202) 546-0738. David Cole, Legal Director. Press, (202) 549-2666.*

General email, media@acludc.org

Web, www.aclu.org/legiupdate

Advocates legislation to guarantee constitutional rights and civil liberties. Monitors agency compliance with the Privacy Act and other access statutes. Produces publications. (Headquarters in New York maintains docket of cases.)

Foundation for Defense of Democracies (FDD), *P.O. Box 33249, 20033-0249; (202) 207-0190. Fax, (202) 207-0191. Clifford D. May, President; Mark Dubowitz, Chief Executive Officer.*

General email, info@fdd.org

Web, www.defenddemocracy.org, Twitter, @FDD and Facebook, www.facebook.com/followFDD

Conducts research and education related to the war on terrorism and the promotion of democracy.

Reporters Committee for Freedom of the Press, *1156 15th St. N.W., #1020, 20005; (202) 795-9300. Fax, (202) 795-9310. Bruce D. Brown, Executive Director, (202) 795-9301. Legal defense hotline, (800) 336-4243.*

General email, info@rcfp.org

Web, www.rcfp.org, Twitter, @rcfp

Legal defense hotline, hotline@rcpf.org

Committee of reporters, news editors, publishers, and lawyers from the print and broadcast media. Maintains a legal defense and research fund for members of the news media involved in freedom of the press court cases; interests include access to information and privacy issues faced by journalists covering antiterrorism initiatives and military actions abroad.

Defense and Homeland Security Budgets

▶**AGENCIES**

Army Dept. *(Defense Dept.), Chief Information Officer / G-6, 107 Army Pentagon, #3E608, 20310-0107; (703) 695-4366. Fax, (703) 695-3091. Gregory L. Garcia, Chief Information Officer.*

Web, http://ciog6.army.mil and Twitter, @ArmyCIOG6

Oversees policy and budget for the Army's information systems and programs.

Defense Contract Audit Agency *(Defense Dept.), 8725 John Jay Kingman Rd., #2135, Fort Belvoir, VA 22060-6219; (703) 767-3200. Fax, (703) 767-3267. Anita Bales, Director. Media, (703) 697-5131. DCAA OIG hotline, (571) 448-3135.*

General email, dcaaweb@dcaa.mil

Web, www.dcaa.mil

Performs all contract audits for the Defense Dept. Provides Defense Dept. personnel responsible for procurement and contract administration with accounting and financial advisory services regarding the negotiation, administration, and settlement of contracts and subcontracts.

Defense Contract Management Agency *(Defense Dept.), 14501 George Carter Way, 2nd Floor, Chantilly, VA 20151; (571) 521-1600. Vice Adm. David H. Lewis (USN), Director. FOIA, (804) 734-1488. Media, (804) 734-1492.*

Web, www.dcma.mil and Twitter, @DCMAnews

Ensures the integrity of the contracting process, and provides a broad range of contract-procurement management services, including cost and pricing, quality assurance, contract administration and termination, and small business support.

Defense Dept. (DoD), *Comptroller, 1100 Defense Pentagon, #3E770, 20301-1100; (703) 695-3237. David L. Norquist, Comptroller.*

Web, http://comptroller.defense.gov

Supervises and reviews the preparation and implementation of the defense budget. Advises the secretary of defense on fiscal matters. Collects and distributes information on the department's management of resources.

Homeland Security Dept. (DHS), *Management Directorate,* 3801 Nebraska Ave. N.W., 20528 (mailing address: 245 Murray Lane, MS 04401, Washington, DC 20528); (202) 447-3400. (202) 447-3106. Fax, (202) 447-3713. Claire M. Grady, Under Secretary.
Web, www.dhs.gov/about-directorate-management

Responsible for department budget, appropriations, expenditure of funds, accounting and finance, procurement, human resources and personnel, information technology systems, facilities, property, equipment and other material resources, and performance measurement.

Office of Management and Budget (OMB) *(Executive Office of the President),* *Homeland Security,* 725 17th St. N.W., #9208, 20503; (202) 395-4892. Fax, (202) 395-0850. James Holm, Chief. Press, (202) 395-7254.
Web, www.whitehouse.gov/omb

Assists and advises the OMB director on budget preparation, proposed legislation, and evaluations of Homeland Security Dept. programs, policies, and activities.

Office of Management and Budget (OMB) *(Executive Office of the President),* *National Security,* 725 17th St. N.W., #10001, 20503; (202) 395-3884. Fax, (202) 395-3307. Robert Blair, Associate Director. Press, (202) 395-7254.
Web, www.whitehouse.gov/omb

Supervises preparation of the Defense Dept., intelligence community, and veterans affairs portions of the federal budget.

►CONGRESS

For a listing of relevant congressional committees and subcommittees, please see pages 608–609 or the Appendix.

Government Accountability Office (GAO), *Defense Capabilities and Management (DCM),* 441 G St. N.W., #4440B, 20548; (202) 512-4300. Cathleen A. Berrick, Managing Director.
Web, www.gao.gov/careers/dcm.html

Audits, analyzes, and evaluates Defense Dept. acquisition, spending, and international programs.

►NONGOVERNMENTAL

Center for Strategic and Budgetary Assessments (CSBA), 1667 K St. N.W., #900, 20006-1659; (202) 331-7990. Fax, (202) 331-8019. Thomas G. Mahnken, President.
General email, info@csbaonline.org
*Web, http://csbaonline.org and Twitter, @CSBA_*

Think tank that promotes deliberation of national security strategy, the future of the U.S. military, and defense investment options. Conducts analyses of defense budget and programmatic analysis. Compares the relative strengths and weaknesses of the United States and potential military competitors. Conducts seminar-style war-games to analyze the operational and strategic levels of conflict, as well as strategy and investment alternatives.

Anticipates future military trends, based on analysis of historical trends.

National Campaign for a Peace Tax Fund, 2121 Decatur Pl. N.W., 20008-1923; (202) 483-3751. Malachy Killbride, Executive Director. Toll-free, (888) 732-2382.
General email, info@peacetaxfund.org
Web, www.peacetaxfund.org

Supports legislation permitting taxpayers who are conscientiously opposed to military expenditures to have the military portion of their income tax money placed in a separate, nonmilitary fund.

Women's Action for New Directions (WAND), *Washington Office,* 810 7th St. N.E., 20002; (202) 459-4769. Fax, (202) 544-7612. Nancy Parrish, Executive Director; Caroline Dorminey, Policy Director.
General email, peace@wand.org
Web, www.wand.org and Twitter, @WomensAction

Seeks to redirect federal spending priorities from military spending toward domestic needs; works to develop citizen expertise through education and political involvement; provides educational programs and material about nuclear and conventional weapons; monitors defense legislation, budget policy legislation, and legislation affecting women. (Headquarters in Arlington, Mass.)

Military Aid and Peacekeeping

►AGENCIES

Bureau of European and Eurasian Affairs *(State Dept.),* *European Security and Political Affairs,* 2201 C St. N.W., #6511, 20520; (202) 647-1626. Fax, (202) 647-1369. Joseph Manso, Director.
Web, www.state.gov/p/eur

Coordinates and advises, with the Defense Dept. and other agencies, the U.S. mission to NATO and the U.S. delegation to the Organization for Security and Cooperation in Europe regarding political, military, and arms control matters.

Bureau of Political-Military Affairs (PM) *(State Dept.),* *Security Assistance,* 2401 E St. N.W., #H1038, 20037; (202) 663-3040. Kevin O'Keefe, Director.
Web, www.state.gov/t/pm/sa

Administers funding for security assistance and capacity-building programs in foreign countries.

Defense Dept. (DoD), *International Security Affairs, European and NATO Policy,* 2000 Defense Pentagon, #5B652, 20301-2000; (703) 695-5553. James J. Townsend, Deputy Assistant Secretary (Acting); Rachel Ellehuus, Principal Director.
Web, www.defense.gov

Advises the assistant secretary for international security affairs on matters dealing with Europe and NATO.

Defense Security Cooperation Agency *(Defense Dept.),* 2800 Defense Pentagon, 20301-2800; (703) 697-9709.

Lt. Gen. Charles Hooper (USN), Director; Gregory Kausner, Deputy Director. Public Affairs, (703) 604-6617.
General email, dsca.ncr.lmo.mbx.info@mail.mil
Web, www.dsca.mil

Administers programs providing defense articles and services, military training and education, humanitarian assistance, and landmine removal to international partners in furtherance of U.S. policies and strategic objectives.

► **CONGRESS**

For a listing of relevant congressional committees and subcommittees, please see pages 608–609 or the Appendix.

► **INTERNATIONAL ORGANIZATIONS**

Inter-American Defense Board, 2600 16th St. N.W., 20441-0002; (202) 939-6041. Fax, (202) 319-2847. Brig. Gen. Luis Rodriguez Bucio, Chair (in Mexico); Brig. Gen. Stephen Lacroix, Director General (in Canada); Maj. Gen. James E. Taylor, Inter-American Defense College Director. Inter-American Defense College, (202) 646-1337.
General email, jid@jid.org
Web, http://iadb.jid.org

Membership: military officers from twenty-eight countries of the Western Hemisphere. Plans for the collective self-defense of the American continents. Develops procedures for standardizing military organization and operations; operates the Inter-American Defense Board and Inter-American Defense College. Advises the Organization of American States on military and defense matters.

► **NONGOVERNMENTAL**

International Stability Operations Assn. (ISOA), 17251 Eye St. N.W., #300, 20006 (mailing address: 1714 Corwin Dr., Silver Spring, MD 20910); (703) 336-3940. Howard (Howie) Lind, President.
General email, howielind@stability-operations.org
Web, www.stability-operations.org

Membership: private-sector service companies involved in all sectors of peace and stability operations around the world, including mine clearance, logistics, security, training, and emergency humanitarian aid. Works to institute standards and codes of conduct. Monitors legislation.

ARMS CONTROL, DISARMAMENT, AND THREAT REDUCTION

General

► **AGENCIES**

Bureau of Arms Control, Verification, and Compliance (AVC) *(State Dept.),* 2201 C St. N.W., #5950, 20520; (202) 647-5315. Yleem Poblete, Assistant Secretary.
Web, www.state.gov/t/avc

Leads development of U.S. arms control, missile defense, and space policies, including negotiation and implementation of international nonproliferation and disarmament agreements.

Bureau of Arms Control, Verification, and Compliance (AVC) *(State Dept.), Emerging Security Challenges (ESC),* 2201 C St. N.W., #5725, 20520; (202) 647-7620. Eric E. Desautels, Director, (202) 647-7620.
Web, www.state.gov/t/avc/c21764.htm

Provides research and recommendations on all policy and threat issues related to missile defense systems and cooperation, outer space security issues and transparency, cyberstability, and Arctic and Antarctic security issues.

Bureau of Arms Control, Verification, and Compliance (AVC) *(State Dept.), Euro-Atlantic Security Affairs (ESA),* 2201 C St. N.W., #5724, 20520; (202) 647-9170. Vacant, Director.
Web, www.state.gov/t/avc/cca

Handles matters relating to existing and prospective European and Euro-Atlantic arms control, nonproliferation, disarmament agreements, and security arrangements.

Bureau of Arms Control, Verification, and Compliance (AVC) *(State Dept.), Strategic Stability and Deterrence Affairs (SSD),* 2201 C St. N.W., #5758, 20520; (202) 736-4467. Wade Boese, Director.
Web, www.state.gov/t/avc/c23758.htm

Promotes stability and reduces nuclear threats through policy development, negotiation, and implementation of arms control to ensure U.S. security.

Bureau of Arms Control, Verification, and Compliance (AVC) *(State Dept.), Verification, Planning, and Outreach (VPO),* 2201 C St. N.W., #5669, 20520; (202) 647-9238. Jody L. Daniel, Director.
Web, www.state.gov/t/avc/vtt

Identifies and prioritizes emerging verification and compliance issues, and recommends the appropriate use of the Bureau's resources for both current and future arms control challenges, including the application of technological and analytical solutions.

Bureau of Economic and Business Affairs (EB) *(State Dept.), Counter Threat Finance and Sanctions (TFS), Threat Finance Countermeasures (TFC),* 2201 C St. N.W., #3843, 20520; (202) 647-5763. Fax, (202) 647-7407. Andrew J. Weinschenk, Director.
Web, www.state.gov/e/eb/tfs/tfc

Seeks to minimize the funding available to groups and individuals that prove a threat to domestic, international, and regional security.

Bureau of Industry and Security (BIS) *(Commerce Dept.),* 14th St. and Constitution Ave. N.W., #3898, 20230; (202) 482-1455. Daniel O. Hill, Deputy Under Secretary (Acting). Export licensing information, (202) 482-4811. Press, (202) 482-2721.
Web, www.bis.doc.gov and Twitter, @BISgov

Administers the Export Administration Act; maintains control lists and performs export licensing for the purposes of national security, foreign policy, and prevention of short supply. Seeks to prevent proliferation of dual-use exports, especially weapons of mass destruction.

Bureau of International Security and Nonproliferation (ISN) *(State Dept.)*, 2201 C St. N.W., #3932, 20520; (202) 647-5999. *Christopher A. Ford, Assistant Secretary.* Web, *www.state.gov/t/isn*, Twitter, *@StateISN* and Facebook, *www.facebook.com/StateDepartment. ISNBureau*

Leads U.S. efforts to prevent the spread of weapons of mass destruction (WMD, including nuclear, chemical, and biological weapons) and their delivery systems; spearheads efforts to promote international consensus on WMD proliferation; supports efforts of foreign partners to prevent, protect against, and respond to the threat or use of WMD by terrorists.

Bureau of International Security and Nonproliferation (ISN) *(State Dept.)*, *Biological Policy Staff (BPS)*, 2201 C St. N.W., #3651, 20520; (202) 647-7903. *Christopher Park, Director.* Web, *www.state.gov/t/isn/offices/bps/index.htm*

Oversees implementation of the Biological Weapons convention with the aim to prevent or regress the threat of acquisition or use of biological weapons by state and non-state actors; supports policies and strategies for countering biological threats, misuse of advances in the life sciences, and use of nonproliferation tools.

Bureau of International Security and Nonproliferation (ISN) *(State Dept.)*, *Conventional Arms Threat Reduction (CATR)*, 2201 C St. N.W., #5528, 20520; (202) 647-2371. *Ann K. Ganzer, Director.* Web, *www.state.gov/t/isn/offices/catr/index.htm*

Works to combat the proliferation of advanced conventional weapons and related dual-use goods and technologies, including tanks, aircraft, missiles, sensor and lasers, man-portable air defense systems, and precision-guided munitions; leads policy on commercial remote-sensing.

Bureau of International Security and Nonproliferation (ISN) *(State Dept.)*, *Cooperative Threat Reduction (CTR)*, 2201 C St. N.W., #3326, 20520; (202) 736-7190. *Alexander Stolar, Director (Acting).* Web, *www.state.gov/t/isn/offices/ctr/index.htm*

Oversees the diplomatic aspects of programs aimed at reducing the threat posed by terrorist organizations or states seeking to acquire weapons of mass destruction expertise, materials, and equipment.

Bureau of International Security and Nonproliferation (ISN) *(State Dept.)*, *Counterproliferation Initiatives (CPI)*, 2201 C St. N.W., #3452, 20520; (202) 647-7895. *Phillip (Tony) Foley, Director.* Web, *www.state.gov/t/isn/offices/cpi/index.htm*

Leads efforts to develop, implement, and improve counterproliferation policies to impede the proliferation of weapons of mass destruction; implements nuclear sanctions; ensures U.S. policy is in accordance with the UN Security Council Resolution 1540.

Bureau of International Security and Nonproliferation (ISN) *(State Dept.)*, *Export Control Cooperation (ECC)*, 2201 C St. N.W., #3317, 20520; (202) 647-1966. *Jason Witow, Director.* Web, *www.state.gov/t/isn/offices/ecc/index.htm*

Provides assistance to foreign governments to ensure strategic trade control systems meet international standards and establish independent capabilities to regulate transfers of weapons of mass destruction, WMD-related items, conventional arms, and related dual-use items, and to detect, interdict, investigate, and prosecute illicit transfers of such items.

Bureau of International Security and Nonproliferation (ISN) *(State Dept.)*, *Nonproliferation and Disarmament Fund (NDF)*, 2201 C St. N.W., #3208, 20520; (202) 647-0094. *Steven Saboe, Director.* Web, *www.state.gov/t/isn/offices/ndf/index.htm*

Responds to high-priority and unanticipated nonproliferation and disarmament issues, frequently in areas where other programs do not have authority.

Bureau of International Security and Nonproliferation (ISN) *(State Dept.)*, *Threat Reduction (TR)*, 2201 C St. N.W., #3310, 20520; (202) 647-6643. *Vacant, Ambassador; Marc Forino, Special Advisor to the Ambassador.* Web, *www.state.gov/t/isn/offices/c34463.htm*

Promotes programs in chemical, biological, nuclear and radiological security; works with domestic and international partners in the security, animal and human health, and law enforcement sectors to ensure coordinated approaches to international implementation.

Bureau of International Security and Nonproliferation (ISN) *(State Dept.)*, *Weapons of Mass Destruction Terrorism (WMDT)*, 2201 C St. N.W., #3733, 20520; (202) 647-8699. Fax, (202) 647-4920. *Renee Sonderman, Director.* Web, *www.state.gov/t/isn/offices/wmdt/index.htm*

Works to reduce the threat of weapons of mass destruction terrorism by establishing, strengthening, and maintaining the capabilities of international partners to prevent, detect, and respond to terrorist attempts to acquire radiological or nuclear materials; helps build capacity to respond to chemical, biological, radiological, and nuclear incidents.

Bureau of Political-Military Affairs (PM) *(State Dept.)*, *Weapons Removal and Abatement (WRA)*, 2025 E St. N.W., #NE2025, 20520; (202) 453-8304. *Stan Brown, Director.* Web, *www.state.gov/t/pm/wra*

Manages programs aimed at reducing and destroying stockpiled, poorly-secured, at-risk, illicitly proliferated, and indiscriminately used conventional weapons of war.

Defense Dept. (DoD), *Homeland Defense and Global Security*, 2600 Defense Pentagon, #3C852A, 20301-2600; (703) 697-7728. Fax, (703) 693-6338. *Kenneth P. Rapuano, Assistant Secretary.* Web, *http://policy.defense.gov/OUSDP-Offices/ASD-for-Homeland-Defense-Global-Security*

Advises the secretary on reducing and countering nuclear, biological, chemical, and missile threats to the United States and its forces and allies; arms control negotiations, implementation, and verification policy; nuclear weapons policy, denuclearization, threat reduction, and nuclear safety and security; and technology transfer and cyber security.

Defense Dept. (DoD), *Plans,* 2400 Defense Pentagon, #5E384, 20301; (703) 614-0462. Fax, (703) 695-7230. Victorino Mercado, Deputy Assistant Secretary. Press, (703) 697-5131.
Web, www.defense.gov

Formulates national policies to prevent and counter the proliferation of nuclear, chemical, and biological weapons; missiles; and conventional technologies. Devises arms control agreements, export controls, technology transfer policies, and military planning policies.

Defense Threat Reduction Agency *(Defense Dept.),* 8725 John Jay Kingman Rd., MS 6201, Fort Belvoir, VA 22060-6201; (703) 767-4883. Vayl Oxford, Director. Press, (703) 767-5870.
General email, dtra.belvoir.JO.mbx.dtra-publicaffairs@mail.mil
Web, www.dtra.mil

Seeks to reduce, eliminate, and counter the threat to the United States and its allies from weapons of mass destruction; conducts technology security activities, cooperative threat reduction programs, arms control treaty monitoring, and on-site inspection; provides technical support on weapons of mass destruction matters to the Defense Dept. components.

Homeland Security Dept. (DHS), *Countering Weapons of Mass Destruction (CWMD),* 1125 15th St., 20221; (202) 254-7799. James F. McDonnell, Assistant Secretary. DHS switchboard, (202) 282-8000.
Web, www.dhs.gov/countering-weapons-mass-destruction-office#

Responsible for countering attempts by terrorists or other threat actors to carry out an attack against the United States or its interests using a weapon of mass destruction.

Joint Improvised-Threat Defeat Organization *(Defense Dept.),* 8725 John J. Kingman Rd., MS 6201, Fort Belvoir, VA 22060-6201; (703) 995-6900. Maj. Gen. Chris Bentley, Director; Vayl Oxford, Senior Executive Service Director, DTRA, (703) 767-4883. Media, (703) 995-6536, ext. 5045. Operational support, (703) 995-5553.
General email, jida.ncr.j3.mbx.operational-support@mail.mil
Web, https://dtra.mil/mission/JIDO

Combat support agency handling actions to counter improvised threats, especially improvised explosive devices (IEDs). It is a subordinate to the Defense Threat Reduction Agency (DTRA).

State Dept., *Nuclear Risk Reduction Center (NRRC),* 2201 C St. N.W., #5635, 20520; (202) 647-0027. Deborah C. Schneider, Staff Director.
Web, www.state.gov/t/avc/nrrc

Supports implementation of arms control and security agreements with foreign governments by operating government-to-government communications systems.

State Dept., *Under Secretary for Arms Control and International Security,* 2201 C St. N.W., #7208, 20520-7512; (202) 647-1049. Andrea L. Thompson, Under Secretary.
Web, www.state.gov/t and Twitter, @UnderSecT

Works with the secretary of state to develop policy on nonproliferation, arms control, regional security and defense relations, and arms transfers and security assistance. Oversees the Bureau of Arms Control, Verification and Compliance, Bureau of International Security and Nonproliferation, and Bureau of Political-Military Affairs.

▶**CONGRESS**

For a listing of relevant congressional committees and subcommittees, please see pages 608–609 or the Appendix.

▶**NONGOVERNMENTAL**

Arms Control Assn., 1200 18th St. N.W., #1175, 20005; (202) 463-8270. Fax, (202) 463-8273. Daryl G. Kimball, Executive Director.
General email, aca@armscontrol.org
Web, www.armscontrol.org and
Twitter, @ArmsControlNow

Nonpartisan organization that seeks to broaden public understanding and support for effective arms control and disarmament in national security policy through education and media programs. Publishes *Arms Control Today.*

Council for a Livable World, 820 1st St. N.E., #LL-180, 20002; (202) 543-4100. John Tierney, Executive Director, ext. 2108; James McKeon, Political Director, ext. 2617.
General email, advocacy@clw.org
Web, https://livableworld.org and Twitter, @Livableworld

Citizens' interest group that supports nuclear arms control treaties, strengthened biological and chemical weapons conventions, reduced military spending, peacekeeping, and tight restrictions on international arms sales.

Federation of American Scientists (FAS), 1112 16th St. N.W., #400, 20036; (202) 546-3300. Fax, (202) 675-1010. Ali Nouri, President.
General email, fas@fas.org
Web, www.fas.org, Twitter, @FAScientists and Facebook, www.facebook.com/fascientists

Opposes the global arms race and supports nuclear disarmament and limits on government secrecy. Promotes learning technologies and conducts studies and monitors legislation on U.S. weapons policy; provides the public with information on arms control and related issues.

GlobalSecurity.org, *300 N. Washington St., #B-100, Alexandria, VA 22314-2540; (703) 548-2700. Fax, (703) 548-2424. John E. Pike, Director.*
General email, info@globalsecurity.org
Web, www.globalsecurity.org

Provides background information and covers developing news stories on the military, weapons proliferation, space, homeland security, and intelligence. Offers profiles of agencies, systems, facilities, and current operations as well as a library of primary documentation.

High Frontier, *500 N. Washington St., Alexandria, VA 22314-2314; (703) 535-8774.*
Amb. Henry (Hank) F. Cooper, Chair.
General email, info@highfrontier.org
Web, www.highfrontier.org and Twitter, @highfrontier

Educational organization that provides information on missile defense programs and proliferation. Advocates development of a single-stage-to-orbit space vehicle, a moon base program, and a layered missile defense system. Operates speakers bureau; monitors defense legislation.

Nonproliferation Policy Education Center (NPEC), *1600 Wilson Blvd., #640, Arlington, VA 22209; (571) 970-3187. Henry D. Sokolski, Executive Director.*
General email, info@npolicy.org
Web, www.npolicy.org, Twitter, @NuclearPolicy and Facebook, www.facebook.com/NuclearPolicy

Conducts and publishes research on strategic weapons proliferation issues and makes it available to the press, congressional and executive branch staff, foreign officials, and international organizations.

Nuclear Threat Initiative (NTI), *1776 Eye St. N.W., #600, 20006; (202) 296-4810. Fax, (202) 296-4811. Joan Rohlfing, President; Ernest J. Moniz, Chief Executive Officer.*
General email, contact@nti.org
Web, www.nti.org, Twitter, @NTI_WMD and Facebook, www.facebook.com/nti.org

Works to reduce threats from nuclear, biological, and chemical weapons; publishes monthly and quarterly e-newsletters.

Peace Action, *8630 Fenton St., #934, Silver Spring, MD 20910-5642; (301) 565-4050. Fax, (301) 565-0850. Kevin Martin, President, ext. 307; John Rainwater, Executive Director, (800) 949-9020, ext. 106. Press, (301) 565-4050, ext. 316.*
Web, www.peace-action.org and Twitter, @PeaceAction

Grassroots organization that supports a negotiated comprehensive test ban treaty. Seeks a reduction in the military budget and a transfer of those funds to nonmilitary programs. Works for an end to international arms trade.

Physicians for Social Responsibility (PSR), *1111 14th St. N.W., #700, 20005; (202) 667-4260. Fax, (202) 667-4201. Jeff Carter, Executive Director.*
General email, psrnatl@psr.org
Web, www.psr.org and Twitter, @psrenvironment

Membership: doctors, nurses, health scientists, and concerned citizens. Works toward the elimination of nuclear weapons and use of nuclear power. Conducts public education programs, monitors policy, and serves as a liaison with other concerned groups.

Union of Concerned Scientists, *Global Security, 1825 K St. N.W., #800, 20006-1232; (202) 223-6133. Fax, (202) 223-6162. David Wright, Co-Director; Lisbeth Gronlund, Co-Director.*
General email, ucs@ucsusa.org
Web, www.ucsusa.org

Combines technical analysis, education and advocacy, and engagement with the public and scientific community to promote policies that enhance national and international security. Focuses on technical issues, including verified reductions of nuclear arsenals, fissile material controls, missile defense, and space security. Plays a role in increasing the number of independent scientists and technical analysts working professionally on security issues worldwide. (Headquarters in Cambridge, Mass.)

Nuclear Weapons and Power

▶**AGENCIES**

Bureau of Arms Control, Verification, and Compliance (AVC) *(State Dept.), Multilateral and Nuclear Affairs (MNA), 2201 C St. N.W., #5751, 20520; (202) 647-2792. Jeffrey L. Eberhart, Director.*
Web, www.state.gov/t/avc/c23757.htm

Coordinates U.S. policy on bilateral and multilateral nuclear arms control and disarmament agreements and commitments, verification, and compliance issues.

Bureau of International Security and Nonproliferation (ISN) *(State Dept.), Multilateral Nuclear and Security Affairs (MNSA), 2201 C St. N.W., #5821, 20520; (202) 647-8136. Kurt G. Kessler, Director.*
Web, www.state.gov/t/isn/offices/mnsa/index.htm

Leads development and implementation of U.S. policies related to global nuclear nonproliferation, including international treaties, protocols, and nuclear-related security assurances. Coordinates U.S. policy regarding International Atomic Energy Agency safeguards.

Bureau of International Security and Nonproliferation (ISN) *(State Dept.), Nuclear Energy, Safety, and Security Affairs (NESS), 2201 C St. N.W., #3320, 20520; (202) 647-4061. Richard K. Stratford, Director, (202) 647-4061.*
Web, www.state.gov/t/isn/offices/ness/index.htm

Advises the secretary on policy matters relating to nonproliferation and export controls, nuclear technology and safeguards, and nuclear safety. Negotiates bilateral and multilateral agreements pertaining to nuclear trade, safety, and physical protection.

Defense Nuclear Facilities Safety Board, *625 Indiana Ave. N.W., #700, 20004-2901; (202) 694-7000. Fax, (202)*

208-6518. Bruce Hamilton, Chair. Information, (202) 694-7000. Toll-free, (800) 788-4016.
General email, mailbox@dnfsb.gov
Web, www.dnfsb.gov

Independent board created by Congress and appointed by the president to provide external oversight of Energy Dept. defense nuclear weapons production facilities and make recommendations to the secretary of energy regarding public health and safety.

Energy Dept. (DOE), Under Secretary for Nuclear Security, 1000 Independence Ave. S.W., #7A049, 20585; (202) 586-5555. Fax, (202) 586-4892. Lisa E. Gordon-Hagerty, Under Secretary.
Web, www.energy.gov/nnsa

Maintains the safety, security, and effectiveness of the U.S. nuclear weapons stockpile without nuclear testing; provides the U.S. Navy with safe and effective nuclear propulsion; provides the nation with nuclear counterterrorism and incident response capability.

Homeland Security Dept. (DHS), Countering Weapons of Mass Destruction (CWMD), Domestic Nuclear Detection (DNDO), 3801 Nebraska Ave. N.W., 20528; (202) 254-7280. James F. McDonnell, Director.
Web, www.dhs.gov/domestic-nuclear-detection-office

Seeks to improve the nation's capability to detect and report unauthorized attempts to import, possess, store, develop, or transport nuclear or radiological material for use against the nation, as well as integration of federal nuclear forensics programs. Oversees the development of an integrated global and domestic nuclear detection program with partners from federal, state, local, and international governments and the private sector, and the deployment of a nuclear detection system.

National Nuclear Security Administration (NNSA) (Energy Dept.), Counterterrorism and Counterproliferation, 1000 Independence Ave. S.W., #7B048, 20585; (202) 586-1734. Jay Tilden, Associate Administrator.
Web, www.energy.gov/nnsa/missions/counterterrorism

Responds and counters nuclear threats through innovative science, technology, and policies. Seeks to reduce danger posed by proliferant nations pursuing a nuclear weapons capability.

National Nuclear Security Administration (NNSA) (Energy Dept.), Defense Nuclear Nonproliferation, 1000 Independence Ave. S.W., #7F075, 20585; (202) 586-5000. Fax, (202) 586-1348. Brent K. Park, Deputy Administrator.
Web, www.energy.gov/nnsa/missions/nonproliferation

Works globally to prevent state and non-state actors from developing nuclear weapons or acquiring nuclear or radiological materials, equipment, technology, and expertise. Researches and develops new technology to monitor overseas nuclear activity.

National Nuclear Security Administration (NNSA) (Energy Dept.), Defense Programs, 1000 Independence Ave. S.W., #4A019, 20585; (202) 586-5000. Fax, (202) 586-

5670. Carlie Verdon, Deputy Administrator. Press, (202) 586-7371.
Web, www.energy.gov/nnsa/missions/maintaining-stockpile

Responsible for maintaining and modernizing the nuclear stockpile through the Stockpile Stewardship and Management Program.

Navy Dept. (Defense Dept.), Naval Reactors, Naval Nuclear Propulsion Program, 1240 Isaac Hull Ave. S.E., MS 8037, Washington Navy Yard, DC, 20376-8037; (202) 781-6172. Fax, (202) 781-6403. Adm. James F. Caldwell Jr. (USN), Deputy Administrator.
Web, www.energy.gov/nnsa/missions/powering-navy

Responsible for naval nuclear propulsion.

State Dept., Nuclear Risk Reduction Center (NRRC), 2201 C St. N.W., #5635, 20520; (202) 647-0027. Deborah C. Schneider, Staff Director.
Web, www.state.gov/t/avc/nrrc

Handles notification regimes for conventional, nuclear, chemical, and cyber arms, including inspection notices, strategic offensive arms data exchanges, major exercises or unit restructuring, and any other treaty-required communications.

► **CONGRESS**

For a listing of relevant congressional committees and subcommittees, please see pages 608–609 or the Appendix.

► **NONGOVERNMENTAL**

Center for Arms Control and Nonproliferation, 820 1st St. N.E., #LL-180, 20002; (202) 546-0795. John Tierney, Executive Director, ext. 2108.
General email, info@armscontrolcenter.org
Web, http://armscontrolcenter.org and Twitter, @nukes_of_hazzard

Advocates reducing nuclear weapon arsenals, preventing the spread of nuclear weapons, and minimizing the risk of nuclear war by educating the public and policymakers about arms control through policy analysis and research.

Center for Strategic and International Studies, Project on Nuclear Issues, 1616 Rhode Island Ave. N.W., 20036; (202) 775-3211. Rebecca Hersman, Director.
Web, www.csis.org/programs/international-security-program/project-nuclear-issues and Twitter, @CSIS_poni

Conducts and publishes research on proliferation reduction, nuclear arms control, and peaceful nuclear energy fuel cycles.

Fourth Freedom Forum, Washington Office, 1101 14th St. N.W., #900, 20005; (202) 802-9393. Eelco Kessels, Executive Director.
General email, globalct@gmail.com
Web, www.globalcenter.org

Conducts research and training to advance global cooperation to address transnational threats, including terrorism, nuclear proliferation, and drug trafficking.

Institute for Science and International Security, *440 1st St. N.W., #800, 20001; (202) 547-3633. David Albright, President. General email, isis@isis-online.org*

Web, www.isis-online.org and Facebook, www.facebook .com/Institute-for-Science-and-International-Security-351457957011/?ref=br_rs

Conducts research and analysis on nuclear weapons production and nonproliferation issues.

Other Weapons

▶ **AGENCIES**

Bureau of Arms Control, Verification, and Compliance (AVC) *(State Dept.), Chemical and Biological Weapons Affairs (CBW), 2201 C St. N.W., #3828, 20520; (202) 647-6693. Laura Gross, Director. Web, www.state.gov/t/avc/c23755.htm*

Responsible for U.S. implementation of the Chemical Weapons Convention, which promotes a global ban on chemical weapons; leads compliance assessment of the Biological and Toxins Weapons Convention.

Bureau of International Security and Nonproliferation (ISN) *(State Dept.), Missile, Biological, and Chemical Nonproliferation (MBC), 2201 C St. N.W., #3758, 20520; (202) 647-4931. Fax, (202) 636-4863. Pamela Durham, Director. Web, www.state.gov/t/isn/offices/mbc/index.htm*

Leads efforts to impede, roll back, and eliminate the proliferation of chemical and biological weapons, missile delivery systems for weapons of mass destruction, and related equipment, materials, and technology; implements missile sanctions; leads U.S. participation in the Australia Group CBW nonproliferation regime, the Hague Code of Conduct Against Ballistic Missile Proliferation, and the Missile Technology Control Regime.

Defense Dept. (DoD), *Nuclear, Chemical, and Biological Defense Programs, 3050 Defense Pentagon, #5B1064, 20301-3050; (703) 693-9410. Fax, (703) 695-0476. David (Chris) Hassel, Deputy Assistant Secretary. General email, osd.pentagon.ousd-atl.mbx.ncb-cb@mail.mil Web, www.acq.osd.mil/ncbdp/cbd*

Provides capabilities to deter, prevent, protect, mitigate, respond, and recover from chemical, biological, radiological, and nuclear threats. Coordinates, integrates, and provides oversight for the Joint Services Chemical and Biological Defense Program.

▶ **NONGOVERNMENTAL**

Center for Arms Control and Nonproliferation, *820 1st St. N.E., #LL-180, 20002; (202) 546-0795. John Tierney, Executive Director, ex. 2108.*

General email, info@armscontrolcenter.org Web, http://armscontrolcenter.org and Twitter, @nukes_of_hazzard

Promotes research and education on all misuse of biology; supports the Biological and Chemical Weapons Conventions. Interests include preventing the development of biochemical disabling agents as weapons, promoting international measures to monitor biological weapons-capable activities, promoting global cooperative measures for combating infectious diseases, ethical education of bioscientists, monitoring U.S. biodefense and anti-bioterrorism activities, and opposing risky or dangerous biological research.

Nuclear Threat Initiative (NTI), *1776 Eye St. N.W., #600, 20006; (202) 296-4810. Fax, (202) 296-4811. Joan Rohlfing, President; Ernest J. Moniz, Chief Executive Officer. General email, contact@nti.org Web, www.nti.org, Twitter, @NTI_WMD and Facebook, www.facebook.com/nti.org*

Works to reduce threats from nuclear, biological, and chemical weapons; publishes monthly and quarterly e-newsletters.

BORDERS, CUSTOMS, AND IMMIGRATION

General

▶ **AGENCIES**

Homeland Security Dept. (DHS), *Citizenship and Immigration Services Ombudsman, MS 0180, 20528-0180; (202) 357-8100. Fax, (202) 357-0042. Julie Kirchner, Ombudsman. Toll-free, (855) 882-8100. General email, cisombudsman@hq.dhs.gov Web, www.dhs.gov/cisombudsman*

Assists individuals and employers in resolving problems with the U.S. Citizenship and Immigration Services (USCIS); proposes changes in the administrative practices of USCIS in an effort to mitigate identified problems.

U.S. Citizenship and Immigration Services (USCIS) *(Homeland Security Dept.), 20 Massachusetts Ave. N.W., 20529; (800) 375-5283. L. Francis Cissna, Director. Customer Service Center, (800) 375-5283. Press, (202) 272-1200. TTY, (800) 767-1833. Web, www.uscis.gov and Twitter, @USCIS*

Responsible for the delivery of immigration and citizenship services. Priorities include the promotion of national security and the implementation of measures to improve service delivery.

U.S. Customs and Border Protection *(Homeland Security Dept.), 1300 Pennsylvania Ave. N.W., #4.4A, 20229; (202) 325-8000. Fax, (202) 344-1380. Kevin K. McAleenan, Commissioner. Information, (877) 227-5511. Press, (202) 344-1700. TTY, (800) 877-8339. Web, www.cbp.gov and Twitter, @cbp*

Immigration Reform and Advocacy Resources

The following agencies, organizations, blogs, and hotlines offer information pertaining to immigrant and refugee advocacy and immigration reform.

ADVOCACY

American Immigration Lawyers Assn., (202) 507-7600; www.aila.org

Amnesty International, (202) 544-0200; www.amnestyusa.org

Ayuda, (202) 387-4848; www.ayuda.com

Capital Area Immigrants' Rights (CAIR) Coalition, (202) 331-3320; www.caircoalition.org

Catholic Legal Immigration Network, Inc., (301) 565-4800; https://cliniclegal.org

Center for Community Change, (202) 339-9300; www.communitychange.org

Commission on Immigration at the American Bar Assn., (202) 662-1000; www.americanbar.org/groups/public_services/immigration.html

Detention Watch Network, www.detentionwatchnetwork.org

Institute for Policy Studies, (202) 234-9382; www.ips-dc.org

United Nations High Commissioner for Refugees Regional Office, (855) 808-6427; www.unrefugees.org

U.S. Committee for Refugees and Immigrants, (703) 310-1130; www.refugees.org

U.S. Conference of Catholic Bishops, Migration, and Refugee Services, (202) 541-3352; www.usccb.org/about/migration-and-refugee-services/index.cfm

Young Professionals in Foreign Policy Refugee Assistance Program, www.ypfp.org/refugees

REFORM

America's Voice, www.americasvoice.org

Center for Immigration Studies, (202) 466-8185; www.cis.org

Federation for American Immigration Reform (FAIR), (202) 328-7004; www.fairus.org

Immigration Equality Action Fund, (212) 714-2904; www.immigrationequality.org

Immigration Policy Center at the American Immigration Council, (202) 507-7500; www.americanimmigrationcouncil.org

Immigration Reform Law Institute, (202) 232-5590; www.irli.org

ImmigrationWorks USA, (202) 506-4541; www.immigrationworksusa.org

Migration Policy Institute, (202) 266-1940; www.migrationpolicy.org

National Immigration Forum, (202) 347-0040; https://immigrationforum.org

UnidosUS, (202) 785-1670; www.unidosus.org

SOCIAL MEDIA AND BLOGS

Borderlines Blog, Transborder Project, CIP Senior Analyst Tom Barry (575) 313-4544; http://borderlinesblog.blogspot.com

Center for Immigration Studies Blog, (202) 466-8185; http://cis.org/ImmigrationBlog

Immigration Equality Action Fund Blog, www.immigrationequality.org/blog

Progressives for Immigration Reform Blog, (202) 543-5325; www.progressivesforimmigrationreform.org/blog

Reform Immigration for America Blog, http://reformimmigrationforamerica.org/on-our-blog

HOTLINES

Office of Special Counsel for Immigration-Related Unfair Employment Practices, U.S. Department of Justice, Civil Rights Division, Worker hotline (800) 255-7688; Employer hotline, (800) 255-8155; TTY, (800) 237-2515

U.S. Immigration and Customs Enforcement (ICE), Detainees' Hotline, (855) 448-6903

U.S. Citizenship and Immigration Services National Customer Service Center, (800) 375-5283

Assesses and collects duties and taxes on imported merchandise; processes persons and baggage entering the United States; controls export carriers and goods to prevent fraud and smuggling. Library open to the public by appointment.

U.S. Customs and Border Protection *(Homeland Security Dept.), Agricultural Program and Trade Liaison Office, 1300 Pennsylvania Ave. N.W., #2.5B, 20229; (202) 344-3298. Fax, (202) 344-1442. Kevin Harriger, Executive Director.*
Web, www.cbp.gov

Responsible for safeguarding the nation's animal and natural resources from pests and disease through inspections at ports of entry and beyond.

U.S. Customs and Border Protection *(Homeland Security Dept.), Border Patrol, 1300 Pennsylvania Ave. N.W., #6.5E, 20229; (202) 344-2050. Fax, (202) 344-3140. Carla L. Provost, Chief.*
Web, www.cbp.gov/border-security/along-us-borders/overview

Mobile uniformed law enforcement arm of the Homeland Security Dept. Primary mission is to detect and

Air Force Department

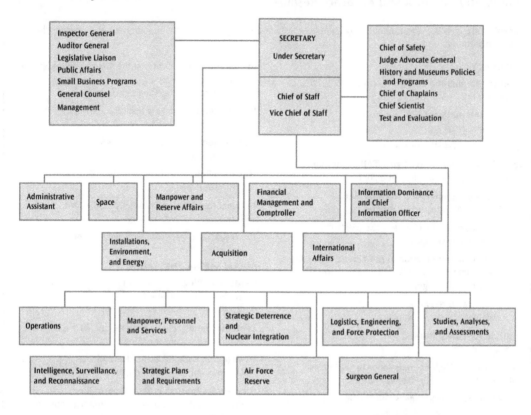

prevent the illegal trafficking of people and contraband across U.S. borders.

U.S. Immigration and Customs Enforcement (ICE)
(Homeland Security Dept.), 500 12th St. S.W., 20536; (202) 732-3000. Fax, (202) 732-3080. Ronald D. Vitiello, Director (Acting). Hotline to report suspicious activity, (866) 347-2423. Press, (202) 732-4242. TTY, (802) 872-6196.
Web, www.ice.gov and Twitter, @ICEgov

Enforces immigration and customs laws within the United States. Focuses on the protection of specified federal buildings and on air and marine enforcement. Undertakes investigations and conducts interdictions.

►CONGRESS

For a listing of relevant congressional committees and subcommittees, please see pages 608–609 or the Appendix.

DEFENSE TRADE AND TECHNOLOGY

General

►AGENCIES

Air Force Dept. *(Defense Dept.), Air Combat Command (ACC), Langley- Eustis Air Force Base, 115 Thompson St.,* #211, Hampton, VA 23665-1987; (757) 764-5741. *Gen. Mike Holmes, Commander. Public Affairs, (757) 764-5007.*
General email, acc.pai@langley.af.mil
Web, www.acc.af.mil, Twitter, @USAF_ACC and Facebook, www.facebook/ACConFB

Primary provider of air combat forces to U.S. warfighting commanders; provides command, control, communications and intelligence systems; conducts global information operations.

Air Force Dept. *(Defense Dept.), Space Command (AF/ SPC), 1670 Air Force Pentagon, 4C855, 20330-1640; (703) 695-0640. Gen. John (Jay) W. Raymond, Commander; Lt. Gen David (DT) W. Thompson, Vice Commander.*
Web, www.afspc.af.mil, Twitter, @AFSPCViceCommander and Facebook, www.facebook.com/ AFSPCViceCommander

Manages the planning, programming, and acquisition of space and cyberspace systems for the Air Force and other military services. (Headquarters in Colo.)

Bureau of Industry and Security (BIS) *(Commerce Dept.), 14th St. and Constitution Ave. N.W., #3898, 20230; (202) 482-1455. Daniel O. Hill, Deputy Under Secretary (Acting). Export licensing information, (202) 482-4811. Press, (202) 482-2721.*
Web, www.bis.doc.gov and Twitter, @BISgov

Assists in providing for an adequate supply of strategic and critical materials for defense activities and civilian needs, including military requirements, and other domestic energy supplies; develops plans for industry to meet national emergencies. Studies the effect of imports on national security and recommends actions. Manages the nation's dual-use export control laws and regulations.

Bureau of Industry and Security (BIS) *(Commerce Dept.), Export Administration (OEA), Strategic Industries and Economic Security, 14th St. and Constitution Ave. N.W., #3876, 20230; (202) 482-4506. Fax, (202) 482-5650. Michael Vaccaro, Director. Web, www.bis.doc.gov/index.php/other-areas/strategic -industries-and-economic-security-sies*

Administers the Defense Production Act and provides industry with information on the allocation of resources falling under the jurisdiction of the act.

Bureau of Industry and Security (BIS) *(Commerce Dept.), Export Enforcement (OEE), 14th St. and Constitution Ave. N.W., #3723, 20230; (202) 482-3618. Douglas R. Hassebrock, Director, (202) 482-1208. Export enforcement hotline, (800) 424-2980. Web, www.bis.doc.gov/index.php/enforcement/oee/7- enforcement*

Enforces dual-use export controls on exports of U.S. goods and technology for purposes of national security, nonproliferation, counterterrorism, foreign policy, and short supply. Enforces the antiboycott provisions of the Export Administration Regulations.

Bureau of Political-Military Affairs (PM) *(State Dept.), 2201 C St. N.W., #6212, 20520; (202) 647-7199. Fax, (202) 736-4779. Mark String, Deputy Assistant Secretary. Web, www.state.gov/t/pm*

Liaison between the State Dept. and Defense Dept. Provides policy direction in the areas of international security, security assistance, military operations, defense strategy and policy, military use of space, and defense trade.

Bureau of Political-Military Affairs (PM) *(State Dept.), Defense Trade Controls (DDTC), 2401 E St. N.W., 1st, 12th and 13th Floors, 20226; (202) 663-2980. Fax, (202) 663-3677. Michael (Mike) F. Miller, Deputy Assistant Secretary (Acting), (202) 663-2861. Web, www.pmddtc.state.gov*

Controls the commercial export of defense articles, services, and related technical data; authorizes the permanent export and temporary import of such items.

Bureau of Political-Military Affairs (PM) *(State Dept.), Regional Security and Arms Transfers (RSAT), 2401 E St. N.W., Room H1012, 20037; (202) 663-3030. Fax, (202) 663-2883. Michael (Mike) F. Miller, Director. Web, www.state.gov/t/pm/rsat*

Manages bilateral and multilateral political-military and regional security relations and the sale and transfer of U.S.-origin defense articles and services to foreign governments.

Defense Dept. (DoD), *Defense Technology Security Administration, 4800 Mark Center Dr., #03D08, Alexandria, VA 22350-1600; (571) 372-2301. Fax, (571) 372-2583. Heidi Grant, Director; Michael Laychak, Deputy Director. Press, (703) 697-5131. Web, www.dtsa.mil and Twitter, @dtsamil*

Develops and implements technology security policy for international transfers of defense-related goods, services, and technologies. Participates in interagency and international activities and regimes that monitor, control, and prevent transfers that could threaten U.S. national security interests.

Homeland Security Dept. (DHS), *Science and Technology Directorate (S&T), 245 Murray Lane, 20528; (202) 254-6006. William N. Bryan, Senior Official Performing the Duties of Under Secretary. Press, (202) 282-8010. Web, www.dhs.gov/st-directorate, Twitter, @dhsscitech and Facebook, www.facebook.com/dhsscitech*

Responsible for oversight and coordination of the development and augmentation of homeland security technology.

National Institute of Standards and Technology (NIST) *(Commerce Dept.), National Security Standards Program, 100 Bureau Dr., MS 8102, Gaithersburg, MD 20898-8102; (301) 975-8610. William Billotte, Program Manager. Web, www.nist.gov/national-security-standards*

Develops technical standards related to national security through federal, state, local and private sector, and international engagement. Focuses on standards for Chemical/Biological/Radiological/Nuclear/Explosive (CBRNE) detection as well as personal protective equipment (PPE), physical infrastructure resilience, and security.

▶**CONGRESS**

For a listing of relevant congressional committees and subcommittees, please see pages 608–609 or the Appendix.

Research and Development

▶**AGENCIES**

Air Force Dept. *(Defense Dept.), Air Force Aquisition (SAF/AQ), 1060 Air Force Pentagon, #4E962, 20330-1060; (703) 697-3039. Fax, (703) 693-6400. Dr. Will Roper, Assistant Secretary. Web, ww3.safaq.hq.af.mil*

Air Force office that directs and reviews Air Force research, development, and acquisition of weapons systems.

Air Force Dept. *(Defense Dept.), Office of Scientific Research (AF/OSR), 875 N. Randolph St., #325, Arlington, VA 22203-1768; (703) 696-7797; Fax, (703) 696-9556. (703) 696-7797. (703) 697-7842. Frederica Darema, Director. General email, info@us.af.mil Web, www.wpafb.af.mil/afrl/afosr, Twitter, @afosr and Facebook, www.facebook.com/afosr*

Sponsors and sustains basic research; assists in the transfer of research results to the war-fighter; supports Air Force goals of control and maximum utilization of air, space, and cyberspace.

Army Corps of Engineers *(Defense Dept.), Research and Development,* 441 G St. N.W., #3417, 20314-1000; (202) 761-1839. Fax, (202) 761-0907. David W. Pittman, SES, Director.
Web, www.usace.army.mil

Supports the research and development efforts of the corps by providing strategic planning and strategic direction and oversight, developing policy and doctrine, developing national program integration, and advising the chief of engineers on science and technology issues.

Army Dept. *(Defense Dept.), Acquisition, Logistics, and Technology,* 103 Army Pentagon, #2E532, 20310-0103; (703) 695-6154. Fax, (703) 697-4003. Ryan D. McCarthy, Assistant Secretary. Press, (703) 697-7592.
Web, www.army.mil/asaalt

Civilian office that directs Army acquisition research and development of weapons systems and missiles.

Army Dept. *(Defense Dept.), Research and Technology,* 103 Army Pentagon, #2E533, 20310-0103; (703) 692-1837. Thomas Russell, Director.
Web, www.army.mil

Sponsors and supports basic research at Army laboratories, universities, and other public and private organizations; assists in the transfer of research and technology to the field.

Defense Advanced Research Projects Agency *(Defense Dept.),* 675 N. Randolph St., Arlington, VA 22203-2114; (703) 526-6630. Steven H. Walker, Director.
Web, www.darpa.mil

Sponsors basic and applied research to maintain U.S. technological superiority and prevent strategic surprise by adversaries. Develops technologically advanced research ideas, assesses technical feasibility, and develops prototypes.

Defense Dept. (DoD), *International Cooperation,* 3070 Defense Pentagon, #5A1062B, 20301-3070; (703) 697-4172. Fax, (703) 693-2026. Joseph Klumpp, Director (Acting).
Web, www.acq.osd.mil/ic

Advises the under secretary of defense for Acquisitions, Technology, and Logistics on cooperative research and development, production, procurement, and follow-up support programs with foreign nations; monitors the transfer of secure technologies to foreign nations.

Defense Dept. (DoD), *Research and Engineering,* 3030 Defense Pentagon, #3E272, 20301-3030; (703) 695-9604. Michael D. Griffin, Under Secretary.
Web, www.acq.osd.mil/chieftechnologist/index.html

Civilian office responsible for policy, guidance, and oversight for the Defense Dept.'s Science and Technology Program. Serves as focal point for in-house laboratories, university research, and other science and technology matters.

Defense Technical Information Center *(Defense Dept.),* 8725 John Jay Kingman Rd., Fort Belvoir, VA 22060-6218;

(703) 767-9100. Christopher E. Thomas, Administrator. Registration, (703) 767-8273. Toll-free, (800) 225-3842.
Web, www.dtic.mil

Acts as a central repository for the Defense Dept.'s collection of current and completed research and development efforts in all fields of science and technology. Disseminates research analysis and development information to contractors, grantees, and registered organizations working on government research and development projects, particularly for the Defense Dept. Users must register with the center.

Marine Corps *(Defense Dept.), Systems Command,* 2200 Lester St., Quantico, VA 22134-6050; (703) 432-3966. Fax, (703) 432-3535. Brig. Gen. Arthur T. Pasagian (USMC), Commanding General.
General email, MCSC.RESUMES@usmc.il
Web, www.amarcorsyscom.marines.mil
Facebook, marcorsyscom

Military office that directs Marine Corps research, development, and acquisition.

Missile Defense Agency *(Defense Dept.),* 5700 18th St., Bldg. 245, Fort Belvoir, VA 22060-5573; (571) 231-8000. Lt. Gen. Samuel A. Greaves (USAF), Director; Rear Adm. Jon A. Hill (USN), Deputy Director. Fraud, waste, and abuse hotline, (800) 424-9098. Press, (256) 450-1599.
General email, mda.info@mda.mil
Web, www.mda.mil

Manages and directs the ballistic missile defense acquisition and research and development programs. Seeks to deploy improved theater missile defense systems and to develop options for effective national missile defenses while increasing the contribution of defensive systems to U.S. and allied security.

Naval Research Laboratory *(Defense Dept.), Research,* 4555 Overlook Ave. S.W., 20375-5320; (202) 767-3301. Fax, (202) 404-2676. Capt. Scott D. Moran (USN), Commanding Officer; Bruce Danly, Director of Research. Personnel locator, (202) 767-3200. Press, (202) 767-2541.
Web, www.nrl.navy.mil, Twitter, @USNRL and Facebook, www.facebook.com/USNRL

Conducts scientific research and develops advanced technology for the Navy. Areas of research include radar systems, radiation technology, tactical electronic warfare, and weapons guidance systems.

Navy Dept. *(Defense Dept.), Naval Research,* 875 N. Randolph St., #1425, Arlington, VA 22203-1995; (703) 696-5031. Fax, (703) 696-5940. Rear Adm. David J. Hahn (USN), Chief; Bob Freeman, Public Affairs Lead.
General email, onrpublicaffairs@navy.mil
Web, www.onr.navy.mil and Twitter, @USNavyresearch

Oversees the offices of Naval Research, Naval Technology, and Advanced Technology; works to ensure transition of research and technology to the fleet; sponsors and supports basic research at Navy laboratories, universities, and other public and private organizations.

Navy Dept. *(Defense Dept.), Research, Development, and Acquisition,* 1000 Navy Pentagon, #4E665, 20350-1000;

Army Department

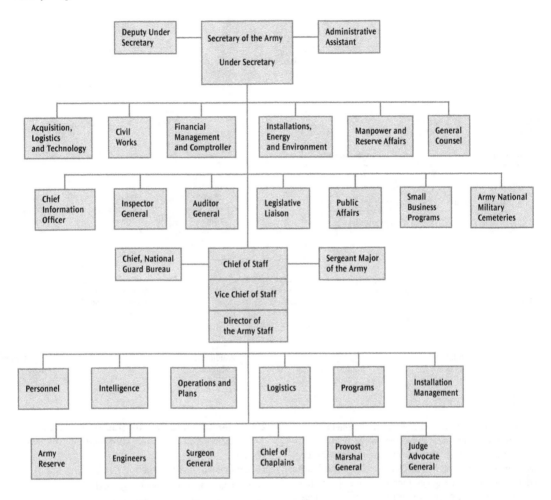

(703) 695-6315. Fax, (703) 697-0172. Col. James Geurts (USN), Assistant Secretary.
Web, www.secnav.navy.mil/rda/pages/ASNRDAorgchart .aspx

Civilian office that directs and reviews Navy and Marine Corps research and development of weapons systems.

Office of Science and Technology Policy (OSTP)

(Executive Office of the President), Eisenhower Executive Office Bldg., 1650 Pennsylvania Ave. N.W., 20504; (202) 456-4444. Fax, (202) 456-6021. Michael Kratsios, Deputy Chief US Chief Technology Officer. Press, (202) 456-6124. General email, info@ostp.gov

Web, www.ostp.gov and Twitter, @WHOSTP

Advises the president on science and technology matters as they affect national security; coordinates science and technology initiatives at the interagency level. Interests include nuclear materials, security, nuclear arms reduction, and counterterrorism.

U.S. Coast Guard (USCG) *(Homeland Security Dept.),* Design and Engineering Standards, CG4, 2703 Martin

Luther King Jr. Ave. S.E., MS 7509, 20593; (202) 372-1366. Vacant, Assistant Commandant.
Web, www.uscg.mil/hq/cg4

Develops and maintains engineering standards for the building of ships, aircraft, shore infrastructure, and Coast Guard facilities. Supports maritime safety, security, mobility, national defense, and protection of natural resources.

►CONGRESS

For a listing of relevant congressional committees and subcommittees, please see pages 608–609 or the Appendix.

►NONGOVERNMENTAL

AFCEA (Armed Forces Communications and Electronics Assn.), 4400 Fair Lakes Court, Fairfax, VA 22033-3899; (703) 631-6100. Fax, (703) 631-6169. Lt. Gen. Robert (Bob) M. Shea (USMC, Ret.), President. Customer Service Center, (703) 631-6158. Toll-free, (800) 336-4583.
General email, service@afcea.org

Web, www.afcea.org/site, Twitter, @AFCEA and Facebook, www.facebook.com/AFCEA.International

Navy Department

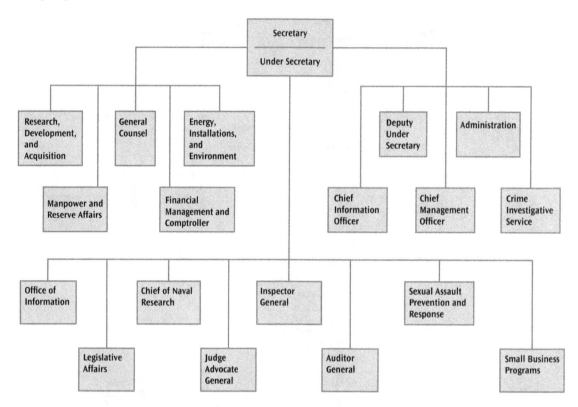

Membership: industrial organizations, scientists, and military and government personnel in the fields of communications, electronics, computers, and electrical engineering. Consults with the Defense Dept. and other federal agencies on design and maintenance of command, control, communications, computer, and intelligence systems; holds events displaying latest communications products.

American Society of Naval Engineers (ASNE), *1452 Duke St., Alexandria, VA 22314-3458; (703) 836-6727. Fax, (703) 836-7491. Capt. Joseph (Ike) Iacovetta (USN, Ret.), Executive Director (Acting), (202) 794-9163.*
General email, asnehq@navalengineers.org

Web, www.navalengineers.org and
Twitter, @NavalEngineers

Membership: civilian, active duty, and retired naval engineers. Provides forum for an exchange of information between industry and government involving all phases of naval engineering.

Analytic Services Inc., *5275 Leesburg Pike, #N5000, Falls Church, VA 22041; (703) 416-2000. Carmen J. Spencer, Chief Executive Officer. Toll-free, (877) 339-4389.*
Web, www.anser.org and Twitter, @ANSERAlerts

Systems analysis organization funded by government contracts. Conducts weapons systems analysis.

Center for Advanced Defense Studies, *1100 H St. N.W., #750, 20005; (202) 289-3332. David Johnson, Executive Director.*
General email, info@c4ads.org
Web, https://c4ads.org, Twitter, @C4ADS
media, communications@c4ads.org

Conducts field research in conflict areas. Awards annual fellowships to experts in weapons trafficking, conflict prevention, terrorism, and global crime.

Institute for Defense Analyses (IDA), *4850 Mark Center Dr., Alexandria, VA 22311-1882; (703) 845-2000. Fax, (703) 845-2588. David S.C. Chu, President; Jennifer Pond, Librarian. Library, (703) 845-2087.*
Web, www.ida.org and Twitter, @IDA_org

Operates three federally funded research and development centers that focus on national security and defense: Systems and Analysis Center, Science and Technology Policy Institute, and Center for Communication and Computing. Conducts research, systems evaluation, and policy analysis for Defense Dept. and other agencies.

Johns Hopkins University Applied Physics Laboratory, *11100 Johns Hopkins Rd., Laurel, MD 20723-6099; (240) 228-5000. Ralph D. Semmel, Director. Public Affairs, (240) 228-5020.*
Web, www.jhuapl.edu, Twitter, @JHUAPL and Facebook, www.facebook.com/JHUAPL

U.S. Coast Guard

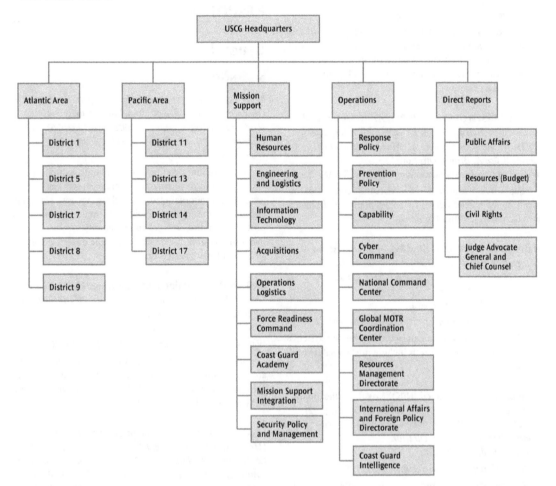

Research and development organization that conducts research for the Defense Dept. and other federal agencies. Interests include defense, national security, and space technologies.

Johns Hopkins University Applied Physics Laboratory, *Research and Exploratory Development, 11100 Johns Hopkins Rd., Laurel, MD 20723-6099; (240) 228-5000. Jim Schatz, Head. Press, (240) 228-5020. Web, www.jhuapl.edu/ourwork/red*

Research and development laboratory that seeks to improve warfighter survivability, sustainment, and performance through battlefield trauma prevention and mitigation, along with medical device evaluation and development. Programs include improvement of soldier protection equipment, the development of a neurally integrated upper extremity prosthetic, and blast-related traumatic brain injury research.

LMI, *7940 Jones Branch Dr., Tysons, VA 22102; (703) 917-9800. Fax, (703) 917-7100. David Zolet, President. Toll-free, (800) 213-4817. Web, www.lmi.org*

Conducts research on military and nonmilitary logistics, including transportation, supply and maintenance, force management, weapons support, acquisition, health systems, international programs, energy and environment, mathematical modeling, installations, operations, and information systems. (Formerly Logistics Management Institute.)

Military Operations Research Society (MORS), *2111 Wilson Blvd., #700, Alexandria, VA 22201; (703) 933-9070. Fax, (703) 933-9066. Susan K. Reardon, Chief Executive Officer, (703) 933-9075. General email, morsoffice@mors.org Web, www.mors.org*

Membership: professional analysts of military operations. Fosters information exchange; promotes professional development and high ethical standards; educates members on emerging issues, analytical techniques, and applications of research.

National Research Council (NRC), *Air Force Studies Board, Keck Center, 500 5th St. N.W., 9th Floor, 20001;*

(202) 334-2000. Gen. Douglas M. Fraser (USAF, Ret.), Chair; Ellen Chou, Director.
Web, http://nationalacademies.org/afsb

Supports activities related to the development of science and technology within the Air Force. Interests of study include fuel efficiency, acquisition processes, and assuring the future scientific and technical qualification of Air Force personnel.

National Research Council (NRC), *Army Science and Technology Board,* 500 5th St. N.W., 9th Floor, 20001; (202) 334-3118. Gen. David M. Maddox (USA, Ret.), Chair; Bruce A. Braun, Director.
Web, http://sites.nationalacademies.org/DEPS/BAST

Supports activities and and advises the Secretary of the Army about policies related to the development of science and technology within the Army.

National Research Council (NRC), *Human-Systems Integration Board,* Keck Center, 500 5th St. N.W., 11th Floor, 20001; (202) 334-3453. Fax, (202) 334-2210. Toby Warden, Director.
General email, bohsi@nas.edu

Web, http://sites.nationalacademies.org/dbasse/bohsi

Conducts studies on human factors and human-systems integration. Areas of research include nuclear safety and military simulation.

National Research Council (NRC), *Naval Studies Board,* Keck Center, 500 5th St. N.W., 9th Floor, 20001; (202) 334-3523. Fax, (202) 334-3695. Gregory K. Crawford, Chair; Charles F. Draper, Director.
General email, nsb@nas.edu

Web, http://sites.nationalacademies.org/DEPS/nsb

Conducts research and supports activites that help provide scientific and technical planning advice to the Navy.

Society of American Military Engineers, 607 Prince St., Alexandria, VA 22314-3117; (703) 549-3800. Fax, (703) 684-0231. Brig. Gen. Joseph Schroedel (USA, Ret.), Executive Director, ext. 110. Press, (703) 548-6153.
General email, editor@same.org

Web, www.same.org and Twitter, @same_hq

Membership: military and civilian engineers, architects, and construction professionals. Conducts workshops and conferences on subjects related to military engineering.

SRI International, *Washington Office,* 1100 Wilson Blvd., #2800, Arlington, VA 22209; (703) 524-2053. Fax, (703) 247-8569. William Jeffrey, Executive Director.
Web, www.sri.com and Twitter, @SRI_Intl

Research organization supported by government and private contracts. Conducts research on military technology, including lasers and computers. Other interests include strategic planning and armed forces interdisciplinary research. (Headquarters in Menlo Park, Calif.)

EMERGENCY PREPAREDNESS AND RESPONSE

General

▶**AGENCIES**

Army Corps of Engineers *(Defense Dept.), Contingency Operations and Office of Homeland Security,* 441 G St. N.W., 20314-1000; (202) 761-4601. Fax, (202) 761-5096. Charles (Ray) R. Alexander Jr., SES, Director.
Web, www.usace.army.mil

Assists military combatant commands, as well as federal, state, and local emergency management and emergency response organizations, with mitigation, planning, training, and exercises to build and sustain capabilities to protect from and respond to any emergency or disaster, including natural disasters and terrorist attacks involving weapons of mass destruction.

Civil Air Patrol National Capital Wing, 200 McChord St. S.W., #111, Joint Base Anacostia-Bolling, 20032; (202) 767-4405. Col. Janon Ellis, Wing Commander.
General email, info@natcapwing.org

Web, www.natcapwg.cap.gov and Twitter, @NatCapWing

Official auxiliary of the U.S. Air Force. Conducts search-and-rescue missions for the Air Force; participates in emergency airlift and disaster relief missions. (Headquarters at Maxwell Air Force Base, Ala.)

Federal Emergency Management Agency (FEMA) *(Homeland Security Dept.),* 500 C St. S.W., 20472; (202) 646-3900. Fax, (202) 212-5889. William B. Long, Administrator. Disaster TTY, (800) 427-5593. FEMA helpline, (800) 621-3362. Locator, (202) 646-2500. Press, (202) 646-3272. Toll-free, 800-621-FEMA. TTY, (800) 462-7585.
General email, femaopa@dhs.gov

Web, www.fema.gov, Twitter, @fema and Facebook, www.facebook.com/FEMA

Manages federal response and recovery efforts following natural disasters, terrorist attacks, and all other kinds of national emergencies. Initiates mitigation activities; works with state and local emergency managers; manages the National Flood Insurance Program.

Federal Emergency Management Agency (FEMA) *(Homeland Security Dept.), Resilience, Federal Insurance and Mitigation Administration,* 400 C St. S.W., 20472; (202) 646-2781. Fax, (202) 646-7970. David I. Maurstad, Deputy Associate Administrator.
Web, www.fema.gov/what-mitigation/federal-insurance-mitigation-administration

Administers federal insurance programs, including the National Flood Insurance Program, to reduce future losses from floods, earthquakes, tornadoes, and other natural disasters. Makes low-cost flood insurance available to eligible homeowners.

Federal Emergency Management Agency (FEMA)
(Homeland Security Dept.), Resilience, Grant Programs,
800 K St. N.W., North Tower, 20001; (800) 368-6498.
Christopher Logan, Assistant Administrator (Acting).
General email, askcsid@fema.gov

Web, www.fema.gov/grants

Administers and manages non-disaster grants to states, local communities, regional authorities, and tribal jurisdictions to mitigate hazards and to prevent, deter, respond to, and recover from terrorism and other threats to national security.

Federal Emergency Management Agency (FEMA)
(Homeland Security Dept.), Resilience, National
Preparedness, Technological Hazards, 400 C St. S.W., MS
3600, 20472-3025; (202) 646-3158. Fax, (703) 308-0324.
Michael Casey, Director.
Web, www.fema.gov/technological-hazards-division

Oversees the Radiological Emergency Preparedness Program to ensure the health and safety of citizens living around commercial nuclear power plants would be adequately protected in the event of a nuclear power plant accident; the Chemical Stockpile Emergency Preparedness Program (CSEPP), a partnership between the FEMA and the U.S. Department of the Army that provides emergency preparedness assistance and resources to communities surrounding the Army's chemical warfare agent stockpiles; and the Federal Radiological Preparedness Coordinating Committee a national-level forum for the development and coordination of radiological prevention and preparedness policies and procedures.

Federal Emergency Management Agency (FEMA)
(Homeland Security Dept.), Response and Recovery
(ORR), 500 C St. S.W., 20472; (202) 212-1946. Fax, (202)
212-1002. Jeffrey Byard, Associate Administrator.
Web, www.fema.gov/office-response-and-recovery

Responsible for coordination of the president's disaster relief program. Comprises the Doctrine and Policy Office, Business Management Office, Response Directorate, Recovery Directorate, Logistics Management Directorate, and Field Operations Directorate.

Health and Human Services Dept. (HHS), *National*
Disaster Medical System (NDMS), 200 Independence Ave.
S.W, #638G, 20201; (202) 475-2479. Ron Miller, Director,
(202) 260-8538. Public Affairs, (202) 205-8114.
General email, NDMSsupprt@hhs.gov

Web, http://phe.gov/ndms

Provides local, state, and tribal governments with medical response, patient movement, and the definitive care of victims of major emergencies and presidentially declared disasters, including those resulting from natural, technological, and human-caused hazards, such as transportation accidents and acts of terrorism involving chemical, biological, radiological, nuclear, and explosive weapons. Maintains a national capability to provide medical, veterinary, and mortuary teams, supplies, and equipment at the sites of disasters, and in transit from the impacted area into participating definitive care facilities.

National Nuclear Security Administration (NNSA)
(Energy Dept.), Emergency Operations, 1000
Independence Ave. S.W., #GH060, 20585; (202) 586-9892.
Fax, (202) 586-3904. Hon. Charles L. Hopkins III, Associate
Administrator.
Web, www.energy.gov/nnsa/nnsa-offices/emergency-operations

Works to ensure coordinated Energy Dept. responses to energy-related emergencies. Recommends policies to mitigate the effects of energy supply crises on the United States; recommends government responses to energy emergencies.

Small Business Administration (SBA), *Disaster*
Assistance, 409 3rd St. S.W., #6050, 20416; (202) 205-6734.
Fax, (202) 205-7728. James Rivera, Associate
Administrator. Service Center, (800) 659-2955. TTY, (800)
877-8339.
Web, www.sba.gov/offices/headquarters/oda

Provides victims of physical disasters with disaster and economic injury loans for homes, businesses, and personal property. Lends funds for uncompensated losses incurred from any disaster declared by the president of the United States or the administrator of the SBA.

U.S. Coast Guard (USCG) *(Homeland Security Dept.),*
Counterterrorism and Defense Policy, CG-ODO, 2703
Martin Luther King Jr. Ave. S.E., MS 7516, 20593-7516;
(202) 372-2101. Fax, (202) 372-8361.
Capt. Clinton Carlson, Director.
Web, www.dco.uscg.mil/Our-Organization/Assistant-Commandant-for-Response-Policy-CG-5R/Office-of-Counterterrorism-Defense-Operations-Policy-CG-ODO/CG

Ensures that the Coast Guard can mobilize effectively during national emergencies, including those resulting from enemy military attack.

U.S. Coast Guard (USCG) *(Homeland Security Dept.),*
National Response Center, 2100 2nd St. S.W., #2111B,
20593-0001; (202) 372-2097. Fax, (202) 267-1322.
Dana S. Tulis, Director. Hotline, (800) 424-8802. Local,
(202) 267-2675. TTY, (202) 267-4477.
General email, NRC@uscg.mil

Web, www.nrc.uscg.mil

Maintains 24-hour hotline for reporting oil, biological, radiological, and chemical discharges in the environment. Notifies appropriate federal officials to reduce the effects of accidents.

U.S. Coast Guard (USCG) *(Homeland Security Dept.),*
Response Policy, CG-5E, 2703 Martin Luther Jr. Ave.
S.W., MS 7516, 20593; (202) 372-2014. (202) 372-2011.
Rear Adm. Anthony (Jack) Vogt, Assistant
Commandant.
Web, www.dco.uscg.mil/Our-Organization/Assistant-Commandant-for-Response-Policy-CG-5R/

Conducts search-and-rescue and polar and domestic ice-breaking operations.

U.S. Fire Administration *(Federal Emergency*
Management Agency), 16825 S. Seton Ave., Emmitsburg,

MD 21727-8998; (301) 447-1000. Fax, (301) 447-1441. G. Keith Bryant, Administrator, (202) 646-4223. Press, (301) 447-1853. Toll-free, (800) 238-3358. Web, www.usfa.fema.gov and Twitter, @usfire

Provides public education, first responder training, technology, and data initiatives in an effort to prevent losses due to fire and related emergencies. Administers the Emergency Management Institute and the National Fire Academy for firefighters and emergency management personnel.

►CONGRESS

For a listing of relevant congressional committees and subcommittees, please see pages 608–609 or the Appendix.

►INTERNATIONAL ORGANIZATIONS

European Union, Delegation to the United States of America, 2175 K St. N.W., 20037; (202) 862-9500. Fax, (202) 429-1766. David O'Sullivan, Ambassador. General email, delegation-usa-info@eeas.europa.eu Web, www.euintheus.org and Twitter, @EUintheUS

Information and public affairs office in the United States for the European Union. Advances collaboration on civilian and military crisis management and conflict prevention initiatives to ensure global security. (Headquarters in Brussels.)

►NONGOVERNMENTAL

American Red Cross, Disaster Preparedness and Response, 431 18th St. N.W., 20006; (202) 303-5214, ext. 1. Gail J. McGovern, President. Donations, 800-RED-CROSS. Press, (202) 303-5551. Toll-free, (800) 733-2767. Web, www.redcross.org, Twitter, @redcross and Facebook, www.facebook.com/redcross and Disaster preparedness, www.redcross.org/about-us/our-work/distaster-relief.html

Chartered by Congress to administer disaster relief. Provides disaster victims with food, shelter, first aid, medical care, and access to other available resources. Feeds emergency workers; handles inquiries from concerned family members outside the disaster area; helps promote disaster preparedness and prevention through training.

National Assn. of State EMS Officials (NASEMSO), 201 Park Washington Ct., Falls Church, VA 22046-4527; (703) 538-1799. Fax, (703) 241-5603. Dia Gainor, Executive Director. General email, info@nasemso.org Web, www.nasemso.org

Supports development of effective emergency medical services (EMS) systems at the local, state, and regional levels. Works to formulate national EMS policy and foster communication and sharing among state EMS officials.

National Emergency Management Assn., Washington Office, 444 N. Capitol St. N.W., #401, 20001-1557; (202) 624-5460. Fax, (202) 624-5452. Brad Richy, President; A. J. Gary, Legislative Committee Chair, (202) 624-5459. Web, www.nemaweb.org and Twitter, @NEMA_DC

Professional association of state emergency managers. Promotes improvement of emergency management through strategic partnerships and innovative programs. (Member of the Council of State Governments; headquarters in Lexington, Ky.)

Salvation Army Disaster Service, 2626 Pennsylvania Ave. N.W., 20037-1618; (202) 756-2600. Fax, (202) 679-5568. Rebecca Chestnutt, Disaster Director. General email, rebecca.chestnutt@uss.salvationarmy.org Web, http://disaster.salvationarmyusa.org and Twitter, @SalArmyEDS

Provides U.S. and international disaster victims and rescuers with emergency support, including food, clothing, and counseling services.

Union of Concerned Scientists, Nuclear Power, 1825 K St. N.W., #800, 20006; (202) 223-6133. Fax, (202) 223-6162. Edwin Lyman, Director (Acting). General email, ucs@ucsusa.org Web, www.ucsusa.org/nuclear-power

An independent public interest group of scientists and citizens concerned with U.S. nuclear power policy and ability to respond to nuclear accidents. Interests include nuclear waste storage, storage facility security measures, safe generation of fissure chain reactions, and reactor design.

Coordination and Partnerships

►AGENCIES

Bureau of Political-Military Affairs (PM) (State Dept.), State-Defense Integration (SDI), 2201 C St. N.W., #2422, 20520; (202) 647-4081. Kathryn Schalow, Director. Web, www.state.gov/t/pm/sdi

Military exercise liaison between State Dept. and Defense Dept. Manages the Foreign Policy Advisor (POLAD) program to advise U.S. military combatant and component commanders about military operations, planning, and exercises. Supports the Military Advisor (MILAD) program to assign U.S. military personnel to State Dept. offices to advise on military operations and exercises, post-conflict reconstruction, counterterrorism, and Pentagon approval processes.

Federal Bureau of Investigation (FBI) (Justice Dept.), National Joint Terrorism Task Force, 935 Pennsylvania Ave. N.W., 20535-0001; (571) 280-5688. Fax, (571) 280-6922. William Callahan, Unit Chief. Web, www.fbi.gov/washingtondc/about/partnerships and www.fbi.gov/about-us/investigate/terrorism/national-joint-terrorism-task-force

Group of more than fifty agencies from the fields of intelligence, public safety, and federal, state, and local law enforcement that collects terrorism information and intelligence and funnels it to the more than five hundred JTTFs

Federal Emergency Management Agency

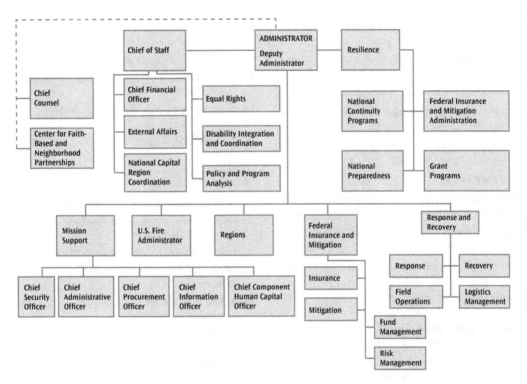

- - - Indicates a support or advisory relationship with the unit rather than a direct reporting relationship

(teams of local, state, and federal agents based at FBI field offices), various terrorism units within the FBI, and partner agencies. Helps the FBI with terrorism investigations.

Federal Bureau of Investigation (FBI) *(Justice Dept.),* *National Security Branch (NSB), Counterterrorism Division,* 935 Pennsylvania Ave. N.W., #4204, 20535; (571) 280-5000. Fax, (202) 324-7050. Michael G. McGarrity, Assistant Director. National security hotline, (202) 324-3000. Press, (202) 324-3691.
Web, www.fbi.gov/about-us/investigate/terrorism

Collects, analyzes, and shares information and intelligence with authorities to combat international terrorism operations within the United States and in support of extra-territorial investigations, domestic terrorism operations, and counterterrorism. Maintains the Joint Terrorism Task Force, which includes representatives from the Defense Dept., Energy Dept., Federal Emergency Management Agency, CIA, U.S. Customs and Border Protection, U.S. Secret Service, and Immigration and Customs Enforcement.

Federal Bureau of Investigation (FBI) *(Justice Dept.),* *National Security Branch (NSB), Terrorist Screening Center,* 935 Pennsylvania Ave. N.W., 20535; (571) 350-5678. Charles K. Kable, Director. Toll-free, (866) 872-5678. Press, (571) 350-6397.
General email, tsc@tsc.gov
Web, www.fbi.gov/about-us/nsb/tsc
Press, media@tsc.gov

Coordinates access to terrorist watch lists from multiple agencies. Provides operational support to federal screeners and state and local law enforcement officials.

Federal Bureau of Investigation (FBI) *(Justice Dept.),* *Partner Engagement,* 935 Pennsylvania Ave. N.W., #7128, 20535; (202) 324-7126. Kerry Sleeper, Assistant Director. General email, olec@leo.gov
Web, www.fbi.gov/about/partnerships/office-of-partner-engagement

Advises FBI executives on the use of state and local law enforcement and resources in criminal, cyber, and counterterrorism investigations. Coordinates the bureau's intelligence-sharing and technological efforts with state and local law enforcement. Serves as a liaison with the Homeland Security Dept. and other federal entities.

Federal Emergency Management Agency (FEMA) *(Homeland Security Dept.), Emergency Management Institute,* 16825 S. Seton Ave., Emmitsburg, MD 21727; (301) 447-1000. Fax, (301) 447-1658. Tony Russell, Superintendent, (301) 447-1286.
Web, www.training.fema.gov/EMI

Provides federal, state, tribal, and local government personnel and some private organizations engaged in emergency management with technical, professional, and vocational training. Educational programs include hazard mitigation, emergency preparedness, and disaster response.

Domestic Disaster Relief Organizations

Adventist Development & Relief Agency International, (800) 424-2372; www.adra.org

American Red Cross, (800) 733-2767 or (202) 303-5214; www.redcross.org

AmeriCares, (203) 658-9500; www.americares.org

Ananda Marga Universal Relief Team, Inc., (301) 738-7122; www.amurt.net

Catholic Charities USA, (703) 549-1390; www.catholiccharitiesusa.org

Catholic Relief Services, (877) 435-7277; www.crs.org

Children's Miracle Network (Osmond Foundation for the Children of the World), (801) 214-7400; www.cmn.org

Children's Network International, (888) 818-4483; www.helpthechildren.org

Church World Service, (800) 297-1516 or (574) 264-3102; www.cwsglobal.org

Direct Relief International, (805) 964-4767, (800) 676-1638; www.directrelief.org

Episcopal Relief & Development, (855) 312-4325; www.episcopalrelief.org

Federal Employee Education and Assistance Fund (FEEA), (202) 554-0007; www.feea.org

Feeding America, (800) 771-2303; www.feedingamerica.org

Feed the Children, (800) 627-4556; www.feedthechildren.org

Habitat for Humanity International, (800) 422-4828; www.habitat.org

Health Right International, (212) 226-9890; www.healthright.org

InterAction, (202) 667-8227; www.interaction.org

International Federation of Red Cross/Red Crescent, (212) 338-0161; www.ifrc.org

International Rescue Committee, (212) 551-3000; www.rescue.org

Islamic Relief USA, (855) 447-1001 or (703) 370-7202; www.irusa.org

Medical Teams International, (425) 454-8326; www.medicalteams.org

Mercy Corps, (202) 463-7383; www.mercycorps.org

Operation Blessing International Relief and Development Corporation, (757) 226-3401; www.ob.org

Operation USA, (800) 678-7255; www.opusa.org

Oxfam America, (800) 776-9326 or (202) 496-1180; www.oxfamamerica.org

Rebuilding Together, Inc., (800) 473-4229; www.rebuildingtogether.org

Save the Children, (800) 728-3843 or (203) 221-4000; www.savethechildren.org

United Methodist Committee on Relief, (800) 554-8583; www.umcor.org

United Way Worldwide, (703) 836-7112; www.unitedway.org

World Health Organization (Pan American Health Organization), (202) 974-3000; www.who.int/en or www.paho.org

World Vision, (888) 511-6548; www.worldvision.org

Federal Emergency Management Agency (FEMA)
(Homeland Security Dept.), Resilience, 500 C St. S.W., 20472; (202) 646-3100. Fax, (202) 786-0851. Daniel Kaniewski, Deputy Administrator. Disaster Assistance, 800-621-FEMA. TTY, (800) 462-7585. Web, www.fema.gov/resilience and National Incident Management System (NIMS), www.fema.gov/national-incident-management-system and Regional NIMS Coordinators, www.fema.gov/fema-regional-nims-contacts

Coordination of preparedness and protection-related activities throughout FEMA, including grants, planning, training, exercises, individual and community preparedness, assessments, lessons learned, continuity of government, and national capital region coordination. Includes the following offices and components: Federal Insurance and Mitigation Administration, Grant Programs Directorate, National Continuity Programs, and National Preparedness Directorate. Oversees the National Incident Management System (NIMS). Integrates federal, state, local, and tribal emergency response and preparedness practices into a national framework. Promotes standardized structures and procedures and interoperable communications systems. Operates ten regional offices.

Federal Emergency Management Agency (FEMA)
(Homeland Security Dept.), Resilience, National Continuity Programs, 500 C St. S.W., #524, 20472; (202) 646-4145. Fax, (202) 646-3921. Daniel Lipka, Assistant Administrator (Acting). Web, www.fema.gov/national-continuity-programs

Responsible for the coordination of all Federal Emergency Management Agency national security programs. Manages Integrated Public Alert Warning System (IPAWS).

Federal Emergency Management Agency (FEMA)
(Homeland Security Dept.), Resilience, National Preparedness, Individual and Community Preparedness, Techworld Bldg., 800 K St. N.W., #5127, 20472-3630; (202) 786-9557. Natalie F. Enclade, Director. Flood insurance information, (888) 379-9531. Storm shelter information, (866) 222-3580. General email, citizencorps@dhs.gov Web, www.ready.gov/citizen-corps

Conducts research on individual, business, and community preparedness. Administers Citizen Corps, a national network of state, territory, tribal, and local councils that coordinate with local first responders to develop community-specific public education, outreach, training, and volunteer opportunities that address community preparedness and resiliency.

Financial Crimes Enforcement Network *(Treasury Dept.), P.O. Box 39, Vienna, VA 22183-0039; (703) 905-3591. Fax, (703) 905-3690. Kenneth A. Blanco, Director. Press, (703) 905-3770. Resource Center, (800) 767-2825. General email, frc@fincen.gov*

Web, www.fincen.gov

Administers an information network in support of federal, state, and local law enforcement agencies in the prevention and detection of terrorist financing, money-laundering operations, and other financial crimes. Administers the Bank Secrecy Act.

Homeland Security Dept. (DHS), *Bombing Prevention (OBP), 3801 Nebraska Ave. N.W., 20528; (703) 235-8147. Fax, (703) 235-9711. Sean Haglund, Deputy Chief, (703) 235-8147.*

General email, OBP@hq.dhs.gov

Web, www.dhs.gov/cisa/office-bombing-prevention-obp

Coordinates national efforts to detect, prevent, and respond to terrorist improvised explosive device (IED) threats and leads the Homeland Security Dept. efforts to implement the National Counter-IED policy. Works with federal agencies, state and local governments, and the private sector to promote information sharing and IED awareness. Maintains database on equipment, training, and assets required for effective response to IED threats. Sponsors Technical Resource for Incident Prevention (TRIPwire), an online information-sharing network for bomb technicians and other law enforcement officials.

Homeland Security Dept. (DHS), *Infrastructure Protection (IP), 1310 N. Courthouse Rd., Arlington, VA 22201; Fax, (202) 235-9757. Christopher C. Krebs, Assistant Secretary. DHS Switchboard, (202) 282-8000. General email, SOPDExecsec@hq.dhs.gov*

Web, www.dhs.gov/about-office-infrastructure-protection

Develops partnerships and communication lines with state and local governments and the private sector.

Homeland Security Dept. (DHS), *Office of Strategy, Policy, and Plans, Bldg. 81, 3801 Nebraska Ave. N.W., #17, 20528; (202) 282-8484. Fax, (202) 282-8679. James D. Nealon, Official for the Office of Assistant Secretary (Acting). DHS Switchboard, (202) 282-8000. Press, (202) 282-8010. General email, private.sector@dhs.gov*

Web, www.dhs.gov/office-policy

Works to facilitate outreach to industry and flow of information between industry and the department on security topics ranging from protecting critical infrastructure from sabotage to securing computer networks from hackers. Administers the Loaned Executive Program to partner with executive-level experts on a volunteer basis for specific needs.

Homeland Security Dept. (DHS), *Operations Coordination, 3801 Nebraska Ave. N.W., Bldg. 3, #01107, 20528; (202) 282-9580. Fax, (202) 282-9811. Richard Chavez, Director (Acting).*

Web, www.dhs.gov/office-operations-coordination

Collects and fuses intelligence and enforcement activities information that may have a terrorist nexus from a variety of federal, state, territorial, tribal, local, and private sector partners to continually monitor the nation's threat environment. Coordinates incident management activities within the department and with state governors, homeland security advisors, law enforcement partners, and critical infrastructure operators in all states and major urban areas nationwide.

Homeland Security Dept. (DHS), *Partnership and Engagement (OPE), 245 Murray Lane S.W., 20528-0075; John H. Hill, Assistant Secretary; David Munro, Director of Tribal Affairs, (202) 447-4239; Bryan Hyer, Director of State Affairs. DHS Switchboard, (202) 282-8000. State and Local Law Enforcement, (202) 282-9545.*

Web, www.dhs.gov/partnership-engagement

Coordinates agency outreach efforts with critical stakeholders nationwide, including state, local, tribal, territorial governments, elected officials, law enforcement, the private sector, and colleges and universities to ensure a unified approach to external engagement.

Transportation Dept. (DOT), *Intelligence, Security, and Emergency Response, 1200 New Jersey Ave. S.E., #56125, 20590; (202) 366-6525. Fax, (202) 366-7261. Richard Chávez, Director.*

Web, www.transportation.gov/mission/administrations/ intelligence-security-emergency-response

Advises the secretary on transportation intelligence and security policy. Develops, coordinates, and reviews transportation emergency preparedness programs for use in emergencies affecting national defense and in emergencies caused by natural and man-made disasters and crisis situations.

Transportation Security Administration (TSA) *(Homeland Security Dept.), Freedom Center, 13555 EDS Dr., Herndon, VA 20171 (mailing address: TSOC Annex, 601 S. 12th St., Arlington, VA 22202); (866) 655-7023. Roderick Allison, Chief of Operations (Acting).*

Web, www.tsa.gov

Operations center that provides continual federal, state, and local coordination, communications, and domain awareness for all of the Homeland Security Dept.'s transportation-related security activities worldwide. Transportation domains include highway, rail, shipping, and aviation.

►CONGRESS

For a listing of relevant congressional committees and subcommittees, please see pages 608–609 or the Appendix.

►INFORMATION SHARING AND ANALYSIS CENTERS

A 1998 decision directive issued by President Bill Clinton defined various infrastructure industries critical to the national economy and public well-being. The directive proposed the creation of Information Sharing and Analysis Centers (ISACs), which would be established by each critical infrastructure industry to communicate with its members, its government partners, and other ISACs about threat indications, vulnerabilities, and protection strategies. Each ISAC is led by a government agency or private entity. ISACs led by Washington-area agencies or companies are listed below.

Communications ISAC *(Homeland Security Dept.), c/o National Coordinating Center for Communications, 245 Murray Lane, MS0615, 20520; (703) 235-5080.*
John O'Connor, Director of National Coordinating Center for Communications; Rear Adm. Ronald (Ron) T. Hewitt (USCG), Assistant Director, Office of Emergency Communications.
General email, ncc@hq.dhs.gov

Web, www.dhs.gov/national-coordinating-center-communications

Communications network that links federal civilian, military, diplomatic, and intelligence agencies with private sector cyber and telecommunications providers to protect the nation's telecommunications infrastructure and restore it from disruptions caused by attacks or natural disasters. Includes the National Cybersecurity and Communications Integration Center, a 24/7 center for protection of computer and communications across federal, state, and local governments; intelligence and law enforcement agencies; and the private sector.

Financial Services ISAC (FS-ISAC), *12020 Sunrise Valley Dr., #230, Reston, VA 20191; (877) 612-2622. Fax, (301) 579-6106. Steven Silberstein, President.*
General email, admin@fsisac.com

Web, www.fsisac.com and Twitter, @FSISAC

Provides a confidential venue for sharing security vulnerabilities and solutions, including data obtained from such sources as other ISACs, law enforcement agencies, technology providers, and security associations. Works to facilitate trust, cooperation, and information sharing among its participants and assesses proactive means of mitigating cybersecurity risks.

Surface Transportation Information Sharing and Analysis Center (ISAC), *c/o EWA Information and Infrastructure Technologies, Inc., 13873 Park Center Rd., #200, Herndon, VA 20171-5406; (703) 478-7600. Fax, (703) 478-7654. Paul G. Wolfe, Director, (703) 478-7656; Todd Steinmetz, Program Manager. Toll-free, (866) 784-7221.*
General email, st-isac@surfacetransportationisac.org

Web, www.surfacetransportationisac.org

Protects physical and electronic infrastructure of surface transportation and public transit carriers. Collects, analyzes, and distributes critical security and threat information from worldwide resources; shares best security

practices and provides 24/7 immediate physical and cyberthreat warnings.

U.S. Fire Administration *(Federal Emergency Management Agency), Emergency Management and Response, 16825 S. Seton Ave., Emmitsburg, MD 21727-8920; (301) 447-1325. Fax, (301) 447-1034. Rick Ziebart, Branch Chief, (301) 447-1821. National Emergency training switchboard, (301) 447-1000.*
General email, fema-nfirshelp@fema.dhs.gov

Web, www.usfa.fema.gov/operations/ops_cip.html and Twitter, @usfire

Collects, analyzes, and disseminates information to support the critical infrastructure protection and resilience efforts of the nation's emergency services sector. Researches current physical and cyber protection issues, operates an information center, issues alerts and messages, and prepares instructional materials relevant to the emergency services community.

WaterISAC, *1620 Eye St. N.W., #500, 20006-4027; (202) 331-0479. Diane VanDe Hei, Executive Director. Toll-free, (866) 426-4722.*
General email, info@waterisac.org

Web, www.waterisac.org and Twitter, @WaterISAC

Gathers, analyzes, and disseminates threat information concerning the water community from utilities' security incident reports and agencies of the federal government. Provides the water community with access to sensitive information and resources about cyber, physical, and contamination threats.

►NONGOVERNMENTAL

International Assn. of Chiefs of Police, *Advisory Committee for Patrol and Tactical Operations, 44 Canal Center Plaza, #200, Alexandria, VA 22314; (703) 836-6767. Sabrina Rhodes, Staff Liaison. Toll-free, (800) 843-4227.*
General email, committees@theiacp.org

Web, www.theiacp.org/workinggroup/Committee/patrol-and-tactical-operations-committee

Membership: foreign and U.S. police executives and administrators. Maintains liaison with civil defense and emergency service agencies in the United States and other nations; prepares guidelines for police cooperation with emergency and disaster relief agencies during emergencies.

National Governors Assn. (NGA), *Center for Best Practices, Homeland Security and Public Safety Division, 444 N. Capitol St. N.W., #267, 20001-1512; (202) 624-5300. Fax, (202) 624-5313. Jeffrey McLeod, Division Director; Mary Ott, Legislature Director.*
Web, www.nga.org/cms/center/hsps

Provides support to governors in responding to the challenges of homeland security through technical assistance and policy research, and by facilitating their participation in national discussion and initiatives. Current issues include cybersecurity, prescription drug abuse, public safety broadband, sentencing and corrections reform, homeland security grant reform, justice information-sharing, and public health preparedness.

National Voluntary Organizations Active in Disaster (NVOAD), 950 North Washington St., Alexandria, VA 22314 (mailing address: P.O. Box 26125, Alexandria, VA 22313); (703) 778-5088. Fax, (703) 778-5091. Gregory Forrester, President; Katherine Boatwright, Director of Operations.
General email, info@nvoad.org

Web, www.nvoad.org and Twitter, @NationalVOAD

Seeks to promote communication, cooperation, coordination, and collaboration among voluntary agencies that participate in disaster response, relief, and recovery nationally.

Emergency Communications

▶ **AGENCIES**

DC Homeland Security and Emergency Management Agency, 2720 Martin Luther King Ave. S.E., 20032; (202) 727-6161. Fax, (202) 715-7288. Chris Rodriguez, Director; Kim McCall, Community Outreach Coordinator. TTY, (202) 730-0488.
General email, hsema.training@dc.gov

Web, http://hsema.dc.gov, Twitter, @DC_HSEMA and Facebook, www.facebook.com/HSEMADC

Leads planning and coordination of homeland security and emergency management efforts to ensure that the District of Columbia is prepared to prevent, protect against, respond to, mitigate, and recover from all threats and hazards. Provides emergency planning services, training, and seminars. Remains updated on potential threats and hazards, and keeps the community informed of hazards and safety planning.

Defense Dept. (DoD), White House Communications Agency, U.S. Naval Station, Anacostia Annex, 2743 Defense Blvd. S.W., #220, 20373-5815; (202) 757-5530. (202) 757-5150. Fax, (202) 757-5529. Col. James F. Riley Jr. (USA), Director.
Web, www.disa.mil/whca

Responsible for presidential communications.

Federal Communications Commission (FCC), Emergency Alert System, 445 12th St. S.W., #7-A807, 20554; (202) 418-1228. Fax, (202) 418-2790. Bonnie Gay, EAS Coordinator. FCC 24/7 Operations Center, (202) 418-1122.
General email, eas@fcc.gov

Web, www.fcc.gov/pshs/services/eas

FCC 24/7 Operations Center, FCCOPCenter@fcc.gov

Develops rules and regulations for the Emergency Alert System, which is the national warning system the president would use to communicate with the public during a national emergency in the event that access to normal media outlets becomes unavailable. It is also used by state and local officials for weather-related and man-made emergencies.

Federal Communications Commission (FCC), Public Safety and Homeland Security Bureau (PSHSB), 445 12th St. S.W., #7C732, 20554; (202) 418-1300. Fax, (202) 418-2817. Lisa M. Fowlkes, Chief. 24-Hour Operations Center, (202) 418-1122. Press, (202) 418-0503.
General email, pshsbinfo@fcc.gov

Web, www.fcc.gov/public-safety-homeland-security

Develops, recommends, and administers the FCC's policies pertaining to public safety communications issues, including 911 and E911. Responsible for the operability and interoperability of public safety communications, communications infrastructure protection and disaster response, and network security and reliability. Administers the Emergency Response Interoperability Network (ERIC), establishing and maintaining a broadband public safety wireless network, including authentication and encryption.

Homeland Security Dept. (DHS), Emergency Communications (OEC), 245 Murray Lane, MS 0615, Arlington, VA 20528-0615; Ron Hewitt, Director. DHS Switchboard, (202) 282-8000.
General email, oec@dhs.gov

Web, www.dhs.gov/office-emergency-communications

Ensures that the federal government has the necessary communications capabilities to permit its continued operation during a national emergency; provides emergency responders and government officials with communications support as it directs the nation's recovery from a major disaster; provides training, coordination, tools, and guidance to help federal, state, local, tribal, territorial, and industry partners develop their emergency communications capabilities.

National Communications System (Homeland Security Dept.), President's National Security Telecommunications Advisory Committee, DHS, 1880 2nd St. S.W., 20024; Renee James, Chair. DHS switchboard, (202) 282-8000.
General email, NSTAC@hq.dhs.gov

Web, www.dhs.gov/national-security-telecommunications-advisory-committee and Twitter, @DHSgov

Advises the president, the National Security Council, the Office of Science and Technology Policy, and the Office of Management and Budget on specific measures to improve telecommunications for the federal government. Areas of major focus include strengthening national security, enhancing cybersecurity, maintaining the global communications infrastructure, assuring communications for disaster response, and addressing infrastructure interdependencies and dependencies.

U.S. Coast Guard (USCG) (Homeland Security Dept.), National Response Center, 2100 2nd St. S.W., #2111B, 20593-0001; (202) 372-2097. Fax, (202) 267-1322. Dana S. Tulis, Director. Hotline, (800) 424-8802. Local, (202) 267-2675. TTY, (202) 267-4477.
General email, NRC@uscg.mil

Web, www.nrc.uscg.mil

Maintains 24-hour hotline for reporting oil, biological, radiological, and chemical discharges in the environment. Notifies appropriate federal officials to reduce the effects of accidents.

Industrial and Military Planning and Mobilization

►AGENCIES

Bureau of Political-Military Affairs (PM) *(State Dept.), State-Defense Integration (SDI), 2201 C St. N.W., #2422, 20520; (202) 647-4081. Kathryn Schalow, Director. Web, www.state.gov/t/pm/sdi*

Military exercise liaison between State Dept. and Defense Dept. Manages the Foreign Policy Advisor (POLAD) program to advise U.S. military combatant and component commanders about military operations, planning, and exercises. Supports the Military Advisor (MILAD) program to assign U.S. military personnel to State Dept. offices to advise on military operations and exercises, post-conflict reconstruction, counterterrorism, and Pentagon approval processes.

Defense Logistics Agency *(Defense Dept.), Logistics Operations, 8725 John Jay Kingman Rd., Fort Belvoir, VA 22060-6221; (703) 767-1600. Fax, (703) 767-1588. Maj. Gen. Mark K. Johnson (USAF), Director. Press, (703) 767-6200. Web, www.dla.mil/HQ/LogisticsOperations.aspx*

Oversees management, storage, and distribution of items used to support logistics for the military services and federal agencies. Synchronizes the Defense Logistics Agency's capabilities with the combatant commands, military services, the joint staff, other combat support defense agencies, and designated federal agencies. Provides logistics policy, with an emphasis on modernizing business systems and maximizing readiness and combat logistics support.

Maritime Administration *(Transportation Dept.), Sealift Operations and Emergency Preparedness, West Bldg., 1200 New Jersey Ave. S.E., W23-302, 20590; (202) 366-1031. Fax, (202) 366-5904. Russell Krause, Chief. Web, www.marad.dot.gov/ports/maritime-emergency-preparedness-and-response*

Plans for the transition of merchant shipping from peacetime to wartime operations under the direction of the National Shipping Authority. Participates in interagency planning and policy development for maritime security-related directives. Coordinates port personnel and the military for deployments through the commercial strategic seaports. Represents the United States at the NATO Planning Board for Ocean Shipping. (The National Shipping Authority is a stand-by organization that is activated upon the declaration of a war or other national emergency.)

Maritime Administration *(Transportation Dept.), Ship Operations, West Bldg., 1200 New Jersey Ave. S.E., MAR-610, MS2-W25-336, 20590; (202) 366-1875.*

Fax, (202) 366-3954. Kevin M. Tokarski, Associate Administrator. Web, www.marad.dot.gov/strategic-sealift/office-ship-operations

Maintains the National Defense Reserve Fleet, a fleet of older vessels traded in by U.S. flag operators that are called into operation during emergencies; manages and administers the National Defense Reserve Fleet, a fleet of ships available for operation within four to twenty days, to meet the nation's sealift readiness requirements.

Maritime Administration *(Transportation Dept.), Strategic Sealift, West Bldg., 1200 New Jersey Ave. S.E., Mar-600, MS 1, W25-330, 20590; (202) 366-5400. Fax, (202) 366-5904. Kevin M. Tokarski, Associate Administrator. Web, www.maritime.dot.gov/national-security/strategic-sealift/strategic-sealift*

Administers strategic sealift programs for the Maritime Administration and ensures that merchant shipping is available in times of war or national emergency.

►CONGRESS

For a listing of relevant congressional committees and subcommittees, please see pages 608–609 or the Appendix.

►NONGOVERNMENTAL

National Defense Industrial Assn. (NDIA), *2101 Wilson Blvd., #700, Arlington, VA 22201-3061; (703) 522-1820. Fax, (703) 522-1885. Gen. Herbert (Hawk) J. Carlisle (USAF, Ret.), President. Web, www.ndia.org, Twitter, @NDIAToday and Facebook, www.facebook.com/NDIAMembership*

Membership: U.S. citizens and businesses interested in national security. Also open to individuals and businesses in nations that have defense agreements with the United States. Provides information and expertise on defense preparedness issues; works to increase public awareness of national defense preparedness through education programs; serves as a forum for dialogue between the defense industry and the government.

National Defense Transportation Assn. (NDTA), *50 S. Pickett St., #220, Alexandria, VA 22304; (703) 751-5011. Fax, (703) 823-8761. Vice Adm. William A. Brown (USN, Ret.), President. Web, www.ndtahq.com and Twitter, @NDTAHQ*

Membership: transportation service companies. Maintains liaison with the Defense Dept., the Transportation Dept., and the Transportation Security Administration to prepare emergency transportation plans.

Infrastructure Protection

►AGENCIES

Army Corps of Engineers *(Defense Dept.), 441 G St. N.W., #3K05, 20314-1000; (202) 761-0001. Fax, (202)*

761-4463. *Lt. Gen. Todd T. Semonite (USA), Chief of Engineers.* Press, *(202) 761-0011.*
General email, hq-publicaffairs@usace.army.mil
Web, *www.usace.army.mil* and *Twitter, @USACEHQ*

Devises hurricane and storm damage reduction infrastructure.

Energy Dept. (DOE), *Electricity Delivery and Energy Reliability (OE), 1000 Independence Ave. S.W., #8H033, 20585; (202) 586-1411. Fax, (202) 586-1472. Bruce Walker, Assistant Secretary.*
General email, OEwebmaster@hq.doe.gov
Web, *https://energy.gov/oe/office-electricity-delivery-and-energy-reliability*

Leads the federal response to energy emergencies, guides technology research and development on the security and reliability of the nation's energy systems, provides training and support for stakeholders, and works to assess and mitigate energy system vulnerabilities. Works in conjunction with the Homeland Security Dept. and other DOE programs, federal groups, state and local governments, and private industry.

Federal Bureau of Investigation (FBI) *(Justice Dept.),* **Cyber Division,** *935 Pennsylvania Ave. N.W., #5835, 20535; (202) 324-7770. Fax, (202) 324-2840. Matt Gorham Jr., Assistant Director.*
Web, *www.fbi.gov/about-us/investigate/cyber*

Coordinates the investigations of federal violations in which the Internet or computer networks are exploited for terrorist, foreign government-sponsored intelligence, or criminal activities, including copyright violations, fraud, pornography, child exploitation, and malicious computer intrusions.

Federal Energy Regulatory Commission (FERC) *(Energy Dept.), Energy Infrastructure Security (OEIS), 888 1st St. N.E., #9M-13, 20426; (202) 502-8867. Fax, (202) 219-2836. Joseph H. McClelland, Director.*
Web, *www.ferc.gov/about/offices/oeis.asp*

Seeks to identify risk and vulnerability to potential physical and cyber attacks and to coordinate collaborative mitigation actions. Formulates and makes recommendations for Commission action with state and federal agencies and the energy industry.

Federal Protective Service (FPS) *(Homeland Security Dept.), 800 N. Capitol St., 5th Floor, 20002; Fax, (202) 732-8109. L. Eric Patterson, Director. Switchboard, (202) 282-8000.*
Web, *www.dhs.gov/about-federal-protective-service*

Works to ensure that appropriate levels of security are in place in General Services Administration–managed facilities throughout the United States. Conducts assessments on all GSA-controlled facilities to evaluate threats and tailor appropriate security countermeasures. Has enforcement capability to detain and arrest people, seize goods or conveyances, obtain arrest and search warrants, respond to incidents and emergency situations, provide protection during demonstrations or civil unrest, and be deputized for law enforcement response in special situations.

Homeland Security Dept. (DHS), *Cybersecurity and Communications (CS&C), 245 Murray Lane S.w., Bldg. 410, MS 8570, 20528-8570; (888) 282-0870. Jeanette Manfra, Deputy Director, (202) 343-1721; Richard Driggers, Deputy Assistant Director, (631) 323-3054. DHS switchboard, (202) 282-8000. Press, (202) 282-8010. TTY, (202) 282-8000.*
General email, info@us-cert.gov
Web, *www.dhs.gov/office-cybersecurity-and-communications*

Works with the public and private sectors as well as international partners to enhance the security of the nation's cyber and communications infrastructure. Works with other federal agencies in developing comprehensive plans to prevent and mitigate cyber-based attacks. Identifies security vulnerabilities and coordinates warning and response procedures.

Homeland Security Dept. (DHS), *Cybersecurity and Infrastructure Security Agency (CISA), 3801 Nebraska Ave., Bldg. 5, 20528; (703) 235-2010. Christopher C. Krebs, Director.*
Web, *www.dhs.gov/CISA*

Identifies and assesses threats to the nation's physical and cyber infrastructure; issues warnings to prevent damage.

Homeland Security Dept. (DHS), *Infrastructure Protection (IP), 1310 N. Courthouse Rd., Arlington, VA 22201; Fax, (202) 235-9757. Christopher C. Krebs, Assistant Secretary. DHS Switchboard, (202) 282-8000.*
General email, SOPDExecsec@hq.dhs.gov
Web, *www.dhs.gov/about-office-infrastructure-protection*

Coordinates the collection and analysis of intelligence and information pertaining to threats against the nation's physical and informational infrastructure, and leads related programs and policy efforts; identifies and assesses vulnerabilities, takes preventive action, and issues timely warnings. Coordinates the National Infrastructure Protection Plan and other programs to respond to and quickly recover from attacks or other emergencies.

Interior Dept. (DOI), *Emergency Management, 1849 C St. N.W., MS 6628, 20240; (202) 208-4679. Fax, (202) 219-3421. Lisa Branum, Director. Watch Office Toll-free, (877) 246-1373. Watch Office (24/7), (202) 208-4108.*
General email, DOI_Watch_Office@ios.doi.gov
Web, *www.doi.gov/emergency*

Establishes and disseminates policy and coordinates the development of Interior Dept. programs for emergency prevention, planning, response, and recovery that affects federal and tribal lands, facilities, infrastructure, and resources. Provides assistance to other units of government under federal laws, executive orders, interagency emergency response plans such as the National Response Framework, and other agreements.

Interior Dept. (DOI), *Law Enforcement and Security (OLES), 1849 C St. N.W., MS 3428-MIB, 20240; (202) 208-6319. Fax, (202) 208-1185. Darren Cruzan, Director. Watch Office, (202) 208-4108.*
Web, *www.doi.gov/pmb/oles*

Provides direction, policy guidance, and oversight and coordination to the Interior Dept.'s law enforcement, intelligence, and security programs. Works to protect critical infrastructure facilities, national icons, and monuments.

National Aeronautics and Space Administration (NASA), *Protective Services, 300 E St. S.W., #6T39, 20546; (202) 358-2010. Fax, (202) 358-3238. Joseph S. Mahaley, Assistant Administrator.*
Web, www.hq.nasa.gov/hq/security.html

Serves as the focal point for policy formulation, oversight, coordination, and management of NASA's security, counterintelligence, counterterrorism, emergency preparedness and response, and continuity of operations programs.

National Cybersecurity and Communications Integration Center *(Homeland Security Dept.), 245 Murray Lane S.W., Bldg. 410, MS 0635, 20598; (888) 282-0870. Fax, (703) 235-5110. Vacant, Deputy Director. Press, (202) 282-8010.*
General email, info@us-cert.gov
Web, www.us-cert.gov

Leads and coordinates efforts to improve the nation's cybersecurity capabilities; promotes cyber information sharing; and manages cyber risks to the nation through detection, analysis, communication, coordination, and response activities.

National Institute of Standards and Technology (NIST) *(Commerce Dept.), Computer Security, 100 Bureau Dr., MS 8930, Gaithersburg, MD 20899-8930; (301) 975-8443. Fax, (301) 975-8670. Patrick O'Reilly, Division Liason, (301) 975-4751.*
General email, inquiries@nist.gov
Web, www.nist.gov/itl/csd

Works to improve information systems security by raising awareness of information technology risks, vulnerabilities, and protection requirements; researches and advises government agencies of risks; devises measures for cost-effective security and privacy of sensitive federal systems.

Pentagon Force Protection Agency, *9000 Defense Pentagon, 20301; (703) 697-1001. Fax, (703) 695-0681. Jonathan H. Cofer, Director. Emergency line, (703) 697-5555.*
General email, pfpa.pentagon.cco.mbx.general@mail.mil
Web, www.pfpa.mil and Twitter, @PFPAofficial

Civilian agency providing protection for Pentagon occupants, visitors, and infrastructure, including law enforcement, security, surveillance, and crisis prevention.

Transportation Security Administration (TSA) *(Homeland Security Dept.), TSA-1, 601 S. 12th St., 7th Floor, Arlington, VA 20598-6001; Fax, (571) 227-1398. David P. Pekoske, Administrator; Huban A. Gowadia, Deputy Administrator. Press, (571) 227-2829. TSA Contact Center, (866) 289-9673.*
General email, TSA-ContactCenter@tsa.dhs.gov
Web, www.tsa.gov and Twitter, @TSA

Responsible for aviation, rail, land, and maritime transportation security. Programs and interests include the stationing of federal security directors and federal passenger screeners at airports, the Federal Air Marshal Program, improved detection of explosives, and enhanced port security.

Transportation Security Administration (TSA) *(Homeland Security Dept.), Intelligence and Analysis, TSA-10, 601 S. 12th St., 6th Floor, Arlington, VA 22202-4220; (703) 601-3100. Fax, (703) 601-3290. Thomas L. Bush, Assistant Administrator.*
Web, www.tsa.gov

Conducts a range of programs designed to ensure that known or suspected terrorists do not gain access to sensitive areas of the nation's transportation system, including the Alien Flight, Registered Traveler, Secure Flight, and Transportation Worker Identification Credential programs and Hazmat Materials Truck Drivers Background Checks.

Treasury Dept., *Domestic Finance, Critical Infrastructure Protection and Compliance Policy, 1500 Pennsylvania Ave. N.W., 20220; (202) 622-2000. Fax, (202) 622-2310. Vacant, Director.*
General email, OCIP@do.treas.gov
Web, www.treasury.gov/about/organizational-structure/offices/Pages/-Office-of-Critical-Infrastructure-Protection-and-Compliance-Policy.aspx

Works with the private sector to protect the nation's financial infrastructure. Maintains privacy protections for personal financial information. Develops regulations against money laundering and terrorism financing. Serves as the department's principal liaison with the Homeland Security Dept. on infrastructure protection issues.

U.S. Coast Guard (USCG) *(Homeland Security Dept.), Deputy for Operations Policy and Capabilities, CG-DCO-D, 2703 Martin Luther King Jr. Ave. S.E., MS 7318, 20593-7318; (202) 372-1001. Fax, (202) 372-2900. Rear Adm. Meredith L. Austin, Deputy.*
Web, www.dco.uscg.mil/Our-Organization/Deputy-for-Operations-Policy-and-Capabilities-DCO-D/

Establishes and enforces regulations for port safety; environmental protection; vessel safety, inspection, design, documentation, and investigation; licensing of merchant vessel personnel; and shipment of hazardous materials.

U.S. Secret Service *(Homeland Security Dept.), 950 H St. N.W., #8000, 20223; (202) 406-5000. Fax, (202) 406-5246. James M. Murray, Director. Information, (202) 406-5708. Press, (202) 406-5708.*
Web, www.secretservice.gov and Twitter, @SecretService

Protects the president and vice president of the United States and their immediate family members, foreign heads of state and their spouses, and other individuals as designated by the president. Investigates threats against these protectees; protects the White House, vice president's residence, and foreign missions; and plans and implements security designs for national special security events.

►CONGRESS

For a listing of relevant congressional committees and sub-committees, please see pages 608–609 or the Appendix.

Government Accountability Office (GAO), *Physical Infrastructure (PI), 441 G St. N.W., #2T23-B, 20548 (mailing address: 441 G St. N.W., #2T23B, Washington, DC 20548); (202) 512-2834. Daniel Bertoni, Managing Director, (202) 512-5988.*
Web, www.gao.gov/careers/physicalinfrastructure.html

Provides guidance to Congress on the efficiency, safety, and security of the nation's infrastructure, including transportation systems, telecommunications networks, oil and gas pipelines, and federal facilities owned, funded, and operated by both the public and private sectors.

►NONGOVERNMENTAL

SANS Institute, *11200 Rockville Pike, #200, North Bethesda, MD 20852; (301) 654-7267. Fax, (301) 951-0140. Alan Paller, President.*
General email, info@sans.org
Web, www.sans.org and Twitter, @SANSInstitute

Develops, maintains, and makes available at no cost the largest collection of research documents about information security. Operates Internet Storm Center, the Internet's early warning system. (Also known as SysAdmin, Audit, Network, Security Institute.)

Public Health and Environment

►AGENCIES

Agency for Toxic Substances and Disease Registry (ATSDR) *(Health and Human Services Dept.), Washington Office, 1200 Pennsylvania Ave. N.W., MC 5202P, 20460; Steve A. Jones, Regional Director, (703) 603-8729. Info, (800) 232-4436.*
Web, www.atsdr.cdc.gov/dro/hq.html,
Twitter, @CDCEnvironment and Facebook, www.facebook .com/ToxZone

Works with federal, state, and local agencies to prevent, minimize, or eliminate adverse effects of exposure to toxic substances at spill and waste disposal sites. Maintains a registry of persons exposed to hazardous substances and of diseases and illnesses resulting from exposure to hazardous or toxic substances. Conducts public health assessments, health studies, surveillance activities and health education training. Maintains inventory of hazardous substances and registry of sites closed or restricted because of contamination by hazardous material. (Headquarters in Atlanta, Ga.)

Assistant Secretary for Health (OASH) *(Health and Human Services Dept.), Global Affairs (OGA), 200 Independence Ave. S.W., #639H, 20201; (202) 690-6174. (202) 260-0399. Fax, (202) 690-7127. Garrett Grigsby, Assistant Secretary (Acting).*
General email, globalhealth@hhs.gov
Web, www.globalhealth.gov and Twitter, @hhsgov

Oversees the Office of Pandemics and Emerging Threats (PET). Works with other U.S. government agencies, foreign governments, and multilateral organizations to prevent, detect, and respond to health threats.

Assistant Secretary for Health (OASH) *(Health and Human Services Dept.), Surgeon General, Commissioned Corps of the U.S. Public Health Service (PHS), Division of Commissioned Corps Personnel and Readiness (DCCPR), 1101 Wootton Pkwy., Plaza Level, #100, Rockville, MD 20852; (240) 453-6000. Fax, (240) 453-6109. Rear Adm. Joan Hunter, Director. Recruitment, (800) 279-1605.*
General email, CCHelpDesk@hhs.gov
Web, www.usphs.gov
Recruitment, Corpsrecruitment@hhs.gov

Responsible for the overall force management, operations, and deployment readiness and response of the Commissioned Corps of the U.S. Public Health Service, uniformed service health professionals with a wide range of specialties who respond to emergencies, conduct research, and care for patients in underserved communities through federal agencies such as the National Institutes of Health, the Centers for Disease Control and Prevention, the Indian Health Service, and the Bureau of Prisons.

Bureau of Oceans and International Environmental and Scientific Affairs (OES) *(State Dept.), International Health and Biodefense (IHB), 2201 C St. N.W., #2734, 20520; (202) 647-1318. Jerry Mallory, Director.*
Web, www.state.gov/e/oes/intlhealthbiodefense

Advances the Global Health Security Agenda and focuses on issues including pandemic preparedness, new outbreaks of disease, new international policy discussions, and the impact of science and technology, medicine, and public health.

Centers for Disease Control and Prevention (CDC) *(Health and Human Services Dept.), Washington Office, 395 E St. S.W., #9100, 20201; (202) 245-0600. Fax, (202) 245-0602. Robert Redfield, Director; Dr. Mitchell (Mitch) Wolfe, Director, Washington Office (Acting). Public inquiries, (800) 232-4636. TTY, (888) 232-6348.*
General email, cdcwashington@cdc.gov
Web, www.cdc.gov/washington and Twitter, @CDCgov

Supports the CDC's Bioterrorism and Preparedness and Response Program, which develops federal, state, and local capacity to respond to bioterrorism. (Headquarters in Atlanta, Ga.)

Environmental Protection Agency (EPA), *Emergency Management, 1200 Pennsylvania Ave. N.W., MC 5104A, 20460; (202) 564-8600. Reggie Cheatham, Director, (202) 564-8003. Toll-free call center, (800) 424-8802.*
Web, www.epa.gov/emergency-response

Responsible for planning for and responding to the harmful effects of the release or dissemination of toxic chemicals. Areas of responsibility include helping state and local responders plan for emergencies, coordinating with key federal partners, training first responders, and providing resources in the event of a terrorist incident. Carries out preparedness and response activities for intentional and accidental CBRN (Chemical, Biological, Radiation, and Nuclear) events.

Health and Human Services Dept. (HHS), *National Disaster Medical System (NDMS), 200 Independence Ave. S.W., #638G, 20201; (202) 475-2479. Ron Miller, Director, (202) 260-8538. Public Affairs, (202) 205-8114.*
General email, NDMSsupprt@hhs.gov

Web, http://phe.gov/ndms

Federally coordinated program that collaborates with other federal agencies; tribal, state, and local governments; private businesses; and civilian volunteers to ensure the delivery of medical resources following a disaster.

Health and Human Services Dept. (HHS), *Preparedness and Response (ASPR), 200 Independence Ave. S.W., #638-G, 20201; (202) 205-2882. Dr. Robert Kadlec, Assistant Secretary.*
Web, www.phe.gov/Preparedness/Pages/default.aspx and Twitter, @PHEgov

Responsible for coordinating U.S. medical and public health preparedness and response to emergencies, including natural disasters, pandemic and emerging infectious disease, and acts of biological, chemical, and nuclear terrorism. Manages advanced research and development of medical countermeasures. Oversees the hospital preparedness grant program, which provides funding to state governments.

Homeland Security Dept. (DHS), *Countering Weapons of Mass Destruction (CWMD), Health Affairs (OHA), 650 Massachusetts Ave. N.W., MS 0020, 20528; (202) 254-6479. Dave Fluty, Deputy Assistant Secretary (Acting). DHS switchboard, (202) 282-8000.*
General email, healthaffairs@dhs.gov

Web, www.dhs.gov/office-health-affairs

Guides DHS leaders on medical and public health issues related to national security; analyzes data and monitors biological and chemical threats and responses to pandemics.

National Institute of Allergy and Infectious Diseases (NIAID) *(National Institutes of Health), 5601 Fishers Lane, MSC 9806, Bethesda, MD 20892-9806; (301) 496-5717. Fax, (301) 402-3573. Dr. Anthony S. Fauci, Director. Press, (301) 402-1663. Toll-free health and research information, (866) 284-4107. TTY health and research information, (800) 877-8339.*
General email, ocpostoffice@niaid.nih.gov

Web, www.niaid.nih.gov, Twitter, @NIAIDNews and Facebook, www.facebook.com/niaid.nih

Responsible for coordinating and administering a medical program to counter radiological and nuclear threats. Works with the National Cancer Institute and other federal agencies, academia, and industry to develop medical measures to assess, diagnose, and care for civilians exposed to radiation.

►**CONGRESS**

For a listing of relevant congressional committees and subcommittees, please see pages 608–609 or the Appendix.

►**NONGOVERNMENTAL**

American Public Health Assn., *800 Eye St. N.W., 20001-3710; (202) 777-2742. Fax, (202) 777-2534. Dr. Georges C. Benjamin, Executive Director. TTY, (202) 777-2500.*
General email, comments@apha.org

Web, www.apha.org and Twitter, @PublicHealth

Membership: health providers, educators, environmentalists, policymakers, and health officials at all levels working both within and outside of governmental organizations and educational institutions. Works to protect communities from serious, preventable health threats. Strives to ensure that community-based health promotion and disease prevention activities and preventive health services are universally accessible in the United States. Develops standards for scientific procedures in public health.

American Red Cross, *Disaster Preparedness and Response, 431 18th St. N.W., 20006; (202) 303-5214, ext. 1. Gail J. McGovern, President. Donations, 800-RED-CROSS. Press, (202) 303-5551. Toll-free, (800) 733-2767.*
Web, www.redcross.org, Twitter, @redcross and Facebook, www.facebook.com/redcross and Disaster preparedness, www.redcross.org/about-us/our-work/distaster-relief.html

Chartered by Congress to administer disaster relief. Provides disaster victims with food, shelter, first aid, medical care, and access to other available resources. Feeds emergency workers; handles inquiries from concerned family members outside the disaster area; helps promote disaster preparedness and prevention through training.

Assn. of Public Health Laboratories, *8515 Georgia Ave., #700, Silver Spring, MD 20910; (240) 485-2745. Fax, (240) 485-2700. Scott J. Becker, Executive Director, (240) 485-2747. Press, (240) 485-2793.*
General email, info@aphl.org

Web, www.aphl.org and Twitter, @APHL

Membership: state and local public health, environmental, agricultural, and food safety laboratories. Offers technical assistance to member laboratories; sponsors educational programs for public health and clinical laboratory practitioners; develops systems for electronic exchange of lab data; develops laboratory system in under-resourced countries. Works with the CDC, FDA, EPA, and other federal partners to support disease detection and surveillance, laboratory response to health crises, quality drinking water, and other public health services.

Assn. of Schools and Programs of Public Health, *1900 M St. N.W., #710, 20036; (202) 296-1099. Fax, (202) 296-1252. Laura Magaña Valladares, President, (202) 296-1099, ext. 120.*
General email, info@aspph.org

Web, www.aspph.org and Twitter, @ASPPHtweets

Membership: deans, faculty, and students of accredited graduate schools of public health. Promotes improved education and training of professional public health personnel; interests include disease prevention, health promotion, and international health.

Assn. of State and Territorial Health Officials, *2231 Crystal Dr., #450, Arlington, VA 22202; (202) 371-9090. Fax, (571) 527-3189. Michael Fraser, Executive Director, (202) 371-3142.*
Web, www.astho.org, www.statepublichealth.org and Twitter, @astho

Membership: executive officers of state and territorial public health departments. Serves as legislative review agency and information source for members. Monitors legislation and regulations.

National Assn. of State EMS Officials (NASEMSO), *201 Park Washington Ct., Falls Church, VA 22046-4527; (703) 538-1799. Fax, (703) 241-5603. Dia Gainor, Executive Director.*
General email, info@nasemso.org
Web, www.nasemso.org

Supports development of effective emergency medical services (EMS) systems at the local, state, and regional levels. Works to formulate national EMS policy and foster communication and sharing among state EMS officials.

National Center for Biodefense and Infectious Diseases *(George Mason University), 10650 Pyramid Pl., MS 1J5, Manassas, VA 20110; (703) 993-4265. Fax, (703) 993-4280. Charles Bailey, Executive Director.*
General email, cbailey2@gmu.edu
Web, http://ncbid.gmu.edu
http://cos.gmu.edu

Researches and develops diagnostics and treatments for emerging infectious diseases as well as those pathogens that could be used as terrorist weapons that require special containment. Manages a graduate education program.

National Research Council (NRC), *Disasters Roundtable, Keck Center, 500 5th St. N.W., 20001; (202) 334-2243. Fax, (202) 334-1393. Ells M. Stanley Sr., Chair; Lauren Alexander Augustine, Director.*
General email, dr@nas.edu
Web, www.dels.nas.edu/dr

Facilitates the exchange of ideas among scientists, practitioners, and policymakers concerned with issues related to natural, technological, and other disasters. Roundtable workshops are held three times a year in Washington, D.C.

National Research Council (NRC), *Global Health Board, Keck Center, 500 5th St. N.W., 20001; (202) 334-3967. Fax, (202) 334-3861. Ann Kerth, Chair; Julie Pavlin, Director.*
General email, HMD-NASEM@nas.edu
Web, www.nationalacademies.org/hmd/About-HMD/ Leadership-Staff/HMD-Staff-Leadership-Boards/Board-on-Global-Health.aspx

Carries out activities related to international health policy and health concerns of developing countries; main focus is public health programs for prevention and control of disease and disability.

National Research Council (NRC), *Population Health and Public Health Practice Board, Keck Center, 500 5th St. N.W., 20001; (202) 334-2383. Fax, (202) 334-2939. Rose Marie Martinez, Director.*
General email, bph@nas.edu
Web, www.nationalacademies.org/hmd

Supports research on public health, including vaccine safety, pandemic preparedness issues, smoking cessation, health disparities, and reducing environmental and occupational hazards.

National Vaccine Information Center, *21525 Ridgetop Circle, #100, Sterling, VA 20166; (703) 938-0342. Fax, (571) 313-1268. Barbara Loe Fisher, President; Theresa Wrangham, Executive Director.*
General email, contactnvic@gmail.com
Web, www.nvic.org, Twitter, @NVICLoeDown and Facebook, www.facebook.com/national.vaccine .information.center

Educates the public and provides research on vaccination safety procedures and effectiveness; supports reform of the vaccination system; publishes information on diseases and vaccines; and monitors legislation and regulations.

Pan American Health Organization, *525 23rd St. N.W., 20037; (202) 974-3000. Fax, (202) 974-3663. Dr. Carissa F. Etienne, Director.*
Web, www.paho.org and Twitter, @PAHOWHO

Works to extend health services to underserved populations of its member countries and to control or eradicate communicable diseases; promotes cooperation among governments to solve public health problems. (Regional Office for the Americas of the World Health Organization, which is headquartered in Geneva, Switzerland.)

Selective Service

▶AGENCIES

Selective Service System, *1515 Wilson Blvd., #400, Arlington, VA 22209-2425; (703) 605-4100. Fax, (703) 605-4106. Donald M. Benton, Director. Locator, (703) 605-4000. Toll-free, (888) 655-1825. TTY, (800) 877-8339. TTY Español, (800) 845-6136.*
General email, information@sss.gov
Web, www.sss.gov and Twitter, @sss_gov

Supplies the armed forces with manpower when authorized; registers male citizens of the United States ages eighteen to twenty-five. In an emergency, would institute a draft and would provide alternative service assignments to men classified as conscientious objectors.

▶CONGRESS

For a listing of relevant congressional committees and subcommittees, please see pages 608–609 or the Appendix.

Strategic Stockpiles

▶**AGENCIES**

Defense Dept. (DoD), *Industrial Policy,* 1400 Defense Pentagon, #3B854, 20301-3300; (703) 697-0051. Fax, (703) 695-4885. David Stapleton, Deputy Assistant Secretary (Acting).
General email, osd.mibp.inquiries@mail.mil
Web, www.businessdefense.gov

Develops and oversees policy, assessment and analysis, and investment programs for mainitaining the U.S. defense industrial base.

Defense Logistics Agency *(Defense Dept.),* **Strategic Materials,** 8725 John Jay Kingman Rd., #3229, Fort Belvoir, VA 22060-6223; (703) 767-5500. Fax, (703) 767-3316. Ronnie Favors, Administrator. Press, (703) 767-6479.
Web, www.dla.mil/HQ/Acquisition/Strategicmaterials.aspx

Manages the national defense stockpile of strategic and critical materials. Purchases strategic materials, including beryllium and newly developed high-tech alloys. Disposes of excess materials, including tin, silver, industrial diamond stones, tungsten, and vegetable tannin.

Fossil Energy (FE) *(Energy Dept.),* **Petroleum Reserves,** Forrestal Bldg., 1000 Independence Ave. S.W., FE-40, 20585; (202) 586-4410. Douglas Macintyre, Deputy Assistant Secretary (Acting).
Web, www.energy.gov/fe/services/petroleum-reserves

Manages programs that provide the United States with strategic and economic protection against disruptions in oil supplies, including the Strategic Petroleum Reserves, the Northeast Home Heating Oil Reserve, and the Naval Petroleum and the Northeast Gasoline Supply Reserve.

▶**CONGRESS**

For a listing of relevant congressional committees and subcommittees, please see pages 608–609 or the Appendix.

INTELLIGENCE AND COUNTERTERRORISM

General

▶**AGENCIES**

Air Force Dept. *(Defense Dept.),* **Intelligence, Surveillance and Reconnaissance (ISR),** 1060 Air Force Pentagon, #4B136, 20330-1060; (703) 695-5613. Lt. Gen VeraLinn (Dash) Jamieson, Chief of Staff.
Web, www.af.mil/ISR.aspx

Collects and analyzes crucial information and data about enemy targets and distributes intelligence to other Air Force departments.

Army Dept. *(Defense Dept.),* **Intelligence,** 1000 Army Pentagon, #2E408, 20310-1000; (703) 695-3033. Fax, (703) 697-7605. Gen. Mark A. Milley (USA), Chief of Staff.
Web, www.army.mil

Military office that directs Army intelligence activities and coordinates activities with other intelligence agencies.

Bureau of Counterterrorism and Countering Violent Extremism (CT) *(State Dept.),* 2201 C St. N.W., #2509, 20520; (202) 647-9892. Fax, (202) 647-9256. Nathan Sales, Coordinator. Press, (202) 647-1845.
Web, www.state.gov/j/ct and *Twitter, @StateDeptCT*

Implements U.S. counterterrorism policy and coordinates activities with foreign governments; responds to terrorist acts; works to promote a stronger counterterrorism stance worldwide through diplomatic engagement, regional capacity building, designations, and information sharing to target specific terrorist networks and branches.

Bureau of Intelligence and Research (INR) *(State Dept.),* 2201 C St. N.W., #6468, 20520-6531; (202) 647-9177. Fax, (202) 736-4688. Ellen E. McCarthy, Assistant Secretary.
Web, www.state.gov/s/inr

Coordinates foreign policy–related research, analysis, and intelligence programs for the State Dept. and other federal agencies.

Central Intelligence Agency (CIA), CIA Headquarters, 930 Dolley Madison Blvd., McLean, VA 20505 (mailing address: CIA Headquarters, Washington, DC 20505); (703) 482-0623. Fax, (571) 204-3800. Gina Haspel, Director.
Web, www.cia.gov and *Twitter, @CIA*

Gathers and evaluates foreign intelligence to assist the president and senior U.S. government policymakers in making foreign policy and national security decisions. Reports directly to the Office of National Intelligence, which coordinates intelligence functions of all government agencies involved with homeland security.

Defense Dept. (DoD), *Intelligence,* 5000 Defense Pentagon, #3E834, 20301-5000; (703) 695-0971. Fax, (703) 693-5706. Joseph Kernan, Under Secretary.
Web, www.defense.gov

Responsible for ensuring the secretary of defense's access to intelligence information.

Defense Dept. (DoD), *Intelligence Oversight,* 7200 Defense Pentagon, #2E1052, 20301-7200; (703) 695-9542. Michael T. Mahar, Senior Official.
General email, osd.pentagon.odcmo.list.dod-sioo-iod@mail.mil
Web, dodsioo.defense.gov

Responsible for the independent oversight of all Defense Dept. intelligence, counterintelligence, and related activities, and for the formulation of intelligence oversight policy; reviews intelligence operations and investigates and reports on possible violations of federal law or regulations.

Counterterrorism Resources and Contacts

The following agencies, organizations, and hotlines offer information pertaining to terrorism and counterterrorism issues.

AGENCIES

Bureau of Counterterrorism, Nathan A. Sales, Coordinator, (202) 647-9892 (State Dept.)

Bureau of Industry and Security, Richard Ashooh, Assistant Under Secretary (202) 482-5491; toll free (800) 424-2980, (Commerce Dept.)

Central Intelligence Agency, Vacant, Director (703) 482-0623, (Justice Dept.)

Defence Intelligence Agency, Lt. Gen. Robert P. Ashley, Jr., (202) 231-5554, (Defense Dept.)

FBI Counterterrorism Division, Bradley "Grant" Mendenhall, Asst. Director, (202) 324-3000, (Justice Dept.)

Homeland Security Council, Rear Admiral Douglas Fears, Assistant to the President for Counterterrorism and Homeland Security, (202) 456-6317 (Executive Office of the President)

Homeland Security Dept., Kevin McAleenan, Secretary (Acting), (202) 282-8000

INTERPOL, Wayne Salzgaber, Director (Acting), (202) 616-9000 (Justice Dept.)

National Counterterrorism Center, Russell "Russ" Travers, Director (Acting), 855-731-3260

National Nuclear Security Administration, Steven C. Erhart, Under Secretary (Acting), (202) 586-5000 (Energy Dept.)

National Security Agency/Central Security Service, Michael S. Rogers, Director, (301) 688-6524 (Defense Dept.)

National Security Council, John Bolton, National Security Advisor, (202) 456-1414, (Executive Office of the President)

National Security Division, Counterterrorism and Espionage, Dana J. Boente, Asst. Attorney General (Acting), (202) 514-2000 (Justice Dept.)

Office of Counterterrorism and Emergency Coordination (FDA), Rosemary Roberts, Director, (301) 796-2210 (Health and Human Services Dept.)

Office of Foreign Assets Control, Andrea Gacki, Director, (202) 622-2510 (Treasury Dept.)

Office of Nuclear Security and Incident Response, Brian Holian, Director, (301) 287-3734

Office of Terrorism and Financial Intelligence, Sigal Mandelker, Under Secretary, (202) 622-8260, (Treasury Dept.)

Office of the Director of National Intelligence, Daniel Coats, Director, (703) 733-8600

Transportation Security Administration, David P. Pekoske, Administrator, (866) 289-9673 (Homeland Security Dept.)

U.S. Immigration and Customs Enforcement, Ronald Vitiello, Director, (202) 732-3000 (Homeland Security Dept.)

U.S. Secret Service, Randolph D. Alles, Director, (202) 406-5708 (Homeland Security Dept.)

ORGANIZATIONS

Foundation for Defense of Democracies, Clifford D. May, Director, (202) 207-0190

International Center for Terrorism Studies, Michael S. Swetnam, Chief Executive Officer, (703) 525-0770

RAND Homeland Security and Defense Center, Michael D. Rich, President, (310) 451-6913

HOTLINES

Federal Bureau of Investigation, (202) 324-3000

Office of Foreign Assets Control, (800) 540-6322

Transportation Security Administration, (866) 289-9673

U.S. Immigration and Customs Enforcement, (866) 347-2423

Defense Dept. (DoD), *Special Operations and Low-Intensity Conflict, 2500 Defense Pentagon, #3C852A, 20301-2500; (703) 695-9667. Fax, (703) 693-6335. Owen West, Assistant Secretary.*
Web, http://policy.defense.gov/OUSDP-Offices/ASD-for-Special-Operations-Low-Intensity-Conflict

Serves as special staff assistant and civilian adviser to the secretary of defense on matters related to special operations and international terrorism.

Defense Information Systems Agency *(Defense Dept.), 6910 Cooper Ave., Fort Meade, MD 20755; (703) 607-6001. Vice Adm. Nancy A. Norton (USA), Director.*
Web, www.disa.mil

The Defense Dept. agency responsible for information technology and the central manager for major portions of the defense information infrastructure. Units include the White House Communications Agency.

Defense Intelligence Agency *(Defense Dept.), 200 MacDill Blvd., 20340; (202) 231-5554. Fax, (202) 231-0851. Lt. Gen. Robert P. Ashley Jr. (USA), Director. General email, DIA-PAO@dia.mil*
Web, www.dia.mil

Collects and evaluates foreign military–related intelligence information to satisfy the requirements of the secretary of defense, Joint Chiefs of Staff, selected components of the Defense Dept., Office of National Intelligence, and other authorized agencies.

Federal Bureau of Investigation (FBI) *(Justice Dept.),* *National Joint Terrorism Task Force,* *935 Pennsylvania Ave. N.W., 20535-0001; (571) 280-5688. Fax, (571) 280-6922. William Callahan, Unit Chief.*
Web, www.fbi.gov/washingtondc/about/partnerships and www.fbi.gov/about-us/investigate/terrorism/national-joint-terrorism-task-force

Group of more than fifty agencies from the fields of intelligence, public safety, and federal, state, and local law enforcement that collects terrorism information and intelligence and funnels it to the more than five hundred JTTFs (teams of local, state, and federal agents based at FBI field offices), various terrorism units within the FBI, and partner agencies. Helps the FBI with terrorism investigations.

Federal Bureau of Investigation (FBI) *(Justice Dept.),* *National Security Branch (NSB), Counterintelligence Division, 935 Pennsylvania Ave. N.W., 20535; (202) 324-4614. Fax, (202) 324-0848. Bill Priestap, Assistant Director. National security hotline, (202) 324-3000.*
Web, www.fbi.gov/about-us/investigate/counterintelligence

Provides centralized management and oversight of all foreign counterintelligence investigations. Integrates law enforcement with intelligence efforts to investigate violations of federal laws against espionage, including economic espionage. Seeks to prevent foreign acquisition of weapons of mass destruction, penetration of the U.S. intelligence community and government agencies and contractors, and compromise of U.S. critical national assets.

Federal Bureau of Investigation (FBI) *(Justice Dept.),* *National Security Branch (NSB), Counterterrorism Division, 935 Pennsylvania Ave. N.W., #4204, 20535; (571) 280-5000. Fax, (202) 324-7050. Michael G. McGarrity, Assistant Director. National security hotline, (202) 324-3000. Press, (202) 324-3691.*
Web, www.fbi.gov/about-us/investigate/terrorism

Collects, analyzes, and shares information and intelligence with authorities to combat international terrorism operations within the United States and in support of extraterritorial investigations, domestic terrorism operations, and counterterrorism. Maintains the Joint Terrorism Task Force, which includes representatives from the Defense Dept., Energy Dept., Federal Emergency Management Agency, CIA, U.S. Customs and Border Protection, U.S. Secret Service, and Immigration and Customs Enforcement.

Federal Bureau of Investigation (FBI) *(Justice Dept.),* *National Security Branch (NSB), Terrorist Screening Center, 935 Pennsylvania Ave. N.W., 20535; (571) 350-5678. Charles K. Kable, Director. Toll-free, (866) 872-5678. Press, (571) 350-6397.*
General email, tsc@tsc.gov
Web, www.fbi.gov/about-us/nsb/tsc
Press, media@tsc.gov

Coordinates access to terrorist watch lists from multiple agencies. Provides operational support to federal screeners and state and local law enforcement officials.

Homeland Security Council *(Executive Office of the President),* *The White House, 20502; (202) 456-6317. Doug Fears, Homeland Security Advisor.*
Web, www.whitehouse.gov

Advises the president on combating global terrorism and homeland security policy.

Homeland Security Dept. (DHS), *3801 Nebraska Ave. N.W., 20528; 301 7th St. S.W., MS0501, 20528; (202) 282-8000. (202) 447-5890. Fax, (202) 447-5437. Kevin K. McAleenan, Secretary (Acting); Claire M. Grady, Deputy Secretary (Acting); Jonathan Hoffman, Communications Director, (202) 282-8852.*
General email, DHSExecSec@hq.dhs.gov
Web, www.dhs.gov and Twitter, @DHSgov

Coordinates the strategy of the executive branch with those of state and local governments and private entities to detect, prepare for, protect against, respond to, and recover from terrorist attacks and other emergencies in the United States. Administers the National Terrorism Advisory System to communicate information about terrorist threats to the public.

Homeland Security Dept. (DHS), *Countering Weapons of Mass Destruction (CWMD), 1125 15th St., 20221; (202) 254-7799. James F. McDonnell, Assistant Secretary. DHS switchboard, (202) 282-8000.*
Web, www.dhs.gov/countering-weapons-mass-destruction-office#

Responsible for countering attempts by terrorists or other threat actors to carry out an attack against the United States or its interests using a weapon of mass destruction.

Homeland Security Dept. (DHS), *Intelligence and Analysis (I&A), 3801 Nebraska Ave. N.W., Bldg. 19, 20528; (202) 447-4154. David J. Glawe, Under Secretary; Brian J. Murphy, Deputy Undersecretary.*
Web, www.dhs.gov/office-intelligence-and-analysis

Uses intelligence from multiple sources to identify and assess current and future threats to the United States; provides guidance to the secretary on homeland security issues.

Marine Corps *(Defense Dept.), Intelligence, 3000 Marine Corps Pentagon, #1A262B, 20350-3000; (703) 614-2522. Fax, (703) 614-5888. Brig. Gen. William Seely (USMC), Director.*
Web, www.hqmc.marines.mil/intelligence

Military office that directs Marine Corps intelligence policy and coordinates activities with other intelligence agencies.

National Aeronautics and Space Administration (NASA), *Protective Services, 300 E St. S.W., #6T39, 20546; (202) 358-2010. Fax, (202) 358-3238. Joseph S. Mahaley, Assistant Administrator.*
Web, www.hq.nasa.gov/hq/security.html

Serves as the focal point for policy formulation, oversight, coordination, and management of NASA's security, counterintelligence, counterterrorism, emergency preparedness and response, and continuity of operations programs.

National Geospatial-Intelligence Agency *(Defense Dept.),* 7500 Geoint Dr., Springfield, VA 22150-7500; (571) 557-5400. Fax, (571) 558-3169. Robert Cardillo, Director. Maps and imagery products, (571) 557-5400.
General email, publicaffairs@nga.mil

Web, www.nga.mil, Twitter, @NGA_GEOINT and Facebook, www.facebook.com/NatlGEOINTAgency

Combat support agency that develops imagery and map-based intelligence in support of national defense objectives.

National Reconnaissance Office (NRO) *(Defense Dept.),* 14675 Lee Rd., Chantilly, VA 20151-1715; (703) 808-5050. Fax, (703) 808-1171. Betty J. Sapp, Director.
General email, publicaffairs@nro.mil

Web, www.nro.gov, Twitter, @NatReconOfc and Facebook, www.facebook.com/NationalReconnaissanceOffice

Researches, develops, and operates intelligence satellites. Gathers intelligence for various purposes, including indications and warnings, monitoring of arms control agreements, military operations and exercises, and monitoring of natural disasters and other environmental issues.

National Security Agency (NSA) *(Defense Dept.),* 9800 Savage Rd., #6272, Fort Meade, MD 20755-6000; (301) 688-6311. Fax, (301) 688-6198. Gen. Paul M. Nakasone (USA), Director; George C. Barnes, Deputy Director. FOIA Public Liaison Office, (301) 688-6527. Public Affairs and Media, (301) 688-6524.
General email, nsapao@nsa.gov

Web, www.nsa.gov, Twitter, @NSAGov and Facebook, www.facebook.com/NSAUSGov

Provides technology, products, and services to secure information and information infrastructure critical to U.S. national security interests. Organizes and controls all foreign signals collection and processing activities of the United States in accordance with requirements established by the Defense Dept., the Office of the Director of National Intelligence, and by national policies with the advice of the National Foreign Intelligence Board.

National Security Division *(Justice Dept.),* 950 Pennsylvania Ave. N.W., #7339, 20530; (202) 514-2401. Fax, (202) 514-9836. John Demers, Assistant Attorney General. Press, (202) 514-2007.
General email, nsd.public@usdoj.gov

Web, www.justice.gov/nsd

Coordinates the Justice Dept.'s intelligence, counterterrorism, counterespionage, and other national security activities.

National Security Division *(Justice Dept.), Counterintelligence and Export Control,* 950 Pennsylvania Ave. N.W., 20530; (202) 514-1057. Fax, (202) 514-8714. Joy Bratt, Chief.
General email, nsd.public@usdoj.gov

Web, www.justice.gov/nsd

Supervises the investigation and prosecution of cases affecting national security, foreign relations, and the export of military and strategic commodities and technology. Has executive responsibility for authorizing the prosecution of cases under criminal statutes relating to espionage, sabotage, neutrality, and atomic energy. Provides legal advice to U.S. Attorney's offices and investigates agencies on federal statutes concerning national security. Coordinates criminal cases involving the application of the Classified Information Procedures Act. Administers and enforces the Foreign Agents Registration Act of 1938 and related disclosure statutes.

National Security Division *(Justice Dept.), Counterterrorism,* 950 Pennsylvania Ave. N.W., 20530; (202) 514-1057. Fax, (202) 514-8714. Michael J. Mullaney, Chief.
General email, nsd.public@usdoj.gov

Web, www.justice.gov/nsd/counterterrorism-section

Responsible for the design, implementation, and support of law enforcement efforts, legislative initiatives, policies, and strategies related to combating international and domestic terrorism.

National Security Division *(Justice Dept.), Intelligence,* 950 Pennsylvania Ave. N.W., 20530; (202) 514-7941. Fax, (202) 514-8714. John C. Demers, Assistant Attorney General.
General email, nsd.public@usdoj.gov

Web, www.justice.gov/nsd/office-intelligence

Seeks to ensure that Intelligence Community agencies have the legal authorities necessary to conduct intelligence operations, particularly operations involving the Foreign Intelligence Surveillance Act (FISA). Oversees various national security activities of Intelligence Community agencies; participates in FISA-related litigation.

National Security Division *(Justice Dept.), Justice for Victims of Overseas Terrorism,* 950 Pennsylvania Ave. N.W., 20530; (202) 233-0701. Heather Cartwright, Director.
General email, nsd.ovt@usdoj.gov

Web, www.justice.gov/nsd-ovt

Responsible for establishing a Joint Task Force with the State Dept. in the event of a terrorist incident against U.S. citizens overseas. Responds to congressional and citizens' inquiries on the department's response to such attacks.

National Security Division *(Justice Dept.), Law and Policy,* 950 Pennsylvania Ave. N.W., 20530; (202) 514-7941. Brad Wiegmann, Deputy Assistant Attorney General.
General email, nsd.justice@usdoj.gov

Web, www.justice.gov/nsd

Develops and implements Justice Dept. policies with regard to intelligence, counterterrorism, and other national security matters.

Office of the Director of National Intelligence (DNI), Intelligence Campus, 1500 Tysons McClean Dr., McLean, VA 22102; (703) 733-8600. Dan Coats, Director; Brian Hale, Public Affairs. Press and public affairs, (703) 275-3637.
Web, www.dni.gov and Twitter, @ODNI

Leads a unified intelligence community and serves as the principal adviser to the president on intelligence matters. Orders the collection of new intelligence to ensure the sharing of information among agencies and to establish common standards for the intelligence community's personnel. Responsible for determining the annual budgets for all national intelligence agencies and for directing how these funds are spent.

Office of the Director of National Intelligence (DNI),
National Counterintelligence and Security Center,
Liberty Crossing, ICC-B, 1500 Tysons McLean Dr.,
McLean, VA 22102; (703) 733-8600. William Evanina,
National Counterintelligence Executive.
Web, www.ncsc.gov

Conducts foreign intelligence threat assessments; promotes collaboration and information sharing throughout the U.S. counterintelligence community through conferences and other outreach and training activities; makes recommendations to decision makers concerning national counterintelligence strategy.

Office of the Director of National Intelligence (DNI),
National Counterterrorism Center, Liberty Crossing, 1500
Tysons McLean Dr., McLean Dr., VA 22102; (571) 280-
6160. Fax, (571) 280-5551. Vice Adm. Joseph Maguire,
Director; Tricia Wellman, Executive Director.
General email, nctcpao@nctc.gov

Web, www.nctc.gov

Serves as a hub for terrorism threat–related information collected domestically and abroad. Responsible for assessing, integrating, and disseminating terrorist threat information and all-source analysis; maintains U.S. government's central database on known and suspected terrorists; and identifies collection requirements related to the terrorist threat. Participates in strategic planning for counterterrorism activities.

Office of the Director of National Intelligence (DNI),
National Intelligence Council, CIA Headquarters,
Langley, VA 20505; (703) 482-6724. Fax, (703) 482-8652.
Amy McAuliffe, Chair.
*Web, www.dni.gov/index.php?option=com_*
content&view=article&id=398&Itemid=776 and
Twitter, @ODNI_NIC

Supports the director of national intelligence and serves as the intelligence community's center for mid- and long-term strategic thinking. Provides a focal point for policymakers' inquiries and needs. Establishes contacts with private sector and academic experts in the intelligence field.

President's Intelligence Advisory Board and
Intelligence Oversight Board *(Executive Office of the*
President), New Executive Office Bldg., #5020, 20502; (202)
456-2352. Fax, (202) 395-3403. Stephen Feinberg, Chair.
Web, www.whitehouse.gov/piab

Members appointed by the president. Assesses the quality, quantity, and adequacy of foreign intelligence collection and of counterintelligence activities by all government

agencies; advises the president on matters concerning intelligence and national security.

State Dept., Global Engagement Center, *2201 C St. N.W.,*
#2429, 20520; (202) 736-7548. Daniel Kimmage,
Coordinator (Acting).
Web, www.state.gov/r/gec

Works to coordinate, orient, and inform government-wide foreign communications activities targeted against terrorism and violent extremism.

Transportation Dept. (DOT), *Intelligence, Security, and*
Emergency Response, 1200 New Jersey Ave. S.E., #56125,
20590; (202) 366-6525. Fax, (202) 366-7261.
Richard Chávez, Director.
Web, www.transportation.gov/mission/administrations/
intelligence-security-emergency-response

Advises the secretary on transportation intelligence and security policy. Acts as liaison with the intelligence community, federal agencies, corporations, and interest groups; administers counterterrorism strategic planning processes.

Transportation Security Administration (TSA)
(Homeland Security Dept.), Intelligence and Analysis,
TSA-10, 601 S. 12th St., 6th Floor, Arlington, VA
22202-4220; (703) 601-3100. Fax, (703) 601-3290.
Thomas L. Bush, Assistant Administrator.
Web, www.tsa.gov

Conducts a range of programs designed to ensure that known or suspected terrorists do not gain access to sensitive areas of the nation's transportation system, including the Alien Flight, Registered Traveler, Secure Flight, and Transportation Worker Identification Credential programs and Hazmat Materials Truck Drivers Background Checks.

Treasury Dept., *Terrorism and Financial Intelligence,*
1500 Pennsylvania Ave. N.W., #4316, 20220; (202)
622-8260. Fax, (202) 622-1914. Sigal Mandelker, Under
Secretary. Press, (202) 622-2960.
Web, www.treasury.gov/about/organizational-structure/
offices/Pages/Office-of-Terrorism-and-Financial-
Intelligence.aspx

Develops and maintains the Treasury Dept.'s strategies to combat terrorist financing domestically and internationally; develops and implements the National Money Laundering strategy as well as other policies and programs to fight financial crimes.

Treasury Dept., *Terrorism and Financial Intelligence,*
Foreign Assets Control, 1500 Pennsylvania Ave. N.W.,
Treasury Annex, 20220; (202) 622-2490. Fax, (202) 622-
1657. Andrea E. Gacki, Director. Hotline, (800) 540-6322.
Licensing Division, (202) 622-2480.
General email, ofac_feedback@do.treas.gov

Web, www.treasury.gov/about/organizational-structure/
offices/Pages/Office-of-Foreign-Assets-Control.aspx

Authorized under the Enemy Act, the International Emergency Economic Powers Act, and United Nations Participation Act, and other relevant statutory authorities

Office of the Director of National Intelligence

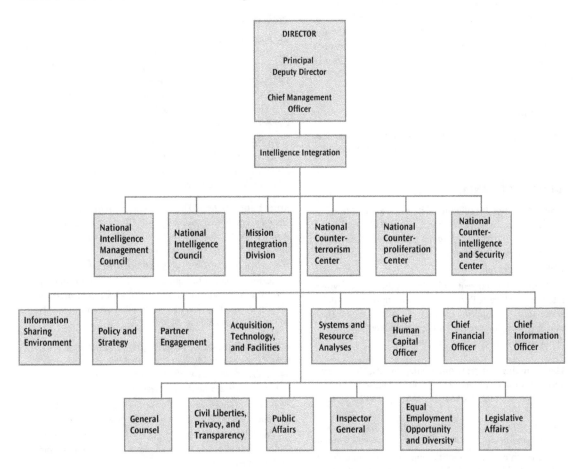

to control financial and commercial dealings with certain countries and their foreign nationals in times of war or emergencies. Regulations involving foreign assets control, narcotics, nonproliferation, and commercial transactions currently apply in varying degrees to the Balkans, Belarus, Burma, Côte d'Ivoire, Cuba, Iran, Iraq, Lebanon, Libya, North Korea, Somalia, Sudan, Syria, Yemen, and Zimbabwe, as well as terrorists wherever located and transnational criminal organizations.

Treasury Dept., *Terrorism and Financial Intelligence, Terrorist Financing and Financial Crime, 1500 Pennsylvania Ave. N.W., 20220; (202) 622-1655. Fax, (202) 622-3915. Marshall Billingslea, Assistant Secretary. Press, (202) 622-2960.*
Web, www.treasury.gov/about/organizational-structure/ offices/Pages/Office-of-Terrorist-Financing-and-Financial-Crimes.aspx

Sets strategy and policy for combating the financing of terrorism both domestically and abroad.

U.S. Coast Guard (USCG) *(Homeland Security Dept.), Counterterrorism and Defense Policy, CG-ODO, 2703 Martin Luther King Jr. Ave. S.E., MS 7516, 20593-7516;*
(202) 372-2101. Fax, (202) 372-8361. Capt. Clinton Carlson, Director. Web, www.dco.uscg.mil/Our-Organization/Assistant-Commandant-for-Response-Policy-CG-5R/Office-of-Counterterrorism-Defense-Operations-Policy-CG-ODO/CG

Provides advanced tactical skills to aid in response to terrorist incidents or to incidents involving weapons of mass destruction.

U.S. Coast Guard (USCG) *(Homeland Security Dept.), Intelligence, CG-2, 2703 Martin Luther King Jr. Ave. S.E., MS 7301, 20593-7301; (202) 372-2700. Fax, (202) 372-2956. Rear Adm. Robert Hayes, Assistant Commandant. Response Center, (800) 424-8802. Web, www.dco.uscg.mil/Our-Organization/Intelligence-CG-2/*

Manages all Coast Guard intelligence activities and programs.

U.S. Customs and Border Protection *(Homeland Security Dept.), Intelligence and Investigative Liaison, 1300 Pennsylvania Ave. N.W., #7.3D, 20229; (202) 344-1150. Jennifer Ley, Assistant Commissioner (Acting).*

Web, www.cbp.gov/about/leadership/assistant-commissioners-office/intelligence-investigative-liaison

Coordinates the effort to prevent the introduction of weapons of mass destruction into the United States and to prevent international terrorists from obtaining weapons of mass destruction materials, technologies, arms, funds, and other support.

►CONGRESS

For a listing of relevant congressional committees and subcommittees, please see pages 608–609 or the Appendix.

►NONGOVERNMENTAL

Assn. of Former Intelligence Officers (AFIO), *7700 Leesburg Pike, #324, Falls Church, VA 22043; (703) 790-0320. Fax, (703) 991-1278. James R. Hughes, President. General email, afio@afio.com*

Web, www.afio.com

Membership: current and former military and civilian intelligence officers. Encourages public support for intelligence agencies; supports increased intelligence education in colleges and universities; and provides guidance to students seeking careers in intelligence.

The Brookings Institution, *Center for 21st Century Security and Intelligence, 1775 Massachusetts Ave. N.W., 20036; (202) 797-6103. Michael E. O'Hanlon, Director.*

Web, www.brookings.edu/center/center-for-21st-century-security-and-intelligence and Twitter, @MichaelEOHanlon

Research center promoting policymaking on defense, arms control and nonproliferation, cybersecurity, arms control, and intelligence.

Fourth Freedom Forum, *Washington Office, 1101 14th St. N.W., #900, 20005; (202) 802-9393. Eelco Kessels, Executive Director. General email, globalct@gmail.com*

Web, www.globalcenter.org

Conducts research and training to advance global cooperation to address transnational threats, including terrorism, nuclear proliferation, and drug trafficking.

Potomac Institute for Policy Studies, *International Center for Terrorism Studies (ICTS), 901 N. Stuart St., #1200, Arlington, VA 22203-1821; (703) 525-0770. Fax, (703) 525-0299. Michael S. Swetnam, Chief Executive Officer; Yonah Alexander, Director. General email, webmaster@potomacinstitute.org*

Web, www.potomacinstitute.org and Twitter, @PotomacInst

Public policy research institute that conducts studies on key science and technology issues. The ICTS focuses on all forms of terrorism and the potential for terrorism, including biological, chemical, or nuclear violence, as well as information warfare and cyberterrorism.

Internal (Agency) Security

►AGENCIES

Air Force Dept. *(Defense Dept.), Special Investigations (AF/OSI), 27130 Telegraph Rd., #W1642, Quantico, VA 22134; (571) 305-8028. Col Kirk B. Stabler, Commander; Jeffrey D. Specht, Executive Director; CMSgt. Karen F. Bierne-Flint, Chief Master Sergeant. Toll Free Crimebusters, (877) 246-1453. General email, hqafosi.watch@us.af.mil*

Web, www.osi.af.mil and Twitter, @AirForceOSI

Develops and implements policy on investigations of foreign intelligence, terrorism, and other crimes as they relate to Air Force security.

Army Dept. *(Defense Dept.), Counterintelligence, Human Intelligence, Security and Disclosure, 1000 Army Pentagon, #2D350, 20310-1000; (703) 695-1007. Fax, (703) 695-3149. Vacant, Director. Web, www.dami.army.pentagon.mil/DAMI-CD.aspx*

Responsible for foreign disclosure, policy formation, planning, programming, oversight, and representation for counterintelligence, human intelligence, and security countermeasures of the Army.

Bureau of Diplomatic Security (DS) *(State Dept.), 2201 C St. N.W., #6316, 20520; (202) 647-6290. Fax, (571) 345-2527. Michael Evanoff, Assistant Secretary. General email, DSPublicAffairs@state.gov*

Web, www.state.gov/m/ds, Twitter, @StateDeptDSS and Facebook, www.facebook.com/StateDeptDSS

Provides a secure environment for conducting U.S. diplomacy and promoting American interests abroad and in the United States.

Bureau of Diplomatic Security (DS) *(State Dept.), Countermeasures, 1801 N. Lynn St., #23L04, Rosslyn, VA 22209; (571) 345-3836. Todd J. Brown, Deputy Assistant Secretary.*

Web, www.state.gov/m/ds

Oversees the Office of Physical Security and Office of Security Technology to direct and develop worldwide physical security standards, policies, procedures, and guidelines for protecting personnel, facilities, and national security information.

Bureau of Diplomatic Security (DS) *(State Dept.), Diplomatic Security Service (DSS), 1801 N. Lynn St., 23rd Floor, Rosslyn, VA 22209; (571) 345-3815. Fax, (202) 647-0122. Christian J. Schurman, Principal Deputy Assistant Secretary. Diplomatic Service Command Center, (571) 345-3146. Public Affairs, (571) 345-2502. Web, www.state.gov/m/ds/c66769.htm*

Conducts background investigations of potential government employees, investigates passport and visa fraud, and warns government employees of any counterintelligence dangers they might encounter.

Bureau of Diplomatic Security (DS) *(State Dept.), International Programs (IP), 1801 N. Lynn St., 22nd*

Floor, #SA20, Rosslyn, VA 22209; (571) 345-3842.
Assiya Asheaf-Miller, Assistant Director.
Web, www.state.gov/m/ds

Provides leadership, support, and oversight of overseas security and law enforcement programs, including local embassy guards, marine security guards, chief of mission and principal officer bodyguards, emergency planning, and surveillance detection.

Bureau of Diplomatic Security (DS) (State Dept.),
Security Infrastructure (SI), 1801 N. Lynn St., 23rd Floor, #SA20, Rosslyn, VA 22209; (571) 345-3791.
Douglas Quiram, Senior Coordinator (Acting).
Web, www.state.gov/m/ds

Manages matters relating to security infrastructure in the functional areas of information security, computer security, and personnel security and suitability.

Bureau of Diplomatic Security (DS) (State Dept.),
Security Technology (ST), 1400 Wilson Blvd., 1st Floor, #SA14, Rosslyn, VA 22209; (703) 312-3667.
John Fitzsimmons, Assistant Director.
Web, www.state.gov/m/ds

Oversees planning, policy development, coordination, and implementation of the technology innovation and cybersecurity programs. Oversees the offices of Cyber Monitoring and Operations, Cyber Threat and Investigations, and Technology Innovation and Engineering.

Bureau of Diplomatic Security (DS) (State Dept.), Threat
Investigations and Analysis (TIA), 1801 N. Lynn St., 23rd Floor, Rosslyn, VA 22209; (571) 345-3809.
Bartle B. Gorman, Assistant Director.
Web, www.state.gov/m/ds

Oversees all threat management programs within the Bureau of Diplomatic Security that analyze, assess, investigate, and disseminate information on threats directed against facilities and personnel overseas and domestically.

Bureau of Diplomatic Security (DS) (State Dept.),
Training, 1801 N. Lynn St., #SA11B, Rosslyn, VA 22209; (571) 226-9760. Robert Weitzel, Assistant Director (Acting).
Web, www.state.gov/m/ds

Trains diplomatic security special agents, prepares personnel to serve at U.S. diplomatic posts in critical and high-threat countries, administers anti-terrorism training to foreign police, and deploys its own agents for training and special protective missions to primarily high-threat overseas posts. Oversees Offices of Antiterrorism Assistance, Training and Performance Support, and Mobile Security Deployments.

Defense Dept. (DoD), *Counterintelligence and Security,*
5000 Defense Pentagon, #3C1088, 20301-5000; (703) 697-5216. Fax, (703) 695-8217. Bill Evanina, Director.
Web, www.defense.gov

Oversees counterintelligence policy and oversight to protect against espionage and other foreign intelligence activities, sabotage, international terrorist activities, and

assassination efforts of foreign powers, organizations, or persons directed against the Defense Dept.

Defense Security Service (Defense Dept.), 27130
Telegraph Rd., Quantico, VA 22134; (571) 305-6083.
Fax, (571) 305-6869. Daniel E. Payne, Director. Public Affairs, (571) 305-6562.
Web, www.dss.mil and Twitter, @DSSPublicAffair

Administers programs to protect classified government information and resources, including the National Industrial Security Program (NISP). Serves the Defense Dept. and other executive departments and agencies. Operates the Center for Development and Security Excellence to educate, train, and enhance awareness of security matters.

Energy Dept. (DOE), *Intelligence and*
Counterintelligence, 1000 Independence Ave. S.W., #2610, 20585; (202) 586-2610. Fax, (202) 287-5999.
Steven K. Black, Director; Charles Durant, Deputy Director of Counterintelligence; Kevin Kremer, Principal Deputy Director of Intelligence.
Web, www.energy.gov/office-intelligence-and-counterintelligence

Identifies and deters intelligence threats directed at Energy Dept. facilities, personnel, information, and technology. Protects nuclear weapons secrets and other sensitive scientific projects.

INTERPOL Washington (Justice Dept.), 950 Pennsylvania Ave., 20530-0001; (202) 616-9000. Fax, (202) 616-8400.
Wayne Salzgaber, Director.
Web, www.justice.gov/interpol-washington,
Twitter, @TheJusticeDept and Facebook, www.facebook.com/DOJ

U.S. representative to INTERPOL; interacts in international investigations of terrorism on behalf of U.S. police. Serves as liaison between foreign and U.S. law enforcement agencies. Headquarters office sponsors forums enabling foreign governments to discuss counterterrorism policy. (Headquarters in Lyons, France.)

National Archives and Records Administration (NARA),
Information Security Oversight (ISOO), 700
Pennsylvania Ave. N.W., #100, 20408-0001; (202) 357-5250. Fax, (202) 357-5907. Mark A. Bradley, Director.
General email, isoo@nara.gov
Web, www.archives.gov/isoo

Receiving guidance from the National Security Council, administers governmentwide security classification program under which information is classified, declassified, and safeguarded for national security purposes. Develops policies and procedures for sensitive unclassified information.

National Nuclear Security Administration (NNSA)
(Energy Dept.), *Defense Nuclear Security (DNS),* 1000
Independence Ave. S.W., #GF261, 20585; (202) 586-8900.
Jeffrey R. Johnson, Associate Administrator.
Web, www.energy.gov/nnsa/nnsa-offices/defense-nuclear-security

Ensures the protective force, physical security, information security, material control and accountability, personnel security, and security program operations and planning measures in agency offices and facilities are effectively being carried out.

National Security Agency (NSA) *(Defense Dept.), 9800 Savage Rd., #6272, Fort Meade, MD 20755-6000; (301) 688-6311. Fax, (301) 688-6198. Gen. Paul M. Nakasone (USA), Director; George C. Barnes, Deputy Director. FOIA Public Liaison Office, (301) 688-6527. Public Affairs and Media, (301) 688-6524.*
General email, nsapao@nsa.gov

Web, www.nsa.gov, Twitter, @NSAGov and Facebook, www.facebook.com/NSAUSGov

Maintains and operates the Defense Dept.'s Computer Security Center; ensures communications and computer security within the government.

Navy Dept. *(Defense Dept.), Naval Criminal Investigative Service, 27130 Telegraph Rd., Quantico, VA 22134; (571) 305-9000. Fax, (571) 305-9115. Andrew Traver, Director. Hotline, (877) 579-3648.*
General email, ncispublicaffairs@ncis.navy.mil

Web, www.navy.mil/local/ncis, Twitter, @RealNCIS and Facebook, www.facebook.com/NCIS.Official

Handles felony criminal investigations, counterintelligence, counterterrorism, and security for the Navy Dept., working with federal, state, local, and foreign agencies to investigate crimes; processes security clearances for the Navy Dept.

MILITARY INSTALLATIONS

General

▶**AGENCIES**

Air Force Dept. *(Defense Dept.), Installations, Environment and Energy (SAF/IEE), Environment, Safety and Infrastructure, 1665 Air Force Pentagon, #4B941, 20330-1665; (703) 697-9297. Fax, (703) 693-7568. Mark A. Correll, Deputy Assistant Secretary. Public Affairs, (703) 697-4936.*
General email, safie.workflow@pentagon.af.mil

Web, www.safie.hq.af.mil/About-Us/Units/Environment-Safety-Infrastructure

Responsible for policy, governance, and oversight of Air Force environmental compliance, natural and cultural resource management, installation energy, facilities and utilities, and occupational health and safety. Interests include radioactive materials management and safety.

Air Force Dept. *(Defense Dept.), Installations, Environment and Energy (SAF/IEE), Installations, 1665 Air Force Pentagon, #4B941, 20330-1665; (703) 695-3592. Jennifer Miller, Deputy Assistant Secretary. Public Affairs, (703) 697-4936.*
Web, www.safie.hq.af.mil/About-Us/Units/Installations

Military office that provides management oversight for Air Force installations, including asset management, base closures, military construction, family housing, community and congressional interface, joint use of airfields, ranges, and disposal of real property.

Air Force Dept. *(Defense Dept.), Installations, Environment and Energy (SAF/IEE), Operational Energy, 1665 Air Force Pentagon, #4B941, 20330-166; (571) 256-4711. Roberto Guerrero, Deputy Assistant Secretary. Public Affairs, (703) 697-4936.*
Web, www.safie.hq.af.mil/About-Us/Units/OpEnergy

Provides policy, governance, and oversight of energy optimization programs, including waste elimination, uninterrupted access to fuel, and improved resiliency.

Army Dept. *(Defense Dept.), Installations, Energy, and Environment, 110 Army Pentagon, #3E464, 20310-0110; (703) 692-9800. Fax, (703) 692-9808. J. Randall Robinson, Assistant Secretary (Acting).*
General email, asaie.webmaster@hqda.army.mil

Web, www.army.mil/asaiee

Civilian office that establishes policy, provides strategic direction and supervises all matters pertaining to infrastructure, Army installations and contingency bases, energy, and environmental programs to enable global Army operations.

Defense Dept. (DoD), *Sustainment, 3400 Defense Pentagon, #1E518, 20301-3500; (703) 697-1369. Fax, (703) 693-0555. Robert H. McMahon, Assistant Secretary.*
Web, www.acq.osd.mil/eie

Oversees and provides guidance on logistics, maintenance, material readiness, strategic mobility, and sustainment for all Defense Dept. domestic and overseas installations.

National Nuclear Security Administration (NNSA) *(Energy Dept.), Naval Nuclear Propulsion Program, Bldg. 197, 1333 Isaac Hull Ave. S.E., MS 1070, 20376; (202) 781-4195. Fax, (202) 781-4588. Adm. James Frank Caldwell Jr., Director.*
Web, www.energy.gov/nnsa/missions/powering-navy

Designs, develops, and operates the militarily effective nuclear propulsion plants and ships. Responsible for maintaining and improving related facilities, radiological controls, and environmental safety.

National Nuclear Security Administration (NNSA) *(Energy Dept.), Safety, Infrastructure, and Operations, 1000 Independence Ave. S.W., #6G092, 20585; (202) 586-4379. James McConnell, Associate Administrator.*
Web, www.energy.gov/nnsa/nnsa-offices/safety-infrastructure-operations

Implements programs, policies, procedures, and new technology to ensure existing facilities are safely operated, managed, and that new facilities are up to safety and quality standards.

▶**CONGRESS**

For a listing of relevant congressional committees and subcommittees, please see pages 608–609 or the Appendix.

Base Closings, Economic Impact

▶AGENCIES

Air Force Dept. *(Defense Dept.), Installations, Environment and Energy (SAF/IEE),* 1665 Air Force Pentagon, #4B941, SAF/IEI, 20330-1665; (703) 695-3592. Fax, (703) 693-7568. John W. Henderson, Assistant Secretary. Public Affairs, (703) 697-4936.
General email, safie.workflow@pentagon.af.mil
Web, www.safie.hq.af.mil

Civilian office that plans and reviews the building, repairing, renovating, and closing of Air Force bases.

Air Force Dept. *(Defense Dept.), Installations, Environment and Energy (SAF/IEE), Installations,* 1665 Air Force Pentagon, #4B941, 20330-1665; (703) 695-3592. Jennifer Miller, Deputy Assistant Secretary. Public Affairs, (703) 697-4936.
Web, www.safie.hq.af.mil/About-Us/Units/Installations

Military office that provides management oversight for implementing base closings and base realignment under the Base Realignment Act (BRAC).

Army Dept. *(Defense Dept.), Employment Policy,* 6010 6th St., #200, Bldg. 1465, Ft. Belvoir, VA 22060-5595; (703) 806-3867. Denetris Winston, Chief.
Web, www.army.mil

Military office responsible for employment policies to assist civilian personnel in cases of Defense Dept. program changes, including base closings.

Defense Dept. (DoD), *Economic Adjustment,* 2231 Crystal Dr., #520, Arlington, VA 22202-4704; (703) 697-2130. Fax, (703) 607-0170. Patrick J. O'Brien, Director, (703) 697-2123.
Web, www.oea.gov and Twitter, @OEAGov

Civilian office that helps community officials develop strategies and coordinate plans to alleviate the economic effect of major defense program changes, including base closings (BRAC) and contract cutbacks.

Defense Dept. (DoD), *Employment and Compensation,* 4800 Mark Center Dr., #06F15, SCTP Division, Alexandria, VA 22350-1100; (703) 882-5196. Hong Miller, Director.
Web, www.dcpas.osd.mil/EC

Manages workforce restructuring programs for Defense Dept. civilians, including downsizing, placement, voluntary early retirement, and transition assistance programs.

Marine Corps *(Defense Dept.), Installation Command, Installation and Logistics Facilities Directorate,* 3000 Marine Corps Pentagon, #2D153A, 20350-3000; (703) 695-8202. Fax, (703) 695-8550. Maj.
Gen. Vincent A. Coglianess (USN), Director.
Web, www.mcicom.marines.mil

Military office that reviews studies on base closings under the Base Realignment Act (BRAC).

Commissaries, PXs, and Service Clubs

▶AGENCIES

Defense Commissary Agency *(Defense Dept.),* 1300 E Ave., Fort Lee, VA 23801-1800; (703) 571-7185. Fax, (703) 571-9297. Robin Schmidt, Washington Office Director; Michael Dowling, Deputy Director.
Web, www.commissaries.com, Twitter, @YourCommissary and Facebook, www.facebook.com/YourCommissary

Serves as a representative for the Defense Commissary Agency in the Pentagon and the Washington, D.C., area. Monitors legislation and regulations.

Defense Dept. (DoD), *Army and Air Force Exchange, Washington Office,* 2530 Crystal Dr., #4158, Arlington, VA 22202; (703) 602-8975. Thomas C. Shull, Director; Gregg Cox, Senior Vice President of Government Affairs, (703) 602-6684. Toll-free, (800) 527-2345. Toll-free store locator, (800) 527-6790.
Web, www.shopmyexchange.com

Delivers goods and services to the military community at competitively low prices. Returns earnings to Army and Air Force to support morale, welfare, and recreation programs. (Headquarters in Dallas, Tex.)

Navy Dept. *(Defense Dept.), Manpower and Reserve Affairs,* 1000 Navy Pentagon, #4E590, 20350-1000; (703) 695-4333. Fax, (703) 614-4103. Gregory J. Slavonic, Assistant Secretary.
Web, www.navy.mil

Civilian office that develops policies for Navy and Marine Corps commissaries, exchanges, and service clubs and reviews their operations.

Navy Dept. *(Defense Dept.), Navy Exchange Service Command,* 701 S. Courthouse Rd., Arlington, VA 22204; (757) 631-4170. Andy Howell, Vice President of Government Affairs. Navy Exchange, (757) 631-4170. Online store, (877) 810-9030.
Web, www.mynavyexchange.com and Facebook, www.facebook.com/NavyExchange

Civilian office that serves as a liaison among the Navy Exchange Service Command, the Navy Supply Systems Command, Congress, and the Defense Dept. (Headquarters in Virginia Beach, Va.)

▶CONGRESS

For a listing of relevant congressional committees and sub-committees, please see pages 608–609 or the Appendix.

▶NONGOVERNMENTAL

American Logistics Assn., 1101 Vermont Ave. N.W., #1002, 20005; (202) 466-2520. Fax, (240) 823-9181. L. Maurice Branch, President, ext. 4162.
General email, membership@ala-national.org
Web, www.ala-national.org

Membership: suppliers of military commissaries and exchanges. Acts as liaison between the Defense Dept. and service contractors; monitors legislation and testifies on issues of interest to members. Monitors legislation.

United Service Organizations (USO), *2111 Wilson Blvd., #1200, Arlington, VA 22201-7677 (mailing address: P.O. Box 96860, Washington, DC 20077); (703) 908-6400. Fax, (703) 908-6402. J.D. Crouch II, President. Toll-free, (888) 484-3876.*
Web, www.uso.org and Twitter, @the_USO

Voluntary civilian organization chartered by Congress. Provides military personnel and their families in the United States and overseas with social, educational, and recreational programs.

Construction, Housing, and Real Estate

▶**AGENCIES**

Air Force Dept. *(Defense Dept.),* **Civil Engineer Center (AFCEC),** *1260 Air Force Pentagon, 20330; (703) 693-4301. Fax, (703) 693-4893. Terry G. Edwards, Director.*
General email, afcec.pa@us.af.mil

Web, www.afcec.af.mil, Twitter, @TheAFCEC and Facebook, www.facebook.com/TheAFCEC

Military office that plans and directs construction of Air Force facilities in the United States and overseas. Oversees the Civil Engineer Center in San Antonio, Texas.

Air Force Dept. *(Defense Dept.),* **Housing,** *1260 Air Force Pentagon, #4C1057, 20330-1260; (703) 693-4193. Sheila Schwartz, Branch Chief.*
Web, www.housing.af.mil

Military office that manages the operation of Air Force housing on military installations in the United States and overseas.

Air Force Dept. *(Defense Dept.),* **Installations, Environment and Energy (SAF/IEE),** *1665 Air Force Pentagon, #4B941, SAF/IEI, 20330-1665; (703) 695-3592. Fax, (703) 693-7568. John W. Henderson, Assistant Secretary. Public Affairs, (703) 697-4936.*
General email, safie.workflow@pentagon.af.mil

Web, www.safie.hq.af.mil

Civilian office that plans and reviews construction policies and programs of Air Force military facilities (including the Military Construction Program), basing of major weapons systems and units, housing programs, and real estate buying, selling, and leasing in the United States.

Air Force Dept. *(Defense Dept.),* **Installations, Environment and Energy (SAF/IEE), Installations,** *1665 Air Force Pentagon, #4B941, 20330-1665; (703) 695-3592. Jennifer Miller, Deputy Assistant Secretary. Public Affairs, (703) 697-4936.*
Web, www.safie.hq.af.mil/About-Us/Units/Installations

Military office that provides management oversight for Air Force installations, including asset management,

military construction, family housing, and disposal of real property.

Army Corps of Engineers *(Defense Dept.),* *441 G St. N.W., #3K05, 20314-1000; (202) 761-0001. Fax, (202) 761-4463. Lt. Gen. Todd T. Semonite (USA), Chief of Engineers. Press, (202) 761-0011.*
General email, hq-publicaffairs@usace.army.mil

Web, www.usace.army.mil and Twitter, @USACEHQ

Military office that establishes policy and designs, directs, and manages civil works and military construction projects of the Army Corps of Engineers; directs the Army's real estate leasing and buying for military installations and civil works projects.

Defense Dept. (DoD), *Facilities Investment and Management, 3400 Defense Pentagon, #5C646, 20301-3400; (703) 697-6195. Fax, (703) 693-2659. Michael McAndrew, Director.*
Web, www.acq.osd.mil/eie/FIM/FIM_index.html

Responsible for military construction and facility-related legislative proposals and policies to manage worldwide defense installations and to acquire, construct, maintain, modernize, and dispose of defense facilities. Prepares the department's annual military construction budget; manages military construction, real property maintenance, and base operations; oversees host nation programs for facilities; and develops procedures for measuring the effect of defense facilities on military readiness.

Marine Corps *(Defense Dept.),* **Installation Command, Installation and Logistics Facilities Directorate,** *3000 Marine Corps Pentagon, #2D153A, 20350-3000; (703) 695-8202. Fax, (703) 695-8550. Maj. Gen. Vincent A. Coglianess (USN), Director.*
Web, www.mcicom.marines.mil

Military office responsible for military construction and the acquisition, management, and disposal of Marine Corps real property.

Marine Corps *(Defense Dept.),* **Installations and Environment,** *3250 Catlin Ave., #235, Quantico, VA 22134-5001; (703) 784-2557. Fax, (703) 784-2332. Kirk Nelson, Director, (703) 784-2557. Emergency maintenance, (703) 784-2072.*
Web, www.mcicom.marines.mil

Control point for the Marine Corps divisions of public works, family housing, and natural resources and environmental affairs.

Navy Dept. *(Defense Dept.),* **Energy, Installations, and Environment,** *1000 Navy Pentagon, #4E731, 20350-1000; (703) 693-4530. Fax, (703) 693-1165. Phyllis L. Bayer, Assistant Secretary.*
Web, www.secnav.navy.mil/eie/pages

Civilian office that monitors and reviews construction of Navy military facilities and housing and the buying and leasing of real estate in the United States and overseas. Interests include environmental planning, protection and restoration; conservation of natural resources.

Navy Dept. *(Defense Dept.), Naval Facilities Engineering Command,* 1322 Patterson Ave. S.E., #100, Washington Navy Yard, DC, 20374-5065; (202) 685-9499. Fax, (202) 685-1463. Rear Adm. John Korka (USN), Commander. Press and public affairs, (202) 685-9232.
Web, www.navy.mil/local/navfachq and
Twitter, @NAVFAC

Military command that plans, designs, and constructs facilities for Navy and other Defense Dept. activities around the world and manages Navy public works, utilities, environmental programs, and real estate.

Navy Dept. *(Defense Dept.), Real Estate,* 1322 Patterson Ave. S.E. #1000, Washington Navy Yard, DC, 20350; (703) 685-9335. Jim Omans, Director.
Web, www.navfac.navy.mil/products_and_services/am/products_and services/real_estate.html and
Twitter, @NAVFAC

Military office that directs the Navy's real estate leasing, buying, and disposition for military installations.

U.S. Coast Guard (USCG) *(Homeland Security Dept.), Housing Programs,* CG-1333, 2703 Martin Luther King Jr. Ave. S.E., MS 7907, 20593-7907; (202) 475-5407. Fax, (202) 475-5927. Melissa Fredrickson, Chief.
General email, HQS-SMB-CG-HOUSING@uscg.mil
Web, www.dcms.uscg.mil

Provides housing and management for uniformed Coast Guard personnel.

Veterans Affairs Dept. (VA), *Construction and Facilities Management,* 425 Eye St. N.W., 6th Floor, 20001 (mailing address: 810 Vermont Ave. N.W., MS 003C, Washington, DC 20420); (202) 632-4607. Anthony E. Costa, Executive Director (Acting), (202) 632-4606.
General email, cfm@va.gov
Web, www.cfm.va.gov

Principal construction and real estate arm of the Veterans Administration. Manages all major VA construction and leasing projects.

▶ **CONGRESS**

For a listing of relevant congressional committees and subcommittees, please see pages 608–609 or the Appendix.

PROCUREMENT, ACQUISITION, AND LOGISTICS

General

▶ **AGENCIES**

Air Force Dept. *(Defense Dept.), Air Force Aquisition (SAF/AQ),* 1060 Air Force Pentagon, #4E962, 20330-1060; (703) 697-3039. Fax, (703) 693-6400. Dr. Will Roper, Assistant Secretary.
Web, ww3.safaq.hq.af.mil

Air Force office that directs and reviews Air Force procurement policies and programs.

Air Force Dept. *(Defense Dept.), Air Force Aquisition (SAF/AQ), Program Executive Office for Combat and Mission Support (PEO-CM),* Joint Base Anacostia-Bolling, 112 Luke Ave., #330, 20032; (202) 404-3207. Fax, (202) 404-6351. Randall D. Culpepper, Executive Officer (Acting).
General email, peocm-shared@pentagon.af.mil
Web, ww3.safaq.hq.af.mil/Organizations/AFPEO-CM

Regulates the acquisition and delivery of the Air Force's operational and mission support services.

Air Force Dept. *(Defense Dept.), Air Force Aquisition, Contracting (SAF/AQC),* 1060 Air Force Pentagon, 20330-1060; (571) 256-2397. Fax, (571) 256-2431.
Pamela C. Schwenke, Associate Deputy Assistant Secretary; Major General Cameron G. Holt, Deputy Assistant Secretary.
Web, ww3.safaq.hq.af.mil/contracting

Develops, implements, and enforces contracting policies on Air Force acquisitions worldwide, including research and development services, weapons systems, logistics services, and operational contracts.

Air Force Dept. *(Defense Dept.), Air Force Aquisition, Global Power Programs (SAF/AQP),* 1060 Air Force Pentagon, #4A122, 20330; (571) 256-0191. Fax, (571) 256-0280. Maj. Gen. Michael A. Fantini, Director. Public inquiries, (703) 697-3039.
Web, ww3.safaq.hq.af.mil/Organizations

Military office that directs Air Force acquisition and development programs within the tactical arena.

Air Force Dept. *(Defense Dept.), Air Force Aquisition, Logistics and Product Support, (SAF/AQD),* 1060 Air Force Pentagon, #4D138, 20330-1060; (703) 693-2185. Fax, (571) 256-0344. Lawrence S. Kingsley, Deputy Assistant Secretary.
Web, ww3.safaq.hq.af.mil/Organizations/SAF-AQD/

Facilitates the supply chain process to provide secure and sustainable resources for the Air Force.

Army Dept. *(Defense Dept.), Procurement,* 103 Army Pentagon, #2D528, 20310-0103; (703) 695-2488. Brig. Gen. Michael Hoskin, Deputy Assistant Secretary (Acting).
Web, www.army.mil

Directs and reviews Army procurement policies.

Defense Acquisition University *(Defense Dept.),* 9820 Belvoir Rd., Fort Belvoir, VA 22060-5565; (703) 805-3360. Fax, (703) 805-2639. James P. Woolsey, President. Toll-free, (866) 568-6924.
General email, DAUhelp@dau.mil
Web, www.dau.mil and Twitter, @DAUNow

Academic institution that offers courses to military and civilian personnel who specialize in acquisition and procurement. Conducts research to support and improve management of defense systems acquisition programs.

Defense Dept. (DoD), *Acquisition, Technology, and Logistics,* 3010 Defense Pentagon, #3E1010, 20301-3010; (703) 697-7021. Ellen Lord, Under Secretary; Alan R. Shaffer, Deputy Under Secretary.
Web, www.acq.osd.mil

Supervises Dept.'s acquisitions; establishes policies for acquisition, including procurement of goods and services, research and development, developmental testing, and contract administration, as well as policies for logistics, maintenance, and sustainment support.

Defense Dept. (DoD), *Defense Acquisition Regulations System (DARS) Directorate and DARS Council,* 3060 Defense Pentagon, #3B941, 20301-3060; (571) 372-6176. Linda Neilson, Deputy Director.
Web, www.acq.osd.mil/dpap/dars

Develops procurement regulations and manages changes to procurement regulations for the Defense Dept.

Defense Dept. (DoD), *Defense Procurement and Acquisition Policy,* 3060 Defense Pentagon, #3C152, 20301-3060; (703) 695-4235. Fax, (571) 256-7004. Kim Herrington, Director (Acting).
Web, www.acq.osd.mil/dpap

Responsible for all acquisition and procurement policy matters for the Defense Dept. Serves as principal adviser to the under secretary of defense for acquisition, technology, and logistics on strategies relating to all major weapon systems programs, major automated information systems programs, and services acquisitions.

Defense Dept. (DoD), *Logistics and Materiel Readiness,* 3500 Defense Pentagon, #1E518, 20301-3500; (703) 697-1369. Fax, (703) 693-0555. Robert H. McMahon, Assistant Secretary.
General email, osd.pentagon.ousd-atl.mxb@mail.mil
Web, www.acq.osd.mil/log

Formulates and implements department policies and programs for the conduct of logistics, maintenance, materiel readiness, strategic mobility, and sustainable support.

Defense Dept. (DoD), *Operational Test and Evaluation,* 1700 Defense Pentagon, #3E1088, 20301-1700; (703) 697-3655. Fax, (703) 693-5248. Robert Behler, Director. Press, (703) 697-5331.
Web, www.dote.osd.mil

Ensures that major acquisitions, including weapons systems, are operationally effective and suitable prior to full-scale investment. Provides the secretary of defense and Congress with independent assessment of these programs.

Defense Logistics Agency *(Defense Dept.),* 8725 John Jay Kingman Rd., #2533, Fort Belvoir, VA 22060-6221; (703) 767-5200. Fax, (703) 767-5207. Lt. Gen. Darrell Williams, Director. Press, (703) 767-6200.
Web, www.dla.mil

Administers defense contracts; acquires, stores, and distributes food, clothing, medical, and other supplies used by the military services and other federal agencies; administers programs related to logistical support for the military services; and assists military services with developing, acquiring, and using technical information and defense materiel and disposing of materiel no longer needed.

Defense Logistics Agency *(Defense Dept.), Energy,* 8725 John Jay Kingman Rd., #4950, Fort Belvoir, VA 22060-6222; (703) 767-5042. Fax, (703) 767-9690. Brig. Gen. Albert G. Miller (USAF), Commander. Public Affairs, (703) 767-4108. Toll-free, (877) 352-2255.
General email, dlaenergypublicaffairs@dla.mil
Web, www.dla.mil/Energy.aspx

Provides the Defense Dept. and other federal agencies with products and services to meet energy-related needs; facilitates the cycle of storage and deployment of fuels and other energy sources, including petroleum, electricity, water, and natural gas, as well as space and missile propellants. Provides information on alternative fuels and renewable energy and serves as the executive agent for the Defense Dept.'s bulk petroleum supply chain.

Defense Logistics Agency *(Defense Dept.), Logistics Operations,* 8725 John Jay Kingman Rd., Fort Belvoir, VA 22060-6221; (703) 767-1600. Fax, (703) 767-1588. Maj. Gen. Mark K. Johnson (USAF), Director. Press, (703) 767-6200.
Web, www.dla.mil/HQ/LogisticsOperations.aspx

Oversees management, storage, and distribution of items used to support logistics for the military services and federal agencies. Synchronizes the Defense Logistics Agency's capabilities with the combatant commands, military services, the joint staff, other combat support defense agencies, and designated federal agencies. Provides logistics policy, with an emphasis on modernizing business systems and maximizing readiness and combat logistics support.

Defense Logistics Agency *(Defense Dept.), Strategic Materials,* 8725 John Jay Kingman Rd., #3229, Fort Belvoir, VA 22060-6223; (703) 767-5500. Fax, (703) 767-3316. Ronnie Favors, Administrator. Press, (703) 767-6479.
Web, www.dla.mil/HQ/Acquisition/Strategicmaterials.aspx

Manages the national defense stockpile of strategic and critical materials. Purchases strategic materials, including beryllium and newly developed high-tech alloys. Disposes of excess materials, including tin, silver, industrial diamond stones, tungsten, and vegetable tannin.

Marine Corps *(Defense Dept.), Contracts,* 701 S. Courthouse Rd., #2000, Arlington, VA 22204; (703) 604-3584. Fax, (703) 604-6675. Vacant, Deputy Director.
Web, www.iandl.marines.mil/divisions/contracts(LB).aspx

Military office that directs Marine Corps procurement programs.

National Nuclear Security Administration (NNSA) *(Energy Dept.), Acquisition and Project Management,* 1000 Independence Ave. S.W., #IJ009, 20585; (202) 586-5627. Fax, (202) 586-6002. Robert B. Raines, Associate Administrator.
Web, www.energy.gov/nnsa/nnsa-offices/acquisition-and-project-management

Monitors necessary federal acquisition and project management policies and regulations. Seeks to improve agency's program cost and scheduling performance.

Navy Dept. *(Defense Dept.)*, *Acquisition and Procurement*, 1000 Navy Pentagon, #BF992A, 20350-1000; (703) 614-9595. Elliott B. Branch, Deputy Assistant Secretary; Capt. John Windom, Executive Director (Acting). Web, www.secnav.navy.mil/rda/Pages/DASN_AP.aspx

Directs and reviews Navy acquisition and procurement policy.

U.S. Coast Guard (USCG) *(Homeland Security Dept.)*, *Acquisition Directorate*, 2703 Martin Luther King Jr. Ave. S.E., MS 7816, 20593-7816; (202) 475-3000. Fax, (202) 372-8432. Rear Adm. Michael J. Haycock, Assistant Commandant.
General email, acquisition@uscg.mil
Web, www.dcms.uscg.mil/Our-Organization/Assistant-Commandant-for-Acquisitions-CG-9/

Administers all procurement made through the Acquisition Contract Support Division.

► **CONGRESS**

For a listing of relevant congressional committees and subcommittees, please see pages 608–609 or the Appendix.

► **NONGOVERNMENTAL**

CompTIA, *Public Advocacy,* 515 2nd St. N.E., 20002; (202) 503-3629. Todd Thibodeaux, President; Elizabeth (Liz) Hyman, Executive Vice President, Public Advocacy, (202) 503-3621. Press, (202) 682-4458. Toll-free, (866) 835-8020.
General email, martes@comptia.org
Web, www.comptia.org

Membership: companies providing information technology and electronics products and services to government organizations at the federal, state, and local levels. Provides information on governmental affairs, business intelligence, industry trends, and forecasts. Monitors legislation and regulation on federal procurement of technology products and services. (Headquarters in Downers Grove, Ill.)

National Defense Transportation Assn. (NDTA), 50 S. Pickett St., #220, Alexandria, VA 22304; (703) 751-5011. Fax, (703) 823-8761. Vice Adm. William A. Brown (USN, Ret.), President.
Web, www.ndtahq.com and Twitter, @NDTAHQ

Membership: transportation users, manufacturers, and mode carriers; information technology firms; and related military, government, and civil interests worldwide. Promotes a strong U.S. transportation capability through coordination of private industry, government, and the military.

16 Science and Technology

GENERAL POLICY AND ANALYSIS

Basic Resources

▶AGENCIES

National Institute of Standards and Technology (NIST) *(Commerce Dept.), Special Programs Office,* 100 Bureau Dr., MS 4701, Gaithersburg, MD 20899-4701; (301) 975-4447. Fax, (301) 975-8972. Richard R. Cavanagh, Director. General information, (301) 975-2756.
Web, www.nist.gov/spo

Fosters collaboration among government, military, academic, professional, and private organizations to respond to critical national needs through science-based standards and technology innovation, including areas of forensic science and information technology.

National Institutes of Health (NIH) *(Health and Human Services Dept.), Science Policy (OSP),* 6705 Rockledge Dr., MSC 7985, Bethesda, MD 20892-7985; (301) 496-9838. Fax, (301) 496-9839. Carrie D. Wolinetz, Associate Director, (301) 496-2122.
General email, sciencepolicy@od.nih.gov
Web, http://osp.od.nih.gov

Advises the NIH director on science policy issues affecting the medical research community. Participates in the development of new policy and program initiatives. Monitors and coordinates agency planning and evaluation activities. Plans and implements a comprehensive science education program. Develops and implements NIH policies and procedures for the safe conduct of recombinant DNA and other biotechnology activities.

National Science Foundation (NSF), 2415 Eisenhower Ave., Alexandria, VA 22314; (703) 292-5111. Fax, (703) 292-9232. France A. Córdova, Director, (703) 292-8000. Government Affairs, (703) 292-8070. Library, (703) 292-7830. Publications, (703) 292-7827. TTY, (703) 292-5090. TTY Toll-free, (800) 281-8749.
General email, info@nsf.gov
Web, www.nsf.gov, Twitter, @NSF,
Facebook, www.facebook.com/US.NSF and
YouTube, www.youtube.com/user/VideosatNSF

Sponsors scientific and engineering research; develops and helps implement science and engineering education programs; fosters dissemination of scientific information; promotes international cooperation within the scientific community; and assists with national science policy planning.

National Science Foundation (NSF), *National Science Board,* 2415 Eisenhower Ave., Room W19200, Alexandria, VA 22134; (703) 292-7000. Fax, (703) 292-9008. John Veysey, Executive Officer. TTY, (800) 281-8749.
General email, NationalScienceBrd@nsf.gov
Web, www.nsf.gov/nsb

Formulates policy for the National Science Foundation; advises the president on national science policy.

Office of Management and Budget (OMB) *(Executive Office of the President), Energy, Science, and Water,* 725 17th St. N.W., #8002, 20503; (202) 395-3404. Fax, (202) 395-3049. Jim Herz, Associate Director. Press, (202) 395-7254.
Web, www.whitehouse.gov/omb

Assists and advises the OMB director in budget preparation; analyzes and evaluates programs in space and science, including the activities of the National Science Foundation and the National Aeronautics and Space Administration; coordinates OMB science, energy, and space policies and programs.

Office of Science and Technology Policy (OSTP) *(Executive Office of the President),* Eisenhower Executive Office Bldg., 1650 Pennsylvania Ave. N.W., 20504; (202) 456-4444. Fax, (202) 456-6021. Michael Kratsios, Deputy Chief US Chief Technology Officer. Press, (202) 456-6124.
General email, info@ostp.gov
Web, www.ostp.gov and Twitter, @WHOSTP

Advises the president and Executive Branch on the scientific, engineering, and technological aspects of the economy, national security, homeland security, health, foreign relations, the environment, and the technological recovery and use of resources, among other topics. Leads interagency science and technology policy coordination efforts.

Office of Science and Technology Policy (OSTP) *(Executive Office of the President), National Science and Technology Council,* Eisenhower Executive Office Bldg., 1650 Pennsylvania Ave. N.W., 20504; (202) 456-4444. Fax, (202) 456-6021. Michael Kratsios, Deputy U.S. Chief Technology Officer.
General email, info@ostp.gov
Web, www.ostp.gov

Coordinates science and technology research, development activities, policies, and programs that involve more than one federal agency. Activities concern earth sciences, materials, forestry research, and radiation policy.

Office of Science and Technology Policy (OSTP) *(Executive Office of the President), Science,* Eisenhower Executive Office Bldg., 1650 Pennsylvania Ave. N.W., 20504; (202) 456-4444. Fax, (202) 456-6027. Lloyd Whitman, Assistant Director.
General email, info@ostp.gov
Web, www.ostp.gov

Advises the president and others within the executive office on the impact of science and technology on domestic and international affairs; coordinates executive office and federal agency actions related to these issues. Analyzes policies on biological, physical, social, and behavioral sciences and engineering; coordinates executive office and federal agency actions related to these issues. Evaluates the effectiveness of government science programs. Provides technical support to Homeland Security Dept.

Office of Science and Technology Policy (OSTP) *(Executive Office of the President), Technology and Innovation,* Eisenhower Executive Office Bldg., 1650 Pennsylvania Ave. N.W., 20504; (202) 456-4444. Fax, (202)

456-6021. *Winter Casey, Senior Policy Advisor.*
Press, engagement@ostp.eop.gov.
General email, info@ostp.gov
Web, www.ostp.gov

Analyzes policies and advises the president on technology and related issues of physical, computational, and space sciences; coordinates executive office and federal agency actions related to these issues. Issues include national broadband access; advancing health IT; modernizing public safety communications; and clean manufacturing.

Office of Science *(Energy Dept.), 1000 Independence Ave.*
S.W., #7B058, 20585; (202) 586-5430. Fax, (202) 586-4120.
Vacant, Director; J. Stephen Binkley, Deputy Director of
Science Programs.
Web, https://science.energy.gov and Twitter, @doescience

Advises the secretary on the department's physical science and energy research and development programs; the management of the nonweapons multipurpose laboratories; and education and training activities required for basic and applied research. Manages the department's high-energy physics, nuclear physics, fusion energy sciences, basic energy sciences, health and environmental research, and computational and technology research. Provides and operates the large-scale facilities required for research in the physical and life sciences.

►CONGRESS

For a listing of relevant congressional committees and subcommittees, please see pages 682–683 or the Appendix.

Government Accountability Office (GAO), *Natural*
Resources and Environment (NRE), 441 G St. N.W.,
#2T23-A, 20548 (mailing address: 441 G St. N.W., #2T23A,
Washington, DC 20548); (202) 512-3841. Mark Gaffigan,
Managing Director.
Web, www.gao.gov/careers/nre.html

Audits, analyzes, and evaluates for Congress federal agriculture, food safety, and energy programs; provides guidance on issues including efforts to ensure a reliable and environmentally sound energy supply, land and water resources management, protection of the environment, hazardous and nuclear wastes threat reduction, food safety, and investment in science.

►NONGOVERNMENTAL

American Assn. for the Advancement of Science (AAAS),
1200 New York Ave. N.W., 12th Floor, 20005; (202) 326-
6400. Rush D. Holt, Chief Executive Officer. Press, (202)
326-6440.
General email, ehr@aaas.org
Web, www.aaas.org, Twitter, @AAAS and Facebook,
www.facebook.com/AAAS-Science

Membership: scientists, affiliated scientific organizations, and individuals interested in science. Promotes science education; the increased participation of women, minorities, and the disabled in the science and technology workforce; the responsible use of science in public policy;

international cooperation in science; and the increased public engagement with science and technology. Sponsors national and international symposia, workshops, and meetings; publishes *Science* magazine.

Center for Strategic and International Studies,
Technology Policy Program, 1616 Rhode Island Ave.
N.W., 20036; (202) 775-3175. Fax, (202) 775-3199.
James Andrew Lewis, Director.
General email, techpolicy@csis.org
Web, www.csis.org/programs/technology-policy-program
and *Twitter, @CyberCSIS*

Conducts and publishes research on emerging technologies, intelligence reform, and space and globalization programs. Interests include cybersecurity, privacy and surveillance, technology and innovation, and Internet governance.

Council of Scientific Society Presidents, *1155 16th St.*
N.W., 20036; (202) 872-6230. David Baltensperger, Chair.
Membership, (254) 776-3550.
General email, info@sciencepresidents.org
Web, http://cssp.us

Membership: presidents, presidents-elect, and immediate past presidents of professional scientific societies and federations. Supports professional science education. Serves as a forum for discussion of emerging scientific issues, formulates national science policy, and develops the nation's scientific leadership.

Federation of American Scientists (FAS), *1112 16th St.*
N.W., #400, 20036; (202) 546-3300. Fax, (202) 675-1010.
Ali Nouri, President.
General email, fas@fas.org
Web, www.fas.org, Twitter, @FAScientists and
Facebook, www.facebook.com/fascientists

Conducts studies and monitors legislation on issues and problems related to science and technology, especially U.S. nuclear arms policy, energy, arms transfer, and civil aerospace issues.

Information Technology and Innovation Foundation,
1101 K St. N.W., #610, 20005; (202) 449-1351. Fax, (202)
638-4922. Robert D. Atkinson, President; Lindsay Bednar,
Communications Director. Press, (202) 626-5744.
General email, mail@itif.org
Web, www.itif.org, Twitter, @ITIFdc and Facebook,
www.facebook.com/innovationpolicy

Nonprofit think tank that supports the advancement of science and technology. Studies and publishes reports on policy. Holds forums for policymakers to discuss issues affecting technological innovation.

National Geographic Society, *Committee for Research*
and Exploration, 1145 17th St. N.W., 20036-4688; (202)
862-8264. Fax, (202) 429-5729. Peter H. Raven, Chair.
TTY, (800) 548-9797.
General email, cre@ngs.org
Web, www.nationalgeographic.org/funding-opportunities/
grants

Sponsors basic research grants in the sciences, including anthropology, archaeology, astronomy, biology, botany, ecology, physical and human geography, geology, oceanography, paleontology, and zoology. To apply for grants, see website.

National Research Council (NRC), *Keck Center, 500 5th St. N.W., 20001; (202) 334-2000. Fax, (202) 334-2419. Marcia McNutt, Chair; C.D. (Dan) Mote Jr., Vice Chair; Victor J. Dzau, Vice Chair; Bruce B. Darling, Executive Officer. Library, (202) 334-2125. Press, (202) 334-2138. Publications, (800) 624-6242.*
General email, news@nas.edu

Web, www.nationalacademies.org, Twitter, @theNASEM and Facebook, www.facebook.com/NationalAcademies

Serves as the principal operating agency of the National Academy of Sciences, National Academy of Engineering, and the National Academy of Medicine. Program units focus on physical, social, and life sciences; applications of science, including medicine, transportation, and education; international affairs; and U.S. government policy. Library open to the public by appointment.

National Research Council (NRC), *Government-University-Industry Research Roundtable (GUIRR), Keck Center, 500 5th St. N.W., #WS516, 20001; (202) 334-3486. Fax, (202) 334-1369. Susan Sauer Sloan, Director; Al Grasso, Co-chair; Lahlrie Leshia, Co-chair.*
General email, guirr@nas.edu

Web, http://sites.nationalacademies.org/pga/guirr

Forum sponsored by the National Academy of Sciences, National Academy of Engineering, and Institute of Medicine. Provides scientists, engineers, and members of government, academia, and industry with an opportunity to discuss ways to catalyze productive cross-sector collaboration, take action on scientific matters of national importance, and improve the infrastructure for science and technology research.

Society for Science and the Public, *1719 N St. N.W., 20036; (202) 785-2255. Fax, (202) 785-3751. Maya Ajmera, Chief Executive Officer. Toll-free, (800) 552-4412.*
Web, www.societyforscience.org, Twitter, @Society4Science
General email, ssp@societyforscience.org

Promotes understanding and appreciation of science and the role it plays in human advancement. Sponsors science competitions and other science education programs in schools; awards scholarships. Publishes *Science News* and *Science News for Kids.* Provides funds and training to select U.S. science and math teachers who serve under-resourced students.

Union of Concerned Scientists, *Washington Office, 1825 K St. N.W., #800, 20006; (202) 223-6133. Fax, (202) 223-6162. Kenneth Kimmell, President.*
General email, ucs@ucsusa.org

Web, www.ucsusa.org, Twitter, @UCSUSA and Facebook, www.facebook.com/unionofconcernedscientists

Science advocacy organization with interests in the areas of clean energy, clean vehicles, food and agriculture, global warming, nuclear power, and nuclear weapons. (Headquarters in Cambridge, Mass.)

Data, Statistics, and References

▶**AGENCIES**

Dibner Library of the History of Science and Technology *(Smithsonian Institution), 12th St. and Constitution Ave. N.W., NMAH 1041, MRC 672, 20560 (mailing address: P.O. Box 37012, MRC 154, Washington, DC 20013-7012); (202) 633-3872. Lilla Vekerdy, Head of Special Collections. Press, (202) 633-1522.*
General email, Dibnerlibrary@si.edu

Web, www.library.si.edu/libraries/dibner-library-history-science-and-technology

Collection includes major holdings in the history of science and technology dating from the fifteenth century to the nineteenth century. Extensive collections in engineering, transportation, chemistry, mathematics, physics, electricity, and astronomy. Open to the public by appointment.

Goddard Space Flight Center *(National Aeronautics and Space Administration), Science Proposal Support Office (SPSO), 8800 Greenbelt Rd., Code 605, Greenbelt, MD 20771; (301) 286-0807. Fax, (301) 286-1772. David T. Leisawitz, Chief, (301) 286-0807.*
General email, spso@gsfc.nasa.gov

Web, http://science.gsfc.nasa.gov/spso

Supports the writing of proposals for NASA, within the Goddard Space Flight Center.

Goddard Space Flight Center *(National Aeronautics and Space Administration), Solar System Exploration Data Services (SSEDSO), 8800 Greenbelt Rd., Code 690.1, Greenbelt, MD 20771; (301) 286-1743. Fax, (301) 286-1771. Thomas Morgan, Head (Acting), (301) 286-1743.*
General email, request@nssdc.gsfc.nasa.gov

Web, http://ssedso.gsfc.nasa.gov

Coordinates data management and archiving plans within NASA's Science Mission. Operates the National Space Science Data Center (NSSDC) as a permanent archive for data associated with NASA's missions, the Crustal Dynamics Data Information System (CDDIS), and the Planetary Data System (PDS).

National Institute of Standards and Technology (NIST) *(Commerce Dept.), 100 Bureau Dr., Bldg. 101, #A1134, Gaithersburg, MD 20899-1000 (mailing address: 100 Bureau Dr., MS 1000, Gaithersburg, MD 20899); (301) 975-2300. Fax, (301) 869-8972. Walter Copan, Under Secretary. TTY, (800) 877-8339.*
General email, director@nist.gov

Web, www.nist.gov

Nonregulatory agency that serves as national reference and measurement laboratory for the physical and engineering sciences.

National Institute of Standards and Technology (NIST) *(Commerce Dept.), Information Services, Research*

SCIENCE AND TECHNOLOGY RESOURCES IN CONGRESS

For a complete listing of congressional committees, including their full contact information, leadership, membership, and jurisdictions, please refer to the Appendix on pages 827–948.

HOUSE:

House Administration Committee, (202) 225-8281.
Web, cha.house.gov

House Agriculture Committee, (202) 225-2171.
Web, agriculture.house.gov

Subcommittee on Biotechnology, Horticulture, and Research, (202) 225-2171.

Subcommittee on Conservation and Forestry, (202) 225-2171.

House Appropriations Committee, (202) 225-2771.
Web, appropriations.house.gov

Subcommittee on Commerce, Justice, Science, and Related Agencies, (202) 225-3351.

Subcommittee on Interior, Environment, and Related Agencies, (202) 225-3081.

Subcommittee on Labor, Health and Human Services, Education, and Related Agencies, (202) 225-3508.

House Armed Services Committee, (202) 225-4151.
Web, armedservices.house.gov

Subcommittee on Emerging Threats and Capabilities, (202) 226-2843.

House Education and the Workforce Committee, (202) 225-4527.
Web, edworkforce.house.gov

Subcommittee on Early Childhood, Elementary, and Secondary Education, (202) 225-4527.

Subcommittee on Higher Education and Workforce Development, (202) 225-4527.

House Energy and Commerce Committee, (202) 225-2927.
Web, energycommerce.house.gov

Subcommittee on Communications and Technology, (202) 225-2927.

House Homeland Security Committee, (202) 226-8417.
Web, homeland.house.gov

Subcommittee on Cybersecurity and Infrastructure Protection, (202) 226-8417.

House Judiciary Committee, (202) 225-3951.
Web, judiciary.house.gov

Subcommittee on Courts, Intellectual Property, and the Internet, (202) 225-5741.

House Natural Resources Committee, (202) 225-2761.
Web, naturalresources.house.gov

Subcommittee on Energy and Mineral Resources, (202) 225-9297.

Subcommittee on Federal Lands, (202) 226-7736.

Subcommittee on Oversight and Investigations, (202) 225-7107.

Subcommittee on Water, Power, and Oceans, (202) 225-8331.

House Oversight and Government Reform Committee, (202) 225-5074.
Web, oversight.house.gov

Subcomittee on Information Technology, (202) 225-5074.

House Science, Space, and Technology Committee, (202) 225-6371.
Web, science.house.gov

Library, 100 Bureau Dr., MS 2500, Gaithersburg, MD 20899-2500; (301) 975-3052. Fax, (301) 869-8071. Susan Makar, Librarian, (301) 975-3054. General email, library@nist.gov

Web, www.nist.gov/nvl

Creates and maintains a virtual knowledge base that supports research and administrative needs for the institute. Includes material on engineering, chemistry, physics, mathematics, materials science, and computer science. Home to NIST museum and history program. Publication and information services available to the public.

National Institute of Standards and Technology (NIST) *(Commerce Dept.), Information Technology Lab, Statistical Engineering, Bldg. 222, 100 Bureau Dr., #A-247, MS 8980, Gaithersburg, MD 20899-8980; (301) 975-2839. Fax, (301) 975-3144. William F. Guthrie, Division Chief, (301) 975-2854.*

Web, www.nist.gov/itl/sed

Promotes the use of effective statistical techniques for planning analysis of experiments in the physical sciences within industry and government; interprets experiments and data collection programs. Offers training courses and workshops in methods and techniques.

National Institute of Standards and Technology (NIST) *(Commerce Dept.), Material Measurement Laboratory, 100 Bureau Dr., Bldg. 227, #A311, MS 8300, Gaithersburg, MD 20899-8300; (301) 975-8300. Fax, (301) 975-3845. Eric Lin, Director, (301) 975-6743. General email, cstlinfo@nist.gov*

Web, www.nist.gov/mml

Serves as the national reference laboratory for measurements in the chemical, biological, and material sciences. Researches industrial, biological, and environmental materials and processes to support development in manufacturing, nanotechnology, electronics, energy, health care, law enforcement, food safety, and other areas.

Subcommittee on Energy, (202) 225-6371.
Subcommittee on Oversight, (202) 225-6371.
Subcommittee on Research and Technology,
(202) 225-6371.
Subcommittee on Space, (202) 225-6371.
House Small Business Committee, (202) 225-5821.
Web, smallbusiness.house.gov
Subcommittee on Health and Technology,
(202) 225-5821.

SENATE:

Senate Agriculture, Nutrition, and Forestry
Committee, (202) 224-2035.
Web, agriculture.senate.gov
Subcommittee on Nutrition, Agricultural
Research, Specialty Crops, (202) 224-2035.
Senate Appropriations Committee, (202) 224-7257.
Web, appropriations.senate.gov
Subcommittee on Commerce, Justice, Science,
and Related Agencies, (202) 224-5202.
Subcommittee on Interior, Environment, and
Related Agencies, (202) 228-0774.
Subcommittee on Labor, Health and Human
Services, Education, and Related Agencies,
(202) 224-9145.
Senate Armed Services Committee, (202) 224-3871.
Web, armed-services.senate.gov
Subcommittee on Emerging Threats and
Capabilities, (202) 224-3871.
Subcommittee on Strategic Forces,
(202) 224-3871.

Senate Commerce, Science, and Transportation
Committee, (202) 224-1251.
Web, commerce.senate.gov
Subcommittee on Aviation Operations, Safety,
and Security, (202) 224-1251.
Subcommittee on Communications, Technology,
Innovation, and the Internet, (202) 224-1251.
Subcommittee on Consumer Protection, Product
Safety, Insurance, and Data Security,
(202) 224-1251.
Subcommittee on Oceans, Atmosphere, Fisheries,
and the Coast Guard, (202) 224-1251.
Subcommittee on Science, Space and
Competitiveness, (202) 224-1251.
Subcommittee on Surface Transportation and
Merchant Marine Infastructure, Safety, and
Security, (202) 224-1251.
Senate Energy and Natural Resources Committee,
(202) 224-4971.
Web, energy.senate.gov
Subcommittee on Energy, (202) 224-4971.
Subcommittee on Public Lands, Forests, and
Mining, (202) 224-4971.
Subcommittee on Water and Power, (202) 224-4971.
Senate Environment and Public Works Committee,
(202) 224-6176.
Web, epw.senate.gov
Subcommittee on Clean Air and Nuclear Safety,
(202) 224-6176.
Subcommittee on Fisheries, Water, and Wildlife,
(202) 224-6176.

Disseminates reference measurement procedures, certified reference materials, and best-practice guides.

National Institute of Standards and Technology (NIST)
(Commerce Dept.), Physical Measurement Laboratory,
100 Bureau Dr., Bldg. 221, #B160, MS 8400, Gaithersburg,
MD 20899-8400; (301) 975-4200. Fax, (301) 975-3038.
Carl J. Williams, Director.
Web, www.nist.gov/pml

Develops and disseminates national standards of measurement for length, mass, force, acceleration, time, wavelength, frequency, humidity, and radiation. Collaborates with industries, universities, and professional and standards-setting organizations.

National Institute of Standards and Technology (NIST)
(Commerce Dept.), Standard Reference Data, 100 Bureau
Dr., MS 8500, Gaithersburg, MD 20899-8500; (301) 975-
2200. Fax, (301) 975-4553. Adam Morey, Supervisory

Measurement Services Product Specialist, (301) 975-3173.
Toll-free, (844) 374-0183.
General email, data@nist.gov
Web, www.nist.gov/srd

Collects and disseminates critically evaluated physical, chemical, and materials properties data in the physical sciences and engineering for use by industry, government, and academic laboratories. Develops databases in a variety of formats, including disk, CD-ROM, and online.

National Museum of American History *(Smithsonian*
Institution), Library, 14th St. and Constitution Ave. N.W.,
R5016, MRC 630, 20560-0630 (mailing address: #5016
Smithsonian Institution, P.O. Box 37012, MRC 360,
Washington, DC 20013-7012); (202) 633-3865. Fax, (202)
633-3427. William Baxter, Head Librarian, (202) 633-2067.
General email, askalibrarian@si.edu
Web, www.library.si.edu/libraries/national-museum-
american-history-library

Online catalogue, http://siris-libraries.si.edu/ipac20/ipac .jsp?profile=liball

Collection includes materials on the history of medicine, science, and technology, with concentrations in engineering, transportation, and applied science. Open to the public by appointment. All library holdings are listed in the online catalog.

National Oceanic and Atmospheric Administration (NOAA) *(Commerce Dept.)*, *Central Library*, *1315 East-West Hwy., SSMC3, 2nd Floor, Silver Spring, MD 20910; (301) 713-2600. Fax, (301) 713-4598. Deirdre Clarkin, Director, (301) 713-2606. Reference service, (301) 713-2600, ext. 157. TTY, (301) 713-2779.*
General email, library.reference@noaa.gov
Web, http://library.noaa.gov

Collection includes electronic NOAA documents, reports, and videos; electronic and print journals; the NOAA Photo Library; bibliographic database of other NOAA libraries; and climate data. Makes interlibrary loans; library open to the public, with two forms of photo ID, Monday through Friday, 9:00 a.m.–4:00 p.m.

National Oceanic and Atmospheric Administration (NOAA) *(Commerce Dept.)*, *National Centers for Environmental Information (NCEI)*, *1315 East-West Hwy., SSMC3, 4th Floor, Silver Spring, MD 20910-3282; (301) 713-3277. Fax, (301) 713-3300. Mary Wohlgemuth, Director, (828) 271-4476.*
General email, ncei.info@noaa.gov
Web, www.nodc.noaa.gov

Responsible for hosting and providing access to comprehensive oceanic, atmospheric, and geophysical data. Provides world's largest collection of freely available oceanographic data, including water temperatures dating back to the late 1700s and measuring thousands of meters deep, scientific journals, rare books, historical photo collections, and maps through the NOAA Central Library, and data management expertise and training. Merger of NOAA's three data centers: National Climatic Data Center, National Geophysical Data Center, and National Oceanographic Data Center, which includes the National Coastal Data Development Center.

National Oceanic and Atmospheric Administration (NOAA) *(Commerce Dept.)*, *National Environmental Satellite, Data, and Information Service (NESDIS)*, *1335 East-West Hwy., SSMC1, 8th Floor, Silver Spring, MD 20910; (301) 713-3578. Fax, (301) 713-1249. Stephen Volz, Assistant Administrator. Press, (301) 713-0214.*
Web, www.nesdis.noaa.gov and Twitter, @NOAASatellites

Acquires and disseminates global environmental (marine, atmospheric, solid earth, and solar-terrestrial) satellite data. Maintains comprehensive data and information referral service.

National Science Foundation (NSF), *National Center for Science and Engineering Statistics, 2415 Eisenhower Ave., Room 1400, Alexandria, VA 22134; (703) 292-8780. Fax, (703) 292-9092. Emilda B. Rivers, Director.*
Web, www.nsf.gov/statistics

Compiles, analyzes, and disseminates quantitative information about domestic and international resources devoted to science, engineering, and technology. Provides information to other federal agencies for policy formulation.

National Technical Information Service (NTIS) *(Commerce Dept.)*, *5301 Shawnee Rd., Alexandria, VA 22312; (703) 605-6000. Fax, (703) 605-6900. Avi Bender, Director, (703) 605-6400. Bookstore, (703) 605-6040. Customer support, (703) 605-6050. Toll-free, (800) 553-6847. Toll-free customer support, (888) 584-8332. TTY, (703) 487-4639.*
General email, info@ntis.gov
Web, www.ntis.gov, Twitter, @NTISInfo and Facebook, www.facebook.com/ NTISCustomerContactCenter

Collects and organizes technical, scientific, engineering, and business-related information generated by U.S. and foreign governments and makes it available for commercial use in the private sector. Makes available approximately 3 million works covering research and development, current events, business and management studies, translations of foreign open source reports, foreign and domestic trade, general statistics, environment and energy, health and social sciences, and hundreds of other areas. Provides computer software and computerized data files in a variety of formats, including Internet downloads. Houses the Homeland Security Information Center, a centralized source on major security concerns for health and medicine, food and agriculture, and biochemical war.

Smithsonian Institution, *Office of the Director, Libraries, National Museum of Natural History, 10th St. and Constitution Ave. N.W., Room 29, 20560 (mailing address: P.O. Box 37012, MRC 154, Washington, DC 20013-7012); (202) 633-2240. Nancy E. Gwinn, Director.*
Web, http://library.si.edu and Twitter, @SILibraries

Maintains collection of general reference, biographical, and interdisciplinary materials; serves as an information resource on institution libraries, a number of which have collections in scientific subjects, including horticulture, botany, science and technology, and anthropology.

U.S. Geological Survey (USGS) *(Interior Dept.)*, *Library Services, 950 National Center, #1D100, Reston, VA 20192 (mailing address: 12201 Sunrise Valley Dr., #1D100, MS 950, Reston, VA 20192); (703) 648-4301. Fax, (703) 648-6373. Catharine (Cate) Canevari, Library Director, (703) 648-7182.*
General email, library@usgs.gov
Web, http://library.usgs.gov

Maintains collection of books, periodicals, serials, maps, and technical reports on geology, mineral and water resources, mineralogy, paleontology, petrology, soil and environmental sciences, biology, and physics and chemistry as they relate to natural sciences. Open to the public Monday–Friday; makes interlibrary loans.

► CONGRESS

For a listing of relevant congressional committees and subcommittees, please see pages 682–683 or the Appendix.

Library of Congress, *Science, Technology, and Business,* *John Adams Bldg., 101 Independence Ave. S.E., #LA 508, 20540-4750; (202) 707-5639. Fax, (202) 707-1925. Ron Bluestone, Chief, (202) 707-0948. Business Reference Services, (202) 707-7934. Science Reference Services, (202) 707-6401. Technical reports, (202) 707-5655.*
Web, www.loc.gov/rr/scitech

Offers reference service by telephone, by correspondence, and in person. Maintains a collection of more than 3 million reports on science, technology, business management, and economics.

▶ **NONGOVERNMENTAL**

American Statistical Assn., *732 N. Washington St., Alexandria, VA 22314-1943; (703) 684-1221. Fax, (703) 684-2037. Ronald Wasserstein, Executive Director. Toll-free, (888) 231-3473.*
General email, asainfo@amstat.org
Web, www.amstat.org

Membership: statistical practitioners in industry, government, and academia. Supports excellence in the development, application, and dissemination of statistical science through meetings, publications, membership services, education, accreditation, and advocacy.

International Programs

▶ **AGENCIES**

Bureau of International Organization Affairs (IO) *(State Dept.), Specialized and Technical Agencies (STA), 2401 E St., Room L409, 20037; (202) 663-3121. Fax, (202) 647-8902. Gregory D. Thome, Director.*
Web, www.state.gov/p/io

Oversees U.S. participation in international specialized and technical organizations, including the International Atomic Energy Agency, the United Nations Environment Programme, and the Commission on Sustainable Development. Works to ensure that United Nations agencies follow United Nations Conference on Environment and Development recommendations on sustainable growth.

Bureau of Oceans and International Environmental and Scientific Affairs (OES) *(State Dept.), 2201 C St. N.W., #3880, 20520-7818; (202) 647-1554. Fax, (202) 647-0217. Marcia Bernicat, Principal Deputy Assistant Secretary.*
Web, www.state.gov/e/oes, Twitter, @StateDeptOES and Facebook, www.facebook.com/StateDepartment.OES

Formulates and implements policies and proposals for U.S. international scientific, technological, environmental, oceanic and marine, Arctic and Antarctic, and space programs; coordinates international science and technology policy with other federal agencies.

Bureau of Oceans and International Environmental and Scientific Affairs (OES) *(State Dept.), Policy and Public Outreach (PPO), 2201 C St. N.W., #2880, 20520; (202) 647-4658. Susan Cleary, Director.*
Web, www.state.gov/e/oes/policy

Integrates oceans, environment, polar, science, technology, and health issues into U.S. foreign policy, and works to address these issues in the media, NGOs, the private sector, and Congress.

Bureau of Oceans and International Environmental and Scientific Affairs (OES) *(State Dept.), Science and Technology Cooperation (STC), 1800 G St. N.W., #10100, 20006; (202) 663-2623. Lisa Brodey, Director.*
Web, www.state.gov/e/oes/stc

Advances U.S. foreign policy through science and technology, and fosters a global environment that supports innovation and transparency in government.

National Institute of Standards and Technology (NIST) *(Commerce Dept.), International and Academic Affairs, 100 Bureau Dr., MS 1090, Gaithersburg, MD 20899-1090; (301) 975-6478. Fax, (301) 975-3530. Claire M. Saundry, Director, (301) 975-2386. TTY, (301) 975-8295.*
General email, inquiries@nist.gov
Web, www.nist.gov/iaao

Represents the institute in international functions involving science and technology; coordinates programs with foreign institutions; assists scientists from foreign countries who visit the institute for consultation. Administers a postdoctoral research associates program and oversees NIST's cooperation with academic institutions and researchers.

National Oceanic and Atmospheric Administration (NOAA) *(Commerce Dept.), National Environmental Satellite, Data, and Information Service (NESDIS), 1335 East-West Hwy., SSMC1, 8th Floor, Silver Spring, MD 20910; (301) 713-3578. Fax, (301) 713-1249. Stephen Volz, Assistant Administrator. Press, (301) 713-0214.*
Web, www.nesdis.noaa.gov and Twitter, @NOAASatellites

Acquires and disseminates global environmental satellite data: marine, atmospheric, solid earth, and solar-terrestrial. Participates, with the National Meteorological Center, in the United Nations World Weather Watch Programme developed by the World Meteorological Organization. Manages U.S. civil earth-observing satellite systems and atmospheric, oceanographic, geophysical, and solar data centers. Provides the public, businesses, and government agencies with environmental data and information products and services.

National Oceanic and Atmospheric Administration (NOAA) *(Commerce Dept.), National Weather Service (NWS), National Centers for Environmental Prediction (NCEP), 5830 University Research Court, College Park, MD 20740; (301) 683-1314. Fax, (301) 683-1325. William M. Lapenta, Director, (301) 683-1315.*
Web, www.ncep.noaa.gov

The National Center for Environmental Prediction and the National Environmental Satellite, Data, and Information Service are part of the World Weather Watch Programme developed by the United Nations World Meteorological Organization. Collects and exchanges data with other nations; provides other national weather service offices, private meteorologists, and government agencies with products, including forecast guidance products.

National Science Foundation (NSF), *International Science and Engineering,* 2415 Eisenhower Ave., Room W17220, Alexandria, VA 22134; (703) 292-8710. Fax, (703) 292-9481. Rebecca L. Keiser, Office Head. Web, www.nsf.gov/dir/index.jsp?org=OISE

Serves as the foundation's focal point for international scientific and engineering activities; promotes new partnerships between U.S. scientists and engineers and their foreign colleagues; provides support for U.S. participation in international scientific organizations from three overseas offices (Paris, Tokyo, and Beijing).

Smithsonian Institution, *International Relations and Global Programs,* 1100 Jefferson Dr. S.W., #3123, 20560 (mailing address: P.O. Box 37012, Quad MRC 705, Washington, DC 20013-7012); (202) 633-4795. Fax, (202) 786-2557. Molly Fannon, Director. General email, global@si.edu

Web, https://global.si.edu and Twitter, @GlobalSI

Fosters the development and coordinates the international aspects of Smithsonian scientific activities; facilitates basic research in the natural sciences and encourages international collaboration among individuals and institutions.

▶**INTERNATIONAL ORGANIZATIONS**

InterAcademy Partnership, *Washington Office,* 500 5th St. N.W., 20001; Teresa Stoepler, Executive Director. General email, iap@twas.org

Web, www.interacademies.org/33326/IAP-R and Twitter, @IAPartnerships

Global network of science, engineering, and medical academies in countries worldwide. Promotes communication among leading authorities in the natural and social sciences; establishes regional networks of academies to identify critical issues, thereby building capacity for advice to governments and international organizations. Interests include science education, the engagement of women in science, and sustainable management of water, energy, and other resources. (Hosted by National Academies of Science, Engineering, and Medicine.)

▶**NONGOVERNMENTAL**

American Assn. for the Advancement of Science (AAAS), *Office of International and Security Affairs,* 1200 New York Ave. N.W., 6th Floor, 20005; (202) 326-6650. Fax, (202) 289-4958. Tom Wang, Chief International Officer. Web, www.aaas.org/oisa

Promotes international cooperation among scientists. Helps build scientific infrastructure in developing countries. Works to improve the quality of scientific input in international discourse.

National Research Council (NRC), *Policy and Global Affairs,* Keck Center, 500 5th St. N.W., #528, 20001; (202) 334-3847. Fax, (202) 334-2139. Anne Petersen, Chair.

General email, pga@nas.edu

Web, http://sites.nationalacademies.org/pga

Serves the international interests of the National Research Council, National Academy of Sciences, National Academy of Engineering, and Institute of Medicine. Promotes effective application of science and technology to the economic and social problems of industrialized and developing countries, and advises U.S. government agencies.

Research Applications

▶**AGENCIES**

Defense Technical Information Center *(Defense Dept.),* 8725 John Jay Kingman Rd., Fort Belvoir, VA 22060-6218; (703) 767-9100. Christopher E. Thomas, Administrator. Registration, (703) 767-8273. Toll-free, (800) 225-3842. Web, www.dtic.mil

Acts as a central repository for the Defense Dept.'s collection of current and completed research and development efforts in all fields of science and technology. Disseminates research analysis and development information to contractors, grantees, and registered organizations working on government research and development projects, particularly for the Defense Dept. Users must register with the center.

Energy Dept. (DOE), *Technology Transitions (OTT),* 1000 Independence Ave. S.W., 20585; (202) 586-5000. Conner Prochaska, Director. General email, OTT@hq.doe.gov

Web, https://energy.gov/technologytransitions/office-technology-transitions

Develops policies and establishes partnerships with the commercial sector to translate agency energy technology research and innovation into products and services for the private sector.

National Aeronautics and Space Administration (NASA), *Science Mission Directorate (SMD),* 300 E St. S.W., #3J28, 20546; (202) 358-3889. Fax, (202) 358-3092. Thomas Zurbuchen, Associate Administrator. General email, science@hq.nasa.gov

Web, http://science.nasa.gov and Twitter, @NASAScienceCast

Sponsors scientific research and analysis. Exchanges information with the international science community. Primary areas of study are astronomy and astrophysics, earth sciences, heliophysics, and planetary science.

National Institutes of Health (NIH) *(Health and Human Services Dept.),* Intramural Research *(IRP),* Technology Transfer *(OTT),* 6011 Executive Blvd., #325, MSC-7660, Rockville, MD 20852-3804; (301) 496-7057. Fax, (301) 402-0220. Karen Rogers, Director (Acting). General email, nihott@mail.nih.gov

Web, www.ott.nih.gov

Evaluates, protects, monitors, and manages the NIH invention portfolio. Oversees patent prosecution, negotiates and monitors licensing agreements, and provides oversight and central policy review of cooperative research and development agreements. Also manages the patent and licensing activities of the Food and Drug Administration (FDA). Responsible for the central development and implementation of technology transfer policies for three research components of the Public Health Service—the NIH, the FDA, and the Centers for Disease Control and Prevention.

National Science Foundation (NSF), *National Nanotechnology Initiative,* 2415 Eisenhower Ave., Room C14016, Alexandria, VA 22134; (703) 292-7032. Mihail C. Roco, Senior Adviser, (703) 292-7032. General email, info@nnco.nano.gov

Web, www.nsf.gov/crssprgm/nano

Coordinates multiagency efforts in understanding nanoscale phenomena and furthering nanotechnology research and development.

▶ NONGOVERNMENTAL

American Assn. for the Advancement of Science (AAAS), *Center of Science, Policy, and Society Programs,* 1200 New York Ave. N.W., 20005; (202) 326-6788. Maureen Kearney, Chief Program Director. Press, (202) 326-6440. Web, www.aaas.org/program/center-science-policy-and-society-programs

Promotes scientific research and applications. Supports dialogue between scientists and communities, including government, ethics, religion, and law.

American Assn. for the Advancement of Science (AAAS), *Scientific Responsibility, Human Rights, and Law Program,* 1200 New York Ave. N.W., 8th Floor, 20005; (202) 326-6604. Fax, (202) 289-4950. Jessica Wyndham, Director. General email, srhrl@aaas.org

Web, www.aaas.org/program/scientific-responsibility-human-rights-law, Twitter, @AAAS-SRHRL and Facebook, www.facebook.com/SRHRL

Engages policymakers and the general public on the ethical, legal, and human-rights issues related to the conduct and application of science and technology. Defends the freedom to engage in scientific inquiry; promotes responsible research practices; advances the application of science and technology to document human rights violations.

American National Standards Institute (ANSI), 1899 L St. N.W., 11th Floor, 20036; (202) 293-8020. Fax, (202) 293-9287. S. Joe Bhatia, President, (202) 331-3605. General email, info@ansi.org

Web, www.ansi.org

Administers and coordinates the voluntary U.S. private sector–led consensus standards and conformity assessment system. Serves as the official U.S. representative to the International Organization of Standardization (ISO) and, via the U.S. National Committee, the International Electrotechnical Commission (IEC), and is a U.S. representative to the International Accreditation Forum (IAF).

The Brookings Institution, *Center for Technology Innovation,* 1775 Massachusetts Ave. N.W., 20036; (202) 797-6090. Darrell M. West, Director, (202) 797-6481. Web, www.brookings.edu/about/center-for-technology-innovation

Research center promoting policymaking and public debate about technology innovation, including digital infrastructure, the mobile economy, e-governance, digital media and entertainment, cybersecurity and privacy, digital medicine, and virtual education.

The Brookings Institution, *Governance Studies,* 1755 Massachusetts Ave. N.W., 20036; (202) 797-6090. Fax, (202) 797-6144. Darrell M. West, Director, (202) 797-6481. Information, (202) 797-6000. Press, (202) 797-6105. Web, www.brookings.edu/governance

Promotes public debate on technology innovation and develops data-driven scholarship to understand the legal, economic, social, and governance impact of technology.

Institute for Alternative Futures (IAF), 2800 Eisenhower Ave., #220, Alexandria, VA 22314-5204; (703) 684-5880. Fax, (703) 684-0640. Jonathan Peck, President. General email, futurist@altfutures.org

Web, www.altfutures.org and Facebook, www.facebook.com/Institute-for-Alternative-Futures-227831155314

Research and educational organization that explores the implications of future developments in various fields and facilitates planning efforts. Works with state and local governments, Congress, international organizations, federal government, and regional associations; conducts seminars. Interests include pharmaceutical research, health care, telecommunications, artificial intelligence, energy, the environment, and sustainability.

National Research Council (NRC), *Behavioral, Cognitive, and Sensory Sciences Board,* Keck Center, 500 5th St. N.W., 11th Floor, 20001; (202) 334-2678. Fax, (202) 334-2210. Barbara A. Wanchisen, Director, (202) 334-2394; Susan T. Fiske, Chair. General email, BBCSS@nas.edu

Web, www.nationalacademies.org/bbcss

Advises government agencies on policies relating to the behavioral, cognitive, and sensory sciences.

Public Technology Institute (PTI), 660 N. Capitol St. N.W., #400, Alexandria, VA 20001; (202) 626-2400. Alan R. Shark, Executive Director, (202) 626-2445. Press, (202) 626-2432. General email, info@pti.org

Web, www.pti.org and Twitter, @Public_Tech

Cooperative research, development, and technology-transfer organization of cities and counties in North America. Applies available technological innovations and develops other methods to improve public services.

RAND Corp., *Washington Office,* 1200 S. Hayes St., Arlington, VA 22202-5050; (703) 413-1100. Fax, (703) 413-8111. Nicholas Burger, Director; Anita Chandra, Director for Social and Economic Well-Being, ext. 5323. Web, www.rand.org

Conducts research on energy, emerging technologies and critical systems, space and transportation, technology policies, international cooperative research, water resources, ocean and atmospheric sciences, and other technologies in defense and nondefense areas. (Headquarters in Santa Monica, Calif.)

SRI International, *Washington Office, 1100 Wilson Blvd., #2800, Arlington, VA 22209; (703) 524-2053. Fax, (703) 247-8569. William Jeffrey, Executive Director.*
Web, www.sri.com and Twitter, @SRI_Intl

Research and consulting organization that conducts basic and applied research for government, industry, and business. Interests include engineering, physical and life sciences, and international research. (Headquarters in Menlo Park, Calif.)

Scientific Research Practices

▶**AGENCIES**

Assistant Secretary for Health (OASH) *(Health and Human Services Dept.), Human Research Protections (OHRP), Tower Bldg., 1101 Wootton Pkwy., #200, Rockville, MD 20852; (240) 453-6900. Fax, (240) 453-6909. Dr. Jerry Menikoff, Director. Toll-free, (866) 447-4777.*
General email, ohrp@hhs.gov

Web, www.hhs.gov/ohrp

Promotes the rights, welfare, and well-being of subjects involved in research conducted or supported by the Health and Human Services Dept.; helps ensure that research is carried out in accordance with federal regulations by providing clarification and guidance, developing educational programs and materials, and maintaining regulatory oversight.

Assistant Secretary for Health (OASH) *(Health and Human Services Dept.), Research Integrity (ORI), Tower Bldg., 1101 Wootton Pkwy., #750, Rockville, MD 20852; (240) 453-8200. Fax, (301) 443-5351. Wanda Jones, Director (Acting).*
General email, askori@hhs.gov

Web, https://ori.hhs.gov

Seeks to promote the quality of Public Health Service extramural and intramural research programs. (Extramural programs provide funding to research institutions that are not part of the federal government. Intramural programs provide funding for research conducted within federal government facilities.) Provides oversight of institutional inquiries and investigations of research misconduct and technical assistance to institutions during these proceedings; reviews institutional findings and process and proposes administrative actions to the Health and Human Services Dept. when the Office of Research Integrity makes a finding of research misconduct; sponsors educational programs and activities for professionals interested in research integrity; sponsors grants for conferences and basic research on research integrity; administers institutional assurance program; and coordinates with institutions to protect from retaliation individuals involved in research misconduct matters.

Education Dept., *Chief Financial Officer (OCFO), Financial Management Operations, 550 12th St. S.W., 6th Floor, 20005; (202) 245-8118. Fax, (202) 205-0765. Gary Wood, Director.*
General email, gary.wood@ed.gov
Web, www2.ed.gov/about/offices/list/ocfo/humansub.html

Advises grantees and applicants for department-supported research on regulations for protecting human subjects. Provides guidance to the Education Dept. on the requirements for complying with the regulations. Serves as the primary Education Dept. contact for matters concerning the protection of human subjects in research.

Food and Drug Administration (FDA) *(Health and Human Services Dept.), Good Clinical Practice (OGCP), White Oak Bldg. 32-5103, 10903 New Hampshire Ave., Silver Spring, MD 20993; (301) 796-8340. Fax, (301) 847-8640. Joanne Less, Director.*
General email, gcp.questions@fda.hhs.gov
Web, www.fda.gov/AboutFDA/CentersOffices/OfficeofMedicalProductsandTobacco/OfficeofScienceandHealthCoordination/ucm2018191.htm

Provides information to the FDA Commissioner about clinical human research trials and impacts on policy.

National Aeronautics and Space Administration (NASA), *Chief Health and Medical Officer, 300 E St. S.W., 20546; (202) 358-2390. Fax, (202) 358-3349. Dr. James D. Polk, Chief Health and Medical Officer.*
Web, www.nasa.gov/offices/ochmo

Monitors human and animal research and clinical practice to ensure that NASA adheres to appropriate medical and ethical standards and satisfies all regulatory and statutory requirements.

National Institutes of Health (NIH) *(Health and Human Services Dept.), Animal Care and Use (OACU), 31 Center Dr., Bldg. 31, #B1C37, MSC 2252, Bethesda, MD 20892-2252; (301) 496-5424. Fax, (301) 480-8298. Stephen Denny, Director (Acting).*
General email, secoacu@od.nih.gov
Web, http://oacu.oir.nih.gov

Provides guidance for the humane care and use of animals in the intramural research program at NIH.

National Institutes of Health (NIH) *(Health and Human Services Dept.), Human Research Protections Program (HRPP), 9000 Rockville Pike, Clinical Center, Bldg. 10, #2C146, MSC 1154, Bethesda, MD 20892-1154; (301) 402-3444. Fax, (301) 402-3443. Heather Bridge, Director (Acting).*
Web, http://ohsr.od.nih.gov

Helps NIH investigators understand and comply with ethical principles and regulatory requirements involved in human subjects research. Assists NIH components in administering and regulating human subjects research activities.

National Institutes of Health (NIH) *(Health and Human Services Dept.)*, *Laboratory Animal Welfare (OLAW)*, *6705 Rockledge Dr., RLK1, #360, MSC 7982, Bethesda, MD 20892-7982; (301) 496-7163. Fax, (301) 480-3394. Patricia A. Brown, Director.*
General email, olaw@mail.nih.gov
Web, https://olaw.nih.gov/home.htm

Develops and monitors policy on the humane care and use of animals in research conducted by any public health service entity.

National Institutes of Health (NIH) *(Health and Human Services Dept.)*, *Stem Cell Task Force, 9000 Rockville Pike, 31 Center Dr., Bldg. 31, #8A52, MSC2540, Bethesda, MD 20892-2540; (301) 496-3167. Dr. Walter J. Koroshetz, Chair.*
General email, stemcell@mail.nih.gov
Web, http://stemcells.nih.gov

Seeks the advice of scientific leaders in stem cell research about the challenges to advancing the stem cell research agenda and strategies for overcoming them.

Office of Science *(Energy Dept.)*, *Biological and Environmental Research (BER), Biological Systems Science Division (BSSD), Human Subjects Protection Program, 19901 Germantown Rd., #SC23.2, Germantown, MD 20874-1290 (mailing address: Germantown Bldg., 1000 Independence Ave. S.W., #SC23.2, Washington, DC 20585); (301) 903-7693. Fax, (301) 903-0567. Elizabeth (Libby) White, Program Manager.*
General email, humansubjects@science.doe.gov
Web, https://science.energy.gov/ber/human-subjects

Works to protect the rights and welfare of human subject research volunteers by establishing guidelines and enforcing regulations on scientific research that uses human subjects, including research that involves identifiable or high-risk data, worker populations or subgroups; humans testing devices, products, or materials; and bodily materials. Acts as an educational and technical resource to investigators, administrators, and institutional research boards.

▶ **NONGOVERNMENTAL**

American Assn. for Laboratory Accreditation (A2LA), *5202 Presidents Court, #220, Frederick, MD 21703; (301) 644-3248. Fax, (240) 454-9449. Lonnie Spires, President, (301) 644-3208.*
General email, info@a2la.org
Web, www.a2la.org, Twitter, @A2LA_ and Facebook, www.facebook.com/a2laaccreditation

Monitors and accredits laboratories that test construction materials and perform acoustics and vibration, biological, calibration, chemical, electrical, environmental, geotechnical, mechanical, nondestructive, and thermal testing. Offers laboratory-related training and programs for accreditation of inspection bodies, proficiency testing providers, and reference material producers.

American Assn. for the Advancement of Science (AAAS), *Scientific Responsibility, Human Rights, and Law*

Program, 1200 New York Ave. N.W., 8th Floor, 20005; (202) 326-6604. Fax, (202) 289-4950. Jessica Wyndham, Director.
General email, srhrl@aaas.org
Web, www.aaas.org/program/scientific-responsibility-human-rights-law, Twitter, @AAAS-SRHRL and Facebook, www.facebook.com/SRHRL

Engages policymakers and the general public on the ethical, legal, and human-rights issues related to the conduct and application of science and technology. Defends the freedom to engage in scientific inquiry; promotes responsible research practices; advances the application of science and technology to document human rights violations.

American Council of Independent Laboratories (ACIL), *1875 Eye St. N.W., #500, 20006; (202) 887-5872 ext. 1. Fax, (202) 887-0021. Richard Bright, Chief Operating Officer, ext. 2.*
General email, info@acil.org
Web, www.acil.org, Twitter, @acilnews and Facebook, www.facebook.com/acil.info

Membership: independent commercial scientific and engineering firms and testing laboratories. Promotes professional and ethical business practices in providing analysis, testing, product certification, and research and consulting services in engineering, food sciences, analytical chemistry, and environmental geosciences.

AOAC International, *2275 Research Blvd., #300, Rockville, MD 20850-3250; (301) 924-7077. Fax, (301) 924-7089. David B. Schmidt, Executive Director. Information, (800) 379-2622.*
General email, aoac@aoac.org
Web, www.aoac.org

International association of analytical science professionals, companies, government agencies, nongovernmental organizations, and institutions. Supports the standards and method development, evaluation, and publication of reliable chemical and biological methods of analysis for foods, drugs, feed, fertilizers, pesticides, water, and other substances. Promotes voluntary consensus standards development for analytical methodology, fit-for-purpose methods, and quality measurements in the analytical sciences.

Humane Society of the United States, *Animal Research Issues, 700 Professional Dr., Gaithersburg, MD 20879; (202) 452-1100. Fax, (301) 258-7760. Kathleen (Katy) Conlee, Vice President.*
General email, ari@humanesociety.org
Web, www.humanesociety.org/about/departments/animals_research.html

Seeks to end the suffering of animals in research. Promotes the use of alternatives that replace, refine, or reduce the use of animals in scientific research, education, and consumer product testing. Conducts outreach programs aimed toward the public and the scientific community.

National Assn. for Biomedical Research, *1100 Vermont Ave. N.W., #1100, 20005; (202) 857-0540. Fax, (202) 659-1902. Matthew Bailey, President.*

General email, info@nabr.org

Web, www.nabr.org

Membership: scientific and medical professional societies, academic institutions, and research-oriented corporations involved in the use of animals in biomedical research. Supports the humane use of animals in medical research, education, and product-safety assessment. Monitors legislation and regulations.

National Research Council (NRC), *Laboratory Assessments Board,* *Keck Center, 500 5th St. N.W., #W900, 20001; (202) 334-3311. Fax, (202) 334-2791. James P. McGee, Director.*

General email, lab@nas.edu

Web, http://sites.nationalacademies.org/deps/lab

Reviews and assesses the quality of internal research conducted at NRC laboratories, including those established by federal agencies at national laboratories and at government-owned, contractor-operated facilities.

Society of Research Administrators International (SRA International), *1560 Wilson Blvd., #310, Arlington, VA 22209; (703) 741-0140. Fax, (703) 741-0142. Ellen Lupinski Quinn, Chief Operating Officer, ext. 213.*

General email, info@srainternational.org

Web, www.srainternational.org and Twitter, @SocietyRAIntl

Membership: scientific and medical research administrators in the United States and other countries. Educates the public about the profession; offers professional development services; sponsors mentoring and awards programs.

BIOLOGY AND LIFE SCIENCES

General

▶**AGENCIES**

National Institute of General Medical Sciences (NIGMS) *(National Institutes of Health), 45 Center Dr., #3AN44E, MSC 6200, Bethesda, MD 20892-6200; (301) 496-7301. Fax, (301) 402-0156. Jon R. Lorsch, Director.*

General email, info@nigms.nih.gov

Web, www.nigms.nih.gov, Twitter, @NIGMS and Facebook, www.facebook.com/nigms.nih.gov

Primarily supports basic biomedical research and training that lays the foundation for advances in disease diagnosis, treatment, and prevention. Areas of special interest include bioinformatics, cell biology, developmental biology, physiology, biological chemistry genetics, and computational biology.

National Museum of Natural History *(Smithsonian Institution), 10th St. and Constitution Ave. N.W., 20560-0106 (mailing address: P.O. Box 37012, MRC 106, Washington, DC 20013-7012); (202) 633-2664. Fax, (202) 633-0169. Kirk Johnson, Director. General Smithsonian information, (202) 633-1000. Library, (202) 633-1680. Press, (202) 633-2950. TTY, (202) 633-5285.*

General email, naturalexperience@si.edu

Web, www.mnh.si.edu and Twitter, @NMNH

Conducts research and maintains exhibitions and collections relating to the natural sciences. Collections are organized into seven research and curatorial departments: anthropology, botany, entomology, invertebrate zoology, mineral sciences, paleobiology, and vertebrate zoology.

National Museum of Natural History *(Smithsonian Institution), Library, 10th St. and Constitution Ave. N.W., East Court, 1st Floor, 20560-0154 (mailing address: P.O. Box 37012, MRC 154, Washington, DC 20013-7012); (202) 633-1680. Barbara P. Ferry, Head.*

General email, askalibrarian@si.edu

Web, www.library.si.edu/libraries/national-museum-natural-history-library

Maintains reference collections covering anthropology, biodiversity, biology, botany, ecology, entomology, ethnology, mineral sciences, paleobiology, and zoology; permits on-site use of the collections. Open to the public by appointment; makes interlibrary loans.

National Oceanic and Atmospheric Administration (NOAA) *(Commerce Dept.), National Marine Fisheries Service (NMFS), 1315 East-West Hwy., 14th floor, Silver Spring, MD 20910; (301) 427-8000. Fax, (301) 713-1940. Chris Oliver, Assistant Administrator. Press, (301) 427-8003.*

Web, www.nmfs.noaa.gov and Twitter, @NOAAFisheries

Conducts research and collects data on marine ecology and biology; collects, analyzes, and provides information through the Marine Resources Monitoring, Assessment, and Prediction Program. Administers the Magnuson-Stevens Fishery Conservation and Management Act and marine mammals and endangered species protection programs. Works with the Army Corps of Engineers on research into habitat restoration and conservation.

National Science Foundation (NSF), *Biological Sciences Directorate, 2415 Eisenhower Ave., Room C12000, Alexandria, VA 22314; (703) 292-8400. Fax, (703) 292-9154. Joanne Tornow, Assistant Director (Acting).*

Web, www.nsf.gov/dir/index.jsp?org=bio

Serves as a forum for addressing biology research issues, sharing information, identifying gaps in scientific knowledge, and developing consensus among concerned federal agencies. Facilitates continuing cooperation among federal agencies on topical issues.

National Science Foundation (NSF), *Environmental Biology Division, 2415 Eisenhower Ave., Room W121000, Alexandria, VA 22134; (703) 292-8480. Fax, (703) 292-9064. Stephanie Hampton, Director.*

Web, www.nsf.gov/bio/deb/about.jsp

Supports research on populations, species, communities, and ecosystems, including biodiversity, phylogenetic systematics, molecular evolution, life history evolution, natural selection, ecology, biogeography, ecosystem services, conservation biology, global change, and biogeochemical cycles.

National Science Foundation (NSF), *Molecular and Cellular Biosciences Division,* 2415 Eisenhower Ave., Room E12400, Alexandria, VA 22134; (703) 292-8440. Fax, (703) 292-9061. Basil J. Nikolau, Director, (703) 292-4986.
Web, www.nsf.gov/div/index.jsp?div=MCB

Supports research and understanding of complex living systems at cellular levels.

Office of Science *(Energy Dept.),* *Biological and Environmental Research (BER),* 19901 Germantown Rd., #SC23, Germantown, MD 20874-1290 (mailing address: Germantown Bldg., 1000 Independence Ave. S.W., #SC23, Washington, DC 20585); (301) 903-3251. Fax, (301) 903-5051. Sharlene Weatherwax, Associate Director.
General email, sc.ber@science.doe.gov

Web, http://science.energy.gov/ber

Advances biological and environmental research and provides scientific user facilities to support innovation in energy security and environmental responsibility.

U.S. Geological Survey (USGS) *(Interior Dept.),* *Ecosystems,* 12201 Sunrise Valley Dr., MS 300, Reston, VA 20192-0002; (703) 648-4051. Fax, (703) 648-7031. Anne E. Kinsinger, Associate Director.
Web, www.usgs.gov/ecosystems

Conducts research and monitoring to develop and convey an understanding of ecosystem function and distributions, physical and biological components, and trophic dynamics for freshwater, terrestrial, and marine ecosystems and the human, fish, and wildlife communities they support. Subject areas include invasive species, endangered species and habitats, genetics and genomics, and microbiology.

▶ **NONGOVERNMENTAL**

American Institute of Biological Sciences, 950 Herndon Parkway, #450, Herndon, VA 20170; (703) 674-2500. Fax, (703) 674-2509. Scott Glisson, Chief Executive Director, (703) 674-2500 ext. 202; Robert Gropp, Executive Director Public Policy, (202) 628-1500 ext. 250.
General email, info@aibs.org

Web, www.aibs.org, Twitter, @AIBSbiology and Facebook, www.facebook.com/AIBSbiology

Membership: biologists, biology educators, and biological associations. Promotes interdisciplinary cooperation among members engaged in biological research and education; conducts educational programs for members; reviews projects supported by government grants. Monitors legislation and regulations.

American Society for Biochemistry and Molecular Biology (ASBMB), 11200 Rockville Pike, #302, Bethesda, MD 20852-3110; (240) 283-6600. Fax, (301) 881-2080. Barbara A. Gordon, Executive Director.
General email, asbmb@asbmb.org

Web, www.asbmb.org, Twitter, @ASBMB and Facebook, www.facebook.com/asbmb

Membership: professional biological chemists. Participates in the International Union of Biochemistry and Molecular Biology. Publishes several journals; holds workshops and webinars. Offers scholarship and awards to minority members. Monitors legislation and regulations.

American Society for Cell Biology, 8120 Woodmont Ave., #750, Bethesda, MD 20814-2762; (301) 347-9300. Fax, (301) 347-9310. Erika Shugart, Executive Officer, ext. 1.
General email, ascbinfo@ascb.org

Web, www.ascb.org, Twitter, @ASCBiology and Facebook, www.facebook.com/ASCBiology

Membership: scientists who have education or research experience in cell biology or an allied field. Promotes scientific exchange worldwide; organizes courses, workshops, and symposia. Monitors legislation and regulations.

American Society for Microbiology, 1752 N St. N.W., 20036-2904; (202) 737-3600. Stefano Bertuzzi, Chief Executive Director, (202) 942-9303. Press, (202) 942-9365.
General email, service@asmusa.org

Web, www.asm.org, Twitter, @ASMicrobiology and Facebook, www.facebook.com/asmfan

Membership: microbiologists. Encourages education, training, scientific investigation, and application of research results in microbiology and related subjects; participates in international research.

American Type Culture Collection, 10801 University Blvd., Manassas, VA 20110-2209 (mailing address: P.O. Box 1549, Manassas, VA 20108); (703) 365-2700. Fax, (703) 365-2701. Raymond H. Cypress, Chief Executive Officer. Toll-free, (800) 638-6597.
General email, sales@atcc.org

Web, www.atcc.org

Provides research and development tools, reagents, and related biological material management services to government agencies, academic institutions, and private industry worldwide. Serves as a bioresource center of live cultures and genetic material.

Carnegie Institute for Science, 1530 P St. N.W., 20005-1910; (202) 387-6400. Fax, (202) 387-8092. Eric D. Isaacs, President; Magaret Moerchen, Science Deputy.
Web, https://carnegiescience.edu and Twitter, @carnegiescience

Conducts research in plant science biology, genetic and developmental biology, earth and planetary sciences, astronomy, and global ecology and matter at extreme states at the Carnegie Institution's six research departments: Dept. of Embryology (Baltimore, Md.); Geophysical Laboratory (Washington, D.C.); Dept. of Global Ecology (Stanford, Calif.); Dept. of Plant Biology (Stanford, Calif.); Dept. of Terrestrial Magnetism (Washington, D.C.); and The Observatories (Pasadena, Calif., and Las Campanas, Chile).

Ecological Society of America, 1990 M St. N.W., #700, 20036; (202) 833-8773. Fax, (202) 833-8775. Catherine O'Riordan, Executive Director, ext. 206.

General email, esahq@esa.org

Web, www.esa.org

Promotes research in ecology and the scientific study of the relationship between organisms and their past, present, and future environments. Interests include biotechnology; management of natural resources, habitats, and ecosystems to protect biological diversity; and ecologically sound public policies.

Federation of American Societies for Experimental Biology (FASEB), *9650 Rockville Pike, Bethesda, MD 20814-3998; (301) 634-7000. Fax, (301) 634-7354. Frank Krause, Executive Director, (301) 634-7290. Toll-free, (800) 433-2732.*
General email, info@faseb.org

Web, www.faseb.org, Twitter, @FASEBopa and Facebook, www.facebook.com/FASEB.org

Advances biological science through collaborative advocacy for research policies that promote scientific progress and education and lead to improvements in human health. Provides educational meetings and publications to disseminate biological research results. Represents 27 scientific societies and more than 120,000 biomedical researchers around the world.

National Research Council (NRC), *Life Sciences Board, Keck Center, 500 5th St. N.W., 6th Floor, 20001; (202) 334-2187. Fax, (202) 334-1289. Fran Sharples, Director; James P. Collins, Chair.*
General email, bls@nas.edu

Web, http://dels.nas.edu/bls

Supports technical and policy research in the life sciences, including bioterrorism, genomics, biodiversity conservation, and basic biomedical research, such as stem cells.

Biotechnology

▶**AGENCIES**

Animal and Plant Health Inspection Service (APHIS) *(Agriculture Dept.), Biotechnology Regulatory Services, 4700 River Rd., Unit 147, Riverdale, MD 20737; (301) 851-3877. Michael J. Firko, Deputy Administrator. Applications and regulatory requirements, (301) 851-3886. Compliance, (301) 851-3935. Press, (301) 851-4100.*
Web, www.aphis.usda.gov/aphis/ourfocus/biotechnology

Regulates genetically engineered organisms as part of the Coordinated Framework for Regulation of Biotechnology to ensure that genetically engineered products are used in a manner that is safe for plant and animal health, human health, and the environment.

National Institutes of Health (NIH) *(Health and Human Services Dept.), Biotechnology Activities (OBA), 6705 Rockledge Dr., #750, MSC 7985, Bethesda, MD 20892; (301) 496-9838. Fax, (301) 496-9839. Dr. Jessica Tucker, Director, (301) 451-4431.*

General email, oba-osp@od.nih.gov

Web, https://osp.od.nih.gov/biosafety-biosecurity-and-emerging-biotechnology/

Reviews requests submitted to the NIH involving genetic testing, recombinant DNA technology, xenotransplantation, and biosecurity; develops and implements research guidelines for safe conduct of DNA-related research. Monitors scientific progress in human genetics.

National Library of Medicine *(National Institutes of Health), National Center for Biotechnology Information, 8600 Rockville Pike, Bldg. 38A, 8th Floor, Bethesda, MD 20892; (301) 435-5978. Fax, (301) 480-4559. Dr. James Ostell, Director.*
General email, info@ncbi.nlm.nih.gov

Web, www.ncbi.nlm.nih.gov and Pub Med Central, www.pubmedcentral.nih.gov

Creates automated systems for storing and analyzing knowledge of molecular biology and genetics. Develops new information technologies to aid in understanding the molecular processes that control human health and disease. Conducts basic research in computational molecular biology. Sponsors PubMed Central, a publicly accessible digital archive of life sciences journal literature.

Office of Science *(Energy Dept.), Biological and Environmental Research (BER), Biological Systems Science Division (BSSD), 19901 Germantown Rd., #SC23.2, Germantown, MD 20874-1290 (mailing address: Germantown Bldg., 1000 Independence Ave. S.W., #SC23.2, Washington, DC 20585); (301) 903-5469. Fax, (301) 903-0567. Todd Anderson, Director.*
Web, http://science.energy.gov/ber/research/bssd

Supports research and technology development to achieve predictive systems-level understanding of complex biological systems, including redesign of microbes and plants for sustainable biofuel production, improved carbon storage, and contaminent remediation. Areas of research include genomic science, bioimaging technology, biological systems, and radiological sciences.

Office of Science *(Energy Dept.), Biological and Environmental Research (BER), Biological Systems Science Division (BSSD), Genomic Science Program, 19901 Germantown Rd., #SC72, Germantown, MD 20874-1290; (301) 903-5469. Fax, (301) 903-0567. Catherine (Cathy) Ronning, Program Manager.*
Web, http://genomicscience.energy.gov

Supports research using microbial and plant genomic data, high-throughput technologies, and modeling and simulation to develop predictive understanding of biological systems behavior relevent to solving energy and environmental challenges.

▶**NONGOVERNMENTAL**

Biotechnology Innovation Organization, *1201 Maryland Ave. S.W., #900, 20024; (202) 962-9200. Fax, (202) 488-6301. James C. Greenwood, President. Press, (202) 962-9505.*

General email, info@bio.org

Web, www.bio.org and Twitter, @IAmBiotech

Membership: U.S. and international companies engaged in biotechnology. Monitors government activities at all levels; promotes educational activities; conducts workshops.

Friends of the Earth (FOE), *1101 15th St. N.W., 11th Floor, 20005; (202) 783-7400. Fax, (202) 783-0444. Erich Pica, President. Toll-free, (877) 843-8687.*
Web, www.foe.org, Twitter, @foe_us and Facebook, www.facebook.com/foe.us

Monitors legislation and regulations on issues related to seed industry consolidation and patenting laws and on business developments in genetic engineering and synthetic biology and their effect on farming, food production, genetic resources, and the environment.

Genetic Alliance, *4301 Connecticut Ave. N.W., #404, 20008-2369; (202) 966-5557. Fax, (202) 966-8553. Sharon Terry, Chief Executive Officer.*
General email, info@geneticalliance.org

Web, www.geneticalliance.org and Twitter, @GeneticAlliance

Coalition of government, industry, advocacy organizations, and private groups that seeks to advance genetic research and its applications. Promotes increased funding for research, improved access to services, and greater support for emerging technologies, tests, and treatments. Acts as an advocate on behalf of individuals and families living with genetic conditions.

J. Craig Venter Institute, *9714 Medical Center Dr., Rockville, MD 20850; (301) 795-7000. J. Craig Venter, Chief Executive Officer.*
Web, www.jcvi.org

Research institute that analyzes genomes and gene products for medical, nutritional, and agricultural uses; studies genomic sciences and their ethical, legal, and economic implications for society. Produces reports; offers courses, workshops, and internships.

Kennedy Institute of Ethics (*Georgetown University***),** *Healy Hall, 37th and O Sts. N.W., 4th Floor, 20057; (202) 687-8099. David Sulmasy, Director (Acting). Library, (202) 687-3885.*
General email, kennedyinstitute@georgetown.edu

Web, https://kennedyinstitute.georgetown.edu, Twitter, @kieatgu and Facebook, www.facebook.com/KennedyInstituteofEthics

Carries out teaching and research on medical ethics, including legal and ethical definitions of death, allocation of health resources, and recombinant DNA and human gene therapy. Sponsors the annual Intensive Bioethics Course. Conducts international programs. Serves as the home of the Bioethics Research Library at Georgetown University (http://bioethics.georgetown.edu) and the National Information Resource on Ethics and Human Genetics (http://genthx.georgetown.edu). Provides free reference assistance and bibliographic databases covering

all ethical issues in health care, genetics, and biomedical research. Publishes the *Kennedy Institute of Ethics Journal.* Library open to the public.

Botany

▶**AGENCIES**

National Arboretum (*Agriculture Dept.***),** *3501 New York Ave. N.E., 20002-1958; (202) 245-4523. Richard T. Olsen, Director, (202) 245-4539.*
Web, www.usna.usda.gov

Maintains public display of plants on 446 acres; provides information and makes referrals concerning cultivated plants (exclusive of field crops and fruits); conducts plant breeding and research; maintains herbarium.

National Arboretum (*Agriculture Dept.***), Floral and Nursery Plants Research,** *3501 New York Ave. N.E., #100, 20002; (301) 504-6848. Fax, (301) 504-5096. Margaret Pooler, Research Leader, (301) 504-5218.*
Web, www.ars.usda.gov/northeast-area/washington-dc/national-arboretum/floral-and-nursery-plants-research

Supports research and implementation of new technologies in florist and nursery industries. Areas of research include development of new floral, nursery, and turf plants; detection and control of pathogens in ornamental plants; ornamental plant taxonomy; improvement of nursery production systems; and curation of woody landscape plant germplasm as part of the National Plant Germplasm System.

National Museum of Natural History (*Smithsonian Institution***), Botany,** *10th St. and Constitution Ave. N.W., 20560-0166 (mailing address: P.O. Box 37012, MRC 166, Washington, DC 20013-7012); (202) 633-0920. Fax, (202) 786-2563. Laurence J. Dorr, Department Chair. Library, (202) 633-1680.*
Web, www.botany.si.edu

Seeks to discover and describe the diversity of plant life in terrestrial and marine environments, interpret the origins of diversity, and explain the processes responsible for diversity. Research includes systematics, phylogenetics, anatomy, morphology, biogeography, and ecology. Studies how humans are affected by, and have altered, plant diversity. Works to manage, grow, and conserve the collection in the United States National Herbarium (more than 5 million specimens) as a global plant resource. Library open to the public Monday through Friday, 10:00 a.m.–4:00 p.m., by appointment only.

Smithsonian Institution, Botany and Horticulture Library, *10th St. and Constitution Ave. N.W., #W422, 20560-0166 (mailing address: P.O. Box 37012, MRC 154, Washington, DC 20013-7012); (202) 633-1685. Fax, (202) 786-2866. Robin Everly, Branch Librarian.*
General email, askalibrarian@si.edu

Web, https://library.si.edu/libraries/botany-and-horticulture-library and Twitter, @SmithsonianLibraries

Collections include taxonomic botany, plant morphology, general botany, history of botany, grasses, and algae. Permits on-site use of collections (9:00 a.m.–4:30 p.m.; appointment necessary); makes interlibrary loans. (Housed at the National Museum of Natural History.)

Smithsonian Tropical Research Institute, *Forest Global Earth Observatory (ForestGEO), 10th St. and Constitution Ave. N.W., MRC 166, 20560; (202) 633-0666. Fax, (202) 786-2563. Stuart J. Davies, Director. General email, ForestGEO@si.edu*

Web, https://forestgeo.si.edu and Twitter, @ForestGEO

Conducts long-term forest research and contributes to the scientific community through training, grants, and partnerships with international organizations. Uses research to monitor impacts of climate change and to guide natural resource policy. (Formerly Center for Tropical Forest Science.)

▶**CONGRESS**

For a listing of relevant congressional committees and subcommittees, please see pages 682–683 or the Appendix.

U.S. Botanic Garden, *100 Maryland Ave. S.W., 20001 (mailing address: 245 1st St. S.W., Washington, DC 20024); (202) 225-8333. Fax, (202) 225-1561. Saharah Moon Chapotin, Executive Director, (202) 225-1110. Horticulture hotline, (202) 226-4785. Press, (202) 226-4145. Program registration information, (202) 225-1116. Special events, (202) 226-7674. Tour line, (202) 226-2055. General email, usbg@aoc.gov*

Web, www.usbg.gov and Twitter, @USBotanicGarden

Collects, cultivates, and grows various plants for public display and study.

▶**NONGOVERNMENTAL**

American Society for Horticultural Science (ASHS), *1018 Duke St., Alexandria, VA 22314; (703) 836-4606. Michael W. Neff, Executive Director, ext. 106. General email, webmaster@ashs.org*

Web, www.ashs.org and Twitter, @ASHA_Hort

Membership: educators, government workers, firms, associations, and individuals interested in horticultural science. Promotes scientific research and education in horticulture, including international exchange of information. Publishes the *Journal of the American Society for Horticultural Science*.

American Society of Plant Biologists, *15501 Monona Dr., Rockville, MD 20855-2768; (301) 251-0560. Fax, (301) 279-2996. Crispin Taylor, Chief Executive Officer, ext. 115. General email, info@aspb.org*

Web, http://my.aspb.org and Twitter, @ASPB

Membership: plant physiologists, plant biochemists, and molecular biologists. Seeks to educate and promote public interest in the plant sciences. Publishes journals; provides job listings for members; sponsors awards, annual conference, meetings, courses, and seminars.

Zoology

▶**AGENCIES**

Animal and Plant Health Inspection Service (APHIS) *(Agriculture Dept.), Veterinary Services, 400 N. 8th St., #726, Richmond, VA 23219-4824; (804) 343-2561. Fax, (804) 343-2599. Dr. Jack Shere, Deputy Administrator. General email, jack.a.shere@aphis.usda.gov*

Web, www.aphis.usda.gov/aphis/ourfocus/animalhealth

Works to protect and improve the health, quality, and marketability of our nation's animals and various wildlife and animal products. Creates priorities, objectives, strategies, and field activities for cattle, avian, swine, aquaculture, sheep and goat, equine, and cervid health. Disseminates regulatory information addressing the interstate and importation requirements of genetically engineered animals and insects that may spread animal diseases. Advises on animal health and public issues, including animal welfare, local and commercial livestock, natural resource conservation, and public health; conducts animal health monitoring and surveillance.

National Agricultural Library *(Agriculture Dept.), National Invasive Species Information Center (NISIC), 10301 Baltimore Ave., Room 109-HH, Beltsville, MD 20705; (301) 504-6454. Joyce Bolton, Coordinator. General email, invasive@ars.usda.gov*

Web, www.invasivespeciesinfo.gov and Twitter, @InvasiveInfo

Serves as a reference gateway to information, organizations, and services about invasive species.

National Museum of Natural History *(Smithsonian Institution), Entomology, 10th St. and Constitution Ave. N.W., 20560-0105 (mailing address: P.O. Box 37012, MRC 187, #CE-723, Washington, DC 20013-7012); (202) 633-1016. Fax, (202) 786-2894. Sean G. Brady, Chair, (202) 633-0997. Library, (202) 633-1680.*

Web, http://entomology.si.edu

Conducts worldwide research in entomology. Maintains the national collection of insects; lends insect specimens to specialists for research and classification; conducts scholarly training and lectures; publishes research; and maintains databases. Library open to the public by appointment.

National Museum of Natural History *(Smithsonian Institution), Invertebrate Zoology, 10th St. and Constitution Ave. N.W., 20560-0163 (mailing address: P.O. Box 37012, MRC 163, Washington, DC 20013-7012); (202) 633-1740. Fax, (202) 633-0182. Ellen Strong, Chair. Library, (202) 633-1680.*

Web, http://invertebrates.si.edu

Conducts research on the identity, morphology, histology, life history, distribution, classification, and ecology of marine, terrestrial, and freshwater invertebrate animals (except insects); maintains the national collection of invertebrate animals; aids exhibit and educational programs; conducts predoctoral and postdoctoral fellowship programs; provides facilities for visiting scientists in the profession.

National Museum of Natural History *(Smithsonian Institution), Paleobiology, 10th St. and Constitution Ave. N.W., 20560-0121 (mailing address: P.O. Box 37012, MRC 121, Washington, DC 20013-7012); (202) 633-1328. Fax, (202) 786-2832. Hans Dieter-Sues, Chair.*
General email, paleodept@si.edu
Web, http://paleobiology.si.edu
Loans and visiting the collections, paleovisits@si.edu

Conducts research worldwide on invertebrate paleontology, paleobotany, sedimentology, and vertebrate paleontology; provides information on paleontology, paleoclimatology, paleoceanography, ecosystem dynamics, and processes of evolution and extinction. Maintains national collection of fossil organisms and sediment samples.

National Museum of Natural History *(Smithsonian Institution), Vertebrate Zoology, 10th St. and Constitution Ave. N.W., 20560-0159 (mailing address: P.O. Box 37012, MRC 163, Washington, DC 20013-7012); (202) 633-0790. Fax, (202) 633-0182. Carole Baldwin, Curator. Library, (202) 633-1680.*
Web, http://vertebrates.si.edu

Conducts research worldwide on the systematics, ecology, evolution, zoogeography, and behavior of mammals, birds, reptiles, amphibians, and fish; maintains the national collection of specimens. Processes, sorts, and distributes to scientists specimens of marine vertebrates; engages in taxonomic sorting, community analysis, and specimen and sample data management.

►NONGOVERNMENTAL

Assn. of Zoos and Aquariums, *8403 Colesville Rd., #710, Silver Spring, MD 20910-3314; (301) 562-0777. Fax, (301) 562-0888. Dan Ashe, President.*
General email, generalinquiry@aza.org
Web, www.aza.org and Twitter, @zoos_aquariums

Membership: interested individuals and professionally run zoos and aquariums in North America. Administers professional accreditation program; participates in worldwide conservation, education, and research activities.

Entomological Society of America, *3 Park Pl., #307, Annapolis, MD 21401-3722; (301) 731-4535. Fax, (301) 731-4538. David Gammel, Executive Director.*
General email, esa@entsoc.org
Web, www.entsoc.org and Twitter, @EntsocAmerica

Scientific association that promotes the science of entomology and the interests of professionals in the field, with branches throughout the United States.

Jane Goodall Institute, *1595 Spring Hill Rd., #550, Vienna, VA 22182; (703) 682-9220. Fax, (703) 682-9312. Carlos Drews, Chief Operating Officer.*
Web, www.janegoodall.org

Seeks to increase primate habitat conservation, expand noninvasive primate research, and promote activities that ensure the well-being of primates. (Affiliated with Jane Goodall Institutes in Canada, Europe, Asia, and Africa.)

ENGINEERING

General

►AGENCIES

National Institute of Standards and Technology (NIST) *(Commerce Dept.), Engineering Laboratory, 100 Bureau Dr., MS 8600, Gaithersburg, MD 20899-8600; (301) 975-5900. Fax, (301) 975-4032. Howard H. Harary, Director.*
General email, el@nist.gov
Web, www.nist.gov/el

Performs analytical, laboratory, and field research in the area of building technology and its applications for building usefulness, safety, and economy; produces performance criteria and evaluation, test, and measurement methods for building owners, occupants, designers, manufacturers, builders, and federal, state, and local regulatory authorities.

National Science Foundation (NSF), *Engineering Directorate, 2415 Eisenhower Ave., Room C14000, Alexandria, VA 22314; (703) 292-8300. Fax, (703) 292-9467. Dawn M. Tilbury, Assistant Director.*
Web, www.nsf.gov/dir/index.jsp?org=eng

Directorate that supports fundamental research and education in engineering through grants and special equipment awards. Programs are designed to enhance international competitiveness and to improve the quality of engineering in the United States.

►NONGOVERNMENTAL

American Assn. of Engineering Societies, *1801 Alexander Bell Dr., Reston, VA 20191; (202) 296-2237. Fax, (202) 296-1151. Melissa Prelewicz, Executive Director.*
General email, info@aaes.org
Web, www.aaes.org

Federation of engineering societies; member associations are in industry, construction, government, academia, and private practice. Advances the knowledge, understanding, and practice of engineering. Serves as delegate to the World Federation of Engineering Organizations.

American Council of Engineering Companies, *1015 15th St. N.W., 8th Floor, 20005-2605; (202) 347-7474. Fax, (202) 898-0068. Linda Bauer Darr, President; Steven Hall, Vice President of Advocacy and External Affairs.*
General email, acec@acec.org
Web, www.acec.org, Twitter, acec_national and Facebook, www.facebook.com/home.php#!/pages/ACEC-National/150339271657089

Membership: practicing consulting engineering firms and state, local, and regional consulting engineers councils. Serves as an information clearinghouse for member companies in such areas as legislation, legal cases, marketing, management, professional liability, business practices, and insurance. Monitors legislation and regulations.

American Society for Engineering Education, *1818 N St. N.W., #600, 20036-2479; (202) 331-3500. Fax, (202) 265-8504. Norman L. Fortenberry, Executive Director, (202) 331-3545. Press, (202) 331-5767.*
Web, www.asee.org and Twitter, @ASEE_DC

Membership: engineering faculty and administrators, professional engineers, government agencies, and engineering colleges, corporations, and professional societies. Conducts research, conferences, and workshops on engineering education. Monitors legislation and regulations.

American Society of Civil Engineers (ASCE), *1801 Alexander Bell Dr., Reston, VA 20191-4400; Washington Office, 101 Constitution Ave., #375E, 20001; (202) 789-7850. Fax, (202) 789-7859. Thomas W. Smith III, Executive Director. Toll-free, (800) 548-2723. Press, (202) 789-7853. General email, customercare.asce.org*
Web, www.asce.org and Twitter, @ascetweets

Membership: professionals and students in civil engineering. Organizes international conferences; maintains technical and professional reference materials; hosts e-learning sites.

American Society of Heating, Refrigerating, and Air Conditioning Engineers (ASHRAE), *Government Affairs, 1255 23rd St. N.W., #825, 20037; (202) 833-1830. Fax, (202) 833-0118. Doug Read, Director.*
General email, ashre@ashrae.org
Web, www.ashrae.org and Twitter, @ashraenews

Membership: engineers and others involved with the heating, ventilation, air conditioning, and refrigeration industry in the United States and abroad, including students. Sponsors research, meetings, and educational activities. Monitors legislation and regulations. (Headquarters in Atlanta, Ga.)

American Society of Mechanical Engineers (ASME), *Government Relations, 1828 L St. N.W., #510, 20036-5104; (202) 785-3756. Fax, (202) 429-9417. Kathryn Holmes, Director of Government Relations, (202) 785-7390.*
General email, grdept@asme.org
Web, www.asme.org and Twitter, @ASMEdotorg

Serves as a clearinghouse for sharing of information between the federal government and the engineering profession. Monitors legislation and regulations. (Headquarters in New York.)

American Society of Naval Engineers (ASNE), *1452 Duke St., Alexandria, VA 22314-3458; (703) 836-6727. Fax, (703) 836-7491. Capt. Joseph (Ike) Iacovetta (USN, Ret.), Executive Director (Acting), (202) 794-9163.*

General email, asnehq@navalengineers.org
Web, www.navalengineers.org and Twitter, @NavalEngineers

Membership: civilian, active duty, and retired naval engineers. Provides forum for an exchange of information between industry and government involving all phases of naval engineering.

Geoprofessional Business Assn., *15800 Crabbs Branch Way, #300, Rockville, MD 20855; (301) 565-2733. Joel G. Carson, Executive Director.*
General email, info@geoprofessional.org
Web, www.geoprofessional.org and Twitter, @GBAssn

Membership: geoprofessional service firms, including firms that perform geotechnical and infrastructure engineering, environmental services, and construction materials engineering and testing. Conducts conferences and a peer review program on quality control policies and procedures in geoprofessional service firms.

Institute of Electrical and Electronics Engineers–USA (IEEE-USA), *Washington Office, 2001 L St. N.W., #700, 20036; (202) 785-0017. Fax, (202) 785-0835. Chris Brantley, Managing Director.*
General email, ieeeusa@ieee.org
Web, www.ieeeusa.org, Twitter, @IEEEUSA and Facebook, www.facebook.com/ieeeusa

U.S. arm of an international technological and professional organization concerned with all areas of electrotechnology policy, including aerospace, computers, communications, biomedicine, electric power, and consumer electronics. (Headquarters in New York.)

Institute of Transportation Engineers (ITE), *1627 Eye St. N.W., #600, 20006; (202) 785-0060. Fax, (202) 785-0609. Jeffrey F. Paniati, Executive Director, ext. 131.*
General email, ite_staff@ite.org
Web, www.ite.org, Twitter, @ITEhq and Facebook, www.facebook.com/ITEHQ

Membership: international professional transportation engineers. Conducts research, seminars, and training sessions; provides professional and scientific information on transportation standards and recommended practices.

International Test and Evaluation Assn., *4400 Fair Lakes Court, #104, Fairfax, VA 22033-3801; (703) 631-6220. Fax, (703) 631-6221. James M. Gaidry, Executive Director, ext. 204.*
General email, info@itea.org
Web, www.itea.org

Membership: engineers, scientists, managers, and other industry, government, and academic professionals interested in testing and evaluating products and complex systems. Provides a forum for information exchange; monitors international research.

National Academy of Engineering, *500 5th St. N.W., 20001; (202) 334-3200. Fax, (202) 334-2290. C.D. Mote Jr., President, (202) 204-3615.*
Web, www.nae.edu and Twitter, @theNAEng

Society whose members are elected in recognition of important contributions to the field of engineering and technology. Shares responsibility with the National Academy of Sciences for examining questions of science and technology at the request of the federal government; promotes international cooperation. (Affiliated with the National Academy of Sciences.)

National Research Council (NRC), *Infrastructure and the Constructed Environment Board*, *Keck Center, 500 5th St. N.W., #WS938, 20001; (202) 334-3505. Fax, (202) 334-3718. Cameron Oskvig, Chair.*
General email, bice@nas.edu

Web, http://sites.nationalacademies.org/deps/bice/index .htm

Advises the government, the private sector, and the public on technology, science, and public policy related to the design, construction, operations, maintenance, security, and evaluation of buildings, facilities, and infrastructure systems; the relationship between the constructed and natural environments and their interaction with human activities; the effects of natural and manmade hazards on constructed facilities and infrastructure; and the interdependencies of infrastructure systems, including power, water, transportation, telecommunications, wastewater, and buildings.

National Research Council (NRC), *National Material and Manufacturing Board*, *Keck Center, 500 5th St. N.W., #WS921, 20001; (202) 334-3505. Fax, (202) 334-3575. James Lancaster, Director; Ben Wang, Chair.*
General email, nmmb@nas.edu

Web, http://sites.nationalacademies.org/DEPS/NMMB

Conducts research on materials and manufacturing, including at the atomic, molecular, and nano scales, and innovative applications of new and existing materials, including pilot-scale and large-scale manufacturing, the design of new devices, and disposal.

National Society of Black Engineers, *205 Daingerfield Rd., Alexandria, VA 22314; (703) 549-2207. Fax, (703) 683-5312. Karl Reid, Executive Director.*
General email, info@nsbe.org

Web, www.nsbe.org and Twitter, @NSBE

Membership: Black engineers and college students studying engineering. Offers leadership training, professional and career development opportunities, technical seminars and workshops, and career fairs. Holds an annual convention.

National Society of Professional Engineers (NSPE), *1420 King St., Alexandria, VA 22314-2794; (703) 684-2800. Fax, (703) 684-2821. Mark Golden, Executive Director. Member services, (888) 285-6773.*
General email, memserv@nspe.org

Web, www.nspe.org

Membership: U.S.-licensed professional engineers from all disciplines. Holds engineering seminars; operates an information center.

The Optical Society, *2010 Massachusetts Ave. N.W., 20036; (202) 223-8130. Fax, (202) 223-1096. Elizabeth Rogan, Chief Executive Officer. Press, (202) 416-1443.*
General email, info@osa.org

Web, www.osa.org and Twitter, @OpticalSociety

Membership: global optics and photonic scientists, engineers, educators, students, technicians, business professionals, and others interested in optics and photonics worldwide. Promotes research and information exchange; conducts conferences; publishes a scientific journal; sponsors technical groups and programming as well as outreach and educational activities.

ENVIRONMENTAL AND EARTH SCIENCES

General

►AGENCIES

National Aeronautics and Space Administration (NASA), *Science Mission Directorate (SMD)*, *300 E St. S.W., #3J28, 20546; (202) 358-3889. Fax, (202) 358-3092. Thomas Zurbuchen, Associate Administrator.*
General email, science@hq.nasa.gov

Web, http://science.nasa.gov and Twitter, @NASAScienceCast

Seeks to understand the integrated functioning of the earth and the sun. Administers space mission programs and mission-enabling programs, including sub-orbital missions. Sponsors scientific research and analysis. Exchanges information with the international science community. Interests include earth climate and environmental change.

National Oceanic and Atmospheric Administration (NOAA) *(Commerce Dept.), National Centers for Environmental Information (NCEI)*, *1315 East-West Hwy., SSMC3, 4th Floor, Silver Spring, MD 20910-3282; (301) 713-3277. Fax, (301) 713-3300. Mary Wohlgemuth, Director, (828) 271-4476.*
General email, ncei.info@noaa.gov

Web, www.nodc.noaa.gov

Responsible for hosting and providing access to comprehensive oceanic, atmospheric, and geophysical data. Provides world's largest collection of freely available oceanographic data, including water temperatures dating back to the late 1700s and measuring thousands of meters deep, scientific journals, rare books, historical photo collections, and maps through the NOAA Central Library, and data management expertise and training. Merger of NOAA's three data centers: National Climatic Data Center, National Geophysical Data Center, and National Oceanographic Data Center, which includes the National Coastal Data Development Center.

National Oceanic and Atmospheric Administration (NOAA) *(Commerce Dept.), National Environmental*

Satellite, Data, and Information Service (NESDIS), 1335 *East-West Hwy., SSMC1, 8th Floor, Silver Spring, MD 20910; (301) 713-3578. Fax, (301) 713-1249. Stephen Volz, Assistant Administrator. Press, (301) 713-0214.*
Web, www.nesdis.noaa.gov and Twitter, @NOAASatellites

Provides satellite observations of the environment by operating polar orbiting and geostationary satellites; develops satellite techniques; increases the utilization of satellite data in environmental services.

National Science Foundation (NSF), *Geosciences Directorate,* 2415 *Eisenhower Ave., Room C8000, Alexandria, VA 22314; (703) 292-8500. Fax, (703) 292-9448. William E. Easterling, Assistant Director.*
Web, www.nsf.gov/div/index.jsp?org=geo

Directorate that supports research about the earth, including its atmosphere, continents, oceans, and interior. Works to improve the education and human resource base for the geosciences; participates in international and multidisciplinary activities, especially to study changes in the global climate.

National Science Foundation (NSF), *Polar Programs,* 2415 *Eisenhower Ave., Room W7100, Alexandria, VA 22134; (703) 292-8030. Fax, (703) 292-9081. Kelly K. Falkner, Director, 7(603) 292-7424.*
Web, www.nsf.gov/div/index.jsp?div=OPP

Funds and manages U.S. activity in Antarctica; provides grants for arctic programs in polar biology and medicine, earth sciences, atmospheric sciences, meteorology, ocean sciences, and glaciology. The Polar Information Program serves as a clearinghouse for polar data and makes referrals on specific questions.

Smithsonian Environmental Research Center *(Smithsonian Institution),* 647 *Contees Wharf Rd., Edgewater, MD 21037-0028 (mailing address: P.O. Box 28, Edgewater, MD 21037-0028); (443) 482-2200. Fax, (443) 482-2380. Anson (Tuck) H. Hines, Director, (443) 482-2208. Press, (443) 482-2325.*
Web, https://serc.si.edu and Twitter, @SmithsonianEnv

Performs laboratory and field research that measures physical, chemical, and biological interactions to determine the mechanisms of environmental responses to humans' use of air, land, and water. Evaluates properties of the environment that affect the functions of living organisms. Maintains research laboratories, public education program, facilities for controlled environments, and estuarine and terrestrial lands. Wildlife sanctuary open to the public Monday through Saturday, 9:00 a.m.–4:30 p.m., except federal holidays.

U.S. Geological Survey (USGS) *(Interior Dept.),* 12201 *Sunrise Valley Dr., MS 100, Reston, VA 20192-0002; (703) 648-4000. Fax, (703) 648-4454. (703) 648-5953. James F. Reilly, Director, (703) 648-7411. Information, 888-ASK-USGS. Library, (703) 648-7182. Press, (703) 648-4460. phone, (703) 648-5953.*
General email, ask@usgs.gov
Web, www.usgs.gov and Twitter, @USGS

Provides reports, maps, and databases that describe and analyze water, energy, biological, and mineral resources; the land surface; and the underlying geological structure and dynamic processes of the Earth.

U.S. Geological Survey (USGS) *(Interior Dept.), Library Services,* 950 *National Center, #1D100, Reston, VA 20192 (mailing address: 12201 Sunrise Valley Dr., #1D100, MS 950, Reston, VA 20192); (703) 648-4301. Fax, (703) 648-6373. Catharine (Cate) Canevari, Library Director, (703) 648-7182.*
General email, library@usgs.gov
Web, http://library.usgs.gov

Maintains collection of books, periodicals, serials, maps, and technical reports on geology, mineral and water resources, mineralogy, paleontology, petrology, soil and environmental sciences, biology, and physics and chemistry as they relate to natural sciences. Open to the public Monday–Friday; makes interlibrary loans.

United States Arctic Research Commission, 4350 *N. Fairfax Dr., #510, Arlington, VA 22203; (703) 525-0111. Fax, (703) 525-0114. John W. Farrell, Executive Director, (703) 525-0113.*
General email, info@arctic.gov
Web, www.arctic.gov and Twitter, @US_ARC

Presidential advisory commission that develops policy for arctic research; assists the interagency Arctic Research Policy Committee in implementing a national plan of arctic research; recommends improvements in logistics, data management, and dissemination of arctic information.

▶**CONGRESS**

For a listing of relevant congressional committees and subcommittees, please see pages 682–683 or the Appendix.

▶**NONGOVERNMENTAL**

American Academy of Environmental Engineers and Scientists, 147 *Old Solomons Island Rd., #303, Annapolis, MD 21401; (410) 266-3311. Fax, (410) 266-7653. Burk Kalweit, Executive Director.*
General email, info@aaees.org
Web, www.aaees.org, Twitter, @AAEESdotORG and Facebook, www.facebook.com/AAEESdotORG

Membership: state-licensed environmental engineers and scientists who have passed examinations in environmental engineering and/or science specialties, including general environment, air pollution control, solid waste management, hazardous waste management, industrial hygiene, radiation protection, water supply, environmental sustainability, and wastewater.

American Geophysical Union, 2000 *Florida Ave. N.W., 20009-1277; (202) 462-6900. Fax, (202) 328-0566. Robin Bell, President; Christine McEntee, Executive Director. Information, (800) 966-2481.*

General email, service@agu.org

Web, http://sites.agu.org, Twitter, @theagu and Facebook, www.fdacebook.com/AmericanGeopphysicalUnion

Membership: scientists and technologists who study the environments and components of the earth, sun, and solar system. Promotes international cooperation; disseminates information.

National Research Council (NRC), *Polar Research Board,* Keck Center, 500 5th St. N.W., #602, 20001; (202) 334-3479. Fax, (202) 334-3825. Julie Brigham-Grette, Chair; Amanda Staudt, Director, (202) 334-3512.
General email, prb@nas.edu

Web, http://dels.nas.edu/prb

Promotes polar science and provides scientific guidance to federal agencies and the nation on issues in the Arctic, the Antarctic, and cold regions in general.

Atmospheric Sciences

► **AGENCIES**

National Oceanic and Atmospheric Administration (NOAA) *(Commerce Dept.),* 1401 Constitution Ave. N.W., #5128, 20230; (202) 482-3436. Fax, (202) 408-9674. Timothy Gallaudet, Under Secretary (Acting). Library, (301) 713-2600. Press, (202) 482-6090.
Web, www.noaa.gov and Twitter, @NOAA

Conducts research in marine and atmospheric sciences; issues weather forecasts and warnings vital to public safety and the national economy; maintains a national environmental center with data from satellite observations and other sources, including meteorological, oceanic, geodetic, and seismological data centers; provides colleges and universities with grants for research, education, and marine advisory services; prepares and provides nautical and aeronautical charts and maps.

National Oceanic and Atmospheric Administration (NOAA) *(Commerce Dept.),* **Climate Program Office (CPO),** 1315 East-West Hwy., SSMC-3, Room 12124, Silver Spring, MD 20910; (301) 734-1263. Fax, (301) 713-0515. Wayne Higgins, Director.
General email, oar.cpo.office@noaa.gov

Web, www.cpo.noaa.gov

Manages NOAA-funded research programs that focus on climate science and assessments on a regional, national, and international scale.

National Oceanic and Atmospheric Administration (NOAA) *(Commerce Dept.),* **Marine and Aviation Operations (OMAO),** 8403 Colesville Rd., #500, Silver Spring, MD 20910-3282; (301) 713-1045. Fax, (301) 713-1541. Rear Adm. Michael J. Silah, Director, (301) 713-7600. Press, (301) 713-7671.
Web, www.omao.noaa.gov

Uniformed service of the Commerce Dept. that operates and manages NOAA's fleet of atmospheric, hydrographic, oceanographic, and fisheries research ships and aircraft. Supports NOAA's scientific programs.

National Oceanic and Atmospheric Administration (NOAA) *(Commerce Dept.),* **National Weather Service (NWS),** 1325 East-West Hwy., #18150, Silver Spring, MD 20910; (301) 713-9095. Fax, (301) 713-0610. Louis W. Uccellini, Assistant Administrator. Library, (301) 683-1307. National Weather Service forecast office, (703) 996-2200.
Web, www.weather.gov and Twitter, @nws

Issues warnings of hurricanes, severe storms, and floods; provides weather forecasts and services for the general public and for aviation and marine interests.

National Oceanic and Atmospheric Administration (NOAA) *(Commerce Dept.),* **National Weather Service (NWS), Climate Prediction Center (CPC),** 5830 University Research Court, College Park, MD 20740; (301) 683-3428. David DeWitt, Director. Press, (301) 427-9000.
Web, www.cpc.ncep.noaa.gov

Provides climate forecasts, assesses the impact of short-term climate variability, and warns of potentially extreme climate-related events.

National Oceanic and Atmospheric Administration (NOAA) *(Commerce Dept.),* **National Weather Service (NWS), National Centers for Environmental Prediction (NCEP),** 5830 University Research Court, College Park, MD 20740; (301) 683-1314. Fax, (301) 683-1325. William M. Lapenta, Director, (301) 683-1315.
Web, www.ncep.noaa.gov

The National Center for Environmental Prediction and the National Environmental Satellite, Data, and Information Service are part of the World Weather Watch Programme developed by the United Nations World Meteorological Organization. Collects and exchanges data with other nations; provides other national weather service offices, private meteorologists, and government agencies with products, including forecast guidance products.

National Oceanic and Atmospheric Administration (NOAA) *(Commerce Dept.),* **Oceanic and Atmospheric Research (OAR),** 1315 East-West Hwy., Silver Spring, MD 20910; (301) 713-2458. Craig N. McLean, Assistant Administrator.
Web, http://research.noaa.gov and Twitter, @NOAAResearch

Researches weather and water information in order to provide better forecasts and earlier warnings for natural disasters. Promotes the understanding of climate change and variability.

National Science Foundation (NSF), *Atmospheric and Geospace Sciences Division,* 2415 Eisenhower Ave., Room W8022, Alexandria, VA 22314; (703) 292-8520. Fax, (703) 292-9022. Anjuli S. Bamzai, Director.
Web, www.nsf.gov/div/index.jsp?div=ags

Supports research on the earth's atmosphere and the sun's effect on it, including studies of the physics, chemistry, and dynamics of the earth's upper and lower atmospheres and its space environment; climate processes and variations; and the natural global cycles of gases and particles in the earth's atmosphere.

Office of Science *(Energy Dept.)*, *Biological and Environmental Research (BER), Climate and Environmental Sciences Division (CESD)*, *19901 Germantown Rd., #SC23.1, Germantown, MD 20874-1290 (mailing address: Germantown Bldg., 1000 Independence Ave. S.W., #SC23.1, Washington, DC 20585); (301) 903-4775. Gerald Geernaert, Director.*
Web, http://science.energy.gov/ber/research/cesd

Supports research on atmospheric systems, terrestrial ecosystems, and subsurface biogeochemistry as well as Earth system modeling and regional and global climate change modeling to improve predictive understanding of Earth's climate and environmental systems in order to inform development of sustainable solutions to energy challenges.

▶**NONGOVERNMENTAL**

Alliance for Responsible Atmospheric Policy, *2111 Wilson Blvd., 8th Floor, Arlington, VA 22201; (703) 243-0344. Fax, (703) 243-2874. Kevin Fay, Executive Director.*
General email, fay@alliancepolicy.org
Web, www.alliancepolicy.org and Twitter, @Atmospolicy

Coalition of users and producers of chlorofluorocarbons (CFCs). Seeks further study of the stratospheric ozone depletion theory. Coordinates industry participation in the development of economically and environmentally beneficial international and domestic atmospheric policies.

Climate Institute, *1201 New York Ave. N.W., #410, 20005; (202) 552-0163. John C. Topping, President.*
General email, info@climate.org
Web, http://climate.org and Twitter, @Climate_Inst

Educates the public and policymakers on climate change, the greenhouse effect, global warming, and the depletion of the ozone layer. Assesses climate change risks and develops strategies on mitigating climate change in developing countries and in North America.

National Research Council (NRC), *Atmospheric Sciences and Climate Board, Keck Center, 500 5th St. N.W., #602, 20001; (202) 334-3512. Fax, (202) 334-3825. Amanda Staudt, Director; A. R. (Ravi) Ravishankara, Chair.*
General email, basc@nas.edu
Web, www.dels.nas.edu/basc

Supports research on climate change, air pollution, and severe weather in order to address environmental policies, human health, emergency management, energy choices, manufacturing decisions, construction codes, and agricultural methods.

Geology and Earth Sciences

▶**AGENCIES**

Interior Dept. (DOI), *Assistant Secretary for Water and Science, 1849 C St. N.W., #6641, MS 6341, 20240; (202) 208-3186. Fax, (202) 208-6948. Timothy (Tim) R. Petty, Assistant Secretary, (202) 513-0535.*
Web, www.doi.gov

Administers departmental water, scientific, and research activities. Directs and supervises the Bureau of Reclamation and the U.S. Geological Survey.

National Museum of Natural History *(Smithsonian Institution), Mineral Sciences, 10th St. and Constitution Ave. N.W., 4th Floor, East Wing, 20560 (mailing address: P.O. Box 37012, MRC 119, Washington, DC 20013-7012); (202) 633-1860. Fax, (202) 357-2476. Jeffrey Post, Chair. Library, (202) 633-1680.*
Web, www.mineralsciences.si.edu

Conducts research on gems, minerals, meteorites, rocks, and ores. Interests include mineralogy, petrology, volcanology, and geochemistry. Maintains the Global Volcanism Network, which reports worldwide volcanic and seismic activity. Library open to the public by appointment.

National Museum of Natural History *(Smithsonian Institution), Paleobiology, 10th St. and Constitution Ave. N.W., 20560-0121 (mailing address: P.O. Box 37012, MRC 121, Washington, DC 20013-7012); (202) 633-1328. Fax, (202) 786-2832. Hans Dieter-Sues, Chair.*
General email, paleodept@si.edu
Web, http://paleobiology.si.edu
Loans and visiting the collections, paleovisits@si.edu

Conducts research worldwide on invertebrate paleontology, paleobotany, sedimentology, and vertebrate paleontology; provides information on paleontology, paleoclimatology, paleoceanography, ecosystem dynamics, and processes of evolution and extinction. Maintains national collection of fossil organisms and sediment samples.

National Science Foundation (NSF), *Earth Sciences Division, 2415 Eisenhower Ave., Room E8300, Alexandria, VA 22314; (703) 292-8550. Fax, (703) 292-9447. Lina Patino, Director (Acting).*
Web, www.nsf.gov/div/index.jsp?div=ear

Provides grants for research in geology, geophysics, geochemistry, and related fields, including tectonics, hydrologic sciences, and continental dynamics.

Office of Science *(Energy Dept.), Biological and Environmental Research (BER), Climate and Environmental Sciences Division (CESD), 19901 Germantown Rd., #SC23.1, Germantown, MD 20874-1290 (mailing address: Germantown Bldg., 1000 Independence Ave. S.W., #SC23.1, Washington, DC 20585); (301) 903-4775. Gerald Geernaert, Director.*
Web, http://science.energy.gov/ber/research/cesd

Supports research on atmospheric systems, terrestrial ecosystems, and subsurface biogeochemistry as well as Earth system modeling and regional and global climate change modeling to improve predictive understanding of Earth's climate and environmental systems in order to inform development of sustainable solutions to energy challenges.

U.S. Geological Survey (USGS) *(Interior Dept.), Coastal and Marine Hazards and Resources,* 12201 Sunrise Valley Dr., MS 905, Reston, VA 20192; (703) 648-6422. Fax, (703) 648-5464. John W. Haines, Program Coordinator.
Web, http://marine.usgs.gov

Handles resource assessment, exploration research, and marine geologic and environmental studies on U.S. coastal regions and the Outer Continental Shelf.

U.S. Geological Survey (USGS) *(Interior Dept.), Earthquake and Geologic Hazards,* 12201 Sunrise Valley Dr., MS905, Reston, VA 20192-0002; (703) 648-6786. Fax, (703) 648-6717. William S. Leith, Senior Science Advisor.
Web, http://earthquake.usgs.gov

Manages geologic, geophysical, and engineering investigations, including assessments of hazards from earthquakes; conducts research on the mechanisms and occurrences of earthquakes worldwide and their relationship to the behavior of the crust and upper mantle; develops methods for predicting the time, place, and magnitude of earthquakes; conducts engineering and geologic studies on ground failures.

U.S. Geological Survey (USGS) *(Interior Dept.), Global Seismographic Network,* 12201 Sunrise Valley Dr., MS 905, Reston, VA 20192-0002; (703) 648-6714. Fax, (703) 648-6717. Cecily J. Wolfe, Associate Program Coordinator.
Web, http://earthquake.usgs.gov/monitoring/gsn

Monitors and researches seismic activity globally through a network of seismological and geophysical sensors.

U.S. Geological Survey (USGS) *(Interior Dept.), Land Change Science Program,* 12201 Sunrise Valley Dr., MS 516, Reston, VA 20192-0002; (703) 648-5320. Fax, (703) 648-6953. Debra A. Willard, Program Co-Coordinator; Brad Reed, Program Co-Coordinator.
Web, http://usgs.gov/land-resources/land-change-science-program?qt-programs-l2-landing-page=0#qt-programs-l2-landing-page

Collects, analyzes, and disseminates information about natural and human-induced changes to the Earth's surface to better understand the rates, causes, and consequences of climate and land use change. Develops methods and processes for the use of land-surface science in public policy.

U.S. Geological Survey (USGS) *(Interior Dept.), National Cooperative Geologic Mapping Program,* 12201 Sunrise Valley Dr., MS 908, Reston, VA 20192; (703) 648-6053. Fax, (703) 648-6937. John C. Brock, Program Coordinator.
Web, http://ncgmp.usgs.gov

Funds the production of geologic maps in the United States. Provides geologic mapping data from across North America to public and private organizations.

U.S. Geological Survey (USGS) *(Interior Dept.), Volcano Hazards Program,* 12201 Sunrise Valley Dr., MS 904, Reston, VA 20192-0002; (703) 648-4773. Fax, (703) 648-5483. Charles W. Mandeville, Program Coordinator.
General email, vscweb@usgs.gov
Web, http://volcanoes.usgs.gov

Manages geologic, geophysical, and engineering investigations, including assessments of hazards from volcanoes; conducts research worldwide on the mechanisms of volcanoes and on igneous and geothermal systems. Issues warnings of potential volcanic hazards.

▶**NONGOVERNMENTAL**

American Geosciences Institute, 4220 King St., Alexandria, VA 22302-1502; (703) 379-2480. Fax, (703) 379-7563. Allyson K. Anderson Book, Executive Director, ext. 202.
General email, agi@americangeosciences.org
Web, www.americangeosciences.org and Twitter, @AGI_Updates

Membership: earth science societies and associations. Maintains a computerized database with worldwide information on geology, engineering and environmental geology, oceanography, and other geological fields (available to the public for a fee). Monitors legislation and regulations.

Carnegie Institute for Science, 1530 P St. N.W., 20005-1910; (202) 387-6400. Fax, (202) 387-8092. Eric D. Isaacs, President; Margaret Moerchen, Science Deputy.
Web, https://carnegiescience.edu and Twitter, @carnegiescience

Conducts research in plant science biology, genetic and developmental biology, earth and planetary sciences, astronomy, and global ecology and matter at extreme states at the Carnegie Institution's six research departments: Dept. of Embryology (Baltimore, Md.); Geophysical Laboratory (Washington, D.C.); Dept. of Global Ecology (Stanford, Calif.); Dept. of Plant Biology (Stanford, Calif.); Dept. of Terrestrial Magnetism (Washington, D.C.); and The Observatories (Pasadena, Calif., and Las Campanas, Chile).

National Research Council (NRC), *Earth Sciences and Resources Board,* Keck Center, 500 5th St. N.W., #616, 20001; (202) 334-2744. Fax, (202) 334-1377. Elizabeth A. Eide, Director; Gene Whitney, Chair.
General email, besr@nas.edu
Web, http://dels.nas.edu/besr

Coordinates activities, oversees research, and advises policymakers on solid-earth sciences issues. Interests include geography, geological and geotechnical engineering, mapping, and seismology and geodynamics.

Oceanography

▶**AGENCIES**

National Museum of Natural History *(Smithsonian Institution), Botany,* 10th St. and Constitution Ave. N.W.,

20560-0166 (mailing address: P.O. Box 37012, MRC 166, Washington, DC 20013-7012); (202) 633-0920. Fax, (202) 786-2563. Laurence J. Dorr, Department Chair.
Library, (202) 633-1680.
Web, www.botany.si.edu

Investigates the biology, evolution, and classification of tropical and subtropical marine algae and sea grasses. Acts as curator of the national collection in this field. Develops and participates in scholarly programs. Library open to the public Monday through Friday, 10:00 a.m.–4:00 p.m., by appointment only.

National Oceanic and Atmospheric Administration (NOAA) (Commerce Dept.), 1401 Constitution Ave. N.W., #5128, 20230; (202) 482-3436. Fax, (202) 408-9674. Timothy Gallaudet, Under Secretary (Acting).
Library, (301) 713-2600. Press, (202) 482-6090.
Web, www.noaa.gov and Twitter, @NOAA

Conducts research in marine and atmospheric sciences; issues weather forecasts and warnings vital to public safety and the national economy; maintains a national environmental center with data from satellite observations and other sources, including meteorological, oceanic, geodetic, and seismological data centers; provides colleges and universities with grants for research, education, and marine advisory services; prepares and provides nautical and aeronautical charts and maps.

National Oceanic and Atmospheric Administration (NOAA) (Commerce Dept.), Marine and Aviation Operations (OMAO), 8403 Colesville Rd., #500, Silver Spring, MD 20910-3282; (301) 713-1045. Fax, (301) 713-1541. Rear Adm. Michael J. Silah, Director, (301) 713-7600. Press, (301) 713-7671.
Web, www.omao.noaa.gov

Uniformed service of the Commerce Dept. that operates and manages NOAA's fleet of atmospheric, hydrographic, oceanographic, and fisheries research ships and aircraft. Supports NOAA's scientific programs.

National Oceanic and Atmospheric Administration (NOAA) (Commerce Dept.), National Ocean Service (NOS), 1305 East-West Hwy., SSMC4, #9149, Silver Spring, MD 20910; (301) 713-3074. Fax, (301) 713-4269. Nicole LaBoeuf, Assistant Administrator (Acting). Press, (301) 713-3066.
General email, nos.info@noaa.gov
Web, www.oceanservice.noaa.gov

Manages charting and geodetic services, oceanography and marine services, coastal resource coordination, and marine survey operations; conducts environmental cleanup of coastal pollution.

National Oceanic and Atmospheric Administration (NOAA) (Commerce Dept.), National Sea Grant College Program, 1315 East-West Hwy., SSMC-3, 11th Floor, Silver Spring, MD 20910; (301) 734-1066. Fax, (301) 713-0799. Jonathan Pennock, Director, (301) 734-1089. General email, SGweb@noaa.gov
Web, www.seagrant.noaa.gov and Twitter, @SeaGrant

Provides institutions with grants for marine research, education, and advisory services; provides marine environmental information.

National Science Foundation (NSF), Ocean Sciences Division, 2415 Eisenhower Ave., Room W8100, Alexandria, VA 22134; (703) 292-8580. Fax, (703) 292-9449. Terence M. Quinn, Director, (703) 292-7240.
Web, www.nsf.gov/div/index.jsp?div=oce

Awards grants and contracts for acquiring, upgrading, and operating oceanographic research facilities that lend themselves to shared usage. Facilities supported include ships, submersibles, and shipboard and shorebased data logging and processing equipment. Supports development of new drilling techniques and systems.

U.S. Geological Survey (USGS) (Interior Dept.), Coastal and Marine Hazards and Resources, 12201 Sunrise Valley Dr., MS 905, Reston, VA 20192; (703) 648-6422. Fax, (703) 648-5464. John W. Haines, Program Coordinator.
Web, http://marine.usgs.gov

Surveys the continental margins and the ocean floor to provide information on the mineral resources potential of submerged lands.

▶**NONGOVERNMENTAL**

Marine Technology Society, 1100 H St. N.W., #LL-100, 20005; (202) 717-8705. Fax, (202) 347-4302. Kathleen Herndon, Executive Director.
General email, membership@mtsociety.org
Web, www.mtsociety.org

Membership: scientists, engineers, technologists, and others interested in marine science, technology, and education.

National Research Council (NRC), Ocean Studies Board, Keck Center, 500 5th St. N.W., MS 607, 20001; (202) 334-2714. Fax, (202) 334-2885. Larry A. Mayer, Chair; Susan Roberts, Director.
General email, osbfeedback@nas.edu
Web, http://dels.nas.edu/osb

Conducts research to understand, manage, and conserve coastal and marine environments. Areas of interest include the ocean's role in the global climate system, technology and infrastructure needs for ocean research, ocean-related aspects of national security, fisheries science and management, and ocean education.

INFORMATION SCIENCE AND TECHNOLOGY

General

▶**AGENCIES**

Defense Information Systems Agency (Defense Dept.), 6910 Cooper Ave., Fort Meade, MD 20755;

(703) 607-6001. Vice Adm. Nancy A. Norton (USA), Director.
Web, www.disa.mil

The Defense Dept. agency responsible for information technology and the central manager for major portions of the defense information infrastructure. Units include the White House Communications Agency.

Health and Human Services Dept. (HHS), *National Coordinator for Health Information Technology (ONC)*, *330 C St. S.W., Floor 7, 20201; (202) 690-7151. Fax, (202) 690-6079. Dr. Don Rucker, National Coordinator.*
General email, onc.request@hhs.gov

Web, www.healthit.gov and Twitter, @ONC_HealthIT

Coordinates nationwide efforts to implement information technology that allows for electronic use and exchange of health information. Goals include ensuring security for patient health information, improving health care quality, and reducing health care costs.

National Institute of Standards and Technology (NIST) *(Commerce Dept.), Information Technology Lab, 100 Bureau Dr., Bldg. 225, #B264, MS 8900, Gaithersburg, MD 20899-8900; (301) 975-2900. Fax, (301) 975-2378. Charles (Chuck) H. Romine, Director.*
General email, itl_inquiries@nist.gov

Web, www.nist.gov/itl and Twitter, @nistcyber

Collaborates with other institute laboratories, other federal agencies, the U.S. private sector, standards development organizations, and other national and international stakeholders in the development and application of new information technologies to help meet national priorities; develops and deploys standards, tests, and metrics to assure secure, reliable, and interoperable information systems; collaborates to develop cybersecurity standards, guidelines, and techniques for federal agencies and U.S. industry; conducts research in computer science and technology.

National Science Foundation (NSF), *Information and Intelligent Systems Division*, *2415 Eisenhower Ave., Room W10100, Alexandria, VA 22134; (703) 292-8930. Fax, (703) 292-9073. Henry A. Kautz, Director, (703) 292-2606.*
Web, www.nsf.gov/div/index.jsp?div=iis

Supports research and education that develop new knowledge about the role people play in the design and use of information technology; advances the ability to represent, collect, store, organize, visualize, and communicate about data and information; and advances knowledge about how computational systems can perform tasks autonomously, robustly, and with flexibility. Awards grants.

Networking and Information Technology Research and Development (NITRD), *National Coordination Office*, *490 L'Enfant Plaza, S.W., #801, 20024 (mailing address: 4201 Wilson Blvd., #II-405, Arlington, VA 22230); (292) 459-9674. Fax, (202) 459-9673. Tamie Roberts, Director.*
General email, nco@nitrd.gov

Web, www.nitrd.gov and Twitter, @NITRDgov

Coordinates multiagency research and development projects that involve computing, networking, and software. Reports to the National Science and Technology Council; provides information to Congress, U.S. and foreign organizations, and the public.

▶CONGRESS

For a listing of relevant congressional committees and subcommittees, please see pages 682–683 or the Appendix.

Government Accountability Office (GAO), *Information Technology (IT)*, *441 G St. N.W., #4T21, 20548; (202) 512-6408. Valerie Melvin, Managing Director, (202) 512-6304.*
Web, www.gao.gov/careers/infotech.html

Audits, analyzes, and evaluates for Congress federal information management and information security programs to improve performance and reduce costs.

▶NONGOVERNMENTAL

Accredited Standards Committee (ASC X12), *8300 Greensboro Dr., #800, McLean, VA 22102; (703) 970-4480. James (Jim) Taylor, Chair.*
General email, info@x12.org

Web, www.x12.org and Twitter, @X12standards

Promotes the development and maintenance of cross-industry Electronic Data Interchange (EDI), XML schemas, and Context Inspired Component Architecture (CICA) standards in electronic commerce that help organizations improve business methods, lower costs, and increase productivity. Provides administrative and technical support. Chartered by the American National Standards Institute. (Formerly Data Interchange Standards Assn.)

American Council for Technology and Industry Advisory Council (ACT/IAC), *3040 Williams Dr., #500, Fairfax, VA 22031; (703) 208-4800. Fax, (703) 208-4805. Kenneth (Ken) Allen, Executive Director, (703) 208-4800, ext. 204.*
General email, ACT-IAC@actiac.org

Web, www.actiac.org, Twitter, @ACTIAC and Facebook, www.facebook.com/act.iac

Brings government and industry IT executives together to enhance government's ability to use information technologies, artificial intelligence, and intelligent automation technologies. Activities include conferences, white papers, professional development programs, and other events to foster education, the exchange of information, and collaboration.

Assn. for Competitive Technology (ACT), *1401 K St. N.W., #501, 20005; (202) 331-2130. Fax, (202) 331-2139. Morgan Reed, President.*
General email, info@actonline.org

Web, www.actonline.org and Twitter, @actonline

Membership: businesses that engage in or support the information technology industry. International education and advocacy organization for information technology companies worldwide. Interests include intellectual property, international trade, e-commerce, privacy, tax policy, antitrust, and commercial piracy issues. Focuses predominantly on the interests of small and midsized entrepreneurial technology companies. Monitors legislation and regulations.

Assn. for Information and Image Management (AIIM), *8403 Colesville Rd., #1100, Silver Spring, MD 20910; (301) 587-8202. Fax, (301) 587-2711. Peggy Winton, President. Information, (800) 477-2446.*
General email, aiim@aiim.org

Web, www.aiim.org and Twitter, @AIIMIntl

Membership: manufacturers and users of image-based information systems. Works to advance the profession of information management; develops training standards on information management and document formats.

Assn. for Information Science and Technology (ASIS&T), *8555 16th St., #850, Silver Spring, MD 20910; (301) 495-0900. Fax, (301) 495-0810. Lydia Middleton, Executive Director.*
General email, asist@asist.org

Web, www.asist.org and Twitter, @assist_org

Membership: information specialists from such fields as computer science, linguistics, management, librarianship, engineering, law, medicine, chemistry, and education. Advocates research and development in basic and applied information science. Offers continuing-education programs.

Coalition for Networked Information, *21 Dupont Circle N.W., #800, 20036; (202) 296-5098. Fax, (202) 872-0884. Clifford A. Lynch, Executive Director.*
General email, info@cni.org

Web, www.cni.org and Twitter, @cni_org

Membership: higher education, publishing, network and telecommunications, information technology, and libraries and library organizations, as well as government agencies and foundations. Promotes networked information technology, scholarly communication, intellectual productivity, and education.

Future of Privacy Forum, *1400 Eye St. N.W., #450, 20005; (202) 768-8950. John Verdi, Vice President of Policy.*
General email, info@fpf.org

Web, www.fpf.org, Twitter, @futureofprivacy and Facebook, www.facebook.com/FutureofPrivacy

Think tank focusing on privacy; encourages consensus on ethical norms, policies, and practices regarding information and technology privacy.

Information Sciences Institute, *Washington Office, 3811 Fairfax Dr., #200, Arlington, VA 22203; (703) 812-3700. Fax, (703) 812-3712. Prem Natarajan, Executive Director.*
General email, info@isi.edu

Web, www.isi.edu and Twitter, @USC_ISI

Conducts basic and applied research in advanced computer, communications, and information processing technologies. Works with public- and private-sector customers to develop diverse information technologies for civilian

and military uses, often bridging multiple technology disciplines. Projects include advanced communications and network research; distributed databases and pattern recognition with applications in law enforcement, inspection systems, and threat detection; and computing architectures and devices. (Headquarters in Marina del Rey, Calif.; part of the University of Southern California.)

Information Technology Industry Council (ITI), *1101 K St. N.W., #610, 20005; (202) 737-8888. Fax, (202) 638-4922. Jason Oxman, President, (202) 626-5753. Press, (202) 524-5543.*
General email, info@itic.org

Web, www.itic.org, Twitter, @ITI_TechTweets and Facebook, www.facebook.com/ITI.dc

Membership: providers of information and communications technology products and services. Acts as advocate for member companies in the areas of privacy, immigration reform, cybersecurity, intellectual property, tax reform, telecommunications, STEM education, trade, accessibility, voluntary standards, sustainability, and internet governance.

Institute of Electrical and Electronics Engineers–USA (IEEE-USA), *Washington Office, 2001 L St. N.W., #700, 20036; (202) 785-0017. Fax, (202) 785-0835. Chris Brantley, Managing Director.*
General email, ieeeusa@ieee.org

Web, www.ieeeusa.org, Twitter, @IEEEUSA and Facebook, www.facebook.com/ieeeusa

U.S. arm of an international technological and professional organization. Interests include computing and information technology and promoting career and technology policy interests of members. (Headquarters in New York.)

Technology CEO Council, *1341 G St. N.W., #1100, 20005; (202) 585-0258. Fax, (202) 393-3031. Bruce Mehlman, Executive Director.*
General email, info@techceocouncil.org

Web, www.techceocouncil.org

Membership: chief executive officers from U.S. information technology companies. Monitors legislation and regulations on technology and trade issues. Interests include health care information technology, telecommunications, international trade, innovation, digital rights management, export and knowledge controls, and privacy.

Computer Science

▶**AGENCIES**

National Institute of Standards and Technology (NIST) *(Commerce Dept.), Information Technology Lab, 100 Bureau Dr., Bldg. 225, #B264, MS 8900, Gaithersburg, MD 20899-8900; (301) 975-2900. Fax, (301) 975-2378. Charles (Chuck) H. Romine, Director.*
General email, itl_inquiries@nist.gov

Web, www.nist.gov/itl and Twitter, @nistcyber

Collaborates in mathematical, statistical, and computer sciences with other institute laboratories, other federal agencies, the U.S. private sector, standards development organizations, and other national and international stakeholders; provides consultations, methods, and research supporting the institute's scientific and engineering projects.

National Science Foundation (NSF), *Advanced Cyberinfrastructure Division,* 2415 Eisenhower Ave., Room E10400, Alexandria, VA 22314; (703) 292-8970. Fax, (703) 292-9060. Manish Parashar, Director.
Web, www.nsf.gov/div/index.jsp?div=OAC

Supports the development of computing and information infrastructure and helps advance all science and engineering domains. Infrastructure is made accessible to researchers and educators nationwide. Interests include computing and communication, network systems, cyberinfrastructure, and information and intelligent systems.

National Science Foundation (NSF), *Computer and Information Science and Engineering Directorate,* 2415 Eisenhower Ave., Room C10000, Alexandria, VA 22314; (703) 292-8900. Fax, (703) 292-9074. James Kurose, Assistant Director.
Web, www.nsf.gov/dir/index.jsp?org=cise

Supports investigator-initiated research in computer science and engineering. Promotes the use of advanced computing, communications, and information systems. Provides grants for research and education.

National Science Foundation (NSF), *Computer and Network Systems Division,* 2415 Eisenhower Ave., Room E10300, Alexandria, VA 22314; (703) 292-8950. Fax, (703) 292-9010. Kenneth L. Calvert, Director, (703) 292-7366.
Web, www.nsf.gov/div/index.jsp?div=CNS

Supports research and education activities that strive to create new computing and networking technologies and that explore new ways to utilize existing technologies. Seeks to foster the creation of better abstractions and tools for designing, building, analyzing, and measuring future systems. Supports the computing infrastructure that is required for experimental computer science and coordinates cross-divisional activities that foster integration of research and education and broadening of participation in the computer, information science, and engineering (CISE) workforce. Awards grants.

National Science Foundation (NSF), *Computing and Communication Foundations Division,* 2415 Eisenhower Ave., Room W10200, Alexandria, VA 22314; (703) 292-8910. Fax, (703) 292-9059. Walter (Rance) Cleaveland, Director.
Web, www.nsf.gov/div/index.jsp?div=ccf

Supports research and educational activities exploring the foundations of computing and communication devices and their usage. Seeks advances in computing and communication theory, algorithms for computer and computational sciences, and architecture and design of computers and software. Awards grants.

Office of Science *(Energy Dept.),* **Advanced Scientific Computing Research (ASCR),** 19901 Germantown Rd., #SC21, Germantown, MD 20874-1290 (mailing address: Germantown Bldg., 1000 Independence Ave. S.W., #SC21, Washington, DC 20585); (301) 903-7486. Fax, (301) 903-4846. Barbara Helland, Associate Director.
General email, sc.ascr@science.doe.gov
Web, http://science.energy.gov/ascr

Supports mathematical, computational, and computer science research on behalf of the Energy Dept.

▶ NONGOVERNMENTAL

CompTIA, *Public Advocacy,* 515 2nd St. N.E., 20002; (202) 503-3629. Todd Thibodeaux, President; Elizabeth (Liz) Hyman, Executive Vice President, Public Advocacy, (202) 503-3621. Press, (202) 682-4458. Toll-free, (866) 835-8020.
General email, martes@comptia.org
Web, www.comptia.org

Trade association for technology companies offering hardware, software, electronics, telecommunications, and information technology products and services. Offers business services and networking programs to members. Monitors legislation and regulations. (Headquarters in Downers Grove, Ill.)

Computer and Communications Industry Assn. (CCIA), 25 Massachusetts Ave. N.W., 20001; (202) 783-0070. Fax, (202) 783-0534. Edward J. Black, President; Heather Greenfield, Director of Communications.
General email, hgreenfield@ccianet.org
Web, www.ccianet.org and Twitter, @ccianet

Membership: Internet service providers, software providers, and manufacturers and suppliers of computer data processing and communications-related products and services. Interests include Internet freedom, privacy and neutrality, government electronic surveillance, telecommunications policy, tax policy, federal procurement policy, communications and computer industry standards, intellectual property policies, encryption, international trade, and antitrust reform.

National Research Council (NRC), *Computer Science and Telecommunications Board,* Keck Center, 500 5th St. N.W., 20001; (202) 334-2605. Fax, (202) 334-2318. Farnam Jahanian, Chair; Jon Eisenberg, Director, (202) 334-2605.
General email, cstb@nas.edu
Web, http://sites.nationalacademies.org/CSTB

Advises the federal government on technical and public policy issues relating to computing and communications. Research includes computer science, cybersecurity, privacy, the Internet, and electronic voting and voter registration.

National Research Council (NRC), *Human-Systems Integration Board,* Keck Center, 500 5th St. N.W., 11th Floor, 20001; (202) 334-3453. Fax, (202) 334-2210. Toby Warden, Director.

General email, bohsi@nas.edu

Web, http://sites.nationalacademies.org/dbasse/bohsi

Conducts studies on human factors and human-systems integration. Areas of research include virtual reality, human–computer interaction, and modeling social networks.

The Software Alliance (BSA), 20 F St. N.W., #800, 20001; (202) 872-5500. Fax, (202) 872-5501. Victoria A. Espinel, President. Toll-free, (888) 667-4722.
General email, info@bsa.org

Web, www.bsa.org and Twitter, @BSAnews

Membership: personal and business computer software publishing companies. Promotes growth of the software industry worldwide; helps develop electronic commerce.

Software and Information Industry Assn. (SIIA), 1090 Vermont Ave. N.W., 6th Floor, 20005-4905; (202) 289-7442. Fax, (202) 289-7097. Jeff (Ken) Joseph, President, (202) 789-4440.
Web, www.siia.net and Twitter, @SIIAPolicy

Membership: software and digital content companies. Promotes the industry worldwide; sponsors conferences, seminars, and other events. Monitors legislation and regulations.

MATHEMATICAL AND PHYSICAL SCIENCES

General

▶**AGENCIES**

National Institute of Standards and Technology (NIST) (Commerce Dept.), 100 Bureau Dr., Bldg. 101, #A1134, Gaithersburg, MD 20899-1000 (mailing address: 100 Bureau Dr., MS 1000, Gaithersburg, MD 20899); (301) 975-2300. Fax, (301) 869-8972. Walter Copan, Under Secretary. TTY, (800) 877-8339.
General email, director@nist.gov

Web, www.nist.gov

Nonregulatory agency that serves as national reference and measurement laboratory for the physical and engineering sciences. Works with industry, government agencies, and academia; promotes U.S. innovation and industrial competitiveness. Research interests include advanced manufacturing, information technology and cybersecurity, energy, health care, environment and consumer safety, and physical infrastructure.

National Institute of Standards and Technology (NIST) (Commerce Dept.), Information Technology Lab, 100 Bureau Dr., Bldg. 225, #B264, MS 8900, Gaithersburg, MD 20899-8900; (301) 975-2900. Fax, (301) 975-2378. Charles (Chuck) H. Romine, Director.
General email, itl_inquiries@nist.gov

Web, www.nist.gov/itl and Twitter, @nistcyber

Collaborates in mathematical, statistical, and computer sciences with other institute laboratories, other federal agencies, the U.S. private sector, standards development organizations, and other national and international stakeholders; provides consultations, methods, and research supporting the institute's scientific and engineering projects.

National Institutes of Health (NIH) (Health and Human Services Dept.), Center for Information Technology (CIT), 6555 Rock Spring Dr., #3G04, Bethesda, MD 20817; (301) 496-4357. Fax, (301) 402-1754. Andrea T. Norris, Director. Toll Free, (888) 319-4357. TTY, (301) 496-8294.
Web, http://cit.nih.gov

Serves as the primary scientific and technological resource for the NIH in the areas of high-performance computing, database applications, mathematics, statistics, laboratory automation, engineering, computer science and technology, telecommunications, and information resources management.

National Science Foundation (NSF), Mathematical and Physical Sciences Directorate, 2415 Eisenhower Ave., Room C9000, Alexandria, VA 22134; (703) 292-8800. Fax, (703) 292-9151. Anne L. Kinney, Assistant Director.
Web, www.nsf.gov/dir/index.jsp?org=mps

Directorate that supports research in the mathematical and physical sciences; divisions focus on physics, chemistry, materials research, mathematical sciences, and astronomical sciences. Works to improve the education and human resource base for these fields; participates in international and multidisciplinary activities.

Office of Science (Energy Dept.), Basic Energy Sciences (BES), 19901 Germantown Rd., #SC22, Germantown, MD 20874-1290 (mailing address: Germantown Bldg., 1000 Independence Ave. S.W., #SC22, Washington, DC 20585); (301) 903-3081. Fax, (301) 903-6594. Harriet Kung, Director.
General email, sc.bes@science.doe.gov

Web, http://science.energy.gov/bes

Supports research to understand, predict, and control matter and energy at electronic, atomic, and molecular levels to provide foundations for new energy technology.

Chemistry

▶**AGENCIES**

National Institute of Standards and Technology (NIST) (Commerce Dept.), Center for Nanoscale Science and Technology, 100 Bureau Dr., MS 6200, Gaithersburg, MD 20899-6200; (301) 975-8001. Fax, (301) 975-8026. B. Robert Ilic, Director (Acting), (301) 975-2639.
General email, cnst@nist.gov

Web, www.nist.gov/cnst

Provides nanoscale measurement and fabrication methods and access to nanoscale construction technologies to NIST labs, universities, and industries. Offers researchers training and use of in-house nanotechnology tools. Researches nanoscale measurement instruments and methods, and promotes collaboration and shared use.

National Institute of Standards and Technology (NIST) *(Commerce Dept.), Center for Neutron Research, 100 Bureau Dr., Bldg. 235, MS 6100, Gaithersburg, MD 20899-8100; (301) 975-6210. Fax, (301) 869-4770. Robert Dimeo, Director.*
General email, ncnr@nist.gov
Web, www.nist.gov/ncnr

Provides neutron measurement capabilities to the U.S. research community, universities, and industry.

National Institute of Standards and Technology (NIST) *(Commerce Dept.), Physical Measurement Laboratory, 100 Bureau Dr., Bldg. 221, #B160, MS 8400, Gaithersburg, MD 20899-8400; (301) 975-4200. Fax, (301) 975-3038. Carl J. Williams, Director.*
Web, www.nist.gov/pml

Conducts molecular and atomic research and research on physics, electromagnetics, and the properties of solids, liquids, and radio waves.

National Science Foundation (NSF), *Chemistry Division, 2415 Eisenhower Ave., Room E9300, Alexandria, VA 22314; (703) 292-8840. Fax, (703) 292-9037. Carol Bessel, Director (Acting).*
Web, www.nsf.gov/div/index.jsp?div=che

Awards grants to research programs in organic and macromolecular chemistry, experimental and theoretical physical chemistry, analytical and surface chemistry, and inorganic, bioinorganic, and organometallic chemistry; provides funds for instruments needed in chemistry research; coordinates interdisciplinary programs. Monitors international research.

National Science Foundation (NSF), *Materials Research Division, 2415 Eisenhower Ave., Room E9400, Alexandria, VA 22134; (703) 292-8810. Fax, (703) 292-9035. Linda S. Sapochak, Director, (703) 292-4932.*
Web, www.nsf.gov/div/index.jsp?div=dmr

Provides grants for research in condensed matter physics; solid-state and materials, chemistry, polymers, metallic materials and nanostructures, ceramics, electronic and photonic materials and condensed matter and materials theory. Supports multidisciplinary research in these areas through Materials Research Science and Engineering Centers (MRSEC) and national facilities such as the National High Magnetic Field Laboratory (NHMFL) and Synchrotron Radiation Center (SRC); funds major instrumentation projects as well as the acquisition and development of instrumentation for research to create new or advance current capabilities; and encourages international collaboration to positively impact the global advancement of materials research.

▶ **NONGOVERNMENTAL**

American Assn. for Clinical Chemistry, *900 7th St. N.W., #400, 20001; (202) 857-0717. Fax, (202) 833-4576.*

Janet Kreizman, Chief Executive Officer. Toll-free, (800) 892-1400.
General email, info@aacc.org
Web, www.aacc.org, Twitter, @_AACC and Facebook, www.facebook.com/AmerAssocforClinChem

International society of chemists, physicians, and other scientists specializing in clinical chemistry. Provides educational and professional development services; presents awards for outstanding achievement. Monitors legislation and regulations.

American Chemical Society, *1155 16th St. N.W., 20036; (202) 872-4600. Fax, (202) 872-4615. Thomas M. Connelly Jr., Executive Director. Information, (800) 227-5558. Library, (202) 872-4513. Press, (202) 872-6042.*
General email, help@services.acs.org
Web, www.acs.org, Twitter, @AmerChemSociety and Facebook, www.facebook.com/AmericanChemicalSociety

Membership: professional chemists and chemical engineers. Maintains educational programs, including those that evaluate college chemistry departments and high school chemistry curricula. Administers grants and fellowships for basic research; sponsors international exchanges; presents achievement awards. Library open to the public by appointment.

American Chemical Society, *Petroleum Research Fund, 1155 16th St. N.W., 20036; (202) 872-4481. Fax, (202) 872-6319. Dean A. Dunn, Assistant Director, (202) 872-4083.*
General email, prfinfo@acs.org
Web, www.acs.org/content/acs/en/funding-and-awards/grants/prf.html and Facebook, www.facebook.com/AmericanChemicalSociety

Makes grants to nonprofit institutions for advanced scientific education and fundamental research related to the petroleum industry in chemistry, geology, and engineering.

American Chemistry Council, *700 2nd St. N.E., 20002; (202) 249-7000. Fax, (202) 249-6100. Calvin (Cal) M. Dooley, President.*
Web, www.americanchemistry.com,
Twitter, @AmChemistry and Facebook, www.facebook.com/AmericanChemistry

Membership: manufacturers of basic industrial chemicals. Provides members with technical research, communications services, and legal affairs counseling. Sponsors research on chemical risk assessments, biomonitoring, and nanotechnology. Interests include environmental safety and health, transportation, energy, and international trade and security. Monitors legislation and regulations.

National Research Council (NRC), *Chemical Sciences and Technology Board, Keck Center, 500 5th St. N.W., 20001; (202) 334-2500. Fax, (202) 334-1393. Jeremy Mathis, Director.*
General email, bcst@nas.edu
Web, http://dels.nas.edu/bcst

Advises policymakers and decisionmakers about matters related to chemistry and chemical engineering.

National Research Council (NRC), *National Material and Manufacturing Board, Keck Center, 500 5th St. N.W., #WS921, 20001; (202) 334-3505. Fax, (202) 334-3575. James Lancaster, Director; Ben Wang, Chair.*
General email, nmmb@nas.edu

Web, http://sites.nationalacademies.org/DEPS/NMMB

Conducts research on materials and manufacturing, including at the atomic, molecular, and nano scales, and innovative applications of new and existing materials, including pilot-scale and large-scale manufacturing, the design of new devices, and disposal.

Society of Chemical Manufacturers and Affiliates (SOCMA), *1400 Crystal Dr., #630, Arlington, VA 22202; (571) 348-5100. Fax, (571) 348-5138. Jennifer L. Abril, President.*
General email, info@socma.com

Web, www.socma.com and Twitter, @socma

Membership: companies that manufacture, distribute, and market organic chemicals; producers of chemical components; and providers of custom chemical services. Interests include international trade, environmental and occupational safety, chemical security, and health issues; conducts workshops and seminars. Promotes commercial opportunities for members. Monitors legislation and regulations.

Mathematics

▶**AGENCIES**

National Institute of Standards and Technology (NIST) *(Commerce Dept.), Information Technology Lab, 100 Bureau Dr., Bldg. 225, #B264, MS 8900, Gaithersburg, MD 20899-8900; (301) 975-2900. Fax, (301) 975-2378. Charles (Chuck) H. Romine, Director.*
General email, itl_inquiries@nist.gov

Web, www.nist.gov/itl and Twitter, @nistcyber

Seeks to develop applied and computational mathematics to solve problems arising in measurement science and engineering applications; collaborates with NIST and external scientists; disseminates related reference data and software; develops and applies statistical and probabilistic methods and techniques supporting research in measurement science, technology, and the production of standard reference materials.

National Science Foundation (NSF), *Mathematical and Physical Sciences Directorate, 2415 Eisenhower Ave., Room C9000, Alexandria, VA 22134; (703) 292-8800. Fax, (703) 292-9151. Anne L. Kinney, Assistant Director.*
Web, www.nsf.gov/dir/index.jsp?org=mps

Provides grants for research in the mathematical sciences in the following areas: classical and modern analysis, geometric analysis, topology and foundations, algebra and number theory, applied and computational mathematics, and statistics and probability. Maintains special projects program, which supports scientific computing equipment for mathematics research and several research

institutes. Sponsors conferences, workshops, and postdoctoral research fellowships. Monitors international research.

National Science Foundation (NSF), *Mathematical Sciences Division, 2415 Eisenhower Ave., Room E9400, Alexandria, VA 22134; (703) 292-8870. Fax, (703) 292-9450. Juan C. Meza, Director, (703) 292-2407.*
Web, www.nsf.gov/div/index.jsp?org=DMS

Supports research on the properties and applications of mathematical structures.

Office of Science *(Energy Dept.), Advanced Scientific Computing Research (ASCR), 19901 Germantown Rd., #SC21, Germantown, MD 20874-1290 (mailing address: Germantown Bldg., 1000 Independence Ave. S.W., #SC21, Washington, DC 20585); (301) 903-7486. Fax, (301) 903-4846. Barbara Helland, Associate Director.*
General email, sc.ascr@science.doe.gov

Web, http://science.energy.gov/ascr

Supports mathematical, computational, and computer science research on behalf of the Energy Dept.

▶**NONGOVERNMENTAL**

Mathematical Assn. of America, *1529 18th St. N.W., 20036-1358; (202) 387-5200. Fax, (204) 396-5647. Michael Pearson, Executive Director. Information, (800) 331-1622.*
General email, maaservice@maa.org

Web, www.maa.org

Membership: mathematics professors and individuals worldwide with a professional interest in mathematics. Seeks to improve the teaching of collegiate mathematics. Conducts professional development programs.

National Research Council (NRC), *Mathematical Sciences and Analytics Board, Keck Center, 500 5th St. N.W., #K960, 20001; (202) 334-2421. Fax, (202) 334-2422. Michelle K. Schwalbe, Director, (202) 334-1682; Stephen M. Robinson, Chair.*
General email, bmsa@nas.edu

Web, http://sites.nationalacademies.org/DEPS/BMSA

Leads NRC mathematical sciences activities. Main interests include core mathematics, applied mathematics, statistics, operations research, scientific computing, and financial and risk analysis.

Physics

▶**AGENCIES**

Goddard Space Flight Center *(National Aeronautics and Space Administration), Heliophysics Science Division (HSD), 8800 Greenbelt Rd., Code 670, Greenbelt, MD 20771; (301) 286-6418. Fax, (301) 286-5348. Holly R. Gilbert, Director.*
Web, http://hsd.gsfc.nasa.gov

Provides scientific expertise necessary to achieve NASA's strategic science goals in solar physics, heliospheric physics, geospace physics, and space weather. Houses the

Solar Physics Laboratory, the Heliospheric Physics Laboratory, the Geospace Physics Laboratory, and the Space Weather Laboratory.

National Institute of Standards and Technology (NIST) *(Commerce Dept.), Physical Measurement Laboratory, 100 Bureau Dr., Bldg. 221, #B160, MS 8400, Gaithersburg, MD 20899-8400; (301) 975-4200. Fax, (301) 975-3038. Carl J. Williams, Director.*
Web, www.nist.gov/pml

Conducts molecular and atomic research and research on physics, electromagnetics, and the properties of solids, liquids, and radio waves.

National Science Foundation (NSF), *Materials Research Division, 2415 Eisenhower Ave., Room E9400, Alexandria, VA 22134; (703) 292-8810. Fax, (703) 292-9035. Linda S. Sapochak, Director, (703) 292-4932.*
Web, www.nsf.gov/div/index.jsp?div=dmr

Provides grants for research in condensed matter physics; solid-state and materials, chemistry, polymers, metallic materials and nanostructures, ceramics, electronic and photonic materials and condensed matter and materials theory. Supports multidisciplinary research in these areas through Materials Research Science and Engineering Centers (MRSEC) and national facilities such as the National High Magnetic Field Laboratory (NHMFL) and Synchrotron Radiation Center (SRC); funds major instrumentation projects as well as the acquisition and development of instrumentation for research to create new or advance current capabilities; and encourages international collaboration to positively impact the global advancement of materials research.

National Science Foundation (NSF), *Physics Division, 2415 Eisenhower Ave., Room W9200, Alexandria, VA 22134; (703) 292-8890. Fax, (703) 292-9078. C. Denise Caldwell, Director, (703) 292-7371.*
Web, www.nsf.gov/div/index.jsp?div=phy

Awards grants for research and special programs in atomic, molecular, and optical physics; elementary particle physics; and nuclear, theoretical, and gravitational physics.

Office of Science *(Energy Dept.), High Energy Physics (HEP), Germantown Bldg., 1000 Independence Ave. S.W., #SC25, 20585; (301) 903-3624. Fax, (301) 903-2597. James L. Siegrist, Associate Director.*
General email, sc.hep@science.doe.gov
Web, http://science.energy.gov/hep

Provides grants and facilities for research in high energy (or particle) physics. Constructs, operates, and maintains particle accelerators used in high energy research.

Office of Science *(Energy Dept.), Nuclear Physics (NP), 19901 Germantown Rd., #SC26, Germantown, MD 20874-1290 (mailing address: Germantown Bldg., 1000 Independence Ave. S.W., #SC26, Washington, DC 20585); (301) 903-3613. Fax, (301) 903-3833. Timothy J. Hallman, Associate Director.*
General email, sc.np@science.doe.gov
Web, http://science.energy.gov/np

Provides grants and facilities for research in nuclear physics. Manages the nuclear data program. Develops, constructs, and operates accelerator facilities and detectors used in nuclear physics research.

▶ NONGOVERNMENTAL

American Institute of Physics, *1 Physics Ellipse, College Park, MD 20740-3843; (301) 209-3100. Michael H. Moloney, Chief Executive Director, (301) 209-3131.*
Web, www.aip.org

Fosters cooperation within the physics community; improves public understanding of science; disseminates information on scientific research.

American Institute of Physics, *Center for History of Physics, 1 Physics Ellipse, College Park, MD 20740-3843; (301) 209-3165. Gregory (Greg) Good, Director, (301) 209-3174. Library, (301) 209-3177.*
General email, chp@aip.org
Web, www.aip.org/history-programs/physics-history, Twitter, @AIPhistory and Facebook, www.facebook.com/AIPhistory

Records and preserves the history of modern physics and allied fields, including astronomy, meteorological studies, and optics. Maintains a documentation program containing interviews, unpublished data, and historical records and photographs. Manages the Niels Bohr Library, which is open to the public.

American Physical Society, *Washington Office, Office of Government Affairs, 529 14th St. N.W., #1050, 20045-2001; (202) 662-8700. Fax, (202) 662-8711. Francis Slakey, Chief Government Affairs Officer; Mark Elsesser, Legislative Affairs, (202) 662-8710. Press Secretary, (202) 662-8702.*
General email, oga@aps.org
Web, www.aps.org, Twitter, @APSphysics and Facebook, www.facebook.com/apsphysics

Scientific and educational society of educators, students, citizens, and scientists, including industrial scientists. Sponsors studies on issues of public concern related to physics, such as reactor safety and energy use. Informs members of national and international developments. (Headquarters in College Park, Md.)

Biophysical Society, *5515 Security Ln., #1110, Rockville, MD 20852; (240) 290-5600. Fax, (240) 290-5555. Jennifer Pesanelli, Executive Director.*
General email, society@biophysics.org
Web, www.biophysics.org and Twitter, @BiophysicalSoc

Membership: scientists, professors, and researchers engaged in biophysics or related fields. Encourages development and dissemination of knowledge in biophysics through meetings, publications, and outreach activities.

National Research Council (NRC), *Physics and Astronomy Board, Keck Center, 500 5th St. N.W., 20001; (202) 334-3520. Fax, (202) 334-3575. Andrew Loem, Chair; James Lancaster, Director.*

General email, bpa@nas.edu

Web, http://sites.nationalacademies.org/BPA

Provides information to the government and public on scientific matters relating to physics and astronomy, including atomic, molecular, and optical sciences, astronomy and astrophysics, plasma science, radio frequencies, and condensed matter and materials.

The Optical Society, *2010 Massachusetts Ave. N.W., 20036; (202) 223-8130. Fax, (202) 223-1096. Elizabeth Rogan, Chief Executive Officer. Press, (202) 416-1443.*

General email, info@osa.org

Web, www.osa.org and Twitter, @OpticalSociety

Membership: global optics and photonic scientists, engineers, educators, students, technicians, business professionals, and others interested in optics and photonics worldwide. Promotes research and information exchange; conducts conferences; publishes a scientific journal; sponsors technical groups and programming as well as outreach and educational activities.

Weights and Measures, Metric System

▶AGENCIES

National Institute of Standards and Technology (NIST) *(Commerce Dept.), Material Measurement Laboratory, 100 Bureau Dr., Bldg. 227, #A311, MS 8300, Gaithersburg, MD 20899-8300; (301) 975-8300. Fax, (301) 975-3845. Eric Lin, Director, (301) 975-6743.*

General email, cstlinfo@nist.gov

Web, www.nist.gov/mml

Serves as the national reference laboratory for measurements in the chemical, biological, and material sciences. Researches industrial, biological, and environmental materials and processes to support development in manufacturing, nanotechnology, electronics, energy, health care, law enforcement, food safety, and other areas. Disseminates reference measurement procedures, certified reference materials, and best-practice guides.

National Institute of Standards and Technology (NIST) *(Commerce Dept.), Physical Measurement Laboratory, 100 Bureau Dr., Bldg. 221, #B160, MS 8400, Gaithersburg, MD 20899-8400; (301) 975-4200. Fax, (301) 975-3038. Carl J. Williams, Director.*

Web, www.nist.gov/pml

Develops and disseminates national standards of measurement for length, mass, force, acceleration, time, wavelength, frequency, humidity, and radiation.

National Institute of Standards and Technology (NIST) *(Commerce Dept.), Quantum Measurement Division, 100 Bureau Dr., MS 8420, Gaithersburg, MD 20899-8420; (301) 975-3210. Fax, (301) 990-3038. Yuri Ralchenko, Chief (Acting).*

Web, www.nist.gov/pml/div684

Applies research to advance measurement instrumentation and the efficiency of electric power transmission and distribution; develops and maintains national electrical reference standards, primarily for power, energy, and related measurements.

National Institute of Standards and Technology (NIST) *(Commerce Dept.), Weights and Measures, 100 Bureau Dr., MS 2600, Gaithersburg, MD 20899-2600; (301) 975-2956. Fax, (301) 975-8091. Douglas Olson, Chief; Barbara Turner, Public Relations, (301) 975-4004.*

General email, owm@nist.gov

Web, www.nist.gov/pml/weights-and-measures

Promotes uniformity in weights and measures law and enforcement. Provides weights and measures agencies with training and technical assistance; assists state and local agencies in adapting their weights and measures to meet national standards; conducts research; sets uniform standards and regulations. As the U.S. representative to the International Organization of Legal Metrology, works to harmonize international standards and regulatory practices.

National Institute of Standards and Technology (NIST) *(Commerce Dept.), Weights and Measures, Laws and Regulations Group, 100 Bureau Dr., MS 2600, Gaithersburg, MD 20899-2600; (301) 975-3690. Fax, (301) 975-8091. Kenneth S. Butcher, Group Leader, (301) 975-4859; Elizabeth Genty, Metric Coordinator.*

General email, owm@nist.gov

Web, www.nist.gov/metric

Coordinates federal metric conversion transition to ensure consistency in the interpretation and enforcement of packaging, labeling, net content, and other laws; provides the public with technical and general information about the metric system; assists state and local governments, businesses, and educators with metric conversion activities.

▶CONGRESS

For a listing of relevant congressional committees and subcommittees, please see pages 682–683 or the Appendix.

SOCIAL SCIENCES

General

▶AGENCIES

National Institutes of Health (NIH) *(Health and Human Services Dept.), Behavioral and Social Sciences Research (OBSSR), Bldg. 31, 31 Center Dr., #B1C19, Bethesda, MD 20892-0183; (301) 402-1146. Fax, (301) 402-1150. Dr. William Riley, Director.*

Web, http://obssr.od.nih.gov and Twitter, @NIHOBSSR

Works to advance behavioral and social sciences training, to integrate a biobehavioral perspective across the NIH, and to improve communication among scientists and with the public. Develops funding initiatives for research and training. Sets priorities for research. Provides training and career development opportunities for behavioral and social scientists. Links minority students with mentors. Organizes cultural workshops and lectures.

National Museum of Natural History *(Smithsonian Institution), Library, 10th St. and Constitution Ave. N.W., East Court, 1st Floor, 20560-0154 (mailing address: P.O. Box 37012, MRC 154, Washington, DC 20013-7012); (202) 633-1680. Barbara P. Ferry, Head.*
General email, askalibrarian@si.edu

Web, www.library.si.edu/libraries/national-museum-natural-history-library

Maintains reference collections covering anthropology, biodiversity, biology, botany, ecology, entomology, ethnology, mineral sciences, paleobiology, and zoology; permits on-site use of the collections. Open to the public by appointment; makes interlibrary loans.

National Science Foundation (NSF), *Social, Behavioral, and Economic Sciences Directorate, 2415 Eisenhower Ave., Room C13000, Alexandria, VA 22134; (703) 292-8700. Fax, (703) 292-9083. Arthur W. Lupia, Assistant Director, (703) 292-9803.*
Web, www.nsf.gov/dir/index.jsp?org=SBE

Directorate that awards grants for research in behavioral and cognitive sciences, social and economic sciences, science resources studies, and international programs. Provides support for workshops, symposia, and conferences.

▶ **NONGOVERNMENTAL**

American Institutes for Research, *1000 Thomas Jefferson St. N.W., 20007; (202) 403-5000. Fax, (855) 459-6213. David Myers, President. Press, (202) 403-6347. TTY, (877) 334-3499.*
General email, inquiry@air.org

Web, www.air.org and Twitter, @AIR_Info

Conducts behavioral and social science research and provides technical assistance both domestically and internationally in the areas of education, health, and workforce productivity.

American Psychological Assn., *750 1st St. N.E., 20002-4242; (202) 336-5500. Fax, (202) 336-5502. Arthur C. Evans Jr., Chief Executive Officer. Library, (202) 336-5640. Toll-free, (800) 374-2721.*
General email, practise@apa.org

Web, www.apa.org, Twitter, @APA and Facebook, www.facebook.com/AmericanPsychologicalAssociation

Membership: professional psychologists, educators, and behavioral research scientists. Supports research, training, and professional services; works toward improving the qualifications, competence, and training programs of psychologists. Monitors international research and U.S. legislation on mental health. Library open to the public by appointment.

American Psychosomatic Society, *6728 Old McLean Village Dr., McLean, VA 22101-3906; (703) 556-9222. Fax, (703) 556-8729. Laura E. Degnon, Executive Director.*

General email, info@psychosomatic.org

Web, www.psychosomatic.org and Twitter, @connectAPS

Advances and disseminates scientific understanding of relationships among biological, psychological, social, and behavioral factors in medicine through publications, annual meetings, conferences, and interest groups. Offers educational resources and sponsors awards and scholarships.

American Sociological Assn., *1430 K St. N.W., #600, 20005; (202) 383-9005. Fax, (202) 638-0882. Nancy Kidd, Executive Officer, (202) 247-9855. TTY, (202) 638-0981. fax, (202) 638-0882.*
General email, asa@asanet.org

Web, www.asanet.org and Twitter, @ASAnews

Membership: sociologists, social scientists, and others interested in research, teaching, and application of sociology in the United States and internationally. Sponsors professional development program, teaching resources center, and education programs; offers congressional fellowships for sociologists with a PhD or substantial work experience, and predoctoral sociology fellowships for minorities.

Consortium of Social Science Assns., *1430 K St. N.W., #550, 20005; (202) 842-3525. Fax, (202) 842-2788. Wendy A. Naus, Executive Director.*
General email, cossa@cossa.org

Web, www.cossa.org and Twitter, @COSSADC

Consortium of more than 100 associations, scientific societies, universities, research centers, and institutions in the fields of criminology, economics, history, political science, psychology, sociology, statistics, geography, linguistics, law, and social science. Advocates support for research and monitors federal funding in the social and behavioral sciences; conducts seminars; publishes a biweekly electronic newsletter.

Linguistic Society of America, *522 21st St. N.W., #120, 20006-5012; (202) 835-1714. Fax, (202) 835-1717. Alyson Reed, Executive Director.*
General email, lsa@lsadc.org

Web, www.linguisticsociety.org

Membership: individuals and institutions interested in the scientific analysis of language. Holds linguistic institutes every other year and an annual meeting.

National Research Council (NRC), *Behavioral, Cognitive, and Sensory Sciences Board, Keck Center, 500 5th St. N.W., 11th Floor, 20001; (202) 334-2678. Fax, (202) 334-2210. Barbara A. Wanchisen, Director, (202) 334-2394; Susan T. Fiske, Chair.*
General email, BBCSS@nas.edu

Web, www.nationalacademies.org/bbcss

Membership: experts in the fields of cognition, human development, sensory sciences, social psychology, cognitive neuroscience, behavioral neuroscience, social neuroscience, medical ethics, evolutionary and economic anthropology, and health psychology.

National Research Council (NRC), *Children, Youth, and Families Board, Keck Center, 500 5th St. N.W., 7th Floor,*

20001; (202) 334-2300. Fax, (202) 334-2201.
Natacha Blain, Director; Angela Diaz, Chair.
General email, bcyf@nas.edu

Web, http://sites.nationalacademies.org/dbasse/bcyf/index
.htm

Interdisciplinary scientific body seeking to analyze the challenges and critical issues facing children, youth, and families. Interests include the intersection of poverty, education, and life expectancy.

Pew Research Center, *1615 L St. N.W., #800, 20036; (202) 419-4300. Fax, (202) 419-4349. Michael Dimock, President. Press, (202) 419-4372.*
General email, info@pewresearch.org

Web, www.pewresearch.org *and Twitter,* @PewResearch

Nonpartisan research organization that studies issues of public interest in America and around the world. Conducts public opinion polling and social science research; reports news; analyzes news coverage; and holds forums and briefings.

Pew Research Center, *Social and Demographic Trends Project, 1615 L St. N.W., #800, 20036; (202) 419-4372. Fax, (202) 419-4349. Kim Parker, Director. Press, (202) 419-4372.*
Web, www.pewsocialtrends.org *and*
Twitter, @allthingscensus

Studies behaviors and attitudes of Americans in key realms of their daily lives, using original survey research and analysis of government data. Topics of study include the racial wealth gap, the millennial generation, population geography, demographics, immigration, and marriage and family needs.

Anthropology

► **AGENCIES**

Anacostia Community Museum *(Smithsonian Institution), 1901 Fort Pl. S.E., 20020 (mailing address: P.O. Box 37012, MRC 0777, Washington, DC 20013-7012); (202) 633-4820. Fax, (202) 287-3183. Lisa Sasaki, Director (Acting). Press, (202) 633-4876. Public programs, (202) 633-4868. Recorded information, (202) 633-1000. Special events, (202) 633-4867.*
General email, ACMinfo@si.edu

Web, http://anacostia.si.edu *and*
Twitter, @AnacostiaMuseum

Explores, documents, and interprets social and cultural issues that impact contemporary urban communities. Presents changing exhibits and programs.

Bureau of Land Management (BLM) *(Interior Dept.), Cultural and Paleontological Resources and Tribal Consultation, 20 M St. S.E., #2134, 20003; (202) 912-7242. Emily Palus, Deputy Division Chief.*
Web, www.blm.gov/programs/cultural-heritage-and-paleontology

Manages scientific research at archaeological sites. Interests include cultural practices and human effects on environmental change.

National Museum of Natural History *(Smithsonian Institution), Anthropology, 10th St. and Constitution Ave. N.W., 20560-0112 (mailing address: P.O. Box 37012, MRC 112, Washington, DC 20013-7012); (202) 633-1920. Fax, (202) 357-2208. Igor Krupnik, Department Chair. General Smithsonian information, (202) 633-1000. Library, (202) 633-1680.*
Web, http://anthropology.si.edu

Studies humanity, past and present. Research tools include human-environmental interactions, population migrations, origins of domestication and agriculture, endangered languages and knowledge, and physical and forensic anthropology. Maintains archaeological, ethnographic, and skeletal biology collections; the National Anthropological Archive; the Human Studies Film Archives; and public exhibitions of human cultures.

National Park Service (NPS) *(Interior Dept.), Cultural Anthropology Program, 1849 C St. N.W., 20240-0001; (202) 354-2090. Jennifer Talken-Spaulding, Chief.*
General email, jennifer_talken-spaulding@nps.gov

Web, www.nps.gov/orgs/1209

Supports cultural anthropological research through funding provided to parks, and by supporting partners in educational institutions.

► **NONGOVERNMENTAL**

American Anthropological Assn., *2300 Claredon Blvd., #1301, Arlington, VA 22201; (703) 528-1902. Fax, (703) 528-3546. Edward (Ed) Liebow, Executive Director, ext. 1168.*
Web, www.americananthro.org,
Twitter, @AmericanAnthro *and Facebook,* www.facebook
.com/AmericanAnthropologicalAsssociation

Membership: anthropologists, educators, students, and others interested in anthropological studies. Publishes research studies of member organizations, sponsors workshops, and disseminates to members information concerning developments in anthropology worldwide. Publishes more than 20 journals, including *Anthropology News.*

Pre-Columbian Society of Washington, D.C., *1701 17th St. N.W., 20009; Kevin Kelly, President.*
Web, www.pcswdc.org *and Facebook,* www.facebook.com/
The-Pre-Columbian-Society-of-Washington-DC-
212117688825149

Educational organization dedicated to understanding pre-Columbian peoples and cultures of the Americas. Hosts monthly lectures.

Society for American Archaeology, *1111 14th St. N.W., #800, 20005-5622; (202) 789-8200. Fax, (202) 789-0284. Joe E. Watkins, President.*
General email, headquarters@saa.org

Web, www.saa.org *and Twitter,* @SAAorg

Promotes greater awareness, understanding, and research of archaeology on the American continents; works to preserve and publish results of scientific data and research; serves as information clearinghouse for members.

Washington Assn. of Professional Anthropologists, *P.O. Box 34684, 20043-4684; Erik Kjeldgaard, President.*
General email, admin@wapadc.org
Web, http://wapa.cloverpad.org, Twitter, @WAPADC and Facebook, www.facebook.com/WAPAdc

Membership: professional anthropologists, students, and individuals interested in the field. Promotes research and the application of anthropological perspectives; provides practical and educational services, including a mentoring program to provide career advice.

Geography and Mapping

▶AGENCIES

Bureau of Intelligence and Research (INR) *(State Dept.), Office of the Geographer and Global Issues (GGI), 2201 C St. N.W., #6722, 20520; (202) 647-1988. Lee R. Schwartz, Director.*
Web, www.state.gov/s/inr

Advises the State Dept. and other federal agencies on geographic and cartographic matters. Furnishes technical and analytical research and advice in the field of geography.

Census Bureau *(Commerce Dept.), Geography, 4600 Silver Hill Rd., 4th Floor, Suitland, MD 20746 (mailing address: 4600 Silver Hill Rd., 4th Floor, Washington, DC 20233-7400); (301) 763-1128. Fax, (301) 763-4710. Deirdre Dalpiaz Bishop, Chief.*
General email, geo.geography@census.gov
Web, www.census.gov/geo

Manages the MAF TIGER system, a nationwide geographic and address database; prepares maps for use in conducting censuses and surveys and for showing their results geographically; determines names and current boundaries of legal geographic units; defines names and boundaries of selected statistical areas; develops geographic code schemes; maintains computer files of area measurements, geographic boundaries, and map features with address ranges.

National Archives and Records Administration (NARA), *Cartographic and Architectural Unit, 8601 Adelphi Rd., #3320, College Park, MD 20740-6001; (301) 837-3200. Fax, (301) 837-3622. Peter F. Brauer, Cartographic Supervisor, (301) 837-2036.*
General email, carto@nara.gov
Web, www.archives.gov/publications/general-info-leaflets/26-cartographic.html

Makes information available on federal government cartographic records, architectural drawings, and aerial mapping films; prepares descriptive guides and inventories of records. Research room open to the public. Records may be reproduced for a fee.

National Geospatial-Intelligence Agency *(Defense Dept.), 7500 Geoint Dr., Springfield, VA 22150-7500; (571) 557-5400. Fax, (571) 558-3169. Robert Cardillo, Director. Maps and imagery products, (571) 557-5400.*
General email, publicaffairs@nga.mil
Web, www.nga.mil, Twitter, @NGA_GEOINT and Facebook, www.facebook.com/NatlGEOINTAgency

Combat support agency that develops imagery and map-based intelligence in support of national defense objectives.

National Oceanic and Atmospheric Administration (NOAA) *(Commerce Dept.), National Geodetic Survey (NGS), 1315 East-West Hwy., SSMC-3, #9340, Silver Spring, MD 20910-3282; (301) 713-3242. Fax, (301) 713-4172. Juliana P. Blackwell, Director, (240) 533-9658.*
General email, ngs.infocenter@noaa.gov
Web, www.ngs.noaa.gov

Develops and maintains the National Spatial Reference System, a national geodetic reference system that serves as a common reference for latitude, longitude, height, scale, orientation, and gravity measurements. Maps the nation's coastal zone and waterways; conducts research and development programs to improve the collection, distribution, and use of spatial data; coordinates the development and application of new surveying instrumentation and procedures.

National Oceanic and Atmospheric Administration (NOAA) *(Commerce Dept.), National Ocean Service (NOS), Coast Survey, 1315 East-West Hwy., #6147, SSMC3, Silver Spring, MD 20910-3282; (301) 713-2770. Fax, (301) 713-4019. Rear Adm. Shepard Smith, Director. Toll-free, (888) 990-6622.*
Web, www.nauticalcharts.noaa.gov and Twitter, @NOAAcharts

Directs programs and conducts research to support fundamental scientific and engineering activities and resource development for safe navigation of the nation's waterways and territorial seas. Prints on demand and distributes nautical charts.

U.S. Board on Geographic Names, *12201 Sunrise Valley Dr., MS 523, Reston, VA 20192-0523 (mailing address: 523 National Center, Reston, VA 20192); (703) 648-4552. Fax, (703) 648-4549. Louis (Lou) Yost, Executive Secretary.*
General email, bgnexec@usgs.gov
Web, http://geonames.usgs.gov

Interagency organization established by Congress to standardize geographic names used by the U.S. government. Board members are representatives from the departments of Agriculture, Commerce, Defense, Homeland Security, Interior, and State; the Central Intelligence Agency; the Government Printing Office; the Library of Congress; and the U.S. Postal Service. Sets policy governing the use of both domestic and foreign geographic names as well as underseas feature names and Antarctic feature names. (Affiliated with the U.S. Geological Survey.)

U.S. Geological Survey (USGS) *(Interior Dept.), 12201 Sunrise Valley Dr., MS 100, Reston, VA 20192-0002; (703)*

648-4000. Fax, (703) 648-4454. (703) 648-5953. *James F. Reilly, Director, (703) 648-7411. Information, 888-ASK-USGS. Library, (703) 648-7182. Press, (703) 648-4460. phone, (703) 648-5953.*
General email, ask@usgs.gov

Web, www.usgs.gov and Twitter, @USGS

Provides reports, maps, and databases that describe and analyze water, energy, biological, and mineral resources; the land surface; and the underlying geological structure and dynamic processes of the Earth.

U.S. Geological Survey (USGS) *(Interior Dept.),* **National Cooperative Geologic Mapping Program,** *12201 Sunrise Valley Dr., MS 908, Reston, VA 20192; (703) 648-6053. Fax, (703) 648-6937. John C. Brock, Program Coordinator.*
Web, http://ncgmp.usgs.gov

Funds the production of geologic maps in the United States. Provides geologic mapping data from across North America to public and private organizations.

U.S. Geological Survey (USGS) *(Interior Dept.),* **National Geospatial Program,** *12201 Sunrise Valley Dr., MS 511, Reston, VA 20192 (mailing address: 511 National Center, Reston, VA 20192); (703) 648-4725. Fax, (703) 648-4722. Michael Allan Tischler, Director.*
Web, www.usgs.gov/ngpo and The National Map, www.usgs.gov/core-science-systems/ngp/tnm-delivery

Provides a foundation of digital geospatial data representing the topography, natural landscape, and built environment of the United States. Provides data downloads at The National Map, an interactive map-based application.

▶**CONGRESS**

For a listing of relevant congressional committees and subcommittees, please see pages 682–683 or the Appendix.

Library of Congress, *Geography and Map Division, James Madison Memorial Bldg., 101 Independence Ave. S.E., #LM B01, 20540-4650; (202) 707-8530. Fax, (202) 707-8531. Paulette Hasier, Chief, (202) 707-3400. Reading room, (202) 707-6277.*
Web, www.loc.gov/rr/geogmap

Maintains cartographic collection of maps, atlases, globes, and reference books. Reference service provided; reading room open to the public. Interlibrary loans available through the library's loan division. Restricted copying privileges. Free copies may be made for personal use only (self-service).

▶**NONGOVERNMENTAL**

Assn. of American Geographers, *1710 16th St. N.W., 20009-3198; (202) 234-1450. Fax, (202) 234-2744. Douglas Richardson, Executive Director.*
General email, gaia@aag.org

Web, www.aag.org and Twitter, @theAAG

Membership: educators, students, business executives, government employees, and scientists in the field of geography. Seeks to advance professional studies in geography

and encourages the application of geographic research in education, government, and business.

Institute of Navigation, *8551 Rixlew Lane, #360, Manassas, VA 20109; (703) 366-2723. Fax, (703) 366-2724. Lisa Beaty, Executive Director.*
General email, membership@ion.org

Web, www.ion.org, Twitter, @ionavigation and Facebook, www.facebook.com/InstituteOfNavigation

Membership: individuals and organizations interested in navigation and position-determining systems. Encourages research in navigation and establishment of uniform practices in navigation operations and education; conducts symposia on air, space, marine, and land navigation, as well as position determination. Sponsors awards celebrating developments in satellite navigation.

National Geographic Maps, *1145 17th St. N.W., 20036-4688; (202) 857-7000. Juan Valdés, Director of Editorial and Cartographic Research. Toll-free and map orders, (800) 962-1643. Toll-free fax, (800) 626-8676.*
General email, maps@ngs.org

Web, www.natgeomaps.com

Produces and sells to the public political, physical, and thematic maps, atlases, and globes. (Affiliated with the National Geographic Society. Headquarters in Evergreen, Colo.)

National Society of Professional Surveyors, *5119 Pegasus Ct., Suite Q, Frederick, MD 21704; (240) 439-4615. Fax, (240) 439-4952. Curtis W. Sumner, Executive Director, ext. 106.*
General email, info@nsps.org

Web, www.nsps.us.com, Twitter, @NSPSINC and Facebook, www.facebook.com/nspsinc

Membership: professionals working worldwide in surveying, cartography, geodesy, and geographic/land information systems (computerized mapping systems used in urban, regional, and environmental planning). Sponsors workshops and seminars for surveyors and mapping professionals; participates in accreditation of college and university surveying and related degree programs; grants scholarships; develops and administers certification programs for hydrographers and survey technicians. Monitors legislation and regulations.

SPACE SCIENCES

General

▶**AGENCIES**

Bureau of Oceans and International Environmental and Scientific Affairs (OES) *(State Dept.),* **Space and Advanced Technology (SAT),** *1800 G St. N.W., #10100, 20006; (202) 663-2398. Kenneth D. Hodgkins, Director.*
Web, www.state.gov/e/oes/sat

Works with U.S. space policies and multilateral science activities to support U.S. foreign policy objectives in order to enhance U.S. space and technological competitiveness.

Goddard Space Flight Center *(National Aeronautics and Space Administration), 8800 Greenbelt Rd., Code 130, Greenbelt, MD 20771; (301) 286-2000. Fax, (301) 286-1707. Christopher J. Scolese, Director. Employee directory, (301) 286-2000. Press, (301) 286-8955. Tours, (301) 286-3978. Visitors Center, (301) 286-3978.*
Web, www.nasa.gov/centers/goddard,
Twitter, @NASAGoddard and Facebook, www.facebook.com/NASAGoddard

Conducts space and earth science research; develops and operates flight missions; maintains spaceflight tracking and data acquisition networks; develops technology and instruments; develops and maintains advanced information systems for the display, analysis, archiving, and distribution of space and earth science data; and develops National Oceanic and Atmospheric Administration (NOAA) satellite systems that provide environmental data for forecasting and research.

Goddard Space Flight Center *(National Aeronautics and Space Administration), Heliophysics Science Division (HSD), 8800 Greenbelt Rd., Code 670, Greenbelt, MD 20771; (301) 286-6418. Fax, (301) 286-5348.*
Holly R. Gilbert, Director.
Web, http://hsd.gsfc.nasa.gov

Provides scientific expertise necessary to achieve NASA's strategic science goals in solar physics, heliospheric physics, geospace physics, and space weather. Houses the Solar Physics Laboratory, the Heliospheric Physics Laboratory, the Geospace Physics Laboratory, and the Space Weather Laboratory.

Goddard Space Flight Center *(National Aeronautics and Space Administration), National Space Science Data Coordinated Archive (NSSDCA), 8800 Greenbelt Rd., Code 690.1, Greenbelt, MD 20771; (301) 286-6695. Fax, (301) 286-1635. David Williams, Head.*
General email, nssdc-request@lists.nasa.gov
Web, http://nssdc.gsfc.nasa.gov

Permanent archive for NASA space science mission data. Acquires, catalogs, and distributes NASA mission data to the international space science community, including research organizations and scientists, universities, and other interested organizations worldwide. Teams with NASA's discipline-specific space science "active archives," which provide researchers and, in some cases, the general public with access to data. Provides software tools and network access, including online information databases about NASA and non-NASA data, to promote collaborative data analysis. (Mail data requests to Coordinated Request User Support Office, Code 690.1, NASA Space Science Data Coordinated Archive, NASA Goddard Space Flight Center, Greenbelt, MD 20771.)

Goddard Space Flight Center *(National Aeronautics and Space Administration), Sciences and Exploration Directorate (SED), 8800 Greenbelt Rd., Code 600,*
Greenbelt, MD 20771; (301) 286-4828. Fax, (301) 286-1772. Mark Clampin, Director, (301) 286-6066.
Web, http://science.gsfc.nasa.gov

Plans, organizes, implements, and evaluates a broad system of theoretical and experimental scientific research in the study of the earth-sun system, the solar system and the origins of life, and the birth and evolution of the universe. Develops technology for space-based research. Activities include modeling and basic research, flight experiment development, and data analysis.

Goddard Space Flight Center *(National Aeronautics and Space Administration), Solar System Exploration Data Services (SSEDSO), 8800 Greenbelt Rd., Code 690.1, Greenbelt, MD 20771; (301) 286-1743. Fax, (301) 286-1771. Thomas Morgan, Head (Acting), (301) 286-1743.*
General email, request@nssdc.gsfc.nasa.gov
Web, http://ssedso.gsfc.nasa.gov

Coordinates data management and archiving plans within NASA's Science Mission. Operates the National Space Science Data Center (NSSDC) as a permanent archive for data associated with NASA's missions, the Crustal Dynamics Data Information System (CDDIS), and the Planetary Data System (PDS).

National Aeronautics and Space Administration (NASA), *300 E St. S.W., #5R30, 20546 (mailing address: 300 E St. S.W., Washington, DC 20546-0001); (202) 358-0001. Fax, (202) 358-4338. Jim Bridenstine, Administrator. Information, (202) 358-0001. Library, (202) 358-0168. TTY, (800) 877-0996.*
General email, public-inquiries@hq.nasa.gov
Web, www.nasa.gov, Twitter, @JimBridenstine and Library, www.hq.nasa.gov/office/hqlibrary

Develops, manages, and has oversight of the agency's programs and missions. Interacts with Congress and state officials and responds to national and international inquiries. Serves as the administrative office for the agency. Library open to the public Monday through Friday, 7:30 a.m.–5:00 p.m.

National Aeronautics and Space Administration (NASA), *Aeronautics Research Mission Directorate (ARMD), 300 E St. S.W., #6B27, 20546; (202) 358-4600. Fax, (202) 358-3640. Jaiwon Shin, Associate Administrator.*
Web, www.nasa.gov/aeroresearch and Twitter, @NASAAero

Conducts research in aerodynamics, materials, structures, avionics, propulsion, high-performance computing, human factors, aviation safety, and space transportation in support of national space and aeronautical research and technology goals. Manages the following NASA research centers: Ames (Moffett Field, Calif.), Dryden (Edwards, Calif.), Langley (Hampton, Va.), and Glenn (Cleveland, Ohio).

National Aeronautics and Space Administration (NASA), *Chief Engineer, 300 E St. S.W., #6N19, 20546; (202) 358-1823. Fax, (202) 358-3296. Ralph R. Roe Jr., Chief Engineer, (757) 864-2400.*
Web, http://oce.nasa.gov

National Aeronautics and Space Administration

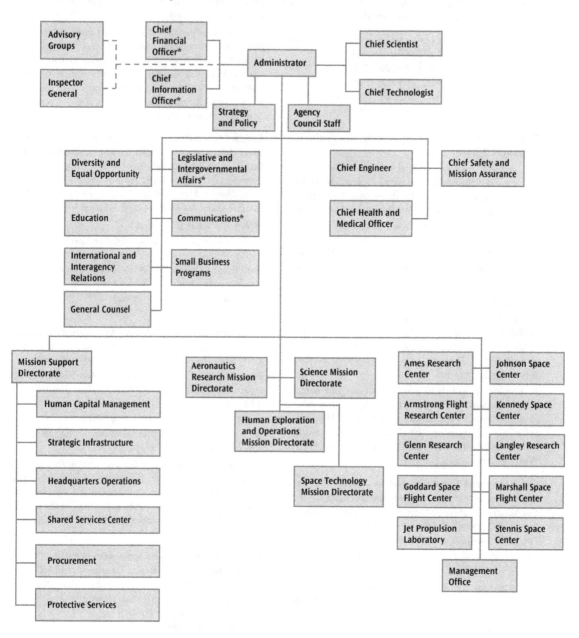

* Center functional office directors report to Agency Associate Administrator. Deputy and below report to center leadership.
– – – – Operate Independently

Serves as the agency's principal adviser on matters pertaining to the technical readiness and execution of programs and projects.

National Aeronautics and Space Administration (NASA), *Chief Health and Medical Officer,* 300 E St. S.W., 20546; (202) 358-2390. Fax, (202) 358-3349. Dr. James D. Polk, *Chief Health and Medical Officer.* Web, www.nasa.gov/offices/ochmo

Ensures the health and safety of NASA employees in space and on the ground. Develops health and medical policy, establishes guidelines for health and medical practices, oversees health care delivery, and monitors human and animal research standards within the agency.

National Aeronautics and Space Administration (NASA), *Education,* 300 E St. S.W., 4th Floor, 20546; (202)

358-0103. Fax, (202) 358-3048. Mike Kincaid, Associate Administrator.

General email, education@nasa.gov

Web, http://nasa.gov/offices/education/about and Twitter, @NASAedu

Coordinates NASA's education programs and activities to meet national educational needs and ensure a sufficient talent pool to preserve U.S. leadership in aeronautical technology and space science.

National Aeronautics and Space Administration (NASA), Human Exploration and Operations Directorate (HEO), 300 E St. S.W., 20546; (202) 358-2015. Fax, (202) 358-2838. William (Bill) H. Gerstenmaier, Associate Administrator. Information, (202) 358-0000.

Web, www.nasa.gov/directorates/heo

Responsible for space operations related to human and robotic exploration, including launch, transport, and communications. Manages the International Space Station, commercial space transportation, and research and development in space life sciences.

National Aeronautics and Space Administration (NASA), NASA Advisory Council, 300 E St. S.W., #2V79, 20546; (202) 358-4510. Lester L. Lyles (USAF, Ret.), Chair; Diane Rausch, Executive Director.

Web, www.nasa.gov/offices/nac

Advises the administrator on programs and issues of importance to NASA. The council consists of nine committees: Aeronautics; Audit, Finance, and Analysis; Commercial Space; Education and Public Outreach; Exploration; Information Technology Infrastructure; Science; Space Operations; and Technology and Innovation.

National Aeronautics and Space Administration (NASA), National Space Council, 300 E St. S.W., #5R30, 20546; (202) 358-2406. Scott Pace, Executive Director. NASA newsroom, (202) 358-1600.

Web, www.nasa.gov/content/national-space-council-users-advisory-group

Advises the president regarding national space policy and strategy. Focuses on space policy, including long-range goals, developing strategies and recommendations on space-related issues, and fostering close coordination, cooperation, and technology and information exchange among the civil, national security, and commercial space sectors.

National Aeronautics and Space Administration (NASA), Protective Services, 300 E St. S.W., #6T39, 20546; (202) 358-2010. Fax, (202) 358-3238. Joseph S. Mahaley, Assistant Administrator.

Web, www.hq.nasa.gov/hq/security.html

Serves as the focal point for policy formulation, oversight, coordination, and management of NASA's security, counterintelligence, counterterrorism, emergency preparedness and response, and continuity of operations programs.

National Aeronautics and Space Administration (NASA), Safety and Mission Assurance (SMA), 300 E St. S.W.,

#5A42, 20546; (202) 358-2406. Fax, (202) 358-2699. Terrence W. Wilcutt, Chief; Bill Loewy, GIDEP Program Manager.

General email, nasa-sma@mail.nasa.gov

Web, https://sma.nasa.gov

Evaluates the safety and reliability of NASA systems and programs. Alerts officials to technical execution and physical readiness of NASA projects.

National Air and Space Museum (Smithsonian Institution), 6th St. and Independence Ave. S.W., 20560; (202) 633-2214. Fax, (202) 633-8174. Gen. J. R. (Jack) Dailey (USMC, Ret.), Director, (202) 633-2350. Education Office, (202) 633-2540. Library, (202) 633-2320. Tours, (202) 633-2563. TTY, (202) 633-5285.

General email, info@si.edu

Web, www.airandspace.si.edu and Twitter, @airandspace

Collects, preserves, and exhibits astronautical objects and equipment of historical interest, including aircraft, spacecraft, and communications and weather satellites. Library open to the public by appointment.

National Air and Space Museum (Smithsonian Institution), Steven F. Udvar-Hazy Center, 14390 Air and Space Museum Pkwy., Chantilly, VA 20151; (703) 572-4118. Gen. John R. Dailey, Director, (202) 633-2350. Public Affairs, (202) 633-1000. TTY, (202) 633-5285.

General email, info@si.edu

Web, www.airandspace.si.edu/visit/udvar-hazy-center

Displays and preserves a collection of historical aviation and space artifacts, including the B-29 Superfortress Enola Gay, the Lockheed SR-71 Blackbird, the prototype of the Boeing 707, the space shuttle Discovery, and a Concorde. Provides a center for research into the history, science, and technology of aviation and space flight. Open to the public daily 10:00 a.m.–5:30 p.m., except December 25.

National Oceanic and Atmospheric Administration (NOAA) (Commerce Dept.), Space Commercialization, 1401 Constitution Ave. N.W., #2518, 20230; (202) 482-6125. Fax, (202) 482-4429. Kevin M. O'Connell, Director (Acting).

General email, space.commerce@noaa.gov

Web, www.space.commerce.gov

The principal unit for space commerce within NOAA and the Commerce Dept. Promotes economic growth and technological advancement of U.S. commercial space industry focusing on sectors including satellite navigation, satellite imagery, space transportation, and entrepreneurial space business. Participates in discussions of national space policy.

▶**CONGRESS**

For a listing of relevant congressional committees and subcommittees, please see pages 682–683 or the Appendix.

►INTERNATIONAL ORGANIZATIONS

European Space Agency (ESA), Washington Office, *1201 F St. N.W., #470, 20004; (202) 488-4158. Johann-Dietrich Wörner, Director General.*
Web, www.esa.int/ESA

Intergovernmental agency that promotes international collaboration in space research and development and the use of space technology for peaceful purposes. Members include Austria, Belgium, Czech Republic, Denmark, Estonia, Finland, France, Germany, Greece, Hungary, Ireland, Italy, Luxembourg, the Netherlands, Norway, Poland, Portugal, Romania, Spain, Sweden, Switzerland, and the United Kingdom. Canada participates in some programs, and Slovenia is a member state. (Headquarters in Paris.)

►NONGOVERNMENTAL

American Astronautical Society, *6352 Rolling Mill Pl., #102, Springfield, VA 22152-2370; (703) 866-0020. Fax, (703) 866-3526. Jim Way, Executive Director.*
General email, aas@astronautical.org
Web, http://astronautical.org, Twitter, @astrosociety and Facebook, www.facebook.com/ AmericanAstrnauticalSociety

Scientific and technological society of researchers, scientists, astronauts, and other professionals in the field of astronautics and spaceflight engineering. Organizes national and local meetings and symposia; promotes international cooperation.

American Institute of Aeronautics and Astronautics (AIAA), *12700 Sunrise Valley Dr., #200, Reston, VA 20191-5807; (703) 264-7500. Daniel (Dan) L. Dumbacher, Executive Director, ext. 1. Information, (800) 639-2422.*
General email, custserv@aiaa.org
Web, www.aiaa.org, Twitter, @aiaa and Facebook, www.facebook.com/AIAAFan

Membership: engineers, scientists, and students in the fields of aeronautics and astronautics. Holds workshops on aerospace technical issues for congressional subcommittees; sponsors international conferences. Offers computerized database through its Technical Information Service.

National Research Council (NRC), Aeronautics and Space Engineering Board, *Keck Center, 500 5th St. N.W., #W932, 9th Floor, 20001; (202) 334-3477. Fax, (202) 334-3701. Colleen Hartman, Director.*
General email, aseb@nas.edu
Web, www.nationalacademies.org/aseb

Membership: aeronautics and space experts. Advises government agencies on aeronautics and space engineering research, technology, experiments, international programs, and policy. Library open to the public by appointment.

National Research Council (NRC), Space Studies Board, *Keck Center, 500 5th St. N.W., 9th Floor, 20001; (202) 334-3477. Fax, (202) 334-3701. Fiona Harrison, Chair; Michael Moloney, Director, (202) 334-2142.*

General email, ssb@nas.edu
Web, www.nationalacademies.org/ssb and Twitter, @SSB_ASEB_News

Provides advice to the government on space policy issues and issues concerning space science activities, including space-based astrophysics, heliophysics, solar system exploration, earth science, and microgravity life and physical sciences. Produces discipline-based "Decadal Surveys," which set priorities for government investments over ten-year time periods.

National Space Society, *11130 Sunrise Valley Dr., #350, Reston, VA 20191 (mailing address: P.O. Box 98106, Washington, DC 20090-8106); (202) 429-1600. Fax, (703) 435-3490. Bruce Pittman, Senior Operating Officer.*
General email, nsshq@nss.org
Web, www.nss.org

Membership: individuals interested in space programs and applications of space technology. Provides information on NASA, commercial space activities, and international cooperation; promotes public education on space exploration and development; conducts conferences and workshops; publishes quarterly magazine. Monitors legislation and regulations.

Resources for the Future, *1616 P St. N.W., 20036-1400; (202) 328-5000. Fax, (202) 939-3460. Richard G. Newell, President. Library, (202) 328-5089. Press, (202) 328-5168.*
General email, info@rff.org
Web, www.rff.org and Twitter, @rff

Examines the economic aspects of U.S. space policy, including policy on communications satellites and space debris. Focuses on the role of private business versus that of government.

Space Policy Institute *(George Washington University), 1957 E St. N.W., #403, 20052; (202) 994-1592. Fax, (202) 994-1639. Henry R. Hertzfeld, Director, (202) 994-6628.*
General email, spi@gwu.edu
Web, https://spi.elliott.gwu.edu

Conducts research on space policy issues; organizes seminars, symposia, and conferences. Focuses on civilian space activities, including competitive and cooperative interactions on space between the United States and other countries.

Astronomy

►AGENCIES

National Aeronautics and Space Administration (NASA), Science Mission Directorate (SMD), *300 E St. S.W., #3J28, 20546; (202) 358-3889. Fax, (202) 358-3092. Thomas Zurbuchen, Associate Administrator.*
General email, science@hq.nasa.gov
Web, http://science.nasa.gov and Twitter, @NASAScienceCast

Seeks to understand the origins, evolution, and structure of the solar system and the universe; to understand the integrated functioning of the earth and the sun; and to ascertain the potential for life elsewhere. Administers space mission programs and mission-enabling programs, including suborbital missions. Sponsors scientific research and analysis.

National Science Foundation (NSF), *Astronomical Sciences Division, 2415 Eisenhower Ave., Room W9100, Alexandria, VA 22314; (703) 292-8820. Fax, (703) 292-9034. Richard F. Green, Director, (703) 292-8063.*
Web, www.nsf.gov/div/index.jsp?div=ast

Provides grants for ground-based astronomy and astronomical research on planetary astronomy, stellar astronomy and astrophysics, galactic astronomy, extragalactic astronomy and cosmology, and advanced technologies and instrumentation. Maintains astronomical facilities; participates in international projects.

U.S. Naval Observatory *(Defense Dept.), 3450 Massachusetts Ave. N.W., 20392-5420; (202) 762-1438. Fax, (202) 762-1489. Capt. Michael Riggins, Superintendent.*
General email, USNO_PAO@navy.mil
Web, www.usno.navy.mil/USNO

Determines the precise positions and motions of celestial bodies. Operates the U.S. master clock. Provides the U.S. Navy and Defense Dept. with astronomical and timing data for navigation, precise positioning, and command, control, and communications. Maintains a library, with the catalog available on the website.

▶ **NONGOVERNMENTAL**

American Astronomical Society, *1667 K St. N.W., #800, 20006; (202) 328-2010. Fax, (202) 234-2560. Kevin B. Marvel, Executive Officer.*
General email, aas@aas.org
Web, https://aas.org, Twitter, @AAS_Office and Facebook, www.facebook.com/ AmericanAstronomicalSociety

Membership: astronomers and other professionals interested in the advancement of astronomy in North America and worldwide. Publishes technical journals; holds scientific meetings; participates in international organizations; awards prizes for outstanding scientific achievements.

American Geophysical Union, *2000 Florida Ave. N.W., 20009-1277; (202) 462-6900. Fax, (202) 328-0566.*

Robin Bell, President; Christine McEntee, Executive Director. Information, (800) 966-2481.
General email, service@agu.org
Web, http://sites.agu.org, Twitter, @theagu and Facebook, www.fdacebook.com/ AmericanGeopphysicalUnion

Membership: scientists and technologists who study the environments and components of the earth, sun, and solar system. Promotes international cooperation; disseminates information.

Assn. of Universities for Research in Astronomy (AURA), *1331 Pennsylvania Ave. N.W., 20004; (202) 483-2101. Fax, (202) 483-2106. Matt Mountain, President.*
Web, www.aura-astronomy.org and Twitter, @AURADC

Consortium of universities. Manages four ground-based observatories and the international Gemini Project for the National Science Foundation and manages the Space Telescope Science Institute for the National Aeronautics and Space Administration.

Carnegie Institute for Science, *1530 P St. N.W., 20005-1910; (202) 387-6400. Fax, (202) 387-8092. Eric D. Isaacs, President; Margaret Moerchen, Science Deputy.*
Web, https://carnegiescience.edu and Twitter, @carnegiescience

Conducts research in plant science biology, genetic and developmental biology, earth and planetary sciences, astronomy, and global ecology and matter at extreme states at the Carnegie Institution's six research departments: Dept. of Embryology (Baltimore, Md.); Geophysical Laboratory (Washington, D.C.); Dept. of Global Ecology (Stanford, Calif.); Dept. of Plant Biology (Stanford, Calif.); Dept. of Terrestrial Magnetism (Washington, D.C.); and The Observatories (Pasadena, Calif., and Las Campanas, Chile).

National Research Council (NRC), *Physics and Astronomy Board, Keck Center, 500 5th St. N.W., 20001; (202) 334-3520. Fax, (202) 334-3575. Andrew Loem, Chair; James Lancaster, Director.*
General email, bpa@nas.edu
Web, http://sites.nationalacademies.org/BPA

Provides information to the government and public on scientific matters relating to physics and astronomy, including atomic, molecular, and optical sciences, astronomy and astrophysics, plasma science, radio frequencies, and condensed matter and materials.

17 ⚖

Social Services and Disabilities

GENERAL POLICY AND ANALYSIS

Basic Resources

▶AGENCIES

Administration for Children and Families (ACF) *(Health and Human Services Dept.)*, **Administration for Native Americans (ANA)**, *330 C St. S.W., Room 4126, 20201; (202) 690-7776. Fax, (202) 690-8145. Jeannie Hovland, Commissioner. Toll-free, (877) 922-9262.*
General email, anacomments@acf.hhs.gov
Web, www.acf.hhs.gov/ana

Awards grants for locally determined social and economic development strategies; promotes Native American economic and social self-sufficiency; funds tribes and Native American and Native Hawaiian organizations; provides grant funding for community development projects. Commissioner chairs the Intradepartmental Council on Indian Affairs, which coordinates Native American–related programs.

Corp. for National and Community Service, *250 E St. N.W., 20525; (202) 606-5000. Fax, (202) 606-3460. Barbara Stewart, Chief Executive Officer. Press, (202) 606-6775. TTY, (800) 833-3722. Volunteer recruiting information, (800) 942-2677.*
General email, info@cns.gov
Web, www.nationalservice.gov and Twitter, @nationalservice

Independent corporation that administers federally sponsored domestic volunteer programs that provide disadvantaged citizens with services, including AmeriCorps, AmeriCorps-VISTA (Volunteers in Service to America), AmeriCorps-NCCC (National Civilian Community Corps), and the Senior Corps.

Food and Nutrition Service *(Agriculture Dept.),* **Supplemental Nutrition Assistance Program (SNAP),** *3101 Park Center Dr., #808, Alexandria, VA 22302-1594; (703) 305-2026. Fax, (703) 305-2454. Jessica Shahin, Associate Administrator, (703) 305-2022.*
Web, www.fns.usda.gov/snap

Administers SNAP through state welfare agencies to provide needy persons with Electronic Benefit Transfer cards to increase food purchasing power. Provides matching funds to cover half the cost of EBT card issuance.

Health and Human Services Dept. (HHS), *200 Independence Ave. S.W., 20201; (202) 690-7000. Fax, (202) 690-7203. Alex M. Azar II, Secretary. Public Affairs, (202) 690-6343. Toll-free, (877) 696-6775. TTY, (800) 877-8339.*
General email, secretary@hhs.gov
Web, www.hhs.gov, Twitter, @HHSGov and Facebook, www.facebook.com/HHS

Acts as principal adviser to the president on health and welfare plans, policies, and programs of the federal government. Encompasses eleven operating divisions, including eight agencies in the U.S. Public Health Service and three human services agencies, including the Centers for Medicare and Medicaid Services, the Administration for Children and Families, the National Institutes of Health, and the Centers for Disease Control and Prevention.

Health and Human Services Dept. (HHS), *Planning and Evaluation (ASPE), 200 Independence Ave. S.W., #415F, 20201; (202) 690-7858. Fax, (202) 690-7383. Brenda Destro, Deputy Assistant Secretary.*
General email, osaspeinfo@hhs.gov
Web, https://aspe.hhs.gov and Twitter, @HHS_ASPE

Advises the secretary on policy development in health, disability, human services, data, and science, and provides advice and analysis on economic policy. Manages strategic and legislative planning and reviews regulations. Conducts research and evaluation studies, develops policy analyses, and estimates the cost and benefits of policy alternatives under consideration by the department or Congress.

Health and Human Services Dept. (HHS), *Planning and Evaluation (ASPE), Disability, Aging, and Long-Term Care Policy (DALTCP), 200 Independence Ave. S.W., #424E, 20201; (202) 690-6443. Fax, (202) 401-7733. Arne W. Owens, Deputy Assistant Secretary.*
Web, http://aspe.hhs.gov/office_specific/daltcp.cfm

Responsible for developing, evaluating, and coordinating department policies and programs that support the independence, productivity, health, and long-term care needs of elderly individuals and people with disabilities. Operates regionally within ten HHS offices.

Health and Human Services Dept. (HHS), *Planning and Evaluation (ASPE), Human Services Policy, Division of Data and Technical Analysis, 200 Independence Ave. S.W., #404E, 20201; (202) 690-7409. Fax, (202) 690-6562. Robin Ghertner, Director.*
Web, https://aspe.hhs.gov/office-human-services-policy

Develops policies and programs concerning low-income and disadvantaged populations. Conducts data collection activities, secondary data analysis, modeling, and cost analyses. Issues annual updates to the poverty guidelines and reports to Congress on welfare dependence indicators.

Health and Human Services Dept. (HHS), *Planning and Evaluation (ASPE), Human Services Policy, Division of Economic Support for Families, 200 Independence Ave. S.W., #404E.5, 20201; (202) 690-7409. Fax, (202) 690-6562. Kelly Kinnison, Director, (202) 690-6850.*
Web, www.aspe.hhs.gov/office-human-services-policy

Develops policies and procedures around low-income populations; conducts research and disseminates information on human services programs that provide nonelderly populations, including families with children, with economic support, employment, training, and related assistance.

▶CONGRESS

For a listing of relevant congressional committees and subcommittees, please see page 723 or the Appendix.

►NONGOVERNMENTAL

American Public Human Services Assn., *1101 Wilson Blvd., 6th Floor, Arlington, VA 22209; (202) 682-0100. Fax, (202) 289-6555. Tracy Wareing Evans, President, ext. 231.*
General email, memberservice@aphsa.org
Web, www.aphsa.org and Twitter, @APHSA1

Membership: state and local human services administrators. Works toward an integrated human services system to improve the health and well-being of individuals and communities. Exchanges knowledge and best practices through conferences and publications; implements policies in partnership with government, businesses, and community organizations; monitors legislation and regulations.

Catholic Charities USA, *2050 Ballenger Ave., #400, Alexandria, VA 22314; (703) 549-1390. Fax, (703) 549-1656. Sister Donna Markham, President.*
General email, info@catholiccharitiesusa.org
Web, https://catholiccharitiesusa.org and Twitter, @CCharitiesUSA

Member agencies and institutions provide assistance to persons of all backgrounds; community-based services include day care, counseling, food, and housing. National office provides members with advocacy and professional support, including networking, training and consulting, program development, and financial benefits. Represents the Catholic community in times of domestic disaster.

Center for Community Change, *1536 U St. N.W., 20009; (202) 339-9300. Fax, (202) 387-4892. Dorian Warren, President.*
General email, info@communitychange.org
Web, https://communitychange.org and Twitter, @communitychange

Works to strengthen grassroots organizations that help low-income people, working-class people, and minorities develop skills and resources to improve their communities and change the policies and institutions that affect their lives. Monitors legislation and regulations.

Center for Law and Social Policy (CLASP), *1200 18th St. N.W., #200, 20036; (202) 906-8000. Fax, (202) 842-2885. Olivia Golden, Executive Director.*
General email, aparker@clasp.org
Web, www.clasp.org and Twitter, @CLASP_DC

Public policy organization with expertise in national, state, and local policy affecting low-income Americans. Seeks to improve the economic security and educational and workforce prospects of low-income children, youth, adults, and families.

Center for the Study of Social Policy, *1575 Eye St. N.W., #500, 20005-3922; (202) 371-1565. Fax, (202) 371-1472. Frank Farrow, President. Press, (202) 454-4140.*
General email, info@cssp.org
Web, www.cssp.org and Twitter, @CtrSocialPolicy

Assists states and communities in organizing, financing, and delivering human services, with a focus on children and families. Helps build capacity for local decision making; helps communities use informal supports in the protection of children; promotes nonadversarial approach to class action litigation on behalf of dependent children.

Center on Budget and Policy Priorities, *820 1st St. N.E., #510, 20002; (202) 408-1080. Fax, (202) 408-1056. Robert Greenstein, President.*
General email, center@cbpp.org
Web, www.cbpp.org and Twitter, @CenterOnBudget

Research group that analyzes changes in federal and state programs, such as tax credits, Medicaid coverage, and food stamps, and their effect on low-income and moderate-income households.

Central American Resource Center (CARECEN), *1460 Columbia Rd. N.W., #C-1, 20009; (202) 328-9799. Fax, (202) 328-7894. Abel Nuñez, Executive Director.*
General email, info@carecendc.org
Web, http://carecendc.org, Twitter, @CarecenDC and Facebook, www.facebook.com/CARECEN.DC

Helps Central American and Latino immigrants obtain and maintain legal status. Seeks to address the legal and social service needs of Latinos in the Washington area; to facilitate Latinos' transition to life in the United States; and to provide Latinos with the resources and leadership skills necessary to promote the community's development. Works closely with other community-based agencies.

Christian Relief Services, *8301 Richmond Hwy., #900, Alexandria, VA 22309; (703) 317-9086. Fax, (703) 317-9690. Paul Krizek, Executive Director. Information, 800-33-RELIEF. TTY, (800) 828-1140.*
General email, info@christianrelief.org
Web, http://christianrelief.org

Promotes economic development and the alleviation of poverty in urban areas of the United States, Appalachia, Native American reservations, Haiti, Mexico, Honduras, Lithuania, the Czech Republic, and Africa. Donates medical supplies and food; administers housing, hospital, and school construction programs; provides affordable housing for low-income individuals and families.

Coalition on Human Needs, *1825 K St. N.W., #411, 20006; (202) 223-2532. Fax, (202) 223-2538. Deborah Weinstein, Executive Director, ext. 111.*
General email, bburnam@chn.org
Web, www.chn.org and Twitter, @CoalitiononHN

Promotes public policies that address the needs of low-income Americans. Members include civil rights, religious, labor, and professional organizations and service providers concerned with the well-being of children, women, the elderly, and people with disabilities.

Community Action Partnership, *1020 19th St. N.W., #700, 20036; (202) 265-7546. Fax, (202) 265-5048. Denise Harlow, Chief Executive Officer, (202) 595-0660.*
General email, info@communityactionpartnership.com
Web, https://communityactionpartnership.com and Twitter, @CAPartnership

SOCIAL SERVICES AND DISABILITIES RESOURCES IN CONGRESS

For a complete listing of congressional committees, including their full contact information, leadership, membership, and jurisdictions, please refer to the Appendix on pages 827–948.

HOUSE:

House Agriculture Committee, (202) 225-2171.
Web, agriculture.house.gov
  Subcommittee on Nutrition, (202) 225-2171.
House Appropriations Committee, (202) 225-2771.
Web, appropriations.house.gov
  Subcommittee on Agriculture, Rural
    Development, Food and Drug
    Administration, and Related Agencies,
    (202) 225-2638.
  Subcommittee on Financial Services and General
    Government, (202) 225-7245.
  Subcommittee on Labor, Health and Human
    Services, Education, and Related Agencies,
    (202) 225-3508.
  Subcommittee on Military Construction,
    Veterans Affairs, and Related Agencies,
    (202) 225-3047.
  Subcommittee on Transportation, Housing and
    Urban Development, and Related Agencies,
    (202) 225-2141.
House Education and the Workforce Committee,
  (202) 225-4527.
Web, edworkforce.house.gov
  Subcommittee on Early Childhood, Elementary,
    and Secondary Education, (202) 225-4527.
  Subcommittee on Health, Employment, Labor,
    and Pensions, (202) 225-4527.
  Subcommittee on Higher Education and
    Workforce Development, (202) 225-4527.
House Energy and Commerce Committee,
  (202) 225-2927.
Web, energycommerce.house.gov
  Subcommittee on Health, (202) 225-2927.
House Small Business Committee, (202) 225-5821.
Web, smallbusiness.house.gov
  Subcommittee on Health and Technology,
    (202) 225-5821.
House Veterans' Affairs Committee, (202) 225-3527.
Web, veterans.house.gov

  Subcommittee on Disability Assistance and
    Memorial Affairs, (202) 225-9164.
House Ways and Means Committee, (202) 225-3625.
Web, waysandmeans.house.gov
  Subcommittee on Health, (202) 225-3943.
  Subcommittee on Social Security, (202) 225-9263.

SENATE:

Senate Agriculture, Nutrition, and Forestry
  Committee, (202) 224-2035.
Web, agriculture.senate.gov
  Subcommittee on Nutrition, Agricultural
    Research, Specialty Crops, (202) 224-2035.
Senate Appropriations Committee, (202) 224-7257.
Web, appropriations.senate.gov
  Subcommittee on Agriculture, Rural
    Development, Food and Drug Administration,
    and Related Agencies, (202) 224-8090.
  Subcommittee on Labor, Health and Human
    Services, Education, and Related Agencies,
    (202) 224-9145.
  Subcommittee on Transportation, Housing and
    Urban Development, and Related Agencies,
    (202) 224-7281.
Senate Finance Committee, (202) 224-4515.
Web, finance.senate.gov
  Subcommittee on Health Care, (202) 224-4515.
  Subcommittee on Social Security, Pensions, and
    Family Policy, (202) 224-4515.
Senate Health, Education, Labor, and Pensions
  Committee, (202) 224-5375.
Web, help.senate.gov
  Subcommittee on Children and Families,
    (202) 224-5375.
  Subcommittee on Primary Health and
    Retirement Security, (202) 224-5375.
Senate Special Committee on Aging, (202) 224-5364.
Web, aging.senate.gov
Senate Veterans' Affairs Committee, (202) 224-9126.
Web, www.veterans.senate.gov

Provides community action agencies with information, training, and technical assistance; acts as advocate, at all levels of government, for low-income people. Interests include Head Start, job training, housing, food banks, energy assistance, and financial education.

Council on Social Work Education, *1701 Duke St., #200, Alexandria, VA 22314-3457; (703) 683-8080. Fax, (703) 683-8099. Darla Spence Coffey, President.*
General email, info@cswe.org
Web, www.cswe.org and Twitter, @CSocialWorkEd

Membership: educational and professional institutions, social welfare agencies, and private citizens. Promotes high-quality education in social work. Accredits social work programs.

Food Research and Action Center (FRAC), *1200 18th St. N.W., #400, 20036; (202) 986-2200. Fax, (202) 986-2525. James D. Weill, President.*
General email, cbsutton@frac.org
Web, www.frac.org, Twitter, @fractweets and Facebook, www.facebook.com/ foodresearchandactioncenter

Public interest advocacy center that works to end hunger and undernutrition in the United States. Offers organizational aid, training, and information to groups seeking to improve or expand federal food programs, including food stamp, child nutrition, and WIC (women, infants, and children) programs; conducts studies relating to hunger and poverty; coordinates network of antihunger organizations. Monitors legislation and regulations.

Jewish Federations of North America, *Washington Office,* *(202) 785-5900. William Daroff, Director.*
General email, dc@JewishFederations.org

Web, www.jewishfederations.org and
Facebook, www.facebook.com/jfederations

Acts as advocate for the 148 Jewish federations across the United States on issues of concern, including long-term care, families at risk, and naturally occurring retirement communities. Offers marketing, communications, and public relations support; coordinates a speakers bureau. (Headquarters in New York.)

National Assn. for the Advancement of Colored People (NAACP), *Washington Bureau, 1156 15th St. N.W., #915, 20005; (202) 463-2940. Fax, (202) 463-2953. Derrick Johnson, President.*
General email, washingtonbureau@naacpnet.org

Web, www.naacp.org and Twitter, @NAACP

Membership: persons interested in civil rights for all minorities. Interests include welfare reform and related social welfare matters. Administers programs that create employment and affordable housing opportunities and that improve health care. Monitors legislation and regulations. (Headquarters in Baltimore, Md.)

National Assn. of Social Workers, *750 1st St. N.E., #800, 20002-4241; (202) 408-8600. Fax, (202) 336-8312. Angelo McClain, Chief Executive Officer; Kathryn Conley, President. Member services, (800) 742-4089. Press, (202) 336-8324.*
General email, membership@socialworkers.org

Web, www.socialworkers.org and Twitter, @nasw

Membership: graduates of accredited social work education programs and students in accredited programs. Promotes the interests of social workers and their clients; promotes professional standards; offers professional development opportunities; certifies members of the Academy of Certified Social Workers; conducts research. Monitors legislation and regulations.

National Community Action Foundation (NCAF), *400 N. Capitol St. N.W., #G80, 20001 (mailing address: P.O. Box 78214, Washington, DC 20013); (202) 842-2092. Fax, (202) 842-2095. David A. Bradley, Chief Executive Officer.*
General email, info@ncaf.org

Web, www.ncaf.org and Twitter, @NCAFNews

Organization for community action agencies concerned with issues that affect the poor. Provides information on Community Services Block Grants, low-income energy assistance, employment and training, weatherization

of low-income housing, nutrition, and the Head Start program.

National Human Services Assembly, *1101 14th St. N.W., #600, 20005; (202) 347-2080. Fax, (202) 393-4517. Lee Sherman, President, (202) 347-2080 ext. 92.*
General email, info@nassembly.org

Web, www.nassembly.org

Membership: national nonprofit health and human service organizations. Provides collective leadership in the areas of health and human service. Provides members' professional staff and volunteers with a forum to share information. Supports public policies, programs, and resources that advance the effectiveness of health and human service organizations and their service delivery.

National Urban League, *Washington Bureau, 2901 14th St. N.W., 20009; (202) 265-8200. George H. Lambert Jr., Affiliate Chief Executive Officer.*
Web, http://nul.iamempowered.com/affiliate/greater-washington-urban-league

Federal advocacy division of social service organization concerned with the social welfare of African Americans and other minorities. (Headquarters in New York.)

Poverty and Race Research Action Council, *740 15th St. N.W., #300, 20005; (202) 866-0703. Fax, (202) 842-2885. Philip Tegeler, Executive Director.*
General email, info@prrac.org

Web, www.prrac.org and Twitter, @PRRAC_DC

Facilitates cooperative links between researchers and activists who work on race and poverty issues. Publishes bimonthly *Poverty & Race* newsletter and a civil rights history curriculum guide. Policy research areas include housing, education, and health disparities.

Public Welfare Foundation, *1200 U St. N.W., 20009-4443; (202) 965-1800. Fax, (202) 265-8851. Candice C. Jones, President. Press, ext. 242.*
General email, info@publicwelfare.org

Web, www.publicwelfare.org and Twitter, @PublicWelfare

Seeks to assist disadvantaged populations in overcoming barriers to full participation in society. Works to end overincarceration of adults and juveniles. Awards grants to nonprofits in the following areas: criminal and juvenile justice and workers' rights.

Salvation Army, *615 Slaters Lane, Alexandria, VA 22313 (mailing address: P.O. Box 269, Alexandria, VA 22313-0269); (703) 684-5500. David Hudson, National Commander. Media, (703) 684-5500. Donating Goods, (800) 728-7825. Toll free, (800) 725-2769.*
Web, www.salvationarmyusa.org and
Twitter, @SalvationArmyUS

International Christian social welfare organization that provides food, clothing, shelter, and social services to the homeless, the elderly, children, and persons with illness or disabilities. (International headquarters in London.)

U.S. Conference of Mayors, *City Human Services Officials, 1620 Eye St. N.W., 4th Floor, 20006; (202)*

293-7330. Fax, (202) 293-2352. Crystal D. Swann, Assistant Executive Director for Children, Health, and Human Services, (202) 861-6707.

General email, info@usmayors.org

Web, www.usmayors.org/the-conference/committees-and-task-forces

Promotes improved social services for specific urban populations through meetings, technical assistance, and training programs for members; fosters information exchange among federal, state, and local governments, human services experts, and other groups concerned with human services issues.

Urban Institute, 500 L'Enfant Plaza S.W., 20024; (202) 833-7200. Fax, (202) 467-5775. Sarah Rosen Wartell, President. Public Affairs, (202) 261-5709.

General email, publicaffairs@urban.org

Web, www.urban.org and Twitter, @urbaninstitute

Nonpartisan public policy research and education organization. Interests include states' use of federal funds; delivery of social services to specific groups, including children of mothers in welfare reform programs; retirement policy, income, and community-based services for the elderly; job placement and training programs for welfare recipients; health care cost reform; food stamps; child nutrition; the homeless; housing; immigration; justice policy and prisoner reentry; federal, state, and local tax policy; and education policy.

Urban Institute, *Center on Labor, Human Services, and Population,* 500 L'Enfant Plaza S.W., 20024; (202) 833-7200. Fax, (202) 463-8522. Signe-Mary McKernan, Vice President.

Web, www.urban.org/policy-centers/center-labor-human-services-and-population

Analyzes employment and income trends, studies how the U.S. population is growing, and evaluates programs dealing with homelessness, child welfare, and job training. Other areas of interest include immigration, mortality, sexual and reproductive health, adolescent risk behavior, child care, domestic violence, and youth development.

Urban Institute, *Income and Benefits Policy Center,* 500 L'Enfant Plaza S.W., 20024; (202) 833-7200. Fax, (202) 833-4388. Gregory Acs, Vice President.

Web, www.urban.org/center/ibp

Retirement policy, http://urban.org/retirement_policy

Studies how public policy influences behavior and the economic well-being of families, particularly the disabled, the elderly, and those with low incomes.

CHILDREN AND FAMILIES

General

▶AGENCIES

Administration for Children and Families (ACF) *(Health and Human Services Dept.),* Mary E. Switzer Bldg., 330

C St. S.W., 20201 (mailing address: 370 L'Enfant Promenade S.W., Washington, DC 20447); (202) 401-9200. Lynn Johnston, Assistant Secretary. Domestic violence hotline, (800) 799-7233; TTY, (800) 787-3224. National runaway safeline, (800) 786-2929. National teen dating abuse helpline, (866) 331-9474. Public Affairs, (202) 401-9215.

Web, www.acf.hhs.gov, Twitter, @ChildrenAndFamilies and Facebook, www.facebook.com/ChildrenAndFamilies

Administers and funds national assistance programs for Native Americans, children, youth, low-income families, and those with intellectual and developmental disabilities to promote stability, economic security, responsibility, and self-support for families; supervises programs and the use of funds to provide the most needy with aid and to increase alternatives to public assistance. Responsible for Social Services Block Grants to the states; coordinates Health and Human Services Dept. policy and regulations on child protection, day care, foster care, adoption services, child abuse and neglect, and special services for those with disabilities. Programs include Temporary Assistance to Needy Families, Child Welfare, Head Start, Child Support Enforcement, Low-Income Home Energy Assistance, Community Services Block Grant, and Refugee Resettlement Assistance.

Administration for Children and Families (ACF) *(Health and Human Services Dept.), Child Care (OCC),* 330 C St. S.W., #4502, 20201; 202- 690-6782. Fax, (202) 690-5600. Shannon Christian, Director.

Web, www.acf.hhs.gov/occ

Press, media@acf.hhs.gov

Supports low-income working families by providing access to affordable, high-quality early care and afterschool programs. Works with state, territory, and tribal governments to provide support for children and their families balancing work schedules with child care programs. Oversees policy implementation to improve and support child care licensing and child care worker training and education.

Administration for Children and Families (ACF) *(Health and Human Services Dept.), Child Support Enforcement (OCSE),* Mary E. Switzer Bldg., 330 C St. S.W., 5th Floor, 20201 (mailing address: 370 L'Enfant Promenade S.W., Washington, DC 20447); (202) 401-9373. Fax, (202) 401-5428. Scott Lekan, Commissioner.

Web, www.acf.hhs.gov/css

Helps states and tribes develop, manage, and operate child support programs. Maintains the Federal Parent Locator Service, which provides state and local child support agencies with information for locating absent parents. State enforcement agencies locate absent parents, establish paternity, establish and enforce support orders, and collect child support payments.

Administration for Children and Families (ACF) *(Health and Human Services Dept.), Children's Bureau (CB),* Mary E. Switzer Bldg., 330 C St. S.W., 3rd Floor, 20201; (202) 205-8618. Fax, (202) 205-9721. Jerry Milner, Associate Commissioner.

*Web, www.acf.hhs.gov/cb and Facebook, www.facebook
.com/thechildrensbureau*

Works with state and local agencies to develop programs that focus on preventing the abuse of children in troubled families, protecting children from further abuse, and finding permanent placements for those who cannot safely return to their homes. Administers grants.

Administration for Children and Families (ACF) *(Health and Human Services Dept.), Community Services (OCS),*
*Mary E. Switzer Bldg., 330 C St. S.W., 5th Floor, 20201
(mailing address: Mail Room 5425); (202) 401-9333.
Fax, (202) 401-5718. Clarence H. Carter, Director (Acting).
Web, www.acf.hhs.gov/ocs*

Administers the Community Services Block Grant and Discretionary Grant programs and the Low-Income Home Energy Assistance Block Grant Program for heating, cooling, and weatherizing low-income households.

Administration for Children and Families (ACF) *(Health and Human Services Dept.), Family and Youth Services Bureau (FYSB),* *Mary E. Switzer Bldg., 330 C St. S.W.,
20201; (202) 205-8102. Fax, (202) 260-9333.
William Wubbenhorst, Associate Commissioner (Acting).
Domestic violence hotline, (800) 799-7233. Runaway
safeline, (800) 786-2929.
Web, www.acf.hhs.gov/fysb and Twitter, @FYSBgov*

Administers federal discretionary grant programs for projects serving runaway and homeless youth and for projects that deter youth involvement in gangs. Provides youth service agencies with training and technical assistance. Monitors federal policies, programs, and legislation. Supports research on youth development issues, including gangs, runaways, and homeless youth. Operates national clearinghouse on families and youth. Issues grants and monitors abstinence education programs.

Administration for Children and Families (ACF) *(Health and Human Services Dept.), Family Assistance (OFA),*
*Mary E. Switzer Bldg., 330 C St. S.W., 3rd Floor, 20201;
(202) 401-9275. Fax, (202) 205-5887. Clarence H. Carter,
Director.
Web, www.acf.hhs.gov/ofa and Twitter, @OFA-ACF*

Provides leadership, direction, and technical guidance to the states, tribes, and territories on administration of the TANF (Temporary Assistance to Needy Families) Block Grant. Focuses efforts to increase economic independence and productivity for families. Provides direction and guidance in collection and dissemination of performance and other data for these programs.

Administration for Children and Families (ACF) *(Health and Human Services Dept.), Human Services, Emergency Preparedness, and Response (OHSEPR),* *Mary E. Switzer
Bldg., 330 C St. S.W., 20201; (202) 401-4966. Fax, (202)
205-8446. Natalie Grant, Director.
General email, ohsepr@acf.hhs.gov
Web, www.acf.hhs.gov/ohsepr*

Oversees human services, such as child care, child welfare, and energy assistance, in preparedness, response, and recovery from disasters and public health emergencies.

Creates emergency plans and provides technical assistance and preparedness training to families and communities. Manages the Immediate Disaster Case Management Program.

Administration for Children and Families (ACF) *(Health and Human Services Dept.), Refugee Resettlement (ORR),* *Mary E. Switzer Bldg., 330 C St.
S.W., Room 5123, 20201; (202) 401-9246. Fax, (202) 401-0981. Jonathan Hayes, Director (Acting). Parent
Hotline, (800) 203-7001.
Web, www.acf.hhs.gov/orr*

Provides critical resources to assist refugees, Cuban and Haitian entrants, asylees, trafficking and torture victims, repatriated U.S. citizens, and unaccompanied alien children. Seeks to help individuals achieve economic self-sufficiency and social adjustment to help them integrate fully into American society. Provides states and nonprofit agencies with grants for refugee social services such as English language and employment training.

Administration for Children and Families (ACF) *(Health and Human Services Dept.), Trafficking in Persons (OTIP),* *Mary E. Switzer Bldg., 330 C St. S.W.,
Washington, DC; (202) 401-9372. Fax, (202) 401-4678.
Katherine Chon, Director. Foreign national adults with
certification helpline, (866) 401-5510. Foreign national
minors with eligibility assistance helpline, (202) 205-4582.
Human trafficking tip hotline, (888) 373-7888.
General email, endtrafficking@acf.hhs.gov*

Web, www.acf.hhs.gov/otip

*Human trafficking tip email,
help@humantraffickinghotline.org*

Develops antitrafficking strategies, policies, and programs to prevent human trafficking; promotes increased health and human service capacity to respond to human trafficking and access to services for survivors.

Assistant Secretary for Health (OASH) *(Health and Human Services Dept.), Adolescent Health (OAH),* *1101
Wootton Pkwy., #700, Rockville, MD 20852; (240) 453-2846. Evelyn Kappeler, Director.
General email, oah.gov@hhs.gov*

Web, www.hhs.gov/ash/oah

Implements the Pregnancy Assistance Fund to assist states and tribes with support services for expectant and parenting teens and their families including student services at high schools, higher education institutions, and community centers and services for pregnant women who are victims of domestic abuse and sexual violence.

Bureau of Indian Affairs (BIA) *(Interior Dept.), Indian Services (OIS),* *1849 C St. N.W., MS 3645-MIB, 20240;
(202) 513-7642. Fax, (202) 208-2648. Debrah McBride,
Deputy Bureau Director (Acting). Public Affairs, (202)
208-3710.
Web, www.bia.gov/bia/ois*

Gives assistance, in accordance with state payment standards, to American Indians and Alaska Natives of federally recognized tribes living on or near reservations and in tribal service areas, and provides family and individual counseling and child welfare services.

Food and Nutrition Service *(Agriculture Dept.)*, *3101 Park Center Dr., #906, Alexandria, VA 22302-1500; (703) 305-2060. Fax, (703) 305-2908. Brandon Lipps, Administrator. Information, (703) 305-2286.*
Web, www.fns.usda.gov and Twitter, @USDANutrition

Administers all Agriculture Dept. domestic food assistance, including the distribution of funds and food for school breakfast and lunch programs (preschool through secondary) to public and nonprofit private schools; the Supplemental Nutrition Assistance Program (SNAP, formerly the food stamp program); and a supplemental nutrition program for women, infants, and children (WIC).

Food and Nutrition Service *(Agriculture Dept.)*, *Chief Communications Officer, 3101 Park Center Dr., #926, Alexandria, VA 22302; (703) 305-2281. Fax, (703) 305-2312. Kate Fink, Director of External and Governmental Affairs; Brooke Hardison, Director of Communications (Acting).*
Web, www.fns.usda.gov/cga

Provides information concerning the Food and Nutrition Service and its fifteen nutrition assistance programs to the media, program participants, advocates, members of Congress, and the general public. Monitors and analyzes relevant legislation.

Food and Nutrition Service *(Agriculture Dept.)*, *Child Nutrition, 3101 Park Center Dr., #640, Alexandria, VA 22302-1500; (703) 305-2054. Cindy Long, Deputy Administrator. Press, (202) 720-4623.*
General email, cndinternet@fns.usda.gov
Web, www.fns.usda.gov/school-meals/child-nutrition-programs

Administers the transfer of funds to state agencies for the National School Lunch Program, the School Breakfast Program, the Special Milk Program, the Child and Adult Care Food Program, and the Summer Food Service Program. These programs help fight hunger and obesity by reimbursing organizations such as schools, child care centers, and after-school programs for providing healthy meals to children.

Food and Nutrition Service *(Agriculture Dept.)*, *Food Distribution, 3101 Park Center Dr., #504, Alexandria, VA 22302-1500; (703) 305-2680. Fax, (703) 305-2964. Laura Castro, Director.*
General email, fdd-pst@fns.usda.gov
Web, www.fns.usda.gov/fdd

Administers the purchasing and distribution of food to state agencies for child care centers, public and private schools, public and nonprofit charitable institutions, and summer camps. Coordinates the distribution of special commodities, including surplus cheese and butter. Administers the National Commodity Processing Program, which facilitates distribution, at reduced prices, of processed foods to state agencies.

Food and Nutrition Service *(Agriculture Dept.)*, *National School Lunch Program, 3101 Park Center Dr.,* *6th floor, Alexandria, VA 22302; (703) 305-2590. Cindy Long, Deputy Administrator. Communications, (703) 305-2281.*
Web, www.fns.usda.gov/nslp/national-school-lunch-program-nslp

Administers the federal assistance meal program operating in public and nonprofit private schools and residential child care institutions. Provides daily nutritionally balanced, low-cost, or free lunches to children.

Food and Nutrition Service *(Agriculture Dept.)*, **Policy Support**, *3101 Park Center Dr., #1014, Alexandria, VA 22302-1500; (703) 305-2017. Fax, (703) 305-2576. Richard Lucas, Deputy Associate Administrator.*
Web, www.fns.usda.gov/ops/research-and-analysis

Evaluates federal nutrition assistance programs; provides results to policymakers and program administrators. Funds demonstration grants for state and local nutrition assistance projects.

Food and Nutrition Service *(Agriculture Dept.)*, **Special Supplemental Nutrition Program for Women, Infants, and Children (WIC)**, *3101 Park Center Dr., #520, Alexandria, VA 22302-1594; (703) 305-2746. Fax, (703) 305-2196. Sarah Widor, Director.*
Web, www.fns.usda.gov/wic

Provides health departments and agencies with federal funding for food supplements and administrative expenses to make food, nutrition education, and health services available to infants, young children, and pregnant, nursing, and postpartum women.

Health and Human Services Dept. (HHS), **Head Start (OHS)**, *330 C St. S.W., 8th Floor, 20201; (202) 205-8573. Deborah Bergeron, Director. Information, (866) 763-6481.*
Web, www.acf.hhs.gov/ohs, Twitter, @HeadStartgov and Facebook, www.facebook.com/HeadStartgov

Awards grants to nonprofit and for-profit organizations and local governments for operating community Head Start programs (comprehensive development programs for children, ages birth to five, of low-income families); manages parent and child centers, Early Childhood Learning and Knowledge Centers (ECLKC), for families with children up to age five. Conducts research and manages demonstration programs, including those under the Comprehensive Child Care Development Act of 1988; administers the Child Development Associate scholarship program, which trains individuals for careers in child development, often as Head Start teachers.

Health and Human Services Dept. (HHS), *Planning and Evaluation (ASPE), Division of Children and Youth Policy, 200 Independence Ave. S.W., #404E, 20201; (202) 690-6806. Fax, (202) 690-6562. Cheri Hoffman, Director.*
Web, www.aspe.hhs.gov/office-human-services-policy

Develops policies and procedures for programs that benefit children, youth, and families. Interests include early care and education, home visiting, youth development and risky behaviors, parenting and family support, child welfare and foster care, and linkages with physical and mental health. (Located within the Office of Human Services Policy.)

Health and Human Services Dept. (HHS), *Planning and Evaluation (ASPE), Human Services Policy,* 200 Independence Ave. S.W., #404E, 20201; (202) 690-7409. Brenda Destro, Deputy Assistant Secretary.
Web, https://aspe.hhs.gov/office-human-services-policy

Conducts policy research, analysis, evaluation, and coordination on issues across the department, including poverty and measurement, vulnerable populations, early childhood education and child welfare, economic support for families, and youth development.

Office of Justice Programs (OJP) *(Justice Dept.), Juvenile Justice and Delinquency Prevention (OJJDP),* 810 7th St. N.W., 20531; (202) 307-5911. Fax, (301) 240-5830. Caren Harp, Administrator.
Clearinghouse, (800) 851-3420.
Web, www.ojjdp.gov, Twitter, @OJPOJJDP and Facebook, www.facebook.com/OJPOJJDP

Coordinates with youth programs of the Agriculture, Education, Housing and Urban Development, Interior, Labor, and Health and Human Services Depts., including the Center for Studies of Crime and Delinquency.

▶**CONGRESS**

For a listing of relevant congressional committees and sub-committees, please see page 723 or the Appendix.

▶**NONGOVERNMENTAL**

Active Minds, 2001 S St. N.W., #630, 20009; (202) 332-9595. Alison Malmon, Executive Director, ext. 101. Press, (202) 332-9595, ext. 109.
General email, info@activeminds.org
Web, www.activeminds.org, Twitter, @active_minds and Facebook, www.facebook.com/activemindsinc

Supports student-run chapters nationwide to help promote youth mental health awareness on college campuses. Offers mental health and mental illness information and resources.

Alliance for Strong Families and Communities, *Public Policy and Mobilization,* 1825 K St. N.W., #600, 20006; (202) 429-0364. Ilana Levinson, Senior Director Government Relations. Toll-free, (800) 221-3726.
General email, policy@alliance1.org
Web, www.alliance1.org, Twitter, @alliancenews and Facebook, www.facebook.com/AllianceForStrongFamiliesAndCommunities

Provides resources and leadership to more than 300 nonprofit child-serving and family-serving organizations in the United States and Canada. Works to strengthen community-based programs and services to families, children, and communities. Monitors legislation.

America's Promise Alliance, 1110 Vermont Ave. N.W., #900, 20005; (202) 657-0600. Fax, (202) 657-0601. John Gomperts, President.

General email, info@americaspromise.org
Web, www.americaspromise.org and Twitter, @americaspromise

Works with national and local organizations to support America's youth. Interests include adult mentoring, safe environments, physical and psychological health, effective education, and opportunities to help others. Seeks to reduce the high school dropout rate.

American Assn. for Marriage and Family Therapy, 112 S. Alfred St., Alexandria, VA 22314-3061; (703) 838-9808. Fax, (703) 838-9805. Tracy A. Todd, Executive Director.
General email, central@aamft.org
Web, www.aamft.org, Twitter, @TheAAMFT and Facebook, www.facebook.com/TheAAFT

Membership: professional marriage and family therapists. Promotes professional standards in marriage and family therapy through training programs; provides the public with educational material and online referral service for marriage and family therapy.

American Bar Assn. (ABA), *Center on Children and the Law,* 1050 Connecticut Ave. N.W., #400, 20036; (202) 662-1720. Vacant, Director; Kathleen McNaught, Assistant Director.
General email, ctrchildlaw@americanbar.org
Web, www.americanbar.org/groups/child_law.html, Twitter, @ABACCL and Facebook, www.facebook.com/abaCCL

Works to increase lawyer representation of children; sponsors speakers and conferences; monitors legislation. Interests include child sexual abuse and exploitation, missing and runaway children, parental kidnapping, child support, foster care, and adoption of children with special needs.

American Humane Assn., 1400 16th St. N.W., #360, 20036; (202) 841-6080. Fax, (202) 450-2335. Robin R. Ganzert, President. Toll-free, (800) 227-4645.
General email, info@americanhumane.org
Web, www.americanhumane.org, Twitter, @AmericanHumane and Facebook, www.facebook.com/americanhumane

Membership: animal shelters, humane organizations, child protection agencies, government agencies, and individuals. Prepares model state legislation on child abuse and its prevention; publishes surveys on child and animal abuse and state abuse laws.

Boys and Girls Clubs of America, *Government Relations,* 440 1st St. N.W., #1020, 20001; (202) 507-6670. Jim Clark, President.
General email, info@bgca.org
Web, www.bgca.org

National network of neighborhood-based facilities that provide programs for underserved children six to eighteen years old, conducted by professional staff. Programs emphasize leadership development, education and career exploration, financial literacy, health and life skills, the arts, sports, fitness and recreation, and family outreach. (Headquarters in Atlanta, Ga.)

The Brookings Institution, *Center on Children and Families, 1775 Massachusetts Ave. N.W., 20036; (202) 797-6138. Richard V. Reeves, Co-Director.*
Web, www.brookings.edu/center/center-on-children-and-families and Twitter, @BrookingsCCF

Research center promoting policies that affect the well-being of America's children, especially children in less advantaged families, and combat issues of poverty, inequality, and lack of opportunity. Interests include education and economic mobility, opportunities for low-income families; single-parent families; and growing elderly population economic challenges.

The Brookings Institution, *Economic Studies, 1775 Massachusetts Ave. N.W., 20036-2188; (202) 797-6000. Fax, (202) 797-6181. Ted Gayer, Director, (202) 797-6230. Press, (202) 797-6105.*
General email, escomment@brookings.edu
Web, www.brookings.edu/economics and Twitter, @BrookingsEcon

Studies policies for the well-being of children and families to address poverty, inequality, and lack of opportunity.

Caregiver Action Network, *1150 Connecticut Ave. N.W., #501, 20036-3904; (202) 454-3970. John Schall, Chief Executive Officer.*
General email, info@caregiveraction.org
Web, www.caregiveraction.org and Twitter, @CaregiverAction

Seeks to increase the quality of life of family caregivers by providing support and information; works to raise public awareness of caregiving through educational activities. (Formerly National Family Caregivers Assn.)

Child Welfare League of America, *727 15th St. N.W., 12th Floor, 20005; (202) 688-4200. Fax, (202) 833-1689. Christine L. James-Brown, President.*
General email, cwla@cwla.org
Web, www.cwla.org and Twitter, @CWLAofficial

Membership: public and private child welfare agencies. Develops standards for the field; provides information on adoption, early childhood education, foster care, group home services, child protection, residential care for children and youth, services to pregnant adolescents and young parents, and other child welfare issues. Monitors and acts as advocate on federal children and family legislation.

ChildFund International, *Washington Office, 1200 18th St. N.W., #718, 20036; (804) 756-2700. Fax, (202) 682-3481. Anne Lynam Goddard, President; Cheri Dahl, Executive Director, U.S. Programs. Toll-free, (800) 776-6767.*
General email, questions@childfund.org
Web, www.childfund.org and Twitter, @ChildFund

Nonsectarian international humanitarian organization that promotes improved child welfare standards and services worldwide by supporting long-term sustainable development. Provides children in emergency situations brought on by war, natural disaster, and other circumstances with education, medical care, food, clothing, and shelter. Provides aid and promotes the development potential of children of all backgrounds. (Headquarters in Richmond, Va.)

Children's Defense Fund, *25 E St. N.W., 20001; (202) 628-8787. Fax, (202) 662-3510. Marian Wright Edelman, President Emerita; Max Lesko, National Executive Director. Toll-free, (800) 233-1200.*
General email, cdfinfo@childrensdefense.org
Web, www.childrensdefense.org and Twitter, @ChildDefender

Advocacy group concerned with programs and policies for children and youth, particularly poor and minority children. Interests include health care, child welfare and mental health, early childhood development, education and youth development, child care, job training and employment, and family support. Works to ensure educational and job opportunities for youth.

Children's Home Society of Minnesota, *Washington Office, 8555 16th St., #600, Silver Spring, MD 20910; (301) 562-6500. Fax, (301) 587-3869. Jodi Harpstead, Director. Toll-free, (888) 904-2229.*
General email, inquire@chlss.org
Web, https://chlss.org and Twitter, @CHLSSAdoption

Provides information on international adoption; sponsors seminars and workshops for adoptive and prospective adoptive parents. (Headquarters in St. Paul, Minn.)

Children's Rights Council (CRC), *720 Eye St. S.E., 20003 (mailing address: 1296 Cronson Blvd., #3086, Crofton, MD 21114); (301) 459-1220. Lesa D. Britt, Chief Executive Officer.*
General email, info@crckids.org
Web, www.crckids.org

Membership: parents and professionals. Works to strengthen families through education and advocacy. Supports family formation and preservation. Conducts conferences and serves as an information clearinghouse. Interests include children whose parents are separated, unwed, or divorced.

Congressional Coalition on Adoption Institute (CCAI), *311 Massachusetts Ave. N.E., 20002; (202) 544-8500. Fax, (202) 544-8501. Bethany Haley, Executive Director (Acting).*
General email, info@ccainstitute.org
Web, http://ccainstitute.org and Twitter, @CCAInstitute

Promotes awareness of children without families. Educates policymakers about foster care and adoption issues.

Council for Professional Recognition, *2460 16th St. N.W., 20009-3547; (202) 265-9090. Fax, (202) 265-9161. Valora Washington, Chief Executive Officer. Toll-free, (800) 424-4310.*
CDA Candidates email, cdafeedback@cda.org,
Web, www.cdacouncil.org and Twitter, @cdacouncil

Promotes high standards for early childhood teachers. Awards credentials to family day care, preschool, home visitor, and infant-toddler caregivers. Administers the Child Development Associate National Credentialing Program, designed to assess and credential early childhood education professionals.

Covenant House, *Washington Office, 2001 Mississippi Ave. S.E., 20020; (202) 610-9600. Madye Henson, President.*
Web, http://covenanthousedc.org and Twitter, @CovenantHouseDC

Protects young people suffering from homelessness, abuse, and neglect. Provides services including transitional housing, GED and adult education, and job readiness. (Affiliated with Covenant House International.)

Cradle of Hope, *8630 Fenton St., #310, Silver Spring, MD 20910; (301) 587-4400. Fax, (301) 588-3091. Linda Perilstein, Executive Director.*
General email, info@cradlehope.org
Web, www.cradlehope.org

International adoption center specializing in the placement of children from China. Offers preadoption and postadoption support services. Sponsors the Bridge of Hope program, a summer camp where older Chinese children meet and spend time with potential host families, in several U.S. locations, including the Washington, D.C., metro region.

Every Child Matters, *660 Pennsylvania Ave. S.E., #303, 20003; (202) 223-8177. Fax, (202) 223-8499. Brian Ahlberg, President.*
General email, info@everychildmatters.org
Web, www.everychildmatters.org and Twitter, @VotingforKids

Works to make children's needs a political priority through public education activities. Interests include prevention of child abuse and neglect, improvement of the health of low-income children, solutions in child care, early childhood education, and after-school programs.

FAIR Girls, *2021 L St. N.W., #254, 20036; (202) 520-9777. Erin Andrews, Executive Director. Crisis hotline, (855) 900-3247. National trafficking hotline, (888) 373-7888.*
General email, info@fairgirls.org
Web, www.fairgirls.org

Provides interventionist holistic care for survivors of trafficking who identify as girls or young women through prevention education and policy advocacy. Works to eradicate human trafficking and create improved outcomes for survivors.

Family and Home Network, *P.O. Box 492, Merrifield, VA 22116; 3110 Landover St., Alexandria, VA 22305; (703) 304-3982. Catherine Myers, Executive Director.*
General email, cmyers@familyandhome.org
Web, www.familyandhome.org and Twitter, @familyhomeorg

Provides information and support for parents who stay home, or who would like to stay home (full or part time), to raise their children, in the United States and abroad. Monitors legislation and regulations relating to family issues.

Generations United, *25 E St. N.W., 3rd Floor, 20001; (202) 289-3979. Fax, (202) 289-3952. Donna M. Butts, Executive Director.*
General email, gu@gu.org
Web, www.gu.org and Twitter, @GensUnited

Membership organization that promotes intergenerational programs and public policies. Focuses on the economic, social, and personal benefits of intergenerational cooperation. Encourages collaboration between organizations that represent different age groups.

Girl Scouts of the U.S.A., *Public Policy and Advocacy, 816 Connecticut Ave. N.W., 3rd Floor, 20006; (202) 659-3780. Fax, (202) 331-8065. Sylvia Acevedo, Chief Executive Officer.*
General email, advocacy@girlscouts.org
Web, www.girlscouts.org/en/about-girl-scouts/advocacy .html

Educational service organization for girls grades K–12 that promotes personal development through development of life skills, the outdoors, leadership, entrepreneurship, and other projects. Areas of advocacy include girls' healthy living, increasing girls' participation in STEM (science, technology, engineering, and math) fields, financial literacy, career education, and supporting girls in underserved communities. (Headquarters in New York.)

Hispanic Access Foundation, *1030 15th St. N.W., Suite B/ 1, #150, 20005; (202) 640-4342. Fax, (202) 640-4343. Maite Arce, President.*
General email, info@hispanicaccess.org
Web, https://hispanicaccess.org, Twitter, @HispanicAccess and Facebook, www.facebook.com/ HispanicAccessFoundation

Nonprofit that partners with faith, community, and grassroots organizations to provide resources and information to Latinos about economics, health, education, and the environment, and connect them to bilingual service providers. Promotes civil engagement and improving the lives of Hispanics.

Kidsave, *4622 Wisconsin Ave. N.W., #202, 20016; (202) 503-3100. Fax, (202) 503-3131. Terry Baugh, President.*
General email, info@kidsave.org
Web, www.kidsave.org, Twitter, @Kidsave_Intl and Facebook, www.facebook.com/KidsaveInternational

Maintains programs that provide children age eight and older in orphanages and foster care the opportunity for weekend visits and short stays with families in the community with the goal of permanent adoption or long-term mentoring. Monitors child welfare legislation and regulations worldwide.

National Assn. for the Education of Young Children, *1313 L St. N.W., #500, 20005; (202) 232-8777. Fax, (202) 328-1846. Rhian Evans Allvin, Chief Executive Officer, ext. 8819. Information, (800) 424-2460.*

General email, help@naeyc.org

Web, www.naeyc.org and Twitter, @NAEYC

Membership: early childhood teachers, administrators, college faculty, and directors of early childhood programs at the state and local levels. Works to improve the quality of early childhood care and education. Administers national accreditation system for early childhood programs. Maintains information service.

National Black Child Development Institute, 8455 Colesville Rd., #910, Silver Spring, MD 20910; (202) 833-2220. Fax, (202) 833-8222. Tobeka G. Green, President. Toll-free, (800) 556-2234.

General email, moreinfo@nbcdi.org

Web, www.nbcdi.org and Twitter, @NBCDI

Advocacy group for Black children, youth, and families. Interests include child care, adoption, and health, and early childhood education. Provides information on government policies that affect Black children, youth, and families.

National Child Support Enforcement Assn., 7918 Jones Branch Dr., #300, McLean, VA 22102; (703) 506-2880. Fax, (703) 506-3266. Ann Marie Ruskin, Executive Director, ext. 4359.

General email, customerservice@ncsea.org

Web, www.ncsea.org and Twitter, @NCSEA1

Promotes enforcement of child support obligations and educates social workers, attorneys, judges, and other professionals on child support issues. Fosters exchange of ideas among child support professionals. Monitors legislation and regulations.

National Collaboration for Youth, 1101 14th St. N.W., #600, 20005; (202) 347-2080. Fax, (202) 393-4517. Brandon Toth, Director of Public Policy.

General email, policy@nassembly.org

Web, www.collab4youth.org, Twitter, @NatlAssembly and Facebook, www.facebook.com/ NationalHumanServicesAssembly

Membership: national youth-serving organizations. Works to improve members' youth development programs through information exchange and other support. Raises public awareness of youth issues. Monitors legislation and regulations. (Affiliate of the National Human Services Assembly.)

National Council for Adoption, 225 N. Washington St., Alexandria, VA 22314-2561; (703) 299-6633. Fax, (703) 299-6004. Charles (Chuck) Johnson, Chief Executive Officer. Press, (301) 751-3750.

General email, ncfa@adoptioncouncil.org

Web, www.adoptioncouncil.org, Twitter, @AdoptionCouncil and Facebook, www.facebook .com/AdoptionCouncil

Organization of individuals, national and international agencies, and corporations interested in adoption. Supports adoption through legal, ethical agencies; advocates the right to confidentiality in adoption. Conducts research and holds conferences; provides information; supports

pregnancy counseling, maternity services, and counseling for infertile couples. Monitors legislation and regulations.

National Fatherhood Initiative, 12410 Milestone Center Dr., #600, Germantown, MD 20876; (301) 948-0599. Fax, (301) 948-6776. Christopher (Chris) Brown, President. Information, (301) 948-4325.

General email, info@fatherhood.org

Web, www.fatherhood.org, Twitter, @thefatherfactor and Facebook, www.facebook.com/nationalfatherhoodinitiative

Works to improve the well-being of children by increasing the proportion of children growing up with involved, responsible, and committed fathers. Provides curricula, training, and assistance to state and community fatherhood initiatives. Conducts public awareness campaigns and research. Monitors legislation.

National Head Start Assn., 1651 Prince St., Alexandria, VA 22314; (703) 739-0875. Fax, (703) 739-0878. Yasmina S. Vinci, Executive Director. Toll-free, (866) 677-8724.

Web, www.nhsa.org

Membership: organizations that represent Head Start children, families, and staff. Recommends strategies on issues affecting Head Start programs; provides training and professional development opportunities. Monitors legislation and regulations.

National Network for Youth (NN4Y), 741 8th St. S.E., 20003; (202) 783-7949. Darla Bardine, Executive Director. National Runaway Safeline, (800) 786-2929.

General email, info@nn4youth.org

Web, www.nn4youth.org

Membership: providers of services related to runaway and homeless youth. Offers technical assistance to new and existing youth projects. Monitors legislation and regulations.

National PTA, 1250 N. Pitt St., Alexandria, VA 22314; (703) 518-1200. Fax, (703) 836-0942. Nathan R. Monell, Executive Director. Toll-free, (800) 307-4782.

General email, info@pta.org

Web, www.pta.org, Twitter, @NationalPTA and Facebook, www.facebook.com/ParentTeacherAssociation

Membership: parent-teacher associations at the preschool, elementary, and secondary levels. Supports school breakfast and lunch programs; works as an active member of the Child Nutrition Forum, which supports federally funded nutrition programs for children.

National Urban League, *Washington Bureau,* 2901 14th St. N.W., 20009; (202) 265-8200. George H. Lambert Jr., Affiliate Chief Executive Officer.

Web, http://nul.iamempowered.com/affiliate/greater-washington-urban-league

Federal advocacy division of social service organization concerned with the social welfare of African Americans and other minorities. Youth Development division provides local leagues with technical assistance for youth programs and seeks training opportunities for youth within Urban League programs. (Headquarters in New York.)

Resources for Older Adults

ADVOCACY

AARP, (888) 687-2277 or (877) 342-2277 (Spanish); www.aarp.org

Alliance for Retired Americans, (202) 637-5399; www.retiredamericans.org

National Council of Gray Panthers Networks (248) 549-5170; http://www.facebook.com/ NationalCouncilofGrayPanthersNetworks

National Caucus and Center on Black Aged, Inc., (202) 637-8400; www.ncba-aged.org

National Committee to Preserve Social Security and Medicare, (800) 966-1935 or (202) 216-0420; www.ncpssm.org

National Consumers League, (202) 835-3323; www.nclnet .org or www.sosrx.org

National Hispanic Council on Aging, (202) 347-9733; www.nhcoa.org

Seniors Coalition, (202) 261-3594; www.senior.org

60 Plus, (703) 807-2070; www.60plus.org

AGENCIES

Administration for Community Living, (202) 401-4634; www.acl.gov

Centers for Medicare and Medicaid Services (CMS), (877) 267-2323; www.cms.gov

Employment and Training Administration, Older Worker Program, (866) 487-2365; www.doleta.gov/seniors

National Assn. of Area Agencies on Aging, Eldercare Locator, (202) 872-0888; www.n4a.org

National Institute on Aging (NIA), (800) 222-2225; www.nia.nih.gov

Social Security Administration (SSA), (800) 772-1213; www.ssa.gov

Veterans Affairs Dept., (800) 827-1000; www.va.gov

HEALTH

Alliance for Aging Research, (202) 293-2856; www.agingresearch.org

Alzheimer's Assn., (800) 272-3900; www.alz.org

Families USA, (202) 628-3030; www.familiesusa.org

Geriatric Mental Health Foundation, (formerly the American Assn. for Geriatric Psychiatry), (703) 556-9222; www.gmhfonline.org

National Osteoporosis Foundation, (800) 231-4222; www.nof.org

HOUSING, NURSING HOMES, ASSISTED LIVING

Armed Forces Retirement Home, (202) 541-7500; www.afrh.gov

Army Distaff Foundation, (202) 541-0400; www.armydistaff.org

B'nai B'rith International, Center for Senior Services, (866) 999 6596; www.bnaibrith.org/ seniors.html

Consumer Consortium on Assisted Living, www.ccal.org

National Consumer Voice for Quality Long-term Care, (202) 332-2275; www.theconsumervoice.org

SERVICES, COMMUNITY SERVICE

American Veterans (AMVETS), (877) 726-8387; www.amvets.org

Jewish Council for the Aging of Greater Washington, (301) 255-4200; www.accessjca.org

National Council on the Aging, (571) 527-3900; www.ncoa.org

National Senior Service Corps, www.seniorcorps.org

Senior Community Service Employment Program, (877) 872-5627; www.doleta.gov/seniors

---

Power to Decide, *1776 Massachusetts Ave. N.W., #200, 20036; (202) 478-8500. Fax, (202) 478-8588. Ginny Ehrlich, Chief Executive Officer.*
General email, info@powertodecide.org

Web, www.powertodecide.org and
Twitter, @powertodecide

Nonpartisan initiative that seeks to reduce the U.S. teen and unplanned pregnancy rates. Provides education and information regarding contraception. (Formerly the National Campaign to Prevent Teen and Unplanned Pregnancy.)

Share Our Strength, *1030 15th St. N.W., #1100W, 20005; (202) 393-2925. Fax, (202) 289-9003. Bill (Billy) Shore, Executive Chair. Toll-free, (800) 969-4767.*
General email, info@strength.org

Web, www.nokidhungry.org and Twitter, @nokidhungry

Works to alleviate and prevent hunger and poverty for children in the United States. Provides food assistance; treats malnutrition; seeks long-term solutions to hunger and poverty through fund-raising, partnerships with corporations and nonprofit organizations, grants, and educational programs.

U.S. Conference of Mayors, *Task Force on Hunger and Homelessness, 1620 Eye St. N.W., 4th Floor, 20006; (202) 293-7330. Fax, (202) 293-2352. Eugene T. Lowe, Assistant Executive Director for Community Development and Housing, (202) 861-6710.*
Web, www.usmayors.org/the-conference/committees-and-task-forces

Tracks trends in hunger, homelessness, and community programs that address homelessness and hunger in U.S. cities; issues reports. Monitors legislation and regulations.

Urban Institute, *Low-Income Working Families Initiative,* 500 L'Enfant Plaza S.W., 20024; (202) 833-7200. Fax, (202) 833-4388. Gregory Arcs, Vice President of Income and Benefits Policy; Genevieve M. Kenney, Vice President of Health Policy; Nancy G. LaVigne, Vice President of Justice Policy.
Web, www.urban.org/center/lwf

Studies low-income families, identifies factors that contribute to poor outcomes, and develops public policy solutions. Interests include economic security, the public programs safety net, better life chances for children, and racial and ethnic disparities.

Older Adults

▶AGENCIES

Administration for Community Living (ACL) *(Health and Human Services Dept.),* Mary E. Switzer Bldg., 330 C St. S.W., 20201; (202) 401-4634. Lance Robertson, Administrator. Eldercare locator, (800) 677-1116.
General email, aclinfo@acl.hhs.gov

Web, https://acl.gov, Twitter, @aclgov and Facebook, www .facebook.com/aclgov

Oversees programs that provide assistance to older adults, persons with disabilities, and family caregivers. Represents and acts as advocate for individuals with disabilities and older adults throughout the federal government, seeking to ensure that these individuals are as involved as appropriate in the development and implementation of policies, programs, and regulations related to community living.

Administration for Community Living (ACL) *(Health and Human Services Dept.), Administration on Aging (AOA),* Mary E. Switzer Bldg., 330 C St. S.W., 20201; (202) 619-0724. Edwin L. Walker, Deputy Assistant Secretary. Eldercare locator, (800) 677-1116. Press, (202) 357-3507. TTY, (800) 877-8339.
Web, www.acl.gov/about-acl/administration-aging

Advocacy agency for older Americans and their concerns. Collaborates with tribal organizations, community and national organizations, and state and area agencies to implement grant programs and services designed to improve the quality of life for older Americans, such as information and referral, adult day care, elder abuse prevention, home-delivered meals, in-home care, transportation, and services for caregivers.

Senior Corps *(Corp. for National and Community Service), Retired and Senior Volunteer Program, Foster Grandparent Program, and Senior Companion Program,* 250 E. St. S.W., 20525; (202) 606-5000. Deborah Cox Roush, Director. National service information hotline, (800) 942-2677. Press, (202) 606-6775. General email, info@cns.gov

Web, www.nationalservice.gov/programs/senior-corps, Twitter, @SeniorCorps and Facebook, www.facebook.com/ SeniorCorps

Network of programs that help older Americans find service opportunities in their communities, including the Retired and Senior Volunteer Program, which encourages older citizens to use their talents and experience in community service; the Foster Grandparent Program, which gives older citizens opportunities to work with exceptional children and children with special needs; and the Senior Companion Program, which recruits older citizens to help homebound adults, especially seniors, with special needs.

▶CONGRESS

For a listing of relevant congressional committees and subcommittees, please see page 723 or the Appendix.

▶NONGOVERNMENTAL

AARP, 601 E St. N.W., 20049; (202) 434-2277. Fax, (202) 434-7946. Jo Ann C. Jenkins, Chief Executive Officer. Library, (202) 434-6233. Membership, (202) 434-7550. Membership, toll-free, (800) 566-0242. Press, (202) 434-2560. Toll-free, (888) 687-2277. TTY, (877) 434-7598. Toll-free Spanish, (877) 342-2277. TTY Spanish, (866) 238-9488.
General email, member@aarp.org

Web, www.aarp.org, Twitter, @AARP and Facebook, www .facebook.com/AARP

Membership: people fifty years of age and older. Conducts educational and counseling programs in areas concerning older adults, such as widowed persons services, health promotion, housing, consumer protection, and food insecurity.

AARP Foundation, 601 E St. N.W., 20049; Fax, (202) 434-6593. Lisa Marsh Ryerson, President. Foundation, (202) 434-6200. Press, (202) 434-2560. Toll-free Foundation, (800) 775-6776. Toll-free TTY, (877) 434-7598.
General email, info@aarpfoundation.org

Web, www.aarp.org/foundation,
Twitter, @AARPFoundation and Facebook, www.facebook .com/AARPFoundation

Foundation email, giving@aarp.org

Seeks to educate the public on aging issues; sponsors conferences and produces publications on age-related concerns. Interests include aging and living environments for older persons. Funds age-related research, educational grants, legal hotlines, senior employment programs, and reverse mortgage projects. (Affiliated with AARP.)

Alliance for Retired Americans, 815 16th St. N.W., 4th Floor, 20006-4104; (202) 637-5399. Fax, (202) 637-5398. Robert Roach Jr., President. Membership, (800) 333-7212.
Web, https://retiredamericans.org, Twitter, @ActiveRetirees and Facebook, www.facebook.com/retiredamericans

Seeks to strengthen benefits to the elderly, including improved Social Security payments, increased employment, and education and health programs. (Affiliate of the AFL-CIO.)

American Seniors Housing Assn., 5225 Wisconsin Ave. N.W., #502, 20015; (202) 237-0900. Fax, (202) 237-1616. David Schless, President, (202) 885-5560.

General email, info@seniorshousing.org

Web, www.seniorshousing.org

Membership: development, finance, and operation professionals working in seniors apartments, independent and assisted living communities, and retirement communities. Promotes the advancement of quality seniors housing and health care through research, education, and monitoring legislation and regulations.

Jewish Council for the Aging of Greater Washington, *12320 Parklawn Dr., Rockville, MD 20852-1726; (301) 255-4200. (703) 425-0999. Fax, (301) 231-9360. David N. Gamse, Chief Executive Officer.*

General email, seniorhelpline@accessjca.org

Web, www.accessjca.org

Nonsectarian organization that provides programs and services throughout the metropolitan D.C. area to help older people continue living independent lives. Offers employment services, computer training, adult day care, social day care, transportation, information services and referrals for transportation and in-home services, and volunteer opportunities.

National Assn. of Area Agencies on Aging, *1730 Rhode Island Ave. N.W., #1200, 20036; (202) 872-0888. Fax, (202) 872-0057. Sandy Markwood, Chief Executive Officer.*

General email, info@n4a.org

Web, www.n4a.org and Twitter, @n4aACTION

Works to establish an effective national policy on aging; provides local agencies on aging and Native American aging programs with training and technical assistance; disseminates information to these agencies and the public. Monitors legislation and regulations.

National Assn. of Area Agencies on Aging, *Eldercare Locator, 1730 Rhode Island Ave. N.W., #1200, 20036; (202) 872-0888. Fax, (202) 872-0057. Patrice Earnest, Director. Toll-free, (800) 677-1116.*

General email, eldercarelocator@n4a.org

Web, www.eldercare.acl.gov and Twitter, @EldercareLoc

National toll-free directory assistance service that connects older people and caregivers with local support resources, including meal services, home care, transportation, housing alternatives, home repair, recreation, social activities, and legal services. Language interpretation service for 150 languages available 9:00 a.m.–8:00 p.m. at the toll-free number. (Provided by the U.S. Administration on Aging and administered by the National Assn. of Area Agencies on Aging.)

National Assn. of States United for Aging and Disabilities, *1201 15th St. N.W., #350, 20005-2842; (202) 898-2578. Fax, (202) 898-2583. Martha Roherty, Executive Director.*

General email, info@nasuad.org

Web, www.nasuad.org

Membership: state and territorial governmental units that work with older adults, people with disabilities, and their caregivers. Provides members with information, technical assistance, and professional training. Monitors legislation and regulations.

National Caucus and Center on Black Aging, Inc., *1220 L St. N.W., #800, 20005-2407; (202) 637-8400. Fax, (202) 347-0895. Karyne Jones, President.*

General email, support@ncba-aged.org

Web, www.ncba-aged.org and Twitter, @NCBADC

Concerned with issues that affect older Black Americans and other minorities. Sponsors employment and housing programs for older adults and education and training for professionals in gerontology. Monitors legislation and regulations.

National Council on Aging, *251 18th St. South, #500, Arlington, VA 22202; (571) 527-3900. Fax, (571) 527-3901. James P. (Jim) Firman, President, ext. 1. Eldercare locator, (800) 677-1116. Press, (571) 527-3914.*

General email, info@ncoa.org

Web, www.ncoa.org, Twitter, @NCOAging and Facebook, www.facebook.com/NCOAging

Serves as an information clearinghouse on training, technical assistance, advocacy, and research on every aspect of aging. Provides information on social services for older persons. Monitors legislation and regulations.

National Hispanic Council on Aging, *2201 12th St. N.W., #101, 20009; (202) 347-9733. Fax, (202) 347-9735. Yanira Cruz, President.*

General email, nhcoa@nhcoa.org

Web, www.nhcoa.org and Twitter, @NHCOA

Membership: senior citizens, health care workers, professionals in the field of aging, and others in the United States and Puerto Rico who are interested in topics related to Hispanics and aging. Provides research training, policy analysis, consulting, and technical assistance; sponsors seminars, workshops, and management internships.

DISABILITIES

General

▶**AGENCIES**

Access Board, *1331 F St. N.W., #1000, 20004-1111; (202) 272-0080. Fax, (202) 272-0081. David M. Capozzi, Executive Director, (202) 272-0010. Toll-free, (800) 872-2253. Toll-free TTY, (800) 993-2822. TTY, (202) 272-0082.*

General email, info@access-board.gov

Web, www.access-board.gov

Develops and maintains accessibility requirements for buildings, transit vehicles, telecommunications equipment, medical diagnostic equipment, and electronic and information technology. Provides technical assistance and training on these guidelines and standards. Enforces access standards for federally funded facilities through the Architectural Barriers Act.

Administration for Community Living (ACL) *(Health and Human Services Dept.),* Mary E. Switzer Bldg., 330 C St. S.W., 20201; (202) 401-4634. Lance Robertson, Administrator. Eldercare locator, (800) 677-1116.
General email, aclinfo@acl.hhs.gov

Web, https://acl.gov, Twitter, @aclgov and Facebook, www .facebook.com/aclgov

Oversees programs that provide assistance to older adults, persons with disabilities, and family caregivers. Represents and acts as advocate for individuals with disabilities and older adults throughout the federal government, seeking to ensure that these individuals are as involved as appropriate in the development and implementation of policies, programs, and regulations related to community living.

Administration for Community Living (ACL) *(Health and Human Services Dept.),* **National Institute on Disability, Independent Living, and Rehabilitation Research (NIDILRR),** Mary E. Switzer Bldg., 330 C St. S.W., Room 1304, 20201 (mailing address: 400 Maryland Ave. S.W., MS 2700, Washington, DC 20202-7100); (202) 795-7398. Fax, (202) 205-0392. Robert Jaeger, Director.
General email, nidilrr-mailbox@acl.hhs.gov

Web, www.acl.gov/about-acl/about-national-institute-disability-independent-living-and-rehabilitation-research

Supports applied research, training, and development to improve the lives of individuals with disabilities from birth to adulthood. Generates new knowledge and promotes its effective use to improve the abilities of people with disabilities to perform activities of their choice in the community, and also to expand society's capacity to provide full opportunities and accommodations for its citizens with disabilities. Awards grants for rehabilitation research programs and scientific, technical, and methodological research; coordinates federal rehabilitation research programs; offers field research fellowships.

Civil Rights Division *(Justice Dept.),* **Disability Rights (DRS),** 950 Pennsylvania Ave. N.W., 20530; (202) 307-0663. Fax, (202) 307-1197. Rebecca Bond, Chief. Information and ADA specialist, (800) 514-0301. TTY, (800) 514-0383.
Web, www.justice.gov/crt/disability-rights-section

Litigates cases under Titles I, II, and III of the Americans with Disabilities Act, which prohibits discrimination on the basis of disability in places of public accommodation and in all activities of state and local government. Provides technical assistance to businesses and individuals affected by the law.

Education Dept., *Special Education and Rehabilitative Services (OSERS),* Lyndon Baines Johnson Bldg., 400 Maryland Ave. S.W., 20202-7100 (mailing address: 400 Maryland Ave. S.W., Washington, DC 20202-7000); (202) 245-7468 (main phone is voice and TTY accessible). Fax, (202) 245-7638. Johnny Collett, Assistant Secretary.
Web, www2.ed.gov/about/offices/list/osers

Provides information on federal legislation and programs and national organizations concerning individuals with disabilities.

Education Dept., *Special Education and Rehabilitative Services (OSERS), Rehabilitation Services Administration (RSA),* Lyndon Baines Johnson Bldg., 400 Maryland Ave. S.W., 20202-7100; (202) 245-7468. Fax, (202) 245-7591. Carol Dobak, Deputy Commissioner (Acting).
Web, www2.ed.gov/about/offices/list/osers/rsa

Coordinates and directs major federal programs for eligible physically and mentally disabled persons. Administers distribution of grants for training and employment programs and for establishing supported-employment and independent-living programs. Provides vocational training and job placement.

Eunice Kennedy Shriver National Institute of Child Health and Human Development (NICHD) *(National Institutes of Health),* **National Center for Medical Rehabilitation Research (NCMRR),** 6710B Rockledge Dr., Bldg. 6710B, Room 2107, MSC 7002, Bethesda, MD 20817; (301) 496-0295. Fax, (301) 480-3854. Alison Cernich, Director.
Web, www.nichd.nih.gov/about/org/ncmrr

Supports research to foster the development of scientific knowledge needed to enhance the health, productivity, independence, and quality of life of persons with disabilities. Supports research and research training on pathophysiology and management of chronically injured nervous and musculoskeletal systems (including stroke, traumatic brain injury, spinal cord injury, and orthopedic conditions); repair and recovery of motor and cognitive function; functional plasticity, adaptation, and windows of opportunity for rehabilitative interventions; rehabilitative strategies; pediatric rehabilitation; secondary conditions associated with chronic disabilities; improved diagnosis, assessment, and outcome measures; and development of orthotics, prosthetics, and other assistive technologies and devices.

John F. Kennedy Center for the Performing Arts, *VSA and Accessibility,* 2700 F St. N.W., 20566 (mailing address: P.O. Box 101510, Arlington, VA 22210); (202) 416-8898. Fax, (202) 416-4840. Betty Siegel, Director.
General email, access@kennedy-center.org

Web, www.kennedy-center.org/education

Initiates and supports research and program development providing arts training and programming for persons with disabilities to make classrooms and communities more inclusive. Provides technical assistance and training to VSA Arts state organizations; acts as an information clearinghouse for arts and persons with disabilities.

Labor Dept. (DOL), *Disability Employment Policy (ODEP),* 200 Constitution Ave. N.W., #S1303, 20210; (202) 693-7880. Fax, (202) 693-7888. Nathan Mehrens, Deputy Assistant Secretary for Policy, (202) 693-5959. Toll-free, 866-ODEP-DOL (633-7365). TTY, (877) 889-5627.
General email, odep@dol.gov

Web, www.dol.gov/odep

Seeks to eliminate physical and psychological barriers to the disabled through education and information programs; promotes education, training, rehabilitation, and employment opportunities for people with disabilities.

National Council on Disability, *1331 F St. N.W., #850, 20004-1107; (202) 272-2004. Fax, (202) 272-2022. Lisa Grubb, Executive Director.*
General email, ncd@ncd.gov

Web, www.ncd.gov, Twitter, @NatCounDis and Facebook, www.facebook.com/NCDgov

Independent federal agency providing advice to the president, Congress, and executive branch agencies to promote policies and programs that ensure equal opportunity for individuals with disabilities and enable individuals with disabilities to achieve self-sufficiency and full integration into society.

Smithsonian Institution, *Accessibility Program, 14th St. and Constitution Ave. N.W., #1050, 20013-7012 (mailing address: P.O. Box 37012, NMAH, MRC 607, Washington, DC 20013-7012); (202) 633-2921. Fax, (202) 633-4352. Elizabeth (Beth) Ziebarth, Director.*
General email, access@si.edu

Web, www.si.edu/Accessibility

Coordinates the Smithsonian's efforts to improve accessibility of its programs and facilities to visitors and staff with disabilities. Serves as a resource for museums and individuals nationwide.

Social Security Administration (SSA), *Disability Determinations, 3570 Annex Bldg., 6401 Security Blvd., Baltimore, MD 21235; (410) 965-1170. Fax, (410) 965-6503. John E. Owens, Associate Commissioner. Information, (800) 772-1213. TTY, (800) 325-0778.*
Web, www.ssa.gov/disability

Administers and regulates the disability insurance program and disability provisions of the Supplemental Security Income (SSI) program.

Workers Compensation (OWCP) *(Labor Dept.), Coal Mine Workers' Compensation, 200 Constitution Ave. N.W., #C3520, 20210 (mailing address: DCMWC, P.O. Box 8307, London, KY 40742-8307); (202) 693-0046. Fax, (202) 693-1395. Michael A. Chance, Director. Toll-free Federal Black Lung Program, (800) 347-2502. TTY, (877) 889-5627.*
General email, DCMWC-public@dol.gov

Web, www.dol.gov/owcp/dcmwc

Provides direction for administration of the black lung benefits program. Adjudicates all black lung claims; certifies benefit payments and maintains black lung beneficiary rolls.

▶**CONGRESS**

For a listing of relevant congressional committees and subcommittees, please see page 723 or the Appendix.

Library of Congress, *National Library Service for the Blind and Physically Handicapped, 1291 Taylor St. N.W., 20542 (mailing address: Library of Congress, Washington,*
DC 20542); (202) 707-5100. Fax, (202) 707-0712. Karen Keninger, Director. Toll-free, (888) 657-7323.
General email, nls@loc.gov

Web, www.loc.gov/nls

Braille email, braille@loc.gov

Administers a national program of free library services for persons with physical disabilities in cooperation with regional and subregional libraries. Produces and distributes full-length books and magazines in recorded form and in Braille. Reference section answers questions relating to blindness and physical disabilities and on library services available to persons with disabilities.

▶**NONGOVERNMENTAL**

American Assn. of People with Disabilities (AAPD), *2013 H St. N.W., 5th Floor, 20006; (202) 521-4316. Helena Berger, President. Toll-free, (800) 840-8844.*
General email, communications@aapd.com

Web, www.aapd.com, Twitter, @AAPD and Facebook, www.facebook.com/DisabilityPowered

Works to organize the disability community to effect political, economic, and social change through programs on employment, independent living, and assistive technology. Seeks to educate the public and policymakers on issues affecting persons with disabilities. Works in coalition with other organizations toward full enforcement of disability and antidiscrimination laws.

American Bar Assn. (ABA), *Commission on Disability Rights, 1050 Connecticut Ave. N.W., #400, 20036; (202) 662-1570. Fax, (202) 442-3439. Amy L. Allbright, Director; Robert T. Gonzales, Chair.*
General email, cdr@americanbar.org

Web, www.americanbar.org/groups/diversity/disabilityrights, Twitter, @ABADisability and Facebook, www.facebook.com/ABA.CDR

Promotes the rule of law for persons with mental, physical, and sensory disabilities and their full and equal participation in the legal profession. Offers online resources, publications, and continuing-education opportunities on disability law topics and engages in national initiatives to remove barriers to the education, employment, and advancement of lawyers with disabilities.

American Counseling Assn., *Rehabilitation, 6101 Stevenson Ave., #600, Alexandria, VA 22304-3300; (703) 823-9800. Richard Yep, Chief Executive Officer, ext. 231. Toll-free, (800) 347-6647. Toll-free fax, (800) 473-2329.*
General email, ryep@counseling.org

Web, www.counseling.org, Twitter, @CounselingViews and Facebook, www.facebook.com/American.Counseling .Association

Membership: counselors, counselor educators, and graduate students in the rehabilitation field, and other interested persons. Establishes counseling and research standards; encourages establishment of rehabilitation facilities; conducts leadership training and continuing education programs; serves as a liaison between counselors and clients. Monitors legislation and regulations.

American Medical Rehabilitation Providers Assn. (AMRPA), *529 14th St., N.W., # 750, 20045; (202) 591-2469. Fax, (202) 223-1925. John Ferraro, Executive Director. Toll-free, (888) 346-4624.*
General email, info@amrpa.org

Web, www.amrpa.org, Twitter, @AMRPA and Facebook, www.facebook.com/ AmericanMedicalRehabilitationProvidersAssociation

Association representing a membership of freestanding rehabilitation hospitals and rehabilitation units of general hospitals, outpatient rehabilitation facilities, skilled-nursing facilities, and others. Provides leadership, advocacy, and resources to develop medical rehabilitation services and supports for persons with disabilities and others in need of services. Acts as a clearinghouse for information to members on the nature and availability of services. Monitors legislation and regulations.

American Network of Community Options and Resources (ANCOR), *1101 King St., #380, Alexandria, VA 22314; (703) 535-7850. Fax, (703) 535-7860. Barbara Merrill, Chief Executive Officer.*
General email, ancor@ancor.org

Web, www.ancor.org and Twitter, @TheRealANCOR

Membership: privately operated agencies and corporations that provide support and services to people with disabilities. Advises and works with regulatory and consumer agencies that serve people with disabilities; provides information and sponsors seminars and workshops. Monitors legislation and regulations.

American Occupational Therapy Assn., *4720 Montgomery Lane, #200, Bethesda, MD 20814-3449; (301) 652-6611. Fax, (301) 652-7711. Sherry Keramidas, Executive Director. TTY, (800) 377-8555.*
Web, www.aota.org and Twitter, @AOTAInc

Provides evidence-based practice resources for disability rehabilitation, including practice guidelines, a critically appraised papers repository and exchange, and podcast series. Publishes the *American Journal of Occupational Therapy.*

American Orthotic and Prosthetic Assn., *330 John Carlyle St., #200, Alexandria, VA 22314-5760 (mailing address: P.O. Box 34711, Alexandria, VA 22334); (571) 431-0876. Fax, (571) 431-0899. Eve Lee, Executive Director, (571) 431-0802.*
General email, info@aopanet.org

Web, www.aopanet.org and Twitter, @AmericanOandP

Membership: companies that manufacture or supply artificial limbs and braces, and patient-care professionals who fit and supervise device use.

American Physical Therapy Assn., *1111 N. Fairfax St., Alexandria, VA 22314-1488; (703) 684-2782. Fax, (703) 684-7343. Justin Moore, Chief Executive Officer. Information, (800) 999-2782.*

General email, memberservices@apta.org

Web, www.apta.org, Twitter, @APTAtweets and Facebook, www.facebook.com/ AmericanPhysicalTherapyAssociation

Membership: physical therapists, assistants, and students. Establishes professional standards and accredits physical therapy programs; seeks to improve physical therapy education, practice, and research.

American Speech-Language-Hearing Assn. (ASHA), *2200 Research Blvd., Rockville, MD 20850-3289; 444 N. Capitol St. N.W., #715, 20001; (202) 624-5951. Fax, (301) 296-8500. Arlene Pietranton, Chief Executive Officer. Press, (301) 296-8732. Toll-free for Action Center, (800) 498-2071 (voice and TTY accessible). Toll-free for nonmembers, (800) 638-8255.*
General email, nsslha@asha.org

Web, www.asha.org and Twitter, @ASHAWeb

Advocates the rights of the communicatively disabled; provides information on speech, hearing, and language problems. Provides referrals to speech-language pathologists and audiologists. Interests include national and international standards for bioacoustics and noise. (National office in Rockville, Md.)

Assn. of University Centers on Disabilities (AUCD), *1100 Wayne Ave., #1000, Silver Spring, MD 20910; (301) 588-8252. Fax, (301) 588-2842. Andrew J. Imparato, Executive Director.*
General email, aucdinfo@aucd.org

Web, www.aucd.org and Twitter, @AUCDNews

Network of facilities that diagnose and treat the developmentally disabled. Trains graduate students and professionals in the field; helps state and local agencies develop services. Interests include interdisciplinary training and services, early screening to prevent developmental disabilities, and development of equipment and programs to serve persons with disabilities.

Brain Injury Assn. of America, *1608 Spring Hill Rd., #110, Vienna, VA 22182; (703) 761-0750. Fax, (703) 761-0755. Susan H. Connors, President. Information, (800) 444-6443.*
General email, info@biausa.org

Web, www.biausa.org and Twitter, @biaamerica

Works to improve the quality of life for persons with traumatic brain injuries and for their families. Promotes the prevention of head injuries through public awareness and education programs. Offers state-level support services for individuals and their families. Monitors legislation and regulations.

Center for Employment and Economic Well-Being, *1133 19th St. N.W., #400, 20036; (202) 682-0100. Fax, (202) 204-0071. Kerry Desjardins, Policy Associate; Russ Sykes, Director.*
Web, https://aphsa.org/CEEWB/default.aspx and Twitter, @APHSA1

Works to identify the best practices and resources that will help move low-income individuals into sustainable careers. Supports public policies that provide the opportunities for individuals, families, and communities to succeed in the workforce. (Affiliated with the American Public Human Services Association.)

Consortium for Citizens with Disabilities (CCD), *820 1st St. N.E., #740, 20002; (202) 567-3516. Fax, (202) 408-9520. Lisa Ekman, Chair.*
General email, info@c-c-d.org
Web, www.c-c-d.org and Twitter, @ccd4pwd

Coalition of national disability organizations. Advocates for a national public policy that ensures the self-determination, independence, empowerment, and integration in all aspects of society for children and adults with disabilities.

Disability Rights International, *1666 Connecticut Ave. N.W., #325, 20009; (202) 296-0800. Fax, (202) 697-5422. Laurie Ahern, President; Eric Rosenthal, Executive Director.*
General email, info@driadvocacy.org
Web, www.driadvocacy.org and Twitter, @DRI_advocacy

Challenges discrimination of and abuse faced by people with disabilities worldwide, with special attention to protecting the rights of children living in orphanages or other institutions. Documents conditions, publishes reports, and trains grassroots advocates.

Disabled American Veterans, *National Service and Legislative Headquarters, 807 Maine Ave. S.W., 20024-2410; (202) 554-3501. Fax, (202) 554-3581. J. Marc Burgess, National Adjutant; Dennis R. Nixon, National Commander. Toll-free, (877) 872-3289.*
Web, www.dav.org

Chartered by Congress to assist veterans with claims for benefits; represents veterans seeking to correct alleged errors in military records. Assists families of veterans with disabilities. (Headquarters in Cold Spring, Ky.)

Disabled Sports USA, *451 Hungerford Dr., #608, Rockville, MD 20850; (301) 217-0960. Fax, (301) 217-0968. Glenn Merry, Executive Director, (301) 217-9838.*
General email, info@dsusa.org
Web, www.disabledsportsusa.org and Twitter, @DisabledSportsUSA

Offers nationwide sports rehabilitation programs in more than forty summer and winter sports; promotes independence, confidence, and fitness through programs for people with permanent disabilities, including wounded service personnel; conducts workshops and competitions through community-based chapters; participates in world championships.

Easter Seals, *Washington Region Office, 1420 Spring St., Silver Spring, MD 20910; (301) 588-8700. Fax, (301) 920-9770. John Horowitch, Executive Officer. Toll-free, (800) 886-3771.*
Web, www.easterseals.com/DCMDVA

Promotes equal opportunity for people with autism, disabilities, and other special needs. Interests include child development, early childhood education, adult medical daycare services, and services aimed to aid military veterans and their families as they reenter their communities. (Headquarters in Chicago, Ill.)

Epilepsy Foundation, *8301 Professional Pl. East, #230, Landover, MD 20785-2356; (301) 459-3700. Fax, (301) 577-2684. Phillip Gattone, Chief Executive Officer. Information, (800) 332-1000. Spanish language, (866) 748-8008.*
General email, contactus@efa.org
Web, www.epilepsy.com and Twitter, @EpilepsyFdn

Promotes research and treatment of epilepsy; makes research grants; disseminates information and educational materials. Affiliates provide direct services for people with epilepsy and make referrals when necessary.

Girl Scouts of the U.S.A., *Public Policy and Advocacy, 816 Connecticut Ave. N.W., 3rd Floor, 20006; (202) 659-3780. Fax, (202) 331-8065. Sylvia Acevedo, Chief Executive Officer.*
General email, advocacy@girlscouts.org
Web, www.girlscouts.org/en/about-girl-scouts/advocacy .html

Educational service organization for girls grades K–12. Promotes personal development through development of life skills, the outdoors, leadership, entrepreneurship, and such programs as Girl Scouting for Handicapped Girls. (Headquarters in New York.)

Helen A. Kellar Institute for Human Disabilities *(George Mason University), 4400 University Dr., MS 1F2, Fairfax, VA 22030; (703) 993-3670. Fax, (703) 993-3681. Linda Mason, Director.*
Web, http://kihd.gmu.edu

Combines resources from local, state, national, public, and private affiliations to develop products, services, and programs for persons with disabilities.

International Code Council, *500 New Jersey Ave. N.W., 6th Floor, 20001-2070; (202) 370-1800. Fax, (202) 783-2348. Dominic Sims, Chief Executive Officer. Toll-free, (888) 422-7233.*
General email, carecenter@iccsafe.org
Web, www.iccsafe.org, Twitter, @IntlCodeCouncil and Facebook, www.facebook.com/InternationalCodeCouncil

Provides review board for the American National Standards Institute accessibility standards, which ensure that buildings are accessible to persons with physical disabilities.

National Assn. of Councils on Developmental Disabilities, *1825 K St. N.W., #600, 20006; (202) 506-5813. Fax, (202) 506-5846. Donna A. Meltzer, Chief Executive Officer, (202) 506-5813 ext. 103.*
General email, info@nacdd.org
Web, www.nacdd.org and Twitter, @NACDD

Membership: state and territorial councils authorized by the Developmental Disabilities Act. Promotes the interests of people with developmental disabilities. Interests include services, supports, and equal opportunity. Monitors legislation and regulations.

National Assn. of States United for Aging and Disabilities, *1201 15th St. N.W., #350, 20005-2842; (202) 898-2578. Fax, (202) 898-2583. Martha Roherty, Executive Director.*
General email, info@nasuad.org
Web, www.nasuad.org

Membership: state and territorial governmental units that work with older adults, people with disabilities, and their caregivers. Provides members with information, technical assistance, and professional training. Monitors legislation and regulations.

National Council on Independent Living, *2013 H St. N.W., 6th Floor, 20006; (202) 207-0334. Fax, (202) 207-0341. Kelly Buckland, Executive Director. Toll-free, (844) 778-7961. TTY, (202) 207-0340.*
General email, ncil@ncil.org
Web, www.ncil.org, Twitter, @NCILAdvocacy and Facebook, www.facebook.com/NationalCouncilonIndependentLiving

Membership: independent living centers, individuals with disabilities, and organizations that act as advocates for the human and civil rights of people with disabilities. Assists member centers in building their capacity to promote social change, eliminate disability-based discrimination, and create opportunities for people with disabilities to participate in the legislative process. Offers members training programs, conducts an annual conference, and disseminates related news and research. Monitors legislation and regulations.

National Disability Institute, *1667 K St. N.W., #480, 20006; (202) 296-2040. Michael Morris, Executive Director, (202) 296-2046.*
General email, info@realeconomicimpact.org
Web, www.nationaldisabilityinstitute.org and Twitter, @RealEconImpact

Advocates public policies that address the economic interests of those with disabilities and their families. Interests include tax education and preparation, asset development, financial education, and employment programs.

National Disability Rights Network, *820 1st St. N.E., #740, 20002; (202) 408-9514. Fax, (202) 408-9520. Curtis L. (Curt) Decker, Executive Director, ext. 107. TTY, (202) 408-9521.*
General email, info@ndrn.org
Web, http://ndrn.org and Twitter, @NDRNadvocates

Membership: agencies working for people with disabilities. Provides state agencies with training and technical assistance; maintains an electronic mail network. Monitors legislation and regulations. (Formerly the National Assn. of Protection and Advocacy Systems and Client Assistance Programs (P&A/CAP).)

National Multiple Sclerosis Society, *Washington Chapter, 1800 M St. N.W., #B50 North, 20036; (202) 296-5363. Fax, (202) 296-3425. Chartese Berry, Chapter President, (202) 375-5616. Toll-free, (800) 344-4867.*

General email, info-dcmd@nmss.org
Web, www.msandyou.org

Provides multiple sclerosis patient services, including individual and family counseling, exercise programs, equipment loans, medical and social service referrals, transportation assistance, back-to-work training programs, and inservice training seminars for nurses, homemakers, and physical and occupational therapists. (Headquarters in New York.)

National Rehabilitation Assn., *8400 Corporate Dr., #500, Landover, MD 20785 (mailing address: P.O. Box 150235, Alexandria, VA 22315); (703) 836-0850. Fax, (703) 836-0848. Greg Mason, President, (979) 220-6754; Fredric K. Schroeder, Executive Director, ext. 303. Toll-free, (888) 258-4295. TTY, (703) 836-0849.*
General email, info@nationalrehab.org
Web, www.nationalrehab.org

Membership: administrators, counselors, therapists, disability examiners, vocational evaluators, instructors, job placement specialists, disability managers in the corporate sector, and others interested in rehabilitation of the physically and mentally disabled. Sponsors conferences and workshops. Monitors legislation and regulations.

National Rehabilitation Information Center (NARIC), *8400 Corporate Dr., #500, Landover, MD 20785; (301) 459-5900. Fax, (301) 459-4263. Mark Odum, Director. Information, (800) 346-2742. TTY, (301) 459-5984.*
General email, naricinfo@heitechservices.com
Web, http://naric.com

Provides information on disability and rehabilitation research. Acts as referral agency for disability and rehabilitation facilities and programs. Website has a Spanish-language link.

Paralyzed Veterans of America, *801 18th St. N.W., 20006-3517; (202) 872-1300. Carl Blake Jr., Executive Director; David Zurfluh, National President. Hotline, (800) 232-1782. Information, (800) 424-8200. TTY, (800) 795-4327.*
General email, info@pva.org
Web, www.pva.org and Twitter, @PVA1946

Congressionally chartered veterans service organization that assists veterans with claims for benefits. Distributes information on special education for paralyzed veterans; acts as advocate for high-quality care, and supports and raises funds for medical research.

Rehabilitation Engineering and Assistive Technology Society of North America (RESNA), *1560 Wilson Blvd., #850, Arlington, VA 22209; (703) 524-6686. Fax, (703) 524-6630. Andrea Van Hook, Executive Director (Acting).*
General email, info@resna.org
Web, www.resna.org and Twitter, @RESNAorg

Membership: engineers, health professionals, assistive technologists, persons with disabilities, and others. Promotes and supports developments in rehabilitation engineering and technology; acts as an information clearinghouse.

(RESNA stands for Rehabilitation Engineering and Assistive Technology Society of North America.)

Special Olympics International Inc., *1133 19th St. N.W., 20036-3604; (202) 628-3630. Fax, (202) 824-0200. Mary Davis, Chief Executive Officer; Timothy P. Shriver, Chair. Toll-free, (800) 700-8585.*
General email, info@specialolympics.org
Web, www.specialolympics.org and Twitter, @SpecialOlympics

Offers individuals with intellectual disabilities opportunities for year-round sports training; sponsors athletic competition for 4 million athletes worldwide in twenty-two individual and Olympic-type team sports.

Spina Bifida Assn., *1600 Wilson Blvd., #800, Arlington, VA 22209 (mailing address: P.O. Box 17427, Arlington, VA 22216); (202) 944-3285. Fax, (202) 944-3295. Sara Struwe, Chief Executive Officer, ext. 12. Information, (800) 621-3141.*
General email, sbaa@sbaa.org
Web, http://spinabifidaassociation.org and Twitter, @SpinaBifidaAssn

Membership: individuals with spina bifida, their supporters, and concerned professionals. Offers educational programs, scholarships, and support services; acts as a clearinghouse; provides referrals and information about treatment and prevention. Serves as U.S. member of the International Federation for Hydrocephalus and Spina Bifida, which is headquartered in Geneva, Switzerland. Monitors legislation and regulations.

TASH, *1101 15th St.N.W., #1212, 20005; (202) 467-5730, ext. 1309. Fax, (202) 540-9019. Ruthie-Marie Beckwith, Executive Director, (202) 467-5730, ext. 1316.*
General email, info@tash.org
Web, www.tash.org and Twitter, @TASHtweet

International human rights advocacy group for people with disabilities. Educates the public and policymakers on issues such as equal education, employment, and community living for people with disabilities. Publishes journals and conducts research to improve living practices for severely disabled people. Monitors legislation and regulations on antidiscrimination measures.

United Cerebral Palsy (UCP), *1825 K St. N.W., #600, 20006; (202) 776-0406. Fax, (202) 776-0414. Armando Contreras, President. Information, (800) 872-5827.*
Web, www.ucp.org and Twitter, @UCPnational

National network of state and local affiliates that assists individuals with cerebral palsy and other developmental disabilities and their families. Provides parent education, early intervention, employment services, family support and respite programs, therapy, assistive technology, and vocational training. Promotes research on cerebral palsy; supports the use of assistive technology and community-based living arrangements for persons with cerebral palsy and other developmental disabilities.

Blind and Visually Impaired

▶ CONGRESS

For a listing of relevant congressional committees and sub-committees, please see page 723 or the Appendix.

Library of Congress, *National Library Service for the Blind and Physically Handicapped, 1291 Taylor St. N.W., 20542 (mailing address: Library of Congress, Washington, DC 20542); (202) 707-5100. Fax, (202) 707-0712. Karen Keninger, Director. Toll-free, (888) 657-7323.*
General email, nls@loc.gov
Web, www.loc.gov/nls
Braille email, braille@loc.gov

Administers a national program of free library services for persons with physical disabilities in cooperation with regional and subregional libraries. Produces and distributes full-length books and magazines in recorded form and in Braille. Reference section answers questions relating to blindness and physical disabilities and on library services available to persons with disabilities.

▶ NONGOVERNMENTAL

American Council of the Blind (ACB), *1703 N. Beauregard St., #420, Alexandria, VA 22311; (202) 467-5081. Fax, (703) 465-5085. Eric Bridges, Executive Director, ext. 12040; Anthony Stephens, Director of Advocacy, ext. 12041. Toll-free, (800) 424-8666.*
General email, info@acb.org
Web, www.acb.org, Twitter, @acbnational and Facebook, www.facebook.com/ AmericanCounciloftheBlindOfficial
Advocacy, advocacy@acb.org

Membership organization serving blind and visually impaired individuals. Interests include telecommunications, rehabilitation services, and transportation. Provides blind individuals with information and referral services; advises state organizations and agencies serving the blind; sponsors scholarships for the blind and visually impaired. Provides information to the public.

American Foundation for the Blind, *Public Policy Center, 1401 S. Clark St., #730, Arlington, VA 22202; (202) 469-6831. Stephanie Enyart, Chief Public Policy and Research Officer. Toll-free, (800) 232-5463.*
General email, afbgov@afb.org
Web, www.afb.org/info/programs-and-services/public-policy-center/12 and Facebook, www.facebook.com/ americanfoundationfortheblind

Advocates equality of access and opportunity for the blind and visually impaired. Conducts research and provides consulting; develops and implements public policy and legislation. Maintains the Helen Keller Archives and M.C. Migel Memorial Library at its headquarters in New York.

Assn. for Education and Rehabilitation of the Blind and Visually Impaired, *1703 N. Beauregard St., #440, Alexandria, VA 22311; (703) 671-4500. Fax, (703) 671-6391. Louis M. Tutt, Executive Director. Toll-free, (877) 492-2708.*
General email, aer@aerbvi.org

Web, www.aerbvi.org and Twitter, @AERBVI

Membership: professionals who work in all phases of education and rehabilitation of children and adults who are blind and visually impaired. Provides support and professional development opportunities through conferences, continuing education, and publications. Issues professional recognition awards and student scholarships. Monitors legislation and regulations.

Blinded Veterans Assn., *125 N. West St., Alexandria, VA 22314; (202) 371-8880. Fax, (202) 371-8258. Joseph Bogart, Executive Director. Toll-free, (800) 669-7079.*
General email, bva@bva.org

Web, www.bva.org and Twitter, @BlindedVeterans

Chartered by Congress to assist veterans with claims for benefits. Seeks out blinded veterans to make them aware of benefits and services available to them.

National Federation of the Blind, *200 E. Wells St., Baltimore, MD 21230 (mailing address: P.O. Box 29141, Washington, D.C. 20017); (410) 659-9314. Fax, (410) 685-5653. Shawn M. Callaway, President.*
General email, nfb@nfb.org

Web, www.nfb.org and Twitter, @nfb_voice

Membership organization providing support networks for the blind and information about blindness and vision loss, assistive technologies, education and employment services.

National Industries for the Blind (NIB), *3000 Potomac Ave., Alexandria, VA 22305; (703) 310-0500. Kevin A. Lynch, Chief Executive Officer.*
General email, communications@nib.org

Web, www.nib.org, Twitter, @NatIndBlind and Facebook, www.facebook.com/NatIndBlind

Works to develop and improve opportunities for evaluating, training, employing, and advancing people who are blind and visually disabled. Develops business opportunities in the federal, state, and commercial marketplaces for organizations employing people who are blind or visually impaired.

Prevention of Blindness Society of Metropolitan Washington, *233 Massachusetts Ave. N.E., 20002; (202) 234-1010. Fax, (202) 234-1020. Caren Forsten, Executive Director.*
General email, communications@youreyes.org

Web, www.youreyes.org, Twitter, @youreyesdc and Facebook, www.facebook.com/youreyesdc

Conducts preschool and elementary school screening program and glaucoma screening; provides information and referral service on eye health care; assists low-income persons in obtaining eye care and provides eyeglasses for a nominal fee to persons experiencing financial stress; conducts macular degeneration support group.

Deaf and Hard of Hearing

▶**AGENCIES**

General Services Administration (GSA), *Federal Relay Service (FedRelay), 10304 Eaton Pl., Fairfax, VA 22030; (703) 306-6308. Tatyana Mezentseva, Customer Relationship Manager. Customer Service, (800) 877-0996 (Voice/TTY, ASCII, Spanish). Speech-to-Speech, (877) 877-8982. TeleBraille, (866) 893-8340. TTY/ASCII, (800) 877-8339. VCO (Voice Carry Over), (877) 877-6280. Voice, (866) 377-8642.*
General email, ITCSC@gsa.gov

Web, www.gsa.gov/fedrelay and www.federalrelay.us

Provides telecommunications services for conducting official business with and within the federal government to individuals who are deaf or hard of hearing or who have speech disabilities. Federal Relay Service features are Voice, Text Telephone (TTY)/ASCII, HCO, Speech-to-Speech (STS), Spanish, Telebraille, Captioned Telephone Service (CTS), IP Relay, Video Relay Service (VRS), and Relay Conference Captioning (RCC)(including Spanish-to-Spanish captioning). For those with limited English proficiency, contact fas.car@gsa.gov, as services are available in Spanish, Vietnamese, Russian, Portuguese, Polish, Haitian, Creole, and Arabic.

National Institute on Deafness and Other Communication Disorders (NIDCD) *(National Institutes of Health), 31 Center Dr., #3C02, MSC 2320, Bethesda, MD 20892-2320; (301) 827-8183. Fax, (301) 402-0018. Judith Cooper Jr., Director (Acting), (301) 402-0900. Evenings and weekends, (301) 496-3315. Interpreter service, (301) 496-1807. Toll-free, (800) 241-1044. TTY, (800) 241-1055.*
General email, nidcdinfo@nidcd.nih.gov

Web, www.nidcd.nih.gov and Twitter, @nidcd

Conducts and supports research and research training and disseminates information on hearing disorders and other communication processes, including diseases that affect hearing, balance, smell, taste, voice, speech, and language. Monitors international research.

▶**NONGOVERNMENTAL**

Alexander Graham Bell Assn. for the Deaf and Hard of Hearing, *3417 Volta Pl. N.W., 20007-2778; (202) 337-5220. Fax, (202) 337-8314. Emilio Alonso-Mendoza, Chief Executive Officer. TTY, (202) 337-5221.*
General email, info@agbell.org

Web, www.agbell.org, Twitter, @AGBellAssoc and Facebook, www.facebook.com/AGBellAssociation

Provides hearing-impaired children in the United States and abroad with information and special education programs; works to improve employment opportunities for deaf persons; acts as a support group for parents of deaf persons.

American Academy of Audiology, *11480 Commerce Park Dr., #220, Reston, VA 20191 (mailing address: Capitol Hill Office: 312 Massachusetts Ave. N.E., Washington, DC 20002); (703) 790-8466. Fax, (703) 790-8631. Tanya Tolpegin, Executive Director, ext. 1050; Lisa Christensen, President. Toll-free, (800) 222-2336. Government Relations, ext. 1060.*
General email, infoaud@audiology.org

Web, www.audiology.org, Twitter, @AcedemyofAud and Facebook, www.facebook.com/ americanacademyofaudiology

Membership: more than 12,000 audiologists. Provides consumer information on testing and treatment for hearing loss and balance care; sponsors research and continuing education for audiologists. Monitors legislation and regulations.

American Speech-Language-Hearing Assn. (ASHA), *2200 Research Blvd., Rockville, MD 20850-3289; 444 N. Capitol St. N.W., #715, 20001; (202) 624-5951. Fax, (301) 296-8500. Arlene Pietranton, Chief Executive Officer. Press, (301) 296-8732. Toll-free for Action Center, (800) 498-2071 (voice and TTY accessible). Toll-free for nonmembers, (800) 638-8255.*
General email, nsslha@asha.org

Web, www.asha.org and Twitter, @ASHAWeb

Advocates the rights of the communicatively disabled; provides information on speech, hearing, and language problems. Provides referrals to speech-language pathologists and audiologists. Interests include national and international standards for bioacoustics and noise. (National office in Rockville, Md.)

Gallaudet University, *800 Florida Ave. N.E., 20002-3695; (202) 651-5000. Roberta (Bobbi) Cordano, President, (202) 651-5005.*
Web, www.gallaudet.edu, Twitter, @GallaudetU and Facebook, www.facebook.com/gallaudetu

Offers undergraduate, graduate, and doctoral degree programs for deaf, hard-of-hearing, and hearing students. Conducts research; maintains the Laurent Clerc National Deaf Education Center and demonstration preschool, elementary (Kendall Demonstration Elementary School), and secondary (Model Secondary School for the Deaf) programs. Sponsors the Center for Global Education, National Deaf Education Network and Clearinghouse, and the Cochlear Implant Education Center. Links to each department's video phone are at www.gallaudet.edu/about_ gallaudet/contact_us.html.

Hearing Industries Assn., *777 6th St., N.W., #09-114, 20001; (202) 975-0905. Kate Carr, President. Hearing helpline, (800) 327-9355.*
General email, info@betterhearing.org

Web, www.hearing.org and Twitter, @better_hearing

Educational and advocacy organization that conducts national public information programs on hearing loss, hearing aids, and other treatments.

Hearing Industries Assn., *777 6th St. N.W., # 09-114, 20001; (202) 975-0905. Kate Carr, President.*
General email, info@hearing.org

Web, www.hearing.org

Membership: hearing aid manufacturers and companies that supply hearing aid components.

Hearing Loss Assn. of America, *7910 Woodmont Ave., #1200, Bethesda, MD 20814; (301) 657-2248. Fax, (301) 913-9413. Barbara Kelley, Executive Director.*
Web, www.hearingloss.org and Twitter, @HLAA

Promotes understanding of the nature, causes, and remedies of hearing loss. Provides hearing-impaired people with support and information. Seeks to educate the public about hearing loss and the problems of the hard of hearing. Provides travelers with information on assistive listening devices in museums, theaters, and places of worship. Holds annual convention for people with hearing loss and professionals.

Laurent Clerc National Deaf Education Center, *Planning, Development, and Dissemination, 800 Florida Ave. N.E., 20002-3695; (202) 651-5000, Voice. Fax, (202) 651-5708. Betsy Meynardie, Executive Director. Cochlear Implant Education Center, (202) 651-5638. Toll-free, (800) 526-9105. TTY, (202) 651-5051.*
Web, www.gallaudet.edu/clerc-center, Twitter, @ClercCenter and Facebook, www.facebook.com/ InsideClercCenter

Provides information on topics dealing with hearing loss and deafness for children and young adults up to age twenty-one, and operates elementary and secondary demonstration schools. Houses the Cochlear Implant Education Center and serves as a clearinghouse for information on questions related to deafness. (Affiliated with Gallaudet University.)

National Assn. of the Deaf, *8630 Fenton St., #820, Silver Spring, MD 20910-3819; (301) 587-1788. Fax, (301) 587-1791. Howard A. Rosenblum, Chief Executive Officer. TTY, (301) 587-1789. Videophone, (301) 587-1788.*
Web, www.nad.org and Twitter, @NAD1880

Membership: state associations, affiliate organizations, and individuals that promote, protect, and preserve the civil, human, and linguistic rights of deaf and hard of hearing individuals in the United States. Provides advocacy and legal expertise in the areas of early intervention, education, employment, health care, technology and telecommunications. Provides youth leadership training. Represents the United States to the World Federation of the Deaf (WFD).

National Captioning Institute, *3725 Concorde Pkwy., #100, Chantilly, VA 20151; Fax, (703) 917-9853. Gene Chao, Chief Executive Officer. Phone/TTY, (703) 917-7600.*
General email, mail@ncicap.org

Web, www.ncicap.org

Captions television, cable, webcasting, home video, and DVD programs for the deaf and hard-of-hearing, and produces audio descriptions for the blind on behalf of public and commercial broadcast television networks, cable networks, syndicators, program producers, government agencies, advertisers, and home video distributors. Offers subtitling and language translation services. Produces and disseminates information about the national closed-captioning service and audio-description services.

Quota International, *1420 21st St. N.W., 20036; (202) 331-9694. Fax, (202) 331-4395. Nancy Fitzpatrick, Executive Director.*
General email, staff@quota.org
Web, www.quotainternational.org and Twitter, @QuotaIntl

International service organization that links members in twelve countries in a worldwide network of service and friendship. Interests include deaf, hard-of-hearing, and speech-impaired individuals and disadvantaged women and children. Maintains the We Share Foundation, a charitable organization.

Registry of Interpreters for the Deaf, *333 Commerce St., Alexandria, VA 22314; (703) 838-0030. Fax, (703) 838-0454. Melvin Walker, President; Elijah Sow, Chief Operating Officer, ext. 205. VP, (571) 257-3957.*
General email, RIDinfo@rid.org
Web, www.rid.org and Twitter, @RID_Inc

Membership: professional interpreters, transliterators, interpretation students, and educators. Trains, tests, and certifies interpreters; maintains registry of certified interpreters; establishes certification standards. Sponsors training workshops and conferences; publishes professional development literature.

TDI, *P.O. Box 8009, Silver Spring, MD 20907; Claude L. Stout, Executive Director. Phone (voice/video), (301) 563-9112.*
General email, info@TDIforaccess.org
Web, https://tdiforaccess.org and Twitter, @TDIforAccess

Membership: individuals, organizations, and businesses that advocate equal access to telecommunications, media, and information technologies for Americans who are deaf and hard of hearing. Interests include closed captioning for television, movies, DVDs, and online videos; emergency access (911); and TTY and Telecommunications Relay Services. Publishes a quarterly magazine and an annual resource directory. Monitors legislation and regulations.

Intellectual and Developmental Disabilities

►AGENCIES

Administration for Community Living (ACL) *(Health and Human Services Dept.), Administration on Disabilities (AoD), Mary E. Switzer Bldg., 330 C St. S.W., 20201; (202) 401-4634, ext. 4. Julie Hocker, Commissioner.*
General email, aclinfo@acl.hhs.gov
Web, https://acl.gov/about-acl/administration-disabilities

Works with states, communities, and partners in disability networks to increase the independence, productivity, and community integration of individuals with disabilities; helps improve opportunities for people with disabilities to access quality services and supports, achieve economic self-sufficiency, and experience equality and inclusion in all facets of community life. Acts as advocate for state protection, offers grants to university centers for research. Funds Projects of National Significance and administers the President's Committee on Intellectual Disabilities.

Eunice Kennedy Shriver National Institute of Child Health and Human Development (NICHD) *(National Institutes of Health), Intellectual and Developmental Disabilities Branch (IDDB), 6710B Rockledge Dr., Bldg. 6710B, Room 2328, MSC 7002, Bethesda, MD 20817; (301) 496-1383. Fax, (301) 480-5665. Dr. Melissa Ann Parisi, Chief.*
Web, www.nichd.nih.gov/about/org/der/branches/iddb

Supports research projects, training programs, and research centers dedicated to understanding, preventing, and ameliorating intellectual and developmental disabilities. Major research areas include common and rare neuromuscular and neurodevelopmental disorders, such as Down, Fragile X, and Rett syndromes; inborn errors of metabolism; autism spectrum disorders; and conditions currently and soon-to-be detectable through newborn screening.

►NONGOVERNMENTAL

American Assn. on Intellectual and Developmental Disabilities (AAIDD), *8403 Colesville Rd., #900, Silver Spring, MD 20910; (202) 387-1968. Fax, (202) 387-2193. Margaret A. Nygren, Executive Director. Bookstore, ext. 216.*
Web, http://aaidd.org, Twitter, @TheAAIDD and Facebook, www.facebook.com/TheAAIDD

Association for professionals who work in the field of intellectual and developmental disabilities. Promotes progressive policy, sound research, effective practices, and human rights for people with intellectual and developmental disabilities. Sponsors conferences and training workshops. Monitors legislation and regulations.

The Arc, *1825 K St. N.W., #1200, 20006; (202) 534-3700. Fax, (202) 534-3731. Peter V. Berns, Chief Executive Officer; Marty Ford, Senior Executive Officer of Public Policy. Information, (800) 433-5255.*
General email, info@thearc.org
Web, www.thearc.org, Twitter, @TheArcUS and Facebook, www.facebook.com/thearcus and Public Policy, www.thearc.org/what-we-do/public-policy

Membership: people with intellectual and developmental disabilities and their service providers. Provides oversight and technical assistance for local groups that provide services and support for individuals with disabilities and their families. Monitors federal legislation, regulations, and legal decisions.

Autism Society of America, *4340 East-West Hwy., #350, Bethesda, MD 20814; (301) 657-0881. Fax, (301) 657-0869. Scott Badesch, President. Information, (800) 328-8476.*

Social Security Administration

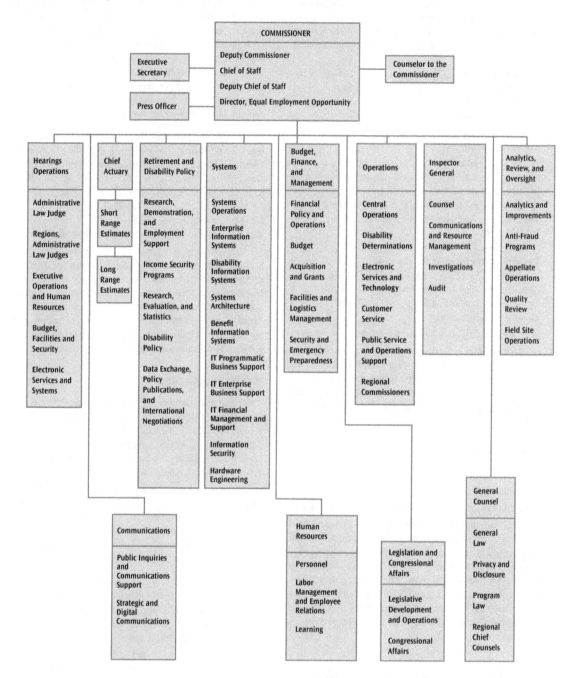

General email, info@autism-society.org

Web, www.autism-society.org and
Twitter, @AutismSociety

Monitors legislation and regulations affecting support, education, training, research, and other services for individuals with autism. Offers referral service and information to the public.

Best Buddies International, *Capitol Region,* 6231 Leesburg Pike, #310, Falls Church, VA 22044; (703)

533-9420. Fax, (703) 533-9423. Karen Glasser, Regional Director. Information, (800) 892-8339.

General email, capitolregion@bestbuddies.org

Web, www.bestbuddies.org/capitolregion and
Twitter, @BestBuddies

Volunteer organization that provides companionship, integrated employment, and leadership development programs to people with intellectual disabilities worldwide. (Headquarters in Miami, Fla.)

Joseph P. Kennedy Jr. Foundation, *1133 19th St. N.W., 12th Floor, 20036-3604; (202) 393-1250. Steve Eidelman, Executive Director.*
General email, jpkjrfdn@gmail.com
Web, www.jpkf.org

Seeks to enhance the quality of life of persons with intellectual disabilities and their families through public policy advocacy. Provides information and training on the policymaking process.

National Assn. of State Directors of Developmental Disabilities Services (NASDDDS), *301 N. Fairfax St., #101, Alexandria, VA 22314-2633; (703) 683-4202.*
Mary Lee Fay, Executive Director, (971) 219-3006.
Web, www.nasddds.org

Membership: chief administrators of state intellectual and developmental disability programs. Coordinates exchange of information on intellectual and developmental disability programs among the states; provides technical assistance to members and information on state programs.

National Children's Center, *8157 Georgia Ave., Silver Spring, MD 20910; (202) 722-2300. Fax, (202) 722-2383. Patricia Browne, President.*
Web, www.nccinc.org

Provides educational, social, and clinical services to infants, children, and adults with intellectual and other developmental disabilities. Services provided through a 24-hour intensive treatment program, group homes and independent living programs, educational services, adult treatment programs, and early intervention programs for infants with disabilities or infants at high risk. Operates a child development center for children with and without disabilities.

Psychiatric Rehabilitation Assn., *7918 Jones Branch Dr., #300, McLean, VA 22101; (703) 442-2078. Fax, (703) 506-3266. Lee K. Lowery, Managing Director.*
General email, info@psychrehabassociation.org
Web, www.uspra.org and Twitter, @PsychRehab

Membership: agencies, mental health practitioners, researchers, policymakers, family groups, and consumer organizations. Supports the community adjustment of persons with psychiatric disabilities. Promotes the role of rehabilitation in mental health systems; opposes discrimination based on mental disability. Certifies psychosocial rehabilitation practitioners.

HOMELESSNESS

General

▶**AGENCIES**

Education Dept., *Career, Technical, and Adult Education (OCTAE), Adult Education and Literacy, 550 12th St. S.W., 11th Floor, 20202-7100 (mailing address: 400 Maryland Ave. S.W., P-OCTAE, DAEL, Washington, DC*
20202); (202) 245-7700. Fax, (202) 245-7838.
Cheryl L. Keenan, Director, (202) 245-7810.
General email, octae@ed.gov
Web, www2.ed.gov/about/offices/list/ovae/pi/AdultEd

Provides state and local agencies and community-based organizations with assistance in establishing education programs for homeless adults.

Education Dept., *Elementary and Secondary Education (OESE), Safe and Healthy Students (OSHS), Education for Homeless Children and Youth Program, Lyndon Baines Johnson Bldg., 400 Maryland Ave. S.W., 20202-6132; (202) 453-6777. Fax, (202) 260-7764.*
John McLaughlin, Program Coordinator.
General email, HomelessEd@ed.gov
Web, www2.ed.gov/programs/homeless

Provides formula grants to education agencies in the states, Puerto Rico, and through the Bureau of Indian Affairs to Native Americans to educate homeless children and youth and to establish an office of coordinator of education for homeless children and youth in each jurisdiction.

Emergency Food and Shelter National Board Program, *701 N. Fairfax St., #310, Alexandria, VA 22314-2064; (703) 706-9660. Fax, (703) 706-9677. Kelly Andreae, Director.*
General email, efsp@uww.unitedway.org
Web, www.efsp.unitedway.org

Public/private partnership created by Congress to help meet the needs of hungry and homeless by allocating federal funds for the provision of food and shelter. Administers the Emergency Food and Shelter Program under the McKinney-Vento Act; gives supplemental assistance to more than 14,000 human service agencies. Does not provide direct assistance to the public.

Health and Human Services Dept. (HHS), *Planning and Evaluation (ASPE), Human Services Policy, Division of Economic Support for Families, 200 Independence Ave. S.W., #404E.5, 20201; (202) 690-7409. Fax, (202) 690-6562. Kelly Kinnison, Director, (202) 690-6850.*
Web, www.aspe.hhs.gov/office-human-services-policy

Develops policies around homelessness and reentry. (Located within the Office of Human Services Policy.)

Housing and Urban Development Dept. (HUD), *Community Planning and Development, 451 7th St. S.W., #7100, 20410; (202) 708-2690. Fax, (202) 708-3336. Neal J. Rackleff, Assistant Secretary; David Woll, Principal Deputy Assistant Secretary.*
Web, www.hud.gov/program_offices/comm_planning

Gives supplemental assistance to facilities that aid the homeless; awards grants for innovative programs that address the needs of homeless families with children.

Housing and Urban Development Dept. (HUD), *Community Planning and Development, Special Needs Assistance Programs, Community Assistance Division, 451 7th St. S.W., #7266, 20410; (202) 708-1234. Fax, (202) 401-0053. Brian Fitzmaurice, Director, (202) 402-4080. HUD locator, (202) 401-0388. fax, (202) 401-0053.*
Web, www.hud.gov

Advises and represents the secretary on homelessness matters; promotes cooperation among federal agencies on homelessness issues; coordinates assistance programs for the homeless under the McKinney Act. Trains HUD field staff in administering homelessness programs. Distributes funds to eligible nonprofit organizations, cities, counties, tribes, and territories for shelter, care, transitional housing, and permanent housing for the disabled homeless. Programs provide for acquisition and rehabilitation of buildings, prevention of homelessness, counseling, and medical care. Administers the Federal Surplus Property Program and spearheads the initiative to lease HUD-held homes to the homeless.

▶NONGOVERNMENTAL

Covenant House, Washington Office, 2001 Mississippi Ave. S.E., 20020; (202) 610-9600. Madye Henson, President.
Web, http://covenanthousedc.org and Twitter, @CovenantHouseDC

Protects young people suffering from homelessness, abuse, and neglect. Provides services including transitional housing, GED and adult education, and job readiness. (Affiliated with Covenant House International.)

D.C. Central Kitchen, 425 2nd St. N.W., 20001; (202) 234-0707. Michael F. Curtin, Chief Executive Officer, (202) 266-2018.
Web, www.dccentralkitchen.org and Twitter, @dcck

Distributes food to D.C.-area homeless shelters, transitional homes, low-income schoolchildren, and corner store "food deserts."

National Alliance to End Homelessness, 1518 K St. N.W., 2nd Floor, 20005; (202) 638-1526. Fax, (202) 638-4664. Nan Roman, President.
General email, info@naeh.org
Web, www.naeh.org and Twitter, @naehomelessness

Policy, research, and capacity-building organization that works to prevent, alleviate, and end problems of the homeless. Provides data and research to policymakers and the public; encourages public-private collaboration for stronger programs to reduce the homeless population, and works with communities to improve assistance programs for the homeless.

National Coalition for Homeless Veterans, 1730 M. St. N.W., #705, 20036; (202) 546-1969. Fax, (202) 546-2063. Kathryn Monet, Executive Director. Toll-free, 800-VET-HELP. Toll-free fax, (888) 233-8582.
General email, info@nchv.org
Web, www.nchv.org and Twitter, @NCHVorg

Faith-based organization providing technical assistance to service providers; advocates on behalf of homeless veterans.

National Coalition for the Homeless, 2201 P St. N.W., 20037-1033; (202) 462-4822. Megan Hustings, Director (Acting).

General email, info@nationalhomeless.org
Web, www.nationalhomeless.org, Twitter, @Ntl_Homeless and Facebook, www.facebook.com/NationalCoalitionfortheHomeless

Advocacy network of persons who are or have been homeless, state and local coalitions, other activists, service providers, housing developers, and others. Seeks to create the systemic and attitudinal changes necessary to end homelessness. Works to meet the needs of persons who are homeless or at risk of becoming homeless.

National Law Center on Homelessness and Poverty, 2000 M St. N.W., #210, 20036; (202) 638-2535. Fax, (202) 628-2737. Maria Foscarinis, Executive Director.
General email, email@nlchp.org
Web, www.nlchp.org and Twitter, @nichphomeless

Legal advocacy group that works to prevent and end homelessness through impact litigation, legislation, and education. Conducts research on homelessness issues. Acts as a clearinghouse for legal information and technical assistance. Monitors legislation and regulations.

Salvation Army, 615 Slaters Lane, Alexandria, VA 22313 (mailing address: P.O. Box 269, Alexandria, VA 22313-0269); (703) 684-5500. David Hudson, National Commander. Press, (703) 684-5500. Donating Goods, (800) 728-7825. Toll free, (800) 725-2769.
Web, www.salvationarmyusa.org and Twitter, @SalvationArmyUS

International religious social welfare organization that provides the homeless with residences and social services, including counseling, emergency help, and employment services. (International headquarters in London.)

U.S. Conference of Mayors, Task Force on Hunger and Homelessness, 1620 Eye St. N.W., 4th Floor, 20006; (202) 293-7330. Fax, (202) 293-2352. Eugene T. Lowe, Assistant Executive Director for Community Development and Housing, (202) 861-6710.
Web, www.usmayors.org/the-conference/committees-and-task-forces

Tracks trends in hunger, homelessness, and community programs that address homelessness and hunger in U.S. cities; issues reports. Monitors legislation and regulations.

SOCIAL SECURITY

General

▶AGENCIES

Social Security Administration (SSA), 6401 Security Blvd., Baltimore, MD 21235; (410) 965-3120. Fax, (410) 966-1463. Nancy A. Berryhill, Commissioner (Acting). Information, (800) 772-1213. Press, (410) 929-4774. TTY, (800) 325-0778.
Web, www.ssa.gov and Twitter, @SocialSecurity

Administers national Social Security programs and the Supplemental Security Income program.

Social Security Administration (SSA), Central Operations, 1500 Woodlawn Dr., Baltimore, MD 21241; (410) 966-7000. Fax, (410) 966-6005. Chris R. Goble, Associate Commissioner. Information, (800) 772-1213.

Reviews and authorizes claims for benefits under the disability insurance program and all claims for beneficiaries living abroad; certifies benefits payments; maintains beneficiary rolls.

Social Security Administration (SSA), Disability Determinations, 3570 Annex Bldg., 6401 Security Blvd., Baltimore, MD 21235; (410) 965-1170. Fax, (410) 965-6503. John E. Owens, Associate Commissioner. Information, (800) 772-1213. TTY, (800) 325-0778. Web, www.ssa.gov/disability

Provides direction for administration of the disability insurance program, which is paid out of the Social Security Trust Fund. Administers disability and blindness provisions of the Supplemental Security Income (SSI) program. Responsible for claims filed under black lung benefits program before July 1, 1973.

Social Security Administration (SSA), Hearings Operations, 5107 Leesburg Pike, #1600, Falls Church, VA 22041-3255; (703) 966-8200. Fax, (703) 605-8201. Theresa L. Gruber, Deputy Commissioner. Toll-free, (800) 772-1213. TTY, (800) 325-0778. Web, www.ssa.gov/appeals/about_us.html

Administers a nationwide system of administrative law judges who conduct hearings and decide appealed cases concerning benefits provisions. Reviews decisions for appeals council action, if necessary, and renders the secretary's final decision. Reviews benefits cases on disability, retirement and survivors' benefits, and supplemental security income.

Social Security Administration (SSA), Operations, 6401 Security Blvd., West High Rise, #1204, Baltimore, MD 21235; (410) 965-3145. Fax, (410) 966-7941. Gracie M. Kim, Deputy Commissioner (Acting). Information, (800) 772-1213. TTY, (800) 325-0778. Web, www.ssa.gov

Issues Social Security numbers, maintains earnings and beneficiary records, authorizes claims, certifies benefits, and makes postadjudicative changes in beneficiary records for retirement, survivors and disability insurance, and black lung claims. Maintains toll-free number for workers who want information on future Social Security benefits.

Social Security Administration (SSA), Quality Review, 6401 Security Blvd., #252, Altmeyer Bldg., Baltimore, MD 21235; Fax, (410) 965-8582. (410) 966-0607. Samara Richardson, Associate Commissioner. Web, www.ssa.gov

Reviews, evaluates, and reports on the integrity and quality of the administration of Social Security programs; conducts broad-based reviews, studies, and analyses of agency operations with emphasis on compliance with laws, regulations, and policies.

Social Security Administration (SSA), Research, Evaluation, and Statistics, 500 E St. S.W., #922, 20254; (202) 358-6020. Fax, (202) 358-6187. Jason D. Brown, Associate Commissioner. Publications, (202) 358-6405. Web, www.ssa.gov/policy/about/ORES.html

Compiles statistics on beneficiaries; conducts research on the economic status of beneficiaries and the relationship between Social Security, the American people, and the economy; analyzes the effects of proposed Social Security legislation, especially on lower-income and middle-income individuals and families; disseminates results of research and statistical programs through publications.

Workers Compensation (OWCP) (Labor Dept.), Coal Mine Workers' Compensation, 200 Constitution Ave. N.W., #C3520, 20210 (mailing address: DCMWC, P.O. Box 8307, London, KY 40742-8307); (202) 693-0046. Fax, (202) 693-1395. Michael A. Chance, Director. Toll-free Federal Black Lung Program, (800) 347-2502. TTY, (877) 889-5627. General email, DCMWC-public@dol.gov Web, www.dol.gov/owcp/dcmwc

Provides direction for administration of the black lung benefits program. Adjudicates all black lung claims; certifies benefit payments and maintains black lung beneficiary rolls.

►CONGRESS

For a listing of relevant congressional committees and subcommittees, please see page 723 or the Appendix.

►NONGOVERNMENTAL

AARP, 601 E St. N.W., 20049; (202) 434-2277. Fax, (202) 434-7946. Jo Ann C. Jenkins, Chief Executive Officer. Library, (202) 434-6233. Membership, (202) 434-7550. Membership, toll-free, (800) 566-0242. Press, (202) 434-2560. Toll-free, (888) 687-2277. TTY, (877) 434-7598. Toll-free Spanish, (877) 342-2277. TTY Spanish, (866) 238-9488. General email, member@aarp.org Web, www.aarp.org, Twitter, @AARP and Facebook, www.facebook.com/AARP

Membership: people fifty years of age and older. Works to address members' needs and interests through education, advocacy, and service. Monitors legislation and regulations and disseminates information on issues affecting older Americans, including issues related to Social Security.

National Academy of Social Insurance, 1200 New Hampshire Ave. N.W., #830, 20036; (202) 452-8097. Fax, (202) 452-8111. William J. Arnone, Chief Executive Officer. General email, nasi@nasi.org Web, www.nasi.org

Promotes research and education on Social Security, Medicare, health care financing, and related public and private programs; assesses social insurance programs and their relationship to other programs; supports research and leadership development. Acts as a clearinghouse for social insurance information.

National Committee to Preserve Social Security and Medicare, *111 K St. N.E., #700, 20002; (202) 216-0420. Fax, (202) 216-0446. Max Richtman, President. Press, (202) 216-8378. Senior hotline/Legislative updates, (800) 998-0180.*

General email, webmaster@ncpssm.org

Web, www.ncpssm.org, Twitter, @NCPSSM and Facebook, www.facebook.com/NationalCommittee

Educational and advocacy organization that focuses on Social Security and Medicare programs and on related income security and health issues. Interests include retirement income protection, health care reform, and the quality of life of seniors. Monitors legislation and regulations.

18

Transportation

GENERAL POLICY AND ANALYSIS

Basic Resources

►AGENCIES

Access Board, 1331 F St. N.W., #1000, 20004-1111; (202) 272-0080. Fax, (202) 272-0081. David M. Capozzi, Executive Director, (202) 272-0010.
Toll-free, (800) 872-2253. Toll-free TTY, (800) 993-2822. TTY, (202) 272-0082.
General email, info@access-board.gov
Web, www.access-board.gov

Develops and maintains accessibility requirements for buildings, transit vehicles, telecommunications equipment, medical diagnostic equipment, and electronic and information technology. Provides technical assistance and training on these guidelines and standards. Enforces access standards for federally funded facilities through the Architectural Barriers Act.

Bureau of Economic and Business Affairs (EB) *(State Dept.), Transportation Affairs (TRA),* 2201 C St. N.W., #3425, 20520-5820; (202) 647-4045. Hugo Y. Yon, Deputy Assistant Secretary (Acting).
Web, www.state.gov/e/eb/tra

Supports the U.S. global transportation industry; negotiates international air services agreements; works with other departments on safe transportation infrastructure policies. Oversees the offices of Aviation Negotiations and Transportation Policy.

Bureau of Economic and Business Affairs (EB) *(State Dept.), Transportation Affairs (TRA), Transportation Policy (OTP),* 2201 C St. N.W., #3425, 20520-5820; (202) 647-9341. Fax, (202) 647-8628. Megan Walklet-Tighe, Director.
Web, www.state.gov/e/eb/tra

Develops and coordinates policy on international civil aviation, maritime, and land transport, including policy research, safety and security, discriminatory and unfair practices, commercial and operational problems encountered abroad, overflight and landing authorizations, port access, environmental protection, and accident investigations.

National Transportation Safety Board (NTSB), 490 L'Enfant Plaza East S.W., 20594-2000; (202) 314-6000. Fax, (202) 314-6018. Robert L. Sumwalt, Chair; Susan Kantrowitz, Director of Administration. Press, (202) 314-6100.
Web, www.ntsb.gov, Twitter, @NTSB and Facebook, www.facebook.com/NTSBgov and YouTube, www.youtube.com/user/NTSBgov

Promotes transportation safety through independent investigations of accidents and other safety problems. Makes recommendations for safety improvement. Operates three regional offices.

National Transportation Safety Board (NTSB), *Research and Engineering,* 490 L'Enfant Plaza East S.W., 20594-2000; (202) 314-6501. Fax, (240) 752-6247. Jim Ritter, Director.
Web, www.ntsb.gov/about/organization/RE

Evaluates effectiveness of federal, state, and local safety programs. Identifies transportation safety issues not being addressed by government or industry. Conducts studies on specific safety problems. Provides technical support to accident investigations. Operates in four divisions: Safety Research and Statistical Analysis; Vehicle Performance; Vehicle Recorder; and Materials Laboratory.

National Transportation Safety Board (NTSB), *Safety Recommendations and Communications,* 490 L'Enfant Plaza East S.W., 20594-2000; (202) 314-6100. Fax, (240) 752-6247. Paul Sledzik, Director.
Web, www.ntsb.gov/about/organization/OC

Makes transportation safety recommendations to federal and state agencies on all modes of transportation. Produces the annual "Most Wanted" list of critical transportation safety projects.

Office of Management and Budget (OMB) *(Executive Office of the President), Transportation,* 725 17th St. N.W., #9002, 20503; (202) 395-6138. Fax, (202) 395-4797. David Connolly, Chief. Press, (202) 395-7254.
Web, www.whitehouse.gov/omb

Assists and advises the OMB director on budget preparation, proposed legislation, and evaluations of Transportation Dept. programs, policies, and activities.

Office of the Assistant Secretary of Research and Technology *(Transportation Dept.),* 1200 New Jersey Ave. S.E., 20590; (202) 366-3282. Fax, (202) 366-3759. Vacant, Assistant Secretary; Vacant, Executive Director; Keith Nelson, Deputy Executive Director. DOT library, (800) 853-1351. Toll-free, (800) 853-1351.
General email, ritainfo@dot.gov
Web, www.transportation.gov/research-technology

Coordinates and manages the department's research portfolio and expedites implementation of innovative technologies. Oversees the Bureau of Transportation Statistics, Volpe National Transportation Systems Center (in Cambridge, Mass.), and the Transportation Safety Institute (in Oklahoma City).

Office of the Assistant Secretary of Research and Technology *(Transportation Dept.), Bureau of Transportation Statistics,* 1200 New Jersery Ave. S.E., #E34-314, 20590; (202) 366-1270. Patricia S. Hu, Director. Information, (800) 853-1351. Press, (202) 366-5568.
General email, btsinfo@dot.gov
Web, www.bts.gov

Works to improve public awareness of the nation's transportation systems. Collects, analyzes, and publishes a comprehensive, cross-modal set of transportation statistics.

Office of the Assistant Secretary of Research and Technology *(Transportation Dept.), Research, Development, and Technology,* 1200 New Jersey Ave. S.E., #E33-304, 20590-0001; (202) 366-1351.

TRANSPORTATION RESOURCES IN CONGRESS

For a complete listing of congressional committees, including their full contact information, leadership, membership, and jurisdictions, please refer to the Appendix on pages 827–948.

HOUSE:

House Appropriations Committee, (202) 225-2771.
Web, appropriations.house.gov
    Subcommittee on Energy and Water Development, and Related Agencies, (202) 225-3421.
    Subcommittee on Financial Services and General Government, (202) 225-7245.
    Subcommittee on Homeland Security, (202) 225-5834.
    Subcommittee on Transportation, Housing and Urban Development, and Related Agencies, (202) 225-2141.
House Energy and Commerce Committee, (202) 225-2927.
Web, energycommerce.house.gov
    Subcommittee on Digital Commerce and Consumer Protection, (202) 225-2927.
House Homeland Security Committee, (202) 226-8417.
Web, homeland.house.gov
    Subcommittee on Border and Maritime Security, (202) 226-8417.
    Subcommittee on Transportation and Protective Security, (202) 226-8417.
House Natural Resources Committee, (202) 225-2761.
Web, naturalresources.house.gov
    Subcommittee on Water, Power, and Oceans, (202) 225-8331.
House Science, Space, and Technology Committee, (202) 225-6371.
Web, science.house.gov
    Subcommittee on Research and Technology, (202) 225-6371.
    Subcommittee on Space, (202) 225-6371.
House Transportation and Infrastructure Committee, (202) 225-9446.
Web, transportation.house.gov
    Subcommittee on Aviation, (202) 226-3220.

    Subcommittee on Coast Guard and Maritime Transportation, (202) 226-3552.
    Subcommittee on Economic Development, Public Buildings, and Emergency Management, (202) 225-3014.
    Subcommittee on Highways and Transit, (202) 225-6715.
    Subcommittee on Railroads, Pipelines, and Hazardous Materials, (202) 226-0727.
    Subcommittee on Water Resources and Environment, (202) 225-4360.

SENATE:

Senate Appropriations Committee, (202) 224-7257.
Web, appropriations.senate.gov
    Subcommittee on Transportation, Housing and Urban Development, and Related Agencies, (202) 224-7281.
Senate Banking, Housing, and Urban Affairs Committee, (202) 224-7391.
Web, banking.senate.gov
    Subcommittee on Housing, Transportation and Community Development, (202) 224-7391.
Senate Commerce, Science, and Transportation Committee, (202) 224-1251.
Web, commerce.senate.gov
    Subcommittee on Aviation Operations, Safety, and Security, (202) 224-1251.
    Subcommittee on Surface Transportation and Merchant Marine Infastructure, Safety, and Security, (202) 224-1251.
Senate Environment and Public Works Committee, (202) 224-6176.
Web, epw.senate.gov
    Subcommittee on Transportation and Infrastructure, (202) 224-6176.
Senate Finance Committee, (202) 224-4515.
Web, finance.senate.gov
    Subcommittee on Energy, Natural Resources, and Infrastructure, (202) 224-4515.

Fax, (202) 366-3759. Kevin Womack, Director.
Toll-free, (800) 853-1351.
Web, www.transportation.gov/research-technology

Supports transportation innovation research, engineering, education, and safety training. Focus includes intermodal transportation; partnerships among government, universities, and industry; and economic growth and competitiveness through use of new technologies. Monitors international research.

Pipeline and Hazardous Materials Safety Administration *(Transportation Dept.), 1200 New Jersey*

Ave. S.E., #E27-300, 20590; (202) 366-4433.
Fax, (202) 366-3666. Howard (Skip) Elliott, Administrator.
Hazardous Materials Information Center, (800) 467-4922.
To report an incident, (800) 424-8802.
General email, phmsa.administrator@dot.gov
Web, www.phmsa.dot.gov and Twitter, @PHMSA_DOT

Oversees the safe and secure movement of hazardous materials to industry and consumers by all modes of transportation, including pipelines. Works to eliminate transportation-related deaths and injuries. Promotes transportation solutions to protect communities and the environment.

Transportation Department

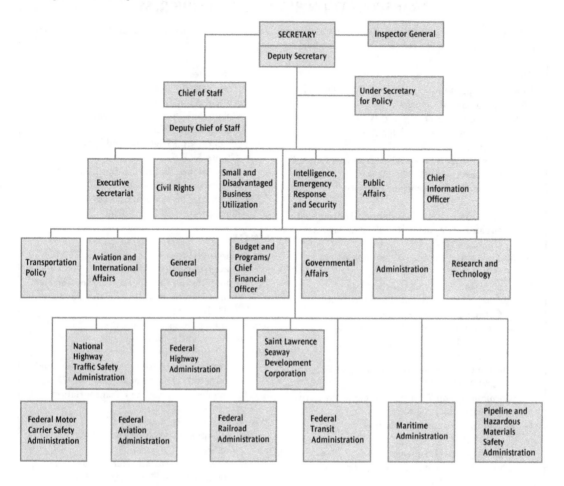

Pipeline and Hazardous Materials Safety Administration *(Transportation Dept.)*, *Hazardous Materials Safety,* 1200 New Jersey Ave. S.E., #E21-317, 20590; (202) 366-4488. Fax, (202) 366-5713. *William S. (Bill) Schoonover, Associate Administrator.* Hazardous Materials Information Center, (800) 467-4922.
General email, phmsa.hmhazmatsafety@dot.gov

Web, https://cms.phmsa.dot.gov/about-phmsa/offices/office-hazardous-materials-safety

Federal safety authority for the transportation of hazardous materials by air, rail, highway, and water. Works to reduce dangers of hazardous materials transportation. Issues regulations for classifications, communications, shipper and carrier operations, training and security requirements, and packaging and container specifications.

Surface Transportation Board (STB), *Public Assistance, Governmental Affairs, and Compliance,* 395 E St. S.W., #1202, 20423-0001; (202) 245-0238. Fax, (202) 245-0461. *Lucille L. Marvin, Director.* Toll-free, (866) 254-1792. TTY, (800) 877-8339.

General email, rcpa@stb.gov

Web, www.stb.gov/stb/about/office_opagac.html

Informs members of Congress, the public, and the media of board actions. Prepares testimony for hearings; comments on proposed legislation; assists the public in matters involving transportation regulations.

Transportation Dept. (DOT), 1200 New Jersey Ave. S.E., 20590; (202) 366-4000. Elaine L. Chao, Secretary; Jeffrey A. Rosen, Deputy Secretary. Press, (202) 366-4570. Toll-free, (855) 368-4200. TTY, (800) 877-8339.
General email, pressoffice@dot.gov

Web, www.transportation.gov and Twitter, @USDOT

Responsible for shaping and administering policies and programs to protect and enhance the transportation system and services. Includes the Federal Aviation Administration, Federal Highway Administration, Federal Motor Carrier Safety Administration, Federal Railroad Administration, Maritime Administration, National Highway Traffic Safety Administration, Pipeline and Hazardous Materials Safety Administration, Federal Transit Administration, and the Saint Lawrence Seaway Development

Corp. The Surface Transportation Board is also administratively affiliated, but decisionally independent.

Transportation Dept. (DOT), *Intelligence, Security, and Emergency Response,* 1200 New Jersey Ave. S.E., #56125, 20590; (202) 366-6525. Fax, (202) 366-7261.
Richard Chávez, Director.
Web, www.transportation.gov/mission/administrations/intelligence-security-emergency-response

Advises the secretary on transportation intelligence and security policy. Acts as liaison with the intelligence community, federal agencies, corporations, and interest groups; administers counterterrorism strategic planning processes.

Transportation Dept. (DOT), *Policy Development, Strategic Planning, and Performance,* 1200 New Jersey Ave. S.E., #W84-310, 20590; (202) 366-4416.
Fax, (202) 366-0263. Barbara McCann, Director.
TTY, (800) 877-8339.
Web, www.transportation.gov/policy/office-policy-planning-performance

Develops, coordinates, and evaluates public policy with respect to safety, environmental, energy, and accessibility issues affecting all aspects of transportation. Assesses the economic and institutional implications of domestic transportation matters. Oversees legislative and regulatory proposals affecting transportation. Provides advice on research and development requirements. Develops policy proposals to improve the performance, safety, and efficiency of the transportation system.

Transportation Security Administration (TSA) *(Homeland Security Dept.),* TSA-1, 601 S. 12th St., 7th Floor, Arlington, VA 20598-6001; Fax, (571) 227-1398. *David P. Pekoske, Administrator; Huban A. Gowadia, Deputy Administrator. Press, (571) 227-2829. TSA Contact Center, (866) 289-9673.*
General email, TSA-ContactCenter@tsa.dhs.gov
Web, www.tsa.gov and Twitter, @TSA

Protects the nation's transportation systems to ensure freedom of movement for people and commerce.

Transportation Security Administration (TSA) *(Homeland Security Dept.), Acquisition,* TSA-25, 601 S. 12th St., Arlington, VA 20598-6025; (571) 227-2161. *Fax, (571) 227-2911. Latetia Anderson, Assistant Administrator.*
Web, www.tsa.gov

Administers contract grants, cooperative agreements, and other transactions in support of TSA's mission. Develops acquisitions strategies, policies, programs, and processes.

Transportation Security Administration (TSA) *(Homeland Security Dept.), Contact Center,* 601 S. 12th St., 7th Floor, Arlington, VA 20598; (866) 289-9673. *Michelle Cartagena, Program Manager.*
General email, tsa-contactcenter@tsa.dhs.gov
Web, www.tsa.gov

Answers questions and collects concerns from the public regarding travel security.

Transportation Security Administration (TSA) *(Homeland Security Dept.), Freedom Center,* 13555 EDS Dr., Herndon, VA 20171 (mailing address: TSOC Annex, 601 S. 12th St., Arlington, VA 22202); (866) 655-7023. *Roderick Allison, Chief of Operations (Acting).*
Web, www.tsa.gov

Operations center that provides continual federal, state, and local coordination, communications, and domain awareness for all of the Homeland Security Dept.'s transportation-related security activities worldwide. Transportation domains include highway, rail, shipping, and aviation.

Transportation Security Administration (TSA) *(Homeland Security Dept.), Intelligence and Analysis,* TSA-10, 601 S. 12th St., 6th Floor, Arlington, VA 22202-4220; (703) 601-3100. Fax, (703) 601-3290. *Thomas L. Bush, Assistant Administrator.*
Web, www.tsa.gov

Oversees TSA's intelligence gathering and information sharing as they pertain to national security and the safety of the nation's transportation systems.

Transportation Security Administration (TSA) *(Homeland Security Dept.), Security Policy and Industry Engagement,* TSA-28, 601 S. 12th St., Arlington, VA 20598-6028; (571) 227-1417. Fax, (571) 227-2932. *Eddie Mayenschein, Assistant Administrator.*
Web, www.tsa.gov

Formulates policy and shares information related to security in various segments of the transportation industry, including commercial airports, commercial airlines, general aviation, mass transit and passenger rail, freight rail, maritime, highway and motor carrier, pipeline and air cargo. Coordinates with the U.S. Coast Guard.

Transportation Security Administration (TSA) *(Homeland Security Dept.), Strategic Communications and Public Affairs,* TSA-4, 601 S. 12th St., Arlington, VA 20598-6028; (571) 227-2829. Fax, (571) 227-2552. *Michael Bifello, Assistant Administrator.*
General email, tsamedia@tsa.dhs.gov
Web, www.tsa.gov/press

Responsible for TSA's communications and public information outreach, both externally and internally.

►CONGRESS

For a listing of relevant congressional committees and subcommittees, please see page 751 or the Appendix.

►NONGOVERNMENTAL

American Public Works Assn., Washington Office, 1275 K St. N.W., #750, 20005; (202) 408-9541. Andrea Eales, *Director of Government Affairs, (202) 218-6730.*
General email, apwa.washington@gmail.com
Web, www.apwa.net and Twitter, @APWATweets

Membership: engineers, architects, and others who maintain and manage public works facilities and services.

Transportation Security Administration

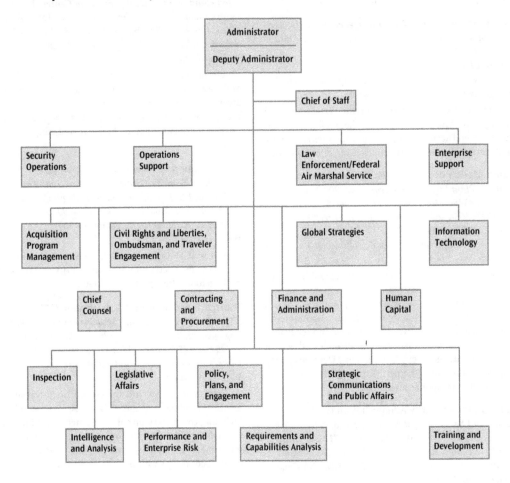

Conducts research and education and promotes exchange of information on transportation and infrastructure-related issues. (Headquarters in Kansas City, Mo.)

Americans for Transportation Mobility Coalition, *U.S. Chamber of Commerce, 1615 H St. N.W., 20062; (202) 463-5842. Thomas W. Smith III, Executive Director. General email, mobility@uschamber.com*

Web, www.fasterbettersafer.org and Twitter, @ATMCoalition

Advocates increased dedicated federal and private sector funding for roads, bridges, and public transportation systems. Members include associations involved in designing, building, or maintaining transportation infrastructure. Monitors legislation. (Affiliated with the U.S. Chamber of Commerce.)

Assn. of Transportation Law Professionals, *P.O. Box 5407, Annapolis, MD 21403; (410) 268-1311. Fax, (410) 268-1322. Lauren Michalski, Executive Director. General email, info@atlp.org*

Web, www.atlp.org

Membership: Transportation attorneys and company counsel, government officials, and industry practitioners.

Interests include railroad, motor, energy, pipeline, antitrust, labor, logistics, safety, environmental, air, and maritime matters.

Conference of Minority Transportation Officials, *100 M St. S.E., #917, 20003; (202) 506-2917. A. Bradley Mims, Chief Executive Officer. General email, info@comto.org*

Web, www.comto.org, Twitter, @COMTO_National and Facebook, www.facebook.com/Conference-Of-Minority-Transportation-Officials-COMTO-330029463789014

Forum for minority professionals working in the transportation sector. Provides opportunities and reinforces networks through advocacy, training, and professional development for minorities in the industry.

Diesel Technology Forum, *5291 Corporate Dr., #102, Frederick, MD 21703-2875; (301) 668-7230. Fax, (301) 668-7234. Allen Schaeffer, Executive Director; Kristen Gifford, Communications. General email, dtf@dieselforum.org*

Web, www.dieselforum.org and Twitter, @DieselTechForum

Membership: vehicle and engine manufacturers, component suppliers, petroleum refineries, and emissions control device makers. Advocates use of diesel engines. Provides information on diesel power technology use and efforts to improve fuel efficiency and emissions control. Monitors legislation and regulations.

Eno Center for Transportation, *1629 K St. N.W., #200, 20006; (202) 879-4700. Robert Puentes, President, (202) 879-4711.*
General email, publicaffairs@enotrans.org
Web, www.enotrans.org

Nonpartisan think tank that seeks continuous improvement in transportation and its public and private leadership in order to increase the system's mobility, safety, and sustainability. Offers professional development programs, policy forums, and publications.

Institute of Transportation Engineers (ITE), *1627 Eye St. N.W., #600, 20006; (202) 785-0060. Fax, (202) 785-0609. Jeffrey F. Paniati, Executive Director, ext. 131.*
General email, ite_staff@ite.org
Web, www.ite.org, Twitter, @ITEhq and Facebook, www.facebook.com/ITEHQ

Membership: international professional transportation engineers. Conducts research, seminars, and training sessions; provides professional and scientific information on transportation standards and recommended practices.

National Defense Transportation Assn. (NDTA), *50 S. Pickett St., #220, Alexandria, VA 22304; (703) 751-5011. Fax, (703) 823-8761. Vice Adm. William A. Brown (USN, Ret.), President.*
Web, www.ndtahq.com and Twitter, @NDTAHQ

Membership: transportation users, manufacturers, and mode carriers; information technology firms; and related military, government, and civil interests worldwide. Promotes a strong U.S. transportation capability through coordination of private industry, government, and the military.

National Governors Assn. (NGA), *Center for Best Practices, Environment, Energy, and Transportation Division, 444 N. Capitol St. N.W., #267, 20001-1512; (202) 624-5300. Fax, (202) 624-7829. Sue Gander, Director.*
General email, webmaster@nga.org
Web, www.nga.org/cms/center/eet

Identifies best practices for energy, land use, environment, and transportation issues and shares these with the states.

National Research Council (NRC), *Transportation Research Board, Keck Center, 500 5th St. N.W., 7th Floor, 20001; (202) 334-2934. Fax, (202) 334-2003. Neil J. Pedersen Jr., Executive Director, (202) 334-2942. Library, (202) 334-2947. Press, (202) 334-3134.*
Web, www.trb.org

Promotes research in transportation systems planning and administration and in the design, construction, maintenance, and operation of transportation facilities. Provides information to state and national highway and transportation departments; operates research information services; conducts studies, conferences, and workshops; publishes technical reports. Library open to the public by appointment.

National Research Council (NRC), *Transportation Research Board Library, Keck Center, 500 5th St. N.W., #439, 20001; (202) 334-2989. Fax, (202) 334-2527. Alexandra Briseno, Senior Librarian. Press, (202) 334-3252.*
General email, TRBlibrary@nas.edu
Web, www.trb.org/library

Primary archive for the Transportation Research Board, Highway Research Board, Strategic Highway Research Program, and Marine Board. Subject areas include transportation, aviation, engineering, rail, roads, and transit. Provides information to transportation-related federal agencies. Library open to the public by appointment.

Surface Transportation Information Sharing and Analysis Center (ISAC), *c/o EWA Information and Infrastructure Technologies, Inc., 13873 Park Center Rd., #200, Herndon, VA 20171-5406; (703) 478-7600. Fax, (703) 478-7654. Paul G. Wolfe, Director, (703) 478-7656; Todd Steinmetz, Program Manager. Toll-free, (866) 784-7221.*
General email, st-isac@surfacetransportationisac.org
Web, www.surfacetransportationisac.org

Protects physical and electronic infrastructure of surface transportation and public transit carriers. Collects, analyzes, and distributes critical security and threat information from worldwide resources; shares best security practices and provides 24/7 immediate physical and cyber-threat warnings.

Freight and Intermodalism

▶**AGENCIES**

Maritime Administration *(Transportation Dept.), Port Infrastructure Development and Congestion Mitigation, West Bldg., 1200 New Jersey Ave. S.E., MAR-510, #W21-308, 20590; (202) 366-5076. Fax, (202) 366-6988. Robert Bouchard, Director.*
Web, www.marad.dot.gov/ports/office-port-infrastructure-development

Provides coordination and management of port infrastructure projects; provides leadership in national congestion mitigation efforts that involve waterway and port issues; promotes the development and improved utilization of ports and port facilities, including intermodal connections, terminals, and distribution networks; and provides technical information and advice to other agencies and organizations concerned with intermodal development. Information and advice include the analysis of intermodal economics, the development of applicable information systems, investigation of institutional and regulatory impediments, and the application of appropriate transportation management systems.

Surface Transportation Board (STB), *395 E St. S.W., #1220, 20423-0001; (202) 245-0245. Fax, (202) 245-0458. Ann D. Begeman, Chair. Library, (202) 245-0288. Press, (202) 245-0238. TTY, (800) 877-8339.*
Web, www.stb.gov/stb/index.html

Regulates rates for water transportation and intermodal connections in noncontiguous domestic trade (between the mainland and Alaska, Hawaii, or U.S. territories). Library open to the public.

▶**NONGOVERNMENTAL**

American Moving and Storage Assn. (AMSA), *2800 Eisenhower Ave., #200, Alexandria, VA 22314-4578; (703) 683-7410. Fax, (703) 683-7527. Scott Michael, President, (703) 683-7418. Information, (888) 849-2672.*
General email, membership_web@moving.org
Web, www.promover.org, Twitter, @AMSAProMover and Facebook, www.facebook.com/amsapromover

Represents members' views before the Transportation Dept. and other government agencies. Conducts certification and training programs. Provides financial support for research on the moving and storage industry. Monitors legislation and regulations.

Intermodal Assn. of North America, *11785 Beltsville Dr., #1100, Calverton, MD 20705-4049; (301) 982-3400. Fax, (301) 982-4815. Joanne F. (Joni) Casey, President, ext. 349.*
General email, info@intermodal.org
Web, www.intermodal.org and Twitter, @Intermodal

Membership: railroads, stacktrain operators, water carriers, motor carriers, marketing companies, and suppliers to the intermodal industry. Promotes intermodal transportation of freight. Monitors legislation and regulations.

International Brotherhood of Teamsters, *25 Louisiana Ave. N.W., 20001-2198; (202) 624-6800. Fax, (202) 624-6918. James P. Hoffa, General President; Christy Bailey, Director of Federal Legislation and Regulation, (202) 624-6993; Bret Caldwell, Director of Communications, (202) 624-6911. Press, (202) 624-6911. General email, communications@teamster.org*
Web, www.teamster.org

Membership: workers in the transportation and construction industries, factories, offices, hospitals, warehouses, and other workplaces. Helps members negotiate pay, benefits, and better working conditions; conducts training programs and workshops. Monitors legislation and regulations.

National Assn. of Chemical Distributors (NACD), *1560 Wilson Blvd., #1100, Arlington, VA 22209; (703) 527-6223. Fax, (703) 527-7747. Eric Byer, President. General email, nacdpublicaffairs@nacd.com*
Web, www.nacd.com and Twitter, @NACD_RD

Membership: firms involved in purchasing, processing, blending, storing, transporting, and marketing of chemical products. Provides members with information on such topics as training, safe handling and transport of chemicals,

liability insurance, and environmental issues. Manages the NACD Chemical Educational Foundation. Monitors legislation and regulations.

National Customs Brokers and Forwarders Assn. of America, *1200 18th St. N.W., #901, 20036; (202) 466-0222. Fax, (202) 466-0226. Megan Montgomery, Executive Vice President.*
General email, recep@ncbfaa.org
Web, www.ncbfaa.org

Membership: customs brokers and freight forwarders in the United States. Fosters information exchange within the industry. Monitors legislation and regulations.

National Industrial Transportation League, *7918 Jones Branch Dr., #300, McLean, VA 22102; (703) 524-5011. Fax, (703) 506-3266. Jennifer Hedrick, Executive Director. General email, info@nitl.org*
Web, www.nitl.org

Membership: air, water, and surface shippers and receivers, including industries, corporations, chambers of commerce, and trade associations. Monitors legislation and regulations.

AIR TRANSPORTATION

General

▶**AGENCIES**

Bureau of Economic and Business Affairs (EB) *(State Dept.), Transportation Affairs (TRA), Aviation Negotiations (AN), 2201 C St. N.W., #3425, 20520-5820; (202) 647-5843. Fax, (202) 647-9143. Paul A. Brown, Director.*
Web, www.state.gov/e/eb/tra

Manages bilateral aviation relationships; works with the Transportation Dept. and private sector to negotiate bilateral agreements to support and improve commercial aviation.

Civil Air Patrol National Capital Wing, *200 McChord St. S.W., #111, Joint Base Anacostia-Bolling, 20032; (202) 767-4405. Col. Janon Ellis, Wing Commander.*
General email, info@natcapwing.org
Web, www.natcapwg.cap.gov and Twitter, @NatCapWing

Official civilian auxiliary of the U.S. Air Force. Primary function is to conduct search-and-rescue missions for the Air Force. Maintains an aerospace education program for adults and a cadet program for junior and senior high school students. (Headquarters at Maxwell Air Force Base, Ala.)

Civil Division *(Justice Dept.), Torts Branch, Aviation and Admiralty Litigation, 1425 New York Ave. N.W., #10100, 20005 (mailing address: P.O. Box 14271, Washington, DC 20044-4271); (202) 616-4100. Fax, (202) 616-4002. Barry Benson, Director.*
Web, www.justice.gov/civil/torts/aa/t-aa.html

Federal Aviation Administration

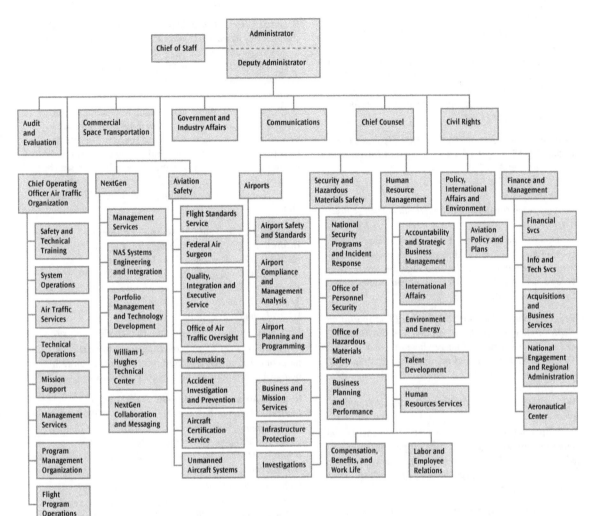

Represents the federal government in civil suits arising from aviation and admiralty incidents and accidents. In aviation, handles tort litigation for the government's activities in the operation of the air traffic control system, regulation of air commerce, weather services, aeronautical charting, and operation of its own civil and military aircraft. In admiralty, defends the government's placement and maintenance of maritime navigational aids, its nautical charting and dredging activities, and its operation and maintenance of U.S. and contract-operated vessels. Brings cases for government cargo damage, pollution cleanups, and damage to U.S. locks, dams, and navaids.

Federal Aviation Administration (FAA) *(Transportation Dept.),* 800 Independence Ave. S.W., 20591; (202) 267-3111. Fax, (202) 267-7887. Dan Elwell, Administrator (Acting). Press, (202) 267-3883. Toll-free, (866) 835-5322.
Web, www.faa.gov, *Twitter,* @FAANews *and Facebook,* www.facebook.com/FAA

Regulates air commerce to improve aviation safety; promotes development of a national system of airports; develops and operates a common system of air traffic control and air navigation for both civilian and military aircraft; prepares the annual National Aviation System Plan.

Federal Aviation Administration (FAA) *(Transportation Dept.), Commercial Space Transportation (AST),* 800 Independence Ave. S.W., #331, AST-1, 20591; (202) 267-7793. Fax, (202) 267-5450. Wayne Monteith, Associate Administrator.
General email, michael.coffman@faa.gov
Web, www.faa.gov/about/office_org/headquarters_offices/ast

Promotes and facilitates the operation of commercial expendable space launch vehicles by the private sector; licenses and regulates these activities.

Federal Aviation Administration (FAA) *(Transportation Dept.), NextGen,* 800 Independence Ave. S.W., 20591;

(202) 267-7111. Fax, (202) 267-5621. Pamela Whitely, Assistant Administrator (Acting).

General email, nextgen@faa.gov

Web, www.faa.gov/about/office_org/headquarters_offices/ang

Plans and develops the Next Generation Air Transportation System infrastructure, which integrates technologies including satellite navigation and advanced digital communications, to reduce air transportation delays, save fuel, and lower carbon emissions.

Federal Aviation Administration (FAA) *(Transportation Dept.), NextGen, Systems Engineering and Integration, 1250 Maryland Ave. S.W., 3rd Floor, 20024; (202) 267-6559. Fax, (202) 385-7105. Joseph Post, Director (Acting).*

Web, www.faa.gov/about/office_org/headquarters_offices/ang/offices

Designs and maintains the National Airspace System (NAS) Enterprise Architecture and provides systems engineering and safety expertise to bridge the gap between today's NAS and the Next Generation Air Transportation System (NextGen).

Federal Aviation Administration (FAA) *(Transportation Dept.), Policy, International Affairs, and Environment (APL), Environment and Energy Research and Development, 800 Independence Ave. S.W., #900W, 20591; (202) 267-3576. Fax, (202) 267-5594. Kevin Welsh, Executive Director.*

Web, www.faa.gov/about/office_org/headquarters_offices/apl/research

Responsible for environmental affairs and energy conservation for aviation, including implementation and administration of various aviation-related environmental acts. Seeks to improve energy efficiency while reducing noise and emission impacts.

Federal Aviation Administration (FAA) *(Transportation Dept.), Policy, International Affairs, and Environment (APL), International Affairs, 600 Independence Ave. S.W., #6E1500, API-1, 20591; (202) 267-1000. Fax, (202) 267-7198. Chris Rocheleau, Executive Director.*

Web, www.faa.gov/about/office_org/headquarters_offices/apl/international_affairs

Coordinates all activities of the FAA that involve foreign relations; acts as liaison with the State Dept. and other agencies concerning international aviation; provides other countries with technical assistance on civil aviation problems; formulates international civil aviation policy for the United States.

International Trade Administration (ITA) *(Commerce Dept.), Industry and Analysis (I&A), Transportation and Machinery (OTM), 1401 Constitution Ave. N.W., #38032, 20230-0001; (202) 482-0572. Fax, (202) 482-0674. Scott Kennedy, Director, (202) 482-4874.*

Web, http://trade.gov/td/otm

Promotes the export of U.S. aerospace, automotive, and machinery products; compiles and analyzes industry data; seeks to secure a favorable position for the U.S. aerospace, auto, and machinery industries in global markets through policy and trade agreements.

National Aeronautics and Space Administration (NASA), *Aeronautics Research Mission Directorate (ARMD), 300 E St. S.W., #6B27, 20546; (202) 358-4600. Fax, (202) 358-3640. Jaiwon Shin, Associate Administrator.*

Web, www.nasa.gov/aeroresearch and Twitter, @NASAAero

Conducts research in aerodynamics, materials, structures, avionics, propulsion, high-performance computing, human factors, aviation safety, and space transportation in support of national space and aeronautical research and technology goals. Manages the following NASA research centers: Ames (Moffett Field, Calif.), Dryden (Edwards, Calif.), Langley (Hampton, Va.), and Glenn (Cleveland, Ohio).

National Air and Space Museum *(Smithsonian Institution), 6th St. and Independence Ave. S.W., 20560; (202) 633-2214. Fax, (202) 633-8174. Gen. J. R. (Jack) Dailey (USMC, Ret.), Director, (202) 633-2350. Education Office, (202) 633-2540. Library, (202) 633-2320. Tours, (202) 633-2563. TTY, (202) 633-5285.*

General email, info@si.edu

Web, www.airandspace.si.edu and Twitter, @airandspace

Maintains exhibits and collections on aeronautics, pioneers of flight, and early aircraft through modern air technology. Library open to the public by appointment.

National Air and Space Museum *(Smithsonian Institution), Steven F. Udvar-Hazy Center, 14390 Air and Space Museum Pkwy., Chantilly, VA 20151; (703) 572-4118. Gen. John R. Dailey, Director, (202) 633-2350. Public Affairs, (202) 633-1000. TTY, (202) 633-5285.*

General email, info@si.edu

Web, www.airandspace.si.edu/visit/udvar-hazy-center

Displays and preserves a collection of historical aviation and space artifacts, including the B-29 Superfortress *Enola Gay*, the Lockheed SR-71 Blackbird, the prototype of the Boeing 707, the space shuttle *Discovery*, and a Concorde. Provides a center for research into the history, science, and technology of aviation and space flight. Open to the public daily 10:00 a.m.–5:30 p.m., except December 25.

National Mediation Board, *1301 K St. N.W., #250E, 20005-7011; (202) 692-5000. Fax, (202) 692-5082. Kyle Fortson, Chair. Information, (202) 692-5050. TTY, (202) 692-5001.*

General email, infoline@nmb.gov

Web, www.nmb.gov

Mediates labor disputes in the airline industry; determines and certifies labor representatives for the industry.

National Oceanic and Atmospheric Administration (NOAA) *(Commerce Dept.), Marine and Aviation Operations (OMAO), 8403 Colesville Rd., #500, Silver Spring, MD 20910-3282; (301) 713-1045. Fax, (301) 713-1541. Rear Adm. Michael J. Silah, Director, (301) 713-7600. Press, (301) 713-7671.*

Web, www.omao.noaa.gov

Operates NOAA's aircraft for hurricane reconnaissance and research, marine mammal and fisheries assessment, and coastal mapping.

Office of the Assistant Secretary of Research and Technology *(Transportation Dept.), Bureau of Transportation Statistics, Airline Information,* 1200 New Jersey Ave. S.E., #E-34, RTS-42, 20590; (202) 366-4373. Fax, (202) 366-3383. William Chadwick, Director. General email, oai-support@bts.gov
Web, www.bts.gov/topics/airlines-and-airports-0

Develops, interprets, and enforces accounting and reporting regulations for all areas of the aviation industry; issues air carrier reporting instructions, waivers, and due-date extensions.

Transportation Dept. (DOT), *Aviation Analysis,* 1200 New Jersey Ave. S.E., #W86-481, 20590; (202) 366-5903. Fax, (202) 366-7638. Todd M. Homan, Director. Press, (202) 366-4570. TTY, (800) 877-8339.
Web, www.transportation.gov/policy/aviation-policy/office-aviation-analysis

Analyzes essential air service needs of communities; directs subsidy policy and programs; guarantees air service to small communities; conducts research for the department on airline mergers, international route awards, and employee protection programs; administers the air carrier fitness provisions of the Federal Aviation Act; registers domestic air carriers; enforces charter regulations for tour operators.

Transportation Dept. (DOT), *Aviation and International Affairs,* 1200 New Jersey Ave. S.E., #W88-322, 20590; (202) 366-8822. Joel Szabat, Deputy Assistant Secretary. Press, (202) 366-4570. TTY, (800) 877-8339.
Web, www.transportation.gov/policy/assistant-secretary-aviation-international-affairs

Develops and implements public policy related to the airline industry and international civil aviation. Administers laws and regulations over a range of aviation trade issues, including U.S. and foreign carrier economic authority to engage in air transportation, small community transportation, the establishment of mail rates within Alaska and in the international market, and access at U.S. airports.

Transportation Dept. (DOT), *Aviation Consumer Protection,* 1200 New Jersey Ave. S.E., 20590; (202) 366-2220. Norman Strickman, Director, (202) 366-5960. Air travelers with disabilities hotline, (800) 778-4838. TTY, (202) 366-0511.
Web, www.transportation.gov/airconsumer

Addresses complaints about airline service and consumer-protection matters. Conducts investigations, provides assistance, and reviews regulations affecting air carriers.

Transportation Dept. (DOT), *International Aviation,* 1200 New Jersey Ave. S.E., #W86-316, 20590; (202) 366-2423. Fax, (202) 366-3694. Brian Hedberg, Director, (202) 366-7783.

Web, www.transportation.gov/policy/aviation-policy/office-international-aviation

Responsible for international aviation regulation and negotiations, including fares, tariffs, and foreign licenses; represents the United States at international aviation meetings.

►CONGRESS

For a listing of relevant congressional committees and subcommittees, please see page 751 or the Appendix.

►NONGOVERNMENTAL

Aeronautical Repair Station Assn., *121 N. Henry St., Alexandria, VA 22314-2903; (703) 739-9543. Fax, (703) 299-0254. Sarah MacLeod, Executive Director, ext. 114.*
General email, arsa@arsa.org
Web, www.arsa.org, Twitter, @ARSAWorks and Facebook, www.facebook.com/AeronauticalRepairStationAssociation

Membership: repair stations that have Federal Aviation Administration certificates or comparable non-U.S. certification; associate members are suppliers and distributors of components and parts. Works to improve relations between repair stations and manufacturers. Interests include establishing uniformity in the application, interpretation, and enforcement of FAA regulations. Monitors legislation and regulations.

Aerospace Industries Assn. (AIA), *1000 Wilson Blvd., #1700, Arlington, VA 22209-3928; (703) 358-1000. Eric K. Fanning, President. Press, (703) 358-1078.*
General email, aia@aia-aerospace.org
Web, www.aia-aerospace.org, Twitter, @aiaspeaks and Facebook, www.facebook.com/AIA.Aerospace

Represents manufacturers of commercial, military, and business aircraft; helicopters; aircraft engines; missiles; spacecraft; and related components and equipment. Interests include international standards and trade.

Air Line Pilots Assn., International, *1625 Massachusetts Ave. N.W., #800, 20036; (703) 689-2270. Capt. Joe DePete, President. Press, (703) 481-4440. Toll-free, (888) 359-2572.*
General email, alpaemail@alpa.org
Web, www.alpa.org, Twitter, @wearealpa and Facebook, www.facebook.com/WeAreAlpa

Membership: airline pilots in the United States and Canada. Promotes air travel safety; assists investigations of aviation accidents. Publishes the *Air Line Pilot Magazine.* Monitors legislation and regulations. (Affiliated with the AFL-CIO and the Canadian Labour Conference.)

Aircraft Owners and Pilots Assn. (AOPA), *Legislative Affairs, 421 Aviation Way, Frederick, MD 21701; (301) 695-2000. Fax, (301) 695-2375. Mark Baker, President; Jim Coon, Senior Vice President of Government Affairs and Advocacy. Toll-free, (800) 872-2672.*

Web, www.aopa.org, Twitter, @AOPA and Facebook, www.facebook.com/AOPApilots

Membership: owners and pilots of general aviation aircraft. Washington office monitors legislation and regulations. Headquarters office provides members with a variety of aviation-related services; issues airport directory and handbook for pilots; sponsors the Air Safety Foundation. (Headquarters in Frederick, Md.)

Airlines for America (A4A), *1275 Pennsylvania Ave. N.W., #1300, 20004; (202) 626-4000. Nicholas E. Calio, President. Press, (202) 821-7513.*
General email, a4a@airlines.org

Web, www.airlines.org, Twitter, @aorlinesdotorg and Facebook, www.facebook.com/AirlinesForAmerica

Membership: U.S. scheduled air carriers. Promotes aviation safety and the facilitation of air transportation for passengers and cargo. Collects data on trends in airline operations. Monitors legislation and regulations.

American Institute of Aeronautics and Astronautics (AIAA), *12700 Sunrise Valley Dr., #200, Reston, VA 20191-5807; (703) 264-7500. Daniel L. (Dan) Dumbacher, Executive Director, ext. 1. Information, (800) 639-2422.*
General email, custserv@aiaa.org

Web, www.aiaa.org, Twitter, @aiaa and Facebook, www .facebook.com/AIAAFan

Membership: engineers, scientists, and students in the fields of aeronautics and astronautics. Holds workshops on aerospace technical issues for congressional subcommittees; sponsors international conferences. Offers computerized database through its Technical Information Service.

Assn. of Flight Attendants–CWA, *501 3rd St. N.W., 20001-2797; (202) 434-1300. Fax, (202) 434-1319. Sara Nelson, President. Press, (202) 550-5520. Toll-free, (800) 424-2401.*
General email, info@afacwa.org

Web, www.afacwa.org and Twitter, @afa_cwa

Membership: approximately 60,000 flight attendants. Helps members negotiate pay, benefits, and better working conditions; conducts training programs and workshops. Monitors legislation and regulations. (Affiliated with the AFL-CIO.)

Cargo Airline Assn., *1620 L St. N.W., #610, 20036-2438; (202) 293-1030. Fax, (202) 293-4377. Stephen A. Alterman, President.*
General email, info@cargoair.org

Web, www.cargoair.org

Membership: cargo airlines and other firms interested in the development and promotion of air freight.

Coalition of Airline Pilots Assns. (CAPA), *444 N. Capitol St., #528, 20001; (202) 624-3535. Fax, (202) 624-3536. Maryanne DeMarco, Executive Director, (202) 624-3538.*
General email, info@capapilots.org

Web, www.capapilots.org and Twitter, @CAPApilots

Trade association of more than 28,000 professional pilots. Addresses safety, security, legislative, and regulatory issues affecting flight deck crew members, as well

as domestic and international policy issues regarding aviation safety and security.

General Aviation Manufacturers Assn. (GAMA), *1400 K St. N.W., #801, 20005-2485; (202) 393-1500. Fax, (202) 842-4063. Peter J. (Pete) Bunce, President.*
General email, info@gama.aero

Web, www.gama.aero, Twitter, @GAManufacturers and Facebook, www.facebook.com/General.Aviation .Manufacturers.Association

Membership: manufacturers of business, commuter, and personal aircraft and manufacturers of engines, avionics, and related equipment. Monitors legislation and regulations; sponsors safety and public information programs.

Helicopter Assn. International, *1920 Ballenger Ave., 4th Floor, Alexandria, VA 22314-2898; (703) 683-4646. Fax, (703) 683-4745. Matthew S. Zuccaro, President.*
General email, rotor@rotor.org

Web, www.rotor.com and Twitter, @HeliAssoc

Membership: owners, manufacturers, pilots, and operator-owners and service suppliers of helicopters and affiliated companies in the civil helicopter industry. Provides information on use and operation of helicopters; offers business management and aviation safety courses; sponsors annual industry exposition. Monitors legislation and regulations.

National Aeronautic Assn., *Reagan Washington National Airport, Hangar 7, #202, 20001-6015; (703) 416-4888. Fax, (703) 416-4877. Greg Principato, President.*
General email, naa@naa.aero

Web, www.naa.aero and Facebook, www.facebook.com/ NationalAeronauticAssociation

Membership: persons interested in development of general and sporting aviation, including skydiving, commercial and military aircraft, and spaceflight. Oversees and approves official U.S. aircraft, aeronautics, and space records. Serves as U.S. representative to the International Aeronautical Federation in Lausanne, Switzerland.

National Agricultural Aviation Assn., *1440 Duke St., Alexandria, VA 22314; (202) 546-5722. Fax, (202) 546-5726. Andrew D. Moore, Executive Director.*
General email, information@agaviation.org

Web, www.agaviation.org

Membership: agricultural pilots; operating companies that seed, fertilize, and spray land by air; and allied industries. Monitors legislation and regulations. (Affiliated with National Agricultural Aviation Research and Education Foundation.)

National Air Carrier Assn., *1735 N. Lynne St., #105, Arlington, VA 22209; (703) 358-8060. Fax, (703) 358-8070. George Novak, President, (703) 358-8065.*
Web, www.naca.cc

Membership: U.S. air carriers certified for nonscheduled and scheduled operations for passengers and cargo in the United States and abroad. Monitors legislation and regulations.

National Air Transportation Assn., *818 Connecticut Ave. N.W., #900, 20006; (202) 774-1535. Fax, (202) 452-0837. Gary Dempsey, President. Information, (800) 808-6282. Web, www.nata.aero and Twitter, @NATAareo*

Membership: companies that provide on-demand air charter, flight training, maintenance and repair, avionics, and other services. Manages an education foundation; compiles statistics; provides business assistance programs. Monitors legislation and regulations. (Affiliated with the National Air Transportation Foundation.)

National Assn. of State Aviation Officials, *1420 New York Ave., 5th Floor NW, 20005; (202) 868-6753. Fax, (202) 280-1080. Shelly Simi, President, (202) 802-9008. General email, info@nasao.org*

Web, www.nasao.org, Twitter, @NASAO1931 and Facebook, www.facebook.com/NASAO1931 and Library, www.nasao.org/resources

Membership: state and territorial aeronautics agencies that deal with aviation issues, including regulation. Seeks uniform aviation laws; manages an aviation research and education foundation. Online library is accessible to non-members.

National Business Aviation Assn. (NBAA), *1200 G St. N.W., #1100, 20005; (202) 783-9000. Fax, (202) 331-8364. Ed Bolen, President. Toll-free, (800) 394-6222. General email, info@nbaa.org*

Web, www.nbaa.org and Twitter, @NBAA

Membership: companies owning and operating aircraft for business use, suppliers, and maintenance and air fleet service companies. Conducts seminars and workshops in business aviation management. Sponsors annual civilian aviation exposition. Monitors legislation and regulations.

Regional Airline Assn., *1201 15th St. N.W., #430, 20005; (202) 367-1170. Fax, (202) 367-2170. Faye Malarkey Black, President; Drew Jacoby Lemos, Director of Government Affairs. Press, (202) 367-2323. General email, raa@raa.org*

Web, www.raa.org

Membership: regional airlines that provide passenger, scheduled cargo, and mail service. Issues an annual report on the industry and hosts an annual convention. Monitors legislation and regulation.

RTCA Inc., *1150 18th St. N.W., #910, 20036; (202) 833-9339. Fax, (202) 833-9434. Terry McVenes, President. General email, info@rtca.org*

Web, www.rtca.org and Twitter, @RTCAInc

Membership: federal agencies, aviation organizations, and commercial firms interested in aeronautical systems. Develops and publishes standards for aviation, including minimum operational performance standards for equipment; conducts research, makes recommendations to FAA, and issues reports on the field of aviation electronics and telecommunications.

Vertical Flight Society, *[American Helicopter Society (AHS International)], [Vertical Lift Consortium (VLC)], 2701 Prosperity Ave., #210, Fairfax, VA 22031; (703) 684-6777. Fax, (703) 739-9279. Michael Hirschberg, Executive Director, ext. 111. Toll-free, (855) 247-4685. General email, staff@vtol.org*

Web, http://vtol.org, Twitter, @VTOLsociety and Facebook, www.facebook.com/VTOLSociety

Membership: individuals and organizations interested in vertical flight. Acts as an information clearinghouse for technical data on helicopter design improvement, aerodynamics, and safety. Awards the Vertical Flight Foundation Scholarship to college students interested in helicopter technology. (Formerly the American Helicopter Society.)

Airports

▶ AGENCIES

Animal and Plant Health Inspection Service (APHIS) *(Agriculture Dept.), Wildlife Services, 1400 Independence Ave. S.W., #1624S, 20250-3402; 4700 River Rd., Riverdale, MD 20737; (202) 799-7095. Fax, (202) 690-0053. Janet Bucknall, Deputy Administrator. Web, www.aphis.usda.gov/wildlife_damage*

Works to minimize damage caused by wildlife to human health and safety. Interests include aviation safety; works with airport managers to reduce the risk of bird strikes. Oversees the National Wildlife Research Center in Ft. Collins, Colo.

Bureau of Land Management (BLM) *(Interior Dept.), Lands, Realty, and Cadastral Survey, 1849 C St. N.W., #2134LM, 20003; (202) 912-7088. Fax, (202) 912-7199. Robert Jolley, Division Chief, (202) 912-7350. Web, www.blm.gov/programs/lands-and-realty*

Operates the Airport Lease Program, which leases public lands for use as public airports.

Federal Aviation Administration (FAA) *(Transportation Dept.), Airport Planning and Environment (APP), 800 Independence Ave. S.W., #619, APP-400, 20591-0001; (202) 267-3263. Fax, (202) 267-5383. Mike Hines, Manager. Aviation safety, (202) 267-3131. Web, www.faa.gov/about/office_org/headquarters_offices/arp/offices/app/app400*

Leads the FAA's strategic policy and planning efforts to provide a safe, efficient, and sustainable national airport system, coordinates the agency's reauthorization before Congress, and is responsible for national aviation policies and strategies in the environment and energy arenas, including aviation activity forecasts, economic analyses, aircraft noise and emissions research and policy, environmental policy, and aviation insurance.

Federal Aviation Administration (FAA) *(Transportation Dept.), Airports (ARP), 800 Independence Ave. S.W., #600E, ARP-1, 20591; (202) 267-9590. Fax, (202) 267-5301. Kirk Shaffer, Associate Administrator.*

Web, www.faa.gov/about/office_org/headquarters_
offices/arp

Makes grants for development and improvement of publicly operated and owned airports and some privately owned airports; inspects and certifies safety design standards for airports; administers the congressional Airport Improvement Program and Passenger Facility Charges Program; ensures that airports receiving federal funding comply with federal regulations. Questions about local airports are usually referred to a local FAA field office.

Maryland Aviation Administration, *Terminal Bldg., P.O. Box 8766, 3rd Floor, BWI Airport, MD 21240-0766; (410) 859-7100. Fax, (410) 850-4729. Edward P. Carey, Chief Administrative Officer, (410) 859-7072. Information, (800) 435-9294. Press, (410) 859-7027. TTY, (410) 859-7227.*
General email, maa@mdot.state.md.us
Web, www.marylandaviation.com and www.bwiairport .com

Responsible for aviation operations, planning, instruction, and safety in Maryland; operates Baltimore/Washington International Thurgood Marshall Airport (BWI) and Martin State Airport.

Metropolitan Washington Airports Authority, *1 Aviation Circle, 20001-2400; (703) 417-8600. John E. Potter, President. Press, (703) 417-8370.*
Web, www.mwaa.com

Independent interstate agency created by Virginia and the District of Columbia with the consent of Congress; operates Washington Dulles International Airport and Ronald Reagan Washington National Airport.

►**NONGOVERNMENTAL**

Airports Council International (ACI), *North America (ACI-NA), 1615 L St. N.W., #300, 20036; (202) 293-8500. Fax, (202) 331-1362. Kevin M. Burke, President; Annie Russo, Senior Vice President of Government and Political Affairs.*
General email, memberservices@airportscouncil.org
Web, www.airportscouncil.org, Twitter, @airportscouncil and Facebook, www.facebook.com/airportscouncil

Membership: authorities, boards, commissions, and municipal departments operating public airports. Represents local, regional, and state governing bodies that own and operate commercial airports in the United States and Canada. Serves as liaison with government agencies and other aviation organizations; works to improve passenger and freight facilitation; acts as clearinghouse on engineering and operational aspects of airport development. Monitors legislation and regulations.

American Assn. of Airport Executives, *Barclay Bldg., 601 Madison St., Alexandria, VA 22314; (703) 824-0504. Fax, (703) 820-1395. Todd Hauptli, President, (703) 578-2514.*
Web, www.aaae.org, Twitter, @aaaedelivers and Facebook, www.facebook.com/AAAEDelivers

Membership: airport managers, superintendents, consultants, government officials, authorities and commissioners, and others interested in the construction, management, and operation of airports. Conducts examination for and awards the professional designation of Accredited Airport Executive.

Aviation Safety and Security

►**AGENCIES**

Federal Aviation Administration (FAA) *(Transportation Dept.), Accident Investigation and Prevention (AVP), 800 Independence Ave. S.W., #840, AVP-1, 20591; (202) 267-9612. Fax, (202) 267-3265. Michael O'Donnell, Director.*
Web, www.faa.gov/about/office_org/headquarters_ offices/avs/offices/avp

Investigates aviation accidents and incidents to detect unsafe conditions and trends in the national airspace system and to coordinate corrective action.

Federal Aviation Administration (FAA) *(Transportation Dept.), Air Traffic Organization (AJO), 800 Independence Ave. S.W., #1018A, AJA-O, 20591; (202) 267-7224. Fax, (202) 267-5085. Teri L. Bristol, Chief Operating Officer. FAA communications, (202) 267-3883.*
Web, www.faa.gov/about/office_org/headquarters_ offices/ato

Operates the national air traffic control system; employs air traffic controllers at airport towers, terminal radar approach controls, en route air traffic control centers, and flight service stations in Alaska; maintains the William J. Hughes Technical Center for aviation research, testing, and evaluation.

Federal Aviation Administration (FAA) *(Transportation Dept.), Air Traffic Organization (AJO), Air Traffic Services, 600 Independence Ave. S.W., #FOB 10-B, #3E1500, 20591; (202) 267-0634. Fax, (202) 493-4306. Jeffrey Vincent, Vice President (Acting).*
Web, www.faa.gov/about/office_org/headquarters_offices/ ato/service_units/air_traffic_services

Provides safe, secure, and efficient management for the National Airspace System and international airspace assigned to U.S. control. Responsible for Airport Traffic Control Towers (federal and contract), Terminal Radar Approach facilities, Air Route Traffic Control Centers, and Combined Center Radar Approach Control facilities to guide aircraft through their various phases of flight.

Federal Aviation Administration (FAA) *(Transportation Dept.), Air Traffic Organization (AJO), Technical Operations, 800 Independence Ave. S.W., #700E-10A, 20591; (202) 267-3366. Fax, (202) 267-6060. Jeffrey Planter, Vice President.*
Web, www.faa.gov/about/office_org/headquarters_offices/ ato/service_units/techops

Conducts research and development programs aimed at providing procedures, facilities, and devices needed for a safe and efficient system of air navigation and air traffic control.

Federal Aviation Administration (FAA) *(Transportation Dept.), Air Traffic Safety Oversight Service (AOV)*, 800 Independence Ave. S.W., 20591; (202) 267-5205. Michael J. O'Donnell, Executive Director. Web, www.faa.gov/about/office_org/headquarters_offices/ avs/offices/aov

Establishes safety standards and provides independent oversight of the Air Traffic Organization.

Federal Aviation Administration (FAA) *(Transportation Dept.), Aviation Safety (AVS), Aerospace Medicine*, 800 Independence Ave. S.W., #800W, AAM-1, 20591; (202) 267-3535. Fax, (202) 267-5399. Dr. Michael A. Berry, Federal Air Surgeon. Web, www.faa.gov/about/office_org/headquarters_offices/ avs/offices/aam

Responsible for the medical activities and policies of the FAA; designates, through regional offices, aviation medical examiners who conduct periodic medical examinations of all air personnel; regulates and oversees drug and alcohol testing programs for pilots, air traffic controllers, and others who hold safety-sensitive positions; maintains a Civil Aerospace Medical Institute in Oklahoma City.

Federal Aviation Administration (FAA) *(Transportation Dept.), Aviation Safety (AVS), Aircraft Certification Service*, 800 Independence Ave. S.W., #800E, AIR-1, 20591-0004; (202) 267-8235. Fax, (202) 267-5364. Earl Lawrence, Director. Aviation safety, (202) 267-3131. Web, ttps://www.faa.gov/about/office_org/headquarters_ offices/avs/offices/air

Certifies all aircraft for airworthiness; approves designs and specifications for new aircraft, aircraft engines, propellers, and appliances; supervises aircraft manufacturing and testing. Directs a fuels program and an international division.

Federal Aviation Administration (FAA) *(Transportation Dept.), Aviation Safety (AVS), Flight Standards Service*, 800 Independence Ave. S.W., #821, AFS-1, 20591; (202) 267-8237. Fax, (202) 267-5230. Ricardo Domingo, Director. Press, (202) 267-3883. Web, www.faa.gov/about/office_org/headquarters_offices/ avs/offices/afx

Sets certification standards for air carriers, commercial operators, air agencies, and air personnel (except air traffic control tower operators); directs and executes certification and inspection of flight procedures, operating methods, air personnel qualification and proficiency, and maintenance aspects of airworthiness programs; manages the registry of civil aircraft and all official air personnel records; supports law enforcement agencies responsible for drug interdiction.

Federal Aviation Administration (FAA) *(Transportation Dept.), Security and Hazardous Materials Safety (ASH)*, 800 Independence Ave. S.W., #300E, 20591; (202) 267-7211. Fax, (202) 267-8496. Claudio Manno, Associate Administrator.

Web, www.faa.gov/about/office_org/headquarters_ offices/ash

Seeks to ensure air transportation safety by preventing hazardous materials accidents aboard aircraft and protecting FAA employees and facilities from criminal and terrorist acts.

Federal Communications Commission (FCC), *Enforcement Bureau (EB)*, 445 12th St. S.W., 3rd Floor, #7C723, 20554; (202) 418-7450. Fax, (202) 418-2810. Rosemary Harold, Chief. Press, (202) 418-0500. Toll-free, (888) 225-5322. Web, www.fcc.gov/enforcement#block-menu-block-4

Provides technical services to aid the Federal Aviation Administration in locating aircraft in distress; provides interference resolution for air traffic control radio frequencies.

National Transportation Safety Board (NTSB), *Aviation Safety*, 490 L'Enfant Plaza East S.W., #5400, 20594-0001; (202) 314-6344. Fax, (240) 752-6257. John DeLisi, Director. Information, (202) 314-6540. Press, (202) 314-6100. Web, www.ntsb.gov/about/organization/AS

Responsible for management, policies, and programs in aviation safety and for aviation accident investigations. Manages programs on special investigations, safety issues, and safety objectives. Acts as U.S. representative in international investigations.

Transportation Security Administration (TSA) *(Homeland Security Dept.)*, TSA-1, 601 S. 12th St., 7th Floor, Arlington, VA 20598-6001; Fax, (571) 227-1398. David P. Pekoske, Administrator; Huban A. Gowadia, Deputy Administrator. Press, (571) 227-2829. TSA Contact Center, (866) 289-9673. General email, TSA-ContactCenter@tsa.dhs.gov Web, www.tsa.gov and Twitter, @TSA

Protects the nation's transportation system. Performs and oversees airport security, including passenger and baggage screeners, airport federal security directors, and air marshals. Questions and concerns regarding travel can be submitted toll-free to the TSA Contact Center.

Transportation Security Administration (TSA) *(Homeland Security Dept.), Office of Law Enforcement, Federal Air Marshal Service*, TSA-18, 601 S. 12th St., Arlington, VA 20598-6018; (703) 487-3400. Fax, (703) 487-3405. Roderick Allison, Director. Web, www.tsa.gov/about-tsa/office-law-enforcement

Protects air security in the United States. Promotes public confidence in the U.S. civil aviation system. Deploys marshals on flights around the world to detect and deter hostile acts targeting U.S. air carriers, airports, passengers, and crews.

▶**NONGOVERNMENTAL**

Aerospace Medical Assn., 320 S. Henry St., Alexandria, VA 22314-3579; (703) 739-2240. Fax, (703) 739-9652. Jeffery C. Sventek, Executive Director.

National Transportation Safety Board

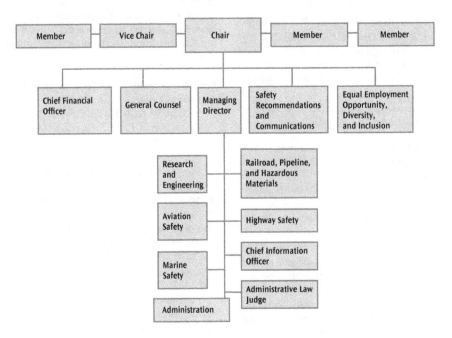

General email, inquiries@asma.org

Web, www.asma.org, Twitter, @Aero_Med and
Facebook, www.facebook.com/
AerospaceMedicalAssociation

Membership: physicians, flight surgeons, aviation medical examiners, flight nurses, scientists, technicians, and specialists in clinical, operational, and research fields of aerospace medicine. Promotes programs to improve aerospace medicine and maintain safety in aviation by examining and monitoring the health of aviation personnel; members may consult in aircraft investigation and cockpit design.

Air Traffic Control Assn. (ACTA), *1101 King St., #300, Alexandria, VA 22314-2963; (703) 299-2430.*
Fax, (703) 299-2437. Peter F. Dumont, President.
General email, info@atca.org

Web, www.atca.org, Twitter, @ATCA-now and
Facebook, www.facebook.com/AirTraffic
ControlAssociation

Membership: air traffic controllers, flight service station specialists, pilots, aviation engineers and manufacturers, and others interested in air traffic control systems. Compiles and publishes information and data concerning air traffic control; provides information to members, Congress, and federal agencies. Provides scholarships to aviation students and children of air traffic controllers.

American Assn. of Airport Executives, *Barclay Bldg., 601 Madison St., Alexandria, VA 22314; (703) 824-0504. Fax, (703) 820-1395. Todd Hauptli, President, (703) 578-2514.*

Web, www.aaae.org, Twitter, @aaaedelivers and
Facebook, www.facebook.com/AAAEDelivers

Maintains the Transportation Security Clearinghouse, which matches fingerprints and other personal information from airport and airline employees against FBI databases.

Flight Safety Foundation, *701 N. Fairfax St., #250, Alexandria, VA 22314-2058; (703) 739-6700. Fax, (703) 739-6708. John Hamilton, Chair; Hassan Shahidi, Chief Executive Officer. Press, (703) 739-6700, ext. 116.*
General email, info@flightsafety.org

Web, www.flightsafety.org, Twitter, @flightsafety and
Facebook, www.facebook.com/FlightSafetyFoundation

Membership: aerospace manufacturers, domestic and foreign airlines, energy and insurance companies, educational institutions, and organizations and corporations interested in flight safety. Sponsors seminars, publishes literature, and conducts studies and safety audits on air safety for governments and industries. Administers award programs that recognize achievements in air safety.

International Society of Air Safety Investigators (ISASI), *107 E. Holly Ave., #11, Sterling, VA 20164-5405; (703) 430-9668. Fax, (703) 430-4970. Toby A. Carroll, U.S. Society President; Ann Schull, International Office Manager.*
General email, isasi@erols.com

Web, www.isasi.org

Membership: specialists who investigate and seek to define the causes of aircraft accidents. Encourages improvement of air safety and investigative procedures through information exchange and educational seminars.

National Air Traffic Controllers Assn., *1325 Massachusetts Ave. N.W., 20005; (202) 628-5451. Fax, (202) 380-9118. Paul Rinaldi, President. Toll-free, (800) 266-0895.*
General email, web_staff@list.natca.net

Web, www.natca.org and Twitter, @NATCA

Seeks to increase air traffic controller staffing levels, improve working conditions, and encourage procurement of more modern, reliable equipment. Concerned with airport safety worldwide.

National Research Council (NRC), *Human-Systems Integration Board, Keck Center, 500 5th St. N.W., 11th Floor, 20001; (202) 334-3453. Fax, (202) 334-2210. Toby Warden, Director.*
General email, bohsi@nas.edu

Web, http://sites.nationalacademies.org/dbasse/bohsi

Conducts studies on human factors and human-systems integration. Research includes air traffic control.

Professional Aviation Safety Specialists, *1200 G St. N.W., #750, 20005; (202) 293-7277. Fax, (202) 293-7727. Mike Perrone, President.*
General email, nationaloffice@passmember.net

Web, www.passnational.org and Twitter, @PASSNational

Membership: FAA and DoD employees who install, maintain, support and certify air traffic control and national defense equipment, inspect and oversee the commercial and general aviation industries, develop flight procedures, and perform quality analyses of complex aviation systems used in air traffic control and national defense in the United States and abroad.

MARITIME TRANSPORTATION

General

▶AGENCIES

Army Corps of Engineers *(Defense Dept.), 441 G St. N.W., #3K05, 20314-1000; (202) 761-0001. Fax, (202) 761-4463. Lt. Gen. Todd T. Semonite (USA), Chief of Engineers. Press, (202) 761-0011.*
General email, hq-publicaffairs@usace.army.mil

Web, www.usace.army.mil and Twitter, @USACEHQ

Provides local governments with navigation, waterway dredging, flood control, disaster relief, and hydroelectric power services.

Civil Division *(Justice Dept.), Torts Branch, Aviation and Admiralty Litigation, 1425 New York Ave. N.W., #10100, 20005 (mailing address: P.O. Box 14271, Washington, DC 20044-4271); (202) 616-4100. Fax, (202) 616-4002. Barry Benson, Director.*
Web, www.justice.gov/civil/torts/aa/t-aa.html

Represents the federal government in civil suits concerning the maritime industry, including ships, shipping, and merchant marine personnel. Handles civil cases arising from admiralty incidents and accidents, including oil spills.

Federal Maritime Commission (FMC), *800 N. Capitol St. N.W., 20573-0001; (202) 523-5725. Fax, (202) 523-0014. Michael A. Khouri, Chair (Acting); Karen V. Gregory, Managing Director. Library, (202) 523-5762. TTY, (800) 877-8339.*
General email, inquiries@fmc.gov

Web, www.fmc.gov and Twitter, @FMC_gov

Regulates the foreign ocean shipping of the United States; enforces maritime shipping laws and regulations regarding rates and charges, freight forwarding, passengers, and port authorities. Library open to the public (Monday–Friday, 8:00 a.m.–4:30 p.m.).

Federal Maritime Commission (FMC), *Certification and Licensing, 800 N. Capitol St. N.W., #970, 20573-0001; (202) 523-5787. Fax, (202) 566-0011. Sandra L. Kusumoto, Director.*
General email, blc@fmc.gov

Web, www.fmc.gov/bureaus_offices/bureau_of_ certification_and_licensing.aspx

Licenses ocean freight forwarders and non-vessel-operating common carriers. Issues certificates of financial responsibility to ensure that cruise lines refund fares and meet their liability in case of death, injury, or nonperformance. Library open to the public (Monday–Friday, 8:00 a.m.–4:30 p.m.).

Federal Maritime Commission (FMC), *Trade Analysis, 800 N. Capitol St. N.W., #940, 20573-0001; (202) 523-5796. Fax, (202) 523-5867. Florence A. Carr, Director. Library, (202) 523-5762.*
General email, tradeanalysis@fmc.gov

Web, www.fmc.gov/bureaus_offices/bureau_of_trade_ analysis.aspx

Analyzes and monitors agreements between terminal operators and shipping companies and agreements among ocean common carriers. Reviews and analyzes service contracts, monitors rates of government-owned controlled carriers, reviews carrier-published tariff systems under the accessibility and accuracy standards, and responds to inquiries or issues that arise concerning service contracts or tariffs. Conducts competition and market analysis to detect activity that is substantially anti-competitive. Library open to the public (Monday–Friday, 8:00 a.m.–4:30 p.m.).

Maritime Administration *(Transportation Dept.), West Bldg., 1200 New Jersey Ave. S.E., 20590; (202) 366-5320. Fax, (202) 366-3890. Rear Adm. Mark H. Buzby, Administrator; Rick Balzano, Deputy Administrator. Press, (202) 366-5705.*
Web, www.marad.dot.gov and Facebook, www.facebook .com/DOTMARAD

Conducts research on shipbuilding and operations; provides financing guarantees and a tax-deferred fund for shipbuilding; promotes the maritime industry; operates the U.S. Merchant Marine Academy in Kings Point, New York.

Maritime Administration *(Transportation Dept.),* **Business and Finance Development,** *West Bldg., 1200 New Jersey Ave. S.E., MAR-750, 20590; (202) 366-5737. David Heller, Associate Administrator (Acting). Web, www.marad.dot.gov*

Works with shipyards, ship owners, operations and labor to aid growth of modern shipyards. Functions include financial approval, marine financing, cargo preference and domestic trade, workforce development and shipyard and marine engineering.

Maritime Administration *(Transportation Dept.),* **Cargo and Commercial Sealift,** *West Bldg., 1200 New Jersey Ave. S.E., MAR-620, MS 2, 20590; (202) 366-4610. Fax, (202) 366-5522. William H. Cahill, Deputy Assoc. Administrator, (202) 366-1875. General email, cargo.marad@dot.gov Web, www.marad.dot.gov/ports/cargo-preference*

Enforces cargo preference laws and regulations. Promotes and monitors the use of U.S. flag vessels in the movement of cargo on international waters.

Maritime Administration *(Transportation Dept.),* **Education, Maritime Training and Careers,** *West Bldg., 1200 New Jersey Ave. S.E., MAR-650, W23-314, 20590; (202) 366-5469. Chris Waller, Director. Workforce Development, (202) 493-0029. General email, careersafloat@dot.gov Web, www.marad.dot.gov/education*

Administers programs for the U.S. Merchant Marine Academy and State Academies. Promotes maritime workforce development.

Maritime Administration *(Transportation Dept.),* **Federal Ship Financing Program (Title XI),** *West Bldg., 1200 New Jersey Ave. S.E., 2nd Floor, 20590; (202) 366-5737. Fax, (202) 366-7901. David Gilmore, Director. General email, marinefinancing@dot.gov Web, www.maritime.dot.gov/grants/title-xi/federal-ship-financing-program-title-xi*

Provides ship financing guarantees for ship construction and shipyard modernization; administers the Capital Construction Fund Program.

Maritime Administration *(Transportation Dept.),* **International Activities,** *West Bldg., 1200 New Jersey Ave. S.E., W28-312, 20590; (202) 366-5493. Lonnie Kishiyama, Director. Web, www.marad.dot.gov/economic-security/international-activities*

Formulates the agency's position on international issues affecting the U.S. maritime industry with the goal of reducing or eliminating international barriers to trade and improving market access.

Maritime Administration *(Transportation Dept.),* **Policy and Plans,** *West Bldg., 1200 New Jersey Ave. S.E., MAR-232, 20590; (202) 366-2145. Fax, (202) 366-3890. Douglas McDonald, Director.*

Web, www.marad.dot.gov/about-us/office-administrator/director-office-policy-and-plans

Supports the agency's policy development process with research, analysis, and documentation. Assesses the effects of legislative and regulatory proposals on maritime programs and maritime industries. Investigates the effects of national and global events on maritime policy and operations.

National Oceanic and Atmospheric Administration (NOAA) *(Commerce Dept.),* **Marine and Aviation Operations (OMAO),** *8403 Colesville Rd., #500, Silver Spring, MD 20910-3282; (301) 713-1045. Fax, (301) 713-1541. Rear Adm. Michael J. Silah, Director, (301) 713-7600. Press, (301) 713-7671. Web, www.omao.noaa.gov*

Operates NOAA's fleet of ships for fisheries research, nautical charting, and ocean and climate studies.

U.S. Coast Guard (USCG) *(Homeland Security Dept.), 2703 Martin Luther King Jr. Ave. S.E., MS 7000, 20593-7000; (202) 372-4000. Fax, (202) 372-8302. Adm. Karl L. Schultz, Commandant. Public Affairs, (202) 372-4600. Web, www.uscg.mil and Twitter, @USCG*

Carries out search-and-rescue missions in and around navigable waters and on the high seas; enforces federal laws on the high seas and navigable waters of the United States and its possessions; conducts marine environmental protection programs; administers boating safety programs; inspects and regulates construction, safety, and equipment of merchant marine vessels; establishes and maintains a system of navigation aids; carries out domestic icebreaking activities; maintains a state of military readiness to assist the Navy in time of war or when directed by the president.

U.S. Coast Guard (USCG) *(Homeland Security Dept.),* **Design and Engineering Standards,** *CG-ENG, 2703 Martin Luther King Jr. Ave. S.E., MS 7509, 20593-7509; (202) 372-1352. Capt. Benjamin Hawkins, Chief. Web, www.dco.uscg.mil/CG-ENG*

Develops and maintains engineering standards for the building of ships, aircraft, shore infrastructure, and Coast Guard facilities. Supports maritime safety, security, mobility, national defense, and protection of natural resources.

U.S. Coast Guard (USCG) *(Homeland Security Dept.),* **Response Policy,** *CG-5E, 2703 Martin Luther Jr. Ave. S.W., MS 7516, 20593; (202) 372-2014. (202) 372-2011. Rear Adm. Anthony (Jack) Vogt, Assistant Commandant. Web, www.dco.uscg.mil/Our-Organization/Assistant-Commandant-for-Response-Policy-CG-5R/*

Regulates waterways under U.S. jurisdiction.

►CONGRESS

For a listing of relevant congressional committees and subcommittees, please see page 751 or the Appendix.

American Maritime Congress, *444 N. Capitol St. N.W., #800, 20001-1570; (202) 347-8020. Fax, (202) 347-1550. James E. (Jim) Caponiti, President.*
General email, info@americanmaritime.org
Web, http://americanmaritime.org

Organization of U.S.-flag carriers engaged in ocean-borne transportation. Conducts research, education, and advocacy on behalf of the U.S.-flag merchant marine.

Chamber of Shipping of America, *1730 Rhode Island Ave. N.W., #702, 20036-4517; (202) 775-4399. Fax, (202) 659-3795. Kathy J. Metcalf, President.*
Web, www.knowships.org and Twitter, @CSAKnowships

Represents U.S.-based companies that own, operate, or charter oceangoing tankers, container ships, and other merchant vessels engaged in domestic and international trade and companies that maintain a commercial interest in the operation of such oceangoing vessels.

Marine Engineers' Beneficial Assn. (MEBA), *444 N. Capitol St. N.W., #800, 20001-1570; (202) 638-5355. Fax, (202) 638-5369. Marshall Ainley, President.*
Web, www.mebaunion.org

Maritime labor union. Represents engineers and deck officers, domestically and internationally. Monitors legislation and regulation.

Maritime Institute for Research and Industrial Development, *1025 Connecticut Ave. N.W., #507, 20036-5412; (202) 463-6505. Fax, (202) 223-9093. C. James (Jim) Patti, President.*
General email, jpatti@miraid.org
Web, www.miraid.org

Membership: U.S.-flagship operators. Promotes the development of the U.S. merchant marine. Interests include the use of private commercial merchant vessels by the Defense Dept., enforcement of cargo preference (Jones Act) laws for U.S.-flagships, and maintenance of cabotage laws.

National Marine Manufacturers Assn., *Government Relations, 650 Massachusetts Ave. N.W., #520, 20001; (202) 737-9750. Fax, (202) 628-4716. Nicole Vasilaros, Vice President, (202) 737-9763.*
Web, www.nmma.org/government and Twitter, @therealNMMA

Membership: recreational marine equipment manufacturers. Promotes boating safety and the development of boating facilities. Monitors legislation and regulations. (Headquarters in Chicago, Ill.)

National Research Council (NRC), *Marine Board, Keck Center, 500 5th St. N.W., 20001; (202) 334-2000. Edward Comstock, Chair.*
Web, www.trb.org/MarineBoard/MarineBoard.aspx

Supports research and provides information relating to new technologies, laws and regulations, economics, the environment, and other issues affecting the marine transportation system, port operations, coastal engineering, and marine governance.

Shipbuilders Council of America, *20 F St. N.W., #500, 20001; (202) 737-3234. Fax, (202) 737-0264. Matthew (Matt) Paxton, President.*
Web, http://shipbuilders.org and Twitter, @ShipbuildersUSA

Membership: U.S. shipyards that repair and build commercial ships and naval and other government vessels; and allied industries and associations. Monitors legislation and regulations.

Transportation Institute, *5201 Auth Way, Camp Springs, MD 20746-4211; (301) 423-3335. Fax, (301) 423-0634. James L. Henry, President.*
General email, info@trans-inst.org
Web, https://transportationinstitute.org and Twitter, @Trans_Inst

Membership: U.S.-flag maritime shipping companies. Conducts research on freight regulation and rates, government subsidies and assistance, domestic and international maritime matters, maritime safety, ports, Saint Lawrence Seaway, shipbuilding, and regulation of shipping.

World Shipping Council, *1156 15th St. N.W., #300, 20005; (202) 589-1230. Fax, (202) 589-1231. John W. Butler, President.*
General email, info@worldshipping.org
Web, www.worldshipping.org

Membership association representing the liner shipping industry. Works with policymakers and other industry groups interested in international transportation issues, including maritime security, regulatory policy, tax issues, safety, the environment, harbor dredging, and trade infrastructure. Monitors legislation and regulations.

Maritime Safety

Maritime Administration *(Transportation Dept.), Environment and Compliance, Security Office, West Bldg., 1200 New Jersey Ave. S.E., W28-340, 20590; (202) 366-1883. Cameron T. Naron, Director.*
General email, maradsecurity@dot.gov
Web, www.maritime.dot.gov/ports/office-security/office-maritime-security

Promotes security throughout the maritime transportation system through maritime information security support, maritime warnings, and advisories for American vessels by using information technology.

Maritime Administration *(Transportation Dept.), Office of Environment, West Bldg., 1200 New Jersey Ave. S.E., W28-342, 20590; (202) 366-1931. Fax, (202) 366-6988. Michael Carter, Associate Administrator (Acting).*
Web, www.maritime.dot.gov/ports/office-environment/office-environment

Focuses on environmental stewardship, maritime safety, and maritime security; maritime research and development; and maritime international and domestic rules, regulations, and standards. Provides environmental support for America's Marine Highway Program and ensures compliance with the National Environmental Policy Act. Advises Maritime Administrator on domestic and international environmental policies that affect maritime transportation.

Maritime Administration *(Transportation Dept.), Sealift Operations and Emergency Preparedness, West Bldg., 1200 New Jersey Ave. S.E., W23-302, 20590; (202) 366-1031. Fax, (202) 366-5904. Russell Krause, Chief. Web, www.marad.dot.gov/ports/maritime-emergency-preparedness-and-response*

Plans for the transition of merchant shipping from peacetime to wartime operations under the direction of the National Shipping Authority. Participates in interagency planning and policy development for maritime security-related directives. Coordinates port personnel and the military for deployments through the commercial strategic seaports. Represents the United States at the NATO Planning Board for Ocean Shipping. (The National Shipping Authority is a stand-by organization that is activated upon the declaration of a war or other national emergency.)

Maritime Administration *(Transportation Dept.), Ship Operations, West Bldg., 1200 New Jersey Ave. S.E., MAR-610, MS2-W25-336, 20590; (202) 366-1875. Fax, (202) 366-3954. Kevin M. Tokarski, Associate Administrator. Web, www.marad.dot.gov/strategic-sealift/office-ship-operations*

Maintains the National Defense Reserve Fleet, a fleet of older vessels traded in by U.S. flag operators that are called into operation during emergencies; manages and administers the National Defense Reserve Fleet, a fleet of ships available for operation within four to twenty days, to meet the nation's sealift readiness requirements.

Maritime Administration *(Transportation Dept.), Strategic Sealift, West Bldg., 1200 New Jersey Ave. S.E., Mar-600, MS 1, W25-330, 20590; (202) 366-5400. Fax, (202) 366-5904. Kevin M. Tokarski, Associate Administrator. Web, www.maritime.dot.gov/national-security/strategic-sealift/strategic-sealift*

Administers strategic sealift programs for the Maritime Administration and ensures that merchant shipping is available in times of war or national emergency.

National Oceanic and Atmospheric Administration (NOAA) *(Commerce Dept.), National Ocean Service (NOS), Coast Survey, 1315 East-West Hwy., #6147, SSMC3, Silver Spring, MD 20910-3282; (301) 713-2770. Fax, (301) 713-4019. Rear Adm. Shepard Smith, Director. Toll-free, (888) 990-6622. Web, www.nauticalcharts.noaa.gov and Twitter, @NOAAcharts*

Directs programs and conducts research to support fundamental scientific and engineering activities and resource development for safe navigation of the nation's waterways and territorial seas. Prints on demand and distributes nautical charts.

National Transportation Safety Board (NTSB), *Marine Safety, 490 L'Enfant Plaza East S.W., #6300, 20594-0001; (202) 314-6456. Fax, (202) 459-9299. Brian Curtis, Director. Web, www.ntsb.gov/about/organization/MS*

Investigates selected marine transportation accidents, including major marine accidents that involve U.S. Coast Guard operations or functions. Determines the facts upon which the board establishes probable cause; makes recommendations on matters pertaining to marine transportation safety and accident prevention.

Occupational Safety and Health Administration (OSHA) *(Labor Dept.), Maritime Enforcement, 200 Constitution Ave. N.W., #N3610, 20210-0001; (202) 693-2399. Fax, (202) 693-2369. Stephen Butler, Director, ext. 32152. Web, www.osha.gov/dts/maritime/dir_maritime.html*

Administers occupational safety and health enforcement program for the maritime industries. Provides comprehensive program guidelines, policies, procedures, technical assistance, and information dissemination.

U.S. Coast Guard (USCG) *(Homeland Security Dept.), Auxiliary and Boating Safety, CG-BSX-2, 2703 Martin Luther King Jr. Ave. S.E., MS 7509, 20593; (202) 372-1507. Fax, (202) 372-1908. Capt. Scott L. Johnson, Chief. General email, CGAUX@uscg.mil Web, www.uscg.mil/Our-Organization/Auxiliary and www.uscgboating.org*

Tracks and analyzes boating accidents; writes and enforces safety regulations for recreational boats and associated equipment; sets boater education standards; coordinates public awareness and information programs; awards grants to states and nongovernmental organizations to improve safety.

U.S. Coast Guard (USCG) *(Homeland Security Dept.), Deputy for Operations Policy and Capabilities, CG-DCO-D, 2703 Martin Luther King Jr. Ave. S.E., MS 7318, 20593-7318; (202) 372-1001. Fax, (202) 372-2900. Rear Adm. Meredith L. Austin, Deputy. Web, www.dco.uscg.mil/Our-Organization/Deputy-for-Operations-Policy-and-Capabilities-DCO-D/*

Establishes and enforces regulations for port safety; environmental protection; vessel safety, inspection, design, documentation, and investigation; licensing of merchant vessel personnel; and shipment of hazardous materials.

U.S. Coast Guard (USCG) *(Homeland Security Dept.), Design and Engineering Standards, CG-ENG, 2703 Martin Luther King Jr. Ave. S.E., MS 7509, 20593-7509; (202) 372-1352. Capt. Benjamin Hawkins, Chief. Web, www.dco.uscg.mil/CG-ENG*

Develops standards; responsible for general vessel arrangements, naval architecture, vessel design and construction, and transport of bulk dangerous cargoes. Supports national advisory committees and national professional organizations to achieve industry standards.

U.S. Coast Guard (USCG) *(Homeland Security Dept.), Investigations and Casualty Analysis, CGINV, 2702*

Martin Luther King Jr. Ave. S.E., MS 7501, 20593-7501; (202) 372-1029. Fax, (202) 372-1907.
Capt. Jason Neubauer, Chief.
Web, www.dco.uscg.mil/Our-Organization/Assistant-Commandant-for-Prevention-Policy-CG-5P/Inspections-Compliance-CG-5PC-/cginv

Handles disciplinary proceedings for merchant marine personnel. Compiles and analyzes records of accidents involving commercial vessels that result in loss of life, serious injury, or substantial damage. Focuses on marine safety and environmental protection through marine inspection activities, including investigation of spills and drug and alcohol testing.

U.S. Coast Guard (USCG) (Homeland Security Dept.), Marine Safety Center, CG-5P, 2703 Martin Luther King Jr. Ave. S.E., MS 7430, 20593; (202) 795-6725. Capt. Scott John J. Kelly, Commanding Officer.
General email, msc@uscg.mil
Web, www.uscg.mil/hq/msc, http://homeport.uscg.mil

Reviews and approves commercial vessel plans and specifications to ensure technical compliance with federal safety and pollution abatement standards.

▶NONGOVERNMENTAL

Cruise Lines International Assn., 1201 F St. N.W., #250, 20004; (202) 759-9370. Fax, (202) 759-9344.
Kelly Craighead, President.
General email, info@cruising.org
Web, www.cruising.org

Membership: more than fifty cruise lines as well as other cruise industry professionals. Advises domestic and international regulatory organizations on shipping policy. Works with U.S. and international agencies to promote safety, public health, security, medical facilities, environmental awareness, and passenger protection. Monitors legislation and regulations.

National Maritime Safety Assn., 1420 New York Ave., 22102; (202) 802-9000. John E. Crowley, Executive Director, (202) 587-4801.
General email, mto@nmsa.us
Web, www.nmsa.us

Represents the marine cargo handling industry in safety and health matters arising under various statutes, including the Occupational Safety and Health Act. Serves as a clearinghouse on information to help reduce injuries and illnesses in the marine cargo handling workplace. Monitors legislation and regulations.

Ports and Waterways

▶AGENCIES

Army Corps of Engineers (Defense Dept.), Civil Works, 441 G St. N.W., 20314-1000; (202) 761-0099.
Fax, (202) 761-0559. James Dalton, Director;

Maj. Gen. Scott A. Spellmon, Deputy Commanding General for Civil and Emergency Operations.
Web, www.usace.army.mil

Coordinates field offices that oversee harbors, dams, levees, waterways, locks, reservoirs, and other construction projects designed to facilitate transportation, flood control, and environmental restoration projects. Major projects include the Mississippi, Missouri, and Ohio Rivers; Bay Delta in California; the Great Lakes; the Chesapeake Bay; the Everglades in Florida; and the Gulf of Mexico.

Federal Maritime Commission (FMC), Agreements, 800 N. Capitol St. N.W., #940, 20573-0001; (202) 523-5793.
Fax, (202) 523-5867. Jason Guthrie, Director.
General email, tradeanalysis@fmc.gov
Web, www.fmc.gov/bureaus_offices/agreements.aspx

Analyzes agreements between terminal operators and shipping companies for docking facilities and agreements among ocean common carriers.

Maritime Administration (Transportation Dept.), Intermodal System Development, West Bldg., 1200 New Jersey Ave. S.E., MAR-500, W21-320, 20590; (202) 366-0678. Lauren K. Brand, Associate Administrator.
General email, pao.marad@dot.gov
Web, www.maritime.dot.gov/aboutus/office-administrator/associate-administrator/intermodal-systems-development

Responsible for direction and administration of port and intermodal transportation development and port readiness for national defense.

Maritime Administration (Transportation Dept.), Port Infrastructure Development and Congestion Mitigation, West Bldg., 1200 New Jersey Ave. S.E., MAR-510, #W21-308, 20590; (202) 366-5076. Fax, (202) 366-6988.
Robert Bouchard, Director.
Web, www.marad.dot.gov/ports/office-port-infrastructure-development

Provides coordination and management of port infrastructure projects; provides leadership in national congestion mitigation efforts that involve waterway and port issues; promotes the development and improved utilization of ports and port facilities, including intermodal connections, terminals, and distribution networks; and provides technical information and advice to other agencies and organizations concerned with intermodal development. Information and advice include the analysis of intermodal economics, the development of applicable information systems, investigation of institutional and regulatory impediments, and the application of appropriate transportation management systems.

Saint Lawrence Seaway Development Corp. (Transportation Dept.), 1200 New Jersey Ave. S.E., #E311, 20590; (202) 366-0091. Fax, (202) 366-7147.
Craig H. Middlebrook, Deputy Administrator.
Toll-free, (800) 785-2779.
General email, slsdc@dot.gov
Web, www.seaway.dot.gov

Operates and maintains the Saint Lawrence Seaway within U.S. territorial limits; conducts development programs and coordinates activities with its Canadian counterpart.

Tennessee Valley Authority, *Government Affairs, 500 N. Capitol St. N.W., #220, 20001; (202) 898-2999. Fax, (202) 898-2998. William D. (Bill) Johnson, President. General email, tvainfo@tva.gov*

Web, www.tva.gov and Twitter, @TVAnews

Coordinates resource conservation, development, and land-use programs in the Tennessee River Valley. Operates the river control system; projects include flood control, navigation development, and multiple-use reservoirs.

U.S. Coast Guard (USCG) *(Homeland Security Dept.), 2703 Martin Luther King Jr. Ave. S.E., MS 7000, 20593-7000; (202) 372-4000. Fax, (202) 372-8302. Adm. Karl L. Schultz, Commandant. Public Affairs, (202) 372-4600.*

Web, www.uscg.mil and Twitter, @USCG

Enforces rules and regulations governing the safety and security of ports and anchorages and the movement of vessels in U.S. waters. Supervises cargo transfer operations, storage, and stowage; conducts harbor patrols and waterfront facility inspections; establishes security zones and monitors vessel movement.

▶NONGOVERNMENTAL

American Assn. of Port Authorities (AAPA), *1010 Duke St., Alexandria, VA 22314-3589; (703) 684-5700. Fax, (703) 684-6321. Kurt J. Nagle, President. General email, info@aapa-ports.org*

Web, www.aapa-ports.org, Twitter, @AAPA-Seaports and Facebook, www.facebook.com/seaportsdeliverprosperity

Membership: public port authorities in the Western Hemisphere. Provides technical and economic information on port finance, environmental issues, construction, operation, and security.

American Waterways Operators, *801 N. Quincy St., #200, Arlington, VA 22203-1708; (703) 841-9300. Fax, (703) 841-0389. Thomas A. Allegretti, President. Web, www.americanwaterways.com and Twitter, @AWOadvocacy*

Membership: operators of barges, tugboats, and towboats on navigable coastal and inland waterways. Acts as liaison with Congress, the U.S. Coast Guard, the Army Corps of Engineers, and other federal agencies. Establishes safety standards and conducts training for efficient, environmentally responsible transportation. Monitors legislation and regulations.

International Longshore and Warehouse Union (ILWU), *Washington Office, 1025 Connecticut Ave. N.W., #507, 20036; (202) 463-6265. Fax, (202) 467-4875. Lindsay McLaughlin, Legislative Director. General email, bianca.blomquist@ilwu.org*

Web, www.ilwu.org

Membership: longshore and warehouse personnel. Helps members negotiate pay, benefits, and better working conditions; conducts training programs and workshops. Monitors legislation and regulations. (Headquarters in San Francisco, Calif.)

International Longshoremen's Assn., *Washington Office, 1101 17th St. N.W., #400, 20036-4704; (202) 955-6304. Fax, (202) 955-6048. John Bowers Jr., Executive Director. General email, iladc@aol.com*

Web, www.ilaunion.org

Membership: approximately 65,000 longshore personnel. Helps members negotiate pay, benefits, and better working conditions; conducts training programs and workshops. Monitors legislation and regulations. (Headquarters in New Jersey; affiliated with the AFL-CIO.)

National Assn. of Waterfront Employers, *8400 Westpark Dr., 2nd Floor, McLean, VA 22102; (202) 587-4800. Fax, (202) 587-4888. John E. Crowley Jr., President, (202) 587-4801. General email, mto@nawe.us*

Web, www.nawe.us

Membership: private sector stevedore companies and marine terminal operators, their subsidiaries, and other waterfront-related employers. Legislative interests include trade, shipping, antitrust issues, insurance, port security, and user-fee issues. Monitors legislation and regulations.

National Research Council (NRC), *Marine Board, Keck Center, 500 5th St. N.W., 20001; (202) 334-2000. Edward Comstock, Chair. Web, www.trb.org/MarineBoard/MarineBoard.aspx*

Supports research and provides information relating to new technologies, laws and regulations, economics, the environment, and other issues affecting the marine transportation system, port operations, coastal engineering, and marine governance.

National Waterways Conference, *1100 N. Glebe Rd., #1010, Arlington, VA 22201; (703) 224-8007. Fax, (866) 371-1390. Amy W. Larson, President, (703) 224-8007. General email, info@waterways.org*

Web, www.waterways.org

Membership: petroleum, coal, chemical, electric power, building materials, iron and steel, and grain companies; port authorities; water carriers; and others interested or involved in waterways. Sponsors educational programs on waterways. Monitors legislation and regulations.

Passenger Vessel Assn., *103 Oronoco St., #200, Alexandria, VA 22314; (703) 518-5005. Fax, (703) 518-5151. John R. Groundwater, Executive Director, ext. 22. Toll-free, (800) 807-8360. General email, pvinfo@passengervessel.com*

Web, www.passengervessel.com

Membership: owners, operators, and suppliers for U.S. and Canadian passenger vessels and international vessel companies. Interests include insurance, safety and security, and U.S. congressional impact upon dinner and excursion boats, car and passenger ferries, overnight cruise ships, and riverboat casinos. Monitors legislation and regulations.

Transportation Institute, *5201 Auth Way, Camp Springs, MD 20746-4211; (301) 423-3335. Fax, (301) 423-0634. James L. Henry, President.*
General email, info@trans-inst.org
Web, https://transportationinstitute.org and Twitter, @Trans_Inst

Membership: U.S.-flag maritime shipping companies. Conducts research on freight regulation and rates, government subsidies and assistance, domestic and international maritime matters, maritime safety, ports, Saint Lawrence Seaway, shipbuilding, and regulation of shipping.

Waterways Council, Inc., *499 S. Capitol St. S.W., #401, 20003; (202) 765-2166. Fax, (202) 765-2167. Michael (Mike) Toohey, President.*
Web, www.waterwayscouncil.org,
Twitter, @WaterwaysCouncil
Press, dcalhoun@waterwayscouncil.org

Membership: port authorities, waterways carriers, shippers, shipping associations, and waterways advocacy groups. Acts as advocate for a modern and well-maintained system of inland waterways and port infrastructure. Monitors legislation and regulations.

MOTOR VEHICLES

General

▶**AGENCIES**

Federal Motor Carrier Safety Administration *(Transportation Dept.), Bus and Truck Standards and Operations, 1200 New Jersey Ave. S.E., #N64-330, 20590; (202) 366-5370. Fax, (202) 366-8842. Chuck Horan, Director, (202) 366-2362.*
Web, www.fmcsa.dot.gov

Regulates motor vehicle size and weight on federally aided highways; conducts studies on issues relating to motor carrier transportation; promotes uniformity in state and federal motor carrier laws and regulations.

▶**CONGRESS**

For a listing of relevant congressional committees and subcommittees, please see page 751 or the Appendix.

▶**NONGOVERNMENTAL**

American Assn. of Motor Vehicle Administrators (AAMVA), *4401 Wilson Blvd., #700, Arlington, VA 22203-1753; (703) 522-4200. Anne S. Ferro, President. Press, (703) 908-2955.*
General email, info@aamva.org
Web, www.aamva.org, Twitter, @AAMVAConnection and Facebook, www.facebook.com/AAMVA

Membership: officials responsible for administering and enforcing motor vehicle and traffic laws in the United States and Canada. Promotes uniform laws and regulations for vehicle registration, driver's licenses, and motor carrier services.

American Automobile Assn. (AAA), *Washington Office, 1405 G. St. N.W., 20005; (202) 481-6820. Fax, (202) 393-5423. John Townsend, Manager of Public Affairs.*
General email, jingrassia@national.AAA.com
Web, www.aaa.com and Twitter, @AAADCNews

Membership: state and local automobile associations. Conducts public outreach and offers publications through the AAA Foundation for Traffic Safety. Interests include all aspects of highway transportation, travel and tourism, safety, drunk driving, and legislation that affects motorists. (Headquarters in Heathrow, Fla.)

American Bus Assn., *111 K St. N.E., 9th Floor, 20002; (202) 842-1645. Fax, (202) 842-0850. Peter J. Pantuso, President, (202) 218-7229; Suzanne Te Beau Rodhe, Vice President Government Affairs and Policy, (202) 218-7224. Press, (202) 218-7220. Toll-free, (800) 283-2877.*
General email, abainfo@buses.org
Web, www.buses.org, Twitter, @AmericanBusAssn and Facebook, www.facebook.com/AmericanBusAssociation
Press email, mhinton@buses.org

Membership: privately owned intercity bus companies, state associations, travel/tourism businesses, bus manufacturers, and those interested in the bus industry. Monitors legislation and regulations.

American Trucking Assns., *950 N. Glebe Rd., #210, Arlington, VA 22203-4181 (mailing address: Washington Office, 430 1st St. S.E., #100, Washington, DC 20003); (703) 838-1700. Fax, (703) 838-1936. Chris Spear, President. Legislative Affairs, (202) 544-6245. Press, (703) 838-1873.*
General email, media@trucking.org
Web, www.trucking.org and Twitter, @TRUCKINGdotORG

Membership: state trucking associations, individual trucking and motor carrier organizations, and related supply companies. Maintains departments on industrial relations, law, management systems, research, safety, traffic, state laws, taxation, communications, legislation, economics, and engineering.

Highway Loss Data Institute, *1005 N. Glebe Rd., #700, Arlington, VA 22201; (703) 247-1600. Fax, (703) 247-1595. David Harkey, President.*
Web, www.iihs.org and Twitter, @IIHS_autosafety

Research organization that gathers, processes, and publishes data on the ways in which insurance losses vary among different kinds of vehicles. (Affiliated with Insurance Institute for Highway Safety.)

International Parking Institute, *1330 Braddock Pl., #350, Alexandria, VA 22314; (571) 699-3011.*

Fax, (703) 566-2267. Shawn D. Conrad, Chief Executive Officer.
General email, ipi@parking-mobility.org
Web, www.parking.org

Membership: operators, designers, and builders of parking lots and structures. Provides leadership to the parking industry; supports professional development; works with transportation and related fields.

Motorcycle Industry Council, *Government Relations,* 1235 South Clark St., #600, Arlington, VA 22202; (703) 416-0444. Fax, (703) 416-2269. Scott Schloegel, Senior Vice President, (703) 416-0444, ext. 3202.
Web, www.mic.org

Membership: manufacturers and distributors of motorcycles, mopeds, and related parts, accessories, and equipment. Monitors legislation and regulations. (Headquarters in Irvine, Calif.)

Motorcycle Riders Foundation, 2221 S. Clark St., Arlington, VA 22202; (202) 546-0983.
Kirk (Hardtail) Willard, President.
General email, mrfoffice@mrf.org
Web, www.mrf.org

Lobby and advocacy group that supports motorcyclist rights. Sponsors seminars for activists. Interests include motorcycle safety, training, and licensing. Monitors legislation and regulations.

National Institute for Automotive Service Excellence, 1503 Edwards Ferry Rd. N.E., #401, Leesburg, VA 20176; (703) 669-6600. Fax, (703) 669-6122. Timothy Zilke, President. Toll-free, (800) 390-6789.
General email, contactus@ase.com
Web, www.ase.com and Facebook, www.facebook.com/ASEtests

Administers program for testing and certifying automotive technicians; researches methods for improving technician training.

National Motor Freight Traffic Assn., 1001 N. Fairfax St., #600, Alexandria, VA 22314-1798; (703) 838-1810.
Fax, (703) 683-6296. Paul Levine, Executive Director.
Toll-free, (866) 411-6632.
General email, customerservice@nmfta.org
Web, www.nmfta.org

Membership: motor carriers of general goods in interstate and intrastate commerce. Publishes *National Motor Freight Classification.*

National Parking Assn., 1112 16th St. N.W., #840, 20036-4880; (202) 296-4336. Fax, (202) 296-3102.
Christine Banning, President, (202) 470-6299.
Toll-free, (800) 647-7275.
General email, info@weareparking.org
Web, www.weareparking.org and Twitter, @weareparking

Membership: parking garage operators, parking consultants, universities, municipalities, medical centers, and vendors. Offers information and research services; sponsors

seminars and educational programs on garage design and equipment. Monitors legislation and regulations.

National Private Truck Council, 950 N. Glebe Rd., #2300, Arlington, VA 22203-4183; (703) 683-1300.
Fax, (703) 683-1217. Gary F. Petty, President, (703) 838-8898.
General email, memberservice@nptc.org
Web, www.nptc.org and Twitter, @NPTC1939

Membership: manufacturers, retailers, distributors, wholesalers, and suppliers that operate their own private truck fleets in conjunction with their nontransportation businesses. Interests include standards, best practices, benchmarking, federal regulatory compliance, peer-to-peer networking, and business economics. Supports economic deregulation of the trucking industry and uniformity in state taxation of the industry. NPTC Institute supports continuing education and certification programs.

National Tank Truck Carriers (NTTC), 950 N. Glebe Rd., #520, Arlington, VA 22203-4183; (703) 838-1960.
Fax, (703) 838-8860. Dan Furth, President.
General email, nttcstaff@tanktruck.org
Web, www.tanktruck.org

Focuses on issues of the tank truck industry and represents the industry before Congress and federal agencies.

NATSO, Inc., 1300 Braddock Pl., #501, Alexandria, VA 22314; (703) 549-2100. Lisa J. Mullings, President.
General email, editor@natso.com
Web, www.natso.com, Twitter, @NATSO_Inc and Facebook, www.facebook.com/NATSOInc

Membership: travel plaza and truck stop operators and suppliers to the truck stop industry. Provides credit information and educational training programs. Monitors legislation and regulations. Operates the NATSO Foundation, which promotes highway safety.

NGVAmerica (Natural Gas Vehicles for America), 400 N. Capitol St. N.W., 20001; (202) 824-7360.
Fax, (202) 824-9160. Daniel Gage, President;
Allison Cunningham, Director of Government Affairs.
General email, pkerkhoven@ngvamerica.org
Web, www.ngvamerica.org, Twitter, @NGVamerican and Facebook, www.facebook.com/NGVAmerica

Membership: natural gas distributors and producers; automobile and engine manufacturers; natural gas vehicle product and service suppliers; research and development organizations; enviromental groups; and state and local government agencies. Advocates installation of natural gas and biomethane fuel stations and development of industry standards. Helps market new products and equipment related to compressed natural gas (CNG), liquefied natural gas (LNG), and biomethane-powered vehicles.

Truckload Carriers Assn., 555 E. Braddock Rd., Alexandria, VA 22314; (703) 838-1950.
Fax, (703) 836-6610. John Lyboldt, President.
General email, tca@truckload.org
Web, www.truckload.org and Twitter, @TCANews

Membership: truckload carriers and industry suppliers. Provides information and educational programs to members. Represents intercity common and contract trucking companies before Congress, federal agencies, courts, and the media.

Union of Concerned Scientists, *Clean Vehicles Program,* *1825 K St. N.W., #800, 20006-1232; (202) 223-6133. Fax, (202) 223-6162. Michelle Robinson, Director.* General email, ucs@ucsusa.org

Web, www.ucsusa.org/clean-vehicles and Twitter, @ucsusa

Develops and promotes strategies for reducing U.S. consumption of oil, including increasing fuel efficiency of cars and trucks, as well as promoting advanced vehicle technology, including battery-electric, hybrid-electric, and fuel-cell vehicles, and next-generation biofuels. (Headquarters in Cambridge, Mass.)

Highways

▶ **AGENCIES**

Federal Highway Administration (FHWA) *(Transportation Dept.), 1200 New Jersey Ave. S.E., 20590-0001; (202) 366-4000. Fax, (202) 366-3244. Vacant, Administrator; Thomas D. Everett, Executive Director. Press and public affairs, (202) 366-0660. Web, www.fhwa.dot.gov, Twitter, @USDOTFHWA and Facebook, www.facebook.com/FederalHighwayAdmin*

Administers federal-aid highway programs with money from the Highway Trust Fund; works to improve highway and motor vehicle safety; coordinates research and development programs on highway and traffic safety, construction costs, and the environmental impact of highway transportation; administers regional and territorial highway building programs and the highway beautification program.

Federal Highway Administration (FHWA) *(Transportation Dept.), Infrastructure, 1200 New Jersey Ave. S.E., #E75-312, 20590; (202) 366-0371. Fax, (202) 493-0099. Derrell Turner, Associate Administrator (Acting). General email, sharon.r.smith@dot.gov*

Web, www.fhwa.dot.gov/infrastructure

Provides guidance and oversight for planning, design, construction, and maintenance operations relating to federal aid, direct federal construction, and other highway programs; establishes design guidelines and specifications for highways built with federal funds.

Federal Highway Administration (FHWA) *(Transportation Dept.), National Highway Institute, 1310 N. Courthouse Rd., Arlington, VA 22201-1555; (703) 235-0500. Fax, (703) 235-0593. Michael Davies, Director. Toll-free, (877) 558-6873. Web, www.nhi.fhwa.dot.gov*

Develops and administers, in cooperation with state highway departments, technical training programs for agency, state, and local highway department employees.

Federal Highway Administration (FHWA) *(Transportation Dept.), Operations, 1200 New Jersey Ave. S.E., #E86-205, 20590-0001; (202) 366-8753. Fax, (202) 366-3225. Martin Knopp, Associate Administrator, (202) 366-9210. Press, (202) 366-4650. Web, www.ops.fhwa.dot.gov*

Fosters the efficient management and operation of the highway system. Responsible for congestion management, pricing, ITS deployment, traffic operations, emergency management, and freight management. Includes offices of Transportation Management, Freight Management and Operations, and Transportation Operations.

Federal Highway Administration (FHWA) *(Transportation Dept.), Planning, Environment, and Realty, 1200 New Jersey Ave. S.E., #E76-306, 20590; (202) 366-0116. Fax, (202) 366-3713. Gloria M. Shepherd, Associate Administrator. Web, www.fhwa.dot.gov/real_estate*

Works with developers and municipalities to ensure conformity with the National Environmental Policy Act (NEPA) project development process.

Federal Highway Administration (FHWA) *(Transportation Dept.), Policy and Governmental Affairs, 1200 New Jersey Ave. S.E., 8th Floor, 20590-0001; (202) 366-9233. Fax, (202) 366-3590. Mala Parker, Associate Administrator. Web, www.fhwa.dot.gov/policy*

Develops policy and administers the Federal Highway Administration's international programs. Conducts policy studies and analyzes legislation; makes recommendations; compiles and reviews highway-related data. Represents the administration at international conferences; administers foreign-assistance programs.

Federal Highway Administration (FHWA) *(Transportation Dept.), Research, Development, and Technology, 6300 Georgetown Pike, #T306, McLean, VA 22101-2296; (202) 493-3999. Fax, (202) 493-3170. Hari Kalla, Associate Administrator. Library, (202) 493-3058. General email, TFHRC.webmaster@dot.gov*

Web, www.fhwa.dot.gov/research

Conducts highway research and development programs; studies safety, location, design, construction, operation, and maintenance of highways; cooperates with state and local highway departments in utilizing results of research. Library access via public library exchange.

U.S. Coast Guard (USCG) *(Homeland Security Dept.), 2703 Martin Luther King Jr. Ave. S.E., MS 7000, 20593-7000; (202) 372-4000. Fax, (202) 372-8302. Adm. Karl L. Schultz, Commandant. Public Affairs, (202) 372-4600. Web, www.uscg.mil and Twitter, @USCG*

Regulates the construction, maintenance, and operation of bridges across U.S. navigable waters.

▶NONGOVERNMENTAL

American Assn. of State Highway and Transportation Officials (AASHTO), *444 N. Capitol St. N.W., #249, 20001-1512; (202) 624-5800. Fax, (202) 624-5806. Jim Tymon, Executive Director, (202) 624-5811.*
General email, info@aashto.org
Web, www.transportation.org, Twitter, @aashtospeaks and Facebook, www.facebook.com/AASHTOspeaks

Membership: the transportation departments of the 50 states, the District of Columbia, and Puerto Rico, and affiliated agencies, including the U.S. Department of Transportation as a nonvoting ex officio member. Maintains committees on all modes of transportation and departmental affairs. Offers technology assistance, web seminars, publications.

American Highway Users Alliance, *1920 L St. N.W., #525, 20036; (202) 857-1200. Fax, (202) 857-1220. Gregory M. Cohen, President.*
General email, info@highways.org
Web, www.highways.org, Twitter, @highwayusers and Facebook, www.facebook.com/highwayusers

Membership: companies and associations representing major industry and highway user groups. Develops information, analyzes public policy, and advocates legislation to improve roadway safety and efficiency and to increase the mobility of the American public. (Affiliated with the Roadway Safety Foundation.)

American Road and Transportation Builders Assn. (ARTBA), *250 E St. S.W., #900, 20024; (202) 289-4434. Fax, (202) 289-4435. David (Dave) Bauer, President.*
General email, klammie@artba.org
Web, www.artba.org, Twitter, @ARTBA and Facebook, www.facebook.com/ARTBAssociation

Membership: highway and transportation contractors; federal, state, and local engineers and officials; construction equipment manufacturers and distributors; and others interested in the transportation construction industry. Serves as liaison with government; provides information on highway engineering and construction developments.

Assn. for Safe International Road Travel (ASIRT), *11769 Gainsborough Rd., Potomac, MD 20854; (240) 249-0100. Fax, (301) 329-8487. Cathy Silberman, Executive Director.*
General email, asirt@asirt.org
Web, www.asirt.org and Facebook, www.facebook.com/ASIRT.org

Promotes road safety through education and advocacy with governments in the United States and abroad. Serves as information resource for governments, study abroad programs, travel organizations, nongovernmental organizations, and individual travelers.

Intelligent Transportation Society of America, *1100 New Jersey Ave. S.E., #850, 20003; (202) 484-4847. Fax, (202) 484-3483. Shailen Bhatt, President.*
General email, info@itsa.org
Web, www.itsa.org, Twitter, @ITS_America and Facebook, www.facebook.com/ITSofAmerica

Advocates application of electronic, computer, and communications technology to make surface transportation more efficient and to improve safety, security, and environmental sustainability. Coordinates research, development, and implementation of intelligent transportation systems by government, academia, and industry.

International Bridge, Tunnel, and Turnpike Assn., *1146 19th St. N.W., #600, 20036-3725; (202) 659-4620. Fax, (202) 659-0500. Patrick D. Jones, Executive Director, ext. 21; Neil Gray, Director of Government Affairs, ext. 14. General email, ibtta@ibtta.org*
Web, www.ibtta.org

Membership: public and private operators of toll facilities and associated industries. Conducts research; compiles statistics.

International Road Federation (IRF), *Madison Pl., 500 Montgomery St., 5th Floor, Alexandria, VA 22314; (703) 535-1001. Fax, (703) 535-1007. C. Patrick Sankey, President.*
General email, info@irfglobal.org
Web, www.irfglobal.org

Membership: contractors, consultants, equipment manufacturers, researchers, and others involved in the road building industry. Administers fellowship program that allows foreign engineering students to study at U.S. graduate schools. Maintains interest in roads and highways worldwide.

The Road Information Program (TRIP), *3000 Connecticut Ave. N.W., #208, 20008; (202) 466-6706. William M. Wilkins, Executive Director. Press, (703) 801-9212.*
General email, wilkins@tripnet.org
Web, http://tripnet.org and Twitter, @TRIP_Inc

Organization of transportation specialists; conducts research on economic and technical transportation issues; promotes consumer awareness of the condition of the national road and bridge system.

Manufacturing and Sales

▶AGENCIES

Energy Efficiency and Renewable Energy (EERE) *(Energy Dept.),* **Vehicle Technologies (VTO),** *1000 Independence Ave. S.W., #5G030, 20585; (202) 586-8055. Fax, (202) 586-7409. David Howell, Deputy Director. Web, www.energy.gov/eere/vehicles/vehicle-technologies-office*

Works with the motor vehicle industry to develop technologies for improved vehicle fuel efficiency and cleaner fuels.

International Trade Administration (ITA) *(Commerce Dept.),* **Industry and Analysis (I&A),** *Transportation* *and Machinery (OTM)*, *1401 Constitution Ave. N.W., #38032, 20230-0001; (202) 482-0572. Fax, (202) 482-0674. Scott Kennedy, Director, (202) 482-4874. Web, http://trade.gov/td/otm*

Promotes the export of U.S. aerospace, automotive, and machinery products; compiles and analyzes industry data; seeks to secure a favorable position for the U.S. aerospace, auto, and machinery industries in global markets through policy and trade agreements.

▶ **NONGOVERNMENTAL**

Alliance of Automobile Manufacturers, *803 7th St. N.W., #300, 20001; (202) 326-5500. Mitch Bainwol, President. Web, www.autoalliance.org, Twitter, @auto_alliance and Facebook, www.facebook.com/autoalliance*

Trade association of major automakers. Provides advocacy on automotive issues focusing primarily on environment, energy, and safety. Seeks to harmonize global automotive standards.

American Automotive Leasing Assn., *122 C. St., #540, 20001; (703) 548-0777. Pamela Sederholm, Executive Director. General email, sederholm@aalafleet.com Web, http://aalafleet.com*

Membership: automotive commercial fleet leasing and management companies. Monitors legislation and regulations.

American International Automobile Dealers Assn., *500 Montgomery St., #800, Alexandria, VA 22314; (703) 519-7800. Fax, (703) 519-7810. Cody Lusk, President, ext. 1. Toll-free, (800) 462-4232. General email, goaiada@aiada.org Web, www.aiada.org, Twitter, @AIADA_News and Facebook, www.facebook.com/AIADA.News President's Twitter, @AIADA_Prez*

Promotes a favorable market for international nameplate automobiles in the United States through education of policymakers and the general public. Monitors legislation and regulations concerning tariffs, quotas, taxes, fuel economy, and clean air initiatives.

Assn. of Global Automakers, *1050 K St. N.W., #650, 20001; (202) 650-5555. John Bozzella, President. General email, info@globalautomakers.org Web, www.globalautomakers.org and Twitter, @ComiAutomkrs*

Membership: automobile manufacturers and parts suppliers. Monitors legislation and regulations.

Auto Care Assn., *7101 Wisconsin Ave., #1300, Bethesda, MD 20814-3415; (301) 654-6664. Fax, (301) 654-3299. Bill Hanvey, President. General email, info@autocare.org Web, www.autocare.org and Twitter, @AutoCareOrg*

Membership: domestic and international manufacturers, manufacturers' representatives, retailers, and distributors in the automotive aftermarket industry, which involves service of a vehicle after it leaves the dealership. Offers educational programs, conducts research, and provides members with technical and international trade services; acts as liaison with government; sponsors annual marketing conference and trade shows. (Formerly Automotive Aftermarket Industry Assn.)

Automotive Parts Remanufacturers Assn., *1602 Belle View Blvd., #3097, Alexandria, VA 22307; (703) 968-2772. Fax, 703-9753-2445. Joe Kripli, President. General email, info@apra.org Web, www.apra.org and Twitter, @buyreman*

Membership: rebuilders and remanufacturers of automotive parts. Conducts educational programs on transmission, brake, clutch, water pump, air conditioning, electrical parts, heavy-duty brake, and carburetor rebuilding.

Automotive Recyclers Assn. (ARA), *9113 Church St., Manassas, VA 20110-5456; (571) 208-0428. Fax, (571) 208-0430. Jonathan Morrow, President. Toll-free, (888) 385-1005. General email, staff@a-r-a.org Web, www.a-r-a.org and Twitter, @AutoRecyclers*

Membership: retail and wholesale firms involved in the dismantling and sale of used motor vehicle parts. Works to increase the efficiency of businesses in the automotive recycling industry. Cooperates with public and private agencies to encourage further automotive recycling efforts.

Certified Automotive Parts Assn., *1000 Vermont Ave. N.W., #1010, 20005; (202) 737-2212. Fax, (202) 737-2214. Jack Gillis, Executive Director. General email, info@CAPAcertified.org Web, www.capacertified.org*

Provides certification of automotive parts used for collision repairs. Evaluates products based on quality standards for fit, materials, and resistance to corrosion. Encourages a competitive market to reduce the price of automobile accident repairs.

Coalition for Auto Repair Equality, *105 Oronoco St., #115, Alexandria, VA 22314-2015; (901) 495-7962. Sandy Bass-Cors, Executive Director. General email, care@careauto.org Web, http://careauto.org*

Works to promote greater competition in the automotive aftermarket repair industry in order to protect consumers. Monitors state and federal legislation that impacts motorists and the automotive aftermarket repair industry.

Electric Drive Transportation Assn. (EDTA), *1250 Eye St., #902, 20005; (202) 408-0774. Fax, (202) 408-7610. Genevieve Cullen, President, ext. 308; Christine Spann, Communications. Press, (202) 408-0774, ext. 312. General email, info@electricdrive.org Web, www.electricdrive.org*

Membership: automotive and other equipment manufacturers, utilities, technology developers, component suppliers, and government agencies. Conducts public policy advocacy, education, industry networking, and international conferences in the areas of battery, hybrid, and fuel cell electric drive technologies and infrastructures.

Japan Automobile Manufacturers Assn. (JAMA), *Washington Office, 888 17th St. N.W., #609, 20036; (202) 296-8537. Fax, (202) 872-1272. Manuel Manriquez, General Director. Press, (202) 803-6828.*
General email, info@jama.org
Web, www.jama.org and Twitter, @JapanAutosUSA

Membership: Japanese motor vehicle manufacturers. Interests include energy, market, trade, and environmental issues. (Headquarters in Tokyo, Japan.)

Manufacturers of Emission Controls Assn., *2200 Wilson Blvd., #310, Arlington, VA 22201; (202) 296-4797. Rasto Brezny, Executive Director.*
General email, asantos@meca.org
Web, www.meca.org and Twitter, @MECAforCleanAir

Membership: manufacturers of motor vehicle emission control equipment. Provides information on emission technology and industry capabilities.

National Automobile Dealers Assn. (NADA), *8400 Westpark Dr., Tysons, VA 22102-3591; (703) 821-7000. Fax, (703) 821-7075. Peter K. Welch, President; David Reagan, Vice President of Legislative Affairs; Jonathan Collegio, Senior Vice President of Public Affairs, (703) 821-7120. Press, (703) 821-7121. Toll-free, (800) 557-6232.*
General email, NADAinfo@nada.org
Web, www.nada.org

Membership: domestic and imported franchised new car and truck dealers. Publishes the *National Automobile Dealers Used Car Guide (Blue Book).*

Recreation Vehicle Dealers Assn. of North America (RVDA), *3930 University Dr., Fairfax, VA 22030-2515; (703) 591-7130. Fax, (703) 591-0734. Phil Ingrassia, President.*
General email, info@rvda.org
Web, www.rvda.org and Twitter, @RVLearningCtr

Membership: recreation vehicle dealers. Interests include government regulation of safety, trade, warranty, and franchising; provides members with educational services, certification programs, and conventions; works to improve service standards for consumers. Monitors legislation and regulations.

Recreation Vehicle Industry Assn. (RVIA), *1896 Preston White Dr., Reston, VA 20191-4363 (mailing address: P.O. Box 2999, Reston, VA 20195-0999); (703) 620-6003. Fax, (703) 620-5071. Frank Hugelmeyer, President, ext. 335.*
Web, www.rvia.org

Membership: manufacturers of recreation vehicles and their suppliers. Compiles shipment statistics and other technical data; provides consumers and the media with information on the industry. Assists members' compliance with American National Standards Institute requirements for recreation vehicles. Monitors legislation and regulations.

Tire Industry Assn., *1532 Pointer Ridge Pl., Suite G, Bowie, MD 20716-1883; (301) 430-7280. Fax, (301) 430-7283. Roy Littlefield, Chief Executive Officer. Toll-free, (800) 876-8372.*
General email, info@tireindustry.org
Web, www.tireindustry.org and Twitter, @thetireindustry

Membership: all segments of the tire industry, including those that manufacture, repair, recycle, sell, service, or use new or retreaded tires and also suppliers that furnish equipment or services to the industry. Interests include environmental and small-business issues. Monitors legislation and regulations.

Truck Renting and Leasing Assn., *675 N. Washington St., #410, Alexandria, VA 22314-1939; (703) 299-9120. Fax, (703) 299-9115. Jake Jacoby, President.*
Web, www.trala.org and Twitter, @TRALAorg

Membership: vehicle renting and leasing companies and suppliers to the industry. Acts as liaison with state and federal legislative bodies and regulatory agencies. Interests include truck security and safety, tort reform, operating taxes and registration fees, insurance, and environmental issues. Monitors state and federal legislation and regulations.

Truck Trailer Manufacturers Assn. (TTMA), *7001 Heritage Village Plaza, #220, Gainesville, VA 20155; (703) 549-3010. Jeff Sims, President.*
Web, www.ttmanet.org

Membership: trailer manufacturing and supply companies. Serves as liaison between its members and government agencies. Publishes technical and industry news reports.

UNITE HERE, *Washington Office, 1775 K St. N.W., #620, 20006-1530; (202) 393-4373. Fax, (202) 223-6213 or (202) 342-2929. Donald Taylor, President.*
Web, www.unitehere.org and Twitter, @unitehere

Membership: workers in the United States and Canada who work in the hotel, gaming, food service, distribution, transportation, manufacturing, textile, laundry, and airport industries. Assists members with contract negotiation and grievances; conducts training programs and workshops. Monitors legislation and regulations. (Headquarters in New York. Formed by the merger of the former Union of Needletrades, Textiles and Industrial Employees and the Hotel Employees and Restaurant Employees International Union.)

United Auto Workers (UAW), *Washington Office, 1757 N St. N.W., 20036; (202) 828-8500. Fax, (202) 293-3457. Josh Nassar, Legislative Director.*
Web, www.uaw.org and Twitter, @uaw

Membership: approximately 400,000 active and 600,000 retired North American workers in aerospace, automotive, defense, manufacturing, steel, technical, and other industries. Assists members with contract negotiations and grievances; conducts training programs and workshops. Monitors legislation and regulations. (Headquarters in Detroit, Mich.)

Traffic Safety

►AGENCIES

Federal Motor Carrier Safety Administration

(Transportation Dept.), 1200 New Jersey Ave. S.E., #W60-300, 20590; (800) 832-5660. Fax, (202) 366-3224. Raymond P. Martinez, Administrator. Consumer complaints, (888) 368-7238. Toll-free hotline, (888) 327-4236. Toll-free information, (800) 832-5660. TTY, (800) 877-8339.
Web, www.fmcsa.dot.gov, Twitter, @FMCSA and Facebook, www.facebook.com/FMCSA

Partners with federal, state, and local enforcement agencies, the motor carrier industry, safety groups, and organized labor in efforts to reduce bus- and truck-related crashes.

Federal Motor Carrier Safety Administration

(Transportation Dept.), Bus and Truck Standards and Operations, 1200 New Jersey Ave. S.E., #N64-330, 20590; (202) 366-5370. Fax, (202) 366-8842. Chuck Horan, Director, (202) 366-2362.
Web, www.fmcsa.dot.gov

Interprets and disseminates national safety regulations regarding commercial drivers' qualifications, maximum hours of service, accident reporting, and transportation of hazardous materials. Sets minimum levels of financial liability for trucks and buses. Responsible for Commercial Driver's License Information Program.

National Highway Traffic Safety Administration

(Transportation Dept.), West Bldg., 1200 New Jersey Ave. S.E., #42300, 20590; (202) 366-1836. Fax, (202) 366-2106. Heidi King, Deputy Administrator. Press, (202) 366-9550. Toll-free 24-hour hotline, (888) 327-4236. TTY, (800) 424-9153.
Web, www.nhtsa.gov, Twitter, @NHTSAgov and Consumer safety information, www.safercar.gov

Implements motor vehicle safety programs; issues federal motor vehicle safety standards; conducts testing programs to determine compliance with these standards; rates vehicles under the 5-star government rating program for crashworthiness and antirollover stability; maintains the website www.safercar.gov, a consumer auto safety information site; funds local and state motor vehicle and driver safety programs; conducts research on motor vehicle safety and equipment, and human factors relating to auto and traffic safety. The Auto Safety Hotline and the website provide safety information and handle consumer problems and complaints involving safety-related defects and noncompliance matters.

National Highway Traffic Safety Administration

(Transportation Dept.), National Driver Register, 1200 New Jersey Ave. S.E., #W55-123, 20590-0001; (202) 366-4800. Fax, (202) 366-2746. Sean H. McLaurin, Chief. Toll-free, (888) 851-0436.
Web, www.nhtsa.gov/Data/National+Driver+Register +(NDR)

Maintains and operates the National Driver Register, a program in which states exchange information on motor vehicle driving records to ensure that drivers with suspended licenses in one state cannot obtain licenses in any other state.

National Transportation Safety Board (NTSB), *490 L'Enfant Plaza East S.W., 20594-2000; (202) 314-6000. Fax, (202) 314-6018. Robert L. Sumwalt, Chair; Susan Kantrowitz, Director of Administration. Press, (202) 314-6100.*
Web, www.ntsb.gov, Twitter, @NTSB and Facebook, www.facebook.com/NTSBgov and YouTube, www.youtube.com/user/NTSBgov

Promotes transportation safety through independent investigations of accidents and other safety problems. Makes recommendations for safety improvement. Operates three regional offices.

National Transportation Safety Board (NTSB), *Highway Safety, 490 L'Enfant Plaza East S.W., 20594-0001; (202) 314-6471. Fax, (202) 459-9334. Robert Molloy, Director. Press, (202) 314-6100.*
Web, www.ntsb.gov/about/organization/HS

In cooperation with states, investigates selected highway transportation accidents to compile the facts upon which the board determines probable cause; works to prevent similar recurrences; makes recommendations on matters pertaining to highway safety and accident prevention.

►NONGOVERNMENTAL

AAA Foundation for Traffic Safety, *607 14th St. N.W., #201, 20005; (202) 638-5944. Fax, (202) 638-5943. C.Y. David Chang, Executive Director.*
General email, info@aaafoundation.org
Web, www.aaafoundation.org

Sponsors "human factor" research on traffic safety issues, including bicycle, pedestrian, and road safety; researches driver behavior and performance, emerging technologies, roadway systems, and drivers and road users; supplies traffic safety educational materials to elementary and secondary schools, commercial driving schools, law enforcement agencies, motor vehicle administrations, and programs for older drivers.

Advocates for Highway and Auto Safety, *750 1st St. N.E., #1130, 20002-8007; (202) 408-1711. Fax, (202) 408-1699. Jacqueline (Jackie) Gillan, President.*
General email, advocates@saferoads.org
Web, www.saferoads.org and Twitter, @SafeRoadsNow

Coalition of insurers, citizens' groups, and public health and safety organizations. Advocates public policy designed to reduce deaths, injuries, and economic costs associated with motor vehicle crashes and fraud and theft involving motor vehicles. Interests include safety belts and child safety seats, drunk driving abuse, motorcycle helmets, vehicle crashworthiness, and speed limits. Monitors legislation and regulations.

American Highway Users Alliance, *1920 L St. N.W., #525, 20036; (202) 857-1200. Fax, (202) 857-1220. Gregory M. Cohen, President.*
General email, info@highways.org

Web, www.highways.org, Twitter, @highwayusers and Facebook, www.facebook.com/highwayusers

Membership: companies and associations representing major industry and highway user groups. Develops information, analyzes public policy, and advocates legislation to improve roadway safety and efficiency and to increase the mobility of the American public. (Affiliated with the Roadway Safety Foundation.)

American Trucking Assns., *Policy and Regulatory Affairs, 950 N. Glebe Rd., #210, Arlington, VA 22203; (703) 838-1996. Fax, (703) 838-1748. Bob Costello, Senior Vice President. Press, (703) 838-1873.*
Web, www.trucking.org

Membership: state trucking associations, individual trucking and motor carrier organizations, and related supply companies. Provides information on safety for the trucking industry. Monitors legislation and regulations.

Center for Auto Safety, *1825 Connecticut Ave. N.W., #330, 20009-5708; (202) 328-7700. Fax, (202) 387-0140. Jason K. Levine, Director.*
General email, contact@autosafety.org

Web, www.autosafety.org and Twitter, @Ctr4AutoSafety

Public interest organization that receives written consumer complaints against auto manufacturers; monitors federal agencies responsible for regulating and enforcing auto and highway safety rules.

Commercial Vehicle Safety Alliance (CVSA), *6303 Ivy Lane, #310, Greenbelt, MD 20770-6319 (mailing address: Policy and Government Affairs: 444 N. Capitol St. N.W., #722, Washington, DC 20001-1534); (301) 830-6143. Fax, (301) 830-6144. Collin B. Mooney, Executive Director; Adrienne L. Gildea, Deputy Executive Director.*
General email, cvsahq@cvsa.org

Web, http://cvsa.org and Twitter, @CVSA

Membership: local, state, provincial, territorial, and federal motor carrier safety officials and industry representatives from the United States, Canada, and Mexico. Promotes improved methods of highway and terminal inspection of commercial vehicles, drivers, and cargo; and uniformity and reciprocity of inspection criteria and enforcement across jurisdictions.

Governors Highway Safety Assn., *660 N. Capitol St. N.W., #220, 20001-1642; (202) 789-0942. Fax, (202) 789-0946. Jonathan Adkins, Executive Director.*
General email, headquarters@ghsa.org

Web, www.ghsa.org and Twitter, @GHSAHQ

Membership: state officials who manage highway safety programs. Interprets technical data concerning highway safety. Represents the states in policy debates on national highway safety issues.

Institute of Transportation Engineers (ITE), *1627 Eye St. N.W., #600, 20006; (202) 785-0060. Fax, (202) 785-0609. Jeffrey F. Paniati, Executive Director, ext. 131.*
General email, ite_staff@ite.org

Web, www.ite.org, Twitter, @ITEhq and Facebook, www.facebook.com/ITEHQ

Membership: international professional transportation engineers. Interests include safe and efficient surface transportation; provides professional and scientific information on transportation standards and recommended practices.

Insurance Institute for Highway Safety, *1005 N. Glebe Rd., #800, Arlington, VA 22201; (703) 247-1500. Fax, (703) 247-1588. David Harkey, President. Highway Loss Data Institute, (703) 247-1600. Vehicle Research Center, (434) 985-4600.*
Web, www.iihs.org, Twitter, @IIHS_autosafety and Facebook, www.facebook.com/iihs.org

Membership: property and casualty insurance associations and individual insurance companies. Conducts research and provides data on highway safety; seeks ways to reduce losses from vehicle crashes. (Operates with Highway Loss Data Institute and the Vehicle Research Center.)

Mothers Against Drunk Driving (MADD), *Government Affairs, 1200 18th St. N.W., #700, 20036; (202) 688-1193. Fax, (972) 869-2206. J.T. Griffin, Chief Government Affairs Officer; Frank Harris, State Legislative Affairs Manager, (202) 688-1194. 24-hour helpline, 877-MADD-HELP. Toll-free, (877) 275-6233.*
General email, policy@madd.org

Web, www.madd.org, Twitter, @MADDOnline and Facebook, www.facebook.com/MADD.Official

Advocacy group that seeks to stop drunk driving and prevent underage drinking. Monitors legislation and regulations. (Headquarters in Irving, Tex.)

Network of Employers for Traffic Safety, *344 Maple Ave. West, #357, Vienna, VA 22180; (703) 755-5350. Joseph L. McKillips, Executive Director.*
General email, sgillies@trafficsafety.org

Web, www.trafficsafety.org

Dedicated to reducing the human and economic cost associated with automobile and highway crashes. Helps employers develop and implement workplace traffic and highway safety programs. Provides technical assistance.

Roadway Safety Foundation, *1920 L St. N.W., #525, 20036; (202) 857-1228. Fax, (202) 857-1220. Gregory M. Cohen, Executive Director.*
General email, info@roadwaysafety.org

Web, www.roadwaysafety.org and Twitter, @roadway_safety

Conducts highway safety programs to reduce automobile-related crashes and deaths. (Affiliated with American Highway Users Alliance.)

U.S. Tire Manufacturers Assn., *1400 K St. N.W., #900, 20005; (202) 682-4800. Fax, (202) 682-4854. Anne Forristall Luke, President.*

General email, info@ustires.org

Web, www.ustires.org and Twitter, @USTireAssoc

Membership: American tire manufacturers. Provides consumers with information on tire care and safety. Develops safety standards for passenger, light truck, and commercial truck tires. Monitors legislation and regulations. (Formerly Rubber Manufacturers Assn.)

United Motorcoach Assn. (UMA), *113 S. West St., 4th Floor, Alexandria, VA 22314-2824; (703) 838-2929. Fax, (703) 838-2950. Stacy Tetschner, Chief Executive Officer. Toll-free, (800) 424-8262.*
General email, info@uma.org

Web, www.uma.org and Twitter, @UMADrives

Membership: professional bus and motorcoach companies and suppliers and manufacturers in the industry. Provides information, offers technical assistance, conducts research, and monitors legislation. Interests include insurance, safety programs, and credit.

RAIL TRANSPORTATION

General

▶**AGENCIES**

Federal Railroad Administration *(Transportation Dept.), 1200 New Jersey Ave. S.E., 3rd Floor, 20590; (202) 493-6014. Fax, (202) 493-6481. Ronald Batory, Administrator. Public Affairs, (202) 493-6024.*
General email, frapa@dot.gov

Web, www.fra.dot.gov, Twitter, @USDOTFRA and Facebook, www.facebook.com/USDOTFRA

Develops national rail policies; enforces rail safety laws; administers financial assistance programs available to states and the rail industry; conducts research and development on improved rail safety. Operates eight regional offices.

Federal Railroad Administration *(Transportation Dept.), Public Engagement, West Bldg., 1200 New Jersey Ave. S.E., MS 10, 20590; (202) 493-6405. Fax, (202) 493-6009. Timothy Barkley Sr., Director, (202) 493-1305.*
General email, frapa@dot.gov

Web, https://www.fra.dot.gov/Page/P0030

Plans, coordinates, and administers activities related to railroad economics, finance, traffic and network analysis, labor management, and transportation planning, as well as intermodal, environmental, emergency response, and international programs.

Federal Railroad Administration *(Transportation Dept.), Railroad Policy and Development, 1200 New Jersey Ave. S.E., 3rd Floor, 20590; (202) 493-6381. Fax, (202) 493-6330. Paul W. Nissenbaum, Associate Administrator.*
General email, OfficeofRPD@dot.gov

Web, www.fra.dot.gov/page/p0031

Administers federal assistance programs for national, regional, and local rail services, including freight service assistance, service continuation, and passenger service. Conducts research on and development of new rail technologies.

Federal Railroad Administration *(Transportation Dept.), Railroad Safety, 1200 New Jersey Ave. S.E., 3rd Floor, 20590; (202) 493-6014. Fax, (202) 493-6216. Robert C. Lauby, Associate Administrator.*
General email, rrswebinquiries@dot.gov

Web, www.fra.dot.gov/Page/P0010

Administers and enforces federal laws and regulations that promote railroad safety, including track maintenance, inspection and equipment standards, operating practices, and transportation of explosives and other hazardous materials. Conducts inspections and reports on railroad equipment facilities and accidents. All safety and/or security issues, such as bomb threats or biochemical threats, are managed by security specialists.

National Mediation Board, *1301 K St. N.W., #250E, 20005-7011; (202) 692-5000. Fax, (202) 692-5082. Kyle Fortson, Chair. Information, (202) 692-5050. TTY, (202) 692-5001.*
General email, infoline@nmb.gov

Web, www.nmb.gov

Mediates labor disputes in the railroad industry; determines and certifies labor representatives for the industry.

National Railroad Passenger Corp. (Amtrak), *1 Massachusetts Ave. N.W., 20001; (202) 906-3000. Richard Anderson, President; Ken Altman, Senior Director of Government Affairs. Emergency, (800) 331-0008. Press, (202) 906-3860. Reservations, (800) 872-7245. TTY, (800) 523-6590.*
Web, www.amtrak.com, Twitter, @amtrak and Facebook, www.facebook.com/Amtrak

Quasi-public corporation created by the Rail Passenger Service Act of 1970 to improve and develop intercity passenger rail service.

Surface Transportation Board (STB), *395 E St. S.W., #1220, 20423-0001; (202) 245-0245. Fax, (202) 245-0458. Ann D. Begeman, Chair. Library, (202) 245-0288. Press, (202) 245-0238. TTY, (800) 877-8339.*
Web, www.stb.gov/stb/index.html

Regulates rail rate disputes, railroad consolidations, rail line construction proposals, line abandonments, and rail car service. Library open to the public.

Surface Transportation Board (STB), *Public Assistance, Governmental Affairs, and Compliance, 395 E St. S.W., #1202, 20423-0001; (202) 245-0238. Fax, (202) 245-0461. Lucille L. Marvin, Director. Toll-free, (866) 254-1792. TTY, (800) 877-8339.*
General email, rcpa@stb.gov

Web, www.stb.gov/stb/about/office_opagac.html

Informs members of Congress, the public, and the media of board actions. Administers the Rail Customer and Public Assistance Program.

U.S. Coast Guard (USCG) *(Homeland Security Dept.)*, *2703 Martin Luther King Jr. Ave. S.E., MS 7000, 20593-7000; (202) 372-4000. Fax, (202) 372-8302. Adm. Karl L. Schultz, Commandant. Public Affairs, (202) 372-4600.*
Web, www.uscg.mil and Twitter, @USCG

Regulates the construction, maintenance, and operation of bridges across U.S. navigable waters, including railway bridges.

▶**CONGRESS**

For a listing of relevant congressional committees and sub-committees, please see page 751 or the Appendix.

▶**NONGOVERNMENTAL**

American Short Line and Regional Railroad Assn. (ASLRRA), *50 F St. N.W., #7020, 20001-1564; (202) 628-4500. Fax, (202) 628-6430. Chuck Baker, President, (202) 585-3440.*
General email, aslrra@aslrra.org
Web, www.aslrra.org, Twitter, @ASLRRA and Facebook, www.facebook.com/aslrra

Membership: independently owned short line and regional railroad systems as well as companies that supply goods and services to short line railroads. Assists members with technical and legal questions; compiles information on laws, regulations, saftey, and other matters affecting the industry.

Assn. of American Railroads, *425 3rd St. S.W., #1000, 20024; (202) 639-2100. Fax, (202) 639-2886. Ian Jefferies, President. Press, (202) 639-2345.*
General email, info@aar.org
Web, www.aar.org and Twitter, @AAR_FreightRail

Membership: major freight railroads in the United States, Canada, and Mexico, as well as Amtrak. Provides information on freight railroad operations, safety and maintenance, economics and finance, management, and law and legislation; conducts research; issues statistical reports.

Brotherhood of Maintenance of Way Employees, *International Brotherhood of Teamsters, National Legislation, 25 Louisiana Ave. N.W., 7th Floor, 20001; (202) 508-6445. Fax, (202) 508-6450. Freddie N. Simpson, President; Charlie Hogue, Director of Government Affairs, (202) 508-6447.*
General email, bmwe-dc@bmwewash.org
Web, www.bmwe.org and Twitter, @BMWEDIBT

Membership: rail industry workers and others. Assists members with contract negotiation and grievances; conducts training programs and workshops. Monitors legislation and regulations. (Headquarters in Novi, Mich.)

International Assn. of Machinists and Aerospace Workers, *Transportation Communications Union, 3 Research Pl., Rockville, MD 20850-3279; (301) 948-4910. Robert A. Scardelletti, President.*
General email, info@iamaw.org
Web, www.goiam.org/index.php/tcunion

Membership: approximately 46,000 railway workers. Assists members with contract negotiation and grievances; conducts training programs and workshops. Monitors legislation and regulations. (Affiliated with the AFL-CIO and Canadian Labour Congress.)

International Brotherhood of Electrical Workers (IBEW), *900 7th St. N.W., 20001; (202) 833-7000. Fax, (202) 728-7676. Lonnie Stephenson, International President; Kenneth Cooper, International Secretary-Treasurer.*
General email, webmaster@ibew.org
Web, www.ibew.org

Membership: workers in utilities, construction, telecommunications, broadcasting, manufacturing, railroads, and government. Helps members negotiate pay, benefits, and better working conditions; conducts training programs and workshops. Monitors legislation and regulations. (Affiliated with the AFL-CIO.)

National Railroad Construction and Maintenance Assn., *410 1st St. S.E., #200, 20003; (202) 715-1264. Fax, (202) 318-0867. Chuck Baker, President, (202) 715-2920.*
General email, info@nrcma.org
Web, www.nrcma.org

Membership: railroad suppliers and contractors. Supports government funding for rail and transit systems. Holds conferences on industry practices, safety, and policy issues.

National Railway Labor Conference, *251 18th St. South, #750, Arlington, VA 22202; (571) 336-7600. Brendan M. Branon, Chair.*
Web, www.nrlc.ws

Assists member railroad lines with labor matters; negotiates with railroad labor representatives.

Rail Passengers Assn., *1200 G St. N.W., #240, 20005; (202) 408-8362. Fax, (202) 408-8287. Jim Mathews, Chief Executive Officer.*
General email, narp@narprail.org
Web, www.railpassengers.org and Twitter, @narprail

Education and advocacy organization. Works to expand and improve U.S. intercity and commuter rail passenger service, increase federal funds for mass transit, and address environmental concerns pertaining to mass transit. Works with Amtrak on scheduling, new services, and fares. (Formerly the National Association of Railroad Passengers.)

Railway Supply Institute (RSI), *425 3rd St. S.W., #920, 20024; (202) 347-4664. Fax, (202) 347-0047. E. Michael O'Malley, President, ext. 103; Nicole Brewin, Vice President of Government Affairs, ext. 104.*
Web, www.rsiweb.org and Twitter, @Railway_Supply

Membership: railroad and rail rapid transit suppliers. Conducts research on safety and new technology; monitors legislation.

Sheet Metal, Air, Rail, and Transportation Workers (SMART), *1750 New York Ave. N.W., 6th Floor, 20006; (202) 662-0880. Joseph Sellers Jr., General President. Toll-free, (800) 457-7694.*
General email, info@smart-union.org
Web, http://smart-union.org and
Twitter, @smartunionworks

Membership: United States, Puerto Rican, and Canadian workers in the building and construction trades, manufacturing, and the railroad and shipyard industries. Assists members with contract negotiation and grievances; conducts training programs and workshops. Monitors legislation and regulations. (Affiliated with the Sheet Metal and Air Conditioning Contractors' Assn., the AFL-CIO, and the Canadian Labour Congress.)

TRANSIT SYSTEMS

General

▶AGENCIES

Federal Transit Administration *(Transportation Dept.),* *1200 New Jersey Ave. S.E., #E57-310, 20590; (202) 366-4043. Fax, (202) 366-9854. K. Jane Williams, Administrator (Acting); Matthew Welbes, Executive Director. Information and press, (202) 366-4043. TTY, (866) 377-8642. TTY, (800) 877-8339.*
Web, www.transit.dot.gov, Twitter, @FTA_DOT and Facebook, www.facebook.com/FTADOT

Responsible for developing improved public transportation facilities, equipment, techniques, and methods; assists state and local governments in financing public transportation systems; oversees the safety of U.S. public transit.

Federal Transit Administration *(Transportation Dept.),* **Budget and Policy,** *1200 New Jersey Ave. S.E., #E52-326, 20590; (202) 366-4050. Fax, (202) 366-7116. Robert Tuccillo, Associate Administrator. Press, (202) 366-4043.*
Web, www.fta.dot.gov

Develops budgets, programs, legislative proposals, and policies for the federal transit program; evaluates program proposals and their potential impact on local communities; coordinates private sector initiatives of the agency.

Federal Transit Administration *(Transportation Dept.),* **Program Management,** *1200 New Jersey Ave. S.E., 4th Floor, 20590; (202) 366-4020. Fax, (202) 366-7951. Bruce Robinson, Associate Administrator (Acting). Information and press, (202) 366-4043.*
Web, www.fta.dot.gov

Administers capital planning and operating assistance grants and loan activities; monitors transit projects in such areas as environmental impact, special provisions for the elderly and people with disabilities, efficiency, and investment.

Federal Transit Administration *(Transportation Dept.),* **Research, Demonstration, and Innovation,** *1200 New Jersey Ave. S.E., #E43-431, 20590; (202) 366-4052. Fax, (202) 366-3765. Vincent Valdes, Associate Administrator. Information and press, (202) 366-4043.*
Web, www.fta.dot.gov

Provides industry and state and local governments with contracts, cooperative agreements, and grants for testing, developing, and demonstrating methods of improved mass transportation service and technology.

Maryland Transit Administration, *6 St. Paul St., Baltimore, MD 21202-1614; (410) 539-5000. Fax, (410) 333-0893. Sean Adgerson, Chief Executive Officer. Information, 866-RIDE-MTA. Mobility/ Paratransit, (410) 764-8181. Press, (410) 767-3936. TTY, (410) 539-3497.*
Web, http://mta.maryland.gov

Responsible for mass transit programs in Maryland; provides MARC commuter rail service for Baltimore, Washington, and suburbs in Maryland and West Virginia.

Surface Transportation Board (STB), *395 E St. S.W., #1220, 20423-0001; (202) 245-0245. Fax, (202) 245-0458. Ann D. Begeman, Chair. Library, (202) 245-0288. Press, (202) 245-0238. TTY, (800) 877-8339.*
Web, www.stb.gov/stb/index.html

Regulates mergers and through-route requirements for the intercity bus industry. Library open to the public.

Virginia Railway Express (VRE), *1500 King St., #202, Alexandria, VA 22314; (703) 684-1001. Fax, (703) 684-1313. Doug Allen, Chief Executive Officer. Press, (703) 838-5416. Toll-free, (800) 743-3873. TTY, (703) 684-0551.*
General email, gotrains@vre.org
Web, www.vre.org and Twitter, @VaRailXpress

Regional transportation partnership that provides commuter rail service from Fredericksburg and Manassas, Va., to Washington, D.C.

Washington Metropolitan Area Transit Authority (Metro), *600 5th St. N.W., 20001; (202) 962-1234. Fax, (202) 962-1133. Paul J. Wiedefeld, General Manager. Information, (202) 637-7000. Lost and found, (202) 962-1195. Metro access (for those with disabilities), (800) 523-7009. Press, (202) 962-1051. TTY (Administration), (202) 962-1000. TTY (Metro access), (301) 588-7535.*
Web, www.wmata.com and Twitter, @wmata

Provides bus and rail transit service to Washington, D.C., and neighboring Maryland and Virginia communities; assesses and plans for transportation needs. Provides fare, schedule, and route information; promotes accessibility for persons with disabilities and the elderly.

▶CONGRESS

For a listing of relevant congressional committees and sub-committees, please see page 751 or the Appendix.

▶NONGOVERNMENTAL

Amalgamated Transit Union (ATU), *10000 New Hampshire Ave., Silver Spring, MD 20903; (301) 431-7100. Fax, (301) 431-7117. Lawrence J. Hanley, President. Toll-free, (888) 240-1196.*
General email, mreza@atu.org
Web, www.atu.org, Twitter, @ATUCOMM and Facebook, www.facebook.com/ATUInternational

Membership: transit workers in the United States and Canada, including bus, van, ambulance, subway, and light rail operators; clerks, baggage handlers, and maintenance employees in urban transit, over-the-road, and school bus industries; and municipal workers. Assists members with contract negotiations and grievances; conducts training programs and seminars. Monitors legislation and regulations. (Affiliated with the AFL-CIO.)

American Bus Assn., *111 K St. N.E., 9th Floor, 20002; (202) 842-1645. Fax, (202) 842-0850. Peter J. Pantuso, President, (202) 218-7229; Suzanne Te Beau Rodhe, Vice President Government Affairs and Policy, (202) 218-7224. Press, (202) 218-7220. Toll-free, (800) 283-2877.*
General email, abainfo@buses.org
Web, www.buses.org, Twitter, @AmericanBusAssn and Facebook, www.facebook.com/AmericanBusAssociation
Press, mhinton@buses.org

Membership: privately owned intercity bus companies, state associations, travel/tourism businesses, bus manufacturers, and those interested in the bus industry. Monitors legislation and regulations.

American Public Transportation Assn. (APTA), *1300 Eye St. N.W., #1200 East, 20005; (202) 496-4800. Fax, (202) 496-4324. Paul P. Skoutelas, President, (202) 496-4889. Press, (202) 496-4816.*
General email, apta@apta.com
Web, www.apta.com and Twitter, @APTA_Info

Membership: public organizations engaged in bus, paratransit, light rail, commuter rail, subways, waterborne passenger services, and high-speed rail, as well as large and small companies that plan, design, construct, finance, supply, and operate bus and rail services worldwide. Compiles data on the industry; promotes research. Monitors legislation and regulations.

Assn. of Metropolitan Planning Organizations, *444 N. Capitol St., #345, 20001; (202) 624-3680. Fax, (202) 624-3685. DeLania Hardy, Executive Director. General email, ampo@ampo.org*
Web, www.ampo.org and Twitter, @ASSOC_MPOS

Membership: more than 385 metropolitan councils of elected officials and transportation professionals responsible for planning local transportation systems. Provides a forum for professional and organizational development; sponsors conferences and training programs.

Community Transportation Assn. of America, *1341 G St. N.W., #250, 20005; Fax, (202) 737-9197. Scott Bogren, Executive Director, ext. 704. Toll-free, (800) 891-0590. Web, http://web1.ctaa.org and Twitter, @OfficialCTAA*

Works to improve mobility for the elderly, the poor, and persons with disabilities; concerns include rural, small-city, and specialized transportation.

National Research Council (NRC), *Infrastructure and the Constructed Environment Board, Keck Center, 500 5th St. N.W., #WS938, 20001; (202) 334-3505. Fax, (202) 334-3718. Cameron Oskvig, Chair.*
General email, bice@nas.edu
Web, http://sites.nationalacademies.org/deps/bice/index.htm

Advises the government, the private sector, and the public on technology, science, and public policy related to the design, construction, operations, maintenance, security, and evaluation of buildings, facilities, and infrastructure systems; the relationship between the constructed and natural environments and their interaction with human activities; the effects of natural and manmade hazards on constructed facilities and infrastructure; and the interdependencies of infrastructure systems, including power, water, transportation, telecommunications, wastewater, and buildings.

Rail Passengers Assn., *1200 G St. N.W., #240, 20005; (202) 408-8362. Fax, (202) 408-8287. Jim Mathews, Chief Executive Officer.*
General email, narp@narprail.org
Web, www.railpassengers.org and Twitter, @narprail

Education and advocacy organization. Works to expand and improve U.S. intercity and commuter rail passenger service, increase federal funds for mass transit, and address environmental concerns pertaining to mass transit. Works with Amtrak on scheduling, new services, and fares. (Formerly the National Association of Railroad Passengers.)

United Motorcoach Assn. (UMA), *113 S. West St., 4th Floor, Alexandria, VA 22314-2824; (703) 838-2929. Fax, (703) 838-2950. Stacy Tetschner, Chief Executive Officer. Toll-free, (800) 424-8262.*
General email, info@uma.org
Web, www.uma.org and Twitter, @UMADrives

Membership: professional bus and motorcoach companies and suppliers and manufacturers in the industry. Provides information, offers technical assistance, conducts research, and monitors legislation. Interests include insurance, safety programs, and credit.

19

U.S. Congress and Politics

ACCESS TO CONGRESSIONAL INFORMATION

Basic Resources

►AGENCIES

National Archives and Records Administration (NARA), *Center for Legislative Archives, 700 Pennsylvania Ave. N.W., #8E, 20408; (202) 357-5350. Fax, (202) 357-5911. Richard H. Hunt, Director, (202) 357-5472. General email, legislative.archives@nara.gov*

Web, www.archives.gov/legislative and Twitter, @CongressArchive

Collects and maintains records of congressional committees and legislative files from 1789 to the present. Publishes inventories and guides to these records.

National Archives and Records Administration (NARA), *Federal Register, 7 G St. N.W., #A-734, 20401 (mailing address: NF, 8601 Adelphi Rd., College Park, MD 20740-6001); (202) 741-6000. Fax, (202) 741-6012. Oliver A. Potts, Director, (202) 741-6100. TTY, (202) 523-5229. General email, fedreg.info@nara.gov*

Web, www.archives.gov/federal_register/the-federal-register and Twitter, @FedRegister

Assigns public law numbers to enacted legislation, executive orders, and proclamations. Responds to inquiries on public law numbers. Assists inquirers in finding presidential signing or veto messages in the *Daily Compilation of Presidential Documents* and the *Public Papers of the Presidents.* Compiles slip laws and annual United States Statutes at Large; compiles indexes for finding statutory provisions. Operates Public Law Electronic Notification System (PENS), which provides information by email on new legislation. Coordinates the functions of the Electoral College and the constitutional amendment process. Publications available from the U.S. Government Printing Office.

►CONGRESS

For a listing of relevant congressional committees and subcommittees, please see page 785 or the Appendix.

Clerk of the U.S. House of Representatives, *H154 CAP, 20515-6601; (202) 225-7000. Karen L. Haas, Clerk. Communications, (202) 225-1908. General email, info.clerkweb@mail.house.gov*

Web, http://clerk.house.gov

Maintains and distributes House bills, reports, public laws, and documents to members' offices, committee staffs, and the general public. Provides daily schedules, when the House is in session, on website. Provides legislative history of all measures reported by House and Senate committees. Provides additional materials in the *Congressional Record* (also available from the Contact Center, Government Printing Office, Washington, D.C., (202) 512-1800 or in electronic format at www.gpoaccess.gov).

Provides video coverage of House floor proceedings through http://houselive.gov.

Senate Executive Clerk, *S138 CAP, 20510; (202) 224-4341. Jennifer Gorham, Executive Clerk.*

Maintains and distributes copies of treaties submitted to the Senate for ratification; provides information on submitted treaties and nominations. (Shares distribution responsibility with Senate Printing and Document Services, [202] 224-7701.)

Senate Historical Office, *201 SHOB, 20510; (202) 224-6900. Betty K. Koed, Historian. General email, historian@sec.senate.gov*

Web, www.senate.gov/art/art_hist_home.htm and Twitter, @SenateHistory

Serves as an information clearinghouse on Senate history, traditions, and members. Collects, organizes, and distributes to the public unpublished Senate documents; collects and preserves photographs and pictures related to Senate history; conducts an oral history program; advises senators and Senate committees on the disposition of their noncurrent papers and records. Produces publications on the history of the Senate.

Senate Office of Conservation and Preservation, *S416 CAP, 20510; (202) 224-4550. Leona Faust, Director, (202) 224-5730.*

Develops and coordinates programs related to the conservation and preservation of Senate records and materials for the secretary of the Senate.

Senate Printing and Document Services, *B04 SHOB, 20510-7106; (202) 224-7701. Fax, (202) 228-2815. Karen Moore, Director. General email, orders@sec.senate.gov*

Web, www.senate.gov/legislative/common/generic/Doc_Room.htm

Maintains and distributes Senate bills, reports, public laws, and documents. To obtain material send a self-addressed mailing label or fax with request. Documents and information may be accessed on the website.

U.S. House of Representatives, *Legislative Resource Center, B81 CHOB, 20515-6612; Fax, (202) 226-4362. Ronald (Dale) Thomas, Chief. Bill status, (202) 226-5200. General email, info.clerkweb@mail.house.gov*

Web, http://clerk.house.gov/about/offices_lrc.aspx

Provides legislative information, records and registration, historical information, and library services to the House and the public. Reading room contains computer terminals where collections may be viewed or printed out. Print publications include a biographical directory, a guide to research collections of former House members, and books on African Americans and women who have served in Congress. Collections include House and Senate journals (1st Congress to present); *Congressional Record* and its predecessors (1st Congress to present); House reports, documents, bills, resolutions, and hearings; Senate reports and documents; U.S. statutes, treaties, the *Federal Register,*

U.S. CONGRESS AND POLITICS RESOURCES IN CONGRESS

For a complete listing of congressional committees, including their full contact information, leadership, membership, and jurisdictions, please refer to the Appendix on pages 827–948.

HOUSE:

House Administration Committee, (202) 225-8281.
Web, cha.house.gov
House Appropriations Committee, (202) 225-2771.
Web, appropriations.house.gov
    Subcommittee on Financial Services and General Government, (202) 225-7245.
    Subcommittee on Legislative Branch, (202) 226-7252.
House Ethics Committee, (202) 225-7103.
Web, ethics.house.gov
House Judiciary Committee, (202) 225-3951.
Web, judiciary.house.gov
    Subcommittee on the Constitution and Civil Justice, (202) 225-2825.
House Oversight and Government Reform Committee, (202) 225-5074.
Web, oversight.house.gov
    Subcommittee on Government Operations, (202) 225-5074.
    Subcommittee on Interior, Energy, and Environment, (202) 225-5074.
House Rules Committee, (202) 225-9191.
Web, rules.house.gov
    Subcommittee on the Legislative and Budget Process, (202) 225-9191.
    Subcommittee on Rules and Organization of the House, (202) 225-9191.
House Transportation and Infrastructure Committee, (202) 225-9446.
Web, transportation.house.gov
    Subcommittee on Economic Development, Public Buildings, and Emergency Management, (202) 225-3014.
House Ways and Means Committee, (202) 225-3625.
Web, waysandmeans.house.gov

JOINT:

Joint Committee on Printing, (202) 225-2061.
Web, cha.house.gov/jointcommittees/joint-committee-on-printing
Joint Committee on the Library of Congress, (202) 225-8281.
Web, cha.house.gov/jointcommittees/joint-committee-library

SENATE:

Senate Appropriations Committee, (202) 224-7257.
Web, appropriations.senate.gov
    Subcommittee on Financial Services and General Government, (202) 224-1133.
    Subcommittee on Legislative Branch, (202) 224-3477.
Senate Finance Committee, (202) 224-4515.
Web, finance.senate.gov
Senate Homeland Security and Governmental Affairs Committee, (202) 224-4751.
Web, hsgac.senate.gov
    Permanent Subcommittee on Investigations, (202) 224-3721.
    Subcommittee on Federal Spending, Oversight, and Emergency Management, (202) 224-7155.
    Subcommittee on Regulatory Affairs and Federal Management, (202) 224-4551.
Senate Judiciary Committee, (202) 224-5225.
Web, judiciary.senate.gov
    Subcommittee on the Constitution, (202) 224-5922.
Senate Rules and Administration Committee, (202) 224-6352.
Web, rules.senate.gov
Senate Select Committee on Ethics, (202) 224-2981.
Web, ethics.senate.gov

U.S. codes, and numerous other documents. (See website or call for a complete list of collections.)

U.S. House of Representatives, *Office of Art and Archives, B53 CHOB, 20515; (202) 226-1300. Fax, (202) 226-4635. Farar P. Elliott, Chief.*
General art email, art@mail.house.gov
General archives email, archives@mail.house.gov
Web, http://history.house.gov and
Twitter, @USHouseHistory

Works with the Office of the Historian to provide access to published documents and historical records of the House. Advises members on the disposition of their records and papers; maintains information on manuscript collections of former members; maintains biographical files on former members; houses photographs and artifacts of former members. Produces publications on Congress and its members.

U.S. House of Representatives, *Office of the Historian, B53 CHOB, 20515; (202) 226-1300.*
Matthew A. Wasniewski, House Historian.
General email, history@mail.house.gov
Web, http://history.house.gov and
Twitter, @ushousehistory

Works with the Office of Art and Archives to provide access to published documents and historical records of the House. Conducts historical research. Advises members on the disposition of their records and papers; maintains information on manuscript collections of former members; maintains biographical files on former members. Produces publications on Congress and its members.

►NEWS SERVICES

CQ Press, 2600 Virginia Ave. N.W., #600, 20037; (202) 729-1800. Fax, (202) 729-1940. Blaise R. Simqu, President. Toll-free, (800) 818-7243.
General email, orders@sagepub.com
Web, https://us.sagepub.com/en-us/nam/cqpress

Publishes books, directories, periodicals, and online products on U.S. government, history, and politics. Products include U.S. Political Stats, CQ Press Encyclopedia of American Government, and CQ Researcher. (An imprint of SAGE Publishing; Headquarters in Thousand Oaks, Calif.)

Washington Post, 1301 K St. N.W., 20071; (202) 334-6000. Frederick J. (Fred) Ryan Jr., Publisher;
Martin (Marty) Baron, Executive Editor. Toll-free, (800) 627-1150.
Web, www.washingtonpost.com and
Twitter, @washingtonpost

Provides news and analysis of congressional activities.

►NONGOVERNMENTAL

White House Correspondents' Assn., 600 New Hampshire Ave. N.W., #800, 20037; (202) 266-7453. Fax, (202) 266-7454. Steven Thomma, Executive Director. General email, director@whca.press

Web, www.whca.net and Twitter, @whca

Membership: reporters with permanent White House press credentials. Acts as a liaison between reporters and White House staff. Sponsors annual WHCA Journalism Awards and Scholarships fund-raising dinner.

Congressional Record

The Congressional Record, *published daily when Congress is in session, is a printed account of proceedings on the floor of the House and Senate. A Daily Digest section summarizes the day's action on the floor and in committees and lists committee meetings scheduled for the following day. An index is published biweekly and at the close of sessions of Congress. Since January 1995, House members have not been allowed to edit their remarks before they appear in the Record, but senators retain this privilege. Material not spoken on the floor may be inserted through unanimous consent to revise or extend a speech and is published in a distinctive typeface. Grammatical, typographical, and technical corrections are also permitted.*

►CONGRESS

For a listing of relevant congressional committees and subcommittees, please see page 785 or the Appendix.

Government Publishing Office (GPO), *Main Bookstore,* 732 N. Capitol St. N.W., 20401; (202) 512-1800. Fax, (202) 512-2104. Lisa Williams, Chief of Distribution and Service Outreach, (202) 512-1065. Bookstore, (202) 512-0132. Toll-free, (866) 512-1800.
General email, ContactCenter@gpo.gov
Web, http://bookstore.gpo.gov

Sells copies of and subscriptions to the Congressional Record. Expert help from government information librarians is available at http://govtinfo.org. Orders may be placed on the website. The Congressional Record from 1994 to the present is available online at www.fdsys.gov.

Library of Congress, *Law Library,* James Madison Memorial Bldg., 101 Independence Ave. S.E., #LM 240, 20540; (202) 707-5065. Fax, (202) 707-1820. Jane Sanchez, Law Librarian, (202) 707-9825. Reading room, (202) 707-5080. Reference, (202) 707-5079.
Web, www.loc.gov/law, Twitter, @LawLibCongress and Facebook, www.facebook.com/lawlibraryofcongress

Copies of the Congressional Record are available for reading. Terminals in the reading room provide access to a computer system containing bill digests from the 93rd Congress to date. The Congressional Record can also be accessed online at www.congress.gov.

►NONGOVERNMENTAL

Martin Luther King Jr. Memorial Library, 901 G St. N.W., 20001-4599; (202) 727-0321. Fax, (202) 727-1129. Richard Reyes-Gavilan, Director. Circulation, (202) 727-1579. TTY, (202) 727-2255.
General email, mlkjrlibrary@dc.gov
Web, www.dclibrary.org/mlk

Maintains collection of the Congressional Record from 1879 to the present, available in various formats (bound volumes, microfilm, microfiche, and electronic). The library is closed until March of 2020 for renovation.

Schedules, Status of Legislation

Information can also be obtained from the Congressional Record *(Daily Digest) and from individual congressional committees (see 116th Congress, p. 827).*

►CONGRESS

For a listing of relevant congressional committees and subcommittees, please see page 785 or the Appendix.

Clerk of the U.S. House of Representatives, H154 CAP, 20515-6601; (202) 225-7000. Karen L. Haas, Clerk. Communications, (202) 225-1908.
General email, info.clerkweb@mail.house.gov
Web, http://clerk.house.gov

Maintains and distributes House bills, reports, public laws, and documents to members' offices, committee staffs, and the general public. Provides daily schedules, when the House is in session, on website. Provides legislative history of all measures reported by House and Senate committees. Provides additional materials in the *Congressional Record* (also available from the Contact Center, Government Printing Office, Washington, D.C., (202) 512-1800 or in electronic format at www.gpoaccess.gov). Provides video coverage of House floor proceedings through http://house live.gov.

House Democratic Cloakroom, *H222 CAP, 20515; (202) 225-7330. Fax, (202) 226-5659. Robert (Bob) Fischer, Manager. House floor action, (202) 225-7400. Legislative program, (202) 225-1600.*
Web, https://democraticcloakroom.house.gov and Twitter, @DemCloakroom

Provides information about House floor proceedings.

House Republican Cloakroom, *H223 CAP, 20515; (202) 225-7350. Fax, (202) 225-8247. Ryan O'Toole, Manager. Web, http://repcloakroom.house.gov and Twitter, @RepCloakroom*

Provides information about House floor proceedings.

Senate Democratic Cloakroom, *S225 CAP, 20510; (202) 224-4691. Nicole Catucci-Brockmeyer, Assistant; Danica Daneshforonz Rodman, Assistant; Stephanie Paone, Assistant; Daniel Tinsley, Assistant; Brad Watt, Assistant. Senate floor action, (202) 224-8541. Web, www.democrats.senate.gov/floor and Twitter, @DSenFloor*

Provides information about Senate floor proceedings.

Senate Republican Cloakroom, *S226 CAP, 20510; (202) 224-6191. Fax, (202) 224-2860. Laura Dove, Secretary. Senate floor action, (202) 224-8601. Twitter, @SenateCloakroom*

Provides information about Senate floor proceedings.

U.S. House of Representatives, *Legislative Resource Center, B81 CHOB, 20515-6612; Fax, (202) 226-4362. Ronald (Dale) Thomas, Chief. Bill status, (202) 226-5200. General email, info.clerkweb@mail.house.gov*
Web, http://clerk.house.gov/about/offices_lrc.aspx

Records, stores, and provides legislative status information on all bills and resolutions pending in Congress.

▶ **NEWS SERVICES**

Associated Press, *Washington Bureau, 1100 13th St. N.W., #500, 20005-4076; (202) 641-9000. Fax, (202) 263-8800. Julie Pace, Bureau Chief. Press, (212) 621-7005. General email, info@ap.org*
Web, www.ap.org and Twitter, @AP

Publishes daybook that lists congressional committee meetings and hearings and their location and subject matter. Fee for services. (Headquarters in New York.)

CQ Roll Call, *1625 Eye St. N.W., #200, 20006-4061; (202) 650-6500. Tim Hwang, Chair. Subscriptions and demonstrations, (202) 650-6599. Toll-free, (800) 432-2250. Web, https://cqrollcall.com and Twitter, @cqrollcall*

Provides nonpartisan online congressional news and analysis, including legislative summaries, votes, testimony, and archival and reference materials. Provides hearing and markup schedules, including time and location, meeting agendas, and full witness listings. Fee for services. (Merger of Congressional Quarterly, Roll Call, and Capitol Advantage; subsidiary of the Economist Group.)

United Press International (UPI), *1133 19th St. N.W., 20036; (202) 898-8000. Fax, (202) 898-8048. Nicholas Chiaia, President; Michael J. Marshall, Editor-In-Chief.*
Web, www.upi.com and Twitter, @UPI

Wire service that lists congressional committee meetings and hearings, locations, and subject matter. Fee for services.

CAMPAIGNS AND ELECTIONS

General

▶ **AGENCIES**

Criminal Division *(Justice Dept.), Election Crimes, 1400 New York Ave. N.W., #12100, 20005; (202) 514-1412. Anna Lou Tirol, Chief (Acting), (202) 514-1178. Press, (202) 514-2007.*
Web, www.justice.gov/criminal/pin

Supervises enforcement of federal criminal laws related to campaigns and elections. Oversees investigation of deprivation of voting rights; intimidation and coercion of voters; denial or promise of federal employment or other benefits; illegal political contributions, expenditures, and solicitations; and all other election violations referred to the division.

Election Assistance Commission, *1335 East-West Hwy., #4300, Silver Spring, MD 20910; (301) 563-3919. Fax, (301) 734-3108. Brian D. Newby, Executive Director. Press, (301) 563-3951. Toll-free, (866) 747-1471. Web, www.eac.gov*

Serves as national information clearinghouse on the administration of federal elections. Responsible for adopting voting system guidelines. Tests and certifies voting system hardware and software. Studies election technology and voting accessibility. Reports data from the states for each federal election and maintains the National Mail Voter registration form.

Federal Communications Commission (FCC), *Media Bureau (MB), Policy Division, 445 12th St. S.W., 20554; (202) 418-2120. Fax, (202) 418-1069. Martha Heller, Chief. Web, www.fcc.gov/media/policy/policy-division*

Handles complaints and inquiries concerning the equal time rule, which requires equal broadcast opportunities for all legally qualified candidates for the same office, and other political broadcast, cable, and satellite rules. Interprets and enforces related Communications Act provisions, including the requirement for sponsorship identification of all paid political broadcast, cable, and satellite announcements

Federal Election Commission

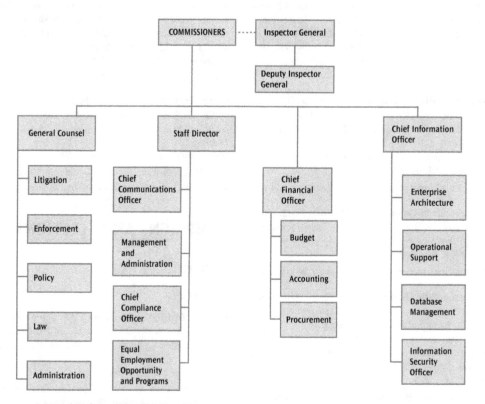

```
COMMISSIONERS ----- Inspector General
                          |
                    Deputy Inspector
                    General
```

- **General Counsel**
  - Litigation
  - Enforcement
  - Policy
  - Law
  - Administration
- **Staff Director**
  - Chief Communications Officer
  - Management and Administration
  - Chief Compliance Officer
  - Equal Employment Opportunity and Programs
  - Chief Financial Officer
    - Budget
    - Accounting
    - Procurement
- **Chief Information Officer**
  - Enterprise Architecture
  - Operational Support
  - Database Management
  - Information Security Officer

---- Denotes independent operation within the agency

and the requirement for broadcasters to furnish federal candidates with reasonable access to broadcast time for political advertising. Administers Equal Employment Opportunity (EEO) matters.

Federal Election Commission (FEC), *1050 1st St. N.E., 20463; (202) 694-1000. Ellen Weintraub, Chair. Press, (202) 694-1220. Information, (202) 694-1100. Public records, (202) 694-1120. Toll-free information, (800) 424-9530. TTY, (202) 219-3336.*
General email, info@fec.gov

Web, www.fec.gov and Twitter, @FEC

Formulates, administers, and enforces policy with respect to the Federal Election Campaign Act of 1971 as amended, including campaign finance disclosure requirements, contribution and expenditure limitations, and public financing of presidential nominating campaigns. Receives campaign finance reports; makes rules and regulations; conducts audits and investigations. Makes copies of campaign finance reports available for inspection.

Federal Election Commission (FEC), *Public Disclosure and Media Relations, 1050 1st St. N.E., 20463; (202) 694-1220. Judith Ingram, Press Officer. Information, (800) 424-9530. TTY, (202) 219-3336.*
General email, press@fec.gov

Web, www.fec.gov/about/offices/press/press.shtml

Makes available for public inspection and copying the detailed campaign finance reports on contributions and expenditures filed by candidates for federal office, their supporting political committees, and individuals and committees making expenditures on behalf of a candidate. Maintains copies of all reports and statements filed since 1972.

►CONGRESS

For a listing of relevant congressional committees and subcommittees, please see page 785 or the Appendix.

House Commission on Congressional Mailing Standards (Franking Commission), *1216 LHOB, 20515-6328; (202) 226-0647. Rep. Bryan Steil, Chair; Tim Sullivan, Minority Staff Director; Matt DeFreitas, Majority Staff Director.*
Web, https://cha.house.gov/franking-commission/about-franking-commission

Issues regulations governing mass mailings by members' offices. Receives complaints, conducts investigations, and issues decisions on disputes arising from the alleged abuse of franked mail by House members.

U.S. House of Representatives, *Legislative Resource Center, Records and Registration, 135 CHOB,*

20515-6612; (202) 226-5200. Fax, (202) 226-5169.
Steve Pingeton, Manager.
Web, http://clerk.house.gov

Receives personal financial disclosure reports for members of the House, candidates for the House, and certain employees. Open for public inspection.

▶ NONGOVERNMENTAL

American Assn. of Political Consultants, 1775 Tysons Blvd., 5th Floor, McLean, VA 22102; (703) 245-8020. Fax, (703) 995-0628. Alana Joyce, Executive Director, (703) 245-8021.
General email, info@theaapc.org

Web, www.theaapc.org, Twitter, @theaapc and Facebook, www.facebook.com/AApcFans

Membership: political consultants, media specialists, campaign managers, corporate public affairs officers, pollsters, public officials, academicians, fund-raisers, lobbyists, college students, and congressional staffers. Focuses on ethics of the profession; provides members with opportunities to meet industry leaders and learn new techniques and emerging technologies.

American Bar Assn. (ABA), *Standing Committee on Election Law,* 1050 Connecticut Ave. N.W., #400, 20036; (202) 662-1694. Fax, (202) 638-3844. Elizabeth M. Yang, Director.
General email, election@americanbar.org

Web, www.americanbar.org/groups/public_services/election_law.html

Studies ways to improve the U.S. election and campaign process.

Campaign Finance Institute, 1775 Eye St. N.W., #1150, 20006; (202) 969-8890. Michael J. Malbin, Executive Director.
General email, info@cfinst.org

Web, www.cfinst.org and Twitter, @cfinst_org

Conducts objective research and educates about campaign financing. Makes recommendations for policy changes in campaign financing.

The Campaign Legal Center, 1411 K St. N.W., #1400, 20005; (202) 736-2200. Fax, (202) 736-2222. Trevor Potter, President.
General email, info@campaignlegalcenter.org

Web, www.campaignlegalcenter.org and Twitter, @CampaignLegal

Works to improve the U.S. democratic process across all levels of government through public education, litigation, policy analysis and debate, participation in regulatory proceedings, and drafting pro-democracy laws and policies and advocating their adoption.

Commission on Presidential Debates, 1200 New Hampshire Ave. N.W., #445, 20036; (202) 872-1020. Fax, (202) 783-5923. Frank J. Fahrenkopf Jr., Co-Chair; Dorothy S. Ridings, Co-Chair; Janet H. Brown, Executive Director.

Web, http://debates.org, Twitter, @debates
Press, media@debates.org

Independent nonpartisan organization established to sponsor general election presidential and vice presidential debates and to undertake educational and research activities related to the debates.

Common Cause, 805 15th St. N.W., #800, 20005; (202) 833-1200. Karen Hobert Flynn, President. Press, (202) 736-5788.
General email, CauseNet@commoncause.org

Web, www.commoncause.org and Twitter, @CommonCause

Nonpartisan national citizens' lobby on behalf of open, honest, and accountable government. Through 400,000 members and supporters, works in Washington and state capitals in support of limits on contributions and spending, high ethical standards in government, voting rights, media reform, and economic justice.

CQ Political MoneyLine, 1625 Eye St. N.W., #200, 20006-4061; (202) 650-6500. Kent Cooper, Editor; Tony Raymond, Editor.
General email, questions@cq.com

Web, www.politicalmoneyline.com and Twitter, @pml_tray

Monitors and reports on money as it is used in campaigns, political action committees, 527s, political parties, and by lobbyists. (Affiliated with CQ Roll Call.)

Electionline.org, 2630 Adams Mill Rd. N.W., #208, 20009; (202) 588-7332. Mindy Moretti, Editor.
General email, mmoretti@electionline.org

Web, www.electionline.org and Twitter, @electiononline

Online resource providing news and analysis on election reform. (Receives support from Hewlett Fund and Democracy Fund.)

Every Voice Center, 1211 Connecticut Ave. N.W., #600, 20036; (202) 640-5600. Fax, (202) 521-0605. David Donnelly, President, (202) 895-2357.
General email, info@everyvoice.org

Web, www.everyvoice.org and Twitter, @EveryVoice

National grassroots organization interested in campaign finance reform. Supports the Fair Election model of campaign finance under which candidates who accept only small donations receive additional money from a public fund sufficient to run a competitive campaign.

OpenSecrets.org / Center for Responsive Politics, 1300 L St. N.W., #200, 20005; (202) 857-0044. Fax, (202) 857-7809. Sheila Krumholz, Executive Director; Brendan Quinn, Press Contact, (202) 354-0110. Press, (202) 354-0111.
General email, info@crp.org; press@crp.org

Web, www.opensecrets.org and Twitter, @opensecretsdc

Conducts research on federal campaign finance and lobbying in connection with congressional and presidential elections.

Election Statistics and Apportionment

►AGENCIES

Census Bureau *(Commerce Dept.), Census Redistricting Data,* 4600 Silver Hill Rd., #4H057, Suitland, MD 20746 *(mailing address: 4600 Silver Hill Rd., #4H057, Washington, DC 20233-0100); (301) 763-4039. Fax, (301) 763-4348. James C.A. Whitehorne, Chief.*
General email, RDO@census.gov

Web, www.census.gov/rdo

Provides state legislatures with population figures for use in legislative redistricting.

Census Bureau *(Commerce Dept.), Customer Liaison and Marketing Services,* North Bldg., 4600 Silver Hill Rd., #8H180, Suitland, MD 20746 *(mailing address: Customer Service, Bureau of the Census, MS 0801, Washington, DC 20233-0500); (301) 763-4636. Fax, (301) 763-6831. Misty Reed, Chief (Acting). Orders, (800) 923-8282. Press, (301) 763-3030.*
General email, clmso.call.center.help@census.gov

Web, www.census.gov/clo/www/clo.html

Main contact for information about the Census Bureau's products and services. Census data and maps on counties, municipalities, and other small areas are available on the website and in libraries.

Census Bureau *(Commerce Dept.), Population,* 4600 Silver Hill Rd., #6H174, Suitland, MD 20746 *(mailing address: 4600 Silver Hill Rd., #6H174, Washington, DC 20233-8800); (301) 763-2071. Fax, (301) 763-2516. Karen Battle, Chief.*
General email, pop@census.gov

Web, www.census.gov/programs-surveys/popproj.html

Computes every ten years the population figures that determine the number of representatives each state may have in the House of Representatives.

►CONGRESS

For a listing of relevant congressional committees and subcommittees, please see page 785 or the Appendix.

Clerk of the U.S. House of Representatives, H154 CAP, 20515-6601; (202) 225-7000. Karen L. Haas, Clerk. Communications, (202) 225-1908.
General email, info.clerkweb@mail.house.gov

Web, http://clerk.house.gov

Publishes biennial compilation of statistics on congressional and presidential elections.

►NONGOVERNMENTAL

Common Cause, *State Organization,* 805 15th St. N.W., #800, 20005; (202) 833-1200. Jenny Rose Flanagan, Vice President for State Operations, (303) 842-1515. Press, (202) 736-5712.
Web, www.commoncause.org

Nonpartisan citizens' lobby on behalf of open, honest, and accountable government. Offices in Washington, D.C., and 35 states. Supports independent redistricting commissions to draw congressional and state legislative districts. Works for laws strengthening voting rights and modern voting equipment.

Voting, Political Participation

►NONGOVERNMENTAL

America Votes, 1155 Connecticut Ave. N.W., #600, 20036; (202) 962-7240. Fax, (202) 962-7241. Greg Speed, President; Sara Schreiber, Managing Director.
Web, www.americavotes.org, Twitter, @AmericaVotes and Facebook, www.facebook.com/AmericaVotesOrg

Coalition that seeks to increase voter registration, education, and participation in electoral politics.

Arab American Institute, 1600 K St. N.W., #601, 20006; (202) 429-9210. Fax, (202) 429-9214. James J. Zogby, President.
General email, communications@aaiusa.org

Web, www.aaiusa.org and Twitter, @AAIUSA

Fosters civic and political empowerment of Americans of Arab descent through research, policy formation, and political activism.

Center for Economic and Policy Research (CEPR), 1611 Connecticut Ave. N.W., #400, 20009; (202) 293-5380. Fax, (202) 588-1356. Eileen Applebaum, Co-Director; Mark Weisbrot, Co-Director.
General email, info@cepr.net

Web, http://cepr.net and Twitter, @ceprdc

Researches economic and social issues and the impact of related public policies. Presents findings to the public with the goal of better preparing citizens to choose among various policy options. Promotes democratic debate and voter education. Areas of interest include health care, trade, financial reform, Social Security, taxes, housing, and the labor market.

Clare Booth Luce Policy Institute, 112 Elden St., Suite P, Herndon, VA 20170; (703) 318-0730. Fax, (703) 318-8867. Michelle Easton, President. Toll-free, (888) 891-4288.
General email, info@cblpi.org

Web, http://cblpi.org and Twitter, @CBLPI

Seeks to engage young women through student programs promoting conservative values and leadership. Offers mentoring, internship, and networking opportunities for young women.

Coalition of Black Trade Unionists, 1155 Connecticut Ave. N.W., #500, 20036 (mailing address: P.O. Box 66268, Washington, DC 20035); (202) 778-3318. Fax, (202) 419-1486. Terrence L. Melvin, President.
General email, cbtu@cbtu.org

Web, http://cbtu.org and Twitter, @CBTU72

Monitors legislation affecting African American and other minority trade unionists. Focuses on equal employment

Resources for Political Participation

NATIONWIDE CAMPAIGNS

Democratic Congressional Campaign Committee,
(202) 863-1500; www.dccc.org

Democratic Governors Assn., (202) 772-5600;
www.democraticgovernors.org

Democratic National Committee (DNC), (202) 863-8000;
www.democrats.org

Democratic Senatorial Campaign Committee,
(202) 224-2447; www.dscc.org

FairVote, (301) 270-4616; www.fairvote.org

Fieldworks, (202) 667-4400; www.fieldworks
.com

Green Party of the United States, (202) 319-7191;
www.gp.org

League of Women Voters (LWV), (202) 429-1965;
www.lwv.org

Libertarian Party, (202) 333-0008; www.lp.org

Mobilize, www.mobilize.org

National Republican Congressional Committee,
(202) 479-7000; www.nrcc.org

National Republican Senatorial Committee,
(202) 675-6000; www.nrsc.org

Republican Governors Assn., (202) 662-4140; www.rga.org

Republican National Committee (RNC), (202) 863-8500;
www.gop.com

Rock the Vote, (202) 719-9910; www.rockthevote.com

IN MARYLAND, VIRGINIA, AND WASHINGTON, D.C.

DC Vote, (202) 462-6000; www.dcvote.org

District of Columbia Board of Elections and Ethics,
(202) 727-2525; www.dcboee.org

Maryland State Board of Elections, (800) 222-8683
or (410) 269-2840; www.elections.state.md.us

Virginia State Board of Elections, (804) 864-8901;
www.elections.virginia.gov

Volunteer on Election Day in Maryland,
www.elections.state.md.us/get_involved

---

opportunity, unemployment, and voter education and registration.

Democracy 21, *2000 Massachusetts Ave. N.W., 20036; (202) 355-9600. Fred Wertheimer, President.*
General email, info@Democracy21.org
Web, www.democracy21.org and
Twitter, @FredWertheimer

Focuses on using the communications revolution to strengthen democracy and on eliminating the influence of big money in American politics.

FairVote, *6930 Carroll Ave., #240, Takoma Park, MD 20912; (301) 270-4616. Fax, (301) 270-4133. Robert Richie, President.*
General email, info@fairvote.org
Web, www.fairvote.org and Twitter, @fairvote

Studies how voting systems affect participation, representation, and governance both domestically and internationally. Advocates electoral reform, ranks choice voting, and multimember districts at the local, state, and national levels. (Formerly the Center for Voting and Democracy.)

Internet Education Foundation, *1440 G St. N.W., 20005; (202) 638-4370. Fax, (202) 637-0968. Tim Lordan, Executive Director.*
General email, tlordan@neted.org
Web, www.neted.org

Sponsors educational initiatives promoting the Internet as a valuable medium for democratic participation, communications, and commerce. Funds the Congressional Internet Caucus Advisory Committee, which works

to inform Congress of important Internet-related policy issues. Monitors legislation and regulations.

Joint Center for Political and Economic Studies, *633 Pennsylvania Ave. N.W., 20004; (202) 789-3500. Fax, (202) 789-6390. Spencer Overton, President.*
General email, info@jointcenter.org
Web, www.jointcenter.org and Twitter, @JointCenter

Documents and analyzes the political and economic status of African Americans, focusing on political participation, economic advancement, and health policy. Publishes *Focus Magazine* annually; disseminates information through forums and conferences.

Labor Council for Latin American Advancement, *815 16th St. N.W., 3rd Floor, 20006; (202) 508-6919. Fax, (202) 508-6922. Hector E. Sanchez, Executive Director.*
General email, headquarters@lclaa.org
Web, www.lclaa.org, Twitter, @LCLAA and
Facebook, www.facebook.com/LCLAA

Membership: Hispanic trade unionists. Encourages equal employment opportunity, voter registration, and participation in the political process. (Affiliated with the AFL-CIO and the Change to Win Federation.)

League of Women Voters (LWV), *1730 M St. N.W., #1000, 20036-4508; (202) 429-1965. Fax, (202) 429-0854. Chris Carson, President; Virginia Kase, Chief Executive Officer.*
General email, lwv@lwv.org
Web, www.lwv.org, Twitter, @LWV and
Facebook, www.facebook.com/leagueofwomenvoters

Membership: women and men interested in nonpartisan political action and study. Works to increase participation in government; provides information on voter registration and balloting. Interests include social policy, natural resources, international relations, and representative government.

National Assn. of Latino Elected and Appointed Officials Educational Fund, Washington Office, 600 Pennsylvania Ave. S.E., #480, 20003; (202) 546-2536. Fax, (202) 546-4121. Arturo Vargas, Executive Director; Rosalind Gold, Senior Director of Policy, Research, and Advocacy.
General email, jgarcia@naleo.org

Web, www.naleo.org, Twitter, @NALEO and Twitter, @ArturoNALEO

Research and advocacy group that provides civic affairs information and assistance on legislation affecting Latinos. Encourages Latino participation in local, state, and national politics. Interests include health care and social, economic, and educational issues. (Headquarters in Los Angeles, Calif.)

National Black Caucus of Local Elected Officials (NBC/LEO), National League of Cities, 660 N. Capitol St. N.W., 20001; (202) 626-3000. Leon Andrews, Director for Race, Equity, and Leadership, (202) 626-3039. Information, (877) 827-2385.
General email, constituencygroups@nlc.org

Web, www.nlc.org

Membership: Black elected officials at the local level and other interested individuals. Seeks to increase Black participation on the National League of Cities' steering and policy committees. Informs members on issues, and plans strategies to achieve objectives through legislation and direct action. Interests include cultural diversity, local government and community participation, housing, economics, job training, the family, and human rights.

National Black Caucus of State Legislators, 444 N. Capitol St. N.W., #622, 20001; (202) 624-5457. Fax, (202) 508-3826. Juanzena Johnson, Executive Director.
Web, www.nbcsl.org

Membership: Black state legislators. Promotes effective leadership among Black state legislators through education, research, and training; serves as an information network and clearinghouse for members.

National Coalition on Black Civic Participation, 1666 K St., #440, 20006; (202) 659-4929. Fax, (202) 659-5025. Melanie L. Campbell, President.
General email, ncbcp@ncbcp.org

Web, www.ncbcp.org and Facebook, www.facebook.com/NCBCP

Seeks to increase Black voter civic participation to eliminate barriers to political participation for Black Americans. Sponsors a variety of voter education, registration, and get-out-the-vote and protect-the-vote activities, including Operation Big Vote, Black Youth Vote, Black Women's Roundtable, the Information Resource Center, Civic Engagement, Voices of the Electorate, and the Unity Black Voter Empowerment Campaign. Monitors legislation and regulations.

National Congress of Black Women, 1250 4th St. S.W., #WG-1, 20024; (202) 678-6788. E. Faye Williams, President.
General email, info@nationalcongressbw.org

Web, www.nationalcongressbw.org

Nonpartisan political organization that encourages Black American women to participate in the political process. Advocates nonpartisan voter registration and encourages Black American women to engage in other political activities. Develops positions and participates in platform development and strategies that address the needs of communities at every level of government.

National Women's Political Caucus, 1001 Connecticut Ave., #1020, 20036 (mailing address: P.O. Box 50476, Washington, DC 20091); (202) 785-1100. Donna Lent, President; Deidre Malone, Communications.
General email, info@nwpc.org

Web, www.nwpc.org, Twitter, @NWPCnational and Facebook, www.facebook.com/NWPC.fb

Advocacy group that seeks greater involvement of women in politics. Seeks to identify, recruit, and train women for elective and appointive political office, regardless of party affiliation; serves as an information clearinghouse on women in politics, particularly during election campaigns; publishes directory of women holding federal and state offices.

Pew Research Center, U.S. Politics and Policy Project, 1615 L St. N.W., #800, 20036; (202) 419-4300. Fax, (202) 419-8562. Carroll Doherty, Director, (202) 419-4363.
Web, http://people-press.org

Studies attitudes toward politics and public policy issues as well as the changing U.S. electorate through public opinion research. Conducts national surveys measuring public attentiveness to major news stories; charts trends in values and political and social attitudes. Makes survey results available online, free of charge.

Republican National Committee (RNC), Political, 310 1st St. S.E., 20003; (202) 863-8500, ext. 6. Fax, (202) 863-8773. Vacant, Political Director; Sarah Nelson, Deputy Political Director; Ronna McDaniel, Chair. Press, (202) 863-8614.
General email, ecampaign@gop.com

Web, https://gop.com

Responsible for electoral activities at the federal, state, and local levels; operates party constituency outreach programs; coordinates voter registration.

Voter Participation Center, 1707 L St. N.W., #300, 20036; (202) 659-9570. Fax, (202) 659-9585. Page S. Gardner, President. Toll-free, (877) 255-6750.
General email, info@voterparticipation.org

Web, www.voterparticipation.org and Twitter, @VoterCenter

Nonpartisan organization that seeks to increase voter participation, especially of unmarried women (single, widowed, divorced, or separated), people of color, and

18-to-29-year-old citizens. (Formerly Women's Voices, Women Vote.)

Women & Politics Institute *(American University)*, *4400 Massachusetts Ave. N.W., Kerwin Hall, #109E, 20016; (202) 885-2903. Fax, (202) 885-2967. Betsy Fischer Martin, Executive Director.*
General email, wpi@american.edu
Web, www.american.edu/spa/wpi and Twitter, @AU_WPI

Research center that encourages women to participate in politics and addresses women's issues. Administers graduate and undergraduate certificates to academics studying women, policy, and political leadership. Assists women in securing employment in the political sphere through leadership training programs.

Younger Women's Task Force, *1310 L St. N.W., #1000, 20005; (202) 785-7700. Fax, (202) 872-1425. Kimberly Churches, Chief Executive Officer. Toll-free, (800) 326-2289. TTY, (202) 785-7777.*
General email, ywtf@aauw.org
Web, www.aauw.org/membership/ywtf and Twitter, @ywtf

Grassroots organization that encourages young women to engage in political activism on issues directly affecting them. Provides leadership training and a local and national network for peer mentoring. (Sponsored by the American Assn. of University Women.)

CAPITOL

Capitol switchboard, (202) 224-3121, and Federal Relay Service (TTY), (800) 877-8339. See also 116th Congress (p. 827) for each member's office.

General

▶CONGRESS

Architect of the Capitol, *SB15 CAP, 20515; (202) 228-1793. Fax, (202) 228-1893. Christine A. Merdon, Architect (Acting). Flag Office, (202) 228-4239.*
Web, www.aoc.gov and Twitter, @uscapitol

Maintains the Capitol and its grounds, the House and Senate office buildings, Capitol power plant, Robert A. Taft Memorial, Thurgood Marshall Federal Judiciary Building, Capitol Police headquarters, and buildings and grounds of the Supreme Court and the Library of Congress; operates the Capitol Visitor Center, and the Botanic Garden and Senate restaurants. Acquires property and plans and constructs buildings for Congress, the Supreme Court, and the Library of Congress. Assists the Congress in deciding which artwork, historical objects, and exhibits are to be accepted for display in the Capitol and is responsible for their care and repair, as well as the maintenance and restoration of murals and architectural elements throughout the Capitol campus. Arranges inaugural ceremonies and other ceremonies held in the buildings or on the grounds. Flag office flies American flags over the Capitol at legislators' request.

Senate Commission on Art, *S411 CAP, 20510; (202) 224-2955. Melinda Smith, Curator of the Senate.*
General email, curator@sec.senate.gov
Web, www.senate.gov/art/art_hist_home.htm

Accepts artwork and historical objects for display in Senate office buildings and the Senate wing of the Capitol. Maintains and exhibits Senate collections (paintings, sculptures, furniture, and manuscripts); oversees and maintains old Senate and Supreme Court chambers.

Superintendent of the House Office Buildings, *2046 RHOB, 20515; (202) 225-4141. William M. (Bill) Weidemeyer, Superintendent.*
Web, www.aoc.gov/organizational-directory/house-superintendent

Oversees construction, maintenance, and operation of House office buildings; assigns office space to House members under rules of procedure established by the Speaker's office and the House Office Building Commission.

Superintendent of the Senate Office Buildings, *G245 SDOB, 20510; (202) 224-3141. Takis Tzamaras, Superintendent.*
Web, www.aoc.gov/organizational-directory/senate-superintendent

Oversees construction, maintenance, and operation of Senate office buildings.

U.S. Botanic Garden, *100 Maryland Ave. S.W., 20001 (mailing address: 245 1st St. S.W., Washington, DC 20024); (202) 225-8333. Fax, (202) 225-1561. Saharah Moon Chapotin, Executive Director, (202) 225-1110. Horticulture hotline, (202) 226-4785. Press, (202) 226-4145. Program registration information, (202) 225-1116. Special events, (202) 226-7674. Tour line, (202) 226-2055.*
General email, usbg@aoc.gov
Web, www.usbg.gov and Twitter, @USBotanicGarden

Collects, cultivates, and grows various plants for public display and study.

U.S. Capitol Police, *119 D St. N.E., 20510; (202) 224-9806. Fax, (202) 228-2592. Matthew R. Verderosa, Chief. Public information, (202) 224-1677.*
General email, PIO@uscp.gov
Web, www.uscapitolpolice.gov

Responsible for security for the Capitol, House and Senate office buildings, and Botanic Garden; approves demonstration permits.

▶NONGOVERNMENTAL

U.S. Capitol Historical Society, *200 Maryland Ave. N.E., 20002; (202) 543-8919. Fax, (202) 525-2790. Jane L. Campbell, President, ext. 12; William C. di Giacomantonio, Chief Historian, ext. 27. Information, (800) 887-9318.*

General email, uschs@uschs.org

Web, https://uschs.org, Twitter, @USCapHis and Twitter, @CapitolHistory

Membership: members of Congress, individuals, and organizations interested in the preservation of the history and traditions of the U.S. Capitol. Conducts historical research; offers tours, lectures, workshops, and films; holds events involving members of Congress; publishes an annual historical calendar.

Tours and Events

▶ CONGRESS

The House and Senate public galleries are open when Congress is in session. The House galleries are also open when the House is not in session. Free gallery passes are available from any congressional office.

Architect of the Capitol, *Congressional Accessibility Services, Crypt of The Capitol, 20510; (202) 224-4048. Fax, (202) 228-4679. David Hauck, Director. TTY, (202) 224-4049.*
Web, www.aoc.gov/accessibility-services

Office works to make the Capitol and its grounds and buildings accessible to members of Congress, staff, and the public.

Sergeant at Arms and Doorkeeper of the U.S. Senate, *S151 CAP, 20510-7200; (202) 224-2341. Michael C. Stenger, Sergeant at Arms and Doorkeeper. Web, www.senate.gov/reference/office/sergeant_at_ arms.htm*

Enforces rules and regulations of the Senate public gallery. Responsible for security of the Capitol and Senate buildings. Approves visiting band performances on the Senate steps. (To arrange for performances, contact your senator.)

Sergeant at Arms of the U.S. House of Representatives, *H124 CAP, 20515-6611; (202) 225-2456. Fax, (202) 225-3233. Paul D. Irving, Sergeant at Arms. General email, saamail@mail.house.gov*
Web, www.house.gov/the-house-explained/officers-and-organizations/sergeant-at-arms

Enforces rules and regulations of the House public gallery. Responsible for the security of the Capitol and House buildings. Approves visiting band performances on the House steps. (To arrange for performances, contact your representative.)

U.S. Capitol Visitor Center, *The Capitol, 20510; (202) 226-8000. Fax, (202) 593-1832. Beth Plemmons, Chief Executive Officer for Visitor Services. Press, (202) 593-1833. Visitor information, (202) 225-6827.*
Web, http://visitthecapitol.gov and Twitter, @visitthecapitol

Offers the general public free guided tours of the interior of the U.S. Capitol. Provides accommodations for visitors with special needs.

▶ NONGOVERNMENTAL

U.S. Capitol Historical Society, *200 Maryland Ave. N.E., 20002; (202) 543-8919. Fax, (202) 525-2790. Jane L. Campbell, President, ext. 12; William C. di Giacomantonio, Chief Historian, ext. 27. Information, (800) 887-9318. General email, uschs@uschs.org*
Web, https://uschs.org, Twitter, @USCapHis and Twitter, @CapitolHistory

Offers tours, lectures, films, publications, and merchandise; maintains information centers in the Capitol.

CONGRESS AT WORK

See 116th Congress (p. 827) for members' offices and committee assignments and for rosters of congressional committees and subcommittees.

General

▶ CONGRESS

For a listing of relevant congressional committees and subcommittees, please see page 785 or the Appendix.

House Recording Studio, *2010 RHOB, 20515; (202) 225-3941. Fax, (202) 225-0707. Patrick Hirsch, Director.*

Assists House members in making tape recordings. Provides daily gavel-to-gavel television coverage of House floor proceedings.

Interparliamentary Affairs, *HC4 CAP, 20515; (202) 226-1766. Kate Knudson, Director.*

Assists the House Speaker with international travel and the reception of foreign legislators.

Interparliamentary Services, *808 SHOB, 20510; (202) 224-3047. Sally Walsh, Director.*

Provides support to senators participating in interparliamentary conferences and other international travel. Responsible for financial, administrative, and protocol functions.

Office of Photography, *U.S. House of Representatives, B302 RHOB, 20515; (202) 225-2840. Fax, (202) 225-5896. Jeff Blakley, Director. Chief Administration Office, (202) 226-6660.*
Web, cao.house.gov

Provides House members with photographic assistance.

Parliamentarian of the U.S. House of Representatives, *H209 CAP, 20515; (202) 225-7373. Thomas J. Wickham Jr., Parliamentarian.*
Web, www.house.gov/the-house-explained/officers-and-organizations/parliamentarian-of-the-house

Advises presiding officers on parliamentary procedures and committee jurisdiction over legislation; prepares and maintains a compilation of the precedents of the House.

Parliamentarian of the U.S. Senate, *S133 CAP, 20510;* *(202) 224-6128. Elizabeth C. MacDonough, Parliamentarian.*

Advises presiding officers on parliamentary procedures and committee jurisdiction over legislation; prepares and maintains a compilation of the precedents of the Senate.

Senate Democratic Policy and Communications Center, *S318 CAP, 20510; (202) 224-3232. Fax, (202) 228-5576. Sen. Debbie Stabenow, Chair; Sen. Joe Manchin, Vice Chair.* Web, www.democrats.senate.gov

Offers radio, television, and Internet services to Senate Democrats and their staffs to more effectively disseminate information to constituents at home.

Sergeant at Arms and Doorkeeper of the U.S. Senate, *Senate Photo Studio, G85 SDOB, 20510; (202) 224-6000. Vacant, Manager.*

Provides Senate members with photographic assistance.

Sergeant at Arms of the U.S. House of Representatives, *Emergency Management Division, 192 FHOB, 20515-6462; (202) 226-0950. Fax, (202) 226-6598. Bob Dohr, Sergeant at Arms Chief Operating Officer.*

Liaises between the House and the Homeland Security Dept., the U.S. Capitol Police, and other responders in the coordination of response to emergency situations.

Leadership

▶ **HOUSE**

See House Leadership and Partisan Committees (p. 911).

House Democratic Caucus, *B245 LHOB, 20515; (202) 225-1400. Rep. Hakeem Jeffries, Chair; Rep. Katherine Clark, Vice Chair; Gideon Bragin, Executive Director.* General email, democratic.caucus@mail.house.gov Web, www.dems.gov and Twitter, @HouseDemocrats

Membership: House Democrats. Selects Democratic leadership; formulates party rules and floor strategy; considers caucus members' recommendations on major issues; votes on the Democratic Steering and Policy Committee's recommendations for Democratic committee assignments.

House Democratic Steering and Policy Committee, *233 CHOB, 20515-6527; (202) 225-0100. Fax, (202) 225-4188. Rep. Nancy Pelosi, Chair; Rep. Eric Swalwell, Co-Chair for Policy; Rep. Rosa L. DeLauro, Co-Chair for Steering.*

Makes recommendations to the Democratic leadership on party policy and priorities and participates in decision making with the leadership.

House Republican Conference, *B245 LHOB, 20515; (202) 225-5107. Rep. Liz Cheney, Chair; Rep. Mark Walker, Vice Chair; Will Henderson, Staff Contact.* Web, www.gop.gov, Twitter, @HouseGOP and Facebook, www.facebook.com/HouseRepublicans

Membership: House Republicans. Selects Republican leadership; formulates party rules and floor strategy, and considers party positions on major legislation; votes on the Republican Committee on Committees' recommendations for House committee chairs and Republican committee assignments; publishes Weekly Floor Briefing and Daily Floor Briefing, which analyze pending legislation.

House Republican Policy Committee, *207 CHOB, 20515-6549; (202) 225-4921. Fax, (202) 225-3382. Rep. Gary Palmer, Chair; Kelsey Law, Staff Director.* General email, policycommittee@mail.house.gov Web, http://republicanpolicy.house.gov, Twitter, @GOPpolicy and Facebook, www.facebook.com/RepublicanPolicyCommittee

Studies legislation and makes recommendations on House Republican policies and positions on proposed legislation.

Majority Leader of the U.S. House of Representatives, *1705 Longworth House Office Building, 20515; (202) 225-4131. Fax, (202) 225-4300. Rep. Steny Hoyer, Majority Leader; Alexis Covey-Brandt, Chief of Staff.* Web, www.majorityleader.gov and Twitter, @LeaderHoyer

Serves as chief strategist and floor spokesperson for the majority party in the House.

Majority Whip of the U.S. House of Representatives, *H329 CAP, 20515; (202) 226-32107. Fax, (202) 225-9253. Rep. James E. Clyburn, Majority Whip; Yelberton Watkins, Chief of Staff.* Web, http://majoritywhip.house.gov and Twitter, @WhipClyburn

Serves as assistant majority leader in the House; helps marshal majority forces in support of party strategy.

Minority Leader of the U.S. House of Representatives, *H204 CAP, 20515-6537; (202) 225-4000. Fax, (202) 225-0781. Rep. Kevin McCarthy, Minority Leader; Barrett Karr, Chief of Staff.* Web, http://republicanleader.gov and Twitter, @GOPLeader

Serves as chief strategist and floor spokesperson for the minority party in the House.

Minority Whip of the U.S. House of Representatives, *1705 LHOB, 20515; (202) 225-3015. Rep. Steve Scalise, Minority Whip.* Web, http://republicanwhip.gov and Twitter, @SteveScalise

Serves as assistant minority leader in the House; helps marshal minority forces in support of party strategy.

Speaker of the U.S. House of Representatives, *Speaker's Office, 1236 LHOB, 20515; (202) 225-4965. Rep. Nancy Pelosi, Speaker; Danny Weiss, Chief of Staff.* Web, www.speaker.gov and Twitter, @SpeakerPelosi

Presides over the House while in session; preserves decorum and order; announces vote results; recognizes members for debate and introduction of bills, amendments, and motions; refers bills and resolutions to committees;

decides points of order; appoints House members to conference committees; votes at own discretion.

▶SENATE

See Senate Leadership and Partisan Committees (p. 927).

Democratic Policy and Communication Center, *419 SHOB, 20510; (202) 224-3232. Fax, (202) 228-3432. Sen. Debbie A. Stabenow, Chair. Web, www.dpcc.senate.gov*

Studies and makes recommendations to the Democratic leadership on legislation for consideration by the Senate; prepares policy papers and develops Democratic policy initiatives.

Democratic Steering and Outreach Committee, *712 SHOB, 20510; (202) 224-9048. Fax, (202) 224-5476. Sen. Amy Klobuchar, Chair. General email, steering@dsoc.senate.gov Web, www.dsoc.senate.gov*

Makes Democratic committee assignments subject to approval by the Senate Democratic Conference. Develops and maintains relationships with leaders and organizations outside of Congress.

Majority Leader of the U.S. Senate, *317 SROB, 20510-1702; (202) 224-2541. Fax, (202) 224-2499. Sen. Mitch McConnell, Majority Leader; Phil Maxson, Chief of Staff. Web, www.mcconnell.senate.gov and Twitter, @senatmajldr*

Serves as chief strategist and floor spokesperson for the majority party in the Senate.

Majority Whip of the U.S. Senate, *517 SHOB, 20510-4305; (202) 224-2934. Fax, (202) 228-2856. Sen. John Cornyn, Majority Whip; Beth Jafari, Chief of Staff. Web, www.cornyn.senate.gov*

Serves as assistant majority leader in the Senate; helps marshal majority forces in support of party strategy.

Minority Leader of the U.S. Senate, *322 SHOB, 20510; (202) 224-6542. Fax, (202) 228-3027. Sen. Charles E. Schumer, Minority Leader; Mike Lynch, Chief of Staff. TTY, (202) 224-0420. Web, www.schumer.senate.gov*

Serves as chief strategist and floor spokesperson for the minority party in the Senate.

Minority Whip of the U.S. Senate, *711 SHOB, 20510-1304; (202) 224-2152. Fax, (202) 228-0400. Sen. Richard J. Durbin, Minority Whip; Patrick J. Souders, Projects Director. TTY, (202) 224-8180. Web, www.durbin.senate.gov and Twitter, @SenatorDurbin*

Serves as assistant minority leader in the Senate; helps marshal minority forces in support of party strategy.

President Pro Tempore of the U.S. Senate, *135 SHOB, 20510-4402; (202) 224-3744. Fax, (202) 224-6020. Sen. Chuck Grassley, President Pro Tempore. Web, www.grassley.senate.gov*

Presides over the Senate in the absence of the vice president.

Senate Democratic Conference, *S309 CAP, 20510; (202) 224-3735. Sen. Charles E. Schumer, Chair; Sen. Elizabeth Warren, Vice Chair; Sen. Tammy Baldwin, Secretary; Sen. Mark R. Warner, Vice Chair. Web, www.democrats.senate.gov and Twitter, @SenateDems*

Membership: Democratic senators. Selects Democratic leadership; formulates party rules and floor strategy and considers party positions on major legislation; votes on the Democratic Steering Committee's recommendations for Democratic committee assignments.

Senate Republican Conference, *405 SHOB, 20510; (202) 224-2764. Fax, (202) 228-4276. Sen. John Thune, Chair; Rep. Roy Blunt, Vice Chair. Web, http://republican.senate.gov and Twitter, @SenateGOP*

Membership: Republican senators. Serves as caucus and central coordinating body of the party. Organizes and elects Senate Republican leadership; votes on Republican Committee on Committees' recommendations for Senate committee chairs and Republican committee assignments. Staff provides various support and media services for Republican members.

Senate Republican Policy Committee, *347 SROB, 20510; (202) 224-2946. Fax, (202) 228-2628. Sen. Roy Blunt, Chair; Stacy McBride, Director. General email, SenateRPC_@RPC.Senate.gov Web, www.rpc.senate.gov and Twitter, @SenateRPC*

Studies and makes recommendations to the Republican leader on the priorities and scheduling of legislation on the Senate floor; prepares policy papers and develops Republican policy initiatives.

Vice President of the United States, *President of the Senate, The White House, 20500; (202) 224-2424. Michael R. Pence, President of the Senate; Jonathan Hiler, Director for Legislative Affairs. General email, vice.president@whitehouse.gov Web, www.whitehouse.gov/administration/vice-president-pence and Twitter, @VP*

Presides over the Senate while in session; preserves decorum and order; announces vote results; recognizes members for debate and introduction of bills, amendments, and motions; decides points of order; votes only in the case of a tie. (President pro tempore of the Senate presides in the absence of the vice president.)

Officers

▶HOUSE

Chaplain of the U.S. House of Representatives, *HB25 CAP, 20515-6655; (202) 225-2509. Fax, (202) 226-4928. Rev. Patrick J. (Pat) Conroy, Chaplain.*

General email, chaplainoffice@mail.house.gov

Web, http://chaplain.house.gov

Opens each day's House session with a prayer and offers other religious services and study groups to House members, their families, and staffs. (Prayer sometimes offered by visiting chaplain.)

Chief Administrative Officer of the U.S. House of Representatives, HB26 CAP, 20515; (202) 226-6660. Philip G. Kiko, Chief Administrative Officer. Press, (202) 226-1091.

Web, https://cao.house.gov

Responsible for House member and staff payrolls; computer system; internal mail, office furnishings and supplies; telecommunications; tour guides; nonlegislative functions of the House printing services, recording studio, and records office; and other administrative areas.

Clerk of the U.S. House of Representatives, H154 CAP, 20515-6601; (202) 225-7000. Karen L. Haas, Clerk. Communications, (202) 225-1908.

General email, info.clerkweb@mail.house.gov

Web, http://clerk.house.gov

Responsible for direction of duties of House employees; receives lobby registrations and reports of campaign expenditures and receipts of House candidates; disburses funds appropriated for House expenditures; responsible for other activities necessary for the continuing operation of the House.

General Counsel of the U.S. House of Representatives, 219 CHOB, 20515; (202) 225-9700. Douglas N. Letter, General Counsel.

Web, https://ogc.house.gov

Advises House members and committees on legal matters.

House Legislative Counsel, H2-337 FHOB, 20515-6721; (202) 225-6060. Fax, (202) 225-3437. Wade Ballou, Legislative Counsel.

General email, legcoun@mail.house.gov

Web, https://legcouncil.house.gov

Assists House members and committees in drafting legislation.

Inspector General of the U.S. House of Representatives, 386 FHOB, 20515-9990; (202) 226-1250. Fax, (202) 225-4240. Michael Ptasienski, Inspector General; Joseph Picolla, Deputy Inspector General. Hotline, (202) 593-0068.

General email, HouseIG@mail.house.gov

Web, www.house.gov/the-house-explained/officers-and-organizations/inspector-general

Conducts periodic audit advisory and investigative services of the financial, administrative, and technology-based operations of the House and joint entities.

Sergeant at Arms of the U.S. House of Representatives, H124 CAP, 20515-6611; (202) 225-2456. Fax, (202) 225-3233. Paul D. Irving, Sergeant at Arms.

General email, saamail@mail.house.gov

Web, www.house.gov/the-house-explained/officers-and-organizations/sergeant-at-arms

Maintains order on the House floor; executes orders from the Speaker of the House. Serves on the Capitol Police Board and Capitol Guide Board; oversees Capitol security (with Senate Sergeant at Arms) and protocol.

Speaker of the U.S. House of Representatives, *Floor Assistant,* 1236 LHOB, 20515; (202) 225-4965. Sarah Coyle, Floor Assistant; Ryan O'Toole, Floor Assistant.

Assists the majority leadership and members on legislative matters.

▶ SENATE

Chaplain of the U.S. Senate, S332 CAP, 20510-7002; (202) 224-2510. Fax, (202) 224-9686. Barry C. Black, Chaplain.

Web, www.senate.gov/reference/office/chaplain.htm

Opens each day's Senate session with a prayer and offers other religious services to Senate members, their families, and staffs. (Prayer sometimes offered by visiting chaplain.)

Legislative Counsel of the Senate, 668 SDOB, 20510-7250; (202) 224-6461. Fax, (202) 224-0567. William Baird, Legislative Counsel.

General email, receptionist@slc.senate.gov

Web, www.slc.senate.gov

Assists Senate members and committees in drafting legislation.

Majority Secretary of the U.S. Senate, S337 CAP, 20510-7024; (202) 224-3837. Fax, (202) 224-2860. Laura Dove, Secretary.

Web, www.senate.gov/senators/leadership.htm

Assists the majority leader and majority party in the Senate.

Minority Secretary of the U.S. Senate, S309 CAP, 20510-7014; (202) 224-3735. Gary B. Myrick, Secretary; Tricia Engle, Assistant Secretary.

Web, www.senate.gov/senators/leadership.htm

Assists the minority leader and the minority party in the Senate.

Secretary of the U.S. Senate, S312 CAP, 20510; (202) 224-3622. Julie E. Adams, Secretary of the Senate.

Web, www.senate.gov/reference/office/secretary_of_senate.htm

Chief legislative, financial, and administrative officer of the Senate. Responsible for direction of duties of Senate employees and administration of oaths; receives lobby registrations and reports of campaign expenditures and receipts of Senate candidates; responsible for other day-to-day Senate activities.

Senate Legal Counsel, 642 SHOB, 20510-7250; (202) 224-4435. Fax, (202) 224-3391. Patricia Mack Bryan, Legal Counsel.

Advises Senate members and committees on legal matters.

Sergeant at Arms and Doorkeeper of the U.S. Senate, *S151 CAP, 20510-7200; (202) 224-2341. Michael C. Stenger, Sergeant at Arms and Doorkeeper. Web, www.senate.gov/reference/office/sergeant_at_ arms.htm*

Oversees the Senate wing of the Capitol; doormen; Senate pages; and telecommunication, photographic, supply, and janitorial services. Maintains order on the Senate floor and galleries; oversees Capitol security (with House Sergeant at Arms); sits on the Capitol Police Board and Capitol Guide Board.

Pay and Perquisites

►**CONGRESS**

For a listing of relevant congressional committees and subcommittees, please see page 785 or the Appendix.

Attending Physician of Congress, *H166 CAP, 20515-8907; (202) 225-5421. Dr. Brian Monahan, Attending Physician; Christopher Picaut, Chief of Staff.*

Provides members with primary care, first aid, emergency care, and environmental/occupational health services; provides House and Senate employees, visiting dignitaries, and tourists with first-aid and emergency care.

Clerk of the U.S. House of Representatives, *H154 CAP, 20515-6601; (202) 225-7000. Karen L. Haas, Clerk. Communications, (202) 225-1908. General email, info.clerkweb@mail.house.gov Web, http://clerk.house.gov*

Prepares and submits quarterly reports covering the receipts and expenditures of the House, including disbursements by each committee and each member's office and staff. Reports available from the Legislative Resource Center.

House Commission on Congressional Mailing Standards (Franking Commission), *1216 LHOB, 20515-6328; (202) 226-0647. Rep. Bryan Steil, Chair; Tim Sullivan, Minority Staff Director; Matt DeFreitas, Majority Staff Director. Web, https://cha.house.gov/franking-commission/about-franking-commission*

Oversight of the use of franked mail by House members.

Secretary of the U.S. Senate, *S312 CAP, 20510; (202) 224-3622. Julie E. Adams, Secretary of the Senate. Web, www.senate.gov/reference/office/secretary_of_ senate.htm*

Prepares and submits semiannual reports covering the receipts and expenditures of the Senate, including data on each committee and each member's office and staff. Reports available from the Government Printing Office.

►**NONGOVERNMENTAL**

National Taxpayers Union, *Communications, 122 C St. N.W., #650, 20001; (703) 683-5700. Peter Sepp, President; Nan Swift, Federal Affairs. General email, ntu@ntu.org Web, www.ntu.org and Twitter, @NTU*

Citizens' interest group that publishes reports on congressional pay and perquisites, including pensions and the franking privilege.

Standards of Conduct

►**AGENCIES**

Criminal Division *(Justice Dept.),* **Public Integrity (PIN),** *1400 New York Ave. N.W., #12000, 20005; (202) 514-1412. AnnaLou Tirol, Chief (Acting). Web, www.justice.gov/criminal/pin*

Conducts investigations of wrongdoing in selected cases that involve alleged corruption of public office or violations of election law by public officials, including members of Congress.

►**CONGRESS**

For a listing of relevant congressional committees and subcommittees, please see page 785 or the Appendix.

Secretary of the U.S. Senate, *Public Records, Ethics, 232 SHOB, 20510-7116; (202) 224-0758. Dana K. McCallum, Superintendent of Public Records. General email, lobby@sec.senate.gov Web, www.senate.gov/legislative/opr.htm*

Receives and maintains the financial disclosure records of Senate members, officers, employees, candidates, and legislative organizations. Receives reports from committee chairs on foreign travel by senators and staff. Records open for public inspection, 9:00 a.m.–5:30 p.m.

U.S. House of Representatives, *Legislative Resource Center, Records and Registration, 135 CHOB, 20515-6612; (202) 226-5200. Fax, (202) 226-5169. Steve Pingeton, Manager. Web, http://clerk.house.gov*

Receives and maintains the financial disclosure records of House members, officers, employees, candidates, and certain legislative organizations. Receives reports from committee chairs on foreign travel by members and staff. Records open for public inspection.

U.S. House of Representatives, *Office of Congressional Ethics, 425 3rd St. S.W., #1110, 20024 (mailing address: P.O. Box 895, Washington, DC 20515-0895); (202) 225-9739. Fax, (202) 226-0997. David Skaggs, Chair. General email, oce@mail.house.gov Web, https://oce.house.gov, Twitter, @CongressEthics and Facebook, www.facebook.com/OfficeofCongressionalEthics*

Independent nonpartisan body charged with reviewing allegations of misconduct against members, officers, and staff of the House of Representatives; refers matters to the House Committee on Ethics.

CONGRESSIONAL SUPPORT GROUPS

General

▶ **CONGRESS**

For a listing of relevant congressional committees and subcommittees, please see page 785 or the Appendix.

Congressional Budget Office, *FHOB, 2nd and D Sts. S.W., 4th Floor, 20515-6925; (202) 226-2600. Keith Hall, Director. Press, (202) 226-2602.*
Web, www.cbo.gov and Twitter, @USCBO

Nonpartisan office that provides the House and Senate with analyses needed for economic and budget decisions, and with the information and estimates required for the congressional budget process.

Congressional Budget Office, *Health, Retirement, and Long-Term Analysis, FHOB, 2nd and D Sts. S.W., 4th Floor, 20515-6925; (202) 226-2676. David Weaver, Assistant Director.*
Web, www.cbo.gov

Analyzes federal programs and policies concerning health care and retirement, including Medicare, Medicaid, subsidies to be provided through health insurance exchanges, and Social Security. Responsible for long-term budget protection and analyses of long-term effects of proposed legislation. Prepares reports to Congress.

Government Accountability Office (GAO), *441 G St. N.W., 20548; (202) 512-5500. Fax, (202) 512-5507. Gene L. Dodaro, Comptroller General. Congressional Relations, (202) 512-4400. Information, (202) 512-3000. Publications and documents, (202) 512-6000. General email, contact@gao.gov*
Web, www.gao.gov and Twitter, @USGAO

Independent, nonpartisan agency in the legislative branch. Serves as the investigating agency for Congress; carries out legal, accounting, auditing, and claims settlement functions; makes recommendations for more effective government operations; makes reports available to Congress and the public.

Government Accountability Office (GAO), *Applied Research and Methods (ARM), 441 G St. N.W., #6H19, 20548; (202) 512-2700. Nancy Kingsbury, Managing Director.*
Web, www.gao.gov/careers/arm.html

Provides technical and specialist expertise to support GAO teams, including specialized reviews and guidance on methodological issues; conducts studies on questions of interest to Congress that require specialized analysis.

Government Accountability Office (GAO), *Defense Capabilities and Management (DCM), 441 G St. N.W., #4440B, 20548; (202) 512-4300. Cathleen A. Berrick, Managing Director.*
Web, www.gao.gov/careers/dcm.html

Provides analyses, recommendations, and policy options to Congress in areas of defense, including planning and force structure, readiness and training, war-fighter support, emerging threats, irregular warfare, homeland defense, strategic human-capital management, logistics, infrastructure, business operations, and budgeting.

Government Accountability Office (GAO), *Education, Workforce, and Income Security (EWIS), 441 G St. N.W., #5910, 20548; (202) 512-7215. Barbara D. Bovbjerg, Managing Director.*
Web, www.gao.gov/careers/ewis.html

Assists Congress in analyzing the efficiency and effectiveness of federal agency programs that foster the development, education, and skill attainment of children and adults; provide benefits and protections for workers, families, veterans, and those with disabilities; ensure an adequate and secure retirement for an aging population.

Government Accountability Office (GAO), *Financial Management and Assurance (FMA), 441 G St. N.W., #5Q24, 20548; (202) 512-2600. Larry Malenich, Managing Director.*
Web, www.gao.gov/careers/fma.html

Helps Congress implement the 1990 Chief Financial Officers Act, the 1994 Government Management Reform Act, the 1996 Federal Financial Management Improvement Act, and other crosscutting financial management legislation.

Government Accountability Office (GAO), *Financial Markets and Community Investment (FMCI), 441 G St. N.W., #5Q24, 20548; (202) 512-8678. Lawrence Evans, Managing Director, (202) 512-4802.*
Web, www.gao.gov/careers/fmci.html

Supports congressional efforts to ensure that U.S. financial markets function smoothly and effectively, identifies fraud and abuse, and promotes sound, sustainable community investment by assessing the effectiveness of federal initiatives aimed at small businesses, state and local governments, and communities.

Government Accountability Office (GAO), *Forensic Audits and Investigative Service (FAIS), 441 G St. N.W., #4T21, 20548; (202) 512-6722. Johana R. Ayers, Managing Director, (202) 512-5741. FraudNet, (800) 424-5454.*
Web, www.gao.gov/careers/fais.html

Provides Congress with forensic audits, investigations of fraud, waste, abuse, and security and vulnerability assessments; manages FraudNet.

Government Accountability Office (GAO), *Health Care (HC), 441 G St. N.W., #5A21, 20548; (202) 512-7114. Nikki Clowers, Managing Director, (202) 512-4010.*
Web, www.gao.gov/careers/healthcare.html

Provides analyses, recommendations, and policy options to Congress and the executive branch for all federal government health programs, including those administered by the Defense (TRICARE), Health and Human Services, and Veterans Affairs Depts.

Government Accountability Office (GAO), *Homeland Security and Justice (HSJ),* *441 G St. N.W., #6H19, 20548; (202) 512-8777. Charles M. Johnson Jr., Managing Director.*
Web, www.gao.gov/careers/hsj.html

Audits, analyzes, and evaluates for Congress federal administration of homeland security and justice areas and national preparedness programs and activities.

Government Accountability Office (GAO), *Information Technology (IT),* *441 G St. N.W., #4T21, 20548; (202) 512-6408. Valerie Melvin, Managing Director, (202) 512-6304.*
Web, www.gao.gov/careers/infotech.html

Audits, analyzes, and evaluates for Congress federal information management and information security programs to improve performance and reduce costs.

Government Accountability Office (GAO), *International Affairs and Trade (IAT),* *441 G St. N.W., #4T21, 20548; (202) 512-4128. Thomas Melito, Managing Director.*
Web, www.gao.gov/careers/iat.html

Audits, analyzes, and evaluates international programs and trade; evaluates economic, political, and security problems worldwide. In addition to federal departments, oversight work includes U.S. Agency for International Development, Office of the U.S. Trade Representative, Broadcasting Board of Governors, North Atlantic Treaty Organization, World Bank, International Monetary Fund, and United Nations.

Government Accountability Office (GAO), *Natural Resources and Environment (NRE),* *441 G St. N.W., #2T23-A, 20548 (mailing address: 441 G St. N.W., #2T23A, Washington, DC 20548); (202) 512-3841. Mark Gaffigan, Managing Director.*
Web, www.gao.gov/careers/nre.html

Audits, analyzes, and evaluates for Congress federal agriculture, food safety, and energy programs; provides guidance on issues including efforts to ensure a reliable and environmentally sound energy supply, land and water resources management, protection of the environment, hazardous and nuclear wastes threat reduction, food safety, and investment in science.

Government Accountability Office (GAO), *Physical Infrastructure (PI),* *441 G St. N.W., #2T23-B, 20548 (mailing address: 441 G St. N.W., #2T23B, Washington, DC 20548); (202) 512-2834. Daniel Bertoni, Managing Director, (202) 512-5988.*
Web, www.gao.gov/careers/physicalinfrastructure.html

Provides guidance to Congress on the efficiency, safety, and security of the nation's infrastructure, including transportation systems, telecommunications networks, oil and gas pipelines, and federal facilities owned, funded, and operated by both the public and private sectors.

House Legislative Counsel, *H2-337 FHOB, 20515-6721; (202) 225-6060. Fax, (202) 225-3437. Wade Ballou, Legislative Counsel.*
General email, legcoun@mail.house.gov
Web, https://legcouncil.house.gov

Assists House members and committees in drafting legislation.

Law Revision Counsel, *H2-308 FHOB, 20515-6711; (202) 226-2411. Fax, (202) 225-0010. Ralph V. Seep, Law Revision Counsel.*
General email, uscode@mail.house.gov
Web, http://uscode.house.gov and Twitter, @uscode

Develops and updates an official classification of U.S. laws. Codifies, cites, and publishes the U.S. Code.

Library of Congress, *Congressional Research Service,* *James Madison Memorial Bldg., 101 Independence Ave. S.E., #LM 203, 20540; (202) 707-5775. Fax, (202) 707-6745. Mary B. Mazanec, Director. Information, (202) 707-5700.*
Web, www.loc.gov/crsinfo

Provides confidential policy and legal research and analysis exclusively to committees and members of the House and Senate, regardless of party affiliation. Using multiple disciplines and research methodologies, assists at every stage of the legislative process, from early considerations that precede bill drafting, through committee hearings and floor debate, to the oversight of enacted laws and various agency activities.

Senate Legal Counsel, *642 SHOB, 20510-7250; (202) 224-4435. Fax, (202) 224-3391. Patricia Mack Bryan, Legal Counsel.*

Advises Senate members and committees on legal matters.

Liaison Offices

▶ CONGRESS

For a listing of relevant congressional committees and subcommittees, please see page 785 or the Appendix.

Agriculture Dept. (USDA), *Congressional Relations (OCR),* *1400 Independence Ave. S.W., #219-A, 20250; (202) 720-7095. Fax, (202) 720-8077. Abbey Fretz, Director, (202) 720-9962.*
Web, www.usda.gov/our-agency/staff-offices/office-congressional-relations-ocr

Advises Congress on agriculture, nutrition, and forestry legislation and budget proposals.

Agriculture Dept. (USDA), *Rural Development, External Affairs,* *1400 Independence Ave. S.W., MS 0705, 20250-0705; Maria Wheat, Director; Freddie Mack, Deputy Director. Congressional inquiries, (202) 720-0999. Press, (202) 690-0498.*
Web, www.rd.usda.gov/about-rd/offices/legislative-public-affairs

U.S. House of Representatives

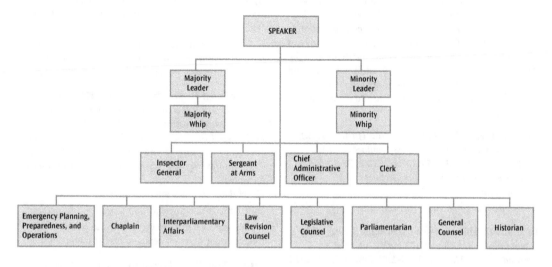

Advises Congress on legislation and policy related to housing, lending, and rural development; coordinates agency testimony before congressional hearings.

Alcohol and Tobacco Tax and Trade Bureau (TTB) *(Treasury Dept.), Congressional and Public Affairs,* 1310 G St. N.W., Box 12, 20005; (202) 453-2180. Fax, (202) 453-2912. Tom Hogue, Congressional Liaison.
Web, www.ttb.gov/offices/media.shtml

Plans, develops, and implements communication regarding TTB affairs.

Animal and Plant Health Inspection Service (APHIS) *(Agriculture Dept.), Legislative and Public Affairs,* South Bldg., 1400 Independence Ave. S.W., #1147, 20250; (202) 799-7030. Bethany Jones, Deputy Administrator, (301) 955-1203. Public Affairs, (301) 851-4100.
Web, www.aphis.usda.gov/aphis/banner/contactus/sa_aphis_contacts/ct_contact_lpa

Advises Congress on legislation related to agriculture, food, natural resources, and wildlife.

Census Bureau *(Commerce Dept.), Congressional and Intergovernmental Affairs,* 4600 Silver Hill Rd., #8H166, Suitland, MD 20746; (301) 763-6100. Fax, (301) 763-3780. Christopher Stanley, Chief.
General email, cao@census.gov

Web, www.census.gov/about/cong-gov-affairs.html

Advises Congress on census policies and programs; provides Census data to Congress.

Commerce Dept., *Legislative and Intergovernmental Affairs,* 1401 Constitution Ave. N.W., 20230; (202) 482-3663. Fax, (202) 482-4420. Mike Platt, Assistant Secretary.
Web, www.commerce.gov//doc/os/office-legislative-and-intergovernmental-affairs

Advises Congress on legislation related to job creation, economic growth, sustainable development, and improved standards of living.

Education Dept., *Legislative and Congressional Affairs (OLCA),* Lyndon Baines Johnson Bldg., 400 Maryland Ave. S.W., #6W315, 20202-3500; (202) 401-0020. Fax, (202) 401-1438. Peter Oppenheim, Assistant Secretary.
General email, olcainquiries@ed.gov

Web, www2.ed.gov/about/offices/list/olca

Advises Congress on policy and legislation related to education.

Energy Dept. (DOE), *Congressional and Intergovernmental Affairs,* 1000 Independence Ave. S.W., #7B138, 20585; (202) 586-5450. Fax, (202) 586-4891. Melissa F. Burnison, Assistant Secretary. Toll-free, (800) 342-5363.
General email, robert.tuttle@hq.doe.gov

Web, www.energy.gov/congressional/office-congressional-and-intergovernmental-affairs

Advises Congress on energy-related policies, programs, and initiatives.

Equal Employment Opportunity Commission (EEOC), *Legislative Affairs,* 131 M St. N.E., Room 6NE25J, 20507; (202) 663-4191. Fax, (202) 663-4912. Patricia Crawford, Director.
General email, legis@eeoc.gov

Web, www.eeoc.gov/eeoc/legislative

Advises Congress on policy and legislation related to equal employment and discrimination in the workplace; coordinates department testimony before congressional hearings.

European Parliament Liaison Office, 2175 K St. N.W., #600, 20037; (202) 862-4734. Antoine Ripoll, Director, (202) 862-4731.
General email, epwashington@ep.europa.eu

Web, www.europarl.europa.eu/us and *Twitter, @EPWashingtonDC*

Acts as the contact point between the European Parliament and the U.S. Congress. Seeks to intensify working relations between the European Parliament and the U.S. Congress at all levels, particularly between corresponding committees of jurisdiction, and between European Parliament lawmakers and U.S. regulators. Represents the Parliament's viewpoint to the U.S. administration and Congress. Principal issues addressed are human rights, the threat of terrorism, economic growth, and environmental protection.

Federal Bureau of Investigation (FBI) *(Justice Dept.)*, *Congressional Affairs*, 935 Pennsylvania Ave. N.W., #7240, 20535; (202) 324-5051. Fax, (202) 324-6490. Jill C. Tyson, Assistant Director (Acting). Web, www.fbi.gov

Advises Congress about FBI activities.

Food and Nutrition Service *(Agriculture Dept.)*, *Chief Communications Officer*, 3101 Park Center Dr., #926, Alexandria, VA 22302; (703) 305-2281. Fax, (703) 305-2312. Kate Fink, Director of External and Governmental Affairs; Brooke Hardison, Director of Communications (Acting). Web, www.fns.usda.gov/cga

Advises Congress on policy and legislation related to food and nutrition programs; coordinates department testimony before congressional hearings.

Government Accountability Office (GAO), *Congressional Relations (CR)*, 441 G St. N.W., Room 7125, 20548; 202-512-4400. Fax, (202) 512-4641. Orice Williams (Kate) Brown, Managing Director, (202) 512-5837. General email, CongRel@gao.gov Web, www.gao.gov

Point of contact within the GAO for contacts with Congress.

Health and Human Services Dept. (HHS), *Legislation*, 200 Independence Ave. S.W., 20201; (202) 690-7627. Fax, (202) 690-7380. Matthew Bassett, Assistant Secretary. Web, www.hhs.gov/about/agencies/asl

Advises Congress on legislation related to health and human services.

Homeland Security Dept. (DHS), *Legislative Affairs*, MS 0020, 20528; (202) 447-5890. Fax, (202) 447-5437. Christine Cassidy, Assistant Secretary; Vince Micone, Deputy Assistant Secretary. General email, CongresstoDHS@hq.dhs.gov Web, www.dhs.gov/about-office-legislative-affairs

Advises Congress about national threat and hazard response as well as safe and secure borders.

Housing and Urban Development Dept. (HUD), *Congressional and Intergovernmental Relations*, 451 7th St. S.W., Room 10120, 20410; (202) 708-0005. Fax, (202) 708-3794. Len Wolfson, Assistant Secretary. Web, www.hud.gov/program_offices/gov_relations/dircir

Advises Congress on policy and legislation related to housing and urban development.

Interior Dept. (DOI), *Congressional and Legislative Affairs*, 1849 C St. N.W., MS 6038-MIB, 20240; (202) 208-7693. Fax, (202) 208-7619. Cole Rojewski, Director. Web, www.doi.gov/ocl

Advises Congress on policy and legislation related to natural resources and tribal communities; coordinates department testimony before congressional hearings.

International Trade Administration (ITA) *(Commerce Dept.)*, *Legislative and Intergovernmental Affairs (OLIA)*, 1401 Constitution Ave. N.W., MS 3424, 20230; (202) 482-3015. Fax, (202) 482-0900. Alexander Stoddard, Legislative and Intergovernmental Director, (202) 482-7917; Andrew Sigmon, Legislative and Intergovernmental Specialist. General email, ITALegislativeAffairs@trade.gov Web, http://trade.gov/olia

Advises Congress on legislation and policies related to international trade matters and export opportunities.

Justice Dept. (DOJ), *Legislative Affairs*, 950 Pennsylvania Ave. N.W., #1145, 20530-0001; (202) 514-2141. Stephen E. Boyd, Assistant Attorney General. Public Liaison, (202) 514-3465. Web, www.justice.gov/ola

Advises Congress on Justice Dept. initiatives; coordinates department testimony before congressional hearings; participates in the Senate confirmation process for federal judges and Justice Dept. nominees.

Labor Dept. (DOL), *Congressional and Intergovernmental Affairs*, 200 Constitution Ave. N.W., #S-2220, 20210; (202) 693-4600. Fax, (202) 693-4642. Vacant, Assistant Secretary. Web, www.dol.gov/agencies/ocia

Advises Congress on policy and legislation related to federal labor matters.

National Institute of Standards and Technology (NIST) *(Commerce Dept.)*, *Congressional and Legislative Affairs*, 100 Bureau Dr., MS 1051, Gaithersburg, MD 20899-1051; (301) 975-5675. Fax, (301) 926-2569. Jim Schufreider, Director. Web, www.nist.gov/director/ocla

Advises Congress on policy related to technology, measurements, and standards; coordinates agency testimony before congressional hearings.

National Marine Manufacturers Assn., *Government Relations*, 650 Massachusetts Ave. N.W., #520, 20001; (202) 737-9750. Fax, (202) 628-4716. Nicole Vasilaros, Vice President, (202) 737-9763. Web, www.nmma.org/government and Twitter, @therealNMMA

Advises Congress on matters related to boating safety and the development of boating facilities.

National Oceanic and Atmospheric Administration (NOAA) *(Commerce Dept.)*, *Legislative and Intergovernmental Affairs*, 1401 Constitution Ave. N.W., #5128, 20230; (202) 482-4981. Wendy Lewis, Director,

U.S. Senate

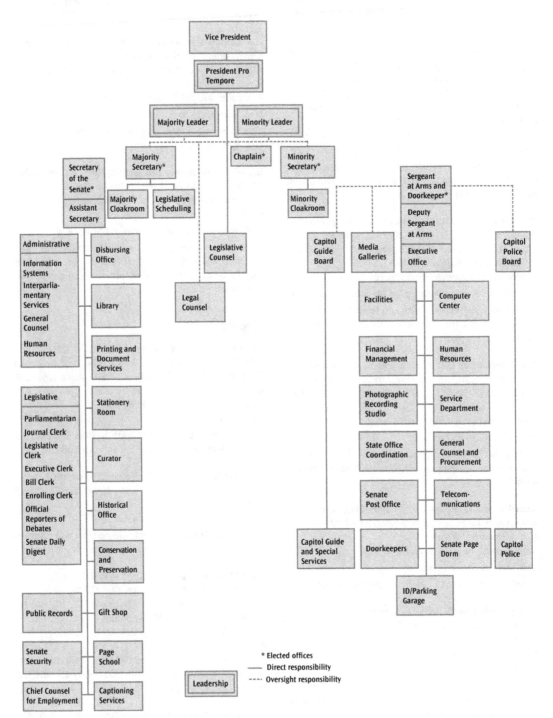

(202) 482-5488; Chris Hayes, Legislative Affairs Specialist, (202) 482-1284.
Web, www.legislative.noaa.gov

Advises Congress on legislation and policy related to climate change, marine commerce, and ocean and coastal resources; coordinates agency testimony before congressional hearings.

Office of Personnel Management (OPM), *Congressional, Legislative, and Intergovernmental Affairs,* 1900 E St. N.W., #6316G, 20415 (mailing address: Constituent Services, B332 RHOB, Washington, DC 20515); (202) 606-1300. Fax, (202) 606-1344. Jonathan Blythe, Director. Constituent services, (202) 225-4955.
Web, www.opm.gov/about-us/our-people-organization/congressional-legislative-intergovernmental-affairs

Advises Congress on federal civil service matters, especially those pertaining to federal employment, retirement, and health benefits programs.

Pension Benefit Guaranty Corp., *Legislative Affairs,* 1200 K St. N.W., 20005-4026; (202) 326-4000. Fax, (202) 326-4224. Alice Maroni, Chief Management Officer. Phone for members and staff, (202) 326-4223.
General email, congressionals@pbgc.gov
Web, www.pbgc.gov/about/pg/pbgc-legislative-affairs.html

Advises Congress on policy and legislation related to pension benefits and private-sector retirement benefit plans.

Postal Regulatory Commission, *Public Affairs and Government Relations,* 901 New York Ave. N.W., #200, 20268; (202) 789-6800. Fax, (202) 789-6891. Ann C. Fisher, Director.
General email, prc-pagr@prc.gov
Web, www.prc.gov/offices/pagr

Advises Congress on policy related to the Postal Service; coordinates commission testimony before congressional hearings.

Securities and Exchange Commission (SEC), *Investor Advocate,* 100 F St. N.E., 20549; (202) 551-3302. Rick A. Fleming, Director.
General email, InvestorAdvocate@sec.gov
Web, www.sec.gov/investorad

Submits reports to Congress concerning SEC activities.

Transportation Dept. (DOT), *Government Affairs,* 1200 New Jersey Ave. S.E., 20590; (202) 366-4573. Adam J. Sullivan, Assistant Secretary.
Web, www.transportation.gov/government-affairs
General email, OSTGovAffairs@dot.gov

Advises Congress on policy and legislation related to transportation and transportation systems; coordinates department testimony before congressional hearings.

Treasury Dept., *Legislative Affairs,* 1500 Pennsylvania Ave. N.W., #3134, 20220; (202) 622-1900. Fax, (202) 622-0534. Vacant, Assistant Secretary.

General email, LegAffairs@do.treas.gov
Web, www.treasury.gov/about/organizational-structure/offices/Pages/Legislative-Affairs.aspx

Advises Congress on legislation and policies related to economics, finance, and financial security; coordinates department testimony before congressional hearings.

U.S. Commission on Civil Rights, *Public Affairs and Congressional Affairs,* 1331 Pennsylvania Ave. N.W., #1150, 20425; (202) 376-8371. Fax, (202) 376-7672. Brian Walch, Director.
General email, publicaffairs@usccr.gov
Web, www.usccr.gov

Advises Congress on legislation and policy related to civil rights issues.

U.S.–China Economic and Security Review Commission, 444 N. Capitol St. N.W., #602, 20001; (202) 624-1407. Fax, (202) 624-1406. Daniel Peck, Executive Director.
General email, contact@uscc.gov
Web, www.uscc.gov and Twitter, @USCC_GOV

Investigates the national security implications of the bilateral trade and economic relationship between China and the United States. Makes recommendations to Congress based on its findings.

▶ HOUSE

Air Force Legislative Liaison, B322 RHOB, 20515-0001; (202) 685-4531. Fax, (202) 685-2592. Col. Thomas Kunkel, Chief, House Liaison Division. Alternate phone, (202) 225-6656.
General email, usaf.pentagon.saf-ll.list.rss-saf-llh-distro-list@mail.mil

Provides House members with services and information on all matters related to the U.S. Air Force.

Army Liaison, 2024 RHOB, 20515; (202) 685-2676. Fax, (202) 256-2674. Col. Timothy Holman (USA), Chief; Jodi Mitchell, Deputy Chief.
Web, http://ocll.hqda.pentagon.mil

Provides House members with services and information on all matters related to the U.S. Army.

Navy–Marine Corps Liaison, B324 RHOB, 20515; Fax, (202) 685-6077. Capt. Scott Farr (USN), Navy Director, House; Col. John A. Ostrowski (USMC), Marine Corps Director, House. Navy (House), (202) 225-7126. Marine Corps (House), (202) 225-7124. fax, (202) 685-6077.

Provides House members with services and information on all matters related to the U.S. Navy and the U.S. Marine Corps.

State Dept., *Capitol Hill House Liaison,* B330 RHOB, 20515; (202) 226-4642. Kem C. Anderson, Director (Acting); Mary Elizabeth Taylor, Assistant Secretary for Legislative Affairs.
Web, www.state.gov/s/h/c26762.htm

Advises House members on foreign policy and legislation; provides services related to consular affairs and travel by members of Congress.

U.S. Coast Guard House Liaison, *B320 RHOB, 20515; (202) 225-4775. Fax, (202) 426-6081. Cmdr. JoAnn Burdian, Chief. General email, house@uscg.mil*

Provides House members with services and information on all matters related to the U.S. Coast Guard.

Veterans Affairs Dept. (VA), *Congressional and Legislative Affairs, 2026 RHOB, 20515; (202) 225-2280. Fax, (202) 273-9988. Annmarie Amaral, Director. General email, ocla-cls@va.gov*

Web, www.va.gov/oca/index.asp

Provides House members with services and information on all matters related to veterans' benefits and services.

White House Legislative Affairs, *White House, 1600 Pennsylvania Ave. N.W., 20502; (202) 456-2230. Ben Howard, Deputy Director, House Liaison; Shahira Knight, Assistant to the President and Director of Legislative Affairs. White House Switchboard, (202) 456-1414.*

Web, www.whitehouse.gov

Press, whopress@who.eop.gov

Serves as a liaison between the president and the House of Representatives.

▶SENATE

Air Force Legislative Liaison (SAF/LL), *182 SROB, 20510; (202) 224-2481. Brig. Gen. Caroline M. Miller, Chief, Senate Liaison Division. General email, usaf.pentagon.saf-ll.mbx.saf-limi=workflow@mail.mil*

Provides senators with services and information on all matters related to the U.S. Air Force.

Army Liaison, *183 RSOB, 20510; (202) 224-2881. Fax, (703) 693-4574. Col. Michael J. Lawson (USA), Chief. Web, http://ocll.hqda.pentagon.mil*

Provides senators with services and information on all matters related to the U.S. Army.

Navy–Marine Corps Liaison, *SR-182, 20510; Fax, (202) 685-6005. Capt. Scott Sciretta (USN), Navy Director, Senate; Col. John Lauder (USMC), Marine Corps Director, Senate. Navy (Senate), (202) 685-6003. Marine Corps (Senate), (202) 224-4681. fax, (202) 685-6005. General email, M_HQMC_OLA_CONGRINT_fct@USMC.mil*

Provides senators with services and information on all matters related to the U.S. Navy and the U.S. Marine Corps.

State Dept., Capitol Hill Senate Liaison, *189 SROB, 20002; (202) 228-1602. Danielle McCartney, Director. Web, www.state.gov/s/h/c26762.htm*

Advises Senate members on foreign policy and legislation; provides services related to consular affairs and travel by members of Congress.

U.S. Coast Guard Senate Liaison, *183 RSOB, 20510; (202) 224-2913. Fax, (202) 755-1695. Cmdr. Brian LeFebvre, Chief. General email, senate@uscg.mil*

Provides senators with services and information on all matters related to the U.S. Coast Guard.

Veterans Affairs Dept. (VA), *Congressional and Legislative Affairs, 189 RSOB, 20510; (202) 224-5351. Fax, (202) 273-9988. Annmarie Amaral, Director. General email, ocla-cls@va.gov*

Web, www.va.gov/oca/index.asp

Provides senators with services and information on all matters related to veterans' benefits and services.

White House Legislative Affairs, *White House, 1600 Pennsylvania Ave. N.W., 20502; (202) 456-2230. Amy Swonger, Deputy Director, Senate Liaison; Shahira Knight, Assistant to the President and Director of Legislative Affairs. White House Switchboard, (202) 456-1414.*

Web, www.whitehouse.gov

Press, whopress@who.eop.gov

Serves as a liaison between the Senate and the president.

Libraries

▶CONGRESS

For a listing of relevant congressional committees and subcommittees, please see page 785 or the Appendix.

Library of Congress, Congressional Research Service, *James Madison Memorial Bldg., 101 Independence Ave. S.E., #LM 203, 20540; (202) 707-5775. Fax, (202) 707-6745. Mary B. Mazanec, Director. Information, (202) 707-5700. Web, www.loc.gov/crsinfo*

Provides members of Congress and committees with research and reference assistance.

Library of Congress, Federal Research Division, *John Adams Bldg., 101 Independence Ave. S.E., #LA 5281, 20540-4840; (202) 707-3900. Fax, (202) 707-3920. Mukta Ohri, Chief. General email, frds@loc.gov*

Web, www.loc.gov/rr/frd

Provides research and analytical support to federal agencies and authorized federal contractors.

Library of Congress, Law Library, *James Madison Memorial Bldg., 101 Independence Ave. S.E., #LM 240, 20540; (202) 707-5065. Fax, (202) 707-1820. Jane Sanchez, Law Librarian, (202) 707-9825. Reading room, (202) 707-5080. Reference, (202) 707-5079. Web, www.loc.gov/law, Twitter, @LawLibCongress and Facebook, www.facebook.com/lawlibraryofcongress*

Provides Congress and the Supreme Court with access to current legal research materials.

Library of the Senate, *B15 SROB, 20510; (202) 224-7106. Fax, (202) 224-0879. Leona Faust, Librarian; Betsy Moon, Catalogue Supervisor, (202) 224-0879.*
General email, betsy_moon@sec.senate.gov

Maintains special collection for Senate private use of primary source legislative materials, including reports, hearing transcripts, prints, documents, and debate proceedings. (Not open to the public.)

U.S. House of Representatives, *Legislative Resource Center, Library Services, 135 CHOB, 20515-6612; (202) 225-9000. Fax, (202) 226-5204. Rae Ellen Best, House Librarian.*
Web, http://library.clerk.house.gov

Serves as the statutory and official depository of House reports, hearings, prints, and documents for the clerk of the House. Includes the divisions of Library Services, Public Information, Records and Registration, and the House Document Room.

Pages

▶ **CONGRESS**

For a listing of relevant congressional committees and subcommittees, please see page 785 or the Appendix.

Senate Page School, *U.S. Senate, 20510-7248; (202) 224-3927. Katherine Wheeden, Principal, (202) 224-3926.*
Web, www.senate.gov/reference/reference_index_subjects/ Pages_vrd.htm

Provides education for pages of the Senate.

Sergeant at Arms and Doorkeeper of the U.S. Senate, *Senate Page Program, Webster Hall, #11, 20510; (202) 228-1291. Elizabeth Roach, Director.*

Oversees and enforces rules and regulations concerning Senate pages after they have been appointed.

Staff

▶ **CONGRESS**

Human Resources, *House Vacancy Announcement and Placement Service, H2-102 FHOB, 20515-6201; (202) 224-3121. John Salamon, Chief Human Resources Officer. TTY, (202) 225-1904.*
Web, www.house.gov/employment/positions-with-members-and-committees

Assists House members and committees fill staff vacancies by posting job vacancies and maintaining a résumé bank of candidates seeking employment.

Senate Placement Office, *116 SHOB, 20510; (202) 224-9167. Brian Bean, Manager. TTY, (202) 224-4215.*

General email, placementofficeinfo@saa.senate.gov
Web, www.senate.gov/visiting/common/generic/ placement_office.htm and Twitter, @SenatePlacement

Provides members, committees, and administrative offices of the Senate with placement and referral services. Compiles Senate Employment Bulletin, an online listing of available jobs.

▶ **NONGOVERNMENTAL**

Congressional Management Foundation, *216 7th St. S.E., 2nd Floor, 20003; (202) 546-0100. Bradford (Brad) Fitch, President.*
General email, cmf@congressfoundation.org
Web, www.congressfoundation.org, Twitter, @CongressFdn and Facebook, www.facebook.com/CongressFoundation

Nonpartisan organization that provides members of Congress and their staffs with management information and services through seminars, consultation, research, and publications.

Federal Bar Assn., *1220 N. Fillmore St., #444, Arlington, VA 22201; (571) 481-9100. Fax, (571) 481-9090. Stacey King, Executive Director.*
General email, fba@fedbar.org
Web, www.fedbar.org, Twitter, @federalbar and Facebook, www.facebook.com/FederalBar

Organization of bar members who are present or former staff members of the House, Senate, Library of Congress, Supreme Court, Government Accountability Office, or Government Printing Office, or attorneys in legislative practice before federal courts or agencies.

House Chiefs of Staff Assn., *2082 RHOB, 20515; (202) 225-6411. Fax, (202) 226-0778. Drew Kent, Chief of Staff.*

Sponsors professional development programs and social activities for current chiefs of staff and staff directors. Promotes bipartisanship.

POLITICAL ADVOCACY

General

▶ **CONGRESS**

For a listing of relevant congressional committees and subcommittees, please see page 785 or the Appendix.

U.S. House of Representatives, *Legislative Resource Center, Records and Registration, 135 CHOB, 20515-6612; (202) 226-5200. Fax, (202) 226-5169. Steve Pingeton, Manager.*
Web, http://clerk.house.gov

Receives and maintains lobby registrations and quarterly financial reports of lobbyists. Administers the statutes of the Federal Regulation of Lobbying Act of 1995 and counsels lobbyists. Receives and maintains agency filings made under the requirements of Section 319 of the Interior Dept. and Related Agencies Appropriations Act for fiscal

Ratings of Members of Congress

The following organizations either publish voting records on selected issues or regularly rate members of Congress.

AFL-CIO, 815 16th St. N.W., 20006; (202) 637-5018; www.aflcio.org

American Conservative Union, 1331 H St. N.W., #500, 20005; (202) 347-9388; Fax: (202) 347-9389; www.conservative.org

American Farm Bureau Federation, 600 Maryland Ave. S.W., #1000W, 20024; (202) 406-3600; www.fb.org

Americans for Democratic Action, 1629 K St. N.W., #300, 20006; (202) 600-7762; Fax: (202) 204-8637; www.adaction.org

Americans for Tax Reform, 722 12th St. N.W., #400, 20005; (202) 785-0266; Fax: (202) 785-0261; www.atr.org

Citizens Against Government Waste, 1100 Connecticut Ave. N.W., #650, 20036; (202) 467-5300; Fax: (202) 467-4253; www.cagw.org

Citizens for Responsibility and Ethics in Washington, 455 Massachusetts Ave. N.W., 6th Floor, 20001; (202) 408-5565; www.citizensforethics.org

The Club for Growth, 2001 L St. N.W., #600, 20036; (202) 955-5500; Fax: (202) 955-9466; www.clubforgrowth.org

Drum Major Institute for Public Policy, 885 Second Ave., 47th Floor, New York, NY 10017; (212) 909-9589; Fax: (212) 909-9489; www.drummajorinst.org

Human Rights Campaign, 1640 Rhode Island Ave. N.W., 20036-3278; (800) 777-4723 or (202) 628-4160; Fax: (202) 347-5323; TTY, (202) 216-1572; www.hrc.org

Leadership Conference on Civil Rights, 1620 L St. N.W., #1100, 20036; (202) 466-3311; www.civilrights.org

League of Conservation Voters, 1920 L St. N.W., #800, 20036; (202) 785-8683; Fax: (202) 835-0491; www.lcv.org

NAACP (National Assn. for the Advancement of Colored People), 4805 Mt. Hope Dr., Baltimore, MD 21215; (410) 580-5777; www.naacp.org

NARAL Pro-Choice America, 1156 15th St. N.W., #700, 20005; (202) 973-3000; Fax: (202) 973-3096; www.prochoiceamerica.org

National Assn. of Social Workers, 750 1st St. N.E., #800, 20002; (202) 408-8600; www.socialworkers.org

National Education Assn., 1201 16th St. N.W., 20036-3290; (202) 833-4000; Fax: (202) 822-7974; www.nea.org

National Federation of Independent Business, 1201 F St. N.W., #200, 20004-1221; (202) 554-9000; www.nfib.com

National Right to Life Committee, 512 10th St. N.W., 20004; (202) 626-8800; www.nrlc.org

National Taxpayers Union, 25 Massachusetts Ave. N.W., #140, 20001; (703) 683-5700; www.ntu.org

Population Connection, 2120 L St. N.W., #500, 20037; (202) 332-2200; Fax: (202) 332-2302; www.populationconnection.org

Public Citizen, Congress Watch, 215 Pennsylvania Ave. S.E., 20003; (202) 546-4996; www.citizen.org

U.S. Chamber of Commerce, Congressional Affairs, 1615 H St. N.W., 20062; (202) 659-6000; www.uschamber.com

U.S. Student Assn., P.O. Box 33486, 20036; (202) 640-6570; www.usstudents.org

---

1990 (known as the Byrd Amendment). Open for public inspection.

▶**NONGOVERNMENTAL**

Bipartisan Policy Center, *1225 Eye St. N.W., #1000, 20005-5977; (202) 204-2400. Fax, (202) 318-0876. Jason S. Grumet, President; G. William Hoagland, Senior Vice President. General email, bipartisaninfo@energycommission.org Web, https://bipartisanpolicy.org and Twitter, @BPC_Bipartisan*

Think tank advocating bipartisanship policymaking. Interests include health, energy, national and homeland security, the economy, housing, immigration, infrastructure, and governance. Monitors legislation and regulations.

The Brookings Institution, *1775 Massachusetts Ave. N.W., 20036; (202) 797-6000. Fax, (202) 797-6004. John R. Allen, President. Press, (202) 797-6105.*

General email, communications@brookings.edu

Web, www.brookings.edu and Twitter, @Brookingsinst

Public policy research organization that seeks to improve the performance of American institutions, the effectiveness of government programs, and the quality of public policy through research and analysis. Sponsors lectures, debates, and policy forums.

Capital Research Center, *1513 16th St. N.W., 20036; (202) 483-6900. Fax, (202) 483-6990. Scott Walter, President; Kristen Eastlick, Vice President for Programs, (202) 462-2052.*

General email, contact@capitalresearch.org

Web, https://capitalresearch.org and Twitter, @capitalresearch

Conservative think tank that researches funding sources, especially foundations, charities, and other nonprofits, of public interest and advocacy groups. Analyzes the impact these groups have on public policy. Publishes findings in newsletters and reports.

Charles F. Kettering Foundation, *Washington Office,*
444 N. Capitol St. N.W., #434, 20001-1512; (202) 393-4478.
David Mathews, President.
Web, www.kettering.org and Twitter, @KetteringFdn

Works to understand democracy and its processes and
improve the domestic policymaking process through citizen deliberation. Supports international programs focusing
on unofficial, citizen-to-citizen diplomacy. Encourages
greater citizen involvement in formation of public policy.
Interests include public education and at-risk youths.
(Headquarters in Dayton, Ohio.)

Citizens United, *1006 Pennsylvania Ave. S.E., 20003-2142;*
(202) 547-5420. Fax, (202) 547-5421. David N. Bossie,
President.
General email, info@citizensunited.org
*Web, http://citizensunited.org and Twitter, @Citizens_*
United

Acts as advocate for key elements of the conservative
legislative and policy agenda.

Eisenhower Institute, *818 Connecticut Ave. N.W., #800,*
20006; (202) 628-4444. Fax, (202) 628-4445.
Susan Eisenhower, Chair Emeritus; Patrick Cochran,
Program Manager.
General email, ei@gettysburg.edu
Web, www.eisenhowerinstitute.org

Nonpartisan research and educational organization
modeled on President Eisenhower's legacy of public policy
formation and leadership, stressing pursuit of facts, respect-
ful dialogue, and a focus on the future. (Affiliated with
Gettysburg College in Gettysburg, Pa.)

National Institute for Lobbying and Ethics, *10340*
Democracy Lane, Fairfax, VA 22030; (703) 383-1330.
Paul Miller, President.
General email, paul@lobbyinginstitute.com
Web, www.lobbyinginstitute.com and
Twitter, @LobbyingInstitute

Membership: professional lobbyists and other professional public relations staff. Works to improve the technical
skills, ethics, and public image of lobbyists. Monitors lobby
legislation and conducts education programs on public
issues, lobbying techniques, and other related issues.

Public Citizen, *1600 20th St. N.W., 20009; (202) 588-1000.*
Fax, (202) 588-7798. Robert Weissman, President.
General email, pcmail@citizen.org
Web, www.citizen.org and Twitter, @Public_Citizen

Public interest consumer advocacy organization comprising the following programs: Congress Watch, Health
Research Group, Energy Program, Litigation Group, Global
Trade Watch, Democracy is for People Project, and Commercial Alert Program.

Women & Politics Institute *(American University),* *4400*
Massachusetts Ave. N.W., Kerwin Hall, #109E, 20016;
(202) 885-2903. Fax, (202) 885-2967. Betsy Fischer Martin,
Executive Director.

General email, wpi@american.edu
Web, www.american.edu/spa/wpi and Twitter, @AU_WPI

Research center that encourages women to participate
in politics and addresses women's issues. Administers graduate and undergraduate certificates to academics studying
women, policy, and political leadership. Assists women in
securing employment in the political sphere through leadership training programs.

Ethnic Group Advocacy

▶**NONGOVERNMENTAL**

American Polish Advisory Council (APAC), *2025 O St.*
N.W., 20036; (202) 630-1714. Darek Barcikowski,
Executive Director.
Web, www.americanpolishadvisorycouncil.org

Promotes Polish Americans' involvement in politics,
public affairs, service, and policymaking. Educates Polish
Americans about the American governmental system and
voting. Researches political, economic, and civil issues facing Polish American communities. Holds an annual conference to discuss the current and future role of Poland's
relationship with the United States.

American–Arab Anti-Discrimination Committee (ADC),
1705 DeSales St. N.W., #500, 20036; (202) 244-2990.
Fax, (202) 333-6470. Samer E. Khalaf, President.
General email, adc@adc.org
Web, www.adc.org and Twitter, @adctweets

Nonpartisan and nonsectarian organization that promotes Arab cultural heritage to the public and policymakers. Sponsors student internships to Washington, D.C.

Arab American Institute, *1600 K St. N.W., #601, 20006;*
(202) 429-9210. Fax, (202) 429-9214. James J. Zogby,
President.
General email, communications@aaiusa.org
Web, www.aaiusa.org and Twitter, @AAIUSA

Fosters civic and political empowerment of Americans
of Arab descent through research, policy formation, and
political activism.

Armenian National Committee of America, *1711 N St.*
N.W., 20036; (202) 775-1918. Fax, (202) 223-7964.
Aram Hamparian, Executive Director.
General email, anca@anca.org
Web, www.anca.org and Twitter, @ANCA_DC

Armenian American grassroots political organization.
Works to advance concerns of the Armenian American
community. Interests include strengthening U.S.–Armenian
relations.

Asian Americans Advancing Justice (AAJC), *1620 L St.*
N.W., #1050, 20036; (202) 296-2300. Fax, (202) 296-2318.
John C. Yang, President.
General email, information@advancingequality.org
Web, www.advancingjustice_aajc.org and
Twitter, @AAAJ_AAJC

Works to advance the human and civil rights of Asian Americans and other minority groups through advocacy, public policy, public education, and litigation. Promotes civic engagement at the local, regional, and national levels. Interests include affirmative action, hate crimes, media diversity, census, broadband and telecommunications, youth advocacy, immigrant rights, language access, and voting rights.

B'nai B'rith International, *1120 20th St. N.W., #300N, 20036; (202) 857-6600. Fax, (202) 857-2700. Daniel S. Mariaschin, Executive Vice President. Press, (202) 857-6699. Toll-free, (888) 388-4224.*
General email, info@bnaibrith.org

Web, www.bnaibrith.org and Twitter, @BnaiBrith

Advocates policies in support of Jews and the State of Israel.

Congressional Black Caucus Foundation, *1720 Massachusetts Ave. N.W., 20036-1903; (202) 263-2800. Fax, (202) 263-0842. Elsie L. Scott, President (Acting). General email, info@cbcfinc.org*

Web, www.cbcfinc.org and Twitter, @CBCFInc

Conducts research and offers programs on public policy issues with the aim of improving the socioeconomic circumstances of African Americans and other underserved populations. Holds issue forums and leadership seminars. Provides elected officials, organizations, and researchers with statistical, demographic, public policy, and political information.

Japanese American Citizens League, *Washington Office, 1629 K St. N.W., #400, 20006; (202) 223-1240. David Inoue, Executive Director. General email, dc@jacl.org*

Web, www.jacl.org

Monitors legislative and regulatory activities affecting the rights of Japanese Americans. Supports civil rights of all Americans, with a focus on Asian and Asian Pacific Americans. (Headquarters in San Francisco, Calif.)

Labor Council for Latin American Advancement, *815 16th St. N.W., 3rd Floor, 20006; (202) 508-6919. Fax, (202) 508-6922. Hector E. Sanchez, Executive Director. General email, headquarters@lclaa.org*

Web, www.lclaa.org, Twitter, @LCLAA and Facebook, www.facebook.com/LCLAA

Membership: Hispanic trade unionists. Encourages equal employment opportunity, voter registration, and participation in the political process. (Affiliated with the AFL-CIO and the Change to Win Federation.)

League of United Latin American Citizens, *1133 19th St. N.W., #1000, 20036; (202) 833-6130. Fax, (202) 833-6135. Sidney Benavides, Chief Executive Officer, ext. 108. General email, info@lulac.org*

Web, www.lulac.org

Seeks full social, political, economic, and educational rights for Hispanics in the United States. Programs include housing projects for the poor, employment and training for

youth and women, and political advocacy on issues affecting Hispanics, including immigration. Affiliated with National Educational Service Centers (LNESCs), which award scholarships. Holds exposition open to the public.

Mexican American Legal Defense and Educational Fund, *National Public Policy, 1016 16th St. N.W., #100, 20036; (202) 293-2828. Thomas A. Saenz, President; Andrea Senteno, Legislative Staff Attorney. General information, (213) 629-2512. General email, info@maldef.org*

Web, www.maldef.org/about/offices/washington_dc

Works with Congress and the White House to promote legislative advocacy for minority groups. Interests include equal employment, voting rights, bilingual education, immigration, and discrimination. Monitors legislation and regulations. (Headquarters in Los Angeles, Calif.)

National Assn. of Latino Elected and Appointed Officials Educational Fund, *Washington Office, 600 Pennsylvania Ave. S.E., #480, 20003; (202) 546-2536. Fax, (202) 546-4121. Arturo Vargas, Executive Director; Rosalind Gold, Senior Director of Policy, Research, and Advocacy. General email, jgarcia@naleo.org*

Web, www.naleo.org, Twitter, @NALEO and Twitter, @ArturoNALEO

Research and advocacy group that provides civic affairs information and assistance on legislation affecting Latinos. Encourages Latino participation in local, state, and national politics. Interests include health care and social, economic, and educational issues. (Headquarters in Los Angeles, Calif.)

National Conference of Puerto Rican Women, *1220 L St. N.W., #100-177, 20005; Michelle Centeno, National President; Milagros V. McGuire, President of the Washington, D.C., Chapter. General email, nacoprw_nationalpress55@aol.com*

Web, www.nacoprw.org

Nonprofit, nonpartisan organization promoting the participation of Puerto Rican and other Hispanic women in their economic, social, and political life. Provides training, mentorship, and leadership development at the local and national level through workshops and institutes; provides scholarships to Hispanic individuals.

National Congress of American Indians, *Embassy of Tribal Nations, 1516 P St. N.W., 20005; (202) 466-7767. Fax, (202) 466-7797. Jacqueline Johnson Pata, Executive Director, ext. 218. General email, ncai@ncai.org*

Web, www.ncai.org and Twitter, @NCAI1944

Membership: American Indian and Alaska Native tribal governments and individuals. Provides information and serves as general advocate for tribes. Monitors legislative and regulatory activities affecting Native American affairs.

National Italian American Foundation, *1860 19th St. N.W., 20009; (202) 387-0600. Fax, (202) 387-0800. Jerry Jones, Chief of Staff, (202) 939-3102. Press, (202) 387-0600.*

General email, information@niaf.org

Web, www.niaf.org

Represents the interests of Italian Americans before Congress.

OCA: Asian Pacific American Advocates, 1322 18th St. N.W., 20036-1803; (202) 223-5500. Fax, (202) 296-0540. Ken Lee, Chief Executive Officer.
General email, oca@ocanational.org

Web, www.ocanational.org, Twitter, @OCANational and Facebook, www.facebook.com/OCAnatl

Advocacy group seeking to advance the social, political, and economic well-being of Asian Pacific Americans in the United States.

Orthodox Union, Advocacy Center, 820 1st St. N.E., #730, 20002; (202) 513-6484. Fax, (202) 513-6497. Nathan Diament, Executive Director.
General email, info@ouadvocacy.org

Web, www.ou.org/public_affairs

Works to protect Orthodox Jewish interests and freedoms through dissemination of policy briefings to government officials. Encourages Jewish law and a traditional perspective on public policy issues. Coordinates grassroots activities. (Headquarters in New York.)

Republican Jewish Coalition, 50 F St. N.W., #100, 20001; (202) 638-6688. Fax, (202) 638-6694. Matthew Brooks, Executive Director; Norm M. Coleman, National Chair.
General email, rjc@rjchq.org

Web, www.rjchq.org and Twitter, @RJC

Legislative interest group that works to build support among Republican party decision makers on issues of concern to the Jewish community; studies domestic and foreign policy issues affecting the Jewish community; supports a strong relationship between the United States and Israel. Monitors legislation and regulations.

Southeast Asia Resource Action Center (SEARAC), 1628 16th St. N.W., 3rd Floor, 20009; (202) 601-2960. Fax, (202) 667-6449. Quyen Dinh, Executive Director.
General email, searac@searac.org

Web, www.searac.org and Twitter, @SEARC

Works to advance Cambodian, Hmong, Laotian, and Vietnamese refugee rights through leadership and advocacy training. Collects and analyzes data on Southeast Asian Americans; publishes reports.

Political Action Committees and 527s

The following are some key political action committees (PACs) based in Washington.

▶AGRICULTURE AND FOOD

Agricultural Retailers Assn. PAC, 1156 15th St. N.W., #500, 20005; (202) 457-0825. Fax, (202) 457-0864.

Richard Gupton, Senior Vice President of Legislative Policy, (202) 595-1699.
General email, info@aradc.org

Web, www.aradc.org/governmentaffairs/arapac and Twitter, @AgRetailers

American Beverage Assn. PAC, 1275 Pennsylvania Ave. N.W., #1100, 20004; (202) 463-6719. Fax, (202) 463-8277. Kevin W. Keane, Vice President of Government and Public Affairs.
General email, info@ameribev.org

Web, www.ameribev.org/initiatives-advocacy, Twitter, @AmeriBev and Facebook, www.facebook.com/AmeriBev

American Sugarbeet Growers Assn. PAC, 1155 15th St. N.W., #1100, 20005; (202) 833-2398. Fax, (240) 235-4291. Dan Younggren, Vice President.
General email, info@americansugarbeet.org

Web, www.americansugarbeet.org

Beer Institute PAC, 440 1st St. N.W., #350, 20001; (202) 737-2337. Fax, (202) 737-7004. Dan Roth, Senior Director of Public Affairs.
General email, droth@beerinstitute.org

Web, www.beerinstitute.org and Twitter, @beerinstitute

CandyPAC, 1101 30th St N.W., #200, 20007; (202) 534-1440. Tod Moore, Manager of Government Affairs; Liz Clark, Senior Vice President of Public Policy.
General email, info@CandyUSA.com

Web, www.candyusa.com/advocacy/candypac and Twitter, @CandyUSA

(Affiliated with the National Confectioners Assn.)

Crop Insurance and Reinsurance Bureau PAC, 440 First St. N.W., #500, 20001; (202) 544-0067. Sarah Hubbart, Director of Communications and Federal Affairs.
General email, www.cropinsurance.org/contact

Web, www.cropinsurance.org/cirb-pac

International Dairy Foods Assn., Ice Cream, Milk, and Cheese PAC, 1250 H St. N.W., #900, 20005; (202) 737-4332. Fax, (202) 331-7820. Colin Newman, Manager of Legislative Affairs.
General email, pac@idfa.org

Web, www.idfa.org/dairycounts/pac, Twitter, @dairyidfa and Facebook, www.facebook.com/dairyIDFA

National Cattleman's Beef Assn. PAC, 1275 Pennsylvania Ave. N.W., #801, 20004; (202) 347-0228. Fax, (202) 638-0607. Kendal Frazier, Chief Executive Officer; Colin Woodall, Senior Vice President of Governmental Affairs; Joe Guild, Treasurer.
General email, alee@beef.org

Web, www.beefusa.org/ncba-pac-onemissiononevoice.aspx, Twitter, @BeefUSA and Facebook, www.facebook.com/BeefUSA

National Corn Growers Assn. PAC, *20 F St. N.W., #600, 20001; (202) 628-7001. Fax, (202) 628-1933. Kat Emerson, Director of Public Policy.*
General email, corninfo@ncga.com
Web, www.ncga.com/about-ncga/cornpac

National Council of Farmer Cooperatives CO-OP/PAC, *50 F St. N.W., #900, 20001; (202) 879-0826. Fax, (202) 626-8722. Kelsey S. Billings, Treasurer.*
General email, kbillings@ncfc.org
Web, www.ncfc.org and Twitter, @FarmerCoop

National Potato Council PAC, *1300 L St. N.W., #910, 20005; (202) 682-9456. Fax, (202) 682-0333. Kam Quarles, Director of Public Policy.*
General email, spudinfo@nationalpotatocouncil.org
Web, www.nationalpotatocouncil.org and Twitter, @ThisSpudsforYou

North American Meat Institute PAC, *1150 Connecticut Ave. N.W., #1200, 20036; (202) 587-4200. Brad McDowell, Treasurer, (202) 587-4235.*
Web, www.meatinstitute.org, Twitter, @MeatInstitute and Facebook, www.facebook.com/AmericanMeatInstitute

The Farm Credit Council PAC, *50 F St. N.W., #900, 20001; (202) 626-8710. Fax, (202) 626-8718. Kim Boscia, Treasurer, (202) 879-0842.*
General email, ask@fccouncil.org
Web, https://farmcredit.com/farm-credit-council and Twitter, @farmcredit

Wine & Spirits Wholesalers of America PAC, *805 15th St. N.W., #1120, 20005; (202) 371-9792. Fax, (202) 789-2405. Catherine McDaniel, Vice President, Federal Affairs.*
General email, info@wswa.org
Web, www.wswa.org/issues/wswa-pac, Twitter, @WSWAMedia and Facebook, www.facebook .com/wswa

▶ **BUSINESS AND ECONOMICS**

American Bankers Assn. BankPAC, *1120 Connecticut Ave. N.W., 20036; (202) 663-5017. Rob Engstrom, Chief Political Strategist; Laura Salameh, BankPac Manager, (202) 663-5331.*
General email, abapac@aba.com
Web, www.aba.com/Advocacy/Pages/BankPac.aspxPoli, Twitter, @ABABankers and Facebook, www.facebook.com/ AmericanBankersAssociation

American Council of Life Insurers PAC, *101 Constitution Ave. N.W., #700 West, 20001-2133; (202) 624-2000. J. Bruce Ferguson, Senior Vice President State Relations, (202) 624-2385.*
General email, pac@acli.com
Web, www.acli.com, Twitter, @ACLINews and Facebook, www.facebook.com/ACLINews

American Hotel and Lodging Assn., *Hotel PAC, 1250 Eye St. N.W., #110, 20005; (202) 289-3132. Fax, (202) 289-3199. Brian Crawford, Executive Vice President of Government Affairs, (202) 289-3130.*
General email, gov.affairs@ahla.com
Web, www.ahla.com/hotelpac

Credit Union Legislative Action Council, *99 M St. S.E., #300, 20003; (202) 638-5777. Fax, (202) 638-7751. Trey Hawkins, Vice President, Political Affairs.*
Toll-free, (800) 356-9655.
General email, hello@cuna.coop
Web, www.cuna.org/culac

Cruise Lines International Assn. PAC, *1201 F St. N.W., #250, 20004; (202) 759-9326. Fax, (202) 759-9344. Christina Perez, Government Affairs Manager.*
General email, info@cruising.org
Web, www.cruising.org/about-the-industry/about-clia/clia-pac and Twitter, @CLIAGlobal

Hardwood Federation PAC, *1101 K St. N.W., #700, 20005; (202) 463-5186. Cary Moon, Policy Manager.*
General email, hardwood.federation@hardwoodfederation .com
Web, www.hardwoodfederation.com

Independent Community Bankers of America PAC, *1615 L St. N.W., #900, 20036; (202) 659-8111. Martina Dashner, Vice President, (202) 821-4418. Toll-free, (800) 422-8439.*
General email, icbpac@icba.org
Web, www.icba.org/advocacy/grassroots-be-heard!/icbpac, Twitter, @ICBA and Facebook, www.facebook.com/icbaorg

Independent Insurance Agents and Brokers of America Political Action Committee (InsurPac), *20 F St. N.W., #610, 20001; (202) 863-7000. Fax, (202) 863-7015. Nathan Riedel, Vice President of Political Affairs.*
General email, InsurPac@iiaba.net
Web, www.independentagent.com/governmentaffairs/ insurPac/default.aspx

Insurance and Financial Advisors PAC, *2901 Telestar Court, Falls Church, VA 22042-1205; (703) 770-8100. Fax, (703) 770-8151. Stephanie Sheridon, Director.*
Toll-free, (877) 866-2432.
General email, mishak@naifa.org
Web, www.naifa.org/advocacy/ifapac and Twitter, @NAIFA

Investment Company Institute PAC, *1401 H St. N.W., #1200, 20005; (202) 326-5800. Peter Gallary, Treasurer. Press, (202) 371-5413.*
Web, www.ici.org, Twitter, @ICI and Facebook, www.facebook.com/ici.org

Mortgage Bankers Assn. PAC, *1919 M St. N.W., 5th Floor, 20036; (202) 557-2777. Rick Arvielo, Chief Executive Officer; William Griffin, Executive Vice President.*

General email, morpac@mba.org

Web, www.mba.org/get-involved/mbas-political-action-committee

The National Assn. of Business Political Action Committees, *101 Constitution Ave. N.W., # L-110, 20001; (202) 341-3780. Fax, (202) 478-0342. Geoff Ziebart, Executive Director.*
General email, nabpac@nabpac.org

Web, www.nabpac.org and Twitter, @nabpc

National Assn. of Real Estate Investment Trusts, Inc. PAC, *1875 Eye St. N.W., #600, 20006; (202) 739-9436. Fax, (202) 739-9401. Steven Lowery, Director.*
General email, reitpac@nareit.com

Web, https://reitpac.org

National Beer Wholesalers Assn. PAC, *1101 King St., #600, Alexandria, VA 22314-2944; (703) 683-4300. Fax, (703) 683-8965. Linda Auglis, Director.*
General email, info@nbwa.org

Web, www.nbwa.org

National Federation of Independent Business, *Federal PAC, 1201 F St. N.W., #200, 20004; (202) 314-2061. (800) 274-6342. Jeff Smith, Treasurer; Sharon Sussin, National Political Director.*
Web, www.nfib.com/advocacy, Twitter, @NFIB and Facebook, www.facebook.com/NFIB

Supports candidates in both federal and state elections who support small business.

National Multifamily Housing Council PAC, *1775 Eye St. N.W., #1100, 20006; (202) 974-2300. Fax, (202) 775-0112. Colin Dunn, Director for Advocacy, (202) 974-2370.*
Web, www.nmhc.org, Twitter, @ApartmentWire and Facebook, www.facebook.com/nmhc

Restaurant PAC of the National Restaurant Assn., *2055 L St. N.W., #700, 20036; (202) 331-5920. Joe Essa, Chair.*
General email, advocacy@restaurant.org

Web, www.restaurant.org/advocacy/Get-Involved/Restaurant-PAC, Twitter, @RestaurantsAct and Facebook, www.facebook.com/RestaurantsAct

Securities Industry and Financial Markets Assn. PAC, *1101 New York Ave. N.W., 8th Floor, 20005; (202) 962-7462. Julia Henson, Political Affairs Associate.*
General email, inquiry@sifma.org

Web, www.sifma.org/resources/general/pac

Service Employees International Union Committee on Political Education (SEIU COPE), *1800 Massachusetts Ave. N.W., 20036; (202) 730-7112. Gerry Hudson, Treasurer; Mary Kay Henry, President. Toll-free, (800) 424-8592.*
Web, www.seiu.org, Twitter, @SEIU and Facebook, www.facebook.com/SEIU

▶ **CIVIL RIGHTS**

American Assn. for Justice PAC, *777 6th St. N.W., #200, 20001; (202) 965-3500. Fax, (202) 338-8709. Elise R. Saguinetti, President; Tad Thomas, Treasurer. Outreach, ext. 8425. Toll-free, (800) 424-2725.*
General email, outreach@justice.org

Web, www.justice.org

(Formerly the Assn. of Trial Lawyers of America.)

BOLD PAC, *220 Eye St. N.E., #280, 20002; (202) 271-9682. Diane Evans, Treasurer.*
General email, admin@evanskatz.com

Web, www.boldpac.com and Twitter, @BOLDPAC

(Affiliated with the Committee for Hispanic Caucus.)

Human Rights Campaign PAC (HRC), *1640 Rhode Island Ave. N.W., 20036; (202) 216-1545. Fax, (202) 347-5323. Mike Mings, Director. TTY, (202) 216-1572.*
General email, hrc@hrc.org

Web, www.hrc.org/issues/pages/federal-pac and Twitter, @HRC

Supports pro-equality candidates for state and federal office who favor lesbian, gay, bisexual, and transgender equality.

JStreetPAC, *(202) 596-5207. Danny Yu, Vice President of Finance.*
General email, info@jstreetpac.org.

Web, https://donate.jstreetpac.org and Twitter, @jstreetdotorg

Focuses on pro-Israel and pro-peace American relationships and supports candidates in favor of a diplomacy-first approach to advancing U.S. interests in the Middle East and promoting peace and security for Israel.

LGBT Victory Fund Federal PAC, *1225 Eye St. N.W., #525, 20005; (202) 842-8679. Fax, (202) 289-3863. Sean Meloy, Political Director; Elliot Imse, Director of Communications.*
General email, communications@victoryfund.org

Web, www.victoryfund.org and Twitter, @VictoryFund

NARAL Pro-Choice America PAC, *1725 Eye St. N.W., #900, 20006; (202) 973-3000. Fax, (202) 973-3096. Ilyse Hogue, President.*
General email, CAN@ProChoiceAmerica.org

Web, www.prochoiceamerica.org and Twitter, @NARAL

National Assn. of Social Workers Political Action for Candidate Election, *750 1st St. N.E., #800, 20002-4241; (202) 408-8600. Fax, (202) 336-8312. Dena Kathener, Senior Political Affairs Associate.*
Web, www.socialworkers.org/advocacy/political-action-for-candidate-election-pace, Twitter, @nasw and Facebook, www.facebook.com/socialworkers

National Rifle Assn. of America–Political Victory Fund, *11250 Waples Mill Rd., Fairfax, VA 22030; (703) 267-1152. Mary R. Adkins, Treasurer; Chris Cox, Chair.*
Web, www.nrapvf.org, Twitter, @NRAPVF and Facebook, www.facebook.com/NationalRifleAssociation

Women's Campaign Fund, *718 7th St. N.W., 2nd Floor, 20001; (202) 796-8259. Betsy Mullins, President; Georgia Berner, Chair.*
General email, info@wcfonline.org
Web, www.wcfonline.org and Twitter, @WCFonline

A national nonpartisan organization dedicated to dramatically increasing the number of women in elected office.

▶ COMMUNICATIONS AND MEDIA

BSA—The Software Alliance PAC, *20 F St. N.W., #800, 20001; (202) 872-5500. Fax, (202) 872-5501. Leticia Lewis, Director of Policy.*
General email, info@bsa.org
Web, www.bsa.org

BSA pioneers compliance programs that promote legal software use and advocates public policies that foster technology innovation and drive growth in the digital economy.

Consumer Technology Assn. PAC, *1919 S. Eads St., Arlington, VA 22202; (703) 907-7600. Fax, (703) 907-7675. Glenda MacMullin, Treasurer; Gary Shapiro, President. Toll-free, (866) 858-1555. Toll-free fax, (866) 858-2555.*
General email, CTA@CTA.tech
Web, https://cta.tech/Policy/CTAPAC.aspx, Twitter, @CTATech and Facebook, www.facebook.com/ConsumerTechnologyAssociation

Dell Technologies PAC, *440 First St. N.W., #820, 20001; (202) 408-5905. Christopher Turner, Treasurer.*
General email, PAC@Dell.com
Web, www.dell.com/learn/is/en/iscorp1/corp-comm/public-policy

National Assn. of Broadcasters Political Action Committee, *1771 N St. N.W., 20036; (202) 429-5314. Jennifer Fleming, Director.*
General email, PAC@nab.org
Web, www.nabpac.com

National Cable and Telecommunications Assn. PAC, *25 Massachusetts Ave. N.W., #100, 20001; (202) 222-2516. Kenneth A. Gross, Treasurer.*
General email, info@ncta.com
Web, www.ncta.com, Twitter, @NCTAitv and Facebook, www.facebook.com/NCTAitv
Press, mediaoutreach@ncta.com

Printing Industries of America PAC, *1001 G St. N.W., #800, 20001; (202) 627-6925. Lisbeth Lyons, Vice President of Government Affairs, ext. 504.*
General email, printing@printing.org
Web, www.printpaconline.org

Verizon Communications Inc., PAC, *1300 Eye St. N.W., #500 East, 20005; (202) 515-2557. Taylor Craig, Treasurer.*
General email, taylor.k.craig@verizon.com
Web, https://vz.epacweb.com

▶ DEFENSE

Council for a Livable World, *820 1st St. N.E., #LL-180, 20002; (202) 543-4100. John Tierney, Executive Director, ext. 2108; James McKeon, Political Director, ext. 2617.*
General email, advocacy@clw.org
Web, https://livableworld.org and Twitter, @Livableworld

Supports congressional candidates who advocate arms control and progressive national security policy.

United Technologies Corp. PAC, *1101 Pennsylvania Ave. N.W., 10th Floor, 20004; (202) 336-7485. Krister J. Holladay, Treasurer.*
General email, pac@corpdc.utc.com
Web, www.utc.com

▶ ENERGY AND NATURAL RESOURCES

Action Committee for Rural Electrification *(National Rural Electric Cooperative Assn.), 4301 Wilson Blvd., Arlington, VA 22203-1860; (703) 907-5500. Fax, (703) 907-5516. Jim Matheson, Chief Executive Officer.*
Web, www.electric.coop

Membership: To power communities and empower members to improve the quality of their lives. Works to promote and support co-ops.

American Forest and Paper Assn. PAC, *1101 K St. N.W., #700, 20005; (202) 463-2755. Laura Pickard, Manager.*
General email, info@afandpa.org
Web, www.bipac.net/afpapac/login.asp

American Gas Assn. PAC (GASPAC), *400 N. Capitol St. N.W., #450, 20001; (202) 824-7231. Katie Tomarchio, Manager of Political Programs, (202) 824-7231.*
Web, www.aga.org/about/advocacy/gaspac, Twitter, @aga_naturalgas and Facebook, www.facebook.com/naturalgas

American Wind Energy Assn. PAC, *1501 M St. N.W., #900, 20005; (202) 383-2500. Fax, (202) 383-2505. Jenna Marinstein, Federal Legislative Affairs Associate.*
General email, jbeckwith@awea.org
Web, www.awea.org

Friends of the Earth PAC, *1101 15th St. N.W., 11th Floor, 20005; (202) 783-7400. Fax, (202) 783-0444. Erich Pica, Treasurer. Toll-free, 1 (877) 843-8687.*
Web, www.foeaction.org and Twitter, @foeaction

International Paper PAC, *1101 Pennsylvania Ave. N.W., #200, 20004; (202) 628-1223. Meaghan Killion Joyce, Political Affairs Manager, (202) 628-1321; Chris Keuleman, Global Vice President for Government Relations.*
General email, ippac@ipaper.com
Web, www.internationalpaper.com

National Alliance of Forest Owners PAC, *122 C St. N.W., #630, 20001; (202) 747-0759. Fax, (202) 824-0770. William (Chip) Murray, Vice President for Policy, (202) 747-0742.*

General email, info@nafoalliance.org

Web, www.nafoalliance.org

National Mining Assn., MINEPAC and COALPAC, 101 Constituion Ave. N.W., #500 East, 20001; (202) 463-2600, ext. 66526. Fax, (202) 463-2666. M. Richardson (Rich) Nolan, Treasurer.
Web, www.nma.org

Solar Energy Industries Assn. PAC, 1425 K St. N.W., #1000, 20005; (202) 682-0556. Fax, (202) 682-0559. Suzanne Farris, Director, (202) 556-2881.
General email, pac@seia.org

Web, www.seia.org/seia-solarpac and Twitter, @SEIA

Sustainable Energy and Environment Coalition PAC, 2463 RHOB, 20515; (202) 226-5034. Maria Laverdiere, Executive Director.
General email, info@seecpac.org

Web, http://seecpac.org, Twitter, @SEEC and Facebook, www.facebook.com/ SustainableEnergyandEnvironmentCoalition

House of Representatives Sustainable Energy & Environment Coalition, https://seec-tonko.house.gov

▶ **HEALTH**

American Assn. of Orthopaedic Surgeons, Orthopaedic PAC, 317 Massachusetts Ave. N.E.,#100, 20002; (202) 546-4430. Fax, (202) 546-5051. Stacie Monroe, Political Affairs Manager, (202) 584-4150.
General email, dc@aaos.org

Web, www.aaos.org/advocacy/pac, Twitter, @AAOSAdvocacy and Facebook, www.facebook .com/AAOS1

American College of Obstetricians and Gynecologists PAC, 409 12th St. S.W., 20024 (mailing address: Government Affairs, P.O. Box 96920, Washington, DC., 20090-6920); (202) 863-2509. Fax, (202) 488-3985. Mary Schilling, Political Advocacy Director, (202) 863-2512.
General email, Govtrel@acog.org

Web, www.obgynpac.org and Twitter, @ACOGAction

American College of Radiology Assn. PAC (RADPAC), 505 9th St. N.W., #910, 20004; Fax, (703) 262-9312. Ted Burnes, Director, (703) 648-8949. Toll-free, (888) 295-8843.
General email, tburnes@acr.org

Web, www.radpac.org and Twitter, @RADPAC

American Health Care Assn. Political Action Committee (AHCA-PAC), 1201 L St. N.W., 20005-4015; Fax, (202) 842-3860. Jennifer Knorr Hahs, Political Action Director, (202) 898-2844. General Phone, (202) 842-4444.
General email, PAC@ahca.org

Web, www.ahcancal.org

Membership: Standing in favor of protecting long term and post acute care. Protects against even more cuts to Medicare and Medicaid. Contacts legislators to help facilitate

health information technology, provide adequate funding. increase Licensure and Oversight of Assisted Living. Monitors legislation and regulations, especially with the Department of Labor.

American Hospital Assn. PAC, Two CityCenter, 800 10th St. N.W., #400, 20001-4956; (202) 638-1100. Tom Nickels, Executive Vice President of Government Affairs, (202) 626-2314. Help Line, (800) 424-4301.
Web, www.aha.org, Twitter, @AHAhospitals and Facebook, www.facebook.com/ahahospitals

American Medical Assn. Political Action Committee (AMPAC), 25 Massachusetts Ave. N.W., #600, 20001; (202) 789-7400. Fax, (202) 789-7469. Kevin L. Walker, Executive Director Public Affairs.
Web, www.ampaconline.org

American Osteopathic Information Assn. PAC, 1090 Vermont Ave. N.W., #500, 20005; (202) 414-0152. Fax, (800) 962-9008. Sean Neal, Director.
General email, opac@osteotech.org

Web, www.osteopathicpac.org and Twitter, @AOAforDOs

American Psychiatric Assn. PAC, 800 Maine Ave. S.W., #900, 20024; (703) 907-7300. David Keen, Chief Financial Officer.
General email, advocacy@psych.org

Web, www.psychiatry.org/psychiatrists/advocacy-apapac

American Veterinary Medical Assn. PAC, 1910 Sunderland Pl. N.W., 20036; (800) 321-1473. Fax, (202) 842-4360. Dr. Kent McClure, Chief Governmental Relations Officer.
General email, avmapac@avma.org

Web, www.avma.org/Advocacy/AVMAPAC/Pages/default .aspx and Twitter, @AVMACAN

Express Scripts Inc. PAC, 300 New Jersey Ave. N.W., #600, 20001; (202) 383-7983. Jonah Houts, Vice President of Government Affairs. Toll-free, (800) 282-2881.
General email, jhouts@express-scripts.com

Web, www.lab.express-scripts.com/about/government-relations

Humana Inc. PAC, 975 F St. N.W., #550, 20004; (202) 467-8682. Doug Stoss, Treasurer.
General email, humanapac@humana.com

Web, www.humana.com/about/public-policy/political-activity-contributions and Twitter, @Humana

National Active and Retired Federal Employees PAC (NARFE), 606 N. Washington St., Alexandria, VA 22314; (703) 838-7780. Fax, (703) 838-7785. John Hatton, Deputy Legislative Director. Member records, (800) 456-8410.
General email, advocacy@narfe.org

Web, www.narfe.org/legislation and Twitter, @narfehq

Supports health care and retirement benefits for current and retired federal employees.

National Committee to Preserve Social Security and Medicare PAC, *10 G St. N.E., #600, 20002-4215; (202) 216-0420. Fax, (202) 216-0446. Phillip Rotondi, Political Director; Dan Adcock, Director of Government Relations and Policy. Press, (202) 216-8378.*
Web, www.ncpssm.org, Twitter, @NCPSSM and Facebook, www.facebook.com/NationalCommittee

Natural Products Assn. PAC, *440 1st St. N.W., #520, 20001; (202) 204-4721. Daniel Fabricant, President, (202) 204-4721.*
General email, PAC@NPAnational.org
Web, www.npanational.org/advocacy/pac and Twitter, @NPANational

Interests include dietary supplements, personal care products, homecare products, and food.

Physical Therapy Political Action Committee (PT-PAC), *1111 N. Fairfax St., Alexandria, VA 22314-1488; (703) 684-2782. Fax, (703) 684-7343. Michael Matlack, Director, ext. 8533. Toll-free, (800) 999-2782.*
General email, ptpac@apta.org
Web, www.ptpac.org and Twitter, @PTPAC

Planned Parenthood Action Fund, *1110 Vermont Ave. N.W., #300, 20005; (202) 973-4800. Fax, (202) 296-3242. Dr. Leana Wen, President. Toll-free, (800) 430-4907.*
General email, actionfund@ppfa.org
Web, www.plannedparenthoodaction.org and Twitter, @PPAct

Nonpartisan organization that supports candidates who advocate for reproductive health care, including sex education, health care reform for women, birth control, and legal abortion access in the United States.

Population Connection Action Fund PAC, *2120 L St. N.W., #500, 20037; (202) 332-2200. Fax, (202) 332-2302. Brian Dixon, Senior Vice President of Media and Government Relations. Toll-free, (800) 767-1956.*
General email, info@popconnectaction.org
Web, www.populationconnectionaction.org and Twitter, @popconnect

Interests include U.S. foreign aid for international family planning, affordable contraceptives access, and population growth education.

Seniors Housing Political Action Committee, *5225 Wisconsin Ave. N.W., #502, 20015; (202) 237-0900. Fax, (202) 237-1616. Jeanne McGlynn Delgado, Vice President of Government Affairs.*
Web, https://seniorshousing.org/sh-pac-steering-committee.php

▶ **LABOR**

Active Ballot Club *(United Food and Commercial Workers International Union, AFL-CIO), 1775 K St. N.W., 20006; (202) 223-3111. Fax, (202) 728-1830. Anthony M. (Marc) Perrone, President; Esther López, Secretary-Treasurer.*

Web, www.ufcwaction.org/abc, Twitter, @UFCW and Facebook, www.facebook.com/ufcwinternational

Advocates for higher wages and paid sick leave, and works toward achieving economic stabilty for workers.

Air Line Pilots Assn. PAC, *1625 Massachusetts Ave. N.W., 8th Floor, 20036; (703) 689-2270. Capt. Joe DePete, President; Capt. Joseph A. Genovese, Jr., Treasurer. Toll-free, (888) 359-2572.*
Web, www.alpa.org/advocacy/alpa-pac

Helps educate decision makers in DC. understand the issues of about pilots, flight concerns and technology; builds pilot partisan majorities in the House and Senate.

Amalgamated Transit Union—COPE (Committee on Political Education), *10000 New Hampshire Ave., Silver Spring, MD 20903; (301) 431-7100. Fax, (301) 431-7117. Oscar Owens, International Treasurer. Toll- Free, (888) 240-1196.*
Web, www.atu.org/action/atu-cope

American Federation of State, County and Municipal Employees (AFSCME), *1625 L St. N.W., 20036-5687; (202) 429-1000. Fax, (202) 429-1293. Lee A. Saunders, President. Press, (202) 429-1145. TTY, (202) 659-0446.*
Web, www.afscme.org, Twitter, @AFSCME and Facebook, www.facebook.com/ASFCME

American Federation of Teachers (AFT), *Political Dept., 555 New Jersey Ave. N.W., 20001; (202) 879-4400. Randi Weingarten, President; Lorretta Johnson, Secretary-Treasurer. Press, (202) 879-4458.*
Web, www.aft.org/position/federal-legislation-and-advocacy, Twitter, @rweingarten and Facebook, www.facebook.com/AFTUnion
Advocacy email, highered@aft.org

American Road and Transportation Builders Assn. PAC, *1219 28th St. N.W., 20007; (202) 289-4434. Fax, (202) 289-4435. Nick Goldstein, Assistant General Counsel, (202) 683-1005.*
General email, ngoldstein@artba.org
Web, www.artba.org/government-affairs/political-action-committee and Twitter, @ARTBA

Associated Builders and Contractors PAC, *440 1st St. N.W., #200, 20001; (202) 595-1505. Chris Singerling, Treasurer.*
General email, gotquestions@abc.org
Web, www.abc.org, Twitter, @ABCNational and Facebook, www.facebook.com/ABCNational

BUILD PAC of the National Assn. of Home Builders, *1201 15th St. N.W., 20005-2800; (202) 266-8259. Fax, (202) 266-8400. Jim Tobin, Executive Vice President. Toll free, (800) 368-5342.*
Web, www.nahb.org/buildpac

Membership: includes building contractors, remodelers, and others who support candidates and issues affecting the home-building industry.

Carpenters Legislative Improvement Committee, *United Brotherhood of Carpenters and Joiners of America,* 101 Constitution Ave. N.W., 10th Floor, 20001; (202) 546-6206. Andris J. Silins, Treasurer; Douglas J. McCarron, President.

General email, webmaster@carpenters.org

Web, www.carpenters.org, Twitter, @UBCJA_Official and Facebook, www.facebook.com/CarpentersUnited

Committee on Letter Carriers Political Education *(National Assn. of Letter Carriers, AFL-CIO),* 100 Indiana Ave. N.W., 20001-2144; (202) 393-4695. Fax, (202) 756-7400. Fredric V. Rolando, President; Brian Renfroe, Executive Vice President. Legislation information, (202) 662-2833.

General email, nalcinf@nalc.org

Web, www.nalc.org and Twitter, @NALC_National

Committee on Political Action of the American Postal Workers Union, 1300 L St. N.W., 20005; (202) 842-4210. Fax, (202) 682-2528. Judy Beard, Legislative and Political Director, (202) 842-4211.

Web, www.apwu.org and Twitter, @apwunational

CWA-COPE Political Contributions Committee *(Communications Workers of America, AFL-CIO),* 501 3rd St. N.W., 20001-2797; (202) 434-1100. Fax, (202) 434-1279. Chris Shelton, President.

Web, www.cwa-union.org

International Assn. of Fire Fighters PAC, 1750 New York Ave. N.W., #300, 20006-5395; (202) 804-1581. Fax, (202) 737-8418. Shannon Meissner, Director of Governmental Affairs.

General email, btimmins@IAFF.org

Web, www.client.prod.iaff.org/#page=governmental

International Assn. of Sheet Metal, Air, Rail, and Transportation Workers, Political Action League, 1750 New York Ave. N.W., 6th Floor, 20006-5386; (202) 662-0800. Fax, (202) 662-0880. John Risch, SMART National Legislative Director, (202) 543-7714; Joe Sellers, President, (202) 662-0845. Toll-free, (800) 457-7694.

General email, info@smart-union.org

Web, http://smart-union.org

International Brotherhood of Electrical Workers PAC, 900 7th St. N.W., 20001; (202) 833-7000. Fax, (202) 728-6144. Austin Keyser, Director of Political and Legislative Affairs, (202) 728-6046. Press, (202) 728-6014.

General email, Political@ibew.org

Web, www.ibew.org/Political

International Brotherhood of Teamsters, *Federal Legislation and Regulation,* 25 Louisiana Ave. N.W., 20001-2194; (202) 624-6993. Fax, (202) 624-6992. Christy Bailey, Director; Ken Hall, General Secretary–Treasurer. Press, (202) 624-6911.

General email, drive@teamster.org

Web, www.teamster.org

International Union of Operating Engineers, *Engineers Political Education Committee,* 1125 17th St. N.W., 20036; (202) 429-9100, ext. 2682. Fax, (202) 778-2688. Brian E. Hickey, Treasurer.

Web, www.iuoe.org/about-iuoe/iuoe-legislative-and-political-affairs

Ironworkers Political Action League, 1750 New York Ave. N.W., #400, 20006; (202) 383-4800. Fax, (202) 638-4856. Ross Templeton, Political and Legislative Director.

General email, iwmagazine@wintl.org

Web, www.ironworkers.org, Twitter, @TheIronworkers and Facebook, www.facebook.com/impactironworkers

Laborers' Political League of Laborers' International Union of North America, 905 16th St. N.W., 20006-1765; (202) 942-2272. Fax, (202) 942-2307. David Mallino, Legislative and Political Director, (202) 942-2273; Armand E. Sabitoni, General Secretary-Treasurer, (401) 751-8010.

General email, dmallino@liuna.org

Web, www.liuna.org

Machinists Non-Partisan Political League *(International Assn. of Machinists and Aerospace Workers, AFL-CIO),* 9000 Machinists Pl., Upper Marlboro, MD 20772-2687; (301) 967-4500. Fax, (301) 967-4595. Rick de la Fuente, Political Action Director; Hasan Solomon, Legislative Director; Dora Cerventes, General Secretary–Treasurer.

General email, info@iamaw.org

Web, www.goiam.org/index.php/mnpl

National Air Traffic Controllers Assn. PAC, 1325 Massachusetts Ave. N.W., 20005; (202) 628-5451. Fax, (202) 628-5767. Michelle Fevola, PAC and Political Representative.

General email, eweaver@natcadc.org

Web, www.natca.org

National Education Assn. Fund for Children and Public Education, 1201 16th St. N.W., #510, 20036-3290; (202) 833-4000. Fax, (202) 822-7309. Mary Kusler, Director. Press, (202) 822-7823.

General Email, neafund@nea.org and Web, www.neafund.org

National Lumber and Building Material Dealers Assn. PAC, 2025 M St. N.W., #800, 20036; (202) 367-1169. Ben Gann, Vice President of Political and Legislative Affairs.

General email, MemberSupport@dealer.org

Web, www.dealer.org/?page=PoliticalAction and Twitter, @NLBMDA

National Roofing Contractors Assn. PAC, 324 4th St. N.E., 20002; (202) 546-7584. Nathan Pick, Director of Advocacy and Political Affairs.

General email, info@nrca.net

Web, www.nrca.net/roofing/ROOFPAC-622 and Twitter, @NRCAnews

National Stone, Sand, and Gravel Assn., *ROCK PAC,* 66 *Canal Center Plazea, #300, Alexandria, VA 22314; (703) 525-8788. Michael Johnson, Treasurer; Jim Riley, President; Laura Hylden Henry, PAC Director. Toll-free, (800) 342-1415.*
Web, www.nssga.org/advocacy/rockpac, Twitter, @NSSGA and Facebook, www.facebook.com/nssga

Professional Aviation Safety Specialists PAC, *1200 G St. N.W., #750, 20005; (202) 293-7277. Fax, (202) 293-7727. Sophie White, Legislative Affairs Director.*
Web, www.passnational.org and Twitter, @passnational

United Mine Workers of America, *Coal Miners PAC,* 18354 *Quantico Gateway Dr., #200, Triangle, VA 22172; (703) 291-2400. Levi D. Allen, Secretary-Treasurer, (703) 291-2401.*
General email, info@umwa.org
Web, www.umwa.org

United Mine Workers of America, *Power PAC,* 18354 *Quantico Gateway Dr., #200, Triangle, VA 22172-1779; (703) 291-2400. Levi D. Allen, Secretary-Treasurer.*
General email, mdelbalzo@umwa.org
Web, www.umwa.org

▶ NONCONNECTED

314 Action Fund PAC, *410 1st St.Washington, DC, 20003 (mailing address: P.O. BOX 14560, Washington, DC 20044); (267) 544-9099. (434) 362-0238. Joshua Morrow, Executive Director.*
General email, info@314action.org
Web, www.314action.org, Twitter, @314action and Facebook, www.facebook.com/314Action

Supports candidates who advocate for innovation in Science, Technology, Engineering, and Mathematics (STEM) education.

America Votes, *1155 Connecticut Ave. N.W., #600, 20036; (202) 962-7240. Fax, (202) 962-7241. Greg Speed, President; Sara Schreiber, Managing Director.*
Web, www.americavotes.org, Twitter, @AmericaVotes and Facebook, www.facebook.com/AmericaVotesOrg

Seeks to mobilize Americans to register and vote around critical issues.

Automotive Free International Trade PAC, *1625 Prince St., #225, Alexandria, VA 22314-2889; (703) 684-8880. Fax, (703) 684-8920. Mary Hanagan, Executive Director. Toll-free, (800) 234-8748.*
General email, information@afitpac.com
Web, www.afitpac.com

Black America's PAC, *1325 G St. N.W., #500, 20005; (202) 552-7422. Fax, (202) 552-7421. Alvin Williams, President.*
General email, www.bampac.org/bampac_contact form.org
Web, www.bampac.org and Twitter, @BAM_PAC

Club for Growth, *2001 L St. N.W., #600, 20036; (202) 955-5500. Fax, (202) 955-9466. David McIntosh, President. Toll-free, (855) 432-0899.*
General email, press@clubforgrowth.org
Web, www.clubforgrowth.org and Twitter, @Club4Growth

Promotes mainly Republican candidates with conservative economic policies and voting records. Interests include limited government, low taxes, estate tax repeal, social security reform, free trade, tax code reform, school choice, and deregulation.

Deloitte and Touche LLP Federal PAC, *P.O. Box 365, 20044; (202) 734-3180. Heidi Green, Treasurer.*
General email, deloittepac@deloitte.com
Web, www.deloittepac.com

EMILY's List, *1800 M St., #375N, 20036; (202) 326-1400. Fax, (202) 326-1415. Stephanie Schriock, President. Toll-free, 800-68-EMILY.*
Web, www.emilyslist.org and Twitter, @emilyslist

Raises money and helps to support pro-choice Democratic women candidates for political office.

Gay & Lesbian Victory Fund and Leadership Institute, *1225 Eye St. N.W., #525, 20005; (202) 842-8679. Fax, (202) 289-3863. Annise Parker, President.*
Web, www.victoryfund.org, Twitter, @VictoryFund and Facebook, www.facebook.com/victoryfund

Identifies, trains, and supports open lesbian, gay, bisexual, transgender, and queer (LGBTQ) candidates and officials at the local, state, and federal levels of government.

Giffords PAC, *P.O. Box 51196, 20091; (571) 295-7807. Peter Ambler, Executive Director.*
General email, info@giffords.org
Web, http://giffords.org and Twitter, @GiffordsCourage

Supports candidates in favor of gun control.

GOPAC, *1201 Wilson Blvd., #2110, Arlington, VA 22209; (703) 566-0376. Jessica Curtis, Executive Director.*
General email, contact@gopac.org
Web, www.gopac.org and Twitter, @GOPAC

Recruits and trains conservative Republican candidates for local and state office.

KPMG PAC, *1801 K St. N.W., #12000, 20006 (mailing address: P.O. Box 18254, Washington, DC 20036-9998); (202) 533-3800. Fax, (202) 533-8516. Lynne Doughtie, Chief Executive Officer; Manal S. Corwin, Principal-in-Charge, in Washington, D.C.*
Web, www.kpmg.com and Twitter, @kpmg_us

Global network of LLP firms providing audit, tax, and advisory services to businesses.

L PAC, *2120 L St. N.W., #850, 20037; 810 7th St. N.E., 20002; (202) 629-0298. Stephanie Sandberg, Executive Director.*
General email, info@teamlpac.com
Web, www.teamlpac.com, Twitter, @TeamLPAC and Facebook, www.facebook.com/teamlpac

Supports candidates who champion LGBTQ rights, women's equality, and social justice.

New Democrat Coalition PAC, *1410 LHOB, Washington, DC, 20515; (202) 225-5916. Ami Bera, Co-Chair; Derek Kilmer, Co-Chair; Helen Milby, Treasurer.*
Web, www.newdempac.com, Twitter, @HouseNewDems and Facebook, www.facebook.com/NewDemocratCoalition

Supports election and reelection of Democrats to the House of Representatives.

PricewaterhouseCoopers PAC, *600 13th St. N.W., #600, 20005; (202) 414-1000. Fax, (202) 414-1301. Gary Price, Chief Administrative Officer; Roz Brooks, Managing Director of Government, Regulatory Affairs, and Public Policy.*
Web, http://pwc.com and Twitter, @PWC_LLP

Value in Electing Women PAC, *701 8th St. N.W., #500, 20001; (703) 801-3465. Julie Conway, Executive Director.*
General email, julie@viewpac.org
Web, www.viewpac.org

Focuses on supporting female Republican congressional candidates.

The Washington PAC, *444 N. Capitol St. N.W., #618, 20001; (202) 347-6613. Fax, (202) 393-7006. Morris J. Amitay, Founder.*
General email, MJA@WashingtonPAC.com
Web, www.washingtonpac.com

Promotes pro-Israel policies.

Women Under Forty PAC, *303 17th St. S.E., 20003; (626) 688-4834. Katie Vlietstra Wonnenberg, Treasurer.*
General email, info@wufpac.org
Web, www.wufpac.org and Twitter, @wufpac

Supports young female congressional candidates.

Airlines for America PAC, *1275 Pennsylvania Ave. N.W., #1300, 20004; (202) 626-4205. Paul E. Archambeault, Treasurer.*
General email, mediarelations@airlines.org
Web, www.airlines.org/about-us and Twitter, @AirlinesDotOrg

Assn. of Global Automakers Inc. PAC (Drive2Action PAC), *1050 K St. N.W., #650, 20001; (202) 650-5555. Damon Porter, Vice President of Government Affairs.*
General email, info@globalautomakers.org
Web, www.globalautomakers.org/advocacy/political-action-committee and Twitter, @GloblAutomkrs

NADA PAC (National Automobile Dealers Assn.), *8484 Westpark Dr., #500, Tysons Corner, VA 22102; (202) 627-6755. Fax, (202) 627-6750. Peter Welch, President. Toll-free, (800) 557-6232.*
General email, nadapac@nada.org
Web, www.nada.org/NADAPAC

Formerly the Dealers Election Action Committee, or DEAC.

Super Political Action Committees

Independent expenditure-only committees, commonly known as SuperPACs, are organizations registered with the Federal Election Commission that may raise unlimited funds from individuals, corporations, businesses, and others to advocate for or against specific candidates for public office. Direct contributions to candidates' campaigns are prohibited.

▶**NONCONNECTED**

America Votes Action Fund, *1555 Connecticut Ave. N.W., #600, 20036; (202) 962-7240. Susan Finkle-Sourlis, Treasurer.*
General email, actionfund@americavotes.org
Web, www.americavotes.org, Twitter, @AmericaVotes and Facebook, www.facebook.com/AmericaVotesOrg

Works with over 400 state and national partner organizations to advance progressive policies, win elections, and protect every American's right to vote.

American Crossroads, *P.O. Box 34413, 20043; (202) 559-6428. Steven Law, President.*
General email, info@americancrossroads.org
Web, www.americancrossroads.org, Twitter, @AmericanCrossroads and Facebook, www.facebook.com/AmericanCrossroads

Promotes Republican candidates who support strong defense, free enterprise, and limited government. Targets voters through television ads, mailings, and phone campaigns.

American Dental Assn. PAC, *1111 14th St. N.W., #1100, 20005; (202) 898-2424. Sarah Milligan, Director, (202) 789-5171; Dr. Tommy Harrison, Chair.*
General email, adpac@ada.org
Web, www.ada.org/en/advocacy/adpac

Nonpartisan organization that promotes congressional candidates who advocate for dentists, oral health, and oral health's connection to overall health. Provides educational resources to dentists interested in seeking public office at local, state, or national levels.

Congressional Leadership Fund, *1747 Pennsylvania Ave. N.W., 5th Floor, 20006; (205) 908-2299. Caleb Crosby, Treasurer.*
General email, contact@congressionalleadershipfund.org
Web, www.congressionalleadershipfund.org, Twitter, @CLFSuperPAC and Facebook, www.facebook .com/CongressionalLeadershipFund

Supports a Republican majority in the House of Representatives.

Defending Main Street Super PAC, *325 7th St. N.W., #610, 20004; (202) 393-4353. Fax, (202) 393-4354. Sarah Chamberlain, Executive Director.*

General email, mainstreetgop@gmail.com

Web, www.mainstreetpac.com, Twitter, @MainStreetGOP and Facebook, www.facebook.com/MainStreetGOP

Represents and supports Republican candidates who work across party lines.

Freedom Partners Action Fund, 2300 Wilson Blvd., #500, Arlington, VA 22201; (202) 557-1398. Thomas F. Maxwell III, Treasurer.
General email, info@fpaction.org

Web, https://fpaction.org, Twitter, @FPActionFund and Facebook, www.facebook.com/fpaction

Supports Senate candidates who promote free markets and a free society.

FreedomWorks for America, 400 N. Capitol St. N.W., #765, 20001; (202) 783-3870. Noah Wall, Executive Director.
Web, www.freedomworksforamerica.org and Twitter, @FWForAmerica

Promotes conservative grassroots candidates who advocate lower taxes and smaller government.

House Majority PAC, 700 13th St. N.W., #600, 20005; (202) 853-9089. Alixandria Lapp, President.
General email, info@thehousemajoritypac.com

Web, www.thehousemajoritypac.com, Twitter, @HouseMajPAC and Facebook, www.facebook .com/HouseMajorityPAC

Supports Democratic candidates for the House of Representatives.

League of Conservation Voters Action Fund, 740 15th St. N.W., 7th Floor, 20005; (202) 785-8683. Fax, (202) 835-0491. Sara Chieffo, Vice President for Government Affairs.
General email, feedback@lcv.org

Web, www.lcv.org, Twitter, @LCVoters and Facebook, www.facebook.com/LCVoters

Supports candidates who implement environmental laws and policies.

Local Voices, 1666 Connecticut Ave. N.W., 5th Floor, 20009; (213) 925-7535. Houston King, Treasurer.
Web, www.localvoices.org, Twitter, @LocalVoicesUS and Facebook, www.facebook.com/LocalVoicesUS

Creates Democratic campaign ads in battleground states featuring local voices sharing their political views.

National Realtors Assn. Political Action Committee, 500 New Jersey Ave. N.W., 20001-2020; (202) 383-1000. Shannon McGahn, Senior Vice President of Government Affairs, (202) 383-1205. Toll-free, (800) 874-6500.
Web, www.nar.realtor/topics/rpac

Nonpartisan organization that promotes federal, state, and local candidates who advocate for private property rights and free enterprise. (Headquarters in Chicago.)

New American Jobs Fund, 740 15th St., 7th Floor, 20005; Patrick Collins, Treasurer. Phon, (202) 785-8683.
General email, info@newamericanjobs.org

Web, www.newamericanjobsfund.org

Supports candidates seeking to build a clean energy economy and create jobs.

Priorities USA Action, 1150 18th St. N.W., 20036; (202) 796-1130. Jim Shesel, Finance Officer; Patrick McHugh, Executive Director.
General email, press@priorities.org

Web, www.prioritiesusaaction.org, Twitter, @prioritiesUSA and Facebook, www.facebook.com/PrioritiesUSA

Voter-centric progressive advocacy organization and service center for the grassroots progressive movement.

Women Speak Out PAC, 2800 Shirlington Rd., #1200, Arlington, VA 22206; (202) 223-8073. Emily Buchanan, Executive Director.
Web, www.sba-list.org/women-speak-out-pac, Twitter, @SBAList and Facebook, www.facebook.com/SusanBAnthonyList

Supports congressional candidates opposed to abortion.

Women Vote!—EMILY's List, 1800 M St. N.W., #375N, 20036; (202) 326-1400. Stephanie Schriock, President. Toll-free, (800) 683-6459.
General email, press@emilyslist.org

Web, http://emilyslist.org/pages/entry/women-vote and Twitter, @emilyslist

Seeks to influence women to vote for pro-choice Democratic women candidates and other Democratic candidates. Targets candidates opposed to these positions.

Working America Coalition, 815 16th St. N.W., 20006; (202) 637-5137. Crystal King, Treasurer.
General email, info@workingamerica.org

Web, www.workingamericavotes.org, Twitter, @WorkingAmericavotes and Facebook, www .facebook.com/WorkingAmerica

Works to elect progressive candidates and pass legislation to improve the lives of working families.

Working for Us PAC, 888 16th St. N.W., #650, 20006; (202) 499-7420. Steve Rosenthal, President.
General email, info@workingforuspac.org

Web, www.workingforuspac.org

Promotes candidates focused on job creation, health care reform, and expanding public services. Campaigns against candidates opposed to these principles. (Affiliated with The Organizing Group.)

Political Interest Groups

►NONGOVERNMENTAL

American Conservative Union (ACU), 1331 H St. N.W., #500, 20005; (202) 347-9388. Fax, (202) 347-9389. Dan Schneider, Executive Director; Michi Iljazi, Director of Government Affairs.
General email, contact@conservative.org

Web, http://conservative.org, Twitter, @ACUConservative and Facebook, www.facebook.com/ACUConservative

Legislative interest organization that focuses on defense, foreign policy, economics, the national budget, taxes, and legal and social issues. Monitors legislation and regulations.

American Family Voices, *1250 Eye St. N.W., #250, 20005; (202) 393-4352. Michael Lux, President; Lauren Windsor, Executive Director.*
General email, admin@americanfamilyvoices.org
Web, http://americanfamilyvoices.org, Twitter, @AFVhq and Facebook, www.facebook.com/AmericanFamilyVoices

Acts as advocate on behalf of middle-class and low-income families dealing with economic, health care, and consumer issues.

American Opportunity, *901 N. Washington St., #206, Alexandria, VA 22314; (703) 837-0030.*
James S. (Jim) Gilmore, President.
General email, contact@americanopportunity.org
Web, www.americanopportunity.org, Twitter, @ameriopp and Facebook, www.facebook.com/americanopportunity .org

Conservative political think tank that promotes traditional values. Primary interests are economic and foreign policy. (Formerly the Free Congress Research and Education Foundation [FCF]).

Americans for Democratic Action, *1629 K St. N.W., #300, 20006; (202) 600-7762. Fax, (202) 204-8637. Don Kusler, National Director.*
General email, info@adaction.org
Web, www.adaction.org and Twitter, @ADAction

Legislative interest organization that seeks to strengthen civil, constitutional, women's, family, workers', and human rights, and promotes grassroots activism. Interests include education, health care, immigration, peace, tax reform, and voter access.

Americans for Prosperity, *1310 N. Courthouse Rd., #700, Arlington, VA 22201; (703) 224-3200. Fax, (703) 224-3201. Emily Seidel, Chief Executive Officer. Toll-free, (866) 730-0150.*
General email, info@AFPhq.org
Web, www.americansforprosperity.org and Twitter, @AFPhq

Grassroots organization that seeks to educate citizens about economic policy and encourage their participation in the public policy process. Supports limited government and free markets on the local, state, and federal levels. Specific interests include Social Security, trade, and taxes. Monitors legislation and regulations.

Cato Institute, *1000 Massachusetts Ave. N.W., 20001-5403; (202) 842-0200. Fax, (202) 842-3490. Peter Goettler, President. Press, (202) 842-5251.*
General email, pr@cato.org
Web, www.cato.org and Twitter, @CatoInstitute

Public policy research organization that advocates limited government and individual liberty. Interests include privatization and deregulation, low and simple taxes, and

reduced government spending. Encourages voluntary solutions to social and economic problems.

Center for American Progress, *1333 H St. N.W., 10th Floor, 20005; (202) 682-1611. Fax, (202) 682-1867. Neera Tanden, President.*
General email, progress@americanprogress.org
Web, www.americanprogress.org and Twitter, @amprog

Nonpartisan research and educational institute that strives to ensure opportunity for all Americans. Advocates policies to create sustained economic growth and new opportunities. Supports fiscal discipline, shared prosperity, and investments in people through education, health care, and workforce training.

Center for Public Justice, *312 Massachusetts Ave. N.E., 20002 (mailing address: P.O. Box 48368, Washington, DC 20002-0368); (202) 695-2667. Stephanie Summers, Chief Executive Officer.*
General email, inquiries@cpjustice.org
Web, www.cpjustice.org and Twitter, @cpjustice

Christian think tank advocating biblical-based solutions to policymakers. Interests include education reform, foreign affairs, welfare policy, and religious freedom.

Christian Coalition of America, *P.O. Box 37030, 20013-7030; (202) 479-6900. Fax, (202) 479-4262. Roberta Combs, President. Press, (202) 549-6257.*
General email, coalition@cc.org
Web, http://cc.org and Twitter, @ccoalition

Membership: individuals who support traditional, conservative Christian values. Represents members' views to all levels of government and to the media.

Christian Science Committee on Publication, *Federal Office, 444 N. Capitol St. N.W., #601, 20001; (202) 296-2190. Tessa E.B. Frost, Director of Federal Government Affairs.*
General email, federal@christianscience.com
Web, www.christianscience.com/member-resources/ committee-on-publication

Works with Congress and regulatory agencies to ensure that the interests of Christian Science are not adversely affected by law or regulations.

Common Cause, *805 15th St. N.W., #800, 20005; (202) 833-1200. Karen Hobert Flynn, President. Press, (202) 736-5788.*
General email, CauseNet@commoncause.org
Web, www.commoncause.org and Twitter, @CommonCause

Nonpartisan citizens' lobby that works for reform in federal and state government and politics. Advocates national and state limits on political spending, small donor-based public financing of election campaigns, high ethical standards and tough ethics enforcement for public officials, strong voting rights laws and modern voting equipment, and free exchange of ideas online.

Concerned Women for America, *1015 15th St. N.W., #1100, 20005; (202) 488-7000. Fax, (202) 488-0806. Penny Young Nance, Chief Executive Officer. Web, https://concernedwomen.org and Twitter, @CWforA*

Public policy organization that seeks to protect the rights of the family and preserve Judeo-Christian values. Monitors legislation affecting family and religious issues.

The Conservative Caucus (TCC), *332 W. Lee Hwy., #221, Warrenton, VA 20816; (540) 219-4536. Peter J. Thomas, Chair. General email, info@conservativeusa.org*

Web, www.conservativeusa.org and Twitter, @ConservCaucus

Legislative interest organization that promotes grass-roots activity on issues such as national defense and economic and tax policy. The Conservative Caucus Research, Analysis, and Education Foundation studies public issues including Central American affairs, defense policy, and federal funding of political advocacy groups.

Eagle Forum, *Washington Office, 316 Pennsylvania Ave. S.E., #203, 20003; (757) 277-4848. Fax, (202) 547-6996. Eunie Smith, President; Colleen Holcomb, Chief Administrator, in Washington, D.C. General email, Eagle@EagleForum.org*

Web, www.eagleforum.org and Twitter, @EagleForum

Supports conservative, pro-family policies at all levels of government. Promotes traditional marriage, pro-life policies, limited government, and American sovereignty. Other concerns include education, national defense, and taxes. (Headquarters in Alton, Ill.)

English First, *8001 Forbes Pl., #202, Springfield, VA 22151-2205; (703) 321-8818. Frank McGlynn, Executive Director. Web, www.englishfirst.org*

Seeks to make English the official language of the United States. Advocates policies that make English education available to all children. Monitors legislation and regulations. Opposes multilingual education and governmental policies, including Clinton Executive Order 13166.

Family Research Council, *801 G St. N.W., 20001-3729; (202) 393-2100. Fax, (202) 393-2134. Tony Perkins, President. Toll-free, (800) 225-4008. Web, www.frc.org, Twitter, @FRCdc and Facebook, www.facebook.com/familyresearchcouncil*

Legislative interest organization that analyzes issues affecting the family and seeks to ensure that the interests of the family are considered in the formulation of public policy.

Feminist Majority, *1600 Wilson Blvd., #801, Arlington, VA 22209-2505; (703) 522-2214. Fax, (703) 522-2219. Eleanor Smeal, President; Alice Cohan, Political Director. General email, feedback@feminist.org*

Web, www.feministmajority.org, Twitter, @femmajority and Facebook, www.facebook.com/FeministMajorityFoundation

Legislative interest group that seeks to increase the number of feminists running for public office; promotes a national feminist agenda.

Food Policy Action, *1436 U St. N.W., #200, 20009; (202) 997-3266. Monica Mills, Executive Director. General email, info@foodpolicyaction.org*

Web, http://foodpolicyaction.org, Twitter, @FPAction and Facebook, www.facebook.com/FoodPolicyAction

Promotes policies that support healthful food options; works to reduce hunger and improve food access; publishes a congressional vote and legislation scorecard.

FreedomWorks, *111 K St. N.E., #600, 20002; (202) 783-3870. Fax, (202) 942-7649. Adam Brandon, President. Toll-free, (888) 564-6273. Web, www.freedomworks.org, Twitter, @FreedomWorks and Facebook, www.facebook.com/FreedomWorks*

Recruits, educates, trains, and mobilizes volunteer activists to promote lower taxes, less government, and greater economic freedom. Maintains scorecards on members of the Senate and House based on adherence to Freedom-Works positions.

Friends Committee on National Legislation (FCNL), *245 2nd St. N.E., 20002-5795; (202) 547-6000. Fax, (202) 547-6019. Diane Randall, Executive Secretary. Recorded information, (202) 547-4343. Toll-free, (800) 630-1330. General email, fcnl@fcnl.org*

Web, www.fcnl.org, Twitter, @FCNL and Facebook, www.facebook.com/quakerlobby

Advocates economic justice, world disarmament, international cooperation, and religious rights. Acts as advocate on behalf of Native Americans in such areas as treaty rights, self-determination, and U.S. trust responsibilities. Conducts research and educational activities through the FCNL Education Fund. Opposes the death penalty. Monitors national legislation and policy. (Affiliated with the Religious Society of Friends [Quakers].)

Frontiers of Freedom, *4094 Majestic Blvd., #380, Fairfax, VA 22033; (703) 246-0110. Fax, (703) 246-0129. George C. Landrith, President. General email, info@ff.org*

Web, www.ff.org, Twitter, @FoF_Liberty and Facebook, www.facebook.com/FrontiersofFreedom

Seeks to increase personal freedom through a reduction in the size of government. Interests include property rights, regulatory and tax reform, global warming, national missile defense, Internet regulation, school vouchers, and Second Amendment rights. Monitors legislation and regulations.

The Heritage Foundation, *214 Massachusetts Ave. N.E., 20002-4999; (202) 546-4400. Fax, (202) 546-8328. Kay Coles James, President. Press, (202) 675-1761. General email, info@heritage.org*

Web, www.heritage.org

Conservative public policy research organization that conducts research and analysis and sponsors lectures, debates, and policy forums advocating individual freedom, limited government, the free market system, and a strong national defense.

Institute on Religion and Democracy, *1023 15th St. N.W., #601, 20005-2601; (202) 682-4131. Fax, (202) 682-4136. Mark Tooley, President.*
General email, info@theird.org

Web, www.theird.org, Twitter, @theIRD and Facebook, www.facebook.com/TheIRD

Interdenominational bipartisan organization that supports democratic and constitutional forms of government consistent with the values of Christianity. Serves as a resource center to promote Christian perspectives on U.S. national and foreign policy questions. Interests include international conflicts, religious liberties, and the promotion of democratic forms of government in the United States and worldwide.

Log Cabin Republicans, *1090 Vermont Ave. N.W., #850, 20005; (202) 420-7873. Jerri Ann Henry, Executive Director.*
General email, info@logcabin.org

Web, www.logcabin.org

Membership: lesbian, gay, bisexual, transgender, and allied Republicans. Educates conservative politicians and voters on LGBT issues; disseminates information; conducts seminars for members. Promotes conservative values among members of the gay community. Raises campaign funds. Monitors legislation and regulations.

National Center for Public Policy Research, *Project 21, 20 F St. N.W., #700, 20001; (202) 507-6398, ext. 11. Fax, (202) 543-5975. David W. Almasi, Vice President.*
General email, project21@nationalcenter.org

Web, www.nationalcenter.org/P21Index.html and Facebook, www.facebook.com/NCPPR

Promotes public policies to counter the disenfranchisement of African Americans. Interests include affirmative action and reparations.

National Jewish Democratic Council, *P.O. Box 65683, 20035; (202) 216-9060. Greg Rosenbaum, Chair.*
General email, info@njdc.org

Web, www.njdc.org and Twitter, @NJDC

Encourages Jewish involvement in the Democratic party and its political campaigns. Monitors and analyzes domestic and foreign policy issues that concern the American Jewish community.

National Organization for Marriage, *2029 K St. N.W., #300, 20006; (888) 894-3604. Brian S. Brown, President.*
General email, contact@nationformarriage.org

Web, www.nationformarriage.org and Twitter, @NOMupdate

Supports marriage-related initiatives at state and local levels, with an emphais on the Northeast and West Coast. Opposes same-sex marriage. Monitors legislation.

National Organization for Women (NOW), *1100 H St. N.W., #300, 20005; (202) 628-8669. Toni Van Pelt, President. TTY, (202) 331-9002.*

General email, now@now.org

Web, www.now.org and Twitter, @NationalNOW

Membership: women and men interested in feminist civil rights. Acts through demonstrations, court cases, and legislative efforts to improve the status of all women. Interests include increasing the number of women in elected and appointed office, improving women's economic status and health coverage, ending violence against women, preserving abortion rights, and abolishing discrimination based on gender, race, age, and sexual orientation.

National Taxpayers Union, *Communications, 122 C St. N.W., #650, 20001; (703) 683-5700. Peter Sepp, President; Nan Swift, Federal Affairs.*
General email, ntu@ntu.org

Web, www.ntu.org and Twitter, @NTU

Citizens' interest group that promotes tax and spending reduction at all levels of government. Supports constitutional amendments to balance the federal budget and limit taxes.

NDN (New Democrat Network), *800 Maine Ave. S.W., #200, 20024; (202) 544-9200. Simon Rosenberg, President.*
General email, info@ndn.org

Web, www.ndn.org

Studies progressive politics as it relates to the rise in conservatism, changing voter trends, and new media strategies for campaigns.

NETWORK (National Catholic Social Justice Lobby), *820 1st St., N.E., #350, 20001-1630; (202) 347-9797. Fax, (202) 347-9864. Sr. Simone Campbell, Executive Director.*
General email, networkupdate@networklobby.org

Web, www.networklobby.org and Facebook, www.facebook.com/NetworkLobby

Catholic social justice lobby that coordinates political activity and promotes economic and social justice. Monitors legislation and regulations.

New America Foundation, *740 15th St., #900, 20036; (202) 986-2700. Fax, (202) 986-3696. Tyra A. Mariania, President; David G. Bradley, Chair.*
Web, www.newamerica.org, Twitter, @NewAmerica and Facebook, www.facebook.com/NewAmerica

Public policy institute that seeks to bring innovative policy ideas to the fore and nurture the next generation of public policy intellectuals. Sponsors research, writing, conferences, and events. Funds studies of government programs. Seeks to stimulate more informed reporting and analyses of government activities.

No Labels, *1130 Connecticut Ave. N.W., #325, 20036 (mailing address: P.O. Box 25429); (202) 588-1990. Fax, (202) 588-7383. Margaret Kimbrell, Executive Director, ext. 235.*
General email, pressoffice@nolabels.org

Web, www.nolabels.org, Twitter, @NoLabelsOrg and Facebook, www.facebook.com/NoLabels

Promotes a bipartisan approach to improving issues such as unemployment, social security and Medicare, the federal budget, and securing energy.

People for the American Way (PFAW), *1101 15th St. N.W., #600, 20005-5002; (202) 467-4999. Fax, (202) 293-2672. Michael B. Keegan, President. Toll-free, (800) 326-7329.*
General email, pfaw@pfaw.org
Web, www.pfaw.org and Twitter, @peoplefor

Nonprofit organization that promotes public policies that reflect the values of freedom, fairness, and equal opportunity; acts as advocate for constitutional protections and civil rights, and for strong democratic institutions, including a federal judiciary that upholds individual rights. Conducts leadership development programs for college students, African American religious leaders, and young elected officials.

Public Affairs Council, *2121 K St. N.W., #900, 20037; (202) 787-5950. Fax, (202) 787-5942. Douglas G. Pinkham, President, (202) 787-5964.*
General email, pac@pac.org
Web, www.pac.org and Twitter, @PACouncil

Membership: public affairs professionals. Informs and counsels members on public affairs programs. Sponsors conferences on election issues, government relations, and political trends. Sponsors the Foundation for Public Affairs.

Public Citizen, *Congress Watch, 215 Pennsylvania Ave. S.E., 20003; (202) 546-4996. Lisa Gilbert, Vice President of Legislative Affairs.*
General email, action@citizen.org
Web, www.citizen.org/congress

Citizens' interest group engaged in public education, research, media outreach, and citizen activism. Interests include campaign finance reform, consumer protection, financial services, public health and safety, government reform, trade, and the environment.

Rainbow PUSH Coalition, *Public Policy Institute, Government Relations and Telecommunications Project, 727 15th St. N.W., #200, 20005; (301) 256-8587. Fax, (202) 393-1495. Jesse L. Jackson Sr., President; Steve Smith, Executive Director; Frank Watkins, Director of Public Policy. Press, (773) 373-3366.*
General email, info@rainbowpush.org
Web, https://rainbowpush.org/washington-dc and Twitter, @RPCoalition

Independent civil rights organization concerned with foreign policy and public policy toward political, economic, and social justice for women, workers, and minorities. Interests include poverty and hunger, peace and justice, gun violence, corporate diversity, and voter registration. (Headquarters in Chicago, Ill.)

Taxpayers for Common Sense, *651 Pennsylvania Ave. S.E., 20003; (202) 546-8500. Ryan Alexander, President.*
General email, info@taxpayer.net
Web, www.taxpayer.net and Twitter, @taxpayers

Nonpartisan organization that works with Congress, the media, and grassroots organizations to reduce government waste and increase accountability for federal expenditures. Disseminates research results to the public via media and Web outreach.

Third Way, *1025 Connecticut Ave. N.W., #400, 20036; (202) 384-1700. Fax, (202) 775-0430. Jonathan Cowan, President.*
General email, contact@thirdway.org
Web, www.thirdway.org and Twitter, @ThirdWayTweet

Think tank that works with moderate and progressive legislators to develop modern solutions to economic, cultural, and national security issues. Conducts studies and polls; develops policy papers and strategy documents.

U.S. Chamber of Commerce, *Political Affairs and Federation Relations, 1615 H St. N.W., 20062-2000; (202) 463-5560. Sara Armstrong, Vice President.*
Web, www.uschamber.com/political-affairs-and-federation-relations

Federation that works to enact pro-business legislation; tracks election law legislation; coordinates the chamber's candidate endorsement program and its grassroots lobbying activities.

Urban Institute, *500 L'Enfant Plaza S.W., 20024; (202) 833-7200. Fax, (202) 467-5775. Sarah Rosen Wartell, President. Public Affairs, (202) 261-5709.*
General email, publicaffairs@urban.org
Web, www.urban.org and Twitter, @urbaninstitute

Nonpartisan research and education organization. Investigates U.S. social and economic problems; encourages discussion on solving society's problems, improving and implementing government decisions, and increasing citizens' awareness of public choices.

Veterans of Foreign Wars of the United States, *National Legislative Service, 200 Maryland Ave. N.E., 20002-5724; (202) 543-2239. Fax, (202) 543-2746. Carlos Fuentes, Director.*
Web, www.vfw.org/VFW-in-DC/National-Legislative-Service

Represents members before Congress and participates in congressional hearings, with a focus on health and quality of life issues. Manages the VFW Action Corps grassroots organization. Monitors legislation and regulations.

Washington Government Relations Group, *1325 G St. N.W., #500, 20005; (202) 449-7651. Fax, (202) 449-7701. Marcus Sebastian Mason, President.*
General email, info@wgrginc.org
Web, www.wgrginc.org

Works to enrich the careers and leadership abilities of African American government relations professionals working in business, financial institutions, law firms, trade associations, and nonprofit organizations. Increases dialogue between members and senior-level policymakers to produce public policy solutions.

Women Legislators' Lobby (WiLL), *Policy and Programs, 810 7th St. N.E., 20002; (202) 459-4769. Jennifer Blemair, Director; Samantha Blake, Program Manager.*
General email, peace@wand.org
Web, www.wand.org/will and Twitter, @WomenLegisLobby

Bipartisan group of women state legislators. Sponsors conferences, training workshops, issue briefings, and seminars; provides information and action alerts on ways federal policies affect states. Interests include federal budget priorities, national security, and arms control. Monitors related legislation and regulations. (National office in Cambridge, Mass. Affiliated with Women's Action for New Directions.)

Women's Action for New Directions (WAND), *Washington Office, 810 7th St. N.E., 20002; (202) 459-4769. Fax, (202) 544-7612. Nancy Parrish, Executive Director; Caroline Dorminey, Policy Director.*
General email, peace@wand.org

Web, www.wand.org and Twitter, @WomensAction

Seeks to empower women to act politically to reduce violence and militarism and redirect excessive military resources toward unmet human and environmental needs. Monitors legislation on federal budget priorities. (Headquarters in Arlington, Mass.)

Women's Congressional Policy Institute, *409 12th St. S.W., #702, 20024; (202) 554-2323. Fax, (202) 554-2346. Cynthia A. (Cindy) Hall, President.*
General email, webmaster@WCPInst.org

Web, www.wcpinst.org and Twitter, @WCPInst

Nonpartisan organization that provides legislative analysis and information services on congressional actions affecting women and their families. Works with congressional women's caucus leaders at federal, state, and local levels, as well as other groups, to provide information pertaining to women's issues. Sponsors Congressional Fellowships on Women and Public Policy for graduate students who are placed in congressional offices from January through August to work on policy issues affecting women.

Women's Research and Education Institute (WREI), *3808 Brighton Court, Alexandria, VA 22305; (703) 302-0754. Susan Scanlan, President, (202) 280-2718.*
General email, wrei@wrei.org

Web, www.wrei.org

Analyzes policy-relevant information on women's issues. Educates the public through reports and conferences. Interests include women's employment and economic status; women in nontraditional occupations; military women and veterans; older women; women's health issues; and women and immigration. Library open to the public.

POLITICAL PARTY ORGANIZATIONS

Democratic

▶NONGOVERNMENTAL

Democratic Congressional Campaign Committee, *430 S. Capitol St. S.E., 20003-4024; (202) 863-1500. Fax, (202) 485-3412. Rep. Cheri Bustos, Chair.*

General email, dccc@dccc.org

Web, www.dccc.org and Twitter, @dccc.org

Provides Democratic House candidates with financial and other campaign services.

Democratic Governors Assn., *1225 Eye St. N.W., #1100, 20005; (202) 772-5600. Fax, (202) 772-5602. Phil Murphy, Chair; Elisabeth Pearson, Executive Director.*
General email, dga@dga.net

Web, www.democraticgovernors.org and Twitter, @DemGovs

Serves as a liaison between governors' offices and Democratic Party organizations; assists Democratic gubernatorial candidates.

Democratic National Committee (DNC), *430 S. Capitol St. S.E., 20003; (202) 863-8000. Fax, (202) 863-8063. Tom Perez, Chair. Press, (202) 863-8148.*
General email, info@democrats.org

Web, www.democrats.org and Twitter, @TheDemocrats

Formulates and promotes Democratic Party policies and positions; assists Democratic candidates for state and national office; organizes national political activities; works with state and local officials and organizations.

Democratic National Committee (DNC), *Assn. of State Democratic Chairs, 430 S. Capitol St. S.E., 20003; (202) 863-8000. Ken Martin, President. Press, (202) 863-8148.*
General email, info@democrats.org

Web, http://asdc.democrats.org and Twitter, @TheDemocrats/StateDemocraticParties

Acts as a liaison between state parties and the DNC; works to strengthen state parties for national, state, and local elections; conducts fund-raising activities for state parties.

Democratic National Committee (DNC), *Communications, 430 S. Capitol St. S.E., 20003; (202) 863-8148. Xochitl Hinojosa, Director.*
General email, DNCPress@dnc.org

Web, www.democrats.org and Twitter, @TheDemocrats

Assists federal, state, and local Democratic candidates and officials in delivering a coordinated message on current issues; works to improve and expand relations with the press and to increase the visibility of Democratic officials and the Democratic Party.

Democratic National Committee (DNC), *Finance, 430 S. Capitol St. S.E., 20003; (202) 863-8000. Fax, (202) 572-7819. Henry R. Munoz III, Chair. Press, (202) 863-8148.*
General email, info@democrats.org

Web, www.democrats.org

Responsible for developing the Democratic Party's financial base. Coordinates fund-raising efforts for and gives financial support to Democratic candidates in national, state, and local campaigns.

Democratic National Committee (DNC), *Research, 430 S. Capitol St. S.E., 20003; (202) 863-8000. Lauren Dillon, Director. Press, (202) 863-8148.*

General email, info@democrats.org

Web, www.democrats.org

Provides Democratic elected officials, candidates, state party organizations, and the general public with information on Democratic Party policy and programs.

Democratic Senatorial Campaign Committee, *120 Maryland Ave. N.E., 20002-5610; (202) 224-2447. Fax, (202) 969-0354. Sen. Catherine Cortez Masto, Chair; Mindy Myers, Executive Director.*
General email, info@dscc.org

Web, www.dscc.org and Twitter, @dscc

Provides Democratic senatorial candidates with financial, research, and consulting services.

Woman's National Democratic Club, *Committee on Public Policy, 1526 New Hampshire Ave. N.W., 20036; (202) 232-7363. Nuchhi Currier, President; Elizabeth (Betsy) Spiro Clark.*
General email, info@democraticwoman.org

Web, www.democraticwoman.org and Twitter, @WNDC_1922

Studies issues and presents views to congressional committees, the Democratic Party Platform Committee, Democratic leadership groups, elected officials, and other interested groups.

Republican

▶**NONGOVERNMENTAL**

College Republican National Committee, *1500 K St. N.W., #325, 20005; (202) 608-1411. Fax, (202) 608-1429. Chandler Thornton, National Chair; Ben Rajadurai, Deputy Executive Director. Information, (888) 765-3564.*
General email, team@crnc.org

Web, www.crnc.org and Twitter, @CRNC

Membership: Republican college students. Promotes grassroots support for the Republican Party and provides campaign assistance.

National Federation of Republican Women, *124 N. Alfred St., Alexandria, VA 22314; (703) 548-9688. Fax, (703) 548-9836. Jody Rushton, President.*
General email, mail@nfrw.org

Web, www.nfrw.org

Organizes volunteers for support of Republican candidates for national, state, and local offices; encourages candidacy of Republican women; sponsors campaign management schools. Recruits Republican women candidates for office.

National Republican Congressional Committee, *320 1st St. S.E., 20003-1838; (202) 479-7000. Fax, (202) 863-0693. Rep. Steve Stivers, Chair; John Rogers, Executive Director. Press, (202) 479-7070.*
General email, website@nrcc.org

Web, www.nrcc.org

Provides Republican House candidates with campaign assistance, including financial, public relations, media, and direct mail services.

National Republican Senatorial Committee (NRSC), *425 2nd St. N.E., 20002-4914; (202) 675-6000. Sen. Cory Gardner, Chair; Chris Hansen, Executive Director.*
General email, info@nrsc.org

Web, www.nrsc.org

Provides Republican senatorial candidates with financial and public relations services.

Republican Governors Assn., *1747 Pennsylvania Ave. N.W., #250, 20006; (202) 662-4140. Gov. Pete Ricketts, Chair; Dave Rexrode, Executive Director.*
General email, info@rga.org

Web, www.rga.org and Twitter, @The_RGA

Serves as a liaison between governors' offices and Republican Party organizations; assists Republican candidates for governor.

Republican Main Street Partnership, *325 7th St. N.W., #610, 20004; (202) 393-4353. Fax, (202) 393-4354. Sarah Chamberlain, President.*
Web, https://republicanmainstreet.org and Twitter, @MainStreetGOP

Membership: centrist Republican Party members of Congress. Develops and promotes moderate Republican policies.

Republican National Committee (RNC), *310 1st St. S.E., 20003; (202) 863-8500. Fax, (202) 863-8820. Ronna McDaniel, Chair; Bob Paduchik, Co-Chair. Press, (202) 863-8614.*
General email, ecampaign@gop.com

Web, https://gop.com and Twitter, @GOP

Develops and promotes Republican Party policies and positions; assists Republican candidates for state and national office; sponsors workshops to recruit Republican candidates and provide instruction in campaign techniques; organizes national political activities; works with state and local officials and organizations.

Republican National Committee (RNC), *Communications, 310 1st St. S.E., 20003; (202) 863-8614. Fax, (202) 863-8773. Ryan Mahoney, Director.*
General email, RNCpress@gop.com

Web, https://gop.com

Assists federal, state, and local Republican candidates and officials in delivering a coordinated message on current issues; works to improve and expand relations with the press and to increase the visibility of Republican officials and the Republican message.

Republican National Committee (RNC), *Counsel, 310 1st St. S.E., 20003; (202) 863-8638. Fax, (202) 863-8654. John Phillippe, Chief Counsel; John Ryder, General Counsel. Press, (202) 863-8614.*
General email, counsel@gop.com

Web, https://gop.com

Responsible for legal affairs of the RNC, including equal time and fairness cases before the Federal Communications Commission. Advises the RNC and state parties on redistricting and campaign finance law compliance.

Republican National Committee (RNC), *Finance, 310 1st St. S.E., 20003; (202) 863-8500, ext. 4. Fax, (202) 863-8690. Richard Walters, Director.*
General email, finance@gop.com

Web, https://gop.com

Responsible for developing the Republican Party's financial base. Coordinates fund-raising efforts for and gives financial support to Republican candidates in national, state, and local campaigns.

Ripon Society, *1155 15th St. N.W., #550, 20005; (202) 216-1008. James K. Conzelman, Chief Executive Officer.*
General email, info@riponsociety.org

Web, www.riponsociety.org and Twitter, @RiponSociety

Membership: moderate Republicans. Works for the adoption of moderate policies within the Republican party.

Other Political Parties

▶**NONGOVERNMENTAL**

Green Party of the United States, *6411 Orchard Ave., #101, Takoma Park, MD 20912 (mailing address: P.O. Box 75075, Washington, DC 20013); (202) 319-7191. Vacant, Office Manager.*
General email, office@gp.org

Web, www.gp.org and Twitter, @greenparty.us

Committed to environmentalism, nonviolence, social justice, and grassroots organizing.

Libertarian Party, *1444 Duke St., Alexandria, VA 22314; (202) 333-0008. Fax, (202) 333-0072. Lauren Daugherty, Executive Director (Acting). Press, (202) 333-0008, ext. 222. Toll-free, (800) 353-2887.*
General email, info@lp.org

Web, www.lp.org

Nationally organized political party. Seeks to bring libertarian ideas into the national political debate. Believes in the primacy of the individual over government; supports property rights, free trade, and eventual elimination of taxes.

116th Congress

Delegations to the 116th Congress

Following are the senators and representatives of state delegations for the 116th Congress. This information is current as of April 12, 2019. Senators are presented first and listed according to seniority. Representatives follow, listed by district. Freshman members appear in italics and "AL" indicates at-large members. # indicates new senators who served in the House of Representatives in the 115th Congress. $ indicates members of the House of Representatives who were elected on Nov. 6, 2018, both to finish the 115th Congress and for a full term in the 116th Congress; they are italicized with the true freshman members.

ALABAMA

Richard C. Shelby (R)
Doug Jones (D)
1. Bradley Byrne (R)
2. Martha Roby (R)
3. Mike Rogers (R)
4. Robert Aderholt (R)
5. Mo Brooks (R)
6. Gary Palmer (R)
7. Terri A. Sewell (D)

ALASKA

Lisa Murkowski (R)
Dan Sullivan (R)
AL Don Young (R)

AMERICAN SAMOA (NON-VOTING DELEGATE)

AL Aumua Amata Coleman
   Radewagen (R)

ARIZONA

Martha McSally (R)
Kyrsten Sinema (D)#
1. Tom O'Halleran (D)
2. *Ann Kirkpatrick (D)*
3. Raúl Grijalva (D)
4. Paul A. Gosar (R)
5. Andy Biggs (R)
6. David Schweikert (R)
7. Rubén Gallego (D)
8. *Debbie Lesko (R)*
9. *Greg Stanton (D)*

ARKANSAS

John Boozman (R)
Tom Cotton (R)
1. Rick Crawford (R)
2. French Hill (R)
3. Steve Womack (R)
4. Bruce Westerman (R)

CALIFORNIA

Dianne Feinstein (D)
Kamala D. Harris (D)
1. Doug LaMalfa (R)
2. Jared Huffman (D)
3. John Garamendi (D)
4. Tom McClintock (R)
5. Mike Thompson (D)
6. Doris O. Matsui (D)
7. Ami Bera (D)
8. Paul Cook (R)
9. Jerry McNerney (D)
10. *Josh Harder (R)*
11. Mark DeSaulnier (D)
12. Nancy Pelosi (D)
13. Barbara Lee (D)
14. Jackie Speier (D)
15. Eric Swalwell (D)
16. Jim Costa (D)
17. Ro Khanna (D)
18. Anna G. Eshoo (D)
19. Zoe Lofgren (D)
20. *Jimmy Panetta (D)*
21. *TJ Cox (D)*
22. Devin Nunes (R)
23. Kevin McCarthy (R)
24. Salud Carbajal (D)
25. *Katie Hill (D)*
26. Julia Brownley (D)
27. Judy Chu (D)
28. Adam Schiff (D)
29. Tony Cárdenas (D)
30. Brad Sherman (D)
31. Pete Aguilar (D)
32. Grace Napolitano (D)
33. Ted Lieu (D)
34. Jimmy Gomez (D)
35. Norma Torres (D)
36. Raul Ruiz (D)
37. Karen Bass (D)
38. Linda Sánchez (D)
39. *Gilbert Ray Cisneros Jr. (D)*
40. Lucille Roybal-Allard (D)
41. Mark Takano (D)
42. Ken Calvert (R)
43. Maxine Waters (D)
44. Nanette Diaz Barragán (D)
45. *Katie Porter (D)*
46. J. Luis Correa (D)
47. Alan Lowenthal (D)
48. *Harley Rouda (D)*
49. *Mike Levin (D)*
50. Duncan Hunter (R)
51. Juan Vargas (D)
52. Scott Peters (D)
53. Susan Davis (D)

COLORADO

Michael F. Bennet (D)
Cory Gardner (R)
1. Diana DeGette (D)
2. Joe Neguse (D)
3. Scott Tipton (R)
4. Ken Buck (R)
5. Doug Lamborn (R)
6. *Jason Crow (D)*
7. Ed Perlmutter (D)

CONNECTICUT

Richard Blumenthal (D)
Chris Murphy (D)
1. John B. Larson (D)
2. Joe Courtney (D)
3. Rosa L. DeLauro (D)
4. Jim Himes (D)
5. *Jahana Hayes (D)*

DELAWARE

Thomas R. Carper (D)
Christopher Coons (D)
AL Lisa Blunt Rochester (D)

DISTRICT OF COLUMBIA (NON-VOTING DELEGATE)

AL Eleanor Holmes Norton (D)

FLORIDA

Rick Scott (R)
Marco Rubio (R)
   1. Matt Gaetz (R)
   2. Neal Dunn (R)
   3. Ted Yoho (R)
   4. John Rutherford (R)
   5. Al Lawson (D)
   6. *Michael Waltz (R)*
   7. Stephanie Murphy (D)
   8. Bill Posey (R)
   9. Darren Soto (D)
   10. Val Demings (D)
   11. Daniel Webster (R)
   12. Gus M. Bilirakis (R)
   13. Charlie Crist (D)
   14. Kathy Castor (D)
   15. *Ross Spano (R)*
   16. Vern Buchanan (R)
   17. *W. Gregory Steube (R)*
   18. Brian Mast (R)
   19. Francis Rooney (R)
   20. Alcee L. Hastings (D)
   21. Lois Frankel (D)
   22. Ted Deutch (D)
   23. Debbie Wasserman
      Schultz (D)
   24. Frederica S. Wilson (D)
   25. Mario Diaz-Balart (R)
   26. *Debbie Mucarsel-Powell (D)*
   27. *Donna E. Shalala (D)*

GEORGIA

Johnny Isakson (R)
David Perdue *(R)*
   1. Buddy Carter (R)
   2. Sanford D.
      Bishop Jr. (D)
   3. A. Drew Ferguson (R)
   4. Hank Johnson
      Jr. (D)
   5. John Lewis (D)
   6. *Lucy McBath (D)*
   7. Robert Woodall (R)
   8. Austin Scott (R)
   9. Doug Collins (R)
   10. Jody Hice (R)
   11. Barry Loudermilk (R)
   12. Rick Allen (R)
   13. David Scott (D)
   14. Tom Graves (R)

GUAM (NON-VOTING DELEGATE)

AL *Michael San Nicolas (D)*

HAWAII

Brian Schatz (D)
Mazie K. Hirono (D)
   1. *Ed Case (D)*
   2. Tulsi Gabbard (D)

IDAHO

Mike Crapo (R)
James E. Risch (R)
   1. *Russ Fulcher (R)*
   2. Mike Simpson (R)

ILLINOIS

Dick Durbin (D)
Tammy Duckworth (D)
   1. Bobby L. Rush (D)
   2. Robin Kelly (D)
   3. Daniel Lipinski (D)
   4. *Jesús G. García (D)*
   5. Mike Quigley (D)
   6. *Sean Casten (D)*
   7. Danny K. Davis (D)
   8. Raja Krishnamoorthi (D)
   9. Jan Schakowsky (D)
   10. Bradley Schneider (D)
   11. Bill Foster (D)
   12. Mike Bost (R)
   13. Rodney Davis (R)
   14. *Lauren Underwood (D)*
   15. John Shimkus (R)
   16. Adam Kinzinger (R)
   17. Cheri Bustos (D)
   18. Darin LaHood (R)

INDIANA

Todd Young (R)
Mike Braun (R)
   1. Peter Visclosky (D)
   2. Jackie Walorski (R)
   3. Jim Banks (R)
   4. *James R. Baird (R)*
   5. Susan W. Brooks (R)
   6. *Greg Pence (R)*
   7. André Carson (D)
   8. Larry Bucshon (R)
   9. Trey Hollingsworth (R)

IOWA

Chuck Grassley (R)
Joni Ernst (R)
   1. *Abby Finkenauer (D)*
   2. David Loebsack (D)
   3. *Cindy Axne (D)*
   4. Steve King (R)

KANSAS

Pat Roberts (R)
Jerry Moran (R)
   1. Roger Marshall (R)
   2. *Steve Watkins (R)*
   3. *Sharice Davids (D)*
   4. Ron Estes (R)

KENTUCKY

Mitch McConnell (R)
Rand Paul (R)
   1. James Comer (R)
   2. S. Brett Guthrie (R)
   3. John A. Yarmuth (D)
   4. Thomas Massie (R)
   5. Harold Rogers (R)
   6. Andy Barr (R)

LOUISIANA

John Kennedy (R)
Bill Cassidy (R)
   1. Steve Scalise (R)
   2. Cedric Richmond (D)
   3. Clay Higgins (R)
   4. Mike Johnson (R)
   5. Ralph Abraham (R)
   6. Garret Graves (R)

MAINE

Susan M. Collins (R)
Angus S. King Jr. (I)
   1. Chellie Pingree (D)
   2. *Jared Golden (D)*

MARYLAND

Chris Van Hollen (D)
Benjamin L. Cardin (D)
   1. Andy Harris (R)
   2. C. A. Dutch Ruppersberger (D)
   3. John P. Sarbanes (D)
   4. Anthony Brown (D)
   5. Steny H. Hoyer (D)
   6. *David Trone (D)*
   7. Elijah Cummings (D)
   8. Jamie Raskin (D)

MASSACHUSETTS

Elizabeth Warren (D)
Edward J. Markey (D)
   1. Richard E. Neal (D)
   2. James McGovern (D)
   3. *Lori Trahan (D)*
   4. Joseph P. Kennedy III (D)
   5. Katherine Clark (D)

6. Seth Moulton (D)
7. *Ayanna Pressley (D)*
8. Stephen F. Lynch (D)
9. William Keating (D)

MICHIGAN

Debbie Stabenow (D)
Gary C. Peters (D)
1. Jack Bergman (R)
2. Bill Huizenga (R)
3. Justin Amash (R)
4. John Moolenaar (R)
5. Daniel Kildee (D)
6. Fred Upton (R)
7. Tim Walberg (R)
8. *Elissa Slotkin (D)*
9. *Andy Levin (D)*
10. Paul Mitchell (R)
11. *Haley Stevens (D)*
12. Debbie Dingell (D)
13. *Rashida Tlaib (D)*
14. Brenda Lawrence (D)

MINNESOTA

Amy Klobuchar (D)
Tina Smith (D)
1. *Jim Hagedorn (R)*
2. *Angie Craig (D)*
3. *Dean Phillips (D)*
4. Betty McCollum (D)
5. *Ilhan Omar (D)*
6. Tom Emmer (R)
7. Collin C. Peterson (D)
8. *Pete Stauber (R)*

MISSISSIPPI

Roger F. Wicker (R)
Cindy Hyde-Smith (R)
1. Trent Kelly (R)
2. Bennie G. Thompson (D)
3. *Michael Guest (R)*
4. Steven Palazzo (R)

MISSOURI

Roy Blunt (R)
Josh Hawley (R)
1. William Lacy Clay Jr. (D)
2. Ann Wagner (R)
3. Blaine Luetkemeyer (R)
4. Vicky Hartzler (R)
5. Emanuel Cleaver (D)
6. Sam Graves (R)
7. Billy Long (R)
8. Jason Smith (R)

MONTANA

Jon Tester (D)
Steve Daines (R)
AL Greg Gianforte (R)

NEBRASKA

Deb Fischer (R)
Ben Sasse (R)
1. Jeff Fortenberry (R)
2. Don Bacon (R)
3. Adrian Smith (R)

NEVADA

Catherine Cortez Masto (D)
Jacky Rosen (D)#
1. Dina Titus (D)
2. Mark Amodei (R)
3. *Susie Lee (D)*
4. *Steven Horsford (D)*

NEW HAMPSHIRE

Jeanne Shaheen (D)
Maggie Hassan (D)
1. *Chris Pappas (D)*
2. Ann Kuster (D)

NEW JERSEY

Robert Menendez (D)
Cory A. Booker (D)
1. Donald Norcross (D)
2. *Jefferson Van Drew (D)*
3. *Andy Kim (D)*
4. Chris Smith (R)
5. Josh Gottheimer (D)
6. Frank Pallone Jr. (D)
7. *Tom Malinowski (D)*
8. Albio Sires (D)
9. Bill Pascrell Jr. (D)
10. Donald Payne Jr. (D)
11. *Mikie Sherrill (D)*
12. Bonnie Watson Coleman (D)

NEW MEXICO

Tom Udall (D)
Martin Heinrich (D)
1. *Debra A. Haaland (D)*
2. *Xochitl Torres Small (D)*
3. Ben Ray Luján (D)

NEW YORK

Charles E. Schumer (D)
Kirsten E. Gillibrand (D)
1. Lee Zeldin (R)
2. Pete King (R)

3. Thomas Suozzi (D)
4. Kathleen Rice (D)
5. Gregory W. Meeks (D)
6. Grace Meng (D)
7. Nydia M.
   Velázquez (D)
8. Hakeem Jeffries (D)
9. Yvette D. Clarke (D)
10. Jerrold Nadler (D)
11. *Max Rose (D)*
12. Carolyn Maloney (D)
13. Adriano Espaillat (D)
14. *Alexandria Ocasio-Cortez (D)*
15. José E. Serrano (D)
16. Eliot Engel (D)
17. Nita Lowey (D)
18. Sean Patrick
    Maloney (D)
19. *Antonio Delgado (D)*
20. Paul D. Tonko (D)
21. Elise Stefanik (R)
22. *Anthony Brindisi (D)*
23. Tom Reed (R)
24. John Katko (R)
25. *Joseph D. Morelle (D)$*
26. Brian Higgins (D)
27. Chris Collins (R)

NORTH CAROLINA

Richard Burr (R)
Thom Tillis (R)
1. G. K. Butterfield (D)
2. George Holding (R)
3. Walter B. Jones (R)
4. David Price (D)
5. Virginia Foxx (R)
6. Mark Walker (R)
7. David Rouzer (R)
8. Richard Hudson (R)
9. Vacant
10. Patrick T. McHenry (R)
11. Mark Meadows (R)
12. Alma Adams (D)
13. Ted Budd (R)

NORTH DAKOTA

John Hoeven (R)
Kevin Cramer (R) #
AL *Kelly Armstrong (R)*

NORTHERN MARIANA ISLANDS (NON-VOTING DELEGATE)

AL Gregorio Kilili Camacho Sablan (D)

OHIO

Sherrod Brown (D)
Rob Portman (R)
   1. Steve Chabot (R)
   2. Brad Wenstrup (R)
   3. Joyce Beatty (D)
   4. Jim Jordan (R)
   5. Robert E. Latta (R)
   6. Bill Johnson (R)
   7. Bob Gibbs (R)
   8. Warren Davidson (R)
   9. Marcy Kaptur (D)
   10. Michael Turner (R)
   11. Marcia L. Fudge (D)
   12. *Troy Balderson (R)*
   13. Tim Ryan (D)
   14. David Joyce (R)
   15. Steve Stivers (R)
   16. *Anthony Gonzalez (R)*

OKLAHOMA

James M. Inhofe (R)
James Lankford (R)
   1. *Kevin Hern (R)*
   2. Markwayne Mullin (R)
   3. Frank Lucas (R)
   4. Tom Cole (R)
   5. *Kendra S. Horn (D)*

OREGON

Ron Wyden (D)
Jeff Merkley (D)
   1. Suzanne Bonamici (D)
   2. Greg Walden (R)
   3. Earl Blumenauer (D)
   4. Peter DeFazio (D)
   5. Kurt Schrader (D)

PENNSYLVANIA

Robert P. Casey Jr. (D)
Patrick J. Toomey (R)
   1. Brian K. Fitzpatrick (R)
   2. Brendan F. Boyle (D)
   3. Dwight Evans (D)
   4. *Madeleine Dean (D)*
   5. *Mary Gay Scanlon (D)$*
   6. *Chrissy Houlahan (D)*
   7. *Susan Wild (D)$*
   8. Matt Cartwright (D)
   9. *Daniel Meuser (R)*
   10. Scott Perry (R)
   11. Lloyd Smucker (R)
   12. Tom Marino (R)
   13. *John Joyce (R)*
   14. *Guy Reschenthaler (R)*
   15. Glenn (GT) Thompson (R)
   16. Mike Kelly (R)
   17. Conor Lamb (D)
   18. Mike Doyle (D)

PUERTO RICO (NON-VOTING DELEGATE)

AL *Jenniffer González-Colón (R)*

RHODE ISLAND

Jack Reed (D)
Sheldon Whitehouse (D)
   1. David Cicilline (D)
   2. Jim Langevin (D)

SOUTH CAROLINA

Lindsey Graham (R)
Tim Scott (R)
   1. *Joe Cunningham (D)*
   2. Joe Wilson (R)
   3. Jeff Duncan (R)
   4. *William Timmons (R)*
   5. Ralph Norman (R)
   6. James E. Clyburn (D)
   7. Tom Rice (R)

SOUTH DAKOTA

John Thune (R)
Mike Rounds (R)
AL *Dusty Johnson (R)*

TENNESSEE

Lamar Alexander (R)
Marsha Blackburn (R)#
   1. Phil Roe (R)
   2. *Tim Burchett (R)*
   3. Chuck Fleischmann (R)
   4. Scott DesJarlais (R)
   5. Jim Cooper (D)
   6. *John Rose (R)*
   7. *Mark E. Green (R)*
   8. David Kustoff (R)
   9. Steve Cohen (D)

TEXAS

John Cornyn (R)
Ted Cruz (R)
   1. Louie Gohmert (R)
   2. *Dan Crenshaw (R)*
   3. *Van Taylor (R)*
   4. John Ratcliffe (R)
   5. *Lance Gooden (R)*
   6. *Ron Wright (R)*
   7. *Lizzie Fletcher (D)*
   8. Kevin Brady (R)
   9. Al Green (D)
   10. Michael T. McCaul (R)
   11. K. Michael Conaway (R)
   12. Kay Granger (R)
   13. Mac Thornberry (R)
   14. Randy Weber (R)
   15. Vicente Gonzalez (D)
   16. *Veronica Escobar (D)*
   17. Bill Flores (R)
   18. Sheila Jackson Lee (D)
   19. Jodey Arrington (R)
   20. Joaquin Castro (D)
   21. *Chip Roy (R)*
   22. Pete Olson (R)
   23. Will Hurd (R)
   24. Kenny Marchant (R)
   25. Roger Williams (R)
   26. Michael Burgess (R)
   27. *Michael Cloud (R)*
   28. Henry Cuellar (D)
   29. *Sylvia Garcia (D)*
   30. Eddie Bernice Johnson (D)
   31. John Carter (R)
   32. *Colin Allred (D)*
   33. Marc Veasey (D)
   34. Filemon Vela (D)
   35. Lloyd Doggett (D)
   36. Brian Babin *(R)*

UTAH

Mike Lee (R)
Mitt Romney (R)
   1. Rob Bishop (R)
   2. Chris Stewart (R)
   3. John R. Curtis (R)
   4. *Ben McAdams (D)*

VERMONT

Patrick J. Leahy (D)
Bernard Sanders (I)
AL Peter Welch (D)

VIRGIN ISLANDS (NON-VOTING DELEGATE)

AL Stacey E. Plaskett (D)

VIRGINIA

Mark R. Warner (D)
Tim Kaine (D)
   1. Robert J. Wittman (R)
   2. *Elaine G. Luria (D)*
   3. Robert C. Scott (D)
   4. A. Donald McEachin (D)
   5. *Denver Riggleman (R)*
   6. *Ben Cline (R)*
   7. *Abigail Spanberger (D)*

8. Don Beyer (D)
9. Morgan Griffith (R)
10. *Jennifer Wexton (D)*
11. Gerald E. (Gerry) Connolly (D)

WASHINGTON

Patty Murray (D)
Maria Cantwell (D)
1. Suzan DelBene (D)
2. Rick Larsen (D)
3. Jaime Herrera Beutler (R)
4. Dan Newhouse (R)
5. Cathy McMorris Rodgers (R)
6. Derek Kilmer (D)
7. Pramila Jayapal (D)
8. *Kim Schrier (D)*

9. Adam Smith (D)
10. Denny Heck (D)

WEST VIRGINIA

Joe Manchin III (D)
Shelley Moore Capito (R)
1. David McKinley (R)
2. Alex Mooney (R)
3. *Carol Miller (R)*

WISCONSIN

Ron Johnson (R)
Tammy Baldwin (D)
1. *Bryan Steil (R)*
2. Mark Pocan (D)
3. Ron Kind (D)

4. Gwen Moore (D)
5. F. James Sensenbrenner (R)
6. Glenn Grothman (R)
7. Sean P. Duffy (R)
8. *Mike Gallagher (R)*

WYOMING

Michael B. Enzi (R)
John Barrasso (R)
AL *Liz Cheney (R)*

House Committees

The standing and select committees of the U.S. House of Representatives follow. Each listing includes the room number, office building, zip code, telephone and fax numbers, web address, minority Web address if available, key majority and minority staff members, jurisdiction for each full committee, and party ratio. Subcommittees are listed under the full committees. Members are listed in order of seniority on the committee or subcommittee. Many committees and subcommittees may be contacted via Web-based email forms found on their Web sites.

Republicans, the current majority, are shown in roman type; Democrats, in the minority, appear in italic. The top name in the italicized list is the Ranking Minority Member. Vacancy indicates that a committee or subcommittee seat had not been filled as of April 12, 2019. The partisan committees of the House are listed on page 851. The area code for all phone and fax numbers is (202). A phone number and/or office number next to either the Majority or Minority Staff Director indicates a change from the full committee's office number and/or phone number. If no numbers are listed, the individual's office number and phone number are the same as for the full committee.

AGRICULTURE

Office: 1301 LHOB 20515-6001
Phone: 225-2171   **Fax:** 225-8510
Web: agriculture.house.gov
Minority Web: republicans-agriculture.house.gov
Majority Staff Director: Anne Simmons
Minority Staff Director: Matt Schertz, 225-0317, 1010 LHOB
   Jurisdiction: (1) adulteration of seeds, insect pests, and protection of birds and animals in forest reserves; (2) agriculture generally; (3) agricultural and industrial chemistry; (4) agricultural colleges and experiment stations; (5) agricultural economics and research; (6) agricultural education extension services; (7) agricultural production and marketing, and stabilization of prices of agricultural products and commodities (not including distribution outside of the United States); (8) animal industry and diseases of animals; (9) commodity exchanges; (10) crop insurance and soil conservation; (11) dairy industry; (12) entomology and plant quarantine; (13) extension of farm credit and farm security; (14) inspection of livestock, poultry, meat products, and seafood and seafood products; (15) forestry in general, and forest reserves other than those created from the public domain; (16) human nutrition and home economics; (17) plant industry, soils, and agricultural engineering; (18) rural electrification; (19) rural development; (20) water conservation related to activities of the Department of Agriculture.
Party Ratio: D 26-R 21

Collin C. Peterson, Minn., Chair
David Scott, Ga.
Jim Costa, Calif.
Marcia L. Fudge, Ohio
James McGovern, Mass.
Filemon Vela, Tex.
Stacey E. Plaskett, V.I.
Alma Adams, N.C.
Abigail Spanberger, Va.
Jahana Hayes, Conn.

K. Michael Conaway, Tex.
Glenn (GT) Thompson, Pa.
Austin Scott, Ga.
Rick Crawford, Ark.
Scott DesJarlais, Tenn.
Vicky Hartzler, Mo.
Doug LaMalfa, Calif.
Rodney Davis, Ill.
Ted Yoho, Fla.
Rick Allen, Ga.
Mike Bost, Ill.

Antonio Delgado, N.Y.
TJ Cox, Calif.
Angie Craig, Minn.
Anthony Brindisi, N.Y.
Jefferson Van Drew, N.J.
Josh Harder, Calif.
Kim Schrier, Wash.
Chellie Pingree, Maine
Cheri Bustos, Ill.
Sean Patrick Maloney, N.Y.
Salud Carbajal, Calif.
Al Lawson, Fla.
Tom O'Halleran, Ariz.
Jimmy Panetta, Calif.
Ann Kirkpatrick, Ariz.
Cindy Axne, Iowa

David Rouzer, N.C.
Ralph Abraham, La.
Trent Kelly, Miss.
James Comer, Ky.
Roger Marshall, Kans.
Don Bacon, Neb.
Neal Dunn, Fla.
Dusty Johnson, S.D.
James R. Baird, Ind.
Jim Hagedorn, Minn.

Subcommittees

Biotechnology, Horticulture, and Research
Office: 1301 LHOB 20515   **Phone:** 225-2171
   Stacey E. Plaskett (Chair), Antonio Delgado, TJ Cox, Josh Harder, Anthony Brindisi, Jefferson Van Drew, Kim Schrier, Chellie Pingree, Salud Carbajal, Jimmy Panetta, Sean Patrick Maloney, Al Lawson, Collin C. Peterson (ex officio)
   Neal Dunn (Ranking Minority Member), Glenn (GT) Thompson, Vicky Hartzler, Doug LaMalfa, Rodney Davis, Ted Yoho, Mike Bost, James Comer, James R. Baird, K. Michael Conaway (ex officio)

Commodity Exchanges, Energy, and Credit
Office: 1301 LHOB 20515   **Phone:** 225-2171
   David Scott (Chair), Jefferson Van Drew, Filemon Vela, Stacey E. Plaskett, Abigail Spanberger, Antonio Delgado, Angie Craig, Sean Patrick Maloney, Ann Kirkpatrick, Cindy Axne, Collin C. Peterson (ex officio)
   Austin Scott (Ranking Minority Member), Rick Crawford, Mike Bost, David Rouzer, Roger Marshall, Neal Dunn, Dusty Johnson, James R. Baird, K. Michael Conaway (ex officio)

Conservation and Forestry
Office: 1301 LHOB 20515   **Phone:** 225-2171

AGRICULTURE (continued)

Abigail Spanberger (Chair), Marcia L. Fudge, Tom O'Halleran, Chellie Pingree, Cindy Axne, Collin C. Peterson (ex officio)

Doug LaMalfa (Ranking Minority Member), Rick Allen, Ralph Abraham, Trent Kelly, K. Michael Conaway (ex officio)

General Farm Commodities and Risk Management
Office: 1301 LHOB 20515   **Phone:** 225-2171

Filemon Vela (Chair), Angie Craig, David Scott, Al Lawson, Jefferson Van Drew, Collin C. Peterson (ex officio)

Glenn (GT) Thompson (Ranking Minority Member), Austin Scott, Rick Crawford, Rick Allen, Ralph Abraham, K. Michael Conaway (ex officio)

Livestock and Foreign Agriculture
Office: 1301 LHOB 20515   **Phone:** 225-2171

Jim Costa (Chair), Anthony Brindisi, Jahana Hayes, TJ Cox, Angie Craig, Josh Harder, Filemon Vela, Stacey E. Plaskett, Salud Carbajal, Cheri Bustos, Collin C. Peterson (ex officio)

David Rouzer (Ranking Minority Member), Glenn (GT) Thompson, Scott DesJarlais, Vicky Hartzler, Trent Kelly, James Comer, Roger Marshall, Don Bacon, Jim Hagedorn, K. Michael Conaway (ex officio)

Nutrition
Office: 1301 LHOB 20515   **Phone:** 225-2171

Marcia L. Fudge (Chair), James McGovern, Alma Adams, Jahana Hayes, Kim Schrier, Jefferson Van Drew, Al Lawson, Jimmy Panetta, Collin C. Peterson (ex officio)

Dusty Johnson (Ranking Minority Member), Scott DesJarlais, Rodney Davis, Ted Yoho, Don Bacon, Jim Hagedorn, K. Michael Conaway (ex officio)

APPROPRIATIONS

Office: H-307 CAP 20515-6015
Phone: 225-2771   **Fax:** 226-0383
Web: appropriations.house.gov
Minority Web: republicans-appropriations.house.gov
Majority Staff Director: Shalanda Young
Minority Staff Director: Anne Marie Chotvacs, 225-3481, 1016 LHOB

Jurisdiction: (1) appropriation of the revenue for the support of the Government; (2) rescissions of appropriations contained in appropriations Acts; (3) transfers of unexpected balances; (4) bills and joint resolutions reported by other Committees that provide new entitlement authority as defined in Section 3(9) of the Congressional Budget Act of 1974 and referred to the Committee under Clause 4 (a)(2).
Party Ratio: D 30-R 23

Nita Lowey, N.Y., Chair	*Kay Granger, Tex.*
Marcy Kaptur, Ohio	*Harold Rogers, Ky.*
Peter Visclosky, Ind.	*Robert Aderholt, Ala.*
José E. Serrano, N.Y.	*Mike Simpson, Idaho*
Rosa L. DeLauro, Conn.	*John Carter, Tex.*
David Price, N.C.	*Ken Calvert, Calif.*

Lucille Roybal-Allard, Calif.	*Tom Cole, Okla.*
Sanford D. Bishop Jr., Ga.	*Mario Diaz-Balart, Fla.*
Barbara Lee, Calif.	*Tom Graves, Ga.*
Betty McCollum, Minn.	*Steve Womack, Ark.*
Tim Ryan, Ohio	*Jeff Fortenberry, Neb.*
C. A. Dutch	*Chuck Fleischmann, Tenn.*
Ruppersberger, Md.	*Jaime Herrera Beutler,*
Debbie Wasserman	*Wash.*
Schultz, Fla.	*David Joyce, Ohio*
Henry Cuellar, Tex.	*Andy Harris, Md.*
Chellie Pingree, Maine	*Martha Roby, Ala.*
Mike Quigley, Ill.	*Mark Amodei, Nev.*
Derek Kilmer, Wash.	*Chris Stewart, Utah*
Matt Cartwright, Pa.	*Steven Palazzo, Mo.*
Grace Meng, N.Y.	*Dan Newhouse, Wash.*
Mark Pocan, Wisc.	*John Moolenaar, Mich.*
Katherine Clark, Mass.	*John Rutherford, Fla.*
Pete Aguilar, Calif.	*Will Hurd, Tex.*
Lois Frankel, Fla.	
Cheri Bustos, Ill.	
Bonnie Watson Coleman, N.J.	
Brenda Lawrence, Mich.	
Norma Torres, Calif.	
Charlie Crist, Fla.	
Ann Kirkpatrick, Ariz.	
Ed Case, Hawaii	

Subcommittees

Agriculture, Rural Development, Food and Drug Administration, and Related Agencies
Office: 2362A RHOB 20515   **Phone:** 225-2638

Sanford Bishop Jr. (Chair), Rosa L. DeLauro, Chellie Pingree, Mark Pocan, Barbara Lee, Betty McCollum, Henry Cuellar

Jeff Fortenberry (Ranking Minority Member), Robert Aderholt, Andy Harris, John Moolenaar

Commerce, Justice, Science, and Related Agencies
Office: H-310 CAP 20515   **Phone:** 225-3351

José E. Serrano (Chair), Matt Cartwright, Grace Meng, Brenda Lawrence, Charlie Crist, Ed Case, Marcy Kaptur

Robert Aderholt (Ranking Minority Member), Martha Roby, Steven Palazzo, Tom Graves

Defense
Office: H-405 CAP 20515   **Phone:** 225-2847

Peter Visclosky (Chair), Betty McCollum, Tim Ryan, C. A. Dutch Ruppersberger, Marcy Kaptur, Henry Cuellar, Derek Kilmer, Pete Aguilar, Cheri Bustos, Charlie Crist, Ann Kirkpatrick

Ken Calvert (Ranking Minority Member), Harold Rogers, Tom Cole, Steve Womack, Robert Aderholt, John Carter, Mario Diaz-Balart

Energy and Water Development, and Related Agencies
Office: 2362B RHOB 20515   **Phone:** 225-3421

Marcy Kaptur (Chair), Peter Visclosky, Debbie Wasserman Schultz, Ann Kirkpatrick, Derek Kilmer, Mark Pocan, Lois Frankel

Mike Simpson (Ranking Minority Member), Ken Calvert, Chuck Fleischmann, Dan Newhouse

Financial Services and General Government
Office: 2000 RHOB 20515   **Phone:** 225-7245
Mike Quigley (Chair), José E. Serrano, Matt Cartwright, Sanford D. Bishop Jr., Norma Torres, Charlie Crist, Ann Kirkpatrick
Tom Graves (Ranking Minority Member), Mark Amodei, Chris Stewart, David Joyce

Homeland Security
Office: 2006 RHOB 20515   **Phone:** 225-5834
Lucille Roybal-Allard (Chair), Henry Cuellar, C. A. Dutch Ruppersberger, David Price, Debbie Wasserman Schultz, Grace Meng, Pete Aguilar
Chuck Fleischmann (Ranking Minority Member), Steven Palazzo, Dan Newhouse, John Rutherford

Interior, Environment, and Related Agencies
Office: 2007 RHOB 20515   **Phone:** 225-3081
Betty McCollum (Chair), Chellie Pingree, Derek Kilmer, José E. Serrano, Mike Quigley, Bonnie Watson Coleman, Brenda Lawrence
David Joyce (Ranking Minority Member), Mike Simpson, Chris Stewart, Mark Amodei

Labor, Health and Human Services, Education, and Related Agencies
Office: 2358B RHOB 20515   **Phone:** 225-3508
Rosa L. DeLauro (Chair), Lucille Roybal-Allard, Barbara Lee, Mark Pocan, Katherine Clark, Lois Frankel, Cheri Bustos, Bonnie Watson Coleman
Tom Cole, (Ranking Minority Member), Andy Harris, Jaime Herrera Beutler, John Moolenaar, Tom Graves

Legislative Branch
Office: H-306 CAP 20515   **Phone:** 226-7252
Tim Ryan (Chair), C. A. Dutch Ruppersberger, Katherine Clark, Ed Case
Jaime Herrera Beutler (Ranking Minority Member), Dan Newhouse

Military Construction, Veterans Affairs, and Related Agencies
Office: HT-2 CAP 20515   **Phone:** 225-3047
Debbie Wasserman Schultz (Chair), Sanford D. Bishop Jr., Ed Case, Tim Ryan, Chellie Pingree, Matt Cartwright, Cheri Bustos
John Carter (Ranking Minority Member), Martha Roby, John Rutherford, Will Hurd

State, Foreign Operations, and Related Programs
Office: HT-2 CAP 20515   **Phone:** 225-2041
Nita Lowey (Chair), Barbara Lee, Grace Meng, David Price, Lois Frankel, Norma Torres
Harold Rogers (Ranking Minority Member), Jeff Fortenberry, Martha Roby

Transportation, Housing and Urban Development, and Related Agencies
Office: 2358A RHOB 20515   **Phone:** 225-2141
David Price (Chair), Mike Quigley, Katherine Clark, Bonnie Watson Coleman, Brenda Lawrence, Norma Torres, Pete Aguilar
Mario Diaz-Balart (Ranking Minority Member), Steve Womack, John Rutherford, Will Hurd

ARMED SERVICES
Office: 2216 RHOB 20515-6035
Phone: 225-4151   **Fax:** 225-9077
Web: armedservices.house.gov
Minority Web: republicans-armedservices.house.gov
Majority Staff Director: Paul Arcangeli
Minority Staff Director: Jen Stewart
Jurisdiction: (1) ammunition depots, forts, arsenals, Army, Navy and Air Force reservations and establishments; (2) common defense generally; (3) conservation, development, and use of naval petroleum reserves and oil shale reserves; (4) the Department of Defense generally, including the Departments of the Army, Navy, and Air Force generally; (5) interoceanic canals generally, including measures relating to the maintenance, operation, and administration of interoceanic canals; (6) Merchant Marine Academy and State Merchant Marine Academies; (7) military applications of nuclear energy; (8) tactical intelligence and intelligence-related activities of the Department of Defense; (9) national security aspects of the merchant marine, including financial assistance for the construction and operation of vessels, the maintenance of the United States shipbuilding and ship repair industrial base, cabotage (trade or transport in coastal waters or air space, or between two points within a country), cargo preference, and merchant marine officers and seamen as these matters relate to the national security; (10) pay, promotion, retirement, and other benefits and privileges of members of the armed services; (11) scientific research and development in support of the armed services; (12) selective service; (13) size and composition of the Army, Navy, Marine Corps, and Air Force; (14) soldiers' and sailors' homes; (15) strategic and critical materials necessary for the common defense; (16) cemeteries administered by the Department of Defense.
Party Ratio: D 31-R 26

Adam Smith, Wash., Chair	Mac Thornberry, Tex.
Susan Davis, Calif.	Joe Wilson, S.C.
Jim Langevin, R.I.	Rob Bishop, Utah
Rick Larsen, Wash.	Michael Turner, Ohio
Jim Cooper, Tenn.	Mike Rogers, Ala.
Joe Courtney, Conn.	K. Michael Conaway, Tex.
John Garamendi, Calif.	Doug Lamborn, Colo.
Jackie Speier, Calif.	Robert J. Wittman, Va.
Tulsi Gabbard, Hawaii	Vicky Hartzler, Mo.
Donald Norcross, N.J.	Austin Scott, Ga.
Rubén Gallego, Ariz.	Mo Brooks, Ala.
Seth Moulton, Mass.	Paul Cook, Calif.
Salud Carbajal, Calif.	Bradley Byrne, Ala.
Anthony Brown, Md.	Sam Graves, Mo.
Ro Khanna, Calif.	Elise Stefanik, N.Y.
William Keating, Mass.	Scott DesJarlais, Tenn.
Andy Kim, N.J.	Ralph Abraham, La.
Chrissy Houlahan, Pa.	Trent Kelly, Miss.
Jason Crow, Colo.	Mike Gallagher, Wisc.
Elissa Slotkin, Mich.	Matt Gaetz, Fla.
Lori Trahan, Mass.	Don Bacon, Neb.
Gilbert Ray Cisneros Jr., Calif.	Jim Banks, Ind.
	Liz Cheney, Wyo.

ARMED SERVICES (continued)

Veronica Escobar, Tex.	*Jack Bergman, Mich.*
Debra A. Haaland, N.M.	*Michael Waltz, Fla.*
Elaine G. Luria, Va.	*Paul Mitchell, Hawaii*
Kendra S. Horn, Okla.	
Xochitl Torres Small, N.M.	
Filemon Vela, Tex.	
Mikie Sherrill, N.J.	
Katie Hill, Calif.	
Jared Golden, Maine	

Subcommittees

Intelligence, Emerging Threats, and Capabilities
Office: 2340 RHOB 20515   **Phone:** 225-4151

Jim Langevin (Chair), Rick Larsen, Jim Cooper, Tulsi Gabbard, Anthony Brown, Ro Khanna, William Keating, Andy Kim, Chrissy Houlahan, Jason Crow, Elissa Slotkin, Lori Trahan

Elise Stefanik (Ranking Minority Member), Sam Graves, Ralph Abraham, K. Michael Conaway, Austin Scott, Scott DesJarlais, Mike Gallagher, Michael Waltz, Don Bacon, Jim Banks

Military Personnel
Office: 2340 RHOB 20515   **Phone:** 225-4151

Jackie Speier (Chair), Susan Davis, Rubén Gallego, Gilbert Ray Cisneros Jr., Veronica Escobar, Debra A. Haaland, Lori Trahan, Elaine G. Luria

Trent Kelly (Ranking Minority Member), Ralph Abraham, Liz Cheney, Paul Mitchell, Jack Bergman, Matt Gaetz

Readiness
Office: 2340 RHOB 20515   **Phone:** 226-4151

John Garamendi (Chair), Tulsi Gabbard, Andy Kim, Kendra S. Horn, Chrissy Houlahan, Jason Crow, Xochitl Torres Small, Elissa Slotkin, Veronica Escobar, Debra A. Haaland

Doug Lamborn (Ranking Minority Member), Austin Scott, Joe Wilson, Rob Bishop, Mike Rogers, Mo Brooks, Elise Stefanik, Jack Bergman

Seapower and Projection Forces
Office: 2340 RHOB 20515   **Phone:** 226-4151

Joe Courtney (Chair), Jim Langevin, Jim Cooper, Donald Norcross, Seth Moulton, Filemon Vela, Gilbert Ray Cisneros Jr., Mikie Sherrill, Katie Hill, Jared Golden, Elaine G. Luria

Robert J. Wittman, (Ranking Minority Member), K. Michael Conaway, Mike Gallagher, Jack Bergman, Michael Waltz, Vicky Hartzler, Paul Cook, Bradley Byrne, Trent Kelly

Strategic Forces
Office: 2340 RHOB 20515   **Phone:** 225-4151

Jim Cooper (Chair), Susan Davis, Rick Larsen, John Garamendi, Jackie Speier, Seth Moulton, Salud Carbajal, Ro Khanna, William Keating, Kendra S. Horn

Michael Turner (Ranking Minority Member), Joe Wilson, Rob Bishop, Mike Rogers, Mo Brooks, Bradley Byrne, Scott DesJarlais, MD, Liz Cheney

Tactical Air and Land Forces
Office: 2340 RHOB 20515   **Phone:** 225-4151

Donald Norcross (Chair), Jim Langevin, Joe Courtney, Rubén Gallego, Salud Carbajal, Anthony Brown, Filemon Vela, Xochitl Torres Small, Mikie Sherrill, Katie Hill, Jared Golden

Vicky Hartzler (Ranking Minority Member), Paul Cook, Matt Gaetz, Don Bacon, Jim Banks, Paul Mitchell, Michael Turner, Doug Lamborn, Robert J. Wittman

BUDGET

Office: 204-E CHOB 20515
Phone: 226-7200   **Fax:** 225-9905
Web: budget.house.gov
Minority Web: republicans-budget.house.gov
Majority Staff Director: Ellen Balis
Minority Staff Director: Dan Keniry, 226-7270, 507 CHOB
Jurisdiction: (1) concurrent resolutions on the budget (as defined in section 3(4) of the Congressional Budget Act of 1974), other matters required to be referred to the committee under titles III and IV of that Act, and other measures setting forth appropriate levels of budget totals for the United States Government; (2) budget process generally; (3) establishment, extension, and enforcement of special controls over the Federal budget, including the budgetary treatment of off-budget Federal agencies and measures providing exemption from reduction under any order issued under part C of the Balanced Budget and Emergency Deficit Control Act of 1985; (4) study on a continuing basis the effect on budget outlays of relevant existing and proposed legislation and report the results of such studies to the House on a recurring basis; (5)(a) review on a continuing basis the conduct by the Congressional Budget Office of its functions and duties; (b) hold hearings and receive testimony from Members, Senators, Delegates, the Resident Commissioner, and such appropriate representatives of Federal departments and agencies, the general public, and national organizations as it considers desirable in developing concurrent resolutions on the budget for each fiscal year; (c) make all reports required of it by the Congressional Budget Act of 1974; (d) study on a continuing basis those provisions of law that exempt Federal agencies or any of their activities or outlays from inclusion in the Budget of the United States Government, and report to the House from time to time its recommendations for terminating or modifying such provisions; (e) study on a continuing basis proposals designed to improve and facilitate the congressional budget process, and report to the House from time to time the results of such studies, together with its recommendations; (f) request and evaluate continuing studies of tax expenditures, devise methods of coordinating tax expenditures, policies, and programs with direct budget outlays, and report the results of such studies to the House on a recurring basis.
Party Ratio: D 19-R 14

John A. Yarmuth, Ky., Chair	*Steve Womack, Ark.*
Seth Moulton, Mass.	*Robert Woodall, Ga.*

Hakeem Jeffries, N.Y.
Brian Higgins, N.Y.
Brendan F. Boyle, Pa.
Ro Khanna, Calif.
Rosa L. DeLauro, Conn.
Lloyd Doggett, Tex.
David Price, N.C.
Jan Schakowsky, Ill.
Daniel Kildee, Mich.
Jimmy Panetta, Calif.
Joseph D. Morelle, N.Y.
Steven Horsford, Nev.
Robert C. Scott, Va.
Sheila Jackson Lee, Tex.
Barbara Lee, Calif.
Pramila Jayapal, Wash.
Ilhan Omar, Minn.

Bill Johnson, Ohio
Jason Smith, Mo.
Bill Flores, Tex.
George Holding, N.C.
Chris Stewart, Utah
Ralph Norman, S.C.
Chip Roy, Tex.
Daniel Meuser, Pa.
William Timmons, S.C.
Dan Crenshaw, Tex.
Kevin Hern, Okla.
Tim Burchett, Tenn.

EDUCATION AND LABOR

Office: 2176 RHOB 2-515
Phone: 225-3725 **Fax:** 225-2350
Web: edlabor.house.gov
Minority Web: republicans-edlabor.house.gov
Majority Staff Director: Véronique Pluviose
Minority Staff Director: Brandon Renz, 225-4527, 2101 RHOB

Jurisdiction: (1) elementary and secondary education initiatives, including the No Child Left Behind Act, school choice for low-income families, special education (the Individuals with Disabilities Education Act), teacher quality and teacher training, scientifically based reading instruction, and vocational and technical education; (2) higher education programs, including the Higher Education Act, which supports college access for low- and middle-income students and helps families pay for college; (3) early childhood care and preschool education programs, including Head Start and the Child Care and Development Block Grant; (4) school lunch and child nutrition programs; (5) financial oversight of the U.S. Department of Education; (6) programs and services for the care and treatment of at-risk youth, child abuse prevention, and child adoption; (7) educational research and improvement; (8) adult education; and (9) antipoverty programs, including the Community Services Block Grant Act and the Low Income Home Energy Assistance Program (LIHEAP); (10) pension and retirement security for U.S. workers; (11) access to quality health care for working families and other employee benefits; (12) job training, adult education, and workforce development initiatives, including those under the Workforce Investment Act (WIA), to help local communities train and retrain workers; (13) continuing the successful welfare reforms of 1996; (14) protecting the democratic rights of individual union members; (15) worker health and safety, including occupational safety and health; (16) providing greater choices and flexibility (including "comp time" or family time options) to working women and men; (17) equal employment opportunity and civil rights in employment; (18) wages and hours of labor, including the Fair Labor Standards Act; (19) workers' compensation, and family and medical leave; (20) all matters dealing with relationships between employers and employees.
Party Ratio: D 28-R 22

Robert C. Scott, Va., Chair
Susan Davis, Calif.
Raúl Grijalva, Ariz.
Joe Courtney, Conn.
Marcia L. Fudge, Ohio
Gregorio Kilili Camacho
  Sablan, Northern
  Mariana Is.
Frederica S. Wilson, Fla.
Suzanne Bonamici, Ore.
Mark Takano, Calif.
Alma Adams, N.C.
Mark DeSaulnier, Calif.
Donald Norcross, N.J.
Pramila Jayapal, Wash.
Joseph D. Morelle, N.Y.
Susan Wild, Pa.
Josh Harder, Calif.
Lucy McBath, Ga.
Kim Schrier, Wash.
Lauren Underwood, Ill.
Jahana Hayes, Conn.
Donna E. Shalala, Fla.
Andy Levin, Mich.
Ilhan Omar, Minn.
David Trone, Md.
Haley Stevens, Mich.
Susie Lee, Nev.
Lori Trahan, Mass.
Joaquin Castro, Tex.

Virginia Foxx, N.C.
Phil Roe, Tenn.
Glenn (GT) Thompson, Pa.
Tim Walberg, Mich.
S. Brett Guthrie, Ky.
Bradley Byrne, Ala.
Glenn Grothman, Wisc.
Elise Stefanik, N.Y.
Rick Allen, Ga.
Francis Rooney, Fla.
Lloyd Smucker, Pa.
Jim Banks, Ind.
Mark Walker, N.C.
James Comer, Ky.
Ben Cline, Va.
Russ Fulcher, Idaho
Van Taylor, Tex.
Steve Watkins, Kans.
Ron Wright, Tex.
Daniel Meuser, Pa.
William Timmons, S.C.
Dusty Johnson, S.D.

Subcommittees

Civil Rights and Human Services
Office: 2176 RHOB 20515 **Phone:** 225-3725
   Suzanne Bonamici (Chair), Raúl Grijalva, Marcia L. Fudge, Kim Schrier, Jahana Hayes, David Trone, Susie Lee
   James Comer (Ranking Minority Member), Glenn (GT) Thompson, Elise Stefanik, Dusty Johnson

Early Childhood, Elementary, and Secondary Education
Office: 2176 RHOB 20515 **Phone:** 225-3725
   Gregorio Kilili Camacho Sablan (Chair), Kim Schrier, Jahana Hayes, Donna E. Shalala, Susan Davis, Frederica S. Wilson, Mark DeSaulnier, Joseph D. Morelle
   Rick Allen (Ranking Minority Member), Glenn (GT) Thompson, Glenn Grothman, Van Taylor, William Timmons

Health, Employment, Labor, and Pensions
Office: 2176 RHOB 20515 **Phone:** 225-3725
   Frederica S. Wilson (Chair), Donald Norcross, Joseph D. Morelle, Susan Wild, Lucy McBath, Lauren Underwood, Haley Stevens, Joe Courtney, Marcia L. Fudge, Josh Harder, Donna E. Shalala, Andy Levin, Tori Trahan
   Tim Walberg (Ranking Minority Member), David P. Roe, Rick Allen, Francis Rooney, Jim Banks, Russ Fulcher, Van Taylor, Steve Watkins Jr., Ron Wright, Daniel Meuser, Dusty Johnson

EDUCATION AND LABOR (continued)

Higher Education and Workforce Development
Office: 2176 RHOB 20515   **Phone:** 225-3725
Susan Davis (Chair), Joe Courtney, Mark Takano, Pramila Jayapal, Josh Harder, Andy Levin, Ilhan Omar, David Trone, Susie Lee, Lori Trahan, Joaquin Castro, Raúl Grijalva, Gregorio Kilili Camacho Sablan, Suzanne Bonamici, Alma Adams, Donald Norcross
Lloyd Smucker (Ranking Minority Member), S. Brett Guthrie, Glenn Grothman, Elise Stefanik, Jim Banks, Mark Walker, James Comer, Ben Cline, Russ Fulcher, Steve Watkins, Daniel Meuser, William Timmons

Workforce Protections
Office: 2176 RHOB 20515   **Phone:** 225-3725
Alma Adams (Chair), Mark DeSaulnier, Mark Takano, Pramila Jayapal, Susan Wild, Lucy McBath, Ilhan Omar, Haley Stevens
Bradley Byrne (Ranking Minority Member), Francis Rooney, Mark Walker, Ben Cline, Ron Wright

ENERGY AND COMMERCE

Office: 2125 RHOB 20515-6115
Phone: 225-2927   **Fax:** 225-5735
Web: energycommerce.house.gov
Minority Web: republicans-energycommerce.house.gov/
Majority Staff Director: Jeffrey Carroll
Minority Staff Director: Mike Bloomquist, 225-3641, 2322 RHOB
Jurisdiction: (1) biomedical research and development; (2) consumer affairs and consumer protection; (3) health and health facilities (except health care supported by payroll deductions); (4) interstate energy compacts; (5) interstate and foreign commerce generally; (6) exploration, production, storage, supply, marketing, pricing, and regulation of energy resources, including all fossil fuels, solar energy, and other unconventional or renewable energy resources; (7) conservation of energy resources; (8) energy information generally; (9) the generation and marketing of power (except by federally chartered or Federal regional power marketing authorities); the reliability and interstate transmission of, and ratemaking for, all power, and siting of generation facilities, except the installation of interconnections between Government water power projects; (10) general management of the Department of Energy and management and all functions of the Federal Energy Regulatory Commission; (11) national energy policy generally; (12) public health and quarantine; (13) regulation of the domestic nuclear energy industry, including regulation of research and development reactors and nuclear regulatory research; (14) regulation of interstate and foreign communications; (15) travel and tourism. The committee shall have the same jurisdiction with respect to regulation of nuclear facilities and of use of nuclear energy as it has with respect to regulation of nonnuclear facilities and of use of nonnuclear energy.
Party Ratio: D 31-R 24

Frank Pallone Jr., N.J., Chair
Bobby L. Rush, Ill.
Anna G. Eshoo, Calif.
Eliot Engel, N.Y.
Diana DeGette, Colo.
Mike Doyle, Pa.
Jan Schakowsky, Ill.
G.K. Butterfield, N.C.
Doris O. Matsui, Calif.
Kathy Castor, Fla.
John P. Sarbanes, Md.
Jerry McNerney, Calif.
Peter Welch, Vt.
Ben Ray Luján, N.M.
Paul D. Tonko, N.Y.
Yvette D. Clarke, N.Y.
David Loebsack, Iowa
Kurt Schrader, Ore.
Joseph P. Kennedy III, Mass.
Tony Cárdenas, Calif.
Raul Ruiz, Calif.
Scott Peters, Calif.
Debbie Dingell, Mich.
Marc Veasey, Tex.
Ann Kuster, N.H.
Robin Kelly, Ill.
Nanette Diaz Barragán, Calif.
A. Donald McEachin, Va.
Lisa Blunt Rochester, Del.
Darren Soto, Fla.
Tom O'Halleran, Ariz.

Greg Walden, Ore.
Fred Upton, Mich.
John Shimkus, Ill.
Michael Burgess, Tex.
Steve Scalise, La.
Robert E. Latta, Ohio
Cathy McMorris Rodgers, Wash.
S. Brett Guthrie, Ky.
Pete Olson, Tex.
David McKinley, W.Va.
Adam Kinzinger, Ill.
Morgan Griffith, Va.
Gus M. Bilirakis, Fla.
Bill Johnson, Ohio
Billy Long, Mo.
Larry Bucshon, Ind.
Bill Flores, Tex.
Susan W. Brooks, Ind.
Markwayne Mullin, Okla.
Richard Hudson, N.C.
Tim Walberg, Mich.
Buddy Carter, Ga.
Jeff Duncan, S.C.
Greg Gianforte, Mont.

Subcommittees

Communications and Technology
Office: 2125 RHOB 20515   **Phone:** 225-2927
Mike Doyle (Chair), Jerry McNerney, Yvette D. Clarke, David Loebsack, Marc Veasey, A. Donald McEachin, Darren Soto, Tom O'Halleran, Anna G. Eshoo, Diana DeGette, G.K. Butterfield, Doris O. Matsui, Peter Welch, Ben Ray Luján, Kurt Schrader, Tony Cárdenas, Debbie Dingell, Frank Pallone Jr. (ex officio)
Robert E. Latta (Ranking Minority Member), John Shimkus, Steve Scalise, Pete Olson, Adam Kinzinger, Gus M. Bilirakis, Bill Johnson, Billy Long, Bill Flores, Susan W. Brooks, Tim Walberg, Greg Gianforte, Greg Walden (ex officio)

Consumer Protection and Commerce
Office: 2125 RHOB 20515   **Phone:** 225-2927
Jan Schakowsky (Chair), Kathy Castor, Marc Veasey, Robin Kelly, Tom O'Halleran, Ben Ray Luján, Tony Cárdenas, Lisa Blunt Rochester, Darren Soto, Bobby L. Rush, Doris O. Matsui, Jerry McNerney, Debbie Dingell Frank Pallone Jr. (ex officio)
Cathy McMorris Rodgers (Ranking Minority Member), Fred Upton, Michael Burgess, Robert E. Latta, S. Brett Guthrie, Larry Bucshon, Richard Hudson, Buddy Carter, Greg Gianforte, Greg Walden (ex officio)

Energy

Office: 2125 RHOB 20515   **Phone:** 225-2927

Bobby L. Rush (Chair), Scott Peters, Mike Doyle, John P. Sarbanes, Jerry McNerney, Paul D. Tonko, David Loebsack, G.K. Butterfield, Peter Welch, Kurt Schrader, Joseph P. Kennedy III, Marc Veasey, Ann Kuster, Robin Kelly, Nanette Diaz Barragán, A. Donald McEachin, Tom O'Halleran, Lisa Blunt Rochester, Frank Pallone Jr. (ex officio)

Fred Upton (Ranking Minority Member), Robert E. Latta, Cathy McMorris Rodgers, Pete Olson, David McKinley, Adam Kinzinger, Morgan Griffith, Bill Johnson, Larry Bucshon, Bill Flores, Richard Hudson, Tim Walberg, Jeff Duncan, Greg Walden (ex officio)

Environment and Climate Change

Office: 2125 RHOB 20515   **Phone:** 225-2927

Paul D. Tonko (Chair), Scott Peters, Yvette D. Clarke, Nanette Diaz Barragán, A. Donald McEachin, Lisa Blunt Rochester, Darren Soto, Diana DeGette, Jan Schakowsky, Doris O. Matsui, Jerry McNerney, Raul Ruiz, Debbie Dingell, Frank Pallone Jr. (ex officio)

John Shimkus (Ranking Minority Member), Cathy McMorris Rodgers, David McKinley, Bill Johnson, Billy Long, Bill Flores, Markwayne Mullin, Buddy Carter, Jeff Duncan, Greg Walden (ex officio)

Health

Office: 2125 RHOB 20515   **Phone:** 225-2927

Anna G. Eshoo (Chair), Eliot Engel, G.K. Butterfield, Doris O. Matsui, Kathy Castor, John P. Sarbanes, Ben Ray Luján, Kurt Schrader, Joseph P. Kennedy III, Tony Cárdenas, Peter Welch, Raul Ruiz, Debbie Dingell, Ann Kuster, Robin Kelly, Nanette Diaz Barragán, Lisa Blunt Rochester, Bobby L. Rush, Frank Pallone Jr. (ex officio)

Michael Burgess (Ranking Minority Member), Fred Upton, John Shimkus, S. Brett Guthrie, Morgan Griffith, Gus M. Bilirakis, Billy Long, Larry Bucshon, Susan W. Brooks, Markwayne Mullin, Richard Hudson, Buddy Carter, Greg Gianforte, Greg Walden (ex officio)

Oversight and Investigations

Office: 2125 RHOB 20515   **Phone:** 225-2927

Diana DeGette (Chair), Jan Schakowsky, Joseph P. Kennedy III, Raul Ruiz, Ann Kuster, Kathy Castor, John P. Sarbanes, Paul D. Tonko, Yvette D. Clarke, Scott Peters, Frank Pallone Jr. (ex officio)

S. Brett Guthrie (Ranking Minority Member), Morgan Burgess, David B. McKinley, Morgan Griffith, Susan W. Brooks, Markwayne Mullin, Jeff Duncan, Greg Walden (ex officio)

ETHICS

Office: 1015 LHOB 20515-6328

Phone: 225-7103   **Fax:** 225-3784

Web: ethics.house.gov

Staff Director and Chief Counsel: Tom Rust

Counsel to the Chair: Dan Taylor

Jurisdiction: (1) recommend administrative actions to establish or enforce standards of official conduct; (2) investigate alleged violations of the Code of Official Conduct or of any applicable rules, laws, or regulations governing the performance of official duties or the discharge of official responsibilities. Such investigations must be made in accordance with Committee rules; (3) report to appropriate federal or state authorities substantial evidence of a violation of any law applicable to the performance of official duties that may have been disclosed in a Committee investigation. Such reports must be approved by the House or by an affirmative vote of two-thirds of the Committee; (4) render advisory opinions regarding the propriety of any current or proposed conduct of a Member, officer, or employee, and issue general guidance on such matters as necessary; (5) consider requests for written waivers of the gift rule (clause 5 of House Rule XXV).

Party Ratio: D 5-R 5

Ted Deutch, Fla., Chair	*Kenny Marchant, Tex.*
Grace Meng, N.Y.	*John Ratcliffe, Tex.*
Susan Wild, Pa.	*George Holding, N.C.*
Dean Phillips, Minn.	*Jackie Walorski, Ind.*
Anthony Brown, Md.	*Michael Guest, Miss.*

FINANCIAL SERVICES

Office: 2129 RHOB 20515-6050

Phone: 225-4247

Web: financialservices.house.gov

Minority Web: republicans-financialservices.house.gov

Majority Staff Director: Charla Ouertatani

Minority Staff Director: Steve Otey, 225-7502, 4340 OHOB

Jurisdiction: (1) banks and banking, including deposit insurance and Federal monetary policy; (2) economic stabilization, defense production, renegotiation, and control of the price of commodities, rents, and services; (3) financial aid to commerce and industry (other than transportation); (4) insurance generally; (5) international finance; (6) international financial and monetary organizations; (7) money and credit, including currency and the issuance of notes and redemption thereof; gold and silver, including the coinage thereof; valuation and revaluation of the dollar; (8) public and private housing; (9) securities and exchanges; (10) urban development.

Party Ratio: D 34-R 26

Maxine Waters, Calif., Chair	*Patrick T. McHenry, N.C.*
Carolyn Maloney, N.Y.	*Pete King, N.Y.*
Nydia M. Velázquez, N.Y.	*Frank Lucas, Okla.*
Brad Sherman, Calif.	*Bill Posey, Fla.*
Gregory W. Meeks, N.Y.	*Blaine Luetkemeyer, Mo.*
William Lacy Clay Jr., Mo.	*Bill Huizenga, Mich.*
David Scott, Ga.	*Sean P. Duffy, Wisc.*
Al Green, Tex.	*Steve Stivers, Ohio*
Emanuel Cleaver, Mo.	*Ann Wagner, Mo.*
Ed Perlmutter, Colo.	*Andy Barr, Ky.*
Jim Himes, Conn.	*Scott Tipton, Colo.*
Bill Foster, Ill.	*Roger Williams, Tex.*
Joyce Beatty, Ohio	*French Hill, Ark.*
Denny Heck, Wash.	*Tom Emmer, Minn.*
Juan Vargas, Calif.	*Lee Zeldin, N.Y.*

FINANCIAL SERVICES (continued)

Josh Gottheimer, N.J.
Vicente Gonzalez
Al Lawson, Fla.
Michael San Nicolas, Guam
Rashida Tlaib, Mich.
Katie Porter, Fla.
Cindy Axne, Iowa
Sean Casten, Ill.
Ayanna Pressley, Mass.
Ben McAdams, Utah
Alexandria Ocasio-Cortez, N.Y.
Jennifer Wexton, Va.
Stephen F. Lynch, Mass.
Tulsi Gabbard, Hawaii
Alma Adams, N.C.
Madeleine Dean, Pa.
Jesús G. García, Ill.
Sylvia Garcia, Tex.
Dean Phillips, Minn.

Barry Loudermilk, Ga.
Alex Mooney, W.Va.
Warren Davidson, Ohio
Ted Budd, N.C.
David Kustoff, Tenn.
Trey Hollingsworth, Ind.
Anthony Gonzalez, Ind.
John Rose, Tenn.
Bryan Steil, Wisc.
Lance Gooden, Tex.
Denver Riggleman, Va.

Subcommittees

Consumer Protection and Financial Institutions
Office: 2129 RHOB 20515   **Phone:** 225-7502

Gregory W. Meeks (Chair), David Scott, Nydia M. Velázquez, William Lacy Clay Jr., Denny Heck, Bill Foster, Al Lawson, Rashida Tlaib, Katie Porter, Ayanna Pressley, Ben McAdams, Alexandria Ocasio-Cortez, Jennifer Wexton

Blaine Luetkemeyer (Ranking Minority Member), Frank Lucas, Bill Posey, Andy Barr, Scott Tipton, Roger Williams, Barry Loudermilk, Ted Budd, David Kustoff, Denver Riggleman

Diversity and Inclusion
Office: 2129 RHOB 20515   **Phone:** 225-7502

Joyce Beatty (Chair), William Lacy Clay Jr., Al Green, Josh Gottheimer, Vicente Gonzalez, Al Lawson, Ayanna Pressley, Tulsi Gabbard, Alma Adams, Madeleine Dean, Sylvia Garcia, Dean Phillips

Ann Wagner (Ranking Minority Member), Frank Lucas, Alex Mooney, Ted Budd, David Kustoff, Trey Hollingsworth, Anthony Gonzalez, Bryan Steil, Lance Gooden

Housing, Community Development, and Insurance
Office: 2129 RHOB 20515   **Phone:** 225-7502

William Lacy Clay Jr. (Chair), Nydia M. Velázquez, Emanuel Cleaver, Brad Sherman, Joyce Beatty, Al Green, Vicente Gonzalez, Carolyn Maloney, Denny Heck, Juan Vargas, Al Lawson, Rashida Tlaib, Cindy Axne

Sean P. Duffy (Ranking Minority Member), Blaine Luetkemeyer, Bill Huizenga, Scott Tipton, Lee Zeldin, David Kustoff, Anthony Gonzalez, John Rose, Bryan Steil, Lance Gooden

Investor Protection, Entrepreneurship, and Capital Markets
Office: 2129 RHOB 20515   **Phone:** 225-7502

Carolyn Maloney (Chair), Brad Sherman, David Scott, Jim Himes, Bill Foster, Gregory W. Meeks, Juan Vargas, Josh Gottheimer, Vicente Gonzalez, Michael San Nicolas, Katie Porter, Cindy Axne, Sean Casten, Alexandria Ocasio-Cortez

Bill Huizenga (Ranking Minority Member), Pete King, Sean P. Duffy, Steve Stivers, Ann Wagner, French Hill, Tom Emmer, Alex Mooney, Warren Davidson, Trey Hollingsworth

National Security, International Development, and Monetary Policy
Office: 2129 RHOB 20515   **Phone:** 225-7502

Emanuel Cleaver (Chair), Ed Perlmutter, Jim Himes, Denny Heck, Brad Sherman, Juan Vargas, Josh Gottheimer, Michael San Nicolas, Ben McAdams, Jennifer Wexton, Stephen F. Lynch, Tulsi Gabbard, Jesús G. García

Steve Stivers (Ranking Minority Member), Pete King, Frank D. Lucas, Roger Williams, French Hill, Tom Emmer, Anthony Gonzalez, John Rose, Denver Riggleman

Oversight and Investigations
Office: 2129 RHOB 20515   **Phone:** 225-7502

Al Green (Chair), Joyce Beatty, Stephen F. Lynch, Nydia M. Velázquez, Ed Perlmutter, Rashida Talib, Sean Casten, Madeleine Dean, Sylvia Garcia, Dean Phillips

Andy Barr (Ranking Minority Member), Bill Posey, Lee Zeldin, Barry Loudermilk, Warren Davidson, John Rose, Bryan Steil

FOREIGN AFFAIRS

Office: 2170 RHOB 20515-6050
Phone: 225-5021   **Fax:** 225-5394
Web: foreignaffairs.house.gov
Minority Web: republicans-foreignaffairs.house.gov
Majority Staff Director:
Minority Staff Director: Brendan Shields, 226-8467, 2066 RHOB

Jurisdiction: (1) foreign assistance (including development assistance, Millennium Challenge Corporation, the Millennium Challenge Account, HIV/AIDS in foreign countries, security assistance, and Public Law 480 programs abroad); (2) the Peace Corps; (3) national security developments affecting foreign policy; (4) strategic planning and agreements; (5) war powers, treaties, executive agreements, and the deployment and use of United States Armed Forces; (6) peacekeeping, peace enforcement, and enforcement of United Nations or other international sanctions; (7) arms control and disarmament issues; (8) the United States Agency for International Development; (9) activities and policies of the State, Commerce and Defense Departments and other agencies related to the Arms Export Control Act, and the Foreign Assistance Act including export and licensing policy for munitions items and technology and dual-use equipment and technology; (10) international law; (11) promotion of democracy; (12) international law enforcement issues, including narcotics control programs and activities; (13) Broadcasting Board of Governors; (14) embassy security; (15) international broadcasting; (16) public diplomacy, including international

communication, information policy, international education, and cultural programs.
Party Ratio: D 26-R 21

Eliot Engel, N.Y., Chair	*Michael T. McCaul, Tex.*
Brad Sherman, Calif.	*Chris Smith, N.J.*
Gregory W. Meeks, N.Y.	*Steve Chabot, Ohio*
Albio Sires, N.J.	*Joe Wilson, S.C.*
Gerald E. (Gerry)	*Scott Perry, Pa.*
Connolly, Va.	*Ted Yoho, Fla.*
Ted Deutch, Fla.	*Adam Kinzinger, Ill.*
Karen Bass, Calif.	*Lee Zeldin, N.Y.*
William Keating, Mass.	*F. James Sensenbrenner,*
David Cicilline, R.I.	*Wisc.*
Ami Bera, Calif.	*Ann Wagner, Mo.*
Joaquin Castro, Tex.	*Brian Mast, Fla.*
Dina Titus, Nev.	*Francis Rooney, Fla.*
Adriano Espaillat, N.Y.	*Brian K. Fitzpatrick, Pa.*
Ted Lieu, Calif.	*John R. Curtis, Utah*
Susan Wild, Pa.	*Ken Buck, Colo.*
Dean Phillips, Minn.	*Ron Wright, Tex.*
Ilhan Omar, Minn.	*Guy Reschenthaler, Pa.*
Colin Allred, Tex.	*Tim Burchett, Tenn.*
Andy Levin, Mich.	*Greg Pence, Ind.*
Abigail Spanberger, Va.	*Steve Watkins, Kans.*
Chrissy Houlahan, Pa.	*Michael Guest, Miss.*
Tom Malinowski, N.J.	
David Trone, Md.	
Jim Costa, Calif.	
Juan Vargas, Calif.	
Vicente Gonzalez, Tex.	

Subcommittees

Africa, Global Health, Global Human Rights, and International Organizations
Office: 2170 RHOB 20515   **Phone:** 225-5021
Karen Bass (Chair), Susan Wild, Dean Phillips, Ilhan Omar, Chrissy Houlahan,
Chris Smith (Ranking Minority Member), F. James Sensenbrenner, Ron Wright, Tim Burchett

Asia, the Pacific, and Nonproliferation
Office: 2170 RHOB 20515   **Phone:** 225-5021
Brad Sherman (Chair), Dina Titus, Chrissy Houlahan, Gerald E. (Gerry) Connolly, Ami Bera, Andy Levin, Abigail Spanberger
Ted Yoho (Ranking Minority Member), Scott Perry, Ann Wagner, Brian Mast, John R. Curtis

Europe and Eurasia, Energy, and the Environment
Office: 2170 RHOB 20515   **Phone:** 225-5021
William Keating (Chair), Abigail Spanberger, Gregory W. Meeks, Albio Sires, Ted Deutch, David Cicilline, Joaquin Castro, Dina Titus, Susan Wild, David Trone, Jim Costa, Vicente Gonzalez
Adam Kinzinger (Ranking Minority Member), Joe Wilson, Ann Wagner, F. James Sensenbrenner, Francis Rooney, Brian K. Fitzpatrick, Greg Pence, Ron Wright, Michael Guest, Tim Burchett

Middle East, North Africa, and International Terrorism
Office: 2170 RHOB 20515   **Phone:** 225-5021
Ted Deutch (Chair), Gerald E. (Gerry) Connolly, David Cicilline, Ted Lieu, Colin Allred, Tom Malinowski, David Trone, Brad Sherman, William Keating, Juan Vargas
Joe Wilson (Ranking Minority Member), Steve Chabot, Adam Kinzinger, Lee Zeldin, Brian Mast, Brian K. Fitzpatrick, Guy Reschenthaler, Steve Watkins

Oversight and Investigations
Office: 2170 RHOB 20515   **Phone:** 225-5021
Ami Bera (Chair), Ilhan Omar, Adriano Espaillat, Ted Lieu, Tom Malinowski, David Cicilline
Lee Zeldin (Ranking Minority Member), Scott Perry, Ken Buck, Guy Reschenthaler

Western Hemisphere, Civilian Security, and Trade
Office: 2170 RHOB 20515   **Phone:** 225-5021
Albio Sires (Chair), Gregory W. Meeks, Joaquin Castro, Adriano Espaillat, Dean Phillips, Andy Levin, Vicente Gonzalez, Juan Vargas
Francis Rooney (Ranking Minority Member), Christopher Smith, Ted Yoho, John R. Curtis, Ken Buck, Michael Guest

HOMELAND SECURITY

Office: H2-176 FHOB 20515-6480
Phone: 226-2616   **Fax:** 447-5437
Web: homeland.house.gov
Minority Web: republicans-homeland.house.gov
Majority Staff Director: Hope Goins
Minority Staff Director: Brendan Shields, 226-8417, H2-117 FHOB
Jurisdiction: (1) overall homeland security policy; (2) organization and administration of the Department of Homeland Security; (3) functions of the Department of Homeland Security relating to the following: (a) border and port security (except immigration policy and non-border enforcement); (b) customs (except customs revenue); (c) integration, analysis, and dissemination of homeland security information; (d) domestic preparedness for and collective response to terrorism; (e) research and development; (f) transportation security.
Party Ratio: D 18-R 13

Bennie G. Thompson,	*Mike Rogers, Ala.*
Miss., Chair	*Pete King, N.Y.*
Sheila Jackson Lee, Tex.	*Michael T. McCaul, Tex.*
Colin Allred	*John Katko, N.Y.*
Jim Langevin, R.I.	*John Ratcliffe, Tex.*
Cedric Richmond, La.	*Mark Walker, N.C.*
Donald Payne Jr., N.J.	*Clay Higgins, La.*
Kathleen Rice, N.Y.	*Debbie Lesko, Ariz.*
J. Luis Correa, Calif.	*Mark E. Green, Tenn.*
Xochitl Torres Small, N.M.	*Van Taylor, Tex.*
Lauren Underwood, Ill.	*John Joyce, Pa.*
Max Rose, N.Y.	*Dan Crenshaw, Tex.*
Elissa Slotkin, Mich.	*Michael Guest, Miss.*
Emanuel Cleaver, Miss.	
Al Green, Tex.	

HOMELAND SECURITY (continued)

Yvette D. Clarke, N.Y.
Dina Titus, Nev.
Bonnie Watson Coleman, N.J.
Nanette Barragán, Calif.
Val Demings, Fla.

Subcommittees

Border Security, Facilitation, and Operations
Office: H2-176 FHOB 20515   **Phone:** 226-2616
Kathleen Rice (Chair), Donald Payne Jr., J. Luis Correa, Xochitl Torres Small, Al Green, Yvette D. Clarke, Bennie G. Thompson (ex officio)
Clay Higgins (Ranking Minority Member), Debbie Lesko, John Joyce, Michael Guest, Mike Rogers (ex officio)

Cybersecurity and Infrastructure Protection
Office: H2-176 FHOB 20515   **Phone:** 226-2616
Cedric Richmond (Chair), Sheila Jackson Lee, Jim Langevin, Kathleen Rice, Lauren Underwood, Elissa Slotkin, Bennie G. Thompson (ex officio)
John Katko (Ranking Minority Member), John Ratcliffe, Mark Walker, Van Taylor, Mike Rogers (ex officio)

Emergency Preparedness, Response, and Recovery
Office: H2-176 FHOB 20515   **Phone:** 226-2616
Donald Payne Jr. (Chair), Cedric Richmond, Max Rose, Lauren Underwood, Al Green, Yvette D. Clarke, Bennie G. Thompson (ex officio)
Pete King (Ranking Minority Member), John Joyce, Dan Crenshaw, Michael Guest, Mike Rogers (ex officio)

Intelligence and Counterterrorism
Office: H2-176 FHOB 20515   **Phone:** 226-2616
Max Rose (Chair), Sheila Jackson Lee, Jim Langevin, Elissa Slotkin, Bennie G. Thompson (ex officio)
Mark Walker (Ranking Minority Member), Pete King, Mark E. Green, Mike Rogers (ex officio)

Oversight, Management, and Accountability
Office: H2-176 FHOB 20515   **Phone:** 226-2616
Xochitl Torres Small (Chair), Dina Titus, Bonnie Watson Coleman, Nanette Diaz Barragán, Bennie G. Thompson (ex officio)
Dan Crenshaw (Ranking Minority Member), Clay Higgins, Van Taylor, Mike Rogers (ex officio)

Transportation and Maritime Security
Office: H2-176 FHOB 20515   **Phone:** 226-2616
J. Luis Correa (Chair), Emanuel Cleaver, Dina Titus, Bonnie Watson Coleman, Nanette Diaz Barragán, Val Demings, Bennie G. Thompson (ex officio)
Debbie Lesko (Ranking Minority Member), John Katko, John Ratcliffe, Mark Green, Mike Rogers (ex officio)

HOUSE ADMINISTRATION

Office: 1316 LHOB 20515-6157
Phone: 225-2061   **Fax:** 225-9957
Web: cha.house.gov
Minority Web: republicans-cha.house.gov

Majority Staff Director: Jamie Fleet
Minority Staff Director: Sean Moran, 225-8281, 309 LHOB
Jurisdiction: (1) appropriations from accounts for committee salaries and expenses (except for the Committee on Appropriations), House Information Resources; and allowance and expenses of Members, Delegates, the Resident Commissioner, officers, and administrative offices of the House; (2) auditing and settling of all accounts described in (1), above; (3) employment of persons by the House, including staff for Members, Delegates, the Resident Commissioner, and committees; and reporters of debates, subject to rule VI; (4) except as provided in clause 1(q)(11), matters relating to the Library of Congress, including management thereof, statuary and pictures, acceptance or purchase of works of art for the United States Capitol, the United States Botanic Garden, and purchase of books and manuscripts; (5) The Smithsonian Institution and the incorporation of similar institutions (except as provided in paragraph (q)(11)); (6) expenditure of accounts described in (1), above; (7) Franking Commission; (8) printing and correction of the Congressional Record; (9) accounts of the House generally; (10) assignment of office space for Members, Delegates, the Resident Commissioner, and committees; (11) disposition of useless executive papers; (12) election of the President, Vice President, and Members of the House of Representatives, Senators, Delegates, or the Resident Commissioner; corrupt practices, contested elections, credentials and qualifications, and federal elections generally; (13) services to the House, including the House Restaurant, parking facilities and administration of the House Office Buildings and of the House wing of the United States Capitol; (14) travel of Members of the House of Representatives, Delegates, and the Resident Commissioner; (15) raising, reporting, and use of campaign contributions for candidates for office of Representative in the House of Representatives, Delegate to the House of Representatives, and of Resident Commissioner; (16) compensation, retirement and other benefits of the Members, Delegates, the Resident Commissioner, officers, and employees of the Congress.
Party Ratio: D 6-R 3

Zoe Lofgren, Calif., Chair	*Rodney Davis, Ill.*
Jamie Raskin, Md.	*Mark Walker, N.C.*
Susan Davis, Calif.	*Barry Loudermilk, Ga.*
G.K. Butterfield, N.C.	
Marcia L. Fudge, Ohio	
Pete Aguilar, Calif.	

JUDICIARY

Office: 2138 RHOB 20515-6216
Phone: 225-3951   **Fax:** 225-7680
Web: judiciary.house.gov
Minority Web: republicans-judiciary.house.gov
Majority Chief of Staff: Perry H. Apelbaum
Minority Staff Director: Shelley Husband, 225-6906, 2142 RHOB
Jurisdiction: (1) judiciary and judicial proceedings, civil and criminal; (2) administrative practice and procedure; (3) apportionment of Representatives; (4) bankruptcy,

mutiny, espionage, and counterfeiting; (5) civil liberties; (6) constitutional amendments; (7) criminal law enforcement; (8) federal courts and judges, and local courts in the Territories and possessions; (9) immigration policy and non-border enforcement; (10) interstate compacts generally; (11) claims against the United States; (12) members of Congress, attendance of members, Delegates, and the Resident Commissioner; and their acceptance of incompatible offices; (13) national penitentiaries; (14) patents, the Patent and Trademark Office, copyrights, and trademarks; (15) presidential succession; (16) protection of trade and commerce against unlawful restraints and monopolies; (17) revision and codification of the Statutes of the United States; (18) state and territorial boundary lines; (19) subversive activities affecting the internal security of the United States.

Party Ratio: D 24-R 17

Jerrold Nadler, N.Y., Chair	Doug Collins, Ga.
Mary Gay Scanlon, Pa.	F. James Sensenbrenner,
Zoe Lofgren, Calif.	Wisc.
Sheila Jackson Lee, Tex.	Steve Chabot, Ohio
Steve Cohen, Tenn.	Louie Gohmert, Tex.
Hank Johnson Jr., Ga.	Jim Jordan, Ohio
Ted Deutch, Fla.	Ken Buck, Colo.
Karen Bass, Calif.	John Ratcliffe, Tex.
Cedric Richmond, La.	Martha Roby, Ala.
Hakeem Jeffries, N.Y.	Matt Gaetz, Fla.
David Cicilline, R.I.	Mike Johnson, La.
Eric Swalwell, Calif.	Andy Biggs, Ariz.
Ted Lieu, Calif.	Tom McClintock, Calif.
Jamie Raskin, Md.	Debbie Lesko, Ariz.
Pramila Jayapal, Wash.	Guy Reschenthaler, Pa.
Val Demings, Fla.	Ben Cline, Va.
J. Luis Correa, Calif.	Kelly Armstrong, N.D.
Sylvia R. Garcia, Tex.	W. Gregory Steube, Fla.
Joe Neguse, Colo.	
Lucy McBath, Ga.	
Greg Stanton, Ariz.	
Madeleine Dean, Pa	
Debbie Mucarsel-Powell,	
Fla.	
Veronica Escobar, Tex.	

Subcommittees

Antitrust, Commercial, and Administrative Law
Office: 6240 OHOB 20024 **Phone:** 226-7680

David Cicilline (Chair), Joe Neguse, Hank Johnson, Jamie Raskin, Pramila Jayapal, Val Demings, Mary Gay Scanlon, Lucy McBath

F. James Sensenbrenner (Ranking Minority Member), Matt Gaetz, Ken Buck, Kelly Armstrong, W. Gregory Steube

Constitution, Civil Rights, and Civil Liberties
Office: 2138 RHOB 20515 **Phone:** 225-3951

Steve Cohen (Chair), Jamie Raskin, Eric Swalwell, Mary Gay Scanlon, Madeleine Dean, Sylvia Garcia, Veronica Escobar, Sheila Jackson Lee

Mike Johnson (Ranking Minority Member), Louie Gohmert, Jim Jordan, Guy Reschenthaler, Ben Cline, Kelly Armstrong

Courts, Intellectual Property, and the Internet
Office: 6240 OHOB 20515-6216 **Phone:** 225-5741

Hank Johnson (Chair), J. Luis Correa, Ted Deutch, Cedric Richmond, Hakeem Jeffries, Ted Lieu, Greg Stanton, Zoe Lofgren, Steve Cohen, Karen Bass, Eric Swalwell

Martha Roby (Ranking Minority Member), Steve Chabot, Jim Jordan, John Ratcliffe, Matt Gaetz, Andy Biggs, Guy Reschenthaler, Ben Cline, Mike Johnson

Crime, Terrorism, and Homeland Security
Office: 6240 OHOB 20515 **Phone:** 225-5727

Karen Bass (Chair), Val Demings, Sheila Jackson Lee, Lucy McBath, Ted Deutch, Cedric Richmond, Hakeem Jeffries, David Cicilline, Ted Lieu, Madeleine Dean, Debbie Mucarsel-Powell, Steve Cohen

John Ratcliffe (Ranking Minority Member), F. James Sensenbrenner, Steve Chabot, Louie Gohmert, Tom McClintock, Debbie Lesko, Guy Reschenthaler, Ben Cline, W. Gregory Steube

Immigration and Citizenship
Office: 6320 OHOB 20515 **Phone:** 225-3926

Zoe Lofgren (Chair), Pramila Jayapal, J. Luis Correa, Sylvia Garcia, Joe Neguse, Debbie Mucarsel-Powell, Veronica Escobar, Sheila Jackson Lee, Mary Gay Scanlon

Ken Buck (Ranking Minority Member), Andy Biggs, Tom McClintock, Debbie Lesko, Kelly Armstrong, W. Gregory Steube

NATURAL RESOURCES

Office: 1324 LHOB 20515-6201
Phone: 225-6065 **Fax:** 225-4273
Web: naturalresources.house.gov
Minority Web: republicans-naturalresources.house.gov
Majority Staff Director: David Watkins
Minority Staff Director: Parish Braden, 225-2761, 1329 LHOB

Jurisdiction: (1) fisheries and wildlife, including research, restoration, refuges, and conservation; (2) forest reserves and national parks created from the public domain; (3) forfeiture of land grants and alien ownership, including alien ownership of mineral lands; (4) Geological Survey; (5) international fishing agreements; (6) interstate compacts relating to apportionment of waters for irrigation purposes; (7) irrigation and reclamation, including water supply for reclamation projects and easements of public lands for irrigation projects; and acquisition of private lands when necessary to complete irrigation projects; (8) Native Americans generally, including the care and allotment of Native American lands and general and special measures relating to claims that are paid out of Native American funds; (9) insular possessions of the United States generally (except those affecting the revenue and appropriations); (10) military parks and battlefields, national cemeteries administered by the Secretary of the Interior, parks within the District of Columbia, and the erection of monuments to the memory of individuals; (11) mineral land laws and claims and entries thereunder; (12) mineral resources of public lands; (13) mining

NATURAL RESOURCES (continued)

interests generally; (14) mining schools and experimental stations; (15) marine affairs, including coastal zone management (except for measures relating to oil and other pollution of navigable waters); (16) oceanography; (17) petroleum conservation on public lands and conservation of the radium supply in the United States; (18) preservation of prehistoric ruins and objects of interest on the public domain; (19) public lands generally, including entry, easements, and grazing thereon; (20) relations of the United States with Native Americans and Native American tribes; (21) Trans-Alaska Oil Pipeline (except ratemaking).
Party Ratio: D 23-R 19

Raúl Grijalva, Ariz., Chair
Grace Napolitano, Calif.
Jim Costa, Calif.
Gregorio Kilili Camacho Sablan, Northern Mariana Is.
Jared Huffman, Calif.
Alan Lowenthal, Calif.
Rubén Gallego, Ariz.
TJ Cox, Calif.
Joe Neguse, Colo.
Mike Levin, Calif.
Debra A. Haaland, N.M.
Jefferson Van Drew, N.J.
Joe Cunningham, S.C.
Nydia M. Velázquez, N.Y.
Diana DeGette, Colo.
William Lacy Clay Jr., Mo.
Debbie Dingell, Mich.
Anthony Brown, Md.
A. Donald McEachin, Va.
Darren Soto, Fla.
Ed Case, Hawaii
Steven Horsford, Nev.
Michael San Nicolas, Guam

Rob Bishop, Utah,
Don Young, Alaska
Louie Gohmert, Tex.
Doug Lamborn, Colo.
Robert J. Wittman, Va.
Tom McClintock, Calif.
Paul A. Gosar, Ariz.
Paul Cook, Calif.
Bruce Westerman, Ark.
Garret Graves, La.
Jody Hice, Ga.
Aumua Amata Coleman Radewagen, Am. Samoa
Daniel Webster, Fla.
Liz Cheney, Wyo.
Mike Johnson, La.
Jenniffer González-Colón, P.R.
John R. Curtis, Utah
Kevin Hern, Okla.
Russ Fulcher, Idaho

Subcommittees

Energy and Mineral Resources
Office: 1522 LHOB 20515   **Phone:** 225-9297
Alan Lowenthal (Chair), Mike Levin, Joe Cunningham, A. Donald McEachin, Diana DeGette, Anthony Brown, Jared Huffman, Raúl Grijalva (ex officio)
Paul A. Gosar (Ranking Minority Member), Doug Lamborn, Bruce Westerman, Garret Graves, Liz Cheney, Kevin Hern, Rob Bishop (ex officio)

National Parks, Forests, and Public Lands
Office: 1328 LHOB 20515   **Phone:** 226-7736
Debra A. Haaland (Chair), Alan Lowenthal, Rubén Gallgo, Diana DeGette, Debbie Dingell, Steven Horsford, Jared Huffman, Ed Case, Joe Neguse, Raúl Grijalva (ex officio)
Don Young (Ranking Minority Member), Louie Gohmert, Tom McClintock, Paul Cook, Bruce Westerman, Jody Hice, Daniel Webster, John Curtis, Russ Fulcher, Rob Bishop (ex officio)

Indigenous Peoples of the United States
Office: 1331 LHOB 20515   **Phone:** 226-9725
Rubén Gallego (Chair), Darren Soto, Michael San Nicolas, Debra A. Haaland, Ed Case, Raúl Grijalva (ex officio)
Paul Cook (Ranking Minority Member), Don Young, Aumua Amata Coleman Radewagen, John R. Curtis, Kevin Hern, Vacancy, Rob Bishop (ex officio)

Oversight and Investigations
Office: H2-186 OHOB 20515   **Phone:** 225-7107
TJ Cox (Chair), Debbie Dingell, Michael San Nicolas, Raúl M. Grijalva (ex officio)
Louie Gohmert (Ranking Minority Member), Paul A. Gosar, Mike Johnson, Jenniffer González-Colón, Rob Bishop (ex officio)

Water, Oceans, and Wildlife
Office: 1332 LHOB 20515   **Phone:** 225-8331
Jared Huffman (Chair), Grace Napolitano, Jim Costa, Gregorio Kilili Camacho Sablan, Jefferson Van Drew, Nydia M. Velázquez, Anthony Brown, Ed Case, Alan Lowenthal, TJ Cox, Joe Neguse, Mike Levin, Joe Cunningham, Raúl Grijalva (ex officio)
Tom McClintock, (Ranking Minority Member), Doug Lamborn, Robert J. Wittman, Garret Graves, Jody Hice, Aumua Amata Coleman Radewagen, Daniel Webster, Mike Johnson, Jenniffer González-Colón, Russ Fulcher, Rob Bishop (ex officio)

OVERSIGHT AND REFORM

Office: 2157 RHOB 20515-6143
Phone: 225-5051   **Fax:** 225-4784
Web: oversight.house.gov
Minority Web: republicans-oversight.house.gov
Majority Staff Director: David Rapallo
Minority Staff Director: Chris Hixon, 225-5074, 2157 RHOB
Jurisdiction: (1) federal civil service, including intergovernmental personnel; and the status of officers and employees of the United States, including their compensation, classification, and retirement; (2) municipal affairs of the District of Columbia in general (other than appropriations); (3) federal paperwork reduction; (4) government management and accounting measures generally; (5) holidays and celebrations; (6) overall economy, efficiency, and management of government operations and activities, including Federal procurement; (7) national archives; (8) population and demography generally, including the Census; (9) Postal Service generally, including transportation of the mails; (10) public information and records; (11) relationship of the Federal Government to the States and municipalities generally; (12) reorganizations in the executive branch of the Government.
Party Ratio: D 24-R 18

Elijah Cummings, Md., Chair
Carolyn Maloney, N.Y.
Eleanor Holmes Norton, D.C.

Jim Jordan, Ohio
Justin Amash, Mich.
Paul A. Gosar, Ariz.
Virginia Foxx, N.C.

William Lacy Clay Jr., Mo.
Stephen F. Lynch, Mass.
Jim Cooper, Tenn.
Gerald E. (Gerry) Connolly, Va.
Raja Krishnamoorthi, Ill.
Jamie Raskin, Md.
Harley Rouda, Calif.
Katie Hill, Calif.
Debbie Wasserman Schultz, Fla.
John P. Sarbanes, Md.
Peter Welch, Vt.
Jackie Speier, Calif.
Robin Kelly, Ill.
Mark DeSaulnier, Calif.
Brenda Lawrence, Mich.
Stacey E. Plaskett, V.I.
Ro Khanna, Calif.
Jimmy Gomez, Calif.
Alexandria Ocasio-Cortez, N.Y.
Ayanna Pressley, Mass.
Rashida Tlaib, Mich.

Thomas Massie, Ky.
Mark Meadows, N.C.
Jody Hice, Ga.
Glenn Grothman, Wisc.
James Comer, Ky.
Michael Cloud, Tex.
Bob Gibbs, Ohio
Ralph Norman, S.C.
Clay Higgins, La.
Chip Roy, Tex.
Carol Miller, W.Va.
Mark E. Green, Tenn.
Kelly Armstrong, N.D.
W. Gregory Steube, Fla.

Subcommittees

Civil Rights and Civil Liberties
Office: 2157 RHOB 20515   **Phone:** 225-5051
Jamie Raskin (Chair), Carolyn Maloney, William Lacy Clay Jr., Debbie Wasserman Schultz, Robin Kelly, Jimmy Gomez, Alexandria Ocasio-Cortez, Ayanna Pressley, Eleanor Holmes Norton
Chip Roy (Ranking Minority Member), Justin Amash, Thomas Massie, Mark Meadows, Jody Hice, Michael Cloud, Carol Miller

Economic and Consumer Policy
Office: 2157 RHOB 20515   **Phone:** 225-5051
Raja Krishnamoorthi (Chair), Mark DeSaulnier, Katie Hill, Ro Khanna, Ayanna Pressley, Rashida Tlaib, Gerald E. (Gerry) Connolly
Michael Cloud (Ranking Minority Member), Glenn Grothman, James Comer, Chip Roy, Carol Miller

Environment
Office: 2157 RHOB 20515   **Phone:** 225-5051
Harley Rouda (Chair), Katie Hill, Rashida Tlaib, Raja Krishnamoorthi, Jackie Speier, Jimmy Gomez, Alexandria Ocasio-Cortez
James Comer (Ranking Minority Member), Paul Gosar, Bob Gibbs, Clay Higgins, Kelly Armstrong

Government Operations
Office: 2157 RHOB 20515   **Phone:** 225-5051
Gerald E. (Gerry) Connolly (Chair), Eleanor Holmes Norton, John P. Sarbanes, Jackie Speier, Brenda Lawrence, Stacey E. Plaskett, Ro Khanna, Stephen F. Lynch, Jamie Raskin
Mark Meadows (Ranking Minority Member), Thomas Massie, Jody Hice, Glenn Grothman, James Comer, Ralph Norman, W. Gregory Steube

National Security
Office: 2157 RHOB 20515   **Phone:** 225-5051
Stephen F. Lynch (Chair), Jim Cooper, Peter Welch, Harley Rouda, Debbie Wasserman Schultz, Robin Kelly, Mark DeSaulnier, Stacey E. Plaskett, Brenda Lawrence
Jody Hice (Ranking Minority Member), Justin Amash, Paul A. Gosar, Virginia Foxx, Mark Meadows, Michael Cloud, Mark E. Green

RULES

Office: H-312 CAP 20515-6269
Phone: 225-9091   **Fax:** 226-9191
Web: rules.house.gov
Minority Web: republicans-rules.house.gov
Majority Staff Director: Don Sisson
Minority Staff Director: Kelly Dixon, 225-9191, H-152 CAP
   Jurisdiction: (1) the rules and joint rules (other than rules or joint rules relating to the Code of Official Conduct), and order of business of the House; (2) recesses and final adjournments of Congress.
Party Ratio: D 9-R 4

James McGovern, Mass., Chair
Alcee L. Hastings, Fla.
Norma Torres, Calif.
Ed Perlmutter, Colo.
Jamie Raskin, Md.
Mary Gay Scanlon, Pa.
Joseph D. Morelle, N.Y.
Donna E. Shalala, Fla.
Mark DeSaulnier, Calif.

Tom Cole, Okla.
Robert Woodall, Ga.
Michael Burgess, Tex.
Debbie Lesko, Ariz.

Subcommittees

Legislative and Budget Process
Office: H-312 CAP 20515   **Phone:** 225-9091
Alcee L. Hastings (Chair), Joseph D. Morelle, Mary Gay Scanlon, Donna E. Shalala, James McGovern
Robert Woodall (Ranking Minority Member), Michael Burgess

Rules and Organization of the House
Office: H-312 CAP 20515   **Phone:** 225-9091
Norma Torres (Chair), Ed Perlmutter, Mary Gay Scanlon, Joseph D. Morelle, James McGovern
Debbie Lesko (Ranking Minority Member), Robert Woodall

SCIENCE, SPACE, AND TECHNOLOGY

Office: 2321 RHOB 20515-6301
Phone: 225-6375   **Fax:** 225-3895
Web: science.house.gov
Minority Web: republicans-science.house.gov
Majority Staff Director: Richard Obermann
Minority Staff Director: Josh Mathis, 225-6371, 394 FHOB

SCIENCE, SPACE, AND TECHNOLOGY
(continued)

Jurisdiction: (1) all energy research, development, and demonstration, and projects therefor, and all federally owned or operated nonmilitary energy laboratories; (2) astronautical research and development, including resources, personnel, equipment, and facilities; civil aviation research and development; (3) environmental research and development; (4) marine research; commercial application of energy technology; (5) National Institute of Standards and Technology, standardization of weights and measures and the metric system; (6) National Aeronautics and Space Administration; (7) National Science Foundation; (8) National Weather Service; (9) outer space, including exploration and control thereof; (10) science scholarships; scientific research, development, and demonstration, and projects therefor; (11) The Committee shall review and study on a continuing basis laws, programs, and Government activities relating to nonmilitary research and development.
Party Ratio: D 22-R 17

Eddie Bernice Johnson, Tex., Chair	Frank Lucas, Okla.
	Mo Brooks, Ala.
Zoe Lofgren, Calif.	Bill Posey, Fla.
Daniel Lipinski, Ill.	Randy Weber, Tex.
Suzanne Bonamici, Ore.	Brian Babin, Tex.
Ami Bera, Calif.	Andy Biggs, Ariz.
Conor Lamb, Pa.	Roger Marshall, Kans.
Lizzie Fletcher, Tex.	Neal Dunn, Fla.
Haley Stevens, Mich.	Ralph Norman, S.C.
Kendra S. Horn, Okla.	Michael Cloud, Tex.
Mikie Sherrill, N.J.	Troy Balderson, Ohio
Brad Sherman, Calif.	Pete Olson, Tex.
Steve Cohen, Tenn.	Anthony Gonzalez, Ohio
Jerry McNerney, Calif.	Michael Waltz, Fla.
Ed Perlmutter, Colo.	James R. Baird, Ind.
Paul D. Tonko, N.Y.	Vacant
Bill Foster, Ill.	Vacant
Don Beyer, Va.	
Charlie Crist, Fla.	
Sean Casten, Ill.	
Katie Hill, Calif.	
Ben McAdams, Utah	
Jennifer Wexton, Va.	

Subcommittees

Energy
Office: 2321 RHOB 20515   **Phone:** 225-6375
Conor Lamb (Chair), Daniel Lipinski, Lizzie Fletcher, Haley Stevens, Kendra S. Horn, Jerry McNerney, Bill Foster, Sean Casten
Randy Weber (Ranking Minority Member), Andy Biggs, Neal Dunn, Ralph Norman, Michael Cloud

Environment
Office: 2321 RHOB 20515   **Phone:** 225-6375
Lizzie Fletcher (Chair), Suzanne Bonamici, Conor Lamb, Paul D. Tonko, Charlie Crist, Sean Casten, Ben McAdams, Don Beyer
Roger Marshall (Ranking Minority Member), Brian Babin, Anthony Gonzalez, James R. Baird, Vacant

Investigations and Oversight
Office: 2321 RHOB 20515   **Phone:** 225-6375
Mikie Sherrill (Chair), Suzanne Bonamici, Steve Cohen, Don Beyer, Jennifer Wexton
Ralph Norman (Ranking Minority Member), Andy Biggs, Michael Waltz

Research and Technology
Office: 2321 RHOB 20515   **Phone:** 225-6375
Haley Stevens (Chair), Dan Lipinski, Mikie Sherrill, Brad Sherman, Paul D. Tonko, Ben McAdams, Steve Cohen, Bill Foster
James R. Baird (Ranking Minority Member), Roger Marshall, Neal Dunn, Troy Balderson, Anthony Gonzalez

Space and Aeronautics
Office: 2321 RHOB 20515   **Phone:** 225-6375
Kendra S. Horn (Chair), Zoe Lofgren, Ami Bera, Ed Perlmutter, Don Beyer, Charlie Crist, Katie Hill, Jennifer Wexton
Brian Babin (Ranking Minority Member), Mo Brooks, Bill Posey, Pete Olson, Michael Waltz

SMALL BUSINESS

Office: 2361 RHOB 20515-6315
Phone: 225-4038   **Fax:** 225-7209
Web: smallbusiness.house.gov
Minority Web: republicans-smallbusiness.house.gov
Majority Staff Director: Adam Minehardt
Minority Staff Director: Kevin Fitzpatrick, 225-5821, 2069 RHOB
Jurisdiction: (1) Assistance to and protection of small business, including financial aid, regulatory flexibility, and paperwork reduction; (2) participation of small-business enterprises in Federal procurement and Government contracts; (3) The Committee on Small Business shall study and investigate on a continuing basis the problems of all types of small business.
Party Ratio: D 13-R 10

Nydia M. Velázquez, N.Y., Chair	Steve Chabot, Ohio
	Aumua Amata Coleman Radewagen, Am. Samoa
Abby Finkenauer, Iowa	Trent Kelly, Miss.
Jared Golden, Maine	
Andy Kim, N.J.	Troy Balderson, Ohio
Sharice Davids, Kans.	Kevin Hern, Okla.
Jason Crow, Colo.	Jim Hagedorn, Minn.
Judy Chu, Calif.	Pete Stauber, Minn.
Marc Veasey, Tex.	Tim Burchett, Tenn.
Dwight Evans, Pa.	Ross Spano, Fla.
Bradley Schneider, Ill.	John Joyce, Pa.
Adriano Espaillat, N.Y.	
Antonio Delgado, N.Y.	
Chrissy Houlahan, Pa.	

Subcommittees

Contracting and Infrastructure
Office: 2361 RHOB 20515   **Phone:** 225-5821
Jared Golden (Chair), Marc Veasey, Judy Chu

Pete Stauber (Ranking Minority Member), Jim Hagedorn, Troy Balderson

Economic Growth, Tax, and Capital Access
Office: 2361 RHOB 20515 **Phone:** 225-5821
Andy Kim (Chair), Sharice Davids, Bradley Schneider, Adriano Espaillat, Antonio Delgado, Jason Crow
Kevin Hern (Ranking Minority Member), Ross Spano, Aumua Amata Coleman Radewagen, Pete Stauber

Innovation and Workforce Development
Office: 2361 RHOB 20515 **Phone:** 225-5821
Jason Crow (Chair), Marc Veasey, Chrissy Houlahan, Abby Finkenauer, Andy Kim, Sharice Davids
Troy Balderson (Ranking Minority Member), Tim Burchett, Kevin Hern

Investigations, Oversight, and Regulations
Office: 2361 RHOB 20515 **Phone:** 225-5821
Judy Chu (Chair), Dwight Evans
Ross Spano (Ranking Minority Member), Trent Kelly, Tim Burchett

Rural Development, Agriculture, Trade, and Entrepreneurship
Office: 2361 RHOB 20515 **Phone:** 225-5821
Abby Finkenauer (Chair), Jared Golden, Jason Crow
John Joyce (Ranking Minority Member), Aumua Amata Coleman Radewagen, Trent Kelly, Jim Hagedorn

TRANSPORTATION AND INFRASTRUCTURE

Office: 2165 RHOB 20515-6256
Phone: 225-4472
Web: transportation.house.gov
Minority Web: republicans-transportation.house.gov
Majority Staff Director: Katherine Dedrick
Minority Staff Director: Paul Sass, 225-9446, 2164 RHOB
Jurisdiction: (1) Coast Guard, including lifesaving service, lighthouses, lightships, ocean derelicts, and the Coast Guard Academy; (2) federal management of emergencies and natural disasters; (3) flood control and improvement of rivers and harbors; (4) inland waterways; (5) inspection of merchant marine vessels, lights and signals, lifesaving equipment, and fire protection on such vessels; (6) navigation and laws relating thereto, including pilotage; (7) registering and licensing of vessels and small boats; (8) rules and international arrangements to prevent collisions at sea; (9) the Capitol Building, the Senate and House Office Buildings; (10) constructions or maintenance of roads and post roads (other than appropriations therefor); (11) construction or reconstruction, maintenance, and care of buildings and grounds of the Botanic Garden, the Library of Congress, and the Smithsonian Institution; (12) merchant marine (except for national security aspects thereof); (13) purchase of sites and construction of post offices, customhouses, Federal courthouses, and Government buildings within the District of Columbia; (14) oil and other pollution of navigable waters, including inland, coastal, and ocean waters; (15) marine affairs, including coastal zone management, as they relate to oil and other pollution of navigable waters; (16) public buildings and occupied or improved grounds of the United States generally; (17) public works for the benefit of the benefit of navigation, including bridges and dams (other than international bridges and dams); (18) related transportation regulatory agencies (except the Transportation Security Administration); (19) roads and the safety thereof; (20) transportation, including civil aviation, railroads, water transportation, transportation safety (except automobile safety and transportation security functions of the Department of Homeland Security), transportation infrastructure, transportation labor, and railroad retirement and unemployment (except revenue measures related thereto); (21) water power.
Party Ratio: D 37-R 30

Peter DeFazio, Ore., Chair	Sam Graves, Mo.
Eleanor Holmes Norton, D.C.	Don Young, Alaska
Eddie Bernice Johnson, Tex.	Rick Crawford, Ark.
Elijah Cummings, Md.	Bob Gibbs, Ohio
Rick Larsen, Wash.	Daniel Webster, Fla.
Grace Napolitano, Calif.	Thomas Massie, Ky.
Daniel Lipinski, Ill.	Mark Meadows, N.C.
Steve Cohen, Tenn.	Scott Perry, Pa.
Albio Sires, N.J.	Rodney Davis, Ill.
John Garamendi, Calif.	Robert Woodall, Ga.
Hank Johnson Jr., Ga.	Brian Babin, Tex.
André Carson, Ind.	Garret Graves, La.
Dina Titus, Nev.	David Rouzer, N.C.
Sean Patrick Maloney, N.Y.	Mike Bost, Ill.
Jared Huffman, Calif.	Randy Weber, Tex.
Julia Brownley, Calif.	Doug LaMalfa, Calif.
Frederica S. Wilson, Fla.	Bruce Westerman, Ark.
Donald Payne Jr., N.J.	Lloyd Smucker, Pa.
Alan Lowenthal, Calif.	Paul Mitchell, Mich.
Mark DeSaulnier, Calif.	John Katko, N.Y.
Stacey E. Plaskett, V.I.	Brian Mast, Fla.
Stephen F. Lynch, Mass.	Mike Gallagher, Wisc.
Salud Carbajal, Calif.	Jenniffer González-Colón, P.R.
Anthony Brown, Md.	
Adriano Espaillat, N.Y.	Ross Spano, Fla.
Tom Malinowski, N.J.	Pete Stauber, Minn.
Greg Stanton, Ariz.	Carol Miller, W.Va.
Debbie Mucarsel-Powell, Fla.	Troy Balderson, Ohio
Lizzie Fletcher, Tex.	Gary Palmer, Ala.
Colin Allred, Tex.	Brian K. Fitzpatrick, Pa.
Sharice Davids, Kans.	Greg Pence, Ind.
Abby Finkenauer, Iowa	
Jesús G. García, Ill.	
Antonio Delgado, N.Y.	
Chris Pappas, N.H.	
Angie Craig, Minn.	
Harley Rouda, Calif.	

Subcommittees

Aviation
Office: 2251 RHOB 20515 **Phone:** 226-3220
Rick Larsen (Chair), André Carson, Stacey E. Plaskett, Stephen F. Lynch, Eleanor Holmes Norton, Daniel Lipsinki, Steve Cohen, Henry C. Johnson Jr., Dina Titus, Julia Brownley, Anthony Brown, Greg Stanton, Colin Allred, Jesús G. García, Eddie Bernice Johnson, Sean

TRANSPORTATION AND INFRASTRUCTURE
(continued)

Patrick Maloney, Donald Payne Jr., Sharice Davids, Angie Craig, Grace Napolitano, Salud Carbajal, Peter DeFazio (ex officio)
Garret Graves (Ranking Minority Member), Don Young, Daniel Webster, Thomas Massie, Scott Perry, Robert Woodall, John Katko, David Rouzer, Lloyd Smucker, Paul Mitchell, Brian Mast, Mike Gallagher, Brian K. Fitzpatrick, Troy Balderson, Ross Spano, Pete Stauber, Sam Graves

Coast Guard and Maritime Transportation
Office: 507 FHOB 20515   **Phone:** 226-3552
Sean Patrick Maloney (Chair), Elijah Cummings, Rick Larsen, Stacey E. Plaskett, John Garamendi, Alan Lowenthal, Anthony Brown, Chris Pappas, Peter DeFazio (ex officio)
Bob Gibbs (Ranking Minority Member), Don Young, Randy Weber, Brian Mast, Mike Gallagher, Carol Miller, Sam Graves

Economic Development, Public Buildings, and Emergency Management
Office: 586 FHOB 20515   **Phone:** 225-3014
Dina Titus (Chair), Debbie Mucarsel-Powell, Sharice Davids, Eleanor Holmes Norton, Henry C. Johnson Jr., John Garamendi, Anthony Brown, Lizzie Fletcher, Peter DeFazio (ex officio)
Mark Meadows (Ranking Minority Member), Gary Palmer, Jenniffer González-Colón, Carol Miller, Greg Pence, Sam Graves

Highways and Transit
Office: 2251 RHOB 20515   **Phone:** 225-6715
Eleanor Holmes Norton (Chair), Eddie Bernice Johnson, Steve Cohen, John Garamendi, Henry C. Johnson. Jr., Jared Huffman, Julia Brownley, Frederica S. Wilson, Alan Lowenthal, Mark DeSaulnier, Salud Carbajal, Anthony Brown, Adriano Espaillat, Tom Malinowski, Greg Stanton, Colin Allred, Sharice Davids, Abby Finkenauer, Jesús G. García, Antonio Delgado, Chris Pappas, Angie Craig, Harley Rouda, Grace Napolitano, Albio Sires, Sean Patrick Maloney, Donald Payne Jr., Daniel Lipinski, Dina Titus, Stacey E. Plaskett, Peter DeFazio (Ex Officio)
Rodney Davis (Ranking Minority Member), Don Young, Rick Crawford, Bob Gibbs, Daniel Webster, Thomas Massie, Mark Meadows, Robert Woodall, John Katko, Brian Babin, David Rouzer, Mike Bost, Doug LaMalfa, Bruce Westerman, Lloyd Smucker, Paul Mitchell, Mike Gallagher, Gary Palmer, Brian K. Fitzpatrick, Troy Balderson, Ross Spano, Pete Stauber, Carol Miller, Greg Pence, Sam Graves

Railroads, Pipelines, and Hazardous Materials
Office: 2029 RHOB 20515   **Phone:** 226-0727
Daniel Lipsinki (Chair), Albio Sires, Donald Payne Jr., Lizzie Fletcher, Elijah Cummings, André Carson, Frederica S. Wilson, Mark DeSaulnier, Stephen F. Lynch, Tom Malinowski, Grace Napolitano, Steve Cohen, Jesús G. García, Eleanor Holmes Norton, Eddie Bernice Johnson,

Alan Lowenthal, Colin Allred, Angie Craig, Peter DeFazio (ex officio)
Rick Crawford (Ranking Minority Member), Scott Perry, Rodney Davis, Brian Babin, Mike Bost, Randy Weber, Doug LaMalfa, Lloyd Smucker, Paul Mitchell, Brian K. Fitzpatrick, Troy Balderson, Ross Spano, Pete Stauber, Greg Pence, Sam Graves

Water Resources and Environment
Office: 585 FHOB 20515   **Phone:** 225-4360
Grace Napolitano (Chair), Debbie Mucarsel-Powell, Eddie Bernice Johnson, John Garamendi, Jared Huffman, Alan Lowenthal, Salud Carbajal, Adriano Espaillat, Lizzie Fletcher, Abby Finkenauer, Antonio Delgado, Chris Pappas, Angie Craig, Harley Rouda, Frederica S. Wilson, Stephen F. Lynch, Tom Malinowski, Peter DeFazio (ex officio)
Bruce Westerman (Ranking Minority Member), Daniel Webster, Thomas Massie, Robert Woodall, Brian Babin, Garret Graves, David Rouzer, Mike Bost, Randy Weber, Doug LaMalfa, Brian Mast, Gary Palmer, Jenniffer González-Colón, Sam Graves

VETERANS' AFFAIRS

Office: B234 LHOB 20515-6335
Phone: 225-9756   **Fax:** 225-2034
Web: veterans.house.gov
Minority Web: republicans-veterans.house.gov
Majority Staff Director: Ray Kelley
Minority Staff Director: Jon Towers, 225-3527, 3460 OHOB
Jurisdiction: (1) veterans' measures generally; (2) pensions of all the wars of the U.S., general and special; (3) life insurance issued by the government on account of service in the Armed Forces; (4) compensation, vocational rehabilitation, and education of veterans; (5) veterans' hospitals, medical care, and treatment of veterans; (6) Soldiers' and Sailors' Civil Relief; (7) readjustment of servicemen to civilian life; (8) National Cemeteries.
Party Ratio: D 16–R 12

Mark Takano, Calif., Chair	*Phil Roe, Tenn.*
Julia Brownley, Calif.	*Gus M. Bilirakis, Fla.*
Kathleen Rice, N.Y.	*Aumua Amata Coleman*
Conor Lamb, Pa.	*Radewagen, Am. Samoa*
Mike Levin, Calif.	*Mike Bost, Ill.*
Max Rose, N.Y.	*Neal Dunn, Fla.*
Anthony Brindisi, N.Y.	*Jack Bergman, Mich.*
Gilbert Ray Cisneros Jr.,	*Jim Banks, Ind.*
Calif.	*Andy Barr, Kans.*
Susie Lee, Nev.	*Daniel Meuser, Pa.*
Lauren Underwood, Ill.	*Steve Watkins, Kans.*
Joe Cunningham, S.C.	*Chip Roy, Tex.*
Elaine G. Luria, Va.	*W. Gregory Steube, Fla.*
Chris Pappas, N.H.	
Colin Allred, Tex.	
Collin C. Peterson, Minn.	
Gregorio Kilili Camacho	
Sablan, Northern	
Mariana Is.	

Subcommittees

Disability Assistance and Memorial Affairs
Office: B234 LHOB 20515   **Phone:** 225-9756
   Elaine G. Luria (Chair), Gilbert Ray Cisneros Jr., Gregorio Kilili Camacho Sablan, Colin Allred, Lauren Underwood
   Mike Bost (Ranking Minority Member), Gus M. Bilirakis, Steve Watkins, W. Gregory Steube

Economic Opportunity
Office: B234 LHOB 20515   **Phone:** 226-9756
   Mike Levin (Chair), Kathleen Rice, Anthony Brindisi, Chris Pappas, Elaine G. Luria, Susie Lee, Joe Cunningham
   Gus M. Bilirakis (Ranking Minority Member), Jack Bergman, Jim Banks, Andy Barr, Daniel Meuser

Health
Office: B234 LHOB 20515   **Phone:** 225-9756
   Julia Brownley (Chair), Conor Lamb, Mike Levin, Anthony Brindisi, Max Rose, Gilbert Ray Cisneros Jr., Collin C. Peterson
   Neal Dunn (Ranking Minority Member), Aumua Amata Coleman Radewagen, Andy Barr, Daniel Meuser, W. Gregory Steube

Oversight and Investigations
Office: B234 LHOB 20515   **Phone:** 225-9756
   Chris Pappas (Chair), Kathleen Rice, Max Rose, Gilbert Ray Cisneros Jr., Collin C. Peterson
   Jack Bergman (Ranking Minority Member), Aumua Amata Coleman Radewagen, Mike Bost, Chip Roy

Technology Modernization
Office: B234 LHOB 20515   **Phone:** 225-9756
   Susie Lee (Chair), Julia Brownley, Conor Lamb, Joe Cunningham
   Jim Banks (Ranking Minority Member), Steve Watkins, Chip Roy

WAYS AND MEANS

Office: 1102 LHOB 20515
Phone: 225-3625   **Fax:** 225-5680
Web: waysandmeans.house.gov
Minority Web: gop-waysandmeans.house.gov
Majority Staff Director: Brandon Casey
Minority Staff Director: Gary Andres, 225-4021, 1139 LHOB
   Jurisdiction: (1) customs revenue, collection districts, and ports of entry and delivery; (2) reciprocal trade agreements; (3) revenue measures generally; (4) revenue measures relating to insular possessions; (5) bonded debt of the United States, subject to the last sentence of clause 4(f). Clause 4(f) requires the Committee on Ways and Means to include in its annual report to the Committee on the Budget a specific recommendation, made after holding public hearings, as to the appropriate level of the public debt that should be set forth in the concurrent resolution on the budget; (6) deposit of public monies; (7) transportation of dutiable goods; (8) tax exempt foundations and charitable trusts; (9) National Social Security (except health care and

facilities programs that are supported from general revenues as opposed to payroll deductions and except work incentive programs).
Party Ratio: D 25-R 17

Richard E. Neal, Mass., Chair	Kevin Brady, Tex.
John Lewis, Ga.	Devin Nunes, Calif.
Lloyd Doggett, Tex.	Vern Buchanan, Fla.
Mike Thompson, Calif.	Adrian Smith, Neb.
John B. Larson, Conn.	Kenny Marchant, Tex.
Earl Blumenauer, Ore.	Tom Reed, N.Y.
Ron Kind, Wisc.	Mike Kelly, Pa.
Bill Pascrell Jr., N.J.	George Holding, N.C.
Danny K. Davis, Ill.	Jason Smith, Mo.
Linda Sánchez, Calif.	Tom Rice, S.C.
Brian Higgins, N.Y.	David Schweikert, Ariz.
Terri A. Sewell, Ala.	Jackie Walorski, Ind.
Suzan DelBene, Wash.	Darin LaHood, Ill.
Judy Chu, Calif.	Brad Wenstrup, Ohio
Gwen Moore, Wisc.	Jodey Arrington, Tex.
Daniel Kildee, Mich.	A. Drew Ferguson, Ga.
Brendan F. Boyle, Pa.	Ron Estes, Kans.
Don Beyer, Va.	
Dwight Evans, Pa.	
Bradley Schneider, Ill.	
Thomas Suozzi, N.Y.	
Jimmy Panetta, Calif.	
Stephanie Murphy, Fla.	
Jimmy Gomez, Calif.	
Steven Horsford, Nev.	

Subcommittees

Health
Office: 1102 LHOB 20515   **Phone:** 225-3625
   Lloyd Doggett (Chair), Mike Thompson, Earl Blumenauer, Ron Kind, Brian Higgins, Terri A. Sewell, Judy Chu, Dwight Evans, Bradley Schneider, Jimmy Gomez, Steven Horsford
   Devin Nunes (Ranking Minority Member), Vern Buchanan, Adrian Smith, Kenny Merchant, Tom Reed, Mike Kelly, George Holding

Oversight
Office: 1102 LHOB 20515   **Phone:** 225-3625
   John Lewis (Chair), Linda Sánchez, Suzan DelBene, Judy Chu, Gwen Moore, Brendan F. Boyle, Thomas Suozzi
   Mike Kelly (Ranking Minority Member), Jackie Walorski, Darin LaHood, Brad Wenstrup

Social Security
Office: 1102 LHOB 20515   **Phone:** 225-3625
   John B. Larson (Chair), Bill Pascrell Jr., Linda Sánchez, Brian Higgins, Daniel Kildee, Brendan F. Boyle, Bradley Schneider
   Tom Reed (Ranking Minority Member), Jodey Arrington, A. Drew Ferguson, Ron Estes

Select Revenue Measures
Office: 1102 LHOB 20515   **Phone:** 225-3625

WAYS AND MEANS (continued)

Mike Thompson (Chair), Lloyd Doggett, John B. Larson, Linda Sánchez, Suzan DelBene, Gwen Moore, Brendan F. Boyle, Don Beyer, Thomas Suozzi
Adrian Smith (Ranking Minority Member), Tom Rice, David Schweikert, Darin LaHood, Jodey Arrington, A. Drew Ferguson

Trade
Office: 1102 LHOB 20515   **Phone:** 225-3625
Earl Blumenauer (Chair), Bill Pascrell Jr., Ron Kind, Danny K. Davis, Brian Higgins, Terri A. Sewell, Suzan DelBene, Don Beyer, Daniel Kildee, Jimmy Panetta, Stephanie Murphy
Vern Buchanan (Ranking Minority Member), Devin Nunes, George Holding, Tom Rice, Kenny Merchant, Jason Smith, David Schweikert

Worker and Family Support
Office: 1102 LHOB 20515   **Phone:** 225-3625
Danny K. Davis (Chair), Judy Chu, Terri A. Sewell, Gwen Moore, Dwight Evans, Stephanie Murphy, Jimmy Gomez
Jackie Walorski (Ranking Minority Member), Brad Wenstrup, Ron Estes, Darin LaHood

PERMANENT SELECT INTELLIGENCE

Office: HVC-304 CAP 20515-6415
Phone: 225-7690   **Fax:** 226-5068
Web: intelligence.house.gov
Minority Web: republicans-intelligence.house.gov
Majority Staff Director: Timothy Bergreen
Minority (Deputy) Staff Director: Carly Blake, 225-4121
Jurisdiction: There shall be referred to the select committee proposed legislation, messages, petitions, memorials and other matters relating to the following: (1) the Central Intelligence Agency, the Director of National Intelligence and the National Intelligence Program as defined in section 3(6) of the National Security Act of 1947; (2) intelligence and intelligence-related activities of all other departments and agencies of the Government, including the tactical intelligence and intelligence-related activities of the Department of Defense; (3) the organization or reorganization of the government to the extent that the organization or reorganization relates to a function or activity involving intelligence or intelligence-related activities; (4) authorizations for appropriations, both direct and indirect, for the following: (a) the Central Intelligence Agency, the Director of National Intelligence, and the National Intelligence Program as defined in section 3(6) of the National Security Act of 1947; (b) intelligence and intelligence-

related activities of all other departments and agencies of the Government, including the tactical intelligence and intelligence-related activities of the Department of Defense; (c) a department, agency, subdivision, or program that is a successor to an agency or program named to or referred to in (a) or (b).
Party Ratio: D 13-R 9

Adam Schiff, Calif., Chair	*Devin Nunes, Calif.*
Jim Himes, Conn.	*K. Michael Conaway, Tex.*
Terri A. Sewell, Ala.	*Michael Turner, Ohio*
André Carson, Ind.	*Brad Wenstrup, Ohio*
Jackie Speier, Calif.	*Chris Stewart, Utah*
Mike Quigley, Ill.	*Rick Crawford, Ark.*
Eric Swalwell, Calif.	*Elise Stefanik, N.Y.*
Joaquin Castro	*Will Hurd, Tex.*
Denny Heck, Wash.	*John Ratcliffe, Tex.*
Peter Welch, Vt.	
Sean Patrick Maloney, N.Y.	
Val Demings, Fla.	
Raja Krishnamoorthi, Ill.	

Subcommittees

Counterterrorism, Counterintelligence, and Counterproliferation
Office: HVC-304 CAP 20515   **Phone:** 225-7690
André Carson (Chair), Jackie Speier, Mike Quigley, Joaquin Castro, Peter Welch, Sean Patrick Maloney
Rick Crawford (Ranking Minority Member), K. Michael Conaway, Brad Wenstrup, Chris Stewart

Department of Defense Intelligence and Overhead Architecture
Office: HVC-304 CAP 20515   **Phone:** 225-7690
Terri A. Sewell (Chair), Jim Himes, Denny Heck, Peter Welch, Sean Patrick Maloney, Val Demings
Brad Wenstrup (Ranking Minority Member), Michael Turner, K. Michael Conaway, Will Hurd

Intelligence Modernization and Readiness
Office: HVC-304 CAP 20515   **Phone:** 225-7690
Eric Swalwell (Chair), Terri A. Sewell, Joaquin Castro, Val Demings, Raja Krishnamoorthi
Will Hurd (Ranking Minority Member), Michael Crawford, Elise Stefanik, John Ratcliffe

Strategic Technologies and Advanced Research
Office: HVC-304 CAP 20515   **Phone:** 225-7690
Jim Himes (Chair), André Carson, Mike Quigley, Denny Heck, Eric Swalwell, Raja Krishnamoorthi
Chris Stewart (Ranking Minority Member), Elise Stefanik, John Ratcliffe, Michael Turner

HOUSE LEADERSHIP AND PARTISAN COMMITTEES

DEMOCRATIC LEADERS

Speaker of the House: Nancy Pelosi, Calif.
Majority Leader: Steny H. Hoyer, Md.
Majority Whip: James E. Clyburn, S.C.
Assistant Speaker: Ben Ray Luján, N.M.

DEMOCRATIC PARTISAN COMMITTEES

Democratic Congressional Campaign Committee
Office: 430 S. Capitol St. S.E. 20003-4024
Phone: 863-1500   **Fax:** 485-3412
Web: www.dccc.org
Email: dccc@dccc.org
Cheri Bustos, Ill., Chair

Other Leadership (in alphabetical order)
Allison Jaslow, Executive Director
Jackie Forte-Mackay, Chief Financial Officer
Jalisa Washington-Price, Chief of Staff
Jared Smith, Communications Director
Reps. Don Beyer and Debbie Dingell, Finance Co-Chairs
Reps. Suzan DelBene, Ami Bera, and Bradley Schneider, Frontline Co-Chairs
Rep. Dan Kildee, Heartland Engagement Chair
Reps. Pete Aguilar, Val Demings, and A. Donald McEachin, Recruitment Co-Chairs
Reps. Lois Frankel, Robin Kelly, and Debra A. Haaland, Women LEAD Co-Chairs

Democratic Caucus
Office: B245 LHOB 20515
Phone: 225-1400   **Fax:** 226-4412
Web: www.dems.gov
Hakeem Jeffries, N.Y., Chair
Katherine Clark, Mass., Vice Chair

Democratic Steering and Outreach Committee
Office: 712 HSOB 20002
Phone: 224-9048
Web: www.dpcc.senate.gov
Email: steering@dsoc.senate.gov
Amy Klobuchar, Minn., Chair
Jeanne Shaheen, N.H., Vice Chair

Democratic Policy and Communications Committee
Office: 419 HSOB 20515
Phone: 224-3232
Web: www.dpcc.senate.gov
Email: dpcc@dpcc.senate.gov
Debbie Stabenow, Mich., Chair
Joe Manchin, W.Va., Vice Chair

REPUBLICAN LEADERS

Minority Leader: Kevin McCarthy, Calif.
Minority Whip: Steve Scalise, La.
Republican Conference Chairman: Liz Cheney, Wyo.

REPUBLICAN PARTISAN COMMITTEES

National Republican Congressional Committee
Office: 320 1st St. S.E. 20003-1838
Phone: 479-7000   **Fax:** 484-2543
Web: www.nrcc.org
Email: website@nrcc.org
Tom Emmer, Minn., Chair

Other Leadership (in alphabetical order)
Caitlin Sutherland, Research Director
John Rogers, Political Director
Rob Jentgens, Chief Financial Officer
Matt Gorman, Communications Director
Parker Hamilton Poling, Executive Director
Rep. Richard Hudson, Finance Chair
Rep. Jackie Walorski, Member Services Chair
Rep. Anthony Gonzalez, Outreach Chair
Rep. John Katko, Patriot Chair
Rep. Susan Brooks, Recruitment Chair
Rep. Mario Diaz-Balart, Redistricting Chair

Republican Conference
Office: 1420 LHOB 20515
Phone: 225-5107 **Fax:**226-0154
Web: www.gop.gov
Email: ecampaign@gop.com
Liz Cheney, Wyo., Chair
Mark Walker, N.C., Vice Chair
Jason Smith, Mo., Secretary

Republican Policy Committee
Office: 207 CHOB 20515
Phone: 225-4921   **Fax:** 225-2082
Web: republicanpolicy.house.gov
Gary Palmer, Ala., Chair

Republican Steering Committee
Office: H-107 CAP 20515-3508
Phone: 225-4000   **Fax:** 225-5117
Web: gop.gov/steering-committee/
Kevin McCarthy, Calif., Minority Leader

House Members' Offices

Listed below are House members and their party, state, and district affiliation, followed by the address and telephone number for their Washington office. The area code for all Washington, D.C., numbers is 202. The top administrative aide, Web address, Facebook page, and Twitter account for each member are also provided, when available. Most members may be contacted via the web-based email forms found on their websites. These are followed by the address, telephone and fax numbers, and name of a key aide in the member's district office(s). Each listing concludes with the representative's committee assignments. For partisan committee assignments, see page 851.

As of April 12, 2019, there were 235 Democrats, 197 Republicans, 0 Independents, 3 vacancies, and 6 nonvoting members in the House of Representatives.

Abraham, Ralph, R-La. (5)

Capitol Hill Office: 417 CHOB 20515-1805; 225-8490; Fax: 225-5639; *Chief of Staff:* Luke Letlow
Web: abraham.house.gov
Facebook: www.facebook.com/CongressmanRalphAbraham
Twitter: @RepAbraham
Instagram: @repabraham
District Offices: 2003 MacArthur Dr., Bldg. 5, Alexandria, LA 73201; 318-445-0818; Fax: 318-445-3776; *Office Manager:* Donna Howe
426 DeSiard St., Monroe, LA 71201; 318-322-3500; Fax: 318-322-3577; *Scheduler:* Emma Herrock
Committee Assignments: Agriculture; Armed Services

Adams, Alma, D-N.C. (12)

Capitol Hill Office: 222 CHOB 20515-3312; 225-1510; Fax: 225-1512; *Chief of Staff:* Rhonda Foxx
Web: adams.house.gov
Facebook: www.facebook.com/CongresswomanAdams
Twitter: @RepAdams
YouTube: www.youtube.com/channel/UCPI9ao1Cr1nxEUD2r-usRjQ
Instagram: @repadams
District Offices: 801 E. Moorehead St., #150, Charlotte NC 28202; 704-344-9950; Fax: 704-344-9971; *District Director:* Phanalphie Rhue
Committee Assignments: Agriculture; Education and Labor; Financial Services

Aderholt, Robert, R-Ala. (4)

Capitol Hill Office: 1203 LHOB 20515; 225-4876; Fax: 225-5587; *Chief of Staff:* Brian Rell
Web: aderholt.house.gov
Facebook: www.facebook.com/RobertAderholt
Twitter: @Robert_Aderholt
YouTube: www.youtube.com/RobertAderholt
Instagram: @robert_aderholt
District Offices: 205 4th Ave. N.E., #104, Cullman, AL 35055-1965; 256-734-6043; Fax: 256-737-0885; *Director of Constituent Services:* Jennifer Butler-Taylor

Federal Bldg., 600 Broad St., #107, Gadsden, AL 35901-3745; 256-546-0201; Fax: 256-546-8778; *Field Rep.:* James Manasco
Carl Elliott Federal Bldg., 1710 Alabama Ave., #247, Jasper, AL 35501-5400; 205-221-2310; Fax: 205-221-9035; *District Field Director:* Paul Housel
1011 George Wallace Blvd., #146, Tuscumbia, AL 35674; 256-381-3450; Fax: 256-381-7659; *Field Rep.:* Kreg Kennedy
Committee Assignments: Appropriations; Commission on Security and Cooperation in Europe

Aguilar, Pete, D-Calif. (31)

Capitol Hill Office: 109 CHOB 20515; 225-3201; Fax: 226-6962; *Chief of Staff:* Becky Cornell
Web: aguilar.house.gov
Facebook: www.facebook.com/reppeteaguilar
Twitter: @RepPeteAguilar
YouTube: www.youtube.com/channel/UCxwbFLOlKDsXrwizV5jah7g
Instagram: @rep.peteaguilar
District Office: 685 E. Carnegie Dr., #100, San Bernardino, CA 92408; 909-890-4445; Fax: 909-890-9643; *Scheduler:* Bidie Aguilar
Committee Assignment: Appropriations

Allen, Rick, R-Ga. (12)

Capitol Hill Office: 2400 RHOB 20515; 225-2823; Fax: 225-3377; *Chief of Staff:* Tim Baker
Web: allen.house.gov
Facebook: www.facebook.com/CongressmanRickAllen
Twitter: @RepRickAllen
YouTube: www.youtube.com/channel/UCZPoYXHFDAV17BGLMzGAmpg
Instagram: @rep_rickallen
District Offices: 2743 Perimeter Pkwy., Bldg. 200, #105, Augusta, GA 30909; 706-228-1980; Fax: 706-228-1954; *District Director:* Brinsley Thigpen
100 S. Church St., Dublin, GA 31021; 478-272-4030; Fax: 478-277-0113.
50 E. Main St., Statesboro, GA 30458; 912-243-9452; Fax: 912-243-9453.
107 Old Airport Rd., Suite A, Vidalia, GA 30475; 912-403-3311; Fax: 912-403-3317.
Committee Assignments: Agriculture, Education and Labor

Allred, Colin, D-Tex. (32)

Capitol Hill Office: 328 CHOB 20515-3515; 225-2231;
Chief of Staff: Paige Hutchinson
Web: allred.house.gov
Facebook: www.facebook.com/RepColinAllred
Twitter: @RepColinAllred
YouTube: www.youtube.com/channel/
UCm3l7ZntoH0EI2vIsvxeVqg
Instagram: @repcolinallred
District Offices: 100 N. Central Expressway, #602,
Richardson, TX 75080; 972-972-7949; Fax: 888-671-
0539; *District Director:*
Committee Assignments: Foreign Affairs; Transportation
and Infrastructure; Veterans' Affairs

Amash, Justin, R-Mich. (3)

Capitol Hill Office: 106 CHOB 20515-2203; 225-3831;
Fax: 225-5144; *Chief of Staff:* Poppy Nelson
Web: amash.house.gov
Facebook: www.facebook.com/justinamash
Twitter: @justinamash
YouTube: www.youtube.com/RepJustinAmash
District Office: 110 Michigan St. N.W., #460, Grand
Rapids, MI 49503-2313; 616-451-8383; Fax: 616-454-
5630; *District Director:* Katherine Condon
Satellite Office: 70 W. Michigan Ave., #212, Battle Creek,
MI 49017; 269-205-3823; *District Director:* Katherine
Condon
Committee Assignment: Oversight and Reform

Amodei, Mark, R-Nev. (2)

Capitol Hill Office: 104 CHOB 20515; 225-6155;
Fax: 225-5679; *Chief of Staff:* Bruce Miller
Web: amodei.house.gov
Facebook: www.facebook.com/MarkAmodeiNV2
Twitter: @MarkAmodeiNV2
YouTube: www.youtube.com/MarkAmodeiNV2
Instagram: @markamodeinv2
District Offices: 905 Railroad St., #104 D, Elko, NV 89801;
775-777-7705; Fax: 775-753-9984; *Rural Rep.:*
Martin Paris
5310 Kietzke Lane, #103, Reno, NV 89511; 775-686-5760;
Fax: 775-686-5711; *District Director:* Stacy Parobek
Committee Assignment: Appropriations

Armstrong, Kelly, R-N.D. (At Large)

Capitol Hill Office: 1004 LHOB 20515; 225-2611; *Chief of
Staff:* Roz Leighton
Web: armstrong.house.gov
Facebook: www.facebook.com/RepArmstrongND
Twitter: @RepArmstrongND
YouTube: www.youtube.com/HouseConference
Instagram: @reparmstrongnd
District Offices: 220 E. Rosser Ave., #228, Bismarck, ND
58501; 701-353-6665; *District Director:* Jeff Rustvang
3217 Fiechtner Dr., Suite D, Fargo, ND 58103; 701-
353-6665; *District Director:* Jeff Rustvang
Committee Assignments: Judiciary; Oversight and
Reform

Arrington, Jodey, R-Tex. (19)

Capitol Hill Office: 1029 LHOB 20515; 225-4005;
Fax: 225-9615; *Chief of Staff:* Chelsea Brown
Web: arrington.house.gov
Facebook: www.facebook.com/JodeyArrington
Twitter: @RepArrington
YouTube: www.youtube.com/channel/
UCzNP7vqSUoqWdPJX3UGco3w
Instagram: @repjodeyarrington
District Offices: 500 Chestnut St., #819, Abilene, TX
79602; 325-675-9779; Fax: 325-675-5038; *District
Director:* Lindley Herring
1312 Texas Ave., #219, Lubbock, TX 79401; 806-763-1611;
Fax: 806-767-9168.
Committee Assignment: Ways and Means

Axne, Cindy, D-Iowa (3)

Capitol Hill Office: 330 CHOB 20515-3515; 225-5476;
Fax: 226-1329; *Chief of Staff:* Joseph Diver
Web: axne.house.gov
Facebook: www.facebook.com/RepCindyAxne
Twitter: @RepCindyAxne
District Offices: 501 5th Ave., Council Bluffs, IA 51503;
712-890-3117; *District Director:* Kaitryn Patchett
208 West Taylor, Creston, IA 50801; (Call Capitol Hill
Office); *District Director:* Kaitryn Patchett
400 East Court Ave #346, Des Moines, IA 50309; 515-400-
8180; *Field Rep.:* Brooke Miller, Chloe Gearhart, Derek
Behnke
Committee Assignments: Agriculture; Financial Services

Babin, Brian, R-Tex. (36)

Capitol Hill Office: 2236 RHOB 20515-4336; 225-1555;
Fax: 226-0396; *Chief of Staff:* Ben Couhig
Web: babin.house.gov
Facebook: www.facebook.com/RepBrianBabin
Twitter: @RepBrianBabin
YouTube: www.youtube.com/repbrianbabin
District Offices: 203 Ivy Ave., #600, Deer Park, TX 77536;
832-780-0966; Fax: 832-780-0964; *District Director:*
Kelly Waterman
1201 S. Childers Rd., Orange, TX 77630-5803; 409-883-
8075; Fax: 409-886-9918; *Director of Community
Relations:* Lanie Brown
Tyler County Courthouse, 100 W. Bluff Dr., Woodville, TX
75979; 409-331-8066; *Director of Community
Relations:* Rachel Iglesias
Cleveland Satellite Office: 844-303-8934
Committee Assignments: Science, Space and Technology;
Transportation and Infrastructure

Bacon, Don, R-Neb. (2)

Capitol Hill Office: 1024 LHOB 20515; 225-4155;
Fax: 226-5452; *Chief of Staff:* Mark Dreiling
Web: bacon.house.gov
Facebook: www.facebook.com/RepDonBacon
Twitter: @RepDonBacon
YouTube: www.youtube.com/channel/
UCR9abI1lZzzAZ6HwQXc-dLFQ

District Office: 13906 Gold Circle, #101, Omaha, NE 68144; 402-938-0300; Fax: 402-763-4947 *District Director:* Ben Ungerman
Committee Assignments: Agriculture; Armed Services

Baird, James R., D-Ind. (4)

Capitol Hill Office: 532 CHOB 20515-3515; 225-5037; Fax: 225-0544; *Chief of Staff:* Ashlee Vinyard
Web: baird.house.gov
Facebook: www.facebook.com/RepJimBaird
Twitter: @RepJimBaird
District Offices: 355 S. Washington St., #210, Danville, IN 46122; 317-563-5567; *District Director:* Quincy Cunningham
Committee Assignments: Agriculture; Space, Science, and Technology

Balderson, Troy, R-Ohio (12)

Capitol Hill Office: 1221 LHOB 20515-3515; 225-5355; *Chief of Staff:* Teri Geiger
Web: balderson.house.gov
Facebook: www.facebook.com/RepTroyBalderson
Twitter: @RepBalderson
District Offices: 250 E. Wilson Bridge Rd., #100, Worthington, OH 43085; 614-523-2555; *Assistant District Director:* Lucas Crumley
Committee Assignments: Science, Space, and Technology; Small Business; Transportation and Infrastructure

Banks, Jim, R-Ind. (3)

Capitol Hill Office: 1713 LHOB 20515; 225-4436; *Chief of Staff:* David Keller
Web: banks.house.gov
Facebook: www.facebook.com/RepJimBanks
Twitter: @RepJimBanks
YouTube: www.youtube.com/RepJimBanks
Instagram: @repjimbanks
District Office: 1300 S. Harrison St., Room 3105, Fort Wayne, IN 46802; 260-702-4750; *District Director:* Tinisha Weigelt
Committee Assignments: Armed Services; Education and Labor; Veterans' Affairs

Barr, Andy, R-Ky. (6)

Capitol Hill Office: 2430 RHOB 20515; 225-4706; Fax: 225-2122; *Chief of Staff:* Mary Rosado
Web: barr.house.gov
Facebook: www.facebook.com/RepAndyBarr
Twitter: @RepAndyBarr
YouTube: www.youtube.com/RepAndyBarr
Instagram: @repandybarr
District Office: 2709 Old Rosebud Rd., Lexington, KY 40509; 859-219-1366; Fax: 859-219-3437; *District Director:* Leslie Small
Committee Assignments: Financial Services; Veterans' Affairs

Barragán, Nanette Diaz, D-Calif. (44)

Capitol Hill Office: 1030 LHOB 20515; 225-8220; Fax: 226-7290; *Chief of Staff:* Robert Primus
Web: barragan.house.gov
Facebook: www.facebook.com/CongresswomanBarragan
Twitter: @RepBarragan
Instagram: @repbarragan
District Offices: 701 E. Carson St., Carson, CA 90745; 310-831-1799; *Field Rep.:* Gabriela Sid
205 S. Willowbrook Ave., Compton, CA 90220; 310-831-1799.
302 W. 5th St., #201, San Pedro, CA 90731; 310-831-1799; *District Director:* Francisco Carrillo
8650 California Ave., South Gate, CA 90280; 310-831-1799
Committee Assignments: Energy and Commerce; Homeland Security

Bass, Karen, D-Calif. (37)

Capitol Hill Office: 2059 RHOB 20515; 225-7084; Fax: 225-2422; *Chief of Staff:* Caren Street
Web: bass.house.gov
Facebook: www.facebook.com/RepKarenBass
Twitter: @RepKarenBass
YouTube: www.youtube.com/RepKarenBass
District Office: 4929 Wilshire Blvd., #650, Los Angeles, CA 90010-3820; 323-965-1422; Fax: 323-965-1113.
Committee Assignments: Foreign Affairs; Judiciary

Beatty, Joyce, D-Ohio (3)

Capitol Hill Office: 2303 RHOB 20515; 225-4324; Fax: 225-1984; *Chief of Staff:* Kimberly Ross
Web: beatty.house.gov
Facebook: www.facebook.com/RepJoyceBeatty
Twitter: @RepBeatty
YouTube: www.youtube.com/repbeatty
Instagram: @repbeatty
District Office: 471 E. Broad St., #1100, Columbus, OH 43215; 614-220-0003; Fax: 614-220-5640; *Deputy District Director:* Larry Seward
Committee Assignment: Financial Services

Bera, Ami, D-Calif. (7)

Capitol Hill Office: 1727 LHOB 20515; 225-5716; Fax: 226-1298; *Chief of Staff:* Chad Obermiller
Web: bera.house.gov
Facebook: www.facebook.com/RepAmiBera
Twitter: @RepBera
YouTube: www.youtube.com/repamibera
District Office: 8950 Cal Center Dr., Bldg. 3, #100, Sacramento, CA 95826; 916-635-0505; Fax: 916-635-0514; *District Director:* Mathew Ceccato
Committee Assignments: Foreign Affairs; Science, Space, and Technology

Bergman, Jack, R-Mich. (1)

Capitol Hill Office: 414 CHOB 20515; 225-4735; Fax: 225-4710; *Chief of Staff:* Tony Lis
Web: bergman.house.gov

Facebook: www.facebook.com/RepJackBergman
Twitter: @RepJackBergman
Instagram: @repjackbergman
District Offices: 1396 Douglas Dr., #22B, Traverse, MI 49696; 231-944-7633; Fax: 231-421-8643; *Communications Dir.:* James Hogge
1500 W. Washington St., #2, Marquette, MI 49855; 906-273-2227; Fax: 906-273-1162; *District Rep.:* Nicholas Emmendorfer
Committee Assignments: Armed Services; Veterans' Affairs

Beyer, Don, D-Va. (8)

Capitol Hill Office: 1119 LHOB 20515; 225-4376; Fax: 225-0017; *Chief of Staff:* Ann O'Hanlon
Web: beyer.house.gov
Facebook: www.facebook.com/RepDonBeyer
Twitter: @RepDonBeyer
YouTube: www.youtube.com/repdonbeyer
Instagram: @repdonbeyer
District Office: 5285 Shawnee Rd., #250, Alexandria, VA 22312; 703-658-5403; Fax: 703-658-5408; *District Director:* Noah Simon
Committee Assignments: Science, Space, and Technology; Ways and Means

Biggs, Andy, R-Ariz. (5)

Capitol Hill Office: 1318 LHOB 20515; 225-2635; Fax: 226-4368; *Chief of Staff:* Deborah Mazol
Web: biggs.house.gov
Facebook: www.facebook.com/RepAndyBiggs
Twitter: @RepAndyBiggsAZ
YouTube: www.youtube.com/channel/UCqSq9kWOxk9yNTeILBCVC1w
Instagram: @repandybiggs
District Office: 2509 S. Power Rd., #204, Mesa, AZ 85209; 480-699-8239; Fax: 480-699-4730; *Deputy Chief of Staff:* Greg Safsten
Committee Assignments: Judiciary; Science, Space, and Technology

Bilirakis, Gus M., R-Fla. (12)

Capitol Hill Office: 2227 RHOB 20515-0909; 225-5755; Fax: 225-4085; *Chief of Staff:* Elizabeth Hittos
Web: bilirakis.house.gov
Facebook: www.facebook.com/GusBilirakis
Twitter: @RepGusBilirakis
YouTube: www.youtube.com/RepGusBilirakis
Instagram: @gusbilirakis
District Offices: 7132 Little Rd., New Port Richey, FL 34654; 727-232-2921; Fax: 727-232-2923; *Director of Casework:* Kristen Sellas
600 Klosterman Rd., Room BB-038, Tarpon Springs, FL 34689-1299; 727-940-5860; Fax: 727-940-5861; *Scheduler:* Daniel Paasch
Committee Assignments: Energy and Commerce; Veterans' Affairs

Bishop, Rob, R-Utah (1)

Capitol Hill Office: 123 CHOB 20515-4401; 225-0453; Fax: 225-5857; *Chief of Staff:* Devin Wiser
Web: robbishop.house.gov
Facebook: www.facebook.com/RepRobBishop
Twitter: @RepRobBishop
YouTube: www.youtube.com/CongressmanBishop
District Office: Federal Bldg., 324 25th St., #1017, Ogden UT 84401; 801-625-0107; Fax: 801-625-0124; *District Director:* Peter Jenks
Committee Assignments: Armed Services; Natural Resources, Chair

Bishop, Sanford D., Jr., D-Ga. (2)

Capitol Hill Office: 2407 RHOB 20515-1002; 225-3631; Fax: 225-2203; *Chief of Staff:* Michael Reed
Web: bishop.house.gov
Facebook: www.facebook.com/sanfordbishop
Twitter: @SanfordBishop
YouTube: www.youtube.com/RepSanfordBishop
Instagram: @repsanfordbishop
District Offices: Albany Towers, 223 Pine Ave., #1400, Albany, GA 31701; 229-439-8067; Fax: 229-436-2099; *District Director:* Kenneth Cutts
18 9th St., #201, Columbus, GA 31901-2778; 706-320-9477; Fax: 706-320-9479; *Support Staff:* Jerald Washington
300 Mulberry St., #502, Macon, GA 31201; 478-803-2631; Fax: 478-803-2637; *Deputy District Director:* Shavonda Hill
Committee Assignment: Appropriations

Blumenauer, Earl, D-Ore. (3)

Capitol Hill Office: 1111 LHOB 20515; 225-4811; Fax: 225-8941; *Deputy Chief of Staff:* David Gillman
Web: blumenauer.house.gov
Facebook: www.facebook.com/blumenauer
Twitter: @repblumenauer
YouTube: www.youtube.com/RepBlumenauer
Instagram: @repblumenauer
District Office: 911 11th Ave. N.E., #200, Portland, OR 97232; 503-231-2300; Fax: 503-230-5413; *Chief of Staff:* Willie Smith
Committee Assignment: Ways and Means

Blunt Rochester, Lisa, D-Del. (At Large)

Capitol Hill Office: 1519 LHOB 20515; 225-4165; *Chief of Staff:* Jacqueline Sanchez
Web: bluntrochester.house.gov
Facebook: www.facebook.com/LisaBluntRochester
Twitter: @RepBRochester
Instagram: @replbr
District Offices: 1105 N. Market St., #400, Wilmington, DE 19801; 302-830-2330; *District Director:* Sylvia Banks
28 The Circle, #2, Georgetown, DE 19947; 302-858-4773; *District Director:* Sylvia Banks
Committee Assignment: Energy and Commerce

Bonamici, Suzanne, D-Ore. (1)

Capitol Hill Office: 2231 RHOB 20515; 225-0855;
Fax: 225-9497; *Chief of Staff:* Rachael Bornstein
Web: bonamici.house.gov
Facebook: www.facebook.com/CongresswomanBonamici
Twitter: @RepBonamici
YouTube: www.youtube.com/RepSuzanneBonamici
Instagram: @repbonamici
District Office: 12725 Millikan Way S.W., #220,
Beaverton, OR 97005; 503-469-6010; Fax: 503-469-
6018; *District Director:* Sarah Baessler
Committee Assignments: Education and Labor; Science,
Space, and Technology

Bost, Mike, R-Ill. (12)

Capitol Hill Office: 1440 LHOB 20515-1312; 225-5661;
Fax: 225-0285; *Chief of Staff:* Matt McCullough
Web: bost.house.gov
Facebook: www.facebook.com/RepBost
Twitter: @RepBost
YouTube: www.youtube.com/channel/
UCxgLCZzKuY7g_8-Iu1PSlPQ
District Offices: 200 Potomac Blvd., Mt. Vernon, IL 62864;
618-513-5294
Hunter Bldg., 300 E. Main St., #4, Carbondale, IL 62901;
618-457-5787; Fax: 618-457-2990; *Constituent Service
Rep.:* Janice Clayton
302 W. State St., O'Fallon, IL 62269; 618-622-0766;
Fax: 618-622-0774; *District Director:* Dave Tanzyus
Committee Assignments: Agriculture; Transportation
and Infrastructure; Veterans' Affairs

Boyle, Brendan F., D-Pa. (2)

Capitol Hill Office: 1133 LHOB 20515-3813; 225-6111;
Fax: 226-0611; *Chief of Staff:* John McCarthy
Web: boyle.house.gov
Facebook: www.facebook.com/CongressmanBoyle
Twitter: @CongBoyle
YouTube: www.youtube.com/channel/
UCMP_Anj7lz4eZuSh8GwFqQQ
Instagram: @congressmanboyle
District Offices: 8572 Bustleton Ave., Philadelphia, PA
19152; 215-335-3355; Fax: 215-856-3734; *District
Director:* Scott Heppard
One & Olney Shopping Center, 5675 N. Front St., #180,
Philadelphia, PA 19120; 267-335-5643; Fax: 267-437-
3886; *Constituent Service Rep.:* Anthony Bellmon
2630 Memphis St., Philadelphia, PA, 19125; 267-519-2252;
Fax: 215-426-7741; *District Director:* Scott Heppard
Committee Assignments: Budget; Ways and Means

Brady, Kevin, R-Tex. (8)

Capitol Hill Office: 1011 LHOB 20515; 225-4901;
Fax: 225-5524; *Chief of Staff:* David Davis
Web: kevinbrady.house.gov
Facebook: www.facebook.com/kevinbrady
Twitter: @RepKevinBrady
YouTube: www.youtube.com/KBrady8
Instagram: @repkevinbrady

District Offices: 200 River Point Dr., #304, Conroe, TX
77304-2817; 936-441-5700; Fax: 936-441-5757; *District
Director:* Heather Washburn
1300 11th St., #400, Huntsville, TX 77340; 936-439-9532;
Fax: 936-439-9546; *Caseworker:* Vita Swares
Committee Assignment: Ways and Means, Chair

Brindisi, Anthony, D-N.Y. (22)

Capitol Hill Office: 329 CHOB 20515-3515; 225-3665;
Chief of Staff: Ellen Foster
Web: brindisi.house.gov
Facebook: www.facebook.com/RepBrindisi
Twitter: @RepBrindisi
Instagram: @repbrindisi
District Offices: 430 Court St., #102, Utica, NY 13502;
315-927-7407; *District Director:* Sarah Bormann
Committee Assignments: Agriculture; Veterans' Affairs

Brooks, Mo, R-Ala. (5)

Capitol Hill Office: 2246 RHOB 20515; 225-4801; *Chief of
Staff:* Mark Pettitt
Web: brooks.house.gov
Facebook: www.facebook.com/RepMoBrooks
Twitter: @RepMoBrooks
YouTube: www.youtube.com/RepMoBrooks
District Offices: 302 Lee St., Room 86, Decatur, AL 35601-
1926; 256-355-9400; Fax: 256-355-9406; *Field Rep.:*
Johnny Turner
102 S. Court St., #310, Florence, AL 35630; 256-718-5155;
Fax: 256-718-5156; *Field Rep.:* Laura Smith
2101 W. Clinton Ave., #302, Huntsville, AL 35805-3109;
256-551-0190; Fax: 256-551-0194; *District Director:*
Tiffany Noel
Committee Assignments: Armed Services; Science, Space,
and Technology

Brooks, Susan W., R-Ind. (5)

Capitol Hill Office: 2211 RHOB 20515; 225-2276;
Fax: 225-0016; *Chief of Staff:* Megan Savage
Web: susanwbrooks.house.gov
Facebook: www.facebook.com/
CongresswomanSusanWBrooks
Twitter: @SusanWBrooks
YouTube: www.youtube.com/SusanWBrooks
Instagram: @susanwbrooks
District Offices: 11611 N. Meridian St., #415, Carmel, IN
46032; 317-848-0201; Fax: 317-846-7306; *District
Director:* Karen Glaser
120 E. 8th St., #101, Anderson, IN 46016; 765-640-5115;
Fax: 765-640-5116; *Deputy District Director:* Kevin
Sulc
Committee Assignment: Energy and Commerce

Brown, Anthony, D-Md. (4)

Capitol Hill Office: 1323 LHOB 20515; 225-8699;
Fax: 225-2848; *Chief of Staff:* Maia Espes
Web: anthonybrown.house.gov
Facebook: www.facebook.com/AnthonyBrown.Maryland
Twitter: @RepAnthonyBrown

YouTube: www.youtube.com/AnthonyBrownMaryland
Instagram: @repanthonybrown
District Office: 9701 Apollo Dr., #103, Largo, MD 20774; 301-458-2600; *District Director:* Nichelle Schoultz
Committee Assignments: Armed Services; Ethics; Natural Resources; Transportation and Infrastructure

Brownley, Julia, D-Calif. (26)

Capitol Hill Office: 2262 RHOB 20515; 225-5811; Fax: 225-1100; *Chief of Staff:* Lenny Young
Web: juliabrownley.house.gov
Facebook: www.facebook.com/RepBrownley
Twitter: @JuliaBrownley26
YouTube: www.youtube.com/RepJuliaBrownley
District Offices: 201 E. 4th St., #209B, Oxnard, CA 93030; 805-379-1779; Fax: 805-379-1799; *District Director:* Carina Armenta
223 E. Thousand Oaks Blvd., #220, Thousand Oaks, CA 91360; 805-379-1779; Fax: 805-379-1799; *Deputy District Director:* Sheri Orgel
Committee Assignments: Transportation and Infrastructure; Veterans' Affairs

Buchanan, Vern, R-Fla. (16)

Capitol Hill Office: 2427 RHOB 20515; 225-5015; Fax: 226-0828; *Chief of Staff:* Dave Karvelas
Web: buchanan.house.gov
Facebook: www.facebook.com/CongressmanBuchanan
Twitter: @VernBuchanan
YouTube: www.youtube.com/VernBuchanan
District Offices: 1051 Manatee Ave. West, #305, Bradenton, FL 34205-4954; 941-747-9081; Fax: 941-748-1564; *Field Rep.:* Gary Tibbetts
111 S. Orange Ave., Floor 2R, #202W, Sarasota, FL 34236-5806; 941-951-6643; Fax: 941-951-2972; *District Director:* Chloe Convoy
Committee Assignment: Ways and Means

Buck, Ken, R-Colo. (4)

Capitol Hill Office: 2455 RHOB 20515-0604; 225-4676; Fax: 225-5870; *Chief of Staff:* Ritika Robertson
Web: buck.house.gov
Facebook: www.facebook.com/repkenbuck
Twitter: @RepKenBuck
YouTube: www.youtube.com/repkenbuck
Instagram: @repkenbuck
District Offices: 900 Castleton Rd., #112, Castle Rock, CO 80109; 720-639-9165; *District Director (Acting):* Robin Coran
1023 39th Ave., Suite B, Greeley, CO 80634; 970-702-2136; Fax: 970-702-2951; *Constituent Services Rep.:* Molly Ford
Committee Assignments: Foreign Affairs; Judiciary

Bucshon, Larry, R-Ind. (8)

Capitol Hill Office: 2313 RHOB 20515; 225-4636; Fax: 225-3284; *Chief of Staff:* Kyle Jackson
Web: bucshon.house.gov
Facebook: www.facebook.com/RepLarryBucshon

Twitter: @RepLarryBucshon
YouTube: www.youtube.com/RepLarryBucshon
Instagram: @replarrybucshon
District Offices: 420 Main St., #1402, Evansville, IN 47708; 812-465-6484; Fax: 812-422-4761; *District Director:* Carol Jones
901 Wabash Ave., #140, Terre Haute, IN 47807-3232; 812-232-0523; Fax: 812-232-0526; *Field Rep.:* Sam Pollock
Committee Assignment: Energy and Commerce

Budd, Ted, R-N.C. (13)

Capitol Hill Office: 118 CHOB 20515; 225-4531; *Chief of Staff:* Andrew Bell
Web: budd.house.gov
Facebook: www.facebook.com/RepTedBudd
Twitter: @RepTedBudd
District Offices: 128 Peachtree Lane, Suite A, Advance, NC 27006; 336-998-1313; *District Director:* Todd Poole
4000 Piedmont Pkwy., #131, High Point, NC 27265; 336-858-5013; *Legislative Director:* Alex Vargo
Committee Assignment: Financial Services

Burchett, Tim, R-Tenn. (2)

Capitol Hill Office: 1122 LHOB 20515-3515; 225-5435; Fax: 225-6440; *Chief of Staff:* Michael Grider
Web: burchett.house.gov
Facebook: www.facebook.com/RepTimBurchett
Twitter: @timburchett
District Offices: 800 Market St., #110 Knoxville, TN 37902; 865-523-3772; *District Director:* Jennifer Linginfelter
341 Court St., Maryville, TN 37804; 865-984-5464
Committee Assignment: Budget; Foreign Affairs; Small Business

Burgess, Michael, R-Tex. (26)

Capitol Hill Office: 2161 RHOB 20515; 225-7772; Fax: 225-2919; *Chief of Staff:* James Decker
Web: burgess.house.gov
Facebook: www.facebook.com/michaelcburgess
Twitter: @michaelcburgess
YouTube: www.youtube.com/MichaelCBurgessMD
District Office: 2000 S. Stemmons Fwy., #200, Lake Dallas, TX 75065; 940-497-5031; Fax: 940-497-5067; *District Director:* Erik With
Committee Assignments: Energy and Commerce; Rules

Bustos, Cheri, D-Ill. (17)

Capitol Hill Office: 1233 LHOB 20515; 225-5905; *Chief of Staff:* Jon Pyatt
Web: bustos.house.gov
Facebook: www.facebook.com/RepCheri
Twitter: @RepCheri
YouTube: www.youtube.com/RepCheri
Instagram: @repcheri
District Offices: 820 Adams St. S.W., Peoria, IL 61602; 309-966-1813; *Constituent Advocate:* Laura Rude

119 N. Church St., #207-208, Rockford, IL 61101; 815-968-8011; *Constituent Advocate/ Field Rep.:* Ricardo Montoya Picazo

2401 4th Ave., Rock Island, IL 61201; 309-786-3406; Fax: 309-786-3720; *District Director:* Kate Jennings-Berber

Committee Assignments: Agriculture; Appropriations

Butterfield, G. K., D-N.C. (1)

Capitol Hill Office: 2080 RHOB 20515-3301; 225-3101; Fax: 225-3354; *Chief of Staff:* Kendra Brown
Web: butterfield.house.gov
Facebook: www.facebook.com/congressmangkbutterfield
Twitter: @GKButterfield
YouTube: www.youtube.com/user/GKBNC01
Instagram: @gkbutterfield
District Offices: 2741 Campus Walk Ave., Bldg. 400, #300, Durham, NC 27705; 919-908-0164; Fax: 919-908-0169; *Director of Constituent Services/Northwest District Outreach:* Dollie Burwell

216 Nash St. N.E., Suite B, Wilson, NC 27893-3802; 252-237-9816; Fax: 252-291-0356; *District Director:* Reginald Speight

Committee Assignments: Energy and Commerce; House Administration; Joint Library

Byrne, Bradley, R-Ala. (1)

Capitol Hill Office: 119 CHOB 20515-0101; 225-4931; Fax: 225-0562; *Chief of Staff:* Chad Carlough
Web: byrne.house.gov
Facebook: www.facebook.com/RepByrne
Twitter: @RepByrne
YouTube: www.youtube.com/RepByrne
Instagram: @repbyrne
District Offices: 502 W. Lee Ave., Summerdale, AL 36580; 251-989-2664; Fax: 251-989-2669; *Constituent Services Rep.:* Allison Clark

11 N. Water St., #15290, Mobile, AL 36602; 251-690-2811; Fax: 251-690-2815; *District Director:* Elizabeth Roney

Committee Assignments: Armed Services; Education and Labor

Calvert, Ken, R-Calif. (42)

Capitol Hill Office: 2205 RHOB 20515; 225-1986; Fax: 225-2004; *Chief of Staff:* Dave Kennett
Web: calvert.house.gov
Facebook: www.facebook.com/CalvertforCongress
Twitter: @KenCalvert
YouTube: www.youtube.com/RepKenCalvert
Instagram: @repkencalvert
District Office: 400 S. Vicentia Ave., #125, Corona, CA 92882; 951-277-0042; Fax: 951-277-0420; *District Director:* Jolyn Murphy

Committee Assignment: Appropriations

Carbajal, Salud, D-Calif. (24)

Capitol Hill Office: 1431 LHOB 20515; 225-3601; Fax: 225-5632; *Chief of Staff:* Jeremy Tittle

Web: carbajal.house.gov
Facebook: www.facebook.com/repsaludcarbajal
Twitter: @RepCarbajal
YouTube: www.youtube.com/repcarbajal
Instagram: @repcarbajal
District Offices: 360 S. Hope Ave., #301C, Santa Barbara, CA 93105; 805-730-1710; *District Director:* Chris Henson

1411 Marsh St., #205, San Luis Obispo, CA 93401; 805-546-8348; Fax: 439-3574; *District Rep.:* Greg Hass

Committee Assignments: Agriculture; Armed Services; Transportation and Infrastructure

Cárdenas, Tony, D-Calif. (29)

Capitol Hill Office: 248 RHOB 20515; 225-6131; Fax: 225-0819; *Chief of Staff:* Miguel Franco
Web: cardenas.house.gov
Twitter: @RepCardenas
YouTube: www.youtube.com/repcardenas
Instagram: @repcardenas
District Office: 9612 Van Nuys Blvd., #201, Panorama City, CA 91402; 818- 221-3718; Fax: 818- 221-3809; *District Director:* Gabriela Marquez

Committee Assignment: Energy and Commerce

Carson, André, D-Ind. (7)

Capitol Hill Office: 2135 RHOB 20515-1407; 225-4011; Fax: 225-5633; *Chief of Staff:* Kimberly Rudolph
Web: carson.house.gov
Facebook: www.facebook.com/CongressmanAndreCarson
Twitter: @RepAndreCarson
YouTube: www.youtube.com/user/RepAndreCarson
Instagram: @repandrecarson
District Office: 300 E. Fall Creek Pkwy. N. Dr., #300, Indianapolis, IN 46205; 317-283-6516; Fax: 317-283-6567; *District Director:* Megan Sims

Committee Assignments: Transportation and Infrastructure; Permanent Select Intelligence

Carter, Buddy, R-Ga. (1)

Capitol Hill Office: 2432 RHOB 20515-1001; 225-5831; Fax: 226-2269; *Chief of Staff:* Chris Crawford
Web: buddycarter.house.gov
Facebook: www.facebook.com/CongressmanBuddyCarter
Twitter: @RepBuddyCarter
YouTube: www.youtube.com/congressmanbuddycarter
Instagram: @repbuddycarter
District Offices: 1510 Newcastle St., #200, Brunswick, GA 31520; 912-265-9010; Fax: 912-265-9013; *District Director:* Brooke Childers

6602 Abercorn St., #105B, Savannah, GA 31405; 912-352-0101; Fax: 912-352-0105; *Staff Asst.:* S.K. Bowen

Committee Assignment: Energy and Commerce

Carter, John, R-Tex. (31)

Capitol Hill Office: 2110 RHOB 20515-4331; 225-3864; Fax: 225-5886; *Chief of Staff:* Jonas Miller

Web: carter.house.gov
Facebook: www.facebook.com/judgecarter
Twitter: @JudgeCarter
YouTube: www.youtube.com/RepJohnCarter
Instagram: @judgecarter
District Offices: 1717 N. IH 35, #303, Round Rock, TX 78664; 512-246-1600; Fax: 512-246-1620; *Texas Chief of Staff:* Jonas Miller
6544B S. General Bruce Dr., Temple, TX 76502; 254-933-1392; Fax: 254-933-1650; *Constituent Liaisons:* Cecilia Ellis and Matthew Key
Committee Assignment: Appropriations

Cartwright, Matthew, D-Pa. (8)

Capitol Hill Office: 1034 LHOB 20515; 225-5546; Fax: 226-0996; *Chief of Staff:* Hunter Ridgway
Web: cartwright.house.gov
Facebook: www.facebook.com/ CongressmanMattCartwright
Twitter: @RepCartwright
YouTube: www.youtube.com/channel/ UCnAOvexSGLBnYidaFzguhTQ
Instagram: @repmattcartwright
District Offices: 226 Wyoming Ave., Scranton, PA 18503; 570-341-1050; Fax: 570-341-1055; *District Director:* Bob Morgan
Satellite Office: 20 N. Pennsylvania Ave., #201, Wilkes-Barre, PA 18711; 570-371-0317; *Caseworker:* Christa Mecadon
Committee Assignment: Appropriations

Case, Ed, D-Hawaii (1)

Capitol Hill Office: 2443 RHOB 20515-3515; 225-2726; Fax: 225-0688; *Chief of Staff:* Tim Nelson
Web: case.house.gov
Facebook: www.facebook.com/RepEdCase
Twitter: @RedEdCase
Instagram: @edcasehawaii
District Offices: 1132 Bishop St., #1910, Honolulu, HI 96813; 808-650-6688; *District Director:* Jacqueline Conant
Committee Assignments: Appropriations; Natural Resources

Casten, Sean, D-Ill. (6)

Capitol Hill Office: 429 CHOB 20515-3515; 225-4561; *Chief of Staff:* Ann Adler
Web: casten.house.gov
Facebook: www.facebook.com/RepSeanCasten
Twitter: @RepCasten
YouTube: www.youtube.com/channel/ UCU3whMb767YV7XDIo0a0y6Q
Instagram: @repseancasten
District Offices: 2700 International Dr., #304, West Chicago, IL 60185; 630-520-9450; *District Director:* Anne Wick
Committee Assignments: Financial Services; Science, Space, and Technology

Castor, Kathy, D-Fla. (14)

Capitol Hill Office: 2052 RHOB 20515-0911; 225-3376; Fax: 225-5652; *Chief of Staff:* Clay Phillips
Web: castor.house.gov
Facebook: www.facebook.com/USRepKathyCastor
Twitter: @USRepKCastor
YouTube: www.youtube.com/RepKathyCastor
Instagram: @usrepkathycastor
District Office: 4144 N. Armenia Ave., #300, Tampa, FL 33607-6435; 813-871-2817; Fax: 813-871-2864; *District Director:* Marcia Mejia
Committee Assignment: Energy and Commerce

Castro, Joaquin, D-Tex. (20)

Capitol Hill Office: 2241 RHOB 20515; 225-3236; Fax: 225-1915; *Chief of Staff:* Danny Meza
Web: castro.house.gov
Facebook: www.facebook.com/JoaquinCastroTX
Twitter: @JoaquinCastrotx
YouTube: www.youtube.com/user/JoaquinCastroTX
Instagram: @joaquincastrotx
District Office: 727 E. Cesar E. Chavez Blvd., #B-128, San Antonio, TX 78206; 210-348-8216; Fax: 210-979-0737; *District Director:* Toni Serna
Committee Assignments: Education and Labor; Foreign Affairs; Permanent Select Intelligence

Chabot, Steve, R-Ohio (1)

Capitol Hill Office: 2408 RHOB 20515; 225-2216; Fax: 225-3012; *Chief of Staff:* Stacy Barton
Web: chabot.house.gov
Facebook: www.facebook.com/RepSteveChabot
Twitter: @RepSteveChabot
YouTube: www.youtube.com/CongressmanChabot
Instagram: @repstevechabot
District Offices: 441 Vine St., Room 3003, Cincinnati, OH 45202-3003; 513-684-2723; Fax: 513-421-8722; *District Director:* Joe Abner
11 S. Broadway, Lebanon, OH 45036; 513-421-8704; Fax: 513-421-8722; *District Rep.:* David McCandless;
Committee Assignments: Foreign Affairs; Judiciary; Small Business, Chair

Cheney, Liz, R-Wyo. (At Large)

Capitol Hill Office: 416 CHOB 20515; 225-2311; Fax: 225-3057; *Chief of Staff:* Kara Ahern
Web: cheney.house.gov
Facebook: www.facebook.com/replizcheney
Twitter: @RepLizCheney
District Offices: 100 E. B St., Room 4003, P.O. Box 44003, Casper, WY 82602; 307-261-6595; Fax: 307-261-6597; *Deputy District Director:* Jackie King
2120 Capitol Ave., #8005, Cheyenne, WY 82001; 307-772-2595; Fax: 307-772-2597; *District Director:* Tammy Hooper
300 S. Gillette Ave., #2001, Gillette, WY 82716; 307-414-1677; Fax: 307-414-1711

45 E. Loucks St., #300F, Sheridan, WY 82801; 307-673-4608; Fax: 307-261-6597; *Communications Director:* Amy Edmonds

325 West Main St., #B, Riverton, WY 82501; 307-463-0482; *Field Rep.:* Lindy Linn

Committee Assignments: Armed Services; Natural Resources

Chu, Judy, D-Calif. (27)

Capitol Hill Office: 2423 RHOB 20515-0532; 225-5464; Fax: 225-5467; *Chief of Staff:* Linda Shim

Web: chu.house.gov

Facebook: www.facebook.com/RepJudyChu

Twitter: @RepJudyChu

YouTube: www.youtube.com/RepJudyChu

Instagram: @repjudychu

District Offices: 527 S. Lake Ave., #250, Pasadena, CA 91101; 626-304-0110; Fax: 626-304-0132; *District Director:* Becky Cheng

415 W. Foothill Blvd., #122, Claremont, CA 91711; 909-625-5394; Fax: 909-399-0198; (open Tuesday/Thursday, 9 a.m.–1 p.m.); *Deputy District Director:* Enrique Robles

Committee Assignments: Small Business; Ways and Means

Cicilline, David, D-R.I. (1)

Capitol Hill Office: 2233 RHOB 20515-3901; 225-4911; Fax: 225-3290; *Chief of Staff:* Peter Karafotas

Web: cicilline.house.gov

Facebook: www.facebook.com/CongressmanDavidCicilline

Twitter: @RepCicilline

YouTube: www.youtube.com/RepDavidCicilline

Instagram: @repdavidcicilline

District Office: 1070 Main St., #300, Pawtucket, RI 02860-2134; 401-729-5600; Fax: 401-729-5608; *District Director:* Christopher Bizzacco

Committee Assignments: Foreign Affairs; Judiciary

Cisneros, Gilbert Ray, Jr., D-Calif. (39)

Capitol Hill Office: 431 CHOB 20515-3515; 225-4111; *Chief of Staff:* Nicholas Jordan

Web: cisneros.house.gov

Facebook: www.facebook.com/RepGilCisneros

Twitter: @GilCisnerosCA

Instagram: @gilcisnerosca

District Offices: 1440 N. Harbor Blvd., #601, Fullerton, CA 92835; 714-459-4575; *District Director:* Martin Medrano

Committee Assignments: Armed Services; Veterans' Affairs

Clark, Katherine, D-Mass. (5)

Capitol Hill Office: 2448 RHOB 20515-2107; 225-2836; Fax: 226-0092; *Chief of Staff:* Brooke Scannell

Web: katherineclark.house.gov

Twitter: @RepKClark

YouTube: www.youtube.com/channel/UCgaI52w7QKI8LtkSeCCmSuw

Instagram: @repkclark

District Office: 701 Concord Ave., #101, Cambridge, MA 02138; 617-354-0292; Fax: 617-354-1456; *District Director:* Kelsey Perkins

Satellite Office: 116 Concord St., #1, Framingham, MA 01702; 508-319-9757; *District Director:* Wade Blackman

Committee Assignment: Appropriations

Clarke, Yvette D., D-N.Y. (9)

Capitol Hill Office: 2058 RHOB 20515; 225-6231; Fax: 226-0112; *Chief of Staff:* Charlyn Stanberry

Web: clarke.house.gov

Facebook: www.facebook.com/repyvettedclarke

Twitter: @RepYvetteClarke

YouTube: www.youtube.com/repyvetteclarke

Instagram: @repyvetteclarke

District Office: 222 Lenox Rd., #1 & 2, Brooklyn, NY 11226-3302; 718-287-1142; Fax: 718-287-1223; *District Director:* Anita Taylor

Committee Assignments: Energy and Commerce; Homeland Security

Clay, William Lacy, Jr., D-Mo. (1)

Capitol Hill Office: 2428 RHOB 20515-2501; 225-2406; Fax: 226-3717; *Chief of Staff:* Yvette Cravins

Web: lacyclay.house.gov

Facebook: www.facebook.com/CongressmanClayMO1

Twitter: @LacyClayMO1

YouTube: www.youtube.com/WilliamLacyClay

District Offices: 111 S. 10th St., #24.344, St. Louis, MO 63102; 314-367-1970; Fax: 314-367-1341; *Community Outreach Coord.:* Sherry Faulkner

6830 Gravois Ave., St. Louis, MO 63116; 314-669-9393; 314-669-9398; *Communications Director; Press Secy.:* Steve Engelhardt

1281 Graham Rd., #202, Florissant, MO 63031; 314-383-5240; Fax: 314-383-8020;

Committee Assignments: Financial Services; Natural Resources; Oversight and Reform

Cleaver, Emanuel, D-Mo. (5)

Capitol Hill Office: 2335 RHOB 20515; 225-4535; Fax: 225-4403; *Chief of Staff:* Jennifer Sapiro

Web: cleaver.house.gov

Facebook: www.facebook.com/emanuelcleaverii

Twitter: @repcleaver

YouTube: www.youtube.com/repcleaver

Instagram: @repcleaver

District Offices: 211 W. Maple Ave., Independence, MO 64050-2815; 816-833-4545; Fax: 816-833-2991; *Deputy District Director:* Manny Abarca

101 W. 31st St., Kansas City, MO 64108-3318; 816-842-4545; Fax: 816-471-5215; *District Director:* Whitney Frost

1923 Main St., Higginsville, MO 64037; 660-584-7373; Fax: 660-584-7227; *Rural Policy Director:* Kyle Wilkens

Committee Assignments: Financial Services; Homeland Security

Cline, Ben, R-Va. (6)

Capitol Hill Office: 1009 LHOB 20515-3515; 225-5431; Fax: 225-9681; *Chief of Staff:* Matt Miller
Web: cline.house.gov
Facebook: www.facebook.com/RepBenCline
Twitter: @RepBenCline
District Offices: 70 N. Mason St., #110, Harrisonburg, VA 22802; 540-432-2391; Fax: 540-432-6593
916 Main St., #300, Lynchburg, VA 24504; 434-845-8306; Fax: (434) 845-8245
10 Franklin Rd., #510, Roanoke, VA 24011; 540-857-2672; Fax: (540) 857-2675
117 S Lewis St., #215, Staunton, VA 24401; 540-885-3861; Fax: (540) 885-3930
Committee Assignments: Education and Labor; Judiciary

Cloud, Michael, R-Tex. (27)

Capitol Hill Office: 1314 LHOB 20515-3515; 225-7742; Fax: 226-1134; *Chief of Staff:* Adam Magary
Web: cloud.house.gov
Facebook: www.facebook.com/RepCloudTX
Twitter: @RepCloudTX
District Offices: 101 N. Shoreline Blvd., #300, Corpus Christi, TX 78401; 361-884-2222; Fax: 361-884-2223; *District Director:* J.D. Kennedy
111 N. Glass St., #102, Victoria, TX 77901; 361-894-6446; Fax: 361-884-2223; *Communications Director:* Brian Cruickshanks
Committee Assignments: Oversight and Reform; Science, Space, and Technology

Clyburn, James E., D-S.C. (6)

Capitol Hill Office: 200 CHOB 20515; 225-3315; Fax: 225-2313; *Chief of Staff:* Yelberton R. Watkins
Web: clyburn.house.gov
Twitter: @ClyburnSC06
YouTube: www.youtube.com/repjamesclyburn
Instagram: @whipclyburn
District Offices: 1225 Lady St., #200, Columbia, SC 29201-3210; 803-799-1100; Fax: 803-799-9060; *District Director:* Robert Nance
130 W. Main St., Kingstree, SC 29556; 843-355-1211; Fax: 843-355-1232; *Caseworker:* Kenneth Barnes
176 Brooks Blvd., Santee, SC 29142; 803-854-4700; Fax: 803-854-4900; *District Director:* Robert Nance
Majority Whip

Cohen, Steve, D-Tenn. (9)

Capitol Hill Office: 2104 RHOB 20515; 225-3265; Fax: 225-5663; *Chief of Staff:* Marilyn Dillihay
Web: cohen.house.gov
Facebook: www.facebook.com/CongressmanSteveCohen
Twitter: @RepCohen
YouTube: www.youtube.com/RepCohen
District Office: Clifford Davis/Odell Horton Federal Bldg., 167 N. Main St., #369, Memphis, TN 38103-1822; 901-544-4131; Fax: 901-544-4329; *District Director:* Marzie Thomas

Committee Assignments: Judiciary; Science, Space, and Technology, Transportation and Infrastructure

Cole, Tom, R-Okla. (4)

Capitol Hill Office: 2207 RHOB 20515-3604; 225-6165; Fax: 225-3512; *Deputy Chief of Staff:* Maria Bowie
Web: cole.house.gov
Facebook: www.facebook.com/TomColeOK04
Twitter: @tomcoleok04
YouTube: www.youtube.com/TomColeOK04
Instagram: @tomcoleok04
District Offices: 100 E. 13th St., #213, Ada, OK 74820-6548; 580-436-5375; Fax: 580-436-5451; *Field Rep.:* Amber Savage
711 D Ave. S.W., #201, Lawton, OK 73501-4561; 580-357-2131; Fax: 580-357-7477; *Field Rep.:* Scott Chance
2424 Springer Dr., #201, Norman, OK 73069-3965; 405-329-6500; Fax: 405-321-7369; *District Director:* Will McPherson
Committee Assignments: Appropriations; Rules

Collins, Chris, R-N.Y. (27)

Capitol Hill Office: 2243 RHOB 20515; 225-5265; Fax: 225-5910; *Chief of Staff:* Michael Hook
Web: chriscollins.house.gov
Facebook: www.facebook.com/RepChrisCollins
Twitter: @RepChrisCollins
YouTube: www.youtube.com/RepChrisCollins
Instagram: @repchriscollins
District Offices: 128 Main St., #2, Geneseo, NY 14454; 585-519-4002; Fax: 585-519-4009; *Field Rep.:* George McNerney
8203 Main St., #2, Williamsville, NY 14221; 716-634-2324; Fax: 716-631-7610
Committee Assignments: None

Collins, Doug, R-Ga. (9)

Capitol Hill Office: 1504 LHOB 20515; 225-9893; Fax: 226-1224; *Chief of Staff:* Brendan Belair
Web: dougcollins.house.gov
Facebook: www.facebook.com/RepresentativeDougCollins
Twitter: @RepDougCollins
YouTube: www.youtube.com/repdougcollins
Instagram: @dougcollinsga
District Office: 210 Washington St. N.W., #202, Gainesville, GA 30501; 770-297-3388; Fax: 770-297-3390; *District Director:* Joel Katz
Committee Assignment: Judiciary

Comer, James, R-Ky. (1)

Capitol Hill Office: 1037 LHOB 20515; 225-3115; Fax: 225-3547; *Chief of Staff:* Caroline Cash
Web: comer.house.gov
Facebook: www.facebook.com/CongressmanComer
Twitter: @KYComer
Instagram: @congressmancomer
District Offices: 300 S. 3rd St., Paducah, KY 42003; 270-408-1865; *Sr. Field Rep:* Martie Wiles

200 N. Main St., Suite F, Tompkinsville, KY 42167; 270-487-9509; Toll-free: 800-328-5629; *District Director:* Sandy Simpson
Committee Assignments: Agriculture; Education and Labor; Oversight and Reform

Conaway, K. Michael, R-Tex. (11)

Capitol Hill Office: 2469 RHOB 20515-4311; 225-3605; Fax: 225-1783; *Chief of Staff:* Mark Williams
Web: conaway.house.gov
Facebook: www.facebook.com/mike.conaway
Twitter: @ConawayTX11
YouTube: www.youtube.com/mikeconaway11
Instagram: @mikeconawaytx11
District Offices: Brownwood City Hall, 501 Center Ave., Brownwood, TX 76801-2809; 325-646-1950; Fax: 325-646-2979; *Field Rep.:* Hilary Stegemoller
132 Houston St., Granbury, TX 76048; 682-936-2577; Fax: 682-936-2567; *Field Rep.:* Dianne Williams
County Annex, 104 W. Sandstone St., Llano, TX 78643-2319; 325-247-2826; Fax: 325-247-2676; *Field Rep.:* Nancy Watson
6 Desta Dr., #2000, Midland, TX 79705-5520; 432-687-2390; Fax: 432-687-0277; *District Director:* Evan Thomas
City Hall, 411 W. 8th St., 5th Floor, Odessa, TX 79761-4422; 432-331-9667; Fax: 432-332-6538; *Field Rep.:* Gloria G. Apolinario
33 E. Twohig Ave., #307, San Angelo, TX 76903-6451; 325-659-4010; Fax: 325-659-4014; *District Director:* Joanne Powell
Committee Assignments: Agriculture, Chair; Armed Services; Permanent Select Intelligence

Connolly, Gerald E. (Gerry), D-Va. (11)

Capitol Hill Office: 2238 RHOB 20515-4611; 225-1492; Fax: 225-3071; *Chief of Staff:* James Walkinshaw
Web: connolly.house.gov
Facebook: www.facebook.com/CongressmanGerryConnolly
Twitter: @GerryConnolly
YouTube: www.youtube.com/RepConnolly
District Offices: 4115 Annandale Rd., #103, Annandale, VA 22003-2500; 703-256-3071; Fax: 703-354-1284; *District Director:* Sharon Stark
2241-D Tacketts Mill Dr., Woodbridge, VA 22192-5307; 571-408-4407; Fax: 571-408-4708; *Prince William County Outreach Rep.:* Marlon Dubuisson
Committee Assignments: Foreign Affairs; Oversight and Reform

Cook, Paul, R-Calif. (8)

Capitol Hill Office: 1027 LHOB 20515; 225-5861; Fax: 225-6498; *Chief of Staff:* John Sobel
Web: cook.house.gov
Twitter: @RepPaulCook
YouTube: www.youtube.com/RepPaulCook
Instagram: @repjimcooper

District Offices: 14955 Dale Evans Pkwy., Apple Valley, CA 92307; 760-247-1815; Fax: 760-247-8073; *District Director:* Dakota Higgins
34282 Yucaipa Blvd., Yucaipa, CA 92399; 909-797-4900; Fax: 909-797-4997; *Field Rep.:* Jan Leja
Committee Assignments: Armed Services; Natural Resources

Cooper, Jim, D-Tenn. (5)

Capitol Hill Office: 1536 LHOB 20515-4205; 225-4311; Fax: 226-1035; *Chief of Staff:* Lisa Quigley
Web: cooper.house.gov
Facebook: www.facebook.com/JimCooper
Twitter: @repjimcooper
YouTube: www.youtube.com/RepJimCooper
Instagram: @repjimcooper
District Office: 605 Church St., Nashville, TN 37219-2314; 615-736-5295; Fax: 615-736-7479; *District Director:* Kathy Buggs
Committee Assignments: Armed Services; Oversight and Reform

Correa, J. Luis, D-Calif. (46)

Capitol Hill Office: 1039 LHOB 20515; 225-2965; *Chief of Staff:* Laurie Saroff
Web: correa.house.gov
Facebook: www.facebook.com/RepLouCorrea
Twitter: @RepLouCorrea
YouTube: www.youtube.com/channel/UCIKJJp4QJIDjnjodc23qKkw
District Office: 2323 N. Broadway, #319, Santa Ana, CA 92706; 714-559-6190; *District Director:* Claudio Gallegos
Committee Assignments: Homeland Security; Judiciary

Costa, Jim, D-Calif. (16)

Capitol Hill Office: 2081 RHOB 20515-0520; 225-3341; Fax: 225-9308; *Chief of Staff:* Juan Lopez
Web: costa.house.gov
Facebook: www.facebook.com/RepJimCosta
Twitter: @RepJimCosta
YouTube: www.youtube.com/RepJimCostaCA20
District Offices: 855 M St., #940, Fresno, CA 93721-2757; 559-495-1620; Fax: 559-495-1027; *District Director:* Kathy Mahan
2222 M St., #305, Merced, CA 95340; 209-384-1620; Fax: 209-304-1629 *District Director:* Kathy Mahan
Committee Assignments: Agriculture; Foreign Affairs; Natural Resources

Courtney, Joe, D-Conn. (2)

Capitol Hill Office: 2332 RHOB 20515; 225-2076; Fax: 225-4977; *Chief of Staff:* Neil McKiernan
Web: courtney.house.gov
Facebook: www.facebook.com/joecourtney
Twitter: @RepJoeCourtney
YouTube: www.youtube.com/RepCourtney
Instagram: @repjoecourtney

District Offices: 77 Hazard Ave., Suite J, Enfield, CT 06082-3890; 860-741-6011; Fax: 860-741-6036; *Field Rep.:* Brianna Dezizo

55 Main St., #250, Norwich, CT 06360; 860-886-0139; Fax: 860-886-2974; *District Director:* Ayanti Grant

Committee Assignments: Armed Services; Education and Labor

Cox, TJ, D-Calif. (21)

Capitol Hill Office: 1728 LHOB 20515-3515; 225-4695; *Chief of Staff:* Francois Genard

Web: cox.house.gov

Facebook: www.facebook.com/RepTJCox/

Twitter: @RepTjCox

YouTube: www.youtube.com/reptjcox

Instagram: @reptjcox

District Offices: 2700 M St., #250B, Bakersfield, CA 93301; 661-864-7736; Fax: 833-284-9090; *District Director:* Gilbert Felix

2117 Selma St., Selma, CA 93662; 559-460-6070; Fax: 833-284-9090

Committee Assignments: Agriculture; Natural Resources

Craig, Angie, D-Minn. (2)

Capitol Hill Office: 1523 LHOB 20515-3515; 225-2271; Fax: 225-; *Chief of Staff:* Mara Kunin

Web: craig.house.gov

Facebook: www.facebook.com/RepAngieCraig

Twitter: @RepAngieCraig

YouTube: www.youtube.com/housedems

Instagram: @housedemocrats

District Offices: 12940 Harriet Ave. South, #238, Burnsville, MN 55337; 651-846-2120

Committee Assignment: Agriculture; Transportation and Infrastructure

Crawford, Rick, R-Ark. (1)

Capitol Hill Office: 2422 RHOB 20515; 225-4076; Fax: 225-5602; *Chief of Staff:* Jonah Shumate

Web: crawford.house.gov

Facebook: www.facebook.com/RepRickCrawford

Twitter: @RepRickCrawford

YouTube: www.youtube.com/RepRickCrawford

Instagram: @reprickcrawford

District Offices: 112 S. 1st St., Cabot, AR 72023-3007; 501-843-3043; Fax: 501-843-4955; *Field Rep.:* Jay Sherrod

2400 Highland Dr., #300, Jonesboro, AR 72401-6229; 870-203-0540; Fax: 870-203-0542; *District Director:* Tammy Davenport

1001 Hwy. 62 E., #9, Mountain Home, AR 72653; 870-424-2075; Fax: 870-424-3149; *Field Rep./Veterans Outreach Liaison:* Stetson Painter

Committee Assignments: Agriculture; Transportation and Infrastructure; Permanent Select Intelligence

Crenshaw, Dan, R-Tex. (2)

Capitol Hill Office: 413 CHOB 20515-3515; 225-6565; Fax: 226-et; *Chief of Staff:* Eliza Baker

Web: crenshaw.house.gov

Facebook: www.facebook.com/RepDanCrenshaw

Twitter: @RepDanCrenshaw

YouTube: www.youtube.com/channel/UC2XDiCjAHtJqnSEzrHAY5IQ

Instagram: @dancrenshawtx

District Offices: 1849 Kingwood Dr., #100, Kingwood, TX 77339; 713-860-1330; *Director:* Sue Walden

Committee Assignments: Budget; Homeland Security

Crist, Charlie, D-Fla. (13)

Capitol Hill Office: 215 CHOB 20515; 225-5961; Fax: 225-9764; *Chief of Staff:* Austin Durrer

Web: crist.house.gov

Facebook: www.facebook.com/RepCharlieCrist

Twitter: @RepCharlieCrist

YouTube: www.youtube.com/RepCharlieCrist

Instagram: @repcharliecrist

District Office: 696 1st Ave. North, #203, St. Petersburg, FL 33701; 727-318-6770; Fax: 727-623-0619; *District Director:* Steven Carey

Committee Assignments: Appropriations; Science, Space, and Technology

Crow, Jason, D-Colo. (6)

Capitol Hill Office: 1229 LHOB 20515-3515; 225-7882; *Chief of Staff:* Alex Ball

Web: crow.house.gov

Facebook: www.facebook.com/RepJasonCrow

Twitter: @RepJasonCrow

District Offices: 3300 S. Parker Rd., #100, Aurora, CO 80014; 720-748-7514; *District Director:* Maytham Alshadood

Committee Assignments: Armed Services; Small Business

Cuellar, Henry, D-Tex. (28)

Capitol Hill Office: 2372 RHOB 20515; 225-1640; Fax: 225-1641; *Chief of Staff:* Vacant; *Legislative Director:* Zack Linick

Web: cuellar.house.gov

Facebook: www.facebook.com/repcuellar

Twitter: @RepCuellar

YouTube: www.youtube.com/henrycuellar

District Offices: 602 E. Calton Rd., #2, Laredo, TX 78041-3693; 956-725-0639; Fax: 956-725-2647; *Outreach Coord.:* Francis Atwell

117 E. Tom Landry St., Mission, TX 78572-4160; 956-424-3942; Fax: 956-424-3936; *Constituent Services Coord.:* Nicole Hernandez

100 N. F.M. 3167, Rio Grande City, TX 78582; 956-487-5603; Fax: 956-488-0952; *Outreach Coord.:* Francis Atwell

615 E. Houston St., #563, San Antonio, TX 78205-2048; 210-271-2851; Fax: 210-277-6671; *Outreach Coord.:* Gilbert La Fuente

Committee Assignment: Appropriations

Cummings, Elijah, D-Md. (7)

Capitol Hill Office: 2163 RHOB 20515-2007; 225-4741; Fax: 225-3178; *Chief of Staff:* Vernon Simms

Web: cummings.house.gov
Facebook: www.facebook.com/elijahcummings
Twitter: @RepCummings
YouTube: www.youtube.com/ElijahECummings
Instagram: @repcummings
District Offices: 1010 Park Ave., #105, Baltimore, MD 21201-5600; 410-685-9199; Fax: 410-685-9399; *District Director:* Harry Spikes

754 Frederick Rd., Catonsville, MD 21228-4504; 410-719-8777; Fax: 410-455-0110; *Special Asst.:* Katie Malone

8267 Main St., #102, Ellicott, MD 21043-9903; 410-465-8259; Fax: 410-465-8740; *Special Asst.:* Amy Stratton
Committee Assignments: Oversight and Reform, Chair; Transportation and Infrastructure

Cunningham, Joe, D-S.C. (1)

Capitol Hill Office: 423 CHOB 20515-3515; 225-3176; *Chief of Staff:* Lane Loften
Web: cunningham.house.gov
Facebook: www.facebook.com/RepJoeCunningham
Twitter: @RepCunningham
District Offices: 530 Johnnie Dodds Blvd., #201, Mt. Pleasant, SC 29464; 843-352-7572; *District Director:* Hollis Infanzon

710 Boundary St., #1D, Beaufort, SC 29902; 843-521-2530
Committee Assignments: Natural Resources; Veterans' Affairs

Curtis, John R., R-Utah (3)

Capitol Hill Office: 125 CHOB 20515; 225-7751; Fax: 225-5629; *Chief of Staff:* Corey Norman
Web: curtis.house.gov
Facebook: www.facebook.com/RepJohnCurtis
Twitter: @RepJohnCurtis
YouTube: www.youtube.com/channel/UChAQ4MD-HigmGnImSoAKBVA
Instagram: @repjohncurtis
District Office: 3549 N. University Ave., #275, Provo, UT 84604; 801-922-5400; *District Director:* Lorie Fowlke
Committee Assignments: Foreign Affairs; Natural Resources

Davids, Sharice, D-Kans. (3)

Capitol Hill Office: 1541 LHOB 20515-3515; 225-2865; Fax: 225-2807; *Chief of Staff:* Allison Teixeira Sulier
Web: davids.house.gov
Facebook: www.facebook.com/RepDavids
Twitter: @RepDavids
YouTube: www.youtube.com/channel/UCNUfpXQeUVdh6oKWVmq3xxQ
Instagram: @repdavids
District Offices: 7325 W. 79th St., Overland Park, KS 66204; 913-621-0832; Fax: 913-621-1533; *District Director:* Danielle Robinson

753 State Ave., #460, Kansas City, KS 66101; 913-766-3993
Committee Assignments: Small Business; Transportation and Infrastructure

Davidson, Warren, R-Ohio (8)

Capitol Hill Office: 1107 LHOB 20515; 225-6205; *Chief of Staff:* Adam Hewitt
Web: davidson.house.gov
Facebook: www.facebook.com/CongressmanWarrenDavidson
Twitter: @WarrenDavidson
YouTube: www.youtube.com/channel/UCMzuyZWzk44YRNesFzPTeUw
Instagram: @instawarrendavidson
District Offices: 20 Dotcom Dr., Troy, OH 45373; 937-339-1524; *District Director:* Ben Thaeler

8857 Cincinnati-Dayton Rd., #102, West Chester, OH 45069; 513-779-5400; *Caseworker:* Sharon Heuss
Satellite Office: 76 E. High St., 3rd Floor, Springfield, OH 45502; 937-322-1120
Committee Assignment: Financial Services

Davis, Danny K., D-Ill. (7)

Capitol Hill Office: 2159 RHOB 20515-1307; 225-5006; Fax: 225-5641; *Chief of Staff:* Yul Edwards
Web: davis.house.gov
Facebook: www.facebook.com/CongressmanDKDavis
Twitter: @RepDannyDavis
District Office: 2813-15 W. 5th Ave., Chicago, IL 60612-2040; 773-533-7520; Fax: 773-533-7530; *District Director:* Cherita Logan
Committee Assignment: Ways and Means

Davis, Rodney, R-Ill. (13)

Capitol Hill Office: 1740 LHOB 20515; 225-2371; Fax: 226-0791; *Chief of Staff:* Bret Manley
Web: rodneydavis.house.gov
Facebook: www.facebook.com/RepRodneyDavis
Twitter: @RodneyDavis
YouTube: www.youtube.com/RepRodneyDavis
Instagram: @reprodneydavis
District Offices: 2004 Fox Dr., Champaign, IL 61820; 217-403-4690; Fax: 217-403-4691; *District Director:* Helen Albert

243 S. Water St., #100, Decatur, IL 62523; 217-791-6224; Fax: 217-791-6168; *Community Outreach:* Candice Trees

15 Professional Park Dr., Maryville, IL 62062; 618-205-8660; Fax: 618-205-8662; *Grants and Projects Coord.:* Philip Lasseigne

108 W. Market St., Taylorville, IL 62568; 217-824-5117; Fax: 217-824-5121; *Constituent Services Rep.:* Meg Kettelkamp
Satellite Offices: 2833 S. Grand Ave., East Springfield, IL 62703; 217-791-6224; Fax: 217-791-6168; (by appointment only); *Community Outreach:* Candice Trees

104 W. North St., Normal, IL 61761; 309-252-8834; (by appointment only); *Deputy District Director:* Tyler Cravens
Committee Assignments: Agriculture; House Administration; Joint Library; Joint Printing; Transportation and Infrastructure

Davis, Susan, D-Calif. (53)

Capitol Hill Office: 1214 LHOB 20515-0553; 225-2040;
Fax: 225-2948; *Chief of Staff:* Lisa Sherman
Web: susandavis.house.gov
Facebook: www.facebook.com/RepSusanDavis
Twitter: @RepSusanDavis
YouTube: www.youtube.com/RepSusanADavis
Instagram: @repsusandavis
District Office: 2700 Adams Ave., #102, San Diego, CA
92116; 619-280-5353; Fax: 619-280-5311; *District Director:* Jessica Mier
Committee Assignments: Armed Services; Education and
Labor; House Administration

Dean, Madeleine, D-Pa. (4)

Capitol Hill Office: 129 CHOB 20515-3515; 225-4731;
Chief of Staff: Koh Chiba
Web: dean.house.gov
Facebook: www.facebook.com/RepMadeleineDean
Twitter: @RepDean
Instagram: @ repmadeleinedean
District Offices: 115 E. Glenside Ave., #1, Glenside, PA
19038; 215-884-4300; Fax: 215-884-3640; *District Director:* Kathleen Joyce
101 E. Main St., Suite A, Norristown, PA 19401; 610-
382-1250; Fax: 610-275-1759; *District Director:*
Kathleen Joyce
Committee Assignments: Financial Services; Judiciary

DeFazio, Peter, D-Ore. (4)

Capitol Hill Office: 2134 RHOB 20515-3704; 225-6416;
Chief of Staff: Kristie Greco
Web: defazio.house.gov
Facebook: www.facebook.com/RepPeterDeFazio
Twitter: @RepPeterDeFazio
YouTube: www.youtube.com/PeterDeFazio
District Offices: 405 E. 8th Ave., #2030, Eugene, OR
97401-2706; 541-465-6732; Fax: 541-465-6458; *District Director:* Dan Whelan
612 S.E. Jackson St., #9, Roseburg, OR 97470-4956; 541-440-
3523; Fax: 541-440-3713; *Field Rep.:* Christine Conroy
125 Central Ave., #350, Coos Bay, OR 97420; 541-269-
2609; Fax: 541-269-5760;
Committee Assignment: Transportation and
Infrastructure, Chair

DeGette, Diana, D-Colo. (1)

Capitol Hill Office: 2111 RHOB 20515; 225-4431;
Fax: 225-5657; *Chief of Staff:* Lisa B. Cohen
Web: degette.house.gov
Facebook: www.facebook.com/DianaDeGette
Twitter: @RepDianaDeGette
YouTube: www.youtube.com/RepDianaDeGette
Instagram: repdianadegette
District Office: 600 Grant St., #202, Denver, CO 80203-
3525; 303-844-4988; Fax: 303-844-4996; *Interim District Director:* Andrea Autobee-Trujillo
Committee Assignment: Energy and Commerce; Natural
Resources

DeLauro, Rosa L., D-Conn. (3)

Capitol Hill Office: 2413 RHOB 20515-0703; 225-3661;
Fax: 225-4890; *Chief of Staff:* Leticia Mederos
Web: delauro.house.gov
Facebook: www.facebook.com/
CongresswomanRosaDeLauro
Twitter: @rosadelauro
YouTube: www.youtube.com/RosaDeLauro
Instagram: @rosa_delauro
District Office: 59 Elm St., New Haven, CT 06510; 203-
562-3718; Fax: 203-772-2260; *District Director:*
Jennifer Lamb
Committee Assignments: Appropriations; Budget

DelBene, Suzan, D-Wash. (1)

Capitol Hill Office: 2330 RHOB 20515; 225-6311;
Fax: 226-1606; *Chief of Staff:* Aaron Schmidt
Web: delbene.house.gov
Facebook: www.facebook.com/RepDelBene
Twitter: @RepDelBene
YouTube: www.youtube.com/channel/
UCd00b7TpKDZIr-Ujhaktvjg
Instagram: @repdelbene
District Offices: 22121 17th Ave. S.E., Bldg. E, #220,
Bothell, WA 98021; 425-485-0085; Fax: 425-485-0083;
District Director: Molly Keenan
204 W. Montgomery St., Mount Vernon, WA 98273; 360-
416-7879; *Outreach Coord.:* Kaylee Galloway
Committee Assignments: Budget; Ways and Means

Delgado, Antonio, D-N.Y. (19)

Capitol Hill Office: 1007 LHOB 20515; 225-5614; *Chief of Staff:* John Bivona
Web: delgado.house.gov
Facebook: www.facebook.com/RepAntonioDelgado
Twitter: @repdelgado
Instagram: @repantoniodelgado
District Offices: 111 Main St., Delhi, NY 13753; 845-443-
2930; *District Director:* Amanda Boomhower
256 Clinton Ave., Kingston, NY 12401; 845-443-2930;
District Director: Amanda Boomhower
189 Main St., #500, Oneonta, NY 13820; 845-443-2930;
District Director: Amanda Boomhower
Committee Assignments: Agriculture; Small Business;
Transportation and Infrastructure

Demings, Val, D-Fla. (10)

Capitol Hill Office: 217 CHOB 20515; 225-2176; Fax: 225-
0999; *Chief of Staff:* Wendy Anderson
Web: demings.house.gov
Facebook: www.facebook.com/
RepresentativeValDemings
Twitter: @RepValDemings
YouTube: www.youtube.com/channel/
UCkcshqwFNJG6XeduOforhig
Instagram: @repvaldemings
District Offices: 2295 S. Hiawassee Rd., #301, Orlando, FL
32835; 321-388-9808; Fax: 202-226-6559; *District Director:* Sonja White

Committee Assignments: Homeland Security; Judiciary; Permanent Select Intelligence

DeSaulnier, Mark, D-Calif. (11)

Capitol Hill Office: 503 CHOB 20515-0511; 225-2095; Fax: 225-5609; *Chief of Staff:* Betsy Arnold Marr
Web: desaulnier.house.gov
Facebook: www.facebook.com/RepMarkDeSaulnier
Twitter: @RepDeSaulnier
YouTube: www.youtube.com/RepDeSaulnier
Instagram: @repdesaulnier
District Offices: 440 Civic Center Plaza, 2nd Floor, Richmond, CA 94804; 510-620-1000; Fax: 510-620-1005; *District Director:* Shanelle Scales-Preston
3100 Oak Rd., #110, Walnut Creek, CA 94597; 925-933-2660; Fax: 925-933-2677; *District Director:* Shanelle Scales-Preston
Committee Assignments: Education and Labor; Oversight and Reform; Transportation and Infrastructure

DesJarlais, Scott, R-Tenn. (4)

Capitol Hill Office: 2301 RHOB 20515; 225-6831; Fax: 226-5172; *Chief of Staff:* Richard Vaughn
Web: desjarlais.house.gov
Facebook: www.facebook.com/ScottDesJarlaisTN04
Twitter: @DesJarlaisTN04
YouTube: www.youtube.com/ScottDesJarlaisTN04
Instagram: @desjarlaistn04
District Offices: 711 N. Garden St., Columbia, TN 38401; 931-381-9920; Fax: 931-381-9945; *Constituent Services Coord.:* Becky Moon
305 W. Main St., Murfreesboro, TN 37130; 615-896-1986; Fax: 615-896-8218; *Caseworker:* Kristen Topping
Satellite Offices: 301 Keith St. S.W., #212, Cleveland, TN 37311; 423-472-7500; Fax: 423-472-7800; *Field Rep.:* Shirley Pond
Federal Bldg., 200 S. Jefferson St., #311, Winchester, TN 37398; 931-962-3180; Fax: 931-962-3435;
Committee Assignments: Agriculture; Armed Services

Deutch, Ted, D-Fla. (22)

Capitol Hill Office: 2447 RHOB 20515-0919; 225-3001; Fax: 225-5974; *Chief of Staff:* Joshua Rogin
Web: teddeutch.house.gov
Facebook: www.facebook.com/CongressmanTedDeutch
Twitter: @RepTedDeutch
YouTube: www.youtube.com/CongressmanTedDeutch
Instagram: @repteddeutch
District Offices: 7900 Glades Rd., #250, Boca Raton, FL 33434; 561-470-5440; Fax: 561-470-5446; *District Director:* Wendi Lipsich
Margate City Hall, 5790 Margate Blvd., Margate, FL 33063-3614; 954-972-6454; Fax: 954-974-3191; *Deputy District Director:* Theresa Brier
9500 W. Sample Rd., #201, Coral Springs, FL 33065; 954-255-8336; *Deputy District Director:* Theresa Brier
Committee Assignments: Ethics; Foreign Affairs; Judiciary

Diaz-Balart, Mario, R-Fla. (25)

Capitol Hill Office: 404 CHOB 20515-0921; 225-4211; Fax: 225-8576; *Chief of Staff:* Cesar A. Gonzalez
Web: mariodiazbalart.house.gov
Facebook: www.facebook.com/mdiazbalart
Twitter: @MarioDB
YouTube: www.youtube.com/MarioDiazBalart
Instagram: @repmariodb
District Offices: 8669 36th St. N.W., #100, Doral, FL 33166-6640; 305-470-8555; Fax: 305-470-8575; *Deputy Chief of Staff:* Miguel A. Otero
4715 Golden Gate Pkwy., #1, Naples, FL 34116; 239-348-1620; Fax: 239-348-3569; *Congressional Aide:* Enrique Padron
Committee Assignment: Appropriations

Dingell, Debbie, D-Mich. (12)

Capitol Hill Office: 116 CHOB 20515-2212; 225-4071; Fax: 226-0371; *Chief of Staff:* Greg Sunstrum
Web: debbiedingell.house.gov
Facebook: www.facebook.com/RepDebbieDingell
Twitter: @RepDebDingell
YouTube: www.youtube.com/channel/UCnoP3KLT-HOvzDfC1-I-9lQ
Instagram: @repdingell
District Offices: 301 W. Michigan Ave., #400, Ypsilanti, MI 48197; 734-481-1100; *Field Rep.:* Ryan Hunter
19855 W. Outer Dr., #103-E, Dearborn, MI 48124; 313-278-2936; Fax: 313-278-3914; *District Director:* Callie Bruley
Committee Assignments: Energy and Commerce; Natural Resources

Doggett, Lloyd, D-Tex. (35)

Capitol Hill Office: 2307 RHOB 20515-4325; 225-4865; Fax: 225-3073; *Chief of Staff:* Michael J. Mucchetti
Web: doggett.house.gov
Facebook: www.facebook.com/RepLloydDoggett
Twitter: @RepLloydDoggett
YouTube: www.youtube.com/doggett
Instagram: @reployddoggett
District Offices: Federal Bldg., 300 E. 8th St., #763, Austin, TX 78701-3224; 512-916-5921; Fax: 512-916-5108; *District Director:* Erin Gurak
217 W. Travis St., San Antonio, TX 78205; 210-704-1080; Fax: 210-299-1442; *District Director:* MaryEllen Veliz
Committee Assignments: Budget; Ways and Means

Doyle, Mike, D-Pa. (18)

Capitol Hill Office: 306 CHOB 20515; 225-2135; Fax: 225-3084; *Chief of Staff:* David G. Lucas
Web: doyle.house.gov
Facebook: www.facebook.com/usrepmikedoyle
Twitter: @USRepMikeDoyle
YouTube: www.youtube.com/CongressmanDoyle

District Offices: 2637 E. Carson St., Pittsburgh, PA 15203-5109; 412-390-1499; Fax: 412-390-2118; *District Director:* Paul D'Alesandro

627 Lysle Blvd., McKeesport, PA 15132; 412-664-4049; Fax: 412-664-4053; *Economic Development Rep.:* Jamie Byrne

4705 Library Rd., Bethel Park, PA 15102; 412-283-4451; Fax: 412-283-4465

Committee Assignment: Energy and Commerce

Duffy, Sean P., R-Wisc. (7)

Capitol Hill Office: 1714 LHOB 20515-4907; 225-3365; Fax: 225-3240; *Chief of Staff:* Pete Meachum
Web: duffy.house.gov
Facebook: www.facebook.com/RepSeanDuffy
Twitter: @RepSeanDuffy
YouTube: www.youtube.com/RepSeanDuffy
Instagram: @repseanduffy
District Office: 502 2nd St., #202, Hudson, WI 54016; 715-808-8160; Fax: 715-808-8167; *District Director:* Jesse Garza
Satellite Offices: 15569 Railroad St., #302, Hayward, WI 54843; 715-392-3984; *District Director:* Jesse Garza

208 Grand Ave., Wausau, WI 54403-6217; 715-298-9344; Fax: 715-298-9348;
Committee Assignment: Financial Services

Duncan, Jeff, R-S.C. (3)

Capitol Hill Office: 2229 RHOB 20515-4003; 225-5301; Fax: 225-3216; *Chief of Staff:* Allen Klump
Web: jeffduncan.house.gov
Facebook: www.facebook.com/RepJeffDuncan
Twitter: @RepJeffDuncan
YouTube: www.youtube.com/CongJeffDuncan
Instagram: @repjeffduncan
District Offices: 303 W. Beltline Blvd., Anderson, SC 29625-1505; 864-224-7401; Fax: 864-225-7049; *District Director:* Rick Adkins

100 Plaza Circle, #A1, Clinton, SC 29325; 864-681-1028; Fax: 864-681-1030; *Field Rep.:* Jan Harman
Committee Assignment: Energy and Commerce

Dunn, Neal, R-Fla. (2)

Capitol Hill Office: 316 CHOB 20515; 225-5235; Fax: 225-5615; *Chief of Staff:* Michael Lowry
Web: dunn.house.gov
Facebook: www.facebook.com/Dr.NealDunnFL2
Twitter: @DrNealDunnFL2
YouTube: www.youtube.com/channel/UCRTGfrYP-RuDzJ2KGok7TRA
District Offices: 840 W. 11th St., #2250, Panama City, FL 32401; 850-785-0812; Fax: 850-763-3764; *District Director:* Will Kendrick

300 S. Adams St., Tallahassee, FL 32301; 850-891-8610; Fax: 850-891-8620; *District Director:* Will Kendrick
Committee Assignments: Agriculture; Science Space, and Technology; Veterans' Affairs

Emmer, Tom, R-Minn. (6)

Capitol Hill Office: 315 CHOB 20515-2306; 225-2331; Fax: 225-6475; *Chief of Staff:* Christopher Maneval
Web: emmer.house.gov
Facebook: www.facebook.com/reptomemmer
Twitter: @reptomemmer
YouTube: www.youtube.com/RepTomEmmer
District Office: 9201 Quaday Ave. N.E., #206, Otsego, MN 55330; 763-241-6848; Fax: 763-241-7955; *Press Secretary:* Abby Rime
Committee Assignment: Financial Services

Engel, Eliot, D-N.Y. (16)

Capitol Hill Office: 2426 RHOB 20515-3217; 225-2464; Fax: 225-5513; *Administrative Asst.:* Ned Michalek
Web: engel.house.gov
Facebook: www.facebook.com/RepEliotLEngel
Twitter: @RepEliotEngel
YouTube: www.youtube.com/Engel2161
District Offices: 3655 Johnson Ave., Bronx, NY 10463-1671; 718-796-9700; Fax: 718-796-5134; *Chief of Staff:* Bill Weitz

6 Gramatan Ave., #205, Mount Vernon, NY 10550-3208; 914-699-4100; Fax: 914-699-3646; *Staff Asst.:* Cynthia Miller

177 Dreiser Loop, Room 3, Bronx, NY 10475; 718-320-2314; Fax: 718-320-2047 *Staff Asst.:* Maxine Sullivan
Committee Assignments: Energy and Commerce; Foreign Affairs, Chair

Escobar, Veronica, D-Tex. (16)

Capitol Hill Office: 1505 LHOB 20515-3515; 225-4831; *Chief of Staff:* Eduardo Lerma
Web: escobar.house.gov
Facebook: www.facebook.com/RepEscobar
Twitter: @RepEscobar
YouTube: www.youtube.com/channel/UC46TX2P8K0CA_4gZv8_R2Og/featured
District Offices: Wells Fargo Plaza, 221 N. Kansas St., #1500, El Paso, TX 79901; 915-541-1400; Fax: 915-501-1407; *District Director:* Susie Byrd
Committee Assignments: Armed Services; Judiciary

Eshoo, Anna G., D-Calif. (18)

Capitol Hill Office: 202 CHOB 20515; 225-8104; Fax: 225-8890; *Scheduler:* Noor Shah
Web: eshoo.house.gov
Facebook: www.facebook.com/RepAnnaEshoo
Twitter: @RepAnnaEshoo
YouTube: www.youtube.com/RepAnnaEshoo
Instagram: @repannaeshoo
District Office: 698 Emerson St., Palo Alto, CA 94301-1609; 650-323-2984 or 408-245-2339 or 831-335-2020; Fax: 650-323-3498; *District Chief of Staff:* Karen Chapman
Committee Assignment: Energy and Commerce

Espaillat, Adriano, D-N.Y. (13)

Capitol Hill Office: 1630 LHOB 20515; 225-4365;
Fax: 226-9731; *Chief of Staff:* Aneiry Batista
Web: espaillat.house.gov
Facebook: www.facebook.com/RepEspaillat
Twitter: @RepEspaillat
YouTube: www.youtube.com/channel/
UCi0niBYFhEY70Dz8InbX5OQ
Instagram: @repadrianoespaillat
District Offices: 2530 Grand Concourse Ave., Ground
Floor, Bronx, NY 10458; 718-450-8241; *District
Director:* David Baily
Harlem State Office Bldg., 163 W. 125th St., #507, New
York, NY 10027; 212-663-3900; *Deputy Chief of Staff:*
David Baily
Satellite Office: 5030 Broadway, Room 702, New York,
NY 10034; 888-216-6147;
Committee Assignments: Foreign Affairs; Small Business;
Transportation and Infrastructure

Estes, Ron, R-Kans. (4)

Capitol Hill Office: 1524 LHOB 20515; 225-6216;
Fax: 225-3489; *Chief of Staff:* Josh Bell
Web: estes.house.gov
Facebook: www.facebook.com/RepRonEstes
Twitter: @RepRonEstes
Instagram: @repronestes
District Office: 7701 E. Kellogg Dr., #510, Wichita, KS
67207; 316-262-8992; Fax: 316-262-5309;
Committee Assignment: Ways and Means

Evans, Dwight, D-Pa. (3)

Capitol Hill Office: 1105 LHOB 20515; 225-4001;
Fax: 225-5392; *Chief of Staff:* Kimberly Turner
Web: evans.house.gov
Facebook: www.facebook.com/RepDwightEvans
Twitter: @RepDwightEvans
Instagram: @repdwightevans
District Office: 7174 Ogontz Ave., Philadelphia, PA 19138;
215-276-0340; Fax: 215-276-2939; *District Director:*
Numa St. Louis
Committee Assignments: Small Business; Ways and
Means

Ferguson, A. Drew, R-Ga. (3)

Capitol Hill Office: 1032 LHOB 20515; 225-5901;
Fax: 225-2515; *Chief of Staff:* Bobby Saparow
Web: ferguson.house.gov
Facebook: www.facebook.com/RepDrewFerguson
Twitter: @RepDrewFerguson
YouTube: www.youtube.com/channel/
UCuK7_j2sREWi_7wBAN477bg
Instagram: @repdrewferguson
District Office: 1601B E. Hwy. 34, Suite B, Newnan, GA
30265; 770-683-2033; Fax: 770-683-2042; *District
Director:* Andy Bush
Committee Assignment: Ways and Means

Finkenauer, Abby, D-Iowa (1)

Capitol Hill Office: 124 CHOB 20515-3515; 225-2911;
Fax: 225-6666; *Chief of Staff:* Elizabeth Kerr
Web: finkenauer.house.gov
Facebook: www.facebook.com/RepAbbyFinkenauer
Twitter: @RepFinkenauer
YouTube: www.youtube.com/repabbyfinkenauer
Instagram: @RebAbbyFinkenauer
District Offices: 308 3rd St. S.E., #200, Cedar Rapids, IA
52401; 319-364-2288; Fax: 202-225-2666; *District
Director:* Jared Mullendore
1050 Main St., Dubuque, IA 52001; 563-557-7789
521A Lafayette St., Waterloo, IA 50703; 319-266-6925
Committee Assignment: Small Business; Transportation
and Infrastructure

Fitzpatrick, Brian K., R-Pa. (1)

Capitol Hill Office: 1722 LHOB 20515; 225-4276;
Fax: 225-9511; *Chief of Staff:* Andrew Renterian
Web: brianfitzpatrick.house.gov
Facebook: www.facebook.com/RepBrianFitzpatrick
Twitter: @RepBrianFitz
YouTube: www.youtube.com/channel/
UCYMNcgHss4_Q5JY2vSvMpgw
Instagram: @repbrianfitz
District Office: 1717 Langhorne Newton Rd., #400,
Langhorne, PA 19047; 215-579-8102; Fax: 215-579-
8109; *District Director:* Sue Simon
Committee Assignments: Foreign Affairs; Transportation
and Infrastructure

Fleischmann, Chuck, R-Tenn. (3)

Capitol Hill Office: 2410 RHOB 20515; 225-3271;
Fax: 225-3494; *Chief of Staff:* Jim Hippe
Web: fleischmann.house.gov
Facebook: www.facebook.com/repchuck
Twitter: @RepChuck
YouTube: www.youtube.com/RepChuck
Instagram: @repchuck
District Offices: 6 E. Madison Ave., Athens, TN 37303;
423-745-4671; Fax: 423-745-6025; *Field Rep.:* Maxine
O'Dell-Gernert
900 Georgia Ave., #126, Chattanooga, TN 37402-2282;
423-756-2342; Fax: 423-756-6613; *District Director:*
Bob White
200 Administration Rd., #100, Oak Ridge, TN 37830-8823;
865-576-1976; Fax: 865-576-3221; *Field Rep.:* Cindy
Boshears
Committee Assignment: Appropriations

Fletcher, Lizzie, D-Tex. (7)

Capitol Hill Office: 1429 LHOB 20515-3515; 225-2571;
Fax: 226-3805; *Chief of Staff:* Sarah Feinmann
Web: fletcher.house.gov
Facebook: www.facebook.com/RepFletcher
Twitter: @RepFletcher
YouTube: www.youtube.com/channel/
UCIWDLoDPvawP118TNWi-9rg
Instagram: @repfletcher

District Office: 5599 San Felipe, #950, Houston, TX 77056; 713-353-8680; *District Director:* Brooke Boyette

Committee Assignments: Science, Space, and Technology; Transportation and Infrastructure

Flores, Bill, R-Tex. (17)

Capitol Hill Office: 2440 RHOB 20515; 225-6105; Fax: 225-0350; *Chief of Staff:* Jon Oehmen

Web: flores.house.gov

Facebook: www.facebook.com/RepBillFlores

Twitter: @RepBillFlores

YouTube: www.youtube.com/RepBillFlores

Instagram: @repbillflores

District Offices: 3000 Briarcrest Dr., #406, Bryan, TX 77802; 979-703-4037; Fax: 979-703-8845; *District Director:* James Edge

400 Austin Ave., #302, Waco, TX 76701-2139; 254-732-0748; Fax: 254-732-1755; *District Director:* Jana Hixson

14205 Burnet Rd., #230, Austin, TX 78728; 512-373-3378; Fax: 512-373-3511; *District Director:* James Edge

Committee Assignment: Budget; Energy and Commerce

Fortenberry, Jeff, R-Neb. (1)

Capitol Hill Office: 1514 LHOB 20515-2701; 225-4806; Fax: 225-5686; *Chief of Staff:* Reyn Archer

Web: fortenberry.house.gov

Facebook: www.facebook.com/jefffortenberry

Twitter: @JeffFortenberry

YouTube: www.youtube.com/JeffFortenberry

District Offices: 301 S. 13th St., #100, Lincoln, NE 68508-2532; 402-438-1598; Fax: 402-438-1604; *District Director:* Marie Woodhead

506 W. Madison Ave., #2, Norfolk, NE 68701; 402-379-2064; Fax: 402-379-2101; *Field Rep.:* Nate Blum

Satellite Office: 641 N. Broad St., P.O. Box 377, Fremont, NE 68026-4932; 402-727-0888; Fax: 402-727-9130; *Field Rep.:* Nate Blum

Committee Assignment: Appropriations

Foster, Bill, D-Ill. (11)

Capitol Hill Office: 2366 RHOB 20515; 225-3515; Fax: 225-9420; *Chief of Staff:* Scott Shewcraft

Web: foster.house.gov

Facebook: www.facebook.com/CongressmanBillFoster

Twitter: @RepBillFoster

YouTube: www.youtube.com/RepBillFoster

Instagram: @repbillfoster

District Offices: 2711 E. New York St., #204, Aurora, IL 60502; 630-585-7672; Fax: 630-585-7689; *District Director:* Hilary Denk

195 Springfield Ave., #102, Joliet, IL 60435; 815-280-5876; Fax: 815-582-4342; *Constituent Services Advocate:* Chris Adams

Committee Assignments: Financial Services; Science, Space, and Technology

Foxx, Virginia, R-N.C. (5)

Capitol Hill Office: 2462 RHOB 20515; 225-2071; Fax: 225-2995; *Chief of Staff:* Cyrus Artz

Web: foxx.house.gov

Facebook: www.facebook.com/RepVirginiaFoxx

Twitter: @virginiafoxx

YouTube: www.youtube.com/RepVirginiaFoxx

Instagram: @repvirginiafoxx

District Offices: 400 Shadowline Dr., #205, Boone, NC 28607-4291; 828-265-0240; Fax: 828-265-0390; *District Director:* Robert Meek

3540 Clemmons Rd., #125, Clemmons, NC 27012-8775; 336-778-0211; Fax: 336-778-2290; *Office Manager:* Patricia Bandy

Committee Assignments: Education and Labor; Oversight and Reform

Frankel, Lois, D-Fla. (21)

Capitol Hill Office: 2305 RHOB 20515; 225-9890; Fax: 225-1224; *Chief of Staff:* Kelsey Moran

Web: frankel.house.gov

Facebook: www.facebook.com/RepLoisFrankel

Twitter: @RepLoisFrankel

YouTube: www.youtube.com/RepLoisFrankel

Instagram: @reploisfrankel

District Office: 2500 N. Military Trail, #490, Boca Raton, FL 33431; 561-998-9045; Fax: 561-998-9048; *District Director:* Felicia Goldstein

Committee Assignment: Appropriations

Fudge, Marcia L., D-Ohio (11)

Capitol Hill Office: 2344 RHOB 20515; 225-7032; Fax: 225-1339; *Chief of Staff:* Veleter Mazyck

Web: fudge.house.gov

Facebook: www.facebook.com/RepMarciaLFudge

Twitter: @RepMarciaFudge

YouTube: www.youtube.com/marcialfudge

Instagram: @repmarciafudge

District Offices: 4834 Richmond Rd., #150, Warrensville Heights, OH 44128-5922; 216-522-4900; Fax: 216-522-4908; *Press Secretary:* Ajashu Thomas

1225 Lawton St., Akron, OH 44320; 330-835-4758; Fax: 330-835-4863; *Outreach Coord.:* Joan M. Williams

Committee Assignments: Agriculture; Education and Labor; House Administration

Fulcher, Russ, R-Idaho (1)

Capitol Hill Office: 1520 LHOB 20515-3515; 225-6611; *Chief of Staff:* Cliff Bayer

Web: fulcher.house.gov

Facebook: www.facebook.com/RepRussFulcher

Twitter: @RussFulcher

Instagram: @russfulcher

District Offices: 33 E. Broadway Ave., #251, Meridian, ID 83642; 208-888-3188; Fax: 208-888-0894; *District Director:* Mike Cunnington

313 D St., #107, Lewiston, Idaho 83501; 208-743-1388; *District Director:* Mike Cunnington

1250 Ironwood Dr., #241, Coeur d'Alene ID 83814; 208-667-0127; Fax: 208-667-0310; *District Director:* Mike Cunnington

Committee Assignments: Education and Labor; Natural Resources

Gabbard, Tulsi, D-Hawaii (2)

Capitol Hill Office: 1433 LHOB 20515; 225-4906; Fax: 225-4987; *Legislative Director:* Adam Schantz

Web: gabbard.house.gov

Facebook: www.facebook.com/RepTulsiGabbard

Twitter: @TulsiPress

YouTube: www.youtube.com/tulsipress

Instagram: @tulsigabbard

District Office: 300 Ala Moana Blvd., Room 5-104, Honolulu, HI 96850; 808-541-1986; Fax: 808-538-0233; *Chief of Staff:* Kainoa Penaroza

Committee Assignments: Armed Services; Financial Services

Gaetz, Matt, R-Fla. (1)

Capitol Hill Office: 1721 LHOB 20515; 225-4136; Fax: 225-3414; *Chief of Staff:* Kevin Talley

Web: gaetz.house.gov

Facebook: www.facebook.com/CongressmanMattGaetz

Twitter: @RepMattGaetz

YouTube: www.youtube.com/channel/UClqXcJew_A3s8qiX-T4a9CA

Instagram: @repmattgaetz

District Office: 226 S. Palafox Pl., 6th Floor, Pensacola, FL 32502; 850-479-1183; Fax: 850-479-9394 *District Director:* Dawn McCardle

Satellite Office: 1170 Martin Luther King Jr. Blvd., Bldg. 4, Room 454, Fort Walton Beach, FL 32547; 850-479-1183; Fax: 850-479-9394; *District Director:* Dawn McCardle

Committee Assignments: Armed Services; Judiciary

Gallagher, Mike, R-Wisc. (8)

Capitol Hill Office: 1230 LHOB 20515; 225-5665; *Chief of Staff:* Taylor Andreae

Web: gallagher.house.gov

Facebook: www.facebook.com/RepMikeGallagher

Twitter: @RepGallagher

Instagram: @repgallagher

District Offices: 333 W. College Ave., Appleton, WI 54911; 920-903-9806; *District Director:* Rick Sense

1915 S. Webster Ave., Suite D, Green Bay, WI 54301; 920-301-4500; Fax: 920-301-4500; *District Director:* Rick Sense

Committee Assignments: Armed Services; Transportation and Infrastructure

Gallego, Rubén, D-Ariz. (7)

Capitol Hill Office: 1131 LHOB 20515-0307; 225-4065; *Chief of Staff:* David Montes

Web: rubengallego.house.gov

Facebook: www.facebook.com/RepRubenGallego

Twitter: @RepRubenGallego

YouTube: www.youtube.com/channel/UCru0REdL016INldtvq6gaLA

Instagram: @reprubengallego

District Office: 411 N. Central Ave., #150, Phoenix, AZ 85004; 602-256-0551; Fax: 602-257-9103; *Director of Constituent Services:* Sandra Ferniza

Committee Assignments: Armed Services; Natural Resources

Garamendi, John, D-Calif. (3)

Capitol Hill Office: 2368 RHOB 20515; 225-1880; Fax: 225-5914; *Chief of Staff:* Bradley Bottoms

Web: garamendi.house.gov

Facebook: www.facebook.com/repgaramendi

Twitter: @RepGaramendi

YouTube: www.youtube.com/garamendiCA10

Instagram: @repgaramendi

District Offices: 412 G. St., Davis, CA 95616; 530-753-5301; Fax: 530-753-5614; *District Director:* Debbi Orta Gibbs

1261 Travis Blvd., #130, Fairfield, CA 94533-6293; 707-438-1822; Fax: 707-438-0523; *Constituent Services Rep.:* Jackie Hartsough

Satellite Office: 795 Plumas St., Yuba City, CA 95991; 530-329-8865; Fax: 530-763-4248; *Deputy District Director.:* Debbi Orta Gibbs

Committee Assignments: Armed Services; Transportation and Infrastructure

García, Jesús G., D-Ill. (4)

Capitol Hill Office: 530 CHOB 20515-3515; 225-8203; Fax: 225-; *Chief of Staff:* Kari Moe

Web: chuygarcia.house.gov

Facebook: www.facebook.com/RepChuyGarcia

Twitter: @RepChuyGarcia

YouTube: www.youtube.com/RepChuyGarcia

Instagram: @repchuygarcia

District Offices: 3240 Fullerton Ave., Chicago, IL 60647; 773-342-0774; *District Director:* Patty Garcia

Committee Assignments: Financial Services; Transportation and Infrastructure

Garcia, Sylvia, D-Tex. (29)

Capitol Hill Office: 1620 LHOB 20515-3515; 225-1688; Fax: 225-9903; *Chief of Staff:* John Gorczynski

Web: sylviagarcia.house.gov

Facebook: www.facebook.com/RepSylviaGarcia

Twitter: @RepSylviaGarcia

District Offices: 11811 E. Freeway, #430, Houston, TX 77029; 832-325-3150; *District Director:* Claudia Ortega Hogue

Committee Assignments: Financial Services; Judiciary

Gianforte, Greg, R-Mont. (At Large)

Capitol Hill Office: 1222 LHOB 20515; 225-3211; Fax: 225-5687; *Chief of Staff:* Christine Heggem

Web: gianforte.house.gov

Facebook: www.facebook.com/RepGianforte

Twitter: @GregForMontana

YouTube: www.youtube.com/channel/UCUnBgcdx383i-Y585zpI_yQ
District Offices: 222 N. 32nd St., #900, Billings, MT 59101; 406-969-1736; Fax: 406-702-1182; *State Director:* Lesley Robinson
710 Central Ave., Great Falls, MT 59401; 406-952-1280; Fax: 406-952-1211; *Field Rep.:* Tory Scribner
7 W. 6th Ave., #3B, Helena, MT 59601; 406-502-1435; *Field Rep.:* Brett Simons
Committee Assignment: Energy and Commerce

Gibbs, Bob, R-Ohio (7)

Capitol Hill Office: 2446 RHOB 20515-3518; 225-6265; Fax: 225-3394; *Chief of Staff:* Hillary Gross
Web: gibbs.house.gov
Facebook: www.facebook.com/RepBobGibbs
Twitter: @repbobgibbs
YouTube: www.youtube.com/RepBobGibbs
Instagram: @repbobgibbs
District Offices: 110 Cottage St., Ashland, OH 44805; 419-207-0650; Fax: 419-207-0655; *District Director:* Kim Ross
110 Central Plaza South, Canton, OH 44702; 330-737-1631; *Field Rep.:* Victoria VanBuskirk
Committee Assignments: Oversight and Reform; Transportation and Infrastructure

Gohmert, Louie, R-Tex. (1)

Capitol Hill Office: 2267 RHOB 20515-4301; 225-3035; Fax: 226-1230; *Chief of Staff:* Connie Hair
Web: gohmert.house.gov
Facebook: www.facebook.com/RepLouieGohmert
Twitter: @replouiegohmert
YouTube: www.youtube.com/GohmertTX01
Instagram: @replouiegohmert
District Offices: 101 E. Methvin St., #302, Longview, TX 75601-7277; 903-236-8597; Fax: 903-561-7110; *Caseworker:* Shannon Crisp
300 E. Shepherd Ave., #210, Lufkin, TX 75901-3252; 936-632-3180; Fax: 903-561-7110; *District Director:* Jonna Fitzgerald
102 W. Houston St., Marshall, TX 75670-4038; 903-938-8386; Fax: 903-561-7110; *District Director:* Jonna Fitzgerald
101 W. Main St., #160, Nacogdoches, TX 75961-4830; 936-715-9514; Fax: 903-561-7110; *District Director:* Jonna Fitzgerald
1121 ESE Loop 323, #206, Tyler, TX 75701-9637; 903-561-6349; Fax: 903-561-7110; *District Director:* Jonna Fitzgerald
Committee Assignments: Judiciary; Natural Resources

Golden, Jared, D-Maine (2)

Capitol Hill Office: 1223 LHOB 20515-3515; 225-6306; Fax: 225-2943; *Chief of Staff:* Aisha Woodward
Web: golden.house.gov
Facebook: www.facebook.com/RepGolden
Twitter: @RepGolden

District Offices: 6 State St., #101, Bangor, ME 04401; 207-249-7400
7 Hatch Dr., #230, Caribou, ME 04736; 207-492-6009; Fax: 207-493-4436; *District Director:* Margaret Reynolds
179 Lisbon St., Lewiston, ME 04240; 207-241-6767; Fax: 207-241-6770; *Field Rep.:* Kathy Cloutier
Committee Assignments: Armed Services; Small Business

Gomez, Jimmy, D-Calif. (34)

Capitol Hill Office: 1530 LHOB 20515-0531; 225-6235; Fax: 225-2202 *Chief of Staff:* Bertha Alisa Guerrero
Web: gomez.house.gov
Facebook: www.facebook.com/RepJimmyGomez
Twitter: @RepJimmyGomez
YouTube: www.youtube.com/channel/UCOmm091WM6D01xTdzsWNvbQ
Instagram: @jimmygomezca
District Office: 350 S. Bixel St., #120, Los Angeles, CA 90017; 213-481-1425; Fax: 213-481-1427; *Chief of Staff:* Bertha Guerrero
Committee Assignments: Oversight and Reform; Ways and Means

Gonzalez, Anthony, R-Ohio (16)

Capitol Hill Office: 1023 LHOB 20515-3515; 225-3876; *Chief of Staff:* Tim Lolli
Web: anthonygonzalez.house.gov
Facebook: www.facebook.com/RepAGonzalez
Twitter: @RepAGonzalez
District Offices: 4150 Belden Village St., #607, Canton, OH 44718; 330-599-7037; *District Director:* Heidi Matthews
13477 Prospect Rd., #212, Strongsville, OH 44149; 440-783-3696
Committee Assignments: Financial Services; Science, Space, and Technology

Gonzalez, Vicente, D-Tex. (15)

Capitol Hill Office: 113 CHOB 20515; 225-2531; Fax: 225-5688; *Chief of Staff:* Jose Borjon
Web: gonzalez.house.gov
Facebook: www.facebook.com/USCongressmanVicenteGonzalez
Twitter: @RepGonzalez
YouTube: www.youtube.com/channel/UC5H6oYLKQ_xIXO5CG7fh4hw
Instagram: @repvicentegonzalez
District Office: 1305 W. Hackberry Ave., McAllen, TX 78501; 956-682-5545; Fax: 956-682-0141; *District Office Manager:* Stephanie Toscano
Committee Assignments: Financial Services, Foreign Affairs

González-Colón, Jenniffer, R-P.R. (At Large)

Capitol Hill Office: 1609 LHOB 20515; 225-2615; Fax: 225-2154; *Chief of Staff:* Gabriella Boffelli
Web: gonzalez-colon.house.gov
Facebook: www.facebook.com/JGOPR51

Twitter: @RepJenniffer
YouTube: www.youtube.com/channel/UCZj99h3-
GNKjGGeyp7AJeXw
Instagram: @repjenniffer
District Office: #157 Avenida de la Constitución, Aniguo
Edificio de Medicina Tropical, segundo piso, Puerta de
Tierra, San Juan, Puerto Rico (mailing address: P.O.
Box 9023958, San Juan, PR 00902-3958); 787-723-
6333; Fax: 787-729-6824 or 787-729-7738; *District
Director:* Narel Colon-Torres
Committee Assignments: Natural Resources;
Transportation and Infrastructure

Gooden, Lance, R-Tex. (5)

Capitol Hill Office: 425 CHOB 20515-3515; 225-3484;
Fax: 226-; *Chief of Staff:* Aaron Harris
Web: gooden.house.gov
Facebook: www.facebook.com/RepGooden
Twitter: @RepLanceGooden
YouTube: www.youtube.com/channel/
UCaEs0pYlL_1cLlPBHfl0RIg
District Offices: 18601 LBJ Fwy., #725, Mesquite, TX
75150; 214-765-6789; *District Director:* Lydia Spaun
Committee Assignment: Financial Services

Gosar, Paul A., R-Ariz. (4)

Capitol Hill Office: 2057 RHOB 20515-0301; 225-2315;
Fax: 226-9739; *Chief of Staff:* Tom Van Flein
Web: gosar.house.gov
Facebook: www.facebook.com/repgosar
Twitter: @RepGosar
YouTube: www.youtube.com/repgosar
Instagram: @repgosar
District Offices: 122 N. Cortez St., #104, Prescott, AZ
86301; 928-445-1683; Fax: 928-445-3414; *Office
Manager:* Julie Schreiner
6499 S. Kings Ranch Rd., #4, Gold Canyon, AZ 85118;
480-882-2697; Fax: 480-882-2698; *District Director:*
Penny Pew
Satellite Office: 220 N. 4th St., Kingman, AZ 86401 (by
appointment only); *District Director:* Penny Pew
Committee Assignments: Natural Resources; Oversight
and Reform

Gottheimer, Josh, D-N.J. (5)

Capitol Hill Office: 213 CHOB 20515; 225-4465; Fax: 225-
9048; *Chief of Staff:* Ashley Lantz
Web: gottheimer.house.gov
Facebook: www.facebook.com/RepJoshG
Twitter: @RepJoshG
YouTube: www.youtube.com/channel/
UCNc_9pTqsP0J3tqNlelh7mA
Instagram: @repjoshg
District Offices: 65 Harristown Rd., #104, Glen Rock, NJ
07452; 201-389-1100; *District Director:* Catherine Best
93 Spring St., #408, Newton, NJ 07860; 973-940-1117;
(open Monday/Wednesday/Friday, 9 a.m.–5 p.m.);
Outreach Community Liaison: Patrick Sheehan
Committee Assignment: Financial Services

Granger, Kay, R-Tex. (12)

Capitol Hill Office: 1026 LHOB 20515; 225-5071;
Fax: 225-5683; *Chief of Staff:* Spencer Freebairn
Web: kaygranger.house.gov
Facebook: www.facebook.com/RepKayGranger
Twitter: @RepKayGranger
YouTube: www.youtube.com/RepKayGranger
Instagram: @repkaygranger
District Office: 1701 River Run Rd., #407, Fort Worth, TX
76107-6548; 817-338-0909; Fax: 817-335-5852; *District
Director:* Kristin Vandergriff
Committee Assignment: Appropriations

Graves, Garret, R-La. (6)

Capitol Hill Office: 2402 RHOB 20515; 225-3901;
Fax: 225-7313; *Chief of Staff:* Paul Sawyer
Web: garretgraves.house.gov
Facebook: www.facebook.com/
CongressmanGarretGraves
Twitter: @RepGarretGraves
YouTube: www.youtube.com/channel/
UCQLg9GGwTDluEFJtXf8seTA
Instagram: @instagravesla
District Offices: 2351 Energy Dr., #1200, Baton Rouge, LA
70808; 225-442-1731 Fax: 225-442-1736; *Staff Asst.:*
Jonathan Smith
29261 Frost Rd., 2nd Floor, Livingston, LA 70754; 225-
686-4413; Fax: 225-442-1736; *Staff Asst.:* Jonathan
Smith
908 E. 1st St., NSU Campus, Candies Hall, #405,
Thibodaux, LA 70301; 985-448-4103; Fax: 225-442-
1736; *Staff Asst.:* Jonathan Smith
Committee Assignments: Natural Resource,
Transportation and Infrastructure

Graves, Sam, R-Mo. (6)

Capitol Hill Office: 1135 LHOB 20515-2506; 225-7041;
Fax: 225-8221; *Chief of Staff:* Tom Brown
Web: graves.house.gov
Twitter: @RepSamGraves
YouTube: www.youtube.com/channel/
UCdg2ybvoHsSW6t7iJnKHlNg/featured
Instagram: @repsamgraves
District Offices: 11724 Plaza Circle N.W., #900, Kansas
City, MO 64153; 816-792-3976; Fax: 816-792-0694;
District Director: Tom Brown
411 Jules St., #111, St. Joseph, MO 64501-2275; 816-749-
0800; Fax: 816-749-0801; *Field Rep.:* Matt Barry
Committee Assignments: Armed Services; Transportation
and Infrastructure

Graves, Tom, R-Ga. (14)

Capitol Hill Office: 2078 RHOB 20515; 225-5211;
Fax: 225-8272; *Chief of Staff:* John Donnelly
Web: tomgraves.house.gov
Facebook: www.facebook.com/reptomgraves
Twitter: @RepTomGraves
YouTube: www.youtube.com/CongressmanGraves
Instagram: @reptomgraves

District Offices: 702 S. Thornton Ave., Dalton, GA 30720-8211; 706-226-5320; Fax: 706-278-0840; *District Director:* Bud Whitmire

600 E. 1st St., #301, Rome, GA 30161; 706-290-1776; Fax: 706-232-7864; *Field Rep.:* Travis Loudermilk

Committee Assignment: Appropriations

Green, Al, D-Tex. (9)

Capitol Hill Office: 2347 RHOB 20515-4309; 225-7508; Fax: 225-2947; *Chief of Staff:* Amena Ross

Web: algreen.house.gov

Facebook: www.facebook.com/repalgreen

Twitter: @RepAlGreen

YouTube: www.youtube.com/RepAlGreen

Instagram: @repalgreen

District Office: 3003 S. Loop West, #460, Houston, TX 77054-1301; 713-383-9234; Fax: 713-383-9202; *District Manager of Administration:* Crystal Webster

Committee Assignments: Financial Services; Homeland Security

Green, Mark E., R-Tenn. (7)

Capitol Hill Office: 533 CHOB 20515-3515; 225-2811; *Chief of Staff:* Stephen Siao

Web: markgreen.house.gov

Facebook: www.facebook.com/RepMarkGreenTN

Twitter: @RepMarkGreen

District Offices: 128 N. 2nd St., #104 Clarksville, TN 37040; 931-266-4483; *Field Rep.:* Mark Crane

305 Public Square, #212, Franklin, TN 37064; 629-223-6050; *District Director:* Steve Allbrooks

Committee Assignments: Homeland Security; Oversight and Reform

Griffith, Morgan, R-Va. (9)

Capitol Hill Office: 2202 RHOB 20515-4609; 225-3861; Fax: 225-0076; *Chief of Staff:* Kelly Lungren-McCollum

Web: morgangriffith.house.gov

Facebook: www.facebook.com/RepMorganGriffith

Twitter: @RepMGriffith

YouTube: www.youtube.com/RepMorganGriffith

Instagram: @hmorgangriffith

District Offices: 323 W. Main St., Abingdon, VA 24210-2605; 276-525-1405; Fax: 276-525-1444; *District Director:* Michelle Jenkins

17 W. Main St., Christiansburg, VA 24073-3055; 540-381-5671; Fax: 540-381-5675; *Constituent Rep.:* Barbara Stafford

Committee Assignment: Energy and Commerce

Grijalva, Raúl, D-Ariz. (3)

Capitol Hill Office: 1511 LHOB 20515-0307; 225-2435; Fax: 225-1541; *Chief of Staff:* Amy Emerick

Web: grijalva.house.gov

Facebook: www.facebook.com/Rep.Grijalva

Twitter: @RepRaulGrijalva

YouTube: www.youtube.com/RaulGrijalvaAZ07

Instagram: @repraulgrijalva

District Offices: 1412 N. Central Ave., Suite B, Avondale, AZ 85323; 623-536-3388; Fax: 623-535-7479; *District Rep.:* Luis Falcon

146 N. State Ave., P.O. Box 4105, Somerton, AZ 85350; 928-343-7933; Fax: 928-343-7949; *District Aide*; *Caseworker:* Martha Garcia

101 W. Irvington Rd, Bldg. 4 and 5, Tucson, AZ 85714; 520-622-6788; Fax: 520-622-0198; *District Director:* Rubén Reyes

Committee Assignments: Education and Labor; Natural Resources, Chair

Grothman, Glenn, R-Wisc. (6)

Capitol Hill Office: 1427 LHOB 20515-4906; 225-2476; Fax: 225-2356; *Chief of Staff:* Rachel Ver Velde

Web: grothman.house.gov

Facebook: www.facebook.com/RepGrothman

Twitter: @RepGrothman

YouTube: www.youtube.com/channel/UCui4k83Cot4aeVW_8T33fgg

Instagram: @repglenngrothman

District Office: 24 W. Pioneer Rd., Fond du Lac, WI 54935; 920-907-0624; *District Director:* Al Ott

Committee Assignments: Education and Labor; Oversight and Reform

Guest, Michael, R-Miss. (3)

Capitol Hill Office: 230 CHOB 20515-3515; 225-5031; Fax: 225-5797; *Chief of Staff:* Jordan Downs

Web: guest.house.gov

Facebook: www.facebook.com/RepMichaelGuest

Twitter: @RepMichaelGuest

Instagram: @repmichaelguest

District Offices: 600 Russell St., #160, Starkville, MS 39759; 662-324-0007; *Deputy District Director:* Kyle Jordan

308B East Government St., Brandon, MS 39042; 769-241-6120; *District Director:* Brady Stewart

2214 5th St., 2179, Meridian, MS 39301; 601-693-6681; *Special Assistant:* Frances White

Committee Assignments: Ethics; Foreign Affairs; Homeland Security

Guthrie, S. Brett, R-Ky. (2)

Capitol Hill Office: 2434 RHOB 20515-1702; 225-3501; Fax: 226-2019; *Chief of Staff:* Eric Bergren

Web: guthrie.house.gov

Facebook: www.facebook.com/CongressmanGuthrie

Twitter: @RepGuthrie

YouTube: www.youtube.com/BrettGuthrie

Instagram: @repguthrie

District Office: 996 Wilkinson Trace, #B2, Bowling Green, KY 42103; 270-842-9896; Fax: 270-842-9081; *District Director:* Mark Lord

Satellite Offices: 411 W. Lincoln Trail Blvd., Radcliff, KY 40160; *Field Rep.:* Brian Smith

2200 Airport Rd., Owensboro, KY 42301; *Field Rep.:* Suzanne Miles

Committee Assignments: Education and Labor; Energy and Commerce

Haaland, Debra A., D-N.M. (1)

Capitol Hill Office: 1237 LHOB 20515-3515; 225-6316;
Chief of Staff: Jennifer Van Der Heide
Web: haaland.house.gov
Facebook: www.facebook.com/RepDebHaaland
Twitter: @RepDebHaaland
YouTube: www.youtube.com/channel/
UCbRtULGdCu5N3NytJUyve3A
Instagram: @RepDebHaaland
District Offices: 400 Gold Ave. S.W., #680, Albuquerque,
NM 87102; 505-346-6781; *District Director:* Scott
Forrester
Committee Assignments: Armed Services; Natural
Resources

Hagedorn, Jim, R-Minn. (1)

Capitol Hill Office: 325 CHOB 20515-3515; 225-2472;
Chief of Staff: Peter Su
Web: hagedorn.house.gov
Facebook: www.facebook.com/RepHagedorn
Twitter: @RepHagedorn
YouTube: www.youtube.com/RepHagedorn
Instagram: @RepHagedorn
District Offices: 11 Civic Center Plaza, #301, Mankato,
MN 56001; 507-323-6090; *District Director:* Carol
Stevenson
1530 Greenview Dr. S.W., #207, Rochester, MN 55902;
507-323-6090
Committee Assignments: Agriculture; Small Business

Harder, Josh, R-Calif. (10)

Capitol Hill Office: 131 CHOB 20515-3515; 225-4540;
Fax: 225-3402; *Chief of Staff:* Rachael Goldenberg
Web: harder.house.gov
Facebook: www.facebook.com/RepJoshHarder
Twitter: @RepJoshHarder
Instagram: @repjoshharder
District Offices: 4701 Sisk Rd., #202 Modesto, CA 95356;
209-579-5458; *District Director:* Karen Warner
Committee Assignments: Agriculture; Education and
Labor

Harris, Andy, R-Md. (1)

Capitol Hill Office: 2334 RHOB 20515; 225-5311;
Fax: 225-0254; *Chief of Staff:* John Dutton
Web: harris.house.gov
Facebook: www.facebook.com/AndyHarrisMD
Twitter: @RepAndyHarrisMD
YouTube: www.youtube.com/RepAndyHarris
District Offices: 15 E. Churchville Rd., #102B, Bel Air, MD
21014-3837; 410-588-5670; Fax: 410-588-5673;
Community Liaison: Danielle Hornberger
100 Olde Point Village, #101, Chester, MD 21619; 410-
643-5425; Fax: 410-643-5429; Fax: 410-643-5429;
Community Liaison: Mike Arntz
100 E. Main St., #702, Salisbury, MD 21801; 443-944-8624;
Fax: 443-944-8625; *Constituent Liaison:* Bill Reddish
Committee Assignment: Appropriations

Hartzler, Vicky, R-Mo. (4)

Capitol Hill Office: 2235 RHOB 20515-2504; 225-2876;
Fax: 225-0148; *Chief of Staff:* Chris Connelly
Web: hartzler.house.gov
Facebook: www.facebook.com/Congresswoman.Hartzler
Twitter: @RepHartzler
YouTube: www.youtube.com/RepVickyHartzler
Instagram: @rephartzler
District Offices: 2415 Carter Lane, #4, Columbia, MO
65201; 573-442-9311; Fax: 573-442-9309; *Press
Secretary:* Steve Walsh
1909 N. Commercial St., Harrisonville, MO 64701-1252;
816-884-3411; Fax: 816-884-3163; *Field Rep.:* Adam
Timmerman
219 N. Adams St., Lebanon, MO 65536-3029; 417-
532-5582; Fax: 417-532-3886; *Field Rep.:* Steve
Walsh
Committee Assignments: Agriculture; Armed Services

Hastings, Alcee L., D-Fla. (20)

Capitol Hill Office: 2353 RHOB 20515-0923; 225-1313;
Fax: 225-1171; *Chief of Staff:* Lale M. Morrison
Web: alceehastings.house.gov
Facebook: www.facebook.com/RepHastingsFL
Twitter: @RepHastingsFL
YouTube: www.youtube.com/RepAlceeHastings
District Offices: 2701 W. Oakland Park Blvd., #200,
Fort Lauderdale, FL 33311; 954-733-2800;
Fax: 954-735-9444; *Florida Chief of Staff:* Art
Kennedy
1755 E. Tiffany Dr., Mangonia Park, FL 33407; 561-469-
7048; Fax: 516-848-6940; *Staff Asst.:* Dan Liftman
Committee Assignment: Rules

Hayes, Jahana, D-Conn. (5)

Capitol Hill Office: 1415 LHOB 20515-3515; 225-4476;
Chief of Staff: Joe Dunn
Web: hayes.house.gov
Facebook: www.facebook.com/RepJahanaHayes
Twitter: @RepJahanaHayes
YouTube: www.youtube.com/channel/
UC1px5TjAdWt5wZSRGWu3z6w
Instagram: @ repjahanahayes
District Offices: 108 Bank St., 2nd Floor, Waterbury, CT
06702; 860-223-8412; Fax: 877-568-9290; *District
Director:* Veronica DeLandro
Committee Assignments: Agriculture; Education and
Labor

Heck, Denny, D-Wash. (10)

Capitol Hill Office: 2452 RHOB 20515; 225-9740;
Fax: 225-0129; *Chief of Staff:* Jami Burgess
Web: dennyheck.house.gov
Facebook: www.facebook.com/CongressmanDennyHeck
Twitter: @RepDennyHeck
YouTube: www.youtube.com/RepDennyHeck
District Offices: 420 College St. S.E., #3000, Lacey, WA
98503; 360-459-8514; Fax: 360-459-8581; *District
Director:* Phil Gardner

6000 Main St. S.W., #3B, Lakewood, WA 98499; 253-533-8332; *Deputy District Director:* Lauren Adler

Committee Assignments: Financial Services, Permanent Select Intelligence

Hern, Kevin, R-Okla. (1)

Capitol Hill Office: 1019 LHOB 20515-3515; 225-2211; *Chief of Staff:* Cameron Foster

Web: hern.house.gov

Facebook: www.facebook.com/repkevinhern

Twitter: @repkevinhern

YouTube: www.youtube.com/channel/UC9XRRGCgGOEtEOwUAo1rYZg

District Office: 2448 E. 81st St., #5150, Tulsa, OK 74137; 918-935-3222; Fax: 918-935-2716; *District Director:* Robert Aery

Committee Assignments: Budget; Natural Resources; Small Business

Herrera Beutler, Jaime, R-Wash. (3)

Capitol Hill Office: 2352 RHOB 20515-4703; 225-3536; Fax: 225-3478; *Chief of Staff:* Casey Bowman

Web: herrerabeutler.house.gov

Facebook: www.facebook.com/herrerabeutler

Twitter: @HerreraBeutler

YouTube: www.youtube.com/RepHerreraBeutler

Instagram: @herrerabeutler

District Office: 750 Anderson St., Suite B, Vancouver, WA 98661-3853; 360-695-6292; Fax: 360-695-6197; *District Director:* Pam Piper

Satellite Office: 350 N. Market Blvd., Chehalis, WA 98532; 360-695-6292; *District Director:* Pam Piper

Committee Assignment: Appropriations

Hice, Jody, R-Ga. (10)

Capitol Hill Office: 409 CHOB 20515; 225-4101; Fax: 226-0776 *Chief of Staff:* David Sours

Web: hice.house.gov

Facebook: www.facebook.com/CongressmanJodyHice

Twitter: @CongressmanHice

YouTube: www.youtube.com/channel/UCzUMsS8DusN2QLpgweFthgQ

Instagram: @rep_hice

District Offices: 100 Court St., Monroe, GA 30655; 770-207-1776; Fax: 770-266-6751; *District Director:* Jessica Hayes

210 Railroad St., #2401, Thomson, GA 30824; 770-207-1776; *Field Rep.:* Beth Goolsby

3015 Heritage Rd., #6, Milledgeville, GA 31061; 478-457-0007; Fax: 478-451-2911; *Field Rep.:* Daniel Lentz

Committee Assignments: Natural Resources; Oversight and Reform

Higgins, Brian, D-N.Y. (26)

Capitol Hill Office: 2459 RHOB 20515-3227; 225-3306; Fax: 226-0347; *Chief of Staff:* Matthew Fery

Web: higgins.house.gov

Facebook: www.facebook.com/RepBrianHiggins

Twitter: @RepBrianHiggins

YouTube: www.youtube.com/CongressmanHiggins

Instagram: @repbrianhiggins

District Offices: 726 Exchange St., #601, Buffalo, NY 14210-1484; 716-852-3501; Fax: 716-852-3929; *District Chief of Staff:* Chuck Eaton

800 Main St., #3C, Niagara Falls, NY 14301; 716-282-1274; Fax: 716-282-2479; *District Director:* Suzanne Macri

Committee Assignments: Budget; Ways and Means

Higgins, Clay, R-La. (3)

Capitol Hill Office: 1711 LHOB 20515; 225-2031; Fax: 225-5724; *Chief of Staff:* Kathee Facchiano

Web: clayhiggins.house.gov

Facebook: www.facebook.com/CongressmanClayHiggins

Twitter: @RepClayHiggins

Instagram: @repclayhiggins

District Offices: 600 Jefferson St., #808, Lafayette, LA 70501; 337-703-6105; *District Director:* Rachel Hammac

1 Lakeshore Dr., #1670, Lake Charles, LA, 70629; 337-656-2833; *Legislative Director:* Ward Cormier

Committee Assignments: Homeland Security; Oversight and Reform

Hill, French, R-Ark. (2)

Capitol Hill Office: 1533 LHOB 20515-0402; 225-2506; Fax: 225-5903; *Chief of Staff:* Brooke Bennett

Web: hill.house.gov

Facebook: www.facebook.com/RepFrenchHill

Twitter: @RepFrenchHill

YouTube: www.youtube.com/repfrenchhill

Instagram: @repfrenchhill

District Offices: 1501 N. University Ave., #630, Little Rock, AR 72207; 501-324-5941; Fax: 501-324-6029; *District Director:* Anushree Jumde

1105 Deer St., #12, Conway, AR 72032; 501-358-3481; Fax: 501-358-3494; *District Director:* Anushree Jumde

Committee Assignment: Financial Services

Hill, Katie, D-Calif. (25)

Capitol Hill Office: 1130 LHOB 20515-3515; 225-1956; Fax: 226-0683; *Chief of Staff:* Emily Burns

Web: katiehill.house.gov

Facebook: www.facebook.com/RepKatieHill

Twitter: @RepKatieHill

Instagram: @ repkatiehill

District Offices: 1008 W. Ave. M14, Suite E, Palmdale, CA 93551; 661-839-0539; *District Director:* Angela Giacchetti

1445 E. Los Angeles Ave., #206, Simi Valley, CA 93065; 661-802-0244; *District Director:* Angela Giacchetti

Committee Assignment: Armed Services; Oversight and Reform; Science, Space, and Technology

Himes, Jim, D-Conn. (4)

Capitol Hill Office: 1227 LHOB 20515-0704; 225-5541; Fax: 225-9629; *Chief of Staff:* Mark Henson

Web: himes.house.gov

Facebook: www.facebook.com/CongressmanJimHimes

Twitter: @jahimes
YouTube: www.youtube.com/congressmanhimes
Instagram: @repjimhimes
District Offices: 211 State St., 2nd Floor, Bridgeport, CT 06604-4808; 866-453-0028; Fax: 203-333-6655; *District Director:* Cara Pavlock
888 Washington Blvd., 10th Floor, Stamford, CT 06901-2902; 203-353-9400; Fax: 203-323-1793; *Constituent Services Rep.:* Gloria DePina
Committee Assignments: Financial Services; Permanent Select Intelligence

Holding, George, R-N.C. (2)

Capitol Hill Office: 1110 LHOB 20515; 225-3032; Fax: 225-0181; *Chief of Staff:* Tucker Knott
Web: holding.house.gov
Facebook: www.facebook.com/CongressmanGeorgeHolding
Twitter: @RepHolding
YouTube: www.youtube.com/RepHolding
District Office: 7200 Falls of Neuse Rd., #204, Raleigh, NC 27615; 919-782-4400; Fax: 919-782-4490; *District Director:* Carol Armstrong
Committee Assignments: Budget; Ethics; Ways and Means

Hollingsworth, Trey, R-Ind. (9)

Capitol Hill Office: 1641 LHOB 20515; 225-5315; *Chief of Staff:* Rebecca Shaw
Web: hollingsworth.house.gov
Facebook: www.facebook.com/RepTrey
Twitter: @RepTrey
YouTube: www.youtube.com/channel/UCTgS8a_zLg8HpUnk5WXY5ag
Instagram: @rep_trey
District Offices: 321 Quartermaster Court, Jeffersonville, IN 47130; 812-288-3999; *District Chief of Staff:* Rachel Jacobs
100 E. Jefferson St., Franklin, IN 46131; 317-851-8710; *Legislative Director:* Connor Lentz
Committee Assignment: Financial Services

Horn, Kendra S., D-Okla. (5)

Capitol Hill Office: 415 CHOB 20515-3515; 225-2132; Fax: 226-1463; *Chief of Staff:* Brady King
Web: horn.house.gov
Facebook: www.facebook.com/KendraHornForCongress
Twitter: @RepKendraHorn
YouTube: www.youtube.com/channel/UCtlkMWxcuPiw3P79ccq-htA
District Offices: 400 N. Walker, #210, Oklahoma City, OK 73102; 405-602-3074; *District Director:* Amanda McLain-Snipes
Committee Assignments: Armed Services; Science, Space, and Technology

Horsford, Steven, D-Nev. (4)

Capitol Hill Office: 1330 LHOB 20515-3515; 225-9894; *Deputy Chief of Staff:* Jason Rodriguez

Web: horsford.house.gov
Facebook: www.facebook.com/RepHorsford
Twitter: @RepHorsford
Instagram: @housedemocrats
District Offices: 2250 N. Las Vegas Blvd., #500, North Las Vegas, NV 89030; 702-963-9360; *Field Rep.:* Ender Austin
Committee Assignments: Budget; Natural Resources; Ways and Means

Houlahan, Chrissy, D-Pa. (6)

Capitol Hill Office: 1218 LHOB 20515-3515; 225-4315; *Chief of Staff:* Michelle Dorothy
Web: houlahan.house.gov
Facebook: www.facebook.com/ChrissyHoulahan
Twitter: @rephoulahan
Instagram: @chrissyhoulahan
District Offices: 815 Washington St., #2-48, Reading, PA 19601; 610-295-0815; *District Director:* Sue Walker
709 E. Gay St., #4, West Chester, PA 19380; 610-883-5050
Committee Assignments: Armed Services; Foreign Affairs; Small Business

Hoyer, Steny H., D-Md. (5)

Capitol Hill Office: 1705 LHOB 20515; 225-4131; Fax: 225-4300; *Chief of Staff:* Alexis Covey-Brandt
Web: hoyer.house.gov
Facebook: www.facebook.com/LeaderHoyer
Twitter: @WhipHoyer
YouTube: www.youtube.com/LeaderHoyer
Instagram: @leaderhoyer
District Offices: U.S. District Courthouse, 6500 Cherrywood Lane, #310, Greenbelt, MD 20770-1287; 301-474-0119; Fax: 301-474-4697; *District Director:* Terrance Taylor
4475 Regency Pl., #203, White Plains, MD 20695; 301-843-1577; Fax: 301-843-1331; *District Director:* Betsy Bossart
Majority Leader

Hudson, Richard, R-N.C. (8)

Capitol Hill Office: 2112 RHOB 20515; 225-3715; Fax: 225-4036; *Chief of Staff:* Chris Carter
Web: hudson.house.gov
Facebook: www.facebook.com/RepRichHudson
Twitter: @RepRichHudson
YouTube: www.youtube.com/reprichhudson
Instagram: @reprichhudson
District Offices: 325 McGill Ave. N.W., #500, Concord, NC 28027-6194; 704-786-1612; Fax: 704-782-1004; *District Director:* Billy Constangy
225 Green St., #202, Fayetteville, NC 28301; 910-997-2070; Fax: 910-817-7202; *Constituent Liaison:* Chris Maples
Committee Assignment: Energy and Commerce

Huffman, Jared, D-Calif. (2)

Capitol Hill Office: 1507 LHOB 20515; 225-5161; Fax: 225-5163; *Chief of Staff:* Ben Miller

Web: huffman.house.gov
Facebook: www.facebook.com/RepHuffman
Twitter: @RepHuffman
YouTube: www.youtube.com/RepHuffman
Instagram: @rephuffman
District Offices: 317 3rd St., #1, Eureka, CA 95501; 707-407-3585; Fax: 707-407-3559; *District Director:* Jenny Callaway

430 N. Franklin St., P.O. Box 2208, Fort Bragg, CA 95437; 707-962-0933; Fax: 707-962-0905; *Field Rep.:* Sheba Brown

999 5th Ave., #290, San Rafael, CA 94901; 415-258-9657; Fax: 415-258-9913; *Field Rep.:* Blake Hooper

206 G St., #3, Petaluma, CA 94952; 707-981-8967; *Field Rep.:* Blake Hooper

559 Low Gap Rd., Ukiah, CA 95482; 707-671-7449; *Field Rep.:* Sheba Brown

Committee Assignments: Natural Resources; Transportation and Infrastructure

Huizenga, Bill, R-Mich. (2)

Capitol Hill Office: 2232 RHOB 20515-2202; 225-4401; Fax: 226-0779; *Chief of Staff:* Jon DeWitte
Web: huizenga.house.gov
Facebook: www.facebook.com/rephuizenga
Twitter: @RepHuizenga
YouTube: www.youtube.com/RepHuizenga
Instagram: @rephuizenga
District Offices: 1 S. Harbor Ave., #6B, Grand Haven, MI 49417; 616-414-5516 Fax: 616-570-0934; *District Director:* Matt Kooiman

4555 Wilson Ave. S.W., #3, Grandville, MI 49418; 616-570-0917; Fax: 616-570-0934; *Legislative Director:* Palmer Rafferty

Committee Assignment: Financial Services

Hunter, Duncan, R-Calif. (50)

Capitol Hill Office: 2429 RHOB 20515-0552; 225-5672; Fax: 225-0235; *Chief of Staff:* Rick Terrazas
Web: hunter.house.gov
Facebook: www.facebook.com/DuncanHunter
Twitter: @Rep_Hunter
YouTube: www.youtube.com/CongressmanHunter
District Office: 1611 N. Magnolia Ave., #310, El Cajon, CA 92020; 619-448-5201; Fax: 619-449-2251; *District Chief of Staff:* Michael Harrison

Satellite Office: 41000 Main St., Temecula, CA 92590; 951-695-5108; *District Chief of Staff:* Michael Harrison

Committee Assignments: None

Hurd, Will, R-Tex. (23)

Capitol Hill Office: 317 CHOB 20515; 225-4511; Fax: 225-2237; *Chief of Staff:* John Byers
Web: hurd.house.gov
Facebook: www.facebook.com/HurdOnTheHill
Twitter: @HurdOnTheHill
YouTube: www.youtube.com/channel/UCjWcn2lgGCZbwPs6lKxlziQ
Instagram: @hurdonthehill

District Offices: 17721 Rogers Ranch Pkwy, #120, San Antonio, TX 78258; 210-921-3130; Fax: 210-927-4903; *District Director:* Justin Hollis

1104 W. 10th St., Del Rio, TX 78840; 830-422-2040; *Field Rep.:* Carmen Gutierrez

100 S. Monroe St., Eagle Pass, TX 78852; 210-784-5023; *Field Rep.:* Stacy Arteaga

124 S. Horizon, Socorro, TX 79927; 915-235-6421; *Field Rep.:* Karina Rivera

1 University Way, #202A, San Antonio, TX 78224; 210-784-5023; *Military and Veterans Liaison:* John Arnold

Pecos County Courthouse, 103 W. Callaghan St., 1st Floor, Fort Stockton, TX 79735; 210-245-1548; *District Rep.:* Cindy Ochoa

Committee Assignments: Appropriations; Permanent Select Intelligence

Jackson Lee, Sheila, D-Tex. (18)

Capitol Hill Office: 2079 RHOB 20515-4318; 225-3816; Fax: 225-3317; *Chief of Staff:* Glenn Rushing
Web: jacksonlee.house.gov
Facebook: www.facebook.com/CongresswomanSheilaJacksonLee
Twitter: @JacksonLeeTX18
YouTube: www.youtube.com/RepJacksonLee
Instagram: @repjacksonlee
District Offices: 1919 Smith St., #1180, Houston, TX 77002-8098; 713-655-0050; Fax: 713-655-1612; *Scheduler/Office Manager:* Martha Hernandez

6719 W. Montgomery Rd., #204, Houston, TX 77091-3105; 713-691-4882; *Caseworker/Field Rep.:* James Doggette

420 W. 19th St., Houston, TX 77008-3914; 713-861-4070; *Caseworker/Field Rep.:* Tonya Williams

4300 Lyons Ave., Houston, TX 77020; 713-227-7740; *Caseworker/Field Rep.:* Tonya Williams

Committee Assignments: Budget; Homeland Security; Judiciary

Jayapal, Pramila, D-Wash. (7)

Capitol Hill Office: 1510 LHOB 20515; 225-3106; Fax: 225-6197; *Chief of Staff:* Gautam Raghavan
Web: jayapal.house.gov
Facebook: www.facebook.com/RepJayapal
Twitter: @RepJayapal
YouTube: www.youtube.com/repjayapal
Instagram: @repjayapal
District Office: 1904 3rd Ave., #510, Seattle, WA 98101; 206-674-0040; *District Director:* Rachel Berkson

Committee Assignments: Budget; Education and Labor; Judiciary

Jeffries, Hakeem, D-N.Y. (8)

Capitol Hill Office: 2433 THOB 20515; 225-5936; Fax: 225-1018; *Chief of Staff:* Tasia Jackson
Web: jeffries.house.gov
Twitter: @RepJeffries
YouTube: www.youtube.com/rephakeemjeffries

Instagram: @repjeffries
District Offices: 445 Neptune Ave., 1st Floor, #2C, Brooklyn, NY 11224; 718-373-0033; Fax: 718-373-1333; *Field Rep.:* Frieda Menos
55 Hanson Pl., #603, Brooklyn, NY 11217; 718-237-2211; Fax: 718-237-2273; *District Director:* Maron Alemu
Committee Assignments: Budget; Judiciary

Johnson, Bill, R-Ohio (6)

Capitol Hill Office: 2336 RHOB 20515; 225-5705; Fax: 225-5907; *Chief of Staff:* Mike Smullen
Web: billjohnson.house.gov
Facebook: www.facebook.com/RepBillJohnson
Twitter: @RepBillJohnson
YouTube: www.youtube.com/RepBillJohnson
Instagram: @repbilljohnson
District Offices: 116 Southgate Pkwy., Cambridge, OH 43725; 740-432-2366; Fax: 740-432-2587; *Field Rep.:* Ashley Karlen
202 Park Ave., Suite C, Ironton, OH 45638-1595; 740-534-9431; Fax: 740-534-9482; *Field Rep.:* Julie Stephens
246 Front St., Marietta, OH 45750-2908; 740-376-0868; Fax: 740-376-0886; *Field Rep.:* Renée Rector
192 E. State St., Salem, OH 44460-2843; 330-337-6951; Fax: 330-337-7125; *Field Rep.:* Don Baker; *District Director:* Sarah Keeler
Committee Assignments: Budget; Energy and Commerce

Johnson, Dusty, R-S.D. (At Large)

Capitol Hill Office: 1508 LHOB 20515; 225-2801; Fax: 225-5823; *Chief of Staff:* Andrew Christianson
Web: dustyjohnson.house.gov
Facebook: www.facebook.com/RepDustyJohnson
Twitter: @RepDustyJohnson
Instagram: @repdustyjohnson
District Offices: 304 6th Ave. S.E., Aberdeen, SD 57401; 605-622-1060; *Northeast Director:* Amiee Kamp
2525 W. Main St., #310, Rapid City, SD 57702; 605-646-6454; Fax: 605-791-4679; *West River Director:* Katie Murray
300 North Dakota Ave., #314, Sioux Falls, SD 57108; 605-275-2868; Fax: 202-275-2875; *State Director:* Courtney Heitkamp
Committee Assignments: Agriculture; Education and Labor

Johnson, Eddie Bernice, D-Tex. (30)

Capitol Hill Office: 2306 RHOB 20515; 225-8885; Fax: 226-1477; *Chief of Staff:* Murat T. Gokcigdem
Web: ebjohnson.house.gov
Facebook: www.facebook.com/CongresswomanEBJtx30
Twitter: @RepEBJ
YouTube: www.youtube.com/RepEddieBJohnson
Instagram: @repebj
District Office: 1825 Market Center Blvd., #440, Dallas, TX 75207; 214-922-8885; Fax: 214-922-7028; *District Director:* Dominique Brown
Committee Assignments: Science, Space, and Technology, Chair; Transportation and Infrastructure

Johnson, Hank, Jr., D-Ga. (4)

Capitol Hill Office: 2240 RHOB 20515; 225-1605; Fax: 226-0691; *Chief of Staff:* Arthur D. Sidney
Web: hankjohnson.house.gov
Facebook: www.facebook.com/RepHankJohnson
Twitter: @RepHankJohnson
YouTube: www.youtube.com/RepHankJohnson
Instagram: @rephankjohnson
District Office: 5240 Snapfinger Park Dr., #130, Decatur, GA 30035; 770-987-2291; Fax: 770-987-8721; *District Director:* Kathy Register
Committee Assignments: Judiciary; Transportation and Infrastructure

Johnson, Mike, R-La. (4)

Capitol Hill Office: 418 CHOB 20515; 225-2777; Fax: 225-8039; *Chief of Staff:* Hayden Haynes
Web: mikejohnson.house.gov
Facebook: www.facebook.com/RepMikeJohnson
Twitter: @RepMikeJohnson
YouTube: www.youtube.com/channel/UCzqBEpeIaDEfvAtsA53Fx2Q
Instagram: @repmikejohnson
District Offices: 2250 Hospital Dr., #248, Bossier City, LA 71111; 318-840-0309; *District Director:* Chip Layton
3329 University Pkwy., #552, Room 24, Leesville, LA 71446; 337-392-3146; *District Director:* Chip Layton
Committee Assignments: Judiciary; Natural Resources

Jordan, Jim, R-Ohio (4)

Capitol Hill Office: 2056 RHOB 20515; 225-2676; Fax: 226-0577; *Chief of Staff:* Kevin Eichinger
Web: jordan.house.gov
Facebook: www.facebook.com/repjimjordan
Twitter: @Jim_Jordan
YouTube: www.youtube.com/RepJimJordan
District Offices: 3121 W. Elm Plaza, Lima, OH 45805-2516; 419-999-6455; Fax: 419-999-4238; *District Director:* Cameron Warner
13B E. Main St., Norwalk, OH 44857; 419-663-1426; Fax: 419-668-3015; *Deputy District Director:* Carolina Bick
Satellite Office: 500 S. Sandusky Ave., Bucyrus, OH 44820; 419-663-1426; (open Tuesday/Thursday, 8 a.m.–4:30 p.m.)
Committee Assignments: Judiciary; Oversight and Reform

Joyce, David, R-Ohio (14)

Capitol Hill Office: 1124 LHOB 20515; 225-5731; Fax: 225-3307; *Chief of Staff:* Anna Alburger
Web: joyce.house.gov
Facebook: www.facebook.com/RepDaveJoyce
Twitter: @RepDaveJoyce
YouTube: www.youtube.com/RepDaveJoyce
Instagram: @repdavejoyce
District Offices: 8500 Station St., Mentor, OH 44060; 440-352-3939; Fax: 440- 266-9004; *District Director:* Nick Ciofani

10075 Ravenna Rd., Twinsburg, OH 44087; 330-357-4139; Fax: 330-425-7071; *District Director:* Nick Ciofani

Committee Assignment: Appropriations

Joyce, John, R-Pa. (13)

Capitol Hill Office: 1337 LHOB 20515-3515; 225-2431; Fax: 225-2486; *Chief of Staff:* Jeremy Shoemarker

Web: johnjoyce.house.gov

Facebook: www.facebook.com/RepJohnJoyce

Twitter: @RepJohnJoyce

YouTube: www.youtube.com/channel/UC6F6PTH33VO_wfqfvNjyuiw

District Offices: 100 Lincoln Way East, Suite B, Chambersburg, PA 17201; 717-753-6344; *District Director:* Chad Reichard

5414 6th Ave., Altoona, PA 16602; 814-656-6081; *District Director:* Chad Reichard

451 Stoystown Rd., #102, Somerset, PA 15501

Committee Assignments: Homeland Security; Small Business

Kaptur, Marcy, D-Ohio (9)

Capitol Hill Office: 2186 RHOB 20515; 225-4146; Fax: 225-7711; *Legislative Director:* Jenny Perrino

Web: kaptur.house.gov

Facebook: www.facebook.com/RepresentativeMarcyKaptur

Twitter: @RepMarcyKaptur

YouTube: www.youtube.com/USRepMarcyKaptur

Instagram: @repmarcykaptur

District Offices: 1 Maritime Plaza, #600, Toledo, OH 43604; 419-259-7500; Fax: 419-255-9623; *Chief of Staff:* Steve Katich

200 W. Erie Ave., #310, Lorain, OH 44052; 440-288-1500; Fax: 419-255-9623; *Legislative Asst.:* Jacob Smith

17021 Lorain Ave., Cleveland, OH 44111, 216-767-5933; Fax: 419-255-9623; *Casework Director:* Nick Turner

Committee Assignments: Appropriations Congressional-Executive Commission on China

Katko, John, R-N.Y. (24)

Capitol Hill Office: 2457 RHOB 20515; 225-3701; Fax: 225-4042; *Chief of Staff:* Zach Howell

Web: katko.house.gov

Facebook: www.facebook.com/RepJohnKatko

Twitter: @RepJohnKatko

YouTube: www.youtube.com/channel/UCNRwSHofKKvDKpL92lZIBiw

Instagram: @repjohnkatko

District Offices: 71 Genesee St., Auburn, NY 13021; 315-253-4068; Fax: 315-253-2435; *District Director:* Isabelle Harris

440 S. Warren St., 7th Floor, #711, Syracuse, NY 13202; 315-423-5657; Fax: 315-423-5604; *District Director:* Isabelle Harris

7376 State Route 31, Lyons, NY 14489; 315-253-4068 (by appointment only)

13 W. Oneida St., 2nd Floor, Oswego, NY 13126; 315-423-5657 (by appointment only)

Committee Assignments: Homeland Security; Transportation and Infrastructure

Keating, William, D-Mass. (9)

Capitol Hill Office: 2351 RHOB 20515; 225-3111; Fax: 225-5658; *Chief of Staff:* Garrett Donovan

Web: keating.house.gov

Facebook: www.facebook.com/USRepKeating

Twitter: @USRepKeating

YouTube: www.youtube.com/RepBillKeating

District Offices: 259 Stevens St., Suite E, Hyannis, MA 02601-5134; 508-771-6868; Fax: 508-790-1959; *District Rep.:* Anthony Morse

128 Union St., #103, New Bedford, MA 02740; 508-999-6462; Fax: 508-999-6468; *District Director:* Michael Jackman

170 Court St., Plymouth, MA 02360; 508-746-9000; Fax: 508-732-0072; *District Director:* Michael Jackman

Committee Assignments: Armed Services; Foreign Affairs

Kelly, Mike, R-Pa. (16)

Capitol Hill Office: 1707 LHOB 20515; 225-5406; Fax: 225-3103; *Chief of Staff:* Matthew Stroia

Web: kelly.house.gov

Facebook: www.facebook.com/MikeKellyPA

Twitter: @MikeKellyPA

YouTube: www.youtube.com/RepMikeKelly

District Offices: 101 E. Diamond St., #218, Butler, PA 16001; 724-282-2557; Fax: 724-282-3682; *District Scheduler:* Marci Mustello

208 E. Bayfront Pkwy., #102, Erie, PA 16507-2405; 814-454-8190; Fax: 814-454-8197; *District Director:* Tim Butler

33 Chestnut Ave., Sharon, PA 16146; 724-342-7170; Fax: 724-342-7242; *Senior Constituent Service Rep.:* Jill Burke

Committee Assignment: Ways and Means

Kelly, Robin, D-Ill. (2)

Capitol Hill Office: 2416 RHOB 20515; 225-0773; Fax: 225-4583; *Chief of Staff:* Brandon Webb

Web: robinkelly.house.gov

Facebook: www.facebook.com/reprobinkelly

Twitter: @RepRobinKelly

YouTube: www.youtube.com/channel/UCLhcNPX2nNQLNzwKW0nEykg

Instagram: @reprobinkelly

District Offices: 600 Holiday Plaza Dr., #505, Matteson, IL 60443; 708-679-0078; Fax: 708-679-0216; *Director of Constituent Services:* Cynthia DeWitt

1000 E. 111th St., Chicago, IL 60628; 773-321-2001; *District Director:* Tony Presta

Satellite Office: 304 S. Indiana Ave., Lower Level, Kankakee, IL 60901; 708-679-0078; *Field Rep.:* Rick Bryant

Committee Assignments: Energy and Commerce; Oversight and Reform

Kelly, Trent, R-Miss. (1)

Capitol Hill Office: 1721 LHOB 20515; 225-4306; Fax: 225-3549; *Chief of Staff:* Paul Howell
Web: trentkelly.house.gov
Facebook: www.facebook.com/RepTrentKelly
Twitter: @RepTrentKelly
YouTube: www.youtube.com/channel/UCtDrz-8tdg4ZgOAQHToSWaQ
Instagram: @reptrentkelly
District Offices: 318 N. 7th St., Suite D, Columbus, MS 39701; 662-328-5982 *Field Rep.:* Robert Smith
2565 Caffey St., #200, P.O. Box 218, Hernando, MS 38632; 662-449-3090; Fax: 662-449-4836; *Field Rep.:* Walt Starr
431 W. Main St., Tupelo, MS 38804; 662-841-8808; Fax: 662-841-8845; *District Director:* Darren Herring
855 S. Dunn St., Eupora, MS 39744; 662-258-7240; Fax: 662-258-7240; *Field Rep.:* Willy Weddle
4135 County Rd., #200, Corinth, MS 38844; 662-687-1525; Fax: 662-841-8845; *Field Rep.:* Melinda Whited
Committee Assignments: Agriculture; Armed Services; Small Business

Kennedy, Joseph P., III, D-Mass. (4)

Capitol Hill Office: 304 CHOB 20515; 225-5931; Fax: 225-0182; *Chief of Staff:* Greg Mecher
Web: kennedy.house.gov
Facebook: www.facebook.com/CongressmanJoeKennedyIII
Twitter: @RepJoeKennedy
YouTube: www.youtube.com/channel/UCgfHlaGqxD8p-2V_YlNIqrA
Instagram: @repkennedy
District Offices: 8 N. Main St., #200, Attleboro, MA 02703; 508-431-1110; Fax: 508-431-1101; *Field Rep.:* Lisa Nelson
29 Crafts St., #375, Newton, MA 02458; 617-332-3333; Fax: 617-332- 3308; *District Director:* Nick Clemons
Committee Assignment: Energy and Commerce

Khanna, Ro, D-Calif. (17)

Capitol Hill Office: 221 CHOB 20515; 225-2631; Fax: 225-2699; *Chief of Staff:* Pete Spiro
Web: khanna.house.gov
Facebook: www.facebook.com/RepRoKhanna
Twitter: @RepRoKhanna
YouTube: www.youtube.com/channel/UCr4KOYv1o1oEQhy1jhhm3pQ
Instagram: @reprokhanna
District Office: 900 Lafayette St., #206, Santa Clara, CA 95050; 408-436-2720; Fax: 408-436-2721; *District Director:* Chris Moylan
Committee Assignments: Armed Services; Budget; Oversight and Reform

Kildee, Daniel, D-Mich. (5)

Capitol Hill Office: 203 CHOB 20515; 225-3611; Fax: 225-6393; *Chief of Staff (Acting):* Mitchell Rivard
Web: dankildee.house.gov

Facebook: www.facebook.com/RepDanKildee
Twitter: @RepDanKildee
YouTube: www.youtube.com/RepDanKildee
Instagram: @repdankildee
District Office: 601 Saginaw St., 4th Floor, Flint, MI 48502; 810-238-8627; Fax: 810-238-8658; *District Director:* Chris Flores
Committee Assignments: Budget; Ways and Means

Kilmer, Derek, D-Wash. (6)

Capitol Hill Office: 1410 LHOB 20515; 225-5916; Fax: 226-3575; *Chief of Staff:* Rachel Kelly
Web: kilmer.house.gov
Facebook: www.facebook.com/derek.kilmer
Twitter: @RepDerekKilmer
YouTube: www.youtube.com/RepDerekKilmer
Instagram: @repderekkilmer
District Offices: 345 6th St., #500, Bremerton, WA 98337; 360-373-9725; *Constituent Services Director:* Cheri Williams
950 Pacific Ave., #1230, Tacoma, WA 98402; 253-272-3515; *District Director:* Andrea Roper
Satellite Office: 332 E. 5th St., Port Angeles, WA 98362; 360-797-3623; *District Rep.:* Mary Jane Robins
Committee Assignment: Appropriations

Kim, Andy, D-N.J. (3)

Capitol Hill Office: 1516 LHOB 20515-3515; 225-4765; Fax: 225-0778; *Chief of Staff:* Amy Pfeiffer
Web: kim.house.gov
Facebook: www.facebook.com/RepAndyKimNJ
Twitter: @RepAndyKimNJ
Instagram: @repandykimnj
District Offices: 535 E. Main St., Marlton, NJ 08053; 856-703-2700; Fax: 856-369-8988; *District Director:* Ben Giovine
33 Washington St., P.O. Box 728, Toms River, NJ 08754; 732-504-0490; Fax: 732-714-4244
Committee Assignment: Armed Services; Small Business

Kind, Ron, D-Wisc. (3)

Capitol Hill Office: 1502 LHOB 20515; 225-5506; Fax: 225-5739; *Chief of Staff:* Hana Greenberg
Web: kind.house.gov
Facebook: www.facebook.com/repronkind
Twitter: @RepRonKind
YouTube: www.youtube.com/RepRonKind
Instagram: @repronkind
District Offices: 131 S. Barstow St., #301, Eau Claire, WI 54701; 715-831-9214; Fax: 715-831-9272; *Congressional Aide:* Mark Aumann
205 5th Ave. South, #400, La Crosse, WI 54601; 608-782-2558; Fax: 608-782-4588; *District Chief of Staff:* Loren Kannenberg
Committee Assignment: Ways and Means

King, Pete, R-N.Y. (2)

Capitol Hill Office: 303 CHOB 20515-3203; 225-7896; Fax: 226-2279; *Chief of Staff:* Kevin C. Fogarty

Web: peteking.house.gov
Facebook: www.facebook.com/reppeteking
Twitter: @RepPeteKing
YouTube: www.youtube.com/RepPeterKing
Instagram: @reppeteking
District Office: 1003 Park Blvd., Massapequa Park, NY
11762-2758; 516-541-4225; Fax: 516-541-6602; *District
Director:* Anne Rosenfeld
Committee Assignments: Financial Services; Homeland
Security

King, Steve, R-Iowa (4)

Capitol Hill Office: 2210 RHOB 20515; 225-4426;
Fax: 225-3193; *Chief of Staff:* Sarah Stevens
Web: steveking.house.gov
Facebook: www.facebook.com/SteveKingIA
Twitter: @SteveKingIA
YouTube: www.youtube.com/SteveKingIA
Instagram: @stevekingia
District Offices: 1421 S. Bell Ave., #102, Ames, IA 50010;
515-232-2885; Fax: 515-232-2844;
723 Central Ave., Fort Dodge, IA 50501; 515-573-2738;
Fax: 515-576-7141; *District Rep.:* Jim Oberhelman
202-1st St. S.E., #126, Mason City, IA, 50401; 641-201-
1624; Fax: 641-201-1523; *District Rep.:* Sandy Hanlon
320 6th St., Room 112, Sioux City, IA 51101-1313; 712-
224-4692; Fax: 712-224-4693; *District Director:* Wiltsie
Cretsinger
306 N. Grand Ave., P.O. Box 650, Spencer, IA 51301-4141;
712-580-7754; Fax: 712-580-3354; *District Rep.:*
Andrea Easter
Committee Assignments: None

Kinzinger, Adam, R-Ill. (16)

Capitol Hill Office: 2245 RHOB 20515-1311; 225-3635;
Fax: 225-3521; *Chief of Staff:* Austin Weatherford
Web: kinzinger.house.gov
Facebook: www.facebook.com/RepKinzinger
Twitter: @RepKinzinger
YouTube: www.youtube.com/RepAdamKinzinger
District Offices: 628 Columbus St., #507, Ottawa, IL
61350; 815-431-9271; Fax: 815-431-9383; *District
Director:* Bonnie Walsh
342 W. Walnut St., Watseka, IL 60970; 815-432-0580 (by
appointment only); *Scheduler:* Patrick Doggett
725 N. Lyford Rd., #3, Rockford, IL 61107; 815-708-8032;
(by appointment only); *Field Rep.:* Peter Simino
Committee Assignments: Energy and Commerce; Foreign
Affairs

Kirkpatrick, Ann, D-Ariz. (2)

Capitol Hill Office: 309 CHOB 20515-3515; 225-2542;
Chief of Staff: Carmen Frias
Web: kirkpatrick.house.gov
Facebook: www.facebook.com/RepAnnKirkpatrick
Twitter: @RepKirkpatrick
Instagram: @repannkirkpatrick
District Offices: 77 Calle Portal, #B160, Sierra Vista, AZ
85635; 520-459-3115; *District Director:* Ron Barber

1636 N. Swan Rd., #200, Tucson, AZ 85712; 520-881-3588;
Committee Assignments: Agriculture; Appropriations

Krishnamoorthi, Raja, D-Ill. (8)

Capitol Hill Office: 115 CHOB 20515; 225-3711; Fax: 225-
7830; *Chief of Staff:* Mark Schauerte
Web: krishnamoorthi.house.gov
Facebook: www.facebook.com/CongressmanRaja
Twitter: @CongressmanRaja
YouTube: www.youtube.com/CongressmanRaja
District Office: 1701 E. Woodfield Rd., #704, Schaumburg,
IL 60173; 847-413-1959; Fax: 847-413-1965; *Deputy
Chief of Staff:* Steve Baskin
Committee Assignments: Oversight and Reform;
Permanent Select Intelligence

Kuster, Ann, D-N.H. (2)

Capitol Hill Office: 320 CHOB 20515; 225-5206; Fax: 225-
2946; *Chief of Staff:* Abby Curran
Web: kuster.house.gov
Facebook: www.facebook.com/
CongresswomanAnnieKuster
Twitter: @RepAnnieKuster
YouTube: www.youtube.com/RepKuster
Instagram: @repanniekuster
District Offices: 18 N. Main St., 4th Floor, Concord, NH
03301; 603-226-1002; Fax: 603-226-1010; *District
Director:* Corey Garry
184 Main St., #222, Nashua, NH 03060; 603-595-2006;
Fax: 603-595-2016; *Constituent Outreach Coord.:*
Tom Giancola
33 Main St., #202, Littleton, NH 03561; 603-444-7700;
Service Coord.: Brian Bresnahan
Committee Assignment: Energy and Commerce

Kustoff, David, R-Tenn. (8)

Capitol Hill Office: 523 CHOB 20515; 225-4714; *Chief of
Staff:* Tyler Threadgill
Web: kustoff.house.gov
Facebook: www.facebook.com/RepDavidKustoff
Twitter: @RepDavidKustoff
YouTube: www.youtube.com/channel/
UCK6U4plOKKMrCjv_h59spGQ
Instagram: @repdavidkustoff
District Offices: 5900 Poplar Ave., #202, Memphis, TN
38119; 901-682-4422; Fax: 901-682-8973; *District
Director:* Maryann Dunavant
117 N. Liberty St., Jackson, TN 38301; 731-423-4848;
Fax: 731-427-1537; *District Director:* Ed Jackson
100 S. Main St., #1, Dyersburg, TN 38024; 731-412-1037;
Fax: 731-285-5008; *Field Rep.:* Ivy Rogers
406 S. Lindell St., Martin, TN 38237; 731-412-1043;
Fax: 731-587-7334; *Field Rep.:* Ivy Rogers
Committee Assignment: Financial Services

LaHood, Darin, R-Ill. (18)

Capitol Hill Office: 1424 LHOB 20515-1318; 225-6201;
Fax: 225-9249; *Chief of Staff:* Steven Pfrang
Web: lahood.house.gov

Facebook: www.facebook.com/replahood
Twitter: @RepLaHood
YouTube: www.youtube.com/channel/
UCVRbtFwaBGcixZIkygtalRw
District Offices: 100 N.E. Monroe St., #100, Peoria, IL
61602-1047; 309-671-7027; Fax: 309-671-7309; *District
Director:* Brad Stotler

235 S. 6th St., Springfield, IL 62071; 217-670-1653;
Fax: 217-670-1806; *Springfield Office Director:* Hal
Smith

201 W. Morgan St., Jacksonville, IL 62650; 217-245-1431;
Fax: 217-243-6852; *Constituent Services Specialist:*
Barbara Baker

3004 G.E. Rd., #1B, Bloomington, IL 61704; 309-205-9556
(open Tuesday and Thursday)
Committee Assignments: Joint Economic; Natural
Resources; Ways and Means

LaMalfa, Doug, R-Calif. (1)

Capitol Hill Office: 322 CHOB 20515; 225-3076; Fax: 226-
0852; *Chief of Staff:* Mark Spannagel
Web: lamalfa.house.gov
Facebook: www.facebook.com/RepLaMalfa
Twitter: @RepLaMalfa
YouTube: www.youtube.com/RepLaMalfa
District Offices: 2399 Rickenbacker Way, Auburn, CA
95602; 530-878-5035; Fax: 530-878-5037; *Chief of
Staff:* Mark Spannagel

120 Independence Circle, Suite B, Chico, CA 95973; 530-
343-1000; *Senior District Coord.:* Laura Page

2885 Churn Creek Rd., Suite C, Redding, CA 96002; 530-
223-5898; Fax: 530-223-5897; *Sr. Caseworker.:*
Stephanie White
Committee Assignments: Agriculture; Transportation
and Infrastructure

Lamb, Conor, D-Pa. (17)

Capitol Hill Office: 1224 LHOB 20515; 225-2301;
Fax: 225-1844; *Chief of Staff:* Craig Kwiecinski
Web: lamb.house.gov
Facebook: www.facebook.com/RepConorLamb
Twitter: @RepConorLamb
YouTube: www.youtube.com/channel/
UC7hX59n_ixS1Bz3f8Je02yA?view_as=subscriber
District Offices: 504 Washington Rd., Pittsburgh, PA
15228-2817; 412-344-5583; Fax: 412-429-5092; *District
Director:* Marcie Callan
3468 Brodhead Rd., Monaca, PA 15061; 724-206-4860
Committee Assignments: Science, Space, and Technology;
Veterans' Affairs

Lamborn, Doug, R-Colo. (5)

Capitol Hill Office: 2371 RHOB 20515; 225-4422;
Fax: 226-2638; *Chief of Staff:* Dale Anderson
Web: lamborn.house.gov
Facebook: www.facebook.com/
CongressmanDougLamborn
Twitter: @RepDLamborn
YouTube: www.youtube.com/CongressmanLamborn

Instagram: @douglamborn
District Office: 1125 Kelly Johnson Blvd., #330, Colorado
Springs, CO 80920-3965; 719-520-0055; Fax: 719-520-
0840; *District Director:* Marcus Breubaker
Satellite Office: 415 Main St., Buena Vista, CO 81211;
719-520-0055 (by appointment only); Fax: 719-520-
0840; *District Director:* Marcus Breubaker
Committee Assignments: Armed Services; Natural
Resources

Langevin, Jim, D-R.I. (2)

Capitol Hill Office: 2077 RHOB 20515; 225-2735;
Fax: 225-5976; *Chief of Staff:* Todd Adams
Web: langevin.house.gov
Facebook: www.facebook.com/CongressmanJimLangevin
Twitter: @JimLangevin
YouTube: www.youtube.com/jimlangevin
Instagram: @repjimlangevin
District Office: 300 Centerville Rd., #200 South, Warwick,
RI 02886-0200; 401-732-9400; Fax: 401-737-2982;
District Director: Seth Klaiman
Committee Assignments: Armed Services; Homeland
Security

Larsen, Rick, D-Wash. (2)

Capitol Hill Office: 2113 RHOB 20515; 225-2605;
Fax: 225-4420; *Chief of Staff:* Kimberly Johnston
Web: larsen.house.gov
Facebook: www.facebook.com/RepRickLarsen
Twitter: @RepRickLarsen
YouTube: www.youtube.com/CongressmanLarsen
Instagram: @repricklarsen
District Offices: Wall Street Bldg., 2930 Wetmore Ave.,
#9F, Everett, WA 98201-4070; 425-252-3188; Fax: 425-
252-6606; *District Director:* Adam LeMieux
119 N. Commercial St., #275, Bellingham, WA 98225-
4452; 360-733-4500; Fax: 360-733-5144; *Community
Liaison:* Laura Gelwicks
Committee Assignments: Armed Services; Transportation
and Infrastructure

Larson, John B., D-Conn. (1)

Capitol Hill Office: 1501 LHOB 20515-0701; 225-2265;
Fax: 225-1031; *Chief of Staff:* David Sitcovsky
Web: larson.house.gov
Facebook: www.facebook.com/RepJohnLarson
Twitter: @RepJohnLarson
YouTube: www.youtube.com/RepJohnLarson
Instagram: @repjohnblarson
District Office: 221 Main St., 2nd Floor, Hartford, CT
06106-1890; 860-278-8888; Fax: 860-278-2111; *District
Director:* Maureen Moriarty
Committee Assignment: Ways and Means

Latta, Robert E., R-Ohio (5)

Capitol Hill Office: 2467 RHOB 20515; 225-6405;
Fax: 225-1985; *Chief of Staff:* Allison Witt Poulios
Web: latta.house.gov
Facebook: www.facebook.com/boblatta

Twitter: @boblatta
YouTube: www.youtube.com/CongressmanBobLatta
District Offices: 1045 N. Main St., #6, Bowling Green, OH
43402-1361; 419-354-8700; Fax: 419-354-8702; *District
Director:* David Wirt
101 Clinton St., #1200, Defiance, OH 43512-2165; 419-782-
1996; Fax: 419-784-9808; *Sr. District Rep.:* Kathy Shaver
318 Dorney Plaza, #302, Findlay, OH 45840; 419-422-7791;
District Rep.: Brian Bauman
Committee Assignment: Energy and Commerce

Lawrence, Brenda, D-Mich. (14)

Capitol Hill Office: 2463 RHOB 20515-2214; 225-5802;
Fax: 226-2356; *Chief of Staff:* Ryan Hedgepeth
Web: lawrence.house.gov
Facebook: www.facebook.com/Rep.BLawrence
Twitter: @RepLawrence
YouTube: www.youtube.com/channel/
UCf0USy9GNigkB8O9sS1dodw
Instagram: @repbrendalawrence
District Offices: 5555 Conner Ave., #2215, Detroit, MI
48213; 313-423-6183; Fax: 313-499-1633; *Sr.
Constituent Outreach Coord.:* James Slaughter
26700 Lahser Rd., #330, Southfield, MI 48033; 248-356-2052;
Fax: 248-356-4532; *District Director:* Jeremy Kaplan
Committee Assignments: Appropriations; Oversight and
Reform

Lawson, Al, D-Fla. (5)

Capitol Hill Office: 1406 LHOB 20515; 225-0123;
Fax: 225-2256; *Chief of Staff:* Tola Thompson
Web: lawson.house.gov
Facebook: www.facebook.com/RepAlLawsonJr
Twitter: @RepAlLawsonJr
Instagram: @repallawsonjr
District Offices: 435 N. Macomb St., Tallahassee, FL
32301; 850-558-9450; Fax: 850-577-0633; *District
Director:* Deborah Fairhurst
1010 N. Davis St., #206, Jacksonville FL 32209; 904-354-
1652; Fax: 904-379-0309; *District Director:* Kortney
Wesley
Committee Assignments: Agriculture; Financial Services

Lee, Barbara, D-Calif. (13)

Capitol Hill Office: 2470 RHOB 20515-0509; 225-2661;
Fax: 225-9817; *Chief of Staff:* Julie Nickson
Web: lee.house.gov
Facebook: www.facebook.com/RepBarbaraLee
Twitter: @RepBarbaraLee
YouTube: www.youtube.com/RepLee
Instagram: @repbarbaralee
District Office: 1301 Clay St., #1000-N, Oakland, CA
94612; 510-763-0370; Fax: 510-763-6538; *District
Director:* Tatyana Kalinga
Committee Assignments: Appropriations; Budget

Lee, Susie, D-Nev. (3)

Capitol Hill Office: 522 CHOB 20515-3515; 225-3252;
Fax: 225-2185; *Chief of Staff:* Brandon Cox

Web: susielee.house.gov
Facebook: www.facebook.com/RepSusieLee
Twitter: @RepSusieLee
Instagram: @repsusielee
District Office: 8872 S. Eastern Ave., #210 & 220, Las
Vegas, NV 89123; 702-963-9336; *District Director:*
Michael Vannozzi
Committee Assignments: Education and Labor; Veterans'
Affairs

Lesko, Debbie, R-Ariz. (8)

Capitol Hill Office: 1113 LHOB 20515-3515; 225-4576;
Chief of Staff: Abby Gunderson-Schwarz
Web: lesko.house.gov
Facebook: www.facebook.com/RepDebbieLesko
Twitter: @RepDLesko
Instagram: @replesko
District Office: 7121 W. Bell Rd., #200, Glendale, AZ
85308; 623-776-7911; Fax: 623-776-7832; *District
Director:* Lisa Gray
Committee Assignments: Homeland Security; Judiciary;
Rules

Levin, Andy, D-Mich. (9)

Capitol Hill Office: 228 CHOB 20515-3515; 225-4961;
Chief of Staff:
Web: andylevin.house.gov
Facebook: www.facebook.com/RepAndyLevin
Twitter: @RepAndyLevin
Instagram: @repandylevin
District Office: 30500 Van Dyke Ave., #306, Warren, MI
48093; 586-498-7122; *District Director:*
Committee Assignments: Education and Labor; Foreign
Affairs

Levin, Mike, D-Calif (49)

Capitol Hill Office: 1626 LHOB 20515-3515; 225-3906;
Chief of Staff: Kara Van Stralen
Web: mikelevin.house.gov
Facebook: www.facebook.com/RepMikeLevin
Twitter: @RepMikeLevin
YouTube: www.youtube.com/channel/
UCYFDRohyZgoPy5rXOaVZO-A
Instagram: @RepMikeLevin
District Offices: 33282 Golden Lantern, #102, Dana Point,
CA 92629; 949-281-2449; *District Director:* Francine
Busby
2204 El Camino Real, #314, Oceanside, CA 92054; 760-
599-5000; *District Director:* Francine Busby
Committee Assignments: Natural Resources; Veterans'
Affairs

Lewis, John, D-Ga. (5)

Capitol Hill Office: 300 CHOB 20515-1005; 225-3801;
Fax: 225-0351; *Chief of Staff, Floor Asst.:* Michael
Collins
Web: johnlewis.house.gov
Facebook: www.facebook.com/RepJohnLewis
Twitter: @repjohnlewis

YouTube: www.youtube.com/repjohnlewis
Instagram: @repjohnlewis
District Office: 100 Peachtree St. N.W., #1920, Atlanta, GA 30303-1906; 404-659-0116; Fax: 404-331-0947; *District Director:* Tuere Butler
Committee Assignment: Ways and Means; Senior Chief Deputy Whip

Lieu, Ted, D-Calif. (33)

Capitol Hill Office: 403 CHOB 20515; 225-3976; Fax: 225-4099; *Chief of Staff:* Marc Cevasco
Web: lieu.house.gov
Facebook: www.facebook.com/RepTedLieu
Twitter: @RepTedLieu
YouTube: www.youtube.com/RepTedLieu
Instagram: @reptedlieu
District Office: 5055 Wilshire Blvd., #310, Los Angeles, CA 90036; 323-651-1040; Fax: 323-655-0502; *District Director:* Nicolas Rodriquez
Satellite Office: 1600 Rosecrans Ave., 4th Floor, Manhattan Beach, CA 90266; 310-321-7664 (by appointment only); Fax: 323-655-0502; *District Director:* Nicolas Rodriquez
Committee Assignments: Foreign Affairs; Judiciary

Lipinski, Daniel, D-Ill. (3)

Capitol Hill Office: 2346 RHOB 20515-1303; 225-5701; Fax: 225-1012; *Chief of Staff:* Eric L. Lausten
Web: lipinski.house.gov
Facebook: www.facebook.com/repdanlipinski
Twitter: @RepLipinski
YouTube: www.youtube.com/lipinski03
District Office: 6245 S. Archer Ave., Chicago, IL 60638-2609; 773-948-6223; Fax: 773-767-9395; *District Chief of Staff:* Brian Oszakiewski
Satellite Offices: Central Square Bldg., 222 E. 9th St., #109, Lockport, IL 60441; 815-838-1990; Fax: 815-838-1993; *Communications Director:* Phil Davidson
5210 W. 95th St., #104, Oak Lawn, IL 60453; 708-424-0853; Fax: 708-424-1855
Orland Park Village Hall, 14700 S. Ravinia Ave., Orland Park, IL 60462; 708-403-4379; Fax: 708-403-5963
Committee Assignments: Science, Space, and Technology; Transportation and Infrastructure

Loebsack, David, D-Iowa (2)

Capitol Hill Office: 1211 LHOB 20515-1502; 225-6576; Fax: 226-0757; *Chief of Staff:* Eric Witte
Web: loebsack.house.gov
Facebook: www.facebook.com/DaveLoebsack
Twitter: @daveloebsack
YouTube: www.youtube.com/CongressmanLoebsack
District Offices: 209 W. 4th St., #104, Davenport, IA 52801; 563-323-5988; Fax: 563-323-5231; *District Director:* Robert Sueppel
125 S. Dubuque St., Iowa City, IA 52240-4000; 319-351-0789; Fax: 319-351-5789; *District Rep.:* David Leshtz
Committee Assignment: Energy and Commerce

Lofgren, Zoe, D-Calif. (19)

Capitol Hill Office: 1401 LHOB 20515; 225-3072; Fax: 225-3336; *Chief of Staff:* Stacey Leavandosky
Web: lofgren.house.gov
Facebook: www.facebook.com/zoelofgren
Twitter: @RepZoeLofgren
YouTube: www.youtube.com/RepZoeLofgren
District Office: 635 N. 1st St., Suite B, San Jose, CA 95112; 408-271-8700; Fax: 408-271-8714; *District Chief of Staff:* Sandra Soto
Committee Assignments: House Administration, Chair; Joint Library; Joint Printing, Chair; Judiciary; Science, Space, and Technology

Long, Billy, R-Mo. (7)

Capitol Hill Office: 2454 RHOB 20515; 225-6536; Fax: 225-5604; *Chief of Staff:* Joe Lillis
Web: long.house.gov
Facebook: www.facebook.com/Rep.Billy.Long
Twitter: @UsRepLong
YouTube: www.youtube.com/MOdistrict7
District Offices: 2727 E. 32nd St., #2, Joplin, MO 64804-3155; 417-781-1041; Fax: 417-781-2832; *Field Rep.:* Jacob Heisten
3232 E. Ridgeview St., Springfield, MO 65804-4076; 417-889-1800; Fax: 417-889-4915; *District Director:* Royce Reding
Committee Assignment: Energy and Commerce

Loudermilk, Barry, R-Ga. (11)

Capitol Hill Office: 422 CHOB 20515-1011; 225-2931; Fax: 225-2944; *Chief of Staff:* Rob Adkerson
Web: loudermilk.house.gov
Facebook: www.facebook.com/RepLoudermilk
Twitter: @RepLoudermilk
YouTube: www.youtube.com/channel/UC2Kfw8fjca8k3w3KpzL5tNg
Instagram: @reploudermilk
District Offices: 9898 Hwy. 92, #100, Woodstock, GA 30188; 770-429-1776; Fax: 770-517-7427; *District Director:* Wayne Dodd
135 W. Cherokee Ave., #122, Cartersville, GA 30120; 770-429-1776; *District Director:* Wayne Dodd
600 Galleria Pkwy., #120, Atlanta, GA 30339; 770-429-1776; Fax: 678-556-5184; *Communications Director:* Brandon Cockerham
Committee Assignments: Financial Services; House Administration; Joint Library; Joint Publishing

Lowenthal, Alan, D-Calif. (47)

Capitol Hill Office: 108 CHOB 20515; 225-7924; Fax: 225-7926; *Chief of Staff:* Tim Hysom
Web: lowenthal.house.gov
Facebook: www.facebook.com/RepLowenthal
Twitter: @RepLowenthal
YouTube: www.youtube.com/RepLowenthal
Instagram: @replowenthal
District Offices: 100 W. Broadway, #600, Long Beach, CA 90802; 562-436-3828; Fax: 562-437-6434; *District Director:* Mark Pulido

12865 Main St., #200, Garden Grove, CA 92840; 714-243-4088; Fax: 562-437-6434; *Field Rep.:* Phong Ly

Committee Assignments: Natural Resources; Transportation and Infrastructure

Lowey, Nita, D-N.Y. (17)

Capitol Hill Office: 2365 RHOB 20515-3218; 225-6506; Fax: 225-0546; *Chief of Staff:* Elizabeth Stanley
Web: lowey.house.gov
Facebook: www.facebook.com/RepLowey
Twitter: @NitaLowey
YouTube: www.youtube.com/nitalowey
Instagram: @nitalowey
District Offices: 67 N. Main St., #101, New City, NY 10956; 845-639-3485; Fax: 845-634-4079; *District Rep.:* Cory Hasson
222 Mamaroneck Ave., #312, White Plains, NY 10605; 914-428-1707; Fax: 914-328-1505; *District Director:* Patricia Keegan
Committee Assignment: Appropriations, Chair

Lucas, Frank, R-Okla. (3)

Capitol Hill Office: 2405 RHOB 20515-3603; 225-5565; Fax: 225-8698; *Chief of Staff:* Stacey Glasscock
Web: lucas.house.gov
Facebook: www.facebook.com/RepFrankLucas
Twitter: @RepFrankLucas
YouTube: www.youtube.com/RepFrankLucas
Instagram: @repfranklucas
District Office: 10952 Expressway N.W., Suite B, Yukon, OK 73099-8214; 405-373-1958; Fax: 405-373-2046; *District Director:* Sherri Gamel
Committee Assignments: Financial Services; Science, Space, and Technology

Luetkemeyer, Blaine, R-Mo. (3)

Capitol Hill Office: 2230 RHOB 20515; 225-2956; Fax: 225-5712; *Chief of Staff:* Chad Ramey
Web: luetkemeyer.house.gov
Facebook: www.facebook.com/BlaineLuetkemeyer
Twitter: @RepBlainePress
YouTube: www.youtube.com/BLuetkemeyer
Instagram: @repblaine
District Offices: 2117 Missouri Blvd., Jefferson City, MO 65109; 573-635-7232; Fax: 573-635-8347; *District Deputy Chief of Staff:* Jeremy Ketterer
113 E. Pearce Blvd., Wentzville, MO 63385; 636-327-7055; Fax: 636-327-3254; *District Rep.:* Christa Montgomery
516 Jefferson St., Washington, MO 63090-2706; 636-239-2276; Fax: 636-239-0478; *District Office Director:* Jim McNichols
Committee Assignment: Financial Services

Luján, Ben Ray, D-N.M. (3)

Capitol Hill Office: 2323 RHOB 20515; 225-6190; Fax: 226-1528; *Chief of Staff:* Angela K. Ramirez
Web: lujan.house.gov

Facebook: www.facebook.com/RepBenRayLujan
Twitter: @repbenraylujan
YouTube: www.youtube.com/Repbenraylujan
Instagram: @repbenraylujan
District Offices: 800 Municipal Dr., Farmington, NM 87401-2663; 505-324-1005; Fax: 505-324-1026; *Field Rep.:* Brian Lee
110 W. Aztec Ave., Gallup, NM 87301-6202; 505-863-0582; Fax: 505-863-0678; *Field Rep.*; Navajo Nation Advisor: Brian Lee
903 University Ave., P.O. Box 1368, Las Vegas, NM 87701; 505-454-3038; Fax: 505-454-3265; *Field Rep.:* Steven Salas
3200 Civic Center Circle N.E., #330, Rio Rancho, NM 87144-4503; 505-994-0499; Fax: 505-994-0550; *Constituent Liaison*: Joseph Casados
1611 Calle Lorca, Suite A, Santa Fe, NM 87505-7640; 505-984-8950; Fax: 505-986-5047; *District Director:* Jennifer Conn-Catechis
404 W. Route 66 Blvd., Tucumcari, NM 88401-3279; 575-461-3029; Fax: 575-461-3192; *Field Rep.:* Ron Wilmot
Committee Assignment: Assistant Speaker, Energy and Commerce

Luria, Elaine G. D-Va. (2)

Capitol Hill Office: 534 CHOB 20515-3515; 225-4215; Fax: 225-4218; *Chief of Staff:* Kathryn Sorenson
Web: luria.house.gov
Facebook: www.facebook.com/RepElaineLuria
Twitter: @RepElaineLuria
District Offices: 283 Constitution Way, One Columbus Center, #900, Virginia Beach, VA 23462; 757-364-7650; Fax: 757-687-8298 *District Director:* Dave Wickershan
25020 Shore Pkwy., #1B, Onley, VA 23418; 757-364-7631
Committee Assignments: Armed Services; Veterans' Affairs

Lynch, Stephen F., D-Mass. (8)

Capitol Hill Office: 2109 RHOB 20515; 225-8273; Fax: 225-3984; *Chief of Staff:* Kevin Ryan
Web: lynch.house.gov
Facebook: www.facebook.com/repstephenlynch
Twitter: @RepStephenLynch
YouTube: www.youtube.com/RepLynch
District Offices: One Harbor St., #304, Boston, MA 02210-2433; 617-428-2000; Fax: 617-428-2011; *District Director:* Bob Fowkes
37 Belmont St., 2nd Floor, #3, Brockton, MA 02301; 508-586-5555; Fax: 508-580-4692; *District Rep.:* Shaynah Barnes
1245 Hancock St., #16, Quincy, MA 02169; 617-657-6305; Fax: 617-773-0995; *District Rep.:* Joe King
Committee Assignments: Financial Services; Oversight and Reform; Transportation and Infrastructure

Malinowski, Tom, D-N.J. (7)

Capitol Hill Office: 426 CHOB 20515-3515; 225-5361; *Chief of Staff:* Colston Reid
Web: malinowski.house.gov

Facebook: www.facebook.com/HouseDemocrats
Twitter: @RepMalinowski
District Office: 58 E. Main St., 1st Floor, Somerville, NJ 08876; 908-547-3307; *District Director:* Mitchelle Drulif
Committee Assignments: Congressional-Executive Commission on China; Foreign Affairs; Transportation and Infrastructure

Maloney, Carolyn, D-N.Y. (12)

Capitol Hill Office: 2308 RHOB 20515-001; 225-7944; Fax: 225-4709; *Chief of Staff:* Michael Iger
Web: maloney.house.gov
Facebook: www.facebook.com/RepCarolynMaloney
Twitter: @RepMaloney
YouTube: www.youtube.com/carolynbmaloney
Instagram: @repmaloney
District Offices: 31-19 Newtown Ave., Astoria, NY 11102-1391; 718-932-1804; Fax: 212-860-0704; *District Rep.:* Edward Babor
1651 3rd Ave., #311, New York, NY 10128-3679; 212-860-0606; Fax: 212-860-0704; *New York Chief of Staff:* Minna Elias
619 Lorimer St., Brooklyn, NY 11211-2228; 718-349-5972; Fax: 212-860-0704 (open Tuesday, 9 a.m.–5 p.m.); *District Rep.:* Mary Odomirok
Committee Assignments: Financial Services; Oversight and Reform

Maloney, Sean Patrick, D-N.Y. (18)

Capitol Hill Office: 2331 RHOB 20515; 225-5441; Fax: 225-3289; *Chief of Staff:* Timothy Persico; *Deputy Chief of Staff:* Ryan Lehman
Web: seanmaloney.house.gov
Facebook: www.facebook.com/repseanmaloney
Twitter: @RepSeanMaloney
YouTube: www.youtube.com/channel/UCNiVzzf4Vz-vCMPBcnjGuXQ
Instagram: @repseanpatrickmaloney
District Office: 123 Grand St., 2nd Floor, Newburgh, NY 12550; 845-561-1259; Fax: 845-561-2890; *District Director:* Joseph Donat
Committee Assignments: Agriculture; Transportation and Infrastructure; Permanent Select Intelligence

Marchant, Kenny, R-Tex. (24)

Capitol Hill Office: 2304 RHOB 20515; 225-6605; Fax: 225-0074; *Chief of Staff:* Brian Thomas
Web: marchant.house.gov
Facebook: www.facebook.com/RepKennyMarchant
Twitter: @RepKenMarchant
YouTube: www.youtube.com/RepKennyMarchant
District Office: 9901 E. Valley Ranch Pkwy., #2060, Irving, TX 75063-7186; 972-556-0162; Fax: 972-409-9704; *Deputy Chief of Staff:* Susie Miller
Committee Assignments: Ethics; Ways and Means

Marshall, Roger, R-Kans. (1)

Capitol Hill Office: 312 CHOB 20515; 225-2715; *Chief of Staff:* Brent Robertson

Web: marshall.house.gov
Facebook: www.facebook.com/RogerMarshallMD
Twitter: @RogerMarshallMD
YouTube: www.youtube.com/channel/UCR3nOFMqBB-kRpKFwgapMaQ
Instagram: @repmarshall
District Offices: 200 E. Iron Ave., Salina, KS 67401; 785-829-9000; *District Director:* Katie Sawyer
816 Campus Dr., #500, Garden City, KS 67846; 620-765-7800; *Deputy Director:* Becca Swender
Committee Assignments: Agriculture; Science, Space, and Technology

Massie, Thomas, R-Ky. (4)

Capitol Hill Office: 2453 RHOB 20515; 225-3465; Fax: 225-0003; *Chief of Staff:* John Ferland
Web: massie.house.gov
Facebook: www.facebook.com/RepThomasMassie
Twitter: @RepThomasMassie
YouTube: www.youtube.com/RepThomasMassie
Instagram: @repthomasmassie
District Offices: 1700 Greenup Ave., #505, Ashland, KY 41101; 606-324-9898; *Field Rep.:* J.R. Reed
541 Buttermilk Pike, #208, Crescent Springs, KY 41017-3924; 859-426-0080; Fax: 859-426-0061; *Staff Asst.:* Kevin Kreft
110 W. Jefferson St., LaGrange, KY 40031; 502-265-9119; Fax: 502-265-9126; *Western District Field Rep.:* Stacey Rockaway
Committee Assignments: Oversight and Reform; Transportation and Infrastructure

Mast, Brian, R-Fla. (18)

Capitol Hill Office: 2182 RHOB 20515; 225-3026; Fax: 225-8398; *Chief of Staff:* James Langenderfer
Web: mast.house.gov
Facebook: www.facebook.com/RepBrianMast
Twitter: @RepBrianMast
YouTube: www.youtube.com/RepBrianMast
Instagram: @repbrianmast
District Offices: 121 Port St. Lucie Blvd. S.W., Port St. Lucie, FL 34984; 772-336-2877; *District Director:* Nick Ciotti
171 Flager Ave. S.W., Stuart, FL 34994; 772-403-0900; *Field Rep.:* Amy Galante
420 U.S. Hwy. 1, #19, North Palm Beach, FL 33408; 561-530-7778; *Field Rep.:* John South
Committee Assignments: Foreign Affairs; Transportation and Infrastructure

Matsui, Doris O., D-Calif. (6)

Capitol Hill Office: 2311 RHOB 20515-0506; 225-7163; Fax: 225-0566; *Chief of Staff:* Kyle Victor
Web: matsui.house.gov
Facebook: www.facebook.com/doris.matsui
Twitter: @DorisMatsui
YouTube: www.youtube.com/channel/UCSqqxVkvskHq3cY2MCbTZsw
Instagram: @repdorismatsui

District Office: 501 Eye St., #12-600, Sacramento, CA 95814-4778; 916-498-5600; Fax: 916-444-6117; *District Director:* Glenda Corcoran

Committee Assignment: Energy and Commerce; Rules

McAdams, Ben, D-Utah (4)

Capitol Hill Office: 130 CHOB 20515-3515; 225-3011; Fax: 225-5638; *Chief of Staff:* Nicole Dunn

Web: mcadams.house.gov

Facebook: www.facebook.com/RepBenMcAdams

Twitter: @RepBenMcAdams

Instagram: @repbenmcadams

District Office: 9067 S. 1300 West, #101, West Jordan, UT, 84088; 801-999-9801; *District Director:* Tiffany Clason

Committee Assignments: Congressional-Executive Commission on China; Financial Services; Science, Space, and Technology

McBath, Lucy, D-Ga. (6)

Capitol Hill Office: 1513 LHOB 20515-3515; 225-4501; Fax: 225-4656; *Chief of Staff:* Joon Suh

Web: mcbath.house.gov

Facebook: www.facebook.com/replucymcbath

Twitter: @RepLucyMcBath

Instagram: @replucymcbath

District Office: 5775 Glenridge Dr., Bldg. B, #380, Atlanta, GA 30328; 202-225-4501; Fax: 202-225-4656; *District Director:* Bianca Keaton

Committee Assignments: Education and Labor; Judiciary

McCarthy, Kevin, R-Calif. (23)

Capitol Hill Office: 2468 RHOB 20515; 225-2915; Fax: 225-2908; *Chief of Staff:* James B. Min

Web: kevinmccarthy.house.gov

Facebook: www.facebook.com/RepKevinMcCarthy

Twitter: @GOPLeader

YouTube: www.youtube.com/RepKevinMcCarthy

Instagram: @repkevinmccarthy

District Office: 4100 Empire Dr., #150, Bakersfield, CA 93309-0409; 661-327-3611; Fax: 661-637-0867; *District Director:* Robin Lake-Foster

Minority Leader

McCaul, Michael T., R-Tex. (10)

Capitol Hill Office: 2001 RHOB 20515-4310; 225-2401; Fax: 225-5955; *Chief of Staff:* Steve Gilleland

Web: mccaul.house.gov

Facebook: www.facebook.com/michaeltmccaul

Twitter: @RepMcCaul

YouTube: www.youtube.com/MichaelTMcCaul

Instagram: @congressman_mccaul

District Offices: 3301 Northland Dr., #212, Austin, TX 78731; 512-473-2357; Fax: 512-473-0514 (by appointment only); *District Director:* Johnna Carlson

Rosewood Professional Bldg., 990 Village Square Dr., Suite B, Tomball, TX 77375-4269; 281-255-8372; Fax: 281-255-0034; *Constituent Liaison/Caseworker:* Sherrie Meicher

Satellite Offices: Katy Commerce Center, 1773 Westborough Dr., #223, Katy, TX 77449; 281-398-1247

(by appointment only); *Eastern District Field Director:* Lorissa Plunto

2000 S. Market St., #303, Brenham, TX 77833-5800; 979-830-8497; Fax: 979-830-1984; (open Tuesday/ Thursday, 8 a.m.–5 p.m.); *Constituent Liaison/ Caseworker:* Marita Mikeska

Committee Assignments: Foreign Affairs; Homeland Security

McClintock, Tom, R-Calif. (4)

Capitol Hill Office: 2312 RHOB 20515-0504; 225-2511; Fax: 225-5444; *Chief of Staff:* Rocky Deal

Web: mcclintock.house.gov

Facebook: www.facebook.com/Congressman-Tom-McClintock-81125319109

Twitter: @RepMcClintock

YouTube: www.youtube.com/McClintockCA04

District Office: 2200A Douglas Blvd., #240, Roseville, CA 95661; 916-786-5560; Fax: 916-786-6364; *District Director:* Rocky Deal

Committee Assignments: Budget; Natural Resources

McCollum, Betty, D-Minn. (4)

Capitol Hill Office: 2256 RHOB 20515-2304; 225-6631; Fax: 225-1968; *Chief of Staff:* Bill Harper

Web: mccollum.house.gov

Facebook: www.facebook.com/repbettymccollum

Twitter: @BettyMcCollum04

YouTube: www.youtube.com/BMcCollum04

Instagram: @repbettymccollum

District Office: 661 LaSalle St., #110, St. Paul, MN 55114; 651-224-9191; Fax: 651-224-3056; *District Director:* Joshua Straka

Committee Assignment: Appropriations

McEachin, A. Donald, D-Va. (4)

Capitol Hill Office: 314 CHOB 20515; 225-6365; Fax: 226-1170; *Sr. Advisor:* Abbi Easter

Web: mceachin.house.gov

Facebook: www.facebook.com/RepMcEachin

Twitter: @RepMcEachin

YouTube: www.youtube.com/channel/ UCMoPYHuZ3fZho0ZixZCfiFg

Instagram: @repmceachin

District Offices: 110 N. Robinson St., #403, Richmond, VA 23220; 804-486-1840; *District Director:* Tara Rountree

131 N. Saratoga St., Suite B, Suffolk, VA 23434; 757-942-6050; *Caseworker:* Mary Burroughs

Committee Assignments: Energy and Commerce; Natural Resources

McGovern, James, D-Mass. (2)

Capitol Hill Office: 408 CHOB 20515-2103; 225-6101; Fax: 225-5759; *Chief of Staff:* Jennifer Chandler

Web: mcgovern.house.gov

Facebook: www.facebook.com/RepJimMcGovern

Twitter: @RepMcGovern

YouTube: www.youtube.com/RepJimMcGovern

Instagram: @repmcgovern

District Offices: 24 Church St., #27, Leominster, MA 01453; 978-466-3552; Fax: 978-466-3973; *District Rep.:* Eladia Romero

94 Pleasant St., Northampton, MA 01060; 413-341-8700; Fax: 413-584-1216; *District Rep.:* John Niedzielski

12 E. Worcester St., #1, Worcester, MA 01604; 508-831-7356; Fax: 508-754-0982; *District Director:* Kathleen Polanowicz

Committee Assignments: Agriculture; Congressional-Executive Commission on China, Chair; Rules, Chair

McHenry, Patrick T., R-N.C. (10)

Capitol Hill Office: 2004 RHOB 20515; 225-2576; Fax: 225-0316; *Chief of Staff:* Jeff Butler

Web: mchenry.house.gov

Facebook: www.facebook.com/CongressmanMcHenry

Twitter: @PatrickMcHenry

YouTube: www.youtube.com/CongressmanMcHenry

Instagram: @reppatrickmchenry

District Offices: 128 W. Main Ave., #115, Gastonia, NC 28052; 704-833-0096; Fax: 704-833-0887; *District Director:* Brett Keeter

1990 Main Ave. S.E., P.O. Box 1830, Hickory, NC 28603; 828-327-6100; Fax: 828-327-8311; *Sr. District Rep.:* Nancy Meek

Satellite Office: 160 Midland Ave., Black Mountain, NC 28711; 828-669-0600; (open Monday/Wednesday, 12 p.m.–5 p.m.); *Regional Director:* Roger Kumpf

Committee Assignment: Financial Services

McKinley, David, R-W.Va. (1)

Capitol Hill Office: 2239 RHOB 20515; 225-4172; Fax: 225-7564; *Chief of Staff:* Mike Hamilton

Web: mckinley.house.gov

Facebook: www.facebook.com/RepMcKinley

Twitter: @RepMcKinley

YouTube: www.youtube.com/RepDavidMcKinley

District Offices: 709 Beechurst Ave., #29, Morgantown, WV 26505-4689; 304-284-8506; Fax: 804-284-8505; *District Director:* Rod Rogers

408 Market St., Parkersburg, WV 26101; 304-422-5972; Fax: 304-422-5974; *Constituent Services Rep.:* Robert Villers

Horne Bldg., 1100 Main St., #101, Wheeling, WV 26003; 304-232-3801; Fax: 304-232-3813; *Constituent Services Rep.:* Chantel Young

Committee Assignment: Energy and Commerce

McMorris Rodgers, Cathy, R-Wash. (5)

Capitol Hill Office: 1035 LHOB 20515; 225-2006; Fax: 225-3392; *Chief of Staff:* Nate Hodson

Web: mcmorris.house.gov

Facebook: www.facebook.com/mcmorrisrodgers

Twitter: @cathymcmorris

YouTube: www.youtube.com/McMorrisRodgers

Instagram: @cathymcmorris

District Offices: 555 S. Main St., Colville, WA 99114-2503; 509-684-3481; Fax: 509-684-3482; *District Rep.:* Andrew Engall

10 N. Post St., #625, Spokane, WA 99201-0706; 509-353-2374; Fax: 509-234-0445; *District Director:* Traci Couture

26 E. Main St., #2, Walla Walla, WA 99362-1925; 509-529-9358; Fax: 509-529-9379; *Deputy Rep.:* Victor Valerio

Committee Assignment: Energy and Commerce

McNerney, Jerry, D-Calif. (9)

Capitol Hill Office: 2265 RHOB 20515-0511; 225-1947; Fax: 225-4060; *Chief of Staff:* Nicole Alioto

Web: mcnerney.house.gov

Facebook: www.facebook.com/jerrymcnerney

Twitter: @RepMcNerney

YouTube: www.youtube.com/RepJerryMcNerney

District Offices: Antioch Community Center, 4703 Lone Tree Way, Antioch, CA 94531; 925-754-0716; Fax: 925-754-0728; *District Director:* Alisa Alva

2222 Grand Canal Blvd., #7, Stockton, CA 95207-6671; 209-476-8552; Fax: 209-476-8587; *District Scheduler:* Emily Owen

Committee Assignments: Energy and Commerce; Science, Space, and Technology

Meadows, Mark, R-N.C. (11)

Capitol Hill Office: 2160 RHOB 20515; 225-6401; Fax: 226-6422; *Chief of Staff:* Paul Fitzpatrick

Web: meadows.house.gov

Facebook: www.facebook.com/Repmarkmeadows

Twitter: @RepMarkMeadows

YouTube: www.youtube.com/RepMarkMeadows

Instagram: @repmarkmeadows

District Office: 200 N. Grove St., #90, Hendersonville, NC 28792; 828-693-5660; Fax: 828-693-5603; *District Director:* Wayne Kane

Committee Assignments: Oversight and Reform; Transportation and Infrastructure

Meeks, Gregory W., D-N.Y. (5)

Capitol Hill Office: 2234 RHOB 20515; 225-3461; Fax: 226-4169; *Chief of Staff:* Sophia Lafargue

Web: meeks.house.gov

Facebook: www.facebook.com/RepGregoryMeeks

Twitter: @RepGregoryMeeks

YouTube: www.youtube.com/repgregorymeeks

Instagram: @repgregorymeeks

District Offices: 67-12 Rockaway Beach Blvd., Arverne, NY 11692; 347-230-4032; Fax: 347-230-4045; *District Director:* Robert Simmons

153-01 Jamaica Ave., 2nd Floor, Jamaica, NY 11432; 718-725-6000; Fax: 718-725-9868; *Executive Director:* Joe Edwards

Committee Assignments: Financial Services; Foreign Affairs

Meng, Grace, D-N.Y. (6)

Capitol Hill Office: 2209 RHOB 20515; 225-2601; Fax: 225-1589; *Chief of Staff:* Justin Oswald

Web: meng.house.gov

Facebook: www.facebook.com/repgracemeng
Twitter: @RepGraceMeng
YouTube: www.youtube.com/channel/
UCHg516zJKbIBtXFAJ0nu3XQ
District Offices: 40-13 159th St., Suite A, Flushing, NY 11358; 718-358-6364; Fax: 718-445-7868; *District Director:* Anthony Lemma
118-35 Queens Blvd., 17th Floor, Forest Hills, NY 11375; 718-358-6364; Fax: 718-445-7868; (by appointment only); *District Director:* Anthony Lemma
Committee Assignments: Appropriations; Ethics

Meuser, Daniel, D-Pa. (9)

Capitol Hill Office: 326 CHOB 20515-3515; 225-6511; *Chief of Staff:* Dante Cutrona
Web: meuser.house.gov
Facebook: www.facebook.com/RepMeuser
Twitter: @RepMeuser
YouTube: www.youtube.com/channel/
UCFBiWT7JNlSyUNuxYqjdUtA
District Offices: 1044 E. Main St., Palmyra, PA 17078; *Caseworker:* Karen Ludwig
121 Progress Ave., #110, Losch Plaza, Pottsville, PA 17901; 570-871-6370; *District Director:* John Gouwer, Katie Hetherington-Cunfer
Committee Assignments: Budget; Education and Labor; Veterans' Affairs

Miller, Carol, R-W.Va. (3)

Capitol Hill Office: 1605 LHOB 20515-3515; 225-3452; *Chief of Staff:* Matthew Donnellan
Web: miller.house.gov
Facebookk: www.facebook.com/RepCarolMiller
Twitter: @RepCarolMiller
Instagram: @repcarolmiller
District Offices: 307 Prince St., Beckley, WV 25801; 304-250-6177, Fax: 304-250-6179; *Deputy District Director:* Kim McMillion
Elizabeth Kee Federal Bldg., 601 Federal St., Bluefield, WV 24701; 304-250-6177
Sidney L. Christie Federal Bldg., 845 5th Ave., Huntington, WV 25701; 304-522-2201; Fax: 304-529-5716; *Director of Constituent Services:* Teri Booth
Committee Assignments: Oversight and Reform; Transportation and Infrastructure

Mitchell, Paul, R-Mich. (10)

Capitol Hill Office: 211 CHOB 20515; 225-2106; Fax: 226-1169; *Chief of Staff:* Kyle Kizzier
Web: mitchell.house.gov
Facebook: www.facebook.com/reppaulmitchell
Twitter: @RepPaulMitchell
YouTube: www.youtube.com/RepPaulMitchell
Instagram: @reppaulmitchell
District Office: 48701 Van Dyke Ave., Shelby Township, MI 48317; 586-997-5010; Fax: 586-997-5013; *District Director:* Tony Forlini
Committee Assignments: Armed Services; Transportation and Infrastructure

Moolenaar, John, R-Mich. (4)

Capitol Hill Office: 117 CHOB 20515-2204; 225-3561; Fax: 225-9679; *Chief of Staff:* Lindsay Ryan
Web: moolenaar.house.gov
Facebook: www.facebook.com/RepMoolenaar
Twitter: @RepMoolenaar
YouTube: www.youtube.com/channel/
UCnMvVN4a8roZu4crE0UW2DA
Instagram: @repmoolenaar
District Office: 200 E. Main St., #230, Midland, MI 48640; 989-631-2552; Fax: 989-631-6271; *District Chief of Staff:* Ashton Bortz
Satellite Office: 201 N. Mitchell St., #301, Cadillac, MI 49601; 231-942-5070; Fax: 231-876-9505; (open Monday/Tuesday/Thursday, 9 a.m.–4 p.m.); *Director or Consituent Services:* Tarin Brunink
Committee Assignment: Appropriations

Mooney, Alex, R-W.Va. (2)

Capitol Hill Office: 2440 RHOB 20515-4802; 225-2711; Fax: 225-7856; *Chief of Staff:* Michael Hough
Web: mooney.house.gov
Facebook: www.facebook.com/CongressmanAlexMooney
Twitter: @RepAlexMooney
YouTube: www.youtube.com/channel/
UCw9CGkF4Re3areluI43TGyA
Instagram: @repalexmooney
District Offices: 405 Capitol St., #306, Charleston, WV 25301; 304-925-5964; Fax: 304-926-8912; *District Director:* Chad Story
300 Foxcroft Ave., #101, Martinsburg, WV 25401; 304-264-8810; Fax: 304-264-8815; *District Director:* Chad Story
Committee Assignment: Financial Services

Moore, Gwen, D-Wisc. (4)

Capitol Hill Office: 2252 RHOB 20515; 225-4572; Fax: 225-8135; *Chief of Staff:* Sean Gard
Web: gwenmoore.house.gov
Facebook: www.facebook.com/GwenSMoore
Twitter: @RepGwenMoore
YouTube: www.youtube.com/RepGwenMoore
Instagram: @repgwenmoore
District Office: 316 N. Milwaukee St., #406, Milwaukee, WI 53202-5818; 414-297-1140; Fax: 414-297-1086; *District Director:* Shirley Ellis
Committee Assignment: Ways and Means

Morelle, Joseph D., D-N.Y. (25)

Capitol Hill Office: 1317 LHOB 20515-3515; 225-3615; *Chief of Staff:* Nicholas Weatherbee
Web: morelle.house.gov
Facebook: www.facebook.com/RepJoeMorelle
Twitter: @RepJoeMorelle
District Office: 3210 Federal Bldg., 100 State St., Rochester, NY 14614; 585-232-4850; Fax: 585-232-1954; *District Director:* Kaleigh Benedict
Committee Assignments: Education and Labor; Rules; Budget

Moulton, Seth, D-Mass. (6)

Capitol Hill Office: 1127 LHOB 20515-2106; 225-8020; Fax: 225-5915; *Chief of Staff:* Alexis L'Heureux
Web: moulton.house.gov
Facebook: www.facebook.com/RepMoulton
Twitter: @teammoulton
YouTube: www.youtube.com/channel/ UC5w5qn7nj5Ljy69LTV7a_fQ
Instagram: @repmoulton
District Office: 21 Front St., Salem, MA 01970; 978-531-1669; Fax: 978-224-2270; *District Director:* Rick Jakious
Committee Assignments: Armed Services; Budget

Mucarsel-Powell, Debbie, D-Fla. (26)

Capitol Hill Office: 114 CHOB 20515-3515; 225-2778; Fax: 225-; *Chief of Staff:* Laura Rodriguez
Web: mucarsel-powell.house.gov
Facebook: www.facebook.com/RepDMP
Twitter: @RepDMP
YouTube: www.youtube.com/repdmp
District Offices: 1100 Simonton St., #1-213, Key West, FL 33010; 305-292-4485; *District Director:* Daniel Horton-Diaz
12851 42nd St. S.W., #131, Miami, FL 33175; 305-222-0160; *District Director:* Daniel Horton-Diaz
404 West Palm Dr., Florida City, FL 33034
Committee Assignments: Judiciary; Transportation and Infrastructure

Mullin, Markwayne, R-Okla. (2)

Capitol Hill Office: 2421 LHOB 20515; 225-2701; Fax: 225-3038; *Chief of Staff:* Mike Stopp
Web: mullin.house.gov
Facebook: www.facebook.com/RepMullin
Twitter: @RepMullin
YouTube: www.youtube.com/channel/UCLQlm-cbGbJj9baZC6oFsag
Instagram: @markwaynemullin
District Offices: 1 E. Choctaw, #175, McAlester, OK 74501; 918-423-5951; Fax: 918-423-1940; *Field Rep.:* Betty Ford
811-A N. York St., Muskogee, OK 74403; 918-687-2533; Fax: 918-686-0128; *Field Rep.:* William Barnes
223 W. Patti Page Blvd., Claremore, OK 74017; 918-283-6262; Fax: 918-923-6451; *Field Rep.:* Debbie Dooley
Committee Assignment: Energy and Commerce

Murphy, Stephanie, D-Fla. (7)

Capitol Hill Office: 1710 LHOB 20515; 225-4035; Fax: 226-0821; *Chief of Staff:* Brad Howard
Web: stephaniemurphy.house.gov
Facebook: www.facebook.com/RepStephMurphy
Twitter: @RepStephMurphy
YouTube: www.youtube.com/channel/ UCmd4mo5owVTGetYcPmkcI1g
Instagram: @repstephmurphy
District Offices: 225 E. Robinson, #525, Orlando, FL 32801; 888-205-5421; *District Director:* Lauren Allen

110 W. 1st St., #210, Sanford, FL 32771; 888-205-5421; *Sanford Office Manager:* Thomas Steenekamp
Committee Assignment: Ways and Means

Nadler, Jerrold, D-N.Y. (10)

Capitol Hill Office: 2132 RHOB 20515; 225-5635; Fax: 225-6923; *Washington Director:* John Doty
Web: nadler.house.gov
Facebook: www.facebook.com/CongressmanNadler
Twitter: @RepJerryNadler
YouTube: www.youtube.com/CongressmanNadler
Instagram: @repjerrynadler
District Offices: 6605 Fort Hamilton Pkwy., Brooklyn, NY 11219; 718-373-3198; Fax: 718-996-0039; *Brooklyn Director:* Robert Gottheim
201 Varick St., #669, New York, NY 10014-7069; 212-367-7350; Fax: 212-367-7356; *Chief of Staff:* Amy Rutkin
Committee Assignment: Judiciary, Chair

Napolitano, Grace, D-Calif. (32)

Capitol Hill Office: 1610 LHOB 20515-0538; 225-5256; Fax: 225-0027; *Chief of Staff:* Daniel S. Chao
Web: napolitano.house.gov
Facebook: www.facebook.com/RepGraceNapolitano
Twitter: @gracenapolitano
YouTube: www.youtube.com/RepGraceNapolitano
Instagram: @repgracenapolitano
District Office: 4401 Santa Anita Ave., #201, El Monte, CA 91731; 626-350-0150; Fax: 626-350-0450; *District Chief of Staff:* Perla Hernandez Trumkul
Committee Assignments: Natural Resources; Transportation and Infrastructure

Neal, Richard E., D-Mass. (1)

Capitol Hill Office: 2309 RHOB 20515-2102; 225-5601; Fax: 225-8112; *Chief of Staff:* William Tranghese
Web: neal.house.gov
Facebook: www.facebook.com/reprichardneal
Twitter: @RepRichardNeal
YouTube: www.youtube.com/RepRichardENeal
District Offices: 78 Center St., Pittsfield, MA 01201; 413-442-0946; Fax: 413-443-2792; *District Director:* William Powers
300 State St., #200, Springfield, MA 01105-1711; 413-785-0325; Fax: 413-747-0604; *Scheduler:* Elizabeth Quigley
Committee Assignment: Ways and Means, Chair

Neguse, Joe, D-Colo. (2)

Capitol Hill Office: 1419 LHOB 20515; 225-2161; *Chief of Staff:* Lisa Bianco
Web: neguse.house.gov
Facebook: www.facebook.com/RepJoeNeguse
Twitter: @RepJoeNeguse
Instagram: @repjohncurtis
District Office: 2503 Walnut St., #300, Boulder, CO 80302; 303-335-1045
1220 S. College Ave., #100A, Fort Collins, CO 80524; 970-372-3971
Committee Assignments: Judiciary; Natural Resources

Newhouse, Dan, R-Wash. (4)

Capitol Hill Office: 1414 LHOB 20515; 225-5816; Fax: 225-3251; *Chief of Staff:* Carrie Meadows
Web: newhouse.house.gov
Facebook: www.facebook.com/RepNewhouse
Twitter: @RepNewhouse
YouTube: www.youtube.com/channel/UCllbsv_aoIaPS6W3aSonZlw
Instagram: @repnewhouse
District Office: 402 E. Yakima Ave., #1000, Yakima, WA 98901; 509-452-3243; Fax: 509-452-3438; *District Director:* Jamie Daniels
3100 George Washington Way, #130, Richland, WA 99354; 509-713-7374; Fax: 509-713-7377; *District Rep.:* Josh Lozano
Committee Assignment: Appropriations

Norcross, Donald, D-N.J. (1)

Capitol Hill Office: 2437 RHOB 20515-3001; 225-6501; Fax: 225-6583; *Chief of Staff:* Michael Maitland
Web: norcross.house.gov
Facebook: www.facebook.com/DonaldNorcrossNJ
Twitter: @DonaldNorcross
YouTube: www.youtube.com/channel/UC7kXK_PyDiOT8YrdP0jYZHw/feed
Instagram: @donald_norcross
District Office: 10 Melrose Ave., #210, Cherry Hill, NJ 08003; 856-427-7000; Fax: 856-427-4109; *District Director:* Mary Cruz
Committee Assignments: Armed Services; Education and Labor

Norman, Ralph, R-S.C. (5)

Capitol Hill Office: 319 CHOB 20515; 225-5501; Fax: 225-0464; *Chief of Staff:* Mark Piland
Web: norman.house.gov
Facebook: www.facebook.com/RepRalphNorman
Twitter: @RepRalphNorman
YouTube: www.youtube.com/channel/UC-vxt0Y_jalfzndsSNkZw1w
District Office: 454 S. Anderson Rd., #302B, Rock Hill, SC 29730; 803-327-1114; Fax: 803-327-4330; *District Director:* David O'Neal
Committee Assignments: Budget; Oversight and Reform, Science, Space, and Technology

Norton, Eleanor Holmes, D-D.C. (At Large)

Capitol Hill Office: 2136 RHOB 20515-5101; 225-8050; Fax: 225-3002; *Chief of Staff:* Raven Reeder
Web: norton.house.gov
Facebook: www.facebook.com/CongresswomanNorton
Twitter: @EleanorNorton
YouTube: www.youtube.com/EleanorHNorton
Instagram: @congresswomannorton
District Offices: 2235 Shannon Pl. S.E., #2032-A, Washington, DC 20020-7005; 202-678-8900; Fax: 202-678-8844; *District Director:* Tristan Breaux
90 K St. N.E., #100, Washington, DC 20001; 202-408-9041; Fax: 202-408-9048; *District Director:* Tristan Breaux

Committee Assignments: Oversight and Reform; Transportation and Infrastructure

Nunes, Devin, R-Calif. (22)

Capitol Hill Office: 1013 LHOB 20515-0521; 225-2523; Fax: 225-3404; *Chief of Staff:* Jilian Plank
Web: nunes.house.gov
Facebook: www.facebook.com/Congressman-Devin-Nunes-376470350795
Twitter: @RepDevinNunes
YouTube: www.youtube.com/RepDevinNunes
District Offices: 264 Clovis Ave., #206, Clovis, CA 93612-1115; 559-323-5235; Fax: 559-323-5528; *Field Rep.:* Crystal Ragan
113 N. Church St., #208, Visalia, CA 93291-6300; 559-733-3861; Fax: 559-733-3865; *District Director:* Melissa Semoes
Committee Assignments: Ways and Means; Permanent Select Intelligence

Ocasio-Cortez, Alexandria, D-N.Y. (14)

Capitol Hill Office: 229 CHOB 20515-3515; 225-3965; *Chief of Staff:* Saikat Chakrabarti
Web: ocasio-cortez.house.gov
Facebook: www.facebook.com/repAOC
Twitter: @RepAOC
District Office: 74-09 37th Ave., #305, Jackson Heights, NY 11372; 718-662-5970; *District Director:* Maribel Hernandez-Rivera
Committee Assignments: Financial Services; Oversight and Reform

O'Halleran, Tom, D-Ariz. (1)

Capitol Hill Office: 324 CHOB 20515; 225-3361; Fax: 225-3462; *Chief of Staff:* Jeremy Nordquist
Web: ohalleran.house.gov
Facebook: www.facebook.com/repohalleran
Twitter: @RepOHalleran
YouTube: www.youtube.com/repohalleran
Instagram: @repohalleran
District Offices: 211 N. Florence St., #1, Casa Grande, AZ 85122; 520-316-0839; *District Director:* Blanca Varela
405 N. Beaver St., #6, Flagstaff, AZ 86001; 928-286-5338; *Deputy District Director:* Chip Davis
3037 W. Ina Rd., #101, Tucson, AZ 85741; 928-304-0131; *Constituent Services Rep.:* Max Dell'Oliver
Committee Assignments: Agriculture; Energy and Commerce

Olson, Pete, R-Tex. (22)

Capitol Hill Office: 2133 RHOB 20515; 225-5951; Fax: 225-5241; *Chief of Staff:* Melissa Kelly
Web: olson.house.gov
Facebook: www.facebook.com/Rep.PeteOlson
Twitter: @RepPeteOlson
YouTube: www.youtube.com/PeteOlsonTX22
Instagram: @reppeteolson

District Offices: 1920 Country Pl. Pkwy., #140, Pearland, TX 77584; 281-485-4855; Fax: 832-617-8569; *Field Rep.:* J.P. Anders

2277 Plaza Dr., #195, Sugar Land, TX 77479; 281-494-2690; Fax: 281-494-2649; *District Director:* Christian Bionat

Committee Assignments: Energy and Commerce; Science, Space, and Technology

Omar, Ilhan, D-Minn. (5)

Capitol Hill Office: 1517 LHOB 20515-3515; 225-4755; Fax: 216-522-4908; *Chief of Staff:* Connor McNutt

Web: omar.house.gov

Facebook: www.facebook.com/RepIlhan

Twitter: @Ilhan

YouTube: www.youtube.com/channel/UC4meVUkgJUxyHE5CifWAumQ

Instagram: @repilhan

District Office: 404 3rd Ave. North, #203, Minneapolis, MN 55401; 613-333-1272; *District Director:* Davis Senseman

Committee Assignments: Budget; Education and Labor; Foreign Affairs

Palazzo, Steven, R-Miss. (4)

Capitol Hill Office: 2349 RHOB 20515-2404; 225-5772; Fax: 225-7074; *Chief of Staff:* Hunter Lipscomb

Web: palazzo.house.gov

Facebook: www.facebook.com/stevenpalazzo

Twitter: @CongPalazzo

YouTube: www.youtube.com/CongressmanPalazzo

Instagram: @congressmanpalazzo

District Offices: 84 48th St., Gulf Port, MS 39505; *District Director:* Michelle Gargiulo

641 Main St., #142, Hattiesburg, MS 39401-3478; 601-582-3246; Fax: 601-582-3452; *Office Manager:* Anita Bourne

3118 Pascagoula St., #181, Pascagoula, MS 39567-4215; 228-202-8104; Fax: 228-202-8105; (by appointment only); *Constituent Liaison:* Debora Hembree

Committee Assignment: Appropriations

Pallone, Frank, Jr., D-N.J. (6)

Capitol Hill Office: 2107 RHOB 20515-3006; 225-4671; Fax: 225-9665; *Deputy Chief of Staff:* Liam Fitzsimmons

Web: pallone.house.gov

Facebook: www.facebook.com/RepFrankPallone

Twitter: @FrankPallone

YouTube: www.youtube.com/RepFrankPallone

Instagram: @repfrankpallone

District Offices: 504 Broadway, Long Branch, NJ 07740-5951; 732-571-1140; Fax: 732-870-3890; *Chief of Staff:* Janice Fuller

67/69 Church St., New Brunswick, NJ 08901; 732-249-8892; Fax: 732-249-1335; *Constituent Services Director:* Alexandra Maldonado

Committee Assignment: Energy and Commerce, Chair

Palmer, Gary, R-Ala. (6)

Capitol Hill Office: 207 CHOB 20515; 225-4921; Fax: 225-2082; *Chief of Staff:* William Smith

Web: palmer.house.gov

Facebook: www.facebook.com/CongressmanGaryPalmer

Twitter: @USRepGaryPalmer

YouTube: www.youtube.com/channel/UCYZfP-cNIvlJY3AcAc9OPpQ

Instagram: @repgarypalmer

District Offices: 703 2nd Ave. North, P.O. Box 502, Clanton, AL 35045; 205-280-6846; Fax: 205-968-1294; *District Director:* Ray Melik

3535 Grandview Pkwy., #525, Birmingham, AL 35243; 205-968-1290; Fax: 205-968-1294; *District Director:* Ray Melick

220 2nd Ave. East, Oneonta, AL 35121; 205-625-4160; *District Director:* Ray Melik

Committee Assignment: Transportation and Infrastructure

Panetta, Jimmy, D-Calif. (20)

Capitol Hill Office: 212 CHOB 20515; 225-2861; Fax: 225-6791; *Chief of Staff:* Joel Bailey

Web: panetta.house.gov

Facebook: www.facebook.com/RepJimmyPanetta

Twitter: @RepJimmyPanetta

YouTube: www.youtube.com/channel/UCmw-aERG51C96edMDPN7fXQ

Instagram: @repjimmypanetta

District Offices: 100 W. Alisal St., Salinas, CA 93901; 831-424-2229; Fax: 831-424-7099; *District Director:* Kathleen Lee

701 Ocean St., Room 318C, Santa Cruz, CA 95060; 831-429-1976; *Congressional Aide:* Taylor Brenis, Emmanuel Garcia

Committee Assignments: Agriculture; Budget, Ways and Means

Pappas, Chris, D-N.H. (1)

Capitol Hill Office: 323 CHOB 20515-3515; 225-5456; *Chief of Staff:*

Web: pappas.house.gov

Facebook: www.facebook.com/RepChrisPappas

Twitter: @RepChrisPappas

District Office: 660 Central Ave., #101, Dover, NH 03820; 603-285-4300

Committee Assignments: Transportation and Infrastructure; Veterans' Affairs

Pascrell, Bill, Jr., D-N.J. (9)

Capitol Hill Office: 2409 RHOB 20515-3008; 225-5751; Fax: 225-5782; *Chief of Staff:* Benjamin Rich

Web: pascrell.house.gov

Facebook: www.facebook.com/pascrell

Twitter: @BillPascrell

YouTube: www.youtube.com/RepPascrell

Instagram: @billpascrell

District Offices: 200 Federal Plaza, #500, Paterson, NJ 07505-1999; 973-523-5152; Fax: 973-523-0637; *District Director:* Ritzy Moralez-Diaz

330 Passaic St., 1st Floor, Passaic, NJ 07055-5815; 973-472-4510; Fax: 973-472-0852; (open Monday/Wednesday, 9 a.m.–5 p.m.); *Field Rep.:* Karlito Almeda

Satellite Offices: 367 Valley Brook Ave., Lyndhurst, NJ 07071; 201-935-2248; (open Wednesday/Friday, 9 a.m.–5 p.m.); *Field Rep.:* Karlito Almeda

2-10 N. Van Brunt St., Englewood, NJ 07631; 201-935-2248; (open Tuesday/Thursday, 9 a.m.–5 p.m.); *Field Rep.:* Ian Godfrey

Committee Assignment: Ways and Means

Payne, Donald, Jr., D-N.J. (10)

Capitol Hill Office: 103 CHOB 20515; 225-3436; Fax: 225-4160; *Chief of Staff:* LaVerne Alexander
Web: payne.house.gov
Facebook: www.facebook.com/DonaldPayneJr
Twitter: @RepDonaldPayne
YouTube: www.youtube.com/channel/UCTG_SeYsOgbngjv1Donyu0w
Instagram: @repdonaldpaynejr
District Offices: 253 Martin Luther King Dr., Jersey City, NJ 07305; 201-369-0392; Fax: 201-369-0395; *Constituent Service Asst.:* Elizabeth Lorenzo

60 Nelson Pl., 14th Floor, Newark, NJ 07102; 973-645-3213; Fax: 973-645-5902; *District Director:* Michael Gray

1455 Liberty Ave., Hillside, NJ 07205; 862-229-2994; Fax: 862-225-294;

Committee Assignments: Homeland Security; Transportation and Infrastructure

Pelosi, Nancy, D-Calif. (12)

Capitol Hill Office: 1236 RHOB 20515-0508; 225-4965; Fax: 225-8259; *Chief of Staff:* Robert Edmonson
Web: pelosi.house.gov
Facebook: www.facebook.com/NancyPelosi
Twitter: @NancyPelosi
YouTube: www.youtube.com/nancypelosi
District Office: 90 7th St., #2-800, San Francisco, CA 94103-6723; 415-556-4862; Fax: 415-861-1670; *District Chief of Staff:* Dan Bernal
Speaker of the House

Pence, Greg, R-Ind. (6)

Capitol Hill Office: 222 CHOB 20515-3515; 225-3021; Fax: 225-3382; *Chief of Staff:* Kyle Robertson
Web: pence.house.gov
Facebook: www.facebook.com/RepGregPence
Twitter: @RepGregPence
Instagram: @repgregpence
District Office: 555 1st St., Suite B, Columbus, IN 47201; 812-799-5230; *District Director:* Ryan Jarmula
Committee Assignments: Foreign Affairs; Transportation and Infrastructure

Perlmutter, Ed, D-Colo. (7)

Capitol Hill Office: 1226 LHOB 20515; 225-2645; Fax: 225-5278; *Chief of Operations:* Alison Inderfurth
Web: perlmutter.house.gov

Facebook: www.facebook.com/RepPerlmutter
Twitter: @RepPerlmutter
YouTube: www.youtube.com/RepPerlmutter
District Office: 12600 W. Colfax Ave., #B-400, Lakewood, CO 80215-3779; 303-274-7944; Fax: 303-274-6455; *Chief of Staff:* Danielle Radovich-Piper
Committee Assignment: Financial Services; Rules; Science, Space, and Technology

Perry, Scott, R-Pa. (10)

Capitol Hill Office: 1207 LHOB 20515; 225-5836; Fax: 226-1000; *Chief of Staff:* Lauren Muglia
Web: perry.house.gov
Facebook: www.facebook.com/repscottperry
Twitter: @RepScottPerry
YouTube: www.youtube.com/RepScottPerry
Instagram: @repscottperry
District Offices: 730 N. Front St., Wormleysburg, PA 17043; 717-635-9504; Fax: 717-635-9861; *Director of Constituent Services:* Tyra Wallace

800 Corporate Circle, #202, Harrisburg, PA 17110; 717-603-4980

2501 Catherine St., #11, York, PA 17408; 717-893-7868

Committee Assignments: Foreign Affairs; Transportation and Infrastructure

Peters, Scott, D-Calif. (52)

Capitol Hill Office: 2338 RHOB 20515-0550; 225-0508; Fax: 225-2558; *Chief of Staff:* Daniel Zawitoski
Web: scottpeters.house.gov
Facebook: www.facebook.com/RepScottPeters
Twitter: @RepScottPeters
YouTube: www.youtube.com/repscottpeters
Instagram: @repscottpeters
District Office: 4350 Executive Dr., #105, San Diego, CA 92121; 858-455-5550; Fax: 858-455-5516; *District Chief of Staff:* MaryAnne Pintar
Committee Assignment: Energy and Commerce

Peterson, Collin C., D-Minn. (7)

Capitol Hill Office: 2204 RHOB 20515; 225-2165; Fax: 225-1593; *Deputy Chief of Staff, Legislative Director:* Adam Durand
Web: collinpeterson.house.gov
Facebook: www.facebook.com/Collin-Peterson-6595227967
Twitter: @collinpeterson
District Offices: 714 Lake Ave., #101, Detroit Lakes, MN 56501; 218-847-5056; Fax: 218-847-5109; *Chief of Staff:* Allison Stock

1420 E. College Dr. SW/WC, Marshall, MN 56258-2065; 507-537-2299; Fax: 507-537-2298; *Staff Asst.:* Meg Louwagie

230 E. 3rd St., Redwood Falls, MN 56283; 507-637-2270; *Staff Asst.:* Meg Louwagie

1700 Technology Dr., #119, Willmar, MN 56201-3696; 320-235-1061; Fax: 320-235-2651; *Staff Asst.:* Mary Bertram

13892 Airport Dr., Thief River Falls, MN 56701; 218-683-5405; Fax: 218-847-5109

Committee Assignments: Agriculture, Chair; Veterans' Affairs

Phillips, Dean, D-Minn. (3)

Capitol Hill Office: 1305, LHOB 20515-3515; 225-2871; Fax: 225-6351; *Chief of Staff:* Tim Bertocci

Web: phillips.house.gov

Facebook: www.facebook.com/RepDeanPhillips

Twitter: @RepDeanPhillips

YouTube: www.youtube.com/channel/UCQ7y_sateDGmnnw1NVuaTvA

Instagram: @repdeanphillips

District Office: 13911 Ridgedale Dr., #200, Minnetonka, MN 55305; 952-563-4593

Committee Assignments: Ethics; Financial Services; Foreign Affairs

Pingree, Chellie, D-Maine (1)

Capitol Hill Office: 2162 RHOB 20515-1901; 225-6116; Fax: 225-5590; *Chief of Staff:* Jesse Connolly

Web: pingree.house.gov

Facebook: www.facebook.com/ChelliePingree

Twitter: @chelliepingree

YouTube: www.youtube.com/CongresswomanPingree

Instagram: @chelliepingree

District Offices: 2 Portland Fish Pier, #304, Portland, ME 04101; 207-774-5019; Fax: 207-871-0720; *Deputy Director of Communications:* Andrew Colvin

1 Silver St., Waterville, ME 04901; 207-873-5713; Fax: 207-873-5717; *Field Rep.:* Pamela Trinward

Committee Assignments: Agriculture; Appropriations

Plaskett, Stacey E., D-Virgin Islands. (At Large)

Capitol Hill Office: 2404 RHOB 20515; 225-1790; Fax: 225-5517; *Chief of Staff:* Erik Prince

Web: plaskett.house.gov

Facebook: www.facebook.com/repstaceyplaskett

Twitter: @StaceyPlaskett

YouTube: www.youtube.com/channel/UC3V7biFZHDFHDFZy6cCSZUA

Instagram: @stacey_plaskett

District Offices: 60 King St., Frederiksted, VI 00840; 340-778-5900; Fax: 340-778-5111; *Caseworker:* Laverne Joseph

9100 Port of Sale Mall, #22, St. Thomas, VI 00802; 340-774-4408; Fax: 340-774-8033; *District Director:* Cletis Clendinen

Committee Assignments: Agriculture, Oversight and Reform; Transportation and Infrastructure

Pocan, Mark, D-Wisc. (2)

Capitol Hill Office: 1421 LHOB 20515; 225-2906; Fax: 225-6942; *Chief of Staff:* Glenn Wavrunek

Web: pocan.house.gov

Facebook: www.facebook.com/repmarkpocan

Twitter: @repmarkpocan

YouTube: www.youtube.com/repmarkpocan

Instagram: @repmarkpocan

District Offices: 10 E. Doty St., #405, Madison, WI 53703-5103; 608-258-9800; Fax: 608-258-0377; *District Director:* Dane Varese

100 State St., 3rd Floor, Beloit, WI 53511; 608-365-8001; *District Director:* Dane Varese

Committee Assignment: Appropriations

Porter, Katie, D-Calif. (45)

Capitol Hill Office: 1117 LHOB 20515-3515; 225-5611; *Chief of Staff:* Amanda Fischer

Web: porter.house.gov

Facebook: www.facebook.com/repkatieporter

Twitter: @RepKatiePorter

YouTube: www.youtube.com/channel/UCRdB2ce4DloCSyuPbWfOZyw

Instagram: @repkatieporter

District Office: 2151 Michelson Dr., #195, Irvine, CA 92612; 949-668-6600; *District Director:* Kelly Jones

Committee Assignment: Financial Services

Posey, Bill, R-Fla. (8)

Capitol Hill Office: 2150 RHOB 20515; 225-3671; Fax: 225-3516; *Chief of Staff:* Stuart Burns

Web: posey.house.gov

Facebook: www.facebook.com/bill.posey15

Twitter: @congbillposey

YouTube: www.youtube.com/CongressmanPosey

District Office: 2725 Judge Fran Jamieson Way, Bldg. C, Melbourne, FL 32940-6605; 321-632-1776; Fax: 321-639-8595; *District Scheduler/District Director:* Patrick Gavin

Committee Assignments: Financial Services; Science, Space, and Technology

Pressley, Ayanna, D-Mass. (7)

Capitol Hill Office: 1108 LHOB 20515-3515; 225-5111; Fax: 225-9322; *Chief of Staff:* Sarah Groh

Web: pressley.house.gov

Facebook: www.facebook.com/RepAyannaPressley

Twitter: @RepPressley

Instagram: @repayannapressley

District Office: 1700 Dorchester Ave., Boston, MA 02122; 617-850-0040; *District Director:* Eric White

Committee Assignments: Financial Services; Oversight and Reform

Price, David, D-N.C. (4)

Capitol Hill Office: 2108 RHOB 20515; 225-1784; Fax: 225-2014; *Deputy Chief of Staff/Office Director:* Justin Wein

Web: price.house.gov

Facebook: www.facebook.com/RepDavidEPrice

Twitter: @RepDavidEPrice

YouTube: www.youtube.com/RepDavidPrice

Instagram: @repdavidprice

District Offices: 1777 Fordham Blvd., #204, Chapel Hill, NC 27514; 919-967-7924; Fax: 919-967-8324; *District Director:* Asher Hildebrand

436 N. Harrington St., #100, Raleigh, NC 27603; 919-859-5999; Fax: 919-859-5998; *Chief of Staff:* Asher Hildebrand

Committee Assignments: Appropriations; Budget

Quigley, Mike, D-Ill. (5)

Capitol Hill Office: 2458 RHOB 20515; 225-4061; Fax: 225-5603; *Chief of Staff:* Juan Hinojosa

Web: quigley.house.gov

Facebook: www.facebook.com/repmikequigley

Twitter: @RepMikeQuigley

YouTube: www.youtube.com/RepMikeQuigley

Instagram: @repmikequigley

District Offices: 3223 N. Sheffield Ave., Chicago, IL 60657; 773-267-5926; *District Director:* Mary Ann Levar

4345 N. Milwaukee Ave., Chicago, IL 60641; 773-267-5926; Fax: 773-267-6583; *District Director:* Mary Ann Levar

Committee Assignments: Appropriations; Permanent Select Intelligence

Radewagen, Aumua Amata Coleman, R-Am. Samoa (At Large)

Capitol Hill Office: 1339 LHOB 20515; 225-8577; Fax: 225-8757; *Chief of Staff:* Leafaina O. Yahn

Web: radewagen.house.gov

Facebook: www.facebook.com/aumuaamata

Twitter: @RepAmata

YouTube: www.youtube.com/channel/UCGdrLQbt1PYDTPsampx4t1A

Instagram: @repamata

District Office: P.O. Box 5859, Pago Pago, AS 96799; 684-633-3601; Fax: 684-633-3607 *District Director:* Pulu Ae Ae

Committee Assignments: Natural Resources; Small Business; Veterans' Affairs

Raskin, Jamie, D-Md. (8)

Capitol Hill Office: 412 CHOB 20515; 225-5341; *Chief of Staff:* Julie Tagan

Web: raskin.house.gov

Facebook: www.facebook.com/RepRaskin

Twitter: @RepRaskin

YouTube: www.youtube.com/RepRaskin

Instagram: @repraskin

District Office: 51 Monroe St., #503, Rockville, MD 20850; 301-354-1000; *District Director:* Kathleen Connor

Committee Assignments: House Administration; Judiciary; Oversight and Reform; Rules

Ratcliffe, John, R-Tex. (4)

Capitol Hill Office: 223 CHOB 20515; 225-6673; Fax: 225-3332; *Chief of Staff:* Dustin Carmack

Web: ratcliffe.house.gov

Facebook: www.facebook.com/RepRatcliffe

Twitter: @RepRatcliffe

YouTube: www.youtube.com/channel/UCo37eRsRga4fUYijDa6j6oA

Instagram: @rep_ratcliffe

District Offices: 6531 Horizon Rd., Suite A, Rockwall, TX 75032; 972-771-0100; Fax: 972-771-1222; *District Director:* Jason Ross

100 W. Houston St., 1st Floor, Sherman, TX 75090; 903-813-5270; Fax: 903-868-8613; *Regional Rep.:* Jamie Baker

2600 N. Robison Rd., #190, Texarkana, TX 75599; 903-823-3173; Fax: 903-832-3232; *Regional Rep.:* Robbin Bass

Committee Assignments: Ethics; Homeland Security; Judiciary; Permanent Select Intelligence

Reed, Tom, R-N.Y. (23)

Capitol Hill Office: 2263 RHOB 20515; 225-3161; Fax: 226-6599; *Chief of Staff:* Drew Wayne

Web: reed.house.gov

Facebook: www.facebook.com/RepTomReed

Twitter: @RepTomReed

YouTube: www.youtube.com/user/CongressmanTomReed

Instagram: @rep.tomreed

District Offices: 89 W. Market St., Corning, NY 14830; 607-654-7566; Fax: 607-654-7568; *District Director:* Alison Hunt

433 Exchange St., Geneva, NY 14456; 315-759-5229; Fax: 315-325-4045; *Finger Lakes Regional Director:* Taryn Windheim

2 E. 2nd St., #208, Jamestown, NY 14701; 716-708-6369; Fax: 716-708-6058; *Caseworker/Field Rep.:* Katrina Fuller

1 Bluebird Square, Olean, NY 14760-2500; 716-379-8434; Fax: 716-806-1069; *Constituent Services Specialist:* Lee James

Committee Assignment: Ways and Means

Reschenthaler, Guy, R-Pa. (14)

Capitol Hill Office: 531 CHOB 20515-3515; 225-2065; *Chief of Staff:* Aaron Bonnaure

Web: reschenthaler.house.gov

Facebook: www.facebook.com/GReschenthaler

Twitter: @GReschenthaler

District Offices: 700 Pellis Rd., Greensburg, PA 15601; 724-219-4200

14 S. Main St., Washington, PA 15301; 724-206-4800

Committee Assignments: Foreign Affairs; Judiciary

Rice, Kathleen, D-N.Y. (4)

Capitol Hill Office: 2435 RHOB 20515-3204; 225-5516; Fax: 225-5758; *Chief of Staff:* Nell Reilly

Web: kathleenrice.house.gov

Facebook: www.facebook.com/RepKathleenRice

Twitter: @RepKathleenRice

YouTube: www.youtube.com/channel/UCLYLmjrGtzzCFXMWPBxHAug

Instagram: @repkathleenrice

District Office: 229 7th St., #300, Garden City, NY 11530; 516-739-3008; Fax: 516-739-2973; *Deputy District Director:* Amanda Walsh

Committee Assignments: Homeland Security; Veterans' Affairs

Rice, Tom, R-S.C. (7)

Capitol Hill Office: 512 CHOB 20515; 225-9895; Fax: 225-9690; *Chief of Staff:* Jennifer Watson

Web: rice.house.gov

Facebook: www.facebook.com/reptomrice

Twitter: @RepTomRice

YouTube: www.youtube.com/RepTomRice

Instagram: @reptomrice

District Offices: 1831 W. Evans St., #300, Florence, SC 29501; 843-679-9781; Fax: 843-679-9783; *Constituent Service Rep.:* Pam Ratliffe

2411 N. Oak St., #405, Myrtle Beach, SC 29577; 843-445-6459; Fax: 843-445-6418; *District Director:* Andrew Mims

Committee Assignment: Ways and Means

Richmond, Cedric, D-La. (2)

Capitol Hill Office: 506 CHOB 20515; 225-6636; Fax: 225-1988; *Chief of Staff:* Virgil A. Miller

Web: richmond.house.gov

Facebook: www.facebook.com/RepRichmond

Twitter: @RepRichmond

YouTube: www.youtube.com/RepCedricRichmond

Instagram: @repcedric

District Offices: 200 Derbigny St., #3200, Gretna, LA 70053-5876; 504-365-0390; *Deputy District Director:* DeShannon Cobb-Russell

2021 Lakeshore Dr., #309, New Orleans, LA 70122-3501; 504-288-3777; Fax: 504-288-4090; *Deputy Chief of Staff:* Enix Smith

1520 Thomas H. Delpit Dr., #126, Baton Rouge, LA 70802; 225-636-5600; Fax: 225-636-5680; *Deputy District Director:* Darlene Fields

Committee Assignments: Homeland Security; Judiciary

Riggleman, Denver, R-Va. (5)

Capitol Hill Office: 1022 LHOB 20515-3515; 225-4711; *Chief of Staff:* Dave Natonski

Web: riggleman.house.gov

Facebook: www.facebook.com/RepRiggleman

Twitter: @RepRiggleman

YouTube: www.youtube.com/channel/UC8mZiEOiWcSVVyMiUmE0AjQ

Instagram: @repriggleman

District Offices: 686 Berkmar Cir., Charlottesville, VA 22901; 434-973-9631; *District Coord.:* Esther Page

308 Craghead St., #102-D, Danville, VA 24541; 434-791-2596; *District Director:* Denise Van Valkenburg

Committee Assignment: Financial Services

Roby, Martha, R-Ala. (2)

Capitol Hill Office: 504 CHOB 20515-0102; 225-2901; Fax: 225-8913; *Chief of Staff:* Mike Albares

Web: roby.house.gov

Facebook: www.facebook.com/Representative.Martha.Roby

Twitter: @RepMarthaRoby

YouTube: www.youtube.com/RepRoby

Instagram: @martharoby

District Offices: 505 E. Three Notch St., #322, Andalusia, AL 36420-3129; 334-428-1129; Fax: 334-222-3342; *Constituent Services Rep.:* Amelia McMahon

217 Graceland Dr., #5, Dothan, AL 36305-7376; 334-794-9680; Fax: 334-671-1480; *District Director:* Barbara Light

401 Adams Ave., #160, Montgomery, AL 36104-4340; 334-262-7718; Fax: 334-262-8758; *Constituent Services Rep.:* Charlotte Bent

Committee Assignments: Appropriations; Judiciary

Roe, Phil, R-Tenn. (1)

Capitol Hill Office: 102 CHOB 20515; 225-6356; Fax: 225-5714; *Chief of Staff:* Matthew Meyer

Web: roe.house.gov

Facebook: www.facebook.com/DrPhilRoe

Twitter: @DrPhilRoe

YouTube: www.youtube.com/drphilroe

Instagram: @drphilroe

District Offices: 205 Revere St., Kingsport, TN 37660; 423-247-8161; Fax: 423-247-0119; *District Director:* Bill Darden

1609 Walters State CC Dr., #4, Morristown, TN 37813; 423-254-1400; Fax: 423-254-1403; *Caseworker:* Cheryl Bennett; *Caseworker:* Angie Jarnagin

Committee Assignments: Education and Labor; Veterans' Affairs

Rogers, Harold, R-Ky. (5)

Capitol Hill Office: 2406 RHOB 20515; 225-4601; Fax: 225-0940; *Chief of Staff:* Megan Bell

Web: halrogers.house.gov

Facebook: www.facebook.com/CongressmanHalRogers

Twitter: @RepHalRogers

YouTube: www.youtube.com/RepHalRogers

District Offices: 48 S. KY Hwy. 15, Hazard, KY 41701; 606-439-0794; Fax: 606-439-4647; *Field Rep.:* Andrea Begley

110 Resource Court, Suite A, Prestonsburg, KY 41653-7851; 606-886-0844; Fax: 606-889-0371; *Field Rep.:* Adam Rice

551 Clifty St., Somerset, KY 42503; 606-679-8346; Fax: 606-678-4856; *District Director:* Karen Kelly

Committee Assignment: Appropriations

Rogers, Mike, R-Ala. (3)

Capitol Hill Office: 2184 RHOB 20515; 225-3261; Fax: 226-8485; *Chief of Staff:* Chris Brinson

Web: mikerogers.house.gov

Facebook: www.facebook.com/MikeRogersforCongress

Twitter: @RepMikeRogersAL

YouTube: www.youtube.com/MikeRogersAL03

Instagram: @repmikerogersal

District Offices: 1129 Noble St., #104, Anniston, AL 36201; 256-236-5655; Fax: 256-237-9203; *District Director:* Sheri Rollins

G.W. Andrews Federal Bldg., 701 Ave. A, #300, Opelika, AL 36801; 334-745-6221; Fax: 334-742-0109; *Field Rep.:* Alvin Lewis

Committee Assignments: Armed Services; Homeland Security

Rooney, Francis, R-Fla. (19)

Capitol Hill Office: 120 CHOB 20515; 225-2536; Fax: 226-3547; *Chief of Staff:* Jessica Carter
Web: francisrooney.house.gov
Facebook: www.facebook.com/RepRooney
Twitter: @RepRooney
YouTube: www.youtube.com/channel/UC5dLBbrW1JwIGs9h248lk6g
District Offices: 3299 Tamiami Trail East, #105, Naples, FL 34112; 239-252-6225; *District Rep.:* Melany Hernandez
1039 S.E. 9th Ave., #308, Cape Coral, FL 33990; 239-599-6033; Fax: 239-573-7629; *District Director:* Tami Holiday
Committee Assignments: Education and Labor; Foreign Affairs

Rose, John, R-Tenn. (6)

Capitol Hill Office: 1232 LHOB 20515-3515; 225-4231; Fax: 615-206-8980; *Chief of Staff:* Van Hilleary
Web: johnrose.house.gov
Facebook: www.facebook.com/repjohnrose
Twitter: @RepJohnRose
District Offices: 321 E. Spring St., #301 Cookeville, TN 38501; 931-854-9430; Fax: 615-206-8980; *District Director:* Rebecca Foster
355 N. Belvedere Dr., #308, Gallatin, TN 37066; 615-206-8204; Fax: 615-206-8980; *Deputy District Director:* Ray Render
Committee Assignment: Financial Services

Rose, Max, D-N.Y. (11)

Capitol Hill Office: 1529 LHOB 20515-3515; 225-3371; Fax: 226-1272; *Chief of Staff:* Anne Sokolov
Web: maxrose.house.gov
Facebook: www.facebook.com/RepMaxRose
Twitter: @RepMaxRose
YouTube: www.youtube.com/channel/UCW0nSIy4fRxysqrFFSkOcVw
District Offices: 265 New Dorp Lane, 2nd Floor, Staten Island, NY 10306; 718-667-3313; *District Director:* Kevin Elkins
Committee Assignment: Homeland Security, Veterans' Affairs

Rouda, Harley, D-Calif. (48)

Capitol Hill Office: 2300 RHOB 20515-3515; 225-2415; Fax: 226-2263; *Chief of Staff:* Emily Crerand
Web: rouda.house.gov
Facebook: www.facebook.com/RepHarley
Twitter: @RepHarley
YouTube: www.youtube.com/HouseDems
Instagram: @repharleyrouda
District Office: 4000 Westerly Pl., #270, Newport Beach, CA 92660; 714-960-6483; Fax: 833-298-8465; *District Director:* Laura Oatman
Committee Assignments: Oversight and Reform; Transportation and Infrastructure

Rouzer, David, R-N.C. (7)

Capitol Hill Office: 3249 RHOB 20515-3307; 225-2731; Fax: 225-5773; *Chief of Staff:* Melissa Murphy
Web: rouzer.house.gov
Facebook: www.facebook.com/RepRouzer
Twitter: @RepDavidRouzer
YouTube: www.youtube.com/channel/UCBvOxpqoGi1HlHjX9v_gHZw
Instagram: @repdavidrouzer
District Offices: 310 Government Center Dr., #1, Bolivia, NC 28422; 910-253-6111; Fax: 910-253-6114; *District Director:* Chance Lambeth
4001 US Hwy. 301 South, #106, Four Oaks, NC 27524; 919-938-3040; Fax: 919-938-3540; *Deputy District Director:* Lisa Littler
230 Government Center Dr., #113, Wilmington, NC 28403; 910-395-0202; Fax: 910-395-0209; *District Director:* Chance Lambeth
Committee Assignments: Agriculture; Transportation & Infrastructure

Roy, Chip, R-Tex. (21)

Capitol Hill Office: 1319 LHOB 20515-3515; 225-4236; Fax: 225-8628; *Chief of Staff:* Wade Miller
Web: roy.house.gov
Facebook: www.facebook.com/RepChipRoy
Twitter: @RepChipRoy
YouTube: www.youtube.com/channel/UCu6wgN7DvYxUMnywD3XE3TQ
District Offices: 1100 410 Loop N.E., #640, San Antonio, TX 78209; 210-821-5024; Fax: 210-821-5947; *District Director:* Nathan McDaniel
5900 Southwest Pkwy., Bldg 2, #201a, Austin, TX 78735; 512-871-5959
125 Lehmann Dr., #201, Kerrville, TX 78028; 830-896-0154
Committee Assignments: Budget; Oversight and Reform; Veterans' Affairs

Roybal-Allard, Lucille, D-Calif. (40)

Capitol Hill Office: 2083 RHOB 20515; 225-1766; Fax: 226-0350; *Chief of Staff:* Victor Castillo
Web: roybal-allard.house.gov
Facebook: www.facebook.com/RepRoybalAllard
Twitter: @RepRoybalAllard
YouTube: www.youtube.com/RepRoybalAllard
Instagram: @reproybalallard
District Office: 500 Citadel Dr., #320, Commerce, CA 90040; 323-721-8790; Fax: 323-721-8789; *District Chief of Staff:* Ana Figueroa
Committee Assignment: Appropriations

Ruiz, Raul, D-Calif. (36)

Capitol Hill Office: 2342 RHOB 20515; 225-5330; Fax: 225-1238; *Chief of Staff:* Tim Del Monico
Web: ruiz.house.gov
Facebook: www.facebook.com/CongressmanRaulRuizMD
Twitter: @CongressmanRuiz
YouTube: www.youtube.com/RepRaulRuiz

District Offices: 445 E. Florida Ave., 2nd Floor, Hemet, CA 92543; 951-765-2304; Fax: 951-765-3784; *District Director:* Jacqueline Lopez

43875 Washington St., Suite F, Palm Desert, CA 92211; 760-424-8888; Fax: 760-424-8993; *Staff Asst.:* Armando Robles

Committee Assignment: Energy and Commerce

Ruppersberger, C. A. Dutch, D-Md. (2)

Capitol Hill Office: 2206 RHOB 20515-2002; 225-3061; Fax: 225-3094; *Chief of Staff:* Tara Linnehan Oursler
Web: ruppersberger.house.gov
Facebook: www.facebook.com/RepDutchRuppersberger
Twitter: @Call_Me_Dutch
YouTube: www.youtube.com/Ruppersberger
Instagram: @dutchruppersberger
District Office: The Atrium, 375 W. Padonia Rd., #200, Timonium, MD 21093-2130; 410-628-2701; Fax: 410-628-2708; *Constituent Liaison:* Lynn Yates
Committee Assignment: Appropriations

Rush, Bobby L., D-Ill. (1)

Capitol Hill Office: 2188 RHOB 20515-1301; 225-4372; Fax: 226-0333; *Chief of Staff:* Yardly Pollas-Kimble
Web: rush.house.gov
Facebook: www.facebook.com/congressmanbobbyrush
Twitter: @RepBobbyRush
YouTube: www.youtube.com/CongressmanRush
District Office: 11750 S. Western Ave., Chicago, IL 60643-4732; 773-779-2400; Fax: 773-779-2401; *District Director:* Robyn Wheeler Grange
Committee Assignment: Energy and Commerce

Rutherford, John, R-Fla. (4)

Capitol Hill Office: 1711 LHOB 20515; 225-2501; *Chief of Staff:* Kelly Simpson
Web: rutherford.house.gov
Facebook: www.facebook.com/RepRutherfordFL
Twitter: @RepRutherfordFL
District Office: 4130 Salsibury Rd., #2500, Jacksonville, FL 32216; 904-831-5205; *District Director:* Jackie Smith
Committee Assignment: Appropriations

Ryan, Tim, D-Ohio (13)

Capitol Hill Office: 1126 LHOB 20515-3517; 225-5261; Fax: 225-3719; *Chief of Staff:* Ron Grimes
Web: timryan.house.gov
Facebook: www.facebook.com/timryan
Twitter: @RepTimRyan
YouTube: www.youtube.com/TimRyanVision
Instagram: @reptimryan
District Offices: 1030 Tallmadge Ave., Akron, OH 44310; 330-630-7311; Fax: 330-630-7314; *Economic Development Coord.:* Catey Breck

197 W. Market St., Warren, OH 44481-1024; 330-373-0074; Fax: 330-373-0098; *District Director:* Rick Leonard

241 W. Federal St., Youngstown, OH 44503-1207; 330-740-0193; Fax: 330-740-0182; *Constituent Liaison:* Matt Vadas

Committee Assignments: Appropriations; Joint Library

Sablan, Gregorio Kilili Camacho, D-Northern Mariana Is. (At Large)

Capitol Hill Office: 2411 RHOB 20515; 225-2646; Fax: 226-4249; *Chief of Staff:* Robert J. Schwalbach
Web: sablan.house.gov
Facebook: www.facebook.com/congressmansablan
Twitter: @Kilili_Sablan
YouTube: www.youtube.com/CongressmanSablan
Instagram: @kilili_sablan
District Offices: P.O. Box 1361, Rota, MP 96951; 670-532-2647; Fax: 670-532-2649; *Staff Asst.:* Harry Masga
P.O. Box 504879, Saipan, MP 96950; 670-323-2647/8; Fax: 670-323-2649; *District Director:* Mike Tenorio
P.O. Box 520394, Tinian, MP 96952; 670-433-2647; Fax: 670-433-2648; *Staff Asst.:* Edward Hofschneider
Committee Assignments: Education and Labor; Natural Resources; Veterans' Affairs

Sánchez, Linda, D-Calif. (38)

Capitol Hill Office: 2329 RHOB 20515-0539; 225-6676; Fax: 226-1012; *Chief of Staff:* Lea Sulkala
Web: lindasanchez.house.gov
Facebook: www.facebook.com/RepLindaSanchez
Twitter: @RepLindaSanchez
YouTube: www.youtube.com/LindaTSanchez
Instagram: @replindasanchez
District Office: 12440 E. Imperial Hwy., #140, Norwalk, CA 90650; 562-860-5050; Fax: 562-924-2914; *District Director:* Yvette Shahinian
Committee Assignment: Ways and Means

Sarbanes, John P., D-Md. (3)

Capitol Hill Office: 2370 RHOB 20515-2003; 225-4016; Fax: 225-9219; *Chief of Staff:* Dvora Lovinger
Web: sarbanes.house.gov
Facebook: www.facebook.com/RepSarbanes
Twitter: @RepSarbanes
YouTube: www.youtube.com/RepJohnSarbanes
District Office: 600 Baltimore Ave., #303, Towson, MD 21204-4022; 410-832-8890; Fax: 410-832-8898; *District Director:* Fred Hassell
Satellite Offices: Arundel Center, 44 Calvert St., #349, Annapolis, MD 21401-1930; 410-295-1679; Fax: 410-295-1682; (open Tuesday, 11 a.m.–1 p.m. or by appointment); *Community Relations Specialist:* Cecilia Simms
14906 Old Columbia Pike, Burtonsville, MD 20866; 301-421-4078; (open Thursday, 11 a.m.–1 p.m. or by appointment); *Community Relations Specialist:* Cecilia Simms
Committee Assignments: Energy and Commerce; Oversight and Reform

Scalise, Steve, R-La. (1)

Capitol Hill Office: 2049 RHOB 20515; 225-3015;
Fax: 226-0386; *Chief of Staff:* Megan Bel Miller
Web: scalise.house.gov
Facebook: www.facebook.com/RepSteveScalise
Twitter: @GeauxScalise
YouTube: www.youtube.com/RepSteveScalise
Instagram: @stevescalise
District Offices: 1514 Martens Dr., #10, Hammond, LA
70401; 985-340-2185; Fax: 985-340-3122; *District
Director:* Charles Henry
8026 Main St., #700, Houma, LA 70360; 985-879-2300;
Fax: 985-879-2306; *Field Rep.:* Ramona Williamson
21454 Koop Dr., #2C, Mandeville, LA 70471; 985-893-
9064; Fax: 985-893-9707; *Field Rep.:* Danielle Evans
110 Veterans Blvd., #500, Metairie, LA 70005; 504-837-
1259; Fax: 504-837-4239; *Field Rep.:* Ramona
Williamson
Committee Assignment: Energy and Commerce

Scanlon, Mary Gay, D-Pa. (5)

Capitol Hill Office: 1535 LHOB 20515-3515; 225-2011;
Fax: 226-0280; *Chief of Staff:* Roddy Flynn
Web: scanlon.house.gov
Facebook: www.facebook.com/RepMGS
Twitter: @RepMGS
Instagram: @repmgs
District Office: 927 E. Baltimore Ave., East Lansdowne, PA
19050; 610-626-1913; *District Director:* Heather Boyd
Committee Assignments: Judiciary; Rules

Schakowsky, Jan, D-Ill. (9)

Capitol Hill Office: 2367 RHOB 20515-1309; 225-2111;
Fax: 226-6890; *Chief of Staff:* Robert Marcus
Web: schakowsky.house.gov
Facebook: www.facebook.com/janschakowsky
Twitter: @janschakowsky
YouTube: www.youtube.com/RepSchakowsky
Instagram: @janschakowsky
District Offices: 5533 N. Broadway St., #2, Chicago, IL
60640-1405; 773-506-7100; Fax: 773-506-9202; *District
Director:* Leslie Combs
820 Davis St., #105, Evanston, IL 60201-4400; 847-328-
3409; Fax: 847-328-3425; *Grants Coord. and
Constituent Advocate:* Andrew Goczkowski
1852 Johns Dr., Glenview, IL 60025; 847-328-3409;
Fax: 847-328-3425; *Constituent Advocate:* Abbey
Eusebio
Committee Assignments: Budget; Energy and Commerce

Schiff, Adam, D-Calif. (28)

Capitol Hill Office: 2269 RHOB 20515; 225-4176;
Fax: 225-5828; *Chief of Staff:* Jeff Lowenstein
Web: schiff.house.gov
Facebook: www.facebook.com/RepAdamSchiff
Twitter: @RepAdamSchiff
YouTube: www.youtube.com/RepAdamSchiff
Instagram: @repadamschiff

District Office: 245 E. Olive Ave., #200, Burbank, CA
91502; 818-450-2900; Fax: 818-450-2928; *District
Director:* Ann Peifer
Satellite Office: 5500 Hollywood Blvd., #416, Los Angeles,
CA 90028; 323-315-5555 (by appointment only);
District Director: Ann Peifer
Committee Assignment: Permanent Select Intelligence

Schneider, Bradley, D-Ill. (10)

Capitol Hill Office: 1432 LHOB 20515; 225-4835;
Fax: 225-0837; *Chief of Staff:* Connor O'Shea
Web: schneider.house.gov
Facebook: www.facebook.com/
CongressmanBradSchneider
Twitter: @RepSchneider
YouTube: www.youtube.com/RepBradSchneider
Instagram: @repschneider
District Office: 111 Barclay Blvd., #200, Lincolnshire, IL
60069; 847-383-4870; Fax: 847-793-0677; *District
Director:* Magen Ryan
Committee Assignments: Small Business; Ways and Means

Schrader, Kurt, D-Ore. (5)

Capitol Hill Office: 2431 RHOB 20515; 225-5711;
Fax: 225-5699; *Chief of Staff:* Paul Gage
Web: schrader.house.gov
Facebook: www.facebook.com/repschrader
Twitter: @RepSchrader
YouTube: www.youtube.com/RepKurtSchrader
District Offices: 621 High St., Oregon City, OR 97045-
2240; 503-557-1324; Fax: 503-557-1981; *District
Director:* Suzanne Kunse
530 Center St. N.E., #415, Salem, OR 97301; 503-588-9100;
Fax: 503-588-5517; *Caseworker:* Mary Ann Smith
Committee Assignment: Energy and Commerce

Schrier, Kim, D-Wash. (8)

Capitol Hill Office: 1123 LHOB 20515-3515; 225-7761;
Fax: 225-4272; *Chief of Staff:* Erin O'Quinn
Web: schrier.house.gov
Facebook: www.facebook.com/RepKimSchrier
Twitter: @RepKimSchrier
Instagram: @repkimschrier
District Office: 1445 Mall St. N.W., #4, Issaquah, WA
98027; 425-657-1001; *District Director:* Maria
Leininger
Committee Assignments: Agriculture; Education and
Labor

Schweikert, David, R-Ariz. (6)

Capitol Hill Office: 2059 RHOB 20515; 225-2190;
Fax: 225-0096; *Chief of Staff:* Katherina Dimenstein
Web: schweikert.house.gov
Facebook: www.facebook.com/repdavidschweikert
Twitter: @RepDavid
YouTube: www.youtube.com/RepDavidSchweikert
Instagram: @repdavid

District Office: 14500 N. Northsight Blvd., #224, Scottsdale, AZ 85260; 480-946-2411; Fax: 480-946-2446; *District Director:* Ernestina Borquez-Smith
Committee Assignment: Ways and Means

Scott, Austin, R-Ga. (8)

Capitol Hill Office: 2417 RHOB 20515-1008; 225-6531; Fax: 225-3013; *Chief of Staff:* Jason Lawrence
Web: austinscott.house.gov
Facebook: www.facebook.com/RepAustinScott
Twitter: @AustinScottGA08
YouTube: www.youtube.com/RepAustinScott
District Offices: 127-B N. Central Ave., Tifton, GA 31794-4087; 229-396-5175; Fax: 229-396-5179; *District Director:* Alice Johnson
230 Margie Dr., #500, Warner Robins, GA 31088; 478-971-1776; Fax: 478-971-1778; *Field Rep.:* Slayten Carter
Committee Assignments: Agriculture; Armed Services

Scott, David, D-Ga. (13)

Capitol Hill Office: 225 CHOB 20515-1013; 225-2939; Fax: 225-4628; *Chief of Staff and Contact:* Gary Woodward
Web: davidscott.house.gov
Facebook: www.facebook.com/RepDavidScott
Twitter: @repdavidscott
YouTube: www.youtube.com/RepDavidScott
Instagram: @repdavidscott
District Offices: 173 N. Main St., Jonesboro, GA 30236-3567; 770-210-5073; Fax: 770-210-5673; *District Director:* Chandra Harris
888 Concord Rd., #100, Smyrna, GA 30080-4202; 770-432-5405; Fax: 770-432-5813; *Deputy District Director:* Isaac Dodoo
Committee Assignments: Agriculture; Financial Services

Scott, Robert C., D-Va. (3)

Capitol Hill Office: 1201 LHOB 20515-4603; 225-8351; Fax: 225-8354; *Chief of Staff:* David Dailey
Web: bobbyscott.house.gov
Facebook: www.facebook.com/RepBobbyScott
Twitter: @BobbyScott
YouTube: www.youtube.com/RepBobbyScott
Instagram: @repbobbyscott
District Office: 2600 Washington Ave., #1010, Newport News, VA 23607-4333; 757-380-1000; Fax: 757-928-6694; *Legislative Asst.:* Demontre Boone
Committee Assignments: Education and Labor, Chair; Budget

Sensenbrenner, F. James, R-Wisc. (5)

Capitol Hill Office: 2449 RHOB 20515-4905; 225-5101; Fax: 225-3190; *Co-Chief of Staff:* Matt Bisenius
Web: sensenbrenner.house.gov
Facebook: www.facebook.com/RepSensenbrenner
Twitter: @JimPressOffice
YouTube: www.youtube.com/RepSensenbrenner
Instagram: @repjimsensenbrenner

District Office: 120 Bishops Way, #154, Brookfield, WI 53005-6249; 262-784-1111; Fax: 262-784-9437; *Co-Chief of Staff/District Director:* Loni Hagerup
Committee Assignments: Foreign Affairs; Judiciary

Serrano, José E., D-N.Y. (15)

Capitol Hill Office: 2354 RHOB 20515; 225-4361; Fax: 225-6001; *Chief of Staff:* Matthew Alpert
Web: serrano.house.gov
Facebook: www.facebook.com/RepJoseSerrano
Twitter: @RepJoseSerrano
YouTube: www.youtube.com/CongressmanSerrano
Instagram: @repjoseserrano
District Office: 1231 Lafayette Ave., 4th Floor, Bronx, NY 10474-5331; 718-620-0084; Fax: 718-620-0658; *District Director:* Anthony R. Jordan
Committee Assignment: Appropriations

Sewell, Terri A., D-Ala. (7)

Capitol Hill Office: 2201 RHOB 20515; 225-2665; Fax: 226-9567; *Chief of Staff:* Cachavious English
Web: sewell.house.gov
Facebook: www.facebook.com/RepSewell
Twitter: @RepTerriSewell
YouTube: www.youtube.com/RepSewell
Instagram: @repterriasewell
District Offices: Two 20th St. North, #1130, Birmingham, AL 35203-4014; 205-254-1960; Fax: 205-254-1974; *Deputy District Director:* Oscar Berry
2501 7th St., #300, Tuscaloosa, AL 35401; 205-752-5380; 205-752-5899; *Constituent Services Rep.:* Reba Love
101 S. Lawrence St., Courthouse Annex 3, Montgomery, AL 36104; 334-262-1919; Fax: 334-262-1921; *Constituent Services Manager/Outreach Coord.:* Melinda Williams
908 Alabama Ave., Federal Bldg., #112, Selma, AL 36701-4660; 334-877-4414; Fax: 334-877-4489; *Constituent Services Rep.:* Dianna Johnson
Committee Assignments: Ways and Means; Permanent Select Intelligence

Shalala, Donna E., D-Fla. (27)

Capitol Hill Office: 1320 LHOB 20515-3515; 225-3931; Fax: 225-5620; *Chief of Staff:* Jessica Killin
Web: shalala.house.gov
Facebook: www.facebook.com/RepShalala
Twitter: @RepShalala
Instagram: @repshalala
District Office: 7700 N. Kendall Dr., #605, Miami, FL 33156; (305) 668-2285; Fax: 305-668-5970; *District Director:* Raul Martinez Jr.
Committee Assignments: Education and Labor; Rules

Sherman, Brad, D-Calif. (30)

Capitol Hill Office: 2181 RHOB 20515; 225-5911; Fax: 225-5879; *Chief of Staff:* Don MacDonald
Web: sherman.house.gov

Facebook: www.facebook.com/
CongressmanBradSherman
Twitter: @BradSherman
YouTube: www.youtube.com/CongressmanSherman
Instagram: @congressmansherman
District Office: 5000 Van Nuys Blvd., #420, Sherman
Oaks, CA 91403; 818-501-9200; Fax: 818-501-1554;
District Chief of Staff: Scott Abrams
Committee Assignments: Financial Services; Foreign
Affairs; Science, Space, and Technology

Sherrill, Mikie, D-N.J. (11)

Capitol Hill Office: 1208 LHOB 20515-3515; 225-5034;
Fax: 225-3186; *Chief of Staff:* Ethan Saxon
Web: sherrill.house.gov
Facebook: www.facebook.com/RepMikieSherrill
Twitter: @RepSherrill
District Office: 8 Wood Hollow Rd., #203, Parsippany, NJ
07054; 718-620-0084; Fax: 718-620-0658; *District
Director:* Jill Hirsch, Kellie Doucette
Committee Assignments: Armed Services; Science, Space,
and Technology

Shimkus, John, R-Ill. (15)

Capitol Hill Office: 2217 RHOB 20515; 225-5271;
Fax: 225-5880; *Chief of Staff:* Craig A. Roberts
Web: shimkus.house.gov
Facebook: www.facebook.com/repshimkus
Twitter: @RepShimkus
YouTube: www.youtube.com/RepShimkus
District Offices: 201 N. Vermilion St., #325, Danville, IL
61832; 217-446-0664; Fax: 217-446-0670; *District
Aides:* Chuck Hantz and Reno Jamison
101 N. 4th St., #303, Effingham, IL 62401; 217-347-7947;
Fax: 217-342-1219; *District Aide:* Michael Hall
110 E. Locust St., Room 12, Harrisburg, IL 62946-1557; 618-
252-8271; Fax: 618-252-8317; *District Aide:* Jenny Pruitt
15 Professional Park Dr., Maryville, IL 62062; 618-288-7190;
Fax: 618-288-7219; *District Director:* Deb Detmers
Committee Assignment: Energy and Commerce

Simpson, Mike, R-Idaho (2)

Capitol Hill Office: 2084 RHOB 20515; 225-5531;
Fax: 225-8216; *Chief of Staff:* Lindsay J. Slater
Web: simpson.house.gov
Facebook: www.facebook.com/Mike-Simpson-
96007744606
Twitter: @CongMikeSimpson
YouTube: www.youtube.com/CongMikeSimpson
District Offices: 802 W. Bannock St., #600, Boise, ID
83702-5843; 208-334-1953; Fax: 208-334-9533; *District
Director, Communications Director:* Nikki Wallace
410 Memorial Dr., #203, Idaho Falls, ID 83402-3600; 208-
523-6701; Fax: 208-523-2384; *Field Rep.:* Brennan
Summers
650 Addison Ave. West, Twin Falls, ID 83301-3392; 208-
734-7219; Fax: 208-734-7244; *Community
Development Coord.:* Linda Culver
Committee Assignment: Appropriations

Sires, Albio, D-N.J. (8)

Capitol Hill Office: 2268 RHOB 20515-3013;
225-7919; Fax: 226-0792; *Chief of Staff:* Gene
Martorony
Web: sires.house.gov
Facebook: www.facebook.com/RepAlbioSires
Twitter: @RepSires
YouTube: www.youtube.com/RepSiresNJ13
Instagram: @repsires
District Offices: 800 Anna St., Elizabeth, NJ 07201; 908-
820-0692; Fax: 908-820-0694; *Deputy Chief of Staff:*
Ada Morell
257 Cornelison Ave., #4408, Jersey City, NJ 07302; 201-
309-0301; Fax: 201-309-0384; *Communications
Director:* Erica Daughtrey
5500 Palisade Ave., Suite A, West New York, NJ 07093-
2124; 201-558-0800; Fax: 201-617-2809; *Congressional
Aides:* Liz Victorin, Rich Barsa
Committee Assignments: Foreign Affairs; Transportation
and Infrastructure

Slotkin, Elissa, D-Mich. (8)

Capitol Hill Office: 1531 LHOB 20515-3515; 225-4872;
Fax: 225-5820; *Chief of Staff:* Mela Louise Norman
Web: slotkin.house.gov
Facebook: www.facebook.com/RepElissaSlotkin
Twitter: @RepSlotkin
Instagram: @repslotkin
District Office: 1100 W. Saginaw St., #3A, Lansing,
MI 48915; 517-993-0510; *Staff Assistant:* Nina
Capuzzi
Committee Assignments: Armed Services; Homeland
Security

Smith, Adam, D-Wash. (9)

Capitol Hill Office: 2264 RHOB 20515-4709; 225-8901;
Fax: 225-5893; *Chief of Staff:* Shana M. Chandler
Web: adamsmith.house.gov
Facebook: www.facebook.com/RepAdamSmith
Twitter: @RepAdamSmith
YouTube: www.youtube.com/Congressmanadamsmith
Instagram: @repadamsmith
District Office: 101 Evergreen Bldg., 15 S. Grady Way,
Renton, WA 98057; 425-793-5180; Fax: 425-793-5181;
District Director: Caitlyn Cole
Committee Assignment: Armed Services, Chair

Smith, Adrian, R-Neb. (3)

Capitol Hill Office: 502 CHOB 20515; 225-6435; Fax: 225-
0207; *Chief of Staff:* Monica Didiuk
Web: adriansmith.house.gov
Facebook: www.facebook.com/AdrianSmithNE
Twitter: @RepAdrianSmith
YouTube: www.youtube.com/RepAdrianSmith
Instagram: @repadriansmith
District Offices: 1811 W. 2nd St., #275, Grand Island, NE
68803; 308-384-3900; Fax: 308-384-3902; *Constituent
Services Director:* Alex Straatmann

416 Valley View Dr., #600, Scottsbluff, NE 69361-1486; 308-633-6333; Fax: 308-633-6335; *Office Coord.:* Lenora Brotzman

Committee Assignments: Ways and Means

Smith, Chris, R-N.J. (4)

Capitol Hill Office: 2373 RHOB 20515-3004; 225-3765; Fax: 225-7768; *Chief of Staff:* Mary Noonan

Web: chrissmith.house.gov

Facebook: www.facebook.com/RepChrisSmith

Twitter: @RepChrisSmith

YouTube: www.youtube.com/USRepChrisSmith

Instagram: @repchrissmith

District Offices: 4573 S. Broad St., Hamilton, NJ 08620; 609-585-7878; Fax: 609-585-9155; *District Director:* Jeff Sagnip

405 Route 539 (Pinehurst Rd.), Plumsted, NJ 08514; 609-286-2571; Fax: 609-286-2630; *District Director:* Jeff Sagnip

Raintree Shopping Center, 112 Village Center Dr., 2nd Floor, Freehold, NJ 07728; 732-780-3035; Fax: 732-780-3079; *Public Policy Advisor and District Director:* Jo Smith Schloeder

Committee Assignments: Congressional-Executive Commission on China; Foreign Affairs

Smith, Jason, R-Mo. (8)

Capitol Hill Office: 2418 RHOB 20515-2508; 225-4404; Fax: 226-0326; *Chief of Staff:* Mark Roman

Web: jasonsmith.house.gov

Facebook: www.facebook.com/repjasonsmith

Twitter: @RepJasonSmith

YouTube: www.youtube.com/RepJasonSmith

Instagram: @repjasonsmith

District Offices: 830 S. Bishop Ave., Suite A, Rolla, MO 65401-4340; 573-364-2455; Fax: 573-364-1053; *Field Rep.:* Bennie Cook

2502 Tanner Dr., #205, Cape Girardeau, MO 63703; 573-335-0101; Fax: 573-335-1931; *Office Manager, Constituent Services Specialist:* Leslie Herbst

22 E. Columbia St., P.O. Box 1165, Farmington, MO 63640; 573-756-9755; Fax: 573-756-9762; *District Office Director:* Donna Hickman

35 Court Square, #300, West Plains, MO 65775; 417-255-1515; Fax: 417-255-2009

2725 N. Westwood Blvd., #5A, Poplar Bluff, MO 63901

Committee Assignments: Budget; Ways and Means

Smucker, Lloyd, R-Pa. (11)

Capitol Hill Office: 127 CHOB 20515; 225-2411; Fax: 225-2013; *Chief of Staff:* Greg Facchiano

Web: smucker.house.gov

Facebook: www.facebook.com/RepSmucker

Twitter: @RepSmucker

YouTube: www.youtube.com/channel/UCs5iMvWy-oTHyf5HuwB7FCg

District Office: 51 S. Duke St., #201, Lancaster, PA 17602; 717-393-0667; Fax: 717-393-0924; *District Director:* Zachary Peirson

Committee Assignments: Education and Labor; Transportation and Infrastructure

Soto, Darren, D-Fla. (9)

Capitol Hill Office: 1507 LHOB 20515; 225-9889; Fax: 225-9742; *Chief of Staff:* Christine Biron

Web: soto.house.gov

Facebook: www.facebook.com/CongressmanDarrenSoto

Twitter: @RepDarrenSoto

YouTube: www.youtube.com/repdarrensoto

Instagram: @repdarrensoto

District Office: 804 Bryan St., Kissimmee, FL 34741; 407-452-1171; *District Director:* Michelle Martinez

Satellite Offices: 620 E. Main St., Haines City, FL 33844; 202-600-0843 or 202-615-1308; (open Wednesday, 9 a.m.–5 p.m.); *District Director:* Michelle Martinez

451 3rd St. N.W., Winter Haven, FL 33881; 202-600-0843 or 202-615-1308; (open Thursday and Friday, 9 a.m.–5 p.m.); *District Director:* Michelle Martinez

VA Medical Center, 13800 Veterans Way, #1F806, Orlando, FL 32327; 202-322-4476; *Field Rep.:* Pablo Alvarado

201 West Central Ave., Lake Wales, FL 33853; 202-600-0843; *Field Rep.:* Leah West and Darren Vierde

Committee Assignments: Energy and Commerce; Natural Resources

Spanberger, Abigail, D-Va. (7)

Capitol Hill Office: 1239 LHOB 20515; 225-2815; Fax: 225-0011; *Chief of Staff:* Roscoe Jones

Web: spanberger.house.gov

Facebook: www.facebook.com/RepAbigailSpanberger

Twitter: @RepSpanberger

YouTube: www.youtube.com/channel/UC66jKgZXnDVGUrOnwHjpvNg

Instagram: @repspanberger

District Offices: 4201 Dominion Blvd., #110, Glen Allen, VA 23060; 804-401-4110; *District Director:* Karen Mask

9104 Courthouse Rd., #249, Spotsylvania, VA 22553; *District Coord.:* Kristi Black

Committee Assignments: Agriculture; Foreign Affairs

Spano, Ross, R-Fla. (15)

Capitol Hill Office: 224 CHOB 20515-3515; 225-1252; Fax: 226-0585; *Chief of Staff:* Jamie Robinette

Web: spano.house.gov

Facebook: www.facebook.com/RepRossSpano

Twitter: @RepRossSpano

YouTube: www.youtube.com/channel/UC76zj2A9kyui_pjJ5Yj7ewA

District Office: 124 S. Florida Ave., #304, Lakeland, FL 33801; 863-644-8215; Fax: 863-648-0749; *District Director:* Blaine Gravitt

Committee Assignments: Small Business; Transportation and Infrastructure

Speier, Jackie, D-Calif. (14)

Capitol Hill Office: 2465 RHOB 20515; 225-3531; Fax: 226-4183; *Chief of Staff:* Josh Connolly

Web: speier.house.gov

Facebook: www.facebook.com/JackieSpeier
Twitter: @RepSpeier
YouTube: www.youtube.com/JackieSpeierCA12
Instagram: @jackiespeier
District Office: 155 Bovet Rd., #780, San Mateo, CA 94402; 650-342-0300; Fax: 650-375-8270; *District Director:* Brian Perkins
Committee Assignments: Armed Services; Oversight and Reform; Permanent Select Intelligence

Stanton, Greg, D-Ariz. (9)

Capitol Hill Office: 128 CHOB 20515-3515; 225-9888; *Chief of Staff:* Seth Scott
Web: stanton.house.gov
Facebook: www.facebook.com/RepGregStanton
Twitter: @RepGregStanton
District Offices: 2944 N. 44th St., #150, Phoenix, AZ 85018; 602-956-2463; *District Director:* Eric Chalmers
Committee Assignment: Judiciary; Transportation and Infrastructure

Stauber, Pete, R-Minn. (8)

Capitol Hill Office: 126 CHOB 20515-3515; 225-6211; Fax: 225-0699; *Chief of Staff:* Desiree Koetzle
Web: stauber.house.gov
Facebook: www.facebook.com/RepPeteStauber
Twitter: @RepPeteStauber
Instagram: @reppetestauber
District Offices: Brainerd City Hall, 501 Laurel St., Brainerd, MN 56401; 218-355-0862; *Field Rep.:* Louis Crombie
Cambridge City Hall, 300 3rd Ave. N.E., Cambridge, MN 55008; 763-552-3359
Chisholm City Hall, 316 W. Lake St., #7, Chisholm, MN 55719; 218-355-0726; *Field Rep.:* Spencer Igo
5094 Miller Trunk Hwy., #900, Hermantown, MN 55811; 218-481-6396; *District Director:* Isaac Schultz
Committee Assignments: Small Business; Transportation and Infrastructure

Stefanik, Elise, R-N.Y. (21)

Capitol Hill Office: 318 CHOB 20515; 225-4611; Fax: 226-0621; *Chief of Staff:* Anthony Pileggi
Web: stefanik.house.gov
Facebook: www.facebook.com/RepEliseStefanik
Twitter: @RepStefanik
YouTube: www.youtube.com/channel/UCHvf42C8Vw6QnjwO2L2ukKA
Instagram: @elisestefanik
District Office: 23 Durkee St., Suite C, Plattsburgh, NY 12901; 518-561-2324; Fax: 518-561-2408; *Regional Director:* Joel Wood
88 Public Square, Suite A, Watertown, NY 13601; 315-782-3150; Fax: 315-782-1291; *Regional Director:* Mary Jo Richards
5 Orange St., #4 Glens Falls, NY 12801; 518-743-0964; Fax: 518-743-1391; *Regional Director:* Halie Northrop
Committee Assignments: Armed Services; Education and Labor; Permanent Select Intelligence

Steil, Bryan, R-Wisc. (1)

Capitol Hill Office: 1408 LHOB 20515-3515; 225-3031; *Chief of Staff:* Ryan Carney
Web: steil.house.gov
Facebook: www.facebook.com/RepBryanSteil
Twitter: @RepBryanSteil
YouTube: www.youtube.com/repbryansteil
Instagram: @repbryansteil
District Offices: 20 S. Main St., #10, Janesville, WI 53545; 608-752-4050; *District Director:* Susie Liston
Somers Village/Town Hall, 7511 12th St., Somers, WI 53171; 262-654-1901; *District Director:* Susie Liston
Racine County Courthouse, 730 Wisconsin Ave., #101, Racine, WI 53403; 262-637-0510; *District Director:* Susie Liston
Committee Assignment: Financial Services

Steube, W. Gregory, R-Fla. (17)

Capitol Hill Office: 521 CHOB 20515-3515; 225-5792; Fax: 225-3132; *Chief of Staff:* Alex Blair
Web: steube.house.gov
Facebook: www.facebook.com/RepGregSteube
Twitter: @RepGregSteube
Instagram: @repgregsteube
District Offices: 304 2nd St. N.W., Okeechobee, FL 34972; 941-575-9101; Fax: 941-575-9103
226 Taylor St., #230, Punta Gorda, FL 33950; 941-575-9101; Fax: 941-575-9103; *District Director:* Sidney Gruters
4507 George Blvd., Sebring, FL 33875; 941-575-9101; Fax: 941-575-9103
Committee Assignments: Judiciary; Oversight and Reform; Veterans' Affairs

Stevens, Haley, D-Mich. (11)

Capitol Hill Office: 227 CHOB 20515-3515; 225-8171; Fax: 225-2267; *Chief of Staff:* Justin German
Web: stevens.house.gov
Facebook: www.facebook.com/RepHaleyStevens
Twitter: @RepHaleyStevens
Instagram: @rephaleystevens
District Office: 37695 Pembroke Ave., Livonia, MI 48152; 734-853-3040; *District Director:* Colleen Pobur
Committee Assignments: Education and Labor; Science, Space, and Technology

Stewart, Chris, R-Utah (2)

Capitol Hill Office: 2242 RHOB 20515; 225-9730; Fax: 225-9627; *Chief of Staff:* Chris Harmer
Web: stewart.house.gov
Facebook: www.facebook.com/RepChrisStewart
Twitter: @RepChrisStewart
YouTube: www.youtube.com/RepChrisStewart
Instagram: @repchrisstewart
District Offices: 420 E. South Temple St., #390, Salt Lake City, UT 84111; 801-364-5550; Fax: 801-364-5551; *District Director:* Gary Webster

253 W. St. George Blvd., #100, St. George, UT 84770; 435-627-1500; Fax: 435-627-1911; *Southern Utah District Director:* Adam Snow
Committee Assignments: Appropriations; Budget; Permanent Select Intelligence

Stivers, Steve, R-Ohio (15)

Capitol Hill Office: 2234 RHOB 20515-3515; 225-2015; Fax: 225-3529; *Chief of Staff:* Courtney Whetstone
Web: stivers.house.gov
Facebook: www.facebook.com/RepSteveStivers
Twitter: @RepSteveStivers
YouTube: www.youtube.com/RepSteveStivers
Instagram: @repstevestivers
District Offices: 3790 Municipal Way, Hilliard, OH 43026; 614-771-4968; Fax: 614-771-3990; *District Director:* Adam Rapien
104 E. Main St., Lancaster, OH 43130; 740-654-2654; Fax: 740-654-2482; *Field Rep.:* Wil Floyd
69 N. South St., Wilmington, OH 45177; 937-283-7049; Fax: 937-283-7052; *Caseworker:* Sherry Stuckert
Committee Assignment: Financial Services

Suozzi, Thomas, D-N.Y. (3)

Capitol Hill Office: 214 CHOB 20515; 225-3335; Fax: 225-4669; *Chief of Staff:* Mike Florio
Web: suozzi.house.gov
Facebook: www.facebook.com/RepTomSuozzi
Twitter: @RepTomSuozzi
YouTube: www.youtube.com/channel/UCHjLmETJ7qXtciV7dlAzzgQ
Instagram: @reptomsuozzi
District Offices: 478A Park Ave., Huntington, NY 11743; 631-923-4100; Fax: 631-923-3660; *District Director:* Cindy Rogers
250-02 Northern Blvd., Little Neck, NY 11362; 718-631-0400; (open Monday/Tuesday/Thursday, 9 a.m.–5:30 p.m. or by appointment); *District Director:* Cindy Rogers
Committee Assignments: Congressional-Executive Commission on China; Ways and Means

Swalwell, Eric, D-Calif. (15)

Capitol Hill Office: 407 CHOB 20515; 225-5065; Fax: 226-3805; *Chief of Staff:* Alex Evans
Web: swalwell.house.gov
Facebook: www.facebook.com/CongressmanEricSwalwell
Twitter: @RepSwalwell
YouTube: www.youtube.com/ericswalwell
Instagram: @repswalwell
District Office: 3615 Castro Valley Blvd., Castro Valley, CA 94546; 510-370-3322; *District Director:* Mallory DeLauro
Committee Assignments: Judiciary; Permanent Select Intelligence

Takano, Mark, D-Calif. (41)

Capitol Hill Office: 420 CHOB 20515; 225-2305; Fax: 225-7018; *Chief of Staff:* Richard McPike
Web: takano.house.gov

Facebook: www.facebook.com/RepMarkTakano
Twitter: @RepMarkTakano
YouTube: www.youtube.com/RepMarkTakano
Instagram: @repmarktakano
District Office: 3403 10th St., #610, Riverside, CA 92501; 951-222-0203; Fax: 951-222-0217; *District Director:* Rafael Elizalde
Committee Assignments: Education and Labor; Veterans' Affairs, Chair

Taylor, Van, R-Tex. (3)

Capitol Hill Office: 1404 LHOB 20515-3515; 225-4201; Fax: 225-1485; *Chief of Staff:* Lonnie Dietz
Web: vantaylor.house.gov
Facebook: www.facebook.com/RepVanTaylor
Twitter: @RepVanTaylor
Instagram: @repvantaylor
District Offices: 5600 Tennyson Pkwy., #275, Plano, TX 75204; 972-202-4150; *District Director:* Sable Jones
Committee Assignment: Education and Labor; Homeland Security

Thompson, Bennie G., D-Miss. (2)

Capitol Hill Office: 2466 RHOB 20515-2402; 225-5876; Fax: 225-5898; *Chief of Staff:* Andrea Lee
Web: benniethompson.house.gov
Facebook: www.facebook.com/CongressmanBennieGThompson
Twitter: @BennieGThompson
YouTube: www.youtube.com/RepBennieThompson
Instagram: @benniegthompson
District Offices: 107 W. Madison St., P. O. Box 610, Bolton, MS 39041; 601-866-9003; Fax: 601-866-9036; *Field Rep.:* Brenda Funches
910 Courthouse Lane, Greenville, MS 38701-3764; 662-335-9003; Fax: 662-334-1304; *Community Development Coord.:* Timla Washington
728 Main St., Suite A, Greenwood, MS 38930; 662-455-9003; Fax: 662-453-0118; *Field Rep.:* Reginald Moore
3607 Medgar Evers Blvd., Jackson, MS 39213-6364; 601-946-9003; Fax: 601-982-5337; *Senior Caseworker:* Stephen Gavin
263 E. Main St., P.O. Box 356, Marks, MS 38646; 662-326-9003; *Caseworker,Field Rep.:* Sandra Jamison
106 Green Ave., #106, P.O. Box 679, Mound Bayou, MS 38762-9594; 662-741-9003; Fax: 662-741-9002; *Caseworker, Field Rep.:* Cedric Watkins
Committee Assignment: Homeland Security, Chair

Thompson, Glenn (GT), R-Pa. (15)

Capitol Hill Office: 400 CHOB 20515-3805; 225-5121; Fax: 225-5796; *Chief of Staff:* Matthew Brennan
Web: thompson.house.gov
Facebook: www.facebook.com/CongressmanGT
Twitter: @CongressmanGT
YouTube: www.youtube.com/CongressmanGT
Instagram: @congressman_gt

District Offices: 3555 Benner Pike, #101, Bellefonte, PA 16823-8474; 814-353-0215; Fax: 814-353-0218; *Office Manager/Caseworker:* Andrea Dubbs

107 S. Center St., Ebensburg, PA 15931; 814-419-8583; Fax: 814-846-5124; *Field Rep.:* Brian Subich

217 Elm St., Suite B, Oil City, PA 16301; 814-670-0432; Fax: 814-670-0868; *District Director:* Brad Moore

Committee Assignments: Agriculture; Education and Labor

Thompson, Mike, D-Calif. (5)

Capitol Hill Office: 406 CHOB 20515-0501; 225-3311; Fax: 225-4335; *Chief of Staff:* Melanie Rhinehart Van Tassell

Web: mikethompson.house.gov
Facebook: www.facebook.com/RepMikeThompson
Twitter: @RepThompson
YouTube: www.youtube.com/CongressmanMThompson
Instagram: @repmikethompson

District Offices: 2721 Napa Valley Corporate Dr., Napa, CA 94558; 707-226-9898; Fax: 707-251-9800; *District Director:* Brad Onorato

2300 County Center Dr., #A100, Santa Rosa, CA 95403; 707-542-7182; Fax: 707-542-2745; *Sr. Field Rep.:* Rebecca Hermosillo

985 Walnut Dr., Vallejo, CA 94592; 707-645-1888; Fax: 707-645-1870; *District Rep.:* Mel Orpilla

Committee Assignment: Ways and Means

Thornberry, Mac, R-Tex. (13)

Capitol Hill Office: 2208 RHOB 20515-4313; 225-3706; Fax: 225-3486; *Chief of Staff:* Josh Martin

Web: thornberry.house.gov
Facebook: www.facebook.com/repmacthornberry
Twitter: @MacTXPress
YouTube: www.youtube.com/RepMacThornberry
Instagram: @macthornberry

District Offices: 620 S. Taylor St., #200, Amarillo, TX 79101-3541; 806-371-8844; Fax: 806-371-7044; *Deputy District Director:* Paul Simpson

2525 Kell Blvd., #406, Wichita Falls, TX 76308-2829; 940-692-1700; Fax: 940-692-0539; *District Director:* Sandra Ross

Committee Assignment: Armed Services

Timmons, William, R-S.C. (4)

Capitol Hill Office: 313 CHOB 20515-3515; 225-6030; *Chief of Staff:* Moutray McLaren

Web: timmons.house.gov
Facebook: www.facebook.com/RepTimmons
Twitter: @reptimmons

District Offices: 104 S. Main St., #801, Greenville, SC 29601; 864-241-0175; *District Director:* Hope Blackley

101 W. St. John St., #303, Spartanburg, SC 29306; 864-583-3264; *District Director:* Hope Blackley

Committee Assignments: Budget; Education and Labor

Tipton, Scott, R-Colo. (3)

Capitol Hill Office: 218 CHOB 20515-0603; 225-4761; Fax: 226-9669; *Chief of Staff:* Joshua Green

Web: tipton.house.gov
Facebook: www.facebook.com/CongressmanScottTipton
Twitter: @RepTipton
YouTube: www.youtube.com/RepScottTipton
Instagram: @repscotttipton

District Offices: 609 Main St., #105, Box 11, Alamosa, CO 81101-2557; 719-587-5105; Fax: 719-587-5137; *Field Rep.:* Brenda Felmlee

835 E. 2nd Ave., #230, Durango, CO 81301-5474; 970-259-1490; Fax: 970-259-1563

225 N. 5th St., #702, Grand Junction, CO 81501-2658; 970-241-2499; Fax: 970-241-3053

503 N. Main St., #658, Pueblo, CO 81003-3132; 719-542-1073; Fax: 719-542-1127; *District Director:* Brian McCain

Committee Assignment: Financial Services

Titus, Dina, D-Nev. (1)

Capitol Hill Office: 2464 RHOB 20515; 225-5965; Fax: 225-3119; *Chief of Staff:* Jay Gertsema

Web: titus.house.gov
Facebook: www.facebook.com/CongresswomanTitus
Twitter: @repdinatitus
YouTube: www.youtube.com/CongresswomanTitus
Instagram: @dinatitusnv

District Office: 495 S. Main St., 3rd Floor, Las Vegas, NV 89101; 702-220-9823; Fax: 702-220-9841; *District Director:* Vinny Spotleson

Committee Assignments: Foreign Affairs; Homeland Security; Transportation and Infrastructure

Tlaib, Rashida, D-Mich. (13)

Capitol Hill Office: 1628 LHOB 20515-3515; 225-5126; Fax: 225-9985; *Chief of Staff:* Ryan Anderson

Web: tlaib.house.gov
Facebook: www.facebook.com/RepRashida
Twitter: @RepRashida

District Office: 10600 W. Jefferson St., River Rouge, MI 48218; 313-203-7540; *District Director:* Larissa Richardson

Committee Assignments: Financial Services; Oversight and Reform

Tonko, Paul D., D-N.Y. (20)

Capitol Hill Office: 2469 RHOB 20515; 225-5076; Fax: 225-5077; *Chief of Staff:* Clinton Britt

Web: tonko.house.gov
Facebook: www.facebook.com/reppaultonko
Twitter: @RepPaulTonko
YouTube: www.youtube.com/reppaultonko
Instagram: @reppaultonko

District Offices: 19 Dove St., #302, Albany, NY 12210; 518-465-0700; Fax: 518-427-5107; *District Director:* Colleen Williams

61 Church St., Room 309, Amsterdam, NY 12010-4424; 518-843-3400; Fax: 518-843-8874; *Constituent Services Rep.:* Kelly Quist-Demars

105 Jay St., Room 15, Schenectady, NY 12305-1970; 518-374-4547; Fax: 518-374-7908; *Sr. Constituent Rep.:* Cora Schroeter
Committee Assignments: Energy and Commerce; Science, Space, and Technology

Torres, Norma, D-Calif. (35)

Capitol Hill Office: 2444 RHOB 20515; 225-6161; Fax: 225-8671; *Chief of Staff:* James Cho
Web: torres.house.gov
Facebook: www.facebook.com/RepNormaTorres
Twitter: @NormaJTorres
YouTube: www.youtube.com/channel/UCvWY4qKP6–o3pIJY7hhKDg
Instagram: @repnormatorres
District Office: 3200 Inland Empire Blvd., #200B, Ontario, CA 91764; 909-481-6474; Fax: 909-941-1362; *District Director:* Daniel Enz
Committee Assignments: Appropriations; Rules

Torres Small, Xochitl, D-N.M. (2)

Capitol Hill Office: 430 CHOB 20515-3515; 225-2365; Fax: 225-9599; *Chief of Staff:* René Muñoz
Web: torressmall.house.gov
Facebook: www.facebook.com/RepTorresSmall
Twitter: @RepTorresSmall
YouTube: www.youtube.com/housedems
Instagram: @housedemocrats
District Office: 240 S. Water St., Las Cruces, NM 88001; 575-323-6384; *District Director:* Nayomi Valdez
Committee Assignments: Armed Services; Homeland Security

Trahan, Lori, D-Mass. (3)

Capitol Hill Office: 1616 LHOB 20515-3515; 225-3411; *Chief of Staff:* Alicia Molt West
Web: trahan.house.gov
Facebook: www.facebook.com/RepLoriTrahan
Twitter: @RepLoriTrahan
Instagram: @reploritrahan
District Offices: Fitchburg State University Center for Professional Studies, 150B Main St., Fitchburg, MA 01420; 978-459-0101 (open Tuesday/Thursday, 8:30 a.m.–12:00 p.m.)
15 Union St., 4th Floor, Lawrence, MA 01840; 978-258-1138 (open Tuesdays/Thursdays, 8 a.m.–12 p.m.)
126 John St., #12, Lowell, MA 01852; 978-459-0101; *District Director:* Emily Byrne
Committee Assignments: Armed Services; Education and Labor

Trone, David, D-Md. (6)

Capitol Hill Office: 1213 LHOB 20515-3515; 225-2721; *Chief of Staff:* Andy Flick
Web: trone.house.gov
Facebook: www.facebook.com/repdavidtrone
Twitter: @RepDavidTrone
YouTube: www.youtube.com/channel/UCkhS5ZuWjqe3YC2xWnXaK5w

Instagram: @davidjtrone
District Office: One Washington Center, 9801 Washingtonian Blvd., Gaithersburg, MD 20878; 301-926-0324; *District Director:* Sunny Holding
Committee Assignments: Education and Labor; Foreign Affairs

Turner, Michael, R-Ohio (10)

Capitol Hill Office: 2082 RHOB 20515-3503; 225-6465; Fax: 225-6754; *Chief of Staff:* Adam Howard
Web: turner.house.gov
Facebook: www.facebook.com/RepMikeTurner
Twitter: @RepMikeTurner
YouTube: www.youtube.com/channel/UCxbpjLbEoYvOIfuRmfR7CWQ
Instagram: @repmiketurner
District Office: 120 W. 3rd St., #305, Dayton, OH 45402-1819; 937-225-2843; Fax: 937-225-2752; *District Director:* Frank DeBrosse
Committee Assignments: Armed Services; Permanent Select Intelligence

Underwood, Lauren, D-Ill. (14)

Capitol Hill Office: 1118 LHOB 20515-3515; 225-2976; Fax: 225-0697; *Chief of Staff:* Andrea R. Harris
Web: underwood.house.gov
Facebook: www.facebook.com/repunderwood
Twitter: @RepUnderwood
District Office: 490 E. Roosevelt Rd., #202, West Chicago, IL 60185; 630-549-2190; Fax: 630-584-2746; *District Director:* Maria Peterson
Committee Assignments: Education and Labor; Homeland Security; Veterans' Affairs

Upton, Fred, R-Mich. (6)

Capitol Hill Office: 2183 RHOB 20515-2206; 225-3761; Fax: 225-4986; *Chief of Staff:* Joan Hillebrands
Web: upton.house.gov
Facebook: www.facebook.com/RepFredUpton
Twitter: @RepFredUpton
YouTube: www.youtube.com/RepFredUpton
Instagram: @repfredupton
District Offices: 350 E. Michigan Ave., #130, Kalamazoo, MI 49007; 269-385-0039; Fax: 269-385-2888; *District Rep:* Nate Henschel
720 Mail St., St. Joseph, MI 49085-2182; 269-982-1986; Fax: 269-982-0237; *District Director:* Mike Ryan
Committee Assignment: Energy and Commerce

Van Drew, Jefferson, D-N.J. (2)

Capitol Hill Office: 331 CHOB 20515-3515; 225-6572; Fax: 225-3318; *Chief of Staff:* Allison Murphy
Web: vandrew.house.gov
Facebook: www.facebook.com/CongressmanJVD
Twitter: @CongressmanJVD
YouTube: www.youtube.com/channel/UCc5AGO_bQLeiv313Bbr35fg?view_as=subscriber
Instagram: @jeffvandrew

District Office: 5914 Main St., #103, Mays Landing, NJ 08330; 609-625-5008; Fax: 609-625-5071; *District Director:* John Kirk

Committee Assignments: Agriculture; Natural Resources

Vargas, Juan, D-Calif. (51)

Capitol Hill Office: 2244 RHOB 20515; 225-8045; Fax: 225-2772; *Chief of Staff:* Tim Walsh

Web: vargas.house.gov

Facebook: www.facebook.com/RepJuanVargas

Twitter: @RepJuanVargas

YouTube: www.youtube.com/RepJuanVargas

Instagram: @repjuanvargas

District Offices: 333 F St., Suite A, Chula Vista, CA 91910-2624; 619-422-5963; Fax: 619-422-7290; *Field Rep.:* Paola Guzman

380 N. 8th St., #14, El Centro, CA 92243; 760-355-9900; Fax: 760-312-9664; *Sr. Field Rep.:* Tomas Oliva

Committee Assignments: Financial Services; Foreign Affairs

Veasey, Marc, D-Tex. (33)

Capitol Hill Office: 2348 RHOB 20515; 225-9897; Fax: 225-9702; *Chief of Staff:* Askia Surma

Web: veasey.house.gov

Facebook: www.facebook.com/CongressmanMarcVeasey

Twitter: @RepVeasey

YouTube: www.youtube.com/marcveasey

Instagram: @repveasey

District Offices: JP Morgan Chase Bldg., 1881 Sylvan Ave., #108, Dallas, TX 75208; 214-741-1387; Fax: 214-741-2026; *District Director:* Anne Hagan

6707 Brentwood Stair Rd., #200, Fort Worth, TX 76112; 817-920-9086; Fax: 817-920-9324; *Director of Constituent Services:* Jennifer Ward

Committee Assignments: Energy and Commerce; Small Business

Vela, Filemon, D-Tex. (34)

Capitol Hill Office: 307 CHOB 20515; 225-9901; Fax: 225-9770; *Chief of Staff:* Perry Brody

Web: vela.house.gov

Facebook: www.facebook.com/UsCongressmanFilemonVela

Twitter: @RepFilemonVela

YouTube: www.youtube.com/RepFilemonVela

Instagram: @repfilemonvela

District Offices: 500 E. Main St., Alice, TX 78332; 361-230-9776; *District Director:* Jose Pereida

333 Ebony Ave., Brownsville, TX 78520; 956-544-8352; *Cameron County District Director:* Marisela Cortez

1390 W. Expressway 83, San Benito, TX 78586; 956-276-4497; Fax: 956-276-4603; *Hidalgo County District Director:* Sally Lara

500 S. Kansas Ave., Weslaco, TX 785596; 956-520-8273; Fax: 956-520-8277; *Caseworker:* Anissa Guajardo

Committee Assignments: Agriculture; Armed Services

Velázquez, Nydia M., D-N.Y. (7)

Capitol Hill Office: 2302 RHOB 20515-3212; 225-2361; Fax: 226-0327; *Chief of Staff:* Adam Minehardt

Web: velazquez.house.gov

Facebook: www.facebook.com/RepNydiaVelazquez

Twitter: @NydiaVelazquez

YouTube: www.youtube.com/nydiavelazquez

Instagram: @rep_velazquez

District Offices: 266 Broadway, #201, Brooklyn, NY 11211-6215; 718-599-3658; Fax: 718-599-4537; *Exec. Asst.:* Lucy Morcelo

16 Court St., #1006, Brooklyn, NY 11241-1010; 718-222-5819; Fax: 718-222-5830; *District Director:* Daniel Wiley

500 Pearl St., #973, New York, NY 10007; 212-619-2606; Fax: 212-619-4969; *Community Liaison:* Iris Quiñones

Committee Assignments: Small Business, Chair; Financial Services; Natural Resources

Visclosky, Peter, D-Ind. (1)

Capitol Hill Office: 2328 RHOB 20515-1401; 225-2461; Fax: 225-2493; *Chief of Staff:* Mark Lopez

Web: visclosky.house.gov

Facebook: www.facebook.com/repvisclosky

Twitter: @RepVisclosky

YouTube: www.youtube.com/PeteVisclosky1

District Office: 7895 Broadway, Suite A, Merrillville, IN 46410-5529; 219-795-1844; Fax: 219-795-1850; *Constituent Services Director:* Greg Gulvas

Committee Assignment: Appropriations

Wagner, Ann, R-Mo. (2)

Capitol Hill Office: 2350 RHOB 20515; 225-1621; Fax: 225-2563; *Chief of Staff:* Charlie Keller

Web: wagner.house.gov

Facebook: www.facebook.com/RepAnnWagner

Twitter: @RepAnnWagner

YouTube: www.youtube.com/channel/UCy2v2DXXvQnbRc8Zx77Dnsg

Instagram: @repannwagner

District Office: 301 Sovereign Court, #201, Ballwin, MO 63011-4442; 636-779-5449; Fax: 636-779-5457; *District Director:* Miriam Stonebraker

Committee Assignments: Financial Services; Foreign Affairs

Walberg, Tim, R-Mich. (7)

Capitol Hill Office: 2266 RHOB 20515; 225-6276; Fax: 225-6281; *Chief of Staff:* R.J. Laukitis

Web: walberg.house.gov

Facebook: www.facebook.com/RepWalberg

Twitter: @RepWalberg

YouTube: www.youtube.com/RepWalberg

Instagram: @repwalberg

District Office: 401 W. Michigan Ave., Jackson, MI 49201; 517-780-9075; Fax: 517-780-9081; *District Director:* Stephen Rajzer

Committee Assignments: Education and Labor; Energy and Commerce

Walden, Greg, R-Ore. (2)

Capitol Hill Office: 2185 RHOB 20515-3702; 225-6730; Fax: 225-5774; *Chief of Staff:* Lorissa Bounds
Web: walden.house.gov
Facebook: www.facebook.com/repgregwalden
Twitter: @repgregwalden
YouTube: www.youtube.com/RepGregWalden
Instagram: @repgregwalden
District Offices: 1051 Bond St. N.W., #400, Bend, OR 97701-2061; 541-389-4408; Fax: 541-389-4452; *Central Oregon Office Director:* Nick Strader
1211 Washington Ave., La Grande, OR 97850-2535; 541-624-2400; *Field Rep.:* Tucker Billman
14 N. Central Ave., #112, Medford, OR 97501-5912; 541-776-4646; Fax: 541-779-0204; *Southern Oregon Office Director:* Katelyn Pay
Committee Assignment: Energy and Commerce

Walker, Mark, R-N.C. (6)

Capitol Hill Office: 1725 LHOB 20515; 225-3065; Fax: 225-8611; *Chief of Staff:* Scott Luginbill
Web: walker.house.gov
Facebook: www.facebook.com/RepMarkWalker
Twitter: @RepMarkWalker
YouTube: www.youtube.com/channel/UC2w0KJe43jr0Hlhi6J5smhg
Instagram: @repmarkwalker
District Offices: 809 Green Valley Rd., #104, Greensboro, NC 27408; 336-333-5005; *District Director:* Julie Emmons
219B W. Elm St., P.O. Box 812, Graham, NC 27253; 336-229-0159; Fax: 336-350-9514; *Constituent Services Liaison:* Janine Osborne
222 Sunset Ave., #101, Asheboro, NC 27203; 336-626-3060; Fax: 336-629-7819; *Constituent Services Liaison:* Janine Osborne
Committee Assignments: Education and Labor; Homeland Security; House Administration

Walorski, Jackie, R-Ind. (2)

Capitol Hill Office: 419 CHOB 20515; 225-3915; Fax: 225-6798; *Chief of Staff:* Mike Dankler
Web: walorski.house.gov
Facebook: www.facebook.com/RepJackieWalorski
Twitter: @RepWalorski
YouTube: www.youtube.com/repwalorski
Instagram: @jackiewalorski
District Office: 202 Lincolnway East, #101, Mishawaka, IN 46544; 574-204-2645; Fax: 574-217-8735; *District Director:* Brian Spaulding
Satellite Office: 709 Main St., Rochester, IN 46975; 574-223-4373; Fax: 574-217-8735; *District Director:* Brian Spaulding
Committee Assignments: Ethics; Ways and Means

Waltz, Michael, R-Fla. (6)

Capitol Hill Office: 216 CHOB 20515-3515; 225-2706; *Chief of Staff:* Micah Ketchel
Web: waltz.house.gov
Facebook: www.facebook.com/repmichaelwaltz
Twitter: @RepMichaelWaltz
YouTube: www.youtube.com/RepMichaelWaltz
Instagram: @repwaltz
District Offices: 120 S. Florida Ave., #324 Deland, FL 32720; 386-279-0707; Fax: 386-279-0874; *District Director:* Ernie Audino
31 Lupi Ct., #130, Palm Coast, FL 32137; 386-302-0442; Fax: 386-283-5164; *District Director:* Ernie Audino
1000 City Center Dr., 2nd Floor, Port Orange, FL 32129; 386-238-9711; Fax: (386) 238-9714; *District Director:* Ernie Audino
Committee Assignments: Armed Services; Science, Space, and Technology

Wasserman Schultz, Debbie, D-Fla. (23)

Capitol Hill Office: 1114 LHOB 20515; 225-7931; Fax: 226-2052; *Chief of Staff:* Tracie Pough
Web: wassermanschultz.house.gov
Facebook: www.facebook.com/RepDWS
Twitter: @RepDWStweets
YouTube: www.youtube.com/RepWassermanSchultz
Instagram: @repdws
District Offices: 19200 W. Country Club Dr., Aventura, FL 33180-2403; 305-936-5724; Fax: 305-932-9664; *Deputy District Director:* Laurie Flink
777 Sawgrass Corporate Pkwy., Sunrise, FL 33325; 954-845-1179; Fax: 954-845-0396; *District Director:* Vivian Piereschi
Committee Assignments: Appropriations; Oversight and Reform

Waters, Maxine, D-Calif. (43)

Capitol Hill Office: 2221 RHOB 20515-0535; 225-2201; Fax: 225-7854; *Chief of Staff:* Twaun Samuel
Web: waters.house.gov
Facebook: www.facebook.com/MaxineWaters
Twitter: @RepMaxineWaters
YouTube: www.youtube.com/MaxineWaters
Instagram: @repmaxinewaters
District Office: 10124 S. Broadway, #1, Los Angeles, CA 90003-4535; 323-757-8900; Fax: 323-757-9506; *District Director:* Blanca Jimenez
Committee Assignment: Financial Services, Chair

Watkins, Steve, R-Kans. (2)

Capitol Hill Office: 1205 LHOB 20515-3515; 225-6601; Fax: 225-7986; *Chief of Staff:* Colin Brainard
Web: watkins.house.gov
Facebook: www.facebook.com/CongressmanSteveWatkins
Twitter: @Rep_Watkins
YouTube: www.youtube.com/channel/UCwBArNt6l7uls9czARQsLtA

District Offices: 1001 N. Broadway St., Suite C, Pittsburg, KS 66762; 620-231-5966; *District Director:* Will Callen
3550 5th St. S.W., Topeka, KS 66606; 785-234-5966; *District Director:* Bill Roe
Committee Assignments: Education and Labor; Foreign Affairs; Veterans' Affairs

Watson Coleman, Bonnie, D-N.J. (12)

Capitol Hill Office: 2442 RHOB 20515; 225-5801; Fax: 225-6025; *Chief of Staff:* James Gee
Web: watsoncoleman.house.gov
Facebook: www.facebook.com/RepBonnie
Twitter: @RepBonnie
YouTube: www.youtube.com/channel/ UCrxEaX0VKZKwg3930du2D5A
Instagram: @repbonnie
District Office: 850 Bear Tavern Rd., #201, Ewing, NJ 08628; 609-883-0026; Fax: 609-883-2093; *District Director:* Kari Osmond
Committee Assignments: Appropriations; Homeland Security

Weber, Randy, R-Tex. (14)

Capitol Hill Office: 107 CHOB 20515; 225-2831; Fax: 225-0271; *Chief of Staff:* Chara McMichael
Web: weber.house.gov
Facebook: www.facebook.com/TXRandy14
Twitter: @TXRandy14
YouTube: www.youtube.com/TXRandy14
Instagram: @txrandy14
District Offices: 350 Pine St., #730, Beaumont, TX 77701; 409-835-0108; Fax: 409-835-0578; *Deputy District Director:* Blake Hopper
122 West Way, #301, Lake Jackson, TX 77566-5245; 979-285-0231; Fax: 979-285-0271; *Community Liaison:* Dodie Armstrong
174 Calder Rd., #150, League City, TX 77573; 281-316-0231; Fax: 281-316-0271; *District Director:* Jed Webb
Committee Assignments: Science, Space, and Technology; Transportation and Infrastructure

Webster, Daniel, R-Fla. (11)

Capitol Hill Office: 1210 LHOB 20515; 225-1002; Fax: 226-6559; *Chief of Staff:* Jaryn Emhof
Web: webster.house.gov
Facebook: www.facebook.com/RepWebster
Twitter: @RepWebster
YouTube: www.youtube.com/repdanwebster
District Office: 318 S. 2nd St., Suite A, Leesburg, FL 34748; 352-241-9220; Fax: 352-241-9181; *District Director:* Christa Pearson
Satellite Offices: 8015 E. County Rd. 466, Suite B, The Villages, FL 32162; 352-383-3552; (open Monday/Wednesday); *District Director:* Christa Pearson
212 W. Main St., #208A, Inverness, FL 34451; 352-241-9204; (open Tuesday/Thursday); *District Director:* Christa Pearson

15 N. Main St., Suite B, Brooksville, FL 34601; 352-241-9230; (open Tuesday/Thursday); *District Director:* Christa Pearson
Committee Assignments: Natural Resources; Transportation and Infrastructure

Welch, Peter, D-Vt. (At Large)

Capitol Hill Office: 2187 RHOB 20515; 225-4115; Fax: 225-6790; *Chief of Staff:* Bob Rogan
Web: welch.house.gov
Facebook: www.facebook.com/PeterWelch
Twitter: @PeterWelch
YouTube: www.youtube.com/RepPeterWelch
Instagram: @reppeterwelch
District Office: 128 Lakeside Ave., #235, Burlington, VT 05401; 802-652-2450; Fax: 802-652-2497; *State Director:* George Twigg
Committee Assignments: Energy and Commerce; Oversight and Reform; Permanent Select Intelligence

Wenstrup, Brad, R-Ohio (2)

Capitol Hill Office: 2419 RHOB 20515; 225-3164; Fax: 225-1992; *Chief of Staff:* Derek Harley
Web: wenstrup.house.gov
Facebook: www.facebook.com/RepBradWenstrup
Twitter: @RepBradWenstrup
YouTube: www.youtube.com/repbradwenstrup
Instagram: @repbradwenstrup
District Offices: 7954 Beechmont Ave., #200, Cincinnati, OH 45255; 513-474-7777; Fax: 513-605-1377; *District Director/Deputy Chief of Staff:* Jeff Groenke
170 N. Main St., Peebles, OH 45660; 513-605-1380; Fax: 937-798-4024; *Sr. Constituent Liaison:* Teresa Lewis
4350 Aicholtz Rd., Cincinnati, OH 45245
Committee Assignments: Ways and Means; Permanent Select Intelligence

Westerman, Bruce, R-Ark. (4)

Capitol Hill Office: 209 CHOB 20515-0404; 225-3772; Fax: 225-1314; *Chief of Staff:* Vivian Moeglein
Web: westerman.house.gov
Facebook: www.facebook.com/RepWesterman
Twitter: @RepWesterman
YouTube: www.youtube.com/channel/ UCNshPbmupCwP5a7Hi79jETQ
Instagram: @repwesterman
District Offices: 101 N. Washington Ave., #406, El Dorado, AR 71730; 870-864-8946; Fax: 870-864-8958; *District Director:* Jason D. McGehee
101 Reserve St., #200, Hot Springs, AR 71901; 501-609-9796; Fax: 501-609-9887; *District Director:* Jason D. McGehee
211 W. Commercial St., Ozark, AR 72949; 479-667-0075; Fax: 501-609-9887; *Field Rep.:* Robert Ballinger
100 E. 8th Ave., Room 2521, Pine Bluff, AR 71601; 870-536-8178; Fax: 870-536-8364; *District Director:* Jason D. McGehee
Committee Assignments: Natural Resources; Transportation and Infrastructure

Wexton, Jennifer, D-Va. (10)

Capitol Hill Office: 1217 LHOB 20515-3515; 225-5136; Fax: 225-0437; *Chief of Staff:* Abby Carter
Web: wexton.house.gov
Facebook: www.facebook.com/CongresswomanWexton
Twitter: @RepWexton
Instagram: @repwexton
District Office: 21351 Gentry Dr., #140, Sterling, VA 20166; 703-234-3800; *District Director:* Erica Constance
Committee Assignments: Financial Services; Science, Space, and Technology

Wild, Susan, D-Pa. (7)

Capitol Hill Office: 1607 LHOB 20515-3515; 225-6411; *Chief of Staff:* Jed Ober
Web: wild.house.gov
Facebook: www.facebook.com/repsusanwild
Twitter: @RepSusanWild
Instagram: @repsusanwild
District Offices: 840 Hamilton St., #303, Allentown, PA 18101; 484-781-6000; *District Director:* Megan Beste
400 Northampton St., #503, Easton, PA 18042; 610-333-1170; *District Director:* Megan Beste
Committee Assignments: Education and Labor; Ethics; Foreign Affairs

Williams, Roger, R-Tex. (25)

Capitol Hill Office: 1708 LHOB 20515; 225-9896; Fax: 225-9692; *Chief of Staff:* Colby Hale
Web: williams.house.gov
Facebook: www.facebook.com/RepRogerWilliams
Twitter: @RepRWilliams
YouTube: www.youtube.com/channel/UCBtfmMMQarjtLB9U_pWMOhw
District Offices: 1005 Congress Ave., #925, Austin, TX 78701; 512-473-8910; Fax: 817-774-2576; *District Director:* John Etue
115 S. Main St., #206, Cleburne, TX 76033; 817-774-2575; Fax: 817-774-2576; *District Rep.:* Robert Camacho
Committee Assignment: Financial Services

Wilson, Frederica S., D-Fla. (24)

Capitol Hill Office: 2445 RHOB 20515; 225-4506; Fax: 226-0777; *Chief of Staff:* Chasseny Lewis
Web: wilson.house.gov
Facebook: www.facebook.com/RepWilson
Twitter: @RepWilson
YouTube: www.youtube.com/RepFredericaWilson
Instagram: @repwilson
District Offices: 18425 2nd Ave. N.W., #355, Miami Gardens, FL 33169-4534; 305-690-5905; Fax: 305-690-5951; *District Chief of Staff:* Alexis Snyder
West Park City Hall, 1965 S. State Rd. 7, West Park, FL 33023; 954-989-2688;
Pembroke Pines City Hall, 10100 Pines Blvd., Bldg. B, Third Floor, Pembroke Pines, FL 33026; 954-450-6767; (open Wednesday 9 a.m.–5 p.m.); *District Director:* Joyce Postell

Committee Assignments: Education and Labor; Transportation and Infrastructure

Wilson, Joe, R-S.C. (2)

Capitol Hill Office: 1436 LHOB 20515; 225-2452; Fax: 225-2455; *Chief of Staff:* Jonathan Day
Web: joewilson.house.gov
Facebook: www.facebook.com/JoeWilson
Twitter: @RepJoeWilson
YouTube: www.youtube.com/RepJoeWilson
Instagram: @repjoewilson
District Offices: 1930 University Pkwy., #1600, Aiken, SC 29801; 803-642-6416; Fax: 803-642-6418; *Special Asst.:* Martha Ruthven
1700 Sunset Blvd. (U.S. 378), #1, West Columbia, SC 29169; 803-939-0041; Fax: 803-939-0078; *District Director:* Butch Wallace
Committee Assignments: Armed Services; Foreign Affairs

Wittman, Robert J., R-Va. (1)

Capitol Hill Office: 2055 RHOB 20515; 225-4261; Fax: 225-4382; *Chief of Staff:* Carolyn King
Web: wittman.house.gov
Facebook: www.facebook.com/RepRobWittman
Twitter: @RobWittman
YouTube: www.youtube.com/RobWittman
Instagram: @reprobwittman
District Offices: 95 Dunn Dr., #201, Stafford, VA 22556; 540-659-2734; Fax: 540-659-2737; *Outreach Coord.:* Karen Klotz
508 Church Lane, P.O. Box 3106, Tappahannock, VA 22560; 804-443-0668; Fax: 804-443-0671; *Deputy District Director:* Chris Jones
6501 Mechanicsville Turnpike, #102, Mechanicsville, VA 23111; 804-730-6595; Fax: 804-730-6597; *District Director:* Joe Schumacher
Committee Assignments: Armed Services; Natural Resources

Womack, Steve, R-Ark. (3)

Capitol Hill Office: 2412 RHOB 20515; 225-4301; Fax: 225-5713; *Chief of Staff:* Beau T. Walker
Web: womack.house.gov
Facebook: www.facebook.com/RepSteveWomack
Twitter: @rep_stevewomack
YouTube: www.youtube.com/CongressmanWomack
Instagram: @rep_stevewomack
District Offices: 60101 Phoenix Ave., #4, Fort Smith, AR 72903; 479-424-1146; Fax: 479-424-2737; *Field Rep.:* Janice Scaggs
303 N. Main St., #102, Harrison, AR 72601-3508; 870-741-6900; Fax: 870-741-7741; *Field Rep.:* Teri Garrett
3333 Pinnacle Hills Pkwy., #120, Rogers, AR 72758-9100; 479-464-0446; Fax: 479-464-0063; *Field Rep.:* Jeff Thacker
Committee Assignments: Appropriations; Budget, Chair

Woodall, Robert, R-Ga. (7)

Capitol Hill Office: 1724 LHOB 20515-1007; 225-4272; Fax: 225-4696; *Chief of Staff:* Derick Corbett

Web: woodall.house.gov
Facebook: www.facebook.com/RepRobWoodall
Twitter: @RepRobWoodall
YouTube: www.youtube.com/RobWoodallGA07
Instagram: @reprobwoodall
District Office: 75 Langley Dr., Lawrenceville, GA 30046-6935; 770-232-3005; Fax: 770-232-2909; *District Director:* Debra Poirot
Committee Assignments: Budget; Rules; Transportation and Infrastructure

Wright, Ron, R-Tex. (6)

Capitol Hill Office: 428 CHOB 20515-3515; 225-2002; Fax: 225-3052; *Chief of Staff:* Ryan Thompson
Web: wright.house.gov
Facebook: www.facebook.com/Congressman-Ron-Wright-594717754318936/?modal=admin_todo_tour
Twitter: @RepRonWright
YouTube: www.youtube.com/channel/UCPcScwg3VXeusn8tUaenkAA
District Office: 5840 W. Ronald Reagan Memorial Hwy., #115, Arlington, TX 76017 *District Director:* Andy Ngyuen
Committee Assignments: Education and Labor; Foreign Affairs

Yarmuth, John A., D-Ky. (3)

Capitol Hill Office: 402 CHOB 20515; 225-5401; Fax: 225-5776; *Chief of Staff:* Julie Carr
Web: yarmuth.house.gov
Facebook: www.facebook.com/RepJohnYarmuth
Twitter: @RepJohnYarmuth
YouTube: www.youtube.com/RepJohnYarmuth
District Offices: Romano L. Mazzoli Federal Bldg., 600 Martin Luther King, Jr. Pl., #216, Louisville, KY 40202; 502-582-5129; Fax: 502-582-5897; *District Director:* Nicole Yates
Southwest Government Center, 7219 Dixie Hwy., Louisville, KY 40258-3756; 502-933-5863; Fax: 502-935-6934; *Congressional Aide:* Shelley Spratt
Committee Assignment: Budget, Chair

Yoho, Ted, R-Fla. (3)

Capitol Hill Office: 1730 LHOB 20515; 225-5744; Fax: 225-3973; *Chief of Staff:* Larry Calhoun
Web: yoho.house.gov
Facebook: www.facebook.com/CongressmanTedYoho
Twitter: @RepTedYoho
YouTube: www.youtube.com/RepTedYoho
Instagram: @reptedyoho
District Offices: 5000 27th Court N.W., Suite A, Gainesville, FL 32606; 352-505-0838; Fax: 352-505-3511; *Deputy Chief of Staff:* Kat Cammack *District Director:* Jessica Norfleet
35 Knight Boxx Rd., #1, Orange Park, FL 32065; 904-276-9626; Fax: 904-276-9336; *Constituent Advocate:* Dorothy Richardson

2509 Crill Ave., #200, Palatka, FL 32177, 386-326-7221; (open Tuesday/Thursday); *District Director:* Jessica Norfleet
Committee Assignments: Agriculture; Foreign Affairs

Young, Don, R-Alaska (At Large)

Capitol Hill Office: 2314 RHOB 20515-0201; 225-5765; Fax: 225-0425; *Chief of Staff:* Pamela A. Day
Web: donyoung.house.gov
Facebook: www.facebook.com/RepDonYoung
Twitter: @repdonyoung
YouTube: www.youtube.com/RepDonYoung
Instagram: @repdonyoung
District Offices: 471 W. 36th Ave., #201, Anchorage, AK 99503-5920; 907-271-5978; Fax: 907-271-5950; *State Director:* Chad Padgett
Key Bank Bldg., 100 Cushman St., #307, Fairbanks, AK 99701; 907-456-0210; Fax: 907-456-0279; *Special Asst.:* Kim Stickler
Committee Assignments: Natural Resources; Transportation and Infrastructure

Zeldin, Lee, R-N.Y. (1)

Capitol Hill Office: 2441 RHOB 20515-3201; 225-3826; Fax: 225-3143; *Chief of Staff:* Eric Amidon
Web: zeldin.house.gov
Facebook: www.facebook.com/RepLeeZeldin
Twitter: @RepLeeZeldin
YouTube: www.youtube.com/repleezeldin
Instagram: @repleezeldin
District Office: 31 Oak St., #20, Patchogue, NY 11772; 631-289-1097; Fax: 631-289-1268; *District Director:* Mark Woolley
Satellite Office: 30 W. Main St., #201, Riverhead, NY 11901; 631-209-4235; (open Tuesday/Wednesday/Thursday, 10 a.m.–2 p.m. by appointment only); *District Director:* Mark Woolley
Committee Assignments: Financial Services; Foreign Affairs

Vacant, N.C. (3)

Capitol Hill Office: 2333 RHOB 20515; 225-3415
District Offices: 1105-C Corporate Dr., Greenville, NC 27858; 252-931-1003

Vacant, N.C. (9)

Capitol Hill Office: 132 CHOB 20515; 225-1976

Vacant, Pa. (12)

Capitol Hill Office: 1717 LHOB 20515; 225-3731
District Offices: 713 Bridge St., #29, Selinsgrove, PA 17870; 570-374-9469; Fax: 570-374-9589; *District Rep.:* Aimee Snyder
181 W. Tioga St., #2, Tunkhannock, PA 18657; 570-996-6550
1020 Commerce Park Dr., #1A, Williamsport, PA 17701-5434; 570-322-3961; Fax: 570-322-3965

Joint Committees of Congress

The joint committees of Congress follow. Each listing includes room number, office building, zip code, telephone number, Web address(es), key staffers, committee jurisdiction, and membership (in order of seniority) for each committee. Members are drawn from the Senate and House and from both parties. This information is current as of April 12, 2019.

Senate Republicans, the current majority in that chamber, are shown in roman type; Democrats, in the minority, appear in italic. On the other hand, House Democrats are shown in roman type due to their majority in that chamber; while House Republicans appear in italics. When a senator serves as chair, the vice chair usually is a representative, and vice versa. The location of the chair usually rotates from one chamber to the other at the beginning of each Congress. The area code for all phone and fax numbers is (202). A phone number and/or office number next to either the Majority or Minority Staff Director indicates a change from the full committee's office number and/or phone number. If no numbers are listed, the individual's office number and phone number are the same as for the full committee.

JOINT ECONOMIC COMMITTEE

Office: G-01 SDOB 20510-6075
Phone: 224-5171; **Fax:** 224-0240
Web: www.jec.senate.gov
Minority Web: www.jec.senate.gov/public/index.cfm/minority
Majority Staff Director: Scott Winship
Minority Staff Director: Harry Gulag
 Jurisdiction: (1) make a continuing study of matters relating to the Economic Report of the President; (2) study means of coordinating programs in order to further the policy of this Act; and (3) as a guide to the several committees of the Congress dealing with legislation relating to the Economic Report, not later than March 1 of each year (beginning with the year 1947) to file a report with the Senate and the House of Representatives containing its findings and recommendations with respect to each of the main recommendations made by the President in the Economic Report, and from time to time to make other reports and recommendations to the Senate and the House of Representatives as it deems advisable.
Party Ratio: R 10-D 10

Senate Members

Mike Lee, Utah, Vice Chair	*Martin Heinrich, N.M.*
Tom Cotton, Ark.	*Amy Klobuchar, Minn.*
Ben Sasse, Neb.	*Gary C. Peters, Mich.*
Rob Portman, Ohio	*Maggie Hassan, N.H.*
Ted Cruz, Tex.	
Bill Cassidy, La.	

House Members

Carolyn Maloney, N.Y., Vice Chair	*David Schweikert, Ariz.*
Don Beyer, Va.	*Darin Lahood, Ill.*
Denny Heck, Wash.	*Kenny Marchant, Tex.*
David Trone, Md.	*Jaime Herrera Beutler,*
Joyce Beatty, Ohio.	*Wash.*
Lois Frankel, Fla.	

JOINT COMMITTEE ON THE LIBRARY

Office: 1307 LHOB 20515-6157
Phone: 225-2061 **Fax:** 226-2061
Web: cha.house.gov/jointcommittees/joint-committee-library
Majority Staff Director: Kyle Anderson

Minority Staff Director: Jen Doulby; 1309 LHOB 20515-6157; 225-8281
 Jurisdiction: considers proposals concerning the management and expansion of the Library of Congress, the development and maintenance of the National Sanctuary Hall Collection and the United States Botanic Garden, the receipt of gifts for the benefit of the Library, and certain matters relating to placing of statues and other works of art in the United States Capitol.
Party Ratio: R 5-D 5

Senate Members

Roy Blunt, Mo., Chair	*Patrick J. Leahy, Vt.*
Richard Shelby, Ala.	*Amy Klobuchar, Minn.*
Pat Roberts, Kans.	

House Members

Zoe Lofgren, Calif., Vice Chair	*Rodney Davis, Ill.*
Tim Ryan, Ohio	*Barry Loudermilk, Ga.*
G.K. Butterfield, N.C.	

JOINT COMMITTEE ON PRINTING

Office: 1307 LHOB 20515
Phone: 225-2061 **Fax:** 226-2061
Web: http://cha.house.gov/jointcommittees/joint-committee-on-printing
Majority Professional Staff Member: Katie Ryan
Minority Professional Staff Member: Jen Doulby; 1309 LHOB; 225-8281
 Jurisdiction: oversight of (1) the functions of the Government Printing Office and general printing procedures of the federal government; and (2) compliance by federal entities with Title 44 of the U.S. Code, and the Government Printing and Binding Regulations.
Party Ratio: R 5-D 5

Senate Members

Roy Blunt, Mo., Vice Chair	*Amy Klobuchar, Minn.*
Pat Roberts, Kans.	*Tom Udall, N.M.*
Roger F. Wicker, Miss.	

House Members

Zoe Lofgren, Calif., Chair	*Rodney Davis, Ill.*
Jamie Raskin, Md.	*Barry Loudermilk, Ga.*
Susan Davis, Calif.	

JOINT COMMITTEE ON TAXATION

Office: 502 FHOB 20515-6453
Phone: 225-3621 **Fax:** 225-0832
Web: www.jct.gov
Chief of Staff: Thomas A. Barthold
Deputy Chief of Staff: Robert P. Harvey; 226-7575
  Jurisdiction: involved with every aspect of the tax legislative process, including: (1) assisting Congressional tax-writing committees and Members of Congress with development and analysis of legislative proposals; (2) preparing official revenue estimates of all tax legislation considered by the Congress; (3) drafting legislative histories for tax-related bills; (4) investigating various aspects of the Federal tax system.
Party Ratio: R 5-D 5

Senate Members

Chuck Grassley, Iowa, Vice Chair
Mike Crapo, Idaho
Michael B. Enzi, Wyo.

Ron Wyden, Ore.
Debbie Stabenow, Mich.

House Members

Richard Neal, Mass., Chair
John Lewis, Ga.
Lloyd Doggett, Tex.

Kevin Brady, Tex.
Devin Nunes, Calif.

COMMISSION ON SECURITY AND COOPERATION IN EUROPE (HELSINKI COMMISSION)

Office: 234 FHOB 20515-6460
Phone: 225-1901 **Fax:** 226-4199
Web: www.csce.gov
Chief of Staff: Alex T. Johnson
Senior Senate Policy Advisor: Kyle Parker
  Jurisdiction: The Commission is authorized and directed to monitor the acts of the signatories that reflect compliance with or violation of the articles of the Final Act of the Conference on Security and Cooperation in Europe, with particular regard to the provisions relating to human rights and Cooperation in Humanitarian Fields. The Commission is further authorized and directed to monitor and encourage the development of programs and activities of the United States Government and private organizations with a view toward taking advantage of the provisions of the Final Act to expand East-West economic cooperation and a greater interchange of people and ideas between East and West.
Party Ratio: R 9-D 8

Senate Members

Roger Wicker, Miss., Co-Chair
John Boozman, Ark.
Marco Rubio, Fla.
Thom Tillis, N.C.
Cory Gardner, Colo.

Benjamin L. Cardin, Md.,
  Ranking Member
Jeanne Shaheen, N.H.
Tom Udall, N.M.
Sheldon Whitehouse, R.I.

House Members

Alcee L. Hastings, Fla., Chair
Steve Cohen, Tenn.
Sheila Jackson Lee, Tex.

Chris Smith, N.J., Ranking
  Member
Robert B. Aderholt, Ala.

Gwen Moore, Wisc.

Michael C. Burgess
Richard Hudson, N.C.

CONGRESSIONAL-EXECUTIVE COMMISSION ON CHINA

Office: 243 FHOB 20515-0001
Phone: 226-3766 **Fax:** 226-3804
Web: www.cecc.gov
CECC Political Prisoner Database: www.cecc.gov/resources/political-prisoner-database
International Human Rights Materials: www.cecc.gov/resources/international-human-rights-materials
Staff Director: Jonathan Stivers, 226-3821
Deputy Staff Director: Vacant, 226-3798
  Jurisdiction: The Commission shall: (a) monitor the acts of the People's Republic of China which reflect compliance with or violation of human rights, in particular, those contained in the International Covenant on Civil and Political Rights and in the Universal Declaration of Human Rights; (b) compile and maintain lists of persons believed to be imprisoned, detained, or placed under house arrest, tortured, or otherwise persecuted by the Government of the People's Republic of China due to their pursuit of the rights described in subsection (a), and exercise appropriate discretion, including concerns regarding the safety and security of, and benefit to, the persons who may be included on the lists and their families; (c) monitor the development of the rule of law in the People's Republic of China; (d) monitor and encourage the development of programs and activities of the United States Government and private organizations with a view toward increasing the interchange of people and ideas between the United States and the People's Republic of China and expanding cooperation in areas; (e) seek out and maintain contacts with nongovernmental organizations, including receiving reports and updates from such organizations and evaluating such reports; (f) cooperate with the Special Coordinator for Tibetan Issues in the Department of State; (g) issue an annual report to the President and the Congress setting forth the findings of the Commission during the preceding 12-month period, in carrying out subsections (a) through (c); (h) include specific information in the report as to the nature and implementation of laws or policies concerning the rights set forth; (i) hold hearings on the contents of the report; (j) submit to the President and the Congress reports that supplement the annual reports, as appropriate.
Party Ratio: R 7-D 9

Senate Members

Marco Rubio, Fla., Co-Chair
James Lankford, Okla.
Tom Cotton, Ark.
Steve Daines, Mont.
Todd Young, Ind.

Dianne Feinstein, Calif.
Jeff Merkley, Ore.
Gary Peters, Mich.
Angus S. King Jr., Maine (I)

House Members

James McGovern, Mass., Chair
Marcy Kaptur, Ohio
Thomas Suozzi, N.Y.
Tom Malinowski, N.J.
Ben McAdams, Utah

Chris Smith, N.J.
Brian Mast, Fla.
Vacant
Vacant

Senate Committees

The standing and select committees of the U.S. Senate follow. This information is current as of April 12, 2019. Each listing includes room number, office building, zip code, telephone and fax numbers, web address, minority web address if available, key majority and minority staff members, jurisdiction for the full committee, and party ratio. Subcommittees are listed under the full committees. Members are listed in order of seniority on the committee or subcommittee. Many committees and subcommittees may be contacted via web-based email forms found on their websites. A phone number and/or office number next to either the Majority or Minority Staff Director indicates a change from the full committee's office number and/or phone number. If no numbers are listed, the individual's office number and phone number are the same as for the full committee.

Republicans, the current majority, are shown in roman type; Democrats, in the minority, appear in italic. The top name in the italicized list is the Ranking Minority Member. Bernard Sanders, I-Vt., and Angus S. King Jr., I-Maine, caucus with the Democrats and accrue committee seniority with Democrats; thus, they are counted with the Democrats in the party ratio, although (I) appears after their names. The partisan committees of the Senate are listed on page 927. The area code for all phone and fax numbers is (202).

AGRICULTURE, NUTRITION, AND FORESTRY

Office: 328A SROB 20510-6000
Phone: 224-2035 **Fax:** 228-2125
Web: www.agriculture.senate.gov
Minority Web: www.agriculture.senate.gov/newsroom/minority-news
Majority Staff Director: James Glueck
Minority Staff Director: Joe Shultz

Jurisdiction: (1) agricultural economics and research; (2) agricultural extension services and experiment stations; (3) agricultural production, marketing, and stabilization of prices; (4) agriculture and agricultural commodities; (5) animal industry and animal diseases; (6) crop insurance and soil conservation; (7) farm credit and farm security; (8) food from fresh waters; (9) food stamp programs; (10) forestry and forest reserves and wilderness areas other than those created from the public domain; (11) home economics; (12) human nutrition; (13) inspection of livestock, meat, and agricultural products; (14) pests and pesticides; (15) plant industry, soils, and agricultural engineering; (16) rural development, rural electrification, and watersheds; (17) school nutrition programs. The committee shall also study and review, on a comprehensive basis, matters relating to food, nutrition, and hunger, both in the United States and in foreign countries, and rural affairs, and report thereon from time to time.

Party Ratio: R 11-D 9

Pat Roberts, Kans., Chair	*Debbie Stabenow, Mich.*
Mitch McConnell, Ky.	*Patrick J. Leahy, Vt.*
John Boozman, Ark.	*Sherrod Brown, Ohio*
John Hoeven, N.D.	*Amy Klobuchar, Minn.*
Joni Ernst, Iowa	*Michael F. Bennet, Colo.*
Cindy Hyde-Smith, Miss.	*Kirsten E. Gillibrand, N.Y.*
Mike Braun, Ind.	*Richard J. Durbin, Ill.*
Chuck Grassley, Iowa	*Robert P. Casey Jr., Pa.*
John Thune, S.D.	*Tina Smith, Minn.*
David Perdue, Ga.	
Deb Fischer, Neb.	

Subcommittees

Commodities, Risk Management, and Trade
Office: 328A SROB 20510 **Phone:** 224-2035
John Boozman (Chair), John Hoeven, David Perdue, Chuck Grassley, John Thune, Cindy Hyde-Smith
Sherrod Brown (Ranking Minority Member), Kirsten E. Gillibrand, Michael F. Bennet, Tina Smith

Conservation, Forestry, and Natural Resources
Office: 328A SROB 20510 **Phone:** 224-2035
Mitch McConnell (Chair), John Boozman, Chuck Grassley, David Perdue, Cindy Hyde-Smith
Michael F. Bennet (Ranking Minority Member), Amy Klobuchar, Patrick J. Leahy, Robert P. Casey Jr.

Livestock, Marketing, and Agriculture Security
Office: 328A SROB 20510 **Phone:** 224-2035
Deb Fischer (Chair), Mitch McConnell, Joni Ernst, John Thune, Chuck Grassley
Kirsten E. Gillibrand (Ranking Minority Member), Patrick J. Leahy, Amy Klobuchar, Robert P. Casey Jr.

Nutrition, Specialty Crops, and Agricultural Research
Office: 328A SROB 20510 **Phone:** 224-2035
David Perdue (Chair), Mitch McConnell, John Boozman, John Hoeven, Joni Ernst, Deb Fischer
Robert P. Casey Jr. (Ranking Minority Member), Patrick J. Leahy, Sherrod Brown, Kirsten E. Gillibrand, Tina Smith

Rural Development and Energy
Office: 328A SROB 20510 **Phone:** 224-2035
Joni Ernst (Chair), John Boozman, John Hoeven, John Thune, Cindy Hyde-Smith, Deb Fischer
Tina Smith (Ranking Minority Member), Sherrod Brown, Amy Klobuchar, Michael F. Bennet

APPROPRIATIONS

Office: S-128 CAP 20510-6025
Phone: 224-7257 **Fax:** 224-2100
Web: www.appropriations.senate.gov

Minority Web: www.appropriations.senate.gov/news/minority

Majority Staff Director: Shannon Hines

Minority Staff Director: Charles Kieffer; S-146A CAP; 224-7363

Jurisdiction: (1) appropriation of the revenue for the support of the government, except as provided in subparagraph (e); (2) rescission of appropriations contained in appropriation acts (referred to in section 105 of title 1, United States Code); (3) the amount of new spending authority described in section 401(c)(2) (A) and (B) of the Congressional Budget and Impoundment Control Act of 1974 which is to be effective for a fiscal year; (4) new spending authority described in section 401(c)(2) (C) of the Congressional Budget and Impoundment Control Act of 1974 provided in bills and resolutions referred to the committee under section 401(b)(2) of that Act.

Party Ratio: R 16-D 15

Richard Shelby, Ala., Chair	*Patrick J. Leahy, Vt.*
Mitch McConnell, Ky.	*Patty Murray, Wash.*
Lamar Alexander, Tenn.	*Dianne Feinstein, Calif.*
Susan M. Collins, Maine	*Richard J. Durbin, Ill.*
Lisa Murkowski, Alaska	*Jack Reed, R.I.*
Lindsey Graham, S.C.	*Jon Tester, Mont.*
Roy Blunt, Mo.	*Tom Udall, N.M.*
Jerry Moran, Kans.	*Jeanne Shaheen, N.H.*
John Hoeven, N.D.	*Jeff Merkley, Ore.*
John Boozman, Ark.	*Christopher Coons, Del.*
Shelley Moore Capito, W.Va.	*Brian Schatz, Hawaii*
James Lankford, Okla.	*Tammy Baldwin, Wisc.*
Steve Daines, Mont.	*Chris Murphy, Conn.*
Marco Rubio, Fla.	*Joe Manchin, W.Va.*
John Kennedy, La.	*Chris Van Hollen, Md.*
Cindy Hyde-Smith, Miss.	

Subcommittees

Agriculture, Rural Development, Food and Drug Administration, and Related Agencies

Office: S-128 CAP 20510   **Phone:** 224-7257

John Hoeven (Chair), Roy Blunt, Mitch McConnell, Susan M. Collins, Jerry Moran, John Kennedy, Cindy Hyde-Smith, Richard Shelby (ex officio)

Jeff Merkley (Ranking Minority Member), Dianne Feinstein, John Tester, Tom Udall, Patrick J. Leahy, Tammy Baldwin

Commerce, Justice, Science, and Related Agencies

Office: S-128 CAP 20510   **Phone:** 224-7257

Jerry Moran (Chair), Lamar Alexander, Susan M. Collins, Lisa Murkowski, Lindsey Graham, John Boozman, Shelley Moore Capito, Marco Rubio, John Kennedy, Richard Shelby

Jeanne Shaheen (Ranking Minority Member), Patrick J. Leahy, Dianne Feinstein, Jack Reed, Christopher Coons, Brian Schatz, Joe Manchin, Chris Van Hollen

Defense

Office: S-128 CAP 20510   **Phone:** 224-7257

Richard Shelby (Chair), Mitch McConnell, Lamar Alexander, Susan M. Collins, Lisa Murkowski, Lindsey

Graham, Roy Blunt, John Boozman, Jerry Moran, John Hoeven

Richard J. Durbin (Ranking Minority Member), Patrick J. Leahy, Dianne Feinstein, Patty Murray, Jack Reed, Jon Tester, Tom Udall, Brian Schatz, Tammy Baldwin

Energy and Water Development

Office: S-128 CAP 20510   **Phone:** 224-7257

Lamar Alexander (Chair), Mitch McConnell, Richard Shelby, Susan M. Collins, Lisa Murkowski, Lindsey Graham, John Hoeven, John Kennedy, Cindy Hyde-Smith

Dianne Feinstein (Ranking Minority Member), Patty Murray, Jon Tester, Richard J. Durbin, Tom Udall, Jeanne Shaheen, Jeff Merkley, Christopher Coons, Patrick J. Leahy (ex officio)

Financial Services and General Government

Office: S-128 CAP 20510   **Phone:** 224-7257

John Kennedy (Chair), John Boozman, Jerry Moran, James Lankford, Steve Daines, Richard Shelby (ex officio)

Christopher Coons (Ranking Minority Member), Richard J. Durbin, Joe Manchin, Chris Van Hollen, Patrick J. Leahy (ex officio)

Homeland Security

Office: S-128 CAP 20510   **Phone:** 224-7257

Shelley Moore Capito (Chair), Richard Shelby, Lisa Murkowski, John Hoeven, James Lankford, John Kennedy, Cindy-Hyde Smith

Jon Tester (Ranking Minority Member), Jeanne Shaheen, Patrick J. Leahy, Patty Murray, Tammy Baldwin, Joe Manchin

Interior, Environment, and Related Agencies

Office: S-128 CAP 20510   **Phone:** 224-7257

Lisa Murkowski (Chair), Lamar Alexander, Roy Blunt, Mitch McConnell, Steve Daines, Shelley Moore Capito, Marco Rubio, Cindy Hyde-Smith, Richard Shelby (ex officio)

Tom Udall (Ranking Minority Member), Jack Reed, Dianne Feinstein, Patrick J. Leahy, Jon Tester, Jeff Merkley, Chris Van Hollen

Labor, Health and Human Services, Education, and Related Agencies

Office: S-128 CAP 20510   **Phone:** 224-7257

Roy Blunt (Chair), Jerry Moran, Richard Shelby, Lamar Alexander, Lindsey Graham, Shelley Moore Capito, James Lankford, John Kennedy, Marco Rubio, Cindy Hyde-Smith

Patty Murray (Ranking Minority Member), Richard J. Durbin, Jack Reed, Jeanne Shaheen, Jeff Merkley, Brian Schatz, Tammy Baldwin, Chris Murphy, Joe Manchin, Patrick J. Leahy (ex officio)

Legislative Branch

Office: S-128 CAP 20510   **Phone:** 224-7257

Cindy Hyde-Smith (Chair), Richard Shelby, James Lankford

Chris Murphy (Ranking Minority Member), Chris Van Hollen, Patrick J. Leahy (ex officio)

APPROPRIATIONS (continued)

Military Construction, Veterans Affairs, and Related Agencies
Office: S-128 CAP 20510   **Phone:** 224-7257
John Boozman (Chair), Mitch McConnell, Susan M. Collins, John Hoeven, Lisa Murkowski, Shelley Moore Capito, Marco Rubio, Steve Daines, Richard Shelby (ex officio)

Brian Schatz (Ranking Minority Member), Jon Tester, Patty Murray, Jack Reed, Tom Udall, Tammy Baldwin, Chris Murphy, Patrick J. Leahy (ex officio)

State, Foreign Operations, and Related Programs
Office: S-128 CAP 20510   **Phone:** 224-7257
Lindsey Graham (Chair), Mitch McConnell, Roy Blunt, John Boozman, Jerry Moran, James Lankford, Steve Daines, Marco Rubio, Richard Shelby (ex officio)

Patrick J. Leahy (Ranking Minority Member), Richard J. Durbin, Jeanne Shaheen, Christopher Coons, Jeff Merkley, Chris Murphy, Chris Van Hollen

Transportation, Housing and Urban Development, and Related Agencies
Office: S-128 CAP 20510   **Phone:** 224-7257
Susan M. Collins (Chair), Richard Shelby, Lamar Alexander, Roy Blunt, John Boozman, Shelley Moore Capito, Steve Daines, Lindsey Graham, John Hoeven

Jack Reed (Ranking Minority Member), Patty Murray, Richard J. Durbin, Dianne Feinstein, Christopher Coons, Brian Schatz, Chris Murphy, Joe Manchin, Patrick J. Leahy (ex officio)

ARMED SERVICES

Office: 228 SROB 20510-6050
Phone: 224-3871   **Fax:** 228-0037
Web: www.armed-services.senate.gov
Majority Staff Director: John Bonsel
Minority Staff Director: Elizabeth L. King
Jurisdiction: (1) aeronautical and space activities peculiar to or primarily associated with the development of weapons systems or military operations; (2) common defense; (3) Department of Defense, the Department of the Army, the Department of the Navy, and the Department of the Air Force, generally; (4) maintenance and operation of the Panama Canal, including administration, sanitation, and government of the Canal Zone; (5) military research and development; (6) national security aspects of nuclear energy; (7) naval petroleum reserves, except those in Alaska; (8) pay, promotion, retirement, and other benefits and privileges of members of the armed forces, including overseas education of civilian and military dependents; (9) selective service system; (10) strategic and critical materials necessary for the common defense. The committee shall also study and review, on a comprehensive basis, matters relating to the common defense policy of the United States.
Party Ratio: R 14-D 13

James M. Inhofe, Okla.,
  Chair

Jack Reed, R.I.
Jeanne Shaheen, N.H.

Roger F. Wicker, Miss.
Deb Fischer, Neb.
Tom Cotton, Ark.
Mike Rounds, S.D.
Joni Ernst, Iowa
Thom Tillis, N.C.
Dan Sullivan, Alaska
David Perdue, Ga.
Kevin Cramer, N.D.
Martha McSally, Ariz.
Rick Scott, Fla.
Marsha Blackburn, Tenn.
Josh Hawley, Mo.

Kirsten E. Gillibrand, N.Y.
Richard Blumenthal, Conn.
Mazie K. Hirono, Hawaii
Tim Kaine, Va.
Angus S. King Jr., Maine (I)
Martin Heinrich, N.M.
Elizabeth Warren, Mass.
Gary C. Peters, Mich.
Joe Manchin, W.Va.
Tammy Duckworth, Ill.
Doug Jones, Ala.

Subcommittees

Airland
Office: 228 SROB 20510   **Phone:** 224-3871
Tom Cotton (Chair), James M. Inhofe, Roger F. Wicker, Dan Sullivan, Thom Tillis, James M. Inhofe (ex officio), Kevin Cramer, Martha McSally, Rick Scott

Angus S. King Jr. (Ranking Minority Member), Richard Blumenthal, Elizabeth Warren, Gary C. Peters, Tammy Duckworth, Doug Jones, Jack Reed (ex officio)

Cybersecurity
Office: 228 SROB 20510   **Phone:** 224-3871
Mike Rounds (Chair), Roger F. Wicker, David Perdue, Rick Scott, Marsha Blackburn, James M. Inhofe (ex officio)

Joe Manchin (Ranking Minority Member), Kristen E. Gillibrand, Richard Blumenthal, Martin Heinrich, Jack Reed (ex officio)

Emerging Threats and Capabilities
Office: 228 SROB 20510   **Phone:** 224-3871
Joni Ernst (Chair), Deb Fischer, Kevin Cramer, Marsha Blackburn, Josh Hawley, James M. Inhofe (ex officio)

Gary C. Peters (Ranking Minority Member), Jeanne Shaheen, Martin Heinrich, Mazie K. Hirono, Jack Reed (ex officio)

Personnel
Office: 228 SROB 20510   **Phone:** 224-3871
Thom Tillis (Chair), Mike Rounds, Martha McSally, Rick Scott, James M. Inhofe (ex officio)

Kirsten E. Gillibrand (Ranking Minority Member), Tammy Duckworth, Elizabeth Warren, Jack Reed (ex officio)

Readiness and Management Support
Office: 228 SROB 20510   **Phone:** 224-3871
Dan Sullivan (Chair), Deb Fischer, Joni Ernst, David Perdue, Martha McSally, Marsha Blackburn, James M. Inhofe (ex officio)

Tim Kaine (Ranking Minority Member), Jeanne Shaheen, Mazie K. Hirono, Tammy Duckworth, Doug Jones, Jack Reed (ex officio)

SeaPower
Office: 228 SROB 20510   **Phone:** 224-3871
David Purdue (Chair), Roger F. Wicker, Joni Ernst, Josh Hawley, Thom Tillis, Dan Sullivan, Tom Cotton, James M. Inhofe (ex officio)

Mazie K. Hirono (Ranking Minority Member), Jeanne Shaheen, Richard Blumenthal, Tim Kaine, Angus S. King Jr., Jack Reed (ex officio)

Strategic Forces
Office: 228 SROB 20510   **Phone:** 224-3871
Deb Fischer (Chair), James M. Inhofe (ex officio), Tom Cotton, Dan Sullivan, Mike Rounds, Kevin Cramer, Josh Hawley
Martin Heinrich (Ranking Minority Member), Angus S. King Jr., Elizabeth Warren, Joe Manchin, Doug Jones, Jack Reed (ex officio)

BANKING, HOUSING, AND URBAN AFFAIRS

Office: 534 SDOB 20510-6075
Phone: 224-7391   **Fax:** 224-5137
Web: www.banking.senate.gov
Minority Web: www.banking.senate.gov/public/index.cfm/democratic-press-releases
Majority Staff Director: Gregg Richard
Minority Staff Director: Laura Swanson
Jurisdiction: (1) banks, banking, and financial institutions; (2) control of prices of commodities, rents, and services; (3) deposit insurance; (4) economic stabilization and defense production; (5) export and foreign trade promotion; (6) export controls; (7) federal monetary policy, including Federal Reserve System; (8) financial aid to commerce and industry; (9) issuance and redemption of notes; (10) money and credit, including currency and coinage; (11) nursing home construction; (12) public and private housing (including veterans' housing) (13) renegotiation of Government contracts; (14) urban development and urban mass transit. The committee shall also study and review, on a comprehensive basis, matters relating to international economic policy as it affects United States monetary affairs, credit, and financial institutions; economic growth, urban affairs and credit, and report thereon from time to time.
Party Ratio: R 13-D 12

Mike Crapo, Idaho, Chair	Sherrod Brown, Ohio
Richard Shelby, Ala.	Jack Reed, R.I.
Patrick J. Toomey, Pa.	Robert Menendez, N.J.
Tim Scott, S.C.	Jon Tester, Mont.
Ben Sasse, Neb.	Mark R. Warner, Va.
Tom Cotton, Ark.	Elizabeth Warren, Mass.
Mike Rounds, S.D.	Brian Schatz, Hawaii
David Perdue, Ga.	Chris Van Hollen, Md.
Thom Tillis, N.C.	Catherine Cortez Masto, Nev.
John Kennedy, La.	Doug Jones, Ala.
Martha McSally, Ariz.	Tina Smith, Minn.
Jerry Moran, Kans.	Kyrsten Sinema, Ariz.
Kevin Cramer, N.D.	

Subcommittees

Economic Policy
Office: 534 SDOB 20510   **Phone:** 224-7391
Tom Cotton (Chair), Patrick J. Toomey, David Perdue, Thom Tillis, John Kennedy, Mike Crapo (ex officio)

Heidi Heitkamp (Ranking Minority Member), Elizabeth Warren, Robert Menendez, Joe Donnelly, Sherrod Brown (ex officio)

Financial Institutions and Consumer Protection
Office: 534 SDOB 20510 Phone: 224-7391
Tim Scott (Chair), Mike Rounds, Thom Tillis, John Kennedy, Jerry Moran, Kevin Cramer, Richard C. Shelby, Patrick J. Toomey, Ben Sasse, Mike Crapo (ex officio)
Elizabeth Warren (Ranking Minority Member), Jack Reed, Mark R. Warner, Jon Tester, Brian Schatz, Catherine Cortez Masto, Chris Van Hollen, Doug Jones, Sherrod Brown (ex officio)

Housing, Transportation, and Community Development
Office: 534 SDOB 20510   **Phone:** 224-7391
David Perdue (Chair), Tom Cotton, Mike Rounds, Richard Shelby, Martha McSally, Jerry Moran, Kevin Cramer, Mike Crapo (ex officio)
Robert Menendez (Ranking Minority Member), Jack Reed, Elizabeth Warren, Catherine Cortez Masto, Doug Jones, Tina Smith, Sherrod Brown (ex officio)

National Security and International Trade and Finance
Office: 534 SDOB 20510   **Phone:** 224-7391
Ben Sasse (Chair), Martha McSally, Jerry Moran, Patrick J. Toomey, Tim Scott, Mike Crapo (ex officio)
Mark Warner (Ranking Minority Member), Kyrsten Sinema, Chris Van Hollen, Brian Schatz, Sherrod Brown (ex officio)

Securities, Insurance, and Investment
Office: 534 SDOB 20510   **Phone:** 224-7391
Patrick J. Toomey (Chair), Martha McSally, Tim Scott, Tom Cotton, Richard Shelby, Thom Tillis, Mike Rounds, John Kennedy, Mike Crapo (ex officio)
Mark R. Warner (Ranking Minority Member), Jack Reed, Robert Menendez, Jon Tester, Elizabeth Warren, Tina Smith, Kyrsten Sinema, Sherrod Brown (ex officio)

BUDGET

Office: 624 SDOB 20510-6100
Phone: 224-0642   **Fax:** 224-4835
Web: www.budget.senate.gov
Minority Web: www.budget.senate.gov/ranking-member/newsroom
Majority Staff Director: Elizabeth McDonald
Minority Staff Director: Warren Gunnels
Jurisdiction: (1) all concurrent resolutions on the budget (as defined in Section 3 (a) (4) of the Congressional Budget Act of 1974) and all other matters required to be referred to that committee under Titles III and IV of that Act, and messages, petitions, memorials, and other matters relating thereto. (2) The committee shall have the duty (A) to report the matters required to be reported by it under Titles III and IV of the Congressional Budget and Impoundment Control Act of 1974; (B) to make continuing studies of the effect on budget outlays of relevant existing and proposed legislation and to report the results of such studies to the Senate on a

BUDGET (continued)

recurring basis; (C) to request and evaluate continuing studies of tax expenditures, to devise methods of coordinating tax expenditures, policies, and programs with direct budget outlays, and to report the results of such studies to the Senate on a recurring basis; and (D) to review, on a continuing basis, the conduct by the Congressional Budget Office of its functions and duties.

Party Ratio: R 11-D 10

Michael B. Enzi, Wyo.,
   Chair
Chuck Grassley, Iowa
Mike Crapo, Idaho
Lindsey Graham, S.C.
Patrick J. Toomey, Pa.
Ron Johnson, Wisc.
David Perdue, Ga.
Mike Braun, Ind.
Rick Scott, Fla.
John Kennedy, La.
Kevin Cramer, N.D.

Bernard Sanders, Vt. (I)
Patty Murray, Wash.
Ron Wyden, Ore.
Debbie Stabenow, Mich.
Sheldon Whitehouse, R.I.
Mark R. Warner, Va.
Jeff Merkley, Ore.
Tim Kaine, Va.
Chris Van Hollen, Md.
Kamala D. Harris, Calif.

COMMERCE, SCIENCE, AND TRANSPORTATION

Office: 512 SDOB 20510-6125
Phone: 224-1251 **Fax:** 224-1259
Web: www.commerce.senate.gov
Minority Web: www.commerce.senate.gov/public/index
  .cfm/minority-dems
Majority Staff Director: John Keast
Minority Staff Director: Kim Lipsky; 425 SHOB; 224-0411
   Jurisdiction: (1) Coast Guard; (2) coastal zone management; (3) communications; (4) highway safety; (5) inland waterways, except construction; (6) interstate commerce; (7) marine and ocean navigation, safety, and transportation, including navigational aspects of deepwater ports; (8) marine fisheries; (9) Merchant Marine and navigation; (10) nonmilitary aeronautical and space sciences; (11) oceans, weather, and atmospheric activities; (12) Panama Canal and interoceanic canals generally, except as provided in subparagraph (c); (13) regulation of consumer products and services, including testing related to toxic substances, other than pesticides, and except for credit, financial services, and housing; (14) regulation of interstate common carriers, including railroads, buses, trucks, vessels, pipelines, and civil aviation; (15) science engineering, and technology research, development, and policy; (16) sports; (17) standards and measurement; (18) transportation; (19) transportation and commerce aspects of Outer Continental Shelf lands. The committee shall also study and review, on a comprehensive basis, all matters relating to science and technology, oceans policy, transportation, communications, and consumer affairs, and report thereon from time to time.

Party Ratio: R 14-D 12

Roger F. Wicker, Miss.,
   Chair
John Thune, S.D.

Maria Cantwell, Wash.
Amy Klobuchar, Minn.
Richard Blumenthal, Conn.

Roy Blunt, Mo.
Ted Cruz, Tex.
Deb Fischer, Neb.
Dan Sullivan, Alaska
Jerry Moran, Kans.
Ron Johnson, Wisc.
Cory Gardner, Colo.
Marsha Blackburn, Tenn.
Shelley Moore Capito,
  W.Va.
Todd Young, Ind.
Mike Lee, Utah
Rick Scott, Fla.

Brian Schatz, Hawaii
Edward J. Markey, Mass.
Tom Udall, N.M.
Gary C. Peters, Mich.
Tammy Baldwin, Wisc.
Tammy Duckworth, Ill.
Jon Tester, Mont.
Jacky Rosen, Nev.
Kyrsten Sinema, Ariz.

Subcommittees

Aviation Operations, Safety and Security
Office: 512 SDOB 20510 **Phone:** 224-1251
   Roy Blunt (Chair), Roger F. Wicker, Ted Cruz, Deb Fischer, Jerry Moran, Dan Sullivan, John Thune (Ex Officio), Cory Gardner, Todd Young, Mike Lee, Shelley Moore Capito
   Maria Cantwell (Ranking Minority Member), Amy Klobuchar, Richard Blumenthal, Brian Schatz, Edward J. Markey, Tom Udall, Gary C. Peters, Tammy Baldwin, Tammy Duckworth, Jon Tester

Communications, Technology, Innovation, and the Internet
Office: 512 SDOB 20510 **Phone:** 224-1251
   Roger F. Wicker (Chair), Roy Blunt, Ted Cruz, Deb Fischer, Jerry Moran, Dan Sullivan, Ron Johnson, Cory Gardner, Mike Lee, Shelley Moore Capito, John Thune (Ex Officio), Todd Young
   Brian Schatz (Ranking Minority Member), Maria Cantwell, Amy Klobuchar, Richard Blumenthal, Edward J. Markey, Tom Udall, Gary C. Peters, Tammy Baldwin, Tammy Duckworth, Jon Tester

Consumer Protection, Product Safety, Insurance, and Data Security
Office: 512 SDOB 20510 **Phone:** 224-1251
   Jerry Moran (Chair), Roy Blunt, Ted Cruz, Deb Fischer, Mike Lee, Shelley Moore Capito, Todd Young, John Thune (Ex Officio)
   Richard Blumenthal (Ranking Minority Member), Amy Klobuchar, Edward J. Markey, Tom Udall, Tammy Duckworth

Oceans, Atmosphere, Fisheries, and Coast Guard
Office: 512 SDOB 20510 **Phone:** 224-1251
   Dan Sullivan (Chair), Roger F. Wicker, Deb Fischer, Ron Johnson, John Thune (Ex Officio), Cory Gardner, Mike Lee, Todd Young
   Tammy Baldwin (Ranking Minority Member), Maria Cantwell, Richard Blumenthal, Brian Schatz, Edward J. Markey, Gary C. Peters

Space, Science, and Competitiveness
Office: 512 SDOB 20510 **Phone:** 224-1251
   Ted Cruz (Chair), Jerry Moran, Dan Sullivan, Cory Gardner, Mike Lee, Ron Johnson, Shelley Moore Capito, John Thune (Ex Officio)

Edward J. Markey (Ranking Minority Member), Brian Schatz, Tom Udall, Gary C. Peters, Tammy Baldwin

Surface Transportation and Merchant Marine Infrastructure, Safety, and Security

Office: 512 SDOB 20510   **Phone:** 224-1251

Deb Fischer (Chair), Roy Blunt, Roger F. Wicker, Todd Young, Cory Gardner, Ron Johnson, Shelley Moore Capito, John Thune (ex officio)

Gary C. Peters (Ranking Minority Member), Richard Blumenthal, Maria Cantwell, Amy Klobuchar, Tom Udall, Tammy Baldwin, Tammy Duckworth

ENERGY AND NATURAL RESOURCES

Office: 304 SDOB 20510-6150
Phone: 224-4971   **Fax:** 224-6163
Web: www.energy.senate.gov
Minority Web: www.energy.senate.gov/public/index.cfm/democratic-news
Majority Staff Director: Brian Hughes
Minority Staff Director: Sarah Venuto

Jurisdiction: (1) coal production, distribution, and utilization; (2) energy policy; (3) energy regulation and energy conservation; (4) energy related aspects of deepwater ports; (5) energy research and development; (6) extraction of minerals from oceans and Outer Continental Shelf lands; (7) hydroelectric power, irrigation, and reclamation; (8) mining education and research; (9) mining, mineral lands, mining claims, and mineral conservation; (10) national parks, recreation areas, wilderness areas, wild and scenic rivers, historic sites, military parks and battlefields, and on the public domain, preservation of prehistoric ruins and objects of interest; (11) naval petroleum reserves in Alaska; (12) nonmilitary development of nuclear energy; (13) oil and gas production and distribution; (14) public lands and forests, including farming and grazing thereon, and mineral extraction therefrom; (15) solar energy systems; (16) territorial possessions of the United States, including trusteeships; international energy affairs and emergency preparedness; nuclear waste policy; privatization of federal assets; Trans-Alaska Pipeline System and other oil or gas pipeline transportation systems within Alaska; Alaska Native Claims Settlement Act of 1971; Alaska National Interest Lands Conservation Act of 1980; Antarctic research and energy development; Arctic research and energy development; Native Hawaiian matters. The Committee shall also study and review, on a comprehensive basis, matters relating to energy and resources development.
Party Ratio: R 11-D 9

Lisa Murkowski, Alaska, Chair	Joe Manchin, W.Va.
John Barrasso, Wyo.	Ron Wyden, Ore.
James E. Risch, Idaho	Maria Cantwell, Wash.
Mike Lee, Utah	Bernard Sanders, Vt. (I)
Bill Cassidy, La.	Debbie Stabenow, Mich.
Cory Gardner, Colo.	Martin Heinrich, N.M.
Cindy Hyde-Smith, Miss.	Mazie K. Hirono, Hawaii
Martha McSally, Ariz.	Angus S. King Jr., Maine (I)

Lamar Alexander, Tenn.	Catherine Cortez Masto, Nev.
Steve Daines, Mont.	
John Hoeven, N.D.	

Subcommittees

Energy
Office: 304 SDOB 20510   **Phone:** 224-4971

Bill Cassidy (Chair), James E. Risch, Mike Lee, Steve Daines, Cory Gardner, Cindy Hyde-Smith, Martha McSally, John Hoeven, Lamar Alexander, Lisa Murkowski (ex officio)

Martin Heinrich (Ranking Minority Member), Ron Wyden, Bernard Sanders, Debbie Stabenow, Mazie K. Hirono, Angus S. King Jr. Catherine Cortez Masto, Maria Cantwell, Joe Manchin (ex officio)

National Parks
Office: 304 SDOB 20510   **Phone:** 224-4971

Steve Daines (Chair), John Barrasso, Mike Lee, Lamar Alexander, John Hoeven, Cory Gardner, Cindy Hyde-Smith, Lisa Murkowski (ex officio)

Angus S. King Jr. (Ranking Minority Member), Bernard Sanders, Debbie Stabenow, Martin Heinrich, Mazie K. Hirono, Joe Manchin (ex officio)

Public Lands, Forests, and Mining
Office: 304 SDOB 20510   **Phone:** 224-4971

Mike Lee (Chair), James E. Risch, John Barrasso, Steve Daines, Bill Cassidy, Cory Gardner, Cindy Hyde-Smith, Martha McSally, John Hoeven, Lisa Murkowski (ex officio)

Ron Wyden (Ranking Minority Member), Debbie Stabenow, Joe Manchin (ex officio), Martin Heinrich, Mazie K. Hirono, Catherine Cortez Masto, Angus S. King Jr., Maria Cantwell

Water and Power
Office: 304 SDOB 20510   **Phone:** 224-4971

Martha McSally (Chair), John Barrasso, James E. Risch, Bill Cassidy, Cory Gardner, Lamar Alexander, Lisa Murkowski (ex officio)

Catherine Masto Cortez (Ranking Minority Member), Ron Wyden, Bernard Sanders, Joe Manchin (ex officio), Maria Cantwell

ENVIRONMENT AND PUBLIC WORKS

Office: 410 SDOB 20510-6175
Phone: 224-6176   **Fax:** 224-1273
Web: www.epw.senate.gov
Minority Web: www.epw.senate.gov/public/index.cfm/latest-updates-democratic
Majority Staff Director: Richard Russell
Minority Staff Director: Mary Frances Repko; 456 SDOB; 224-8832

Jurisdiction: (1) air pollution; (2) construction and maintenance of highways; (3) environmental aspects of Outer Continental Shelf lands; (4) environmental effects of toxic substances, other than pesticides; (5) environmental policy; (6) environmental research and development; (7) fisheries and wildlife; (8) flood control and improvements of rivers and harbors, including environmental

ENVIRONMENT AND PUBLIC WORKS
(continued)

aspects of deepwater ports; (9) noise pollution; (10) non-military environmental regulation and control of nuclear energy; (11) ocean dumping; (12) public buildings and improved grounds of the United States generally, including Federal buildings in the District of Columbia; (13) public works, bridges, and dams; (14) regional economic development; (15) solid waste disposal and recycling; (16) water pollution; (17) water resources. The committee shall also study and review, on a comprehensive basis, matters relating to environmental protection and resource utilization and conservation. The committee shall also study and review, on a comprehensive basis, matters relating to environmental protection and resource utilization and conservation, and report thereon from time to time.

Party Ratio: R 11-D 10

John Barrasso, Wyo., Chair	Thomas R. Carper, Del.
James M. Inhofe, Okla.	Benjamin L. Cardin, Md.
Shelley Moore Capito, W.Va.	Bernard Sanders, Vt. (I)
	Sheldon Whitehouse, R.I.
Kevin Cramer, N.D.	Jeff Merkley, Ore.
Mike Braun, Ind.	Kirsten E. Gillibrand, N.Y.
John Boozman, Ark.	Cory A. Booker, N.J.
Roger F. Wicker, Miss.	Edward J. Markey, Mass.
Mike Rounds, S.D.	Tammy Duckworth, Ill.
Joni Ernst, IA.	Chris Van Hollen. Md.
Dan Sullivan, Alaska	
Richard Shelby, Ala.	

Subcommittees

Clean Air and Nuclear Safety
Office: 410 SDOB 20510   **Phone:** 224-6176
Shelley Moore Capito (Chair), James M. Inhofe, John Boozman, Roger F. Wicker, John Barrasso (Ex officio), Joni Ernst, Richard Shelby
Sheldon Whitehouse (Ranking Minority Member), Benjamin L. Cardin, Bernard Sanders, Jeff Merkley, Kirsten E. Gillibrand, Edward J. Markey, Tammy Duckworth, Thomas R. Carper (ex officio)

Fisheries, Water, and Wildlife
Office: 410 SDOB 20510   **Phone:** 224-6176
John Boozman (Chair), James M. Inhofe, Shelley Moore Capito, Roger F. Wicker, Mike Rounds, Dan Sullivan, Richard Shelby, John Barrasso (Ex officio)
Tammy Duckworth (Ranking Minority Member), Benjamin L. Cardin, Sheldon Whitehouse, Jeff Merkley, Kirsten E. Gillibrand, Edward J. Markey, Chris Van Hollen, Thomas R. Carper (ex officio)

Superfund, Waste Management, and Regulatory Oversight
Office: 410 SDOB 20510   **Phone:** 224-6176
Mike Rounds (Chair), Joni Ernst, Dan Sullivan, John Barrasso (ex officio)
Cory A. Booker (Ranking Minority Member), Bernard Sanders, Chris Van Hollen, Thomas R. Carper (ex officio)

Transportation and Infrastructure
Office: 410 SDOB 20510   **Phone:** 224-6176
James M. Inhofe (Chair), Shelley Moore Capito, John Boozman, Roger F. Wicker, Jerry Moran, Joni Ernst, Dan Sullivan, Richard Shelby, John Barrasso (ex officio)
Benjamin L. Cardin (Ranking Minority Member), Bernard Sanders, Sheldon Whitehouse, Jeff Merkley, Kirsten E. Gillibrand, Edward J. Markey, Tammy Duckworth, Cory A. Booker, Thomas R. Carper (ex officio)

FINANCE

Office: 219 SDOB 20510-6200
Phone: 224-4515 **Fax:** 228-0554
Web: www.finance.senate.gov
Minority Web: www.finance.senate.gov/ranking-members-news
Majority Staff Director: Kolan Davis
Minority Staff Director: Joshua Sheinkman
Jurisdiction: (1) bonded debt of the United States, except as provided in the Congressional Budget Act of 1974; (2) customs, collection districts, and ports of entry and delivery; (3) deposit of public moneys; (4) general revenue sharing; (5) health programs under the Social Security Act and health programs financed by a specific tax or trust fund; (6) national social security; (7) reciprocal trade agreements; (8) revenue measures generally, except as provided in the Congressional Budget Act of 1974; (9) revenue measures relating to the insular possessions; (10) tariffs and import quotas, and matters related thereto; (11) transportation of dutiable goods.

Party Ratio: R 15-D 13

Chuck Grassley, Iowa, Chair	Ron Wyden, Ore.
	Debbie Stabenow, Mich.
Patrick J. Toomey, Pa.	Maria Cantwell, Wash.
Mike Crapo, Idaho	Robert Menendez, N.J.
Pat Roberts, Kans.	Thomas R. Carper, Del.
Michael B. Enzi, Wyo.	Benjamin L. Cardin, Md.
John Cornyn, Tex.	Sherrod Brown, Ohio
John Thune, S.D.	Michael F. Bennet, Colo.
Richard Burr, N.C.	Robert P. Casey Jr., Pa.
Johnny Isakson, Ga.	Mark R. Warner, Va.
Rob Portman, Ohio	Sheldon Whitehouse, R.I.
James Lankford, Okla.	Maggie Hassan, N.H.
Steve Daines, Mont.	Catherine Cortez Masto, Nev.
Tim Scott, S.C.	
Bill Cassidy, La.	
Todd Young, Ind.	

Subcommittees

Energy, Natural Resources, and Infrastructure
Office: 219 SDOB 20510   **Phone:** 224-4515
Tim Scott (Chair), Chuck Grassley, Mike Crapo, Pat Roberts, Steve Daines, Michael B. Enzi, John Cornyn, Richard Burr
Michael F. Bennet (Ranking Minority Member), Maria Cantwell, Thomas R. Carper, Sheldon Whitehouse, Maggie Hassan, Ron Wyden

Fiscal Responsibility and Economic Growth
Office: 219 SDOB 20510   **Phone:** 224-4515

Tim Scott (Chair), James Lankford

Maggie Hassan (Ranking Minority Member), Ron Wyden

Health Care
Office: 219 SDOB 20510   **Phone:** 224-4515

Patrick J. Toomey (Chair), Chuck Grassley, Pat Roberts, Michael B. Enzi, Richard Burr, John Thune, Johnny Isakson, Tim Scott, Bill Cassidy, James Lankford, Steve Daines, Todd Young

Debbie Stabenow (Ranking Minority Member), Maria Cantwell, Robert Menendez, Benjamin L. Cardin, Sherrod Brown, Robert P. Casey, Maggie Hassan, Catherine Cortez Masto, Mark R. Warner, Thomas R. Carper, Sheldon Whitehouse

International Trade, Customs, and Global Competitiveness
Office: 219 SDOB 20510   **Phone:** 224-4515

John Cornyn (Chair), Mike Crapo, Rob Portman, Patrick J. Toomey, Tim Scott, Bill Cassidy, Steve Daines, Johnny Isakson, Chuck Grassley, Pat Roberts, John Thune, Todd Young

Robert P. Casey Jr. (Ranking Minority Member), Debbie Stabenow, Benjamin L. Cardin, Ron Wyden, Maria Cantwell, Robert Menendez, Sherrod Brown, Mark R. Warner, Catherine Cortez Masto

Social Security, Pensions, and Family Policy
Office: 219 SDOB 20510   **Phone:** 224-4515

Rob Portman (Chair), Chuck Grassley, Bill Cassidy, James Lankford, Todd Young

Sherrod Brown (Ranking Minority Member), Robert P. Casey Jr., Michael F. Bennet, Catherine Cortez Masto

Taxation and IRS Oversight
Office: 219 SDOB 20510   **Phone:** 224-4515

John Thune (Chair), Mike Crapo, Michael B. Enzi, John Cornyn, Richard Burr, Johnny Isakson, Rob Portman, Patrick J. Toomey

Mark R. Warner (Ranking Minority Member), Michael F. Bennet, Robert Menendez, Thomas R. Carper, Benjamin L. Cardin, Sheldon Whitehouse

FOREIGN RELATIONS

Office: 423 SDOB 20510-6225
Phone: 224-4651   **Fax:** 224-0836
Web: www.foreign.senate.gov
Minority Web: www.foreign.senate.gov/press/ranking
Majority Staff Director: Chris Socha
Minority Staff Director: Jessica Lewis; Fax: 228-3612

Jurisdiction: (1) acquisition of land and buildings for embassies and legations in foreign countries; (2) boundaries of the United States; (3) diplomatic service; (4) foreign economic, military, technical, and humanitarian assistance; (5) foreign loans; (6) international activities of the American National Red Cross, and the International Committee of the Red Cross; (7) international aspects of nuclear energy, including nuclear transfer policy; (8) international conferences and congresses; (9) international law as it relates to foreign policy; (10) International Monetary Fund and other international organizations established primarily for international monetary purposes (except that, at the request of the Committee on Banking, Housing, and Urban Affairs, any proposed legislation relating to such subjects reported by the Committee on Foreign Relations shall be referred to the Committee on Banking, Housing, and Urban Affairs); (11) intervention abroad and declarations of war; (12) measures to foster commercial intercourse with foreign nations and to safeguard United States business interests abroad; (13) national security and international aspects of trusteeships of the United States; (14) ocean and international environmental and scientific affairs as they relate to foreign policy; (15) protection of United States citizens abroad and expatriation; (16) relations of the United States with foreign nations generally; (17) treaties and executive agreements, except reciprocal trade agreements; (18) the United Nations and its affiliated organizations; (19) World Bank group, the regional development banks, and other international organizations established primarily for development assistance purposes. The committee shall also study and review, on a comprehensive basis, matters relating to national security policy, foreign policy, and international economic policy as they relate to the foreign policy of the United States, and matters relating to food, hunger and nutrition in foreign countries.

Party Ratio: R 12-D 10

James E. Risch, Idaho, Chair	Robert Menendez, N.J.
Marco Rubio, Fla.	Benjamin L. Cardin, Md.
Ron Johnson, Wisc.	Jeanne Shaheen, N.H.
Cory Gardner, Colo.	Christopher Coons, Del.
Lindsey Graham, S.C.	Tom Udall, N.M.
Johnny Isakson, Ga.	Chris Murphy, Conn.
Rand Paul, Ky.	Tim Kaine, Va.
John Barrasso, Wyo.	Edward J. Markey, Mass.
Todd Young, Ind.	Jeff Merkley, Ore.
Rob Portman, Ohio	Cory A. Booker, N.J.
Ted Cruz, Tex.	
Mitt Romney, Utah	

Subcommittees

Africa and Global Health Policy
Office: 423 SDOB 20510   **Phone:** 224-4651

Lindsey Graham (Chair), Johnny Isakson, Rob Portman, Ron Johnson, Ted Cruz, James E. Risch (ex officio)

Tim Kaine (Ranking Minority Member), Christopher Coons, Cory A. Booker, Christopher Murphy, Robert Menendez (ex officio)

East Asia, the Pacific, and International Cybersecurity Policy
Office: 423 SDOB 20510   **Phone:** 224-4651

Cory Gardner (Chair), Marco Rubio, Ron Johnson, Johnny Isakson, James E. Risch (ex officio), Todd Young

Edward J. Markey (Ranking Minority Member), Jeff Merkley, Christopher Coons, Tom Udall, Robert Menendez (ex officio)

FOREIGN RELATIONS (continued)

Europe and Regional Security Cooperation
Office: 423 SDOB 20510 **Phone:** 224-4651
Ron Johnson (Chair), John Barrasso, Rand Paul, James E. Risch, Rob Portman, Mitt Romney
Jeanne Shaheen (Ranking Minority Member), Christopher Murphy, Benjamin L. Cardin, Christopher Coons, Robert Menendez (ex officio)

Multilateral International Development, Multilateral Institutions, and International Economic, Energy, and Environmental Policy
Office: 423 SDOB 20510 **Phone:** 224-4651
Todd Young (Chair), Mitt Romney, Paul Rand, John Barrasso, Lindsey Graham, James E. Risch (ex officio)
Jeff Merkley (Ranking Minority Member), Edward J. Markey, Tom Udall, Cory A. Booker, Robert Menendez (ex officio)

Near East, South Asia, Central Asia, and Counterterrorism
Office: 423 SDOB 20510 **Phone:** 224-4651
Mitt Romney (Chair), Ted Cruz, Lindsey Graham, Cory Gardner, Rand Paul, James E. Risch (ex officio)
Christopher Murphy (Ranking Minority Member), Benjamin Cardin, Jeanne Shaheen, Tim Kaine, Robert Menendez (ex officio)

State Department and USAID Management, International Operations, and Bilateral International Development
Office: 423 SDOB 20510 **Phone:** 224-4651
Johnny Isakson (Chair), James E. Risch, Marco Rubio, Rob Portman, Rand Paul, Todd Young
Cory A. Booker (Ranking Minority Member), Edward J. Markey, Jeff Merkley, Tom Udall, Robert Menendez (ex officio)

Western Hemisphere, Transnational Crime, Civilian Security, Democracy, Human Rights, and Global Women's Issues
Office: 423 SDOB 20510 **Phone:** 224-4651
Marco Rubio (Chair), Rob Portman, Ted Cruz, Cory Gardner, John Barrasso, James E. Risch (ex officio)
Benjamin L. Cardin (Ranking Minority Member), Tom Udall, Tim Kaine, Jeanne Shaheen, Robert Menendez (ex officio)

HEALTH, EDUCATION, LABOR, AND PENSIONS

Office: 428 SDOB 20510-6300
Phone: 224-5375 **Fax:** 228-5044
Web: www.help.senate.gov
Minority Web: www.help.senate.gov/ranking/newsroom
Majority Staff Director: David Cleary
Minority Staff Director: Evan Schatz
Jurisdiction: (1) measures relating to education, labor, health, and public welfare; (2) aging; (3) agricultural colleges; (4) arts and humanities; (5) biomedical research and development; (6) child labor; (7) convict labor and the entry of goods made by convicts into interstate commerce; (8) domestic activities of the American National Red Cross; (9) equal employment opportunity; (10) Gallaudet University (Washington, D.C.), Howard University (Washington, D.C.), and St. Elizabeth's Hospital (Washington, D.C.); (11) individuals with disabilities; (12) labor standards and labor statistics; (13) mediation and arbitration of labor disputes; (14) occupational safety and health, including the welfare of miners; (15) private pension plans; (16) public health; (17) railway labor and retirement; (18) regulation of foreign laborers; (19) student loans; (20) wages and hours of labor. The committee shall also study and review, on a comprehensive basis, matters relating to health, education and training, and public welfare, and report thereon from time to time.
Party Ratio: R 12-D 11

Lamar Alexander, Tenn., Chair	Patty Murray, Wash.
	Bernard Sanders, Vt. (I)
Michael B. Enzi, Wyo.	Robert P. Casey Jr., Pa.
Richard Burr, N.C.	Tammy Baldwin, Wisc.
Johnny Isakson, Ga.	Chris Murphy, Conn.
Rand Paul, Ky.	Elizabeth Warren, Mass.
Susan M. Collins, Maine	Tim Kaine, Va.
Lisa Murkowski, Alaska	Maggie Hassan, N.H.
Tim Scott, S.C.	Tina Smith. Minn.
Mitt Romney, Utah	Doug Jones, Ala.
Mike Braun, Ind.	Jacky Rosen, Nev.
Pat Roberts, Kans.	
Bill Cassidy, La.	

Subcommittees

Children and Families
Office: 428 SDOB 20510 **Phone:** 224-5375
Rand Paul (Chair), Lisa Murkowski, Richard Burr, Pat Roberts, Bill Cassidy, Tim Scott, Lamar Alexander (ex officio), Mitt Romney
Robert P. Casey Jr. (Ranking Minority Member), Bernard Sanders, Chris Murphy, Tim Kaine, Maggie Hassan, Patty Murray, Tina Smith

Employment and Workplace Safety
Office: 428 SDOB 20510 **Phone:** 224-5375
Johnny Isakson (Chair), Rand Paul, Tim Scott, Mitt Romney, Mike Braun, Richard Burr, Bill Cassidy, Lamar Alexander (ex officio)
Tammy Baldwin (Ranking Minority Member), Robert P. Casey Jr., Elizabeth Warren, Patty Murray (ex officio), Tina Smith, Doug Jones, Jacky Rosen

Primary Health and Retirement Security
Office: 428 SDOB 20510 **Phone:** 224-5375
Michael B. Enzi (Chair), Richard Burr, Susan M. Collins, Tim Scott, Mitt Romney, Mike Braun, Pat Roberts, Bill Cassidy, Lisa Murkowski, Tim Scott, Lamar Alexander (ex officio)
Bernard Sanders (Ranking Minority Member), Tammy Baldwin, Chris Murphy, Elizabeth Warren, Tim Kaine, Maggie Hassan, Doug Jones, Patty Murray, Jacky Rosen

HOMELAND SECURITY AND GOVERNMENTAL AFFAIRS

Office: 340 SDOB 20510-6250
Phone: 224-4751   **Fax:** 224-9603
Web: www.hsgac.senate.gov
Minority Web: www.hsgac.senate.gov/media/minority-media
Majority Staff Director: Gabrielle D'Adamo
Minority Staff Director: David Weinberg; 442 SHOB; 224-2627

Jurisdiction: (1) Department of Homeland Security, except matters relating to the Coast Guard, the Transportation Security Administration, the Federal Law Enforcement Training Center, or the Secret Service; and the United States Citizenship and Immigration Service; or the immigration functions of the United States Customs and Border Protection or the United States Immigration and Custom Enforcement or the Directorate of Border and Transportation Security; and the following functions performed by any employee of the Department of Homeland Security: any customs revenue function, including any function provided for in Section 415 of the Homeland Security Act of 2002; any commercial function or commercial operation of the Bureau of Customs and Border Protection or Bureau of Immigration and Customs Enforcement, including matters relating to trade facilitation and trade regulation; or any other function related to the above items that was exercised by the United States Customs Service on the day before the effective date of the Homeland Security Act of 2002; (2) archives of the United States; (3) budget and accounting measures, other than appropriations, except as provided in the Congressional Budget Act of 1974; (4) census and collection of statistics, including economic and social statistics; (5) congressional organization, except for any part of the matter that amends the rules or orders of the Senate; (6) federal civil service; (7) government information; (8) intergovernmental relations; (9) municipal affairs of the District of Columbia, except appropriations therefor; (10) organization and management of United States nuclear export policy; (11) organization and reorganization of the executive branch of the Government; (12) United States Postal Service; (13) status of officers and employees of the United States, including their classification, compensation, and benefits. The committee shall have the duty of (A) receiving and examining reports of the Comptroller General of the United States and of submitting such recommendations to the Senate as it deems necessary or desirable in connection with the subject matter of such reports; (B) studying the efficiency, economy, and effectiveness of all agencies and departments of the Government; (C) evaluating the effects of laws enacted to reorganize the legislative and executive branches of the Government; and (D) studying the intergovernmental relationships between the United States and the States and municipalities, and between the United States and international organizations of which the United States is a member.
Party Ratio: R 8-D 6

Ron Johnson, Wisc., Chair	*Gary C. Peters, Mich.*
Rob Portman, Ohio	*Thomas R. Carper, Del.*
Rand Paul, Ky.	*Maggie Hassan, N.H.*
James Lankford, Okla.	*Kamala D. Harris, Calif.*
Mitt Romney, Utah	*Kyrsten Sinema, Ariz.*
Rick Scott, Fla.	*Jacky Rosen, Nev.*
Michael B. Enzi, Wyo.	
Josh Hawley, Mo.	

Subcommittees

Federal Spending Oversight and Emergency Management
Office: SD-342 SDOB 20510   **Phone:** 224-2254
Rand Paul (Chair), James Lankford, Michael B. Enzi, John Hoeven
Gary C. Peters (Ranking Minority Member), Kamala D. Harris, Doug Jones

Permanent Investigations
Office: SD-342 SDOB 20510   **Phone:** 224-3721
Rob Portman (Chair), Rand Paul, James Lankford, Mitt Romney, Josh Hawley, Ron Johnson (ex officio)
Thomas R. Carper (Ranking Minority Member), Maggie Hassan, Kamala D. Harris, Jacky Rosen

Regulatory Affairs and Federal Management
Office: SD-342 SDOB 20510   **Phone:** 224-4551
James Lankford (Chair), Rob Portman, Mitt Romney, Rick Scott, Michael B. Enzi, Ron Johnson (ex officio)
Kyrsten Sinema (Ranking Minority Member), Thomas R. Carper, Jacky Rosen

INDIAN AFFAIRS

Office: 838 SHOB 20510-6450
Phone: 224-2251   **Fax:** 224-5429
Web: www.indian.senate.gov
Majority Staff Director: Mike Andrews
Minority Staff Director: Jennifer Romero; Fax: 228-2589

Jurisdiction: (1) all proposed legislation, messages, petitions, memorials, and other matters relating to Indian affairs shall be referred to the committee; (2) study any and all matters pertaining to problems and opportunities of Indians, including but not limited to, Indian land management and trust responsibilities, Indian education, Indian health, special services, and Indian loan programs, the National Indian Gaming Regulatory Act of 1988, the National Indian Gaming Commission, and Indian claims against the United States.
Party Ratio: R 7-D 6

John Hoeven, N.D., Chair	*Tom Udall, N.M.*
John Barrasso, Wyo.	*Jon Tester, Mont.*
Lisa Murkowski, Alaska	*Maria Cantwell, Wash.*
James Lankford, Okla.	*Brian Schatz, Hawaii*
Steve Daines, Mont.	*Catherine Cortez Masto, Nev.*
Martha McSally, Ariz.	
Jerry Moran, Kans.	*Tina Smith, Minn.*

JUDICIARY

Office: 224 SDOB 20510-6275
Phone: 224-5225   **Fax:** 224-9102
Web: www.judiciary.senate.gov
Majority Staff Director: Lee Holmes

JUDICIARY (continued)

Minority Staff Director: Jennifer Duck; 152 SDOB; 224-7703; Fax: 224-9516

Jurisdiction: (1) apportionment of Representatives; (2) bankruptcy, mutiny, espionage, and counterfeiting; (3) civil liberties; (4) constitutional amendments; (5) federal courts and federal judges; (6) government information; (7) holidays and celebrations; (8) immigration and naturalization; (9) interstate compacts generally; (10) judicial proceedings, civil and criminal, generally; (11) local courts in United States territories and possessions; (12) measures relating to claims against the United States; (13) national penitentiaries; (14) Patent Office; (15) patents, copyrights, and trademarks; (16) protection of trade and commerce against unlawful restraints and monopolies; (17) revision and codification of the statutes of the United States; (18) state and territorial boundary lines.

Party Ratio: R 12-D 10

Lindsey Graham, S.C., Chair	Dianne Feinstein, Calif.
Chuck Grassley, Iowa	Patrick J. Leahy, Vt.
John Cornyn, Tex.	Richard J. Durbin, Ill.
Mike Lee, Utah	Sheldon Whitehouse, R.I.
Ted Cruz, Tex.	Amy Klobuchar, Minn.
Thom Tillis, N.C.	Christopher Coons, Del.
Josh Hawley, Mo.	Richard Blumenthal, Conn.
Joni Ernst, Iowa	Mazie K. Hirono, Hawaii
Marsha Blackburn, Tenn.	Cory A. Booker, N.J.
Ben Sasse, Neb.	Kamala D. Harris, Calif.
John Kennedy, La.	
Mike Crapo, Idaho	

Subcommittees

Antitrust, Competition Policy and Consumer Rights
Office: 224 SDOB 20510 **Phone:** 224-5225
Mike Lee (Chair), Chuck Grassley, Josh Hawley, Mike Crapo, Marsha Blackburn, Lindsey Graham (ex officio)
Amy Klobuchar (Ranking Minority Member), Richard Blumenthal, Patrick J. Leahy, Cory A. Booker, Dianne Feinstein (ex officio)

The Constitution
Office: 224 SDOB 20510 **Phone:** 224-5225
Ted Cruz (Chair), John Cornyn, Lindsey Graham (ex officio), Mike Lee, Mike Crapo, Ben Sasse, Marsha Blackburn
Mazie K. Hirono (Ranking Minority Member), Richard J. Durbin, Christopher Coons, Kamala D. Harris, Sheldon Whitehouse, Dianne Feinstein (ex officio)

Crime and Terrorism
Office: 224 SDOB 20510 **Phone:** 224-5225
Josh Hawley (Chair), Lindsey Graham, John Cornyn, Ted Cruz, John Kennedy, Thom Tillis, Joni Ernst
Sheldon Whitehouse (Ranking Minority Member), Amy Klobuchar, Christopher Coons, Richard J. Durbin, Cory A. Booker, Dianne Feinstein

Border Security and Immigration
Office: 224 SDOB 20510 **Phone:** 224-5225

John Cornyn (Chair), Lindsey Graham, Chuck Grassley, Mike Lee, Ted Cruz, Josh Hawley, Thom Tillis, John Kennedy, Joni Ernst
Richard J. Durbin (Ranking Minority Member), Patrick J. Leahy, Dianne Feinstein, Amy Klobuchar, Christopher Coons, Richard Blumenthal, Mazie K. Hirono, Cory A. Booker

Oversight, Agency Action, Federal Rights, and Federal Courts
Office: 224 SDOB 20510 **Phone:** 224-5225
Ben Sasse (Chair), Chuck Grassley, Thom Tillis, Joni Ernst, John Kennedy, Mike Crapo, Lindsey Graham (ex officio)
Richard Blumenthal (Ranking Minority Member), Sheldon Whitehouse, Amy Klobuchar, Patrick J. Leahy, Mazie K. Hirono, Dianne Feinstein (ex officio)

Intellectual Property
Office: 224 SDOB 20510 **Phone:** 224-5225
Thom Tillis (Chair), Lindsey Graham, Chuck Grassley, John Cornyn, Mike Lee, Ben Sasse, Mike Crapo, Marsha Blackburn
Christopher Coons (Ranking Minority Member), Patrick J. Leahy, Richard J. Durbin, Sheldon Whitehouse, Richard Blumenthal, Mazie K. Hirono, Kamala D. Harris

RULES AND ADMINISTRATION

Office: 305 SROB 20510-6325
Phone: 224-6352 **Fax:** 224-1912
Web: www.rules.senate.gov
Minority Web: www.rules.senate.gov/news/minority-news
Majority Staff Director: Fitzugh Elder, IV
Minority Staff Director: Elizabeth Peluso
Jurisdiction: (1) administration of the Senate office Buildings and the Senate wing of the United States Capitol, including the assignment of office space; (2) Congressional organization relative to rules and procedures, and Senate rules and regulations, including Senate floor rules and Senate gallery rules; (3) corrupt practices; (4) credentials and qualifications of Members of the Senate, contested elections, and acceptance of incompatible offices; (5) federal elections generally, including the election of the President, Vice President, and Members of the Congress; (6) Government Printing Office, and the printing and correction of the Congressional Record, as well as those matters provided for under Rule XI; (7) meetings of the Congress and attendance of Members; (8) payment of money out of the contingent fund of the Senate or creating a charge upon the same (except that any resolution relating to substantive matter within the jurisdiction of any other standing committee of the Senate shall be first referred to such committee); (9) Presidential Succession; (10) purchase of books and manuscripts and erection of monuments to the memory of individuals; (11) Senate Library and statuary, art, and pictures in the United States Capitol and Senate office buildings; (12) services to the Senate, including the Senate restaurant; (13) United States Capitol and congressional office buildings, the Library of Congress, the Smithsonian Institution (and the incorporation of similar institutions), and the United States Botanic Garden. The

committee shall also (A) make a continuing study of the organization and operation of the Congress of the United States and shall recommend improvements in such organization and operation with a view toward strengthening the Congress, simplifying its operations, improving its relationships with other branches of the United States Government, and enabling it better to meet its responsibilities under the Constitution of the United States; (B) identify any court proceeding or action which, in the opinion of the Committee, is of vital interest to the Congress as a constitutionally established institution of the Federal Government and call such proceeding or action to the attention of the Senate; (C) develop, implement, and update as necessary a strategic planning process and a strategic plan for the functional and technical infrastructure support of the Senate and provide oversight over plans developed by Senate officers and others in accordance with the strategic planning process.

Party Ratio: R 10-D 9

Roy Blunt, Mo., Chair	*Amy Klobuchar, Minn.*
Richard Shelby, Ala.	*Charles E. Schumer, N.Y.*
Lamar Alexander, Tenn.	*Dianne Feinstein, Calif.*
Mitch McConnell, Ky.	*Richard J. Durbin, Ill.*
Pat Roberts, Kans.	*Tom Udall, N.M.*
Ted Cruz, Tex.	*Mark R. Warner, Va.*
Shelley Moore Capito, W.Va.	*Patrick J. Leahy, Vt.*
Roger F. Wicker, Miss.	*Angus S. King Jr., Maine (I)*
Deb Fischer, Neb.	*Catherine Cortez Masto,*
Cindy Hyde-Smith, Miss.	*Nev.*

SMALL BUSINESS AND ENTREPRENEURSHIP

Office: 428A SROB 20510-6350
Phone: 224-5175 **Fax:** 224-5619
Web: www.sbc.senate.gov
Minority Web: www.sbc.senate.gov/public/index.cfm?
  p=RankingMember
Majority Staff Director: Mike Needham
Minority Staff Director: Sean Moore
  Jurisdiction: (1) all proposed legislation, messages, petitions, memorials and other matters relating to the Small Business Administration; (2) any proposed legislation reported by such committee that relates to matters other than the functions of the Small Business Administration shall, at the request of the chair of any standing committee having jurisdiction over the subject matter extraneous to the functions of the Small Business Administration, be considered and reported by such standing committee prior to its consideration by the Senate; and likewise measures reported by other committees directly relating to the Small Business Administration shall, at the request of the chair of the Committee on Small Business and Entrepreneurship, be referred to the Committee on Small Business and Entrepreneurship for its consideration of any portions of the measure dealing with the Small Business Administration, and be reported by this Committee prior to its consideration by the Senate; (3) study and survey by means of research and investigation all problems of small business enterprises.

Party Ratio: R 10-D 9

Marco Rubio, Fla., Chair	*Benjamin L. Cardin, Md.*
James E. Risch, Idaho	*Jeanne Shaheen, N.H.*
Tim Scott, S.C.	*Maria Cantwell, Wash.*
Rand Paul, Ky.	*Edward J. Markey, Mass.*
Joni Ernst, Iowa	*Cory A. Booker, N.J.*
Mike Rounds, S.D.	*Christopher Coons, Del.*
Mitt Romney, Utah.	*Mazie K. Hirono, Hawaii*
John Kennedy, La.	*Tammy Duckworth, Ill.*
James M. Inhofe, Okla.	*Jacky Rosen, Nev.*
Todd Young, Ind.	

VETERANS' AFFAIRS

Office: 412 SROB 20510-6375
Phone: 224-9126 **Fax:** 224-8908
Web: www.veterans.senate.gov
Minority Web: www.veterans.senate.gov/newsroom/
  minority-news
Majority Staff Director: Robert Henke
Minority Staff Director: Tony McClain; 825A SHOB; 224-2074
  Jurisdiction: (1) compensation of veterans; (2) life insurance issued by the government on account of service in the Armed Forces; (3) national cemeteries; (4) pensions of all the wars of the United States; (5) readjustment of service personnel to civil life; (6) soldiers' and sailors' civil relief, including oversight of and appropriate modifications to the Soldiers' and Sailors' Civil Relief Act of 1940; (7) veterans' hospitals, medical care and treatment of veterans; (8) veterans' measures generally; (9) vocational rehabilitation and education of veterans.

Party Ratio: R 9-D 8

Johnny Isakson, Ga., Chair	*Jon Tester, Mont.*
Jerry Moran, Kans.	*Richard Blumenthal, Conn.*
John Boozman, Ark.	*Patty Murray, Wash.*
Kevin Cramer, N.D.	*Bernard Sanders, Vt. (I)*
Bill Cassidy, La.	*Sherrod Brown, Ohio*
Mike Rounds, S.D.	*Mazie K. Hirono, Hawaii*
Thom Tillis, N.C.	*Joe Manchin, W.Va.*
Dan Sullivan, Alaska	*Kyrsten Sinema, Ariz.*
Marsha Blackburn, Tenn.	

SELECT ETHICS

Office: 220 SHOB 20510-6425
Phone: 224-2981 **Fax:** 224-7416
Web: www.ethics.senate.gov
Staff Director: Deborah Mayer
  Jurisdiction: (1) receive and investigate allegations of improper conduct that may reflect upon the Senate, violations of law, violations of the Senate Code of Official Conduct, and violations of rules and regulations of the Senate; (2) recommend disciplinary action; (3) recommend additional Senate rules or regulations to ensure proper standards of conduct; (4) report violations of any law to the proper Federal and State authorities; (5) sets out ten standards of conduct that should be adhered to by all government employees, including office holders; (6) investigate unauthorized disclosures of intelligence information by a Member, officer, or employee of the Senate and to report to the Senate on any substantial allegation; (7) provide guidance and promulgate

SELECT ETHICS (continued)

rules regarding the frank and may investigate complaints involving a violation of the Franking statute; (8) responsible for Financial Disclosure Statements (Title I) and for Outside Employment (Title V) with respect to members, officers, and employees of the Senate; (9) administer the provisions of the Foreign Gifts and Decorations Act with respect Members, officers, and employees of the United States Senate; (10) as the "supervising ethics office" for the Senate, the Committee is responsible for the statutory prohibitions against Members, officers, and employees of the Senate giving gifts to an official superior or receiving gifts from employees with a lower salary level, or soliciting or receiving gifts.

Party Ratio: R 3-D 3

Johnny Isakson, Ga., Chair	Christopher Coons, Del.,
Pat Roberts, Kans.	Vice Chair
James E. Risch, Idaho	Brian Schatz, Hawaii
	Jeanne Shaheen, N.H.

SELECT INTELLIGENCE

Office: 211 SHOB 20510-6475
Phone: 224-1700 **Fax:** 224-1772
Web: www.intelligence.senate.gov
Majority Staff Director: Christopher A. Joyner
Minority Staff Director: Michael Casey

Jurisdiction: (1) oversee and make continuing studies of the intelligence activities and programs of the United States Government, including, but not limited to, the Central Intelligence Agency Act of 1949, Classified Information Procedures Act of 1980, classified national security information, foreign intelligence electronic surveillance, Foreign Intelligence Surveillance Act of 1978, National Security Act of 1947, National Security Agency Act of 1959, national security information, President's Foreign Intelligence Advisory Board (Executive Office of the President), Provide Appropriate Tools Required to Intercept and Obstruct Terrorism (PATRIOT) Act of 2001, security requirements for government employment; (2) submit to the Senate appropriate proposals for legislation; (3) report to the Senate concerning such intelligence activities and programs; (4) provide vigilant legislative oversight over the intelligence activities of the United States to assure that such activities are in conformity with the Constitution and laws of the United States.

Party Ratio: R 10-D 9

Richard Burr, N.C., Chair	Mark R. Warner, Va.,
James E. Risch, Idaho	Vice Chair
Marco Rubio, Va.	Dianne Feinstein, Calif.
Susan M. Collins, Maine	Ron Wyden, Ore.
Roy Blunt, Mo.	Martin Heinrich, N.M.
Tom Cotton, Ark.	Angus S. King Jr., Maine (I)
John Cornyn, Tex.	Michael F. Bennet, Colo.
Ben Sasse, Neb.	Kamala D. Harris, Calif.
Mitch McConnell	Charles E. Schumer
(ex officio)	(ex officio)
James M. Inhofe, Okla.	Jack Reed (ex officio)
(ex officio)	

SPECIAL AGING

Office: G-31 SDOB 20510-6050
Phone: 224-5364 **Fax:** 224-8660
Web: www.aging.senate.gov
Minority Web: www.aging.senate.gov/press-room/
  minority
Majority Staff Director: Kevin Kelley
Minority Staff Director: Kate Mevis; 628 SHOB; 224-0185;
  Fax: 224-9920

Jurisdiction: (1) conduct a continuing study of any and all matters pertaining to problems and opportunities of older people, including, but not limited to, problems and opportunities of maintaining health, of assuring adequate income, of finding employment, of engaging in productive and rewarding activity, of securing proper housing, and when necessary, of obtaining care or assistance. No proposed legislation shall be referred to such committee, and such committee shall not have power to report by bill, or otherwise have legislative jurisdiction. (2) The special committee shall, from time to time (but not less often than once each year), report to the Senate the results of the study conducted pursuant to paragraph (1), together with such recommendation as it considers appropriate.

Party Ratio: R 8-D 7

Susan M. Collins, Maine,	Robert P. Casey Jr., Pa.
Chair	Kirsten E. Gillibrand, N.Y.
Tim Scott, S.C.	Richard Blumenthal, Conn.
Richard Burr, N.C.	Elizabeth Warren, Mass.
Martha McSally, Ariz.	Doug Jones, Ala.
Marco Rubio, Fla.	Kyrsten Sinema, Ariz.
Josh Hawley, Mo.	Jacky Rosen, Nev.
Mike Braun, Ind.	
Rick Scott, Fla.	

INTERNATIONAL NARCOTICS CONTROL CAUCUS

Office: 818-C SHOB 20510
Phone: 224-9032
Web: www.drugcaucus.senate.gov

Purpose: The Senate Caucus on International Narcotics Control was created to "monitor and encourage United States Government and private programs seeking to expand international cooperation against drug abuse and narcotics trafficking" and to "monitor and promote international compliance with narcotics control treaties." As a formal organization of the U.S. Senate, the Caucus has the status of a standing committee. The Caucus exercises oversight on a wide range of issues, including international counternarcotics assistance and domestic drug prevention and treatment programs. The Caucus has held numerous hearings over the years and has issued a number of reports on U.S. narcotics control policy.

Party Ratio: R 4-D 3

John Cornyn, Tex., Chair	Dianne Feinstein, Calif.,
Chuck Grassley, Iowa	Co-Chair
James E. Risch, Idaho	Jacky Rosen, Nev.
David Perdue, Ga.	Sheldon Whitehouse, R.I.

SENATE LEADERSHIP AND PARTISAN COMMITTEES

REPUBLICAN LEADERS

Majority Floor Leader: Mitch McConnell, Ky.
Majority Whip: John Thune, S.D.

REPUBLICAN PARTISAN COMMITTEES

National Republican Senatorial Committee
Office: 425 2nd St. N.E. 20002-4914
Phone: 675-6000   **Fax:** 675-4730
Web: www.nrsc.org
Todd Young, Ind., Chair
Vacant, Vice Chair
Kevin McLaughlin, Executive Director

Republican Conference
Office: 405 SHOB 20510-7060
Phone: 224-2764   **Fax:** 228-4276
Web: www.republican.senate.gov
John Barrasso, Wyo., Chair
Joni Ernst, Iowa, Vice Chair

Republican Policy Committee
Office: 347 SROB 20510-7064
Phone: 224-2946   **Fax:** 228-2628 and 224-1235
Web: www.rpc.senate.gov
Roy Blunt, Mo., Chair

DEMOCRATIC LEADERS

Minority Floor Leader: *Charles E. Schumer, N.Y.*
Minority Whip: *Richard J. Durbin, Ill.*

DEMOCRATIC PARTISAN COMMITTEES

Democratic Policy and Communications Center
Office: S-318 CAP 20510
Phone: 224-2939   **Fax:** 228-5576
Web: www.dpcc.senate.gov
Debbie Stabenow, Mich., Chair
Joe Manchin, W.Va., Vice Chair

Democratic Senatorial Campaign Committee
Office: 120 Maryland Ave. N.E. 20002-5610
Phone: 224-2447   **Fax:** 969-0354
Web: www.dscc.org
Email: info@dscc.org
Catherine Cortez Masto, Nev., Chair
Scott Fairchild, Executive Director

Democratic Steering and Outreach Committee
Office: 712 SHOB 20510
Phone: 224-9048   **Fax:** 224-5476
Web: www.dsoc.senate.gov
Email: steering@dsoc.senate.gov
Amy Klobuchar, Minn., Chair
Jeanne Shaheen, N.H., Vice Chair

Senate Members' Offices

The following list gives Senate members and their party and state affiliation, followed by the address and telephone and fax numbers for their Washington office. The area code for all Washington, D.C., numbers is 202. A top administrative aide, a Web address, and social media for each senator are also provided, when available. Most members may be contacted via the Web-based email forms found on their Web sites. These are followed by the address, telephone and fax numbers, and name of a key aide for the senator's district office(s). Each listing concludes with the senator's Committee Assignments. For partisan Committee Assignments, see page 927.

As of April 12, 2019, there were 53 Republicans, 45 Democrats, 0 vacancies, and 2 Independents who caucus with the Democrats in the Senate.

Alexander, Lamar, R-Tenn.

Capitol Hill Office: 455 SDOB 20510-4206; 224-4944; Fax: 228-3398; *Chief of Staff:* David Cleary
Web: www.alexander.senate.gov
Facebook: www.facebook.com/senatorlamaralexander
Twitter: @SenAlexander
Instagram: @senalexander
YouTube: www.youtube.com/lamaralexander
District Offices: 2525 Hwy. 75, #101, Blountville, TN 37617-6366; 423-325-6240; Fax: 423-325-6236; *Field Rep.:* Lana Moore
Joel E. Soloman Federal Bldg., 900 Georgia Ave., #260, Chattanooga, TN 37402-2240; 423-752-5337; Fax: 423-752-5342; *Field Rep.:* Jeff Lewis
111 Murray Guard Dr., Suite D, Jackson, TN 38305-3628; 731-664-0289; Fax: 731-664-3129; *Field Rep.:* Matt Varino
Howard H. Baker Jr. U.S. Courthouse, 800 Market St., #112, Knoxville, TN 37902-2303; 865-545-4253; Fax: 865-545-4252; *State Director:* Patrick Jaynes
Clifford Davis-Odell Horton Federal Bldg., 167 N. Main St., #1068, Memphis, TN 38103-1858; 901-544-4224; Fax: 901-544-4227; *Field Rep.:* Chris Connolly
3322 W. End Ave., #120, Nashville, TN 37203-6821; 615-736-5129; Fax: 615-269-4803; *State Scheduler and Office Manager:* Faye Head
Committee Assignments: Appropriations; Energy and Natural Resources; Health, Education, Labor, and Pensions, Chair; Rules and Administration

Baldwin, Tammy, D-Wisc.

Capitol Hill Office: 709 SHOB 20510; 224-5653; Fax: 224-9787; *Chief of Staff:* Bill Murat
Web: www.baldwin.senate.gov
Facebook: www.facebook.com/senatortammybaldwin
Twitter: @SenatorBaldwin
Instagram: @senatorbaldwin
YouTube: www.youtube.com/senatortammybaldwin
District Offices: 500 S. Barstow St., #LL2, Eau Claire, WI 54701-3608; 715-832-8424; *Field Rep.:* Kelly Westlund
205 5th Ave. South, Room 216, La Crosse, WI 54601; 608-796-0045; Fax: 608-796-0089; *Regional Rep.:* Gregg Wavrunek

30 W. Mifflin St., #700, Madison, WI 53703-2568; 608-264-5338; Fax: 608-264-5473; *State Director:* Janet Piraino
633 W. Wisconsin Ave., #1920, Milwaukee, WI 53203-2205; 414-297-4451; Fax: 414-297-4455; *Field Rep.:* Tiffany Henry
2100 Stewart Ave., #250B, Wausau, WI 54401; 715-261-2611; *Outreach Rep:* Doug Hill
1039 W. Mason St. #119, Green Bay, WI 54303; 920-498-2668; *Regional Rep:* Jennifer Garner
Committee Assignments: Appropriations; Commerce, Science, and Transportation; Health, Education, Labor, and Pensions

Barrasso, John, R-Wyo.

Capitol Hill Office: 307 SDOB 20510-5005; 224-6441; Fax: 224-1724; *Chief of Staff:* J. Dan Kunsman
Web: www.barrasso.senate.gov
Facebook: www.facebook.com/johnbarrasso
Twitter: @senjohnbarrasso
Instagram: @senjohnbarrasso
YouTube: www.youtube.com/barrassowyo
District Offices: 100 E. B St., #2004, Casper, WY 82601-7021; 307-261-6413; Fax: 307-265-6706; *Field Rep.:* Nolan Rap
2120 Capitol Ave., #2013, Cheyenne, WY 82001-3631; 307-772-2451; Fax: 307-638-3512; *State Director:* Jinx Clark
324 E. Washington Ave., Riverton, WY 82501-4342; 307-856-6642; Fax: 307-856-5901; *Field Rep.:* Pam Buline
1575 Dewar Dr., #218, Rock Springs, WY 82901-5972; 307-362-5012; Fax: 307-362-5129; *Field Rep.:* Andrew Holcomb
2 N. Main St., #206, Sheridan, WY 82801-6322; 307-672-6456; Fax: 307-672-8227; *Field Rep.:* Christy Stofferf
Committee Assignments: Energy and Natural Resources; Environment and Public Works, Chair; Foreign Relations; Indian Affairs

Bennet, Michael F., D-Colo.

Capitol Hill Office: 261 SROB 20510-0608; 224-5852; Fax: 228-5097; *Chief of Staff:* Jonathan Davidson
Web: www.bennet.senate.gov
Facebook: www.facebook.com/senbennetco

Twitter: @senbennetco
Instagram: @senatorbennet
YouTube: www.youtube.com/senatorbennet
District Offices: 609 Main St., #110, Alamosa, CO 81101-2557; 719-587-0096; Fax: 719-587-0098; *Regional Rep.:* Erin Minks

409 N. Tejon St., #107, Colorado Springs, CO 80903-1163; 719-328-1100; Fax: 719-328-1129; *Regional Director:* Annie Oatman-Gardner

1244 Speer Blvd., Denver, CO 80204; 303-455-7600; Fax: 303-455-8851; *State Director:* Julie Duvall

835 E. 2nd Ave., #206, Durango, CO 81301-5475; 970-259-1710; Fax: 970-259-9789; *Regional Director:* John Whitney

1200 S. College Ave., #211, Fort Collins, CO 80524-3746; 970-224-2200; Fax: 970-224-2205; *Regional Director:* James Thompson

129 W. B St., Pueblo, CO 81003-3400; 719-542-7550; Fax: 719-542-7555; *Regional Director:* Dwight Gardner

225 N. 5th St., #511, Grand Junction, CO 81501; 970-241-6631; *Constituent Advocate:* Alyssa Logan
Committee Assignments: Agriculture, Nutrition, and Forestry; Finance; Select Intelligence

Blackburn, Marsha, R-Tenn.

Capitol Hill Office: B40B SDOB 20510-5005; 224-3344; Fax: 228-0566; *Chief of Staff:* Chuck Flint
Web: www.blackburn.senate.gov
Facebook: www.facebook.com/marshablackburn
Twitter: @MarshaBlackburn
Instagram: @marshablackburn
YouTube: www.youtube.com/channel/UCK_JQCLG1Zzea10S9oHAIOA
District Offices: 800 Market St., #121, Knoxville, TN 37902; 865-540-3781; Fax: 865-540-7952; *Lead Constituent Services Director:* Rhonda Smithson; *Constituent Services Rep.:* Kristin Rosa

91 Stonebridge Blvd., #103, Jackson, TN 38305; 731-660-3971; Fax: 731-660-3978; *State Constituent Services Coordinator:* Dana Magneson

1105 E. Jackson Blvd., #4, Jonesborough, TN 37659; 423-753-4009; Fax: 423-788-0250; *Constituent Services Rep.:* Kim Cordell

10 W. Martin Luther King Blvd., 6th Floor, Chattanooga, TN 37402; 423-541-2939; Fax: 423-541-2944; *Office Administrator, Constituent Services Rep.:* Kelly Puckett

100 Peabody Pl., #1125, Memphis, TN 38103; 901-527-9199; Fax: 901-527-9395; *Constituent Services Rep.:* Jerri Wheeler
Committee Assignments: Armed Services, Commerce, Science, and Transportation; Judiciary; Veterans' Affairs

Blumenthal, Richard, D-Conn.

Capitol Hill Office: 706 SHOB 20510-0704; 224-2823; Fax: 224-9673; *Chief of Staff:* Joel Kelsey
Web: www.blumenthal.senate.gov

Facebook: www.facebook.com/SenBlumenthal
Twitter: @SenBlumenthal
Instagram: @senblumenthal
YouTube: www.youtube.com/senatorblumenthal
District Offices: 90 State House Square, 10th Floor, Hartford, CT 06103; 860-258-6940; Fax: 860-258-6958; *State Director:* Rich Kehoe

915 Lafayette Blvd., Room 304, Bridgeport, CT 06604; 203-330-0598; Fax: 203-330-0608; *State Director:* Rich Kehoe
Committee Assignments: Armed Services; Commerce, Science, and Transportation; Judiciary; Special Aging; Veterans' Affairs

Blunt, Roy, R-Mo.

Capitol Hill Office: 260 SROB 20510-2508; 224-5721; *Chief of Staff:* Stacy McBride
Web: www.blunt.senate.gov
Facebook: www.facebook.com/SenatorBlunt
Twitter: @RoyBlunt
Instagram: @royblunt
YouTube: www.youtube.com/SenatorBlunt
District Offices: 338 Broadway, #303, Cape Girardeau, MO 63701; 573-334-7044; *Office Director:* Caroline Yielding

111 S. 10th St., #23.305, St. Louis, MO 63102; 314-725-4484; *Office Director:* Mary Beth Luna Wolf

1123 Wilkes Blvd., #320, Columbia, MO 65201-7931; 573-442-8151; *State Director:* Derek Coats

1000 Walnut St., #1560, Kansas City, MO 64106; 816-471-7141; *Office Director:* Brandt Shields

2740B E. Sunshine St., Springfield, MO 65804-2016; 417-877-7814; *District Office Director:* Joelle Cannon
Committee Assignments: Appropriations; Commerce, Science, and Transportation; Joint Library, Chair; Joint Printing, Vice Chair; Rules and Administration, Chair; Select Intelligence

Booker, Cory A., D-N.J.

Capitol Hill Office: 359 SDOB 20510; 224-3224; Fax: 224-8378; *Chief of Staff:* Matt Klapper
Web: booker.senate.gov
Facebook: www.facebook.com/corybooker
Twitter: @corybooker
Instagram: @corybooker
YouTube: www.youtube.com/sencorybooker
District Offices: One Port Center, 2 Riverside Dr., #505, Camden, NJ 08101; 856-338-8922; Fax: 856-338-8936 *South Jersey Director:* Bill Moen

One Gateway Center, 23rd Floor, Newark, NJ 07102; 973-639-8700; Fax: 973-639-8723; *State Director:* George Helmy
Committee Assignments: Environment and Public Works; Foreign Relations; Judiciary; Small Business and Entrepreneurship

Boozman, John, R-Ark.

Capitol Hill Office: 141 SHOB 20510-0406; 224-4843; Fax: 228-1371; *Chief of Staff:* Toni-Marie Higgins
Web: www.boozman.senate.gov

Facebook: www.facebook.com/JohnBoozman
Twitter: @JohnBoozman
Instagram: @johnboozman
YouTube: www.youtube.com/BoozmanPressOffice
District Offices: 106 W. Main St., #104, El Dorado, AR 71730-5634; 870-863-4641; Fax: 870-863-4105; *Constituent Services Rep.:* Chase Emerson

1120 Garrison Ave., #2B, Fort Smith, AR 72901-2617; 479-573-0189; Fax: 479-573-0553; *Casework Coord.:* Kathy Watson

300 S. Church St., #400, Jonesboro, AR 72401-2911; 870-268-6925; Fax: 870-268-6887; *Caseworker:* Amanda Blaylock

1401 W. Capitol Ave., #155, Little Rock, AR 72201-2942; 501-372-7153; Fax: 501-372-7163; *Grants Coord.:* Jimmy Harris

213 W. Monroe Ave., Suite N, Lowell, AR 72745-9451; 479-725-0400; Fax: 479-725-0408; *State Director:* Stacey McClure

1001 Hwy 62 East, #11, Mountain Home, AR 72653-3215; 870-424-0129; Fax: 870-424-0141; *Caseworker, Social Security Medicare:* Sherry Slippo

620 E. 22nd St., #204, Stuttgart, AR 72160-9007; 870-672-6941; Fax: 870-672-6962; *Field Rep.:* Ty Davis

Committee Assignments: Agriculture, Nutrition, and Forestry; Appropriations; Environment and Public Works; Veterans' Affairs; Commission on Security and Cooperation in Europe

Braun, Mike, R-Ind.

Capitol Hill Office: B-85 SROB 20510; 202-224-4814; *Chief of Staff:* Joshua Kelley
Web: www.braun.senate.gov
Facebook: www.facebook.com/SenatorBraun
Twitter: @SenatorBraun
YouTube: www.youtube.com/channel/UCQ02jR4CJErAbv3522PJffA
District Offices: 115 N. Pennsylvania St., Indianapolis, IN 46204; 317-822-8240; Fax: 317-822-8353; *State Director:* Jason Johnson

203 E. Berry St., #702B, Fort Wayne, IN 46802; 260-427-2164; Fax: 260-427-2167; *Regional Director:* Mary Martin

5400 Federal Plaza, #3200, Hammond IN 46320; 219-937-9650; Fax: 219-937-9665; *Regional Rep.:* Anthony Ferraro

205 W. Colfax Ave., South Bend, IN 46601; 574-288-6302; Fax: 574-288-6450

Committee Assignments: Agriculture, Nutrition, and Forestry; Environment and Public Works; Health, Education, Labor, and Pensions; Budget, Special Aging

Brown, Sherrod, D-Ohio

Capitol Hill Office: 713 SHOB 20510-3505; 224-2315; Fax: 228-6321; *Chief of Staff:* Sarah Benzing
Web: www.brown.senate.gov
Facebook: www.facebook.com/sherrod
Twitter: @sensherrodbrown

Instagram: @sensherrodbrown
YouTube: www.youtube.com/SherrodBrownOhio
District Offices: 425 Walnut St., #2310, Cincinnati, OH 45202-3915; 513-684-1021; Fax: 513-684-1029; *Southwest Regional Director:* Alea Brown

801 W. Superior Ave., #1400, Cleveland, OH 44114-1869; 216-522-7272; Fax: 216-522-2239; *State Director:* John Ryan

200 N. High St., Room 614, Columbus, OH 43215-2408; 614-469-2083; Fax: 614-469-2171; *Central Ohio Regional Director:* Joe Gilligan

200 W. Erie Ave., #312, Lorain, OH 44052; 440-242-4100; Fax: 440-242-4108; *Constituent Advocate:* Margaret Molnar

Committee Assignments: Agriculture, Nutrition, and Forestry; Banking, Housing, and Urban Affairs, Ranking Minority Member; Finance; Veterans' Affairs

Burr, Richard, R-N.C.

Capitol Hill Office: 217 SROB 20510-3308; 224-3154; Fax: 228-2981; *Chief of Staff:* Natasha Hickman
Web: www.burr.senate.gov
Facebook: www.facebook.com/SenatorRichardBurr
Twitter: @senatorburr
Instagram: @senatorburr
YouTube: www.youtube.com/SenatorRichardBurr
District Offices: Federal Bldg., 151 Patton Ave., #204, Asheville, NC 28801-2689; 828-350-2437; Fax: 828-350-2439; *State Director:* Dean Myers

100 Coast Line St., Room 210, Rocky Mount, NC 27804-5849; 252-977-9522; Fax: 252-977-7902; *Field Rep.:* Betty Jo Shepheard

201 N. Front St., #809, Wilmington, NC 28401-5089; 910-251-1058; Fax: 910-251-7975; *Constituent Advocate:* Brandon Hawkins

2000 W. 1st St., #508, Winston-Salem, NC 27104-4225; 336-631-5125; Fax: 336-725-4493; *State Director:* Dean Myers

Committee Assignments: Finance; Health, Education, Labor, and Pensions; Select Intelligence, Chair; Special Aging

Cantwell, Maria, D-Wash.

Capitol Hill Office: 511 SHOB 20510-4705; 224-3441; Fax: 228-0514; *Chief of Staff:* Travis Lumpkin
Web: www.cantwell.senate.gov
Facebook: www.facebook.com/senatorcantwell
Twitter: @SenatorCantwell
Instagram: @senatormariacantwell
YouTube: www.youtube.com/SenatorCantwell
District Offices: 2930 Wetmore Ave., #9B, Everett, WA 98201-4044; 425-303-0114; Fax: 425-303-8351; *Northwest Outreach Director:* Cameron Caldwell

825 Jadwin Ave., #206, Richland, WA 99352-3562; 509-946-8106; Fax: 509-946-6937; *Central Washington Director:* Richard Evans

915 2nd Ave., #3206, Seattle, WA 98174-1011; 206-220-6400; Fax: 206-220-6404; *Staff Director:* Nate Caminos

920 W. Riverside Ave., #697, Spokane, WA 99201-1008; 509-353-2507; Fax: 509-353-2547; *Eastern Outreach Director:* Alex Scott

950 Pacific Ave., #615, Tacoma, WA 98402-4431; 253-572-2281; Fax: 253-572-5879; *Olympic Peninsula and Pierce County Director:* Rosa McLeod

1313 Officers Row, Vancouver, WA 98661-3856; 360-696-7838; Fax: 360-696-7844; *Southwest Outreach Director:* Dena Horton

Committee Assignments: Commerce, Science, and Transportation; Energy and Natural Resources; Finance; Indian Affairs; Small Business and Entrepreneurship

Capito, Shelley Moore, D-W.Va.

Capitol Hill Office: 172 SROB 20510; 224-6472; Fax: 224-7665; *Chief of Staff:* Joel Brubaker

Web: www.capito.senate.gov

Facebook: www.facebook.com/senshelley

Twitter: @SenCapito

Instagram: sencapito

YouTube: www.youtube.com/channel/ UCbiXdR4XQ3vD9Xp5lfR9QXw

District Offices: 500 Virginia St. East, #950, Charleston, WV 25301; 304-347-5372; Fax: 304-347-5371; *State Director:* Mary Elisabeth Eckerson

300 Foxcroft Ave., #202A, Martinsburg, WV 25401; 304-262-9285; Fax: 304-262-9288; *Field Rep:* Chris Strovel

48 Donley St., #504, Morgantown, WV 26401; 304-292-2310; *Field Rep.:* Jessicah Cross

220 N. Kanawha St., #1, Beckley, WV 25801; 304-347-5372

Committee Assignments: Appropriations; Commerce, Science, and Transportation; Environment and Public Works; Rules and Administration

Cardin, Benjamin L., D-Md.

Capitol Hill Office: 509 SHOB 20510-2004; 224-4524; Fax: 224-1651; *Chief of Staff:* Christopher W. Lynch

Web: www.cardin.senate.gov

Facebook: www.facebook.com/senatorbencardin

Twitter: @SenatorCardin

Instagram: @senatorcardin

YouTube: www.youtube.com/SenatorCardin

District Offices: 100 S. Charles St., Tower 1, #1710, Baltimore, MD 21201-2788; 410-962-4436; Fax: 410-962-4156; *State Director:* Carleton Atkinson

10201 Martin Luther King Jr. Hwy., #210, Bowie, MD 20720-4000; 301-860-0414; Fax: 301-860-0416; *Field Rep.:* Ryan Middleton

13 Canal St., Room 305, Cumberland, MD 21502-3054; 301-777-2957; Fax: 301-777-2959; *Field Rep.:* Robin Summerfield

451 Hungerford Dr., #210, Rockville, MD 20850-4187; 301-762-2974; Fax: 301-762-2976; *Field Rep.:* Ken Reichard

212 W. Main St., #301C, Salisbury, MD 21801-4920; 410-546-4250; Fax: 410-546-4252; *Field Rep.:* Kim Kratovil

Committee Assignments: Environment and Public Works; Finance; Foreign Relations; Small Business and Entrepreneurship, Ranking Minority Member; Commission on Security and Cooperation in Europe

Carper, Thomas R., D-Del.

Capitol Hill Office: 513 SHOB 20510-0803; 224-2441; Fax: 228-2190; *Chief of Staff:* Bill Ghent

Web: www.carper.senate.gov

Facebook: www.facebook.com/tomcarper

Twitter: @senatorcarper

YouTube: www.youtube.com/user/SenatorCarper

District Offices: 500 W. Loockerman St., #470, Dover, DE 19904-3298; 302-674-3308; Fax: 302-674-5464; *State Director:* Lori James

12 The Circle, Georgetown, DE 19947-1501; 302-856-7690; Fax: 302-856-3001; *Sussex County Regional Director:* Karen McGrath

301 N. Walnut St., #102L-1, Wilmington, DE 19801-3974; 302-573-6291; Fax: 302-573-6434; *New Castle County Regional Director:* Bonnie Wu

Committee Assignments: Environment and Public Works, Ranking Minority Member; Finance; Homeland Security and Governmental Affairs

Casey, Robert P. Jr., D-Pa.

Capitol Hill Office: 393 SROB 20510-3805; 224-6324; Fax: 228-0604; *Acting Chief of Staff:* Kristen Gentile

Web: www.casey.senate.gov

Facebook: www.facebook.com/SenatorBobCasey

Twitter: @SenBobCasey

Instagram: @senbobcasey

YouTube: www.youtube.com/SenatorBobCasey

District Offices: 840 Hamilton St., #301, Allentown, PA 18101-2456; 610-782-9470; Fax: 610-782-9474; *Regional Manager:* Connor Corpora

817 E. Bishop St., Suite C, Bellefonte, PA 16823-2321; 814-357-0314; Fax: 814-357-0318; *Regional Manager:* Kim Bierly

17 S. Park Row, #B-150, Erie, PA 16501-1162; 814-874-5080; Fax: 814-874-5084; *Regional Manager:* Kyle Hannon

200 N. 3rd St., #14A, Harrisburg, PA 17101-2105; 717-231-7540; Fax: 717-231-7542; *Director of Constituent Services:* Teresa Dennis

2000 Market St., #610, Philadelphia, PA 19103; 215-405-9660; Fax: 215-405-9669; *State Director:* Erin Wilson

Grant Bldg., 310 Grant St., #2415, Pittsburgh, PA 15219; 412-803-7370; Fax: 412-803-7379; *Southwestern PA Regional Director:* Elizabeth Fishback

417 Lackawanna Ave., #303, Scranton, PA 18503-2013; 570-941-0930; Fax: 570-941-0937; *State Scheduler:* Jessica Butherus

Committee Assignments: Agriculture, Nutrition, and Forestry; Finance; Health, Education, Labor, and Pensions; Special Aging, Ranking Minority Member

Cassidy, Bill, R-La.

Capitol Hill Office: 520 SHOB 20510-1804; 224-5824; Fax: 224-6161; *Chief of Staff:* James Quinn

Web: www.cassidy.senate.gov

Facebook: www.facebook.com/billcassidy

Twitter: @billcassidy

YouTube: www.youtube.com/DrBillCassidy

District Offices: 3600 Jackson St., #115A, Alexandria, LA 71301; 318-448-7176; Fax: 318- 448-5175; *Central Louisiana State Director:* Tommie Seaton

5555 Hilton Ave., #100, Baton Rouge, LA 70808; 225-929-7711; Fax: 225-292-7688; *State Director:* Brian McNabb

101 La Rue France, #505, Lafayette, LA 70508; 337-261-1400; Fax: 337-261-1490; *South Western Regional Director:* Lauren Casanova

1 Lakeshore Dr., #1155, Lake Charles, LA 70629; 337-493-5398; Fax: 225-247-5629; *South Western Regional Director:* Lauren Casanova

3421 N. Causeway Blvd., #204, Metairie, LA 70002; 504-838-0130; Fax: 504-838-0133; *Regional Director:* Rachel Perez

1651 Louisville Ave., #123, Monroe, LA 70120; 318-324-2111; Fax: 318-324-2197; *Regional Director:* Angie Robert

6425 Youree Dr., #415, Shreveport, LA 71105; 318-798-3215; Fax: 318-798-8471; *Regional Director:* Stephanie McKenzie

Committee Assignments: Energy and Natural Resources; Finance; Health, Education, Labor, and Pensions; Veterans' Affairs; Joint Economic

Collins, Susan M., R-Maine

Capitol Hill Office: 413 SDOB 20510-1904; 224-2523; Fax: 224-2693; *Chief of Staff:* Steve Abbott
Web: www.collins.senate.gov
Facebook: www.facebook.com/susancollins
Twitter: @senatorcollins
Instagram: @sensusancollins
YouTube: www.youtube.com/SenatorSusanCollins
District Offices: 68 Sewall St., Room 507, Augusta, ME 04330-6354; 207-622-8414; Fax: 207-622-5884; *State Office Rep.:* Mark Winter

202 Harlow St., Room 20100, Bangor, ME 04401; 207-945-0417; Fax: 207-990-4604; *State Office Rep.:* Carol Woodcock

160 Main St., Biddeford, ME 04005-2580; 207-283-1101; Fax: 207-283-4054; *State Office Rep.:* Alexandria Pelczar

25 Sweden St., Suite A, Caribou, ME 04736-2149; 207-493-7873; Fax: 207-493-7810; *State Office Rep.:* Trisha House

55 Lisbon St., Lewiston, ME 04240-7117; 207-784-6969; Fax: 207-782-6475; *State Office Rep.:* Carlene Tremblay

One Canal Plaza, #802, Portland, ME 04101-4083; 207-780-3575; Fax: 207-828-0380; *State Office Rep.:* Kate Simpson

Committee Assignments: Appropriations; Health, Education, Labor, and Pensions; Select Intelligence; Special Aging, Chair

Coons, Christopher, D-Del.

Capitol Hill Office: 127A SROB 20510-0805; 224-5042; Fax: 228-3075; *Chief of Staff:* Jonathan Stahler
Web: www.coons.senate.gov

Facebook: www.facebook.com/senatorchriscoons
Twitter: @ChrisCoons
Instagram: @senatorchriscoons
YouTube: www.youtube.com/senatorchriscoons
District Offices: 500 W. Loockerman St., #450, Dover, DE 19904-3298; 302-736-5601; Fax: 302-736-5609; *Kent/Sussex Coord.:* Kate Rorher

1105 N. Market St., #100, Wilmington, DE 19801-1233; 302-573-6345; Fax: 302-573-6351; *State Director:* Jim Paoli

Committee Assignments: Appropriations; Foreign Relations; Judiciary; Select Ethics, Vice Chair; Small Business and Entrepreneurship

Cornyn, John, R-Tex.

Capitol Hill Office: 517 SHOB 20510-4305; 224-2934; Fax: 224-5220; *Chief of Staff:* Beth Jafari
Web: www.cornyn.senate.gov
Facebook: www.facebook.com/Sen.JohnCornyn
Twitter: @JohnCornyn
Instagram: @johncornyn
YouTube: www.youtube.com/SenJohnCornyn
District Offices: Chase Tower, 221 W. 6th St., #1530, Austin, TX 78701-3403; 512-469-6034; Fax: 512-469-6020; *State Field Director:* David James

5001 Spring Valley Rd., #1125E, Dallas, TX 75244-3916; 972-239-1310; Fax: 972-239-2110; *Regional Director:* Collin McLochlin

222 E. Van Buren. Ave., #404, Harlingen, TX 78550-6804; 956-423-0162; Fax: 956-423-0193; *Regional Director:* Ana Garcia

5300 Memorial Dr., #980, Houston, TX 77007; 713-572-3337; Fax: 713-572-3777; *Regional Director:* Jay Guerrero

Wells Fargo Center, 1500 Broadway, #1230, Lubbock, TX 79401-3114; 806-472-7533; Fax: 806-472-7536; *Regional Director:* Jaci Glover

600 Navarro St., #210, San Antonio, TX 78205; 210-224-7485; Fax: 210-224-8569; *Regional Director:* Jonathan Huhn

100 E. Ferguson St., #1004, Tyler, TX 75702; 903-593-0902; Fax: 903-593-0920; *Regional Director:* Kathy Comer

Committee Assignments: Finance; International Narcotics Control Caucus, Chair; Judiciary; Select Intelligence

Cortez Masto, Catherine, D-Nev.

Capitol Hill Office: 204 SROB 20510; 224-3542; *Chief of Staff:* Reynaldo Benitez
Web: www.cortezmasto.senate.gov
Facebook: www.facebook.com/SenatorCortezMasto
Twitter: @SenCortezMasto
Instagram: @catherinecortezmastofornv
YouTube: www.youtube.com/channel/ UCip_83SiKUqwnUT57VOXrCg
District Offices: 333 Las Vegas Blvd. South, #8016, Las Vegas, NV 89101; 702-388-5020; Fax: 702-388-5030 *State Director:* Zach Varagova

Courthouse and Federal Bldg., 400 S. Virginia St., #902, Reno, NV 89501; 775-686-5750; Fax: 775-686-5757; **Regional Rep.:** Gillian Block and Kerry Durmick
Committee Assignments: Banking, Housing, and Urban Affairs; Finance; Energy and Natural Resources; Indian Affairs; Rules and Administration

Cotton, Tom, R-Ark.

Capitol Hill Office: 124 SROB 20510; 224-2353; **Chief of Staff:** Doug Coutts
Web: www.cotton.senate.gov
Facebook: www.facebook.com/SenatorTomCotton
Twitter: @SenTomCotton
Instagram: @tomcottonar
YouTube: www.youtube.com/channel/
UCxrZsasJfxOVUEOnhed5doA
District Offices: 1401 W. Capitol Ave., #235, Little Rock, AR 72201; 501-223-9081; Fax: 501-223-9105; **State Director:** Vanessa Moody
1108 S. Old Missouri Rd., Suite B, Springdale, AR 72764; 479-751-0879; Fax: 479-927-1092; **Field Rep.:** Kaci Sturgeon
106 W. Main St., #410, El Dorado, AR 71730; 870-864-8582; Fax: 870-864-8571; **Communications:** Trent Garner
300 S. Church St., #338, Jonesboro, AR 72401; 870-933-6223; Fax: 870-933-6596; **Projects Director:** Jeff Morris
Committee Assignments: Armed Services; Banking, Housing, and Urban Affairs; Congressional-Executive Commission on China; Select Intelligence; Joint Economic

Cramer, Kevin, R-N.D.

Capitol Hill Office: B40C SDOB 20510-1205; 224-2043; **Chief of Staff:** Mark Gruman
Web: www.cramer.senate.gov
Facebook: www.facebook.com/SenatorKevinCramer
Twitter: @SenKevinCramer
Instagram: @senatorkevincramer
YouTube: www.youtube.com/c/Senkevincramer
District Offices: 306 Federal Bldg., 657 2nd Ave. North, Fargo, ND 58102; 701-232-5094; **State Director:** Lisa Gibbens; **Southeast Regional Rep.:** Cody Morschinger
105 Federal Bldg., 100 1st St. S.W., Minot, ND 58701; 701-837-6141; **Northwest Regional Rep., Policy Advisor:** Kaitlyn Weidert
Committee Assignments: Armed Services; Banking, Housing, and Urban Affairs, Environment and Public Works; Budget; Veterans' Affairs

Crapo, Mike, R-Idaho

Capitol Hill Office: 239 SDOB 20510-1205; 224-6142; Fax: 228-1375; **Chief of Staff:** Susan Wheeler
Web: www.crapo.senate.gov
Facebook: www.facebook.com/mikecrapo
Twitter: @mikecrapo
Instagram: @mikecrapo
YouTube: www.youtube.com/senatorcrapo

District Offices: 251 E. Front St., #205, Boise, ID 83702-7312; 208-334-1776; Fax: 208-334-9044; **Regional Chief of Staff:** John Hoehne
610 W. Hubbard St., #209, Coeur d'Alene, ID 83814-2287; 208-664-5490; Fax: 208-664-0889; **Regional Director:** Karen Roetter
410 Memorial Dr., #204, Idaho Falls, ID 83402-3600; 208-522-9779; Fax: 208-529-8367; **Regional Director:** Kathryn Hitch
313 D St., #105, Lewiston, ID 83501-1894; 208-743-1492; Fax: 208-743-6484; **State Director:** Tony Fnodderly
275 S. 5th Ave., #100, Pocatello, ID 83201; 208-236-6775; Fax: 208-236-6935; **Regional Director:** Farhana Hibbert
202 Falls Ave., #2, Twin Falls, ID 83301-3372; 208-734-2515; Fax: 208-733-0414; **Regional Director:** Samantha Marshall
Committee Assignments: Banking, Housing, and Urban Affairs, Chair; Budget; Finance; Indian Affairs; Joint Taxation; Judiciary

Cruz, Ted, R-Tex.

Capitol Hill Office: 404 SROB 20510; 224-5922; **Chief of Staff:** Prerak Shah
Web: www.cruz.senate.gov
Facebook: www.facebook.com/SenatorTedCruz
Twitter: @SenTedCruz
Instagram: @sentedcruz
YouTube: www.youtube.com/SenTedCruz
District Offices: 300 E. 8th St., #961, Austin, TX 78701-3226; 512-916-5834; Fax: 512-916-5839; **State Director:** Carl Mica
Lee Park Tower II, 3626 N. Hall St., #410, Dallas, TX 75219; 214-599-8749; **Regional Director:** Michael Flusche
1919 Smith St., #9047, Houston, TX 77002; 713-718-3057; **Regional Director:** Jason Fuller
9901 IH-10W, #950, San Antonio, TX 78230; 210-340-2885; **Regional Director:** Javier Salinas
305 S. Broadway, #501, Tyler, TX 75702; 903-593-5130; **Regional Director:** Daniel Alders
200 S. 10th St., #1603, McAllen, TX 78501; 956-686-7339; Fax: 956-61-3692; **Regional Director:** Casandra Meade
Committee Assignments: Foreign Relations; Commerce, Science, and Transportation; Judiciary; Rules and Administration; Joint Economic

Daines, Steve, R-Mont.

Capitol Hill Office: 320 SHOB 20510-2605; 224-2651; Fax: 228-1236; **Chief of Staff:** Jason Thielman
Web: www.daines.senate.gov
Facebook: www.facebook.com/SteveDainesMT
Twitter: @SteveDaines
Instagram: @stevedaines
YouTube: www.youtube.com/SteveDainesMT
District Offices: 218 E. Front St., #103, Missoula, MT 59802; 406-549-8198; Fax: 406-549-0905; **Caseworker:** Sharon Parks-Banda
13 S. Willson Ave., #18, Bozeman, MT 59715; 406-587-3446; Fax: 406-587-3951; **State Director:** Liz Dellwo

222 N. 32nd St., #100, Billings, MT 59101; 406-245-6822; Fax: 406-702-1182; *Administrative Director:* Amber Heinz

104 4th St. North, #302, Great Falls, MT 59401; 406-453-0148; *Liaison:* Robin Baker

30 W. 14th St., #206, Helena, MT 59601; 406-443-3189; *Field Rep.:* Gilda Clancy

40 2nd St. East, #211, KM Bldg., Kalispell, MT 59901; 406-257-3765; *Field Rep:* Ron Catlett

310 N. Center, Hardin, MT 59034; 406-665-4126; *Tribal Liaison:* Amanda Peterman

609 S. Central Ave., #4, Central Plaza Bldg., Sidney, MT 59270; 406-482-9010; *Field Rep.:* Kenneth Bogner

Committee Assignments: Appropriations; Congressional-Executive Commission on China; Energy and Natural Resources; Indian Affairs; Finance

Duckworth, Tammy, D-Ill.

Capitol Hill Office: 524 SHOB 20510, 224-2854; Fax: 228-4611; *Chief of Staff:* Kaitlin Sahey
Web: www.duckworth.senate.gov
Facebook: www.facebook.com/SenDuckworth
Twitter: @SenDuckworth
Instagram: @senduckworth
YouTube: www.youtube.com/SenDuckworth
District Offices: 230 S. Dearborn St., #3720, Chicago, IL 60604; 312-886-3506; Fax: 312-583-0374; *State Director:* Marina Saz-Huppert

441 E. Willow St., Carbondale, IL 62901; 618-677-7000; Fax: 618-351-1551; *Southern Community Outreach Coordinator:* Jim Kirkpatrick and Katie Foley

8 S. Old State Capitol Plaza, Springfield, IL 62701; 217-528-6124; Fax: 217-528-7043; *State Director:* Cameron Joost

23 Public Square, #460, Belleville, IL 62220; 618-722-7070; Fax: 618-235-4011; *Office Manager:* Robin Cromer

1823 2nd Ave., #2, Rock Island, IL 61201; 309-606-7060; Fax: 309-786-1799; *Community Outreach Coordinators:* Courtney Loftin and Halle O'Connor

Committee Assignments: Commerce, Science, and Transportation; Armed Services; Environment and Public Works; Small Business and Entrepreneurship

Durbin, Richard J., D-Ill.

Capitol Hill Office: 711 SHOB 20510-1304; 224-2152; Fax: 228-0400; *Chief of Staff:* Patrick J. Souders
Web: www.durbin.senate.gov
Facebook: www.facebook.com/SenatorDurbin
Twitter: @SenatorDurbin
YouTube: www.youtube.com/SenatorDurbin
District Offices: 250 W. Cherry St., #115-D, Carbondale, IL 62901-2856; 618-351-1122; Fax: 618-351-1124; *Staff Asst.:* Susan Watson

230 S. Dearborn St., #3892, Chicago, IL 60604-1505; 312-353-4952; Fax: 312-353-0150; *Office Manager:* Tom Bride

1504 3rd Ave., #227, Rock Island, IL 61201-8612; 309-786-5173; Fax: 309-786-5404 *Western Illinois Outreach Coord.:* Awisi Quartey

525 S. 8th St., Springfield, IL 62703-1606; 217-492-4062; Fax: 217-492-4382; *State Director:* Bill Houlihan

Committee Assignments: Agriculture, Nutrition, and Forestry; Appropriations; Judiciary; Rules and Administration

Enzi, Michael B., R-Wyo.

Capitol Hill Office: 379A SROB 20510-5004; 224-3424; Fax: 228-0359; *Chief of Staff:* Tara Shaw
Web: www.enzi.senate.gov
Facebook: www.facebook.com/mikeenzi
Twitter: @SenatorEnzi
Instagram: @senatorenzi
YouTube: www.youtube.com/SenatorEnzi
District Offices: 100 E. B St., #3201, P.O. Box 33201, Casper, WY 82602; 307-261-6572; Fax: 307-261-6574; *Field Rep.:* Justin Rogers

2120 Capitol Ave., #2007, Cheyenne, WY 82001-3631; 307-772-2477; Fax: 307-772-2480; *Field Rep.:* Dianne Kirkbride; Martha Wilson

1285 Sheridan Ave., #210, Cody, WY 82414-3653; 307-527-9444; Fax: 307-527-9476; *State Director:* Karen McCreery

222 S. Gillette Ave., #503, Gillette, WY 82716-3803; 307-682-6268; Fax: 307-682-6501; *Field Rep.:* DeAnna Kay

1110 Maple Way, Suite G, P.O. Box 12470, Jackson, WY 83002-2470; 307-739-9507; Fax: 307-739-9520; *Field Rep.:* Nikki Brunner

Committee Assignments: Budget, Chair; Finance; Health, Education, Labor, and Pensions; Homeland Security and Governmental Affairs

Ernst, Joni, R-Iowa

Capitol Hill Office: 111 SROB 20510-1502; 224-3254; Fax: 224-9369; *Chief of Staff:* Lisa Goeas
Web: www.ernst.senate.gov
Facebook: www.facebook.com/senjoniernst
Twitter: @SenJoniErnst
Instagram: @senjoniernst
YouTube: www.youtube.com/channel/UCLwrmtF_84FIcK3TyMs4MIw
District Offices: 733 Federal Bldg., 210 Walnut St., Des Moines, IA 50309; 515-284-4574; Fax: 515-284-4937; *State Director:* Clarke Scanlon

111 7th Ave. S.E., #480, Cedar Rapids, IA 52401-2101; 319-365-4504; Fax: 319-365-4683; *Field Rep.:* Justin Jensen

201 W. 2nd St., #806, Davenport, IA 52803; 563-322-0677; Fax: 563-322-0854; *Regional Director:* Joe Krenzelok

194 Federal Bldg., 320 6th St., Sioux City, IA 51101; 712-252-1550; Fax: 712-252-1638 *Regional Director:* Jerry Felf

221 Federal Bldg., 8 S. 6th St., Council Bluffs, IA 51501; 712-352-1167; Fax: 712-352-0087; *Constituent Service Director:* Emily McKern

Committee Assignments: Agriculture, Nutrition, and Forestry; Armed Services; Environment and Public Works; Small Business and Entrepreneurship; Judiciary

Feinstein, Dianne, D-Calif.

Capitol Hill Office: 331 SHOB 20510-0504; 224-3841; Fax: 228-3954; *Chief of Staff:* David Grannis
Web: www.feinstein.senate.gov
Facebook: www.facebook.com/SenatorFeinstein
Twitter: @senfeinstein
YouTube: www.youtube.com/SenatorFeinstein
District Offices: 2500 Tulare St., #4290, Fresno, CA 93721-1331; 559-485-7430; Fax: 559-485-9689; *District Director:* Shelly Abajian
11111 Santa Monica Blvd., #915, Los Angeles, CA 90025-3343; 310-914-7300; Fax: 310-914-7318; *Deputy State Director:* Peter Muller
880 Front St., #4236, San Diego, CA 92101; 619-231-9712; Fax: 619-231-1108; *District Director:* Bill Kratz
One Post St., #2450, San Francisco, CA 94104-5240; 415-393-0707; Fax: 415-393-0710; *State Director:* Jim Lazarus
Committee Assignments: Appropriations; Congressional-Executive Commission on China; International Narcotics Control Caucus, Vice Chair; Judiciary, Ranking Minority Member; Rules and Administration; Select Intelligence

Fischer, Deb, R-Neb.

Capitol Hill Office: 454 SROB 20510; 224-6551; Fax: 228-1325; *Chief of Staff:* Joe Hack
Web: www.fischer.senate.gov/public
Facebook: www.facebook.com/senatordebfischer
Twitter: @SenatorFischer
YouTube: www.youtube.com/SenatorDebFischer
District Offices: 440 N. 8th St., #120, Lincoln, NE 68508; 402-441-4600; Fax: 402-476-8753; *State Director:* Holly Baker
11819 Miracle Hills Dr., #205, Omaha, NE 68154; 402-391-3411; Fax: 402-391-4725; *Outreach Coord.:* Denise Barrett
20 W. 23rd St., Kearney, NE 68847; 308-234-2361; Fax: 308-234-3684; *Constituent Services Director:* Julie Booker
120 E. 16th St., #2013, Scottsbluff, NE 69361; 308-630-2329; Fax: 308-630-2321; *Constituent Services Director:* Brandy McCaslin
Committee Assignments: Agriculture, Nutrition, Forestry; Armed Services; Commerce, Science, and Transportation; Environment and Public Works; Rules and Administration

Gardner, Cory, R-Colo.

Capitol Hill Office: 354 SROB 20510-0608; 224-5941; Fax: 224-6524; *Chief of Staff:* Curtis Swager
Web: www.gardner.senate.gov
Facebook: www.facebook.com/SenCoryGardner
Twitter: @SenCoryGardner
Instagram: @sencorygardner
YouTube: www.youtube.com/channel/UC7Vi5vAFb7piu_BNwrYDBxQ
District Offices: 102 S. Tejon St., #930, Colorado Springs, CO 80903; 719-632-6706; Fax: 202-228-7176; *Caseworker:* Rebecca Rudder

721 19th St., #150, Denver, CO 80202; 303-391-5777; Fax: 202-224-6524; *State Director:* Andy Merret
2001 S. Shields St., Bldg. H, #104, Fort Collins, CO 80524; 970-484-3502; *Regional Director:* Dan Betts
801 8th St., #140A, Greeley, CO 80631; 970-352-5546; Fax: 202-228-7172; *Regional Director:* Maria Secrest
400 Rood Ave., Federal Bldg., #220, Grand Junction, CO 81501; 970-245-9553; Fax: 202-228-7173; *Regional Director:* Betsy Bair
503 N. Main St., #426, Pueblo, CO 81003; 719-543-1324; Fax: 202-228-7174; *Regional Director:* Cathy Garcia
529 N. Albany St., #1220, Yuma, CO 80759; 970-848-3095; Fax: 202-228-7175; *Regional Director:* Darlene Carpio
329 S. Camino del Rio, Suite I, Durango, CO 81303; 970-415-7416; *Regional Director:* Ann McCoy-Harold
Committee Assignments: Commerce, Science, and Transportation; Energy and Natural Resources; Foreign Relations; Commission on Security and Cooperation in Europe

Gillibrand, Kirsten E., D-N.Y.

Capitol Hill Office: 478 SROB 20510-3205; 224-4451; Fax: 228-0282; *Chief of Staff:* Joi Chaney
Web: www.gillibrand.senate.gov
Facebook: www.facebook.com/KirstenGillibrand
Twitter: @SenGillibrand
Instagram: @kirstengillibrand
YouTube: www.youtube.com/KirstenEGillibrand
District Offices: Leo W. O'Brien Federal Office Bldg., 11A Clinton Ave., Room 821, Albany, NY 12207-2202; 518-431-0120; Fax: 518-431-0128; *Regional Director:* David Connors
Larkin At Exchange, 726 Exchange St., #511, Buffalo, NY 14210-1485; 716-854-9725; Fax: 716-854-9731; *Regional Director:* James Kennedy
P.O. Box 273, Lowville, NY 13367; 315-376-6118; Fax: 315-376-6118; *Regional Director:* Susan Merrell
P.O. Box 749, Yonkers, NY 10710; 845-875-4585; Fax: 845-875-9099; *Regional Director:* Lisa Hofflich
155 Pinelawn Rd., #250 N., Melville, NY 11747-3247; 631-249-2825; Fax: 631-249-2847; *Regional Director:* Magdalonie Campbell
780 3rd Ave., #2601, New York, NY 10017-2177; 212-688-6262; Fax: 866-824-6340; *State Director:* Emily Arsenault
Kenneth B. Keating Federal Office Bldg., 100 State St., Room 4195, Rochester, NY 14614-1318; 585-263-6250; Fax: 585-263-6247; *Deputy State Director:* Sarah Clark
James M. Hanley Federal Bldg., 100 S. Clinton St., Room 1470, P.O. Box 7378, Syracuse, NY 13261; 315-448-0470; Fax: 315-448-0476; *Regional Director:* Jarred Jones
Committee Assignments: Agriculture, Nutrition, and Forestry; Armed Services; Environment and Public Works; Special Aging

Graham, Lindsey, R-S.C.

Capitol Hill Office: 290 SROB 20510-4003; 224-5972; Fax: 224-3808; *Chief of Staff:* Richard S. Perry
Web: www.lgraham.senate.gov

Facebook: www.facebook.com/USSenatorLindseyGraham
Twitter: @GrahamBlog
Instagram: @lindseygrahamsc
YouTube: www.youtube.com/channel/
UClLGZMA5Ei2Z8fR1PLEx6yQ
District Offices: 508 Hampton St., #202, Columbia, SC 29201-2718; 803-933-0112; Fax: 803-933-0957; *Midlands Regional Director:* Yvette Rowland

McMillan Federal Bldg., 401 W. Evans St., #111, Florence, SC 29501-3460; 843-669-1505; Fax: 843-669-9015; *Pee Dee Regional Director:* Celia Urquhart

130 S. Main St., 7th Floor, Greenville, SC 29601-4870; 864-250-1417; Fax: 864-250-4322; *State Director:* Van Cato

530 Johnnie Dodds Blvd., #202, Mt. Pleasant, SC 29464-3029; 843-849-3887; Fax: 843-971-3669; *Low Country Regional Director:* Dan Head

124 Exchange St., Suite A, Pendleton, SC 29670-1312; 864-646-4090; Fax: 864-646-8609; *Sr. Advisor:* Denise Bauld

235 E. Main St., #100, Rock Hill, SC 29730-4891; 803-366-2828; Fax: 803-366-5353; *Piedmont Regional Director:* Teresa Thomas
Committee Assignments: Appropriations; Foreign Relations; Budget; Judiciary, Chair

Grassley, Chuck, R-Iowa

Capitol Hill Office: 135 SHOB 20510-1501; 224-3744; Fax: 224-6020; *Chief of Staff:* Aaron Cummings
Web: www.grassley.senate.gov
Facebook: www.facebook.com/grassley
Twitter: @chuckgrassley
Instagram: @senatorchuckgrassley
YouTube: www.youtube.com/SenChuckGrassley
District Offices: 111 7th Ave. S.E., Box 13, #6800, Cedar Rapids, IA 52401; 319-363-6832; Fax: 319-363-7179; *Regional Director:* Fred Schuster

307 Federal Bldg., 8 S. 6th St., Council Bluffs, IA 51501; 712-322-7103; Fax: 712-322-7196; *Regional Director; Constituent Services Specialist:* Donna Barry

201 W. 2nd St., #720, Davenport, IA 52801-1419; 563-322-4331; Fax: 563-322-8552; *Regional Director:* Penny Vacek

721 Federal Bldg., 210 Walnut St., Des Moines, IA 50309-2140; 515-288-1145; Fax: 515-288-5097; *State Director:* Carol Olson

120 Federal Bldg., 320 6th St., Sioux City, IA 51101-1244; 712-233-1860; Fax: 712-233-1634; *Regional Director:* Jacob Bossman

210 Waterloo Bldg., 531 Commercial St., Waterloo, IA 50701-5497; 319-232-6657; Fax: 319-232-9965; *Regional Director:* Jason Mohr
Committee Assignments: Agriculture, Nutrition, and Forestry; Budget; Finance, Chair; International Narcotics Control Caucus; Judiciary; Joint Taxation

Harris, Kamala D., D-Calif.

Capitol Hill Office: 112 SHOB 20510; 224-3553; Fax: 202-224-2200; *Chief of Staff:* Rohini Kosoglu
Web: www.harris.senate.gov

Facebook: www.facebook.com/KamalaHarris
Twitter: @SenKamalaHarris
Instagram: @kamalaharris
YouTube: www.youtube.com/kamalaharrisdotorg
District Offices: 501 I St., #7-800, Sacramento, CA 95814; 916-448-2787; Fax: 202-228-3865; *State Deputy Director:* Julie Rodriguez

2500 Tulare St., #5290, Fresno, CA 93721; 559-497-5109; Fax: 202-228-3864; *District Director:* Matt Rogers

11845 W. Olympic Blvd., #1250W, Los Angeles, CA 90064; 310-231-4494; Fax: 202-224-0357; *Special Assistant:* Josh Wodka

333 Bush St., #3225, San Francisco, CA 94104; 415-981-9369; Fax: 202-224-0454; *Staff Assistant:* Matt Bedinger; *District Director:* Adam Mehis

600 B St., #2240, San Diego, CA 92101; 619-239-3884; Fax: 202-228-3863; *Staff Assistant:* Serena Hendle
Committee Assignments: Budget; Homeland Security and Governmental Affairs; Judiciary; Select Intelligence

Hassan, Maggie, D-N.H.

Capitol Hill Office: 330 SHOB 20510; 224-3324; Fax: 228-0581; *Chief of Staff:* Marc Goldberg
Web: www.hassan.senate.gov
Facebook: www.facebook.com/SenatorHassan
Twitter: @SenatorHassan
Instagram: @senatorhassan
YouTube: www.youtube.com/SenatorHassan
District Offices: 1589 Elm St., 3rd Floor, Manchester, NH 03101; 603-622-2204; Fax: 603-622-2248; *State Director:* Mike Ollen

142 Main St., #520, Nashua, NH 03060; 603-880-3314; *Constituent Services Rep.:* William Bateson

14 Manchester Square, #140, Portsmouth, NH 03801; 603-433-4445

Berlin City Hall, Lower Level, 168 Main St., Berlin, NH 03570; 603-752-6190

James C. Cleveland Federal Bldg., 53 Pleasant St., Concord, NH 03301; 603-622-2204
Committee Assignments: Commerce, Science, and Transportation; Health, Education, Labor, and Pensions; Homeland Security and Governmental Affairs; Joint Economic; Finance

Hawley, Josh, R-Mo.

Capitol Hill Office: B40A SDOB 20510; 224-6154; *Chief of Staff:* Kyle Tlotkin
Web: www.hawley.senate.gov
Facebook: www.facebook.com/HawleyMO
Twitter: @HawleyMO
Instagram: @senatorhawley
YouTube: www.youtube.com/channel/
UCMzt8xq6qQ3XQ_DlNfJx0-w
District Offices: Constituent Services Office, 816-960-4694
Committee Assignments: Armed Services; Homeland Security and Governmental Affairs; Small Business and Entrepreneurship; Judiciary; Special Aging

Heinrich, Martin, D-N.M.

Capitol Hill Office: 303 SHOB 20510; 224-5521; Fax: 228-2841; *Chief of Staff:* Joe Britton

Web: www.heinrich.senate.gov

Facebook: www.facebook.com/MartinHeinrich

Twitter: @martinheinrich

Instagram: @senatormartinheinrich

YouTube: www.youtube.com/SenMartinHeinrich

District Offices: 400 Gold Ave. S.W., #1080, Albuquerque, NM 87102; 505-346-6601; Fax: 505-346-6780; *Constituent Services Director:* Miguel Negrete

7450 E. Main St., Suite A, Farmington, NM 87402; 505-325-5030; Fax: 505-325-6035; *Field Rep.:* Jim Dumont

Loretto Towne Center, 505 S. Main St., #148, Las Cruces, NM 88001-1200; 575-523-6561; Fax: 575-523-6584; *Field Rep:* Dara Parker

200 E. 4th St., #300, Roswell, NM 88201; 575-622-7113; Fax: 575-622-3538; *Constituent Services Rep.:* Iris Karges

123 E. Marcy St., #103, Santa Fe, NM 87501-2046; 505-988-6647; Fax: 505-992-8435; *Field Rep.:* Patricia Dominguez

Committee Assignments: Armed Services; Energy and Natural Resources; Select Intelligence; Joint Economic

Hirono, Mazie K., D-Hawaii

Capitol Hill Office: 730 SHOB 20510; 224-6361; Fax: 224-2126; *Chief of Staff:* Alan Yamamoto

Web: www.hirono.senate.gov

Facebook: www.facebook.com/senatorhirono

Twitter: @maziehirono

Instagram: @maziehirono

YouTube: www.youtube.com/CongresswomanHirono

District Office: 300 Ala Moana Blvd., Room 3-106, Honolulu, HI 96850; 808-522-8970; Fax: 808-545-4683; *State Director:* Alan Yamamoto

Committee Assignments: Armed Services; Energy and Natural Resources; Judiciary; Small Business and Entrepreneurship; Veterans' Affairs

Hoeven, John, R-N.D.

Capitol Hill Office: 338 SROB 20510-3406; 224-2551; Fax: 224-7999; *Chief of Staff:* Cassie Bladow

Web: www.hoeven.senate.gov

Facebook: www.facebook.com/SenatorJohnHoeven

Twitter: @SenJohnHoeven

Instagram: @senjohnhoeven

YouTube: www.youtube.com/SenatorJohnHoevenND

District Offices: U.S. Federal Bldg., 220 E. Rosser Ave., Room 312, Bismarck, ND 58501-3869; 701-250-4618; Fax: 701-250-4484

123 Broadway North, #201, Fargo, ND 58103; 701-239-5389; Fax: 701-239-5112; *State Director:* Jessica Lee

Federal Bldg., 102 N. 4th St., Room 108, Grand Forks, ND 58203-3738; 701-746-8972; Fax: 701-746-5613; *Field Rep.:* Tom Brusegaard

100 1st St. S.W., #107, Minot, ND 58701; 701-838-1361; Fax: 701-838-1381; *Regional Director:* Sally Johnson

Committee Assignments: Agriculture, Nutrition, and Forestry; Appropriations; Energy and Natural Resources; Indian Affairs, Chair

Hyde-Smith, Cindy, Miss.

Capitol Hill Office: 113 SDOB 20510-2402; 224-5054; Fax: 224-5321; *Chief of Staff:* Brad White

Web: www.hydesmith.senate.gov

Twitter: @SenHydeSmith

Instagram: @sencindyhydesmith

YouTube: www.youtube.com/channel/UCJHxkJhGST0NTlkzJHWV03Q

District Offices: 2012 15th St., #451, Gulfport, MS 39501-2036; 228-867-9710; Fax: 228-867-9789; *Southern District Director:* Myrtis Franke

190 E. Capitol St., #550, Jackson, MS 39201-2137; 601-965-4459; Fax: 601-965-4919; *Central District Director:* Brad White

911 Jackson Ave., #249, Oxford, MS 38655-3652; 662-236-1018; Fax: 662-236-7618; *Northern District Director:* Mindy Maxwell

Committee Assignments: Agriculture, Nutrition, and Forestry; Appropriations; Rules and Administration; Energy and Natural Resources

Inhofe, James M., R-Okla.

Capitol Hill Office: 205 SROB 20510-3603; 224-4721; Fax: 228-0380; *Chief of Staff:* Luke Holland

Web: www.inhofe.senate.gov

Facebook: www.facebook.com/jiminhofe

Twitter: @InhofePress

YouTube: www.youtube.com/JimInhofePressOffice

District Offices: 302 N. Independence St., #104, Enid, OK 73701-4025; 580-234-5105; Fax: 580-234-5094; *Field Rep.:* Ryan Sproul

215 E. Choctaw Ave., #106, McAlester, OK 74501-5069; 918-426-0933; Fax: 918-426-0935; *State Director:* Brian Hackler

3817 N.W. Expressway, #780, Oklahoma City, OK 73112; 405-608-4381; Fax: 405-604-0917; *State Director:* Brian Hackler

1924 S. Utica Ave., #530, Tulsa, OK 74104; 918-748-5111; Fax: 918-748-5119; *Field Rep.:* Jed Cochran

Committee Assignments: Armed Services, Chair; Environment and Public Works; Small Business and Entrepreneurship

Isakson, Johnny, R-Ga.

Capitol Hill Office: 131 SROB 20510-1008; 224-3643; Fax: 228-0724; *Chief of Staff:* Joan Kirchner

Web: www.isakson.senate.gov

Facebook: www.facebook.com/isakson

Twitter: @SenatorIsakson

Instagram: @senatorisakson

YouTube: www.youtube.com/SenatorIsakson

District Offices: One Overton Park, 3625 Cumberland Blvd., #970, Atlanta, GA 30339-6406; 770-661-0999; Fax: 770-661-0768; *Deputy Chief of Staff:* Trey Kilpatrick

Committee Assignments: Finance; Foreign Relations; Health, Education, Labor, and Pensions; Select Ethics, Chair; Veterans' Affairs, Chair

Johnson, Ron, R-Wisc.

Capitol Hill Office: 328 SHOB 20510-4905; 224-5323; Fax: 228-6965; *Chief of Staff:* Tony Blando
Web: www.ronjohnson.senate.gov
Facebook: www.facebook.com/senronjohnson
Twitter: @SenRonJohnson
Instagram: @senronjohnson
YouTube: www.youtube.com/SenatorRonJohnson
District Offices: 517 E. Wisconsin Ave., #408, Milwaukee, WI 53202-4510; 414-276-7282; Fax: 414-276-7284; *Regional Director:* Ginger Kollmansderger
219 Washington Ave., #100, Oshkosh, WI 54901; 920-230-7250; Fax: 920-230-7262; *State Director:* Julie Leschke
5315 Wall St., #110, Madison, WI 53718; 608-240-9629; Fax: 608-240-9646
Committee Assignments: Budget; Commerce, Science, and Transportation; Foreign Relations; Homeland Security and Governmental Affairs, Chair

Jones, Doug, D-Ala.

Capitol Hill Office: 326 SROB 20510; 224-4124; Fax: 224-3149; *Chief of Staff:* Dana Gresham
Web: www.jones.senate.gov
Facebook: www.facebook.com/senatordougjones
Twitter: @SenDougJones
Instagram: @dougjonesbama
YouTube: www.youtube.com/channel/ UCL8akobkoN2lB5U3kaEjdBw
District Offices: Vance Federal Bldg., 1800 5th Ave. North, Birmingham, AL 35203; 205-731-1500; Fax: 205-731-0221; *Regional Director:* Jose Perry
200 Clinton Ave. N.W., Huntsville, AL 35801; 256-533-0979; Fax: 256-533-0745; *Caseworker:* Shandela McMillian
41 W. I-65 Service Rd. North, #2300-A, Mobile, AL 36608; 251-414-3083; Fax: 251-414-5845; *Field Rep:* Beau Bowden
Federal Courthouse, 1 Church St., #500-B, Montgomery, AL 36014; 334-230-0698; Fax: 334-293-9349; *State Director:* Brantley Fry
100 W. Troy St., #302, Dothan, AL 36303; 334-792-4924; Fax: 334-792-4928
Committee Assignments: Banking, Housing, and Urban Affairs; Health, Education, Labor, and Pensions; Armed Services, Special Aging

Kaine, Tim, D-Va.

Capitol Hill Office: 231 SROB 20510; 224-4024; Fax: 228-6363; *Chief of Staff:* Mike Henry
Web: www.kaine.senate.gov
Facebook: www.facebook.com/SenatorKaine
Twitter: @timkaine
Instagram: @timkaine
YouTube: www.youtube.com/SenatorTimKaine

District Offices: 121 Russell Road, #2, Abingdon, VA 24210; 276-525-4790; Fax: 276- 525-4792; *Regional Director:* Laura Blevins
919 E. Main St., #970, Richmond, VA 23219; 804-771-2221; Fax: 804-771-8313; *State Director:* Keren Dongo
222 Central Park Dr., #120, Virginia Beach, VA 23462; 757-518-1674; Fax: 757-518-1679; *Regional Director:* Diane Kaufman
308 Craghead St., #102A, Danville, VA 24541; 434-792-0976; Fax: 434-792-0978; *Regional Director:* Gwen Mason
611 S. Jefferson St., #5B, Roanoke, VA 24011; 540-682-5693; Fax: 540-682-5697; *Regional Director:* Gwen Mason
9408 Grant Ave., #202, Manassas, VA 20110; 703-361-3192; Fax: 703-361-3198; *Regional Director:* Gaston Araoz-Riveros
Committee Assignments: Armed Services; Budget; Foreign Relations; Health, Education, Labor, and Pensions

Kennedy, John, R-La.

Capitol Hill Office: 383 SROB 20510; 224-4623; Fax: 228-0447; *Chief of Staff:* Preston Robinson
Web: www.kennedy.senate.gov
Facebook: www.facebook.com/JohnKennedyLouisiana
Twitter: @SenJohnKennedy
Instagram: @senjohnkennedy
YouTube: www.youtube.com/channel/ UCDgjkA5Y_npoxeUiSW18JZQ
District Offices: 101 La Rue France, #503, Lafayette, LA 70508; 337-269-5980; *State Director:* Michael Wong
1651 Louisville Ave., #108, Monroe, LA 71201; 318-361-1489; *Regional Rep.:* Hannah Livingston
6501 Coliseum Blvd., #700A, Alexandria, LA 71303; 318-445-2892; *Regional Rep.:* Hannah Livingston
7932 Wrenwood Blvd., Suite A & B, Baton Rouge, LA 70809; 225-926-8033; *State Director:* Michael Wong
401 Market St., #1050, Shreveport, LA 71101; 318-670-5192; *Regional Director:* John Barr
500 Poydras St., #364, New Orleans, LA 70113; 504-581-6189; *State Director:* Michael Wong
21490 Koop Dr., Bldg. A, Mandeville, LA 70471; *Regional Rep.:* Ross White; 985-809-8153
1 Lakeshore Dr., #530, Lake Charles, LA 70629; *Regional Rep.:* Emily Stine; 337-436-6255
Government Towers, 8026 Main St., #700, Houma, LA 70360; *Regional Rep.:* Elise Mary Schlesinger; 985-851-0956
Committee Assignments: Appropriations; Banking, Housing, and Urban Affairs; Budget; Judiciary; Small Business and Entrepreneurship

King, Angus S. Jr., I-Maine

Capitol Hill Office: 133 SHOB 20510; 224-5344; Fax: 224-1946; *Chief of Staff:* Kathleen Connery Dawe
Web: www.king.senate.gov
Facebook: www.facebook.com/SenatorAngusSKingJr
Twitter: @SenAngusKing

Instagram: @anguskingmaine
YouTube: www.youtube.com/senatorangusking
District Offices: 4 Gabriel Dr., #3, Augusta, ME 04330; 207-622-8292; Fax: 207-621-0286; *Regional Rep.:* Chris Rector; Ben Tucker

202 Harlow St., #20350, Bangor, ME 04401; 207-945-8000; *Regional Rep.:* Edie Smith

169 Academy St., Suite A, Presque Isle, ME 04769; 207-764-5124; *Regional Rep.:* Barbara Hayflett

383 US Route 1, #1C, Scarborough, ME 04074; 207-883-1588; *Regional Rep.:* Gail Kezer

Committee Assignments: Armed Services; Congressional-Executive Commission on China; Energy and Natural Resources; Rules and Administration; Select Intelligence

Klobuchar, Amy, D-Minn.

Capitol Hill Office: 425 SDOB 20510-2307; 224-3244; Fax: 228-2186; *Chief of Staff:* Bridgit Helgen
Web: www.klobuchar.senate.gov
Facebook: www.facebook.com/amyklobuchar
Twitter: @amyklobuchar
Instagram: @amyklobuchar
YouTube: www.youtube.com/user/KlobucharForMN
District Offices: 1200 Washington Ave. South, Room 250, Minneapolis, MN 55415-1588; 612-727-5220; Fax: 612-727-5223; *State Director:* Ben Hill

121 4th St. South, Moorhead, MN 56560-2613; 218-287-2219; Fax: 218-287-2930; *Regional Outreach Director:* Andy Martin

1130 1/2 7th St. N.W., Room 212, Rochester, MN 55901-2995; 507-288-5321; Fax: 507-288-2922; *Regional Outreach Director:* Chuck Ackman

Olcott Plaza, Room 105, 820 9th St. North, Virginia, MN 55792-2300; 218-741-9690; Fax: 218-741-3692; *Regional Outreach Director:* Ida Ruckavina

Committee Assignments: Agriculture, Nutrition, and Forestry; Commerce, Science, and Transportation; Joint Economic; Judiciary; Rules and Administration, Ranking Minority Member; Joint Library; Joint Printing

Lankford, James, R-Okla.

Capitol Hill Office: 316 SHOB 20510-3604; 224-5754; Fax: 228-1015; *Chief of Staff:* Michelle Altman
Web: www.lankford.senate.gov
Facebook: www.facebook.com/SenatorLankford
Twitter: @SenatorLankford
Instagram: @senatorlankford
YouTube: www.youtube.com/channel/UCz8T6sK5fEycyWmVz6Vpe5Q
District Offices: 1015 N. Broadway, #310, Oklahoma City, OK 73102; 405-231-4941; *Scheduler:* Kristen Adams

224 S. Boulder, #210, Tulsa, OK 74103; 918-581-7651; *Constituent Services Rep.:* Maggie Collins

Committee Assignments: Appropriations; Congressional-Executive Commission on China; Homeland Security and Governmental Affairs; Indian Affairs; Finance

Leahy, Patrick J., D-Vt.

Capitol Hill Office: 437 SROB 20510-4502; 224-4242; Fax: 224-3479; *Chief of Staff:* John P. Dowd
Web: www.leahy.senate.gov
Facebook: www.facebook.com/SenatorPatrickLeahy
Twitter: @SenatorLeahy
Instagram: @senatorleahy
YouTube: www.youtube.com/SenatorPatrickLeahy
District Offices: 199 Main St., 4th Floor, Burlington, VT 05401; 802-863-2525; Fax: 802-658-1009; *State Director:* John Tracy

87 State St., Room 338, Montpelier, VT 05602-9505; 802-229-0569; Fax: 802-229-1915; *Office Manager:* Diane Derby

Committee Assignments: Agriculture, Nutrition, and Forestry; Appropriations, Ranking Minority Member; Joint Library; Judiciary; Rules and Administration

Lee, Mike, R-Utah

Capitol Hill Office: 361A SROB 20510-4404; 224-5444; Fax: 228-1168; *Chief of Staff:* Allyson Bell
Web: www.lee.senate.gov
Facebook: www.facebook.com/senatormikelee
Twitter: @SenMikeLee
Instagram: @senmikelee
YouTube: www.youtube.com/senatormikelee
District Offices: Wallace F. Bennett Federal Bldg., 125 S. State St., #4225, Salt Lake City, UT 84138-1188; 801-524-5933; Fax: 801-524-5730; *State Director:* Rob Axson

285 W. Tabernacle St., #200, St. George, UT 84770-3474; 435-628-5514; Fax: 435-628-4160; *Southern Utah Director:* Bette Arial

James V. Hansen Federal Bldg., 324 25th St., #1410, Ogden, UT 84401; 801-392-9633; Fax: 801-392-9630; *Northern Utah Director:* Nathan Jackson

Committee Assignments: Commerce, Science, and Transportation; Energy and Natural Resources; Judiciary; Joint Economic, Chair

Manchin, Joe, D-W.Va.

Capitol Hill Office: 306 SHOB 20510-4803; 224-3954; Fax: 228-0002; *Chief of Staff:* Patrick Hayes
Web: www.manchin.senate.gov
Facebook: www.facebook.com/JoeManchinIII
Twitter: @Sen_JoeManchin
YouTube: www.youtube.com/SenatorJoeManchin
District Offices: 900 Pennsylvania Ave., #629, Charleston, WV 25302; 304-342-5855; Fax: 304-343-7144; *State Director:* Mara Boggs

261 Aikens Center, #305, Martinsburg, WV 25404-6203; 304-264-4626; Fax: 304-262-3039; *State Director:* Mara Boggs

230 Adams St., Fairmont, WV 26554; 304-368-0567; Fax: 304-368-0198 *State Director:* Mara Boggs

Committee Assignments: Appropriations; Energy and Natural Resources, Ranking Minority Member; Armed Services; Veterans' Affairs

Markey, Edward J., D-Mass.

Capitol Hill Office: 255 SDOB 20510; 224-2742; *Chief of Staff:* Paul Tencher; *Director of Scheduling and Operations:* Sarah Butler
Web: www.markey.senate.gov
Facebook: www.facebook.com/EdJMarkey
Twitter: @SenMarkey
YouTube: www.youtube.com/repmarkey
District Offices: 975 JFK Federal Bldg., 15 New Sudbury St., Boston, MA 02203; 617-565-8519; Fax: 616-570-9081; *State Director:* Jim Cantwell
222 Milliken Blvd., #312, Fall River, MA 02721; 508-677-0523; *Regional Director:* Christine Pacheco
1550 Main St., 4th Floor, Springfield, MA 01103; 413-785-4610; *Regional Director:* Vanessa Gatling
Committee Assignments: Commerce, Science, and Transportation; Environment and Public Works; Foreign Relations; Small Business and Entrepreneurship

McConnell, Mitch, R-Ky.

Capitol Hill Office: 317 SROB 20510-1702; 224-2541; Fax: 224-2499; *Chief of Staff:* Phil Maxson
Web: www.mcconnell.senate.gov
Facebook: www.facebook.com/mitchmcconnell
Twitter: @McConnellPress
Instagram: @mcconnellpress
YouTube: www.youtube.com/RepublicanLeader
District Offices: Federal Bldg., 241 E. Main St., Room 102, Bowling Green, KY 42101-2175; 270-781-1673; Fax: 270-782-1884; *Field Rep.:* Tim Thomas
1885 Dixie Hwy., #345, Fort Wright, KY 41011; 859-578-0188; Fax: 859-578-0488; *Field Rep.:* Kim Kraft
771 Corporate Dr., #108, Lexington, KY 40503-5439; 859-224-8286; Fax: 859-224-9673; *Field Rep.:* Stephanie Nelson
300 S. Main St., #310, London, KY 40741; 606-864-2026; Fax: 606-864-2035; *Field Rep.:* Donna McClure
601 W. Broadway, Room 630, Louisville, KY 40202-2228; 502-582-6304; Fax: 502-582-5326; *State Director:* Terry Carmack
100 Fountain Ave., #300, Paducah, KY 42001; 270-442-4554; Fax: 270-443-3102; *Field Rep.:* Sue Tharp
Committee Assignments: Agriculture, Nutrition, and Forestry; Appropriations; Rules and Administration; Select Intelligence; Majority Floor Leader

McSally, Martha, R-Ariz.

Capitol Hill Office: B40D SDOB 20515; 224-2235; *Chief of Staff:* Justin Roth
Web: www.mcsally.senate.gov
Facebook: www.facebook.com/SenMarthaMcSally
Twitter: @SenMcSallyAZ
Instagram: @senmcsallyaz
YouTube: www.youtube.com/channel/UCfHMG2Db0TJ_RatSBHuH8NA
District Offices: 2201 E. Camelback Rd., #115, Phoenix, AZ 85016; 602-952-2410; *Outreach Coordinator:*

Chase Kassel; *Casework Manager:* Gina Fong, Rosa Ruiz
407 W. Congress St., #10, Tucson, AZ 85701; 520-670-6334; *Casework Manager:* Rosa Ruiz
Committee Assignments: Armed Services; Banking, Housing, and Urban Affairs; Energy and Natural Resources; Indian Affairs; Special Aging

Menendez, Robert, D-N.J.

Capitol Hill Office: 528 SHOB 20510; 224-4744; Fax: 224-2197; *Chief of Staff:* Fred Turner
Web: www.menendez.senate.gov
Facebook: www.facebook.com/senatormenendez
Twitter: @SenatorMenendez
Instagram: @senatormenendez
YouTube: www.youtube.com/SenatorMenendezNJ
District Offices: 208 White Horse Pike, #18, Barrington, NJ 08007-1322; 856-757-5353; Fax: 856-546-1526; *State Director:* Frank Schultz
One Gateway Center, #1100, Newark, NJ 07102; 973-645-3030; Fax: 973-645-0502; *State Director:* Frank Schultz
Committee Assignments: Banking, Housing, and Urban Affairs; Finance; Foreign Relations, Ranking Minority Member

Merkley, Jeff, D-Ore.

Capitol Hill Office: 313 SHOB 20510-3705; 224-3753; Fax: 228-3997; *Chief of Staff:* Michael S. Zamore
Web: www.merkley.senate.gov
Facebook: www.facebook.com/jeffmerkley
Twitter: @SenJeffMerkley
Instagram: @senjeffmerkley
YouTube: www.youtube.com/SenatorJeffMerkley
District Offices: 131 Hawthorne Ave. N.W., #208, Bend, OR 97701-2958; 541-318-1298; Fax: 541-318-1396; *Field Rep.:* B.J. Westlund
405 E. 8th Ave., #2010, Eugene, OR 97401-2730; 541-465-6750; *Field Rep.:* Courtney Flathers
10 S. Bartlett St., #201, Medford, OR 97501-7204; 541-608-9102; *Field Rep.:* Amy Amrhein
310 2nd St. S.E., #105, Pendleton, OR 97801-2263; 541-278-1129; Fax: 541-278-4109; *Field Rep.:* Jessica Keyes
121 Salmon St. S.W., #1400, Portland, OR 97204-2948; 503-326-3386; Fax: 503-326-2900; *State Director:* Jessica Stevens
161 High St. S.E., #250, Salem, OR 97301; 503-362-8102; *Field Rep.:* Stacey Jochimsen
Committee Assignments: Appropriations; Budget; Congressional-Executive Commission on China; Environment and Public Works; Foreign Relations

Moran, Jerry, R-Kans.

Capitol Hill Office: 521 SDOB 20510-1606; 224-6521; Fax: 228-6966; *Chief of Staff:* Brennon Britton
Web: www.moran.senate.gov/public
Facebook: www.facebook.com/jerrymoran
Twitter: @jerrymoran
YouTube: www.youtube.com/SenatorJerryMoran

District Offices: 1200 Main St., #402, Hays, KS 67601-3649; 785-628-6401; Fax: 785-628-3791; *Constituent Services Director*: Chelsey Ladd

923 Westport Pl., #210, Manhattan, KS 66502; 785-539-8973; Fax: 785-587-0789; *District Rep.:* Kristin Little

23600 College Blvd., #201, Olathe, KS 66061-8709; 913-393-0711; Fax: 913-768-1366; *State Director:* Alex Richard

306 N. Broadway St., #125, P.O. Box 1372, Pittsburg, KS 66762-4836; 620-232-2286; Fax: 620-232-2284; *District Rep.:* Pam Henderson

100 N. Broadway, #210, Wichita, KS 67226-1352; 316-269-9257; Fax: 316-269-9259; *Deputy State Director:* Mike Zamrzla

Committee Assignments: Appropriations; Banking, Housing, and Urban Affairs; Commerce, Science, and Transportation; Indian Affairs; Veterans' Affairs

Murkowski, Lisa, R-Alaska

Capitol Hill Office: 522 SHOB 20510; 224-6665; Fax: 224-5301; *Chief of Staff:* Michael Pawlowski

Web: www.murkowski.senate.gov

Facebook: www.facebook.com/SenLisaMurkowski

Twitter: @lisamurkowski

Instagram: @senlisamurkowski

YouTube: www.youtube.com/Lisa4Senate

District Offices: 510 L St., #600, Anchorage, AK 99501; 907-271-3735; Fax: 877-857-0322; *State Director:* Leila Kimbrell

Court House Square, 250 Cushman Ave., #2D, Fairbanks, AK 99701; 907-456-0233; Fax: 877-857-0322; *Special Asst.:* Trina Bailey

800 Glacier Ave., #101, Juneau, AK 99801; 907-586-7277; Fax: 877-857-0322; *Delegation Rep.:* Dana Herndon

44539 Sterling Hwy, #203, Soldotna, AK 99669; 907-262-4220; Fax: Fax: 877-857-0322; *Special Asst.:* Michelle Blackwell

1900 First Ave., #225, Ketchikan, AK 99901; 907-225-6880; Fax: Fax: 877-857-0322; *Special Asst.:* Chere Klein

851 E. Westpoint Dr., #307, Wasilla, AK 99654-7183; 907-376-7665; Fax: 877-857-0322; *Special Asst.:* Gerri Sumpter

Committee Assignments: Appropriations; Energy and Natural Resources, Chair; Health, Education, Labor, and Pensions; Indian Affairs

Murphy, Chris, D-Conn.

Capitol Hill Office: 136 SHOB 20510; 224-4041; Fax: 224-9750; *Chief of Staff:* Allison Herwitt

Web: www.murphy.senate.gov

Facebook: www.facebook.com/ChrisMurphyCT

Twitter: @SenMurphyOffice

Instagram: @chrismurphyct

YouTube: www.youtube.com/SenChrisMurphy

District Offices: Colt Gateway, 120 Huyshope Ave., #401, Hartford, CT 06106; 860-549-8463; Fax: 860-541-4104; *State Director:* Kenny Curran

Committee Assignments: Appropriations; Foreign Relations; Health, Education, Labor, and Pensions

Murray, Patty, D-Wash.

Capitol Hill Office: 154 SROB 20510; 224-2621; Fax: 224-0238; *Chief of Staff:* Mike Spahn

Web: www.murray.senate.gov

Facebook: www.facebook.com/pattymurray

Twitter: @pattymurray

Instagram: @senpattymurray

YouTube: www.youtube.com/user/SenatorPattyMurray

District Offices: 2930 Wetmore Ave., #9D, Everett, WA 98201; 425-259-6515; Fax: 425-259-7152; *Regional Director:* Ann Seabott

2988 Jackson Federal Bldg., 915 2nd Ave., Seattle, WA 98174-1003; 206-553-5545; Fax: 206-553-0891; *State Director:* Shawn Bills

10 N. Post St., #600, Spokane, WA 99201-0712; 509-624-9515; Fax: 509-624-9561; *Eastern Washington Director:* John Culton

950 Pacific Ave., #650, Tacoma, WA 98402; 253-572-3636; Fax: 253-572-9488; *South Sound Director:* Christine Nahn

The Marshall House, 1323 Officers Row, Vancouver, WA 98661-3856; 360-696-7797; Fax: 360-696-7798; *Southwest Washington Regional Director:* David Hodges

402 E. Yakima Ave., #420, Yakima, WA 98901; 509-453-7462; Fax: 509-453-7731; *Central Washington Director:* Raquel Crowley

Committee Assignments: Appropriations; Budget; Health, Education, Labor, and Pensions, Ranking Minority Member; Veterans' Affairs

Paul, Rand, R-Ky.

Capitol Hill Office: 167 SROB 20510; 224-4343; *Chief of Staff:* William Henderson

Web: www.paul.senate.gov

Facebook: www.facebook.com/SenatorRandPaul

Twitter: @RandPaul

Instagram: @senatorrandpaul

YouTube: www.youtube.com/SenatorRandPaul

District Offices: 1029 State St., Bowling Green, KY 42101-2652; 270-782-8303; *Constituent Services Director:* Bobette Franklin

Committee Assignments: Foreign Relations; Health, Education, Labor, and Pensions; Homeland Security and Governmental Affairs; Small Business and Entrepreneurship

Perdue, David, D-Ga.

Capitol Hill Office: 455 SROB 20510; 224-3521; Fax: 228-1031; *Chief of Staff:* Derrick Dickey

Web: www.perdue.senate.gov

Facebook: www.facebook.com/SenatorDavidPerdue

Twitter: @sendavidperdue

Instagram: @sendavidperdue

YouTube: www.youtube.com/channel/UCXHsrkPP4TAm0s0qB1C31Lw

District Offices: 3280 Peachtree St. N.E., #2640, Atlanta, GA 30339; 404-865-0087; Fax: 404-816-3435; *Communications Director:* Cherie Gillan

Committee Assignments: Agriculture, Nutrition, and Forestry; Armed Services; Banking, Housing, and Urban Affairs; Budget; International Narcotics Control Caucus

Peters, Gary C., D-Mich.

Capitol Hill Office: 724 SHOB 20510; 224-6221; Fax: 224-7387; *Chief of Staff:* Eric Feldman
Web: www.peters.senate.gov
Facebook: www.facebook.com/SenGaryPeters
Twitter: @SenGaryPeters
Instagram: @sengarypeters
YouTube: www.youtube.com/channel/UC7LYNbnKSK2VZqQ98YROWHQ
District Offices: Patrick V. McNamara Federal Bldg., 477 Michigan Ave., #1837, Detroit, MI 48226; 313-226-6020; Fax: 313-226-6948; *Scheduler:* Angeli Chawla
124 W. Allegan St., #1400, Lansing, MI 48933; 517-377-1508; *State Director:* Elise Lancaster
Gerald R. Ford Federal Bldg., 110 Michigan Ave. N.W., #720, Grand Rapids, MI 49503; 616-233-9150; *Regional Director:* Peter Dikow
857 W. Washington St., #308, Marquette, MI 49855; 906-226-4554; *Regional Director:* Vacant
407 6th St., Suite C, Rochester, MI 48307; 248-608-8040; *Regional Director:* James Jackson
515 N. Washington Ave., #401, Saginaw, MI 48607; 989-754-0112; *Regional Director:* Montel Menifee
818 Red Dr., #40, Traverse City, MI 49684; 231-947-7773; *Regional Director:* Eric Keller
Committee Assignments: Armed Services; Commerce, Science, and Transportation; Congressional-Executive Commission on China; Homeland Security and Governmental Affairs, Ranking Minority Member; Joint Economic

Portman, Rob, R-Ohio

Capitol Hill Office: 448 SROB 20510; 224-3353; Fax: 224-9075; *Chief of Staff:* Mark Isakowitz
Web: www.portman.senate.gov
Facebook: www.facebook.com/senrobportman
Twitter: @senrobportman
YouTube: www.youtube.com/user/SenRobPortman
District Offices: 312 Walnut St., #3425, Cincinnati, OH 45202; 513-684-3265; *Southwest Ohio District Director:* Nan Cahall
1240 E. 9th St., Room 3061, Cleveland, OH 44199-2001; 216-522-7095; Fax: 216-522-7097; *Northeast Ohio District Director:* Caryn Candisky
37 W. Broad St., Room 300, Columbus, OH 43215; 614-469-6774; Fax: 614-469-7419; *State Director:* Kevin Hoggatt
420 Madison Ave., Room 1210, Toledo, OH 43604-1221; 419-259-3895; Fax: 419-259-3899; *North West District Director:* Kelsey Krull
Committee Assignments: Finance; Foreign Relations; Homeland Security and Governmental Affairs; Joint Economic

Reed, Jack D., D-R.I.

Capitol Hill Office: 728 SHOB 20510-3903; 224-4642; Fax: 224-4680; *Chief of Staff:* Neil D. Campbell
Web: www.reed.senate.gov
Facebook: www.facebook.com/SenJackReed
Twitter: @SenJackReed
YouTube: www.youtube.com/senatorreed
District Offices: 1000 Chapel View Blvd., #290, Cranston, RI 02920-5602; 401-943-3100; Fax: 401-464-6837; *Deputy Chief of Staff:* Raymond Simone
U.S. District Courthouse, One Exchange Terrace, #408, Providence, RI 02903-1773; 401-528-5200; Fax: 202-224-4680; *Deputy Chief of Staff:* Raymond Simone
Committee Assignments: Appropriations; Armed Services, Ranking Minority Member; Banking, Housing, and Urban Affairs; Select Intelligence

Risch, James E., R-Idaho

Capitol Hill Office: 483 SROB 20510-1206; 224-2752; Fax: 224-2573; *Chief of Staff:* John A. Sandy
Web: www.risch.senate.gov
Facebook: www.facebook.com/SenatorJimRisch
Twitter: @SenatorRisch
YouTube: www.youtube.com/SenatorJamesRisch
District Offices: 350 N. 9th St., #302, Boise, ID 83702-5409; 208-342-7985; Fax: 208-343-2458; *Regional Director:* Rachel Burkett
Harbor Plaza, 610 Hubbard St., #213, Coeur d'Alene, ID 83814-2288; 208-667-6130; Fax: 208-765-1743; *Regional Director:* Sid Smith
901 Pier View Dr., #202A, Idaho Falls, ID 83402-5070; 208-523-5541; Fax: 208-523-9373; *Regional Director:* Amy Taylor
313 D St., #106, Lewiston, ID 83501-1894; 208-743-0792; Fax: 208-746-7275; *Regional Director:* Mike Hanna
275 S. 5th Ave., #290, Pocatello, ID 83201-6410; 208-236-6817; Fax: 208-236-6820; *Regional Director:* Renee Richardson
1411 Falls Ave. East, #201, Twin Falls, ID 83301-3455; 208-734-6780; Fax: 208-734-3905; *State Director:* Mike Matthews
Committee Assignments: Energy and Natural Resources; Foreign Relations, Chair; International Narcotics Control Caucus; Select Ethics; Select Intelligence; Small Business and Entrepreneurship, Chair

Roberts, Pat, R-Kans.

Capitol Hill Office: 109 SHOB 20510-1605; 224-4774; Fax: 224-3514; *Chief of Staff:* Jackie Cottrell
Web: www.roberts.senate.gov
Facebook: www.facebook.com/SenPatRoberts
Twitter: @senpatroberts
Instagram: @senpatroberts
YouTube: www.youtube.com/SenPatRoberts
District Offices: 100 Military Plaza, P.O. Box 550, Dodge City, KS 67801-4990; 620-227-2244; Fax: 620-227-2264; *District Rep.:* Martha Ruiz-Martinez
11900 College Blvd., #203, Overland Park, KS 66210-3939; 913-451-9343; *State Director:* Chad Tenpenny

Frank Carlson Federal Bldg., 444 S.E. Quincy St., #392, Topeka, KS 66683-3599; 785-295-2745; Fax: 785-235-3665; *District Director:* Gilda Lintz

125 N. Market St., #1120, Wichita, KS 67202-1802; 316-263-0416; Fax: 316-263-0273; *District Director:* Tamara Woods

Committee Assignments: Agriculture, Nutrition, and Forestry, Chair; Finance; Health, Education, Labor, and Pensions; Select Ethics; Joint Library; Joint Printing; Rules and Administration

Romney, Mitt, R-Utah

Capitol Hill Office: B33 SROB 20510; 224-5251; Fax: 228-0836; *Chief of Staff:* Matt Waldrip

Web: www.romney.senate.gov

Facebook: www.facebook.com/senatorromney

Twitter: @SenatorRomney

Instagram: @senatorromney

YouTube: www.youtube.com/channel/UCEnG85eZBypPpcmbKUJNdng

District Offices: 125 S. State St., #8402, Salt Lake City, UT 84138; 801-524-4380; *State Director:* Adam Gardiner

Committee Assignments: Foreign Relations; Health, Education, Labor, and Pensions; Homeland Security and Governmental Affairs; Small Business and Entrepreneurship

Rosen, Jacky, D- Nev.

Capitol Hill Office: G12 SDOB 20510; 224-6244; *Chief of Staff:* Dara Cohen

Web: www.rosen.senate.gov

Facebook: www.facebook.com/SenJackyRosen

Twitter: @SenJackyRosen

Instagram: @senjackyrosen

District Offices: 8930 W. Sunset Rd., #230, Las Vegas, NV 89148; 702-388-0205; *State Director:* Nelson Araujo

Bruce Thompson Federal Bldg., 400 S. Virginia St., #738, Reno, NV 89501; 775-337-0110; *Northern Nevada Director:* Natalie Okelson

Committee Assignments: Commerce, Science, Transportation; Health, Education, Labor, and Pensions; Homeland Security and Governmental Affairs; Business and Entrepreneurship; Special Aging; Caucus on International Narcotics Control

Rounds, Mike, R-S.D.

Capitol Hill Office: 502 SHOB 20510-4104; 224-5842; Fax: 224-7482; *Chief of Staff:* Mark Johnston

Web: www.rounds.senate.gov

Facebook: www.facebook.com/SenatorMikeRounds

Twitter: @senatorrounds

YouTube: www.youtube.com/channel/UC-pvzimyBdpdkcIfsicrfrQ

District Offices: 1313 W. Main St., Rapid City, SD 57701; 605-343-5035; Fax: 605-343-5348; *West River Director:* Jeff Marlette

320 N. Main Ave., Suite A, Sioux Falls, SD 57104; 605-336-0486; Fax: 605-336-6624; *East River Director:* Tyler Tordsen

514 S. Main St., #100, Aberdeen, SD 57401; 605-936-0366; *Senior Field Manager:* Josh Haeder

111 W. Capitol Ave., #210, Pierre, SD 57501; 605-224-1450; Fax: 605-224-1397; *Central South Dakota Director:* Kim Olsen

Committee Assignments: Armed Services; Banking, Housing, and Urban Affairs; Environment and Public Works; Veterans' Affairs

Rubio, Marco, R-Fla.

Capitol Hill Office: 284 SROB 20510; 224-3041; Fax: 228-0285; *Chief of Staff:* Mike Needham

Web: www.rubio.senate.gov

Facebook: www.facebook.com/SenatorMarcoRubio

Twitter: @SenRubioPress

Instagram: @marcorubiofla

YouTube: www.youtube.com/SenatorMarcoRubio

District Offices: 300 N. Hogan, #8-111, Jacksonville, FL 32202; 904-398-8586; *Regional Director:* Ashley Cook

201 S. Orange Ave., #350, Orlando, FL 32801-3499; 407-254-2573; Fax: 844-762-1556; *State Director:* Todd Reid

7005 Palafox St., #125, Pensacola, FL 32502-5658; 850-433-2603; *Regional Director:* Marybeth Barrows

402 S. Monroe St., #2105E, Tallahassee, FL 32399-6526; 850-599-9100; *Regional Director:* Joshua Gabel

Sam M. Gibbons U.S. Courthouse, 801 N. Florida Ave., #1130, Tampa, FL 33602; 813-853-1099; *Regional Director:* Johnathan Torres

4580 PGA Blvd., #201, Palm Beach Gardens, FL 33418; 561-775-3360; *Regional Director:* Greg Langowski

7400 87th Ave. S.W., #270, Miami, FL 33173; 305-596-4224; Fax: 305-596-4345; *Regional Director:* Alyn Fernandez

2120 Main St., Room 200, Fort Myers, FL 33901; 866-630-7106; *Regional Director:* Elaine Sarlow

Committee Assignments: Appropriations; Congressional-Executive Commission on China, Co-Chair; Foreign Relations; Small Business and Entrepreneurship, Chair; Select Intelligence; Special Aging; Commission on Security and Cooperation in Europe

Sanders, Bernard, I-Vt.

Capitol Hill Office: 332 SDOB 20510-4504; 224-5141; Fax: 228-0776; *Chief of Staff:* Caryn Compton

Web: www.sanders.senate.gov

Facebook: www.facebook.com/senatorsanders

Twitter: @SenSanders

Instagram: @berniesanders

YouTube: www.youtube.com/user/SenatorSanders

District Offices: 1 Church St., 3rd Floor, Burlington, VT 05401-4451; 802-862-0697; Fax: 802-860-6370; *State Director:* David Weinstein

357 Western Ave., #1B, St. Johnsbury, VT 05819; 800-339-9834; Fax: 802-860-6370; *Outreach Director:* Sheila Reed

Committee Assignments: Budget, Ranking Minority Member; Energy and Natural Resources; Environment and Public Works; Health, Education, Labor, and Pensions; Veterans' Affairs

Sasse, Ben, R-Neb.

Capitol Hill Office: 136 SROB 20510-2707; 224-4224; Fax: 228-1325; *Chief of Staff:* Joe Hack
Web: www.sasse.senate.gov
Facebook: www.facebook.com/SenatorSasse
Twitter: @sensasse
Instagram: @senatorsasse
YouTube: www.youtube.com/channel/
UCYaNGwcM2Dl5yDcDqS6xV2g
District Offices: 115 Railway St., #C102, Scottsbluff, NE 69361; 308-632-6032; Fax: 308-630-2321; *Director of Constituent Services:* Cassie Nichols
4111 4th Ave., #26, Kearney, NE 68845; 308-233-3677; *State Outreach Director:* Ryan Broker
1128 Lincoln Mall, #305, Lincoln, NE 68508; 402-476-1400; *Deputy Chief of Staff:* Shelley Blake
304 N. 168th Circle, #213, Omaha, NE 68118; 402-550-8040; *Director of Military and Veterans Affairs:* Jim Kuester
Committee Assignments: Select Intelligence; Banking, Housing, and Urban Affairs; Judiciary; Joint Economic

Schatz, Brian, D-Hawaii

Capitol Hill Office: 722 SHOB 20510; 224-3934; Fax: 228-1153; *Chief of Staff:* Andrew Winer
Web: www.schatz.senate.gov
Facebook: www.facebook.com/SenBrianSchatz
Twitter: @senbrianschatz
Instagram: @brianschatz
YouTube: www.youtube.com/senbrianschatz
District Offices: 300 Ala Moana Blvd., Room 7-212, Honolulu, HI 96850; 808-523-2061; Fax: 808-523-2065; *Deputy Chief of Staff:* Malia Paul
Committee Assignments: Appropriations; Banking, Housing, and Urban Affairs; Commerce, Science, and Transportation; Indian Affairs; Select Ethics

Schumer, Charles E., D-N.Y.

Capitol Hill Office: 322 SHOB 20510; 224-6542; Fax: 228-3027; *Chief of Staff:* Mike Lynch
Web: www.schumer.senate.gov
Facebook: www.facebook.com/senschumer
Twitter: @senschumer
Instagram: @chuckschumer
YouTube: www.youtube.com/ChuckSchumer
District Offices: Leo O'Brien Bldg., Room 420, Albany, NY 12207; 518-431-4070; Fax: 518-431-4076; *Regional Director:* Steve Mann
15 Henry St., Room 100 A-F , Binghamton, NY 13901; 607-772-6792; Fax: 607-772-8124; *Regional Rep.:* Amanda Spellicy
130 S. Elmwood Ave., #660, Buffalo, NY 14202-2371; 716-846-4111; Fax: 716-846-4113; *Regional Rep.:* Jordan Nicholson
145 Pine Lawn Rd., #300, Melville, NY 11747; 631-753-0978; Fax: 631-753-0997; *Regional Rep.:* Gary Armwood
780 3rd Ave., #2301, New York, NY 10017; 212-486-4430; Fax: 202-228-2838; *State Director:* Martin Brennan

One Park Pl., #100, Peekskill, NY 10566; 914-734-1532; Fax: 914-734-1673; *Regional Rep.:* Lori Nguyen
100 State St., Room 3040, Rochester, NY 14614; 585-263-5866; Fax: 585-263-3173; *Regional Rep.:* Christopher Zeltmann
100 S. Clinton St., Room 841, Syracuse, NY 13261-7318; 315-423-5471; Fax: 315-423-5185; *Regional Rep.:* Joe Nehme
Committee Assignments: Rules and Administration; Select Intelligence; Minority Floor Leader

Scott, Rick, R-Fla.

Capitol Hill Office: 716 SHOB 20510; 224-5274; *Chief of Staff:* Jackie Schutz-Zeckman
Web: www.rickscott.senate.gov
Facebook: www.facebook.com/RickScottSenOffice
Twitter: @SenRickScott
Instagram: @flsenrickscott
YouTube: www.youtube.com/channel/UC-Y9pFmW4PYGZHkC8lcqSkQ
District Offices: 111 N. Adams St., #208, Tallahassee FL 32301; 850-942-8415; *Northwest Florida Regional Director:* Sierra Anderson; *State Director:* Leda Kelly; *Director of Constituent Services:* Lisa Meyer
801 N. Florida Ave., #421, Tampa FL 33602; 813-225-7040
Committee Assignments: Armed Services; Commerce, Science, and Transportation; Homeland Security and Governmental Affairs; Budget; Special Aging

Scott, Tim, R-S.C.

Capitol Hill Office: 104 SHOB 20510-4004; 224-6121; Fax: 228-5143; *Chief of Staff:* Jennifer DeCasper
Web: www.scott.senate.gov
Facebook: www.facebook.com/SenatorTimScott
Twitter: @SenatorTimScott
Instagram: @senatortimscott
YouTube: www.youtube.com/SenatorTimScott
District Offices: 1901 Main St., #1425, Columbia, SC 29201; 803-771-6112; Fax: 855-802-9355; *Regional Director:* Margaret Spaulding
104 S. Main St., #803, Greenville, SC 29601; 864-233-5366; Fax: 855-802-9355; *Constituent Services Director:* Deb Blickenstaff
2500 City Hall Lane, 3rd Floor, North Charleston, SC 29406; 843-727-4525; Fax: 855-802-9355; *State Director:* Joe McKeown
Committee Assignments: Banking, Housing, and Urban Affairs; Finance; Health, Education, Labor, and Pensions; Small Business and Entrepreneurship; Special Aging

Shaheen, Jeanne, D-N.H.

Capitol Hill Office: 506 SHOB 20510-2906; 224-2841; Fax: 228-3194; *Chief of Staff:* Maura Keefe
Web: www.shaheen.senate.gov
Facebook: www.facebook.com/SenatorShaheen
Twitter: @SenatorShaheen
Instagram: @senatorshaheen
YouTube: www.youtube.com/SenatorShaheen

District Offices: 961 Main St., Berlin, NH 03570-3031; 603-752-6300; Fax: 603-752-6305; *Special Asst. for Constituent Services/Policy Projects:* Chuck Henderson

50 Opera House Square, Claremont, NH 03743-5407; 603-542-4872; Fax: 603-542-6582; *Special Asst. for Constituent Services/Outreach:* Bethany Yurek

340 Central Ave., #205, Dover, NH 03820-3770; 603-750-3004; *Special Asst. for Constituent Services/Outreach:* Cara Wry

2 Wall St., #220, Manchester, NH 03101-1261; 603-647-7500; Fax: 647-935-2603; *State Director:* Sarah Holmes

60 Main St., #217, Nashua, NH 03060-2720; 603-883-0196; *Special Asst. for Constituent Services/Outreach:* Letizia Ortiz

12 Gilbo Ave., Suite C, Keene, NH 03431; 603-358-6604; *Special Asst. for Constituent Services/Outreach:* Pam Slack

Committee Assignments: Appropriations; Armed Services; Foreign Relations; Select Ethics; Small Business and Entrepreneurship; Commission on Security and Cooperation in Europe

Shelby, Richard, R-Ala.

Capitol Hill Office: 304 SROB 20510; 224-5744; Fax: 224-3416; *Chief of Staff:* Dayne Cutrell

Web: www.shelby.senate.gov

Facebook: www.facebook.com/RichardShelby

Twitter: @SenShelby

Instagram: @senatorshelby

YouTube: www.youtube.com/SenatorRichardShelby

District Offices: 321 Federal Bldg., 1800 5th Ave. North, #321, Birmingham, AL 35203-2113; 205-731-1384; Fax: 205-731-1386; *District Rep.:* Christian Sanford

1000 Glenn Hearn Blvd., #20127, Huntsville, AL 35824; 256-772-0460; Fax: 256-772-8387; *District Rep.:* Carrie Suggs

445 U.S. Federal Courthouse, 113 St. Joseph St., Mobile, AL 36602-3606; 251-694-4164; Fax: 251-694-4166; *District Rep.:* Tera Johnson

FMJ Federal Courthouse, 15 Lee St., #208, Montgomery, AL 36104-4054; 334-223-7303; Fax: 334-223-7317; *District Rep.:* Vera Jordan

2005 University Blvd., #2100, Tuscaloosa, AL 35401; 205-759-5047; Fax: 205-759-5067; *State Director:* Jonathan Graffeo

Committee Assignments: Appropriations, Chair; Banking, Housing, and Urban Affairs; Environment and Public Works; Rules and Administration; Joint Library

Sinema, Kyrsten, D- Ariz.

Capitol Hill Office: 825 B&C SHOB 20510; 224-4521; *Chief of Staff:* Meg Joseph

Web: www.sinema.senate.gov

Facebook: www.facebook.com/senatorsinema

Twitter: @SenatorSinema

Instagram: @senatorsinema

YouTube: www.youtube.com/user/RepSinema

District Offices: 2200 E. Camelback Rd., #120, Phoenix, AZ 85016; 602-598-7327; *State Director:* Michelle Davidson

Committee Assignments: Banking, Housing, and Urban Affairs; Commerce, Science, and Transportation; Homeland Security and Governmental Affairs; Special Aging

Smith, Tina, D-Minn.

Capitol Hill Office: 309 SHOB 20510; 224-5641; Fax: 224-0044; *Chief of Staff:* Jeff Lomonaco

Web: www.smith.senate.gov

Facebook: www.facebook.com/USSenTinaSmith

Twitter: @SenTinaSmith

Instagram: @tinasmithmn

District Offices: 819 Center Ave., #2A, Moorhead, MN 56560; 218-284-8721; Fax: 218-284-8722; *Outreach Director:* Carson Ouelletpe

515 W. 1st St., #104, Duluth, MN 55802; 218-722-2390; Fax: 218-722-4131; *Outreach Director:* Kyle Vanderflute

60 Plato Blvd. East, #220, Saint Paul, MN 55107; 651-221-1016; Fax: 651-221-1078; *Chief of Staff:* Alana Peterson

1202-1/2 7th St. N.W., #213, Rochester, MN 55901; 507-288-2003; Fax: 507-288-2217; *Outreach Director:* Bree Maki

Committee Assignments: Agriculture, Nutrition, and Forestry; Banking, Housing, Urban Affairs; Health, Education, Labor, and Pensions; Indian Affairs

Stabenow, Debbie, D-Mich.

Capitol Hill Office: 731 SHOB 20510-2204; 224-4822; Fax: 228-0325; *Chief of Staff:* Matt VanKuiken

Web: www.stabenow.senate.gov

Facebook: www.facebook.com/stabenow

Twitter: @SenStabenow

Instagram: @senatordebbiestabenow

YouTube: www.youtube.com/SenatorStabenow

District Offices: 719 Griswold St., #700, Detroit, MI 48226; 313-961-4330; Fax: 313-961-7566; *Regional Manager:* Terry Campbell

221 W. Lake Lansing Rd., #100, East Lansing, MI 48823-8661; 517-203-1760; Fax: 517-203-1778; *State Director:* Teresa Plachetka

432 N. Saginaw St., #301, Flint, MI 48502; 810-720-4172; Fax: 810-720-4178; *Regional Manager:* Derrick Mathis

3280 E. Beltline Court N.E., #400, Grand Rapids, MI 49525; 616-975-0052; Fax: 616-975-5764; *Regional Manager:* Mary Jutnich

1901 W. Ridge, #7, Marquette, MI 49855-3198; 906-228-8756; Fax: 906-228-9162; *Regional Manager:* Jay Gage

3335 S. Airport Rd. West, #6B, Traverse City, MI 49684-7928; 231-929-1031; Fax: 231-929-1250; *Regional Manager:* Brandon Fewins

Committee Assignments: Agriculture, Nutrition, and Forestry, Ranking Minority Member; Budget; Energy and Natural Resources; Finance; Joint Taxation

Sullivan, Dan, R-Alaska

Capitol Hill Office: 702 SHOB 20510; 224-3004; Fax: 228-6801; *Chief of Staff:* Larry Burton
Web: www.sullivan.senate.gov
Facebook: www.facebook.com/SenDanSullivan
Twitter: @sendansullivan
Instagram: @sen_dansullivan
YouTube: www.youtube.com/channel/ UC7tXCm8gKlAhTFo2kuf5ylw
District Offices: 851 E. Westpoint Dr., #309, Wasilla, AK 99654; 907-357-9956; Fax: 907-357-9964; *Regional Director:* Margaret Sharp
Federal Bldg. 101, 12th Ave., #328, Fairbanks, AK 99701; 907-456-0261; Fax: 907-451-7290; *Special Assistant:* Leslie Hajdukovich
805 Frontage Rd., #101, Kenai, AK 99611; 907-262-4040; Fax: 907-283-4401; *Field Director:* Elaina Spraker
44539 Sterling Hwy., #204, Soldotna, AK 99669; 907-262-4040; Fax: 907-262-4224; *Field Director:* Elaina Spraker
1900 1st Ave., #225, Ketchikan, AK 99901; 907-225-6880; Fax: 907-225-0390; *Field Rep.:* Chere Klein
510 L St., #750, Anchorage, AK 99501; 907-271-5915; Fax: 907-258-9305; *State Director:* Renee Limoge Reeve
800 Glacier Ave., #101, Juneau, AK 99801; 907-586-7277; Fax: 907-586-7201; *Staffer:* Dana Herndon
Committee Assignments: Armed Services; Commerce, Science, and Transportation; Environment and Public Works; Veterans' Affairs

Tester, Jon, D-Mont.

Capitol Hill Office: 311 SHOB 20510; 224-2644; Fax: 224-8594; *Chief of Staff:* Aaron Murphey
Web: www.tester.senate.gov
Facebook: www.facebook.com/senatortester
Twitter: @SenatorTester
Instagram: @senatorjontester
YouTube: www.youtube.com/SenatorJonTester
District Offices: Judge Jameson Federal Bldg., 2900 4th Ave. North, #201, Billings, MT 59101; 406-252-0550; Fax: 406-252-7768; *State Scheduler:* Trina Newton
1 E. Main St., #202, Bozeman, MT 59715-6248; 406-586-4450; Fax: 406-586-7647; *Regional Director:* Jenna Rose
Silver Bow Center, 125 W. Granite St., #200, Butte, MT 59701-9215; 406-723-3277; Fax: 406-782-4717; *Regional Director:* Erik Nylund
119 1st Ave. North, #102, Great Falls, MT 59401-2568; 406-452-9585; Fax: 406-452-9586; *Regional Director:* Cheryl Ulmer
Capital One Center, 208 N. Montana Ave., #202, Helena, MT 59601-3837; 406-449-5401; Fax: 406-449-5462; *Veteran Liaison:* Bruce Knutson
8 3rd St. East, #230, Kalispell, MT 59901-4588; 406-257-3360; Fax: 406-257-3974; *Regional Director:* Chad Campbell
130 W. Front St., Missoula, MT 59802; 406-728-3003; Fax: 406-728-2193; *State Director:* Dayna Swanson
Committee Assignments: Appropriations; Banking, Housing, and Urban Affairs; Commerce, Science, and Transportation; Indian Affairs; Veterans' Affairs, Ranking Minority Member

Thune, John, R-S.D.

Capitol Hill Office: 511 SDOB 20510-4105; 224-2321; Fax: 228-5429; *Chief of Staff:* Ryan P. Nelson
Web: www.thune.senate.gov
Facebook: www.facebook.com/johnthune
Twitter: @senjohnthune
Instagram: @senjohnthune
YouTube: www.youtube.com/JohnThune
District Offices: 320 S. 1st St., #101, Aberdeen, SD 57401; 605-225-8823; Fax: 605-225-8468; *Northeast Regional Director:* Judy Vrchota
246 Founders Park Dr., #102, Rapid City, SD 57701; 605-348-7551; Fax: 605-348-7208; *West River Regional Director:* Mark Haugen
5015 S. Bur Oak, Sioux Falls, SD 57108; 605-334-9596; Fax: 605-334-2591; *Chief of Staff; State Director:* Ryan Nelson
Committee Assignments: Agriculture, Nutrition, and Forestry; Commerce, Science, and Transportation; Finance

Tillis, Thom, R-N.C.

Capitol Hill Office: 185 SDOB 20510-3309; 224-6342; Fax: 228-2563; *Chief of Staff:* Ted Lehman
Web: www.tillis.senate.gov
Facebook: www.facebook.com/SenatorThomTillis
Twitter: @SenThomTillis
Instagram: @senthomtillis
YouTube: www.youtube.com/channel/ UCUD9VGV4SSGWjGdbn37Ea2w
District Offices: 9300 Harris Corners Pkwy., #170, Charlotte, NC 28269; 704-509-9087; Fax: 704-509-9162; *State Director:* Kim Candey Barns
1694 E. Arlington Blvd., Suite B, Greenville, NC 27858; 252-329-0371; Fax: 252-329-0290; *Regional Rep.:* Brian Brown
1840 Eastchester Dr., #200, High Point, NC 27265; 336-885-0685; Fax: 336-885-0692; *Regional Rep.:* Nick Wilkinson
310 New Bern Ave., #122, Raleigh, NC 27601; 919-856-4630; Fax: 919-856-4053; *Regional Rep.:* Austen Shearer
1 Historic Courthouse Square, #112, Hendersonville, NC 28792; 828-693-8750; Fax: 828-693-9724
Committee Assignments: Armed Services; Banking, Housing, and Urban Affairs; Judiciary; Veterans' Affairs; Commission on Security and Cooperation in Europe

Toomey, Patrick J., R-Pa.

Capitol Hill Office: 248 SROB 20510-3806; 224-4254; Fax: 228-0284; *Chief of Staff:* Dan Brandt
Web: www.toomey.senate.gov
Facebook: www.facebook.com/senatortoomey
Twitter: @sentoomey
Instagram: @senpattoomey
YouTube: www.youtube.com/sentoomey
District Offices: 1150 S. Cedar Crest Blvd., #101, Allentown, PA 18103; 610-434-1444; Fax: 202-228-2727; *Deputy State Director:* Sue Zimskind

U.S. Federal Bldg., 17 S. Park Row, #B-120, Erie, PA 16501-1156; 814-453-3010; Fax: 814-455-9925; *Northwest Pennsylvania Regional Manager:* Sheila Sterrett

320 Market St., #475E, Harrisburg, PA 17101; 717-782-3951; Fax: 717-782-4920; *State Director:* Bob DeSousa

Richland Square III, 1397 Eisenhower Blvd., #302, Johnstown, PA 15904-3267; 814-266-5970; Fax: 814-266-5973; *Greater Johnstown Regional Manager:* John Frick

U.S. Custom House, 200 Chestnut St., #600, Philadelphia, PA 19106; 215-241-1090; Fax: 202-224-4442; *Southeast Regional Manager:* Katie Schramm

310 Grant St., #1440, Pittsburgh, PA 15219; 412-803-3501; Fax: 412-803-3504; *Western Pennsylvania Director:* Matthew Blackburn

7 N. Wilkes-Barre Blvd., #406, Wilkes-Barre, PA 18702; 570-820-4088; Fax: 570-820-6442; *Eastern Pennsylvania Director:* Brian Langan

Committee Assignments: Banking, Housing, and Urban Affairs; Budget; Finance

Udall, Tom, D-N.M.

Capitol Hill Office: 531 SHOB 20510-3103; 224-6621; Fax: 228-3261; *Chief of Staff:* Bianca Ortiz Werthein

Web: www.tomudall.senate.gov

Facebook: www.facebook.com/senatortomudall

Twitter: @SenatorTomUdall

Instagram: @senatortomudall

YouTube: www.youtube.com/SenatorTomUdall

District Offices: 400 Gold Ave., S.W., #300, Albuquerque, NM 87102; 505-346-6791; Fax: 505-346-6720; *State Director:* Greg Bloom

102 W. Hagerman St., Suite A, Carlsbad, NM 88220; 575-234-0366; Fax: 575-234-1507; *Field Rep.:* Beverly Allen

201 N. Church St., #201B, Las Cruces, NM 88001; 575-526-5475; Fax: 575-523-6589; *Field Rep.:* Marco Grajeda; Rene Romo and Melanie Goodman

120 S. Federal Pl., #302, Santa Fe, NM 87501; 505-988-6511; Fax: 505-988-6514; *Field Rep.:* Michele Jacquez-Ortiz

100 S. Ave. A, #113, Portales, NM 88130; 575-356-6811; Fax: 575-356-6814; *Field Rep.:* Jack Carpenter

Committee Assignments: Appropriations; Commerce, Science, and Transportation; Foreign Relations; Indian Affairs, Vice Chair; Rules and Administration; Joint Printing; Commission on Security and Cooperation in Europe

Van Hollen, Chris, D-Md.

Capitol Hill Office: 110 SHOB 20510; 224-4654; Fax: 228-0629; *Chief of Staff:* Karen Robb

Web: www.vanhollen.senate.gov

Facebook: www.facebook.com/chrisvanhollen

Twitter: @chrisvanhollen

Instagram: @chrisvanhollen

YouTube: www.youtube.com/RepChrisVanHollen

District Offices: 111 Rockville Pike, #960, Rockville, MD 20850; 301-545-1500; Fax: 301-545-1512

32 W. Washington St., #203, Hagerstown, MD 21740; 301-797-2826; *Constituent Services:* Julianna Albowicz

1900 N. Howard St., #100, Baltimore, MD 21218; 667-212-4610; Fax: 301-545-1512; *State Staffer:* Charles Conner

1101 Mercantile Lane, #210, Largo MD 20774; 301-322-6560; Fax: 301-545-1512; *State Staffer:* PK Owusu-Acheaw

204 Cedar St., #200C, Cambridge, MD 21613; 410-221-2074; Fax: 301-545-1512; *State Staffer:* Melissa Kelly

60 W. St., #107, Annapolis, MD 21401; 410-263-1325; Fax: 301-545-1512

Committee Assignments: Appropriations; Banking, Housing, and Urban Affairs; Budget; Environment and Public Works

Warner, Mark R., D-Va.

Capitol Hill Office: 703 SHOB 20510-4606; 224-2023; *Chief of Staff:* Mike Harney

Web: www.warner.senate.gov

Facebook: www.facebook.com/MarkRWarner

Twitter: @MarkWarner

Instagram: @senatorwarner

YouTube: www.youtube.com/SenatorMarkWarner

District Offices: 180 W. Main St., Room 235, Abingdon, VA 24210-2844; 276-628-8158; Fax: 276-628-1036; *Regional Director:* Shane Clem

101 W. Main St., #7771, Norfolk, VA 23510-1690; 757-441-3079; Fax: 757-441-6250; *Regional Director:* Drew Lumpkin

919 E. Main St., #630, Richmond, VA 23219-4600; 804-775-2314; Fax: 804-775-2319; *State Director (Acting):* Lou Kadiri

110 Kirk Ave. S.W., Roanoke, VA 24011; 540-857-2676; Fax: 540-857-2800; *Casework Director:* Chris Monioudis

8000 Towers Crescent Dr., #200, Vienna, VA 22182; 703-442-0670; Fax: 703-442-0408; *Regional Director:* Scott Price

Committee Assignments: Banking, Housing, and Urban Affairs; Budget; Finance; Rules and Administration; Select Intelligence, Vice Chair

Warren, Elizabeth, D-Mass.

Capitol Hill Office: 317 SHOB 20510; 224-4543; Fax: 228-2072; *Chief of Staff:* Anne Reid

Web: www.warren.senate.gov

Facebook: www.facebook.com/senatorelizabethwarren

Twitter: @senwarren

Instagram: @elizabethwarren

YouTube: www.youtube.com/senelizabethwarren

District Offices: 2400 JFK Federal Bldg., 15 New Sudbury St., Boston, MA 02203; 617-565-3170; Fax: 617-227-1875; *State Director:* Mikko Mendoza

1550 Main St., #406, Springfield, MA 01103; 413-788-2690; *Regional Director:* Everett Handford

Committee Assignments: Armed Services; Banking, Housing, and Urban Affairs; Health, Education, Labor, and Pensions; Special Aging

Whitehouse, Sheldon, D-R.I.

Capitol Hill Office: 530 SHOB 20510; 224-2921; Fax: 228-6362; *Chief of Staff:* Sam Goodstein

Web: www.whitehouse.senate.gov

Facebook: www.facebook.com/SenatorWhitehouse

Twitter: @SenWhitehouse
Instagram: @senwhitehouse
YouTube: www.youtube.com/SenatorWhitehouse
District Offices: 170 Westminster St., #200, Providence, RI 02903; 401-453-5294; Fax: 401-453-5085; *State Director:* George Carvalho
Committee Assignments: Budget; Environment and Public Works; International Narcotics Control Caucus; Judiciary; Finance; Commission on Security and Cooperation in Europe

Wicker, Roger F., R-Miss.

Capitol Hill Office: 555 SDOB 20510-2404; 224-6253; Fax: 228-0378; *Chief of Staff:* Michelle Barlow Richardson
Web: www.wicker.senate.gov
Facebook: www.facebook.com/senatorwicker
Twitter: @senatorwicker
Instagram: @senatorwicker
YouTube: www.youtube.com/SenatorWicker
District Offices: 2909 13th St., 3rd Floor, #303, Gulfport, MS 39501; 228-871-7017; Fax: 228-871-7196; *Southern Regional Director:* Brad Ferguson
321 Losher St., P.O. Box 385, Hernando, MS 38632-2124; 662-429-1002; Fax: 662-429-6002; *Constituent Liaison:* Kim Chamberlin and Ladonna Worthing
U.S. Federal Courthouse, 501 E. Court St., #3-500, Jackson, MS 39201; 601-965-4644; Fax: 601-965-4007; *State Director:* Ryan Annison
330 W. Jefferson St., Suite B, Tupelo, MS 38804; 662-844-5010; Fax: 662-844-5030; *Constituent Liaison:* Mattie Wilson
Committee Assignments: Armed Services; Commerce, Science, and Transportation, Chair; Environment and Public Works; Rules and Administration; Joint Printing; Commission on Security and Cooperation in Europe, Chair

Wyden, Ron, D-Ore.

Capitol Hill Office: 221 SDOB 20510; 224-5244; *Chief of Staff:* Jeff Michels
Web: www.wyden.senate.gov
Facebook: www.facebook.com/wyden

Twitter: @ronwyden
Instagram: @ronwyden
YouTube: www.youtube.com/SenRonWyden
District Offices: The Jamison Bldg., 131 Hawthorne Ave. N.W., #107, Bend, OR 97701; 541-330-9142; Fax: 541-330-6266; *Field Rep.:* Jacob Egler
405 E. 8th Ave., #2020, Eugene, OR 97401; 541-431-0229; *Field Rep.:* Juine Chada
SAC Annex Bldg., 105 Fir St., #201, La Grande, OR 97850-2661; 541-962-7691; *Field Rep.:* Kathleen Cathey
Federal Courthouse, 310 W. 6th St., #118, Medford, OR 97501-2700; 541-858-5122; Fax: 541-858-5126; *Field Rep.:* Molly McCarthy
911 11th Ave. N.E., #630, Portland, OR 97232; 503-326-7525; *State Director:* Lisa Rockower
707 13th St. S.E., #285, Salem, OR 97301; 503-589-4555; *Field Rep.:* Fritz Graham
Committee Assignments: Budget; Energy and Natural Resources; Finance, Ranking Minority Member; Select Intelligence; Joint Taxation

Young, Todd, R-Ind.

Capitol Hill Office: 400 SROB 20510; 224-5623; Fax: 224-1845; *Chief of Staff:* John Connell
Web: www.young.senate.gov
Facebook: www.facebook.com/SenatorToddYoung
Twitter: @SenToddYoung
Instagram: @sentoddyoung
YouTube: www.youtube.com/channel/UC0vPqS6JHqPoptRGdyja9Lw
District Offices: 251 N. Illinois St., #120, Indianapolis, IN 46204; 317-226-6700; *State Director:* Andrew Kossack
3602 N. Gate Court, #15, New Albany, IN 47150; 812-542-4820; Fax: 812-542-4826; *District Rep.:* Melissa Acton
Satellite Office: 101 Martin Luther King Jr. Blvd., #110, Evansville, IN 47708; *Field Staff:* Brenda Goff
1300 S. Harrison St., #3161, Fort Wayne, IN 46802; *District Director:* Justin Busch
Committee Assignments: Commerce, Science, and Transportation; Congressional-Executive Commission on China; Foreign Relations; Small Business and Entrepreneurship

House and Senate Caucuses

The following is a compilation of the most active caucuses in the House and Senate. A general staff contact is listed along with the phone number as well as a Web address when available. The area code for all phone numbers is (202). This information is current as of April 12, 2019.

HOUSE CAUCUSES

Agriculture and Rural America Task Force, Elliot Guffin, 225-3715

Americans Abroad Caucus, Max Whitcomb, 225-1491; Web, www.americansabroad.org/americans-abroad-caucus

American Sikh Congressional Caucus, Erik Olsen, 225-1880

Bipartisan Congressional Pro-Life Caucus, Rebecca Duberstein, 225-3765

Bipartisan Congressional Task Force to Combat Identity Theft and Fraud, Hart Thompson, 225-5831

Bipartisan Disabilities Caucus, Katherine Lee, 225-2735; Web, http://disabilitiescaucus.langevin.house.gov

Bipartisan Heroin Task Force, Kevin Diamond, 225-5206

Bipartisan Historically Black Colleges and Universities Caucus, John Christie, 225-1510; Web, https://adams.house.gov/bipartisan-historically-black-colleges-and-universities-hbcu-caucus

Bipartisan Taskforce for Combating Anti-Semitism, Nathaniel Hurd, 225-1901

Blue Dog Coalition, Jared Feldman, 225-3341; Web, https://bluedogcaucus-costa.house.gov/

Climate Solutions Caucus, Courtney Fotwell, 225-2778

Congressional 21st-Century Skills Caucus, Erin Schnell, 225-6576; Web, www.p21.org/our-work/advocacy

Congressional Access to Civil Legal Service Caucus, Eric Fins, 225-5931

Congressional Addiction, Treatment, and Recovery Caucus, Ryan Keating, 225-5261; Web, https://timryan.house.gov/about/committees-and-caucuses/congressional-addiction-treatment-and-recovery-caucus

Congressional Adult Literacy Caucus, Alex Mackey, 225-6356; Web, http://national-coalition-literacy.org/house-adult-literacy-caucus

Congressional Affordable Medicine Caucus, Isaac Loeb, 225-4115

Congressional Air Force Caucus, Jett Thompson, 225-4201; Web, http://secure.afa.org/grl/caucus.asp

Congressional Albanian Issues Caucus, Tim Mulvey, 225-2464

Congressional Aluminum Caucus, Shantanu Tata, 225-6311, Web, www.aluminum.org/advocacy/congressional-aluminum-caucus

Congressional American Religious Freedom Caucus, Scott Rausch, 225-2711

Congressional Animal Protection Caucus, Kevin Stockert, 225-4811; Web, https://blumenauer.house.gov/congressional-animal-protection-caucus

Congressional Arctic Working Group, Alex Ortiz, 225-5765; Web, http://congressionalarcticworkinggroup-larsen.house.gov

Congressional Army Caucus, Karl Yurik, 225-3864; https://carter.house.gov/house-army-caucus

Congressional Army Aviation Caucus, Caryn Hamner, 225-4801

Congressional Arthritis Caucus, Rachel Fybel, 225-8104

Congressional Arts Caucus, Maria Oparil, 225-3615

Congressional Assisting Caregivers Today Caucus, Kelsey Griswold, 225-3765

Congressional Asthma and Allergy Caucus, Hannah Aiken, 225-2464

Congressional Baby Caucus, Elizabeth Albertine, 225-3661

Congressional Balanced Budget Amendment Caucus, Paul Johnson, 225-0453

Congressional Baseball Caucus, Zack Barth, 225-9896

Congressional Beef Caucus, Zack Linick, 225-1640

Congressional Bike Caucus, Lewis Plush, 225-5015; Web, https://blumenauer.house.gov/congressional-bike-caucus

Congressional Biofuels Caucus, Janie Costa, 225-2371

Congressional Biomedical Research Caucus, Drew Hatter, 225-2015

Congressional Black Caucus, Kevin Harris, 225-7084; Web, https://cbc.house.gov/

Congressional Blue Collar Caucus, Helena Mastrogianis, 225-6111

Congressional Border Caucus, Norma Salazar, 225-2435

Congressional Border Security Caucus, Maggie Harrel, 225-4236

Congressional Bourbon Caucus, Elaina Murphy, 225-3501

Congressional Brain Injury Task Force, Elina Houser, 225-5751; Web, http://pascrell.house.gov/issues/brain-injury-task-force

Congressional Building Trades Caucus, Mike Hamilton, 225-4172

Congressional Buy American Caucus, Sofya Leonova, 225-5701

Congressional Cambodia Caucus, Ngoc Nguyen, 225-7924

Congressional Cancer Prevention Caucus, Joe McNally, 225-4071

Congressional Cannabis Caucus, Laura Thrift, 225-4811; Web, https://blumenauer.house.gov/cannabis-caucus

Congressional Carbon Dioxide Enhanced Oil Recovery (CO2-EOR)Caucus, Michael Horder, 225-3605

Congressional Career & Technical Education Caucus, Nick Rockwell, 225-5121; Web, https://careerand technicaleducationcaucus-langevin.house.gov

Congressional Caribbean Caucus, Kathleen Sengstock, 225-2201

Congressional Caucus on the Association of Southeast Asian Nations (ASEAN), Rachel Wagley, 225-1621

Congressional Caucus for Competitiveness in Entertainment Technology (E-TECH), Harry Baumgarten, 225-7931

Congressional Caucus for Effective Foreign Assistance, James Walsh, 225-5744

Congressional Caucus for Women's Issues, Yana Mayayeva, 225-9890

Congressional Caucus on Black Women and Girls, Courtney Cochran, 225-5801; Web, https:// watsoncoleman.house.gov/cbwgcaucus

Congressional Caucus on Bosnia, Piero Pozzi, 225-3765

Congressional Caucus on Brazil, Florence Akinyemi, 225-3461

Congressional Caucus on California High-Speed Rail, Matt Weiner, 225-3072

Congressional Caucus on the Deadliest Cancers, Rachel Fybel, 225-8104

Congressional Caucus on Ethnic and Religious Freedom in Sri Lanka, Laura Wilson, 225-5705

Congressional Caucus on Foster Youth, Nina Dejonghe, 225-7084; Web, http://fosteryouthcaucus-karenbass. house.gov

Congressional Caucus on Hellenic Issues, Shayne Woods, 225-5755

Congressional Caucus on India and Indian-Americans, Curtis Rhyne, 225-3032

Congressional Caucus on Intellectual Property Promotion and Piracy Prevention, Julian Purdy, 225-8901

Congressional Caucus on International Exchange and Study, Sean Higgins, 225-5541

Congressional Caucus on Korea, Calli Shapiro, 225-4561

Congressional Caucus on Long-Range Strike, Chrissi Lee, 225-2876

Congressional Caucus on Macedonia and Macedonian-Americans, Derek Judd, 225-2106

Congressional Caucus on Maternity Care, Anna Breen, 225-3536

Congressional Caucus on Modern Agriculture, Doug Stout, 225-6435

Congressional Caucus on Multicultural Media, Charlyn Stanberry, 225-6231

Congressional Caucus on the Netherlands, Trevor Tenbrink, 225-4401

Congressional Caucus on Parkinson's Disease, Christina Parisi, 225-7944

Congressional Caucus on Poland, Joel Creswell, 225-5701

Congressional Caucus on Public-Private Partnerships (Congressional P3 Caucus), Joshua Ronk, 225-3261

Congressional Caucus on Prescription Drug Abuse, Mariana Osorio, 225-8273

Congressional Caucus on Vietnam, Arlet Abrahamian, 225-3072

Congressional Caucus on Youth Sports, Jared Dilley, 225-2676

Congressional Central America Caucus, Clay Boggs, 225-6161

Congressional Chemistry Caucus, Eva Cline, 225-3561

Congressional Chicken Caucus, Allison Crittenden, 225-4076

Congressional Childhood Cancer Caucus, Thomas Rice, 225-2401; Web, https://childhoodcancer-mccaul. house.gov

Congressional Children's Health Care Caucus, Elizabeth Brown, 225-3376; Web, https://castor.house.gov/ homepage/childrenshealth.htm

Congressional Clean Water Caucus, Zach Dooley, 225-5435

Congressional Coal Caucus, Brian Garand, 225-4172

Congressional Coalition on Adoption, Annie Clark, 225-4576; Wewww.ccainstitute.org

Congressional Coastal Communities Caucus, Roberto Sada, 225-4671

Congressional Coast Guard Caucus, Gabriel Sehr, 225-2076

Congressional Community College Caucus, Alexa Combelic, 225-2076

Congressional Congenital Heart Caucus, Shayne Woods, 225-5755

Congressional Cooperative Business Caucus, Emma Norvell, 225-4111

Congressional Coastal Communities Caucus, David Marten, 225-9740

Congressional Creative Rights Caucus, Linda Shim, 225-5464; Web, http://creativerightscaucus-chu.house.gov

Congressional Cybersecurity Caucus, Nick Leiferson, 225-2735; Web, http://cybercaucus.langevin.house.gov

Congressional Cystic Fibrosis Caucus, Saundrea Shropshire, 225-6101, Web, www.cff.org/ Get-Involved/Advocate/Our-Advocacy-Work/ Congressional-Cystic-Fibrosis-Caucus

Congressional Czech Caucus, Timothy Huebner, 225-4071

Congressional Dairy Farmer Caucus, Mark Fowler, 225-4115

Congressional Deaf Caucus, Justin Maturo, 225-2305

Congressional Diabetes Caucus, Sahil Chaudhary, 225-4431; Web, https://diabetescaucus-degette.house .gov

Congressional Dietary Supplement Caucus, Liz Mann, 225-7751

Congressional Digital Trade Caucus, Shantanu Tata, 225-6311

Congressional Direct Selling Caucus, Preston Bell, 225-3715; Web, www.dsa.org/advocacy/caucus

Congressional Directed Energy Caucus, Peter Lafountain, 225-2735

Congressional Diversifying Tech Caucus, Matt McMurray, 225-0773

Congressional Dyslexia Caucus, Courtney Butler, 225-4236; Web, https://dyslexiacaucus-brownley. house.gov

Congressional E-Learning Caucus, Bo Morris, 225-2161

Congressional Electromagnetic Pulse (EMP)Caucus, David Dorfman, 225-6231

Congressional Electronic Warfare Working Group, Michael Tehrani, 225-6531

Congressional Emergency Medical Services (EMS) Caucus, Lauren Ziegler, 225-1555

Congressional Energy Storage Caucus, Yuri Beckelman, 225-2305

Congressional Estuary Caucus, Valentina Valenta, 225-3671

Congressional Everglades Caucus, Chris Sweet, 225-4211; Web, http://mariodiazbalart.house.gov/issues/ everglades-restoration

Congressional Explosive Ordnance Disposal (EOD) Caucus, Abbi Burgess, 225-4076; Web, http://crawford. house.gov/news/documentsingle.aspx?DocumentID= 398483

Congressional Fertilizer Caucus, Travis Martinez, 225-5816; Web, www.tfi.org/policy-center/get-involved/fertilizer-caucus

Congressional Financial Security and Life Insurance Caucus, Elizabeth O'Hara, 225-5601

Congressional Fintech and Payments Caucus, Catherine Kuerbitz, 225-2939

Congressional Flat Tax Caucus, Rachel Huggins, 225-7772

Congressional Food Safety Caucus, Christian Lovell, 225-3661

Congressional Former Mayors Caucus, Dan Hare, 225-6465

Congressional Fragile X Caucus, Elizabeth Joseth, 225-5031; Web, http://harper.house.gov/about-gregg/ fragile-x

Congressional Franchise Caucus, Richard Lee, 225-2165

Congressional Freshmen Working Group on Addiction, Christina Tsafoulias, 225-272

Congressional Friends of Denmark Caucus, Daniel Silverberg, 225-3130

Congressional Friends of Egypt Caucus, Guido Weiss, 225-4906

Congressional Friends of Ireland Caucus, William Tranghese, 225-5601

Congressional Friends of Liechtenstein Caucus, Susey Davis, 225-4636

Congressional Friends of New Zealand Caucus, Terra Sabag, 225-2605

Congressional Friends of Norway Caucus, Erik Kinney, 225-5101

Congressional Friends of Wales Caucus, Kevin Baird, 225-3861

Congressional Full Employment Caucus, Jenny Perrino, 225-4146

Congressional Future Caucus, Michael Mansour, 225-3635

Congressional German-American Caucus, Scott Nulty, 225-5121

Congressional Global Health Caucus, Libby Foley, 225-6631

Congressional Global Road Safety Caucus, Evan N. Polisar, 225-1313

Congressional Green Schools Caucus, Shane Trimmer, 225-7924; Web, www.centerforgreenschools.org/ congressional-green-schools-caucus

Congressional Grid Innovation Caucus, Teresa Frison, 225-1947

Congressional Gun Violence Prevention Taskforce, Jennifer Goedke, 225- 3311

Congressional Hearing Health Caucus, Christopher Buki, 225-4172

Congressional Heart and Stroke Caucus, Kelsey Griswold, 225-3765

Congressional Hellenic-Israel Alliance, Shayne Woods, 225-5755

Congressional Higher Education Caucus, Charlie Arnowitz, 226-7757

Congressional Home Health Caucus, Saundrea Shropshire, 225-6101

Congressional Homelessness Caucus, Jonathan Jackson, 225-8885

Congressional House Cancer Caucus, Tom Seaman, 225-5916

Congressional House Manufacturing Caucus, Ryan Keating, 225-5261; Web, http://timryan.house.gov/ manufacturing-caucus

Congressional Human Trafficking Caucus, Christina Parisi, 225-7944

Congressional Humanities Caucus, Leigh Whittaker, 225-1784

Congressional Hungarian Caucus, Tim Daniels, 225-5311

Congressional Immigration Reform Caucus, Megan Medley, 225-4876

Congressional Independent Colleges Caucus, Mike Albares, 225-2901

Congressional Innovation Caucus, Taylor Hittler, 225-2701

Congressional International Basic Education Caucus, Mace Flitter, 225-4276

Congressional International Conservation Caucus, Alan Feyerherm, 225-4806

Congressional International Religious Freedom Caucus, Annie Clark, 225-4576

Congressional Internet Caucus, Asad Ramzanali 225-8104

Congressional Interstate 11 Caucus, Rory Burke, 225-2315

Congressional Invasive Species Caucus, Wendy Zirngibl, 225-3311

Congressional Inventions Caucus, Samantha Warren, 225-3515

Congressional Iraq Caucus, Michael Mansour, 225-3635

Congressional Labor and Working Families Caucus, Natasha Silva, 225-8273; Web, https://lynch.house.gov/issue/labor-working-families

Congressional LGBT Equality Caucus, Sarah Trister, 226-4911; Web, https://lgbt-cicilline.house.gov/mission; Twitter, @LGBTEqCaucus

Congressional Life Sciences Caucus, Molly Fischman, 225-3531

Congressional Long Island Sound Caucus, Sarah Talemage, 225-3826

Congressional Lung Cancer Caucus, Merrilee Rogers, 225-3265

Congressional Lupus Caucus, Michael Wertheimer, 225-3111

Congressional Maker Caucus, Ryan Keating, 225-5261; Twitter, @MakerCaucus

Congressional Media Fairness Caucus, Scott Rausch, 225-2711

Congressional Men's Health Caucus, Taylor Hittle, 225-2701; Web, www.menshealthcaucus.net

Congressional Mental Health Caucus, Jennifer Wood, 225-3701

Congressional Mentoring Caucus, Brandon Mendoza, 225-2040

Congressional Middle Class Jobs Caucus, Rachel Sorensen, 225-3712

Congressional Microbusiness Caucus, Ryan Keating, 225-5261

Congressional Military Family Caucus, Matt Neighbors, 225-2006; Web, https://mcmorris.house.gov/congressional-military-family-caucus

Congressional Military Mental Health Caucus, Zach Prager, 225-5261; Web, http://militarymentalhealthcaucus-ryan.house.gov

Congressional Military Sexual Assault Prevention Caucus, Tyler Fitzgerald, 225-6465; Web, https://turner.house.gov/issues/military-sexual-assault-prevention

Congressional Military Veterans Caucus, Suzanne Dodge, 225-3311; Web, http://caucus.militarytimes.com

Congressional Military Youth Programs Caucus, John Shelson, 225-2452

Congressional Missing and Exploited Children's Caucus, John Porter, 225-4901

Congressional Mississippi River Caucus, Ashley Shelton, 225-4076

Congressional Modeling and Simulation Caucus, David Dailey, Christina Ingram, Allen Jones 225-8351

Congressional Morocco Caucus, Molly Cole, 225-1492

Congressional Motorcycle Caucus, Rachel Huggins, 225-7772; Web, https://motorcyclecaucus-burgess.house.gov/

Congressional Motorsports Caucus, Rick Podliska, 225-3671

Congressional Multiple Sclerosis Caucus, Nora Blalock, 225-1784

Congressional National Guard and Reserve Components Caucus, Patrick Large, 225-5772; Web, https://palazzo.house.gov/ngrcc

Congressional National Parks Caucus, Olivia Kirchberg, 225-5506

Congressional Native American Caucus, Rebecca Taylor, 225-6631, Web, https://mccollum.house.gov/about-betty/committees-caucuses/congressional-native-american-caucus

Congressional Natural Gas Caucus, John Busovsky, 225-5121; Web, https://thompson.house.gov/issues/natural-gas-caucus

Congressional Navy and Marine Corps Caucus, Ian Staples, 225-2040

Congressional Neuroscience Caucus, Martha Cramer, 225-4811

Congressional New Americans Caucus, Justin Vogt, 225-6161

Congressional Nigeria Caucus, Glenn Rushing, 225-3816

Congressional Nuclear Security Working Group, Alan Feyerherm, 225-4806

Congressional Oceans Caucus, Kevin Rieg, 225-5765

Congressional Ohio River Basin Caucus, Katy Rowley, 225-5401

Congressional Opportunity Action Group, Miriam Fry, 225-4931

Congressional Oral Health Caucus, Marc Brody, 225-4741; Web, http://simpson.house.gov/issuestatements/oralhealth.htm

Congressional Organ and Tissue Donation and Transplantation Awareness Caucus, Ben Goldeen, 225-3341

Congressional Out of Poverty Caucus, Emma Mehrabi, 225-2661; Web, http://outofpovertycaucus-lee.house.gov

Congressional Peace Corps Caucus, Betsy Thompson, 225-1880

Congressional Peanut Caucus, Michael Albares, 225-2901; Web, http://roby.house.gov/roby-news/congressional-peanut-caucus-formed

Congressional Pediatric & Adult Hydrocephalus Caucus, Charlie Arnowitz, 225-4011; Web, www.hydroassoc.org/congressional-pediatric-and-adult-hydrocephalus-caucus

Congressional Pension Protection for Working Americans Caucus, Will Mitchell, 225-6211

Congressional PFAS Task Force, Jordan Dickinson, 225-3611

Congressional Pilots Caucus, Nick Grimes, 225-7041

Congressional Pollinator Protection Caucus, Lindesy Garber, 225-1313

Congressional Portuguese Caucus, Sarah Trister, 225-4911

Congressional PORTS Caucus, Chris Gorud, 225-7924

Congressional Prayer Caucus, Diem-mi Lu, 225-3515

Congressional Pre-K Caucus, Kaitlyn Montan, 225-3236; Web, https://prekcaucus-castro.house.gov

Congressional Primary Care Caucus, Maria Costigan, 225-2076

Congressional Privacy Caucus, Thomas Woodburn, 225-4431

Congressional Progressive Caucus, Michael Darner, 225-2435; Web, https://cpc-grijalva.house.gov

Congressional Public Broadcasting Caucus, Jon Bosworth, 225-4811; Web, https://blumenauer.house .gov/public-broadcasting-caucus

Congressional Public Health Caucus, Katie Mazzola, 225-4261; Web, www.congressionalpublichealthcaucus .org

Congressional Public Housing Caucus, Helena Schwarc, 225-6111

Congressional Public Transport Caucus, Alex Beckmann, 225-5701

Congressional Puget Sound Recovery Caucus, Jaxon Wolfe, 225-9740; Web, http://dennyheck.house.gov/ legislative-work/puget-sound-recovery

Congressional Range and Testing Center Caucus, Richard Wilkins, 225-6831; Web, https:// rangeandtestingcaucus-desjarlais.house.gov

Congressional Ready Mixed Concrete Caucus, Daniel Tidwell, 225-3271

Congressional Recycling Caucus, Jordan Haverly, 225-5271

Congressional Refinery Caucus, Richard England, 225-5951; Web, http://olson.house.gov/congressional-refinery-caucus

Congressional Research and Development Caucus, Samantha Warren, 225-3515; Web, http:// researchcaucus.org

Congressional Rural Caucus, Doug Stout, 225-6435; Web, http://ruralcaucus-adriansmith.house.gov

Congressional Rural Healthcare Coalition, Nolan Ahern, 225-6730; Web, http://walden.house.gov/rural-health-care

Congressional Safe Climate Caucus, Emily Strombom, Shane Trimmer, 225-7924; Web, http:// safeclimatecaucus-lowenthal.house.gov

Congressional School Choice Caucus, Sarah Feldpausch, 225-2106

Congressional Scouting Caucus, Kevin Gannon, 225-5265

Congressional Science, Technology, Engineering and Mathematics (STEM)Education Caucus, Joel Creswell, 225-5701; Web, http://stemedcaucus2.org

Congressional Second Amendment Caucus, Nino Marchese, 226-6816

Congressional Semiconductor Caucus, Arlet Abrahamian, 225-3071

Congressional Serbian Caucus, Christina Mahoney, 225-4535

Congressional Sharing Economy Caucus, Andrew Ginsburg, 225-5065

Congressional Shellfish Caucus, Wendy Zirngibl, 225-3311

Congressional Shipbuilding Caucus, Chris Ragsdale, 225-4261; Web, http://shipbuilding-wittman.house.gov

Congressional Singapore Caucus, Mariam Fry, 225-4931

Congressional Skin Cancer Caucus, Ella Mathews, 225-4311

Congressional Slovak Caucus, Nathaniel Sans, 225-2461

Congressional Small Business Caucus, Todd Stein, 225-6116

Congressional Smart Transportation Caucus, Kevin Rambosk, 225-4071

Congressional Social Work Caucus, Emma Mehrabi, 225-2661; Web, http://socialworkcaucus-lee.house.gov

Congressional Solar Caucus, Hillary Caron, 225-3711

Congressional Special Operations Forces Caucus, Ray Celeste, 225-3415

Congressional Sportsmen's Caucus, Elise Karkorian, 225-5301, Web, http://congressionalsportsmen.org/ caucuses/congressional

Congressional STEAM Caucus, Julia Angelotti, 225-4611

Congressional Submarine Caucus, Gabe Sehr, 225-2076

Congressional Sudan and South Sudan Caucus, Diala Jadallah, 225-2661

Congressional Taiwan Caucus, Chris Sweet, 225-4211

Congressional Task Force on Alzheimer's Disease, Jayme Holliday, 225-4001

Congressional Task Force on Childhood Obesity, Sarah Nasta, 225-7032

Congressional Task Force on Terrorism and Unconventional Warfare, Katherine Stewart, 225-1510

Congressional Technology Transfer Caucus, Chris Jones, 225-5755

Congressional Term Limits Caucus, Tim Cummings, 225-4005

Congressional Tourette Syndrome Caucus, Merrilee, 225-3265; Web, http://cohen.house.gov/congressional-tourette-syndrome-caucus

Congressional Transparency Caucus, Hannah Mansbach, 225-4061; Web, https://transparencycaucus-quigley. house.gov

Congressional Travel and Tourism Caucus, Chris Jones, 225-5755

Congressional U.S.–Lebanon Friendship Caucus, Ryan McGuire, 225-5961

Congressional U.S.–China Working Group, Terra Sabag, 225-2605; Web, https://uschinaworkinggroup-larsen. house.gov

Congressional U.S.–Mexico Friendship Caucus, Devin Kolb, 225-6131

Congressional Unmanned Systems Caucus, Alex Beckmann, 225-5701

Congressional Urban Caucus, Jeffrey Wilson, 225-6465

Congressional Values Action Team, Katie Doherty, 225-2876

Congressional Veterans Jobs Caucus, Molly Lowe, 225-6155

Congressional Victims' Rights Caucus, Richard England, 225-5951

Congressional Vision Caucus, Nora Blalock, 225-1784; Web, www.preventblindness.org/congressional-vision-caucus

Congressional Voting Rights Caucus, Nicole Varner, 225-9897; Web, https://votingrightscaucus-veasey. house.gov

Congressional Western Caucus, Jeff Small, 225-2315; Web, https://westerncaucus.house.gov

Congressional Wildlife Refuge Caucus, Olivia Kirchberg, 225-5506

Congressional Wine Caucus, Wendy Zirngibl, 225-3311, Web, https://winecaucus-mikethompson.house.gov/

Congressional Working Forests Caucus, Will Layden, 225-3772

Congressional Youth Challenge Caucus, Joseph Ciccone, 225-5256; Web, http://napolitano.house.gov/issue/youth-challenge

Congressional Zoo and Aquarium Caucus, Alan Feyerherm, 225-4806

Connecting the Americas Caucus, Devin Kolb, 225-6131

Conservative Opportunity Society, Chris Stevens, 527-2456; Web, https://conservativeopportunity society-king.house.gov

Creative Rights Caucus, Sally Larson, 225-9893; Web, http://creativerightscaucus-chu.house.gov

Crime Prevention and Youth Development Caucus, Meghann Galloway, 225-6131; Web, http://crimepreventionandyouthdevelopmentcaucus-cardenas.house.gov

Democratic Israel Working Group, Casey Kustin, 225-3001

European Union Caucus, Oren Adaki, 225-2452

Financial and Economic Literacy Caucus, Mark Gilbride, 225-2015; Web, https://financialandeconomicliteracycaucus-stivers.house.gov

Friends of Finland Caucus, Ryan McCormack, 225-3365

Friends of Kazakhstan Caucus, Megan Medley, 225-4876; Web, http://kafcouncil.org/congress/friends-of-kazakhstan-caucus

Friends of Norway Caucus, Libby Foley, 225-6631

Global Investment in America Caucus, Curtis Ryhne, 225-3032

Historic Preservation Caucus, Jeffrey Wilson, 225-6465

House Aerospace Caucus, Patrick Large, 225-5772

House Auto Caucus, Jenny Perrino, 225-4146

House Baltic Caucus, Ari Kirsh 225-5271; Web, http://housebalticcaucus.webs.com

House Decentralized Wastewater Recycling Caucus, Nick Grimes, 225-7041

House Farmer's Cooperative Caucus, Nick Grimes, 225-7041

House Freedom Caucus, Chad Yelinksi, 225-6401; Web, www.facebook.com/freedomcaucus

House General Aviation Caucus, Nick Grimes, 225-7041

House Liberty Caucus, Poppy Nelson, 225-3831

House Paper and Packaging Caucus, Chris Huckleberry, 225-5711

House Republican Israel Caucus, Lindsay Schneider, 225-4422

House Retirement Caucus, Lori Prater, 225-5406

House Rural Education Caucus, Nick Grimes, 225-7041

House Sugar Caucus, Lindsey Garber, 225-1313

House Textile Caucus, Doug Nation, 225-2576

House UK Caucus, Curtis Rhyne, 225-3032

House Whistleblower Protection Caucus, Steven Coyle, 225-5516

Immigrant Servicemembers and Veterans Caucus, Eddie Meyer, 225-8045

Israel Allies Caucus, Jason Steinbaum, 225-2464

Law Enforcement Caucus, Dylan Sodaro, 225-5751, Web, https://pascrell.house.gov/legislation/congressional-law-enforcement-caucus.htm

Lyme Disease Caucus, Monica Herman, 225-3765; Web, http://chrissmith.house.gov/lymedisease

Medical Technology Caucus, Rachel Fybel, 225-8104

Mental Health Caucus, Joseph Cunningham, 225-5256

Missile Defense Caucus, Guido Weiss, 225-4906

Municipal Finance Caucus, Bill Hulse, 225-3061; Web, https://ruppersberger.house.gov/legislative-work/congressional-municipal-finance-caucus

National Guard and Reserve Components Caucus, Patrick Large, 225-5772; Web, http://palazzo.house. gov/ngrcc

National Heritage Area Caucus, Zach Fowler, 225-6411

National Service Caucus, Andrew Heineman, 225-7163

New Democratic Coalition, J.D. Grom, 225-5916, Web, https://newdemocratcoalition-himes.house.gov

Northeast-Midwest (NEMW) Congressional Coalition, Catherine Wilson, 225-5731

Northern Border Caucus, Kayla Williams, 225-3306

Oil and National Security Caucus, Brian Skretny, 225-2464

Problem Solvers Caucus, Drew Wayne, 225-3161

Public Works and Infrastructure Caucus, Dante Cutrona, 225-5965

Purple Heart Caucus, Cory Kastl, 225-5861

Rare Disease Caucus, Dennis Sills, 225-3101

Real Estate Caucus, Dan Hare, 225-6465

Recording Arts and Sciences Congressional Caucus, James Min, 225-4000

Republican Study Committee, Ainsley Holyfield, 226-9717; Web, http://rsc-walker.house.gov

Republican Women's Policy Committee, Suzi Plasencia, 225-5071

Skilled American Workforce Caucus, Alex Huang, 225-5802

Space Power Caucus, Andrew Braun, 225-4422

Sustainable Energy and Environment Coalition, Jamie Smith, 226-1492; Web, http://seec-tonko.house.gov

Task Force on Anti-Terrorism & Proliferation Financing, Mariana Osorio, 225-8273; Web, http://anti-terrorismcaucus-lynch.house.gov

Tuberculosis (TB)Elimination Caucus, Ned Michalek, 225-2464

Tunisia Caucus, Tom Carnes, 225-1313

U.S.-Japan Caucus, Danny Meza, 225-3236 Web, https://usjapancaucus-castro.house.gov

Veterinary Medicine Caucus, Zach Stokes, 225-5711; Web, http://schrader.house.gov/committees/veterinary-medicine-caucus.htm

Work for Warriors Caucus, Colby Kuhns, 225-5861; Web, http://workforwarriorscaucus-takano.house.gov/

SENATE CAUCUSES

Senate Auto Caucus, Sam Mulopulos, 224-3353

Senate Cancer Coalition, Megan Thompson, 224-3841

Senate Caucus on International Narcotics Control, Kelly Lieupo, 224-3841; Web, http://drugcaucus.senate.gov

Senate Cultural Caucus, Doug Dziak, 224-3424

Senate Republican High Tech Task Force, Michael Black, 224-3643

Senate Western Caucus, Kaitlynn Glover, 224-6441; Web, www.barrasso.senate.gov/public/index.cfm/members-swc

HOUSE AND SENATE CAUCUSES

Coalition for Autism Research and Education (CARE), Kate Rowley, 225-2135; Web, http://doyle.house.gov/issue/autism-caucus

California Democratic Congressional Delegation, Matt Weiner, 225-3072; Web, www.cadem.org

Congressional Air Force Caucus, Michael Calcagni, 225-6465; Web, http://secure.afa.org/grl/caucus.asp

Congressional Asian Pacific American Caucus (CAPAC), Krystal Kaai, 225-5464; Web, http://capac-chu.house.gov

Congressional Automotive Performance and Motorsports Caucus, Jennifer Perrino, 225-4146

Congressional Bicameral High-Speed & Intercity Passenger Rail Caucus (HSIPR), Alex Beckmann, 225-5701

Congressional Biomedical Research Caucus, Drew Hatter, 225-2015

Congressional Black Caucus, Peter Hunter, 225-6636; Web, https://cbc.house.gov

Congressional Farmer Cooperative Caucus, Lynn Tjeerdsma, 224-2321

Congressional Fire Services Caucus, Dylan Sadaro, 225-5751; Web, www.cfsi.org/legislation-advocacy/congressional-fire-services-caucus

Congressional Fire Services Institute, William Webb, Executive Director, 371-1277; Web, www.cfsi.org

Congressional Hispanic Caucus, Elena Pino, 225-3236; Web, www.chci.org

Congressional HIV/AIDS Caucus, Diala Jadallah, 225-2661; Web, http://hivaidscaucus-lee.house.gov

Congressional Internet Caucus, Asad Ramzanali, 225-8104; Web, www.netcaucus.org

Congressional NexGen 9-1-1 Caucus, Brian Looser, 225-5271

Congressional Veterans Jobs Caucus, Collen Lewis, 225-3954

United States Association of Former Members of Congress, Peter M. Weichlein, Chief Executive Officer, 222-0972; Web, http://usafmc.org

Ready Reference

Government Hotlines

DEPARTMENTS

Agriculture,
Fraud, waste, and abuse hotline, (800) 424-9121
Meat and poultry safety inquiries, (800) 674-6854

Commerce,
Export enforcement hotline, (800) 424-2980
Fraud, waste, and abuse hotline, (800) 424-5197
Trade Information Center, (800) 872-8723

Defense,
Army Department's Casualty and Mortuary Affairs
Information Center, (800) 626-3317
Fraud, waste, and abuse hotline, (800) 424-9098
Military OneSource, (800) 342-9647

Education,
Fraud, waste, and abuse hotline, (800) 647-8733
Student financial aid information, (800) 433-3243

Energy,
Energy Efficiency and Renewable Energy Information
Center, (877) 337-3463
Fraud, waste, mismanagement, and abuse hotline,
(800) 541-1625

Health and Human Services,
Child Welfare Information Gateway, (800) 394-3366
Fraud hotline, (800) 447-8477
General health information, (800) 336-4797
HIV/AIDS, STDs, and immunization information,
including pandemic flu, (800) 232-4636
Medicare hotline (including prescription drug discounts),
(800) 633-4227
National Adoption Center, (800) 862-3678
National Cancer Institute cancer information,
(800) 422-6237
National Runaway Safeline, (800) 786-2929
Traveler's health information, (800) 232-4636

Homeland Security,
Disaster assistance, (800) 621-3362
Fraud, abuse, and mismanagement, (800) 323-8603
Investigations Tip Line, (866) 347-2423
National Emergency Training Center, (800) 238-3358
Security breaches, hazardous material, chemical, and oil
spills, (202) 267-2675
U.S. Immigration and Customs Enforcement suspicious
activity, (866) 347-2423, detainees' rights, (855) 448-6903

Housing and Urban Development,
Fair Housing Complaints, (800) 669-9777

Justice,
Americans With Disabilities Act information,
(800) 514-0301, TTY, (800) 514-0383
Arson hotline, (888) 283-3473
Bomb information hotline (ATF), (888) 283-2662
Fraud, abuse, or misconduct hotline, (800) 869-4499
Illegal firearms activity hotline, (800) 283-4867
National Criminal Justice Reference Service, (800) 851-3420
National Institute for Corrections Information Center,
(800) 877-1461
Stolen firearms hotline, (888) 930-9275
Unfair employment practices hotline (immigration
related), (800) 255-7688

Transportation,
Auto safety hotline, (800) 424-9393
Aviation safety hotline, (800) 255-1111
Federal Aviation Administration consumer hotline,
(866) 835-5322

Treasury,
Comptroller of the Currency customer assistance hotline,
(800) 613-6743
Fraud, waste, mismanagement, and abuse hotline (IRS
programs), (800) 366-4484
Identity Theft hotline, (800) 908-4490
Tax forms, tax refund information, and general
information, (800) 829-3676
Tax refund status, (800) 829-1954
Taxpayer Advocate Service, (877) 777-4778
Taxpayer assistance, (800) 829-1040

Veterans Affairs,
Benefits hotline, (800) 827-1000
Debt Management Center, (800) 827-0648
Fraud, waste, abuse, and mismanagement hotline,
(800) 488-8244
Insurance policy information, (800) 669-8477

AGENCIES

Consumer Product Safety Commission,
Product safety information, (800) 638-2772

Environmental Protection Agency,
Asbestos and small business hotline, (800) 368-5888
Endangered species hotline, (800) 447-3813
National Lead Information Center, (800) 424-5323
National Pesticides Information Center, (800) 858-7378
National Radon hotline, (800) 767-7236
Ozone Protection hotline, (800) 296-1996
Safe drinking water hotline, (800) 426-4791
Superfund hotline, (800) 424-9346, (703) 412-9810
in Washington
Wetlands information hotline, (800) 832-7828

Export-Import Bank,
Export finance hotline, (800) 565-3946
(202) 565-3946 in Washington

Federal Deposit Insurance Corporation,
Banking complaints and inquiries, (877) 275-3342

Federal Election Commission,
Campaign finance law information, (202) 694-1100

General Services Administration,
Federal Citizen Information Center, (800) 333-4636

Office of Special Counsel,
Prohibited personnel practices information,
(800) 872-9855

Small Business Administration,
Fraud, waste, abuse, and mismanagement hotline,
(800) 767-0385
Small business assistance, (800) 827-5722

Social Security Administration,
Fraud and abuse hotline, (800) 269-0271
Social Security benefits (including Medicare) information,
(800) 772-1213

Directory of Government Information on the Internet

Listed below are Web addresses that lead to executive, legislative, and judicial information on the Internet. These links were active as of April 20, 2018. Government information can also be explored online through the www.usa.gov, which is the U.S. government's official Internet portal to Web pages for federal and state governments, the District of Columbia, and U.S. territories.

EXECUTIVE BRANCH

The White House

Main: www.whitehouse.gov
Twitter: @whitehouse
Facebook: www.facebook.com/WhiteHouse
News: www.whitehouse.gov/articles
President's Bio: www.whitehouse.gov/people/donald-j-trump
Vice President's Bio: www.whitehouse.gov/people/mike-pence
First Lady's Bio: www.whitehouse.gov/people/melania-trump
Contacting the White House: www.whitehouse.gov/contact

Agriculture Dept.

Main: www.usda.gov
Twitter: @usda
Facebook: www.facebook.com/USDA
About the Agriculture Dept.: www.usda.gov/our-agency/about-usda
News: www.usda.gov/media
Secretary's Bio: www.usda.gov/our-agency/about-usda/our-secretary
Employee Directory: https://offices.sc.egov.usda.gov/employeeDirectory/app
Link to Regional Offices: https://offices.sc.egov.usda.gov/locator/app
Department Budget: www.usda.gov/our-agency/about-usda/budget
Blog: www.usda.gov/media/blog
Video: www.youtube.com/user/usda

Commerce Dept.

Main: www.commerce.gov
Twitter: @CommerceGov
Facebook: www.facebook.com/Commercegov
About the Commerce Dept.: www.commerce.gov/about
News: www.commerce.gov/news
Secretary's Bio: www.commerce.gov/directory/wilburross
Employee Directory: www.commerce.gov/directory
Links to State and Regional Offices:
    Census Bureau: www.census.gov/regions
    Commerce Dept.: www.census.gov/regions
    Economic Development Administration: www.eda.gov/contact
Department Budget: www.osec.doc.gov/bmi/budget
Blog: www.commerce.gov/news/the-commerce-blog
Photos: www.flickr.com/photos/commercegov
Video: www.youtube.com/user/CommerceNews

Defense Dept.

Main: www.defense.gov
Twitter: @deptofdefense
Facebook: www.facebook.com/DeptofDefense
About the Defense Dept.: www.defense.gov/about
News: www.defense.gov/newsroom
Secretary's Bio: www.defense.gov/About/Biographies/Biography-View/Article/1055835/james-mattis
Directory of Senior Defense Officials: www.defense.gov/About/Biographies
Department Budget: https://comptroller.defense.gov/Budget-Materials
Live Blog: www.dodlive.mil
Video: www.youtube.com/deptofdefense

Education Dept.

Main: www.ed.gov
Twitter: @usedgov
Facebook: www.facebook.com/ED.gov
About the Education Dept.: www2.ed.gov/about/landing.jhtml
News: www2.ed.gov/news/landing.jhtml
Secretary's Bio: www2.ed.gov/news/staff/bios/devos.html?src=hp
Employee Directory: www2.ed.gov/about/contacts/gen/index.html
State Contacts and Information: www2.ed.gov/about/contacts/state/index.html
Department Budget: www2.ed.gov/about/overview/budget/index.html
Blog: https://blog.ed.gov
Video: www.youtube.com/usedgov

Energy Dept.

Main: www.energy.gov
Twitter: @energy
Facebook: www.facebook.com/energygov
About the Energy Dept.: www.energy.gov/about-us
News: www.energy.gov/news-blog
Secretary's Bio: www.energy.gov/contributors/rick-perry
Employee Directory: www.energy.gov/about-us/staff-and-contractors
Link to Regional Offices: www.energy.gov/contact-us/mailing-addresses-and-information-numbers-operations-field-and-site-offices
Department Budget: www.energy.gov/budget-performance
Video: www.youtube.com/user/USdepartmentofenergy

Health and Human Services Dept.

Main: www.hhs.gov
Twitter: @HHSGov
Facebook: www.facebook.com/HHS
About the Health and Human Services Dept.: www.hhs.gov/about
News: www.hhs.gov/about/news/index.html
Secretary's Bio: www.hhs.gov/about/leadership/secretary/alex-m-azar/index.html
Employee Directory: www.hhs.gov/ohrp/about-ohrp/staff/index.html
Link to Regional Offices: www.hhs.gov/about/agencies/regional-offices
Department Budget: www.hhs.gov/budget
Video: www.youtube.com/user/USGOVHHS

Homeland Security Dept.

Main: www.dhs.gov
Twitter: @DHSgov
Facebook: www.facebook.com/homelandsecurity
About the Homeland Security Dept.: www.dhs.gov/about-dhs
News: www.dhs.gov/news
Secretary's Bio: www.dhs.gov/secretary
Leadership Directory: www.dhs.gov/leadership
Links to Regional Offices:
Federal Emergency Management Agency: www.fema.gov
U.S. Citizenship and Immigration Services: www.uscis.gov
U.S. Secret Service: www.secretservice.gov/field_offices.shtml
Department Budget: www.dhs.gov/dhs-budget
Video: www.youtube.com/ushomelandsecurity

Housing and Urban Development Dept.

Main: www.hud.gov
Twitter: @HUDgov
Facebook: www.facebook.com/HUD
About the Housing and Urban Development Dept.: www.hud.gov/about
News: www.hud.gov/press

Interactive Self-Assessment Tool: www.makinghomeaffordable.gov
Secretary's Bio: www.hud.gov/about/leadership/ben_carson
Employee Directory: https://peoplesearch.hud.gov/po/i/netlocator
Link to Regional Offices: https://portal.hud.gov/hudportal/HUD?src=/states
Department Budget: www.hud.gov/program_offices/cfo/budget
Video: www.youtube.com/hudchannel

Interior Dept.

Main: www.doi.gov
Twitter: @Interior
Facebook: www.facebook.com/USInterior
About the Interior Dept.: www.doi.gov/whoweare
News: www.doi.gov/news
Secretary's Bio: www.doi.gov/whoweare/asbernhardt
Employee Directory: www.doi.gov/employees
Links to Regional Offices:
Bureau of Indian Affairs: www.bia.gov
Bureau of Land Management: www.blm.gov
Bureau of Ocean Energy Management: www.boem.gov
Bureau of Reclamation: www.usbr.gov
National Park Service: www.nps.gov
Office of Surface Mining: www.osmre.gov
U.S. Fish and Wildlife Service: www.fws.gov
U.S. Geological Survey: www.usgs.gov
Department Budget: www.doi.gov/budget
Video: www.youtube.com/USInterior

Justice Dept.

Main: www.justice.gov
Twitter: @TheJusticeDept
Facebook: www.facebook.com/DOJ
About the Justice Dept.: www.justice.gov/about
News: www.justice.gov/briefing-room
Attorney General's Bio: www.justice.gov/ag/staff-profile/meet-attorney-general
Links to Regional Offices:
Drug Enforcement Administration: www.dea.gov/contact.shtml
Federal Bureau of Investigation: www.fbi.gov/contact-us/contact-us
Federal Bureau of Prisons: www.bop.gov/contact
Department Budget: www.justice.gov/doj/fy-2019-budget-and-performance-summary
Video: www.youtube.com/thejusticedepartment

Labor Dept.

Main: www.dol.gov
Twitter: @USDOL
Facebook: www.facebook.com/departmentoflabor
About the Labor Dept.: www.dol.gov/general/aboutdol
News: www.dol.gov/newsroom
Secretary's Bio: www.dol.gov/agencies/osec
Employee Directory: www.dol.gov/general/contact/contact-phonekeypersonnel

Links to Regional Offices:

Bureau of Labor Statistics: www.bls.gov/bls/regnhome.htm

Employment and Training Administration: https://wdr.doleta.gov/contacts

Occupational Safety and Health Administration: www.osha.gov/dcsp/osp/index.html

Department Budget: www.dol.gov/general/aboutdol#Budget

Video: www.youtube.com/usdepartmentoflabor

State Dept.

Main: www.state.gov

Twitter: @StateDept

Facebook: www.facebook.com/usdos

About the State Dept.: www.state.gov/aboutstate

News: www.state.gov/media

Secretary's Bio: www.state.gov/secretary/20172018tillerson/bio/index.htm

Employee Directory: www.state.gov/m/a/gps/directory

Link to Regional Offices: www.state.gov/ofm/ro

Passport Services: https://iafdb.travel.state.gov

Department Budget: www.state.gov/s/d/rm/rls

Blog: https://blogs.state.gov

Video: www.youtube.com/statevideo

Transportation Dept.

Main: www.transportation.gov

Twitter: @usdot

Facebook: www.facebook.com/USDOT

About the Transportation Dept.: www.transportation.gov/about

News: www.transportation.gov/press-releases

Secretary's Bio: www.transportation.gov/mission/secretary-elaine-l-chao

Links to Regional Offices:

Federal Aviation Administration: www.faa.gov/about/office_org

Federal Highway Administration: www.fhwa.dot.gov/about/field.cfm

Federal Railroad Administration: www.fra.dot.gov/Page/P0001

Federal Transit Administration: www.transit.dot.gov/about/regional-offices/regional-offices

Maritime Administration: www.marad.dot.gov

National Highway Traffic Safety Administration: www.nhtsa.gov

Department Budget: www.transportation.gov/budget

Video: www.youtube.com/user/usdotgov

Treasury Dept.

Main: www.treasury.gov

Twitter: @USTreasury

Facebook: www.facebook.com/ustreasury

About the Treasury Dept.: www.treasury.gov/about

News: www.treasury.gov/press-center

Interactive Self-Assessment Tool: www.makinghomeaffordable.gov

Secretary's Bio: https://home.treasury.gov/about/general-information/the-secretary

Directory of Treasury Officials: https://home.treasury.gov/about/general-information/organizational-chart

Links to Regional Offices:

Veterans Benefits Administration: https://benefits.va.gov/benefits/offices.asp

Comptroller of the Currency: www.occ.gov/about/who-we-are/district-and-field-offices/index-organization.html

Financial Management Service: www.fiscal.treasury.gov

Internal Revenue Service: www.irs.gov/uac/Contact-Your-Local-IRS-Office-1

Department Budget: www.treasury.gov/about/budget-performance

Video: www.youtube.com/USTreasGov

Veterans Affairs Dept.

Main: www.va.gov

Twitter: @DeptVetAffairs

Facebook: www.facebook.com/VeteransAffairs

About the Veterans Affairs Dept.: www.va.gov/about_va

News: www.va.gov/opa/pressrel

Secretary's Bio: www.va.gov/opa/bios/secva.asp

Link to Regional Offices: www.va.gov/directory/guide/division.asp?dnum=3&isFlash=0

Department Budget: www.va.gov/budget/products.asp

Video: www.youtube.com/deptvetaffairs

Blog: www.blogs.va.gov/VAntage

LEGISLATIVE BRANCH

Congress

Main: www.congress.gov

Twitter: @congressdotgov

U.S. Constitution: www.archives.gov/founding-docs

Legislative Process: https://rules.house.gov; www.congress.gov

How Laws Are Made: www.congress.gov/resources/display/content/How+Our+Laws+Are+Made+-+Learn+About+the+Legislative+Process

Biographical Directory of the U.S. Congress: http://bioguide.congress.gov/biosearch/biosearch.asp

Election Statistics (1920-present): https://history.house.gov/Institution/Election-Statistics/Election-Statistics/

Video: www.congress.gov/video

Blog: https://blogs.loc.gov/law

House

Main: www.house.gov

Twitter: @HouseGOP, @HouseDemocrats

Schedule: www.house.gov/legislative/

Daily Business: https://clerk.house.gov/floorsummary/floor.aspx

Committees: https://clerk.house.gov/committee_info

Committee Hearing Schedules: https://docs.house.gov/Committee/Committees.aspx

Government of the United States

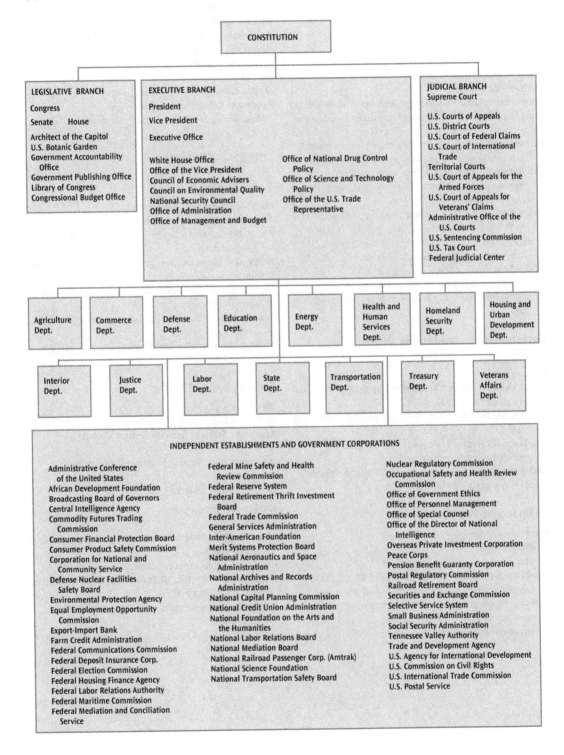

CONSTITUTION

LEGISLATIVE BRANCH

Congress

Senate   House

Architect of the Capitol
U.S. Botanic Garden
Government Accountability
    Office
Government Publishing Office
Library of Congress
Congressional Budget Office

EXECUTIVE BRANCH

President

Vice President

Executive Office

White House Office
Office of the Vice President
Council of Economic Advisers
Council on Environmental Quality
National Security Council
Office of Administration
Office of Management and Budget

Office of National Drug Control
    Policy
Office of Science and Technology
    Policy
Office of the U.S. Trade
    Representative

JUDICIAL BRANCH
Supreme Court

U.S. Courts of Appeals
U.S. District Courts
U.S. Court of Federal Claims
U.S. Court of International
    Trade
Territorial Courts
U.S. Court of Appeals for the
    Armed Forces
U.S. Court of Appeals for
    Veterans' Claims
Administrative Office of the
    U.S. Courts
U.S. Sentencing Commission
U.S. Tax Court
Federal Judicial Center

Agriculture Dept.	Commerce Dept.	Defense Dept.	Education Dept.	Energy Dept.	Health and Human Services Dept.	Homeland Security Dept.	Housing and Urban Development Dept.

Interior Dept.	Justice Dept.	Labor Dept.	State Dept.	Transportation Dept.	Treasury Dept.	Veterans Affairs Dept.

INDEPENDENT ESTABLISHMENTS AND GOVERNMENT CORPORATIONS

Administrative Conference
    of the United States
African Development Foundation
Broadcasting Board of Governors
Central Intelligence Agency
Commodity Futures Trading
    Commission
Consumer Financial Protection Board
Consumer Product Safety Commission
Corporation for National and
    Community Service
Defense Nuclear Facilities
    Safety Board
Environmental Protection Agency
Equal Employment Opportunity
    Commission
Export-Import Bank
Farm Credit Administration
Federal Communications Commission
Federal Deposit Insurance Corp.
Federal Election Commission
Federal Housing Finance Agency
Federal Labor Relations Authority
Federal Maritime Commission
Federal Mediation and Conciliation
    Service

Federal Mine Safety and Health
    Review Commission
Federal Reserve System
Federal Retirement Thrift Investment
    Board
Federal Trade Commission
General Services Administration
Inter-American Foundation
Merit Systems Protection Board
National Aeronautics and Space
    Administration
National Archives and Records
    Administration
National Capital Planning Commission
National Credit Union Administration
National Foundation on the Arts and
    the Humanities
National Labor Relations Board
National Mediation Board
National Railroad Passenger Corp. (Amtrak)
National Science Foundation
National Transportation Safety Board

Nuclear Regulatory Commission
Occupational Safety and Health Review
    Commission
Office of Government Ethics
Office of Personnel Management
Office of Special Counsel
Office of the Director of National
    Intelligence
Overseas Private Investment Corporation
Peace Corps
Pension Benefit Guaranty Corporation
Postal Regulatory Commission
Railroad Retirement Board
Securities and Exchange Commission
Selective Service System
Small Business Administration
Social Security Administration
Tennessee Valley Authority
Trade and Development Agency
U.S. Agency for International Development
U.S. Commission on Civil Rights
U.S. International Trade Commission
U.S. Postal Service

Link to Roll Call Votes: https://clerk.house.gov/legislative/legvotes.aspx
Leadership: www.house.gov/leadership
Media Galleries: https://houselive.gov

Senate

Main: www.senate.gov
Twitter: @SenateFloor
Annual Calendar: www.senate.gov/legislative/calendars.htm
Daily Calendar: www.senate.gov/legislative/LIS/executive_calendar/xcalv.pdf
Committees: www.senate.gov/pagelayout/committees/d_three_sections_with_teasers/committees_home.htm
Committee Hearing Schedules: www.senate.gov/pagelayout/committees/b_three_sections_with_teasers/committee_hearings.htm
Link to Roll Call Votes: www.senate.gov/pagelayout/legislative/a_three_sections_with_teasers/votes.htm
Leadership: www.senate.gov/pagelayout/senators/a_three_sections_with_teasers/leadership.htm
Media Galleries: www.senate.gov/galleries
Executive Nominations: www.senate.gov/pagelayout/legislative/a_three_sections_with_teasers/nominations.htm

Government Accountability Office

Main: www.gao.gov
Twitter: @usgao
About the Government Accountability Office: www.gao.gov/about/index.html
Comptroller General's Bio: www.gao.gov/cghome/gdbiog.html
Employee Directory: www.gao.gov/about.gao/phonebook/orgphonebook.pdf
GAO Reports: www.gao.gov/docsearch/repandtest.html
Media: www.gao.gov/multimedia/video

Government Publishing Office

Main: www.gpo.gov
Twitter: @usgpo
Facebook: www.facebook.com/USGPO
About the Government Printing Office: www.gpo.gov/who-we-are/our-agency/mission-vision-and-goals
News: www.gpo.gov/who-we-are/news-media/news-and-press-releases
Video: www.youtube.com/gpoprinter

Library of Congress

Main: www.loc.gov
Twitter: @librarycongress
Facebook: www.facebook.com/libraryofcongress
About the Library of Congress: www.loc.gov/about
Employee Directory: www.loc.gov/flicc/Staff/staff2new.html
Online Catalog: https://catalog.loc.gov
Copyright Office: www.copyright.gov
Video: www.youtube.com/libraryofcongress

JUDICIAL BRANCH

The Supreme Court

Main: www.supremecourt.gov
Twitter: @USSupremeCourt
About the Supreme Court: www.supremecourt.gov/about/about.aspx
News: www.supremecourt.gov/opinions/slipopinions.aspx
Media: www.supremecourt.gov/publicinfo/publicinfo.aspx
Biographies of the Justices: www.supremecourt.gov/about/biographies.aspx
Supreme Court Docket: www.supremecourt.gov/docket/docket.aspx
Visiting the Supreme Court: www.supremecourt.gov/visiting/visiting.aspx

Federal Judicial Center

Main: www.fjc.gov
History: www.fjc.gov/history/home.nsf
About the Federal Judicial Center: www.fjc.gov/about
Directors: www.fjc.gov/about/board-members

U.S. Federal Courts

Main: www.uscourts.gov
Twitter: @uscourts
About the U.S. Federal Courts: www.uscourts.gov/about-federal-courts
News: www.uscourts.gov/judiciary-news
Biographical Directory of Federal Judges: www.uscourts.gov/judges-judgeships
Publications: www.uscourts.gov/statistics-reports/publications
Video: www.youtube.com/user/uscourts

Governors and Other State Officials

Political affiliations, when available, are indicated by (D) for Democrat, (R) for Republican, and (I) for Independent. For key officials of the District of Columbia and other Washington-area localities, see page 355. This information is current as of April 12, 2019.

Alabama   Web, www.alabama.gov

Gov. Kay Ivey (R), State Capitol, 600 Dexter Ave., #S-104, Montgomery 36130; (334) 242-7100; Fax, (334) 353-0004; Web, www.governor.alabama.gov; Facebook, www.facebook.com/KayIveyAL; Twitter, @GovernorKayIvey; YouTube, www.youtube.com/user/ltgovernorkayivey; Instagram, @governorkayivey

Lt. Gov. Will Ainsworth (R), 11 S. Union St., #S-725, Montgomery 36130; (334) 261-9590; Facebook, www.facebook.com/willainsworthAL; Twitter, @willainsworthAL

Secy. of State John H. Merrill (R), State Capitol Bldg., 600 Dexter Ave., #S-105, Montgomery 36130, P.O. Box 5616, Montgomery 36103-5616; (334) 242-7200; Fax, (334) 242-4993; Web, www.sos.alabama.gov; Facebook, www.facebook.com/alasecretaryofstate; Twitter, @alasecofstate

Atty. Gen. Steve Marshall (R), Alabama State House, 501 Washington Ave., Montgomery 36104; P.O. Box 300152, Montgomery, AL 36130-0152; (334) 242-7300; Fax, (334) 242-4891; Web, www.ago.state.al.us; Facebook, www.facebook.com/AGSteveMarshall

Treasurer John McMillan (R), State Capitol, 600 Dexter Ave., #S-106, Montgomery 36104; (334) 242-7500; Web, www.treasury.alabama.gov; Email, alatreas@treasury.alabama.gov; Facebook, www.facebook.com/JohnMcMillan4; Twitter, @JohnMcMillan4

Washington, DC Representative: Liz Filmore, Washington Representative; Washington Office of the Governor, State of Alabama, 444 N. Capitol St. N.W., #382A, 20001; (334) 242-7438

Alaska   Web, http://alaska.gov

Gov. Michael J. Dunleavy (R), State Capitol, 120 4th St., 3rd Floor, P.O. Box 110001, Juneau 99811-0001; (907) 465-3500; Fax, (907) 465-3532; Web, www.gov.alaska.gov; Facebook, www.facebook.com/GovDunleavy; Twitter, @GovDunleavy; YouTube, www.youtube.com/channel/UCV-aZVxBDQ-SZU6KPSzG4Pg; Instagram, @govdunleavy

Lt. Gov. Kevin Meyer (R), State Capitol,120 4th St., 3rd Floor, Juneau 99811-0015; (907) 465-3520; Fax, (907) 465-3532; Web, www.ltgov.alaska.gov; Facebook, www.facebook.com/LtGovMeyer; Twitter, @ltgovmeyer

(No office of Secretary of State)

Atty. Gen. Kevin G. Clarkson (R), 1031 W. 4th Ave., #200, Anchorage 99501-1994; (907) 269-5100; Fax, (907) 276-3697; Web, www.law.alaska.gov; Email, attorney.general@alaska.gov

(No office of Treasurer)

In Washington, DC: John Crowther, Director, Washington, Office of the Governor, State of Alaska, 444 N. Capitol St. N.W., #336, 20001-1512, (202) 624-5988; Fax, (202) 624-5857

Arizona   Web, http://az.gov

Gov. Doug Ducey (R), State Capitol, 1700 W. Washington St., 9th Floor, Phoenix 85007-2808; (602) 542-4331; Fax, (602) 542-7601; Web, www.azgovernor.gov; Facebook, www.facebook.com/dougducey; Twitter, @DougDucey; YouTube, www.youtube.com/channel/UCi_TVbfG4I5SK6GhjYEfyVQ; Instagram, @dougducey

(No office of Lieutenant Governor)

Secy. of State Katie Hobbs (R), State Capitol, 1700 W. Washington St., 7th Floor, Phoenix 85007-2808; (602) 542-4285; Fax, (602) 542-1575; Web, www.azsos.gov; Facebook, www.facebook.com/SecretaryHobbs; Twitter, @SecretaryHobbs; Instagram, @azsecretartyhobbs

Atty. Gen. Mark Brnovich (R), 2005 N. Central Ave., Phoenix 85004-2926; (602) 542-5025; Fax, (602) 542-4085; Web, www.azag.gov; Facebook, www.facebook.com/GeneralBrnovich; Twitter, @GeneralBrnovich; YouTube, www.youtube.com/user/ArizonaAGO

Treasurer Kimberly Yee (R), 1700 W. Washington St., #102, Phoenix 85007-2808; (602) 542-7800; Fax, (602) 542-7176; Web, www.aztreasury.gov; Twitter, @KimberlyYeeAZ

(No Washington, D.C., representative)

Arkansas   Web, www.arkansas.gov

Gov. Asa Hutchinson (R), State Capitol, 500 Woodlane St., #250, Little Rock 72201-1061; (501) 682-2345; Fax, (501) 682-1382; TTY, (501) 682-7515; Web, www.governor.arkansas.gov; Facebook, www.facebook.com/asaforarkansas; Twitter, @AsaHutchinson; YouTube, www.youtube.com/channel/UCLJcNdgp2PMEmiqJEoYzqwQ?_ga=2.179473956.1425565623.1548966350-1965876865.1548966350

Lt. Gov. Tim Griffin (R), State Capitol, #270, 500 Woodlane St., Little Rock 72201-1061; (501) 682-2144; Fax, (501) 682-2894; Web, www.ltgovernor.arkansas.gov; Email, lg.staff@arkansas.gov; Facebook, www.facebook.com/LtGovTimGriffin; Twitter, @LtGovTimGriffin

Secy. of State John Thurston (R), State Capitol, 500 Woodlane St., #256, Little Rock 72201-1094; (501) 682-1010; Fax, (501) 682-3510; Web, www.sos.arkansas.gov; Email, arsos@sos.arkansas.gov; Facebook, www.facebook.com/ARSecofState; generalinfo@sos.arkansas.gov; Twitter, @ARSecofState; YouTube, www.youtube.com/user/ArkansasSOS; Instagram, @arsecofsate

Atty. Gen. Leslie C. Rutledge (R), Tower Bldg., 323 Center St., #200, Little Rock 72201-2610; (501) 682-2007; Fax, (501) 682-8084; Toll-free, (800) 482-8982; Web, www.ag.arkansas.gov; Facebook, www.facebook.com/AGLeslieRutledge; Twitter, @AGRutledge; YouTube, www.youtube.com/channel/UCHM7qdWTTF4aFybeC0qdtaA; Instagram, @agleslierutledge

Treasurer Dennis Milligan (R), State Capitol, 500 Woodlane, #S-220, Little Rock 72201-1061; (501) 682-5888; Fax, (501) 682-9692; Web, www.artreasury.gov; Email, info@artreasury.gov

Washington, DC, Representative: Katie Beck, Director of State-Federal Relations, Office of Governor Asa Hutchinson, 444 N. Capitol St. N.W., #365, 20001 (202) 220-1329; Email, Katie.beck@governor.arkansas.gov

California   Web, www.ca.gov

Gov. Gavin Newsom (D), State Capitol, #1173, Sacramento 95814; (916) 445-2841; Fax, (916) 558-3160; TTY (916) 464-1580; Web, www.gov.ca.gov; Email, Facebook, www.facebook.com/GavinNewsom; Twitter, @GavinNewsom

Lt. Gov. Eleni Kounalakis (D), State Capitol, #1114, Sacramento 95814; (916) 445-8994; Fax, (916) 323-4998; Web, www.ltg.ca.gov; Twitter, @EleniForCA; Instagram, @eleniforca

Secy. of State Alex Padilla (D), 1500 11th St., #600, Sacramento 95814; (916) 653-6814; Fax, (916) 653-4795; Web, www.sos.ca.gov; Email, secretary.padilla@sos.ca.gov; Facebook, www.facebook.com/CaliforniaSOS; Twitter, @AlexPadilla4CA

Atty. Gen. Xavier Becerra (D), 1300 Eye St., Sacramento 95814-2919; P.O. Box 944255, Sacramento 94244-2550; (916) 445-9555; Fax, (916) 323-534 Toll-free, (800) 952-5225; TTY, (800) 735-2929; TTY Spanish, (800) 855-3000; Web, www.oag.ca.gov

Treasurer Fiona Ma (D), 915 Capitol Mall, #110, C-15, Sacramento 95814; P.O. Box 942809, Sacramento 94209-0001; (916) 653-2995; Fax, (916) 653-3125; Web, www.treasurer.ca.gov; Facebook, www.facebook.com/CaliforniaSTO

In Washington, DC: Katie Mathews, Deputy Director, Washington Office of the Governor, State of California, 444 N. Capitol St. N.W., #134, 20001; (202) 624-5270; Fax, (202) 624-5280

Colorado   Web, www.colorado.gov

Gov. Jared Polis (D), 136 State Capitol, Denver 80203; (303) 866-2471; Fax, (303) 866-2003; Web, www.colorado.gov/governor; Facebook, www.facebook.com/jaredpolis; Twitter, @GovofCO; Instagram, @govofcol

Lt. Gov. Dianna Primavera (D), 130 State Capitol, Denver 80203; (303) 866-2087; Web, www.colorado.gov/ltgovernor; Facebook, www.facebook.com/LtGovofCO; Twitter, @LtGovofCO; Instagram, Itgovofco

Secy. of State Jena Griswold (D), 1700 Broadway, #200, Denver 80290; (303) 894-2200; Fax, (303) 869-4860; Web, www.sos.state.co.us; Facebook, www.facebook.com/Jenaforcolorado; Twitter, @JenaGriswold

Atty. Gen. Phil Weiser (D), Ralph L. Carr Judicial Bldg., 1300 Broadway 10th Floor, Denver 80203; (720) 508-6000; Fax, (720) 508-6030; Web, coag.gov; Facebook, www.facebook.com/ColoradoAttorneyGeneral; Twitter, @COAttnyGeneral

Treasurer Dave Young (D), State Capitol, 220 E. Colfax Ave., #140, Denver 80203-1722; (303) 866-2441; Fax, (303) 866-2123; Web, www.colorado.gov/treasury; Email, treasurer.stapleton@state.co.us; Twitter, @RepDaveYoung

(No Washington, D.C., representative)

Connecticut   Web, www.portal.ct.gov

Gov. Ned Lamont (D), State Capitol, 210 Capitol Ave., Hartford 06106; (860) 566-4840; Fax, (860) 524-7396; Toll-free, (800) 406-1527; TTY, (860) 524-7397; Web, www.governor.ct.gov; Facebook, www.facebook.com/NedLamontCT; Twitter, @GovNedLamont

Lt. Gov. Susan Bysiewicz (D), State Capitol, 210 Capitol Ave., #304, Hartford 06106; (860) 524-7384; Fax, (860) 524-7304; TTY, (860) 524-7397; Web, www.portal.ct.gov/ltgovernor; Email, Lt.GovernorBysiewicz@ct.gov; Facebook, www.facebook.com/SusanBysiewicz; Twitter, @LGSusanB

Secy. of State Denise Merrill (D), 30 Trinity St., Hartford 06106; (860) 509-6200; Fax, (860) 509-6209; Web, www.portal.ct.gov/sots; Facebook, www.facebook.com/SOTSMerrill; Twitter, @sotsmerrill

Atty. Gen. William Tong (D), 55 Elm St., Hartford 06106; (860) 808-5318; Fax, (860) 808-5387; Web, www.portal.ct.gov/ag; Email, attorney.general@ct.gov; Facebook, www.facebook.com/teamtong2018; Twitter, @WilliamTongCT; YouTube, www.youtube.com/user/WilliamTongCT

Treasurer Shawn T. Wooden (D), 55 Elm St., Hartford 06106-1773; (860) 702-3010; Fax, (860) 702-3043; Information, (860) 702-3000; Toll-free, (800) 618-3404; Web, www.ott.ct.gov; Email, state.treasurer@ct.gov; Facebook, www.facebook.com/ShawnTWooden; Twitter, @ShawnTWooden

In Washington, DC: Dan DeSimone, Director, Washington Office of the Governor, State of Connecticut, 444 N. Capitol St. N.W., #317, 20001; (202) 403-8654

Delaware   Web, http://delaware.gov

Gov. John Carney (D), 150 Martin Luther King Jr. Blvd. S., 2nd Floor, Dover 19901; (302) 744-4101; Fax, (302) 577-3210; Web, www.governor.delaware.gov;

Facebook, www.facebook.com/JohnCarneyDE; Twitter, @johncarneyde; Instagram, @johncarneyde

Lt. Gov. Bethany Hall-Long (D), 150 Martin Luther King Jr. Blvd. South, 3rd Floor, Dover 19901; (302) 744-4333; Fax, (302) 577-8787; Web, www.ltgov.delaware .gov; Email, ltgov@state.de.us; Facebook, www .facebook.com/LtGovernorDE; Twitter, @bethanyhalllong

Secy. of State Jeffrey W. Bullock (D), Townsend Building, 401 Federal St., Dover 19901; (302) 857-3037; Fax, (302) 739-3811; Web, www.sos.delaware.gov; Facebook, www.facebook.com/DEDeptState; Twitter, @SecretaryDE

Atty. Gen. Kathy Jennings (D), Carvel State Office Bldg., 820 N. French St., Wilmington 19801; (302) 577-8400; Fax, (302) 577-6630; TTY (302) 577-5783; Web, www .attorneygeneral.delaware.gov; Email, attorney. general@state.de.us; Facebook, www.facebook.com/ DE.AttorneyGeneral; Twitter, @KatheyJenningsDE, @DE_DOJ; YouTube, www.youtube.com/user/ DelawareDOJ

Treasurer Colleen Davis (D), 820 Silver Lake Blvd., #100, Dover 19904; (302) 672-6700; Fax, (302) 739-5635; Web, treasurer.delaware.gov; Email, statetreasurer@ state.de.us

In Washington, DC: Shelia Grant, Deputy Chief of Staff, Washington Office of the Governor, State of Delaware, 444 N. Capitol St. N.W., #542, 20001; (202) 624-7724; Fax, (202) 624-5495

Florida   Web, www.flgov.com

Gov. Ron DeSantis (R), The Capitol, 400 S. Monroe St., Tallahassee 32399-0001; (850) 488-7146; Fax, (850) 488-4042; TTY, (850) 922-7795; Web, www.flgov.com; Facebook, www.facebook.com/RonDeSantisFlorida; Twitter, @RonDeSantisFL; Instagram; @rondesantisfl

Lt. Gov. Jeanette Nuñez (R), The Capitol, 400 S. Monroe St., PL-05, Tallahassee 32399-0001; (850) 717-9331; Web, www.flgov.com; Facebook, www.facebook.com/ LtGovNunez; Twitter, @LtGovNunez

Secy. of State Michael Ertel (R), R.A. Gray Bldg., 500 S. Bronough, Tallahassee 32399-0250; (850) 245-6500; Fax, (850) 245-6125; Web, www.dos.myflorida.com; Email, SecretaryofState@DOS.MyFlorida.com; Twitter, @MikeErtel; YouTube, www.youtube.com/user/ FloridaDeptOfState

Atty. Gen. Ashley Moody (R), The Capitol, PL-01, 500 S. Bronough St., Tallahassee 32399-1050; (850) 414-3300; Fax, (850) 410-1630; Toll-free, (866) 966-7226; Web, www.myfloridalegal.com; Twitter, @AshleyMoodFL

Chief Financial Officer Jimmy Patronis (R), 200 E. Gaines St., Tallahassee 32399-0301; (877) 693-5236; Fax, (850) 413-4993; Out of state, (850) 413-3089; Web; www .myfloridacfo.com; Facebook, www.facebook.com/ FLDFS; Twitter, @JimmyPatronis

In Washington, DC: John Patrick Walsh, Washington Representative, Washington Office, State of Florida, 444 N. Capitol St. N.W., #349, 20001; (202) 624-5885; Fax, (202) 624-5886

Georgia   Web, www.georgia.gov

Gov. Brian P. Kemp (R), State Capitol, 206 Washington St., #203, Atlanta, 30334; Press, Brian Robinson, (404) 656-1776; Fax, (404) 657-7332; Web, www.gov.georgia.gov; Facebook, www.facebook.com/GovKemp; Twitter, @GovKemp; Instagram, @govkemp

Lt. Gov. Geoff Duncan (R), 240 State Capitol, Atlanta, 30334; (404) 656-5030; Fax, (404) 656-6739; Web, www.ltgov.georgia.gov; Twitter, @Geoff DuncanGA

Secy. of State Brad Raffensperger (R), 214 State Capitol, Atlanta, 30334; (404) 656-2881; Fax, (404) 656-0513; Web, www.sos.ga.gov; Email, soscontact@sos.ga.gov; Facebook, www.facebook.com/BradForGeorgiaSOS

Atty. Gen. Chris Carr (R), 40 Capitol Square S.W., Atlanta 30334; (404) 656-3300; Fax, (404) 657-8733; Web, www.law.ga.gov; Email, AGOlens@law.ga.gov; Facebook, www.facebook.com/ GeorgiaAttorneyGeneral; Twitter, @georgia_ag

Treasurer Steve McCoy (R), 200 Piedmont Ave., West Tower, #1204, Atlanta 30334; (404) 656-2168; Fax, (404) 656-9048; Web, www.ost.georgia.gov; Email, ostweb@treasury.ga.gov

In Washington, DC: Mark Hamilton, Policy Director, Washington Office of the Governor, State of Georgia, 1455 Pennsylvania Ave. N.W., #400, 20004; (202) 652-2299; Fax, (202) 347-1142

Hawaii   Web, www.hawaii.gov

Gov. David Ige (D), State Capitol, 415 S. Beretania St., Honolulu 96813; (808) 586-0034; Fax, (808) 586-0006; Web, www.governor.hawaii.gov; Facebook, www .facebook.com/GovernorDavidIge; Twitter, @GovHawaii; YouTube, www.youtube.com/ channel/UC0lxM5Gc2XzEvfIh-UwAxsA

Lt. Gov. Josh Green (D), State Capitol, 415 S. Beretania St., Honolulu 96813; (808) 586-0255; Fax, (808) 586-0231; Web, www.ltgov.hawaii.gov; Facebook, www.facebook .com/LtGovJoshGreen

(No office of Secretary of State)

Atty. Gen. Clare E. Connors (D), 425 Queen St., Honolulu 96813; (808) 586-1500; Fax, (808) 586-1239; Web, www.ag.hawaii.gov; Email, hawaiiag@hawaii.gov

Budget and Finance Director Roderick K. Becker (D), 1 Capitol District Bldg., 250 S. Hotel St., Honolulu 96813; P.O. Box 150, Honolulu 96810; (808) 586-1518; Fax, (808) 586-1976; Web, www.budget.hawaii.gov; Email, hi.budgetandfinance@hawaii.gov

(No Washington, D.C., representative)

Idaho   Web, www.idaho.gov

Gov. Brad Little (R), State Capitol, West Wing., 2nd Floor, Boise 83720-0034; (208) 334-2100; Fax, (208) 334-3454; Web, www.gov.idaho.gov; Email, governor@gov .idaho.gov; Facebook, www.facebook.com/ governorbradlittle; Twitter, @GovernorLittle; Instagram, @governorbradlittle

Lt. Gov. Janice McGeachin (R), State Capitol, #225, Boise 83720-0057; (208) 334-2200; Fax, (208) 334-3259; Web, lgo.idaho.gov; Twitter, @JaniceMcGeachin

Secy. of State Lawerence Denney (R), 700 W. Jefferson, #E205, P.O. Box 83720, Boise 83720-0080; (208) 334-2300; Fax, (208) 334-2282; Web, www.sos.idaho.gov; Facebook, www.facebook.com/IDSecOfState; Twitter, @IDSecofState

Atty. Gen. Lawrence G. Wasden (R), 700 W. Jefferson St., #210, P.O. Box 83720, Boise 83720-0010, (208) 334-2400; Fax, (208) 854-8071; Web, www.ag.idaho.gov; Twitter, @lawrencewasden

Treasurer Julie A. Ellsworth (R), 700 W. Jefferson St., #E126, P.O. Box 83720, Boise 83720; (208) 334-3200; Fax, (208) 332-2959; Web, sto.idaho.gov

(No Washington, D.C., representative)

Illinois   Web, www.illinois.gov

Gov. JB Pritzker (D), 207 State House, Springfield 62706; (217) 782-0244; TTY, (888) 261-3336; Web, www.illinois.gov/gov; Facebook, www.facebook.com/GovPritzker; Twitter, @JBPritzker; Instagram, @govpritzker

Lt. Gov. Juliana Stratton (D), 214 State House, Springfield 62706; (217) 558-3085; Fax, (217) 558-3086; TTY, (866) 383-1866; Web, www.illinois.gov/ltg; Facebook, www.facebook.com/ltgovstratton; Twitter, @LtGovStratton

Secy. of State Jesse White (D), 213 State Capitol Springfield 62756; (217) 785-3000; Fax, (217) 524-0251; Toll-free (in-state only), 800-252-8980; Web, www.cyberdriveillinois.com; Facebook, www.facebook.com/JesseWhiteSOS; Twitter, @ILSecOfState; YouTube, www.youtube.com/user/ILSECSTATE

Atty. Gen. Kwame Raoul (D), 500 S. 2nd St., Springfield 62706-1771; (217) 782-1090; TTY, (877) 844-5461; Web, www.illinoisattorneygeneral.gov; Facebook, www.facebook.com/kwame.raoul.illinois; Twitter, @KwameRaoul

Treasurer Michael W. Frerichs (R), Capitol Bldg., 219 State House, Springfield 62706-1000; (217) 782-2211; Fax, (217) 785-2777; Web, www.illinoistreasurer.gov; Facebook, www.facebook.com/TreasurerMichael Frerichs; Twitter, @ILTreasurer; YouTube, YouTube.com/channel/UCqZXaLI5po2MJSTAgoxA6rw

In Washington, DC: Pat Collier, Director, Washington Office of the Governor, State of Illinois, 444 N. Capitol St. N.W., #400, 20001; (202) 624-7760; Fax, (202) 724-0689

Indiana   Web, www.in.gov

Gov. Eric J. Holcomb (R), 206 State House, 200 W. Washington St., Indianapolis 46204; (317) 232-4567; Fax, (317) 232-3443; Web, www.in.gov/gov; Facebook, www.facebook.com/HolcombForIndiana; Twitter, @GovHolcomb; YouTube, www.youtube.com/channel/UCmcggUX5rA1za_ya16joSKA

Lt. Gov. Suzanna Crouch (R), 333 State House, 200 W. Washington St., Indianapolis 46204-2790; (317) 232-4545; Fax, (317) 232-4788; Web, www.in.gov/lg; Facebook: www.facebook.com/LGSuzanneCrouch; Twitter, @LGSuzanneCrouch; YouTube, www.youtube.com/channel/UCb0WJ4-crAzPBsl0zDq5xhw

Secy. of State Connie Lawson (R), 200 W. Washington St., #201, Indianapolis 46204-2790; (317) 232-6531; Fax, (317) 233-3283; Web, www.in.gov/sos; Email, constituent@sos.IN.gov; Facebook, www.facebook.com/sosconnielawson; Twitter, @SecretaryLawson

Atty. Gen. Curtis T. Hill, Jr. (R), Indiana Government Center South, 302 W. Washington St., 5th Floor, Indianapolis 46204-2770; (317) 232-6201; Fax, (317) 232-7979; Web, www.in.gov/attorneygeneral; Facebook, www.facebook.com/curtishillforindiana; Twitter, @AGCurtisHill; YouTube, www.youtube.com/user/INAttorneyGeneral

Treasurer Kelly Mitchell (R), 242 State House, 200 W. Washington St., Indianapolis 46204; (317) 232-6386; Fax, (317) 233-1780; Web, www.in.gov/tos; Email, tosstaff@tos.state.in.us; Facebook, www.facebook.com/TOSMitchell; Twitter, @tos_mitchell; Instagram, @kellyforindiana

In Washington, DC: Debbie Hohlt, Federal Representative, Washington Office of the Governor, State of Indiana, 444 N. Capitol St. N.W., #411, 20001; (202) 445-8999; Fax, (202) 833-1587

Iowa   Web, www.iowa.gov

Gov. Kim Reynolds (R), State Capitol, 1007 E. Grand Ave., Des Moines 50319; Press, Tim Albrecht, (515) 281-5211; Fax, (515) 725-3527; Web, www.governor.iowa.gov; Facebook, www.facebook.com/IAGovernor; Twitter, @IAGovernor; YouTube, www.youtube.com/channel/UCJmyWoQxfqO-qC0NtHu0VlA

Lt. Gov. Adam Gregg (R), State Capitol, 1007 E. Grand Ave., Des Moines 50319; (515) 281-5211; Fax, (515) 725-3527; Web, www.ltgovernor.iowa.gov; Facebook, www.facebook.com/IaLtGov; Twitter, @IALtGov

Secy. of State Paul D. Pate (R), 1st Floor, Lucas Bldg., 321 E. 12th St., Des Moines 50319; (515) 281-5204; Fax, (515) 242-5952; Web, sos.iowa.gov; Email, sos@sos.iowa.gov; Facebook, www.facebook.com/IASecretaryofState; Twitter, @IowaSOS; YouTube, www.youtube.com/channel/UCIeockCHC47J2xvZDfgTmew

Atty. Gen. Tom Miller (D), Hoover State Office Bldg., 2nd Floor, 1305 E. Walnut St., Des Moines 50319; (515) 281-5164; Fax, (515) 281-4209; Web, www.iowaattorneygeneral.gov; Email, webteam@ag.iowa.gov; Facebook, www.facebook.com/AGIowa; Twitter, @AGIowa; YouTube, www.youtube.com/user/AGIowa

Treasurer Michael L. Fitzgerald (D), Capitol Bldg., 1007 E. Grand Ave., Des Moines 50319; (515) 281-5368; Fax, (515) 281-7562; Web, www.iowatreasurer.gov; Email, treasurer@iowa.gov; Facebook, www.facebook.com/IowaTreasurer; Twitter, @IowaTreasurer; YouTube, www.youtube.com/channel/UCWExS91KSnI1jFt_34FxvRg

In Washington, DC: Stephanie Groen, Director, Washington Office of the Governor, State of Iowa, 400 N. Capitol St. N.W., #359, 20001; (202) 624-5442; Fax, (202) 624-8189

Kansas   Web, www.kansas.gov

Gov. Laura Kelly (D), Capitol, 300 10th Ave. S.W., #241S, Topeka 66612-1590; (785) 368-8500; Toll-free, (877) 579-6757; Web, www.governor.ks.gov; Facebook, www.facebook.com/GovLauraKelly; Twitter, @GovLauraKelly

Lt. Gov. Lynn Rogers (D), Capitol, 300 10th Ave. S.W., #241S, Topeka 66612-1590; (785) 296-2213; Web, https://governor.kansas.gov/about-the-office/lt-governor; Facebook, www.facebook.com/lynnrogersforkansas; Twitter, @LynnRogers4KS

Secy. of State Scott Schwab (R), Memorial Hall, 1st Floor, 120 10th Ave. S.W., Topeka 66612-1594; (785) 296-4564; Fax, (785) 296-4570; Web, sos.kansas.gov; Facebook, www.facebook.com/Kansas-Secretary-of-State-110068102381195; Twitter, @KansasSOS

Atty. Gen. Derek Schmidt (R), Memorial Hall, 120 10th Ave. S.W., 2nd Floor, Topeka 66612-1594; (785) 296-2215; Fax, (785) 296-6296; Toll-free, (888) 428-8436; Web, www.ag.ks.gov; Facebook, www.facebook.com/DerekSchmidtKS; Twitter, @KSAGOffice; YouTube, www.youtube.com/user/AGKansas

Treasurer Jacob LaTurner (R), Landon State Office Bldg., 900 S.W. Jackson St., #201, Topeka 66612-1235; (785) 296-3171; Fax, (785) 296-7950; Web, www.kansasstatetreasurer.com; Facebook, www.facebook.com/LaTurnerForKansas; Twitter, @KansasTreasurer

In Washington, DC: Adam Nordstrom, Washington Representative, Washington Office of the Governor, State of Kansas, 500 New Jersey Ave. N.W., #400, 20001; (202) 258-2084; Fax, (202) 638-1045

Kentucky   Web, www.kentucky.gov

Gov. Matt Bevin (R), The Capitol Bldg., 700 Capitol Ave., #100, Frankfort 40601; (502) 564-2611; Fax, (502) 564-2517; TTY, (502) 564-9551; Web, www.governor.ky.gov; Facebook, www.facebook.com/GovMattBevin; Twitter, @GovMattBevin; YouTube, www.youtube.com/channel/UCDSVVIYqlr023il6THfJy8Q

Lt. Gov. Jenean Hampton (R), The Capitol Bldg., 700 Capitol Ave., #142, Frankfort 40601; (502) 564-2611; Fax, (502) 564-2849; Web, www.ltgovernor.ky.gov; Facebook, www.facebook.com/Kentucky-women-for-Jenean-Hampton-Lt-Governor-337880993067915; Twitter, @ltgovhampton

Secy. of State Alison Lundergan Grimes (D), The Capitol Bldg., 700 Capitol Ave., #152, Frankfort 40601-3493; (502) 564-3490; Fax, (502) 564-5687; Web, www.sos.ky.gov; Facebook, www.facebook.com/kysecretaryofstate; Twitter, @KySecofState; YouTube, www.youtube.com/channel/UCy4JntShb1e_gUdZiyNrFHA

Atty. Gen. Andy Beshear (D), State Capitol, 700 Capitol Ave., #118, Frankfort 40601-3449; (502) 696-5300; Fax, (502) 564-2894; Web, www.ag.ky.gov; Facebook, www.facebook.com/kyoag; Twitter, @kyoag; YouTube, www.youtube.com/kyoag

Treasurer Allison Ball (R), 1050 U.S. Hwy 127 South, #100, Frankfort 40601; (502) 564-4722; Fax, (502) 564-6545; Web, www.treasury.ky.gov/Pages/index.aspx; Email, treasury.web@ky.gov; Facebook, www.facebook.com/treasurerball; Twitter, @KYTreasurer

In Washington, DC: Leeann Veatch, Director, Washington Office of the Governor, State of Kentucky, 444 N. Capitol St. N.W., #380, 20001; (202) 220-1350

Louisiana   Web, www.louisiana.gov

Gov. John Bel Edwards (R), State Capitol, 900 N. 3rd St., 4th Floor, Baton Rouge 70802-9004; P.O. Box 94004, Baton Rouge 70804-9004; (225) 342-7015; Fax, (225) 342-7099; Toll-free, (866) 366-1121; Web, www.gov.louisiana.gov; Facebook, www.facebook.com/LouisianaGov; Twitter, @LouisianaGov; YouTube, www.youtube.com/user/JohnBelForLouisiana; Instagram, @louisiana_gov

Lt. Gov. Billy Nungesser (R), Capitol Annex, Bldg. 1051 N. 3rd St., Baton Rouge 70802; P.O. Box 44243, Baton Rouge, 70804-4242; (225) 342-7009; Fax, (225) 342-1949; Web, www.crt.state.la.us/lt-governor; Email, ltgov@crt.la.gov; Facebook, www.facebook.com/LouisianaLtGov; Twitter, @LouisianaLtGov, @BillyNungesser; Instagram, @louisianaltgov

Secy. of State Tom Schedler (R), 8585 Archives Ave., Baton Rouge 70809; P.O. Box 94125, Baton Rouge 70804-9125; (225) 922-2880; Fax, (225) 922-2003; Web, www.sos.la.gov; Email, admin@sos.louisana.gov; Facebook, www.facebook.com/Louisianasos; Twitter, @Louisiana_sos; YouTube, www.youtube.com/user/SofState; Instagram, @Louisianasos

Atty. Gen. Jeff Landry (R), 1885 N. 3rd St., Baton Rouge 70802, P.O. Box 94005, Baton Rouge 70804; (225) 326-6079; Fax, (225) 326-6793; Web, www.ag.state.la.us; Email, Admininfo@ag.state.la.us; Facebook, www.facebook.com/LandryforLA; Twitter, @AGJeffLandry; Instagram, @agjefflandry

Treasurer John M. Schroder, Sr. (R), 900 N. 3rd St., 3rd Floor, State Capitol, Baton Rouge 70802; P.O. Box 44154, Baton Rouge 70804; (225) 342-0010; Fax, (225) 342-0046; Web, www.treasury.state.la.us; Facebook, www.facebook.com/LouisianaTreasury; Twitter, @LATreasury

Washington, DC Representative: Erin Monroe Wesley, Special Counsel, P.O. Box 94004, Baton Rouge, LA 70804; (225) 342-0312

Maine   Web, www.maine.gov

Gov. Janet T. Mills (D), 1 State House Station, Augusta 04333-0001; (207) 287-3531; Fax, (207) 287-1034; Toll-free, (855) 721-5203; TTY, (207) 287-6548; Web, www.maine.gov/governor/mills; Email, governor@maine.gov; Facebook, www.facebook.com/GovernorJanetMills; Twitter, @GovJanetMills

Secy. of State Matthew Dunlap (D), Nash School Bldg., 103 Sewall St., 2nd Floor, Augusta 04333; Mailing address, 148 State House Station, Augusta 04333-0148; (207) 626-8400; Fax, (207) 287-8598; Web, www.maine.gov/sos; Email, sos.office@maine.gov; Facebook, www.facebook.com/MaineSOS; Twitter, @MESecOfState;

YouTube, www.youtube.com/channel/UCnZ7LSdDcYOIbCQgSeAwisQ

Atty. Gen. Aaron Frey (D), Burton M. Cross Bldg., 6th Floor, 111 Sewall St., Augusta 04333; Mailing address, 6 State House Station, Augusta 04333-0006; (207) 626-8800; TTY, (207) 626-8865; Web, www.maine.gov/ag

Treasure Henry Beck (D), Burton M. Cross Bldg., 3rd Floor, 111 Sewall St., Augusta 04333; Mailing address, 39 State House Station, Augusta 04333-0039; (207) 624-7477; Fax, (207) 287-2367; Toll free (in-state only), 888-283-2808; Web, www.maine.gov/treasurer; Email, state.treasurer@maine.gov; Twitter, @HenryBeckMaine

(No Washington, D.C., representative)

Maryland   Web, www.maryland.gov

Gov. Larry Hogan (R), State House, 100 State Circle, Annapolis 21401; (410) 974-3901; Toll-free, (800) 811-8336; Web, www.governor.maryland.gov; Facebook, www.facebook.com/larryhoganmd; Twitter, @LarryHogan; YouTube, www.youtube.com/channel/UCBheDE_LMwHyl3VShzU73wA

Lt. Gov. Boyd K. Rutherford (R), State House, 100 State Circle, Annapolis 21401-1925; (410) 974-2461; Fax, 410-974-5882; Toll free, 1-800-811-8336; Web, www.governor.maryland.gov/ltgovernor; Facebook, www.facebook.com/BoydKRutherford; Twitter, @BoydKRutherford

Secy. of State John C. Wobensmith (R), Fred L. Wineland Bldg., 16 Francis St., Annapolis 21401; (410) 974-5521; Fax, (410) 974-5190; Web, www.sos.state.md.us; Facebook, www.facebook.com/mdsecretaryofstate; Twitter, @SOSMaryland

Atty. Gen. Brian E. Frosh (R), 200 St. Paul Pl., Baltimore 21202; (410) 576-6300; TTY, (410) 576-6372; Web, www.oag.state.md.us; oag@oag.state.md.us; Facebook, www.facebook.com/MarylandAttorneyGeneral; Twitter, @BrianFrosh; YouTube, www.youtube.com/channel/UCo_Cs5Hn4r5rdArhSPz6XIQ

Treasurer Nancy K. Kopp (D), Goldstein Treasury Bldg. 80 Calvert St., Annapolis 21401; (410) 260-7160; Fax, (410) 974-3530; Toll-free, (800) 974-0468; Web, www.treasurer.state.md.us; Email, treasurer@treasurer.state.md.us

In Washington, DC: Tiffany Waddell, Director, Washington Office of the Governor, State of Maryland, 444 N. Capitol St. N.W., #311, 20001; (202) 624-1430; (202) 624-1432

Massachusetts   Web, www.mass.gov

Gov. Charlie Baker (R), Executive Office, State House, 24 Beacon St., #280, Boston 02133; (617) 725-4005; Fax, (617) 727-9725; Toll-free (in-state only), (888) 870-7770; TTY, (617) 727-3666; Web, www.mass.gov/governor; Facebook, www.facebook.com/CharlieBakerMA; Twitter, @MassGovernor; YouTube, www.youtube.com/user/MassGovernor

Lt. Gov. Karyn Polito (R), State House, 24 Beacon St, #360, Boston 02133; (617) 725-4005; Fax, (617) 727-9725; Web, www.mass.gov/person/karyn-polito-lieutenant-governor; Facebook, www.facebook.com/karynpolitoMA; Twitter, @MassLtGov; Instagram, @massltgov

Secy. of the Commonwealth William Francis Galvin (D), 1 Ashburton Pl., #1611, Boston 02108-1512; (617) 727-7030; Fax, (617) 742-4528; Toll-free (in-state only), (800) 392-6090; TTY, (617) 878-3889; Web, www.sec.state.ma.us; Email, cis@sec.state.ma.us; Twitter, @BillGalvin4MA

Atty. Gen. Maura Healey (D), McCormack Bldg., 1 Ashburton Pl., #2010, Boston 02108-1518; (617) 727-2200; TTY, (617) 727-4765; Web, www.mass.gov/orgs/office-of-attorney-general-maura-healey; Email, ago@state.ma.us; Facebook, www.facebook.com/MassAttorneyGeneral; Twitter, @MassAGO; YouTube, www.youtube.com/user/MassAttorneyGeneral; Instagram, @mass_ago

Treasurer Deborah B. Goldberg (D), State House, 24 Beacon St., #227, Boston, 02133; (617) 367-6900; Fax, (617) 248-0372; Web, www.mass.gov/treasury; Facebook, www.facebook.com/masstreasury; Twitter, @MassTreasury; Instagram, @mass_treasury

In Washington, DC: David Garriepy, Director of State and Federal Relations, Washington Office of the Governor, Commonwealth of Massachusetts, 444 N. Capitol St. N.W., #208, 20001; (202) 624-7713; Fax, (202) 624-7714

Michigan   Web, www.michigan.gov

Gov. Gretchen Whitmer (D), Romney Bldg., 111 S. Capitol Ave., P.O. Box 30013, Lansing 48909; (517) 373-3400; Fax, (517) 335-6863; Web, www.michigan.gov/whitmer; Facebook, www.facebook.com/Gretchen Whitme; Twitter, @gretchenwhitmer; Instagram, @gewhitmer

Lt. Gov. Garlin GilChrist II (D), Romney Bldg., 111 S. Capitol Ave., 5th Floor, P.O. Box 30013, Lansing 48909; (517) 373-6800; Fax, (517) 241-3956; Web, www.michigan.gov/whitmer/0,9309,7-387-90502—,00.html; Facebook, www.facebook.com/garlingilchristM; Twitter, @garlin; Instagram, @garlinii;

Secy. of State Jocelyn Benson (D), Treasury Bldg., 430 W. Allegan St., 1st Floor, Lansing 48918-9900; (517) 322-1460; Fax, (517) 373-0727; Toll-free, (888) 767-6424; Web, www.michigan.gov/sos; Facebook, www.facebook.com/MichiganSoS; Twitter, @MichSos; YouTube, www.youtube.com/user/MichSoSOffice; Instagram, @michigansos

Atty. Gen. Dana Nessel (D), G. Mennen Williams Bldg., 525 W. Ottawa St., 7th Floor, P.O. Box 30212, Lansing 48909; (517) 373-1110; Fax, (517) 373-3042; Web, www.michigan.gov/ag; Email, miag@michigan.gov; Facebook, www.facebook.com/MIAttorneyGeneral; Twitter, @MIAttyGen

Treasurer Rachel Eubanks (D), Treasury Bldg., 430 W. Allegan St., Lansing 48922; (517) 373-3223; Fax, (517) 373-4968; TTY, (517) 636-4999; Web, www.michigan.gov/treasury; Email: StateTreasurer@michigan.gov

In Washington, DC: Jessica Brousseau, Deputy Director, Washington Office of the Governor, State of Michigan,

444 N. Capitol St. N.W., #411, 20001; (202) 624-5840; Fax, (202) 624-5841

Minnesota   Web, www.mn.gov

Gov. Tim Walz (D), 130 State Capitol, 75 Rev. Dr. Martin Luther King Jr. Blvd., St. Paul 55155; (651) 201-3400; Fax, (651) 797-1850; Toll-free, (800) 657-3717; Web, www.mn.gov/governor; Facebook, www.facebook.com/GovTimWalz; Twitter, @GovTimWalz; Instagram, @mngovernor

Lt. Gov. Peggy Flanagan (D), 130 State Capitol, 75 Rev. Dr. Martin Luther King Jr. Blvd., St. Paul 55155; (651) 201-3400; Fax, (651) 797-1850; Web, www.mn.gov/governor; Facebook, www.facebook.com/reppeggyflanagan; Twitter, @LtGovFlanagan;

Secy. of State Steve Simon (D), 180 State Office Bldg., 100 Rev. Dr. Martin Luther King Jr. Blvd., St. Paul 55155; (651) 296-2803; Fax, (651) 297-7067; Toll-free, (877) 551-6767; Web, www.sos.state.mn.us; Email, secretary.state@state.mn.us; Facebook, www.facebook.com/MNSteveSimon; Twitter, @MNSteveSimon

Atty. Gen. Keith Ellison (D), 445 Minnesota St., #1400, St. Paul 55101; (651) 296-3353; Toll-free, (800) 657-3787; TTY, (800) 366-4812; Web, www.ag.state.mn.us; Facebook, www.facebook.com/Keith.Ellison; Twitter, @Keithellison

Commissioner of Minnesota Myron Frans, 400 Centennial Bldg., 658 Cedar St., St. Paul, 55155; (651) 201-8000; Fax, (651) 296-8685; TTY, (800) 627-3529; Web, www.mn.gov/mmb; Email, info.mmb@state.mn.us; Facebook, www.facebook.com/MinnesotaManagementandBudget; Twitter, @MMBCommunicates; YouTube, www.youtube.com/channel/UCsuMfatx17HblWBZDwoeLlw

Washington, DC, Representative: Krista Broton, Washington Representative, 130 State Capitol, 75 Rev. Dr. Martin Luther King Jr. Blvd., St. Paul 55155; (651) 201-3400

Mississippi   Web, www.ms.gov

Gov. Phil Bryant (R), P.O. Box 139, Jackson 39205; (601) 359-3150; Fax, (601) 359-3741; Toll-free, (877) 405-0733; Web, www.governorbryant.ms.gov; Email, governor@governor.state.ms.us; Facebook, www.facebook.com/im4phil; Twitter, @PhilBryantMS; YouTube, www.youtube.com/user/GovernorPhilBryant

Lt. Gov. Tate Reeves (R), New Capitol Bldg., #315, 400 High St., P.O. Box 1018, Jackson 39215-1018; (601) 359-3200; Fax, (601) 359-4054; Web, www.ltgovreeves.ms.gov; Email, ltgov@senate.ms.gov; Facebook, www.facebook.com/tatereeves; Twitter, @tatereeves; YouTube, www.youtube.com/user/friendsoftatereeves

Secy. of State Delbert Hosemann (R), 401 Mississippi St., Jackson 39201, (601) 359-1350; Fax, (601) 359-1499; Web, www.sos.ms.gov; Facebook, www.facebook.com/MississippiSecretaryofState; Twitter, @MississippiSOS

Atty. Gen. Jim Hood (D), Walter Sillers Bldg., 550 High St., #1200, Jackson 39201, P.O. Box 220, Jackson 39205;

(601) 359-3680; Fax, (601) 359-3796; Web, www.ago.state.ms.us; Facebook; www.facebook.com/mississippiattorneygeneral; Twitter, @MississippiAGO; YouTube; www.youtube.com/channel/UCa3_7VnsUf_EMZuNPpKFOnA

Treasurer Lynn Fitch (R), 1101-A Woolfolk Bldg., 501 N. West St., Jackson 39201, P.O. Box 138, Jackson 39205; (601) 359-3600; Fax, (601) 359-2001; Web,; Facebook, www.facebook.com/Lynn-Fitch-159825444064888; Twitter, @LynnFitch; YouTube, www.youtube.com/channel/UCcLdk5zzJIoMSD7ba69VD6g; Instagram, @lynnfitchtreasurer

Washington, DC, Representative: Joey Songy, Chief of Staff, P.O. Box 139, Jackson, MS 39205; (601) 359-3150

Missouri   Web, www.mo.gov

Gov. Michael L. Parson (R), State Capitol, #216, Jefferson City 65101; P.O. Box 720, Jefferson City 65102; (573) 751-3222; Web, www.governor.mo.gov; Facebook, www.facebook.com/GovMikeParson; Twitter, @GovParsonMO

Lt. Gov. Mike Kehoe (R), State Capitol, #224, Jefferson City 65101; (573) 751-4727; Fax, (573) 751-9422; Web, ltgov.mo.gov; Email, ltgovinfo@ltgov.mo.gov; Facebook, www.facebook.com/MoLtGovMikeKehoe; Twitter, @LtGovMikeKehoe; YouTube, www.youtube.com/channel/UCwNFEbJTmALdxa3mfuSc3Ig

Secy. of State John R. Ashcroft (R), 600 W. Main St., Jefferson City 65101; (573) 751-4936; Fax, (573) 751-2490; Web, www.sos.mo.gov; Email, Info@sos.mo.gov; Facebook, www.facebook.com/AshcroftForMO; Twitter, @MissouriSOS

Atty. Gen. Eric Schmitt (R), Supreme Court Bldg., 207 W. High St., P.O. Box 899, Jefferson City 65102; (573) 751-3321; Fax, (573) 751-0774; Web, www.ago.mo.gov; Facebook, www.facebook.com/AttorneyGeneralSchmitt; Twitter, @AGEricSchmitt; YouTube, www.youtube.com/user/moagoffice; Instagram, @agericschmitt

Treasurer Scott FitzPatrick (R), P.O. Box 210, Jefferson City 65102, (573) 751-8533; Fax, (573) 751-0343; Web, www.treasurer.mo.gov; Facebook, www.facebook.com/MOTreasurer; Twitter, @MOTreasurer

(No Washington, D.C., representative)

Montana   Web, http://mt.gov

Gov. Steve Bullock (D), State Capitol, #204, P.O. Box 200801, Helena 59620-0801; (406) 444-3111; Fax, (406) 444-5529; Toll free, 855-318-1330; Web, www.governor.mt.gov; Facebook, www.facebook.com/GovernorBullock; Twitter, @GovernorBullock; YouTube, www.youtube.com/user/GovernorBullock

Lt. Gov. Mike Cooney (D), State Capitol, #207, P.O. Box 200801, Helena 59620-1901; (406) 444-5665; Fax, (406) 444-5529; Web, www.governor.mt.gov/Home/LTGovernor

Secy. of State Corey Stapleton (R), State Capitol Bldg., 1301 6th Ave., #260, Helena 59601; P.O. Box 202801, Helena, 59620; (406) 444-2034, Fax, (406) 444-3976;

TTY, (406) 444-9068; Web, www.sos.mt.gov; Email, secretary@mt.gov; Twitter, @Stapleton_MT

Atty. Gen. Tim Fox (R), Justice Bldg., 215 N. Sanders St., 3rd Floor, P.O. Box 201401, Helena 59620-1401; (406) 444-2026; Fax, (406) 444-3549; Web, www.dojmt.gov/ agooffice; Email, contactdoj@mt.gov; Twitter, @AGTimFox

Director of Dept. of Administration John Lewis, 125 N. Roberts St., P.O. Box 200101, Helena 59620-0101; (406) 444-2511 or (406) 444-2023; Fax (406) 444-6194; Web, www.doa.mt.gov; Facebook, www.facebook.com/ mtdoa; Twitter, @MTDeptofAdmin

(No Washington, D.C., representative)

Nebraska   Web, www.nebraska.gov

Gov. Pete Ricketts (R), State Capitol, 1445 K St., #2316, P.O. Box 94848, Lincoln 68509; (402) 471-2244; Fax, (402) 471-6031; Web, www.governor.nebraska .gov; Facebook, www.facebook.com/GovernorPete Ricketts; Twitter, @GovRicketts; YouTube, www .youtube.com/channel/UCcDw3_ CGhTVcVtxoGKRkjlQ; Instagram, @govricketts

Lt. Gov. Mike Foley (R), State Capitol, #2315, P.O. Box 94848, Lincoln 68509; (402) 471-2256; Fax, (402) 471-6031; Web, www.ltgov.nebraska.gov

Secy. of State Robert B. Evnen (R), State Capitol, 1445 K St., #2300, Lincoln; P.O. Box 94608, Lincoln 68509; (402) 471-2554; Fax, (402) 471-3237; Web, www.sos.ne .gov; Facebook, www.facebook.com/ bobevnenfornebraska

Atty. Gen. Doug Peterson (R), 2115 State Capitol, Lincoln 68509; (402) 471-2683; Fax, (402) 471-3297; Web, www.ago.nebraska.gov; Email, ago.info.help@nebraska .gov; Facebook, www.facebook.com/AGDougPeterson; Twitter, @AGDougPeterson

Treasurer John Murante (R), State Capitol, #2005, P.O. Box 94788, Lincoln 68509; (402) 471-2455; Fax, (402) 471-4390; Web, www.treasurer.nebraska.gov; Facebook, www.facebook.com/NebraskaTreasurer; Twitter, @NeTreasurer; YouTube, www.youtube.com/ user/nstovideos

Washington, DC, Representative: Lauren Kintner, Policy Director and General Counsel, State Capitol, #1319, Lincoln, NE 68509 (402) 471-2414

Nevada   Web, www.nv.gov

Gov. Steve Sisolak (D), State Capitol Bldg., 101 N. Carson St., Carson City 89701; (775) 684-5670; Fax, (775) 684-5683; Web, www.gov.nv.gov; Twitter, @SteveSisolak

Lt. Gov. Kate Marshall (D), State Capitol Bldg., 101 N. Carson St., #2, Carson City 89701; (775) 684-7111; Fax, (775) 684-7110; Web, www.ltgov.nv.gov; Email, Ltgov@ltgov.nv.gov; Facebook, www.facebook.com/ KateMarshallNV; Twitter, @KateMarshallNV

Secy. of State Barbara Cegavske (R), State Capitol Bldg., 101 N. Carson St., Carson City 89701-4786; (775) 684-5708; Fax, (775) 684-5725; Web, www.nvsos.gov; Email, sosmail@sos.nv.gov; Facebook, www.facebook .com/NVSOS; Twitter, @NVSOS

Atty. Gen. Aaron Ford (D), Capitol Complex, 100 N. Carson St., Carson City 89701-4717; (775) 684-1100; Fax, (775) 684-1108; Web, ag.nv.gov; Email, aginfo@ag .nv.gov; Facebook, www.facebook.com/ NVAttorneyGeneral; Twitter, @NevadaAG; YouTube, www.youtube.com/user/NevadaAG

Treasurer Zach Conine (D), Capitol Bldg., 101 N. Carson St., #4, Carson City 89701-4786; (775) 684-5600; Fax, (775) 684-5781; Web, www.nevadatreasurer.gov; Twitter, @ZConine

(No Washington, D.C., representative)

New Hampshire   Web, www.nh.gov

Gov. Chris Sununu (R), State House, 107 N. Main St., Concord 03301; (603) 271-2121; Fax, (603) 271-7640; Web, www.governor.nh.gov; Facebook, www.facebook .com/GovernorChrisSununu; Twitter, @GovChrisSununu; YouTube, www.youtube.com/ channel/UC5miBopIJbVV0Zt7NXNYWhQ

(No office of Lieutenant Governor)

Secy. of State William M. Gardner (D), State House, #204, 107 N. Main St., Concord 03301; (603) 271-3242; Fax, (603) 271-6316; Web, www.sos.nh.gov; Email, Administration@sos.nh.gov

Atty. Gen. Gordon MacDonald (R), 33 Capitol St., Concord 03301; (603) 271-3658; Fax, (603) 271-2110; TTY, (800) 735-2964; Web, www.doj.nh.gov; Email, attorneygeneral@doj.nh.gov

Treasurer William F. Dwyer (D), State House Annex, 25 Capitol St., #121, Concord 03301; (603) 271-2621; Fax, (603) 271-3922; Web, www.nh.gov/treasury; Email, treasury@treasury.state.nh.us

Washington, DC, Representative: Paul Collins, Senior Advisor, State House, 107 N. Main St., #208, Concord, NH 03301; (603) 271-2121

New Jersey   Web, www.newjersey.gov

Gov. Phil Murphy (D), State House, 125 W. State St., P.O. Box 001, Trenton 08625; (609) 292-6000; Fax, (609) 292-3454; Web, www.state.nj.us/governor; Facebook, www.facebook.com/governorphilmurphy; Twitter, @GovMurphy; Instagram, @govmurphy

Lt. Gov. Sheila Oliver (D), 225 W. State St., P.O. Box 300, Trenton 08625; (609) 292-6000; Fax, (609) 777-1764; Web, www.nj.gov/governor/admin/lt; Email, Feedback@sos.state.nj.us; Facebook, www.facebook .com/LtGovOliver; Twitter, @LtGovOliver

Secy. of State Tahesha Way (D), New Jersey Dept. Of State, 225 W. State St., 4th floor, P.O. Box 300, Trenton 08625; (609)-777-2581; Web, www.state.nj.us/state; Facebook, www.facebook.com/SecretaryWay; Twitter, @SecretaryWay; YouTube, www.youtube.com/channel/ UCpra_Xk_0KhMXhiJwCc6hzw

Atty. Gen. Gurbir Grewal (D), 25 Market St., 8th Floor, West Wing, P.O. Box 080, Trenton 08625-0080; (609) 292-4925; Fax, (609) 292-3508; Web, www.nj.gov/oag; Facebook, www.facebook.com/NJAttorneyGenerals Office; Twitter, @NewJerseyAG; YouTube, www .youtube.com/user/NewJerseyGovernment

Treasurer Elizabeth Muoio (D), State House, 225 W. State St., Trenton 08625; P.O. Box 002, Trenton 08625; (609) 292-6748; Web, www.state.nj.us/treasury

In Washington, DC: Kirtan Mehta, Director, Washington Office of the Governor, State of New Jersey, 444 N. Capitol St. N.W., #201, 20001; (202) 638-0631; Fax, (202) 638-2296

New Mexico   Web, www.newmexico.gov

Gov. Michelle Lujan Grisham (D), State Capitol Bldg., 490 Old Santa Fe Trail, #400, Santa Fe 87501; (505) 476-2200; Fax, (505) 476-2226; Web, www.governor.state .nm.us; Facebook, www.facebook.com/GovMLG; Twitter, @GovMLG

Lt. Gov. Howie Morales (D), State Capitol Bldg., 490 Old Santa Fe Trail, #417, Santa Fe 87501; (505) 476-2250; Fax, (505) 476-2257; Web, www.ltgov.state.nm.us; Twitter, @Morales4LtGovNM

Secy. of State Maggie Toulouse Oliver (D), State Capitol, North Annex, 325 Don Gaspar Ave., #300, Santa Fe 87501; (505) 827-3614; Fax, (505) 827-3611; Toll-free, (800) 477-3632; Web, www.sos.state.nm.us; Facebook, www.facebook.com/NMSecofState; Twitter, @NMSecOfState

Atty. Gen. Hector Balderas (D), Villagra Bldg., 408 Galisteo St., Santa Fe 87501; P.O. Drawer 1508, Santa Fe 87504-1508; (505) 490-4060; Fax, (505) 490-4833; Toll free, 844-255-9210; Web, www.nmag.gov; Facebook, www.facebook.com/NMAttorneyGeneral; Twitter, @NewMexicoOAG

Treasurer Tim Eichenberg (D), State Treasurer's Office, 2055 S. Pacheco St., #100 & 200, Santa Fe 87505-5135; (505) 955-1120; Fax, (505) 955-1195; Web, www.nmsto .gov; Facebook, www.facebook.com/NMStateTreasurer; Twitter, @NM_Treasurer

(No Washington, D.C., representative)

New York   Web, www.ny.gov

Gov. Andrew Cuomo (D), NYS State Capitol Bldg., Albany 12224; (518) 474-8390; Web, www.governor.ny.gov; Facebook, www.facebook.com/GovernorAndrew Cuomo; Twitter, @NYGovCuomo; YouTube, www .youtube.com/user/nygovcuomo; Instagram, @nygovcuomo

Lt. Gov. Kathy Hochul (D), Executive Chamber, State Capitol, Albany 12224-0341; (518) 474-8390; Fax, (518) 474-1513; Web, www.governor.ny.gov/meet-lieutenant-governor-kathy-hochul; Facebook, www .facebook.com/ltgovhochulny; Twitter, @LtGovHochul NY; YouTube, www.youtube.com/channel/UCNgh6 Me2UyKXOuNDCnsCzPg

Secy. of State Rossana Rosado (D), 1 Commerce Plaza, 99 Washington Ave., Albany 12231-0001; (518) 473-3355; Fax, (518) 474-6572; Web, www.dos.ny.gov; Facebook, www.facebook.com/NewYorkDepartmentOfState; Twitter, @NYSDOS; YouTube, www.youtube.com/ user/nysdosvideos

Atty. Gen. Letitia James (D), State Capitol, Albany 12224-0341; (518) 776-2307; Toll-free, (800) 771-7755; Web,

www.ag.ny.gov; Facebook, www.facebook.com/ newyorkstateag; Twitter, @NewYorkStateAG; Instagram, @newyorkstateag

Treasurer Christopher Curtis (D), 110 State St., 2nd Floor, P.O. Box 22119, Albany 12201-2119; (518) 474-4250; Fax, (518) 402-4118; Web, www.tax.ny.gov; Email, Christopher.curtis@tax.ny.gov; Facebook, www .facebook.com/NYSTaxDept; Twitter, @NYSTaxDept; YouTube, www.youtube.com/user/ NYSTaxDepartment

In Washington, DC: Alexander Cochran, Director, Washington Office of the Governor, State of New York, 444 N. Capitol St. N.W., #301, 20001; (202) 434-7112; Fax, (202) 434-7110

North Carolina   Web, www.nc.gov

Gov. Roy Cooper (D), State Capitol, Raleigh 27699; Mailing address, 20301 Mail Service Center, Raleigh 27699; (919) 814-2000; Fax, (919) 733-2120; Web, www .governor.nc.gov; Facebook, www.facebook.com/ NCgovernor; Twitter, @NC_Governor; Instagram, @nc_governor

Lt. Gov. Dan Forest (R), 310 N. Blount St., Raleigh 27601; Mailing address, Mail Service Center, Raleigh, 27699-0401; (919) 814-3680; Fax, (919) 733-6595; Web, www .ltgov.nc.gov; Facebook, www.facebook.com/ OfficialDanForest; Twitter, @LtGovDanForest; YouTube, www.youtube.com/user/NCLtGovDanForest

Secy. of State Elaine F. Marshall (D), 2 S. Salisbury St., Raleigh, 27601; Mailing address, P.O. Box 29622, Raleigh 27626-0622; (919) 814-5400; Fax, (919) 807-2039; Web, www.sosnc.gov; Facebook, www .facebook.com/NCSecState; Twitter, @NCSecState; YouTube, www.youtube.com/channel/ UCurvEHnuVpW_4wUgg6jqZOw

Atty. Gen. Josh Stein (D), 114 W. Edenton St., Raleigh 27603; Mailing address, 9001 Mail Service Center, Raleigh 27699-9001; (919) 716-6400; Fax, (919) 716-6750; Web, www.ncdoj.gov; Facebook, www.facebook .com/NCDOJ; Twitter, @NCAGO

Treasurer Dale R. Folwell (R), 3200 Atlantic Ave., Raleigh 27603-1385; (919) 814-4000; Web, www.nctreasurer .com; Facebook, www.facebook.com/NCDST

In Washington, DC: Jim McCleskey, Director, North Carolina Washington Office of the Governor, 444 N. Capitol St. N.W., #332, 20001; (202) 624-5833

North Dakota   Web, www.nd.gov

Gov. Doug Burgum (R), State Capitol, 600 E. Boulevard Ave., Bismarck 58505-0100; (701) 328-2200; Fax, (701) 328-2205; Web, www.governor.nd.gov; Facebook, www.facebook.com/GovernorDougBurgum; Twitter, @DougBurgum

Lt. Gov. Brent Sanford (R), State Capitol, 600 E. Boulevard Ave., Dept. 101, Bismarck 58505-0100; (701) 328-2200; Fax, (701) 328-2205; Web, www.governor.nd.gov/ lieutenant-governor-brent-sanford; Facebook, www .facebook.com/NDLtGovBrentSanford; Twitter, @BrentSanfordND

Secy. of State Al Jaeger (R), State Capitol, 600 E. Boulevard Ave., Dept. 108, Bismarck 58505-0500; (701) 328-2900; Fax, (701) 328-2992; Toll-free, (800) 352-0867; TTY, (800) 366-6888; Web, www.sos.nd.gov; Email, sos@nd.gov; Facebook, www.facebook.com/NDSOS

Atty. Gen. Wayne Stenehjem (R), State Capitol, 600 E. Boulevard Ave., Dept. 125, Bismarck 58505; (701) 328-2210; Fax, (701) 328-2226; TTY, (800) 366-6888; Web, attorneygeneral.nd.gov; Email, ndag@nd.gov; Facebook, www.facebook.com/StenehjemforAG

Treasurer Kelly L. Schmidt (R), State Capitol, 3rd Floor, 600 E. Boulevard Ave., Dept. 120, Bismarck 58505-0660; (701) 328-2643; Fax, (701) 328-3002; Web, www.nd.gov/treasurer; Email, treasurer@nd.gov

Washington, DC, Representative: Levi Bachmeier, Policy Advisor, Washington Office of the Governor, 211 N. Union St., #100, Alexandria, VA 22314; (701) 328-2200; Fax, (202) 478-0811

Ohio   Web, www.ohio.gov

Gov. Mike DeWine (R), Vern Riffe Center, 30th Floor, 77 S. High St., Columbus 43215-6117; (614) 466-3555; Fax, (614) 466-9354; Web, www.governor.ohio.gov; Facebook, www.facebook.com/MikeDeWine; Twitter, @MikeDeWine

Lt. Gov. Jon Husted (R), Vern Riffe Center, 30th Floor, 77 S. High St., Columbus 43215-6117; (614) 466-3555; Fax, (614) 644-9345; Web, www.governor.ohio.gov/About/LtGovernor; Facebook, www.facebook.com/hustedforohio; Twitter, @LtGovHusted

Secy. of State Frank LaRose (R), 180 E. Broad St., 16th Floor, Columbus 43215; (614) 466-2655; Fax, (614) 466-3899; TTY, (614) 466-0562; Web, www.sos.state.oh.us; Facebook, www.facebook.com/franklarose; Twitter, @FrankLaRose

Atty. Gen. Dave Yost (R), 30 E. Broad St., 14th Floor, Columbus 43215-3428; (614) 466-4320; Help line, (614) 466-4986; Toll free, 800-282-0515; Web, www.ohioattorneygeneral.gov; Facebook, www.facebook.com/OhioAttorneyGeneral; Twitter, @OhioAG; YouTube, www.youtube.com/user/OhioAttorneyGeneral

Treasurer Robert Sprague (R), 30 E. Broad St., 9th Floor, Columbus 43215; (614) 466-2160; Fax, (614) 644-7313; TTY, (800) 228-1102; Web, www.tos.ohio.gov; Email, treasurer@tos.ohio.gov; Facebook, www.facebook.com/OhioTreasurer; Twitter, @Ohiotreasurer; YouTube, www.youtube.com/user/OhioTreasurer?ob=5

(No Washington, D.C., representative)

Oklahoma   Web, www.ok.gov

Gov. J. Kevin Stitt (R), State Capitol, 2300 N. Lincoln Blvd., #212, Oklahoma City 73105; (405) 521-2342; Fax, (405) 521-3353; Web, www.ok.gov/governor; Facebook, www.facebook.com/GovStitt; Twitter, @GovMaryFallin

Lt. Gov. Matt Pinnell (R), State Capitol, 2300 N. Lincoln Blvd., #211, Oklahoma City 73105; (405) 521-2161;

Fax, (405) 522-8694; Web, www.ok.gov/ltgovernor; Facebook, www.facebook.com/MattPinnellOK

Secy. of Michael Rogers (R), State Capitol, 2300 N. Lincoln Blvd., #122, Oklahoma City 73105; (405) 521-3912; Web, www.sos.ok.gov

Atty. Gen. Mike Hunter (R), 313 21st St. N.E., Oklahoma City 73105; (405) 521-3921; Fax, (405) 521-6246; Web, www.ok.gov/oag; Facebook, www.facebook.com/AttorneyGeneralMikeHunter; Twitter, @AGMikeHunter;

Treasurer Randy McDaniel (R), State Capitol, 2300 N. Lincoln Blvd., #217, Oklahoma City 73105; (405) 521-3191; Web, www.ok.gov/treasurer; Facebook, www.facebook.com/OKTreasurer; Twitter, @OKTreasurer

Washington, DC, Representative: Michael Junk, Chief of Staff, Washington Office of the Governor, State of Oklahoma, 2300 N. Lincoln Blvd., #212, Oklahoma City, OK 73105; (405) 521-2342

Oregon   Web, www.oregon.gov

Gov. Kate Brown (D), 160 State Capitol, 900 Court St. N.E., Salem 97301-4047; (503) 378-4582; Fax, (503) 378-6827; Web, www.governor.oregon.gov; Facebook, www.facebook.com/OregonGovernor; Twitter, @OregonGovBrown; YouTube, www.youtube.com/channel/UCIvf0TD6Lo0L6_lQEBhGYkQ

(No office of Lieutenant Governor)

Secy. of State Dennis Richardson (R), Capitol Rm. 136, 900 Court St. NE, Salem 97301-0722; (503) 986-1523; Fax, (503) 986-1616; Web, sos.oregon.gov; Email, oregon.sos@oregon.gov; Facebook, www.facebook.com/DennisRichardsonforOregon; Twitter, @OregonSoS

Atty. Gen. Ellen F. Rosenblum (D), Justice Bldg., 1162 Court St. N.E., Salem 97301-4096; (503) 378-4400; Fax, (503) 378-4017; Web, www.doj.state.or.us; Facebook, www.facebook.com/EllenforAG; Twitter, @ORDOJ

Treasurer Tobias Read (D), 900 Court St. N.E., #159 Salem 97301-4043; (503) 378-4329; Fax, (503) 373-7051; Web, www.Oregon.gov/treasury; Email, oregon.treasurer@state.or.us; Facebook, www.facebook.com/oregonstatetreasury; Twitter, @OregonTreasury

Washington, DC, Representative: Drew Johnston, Washington Office of the Governor State of Oregon, 444 N. Capitol St., #134, 20001; (202) 508-3847

Pennsylvania   Web, www.pa.gov

Gov. Tom Wolf (D), 508 Capitol Bldg., 501 N. 3rd St., Harrisburg 17120; (717) 787-2500; Fax, (717) 772-8284; Web, www.governor.pa.gov; Email, governor@pa.gov; Facebook, www.facebook.com/GovernorWolf; Twitter, @GovernorTomWolf; YouTube, www.youtube.com/channel/UC8cXXCdLzcYoYGa_BqaPsgA; Instagram, @governotomwolf

Lt. Gov. John Fetterman (D), 200 Capitol Bldg., 501 N. 3rd St., Harrisburg 17120-0002; (717) 787-3300; Fax, (717) 783-0150; Web, www.governor.pa.gov/

lieutenant-governor; Facebook, www.facebook.com/
JohnFettermanPA; Twitter, @JohnFetterman

**Secy. of the Commonwealth Kathy Boockvar,
Acting (D)**, 302 North Office Bldg., Harrisburg
17120; (717) 787-6458; Fax, (717) 787-1734; Web,
www.dos.pa.gov; Facebook, www.facebook.com/
PADepartmentofState; Twitter, @PAStateDept

Atty. Gen. Josh Shapiro (D), 11 N. 3rd St., General
Strawberry Square, 16th Floor, Harrisburg 17120; (717)
787-3391; Fax, (717) 783-8242; Web, www
.attorneygeneral.gov; Facebook, www.facebook.com/
PaAttorneyGen; Twitter, @PAAttorneyGen; YouTube,
www.youtube.com/channel/UC13KvRB_
Bca8NbMtkLCaRQg

Treasurer Joe Torsella (D), 129 Finance Bldg., Harrisburg
17120; (717) 787-2465; Fax, (717) 783-9760; Web,
www.patreasury.gov; Facebook, www.facebook.com/
PATreasury; Twitter, @PATreasury; YouTube, www
.youtube.com/channel/UCcCoeilgt3uUOSTL1Jzcn8g

(No Washington, D.C., representative)

Rhode Island   Web, www.ri.gov

Gov. Gina Raimondo (D), State House, 82 Smith St.,
Providence 02903-1196; (401) 222-2080; Fax (401)
228-8096; Web, www.governor.ri.gov; Email,
governor@governor.ri.gov; Facebook, www.facebook
.com/GinaMRaimondo; Twitter, @ginaraimondo;
YouTube, www.youtube.com/channel/
UCIhGaDwb9UwW4zWlGOH4u5g

Lt. Gov. Daniel J. McKee (D), State House, #116, 82 Smith
St., Providence 02903; (401) 222-2371; Fax, (401) 222-
2012; Web, www.ltgov.ri.gov; Email, info@ltgov.state.ri
.us; Facebook, www.facebook.com/LGDanMcKee;
Twitter, @LGDanMcKee

Secy. of State Nellie M. Gorbea (D), 82 Smith St., State
House, #218, Providence 02903-1120; (401) 222-2357;
Fax, (401) 222-1356; TTY, (711)-222-2357; Web,
www.sos.ri.gov; Email, secretarygorbea@sos.ri.gov;
Facebook, www.facebook.com/RIDepartmentOfState;
Twitter, @RISecState

Atty. Gen. Peter F. Neronha (D), 150 S. Main St.,
Providence 02903-2856; (401) 274-4400; Fax, (401)
222-1302; Web, www.riag.ri.gov

Treasurer Seth Magaziner (D), State House, 82 Smith St.,
#102, Providence 02903; (401) 222-2397; Fax, (401) 222-
6140; Web, www.treasury.ri.gov; Twitter, @RITreasury

(No Washington, D.C., representative)

South Carolina   Web, www.sc.gov

Gov. Henry McMaster (R), State House, 1100 Gervais St,
Columbia 29201; Press, Rob Godfrey, (803) 734-2100;
Fax, (803) 734-5167; Web, www.governor.sc.gov;
Facebook, www.facebook.com/HenryMcMaster;
Twitter, @henrymcmaster

Lt. Gov. Pamela Evette (R), State House, 1st Floor,
Columbia 29202; P.O. Box 142, Columbia 29202; (803)
734-2100; Fax, (803) 734-2082; Web, www.ltgov.sc.gov;
Email, LtGovernor@scstatehouse.gov; Facebook, www
.facebook.com/pamelaevettesc; Twitter, @PamelaEvette

Secy. of State Mark Hammond (R), 1205 Pendleton St.,
#525, Columbia 29201; P.O. Box 11350, Columbia
29211; (803) 734-2170; Fax, (803) 734-1661; Web,
www.sos.sc.gov; Facebook, www.facebook.com/
SecretaryofStateMarkHammond

Atty. Gen. Alan Wilson (R), Rembert Dennis Bldg., 1000
Assembly St., #519, Columbia 29201; P.O. Box 11549,
Columbia 29201; (803) 734-3970; Fax, (803) 253-6283;
Web, www.scag.gov; Facebook, www.facebook.com/
AGAlanWilson; Twitter, @SCAttyGenOffice;
YouTube, www.youtube.com/user/AlanWilsonAG

Treasurer Curtis M. Loftis Jr. (R), Wade Hampton Bldg.,
1200 Senate St., #214, Columbia 29201; P.O. Box
11778, Columbia 29211; (803) 734-2101; Fax, (803)
734-2690; Web, www.treasurer.sc.gov; Email,
treasurer@sto.sc.gov; Facebook, www.facebook.com/
SCStateTreasurer; Twitter, @TreasurerLoftis;
YouTube, www.youtube.com/user/treasurerloftis

(No Washington, D.C., representative)

South Dakota   Web, sd.gov

Gov. Kristi Noem (R), Capitol Bldg., 500 E. Capitol Ave.,
Pierre 57501; (605) 773-3212; Fax, (605) 773-4711;
Web, www.sd.gov/governor; Facebook, www.facebook
.com/kristiforgovernor; Twitter, @KristiNoem

Lt. Gov. Larry Rhoden (R), Capitol Bldg., 500 E. Capitol
Ave., Pierre 57501-5070; (605) 773-3212; Fax, (605) 773-
4711; Web, sd.gov/governor/ltgovernor/default.aspx;

Secy. of State Steve Barnett (R), Capitol Bldg., 500 E.
Capitol Ave., #204, Pierre 57501-5070; (605) 773-3537;
Fax, (605) 773-6580; Web, www.sdsos.gov; Email,
sdsos@state.sd.us;

Atty. Gen. Jason Ravnsborg (R), 1302 E. Hwy. 14, #1,
Pierre 57501-8501; (605) 773-3215; Fax, (605)
773-4106; TTY, (605) 773-6585; Web, www.atg.sd.gov;
Twitter, @JasonRavnsborg

Treasurer Josh Haeder (R), State Capitol, 500 E. Capitol
Ave., #212, Pierre 57501-5070; (605) 773-3378;
Fax, (605) 773-3115; Web, www.sdtreasurer.gov;
Facebook, www.facebook.com/joshforsd

Washington, DC, Representative: Kennedy Noem,
Washington Representative, State Capitol, 500 E.
Capitol Ave., Pierre, SD 57501; (605) 773-3212

Tennessee   Web, www.tn.gov

Gov. Bill Lee (R), State Capitol, 1st Floor, 600 Dr. Martin L.
King Jr. Blvd., Nashville 37243-0001; (615) 741-2001;
Fax, (615) 532-9711; Web, www.tn.gov/governor;
Facebook, www.facebook.com/BillLeeTN; Twitter,
@GovBillLee; Instagram, @govbilllee

Lt. Gov. Randy McNally (R), 700 Cordell Hull Bldg., 425
5th Ave. North, Nashville 37243-0202; (615) 741-6806;
Fax, (615) 253-0197; Web, www.capitol.tn.gov/senate/
speaker.html; Email, lt.gov.ron.ramsey@capitol.tn.gov;
Facebook, www.facebook.com/ltgovmcnally; Twitter,
@ltgovmcnally

Secy. of State Tre Hargett (R), State Capitol, 312 Rosa L.
Parks Ave., Nashville 37243-1102; (615) 741-2286;
Fax, (615) 741-5962; Web, sos.tn.gov; Facebook,

www.facebook.com/TennesseeSecretaryofState; Twitter, @SecTreHargett; YouTube, www .youtube.com/c/sectrehargett; Instagram, @sectrehargett

Atty. Gen. Herbert H. Slattery III (R), Cordell Hull Bldg., 425 5th Ave. North, Nashville 37243-0485; P.O. Box 20207, Nashville 37202-0207; (615) 741-3491; Fax, (615) 741-2009; Web, www.tn.gov/ attorneygeneral.html; Facebook, www.facebook.com/ Tennessee-Attorney-General-1436615396648529; Twitter, @TNattygen

Treasurer David H. Lillard Jr. (R), Tennessee State Capitol, 1st Floor, 600 Charlotte Ave., Nashville 37243-0225; (615) 741-2956; Web, treasury.tn.gov; Facebook, www.facebook.com/TNTreasury; Twitter, @TNTreasury; YouTube, www.youtube.com/user/ TNTreasury

(No Washington, D.C., representative)

Texas   Web, www.texas.gov

Gov. Greg Abbott (R), State Insurance Bldg., 1100 San Jacinto Blvd., #151B, Austin 78701; P.O. Box 12428, Austin 78711; (512) 463-2000; Fax, (512) 463-1849; Web, www.governor.state.tx.us; Facebook, www .facebook.com/TexasGovernor; Twitter, @GovAbbott; YouTube, www.youtube.com/channel/ UCqTttg2CGGqDmMYR1S0q5Hw; Instagram, @govabbott

Lt. Gov. Dan Patrick (R), Capitol Station, P.O. Box 12068, Austin 78711-2068; (512) 463-0001; Fax, (512) 463-0677; Web, www.ltgov.state.tx.us; Email, LTGConstituent.Affairs@ltgov.texas.gov; Facebook, www.facebook.com/ltgovtx; Twitter, @LTGovTX; Instagram, @ltgovtx

Secy. of State David Whitley (R), 1100 Congress Capitol Bldg., #1E.8, Austin 78701; P.O. Box 12887, Austin 78711-2887; (512) 463-5770; Fax, (512) 475-2761; Web, www.sos.state.tx.us; Email, secretary@ sos.texas.gov; Facebook, www.facebook.com/ txsecretary; Twitter, @TXsecofstate; Instagram, @texassecretary

Atty. Gen. Ken Paxton (R), 300 W. 15th St., 8th Floor, Austin 78701; P.O. Box 12548, Austin 78711; (512) 463-2100; Fax, (512) 475-2994; Toll free, (800) 735-2989; Web, www.oag.state.tx.us; Facebook, www .facebook.com/TexasAttorneyGeneral; Twitter, @TXAG; YouTube, www.youtube.com/user/ TexasAttorneyGeneral

Comptroller Glenn Hegar (R), Lyndon B. Johnson Bldg., 111 E. 17th St., 1st St., Austin 78774-0100; P.O. Box 13528 Capitol Station, Austin 78711-3528; (512) 463-4000; Fax, (512) 475-0352; Web, www.comptroller. texas.gov; Email, texas.comptroller@cpa.state.tx.us; Facebook, www.facebook.com/txcomptroller; Twitter, @txcomptroller; YouTube, www.youtube.com/user/ txcomptroller

In Washington, DC: Jerry Strickland, Director, Office of State-Federal Relations, State of Texas, 10 G St. N.E., #650, 20001; (202) 638-3927; Fax, (202) 628-1943

Utah   Web, www.utah.gov

Gov. Gary Herbert (R), Utah State Capitol Complex, 350 N. State St., #200, P.O. Box 142220, Salt Lake City 84114-2220; (801) 538-1000; Fax, (801) 538-1528; Toll-free, (800) 705-2464; Web, www.utah.gov/ governor; Facebook, www.facebook.com/GovGary Herbert; Twitter, @GovHerbert; YouTube, www .youtube.com/channel/UCsHi3azbJqzuOLA0IQ3J HCA; Instagram, @governorherbert

Lt. Gov. Spencer J. Cox (R), Utah State Capitol Complex, #220, P.O. Box 142325, Salt Lake City 84114-2220; (801) 538-1041; Fax, (801) 538-1133; Web, www.utah .gov/ltgovernor; Facebook, www.facebook.com/ ltgovernorcox; Twitter, @SpencerJCox

(No office of Secretary of State)

Atty. Gen. Sean D. Reyes (R), State Capitol Complex, 350 N. State St., #230, P.O. Box 142320, Salt Lake City 84114-2320; (801) 366-0260; Fax, (801) 538-1121; Toll free, (800) 244-4636 Web, attorneygeneral.utah.gov; Email, uag@agutah.gov; Facebook, www.facebook.com/ UtahAttorneyGeneral; Twitter, @UtahAG; YouTube, www.youtube.com/user/UtahAGoffice

Treasurer David Damschen (R), State Capitol Complex, 350 N. State St., #180, P.O. Box 142315, Salt Lake City 84114-2315; (801) 538-1042; Fax, (801) 538-1465; Web, www.treasurer.utah.gov; Email, sto@utah.gov; Facebook, www.facebook.com/UtahTreasurer; Twitter, @UtahTreasurer

Washington, DC, Representative: Gordon Larson, Director, State and Federal Regulations, 350 N. State St., #200, Salt Lake City, UT 84114; (202) 577-6355

Vermont   Web, www.vermont.gov

Gov. Phil Scott (R), Pavilion Office Bldg., 109 State St., Montpelier 05609-0101; (802) 828-3333; Fax, (802) 828-3339; TTY, (800) 649-6825; Web, www.governor .vermont.gov; Facebook, www.facebook.com/ GovPhilScott; Twitter, @GovPhilScott

Lt. Gov. David Zuckerman (D), 115 State St., Montpelier 05633-5401; (802) 828-2226; Fax, (802) 828-3198; Cell, (802) 622-4136; Web, www.ltgov.vermont.gov; Facebook, www.facebook.com/VTLtGov; Twitter, @VTLgGov; YouTube, www.youtube.com/channel/ UCstjBPsg1MXm5Q-FvMdWG9Q

Secy. of State Jim Condos (D), 128 State St., Montpelier 05633-1101; Information, (802) 828-2363; Fax, (802) 828-2496; Web, www.sec.state.vt.us; Email, jim .condos@sec.state.vt.us; Facebook, www.facebook.com/ SecretaryOfStateJimCondos; Twitter, @VermontSOS; YouTube, www.youtube.com/channel/UCdy2e0Ew W59oMye-Odnh3rQ

Atty. Gen. TJ Donovan (D), Pavilion Office Bldg., 109 State St., Montpelier 05609-1001; (802) 828-3171; Fax, (802) 304-1014; TTY, (802) 828-3665; Web, www.ago .vermont.gov; Email, ago.info@.state.vt.us; Facebook, www.facebook.com/tjdonovanVT; Twitter, @VTAttorneyGen

Treasurer Elizabeth (Beth) Pearce (D), Pavilion Office Bldg., 109 State St., 4th Floor, Montpelier 05609-6200;

(802) 828-2301; Fax, (802) 828-2772; TTY, (800) 253-0191; Web, www.vermonttreasurer.gov; Email, Treasurers.Office@vermont.gov; Facebook, www.facebook.com/Beth-Pearce-343317092414108; Twitter, @TreasurerPearce

(No Washington, D.C., representative)

Virginia   Web, www.virginia.gov

Gov. Ralph S. Northam(D), Patrick Henry Bldg., 3rd Floor, 1111 E. Broad St., Richmond 23219; P.O. Box 1475, Richmond, 23218 (804) 786-2211; Fax, (804) 371-6351; TTY, (800) 828-1120; Web, www.governor.virginia.gov; Facebook, www.facebook.com/GovernorVA; Twitter, @GovernorVA; Instagram, @governorralphnortham

Lt. Gov. Justin E. Fairfax (D), 102 Governor St., Richmond, P.O. Box 1195, Richmond 23218; (804) 786-2078; Fax, (804) 786-7514; Web, www.ltgov.virginia.gov; Email, ltgov@ltgov.virginia.gov; Facebook, www.facebook.com/JustinEFairfax; Twitter, @FairfaxJustin

Secy. of the Commonwealth Kelly Thomasson (D), 1111 E. Broad St., 4th Floor, Richmond 23219; P.O. Box 2454, Richmond 23218; (804) 786-2441; Fax, (804) 371-0017; Web, www.commonwealth.virginia.gov; Facebook, www.facebook.com/SecOfCommonwealth

Atty. Gen. Mark R. Herring (D), 202 N. 9th St., Richmond 23219; (804) 786-2071; Web, www.oag.state.va.us; Email, contact@Virginia.gov; Facebook, www.facebook.com/markherringva; Twitter, @AGMarkHerring; YouTube, www.youtube.com/user/AGMarkHerring

Treasurer Manju Ganeriwala (D), James Monroe Bldg., 3rd Floor, 101 N. 14th St., Richmond 23219; (804) 225-2142; Fax, (804) 225-3187; Web, www.trs.virginia.gov

In Washington, DC: Stacy Brayboy, Director of Intergov. Affairs, Virginia Office of Intergovernmental Affairs, Commonwealth of Virginia, 444 N. Capitol St. N.W., #214, 20001; (202) 783-1769; Fax, (202) 783-7687

Washington   Web, www.access.wa.gov

Gov. Jay Inslee (D), Legislative Bldg., 2nd Floor, 1143 Capitol Way South, P.O. Box 40002, Olympia 98504-0002; (360) 902-4111; Fax, (360) 753-4110; TTY (WA only), (800) 833-6388; Web, www.governor.wa.gov; Facebook, www.facebook.com/WaStateGov; Twitter, @GovInslee

Lt. Gov. Cyrus Habib (D), Legislative Bldg., #220, 416 Sid Snyder Ave. S.W., P.O. Box 40400, Olympia 98504-0400; (360) 786-7700; Fax, (360) 786-7749; Web, www.ltgov.wa.gov; Email, ltgov@ltgov.wa.gov; Facebook, www.facebook.com/waltgov; Twitter, @waltgov

Secy. of State Kim Wyman (R), Legislative Bldg., 2nd Floor, 416 Sid Snyder Ave. S.W., P.O. Box 40220 Olympia 98504-0220; (360) 902-4151; Fax, (360) 586-5629; TTY, (800) 422–8683; Web, www.sos.wa.gov; Email, secretaryofstate@sos.wa.gov; Facebook, www.facebook.com/WaSecretaryOfState; Twitter, @secstatewa; YouTube, www.youtube.com/user/secstatewa

Atty. Gen. Bob Ferguson (D), 1125 Washington St. S.E., P.O. Box 40100, Olympia 98504-0100; (360) 753-6200; Fax, (360) 664-0228; Toll free (in-state only), (800) 551-4636; TTY, (800) 833-6388; Web, www.atg.wa.gov; Facebook, www.facebook.com/WAStateAttorney General; Twitter, @AGOWA; YouTube, www.youtube.com/user/WashingtonAGO

Treasurer Duane A. Davidson (D), Legislative Bldg., 416 Sid Synder Ave. S.W., #230, P.O. Box 40200, Olympia 98504; (360) 902-9000; Fax, (360) 902-9037; TTY, (360) 902-8963; Web, www.tre.wa.gov; Facebook, www.facebook.com/electduanedavidson; Twitter, @WaTreasurer

In Washington, DC: Casey Katims, Director, Washington Office of the Governor, State of Washington, 444 N. Capitol St. N.W., #411, 20001; (202) 624-3546

West Virginia   Web, www.wv.gov

Gov. Jim Justice (D), State Capitol, 1900 Kanawha Blvd. East, Charleston 25305-0370; (304) 558-2000; Toll-free, (888) 438-2731; Web, www.governor.wv.gov; Facebook, www.facebook.com/WVGovernor; Twitter, @WVGovernor; YouTube, www.youtube.com/channel/UCnjhqLLesIzuw2V2i-Mg0ww

Senate Pres. Mitch Carmichael (R), Capitol Complex, Bldg. 1, #227M, Charleston 25305; (304) 357-7801; Fax, (304) 357-7839; Web, www.legis.state.wv.us; Email, mitch.carmichael@wvsenate.gov; Facebook, www.facebook.com/mitchcarmichaelwv; Twitter, @SenCarmichaelWV

Secy. of State Mac Warner (R), Capitol Complex, Bldg. 1, #157-K, 1900 Kanawha Blvd. East, Charleston 25305-0770; (304) 558-6000; Fax, (304) 558-0900; Web, www.sos.wv.gov; Facebook, www.facebook.com/wvsos Twitter, @wvsosoffice

Atty. Gen. Patrick Morrisey (R), Capitol Complex, Bldg. 1, #E-26, 1900 Kanawha Blvd. East, Charleston 25305; (304) 558-2021; Fax, (304) 558-0140; Web, www.ago.wv.gov; Facebook, www.facebook.com/agwestv; Twitter, @WestVirginiaAG; YouTube, www.youtube.com/user/Morrisey4AG

Treasurer John D. Perdue (D), Capitol Complex, Bldg. 1, #E-145, 1900 Kanawha Blvd. East, Charleston 25305; (304) 558-5000; Toll-free, (800) 422-7498; TTY, (304) 340-1598; Web, www.wvsto.gov; Email, wvtreasury@wvsto.gov; Facebook, www.facebook.com/WVTreasury; Twitter, @WVTreasury; YouTube, www.youtube.com/user/WVTreasury

(No Washington, D.C., representative)

Wisconsin   Web, www.wisconsin.gov

Gov. Tony Evers (D), 115 E. Capitol, P.O. Box 7863, Madison 53702-7863; (608) 266-1212; Fax, (608) 267-8983; TTY, (608) 267-6790; Web, www.evers.wi.gov/Pages/Home.aspx; Email, EversInfo@wisconsin.gov; Facebook, www.facebook.com/governorscottwalker; Twitter, @Tony4WI

Lt. Gov. Mandela Barnes (D), 19 E. Capitol, Madison 53702, P.O. Box 2043, Madison 53702; (608) 266-3516;

Fax, (608) 267-3571; Web, www.ltgov.wisconsin.gov; Email, ltgov@wisconsin.gov; Facebook, www.facebook.com/theothermandela; Twitter, @TheOtherMandela

Secy. of State Douglas La Follette (D), B41 W., State Capitol, P.O. Box 7848, Madison 53703; (608) 266-8888 X3; Fax, (608) 266-3159; Web, www.sos.state.wi.us; Email, statesec@sos.state.wi.us; Facebook, www.facebook.com/sosdoug; Twitter, @DougLaFollette

Atty. Gen. Josh Kaul (D), 17 W. Main St., Madison 53702, P.O. Box 7857, Madison 53707-7857; (608) 266-1221; Fax, (608) 267-2779; Web, www.doj.state.wi.us; Facebook, www.facebook.com/JoshKaulW; Twitter, @WisDOJ; YouTube, www.youtube.com/user/WisconsinDOJ

Treasurer Sarah Godlewski (D), B41 W. State Capitol, Madison 53703; P.O. Box 2114, Madison 53701; (608) 266-1714; Fax, (608) 261-6799; Web, www.statetreasury.wisconsin.gov; Email, Sarah.Godlewski@wisconsin.gov; Twitter, @SarahforWI

(No Washington, D.C., representative)

Wyoming   Web, www.wyo.gov

Gov. Mark Gordon (R), Idelman Mansion, 2323 Carey Ave., Cheyenne 82002-0010; (307) 777-7434; Fax, (307) 632-3909; Web, www.governor.wyo.gov; Facebook, www.facebook.com/governormarkgordon; Twitter, @GordonGovernor

(No office of Lieutenant Governor)

Secy. of State Edward A. Buchanan (R), 2020 Carey Ave., #600, Cheyenne 82002-0020; (307) 777-7378; Fax, (307) 777-6217; Web, www.soswy.state.wy.us; Email, SecOfState@wyo.gov; Facebook, www.facebook.com/wyosos;

Atty. Gen Peter K. Michael (R), Kendrick Bldg., 2320 Capitol Ave., Cheyenne 82002; (307) 777-7841; Fax, (307) 777-6869; TTY, (307) 777-5351; Web, ag.wyo.gov; Email, attorneygeneral.state.wy.us

Treasurer Curtis E. Meier, Jr. (R), 2020 Carey Ave., 4th Floor, Cheyenne 82002; (307) 777-7408; Fax, (307) 777-5411; Web, treasurer.state.wy.us; Email, treasurer@wyo.gov;

(No Washington, D.C., representative)

U.S. TERRITORIES

American Samoa   Web, www.americansamoa.gov

Gov. HTC Lolo Matalasi Moliga (I), P. Lutali Executive Office Bldg., Pago Pago, American Samoa 96799; (011) 684-633-4116; Fax, (011) 684-633-2269; Email, info@as.gov; Facebook, www.facebook.com/americansamoagov.gov

Lt. Gov. HC Lemanu Peleti Mauga (I), P. Lutali Executive Office Bldg., Pago Pago, American Samoa 96799; (011) 684-633-4116; Fax, (011) 684-633-2269

(No Washington, D.C., representative)

Guam   Web, www.guam.gov

Gov. Lourdes A. Leon Guerrero (R), Ricardo J. Bordallo Governor's Complex, Adelup, Guam 96910; (671) 472-8931, (671) 472-8936; Fax, (671) 472-4826; Web, www.governor.guam.gov;

Lt. Gov. Joshua J. Bordallo (R), Ricardo J. Bordallo Governor's Complex, Adelup, Guam 96910; P.O. BOX 2950, Hagåtña, Guam 96932; (671) 475-9380; Fax, (671) 477-2007; Web, www.lt.guam.gov; Facebook, ltgov.ray.tenorio

In Washington, DC: Margaret Metcalfe, Director, Washington Office, Governor of Guam, 444 N. Capitol St. N.W., #619, 20001; (202) 434-4855; Fax (202) 434-4856

Northern Mariana   Islands Web, gov.mp

Gov. Ralph Torres (R), Memorial Bldg., Capitol Hill, Caller Box 10007, Saipan, MP 96950; (670) 664-2280; Web, gov.mp/biographies-2/governor-2; Facebook, www.facebook.com/ralphdlg.torres; Twitter, @ltcnmi

Lt. Gov. Victor Hocog (R), Memorial Bldg., Capitol Hill, Caller Box 10007, Saipan, MP 96950; (670) 664-2280; Web, gov.mp/biographies-2/lt-governor

(No Washington, D.C., representative)

Puerto Rico   Web, www2.pr.gov

Gov. Ricardo Rosselló (New Progressive Party), Calle Fortaleza #63, Viejo San Juan, P.O. Box 9020082, San Juan, PR 00901-0082; (787) 721-7000; Fax (787) 723-3287; Facebook, www.facebook.com/rrossello; Twitter, @ricardorossello

Lt. Gov. and Secretary of State Luis G. Rivera Marín (New Progressive Party), Calle San José Esq. San Francisco Viejo San Juan, P.O. Box 9023271, San Juan, PR 00902-3271; (787) 722-2121; Fax, (787) 725-7303; Web, estado.pr.gov/es

In Washington, DC: Juan Eugenio Hernandez, Executive Director, Puerto Rico Federal Affairs Administration, 1100 17th St., N.W., #800, 20036; (202) 778-0710; Fax, (202) 822-0916

Virgin Islands   Web, www.vi.gov.

Gov. Albert Bryan Jr. (D), St. Thomas and Water Island, 21-22 Kongens Gade, Charlotte Amalie, St. Thomas, VI 00802; (340) 774-0001; Fax, (340) 693-4309; Web, www.vi.gov/governor-bryan; Twitter, @albertbjr

Lt. Gov. Tregenza Roach (D), 5049 Kongens Gade, St. Thomas, VI 00802; (340) 774-2991; Fax, (340) 774-6953; Web, ltg.gov.vi; Facebook, www.facebook.com/Office-of-the-Lieutenant-Governor-US-Virgin-Islands-1465335007120296

(No Washington, D.C., representative)

Foreign Embassies, U.S. Ambassadors, and Country Desk Offices

Following are key foreign diplomats in the United States, U.S. ambassadors or ranking diplomatic officials abroad, and country offices of the State Department that follow political, cultural, and economic developments. Also included is the African Union Commission. This information is current as of April 12, 2019.

For information on investing or doing business abroad, contact the Commerce Department's Trade Information Center at (800) USA-TRAD(E) (800-872-8723) or visit www.export.gov. The Office of the United States Trade Representative also offers trade information by region at www.ustr.gov/countries-regions.

Afghanistan   Web, www.afghanembassy.us

Ambassador: Roya Rahmani
Chancery: 2341 Wyoming Ave. N.W. 20008; (202) 483-6410; Fax, (202) 483-6488; Email, info@afghan embassy.us
Social Media: Facebook, www.facebook.com/embassyof afghanistan; Twitter, @Embassy_of_AFG; YouTube, www.youtube.com/channel/UCS8XU0p8jsDMQQzJz UcWuGg; Instagram, @afghanistanembassydc
U.S. Ambassador in Kabul: John Bass
State Dept. Country Office: (202) 647-5175

African Union Commission

Web, www.au.int/en/commission

Chair: H.E. Moussa Faki Mahamat
Ambassador: Dr. Arikana Chihombori-Quao
Chancery: 1640 Wisconsin Ave. N.W. 20007; (202) 342-1100; Fax, (202) 342-1114
Social Media: Facebook, www.facebook.com/ AfricanUnionCommission; Twitter, @_AfricanUnion; YouTube, www.youtube.com/user/AUCommission
U.S. Ambassador in Addis Ababa, Ethiopia: Michael Raynor
State Dept. Country Office: (202) 647-0553

Albania   Web, www.ambasadat.gov.al/usa/en

Ambassador: Floreta Faber
Chancery: 2100 S St. N.W. 20008; (202) 223-4942; Fax, (202) 628-7342; Email, embassy.washington@ mfa.gov.al
Social Media: Facebook, www.facebook.com/albanian embassyusa; Twitter, @FloretaFaber, @AlEmbassyUSA
U.S. Ambassador in Tirana: Donald Lu
State Dept. Country Office: (202) 647-1739

Algeria   Web, www.algerianembassy.org

Ambassador: Madjid Bouguerra
Chancery: 2118 Kalorama Rd. N.W. 20008; (202) 265-2800; Fax, (202) 986-5906; Email, mail@algerianembassy.org
U.S. Ambassador in Algiers: John Desrocher
State Dept. Country Office: (202) 647-4371

Andorra

Web, www.exteriors.ad/en/embassies-of-andorra/ andorra-usa-embassy

Ambassador: Elisenda Vives Balmaña
Chancery: 2 United Nations Plaza, 27th Floor, New York, NY 10017; (212) 750-8064; Fax, (212) 750-6630; Email, contact@andorraun.org
U.S. Ambassador: Richard Duke Buchan III
State Dept. Country Office: (202) 647-3151

Angola   Web, www.angola.org

Ambassador: Agostinho Tavares da Silva Neto
Chancery: 2100-2108 16th St. N.W. 20009; (202) 785-1156; Fax, (202) 822-9049
Social Media: Facebook, www.facebook.com/ embaixadadeangolawashington
U.S. Ambassador in Luanda: Nina Fite
State Dept. Country Office: (202) 647-9858

Antigua and Barbuda

Web, www.embassyantiguabarbudadc.com

Ambassador: Ronald Sanders
Chancery: 3234 Prospect St. N.W. 20007; (202) 362-5122; Fax, (202) 362-5225; Email, info@ embassyantiguabarbudadc.com
U.S. Ambassador: Linda S. Taglialatela (resident in Bridgetown, Barbados)
State Dept. Country Office: (202) 647-4384

Aruba   (See The Netherlands)

Argentina   Web, www.eeeuu.mrecic.gov.ar/en

Ambassador: Fernando Oris de Roa
Chancery: 1600 New Hampshire Ave. N.W. 20009; (202) 238-6400; Fax, (202) 332-3171; Email, eeeuu@mrecic.gov.ar
Social Media: Facebook, www.facebook.com/ARGinUSA; Instagram, @arginusa; Twitter, @ARGinUSA
U.S. Ambassador in Buenos Aires: Edward C. Prado
State Dept. Country Office: (202) 647-4994

Armenia   Web, http://usa.mfa.am/en

Ambassador: Varuzhan Nersesyan
Chancery: 2225 R St. N.W. 20008; (202) 319-1976; Fax, (202) 319-2982; Email, armembassyusa@mfa.am
U.S. Ambassador in Yerevan: Lynne Tracy (Chargé d'Affaires)
State Dept. Country Office: (202) 647-9611

Australia   Web, www.usa.embassy.gov.au

Ambassador: Joe Hockey
Chancery: 1601 Massachusetts Ave. N.W. 20036; (202) 797-3000; Fax, (202) 797-3168
Social Media: Facebook, www.facebook.com/AusInTheUS; Twitter, @AusintheUS; Youtube, www.youtube.com/channel/UCEoD8gsW65cF78Cx5NSXd6Q; Instagram, @ausintheus
U.S. Ambassador in Canberra: James Carouso (Chargé d'Affaires)
State Dept. Country Office: (202) 647-7828

Austria   Web, www.austria.org

Ambassador: Wolfgang A. Waldner
Chancery: 3524 International Court N.W. 20008; (202) 895-6700; Fax, (202) 895-6750; Email, inbox@austria.org
Social Media: Facebook, www.facebook.com/austrianembassy; Twitter, @AustriainUSA; Instagram, @austriainusa
U.S. Ambassador in Vienna: Traina D. Traina
State Dept. Country Office: (202) 647-4782

Azerbaijan   Web, washington.mfa.gov.az

Ambassador: Elin Suleymanov
Chancery: 2741 34th St. N.W. 20008; (202) 337-3500; Fax, (202) 337-5911; Email, azerbaijan@azembassy.us
Social Media: Facebook, www.facebook.com/azembassy.us; Twitter, @azembassyus; Instagram, @azembassyus
U.S. Ambassador in Baku: William R. Gill (Chargé d'Affaires)
State Dept. Country Office: (202) 647-9677

Bahamas   Web, www.bahamasembdc.org

Ambassador: Sidney S. Collie
Chancery: 2220 Massachusetts Ave. N.W. 20008; (202) 319-2660; Fax, (202) 319-2668; Email, embassy@bahamasembdc.org
Social Media: Facebook, www.facebook.com/Embassy-of-the-Commonwealth-of-The-Bahamas-Washington-DC-260374077395076
U.S. Ambassador in Nassau: Doug Manchester (Chargé d'Affaires)
State Dept. Country Office: (202) 736-4322

Bahrain

Web, www.mofa.gov.bh/washington/Home.aspx

Ambassador: Shaikh Abdullah bin Mohammed bin Rashid Al Khalifa
Chancery: 3502 International Dr. N.W. 20008; (202) 342-1111; Fax, (202) 362-2192; Email, ambsecretary@bahrainembassy.org
Social Media: Twitter, @bahdiplomatic; YouTube, www.youtube.com/user/bahrainvideo
U.S. Ambassador in Manama: Justin Siberell
State Dept. Country Office: (202) 647-4709

Bangladesh   Web, www.bdembassyusa.org

Ambassador: Mohammad A. Ziauddin
Chancery: 3510 International Dr. N.W. 20008; Ambassador, (202) 244-2745; Main, (202) 244-0183; Fax, (202) 244-7830
Social Media: Facebook, www.facebook.com/BangladeshEmbassyUSA; YouTube, www.youtube.com/playlist?list=PLby_EWM1TmhnIL4ilf_RqZAjLa1WR5TSW
U.S. Ambassador in Dhaka: Earl R. Miller
State Dept. Country Office: (202) 647-2472

Barbados   Web, www.foreign.gov.bb

Ambassador: Selwin Hart
Chancery: 2144 Wyoming Ave. N.W. 20008; (202) 939-9200; Fax, (202) 332-7467; Email, washington@foreign.gov.bb
Social Media: Facebook, www.facebook.com/BarbadosEmbassy
U.S. Ambassador in Bridgetown: Linda S. Taglialatela
State Dept. Country Office: (202) 647-4384

Belarus   Web, www.usa.mfa.gov.by

Ambassador: Pavel Shidlovsky (Special Chargé d'Affaires)
Chancery: 1619 New Hampshire Ave. N.W. 20009; (202) 986-1606; Fax, (202) 986-1805; Email, usa@mfa.gov.by
U.S. Ambassador in Minsk: Jenifer H. Moore (Chargé d'Affaires)
State Dept. Country Office: (202) 736-4443

Belgium

Web, http://unitedstates.diplomatie.belgium.be/en

Ambassador: Dirk Wouters
Chancery: 3330 Garfield St. N.W. 20008; (202) 333-6900; Fax, (202) 333-4960; Email, washington@diplobel.fed.be
Social Media: Facebook, www.facebook.com/BelgiumintheUSA; Twitter, @BelgiumintheUSA
U.S. Ambassador in Brussels: Ronald J. Gidwitz
State Dept. Country Office: (202) 647-5674

Belize   Web, www.belizeembassyusa.mfa.gov.bz

Ambassador: Daniel Gutierez
Chancery: 2535 Massachusetts Ave. N.W. 20008; (202) 332-9636; Fax, (202) 332-6888
Social Media: Twitter, @MFABelize
U.S. Ambassador in Belmopan: Keith R. Gilges (Chargé d'Affaires)
State Dept. Country Office: (202) 647-3519

Benin   Web, www.beninembassy.us

Ambassador: Hector Posset
Chancery: 2124 Kalorama Rd. N.W. 20008;
(202) 232-6656; Fax, (202) 265-1996;
Email, info@beninembassy.us
U.S. Ambassador in Cotonou: Laura Hruby (Chargé d'Affaires)
State Dept. Country Office: (202) 647-6046

Bhutan

The United States and Bhutan do not maintain formal
diplomatic relations. Informal contact is made between
the U.S. embassy and the Bhutanese embassy in New
Delhi, India.
State Dept. Country Office: (202) 647-2941

Bolivia   Web, www.boliviawdc.org

Chief of Mission: General Pablo Canedo
Chancery: 3014 Massachusetts Ave. N.W., #2, 20008;
Chief of Mission, (202) 483-4410; Main, (202) 482-
4410; Fax, (202) 328-3712
U.S. Ambassador in La Paz: Bruce Williamson (Chargé d'Affaires)
State Dept. Country Office: (202) 647-4193

Bosnia and Herzegovina

Web, www.bhembassy.org

Ambassador: Haris Hrle
Chancery: 2109 E St. N.W. 20037; (202) 337-1500;
Fax, (202) 337-1502; Email, info@bhembassy.org
Social Media: Facebook, www.facebook.com/BHembassy.
WashingtonDC
U.S. Ambassador in Sarajevo: Ellen Germain (Chargé d'Affaires)
State Dept. Country Office: (202) 647-4277

Botswana   Web, www.botswanaembassy.org

Ambassador: David John Newman
Chancery: 1531-1533 New Hampshire Ave. N.W. 20036;
(202) 244-4990; Fax, (202) 244-4164;
Email, info@botswanaembassy.org
U.S. Ambassador in Gaborone: Kali Jones (Chargé d'Affaires)
State Dept. Country Office: (202) 647-9852

Brazil   Web, http://washington.itamaraty.gov.br/en-us

Ambassador: Sergio Silva Do Amaral
Chancery: 3006 Massachusetts Ave. N.W. 20008; (202)
238-2700; Fax, (202) 238-2827;
Email, pd.washington@itamaraty.gov.br
Social Media: Facebook, www.facebook.com/
BrazilianEmbassy; Twitter, @BrazilinUSA; YouTube,
www.youtube.com/user/EmbassyofBrazilDC;
Instagram, @brazilinusa
U.S. Ambassador in Brasilia: William Popp (Chargé d'Affaires)
State Dept. Country Office: (202) 649-1249

Brunei   Web, www.bruneiembassy.org

Ambassador: Dato Paduka Haji Serbini bin Haji Ali
Chancery: 3520 International Court N.W. 20008; (202)
237-1838; Fax, (202) 885-0560; Email, info@
bruneiembassy.org
Social Media: Facebook, www.facebook.com/people/
Embassy-Brunei-Darussalam/100007977555585
U.S. Ambassador in Bandar Seri Begawan: Scott E.
Woodard (Chargé d'Affaires)
State Dept. Country Office: (202) 647-4393

Bulgaria   Web, www.bulgaria-embassy.org

Ambassador: Tihomir Stoytchev
Chancery: 1621 22nd St. N.W. 20008, Dimitar Peshev
Plaza; (202) 387-0174; Fax, (202) 234-7973; Email,
office@bulgaria-embassy.org
Social Media: Facebook, www.facebook.com/Bulgarian-
Embassy-in-Washington-DC-156060414441918
U.S. Ambassador in Sofia: Eric Rubin
State Dept. Country Office: (202) 647-1457

Burkina Faso   Web, www.burkina-usa.org

Ambassador: Seydou Sinka (Special Chargé d'Affaires)
Chancery: 2340 Massachusetts Ave. N.W. 20008; (202)
332-5577; Fax, (202) 667-1882; Email, ambawdc@
verizon.net
Social Media: Facebook, www.facebook.com/BURKINA-
EMBASSY-IN-WASHINGTON-DC-
193137697424729
U.S. Ambassador in Ouagadougou: Andrew Young
State Dept. Country Office: (202) 647-2637

Burma   (See Myanmar)

Burundi   Web, www.burundiembassydc-usa.org

Ambassador: Benjamin Manirakiza (Chargé d'Affaires)
Chancery: 2233 Wisconsin Ave. N.W., #408, 20007; (202)
342-2574; Fax, (202) 342-2578; Email,
burundiembusadc@gmail.com
U.S. Ambassador in Bujumbura: Anne Casper
State Dept. Country Office: (202) 647-4965

Cambodia   Web, www.embassyofcambodiadc.org

Ambassador: Chum Bunrong
Chancery: 4530 16th St. N.W. 20011; (202) 726-7742;
Fax, (202) 726-8381; Email, camemb.usa@mfa.gov.kh
U.S. Ambassador in Phnom Penh: Michael Newbill
(Chargé d'Affaires)
State Dept. Country Office: (202) 647-3095

Cameroon   Web, www.cameroonembassyusa.org

Ambassador: Henri Etoundi Essomba
Chancery: 2349 Massachusetts Ave. N.W. 20008; (202)
265-8790; Fax, (202) 387-3826; Email, cs@
cameroonembassyusa.org
U.S. Ambassador in Yaounde: Peter Henry Barlerin
State Dept. Country Office: (202) 647-3139

Canada

Web, https://international.gc.ca/world-monde/country-pays/united_states-etats_unis/washington.aspx?

Ambassador: David MacNaughton
Chancery: 501 Pennsylvania Ave. N.W. 20001; (202) 682-1740; Fax, (202) 682-7726
Social Media: Twitter, @CanEmbUSA
U.S. Ambassador in Ottawa: Kelly Craft
State Dept. Country Office: (202) 647-2170

Cape Verde   Web, www.embcv-usa.gov.cv

Ambassador: Carlos Wahnon Veiga
Chancery: 3415 Massachusetts Ave. N.W. 20007; (202) 965-6820; Fax, (202) 965-1207; Email, admin@caboverdeus.net
U.S. Ambassador in Praia: Donald Heflin
State Dept. Country Office: (202) 647-1540

Central African Republic

Web, www.rcawashington.org

Ambassador: Charles Armel Doubane (Chargé d'Affaires)
Chancery: 2704 Ontario Rd. 20009; (202) 483-7800; Fax, (202) 332-9893
U.S. Ambassador in Bangui: Lucy Tamlyn
State Dept. Country Office: (202) 647-4514

Chad   Web, https://chadembassy.us

Ambassador: Ngote Gali Koutou
Chancery: 2401 Massachusetts Ave. N.W. 20008; (202) 652-1312; Fax, (202) 758-0431
U.S. Ambassador in N'Djamena: Richard K. Bell (Chargé d'Affaires)
State Dept. Country Office: (202) 647-2973

Chile   Web, http://chile.gob.cl/estados-unidos/en

Ambassador: Silva Navarro
Chancery: 1732 Massachusetts Ave. N.W. 20036; (202) 785-1746; Fax, (202) 887-5579; Email, echile.eeuu@minrel.gov.cl
U.S. Ambassador in Santiago: Carol Z. Perez
State Dept. Country Office: (202) 647-2575

China   Web, www.china-embassy.org/eng

Ambassador: Cui Tiankai
Chancery: 3505 International Pl. N.W. 20008; (202) 495-2266; Fax, (202) 495-2138; Email, chinaembpress_us@mfa.gov.cn
U.S. Ambassador in Beijing: Terry Branstad
State Dept. Country Office: (202) 647-9141

Colombia   Web, www.colombiaemb.org

Ambassador: Francisco Santos
Chancery: 1724 Massachusetts Ave. N.W. 20036; (202) 387-8338; Fax, (202) 232-8643; Email, embassyofcolumbia@columbiaemb.org
Social Media: Facebook, www.facebook.com/ColombiaEmbassyUS;

U.S. Ambassador in Bogotá: Kevin Whitaker
State Dept. Country Office: (202) 647-3142

Comoros   Web, www.un.int/comoros

Ambassador: Soilih Mohamed Soilih (in New York)
Chancery: 866 UN Plaza, #418, New York, NY 10017; (212)-750-1637; Fax, (212) 750-1657; Email, comoros@un.int
U.S. Ambassador in Comoros: Stuart R. Wilson (Chargé d'Affaires)
State Dept. Country Office: (202) 736-9048

Congo, Democratic Republic of the (DRC)

Web, www.ambardcusa.org

Ambassador: François Nkuna Balumuene
Chancery: 1100 Connecticut Ave. N.W., #725, 20036; (202) 234-7690; Fax, (202) 234-2609
Social Media: Twitter, @DrcNotes
U.S. Ambassador in Kinshasa: Mike Hammer
State Dept. Country Office: (202) 647-2216

Congo, Republic of the

Web, www.ambacongo-us.org

Ambassador: Serge Mombouli
Chancery: 1720 16th St. N.W. 20009; (202) 726-5500; Fax, (202) 726-1860; Email, info@ambacongo-us.org
Social Media: Facebook, www.facebook.com/AmbaCongoUs; Twitter, @AmbaCongoUs
U.S. Ambassador in Brazzaville: Todd Haskell
State Dept. Country Office: (202) 647-3138

Costa Rica   Web, www.costarica-embassy.org

Ambassador: Fernando Llorca Castro
Chancery: 2114 S St. N.W. 20008; (202) 499-2991; Fax, (202) 265-4795; Email, concr-us-wa@rree.go.cr
Social Media: Facebook, www.facebook.com/EmbajadadeCostaRicaenlosEEUU
U.S. Ambassador in San Jose: Sharon Day
State Dept. Country Office: (202) 647-3519

Côte d'Ivoire   Web, www.ambaciusa.org/Site

Ambassador: Diabaté Daouda
Chancery: 2424 Massachusetts Ave. N.W. 20008; (202) 797-0300; Fax, (202) 204-3967
U.S. Ambassador in Abidjan: Katherine Brucker (Chargé d'Affaires)
State Dept. Country Office: (202) 647-2791

Croatia   Web, us.mvep.hr

Ambassador: Pjer Šimunović
Chancery: 2343 Massachusetts Ave. N.W. 20008; (202) 588-5899; Fax, (202) 588-8936; Email, Washington@mvep.hr
Social Media: Facebook, www.facebook.com/Ministarstvo-vanjskih-i-europskih-poslova-506453726037312; Twitter, @MVEP_hr; YouTube, www.youtube.com/user/MVEPRH

U.S. Ambassador in Zagreb: W. Robert Kohorst
State Dept. Country Office: (202) 647-4297

Cuba   Web, misiones.minrex.gob.cu/en/usa

Ambassador: José Ramón Cabañas Rodríguez
Chancery: 2630 16th St. N.W. 20009; (202) 797-8518, ext. 20; Fax, (202) 797-8521; Email, recepcion@sicuw.org
U.S. Ambassador in Havana: Mara Tekach (Chargé d'Affaires)
State Dept. Country Office: (202) 647-9272

Curacao   (See The Netherlands)

Consul General: Margaret Hawthorne
State Dept. Country Office: (202) 647-4719

Cyprus   Web, www.cyprusembassy.net

Ambassador: Marios Lysiotis
Chancery: 2211 R St. N.W. 20008; (202) 462-5772; Fax, (202) 483-6710; Email, info@cyprusembassy.net
U.S. Ambassador in Nicosia: Kathleen A. Doherty
State Dept. Country Office: (202) 647-6976

Czech Republic   Web, www.mzv.cz/washington

Ambassador: Hynek Kmnonicek
Chancery: 3900 Spring of Freedom St. N.W. 20008; (202) 274-9100; Fax, (202) 966-8540; Email, Washington@embassy.mzv.cz
Social Media: Facebook, www.facebook.com/Czechembassydc; Twitter, @CzechEmbassyDC
U.S. Ambassador in Prague: Stephen B. King
State Dept. Country Office: (202) 647-3191

Denmark   Web, www.usa.um.dk

Ambassador: Lars Gert Lose
Chancery: 3200 Whitehaven St. N.W. 20008; (202) 234-4300; Fax, (202) 328-1470; Email, wasamb@um.dk
Social Media: Twitter, @DenmarkinUSA
U.S. Ambassador in Copenhagen: Carla Sands
State Dept. Country Office: (202) 647-8431

Djibouti   Web, www.djiboutiembassyus.org

Ambassador: Mohamed Siad Doualeh
Chancery: 1156 15th St. N.W., #515, 20005; (202) 331-0270; Fax, (202) 331-0302
Social Media: Twitter, @AmbDoualeh
U.S. Ambassador in Djibouti: Larry Edward André
State Dept. Country Office: (202) 647-6453

Dominica   Web, www.dominicaembassy.com

Ambassador: Judith Anne Rolle (Chargé d'Affaires)
Chancery: 3216 New Mexico Ave. N.W. 20016; (202) 364-6781; Fax, (202) 364-6791; Email, embdomdc@aol.com
U.S. Ambassador: Linda S. Taglialatela (resident in Bridgetown, Barbados)
State Dept. Country Office: (202) 647-4384

Dominican Republic   Web, drembassyusa.org

Ambassador: José Tomás Pérez
Chancery: 1715 22nd St. N.W. 20008; (202) 332-6280; Fax, (202) 265-8057; Email, embassy@us.serex.gov.do
Social Media: Facebook, www.facebook.com/DominicanEmbassy; Twitter, @DREmbassy
U.S. Ambassador in Santo Domingo: Robin S. Bernstein
State Dept. Country Office: (202) 647-5088

East Timor   (See Timor-Leste)

Ecuador   Web, www.ecuador.org/nuevosite

Ambassador: Francisco Carrión Mena
Chancery: 1990 M St. N.W., 3rd Floor, #310, 20036; (202) 234-7200; Fax, (202) 333-2893; Email, embassy@ecuador.org
U.S. Ambassador in Quito: Todd C. Chapman
State Dept. Country Office: (202) 647-2807

Egypt   Web, www.egyptembassy.net

Ambassador: Yasser Reda
Chancery: 3521 International Court N.W. 20008; (202) 895-5400; Fax, (202) 244-5131; Email, embassy@egyptembassy.net
Social Media: Facebook, www.facebook.com/EgyptEmbassyUSA; Twitter, @EgyptEmbassyUSA; Instagram, @egpytembassyusa
U.S. Ambassador in Cairo: Thomas H. Goldberger
State Dept. Country Office: (202) 647-4680

El Salvador   Web, www.elsalvador.org

Ambassador: Claudia Ivette Canjura de Centeno
Chancery: 1400 16th St. N.W., #100, 20036; (202) 595-7500; Fax, (202) 232-3763; Email, correo@elsalvador.org
Social Media: YouTube, www.youtube.com/user/embelsalvadorusa
U.S. Ambassador in San Salvador: Jean Elizabeth Manes
State Dept. Country Office: (202) 647-4161

Equatorial Guinea   Web, www.egembassydc.com

Ambassador: Miguel Ntutumu Evuna Andeme
Chancery: 2020 16th St. N.W. 20009; (202) 518-5700; Fax, (202) 518-5252; Email, secretary@egembassydc.com
Social Media: Facebook, www.facebook.com/egembassydc; Twitter, @EGEmbassy; YouTube, www.youtube.com/channel/UC1zn99_azfsWRfAue-uvr5Q
U.S. Ambassador in Malabo: Julie Furuta-Toy
State Dept. Country Office: (202) 647-4514

Eritrea   Web, www.embassyeritrea.org

Ambassador: Ghirmai Ghebremariam
Chancery: 1708 New Hampshire Ave. N.W. 20009; (202) 319-1991; Fax, (202) 319-1304; Email, embassyeritrea@embassyeritrea.org

U.S. Ambassador in Asmara: Natalie E. Brown (Chargé d'Affaires)
State Dept. Country Office: (202) 647-6453

Estonia   Web, www.estemb.org

Ambassador: Jonatan Veseviov
Chancery: 2131 Massachusetts Ave. N.W. 20008; (202) 588-0101; Fax, (202) 588-0108; Email, Embassy. Washington@mfa.ee
Social Media: Facebook, www.facebook.com/estemb .washington; Twitter, @Estonia_in_US
U.S. Ambassador in Tallinn: Elizabeth Horst (Chargé d'Affaires)
State Dept. Country Office: (202) 647-6582

Ethiopia   Web, www.ethiopianembassy.org

Ambassador: Kassa Tekleberhan
Chancery: 3506 International Dr. N.W. 20008; (202) 364-1200; Fax, (202) 587-0195; Email, ethiopia@ ethiopianembassy.org
U.S. Ambassador in Addis Ababa: Michael Raynor
State Dept. Country Office: (202) 647-6473

European Union   Web: www.euintheus.org

Ambassador: David O'Sullivan
Chancery: 2175 K. St., 20037; (202) 862-9500; Fax, (202) 429-1766
Social Media: Facebook, www.facebook.com/EUintheUS; Twitter, @EUintheUS; YouTube, www.youtube.com/ user/EUintheUS; Instagram, @euintheus
U.S. Ambassador to the EU: Gordon Sondland
State Dept. Country Office: (202) 647-1708

Fiji   Web, www.fijiembassydc.com

Ambassador: Naivakarurubalavu Solo Mara
Chancery: 1707 L. St. N.W., #200, 20036; (202) 466-8320; Fax, (202) 466-8325; Email, info@fijiembassydc.com
Social Media: Facebook, www.facebook.com/ FijiEmbassyWashingtonDC; Twitter, @FijiEmbassyUS
U.S. Ambassador in Suva: Michael Goldman (Chargé d'Affaires)
State Dept. Country Office: (202) 647-2349

Finland   Web, www.finland.org

Ambassador: Kirsti Kauppi
Chancery: 3301 Massachusetts Ave. N.W. 20008; (202) 298-5800; Fax, (202) 298-6030; Email, sanomat.was@ formin.fi
Social Media: Facebook, www.facebook.com/ FinnEmbassyDC; Twitter, @FinnEmbassyDC
U.S. Ambassador in Helsinki: Donna Ann Welton (Chargé d'Affaires)
State Dept. Country Office: (202) 647-6582

France   Web, www.franceintheus.org

Ambassador: Gérard Araud

Chancery: 4101 Reservoir Rd. N.W. 20007; (202) 944-6000; Fax, (202) 944-6166; Email, info@ambafrance-us.org
Social Media: Facebook, www.facebook.com/ FranceInTheUs; Twitter, @franceintheus; YouTube, www.youtube.com/user/franceintheus
U.S. Ambassador in Paris: Jamie McCourt
State Dept. Country Office: (202) 647-4372

Gabon   Web, www.gabonembassyusa.org

Ambassador: Michael Moussa-Adamo
Chancery: 2034 20th St. N.W., 20009; (202) 797-1000; Fax, (202) 332-0668; Email, info@gabonembassy.org
Social Media: Facebook, www.facebook.com/gabon .embassy.1; Twitter @GabonEmbassyDC
U.S. Ambassador in Libreville: Joe Daines
State Dept. Country Office: (202) 647-3138

The Gambia   Web, www.gambiaembassydc.us

Ambassador: Dawda D. Fadera
Chancery: 5630 16th St. N.W. 20011; (202) 785-1399; Fax, (202) 342-0240; Email, info@gambiaembassy.us
Social Media: Facebook, www.facebook.com/ thegambiaembassyindc; Twitter, @dcgambiaembassy; YouTube, www.youtube.com/channel/ UCsBa3CkuMgBxn6dtpuZOFKg
U.S. Ambassador in Banjul: Shelly Seaver (Chargé d'Affaires)
State Dept. Country Office: (202) 647-2637

Georgia   Web, http://georgiaembassyusa.org

Ambassador: David Bakradze
Chancery: 1824 R St. N.W. 20009; (202) 387-2390; Fax, (202) 387-0864; Email, embgeo.usa@mfa.gov.ge
Social Media: Facebook, www.facebook.com/tbilisi .usembassy; Twitter, @GeorgianEmbassy
U.S. Ambassador in Tbilisi: Ross Wilson (Chargé d'Affaires)
State Dept. Country Office: (202) 647-6048

Germany   Web, www.germany.info

Ambassador: Emily Haber
Chancery: 4645 Reservoir Rd. N.W. 20007; (202) 298-4000; Fax, (202) 298-4249
Social Media: Facebook, www.facebook.com/ GermanyinUSA; Twitter, @GermanyinUSA
U.S. Ambassador in Berlin: Richard A. Grenell
State Dept. Country Office: (202) 647-4361

Ghana   Web, www.ghanaembassydc.org

Ambassador: Dr. Barfour Adjei-Barwuah
Chancery: 3512 International Dr. N.W. 20008; (202) 686-4520; Fax, (202) 686-4527; Email, info@ ghanaembassydc.org
U.S. Ambassador in Accra: Stephanie S. Sullivan
State Dept. Country Office: (202) 647-6046

Greece   Web, www.mfa.gr/washington

Ambassador: Haris Lalacos

Chancery: 2217 Massachusetts Ave. N.W. 20008; (202) 939-1300; Fax, (202) 939-1324; Email, gremb.was@mfa.gr

Social Media: Facebook, www.facebook.com/GreeceInWashington; Twitter, @GreeceinUSA; YouTube, www.youtube.com/user/GreeceInWashington

U.S. Ambassador in Athens: Geoffrey R. Pyatt

State Dept. Country Office: (202) 647-6948

Greenland   (See Denmark)

Grenada   Web, www.grenadaembassyusa.org

Ambassador: Yolande Y. Smith

Chancery: 1701 New Hampshire Ave. N.W. 20009-2501; (202) 265-2561; Fax, (202) 265-2468; Email, embassy@grenadaembassyusa.org

U.S. Ambassador in Grenada: Stephen T. Frahm (Chargé d'Affaires)

State Dept. Country Office: (202) 647-4384

Guatemala   Web, http://guatemalaembassyusa.org

Ambassador: Manuel Espina

Chancery: 2220 R St. N.W. 20008; (202) 745-4953; Fax, (202) 745-1908; Email, info@guatemala-embassy.org

Social Media: Twitter, @EmbaGuateUSA; YouTube, www.youtube.com/channel/UCVXhb1KKTBbI2SCs6CpzOoQ

U.S. Ambassador in Guatemala City: Luis E. Arreaga

State Dept. Country Office: (202) 647-3727

Republic of Guinea

Web, http://guineaembassyusa.org/en/welcome-to-the-embassy-of-guinea-washington-usa

Ambassador: Kerfalla Yansané

Chancery: 2112 Leroy Pl. N.W. 20008; (202) 986-4300; Fax, (202) 986-3800; Email, acamara@guineaembassyusa.com

U.S. Ambassador in Conakry: Hugues Ogier

State Dept. Country Office: (202) 647-0252

Guinea-Bissau

There have been several attempts to establish diplomatic relations in recent years.

Contact: P.O. Box 33813, 20033; (301) 947-3958

U.S. Ambassador: Tulinabo Salama Mushingi; resident in Dakar, Senegal; covers matters pertaining to Guinea-Bissau)

State Dept. Country Office: (202) 647-0033

Guyana   Web, www.guyanaembassyusa.org

Ambassador: Riyad Insanally

Chancery: 2490 Tracy Pl. N.W. 20008; (202) 265-6900; Fax, (202) 232-1297; Email, guyanaembassydc@verizon.net

U.S Ambassador in Georgetown: Terry Steers-Gonzalez (Chargé d'Affaires)

State Dept. Country Office: (202) 647-4719

Haiti   Web, www.haiti.org

Ambassador: Paul G. Altidor

Chancery: 2311 Massachusetts Ave. N.W. 20008; (202) 332-4090; Fax, (202) 745-7215; Email, amb.washington@diplomatie.ht

Social Media: Facebook, www.facebook.com/EmbassyofHaiti; Twitter, @EmbassyOfHaiti; Instagram, @embassyofhaiti

U.S. Ambassador in Port-au-Prince: Michele Sison

State Dept. Country Office: (202) 647-9510

The Holy See   Web, www.nuntiususa.org

Apostolic Nuncio: Christophe Pierre

Office: 3339 Massachusetts Ave. N.W. 20008; (202) 333-7121; Fax, (202) 337-4036; Email, nuntiususa@nuntiususa.org

U.S. Ambassador in Rome: Callista Gingrich

State Dept. Country Office: (202) 647-3746

Honduras   Web, www.hondurasemb.org

Ambassador: Marlon Tábora Muñoz

Chancery: 3007 Tilden St. N.W. 20008; (202) 966-7702; Fax, (202) 966-9751

Social Media: Facebook, www.facebook.com/Embajada-de-Honduras-en-los-Estados-Unidos-de-América-188645814515193

U.S. Ambassador in Tegucigalpa: Heide B. Fulton (Chargé d'Affaires)

State Dept. Country Office: (202) 647-3505

Hong Kong   (See China)

State Dept. Country Office: (202) 647-6300

Hungary   Web, www.washington.kormany.hu

Ambassador: László Szabó

Chancery: 3910 Shoemaker St. N.W. 20008; (202) 362-6730; Fax, (202) 966-8135; Email, informacio.was@mfa.gov.hu

Social Media: Facebook, www.facebook.com/Embassy-of-Hungary-in-Washington-DC-102507676462147; Twitter, @HungaryinUSA

U.S. Ambassador in Budapest: David B. Cornstein

State Dept. Country Office: (202) 647-0425

Iceland   Web, www.iceland.is/iceland-abroad/us/wdc

Ambassador: Geir H. Haarde

Chancery: House of Sweden, 2900 K St. N.W., #509, 20007-1704, (202) 265-6653; Fax, (202) 265-6656; Email, icemb.wash@utn.stjr.is

Social Media: Facebook, www.facebook.com/Icelandic.Embassy; Twitter, @IcelandInUS

U.S. Ambassador in Reykjavík: Jill Esposito (Chargé d'Affaires)
State Dept. Country Office: (202) 647-8431

India   Web, www.indianembassy.org

Ambassador: Harsh Vardhan Shringla
Chancery: 2107 Massachusetts Ave. N.W. 20008; (202) 939-7000; Fax, (202) 265-4351
Social Media: Facebook, www.facebook.com/IndiaInUSA; Twitter, @IndianEmbassyUS; YouTube, www.youtube.com/user/indiausrelations
U.S. Ambassador in New Delhi: Kenneth I. Juster
State Dept. Country Office: (202) 647-1112

Indonesia   Web, www.embassyofindonesia.org

Ambassador: Budi Bowoleksono
Chancery: 2020 Massachusetts Ave. N.W. 20036; (202) 775-5200; Fax, (202) 775-5365
Social Media: Twitter, @KBRIWashDC
U.S. Ambassador in Jakarta: Joseph R. Donovan
State Dept. Country Office: (202) 647-2301

Iran   Web, www.daftar.org

The United States severed diplomatic relations with Iran in April 1980. Iran's interests in the United States are represented by the Pakistani embassy.
Iranian Interests Section: 1250 23rd St. N.W., #200, 20037; (202) 965-1073; Fax, (202) 965-4990; Email, info@daftar.org
U.S. interests in Iran are represented by the Swiss embassy in Tehran.
State Dept. Country Office: (202) 647-2520

Iraq   Web, www.iraqiembassy.us

Ambassador: Fareed Yasseen
Chancery: 3421 Massachusetts Ave. N.W. 20007; (202) 742-1600; Fax, (202) 333-1129 **Consulate:** 1801 P St. N.W. 20036; (202) 483-7500; Fax, (202) 462-8815
Social Media: Facebook, www.facebook.com/IraqiEmbassyUSA; Twitter, @IraqiEmbassyUSA
U.S. Ambassador to Baghdad: Douglas Silliman
State Dept. Country Office: (202) 647-6351

Ireland   Web, www.embassyofireland.org

Ambassador: Daniel Mulhall
Chancery: 2234 Massachusetts Ave. N.W. 20008; (202) 462-3939; Fax, (202) 232-5993
Social Media: Facebook, www.facebook.com/embassyofirelandusa; Twitter, @IrelandEmbUSA
U.S. Ambassador in Dublin: Reece Smyth (Chargé d'Affaires)
State Dept. Country Office: (202) 647-6591

Israel   Web, www.israelemb.org

Ambassador: Ron Dermer
Chancery: 3514 International Dr. N.W. 20008; (202) 364-5500; Fax, (202) 364-5423

Social Media: Facebook, www.facebook.com/IsraelinUSA; Twitter, @IsraelinUSA; Instagram, @israelinusa
U.S. Ambassador in Tel Aviv: David Melech Friedman
State Dept. Country Office: (202) 647-3672

Italy   Web, www.ambwashingtondc.esteri.it

Ambassador: Armando Varricchio
Chancery: 3000 Whitehaven St. N.W. 20008; (202) 612-4400; Fax, (202) 518-2152; Email, stampa.washington@esteri.it
Social Media: Facebook, www.facebook.com/ItalyInUs.org; Twitter, @ItalyinUS; YouTube, www.youtube.com/user/italianembassy; Instagram, @italyinus
U.S. Ambassador in Rome: Lewis M. Eisenberg
State Dept. Country Office: (202) 647-3746

Jamaica   Web, www.embassyofjamaica.org

Ambassador: Audrey Patrice Marks
Chancery: 1520 New Hampshire Ave. N.W. 20036; (202) 452-0660; Fax, (202) 452-0036; Email, firstsec@jamaicaembassy.org
U.S. Ambassador in Kingston: Eric Khant (Chargé d'Affaires)
State Dept. Country Office: (202) 736-4322

Japan   Web, www.us.emb-japan.go.jp

Ambassador: Shinsuke J. Sugiyama
Chancery: 2520 Massachusetts Ave. N.W. 20008; (202) 238-6700; Fax, (202) 328-2187
Social Media: Facebook, www.facebook.com/JapanEmbDC; Twitter, @JapanEmbDC
U.S. Ambassador in Tokyo: William Hagerty
State Dept. Country Office: (202) 647-3152

Jordan   Web, www.jordanembassyus.org

Ambassador: Dina Kawar
Chancery: 3504 International Dr. N.W. 20008; (202) 966-2664; Fax, (202) 966-3110; Email, hkjconsular@jordanembassyus.org
Social Media: Facebook, www.facebook.com/JoEmbassyUS; Twitter, @JoEmbassyUS
U.S. Ambassador in Amman: Paul Malik (Chargé d'Affaires)
State Dept. Country Office: (202) 647-1286

Kazakhstan   Web, www.kazakhembus.com

Ambassador: Erzhan Kazykhanov
Chancery: 1401 16th St. N.W. 20036; (202) 232-5488; Fax, (202) 232-5845
Social Media: Facebook, www.facebook.com/KazakhEmbassyDC; Twitter, @KazakhEmbassy; YouTube, www.youtube.com/user/kazembus
U.S. Ambassador in Astana: George A. Krol
State Dept. Country Office: (202) 647-6859

Kenya   Web, www.kenyaembassydc.org

Ambassador: Robinson Njeru Githae

Chancery: 2249 R St. N.W. 20008; (202) 387-6101; Fax, (202) 462-3829; Email, information@ kenyaembassy.com

Social Media: Facebook, www.facebook.com/ kenyaembassyusa; Twitter, @KenyaembassyDC

U.S. Ambassador in Nairobi: Mirembe Nantongo (Chargé d'Affaires)

State Dept. Country Office: (202) 647-8913

Kiribati

Kiribati maintains a Permanent Mission to the United Nations.

Her Excellency: Makuritan Baaro

UN Chancery: 865 44th St., #1109, New York, NY 10017; (212) 867-3310; Fax, (212) 867-3320

Social Media: Facebook, www.facebook.com/ usembassysuva; Twitter, @USEmbassySuva

U.S. Ambassador: Judith Beth Cefkin (resident in Suva, Fiji)

State Dept. Country Office: (202) 647-5156

Korea, Democratic People's Republic of (North)

North Korea maintains a Permanent Mission to the United Nations.

UN Chancery: 515 E. 72nd St., #38F, New York, NY 10021; (212) 772-0712; Fax, (212) 772-0735

The United States does not maintain diplomatic relations with North Korea. The Swedish Embassy in Pyongyang represents the U.S. as a consular protecting power.

State Dept. Country Office: (202) 647-7717

Korea, Republic of (South)   Web, usa.mofa.go.kr

Ambassador: Cho Yoon-je

Chancery: 2450 Massachusetts Ave. N.W. 20008; (202) 939-5600; Fax, (202) 797-0595; Email, consular.usa@ mofa.go.kr

Social Media: Facebook, www.facebook.com/mofakr.eng; Twitter, @MOFAkr_eng

U.S. Ambassador in Seoul: Harry Harris

State Dept. Country Office: (202) 647-7717

Kosovo   Web, www.ambasada-ks.net/us

Ambassador: Vlora Çitaku

Chancery: 2175 K St. N.W. #300, 20037; (202) 450-2130; Fax, (202) 735-0609; Email, consulategeneral.ny@rks-gov.net

Social Media: Facebook, www.facebook.com/MFAKosovo

U.S. Ambassador in Pristina: Philip S. Kosnett

State Dept. Country Office: (202) 647-0608

Kuwait   Web, www.kuwaitembassy.us

Ambassador: Salem Abdullah Al-Jaber Al-Sabah

Chancery: 2940 Tilden St. N.W. 20008; (202) 966-0702; Fax, (202) 364-2868

Social Media: Facebook, www.facebook.com/ MOFAKuwai; Twitter, @MOFAKuwait; Instagram, @mofakuwait

U.S. Ambassador in Kuwait City: Lawrence R. Silverman

State Dept. Country Office: (202) 647-9005

Kyrgyzstan, Republic of Kyrgyz

Web, www.kgembassy.org

Ambassador: Otunbaev Bolot Isakovich

Chancery: 2360 Massachusetts Ave. N.W. 20008; (202) 449-9822; Fax, (202) 386-7550; Email, kgconsul@ kgembassy.org

Social Media: Facebook, www.facebook.com/ kgembassyusa; Twitter, @kgembassy; Instagram, @kgembassy

U.S. Ambassador in Bishkek: Donald Lu

State Dept. Country Office: (202) 647-9119

Laos   Web, www.laoembassy.com

Ambassador: Mai Sayavongs

Chancery: 2222 S St. N.W. 20008; (202) 328-9148; Fax, (202) 332-4923; Email, embasslao@gmail.com

U.S. Ambassador in Vientiane: Rena Bitter

State Dept. Country Office: (202) 647-2459

Latvia   Web, www.mfa.gov.lv/en/usa

Ambassador: Andris Teikmanis

Chancery: 2306 Massachusetts Ave. N.W. 20008; (202) 328-2840; Fax, (202) 328-2860; Email, embassy.usa@ mfa.gov.lv

Social Media: Facebook, www.facebook.com/ EmbassyofLatviainUS; Twitter, @Latvia_USA

U.S. Ambassador in Riga: Nancy Bikoff Pettit

State Dept. Country Office: (202) 647-9980

Lebanon   Web, www.lebanonembassyus.org

Chargé d'Affaires: Gabriel Issa

Chancery: 2560 28th St. N.W. 20008; (202) 939-6300; Fax, (202) 939-6324; Email, info@lebanonembassyus .org

U.S. Ambassador in Beirut: Elizabeth Richard

State Dept. Country Office: (202) 647-1030

Lesotho, Kingdom of

Web, www.lesothoemb-usa.gov.ls

Ambassador: Sankatana Gabriel Maja

Chancery: 2511 Massachusetts Ave. N.W. 20008; (202) 797-5533; Fax, (202) 234-6815; Email, lesothoembassy@verizon.net

U.S. Ambassador in Maseru: Rebecca E. Gonzales

State Dept. Country Office: (202) 647-9838

Liberia   Web, www.liberianembassyus.org

Ambassador: George S. W. Patten

Chancery: 5201 16th St. N.W. 20011; (202) 723-0437; Fax, (202) 723-0436

U.S. Ambassador in Monrovia: Christine Elder

State Dept. Country Office: (202) 647-3469

Libya   Web, www.embassyoflibyadc.org

Chargé d'Affaires: Wafa Bughaighis

Chancery: 1460 Dahlia St. N.W. 20012; (202) 944-9601; Fax, (202) 944-9606

The U.S. Embassy in Tripoli, Libya, closed on July 26, 2014. Ambassador and diplomatic personnel work from the U.S. Embassy in Tunis, Tunisia.

U.S. Ambassador to Tripoli: Peter Bodde (Chargé d'Affaires, in Tunis, Tunisia, the Libya External Office)

State Dept. Country Office: (202) 647-4674

Liechtenstein   Web, www.liechtensteinusa.org

Ambassador: Kurt Jäger

Chancery: 2900 K St. N.W., #602B, 20007; (202) 331-0590; Fax, (202) 331-3221

Social Media: Facebook, www.facebook.com/Embassy-of-Liechtenstein-Washington-DC-263046272021; Twitter, @EmbassyLI

U.S. Ambassador: Edward T. McMullen (resident in Bern, Switzerland)

State Dept. Country Office: (202) 647-0425

Lithuania   Web, www.usa.mfa.lt

Ambassador: Rolandas Kriščiūnas

Chancery: 2622 16th St. N.W. 20009; (202) 234-5860; Fax, (202) 328-0466; Email, amb.us@urm.lt or info@usa.mfa.lt

Social Media: Facebook, www.facebook.com/LTinUSA; Twitter, @LTembassyUS; YouTube, www.youtube.com/channel/UCE0EQy77dzQ1SnA59wSRV7w

U.S. Ambassador in Vilnius: Anne Hall

State Dept. Country Office: (202) 647-8378

Luxembourg   Web, washington.mae.lu

Ambassador: Sylvie Lucas

Chancery: 2200 Massachusetts Ave. N.W. 20008; (202) 265-4171; Fax, (202) 328-8270; Email, luxembassy.was@mae.etat.lu

U.S. Ambassador in Luxembourg: Kerri S. Hannan (Chargé d'Affaires)

State Dept. Country Office: (202) 647-5674

Macau   (See China)

State Dept. Country Office: (202) 647-6300

Macedonia   Web, www.mfa.gov.mk/washington

Chargé d'Affaires: Oliver Krliu (Chargé d'Affaires)

Chancery: 2129 Wyoming Ave. N.W. 20008; (202) 667-0501; Fax, (202) 667-2131; Email, washington@mfa.gov.mk

U.S. Ambassador in Skopje: Jess L. Baily

State Dept. Country Office: (202) 647-3747

Madagascar   Web, www.us-madagascar-embassy.org

Chargé d'Affaires: Velotiana Rakotoanosy Raobelina

Chancery: 2374 Massachusetts Ave. N.W. 20008; (202) 265-5525; Fax, (202) 265-3034; Email, Madagascar.embassy.dc@gmail.com

U.S. Ambassador in Antananarivo: Stuart R. Wilson (Chargé d'Affaires)

State Dept. Country Office: (202) 647-9048

Malawi   Web, www.malawiembassy-dc.org

Ambassador: Edward Yakobe Sawerengera

Chancery: 2408 Massachusetts Ave. N.W., 20008; (202) 721-0270; Fax, (202) 721-0288

U.S. Ambassador in Lilongwe: Virginia E. Palmer

State Dept. Country Office: (202) 647-9856

Malaysia

Web, www.kln.gov.my/web/usa_washington

Ambassador: Zulhasnan Rafique

Chancery: 3516 International Court N.W. 20008; (202) 572-9700; Fax, (202) 572-9882; Email, mwashington@kln.gov.my

U.S. Ambassador in Kuala Lumpur: Kamala Shirin Lakhdhir

State Dept. Country Office: (202) 647-4932

Maldives   Web, www.maldivesmission.com

Ambassador: Ali Naseer Mohamed (in New York)

Chancery: 801 2nd Ave., #202E, New York, NY 10017; (212) 599-6194; Fax, (212) 661-6405

U.S. Ambassador: Atul Keshap (resident in Colombo, Sri Lanka)

State Dept. Country Office: (202) 647-1078

Mali   Web, www.maliembassy.us

Ambassador: Mamdou Nimaga

Chancery: 2130 R St. N.W. 20008; (202) 332-2249; Fax, (202) 332-6603

Social Media: Twitter, @EmbassyofMali

U.S. Ambassador in Bamako: Gregory L. Garland (Chargé d'Affaires)

State Dept. Country Office: (202) 647-3469

Malta

Web, https://foreignaffairs.gov.mt/en/Embassies/Me_United_States

Ambassador: Keith Azzopardi

Chancery: 2017 Connecticut Ave. N.W. 20008; (202) 462-3611; Fax, (202) 387-5470; Email, maltaembassy.washington@gov.mt

U.S. Ambassador in Valletta: Mark A. Schapiro (Chargé d'Affaires)

State Dept. Country Office: (202) 647-3151

Marshall Islands   Web, www.rmiembassyus.org

Ambassador: Gerald M. Zackios

Chancery: 2433 Massachusetts Ave. N.W. 20008; (202) 234-5414; Fax, (202) 232-3236; Email, info@rmiembassyus.org

U.S. Ambassador in Majuro: Karen B. Stewart

State Dept. Country Office: (202) 736-4683

Mauritania

Ambassador: Mohamedoun Daddah

Chancery: 2129 Leroy Pl. N.W. 20008; (202) 232-5700; Fax, (202) 319-2623

U.S. Ambassador in Nouakchott: Michael J. Dodman
State Dept. Country Office: (202) 647-3468

Mauritius

Web, www1.govmu.org/portal/sites/mfamission/
washington/index.htm

Ambassador: Sooroojdev Phokeer
Chancery: 1709 N St. N.W. 20036; (202) 244-1491;
Fax, (202) 966-0983; Email, mauritius.embassy@
verizon.net or washingtonemb@govmu.org
U.S Ambassador in Port Louis: David Reimer
State Dept. Country Office: (202) 736-9048

Mexico   Web, www.embassyofmexico.org

Ambassador: Martha Bárcena Coqui
Chancery: 1911 Pennsylvania Ave. N.W. 20006; (202)
728-1600; Fax, (202) 728-1698; Email, mexembusa@
sre.gob.mx
Social Media: Facebook, www.facebook.com/
EmbamexEUA; Twitter, @EmbamexEUA
U.S. Ambassador in Mexico City: Roberta S. Jacobson
State Dept. Country Office: (202) 647-8766

Micronesia   Web, www.fsmembassydc.org

Ambassador: Akillino H. Susaia
Chancery: 1725 N St. N.W. 20036; (202) 223-4383;
Fax, (202) 223-4391
U.S. Ambassador in Kolonia: Robert A. Riley
State Dept. Country Office: (202) 736-4683

Moldova   Web, www.sua.mfa.md/about-embassy-en

Ambassador: Cristina Balan
Chancery: 2101 S St. N.W. 20008; (202) 667-1130;
Fax, (202) 667-2624; Email, washington@mfa.md
Social Media: Facebook, www.facebook.com/
MoldovainUS; Twitter, @MoldovaEmbUS
U.S. Ambassador in Chisinau: Dereck J. Hogan
State Dept. Country Office: (202) 647-6733

Monaco   Web, www.monacodc.org

Ambassador: Maguy Maccario Doyle
Chancery: 888 17th St. N.W., #500, 20006; (202) 234-1530;
Fax, (202) 244-7656; Email, info@monacodc.org
Social Media: Facebook; www.facebook.com/
EmbassyofMonacoDC; Twitter, @MonacoEmbassyDC
U.S. Ambassador: Jamie McCourt (resident in Paris,
France)
State Dept. Country Office: (202) 647-3072

Mongolia   Web, www.mongolianembassy.us

Ambassador: Bugaa Altangerel
Chancery: 2833 M St. N.W. 20007; (202) 333-7117;
Fax, (202) 298-9227; Email, washinton@mfa.gov.mn
U.S. Ambassador in Ulaanbaatar: Manuel P. Micaller
(Chargé d'Affaires)
State Dept. Country Office: (202) 647-7628

Montenegro

Ambassador: Nebojša Kaluđerović
Chancery: 1610 New Hampshire Ave. N.W. 20009; (202)
234-6108; Fax, (202) 234-6109; Email, usa@mfa.gov.me
U.S. Ambassador in Podgorica: Judy Rising Reinke
State Dept. Country Office: (202) 647-7660

Morocco   Web, www.embassyofmorocco.us

Ambassador: Lalla Joumala Alaoui
Chancery: 3508 International Dr. N.W., 20008; (202) 462-
7979; Fax, (202) 462-7643
Social Media: Twitter, @Morocco_usa
U.S. Ambassador in Rabat: Stephanie Miley (Chargé
d'Affaires)
State Dept. Country Office: (202) 647-1724

Mozambique

Ambassador: Carlos Dos Santos
Chancery: 1525 New Hampshire Ave. N.W. 20036;
(202) 293-7146; Fax, (202) 835-0245;
Email, embamoc@aol.com
U.S. Ambassador in Maputo: H. Dean Pittman
State Dept. Country Office: (202) 647-9857

Myanmar (Burma)

Web, www.mewashingtondc.org

Ambassador: Aung Lynn
Chancery: 2300 S St. N.W. 20008; (202) 332-3344;
Fax, (202) 332-4351; Email, pyi.thayar@verizon.net
U.S. Ambassador in Rangoon: Scot Marciel
State Dept. Country Office: (202) 647-0056

Namibia   Web, www.namibianembassyusa.org

Ambassador: Monica N. Nashandi
Chancery: 1605 New Hampshire Ave. N.W. 20009; (202)
986-0540; Fax, (202) 986-0443; Email, info@
namibiaembassyusa.org
Social Media: Facebook, www.facebook.com/
namibiaembassyusa
U.S. Ambassador in Windhoek: Lisa Johnson
State Dept. Country Office: (202) 647-9858

Nauru   Web, www.un.int/nauru

Ambassador: Marlene I. Moses (in New York)
Chancery: 801 2nd Ave., 3rd Floor, New York, NY 10017;
(212) 937-0074; Fax, (212) 937-0079; Email, nauru@
onecommonwealth.org
U.S. Ambassador: Judith Beth Cefkin (resident in Suva,
Fiji)
State Dept. Country Office: (202) 647-5156

Nepal   Web, us.nepalembassy.gov.np

Ambassador: Arjun Kumar Karki
Chancery: 2131 Leroy Pl. N.W. 20008; (202) 667-4550;
Fax, (202) 667-5534; Email, eonwashington@mofa
.gov.np

Social Media: Facebook, www.facebook.com/
    nepalembassyUSA; Twitter, @nepalembassyusa
U.S. Ambassador in Kathmandu: Randy Berry
State Dept. Country Office: (202) 647-2941

The Netherlands   Web, http://nlintheusa.com

Ambassador: Henne Schuwer
Chancery: 4200 Linnean Ave. N.W. 20008; (202) 244-
    5300; Fax, (202) 362-3430; Email, was-ppc@
    minbuza.nl
Social Media: Facebook, www.facebook.com/
    NLintheUSA; Twitter, @NLintheUSA
U.S. Ambassador at The Hague: Peter Hoekstra
State Dept. Country Office: (202) 647-6555

New Zealand

Web, www.mfat.govt.nz/en/countries-and-regions/
    north-america/united-states-of-america/new-zealand-
    embassy-washington

Ambassador: Rosemary Banks
Chancery: 37 Observatory Circle N.W. 20008; (202)
    328-4800; Fax, (202) 667-5227; Email, wshinfo@
    mfat.govt.nz
Social Media: Facebook, www.facebook.com/
    NZEmbassyUS; Twitter, @NZAmbassadorUS
U.S. Ambassador in Wellington: Scott Brown
State Dept. Country Office: (202) 736-4745

Nicaragua   Web, www.consuladodenicaragua.com

Ambassador: Francisco Obadiah Campbell Hooker
Chancery: 1627 New Hampshire Ave. N.W. 20009; (202)
    939-6570; Fax, (202) 939-6542; Email, mperalta@
    cancilleria.gob.ni
U.S. Ambassador in Managua: Kevin K. Sullivan
State Dept. Country Office: (202) 647-1510

Niger   Web, www.embassyofniger.org

Ambassador: Hassana Alidou
Chancery: 2204 R St. N.W. 20008; (202) 483-4224;
    Fax, (202) 483-3169; Email, communication@
    embassyofniger.org
U.S. Ambassador in Niamey: Eric P. Whitaker
State Dept. Country Office: (202) 647-2791

Nigeria   Web, www.nigeriaembassyusa.org

Ambassador: Sylvanus Adiewere Nsofor
Chancery: 3519 International Court N.W. 20008; (202)
    800-7201; Email, info@nigeriaembassyusa.org
U.S. Ambassador in Abuja: W. Stuart Symington
State Dept. Country Office: (202) 647-3469

Norway   Web, www.norway.no/en/usa

Ambassador: Kåre R. Aas
Chancery: 2720 34th St. N.W. 20008; (202) 333-6000;
    Fax, (202) 469-3990; Email, emb.washington@mfa.no

Social Media: Facebook, www.facebook.com/
    NorwegianEmbassyinWashington;
    Twitter, @NorwayUS; Instagram, @norwayinus
U.S. Ambassador in Oslo: Kenneth J. Braithwaite
State Dept. Country Office: (202) 647-8178

Oman   Web, www.omani.info

Ambassador: Hunaina Al-Mughairy
Chancery: 2535 Belmont Rd. N.W. 20008; (202) 387-1980;
    Fax, (202) 745-4933; Email, inquiries@mofa.gov.om
U.S. Ambassador in Muscat: Marc J. Sievers
State Dept. Country Office: (202) 647-8821

Pakistan   Web, www.embassyofpakistanusa.org

Ambassador: Asad Majeed Khan
Chancery: 3517 International Court N.W. 20008; (202)
    243-6500; Fax, (202) 686-1534; Email, info@
    embassyofpakistanusa.org
Social Media: Facebook, www.facebook.com/
    PakistanEmbassyDC; Twitter, @PakEmbassyDC;
    YouTube, www.youtube.com/user/pakistanembassy
U.S. Ambassador in Islamabad: Paul W. Jones (Chargé
    d'Affaires)
State Dept. Country Office: (202) 647-9823

Palestine Liberation Organization

On September 10, 2018, the U.S. government ordered the
    PLO mission to the U.S. to close.
On October 18, 2018, the U.S. government merged its
    diplomatic mission serving Palestinians with the U.S.
    embassy in Israel.

Palau   Web, www.palauembassy.org

Ambassador: Hersey Kyota
Chancery: 1701 Pennsylvania Ave. N.W., #200, 20006;
    (202) 349-8598; Email, info@palauembassy.com
Social Media: Facebook, www.facebook.com/
    PalauEmbassyDC
U.S. Ambassador in Koror: Amy J. Hyatt
State Dept. Country Office: (202) 736-4683

Panama   Web, www.embassyofpanama.org

Ambassador: Emanuel Gonzalez-Revilla
Chancery: 2862 McGill Terrace N.W. 20008; (202)
    483-1407; Fax, (202) 483-8413; Email, info@
    embassyofpanama.org
Social Media: Facebook, www.facebook.com/
    EmbassyofPanama; Twitter, @EmbPanama_US
U.S. Ambassador in Panama City: Roxanne Cabral
    (Chargé d'Affaires)
State Dept. Country Office: (202) 647-4992

Papua New Guinea   Web, www.pngembassy.org

Ambassador: Rupa Abraham Mulina
Chancery: 1825 K St. N.W., #1010, 20006; (202) 745-3680;
    Fax, (202) 745-3679; Email, info@pngembassy.org
U.S. Ambassador in Port Moresby: Catherine Ebert-Gray
State Dept. Country Office: (202) 647-5156

Paraguay   Web, www.mre.gov.py/embaparusa

Ambassador: Manuel María Cáceres

Chancery: 2209 Massachusetts Ave. N.W. 20008; (202) 483-6960; Fax, (202) 234-4508; Email, gabineteembaparusa@mre.gov.py

Social Media: Facebook, www.facebook.com/Embajada-del-Paraguay-en-los-Estados-Unidos-1601585323408266

U.S. Ambassador in Asunción: Hugo F. Rodriguez Jr. (Chargé d'Affaires)

State Dept. Country Office: (202) 647-1551

Peru   Web, www.embassyofperu.org

Ambassador: Agustín de Madalengoitia (Chargé d'Affaires)

Chancery: 1700 Massachusetts Ave. N.W. 20036; (202) 833-9860; Fax, (202) 659-8124; Email, digitaldiplomacy@embassyofperu.us

Social Media: Facebook, www.facebook.com/EmbassyPeruInTheUSA; Twitter, @PeruInTheUSA; YouTube, www.youtube.com/user/TheEmbassyofPeru; Instagram, @peruintheusa

U.S. Ambassador in Lima: Krishna R. Urs

State Dept. Country Office: (202) 647-4177

Philippines   Web, www.philippineembassy-usa.org

Ambassador: Jose Manuel G. Romualdez

Chancery: Bataan St., 1600 Massachusetts Ave. N.W. 20036; (202) 467-9300; Fax, (202) 467-9417; Email, ambassador@phembassy-us.org

Social Media: Twitter, @philippinesusa; YouTube, www.youtube.com/user/philippineembassyusa

U.S. Ambassador in Manila: Sung Kim

State Dept. Country Office: (202) 647-2927

Poland   Web, http://washington.mfa.gov.pl/en

Ambassador: Piotr Wilczek

Chancery: 2640 16th St. N.W. 20009; (202) 499-1700; Fax, (202) 328-6271; Email, washington.amb@msz.gov.pl

Social Media: Facebook, www.facebook.com/EmbassyofPolandWashingtonDC; Twitter, @PolishEmbassyUS; YouTube, www.youtube.com/user/PolishEmbassyDC

U.S. Ambassador in Warsaw: Georgette Mosbacher

State Dept. Country Office: (202) 647-4139

Portugal   Web, www.embassyportugal-us.org

Ambassador: Domingos Fezas Vital

Chancery: 2012 Massachusetts Ave. N.W. 20036; (202) 350-5400; Fax, (202) 462-3726; Email, info@embassyportugal-us.org

Social Media: Facebook, www.facebook.com/PortugalintheUS

U.S. Ambassador in Lisbon: George E. Glass

State Dept. Country Office: (202) 647-3151

Qatar   Web, http://washington.embassy.qa/en

Ambassador: Sheikh Meshal Bin Hamad Al-Thani

Chancery: 2555 M St. N.W. 20037; (202) 274-1600; Fax, (202) 237-0061; Email, washington@mofa.gov.qa

Social Media: Twitter, @QatarEmbassyUSA; Instagram, @qatarembassyusa

U.S. Ambassador in Doha: William Grant (Chargé d'Affaires)

State Dept. Country Office: (202) 647-2129

Romania   Web, http://washington.mae.ro/en

Ambassador: George Cristian Maior

Chancery: 1607 23rd St. N.W. 20008; (202) 332-4829; (202) 332-4846; Email, washington@mae.ro

Social Media: Facebook, www.facebook.com/romanian.embassy.us

U.S. Ambassador in Bucharest: Hans Klemm

State Dept. Country Office: (202) 736-7152

Russia   Web, https://washington.mid.ru/en

Ambassador: Anatoly I. Antonov

Chancery: 2650 Wisconsin Ave. N.W. 20007; (202) 939-8907; Fax, (202) 298-5735; Email, rusembusa@mid.ru

Social Media: www.facebook.com/RusEmbUSA; Instagram, @rusembusa; Twitter, @RusEmbUSA

U.S. Ambassador in Moscow: Jon M. Huntsman

State Dept. Country Office: (202) 647-9806

Rwanda   Web, www.rwandaembassy.org

Ambassador: Mathilde Mukantabana

Chancery: 1714 New Hampshire Ave. N.W., 20009; (202) 232-2882; Fax, (202) 232-4544; Email, info@rwandaembassy.org

Social Media: Twitter, @RwandaInUSA; Instagram, @rwandainusa

U.S. Ambassador in Kigali: Peter H. Vrooman

State Dept. Country Office: (202) 647-4965

Saint Kitts and Nevis   Web, http://embassy.gov.kn

Ambassador: Dr. Everson Hull

Chancery: 1627 K St. N.W., 20006; (202) 686-2636; Fax, (202) 686-5740; Email, stkittsnevis@embskn.com

U.S. Ambassador: Linda S. Taglialatela (resident in Bridgetown, Barbados)

State Dept. Country Office: (202) 647-4384

Saint Lucia   Web, www.embassyofstlucia.org

Ambassador: Anton Edmunds

Chancery: 1629 K St. N.W., #1250, 20006; (202) 364-6792 or (571) 527-1375; Fax, (202) 364-6723 or (571) 384-7930; Email, embassydc@gosl.govt.lc

U.S. Ambassador: Linda S. Taglialatela (resident in Bridgetown, Barbados)

State Dept. Country Office: (202) 647-4384

Saint Vincent and the Grenadines

Web, www.embsvg.com

Ambassador: Lou-Anne Gaylene Gilchrist
Chancery: 1627 K St. N.W., #1202, N.W. 20006; (202) 364-6730; Email, mail@embsvg.com
U.S. Ambassador: Linda S. Taglialatela (resident in Bridgetown, Barbados)
State Dept. Country Office: (202) 647-4384

Samoa

Ambassador: Aliioaiga Feturi Elisaia (in New York)
Chancery: 685 3rd Ave., #11021, New York, NY 10017; (212) 599-6196; Fax, (212) 599-0797; Email, samoa@un.int
U.S. Ambassador to Apia: Scott Brown
State Dept. Country Office: (202) 736-4745

San Marino

Ambassador: Paolo Rondelli
Chancery: 1711 N St. N.W., 2nd Floor 20036; (202) 223-2418; Email, smrassistant@gmail.com
San Marino is also represented by the Consul General Abigail (Abby) Rupp.
U.S. Ambassador (Virtual Embassy): Lewis Eisenberg
State Dept. Country Office: (202) 647-3072

São   Tomé and Príncipe

Ambassador: Ovidio Manuel Barbosa Pequeno
Chancery: 1211 Connecticut Ave. N.W., #300, 20036; (202) 775-2075, 2075; Fax, (202) 775-2077; Email, embstpusa@verizon.net
U.S. Ambassador: Cynthia Akuetteh (resident in Libreville, Gabon)
State Dept. Country Office: (202) 647-3138

Saudi Arabia   Web, www.saudiembassy.net

Ambassador: Prince Khalid bin Salman bin Abdulaziz
Chancery: 601 New Hampshire Ave. N.W. 20037; (202) 342-3800; Fax, (202) 944-5983
Social Media: Twitter, @SaudiEmbassyUSA; YouTube, www.youtube.com/user/saudiembassyusa
U.S. Ambassador in Riyadh: Christopher Henzel (Chargé d'Affaires)
State Dept. Country Office: (202) 647-7550

Senegal   Web, www.ambasenegal-us.org

Ambassador: Momar Diop
Chancery: 2215 M St. N.W. 20037; (202) 234-0540; Fax, (202) 629-2961; Email, contact@ambasenegal-us.org
U.S. Ambassador in Dakar: Tulinabo Salama Mushingi
State Dept. Country Office: (202) 647-0033

Serbia   Web, www.serbiaembusa.org

Ambassador: Djerdj Matkovic

Chancery: 2233 Wisconsin Ave., N.W. #410 20007; (202) 332-0333; Fax, (202) 332-3933; Email, contact@ambasenegal-us.org
Social Media: Facebook, www.facebook.com/SerbiaEmbWashin; Twitter, @SerbiaEmbWashin
U.S. Ambassador in Belgrade: Kyle Scott
State Dept. Country Office: (202) 647-0310
Seychelles Web, www.mfa.gov.sc
Ambassador: Marie Louise Cecile Potter (in New York)
Chancery: 685 3rd Ave., 11th Floor, #1107, New York, NY 10017; (212) 687-9766, Fax, (212) 972-1786; Email, Seychelles@un.int
Social Media: Twitter, @SeychellesMFA
U.S. Ambassador: David Reimer
State Dept. Country Office: (202) 647-2791

Sierra Leone   Web, www.embassyofsierraleone.net

Ambassador: Sidique Abou-Bakarr Wai
Chancery: 1701 19th St. N.W. 20009-1605; (202) 939-9261; Fax, (202) 483-1798; Email, info@embassyofsierraleone.net
Social Media: Facebook, www.facebook.com/sierraleoneembassy; Twitter, @slembassy_usa
U.S. Ambassador in Freetown: Maria E. Brewer
State Dept. Country Office: (202) 647-1540

Singapore   Web, www.mfa.gov.sg/washington

Ambassador: Ashok Kumar Mirpuri
Chancery: 3501 International Pl. N.W. 20008; (202) 537-3100; Fax, (202) 537-0876; Email, singemb_was@mfa.sg
Social Media: Facebook, www.facebook.com/SingaporeEmbassyDC; Twitter, @SingaporeEmbDC
U.S. Ambassador in Singapore: Stephanie Syptak-Ramnath (Chargé d'Affaires)
State Dept. Country Office: (202) 647-1823

Slovakia   Web, www.mzv.sk/washington

Ambassador: Ivan Korčok
Chancery: 3523 International Ct. N.W. 20008; (202) 237-1054; Fax, (202) 237-6438; Email, emb.washington@mzv.sk
Social Media: Facebook, www.facebook.com/SlovakEmbassyUS?fref=pb&hc_location=profile_browser; Twitter, @SlovakEmbassyUS; YouTube, www.youtube.com/user/mzvsr
U.S. Ambassador in Bratislava: Adam Sterling
State Dept. Country Office: (202) 647-3191

Slovenia   Web, http://washington.embassy.si

Ambassador: Stanislav Vidovič
Chancery: 2410 California St. N.W., 20008; (202) 386-6601; Fax, (202) 386-6633; Email, sloembassy.washington@gov.si
Social Media: Facebook, www.facebook.com/SLOembassyUSA; Twitter, @SLOinUSA
U.S. Ambassador in Ljubljana: Gautam Rana (Chargé d'Affaires)
State Dept. Country Office: (202) 647-4782

Solomon Islands   Web, www.mfaet.gov.sb

Ambassador: Robert Sisilo (in New York)
Chancery: 800 2nd Ave., #400L, New York, NY 10017; (212) 599-6192; Fax, (212) 661-8925; Email, simun@solomons.com
U.S. Ambassador: Catherine Ebert-Gray (resident in Port Moresby, Papua New Guinea)
State Dept. Country Office: (202) 647-5156

Somalia   Web, www.somaliembassydc.net

Ambassador: Ahmed Isse Awad
Chancery: 1705 DeSales St. N.W. #300 20036-4421; (202) 296-0570; Fax, (202) 833-1523;
Social Media: Twitter, @SomaliEmbDC
The Washington embassy ceased operations May 1991. The U.S. embassy in Mogadishu is unstaffed. Diplomatic relations are handled out of the U.S. Embassy in Nairobi, Kenya.
U.S. Ambassador in Mogadishu: Donald Y. Yamamoto
State Dept. Country Office: (202) 647-8284

South Africa   Web, www.saembassy.org

Ambassador: Mninwa Mahlangu
Chancery: 3051 Massachusetts Ave. N.W. 20008; (202) 232-4400; Fax, (202) 265-1607
Social Media: Facebook, www.facebook.com/The-Embassy-of-the-Republic-of-South-Africa-in-the-United-States-497986973581493; Twitter, @SAEmbassyUS
U.S. Ambassador in Pretoria: Jessye Lapenn (Chargé d'Affaires)
State Dept. Country Office: (202) 647-9862

South Sudan   Web, www.southsudanembassyusa.org

Ambassador: Phillip Jada Natana
Chancery: 1015 31st St. N.W., #300, 20007; (202) 293-7940; Fax, (202) 293-7941; Email, info@southsudanembassydc.com
U.S. Ambassador in Juba: Thomas Hushek
State Dept. Country Office: (202) 647-4531

Spain

Web, www.exteriores.gob.es/Embajadas/WASHINGTON

Ambassador: Santiago Cabanas Ansorena
Chancery: 2375 Pennsylvania Ave. N.W. 20037; (202) 452-0100; Fax, (202) 833-5670; Email, emb.washington@maec.es
Social Media: Facebook, www.facebook.com/SpainInTheUSA; Twitter, @SpainInTheUSA; YouTube, www.youtube.com/channel/UCNHaRlVcSvDhoGIaZY8Wz0A; Instagram, @spainintheusa
U.S. Ambassador in Madrid: Richard Duke Buchan III
State Dept. Country Office: (202) 647-3151

Sri Lanka   Web, www.slembassyusa.org

Ambassador: Sarath Dissanayake (Chargé d'Affaires)
Chancery: 3025 Whitehaven St. N.W. 20008; (202) 483-4025; Fax, (202) 232-7181; Email, slembassy@slembassyusa.org
Social Media: Facebook, www.facebook.com/slembassyusa; Twitter, @EmbassyofSL
U.S. Ambassador in Colombo: Alaina Teplitz
State Dept. Country Office: (202) 647-1078

Sudan   Web, www.sudanembassy.org

Ambassador: Maowia Osman Khalid
Chancery: 2210 Massachusetts Ave. N.W. 20008; (202) 338-8565; Fax, (202) 667-2406
U.S. Ambassador in Khartoum: Steven Koutsis (Chargé d'Affaires)
State Dept. Country Office: (202) 647-4531

Suriname   Web, www.surinameembassy.org

Ambassador: Niermala Badrising
Chancery: 4201 Connecticut Ave. N.W., #400, 20008; (202) 629-4302; Fax, (202) 629-4769; Email, amb.vs@foreignaffairs.gov.sr
U.S. Ambassador in Paramaribo: Karen L. Williams
State Dept. Country Office: (202) 647-4719

Swaziland

Ambassador: Njabuliso Gwebu
Chancery: 1712 New Hampshire Ave. N.W. 20009; (202) 234-5002; Fax, (202) 234-8254; Email, info@swazilandembassyus.com or embassy@swaziland-usa.com
U.S. Ambassador in Mbabane: Lisa Peterson
State Dept. Country Office: (202) 647-9852

Sweden

Web, www.swedenabroad.se/en/embassies/usa-washington

Ambassador: Karin Olofsdotter
Chancery: 2900 K St. N.W. 20007; (202) 467-2600; Fax, (202) 467-2699; Email, ambassaden.washington@gov.se
Social Media: Facebook, www.facebook.com/swedeninusa; Twitter, @SwedeninUSA; Instagram, @swedeninusa
U.S. Ambassador in Stockholm: Clifford G. Bond (Chargé d'Affaires)
State Dept. Country Office: (202) 647-9980

Switzerland   Web, www.eda.admin.ch/washington

Ambassador: Martin Dahinden
Chancery: 2900 Cathedral Ave. N.W. 20008; (202) 745-7900; Fax, (202) 387-2564; Email, was.information@eda.admin.ch
Social Media: Facebook, www.facebook.com/SwissEmbassyUSA; Twitter, @SwissEmbassyUSA; YouTube, www.youtube.com/user/ThinkSwiss

U.S. Ambassador in Bern: Edward T. McMullen
State Dept. Country Office: (202) 647-3238

Syria

The U.S. Embassy in Damascus suspended operations in February 2012, and no longer provides routine consular services. Emergency assistance to U.S. citizens is available through the U.S. Interests Section of the Embassy of the Czech Republic in Damascus or the U.S. Embassy in Amman, Jordan.
Chancery (currently closed): 2215 Wyoming Ave. N.W. 20008; (202) 232-6313; Fax, (202) 234-9548; Email, info@syrembassy.net
U.S. Special Envoy: James F. Jeffrey
State Dept. Country Office: (202) 647-2670

Taiwan   Web, www.taiwanembassy.org/us_en

Representation is maintained by the Taipei Economic and Cultural Representatives Office in the United States: 4201 Wisconsin Ave. N.W. 20016; (202) 895-1800; Email, usa@mofa.gov.tw
Social Media: Facebook, www.facebook.com/TECRO.USA; Twitter, @TECRO_USA
Representative of the Republic of China (in Taiwan): Stanley Kao
The United States maintains unofficial relations with Taiwan through the American Institute in Taiwan.
American Institute: 1700 N. Moore St., #1700, Arlington, VA 22209-1385; (703) 525-8474; Kin W. Moy, Director
State Dept. Country Office: (202) 647-7711

Tajikistan   Web, www.tjus.org

Ambassador: Abdujabbor Shirinov
Chancery: 1005 New Hampshire Ave. N.W. 20037; (202) 223-6090; Fax, (202) 223-6091; Email, tajikistan@verizon.net
U.S. Ambassador in Dushanbe: Kevin Covert (Chargé d'Affaires)
State Dept. Country Office: (202) 647-6757

Tanzania   Web, www.tanzaniaembassy-us.org

Ambassador: Wilson Masilingi
Chancery: 1232 22nd St. N.W. 20037; (202) 884-1080; Fax, (202) 797-7408; Email, ubalozi@tanzaniaembassy-us.org
Social Media: Facebook, www.facebook.com/TanzaniaEmbassyUS
U.S. Ambassador in Dar es Salaam: Immi Patterson (Chargé d'Affaires)
State Dept. Country Office: (202) 647-8295

Thailand   Web, www.thaiembdc.org

Ambassador: Virachai Plasai
Chancery: 1024 Wisconsin Ave. N.W. 20007; (202) 944-3600; Fax, (202) 944-3611
Social Media: Facebook, www.facebook.com/Thaiembdc; Twitter, @ThaiEmbDC; YouTube, www.youtube.com/channel/UCEo3cdhO2qv6Ql1R7e6qZsQ

U.S. Ambassador in Bangkok: Peter Haymond (Chargé d'Affaires)
State Dept. Country Office: (202) 647-0036

Timor-Leste   Web, www.timorlesteembassy.org

Ambassador: Domingos Sarmento Alves
Chancery: 4201 Connecticut Ave. N.W., #504, 20008; (202) 966-3202; Fax, (202) 966-3205; Email, info@timorlesteembassy.org
Social Media: Facebook, www.facebook.com/Embassy-of-Timor-Leste-in-Washington-DC-USA-171109652252
U.S. Ambassador in Dili: Kathleen M. Fitzpatrick
State Dept. Country Office: (202) 647-2769

Togo   Web, http://embassyoftogousa.com

Ambassador: Frédéric Edem Hegbe
Chancery: 2208 Massachussetts Ave., N.W. 20008; (202) 234-4212; Fax, (202) 232-3190; Email, embassyoftogo@hotmail.com
U.S. Ambassador in Lomé: David R. Gilmour
State Dept. Country Office: (202) 647-4412

Tonga

Web, http://tongaconsul.com, www.un.int/tonga

Consul General (in California): Sela Tukia
Consulate-General: 1350 Old Bayshore Hwy, #610, Burlingame, CA 94010; (650) 685-1001; Email, consulategeneraloftonga@gmail.com
Tonga maintains a Permanent Mission to the United Nations.
Ambassador to the UN: Mahe 'Uli'uli Sandhurst Tupouniua
UN Chancery: 250 E. 51st St., New York, NY 10022; (917) 369-1025; Fax, (917) 369-1024; Email, tongaunmission@aol.com
U.S. Ambassador: Judith Beth Cefkin (resident in Suva, Fiji)
State Dept. Country Office: (202) 647-5156

Trinidad and Tobago

Web, https://foreign.gov.tt/missions-consuls/tt-missions-abroad/diplomatic-missions/embassy-washington-dc-us

Ambassador: Anthony Phillips-Spencer
Chancery: 1708 Massachusetts Ave. N.W. 20036; (202) 467-6490; Fax, (202) 785-3130; Email, embdcinfo@foreign.gov.tt
U.S. Ambassador in Port-of-Spain: Joseph N. Mondello
State Dept. Country Office: (202) 647-4384

Tunisia   Web, www.tunisianembassy.org

Ambassador: Fayçal Gouia
Chancery: 1515 Massachusetts Ave. N.W. 20005; (202) 862-1850; Fax, (202) 862-1858; Email, info@tunconsusa.org
Social Media: Facebook, www.facebook.com/TUNISIANEMBASSYUSA; Twitter, @TuniEmbassy

U.S. Ambassador in Tunis: Donald Blome
State Dept. Country Office: (202) 647-4676

Turkey   Web, http://vasington.be.mfa.gov.tr

Ambassador: Serdar Kiliç
Chancery: 2525 Massachusetts Ave. N.W. 20008; (202) 612-6701; Fax, (202) 612-6744; Email, embassy .washingtondc@mfa.gov.tr
Social Media: Facebook, www.facebook.com/ turkishembassy; Twitter, @TurkishEmbassy
U.S. Ambassador in Ankara: Jeffrey M. Hovenier (Chargé d'Affaires)
State Dept. Country Office: (202) 647-9749

Turkmenistan   Web, http://usa.tmembassy.gov.tm

Ambassador: Meret B. Orazov
Chancery: 2207 Massachusetts Ave. N.W. 20008; (202) 588-1500; Fax, (202) 280-1003; Email, turkmenembassyus@verizon.net
U.S. Ambassador in Ashgabat: Allen Mustard
State Dept. Country Office: (202) 647-9024

Tuvalu   Web, www.un.int/tuvalu/tuvalu/embassies

Ambassador: Samuelu Laloniu (in New York)
Chancery: 800 E. 2nd Ave., #400B, New York, NY 10017; (212) 490-0534; Fax, (212) 808-4975; Email, Tuvalu. un@gmail.com
U.S. Ambassador: Judith Beth Cefkin (resident in Suva, Fiji)
State Dept. Country Office: (202) 647-2349

Uganda   Web, https://washington.mofa.go.ug

Ambassador: Mull Ssebujja Katende
Chancery: 5911 16th St. N.W. 20011; (202) 726-7100; Fax, (202) 726-1727; Email, washington@mofa.go.ug or info@ugandaembassy.org
U.S. Ambassador in Kampala: Deborah R. Malac
State Dept. Country Office: (202) 647-9742

Ukraine   Web, http://usa.mfa.gov.ua

Ambassador: Valeriy Chaly
Chancery: 3350 M St. N.W. 20007; (202) 349-2963; Fax, (202) 333-0817; Email, emb_us@mfa.gov.ua
Social Media: Facebook, www.facebook.com/ukr.embassy .usa; Twitter, @UKRintheUSA
U.S. Ambassador in Kyiv: Marie L. Yovanovitch
State Dept. Country Office: (202) 647-8671

United Arab Emirates

Web, www.uae-embassy.org

Ambassador: Yousef Al Otaiba
Chancery: 3522 International Court N.W., #400, 20008; (202) 243-2400; Fax, (202) 243-2432
Social Media: Facebook, www.facebook.com/UAEmbassy US; Twitter, @UAEEmbassyUS; YouTube, www .youtube.com/channel/UCAtFXa5-B8SP7zdBMqipEnQ
U.S. Ambassador in Abu Dhabi: Steve C. Bondy
State Dept. Country Office: (202) 647-6562

United Kingdom

Web, www.gov.uk/government/world/organisations/ british-embassy-washington

Ambassador: Sir Nigel Kim Darroch
Chancery: 3100 Massachusetts Ave. N.W. 20008; (202) 588-6500; Fax, (202) 588-7870; Email, britishembassyenquiries@gmail.com
Social Media: Facebook, www.facebook.com/ukinusa; Twitter, @UKinUSA
U.S. Ambassador in London: Robert Wood Johnson
State Dept. Country Office: (202) 647-2441

United Nations   Web, https://unicwash.org

Secretary-General: António Guterres
Information Center: 1775 K St. N.W., #500, 20006; (202) 331-8670; Fax, (202) 331-9191; Email, unicdc@unic.org
Social Media: Facebook, www.facebook.com/ UNWashington; Twitter, @unicdc; YouTube, www.youtube.com/user/UNWashington; Instagram, @unicdc
U.S. Ambassador: Jonathan Cohen
State Dept. Country Office: (202) 736-7555

Uruguay

Web, www.mrree.gub.uy/frontend/page?1,7,442,P,E,0

Ambassador: Carlos Gianelli Derois
Chancery: 1913 Eye St. N.W. 20006; (202) 331-1313; Fax, (202) 331-8142; Email, urueeuu@mrree.gub.uy
U.S. Ambassador in Montevideo: Kelly Keiderling
State Dept. Country Office: (202) 647-1551

Uzbekistan   Web, www.uzbekistan.org

Ambassador: Javlon Vakhabov
Chancery: 1746 Massachusetts Ave. N.W. 20036; (202) 887-5300; Fax, (202) 293-6804; Email, info.washington@mfa.uz
Social Media: Facebook, www.facebook.com/ UZEmbassyDC; Twitter, @UZEmbassyDC
U.S. Ambassador in Tashkent: Alan D. Meltzer (Chargé d'Affaires)
State Dept. Country Office: (202) 647-6765

Vanuatu   Web, www.un.int/vanuatu

Vanuatu maintains a Permanent Mission to the United Nations.
Ambassador to the UN: Odo Tevi
UN Chancery: 800 E. 2nd Ave., #400B, New York, NY 10017; (212) 661-4303; Fax, (212) 661-5544; Email, vanunmis@aol.com
U.S. Ambassador: Catherine Ebert-Gray (resident in Port Moresby, Papua New Guinea)
State Dept. Country Office: (202) 647-5156

Vatican City   (See The Holy See)

Venezuela   Web, eeuu.embajada.gob.ve

Chargé d'Affaires: Carlos J. Ron

Chancery: 1099 30th St. N.W. 20007; (202) 342-2214; Fax, (202) 342-6820; Email, despacho.embveus@ mppre.gob.ve

Social Media: Facebook, www.facebook.com/ VenezuelaInUS; Twitter, @VenezuelaInUS; Instagram, @venezuelainus

U.S. Ambassador in Caracas: James Story (Chargé d'Affaires)

State Dept. Country Office: (202) 647-4984

Vietnam   Web, http://vietnamembassy-usa.org

Ambassador: Ha Kim Ngoc

Chancery: 1233 20th St. N.W., #400, 20036; (202) 861-0737; Fax, (202) 861-0917; Email, info@ vietnamembassy.us

U.S. Ambassador in Hanoi: Dan Kritenbrink

State Dept. Country Office: (202) 647-4023

Western Samoa   (See Samoa)

Yemen   Web, www.yemenembassy.org

Ambassador: Ahmed Awad Binmubarak

Chancery: 2319 Wyoming Ave. N.W. 20008; (202) 965-4760; Fax, (202) 337-2017; Email, information@ yemenembassy.org

Social Media: Facebook, www.facebook.com/ Yemenembassy.DC; Twitter, @YemenEmbassy_DC

U.S. Ambassador in Sana'a: Matthew H. Tueller

State Dept. Country Office: (202) 647-6558

Zambia   Web, www.zambiaembassy.org

Ambassador: Ngosa Simbyakula

Chancery: 2200 R St. N.W. 20008; (202) 234-4111; Fax, (202) 332-0826; Email, info@zambiaembassy.org

Social Media: Facebook, www.facebook.com/ EmbassyOfTheRepublicOfZambia

U.S. Ambassador in Lusaka: Daniel L. Foote

State Dept. Country Office: (202) 647-9857

Zimbabwe   Web, www.zimembassydc.gov.zw

Ambassador: Ammon M. Mutembwa

Chancery: 1608 New Hampshire Ave. N.W. 20009; (202) 332-7100; Fax, (202) 483-9326; Email, infor33@ zimembassydc.gov.zw

U.S. Ambassador in Harare: Brian A. Nichols

State Dept. Country Office: (202) 647-9852

Freedom of Information Act

Access to government information remains a key issue in Washington. In 1966, Congress passed legislation to broaden access: the Freedom of Information Act, or FOIA (PL 89-487; codified in 1967 by PL 90-23). Amendments to expand access even further were passed into law over President Gerald Ford's veto in 1974 (PL 93-502).

Several organizations in Washington specialize in access to government information. See the "Freedom of Information" section in the Communications and the Media chapter for details (p. 110). The Justice Department electronically publishes a clearinghouse of FOIA information at www.justice.gov/oip/foia-resources.

1966 Act

The 1966 act requires executive branch agencies and independent commissions of the federal government to make records, reports, policy statements, and staff manuals available to citizens who request them, unless the materials fall into one of nine exempted categories:

- secret national security or foreign policy information

- internal personnel practices

- information exempted by law (e.g., income tax returns)

- trade secrets, other confidential commercial or financial information

- inter-agency or intra-agency memos

- personal information, personnel or medical files

- law enforcement investigatory information

- information related to reports on financial institutions

- geological and geophysical information

1974 Amendments

Further clarification of the rights of citizens to gain access to government information came in late 1974, when Congress enacted legislation to remove some of the obstacles that the bureaucracy had erected since 1966. Included in the amendments are provisions that:

- Require federal agencies to publish their indexes of final opinions on settlements of internal cases, policy statements, and administrative staff manuals. If, under special circumstances, the indexes are not published, they are to be furnished to any person requesting them for the cost of duplication. The 1966 law simply required agencies to make such indexes available for public inspection and copying.

- Require agencies to release unlisted documents to someone requesting them with a reasonable description (a change designed to ensure that an agency could not refuse to provide material simply because the applicant could not give its precise title).

- Direct each agency to publish a uniform set of fees for providing documents at the cost of finding and copying them. The amendment allows waiver or reduction of those fees when in the public interest.

- Set time limits for agency responses to requests: ten working days for an initial request; twenty working days for an appeal from an initial refusal to produce documents; a possible ten-working-day extension that can be granted only once in a single case.

- Set a thirty-day time limit for an agency response to a complaint filed in court under the act; provide that the courts give such cases priority attention at the appeal, as well as the trial, level.

- Empower federal district courts to order agencies to produce withheld documents and to examine the contested materials privately (in camera) to determine if they are properly exempted.

- Require annual agency reports to Congress, including a list of all agency decisions to withhold information requested under the act; the reasons; the appeals; the results; all relevant rules; the fee schedule; and the names of officials responsible for each denial of information.

- Allow courts to order the government to pay attorneys' fees and court costs for persons winning suits against them under the act.

- Authorize a court to find that an agency employee has acted capriciously or arbitrarily in withholding information; stipulate that disciplinary action is determined by Civil Service Commission proceedings.

- Amend and clarify the wording of the national defense and national security exemption to make clear that it applies only to properly classified information.

- Amend the wording of the law enforcement exemption to allow withholding of information that, if disclosed, would interfere with enforcement proceedings, deprive someone of a fair trial or hearing, invade personal privacy in an unwarranted way, disclose the identity of a confidential source, disclose investigative techniques, or endanger law enforcement personnel; protect from disclosure all information from a confidential source obtained by a criminal law enforcement agency or a lawful national security investigation.

• Provide that separable non exempt portions of requested material be released after deletion of the exempt portions.

• Require an annual report from the attorney general to Congress.

1976 Government in the Sunshine Act

Passed in 1976 to bolster the FOIA, the Government in the Sunshine Act was designed to further government transparency. In due course, the following amendments were made to Exemption 3 of the FOIA:

• Information pertaining to national defense,

• Related exclusively to internal personnel rules and practices,

• Related to accusation of a crime,

• Related to information where disclosure would constitute a breach of privacy,

• Related to investigatory records where the information would harm the proceedings,

• Related to information that would lead to financial speculation or endanger the stability of any financial institution, and

• Related to the agency's participation in legal proceedings.

1984 Amendments

In 1984 Congress enacted legislation that clarified the requirements of the Central Intelligence Agency (CIA) to respond to citizen requests for information. Included in the amendments are provisions that:

• Authorize the CIA to close from FOIA review certain operational files that contain information on the identities of sources and methods. The measure removed the requirement that officials search the files for material that might be subject to disclosure.

• Reverse a ruling by the Justice Department and the Office of Management and Budget that invoked the Privacy Act to deny individuals FOIA access to information about themselves in CIA records. HR 5164 required the CIA to search files in response to FOIA requests by individuals for information about themselves.

• Require the CIA to respond to FOIA requests for information regarding covert actions or suspected CIA improprieties.

All agencies of the executive branch have issued regulations to implement the Freedom of Information Act. To locate a specific agency's regulations, consult the general index of the *Code of Federal Regulations* under "Information availability" or search in www.USA.gov, "FOIA Regulations."

Electronic Freedom of Information Act of 1996

In 1996 Congress enacted legislation clarifying that electronic documents are subject to the same FOIA disclosure rules as are printed documents. The 1996 law also requires federal agencies to make records available to the public in various electronic formats, such as email, compact disc, and files accessible via the Internet. An additional measure seeks to improve the government's response time on FOIA requests by requiring agencies to report annually on the number of pending requests and how long it will take to respond.

Homeland Security Act of 2002

In 2002 Congress passed legislation that established the Homeland Security Department and exempted from FOIA disclosure rules certain information about national defense systems. Included in the act are provisions that:

• Grant broad exemption from FOIA requirements to information that private companies share with the government about vulnerabilities in the nation's critical infrastructure.

• Exempt from FOIA rules and other federal and state disclosure requirements any information about the critical infrastructure that is submitted voluntarily to a covered federal agency to ensure the security of this infrastructure and protected systems; require accompanying statement that such information is being submitted voluntarily in expectation of nondisclosure protection.

• Require the secretary of homeland security to establish procedures for federal agencies to follow in receiving, caring for, and storing critical infrastructure information that has been submitted voluntarily; provide criminal penalties for the unauthorized disclosure of such information.

Executive Order 13392: Improving Agency Disclosure of Information

On December 14, 2005, President George W. Bush issued Executive Order 13392: Improving Agency Disclosure of Information. The order sought to streamline the effectiveness of government agencies in responding to FOIA requests and to reduce backlogs of FOIA requests. The order did not expand the information available under FOIA. The executive order provided:

• A chief FOIA officer (at the assistant secretary or equivalent level) of each government agency to monitor FOIA compliance throughout the agency. The chief FOIA officer must inform agency heads and the attorney general of the agency's FOIA compliance performance.

- A FOIA Requester Service Center that would serve as the first point of contact for a person seeking information concerning the status of a FOIA request and appropriate information about the agency's FOIA response.

- FOIA public liaisons, supervisory officials who would facilitate further action if a requester had concerns regarding how an initial request was handled by the center staff.

- Requirement that the chief FOIA officer review and evaluate the agency's implementation and administration of FOIA pursuant to the executive order. The agency head was mandated to report the findings to the attorney general and to the director of the Office of Management and Budget. The report also must be published on the agency's Web site or in the *Federal Register*. Initial reports were submitted in June 2006, with follow-up plans included in each agency's annual FOIA reports for fiscal years 2006 and 2007 and continuing thereafter.

- The attorney general shall review the agency-specific plans and submit to the president a report on government-wide FOIA implementation. The initial report was submitted in October 2006. The Justice Department publishes annual reports of federal agency compliance on its Web site.

Open Government Act of 2007

On December 31, 2007, President George W. Bush signed the "Openness Promotes Effectiveness in our National (OPEN) Government Act of 2007." The OPEN Government Act amends the Freedom of Information Act (FOIA) by:

- defining "a representative of the news media";

- directing that required attorney fees be paid from an agency's appropriation rather than from the U.S. Treasury's Claims and Judgment Fund;

- prohibiting an agency from assessing search and duplication fees if it fails to comply with FOIA deadlines; and establishing an Office of Government Information Services within the National Archives and Records Administration to review agency compliance with FOIA.

Executive Order 13526: Classified National Security Information

On December 29, 2009, an Executive Order on Classified National Security Information was issued. The Executive Order contains two parts:

- The government may classify certain types of information pertaining to the National Security interests of the United States, even after a FOIA request has been submitted. It may do so if officials believe that keeping the information secret is necessary for National Security.

- Additionally, the order sets a timeline for automatic declassification of old information that has not been specifically tagged as needing to remain secret.

H.R. 4173: The Dodd–Frank Wall Street Reform and Consumer Protection Act

H.R. 4173 was passed in both the House and Senate and signed by President Barack Obama on July 21, 2010. The law has specific implications for the FOIA, and they are as follows:

- Section 9291 of the statute shields the Securities and Exchange Commission (SEC) from FOIA requests, because of the worry that FOIA requests could potentially hinder SEC investigations.

S. 3717, a Bill to Amend the Securities Exchange Act of 1934, the Investment Company Act of 1940, and the Investment Advisers Act of 1940 to Provide for Certain Disclosures Under Section 552 of Title 5, United States Code, (Commonly Referred to as the Freedom of Information Act), and for Other Purposes

This legislation passed both the House and Senate in late September 2010, and it was signed by President Obama on October 5, 2010. The laws FOIA applications are as follows:

- The provision in S. 3717 essentially rolls back the shielding of the SEC from FOIA requests, as previously mandated by Section 9291 of H.R. 4173.

FOIA Oversight and Implementation Act of 2014 (the FOIA Act)

A bill introduced by the House on March 15, 2013, to amend the Freedom of Information Act to make it easier to request and receive information. This bill passed the House unanimously on February 25, 2014. Under the amendment, the Office of Management and Budget would be required to operate a free website where users could submit requests for records and receive information on the status of said request. The bill would also:

- Require agencies to determine whether the release of agency records would contribute significantly to public understanding of the operations or activities of government

- Require agencies to document additional search or duplication fees

- Require agencies to submit annual FOIA reports to the Director of the Office of Government Information Services, in addition to the Attorney General

- Expand the duties of the Chief FOIA Officer of each agency to require an annual compliance review of FOIA requirements

- Establish the Chief FOIA Officers Council to develop recommendations for increasing compliance with FOIA requirements

- Require each agency to update its FOIA regulations within 180 days of the enactment of this Act

- Require the Inspector General of each federal agency to:
   ♦ Periodically review compliance with FOIA disclosure requirements, including the timely processing of requests, assessment of fees and fee waivers, and the use of disclosure exemptions; and

   ♦ Make recommendations to the head of an agency, including recommendations for disciplinary action. Make the improper withholding of information under FOIA a basis for disciplinary action

FOIA Improvement Act of 2014

A bill introduced by the Senate on June 24, 2014, to improve the Freedom of Information Act. This bill passed the Senate unanimously on December 8, 2014. However, it was not brought to a vote by the House despite its resemblance to the FOIA Act. The legislation would:

- Require agencies to electronically make available disclosed agency records to the public

- Reduce the ability of an agency to charge fees for a request if the agency does not meet the FOIA deadline

- Limit the terms by which an agency can determine records exempt from FOIA

- Put a time limit of twenty-five years on Exemption 5 (b5)

- Expand the duties of the Chief FOIA Officer of each agency to require an annual compliance review of FOIA requirements

- Expand the duties of the Chief FOIA Officer of each agency to require an annual compliance review of FOIA requirements

- Establish the Chief FOIA Officers Council to develop recommendations for increasing compliance with FOIA requirements

- Require each agency to update its FOIA regulations within 180 days of the enactment of this Act

- Require the Inspector General of each federal agency to:
   ♦ Periodically review compliance with FOIA disclosure requirements, including the timely processing of requests, assessment of fees and fee waivers, and the use of disclosure exemptions; and

   ♦ Make recommendations to the head of an agency, including recommendations for disciplinary action. Make the improper withholding of information under FOIA a basis for disciplinary action

Justice Dept. "Proactive Disclosure Pilot" of 2015

On July 4, 2015, the Justice Dept. announced a new pilot program at seven agencies designed to test the feasibility of posting online FOIA responses so that they are available to the individual requester as well as the general public. Agencies involved in the pilot program are the Millennium Challenge Corporation, the Office of the Director of National Intelligence, the Environmental Protection Agency, and sections of the Defense, Homeland Security and Justice Depts., the National Archives and Records Administration and the Office of Information Policy. The purpose of the pilot is to determine the policy implementation costs, the effect on staff, and the effect on government stakeholders, as well as the justifications for exceptions.

FOIA Improvement Act of 2016

The act, passed by the House and unanimously by the Senate on June 13, 2016, was signed into law on June 30, 2016. Issues addressed in the act include:

- Requirement for agencies to make available for public inspection in an electronic format records that have been requested three or more times

- Requirement for agencies to establish a minimum of 90 days to file an administrative appeal

- Codification of the "foreseeable harm" standard in that agencies
   ♦ shall withhold information only if the agency reasonably foresees that disclosure would harm an interest protected by an exemption, or if disclosure is prohibited by law
   ♦ shall consider whether partial disclosure of information is possible whenever the agency determines that a full disclosure of a requested record is not possible
   ♦ shall take reasonable steps necessary to segregate and release nonexempt information

● Amendment to Exception 5 stating that the Deliberative process privilege will not apply to records created 25 years or more before the date on which the records were requested

● Notification of the requester, upon extension of a deadline beyond ten days, of right to seek dispute resolution services

● Creation of a new FOIA Council supported by GSA that will consult on a regular basis with requesters

● Addition of the following elements to agency Annual FOIA Reports:

♦ The number of times the agency denied a request for records under subsection (c)

♦ The number of records made available for public inspection in an electronic format under subsection (a)(2)

Justice Dept. "Proactive Disclosure Pilot" Assessment of 2016

Throughout the 2015 Pilot, the Office of Information Policy maintained a collection of data including communications between the involved agencies and OIP, as well as feedback from the public. This information and the findings from its analysis were presented on the DOJ website on June 30, 2016.

Privacy Legislation

Privacy Act

To protect citizens from invasions of privacy by the federal government, Congress passed the Privacy Act of 1974 (PL 93-579). The act permitted individuals for the first time to inspect information about themselves contained in federal agency files and to challenge, correct, or amend the material. The major provisions of the act:

• Permit an individual to have access to personal information in federal agency files and to correct or amend that information.

• Prevent an agency maintaining a file on an individual from making it available to another agency without the individual's consent.

• Require federal agencies to keep records that are necessary, lawful, accurate, and current, and to disclose the existence of all databanks and files containing information on individuals.

• Bar the transfer of personal information to other federal agencies for non-routine use without the individual's prior consent or written request.

• Require agencies to keep accurate accountings of transfers of records and make them available to the individual.

• Prohibit agencies from keeping records on an individual's exercise of First Amendment rights unless the records are authorized by statute, approved by the individual, or within the scope of an official law enforcement activity.

• Permit an individual to seek injunctive relief to correct or amend a record maintained by an agency and permit the individual to recover actual damages when an agency acts in a negligent manner that is "willful or intentional."

• Exempt from disclosure records maintained by the Central Intelligence Agency; records maintained by law enforcement agencies; Secret Service records; statistical information; names of persons providing material used for determining the qualification of an individual for federal government service; federal testing material; and National Archives historical records.

• Provide that an officer or employee of an agency who violates provisions of the act be fined no more than $5,000.

• Prohibit an agency from selling or renting an individual's name or address for mailing list use.

• Require agencies to submit to Congress and to the Office of Management and Budget any plan to establish or alter records. Virtually all agencies of the executive branch have issued regulations to implement the Privacy Act.

• Protections exclude foreigners living in the United States as enacted by President Trump in section 14 of the "Enhancing Public Safety" executive order.

To locate a specific agency's regulations, consult the general index of the Code of Federal Regulations under "Privacy Act" or search in www.USA.gov, "Privacy Act."

USA PATRIOT Act

Following the terrorist attacks of September 11, 2001, Congress passed the USA PATRIOT Act (Uniting and Strengthening America by Providing Appropriate Tools Required to Intercept and Obstruct Terrorism; PL 107-56). Included in the USA PATRIOT Act are provisions that:

• Amend the federal criminal code to authorize the interception of wire, oral, and electronic communications to produce evidence of chemical weapons, terrorism, and computer fraud and abuse.

• Amend the Foreign Intelligence Surveillance Act of 1978 (FISA) to require an application for an electronic surveillance order or search warrant certifying that a significant purpose (formerly, the sole or main purpose) of the surveillance is to obtain foreign intelligence information. The administration of President George W. Bush aggressively defended its use of wiretaps approved by the Foreign Intelligence Surveillance Court, which handles intelligence requests involving suspected spies, terrorists, and foreign agents. Established under FISA, this court operates secretly within the Justice Department.

USA Patriot Improvement and Reauthorization Act of 2005 and USA Patriot Act Additional Reauthorizing Amendments Act of 2006

Some provisions of the USA PATRIOT Act were set to expire at the end of 2005. After a lengthy battle Congress voted to reauthorize the act with some of the more controversial provisions intact, including the FISA amendments and the electronic wiretap provisions. Civil libertarians were concerned with issues regarding four provisions: sections 206 (roving wiretaps), 213 (delayed notice warrants), 215 (business records), and 505 (national security letters).

The Senate addressed some of these concerns in a separate bill, S. 2271, USA PATRIOT Act Additional Reauthorizing Amendments Act of 2006.

On March 9, 2006, the president signed into law the USA PATRIOT Improvement and Reauthorization Act of 2005 as well as the USA PATRIOT Act Additional Reauthorizing Amendments Act of 2006.

The reauthorized USA PATRIOT Act allows for greater congressional oversight and judicial review of section 215 orders, section 206 roving wiretaps, and national security letters. In addition, the act included requirements for high-level approval for section 215 FISA orders for library, bookstore, firearm sale, medical, tax return, and educational records. The act also provided for greater judicial review for delayed notice ("sneak and peek") search warrants. Fourteen of sixteen USA PATRIOT Act provisions were made permanent, and a new sunset date of December 31, 2009, was enacted for sections 206 and 215.

On February 27, 2010, President Barack Obama signed a one-year extension of sections 206 and 215 of the USA PATRIOT Act.

On May 26, 2011, President Barack Obama signed three expiring provisions of the USA PATRIOT Act into law for four more years. These expiring provisions included sections 215, 206, and 6001.

Homeland Security Act of 2002

The Homeland Security Act of 2002 was also passed in the aftermath of the September 11, 2001, terrorist attacks. It contains provisions that:

- Establish the Homeland Security Department.

- Exempt from criminal penalties any disclosure made by an electronic communication service to a federal, state, or local government. In making the disclosure, the service must believe that an emergency involving risk of death or serious physical injury requires disclosure without delay. Any government agency receiving such disclosure must report it to the attorney general.

- Direct the secretary of homeland security to appoint a senior department official to take primary responsibility for information privacy policy.

Protect America Act and Subsequent Follow-Up Legislation

On August 5, 2007, President George W. Bush signed the Protect America Act, which amended the Foreign Intelligence Surveillance Act of 1978 (FISA), declaring that nothing under its definition of "electronic surveillance" shall be construed to encompass surveillance directed at a person reasonably believed to be located outside the United States. Prior to this act, no court permission was obtained for surveillance of parties located outside the United States, though a warrant was required for electronic surveillance of targets within the United States. The Protect America Act allowed the Attorney General or the Director of National Intelligence to direct a third party (i.e., telecommunications provider) to assist with intelligence gathering about individuals located outside the United States and shields such parties from liability without a warrant from the FISA Court. The act did provide FISA Court oversight via requiring the Attorney General to submit to the FISA Court the procedures by which the government determines that such acquisitions do not constitute electronic surveillance. The Attorney General was required to report to the congressional intelligence and judiciary committees semiannually concerning acquisitions made during the previous six-month period.

The Protect America Act was designed as a temporary act to allow intelligence policy officials six months to establish a permanent law. The act expired 180 days later in January; it was briefly reauthorized and expired in February 2008. The Senate passed the FISA Amendments Act of 2007 (S. 2248) in February, which would make many of the provisions of the Protect America Act permanent. However, House leadership objected to many of the provisions. Instead, the House supported its version, the Respected Electronic Surveillance That is Overseen, Reviewed and Effective (RESTORE) Act (H. 3773). This act authorizes the Attorney General and the Director of National Intelligence to conduct electronic surveillance of persons outside the United States in order to acquire foreign intelligence, but places limitations, including the following: The methods must be conducted in a manner consistent with the Fourth Amendment to the U.S. Constitution. The act prohibits targeting of persons reasonably believed to be in the United States (with exceptions). As amended, the bill allowed for limited retroactive immunity for telecommunications service providers. It provided for greater court oversight for targeting procedures, minimization procedures, and guidelines for obtaining warrants. The act expired December 31, 2009, when certain provisions of the PATRIOT Act expired.

Cybersecurity and Infrastructure Security Agency Act of 2018

Signed by President Donald Trump on November 20, 2018, this bill is an amendment to the Homeland Security Act of 2002. It:

- Establishes the Cybersecurity and Infrastructure Security Agency (CISA), a new agency within the Department of Homeland Security tasked with protecting the United States against cyber threats.

- Replaces the National Protection and Programs Directorate (NPPD) with the CISA.

- Creates the position of Director of National Cybersecurity and Infrastructure Security to oversee this agency.

2014–2019 Supreme Court Cases Affecting Privacy

Fernandez v. California

Holding: The Court's decision in *Georgia v. Randolph*, holding that the consent of one occupant is insufficient to authorize police to search a premises if another occupant is present and objects to the search, does not apply when an occupant provides consent well after the objecting occupant has been removed from the premises.

Judgment: Affirmed, 6–3, in an opinion by Justice Alito on February 25, 2014. Justice Scalia and Justice Thomas filed concurring opinions. Justice Ginsburg filed a dissenting opinion in which Justice Sotomayor and Justice Kagan joined.

Navarette v. California

Issue: Whether the Fourth Amendment requires an officer who receives an anonymous tip regarding a drunken or reckless driver to corroborate dangerous driving before stopping the vehicle.

Judgment: Affirmed, 5–4, in an opinion by Justice Thomas on April 22, 2014. Justice Scalia filed a dissenting opinion, in which Justice Ginsburg, Justice Sotomayor, and Justice Kagan joined.

Riley v. California

Issue: Whether evidence admitted at petitioner's trial was obtained in a search of petitioner's cell phone that violated petitioner's Fourth Amendment rights. (Riley's petition had posed a general question about whether the Fourth Amendment allowed police without a warrant to search "the digital contents of an individual's cellphone seized from the person at the time of arrest." In granting review, the Court said it would only rule on this issue: "Whether evidence admitted at [his] trial was obtained in a search of [his] cellphone that violated [his] Fourth Amendment rights.")

Judgment: Reversed and remanded, 9–0, in an opinion by Chief Justice Roberts on June 25, 2014. Justice Alito filed an opinion concurring in part and concurring in the judgment.

United States v. Wurie

Issue: Whether the Fourth Amendment permits the police, without obtaining a warrant, to review the call log of a cellphone found on a person who has been lawfully arrested.

Judgment: Affirmed, 9–0, in an opinion by Chief Justice Roberts on June 25, 2014. Justice Alito filed an opinion concurring in part and concurring in the judgment.

Birchfield v. North Dakota

Issue: A state statute may not criminalize the refusal to submit to a blood test in the absence of a warrant because, while the Fourth Amendment allows for warrantless breath tests incident to an arrest for drunk driving, warrantless blood tests incident to an arrest violate the Fourth Amendment.

Judgment: Affirmed 5–3, in an opinion by Justice Alito, on June 23, 2016. Justice Sotomayor concurred in part and dissented in part, and was joined by Justice Ginsburg. Justice Thomas filed an opinion concurring in the judgment in part and dissenting in part.

Grady v. North Carolina

Issue: Whether or not a search resulting from participation in a North Carolina monitoring program requiring the petitioner to wear a bracelet tracking his whereabouts was reasonable under the Fourth Amendment.

Judgment: Granted, the judgment of the Supreme Court of North Carolina vacated, and the case remanded for further proceedings not inconsistent with this opinion.

Delaware Strong Families v. Matthew Denn

Issue: Whether a state's interest in increasing information concerning those who support the candidates permits it to condition a charity's publication of a nonpartisan voter education guide, which lists all candidates equally and makes no endorsements, upon the immediate and public disclosure of the names and addresses of individuals making unrelated donations over the previous four years.

Judgment: Denied certiorari, 8–1, in an opinion by Justice Thomas on June 28, 2016. The decision upheld Delaware's disclosure of "third party advertisements."

Carpenter v. United States

Issue: Whether the government is violating the Fourth Amendment by accessing individual's historical cell phone location records via third-party communication providers without a warrant.

Judgment: Affirmed, 5–4, in an opinion by Justice Roberts on June 22, 2018. Justices Kennedy, Thomas, Alito and Gorsuch all filed dissenting opinions on the ruling.

State Laws Regarding Privacy Legislation Passed since 2018

Alabama Data Breach Notification Act of 2018

On March 28, 2018, Governor Kay Ivey signed the Alabama Data Breach Notification Act into law, making Alabama the last state to pass legislature requiring data breach notifications. This law, which went into effect on June 1, 2018, mandates that "covered entities" and "third-party agents" must inform individuals of security breaches concerning their personal information.

California Consumer Privacy Act

On June 28, 2018, Governor Jerry Brown signed the California Consumer Privacy Act, designed to protect the personal information of consumers. The four basic rights afforded to citizens under this act are 1) the right to understand what information a business has gathered, 2) the right to prevent businesses from selling their information, 3) the right to demand that their information be deleted by businesses, and 4) the right to guarantee that their services are not impacted by a decision to not share their personal information. Introduced on January 3, 2018, by State Senator Robert Hertzberg and State Assembly Member Ed Chau, the new law will go into effect in 2020.

Colorado Protections for Consumer Data Privacy Law

The Colorado Protections for Consumer Data Privacy Law, signed on May 29, 2018, went into effect on September 1, 2018. This new law specifies what constitutes Personal Identifiable Information (PII) and tasks personal data companies to create security protocols to protect the PII of their customers. It also gives companies up to 30 days to notify individuals about breaches of security that concern their personal information.

South Carolina Insurance Data Security Act

The South Carolina Insurance Data Security Act was signed by Governor Henry McMaster on May 14, 2018, making it the first state law concerning cybersecurity of insurance information. Going into effect on January 1, 2019, the law gives anyone licensed by the South Carolina Department of Insurance to draft a security program.

Vermont's Act 171 of 2018

Approved by Governor Phil Scott on May 22, 2018, Act 171 is the first state law to impose regulations on data brokers who selling or purchasing personal information. Data brokers are now required to annually register with Vermont's Secretary of State and abide by new security requirements when dealing with personal information. The law went into effect on January 1, 2019.

Name Index

Organization Index

Subject Index

NOTE: Entries in **CAPITALS** are chapters.